The ENCYCLOPEDIA of the MUSICAL THEATRE

SECOND EDITION

The ENCYCLOPEDIA of the MUSICAL THEATRE

SECOND EDITION

3

O-Z

Kurt Gänzl

Schirmer Books

an imprint of the Gale Group

New York • Detroit • San Francisco • London • Boston • Woodbridge, CT

First edition published 1994 by Schirmer Books and in Great Britain by Blackwell Publishers

Schirmer Books
1633 Broadway
New York, NY 10019

Gale Group
27500 Drake Road
Farmington Hills, MI 48331

Library of Congress Cataloging-in-Publication Data

Gänzl, Kurt.
The encyclopedia of the musical theatre / Kurt Gänzl. — 2nd ed.
p. cm.
Includes bibliographical references and discographies.
ISBN 0-02-864970-2 (set)
1. Musicals—Encyclopedias. I. Title.

ML 102.M88 G3 2001
782.1'4'03—dc21 2001018361

Printed in the United States of America

Printing number
1 2 3 4 5 6 7 8 9 10

This book is printed on acid-free paper

FRONT COVER, CLOCKWISE: Josephine Cook in a Landestheater, Coburg, production of *Giuditta*, *No, No, Nanette* sheet music cover, photograph of the bride in her frock in *Rose Marie*, *The Mikado* poster, *Là-Haut* sheet music cover.

Contents

Organization of the Encyclopedia

Alphabetization

Entries are arranged in a single alphabetical sequence, using a letter-by-letter system, as follows:

> **MANNEQUINS**
> **DER MANN MIT DEN DREI FRAUEN**
> **MANNSCHAFT AN BORD**
> **MANNSTADT, William**
> **MAN OF LA MANCHA**

For alphabetization purposes, the following conventions have been followed:

- the definite and indefinite articles A, The, L', Le, La, Les, Das, Der, Die, etc. are ignored where they appear at the beginning of show headwords;
- the Scots or Irish prefixes "Mac," "Mc" and "M'" are alphabetized letter-by-letter rather than treated as if they were spelt out "Mac";
- and all accented letters are treated as English unaccented letters.

Cross references appear as follows:

> **MAYTIME** *see* WIE EINST IM MAI

with the capital letter indicating the letter under which the entry may be found.

Introductory and supplementary sections to people entries

The articles are written and ordered under the name in which their subject was active in the theatre. When that name is simply an easily shortened version of the subject's real full name, the rest of that real name is given in square brackets.

> **BROWN, Jon[athan Frederick]**

When the bold headword is not simply a shortened form of the real full name or when the nom de théâtre/nom de plume is not that with which the subject was born, the real full name (where known) is given separately, again in square brackets.

> **BROWN, John [BROWN, Jonathan Frederick]**
>
> **BROWN, John [BRAUNSTEIN, Johann Friedrich]**

The name is followed by the places and dates of birth and death, where known, in parentheses. If the date of death (or birth) is not known it is simply not included.

> (b London, 6 February 1933)

On a number of occasions, a birth year is included but is marked with a query. This is generally where a death certificate or obituary has given the subject's age at death, but a birth certificate and/or date has not been found to confirm that information.

> (b Paris, ?1946; d Nice, 10 August 1980).

The bibliographies given at the end of entries include a representative selection of biographies, autobiographies or other significant literature devoted to the subject. I have not attempted to list every published work—not least because many of the people who have the most works written about them are those whose principal activity was not the musical theatre.

Introductory and supplementary sections to show entries

The introductory sections to show entries give the title (and subtitle where relevant) under which the show was normally played, followed by any considerably used alternative title, then the credits as given on the playbill, and the date and place of the first production. As in the worklists that appear at the end of people articles (see below), this information refers to the first metropolitan performance. In the case of modern works, the date of the official "first night," rather than that of the first preview performance, is given. Out-of-town tryout dates are shown only when there is an appreciable gap between the initial out-of-town production and any later metropolitan production, or when the show failed to find its way to town at all.

NO, NO, NANETTE Musical comedy in 3 acts by Frank Mandel, Otto Harbach and Irving Caesar based on *My Lady Friends* by Mandel and Emil Nyitray (and *Oh, James!* by May Edgington). Music by Vincent Youmans. Garrick Theater, Detroit, 23 April 1923; Harris Theater, Chicago, 7 May 1923; Globe Theater, New York, 16 September 1925.

The supplementary sections at the end of the show entries consist of a record of the dates and places of the first productions of the show in what, for the purposes of this book, are treated as the "main centers" (Berlin, Budapest, London, Melbourne, New York, Paris, Sydney, Vienna) other than that in which it was first performed. When the show was, on these occasions, given in France, Austria, Britain, America, Australia, Hungary or Germany under a title other than its original, the altered or translated title is given, along with the date and place of the production.

Austria: Theater in der Josefstadt 15 May 1952; France: Theatre Marigny *Feu d'artifice* 1952; UK: Bristol Old Vic *Oh, My Papa!* 2 April, Garrick Theatre, London 17 July 1957

Recordings: selection (Ariola-Eurodisc), selection in English (Parlophone EP)

Mention is also made of films and recordings of, and books on, individual shows. I have made no attempt to give details of recordings, as labels and serial numbers of recordings vary from country to country and a complete list of all the show recordings in question would fill a vast volume. I have merely tried to indicate which of the shows dealt with can be found on record, at least some of the labels that have been responsible for those recordings, and whether "original cast" or foreign-language recordings are included amongst them. Similarly, I have mentioned books only in the rare instances where a book is wholly, or very largely, devoted to the show in question.

Authors' and composers' worklists

The worklists attached to the articles on librettists, lyricists and composers are intended to include all of each writer's credited works for the book musical theatre.

Works for which a writer was not credited on the playbills are not included, and neither are works written for such adjacent musical and theatrical areas as opera, ballet, pantomime and revue.

The original works in the list are given in chronological order of their first production.

When a show has been played under more than one title, the title in bold type is the title under which its main metropolitan run was given, with alternative titles in italic type in parentheses. Titles discarded in tryout are noted as "ex-."

1988 **Ain't Broadway Grand** (ex- *Mike*)

Post-metropolitan changes of title are indicated by the prefix "later-." Where the title change was part of a significant rewrite, the rewrite will have a separate entry as "revised version of [original title]."

The year and title of the piece are followed by the names of the writer's credited collaborators on the show in question, in the order: composer(s)/lyricist(s)/librettist(s). Writers who collaborated with the writer in his or her area are shown by a "w" indicating "with." Thus (Smith/w Brown/w Green) would mean that the person who is the subject of the article worked on the show's lyrics with Brown and its book with Green, and the music was by Smith. The names of the subject's collaborators are given in full on their first mention in a worklist, and thereafter by surname only except where a duplicated surname could lead to confusion, such as in the case of contemporaneous text-writers H B Smith, R B Smith and E Smith. Any variants occurring in a show's author/composer credits are included in square brackets. Major revisions of a show are credited separately in the worklist.

In the case of short works only, the names of the authors are followed by an indication such as "1 act" or "3 scenes." Otherwise all works are "full-length" pieces (in the loosest possible meaning of the term when some works from the 19th-century days of very long evenings are in question) in a minimum of two acts.

Each original work entry on the worklist ends with the place and date of the first metropolitan performance. In the case of modern works, the date of the official "first night" rather than that of the first preview performance is used. Out-of-town tryout dates are shown only when there is an appreciable gap between the initial out-of-town production and any later metropolitan production, or when the show failed to find its way to town at all. In the case of shows initially staged in other cities and subsequently remounted in what, for the purposes of this book, are accounted the "main centers" (Berlin, Budapest, London, Melbourne, New York, Paris, Sydney, Vienna), both dates are given. When the theatre in which the show's premiere is given is not based in the city that may be regarded as being/having been the writer's base, the name of the city is included alongside the theatre. So, for example, a Vienna-centered author will be credited with works at the Carltheater, the Theater an der Wien or the Raimundtheater without further elaboration, but for productions at the Theater am Gärtnerplatz, Munich, the Népszínház, Budapest, or the Thalia-Theater, Berlin, the cities would be specified.

1890 **Erminy** (*Erminie*) German version w Heinrich von Waldberg (Carltheater)

1890 **Der bleiche Gast** (Josef Hellmesberger, Zamara/w von Waldberg) Carl-Schultze Theater, Hamburg 6 September

Shows which are not the original work of the writer in question, but simply adaptations of a musical originally written and produced by other writers in another language, are listed under the year of their production in the version by the subject of the worklist. The year is followed by the title given to the piece in the subject's adaptation, followed in parentheses by the title of the original piece in its original language, a description of the nature of the adaptation (where applicable) and the theatre where the adaptation was first staged.

1889 **Capitän Wilson** (*The Yeomen of the Guard*) German version w Carl Lindau (Carltheater)

On the occasions where I have been unable to trace or to confirm that a show credited to a writer was in fact produced, rather than just being announced for production, I have listed the title at the end of the worklist under the heading "Other titles attributed." Conversely, shows which were definitely produced, but for which my details are incomplete, are included in the worklist, with their details as complete as I have been able to make them. Any dubious dates, places or credits are indicated with a question mark, thus, ?1849.

Occasionally circumstances arose which could not be adequately dealt with by the arrangements described above. In these cases, it has been my main care simply to make whatever the situation and credits might be as clear as possible without clinging too unbendingly to a "standard" layout.

Abbreviations

(X) ad (Y)	the work of (X) adapted by (Y), adapter
add	additional
aka	also known as
(X) arr (Y)	the work of (X) arranged by (Y), arranger
b	born
ch	choreographed by, choreographer
d	died
dir	directed by, director
Eng	English/England
fr	from
Fr	French/France
Frln	Fraulein
Ger	German/Germany
Hun	Hungarian/Hungary
ka	known as
jr	junior
Lat	Latin
lib	libretto
ly	lyric(s)
md	musical director
mus	music
nd	no date known
np	no place known
posth	posthumous
rev	revival
scr	screenplay
Sp	Spanish/Spain
sq/sqq	and that/those following
sr	senior
t/o	takeover (of a role)
UK	United Kingdom
u/s	understudy
USA	United States of America

OATES, Alice [A] [née MERRITT] (b Nashville, Tenn, 22 September 1849; d Philadelphia, 24 February 1887). Lively little 19th-century touring producer and performer who took opéra-bouffe in English to all corners of America.

Budding ballad singer Alice Merritt became the wife of actor James A Oates, stage manager at the Nashville Adelphi Theater under Augusta Dargon, at the age of something like 15, and made her first appearance on the stage in his benefit as Paul in *The Pet of the Petticoats.* While still making occasional concert appearances under the name of ''Mdlle Orsini,'' she began working alongside her husband as a soubrette in shows in Nashville (1867), then in Cincinnati, Chicago and St Paul (where her husband took a theatre), playing such roles as Idex in *Undine,* Fianetta in *The White Fawn,* Darnley in *The Field of the Cloth of Gold* and Abdallah in *The Female Forty Thieves.* She subsequently toured ''Mrs James A Oates' Burlesque Troupe'' with the burlesques *The Field of the Cloth of Gold, Rip van Winkle* and *Pocahontas* around America and in May 1870 made her way to New York's Olympic Theater to play Broadway for the first time in *The Fair One in the Golden Wig* (Little Graceful), a burlesque of the old musical drama *The Daughter of the Regiment, or The 800 Fathers* (Josephine) and *The Field of the Cloth of Gold.* She returned to the Olympic in the same August with her first attempt at opéra-bouffe, a seriously botched version of London's already pretty botched version of Hervé's *Little Faust* (playing both Méphisto and the Street Arab!) which met with little favor. However, within a few years the vibrant little actress-manager had entirely swapped her repertoire of old-style British burlesques for one featuring examples of the newest French fashion in musical theatre, and she went on to become one of the most adventurous and durable managers successfully to produce and play English-language opéra-bouffe and opéra-comique around America. The *Little Faust* manner of staging, however, remained her manner throughout. The pieces were heavily botched, their comedy swingeingly lowered, their musical scores spattered with topical and local ditties, and the programs perforated with variety acts, until they resembled far more the old English burlesques the lady had forsaken than the very much more sophisticated French article.

Mrs Oates toured indefatigably throughout America, playing large dates, small dates and (especially as the years went on) a vast number of one-night stands for nearly a decade and making herself and her company a feature of the country's touring circuits. She made, however, only rare appearances on Broadway with her versions of such pieces as *Giroflé-Girofla, Le Petit Duc, La Fille de Madame Angot, La Jolie Parfumeuse, La Princesse de Trébizonde, Les Bavards, Les Prés Saint-Gervais* and *La Grande-Duchesse,* treating New York by and large as another, and usually rather brief, tour date. Her style and her adaptations were found too broad—too obvious and ''provincial''—by the city sophisticates, who liked their opéra-bouffe as given by Aimée or Tostée and in French, or, if it had to be in English, by the likes of the lavish and intelligent Emily Soldene, and without a bundle of music-hall songs or ''nigger sketches'' thrown into the middle of the proceedings. She maintained a decade-long and unbroken popularity with her own audiences, until the early 1880s, when her career began to waver (Electra Mnemosyne Bracegirdle in *Long Branch,* 1880), then to wilt. She faded away into playing variety, burlesque and extravaganza with her name attached to often poor and ill-managed companies, which all too often stranded or broke up on the road.

A contemporary summed up her appeal in her heyday: ''She offers a kind of compromise between the downright deviltry of Aimée and the mild indelicacy of other opéra-bouffe artists. Never insipid, never outrageous, she gravitates nicely between high opera and low comedy, never approaching close enough to either to attract largely.''

Mrs Oates was the first manager to produce a Gilbert and Sullivan work in America when she staged a rather approximate *Trial by Jury* at Philadelphia's Arch Street Theatre in 1875, and she was quickly on the boards with

Plate 282. **Alice Oates** *in* Little Faust.

a botched version of *HMS Pinafore* (with herself as a travesty Ralph Rackstraw) at the Bush Theatre in San Francisco shortly after the show's Boston premiere and before the piece had reached New York. However, the not easy to fiddle with works of Gilbert and Sullivan proved less to her and her audience's tastes than Alice-ized opéra-bouffe, and her repertoire throughout her career was made up largely of stringently lowered from-the-French shows.

Mrs Oates gave early opportunities to a number of people who later became important in the American musical theatre, notably *Evangeline* librettist J Cheever Goodwin, who performed in her company and confirmed his career as a stage author Alice-izing French opéras-bouffes for his employer, and the beautiful Pauline Hall of *Erminie* fame. She also employed a number of the finest established performers of the English musical stage, such as J G Taylor, E D Beverly, Edward Connell and John Howson, in companies that were, in her best days, something just a little more than a setting for their manageress and her performances. She also produced one original comic opera in Blanche Reeves and Jesse Williams's *Mignonette* (Ford's Grand Opera House, Baltimore 9 October 1874).

After the death of her husband, she married her agent, Tracy W Titus, but they quickly separated, and Alice's subsequent series of amorous adventures became a rather embarrassing running newspaper feature.

Mrs Oates never performed outside the American continent. On several occasions it was announced that her troupe would visit Australia, but the trip never eventuated, and after Emily Soldene, with her very much more legitimate productions of opéra-bouffe in English, had stunned the southern colonies in the late 1870s, there were few crumbs left for anyone who might follow.

She died after taking cold in a damp and dreary dressing room in a regional theatre, at the age of 37.

DER OBERSTEIGER Operette in 3 acts by Moritz West and Ludwig Held. Music by Carl Zeller. Theater an der Wien, Vienna, 5 January 1894.

Carl Zeller never succeeded in composing another Operette that found the same enormous success as his delightfully melodious, countryside-and-court show *Der Vogelhändler,* but he nevertheless turned out several other winning scores, of which that for *Der Obersteiger,* attached to a libretto which, above all, created a large and cornucopic Girardi role for the megastar of the Viennese Operette stage, was one of the most attractive.

Alexander Girardi was cast as Martin, the loose-living, work-shy foreman of a mine in a little village somewhere on the Austro-German border. Engaged to pretty Nelly (Therese Biedermann), he nevertheless chases after her cousin, Julie Fahnenschwinger (Jenny Pohlner), but he gets tetchily suspicious and openly accusing when he sees Nelly richly dressed. When he is put in charge of a mineworkers' strike for ''less work, more pay,'' he uses his position to his own financial profit, and he is not above making love to the overseer's wife (Lori Stubel) to get a job for his on-the-side miners' band. However, Martin gets his brownie points when the ''enemy,'' the mine overseer Zwack (Carl Lindau), is made to look ridiculous: having admitted that ''Julie'' is his illegitimate daughter, he sees it revealed that she is actually a Countess in disguise. Before the show is over, she has paired off with the local Count Roderich (Karl Streitmann), and Martin goes back to the soft Nelly.

Der Obersteiger was a less agreeable libretto than that of *Der Vogelhändler,* even though the characters were lined up in almost a repeat of the first show: the country lad, his betrayed country girl, the aristocratic lady whom he runs after and who finally marries one of her own kind, and even two crazy mining officials as equivalents to the two professors of the earlier piece. And the role of Martin, whilst certainly large and equipped with one magnificent hit number, the obligatory Girardi waltz ''Sei nicht bös,'' had none of the appeal of *Der Vogelhändler*'s Adam: he was a fairly despicable boor, and it needed all the charm of a Girardi to make him anything else.

Alexandrine von Schönerer's production of *Der Obersteiger* at the Theater an der Wien was well received, and the piece was given a first run of 61 performances in two months. It was retained in the repertoire throughout the year, making regular reappearances, passing its 100th night on 21 October, and still putting in the occasional matinée performance in 1897. In 1901 it was revived at the Carltheater (15 November) with Mizzi Zwerenz as Nelly, and it remained thereafter on the fringe of the revivable repertoire, reappearing at the Theater an der Wien in 1919 and in 1953 at the Raimundtheater (18 December).

The show's Austrian success was repeated in Germany, where, again without equaling *Der Vogelhändler,* it was for a number of years a highly popular piece in provincial houses, and also in Hungary. First produced there at the Népszínház (ad József Márkus) with Pál Vidor starred as Martin, Aranka Hegyi (''Julie''), Mariska Komáromi (Nelly) and Sándor Dardai (Roderich), it had a very fine first run of 35 performances and was played throughout the country.

If the show did not travel noticeably beyond central Europe—performances given at New York's German-language Terrace-Garten by the Ferenczy troupe from Germany in 1895 and 1896 being the only exceptions I can find—the same could not be said for its star song. ''Sei nicht bös'' (aka ''The Obersteiger Waltz,'' aka ''Don't Be Cross'') went quickly around the world, becoming, curiously, a concert favorite with sopranos. London's George Edwardes snapped it up, had Adrian Ross write some English words and popped it into his *An Artist's Model* as a duet for Hayden Coffin and Marie Tempest under the title ''Music and Laughter,'' but he was forced to withdraw it when the publishers objected. They didn't have quite the same success with Broadway's Richard Mansfield, who had it inserted into his *Trilby* burlesque, where it was sung by Adele Ritchie as Little Willie. Since *Der Obersteiger* never crossed the Channel, the publishers' prohibition did them little good, but they duly made their hit with the song, which is sung to this day in English.

Germany: Theater Unter den Linden 27 January 1894; Hungary: Népszínház *A banyamester* 15 September 1894; USA: Terrace-Garten *The Master Miner* 14 May 1895

THE O'BRIEN GIRL Musical comedy in 2 acts by Frank Mandel and Otto Harbach. Lyrics by Harbach. Music by Louis Hirsch. Liberty Theater, New York, 3 October 1921.

George M Cohan brought back the team that had given him a hit show in *Mary* to attempt a repeat the following year with *The O'Brien Girl.* Once again Frank Mandel and Otto Harbach turned out plot and words on a Cinderellie line with yet another poor, Irish-American lassie singing and dancing her way into the hands, the arms and ultimately the family tree of a handsome, wealthy (or should that be wealthy, handsome?) upper-class, thoroughly American version of a fairy-tale prince. This time the little heroine was a typist called Alice O'Brien (Elisabeth Hines), her reward was called Larry Patten (Truman Stanley) and the obstacles were her employer, Mr Drexel (Robinson Newbold), and his not unreasonably suspicious wife (Georgia Caine), who had destined Larry as a mate for her own daughter, Eloise. Fairyland was an hotel in the Adirondacks, where little Alice had gone to spend her savings on one glorious blowout and where she ran into all the rest of the principals. One critic remarked, perhaps naively, that the tale seemed to be borrowed from the successful play *Diana of Dobson's*—it could, of course, have been borrowed from any one of a dozen recent musical plays, but it was none the worse nor any the less popular for that.

If Hirsch's score didn't produce anything that caught on like the big numbers of *Mary* had done, songs such as ''Learn to Smile,'' ''The O'Brien Girl,'' ''I Wonder How I Ever Passed You By'' and a new ''My Little Canoe'' (Billie Burke's prewar hit must have been forgotten) illustrated the story happily alongside a bevy of the period's obligatory dance numbers (The Indian Prance, The Conversation Step, ''The Last Dance'').

The O'Brien Girl ran for a more than respectable 164 Broadway performances, then toured, but only Australia showed any overseas interest in taking it up. It proved a good decision. Budding producer Hugh J Ward used *The O'Brien Girl* to open the New Princess Theatre in Melbourne and mounted it with Mamie Watson (Alice), Leyland Hodgson (Larry), Mark Daly (Drexel) and May Beatty (Mrs Drexel) featured, and with dancer June Roberts in the role of Eloise and soprano Ena Dale (Miss Hope) tacked in to do their specialities. It ran for an outstanding 202 performances in five and a half months at the Princess, followed up with a hit season in Sydney (Grand Opera House 15 September 1923), where Ward played twice daily to cash in on his show's vogue through a further three months, becoming one of the longest running hits of the 1920s on the Australian musical stage. It was brought back to Melbourne as late as 1936, when Benjamin Fuller and the young Garnet Carroll mounted a revival at the Apollo Theatre (8 August), with Charles Norman and Catherine Stewart featured.

Australia: New Princess Theatre, Melbourne 26 December 1922

AZ OBSITOS Enekes színjatek (play with songs) in 3 acts by Károly Bakonyi. Music by Emmerich Kálmán. Vígszínház, Budapest, 16 March 1910.

Produced at Budapest's Vígszínház, as Kálmán's previous piece, the internationally successful *Tatárjárás,* had been, *Az obsitos* was, like that work, a collaboration with playwright Károly Bakonyi. Unlike the earlier piece, however, it was not described as an ''operett'' but as an ''enekes színjatek,'' and the text to the piece was indeed no Ruritanian operetta tale of soubrettes and so forth, but a period play ''part serious drama, part folk play, part tale,'' which, whilst far from being a fantasy, had some of the characteristics of Bakonyi's great *János vitéz* to it, and to which the musical part was a support.

In an Hungarian village a mother (a nemzetes asszony, *Hermin Haraszthy*) and her daughter, Malcsika (Irén Varsányi), wait. They are waiting for their soldier son and brother to come home from Italy, whither he went during the Hungarian uprisings of 1848. They cannot know that he will not return, for he is dead. The news of his death is to be brought to them by his friend, András Dömötör (Gyula Hegedüs). But András is very close, in physical appearance, to his dead friend, and when he arrives both the mother and, at first, the daughter mistake him for their boy returned home. András cannot undeceive the old lady, and he will not allow himself, under such conditions, to accept the fact that Malcsika is falling in love with him. But, eventually, the secret has to come out. The nemzetes asszony accepts that she has lost her son, but she has the consolation of a new son, for András will marry Malcsika.

The Budapest public, expecting another brightly operettic piece in the style of *Tatárjárás,* were taken aback by the new Kálmán/Bakonyi product, but the show soon found its audience and appreciation. *Az obsitos* was no *János vitéz,* but, following its initial 25 performances at the Vígszínház, it nevertheless had a remarkable career. That career was not simply in Hungary but, in an amazing series of transformations, in a whole series of other countries.

The first of these was Austria. Librettist Victor Léon took up the show, combined with Kálmán on some alterations—one of which was the shifting of the action from its Hungarian setting to an Upper Austrian one, in the year 1859—and directed the resultant *Der gute Kamerad* (now described curiously as ''ein Theaterstück für Musik'') under the management of Oskar Fronz, and with the composer conducting, at the Wiener Bürgertheater. Willy Strehl was Alwin von Kammerer, with Viktoria Pohl-Meiser (Stanzi), Franz Mainau (Baron Martin von Schenkenbach) and Erna Fiebinger (Marlene) in support.

Der gute Kamerad had a respectable run of 53 performances, but it didn't get a look-in after the end of its first run, for the Bürgertheater then began its great run of Eysler Operetten, and the Austro-Hungarian piece was forgotten. Not wholly, however, for in 1914 Wilhelm Karczag decided that *Der gute Kamerad* would be a good piece with which to reopen his theatre after the outbreak of war. Léon rewrote his text (now advertised as being ''freely based on an idea by'' Bakonyi) to make this a Kriegsoperette, a frankly patriotic piece set in the present day, and retitled it *Gold gab ich für Eisen.* Karczag cast the piece with Ernst Tautenhayn (Rabenlechner), Luise Kartousch repeating her *Herbstmanöver* travesty as the young Xaver, alongside Therese Tautenhayn also in travesty as von Kammerer, Betty Fischer in her Theater an der Wien debut as Marlene, and such fine veterans as Paul Guttmann and Karl Tuschl. Vienna showed only a limited interest, however, in being stirred up by a Kriegsoperette. *Gold gab ich für Eisen* passed its 50th performance on 4 December, and little more than three weeks later Karczag remounted the decidedly escapist *Der Opernball* in replacement. *Auf Befehl der Kaiserin* and, above all, *Die Rose von Stambul* soon confirmed that good-old-days entertainment and colorful, ringing Operette were what the wartime Viennese (like their brethren everywhere else) really wanted. *Gold gab ich für Eisen* ended up with a total of 82 showings, during which Frln Kartousch gave up her role to the very untravestied Viktor Flemming.

Germany had earlier picked up *Der gute Kamerad,* without particular enthusiasm, and although it had a veritable factory of Kriegsoperetten of its own, the revised *Gold gab ich für Eisen* was pulled in to add its weight to the war effort. What was good for one side, however, could apparently also be good for the other. Shortly after what remained of *Az obsitos* had done its new rounds in Austria and Germany, it turned up on Broadway. Done over by Rida Johnson Young, its tale was now a semi-weepie, studded with conventional musical-comedy comedy (although no travesty), set in Belgium and with an improbable happy ending. After the soldier hero (John Charles Thomas) had pretended to be his buddy (Frank Ridge) to save the dead man's family pain, he not only won the buddy's sister (Beth Lydy) but saw the undead buddy return safely home. Clifton Crawford and Adele Rowland were the comedy. Kálmán's score now included a bundle of Sigmund Romberg music, plus a handful of other of-the-moment pieces including Miss Rowland's rendition of ''Pack Up Your Troubles in Your Old Kit Bag.'' The Shuberts' production of *Her Soldier Boy* bore no family resemblance at all to *János vitéz,* which probably helped it to its 204 performances at the Astor and Shubert Theaters.

Kálmán's name appeared nowhere on the bills when *Soldier Boy* was produced in London, right under the nose of the self-appointed wartime guardian of the racial purity of the nation's musical stages, J M Glover, whose much-boasted knowledge of music and musical shows apparently didn't reach to knowing from where this show had originally sprung. Edgar Wallace revised Mrs Johnson's book, Frederic Chapelle had his go at the score, and the combination of the heart-tugging tale and songs with titles such as "Song of Home," "I'm Going Home," "He's Coming Home," "The Battle Front at Home," "Mother," "Lonely Princess," "March Along" and "The Military Stamp" ensured the show its longest run of all: 372 performances, which straddled Armistice Day with great advantage to the box office. *Az obsitos,* although barely recognizable, had the distinction of being the only "Germanic" piece (Charles Cuvillier's *The Lilac Domino* apparently counted as "French") to play the West End in the war years. France, however, did not play it, in any version.

Austria: Wiener Bürgertheater *Der gute Kamarad* 27 October 1911, Theater an der Wien *Gold gab ich für Eisen* 18 October 1914; Germany: *Der gute Kamerad* Neues Operetten-Theater, Leipzig *Gold gab ich für Eisen* 28 November 1915; USA: Astor Theater *Her Soldier Boy* 6 December 1916; UK: Apollo Theatre *Soldier Boy* 26 June 1918

Plate 283. **L'Oeil crevé**

L'OEIL CREVÉ Folie musicale in 3 acts by Hervé. Théâtre des Folies-Dramatiques, Paris, 12 October 1867.

Hervé's second attempt, after *Les Chevaliers de la table ronde* (1866), to produce a full-length burlesque opérette to challenge the all-consuming works of Offenbach, *L'Oeil crevé* did precisely that, proving itself one of the most successful opéras-bouffes of the greatest era of burlesque entertainments.

Fleur de Noblesse (Julia Baron) is, in accordance with her name, a flower of a noble family, the daughter of the local Marquis (Berret) and Marquise de Haut-en-Truffes (Adìle Cuinet). However, she has been attacked by a grotesque passion for carpentry and, not coincidentally, for the young cabinetmaker Ernest. The hand of this noble maiden is put up as the prize in an archery contest, which is the highlight of the piece, so she uses her woodworking talents to "fix" the targets. Thus, Ernest seems to hit the bull's-eye, but his triumph and his prize are postponed when the Robin Hoodish forester Alexandrivoire (Marcel), the beloved of the peasant girl Dindonette (Mlle Berthal), arrives on the scene with a challenge. However, Fleur de Noblesse gives the target a shove at the critical moment and, far from splitting his rival's shaft, or marking his announced bull's-eye, Alexandrivoire instead puts his arrow in the eye of the noble maiden. The one gendarme, Geromé (Milher), who constitutes the whole of the Marquisal army, arrests the miscreant and plunges him into a dungeon tower. But Dindonette organizes the extraction of the arrow and, an actful of disguises, doctors, duets and long-lost-babytalk later, everything can end happily.

The tale gave opportunities for a whole series of particular burlesques, from the *Robin Hood, William Tell* and *Lucia di Lammermoor* moments of the archery contest, to musical mockeries of *Der Freischütz* (a hunters' chorus) and *Il trovatore* (a miserere duo for Dindonette and her imprisoned swain), but the favorite portions of Hervé's brightly comical score were a duo for the Marquis d'Enface and Dindonette: the Légende de la langouste atmospherique, an auvergant dialect tale about a chap who used the magic herb of brotherly love to spice his cooked lobster instead of spreading it around the world, Alexandrivoire's La Polonaise et l'hirondelle ("Un jour passant par Meudon"), his third act tyrolienne ("Tournes, tournes, petits batons"), Geromé's comical military number equipped with drum imitations, and the septet, chorus and finale of the second act, which culminated in a crazy, concerted massed effect much like the more famous first-act closing of the author's subsequent *Chilpéric* with its umbrellas and horses.

L'Oeil crevé was an enormous hit. It ran a remarkable 345 performances in its first year, and it returned regularly to the Parisian stage thereafter. It was seen again at the Folies-Dramatiques in 1872 (May) and again in 1876, with Mme Prelly (Dindonette), Simon-Max (Alexandrivoire), Noémie Vernon (Fleur de Noblesse) and Milher in his original role, revised by Hector Crémieux for a royally cast production at the Théâtre de la Renaissance in 1881 (24 September, ''an entirely new libretto''), which interpolated a new role for star soubrette Mily-Meyer, mounted at the Théâtre des Menus-Plaisirs in 1889, 1890 and 1892, and at the Variétés in 1896 (18 April), where Albert Brasseur (Marquis d'Enface), Germaine Gallois (Fleur de Noblesse), Juliette Méaly (Dindonette), Ève Lavallière (Ernest), Paul Fugère, Jane Pernyn (Alexandrivoire), Guy (Marquis d'Enface), Baron (Bailli) and Milher, again, headed the starry cast. It came back to the Variétés again in 1904 (30 December), well after the vogue for genuine opéra-bouffe had faded, with Anna Tariol-Baugé playing Dindonette alongside Albert Brasseur and Mlle Pernyn, now promoted to Fleur de Noblesse. In 1999, in a France just beginning to once again show interest in the great works of its burlesque-theatrical past, a fiddled-with version of the piece was staged at the Opéra-Comique (21 December) under the aegis of Péniche Opéra and the title *Vlan! dans l'oeil* (which, it was insisted, was Hervé's original intention to call the piece), bringing something approximating *L'Oeil crevé* back to the Paris stage after almost a century of absence.

L'Oeil crevé was a burlesque piece in Hervé's furthest-out style, and if the Paris of 1867 found that style hilarious, it was by no means sure that other centers would—presuming that an adapter could be found who would and could repeat the flavor of the original in another language. Vienna gave *Der Pfeil im Auge* (ad Julius Hopp) just four hearings, and an equally uncomprehending New York, which got the piece in its original French from Maurice Grau's company, with Rose Bell (Dindonette), Marie Desclauzas (Fleur de Noblesse), Carrier (Alexandrivoire), Beckers (Marquis d'Enface) and Gabel (Geromé) featured, also gave it the thumbs down with sufficient firmness to ensure that the show was never produced in New York (or, as far as I can see, anywhere else in America) in English.

England, however, which was to repeatedly prove the most receptive among ''foreign'' countries to Hervé's extravagant comicalities, was pleased enough with its first glimpse of his work when F C Burnand's rather approximate adaptation of *L'Oeil crevé* was produced at the Olympic Theatre as *Hit or Miss, or All My Eye and Betty Martin* in 1868 (''the music puts to shame the music-hall stuff accepted in burlesque''). Emily Pitt played Peter (ie, Alexandrivoire), Louisa Moore was Lady Betty Martin (Fleur de Noblesse), Lennox Grey was the equivalent of Dindonette and Robert Soutar and J G Taylor were the Marquis and Marchioness. John Clarke made a feature of the Marquis d'Enface, neatly Burnandized as ''the Duke of Totherside.'' After the huge success of *Chilpéric* in London, the city was happy to see the older show again. It got it both in French (''as played in Paris for 345 nights''), from the visiting Folies-Dramatiques Company (who also did *Chilpéric* and *Le Canard à trois becs* but won greatest applause for this piece), featuring Paola Marié (Dindonette), Blanche d'Antigny (Fleur de Noblesse) and Vauthier (Marquis d'Enface), then in a new H B Farnie version at the Opera Comique (*L'Oeil crevé or the Merry Toxophilites* 21 October 1872) produced under the management of E P Hingston. Julia Mathews (Fleur de Noblesse), Mlle Clary (Alexandrivoire), Pattie Laverne (Dindonette), Richard Temple (Geromé) and David Fisher (Marquis) headed the cast in which Richard Barker, the director, appeared as ''the Sentry,'' and the piece scored a fine success, running through November and December and into the New Year. Yet another version of the piece—the fourth in a decade—returned to the West End in 1877 when a five-scene reduction of Farnie's text was added to Alexander Henderson's triple bill (*La Créole, Up the River*) at the Folly Theatre (as *Shooting Stars* 22 November) with Kate Munroe (Dindonette), Lizzie Beaumont (Fleur de Noblesse), Violet Cameron (Alexandrivoire), John Howson (Gerome) and C H Drew (Marquis) featured.

Australia got the Farnie version.

Austria: Theater an der Wien *Der Pfeil im Auge* 29 February 1868; Germany: Friedrich-Wilhelmstädtisches Theater *Fleur de Noblesse* 22 May 1868; USA: Théâtre Français (Fr) 11 January 1869; UK: Olympic Theatre *Hit or Miss, or All My Eye and Betty Martin* 13 April 1868, Globe Theatre (Fr) 15 June 1872; Australia: Opera House, Melbourne *L'Oeil crevé or the Merry Toxophilites* 28 February 1874

OFFENBACH, Jacques [EBERST, Jacob] (b Cologne, 20 June 1819; d Paris, 3 October 1880). The 19th century's most popular musical-theatre composer.

The son of a German bookbinder, music teacher and cantor named Eberst, but known as Offenbach, the young Jacob was given a good musical education from an early age. When he was 14 years old, his father took him to Paris, where he secured a place at the Conservatoire (becoming Jacques instead of Jacob), but, after a year of studies, he left to earn a living as an orchestral 'cellist, ultimately in the orchestra of the Opéra-Comique. He progressed from orchestral playing to solo work and, in the 1840s, gave concert performances in several of the world's musical capitals.

Offenbach began writing music almost at the same time that he began performing it, at first producing occasional pieces, orchestral dances and instrumental and vocal music before, in 1839, he was given the opportunity to compose for the stage for the first time with a song for the one-act vaudeville *Pascal et Chambord,* produced at the Palais-Royal. That commission, however, had no tomorrow and, although Offenbach began writing with serious intent for the stage in the 1840s, he found that he was unable to get his works staged. The Opéra-Comique, the principal producer of lighter musical works, rejected his efforts and although *Pépito,* a pretty if slightly self-conscious little opérette housing some parody of Rossini, was played briefly at the Théâtre des Variétés, he was obliged to mount performances of his other short pieces under fringe theatre conditions to win a hearing. Not even when he was nominated conductor at the Théâtre Français in 1850, a post that led him to be called upon to supply such scenic and incidental music and/or songs as might be required for that theatre's productions, did he succeed in getting one of his opérettes produced. Then, in 1855, he launched himself on the Parisian stage from two different fronts.

On the one hand, with the help of a finely imagined and funny text by Jules Moinaux, he managed to place one of his opérettes at Hervé's Folies-Nouvelles. This piece, *Oyayaïe, ou La Reine des îles,* was in a different vein from his previous works, works that had been written rather in the style of a Massé or an Adam with the polite portals of the Opéra-Comique in sight. *Oyayaïe* was written in the new burlesque style initiated and encouraged by Hervé, and it rippled with ridiculous and extravagantly idiotic fun. There was not a milkmaid or a Marquis in sight, and the show was peopled instead by the folk of burlesque, with Hervé himself at their head, in travesty, as the titular and cannibalistic Queen of the Islands.

By the time that *Oyayaïe* had found its way to the stage, however, Offenbach had already set another project on its way. The year 1855 was the year of the Paris Exhibition, and the city's purveyors of entertainment were preparing for lucratively larger audiences than were usual as visitors from out of town and overseas poured into Paris. It seemed like a good time to be in the business. Thus, Offenbach, who had managed the production of his early unwanted works himself and who now saw Hervé presenting his own works successfully at the Folies-Nouvelles, decided to become a manager. He took up the lease of the little Théâtre Marigny in the Champs-Élysées, rechristened it the Théâtre des Bouffes-Parisiens and opened with a program made up of four short pieces by J Offenbach: a little introductory scena *Entrez Mesdames, Messieurs,* a virtual two-hander for two comics *Les Deux Aveugles,* the three-handed opéra-comique *Une nuit blanche* and the pantomime *Arlequin barbier. Les Deux Aveugles* proved a major Parisian (and later international) hit, *Une nuit blanche* (which subsequently became much favored in English under the title *Forty Winks*) supported it happily, and Offenbach's theatre and its program became one of the most successful entertainments

Plate 284. **Jacques Offenbach**

of the Exhibition season. Thus launched, the composer/producer began to vary his program, taking in some pieces by other writers, writing himself four more opérettes and two more pantomimes and scoring a second significant success with the sentimental scena (''légende bretonne'') *Le Violoneux,* in which the young Hortense Schneider made her first Paris appearances.

Once the end of the summer season arrived, however, accompanied by the closing of the Exhibition, it soon became clear that the little theatre way out in the Champs-Élysées was no longer a good proposition. Offenbach needed to shift his activities to a more central location if he were to continue as he had begun. He leased an auditorium in the Passage Choiseul, gained a permit in which the limit to the number of characters allowed in his pieces was raised from three to four, and opened, still as the ''Bouffes-Parisiens,'' at the end of December with a program that featured but one piece of his own. However, that one piece was a winner. *Ba-ta-clan* was a return to the burlesque genre of *Oyayaïe,* and it gave Offenbach the producer and Offenbach the musician a fresh success comparable to that of *Les Deux Aveugles.* The new house was rocketed off to the same kind of start as the old one had been. The successes of his winter season included Offenbach's melodrama burlesque *Tromb-al-ca-zar* and an adaptation of Mozart's little *Der Schauspieldirektor* as well as the prize-winning efforts of two neophyte composers, Georges Bizet and Charles Lecocq, before the happy manager moved back to the Champs-Élysées for the summer with a program including such new pieces as *La Rose de Saint-Flour*—a piece in the rustic opérette vein of Massé's *Les Noces de Jeannette* or of Offenbach's own *Le Violoneux*—and *Le 66.*

At the end of this second summer, Offenbach abandoned his first little home and established himself on a full-time basis at the Passage Choiseul, now the one-and-only Théâtre des Bouffes-Parisiens. There he continued to mount an ever-changing program of short pieces, through 1857 (*Croquefer* with a fifth character semi-mute, *Une demoiselle en loterie, Le Mariage aux lanternes,* etc) and into 1858 (*Mesdames de la Halle,* with a full-sized cast at last permitted, and a musical version of Scribe and Mélesville's little vaudeville *La Chatte métamorphosée en femme*), whilst taking the company and its repertoire on tour to Britain and to Lyon, to command performances, and managing to lose money all the while.

The restrictions as to the size of his productions having finally been withdrawn, Offenbach now stretched out for the first time into a more substantial work. October 1858 saw the Bouffes-Parisiens's first production of a full-sized, two-act opéra-bouffe, a piece written in an extension of the Hervé-style, which Offenbach and his librettists had carried so successfully through from *Ba-ta-clan* to *Tromb-al-ca-zar* and *Croquefer.* This style blossomed into something on a different scale in *Orphée aux enfers,* a gloriously imaginative parody of classic mythology and of modern events decorated with Offenbach's most laughing bouffe music. The triumph of *Orphée aux enfers* put the Bouffes-Parisiens on a steady footing, and those corners of the international theatrical world that had not yet taken more notice of Offenbach than to pilfer such of his tunes as they fancied for their pasticcio entertainments began to wake up to the significance of the new hero of the Paris musical theatre and his work.

However, in spite of its great home success (228 successive performances at the Bouffes) and the widespread popularity of its music, *Orphée* did not, at the time, produce the major change of emphasis in the international musical theatre that, in retrospect, might have been expected. It took a number of years, further shows (and not always the same one for every area) for the Offenbach pen to do that.

In the meanwhile, there were further successes—financial, or at least artistic—to come. The year 1859 brought two more: the short *Un mari à la porte* and Offenbach's second full-length piece, the hilarious burlesque of all things medieval *Geneviève de Brabant,* which, although it was a financial loser, confirmed the triumph of *Orphée* at the Bouffes-Parisiens. But there were also some real and substantial failures. When Offenbach moved outside his usual genre and finally forced the gates not only of the Opéra-Comique (*Barkouf,* to a libretto co-written by Scribe) but also of the Opéra (the ballet *Le Papillon*), he had two thorough flops. Back at the Bouffes, however, he produced in 1861 a third triumphant full-length work, the Venetian burlesque *Le Pont des soupirs,* the shorter but no less successful *La Chanson de Fortunio* and the Duc de Morny's delightful *M Choufleuri restera chez lui le . . . ,* followed in 1862 by the sparkling musical comedy *Le Voyage de MM Dunanan père et fils,* the little *M et Mme Denis* and, at his preferred spa town of Ems, *Bavard et Bavarde,* a little piece which he subsequently worked up into a larger one as *Les Bavards.* But, whilst the successes piled up, the money did not. The dizzily spending Offenbach was not a talented manager, and the series of outstandingly popular shows that should have made his fortune instead left the Bouffes-Parisiens almost permanently in the red. After the production of *M et Mme Denis* he was obliged to give up the theatre he had begun, and in 1863 the only fresh Offenbach music premiered in Paris was a song written for a Palais-Royal vaudeville, *Le Brésilien,* by his old collaborator, Ludovic Halévy, and the librettist's newest partner, Henri Meilhac.

Ems, again, was the venue for one of his tiniest and sweetest pieces, *Lischen et Fritzchen,* and Vienna—where his works had begun to raise interest—the chosen city for his next venture into the area that had suited him so ill in 1860; *Die Rheinnixen,* an opéra-comique produced at the Vienna Hofoper, proved as total a failure as had *Barkouf* in Paris. Offenbach returned to the Parisian theatre with *Les Géorgiennes,* less successful perhaps than his previous three-act shows but still back in his "own" world, and then, at what was clearly a crucial point in his career, he began the collaboration that would lead him to an even more outstanding position in the musical theatre than that he had already conquered with *Orphée, Geneviève* and *Le Pont des soupirs.*

Halévy and Meilhac joined the composer to write his second burlesque of classic antiquity, *La Belle Hélène.* Produced by Cogniard at the Théâtre des Variétés in December 1864, the piece won its trio of authors a ringing success such as Paris had not seen in years. And now Offenbach began his real takeover of the world's stages: Vienna was conquered in 1865 with Maric Geistinger's *Die schöne Helena,* and as Offenbach, Halévy and Meilhac swept the stage of the Variétés with further burlesque triumphs in *Barbe-bleue* (1866), *La Grande-Duchesse de Gérolstein* (1867), *Les Brigands* (1869) and the rather less burlesque but ultimately equally successful *La Périchole* (1868), London fell belatedly before Emily Soldene in *Geneviève de Brabant* and Julia Mathews's *La Grande-Duchesse,* whilst in America Lucille Tostée's *La Grande-Duchesse* gave serious impetus to a craze for opéra-bouffe in general and for the works of Offenbach in particular. At home, the composer continued to turn out successes: the glittering comedy-cum-opérette *La Vie parisienne* for the Palais-Royal, the frivolous *La Princesse de Trébizonde* premiered at Baden-Baden before taking over the stage of the Bouffes-Parisiens, and the little bouffonnerie *L'Île de Tulipatan. Les Bergers,* a sardonic three-part look at fidelity in love through the ages, and *La Diva,* a vehicle for Schneider, both staged at the Bouffes, and two further pieces for the Opéra-Comique, *Robinson Crusoe* and *Vert-Vert,* proved less popular.

Les Brigands was playing at the Variétés when the Prussian army marched into Paris. Offenbach, like his chief competitors of times before and after, Hervé and Lecocq, marched quickly out, and he spent the year of the conflict capitalizing on his now thoroughly spread fame around the world. When he returned, however, things did not take up where they had left off. The days of opéra-bouffe were done, and so were the days when Offenbach, Halévy, Meilhac and their star, Hortense Schneider, reigned over the Paris musical theatre and its glittering audiences. Hervé-esque burlesque with its weirdly extravagant tales and laughing music was no longer the order of the day, the dazzling gaiety of the Variétés shows was of yesterday. The fashion, like the régime, had changed. Offenbach still found hits: the grand opéra-bouffe féerie *Le Roi Carotte* owed both some of its success and its truncated run to an extravagant production that made it impossible to balance the books, *La Jolie Parfumeuse* (1873) and *Madame l'Archiduc* (1874), both found genuine international successes one level below his greatest opéras-bouffes, and a Christmas show for London, *Whittington,* fared much better than a Vienna one, *Der schwarze Korsar* (23 performances). But none was a *Grande-Duchesse* or a *Belle Hélène.*

At the same period, however, Offenbach decided almost perversely to go back into management. He took the Théâtre de la Gaîté and there staged revivals of his two earliest Bouffes-Parisiens successes, *Orphée aux enfers* and *Geneviève de Brabant,* and of *La Périchole,* each of which he expanded to larger proportions, with mixed results: if the *Orphée* took least well to having additional songs and scenes stuck into its fabric, it did best at the box office. However, box office proved Offenbach's downfall once again, and a distastrously expensive flop with Sardou's play *La Haine* found him once more an ex-theatre manager and financially in a parlous state.

He was also, now, for the first time for many years, not alone at the head of the French light-musical theatre. The emergence of Charles Lecocq and, above all, the younger man's triumphs in 1872 with *La Fille de Madame Angot* and in 1874 with *Giroflé-Girofla* had rather overshadowed Offenbach's works of the same period, whilst the success of Robert Planquette's *Les Cloches de Corneville* in 1877 was the kind that Offenbach had not known for nearly a decade. Against these works, the long run of the spectacular opéra-bouffe féerie *Le Voyage dans la lune,* the at-best semi-successes of *La Boulangère a des écus* and *La Créole* and the utter failures of *La Boîte au lait* and *Maître Péronilla* weighed sadly light.

However, Offenbach was by no means done. In 1878, the year of Lecocq's latest triumph with *Le Petit Duc,* he found himself in tandem with one of the most efficacious and talented pairs of librettists of the day, Henri Chivot and Alfred Duru, and to their brilliant, action-packed text for *Madame Favart* he composed a score that more than did it justice. *Madame Favart* was no opéra-bouffe, and the music the 60-year-old Offenbach wrote for it had none of the brilliant fireworks of the scores of *Orphée, Geneviève* and *Barbe-bleue.* It was a period comic opera, a farcical tale of sexual hide-and-seek with a series of fine roles and fine songs, and with both something of *La Fille de Madame Angot* and something of the Palais-Royal comedy about it. It was also a hit. The team repeated their success the following year with the splendid *La Fille du tambour-major,* the hit of the Parisian season, and thus Offenbach, who had known so many years at the top of his profession, was able to go out of it at the top. He died the following year of heart trouble, exacerbated by the gout and rheumatics that had dogged him throughout his adult life.

Following his death, his opérette *Belle Lurette* (completed by Delibes) was produced at the Théâtre de la Renaissance and overseas, and the opera *Les Contes d'Hoffmann* (completed by Guiraud) at the Opéra-Comique. This last piece finally gave him, posthumously, the success at the Opéra-Comique that he had always wanted so much, but that he had never been able to win during his lifetime.

Inevitably, after his death, and more particularly following the expiry of his legal copyrights, Offenbach's shows and his music became carrion for the compilers of pasticcio shows in the same way that they had been in his earliest years. One of these, in the wake of the huge success of the Schubert biomusical *Das Dreimäderlhaus,* even attempted to set his music to a version of his life. *Offenbach* (arr Mihály Nádor/Jenő Faragó), produced at Budapest's Király Színház (24 November 1920), fabricated a romance between the composer (song-and-dance comedy player Márton Rátkai) and Hortense Schneider (Juci Lábass), which seemed a little unnecessary, given the fact that he had allegedly had a long liaison with his other principal star, Zulma Bouffar, amongst others. It won a considerable success, racking up 150 performances in Budapest by 25 April 1921, being very soon revived (20 September 1922) and then exported in various versions to Vienna's Neues Wiener Stadttheater (ad Robert Bodanzky, Bruno Hardt-Warden), with Otto Tressler as the composer and Olga Bartos Trau as Hortense, to Germany variously as *Der Meister von Montmartre* and *Pariser Nächte* and, under the title *The Love Song,* to America (13 January 1925), where Allan Prior impersonated the composer alongside Odette Myrtil as Hortense and Evelyn Herbert as his wife, Herminie.

The English-speaking theatre, which made merry pasticcio with the composer's music in the 1860s and 1870s, to the extent of inventing a handful of Offenbach opérettes to texts the composer had never seen (including that of Lecocq's *Fleur de thé*) has, in later years, largely preferred to play the unadventurously small group of his most favored opérettes that have been kept in their repertoire rather than manufacture its own. Broadway, however, was treated to a piece called *The Happiest Girl in the World* (Martin Beck Theater 3 April 1961), which mixed bits of Offenbach with bits of Aristophanes and little success, and London to a piece called *Can-Can* (Adelphi Theatre 8 May 1946), another called *Music at Midnight* (His Majesty's Theatre 10 November 1950) and a new opéra-bouffe, well in the spirit of the old ones, *Christopher Columbus.*

The French musical theatre, too, even at its nadir of recent decades, has still found the space to give revivals of many of Offenbach's works rather than to paste up "new" ones. It is the German-speaking theatre that, by and large, has been responsible not only for the most drastic remakes of the original works but also for the largest number of pasticcio shows. From the very earliest days when Karl Treumann rewrote and had reorchestrated Offenbach's pieces to suit the personnel of his company and local tastes in comedy, Viennese managers concocted their own Offenbach shows, but, after the turn-of-the-century years, even though there were plenty of Offenbach shows to play, the new "make your own Offenbach copyright" shows began in earnest. Amongst them were numbered *Die Heimkehr des Odysseus* (Carltheater 23 March 1917), a version of *L'Île de Tulipatan* with a pasticcio score as *Die glückliche Insel* (1 act, Volksoper 8 June 1918), a composite of music from *Der schwarze Korsar* and elsewhere and an E T A Hoffmann tale made by Julius Stern and Alfred Zamara as *Die Goldschmied von Toledo* (Volksoper 20 October 1920), *Fürstin Tanagra* (Volksoper 1 February 1924), *Der König ihres Herzens* (Johann Strauss-Theater 23 December 1930), a remade version of *Robinson Crusoe* as *Robinsonade* (ad Georg Winckler, Neues Theater, Leipzig 21 September 1930), an *Italian Straw Hat* musical *Hochzeit mit Hindernissen* (Altes Theater, Leipzig 16 February 1930), *Das blaue Hemd von Ithaka* (Admiralspalast, Berlin 13 February 1931), *Die lockere Odette* (Edwin Burmester, Staatstheater, Oldenburg 25 February 1950), *Die Nacht mit Nofretete* (Romain Clairville, Theater am Rossmarkt, Frankfurt 13 November 1951), *Hölle auf Erden* (Georg Kreisler, Hans Haug, Nuremberg 21 January 1967) and *Die klassiche Witwe* (1 act, Cologne 20 June 1969).

In Italy, as early as 1876, a certain Sgr Scalvini brought out an extravaganza called *L'Amore dei tre Melarancie* at Rome's Politeama with a score of pilfered Offenbach music.

1847 **L'Alcôve** (Pittaud de Forges, Adolphe de Leuven) 1 act Salle de la Tour d'Auvergne 24 April

1853 **Le Trésor à Mathurin** (Léon Battu) 1 act Salle Herz 7 May

1853 **Pépito** (Battu, Jules Moinaux) 1 act Théâtre des Variétés 28 October

1854 **Luc et Lucette** (de Forges, Eugène Roche) 1 act Salle Herz 2 May

1855 **Le Decameron** (Jules Méry) 1 act Salle Herz May

1855 **Entrez Messieurs, Mesdames** (Méry, Ludovic Halévy) 1 act Théâtre des Bouffes-Parisiens 5 July

1855 **Les Deux Aveugles** (Moinaux) 1 act Théâtre des Bouffes-Parisiens 5 July

1855 **Une nuit blanche** (Édouard Plouvier) 1 act Théâtre des Bouffes-Parisiens 5 July

1855 **Le Rêve d'une nuit d'été** (Étienne Tréfeu) 1 act Théâtre des Bouffes-Parisiens 30 July

1855 **Oyayaïe, ou La Reine des îles** (Moinaux) 1 act Folies-Nouvelles 4 August

1855 **Le Violoneux** (Eugène Mestépès, Émile Chevalet) 1 act Théâtre des Bouffes-Parisiens 31 August

1855 **Madame Papillon** (Halévy) 1 act Théâtre des Bouffes-Parisiens 3 October

1855 **Paimpol et Périnette** ("De Lussan," ie, de Forges) 1 act Théâtre des Bouffes-Parisiens 29 October

1855 **Ba-ta-clan** (Halévy) 1 act Théâtre des Bouffes-Parisiens 29 December

1856 **Un postillon en gage** (Plouvier, Jules Adenis) 1 act Théâtre des Bouffes-Parisiens 9 February

1856 **Tromb-al-ca-zar, ou Les Criminels dramatiques** (Charles Dupeuty, Ernest Bourget) 1 act Théâtre des Bouffes-Parisiens 3 April

1856 **La Rose de Saint-Flour** (Michel Carré) 1 act Théâtre des Bouffes-Parisiens 12 June

1856 **Les Dragées du baptême** (Dupeuty, Bourget) 1 act Théâtre des Bouffes-Parisiens 18 June

1856 **Le 66** (de Forges, Laurencin) 1 act Théâtre des Bouffes-Parisiens 31 July

1856 **Le Financier et le savetier** (Hector Crémieux [Edmond About, uncredited]) 1 act Théâtre des Bouffes-Parisiens 23 September

1856 **La Bonne d'enfant[s]** (Eugène Bercioux) 1 act Théâtre des Bouffes-Parisiens 14 October

1857 **Les Trois baisers du Diable** (Mestépès) 1 act Théâtre des Bouffes-Parisiens 15 January

1857 **Croquefer, ou le dernier des Paladins** (Adolphe Jaime, Tréfeu) 1 act Théâtre des Bouffes-Parisiens 12 February

1857 **Dragonette** (Mestépès, Jaime) 1 act Théâtre des Bouffes-Parisiens 30 April

1857 **Vent du soir, ou l'horrible festin** (Philippe Gille) 1 act Théâtre des Bouffes-Parisiens 16 May

1857 **Une demoiselle en loterie** (Jaime, Crémieux) 1 act Théâtre des Bouffes-Parisiens 27 July

1857 **Le Mariage aux lanternes** revised *Le Trésor à Mathurin* (Carré, Battu) 1 act Théâtre des Bouffes-Parisiens 10 October

1857 **Les Deux Pêcheurs** (Dupeuty, Bourget) 1 act Théâtre des Bouffes-Parisiens 13 November

1858 **Mesdames de la Halle** (Armand Lapointe) 1 act Théâtre des Bouffes-Parisiens 3 March

1858 **La Chatte métamorphosée en femme** (Eugène Scribe, Mélesville) 1 act Théâtre des Bouffes-Parisiens 19 April

1858 **Orphée aux enfers** (Crémieux, Halévy) Théâtre des Bouffes-Parisiens 21 October

1859 **Un mari à la porte** (Alfred Delacour, Léon Morand) 1 act Théâtre des Bouffes-Parisiens 22 June

1859 **Les Vivandières de la grande armée** (Jaime, de Forges) 1 act Théâtre des Bouffes-Parisiens 6 July

1859 **Geneviève de Brabant** (Tréfeu) Théâtre des Bouffes-Parisiens 19 November

1860 **Daphnis et Chloë** (Clairville, Jules Cordier) 1 act Théâtre des Bouffes-Parisiens 27 March

1860 **Barkouf** (Scribe, Henry Boisseaux) Opéra-Comique 24 December

1861 **La Chanson de Fortunio** (Crémieux, Halévy) 1 act Théâtre des Bouffes-Parisiens 5 January

1861 **Le Pont des soupirs** (Crémieux, Halévy) Théâtre des Bouffes-Parisiens 23 March

1861 **M Choufleuri restera chez lui le . . .** (''Saint-Remy,'' Crémieux, Halévy) 1 act Présidence du Corps-legislatif 31 May; Théâtre des Bouffes-Parisiens 14 September

1861 **Apothicaire et perruquier** (Élie Frébault) 1 act Théâtre des Bouffes-Parisiens 17 October

1861 **Le Roman comique** (Crémieux, Halévy) Théâtre des Bouffes-Parisiens 10 December

1862 **M et Mme Denis** (Laurençin, Michel Delaporte) 1 act Théâtre des Bouffes-Parisiens 11 January

1862 **Le Voyage de MM Dunanan père et fils** (Paul Siraudin, Moinaux) Théâtre des Bouffes-Parisiens 23 March

1862 **Les Bavards** (ex- *Bavard et Bavarde*) (Charles Nuitter) 1 act Ems 11 June; revised version in 2 acts Théâtre des Bouffes-Parisiens 20 February 1863

1862 **Jacqueline** (Crémieux, Halévy) 1 act Théâtre des Bouffes-Parisiens 14 October

1863 **Il Signor Fagotto** (Nuitter, Tréfeu) 1 act Ems 11 July

1863 **Lischen et Fritzchen** (Paul Boisselot) 1 act Ems 21 July; Théâtre des Bouffes-Parisiens 5 January 1864

1864 **L'Amour chanteur** (Nuitter, Ernest L'Épine) 1 act Théâtre des Bouffes-Parisiens 5 January

1864 **Die Rheinnixen** (Nuitter, Tréfeu) Hofoper, Vienna 4 February

1864 **Les Géorgiennes** (Moinaux) Théâtre des Bouffes-Parisiens 16 March

1864 **Le Fifre enchante** (aka *Le soldat magicien*) (Nuitter, Tréfeu) 1 act Ems 9 July; Théâtre des Bouffes-Parisiens 30 September 1868

1864 **Jeanne qui pleure et Jean qui rit** (Nuitter, Tréfeu) 1 act Ems 19 July; Théâtre des Bouffes-Parisiens 3 November 1865

1864 **La Belle Hélène** (Meilhac, Halévy) Théâtre des Variétés 17 December

1865 **Coscoletto** (aka *Le Lazzarone*) (Nuitter, Tréfeu) Ems 24 July

1865 **Les Bergers** (Crémieux, Gille) Théâtre des Bouffes-Parisiens 11 December

1866 **Barbe-bleue** (Meilhac, Halévy) Théâtre des Variétés 5 February

1866 **La Vie parisienne** (Meilhac, Halévy) Palais-Royal 31 October

1867 **La Grande-Duchesse [de Gérolstein]** (Meilhac, Halévy) Théâtre des Variétés 12 April

1867 **La Permission de dix heures** (Mélesville, P Carmouche) 1 act Ems 9 July; Théâtre de la Renaissance 4 September 1873

1867 **Le Leçon de chant electromagnétique** (Bourget) 1 act Ems August

1867 **Robinson Crusoe** (Eugène Cormon, Crémieux) Opéra-Comique 23 November

1868 **Le Château à Toto** (Meilhac, Halévy) Palais-Royal 6 May

1868 **L'Île de Tulipatan** (Henri Chivot, Alfred Duru) 1 act Théâtre des Bouffes-Parisiens 30 September

1868 **La Périchole** (Meilhac, Halévy) Théâtre des Variétés 6 October

1869 **Vert-Vert** (Meilhac, Nuitter) Opéra-Comique 10 March

1869 **La Diva** (Meilhac, Halévy) Théâtre des Bouffes-Parisiens 22 March

1869 **La Princesse de Trébizonde** (Nuitter, Tréfeu) Baden-Baden 31 July; Théâtre des Bouffes-Parisiens 7 December

1869 **Les Brigands** (Meilhac, Halévy) Théâtre des Variétés 10 December

1869 **La Romance de la Rose** (Tréfeu, Jules Prével) 1 act Théâtre des Bouffes-Parisiens 11 December

1871 **Boule de neige** revised *Barkouf* Théâtre des Bouffes-Parisiens 14 December

1872 **Le Roi Carotte** (Victorien Sardou) Théâtre de la Gaîté 15 January

1872 **Fantasio** (Paul de Musset) Opéra-Comique 18 January

1872 **Fleurette** (*Trompeter und Näherin*) (de Forges, Laurençin) 1 act Carltheater, Vienna 8 March

1872 **Der schwarze Korsar** (Nuitter, Tréfeu) Theater an der Wien, Vienna 21 September

1873 **Les Braconniers** (Chivot, Duru) Théâtre des Variétés 29 January

1873 **Pomme d'api** (William Busnach, Halévy) 1 act Théâtre de la Renaissance 4 September

1873 **La Jolie Parfumeuse** (Crémieux, Ernest Blum) Théâtre des la Renaissance 29 November

1874 **Bagatelle** (Crémieux, Blum) 1 act Théâtre des Bouffes-Parisiens 21 May

1874 **Madame l'Archiduc** (Albert Millaud, Halévy) Théâtre des Bouffes-Parisiens 31 October

1874 **Whittington** (H B Farnie) Alhambra, London 26 December

1875 **La Boulangère a des écus** (Meilhac, Halévy) Théâtre des Variétés 19 October

1875 **Le Voyage dans la lune** (Eugène Leterrier, Albert Vanloo, Arnold Mortier) Théâtre de la Gaîté 26 October

1875 **La Créole** (Millaud, Meilhac) Théâtre des Bouffes-Parisiens 3 November

1875 **Tarte à la crème** (Millaud) 1 act Théâtre des Bouffes-Parisiens 14 December

1876 **Pierrette et Jacquot** (Jules Noriac, Gille) 1 act Théâtre des Bouffes-Parisiens 13 October

1876 **La Boîte au lait** (Grangé, Noriac) Théâtre des Bouffes-Parisiens 3 November

1877 **Le Docteur Ox** (Mortier, Gille) Théâtre des Variétés 26 January

1877 **La Foire Saint-Laurent** (Crémieux, Albert Saint-Albin [Ernest Blum, uncredited]) Théâtre des Folies-Dramatiques 10 February

1878 **Maître Péronilla** (Offenbach, Nuitter, Paul Ferrier) Théâtre des Bouffes-Parisiens 13 March

1878 **Madame Favart** (Chivot, Duru) Théâtre des Folies-Dramatiques 28 December

1879 **La Marocaine** (Ferrier, Halévy) Théâtre des Bouffes-Parisiens 13 January

1879 **La Fille du tambour-major** (Chivot, Duru) Théâtre des Folies-Dramatiques 13 December

1880 **Belle Lurette** (Blum, Édouard Blau, Raoul Toche) Théâtre de la Renaissance 30 October

1881 **Mademoiselle Moucheron** (Leterrier, Vanloo) 1 act Théâtre de la Renaissance 10 May

Memoirs: *Offenbach en Amerique: Notes d'un musicien en voyage* (Calmann-Levy, Paris, 1877); Biographies and Literature: Schneider, L: *Offenbach* (Librairie Académique Perrin, Paris, 1923), Martinet, A: *Offenbach* (Dentu, Paris, 1887), Decaux, A: *Offenbach* (Pierre Amiot, Paris, 1958), Brindejoint-Offenbach, J: *Offenbach, mon grand-père* (Plon, Paris, 1940), Faris, A: *Jacques Offenbach* (Scribner, New York, 1980), Pourvoyeur, R: *Offenbach* (Editions du Seuil, 1994), Durfresne, C: *Offenbach ou la gaîté parisienne* (Criterion, Paris, 1992), Dufresne, C: *Offenbach ou la joie de vivre* (Perrin, 1998), Schipperges, T, Dohr, C, and Rüllke, K: *Bibliotheca Offenbachiana* (Verlag Dohr, Cologne, 1998), Hawig, P: *Jacques Offenbach: Facetten zu Leben und Werk* (Verlag Dohr, Cologne, 1999), Harding, J: *Jacques Offenbach: A Biography* (John Calder, London, 1980), Brancour, R: *Offenbach* (Henri Laurens, Paris, 1929), Rissin, D: *Offenbach ou le rire en musique* (Fayard, 1980), Moss, A, Marvel, E: *Cancan and Barcarolle: Life and Times of Jacques Offenbach* (Exposition Press, New York, 1954), Kracauer, S: *Orpheus in Paris: Offenbach and the Paris of His Time* (Knopf, New York, 1938), Renaud, M, Barrault, J-L (eds): *Le Siècle d'Offenbach* (René Julliard, Paris, 1959), Schneidereit, O: *Jacques Offenbach* (VEB Bibliographisches Institut, Leipzig, 1966), Yon, J-C: *Offenbach* (Biographies Gallimard, Paris, 2000), etc

THE OFFICERS' MESS (and how they got out of it) Musical farce in 3 acts by Sydney Blow and Douglas Hoare. Music by Philip Braham. St Martin's Theatre, London, 7 November 1918.

One of the rarely successful attempts by revue producer André Charlot to stage a book musical, *The Officers' Mess* was a follow-up to its authors' *Telling the Tale.* Unlike that show, however, the new one was not a French farce adaptation, but an attempt at an English equivalent. Three soldiers (it was wartime, and all good musical-comedy heroes were soldiers), played by head comic Ralph Lynn, Herbert Sparling and Evan Thomas, place a newspaper advertisement devised to lure some nice girls to a ''borrowed'' apartment. The advertisement instead attracts jewel robbers, police, Odette Myrtil as a French actress, the owner of the flat, and, in the second act, an ingenue for each man. Phil Braham's lively score included a ragtime version of Tchaikovsky's ''1812'' for Miss Myrtil, as well as songs both comical (''I Am the APM,'' ''The Major, the Captain and the Loot'') and crooning (''Float with the Tide'') in the new mode, conducted by the composer of ''In a Persian Market,'' Alfred Ketélby. The show ran 200 West End performances with a shift to the larger Prince's Theatre in mid-run, and its story was subsequently made into a film without its songs.

The songs were still reasonably intact, however, for an Australian season played on Hugh D McIntosh's Tivoli circuit with Vera Pearce (Kitty) delivering ''Give Me a Cozy Little Corner'' and dancing the Charleston alongside Claude Flemming (APM), Bert Clarke (Tony), Marie La Varre (Cora), Ellis Holland, Hugh Steyne and assorted specialities and interpolated songs. It played 10 weeks in Melbourne and a fine 90 nights in Sydney (Tivoli 23 August 1919) to end its Australian life well on the credit side.

Australia: Tivoli, Melbourne 7 June 1919

OF THEE I SING Musical comedy in 2 acts by George S Kaufman and Morrie Ryskind. Lyrics by Ira Gershwin. Music by George Gershwin. Music Box Theater, New York, 26 December 1931.

George S Kaufman and the Gershwin brothers had ventured into the mirth-provoking world of national poli-

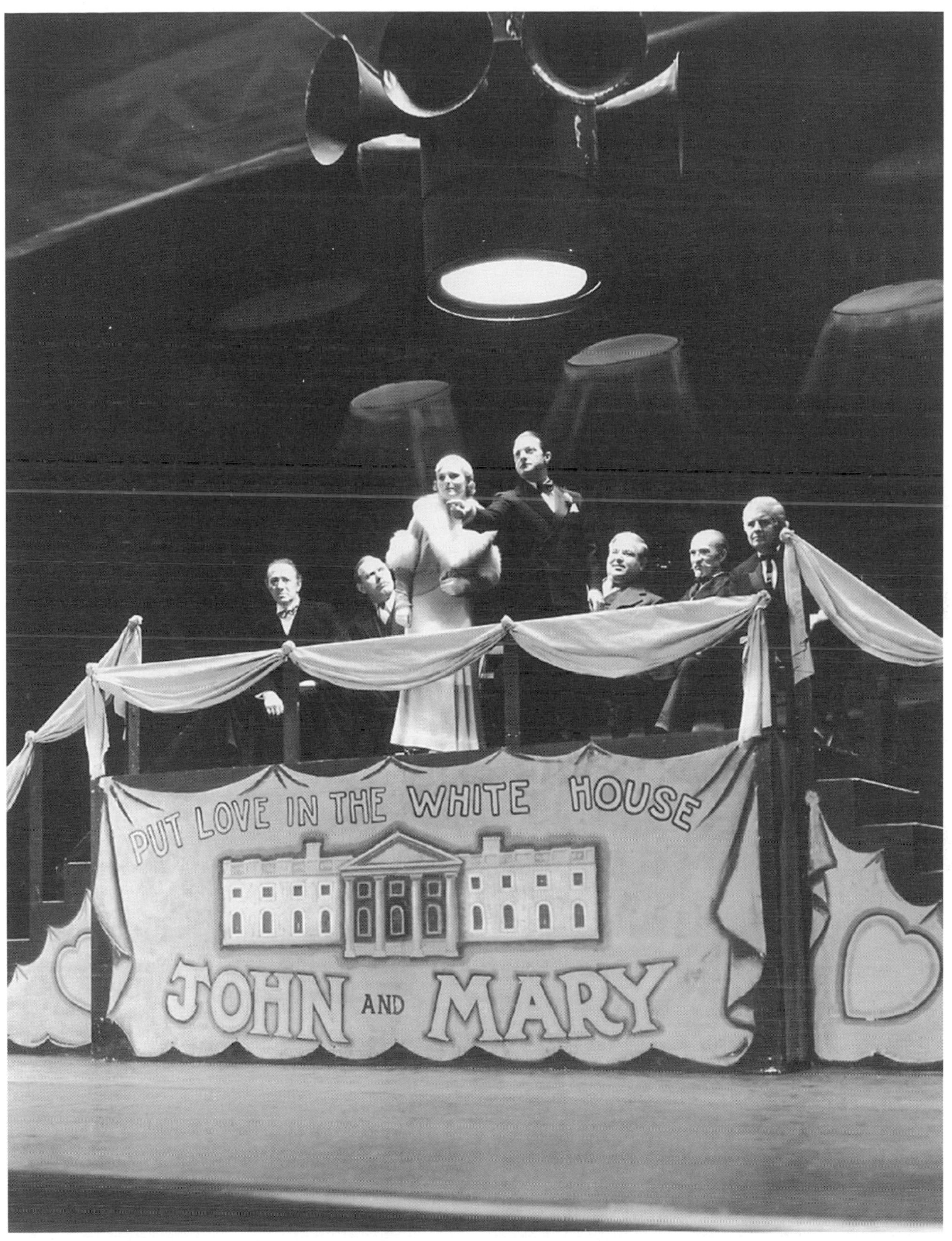

Plate 285. **Of Thee I Sing.** *John P Wintergreen (William Gaxton) running for the Presidency on a platform of love.*

tics for the first time in 1927 with their musical *Strike Up the Band.* The show had folded on the road to New York, but a second version, with its libretto remolded by Morrie Ryskind and remounted in 1930, did better, and the new *Strike Up the Band*'s 191 Broadway performances were sufficient to encourage the collaborators to write another piece with an off–White House tinge, to have another try at burlesquing those most popular burlesque subjects in the world—those rapacious numbskulls in political power and the insane system that put them there.

In fact, what the authors turned out this time around was a delicious piece of on-the-mark foolery in the best vein of such pieces as *La Grande-Duchesse de Gérolstein* or *Chilpéric*: an opéra-bouffe full of endearingly exaggerated and theatrical characters who get themselves involved in a series of almost surreal events as they struggle for wealth and/or marriage and their country's throne. The difference was, of course, that this being the United States of America, the throne in question was not that of Merovingia or Gérolstein, but that seat of power at 1600 Pennsylvania Avenue, Washington, DC.

John P Wintergreen (William Gaxton) has been chosen to represent his party in the election for United States President at one of those hilarious mock-democratic affairs called a Convention. Convention has also given him a running mate—if anyone can remember the fellow's name. Oh yes, it's Alexander Throttlebottom (Victor Moore). In planning their man's campaign for the top job, Wintergreen's party committee sound out a Common Person and discover that what interests the Average American most (after money, of course) is Love. So they decide to base their campaign on love. Bachelor Wintergreen must have a romance and a wedding—these will provoke votes. To find the girl, they hold a contest, and the luscious Miss Diana Devereaux (Grace Brinkley) is announced the winner. Unfortunately for the committee, Wintergreen has decided, in the meantime, that he's going to marry nice, homely secretary Mary Turner (Lois Moran), who can bake corn muffins and sew. Mary and John sweep to victory and the White House on their love ticket, but Diana Devereaux will not be balked. She sues, then (since she is called Devereaux) she gets hold of the French ambassador and turns the whole thing into an international incident. She looks like the winner, but Mary comes up with a case breaker: she has a baby. Diplomatic relations hang on an umbilical cord until a logical answer of Gilbertian proportions is found. When the President is unable to fulfill his duty, it falls to the Vice President to deputize. Someone must find what's his name, who will marry Diana Devereaux and allow the occupants of the White House to get on with ruling their country and eating their corn muffins in peace.

The Gershwins supplied a score for *Of Thee I Sing* that was in the same bouffe manner as the libretto, characterized by the use of the phrase ''of thee I sing'' from the American anthem, which was thrilled out before the crowds at Madison Square on election night, only to be deliciously defused: ''Of thee I sing, baby. . . .'' The campaign zoomed to triumph on ''Love Is Sweeping the Country,'' Mary trilled out a veritable opéra-bouffe waltz scena ''I'm About to Be a Mother,'' and Mlle Devereaux pulled off her petals in rejected despair in ''I Was a Beautiful Blossom'' among a series of concerted pieces that bubbled with musical and textual humor, and a jolly jumble of reminiscences of everything from Gilbert and Sullivan to *Florodora* to Vienna.

Of Thee I Sing had fun with its music, but it also had fun with its subject and its characters, of whom the Vice President whose name and face no one can ever remember (well, how many Vice Presidents do you remember? Or want to remember?) proved the biggest winner, particularly as played by Moore. There was the occasional touch of personal or particular parody—various of the senatorial and political characters were made to resemble physically current incumbents in the old, traditional manner, without those people being personally parodied in the text—but mostly *Of Thee I Sing* was blossoming burlesque and not biting, or even nibbling satire. Of course, it succeeded very much better as such. The show stayed for 411 performances on Broadway, and the text was awarded a Pulitzer Prize for Drama (the first musical libretto thus to be favored) before *Of Thee I Sing* went out on the road with Oscar Shaw, Donald Meek and Harriette Lake at the head of its cast.

Perhaps surprisingly, given its very general fun, the show did not get taken up outside America. Equally surprisingly, given the praise it won from critics and discerning audiences early on, it has had a disappointing career since. A 1952 revival (Ziegfeld Theater 5 May) with Jack Carson (John), Paul Hartman (Throttlebottom), Betty Oakes (Mary) and Lenore Lonergan (Diana) featured, and with author Kaufman as director, failed in 72 performances, and although a version of the show was seen on CBS television in 1972 with Carroll O'Connor, Jack Gilford, Chloris Leachman and Michele Lee in the leading roles, *Of Thee I Sing*'s subsequent theatre life has been limited to intermittent productions in regional theatres. Even in the 1980s and 1990s, with the great vogue for and promotion of Gershwin productions and for anything with a whiff of politics to it, the best that *Of Thee I Sing* managed was a recorded concert performance, given in tandem with a similar performance of its sequel *Let 'em Eat Cake.*

That sequel may, in fact, have been partly responsible for the eclipse of *Of Thee I Sing.* Produced two seasons after the original piece, it went further into surreality, in a tale that had John (Gaxton), Mary (Miss

Moran) and Throttlebottom (Moore) bumped from their presidential positions and leading a revolution to get back in by force. At one point Throttlebottom is sentenced to the guillotine, but by the end of the evening he is President, and John and Mary are working in the clothing business. Some incoherent plotting and a wholesale lack of the joyous tone that had made the first show such a treat contributed to this rather bilious piece shuttering after 90 performances, and perhaps taking something of the shine off its predecessor at the same time.

Whatever the reason, *Of Thee I Sing* remained more spoken of than played through an era where the Gershwins' more lazily digestible works were all the fashion, although concert performances were given in America at the Brooklyn Academy of Music (paired with *Let 'em Eat Cake*) with Jack Gilford as Throttlebottom, and in Britain (''semi-staged concert performance'') by Opera North, during its continuing run of productions of foreign musicals by upmarketed composers. Confusingly billed as ''a centenary production'' (the musical was only 67; it was the centennial of the composer's birth that was being ''celebrated''), it featured William Dazeley as Wintergreen, Rebecca Caine as Mary and Steven Beard in the plum role of Throttlebottom. Finally, however, just before the dawn of the 2000s, the enterprising little Bridewell Theatre in London gave *Of Thee I Sing* its British stage premiere in a month-long season in which Gavin Lee (Wintergreen), Fiona Benjamin (Mary) and Michael Winsor (Throttlebottom) took the leading roles.

UK: Bridewell Theatre 4 August 1999

Recordings: revival cast (Capitol), TV cast (Columbia), Brooklyn Academy of Music concert (w *Let 'em Eat Cake*) (CBS), etc

Literature: Wintergreen, J P (Ryskind, M, ed): *The Diary of an ex-President* (Minton, Balch & Company, New York, 1932)

OH, BOY! Musical comedy in 2 acts by Guy Bolton and P G Wodehouse. Music by Jerome Kern. Princess Theater, New York, 20 February 1917.

Librettist Guy Bolton and songwriter Jerome Kern, this time with the collaboration of novelist-cum-lyricist P G Wodehouse, followed up their successful small-stage ventures *Nobody Home* and *Very Good Eddie* with another piece in the same vein. *Oh, Boy!,* unlike its two predecessors, was not an adaptation, but Bolton took his inspiration from the French vaudeville stage, and from such winningly translated versions of its products as *The Girl from Kays* and *Oh! Oh! Delphine,* in constructing a libretto based on well-used Continental comedy characters: the lady discovered in the rooms of the married (or almost married) man, the bride's pompous parents and the nice-but-strict wealthy relative who needs to be convinced and/or placated before a happy and moneyed ending can be reached.

On this occasion the feminine intruder into the home of George Budd (Tom Powers) and his secretly new little wife, Lou Ellen (Marie Carroll), is one Jackie Sampson (Anna Wheaton), who is fleeing from the law after landing one on an over-amorous gentleman (Frank McGinn) in a cabaret bar. Amongst the farcical events that follow, Jackie masquerades both as George's wife and as his Quaker aunt. Events wind up to their comic pitch when real Aunt Penelope (Edna May Oliver) turns up and knocks back a couple of courage-maintaining Bronxes intended for the phony aunt, Jackie's over-amorous gent turns out to have been the disapproving father of George's covert bride, and a comical policeman appears on the scene to stir and shake up all the elements of the action until they come out into a joyfully predictable denouement. Hal Forde added to the high spirits of the piece as Jim, one of those ''amusing'' best friends whom you wouldn't want for a friend in a thousand years, whilst the two most forward of the floosies whom he smuggles into George's flat for a rave-up were played by girls who would make their name in another medium: Marion Davies and Justine Johnstone. Dance pair Dorothy Dickson and Carl Hyson performed a speciality.

Kern's score for *Oh, Boy!* included some attractive numbers, of which the ringing duo ''Till the Clouds Roll By'' (George/Jackie) proved the most popular, alongside a winsome waltz for Lou Ellen about being ''An Old-Fashioned Wife'' and an interestingly Leslie Stuartish, long-lined number for the comic heroine about her eclectic tastes, ''Rolled into One.'' The comedy was served by Jackie and Jim's dream of ''Nesting Time in Flatbush'' and by one of the handful of songs popped in purely for decoration, telling the tale of ''Flubby Dub, the Caveman.''

If *Oh, Boy!* was made up of familiar elements, it was extremely well made up, and its combination of good, well worked out comic situations and winning songs and dances were precisely what was needed for the kind of small auditorium for which it was designed. The show was greeted with delighted notices and ran in New York for a very fine 463 performances. It shifted from the little Princess to the Casino Theater in the latter days of this run to take advantage of the additional low-price seating the larger theatre offered, before setting out on a long and large series of touring productions.

Australia welcomed the show, in quick time, and in July 1918 J C Williamson Ltd opened their production of *Oh, Boy!* in Sydney with Maud Fane (Jackie), William Green (Jim), George Willoughby (Judge) and London's Gaiety star Connie Ediss as Aunt Penelope. It played seven weeks before being replaced by a revival of *So Long, Letty!,* then five more weeks in Melbourne (Theatre Royal 14 September 1919) before *High Jinks* was brought back as a substitute, compiling a fair record but not one to equal those of those two established favorites.

London's Grossmith and Laurillard took up the British rights to the piece and, after having had the good idea of casting revue comedienne Beatrice Lillie as Jackie opposite Broadway's Powers, had the less good idea of housing the show in the out-of-the-mainstream Kingsway Theatre. Another rising actress, Isabel Jeans, played the obviously good-luck-bringing part of the foremost floosie, and one Harry Tierney number, ''Wedding Bells,'' was slipped into the show's score. The producers also rechristened the piece *Oh, Joy!,* which seemed unneccesary as, in the fashion of the time, it was just as irrelevant as the original title. A fair run of 167 performances was followed by one tour.

Oh, Boy! was revived at the Goodspeed Opera House in 1964 and again in 1984, and it was presented in New York in 1979 by the New Princess Theatre Company, with Judith Blazer starred.

A 1919 film version, made by Albert Capellani, featured Creighton Haley, June Caprice and Joseph Conyers but, of course, not the songs. Or the dialogue.

Australia: Her Majesty's Theatre, Sydney 14 September 1918; UK: Kingsway Theatre *Oh, Joy!* 27 January 1919

Film: 1919

Recording: London cast recording (WRC)

OH, I SAY! Musical comedy in 2 acts by Sydney Blow and Douglas Hoare based on their play of the same name and its original *Une nuit de noces* by Henri Kéroul and Albert Barré. Lyrics by Harry B Smith. Music by Jerome Kern. Casino Theater, New York, 30 October 1913.

Kéroul and Barré's play *Une nuit de noces* (Théâtre des Folies-Dramatiques 2 February 1904) was enjoying a fine London run that would eventually total no fewer than 288 performances in Blow and Hoare's adaptation at the Criterion Theatre (28 May 1913) when the adapters engaged hired to musicalize the piece for the Shuberts. Jerome Kern was given the job of providing the music, and Cecil Cunningham was cast as the actress Sidonie de Mornay whose naughty maid (Clara Palmer) leases her apartment to a pair of newlyweds (Charles Meakins, Alice Yorke) only to have her mistress return unexpectedly and to discover the bridegroom is her old boyfriend. Joseph Herbert was cast as the bride's father.

Kern provided some catchy numbers, notably the unusual, loping love duo ''Alone at Last'' and the hammering dance-song ''Katy-Did'', and *Oh, I Say!* opened at the Harmanus Bleecker Hall in Albany and then at Broadway's Casino Theater whilst the play ran on in London. It did not succeed. It closed after 68 performances and was put out on the road under the theoretically more alluring title of *Their Wedding Night.*

However, five years later the authors took up their text again, threw out the score, replaced it with some songs by the newly popular Phil Braham, then Britain's most adept practitioner of the new dance-time style of music, and had it produced in London by Gerald Kirby and John Wyndham under the title *Telling the Tale* (Ambassadors Theatre 31 August 1918). Marie Blanche played Sidonie, Lucienne Dervyle had the most successful song about ''Rin Tin Tin and Ninette,'' and the production was filled with wartime references and patriotic bits and pieces. It ran 90 performances before being taken into the country by a touring company that had agreed to stop touring the non-musical version of the show before *Telling the Tale* opened in exchange for the rights.

OH, KAY! Musical comedy in 2 acts by Guy Bolton and P G Wodehouse. Lyrics by Ira Gershwin. Additional lyrics by Howard Dietz. Music by George Gershwin. Imperial Theater, New York, 8 November 1926.

Although the play in question had been around for nearly a quarter of a century, and French comedies—credited and uncredited—had been the raw material for Broadway libretti for some two decades, the 1926–27 season saw the announcement and production of two musical comedies based on Maurice Hennequin and Pierre Veber's hit French comedy *La Présidente* (Théâtre des Bouffes-Parisiens 12 September 1902). One of the two musicals was called *Oh, Please!,* was produced by Charles Dillingham and starred British revue star Beatrice Lillie; the other was called *Cheerio!,* was produced by Aarons and Freedley and starred British revue star Gertrude Lawrence. Both had fine authorial credits: *Oh, Please!* was the work of Anne Caldwell and of *No, No, Nanette*'s Otto Harbach and composer Vincent Youmans; *Cheerio!* was written by Guy Bolton, Plum Wodehouse and the Gershwin brothers.

Cheerio! opened at Philadelphia on 18 October, whilst *Oh, Please!,* already into rewrites, pitched camp at the Forrest Theater in the same city. If the battle of the *Présidentes* was on, it was soon looking like a pretty one-sided battle, for the unready *Oh, Please!* suffered a series of postponements and by the time it opened on 19 November, *Cheerio!,* with its title switched now to *Oh, Kay!,* was already out of Philadelphia and on Broadway. The show by now had given up saying that it was based on *La Présidente,* and, indeed, their resemblance between the two pieces was no longer precisely startling.

Whilst Jimmy Winter (Oscar Shaw) is away, a bunch of rum runners have been using his Long Island home as a depot. The chief criminals are a tax-paupered aristocratic British pair, the Duke of Durham (Gerald Oliver Smith) and his sister, Lady Kay (Miss Lawrence), who are being assisted by a couple of local bootleggers, Shorty McKee (Victor Moore) and Larry Potter (Harland Dixon). When Jimmy returns, he brings a bride, the acidulous Judge's daughter, Constance (Sascha Beaumont). But Constance is not around for long, for there has been a legal hitch in the marriage and, of course, whilst she is chastely spending the night in an hotel prefatory to being properly remarried the next day, rum-running Lady Kay blunders into Jimmy's now occupied bedroom. By the time Kay has impersonated Mrs Winter and Jane, the maid, and Shorty has done service as both a butler and a revenue officer, and the plot has taken a bundle of comic turns and back-turns, Kay, rather than Constance, ends up as the ultimate Mrs Winter. Harry T Shannon played a ubiquitous revenue officer who is not what he seems, whilst twins Marion and Madeleine Fairbanks were a couple of incidental twins who provided another running gag and a couple of numbers with Dixon (who had equally little to do with the plot) in what was otherwise a pretty tight-knit show.

The songs for *Oh, Kay!* included several that would became favorites. Miss Lawrence cooed over the thought of "Someone to Watch Over Me" and duetted "Maybe" and then "Do, Do, Do" with Jimmy as a part of their pretense at being husband and wife in the presence of the ever-snooping revenue officer, whilst Dixon scored with his two pasted-in pieces, the for-no-particular-reason instruction to "Clap Yo' Hands" and a description of his "Fidgety Feet." There was also a jolly title song, to which Howard Dietz supplied the late lyric in place of an indisposed Ira Gershwin.

Oh, Kay! proved a splendid vehicle for Miss Lawrence, Moore and Shaw, all of whom had delightful roles in what was certainly one of the best musical-comedy libretti that Bolton and/or Wodehouse manufactured, together or separately, in their long careers. And Miss Lawrence and Shaw were also provided with some delicious musical moments. The public proved swift to appreciate both the performers and their material, and *Oh, Kay!* remained at Broadway's Imperial Theater for 256 performances, whilst the rather bedraggled *Oh, Please!* came and went in 75 nights.

The following year the producers tied up with London's Musical Plays Ltd and exported their show and its star to Britain. Harold French (Jimmy), John Kirby (Shorty), Eric Coxon (Larry) and Claude Hulbert (Duke) supported Miss Lawrence with rather less star power than Moore and Shaw had done, and *Oh, Kay!* was rewarded with a good 214 performances in the West End, before going on the road in two companies in 1928–29 as part of a rush of musical-comedy productions that included two *Hit the Decks*, three *So This Is Loves*, two *No, No, Nanettes*, two *Lady Lucks*, a *Mercenary Mary*, an *Oh, Letty!*, a *Good News*, a *Girl Friend* and a *Tip-Toes*. In the same season, First National put out a silent film version of the plot, with Colleen Moore, Lawrence Gray, Alan Hale and Ford Sterling featured.

Although *Oh, Kay!* apparently went no further (Australia took *Queen High, Castles in the Air, Katja the Dancer, The Desert Song, Hit the Deck* and *Rio Rita* from the Broadway season's crop, but not *Oh, Kay!*), it remained a favorite in both America and Britain in the years that followed, winning regular regional productions and establishing itself, behind *No, No, Nanette,* as one of the flagbearers of 1920s musical comedy to theatregoers of later decades. It was also mounted for a number of more metropolitan revivals, in a series of altered versions, beginning with a mounting at off-Broadway's East 74th Street Theater in 1960 (19 April). Marti Stevens (Kay), Bernie West (Shorty) and David Daniels (Jimmy) starred in a version for which Wodehouse reorganized the score, relyricking two numbers, adding two from Gershwin's early *Primrose* with fresh words attached, and others from Gershwin's film score *Damsel in Distress* and *Lady, Be Good!* The revival played 89 performances. Another, 1978 revival, mounted in Toronto (Royal Alexandra Theater 20 July, ad Thomas Meehan), ended its Broadway-bound life in Washington.

A lightweight London revival played 228 times in the specially receptive surroundings of the Westminster Theater in 1974 (7 March), but another production mounted at the Chichester Festival Theatre (17 May 1984, ad Ned Sherrin, Tony Geiss), with a cast headed by Geoffrey Hutchings, Michael Siberry and Jane Carr, did not make the intended move to London. However, more than 60 years after Moore and Lawrence's triumph, a version of *Oh, Kay!* did return to Broadway, when David Merrick transferred an updated production (ad James Racheff, Dan Siretta) with a racially limited cast from Connecticut's Goodspeed Opera House to New York's Richard Rodgers Theater (25 October 1990). It closed after 77 performances, and an attempt at a return (2 April Lunt-Fontanne Theater) shuttered after 16 previews, but left one or two folk wondering whether a skillful, unbutchered, racially oblivious reproduction of the original show mightn't have proved a winner.

UK: His Majesty's Theatre 21 September 1927

Film: First National 1928

Recordings: original London cast (Smithsonian), off Broadway revival cast (20th Fox/DRG), studio cast (Columbia), etc

OH, LADY! LADY!! Musical comedy in 2 acts by Guy Bolton and P G Wodehouse. Music by Jerome Kern. Princess Theater, New York, 1 February 1918.

Built to follow the same team's successful *Oh, Boy!* into the small Princess Theater, *Oh, Lady! Lady!!* (the title was a minstrel catchline that had characteristically little to do with anything) did not come up to its predecessor in anything but its number of exclamation points. After the brightly knit vaudeville-libretti of *Nobody Home* and *Oh, Boy!,* and the ingenuous good cheer of the play-based *Very Good Eddie* and *Leave It to Jane,* the new show plunged back into worn-out stage cliché with its tale of stolen jewels and temporarily broken romances. Rich Mollie (Vivienne Segal) is going to wed Willoughby Finch (Carl Randall) when Fanny (Florence Shirley), the girlfriend of his valet, Spike (Edward Abeles), steals the family jewels. Mollie's mother suspects Bill—whose old girlfriend (Carroll McComas) has also come on the scene—and she is eager to call the wedding off, but the valet steals the jewels back and everything is all right. Bride and groom shared the most attractive number in Kern's made-for-dancing score, a catchily scooping 2/4 duet, ''Not Yet,'' remade from a number previously interpolated into the out-of-town flop version of the German hit *Polnische Wirtschaft.* However, the number that eventually proved the most durable, Miss Segal's song in praise of her ''Bill,'' was relegated to a moment in the first-act finale on the road to town and had to wait another decade to become a favorite.

First put on the stage at Albany's Harmanus Bleeker Hall on 7 January, *Oh, Lady! Lady!!* took its time coming to town, arrived in well-worked condition and was well received, but its run of 219 performances in its tiny house was much less than was expected of it. Indeed, from a producer's point of view, it was a disappointment all around, for it toured unproductively and failed to win any major overseas productions beyond a season for J C Williamson Ltd in Australia. There, Dorothy Brunton, who somehow managed to find the opportunity to sing ''My Mammy'' during the course of the evening, was featured above the title, with Alfred Frith and Edith Drayson supporting her for just five weeks in Melbourne and another under-par run in Sydney.

Although the musical itself was never filmed, Wodehouse later made over his libretto as a novel and a screenplay called *The Small Bachelor* (1927).

Australia: Her Majesty's Theatre, Melbourne 11 June 1921

OH! OH! DELPHINE Musical comedy in 2 acts by C M S McLellan based on *La Grimpette* by Georges Berr and Marcel Guillemaud. Music by Ivan Caryll. Knickerbocker Theater, New York, 30 September 1912.

McLellan and Caryll had scored a grand international success with their adaptation of Berr and Guillemaud's 1907 Parisian comedy *Le Satyre* as *The Pink Lady,* and they decided to follow it with another musical based on an earlier work by the same authors, *La Grimpette* (Palais-Royal 7 February 1906).

The plot of the show was a wife-swapping one, in which Victor Jolibeau (Scott Welsh), an artist in search of a model with a perfect left shoulder, and his estranged wife, Delphine (Grace Edmond), agree to change partners with Alphonse Bouchotte (Frank McIntyre) and his wife Simone (Stella Hoban). A Persian lady of some charms called Bimboula (Octavia Broske) was also mixed up in the swappings. However, one of those rich uncles (George A Beane) who hold power over the life and love life of their juniors through their wallets and their wills turns up, and propriety has, at least, to seem to be restored. But when the two pairs get temporarily back in their old combinations they find they like it, and the swap is called off. The action was set at the Hotel Beaurivage in the naval port of Brest, allowing some dashing uniforms to sweep by, and the title, unlike most of the *Oh!* titles that littered the theatre of the time, actually had a point to it. One of the prominent characters of the piece (it was even the poster for the show) was Delphine's pet parrot, whose warning cry ''Oh! Oh! Delphine'' perforated the action at the slightest hint of anything feather-raising.

Caryll supplied another delightful score, topped by a particularly bubbly title duo for Delphine and Bouchotte, assisted by the chorus and the parrot, Bouchotte's comical complaint ''Everything's at Home Except Your Wife, the husband-and-wife waltz duet ''Can We Forget?,'' a concerted ''Poor Bouchotte'' and a broadly'' gliding ''The Venus Waltz'' for Jolibeau and Bimboula, the last two of which would have seemed even finer had they resembled *The Pink Lady*'s ''Donny Did'' and ''Beautiful Lady'' just a little less clearly.

Klaw and Erlanger's Broadway production was enthusiastically received (''hit the bull's eye again'') and if it ran a little less long than its predecessor (258 performances) that was perhaps partly because it came along second, and partly because it produced no new star from its ranks as *The Pink Lady* had done with Hazel Dawn. In any case, it was the best run put up by any new show of its season. The following year Klaw and Erlanger put the show on the road prefatory to a return season on Broadway, whilst Robert Courtneidge produced a British *Oh! Oh! Delphine* in London with a cast headed by Harry Welchman (Jolibeau), Iris Hoey (Delphine), Walter Passmore (Bouchotte), Nan Stuart (Simone) and veteran Courtice Pounds as Colonel Pomponnet. Its subject matter caused a little indignant stir in London, and cries of ''censor'' were heard on the first night, but the show lived up to its US reputation with a 174-performance run in the West End before two companies took it on the road.

It was a few years before *Oh! Oh! Delphine* reached Australia, and when it did it seemed to have missed its moment. Reginald Roberts (Jolibeau), Phil Smith (Bouchotte), Gladys Moncrieff (Delphine), Olive Goodwin (Simone) and Florence Young (Bimboula) headed the

Plate 286. **Oh! Oh! Delphine.** *Victor Jolibeau (Scott Welsh) and the ladies of the chorus.*

J C Williamson Ltd company that played four weeks in Melbourne and six in Sydney—a regular run, but nothing exciting.

Coming on the heels of *The Pink Lady, Oh! Oh! Delphine* and the success that it won confirmed the coming of the more textually substantial musical comedy of the *Die geschiedene Frau* type to the Broadway stage. It was a trend that would soon find a following, particularly in less oversized theatres of the Princess and Vanderbilt Theatre type, where genuine comic plots and dialogue and lyrics that occasionally needed to be heard could be displayed.

UK: Shaftesbury Theatre 18 February 1913; Australia: Her Majesty's Theatre, Melbourne 7 September 1918

O'HORGAN, Tom (b Chicago, 3 May 1926).

The director of shows for the off-Broadway Café La Mama Theatre Group and Stage 73, O'Horgan came into the limelight with his direction of the original production of *Hair* (1968) at the New York Shakespeare Festival. He subsequently introduced a second hit when he provided the highly colored original production of *Jesus Christ Superstar* (1971) on Broadway, and he also directed Canada/France's attempt to follow in the *Hair* trail with the futuristic teeny-musical *Starmania* (1979).

O'Horgan directed several other musicals including Broadway's shortlived *Dude* (1972) and a number of off- and off-off-Broadway and regional pieces, both dramatic and musical.

He also put his hand to writing, composing and arranging music for several plays at La Mama, and he had a hand in the creation of several shows, including *Lenny*, Julian Barry's 1971 play on the life and works of Lenny Bruce (incidental music), and a 1989 musical about Senator Joseph McCarthy, produced by Adela Holzer, which closed after three previews.

1971 **Inner City** (Helen Miller/w Eve Merriam) Ethel Barrymore Theater 19 December

1989 **Senator Joe** (Perry Arthur Kroeger) Neil Simon Theater 5 January

OH! PAPA . . . Opérette in 3 acts by André Barde. Music by Maurice Yvain. Théâtre des Nouveautés, Paris, 2 February 1933.

By the time they wrote *Oh! Papa . . .* in 1933, Maurice Yvain and André Barde, two of the most outstanding contributors to the Jazz Age musical-comedy genre that had been the joy of the French 1920s, were approaching the end of their work together, before the composer set out to follow newer and more expansive fashions in the musical theatre. Benoît-Léon Deutsch's production of this, their next-to-last piece as a partnership, ensured that they added one more full-sized hit to their already bulging records.

Nane (Jacqueline Francell) was a happy little poule with an almost-permanent sugar daddy (Carol) until the day that sugar daddy presented her with a lovely diamond, a big check, told her he had just got married as well as goodbye. Modern young girls with their forward know-how are spoiling the market for the professional mistress these days, so Nane decides to change professions and become a modern young girl instead of a ''mistress.'' She frocks up and sets off for the social high spot of Bandol, with her pal Julia (Suzanne Dehelly) pretending to be her maid and Godin (Boucot), the pianist from their dance bar, masquerading as her industrialist papa. Nane plays her part so well that she outclasses Monique, the real industrialist's daughter (Davia), and attracts herself an eligible young man (Germain Champell). Of course, her old lover, Thibaudet, is there, too, with his new wife, Danièle (Christiane Nere), and Danièle just happens to be Nane's young man's sister. But, in the third-act finale, Godin resigns his position as ''papa.''

Yvain's score was made up of the same delicious mix of sexy ballads, tongue-in-cheek romance and blatant comedy that his earlier shows had established. Boucot demonstrated his versatility as ''L'Homme orchestre,'' unblushingly shrugged off his tiny stature in ''Je suis petit,'' and told a woeful tale of mistimed love in ''Contradictions,'' soubrette Davia led a physical jerks number in bathing suits, mused on the values of a mature husband and declared (already!) that she was who she was (''Comme je suis''), while Mlle Dehelly provided the comedy with two music-hally numbers, ''Avec un bruit sec'' and the tale of a ladies' wrestling match (''Qu'est-ce que m'a mis Mimi''). Nane and her young man waltzed sensuously to ''Rien qu'en se frolant,'' and Robert Darthez sang of the useful properties of ''Le Gigolo,'' whilst Danièle built up a bluesy description of her ''Nuit de noces'' and the orgasm that never came and joined Nane in a duo describing how to marry a man first and change his ways thereafter (''Tambour battant''). And alongside this battery of happy songs, Yvain provided some concerted finales and also a magnificent quintet (''Allons aux eaux'').

The show ran through five months in Paris and was swiftly carried off to the provinces and to Hungary (ad Adorján Stella, Imre Harmath)—the country that had shown itself most apt to appreciate France's knuckly Jazz Age musicals—but, in spite of the general worldwide famine in musical theatre at the time, it went no further beyond French frontiers. Within them, however, it stayed alive for some time, and it returned to Paris and the Théâtre de la Republique for a fresh season in 1950.

Hungary: Andrássy-uti Színház 6 January 1934

OKLAHOMA! Musical play in 2 acts by Oscar Hammerstein II based on *Green Grow the Lilacs* by Lynn Riggs. Music by Richard Rodgers. St James Theater, New York, 31 March 1943.

Oklahoma! is one of those shows that—like *The Shop Girl* or *Orphée aux enfers* or even *The Beggar's Opera*—has, over the years since its production, become laden down with the responsibility of being labeled a ''landmark.'' Like all landmarks, real or the product of a publicist's imaginings, it has became endowed with all sorts of significances, that dangerous word ''first'' has been waved around a whole lot (including by some folk who ought to know better), and picked up on by the repeaters of easy phrases. But that's how a lot of theatrical ''history'' (with the help of the publicists) gets made.

Oklahoma! was a first. It was the first Broadway musical that the celebrated team of composer Richard Rodgers and librettist and lyricist Oscar Hammerstein II wrote together. And that is quite enough of a landmark to be going on with. It should have been a Rodgers and Hart show, however, for Rodgers had worked on every single one of his nearly 30 stage shows up to the time of *Oklahoma!* with his partner of 20 years and more, Lorenz Hart. However, Hart's increasing unreliability in both his private and professional lives had meant that Rodgers had to seriously consider a new alliance, and when the Theatre Guild approached him with the proposal to turn their play-with-songs *Green Grow the Lilacs* into a full-sized musical, Rodgers asked Hammerstein, a friend and colleague from his earliest days, to work with him on the project.

Green Grow the Lilacs was an unpretentious, countrified tale of romance, and Rodgers and Hammerstein kept that same tone in their musical version, a musical version that was built solidly on the classic tenets and personnel of the romantic musical theatre: one pair of strong-singing juvenile lovers, one pair of soubrets, one low (preferably accented) comic, one villain and a tale

Plate 287. **Oklahoma!** *"The Surrey with the fringe on top" poses with the show's original cast.*

that separated the lovers at the half-way mark, before getting them together for the Act II finale.

Laurey Williams (Joan Roberts) is keen on cowhand Curly (Alfred Drake) and is counting on him asking her to the box social at the Skidmore place, but a girl has her pride and she's not going to let him know she's keen and counting. Unfortunately, she plays her cards wrong, loses her temper and ends up spitedly accepting the offer of the surly Jud Fry (Howard Da Silva) instead. Even though Laurey is quickly aware that she's been foolish, Jud holds to the girl's promise, and Curly drives Laurey's Aunt Eller (Betty Garde) to the dance in the buggy he'd hired for the occasion. The time comes when the lads bid for the girls' picnic hampers to get themselves a partner for the night, and when it is Laurey's turn Curly outbids Jud for the now frightened girl's hand. But not before he's had to hock his horse, his saddle and his gun to raise the cash. Laurey has learned her lesson now, and when Curly proposes to her she is happy to accept. A few weeks later they are wed, but on the wedding night Jud Fry turns up for his revenge. A fight ensues, Curly throws Jud and the villain falls on the knife he had been ready to use on his rival. Curly is technically guilty of killing Jud, but Aunt Eller is equal to the occasion. The local justices are all here for the festivities, so they can just declare the boy innocent right away and let him get on with his married life and the finale.

The tiny, fresh tale of country romance was counterpointed with its parallel soubret story—the off-and-on affair between cowboy Will Parker (Lee Dixon) and the bouncing, unresisting Ado Annie Carnes (Celeste Holm). Annie's father has promised the boy he can wed Annie when he's got $50, but, unfortunately, each time Will manages to earn the $50 he goes right on and spends it and he has to start again. And Annie isn't much good at waiting. As soon as Will is out of sight, she's off necking with the Jewish peddler Ali Hakim (Joseph Buloff). Ali doesn't have weddings in mind, but Pop Carnes (Ralph Riggs) does. When Will goes mad bidding for Annie's hamper at the social, Ali has to spend all his profits outbidding him just so that Will will still have his $50 and Annie, and Ali won't have to wed her himself.

Both sides of the show were equipped with a barrel of winning songs. At the opening of the piece, Curly hailed the country sunrise with the simple, optimistic "Oh What a Beautiful Mornin'," then described the buggy he's hired for the ball to the trotting rhythms of "The Surrey with the Fringe on Top" and duetted, fencingly, with Laurey on the things they oughtn't to do otherwise "People Will Say We're in Love." She pouted and pretended not to care as she declared ''Many a New Day'' would dawn before she'd worry over a boy, then dreamed longingly of him, under the effect of too deep a sniff of sal volatile, to the strains of ''Out of My Dreams.'' All these pieces came in the first act: when the fun and the action began in Act II, there was no more time for sentimental songs, and Curly's contribution to the later stages of the show came in leading the driving paean to ''Oklahoma!''—the brand-new state in which the show was set, the future of which was paralleled with that of the newlyweds. Amongst the comical pieces, Annie squawked out her excuses for congenital infidelity in ''I Cain't Say No!,'' Will poured out a catalogue of the horrors of great big ''Kansas City'' and demanded of Annie ''All er Nuthin',' whilst Curly painted a picture of Jud's funeral (''Pore Jud Is Daid'') as part of a curious conversation with his rival as he confronts him in the smokehouse where he lodges. The villain had a darkly moody soliloquy (''Lonely Room'') and there were some lively moments for the chorus, notably a dancing opening to the second act that centered on the rivalries between ''The Farmer and the Cowman.''

The Theatre Guild's production of *Oklahoma!* was a huge success. Once again wartime audiences flocked to see a native, good-old-days musical as they had been doing in wartime all over the world ever since there had been wars and musicals to flock to. But this all-American romantic operetta was one with an undeniable freshness to it, and it was hard to credit that its book and lyrics came from the same pen as the last American romantic operetta seen on Broadway, the Hammerstein/Romberg *Sunny River* with its overused tale of the self-sacrificing café singer and the high-born youth. Laurey Williams certainly wasn't going to conclude *Oklahoma!* by becoming the umpteenth famous prima donna of operettic last acts.

Everything about the show was enthused over: the gay, unpretentious story with its recognizably American—if operettically idealized—setting and characters; the matching songs—so often in a vernacular that sounded almost like a real vernacular (give or take a ''rose and a glove'') and neatly fitting their places in the play; Agnes de Mille's dream-sequence ballet scene; the simple opening with no chorus girls—just Aunt Eller sitting alone on stage churning butter and Curly's off-stage voice bringing his ''Oh What a Beautiful Mornin''' closer until he came swaggering on stage. Enthusiasm reigned: it was only long afterwards that that enthusiasm started being expressed in ''firsts'' and ''never befores,'' and someone somewhere picked up the deadly term ''integrated'' and started proselytizing with it. Contemporary opinion was satisfied with noting that it was nice, for a change, not to have the revusical kind of low-comic plus dancing-girl-star type of show where everything stops ''for the introduction of songs and bits of funny dialogue, not to mention the complete sweeping away of the story to make way for a chorus intended to catch public fancy rather than help along the show as a whole.''

When *Oklahoma!* first arrived on Broadway it was just a vast hit, a splendid musical play, well made from top to bottom (even if Jud's revenge and death seemed just a touch tacked on, in the ''ah-ha me proud beauty'' tradition), full of entertainment—romance, comedy, song, dance, visuals—in the shapeliest of proportions. It was also, on a Broadway long starved of outstanding new works, the first really top-class romantic native musical (*Pal Joey* and *Lady in the Dark* not really fitting that bill) since the far-off days of *Show Boat.*

Oklahoma! ran at the St James Theater for 2,212 performances, becoming in the process far, far and away the longest-running musical in Broadway history—a record it held for 15 years until the coming of *My Fair Lady.* But it did more than just break a record. It gave a whole impetus to the musical theatre in America, an impetus that *Pal Joey* and *Lady in the Dark* had not—for all their qualities—given. As it sat royally in place at the St James Theater, *Oklahoma!* became the focal point for a fresh round of romantic musical plays on Broadway. Some—like *Bloomer Girl*—copied almost slavishly and were successful; others followed only in part and were also successful. For years *Oklahoma!*-style dance scenes became the sine qua non and eventually a cliché of the contemporary musical stage. Rodgers and Hammerstein themselves went on to build on their first collaboration with a series of outstanding, colorful romantic musicals that didn't slavishly imitate their own previous work except in their tone and their quality, but *Oklahoma!* proved to be the coccyx to the backbone of the next decade and a half of Broadway operettas.

The first American touring company went out on the road little more than half a year into the run with Harry Stockwell (Curley), Evelyn Wyckoff (Laurey), Pamela Britton (Annie) and David Burns (Ali) featured, at the beginning of more than a decade of traveling the country, but it was not until the war was well and truly over that the show began to be seen in other countries. Britain came first. The Theatre Guild mounted the show at London's Theatre Royal, Drury Lane, with local firm H M Tennent Ltd managing on its behalf and a cast headed by Harold (later to be Howard) Keel (Curly), Betty Jane Watson (Laurey), Dorothea MacFarland (Annie), Walter Donahue from the American tour company (Will) and Marek Windheim (Ali). Most of London had, by now, heard of *Oklahoma!* and knew and loved its songs: pretty soon they loved the show too. The postwar musical stage in London blossomed as, within a matter of weeks, *Oklahoma!, Annie Get Your Gun* and *Bless the Bride* all swept into town. Enthusiasm raced as fans lined themselves up as the champions of one or other of the three great hits—but how good it was to have three such hits to champion! *Oklahoma!* ultimately had the longest run of the three (although *Annie* was housed in the biggest auditorium), even though it ran out the last of its 1,543 performances in the unloved Stoll Theatre (from 29 May 1950) after being displaced from Drury Lane by none other than Rodgers and Hammerstein's next musical: *Carousel.*

Australia did not see *Oklahoma!* until 1949, although J C Williamson Ltd had bought the show some time before. Williamson manager E J Tait was an *Annie* fan and, having purchased both shows from the Rodgers and Hammerstein office, he decided that *Annie Get Your Gun* was the better proposition. The huge success of that piece around Australia and New Zealand proved him right, but *Oklahoma!* didn't do too badly either when it came along behind nearly two years later. Robert Reeves (Curly), Carolyn Adair (Laurey) and Louise Barnhardt (Annie) headed the cast, which played 231 performances in Melbourne and seven and a half months in Sydney (Theatre Royal 29 November 1949).

A film version was produced in 1955 that cast Gordon MacRae (Curly), Shirley Jones (Laurey), Gloria Grahame (Annie), Gene Nelson (Will), Eddie Albert (Ali), Charlotte Greenwood (Aunt Eller) and Rod Steiger (Jud) in a Fred Zinneman production of rosy cheeks and haystacks that remains the classic *Oklahoma!* for many who saw it. The score was kept largely intact, and the peremptory ending was made more dramatically satisfying by the resetting of the wedding-night high-jinks in a haystack to which Jud attempts to set fire. The film succeeded just as each and every *Oklahoma!* up to the time had done.

In the same year, *Oklahoma!* went further afield when a touring company sent out by the State Department and headed by Jack Cassidy (Curly) and the film version's Shirley Jones (Laurey) took the show to Paris and to Rome (Teatro Quattro Fontane, August 1955), but it was some time before the piece—by then a solid part of the standard repertoire in every corner of the English-language theatre—was given foreign-language stagings. The first French version was seen in Belgium, at the Opéra Royal de Wallonie in Liège (22 December 1972), where the company has made a speciality of producing French versions of the classic works of the English-language musical stage.

Regularly played in the half-century since its first production, *Oklahoma!* had its most important round of revivals from 1979, when the piece was remounted on Broadway under the aegis of Zev Bufman and James M Nederlander (Palace Theater 13 December 1979) with Laurence Guittard (Curly), Christine Andreas (Laurey), Christine Ebersole (Annie), Harry Groener (Will) and Bruce Adler (Ali) featured and the now-revered choreography reproduced. A 301-performance run was followed by a British provincial and London mounting under the management of Cameron Mackintosh (Palace Theater 17 September 1980, 419 performances) with John Diedrich (Curly), Rosamund Shelley (Laurey), Jillian Mack (Annie), Linal Haft (Ali) and Mark White (Will) and by an especially successful Australian reproduction (Festival Theatre, Adelaide 1 May 1982) in which Diedrich teamed with Sally Butterfield, Donna Lee, Henri Széps and Peter Bishop. In 1998 (Olivier Theatre 15 July) the piece became the latest in the series of exclusively trans-atlantic-bred musicals staged by Britain's increasingly un-British Royal National Theatre. Hugh Jackman was Curly, alongside Josefina Gabrielle (Laurey), Vicki Simon (Annie) and Jimmy Johnston (Will) and Maureen Lipman featured as Aunt Eller in a Trevor Nunn production that made a virtue of the piece's simplicity and confirmed it as a classic of the musical stage. After its Olivier Theatre season, the show moved to the Lyceum (20 January 1999), where it played for a further eight months. This version was also televised (24 September 1999).

The title *Oklahoma!* had been used on the American stage prior to the arrival of the *Oklahoma!* we all know so well. In 1915 the George Scarborough play *The Girl,* originally produced by David Belasco, was rewritten. The new version was produced under the title *Oklahoma.* However, not long after opening it was felt that the title was too unattractive, and it was dropped, the play going on its way as *The Heart of Wetona* instead.

UK: Theatre Royal, Drury Lane 29 April 1947; Australia: Her Majesty's Theatre, Melbourne 19 February 1949; Germany: Berlin (Eng) 1951, Münster 1973, Theater des Westens 27 January 1982; France: Théâtre des Champs Élysées 20 June 1955

Films: Magna 1955, TV film (UK) 1999

Recordings: original cast (Decca/MCA), revival cast (RCA), London revival cast 1980 (Stiff), Australian revival cast (RCA), National Theatre production (First Night), film soundtrack (Capitol/EMI), selection in German (Ariola), etc

Literature: Wilk, M: *OK!: The Story of ''Oklahoma!''* (Grove Press, New York, 1993)

OKONKOWSKI, Georg (b Hohensalza, 11 February 1863; d Berlin, 25 March 1926).

A prolific author of plays and libretti for the German stage, Okonkowski came to the fore at the same time as composer Jean Gilbert, as the author of their long-running Posse *Polnische Wirtschaft.* Thereafter he collaborated on the writing of many of Gilbert's most successful pieces, notably his two most significant international hits of the 1910s, *Die keusche Susanne* and *Die Kino-Königin.* In the later part of his career he also worked with Walter Bromme and supplied the text for the manager-composer's most successful work, *Mascottchen.*

Apart from his two big successes, a number of Okonkowski's other works traveled beyond Germany, *Polnische Wirtschaft* and *Die moderne Eva* being produced both in America as well as in Vienna, where *Madame Serafin* (Johann Strauss-Theater 3 September 1911), *Zwischen zwölf und eins* (Theater in der Josefstadt 29 March 1914), *Das Fräulein vom Amt* (Wiener Stadttheater 1 February 1916) and *Mascottchen* (Carltheater 26 September 1924) also got a showing. Alongside *A mozitündér* (*Kino-Königin*), *Az ártatlan Zsuzsi* (*Die keusche Susanne*), *Lengyel menyecske* (*Polnische Wirtschaft*) and *Ő Teréz!* (*Das Fräulein vom Amt*), Hungary saw versions of *Zwischen zwölf und eins* (*Éjfélkor* Népopera 11 April 1914) and *Der brave Hendrik* (*A derék Fridolin* Budai Színkör 7 July 1916), and London welcomed *The Girl in the Taxi, The Cinema Star* and *Mam'selle Tralala.*

1897 **1842 (Der grosse Brand in Hamburg)** (Leo Fall) Centralhallen-Theater, Hamburg 1 August

1899 **Der Brandstifter** (Fall) Ostendtheater 1 January

1899 **Der griechische Sklave** (*A Greek Slave*) German version w C M Rohr

1899 **Die Venus von der Markthalle** (Franz Wagner/w Emil Sondermann) Viktoria-Theater 4 December

1900 **Berliner Bilder** (*Berlin nach Elf*) (Wagner/w Sondermann) Centraltheater 14 April

1901 **Diana im Bade** (Max Gabriel) Centralhallen-Theater, Hamburg October

1903 **Der Sonnenvogel** (aka *Der Phönix*) (Viktor Holländer/w Rudolf Schanzer) St Petersburg (Wiener Operetten Ensemble) 22 August; Centraltheater, Berlin April 1904

1905 **Der Strohwitwer** (Wagner/w Fritz Friedmann-Friedrich) Apollotheater, Nuremberg 27 June

1907 **Der Milliardär** (Ferdinand Gradl/w Arthur Lippschitz) Centraltheater 16 February

1908 **Doktor Klapperstorch** (Max Schmidt/Alfred Schönfeld/w Jean Kren) Thalia-Theater 28 March

1909 **Wo wohnt sie denn?** (Holländer/Schönfeld/w Kren) Thalia-Theater 12 February

1909 **Polnische Wirtschaft** (Jean Gilbert/Schönfeld/w Kurt Kraatz) Stadttheater, Cottbus 26 December; Thalia-Theater, Berlin 6 August 1910

1910 **Die keusche Susanne** (J Gilbert) Wilhelm Theater, Magdeburg 26 February; Neues Operettentheater, Berlin 6 August 1911

1911 **Die Luxusweibchen** (Gabriel) Tivoli-Theater, Bremen 5 August

1911 **Madame Serafin** (Robert Winterberg/w Bruno Granichstaedten) Neues Operettentheater, Hamburg 1 September

1911 **Königin Loanda** (Oskar Malata) Stadttheater, Chemnitz 29 October

1911 **Die moderne Eva** (J Gilbert/Schönfeld) Neues Operetten-Theater 11 November

1912 **Die elfte Muse** (J Gilbert) Operettenhaus, Hamburg 22 November

1913 **Zwischen zwölf und eins** (Walter Goetze/w Max Neal, M Ferner) Neues Operetten-Theater, Leipzig 9 February

1913 **Die Kino-Königin** (revised *Die elfte Muse*) (J Gilbert/ad Julius Freund) Metropoltheater 8 March

1913 **Das Farmermädchen** (Georg Jarno) Grosses Operetten-Theater 22 March

1913 **Das Gassenmädel** (Paul Freund) Schauspielhaus, Breslau 2 May

1913 **Fräulein Tralala** (J Gilbert/w Leo Leipziger) Neues Luisen-Theater, Königsberg 15 November

1914 **Die schöne Kubanerin** (Gabriel) Rembrandt Theater, Amsterdam 17 January

1914 **Wenn der Frühling kommt!** (J Gilbert/Schönfeld/w Kren) Thalia-Theater 28 March

1914 **Kam'rad Manne** (J Gilbert/Schönfeld/w Kren) Thalia-Theater 3 August

1915 **Der brave Hendrik** (aka *Der brave Fridolin*) (Gabriel) Rembrandt Theater, Amsterdam 3 April; Theater des Westens 23 May

1915 **Das Fräulein vom Amt** (J Gilbert/w Ernst Arnold) Theater des Westens 13 November

1916 **Die Perle der Frauen** revised *Die Luxusweibchen* Central-Theater, Magdeburg 21 May

1916 **Die stolze Thea** (Gabriel) Rembrandt Theater, Amsterdam 16 September; Theater des Westens 1 May 1917

1917 **Der verliebte Herzog** (aka *Der verliebte Prinz*) (J Gilbert/w Hans Bachwitz) Theater des Westens 1 September

1917 **Senorita Pif-Paf** (Gabriel) Rembrandt Theater, Amsterdam 22 December

1919 **Die Schönste von allen** (J Gilbert) Centraltheater 22 March

1920 **Eine Nacht im Paradies** (Walter Bromme/w Willy Steinberg) Theater am Nollendorfplatz 30 April

1921 **Mascottchen** (Bromme/w Steinberg) Thalia-Theater 15 January

1921 **Scham' dich, Lotte** (Bromme/w Steinberg) Berliner Theater 2 September

1921 **Die Kleine aus der Hölle** (Tilmar Springfield/w Steinberg)

1922 **Madame Flirt** (Bromme/w Steinberg) Berliner Theater 15 April

1923 **Die schöne Rivalin** (Hans Linne/w Steinberg) Theater am Nollendorfplatz 28 March

1923 **Die Tugendprinzessin** (Richard Bars/Kurt Zorlig) Deutsches Künstlertheater ?May

1923 **Schönste der Frauen** (Bromme/w Steinberg) Metropoltheater May

1923 **Casino-Girls** (Eduard Künneke) Metropoltheater 15 September

1923 **Die blonde Geisha** (Hans Ailbout/L Czerney)

1923 **Charlie** (Goetze)

1925 **Tausend süsse Beinchen** (Bromme/Steinberg) Metropoltheater 28 March

1925 **Der Stern von Assuan** (Richard Goldberger/w Ralph A Roberts) Opernhaus am Königplatz 1 July

1925 **Annemarie** (J Gilbert, Robert Gilbert/w Martin Zickel) Schillertheater 2 July

1926 **Lene, Lotte, Liese, Josefinens Tochter** (J Gilbert, R Gilbert) Thalia-Theater 14 January

1926 **Miss Amerika** (Bromme/Kurt Schwabach/w Steinberg) Berliner Theater 20 August

OLCOTT, Chauncey [OLCOTT, Chancellor John] (b Buffalo, NY, 21 July 1860; d Monte Carlo, 18 March 1932). American tenor who turned temporarily comic, then romantic Irish, becoming the classic stage-Irish performer of his era.

Olcott began his performing career singing tenor music in minstrel shows and variety (Haverly's Minstrels, Thatcher's Minstrels, Primrose and West, Carncross's Minstrels in Philadelphia, Denman Thompson Company), and he made his first, rather stiff musical-theatre appearance only in 1886 in Teddy Solomon's *Pepita* (Pablo) alongside Lillian Russell. He later (May 1887) toured for two years as a member of the singing quartet (Frank Hopkins) in the play *The Old Homestead,* before going on to be seen in lead tenor roles in several Broadway productions of English works, ranging from Gilbert and Sullivan for John Duff's company (Ralph Rackstraw, Nanki-Poo) to Edward Jakobowski's *Paola* (1889, Lucien). He also was featured in John McCaull's productions of Suppé's *Clover* and Millöcker's *Die sieben Schwaben* (1890) and the post-McCaull produtcion of *The Tar and the Tartar,* and appeared at the San Francisco Orpheum in opera before, in 1891, he left for Europe to study for the operatic stage. Seasick, he got off in Britain. There he soon got himself a job playing a character tenor role in London's *Miss Decima* (*Miss Helyett,* Chevalier Patrick Julius O'Flannagan), then another in the burlesque *Blue-Eyed Susan* (1892, Gnatbrain), but he soon headed back to America, and landed on his feet. The American stage had recently been bereft of its favorite ''Irish'' touring hero, the much-loved Scanlan, and Olcott's pudgy good looks and attractive tenor led him first to one ''Scanlan'' part, touring in George Jessop's *Mavourneen,* then to a whole series of long-traveling Irish musical plays in which, although he was in no manner an Irishman, he made himself a career and a name as popular as that of his predecessor.

By 1894 Olcott was well enough established to have a first piece, *The Irish Artist,* made to measure for him, and *The Irish Artist* set the successful pattern for those to come. In a quarter of a century of indefatigable touring, he followed up in *The Minstrel of Clare* (1896, ''Olcott's Love Song,'' ''Love Remains the Same''), *Sweet Inniscarra* (1897, ''The Old Fashioned Mother,'' ''Olcott's Fly Song''), *A Romance of Athlone* (1899, ''Olcott's Lullaby,'' ''My Wild Irish Rose''), *Garret O'Magh* (1901, ''Paddy's Cat,'' ''The Lass I Love,'' ''My Sweet Queen,'' ''Ireland! a gra ma chee''), *Old Limerick Town* (1902, ''The Voice of the Violet,'' ''Every Little Dog Must Have His Day''), *Terrence* (Metropolitan Theater, St Paul 27 August 1903, ''My Sonny Boy,'' ''Tick, Tack, Toe,'' ''The Girl I Used to Know,'' ''My Own Dear Irish Queen''), *Edmund Burke* (1905, ''Your Heart Alone Must Tell,'' ''You Can Sail in My Boat''), *Eileen Asthore* (1906, ''For Love of Thee,'' ''Wearers of the Green,'' ''Eileen Asthore''), *O'Neill of Derry* (1907), *Ragged Robin* (1908), *Barry of Ballymore* (1910, ''Mother Machree,'' ''When Irish Eyes Are Smiling''), *Macushla* (1911, ''Macushla''), *The Isle o' Dreams* (1912), *Shameen Dhu* (1913), *The Heart of Paddy Whack* (1914), *Honest John O'Brien* (1916), *Once Upon a Time* (1917) and *The Voice of McConnell* (1920).

Olcott remained a favorite star of the American country circuits until he was 60 years old, delivering annually precisely the combinations of homespun Irishy sentiment, comedy and tenorizing that were expected of him. His sometimes creaky vehicles each introduced a number of songs, and those songs produced a remarkable number of enduring hits, the most notable of which were ''When Irish Eyes Are Smiling'' (for which he shared writer's credit with George Graff and Ernest Ball), ''Mother Machree'' (Ball/Olcott/Rida Johnson Young), and ''Macushla'' (Josephine Rowe/Dermot MacMurrough).

Olcott was the subject of a Hollywood biopic, *My Wild Irish Rose* (1947), in which he was portrayed by Dennis Morgan.

Biography: Olcott, R: *A Song in His Heart* (House of Field, New York, 1939)

OLD CHELSEA Musical romance in 3 acts by Walter Ellis. Lyrics by Walter Ellis and Fred Tysh. Music by Richard Tauber. Additional numbers by Bernard Grün. Birmingham, 21 September 1942; Prince's Theatre, London, 17 February 1943.

A wartime operetta of the most florid olde-worlde kind, *Old Chelsea* was composed by and for the Austrian tenor Richard Tauber, whose librettists for some reason cast him as a poor 18th-century British composer with an opera he longs to have produced. Australian soprano Nancy Brown played the opera singer who sings his music and falls in love with him, and Carol Lynne was the little milliner who helps him through his hard days and steps in to sing the opera to triumph when the prima donna returns to her lordly lover. The light comedy was provided by the young Charles Hawtrey, later to find fame in the *Carry On . . .* films. The music of the piece was mostly unimpressive, but it did produce one hit in the star's big solo, ''My Heart and I,'' to set alongside an enjoyably catty quartet (''A Little Gossip''), which was part of the contribution of another expatriate European, Bernard Grün.

Originally played for three months on the road (with Tauber proving more reliable than he had in his London appearances), it was then taken to London, but it survived only 95 performances there before returning to the provinces, where it later found several revivals. *Old Chelsea* marked both the last West End appearance of Tauber and the first London musical production for its young producer, Bernard Delfont.

Recording: radio broadcast by original cast w Tauber (Sounds Rare)

OLDHAM, Derek [OLDHAM, John Stephens] (b Accrington, 29 March 1887; d Portsmouth, 20 March 1968). Lead tenor of the D'Oyly Carte Company and a string of West End shows.

Lancashire vocalist Oldham had been a bank clerk before he made his London debut as a performer in Heinrich Reinhardt's one-act operetta *The Daring of Diane* (*Die süssen Grisetten*) at the Tivoli music hall. He had his first regular West End part when he appeared in the title role of a revival of *The Chocolate Soldier* in 1914 and, after the First World War, he became principal tenor with the D'Oyly Carte Opera Company for three years. He later played leading roles in *Whirled into Happiness* (*Der Tanz ins Glück*) and a revival of *The Merry Widow* (Camille), then starred in three major imported successes in the West End: opposite Evelyn Laye as René in Fall's *Madame Pompadour,* as Jim Kenyon to the Rose Marie of Edith Day in *Rose Marie* and in the title role of *The Vagabond King.*

Oldham subsequently returned on several occasions to the D'Oyly Carte Company, during which time he sang the tenor roles in the first comprehensive recordings of the Gilbert and Sullivan repertoire, interleaving these periods with further musical theatre roles—*Blue Eyes, The Song of the Drum, The Merry Widow* revival, *The Desert Song* tour, *Lilac Time, The Dancing City* (t/o from Franco Foresta as Archduke Franz), *White Horse Inn* revival, *Monsieur Beaucaire* tour, *A Waltz Dream* tour, *I Call It Love*—and some film appearances. At the age of 53 (but already knocking more years off his age than any other male performer on record), he played Dick Warrington in the British premiere of *Naughty Marietta* (tour), and he continued performing into the 1950s.

Oldham was married to soprano Winnie Melville, who appeared alongside him in *Whirled into Happiness* (t/o Florrie), starred in London's *The Student Prince* (Kathie), *Princess Charming* (Elaine) and, opposite Oldham, *The Vagabond King* (Katharine), and played leading soprano roles with the D'Oyly Carte Company.

OLIAS, Lothar (b Königsberg, 23 December 1913).

Prussian-born Olias studied in Berlin, and worked as a musician and as a music publisher before, in the years after the war, basing himself in Hamburg. There he began to supply music first for cabaret and revue, then for the first of the many films that would make up the large part of his work. He made his first appearance as a musical-comedy composer when he wrote the score for the sailory *Heimweh nach St Pauli,* produced in Hamburg in 1954 with singing star Freddy Quinn top-billed in the role apparently based on himself. The show was later revised with considerable success for Berlin, played in Vienna and ultimately filmed. Another piece, the spoof Western *Prairie-Saloon,* originally written for Hamburg, was also enlarged and rearranged for a successful Berlin production (Berliner Theater 10 November 1961) and later also staged on the other side of the Wall (Erfurt 30 September 1973). In 1965 Olias provided the score for a piece loosely based on some events from Brandon Thomas's *Charley's Aunt,* and in 1967 wrote the songs for a crook musical, set in modern New York, *Millionen für Penny* (Penny being the heroine, not a coin), which was subsequently also played in Eastern Germany (Plauen 18 May 1968) and revived as recently as 1994 at Hannover, 1997 at Esslingen and Parchim and 1998 at Detmold.

1954 **Heimweh nach St Pauli** (Rothenburg) Operettenhaus, Hamburg 3 February (revised version Operettenhaus, Hamburg 18 October 1962); Theater des Westens 7 January 1967

1958 **Prairie-Saloon** (Heinz Wunderlich, Kurt Schwabach) Junges Theater, Hamburg 31 December

1965 **Charley's neue Tante** (Gustav Kampendonk) Hamburg

1967 **Millionen für Penny** (Max Colpet) Theater am Gärtnerplatz, Munich 5 February

1971 **Der Geldschrank steht im Fenster** (*Eine feine Familie*) (Colpet, Wunderlich) Niedert Theater, Bremen 6 February

OLIVER! Musical in 2 acts by Lionel Bart founded on *Oliver Twist* by Charles Dickens. New Theatre, London, 30 June 1960.

When Lionel Bart first thought of making a musical out of Charles Dickens's *Oliver Twist,* he had not actually read the book, and his initial idea was that it would make a good vehicle for his rock-and-rolling friend Tommy Steele. However, the misconception was set right and, without trying to cram in every bit of the original tale, Bart fashioned a libretto out of the essentials of Dickens's narrative, following the life of little Oliver (Keith Hamshere) through his expulsion from the workhouse by the beadle (Paul Whitsun-Jones) for asking for a second helping of gruel, his hateful apprenticeship to the undertaking Sowerberrys (Barry Humphries, Sonia Fraser), his flight to London, his encounter with the Artful Dodger (Martin Horsey) and his induction into the gang of thieves run by the grim Fagin (Ron Moody) up to his ultimate discovery of his wealthy birth and comfortable family. The outline of the original story was well adhered to, although, given the age of the leading character, it was necessary—as it had been in every *Oliver Twist* adaptation through the ages—for female and romantic interest, to build up the prominence of the brutish love affair between the East End villain Bill Sikes (Danny Sewell) and the kind-hearted Nancy (Georgia Brown). Sikes's murder of Nancy and his own death were included in the text in all their dark drama, but in general the colors of Dickens's tale were jollified up. *Oliver!* presented a patter-song Fagin who was a musical-comedy "loveable" villain, on the one hand, and a set of sweet stage children doing a jolly cockney knees-up, on the other.

The simple-sounding songs that Bart supplied to illustrate *Oliver!* were a standard mixture of sentimental and comic, lively and pensive, but they proved to be songs that were made of the stuff that catches and the stuff that endures. The little boy, wondering in his frail soprano "Where Is Love?" in words of touching, unashamed simplicity; the ill-treated Nancy, sticking doggedly by the man she knows may very well kill her, and pouring out her reason in "As Long as He Needs Me"; the beadle's plump paramour simperingly threatening "I Shall Scream" as she sits on his over-padded knee; and the Artful Dodger's walloping "Consider Yourself (at home)" were amongst the musical high spots of a show in which almost every song was a winner.

Bart touted his show around town until producer Donald Albery took it on. Peter Coe and Sean Kenny, director and designer of Bart's previous show, *Lock Up Your Daughters,* were engaged to fulfill the same functions on this one, and the original idea of a production at East London's Theatre Royal, Stratford East, was abandoned when Kenny produced his designs: a revolving complex of multi-purpose dark platforms, stairs and arches that were to win him excited praise and to influence theatre design in Britain for a number of years. *Oliver!* opened instead at Wimbledon, prior to the West End's New Theatre. If there were problems in the suburb, however, they were all ironed out before the in-town opening, and *Oliver!* had a triumphant first night in its West End home.

The show remained at the New Theatre for six years and 2,618 performances, during which time it made its first appearance in the Netherlands, Sweden, Australia, South Africa and Israel, as well as on Broadway, where it arrived, after seasons in both Los Angeles and Toronto, with several of the original London cast, including Miss Brown, featured alongside British juveniles as Oliver (Bruce Prochnik) and the Dodger (David Jones, later to be known as a Monkee) and Clive Revill as Fagin. Once again, the show opened triumphantly, proved the hit of the 1962–63 season and settled in for a 774-performance run, which eclipsed the totals established by *The Boy Friend, Florodora* and *Erminie* and made it the longest-running British-bred musical to have been seen on Broadway up to that time.

Plate 288. *Ron Moody as Fagin in London's* **Oliver!**

In Australia it found equivalent success. Mounted by J C Williamson Ltd in Melbourne with Johnny Lockwood (Fagin), Sheila Bradley (Nancy), Richard Watson (Bumble), John Maxim (Sikes) and former star of operetta and silent screen, Nancy Brown, as Mrs Bumble, it played there for four and a half months, then for four further months in Sydney (Theatre Royal 17 February 1962), returning for a second showing in 1966 (Her Majesty's, Melbourne 22 July, Theatre Royal, Sydney 26 August).

In Britain, the show went on the road in 1965 with Richard Easton and Marti Webb starred. Just seven months after the original New Theatre production had closed, Miss Webb paired with Barry Humphries—promoted now from Sowerberry to Fagin—in a quick revival at the Piccadilly Theatre, which added another 331 performances to the show's remarkable total.

In 1968, whilst *Oliver!* continued its life as one of the most popular new musicals of the postwar years, a film version was made, with Moody repeating his original role alongside Shani Wallis (Nancy), Mark Lester (Oliver), Jack Wild (Dodger), Oliver Reed (Sikes), Leonard Rossiter (Sowerberry) and Harry Secombe (Bumble), and, within a decade, it was back in the West End again. The 1977 revival, which toured for five months under the banner of Cameron Mackintosh before settling into its old home at the Albery (ex-New) Theatre, continued the show's impeccable record of success. With a cast initially headed by Roy Hudd as an outstanding Fagin and Gillian Burns (Nancy), it ran for nearly three years (1,139 performances), taking the show past its 4,000th metropolitan performance and culling appreciable royalties for the property company to which Bart, in a time of need, had sold out his interest in the show. In 1977 *Oliver!* got its first European performance, in Belgium (Antwerp 12 November).

Mackintosh put *Oliver!* back on the road again following its London run, bringing it back for a brief Christmas season in 1983–84. Moody repeated his original role on the original Kenny settings under the distracted direction of original director Coe, and all three showed the signs of having been dragged out once too often. The feeling was confirmed when all three were used on a Broadway repeat *Oliver!* (29 April 1984), which also featured Patti LuPone (Nancy) and Braden Danner (Oliver), for a sad handful of performances. Australia, which was intended to receive the production, did not, when down-under unions there insisted on remaking all the now-famous scenery and originally taken-from-stock but faithfully reproduced-thereafter costumes.

These failures, however, did not dim the popularity of the piece, which continued to be widely played on English-language stages. In the 1980s, as the English-language musical began to make inroads into Europe and as Mackintosh, who had now virtually adopted *Oliver!,* became established as internationally the most successful and wide-reaching producer of musicals, it also made its way into Continental houses. A German-language version (ad Wilfried Steiner) was first produced at Salzburg in 1985, and continues to win productions in central Europe, and Hungary was introduced to a local language version the following year (ad Lia Bassa, György Denes) as *Oliver!* began a belated invasion of the European continent.

In 1990 Britain's National Youth Theatre brought the piece back to London once more, and a large cash gift from Mackintosh to the Royal National Theatre for the production of musicals led to rumors that *Oliver!* would be the first modern British musical to play at the country's most subsidized theatre. However, the National Theatre confirmed its historic disdain for the homemade musical-theatre product, and *Oliver!* returned instead to its biggest British stage yet, at the London Palladium (8 December 1994), for another two and a half profitable years. Jonathan Pryce was a curiously de-semitized Fagin, until succeeded by patented musical-theatre stars Jim Dale and Robert Lindsay, the now famous Barry (''Dame Edna Everage'') Humphries, and in a piece of inspired casting, versatile comedian Russ Abbott, while Sally Dexter, Claire Moore, Ruthie Henshall and Sonia Swaby were the Nancys of the season. The famous designs, having served their time, gave way to a new, more modern set by Anthony Ward. Following a fine London run of 1,352 performances, the piece went once more round Britain, with Abbott and Gary Wilmot sharing the role of Fagin, confirming *Oliver!* as the best-loved British musical of the 1960s.

A French version, scheduled for an apparently unauthorized production at the Opéra de Lyon some 40 years after the show's birth, had the plug pulled on it, but France got its *Oliver* the following year, in the less likely surroundings of Paris's Amphithéâtre Bastille. A chopped up and down libretto, in French (ad Claude Tabet), teamed with songs in English, was performed by a company headed by Bill Dunn (Fagin) and Sabina Benaziz (Nancy) for eight nights.

Oliver Twist was first put on the stage at the Adelphi Theatre in 1839, with Mrs Keeley playing Oliver, and John Oxenford supplied a version to the Queens' in 1868 (11 April) in which Irving (Sikes), Toole (Artful Dodger) and Lionel Brough (Bumble) took part, but this first and only attempt to set the tale as a musical has proved far and away the most enduring version of Dickens's workhouse and Limehouse weepie.

Australia: Her Majesty's Theatre, Melbourne 23 September 1961; USA: Imperial Theater 6 January 1963; Austria: Landestheater, Salzburg 8 January 1985; Germany: Theater am Gärtnerplatz, Munich 29 May 1986; Hungary: Arany János Színház 27 November 1986

Recordings: original cast (RCA), Broadway cast (RCA), Israeli cast (CBS), Dutch cast (Philips), South African cast (RCA), Danish cast (Radius), Hungarian version (Qualiton), Norwegian version (Polygram), London revival 1994 (First Night), German school recording, studio casts (Capitol, World Records, TER etc), film soundtrack (RCA), etc

ON A CLEAR DAY YOU CAN SEE FOREVER Musical in 2 acts by Alan Jay Lerner. Music by Burton Lane. Mark Hellinger Theater, New York, 17 October 1965.

Originally intended, following the end of the Lerner/Loewe partnership, to be a collaboration, under the title *I Picked a Daisy,* between the author and Richard Rodgers, *On a Clear Day You Can See Forever* was rescheduled with Burton Lane as composer when the original pair found themselves incompatible. Lerner's libretto provided a novel twist on the familiar dream-sequence and through-the-generations conventions of the musical theatre. Its heroine, Daisy (Barbara Harris) suffers from extrasensory perception to a degree that arouses the fascinated attention of her psychiatric lecturer, Mark Bruckner

(John Cullum, replacing the tryout's Louis Jourdan). When she agrees to be a subject for his research, she reaches back into an earlier life and brings out an alter ego called Melinda, an 18th-century damsel caught up in the gay-dog life of London and with the raffish Sir Edward Moncrieff (Clifford David). As they work, Daisy's personal interest in Mark grows; at the same time, he takes a shine to her—but in her alter ego as Melinda. When she discovers that she is becoming a cause celèbre in the psychiatric world, Daisy runs away, but by the final curtain she is back to cement her relationship with Mark. Lane's score brought up two numbers that had a considerable life outside the show, Cullum's comforting explanation of Daisy's extraordinary powers in the title song, and his own effort at extrasensory power as, in the final scene, he wills the vanished girl to "Come Back to Me."

Lerner's production of *On a Clear Day* ran for 280 performances and toured briefly, with John Raitt, with Howard Keel and with a revised libretto and song list, before being adapted for a film version, produced again by its author (w Howard W Koch), who had rewritten his stage libretto to give Melinda (Barbra Streisand) multiple reincarnations and no final button with Marc ([*sic*], because it was the Gallic Yves Montand). Miss Streisand had two new numbers to add to two of her own and two of other people's from the stage show, whilst Montand sang the three songs from his stage role and no one else sang anything.

Film: Paramount 1970

Recordings: original cast (RCA Victor), film soundtrack (Columbia)

Video: Japanese (Takarazuka) production

ONCE ON THIS ISLAND Musical by Lyn Ahrens based on the novel *My Love, My Love* by Rosa Guy. Music by Stephen Flaherty. Playwrights Horizons, New York, 6 May 1990; Booth Theater, 18 October 1990.

A Caribbean island musical, with a story that is a variant on Hans Christian Andersen's *The Little Mermaid, Once on This Island* told the tale of an orphan girl, Ti Moune (La Chanze), who rescues the rich Daniel Beauxhomme (Jerry Dixon) from drowning when his car crashes. As Daniel convalesces, the two young people become lovers, but when he is again well he has to return to his family and his home, and to the bride who awaits him there. Papa Ge, the god of death, whom Ti Moune cheated to save the boy, comes to claim his own. Either she must kill Daniel, or her own soul is forfeit to the devil. She chooses to die. But the gods take pity on the girl, and she is transformed into a tree, to guard over Daniel as long as he shall live.

The show's storybook tale, framed as if recounted by the island's storytellers, was accompanied by music in a West Indian vein, a score full of irresistibly rhythmic numbers in which, refreshingly, the rhythm came not from the usual pounding pop battery of electro-percussive instruments but from inside the music itself. Ti-Moune had the best of it, with the warm "Waiting for Life to Begin" and the heartfelt "Forever Yours," and "Mama" Euralie (Sheila Gibbs) the showiest in the zingy "Mama Will Provide."

First produced at Playwrights Horizons (60 performances), in a staging by Graciela Daniele, the show was subsequently taken to Broadway, where its simple pleasures and unpretentious production provided a good deal of pleasure through 487 performances.

The piece was subsequently produced in Britain, with a cast including a number of West Indian born or backgrounded performers, and with Lorna Brown (Ti Moune) and Anthony Corriette (Daniel) in the roles of the lovers. Mounted at the Royalty Theatre, renamed the Island Theatre for the occasion and decked out with all sorts of "atmospheric" Caribbean carnival trimmings, it failed to appeal and shuttered in 145 performances.

UK: Birmingham Repertory Theatre 2 July 1994, Island [Royalty] Theater 28 September 1994

Recordings: original cast (RCA Victor), London cast (TER)

ONCE UPON A MATTRESS Musical comedy in 2 acts by Jay Thompson, Marshall Barer and Dean Fuller based on *The Princess and the Pea.* Lyrics by Marshall Barer. Music by Mary Rodgers. Phoenix Theater, New York, 11 May 1959.

A burlesque fairy tale of a kind, and on a scale, rarely written since the turn of the century, *Once Upon a Mattress* began its life as a rather smaller Barer-Thompson-Rodgers collaboration produced at the Tamiment resort in Pennsylvania in August of 1958. Fuller joined the team to aid in the expansion, which was undertaken before *Once Upon a Mattress* was brought to New York's Phoenix Theater, under the management of Edward Hambleton, Norris Houghton and the show's designers, William and Jean Eckhart, nine months later.

This retelling of the tale of the *Princess and the Pea* introduced Carol Burnett as the Princess Winnifred (pet name not Winnie, but Fred), a lusty, booming nymphet from the outer swamps, who swims the moat to get to her appointment with the daunting Queen Aggravaine (Jane White) to audition for the post of wife to the royal lady's progeny, Dauntless (Joe Bova). No one else in court is allowed to wed until the prince does, so all, particularly the longing Lady Larken (Anne Jones) and her beau, Sir Harry (Allen Case), are on Fred's side. When the Queen's secret test—the famous pea under the mattresses—is sussed out by the court minstrel (Harry Snow) and Jester (Matt Mattox), they provide a little extra help to make

Plate 289. **Once Upon a Mattress.** *Buster Keaton and Dody Goodman as the royals of America's touring production.*

sure that Winnifred passes, and all is prepared for a happy ending in which Dauntless gets his bride and the once mute King Sextimus (Jack Gilford) is restored to connubial and royal power.

Miss Rogers's score caught the mood of burlesque neatly as Miss Burnett explained how "Shy" she was, yodeled out a description of "The Swamps of Home" and mused voluminously over her "Happily Ever After," and the prevented pair of Larken and Harry promised themselves a married life "In a Little While." The Jester wooed the Queen's secret from the Wizard (Robert Weil) with reminiscences of showbiz in the soft-shoe "Very Soft Shoes," and the other dance highlight of the evening came in Joe Layton's staging of "The Spanish Panic," the exhausting dance intended by the Queen to wear Winnifred out before bedtime. The most charming moment of the night's entertainment, however, came when the mute little king decides it is his duty to tell his innocent son about the birds and the bees: his "Man to Man Talk" has to be conducted in mime, whilst the amazed boy translates.

Once Upon a Mattress ran for 216 performances at the Phoenix Theatre and 244 more performances on Broadway, followed by a tour, with a company headed by Buster Keaton, Dody Goodman and Cy Young, a two-month Australian Christmas-season production at Melbourne's Princess Theatre and an oversized London production. Sponsored by the Rodgers and Hammerstein organization (as Williamson Productions) in the spacious Adelphi Theatre, with Jane Connell (Winnifred), Milo O'Shea (King), Thelma Ruby (Queen) and Max Wall (Jester) featured, it proved a 38-performance failure.

Sydney saw *Once Upon a Mattress* for a couple of months at the Palace Theatre in 1962 (3 August), the piece was twice televised with Miss Burnett each time repeating her role, and a British revival, staged nearly 30 years later by Wendy Toye on the tiny stage of the Watermill Theatre in provincial Newbury, confirmed the small-scale delights of the piece. The show finally made its first incursion into Europe in 1990, played in a German version as *Winnifred,* and in 1996 (Broadhurst Theater 19 December) it made a Broadway reappearance, with Sarah Jessica Parker in the role of Winnifred and Heath Lamberts as King Sextimus (187 performances).

Australia: Princess Theatre, Melbourne 4 December 1959; UK: Adelphi Theatre 20 September 1960; Germany: Stadttheater, Hildesheim *Winnifred* 30 December 1990

Recordings: original cast (Kapp/MCA), London cast (HMV), New York revival cast (RCA)

L'ONCLE CÉLESTIN Opérette-bouffe in 3 acts by Maurice Ordonneau and Henri Kéroul. Music by Edmond Audran. Théâtre des Menus-Plaisirs, Paris, 24 March 1891.

Audran followed up the splendid success of *Miss Helyett* (1890) with a similarly lively, vaudevillesque piece of musical comedy that won its composer another ringing Parisian success through a first run of 150 performances, followed by a revival in 1895 for a further 50 performances, and by productions around the world.

Ordonneau and Kéroul's story was another variation on the musical-comedy will theme. The provincial lawyer Pontaillac (Vandenne) and his wife, Paméla (Yvonne Stella), are peacocking their way into Parisian society as Baron and Baronne, on the proceeds of a forthcoming legacy from their despised aubergiste Uncle Célestin. Their aim is to marry their daughter Célestine (Mme Augier) to Gontran des Accacias (Ternet), son of the noble des Accacias (Vavasseur) and his lofty wife (Fanny Genat). Célestine, however, is determined to wed none but her little cousin Gustave (Verneuil). The Pontaillacs are well into their act when the terms of Célestin's will are revealed, and they are shocked in their tracks. It doesn't stop them from inheriting, but it obliges them to go through six months' work in Célestin's inn before doing so. Thus, whilst the ''Baron'' and ''Baronne,'' working themselves into a lather as deeply disguised innkeeping Lenglumes, have their mail phonily redirected to their ''holiday in Switzerland,'' the actually penniless Accacias are busy having false letters redirected to them from their ''holiday in Naples and Monte Carlo.'' Inevitably they turn up at the inn, on the last day of the Pontaillacs' six months, and all sorts of farcical scenes occur with the result that when the notary (F Constance) comes to check up on the fulfillment of the will's conditions, the Pontaillacs deny their identity and lose all. When all seems darkest, a codicil turns up that makes Célestine the heir and allows her to get her man. Discomforture of the Accacias, reform of the foolish Pontaillacs, and all ends happily. Montcavrel played the role of Moreau, Célestin's old pal, who helps the action of the piece in its rebounds.

The songs of the piece fell largely to Célestine, who had a number about her late uncle (''Il aurait fait bien pitieuse mine'') and a love duo (''L'amour, ô mon cousin Gustave'') in the first act, delivered a Chanson de Langlois (''Langlois qu'était au clou'') and a duetto des Cauchois with Gustave (''Nous sommes nés natifs tous les deux'') in her disguise as a Normand serving wench, and topped off the third act with an angry Couplets du jeu de massacre, tearing the foolish Gontran to bits, and a post-codicil letter song in which she begins to bring home the truth to her parents. Gustave had a first-act air, the notary a comic song (''Vous appelez-vous Bernard?'') in the midst of a situation when neither the disguised Pontaillacs nor the disguised Accacias will admit to having a name, and they all joined in moments of buffo ensemble in a score that was, although sizeable, largely an accompaniment to the comedy of the evening.

Following its Parisian success, *L'Oncle Célestin* took off, in the wake of *Miss Helyett,* for all the main musical-theatre centers, but it fared rather less well than the earlier show had done. The German version appeared first, at Berlin's Friedrich-Wilhelmstädtisches Theater, followed by an American version (ad Georges Millet, ly: Fred Lyster), with Jefferson de Angelis (Pontaillac), Jennie Reiffarth (Paméla), Annie Meyers (Célestine), Harry Macdonough (Gontran) and Jennie Weathersby (Mme des Accacias) featured, and dancer Loie Fuller and Mabel Stephenson, the ''American Bird Warbler,'' interpolated into the action, which played through two months at Broadway's Casino Theater. London's production did little better. The score was altered with additional numbers by Meyer Lutz and Leslie Stuart and the old heroes of *Erminie,* Harry Paulton (Marreau) and Frank Wyatt (Acacia), were joined by Gaiety stars E J Lonnen (Golosh) and Sylvia Grey (Countess Acacia) and the Savoy's Scott Russell (Gustave) and Florence Perry (Clementine) at the head of the cast. It failed to take, and the replacement of Miss Grey with Ada Reeve and Paulton by Charles Danby, the addition of William Vokes as ''an india-rubber waiter'' and the wholesale remake of the score after seven weeks could not help enough to get the show through the summer. Budapest's *Celesztin apo* (ad Emil Makai, Ferenc Reiner) was played just six times and, in all, *L'Oncle Célestin* failed to live up to its home success in its various translated and ''adapted'' versions.

Paris saw a revival at the Folies-Dramatiques in April 1895.

Germany: Friedrich-Wilhelmstädtisches Theater *Onkel Cyprian* 26 September 1891; USA: Grand Opera House, St Louis *Uncle Celestin* 30 November 1891, Casino Theater 15 February 1892; UK: Trafalgar Square Theatre *Baron Golosh* 25 April 1895; Hungary: Népszínház *Celesztin apo* 8 January 1897

O'NEAL, Zelma [SCHRAEDER, Zelma] (b Rock Falls, Ill, 29 May 1907; d Largo, Fla, 5 November 1989).

A telephonist turned song-and-dance girl in musical theatre and vaudeville, Miss O'Neal struck oil first time on Broadway when she appeared as a bouncing incidental soubrette with a song in De Sylva, Brown and Henderson's *Good News* (1927, Flo). She repeated her role and ''The Varsity Drag'' in the show's London production the following year before going on to play another similar role in the same team's *Follow Thru* (1929, Angie Howard) and being gratified with a second hit song in ''Button Up Your Overcoat.''

Plate 290. **Zelma O'Neal,** *Roberston Hare, Sidney Fairbrother, Leslie Henson and David Hutcheson are all involved in the ''goings on'' of Bach and Arnold's* Nice Goings On.

She appeared in the film version of *Follow Thru* (1930) and in *Paramount on Parade* (1930), contributed to Broadway's *The Gang's All Here* (1931, Willy Wilson), and in 1932 returned to Britain, where, for several years, she appeared in supporting soubrette roles in the London musical theatre. She was seen in *Nice Goings On* (1933, Tutti) with Leslie Henson, in *Jack o'Diamonds* (1935, Peggy Turner), for which she was also choreographer, and in Henson's *Swing Along* (1936, Miami), as well as in a number of British film musicals (*Give Her a Ring, Mr Cinders* in Binnie Hale's role of Jill, etc), before disappearing from the world's playbills.

110 IN THE SHADE Musical in 2 acts by N Richard Nash based on his play *The Rainmaker.* Lyrics by Tom Jones. Music by Harvey Schmidt. Broadhurst Theater, New York, 24 October 1963.

The musical *110 in the Shade* was made up of a slimmed version of Nash's enjoyable and touching 1954 play (Cort Theater 28 October, 124 performances) and a score by the successful songwriters of *The Fantasticks.* Inga Swenson played Lizzie Curry, the plain and tough-tongued daughter of a country family whose livelihood is threatened by drought. The charlatan ''rainmaker,'' Starbuck (Robert Horton), who promises to save them, at a price, does not fool her, but she does find in his arms the regard, real or faked, that she cannot win from the divorced sheriff, File (Stephen Douglass). When rain does not come, and Starbuck is forced from town, the musical version puts Lizzie into File's arms. And then the rain comes.

The score for the piece produced no take-away number to rival the hit of *The Fantasticks,* but Horton's set piece ''Rain Song,'' his Quarrel Duet with Lizzie (''You're Not Fooling Me'') and a lively, incidental ''Poker Polka'' all fitted the play well, which a curiously off-character piece for the sensible Lizzie about being ''Raunchy'' did rather less.

David Merrick's production of *110 in the Shade* ran for 331 performances on Broadway, but a London presentation by Merrick and Emile Littler, with Miss Swenson and Douglass repeating their roles and Ivor Emmanuel as File, lasted only a disappointing 101 nights. However, a German version (ad Max Colpet) was premiered at Kassel in 1971, and the show, fortified by its fine leading roles and sympathetic tale, has continued to find regional and secondary productions in America over the 30 years since its first staging. A revised version was mounted by the New York City Opera in 1992 (18 July), with Brian Sutherland, Richard Muenz and Karen Ziemba featured.

UK: Palace Theatre 8 February 1967; Germany: Staatstheater, Kassel 27 February 1971

Recordings: original cast (RCA Victor), London cast (Columbia), studio cast (TER), etc

ONE TOUCH OF VENUS Musical in 2 acts by S J Perelman and Ogden Nash based on *The Tinted Venus* by F Anstey. Lyrics by Ogden Nash. Music by Kurt Weill. Imperial Theater, New York, 7 October 1943.

The whimsical 1885 *The Tinted Venus* of ''F Anstey'' [Thomas Anstey Guthrie, 1856–1934] told the comical story of a 19th-century London hairdresser, Leander Tweddle, who brings a statue of Aphrodite to life. Statues had been coming to life regularly on the musical stage since the days of *Galathee* and *Adonis,* but Anstey's book proved nonetheless a fine basis for a spectacular musical comedy, and the use of accredited and classy humorists Perelman and Nash as authors ensured a libretto and lyrics of bristling humor for what would be Kurt Weill's most brightly comical musical play.

New York art collector Whitelaw Savory (John Boles) has bought and imported an Anatolian statue of Venus (the name must have rhymed more easily than Aphrodite) that reminds him of his long-lost love. However, when the statue (Mary Martin) comes to life, she attaches herself not to her owner but to Savory's barber, Rodney Hatch (Kenny Baker), who has been the unintentional instrument of her awakening. Savory is miserable, Rodney is aghast and his fiancée, Gloria (Ruth Bond), and her mother are simply furious, as Venus and Rodney, with a touch of classic magic to aid them, go on to cause havoc throughout Manhattan. Venus magicks ghastly Gloria off to the North Pole when the girl gets too much to take and Rodney is suspected of murder, but when the Grecian goddess finally realizes that marriage to her awakener means a life as an American suburban housewife, she decides she prefers to change back to stone. The little fellow gets a happy ending, however, when a nice, suburban Venus-double arrives in time for the final curtain.

Weill's score produced several romantic numbers that became favorites—Venus's smooth, exploratory ''I'm a Stranger Here Myself,'' her seduction of Rodney to the strains of ''Speak Low'' and Savory's rueful, reflective ''West Wind''—whilst the comical side of affairs was highlighted by a wordful description of the trip of Gloria and her mother ''Way Out West in Jersey'' and Rodney's description of ''The Trouble with Women.'' Two set-piece Agnes de Mille ballets, one illustrative of New York's midday rush (''Forty Minutes for Lunch'') and the other showing Venus the delights of lower-middle-class life and tempting her back to Olympus (''Venus in Ozone Heights'') were inset into the action, along with a pageant number about ''Dr Crippen.''

Cheryl Crawford and John Wildberg's production of *One Touch of Venus,* directed by Elia Kazan, gave Weill the longest Broadway run of his career with a fine record of 567 performances, but although the show was subsequently made over into a film with a truncated and infiltrated score, and with Ava Gardner and the singing voice of Nan Wynn starring as Venus, it did not travel into a first-class production beyond America. It was televised in 1955 and revived at the Goodspeed Opera House on 22 April 1987, with Lynette Perry (Venus) and Michael Piontek (Rodney) in the principal roles.

A German edition (ad Richard Wiehe) was given at Meiningen in 1994, with Dagmar Hauser and Frank Sonnberger featured.

The Tinted Venus has served as a basis for at least five other musicals. The first to hit the stage was a British one written by Willie (brother of Oscar) Wilde for Rosina Vokes (*The Tinted Venus* Prince of Wales Theatre, Liverpool 7 September 1885, Globe Theater, Boston 5 October 1885), which featured its star in some ''sensational dancing'' as Venus and Weedon Grossmith as Leander Tweedle. It was swiftly followed by Charles D Blake and Thomas Addison's *Aphrodite, or Venus on a Lark,* produced at Poli's Theater, Waterbury, Conn, 8 December 1885 with Harry Crandall as Tweedle and Lillie Bate as Aphrodite (''the dialogue of the novel is followed pretty closely''), and by Willie Gill and George Jessop's *Aphrodite Still in the Ring,* produced at Pittsburgh's Library Hall (25 January 1886) and toured from there with Gussie de Forrest in the star role. Just weeks later, in Montreal (22 February 1886) W H Fuller and Richard Golden's version, *A Barber's Scrape,* with Golden starred, followed suit; in 1887 Charles Atkinson's Jollities presented what appears to have been a remade version of Blake and Addison's piece at Boston Museum (1 August) with Atkinson playing ''Cupid Smith''; whilst a fifth—or was it a sixth—effort, which again just called itself *The Tinted Venus* was played at Boston's Point of Pines, 3 August 1903, with Marion Manola as the goddess. None of them seems to have made much of a mark. In Britain, the tale was borrowed a second time for the musical play *Juno* (Woolwich 20 July 1908, J S Barker/H G French/George Roberts).

Anstey's works were also plundered for other musicals. His 1900 fantasy *The Brass Bottle* was turned into *Out of the Bottle* for London (London Hippodrome 11 June 1932, Vivian Ellis, Oscar Levant/Fred Thompson, Clifford Grey), while *Vice Versa* was made, with considerable success, into the touring American musical *Little Puck* (Academy of Music, Buffalo 20 September 1887, ad A C Gunter, Fred Maeder, Robert Fraser, Howard P Taylor), in which Frank Daniels scored an early career hit, and much later into Charles W Chase's farcical musical comedy *Where the Laugh Comes In* (1901).

Germany: Staatstheater, Meiningen 24 June 1994

Film: Universal 1948

Recordings: original cast (Decca/MCA), film soundtrack (Ariel), etc

THE ONLY GIRL Musical farcical comedy in 3 acts by Henry Blossom based on the play *Our Wives* by Frank Mandel and Helen Craft, a version of *Jugendfreude* by Ludwig Fulda. Music by Victor Herbert. 39th Street Theater, New York, 2 November 1914.

A piece in the small-scale musical comedy genre with a book taken this time from the German rather than from the French, *The Only Girl* had three of its once relatively confirmed bachelors (Jed Prouty, Richard Bartlett, Ernest Torrence) falling into marriage quickly and happily enough to be singing a sextet on ''Connubial Bliss'' in the second act, but to be already warning their surviving chum, who practices the profession of librettist (Thurston Hall), about ''When You're Wearing the Ball and Chain'' in the third. Nevertheless, it is not long before the writer gets around to singing ''You're the Only One for Me'' with his lady composer partner, Ruth (Wilda Bennett), who has been playing and singing the show's love theme in the wings since the first act.

The show's largest singing role (a third of the songs), however, fell to none of these reasonably plotworthy folk but to an incidental soubrette called Patsy (Adele Rowland), who opened up proceedings with what Herbert billed as ''an imitation of the present-day ragtime song'' called ''The More I See of Others, Dear, the Better I Like You,'' delivered a piece about ''Personality,'' slipped in a marching song with wartime sentiments (''Here's to the Land We Love, Boys'') and a theatrical song redolent of old comic-opera days (''You Have to Have a Part to Make a Hit'') and joined a sextet of girls, accompanying themselves with the clash of knives, forks and plates, to open the last act. Another incidental lassie had a song and dance routine about someone called ''Antoinette,'' but it was Ruth's soprano solo ''When You're Away,'' a waltz song with a Victorian parlor-song lyric that ended on a top B-natural, which proved the best-liked piece of *The Only Girl*'s score, over and above all the composer's more modernly made numbers.

Joe Weber's production of *The Only Girl* gave Herbert another fine success to follow up that of *Sweethearts* the previous year. It ran through 240 performances, moving up to a larger house from its tiny original theatre when success was clear, before heading to a fine life of some two years on the road.

Grossmith and Laurillard's London production of *The Only Girl* did less well, notching up 107 performances in the small Apollo Theatre with Mabel Russell as Patsy and Kenneth Douglas and Fay Compton featured as the last-wed couple. It did, however, give Herbert the longest run he would achieve from his five shows that were played in London (*The Wizard of the Nile, The Fortune Teller, The Red Mill, Angel Face*).

A 1933–34 San Francisco production, with its score titivated with Herbert favorites from other shows and Guy Robertson as a star, provoked a Shubert revival on Broadway with Robert Halliday and Bettina Hall in the cast (44th Street Theater 21 May 1934), but neither it nor a second West Coast revival, put up in the mid-1940s on the strength of the success of the Broadway revival of Herbert's *The Red Mill,* and which replaced the book with a new one by Alonzo Price, managed to establish *The Only Girl* alongside the best-loved Herbert shows.

UK: Apollo Theatre 25 September 1915

ON THE TOWN Musical in 2 acts by Betty Comden and Adolph Green based on the ballet *Fancy Free.* Music and additional lyrics by Leonard Bernstein. Adelphi Theater, New York, 28 December 1944.

The musical *On the Town* had its genesis in the ballet *Fancy Free,* a work composed (with one sung number, ''Big Stuff'') by Leonard Bernstein and staged by Jerome Robbins for the Ballet Theater (18 April 1944). Under the aegis of producers Oliver Smith and Paul Feigay, Bernstein and Robbins—joined for the text by Bernstein's friends Betty Comden and Adolph Green—took the ballet's basic premise of three sailors on shore leave going out in New York in search of girls and made it into a musical.

Sailors Gabey (John Battles), Ozzie (Green) and Chip (Cris Alexander) get off their ship ready to enjoy a day off in New York, but, when Gabey flips his lid over a poster of a lass billed as the subways' ''Miss Turnstiles'' of the month, his pals agree to spend their day helping him to track down his dream girl. Chip gets waylaid by an extrovert lady cabdriver (Nancy Walker), Ozzie runs into a lass (Betty Comden) with unstoppable impulses and a martyrized fiancé in a museum, but Gabey finally runs his heroine (Sono Osato) to earth, only to finally find out that she is not some kind of a star but a cooch dancer at Coney Island. Then it is time for the boys to go back to their ship and, as they get ready to set off to sea again, three other bright-eyed sailors bounce onto the quay for their day ''on the town.''

Bernstein's score, which was a wholly new one and did not include the music from *Fancy Free,* mixed a series of lively, revusical songs that ranged from the sailors' leaping welcome to ''New York, New York'' to the cabdriver's enthusiastic promise ''I Can Cook, Too'' and Comden and Green's paroxysmically unleashed ''I Get Carried Away,'' with some large and distinctly superior pieces of dance music as accompaniment to the important dance sequences of the show: Gabey's fantasy of ''Miss Turnstiles,'' his wander through the ''Lonely Town,'' the second-act ''Times Square Ballet'' and Gabey's imaginings of Coney Island as ''The Playground of the Rich,'' in which the dancing Miss Osato featured as a glamorous man-tamer.

The fresh and lively *On the Town,* with its semi-revue, semi-dance-and-laughter-show construction, its funny songs, its zippy Robbins dances and unfussy George Abbott staging, proved an immediate success, and the initial Broadway production ran for 463 performances. A 1949 film version, with a cast headed by Frank Sinatra, Gene Kelly, Jules Munshin, Vera-Ellen, Betty Garrett and Ann Miller, although it varied significantly from the original show musically (five new numbers were introduced), successfully recaptured the taking brightness and innocence of the original. The show did not, however, attract foreign takers, and subsequent attempts to reproduce it in later and less innocent days in New York proved failures.

A 1959 off-Broadway production (Carnegie Hall Playhouse 15 January) with Harold Lang (Gabey), Joe Bova (Ozzie) and Joe Layton as choreographer played 70 performances and sparked a first staging (also by Layton) in London, where Don McKay (Gabey), Elliott Gould (Ozzie), Gillian Lewis (Claire) and Andrea Jaffe (Ivy) featured through 53 performances. A 1971 New York revival (Imperial Theater 31 October), with a cast including Ron Husmann (Gabey), Donna McKechnie (Ivy), Phyllis Newman (Claire) and Bernadette Peters (Hildy), folded in 73 performances.

A German version (ad Rolf Merz, Gerhard Hagen) was premiered in Kaiserslautern in 1977, and in 1991, following the Stuttgart Ballet's successful production of *On Your Toes,* the Hamburg Ballet turned its attentions to classic Broadway and produced a version (ad Claud H Henneberg, John Neumeier) of *On the Town* (Hamburg Staatsoper 15 December 1991).

On the Town was played again in New York under the auspices of the New York Shakespeare Festival in 1997 (Delacorte Theater 31 July) and in a shortlived revival at the Gershwin Theater in 1998 (15 November, 65 performances).

UK: Prince of Wales Theatre 30 May 1963; Germany: Pfalztheater, Kaiserslautern 11 September 1977

Film: MGM 1949

Recordings: selections (Columbia, Decca/MCA, etc), London cast (CBS), concert recording (DG) film soundtrack (Show Biz), etc

ON THE TWENTIETH CENTURY Musical in 2 acts by Adolph Green and Betty Comden based on *Twentieth Century* by Ben Hecht, Charles McArthur and Bruce Millholland. Lyrics by Betty Comden and Adolph Green. Music by Cy Coleman. St James Theater, New York, 19 February 1978.

The play *Twentieth Century* (the title referred to the famous luxury train linking New York and Chicago) had a successful 152-performance run at Broadway's Broadhurst Theater in 1932–33 with Moffatt Johnstone and Eugenie Leontovich in the lead roles, was made into an even more successful film with John Barrymore and Carole Lombard as its stars, and returned to Broadway and further success in 1950 with Gloria Swanson and José Ferrer, before it was made into a musical, in 1978, with perhaps the most success of all.

The flamboyant but financially frowsy impresario Oscar Jaffee (John Cullum) books a compartment on the long-distance train from west to east. Not any compartment, but the one next to the fabulous film star Lily Garland (Madeleine Kahn), now a household name but originally his ''discovery'' and once his mistress. Jaffee plans to woo Lily back to his management, and the bait he uses is the role of Mary Magdalene in a spectacular epic that will be financed by an elderly and religious heiress (Imogene Coca) he has encountered on the trip. He has to battle against a more conventional producer equipped with a Somerset Maugham play, against Lily's resident bit of bruisable beefcake, Bruce Granit (Kevin Kline), and the ultimate revelation that his backer is an escaped lunatic, before—at the final curtain—the two fall, laughing, into each other's arms.

Astutely slimmed, the original (male) lunatic happily resexed for the benefit of Miss Coca, and equipped with a volley of witty lyrics, the piece was set by Coleman as a burlesque comic opera. A series of musically dazzling and hilarious solos and ensembles was highlighted by a dilemma scena for Lily, torn between Oscar and the Magdalene on the one hand and the role of Somerset Maugham's ''Babette'' on the other, in a musical monologue that raced from the depths of chest voice to the most distant soprano leger lines, demanding a vocal and dramatic virtuosity rare in any kind of musical theatre. Another scene, in which little Miss piano-playing Plotka, having devastated an incompetent leading lady's singing audition, is transformed by Oscar into a star in the musico-patriotico-weepie ''Véronique,'' helped make the role of Lily one of the outstanding comedy/singing vehicles in musical theatre history, whilst Oscar's extravagantly baritonic hymn of self-confidence ''I Rise Again,'' his fake farewell ''The Legacy,'' and their too-good-to-be-true duo about ''Our Private World'' ensured that her co-star was never left behind. The other musical high spots include a manic sextet in which Oscar and his allies try to get Lily to ''Sign'' a contract, a burlesque death duo (''Lily, Oscar'') and the plotters' harmonized glee at getting a check with ''Five Zeros'' on it.

Hal Prince's direction heightened the burlesque fun of the script and score without ever over-exaggerating it, Robin Wagner's train sets (inside and outside, still and moving) won delighted acclaim and *On the Twentieth Century* gathered a handful of Tony Awards, including Best Musical. Its soon-in-difficulties leading lady was replaced by Judy Kaye, as the piece ran through 460 performances on Broadway before going on the road with Miss Kaye starred opposite Rock Hudson. Harold Fielding's London production, with Keith Michell and Julia McKenzie starred and Mark Wynter as the maltreated Granit, took a couple of nips in the show (two numbers were cut) but, after playing to bulging houses for several months, found its audience vanish almost overnight and closed after 165 performances.

The piece was revived in 1996 at London's Bridewell Theatre (14 August), and at the Goodspeed Opera House in 1999 (April 9).

The ''Twentieth Century'' had featured many years previously in *Fun on the Twentieth Century Limited,* a burlesque-style musical comedy apparently modeled on the durable trainboard *The Tourists in a Palace Pullman Car* and produced in 1902 as a variety theatre entertainment.

UK: Her Majesty's Theatre 19 March 1980

Recording: original cast (Columbia)

ON YOUR TOES Musical comedy in 2 acts by Richard Rodgers, Lorenz Hart and George Abbott. Lyrics by Lorenz Hart. Music by Richard Rodgers. Imperial Theater, New York, 11 April 1936.

Hollywood provided Rodgers and Hart with material for several of their musicals. *America's Sweetheart* used filmland as its subject matter, but two others of the partners' shows were developed from material that had been originally envisaged as the stuff of a film musical. One was *I Married an Angel,* and the other, which found its way to the stage the first, was *On Your Toes,* a dance-based piece set around some amorous and comical situations in a ballet company, initially dreamed up as a movie vehicle for Fred Astaire.

Junior Dolan (Ray Bolger), once a vaudeville performer, is now a music teacher with a couple of promising pupils in composer Sidney Cohn (David Morris) and songwriter Frankie Frayne (Doris Carson). Sidney has composed a jazz ballet, and when Frankie lets out that ballet Maecenas Peggy Porterfield (Luella Gear) is a family friend, Junior wangles an introduction, determined to get Sidney's piece produced. Peggy is all for something new, artistic director Sergei Alexandrovitch (Monty Woolley) is all against and company star Vera Barnova (Tarmara Geva), who has quarreled with Morrosine (Demetrios Vilan), her leading man, is all for Junior (who has just admitted love to Frankie). Peggy's money wins *Slaughter on Tenth Avenue* a production, but since Morrosine can't do the modern steps, Junior steps in to dance the lead male role opposite Vera. The furious Morrosine hires a gunman to shoot him down on opening night, but Junior keeps himself a moving target until the police arrive and he can relax into a fairly improbable happy ending.

The ballet choreographer George Balanchine was hired to do the dances that made up an important part of the show. The first act featured the ballet company's *Princess Zenobia* in which Junior, shoved on at the last minute to replace a missing member of the corps de ballet, manages (equally improbably) to bungle every step and cause havoc with his ineptitudes, whilst the second act included a title song and dance in which phalanxes of ballet performers and tap-dancing students faced up to each other in a confrontation of the two styles that were to be blended in Sidney's ballet. The show came to its climax with the performance of the story ballet *Slaughter on Tenth Avenue,* which began as a dramatic dance piece about a sleazy dance-hall girl (Vera) and a vaudeville hoofer (Junior) before developing into a piece of wild comedy as the hero danced exhaustingly around the stage (why didn't he just run off?), keeping out of the way of the killer's bullets.

In consequence of the large dance element, the song list of *On Your Toes* was shorter than usual, but it still brought out several pieces that would become Rodgers and Hart favorites. Frankie presented ''It's Got to be Love'' as an example of her songwriting, and another pupil showed off his homework in ''Quiet Night,'' whilst Frankie and Junior slipped in the wishful ''There's a Small Hotel'' as their love blossomed, and she torched wistfully that she was ''Glad to Be Unhappy'' when he neglected her to make a fuss over Vera. Peggy had the stand-up numbers of the night, insisting that ''The Heart Is Quicker Than the Eye'' and joining Sergei in ''Too Good for the Average Man.''

If the show's plot was frequently improbable and incoherent, its contents—song, dance and a large dash of comedy—were grand entertainment, and Dwight Deere Wiman's production of *On Your Toes* had a fine Broadway career of 315 performances in 1936–37. Whilst it ran on, Wiman and Lee Ephraim mounted a London production whose comedy element was emphasized in their choice of director: laughter star Leslie Henson. Jack Whiting played Junior, Vera Zorina was Vera and Gina Malo sang Frankie, with Jack Donohue (Morrosine), songwriter Eddie Pola (Sidney) and Oliver Blakeney (Peggy) amongst the supporting cast. The piece did not win the same popularity in London as it had in New York, and it was shuttered after six weeks and sent on the road. The producers decided, however, to have a second go, and on 19 April they reopened the show at the London Coliseum. The original verdict was confirmed, and *On Your Toes* folded a second time after 54 additional performances.

On Your Toes made its way back to Hollywood in 1939, to be filmed with Vera Zorina (but without its songs), and it was given a second Broadway showing in 1954 when, following the success of the 1952 revival of *Pal Joey,* George Abbott mounted a new production with Zorina, Bobby Van (Junior) and Kay Coulter (Frankie) featured. Elaine Stritch played Peggy and was given an additional number, ''You Took Advantage of Me,'' plucked from the score of *Present Arms.* If this revival lasted only 64 performances, a further mounting in 1983 won an altogether different level of appreciation. Ballet star Natalia Makarova was featured in a version that used much of Balanchine's original choreography for its ballet sections (add ch: Peter Martins, Donald Saddler), alongside Lara Teeter (Junior), George S Irving (Sergei), Christine Andreas (Frankie), Dina Merrill (Peggy) and another ballet name, George de la Pena, as Morrosine. The aged Abbott directed (which he had not officially done first time round in spite of being involved in the project almost from the start), and the revival had a grand New York run of 505 performances.

This revival set the show up for the future. The production was exported to London (1984), where Makarova starred alongside Tim Flavin (Junior) and Siobhan McCarthy (Frankie), and the show more than compensated for its unimpressive first visit to the West End by winning a 539-performance run at the same Palace Theatre, which it had visited briefly in 1937. And with the role of Vera now established as okay for a real, live ballet name (Makarova had been followed in America by Galina Panova, and in London by Doreen Wells), new horizons opened for *On Your Toes.* Opera houses had been making back some of the money lost on unpopular operas on productions of operettas and musical plays for some years: *On Your Toes*—even if much of its dance content was unballetic and comic—was splendid meat for the ballet world. In 1991 the Stuttgart Ballet mounted an *On Your Toes* with choreography newly done by Larry Fuller and with Marcia Haydée and Richard Cragun starring, as Rodgers and Hart's show found itself, for a few years, more popularity than it had at any time since the war.

Plate 291. **On Your Toes.** *Tamara Geva (left) and Ray Bolger (kneeling) in Broadway's famous dance musical.*

UK: Palace Theatre 5 February 1937; Germany: Theater im Forum, Ludwigsburg (Eng) 16 September 1990

Recordings: Broadway 1954 revival cast (Decca/DRG), Broadway 1983 revival cast (TER/Polydor), selections (Columbia), etc

OPERETTE In 2 acts by Noël Coward. His Majesty's Theatre, London, 16 March 1938.

After the successes of *Bitter-Sweet* and *Conversation Piece,* Coward persisted in writing romantic operettas without ever again winning the same success. Having successfully imported the queen of the Parisian musical theatre, Yvonne Printemps, for *Conversation Piece,* Coward this time created a role for Berlin's longtime favorite Operette star, Fritzi Massary. Massary featured as a Viennese singing star dispensing song and advice alongside Irene Vanbrugh as the mother of the lovestruck Nigel Vaynham (Griffith Jones), who has to be stopped from the socially suicidal course of marrying Rozanne

Grey (Peggy Wood), the chorine promoted to star of *Operette*'s show-within-a-show, *The Model Maid.* Much of *Operette*'s score was the score of *The Model Maid* in which Coward had fun with pastiches of turn-of-the-century musical styles: the *Florodora* sextet, Gaiety low comedy, and a good ration of soprano solos. However, the enduring success of the score was another of Coward's revusical comedy jeux d'esprit, a male quartet about ''The Stately Homes of England.''

Operette hit trouble on the road and its author/composer/producer/director (and, briefly, musical director after he sacked the original one) made alterations before town, but they were not sufficient and the show, which Coward later counted his least satisfactory, lasted only 133 performances in London before going out on tour with Ivy St Helier playing a remade version of Massary's role.

Recording: original cast (part-record) (WRC)

DER OPERNBALL Operette in 3 acts by Victor Léon and Heinrich von Waldberg based on the comedy *Les Dominos roses* by Alfred Hennequin and Alfred Delacour. Music by Richard Heuberger. Theater an der Wien, Vienna, 5 January 1898.

One of the most internationally successful comedies of its era, Hennequin and Delacour's *Les Dominos roses* (Théâtre du Vaudeville 17 April 1876) was made over as a musical play in three languages—none of which was French—of which the most enduring has turned out to be the Viennese *Der Opernball.* The adaptation, which kept the setting French, was musically set by the Operettic novice Heuberger, with whom co-librettist Léon had earlier collaborated on a ballet, *Struwwelpeter,* for Dresden, and who apparently took his time over it. *Der Opernball* was cited in the production schedules for several years before it appeared on the stage, but when it was produced by Alexandrine von Schönerer at the Theater an der Wien in 1898, it achieved the kind of success that was worth waiting for.

Georges Duménil (Karl Streitmann) offers to take his country friend Paul Aubier (Josef Joseffy) to the Opera Ball in search of a little feminine adventure, and is delighted when opportunity effortlessly presents itself even before the event, in the form of anonymous billets-doux arranging a ball-night rendezvous apiece with an unknown lady disguised in a pink domino. Duménil's pubescent nephew, Henri (Fr Frey), who is aching for his first experiences of the demi-monde, gets a letter too. They are not to know, of course, that the letters come from the female members of their own suspicious household. All three men meet their mystery ladies, and Beaubuisson (Karl Blasel), Mme Duménil's aging uncle, joins in the farcical fun on the arm of a pretty danseuse (Therese Biedermann), as the gentlemen and their pink-dominoed ladies pop in and out of ''private'' boxes (the traditional place for bal masqué hanky-panky). In the course of all this ''popping'' the pairings get rather mixed up and instead of the men romancing their own wives (Fr Ottmann, Fr Reichsberg), as the plotting ladies had intended, each, in turn, ends up making advances to Henri's partner, who is none other than the Duménils' obliging maid, Hortense (Annie Dirkens). When the men, having discovered the plot, make a joke of the whole business with their wives the next day, it is the ladies' turn to be hoist—each suspects her husband of having flirted perhaps too heavily with the other's wife—but all is finally assuaged when Hortense owns up, and it is chastenedly agreed all around that no harm has been done.

Heuberger's score was one of dances—polka, mazurka, march and waltz—combined in three acts of music (including only a single chorus number, subsequently cut) from which one song, Hortense's waltzing invitation to little Henri, ''Geh'n wir in's Chambre separée,'' emerged as an enduring Operette standard.

Frau von Schönerer's production of *Der Opernball* was one of her greatest successes. It was played 56 times en suite and brought back regularly in the Theater an der Wien repertoire thereafter, passing its 100th performance on 29 March 1899, and playing on into 1900, during which time one of the cast changes brought in Ilka Pálmay as Henri. It was then taken into the Carltheater (14 April 1901), where Blasel repeated his Beaubuisson alongside Mizzi Günther (Hortense) and young Louis Treumann (Philippe, the butler) and where it passed its 200th night on 14 December 1902 with Dirkens, Blasel and Streitmann all in their original roles. It played at the Raimundtheater (7 May 1901), made its first appearance at the Volksoper in 1908 (12 February) and in 1914 returned for a month in a starry new production to the Theater an der Wien (30 December), with Luise Kartousch (Henri), Ernst Tautenhayn (Paul), Paul Guttmann (Beaubuisson), Hubert Marischka (Duménil), Betty Fischer (Hortense) and Cordy Millowitsch (Angèle) in the cast.

In 1920 *Der Opernball* was played at the Bürgertheater, in 1922 at the Johann Strauss-Theater, whilst in 1931 the Staatsoper presented a version (ad Rohr, 24 January) with a cast including Leo Slezak (Beaubuisson), Adele Kern (Henri) and Lotte Lehmann (Angèle), which was revived in 1938. In 1952 the Volksoper presented another revised version (ad O T Schuh), with the music done over by Anton Paulik and Rudolf Kattnigg. That version was abandoned for the Volksoper productions of 1985 (27 October) and 1995 (25 February) of an Operette that has remained a solid item of the Viennese repertoire, in the shadow only of the most international of favorites.

Berlin got its first production hot on the heels of Vienna's, with Siegmund as Beaubuisson and Steiner as

Plate 292. **Der Opernball.** *A little bit of feminine plotting sets up a little bit of masculine undoing in Ulmer Theater's production of the musicalized* Dominos roses.

Duménil, alongside Ottilie Collin (Hortense), Frln Erich (Henri) and Frln Asle (Angèle) at the head of the ladies, but although it proved as popular in Germany as in Austria, *Der Opernball* didn't do as well in the other main centers. It was not given in America until more than a decade after its first production, after the fashion for Viennese Operette had been aroused by *Die lustige Witwe.* The intial performances were played at the German-language Yorkville Theater, with Emil Berla (Beaubuisson), Minnie Landau (Angèle), Wilhelm Nikow (Duménil), Mizi Raabe (Henri) and Louise Barthel (Hortense) amongst the cast, but, although a subsequent English version was originally announced as a vehicle for Lillian Russell, it ended up being produced, in a version by Sydney Rosenfeld and Clare Kummer, with Marie Cahill top-billed as Céleste (ex- Hortense) singing "What Are We Coming To?" and dancing the Turkey Trot. Harry Fairleigh (Dumesnil), George Lydecker (Aubier), Harry Conor (Beaubuisson), Olive Ulrich (Angèle) and Burrell Barbarette in the role of a non-travesty Henry supported the star through just 32 performances of *The Opera Ball* on Broadway.

Shortly after, Grossmith and Laurillard brought to Broadway their English musical-comedy version of the *Pink Dominos* tale, *Tonight's the Night.* This very much musically lighter show proved altogether more to Broadway's tastes and, after a successful season in America, was duly taken back to be played for a long run in London, where *Der Opernball* had been ignored. Paris passed on both pieces, and Budapest had its own *Dominos roses* musical produced whilst Heuberger was still getting round to completing his score (*Három légyott* text and music by József Bokor, Népszínház 22 October 1897). *Der Opernball* was, nevertheless, mounted in Budapest, at the Magyar Színház (ad Jenő Faragó) in 1899, and revived at the Népopera in 1916 (16 December).

In 1970 a musical version of James Albery's English adaptation of the original play, *Pink Dominos,* was produced at Britain's Salisbury Playhouse (mus: John Gould, 17 March) under the title *Who Was That Lady?*

Der Opernball has been thrice filmed for the cinema, first by Max Neufeld, with Liane Haid and George Alexander, then by Géza von Bolvary with Marte Harell and Paul Hörbiger as stars, and again by Ernst Marischka (who had also written the screenplay of the 1939 version) and reset in Vienna, featuring a cast including Josef Meinrad (Paul), Johannes Heesters (Georg), Sonja Ziemann (Helene), Herta Feiler (Elisabeth) and Hans Moser, who had also appeared in the first film, in a typical Moser role as the comically all-arranging Oberkellner. A German television version was produced in 1971.

Germany: Theater Unter den Linden 11 March 1898; Hungary: Magyar Színház *Az operabál* 16 May 1899; USA: Yorkville Theater 24 May 1909, Liberty Theater *The Opera Ball* 12 February 1912

Films: Max Neufeld 1931, Géza von Bolvary 1939, Ernst Marischka 1956

Recording: selections (Philips)

ORBACH, Jerry (b New York, 20 October 1935). American actor-singer who has created several major Broadway musical roles.

Orbach made his first notable musical-theatre appearance in succession to Scott Merrill as Macheath in the long-running 1958 revival of *The Threepenny Opera.* In 1960 he created the role of the adventurer, El Gallo, in *The Fantasticks,* introducing the show's hit song "Try to Remember," and the following year created the part of the misanthropic, many-voiced puppeteer in *Carnival,* opposite Anna-Maria Alberghetti. He appeared in revivals of *The Cradle Will Rock, Annie Get Your Gun* (Charlie Davenport) and *Carousel* (Jigger) in the 1960s and, in 1969, created the leading role of the too-obliging apartment owner, Chuck Baxter, in another highly successful musical, *Promises, Promises.*

In 1975 Orbach starred with Gwen Verdon and Chita Rivera as the glint-toothed lawyer Billy Flynn in *Chicago* ("All I Care About Is Love") and in 1980 as the magnetic Julian Marsh in the stage version of *42nd Street,* compiling an impressive list of major new musical roles for an era when many a star artist is credited with only one or two such parts in (or as) an entire career.

Orbach supplied the voice of the candlestick, Lumière, in the Disney film *Beauty and the Beast.*

THE ORCHID Musical play in 2 acts by James T Tanner. Lyrics by Adrian Ross and Percy Greenbank. Music by Ivan Caryll and Lionel Monckton. Gaiety Theatre, London, 28 October 1903.

The Orchid continued the run of world-famous musical comedies that George Edwardes had produced at the old Gaiety Theatre in the Strand when the producer moved his operation to the newly built Gaiety, further along the same thoroughfare. But if the theatre was new and different, the show was not: *The Orchid* maintained the same formulae, the same writers and the same stars that had given the older house its vast vogue, and it won its reward with a 559-performance run (including an official "second edition").

The plot concerned the precious flower of the title and the efforts of British (Harry Grattan) and French (Robert Nainby) politicians to get their hands on it. The bloom discovered by Peruvian flower hunter Zaccary (Fred Wright jr) gets destroyed, but little Meakin (Edmund Payne), a gardener at a horticultural college, has grown another, and he becomes the object of the politicians' pursuit. That pursuit became mixed up with another, of two young couples who have just been married in Paris but, through the vagueness of the registrar, to the wrong mates (Lionel Mackinder and Ethel Sydney, Gertie Millar and George Grossmith). Connie Ediss was Caroline Twining, a lady mad to marry who ended up sporting the orchid in her hat, and Gabrielle Ray was the secretary to the British minister.

Amongst all the fun—Payne equipped with armor and broadsword (accompanied by the strains of the sabre song from *La Grande-Duchesse*) and challenged to a duel for his flower by the fire-breathing Frenchman, Grattan, touching on a caricature of Joseph Chamberlain, and Gabs Ray making his relationship with his secretary so pointed that it had to be rewritten—came the Gaiety songs. Miss Millar sang of "Little Mary" in reference to J M Barrie's recent play and waxed northern in "Liza Ann," Connie Ediss in a comical get-up sang of "Fancy Dress" and Grossmith and Payne gave their opinion of "The Unemployed" immortalizing Ross's version of the dole-bludger's creed ("It ain't much enjoyment to ask for employment and only get work instead"), but the hit of the show was, as so often in these days, an interpolated number. Grossmith popped in Blanche Ring's Broadway hit "Bedelia" and made as big a success of it in London as she had done on the other side of the Atlantic.

The Orchid duly made its way to the other English-speaking stages of the world that had reveled in the earlier Gaiety musicals. J C Williamson Ltd promptly mounted a version in Australia, with Evelyn Scott and Florence Young playing the two young ladies, George Lauri as Meakin and Clara Clifton as Caroline, while the Gaiety version still ran on in London and while two companies purveyed the piece to the British provinces at the beginning of a series of tours that would last for several years. In 1905 the Edwardes-Wheeler repertory company introduced the show to South Africa at the Cape Town Opera House (1 August), but Edwardes stepped in with an injunction to prevent *The Orchid* and a bundle of his other shows being played on the Far East circuits when royalties were not forthcoming. Only after all this did *The Orchid* make its appearance on Broadway.

The Shuberts' American production hit a problem on the run into town when its top-billed star Eddie Foy (Meakin) threatened to walk out if the part of his co-star, Trixie Friganza (Caroline), were not reduced. In spite of the fact that his own role had been beefed up with such pieces as Bryan and Goetz's hit ''He Goes to Church on Sundays,'' his worries proved justified, for Miss Friganza (who stayed) was a great success, but so was *The Orchid.* It put up a Broadway run of 178 performances, and proved the most popular of all the Gaiety shows that had been transported—in variously ''localized'' and ''intepolated into'' forms—to Broadway. Indeed, so successful was it that the producers announced that they would take their version of the piece back to London and let British audiences compare Foy and Miss Friganza with Payne and Miss Ediss. Foy refused the challenge, however, and it was not for nearly another decade that a remade American version of a London musical braved (very briefly) the West End.

Australia: Her Majesty's Theatre, Melbourne 29 October 1904; USA: Herald Square Theater 8 April 1907

ORDONNEAU, [Jean Léon] Maurice (b Saintes, 18 June 1854; d Paris, December 1916).

Journalist and dramatic critic Ordonneau began writing for the theatre in his early twenties, making an early appearance on a Paris playbill teamed with the established Eugène Grangé and Victor Bernard as an author of the Folies-Marigny revue *Les Cri-cris de Paris* (1876). Over the next four decades, working more often alone than was usually the case in this age of authorial pairings, he contributed liberally to both the straight and musical stage in Paris. Many of his earliest musical collaborations were with composer Edmond Audran, with whom he paired on a first success with *Serment d'amour* in 1886 and again with the amusingly vaudevillesque *L'Oncle Célestin* and with *Madame Suzette* before the two produced their biggest success together in the comical story of *La Poupée* (1896). Ordonneau combined with other prominent composers such as Gaston Serpette (*Cousin-cousine*), Louis Varney (*La Falote*), Victor Roger (*L'Auberge du Tohu-bohu*) and Louis Ganne (*Les Saltimbanques*) on pieces that found success mainly in their country of origin, but he also had a hand in several other pieces that, like *La Poupée,* found greater favor in other countries and in other languages than their original.

The most striking example of this was his text for *Madame Sherry,* a piece in a straightforward French vaudeville mode, which made a considerable hit when it was produced in Germany, with a score by the Austrian composer Hugo Felix, and was then turned into an equally successful American musical comedy with songs by Karl Hoschna and Otto Harbach. His *Les Hirondelles,* set to music by Henri Hirschmann, also had its first production in Germany, whilst his vaudeville *Le Jockey malgré lui,* played in France with a score by Victor Roger, became *The Office Boy* (Victoria Theater 2 November 1903) in America, with the piece's original music replaced by some new songs by Ludwig Englander. The Henry Blossom/Raymond Hubbell musical comedy *The Man from Cook's* (New Amsterdam Theater 25 March 1912) was said to be based on an Ordonneau original (maybe only a story line, but Ordonneau was red-hot beyond the Atlantic at the time because of *Madame Sherry*), which was probably the 1907 ''grosse bouffonerie'' *L'Agence Cook et cie.* Vienna's Theater in der Josefstadt staged a homemade Posse mit Gesang *Wien über alles* (1 January 1901), which credited Ordonneau (w Grenet-Dancourt) as author of its source, which was probably their *Paris, quand-même, ou les deux Bigorret* (Théâtre Cluny 31 March 1896), and Düsseldorf's Lustspielhaus staged a musical version of his *Une affaire scandaleuse* (w Gavault) as *Eine kitzliche Geschichte* (31 October 1912, Hugo Hirsch/Rudolf Schanzer). His *La Petite Vénus,* written with Justin Clérice, though never produced in France, made it to the British stage as *The Royal Star.*

In the later part of his career Ordonneau adapted an increasing number of foreign pieces for the French stage—Spanish, English and Viennese—amongst which were *Charley's Aunt* (equipped with some songs by Ivan Caryll) and Harry Paulton's *Niobe,* as well as a run of musical shows, and he had one final sizeable success with an original libretto the year before his death, with the patriotic wartime musical *La Cocarde de Mimi-Pinson.*

1875 **Les Diamants de Florinette** (Louis Desormes/w Ernest Hamm) 1 act La Pepinière 20 March

1880 **Madame Grégoire** (Édouard Okolowicz, et al/w Paul Burani) Théâtre des Arts 20 May

1882 **Mimi-Pinson** (Gustave Michiels/w Arthur Verneuil [and Paul Burani uncredited]) Théâtre Cluny 14 March

1886 **Serment d'amour** (Edmond Audran) Théâtre des Nouveautés 19 February

1886 **La Princesse Colombine** (*Nell Gwynne*) French version w Émile André (Théâtre des Nouveautés)

1887 **La Fiancée des verts-poteaux** (Audran) Théâtre des Menus-Plaisirs 8 November

1888 **Babette** (*La Grappe d'amour*) (Michiels/w Verneuil ad Alfred Murray, J G Mosenthal) Strand Theatre, London 26 January

1888 **Miette** (Audran) Théâtre de la Renaissance 24 September

1891 **La Petite Poucette** (Raoul Pugno/w Maurice Hennequin) Théâtre de la Renaissance 5 March

1891 **L'Oncle Célestin** (Audran/w Henri Kéroul) Théâtre des Menus-Plaisirs 24 March

1892 **La Cocarde tricolore** (Robert Planquette/Hippolyte Cogniard, Theodore Cogniard ad) Théâtre des Folies-Dramatiques 12 February

1893 **Madame Suzette** (Audran/w André Sylvane) Théâtre des Bouffes-Parisiens 29 March

1893 **Mademoiselle ma femme** (Frédéric Toulmouche/w Octave Pradels) Théâtre des Menus-Plaisirs 5 May

1893 **Cousin-cousine** (Gaston Serpette/w Kéroul) Théâtre des Folies-Dramatiques 23 December

1894 **La Plantation Thomassin** (Albert Vizentini/w Albin Valabrègue) Eden-Theatre, Vichy 24 July

1895 **La Perle du Cantal** (Toulmouche) Théâtre des Folies-Dramatiques 2 March

1895 **La Saint-Valentin** (Toulmouche/w Fernand Beissier) Théâtre des Bouffes-Parisiens 28 March

1896 **La Gran Via** French version (L'Olympia)

1896 **La Falote** (Louis Varney/w Armand Liorat) Théâtre des Folies-Dramatiques 17 April

1896 **La Poupée** (Audran) Théâtre de la Gaîté 21 October

1896 **La Demoiselle de magasin** (*The Shop Girl*) French version (Olympia)

1897 **L'Auberge du Tohu-bohu** (Victor Roger) Théâtre des Folies-Dramatiques 10 February

1897 **La Chula** (d'Hidalgo/w Ensenat, ''G Pollonnais'' [ie, Hubert Desvignes]) 1 act L'Olympia 30 September

1898 **L'Agence Crook et cie** (Roger) Théâtre des Folies-Dramatiques 28 January

1898 **The Royal Star** (*La Petite Vénus*) (Justin Clérice/ad Francis Richardson) Prince of Wales Theatre, London 16 September

1899 **Les Soeurs Gaudichard** (Audran) Théâtre de la Gaîté 21 April

1899 **Les Saltimbanques** (Louis Ganne) Théâtre de la Gaîté 30 December

1901 **Le Curé Vincent** (Audran) Théâtre de la Gaîté 25 October

1902 **Madame Sherry** (Hugo Felix/w Paul Burani ad Benno Jacobson) Centraltheater, Berlin 1 November

1902 **Le Jockey malgré lui** (Roger/w Paul Gavault) Théâtre des Bouffes-Parisiens 4 December

1904 **Les Hirondelles** (*Das Schwalbennest*) (Henri Hirschmann/ad Maurice Rappaport) Centraltheater, Berlin 9 January

1904 **Le Voyage de la mariée** (Clérice, Edmond Diet/w Paul Ferrier) Galeries Saint-Hubert, Brussels 9 December

1905 **Les Filles Jackson et Cie** (Clérice) Théâtre des Bouffes-Parisiens 29 November

1907 **Miss Zozo** (Georges A Haakman/w André Alexandre) Théâtre des Capucines 19 March

1908 **La Môme Flora** (Toulmouche/w Pradels) Théâtre de la Scala 26 December

1910 **La Demoiselle du tabarin** (Edmond Missa, Diet, Toulmouche/w Alexandre) Nouveau Théâtre du Château d'Eau 25 March

1911 **La Marquise de Chicago** (Toulmouche/w Beissier, Louis Herel) Enghien 26 September

1911 **Les Trois Amoureuses** (*Libellentanz*) French version (Théâtre Molière, Brussels)

1912 **Eva** French version w Jean Bénédict (Alhambra, Brussels)

1913 **Coeur de Créole** (*Kreolenblut*) French version w Bénédict (Lille)

1913 **Le Roi des montagnes** (*Das Fürstenkind*) French version w Bénédict (Théâtre Molière, Brussels)

1913 **La Petite Manon** (Hirschmann/w Henze) Theatre Royal, Ghent 15 March

1914 **La Fauvette envolée** (Georges de Seynes/w Bénédict) Marseille

1915 **La Cocarde de Mimi-Pinson** (Henri Goublier/w Francis Gally) Théâtre de l'Apollo 25 November

1916 **La Demoiselle du Printemps** (Goublier) Théâtre de l'Apollo 17 May

1923 **J'épouse Cendrillon** (Guy de Pierreu, A Rachet) Avignon 17 February

DER ORLOW Operette in 3 acts by Ernst Marischka and Bruno Granichstaedten. Music by Granichstaedten. Theater an der Wien, Vienna, 3 April 1925.

One of the most successful musicals to come from the Viennese theatre in the 1920s, *Der Orlow* curiously crept out of the general repertoire thereafter whilst other, less popular, lusher pieces with more fashionable names than that of Bruno Granichstaedten attached to them won revivals and a regular place on the schedules.

Der Orlow is set in the Ruritanian land of modern America, where the once-Grand Duke Alexander, now just plain Alex Doroschinsky (Hubert Marischka), works as a machinist in a car factory owned by John Walsh (Richard Waldemar) and Jolly Jefferson (Fritz Steiner). The two most important elements of a fairly slim plot were the beautiful Russian ballerina Nadja Nadjakowska (Betty Fischer) and the regal diamond of inestimable value, known as Der Orlow, which the ex-Duke has smuggled out of war-torn Europe. Both ballerina and diamond are coveted by Walsh. After interludes at Walsh's mansion and at the Alhambra variety theatre, it is, of course, Alex who gets the girl who gets the jewel. Elsie Altmann was the soubrette who gets the boss, and Hans Moser had one of his famous character cameos as a commissaire at the Alhambra.

Granichstaedten's light and bright, slightly jazzy score began with a shimmy, to which it returned as soon as the soubrets came in sight and the lovers of the tale had finished romancing to more traditional rhythms. Several sections of the show's music were, in fact, scored for jazz band (alto and tenor sax, two trombones, banjo, piano and drums), but Alex still sang sentimentally over his balalaika, Nadja moved regularly into valse lente tempo, and the men of the piece sang of love in march time when the band was not making the most of the shimmy, the Boston, the tango or Moser's comic song in fox-trot time. The most successful single number, however, was the hero's

12/8 Cigarette Song, which, joyously plugged by the Austrian State Tobacco Company, made some very dubious claims for the properties of nicotine (''Was tät das arme Herz, wenn es nicht hätte Das süsse Guft, ein kleines bissel Nikotin!'').

Der Orlow was a hit of the kind of proportions that only *Die lustige Witwe* and *Die Rose von Stambul* had previously been at the Theater an der Wien. It ran through 403 performances to 25 March 1926. When *Die Zirkusprinzessin* took over its stage, it moved on to the Bürgertheater (5 June 1926) for a further six weeks and then to the Raimundtheater, where it passed its 600th performance on 6 May 1927 before returning to the Theater an der Wien (23 July 1927), with Anny Coty and Ernst Nadherny now in its lead roles. It announced the 2 August performance as its 650th. The show was played again intermittently in repertoire until 1930, by which time it had done the rounds of Europe.

Az orlov was well received in its Hungarian version (ad Zsolt Harsányi) with Juci Lábass, Tibor Halmay and Jenő Nádor starred at the Fővárosi Operettszínház, and stayed for 75 nights at Berlin's Theater des Westens, but an English version, adapted by P G Wodehouse and Lauri Wylie under the not-unreasonable title of *Hearts and Diamonds,* was a disappointment in just 46 performances at London's Strand Theatre. *Hearts and Diamonds* featured a strong cast headed by Georges Metaxa, operatic star Louise Edvina and comic Lupino Lane under the direction of Theodore Komisarjevsky, and used some additional numbers by Max Darewski inserted into Granichstaedten's score.

In Paris the piece was produced by Victor de Cottens at the Folies-Wagram in an adaptation by Roger Ferréol and Georges Merry with André Baugé (Alex), Marthe Ferrare (Nadja) and with Boucot in Moser's comic spot, but Broadway passed *Der Orlow* by and its principal success remained its stunning first run in the Austrian capital, where it returned as late as 1959 in a Raimundtheater revival with Johannes Heesters, Margit Bollmann and Rudolf Carl at the head of its cast.

Hungary: Fővárosi Operettszínház *Az orlov* 23 September 1925; Germany: Theater des Westens 7 October 1925; UK: Strand Theatre *Hearts and Diamonds* 1 June 1926; France: Folies-Wagram *L'Orloff* 7 December 1928

ORME, Denise [SMITHER, Gertrude Jessie] (b London, 26 August 1884; d London, 20 October 1960). Edwardian ingenue who married two peers.

Daughter of a musical director, Alfred Smither, and his pianist wife, Jessie Morison, Miss Orme studied violin at the Royal Academy of Music and singing at the Royal College, before taking to the stage, at the age of 22, at the Alhambra and then in the chorus of George Edwardes's production of *Les P'tites Michu* at Daly's Theatre. She was promoted to the role of Blanche-Marie during the run, and she followed up by creating several leading roles for the famous musical play producer, including the title role of *See See* (1906) and a leading soprano part in *Les Merveilleuses* (1906, Illyrine). An accomplished violinist, she managed to have a display of her talent on the instrument inserted into most of her musical roles. During the run of *Les Merveilleuses* her first aristocratic engagement, to Baron Ernsthausen, was announced, but in April of the following year she married instead the Hon John Yarde-Buller, only son and heir to Lord Churston. She subsequently appeared in *Our Miss Gibbs* (1909, Lady Elizabeth Thanet), took over from Gertie Millar in the part of Franzi in *A Waltz Dream* (1908) and appeared alongside George Huntley in the less fortunate *The Hon'ble Phil* (1908, Marie Martinet). She was appearing at the Coliseum Music Hall when her husband succeeded to his title, and she briskly retired from the theatre. Having been first the Baroness Churston, she later rose to the rank of Duchess of Leinster, apparently the only ex-Edwardes employee to wed not one peer of the realm, but two.

It was, however, a talent that apparently ran in the family, for a cousin, who worked as Eileen Orme, came out of the line of grisettes in Edwardes's production of *The Merry Widow* to marry Maurice Hood, the heir to Viscount Bridport.

ORNADEL, [Simon] Cyril (b London, 2 December 1924).

A West End conductor of mostly Broadway musicals (*My Fair Lady, Kiss Me, Kate, Call Me Madam, Paint Your Wagon, Pal Joey, Kismet, The King and I, The Sound of Music,* etc) from the 1950s to the 1980s, Ornadel also composed and arranged much film and television music and wrote both popular songs (''Portrait of My Love,'' 1961 w Norman Newell) and the scores for several stage musicals. These were mostly adaptations of English classic literature, and of them *Pickwick* (''If I Ruled the World'') was easily the most successful. A musical version of Robert Louis Stevenson's *Treasure Island* proved a repeatable seasonal entertainment at London's Mermaid Theatre and was later staged in Germany, whilst an adaptation of *And So to Bed* was produced by British television as *Pepys.*

- 1956 **Starmaker** (David Croft/Ian Stuart Black) King's Theatre, Glasgow 13 February
- 1958 **The Pied Piper** (Croft) Connaught Theatre, Worthing 24 December
- 1963 **Pickwick** (Leslie Bricusse/Wolf Mankowitz) Saville Theatre 4 July
- 1969 **Ann Veronica** (Croft/Frank Wells, Ronald Gow) Cambridge Theatre 17 April

1973 **Treasure Island** (Hal Shaper/Bernard Miles, Josephine Wilson) Mermaid Theatre 17 December

1975 **Great Expectations** (Shaper/Trevor Preston) Yvonne Arnaud Theatre, Guildford 24 December

1978 **Once More Darling** (Norman Newell/Ray Cooney, John Chapman) Churchill Theatre, Bromley 5 June

ORPHÉE AUX ENFERS Opéra-bouffon in 2 acts by Hector Crémieux [and Ludovic Halévy]. Music by Jacques Offenbach. Théâtre des Bouffes-Parisiens, Paris, 21 October 1858. Revised 4-act version, Théâtre de la Gaîté, Paris, 7 February 1874.

Orphée aux enfers was Offenbach's first venture into mounting a full-scale opéra-bouffe at his blossoming little Théâtre des Bouffes-Parisiens, where it marked a significant advance on the three-, four- and five-handed short pieces that, because of legal restrictions on the size and kind of entertainments allowable under his license, had been the house's diet since its inception. The idea of a burlesque of the Orpheus legend, particularly familiar to theatregoers of the time as the subject of Glück's revered opera, *Orfeo* [*ed Eurydice*], had been nurtured some time in the brains of librettists Crémieux and Halévy, but whilst Offenbach was forced to work inside a format that allowed him a maximum of four or five characters, there was little chance of producing a piece that aspired to show Olympus and its inhabitants in all their parodied glory. The dissolution of the prohibitive restrictions in 1858 allowed the collaborators finally to go to work on their *Orphée,* although Halévy, now making advances in the diplomatic world, decided against allowing his name to go on the credits. By October *Orphée aux enfers* was on the stage.

Orpheus (Tayau) is a boring Theban music teacher with an eye for a nymph, and his flirtatious wife, Eurydice (Lise Tautin), in her turn, makes sheep's eyes at the handsome shepherd Aristaeus (Léonce). What Eurydice doesn't know, however, is that her new boyfriend is no less than Pluto, King of the Underworld, in earthly disguise. He wants to have her around more permanently, so he fixes it that she treads on a nasty asp in a cornfield and, having duly mortally expired, is consigned to a comfy boudoir in his nether regions. Orpheus is rid of Eurydice, Pluto has her, and everyone would now be quite happy were it not for that nosy, hectoring creature called Public Opinion (Marguerite Macé-Montrouge). She bullies the unwilling Orpheus into going up to see Jupiter (Desiré) on Olympus, to demand the return of his stolen wife. As a result, the Olympian deities, all thrilled at the thought of a bit of subterranean slumming, descend to Hades en masse, and there Jupiter winkles out the hiding place of Eurydice. Enchanted by her, he proposes that she swap Hades for Olympus. But there is still Orpheus to account to and, worse, the dreadful Public Opinion, who seems to have the silly musician mesmerized. When she gets the traditional story back on its rails, and forces Pluto to make Eurydice follow Orpheus back to earth, Jupiter uses a little thunderbolt to make the musician follow mythology, look back, and lose forever the wife he is longing to lose forever. But that is where mythology must stop. For, if he can't have Eurydice himself, Jupiter is not going to leave her with Pluto and so, in defiance of the classics and of Glück, he turns her into a Bacchante. A highly suitable ending for the girl.

The music with which the composer illustrated this bouquet of comical and satirical fireworks was the most dazzling display of light, comic theatre music in the history of the genre. From the earliest moments of the score, with Eurydice mooning over her shepherd, or screeching insults at her husband's music making, from Aristaeus' mocking entry song, and the lady's melodramatic parody of an operatic death (''La mort m'apparaît souriante'') the score bounced along on a bubble of laughter and melody. The Olympian scene introduced Diana with some fleet-footed hunting couplets and a trio of godly offspring chiding their father over his amorous adventures (Rondeau des Transformations), as well as a quote from Glück's most famous Orpheic moment, the aria ''Che faro senza Eurydice?,'' in Orpheus' unwilling exposure of his case before Jupiter. Hades helped pile up the total of memorable moments with a solo for the lugubrious comic Bache as the dead King of Boeotia (''Quand j'étais roi de Béotie''), Jupiter's attempts to seduce Eurydice whilst disguised as a fly (''Il me semble que sur mon épaule'') and the famous galop infernale, which was to come to be known as ''the can-can.''

The show was quickly a major hit (although Offenbach apparently continued well after the opening to operate cuts and rewrites), and by the time it was removed in the following June it had run for no fewer than 228 nights, and its music was being played throughout the country and even beyond. The first production of the show outside France seems to have been at Breslau (ad L Kalisch) in November 1859 before Prague, then Vienna took up the show. Johann Nestroy, at that time in charge of the Carltheater and already the producer of Vienna's early versions of the short Offenbach works, produced the first Vienna *Orpheus in der Unterwelt* in his own adaptation with himself playing Jupiter, equipped with enough extra satirical dialogue to make his role into something like a meneur de revue. Karl Treumann was Pluto, Philipp Grobecker played Orpheus, Therese Schäfer was Eurydice, Anna Grobecker Public Opinion and Wilhelm Knaack a memorable Styx. *Orpheus* was a distinct hit, and it was brought back at the Carltheater again the following year, by which time Berlin and New

York's German-speaking theatre had also welcomed Nestroy's version with equally happy results. In Berlin, the piece was popular enough to provoke a burlesque of its burlesque—*Orpheus in der Oberwelt*—produced at Meysels Theater. In the meantime, *Orphée aux enfers* had continued its cavalcade around Paris, where, on one famous occasion (1867), the celebrated courtesan Cora Pearl (in her earlier life a London music-hall singer called Louie Crouch) appeared as Cupid.

Many other centers soon had their versions—more or less faithful—of *Orphée,* amongst them Stockholm, Brussels, Copenhagen, Warsaw and St Petersburg, but some places took longer than others to take up this novel kind of entertainment. Although *Orpheus in der Unterwelt* was played in German at several Budapest theatres and in Hungarian at Kassa (ad Endre Latabár) in 1862, the show was not played in the vernacular in Budapest until 1882. When it was (ad Lajos Evva), it was produced with a starry cast toplining Ilka Pálmay (Eurydice), Elek Solymossy (Jupiter), János Kápolnai (Orpheus), Pál Vidor (Pluto), Vidor Kassai (Styx) and Mariska Komáromi (Cupid), scored a grand success, and quickly began to make up for lost time with revivals in 1885, 1889 and 1895.

In England, although the *Orphée* score was swiftly and thoroughly plundered to supply music for burlesque scores, it was not until seven years had gone by, and the Oxford Music Hall had scored a triumph with a potted *Orphée,* that J B Buckstone produced a (rhymed couplet!) English version, *Orpheus in the Haymarket,* churned out by the old master of extravaganza J R Planché at the Haymarket Theatre, with a cast including Louise Keeley (Eurydice), William Farren (Jupiter) and David Fisher (Orpheus). Well enough received, this stiff-necked version was by no means the sensation that might have been expected and played out a slightly shorter than intended season before getting the odd brief reprise in the provinces and colonies. The provinces, in fact, put out a much more interesting version four years later when H C Cooper's traveling opera troupe mounted a more faithful and free-toned version by Arthur Baildon (Theatre Royal, Bath 8 January 1870) with Ledril Ryse (Pluto), Annie Tonnellier (Eurydice), Francis Gaynar (Orpheus) and Henry Lewens (Jupiter) in the leading roles. The provinces of Britain thus got a better introduction to *Orphée* than London had done.

Bits of Offenbach's score got a second metropolitan showing at the Strand burlesque house, where an Orphean burlesque was produced in 1871 as *Eurydice,* with Harry Paulton as Aristaeus, and most of it at the Royal Surrey Gardens in 1873, when another adaptation of the piece, *Eurydice* (ad William F Vandervell), was given a hearing for more than 50 nights before going on to be seen at the National Theatre, Holborn in November. Later, after Hortense Schneider had played two London seasons with *Orphée* in her repertoire, and after Offenbach's subsequent full-sized works had made a more considerable mark, it was brought back again in two further English versions. One, produced by Kate Santley (Royalty Theatre, December 1876), starred its manageress as a Eurydice who expanded her role with a few cockney music-hall songs, alongside the more conventional Pluto of Henry Hallam and the Jupiter of J D Stoyle; a second, a few months later (ad H S Leigh), was a spectacular mounting at the Alhambra (30 April 1877) in a version this time advertised as ''altered by the composer'' (ie, Offenbach's extended rewrite of 1874). Kate Munroe/Cornélie d'Anka (Eurydice), W H Woodfield (Pluto) and Harry Paulton (Jupiter) starred, with the rising J H Ryley as Mercury and a ''grand procession of 300'' and several ballets interpolated. The piece ran almost four months and was one of the Alhambra's most successful productions to date.

Australian managers waited even longer to pick up the show, although Offenbach's score was heard there almost in toto played in Pringle's and Cellier's concerts, but, when *Orpheus* did finally appear on stage in the ''underworld,'' two different productions were mounted within 48 hours of each other. William S Lyster produced Planché's version in Melbourne with top vocalists Alice May (Eurydice), Armes Beaumont (Pluto) and Georgina Hodson (Public Opinion) and with Richard Stewart as Jupiter, whilst two nights later the burlesque actress Lydia Howard presented her production of the same adaptation at Sydney's Royal Victoria Theatre, herself playing Eurydice to the Pluto of J J Welsh and the Jupiter of W Andrews in repertoire with two contrasting pasticcio British burlesques, Byron's *Fra Diavolo* and *[The Nymph of the] Lurleyburg.*

New York, though initially quicker to see the show than Britain—several times in German and then at both the Theatre Français and from Lucille Tostée's company in the original French—took a very long time to get a vernacular production. Both the Kelly and Leon minstrels (2 November 1868, with Edwin Kelly as Jupiter and Francis Leon as Eurydice with ''the entire music'') and Bryant's minstrels (*Red Hot* by John Brougham, 5 April 1869) came out with burlesques during the Tostée season, but it was not until 1883 that something like a real *Orphée* was finally given a Broadway presentation in English. It was a decidedly hacked-up version (ad Max Freeman, Sydney Rosenfeld), filled with low comedy, German jokes and local topical songs, produced by E E Rice at the Bijou Theater, and the cast for the occasion included Digby Bell (Jupiter), Marie Vanoni (Eurydice), Pauline Hall (Venus) and D'Oyly Carte contralto Augusta Roche

(Public Opinion). This Englished *Orphée* was, however, far from the first to have been seen in America. As early as 1869 the adventurous singer-manager George Holman himself translated and mounted the show at Toronto's Lyceum Theater (15 October) with his daughter Sallie as Eurydice to the Jupiter of the not yet famous W H Crane, the Orpheus of the then barely known Charles Drew and the Pluto of George Barton. The piece was played thereafter in the Holman troupe's long and many tours throughout America. As in Britain, the tour circuits were better served than the metropolis.

In 1874, when Offenbach had launched himself on a new period as a theatrical manager, this time at the Théâtre de la Gaîté, he decided to mount a new production of *Orphée.* To fit it for this considerably larger stage, he remade the show, making it both more spectacular (chorus of 120, orchestra of 60, ballet of 60) but also longer and much more full of "items." The new *Orphée* stretched to four acts and included a considerable amount of new vocal material, both solo and choral, let in to the script like so many undone pleats. Eurydice (Marie Cico, who had been the original Minerva) and Pluton (Montaubry) each got an extra song, and Mercury (Grivot), Mars and Cupid all got solos to add to what virtually became a divine variety show on Olympus. There were now four ballets, a children's choir and an interpolated violin piece played by a young Conservatoire pupil. The final act was extended with a piece for the Judges of the Underworld and a comical policemen's chorus, a 10-tableaux visit to "The Kingdom of Neptune," including "Toads and Chinese fish, prawns and shrimps, a march of the Tritons, a sea-horses' polka, a pas de trois by seaweed, and a pas de quatre by Flowers (?!) and flying fish." Christian was seen as Jupiter, and Alexandre was John Styx. If the alterations did little for *Orphée* as a work (the piece has mostly since been played in its original rather than its expanded version), they served their purpose in giving a "second edition" to the Paris public, who came to the Gaîté in their enthusiastic numbers, giving Offenbach a success (d'éstime at least—the vastly expensive production actually lost almost its whole investment in spite of taking a huge 811,436 francs in its first 100 performances), which encouraged him to mete out the same bullfrog treatment to several other of his early works for the same stage. The expanded *Orphée* was, however, brought out at the Gaïté again in 1878 (August), with Hervé in the role of Jupiter, Mme Peschard as Eurydice and Léonce in his original role, and again in 1887 (19 February) with Vauthier (Jupiter), Jeanne Granier (Eurydice), Alexandre (Pluton) and Tauffenberger (Orphée) featured. This last revival disappointed and was quickly replaced by a rerun of *Le Petit Duc.*

Expanded *Orphées*, potted *Orphées*—and in Amsterdam in 1865 an *Orphée* where one greedy actor annexed to himself the roles of Pluto, Orpheus, Jupiter and Styx—but it is, by and large, the original *Orphée aux enfers* that has survived—with intermittent fallow periods—in the international repertoire through all the changes in musical theatre tastes of the past 140 years. It has moved from the commercial theatre into the subsidized theatre, and more specifically the opera houses of the world, as one of the handful of classic musical pieces that are repeatedly reprised, taking precedence virtually everywhere even over those later Offenbach pieces that, originally, had a notably greater popularity in various countries: *Die schöne Helena* in Austria and Hungary, *Geneviève de Brabant* in Britain, *La Grande-Duchesse* in America. In Germany, however, it has from the start been the favorite Offenbach work.

Orphée was regularly revived in France until it reached first the Opéra-Comique and then the Paris Opéra itself (19 January 1988) and, amongst countless other productions, was given a large and glitzy German revival under Max Reinhardt at the Grosses Schauspielhaus in 1922. It was produced again in London in a fiddled-with version by Berboohm Tree and Alfred Noyes, in 1911 (20 December), under the title *Orpheus in the Underground* with bits of spare Offenbach tacked into the score and with Courtice Pounds (Orpheus), Lottie Venne (Mrs Grundy, ie, Public Opinion) and Lionel Mackinder (Pluto) at the head of the cast, but got a major boost in 1960 through Wendy Toye's production of Geoffrey Dunn's hilarious if unsatirical new translation for the Sadler's Wells Opera. That company's successor, English National Opera, did very much less well when (5 September 1985) it attempted a rather incoherent and gimmicky staging of the expanded version (ad Snoo Wilson).

Orphée aux enfers has been filmed for television in Britain (including the memorable Sadler's Wells production of 1962), Germany and Japan.

Austria: Carltheater *Orpheus in der Unterwelt* 17 March 1860; Germany: Breslau 17 November 1859, Friedrich-Wilhelmstädtisches Theater *Orpheus in der Hölle* 23 June 1860; USA: Stadttheater (Ger) March 1861, Théâtre Français (Fr) 17 January 1867, Bijou Theater *Orpheus in the Underworld* 1 December 1883; Hungary: Kassa (Hun) 16 March 1862, Budai Színkör (Ger) 6 May 1862, Népszínház, Budapest *Orfeuz az alvilágban* (or *Orfeuz a pokolban*) 12 May 1882; UK: Haymarket Theatre *Orpheus in the Haymarket* 26 December 1865; Australia: Princess Theatre, Melbourne 30 March 1872

Recordings: complete (Musidisc Festival, EMI-Pathé, Golden Age), selections (EMI-Pathé), selections in English (HMV, TER), selections in German (Philips), etc

Videos: Sadler's Wells 1962, German TV 1968, East German TV 1974, Brent-Walker 1983, HDTV (Japan) 1990

ÖSTERREICHER, Rudolf (b Vienna, 19 July 1881; d Vienna, 23 October 1966).

Performer, author and playwright, Österreicher had a long and wide career in most areas of show business, performing in cabaret, writing for both the musical and the non-musical stage, and authoring the standard biography of Emmerich Kálmán during a career in which he had some 40 musical comedies and Operetten produced in European theatres.

His first pieces to appear on the Vienna stage were the Possen mit Gesang, *Der Gummiradler* and *Bediene dich selbst!,* produced at the Raimundtheater when its author was in his early twenties. He had already turned out the comic *Die Spottvogelwirtin,* with music by Carl Michael Ziehrer, for the same house before he had his first Operettic success with the text to Robert Winterberg's *Ihr Adjutant,* a piece which was played for 46 nights at the Theater an der Wien in 1911 with Fritz Werner starred, and subsequently in Germany and in Hungary (*Az Adjutáns,* ad Frigyes Hervay). A collaboration with Ziehrer on *Das dumme Herz* was worth 68 nights at the Johann Strauss-Theater, Hienrich Reinhardt's *Die erste Frau* ran for over two months at the Carltheater, and Österreicher then followed up with wartime hits around central Europe, having his most successful moments to date with Carl Weinberger on *Drei arme Teufel,* with Edmund Eysler on *Graf Toni,* and with A M Willner on the refitting of chunks of Kálmán's *Zsuzsi kisasszony* score with a new libretto as *Die Faschingsfee.* However, he won his first and only major international success, after nearly 20 years as a librettist, when he supplied the book to Jean Gilbert's *Katja, die Tänzerin.*

Österreicher had further home successes with his texts for Gilbert's *Das Weib in Purpur,* and Robert Stolz's *Eine einzige Nacht, Der Mitternachtswalzer* and *Drei von der Donau,* the first beginning its career with 160 nights at the Carltheater, the second topping 100 nights at the Bürgertheater and the last, a version of Johann Nestroy's *Lumpacivagabundus,* being produced under his own management during a period of management at the Wiener Stadttheater between 1945 and 1947. In the 1950s he collaborated with Hubert Marischka on two last stage musicals.

Österreicher also supplied the screenplays for a number of Operette films.

1903 **Der Gummiradler** (Rudolf Raimann) Raimundtheater 22 December

1905 **Bediene dich selbst!** (Arthur von Henriques) Raimundtheater 14 October

1906 **Die Spottvogelwirtin** (Carl Michael Ziehrer) Raimundtheater 30 October

1911 **Ihr Adjutant** (Robert Winterberg/w Franz von Schonthan) Theater an der Wien 3 March

1911 **Vielliebchen** (Ludwig Englander/w Carl Lindau) Venedig in Wien 5 May

1914 **Das dumme Herz** (Ziehrer/w Wilhelm Sterk) Johann Strauss-Theater 27 February

1914 **Der Kriegsberichterstatter** (many/w Sterk) Apollotheater 9 October

1914 **Das Mädchen im Mond** (Karl Stigler/w Sterk) Carltheater 7 November

1914 **Der Durchgang der Venus** (Edmund Eysler/w A M Willner) Apollotheater 28 November

1915 **Liebesgeister** (Ernst Steffan/w Béla Jenbach) 1 act Apollotheater 1 March

1915 **Der künstliche Mensch** (Leo Fall/w Willner) Theater des Westens, Berlin 2 October

1915 **Die erste Frau** (Heinrich Reinhardt/Willner) Carltheater 22 October

1916 **Drei arme Teufel** (Carl Weinberger/w Heinz Reichert) Theater am Gärtnerplatz, Munich 11 March

1917 **Graf Toni** (Eysler) Apollotheater 2 March

1917 **Die Faschingsfee** (Emmerich Kálmán/w Willner) Johann Strauss-Theater 21 September

1918 **Johann Nestroy** (arr Ernst Reiterer/w Willner) Carltheater 4 December

1919 **Der Künstlerpreis** (Leo Ascher/w Julius Horst) Apollotheater 1 October

1921 **Das Nixchen** (Oscar Straus/w Willner) Wallner-Theater, Berlin 10 September

1921 **Rinaldo** (*Gróf Rinaldo*) German version w Jenbach (Johann Strauss-Theater)

1923 **Katja, die Tänzerin** (Jean Gilbert/w Leopold Jacobson) Johann Strauss-Theater 5 January

1923 **Vierzehn Tage Arrest** (Eysler/w Horst) Raimundtheater 16 June

1923 **Das Weib im Purpur** (Gilbert/w Jacobson) Wiener Stadttheater 21 December

1924 **Ein Ballroman** (*Der Kavalier von zehn bis vier*) (Robert Stolz/w Willner, Fritz Rotter) Apollotheater 29 February

1924 **Geliebte seiner Hoheit** (Gilbert/w Bernauer) Theater am Nollendorfplatz, Berlin 24 September

1925 **[Das Abenteuer des Herrn] Maiermax** (Hugo Hirsch/w Jacobson) Lessing-Theater 31 December

1926 **Der Mitternachtswalzer** (Stolz/w Willner) Wiener Bürgertheater 30 October

1927 **Yvette und ihre Freunde** (Michael Krasznay-Krausz/w Sterk) Wiener Bürgertheater 18 November

1927 **Eine einzige Nacht** (Stolz/w Jacobson) Carltheater 23 December

1930 **Peppina** (Stolz/w Jacobson) Komische Oper, Berlin 22 December

1931 **Das Spitzentuch der Königin** new version w Julius Wilhelm (Johann Strauss-Theater)

1933 **Zwei lachende Augen** (Straus/w Ludwig Hirschfeld) Theater an der Wien 22 December

1943 **Brillanten aus Wien** (Alexander Steinbrecher) Theaterakademie

1947 **Drei von der Donau** (Stolz/w Robert Gilbert) Wiener Stadttheater 24 September

1948 **Ohne Geld war ich reich** (Karl Loube) Raimundtheater 9 January

1955 **Liebesbriefe** (Nico Dostal/w Hubert Marischka) Raimundtheater 23 November

1958 **Deutschmeisterkapelle** (Ziehrer arr/w H Marischka) Raimundtheater 31 May

OTTENHEIMER, Paul (b Stuttgart, 1 March 1873; d Darmstadt, 1951).

Ottenheimer studied in Stuttgart and subsequently became a conductor in Augsburg, Trier, Linz, Graz, Prague, Nuremberg and then, from 1913, at the Hoftheater in Darmstadt. He had a considerable success as a theatre composer when his Operette *Heimliche Liebe* (1911) proved a highly appreciated Viennese vehicle for Alexander Girardi and ran through a first series of 200 performances at the Johann Strauss-Theater in 1911–12 before going on to be seen in Germany and in Hungary (*A kis dobos* Sopron 1 April 1912). This success won him the chance to compose the score to another Julius Bauer text, *Der arme Millionär,* for the same theatre and the same megastar. Erich Müller's production of this second piece lasted a more modest 62 performances, but *Der arme Millionär* followed *Heimliche Liebe* on to further performances in Germany. Another star vehicle, *Hans im Glück,* written this time for Max Pallenberg, was played at the composer's home base in Darmstadt but went no further.

1911 **Heimliche Liebe** (Julius Bauer) Johann Strauss-Theater 13 October

1913 **Der arme Millionär** (Bauer) Johann Strauss-Theater 17 October

1914 **Hans im Glück** (E Rudy) Hoftheater, Darmstadt 7 June

1916 **Des Burschen Heimkehr** (aka *Der tolle Hund*) (Ernst Elias Niedergall) Hoftheater, Darmstadt 30 January

OUR MISS GIBBS Musical comedy in 2 acts by ''Cryptos'' and James T Tanner. Lyrics by Adrian Ross and Percy Greenbank. Music by Ivan Caryll and Lionel Monckton. Gaiety Theatre, London, 23 January 1909.

Fifteen years after the Gaiety Theatre had launched its first modern musical comedy, *The Shop Girl,* about a little vendeuse who wins her way to wealth and social position, George Edwardes's famous and hugely successful house was still turning out tales of the same kind. And, by and large, they were still being compiled and decorated by the same team of writers who had, for more than a decade, been London's and the world's favorite purveyors of the kind of brightly comical song and dance shows in which the Gaiety specialized. *Our Miss Gibbs,* written by the famous five under the pseudonym of ''Cryptos,'' and again telling the tale of a little vendeuse who wins her way to wealth and social position, turned out to be one of the best made and most popular of the series.

Gertie Millar, now the certified star of the Gaiety, played Mary Gibbs, a nice, no-nonsense Yorkshire lass (like Gertie) who sells sweets in Garrods department store, and Teddy Payne, her comical co-star, was her brother Timothy. Mary falls in love with a bank clerk who turns out to be an earl (J Edward Fraser), whilst Timothy accidentally gets mixed up with the attempt by Hughie Pierrepoint (George Grossmith), an aspiring aristocratic criminal, to pinch the Ascot Gold Cup. Robert Hale played Hughie's crook tutor, Slithers, Denise Orme was the ingenue and Hughie's ultimate partner, and Maisie Gay, Gladys Homfrey and Jeannie Aylwin had supporting roles in which they were predictably soubrettish, dragonistic and Scottish-with-songs, respectively. The Gaiety Girls got to parade about glamorously at the White City in the second act.

Caryll and Monckton's score was as lively and pretty as usual, with Monckton's solo for his leading lady/wife proving the hit of the evening. Gertie sang ''Moonstruck,'' prettily done up in pierrot costume, à propos of very little, but probably of just slightly more than the show's other major song success, Grossmith's latest interpolation from America. ''Yip! I-addy! I-ay!'' had nothing at all to do with Yorkshire, the Ascot Gold Cup or *Our Miss Gibbs,* but it was a hit for its performer, as the show ran on for a London season of 636 performances, a score better than any but *The Toreador* of the 15 years of Gaiety musicals. *Our Miss Gibbs* also remained thereafter the best-loved and most often repeated of the group.

Soon on the road in England, it also began its overseas travels before the London run was done. Gabor Steiner transported the show swiftly to Vienna (ad Carl Lindau, Max Baer, Leopold Krenn, Julius Freund), along with the Gaiety's Fred Wright, who played Timothy in German opposite the Miss Gibbs of a tiny teenaged Hungarian soubrette named Mizzi Hajós. As just plain Mitzi, she was soon to find fame and a long musical comedy career in America. The supporting cast included such names as Gisela Werbezirk, Karl Tuschl (Slithers), Betti Seidl and Josef Victora (Hughie), whilst Gracia Soria from the Royal Opera of Madrid headed an interpolated ''Liebesfest'' concert in the second act, in one of the four songs of which a young artist named Betty Fischer was given her chance.

From Vienna, Wright moved on to America to star in Charles Frohman's Broadway production of the show, opposite former Gaiety chorine Pauline Chase, but 57 performances were all the much tampered with show managed in New York. It was much better received in Australia, where J C Williamson billed it, with what eventually proved to be splendid foresight, as ''the greatest musical success of our generation.'' His production featured another of the Wright family, brother Bertie, as Timothy, alongside Blanche Browne (Mary) and Lang-

Plate 293. **Our Miss Gibbs.** *The Gaiety front line disport themselves in front of a reproduction of the White City.*

ford Kirby (Hughie) and with an Australian dancer-actor named Fred Leslie who was in no way related to the famous Gaiety actor doubling as Slithers and choreographer. *Our Miss Gibbs* quite simply broke every long-run record in the Australian theatre. At a time when six weeks was considered a good run, it ran for an amazing seven-and-a bit months at Sydney's Her Majesty's and the Theatre Royal (230 performances), smashing Sydney's long-run record before going on to seasons around Australia and regular revivals for half a dozen years. The eclipse of Gaiety musical comedy by modern Viennese and American shows led it to drop from the repertoire after the First World War, but its record remained solid until the coming of *Rose Marie* 16 years later.

Austria: Wiener Stadttheater *Miss Gibbs* 12 November 1909; USA: Knickerbocker Theater 29 August 1910; Australia: Her Majesty's Theatre, Sydney 24 September 1910

OUT OF THIS WORLD Musical in 2 acts by Dwight Taylor and Reginald Lawrence. Music and lyrics by Cole Porter. New Century Theater, New York, 21 December 1950.

The Cole Porter successor to *Kiss Me, Kate* was allegedly based on the Amphytrion legend, but in fact it had less in common with that specific tale than with bedroom farce in general, and with the many musical plays that had happily mixed immortals and mortals in comical fantasy since the 18th-century *Midas.* The most Amphytrionic bit of the libretto had Jupiter (George Jongeyans, ie, George Gaynes) lusting after a young American tourist (Priscilla Gilette) whilst in the shape of her husband (William Eythe), but top-billing (with four and two shared songs) went to comedienne Charlotte Greenwood, cast in the normally peripheral part of the jealous Juno. Mercury (William Redfield) played his traditional role as Jupiter's pander, David Burns appeared as a Greek gangster and Barbara Ashley as an incidental nymph with a song. The song that caused the most enjoyment in the show was Miss Greenwood's loose-limbed rendition of the plain girl's lament ''Nobody's Chasing Me'' with its typical Porter catalogue of things that were being chased whilst she wasn't. However, the song that lasted the best was one that didn't last in the show as far as Broadway: the surging ''From This Moment On.'' The show itself, under the management of *Kiss Me, Kate*'s Saint Subber and Lemuel Ayers, didn't last either, playing only 157 Broadway performances.

It did, however, get some brief later showings on stage, being seen off-Broadway in 1956 and at New York's Equity Library Theatre in a revamped version (ad

George Oppenheimer) in 1973, turning up in Australia in 1967 in a production mounted at the Menzies Theatre Restaurant in Sydney with Rosina Raisbeck, Colin Croft and Roslyn Dunbar featured through a short season, and most recently putting in an appearance in San Francisco (42nd Street Moon ad Greg McKellen 13 July 2000) as a ''musical comedy farce of Greek Gods and Hollywood Movie Stars on the loose in 1950s Athens.''

Australia: Menzies Theatre Restaurant, Sydney 4 January 1967

Recording: original cast (Columbia)

OVER HERE! America's big band musical by Will Holt. Music and lyrics by Richard M Sherman and Robert B Sherman. Shubert Theater, New York, 6 March 1974.

A 1940s nostalgia show that featured the two surviving members of the Andrews Sisters—Patti and Maxene—in a tongue-in-cheek wartime story. Janie Sell made up the team as the ring-in to the act who turns out to be a rotten German spy. The Sherman brothers, better known for their contribution to filmland musicals such as *Mary Poppins,* provided a 1940s pastiche score arranged by period specialist Louis St Louis and played by a big band, which was topped by a ''best of'' selection of Andrews Sisters favorites. The supporting cast included Ann Reinking and a young man named John Travolta, and *Over Here!* ran through 341 Broadway performances.

Recordings: original cast (Columbia), concert cast 1995 (DRG)

OVER SHE GOES Musical tantivy in 2 acts by Stanley Lupino. Additional dialogue by Arty Ash. Lyrics by Desmond Carter and Frank Eyton. Music by Billy Mayerl. Saville Theatre, London, 23 September 1936.

Continuing their series of dance-and-laughter shows, Laddie Cliff and Stanley Lupino scored a fresh success and a 248-performance run with the jollities of *Over She Goes.* The pair played a couple of vaudevillians whose chum (Eric Fawcett) inherits a title, then finds an opportunistic old fiancée (Barbara Francis) on the doormat. Lupino pretends to be the late Uncle come back to life, the Dowager (Doris Rogers) promptly appears, and complications thicken until the uncle really does turn up. Adele Dixon, Teddie St Denis and Sally Grey were the boys' partners, whilst Syd Walker and Richard Murdoch scored a supporting hit as a pair of policemen called in to help tidy up the mess. Billy Mayerl produced one of his catchiest handfuls of songs for the moments between the fun, with the three boys' version of the title song, Fawcett and Miss Dixon's bandworthy ''I Breathe on Windows'' and Murdoch's silly-ass copper singing about a ''Speed Cop'' proving the highlights.

The show turned out to be the high point of the Lupino/Cliff association and also, sadly, its end. Before the next of their shows appeared Cliff had become too ill to take part. He did, however, appear with Lupino and Murdoch in the film version of the piece, alongside Bertha Belmore as the dowager, Claire Luce and Gina Malo.

Australia took a glimpse at the new-style Gaiety musical with seasons of *Over She Goes* and *Swing Along* in 1937. George Gee, Donald Burr, Valerie Hay, Percy Le Fre, Lois Green and Billie Worth were the principals of the company, and *Over She Goes* did better than its companion piece, with seven-week seasons in both Melbourne and Sydney (Theatre Royal 25 September).

Australia: Her Majesty's Theatre, Melbourne 10 July 1937

Film: Associated British Picture Corp 1937

P

PACIFIC 1860 Musical romance in 3 acts by Noël Coward. Theatre Royal, Drury Lane, London, 19 December 1946.

Coward's romantic costume operetta *Pacific 1860* reopened the Theatre Royal, Drury Lane after its reconversion from its wartime use as the headquarters of the troops' entertainment organization. Set in a fictional South Seas island, it had a main story line that followed the romance of the son of a socially striving expatriate family, Kerry Stirling (Graham Payn), and the therefore unacceptable opera singer Elena Salvador (Mary Martin) through three acts and a couple of minor hiccups to a happy ending. If the show's story was flimsy, its trappings were much less so, and in the score to *Pacific 1860* Coward produced some of his best writing. None of it, however, was for the two leading characters. Sylvia Cecil as the heroine's duenna had a vintage Coward waltz song (''This Is a Changing World'') and joined two maids in a beautiful trio (''This Is a Night for Lovers''), whilst the comical part of the proceedings included the young society folks' tongue-poking ''His Excellency Regrets,'' the tale of naughty ''Uncle Harry'' who tried to be a missionary (cut, then replaced), a plump lassie's bewailing ''I Wish I Wasn't Quite Such a Big Girl,'' a grim lament for three uncomfortably aging mammas (''Here in the Twilight of Our Days'') and another cut number describing how ''Alice Is at It Again.'' The incidentals, however, were not enough to compensate for the show's very soft center and the miscasting of Miss Martin, and *Pacific 1860* closed in 129 performances. Coward later rescued Miss Cecil's two numbers and put them into the original text of *Sail Away,* but they were cut out of that show when the soprano role was excised on the road.

Recording: original cast (TER)

PACIFICO Opérette in 3 acts by Paul Nivoix. Lyrics by Camille François and Robert Chabrier. Music by Jo Moutet. Théâtre de la Porte-Saint-Martin, Paris, 10 December 1958.

Pacifico brought back to the Paris stage the effective team of matinée idol vocalist George Guétary and celebrated ''paysan'' actor and comedian Bourvil, which had triumphed in the long-running *La Route fleurie.* Guétary rejoiced in ''Réveillon à Paris,'' topped off the title song, and soupily romanced ''Marilyn'' (Corinne Marchand), whilst the comic crinkled his way inimitably through ''C'est du nanar,'' assured the world that ''C'est pas si mal que ça chez nous,'' and also got together with his soubrette partner, Pierrette Bruno, in a couple of duets and with Guétary in one of the less wallpapery numbers of the score, ''Casimir.'' If the jolly material was far from exceptional, the performers, and Bourvil in particular, were, and they kept *Pacifico* in Paris for three seasons.

Recording: original cast (Pathé)

PACIFIC OVERTURES Musical in 2 acts by John Weidman. Music and lyrics by Stephen Sondheim. Additional material by Hugh Wheeler. Winter Garden Theater, New York, 11 January 1976.

Stephen Sondheim's successor to *A Little Night Music* swapped the earlier show's mixture of acerbic old-world tale and brilliant dance-rhythmed music for a purposely undemonstrative and stylized manner in a musical pageant that told, in a semi-revusical style and from a Japanese point of view, the tale of the forcible opening up of Japan to the West under the initial prodding of Commodore Perry and his American ''invaders.'' The show's score mixed textually and musically laconic, often formal and even opaque utterances from some of the Japanese characters, with such items as the witty poisoning of the Shogun by ''Chrysanthemum Tea,'' some national parodies in the invading ''Please, Hallo,'' a part-song for some British sailors attempting to make unwelcome advances to a ''Pretty Lady,'' and a final scene, ''Next,'' showing the more-Western-than-Western result of the outside world's interference.

Produced by Harold Prince, and staged by him in a style that took in elements of Japanese traditional theatre, *Pacific Overtures* was played by a cast of Asian performers headed by Mako as the Reciter, Sab Shimono as Manjiro, the fisherman with experience of the West who attempts to maintain the old Japan, and Isao Sato as Kayama, the samurai who rises to political power on an opportunistic pro-Western line. The production and the show failed to please, and *Pacific Overtures* closed in 193 Broadway performances. It was given an off-Broadway revival by the York Players in 1984 (22 March, 20 performances) and subsequently a more determined one, with such names as the Shuberts and Nugent and McCann attached to its billhead, at the Promenade Theater (25 October 1984), which lasted 109 performances.

In Britain, *Pacific Overtures* was first staged in Manchester with a Caucasian cast and in a production which swapped the formal style of the original staging for a much coloured-up presentation. It pleased its public much better than a subsequent, grayly plodding performance by operatic vocalists which was quickly swept from its unlikely place in the repertoire of the subsidized English National Opera, and it was given a second Manchester season later the same year (1 October 1986). In 1994 it was seen once more at London's Bridewell Theatre (25 April).

UK: Forum Theatre, Wythenshawe, Manchester 29 April 1986, London Coliseum 10 September 1987

Recordings: original cast (RCA), English National Opera cast (TER)

PADILLA [Sánchez], José (b Almeria, 28 May 1889; d Madrid, 25 October 1960).

Best known internationally as the composer of the popular songs ''El relicario,'' ''La violetera'' and ''Valencia,'' Padilla wrote a considerable number of zarzuelas for the Spanish stage as well as providing songs for Parisian revue—''Ça, c'est Paris'' (ad Lucien Boyer, Jacques-Charles, from *La bien amada*), ''Le Tango de Miss'' (performed by Mistinguett at the Moulin-Rouge)—and the scores for two Paris opérettes. His first Parisian piece, *Pépète,* a musical-comedy tale of an aunt's attempts to arrange the devirginizing of an apparently uninterested lad, was produced by Dupont and Baudry at the Théâtre de l'Avenue, with Edmée Favart (Monique), Félix Oudart (Leblairois, director) and Robert Burnier (Gilbert) heading the cast. The second, *Symphonie Portugaise,* 25 years later, was an opérette à grand spectacle in the style of its period produced by and played by Germaine Roger at the Gaîté-Lyrique, and subsequently played in the French provinces without notable success.

Padilla's ''My Spanish Rose'' was interpolated in the Broadway score of Jerome Kern's *The Night Boat,* ''El relicario'' was featured in the Broadway revue *Snapshots of 1921* and ''La violetera'' was performed by Irene Bordoni in *Little Miss Bluebeard.*

1906 **La mala hembra** (Ventura de la Vega) 1 act Teatro Barbieri 24 March

1907 **Las palomas blancas** (Justo Huste) Teatro Apolo, Almeria 31 October

1908 **El centurión** (Miguel Mihura, Navarro, Cumbrearas) 1 act Teatro Lux-Eden 5 October

1908 **La Titiritera** (Garcia Revenga, E Zaballos) 1 act Teatro Lux-Eden 12 October

1909 **Los tres reyes** (L Ferreiro) 1 act Teatro la Latina 5 January

1909 **La copla gitana** (w Quislant/Juan Tavares) 1 act Teatro Barbieri 8 January

1909 **De los barrios bajos** (w Franco) 1 act

1909 **Juan Miguel** (Ventura de la Vega) 1 act Teatro Barbieri 1 October

1909 **El decir de la gente** (Mihura, Ricardo Gonzales de Toro) 1 act Teatro Martin 5 November

1909 **La presidaria** (Ventura de la Vega) 1 act Teatro Barbieri 19 November

1909 **Los viejos verdes** (Manuel de Lara, Joaquín Valverde) Teatro Barbieri 14 December

1910 **Los hombres de empuje** 1 act Teatro Benvenuto June

1910 **Pajaritos y flores** (Mihura, Gonzalez de Toro) 1 act Teatro de Apolo 28 September

1911 **Almas distintas** (Ventura de la Vega) 1 act

1911 **Mirando à la Alhambra** 1 act

1911 **El pueblo del Peleon** (Mihura, Gonzalez de Toro) 1 act

1911 **El divino jugete** (Quiles Pastor) 1 act Teatro Novedades December

1912 **El principe celoso** (Soler Mugica) 1 act Madrid 8 November

1913 **La plebe** (M Fernandez Palomero) 1 act Teatro Novedades, Barcelona 13 December

1914 **De España al cielo** (w Jeronimo Jimenez) 1 act Barcelona February

1914 **El suspiro del moro** (Serrano Clavero) Teatro Comedia, Buenos Aires 24 December

1915 **El manton roja** (Mihura) 1 act Teatro Barbieri 18 December

1916 **La oracion de la vida** (Fernandez Palomero) 1 act Teatro Martin 24 June

1916 **La corte del amor** (Fernandez Palomero) Teatro Comedia, Buenos Aires 24 June

1916 **Marcial Hotel** (Mihura, Gonzales de Toro) 1 act Teatro Martin 4 October

1916 **Miguelin** (Armando Oliveros, José María Castell) Teatro Tivoli, Barcelona 20 October

1917 **Judith, la viuda hebrea** (Gonzalo Jover, Juan Eugenio Morant) 1 act Teatro Victoria, Barcelona 21 September

1917 **Luzbel** (José Aguado, Miguel Nieto) 1 act Teatro Tivoli, Barcelona 7 November

1917 **Sabino el trapisondista** (*El saber todo lo puedo*) 1 act (Oliveros, Castell) Teatro Victoria, Barcelona 21 December

1918 **El secreto de la paz** (José Ramon Franquet) 1 act Teatro Comico, Barcelona 30 March; Teatro Prince, Madrid March 1920

1919 **Reyes, la Jerezana** (F Perez Capo) 1 act Teatro Martin 30 January

1924 **Pépète** (Didier Gold, Dieudonné [ie, Robert Sorre], Charles-Antoine Carpentier) Théâtre de l'Avenue, Paris 3 February

1924 **Sol de Sevilla** (José Andres de la Prada) Teatro Tivoli, Barcelona 18 March

1924 **La bien amada** (de la Prada) Teatro Tivoli, Barcelona

1924 **La mayorala** (de la Prada) Teatro Tivoli, Barcelona

1933 **Con el pelo suelto** (José Silva Aramburu) Teatro Zarzuela 29 November

1934 **Las inviolables** (Aramburu) Principal Palace, Barcelona 19 July

1934 **La bella burlada** (de la Prada) Teatro Nuevo, Barcelona 9 November

1934 **El duende** (Aramburu) 1 act Teatro Comico, Barcelona 28 December

1935 **Mucho ciudado con la Lola** (T Borras) Teatro Comedia, Barcelona 11 March

1935 **Los maridos de Lydia** (Aramburu) Teatro de la Comedia, Barcelona 28 June

1935 **La canción del desierto** (Aramburu) Teatro Nuevo, Barcelona 8 November

1935 **La dama del sol** (de la Prada) Teatro Victoria, Barcelona 23 December

1939 **La giralda** (Serafin Alvarez Quintero, Joaquín Alvarez Quintero) Teatro Victoria, Barcelona 22 September

1939 **Lo que fue de la Dolores** (José Maria Acevedo) Teatro Victoria, Barcelona 2 December

1940 **Repoker de corazones** (Rafael Fernández Shaw) Teatro de la zarzuela 13 October

1941 **La Violetera** (de la Prada) Teatro Comico, Barcelona 17 February

1943 **Nené** (de la Prada, Gonzales de Toro) Principal Palace, Barcelona 12 March

1943 **¡Oh, Tiro liro!** (Aramburu) Principal Palace, Barcelona 7 May

1949 **Symphonie Portugaise** (aka *Romance au Portugal*) (Marc-Cab, Raymond Vincy) Théâtre de la Gaîté-Lyrique 9 October

1950 **La hechicera en Palacio** (Rigel, A Ramos de Castro) Teatro Alcazar 23 November

1952 **Peligro de Marte** (Alvaro de la Iglesia, Rigel) Teatro Lope de Vega 13 September

1956 **La chacha, Rodriguez y su padre** (José Munoz Roman) Teatro Martin 19 October

Many other titles attributed

Biography: Montero, E: *José Padilla* (Fundacíon Baco Exterior, Madrid, 1990)

THE PADLOCK Comic opera in 2 acts by Isaac Bickerstaff based on *El celoso estremeño* by Miguel de Cervantes. Music by Charles Dibdin. Theatre Royal, Drury Lane, 3 October 1768.

One of the most successful of all the English-language musical plays of its era, Bickerstaff and Dibdin's little piece found itself worldwide audiences for many years after its first production.

Don Diego (Charles Bannister) is an aging bachelor who is about to wed the 16-year-old Leonora (Mrs Arne), a penniless lass who has spent the last three months in his home, under lock and key, "on approval." However, on the very night that he goes out to meet the girl's father to confirm that he will take her to wife, the amorous student Leander (Joseph Vernon) woos his way past the comic servant Mungo (Dibdin) and the key-holding duenna, Ursula (Mrs Dorman), scrambling over the garden wall to Leonora's side. Diego returns unexpectedly and, confronted with the sight of the two young people together, realizes that he is foolish to be thinking of taking a young wife. He hands over Leonora to Leander, but he is less magnanimous with the untrustworthy servants: Ursula is fired, and Mungo is sentenced to the bastinado. The padlock of the title was the extra lock that Diego fastened on his house's gate before leaving, a fact that arouses the indignation of the hitherto punctilious Ursula to whom he has not entrusted the key.

The 13 musical numbers that made up the score of the show were largely the brief solos typical of the period, but there was a quartet to end the first act and a finale to the second, as well as a "Good Night" duo for the young pair. However, the numbers which became most popular were those given to Mungo, and most particularly his opening song, bemoaning "Dear heart, what a terrible life am I led," with its catchphrase refrain "Mungo here, Mungo there, Mungo everywhere."

It was Mungo, in fact, who was the key to the show's success for, although notably well written and tuneful, *The Padlock* had otherwise little about it of originality. Its plot lines were overused although they still had many more years life and success in such pieces as *The Quaker* and *The Duenna* to come and its characters—the innocent bride, the aged bridegroom, the amorous student and the duenna—wholly stock ones. But Mungo was something else. To the standard comic servant role, Bickerstaff added a fresh element—the West Indian negro accent, with all its potential for dialect comedy—and this proved a winner. The role was originally written for actor John Moody, but Moody dropped out of the show during rehearsals and composer Dibdin, suitably blacked-up, stepped in to a part that he was convinced should have been his from the start. He was proven right when he made an enormous personal hit inside the general success of *The Padlock,* and the show went on to play a remarkable 54 performances in its first season at Drury Lane.

The play and its famous part were taken up throughout the English-speaking world, and *The Padlock* was seen in every outpost of Empire that possessed anything resembling a theatre. In America, Lewis Hallam jr introduced Mungo to New York audiences. Ultimately, it also made it into other languages. A German version (ad Carl

Bruno), apparently equipped with a different score of music by Carl Binder, was produced as a one-act Posse mit Gesang at Vienna's Carltheater in 1857 with Karl Treumann playing Mungo and Albin Swoboda as Leander, and it was later played, by Treumann's visiting company, in Budapest. An Hungarian version had previously been mounted at the Nemzeti Színház.

In Britain, America and the other colonies the show won repeated revivals, including a number with variations. The ''African Roscius,'' Ira Aldridge, took a break from his Othellos and suchlike and appeared throughout Britain and Europe as Mungo in a performance rather different from that given by Dibdin, and in 1894 J C Bond Andrews and Walter Parke put out a rewritten version under the title *The Keys of Castle* (Lyric Theatre, Hammersmith 10 July). The show was seen in a more pristine form at London's Old Vic as recently as 1979, played in a double bill with *Miss in Her Teens.* Nickolaus Grace appeared as Mungo.

USA: John Street Theater 29 May 1769; Australia: Emu Plains Theatre 20 November 1830; Austria: Carltheater (Eng) 19 February 1853, Carltheater *Das Vorhängeschloss* 18 April 1857; Hungary: Nemzeti Színház *A lakat* 30 August 1853, Budai Színkör *Das Vorhängeschloss* 29 May 1857

PAGANINI Operette in 3 acts by Paul Knepler and Béla Jenbach. Music by Franz Lehár. Johann Strauss-Theater, Vienna, 30 October 1925.

The text to *Paganini* was written by Paul Knepler, the librettist and composer who had scored a fine success with his romanticized biomusical of the Viennese actress and singer *Josefine Gallmeyer* at Vienna's Bürgertheater in 1921. He again composed his own score for his second piece, *Wenn der Hollunder blüht* (w Ignaz M Welleminsky), for the Berlin Bundestheater, but he sent a third book (which a friend persuaded him not to set himself), constructed on the same kind of show biz biography lines, to Lehár. The artist whose name was this time tacked on to a fictional romance was the violinist Niccolo Paganini—whose putative love life had already been plumbed in several plays including a 1915 one by Eddie Knoblock—and the lady in the case was Maria Anna Elisa, Princess of Lucca and Piombino and, for good measure, sister of the Emperor Napoléon. The lady (Emmi Kosáry) hears Paganini (Carl Clewing) playing his violin while she is having lunch in a country inn, without her husband (Peter Hoenselaers), who is off wooing the prima donna of his Court Opera (Gisa Kolbe). A romance begins, and the lady is able to use her knowledge of the Prince's little affair to stop him from expelling her violinist from Lucca and, indeed, to force him to appoint Paganini to a court position. But Napoléon gets annoyed at the international gossip over his sister's indiscreet love affair and sends a general (Felix Dombrowski) to remove Paganini. Although Anna Elisa protects him, the violinist finally convinces her that he must leave her to go to his only real love, his music.

Lehár was delighted with Knepler's offering, had Béla Jenbach, the experienced librettist of his recent *Clo-clo,* help give the piece a final form, and set it with some of the lushest music he had yet provided for the theatre, with the large bulk of that music contained in the two extremely showy, sentimental leading roles. The tenor's bonbon was the pretty ''Gern hab' ich die Frau'n geküsst'' (widely known in English as ''Girls Were Made to Love and Kiss''), but the part of Paganini also had many other big musical moments including a showy entrance number, ''Schönes Italien,'' and the sizeable duo ''Was ich denke,'' shared with his soprano, whose own most expansive raptures came in the aria ''Liebe, du Himmel auf Erden.'' Bella, the prima donna, and Pimpinelli, the princess's chamberlain (Fritz Imhoff), provided some slightly lighter numbers, but it was only really in a jolly rustic opening to the final act that the Operette turned very far from the staunchly romantic.

Textually and musically far in temper from Lehár's *Die lustige Witwe* style, *Paganini* laid a heavy accent on its lead tenor role. This is said to have been due to the composer's wish to build a star role for the favorite tenor, Richard Tauber, but, as it happened, Tauber did not create the role of Paganini. When it was decided to produce the piece at Vienna's Johann Strauss-Theater, rather than in Berlin, Kammersänger Carl Clewing, the 40-year-old actor-turned-heldentenor of the Staatsoper Unter den Linden and Bayreuth's Walther von Stolzing (*Die Meistersinger von Nürnberg*) of the previous season, was selected for the star role. He was paired with the Hungarian soprano Emmi Kosáry, who had so delighted Lehár with her creation of his *Wo die Lerche singt* in Budapest, as his Anna Elisa. Clewing, a rare visitor to the Operette stage, soon moved on, and when Peter Hoenselaers took over as Paganini, the show's posters provided the unusual spectacle of top-billing Kosáry above the show's masculine title. Before *Paganini* reached its 138th and last performance, she too had given over her role, to Lola Grahl.

It was a fair run rather than a fine one (less, for example, than Ralph Benatzky's *Adieu Mimi,* which followed in the same year), but one that was bettered only marginally (apparently for salary reasons) in Berlin when Tauber took up the title role alongside operatic soprano Vera Schwarz, Eugen Rex and Edith Schollwer in Heinz Saltenberg's production at the Deutsches Künstlertheater. In Budapest (ad Ernő Kulinyi), Jenő Nádor and the newest star of Hungarian operettic stage, Gitta Alpár, sang their way to a fine success, whilst in France baritone André Baugé—who was as popular in Paris as Tauber in Berlin—tackled the show's title role when André Rivoire's version was produced at the Théâtre de la Gaîté-Lyrique a couple of years later. Louise Dhamarys (Anna-Elisa), Renée Camia (Bella) and Robert Allard (Pimpinelli) played the other principal roles, and Baugé and the show won a good Parisian season that established *Paganini* as a repertoire piece in France. Subsequent French productions have often followed Baugé's casting by using a high baritone rather than a tenor in the role of Paganini.

Two German-language films were made of *Paganini,* one, as *Gern hab' ich die Frau'n geküsst,* in 1926 (silent!) and a second in 1934, but *Paganini* did not make its way beyond Europe until 1937, when Tauber encouraged a C B Cochran production in London (ad A P Herbert, Reginald Arkell). The tenor starred opposite Evelyn Laye, with Charles Heslop and Joan Panter in support, and found London indifferent.

Excuses have been advanced and readvanced for this failure, just as they have been for the other fair but not fine runs of *Paganini,* but the fact remains that, like any other good but not outstanding piece with a big starring role, it mostly (but not always) did well enough when it was cast with a large and fine-voiced star name, but otherwise provoked limited interest. That big starring role has ensured that it has won, in particular, several recordings, a further German filming for TV (1972 w Teresa Stratas, Joannes Heesters, Peter Kraus) and some revivals, particularly in its French version.

Paganini was not Lehár's first romantic Operette, nor was it Tauber's first essay into Operette, nor his first performance of a Lehár role, nor even did he create the part, but—with more trend-setting help from Knepler and his celebrity-based, ''unhappy-ending'' libretto than is generally acknowledged—it led Lehár and Tauber into the first stages of the series of colorful, romantic Operetten (several others also tenuously attached to famous names and all, bar one remake of an old piece, with unhappy endings) with which they would be involved together in the years that followed.

Germany: Deutsches Künstlertheater 30 January 1926; Hungary: Városi Színház 7 May 1926; France: Théâtre de la Gaîté-Lyrique 3 March 1928; UK: Lyceum Theatre 20 May 1937

Recordings: complete (EMI), complete in French (Decca), selections (RCA, Eurodisc, etc), selections in French (EMI-Pathé)

PAIGE, Elaine [BICKERSTAFF, Elaine J] (b Barnet, Herts, 5 March 1948). *Evita* original who, in a well-paced career, turned herself into Britain's biggest musical-theatre star.

Elaine Paige made her earliest musical theatre appearances as one of the Urchins in the pre-London cast of *The Roar of the Greasepaint . . . the Smell of the Crowd* (1964), as a takeover in the West End's *Hair,* as Eadie in *Maybe That's Your Problem* (1971), as Michelle (ie, Micaëla) in *Rock Carmen* (1972), as a replacement ensemble player in *Jesus Christ Superstar,* and in *Nuts* (Theatre Royal, Stratford East). She subsequently took over from Stacey Gregg as Sandy (to the Danny of Paul Nicholas) in the West End production of *Grease* before creating her first important London musical role as rough-as-guts Rita to the Billy Liar of Michael Crawford in the musical *Billy* at the Theatre Royal, Drury Lane, in 1974 (''Any Minute Now'').

In 1978 she rocketed into the general public's eye when, after a hugely publicized casting, she created the title role in the stage production of *Evita* (''Don't Cry for Me, Argentina,'' ''Rainbow High'') and won overnight fame in a kind of way that had virtually died out in the London theatre world. She compounded that fame when she stepped in during rehearsal to replace the injured Judi Dench as Grizabella, the Glamour Cat of *Cats,* creating the song ''Memory.'' In a subsequent career balanced between recording and the stage, she appeared as the Witch in *Abbacadabra* (1983), created both on record and then in the theatre the role of Florence Dassy in *Chess* (''I Know Him So Well,'' ''Heaven Help My Heart''), appeared again at the Prince Edward Theatre (which had housed her successes in both *Evita* and *Chess*) as Reno Sweeney in the London edition of the latest Broadway adaptation of *Anything Goes,* took the title role in a revival of *Piaf* (1993) , played seasons in the role of Norma Desmond in *Sunset Boulevard* at London's Adelphi Theatre (1995) and again on Broadway (1996), and starred in a revival of *The King and I* (1999) at the Dominion Theatre. She also re-created her still unequaled Grizabella, nearly 20 years on, in the video recording of *Cats.*

PAINTER, Eleanor (b Walkerville, Iowa, 12 September 1891; d Bratenahl, Ohio, 4 November 1947). Prima donna of 1910s and 1920s Broadway.

Miss Painter sang as a church chorister in New York City before going to Europe to study voice under Lilli Lehmann. She made her stage debut as an operatic singer in 1912 as Cio Cio San in *Madama Butterfly.* She appeared in Germany (as Eleanor Painter-Schmidt) in other less expansive operatic roles (Mignon, Micaëla, etc) as well as in the role of Yum-Yum in *Der Mikado* (May 1913) before Andreas Dippel brought her back to America in 1914 to star as Georgine in the Broadway production of Charles Cuvillier's *The Lilac Domino.* She subsequently created the title roles of Victor Herbert's *The Princess Pat* (1915, Patrice Montaldo) and the Catherine Cushing/Rudolf Friml *Glorianna* (1918) and starred in the play (with two songs) *Art and Opportunity* (1917), played in London by Marie Tempest, and as Dolores in the 1920 revival of *Florodora.*

Miss Painter walked out in rehearsals for the American production of Jean Gilbert's *The Lady in Ermine* on

Plate 294. **Paint Your Wagon.** *James Barton starred as Ben Rumson in Broadway's production of Lerner and Loewe's musical.*

the grounds that her character spent too long off stage in the third act, but she returned to Broadway to score a further success as Vera Elizaweta in the American version of Oscar Straus's *Der letzte Walzer,* and to appear in two less memorable musicals, *The Chiffon Girl* (1924) and, after another period working in Germany, in an on-the-road replacement, as Jenny Lind in the biomusical *The Nightingale* (1927). In the later days of her performing career she returned to the operatic stage in San Francisco and Philadelphia.

PAINT YOUR WAGON Musical play in 2 acts by Alan Jay Lerner. Music by Frederick Loewe. Shubert Theater, New York, 12 November 1951.

Paint Your Wagon appeared on the stage some four years after Lerner and Loewe's first big success with *Brigadoon,* and, if its Broadway run did not approach that of its predecessor, it nevertheless confirmed all the good that the earlier piece had promised. The show was as far away from *Brigadoon* in feeling and in style as could be: the fantastical Scots tale of the earlier show was replaced by a rumbustious and throughly American tale of pioneering days, set with songs to match.

Ben Rumson (James Barton) discovers gold whilst burying a fellow prospector, and he and his daughter, Jennifer (Olga San Juan), settle down in the mushrooming Rumson Town as get-rich-quick miners flock in from all over. Widower Ben takes as a wife the divorced Mormon Elizabeth, and, when Jennifer gets old enough, she falls for the handsome Mexican prospector Julio (Tony Bavaar). Her father promptly decides she needs to go back east for some schooling, but, soon after her departure, it becomes clear that Rumson's mines are fading. The miners start to move away to more promising grounds, Elizabeth deserts Ben, and Julio goes into the hills in search of fabled riches. When Jennifer returns, she finds Ben almost alone. He will not leave his town and neither will she, for she will wait there for the day when Julio returns.

When he finally does he is a different man, with all the dreaming knocked out of him. But whilst they may not have the green future they once hoped for, at least they have a future together.

The songs included some charming ballads for Julio (''I Talk to the Trees'') and for Jennifer (''How Can I Wait?''), but it was the songs of the mining men that made up the backbone of the score: the driving, crazy rush for the goldfields in ''I'm On My Way,'' the rough, round-the-fire land-shanty ''They Call the Wind Maria'' (introduced by Rufus Smith) and Ben's crumpled memories of his dead wife (''I Still See Elisa'') and his reflective ''Wand'rin' Star.'' The introduction of a gold-town music-hall saloon provided the opportunity for the required dance routines of the period (ch: Agnes de Mille), first in anticipation of the girls who will come to town, then in their fact.

Cheryl Crawford's production of *Paint Your Wagon* had a fair but insufficient Broadway run of 289 performances, but London gave the show a warmer welcome in a Jack Hylton production that featured Bobby Howes, long exiled from London since an unfortunate confrontation with an audience, as Ben, his real-life daughter, Sally Ann Howes, as Jennifer and Ken Cantril as Julio. It played 477 West End performances before going on the road in 1954. *Paint Your Wagon* was given an overdue reshowing at the Goodspeed Opera House in 1992, with George Ball as Ben, and in 1996 it was seen again in London when Open Air Theatre in Regent's Park mounted it for a summer season (23 July), with Tony Selby playing Ben, prior to taking the show on tour.

In Australia, Alec Kellaway, Lynne Lyons, Richard Curry and Jill Perryman played a good four months in Melbourne, followed by a Sydney season (Her Majesty's Theatre 8 April 1955).

A 1969 film version with a curiously twisted story and a fragmented score (eight numbers, with five fresh ones by André Previn and Lerner interpolated) starred Western heroes Lee Marvin and Clint Eastwood, with Jean Seberg (dubbed by Anita Gordon) and vocalist Harve Presnell as the lovers, and launched Marvin's double-bass growled version of ''Wan'drin' Star'' as hit-parade material.

UK: Her Majesty's Theatre 11 February 1953; Australia: Her Majesty's Theatre, Melbourne 27 November 1954

Film: Paramount 1969

Recordings: original cast (RCA), London cast (Columbia), film soundtrack (Paramount), selections (Fontana)

THE PAJAMA GAME Musical in 2 acts by George Abbott and Richard Bissell based on Bissell's novel *7 1/2 Cents.* Music and lyrics by Richard Adler and Jerry Ross. St James Theater, New York, 13 May 1954.

Many of the names attached to *The Pajama Game,* both above and below the title, were new ones to Broadway: the producing team of Freddie Brisson, Harold Prince and Robert Griffith were mounting their first show in New York, Jerome Robbins was directing and Bob Fosse choreographing on Broadway for the first time, and songwriters Adler and Ross were offering their first score for a book musical. The wisdom of the ages was represented by veteran musical man George Abbott, who had half credits with Robbins and with Richard Bissell, the author of the novel on which the show was based, on the libretto.

Sid Sorokin (John Raitt), the new foreman in the Sleep Tite pajama factory, gets attracted to a tart little dolly bird called Babe (Janis Paige), who is boss of the Grievance Committee of the firm's union. Babe professes to return his feelings, but her priority is with fouling up production at the factory to try to blackmail the Boss into raising wages. Sid has to sack her, but her ethics have rubbed off on him, and he manages to get the Boss's secretary drunk and amorous enough to give him the keys to the firm's confidential ledgers. Equipped with Sleep Tite's figures and projections, he himself moves into the blackmailing business and gets a compromise out of the Boss that looks sufficiently like a ''win'' to Babe and her pals for Sid to ''win'' Babe. If Babe was motivated mostly by money, the other principal characters of the piece operated mainly on lust: the lubricious Prez of the Union (Stanley Prager) chasing after secretary Gladys Hotchkiss (Carol Haney), who is the promised preserve of Time-and-Motion man Hines (Eddie Foy jr), or alternatively after her co-worker Mabel (Reta Shaw).

The songs that illustrated the story were a particularly bright and bounding lot: Babe scornfully denying Sid's attractions in the waltzing ''I'm Not at All in Love,'' Gladys's burlesque description of the passion pit ''Hernando's Hideaway,'' the ''Once a Year Day'' of the firm's picnic, Hines's impossible promise ''I'll Never Be Jealous Again'' and his job description, ''Think of the Time I Save'' and, at the top of the lot, Sid's winning soliloquy, sung to his dictaphone—''Hey There (you with the stars in your eyes).'' The two second-act set dance pieces both featured Carol Haney, as Gladys, opening the half with the sexy ''Steam Heat'' (introduced as an entertainment at a union meeting!) and later, in a Jealousy Ballet depicting the alarmed imaginings of Hines over Gladys's tipsy episode with Sid.

The songs and dances and the colorful, high-spirited staging served to take the distasteful edge off the plot and characters of this long-distance successor to the Garment Workers' revue *Pins and Needles* (1937) in the line of musical shows about garment workers, and *The Pajama Game* had a magnificent Broadway run of 1,063 performances, as well as spending two seasons on the road with Larry Douglas and Fran Warren starring.

In London, Rodgers and Hammerstein's Williamson Music found considerable success when they joined Prince Littler to present Edmund Hockridge (Sid), Joy Nichols (Babe), Max Wall (Hines), Joan Fred Emney (Mabel) and Elizabeth Seal (Gladys) in a restaging of the Broadway production at the huge London Coliseum through a very fine 588 performances. In Australia, too, where J C Williamson Ltd took the then unusual step of casting the piece wholly with native Australians (Bill Newman, Toni Lamond, Tikki Taylor, Keith Peterson) instead of imported ''stars'' (who usually weren't), *The Pajama Game* scored a fine success, beginning with a four-month initial Melbourne season, and in 1957, on the heels of *Kiss Me, Kate,* the show even reached Austria, where, at that point, no other modern Broadway shows had been produced.

In the same year, a Warner Brothers film cast Doris Day as Babe alongside the principals of the original stage production in a version that used virtually all the score, the notable cut being ''Think of the Time I Save.''

The piece has had regular playing in regional American theatres since its production, and in 1973 it returned to Broadway (Lunt-Fontanne Theater 9 December) under the management of composer Adler. Hal Linden, Barbara McNair, Cab Calloway and Sharron Miller headed the cast of a version that attempted to lift the libretto into a different area by introducing a question of race into the central romance (she was black and he white), through only 65 performances. In the 1980s *The Pajama Game* was still to be found on the production schedules, and during that decade it got a couple of very different treatments on the two sides of the Atlantic: in America Richard Muenz, Judy Kaye, Avery Saltzman and Leonora Nemetz featured in a very thoroughly sung production sponsored by the New York City Opera (4 March 1989), while in Britain an undersung provincial mounting, with Paul Jones and Fiona Jane Hendley featured, stopped short of its intended berth in the West End. This did not prevent a fresh British mounting of this strangely recurrent musical, which dropped anchor at the Victoria Palace in the post–trades union era (21 September 1999), advertised desperately as ''a classic feelgood musical.'' Graham Bickley and Leslie Ash took the lead roles in a piece whose age and limitations showed too clearly to allow success.

UK: London Coliseum *The Pyjama Game* 13 October 1955; Australia: Her Majesty's Theatre, Melbourne *The Pyjama Game* 2 February 1957; Austria: Stadttheater, Klagenfurt *Herz im Pajama* 8 November 1957

Film: Warner Bros 1957

Recordings: original cast (Columbia), original London cast (HMV), film soundtrack (Columbia), etc

PAL JOEY Musical in 2 acts by John O'Hara based on his own short stories. Lyrics by Lorenz Hart. Music by Richard Rodgers. Ethel Barrymore Theater, New York, 25 December 1940.

Rodgers and Hart had been mixing their musicals with some agility since their return from Hollywood to Broadway, ranging from the elephantine spectacularities of *Jumbo* to the dance-based *On Your Toes,* the kiddie-concert tale of *Babes in Arms,* the fantasy of *I Married an Angel,* the classic burlesque of *The Boys from Syracuse* and the college high-jinks of *Too Many Girls,* and almost everywhere with success. The question Where do we go next? was answered when author John O'Hara suggested they look at his ''Pal Joey'' pieces in the *New Yorker* magazine with the idea of using the character of the cheap cabaret compère as a starting point for a show. O'Hara was a different kind of writer from those the partners had worked with until now, and it was no surprise that *Pal Joey* turned out to be a different kind of show. As Rodgers later said, ''There wasn't one decent character in the entire play except for the girl who briefly fell for Joey—her trouble was simply that she was stupid.'' But indecent and/or stupid, the characters of *Pal Joey* made up a tough and effective tale.

Joey Evans (Gene Kelly) is compère at a tacky nightclub in Chicago. He's also full of himself, empty-headed and -hearted, and more than eager to drop the dumb Linda English (Leila Ernst), when wealthy, randy Vera Simpson (Vivienne Segal) prowls by the club one evening and flicks her fingers at him. Vera's not interested in Joey's head or heart; her sights are rather lower down. While she's getting what she wants from the boy, she's happy enough to spend the cash to let him run his own club, and rig himself out like a spiv, but when blackmail rears its head, she shuts her purse, shrugs him off and calls up a friend at the police department. Its over, and Joey's back where he started, still emptily talking the big time.

The show's score mixed a bundle of deliberately second-rate cabaret numbers, performed in the club, with a set of ballads that eschewed all that was in that bundle. Joey wooed Linda with the phoney sentiment of ''I Could Write a Book,'' Vera delightedly found herself ''Bewitched (bothered and bewildered)'' by a young man all over again, and joined in a clear-headed tit-for-tat with Linda as each told the other to ''Take Him.'' Pasted into the middle of all this was a revusical number for an incidental journalist, Melba (Jean Casto), ''Zip,'' detailing what a stripper thinks about as she does. June Havoc played club chorine Gladys Bumps, who led the routines, the plotting and a bit of the comedy, and the supporting cast included Van Johnson and Stanley Donen.

Some folk found the shabby characters of Pal Joey and their shabby behavior didn't make much of an evening in the theatre, but musicals with unpleasant lead characters had been successful before (remember *Der Obersteiger*?) and *Pal Joey* found plenty of fans. George Abbott's production ran for 374 performances on Broadway—more than *Jumbo,* more than *I Married an Angel* or *On Your Toes,* more, in fact, than any other Rodgers and Hart show in 20 years except the small-house *A Connecticut Yankee.* It followed up Broadway with a three-month tour, then was put aside.

That might have been all, but in 1950 Columbia put out a long-playing record of the songs from *Pal Joey,* with Vivienne Segal singing her original numbers and dancer Harold Lang as Joey. The record had a remarkable success, and songwriter-producer Jule Styne decided to put the show back on the Broadway stage. Miss Segal and Lang were supported by Patricia Northrop (Linda), Helen Gallagher (Gladys) and Elaine Stritch (Melba), the revival was mounted at the Broadhurst Theater (3 January 1952) and it gave Rodgers and Hart their best run ever: 542 performances. This time, other folk paid attention. Jack Hylton imported *Pal Joey* and Lang into Britain and, with Carol Bruce (Vera) and Sally Bazely (Linda) in the principal female roles, watched his production run up a pretty fair 245 performances at London's Prince's Theatre. Hollywood came next with a film that used a large amount of the original music, supplemented by four Rodgers and Hart hits from earlier shows. It also used Frank Sinatra as a less-dancing, thoroughly convincing Joey, alongside a brace of glamorous co-stars: Rita Hayworth (Vera, sung by Jo Ann Greer) and Kim Novak (Linda, sung by Trudy Ewen).

Pal Joey's revival fixed it firmly in the American repertoire, and it won regular productions thereafter. Bob Fosse (Lang's cover in the 1952 show) played Joey in 1961 and 1963 revivals at the City Center, and in 1976 Christopher Chadman and Joan Copeland featured in a revival at New York's Circle in the Square (27 June 1976, 73 performances), but a 1978 production with Lena Horne and Clifford Davis ended its pre-Broadway life in Los Angeles. Australia saw its only metropolitan *Pal Joey* to date in 1967 at a Sydney dinner theatre, but in 1980 London got a new production (25 September), brought to the West End from the small fringe Half Moon Theatre. Denis Lawson's dazzling Joey, supported by Danielle Carson (Linda) and Sîan Phillips (Vera), headed the cast of a genuinely shabby production (with genuinely shabby chorus girls for its club) through a fine 415 performances.

In 1982 the ever-enterprising Opéra Royal de Wallonie in Belgium gave the first French-language *Pal Joey* (Liège 15 October).

One of the few musicals of its period that survived into the 1970s and 1980s as an at least partly verismo piece, *Pal Joey* has found more partisans and productions in the years since its relaunch than it did in its first decade of life.

Plate 295. **Pal Joey.** *Joey (Harold Lang) faces up to the scheme-team of Ludlow Lowell (Lionel Stander) and Gladys Bumps (Helen Gallagher).*

UK: Prince's Theatre 31 March 1954; Australia: Menzies Theatre Restaurant, Sydney June 1967; Germany: Opernhaus, Essen *Darling Joe* 21 October 1980

Film: Columbia 1957

Recordings: 1950 studio cast w Vivienne Segal (Columbia), part-revival cast w Jane Froman (Capitol/EMI), London 1980 revival cast (TER), studio cast (DRG), film soundtrack (Capitol), etc

PALLENBERG, Max (b Vienna, 18 December 1877; d nr Carlsbad, 20 June 1934).

Regarded for many years as Germany's finest player of classic character and comedy roles, in works by Molière, Shakespeare, Schiller, Goethe, Ibsen, Pirandello, as Molnár's Liliom or the Good Soldier Schweik, Pallenberg also made regular appearances on the musical stage.

He took his first steps to fame when he scored a great success in the role of the comical Wallerstein in the Theater an der Wien's production of *Herbstmanöver* (1909), appeared as Lindoberer in Vienna's *Der fidele Bauer,* and created the parts of Peter Walperl in *Die Förster-Christl* (1907) at the Theater in der Josefstadt, Gregorio in *Der*

Plate 296. **Max Pallenberg** *as Basil Basilowitsch in* Der Graf von Luxemburg.

Frauenjäger (1908), Oberst Kasimir Popoff in *Der tapfere Soldat* (1908) and Basil Basilowitsch in *Der Graf von Luxemburg* (1909) in the years before quitting his home town to play, at first, in Munich, and later in Berlin.

During his career in Berlin he appeared in versions of several classic musical plays—as Menelaos in the chopped-around Metropoltheater *Die schöne Helena,* as Jupiter in *Orpheus in der Unterwelt,* as Ko-Ko in Charell's mashed-up *Mikado* of 1927 and as Calicot to the Pompadour of his wife, Fritzi Massary. He was also seen alongside his wife in Jean Gilbert's Posse *So bummeln wir!* (1912) at the Theater Gross-Berlin am Zoo and created the role of the tribune, Marc Antonius, in Massary's Oscar Straus Operette *Die Perlen der Cleopatra* (1923) at Vienna's Theater an der Wien.

Effectively exiled from Berlin by the anti-Jewish measures of 1933, Pallenberg was killed in an air crash soon after, at the age of 56.

PÁLMAY, Ilka [PETRÁSS, Ilona Pálmay] [aka SZIGLIGETINÉ, Ilka] (b Ungvár, 21 September 1859; d Budapest, 17 February 1945).

The 18-year-old (or 13-year-old if you believe the dates given in some biographies) Ilka Szigligetiné, who had first trod the boards at Kaschau, shot to the theatrical forefront when she appeared at Budapest's Népszínház as Serpolette in the Hungarian premiere of *A Cornevillei harangok* (*Les Cloches de Corneville,* 1878). Over the next decade, during which she shed her first husband, József Szigligeti (1851–1889), and his name, she shared with Aranka Hegyi the major operettic roles—prima donna, soubrette and travesty—at the Népszínház, Budapest's principal musical theatre, as well as taking leads in many of the straight plays that made up the theatre's programs.

Among the 48 different musical pieces and roles she played there were *A királykisasszony babui* (*Les Poupées de l'Infante*), Manola in *Nap és hold* (*Le Jour et la nuit*), Sora in *Gasparone,* Lisbeth (ie, Gretchen) in *Rip,* Offenbach's Eurydice, his Belle Hélène and Gabrielle in *Párizsi élet* (*La Vie parisienne*), Micaëla in A *kertészleány* (*Le Coeur et la Main*), Bronislawa in *Koldusdiák* (*Der Bettelstudent*), a travesty Barinkay in *A cigánybáró* (*Der Ziegunerbaron*), the title role of *A béárni leány* (*La Béarnaise*), the Queen in *A királynő csipkekend ője* (*Das Spitzentuch der Königin*), the title roles of the local versions of *Les Noces d'Olivette, La Grande-Duchesse de Gérolstein, Donna Juanita, Marjolaine, Le Petit Duc, Niniche* and *Boccaccio,* Clairette in *La Fille de Madame Angot,* both Yum-Yum and Nanki-Poo in different productions of *The Mikado,* Denise de Flavigny in *Nebántsvirág* (*Mam'zelle Nitouche*), Benjaminc in *Jozéfu Egyiptomban* (*Joséphine vendue par ses soeurs*), Tilly in *Simplicius,* Nell Gwynne in *A komédiás hercegnő* (Robert Planquette's *Nell Gwynne*), Phryne (apparently Phoebe) in *A gárdista* (*The Yeomen of the Guard*) and Borka (presumably Patience) in *Fejő leány* (*Patience*).

She created starring roles in several early Hungarian operetts including the remake of *L'Étoile* as *Uff király* (1887, Lazuli) and Béla Hegyi and Szidor Bator's *A titkos csók* (1888, Lolotte) and the musical plays *A piros bugyelláris* (1878, Török Zsófi) and *Csókon szerzett vőlegeny* (1883, Irén Abrai), and also played such non-singing roles as that of Zola's *Nana* (1882). In 1883 she appeared with the Budapest company as Micaëla, Manola and Serpolette in a season in Vienna, and she returned there in 1891 to spend more than two years as leading lady at the Theater an der Wien. During that time she created the role of the postmistress Christel in Zeller's *Der Vogelhändler* (1891, "Ich bin der Christel von der Post"), Ilona in the farcical *Heisses Blut* (1892, "written especially for her by Krenn and Lindau"), Lady Sylvia Rockhill in Millöcker's *Das Sonntagskind* (1892) and the title role in Johann Strauss's *Fürstin Ninetta* (1893), as well as appearing as Hélène, Javotte in *Fanchon's Leyer* (*La Fille de Fanchon la vielleuse*), in German versions of Anna Judic's roles of Denise de Flavigny (*Mam'zelle Nitouche*) and Princess Anna Semionowna Machinstoff

(*Die Kosakin*) and introducing the little Operette *La Stupida* (1893 aka *Das Mädchen vom Mirano*). She also played at Berlin's Thomas-Theater (1892, *Heisses Blut,* etc) and Friedrich-Wilhelmstädtisches Theater (1893, *Das Mädchen vom Mirano, Der Bettelstudent, Mam'zelle Nitouche, Schöne Helena).*

After a brief retirement from the stage to become the Gräfin Eugen Kinsky, she moved on to appear at the Theater Unter der Linden in Adolphe Ferron's Operette *Sataniel* (1893) and, to the annoyance of Arthur Sullivan, who tried to stop it, as Nanki-Poo, returning to Vienna in 1895 to star in travesty as Hector in *Die Karlsschülerin* and appearing in London, with the Saxe-Coburg Company, in *Der Vogelhändler* at the Theatre Royal, Drury Lane. This visit resulted in her being offered a contract by D'Oyly Carte, and in 1896–97 she created the roles of Julia Jellicoe in Gilbert and Sullivan's *The Grand Duke* and Felice in *His Majesty* and appeared as Elsie Maynard in a revival of *The Yeomen of the Guard* at the Savoy Theatre.

In 1898–99 she played again in Vienna, starring at the Theater an der Wien in a series of largely new but not very impressive Operetten: *Die Küchen-Comtesse* (Lisa Schwarzen), von Taund's *Der Dreibund* (Lydia), Adolf Müller jr's *Der Blondin von Namur* (Blondin), Josef Bayer's *Fräulein Hexe* (Magdalene), and as the Principessa Santiago de Merimac in Heuberger's version of *Niniche, Ihre Excellenz.*

The later part of her career was spent mostly in Budapest (where in 1901 she played Belasco's non-musical *Madame Butterfly*), although she visited New York in 1905 and appeared there in the multi-parted role of Ilona in *Heisses Blut* in the German-language theatre. In some of her latter-day appearances in Budapest she appeared as the old Countess Irini in the local production of *Der Zigeunerprimás* (1913) and as the elder Hannerl in *Médi* (1918), the Hungarian version of *Hannerl.* She did not officially retire from the stage until 1928 after a career of 50 years in which she had compiled one of the most remarkable careers in the European musical theatre—a career that held the unusual distinction of including the creation of leading roles both for Johann Strauss and for Gilbert and Sullivan.

Autobiography: *Meine Errinerung* (Verlag von Richard Bong, Berlin, 1911)

Plate 297. **Ilka Pálmay** *as Yum Yum.*

PALMER, Minnie (b Philadelphia, 31 March ?1857; d East Islip [Bay Shore], Long Island, NY, 21 May 1936). ''A great favorite, if not much of an actress.''

Diminutive Minnie Palmer, daughter of a sometime actress, made her first appearances on the stage at Ford's and the Abbey Theater in Baltimore. At the age of what was probably 17 she made early attempts at starring in the ''protean comedy'' *Satan in Paris* (1874, playing five roles, including two male), *Maude's Faith, Pepina the Waif* and the romantic drama *Pavillon Rouge* (Brooklyn, 1874, Nanine). She subsequently toured as a star to stock companies (1875), playing everything from Louise in *The Two Orphans* to *Bob* and *Little Silver.* She played in Baltimore as Titania in *A Midsummer Night's Dream* (1875) and a made-to-measure romantic piece called *Gertrude the Belle,* starred in a piece called *Laughing Eyes* (1876) and made her Broadway debut when she donned breeches to play alongside Nat Goodwin, in the burlesques *The Pique Family* (1876, Jimmy Loose), *Black-Eyed Susan* (1876, Susan) and *Ferry O* (1876). Profiting from her very young looks, she played in Boston as Laura in the musical farce *The Little Rebel* (as *Home from School* ''she sings nicely, dances neatly and has made quite a success''), appeared in the unfortunate drama *Kisses* (1876), as Meenie to the Rip of Joseph Jefferson, featured as *The Little Rebel* again at Booth's, played little Dorothy in W S Gilbert's *Dan'l Druce* and Minnie Symperson in his *Engaged,* and took the roles of

Plate 298. *American actress* **Minnie Palmer** *at 40, going on 12.*

Dot in *Dot,* Blanche in *Hurricanes* and Josephine Onyx in *Blondes and Bombshells* (1878). She also appeared in Philadelphia as Amourette in the spectacle *Baba* (1877), as Katharine Schulz to the Fritz of J K Emmet in *The New Fritz* (1878) and created the role of Grace Brandon in Bartley Campbell's drama *My Partner* (1879). In 1879–80 she toured America as Jessie Fairlove in a tailor-made vehicle called *Minnie Palmer's Boarding School* (Norwalk, Conn 5 December 1879, Gaiety, Boston 8 December) and the following season in a disastrous piece called *Pigeon, the Torment* (English's Opera House, San Francisco 31 December 1880) before on 29 August 1881 at Buffalo's Academy of Music she appeared for the first time as the good-as-gold Tina in the low-comedy-cum-sentimental drama *My Sweetheart,* a portmanteau piece of Dutch-accented ''musical comedy'' that was tricked out with narrow-range songs and speciality acts, inserted to showcase its girlish star's various talents. It did so to great effect, and for a long time.

In 1883 (slicing at this stage eight years—though later only three—off her age for the benefit of the press) she took *My Sweetheart* to Britain, where she opened at the Princess's Theatre in Glasgow (4 June 1883) and quickly established herself as a phenomenally popular touring attraction. She easily overran the six months of her announced tour and, to the accompaniment of a stream of preposterous and phony publicity stories kept continually bubbling by her manager husband, John Rogers (although married to Rogers for several years she ''admitted'' to the press that she was bound by a $15,000 bond not to marry and leave the stage for five years, etc), producer H Cecil Beryl kept *My Sweetheart* and its ''juvenile'' star profitably on the road and even essayed a daring visit to London (Strand Theatre 14 January 1884) without the notices being too desperately scalding and with audiences mobbing the house for two hundred performances.

Miss Palmer then went back to America for ''unavoidable engagements,'' but she returned to Britain to play more *My Sweetheart* before, in 1886, she took her show to Australia (Princess, Melbourne 31 January 1886) for a 32-week tour. There she repeated her British success, in spite of the press remarking on the show's similarity to the J C Williamsons' celebrated *Struck Oil.* She followed up in several similar if less successful vehicles, such as Fred Maeder's *Pert and Her Stepmother* (Bush Theater, San Francisco 15 August 1887), *My Brother's Sister* (1889 New York, 1890 London), in which she appeared successively as two boys and two girls, and which was ventured at a matinée at the Gaiety Theatre, *A Mile a Minute* (Nelly Sparkle, People's Theatre, New York 9 February 1891), another remake of *The Little Rebel* called *The School Girl* (Cardiff 2 September 1895, New York, December 1895, Little Miss Loo), *The Showman's Sweetheart* (Belle Hawker, Queen's Theatre, Crouch End 29 August 1898) and *Rose Pompon* (1899), but none held up for long and she returned ultimately and always to *My Sweetheart.*

She made one brief appearance in a slightly more regular form of musical theatre when she took over Letty Lind's role of Maude Sportington in the London production of the variety musical *Morocco Bound* and interpolated her own material, and also starred, on one occasion, in an almost genuine comic opera, Oscar Weil's remake of *La Dormeuse éveillée* as *Suzette,* with the ''Minnie Palmer Opera Company''at the Trenton Opera House (30 September 1890) and New York's Hermann's Theater, playing alongside vocalists of the calibre of Bertha Ricci. She also made what should have been a lucrative London appearance (at £75 per week and 2 percent of the gross) as Cinderella in Henry Leslie's carelessly spectacular and financially disastrous pantomime of 1889. In 1899 she returned to America and took to the vaudeville houses playing a 1-act play called *Rose Pompon* into which she introduced "the specialities of dancing and singing with which she has always been identified." She remained throughout, however, a personality performer whose appeal was not to audiences with any degree of sophistication.

Minnie Palmer stuck to the stage even after her large number of days playing very young girls was over. In 1908 she was still to been seen on the vaudeville circuits playing a J M Barrie sketch called *A Woman's Curiosity,* and she made her final appearance in 1918 in a supporting role in the Broadway play *Lightnin'* (Mrs Jordan). In 1927 she was taken into the Actor's Fund home in Long Island and died there in 1936, admitting to an age of 71.

PANAMA HATTIE Musical comedy in 2 acts by Herbert Fields and B G De Sylva. Music and lyrics by Cole Porter. 46th Street Theater, New York, 30 October 1940.

The fourth of five teamings of songwriter Cole Porter and star Ethel Merman, *Panama Hattie* followed behind *Anything Goes,* which had cast its star as a nightclub-singer-cum-evangelist, *Red, Hot and Blue!* in which she had played a kookie millionairess, and *Dubarry Was a Lady,* which had presented her as a nightclub singer dreamed into antique France. Since the nightclub gals had done much better than the millionairess, it was not so much of a surprise that *Panama Hattie* had for its heroine a bright-as-a-button, hard-as-a-hamstring nightclub hostess. Hattie Maloney (Miss Merman), who runs a classy joint in Panama City, has pulled herself a proposal from a classy gent. Nick Bullett (James Dunn) is a real Mayflower type, even if he is slightly used. That is to say, he's been married before, and he has an eight-year-old daughter named Geraldine, known as Jerry (Jean Carroll), to prove it. This makes Hattie a touch uneasy, but by the end of the evening she's got the kiddie on her side and the wedding can go ahead. Betty Hutton supported as soubrette-comic Florrie, Rags Ragland (Woozy Hogan), Pat Harrington (Skat Briggs) and Frankie Hyers (Windy Deegan) were three comedy sailors out on the town looking for girls, and Englishman Arthur Treacher completed the principal cast as Florrie's opposite number, Englishman Vivian Budd.

The score of *Panama Hattie* included the usual bundle of Porterish name-dropping songs. Miss Merman's "I've Still Got My Health" got in the Astors, Lucius Beebe, Fred Astaire, L B Mayer, Ethel Barrymore, Ina Claire and Billy Rose, and her "I'm Throwing a Ball Tonight" plugged Monty Woolley, Clifford Odets, Grace Moore, Mae West, Bert Lahr, Fanny Brice, Gracie Allen and a few more local luminaries. But it was perhaps no coincidence that the most popular number to emerge from the set was none of these backscratchers, but the star's rueful torch song to the curative value of booze,

Plate 299. **Panama Hattie.** *Ethel Merman outfaces the fleet.*

"Make It Another Old-Fashioned, Please." Among the other songs, Miss Merman informed her chap off-puttingly "My Mother Would Love You" and shared a "Let's Be Buddies" with the child, Miss Hutton bounced out a couple of hunting numbers ("All I've Got to Get Now Is My Man," "They Ain't Done Right by Our Nell") and the sailors jollied forth a couple of songs.

Panama Hattie was a happy, other-folks'-wartime hit. By the time it shuttered on Broadway it had statistically outdone the initial records of *Anything Goes* and *Dubarry Was a Lady* with its 501 performances, as it headed on to the rest of the country, with Dunn and Frances Williams in the lead roles, and for Hollywood, where Ann Sothern took up the part of Hattie for her celluloid incarnation alongside Red Skelton, Ben Blue, Lena Horne, Dan Dailey, Ragland and Virginia O'Brien. The film version took in half a dozen other Porter and non-Porter numbers to add to four of the original songs.

Panama Hattie brought its share of cheer to wartime London, too, as part of what local producers voted the most prosperous theatrical year in memory. Emile Littler, Tom Arnold and Lee Ephraim's production, with Bebe Daniels as a Hattie who (like all good Panamanian nightclub hostesses) was costumed by Hartnell, Ivan Brandt as her man, and Richard Hearne (Loopy) and Claude Hulbert (Budd) among the support, ran up a bomb-bisected

308 performances at the Piccadilly and Adelphi Theatres between 1943 and 1945.

Miss Merman reprised her role alongside Ray Middleton in 1954 for a potted television version that used her three main songs (plus a couple from her other Porter shows), and the show has been given the occasional reshowing, notably at Equity Library Theatre and the Paper Mill Playhouse in 1976, but in spite of its top statistical score in the Porter-Merman stakes first time around, *Panama Hattie* has been eclipsed by *Anything Goes* as a long-term survivor.

UK: Piccadilly Theatre 4 November 1943

Film: MGM 1942

Recording: original cast (Decca/MCA)

LE PAPA DE FRANCINE Opérette à grand spectacle in 4 acts by Victor de Cottens and Paul Gavault. Music by Louis Varney. Théâtre Cluny, Paris, 5 November 1896.

''A rattling, vulgar farce, but amusing and unpretentious,'' commented one usually slightly white-lipped critic after the opening of *Le Papa de Francine,* without yet mentioning all the other elements—from a hit song and a lively score, to as many lavish scenic and costume values as could be fitted on to the little Cluny stage—that went to make up a show, built much on *Voyage de Suzette* lines, which proved a jolly Parisian hit.

Francine's Papa is an American named Burnett (Allart), whom she has never met, for after his progeny-productive French idyll with the danseuse Palmyre Plumet (Adèle Cuinet), he nipped off back across the Atlantic into anonymity. Eighteen years later, having struck both oil and the melancholy remorse of middle age, he has now decided to try to find his child (Mary Lebey) and to that effect hires a secret agent, Mongrapin (Dorgat), who sets off in search of the now plump and plain Palmyre and her daughter. The spectacle of the evening is ensured by the fact that young Francine is working at the Moulin-Rouge as an ''equestrian chanteuse,'' and it is there that Mongrapin tracks her down. However, although Francine has the support of her devoted noble lover, Gontran (Conradin), who has turned circus clown for love of her, there is opposition to the father and daughter reunion from the masher, cousin Adhémar (Hamilton), and his mistress, Diane de Pontivy (Mlle Manuel), who stand to profit if the missing heiress is not found. Disguises and impostures abound as the baddies try to sandbag the goodies on their way to the all-important meeting point at Saint-Germain, via the rowing-club bar in Asnières, a rosière ceremony in Nanterre, the ''sinking of Mme Plumet'' at Chatou, and a villa in Le Vésinet, where Adhémar and Diane impersonate Brazilians and the place becomes the scene for a confrontation between a band of burglars and the gendarmerie. Needless to say, the goodies get there just in time for the happy ending.

The hit of *Le Papa de Francine* was the burglary scene, an item inserted to feature the Price family of pantomimists as the burglars, and highlighted by a delightful waltz trio (''Faire la montre et la chaîne'') in praise of pilfering, performed by the singing burglars La Puce (Mlle Norcy), Galoppe-Chopine (Prévost) and Lilas-Blanc (Houssaye), which became the number of the night. Francine rode onto the stage on a live horse (at the Cluny!) and delivered a Chanson du petit jockey; her mother had her moment in the scene in which she was dropped in the Seine and then, clad in male underwear, fought a duel; and the detective let loose with a comical madrigal (''Vous êtes la rose embaumée'') amongst a whole plethora of jokes about pompiers (an untranslateable speciality of Nanterre) putting out the flames evident in the local virgins. The baddies took time off from being bad to perform a strenuous boléro and a polka.

Le Papa de Francine drew the public to its little theatre for more than two hundred nights in its first run, before being taken up for other center—but without its title. In Vienna, instead of Francine's father having the title role it was *Lolas Cousin,* otherwise the wicked Adhémar, who was promoted. Lola (still ''eine Sängerin zu Pferde'') was played by Frau Wittels-Moser, with Viktoria Pohl-Meiser (Mme Plumet), Otto Maran (Mongrapin), Adele Moraw (Diane), Rauch (Adhémar) and Karl Pfann (Bob Smitting, ex- Gontran) in the other main roles of a version (ad Julius Horst) that actually kept the jokes about the pompiers of Nanterre (surely not very funny outside France?) but reduced the piece from seven scenes to five. Without coming near the huge totals secured by the French *Toto* and *Les Fêtards* at the Theater in der Josefstadt, *Lolas Cousin* confirmed nicely the success of Varney's *Les Petites Brebis* at the same house three years earlier with a useful season of 30 nights.

Hungary got papa back in the title, without Francine, in a version entitled *Utazás egy apa körül* (voyage around a father, ad Emil Makai) staged just a few months later at the Magyar Színház, whilst an English-language version eventually dropped papa, and simply called Francine *A Lucky Girl* (ad Wallace Erskine, Adeline Stuart). Mounted by Erskine for a provincial tour under the title *In Search of a Father* with Miss Stuart starred as Diane to his Charles (ex- Adhémar), Edith Armstrong as Stella (ex- Francine), Maitland Marler as Adolphus Raveller and the cast's only ''name,'' Florence Vie, as mother, it reduced the company's touring baggage by making Stella a ''descriptive vocalist,'' thus cutting the horse, and setting the whole thing in England. The first scene was now ''the Winter Gardens, Brightpool,'' the May Queen Festival was at Cobford, and mama got dumped in Mrs Plummer's baths, Eastbourne, instead of in the Seine. The famous Fred Evans troupe (without their deceased namesake) were the burglars. After an initial production at West Hartlepool the piece was revised and sent out again as *A Lucky Girl.*

Paris saw a revival of the piece in 1898 (3 June, Folies-Dramatiques), with Berthe Legrand as Mme Plumet and Vavasseur as Mongrapin, and another in 1901 at the former music hall, Parisiana, in each of which the speciality-act quotient was once again topped by the clown team, the Prices, who had invented the celebrated burglar scene.

Austria: Theater in der Josefstadt *Lolas Cousin* 11 January 1898; Hungary: Magyar Színház *Utazás egy apa körül* 22 April 1898; UK: *In Search of a Father* Alhambra Theatre, West Hartlepool 16 May 1898, *A Lucky Girl* Grand Theatre, Derby 1 August 1898

PAPP, Joseph [PAPIROFSKY, Yosi] (b Brooklyn, NY, 22 June 1921; d New York, 31 October 1991).

Originally a theatre stage manager, then a producer, Papp was from 1956 the director of the New York Shakespeare Festival, which, progressively belying its title after its first decade of activity, was responsible for the production of a considerable number of original musicals. The enormously successful *Hair* (1967) was the first of these, but although a second Galt MacDermot musical, *Two Gentlemen of Verona,* found some success and a Tony Award, it was the 1975 production of the record-breaking *A Chorus Line* that remained Papp's most outstanding and outstandingly profitable producing achievement. A further major success was won with a lively version of Gilbert and Sullivan's *The Pirates of Penzance* (1980) which, reorchestrated and performed by modern pop voices, totted up the longest run of any Gilbert and Sullivan work in Broadway history and gave the show a new round of international productions and even a film, whilst an effective musical retelling of *The Mystery of Edwin Drood* (1985), equipped with alternative endings, also moved to longish-running success on Broadway (Tony Award).

Other Papp/New York Shakespeare Festival musical theatre productions included *Stomp* (1969), *Sambo* (1969), *Mod-Donna* (1970), *The Wedding of Iphigenia* (1971), *Lotta, or The Best Thing Evolution's Ever Come Up With* (1973), *More Than You Deserve* (1973), *Apple Pie* (1976), *On the Lock-In* (1978), *Dispatches* (1979), a stage adaptation of the French film musical *Les Parapluies de Cherbourg* as *The Umbrellas of Cherbourg* (1979), *Leave It to Beaver Is Dead* (1979), *The Haggadah* (1980), *The Death of von Richthofen as Witnessed from Earth* (1982), *Lullaby and Goodnight* (1982), *Lenny and the Heartbreakers* (1983), *The Human Comedy* (1983), a *Non Pasquale* (1983) and a *La Bohème* (1984) that attempted to take the same trail as *The Pirates of Penzance* without the same success, *The Knife* (1987), *A Stranger Here Myself* (1988), *Genesis* (1989), *Songs of Paradise* (1989), *Romance in Hard Times* (1989), *Up Against It* (1989) and *Jonah* (1990).

Biographies: Little, S: *Enter Joseph Papp* (Coward, McCann & Geoghegan, New York, 1974), Epstein, H: *Joe Papp, an American Life* (Little, Brown, Boston 1994)

PAPP, Mihály (b Makó, 22 November 1875; d Budapest, 20 September 1915).

In his short life and career, character-actor Papp worked at first in provincial theatres, before moving in 1903 from Kolozsvár to Budapest's Király Színház. After two years he left to join the company at the Vígszínház, but he returned to the Király Színház for a second period before moving on to the Magyar Színház. Although his career was made largely on a diet of non-musical plays, he did appear in a number of musical pieces, notably in the Hungarian productions of Lincke's *Lysistrata,* as Prince Paul in *La Grande-Duchesse,* as Scrop in *Die geschiedene Frau,* as Coucy-Couca in the local version of Claude Terrasse's *Le Sire de Vergy* (*Én, te, ő*) and, in particular, created the role of the pathetic Bagó in Hungary's most enduring musical play, *János vitéz.*

LE PARADIS DE MAHOMET Opérette in 3 acts by Henri Blondeau. Music by Robert Planquette. Additional music by Louis Ganne. Théâtre des Variétés, Paris, 15 May 1906.

Planquette's final stage work, completed after his death by Louis Ganne, was produced by Fernand Samuel at the Théâtre des Variétés in 1906. Henri Blondeau's libretto was set in modern Trébizonde, and it took good care continually to take the mickey out of the old Turkish-set opérettes and their characters, while yet employing a plot that might well have served for one of them.

Prince Bredindin (Henri Defreyn), who fancies himself as the Don Juan of his age, wagers with the lovely and uncompliant widow Bengaline (Juliette Méaly) that she will be his within 24 hours. Having failed to stop her marriage to the young merchant Baskir (Jeanne Saulier), he resorts to spiking the reception wine and carries off the sleeping bride to his harem. There, his wives convince the ''dead'' Bengaline that she is in Mahomet's paradise, and the Prince comes to the widow disguised as the spirit of her adored deceased huband, the slaver and sea captain Musaor. ''Paradise'' fills up farcically with ''deceased'' folk: Baskir, Uncle Maboul (Baron), Aunt Sélika (Mme Gilberte), Baskir's little mistress Fathmé (Amélie Diéterle) and her protective brother (Lise Berty), all under the eye of the Prince's myopic secretary, Radaboum (Max

Dearly), who is disguised as the Turkish equivalent of Saint Peter. The Prince's trick falls apart when his moustache falls off in the midst of an embrace, but, when the disgusted Baskir calls in the law to rid him of his unfaithful new wife, that law condemns Bredindin and Bengaline to wed.

Planquette's score gave everyone a sing: The Prince advertised his qualities (''Je fus toujours un homme aimable''), did his impersonation with gusto (''Mes chers amis, je le proclame'') and intimated to his beloved ''Je voudrais être escarpolette'' (I'd like to be a swing!) in order to enfold her the better. Bengaline declared unequivocally ''Il est trop dur de supporter les abstinences du veuvage,'' tossed off a bridal Brindisi, pondered her dilemma in the presence of two ''dead'' husbands (''Je dois contenter mon premier'') and let loose with a ''Toast à l'amour.'' Baskir celebrated his wedding day (''Ah! mes amis, quelle journée'') and duetted with Fathmé, who was in turn well supplied with an aubade and a yodeling song as well as a duet with Dearly, who had his best moment in his impersonation of ''le grand muphti'' sung to the accompaniment of a little dance. In retrospect, however, the melody that won the most attention was a waltz tune that bore the most amazing resemblance to the principal waltz from *Die lustige Witwe,* which had premiered five months earlier (but of course well after Planquette's death) at the Theater an der Wien.

The show was received with enthusiasm and played some 70 times at the Variétés. It was subsequently produced in Hungary (ad Andor Gábor) and in a German version (ad C A Raida) at Dortmund. In America it had a rather stop-go life. After an aborted 1908 tryout with Blanche Ring and Jeff de Angelis featured, and a second false start in 1909, under the Shubert mangement, and the title *The Widow's Paradise,* this time with Adele Ritchie, Eva Davenport, Ralph Herz and Vera Michelena in the lead roles (Hyperion Theater, New Haven 9 September), the show was announced yet again in 1910, first as *The Widow,* then as *A Bridal Trap* under which title it was produced a third time in Scranton, Pa (11 November) with Planquette's music ''arranged'' by Silvio Hein. By the time Dan V Arthur's production finally turned up on Broadway a couple of months later, it starred Grace van Studdiford as Bengaline and George Leon Moore as Prince Bredindin, and had gone back to the original title. It lasted 23 performances in New York before Miss van Studdiford took it off around America. The famous copycat waltz got a wider showing, when a production that claimed it was not *Die lustige Witwe* used it as its big tune.

Le Paradis de Mahomet was revived in Paris, at the Trianon-Lyrique, in 1922.

An earlier *Le Paradis de Mahomet,* a three-act opéra-comique by Eugène Scribe and Mélesville, with music by MM Kreube and Kreutzer, was produced at Paris's Théâtre Feydeau in 1822 (23 March).

Hungary: Király Színház *Mohamed paradicsoma* 10 September 1909; Germany: Stadttheater, Dortmund *Im Paradies Mahomets* 8 February 1910; USA: Lyric Theater, Philadelphia 24 January 1908, Herald Square Theater *The Paradise of Mahomet* 17 January 1911

LES PARAPLUIES DE CHERBOURG Musical comedy in 2 acts by Jacques Demy based on his film screenplay of the same name. Music by Michel Legrand. Public Theater, New York, 1 February 1979.

A sweetly romantic 1963 French film, which presented the particularity for its time of being sung through, Jacques Demy and Michel Legrand's *Les Parapluies de Cherbourg* told the *Fanny*-like tale of an umbrella-merchant's daughter, Geneviève (Catherine Deneuve), who settles for marrying her mother's choice when Guy (Nino Castelnuovo), who has got her pregnant, does not return from the war in Algeria. A surprise screen success, the piece was subsequently adapted for the stage by its author, but its first production was given not in French but in English (ad Sheldon Harnick, Charles Burr) when it was workshopped and then produced by Joseph Papp and the New York Shakespeare Festival for a series of 78 performances in 1979.

Later the same year, the French version was mounted at Paris's Théâtre Montparnasse, directed by Raymond Gérôme, with an orchestra of 11 and a cast of 13, headed by Bee Michelin (Geneviève) and France's *Jesus Christ Superstar* star Daniel Beretta (Guy). Although it was not successful, a London production followed the next year. Susan Gene, Martin Smith and Sheila Matthews headed the cast through 12 sad performances, which lost £140,000.

Michel Legrand is also the composer of a musical version of *Le Comte de Monte Cristo* (Jean Cosmos, Eddie Marnay, Théâtre de la Monnaie, Brussels 18 September 1975) and *Passe-Muraille* (Nantes 6 November 1996, Théâtre des Bouffes-Parisiens 15 January 1997).

France: Théâtre Montparnasse 14 September 1979; UK: Phoenix Theatre *The Umbrellas of Cherbourg* 10 April 1980

Recording: original French cast (Accord)

PARÈS, Philippe (b Paris, 3 May 1901; d Provence, 1979). French composer whose stage successes came in the 1920s and early 1930s.

The son of a musician, Gabriel Parès, the young Philippe began his friendship and his collaboration with Georges van Parys during the years of their studies, and the pair subsequently composed together the scores for a number of films, including René Clair's version of Berr and Verneuil's *Le Million* (1931) and Barnoncelli's screenic *La Femme et le pantin* (''Conchita''), and above all for half a dozen opérettes in the Jazz Age vein played on the Paris stage within a four-year period.

Their first Parisian venture with *Lulu* resulted in a singular success, and the Théâtre Daunou followed it the next year with another dancing comedy, *L'Eau à la bouche,* with a cast headed by Paris's Nanette, Loulou Hégoburu and Fernand Graavey. A transfer of their Brussels production of *La Petite Dame du train bleu,* the comical filmland tale of *Louis XIV* with Dranem at the Théâtre de la Scala, and *Le Coeur y est* confirmed the partnership's vogue. *Couss-couss,* however, marked the end of their Parisian theatre career, and Parès's only subsequent metropolitan venture, alone, was with the postwar piece *La Bride sur le cou.*

A final collaboration with van Parys, another decade on and 30 years after their first success together, produced *Le Moulin sans-souci.* A costume opérette that delved back in time for a plot involving a girl brought up as a boy who makes a heroic soldier, attracts a King's mistress and finally weds a baritonic lieutenant with whom, in her male guise, she has been forced to fight a duel, *Le Moulin sans-souci* found the composers far from the fox-trots and one-steps of their most successful days. Although the show followed the newer fashion for romantic musicals adeptly, its life was limited to the French provinces.

1927 **La Petite Dame du train bleu** (*Quand y-en a pour deux*) (w Georges van Parys/Léo Marchès, Georges Lignereux) Galeries Saint-Hubert, Brussels May; Eldorado, Paris 22 October

1927 **Lulu** (w van Parys/Serge Veber) Théâtre Daunou 14 September

1928 **L'Eau à la bouche** (w van Parys/S Veber) Théâtre Daunou 5 September

1929 **Louis XIV** (w van Parys/S Veber) Théâtre de la Scala

1930 **Le Coeur y est** (w van Parys/Roger Bernstein, Fernand Vimont/Raoul Praxy) Théâtre de l'Athénée 20 May

1931 **Couss-couss** (w van Parys/Jean Guitton) Théâtre de la Scala 26 February

1947 **La Bride sur le cou** (Henry Lemarchand/André Huguet, Max Eddy) Théâtre de la Potinière

1958 **Le Moulin sans-souci** (w van Parys/Marc-Cab/S Veber, Marc-Cab) Opéra, Strasbourg 24 December

A PARISIAN MODEL Musical comedy in 2 acts by Harry B Smith. Music by Max Hoffman. Broadway Theater, New York, 27 November 1906.

A libretto borrowed from the early George Edwardes success *An Artist's Model* and a few other pieces of a similar shape—not excepting the brand-new and not-yet-seen-in-New York *Die lustige Witwe*—put into shape by Harry B Smith, a basic score by the workaday Max Hoffman studded with interpolations as required and a dazzling Florenz Ziegfeld production equipped with a host of girls marshalled by top director/choreographer Julian Mitchell provided the setting for Anna Held in her 1906 starring vehicle on Broadway. Miss Held played an artist's model whose painter lover (Henri Leoni) does not trust her rise to riches and goes off with another girl (Truly Shattuck) until just before the final curtain, and she performed two of her biggest song hits during the course of the evening—her Americanized version of the Scotto/Christiné ''La Petite Tonkinoise'' entitled ''It's Delightful to Be Married'' and Gus Edwards and Will Cobb's ''I Just Can't Make My Eyes Behave.'' Charles Bigelow provided the traditional low comedy, and the entertainment prospered through 222 performances and a tour that included a three-week return (in a ''second edition'') to the Broadway Theater. The two hit songs were reused for the 1989 London revue *Ziegfeld,* performed by Fabienne Guyon in the role of Anna Held.

PARIS, OU LE BON JUGE Opéra-bouffe in 2 acts by Robert de Flers and Gaston de Caillavet. Music by Claude Terrasse. Théâtre des Capucines, Paris, 18 March 1906.

Introduced as part of a two-part program at the tiny Théâtre des Capucines, paired with a vaudeville by the same authors, the classical burlesque *Paris, ou le bon juge* followed, on a smaller scale (and to piano-only accompaniment), the style that de Flers and de Caillavet had successfully used in their earlier collaborations with composer Claude Terrasse, *Les Travaux d'Hercule, Le Sire de Vergy* and *Monsieur de la Palisse.*

The libretto quite simply reversed the classical tale of the judgment of Paris. Venus (Germaine Gallois), Minerva (Mlle Derys) and Juno (Mlle Desprez), sent down from Olympus by an annoyed Jupiter to cool their heels and their ardors on the slopes of Mount Ida, terrorize the shy satyr Sylvain (Victor Henry) with their excesses of femininity, then turn their attentions to the very plain shepherd Paris (Charles Lamy) in whose power lies the gift of the apple. Minerva and Juno, up-to-date goddesses both, offer the boy a good time, but to their amazement, he gives his famous apple to Venus, who has made herself irresistible by refusing herself to him. Minerva and Juno realize they are not so up-to-date after all. Venus gives the apple to Paris's wife, Glycère (Alice Bonheur), whose moribund interest in her husband as a sex object has been reawakened by seeing him the center of all this feminine attention.

The work, and Terrasse's score, with its waltzing music for Venus and its comical pieces for the two men (a satyr singing ''Je suis timide''), won delighted responses, and the little piece was given two series of performances at the Capucines before it was picked up for a selection of productions outside France. In Vienna (ad August Neidhart) it was seen first for a month as part of the program at Danzers Orpheum with Flora Siding featured, later at the same house in a bill with the revue *Wien bei Nacht* (16 March 1907) and then in the smaller Hölle (29 September 1911), the studio theatre of the Theater an der Wien; in Budapest (ad Adolf Mérei) it was the last opérette to be produced at the Népszínház before the great theatre's closure, after which it was taken up by the Royal Orfeum (*A jó biró* 12 August 1911), and in Berlin it was produced at the little Figaro-Theater in a different German adaptation by Waldemar Westland.

In Paris, the piece was brought back to the Capucines in 1908 (21 May) with all but one of the original cast, and it was later played in an enlarged version with an orchestra and chorus and a cast headed by Mlle Gallois, Edmée Favart and the comedian Polin at the Scala in 1911 (9 April), then again at the Théâtre Michel (4 March 1922) with Germaine Huber featured alongside Lamy and Mlle Favart. Thereafter, however, like the other principal works of Terrasse, it drifted from the repertoire as first the Jazz Age musical and then the opérette à grand spectacle took preference over such small-scale and soigné burlesque as the town's preferred entertainment. It has remained, however, a connoisseur's favorite among the French works of its period.

Austria: Danzers Orpheum *Paris der gute Richter* 12 October 1906; Germany: Figaro-Theater *Paris* 7 March 1906; Hungary: Népszínház-Vigopera *Paris almaja* 23 May 1908

PARYS, Georges van (b Paris, 7 June 1902; d Paris, 25 June 1971). French stage and film composer.

Georges van Parys formed an early partnership with Philippe Parès that resulted in some considerable work for the screen and, most notably, a half-dozen mostly successful Jazz Age musical comedies for the Paris stage in the late 1920s and early 1930s. After the two men had gone their separate ways after their sixth show together, it was van Parys who notched up the more significant theatrical contribution, scoring a success with the wartime musical comedy *Une femme par jour* (subsequently played in Britain), with his contribution to the music of the Fernandel spectacular *Les Chasseurs d'images* at the Châtelet, and with the songs for *Minnie Moustache,* a spoof western manufactured to feature the popular singing group the Compagnons de la Chanson.

He rejoined Parès once more, 30 years later, to compose a costume opérette, *Le Moulin sans-souci,* but reverted to the small-scale with *Le Jeu de dames* before signing his last Paris score to a grandiose production, *La Belle de Paris,* produced with insufficient success at the Opéra-Comique.

The partners also wrote music for several musical films (*Le Million, La Femme et le pantin,* etc), and van Parys also provided additional music to Hervé's score for the Fernandel film version of *Mam'zelle Nitouche.*

1922 **Madame la Comtesse** (M Mauday) Théâtre des jeunes artistes 29 April

1927 **La Petite Dame du train bleu** (*Quand y-en a pour deux*) (w Philippe Parès/Léo Marchès, Georges Lignereux) Galeries Saint-Hubert, Brussels May; Eldorado, Paris 22 October

1927 **Lulu** (w Parès/Serge Veber) Théâtre Daunou 14 September

1928 **L'Eau à la bouche** (w Parès/S Veber) Théâtre Daunou 5 September

1929 **Louis XIV** (w Parès/S Veber) Théâtre de la Scala

1930 **Le Coeur y est** (w Parès/Roger Bernstein, Fernand Vimont/Raoul Praxy) Théâtre de l'Athénée 20 May

1931 **Couss-couss** (w Parès/Jean Guitton) Théâtre de la Scala 26 February

1937 **Ma petite amie** (S Veber) Théâtre des Bouffes-Parisiens 31 January

1943 **Une femme par jour** (S Veber, Jean Boyer) Théâtre des Capucines

1946 **Virginie Déjazet** (Jean Marsan, Raymond Vogel) Théâtre des Champs-Élysées

1946 **Les Chasseurs d'images** (w Roger Dumas/Jean Manse/André Mouëzy-Éon) Théâtre du Châtelet 26 October

1956 **Minnie Moustache** (Jean Broussolle, André Hornez) Théâtre de la Gaîté-Lyrique 13 December

1958 **Le Moulin sans-souci** (w Parès/Marc-Cab/S Veber, Marc-Cab) Opéra, Strasbourg 24 December

1961 **La Belle de Paris** (Jean-Jacques Etchevery, Louis Ducreux) Opéra-Comique 9 February

1961 **Le Jeu de dames** (Albert Willemetz, Georges Manoir) Théâtre Moderne 2 December

Autobiography: *Les Jours comme ils viennent* (Plon, Paris, 1969)

PASCAL, Florian [WILLIAMS, Joseph Benjamin] (b Dalston, London, c1849; d Worthing, 12 July 1923). Victorian composer and music publisher.

The son of the important London music publisher Joseph Williams, and himself a member of the board of the family firm, ''Florian Pascal'' was a fluid composer of parlor music and light theatre works in an attractive if scarcely very individual style. His theatre ventures did not earn him celebrity, in spite of his being in the right places at almost the right times. He combined with Harry Paulton on *Cymbia* in 1882, but it was Procida Bucalossi (*Manteaux Noirs*) in the same year and Edward Jakobowski a few years later with *Erminie* (although Pascal apparently composed an unused score this piece) who profited by the author's best comic libretti. He was the composer of *The Vicar of Wide-awake-field,* the piece that heralded the coming of the new burlesque at the Gaiety, but when the inaugural *Little Jack Sheppard* followed, he contributed only five numbers to a score organized by Meyer Lutz, and it was Lutz who went on to score the famous series of burlesques. He did, however, have the consolation that every piece he wrote, whether produced professionally or by amateurs or not at all, and some, such as Gilbert's *Eyes and No Eyes,* which he had not written, but for which he composed a fresh score, was published . . . by Joseph Williams Ltd.

1883 **Cymbia, or the Magic Thimble** (Harry Paulton) Royal Strand Theatre 24 March

1885 **The Vicar of Wide-awake-field, or The Miss-Terryous Uncle** (Henry Pottinger Stephens, William Yardley) Gaiety Theatre 8 August

1887 **Gipsy Gabriel** (Walter Parke, William Hogarth) Theatre Royal, Bradford 3 November

1890 **Tra-la-la Tosca, or The High-Toned Soprano and the Villain Bass** (F C Burnand) Royalty Theatre 9 January

1896 **The Black Squire** (Stephens) Torquay 5 November

1897 **The Golden Age, or Pierrot's Sacrifice** (Henry Byatt) 1 act Savoy Theatre 5 July

1898 **Lady Laura's Arcadia** (F Broughton) 1 act Bijou Theatre 10 July

1899 **Tempests in Teacups** (C Pirkiss, Adrian Ross) 1 act St George's Parish Hall, Forest Hill

PASSION Musical in 1 act by James Lapine based on the film *Passion d'amore* by Ettore Scuola and the novel *Fosca* by I U Tarchetti. Music and lyrics by Stephen Sondheim. Plymouth Theater, New York, 9 May 1994.

A smallish-scale musical play with a triangle of thoroughly human beings at the center of its story and its score, *Passion* marked the return of composer-lyricist Sondheim, after a long absence illustrating the fretwork figures of grand guignol, fairy tale and fancy, to the musical play of real people with real feelings, involved in a real of-this-world story. The result was a piece of a welcome warmth and humanity, with a heart of truly violent passion to it, which nevertheless, in the age of the super-spectacular musical, was able to find itself only limited audiences.

The soldier Giorgio (Jere Shea) is quartered in Milan, where he carries on an easy romance with a pretty young married woman, Clara (Marin Mazzie), until the time comes when he is reassigned to a sunless provincial outpost. There he encounters his Colonel's invalid cousin, Fosca (Donna Murphy). This plain, tortured woman develops an obsessional passion for the uncomplicated and startled Giorgio, but although he uncomprehendingly repulses her for months, finally he finds that the strength of her passion has awakened depths in him that his light love with Clara had never stirred. Although she knows it may kill her, he and Fosca make love. Three days later, she is dead.

The music of the piece ranged from the tripping description of what Giorgio and Clara take as ''Happiness'' to the black tones of Fosca's depairing love and the deep wonderment of Giorgio's realization (''No One Has Ever Loved Me,'' added for the London production), the moods corkscrewing through one another as sung letters fly from the city to the provinces and back, and the whole romantic whirlwind brought intermittently down to common earth by the vulgar banalities of the shallow gossip of Giorgio's fellow soldiers.

Passion took its season's Tony Awards for musical, book and score, as well as for Miss Murphy's powerful performance as Fosca, but closed after only 280 performances whilst ''easier'' pieces ran on.

A London production, mounted by Bill Kenwright, featured Michael Ball as Giorgio, with Helen Hobson (Clara) and Maria Friedman (Fosca) as the women in his life. It, like the Broadway production, failed to find the public for its unspectacular (bar a *Hair*-type glimpse of gratuitous near nudity) kind, and struggled on to a run of 232 performances.

UK: Queens Theatre 26 March 1996

Recordings: original cast (Angel), London cast (First Night)

PASSIONNÉMENT! Comédie musicale in 3 acts by Maurice Hennequin and Albert Willemetz. Music by André Messager. Théâtre de la Michodière, Paris, 15 January 1926.

One of the most successful of Messager's latter-day works, the ''comédie musicale'' *Passionnément!* was composed to an up-to-date libretto in which the virtual inventor of the Jazz Age musical comedy, Albert Willemetz, had a half-share. It told of how the Machiavellian American millionaire William Stevenson (René Koval) yachts his way across the Atlantic to find the dissolute young gambler Robert Perceval (Géo Bury) in order to persuade him to cash in on some land that he has inherited in Colorado. Stevenson knows the land contains oil. He brings with him his pretty young ex-actress wife, Ketty (Jeanne Saint-Bonnet), but, mistrustful of the reputation of French men, he insists that she disguise herself in dark glasses and a gray wig. His mistrust is well placed, for when Perceval spies Ketty without her disguise he falls in love with her. She keeps up the double role of aged wife and her own young niece until she falls in her turn, and warns the young man of her husband's intentions. That way, Perceval ends up, in the best tradition, with both the money and the girl. Renée Duler was Hélène Le Barrois, Perceval's discarded (between Acts I and II) mistress, whilst Denise Grey as Julia, Ketty's oversexed maid, spent the evening with the captain of the yacht (Lucien Baroux) before finding ultimate satisfaction with her employer's ultimately ex-husband. Hélène's husband (who gets her back, one abandonment and three solos later) and two servants completed the cast.

Messager's 21-piece score was topped by solos for Perceval (the title waltz ''Passionnément''), Hélène (the reconciliatory rondeau ''N'imaginez pas'' with which she returns to married something-like-bliss), Julia (three, including the comical prayer for a man ''Vous avez comblé ma patronne'') and Ketty, demanding in ''Ah! pourquoi les bons moments'' why the peak of pleasure has to be so short. Stevenson had a comical piece crediting America's success to ''le régime sec'' (teetotalism), but after discovering ''le bon vin français'' and a new personality between the second and third acts, had a much more amorous solo for the final act. Duets, trios and ensembles played their part in a soigné modern score that won the 73-year-old composer outstanding reviews and a major success.

The original production of the show, mounted by Gustave Quinson and directed by Edmond Roze—all the most experienced the city had to offer—was a grand success. After its initial Paris season it went on the road, with Bury playing his original role, and in 1932 it was seen again in Paris at the Trianon-Lyrique. In the meanwhile, it had made a small excursion abroad. In Hungary, which showed the most enterprise towards the French musical comedy of the 1920s, Jenő Molnár's version of *Nászéjszaka* (wedding night) was a great success at the Belvárosi Színház, running more than one hundred performances in its first run. Another version, *A legszebb éjszaká* (the most wonderful night), which credited new music by Béla Csanak and a book done over by Andor Pünkösti, was played at the Márkus Park Színház in 1943.

The piece traveled little otherwise, although it was seen briefly in New York as played by a visiting French repertoire company with Sonia Alny and Georges Foix featured. A René Guissart film, with Fernand Graavey as its star and Koval repeating his stage role, was produced in 1932, and *Passionnément!* has continued to make regular regional appearances in France through to the present day.

Hungary: Belvárosi Színház *Nászéjszaka* 16 December 1927; USA: Jolson Theater (Fr) 7 March 1929

Film: Mercant & Guissart 1932

Recording: complete (Gaîté-Lyrique)

PASSMORE, Walter [Henry] (b London, 10 May 1867; d London, 29 August 1946). D'Oyly Carte star comic who transferred successfully to the musical-comedy stage.

Apprenticed as a piano maker at Cramer's, Passmore left that business at the end of his indentures and appeared variously as a pianist with concert parties, on tour with the ventriloquist Lieutenant Cole, with the Majiltons and the Milton-Ray combination and with the European production of *Carmen fin de siècle* (1892, José), before he was engaged by D'Oyly Carte in 1893 to appear in a supporting role in *Jane Annie* (Greg) at the Savoy. He stayed with Carte to create the roles of Tarara, the public exploder in *Utopia (Ltd),* and Bobinet in André Messager's *Mirette,* and he was promoted to principal comedian to play the part of Grigg in *The Chieftain* (1894).

Passmore remained chief comic at the Savoy for a decade, starring in the Gilbert and Sullivan repertoire (Ko-Ko, the Grand Duke, Grand Inquisitor, Jack Point, John Wellington Wells, Joseph Porter, Bunthorne, Sergeant of Police, Lord Chancellor) and also in the theatre's productions of *His Majesty* (Boodel), *La Grande-Duchesse* (General Boum), *The Beauty Stone* (The Devil), *The Lucky Star* (King Ouf), *The Rose of Persia* (Hassan), *The Emerald Isle* (Professor Bunn), *Merrie England* (Walter Wilkins) and *A Princess of Kensington* (Puck). He remained with Carte's successor, William Greet, when he switched away from comic opera, to appear as the little dog trainer, Jim Cheese, in the musical comedy *The Earl and the Girl* (1903), and he subsequently played lead comedy roles, more often in a legitimate and farcical vein than in the old-fashioned low style, in London's *The Talk of the Town* (1904, Jerry Snipe), *The Blue Moon* (1905, Private Taylor), *The Dairymaids* (1906, Sam Brudenell), *Lady Tatters* (1907, Seth Lewys), *The Three Kisses* (1907, Garibaldi Pimpinello) and *The Belle of Britanny* (1908, Baptiste Boubillon).

He went on the road playing his original role in *Merrie England* and Simplicitas in *The Arcadians* in 1909–10, and spent several periods playing in homemade musical playlets (*Chicks in the Woods, Sweet William, Queer Fish, The Soldier's Mess, Ducks and Quacks,* etc) on the halls with his second wife, Savoy soprano Agnes Fraser, but he returned to the London stage to play in *Die Fledermaus* (1910, Frank), *Baron Trenck* (1911, Nikola), *Oh! Oh! Delphine* (1913, Alphonse Bouchotte), *Young England* (1916, Tom Moon) and *Valentine* (1918, Gastricus) before moving into the provinces for several years in *Betty* (Achille Jotte), *Petticoat Fair* (1918, Tom), *Fancy Fair* (1919), *Too Many Girls* (1920, Tim Grogan) and *The Purple Lady* (1920, Mooney).

He was seen in London again in the chief comedy role of the light opera *The Rebel Maid* (1921, Solomon Hooker), with José Collins in *Our Nell* (1923, Jericho Mardyke) and in *The Damask Rose* (1930, Count Theodore Volny), interspersing his town dates with tours in *Madame Pompadour* (Calicot), *Princess Charming* (Chubby), *The First Kiss* (Bene Ben) and, at the age of 63, alongside an even older-timer, Amy Augarde, in Courtneidge's tour of *Lavender* (1930).

Passmore and Agnes Fraser were the parents of vocalist Nancy Fraser. His first wife was the dancer Katie Nanton.

1912 **A Queer Fish** (Dudley Powell/w Percy Bradshaw) 1 act New Cross Empire 19 August

1914 **The Soldier's Mess** (Herbert C Sargent) 1 act Nottingham 22 June

PAS SUR LA BOUCHE Opérette in 3 acts by André Barde. Music by Maurice Yvain. Théâtre des Nouveautés, Paris, 17 February 1925.

Following the huge successes of *Ta bouche* (1922) and *Là-haut* (1923), which had placed their composer alongside Henri Christiné at the top of the honors list of the new French musical comedy era, Maurice Yvain paired with André Barde (who, likewise, had joined Albert Willemetz at the head of the librettists' ranks) to turn out another major success with the années folles story of sex and marriage called *Pas sur la bouche.*

Gilberte (Régine Flory) is happily wed to industrialist Georges Valandray (Berval), but she and her companion aunt, Mlle Poumaillac (Jeanne Cheirel), have taken care to hide the fact that Gilberte has been married before, for Georges has metallurgical theories on marriage: the first man who ''puts his mark'' on a woman can never be deceived by her. Unfortunately, when Georges invites an American associate to the house, that associate turns out to be Gilberte's ex, Eric Thomson (René Koval), all anxious to resume their relationship hors mariage. Mlle Poumaillac and Gilberte plot to distract him. Thomson has a weakness—he will not allow himself to be kissed on the lips since the day, when he was 12 years old, that his governess did just that and aroused ungovernable passions in him—so they set every available female on to him. Two acts of dizzyingly farcical complications later, Mlle Poumaillac is forced by circumstances to supply the kiss herself.

The jaunty score included an irrepressibly bouncing title song, delivered by the American, a stand-up number for the low-comic concièrge (Pauline Carton) of the garçonnière where the last act takes place, describing what she sees through keyholes (''Par le trou''), Georges's topical song ''Je me suis laissé embouteiller,'' and Mlle Poumaillac's good advice ''Quand on n'a pas ce qu'on aime,'' all of which became popular, alongside a varied group of numbers for Gilberte—from the waltz ''Comme j'aimerais mon mari'' to the South American strains of ''La Peruvienne'' and ''Soirs de Mexique''—a pair of taking duos for the juveniles of the piece (Pierrette Madd, Robert Darthez) and a hiccuping song for the comically sighing Faradel (Germain Champell), who completed the principal cast. The rest of the show's forces comprised five chorines and a band of a surprising 17 players.

Plate 300. **Pas sur la bouche.** *Lestelly and Marina Hotine in the 1948 revival.*

Produced by Benoît-Léon Deutsch at the Nouveautés, *Pas sur la bouche* was a major hit. Its tunes bubbled to the top of the popular music market, and the show stayed in its Paris home for a first run of more than a year and a half. It got the supreme accolade when one of the year's topical revues gleefully picked up its title to parody as *Pas sous la douche.* The show was taken up and produced in Britain as *Just a Kiss* before that original run was done. However, *Just a Kiss* (ad Frederick Jackson) was a deodorized version of the original that reset the action in Windsor and Mayfair and that interpolated songs by Vivian Ellis (five) and Phil Charig (two) as well as some pieces of *Ta bouche,* which had not been played in Britain, into the remnants of Yvain's score. Marjorie Gordon was wife Valerie, American soubrette Marie George played the aunt, Miss Trask, light-opera vocalist Frederick Ranalow was husband number two and Arthur Margetson his predecessor, through a run (93 performances) at the Shaftesbury and Gaiety Theatres that was as messed about as the show had been.

Hungary continued its fidelity to Yvain's musicals with a production (ad Jenő Heltai) at the Magyar Színház, and the show was seen in its original form in America as played in the repertoire of a French musical-comedy company touring Canada and America. Sonia Alny and Georges Foix appeared as the married couple, with Jane de Poumeyrac as the spunky aunt.

A film version mounted by Nicolas Rimsky and Nicolas Evreïmof in 1930 starred Mireille Perrey (Gilberte), Jacques Grétillat (Georges), Alice Tissot (Mlle Poumaillac) and Nicolas Rimsky (Eric), and *Pas sur la bouche* has continued an episodic life in the French regions up to the present day, marked by a return to Paris and the Théâtre des Bouffes-Parisiens in 1948 with a cast headed by Lestelly, Martina Hotine, Spinelly and Gerald Castrix.

UK: Shaftesbury Theatre *Just a Kiss* 8 September 1926; Hungary: Magyar Színház *Csókról csókra* 4 March 1927; USA: Jolson Theater (Fr) 25 March 1929

Film: Rimsky & Evreïmof 1930

Recordings: original cast selections on *L'Opérette française par ses créateurs* (EPM), selections (Decca)

PASTOR, Tony [PASTOR, Antonio] (b New York, 28 May 1837; d Elmhurst, NY, 26 August 1908). Baron of Broadway variety.

The son of a theatre violinist, Pastor himself performed as a child in a minstrel show at Barnum's Museum, then later in other minstrel shows and in circuses as a rider, tumbler, actor and ultimately ringmaster and, on occasion, clown. He made his first appearances in variety at Rivers Melodeon, Philadelphia, in 1860, and on the theatrical stage in a pantomime at the Bowery Theater in the same year, before starting a new career as a performer of comic songs in appearances at the Broadway Music Hall and the American Theater.

In 1865 Pastor took his own company on the road and, on returning to New York, opened a variety theatre at 201 The Bowery with the avowed aim of running a cleaner house than the majority of dives in which he had worked, a house with less emphasis on drink and blue jokes and with the lucrative prospect of providing family entertainment. His programs at ''Tony Pastor's Opera House'' included a long run of original extravaganzas such as John F Poole's *The Fairies of the Hudson* (19 November 1866) and *Wide-awake, or A New York Boy in China* (23 September 1868, with Pastor as Washington Wide-awake). He had sufficient success that a decade later he was able to move to larger premises (Tony Pastor's New Broadway Theater 585–587 Broadway) and, finally, in 1881, to the house on 14th Street that had once been the German-language Germania Theater and that was to become famous as Tony Pastor's Music Hall.

There he produced variety bills that, moving with the times, included musical playlets, parodies and later farce-comedies as part of the entertainment, and many later well-known figures of the musical-comedy stage from Lillian Russell and May Irwin to Joe Weber and Lew Fields appeared in his bills. His theatre was destroyed by fire in early June 1888, but by the end of October a new theatre had arisen on the site and he was able to reopen for the sterling business, which he continued to find for many years until new ways and new ethics in the vaudeville business pushed him to the side.

Biography: Zellers, P: *Tony Pastor: Dean of the Vaudeville Stage* (Eastern Michigan University Press, Ypsilanti, 1971)

PÁSZTOR, Árpád (b Ungvár, 12 April 1877; d Budapest, 26 October 1940).

Pásztor's earliest important stage work was the translation of Sidney Jones's *A Greek Slave* for Budapest's Népszínház, but he subsequently wrote and rewrote libretti for most of the front guard of contemporary Hungarian composers, notably József Konti, for whom he adapted Alexander Dumas's *Les Demoiselles de Saint-Cyr* as the libretto for *A fecskék,* Pongrác Kacsoh and Ákos Buttykay. He adapted Harry and Edward Paulton's famous comedy *Niobe* as a libretto for an operett by Károly Stoll, and provided the Hungarian version of Reginald De Koven's *Robin Hood,* but his greatest single musical theatre success came with his adaptation of Gergely Csiky's famous Hungarian play *A nagymama* for the Raoul Mader musical of the same name. His text for the ''legend'' *A harang* was subsequently used as the basis for the libretto of Eduard Künneke's Berlin Singspiel *Das Dorf ohne Glocke.*

Pásztor also wrote and adapted several operatic libretti, notably the Hungarian version of Richard Strauss's *Salome,* and, in the second part of his career, devoted himself entirely to straight plays, of which the most widely successful, the 1912 piece *Innocent,* was played on Broadway (Eltinge Theater 9 September 1914) for 109 performances.

1899 **A görög rabszolga** (*A Greek Slave*) Hungarian version w Emil Makai (Népszínház)

1900 **Kadétkisasszony** (Raoul Mader) Népszínház 10 January

1900 **A csillag fia** (*Bar Kochba*) Hungarian version w László Beothy (Népszínház)

1900 **Primadonnák** (Mader) Magyar Színház 29 December

1902 **Niobe** (Károly Stoll) Nepszínház 7 November

1903 **A fecskék** (József Konti) Király Színház 20 January

1904 **Robin Hood** Hungarian version (Király Színház)

1904 **A kis császár** (Stoll) Népszínház 2 March

1905 **A bolygó görög** (Ákos Buttykay) Király Színház 19 October

1906 **Rákóczi** (Pongrác Kacsoh/Sándor Endrődi/w Károly Bakonyi) Király Színház 20 November

1907 **A harang** (Kacsoh, Buttykay) Király Színház 1 February

1908 **A nagymama** (Mader) Népszínház-Vígopera 11 February

PATIENCE, or Bunthorne's Bride Aesthetic comic opera in 2 acts by W S Gilbert. Music by Arthur Sullivan. Opera Comique, London, 23 April 1881.

After the nautical burlesque of *HMS Pinafore* and the melodrama burlesque of *The Pirates of Penzance,* Gilbert and Sullivan turned to a more specific and up-to-date subject with which to make their fun in *Patience.* Their target was the aesthetic movement and its acolytes, the flower-power people of their day, with their willfully refined sensibilities and other-worldly attitudes, and their professed return to the modes and manners of ancient, simple days before the debauchery of the world and its people began. Gilbert chose the more extreme end of the movement, as personifed by such of its devotees as Oscar Wilde, as the very easy target for his darts.

Every lass of the village is sighing medievally at the feet of the pretentious poet Reginald Bunthorne (George Grossmith), rebuffing the 35th Dragoon Guards, who were their last year's delight. Only the milkmaid Patience (Leonora Braham) remains innocently aloof, equating love with the feeling one has for an aunt, until she is informed by her more experienced sisters of the sentiment's sublime unselfishness. Dutifully she determines to love, but to love her handsome childhood sweetheart Archibald Grosvenor (Rutland Barrington) cannot be considered unselfish, so she regretfully agrees to love the boring but smitten Bunthorne, who has secretly admitted to her that his persona is nothing but an attention-grabbing sham. But now that Reginald has declared a preference for Patience, the other maidens promptly desert him to adulate Grosvenor instead, and Bunthorne becomes morbidly miserable at being insufficiently admired. He forces the usurper to deaestheticize and become commonplace, and he himself takes up his rival's blithely poetic and agreeable manner. Since Bunthorne is now perfectly agreeable, Patience feels duteously able to desert him for Grosvenor, and since the other girls return to the Dragoons rather than to dear Reginald, the foolish fellow is the only one left without a partner at the final curtain.

Sullivan's score included many gems: Patience's pretty soubrette solos ''I Cannot Tell What This Love May Be'' and ''Love Is a Plaintive Song''; the over-super-virile songs of Dragoon Colonel Calverley (Richard Temple) (''When I First Put This Uniform On,'' ''If You Want a Receipt for a Popular Mystery''), the aging longings of the booming Lady Jane (Alice Barnett), accompanying herself on the violoncello in ''Silvered Is the Raven Hair,'' and the comical pieces for the rival poets—Bunthorne's recipe for aestheticism (''If You're Anxious for to Shine''), Grosvenor's nursery-rhyme tale of ''The Magnet and the Churn,'' and their pairing in ''When I Go Out of Doors''—as well as Bunthorne and Jane's vengeful anti-Grosvenor duo ''So Go to Him and Say to Him.''

Owing to the loquacity of friend Freddie Clay, the eternally anti-Gilbert F C Burnand discovered that the librettist was working on an ''aesthetic'' piece, and he hurried *The Colonel,* his own from-the-French play burlesquing the same phenomenon, into production. Its enormous success—Burnand's biggest ever—prompted Gilbert and Richard D'Oyly Carte publicly to announce that their piece had been written earlier, but they need not

Plate 301. **Patience.** *Bunthorne (Dennis Olsen) risks a rapprochement with Lady Jane (Heather Begg) (Australian Opera, 1987).*

have worried. The two shows were very different, and the success of one did not harm the other. *Patience*'s London run mounted to 20 months and 578 performances. Only 170 of these, however, were in the Opera Comique, the bedraggled old house that had shot back to popularity as the home of *HMS Pinafore* and *The Pirates of Penzance.* Part way through the run, Carte shifted the show into his brand-new Savoy Theatre, built down Adelphi way on the profits of the earlier shows. As the opening attraction at the Savoy, *Patience* ran on for more than an additional year.

On the other side of the Atlantic, as soon as the subject and target of the new Gilbert and Sullivan work were known, the copycats leaped into action. John Howson brought out a Burnand sketch called *Mary's Canary,* which allowed him to burlesque aesthetics, and Charles F Pidgin, the striving botcher of *La Poupée de Nuremberg* the previous year, announced his ''new comic opera'' *Aesthetica* ''with music by five American composers.'' He doesn't, however, seem to have got it produced.

The show was soon on the British road, and J C Williamson briskly brought it to the Australian stage with Alys Rees (Patience), Howard Vernon (Bunthorne),

George Verdi (Grosvenor) and Maggie Moore (Lady Jane) in the leading roles but, in spite of the fact that the piece had been published and, thus, made free to producers in America, few transatlantic pirates leaped in to take advantage in the way they had with *HMS Pinafore.* The management of St Louis's Uhrig's Cave summer season of comic opera, which had pulled the same trick with several other new and newsworthy foreign musicals, was the first to produce what it claimed to be *Patience,* and St Louis believed them, until the genuine article finally hit the touring circuits and America saw *Patience* in something more like its pristine form. New York, however, waited for the real thing, and when Carte opened his official production on Broadway nine months after the London opening, he was the first to show the city the piece that had not until then won a mounting not through any misplaced sense of honor, but simply because local managers had, apparently, considered the show and its subject a dubious prospect. Aestheticism in all its glory had not, at that stage, reached America. Not, that is, until Oscar Wilde arrived full willingly on a lecture tour sponsored by Mr Richard D'Oyly Carte.

J H Ryley (Bunthorne), James Barton (Grosvenor), Carrie Burton (Patience) and Augusta Roche (Jane) headed Carte's Broadway cast. New York soon caught on to the extravagances that were being parodied, as well as to the general wit and charm of the piece's words and music, and *Patience* briskly became a decided hit. When the theatre's obligations forced a new production, they avoided having to close their newest hit immediately by playing split weeks of *Patience* and the new show until 177 performances had been reached. Other managers had by now got their versions of the New York–approved *Patience* on the go (one splashy version boasted 50 lovesick maidens instead of the regulation 20, and changed the lyrics accordingly) and the comic opera was soon to be seen in all corners of the country. It also made regular Broadway appearances over the next 15 years, the most substantial of which was an 1896 revival (Herald Square Theater 13 July 1896) in which Lillian Russell played the role of Patience, a role she had first played 13 years previously in Fred Intropdi's burlesque of the burlesque entitled *Patience, or The Stage-Struck Maidens* (Tony Pastor's Opera House 23 January 1882). Henry Dixey was her Bunthorne, and Sadie Martinot caused a déshabille sensation in the little role of Angela.

Carte's Englische-Opern-Gesellschaft took *Patience* to Germany (with David Fisher as Bunthorne and Ada Bemister as Patience) and Austria (including 10 performances at the Carltheater with Josephine Findlay as Patience and James Muir as Bunthorne), in a company whose main baggage was the enormously popular *The Mikado.* Hungary ventured a translated version (ad Lajos Evva, Béla J Fái), with Ilka Pálmay starred, and Spain later staged a vernacular version of the show, but by and large *Patience* stuck to the English-speaking areas of the world, where it found a continued popularity and a prominent, enduring place in the D'Oyly Carte and Williamson repertoires to go alongside its American successes. After the expiry of the Gilbert and Sullivan copyrights, this least "operatic" of their works even went opera-house-wards, and *Patience* was staged by London's English National Opera at Sadler's Wells Theatre in 1969 and again at the Coliseum in 1984, the latter production being also played at New York's Metropolitan Opera House.

In 1931 British radio broadcast a sequel to *Patience* entitled *Out of Patience, or Bunthorne Avenged* written by St John Hawkins (16 January).

Australia: Theatre Royal, Sydney 19 December 1881; USA: Uhrig's Cave, St Louis 28 July 1881, Standard Theater, New York 22 September 1882; Germany: Krolls Theater *Sanfthilde* (Eng) 30 April 1887; Austria: Carltheater *Patience (Dragoner und Dichter)* (Eng) 28 May 1887; Hungary: Népszínház *Fejő leány, vagy Költőimádás* 5 November 1887

Recordings: complete (Decca, HMV), etc

Video: Brent-Walker 1982

PATINKIN, Mandy [PATINKIN, Mandel] (b Chicago, 30 November 1952). Strong-voiced American leading man.

In a stage and film acting career that has included more than intermittent appearances in the musical theatre, Patinkin made his two most prominent Broadway appearances in the role of Che in the American production of *Evita* (1980, Tony Award) and as the artists called George in Stephen Sondheim and James Lapine's *Sunday in the Park with George* (1984). Amongst his other musical credits, he appeared in Joseph Papp's production of *The Knife* (1987, Peter), at Britain's 1990 Chichester Festival as Martin in *Born Again,* an unsuccessful musical version of Ionesco's *Rhinoceros,* and the following year, in a return to Broadway, as Archibald in the musicalized kiddie-classic *The Secret Garden.*

In 1989 he appeared at the Public Theater, and subsequently at Broadway's Helen Hayes Theater, in *Mandy Patinkin in Concert: Dress Casual* (25 July, 56 performances), which he later performed throughout America. In 1993 he took over the leading role in *Falsettos* in New York, but subsequently concentrated largely on solo performances notably a one-man show of Yiddish songs, entitled *Mamaloshen,* with which he briefly visited Broadway in 1998. He returned to the musical theatre in 2000, starring with Toni Collette and Eartha Kitt in a musical version of *The Wild Party* (Burrs).

PAUL, Mrs Howard [HILL, Isabelle] (b Dartford, Kent, ?1833; d Turnham Green, London, 6 June 1879). Outstanding singer-actress of the early Victorian stage.

The daughter of a Dartford leather merchant, the soon-to-be-celebrated and dazzlingly versatile Isabelle Hill (original nom de théâtre ''Miss Featherstone'') made her first appearance on the London stage, apparently without any provincial prelude, at the Strand Theatre in the opening weeks of 1853 playing Tom Tug in *The Waterman.* She was subsequently seen in the farcical old Vestris piece *The Invincibles,* as Madge in *Love in a Village,* Floretta in *The Quaker,* Dorothy in *No Song, No Supper,* William in *Rosina,* Lady Macbeth in the burlesque *Macbeth According to Act of Parliament,* Lucy to the Macheath of Adam Leffler in *The Beggar's Opera* (theatrical mythology says she played Macheath), Mrs Verdant Green in *The Black Swan,* in *The Poor Soldier* and in *Guy Mannering* at the Strand (1853), before moving on to Glasgow, where she did play Macheath, Charlotte in *Captain Charlotte,* etc. She returned to town to play at Drury Lane with Brooke (Ophelia, etc), and in the burlesque *The Fountain of Beauty* (1853), and to play Macheath, Apollo in *Midas* and the comic operas *Love's Alarms* and *Any Port in a Storm* at the Haymarket (1853). She appeared that Christmas at Drury Lane as Novelty in the pantomime *King Hummingtop,* and in the new year created the principal male role in G M Layton's new opera *Leone* (1854) before returning to the Haymarket for Planché's revusical *Mr Buckstone's Voyage Round the Globe* (1854) and to play Lady Gay Spanker in *London Assurance.* She subsequently appeared at Sheffield in the extravaganza *Ye Loves of Lord Bateman,* at Leeds in several burlettas and at the Surrey Theatre in Planché's *The Sleeping Beauty* (1855) before visiting Dublin, where she starred in *Cinderella* and in a play written by her recently acquired husband, the thanks-to-her equally well-known (but very, very much less talented) American journalist-cum-performer **[Henry] Howard PAUL** (b Philadelphia, December 1830; d Christchurch, UK, 9 December 1905). *Thrice Married* allowed her to take on four different characters.

Howard Paul subsequently put together a drawing room entertainment for his wife under the title *Patchwork* (Rotunda Room, Dublin December 1855). He also took part, but largely to fill in whilst she changed costumes and makeup between her various characters. *Patchwork* proved an enormous success, and as a result Mrs Paul spent the very large part of the rest of her career as a performer touring ever-changing versions of the entertainment around Britain. Amongst the items that she performed were a celebrated burlesque of the famous tenor Sims Reeves performing ''Come into the Garden, Maud'' (or whatever new song he happened to have introduced), and a potted version of *Fra Diavolo* in which, with the assistance of one soprano, Mrs Paul performed (nearly) all the roles, male and female, of Auber's opéra-comique.

Plate 302. **Mrs Howard Paul.** *One of the great performers of the Victorian stage and salon.*

Although ''Mrs and Mrs Howard Paul's Entertainment'' (later just ''Mrs Howard Paul's'') became the centerpiece of her performing life, she did return from time to time to the stage, almost always to enthusiastic audiences and superlative notices. In 1858 she played at the Lyceum in the extravaganza *The Lancashire Witches,* and with the coming of opéra-bouffe, she appeared on both sides of the Atlantic in the title role of *La Grande-Duchesse de Gérolstein* (Olympic, London, 1868; Théâtre Français, New York, 1870), and in New York as Drogan in *Geneviève de Brabant* (1870). She appeared in comic opera in Paris, played Lady Macbeth and Hecate in Shakespeare's play at Boston and sang Azucena alongside Brignoli and Clara Louise Kellogg in New York, succeeded Hervé in the title role of *Le Petit Faust* at Holborn, and appeared in Farnie's burlesque *Little Gil Blas* (1870) at the Royal Princess's in a busy career that always returned to long tours of the ''Entertainment.''

Her last appearances on the London musical stage were as the glamorous spirit Mistigris in Dion Boucicault's spectacular *Babil and Bijou* at Covent Garden

(1872) and as Lady Sangazure in the original production of *The Sorcerer* (1877). In spite of having to drop out with ''nervous depression and severe flu'' during the run of that show, she was hired to create the next of Gilbert and Sullivan's dragonistic ladies, Sir Joseph Porter's fearsome cousin Hebe, in *HMS Pinafore,* but she was not sufficiently well to make it to opening night. The role was all but cut from the show, leaving the piece with no heavy lady and the secondary contralto role of Little Buttercup as prima contralto. Mrs Paul died the following year whilst playing in *The Crisis* at the Alexandra, Liverpool.

Although she had separated from her husband several years earlier, he (undoubtedly with the vast amounts of money she had earned and he with husbandly right had appropriated) built an elaborate seven-foot marble memorial ''executed by Raemaeckers, the famous Belgian sculptor'' over her grave in Brompton Cemetery. The inscription was from the *Faërie queen,* in the ''ease after warre'' vein. Well, he knew.

PAUL JONES *see* SURCOUF

PAULSEN, Harald (b Elmshorn, 26 August 1895; d Altona, 4 August 1954).

On the stage from the age of 16 as a dancer and actor in provincial German theatres, Paulsen was engaged at the Deutsches Theater in Berlin in 1919. He played there, and later in other Berlin theatres, in a variety of productions from opera and Operette to revue and plays, as well as building a substantial career in more than 150 German films as a bon vivant and character actor (Falke in *Die Fledermaus,* Carnero in *Der Zigeunerbaron, Eine Nacht in Venedig,* etc). In a busy career including hundreds of credits, he appeared in Hugo Hirsch's *Der Fürst von Pappenheim* with Lea Seidl, and as Tom Flips in Bruno Granichstaedten's *Evelyne* in Berlin and in Vienna (1928), was the original Macheath in *Die Dreigroschenoper* (1928) at the Theater am Schiffbauerdamm and at Vienna's Raimundtheater, and played the role of Harald Stone, opposite Anny Ahlers, in the Berlin Metropoltheater premiere of Abraham's *Die Blume von Hawaii* (1931) and that of Leander Bill in Berlin's *Katja, die Tänzerin.*

Between 1938 and 1945 Paulsen ran the Theater am Nollendorfplatz in Berlin before moving on to take up the direction of the Schauspielhaus in Hamburg in his later years.

PAULTON, Harry [PAULTON, Henry] (b Wolverhampton, 16 March 1841; d London, 17 April 1917).

A prominent figure as a performer in the days of opéra-bouffe in Britain, Harry Paulton was also significantly involved as writer, actor and director in the early days of the modern British musical theatre.

After beginning as a small-time actor in his native Wolverhampton and, along with his wife, Rosina, in seasons in the stock companies at Whitehaven (1864), Ryde (1865) and Glasgow's Theatre Royal (1866), Paulton first appeared in London at the Surrey Theatre in the play *The Lottery Ticket* in 1867. Three years later, after stints as principal comedian at the Birmingham Royal, at the Liverpool Prince of Wales and with Francis Fairlie on the road, he was engaged by the Swanborough family at the Strand Theatre. He made an immediate success as a burlesque comedian in the role of Blueskin in *The Idle Prentice* (September 1870). The following year he made his London debut as a writer at the same theatre when, in collaboration with his brother Joseph and musical director John Fitzgerald, he turned out a burlesque of Alexandre Dumas entitled *The Three Musket-Dears (And a Little One In),* which he co-directed and in which he starred as Athos to the Lady de Winter of Edward Terry. The show went on to be seen on Broadway as *The Three Musketeers* (Wood's Museum 21 October 1872). He also appeared at the Strand in the burlesques *Coeur de Lion* (1870, Archduke of Austria, ''Stubborn Leedle Hans''), *Eurydice* (1871, Aristaeus), *Miss Eily O'Connor* revival (1871, Danny Mann), *Ivanhoe* (1871, Isaac of York), *Arion* (1871, Molasses), *Esmeralda or the Sensation Goat* (1871) and *Pygmalion, or The Statue Fair* (1872 rev, King), as well as in the comedies that ran alongside and with those pieces.

In 1872 he was engaged for the piece *Clodhopper's Fortune* at the Alhambra Theatre, which, after a period running composite programs including operetta and burlesque, was about to launch into what would be its most famous period as a theatre with the grandiose production of *Le Roi Carotte.* Paulton was cast in the title role of Offenbach's grand opéra-bouffe féerie and quickly became a great favorite in this theatre, where his brand of broad comedy was well suited. For the next five and a half years he played in virtually every one of the Alhambra's productions, reigning supreme as chief comedian even when the battles between the Alhambra's rival prima donnas Kate Santley and Rose Bell were at their height. Between 1872 and 1877 he appeared in Offenbach's *La Belle Hélène* (Menelaos), *La Jolie Parfumeuse* (La Cocadière), *Whittington* (Sergeant of the Patrol), *Le Voyage dans la lune* (King Cosmos) and *Orpheus in the Underworld* (Jupiter), in Strauss's *King Indigo* (Indigo), in *Chilpéric* (Physician) and in several pasticcio extravaganzas (Leporello in *Don Juan,* Max Doppeldick in *Spectresheim,* Rhadamanthus John in *Lord Bateman,* Kit in *Wildfire*), as well as original works including *The Demon's Bride* (Filastenish), his own imitation of the grand opéra-bouffe féerie, *[The] Black Crook* (Dandelion), a spectacular version of the *Biche au bois* tale in which he co-starred with Kate Santley, and the grand opéra-bouffe *Don Quixote,*

Plate 303. **Harald Paulsen** *as Mackie Messer in the original production of* Die Dreigroschenoper.

written with Frederic Clay, in which he wrote for himself the very large role of Sancho Panza.

In 1878 he left the Alhambra to appear as Frimousse in the British production of *Le Petit Duc,* and he subsequently took leading comic roles in burlesque at the Globe (Dame Tiller to the May Maybud of Mrs Wood in *My Poll and Partner Joe*), and in a further series of Continental pieces including *Stars and Garters* (*L'Étoile,* Zadkiel), *Les Cloches de Corneville* (t/o Bailie, which he built up to a much larger comedy part), *Der Seekadett* (Don Prolixio), *Les Mousquetaires au couvent* (Abbé Bridaine), *La Belle Normande* (Épinard) and *La Boulangère* (Flam). He also made return visits to the Alhambra for *La Petite Mademoiselle* (Taboureau), the English version of *Rothomago* (Rothomago) and *Le Cheval de bronze* (Great Bamboo), before starring there in revised versions of his own *The Black Crook* and of another fairy-tale spectacular *Babil and Bijou* (Auricomus).

During the run of this last piece, he directed the production of the comic opera *Manteaux Noirs* (1882), which he had adapted from Scribe's *Giralda* in collaboration with Walter Parke. The success of the piece was such that Paulton took over the lead comedy role of Dromez at the end of his Alhambra season, but he had less luck with another writing/directing/performing combination when his *Cymbia* (1883, Arthur), an Alhambra piece in all but size, was produced at the Strand. As an author he also supplied two long-lasting pieces, *The Babes* and the short *The Japs,* to comedian Willie Edouin's touring repertoire. As a performer, he returned to established successes to play in *Falka* (Folbach), *Chilpéric* (Ricin) and *Rip van Winkle* (Nick Vedder) whilst preparing his next productions, a musical play called *Lilies* in which he toured during 1885, and a comic opera version of *L'Auberge des Adrets* staged at the Comedy Theatre as *Erminie.*

Erminie proved to be the biggest success of Paulton's career, both as a writer and as a director as well as as a comedy star. He played his showy self-written role as the buffoonish thief Cadeau through the London run, then traveled to America to stage the Broadway production, a production which was to prove the outstanding Broadway musical comedy of the era. He then turned producer to bring the piece back for a second London season before taking it on tour. He also mounted a musical farcical comedy called *Larks* (1886, Dr Theodore Lamb), which he toured round Britain for a number of seasons.

Erminie producer Violet Melnotte produced Paulton's "riotous, socialistic travestie" *Masse-en-yell-oh* (1886, Thomaso Aniello) and another piece modeled on

Plate 304. **Harry Paulton.** *Victorian comedian and librettist who launched* Erminie *towards international success.*

Erminie lines, *Mynheer Jan,* but this production was sabotaged by internal management wranglings. Paulton returned to America, where he was much celebrated as "the author of *Erminie,*" and took starring roles on Broadway in *Dorothy* (Lurcher) and in his own version of Lecocq's *La Princesse des Canaries* (*The Queen's Mate*) opposite his preferred leading lady, Camille D'Arville, and Lillian Russell. He also played the chief comic role of Sapolo Baroni in his *Paola* (1889), which confined itself to a run round the country.

During his American stay Paulton also premiered a comedy with music called *Dorcas,* which was toured with *Erminie* heroine Pauline Hall in its title role. *Dorcas,* like the pieces Paulton had written for Edouin, was a briskly comic show with a score concocted from a variety of sources, made for the less highbrow out-of-town audiences, and, as such, it succeeded largely. Like another similar if mostly non-musical piece, the *schöne Galathee*–like tale of *Niobe,* which traveled the world, was played in a multitude of languages and was made into a musical, with a score by Károly Stoll in Hungary, it had a long life on the touring circuits in both America and Britain. Another farce-comedy, *The Flams,* written for William Hoey, proved adequate to its purpose. However, a further piece, *By Order of the King,* built on similar lines as a vehicle for Fannie Rice and a very strong supporting cast, was folded away after only a handful of provincial performances.

Back in Britain, Paulton played both *Dorcas* and *Niobe* with success, toured in the burlesque *Jaunty Jane Shore* (1894, Richard, Duke of Glo'ster) and also turned to appearing again in comedy, but the biggest moments of his multiple career were now in the past. In 1895 he made his last appearances on the regular West End musical stage when he appeared briefly in *The Taboo* (Papkaio) and in Audran's *L'Oncle Célestin* (*Baron Golosh*) equipped with a rewrite of William Courtright's decidedly un-French old song "Johnny, My Old Friend John," before taking a trip to Australia and New Zealand, where he directed and appeared in the Paulton-Stanley Company with statuesque Alma Stanley playing *A Night Out, My Friend from India, Niobe,* his own *In a Locket* and *Too Much Johnson.* He was later seen in London only in Percy French's fairy play *Noah's Ark* (1906, Jamboree the Pirate King), and in straight plays, latterly as Sir Toby Belch in *Twelfth Night* at Her Majesty's Theatre and as Grumio (*The Taming of the Shrew*) with Martin Harvey in 1913.

His last writings included an adaptation of the French opérette *Les Petites Brebis* (*The Little Innocents*) for the British touring circuits and another collaboration with *Erminie*'s Edward Jakobowski on a piece for the Shuberts, Nixon and Zimmerman called *Winsome Winnie. Winsome Winnie* went through sackings, rewrites and failure (by which time it was credited to Kerker and Ranken but still billed as "as great a success as *Erminie*"), and although Paulton went on to supply several more plays to both London and New York, he dipped no more into the musical theatre.

Paulton was the most consistently popular comedian of the British opéra-bouffe stage, but, more significantly, he was largely responsible as a director and a writer for the success in Britain of a style of musical theatre based on the French opéra-comique with the low-comedy portion heavily emphasized for his own benefit as a performer. *Erminie* was the crowning success of his career, but *Manteaux Noirs* was also a notable achievement.

1870 **The Gay Musketeers, or All For Number One** (pasticcio/w Joseph Eldred) Prince of Wales Theatre, Liverpool 18 April

1871 **The Three Musket-Dears and a Little One In** (pasticcio/w J Paulton) revised *The Gay Musketeers* in 5 scenes Strand Theatre 5 October

1872 **The Black Crook** (Frederic Clay, Georges Jacobi) Alhambra Theatre 23 December

1875 **Una** (Charles Lecocq pasticcio) Queen's Theatre, Dublin 4 April

1876 **Don Quixote** (Clay/w Alfred Maltby) Alhambra Theatre 25 September

1881 **The Black Crook** revised version (Alhambra Theatre)

1882 **(Les) Manteaux Noirs** (Procida Bucalossi/w Walter Parke) Avenue Theatre 3 June

1883 **Cymbia** (Florian Pascal) Strand Theatre 24 March

1884 **The Babes, or Whines from the Woods** (William C Levey) Theatre Royal, Birmingham 8 June; Toole's Theatre 9 September

1884 **Lilies, or Hearts and Actresses** (various) Prince of Wales Theatre, Liverpool 10 November; Avenue Theatre 22 November

1885 **The Japs** (Meyer Lutz/w Mostyn Tedde) Prince's Theatre, Bristol 31 August

1885 **Erminie** (Edward Jakobowski/w Claxson Bellamy) Comedy Theatre 9 November

1886 **Masse-en-yell-oh** (pasticcio/w Mostyn Tedde) 1 act Comedy Theatre 23 March

1887 **Mynheer Jan** (Jakobowski/w Mostyn Tedde) Comedy Theatre 14 February

1888 **MD** English version w Mostyn Tedde (Theatre Royal, Doncaster)

1888 **The Queen's Mate** (*La Princesse des Canaries*) American version (Broadway Theater, New York)

1889 **Paola** (Jakobowski/w Mostyn Tedde) Grand Opera House, Philadelphia and Royalty Theatre, Chester 14 May; Fifth Avenue Theater, New York 26 August

1891 **The Sheik** (''Salvator Sylvain''/w Edward Paulton) Havlin's Theater, Chicago 20 July

1894 **The Flams** (w E Paulton), Grand Opera House, Columbus, Ohio 13 August; Grand Opera House 8 February 1895

1894 **Dorcas** (comp/arr Clement Locknane, Watty Hydes, et al/w Paulton) New Lyceum, Elizabeth, NJ 30 September; Lyceum, Ipswich 31 December; Lyric Theater, New York 28 December 1896

1896 **By Order of the King** (pasticcio/w E Paulton) Lyceum, Cleveland 21 December

1899 **The Dear Girls** revised *Lilies* (Locknane, et al/w Mostyn Tedde) Regent Theatre, Salford 11 September

1901 **The Whirl of the Town** revised English version (Century Theatre)

1901 **The Little Innocents** (*Les Petites Brebis*) English version (Richmond Theatre)

1903 **Winsome Winnie** (Jakobowski) Academy of Music, Baltimore 28 September

A good number of Paulton's works were written in collaboration with his son **Edward A[ntonio] PAULTON** (b Glasgow, ?March 1866; d Hollywood, Calif, 20 March 1939), who wrote in Britain under the name of ''Mostyn Tedde'' and who continued a subsequent career as a prolific author and adapter of comedy, lyrics (''Naughty Banana Peel'') and libretti under his given name in America. He had a hand in several reasonably successful Broadway pieces (the adaptations of Berény's *Little Boy Blue,* for which he also wrote additional songs, and of Adolf Philipp's *Adele, Flo-Flo*) without ever approaching a hit like *Erminie* in the lyrics of which he (and his father) claimed that he had an (uncredited) authorial hand whilst still in fairly short pants. It would not be the last time that Paulton jr went uncredited, for most of his career in the theatre was as a rewriter rather than a writer.

Ted Paulton formed a useful writing (or rewriting) partnership with the German actor-singer-playwright-composer-producer Adolf Philipp when that Proteus of the New York German-language stage ventured into the English-language musical theatre, and together they turned out a series of musicals and plays of which one, *Adele,* also won a brief London production. He, similarly, adapted the lyrics and sometimes the libretti of a number of Continental works, including Oscar Straus's *Die schone Unbekannte* and *Mein junger Herr* for the American stage, but without success.

He also appeared on the stage as a performer, touring at 22 in the title role of the sham doctor in his father's production of the German comic opera *M.D.* (1888). He played in America, under another pseudonym, ''Edward Lowe'' (*The Queen's Mate* 1888, *Turned Up* 1889, Mussa Bey in *The Sheik* 1891, etc). When his last Broadway musical, *Cherry Blossoms,* was produced in 1926 the author appeared in the cast as an elderly Chinaman, nearly 40 years after his first stage appearance. Paulton's last eight years were spent in Hollywood as a scenarist and dialogue writer to the newly talking films.

The libretto to Ivan Caryll's Broadway musical *Kissing Time* (1920) was based on a musical comedy, *Mimi,* written by Paulton and Adolf Philipp, which had closed out of town.

1885 **The Japs** (Meyer Lutz/w Harry Paulton) Prince's Theatre, Bristol 31 August

1886 **Masse-en-tell-oh** (Edward Jakobowski/w H Paulton) 1 act Comedy Theatre 23 March

1886 **Pepita** (*La Princesse des Canaries*) English version (Royal Court Theatre, Liverpool)

1887 **Mynheer Jan** (Jakobowski/w H Paulton) Comedy Theatre 14 February

1888 **MD** English version w H Paulton (Theatre Royal, Doncaster)

1889 **Paola** (Jakobowski/w H Paulton) Grand Opera House, Philadelphia and Royalty Theatre, Chester 14 May; Fifth Avenue Theater, New York 26 August

1891 **The Sheik** (''Salvator Sylvain''/w H Paulton) Havlin's Theater, Chicago 20 July

1892 **Geneviève de Brabant** new English version (Park Theater, Philadelphia)

1892 **The Sea Cadet** (*Der Seekadett*) new English version (Park Theater, Philadelphia)

1893 **Miss Innocence Abroad** (various) Hagan Theater St Louis 20 November; Bijou Theater 25 August 1894

1894 **Dorcas** (comp/arr Clement Locknane, Watty Hydes, et al/w H Paulton) New Lyceum, Elizabeth, NJ 30 September; Lyceum, Ipswich 31 December; Lyric Theater, New York 28 December 1896

1895 **The Flams** (pasticcio/w H Paulton) Tremont Theater, Boston 14 January; Grand Opera House 8 February

1896 **By Order of the King** (pasticcio/w H Paulton) Lyceum, Cleveland 21 December

1899 **The Dear Girls** (Locknane & pasticcio/w H Paulton) Regent Theatre, Salford 11 September

1903 **All at Sea** (Wilfred Arthur) Llandudno 21 May; Prince of Wales Theatre, Liverpool 25 May

1904 **My Lady's Maid** (*Lady Madcap*) American version w R H Burnside, Percy Greenbank (Casino Theater)

1906 **The Princess Beggar** (Alfred Robyn) Majestic Theater, Utica, NY 18 January; Casino Theater, New York 7 January 1907

1908 **The Naked Truth** (various) 1 act Fifth Avenue Theater 22 June

1908 **The Widow's Mite** 1 act Orpheum, Allentown, Pa 14 December

1909 **The Yankee Mandarin** (Reginald de Koven) Opera House, Providence 11 June; Majestic, Boston 14 June

1911 **Little Boy Blue** (*Lord Piccolo*) American version w A E Thomas, Grant Stewart (Lyric Theatre)

1912 **The Rose of Kildare** (various/w Charles Bradley) Hammond, Ind 25 August

1913 **The Midnight Girl** (*Das Mitternachtsmädel*) English version (44th Street Theater)

1913 **Adele** (Adolf Philipp/w Philipp) Longacre Theater, New York 28 August

1913 **Two Lots in the Bronx** (Philipp/w Philipp) Adolf Philipp's 57th Street Theater 27 November

1914 **Auction Pinochle** English version w Adolf Philipp Burbank Theater, Los Angeles 5 April

1914 **Madame Moselle** (Ludwig Englander) Shubert Theater, New York 23 May

1914 **Castle Romance** (various) sketch New Brighton Theater, Brighton Beach 19 July

1914 **The Queen of the Movies** (*Die Kino-Königin*) American version w Glen MacDonough (Globe Theater)

1915 **The Girl of Girls** (Oreste Vessella) Columbia Theater, Washington, DC 4 January

1915 **The Girl Who Smiles** (Philipp/w Philipp) Lyric Theater, New York 9 August; revised version Bronx Opera House 14 February 1916

1915 **Two Is Company** (Philipp/w Philipp) Lyric Theatre 22 September

1917 **The Beautiful Unknown** (*Die schöne Unbekannte*) English version (Parsons' Theater, Hartford) (later played on Broadway in a rewritten version as *My Lady's Glove*)

1917 **Boys Will Be Boys** (*Mein junger Herr*) English version w Ferdinand Stollberg (Playhouse, Wilmington, Del)

1917 **Flo-Flo** (Silvio Hein/Fred de Gresac) Cort Theatre 20 December

1919 **Daly Dreams** (Hein) 1 act Lambs Gambol, Metropolitan Opera House 8 June

1920 **Lady Kitty, Inc** (Paul Lannin/Melville Alexander, Irving Caesar) Ford's Opera House, Baltimore 16 February

1920 **Look Who's Here** (Hein/Frank Mandel) 44th Street Theater 2 March

1920 **Mimi** (w Adolf Philipp, Frank Tours/ w Philipp) Shubert Belasco Theater, Washington, DC 13 March

1920 **It's Up to You** (ex- *High and Dri*) (Klein, John C McManus/w Harry Clarke/Douglas Leavitt, Augustus McHugh) Trenton, NJ 8 November

1920 **All for the Girls** (revised *It's Up to You*) Cincinnati 12 December

1921 **It's Up to You** new version Casino Theater 28 March

1924 **That's My Boy** (Robert Simmonds, Billy Duval/Karyl Norman) Auditorium, Baltimore 10 November

1926 **Cherry Blossoms** (Bernard Hamblen) Syracuse 18 January

Harry Paulton's first burlesque and *The Black Crook* were written with an elder brother, **Joseph Paulton** (d Birmingham, 31 October 1875), whose career as an actor was centered largely on Birmingham. Another brother, **Thomas G[oulde] Paulton** (b 1838; d 25 March 1914), also wrote for the stage (*Princess Amaswanee* Pier, Eastbourne 15 April 1895, etc), was for a time director of Greenwich Theatre and was active as an actor, appearing in a touring company of *Erminie* in Harry's role of Cadeau, and alongside him in *Mynheer Jan.* His second son, **Harry Paulton jr**, also worked as a performer and a director (*The Sheik,* 1891, etc), and several other members of the family were also engaged in the theatrical profession.

PAYNE, Edmund [James] (b Hoxton, London, 14 December 1863; d London, 1 July 1914). Star comedian of George Edwardes's greatest years of Gaiety Theatre musical comedy.

Son of a Hackney chairmaker, and one of a large family, 5-foot, 4-inch Teddy liked to relate that he made his first appearance on the stage at Leighton Buzzard, playing a snowball in a pantomime. He spent the early part of his theatre career as a theatrical comedian in the provinces, appeared in suburban pantomime (Friday in *Robinson Crusoe,* Greenwich 1886) and got his first proper London break when he was hurried on to replace Charles H Kenney as Mephistopheles in a brief stopgap season of *Faust Up-to-Date* (1889), being played by Auguste van Biene's touring company at the Gaiety Theatre. He returned to the road for several years of burlesque and pantomime, reminded London of his existence when van Biene played another stopgap *Faust* season, and finally made it to town when he was brought in as second takeover to the role of the little call-boy Shrimp in George Edwardes's musical farce *In Town,* in succession to Jenny Rogers and Florence Thropp. He had his first own part at the Gaiety in a supporting comedy role in the burlesque *Don Juan* (1893, Lambro's Lieutenant), but made the move to stardom when he was featured as the shopboy Miggles in the next show, *The Shop Girl* (1894).

As chief comedian of the Gaiety Theatre for the next two decades, the little man established himself as one of London's most popular theatrical stars, through top-billed roles in *The Circus Girl* (1896, Biggs), *A Runaway Girl* (1898, Flipper), *The Messenger Boy* (1900, Tommy Bang), where, in deference to his seniority, the ''girl'' element of the title switched sexes, *The Toreador* (1901, Sammy Gigg), *The Orchid* (1903, Meakin), *The Spring Chicken* (1905, Girdle), *Two Naughty Boys* (1906, Max), *The New Aladdin* (1906, Tippin), *The Girls of Gottenberg* (1907, Max Moddelkopf), *Our Miss Gibbs* (1909, Timothy), *Peggy* (1911, Albert Umbles), *The Sunshine Girl* (1912, Floot) and (after a brief absence during which he attempted to become a producer) once more with *The Girl from Utah* (1913, Trimmit).

Payne was forced out of this last show by the illness that led to his death at the age of 49, not long before that of his mentor, Edwardes. The two passings marked, even more than the war and the coming of revue, the end of an era in the British musical theatre.

1892 **Richard Whittington, Esq** (George Dixon, Fred H Graham) Theatre Royal, Bury 9 September

PEARCE, Vera (b Broken Hill, Australia, ?1895; d London, 18 January 1966). Australian beauty turned chorus girl, turned film star, turned musical leading lady, turned character comedienne in an eventful international career.

The extremely beautiful Miss Pearce was first seen in the Australian theatre as a child, appearing in a juvenile sextet in *Florodora.* She was playing in the chorus of Australia's *Our Miss Gibbs* when she won West's Beauty Competition, and was soon to be seen starred in Australian silent films (*The Shepherd of the Southern Cross Nurse Edith Cavell,* etc). In her twenties, with the development of a strong, rich soprano voice, she became one of Australia's leading musical-comedy performers, appearing in star roles in Hugh D McIntosh's productions of *My Lady Frayle* (1919, Lady Frayle, billed as ''Australia's own beauty actress''), *The Officer's Mess* (1919), *His Little Widows* (1920, Blanche), *Maggie* (1920, Maggie) and *Chu Chin Chow* (1920, Zahrat), at the same time exercising another talent in choreographing several musical shows, including Australia's production of *The Lads of the Village* (1919).

She switched from playing leading ladies when she moved to Britain and utilized her increasingly buxom talents in the West End in comical-vocal roles. The first of these was in the brief run of *Love's Awakening* (1922, Marietta), the first successful one as the big and bosomy Flora in London's *No, No, Nanette.* During the 1920s she appeared with Billy Merson in *My Son John* (1926, Clare), as the operatic Sunya Berata in Jack Buchanan's *That's a Good Girl* (1928), as Clotilde in *The New Moon* at the Theatre Royal, Drury Lane (1929), in the disastrous *Open Your Eyes* (1929, Rosalie Symes), the road-closing import *Two Little Girls in Blue,* and in the semi-operatic *Dear Love* (1929, Jeanette), both in London and, in her first American appearance, in its Shubertized girly show version on Broadway under the title *Artists and Models.*

In the 1930s she attacked Jack Buchanan in song-and-dance in *Stand Up and Sing* (1931, Princess Amaris), toured as Auguste in *Wild Violets,* loomed over Bobby Howes in *Yes, Madam?* (1934, Pansy Beresford, ''Czechoslovakian Love'') and galumphed about as the gymnastic teacher, Miss Trundle, in *Please, Teacher!* (1935). Further monstrous ladies followed in *Big Business* (1937, Annabelle Ray), *Wild Oats* (1938, Maria Cloppitt), and *Sitting Pretty* (1939, Clementina Tuttle), before she co-starred with Leslie Henson in *Bob's Your Uncle,* then appeared one last time in the musical theatre in *Rainbow Square* (1951) before taking a number of straight theatre comedy roles in Britain and in America.

She appeared on film—with sound this time—in her original stage role in the screen version of *Please, Teacher!*

Her brother, Harold E Pearce, also worked on the musical stage.

THE PEARL GIRL Musical comedy in 3 acts by Basil Hood. Music by Howard Talbot and Hugo Felix. Shaftesbury Theatre, London, 25 September 1913.

Robert Courtneidge assembled an authorial team for *The Pearl Girl* that glittered with both marquee and real value: Basil Hood, the classiest lyricist and librettist of the Edwardian age, Howard Talbot, composer of *A Chinese Honeymoon* and of half *The Arcadians,* and Hugo Felix, composer of the hit *Madame Sherry* and George Edwardes's *Les Merveilleuses.* His reward was a fine musical play whose 254-performance London run would undoubtedly have been greater had it been produced a few years earlier for, although Felix turned out a company number (''Over There!'') in the newly fashionable tango rhythm, *The Pearl Girl* was, in the early days of the rage for transatlantic rhythms, written textually and musically staunchly in the Edwardian style.

When the fabulously wealthy Mme Alvarez (Marjorie Maxwell) decides to do the London season, she resolves to wear not her famous pearls, but imitation ones fabricated by the London firm of Palmyra Pearls. Palmyra boss Jecks (Lauri de Frece) is thrilled until, with all the puff done, Mme Alvarez cancels her trip. Jecks's secretary, Miranda Peploe (Iris Hoey), saves the day by taking to the salons of Mayfair as Mme Alvarez, winning the desired publicity for her boss and a duke (Harry Welchman) for herself. Alfred Lester was a lovelorn shopboy, Cicely Courtneidge and Jack Hulbert (who became engaged during the show's run) had a soubret romance and songs (''At the Zoo,'' etc) to match, and Ada Blanche played a parvenue socialite who paired off at the curtain with Mr Jecks, who had spent most of the evening disguised as a Spaniard comically shepherding his secretary through the social shoals.

Fay Compton and Marie Blanche succeeded to the role of Miranda, but Miss Hoey took it up again for the road, succeeded by Ruby Vyvyan as the tour ran into 1915. A second company took to the road for part of 1915, and *The Pearl Girl* was seen in the British provinces again in 1916 and 1917.

PEGGY Musical play in 2 acts by George Grossmith jr based on *L'Amorçage* by Léon Xanrof and Gaston Guérin. Lyrics by C H Bovill. Music by Leslie Stuart. Gaiety Theatre, London, 4 March 1911.

When George Edwardes decided to redeploy his forces and introduce a little novelty at the Gaiety Theatre, where the team of Tanner, Ross, Greenbank, Caryll and Monckton had steadily supplied him with hits for so many years, he turned to *Florodora* composer, Leslie Stuart, who had already been tried at the Gaiety with some success with *Havana.* Longtime Gaiety comedy star and *Havana* co-librettist George Grossmith adapted the French comedy *L'Amorçage* as the libretto for a piece that needed to supply good roles for himself and Teddy Payne, but no longer for longtime Gaiety star Gertie Millar, who had gone with her husband, Lionel Monckton, to the Adelphi and *The Quaker Girl.*

Phyllis Dare played Peggy, the manicurist with whom rich James Bendoyle (Robert Hale) falls in love. In order to detach her from her hairdresser fiancé, Albert Umbles (Payne), Bendoyle adopts the principle of ground bait: he hires an impecunious friend, Auberon Blow (Grossmith), to impersonate Albert's long-lost rich uncle and to pour gifts and high-living on to the pair until Peggy becomes used to having nice things. When the supply is suddenly cut off, she will, so he judges, see the advantage of wedding Bendoyle rather than Umbles. Complications include the arrival of a real uncle (Herbert Jarman) with a gorgeous daughter (Olive May), and the fact that Auberon and Peggy fall in love. Grossmith's role allowed him to play the usual comic dandy, but this time also the phony rich uncle and, to his undoubted delight, to get the girl. Auberon and Peggy duly pair off, leaving Bendoyle with the gorgeous Doris, whilst Umbles is given a French danseuse (Gabrielle Ray) as a consolation prize.

Stuart's score mixed waltzes and comical songs for his principals in standard Gaiety style with, as so often, a number for a supporting character proving the best liked. In this case it was Olive May's rope-swinging description of herself as ''The Lass With the Lasso.'' Edwardes kept *Peggy* infused with new items: Grossmith was given a topical song about ''Mr Edison'' and Connie Ediss was written into the script and given two fine and funny Phil Braham/Arthur Wimperis numbers (''Which He Didn't Expect from a Lady,'' ''A Little Bit On''), but in spite of mostly good reviews, the piece did not come up to *Our Miss Gibbs* in popularity and closed after a good-but-not-grand 270 performances.

In America, Thomas W Ryley, who had made a fortune with *Florodora,* lost what remained of it on 37 Broadway performances of a version of what had started out as *Peggy* with Renée Kelly (Peggy), Charles Brown (Blow), Joe Farren Soutar (Bendoyle) and Harry Fisher as Umbles, now called Cecil Custard Carruthers, into which he popped some favorite old bits from *Florodora* and *Havana* amongst a welter of other ''improvements.'' The British provinces, however, welcomed the show: in early 1912 there were three *Peggy*s on the road, the A company richly topped by May de Souza, Millie Hylton and W Louis Bradfield, but the results were apparently not good enough for Edwardes. He canceled Stuart's three-play contract, ending the composer's theatrical career, and turned to Paul Rubens for the next Gaiety shows.

USA: Casino Theater 7 December 1911

PEGGY-ANN Musical comedy in 2 acts by Herbert Fields based on the libretto *Tillie's Nightmare* by Edgar Smith. Lyrics by Lorenz Hart. Music by Richard Rodgers. Vanderbilt Theater, New York, 27 December 1926.

For *Peggy-Ann,* Herbert Fields took the good old ''dream sequence'' gimmick of 19th-century extravaganza, which had been reused with great success in his father's production of the daydreamy musical comedy *Tillie's Nightmare* (1910), tricked it out with some up-to-date references to Freud, and tried to fool folk that the resultant show was daring and meaningful in an avant-garde way. Perhaps a few folk were fooled, but most just enjoyed a musical whose well-proven convention meant that it was able to let itself go with joyfully unreal absurdity in a manner little seen since the days of the more unbounded burlesques had passed away.

Like the heroine of *Tillie's Nightmare,* Peggy-Ann (Helen Ford) is a slavey in a boardinghouse, and her daydreams take her off into glamorous and ridiculous situations in society New York, on an ocean-going yacht complete with shipwreck and on a version of the island of Cuba. The dream was peopled by her mother (Edith

Meiser), Mr (Grant Simpson) and Mrs Frost (Lulu McConnell) and their daughter Alice (Betty Starbuck), Guy Pendelton (Lester Cole), Arnold Small (Fuller Mellish jr), Patricia Seymour (Margaret Breen), Freddie Shawn (Jack Thompson), 12 chorus girls, six chorus boys and a fish (Howard Mellish).

During the musical part of the evening Peggy delivered ''In His Arms'' and ''A Little Birdie Told Me So'' and joined Guy in ''A Tree in the Park'' and Patricia in ''Where's That Rainbow?,'' whilst Mrs Frost encouraged ''Give This Little Girl a Hand'' and Patricia and Freddie sang about ''Havana.''

Fields's production had a sticky start when it hit leading lady troubles. Ona Munson and Ada Mac Weeks were both announced, and Dorothy Dilley, star of *Kitty's Kisses,* actually began rehearsals before being replaced by Miss Ford, the leading lady of Rodgers and Hart's first successful musical, *Dearest Enemy.* The title, too, was changed, as *Peggy* (perhaps because of Leslie Stuart's prewar musical) became *Peggy-Ann.* The changes clearly didn't harm it, for in spite of the fact that the score, unlike that of *Tillie's Nightmare* (which had brought forth ''Heaven Will Protect the Working Girl''), produced no songs that proved take-away hits, the show had a fine run of 333 Broadway performances, a four-month post-Broadway tour and a London production. Alfred Butt's London version, directed by the elder Fields, with Dorothy Dickson as the dreamy and now anglicized heroine, did less well and closed in 134 performances.

UK: Daly's Theatre 27 July 1927

DAS PENSIONAT Comic opera (Operette) in 2 acts by ''C K.'' Music by Franz von Suppé. Theater an der Wien, Vienna, 24 November 1860.

Generally quoted (in preference to Carl Ferdinand Conradin's burlesque *Flodoardo Wuprahall*) as the first significant musical play of the modern era to come out of Vienna, Suppé's little ''komische Oper in zwei Bildern'' followed the model supplied by the one-act works of Offenbach and his French contemporaries, which the Carltheater had been so successfully playing for the past couple of years. The unsigned libretto was assumed to be ''from the French.'' This may very well have been so, but, whether it was following or faking the fashion, it served its purpose well, providing a comical story that allowed plenty of girls on the stage.

The law student Karl (Albin Swoboda) wants to marry Helene (Laura Rudini), but her father will only permit this if Karl finds a job within 48 hours. Karl has his eye on the administrator's post at Helene's school, but it seems that the headmistress, Brigitte (Friederike Fischer), will give it to her cousin. With the help of his comical servant, Florian (Josef Röhring), Karl lures Helene's schoolfriends to a midnight rendezvous where they become witnesses to his passionate declaration to the headmistress and to her not-indifferent response. To save her good name, Brigitte is obliged to give Karl the job, which ensures him his Helene.

Suppé's short score included a good dose of ensemble and choral music—the opening Praeludium and Kirchen Chor (''Mutter von deinem Bild'') and a quartet (''Gute Nacht'') in the first scene, and the second scene's septet (''Hör meiner Lieder tiefen Liebslaut'') and Spottchor (''Eilet schnell wir müssen sehen'')—alongside a Ballade and dance number for a schoolgirl named Amalie (Frln Wiener), a serenade with schoolgirl accompaniment for Karl (''Wenn des Mondes Licht durch die Büsche bricht'') and a duo for Karl and Helene (''O Pein! Ach der Gedanke bring mich um!'').

Das Pensionat was a grand success at the Theater an der Wien, where it was played for 20 nights in succession, and 34 times in all in the six months it remained in the repertoire. It was played immediately afterwards in Hungary—first in German, then at the Nemzeti Színház in an Hungarian translation (ad Lajos Csepreghi), with Károly Huber, Ilka Markovits and Vilma Bognár featured—in Germany, and in the German theatres of America, notably at New York's Stadttheater, where it was first mounted in 1867 with Richard Kaps, Herr Herrmann and Hedwig L'Arronge supported by rather more schoolgirls than the original half-dozen. In Vienna, it was soon taken up by the Carltheater, where it was given a new production in 1879 (27 December), with Karl Blasel as Florian, but although the piece was occasionally reprised thereafter, it was largely bypassed by producers in favor of Suppé's progressively more substantial and more popular works, beginning with *Flotte Bursche, Leichte Kavallerie* and *Die schöne Galathee.*

Although the show did not, apparently, get seen in Britain first time around, it put in an appearance there a century and more on. An English-language version has been played in London by the Guildhall School of Music and Drama and, in 1993, by Morley College.

Hungary: Budai Színkör (Ger) 1 June 1861, Nemzeti Színház *A nőnövelde* 14 April 1862; USA: Stadttheater 18 November 1867

PEPITA

A popular title in the 19th-century musical theatre, it was given first to Edward A Paulton's long-touring British adaptation of Lecocq's *La Princesse des Canaries* (Liverpool 1886). A Broadway comic opera *Pepita* (Edward Solomon/Alfred Thompson), in which Lillian Russell—at that time the composer's sort-of-wife—starred in a version of the old E T A Hoffman doll-girl tale through a fair 88 performances, subtitled itself uncomfortably ''the girl with the glass eyes,'' whilst Hungary's *Pepita* was an operett composed by the successful local musician Béla Hegyi (Népszínház 2 January 1890) and said to be based on Théophile Gauthier's *Ne touchez pas à la reine.*

PÉPITO Opéra-comique in 1 act by Léon Battu and Jules Moinaux. Music by Jacques Offenbach. Théâtre des Variétés, Paris, 28 October 1853.

The first Offenbach opéra-comique to be produced in a regular Paris theatre, *Pépito* was a little piece part rural light opera and part operatic parody. The Pépito of the title does not appear, but he is the background to the action as much as its Basque village. The pretty innkeeper Manuelita (Mlle Larcéna) rebuffs the advances of her Figaroesque competitor Vertigo (Leclère) as she saves up her meager profits for the day when her Pépito returns from the army to wed her. Their childhood friend Miguel (Biéval) comes back to his native village, is attracted by Manuelita, and when (having been ill-informed by the hopeful Vertigo as to the level of her virtue) he makes a rude pass at her he gets soundly turned down. Repentant, he offers to take Pépito's place in the army to allow him to return home, but it turns out that Pépito has married a cantinière and Manuelita is not too unhappy to take the gallant Miguel instead. The parody came mostly in the role of Vertigo, whose Rossinian character was given some Rossini-ish music in an eight-number score that mixed pretty country strains, in the solos and duos for Manuelita and Miguel, with rather formal opera buffa moments, as in Vertigo's air bouffe, without attaining the freedom of musical expression that would later be Offenbach's trademark.

The production of *Pépito* at the Variétés was a fiasco. It lasted just one performance. Nevertheless, Offenbach staged it again himself and brought it back to the Paris boards during the first year of operation of his Bouffes-Parisiens (10 March 1856) to a rather better reception and a place in the Bouffes repertoire at home and in the company's 1850s travels abroad. However, the show ultimately found its main popularity not in France but in Austria. Following the great success of his first Viennese Offenbach presentation, *Hochzeit bei Laternenscheine* (*Le Mariage aux lanternes*), Johann Nestroy staged a slimmed and remade (textually by Karl Treumann, musically by Carl Binder) version of *Pépito* under the title *Das Mädchen von Elisonzo* (later *Elizondo*) on his Carltheater program. Treumann played Vertigo, Therese Braunecker-Schäfer was Manuelita and Anna Grobecker was a travesty Vasco (ex- Miguel). The show gave Nestroy a second Offenbach hit, which Treumann later reproduced at his Theater am Franz-Josefs-Kai. This reshaped version was soon seen in Germany and in Hungary, first in German and soon after at the Nemzeti Színház (ad Lajos Csepreghi) in Hungarian, with Ilka Markovits, Vilma Bognár and Kószeghy featured, and it won numerous repeats in both countries and in Austria over the following years.

Pépito was seen in Britain as played by Offenbach's Bouffes-Parisiens company in 1857, and it was given an American viewing, in English, when put into the repertoire of the number-two-date touring Payson Opera Company, under the title *Vertigo,* in 1876.

UK: St James's Theatre 24 June 1857; Austria: Carltheater *Das Mädchen von Elisonzo* 18 December 1858; Hungary: Budai Színkör (Ger) 1 June 1859, Nemzeti Színház *Az elizondoi lány* 30 September 1861; Germany: *Das Mädchen von Elizondo* 8 November 1859, Flora-Theater 27 July 1894; USA: *Vertigo* November (?) 1876

PEPÖCK, August (b Gmunden, 10 May 1887; d Gmunden, 5 September 1967). Austrian composer of vocal and choral music, of film and stage scores.

A chorister as a child, Pepöck moved to Vienna to make music his study and, after the war, worked for a number of years as a theatre conductor in Germany and in Austria. However, he did not make his first contribution to the lyric stage until he had left the podium and returned to base himself in his hometown of Gmunden. His first piece, *Mädel ade!,* originally produced in Leipzig, was subsequently picked up for the Wiener Bürgertheater. It ran there just under a month. He had more success with the 1937 German production of *Hofball im Schönbrunn,* a good-old-days Operette that dragged the poor old Herzog von Reichstadt on to the Operettic stage one more time for a romance with the equally over-operetticized ballerina Fanny Elssler, and he subsequently collaborated with librettist Bruno Hardt-Warden on another Operette, on the Posse *Eine kleine Liebelei* and on a revision of Ernst Reiterer's successful *Coquin de printemps* pastiche of Josef Strauss music. Like these last two, Pepöck's *Der Reiter der Kaiserin,* a collaboration with singer Robert Nästlberger, was produced in composer-starved wartime Vienna.

1930 **Mädel ade!** (Bruno Hardt-Warden) Operettenhaus, Leipzig 14 January; Wiener Bürgertheater 5 October

1934 **Trompeterliebe** Leipzig

1937 **Hofball im Schönbrunn** (Josef Wentner, Hardt-Warden) Theater des Volkes, Berlin 4 September

1938 **Drei Wochen Sonne** (Hardt-Warden) Städtische Bühnen, Nuremberg 15 November

1941 **Der Reiter der Kaiserin** (Robert Nästlberger, A von Czibulka) Raimundtheater 30 April

1942 **Eine kleine Liebelei** (Hardt-Warden, E A Iberer) Exlbühne 3 July

1944 **Frühlingsluft** revised version w Hardt-Warden (Bürgertheater)

1949 **Der verkaufte Spitzbub** (A von Hamik) Exlbühne, Innsbruck 3 September

1951 **Geschichten aus dem Salzkammergut** Linz 14 December

PERCHANCE TO DREAM Musical play in 3 acts by Ivor Novello. London Hippodrome, 21 April 1945.

One of the most successful of the series of romantic musical plays written by Ivor Novello for the larger theatres of London in the 1930s and 1940s, *Perchance to Dream* followed the multiple-generation format used with such success by Bernauer and Schanzer in *Wie einst im Mai* (1913) and, more recently, by Armin Robinson and Paul Knepler in *Drei Walzer* (1935). In Novello's story the first generation were the aristocratic highwayman, Sir Graham Rodney (Novello), his mistress, Lydia (Muriel Barron), and Melinda (Roma Beaumont), the hated relative whom, in *Lilac Domino* fashion, he wagers he will bed, before falling in love with her. To pay the debt he must lose, he rides to rob one last time and is killed. The second generation are the music teacher Valentine Fayre (Novello), his wife, Veronica (Barron), and Melanie (Beaumont), the passionate girl who cannot prevent herself coming between them. When Veronica discovers she is pregnant, Melanie knows that Valentine will now never leave his wife, and kills herself. In the final, modern generation, the descendants of the families of the unhappy Graham/Valentine and Melinda/Melanie finally get together. The tales were linked by their setting, the mansion called Huntersmoon, where the Rodney/Fayre family live and quarrel and die, and the first two acts both featured Margaret Rutherford as the dowager of the family.

The score of *Perchance to Dream* was once again, given its necessarily non-singing leading male character, written largely for the soprano (Barron) and contralto Olive Gilbert as the blowsy actress Ernestine in the first act and a stout incidental dame in the second. It produced one of Novello's biggest hits in the two women's duet ''We'll Gather Lilacs,'' alongside Lydia's waltz song ''Love Is My Reason for Living,'' the richly contralto ''Highwayman Love'' and some attractive parlor music. Melanie/Melinda was supplied with some gently girlish numbers (''The Night That I Curtsied to the King,'' ''The Glo-Glo'') made to the measure of the vocally light Miss Beaumont.

Tom Arnold's production at the London Hippodrome was a huge success. *Perchance to Dream* played in the West End for more than two and a half years (1,022 performances) before the company took the show to South Africa, then toured it through Britain whilst Novello prepared his next musical. Like Novello's other shows, although its favorite songs became worldwide concert pieces, it was seen little outside Britain, but there it kept up a regular presence, being played in several regional theatres in the 1980s and also being taken on tour with Simon Ward and Diana Martin starred as Rodney/Valentine and Melanie/Melinda.

Recordings: original cast (Decca), selections (EMI)

LA PÉRICHOLE Opéra-bouffe in 2 acts by Ludovic Halévy and Henri Meilhac based on *Le Carrosse du Saint-Sacrement* by Prosper Mérimée. Music by Jacques Offenbach. Théâtre des Variétés, Paris, 6 October 1868. Revised 4-act version, Théâtre des Variétés, 25 April 1874.

In some ways, *La Périchole* represented a departure for Offenbach, Meilhac and Halévy, the trio of collaborators who had made themselves the world's most famous authors in the musical theatre in the five years and four enormous hits (and just one comparative failure) since their first teaming. Although it was still labeled an ''opéra-bouffe,'' and although it still contained some of the extravagant elements of the kind of burlesque humor displayed in the earlier pieces, *La Périchole* was inherently of a different tone to the purely bouffe *La Belle Hélène, Barbe-bleue* and *La Grande-Duchesse de Gérolstein,* and also to the paper-sharp comedy of mores *La Vie parisienne.* Its colorfully comical south-of-the-border tale was even based (albeit very sketchily) on someone's else work, and not as a parody of that work: *La Périchole* was, for all its appellation, a genuine comic opera.

When the penniless Peruvian busker La Périchole (Hortense Schneider) collapses at the end of a day's work and her companion, Piquillo (José Dupuis), goes off to earn some food, she falls easy prey to the libidinous Viceroy, Don Andrès de Ribeira (Grenier), his offer of dinner and a place as lady-in-waiting to his deceased wife. She pens a sad farewell to Piquillo and goes where food awaits her. However, court etiquette insists that the Viceregal ''lady-in-waiting'' must for decency's sake be a married woman, and so, after some liquid persuasion, Périchole agrees to a marriage of convenience. The Viceroy's minions bring in a convenient husband, a fellow found trying to hang himself from despair: a very drunk Piquillo.

When Piquillo finds out the next day what he has done and why, he berates his new wife hideously (and unfairly, for she, at least, knew whom she was marrying!), gets thrown in prison, then released to perform his duty by presenting his wife at court. But at the presentation Périchole offers back all the Viceroy's rich gifts and tells her tale, and that of Piquillo, with such affecting sincerity that Don Andrès gives up his untouched new mistress to her husband and sends them richly on their way.

Offenbach's music to *La Périchole* reflected the difference in the tale's tone. There were jolly pieces, such as the trio of the three innkeeping ladies (''Au Cabaret des trois cousines'') and the Viceroy's description of his

''Incognito,'' and there was high comedy in the first-act finale, overflowing with hard liquor, with a group of wobbly notaries summoned from their supper to perform the ceremony, Périchole's replete ''Ah! quel dîner je viens de faire'' and poor Piquillo's blind-drunk declaration of love (''Je dois vous prévenir, madame''), but the popular highlights of *La Périchole*'s score were the simple song of the strolling minstrels (''L'Espagnol et la jeune Indienne'') with its famous cockeyed refrain ''Il grandira, car il est espagnol,'' and the wholly sentimental and sincere letter song, in which Périchole bids her Piquillo farewell (''O mon cher amant, je te jure''). Sentimental and sincere, and just a little bouffe, for to those who knew their *Manon Lescaut,* Périchole's letter of regrets had a familiar ring.

Critics and early audiences alike refused initially to admit that Offenbach and his librettists had given them another fine, funny and melodious work, instead of one that was solely crazy fun. Groups were even formed to whistle down the unfamiliarly cast Schneider. But *La Périchole* was stronger than them. It held its place at the Variétés through a fine run and was soon exported to every corner of the musical theatre world at the beginning of what was to be a long and strong career.

The first significant revival of *La Périchole* in Paris was in 1874 (25 April), and for that revival, which featured the three stars of the original production, Offenbach and his librettists enlarged the show. Unusually, it ''enlarged'' very well indeed. Unlike their remake of *Orphée,* where the expansion had consisted simply of sticking showy bits and pieces in here and there throughout the work, the new *Périchole* left its highly satisfactory first act pretty well alone and attacked the notably weaker second part of the show. The authors, who had already made alterations and extensions to their book during the first run, now introduced a whole new plot turning, taking a much more burlesque tone in a preposterous new dungeon scene in which the Viceroy appeared in fantastical disguise as a jailor for a whole series of neatly worked-out high jinks. The comic actor Bac featured in this same act, in a burlesque of *Monte Cristo,* as a crazed old prisoner who is digging his way out of prison with a penknife. Offenbach added no fewer than 10 extra numbers to his score to suit the rearranged text, one of which was a delightful—and again unburlesquey—solo for his heroine, ''Je t'adore, ô brigand.'' Even though its critical reception was muted, the new *Périchole,* now in four acts, subsequently got productions around the world.

Other top Parisian prima donnas later took turns at *La Périchole.* In 1877 Anna Judic made a Parisian appearance in the role and in 1895 Jeanne Granier was also seen as Périchole, with Guy as her Piquillo, at the Variétés, but although the show persisted in the late-19th-century and early-20th-century repertoire, it did not do so with quite the vigor that its more exuberant predecessors did. However, in more recent years, as the fashion for theatrical sentimentality has won out over the old fondness for high and/or low comedy, *La Périchole* has found itself progressively more popular amongst the list of Offenbach's works. In the later years of the twentieth century *La Périchole* held a position and a popularity in the Offenbach canon greater than at perhaps any other time, a popularity witnessed by several recordings and by Paris revivals in 1969 (Théâtre de Paris), 1979 (Théâtre Mogador 19 May) and 1984 (Théâtre des Champs-Élysées 17 September).

America was the first foreign country to see the show when *La Périchole* was introduced to New York by H L Bateman's company, with Mlle Irma starring as the street singer alongside Aujac (Piquillo) and Leduc (Don Andrès). It had to struggle against the stiff competition offered by Marie Desclauzas and Rose Bell in *Geneviève de Brabant* up the street at the Théâtre Français, and a few days after the opening Bateman gave up and sold out his lease and company to the adventurous James Fisk. Although this first production was only a partial success, *La Périchole* soon established itself amongst the most popular items in the American opéra-bouffe repertoire, and it became part of the baggage of all the touring French opéra-bouffe companies, making regular New York appearances during their Broadway dates. English versions followed—the burlesque players the Wallace Sisters advertised an English version as early as 1871, the Holman company were playing it by 1872, with Sallie Holman in the title role, Susan Galton appeared as Périchole to John Howson's Panatellas at San Francisco's Opera House in 1873, Emilie Melville introduced it to San Francisco in a version by Fred Lyster, Alice Oates (the four-act version) and Adah Richmond both included it in their repertoire from 1878, and Jeannie Winston in 1882—but it was some time before a vernacular version hit Broadway. In 1895 Lillian Russell appeared in a production at Abbey's Theater (29 April), a Shubert presentation at the Jolson in 1925 was played in Russian and featured Olga Baclanova (21 December), and in 1956 the Metropolitan Opera played a severely damaged version with Patrice Munsel, Theodore Uppman and Cyril Ritchard in the leading roles.

Just a few days after Irma's American opening, Friedrich Strampfer produced *Périchole, die Strassensängerin* (ad Richard Genée) at Vienna's Theater an der Wien. Once again, the piece did not find the triumph of the composer's earlier works, and its record at the house closed at 48 performances. However, the piece survived to return to the Vienna stage as recently as 1996 (14 December) in a new production at the Volksoper.

London saw Schneider herself as Périchole, in repertoire at the Princess's Theatre in 1870, and Henry C Cooper and his touring opera company showed a first English-language version of the piece to the British provinces just three months later with Annie Tonnellier (Mrs Cooper), W Haydon Tilla (Piquillo) and Henry Lewens (Viceroy) in the leading roles, but it was not until five years later that Selina Dolaro presented herself in London in what *The Era* described as "the racy opéra-bouffe" (ad Frank Desprez) with Walter Fisher as her Piquillo and Fred Sullivan (brother of Arthur) as the Viceroy. "A pity that such melody was ever united to so worthless a story," huffed the same paper, complaining that if the sex was taken out of the adaptation there would be nothing left. Dolaro played the show for a fine three months before switching to *La Fille de Madame Angot,* brought it back again in October and again in 1879, by which time Londoners had also seen Emily Soldene in the role in a large production of the four-act version, which she had previously introduced in Australia, at the Alhambra (9 November 1878). In 1887 Mme Humberta and Dekernel played in a revival at the French Theatre (Royalty Theatre 6 December), in 1897 Florence St John played a further English *La Périchole* (Garrick Theatre 14 September), and the show has returned to British stages intermittently over the century since.

Oddly enough, Australia seems to have heard *La Périchole* in English before either London or New York. Lyster's opéra-bouffe company introduced it into its repertoire in May 1875 with Henry Bracy and Clara Thompson starred. Emilie Melville followed up just months behind with her version (and also with Bracy), Fannie Simonsen gave her very sung version of the heroine, and the piece was seen regularly through the 1880s as Melville with the four-act version and Gracie Plaisted (with Majeroni and Wilson's Company, then with Searelle and Harding) trouped their productions through the colonies and the Orient.

Le Carrosse du Saint-Sacrement has served for several other stage pieces, including a comic opera by Henry Busser, *Der Vizekönig von Peru,* mounted at St Gallen's Stadttheater, 27 March 1957.

USA: Pike's Opera House (Fr) 4 January 1869, Abbey's Theater (Eng) 29 April 1895; Austria: Theater an der Wien *Périchole, die Strassensängerin* 9 January 1869; Germany: Friedrich-Wilhelmstädtisches Theater *Périchole, die Strassensängerin* 6 April 1870; Hungary: Budai Színkör (Ger) 12 September 1869 and (Hun) 21 July 1871; UK: Princess's Theatre (Fr) 27 June 1870, Tyne Theatre, Newcastle (Eng) 19 September 1870, Royalty Theatre (Eng) 30 July 1875; Australia: Prince of Wales Theatre, Melbourne 1 May 1875

Recordings: complete (EMI-Pathé, Erato, EMI), complete in German, complete in Russian (Melodiya), Metropolitan Opera excerpts (RCA), etc

Plate 305. **Jean Périer** *of the Opéra-Comique.*

PÉRIER, Jean [Alexis] (b Paris, 2 January 1869; d Paris, 3 November 1954). Star baritone of the Parisian operatic and musical stage.

The son of an opera singer and répétiteur, and the brother of the music-hall artist known as Ram-Hill, Jean Périer soon got himself out of his earliest employment with the Crédit Lyonnais and into the Paris Conservatoire. He quickly made himself known in the Paris musical theatre as a young leading man with an exceptionally fine baritone voice, appearing at the Opéra-Comique as Monostatos, Cantarelli (*Le Pré-aux-clercs*), in *Le Dîner de Pierrot* and as Agoragine in Saint-Saëns's *Phryne* (1893) before going out into the commercial theatre. He featured as Boslard in *Mam'selle Carabin* (1893) and Maître Crabbe in *Le Bonhomme de neige* (1894) at the Bouffes-Parisiens, played alongside Mily-Meyer as Maxime Lambert in Wenzel's *L'Élève de conservatoire* (1894) and took leading roles in the Folies-Dramatiques productions of *La Fiancée en loterie* (1896, Angelin), *La Falote* (1896, Pierre), *Rivoli* (1896), *L'Auberge du tohu-bohu* (1897, Paul Blanchard) and *La Carmagnole* (1897), as well as in revivals of such pieces as *François les bas-bleus* (François) and *Mam'zelle Nitouche* (Champlâtreux).

One of Périer's most important creations came when he moved back to the Bouffes-Parisiens, where in 1898 he introduced the role of Florestan, the hero of Messager's *Véronique* (''Poussez l'ecarpolette,'' Duo de l'âne). He was seen subsequently on the commercial stage in *Shakespeare!* (1899, Brutus), *La Demoiselle aux camélllias* (1899, Robert Delmont), *La Belle au bois dormant* (1900, Olivier), as Montosol in a revival of *Josephine vendue par ses soeurs* (1900) and Gaston in a repeat of *Les P'tites Michu* (1900), and as François again, in *Les 28 Jours de Clairette* and in the Châtelet spectacular *Les Aventures du Capitaine Corcoran* (1902). For a number of years, from 1901 on, however, the bulk of his time was spent appearing at the Salle Favart, where he created, amongst others, the role of Pelléas in Debussy's *Pelléas et Melisande,* Giorgio d'Ast in Leroux's *La Reine Fiamette* and that of Landry in *Fortunio.*

In 1906 Périer created another important musical-theatre part when he appeared in the title role of Louis Ganne's *Hans, le joueur de flûte* at Monte Carlo. In 1910 he repeated his Hans in Paris, but each time returned to the Opéra-Comique. In 1918 he played in revue with Yvonne Printemps, and in 1920 he repeated his Florestan at the Gaîté-Lyrique, where he also appeared as Falsacappa in *Les Brigands.* In 1921 he played the Podesta in a revival of *La Petite Mariée* at the Mogador and appeared at the Théâtre des Champs-Élysées in *La Rose de Roseim.* And in 1923 he created another memorable role as Duparquet, the aging Rodolphe of *La Vie de Bohème,* in the Reynaldo Hahn opéra-comique *Ciboulette.*

Now well and truly into playing ''father'' roles, he spent several years appearing in Paris's more intimate musical houses, pairing with Edmée Favart in the successful *Quand on est trois* (1925) and *Mannequins* (1925, Le Marquis), and creating the part of Cardot in Joseph Szulc's *Divin mensonge* (1926) at the little Théâtre des Capucines. He also appeared on the variety stage, and was to be seen as late as 1938 in the role of the aged Prince Karagin in the Théâtre Mogador's French mounting of the musical *Balalaïka.*

Périer also appeared in musical film and can be seen in a small role in the famous Ludwig Berger film version of *Trois Valses* (1938).

DIE PERLEN DER CLEOPATRA Operette in 3 acts by Julius Brammer and Alfred Grünwald. Music by Oscar Straus. Theater an der Wien, Vienna, 17 November 1923.

A vehicle for Fritzi Massary, Germany's favorite operettic star of the pre-Nazi era, *Die Perlen der Cleopatra* cast her as a more than slightly comical soubrette of an Egyptian sex cat alongside her celebrated comedian husband, Max Pallenberg, in the role of a Marc Antonius who, in this version of the tale, got rather cut out by a younger and more tenorious Roman. The couple were supported by Robert Nästlberger (Prinz Beladonis), Richard Tauber (the Roman Victorian Silvius), Franz Glawatsch (Pampylos, Cleopatra's minister) and Mizzi Mader-Anzengruber (Charmian), and the production was directed by perhaps the most skilled musical stager of his era, Miksa Preger, not in Berlin, but on the stage of the Theater an der Wien.

Straus's score, not angled quite as violently towards its star as might have been expected, was a mixture of vaguely foreign-sounding tones and Viennoiseries. The flavor of the evening was set when Cleopatra introduced herself in song: ''Mir fehlt nicht als ein kleiner ägyptischer Flirt.'' She carried on to sing about ''Der König Tutenkhamen,'' reminding at the end of each verse ''So war ich bin Cleopatra,'' and let loose in her main arietta ''Für euch allein musst es geschehen,'' in which the Queen of the Nile was heard to disport herself in some distinctly un-Egyptian Ländler measures. She also joined in duet with her Roman officer (''Ich bring' mein Herz,'' ''Ja so ein Frauenherz'') without being required to linger long above the stave. The showiest music of the evening was allotted to the young Tauber, who was given a ''Ja, ja so soll es sein'' which was pasted into the second act like a foil-wrapped bonbon (it even had a gift tag: in the printed score the number was separately dedicated to ''mein Freund Richard Tauber'').

Die Perlen der Cleopatra had only a measure of success. It played for two months (61 performances) at the Theater an der Wien, and was subsequently exported to London, where Jimmy White staged it with vast splendor, and some botching by Arthur Wood, at Daly's Theatre (ad J Hastings Turner, Harry Graham). Evelyn Laye was a truly fair Cleopatra, with Shayle Gardner as Mark Antony, Alec Fraser as Silvius, John E Coyle as Beladonis and Jay Laurier as Pamphylos. However, all the splendor (and White ladled in more of everything when the thing refused to go) could not make *Cleopatra* a success, and it sank after just 110 forced nights.

A revised version of the piece by Erwin Straus was presented at the Stadttheater, Zürich, on 31 December 1957.

Since what seems to have been her first operatic appearance in a 1662 Venetian work by Castrovilli, Cleopatra has made a number of appearances on the musical stage, but with very limited fortune. The Hungarian theatre housed perhaps the most successful operettic tale of the Nile Queen in a *Kleopatra* composed by György Verő (6 March 1900, Magyar Színház) and played later in Germany as *Die Bettelgräfin* (which seems to suggest that it wasn't hugely about Egypt and the Ptolemys). In other parts of Europe, Adolf A Philipp and Alexander Neumann's ''Ausstatungsoperette,'' produced at Hamburg's Carl-Schultze Theater in 1897 (24 January), Wilhelm Freudenberg's operatic *Kleopatra* (Magdeburg 12 January 1882) and another by August Enna (Copenhagen 7 February 1894) all left little trace. The Neumann piece, however, nearly got a wider showing. In 1894 it was purchased by Lillian Russell and announced for Broadway with a replacement score variously by Englander or Herman Bemberg. But America's burlyqueen of comic opera never got round to playing Cleopatra.

A musical version of G B Shaw's *Caesar and Cleopatra* as *Her First Roman* (ad Ervin Drake), which featured Leslie Uggams as a Shavianally girlish Cleopatra, was a 17-performance Broadway flop (Lunt-Fontanne Theater 20 October 1968), and an attempt to operaticize Shakespeare as *Antonius und Cleopatra* by the Graf von Wittgenstein (lib: Mosenthal) in Graz, 1 December 1883, seems to have gone no further. The lady presumably put in an appearance in Goetze's 1940 *Kleopatra die zweite* (*Die zwei Gesichte einer Königin*), another piece that had apparently no future.

The longest stage run that the famous Queen has achieved, however, is undoubtedly that compiled through the more than 2,000 nights of Julian Slade and Dorothy Reynolds's *Salad Days* in which, each night, the Manager of the Nightclub sang the comical praises of ''Cleopatra'' in marginally more grammatical manner than the comedienne of the evening had done in *Leave It to Jane* (''Cleopatterer'').

UK: Daly's Theatre *Cleopatra* 2 June 1925

LA PERMISSION DE DIX HEURES Opérette in 1 act by Mélesville and Pierre Carmouche. Music by Jacques Offenbach. Bad Ems, 9 July 1867.

A little military opérette that managed to cram enough farcical content for two pieces into its action, *La Permission de dix heures* dealt with the attempts of Larose Pompon (Grillon) and his beloved Nicole (Marie Lemoine) to pair off the girl's maiden aunt (Mme Colas) with Pompon's sergeant, Lanternick (E Gourdon), thus leaving the way free for their own wedding. A ''ten-hour leave'' intended for Lanternick is issued, by Nicole's machination, to Pompon, and the sergeant, who has started wooing the niece instead of the aunt, gets whisked back to the barracks. In the second part of the entertainment some in-the-dark wooing leads to proposals and beribboned tokens being exchanged, and Lanternick, who thinks he has been promised Nicole, duly ends up with Madame Jobin.

First produced, like a number of Offenbach's smaller pieces, at his preferred spa town of Ems, *La Permission de dix heures* followed another group of Offenbach opérettes by becoming more popular in its German-language version than in the original French. *Urlaub nach Zapfenstreich,* as adapted by Karl Treumann, was produced at the Carltheater the year after its premiere, and reprised there in 1873 with Hermine Meyerhoff as Madame Jobin, Josef Matras as Lanternik and Franz Eppich as Larose Pompon. It also went on to be seen in Hungary before finally making its appearance in Paris, six years after its Ems debut. Mme Dartaux (Mme Jobin), Laurence Grivot (Nicole), Falchieri (Pompon) and Bonnet (Lanternick) headed the cast of the performances at the Théâtre de la Renaissance.

Austria: Carltheater *Urlaub nach Zapfenstreich* 13 February 1868; Hungary: Budai Szinkör *Takarodo után* 13 June 1871; France: Théâtre de la Renaissance, Paris 4 September 1873

PERREY, Mireille [PERRET, Camille] (b Bordeaux, 3 February 1904; d Fontainebleau, 8 May 1991). Parisian stage and screen soubrette.

Mlle Perrey studied at the Paris Conservatoire, made her first stage appearances at the Odéon and the Comédie Française, and went on to play leading juvenile roles on both the Parisian musical stage (*La Térésina, Déshabillez-vous, Arthur,* the title role in *Rosy*) and then in London, where she appeared in the ''French'' role of Yvonne (created on Broadway by Lili Damita) in *Sons o' Guns* (1930), in the title role of *Paulette* (1932) and in Marilyn[n] Miller's role of Madelon in *The One Girl* (ex-*Smiles,* 1932). In a long career, which included five years at the head of Paris's Comédie Wagram, she appeared in a long series of light comedies and in both non-musical and musical film. Her notable musical screen credits included the screenic *Pas sur la bouche* (1931, Gilberte) and *Dédé* (1934), George van Parys's *L'Homme à l'imperméable* (1956) with Fernandel, and the role of Aunt Élise in *Les Parapluies de Cherbourg* (1964). She was still working in the cinema in the early 1980s.

PESSARD, Émile [Louis Fortuné] (b Montmartre, Seine, 29 May 1843; d Paris, 10 February 1917).

The winner of the Paris Conservatoire's top composition prize, the Prix de Rome, in 1866, Pessard did not rise to the classical heights of some other winners. He held the post of inspector of singing tuition for Paris and from 1881 taught harmony at the Conservatoire. Amongst his theatrical compositions were the scores for a number of tidily elegant opéras-comiques, large (*Le Capitaine Fracasse, Les Folies amoureuses*) and small (*La Cruche cassée, Le Char*), a cantata, *Dalila* (1867), an opera, *Tabarin* (Paul Ferrier, Opéra 12 January 1885), a féerie for the Gaîté, the incidental music for the drama *Une Nuit de Noël* (1893) and a mimodrama, *Le Muet* (1894).

In later years, he shifted his sights and composed several opérettes, of which his first venture into the commercial musical field, *Mam'zelle Carabin,* was his most successful. The others won more praise for the distinction of their music than public popularity.

1870 **La Cruche cassée** (Hippolyte Lucas, Émile Abraham) 1 act Opéra-Comique 21 February
1878 **Le Char** (Alphonse Daudet, Paul Arene) 1 act Opéra-Comique 18 January
1878 **Le Capitaine Fracasse** (Catulle Mendès) Théâtre Lyrique 2 July
1888 **Tartarin sur les Alpes** (Henri Bocage, Charles de Courcy) Théâtre de la Gaîté 17 November
1889 **Don Quichotte** (Jules Deschamps) 1 act Théâtre des Menus-Plaisirs 4 July
1891 **Les Folies amoureuses** (André Lénéka, Émmanuel Matrat) Opéra-Comique 15 April
1893 **Mam'zelle Carabin** (Fabrice Carré) Théâtre des Bouffes-Parisiens 3 November
1897 **Gifles et baisers** (Paul Barbier) 1 act Théâtre Luxembourg 16 December
1898 **La Dame de trèfle** (Charles Clairville, Maurice Froyez) Théâtre des Bouffes-Parisiens 13 May
1902 **L'Armée des vierges** (Ernest Depré, Louis Hérel) Théâtre des Bouffes-Parisiens 15 October
1903 **L'Épave** (Depré, Hérel) 1 act Théâtre des Bouffes-Parisiens 17 February
1909 **Mam'zelle Gogo** (Léon Xanrof, Maxime Boucheron) Théâtre Molière, Brussels 27 February

PETER PAN Musical based on the play in 2 acts by J M Barrie. Lyrics by Carolyn Leigh, Betty Comden and Adolph Green. Music by Mark Charlap and Jule Styne. Winter Garden Theater, New York, 20 October 1954.

J M Barrie's much-loved play was originally produced with a substantial score of incidental music and of small songs, composed by John Crook to the author's own words. Other musicians have since composed the same kind of accompanying music and songs for subsequent productions of the play, the best-known set amongst them being those by Leonard Bernstein (Imperial Theater, New York 24 April 1950, six musical pieces), but without inflating the show to a degree that necessitated any filleting of the play's text.

The extent of music that was involved in Crook's score was the musical limit as far as Barrie was concerned. Although he himself wrote for the musical stage, he did not want *Peter Pan* turned into a conventional musical. In his lifetime, he both firmly refused to do the job himself and refused permission for an adaptation of his play by other hands. This veto did not stop some producers from going ahead in any case, at least partially. Charles Dillingham popped two secondhand Jerome Kern numbers (ly: B G De Sylva, Paul West) into his 1924 production with Marilyn[n] Miller, and he was neither the first nor the last to act in such a cavalier fashion.

After Barrie's death, his estate at first continued, in line with his wishes, to refuse permission to musicalize *Peter Pan,* but some piece of unrecorded ''persuasion'' (which, in line with the very dubious management of the Barrie legacy, doubtless had a few dollar signs attached to it) eventually made them change their minds. After first being made into an animated musical film (1953), with a score by Sammy Fain and Sammy Cahn (''Never Smile at a Crocodile,'' ''The Second Star to the Right'') and a surprising degree of success, Barrie's piece was then transformed from the original, oddly atmospheric fairy play into a primary-colored song-and-dance show for Broadway. It was a show that used only some of the play's scenes, topped them up with a series of musical numbers in a different mode from either Crook's melodies or the film songs, and immersed them in a large amount of incidental dancing, principally for a Tiger Lily whose transformation from the heroic huntress of the original into a tiny figure of low-comic fun characterized the spirit of the adaptation.

This production had, apparently, been originally intended by director Jerome Robbins to be a more conventional *Peter Pan,* with Mary Martin (Peter) and Cyril Ritchard (Hook) starred and a Crook-sized score by Charlap and Carolyn Leigh. The expansion into a conventionally sized and shaped musical occurred en route to and from the original West Coast mounting, and on that same route a number of Charlap and Leigh's songs were replaced and/or complemented by some by Styne, Comden and Green. The first team's contribution included Peter's ''I Gotta Crow,'' ''I Won't Grow Up'' and ''I'm Flying,'' the second team provided a piece about ''Never, Never Land.''

This musical comedy *Peter Pan* played only 152 performances on Broadway, but it was transmitted on television the two years following, with most of its stage cast, and it was ultimately made into a television film, which, over the years, won Miss Martin America-wide identification with this version of the role of Peter. Thus kept alive, the musical was toured and eventually won a Broadway revival (Lunt-Fontanne Theatre 6 September 1979), with Sandy Duncan as a memorably agile Peter, George Rose perpetuating the curious local tradition for playing Hook as an effeminate English fop, some expertly designed and performed flying into the auditorium and an extra song. All, apparently, with permission.

This highly successful revival (554 performances) prompted a British production at Plymouth's Theatre Royal, with Bonnie Langford as a very much younger and boyish Peter and Joss Ackland a Hook in the more traditional (masculine) English vein, but British audiences were less happy with such non-Barrie material as a ''Mysterious Lady'' song-scena filled with old-fashioned pantomime business and a menagerie of peluche animals hopping through Neverland, and the show played only a 73-performance festive season in London. The following season Lulu was the song-and-dance Peter with similarly unsatisfactory results.

This *Peter Pan* was subsequently given in Germany (ad Erika Gesell, Christian Severin), with Ute Lemper in the leading role (67 performances) and in 1990 returned to Broadway again (Lunt-Fontanne Theater 11 December), as part of a long nationwide tour, with former Olympic gymnast Cathy Rigby as an athletic (if, again, not very young) Peter in a version that restored some of the play and omitted the ''Mysterious Lady'' double-act.

These revivals resulted in France also putting out a version of this musical comedy *Peter Pan* (ad Alain Marcel). Cast on English lines, with a Peter both young and femininely boyish (Fabienne Guyon) and a handsome, vigorous Capitaine Crochet (Bernard Alane), it also failed to run, but all the time the American company—proudly maintaining Tiger Lily and her ''Ugg a Wugg'' while the craven *Annie Get Your Gun* up the road censored out ''I'm an Indian Too''—continued to tour, putting in several further stops on Broadway as part of that tour, and establishing further a primary-colored image of *Peter Pan* that is special to America, and in considerable contrast to the more ''fairy-play'' image held and preferred elsewhere.

A television musical based on *Peter Pan* was produced by NBC in 1976 (12 December). Jack Burns and Andrew Birkin were credited with the book, rather than Barrie, and Leslie Bricusse and Anthony Newley the songs.

Since the expiry of the copyright on *Peter Pan,* and in spite of a staggeringly unjust (and illegal?) move by the British authorities to reverse that expiry, several other more or less musical versions of the play have been produced, including one by Piers Chater-Robinson that played London's Cambridge Theatre in 1994, with Ron Moody as Captain Hook and Nicola Stapleton as Peter, and another by Britons George Stiles and Anthony Drewe mounted in Denmark in 1999 (Det Ny Teater 21 December).

UK: Theatre Royal, Plymouth 7 November 1985, Aldwych Theatre, London 20 December 1985; Germany: Theater des Westens 21 December 1984; France: Casino de Paris 28 September 1991

Recordings: original cast (RCA), French cast (Carrère), Hong Kong cast (Crown/HMI), American touring cast (JAY), *The Musical Adventures of Peter Pan* (compilation) (Varèse Sarabande), etc

PETERS, Bernadette [LAZZARA, Bernadette] (b Ozone Park, NY, 28 February 1948). Favorite Broadway ingenue with an off-the-wall air.

After a juvenile appearance in *The Most Happy Fella* (1959) and teenage performances off-Broadway as the Cinderella heroine of the J M Barrie musical adaptation *The Penny Friend* (1966) and in the original cast of the long-running *Curley McDimple* (1967, Alice), Miss Peters played her first Broadway role as Josie Cohan in the biomusical *George M* (''Oh, You Wonderful Boy,'' ''Ring to the Name of Rose''). Her next musical, *A Mother's Kisses,* folded in Baltimore on its pre-broadway run, but she won notice and some of the season's kudos with a wide-eyed Ruby Keeler parody in the super-ingenue role of off-Broadway's *Dames at Sea* (1968, Ruby).

She appeared briefly in the ill-fated *La Strada* (1969, Gelsomina), in the five performances of the off-Broadway *Nevertheless They Laugh* (1971, Consuelo) and as Carlotta Monti in the pre-Broadway life of the oddly titled *WC,* a musical about Fields that starred Mickey Rooney and did not make it to New York, and appeared in the comedy role of Hildy in the 1971 revival of *On the Town* before making a second personal hit, opposite Robert Preston, as Mabel Normand in *Mack and Mabel* (1974, ''Look What Happened to Mabel,'' ''Wherever He Ain't,'' ''Time Heals Everything'').

Miss Peters subsequently appeared on Broadway as the vocal soloist for the American adaptation of *Song and Dance,* created two leading roles in Stephen Sondheim musicals—as the mistress of one George and the grandmother of the other in *Sunday in the Park with George* (1984, Dot), and as the Witch in *Into the Woods* (''The Last Midnight'')—introduced the title role of *The Goodbye Girl* (1993, Paula) and appeared as the politically corrected Annie in the 1999 revival of *Annie Get Your Gun* (Tony Award).

She also played the part of Lily in the screen version of *Annie* and voiced the role of Sophie in the cartoon version of *Anastasia* (1998).

LE PETIT CHOC Opérette in 3 acts by P-L Flers. Music by Josef Szulc. Théâtre Daunou, Paris, 25 May 1923.

The composer of *Flup..!* had a further success with his light, up-to-date songs for the musical comedy *Le Petit Choc,* produced in 1923 by Jane Renouardt at the little Théâtre Daunou, one of the most successful of the houses specializing in the small-scale Parisian musical comedies that were the Jazz Age rage. Flers's text featured Régine Flory as the virtuous music-hall star Féfé Mimosa, who is still awaiting ''le petit choc'' before giving herself to a man, and Paul Ville as a young and thoroughly affianced businessman, Maurice Pardeval, off to America on a big business deal. The two are banned from entering America by a morality official when a mix-up makes it appear they are pretending to be husband and wife and, desperate to make their respective appointments, they hurriedly marry each other. After two acts of quiproquos, they find that they like the situation. Maurice's Suzette (Christiane Dor) weds his best friend, Alfred (Adrien Lamy), and the all-important American millionaire, Eusebius Rubbish, is charmed by Féfé into doing business with her husband.

The show's score was topped by Féfé's ''On a toujours ce qu'on ne veut pas,'' her description of ''Le Petit Choc'' and the realization ''J'aime!,'' alongside the well-intentioned ''Copain-copine'' (Féfé/Maurice), the masculine ''Il faut savoir prendre les femmes'' (Alfred) and the tale of six little English girls in search of husbands which signaled ''L'ouverture de la pêche'' as described by the very prominent Alfred.

Seven months of *Le Petit Choc* in Paris were followed by a good touring life, during which the young Gabrielle Ristori appeared as Féfé Mimosa, and a production in Hungary (ad Zsolt Harsányi), where the sexy sophistications, jazzy music and small actor-singer casts of the French 1920s musicals found their readiest and most unembarrassed export market.

Hungary: Belvárosi Színház *Le Jolly Joker* 29 September

LE PETIT DUC Opéra-comique in 3 acts by Henri Meilhac and Ludovic Halévy. Music by Charles Lecocq. Théâtre de la Renaissance, Paris, 25 January 1878.

The most successful and enduring of the highly successful (and in some cases enduring) series of musical plays that Lecocq composed for, and Victor Koning produced at, the Théâtre de la Renaissance in the late 1870s, *Le Petit Duc* combined a shapely and, by and large, gently comical libretto, touched with just sufficient endearing sentiment, with some of Lecocq's most ravishing soprano music, mostly dedicated to the travesty role of the teenaged Duc de Parthenay, devised for the theatre's enormously popular star, Jeanne Granier.

For reasons of state, and the benefit of others generally, the ''little'' teenaged Duc de Parthenay is married to the even younger Blanche de Cambrai (Mily-Meyer), only to find that their elders, decreeing them too young for such things, will not allow them to consummate their marriage. The little Duchesse is sent off to a school at Lunéville, but the disconsolate Duc is, as a consolation, permitted to quit the tutelage of the musty Frimousse (Berthelier) and, thanks to his friendly master of arms, Montlandry (Vauthier), is put at the head of his own regiment. He may be too young for sex, but he's old enough to send men into battle. The Duc, however, has his preoccupations in order. He promptly orders his regiment to Lunéville, besieges the school and disguises himself as a peasant girl to get inside and meet his Blanche. Alas, he is forced to withdraw when his regiment is called to battle. When the dallying French are almost caught unawares by an enemy attack, the Duc banishes women from the encampment only to be exposed for breaking his own commands when Blanche escapes from Lunéville and comes to find him. All is forgiven, however, in the following victory, and the little Duc and his little Duchesse are permitted to become husband and wife for real. The comedy of the piece was enhanced by a ''role de Desclauzas,'' the comico-aristocratic headmistress of the second-act school, which was played and played to the low-comic hilt by none other than Marie Desclauzas herself.

The romantic part of Lecocq's score was of a rare delicacy, notably the first-act soprano duet for the Duc and his bride in which he tries to encourage her to exchange the formal ''vous'' for the more intimate ''tu'' as in ''Je t'aime'' in addressing him, their no-less-innocent reunion on the battlefield in the final act (''Ah, qu'on est bien'') and the Duc's sweet explanation that ''on a l'âge du mariage quand on a l'âge d'amour'' (you are old enough to be wedded and bedded when you are old enough to be in love). The comical part of the musical proceedings, topped by the Duc's peasant-girl tale (''Mes bell' madam', écoutez-ça!'') of the hazards of crossing the army lines (she lost her eggs but saved her virtue) and the old tutor's creaky wooing of the disguised boy (''C'est un idylle''), was equally successful, as was the lively dash of military music that the settings permitted: Montlandry's jolly Chanson du petit bossu, the regiment's choral greeting of ''Mon colonel'' in the first-act finale and the final hailing of the Duc as ''Le plus bel officier du monde.''

Le Petit Duc was a vast success. Granier found in the Duc her greatest role, little Mily-Meyer won her first triumph and one that would only be equaled when she turned to comedy roles, Berthelier and Vauthier both gave anthology performances, and Desclauzas made of the Directrice, Mlle Diane de Château-Lansac, the most memorable character of her memorable career as a character lady. After a first run, which took it through the season, the piece remained solidly in the Renaissance repertoire for five years, and Mlle Granier subsequently repeated her role at the Théâtre de l'Éden in 1888 and again at the Variétés in 1890, each time with José Dupuis as a famous Frimousse.

Marcelle Dartoy (Bouffes-Parisiens, 1897, with Desclauzas and Vauthier repeating their original roles 20 years on), Jeanne Saulier (Variétés, 1904), Anne Dancrey (Gaîté-Lyrique, 1912), Gina Féraud (ibid, 1915), Edmée Favart (Mogador, 1921), Louise Dhamarys (Gaîté-Lyrique, 1926) and Fanély Revoil (Châtelet, 1933) succeeded to Mlle Granier's role on the Paris stage whilst *Le Petit Duc* kept up a regular presence in French theatres as an important part of the heart of the French opérette repertoire. Only with the decline of the Parisian musical theatre did it, too, decline and become limited to occasional regional performances in theatres where charm still had a place alongside romantic spectacle.

By the end of the year of its production, *Le Petit Duc* had been played in all the main centers. Uncharacteristically, Britain was the first to produce its *The Little Duke* (ad B C Stephenson, Clement Scott), perhaps because the venue was Islington's Philharmonic Theatre, the house that had been responsible for launching the vastly profitable English versions of *La Fille de Madame Angot* and *Giroflé-Girofla.* Alice May, the original prima donna of *The Sorcerer,* was whisked out of that show to play the Duc, Alice Burville (London's most recent Geneviève de Brabant) the Duchess, top comic Harry Paulton played Frimousse and Australian actress and singer Emma Chambers was the Directrice, and Lecocq supplied a fresh entr'acte for the slightly rearranged show, which opened one week before the newest local show, *HMS Pinafore.* But something went wrong. *The Little Duke* was put on ill-prepared, and its run in Islington was horrifyingly short. The piece's publishers snatched it back from the incompetent management (bookmaker Charles Head and Richard D'Oyly Carte) and arranged a West End season at the St James's Theatre (16 June 1878), with Ethel Pierson replacing as the Duchess and J D Stoyle as Frimousse. It didn't go either. *The Little Duke* had missed its chance. Londoners later had a chance to see the original version when Mlles Granier, Mily-Meyer and Desclauzas played some performances of *Le Petit Duc* at the Gaiety Theatre in 1881.

Budapest gave an enthusiastic greeting to *A kis herceg* (ad Jenő Rákosi) when it was produced with the great Lujza Blaha (then ka Soldosné) as the Duc paired with little Mariska Komáromi and with Elek Solymossy as Montlandry, at the Népszínház (where it was revived in 1881 and again in 1889), and a month later Vienna's Carltheater produced its German version. Antonie Link (Duc), Rosa Streitmann (Duchesse) and Josef Matras (Frimousse) headed the cast for a disappointing 20 performances. The following year, however, the Carltheater remounted the piece with Frlns Klein and Streitmann and with the Austrian Desclauzas, Therese Schäfer, as Diane (6 September 1879).

In America there was no such diffidence. *Petit Duc* descended on the country's stages en masse just as soon as the performance materials were available. San Francisco got there first, thanks to the determined Alice Oates, who got her version on at the Bush Street Theatre in November 1878. Alice played the Duke to the Duchess of Lulu Stevens, alongside English players J G Taylor (Frimousse) and Edward Connell (Montlandry), while—in typical Oates style—James Meade donned skirts to take the role of the Directrice.

The first East Coast showing was supposed to have been in Philadelphia, where J Cheever Goodwin's version was announced for production a week ahead of Boston's (ad T R Sullivan, Fred Williams). However the Philadelphia company was raking in such shekels with the brand-new *HMS Pinafore* that it postponed its *Petit Duc,* and so Boston got in first (Boston Museum 10 February 1879), giving Alice Harrison (Duke) and Rose Temple (Duchess) the honors of what they claimed as a US premiere. James C Duff mounted this very flung-together-so-as-to-be-first version, starring Florence Ellis and Louise Beaudet, "at popular prices" at Booth's Theatre a few weeks later. It played only three indifferent weeks, but before he was finished Alice Oates had brought her production up from the Philadelphia Arch Street Theater to pitch camp at the Lyceum. When Duff closed, Mlle Beaudet stayed on to sing her role of the Duchess opposite Marie Aimée's Duke in French at the same theatre (5 May). There was no doubt that the show suffered very much from the giant shadow of *HMS Pinafore,* but it nevertheless established itself thoroughly on the American stage. The following year Paola Marié gave Broadway her little Duke, by which time the piece was being liberally played throughout the country in touring opéra-bouffe companies' repertoires and in summer season. It returned for a substantial revival at the Casino Theater (4 August 1884, ad H C Bunner, W J Henderson), in which J H Ryley played the role of Frimousse and Georgine von Januschowsky the Duke, and again in 1896 when Lillian Russell was seen as the Duke in a production at Abbey's Theatre.

Australia got its first hearing of *Le Petit Duc* in the Williams/Sullivan version as played by Horace Lingard's company, with Lingard himself playing Frimousse, his wife, Alice Dunning, as the Duke and Mrs J H Hall and Alma Stanton taking turns as the Duchess. However, none of the favorite touring opéra-bouffe stars chose to include Granier's best vehicle in their repertoire, and although the show was seen again at Melbourne's Alexandra Theatre in 1887 with Marion Norman starred (21 May), it got little other exposure down under.

Brussels, Amsterdam, Madrid, Turin, Stockholm and Prague all presented *Petit Duc*s in the same period, and both South America and other European centers soon followed, confirming the piece—in spite of Vienna's reaction (or translation)—as one of the outstanding opérettes of its period.

UK: Philharmonic Theatre, Islington *The Little Duke* 27 April 1878; Hungary: Népszínház *A kis herceg* 11 October 1878; Austria: Carltheater *Der kleine Herzog* 9 November 1878; Germany: Friedrich-Wilhelmstädtisches Theater *Der kleine Herzog* 24 November 1878, Frankfurt-am-Main *Der fidele Herzog* 7 December 1878; USA: Bush Street Theater, San Francisco 21 October 1878, Booth's Theater 17 March 1879; Australia:

Academy of Music, Melbourne *Fabrice, the Little Duke* 11 August 1879

Recordings: selections (EMI-Pathé, Decca)

LA PETITE BOHÈME Opérette in 3 acts by Paul Ferrier based on *La Vie de Bohème* by Henri Murger. Music by Henri Hir(s)chmann. Théâtre des Variétés, Paris, 19 January 1905.

Ferrier and Hirschmann's version of Murger's famous tale took an altogether different tone from that which Giacosa, Ilica and Puccini had taken less than a decade earlier in their celebrated operatic adaptation of the same piece as *La Bohème* (1896). The piece was not a burlesque (which didn't stop its authors beginning one number "je m'appelle Mimi") but simply a conventional musical-comedy version of the tale where the main focus was on the on-again, off-again, romance of Musette (Jeanne Saulier) and Marcel (Alberthal) and on the comical Barbemuche (Paul Fugère), and in which Mimi (Ève Lavallière) was still well and truly alive for a finale that tried to convince its audience that the so-called bohemian life, lived on bread and water (not evident in the course of the show), was "la terre de génie et le paradis de l'amour." Mimi gushed "C'est mon dada," and got into carnival travesty alongside Barbemuche, who camped a coloratura Catherine the Great, Musette flirted with a vicomte (Prince) but returned to join Marcel in the lyrical "Nous n'avons qu'un temps à vivre" in the third act, and everyone said "vive la Bohème" a dreadful lot, whether they were invading an aristocratic home and drinking its champagne (presumably as a change from all that bread and water) or galloping off to the country.

Fernand Samuel's production at the Variétés had a 16-performance first run, but the piece (ad Benno Jacobson) was subsequently picked up by Berlin's Centraltheater, where the composer had launched his *Les Hirondelles* the year before, and by the voracious Budapest theatre (ad Jenő Heltai), as well as throughout France. The Bouffes-Parisiens brought it back for a season (3 February 1907), with Mariette Sully (Musette) and Simon-Max (Barbemuche) featured, and it was seen once more in Paris in 1921, with Mme Mathieu-Lutz as Musette and Jeanne Saint-Bonnet as Mimi.

Germany: Centraltheater *Musette* 11 November 1905; Hungary: Magyar Színház *Bohémszerelem* (*Musette*) 1 December 1905

LA PETITE MADEMOISELLE Opérette in 3 acts by Henri Meilhac and Ludovic Halévy. Music by Charles Lecocq. Théâtre de la Renaissance, Paris, 12 April 1879.

After having been le petit duc (not to mention la petite mariée), Jeanne Granier—in the hands of the same librettists and the same composer who had given her the earlier triumph—became la petite mademoiselle. The Comtesse Cameroni was the "petite" mademoiselle, thus called in reference to the historical "grande mademoiselle," otherwise Anne-Marie Louise d'Orléans, Duchesse de Montpensier, the 17th-century aristocrat who sided with the Condé-Bourbons and Spain in their ill-fated rebellion against Cardinal Mazarin.

The plottings of the petite mademoiselle involve her in a regulation operettic quantity of disguises. In the first act she takes on the identity of a certain Mlle Douillet, a notary's wife from Angoulème and, when one of that frequently unfaithful wife's military lovers, the young vicomte de Manicamp (Vauthier), comes to seek out his old flame, she accidentally finds true love. She does not find political success, however. In spite of spending the second act disguised, Madame Favart-like, as a serving wench named Trompette (Manicamp is at the same time impersonating an apprentice sausage maker and calling himself Lambin) amongst a bevy of aristocrats all pretending to be what they are not, such contribution as she has made to the cause goes down with the victory of Mazarin's troops. A further act is necessary for her finally to escape the "royal" dictates and to be allowed to wed her little vicomte rather than the elderly brother of her equally elderly deceased husband. Mily-Meyer (Jacqueline Taboureau) and Marie Desclauzas (the tripière, Madelon) from the *Petit Duc* cast again had fine roles as the employers of the two disguised stars, Berthelier was the innkeeper Taboureau, and Lary (Boisvilette) and Urbain (Juvigné) were the other principals.

All the girls had good numbers—Granier describing herself as "Arrivée dans Bordeaux" or, in her serving-maid disguise, swinging in with "Notre patron, homme estimable," Mily-Meyer summoning "Jeunes et vieux" and Desclauzas doing particularly well with her "Quand le cervelas va, tout va!" and "Pauvre peuple, pauvre pays." Manicamp, disguised as Lambin, pretended "Me v'là, j'arriv' de Normandie," whilst Taboureau had his moment in his Couplets du cabaretier ("Ces bons parisiens"). The Mazarinade and its call to arms that ended the second act, a conspiracy septet and a number with an old "Faridondaine" refrain all went to add to a substantial score, which was amongst Lecocq's favorites of his own works.

Without in any way demeriting, *La Petite Mademoiselle,* whether because it followed a touch too closely the recipe as before, whether because of a post–Paris Exhibition kind of decompression, or simply because it just didn't tickle the public quest for novelty, did not score the same kind of long-running success as its predecessors. By the time it was withdrawn in September it had reached a total of 83 performances, which was to be its Parisian career. This comparative disappointment did not stop it from making its way to the many other cities and countries where Meilhac, Halévy and Lecocq's names were potent theatrical attractions, but it did not become a notable hit in any of them. Even in Budapest (ad Béla J Fái), where Lujza Blaha took on another Granier role, it did not repeat the Hungarian successes of *La Petite Mariée, La Marjolaine, Le Petit Duc* and *La Camargo,* whilst in London (ad Robert Reece, H S Leigh), where Constance Loseby took Granier's role, alongside Harry Paulton (Taboureau), Alice May (Madelon), Emma Chambers (Jacqueline) and the young Fred Leslie (Manicamp), it played only a slightly satisfactory 75 performances at the vast Alhambra before being displaced by the year's Christmas show.

Neither country had thought it worthwhile to do much about the title (which meant precious little to those who didn't know about Madame de Montpensier), but in Germany the little miss, as played by one of the Stubel sisters (it seems to have been Lori, but I'm not sure it wasn't Jenny), became, more interestingly, *Die Feinden des Cardinals,* or the Cardinal's enemy. Swoboda, Schulz and Frln Kopka supported, and again the show did just all right. Broadway also saw the piece in German, under the less interesting title of *Trompette,* but with no less a star than Marie Geistinger cast as the Countess Cameroni alongside Adolf Link (Taboureau) and Frau Haubrich (Madelon). Geistinger later played the show in repertoire in Philadelphia, Chicago and elsewhere.

New York got a second helping of *La Petite Mademoiselle* six years later, when the Casino Theater mounted the piece in English under yet another title, *Madelon.* Max Freeman's version seemed to owe something to the German (in spite of his name, Freeman was a German) and English versions before him, but it did seem a little strange to take the title role away from the prima donna and give it to the comedienne. Bertha Ricci was the heroine, and Lillie Grubb played Madelon, alongside James T Powers (Taboureau), Courtice Pounds (Jolivet), Isabelle Urquhart (Pompanon) and Mark Smith (Rabicamp), for a run of six weeks.

Australia, like Britain, retained *La Petite Mademoiselle* as the title of what seemed to be a revamped version of London's text—credited to Leigh and to W H Harrison. Nellie Stewart appeared in the Royal Comic Opera Company's production as the Countess Cameroni, with her sister Docy Stewart as Madelon, Emma Chambers repeating her London Jacqueline, Sgr Broccolini/W H Woodfield (Manicamp) and H R Harwood/Robert Brough (Taboureau) through a good season of six Melbourne weeks and onwards.

Hungary: Népszínház *A kis nagysam* 5 September 1879; UK: Alhambra Theatre 6 October 1879; Germany: Friedrich-Wilhelmstädtisches Theater *Die Feinden des Cardinals* 20 March 1880; USA: Germania Theater *Trompette* (Ger) 13 October 1882, Casino Theater *Madelon* 5 December 1887; Australia: Theatre Royal, Melbourne 14 April 1885

LA PETITE MARIÉE Opéra-comique in 3 acts by Eugène Leterrier and Albert Vanloo. Music by Charles Lecocq. Théâtre de la Renaissance, Paris, 21 December 1875.

When Victor Koning went into management at the Théâtre de la Renaissance on the proceeds of *La Fille de Madame Angot,* he made his start with the enormously successful Paris transfer of Lecocq's *Giroflé-Girofla,* and it was to his old "collaborator" (and, just coincidentally, the hottest composer in town), and the librettists and star of *Giroflé-Girofla* that he turned for his theatre's first new piece. The result was another splendid success, which set the Renaissance off on a six-year, eight-show cycle of Lecocq/Koning shows.

Leterrier and Vanloo supplied a delightfully sexfarcical libretto, with a fine central role made specially to suit Jeanne Granier as Graziella, the "little wife" of the title. Graziella is secretly marrying San Carlo (Félix Puget), the great friend of the local Podesta (Vauthier). The reason for the secrecy is that, once upon a time, San Carlo and the Podesta's wife erred together and got caught, and the great man, rather than expel his friend from court, simply told him that the day that he married he would feel free to take a similar liberty with his wife. The best man for this hush-hush occasion is the bridegroom's other best friend, Montefiasco (Dailly), a man who is kept close tabs on by his wife, the buxom Lucrezia (Mlle Alphonsine), who is inclined to illustrate her congenitally jealous points of view with a horsewhip. All four are together, after the ceremony, when—alas!—the Podesta turns up and, after little dissembling, a touch of lying and a small swap of identity, the farce begins. Two acts and many twists later, the Podesta has had his revenge: San Carlo is made to weep with doubt and with jealousy before he is allowed a happy ending. But the revenge has its underside for, as events unwind, the Podesta finds out more about his late wife and her systematic lack of fidelity than he might, for self-esteem's sake, have wished to know.

Graziella-Granier had the lion's share of the music, amongst which were included the waltz couplets of the first act as she showed off her bridal gown before her husband ("Je tenais, monsieur mon époux"), the little fable of the nightingale, which she recites to and with the Podesta, her high-speed Couplets de l'enlèvement, a pretty Ronde de la petite mariée in the second-act finale and the Couplets des reproches and sobbing duo of the final act, which lead to the denouement. Vauthier, also well served, had a fine basso rondo in the first act, teasingly reminding his friend of his promise ("Le jour ou tu te marieras"), and Lucrezia snapped out her Valse de la cravache, with whiplash accompaniment, as a further musical highlight.

La Petite Mariée was a full-scale success that filled the Renaissance for 10 months. During this time Koning's old associate Humbert mounted it in Brussels, then exported it to London's Opera Comique with Marie Harlem starred as the little bride. Thereafter it went on to be seen in Portugal, Spain, Egypt and, in its first foreign-language production, in Hungarian in Budapest (ad Jenő Rákosi). In its initial season at the Népszínház *La Petite Mariée* became the first opérette to have a major success there without the theatre's overwhelming star, Lujza Blaha, in its lead role. Erzi Vidmár played Graziella, and the show did well enough to be brought back for a second season in 1880.

Marie Aimée introduced *La Petite Mariée* to Broadway, and was seen as Graziella in two successive seasons in New York in between which she purveyed the piece throughout America with her touring company, and London was also given a second showing of the piece in French when Jeanne Granier and the Renaissance company played a season at the Gaiety in 1881. Perhaps because of the impossibility of sterilizing a plot that rested entirely on things sexual, no English version of this sizeable hit appeared in either London or New York, but Australia—not for the first or last time—did not wait for those two main centers of English-language theatre. William S Lyster produced an English *La Petite Mariée* in Melbourne, in a version that seems to have been done by brother Fred Lyster, with Catherine Lewis starred as Graziella. It was another Australian, George Musgrove, who 20 years later finally mounted Harry Greenbank's adaptation of the show, *The Scarlet Feather,* at London's Shaftesbury Theatre. Decima Moore was the little bride, but the score had been rearranged and peppered with additional numbers by Lionel Monckton and Alfred Plumpton, mostly for the benefit of Musgrove's other half, soprano Nellie Stewart, featured in a large inserted role as a page named Pippo. *The Scarlet Feather* was not a success either in Britain or when Musgrove remounted it, with much fanfare, back home. An American version of the piece (ad George Lash) was announced at San Francisco's Tivoli in October 1897, under the title *Complexities,* but it does not seem ever to have got to the stage.

Berlin's production of *Graziella* was followed by several others throughout Germany, but Vienna's *Graziella* (ad Karl Treumann), in spite of a fine cast headed by Karoline Finaly, Karl Blasel (Montefiasco), Josefine Gallmeyer (Lucrezia) and Wilhelm Knaack as the bride's comical father, was played only a so-so 14 times. On the home front, however, in spite of the wash of famous Lecocq opérettes that followed it, *La Petite Mariée* remained a favorite and was brought back to Paris on a number of occasions. It returned to the Renaissance in 1877 with Jane Hading (Mme Koning) starred, and in 1880 with Granier taking up her old role once more. Clara Lardinois (Graziella) and Jacquin (Podesta) featured at the Menus-Plaisirs in 1887. Nearly 30 years later it was played again at the Théâtre Moncey (6 August 1915) and finally, at the Mogador in 1921, with Mme Mathieu-Lutz, Jean Périer and Adrien Lamy at the head of its cast, before slipping, with most of the rest of the shows of the period, from the repertoire.

UK: Opera Comique (Fr) 6 May 1876, Shaftesbury Theatre *The Scarlet Feather* 17 November 1897; Hungary: Népszínház *A kis menyecske* 21 September 1876; Austria: Carltheater *Graziella* 11 November 1876; USA: Eagle Theater (Fr) 6 February 1877; Germany: Friedrich-Wilhelmstädtisches Theater *Graziella* 23 August 1877; Australia: Prince of Wales Theatre, Melbourne 6 December 1876, Princess Theatre, Melbourne *The Scarlet Feather* 26 November 1900

LA PETITE MUETTE Opérette in 3 acts by Paul Ferrier. Music by Gaston Serpette. Théâtre des Bouffes-Parisiens, Paris, 3 October 1877.

Ferrier's story told of pretty 17th-century Spanish Mercedes (Louise Théo), struck dumb on the day of her wedding to Don José d'Albatros (Daubray), the disgraced ex-governor of Burgos, and diagnosed by his doctor Camomillas (Alfred Jolly) as able to recover her voice only when love (or, more to the point, sex) comes along. Her husband is constitutionally unable to effect the cure, and is in despair when, as a mark of his potential recall to favor, his mute wife is given the honor of being named reader to the Infanta. Raphaël (Mme Peschard), the handsome envoy who brings the news of the appointment, not only drives Mercedes to court but also operates the necessary cure on the way there.

The comedy of the piece was accompanied by some lightsome Serpette music (''it is light and gay without being trivial'') of which a certain amount, in spite of her plot line inability to speak until half-way through the second act, fell to Théo. She burst forth, in the 11th number of the score, with an understandable ''Ah! que c'est bon de parler!,'' and promptly followed up with an eight-page duet, a trio and, in spite of doctor's orders, a waltz song (''J'accorde que c'est malaisé''). In the last act, in the course of her work, instead of reading the baby monarch the classics she sings it a kiddie song. Théo had the soubretteries, the winks and nods, and the fun, but the bravura music of the piece was the province of Mme Peschard. She entered with a love song (''Oui, je vous aime''), which scooted up to high C, followed up with a virtuoso coloratura showpiece habañera (''Déjà vos mules rapides''), and negotiated a showy waltz chantée drinking song in the second act (''Plus de tristesse'') and an aubade (''Reveillez-vous belle endormie'') in the third. The other principal roles were played by Mlle Luce (Casilda), the comedian Scipion (Don Gill) and the tenors Minart (Henrique, with a chanson militaire) and Jannin (Pédrille).

After 56 Parisian performances under Charles Comte's management, the piece was played both in Budapest (ad Jenő Rákosi) ("to a cold reception") and in New York by Maurice Grau's opéra-bouffe company, with Paola Marié in the role of Mercedes.

Hungary: Népszínház *A kis néma* 12 February 1878; USA: New Fifth Avenue Theater (Fr) 24 March 1880

LES PETITES BREBIS Opérette in 2 acts by Armand Liorat. Music by Louis Varney. Théâtre Cluny, Paris, 5 June 1895.

Les Petites Brebis was a not-very-far-distant relation of *Das Pensionat,* which was of course just one member of the large family of French and French-derived comedies and opérettes that dealt with chaps chasing after their beloved girls inside the girls' boarding schools. The chaps in this case were the noble Christian (Moïzard) and his comical pal Fifrelin Grobichon (Hamilton), the girls were Alice von Stahlberg (Mlle Azimont) and Fifrelin's sister, Fanny (Mlle Norcy), and Adèle Cuinet featured as Mlle Emeraldine Mouton, the headmistress of the establishment.

Of the 15 numbers in Varney's score, the couplets "Y a de la femme" for Christian and Fifrelin, the Couplets de la lecture as performed by Fanny, Alice, the headmistress and the schoolgirls, Alice's "Dieu que c'est bon" ("lorsque je me retrouve seule") with its shivering "brrrr" refrain, the schoolgirls' bedtime Prière des anges gardiens, and the Christian/Fifrelin rondo Couplets de l'amour, celebrating the happy ending to all the gallivanting, proved the most appreciated.

Les Petites Brebis played for more than one hundred performances at the little Théâtre Cluny on its first run, and promptly set off round Europe, where it found distinct favor among the parade of similar French musical comedies of the 1890s and 1900s.

Heinrich Bolten-Bäckers's German adaptation was a decided hit at Berlin's Alexanderplatz-Theater, and it was promptly picked up by Vienna's Theater in der Josefstadt, the Viennese center of French vaudeville and the recent home of Banès's *Toto* and Varney's *Le Brillant Achille.* Karl Pfann (Christian), Rauch (Fifrelin), Viktoria Pohl-Meiser (Emeraldine), Frln Peroni (Alice) and Frln Grünert (Fanny) headed the cast through a fine 49 consecutive performances, making the show the theatre's most successful piece of the year. Two seasons later it was given a showing in New York's German-language theatre, and Budapest's Magyar Színház produced their version (ad Emil Makai) with the British operetta *Weather or No* as an afterpiece. It was brought back to Berlin, at the Theater des Westens, in 1904 (20 October, 15 per formances), with Hansen (Christian), Frln Gaston (Emeraldine), Wellhof (Badurel) and Below (Fifrelin). Brussels, too, saw the show on several occasions.

In spite of its European popularity, however, the show did not make its way into the English-language main centers. When *The Little Innocents* was finally seen in Britain, in an adaptation by veteran comedian/author Harry Paulton, in 1901, it played only a minor tour.

Germany: Alexanderplatz-Theater *Die kleine Lämmer* 27 October 1895; Austria: Theater in der Josefstadt *Die kleinen Schafen* 22 November 1895; Hungary: Magyar Színház *A baranykak* 10 November 1897; USA: Irving Place Theater *Die kleine Lämmer* 2 April 1898; UK: Richmond Theatre *The Little Innocents* 17 November 1901

LE PETIT FAUST Opéra-bouffe in 3 acts by Hector Crémieux and Adolphe Jaime. Music by Hervé. Théâtre des Folies-Dramatiques, Paris, 28 April 1869.

Of Hervé's three most successful full-scale opéras-bouffes, it was *Le Petit Faust,* the only one of the three to parody another specific work (*L'Oeil crevé* more or less burlesqued *William Tell* but only amongst a whole quiverful of other targets, and *Chilpéric* burlesqued medieval history) in Goethe's *Faust* and Gounod's operatic version thereof, which ultimately proved the most successful and the most enduring, in France if not always beyond. Allegedly written with the Variétés company in view, with Schneider and Dupuis tagged for the roles of Marguerite and Faust, and at one stage mooted for the Palais-Royal, where it was suggested that the vast-nosed comic Hyacinthe might play Siebel, the piece was ultimately mounted at the Folies-Dramatiques with no such starry casting.

Marguerite (Blanche d'Antigny) is brought to the academy for young persons run by Doctor Faust (Hervé) by her brother Valentin (Milher), who is off to the wars. Faust is elderly and immune to girls, but the combination of Marguerite's determined teenage vamping and the interference of the cocky Méphisto (Anna van Ghell) sets the pedagogue in a whirl. Having awakened desire in Faust, Méphisto now has fun helping him assuage it, at the usual price. The artificially rejuvenated Faust, rich and handsome, goes to Paris in search of Marguerite and, having disposed of the interfering Valentin in a duel, prepares to wed the willing girl. Méphisto makes sure that Faust suffers first jealousy, then disappointment when he discovers that his beloved is only after his money, then remorse when the ghost of Valentin turns up inopportunely in the wedding soup, and at last he carries both the foresworn Faust and his ill-behaved bride off to Hell.

The extravagances of Crémieux and Jaime's libretto were not so much in the tale but in the telling of it. The authors indulged in the most far-fetched, zany scenes and speeches, highlighted by the burlesque duel between Valentin and Faust, waged with vegetable knives and won by chicanery when the devil offers the soldier a pinch of snuff in mid-fight. The craziness extended to the songs in pieces such as the gobbledygook Trio de Vaterland and Valentin's burlesque operatic death, whilst still leaving place for lashings of the suggestive, as in Marguerite's insistence on mock-childishly showing Faust her well-placed bruises (''C'est tout bleu'') and her trouser-dropping tale of ''Le Roi de Thune,'' and even the picturesque, as in the parade of the Margarets of all nations in Faust's search for his love. Méphisto had a lively rondeau with which to introduce himself, Marguerite a winsome tyrolienne and Valentin a martial soldier song, and grotesque echoes of the most famous elements of Gounod's score were everywhere. A later addition to the score was a waltz contest, parodying ''the music of the future'' as represented by Wagner's *Die Meistersinger.*

Following its highly successful Paris creation, *Le Petit Faust* followed the most successful works of the French opéra-bouffe stage around the world. Hervé, who had rocked London with his Chilpéric, decided not to play the follow-up season of *Faust* as well, and it was Scots music-hall comic Tom Maclagan who introduced the English version, done by H B Farnie after Dion Boucicault withdrew, with Marguerite Debreux as his Méphisto and Emily Soldene as a buxom Marguerite. Mons Marius was a downy Siebel, Tom Aynsley Cook a booming Valentine, and the young Jennie Lee scored a star-making hit as a little street arab with one scene to play. A fair to fine success, even though it did not begin to compare with *Chilpéric* in London popularity, the production ran through its fixed season from mid-April to the beginning of July. By that time *Doktor Faust junior* (ad Richard Genée and, like London, including the Wagnerian parody) had made its appearance on the Vienna stage with sufficient success to be repeated 40 times during the two seasons it remained in the repertoire. Budapest was given an Hungarian version (ad Endre Latabár, Solymossy), St Petersburg a Russian one and Belgium, Italy and South America saw the show in its original French, but it was New York that got the most curious versions of all.

It was Kelly and Leon's Minstrels who were the first to bring a version *Le Petit Faust* to the American stage, and they altered the casting (and potted the show) in their usual way. In a Kelly and Leon show, Leon was always prima donna. Alice Oates, in her opéra-bouffe debut, followed behind them with a no less personal version. She used the London text as her starting point, but by the time it made it to the stage it had been readapted (allegedly by London conductor Frank Musgrave), localized, and generally mutilated and Mrs Oates (who had sacked Martha Wren in rehearsals when she began to covet her role) had grabbed the parts of both Méphisto and the Street Arab for herself. H T Allen (Faust), Marion Taylor (Marguerite), W H Crane (Valentine), George L Fox (Martha) and Charles H Drew (Siebel) supported through a forced five weeks.

Kelly and Leon promptly came out with a superior, unpotted version in competition. Soon after this, however, the entrepreneurial James Fisk introduced his newly imported set of Parisian opéra-bouffe stars to Broadway in a more conventional *Petit Faust,* and, at last, Broadway got to see something like the real thing. Léa Silly played Méphisto and Céline Montaland was Marguerite, with Constant Gausins as Faust. If the stars proved to be not as popular as their predecessors in the booming line of opéra-bouffe importations, the piece, which ran three straight weeks at the Grand Opera House, pleased well. Marie Aimée followed up with her version in the same season, Coralie Geoffroy and the Worrell Sisters (another English *Little Faust*) all followed suit, Mrs Oates took the piece on the road—and when Marion Taylor departed the cast, replaced her as Marguerite with . . . Harry Allen!—and Lisa Weber had it revamped as *Little Mephistopheles* for her touring company, which featured Miss Taylor as Faust, a male Marguerite and some fresh music by the star's husband, W S Mullaly. Finally, Paola Marié appeared at the Fifth Avenue Theater in the role of Méphisto, which she had taken over in the original Paris production and played on several occasions in Brussels. All in all, New York and America had a fair go at *Le Petit Faust* . . . in one shape or another.

Le Petit Faust was brought back to the Paris Folies-Dramatiques in 1872, and again in September 1876, with Simon-Max, Coralie Geoffroy and Mlle Prelly starred. In 1881 a revised and expanded version, which featured Mlle Raffaele as Marguerite, stretched the role of Siebel (played as a tiresomely smart schoolboy) as a vehicle for Marie Gélabert and that included two great chunks of ballet for spectacle's sake, was mounted at the larger Théâtre de la Porte-Saint-Martin. Cooper and Jeanne Granier starred in an 1891 (16 May) reprise at the same theatre, with Mlle Samé as Méphisto and Sulbac as Valentin, and Guy and Juliette Méaly were featured in yet another at the Variétés in 1897. Both London and New York also mounted later and larger versions of the show during this period. In London, the Alhambra Theatre's *Mefistofele II* (ad Alfred Maltby) gave Lizzie St Quentin as the devil the title role alongside Fred Leslie (Faust), Lionel Brough (Valentine) and Constance Loseby (Marguerite) , whilst an 1897 New York version, played under the title of *Very Little Faust and Much Marguerite,* written by Richard Carroll and Clement King and musically souped up by Fred Eustis, was produced at Hammerstein's Olympia (23 August). Truly Shattuck was Mephisto, chief comic Richard Carroll played Valentine, and Harry Luckstone and Dorothy Morton took the title roles. The show was seen once more in New York, in French, in the repertoire of New Orleans's Roberval company in 1902.

Le Petit Faust won further revivals in Paris in 1908 (Folies-Dramatiques 1 December) and 1934 (Porte-Saint-Martin 19 December with Boucot as Faust and Dranem as Valentin), and it has remained on the fringe of the played repertoire for more than a century, returning in a production at Metz in 1990, and a full-scale revival at Auvers-sur-Oise (26 June 1997) and Paris's Théâtre Déjazet in 1998 (3 November) with with Marion Sylvestre (Marguerite), Jean-François Vinciguerra (Valentin) and Thomas Morris (Faust).

In December 1900 the show's music was used to compile a ballet, *Faust à l'Olympe,* produced by the Isola brothers at Paris's Olympia Music-Hall, with Émilienne d'Alençon (Marguerite) and Jane Thylda (Méphisto) featured, but the record for enterprise must go to the theatre in Besançon which, in 1873, played in one evening—with the same scenery and cast—both Gounod's opera of *Faust* and the whole of *Le Petit Faust.*

UK: Lyceum Theatre *Little Faust* 18 April 1870, Alhambra Theatre *Mefistofele II* 20 December 1880; Austria: Theater an der Wien *Doktor Faust junior* 4 May 1870; USA: Kelly and Leon's Opera House *Le Petit Faust* 15 February 1870; Olympic Theater, *Little Faust* 22 August, Grand Opera House (Fr) 26 September 1870; Hungary: Budai Színkör *Kis Faust* 10 June 1871; Germany: Friedrich-Wilhelmstädtisches Theater 30 June 1871; Australia: Opera House, Melbourne 15 February 1875

Recordings: complete (Clio, Rare Recorded Editions)

PETRÁSS, Sári [Gabrielle] (b Budapest, 5 November 1888; d Sainte-Anne, Belgium, 7 September 1930). Hungarian musical star of five countries' stages.

A niece of Hungary's internationally famous musical star, Ilka Pálmay, Sári Petráss began what was to be a similarly international career as a teenager when she appeared at Budapest's Vígszínház in Offenbach's *Ancsi sír, Jancsi nevet* (*Jeanne qui pleure et Jean qui rit*). She played at the Népszínház in the musicals *Két Hippolit* (Nanett), *Sportlovagok* (Böske), *Külteleki hercegnő* (Willibald), in Izsó Barna's *A mádi zsidó* (Evike) and Jenő Sztojanovits's *Papa lánya,* then moved on in 1907 to the Király Színház, where, over the following years, she appeared as the original Hungarian Helene in Straus's *Ein Walzertraum,* in the British *Hollandi-lány* (*Miss Hook of Holland*), the American *A sogun* (*The Sho-Gun*), as *Die Dollarprinzessin,* Bronislawa in *Der Bettelstudent* and Angèle Didier in *Der Graf von Luxemburg* (1910) and where she also created the ingenue role of Lucy in Victor Jacobi's important *Leányvásár* (1911).

Petráss subsequently appeared in Vienna and in Berlin, where she made a considerable success at the Neues Operettenhaus in *Die keusche Suzanne,* then moved on to Britain and to the management of George Edwardes for whom she played the romantic lead of Ilona (ex- Zorika) in *Gipsy Love* (1912) and her original role in his production of *Marriage Market* (*Leányvásár*). Edwardes described her prior to her British debut as "a personality that fascinates you at once. She is not a great singer, but her phrasing is perfect. She speaks English well. She is quiet, demure, an Edna May with differences." And, I suspect, with rather more singing talent.

Petráss returned to Hungary to star as Helena in *Polenblut* at the Király Színház before going on her travels again, this time to America. There she starred in the American version of the Hungarian operett *Zsuzsi kisasszony* entitled *Miss Springtime* (1916, Rószika Wenzel), and in Oscar Straus's *The Beautiful Unknown* (1917) pre-Broadway. She was replaced before it moved to Broadway and flopped as *My Lady's Glove.* She was seen again in London when she appeared as Sylva Varescu in *The Gipsy Princess* at the Prince of Wales Theatre in 1921, then back in Hungary, where she created the role of Őrzse in Szirmai's *Mezeskalacs* (1923) and played, amongst others, the title role in *Marinka a táncosnő* (*Katja die Tänzerin,* 1923), in Jacobi's posthumous *Miami* (1925), in *Hamburgi menyasszony* (1926) and as Anna Barothy in *Cigánykirály* (Városi Színház, 1927). In 1930 she was drowned in the River Scheldt, in Belgium, in a motoring accident, at the age of 41.

Petráss's second husband was the British vocalist Gordon Crocker.

PFINGSTEN IN FLORENZ Operette in 3 acts by Richard Genée and Julius Riegen. Music by Alfons Czibulka. Theater an der Wien, Vienna, 20 December 1884.

The most generally successful of Czibulka's stage works, *Pfingsten in Florenz* was produced at the Theater an der Wien under the management of Camillo Walzel. Girardi was cast as Fra Bombardo, the dictator of the 16th-century republic of Florence, and Ottilie Collin was Rita, the daughter of the fur merchant Aldo Castrucci (Rotter) and his wife, Perpetua (Katharina Herzog), on whom he casts his nasty potentate's eye. Marie Theresia Massa got into breeches to play the young Angelo Malanotti, a sculptor (and, thus, inevitably a goodie), whilst Karl Blasel as the letter-writer Sparacani and Carl Lindau as the physician Lorenzi shared the comicalities.

Pfingsten in Florenz was played 31 times at the Theater an der Wien before moving on to productions in Prague, Bremen, Dresden, Budapest, Berlin and, most notably, in America (ad Sydney Rosenfeld, Leo Goldmark). For the Casino Theater's production the heroine grew from being Rita to being Amorita and, as played by ex-English chorine, soon-to-be-authoress Madeleine Lucette, gave her name to the English version as its title. Frank H Celli was Bombardo, alongside Francis Wilson (Castrucci), W H Fitzgerald (Sparacani) and Pauline Hall (Angelo), for a run of three months, prior to a McCaull

Plate 306a. **The Phantom of the Opéra** *goes Japanese.*

tour. Pauline Hall took the show on the road with her own company in 1890, and *Amorita* found itself a long series of repertoire and summer season productions around America thereafter.

Germany: Residenztheater, Dresden 15 February 1885, Walhalla-Theater 9 April 1887; USA: Casino Theater *Amorita* 16 November 1885; Hungary: *Punközd Florenzben* 27 February 1886, Budai Színkör 5 May 1886

THE PHANTOM OF THE OPÉRA Musical in a prologue and 2 acts by Andrew Lloyd Webber and Richard Stilgoe based on the novel by Gaston Leroux. Lyrics by Charles Hart. Music by Andrew Lloyd Webber. Her Majesty's Theatre, London, 9 October 1986.

Following the remarkable success of the youth-orientated spectacle of *Starlight Express,* composer Lloyd Webber changed direction thoroughly for his next stage work and entered the realm of the romantic melodrama. The impetus for this change in direction was given by a production of a stage adaptation of *Le Fantôme de l'Opéra,* Gaston Leroux's famous and much-filmed novel, written by Ken Hill, the author of a long list of happy musical plays for the British stage, illustrated by a pasticcio opera score and produced at London's suburban Theatre Royal, Stratford East. Lloyd Webber's original thought was to have his production company mount a piece on similar lines as a vehicle for his then wife, Sarah Brightman, in whom he thought he discerned operatic possibilities, but, as the project advanced, the idea of a pasticcio score was abandoned and Lloyd Webber decided to compose original music for the piece.

Christine Daäé (Miss Brightman), a chorister at the Paris Opéra, receives inspiration and vocal coaching from an unseen ''spirit'' voice, which she superstitiously believes to be that of the angel of music promised to her as a guardian by her dying father. The voice, however, is that of the Phantom of the Opéra (Michael Crawford), a horribly disfigured genius who has made his home deep in the sous-sols of the Opéra building and who has fallen in love with the young woman and her voice. He blackmails and frightens the lessees of the theatre (John Savident, David Firth) into giving her leading roles at the expense of their prima donna, Carlotta (Rosemary Ashe), and into producing an unconventional opera, *Don Juan Triumphant,* which he has written for her. He cannot, however, support Christine's love for the young Raoul de Chagny (Steve Barton), and tragedy threatens to engulf both the lovers and the theatre as a result of his jealousy. But when the young aristocrat pursues the Phantom and the captured Christine to his underground home, it proves

Plate 306b.

that the anguished man is ultimately unable to harm the girl and the one she loves.

The score of the piece produced Lloyd Webber's lushest and most romantic music to date, from which three of the principal numbers, ''The Phantom of the Opéra,'' Raoul and Christine's duet ''All I Ask of You'' and the Phantom's monologue ''Music of the Night,'' all made their way into the top 10 of the hit parades. Alongside these pieces were ranged a series of operatic parodies, the Meyerbeerish opera *Hannibal,* with its coloratura excrescences, the classical Italianate *Il Muto,* which the Phantom's tricks turn into Carlotta's downfall, and the Phantom's own intermittently ''difficult'' *Don Juan Triumphant,* which moves into the climactic, non-operatic duet between the Phantom and Christine (''Past the Point of No Return''). The score also included some vocal ensemble music of a kind and a quality rarely attempted in the postwar musical theatre (''Prima Donna'').

Unable to occupy Lloyd Webber's own theatre, the Palace, which had been leased to the unexpectedly (to some) long-running *Les Misérables,* the Cameron Mackintosh/Really Useful Company production was mounted instead at the slightly undersized (for profitability) Her Majesty's Theatre. Staged with all the colorful romanticism of the 19th-century stage that its text and music encouraged, with a sea of candelabra rising from the stage to light the Phantom and Christine on their journey through the sewers of Paris to the Phantom's home, and the auditorium's central chandelier tumbling to the stage at the Phantom's command, *The Phantom of the Opéra* proved a triumphant London success and settled in for a long and, a decade and more later, still-continuing run. Crawford and Miss Brightman repeated their roles when the piece was produced, with equivalent success and longevity, on Broadway in 1988, and subsequently appeared at the head of the Los Angeles company as *The Phantom of the Opéra* went on to its earliest foreign-language productions at Vienna's Theater an der Wien, with Alexander Goebel and Luzia Nistler featured in the leading roles, in Japan, in Australia (with ex-Australian Opera baritone Anthony Warlowe as the Phantom) and in Hamburg, where operatic vocalist Peter Hoffmann starred initially as the most Wagnerian Phantom to date. In each and every venue the show proved a major hit.

In the wake of the success of the show, Ken Hill's much less elaborate version won further productions in Britain, including an ill-judged West End season in opposition to the sellout Her Majesty's Theatre production, in America and around the Continent (including a visit to Paris's Salle Favart in 1992), whilst a number of other writers jumped swiftly on to the non-copyright Leroux tale, turning out shows under the same or very similar titles in a despairing-seeming copycat manner of a kind that had not been seen in the professional theatre for decades. Several American musicalizations of *The Phantom of the Opéra* tale were launched, including a pasticcio piece initiated at Akron's Carousel Dinner Theater in 1989, a version played at Texas's Theatre Under the Stars (*Phantom* 31 January 1991) with the Broadway-proven names of composer Maury Yeston and author Arthur Kopit attached to it, and another at Miami Beach's Al Hirschfeld Theater (Paul Schierhorn, Lawrence Rosen/ Bruce Falstein, Stan Barber 5 February 1990). All went on to further sites, but none, any more than the original Hill piece, proved likely to be genuinely mistaken for the show that was filling houses across a handful of continents.

A more pleasant ''tribute'' came from the Tiroler Theater, Innsbrück, who instead of copycatting, burlesqued the original tale in good 19th-century fashion in *Das Phantom der Operette, oder Wer hat die Diva erwügt* (6 May 1995). Roberta Cunningham played Christine Nachtigall von Trappsen and Dale Albright was Ekkehard XIV, Graf Broncho von Lungenfels aka Das Phantom. The score was made up of 19th-century Operette music, including three pieces of *The Pirates of Penzance* and the Gavotte from *The Gondoliers.*

USA: Majestic Theater 26 January 1988; Austria: Theater an der Wien 20 December 1988; Australia: Princess Theatre, Melbourne 1990; Germany: Neue Flora-Theater, Hamburg *Das Phantom der Opera* 29 June 1990

Recordings: original cast (Polydor), Austrian cast (Polydor), German cast (Polydor), Japanese cast (Pony Canyon), Canadian cast (Polydor), Netherlands cast (Polydor), Swedish cast (Polydor), Swiss cast (Polydor), studio cast (TER), etc

Literature: Perry, G: *The Complete ''Phantom of the Opera''* (Pavilion, London, 1987)

PHILIPP, Adolf (b Lübeck, 29 January 1864; d New York, 30 July 1936). Eclectic leading light of the German-language stage in turn-of-the-century America.

The young Adolf Philipp ran away from home at the age of 17 (when he remembered, he said it was 14), joined a German provincial stock company and went on to make himself a career as a performer in both straight and musical theatre (''sometimes as a tenor singer, sometimes as a heavy tragedian, but mostly in light comedy''). This career led him first to Vienna, then to Hamburg and, in the 1891–92 season, to New York for an engagement as principal tenor at Gustav Amberg's German-language theatre (Duncan in Adolf von Neuendorff's original operetta *Der Minstrel* 18 May 1892, etc). Following Amberg's collapse, he went on to star in other German pieces at the Terrace Garten and quickly became a local star in roles such as Vandergold in *Der arme Jonathan,* the hero of Carl Zeller's *Der Vagabund,* Simon in *Der Bettelstudent,* Georg in *Der Waffenschmied,* in *Nanon, Der Feldprediger, Apajune der Wassermann,* the title role of *Le Postillon de Longjumeau,* his own *Die Royalisten* and *Der verwunschene Prinz.* In September 1893 he took on the management of the Germania Theater, and there he embarked on a memorable career as manager, star and author, writing and appearing in the large central roles of a series of often long-running German-Jewish comedies (''written in a queer composite of English slang and true German''), each and all equipped with plenty of songs for their leading man. This series gained him in some quarters the nickname of ''the German Harrigan'' (''His stage productions put one in mind of a Harrigan play with the locale transferred''), and his *The Corner Grocer of Avenue A* (Hein Snut, 750 performances) and *A New York Brewer* (Hein Lemkuhl, 856 performances) became classics of the German-American stage.

Philipp gained his first mainstream Broadway credit, when the hugely popular *The Corner Grocer* was anglicized, stuck full of variety acts (''music selected and arranged by Alexander Haig'') and mounted by Russell's Comedians at the Casino Theater under the title *About Town.* Jacques Kruger starred in the author's role for the three weeks of the run. In 1896 he was again represented on the Broadway stage by an English adaptation of his *Mein New York* (Herald Square Theater 14 April) and won considerable praise for his ''beautifully conceived'' piece. ''By adroit handling of his characters the author gives us something of the same impression of largeness and reality which Harrigan's genius used to contrive as a study of familiar American types. Mr Philipp's play cannot be too highly praised [. . .] there is a scene in a fast-house which the author treats with the skill and hardihood of a Zola.''

In 1897 he staged a season (w Leo von Raven) at the Terrace-Garten, appearing in the title role in *Fra Diavolo,* in a German version of Herbert's *The Wizard of the Nile* (19 May 1897) and in *Die Royalisten,* and in 1899 he built a new Arch Street Theater in Philadelphia, which eventually fell into other hands.

In 1900 (23 April), having—after a barney with theatre-owner Amberg that resulted in his being arrested—purchased the Germania on the proceeds of his successes, he produced a set of musical comedies for which he acted as producer, director, overwhelming star, author and co-composer. *Geheimnisse von New York* (played Jochen Kluckhuhn) ran for 102 performances, *Der Millionen-Schwab* for 104 and the musical comedy *Der Kartoffelkönig,* which, half a century before *The King and I,* used a play-within-a-play *Uncle Tom's Cabin* to make a point, equaled their records, records that—in spite of the obviously limited audience pool on which Philipp had to draw—compared well with on-Broadway's productions. The advised press kept an appreciative eye on what was going on at the Germania and put their appreciation into print. Philipp's comic abilities won high praise as being ''above the usual Broadway horseplay,'' and his music was noticed as ''uncommonly good, often excellent,'' but for the moment his original and idiosyncratic productions did not flow into the Broadway mainstream.

The Germania was closed and knocked down in April 1902, to allow for the extension of the subway and the building of Wanamaker's department store, and Philipp—having bankrupted himself attempting to tour—then returned temporarily to Germany. There, with his brother Paul Philipp (d New York, 21 May 1923) as administrator, himself as artistic director and Oberregisseur and one Ludwig Stein providing the necessary, he opened the 1,000-seater Deutsch-Amerikanische Theater in Berlin (29 August 1903). There, between 1903 and 1907 he staged and starred in a variety of pieces depicting the lives of German immigrants in America, nearly all with more (usually) or less music involved and including his own *New York in Wort und Bild, Im wilden Westen* (in which he appeared as a Crocodile Dundeeish cowboy in Berlin), *Der Teufel ist los* (as Heinrich Dabelstein), *Im Lande der Freiheit, Aber, Herr Herzog!* (Lied des schwarzen Katze) and *Er und ich.* His recipe was ''a potpourri of fun with touches of pathos sandwiched in,'' not to forget the inevitable ration of songs. In February 1906, with some small fanfare, he feted his 25 years on the stage. In mid-1907, however, after a rather iffy season with their troupe at the Carl-Schultze Theater in Hamburg, the brothers threw in their hand and returned to America, where they again attempted a Deutsch-Amerikanische Theater, this time in collaboration with the finances of a certain Herr Adolf Geller, manager of the ''zum schwarzen Adler'' music hall on East 86th and 3rd Avenue.

Philipp mounted an English-language production of his *New York in Wort und Bild,* already played not only in Berlin, where it topped four hundred nights, but also in a Viennese version as *Uber'n grossen Teich* (Theater an der Wien 2 September 1906, mus: Ziegler), under the title *From Across the Big Pond* (w Mortimer Theise, Circle Theater 7 September 1907, revised version *Two Islands* 14 October) with himself starred as Louis Strumkohl alongside Anna Boyd, and without luck, but he scored a genuine hit at Geller's ''zum schwarzen Adler'' (now converted into a 900-seater and dubbed ''Wintergarten'') when, after a long-running revival of *Der Corner Grocer* he wrote and produced the slightly scandalous musical comedy *Alma, wo wohnst du?* (1909, credited ''w Paul Hervé and Jean Briquet''). This piece gave him a long run as author and star, got him hauled up on a delightfully publicity-worthy morals charge and was subsequently translated into English and produced with further success on the regular Broadway stage (Weber's Theater, New York 26 September 1910, 232 performances). However, if he got away with his ''naughtinesses'' this time, when he subsequently produced *Hetty macht alles* the guardians of New York's morality decided he had gone too far, the proprietor and star were hauled off to the police courts and the merry musical farce was closed down. They got them for selling alcohol in the auditorium, too. *Hetty* was anglicized by Leon da Costa in 1915 as *That's the Limit,* and apparently she was the limit, for I can find no record of her having found her saucy way back to the New York stage. Still, she got to the Grand, Pennsylvania, to the Lyceum, Rochester, and elsewhere (April 1911), where limits and drinking rules were apparently different.

The success of *Alma,* however, widened Philipp's horizons, and his new piece, *Therese sei nicht böse* (daintily translated as *Therese, Be Mine*), was actually put into rehearsal shortly before *Alma*'s Broadway opening in both German and English versions. The ubiquitous Adolf, of course, directed both companies, and starred in the German one. And while *Therese* opened up at New York's Wintergarten, *Theresa* set out from Toledo, Ohio, to install herself at the Chicago Opera House (27 September 1910). It didn't prove as successful as *Alma* had, but Philipp persisted, and whilst *Alma* still ran on Broadway he brought out *Hetty.* That show's fate didn't deter him either, and in 1912 Philipp established himself as The Adolf Philipp Company, headquartered at the newly built 500-seat 57th Street Theater (later to be better known as the Bandbox), and carried on turning out more musical plays in the *Alma* vein, both in German and for the more competitive English field.

His first production at his new house, the musical *Auction Pinochle,* with its author starring as Harry Schlesinger, played for 150 nights before being sent out in an anglicized version (Burbank Theater, Los Angeles 5 April 1914). It was followed by *Das Mitternachtsmädel,* another piece that was written, like the first, in collaboration with composer ''Jean Briquet'' and original author ''Paul Hervé.'' Both these gentlemen may have existed—perhaps minor figures on the Paris and Berlin theatre scene—but their names served here only to mask the fact that the producer-author-star had written and composed his shows single-handedly. He kept his triple identity secret for some five years before being discovered, and going confessionally into print, at the end of 1915. As *Alma* had done, *The Midnight Girl* shifted to Broadway, and there, under the management of the Shubert brothers and with George Macfarlane starred, it notched up a splendid run of 104 performances (44th Street Theater 23 February 1914) before going on to the rest of the country.

Philipp mounted and starred in a German-language revival of *Alma* (17 April 1913), followed up with another local-comic musical, *Two Lots in the Bronx,* which proved good for one hundred nights in German and more in English, and served the author-producer for his debut in the English-speaking and singing theatre. Then, without previous German production, he brought what he again tried to fool public and press was ''a French operetta'' (though again homemade with the English aid of the usefully hacking Edward Paulton), called *Adele,* to the Longacre. *Adele* set Broadway aghast—it had no girlie chorus! But the girls clearly weren't missed, for *Adele,* praised thoroughly for its ''beautiful music,'' not only ran 196 performances on Broadway before going to the country for a good number of tours, but even crossed the Atlantic and was given a brief production at London's famed Gaiety Theatre. London, however, hadn't yet learned to cope with the small-scale book-based musical, especially without chorus girls. Especially at the Gaiety. *Adele* was a short-lived West End failure.

At home, however, Philipp's style of show, genuine small-theatre musical comedies in the German Posse vein, without spectacle or (mostly) chorus girls, and the attention firmly fixed on the action, the comedy and the songs, had proven itself undeniably popular, and it was no coincidence that it was soon after followed by a local attempt in a similar vein (but with chorus girls) in a popular handful of shows at Broadway's little Princess Theater.

Philipp subsequently joined Saul Rechmann in running the Yorkville Theater as a home for German-language plays and musicals (*Wie einst im Mai, Die schöne vom Strande,* etc) and, with the coming of the First World War, authored (under an umpteenth pseudonym, ''F Schumacher'') and mounted a typically outspoken play called *Zabern,* which provoked the German ambassador in New York to demand its closure as being insulting to Kaiser Wilhelm II. He also authored, produced and starred in a patriotic American comedy-drama called *Tell It to the Marines,* whilst continuing with his run of allegedly adapted musicals. *The Girl Who Smiles* topped the one-hundred-performance mark, but *Two Is Company* was a 29-performance failure. *Mimi,* yet another piece built on the lines of *Alma* and produced in Washington with the equally fake-French Chapine (real name: Helen Benedeck) starred, failed to make it to town in its original production, but Philipp's play was adapted and remusicked by another specialist of the book-based comedy musical, composer Ivan Caryll, and George Hobart, and the result was later produced in New York as *Kissing Time* (Lyric Theater 11 October 1920).

Although he thereafter went quiet on the musical front, Philipp did not remain inactive. The intriguingly titled play *Tin Pajamas* (w Paulton) closed on the road but, having insulted the Kaiser in the First World War, in 1933 this up-front Jewish author turned out, as his last Broadway effort, a very early anti-Hitler play, *Kultur.* Then he finally went into retirement. He died in New York at the age of 72.

An accurate list of Philipp's early German credits is hard to establish, as a second Adolf Philipp was, like him, operating out of Hamburg around the same time as the semi-American one was authoring his earliest Operetten. However, his claim of ''hundreds of performances'' in Germany make it likely—even allowing for his penchant for fibbing about his identity and fictionalizing his curriculum vitae—that he was the author of the musical shows listed below. As opposed to ''*Kleopatra* by Adolf A Philipp,'' et al.

1885 **Die Brieftaube** (Karl Stix) Klagenfurt 21 January

1888 **Die Royalisten** (Josef Manas) Braunschweig 19 July; Terrace-Garten, New York 8 June 1893

1889 **Der Abenteuerer** (Stix/w Emil Sondermann) Carl-Schultze Theater, Hamburg 14 September

1892 **Der arme Edelmann** (Aurel Donndorf/w Sondermann) Carl-Schultze Theater, Hamburg 29 November

1893 **Der Corner Grocer von Avenue A** (Karl von Wegern) Germania Theater 19 October

1893 **About Town** Chicago Opera House 25 December; Casino Theater 26 February 1894

1894 **Der Pawnbroker von der East Side** (von Wegern) Germania Theater 1 March

1894 **Doktor Darkhorst** Germania Theater 30 April

189- **Mein New York** Germania Theater

1895 **Der New Yorker Brauer und seine Familie** Germania Theater 15 September

1896 **Der Butcher aus der erste Avenue** Germania Theater 17 April

1897 **Klein Deutschland** Germania Theater 10 February

1897 **Dollars and Cents** Germania Theater 29 September

1898 **A Day in Manila** Germania Theater (von Wegern) 6 October

189- **New York in Wort und Bild**

189- **The Landlady**

189- **New York bei Nacht**

189- **Die Reise nach America**

1900 **Geheimnisse von New York** Germania Theater 15 September

1900 **Der Millionen-Schwab** Germania Theater 25 December

1901 **Der Kartoffelkönig** (w Edward A Weber) Germania Theater 19 April

1901 **Im Lande der Freiheit** Germania Theater 21 September

1901 **Der Teufel ist los** (w Edward A Weber) Germania Theater 31 December

1903 **Uber'n grossen Teich** (*Der New York Brauer*) Deutsch-Amerikanische Theater, Berlin 29 August

1904 **New York** Deutsch-Amerikanische Theater, Berlin 22 November

1905 **Aber, Herr Herzog!** Deutsch-Amerikanische Theater, Berlin 2 September

1906 **Im wilden Westen** Deutsch-Amerikanische Theater, Berlin 23 October

1906 **Der Sorgenbrecher** Deutsch-Amerikanische Theater, Berlin 22 December

1909 **Alma, wo wohnst du?** Wintergarten ''zum schwarzen Adler'' 25 October

1910 **Therese, sei nicht böse** Wintergarten ''zum schwarzen Adler'' 1 September

1911 **Hetty macht alles** Wintergarten ''zum schwarzen Adler'' 14 January

1912 **Das Mitternachtsmädel** Adolf Philipp's 57th Street Theater 1 September

1912 **Auction Pinochle** Adolf Philipp's 57th Street Theater 12 November

1913 **Adele** (Edward Paulton/w Paulton) Longacre Theater 28 August

1913 **Two Lots in the Bronx** (Paulton/w Paulton) Adolf Philipp's 57th Street Theater 27 November

1914 **The Midnight Girl** English version w Paulton 44th Street Theater 23 February

1915 **The Girl Who Smiles** (Paulton/w Paulton) Lyric Theatre 9 August

1915 **Two Is Company** (Paulton/w Paulton) Lyric Theater 22 September

1918 **Oh Emilie!** Yorkville Theater 9 March

1920 **Mimi** (w Frank E Tours/Paulton/w Paulton) Shubert Belasco Theater, Washington, DC 13 March

Plate 307. **Phi-Phi.** *A 1980 version of the 1918 opérette which seems a little more ''dressed'' than the original.*

Other title credited: *The Masked Marvel* (1916)

PHI-PHI Opérette legère in 3 acts by Albert Willemetz and Fabien Sollar. Music by Henri Christiné. Théâtre des Bouffes-Parisiens, Paris, 12 November 1918.

Although it was not the first small-scale modern musical comedy to visit the Paris stage of the 1910s (Barde and Cuvillier and the Théâtre des Capucines had been at it for years), *Phi-Phi* is generally accepted as the landmark show that launched the postwar craze for small-scale, snappily up-to-date, dance-melodied musical comedy in the French theatre. Once again, as with *Midas, Olympic Revels, Orphée aux enfers, Die schöne Galathee* and *Thespis,* the (almost) infallible classical burlesque turned up in an important position in theatre history. In many ways, *Phi-Phi* was indeed the Jazz Age equivalent of an *Orphée aux enfers* or a *Die schöne Galathee,* for it used its ostensibly ancient Greek story as an often anachronistic vehicle for witty modern chat and the comical portraying of current (and, of course, eternal) social mores and preoccupations, most particularly and naturally sexual ones. Like the earlier pieces, it also decorated its comical tale with the popular light music of the moment but, whereas for the older shows that meant waltzes and galops, in 1918 the fashion called for the fox-trot, the one-step and waltzes of a rather different flavor from those of half a century earlier.

Initially intended for production at Gustave Quinson's 210-seat, underground Théâtre de l'Abri, *Phi-Phi* was written on an economical scale: six principals, eight chorus girls, two dancers and a small band. The chief comic role was that of Phi-Phi (Urban), otherwise that ancient Greek marble chipper Phidias, who picks up and brings home an ostensibly virginal little lass called Aspasie (Alice Cocéa) to serve as the model for ''Virtue'' in his new statue. He also has other designs for her, which his wife (Pierrette Madd) would be more concentrated on dampening down were she herself not involved in sort of dissuading the attentions of a beautiful young man named Ardimédon (Ferréal), who has followed her home from the Portes de Trézène. Ardimédon's presence chez Phidias is justified when—after a quick strip-off (oh, yes) audition—he is chosen to model for ''Love'' in the group statue. Chlamyses and stolai drop with more ease than sex-farcical pants and frocks in a fury of Greek-French comic action, but, of course, in the end Phi-Phi has to share Aspasie (who, as our history books tell us, was no virgin but a particularly skilled street-walker) with his patron, Péricles. A ménage à cinq on the best French (and probably Greek) principles (husband, wife, his mistress, her young lover, mistress's wealthy protector) brings down the curtain. The sixth character of the play was the traditional comic servant (Dréan), who managed to get mixed up with most of the plot without indulging in anything more immoral than a touch of pandering, a lot of gambling and a little unsecured ''borrowing.''

Christiné's sparkling score to this sparkling little tale (a tale that certainly in some of its principles recalled Auguste Germain's *Phryne* of a decade earlier) was arguably the gayest, most dazzling shower of music to have decorated a French opérette since the early days of Offenbach. Phi-Phi himself gurgled rhapsodically over Aspasie's charms in general (''C'est une gamine charmante'') and over her breasts in particular (Chanson des petits païens), whilst the lady in question waltzed through a catalogue of all the lines she'd ever been spun (''Je connais toutes les historiettes''), gasped out an innocent introduction to Péricles (''Ah! cher monsieur!''), justified the importance of a good wardrobe for a woman with ambition (''Bien chapeautée'') and got topical in a description of newspaper novelettes in a number in which Douglas Fairbanks and Mabel Normand got a mention. Madame Phidias, determined herself to model for ''Virtue'' rather than let the wench do so, presented her naked (oh, yes, again) self in a mock operatic Prayer to Pallas, comically described her pursuit by Ardimédon (''J'sortais des portes de Trézène''), waltzed through her seduction in duo with her seducer (''Ah! Tais-toi''), then looked back on it all over again (Duo des souvenirs), whilst her young man joined in the duets and also in the delicious ensembles and finales that completed an 18-number score.

Quinson's production, ultimately shifted from the Abri to the larger Théâtre des Bouffes-Parisiens when that stage went suddenly vacant, proved at first a fair and then—in the celebratory days of ''la victoire''—a huge success. Although he removed it, at one stage, from the Bouffes and sublet the show to Alphonse Franck at the Théâtre Édouard VII, in order to mount another piece, the producer quickly realized his error and hastened the hit-like-no-other little musical back to its original home, as the revue writers acclaimed it in the only way they knew how, by parodying it and its title in such pieces as the Concert Mayol's *Phi-Fi-Fi-Tie* (Jules Bastin/Gibet, Devere). *Phi-Phi* passed its 1,000th performance on 24 January 1921, and it ran on for a further three months before being finally replaced. That replacement was, however, again temporary, and a little more than a month later *Phi-Phi* was back for a second run, and the following year for a third. In 1933 and then, in the wake of the Second War as of the First, in 1947, Urban again appeared on the Paris stage as Phi-Phi, and the Bouffes continued thereafter to host regular fresh productions (1949, 1957, 1980, 1983) of a piece whose delights and tidy proportions made it a practical proposition even in a French commercial theatre that had largely renounced anything but mega-spectacular opérette productions. Most recently, a rather battered version (with a program full of directorial apologies for doing anything so base as producing a musical comedy) was seen at Paris's Nouveau Théâtre Mouffetard in 1989 (31 October), whilst almost every season brings further *Phi-Phi*s (nudity not obligatory) in the French provinces.

If *Phi-Phi* were the rage of the French stage in the years following the war, its export possibilities were, however, quite clearly very limited. How did one translate Willemetz and Sollar's pun-spiked dialogue? And if one could, how would the theatregoers and critics of certain other nationalities react to the bright blue content of the piece? Not to mention all that nudity (male and female). The British, who had already massacred Barde's much less demanding *Son p'tit frère* in the name of ''decency,'' needless to say, cowered out. C B Cochran produced a piece called *Phi-Phi,* but it was unrecognizable. The story (Fred Thompson, Clifford Grey) was altered, the characters were altered, the lyrics were thrown out, the tunes that were left were given to the wrong voices and the score was larded with interpolations by Herman Darewski (''Beautiful Greece,'' ''There's Another One Gone,'' ''The Chicken''), Nat D Ayer and Cole Porter (''The Ragtime Pipes of Pan''), as well as a quintet and a trio by Chantrier, a ballet by Dvořák and a dance by Eugene Goossens. Evelyn Laye, Clifton Webb, Arthur Roberts, Stanley Lupino and June held up a mediocre show that was not *Phi-Phi* for 132 performances.

In America, things went even worse. The Shuberts' production of a version by Glen MacDonough and Harry Wagstaffe Gribble, which featured Frances White as Miss Myrtle Mink, alias Aspasia, and Frank Lalor as Abel Carver (get it?), otherwise Phidias, did not even make it to Broadway. It was perhaps just as well, as the adaptors and lyricist E Ray Goetz had had a fine time with the original, sticking on a prologue and an epilogue, bringing Venus (in a Greek setting? Where did they go to school?) into the proceedings, and generally shuffling the work up alarmingly. Only one piece of music, a ballet-pantomime in Act III, was credited to musical director Arthur H Guttman, but Christiné's melodies had been made to do work other than that for which they were intended.

Hungary's Jenő Heltai did a better job of adaptation than his English-speaking colleagues, and Budapest's *Fi-Fi,* as produced at the Lujza Blaha Színház with Hanna Honthy starried, was a great success. In a city that reveled in the product of the French Jazz Age stage throughout its decade and a bit of prominence, the show ran for more than two hundred performances and earned a revival at the Király Színház in 1930. *Phi-Phi* also, apparently, reached Germany, where it left a sufficient mark to be revived in a new German version (ad Walter Brandin, Artur Maria Rabenalt), which was played at the Deutsches Theater, Munich in 1963–64.

A silent film version was released in 1927 with Georges Gauthier in the title role.

Germany: 1921?; Hungary: Lujza Blaha Színház *Fi-Fi* 7 October 1921; UK: London Pavilion 16 August 1922; USA: Globe Theater, Atlantic City ?1921/22

Film: (silent) Georges Pallu 1927

Recordings: complete (Decca), selections (EMI-Pathé, Westminster), etc

PICCALUGA, [Albert]

Baritone Piccaluga was whisked straight from his ''deuxième prix'' (only!) at the Conservatoire in October 1880 to take over in *Le Bois* at the Opéra-Comique, and he remained several years a member of the company there before turning to the commercial musical theatre. He made his first appearance on the musical-comedy stage at the Menus-Plaisirs in the role of Prince Doriando in a revised version of *Les Pommes d'or* in February 1883, and his fine voice and superior style swiftly won him an engagement at the Bouffes-Parisiens and leading roles in a long series of opérettes. His most successful creations, in a career covering more than 20 years, were the parts of lubricious Annibal de Tourendor with a passion for *Madame Boniface* (1883), the young painter, Paul, who sketches the bits of the inverted *Miss Helyett* (1890) that only a husband ought to see and the opera-singing hero Montosol in *Joséphine vendue par ses soeurs* (1893).

Piccaluga also appeared, amongst others, in the original productions of *La Dormeuse éveillée* (1883, Octave), *Le Diable au corps* (1884, Franz), *Pervenche* (1885), *Les Grenadiers de Mont-Cornette* (1887, Bel-Amour), *La Gamine de Paris* (1887, Romulus), the vaudeville *Le Microbe* (1887, Gustave), *Mam'zelle Crénom* (1888, Alexis), *Oscarine* (1888, Philibert), *La Vénus d'Arles* (1889, Prosper), *Le Mari de la reine* (1889, Florestan), *Cendrillonnette* (1890), *Sainte-Freya* (1892, Captain Ludwig), *Madame Suzette* (1893, William Robiquet), *Mam'zelle Carabin* (1893, Ferdinand), *Le Bonhomme de Neige* (1894, Dr Franz), *Ninette* (1896, Cyrano de Bergerac), *Le Petit Moujik* (1896, Fleury), *Mariage princier* (1900, Médéric), *Les Petites Vestales* (1900) and *La Bouquetière du Château d'Eau* (1902).

He also appeared in many of the classic baritone roles, notably several times as Brissac in *Les Mousquetaires au couvent*, as Athos in *Les Petits Mousquetaires* (1887, with an extra song composed by Varney for the occasion), as Favart, Roger in *Gillette de Narbonne* and Miguel in *Le Jour et la nuit*, as well as playing Frank Abercoed in the French production of *Florodora* (1903) and Duparquet (ie, Falke) in the belated French premiere of *La Chauve-souris*.

PICKWICK Musical in 2 acts by Wolf Mankowitz based on Charles Dickens's *Posthumous Papers of the Pickwick Club*. Lyrics by Leslie Bricusse. Music by Cyril Ornadel. Saville Theatre, London, 4 July 1963.

In the wake of the success of *Oliver!*, the works of Charles Dickens became ripe for rifling by musical writers. In this case it was a performer, the bulky Goon Show comedian-cum-tenor Harry Secombe, who conceived the idea of a musical *Pickwick Papers* built all the way around himself in the role of Samuel Pickwick. The idea was taken up by author Mankowitz and producer Bernard Delfont (later joined by Tom Arnold), with Leslie Bricusse and Cyril Ornadel, who had written pantomime songs for Secombe, allotted the music, and *Oliver!* director and designer, Peter Coe and Sean Kenny, hired for the making of more musical Dickens.

The text ran through the favorite Pickwick episodes—Mrs Bardell's (Jessie Evans) breach of promise suit, the Eatanswill election, the skating party, the Jingle and Rachel Wardle (Hilda Braid) business—in what one critic called ''comic-strip Dickens'' style, accompanied by some jolly songs, most of the best of which were not for the star. Sam Weller (Teddy Green) sang of how he could ''Talk'' his way out of things, and joined Tony Weller (Robin Wentworth) discoursing on ''The Trouble with Women,'' whilst Jingle (Anton Rodgers) described himself as ''A Bit of a Character'' and pattered through an enjoyably concerned ''Very.'' The most successful number, however, did fall to Secombe, tenoriously describing to the electors, in the Eatanswill scene, what he would do ''If I Ruled the World.'' The song ran 17 weeks in the top 20, the show for a year and a half (694 performances) in the West End. *Pickwick* subsequently got several provincial productions, and a less bulky Secombe returned to his role 30 years later in a production at Chichester's Festival Theatre.

David Merrick produced *Pickwick* for America, with Secombe and Rodgers repeating their roles alongside David Jones (Sam) and Charlotte Rae (Mrs Bardell), but, after a fine pre-Broadway season in which it recouped its entire investment, it failed in only 56 performances in New York.

Mr Pickwick was put fairly quickly to music after his appearance on the printed page. In 1842 Messrs George Soane (text) and G Le Jeune (music) put out a song cycle *Pickwick set to Music*, and over the years they had a series of followers. In 1889 a one-act musical called *Pickwick* (Edward Solomon/F C Burnand), which concentrated on the favorite Mrs Bardell episode, so often seen in John Hollingshead's sketch *Bardell v Pickwick* at the Gaiety (24 January 1871 sq), was produced at London's Comedy Theatre. Arthur Cecil (Pickwick), Lottie Venne (Mrs Bardell) and Rutland Barrington (Baker) featured in the first showing of a piece later played at the Trafalgar Square Theatre (13 December 1893) with C P Little, Jessie Bond and Charles Hawtrey, and also produced both in New Zealand (City Hall, Dunedin 18 September 1890) and in Australia.

Pickwick also got a showing on Broadway when De Wolf Hopper starred as a very tall and not at all plump *Mr Pickwick* (Herald Square Theater 19 January 1903) in a musical comedy written by the British-born (but Russian-parented and American resident) Klein brothers, and he was also operaticized by Albert Coates (BBC-TV 13 November 1936, Theatre Royal Covent Garden 23 November 1936).

USA: 46th Street Theater 4 October 1965

Recordings: original cast (Philips, WRC), Chichester revival (TER)

PICON, Molly (b New York, 28 February 1898; d Lancaster, Pa, 5 April 1992).

Molly Picon spent much of the first 40 years of her performing career playing in the Yiddish theatre, where she established herself as a considerable star, and she only subsequently turned to English-language and Broadway theatre. Although she had appeared in a number of original Yiddish musical pieces at the 2nd Avenue Theater and the Molly Picon Theater (*The Jolly Orphan* 1929, also lyrics, *The Kosher Widow* 1959, etc) and made her first regular Broadway appearance in 1940, her first musical part on Broadway was as Clara Weiss, the husbandless American tripper in Israel, in *Milk and Honey.* She scored a sizeable personal success in the role both on Broadway and on tour (1961–64). She later played briefly in the road-folding *Chu Chem* (1966) and in the musical *How to Be a Jewish Mother* (1967), toured in *Funny Girl* and in the title role of *Hello, Dolly!* (1970), and appeared in the film version of *Fiddler on the Roof* as the matchmaking Yente.

Autobiographies: w Rosenberg, E: *So Laugh a Little* (Messner, New York, 1962), w Bergantini, J: *Molly!* (Simon & Schuster, New York, 1980)

PIERNÉ, [Henri Constant] Gabriel (b Metz, 16 August 1863; d Ploujean, 17 July 1937).

As a student at the Paris Conservatoire, Pierné was the winner of the Prix de Rome of 1882. He subsequently became a celebrated conductor, notably at the head of the Concerts Colonne, and was the composer of a number of varied theatre pieces of which the earliest included the mimodrame *Le Docteur Blanc,* written to a livret by Catulle Mendès and produced at the Théâtre des Menus-Plaisirs in 1893, the spectacular ''fantaisie lyrique'' *Bouton d'or,* the pantomime *Salomé* (1895) and the incidental music to Rostand's *La Princesse lointaine* (1895) and *La Samaritaine* (1897).

His ''comédie-lyrique'' *La Fille du Tabarin* (1901), a version of Alfred de Musset's *On ne badine pas avec l'amour* (1910), the one-act opéra-comique adaptation of La Fontaine and Champmesle's *La Coupe enchantée* (1905, *Der Zauberbecher* Stuttgart 1907) and *Sophie Arnould* (1927), were all produced at the Opéra-Comique, but his one full-scale light lyric work for the commercial theatre, *Fragonard,* produced first in Belgium and then at Paris's Théâtre de la Porte-Saint-Martin, won more connoisseur's praise than performances. It was taken into the repertoire of the Opéra-Comique in 1946 for 18 performances.

Pierné also composed the ''impressive incidental music'' for Sarah Bernhardt's production of *Hamlet* (1899).

1893 **Bouton d'or** (Michel Carré) Nouveau Théâtre 4 January

1895 **La Coupe enchantée** (Emmanuel Matrat) 1 act Casino, Royan 24 August; Opéra-Comique, Paris 20 December 1905

1901 **La Fille du Tabarin** (Victorien Sardou, Paul Ferrier) Opéra-Comique 20 February

1910 **On ne badine pas avec l'amour** (Alfred de Musset ad Louis Leloir, Gabriel Nigond) Opéra-Comique 30 May

1927 **Sophie Arnould** (Nigond) 1 act Opéra-Comique 21 February

1933 **Fragonard** (André Rivoire, Romain Coolus) Théâtre de la Monnaie, Brussels nd; Théâtre de la Porte-Saint-Martin 16 October 1934

PIETRI, Giuseppe (b Sant' Ilario in Campo, Elba, 6 May 1886; d Milan, 11 August 1946). Composer of several of the most successful Italian operettas.

The young Pietri was sent to study in Milan under the patronage of an Elban music lover who had heard him playing the organ in the local church, and he made his debut as a composer in the theatre in 1910 with a one-act operatic scena, *Calendimaggio.* His first contribution to the light lyric stage came three years later, and his first significant success in 1915 with the score for the operetta *Addio giovinezza.* Pietri subsequently became one of the most popular Italian theatre composers, through further successes with such pieces as *L'acqua cheta* (1920), a musical version of de Flers and de Caillavet's play *Primerose* (*Primarosa,* 1926), and *Rompicollo* (1928), which became one of the few Italian musical shows to win a production outside Italy when it was played at Berlin's Theater des Volkes under the title *Das grosse Rennen* (27 November 1938, ad Rudolf Frank, Rolf Sievers).

He later turned back to operatic writing and had an opera, *Maristella,* produced with Benjimano Gigli in its leading role in 1934.

1913 **In Flemmerlandia** (Antonio Rubino) Teatro Fossati, Milan 24 September

1915 **Addio giovinezza** (Camasio, Oxilia) Politeama Goldoni, Livorno 20 January; Teatro Diana, Rome 20 April

1916 **Il Signore di Ruy Blas** Bologna

1917 **La Modella** (Antonio Lega) Teatro Quirino, Rome 29 January

1919 **La Lucciola** (Carlo Veneziani) Politeama Goldoni, Livorno 26 March

1920 **L'acqua cheta** (Angelo Nessi/Augusto Novelli) Teatro Nazionale, Rome 27 November

1922 **L'ascensione** (Novelli) Teatro della Pergola, Florence 17 May

1923 **Guarda, guarda la mostarda** (Giovanni Colonna di Cesaro) Teatro dei Piccoli 4 April

1923 **La donna perduta** (Guglielmo Zorzi, Guglielmo Giannini) Teatro degli Italiani 26 September

1924 **Quartetto vagabondo** Teatro Eliseo 4 December

1926 **Namba Zaim** (Veneziani) Teatro Lirico, Milan

1926 **Primarosa** (Carlo Lombardo, Renato Simoni) Teatro Lirico, Milan 29 October

1927 **Tuffolina** (Novelli) Politeama Genovese, Genoa 26 October

1928 **Rompicollo** (Luigi Bonelli, Ferdinando Paoleri) Teatro dal Verme 29 December

1929 **L'isola verde** (Lombardo, Bonelli) Teatro Lirico, Milan 16 October

1930 **Casa mia, casa mia** (Nessi, Novelli) Teatro Quirino, Rome 5 October

1930 **Gioconda Zapaterra** (Giulio Bucciolini) Teatro Alfieri, Florence 10 December

1931 **La dote di Jeannette** (Rossato) Teatro Principe 4 July

1932 **Vent' anni** (Bonelli) Teatro Quirino 2 April

Biography: Carli, R: *Giuseppi Pietri cantore dei goliardi* (Soc Ed Italiana Demetra, Livorno, 1955)

PIFF! PAFF! POUF! Musical cocktail in 2 acts by Stanislaus Stange. Lyrics by William Jerome. Music by Jean Schwartz. Casino Theater, New York, 2 April 1904.

Thomas Q Seabrooke appeared at the top of the bill for *Piff! Paff! Pouf!* as Mr Augustus Melon, a widower, anxious to tie a second knot with the widowed Mrs Montague (Alice Fischer). However, Melon's financial situation is precarious, as he inherits his late wife's fortune only if and when he has successfully married off his four daughters, Nora (Mabel Hollins), Cora (Grace Cameron), Encora (Hilda Hollins) and Rose (Frances Gibsone). Fortunately, there are pretendants at hand: chief comedian Eddie Foy as Peter Pouffle, British baritone Templar Saxe as Lord George Piffle, John Hyams as Macaroni Paffle, and a journalist with the alarmingly burlesquey name of Dick Daily (Harry Stuart).

Plate 308. **Molly Picon** *in a role in a Yiddish musical-comedy at Kessler's Second Avenue Theater.*

Stanislaus Stange's low-vaudevillesque book was illustrated by a score by successful songwriters Jean Schwartz and William Jerome from which Foy pulled out a jolly success as, aided by the Pony Ballet, he described himself as "The Ghost That Never Walked" ("Ghost of a troupe that disbanded in Peoria "), but out of which Seabrooke drew the most enduring number in "Cordalia Malone." Cordalia was represented as being the sister of "Bedelia," the heroine of the song that had won its writers their biggest ever hit, and if she didn't quite repeat her relative's success, she nevertheless proved popular both in America (the song was reused in *Glittering Gloria*) and in Britain, where she was interpolated into the Gaiety Theatre's *The Orchid.* Mabel Hollins tootsie-wootsied through "Under the Goo-Goo Tree," Miss Cameron contributed the topically showbizzy saga "Since Little Dolly Dimple's Made a Hit" and the Pony Ballet performed a "Radium Dance" with luminous frocks and skipping-ropes.

The whole made up an entertainment which drew happily through 264 performances on Broadway for producer Fred C Whitney, before going into the country.

The show's title—a common enough bit of onomatopoeic French for a volley of shot that had been highlighted in song from *Les Huguenots* to *La Grande-Duchesse de Gérolstein*—was used in Paris soon after as the title of Victor de Cottens and Victor Darlay's 1906 Châtelet Christmas spectacular (*Pif! Paf! Pouf!, ou un voyage endiablé* 6 December, mus: Marius Baggers).

PINERO, Arthur Wing (Sir) (b London, 24 May 1855; d London, 23 November 1934).

In a high-profile career as a playwright, initially of comedies and later of more serious dramatic works, Pinero was only once drawn into the musical theatre, when he collaborated with Arthur Sullivan and J Comyns Carr on a ''romantic musical drama'' for Richard D'Oyly Carte and the Savoy Theatre. The obtrusively uncomic opera *The Beauty Stone* was bundled out of the Savoy in 50 stretched performances.

Pinero, however, had a much more profitable connection with the musical stage when, with the coming to English-speaking stages of the equivalent of the French vaudeville—a coherent and often complex comedy with songs—not only established French comedies but also British ones, became the raw material for the musical plays of the day. The first such adaptation of a Pinero play came not in Britain but in Vienna, where his 1885 *The Magistrate* was made into a musical comedy by Heinz von Waldberg and A M Willner, music by Richard Heuberger, under the title *The Baby* (Carltheater 3 October 1909), but the most outstanding success amongst the morceaux of musicalized Pinero was *The Boy* (Adelphi Theatre 14 September 1917), a British version of the same play adapted by Fred Thompson with songs by Lionel Monckton and Howard Talbot. After its two-year London run, it appeared in America as *Good Morning, Judge*. An American musical of 1912, produced by George Lederer as *Mama's Baby Boy* (Lyric Theater, Philadelphia 29 April) and credited to Junie McCree as author, professed to be based on George Hobart's *Mrs Black Is Back,* but also followed much of Pinero's plot.

The success of *The Boy* prompted the same management to adapt the playwright's *In Chancery* (1884) as *Who's Hooper?* (ad Thompson, mus: Talbot, Ivor Novello, 13 September 1919), also with considerable success (349 performances), and Donald Calthrop to mount a version of *The Schoolmistress* under the title *My Nieces* (ad Percy Greenbank, mus: Talbot, Phil Braham, 19 August 1921) with slightly less. After this little splurge, there was a moratorium on Pinero for half a century until the fashion of book-strong shows returned. Michael Stewart, David Heneker and John Addison combined on a musical version of *The Amazons* (1893), produced at the Nottingham Playhouse (7 April 1971), and Julian Slade composed two Pinero pieces: *Trelawny* (Sadler's Wells 27 June 1972), a version of the author's more sentimental *Trelawny of the Wells* (1898), and a second *Schoolmistress* musical, *Out of Bounds* (Theatre Royal, Bristol 26 December 1973).

Early in his career, Pinero worked as a performer, and he was seen in the part of Fripperifoo in the Liverpool pantomime of *Sinbad* in 1875.

1898 **The Beauty Stone** (Arthur Sullivan/J Comyns Carr) Savoy Theatre 28 May

PINKIE AND THE FAIRIES Fairy play in 3 acts by W Graham Robertson. Music by Frederic Norton. Her Majesty's Theatre, London, 19 December 1908.

Robertson's enchantingly poetic little fantasy, first published in book form, found itself a stage production of an unlooked-for kind when Beerbohm Tree mounted it at Her Majesty's Theatre as a Christmas entertainment. It got an even more classy look when Ellen Terry decided that she would like to play one of the adult roles, and Tree cast several other established and coming names as the piece's other characters. Marie Löhr was a chatty, society Cinderella, Viola Tree a dozy Sleeping Beauty, Frederick Volpe and Augusta Havilland were the other two adults, while Stella Patrick Campbell played teenaged Molly, who is taken off to a fairy party by her two little cousins (Iris Hawkins, Philip Tonge). An 11-year-old named Hermione Gingold made her first stage appearance as a fairy herald, but when Montesole and McLeod sent out a touring company the following year she was promoted to the title role.

At a time when children's entertainments such as the very successful *Bluebell in Fairyland* were more inclined to be juvenile versions of adult shows, full of up-to-date songs and sentiments, *Pinkie* was a return to the fairyland of Victorian picture books, and it was much appreciated as such. Tree revived the show for a second Christmas, and it was subsequently seen in regular provincial productions for a number of years thereafter.

Australia: Metropolitan Theatre, Sydney 16 January 1955

THE PINK LADY Musical comedy in 3 acts by C M S McLellan based on *Le Satyre* by Georges Berr and Marcel Guillemaud. Music by Ivan Caryll. New Amsterdam Theater, New York, 13 March 1911.

A frequent visitor to France (where he had studied and where he kept a magnificent second home), the composer Caryll had also written from time to time for the Paris stage and, in his *S.A.R.,* had turned out the kind of substantial vaudeville/musical comedy fare that he could not give to his London employers at the Gaiety Theatre, where the shows had to be built around the stars and to the style of the house. When he quit London to settle and work in New York, it was this French style of piece, rather than the very much less coherent British kind, that he offered to a Broadway which itself had had only a very little experience of such thoroughly legitimate comedies with music. If the first of his contributions in such a style, *Marriage à la Carte,* had only an indifferent run, the second, *The Pink Lady,* a musicalized version of the Parisian farce *Le Satyre,* was a different proposition. It proved to be both a classy piece of work and a major hit and helped give an important impetus toward a better book content in local musicals.

Some light-fingered fellow has been on the loose in the Bois de Compiègne, snatching kisses and pinching bottoms, and he is all the talk at ''Le Joli Coucou'' restaurant, where the action of the first act of the play takes place. Lucien Garidel (William Elliott) comes there to have a last premarital fling with his mistress, Claudine (Hazel Dawn), but unfortunately for him his fiancée, Angèle (Alice Dovey), choses the ''Coucou'' to have a quiet lunch with Maurice d'Uzac (Craufurd Kent) on the very same day. Lucien pretends that Claudine is the wife of the antique dealer Dondidier (Frank Lalor), and is busy setting up this alibi when the Countess of Montanvert (Louise Kelley) is ''got'' by the hot-lipped ''satyr.'' She accuses Dondidier and calls the police, but all the ladies take the funny little chap's side and, as the events of the evening wind up to their climax, he finds himself a sudden celebrity. Amongst all the brouhaha, Lucien and Angèle are happily reunited and Claudine glides equally happily back into the demi-monde.

Caryll's score (five songs, three choruses, three concerted numbers, three finales, four duets) was as sparkling as the comedy, and its principal number, Claudine's richly romantic ''The Kiss Waltz,'' reintroduced in the last act as a duet with Angèle as ''My Beautiful Lady,'' turned out to be one of the biggest hits not only of the season but of the period. A second major hit came with the jaunty, tuneful ''By the Banks of the Saskatchewan,'' sung by two subsidiary characters (Flora Crosbie, Scott Welsh), whilst Dondidier, basking in his ''infamy,'' admitted his little escapades and also admitted ''I Like It!,'' and the ensembles were topped by a brilliantly babbling ensemble of accusation (''Donny Didn't, Donny Did'').

Klaw and Erlanger's production of *The Pink Lady* was a Broadway hit of the first order, playing 316 performances at the New Amsterdam before Charles Frohman took the entire company and production (with Jack Henderson replacing Elliott) across the Atlantic. London's production was as big a success as Broadway's had been, but unfortunately Klaw and Erlanger's economics did not work in the West End in the same way they did in New York, and even full houses at the undersized Globe Theatre could not keep the books buoyant. After 124 performances the London season was closed down and the company transported back to Broadway, where, a month after the last British performances, they reopened at the New Amsterdam Theater (26 August 1912) for a further 24 performances before taking to the road.

From there on, the show moved slowly but surely around the world. In 1917 J C Williamson produced *The Pink Lady* in Australia with Phil Smith (Dondidier), Minnie Love (Claudine) and Ethel Cadman (Angèle) starred through two months in Sydney and a month and a half in Melbourne (Her Majesty's Theatre 9 June 1917), but a scheduled French production, with the original French play somewhat revamped by Louis Verneuil and some Caryll numbers from other shows introduced, hit all sorts of problems. *La Dame en rose* was actually put into rehearsal on more than one occasion before Gustave Quinson finally got it on the stage in 1921. The ''Valse de la Dame en Rose'' was now sung by Odette (Lucette Darbelle) and Garidel (Henri Defreyn), ''Saskatchewan'' was allotted to Henri Vilbert as Dondidier (now called Verdousier), and Caryll's *Chin-Chin* song ''Goodbye, Girls, I'm Through'' was metamorphosed into a piece called ''Charmante!,'' which Defreyn made the hit of the night. Unfortunately for all concerned, Quinson had removed his *Phi-Phi* from the Bouffes-Parisiens to produce *La Dame en rose* and, when it became evident that *Phi-Phi* was still performing in the manner of a big, big hit down at the Édouard VII, the producer promptly took Caryll's piece off and brought *Phi-Phi* back. If one month was all the show got in Paris, this production was nevertheless responsible for *The Pink Lady* being spotted and taken on to one further production, in Hungary, where *A rózsalány* (ad István Zágon, from Verneuil's version) was produced in 1923.

''The Kiss Waltz,'' which became popularly known as ''The Pink Lady Waltz,'' was borrowed by Florenz Ziegfeld for his 1931 *Ziegfeld Follies,* and it was given a fresh whirl across the musical stage when it was prominently featured, well over half a century later, in the score of the London extravaganza *Ziegfeld.*

UK: Globe Theatre 11 April 1912; Australia: Her Majesty's Theatre, Sydney 17 February 1917; France: Théâtre des Bouffes-Parisiens *La Dame en rose* 30 April 1921; Hungary: Lujza Blaha Színház *A rózsalány* 13 October 1923

Recording: selections (AEI)

PINZA, [Fortunato] Ezio (b Rome, 18 May 1892; d Stanford, Conn, 9 May 1957).

After a highly successful international career in opera, the celebrated basso was engaged by Edwin Lester of the Los Angeles Light Opera Company to make a musical comedy debut. Lester, unable to find a suitable vehicle, shared his problem with Richard Rodgers; thus, Pinza made his first Broadway musical appearance in the specially tailored star role of Rodgers and Hammerstein's *South Pacific,* creating ''Some Enchanted Evening,'' ''This Nearly Was Mine'' and a sensation. In 1954 he starred on Broadway a second time in the role of César in a potted musical version of Marcel Pagnol's Marseillais trilogy entitled *Fanny.*

Pinza also appeared in several films, notably as Chaliapin in *Tonight We Sing.*

Autobiography: *Ezio Pinza* (Rinehart, New York, 1959)

PIPE DREAM Musical in 2 acts by Oscar Hammerstein II based on the novel *Sweet Thursday* by John Steinbeck. Music by Richard Rodgers. Shubert Theater, New York, 30 November 1955.

After the international successes of their colorful romantic operettas, Rodgers and Hammerstein brought the rather less colorful down-and-outs of Steinbeck's *Sweet Thursday* to the stage in a musical whose central love story was between a marine biologist without a microscope (Bill Johnson) and a thieving layabout (Judy Tyler) and whose top-billed star, opera's Helen Traubel, played a good-hearted brothel keeper. The two other principal characters of the piece were other vagrants (Mike Kellin, G D Wallace), one of whom organizes a dubious raffle to get Doc his microscope, the other of whom breaks Doc's arm to get the girl to return to him after a squabble.

Rodgers and Hammerstein's score brought forth no numbers to help stock their big, big book of standards, and their production ran through a comparatively poor, and certainly unprofitable, 246 performances, which sent them back promptly to more romantic locations and characters for their next works.

Recording: original cast (RCA)

PIPPIN Musical in 2 acts by Roger O Hirson. Music and lyrics by Stephen Schwartz. Imperial Theater, New York, 23 October 1972.

Originally produced, in an earlier version with a libretto by Ron Strauss and music and lyrics by Schwartz, at the Carnegie-Mellon University in Pittsburgh in 1967, *Pippin* was brought to Broadway in 1972 after the notable success of Schwartz's *Godspell* the previous year. Like that show, *Pippin* was a piece very much of the 1960s, sporting a hero who could have stepped out of the cast of *Godspell,* and period love and war sentiments to match, but this time, under the influence and the remaking of director-choreographer Bob Fosse, the original small piece was worked up into something decidedly larger.

The basic tale of *Pippin* was set in a kind of frame, in the fashion that, though normally used to take the curse off unconfident material, had been successfully used a few seasons earlier by *Man of La Mancha.* Ben Vereen played a compèring character called the Leading Player, at the head of a group of white-faced utility players of the *Godspell* brand, introducing the tale of Pippin (John Rubenstein), son of King Charlemagne, who goes out from Home looking for Himself. On his way, he finds War, The Flesh, Revolution, Encouragement, The Hearth (inclusive of Jill Clayburgh as Catherine) and The Finale, as well as some agreeable songs. The Players' introduction, ''Magic to Do,'' and Pippin's opening solo ''Corner of the Sky'' both became popular out of the show, but the catchy if preachy ''Spread a Little Sunshine'' (introduced by Leland Palmer as Fastrada), ''No Time at All'' (sung by Irene Ryan as Berthe) and the more masculine ''War Is a Science,'' sung by Pippin and his father (Eric Berry), also did well in situ.

Pippin proved a worthy successor to *Godspell* and, aided by some charming sets and a television advertising campaign that has gone down in Broadway history as a classic of efficacy, it established itelf as a long-running hit. Stuart Ostrow's production remained at the Imperial Theatre for 1,944 performances.

In Britain, where television advertising was unheard of, Robert Stigwood's production with Paul Jones (Pippin), Northern J Calloway (Leading Player), Patricia Hodge, Diane Langton, John Turner and Elisabeth Welch featured ran 85 performances. Popular singer Johnny Farnham starred in Kenn Brodziak's Australian production in Melbourne and Sydney (Her Majesty's Theatre 10 August 1974), South Africa saw *Pippin* in 1985 (Her Majesty's Theatre, Johannesburg 10 June), and a German-language version (ad Robert Gilbert) was launched at the Theater an der Wien with Joachim Kemmer as the Leading Player, Béla Erny as Pippin and Grete Keller as Berthe (75 performances) in 1974. In 1981 the show was televised with Fosse directing and choreographing and Vereen repeating the role that had earned him a Tony Award a decade earlier, by which time it showed up already as a period piece.

In 1993 a first Hungarian production (ad György Emőd) made its way to the stage, and *Pippin* was seen again in London in 1998 when it was revived at the Bridewell Theatre (28 May).

Pippin had already served as subject matter for an earlier, German musical comedy, *Pippin der kleine,* produced in the 1920s with a score by Hugo Hirsch.

UK: Her Majesty's Theatre 30 October 1973; Australia: Her Majesty's Theatre, Melbourne 23 February 1974; Austria: Theater an der Wien 6 February 1974; Hungary: Kisvárdai Várszínház,Kisvárda 6 August 1993

Recordings: original cast (Motown), Australian cast (EMI), South African cast (Satbel)

THE PIRATES OF PENZANCE, or The Slave of Duty Comic opera in 2 acts by W S Gilbert. Music by Arthur Sullivan. Bijou Theatre, Paignton, 30 December 1879; Fifth Avenue Theater, New York, 31 December 1879.

Gilbert and Sullivan's successor to the phenomenal *HMS Pinafore* proved to be another enormous international opéra-bouffe hit. Where the former piece had burlesqued things theatrico-naval, the new one, developed from an original scenario about some burglars combined with some elements of an earlier Gilbert operetta, *Our Island Home,* used the highly colored characters and conventions of the melodrama stage as the butt of its fun.

Owing to an error by his childhood nurse, Ruth (Alice Barnett), Frederic (Hugh Talbot) was accidentally apprenticed to the Pirate King (Sgr Broccolini). Now, after having faithfully served his indentures to the age of 21, he is free and his well-pronounced sense of duty drives him to join the police force and devote himself to the extermination of his old skull-and-crossbone mates. Back in the unpiratical world, Frederic falls in love with the first soprano he sees: Mabel (Blanche Roosevelt), daughter of Major General Stanley (J H Ryley). Unfortunately, the pirates are out for revenge on Stanley, who has unfeelingly fibbed himself out of a confrontation with them just as they were about to wed his daughters en masse. Frederic is preparing to lead the police in a raid against the buccaneers, but he is stopped when it is revealed that by a strict reading of the wording of his indentures he is still bound in loyalty to his old master. Battle is joined between pirates and police, and, with the duty-bound Frederic helpless to prevent them, the pirates are victorious—until the police bring out their secret weapon: the name of Queen Victoria. As loyal subjects, the pirates surrender. Then Ruth comes out with the truth: they are all actually errant peers in disguise, so their youthful naughtinesses can all be forgiven and they can mass marry General Stanley's daughters after all.

Sullivan's score echoed the burlesque fun of the script, whether in a rousing song for the Pirate King (''Oh, Better Far to Live and Die''), the merry parody of operatic coloratura in Mabel's ''Poor, Wandering One'' or her extravagantly dramatic farewell (''Go, Ye Heroes'') to the counter-melodied police forces, off to die in battle. As in *HMS Pinafore,* there was a wordful self-descriptive set piece for Stanley (''I Am the Very Model of a Modern Major General''), introducing himself much as Sir Joseph Porter had done in the earlier show, a lugubrious comic number for the Sergeant of Police (Fred Clifton), a song of confession for Ruth, the successor of Little Buttercup's confession from the previous show (''When Frederic Was a Little Lad''), and some rather less burlesque material for Frederic and Mabel, initiating their romance whilst Mabel's sisters gossip tactfully about the weather or, in particular, bidding each other farewell with seeming sincerity before Frederic is forced to change sides again (''Ah! Leave Me Not to Pine Alone''). The whole was topped by ensemble and chorus music in turn pretty, parodic and atmospheric.

Produced under the management of Richard D'Oyly Carte, now acting as an independent producer for the first time after his battles with his consortium of backers over *Pinafore, The Pirates* was mounted almost simultaneously in New York and in Britain, in order to protect the copyright of the piece in both countries. But the continuing run of *HMS Pinafore* at the London Opera Comique meant that whilst a first-class production was staged on Broadway (with the cast given above), the British end was secured by a mocked-up approximation of the show put on at Paignton, Devon, by one of Carte's touring companies. It took place, because of the time difference, slightly before the other, so Richard Mansfield (Stanley), Emilie Petrelli (Mabel), Lyn Cadwaladr (Frederic) and Fred Federici (Pirate King), in theory, ''created'' their roles. Except that what they ''created'' was scarcely what is known today as *The Pirates of Penzance.*

The Pirates of Penzance was a great hit in New York (''one of the greatest financial successes of this or any season, the Fifth Avenue Theatre is positively jammed to the doors every night while the sale of seats in advance continues unprecedented''), but some uncharacteristic mismanagement by Carte meant that its Broadway run was a messy one, in three different theatres over five months. But by the time it closed and the myriad companies around America that had earned a fortune on *Pinafore* had leaped onto the firmly in-copyright *The Pirates of Penzance,* Carte had opened his London version with a lead cast made up largely of the *Pinafore* veterans for whom the roles in its successor had been conceived. Grossmith was Stanley, Richard Temple the Pirate King and tenor George Power played Frederic. There was a pretty new Liverpudlian-Jewish soprano named Marian Hood to play Mabel, Emily Cross stepped in to play Ruth when *Pinafore*'s Harriet Everard was injured by falling scenery in rehearsal, and Rutland Barrington, who hadn't been included in the lineup, asked for and got the role of the Police Sergeant originally planned for Clifton.

The Pirates of Penzance repeated its Broadway success in London (3 April 1880), playing exactly a year and 363 performances at the Opera Comique before giving place to the next Gilbert and Sullivan show and thereafter it had an uneventfully successful life as a prominent part of Carte's repertoire, being toured incessantly and brought back for regular revivals by his principal London-based company. The rest of the English-speaking world also snapped up the new Gilbert and Sullivan show, and Australia's J C Williamson introduced his production, without the unlawful challenges he had suffered on *HMS Pinafore,* in 1881. James South was the Major General, Armes Beaumont played Frederic and Josephine Deakin/Elsa May shared Mabel whilst J C Williamson himself played the Sergeant of Police, soon joined by his wife, Maggie Moore, in the role of Ruth. *The Pirates of Penzance* became a huge Australian favorite and was revived regularly over the next century.

Like the bulk of Gilbert and Sullivan's works, *The Pirates of Penzance* got little exposure in any language but its own, but, following the success of *The Mikado* in Austria, Richard Genée and Camillo Walzel did the piece over into German for the Theater an der Wien. ''The libretto was entirely rearranged, not altogether to advantage, and selections from Sullivan's other operettas interpolated into the score.'' It was voted ''an undoubted success'' but proved to have none of the attractions for Austrian audiences that *The Mikado* had, and was played only 16 times.

The show was given a major re-lease of life in 1980 when the New York Shakespeare Festival produced an uninhibitedly high-spirited version of the piece, which, in spite of tacking in some unfortunate outcuts and clumsily interpolating two numbers from other shows, stayed fairly close to Gilbert's text. The music was partly reorchestrated for a modern band whilst retaining the spirit of the original. With Linda Ronstadt (Mabel), George Rose (Stanley), Rex Smith (Frederic) and Kevin Kline (Pirate King) in the leading roles, this production played 787 performances on Broadway—the longest run anywhere and ever of a Gilbert and Sullivan show—and was reproduced at London's Theatre Royal, Drury Lane, with Pamela Stephenson, George Cole, Michael Praed and Tim Curry with similar success (601 performances) before being taken up around the world. It was also filmed, toured Britain endlessly and got a further London season, at the Palladium with Bonnie Langford (Mabel) and Paul Nicholas (Pirate King), whilst the original version—with no royalties attached—continued to be played as often and elsewhere as it had over the century and a bit past. A German version (ad Klaus Straube), wrongly advertised as a ''deutschsprachige Erstaufführung,'' and based on this production, was given in Dortmund in 1994 (Opernhaus 5 February) and at Berlin's Theater des Westens in 1996 (139 performances) as *The Pirates of Penzance* began to find its way into the theatres of Europe more than a century after its first production.

Earlier filmed versions included television recordings, two brief 1955 efforts by members of the D'Oyly Carte Company, and a video in the Brent-Walker series of recordings of the Gilbert and Sullivan opus.

Australia: Theatre Royal, Sydney 19 March 1881; Austria: Theater an der Wien *Die Piraten* 1 March 1889; Germany: Düsseldorf 1 December 1936, Theater des Westens 16 June 1996

Film: (new version) 1982

Videos: Straftford Festival 1991, 1985, Brent-Walker 1982, etc

PIXLEY, Frank (b Richfield, Ohio, 21 November 1867; d San Diego, 30 December 1919). Librettist to some of the happiest early American comic operas.

Akron, Ohio, schoolteacher turned Chicago (*Times Herald*), Illinois, journalist Pixley made his first original contribution to the musical theatre when he teamed with composer Gustave Luders to write the musical comedy *King Dodo.* The pair were initially unable to find a producer for this piece, but a second effort, *The Burgomaster,* was a major Chicago success, had a brief Broadway run and proved highly popular on tour. As a result, *King Dodo* was snapped up by Henry Savage to follow a similar path.

The third Luders/Pixley work, *The Prince of Pilsen,* turned out to be their best and their most successful. This time even Broadway took notice of the happily American-Continental comic opera with its fine ''Stein Song'' and its pretty ''The Message of the Violet,'' and the piece, certainly one of the best of early American comic operas, not only lived out many years on the road thereafter but returned to New York for several revivals and even traveled to London and to Paris with some success.

This success prompted a call east from Florenz Ziegfeld for Luders, but he continued to work with the Chicago-based Pixley, and the pair turned out a further, if more limited, success in the pretty fantasy *Woodland* (83 performances). Pixley was announced to follow this with a collaboration with Victor Herbert, *The Isle of Enchantment,* but the piece never eventuated, and the remainder of his stageworks were all written in collaboration with his partner of always. However, the last of the team's shows, Klaw and Erlanger's production of the old-fashioned Hawaiian tale of the balloon-blown American who becomes *The Grand Mogul* (40 performances), Louise Gunning's impersonation of *Marcelle* (68 performances) and the disastrous *The Gypsy* (12 performances), which looked far enough back in time to base its plot on a baby swap—all built on the same format of old-fashioned comedy and pretty straightforward songs—did progressively less well and, after the thorough failure of *The Gypsy,* Pixley retired from the theatre and devoted his writing talents to cinematic screenplays. He died in San Diego, whilst only in his early fifties, as the consequence of a fall aboard a steamship.

1900 **The Burgomaster** (Gustave Luders) Dearborn Theater, Chicago 17 June; Manhattan Theater 31 December

1901 **King Dodo** (Luders) Studebaker Theater, Chicago 27 May; Daly's Theater 12 May 1902

1902 **The Prince of Pilsen** (Luders) Tremont Theater, Boston 12 May; Broadway Theater 17 March 1903

1904 **Woodland** (Luders) Tremont Theater, Boston 25 April; New York Theater 21 November

1905 **Florodora** revised book (Broadway Theater)

1906 **The Grand Mogul** (Luders) Colonial Theater, Chicago 7 December; New Amsterdam Theater 25 March 1907

1908 **Marcelle** (ex- *The Baron of Berghof*) (Luders) Casino Theater 1 October

1912 **The Gypsy** (Luders) Park Theater 14 November

PLAIN AND FANCY Musical in 2 acts by Joseph Stein and Will Glickman. Lyrics by Arnold B Horwitt. Music by Albert Hague. Mark Hellinger Theater, New York, 27 January 1955.

A musical set amongst the Amish community of Pennsylvania, *Plain and Fancy* did not make foolish fun of the virtues of the simple life as some turn-of-the-century musicals had done with, for example, the Quaker way of life, even if it presented it as a quaint and picturesque contrast to modern American mores. That modern way of life was represented by Dan (Richard Derr) and Ruth (Shirl Conway), who come to Pennsylvania to sell Dan's farm to Papa Yoder (Stefan Schnabel). The farm will be a dowry for Papa's daughter Katie (Gloria Marlowe), who is to be married to Ezra Reber (Douglas Fletcher Rodgers). But Ezra's brother, Katie's childhood sweetheart Peter (David Daniels), who was cast out of the community for failing its standards, returns and, saving Ezra from a disgrace fueled by the alcohol introduced into the house by the outsiders, wins Katie for himself. Barbara Cook appeared as soubrette Hilda, who ventures into the ''real'' world as represented by a local fair, and returns wiser and, fortunately, not sadder.

The show's highlight came in a representation of an Amish barn raising and its most successful musical moment in Peter and Katie's duet, reminiscing over the days when they were ''Young and Foolish.'' The song became a hit-parade success, and the show played through a fine 461 Broadway performances. A London production, mounted under the management of music publishers Chappell and theatre owner Prince Littler, teamed Derr and Miss Conway with Grace O'Connor (Katie), Malcolm Keen (Yoder) and Jack Drummond (Peter) through a disappointing, forced run of 315 performances.

UK: Theatre Royal, Drury Lane 25 January 1956

Recordings: original cast (Capitol, EMI), London cast (part record) (Dot, Oriole, WRC)

PLANCHÉ, James Robinson (b London 27 February 1796; d London 30 May 1880).

The prolific author of all kinds of musical entertainments from operas (many of which were adaptations or pastiches of Continental pieces) and music dramas [*sic*] to operetta, burletta, musical farce and extravaganza on the one theatrical hand, and pantomimes, dramas and comedies on the other, Planché has survived as the name to grab on to in the English-language light-musical theatre of the first half of the 19th century.

His first staged work was a burlesque, *Amoroso, King of Little Britain,* but in the more than a decade following, the operatic world held most of his attention. Amongst a long list of writings, he adapted Scott's *Guy Mannering* as the text for William Reeve's *The Witch of Derncleugh* (1821); provided texts for the ''operatic drama'' *The Pirate* (1822) and Henry Bishop's *Maid Marian, or The Huntress of Arlingford* (1822), some of the lyrics for *Clari, or The Maid of Milan* (1823, and maybe including ''Home, Sweet Home'') and *Cortez, or The Conquest of Mexico* (1823); wrote the original English libretto for Weber's *Oberon* (1826, ''Ocean, Thou Mighty Monster''); did English versions of Auber's *La Neige* (*The Frozen Lake,* 1824), *Le Maçon* (*The Mason of Buda,* 1828), *L'Ambassadrice* (*Manoeuvring,* 1829), *La Fiancée* (*The National Guard,* 1830), *Le Philtre* (*The Love Charm, or The Village Coquette,* 1831) and *Gustavus III* (1833); adapted Marschner's *Der Vampyr* (1829), Rossini's *Guilliame Tell* as *Hofer or Tell of the Tyrol* (1830), Hérold 's *Le Pré aux Clercs* as *The Court Masque* (1833) and Marliani's *Il Bravo* as *The Red Mask*; and wrote the English versions of *The Marriage of Figaro,* Rossini's *The Siege of Corinth, Norma, The Magic Flute* and *Der Freischütz.*

Planché provided texts, original, borrowed or adapted for a series of burlettas, burlesques and extravaganzas with pasticcio scores, but made his historical mark when he co-wrote the classical burlesque *Olympic Revels* (1831 w Charles Dance), a piece that set in motion a highly successful series of extravaganzas that, interspersed with such revues as *The Drama's Levée, or a Peep at the Past* (1838), *The Drama at Home* (1844), *The New Planet, Mr Buckstone's Ascent of Parnassus, The Camp at the Olympic* (1853), *Mr Buckstone's Voyage Round the Globe* (1854) and *The New Haymarket Spring Meeting* (1855), were mounted initially at the Olympic Theatre and later at the Haymarket and the Lyceum.

Planché's principal fame, however, was won by his poetic stage musical adaptations of classic tales and, above all, of the fairy stories of the French canon, which he also translated in book form. Pieces such as *Fortunio, or The Seven Gifted Servants, The Fair One with the Golden Locks, The Golden Fleece, The Invisible Prince, The King of the Peacocks* and *The Prince of Happy Land* were played throughout the English-speaking world and revived regularly in Britain, America and Australia, the most celebrated of them holding a place in the repertoire even through that later and great period of extravaganza and burlesque writing in the middle years of the 19th century, during which authors such as the Brough brothers, a' Beckett and, later, Byron and Burnand flooded the stage with works based on similar areas of literature.

In his later years, Planché was reponsible for the original English version of Offenbach's *Orphée aux enfers* and provided the lyrics for Dion Boucicault's huge imitation of the French grand opéra-bouffe féerie, *Babil and Bijou,* at Covent Garden.

A number of his non-musical pieces were subsequently adapted to the musical stage by other writers. The 1875 Alhambra extravaganza bouffe *Spectresheim* was based on his *A Romantic Idea,* the 1882 musical comedy *Frolique* (Strand Theatre 18 November), the 1892 comic opera *The Duke's Diversion* and Mrs Pyne Galton's Offenbach pasticcio *The Little Duchess* (Chestnut Street Theatre, Philadelphia 24 January 1870) all on *The Follies of a Night* (itself an adaptation from the French), and Bucalossi's 1894 light opera *Massaroni* on his *The Brigand.*

1818 **Amoroso, King of Little Britain** (pasticcio arr Tom Cooke) 1 act Theatre Royal, Drury Lane 21 April

1819 **The Caliph and the Cadi, or Rumbles in Baghdad** 1 act Sadler's Wells Theatre 16 August

1819 **Fancy's Sketch, or Look Before You Leap** Adelphi Theatre 29 October

1819 **Odds and Ends, or Which Is the Manager?** 1 act Adelphi Theatre 19 November

1820 **A Burletta of Errors, or Jupiter and Alcmena** Adelphi Theatre 6 November

1820 **Who's to Father Me?, or What's Bred in the Bone Won't Come Out in the Flesh** Adelphi Theatre 13 November

1820 **The Deuce Is in Her, or Two Nights at Madrid** Adelphi Theatre 27 November

1821 **Giovanni the Vampire, or How Shall We Get Rid of Him?** Adelphi Theatre 15 January

1821 **Lodgings to Let** Adelphi Theatre 19 February

1821 **Half an Hour's Courtship, or Le Chambre à coucher** 1 act Adelphi Theatre 27 February

1821 **Sherwood Forest, or The Merry Archers** Adelphi Theatre 12 March

1821 **Capers at Canterbury** Adelphi Theatre 1 October

1821 **Love's Alarum** Adelphi Theatre 8 November

1822 **(Henri IV and) the Fair Gabrielle** (Barham Livius) 1 act English Opera House (Lyceum) 5 September

1823 **I Will Have a Wife** (William Reeve) English Opera House (Lyceum) 7 August

1825 **Success, or A Hit if You Like It** 1 act Adelphi Theatre 12 December

1827 **Pay to My Order, or A Chaste Salute** 1 act Royal Gardens, Vauxhall 9 July

1827 **The Rencontre, or Love Will Find a Way** (Henry Bishop) Theatre Royal, Haymarket 12 July

1828 **Paris and London, or A Trip Across the Herring Pond** Adelphi Theatre 21 January

1828 **The Green Eyed Monster** Theatre Royal, Haymarket 18 August

1829 **Theirna-na-oge, or The Prince of the Lakes** (Cooke) Theatre Royal, Drury Lane 20 April

1831 **Olympic Revels, or Prometheus and Pandora** (w Charles Dance) Olympic Theatre 3 January

1831 **Olympic Devils, or Orpheus and Eurydice** (w Dance) Olympic Theatre 26 December

1832 **The Paphian Bower, or Venus and Adonis** (w Dance) Olympic Theatre 26 December

1833 **Promotion, or A Morning in Versailles in 1750** Olympic Theatre 18 February

1833 **The Students of Jena, or The Family Concert** (*La Table et le Logement*) English version (Theatre Royal, Drury Lane)

1833 **High, Low, Jack and the Game, or The Card Party** (w Dance) 1 act Olympic Theatre 30 September

1833 **The Deep, Deep Sea, or Perseus and Andromeda** (w Dance) Olympic Theatre 26 December

1834 **The Loan of a Lover** 1 act Olympic Theatre 29 September

1834 **My Friend the Governor** 1 act Olympic Theatre 29 September

1834 **Telemachus, or The Island of Calypso** (w Dance) 1 act Olympic Theatre 26 December

1835 **The Court Beauties** 1 act Olympic Theatre 14 March

1836 **The Two Figaros** (*Les Deux Figaro*) Olympic Theatre 30 November

1836 **Riquet with the Tuft** (w Dance) 1 act Olympic Theatre 26 December

1837 **A New Servant** 1 act Olympic Theatre 29 September

1837 **Puss in Boots** (w Dance) Olympic Theatre 26 December

1839 **Blue Beard** (w Dance) 1 act Olympic Theatre 2 January

1840 **The Sleeping Beauty in the Wood** Theatre Royal, Covent Garden 20 April

1841 **Beauty and the Beast** Theatre Royal, Covent Garden 12 April

1842 **The White Cat** (arr J H Tully) Theatre Royal, Covent Garden 28 March

1842 **The Follies of a Night** (Cooke) Theatre Royal, Drury Lane 5 October

1843 **Fortunio, or The Seven Gifted Servants** Theatre Royal, Drury Lane 17 April

1843 **The Fair One with the Golden Locks** 1 act Theatre Royal, Haymarket 26 December

1844 **Graciosa and Percinet** 1 act Theatre Royal, Haymarket 26 December

1845 **The Golden Fleece, or Jason and Medea** Theatre Royal, Haymarket 24 March

1845 **The Bee and the Orange Tree, or The Four Wishes** 1 act Theatre Royal, Haymarket 26 December

1846 **The Birds of Aristophanes** 1 act Theatre Royal, Haymarket 18 April

1846 **The Invisible Prince, or The Island of Tranquil Delights** 1 act Theatre Royal, Haymarket 26 December

1847 **The Golden Branch** Theatre Royal, Lyceum 27 December

1848 **Theseus and Ariadne, or The Marriage of Bacchus** Theatre Royal, Lyceum 25 April

1848 **The King of the Peacocks** Theatre Royal, Lyceum 26 December

1849 **The Seven Champions of Christendom** Theatre Royal, Lyceum 9 April

1849 **The Island of Jewels** (arr J H Tully) Theatre Royal, Lyceum 26 December

1850 **Cymon and Iphigenia** (arr Michael Arne/David Garrick ad) 1 act Theatre Royal, Lyceum 1 April

1850 **King Charming, or The Blue Bird of Paradise** (comp/arr Tully) Theatre Royal, Lyceum 26 December

1851 **The Queen of the Frogs** (arr Tully) Theatre Royal, Lyceum 21 April

1851 **The Prince of Happy Land, or The Fawn in the Forest** (arr Tully) Theatre Royal, Lyceum 26 December

1852 **The Good Woman in the Wood** (arr Tully) Theatre Royal, Lyceum 27 December

1853 **Once Upon a Time There Were Two Kings** Theatre Royal, Lyceum 26 December

1854 **The Yellow Dwarf, and the King of the Gold Mines** 1 act Olympic Theatre 26 December

1855 **The Discreet Princess, or Three Glass Distaffs** 1 act Olympic Theatre 26 December

1856 **Young and Handsome** 1 act Olympic Theatre 26 December

1859 **Love and Fortune** (Jacques Offenbach arr) 1 act Princess's Theatre 24 September

1865 **Orpheus in the Haymarket** (*Orphée aux enfers*) English version (Theatre Royal, Haymarket)

1871 **King Christmas** 1 act Gallery of Illustration 26 December

1872 **Babil and Bijou** (Hervé, Frederic Clay, Jules Riviere, et al/ Dion Boucicault) Theatre Royal, Covent Garden 29 August

Autobiography: *Recollections and Reflections* (Tinsley Bros, London, 1872)

PLANQUETTE, [Jean] Robert (b Paris, 31 March 1848; d Paris, 28 January 1903). One of the foremost composers of Parisian opérette in the last decades of the 19th century.

Born in Paris, of Norman stock, Planquette attended the Paris Conservatoire, but he left after one year of study and, still in his teens, launched himself into the world of popular songwriting. He performed a number of his works himself, working in the cafés-concerts as a vocalist at the piano, but he had his first memorable success when Lucien Fugère introduced his march song "Le Régiment de Sambre-et-Meuse" at the Ba-ta-clan in 1867. Over the next decade, beyond a steady supply of songs, he produced a handful of little opérettes and musical monologues (*La Confession de Rosette, On demande une femme de chambre* performed by Anna Judic) for the cafés-concerts, and eased himself into a theatrical production for the first time with the production of the one-act *Paille d'avoine* at the Délassements-Comiques. Finally, Louis Cantin, the manager of the Théâtre des Folies-Dramatiques, gave in to the persistent plugging of Pierre Véron, the editor of the journal *Charivari* and Planquette's sometime librettist and permanent champion, and gave the composer the opportunity to see his first full-length opérette mounted at a major theatre. *Les Cloches de Corneville,* with its lively, colorful and catchy score, won a horrified response from the more snobbish elements of the French musical establishment, glued squarely in the formalities of yesteryear, but a delighted one from the theatregoing public, which gave it a long Paris run and a permanent place in the forefront of the French opérette repertoire as it went on to establish a European and overseas record that made it the most popular French work of its age.

The works with which Planquette followed his great triumph did not evoke the same extravagant response, but they did not do too badly. *Les Voltigeurs de la 32ème,* a military opérette produced as part of the series of Lecocq pieces at the Théâtre de la Renaissance, with that theatre's resident star, Jeanne Granier, in its lead role, racked up 73 performances, and *La Cantinière,* another piece on a military theme, with Berthelier, Brasseur and Léa Silly featured, managed 80, before both pieces went on to other productions in other countries. Planquette's second major hit, however, was not long in coming. The British producer Alexander Henderson, who had made a fortune out of the record-breaking run of *Les Cloches de Corneville* in London, commissioned Planquette to write the score for a musical version of the *Rip van Winkle* story, which he and his inseparable librettist/director, Henry Farnie, were preparing as a vehicle for the young singing comedian Fred Leslie. Planquette popped across from Paris and took lodgings with costumier Charles Alias in London, and there he turned out the made-to-measure score for a *Rip van Winkle* that proved one of the most successful British productions of its time, both at home and abroad. A second collaboration with Farnie and Henderson produced a *Nell Gwynne* that, if its London run was a little disappointing, nevertheless went round the world, and did very much better than the composer's next Paris endeavour, a disastrous piece called *La Cremaillère,* cowritten by Albert Brasseur, the son of the manager of the Nouveautés, and was played there for just a handful of performances.

The Parisian success of *Rip* (shorn of his van Winkle) in 1884 and an indifferent hometown run for a version of *La Princesse Colombine* (*Nell Gwynne*) preceded another fine success for the composer with a swashbuckling, comical opérette about the buccaneer *Surcouf* (1887). Planquette hit the target simultaneously on the other side of the Channel when Farnie, deprived of his fashionable collaborator when Planquette returned to France after *Nell Gwynne,* turned out a heavily reorganized version of *Les Voltigeurs de la 32ème,* which had never been seen in English in Britain, under the title *The Old Guard.* The remake proved enormously popular. *The Old Guard* trouped Britain and the colonies for many years, and Farnie engaged himself in doing a similar job on *Surcouf.* As he had for *The Old Guard,* Planquette supplied such extra music as was deemed necessary, and the result was an almost new opérette called *Paul Jones,* which, mounted by the newly set up Carl Rosa Light Opera Company, proved another long-lived success for its librettist and for its composer, who was finding that his works were, in fact, more successful in Britain than they were in his home country. The run of big London successes, however, came to an end when the Carl Rosa production of *Captain Thérèse* (originally written in French, by Alexandre Bisson, and adapted not by Farnie but by the less popular-touched F C Burnand) lasted a comparatively indifferent 104 performances on its British production and failed totally in Paris.

Amongst the composer's subsequent Paris productions, *Le Talisman* (130 performances) and *Mam'zelle Quat' Sous* both had good home runs and, like the posthumously completed *Le Paradis de Mahomet* (1906), found productions outside France, but they did not get anywhere near equaling the popularity of the happiest of his previous pieces, of which *Les Cloches de Corneville,* in particular, and *Rip* and *Surcouf* less prominently, have remained in the French repertoire in the century and more since their composition.

It has been repeatedly written that Planquette's music was that of a popular songwriter (understood, as opposed to the more soigné work of his theatrical contemporaries), that he was obliged to have his orchestrations done by others and that he borrowed melodies from and/or was reminiscent of his famous predecessors (a comment that scarcely fitted with the first accusation). Looking at his scores alongside the successful shows of his contemporaries, in a Parisian theatre world in which many a Prix de Rome winner and star Conservatoire pupil had failed to make a memorable career, the first is scarcely obvious, unless tunefulness is regarded as the preserve of "popular song"; the second is hardly a crime to a listening public; and the third is no more provable in his case than in all the others. Planquette quite simply caught the mood of his time, wrote some of the most enjoyable show music of his era and had the hits to prove it.

Amongst the foreign remakes of his shows, Planquette's most curious credit was undoubtedly one that came from America. The 1916 musical play *The Amber Express,* for which the score was apparently largely written by Zoel Parenteau, credited him as having composed it "with R Planquette." A difficult feat, 13 years after the composer's death, but *The Amber Express* didn't make sufficient impression for Planquette's contribution to be able now to be evaluated.

1872 **Méfie-toi de Pharaon** (Germain Villemer, Lucien Delormel) 1 act Eldorado 12 October

1874 **Paille d'avoine** (Lemonnier, Adolphe Jaime, Rozale) 1 act Délassements-Comiques 12 March

1874 **Le Serment de Madame Grégoire** (Louis Péricaud, Delormel) 1 act Eldorado 12 October

1875 **Le Zénith** (Adolphe Perreau) 1 act Eldorado 24 April

1875 **Le Valet de coeur** (Péricaud, Delormel) 1 act Alcazar 1 August

1875 **Le Clé du serail** (?w Frédéric Barbier/Mathieu, Fuchs) 1 act Alcazar 1 August

1876 **Le Péage** (Émile André) 1 act Théâtre de la Porte-Saint-Martin 21 October

1877 **Les Cloches de Corneville** (Clairville, Charles Gabet) Théâtre des Folies-Dramatiques 19 April

1879 **Le Chevalier Gaston** (Pierre Véron) 1 act Théâtre de Monte-Carlo, Monaco 3 March

1880 **Les Voltigeurs de la 32ème** (Edmond Gondinet, Georges Duval) Théâtre de la Renaissance 7 January

1880 **La Cantinière** (Paul Burani, Félix Ribeyre) Théâtre des Nouveautés 26 October

1881 **Les Chevau-légers** (Péricaud, Delormel) 1 act Eldorado 15 December

1882 **Rip van Winkle** (H B Farnie) Comedy Theatre, London 14 October

1884 **Nell Gwynne** (Farnie) Avenue Theatre, London 7 February

1885 **La Cremaillère** (Burani, Albert Brasseur) Théâtre des Nouveautés 28 November

1887 **Surcouf** (Henri Chivot, Albert Duru) Théâtre des Folies-Dramatiques 6 October

1887 **The Old Guard** revised English version of *Les Voltigeurs de la 32ème* by Farnie (Avenue Theatre, London)

1889 **Paul Jones** revised English version of *Surcouf* by Farnie (Prince of Wales Theatre, London)

1890 **Captain Thérèse** (Gilbert a' Beckett, F C Burnand/ Alexandre Bisson ad Burnand) Prince of Wales Theatre, London 25 August

1892 **La Cocarde tricolore** (Maurice Ordonneau) Théâtre des Folies-Dramatiques 12 February

1893 **Le Talisman** (Adolphe d'Ennery, Burani) Théâtre de la Gaîté 20 January

1895 **Les Vingt-huit Jours de Champignolette** (Burani) Théâtre de la Republique 17 September

1895 **Panurge** (Henri Meilhac, Albert de Saint-Albin) Théâtre de la Gaîté 22 November

1896 **La Leçon de danse** (Mlle Mariquita) 1 act Théâtre de la Gaîté 9 April

1897 **Mam'zelle Quat' Sous** (Antony Mars, Maurice Desvallières) Théâtre de la Gaîté 5 November

1906 **Le Paradis de Mahomet** (completed by Louis Ganne/ Henri Blondeau) Théâtre des Variétés 14 May

Other title credited: *Le Fiancé de Margot*

PLAYFAIR, Nigel [Ross] (Sir) (b London, 1 July 1874; d London, 19 August 1934).

Barrister-turned-actor Playfair appeared, in the early part of his career, in London's ill-fated production of *Madame Sherry* and in the revue *Pell Mell* in a life otherwise conducted almost wholly in the non-musical theatre.

In 1918 he took over the management of the Lyric Theatre, Hammersmith and was there responsible for a 1920 production of *The Beggar's Opera* that won a memorable success and prompted him to mount (and often play in) further versions of ballad operas and 18th-century musical plays including *Lionel and Clarissa* (Colonel Oldboy), *Love in a Village, Polly* and *The Duenna.* He also produced several original, but less successful, musical shows (*Midsummer Madness, Tantivy Towers, The Fountain of Youth, Derby Day*), a badly mangled remake of *La Vie parisienne* and the admired revue *Riverside Nights,* before retiring from management in 1932.

Playfair had a hand in the writing of a children's musical farce, *Shock-Headed Peter* (w Philip Carr, mus: Walter Rubens) produced at the Garrick Theatre for the Christmas seasons of 1900 and 1901.

Autobiography: *Hammersmith Hoy* (Faber & Faber, London, 1930); Biography: Playfair, G: *My Father's Son* (G Bles, London, 1937)

PLEASE, TEACHER! Musical comedy in 2 acts by K R G Brown, R P Weston and Bert Lee. Lyrics by Weston and Lee. Music by Jack Waller and Joseph Tunbridge. London Hippodrome, 2 October 1935.

A successor to Jack Waller's successful *Yes, Madam?, Please, Teacher!* employed the same writers and most of the same principal cast as its predecessor. Bobby Howes was broke Tommy, masquerading as the explorer brother of schoolgirl Ann Trent (Sepha Treble) in order to get into her school (which was once his family home) to look for documents that could bring him an inheritance. Unfortunately, Ann's real brother has carried off a sacred object from an Oriental shrine, so Tommy has to befuddle a collection of malevolent Chinese as well as headmistress Bertha Belmore, bosomy gym mistress Vera Pearce and music master Wylie Watson as he gambols through the Boy's Own Mag plot and jolly songs of the evening.

Former concert party man Watson scored with a self-accompanied "Song of the 'Cello," Howes told Miss Treble "You Give Me Ideas" and instructed "Mind How You Go Across the Road," and there were comedy ensembles in the burlesque Indian style and for the school pageant. The piece was expertly constructed around the Waller team, and the result was a 301-performance run and a good touring life (it was seen on the road as late as 1950). The show was also compressed into a film musical with its four stars teamed with juvenile girl René Ray.

Film: Associated British 1937

P.L.M. Opérette in 3 acts by Rip. Music by Henri Christiné. Théâtre des Bouffes-Parisiens, Paris, 21 April 1925.

The P.L.M. is the Paris-Lyon-Mediterranee—the French railway system—and the action of *P.L.M.* actually takes place in a railway carriage, which, when the curtain goes up, is in Menton station. Rip's text cast the evening's top-liner, Dranem, as the contrôleur of the train, taking charge like a meneur de revue of a succession of the kind of amorous events and mistakes of identity that are usually set in a seaside hotel. Dranem's feminine co-star was Marguerite Deval, playing the sexually deprived Mme de la Pimprenelle, who takes advantage of a short-circuit blackout between stations to fall into the arms of young Candide (George) without results! However, the voyage does see Candide deflowered by the cocotte Cricri (Suzette O'Nil), who had started out the journey as the little bit of fluff of the minister, Anatole Limace (Jean Gabin). The youngsters of the piece were played by Max de Rieux (Pierre Limace) and Marie Dubas (Madame's niece, Paule). This pair went skinny-dipping in the Mediterranean and ended up clad in each other's overcoats and unable to change back because underneath they were "tout nus." Madame de la Pimprenelle thinks Anatole is the contrôleur, he thinks she is the cleaning lady and Dranem nearly but nearly ends up having . . . if it weren't for an inopportune firecracker in his pocket going off at the wrong time and bringing everyone running, thinking they had heard gunshots.

The comicalities and the sexy imbroglios—perhaps slightly less slick and witty than if they had come from a Barde or a Willemetz—were accompanied by a typical Christiné score of songs and ensembles, from which Dranem's stand-up piece about being "trop nerveux" (to be able to get it up at the right times), his "On s'y fait" and his lecture to Candide about his disgraceful behavior in the blackout ("Ça ne se fait pas") in NOT taking advantage of a lady, Mlle Deval's deploring of her husband's lack of amorous expertise ("J'en veux") and her amazement at her own uncontrollable and indiscriminate desires ("Mais qu'est-ce que j'ai?") and the Java duo for the star pair, "Ça changerait," all gave their performers splendid opportunities. The two youngsters admitted to music to being "Tout nus!," Dranem took the railway analogies a touch further in "Mon coeur est un compartiment" and Candide went on about "Quand une femme vous court après'' amongst the rest of a jolly, dancing set of Jazz Age numbers.

Produced at the Bouffes by Gustave Quinson and Edmond Roze (also director), the show ran for more than seven months and added to the heap of 1920s hits already compiled by its composer and its star.

POCAHONTAS

The (Red) Indian Princess who got herself involved with an Englishman who said he was called John Smith, and via him a whole lot of trouble, has made her way onto the musical stage a number of times. The first important, and by far the most successful, among these was a five-scene burlesque written by actor-playwright John Brougham, with music composed and arranged by James Gaspard Maeder, subtitled *The Gentle Savage,* and produced in New York in 1855 (Wallack's Theater 24 December). Charles Walcot (Smith) and Georgina Hodson (Po-ca-hon-tas) were the principals of the tale, with Brougham himself appearing as the Indian King, Pow-Ha-Tan. The piece was principally a burlesque of the well-known story of the far-from-home military man and the aboriginal maid, with its dialogue phrased in parody of Longfellow's ''Hiawatha,'' but it also served as a vehicle for any movable bits of current, topical burlesque required. Its songs were made up, in the fashion of traditional English burlesque, from popular tunes. The piece had a splendid two-month original run at Wallack's, and it was revived regularly thereafter, both by Brougham himself (in America and at London's Princess Theatre) and by a multitude of others, not to mention with a multitude of up-dating changes, whilst going around the English-speaking stages of the world in a way that no other American-originated burlesque of the period did.

A version of Brougham's *Po-ca-hon-tas* was given by William S Lyster's company in Melbourne in 1862 (21 April, mus arr: Fred Lyster), and Louise Keeley appeared first as the parodied Princess in Britain (Princess Theatre 19 October 1861), but the biggest success won by the piece on that side of the Atlantic came when Mrs John Wood, Brougham's partner on the American stage for some time, appeared as a jolly, plumpish Indian maid in a revival of a revised (by Brougham) version of the piece made for Lydia Thompson and called *La Belle Sauvage* (mus arr: W H Montgomery) at the St James's Theatre (27 November 1869). The show now burlesqued the Bancrofts' hit comedy *School,* took swipes at various popular newspapers and at the current controversy on the writings of Harriet Beecher Stowe, and included one song, ''The Dutchman's Wee Little Dog'' (Barton Hill/W H Montgomery), which became a distinct success as the burlesque ran up a remarkable series of nearly two hundred London performances.

Like only the very most successful of burlesques, *Po-ca-hon-tas* was itself burlesqued when a Mr J H Rathbone put out a *Pocahontas in Black* at Washington's Wall's Opera House on 12 February 1869. The real piece was playing at the city's principal house, the National, the same night. Miner's Eighth Avenue played *Her Royal Highness,* with Sam Villa as a grotesque little Indian (August 1884) and a further burlesque, written by Harry Le Clair, was produced at Koster & Bial's in 1892 (30 May *Pocahontas Up to Date*) with Madge Lessing in the title role.

American divette Lillian Russell had the opportunity to play the part of Pocahontas when her ''husband,'' Teddy Solomon, composed a comic opera, to a text by Sydney Grundy, under that title (subtitled *The Great White Pearl*), which she introduced in 1884 at London's Empire Theatre. Frank Celli was her John Smith, and there was a bundle of comical characters (Robert Brough, Alice Barnett, Herny Ashley, John L Shine) to support the soprano and baritone. This *Pocahontas* was a 24-performance flop. That was still better, however, than either a comic opera *Pow-ha-tan* by W A Baker produced at Des Moines in 1889 (Foster's Opera House 9 November) or a burlesquey *Miss Pocahontas,* a Boston Cadets amdram show written by R A Barnet and R M Baker (et al), which played just 15 performances at Broadway's Lyric Theater from 28 October 1907. The run of flop *Pocahontas*es continued the following year with a Kiralfy spectacular mounted for the Jamestown Exhibition and brought with great fanfare to Philadelphia. It closed after just one week. That same year Thomas Edison put *Pocahontas* on very silent film. Yet another and more modern Indian princess sank swiftly when an inept imported (*Princess*) *Pocahontas* (Goell) produced at Glasgow (8 October) and brought to London's Lyric, Hammersmith in 1963 (14 November), foundered in 12 nights, and in 1995 a cutesie-pie little PC Pocahontas made her way to the animated musical screen (Menken/Schwarz). She too was received with (much) less than wholehearted enthusiasm and ended her career on ice, touring as *The Spirit of Pocahontas* in a mounting by Disney on Ice.

Undoubtedly the most fun and distinctly un-PC Pocahontas, however, would have been that delivered by Fanny Brice in an Eddie Cantor sketch in the *Ziegfeld Follies of 1923.* Miss Brice also managed to play Queen Isabella of Spain in the same sketch.

And so, some century and a half down the line, John Brougham's burlesque maintains its records not only as the most successful American burlesque of the heyday of the burlesque genre but also as the only thoroughly successful representation of the story of the unlikely Mrs Smith to have made it to the musical boards.

Plate 309. **Polenblut.** *Gerti Gordon and Melanie Holliday in the Vienna Volksoper production.*

POLENBLUT Operette in 3 scenes by Leo Stein. Music by Oskar Nedbal. Carltheater, Vienna, 25 October 1913.

The most successful of Oskar Nedbal's stage compositions, and the only one that has remained in the played repertoire, *Polenblut* was a bright, uncomplicated Operette, composed to a conventional but lively libretto by Leo Stein (alleged, though not by Stein, to be based on a bit of Pushkin) set in the present day, in city and country Poland.

The estates of the overly high-living Count Boleslaw Baranksi (Karl Pfann) are so run down that the only way for him to restore his fortunes and save his lands is to make a rich marriage. However, he refuses to even meet Helena, (Mizzi Zwerenz), the daughter of the wealthy but unaristocratic Pan Jan Zarémba (Richard Waldemar), and carries on instead with the ballet girl Wanda (Käthe Ehren), after whom his friend Popiel (Josef König) has been sighing. With the aid of Popiel, the insulted Helena sets out for revenge. She becomes ''Marynia,'' Bolo's new housekeeper, and by her sense, thrift and hard work gets him and the farms working and his worthless friends out of the house. When the truth comes out, Bolo has enough sense to realize that Helena will make a better Countess Baranksi than the ballet girl.

Nedbal's score did not produce any hits, but a colorful set of numbers in the most popular of rhythms—the waltz duos ''Ich seid ein Kavalier'' (Bolo/Helena) and ''Hören Sie, wie es singt und klingt'' (Bolo/Wanda), the big waltz of the second-act finale, ''Mädel, dich hat mir die Glücksfee gebracht,'' Bolo's marching raptures over Wanda, ''Ich kenn' ein süsses Frauchen''—backed up by some mazurka and polka strains, some touches of what passed for Polish color, and some fine ensembles, of which a comical trio (Helena/Popiel/Zarémba) in which Helena's father boasts of his tactfulness (''Ich bin ein Diplomate'') proved one of the most enjoyable items of the evening.

Produced at Vienna's Carltheater by Sigmund Eibenschütz, *Polenblut* had a fine first run of 185 performances, before going into the repertoire. It was played frequently in 1914 and 1915, passed its 250th performance on 26 January 1916 and was given regular performances, with Mizzi Zwerenz retaining her role of Helena, at the Carltheater for more than a decade.

Berlin's *Polenblut,* mounted at the Theater des Westens with Käthe Dorsch starred, was also a fine success through two seasons and 302 performances, whilst Sári Petráss returned from her overseas starring assignments to play Helena in a Budapest production (ad Andor

Gábor), the success of which helped the Király Színház through the difficult early days of the war. However, the same war meant that *Polenblut,* although it won returns in central Europe, did not, by and large, travel further. The one exception was America, where reaction against Germany had not, as in Britain, led to a wholesale rejection of German-language theatre. Comstock and Gest, soon joined by the Shuberts, picked up *Polenblut* and produced it, with some additional numbers by Rudolf Friml, as a vehicle for Emma Trentini. When the show set out from Albany, it was entitled *The Ballet Girl,* said to be adapted from an Hungarian source, and musically credited wholly to Friml. John Charles Thomas was Bolo, Clifton Crawford was Popiel and Letty Yorke played Wanda. When Trentini and Friml began a professionally disruptive affair, the producers threw out the composer and his songs, but the prima donna (having first got the duo ''The Flame of Love'' and ultimately a whole half-dozen of her boyfriend's songs reinstated) had her revenge. When what was now called *The Peasant Girl* (ad Edgar Smith, Harold Atteridge, Herbert Reynolds) proved a hit and she was asked to extend her eight-week Broadway contract, Trentini refused. She was going to Japan with Friml. Her understudy went on, and the show ran another month in New York before going on tour. The turtledoves didn't have time to go to Japan before they broke up.

One of the most popular pieces on the German-language stage during and after the First World War, *Polenblut* was filmed in 1934, with Ivan Petrovich, Anny Ondra and Hans Moser starred, and subsequently taken into the repertoire of the Volksoper (ad Haberland, 10 October 1954), where it was given a new production in 1986 (1 February) with Kurt Schreibmayer and Mirjana Irosch in the leading roles.

Germany: Theater des Westens 1 November 1913; Hungary: Király Színház *Lengyelvér* 22 December 1914; USA: 44th Street Theater *The Peasant Girl* 2 March 1915

Film: Carl Lamac 1934

Recording: selections (Ariola/Philips)

LA POLKA DES LAMPIONS Comédie musicale in 2 acts by Marcel Achard taken from the screenplay *Some Like It Hot.* Music by Gerard Calvi. Théâtre du Châtelet, Paris, 20 December 1961.

A French stage musical version of *Some Like It Hot,* produced at the Théâtre du Châtelet with Georges Guétary (Charles Courtois) and Jean Richard (Blaise Charignon) playing French versions of the two lads disguised, by the necessity to earn a living, as members of a ladies' orchestra, and Nicole Broissin (pianist Nicole) and Annie Duparc (conductor Marie Prévost) in the principal female roles.

The piece went somewhat against the Châtelet's reputation for romantic costume opérette à grand spectacle, but even if the period was the unusually recent 1920s and the setting Deauville and other French venues, there was a good Châtelet total of 20 scenes in the way of spectacle, as well as a lively singing and dancing score including Mlle Broissin's ''Enfin, voici l'amour,'' the boys' conviction that ''Ça ira demain,'' their Prohibition Tango, a ''Cha-cha-charleston'' and a polka title song for Mlle Duparc, and a regular ration of tenor numbers (''Marie et Charles,'' ''Quelle qu'elles soient,'' etc) for Guétary.

La Polka des lampions proved a fine success and, with a record of 534 performances in its vast auditorium, it outran its Broadway alter ego, *Sugar,* as it rang in the centenary of the famous theatre.

Recording: original cast (Pathé)

POLLY

The passion for using girls' names as the titles for musical shows from *Dafne* to *Evita* has, not unnaturally, resulted in one or two of these girls and their names being given more than one show. *Polly* has had (at least) three. The first of these was John Gay's musequel to *The Beggar's Opera,* which promoted Miss Peachum (or Mrs Macheath as she now was) to the title. Originally banned in 1728 as being of too ''satirical'' a nature, *Polly* ultimately made it to the stage, nearly 50 years after it had been written, at the Haymarket Theatre in 1777, and it flopped. It was nevertheless brought back for revivals in 1782 and in 1813 at Drury Lane and, following the great success of the 1920 *Beggar's Opera* revival in London, it was given two rival productions in 1922, one at Chelsea (mus: Hubert Bath, Norman Slee) and the other at the Kingsway Theatre (ad Clifford Bax, 30 December) with Lilian Davies as Polly. Olde Englishe was clearly fashionable, for this time the latter version of the piece lasted 324 performances. It was subsequently given at New York's Cherry Lane Theater (10 October 1925) with Dorothy Brown in the name part. New York took olde Englande's attitude, and *Polly* folded in a month.

The second *Polly,* subtitled *The Pet of the Regiment,* was a comic opera by James Mortimer, with music by Edward Solomon, produced at the Novelty Theatre, London, 4 October 1884. Lillian Russell was Polly, orphan mascot of a regiment and, apparently, the illegitimate daughter of the general's unmarried sister. When it turns out she actually isn't, she can marry her Private Mangel, who is—would you believe it—really and truly a prince. Teetering on the edge of burlesque and of the Gilberty and Sullivanish, *Polly* (with the help of Miss Russell's hit song, ''The Silver Line,'' borrowed from Solomon's last flop, *Lord Bateman*) had a 69-performance run in London, and played 79 Broadway performances for J C Scanlan and E E Rice (Casino Theater 17 April 1885).

Between hosting two foreign *Pollys*, Broadway finally brought out its own. *Polly* Mark III was a musical version of Guy Bolton and George Middleton's successful play *Polly with a Past* (Belasco Theater 6 September 1917, 315 performances). Lyrics by Irving Caesar and music by Phil Charig and Herbert Stothart, however, did nothing to ensure this Polly a future as well as a past, and Arthur Hammerstein's production (Lyric Theater, New York 8 January 1929) with June as Polly folded in 15 performances. Two less abbreviated American Pollys, *Polly of the Circus,* Margaret Mayo's own adaptation of her successful 1907 play (Liberty Theater 23 December, 160 performances), set with Hugo Felix music, which stopped short of New York, and *Polly of Hollywood,* another little lassie who went into films in a Harry Cort production (Cohan Theater 21 February 1927) but did so only for 24 nights, didn't help to lift the Polly-average.

POLNISCHE WIRTSCHAFT Vaudeville-Posse in 3 acts by Kurt Kraatz and Georg Okonkowski. Lyrics by Alfred Schönfeld. Music by Jean Gilbert. Stadttheater, Cottbus, 26 December 1909; Thalia-Theater, Berlin, 6 August 1910.

The first collaboration of playwright Okonkowski and composer Gilbert, and both the playwright's and the composer's first big success, *Polnische Wirtschaft* was produced at Cottbus at the end of 1909, scoring an enormous hit that resulted in its making its way in the new year to Berlin's Thalia-Theater.

The libretto bundled together many familiar and farcical elements, from the musical-comedy will to a comedian in women's clothes, but the mixture proved a well-made and extremely successful one. Polish Marga Hegewaldt, heiress to the Gross-Karschau estates, and her husband, Willy, are paid an annual legacy as long as they remain happily married. They haven't been effectively so for five years, but each year they go lovingly together to pick up the cash. The Graf Kasimir Schofinsky, who stands to gain if Marga's marriage fails, watches their every move. And he has something to watch, for the now-liberated Marga is not only pursued by an aviator named Fritz Sperling, she has also had a little adventure with a certain ''Herr Krause,'' whilst Willy has lined up a second wealthy wife in Erika Mangelsdorf, whose father is none other than the pretended ''Herr Krause.'' In fact, although each of this pair thinks the other wealthy, neither is. Add a blackmailing photographer to the proceedings, and the legacy looks thoroughly threatened. All comes right, however, when Marga and Willy fall back in love and Erika and their funny friend Hans, who inherits a fortune in timely fashion, find they are made for each other. The second and third acts were made up largely of farcical comedy with ''Herr Krause'' avoiding recognition in Polish disguise and Hans dressed up as a girl to flirt with Willy and thus put Erika off his rival. Polish jokes were rife, with Schofinski and his four pretty Polish daughters supplying many of them.

Plate 310. **Polnische Wirtschaft.** *''Und die Clarinette spielt. Di-didi-da . . .'': Helene Ballot and Arnold Rieck in the Thalia-Theater's hit production of Gilbert's musical comedy.*

Gilbert's score favored waltz rhythms—Mangelsdorf leading a 3/4 trio in praise of Berlin (''Wie schön bist du, Berlin''), Hans and Erika's Dorfmusik waltz (''Es bläst ein Trompeter'') with its imitation of orchestral instruments, and the duet for Willy and Marga ''Wer kann dafur?''—but the first act ended with a big march number as everyone decided to go off to the amusement park (''Komm, mein Schatz, in den Lunapark'') and Erika and Hans shared a comical last act Rheinländer-Couplet ''Männe, hak' mir 'mal die Taille auf'' in contrast.

Jean Kren, manager of the Thalia and a successful playwright, added his own touches and his name to the authorial credits before *Polnische Wirtschaft* opened at his theatre, his partner Alfred Schönfeld restaged the show, Emil Sondermann (Mangelsdorf), Arnold Rieck (Hans), Lotte Reinecken (Auguste, the maid), Helene Ballot (Erika), Eugenie della Donna (Marga), Fritz Junkermann (Fritz Sperling) and Paul Bechert (Willy) headed the cast, and among them all they turned up a major hit. *Polnische Wirtschaft* ran at the Thalia until the next of what would become a series of Gilbert Possen, *Autoliebchen,* took its place a year and a half later. It was revived in 1918 (6 December) for a three-month season, during which time it passed its 700th Berlin performance (21 February 1919).

A favorite for many years and through many productions in Germany (during which time the score became decorated with such favorite Gilbert numbers from other sources as *Puppchen*'s ''Puppchen, du bist mein Augenstern!'' and *Autoliebchen*'s ''Ja, das haben die Mädchen so gerne''), the show had, considering the worldwide exposure of Gilbert's almost contemporary *Die keusche Susanne,* a curiously limited life outside that country. Austria, of course, took the Berlin hit up quickly, and it was seen in Vienna (as *Tolle Wirtschaft*—the marriage was now ''crazy'' instead of ''Polish''), played first by the Thalia-Theater company at the Lustspieltheater, complete with almost all its original stars, then in a local production at Ronacher. Frln Ballot was again Erika, alongside Käthe Krenn (Marga), Ferdinand Stein (Willy), Gustav Müller (Mangelsdorf), Karl König (Hans) and director Karl Tuschl (Graf Kasimir). Nowhere, however, did the show win the success it had found at home. In Hungary, where Jenő Faragó's localized adaptation turned the hit waltz about Berlin into ''Ah, ilyen Budapest'' and Willy and Marga pinched the Rheinländer, *Lengyel menyecske* caused no great stir, whilst in America a version adapted by George V Hobart, peppered with additional numbers by Jerome Kern, produced by George M Cohan and Sam Harris, and with Valli Valli (Marga), Mathilde Cottrelly (Gabrielle), Sydney Bracy (Rudolf) and Armand Kalisch (Willy) featured, made it to the Grand Opera House, Chicago (8 September 1912) but not to New York. New York made do with a German-language production mounted at the Irving Place Theater with Georgine Neuendorff and Adolf Kühn featured. Paris saw a Claude Rold/J de Berys *Ménage polonais* at the Château d'Eau in 1914, but the piece never made it to London.

Another piece under the title of *Polnische Wirtschaft* (a double-meaning one, for the expression colloquially means ''a real mess''), written by Richard Genée and Moritz West, with music by Hermann Zumpe, had been previously produced at Berlin's Friedrich-Wilhelmstädtisches Theater on 26 November 1891.

Austria: Lustspieltheater *Tolle Wirtschaft* 14 October 1910; Hungary: Városligeti Színkör *Lengyel menyecske* 18 November 1911; USA: Irving Place Theater *A Nice Mess* 14 December 1910, Empire Theater, Syracuse *A Polish Wedding* 31 August 1912; France: Château d'Eau *Ménage polonais* 6 March 1914

POMME D'API Opérette in 1 act by Ludovic Halévy and William Busnach. Music by Jacques Offenbach. Théâtre de la Renaissance, Paris, 4 September 1873.

Of the handful of one-act opérettes that Offenbach wrote alongside the more substantial pieces of the last decade of his life, the pretty three-handed *Pomme d'api,* helped along by the Parisian debut of Louise Théo in the title role, was the most successful.

Womanizing Uncle Amilcar Rabastens (Daubray) has threatened to cut off Gustave's (Mlle Dartaux) allowance because the silly young fellow has kept the same mistress too dangerously long. He has also sacked his maid, and ordered a nice new young one. The new maid is, of course, Gustave's Pomme d'api, otherwise Catherine (Louise Théo), and the young man has to watch his uncle making purposeful passes at her before the comedy is ended happily. Although Gustave had two numbers and Uncle Amilear one, it was Catherine to whom the bulk of the musical opportunities fell. But the highlight of the evening was the most bouffe part of the entertainment, a comical trio constructed (with a slight reminiscence of *Cox and Box*) around a grill pan and some chops.

Played regularly in France—most recently as part of a spectacle coupé with *Mesdames de la Halle* and *Monsieur Choufleuri* in several Paris seasons—*Pomme d'api* also won productions in its earlier days in London, first at John Hollingshead's Gaiety Theatre and nearly 20 years later in a new translation (ad A Schade, Percy Reeve) as a forepiece at the Criterion, at Vienna's Theater an der Wien as *Nesthäkchen* and in a later German version as *Der Onkel hat gesagt.* It was also seen in America, played in its original French, in the repertoire of Maurice Grau's company.

UK: Gaiety Theatre *Love Apple* 24 September 1874, Criterion Theatre *Poor Mignonette* 2 August 1892; Austria: Theater an der Wien *Nesthäkchen* 22 November 1877; USA: Academy of Music (Fr) 20 May 1880

Recordings: EMI, Bourg

LE POMPON Opérette in 3 acts by Henri Chivot and Alfred Duru. Music by Charles Lecocq. Théâtre des Folies-Dramatiques, Paris, 10 November 1875.

It is Palermo and carnival time, and the brigand Tivolini is going to be there, identifiable by a red-and-white pompon on his hat. Unfortunately, the innocent little doctor Piccolino (Mme Matz-Ferrare), the darling of the ladies and the beloved of the flower girl Fioretta (Mlle Caillot), wears a fatally matching pompon, is arrested and condemned to prison by the viceroy, Melchior (Ange Milher). Worse is to come. The viceroy's fiancée, the Duchesse Ortensia Cazadores y Florida (Mlle Toudouze), is an old flame of the little doctor, and when it gets known that she has visited the prisoner in his cell things look like getting even hotter for our hero. It takes another whole act for everything, with a little help from a blush-making fib from Fioretta, to be sorted out in time for a happy ending. Luco played Barabino, the minister of police, Didier was Castorini and Mlle Paurelle completed the principal cast as Béatrice.

Lecocq's long score, heavy in choral work and in showy vocalizing for the principal singers, included amongst its most favored pages a brindisi for Piccolo, a barcarolle and a virtuoso chanson de la folie for Fioretta.

After the great successes of *La Fille de Madame Angot* and *Giroflé-Girofla* and the semi-succás d'estime of *Les Prés Saint-Gervais, Le Pompon* gave Lecocq the first real Paris flop of his career. It was played just 14 times. This, however, was not the end of its career for, in spite of the Paris failure, Vienna's Carltheater mounted the piece as *Tivolini, der Bandit von Palermo,* the Teatro dal Verme in Milan made a fine success out of it, and Turin and Lyon both nodded approval as well. Budapest's Népszínház produced the show as *A kis doktor* (ad Lajos Tinódy, István Toldy). With Erzsi Vidmár, Emilia Sziklai, János Kápolnai, Miklós Tihanyi and Elek Solymossy at the head of its cast, the Hungarian "little doctor" was played a highly satisfactory 29 times in its first series, and it went on to a number of further productions and performances, outrunning many of the composer's elsewhere-more-successful works in the Hungarian repertoire.

A British version, prepared by Robert Reece, doesn't ever seem to have got to the stage.

Hungary: Népszínház *A kis doktor* 18 November 1876; Austria: Carltheater *Tivolini, der Bandit von Palermo* 3 November 1877; Germany: *Tivolini* 12 January 1878

LE PONT DES SOUPIRS Opéra-bouffe in 4 acts by Hector Crémieux and Ludovic Halévy. Music by Jacques Offenbach. Théâtre des Bouffes-Parisiens, Paris, 23 March 1861; revised version, Théâtre des Variétés, Paris, 8 May 1868.

An opéra-bouffe in the most thoroughly burlesque manner, *Le Pont des soupirs* saw Offenbach and his librettists returning to the style so successfully employed in *Orphée aux enfers* and *Geneviève de Brabant,* after the composer's abortive attempt to take the Opéra-Comique with the more sedately silly *Barkouf.* From Olympus and the French medieval world, he now turned to another favorite funspot of the spectacular-dramatic stage, the watery ways of the city of Venice with its Doges and Council of Ten and other such picturesque and easily burlesqued accoutrements. The librettists of *Orphée* fashioned another wildly extravagant tale around characters heretofore treated more dramatically in operatic pieces such as the 1841 *Katharina Cornaro, Königin von Cypern* (Franz Lachner/Alois Bussel), Halévy's *Reine de Chypre,* Balfe's *The Daughter of St Mark* (1844) or Pacini's *Regina di Cipro* (1846).

Cornarino Cornarini (Desiré), Doge of Venice in this year of 1321, has fled from his foundering fleet and, accompanied by his faithful Baptiste (Bache), arrived back home in deepest disguise and disgrace. He has to watch, powerless, as his wife, Catarina (Lise Tautin), is serenaded by her pretty pageboy, Amoroso (Lucille Tostée), and purposefully courted by the vile and powerful Malatromba (Potel), a dramatically lecherous monster who aspires to the post of Doge. Melodrama rises to farcical heights as Cornarino tries to make contact with his wife and avoid his rival, and the disguised Doge is finally dragged before a very eccentric version of the Council of Ten to give a report on his own death. Malatromba quickly gets himself elected in the "deceased" Doge's place, but then the news comes—Cornarino left too soon, and his fleet won the battle! He is reprieved and can come back to life, but—hang on—now who is Doge? The old or the new? There is nothing left for it but to have a contest. Since this is Venice it is a sea duel, and Cornarino comes out on top thanks to a bit of cheating by Amoroso.

Offenbach's score was in his best bouffe manner and, even if it had not the one big hit number, such as *Orphée*'s galop infernale or the page's serenade in *Geneviève* there was a long list of sparkling and funny musical pieces to be found in the new burlesque: the first-act multiple serenade under the Dogaressa's balcony ("Catarina, je chante"), the comical tale of the loss of the fleet (Complainte de Cornarino), Catarina's parody of an operatic mad scene, staged to keep Malatromba's malevolent fingers from doing fate-worse-than things to her hooks-and-eyes, the crazy Quattuor des poignards staged amongst the bodies and hiding places of the boudoir-farcical second act, as well as some solos that, in typical Offenbachian fashion, verged on being too charming to be properly burlesque.

Produced by Offenbach himself at the Bouffes-Parisiens, with several of the original *Orphée* cast—Mlle Tautin, ex-Eurydice now Catarina, Desiré, formerly Jupiter now Doge of Venice, and Bache, the lugubrious Styx now Baptiste—*Le Pont des soupirs* was not a great success, but it was by no means a failure.

Karl Treumann, now established at his Theater am Franz-Josefs-Kai, was the first foreign manager to host the show, when Offenbach's company visited Vienna in June 1861 with *Le Pont des soupirs* in its baggage, and he was also the first to mount a foreign-language version when his uncredited adaptation of *Die Seufzerbrücke* was produced, just under a year later. Treumann himself played the Doge, alongside Knaack (Baptiste), Markwordt (Malatromba), Anna Marek (Catarina) and Helene Weinberger (Amoroso). Treumann's biggest female star, Anna Grobecker, however, played Cascadetto, and her role was enlarged by a song composed (along with a fourth-act chorus, pierrot dance and Schluss-Galoppade, "based on original Venetian motifs") by the theatre's musical director, Franz von Suppé. Close behind Vienna, Berlin mounted its version of *Die Seufzerbrücke* with sufficient success for it to be given some 50 times over the next 18 months, and the French (Bouffes company tour) and German versions were also both played in Budapest.

In 1868 *Le Pont des soupirs* was given a major revival at Paris's Théâtre des Variétés (8 May). Mlle Tautin was again Catarina, Thiron was Cornarino, Lise Garait played Amoroso and José Dupuis himself was the mean Malatromba. For the occasion, Offenbach reorganized his score, replaced some numbers and added others, and the librettists took the opportunity incomprehensibly to change the ending of their show. In the new version, the contest became a banal shimmy up a pole with a goblet at the end, and Cornarino is defeated. Whilst Malatromba takes over the empire, the ex-Doge, his wife and, of course, his wife's pretty page are sent off to an ambassadorial post in deepest Spain.

Although the revival did no better, as far as a run was concerned, than the original, it nevertheless sparked revivals and productions of its own. Vienna's Carltheater staged its *Seufzerbrücke* (8 February 1873) with Hermine Meyerhoff as Catarina (11 performances), Hungary now got round to an Hungarian version, Marie Aimée and her company introduced the show to America (in French), whilst in London Henry S Leigh's English version was mounted by Richard Mansell at the St James's Theatre (after a short postponement to replace an unsatisfying French Amoroso by a local one), with Edmund Rosenthal as Cornarino, Frank Celli, Augusta Thompson, J A Shaw and Annie Beauclerc. It had to be closed after six weeks when the (unpaid) orchestra walked out, but, in a reversal of the French procedure, *The Bridge of Sighs* was brought out again in London in 1873, this time in a cut-down version.

In spite of this clumsy beginning, London persevered longer with the show than most other cities, for in 1879 another version, enlarged again, and expanding Offenbach's score with music by Hérold, Waldteufel, Campana and Georges Jacobi, was spectacularly produced at the Alhambra under the title *Venice* (ad Charles Searle). Herbert Campbell (Cornarino), Mme Zimeri (Catarina), Constance Loseby (Angelo, ex- Amoroso) and Ambrose Collini (Magnifico, ex- Malatromba) headed a cast that also included such celebrities as Arthur Williams, Emma Chambers and the pantomimic Conquests, through two months. Long in the wake of this, America saw its first English-language *Pont des soupirs* when the ever-adventurous Tivoli in San Francisco mounted a version in 1883, and New York had its first regular English-language performance in 1885 in Brooklyn, where Selina Dolaro headed the cast, alongside Florence Vallière, Lillie West and Harry Brown, for the few nights until the management went bust.

After many years of silence, during which it languished in the shadows of Offenbach's better-liked pieces, *Le Pont des soupirs* resurfaced intermittently in the 20th century. A new German version (ad Otto Maag) was staged in Basle (26 March 1933) and Wiesbaden (31 January 1965), and several French regional theatres, as well as the then ever-enterprising French radio, reprised the work, before a major stage and television revival was mounted in France in 1987 and played at the Théâtre de Paris (10 November 1987) with alternating casts. Directed with a truly bouffe vigor, the production was distinctly successful both in itself and in bringing *Le Pont des soupirs* back to general notice.

Austria: Theater am Franz-Josefs-Kai (Fr) 15 June 1861, *Die Seufzerbrücke* 12 May 1862; Hungary: Nemzeti Színház (Fr) 18 July 1861, Budai Színkör *Seufzerbrücke* 24 June 1865, Budai Színkör *A sóhajok hidja* 27 August 1871; Germany: Friedrich-Wilhelmstädtisches Theater 17 May 1862; UK: St James's Theatre *The Bridge of Sighs* 18 November 1872, Alhambra Theatre *Venice* 5 May 1879; USA: Lina Edwin's Theater (Fr) 27 November 1871, Tivoli Opera House, San Francisco 8 February 1883, Grand Opera House, Brooklyn *The Bridge of Sighs* 20 April 1885

Recording: complete (Bourg)

POPPY Musical comedy in 3 acts by Dorothy Donnelly. Music by Stephen Jones and Arthur Samuels. Apollo Theater, New York, 3 September 1923.

Yet another piece in the Broadway Cinderella series of the early 1920s, *Poppy* joined *Irene, Mary, Sally* and the rest in following the fortunes of its winsome heroine from pauperish obscurity to wealth and a wedding ring. This one had a ring of Maurice Ordonneau's *Les Saltimbanques* about it, as Poppy (Madge Kennedy) started life in a circus, only to discover, when skies seemed darkest, that her long-lost mother was an heiress. The star turn of the show was, however, not Poppy but comedian W C Fields, cast in the role of the little heroine's guardian.

From amongst the songs of the show two pieces, "What Do You Do Sunday(s), Mary?" and "Alibi Baby" (Samuels/Howard Dietz), found some success and the mixture, if almost wearyingly the same as before, proved sweet and savory enough to win *Poppy* a 344-performance run on Broadway, as well as a British production. In London, staged at the Gaiety Theatre with Anne Croft as Poppy and the town's favorite clown, W H Berry, taking Fields's role, *Poppy* notched up a fair run of 188 performances—which was more than her trans-Atlantic sisters *Mary* and *Tip-Toes* had managed, but significantly less than *Irene, Sally, Sunny* and, particularly, the less winsome *Mercenary Mary.*

The same title, with trendily druggy overtones, was used for a breast-beating British musical by Peter Nichols, music by Monty Norman (Barbican Theatre, London 25 September 1982), which used British pantomime conventions and extravagant production values to preach of how the spotlessly noble Orient was debauched by the vile colonizing Victorian British. It had a much shorter life in its original Royal Shakespeare Company production than the Cinderella-with-comedy American show, was remounted with transatlantic money and intent in the West End, and failed a second time, but was later played without its spectacular accoutrements in a small-stage version on the London fringe.

UK: Gaiety Theatre 4 September 1924

Recordings: US show: radio dialogue by Fields (Columbia); UK show: London cast (WEA)

PORGY AND BESS Folk opera in 3 acts by Du Bose Heyward based on the play *Porgy* by Du Bose and Dorothy Heyward. Lyrics by Du Bose Heyward and Ira Gershwin. Music by George Gershwin. Alvin Theater, New York, 10 October 1935.

Initially produced by the Theater Guild as a commercial production on Broadway, the "folk opera" *Porgy and Bess* has subsequently found much of its future in the opera houses of the world.

Adapted from Heyward's novel and play, itself also a Theater Guild production, the musicalized *Porgy,* set in Catfish Row, amongst low-living negro folk, centered on the love affair between the crippled Porgy (Todd Duncan) and Bess (Anne Brown), the flashy mistress of the uncouth Crown (Warren Coleman). Crown kills a man in a gambling brawl and flees the area, leaving the unlikely pair to get together in his absence, and when he manages to come out from hiding to reclaim his woman, Porgy murders him. When he gets out of prison, he finds that Bess has gone to New York with the drug peddler Sportin' Life (John W Bubbles), and he sets off in his donkey cart to find her.

George Gershwin's score illustrated this dramatic tale with great force in a range of musical pieces that brought more individual numbers to the peaks of popularity than any similar work since *Carmen*: the reaching, spun-soprano lullaby "Summertime," Porgy's song of the satisfied vagabond, "I Got Plenty o' Nuttin'," his proud duet with Bess, "Bess, You Is My Woman Now," the harshly comical song of the evil dandy, Sportin' Life ("It Ain't Necessarily So"), and perhaps the most beautiful piece of all, the despairing "My Man's Gone Now," sung by the bereft Serena over her murdered husband's body.

Although its merits were quickly recognized by some (but not all), as a commercial proposition *Porgy and Bess* was a first-time failure, its initial production lasting only 124 performances on Broadway. A revival, bravely sponsored by Cheryl Crawford (Majestic Theater 22 January 1942), with Duncan and Miss Brown again starred, did better (286 performances), and *Porgy and Bess* was picked up for a number of overseas productions, beginning with one in Denmark. However, the piece got its most significant exposure not from a regular theatre season but from two other sources. The first of these was a four-year international tour, played under the aegis of the US State Department, which took *Porgy and Bess* to Vienna, Berlin, London and Paris, with William Warfield and Leontyne Price starred before bringing the show back to Broadway (Ziegfeld Theater 10 March 1953, 305 performances), then continuing on to Europe, Arabia and South America, as well as through America and Canada. The other was a 1959 film version in which Sidney Poitier and Dorothy Dandridge (and the voices of Robert McFerrin and Adele Addison) starred alongside Pearl Bailey and Sammy Davis jr.

Now thoroughly established as a classic of the American light-opera stage, inhabiting that same area between opera and musical theatre most famously occupied by *Carmen* and other classics of the opéra-comique stage, *Porgy and Bess* has subsequently been given a multitude of stagings, principally in America but also throughout the rest of the world. It has played further seasons on Broadway in a Houston Grand Opera production (Uris Theater 25 September 1976, 122 performances) and at the Radio City Music Hall, and has been produced at the Metropolitan Opera House (1985 w Grace Bumbry, Simon Estes) and at Britain's Glyndebourne Festival Opera (1986 w Willard White, Cynthia Hayman) and Royal Opera House, Covent Garden (1992), as it has become accepted as part of the modern operatic repertoire.

All the major American and British productions of *Porgy and Bess* have been played with racially limited casts, and although a New Zealand Opera Company production starring Inia te Wiata as Porgy was staged in New Zealand and Australia with mostly maori players, and some Continental houses have, forcibly, mounted productions without regard to race, even in times that can produce such events as the *Miss Saigon* casting fiasco the first color-blind *Porgy and Bess* on an American or British stage is yet to come.

Austria: Volksoper 7 September 1952; Germany: Titaniapalast 18 September 1952; UK: Stoll Theatre 9 October 1952; France: Théâtre de l'Empire February 1953

Film: Otto Preminger 1959

Recordings: original 1935 cast selection (Mark 56), 1942 revival cast (Decca/MCA), London 1953 cast (RCA Victor), 1976 revival cast (RCA Victor), film soundtrack (Columbia), Glyndebourne cast 1988 (EMI), complete (Columbia/Odyssey), selections in Swedish (SR), etc

Literature: Alpert, H: *The Life and Times of Porgy and Bess* (Knopf, New York, 1990)

Video: EMI (Glyndebourne) 1989

Plate 311. **Cole Porter.** *Fame had yet to come—London's music publishers clearly hadn't heard of Cole Porter when they issued the sheet music to* The Eclipse, *but ''Col'' Porter lasted a good deal longer than their show.*

PORTER, Cole [Albert] (b Peru, Ind, 9 June 1891; d Santa Monica, Calif, 15 October 1964). Broadway songwriter for a series of successful and a handful of enduring shows.

Wealthy and well-living, Cole Porter purveyed from his early writing days a kind of songwriting that reflected his lifestyle: self-aware and crisply suave (if not always so very sophisticated) lyrics blended with smoothly insinuating melodies or comical blips of tune to produce material of a kind that, particularly given its overwhelming devotion to things sexual and/or social, would frequently have seemed more suitable to the then newly popular cabaret world than to that of the theatre. However, although he turned out a number of successful single songs that were not conceived as part of any stage show, it was as a writer of songs and collections of songs for the musical theatre that Porter made his greatest success.

Porter seemed destined for a quick introduction to Broadway when, following several years of supplying songs to college shows, he was booked as ''principal composer'' to Lew Fields's musico-comico-filmico-melodrama *Hands Up. Hands Up* was put on stage at New Haven and promptly pulled. Fields put it back into the pot, called in Harry B Smith and Sigmund Romberg to redo script and songs, and by the time the show got to Broadway, Porter's part in the proceedings was limited to one song, ''Esmeralda.'' However, he had not long to wait. After supplying one further interpolatable song, sung by Irene Bordoni in *Miss Information,* he had his first full-frontal exposure to Broadway at the age of 24, with the ''comic opera'' *See America First,* written with his college chum Lawrason Riggs and produced by top-flight agent Elisabeth Marbury. It was not an auspicious beginning. The show lasted 15 performances, and it was to be another dozen years before Porter would again essay the score for a book musical.

The young man had other things to occupy his salad days, and most of them were not in America. He took to the society circuits of Europe, where he played gaily through the final part of the First World War and through the 1920s, living the life of the high-flying rich (and even more richly wed) and turning out, on the way, a regular supply of brisk and bright songs that found their way into such London shows as Jerome Kern's exported *Very Good Eddie,* the musical farce *Telling the Tale, The Eclipse,* the formerly French revue *As You Were, A Night Out* (ly: Clifford Grey), C B Cochran's revue *Mayfair to Montmartre* and his heavily botched version of the French ''victory'' hit, *Phi-Phi.* For the American stage, he supplied the full scores for Raymond Hitchcock's revusical *Hitchy Koo of 1919* (56 performances) and the Shuberts' sequel *Hitchy-Koo of 1922* (which closed out of town), as well as for John Murray Anderson's longer-lived *Greenwich Village Follies* (1924, 127 performances). For Paris he composed the dance piece *Within the Quota* (1923) and supplied the songs for a 1928 revue at Les Ambassadeurs.

Porter's return to the Broadway book-musical stage was made on a reduced scale, when he provided the six songs (new and recycled) required to top up those borrowed from the Continent by producer E Ray Goetz to make up the musical part of *Paris,* his latest vehicle (w Gilbert Miller) for Irene Bordoni (Mrs Goetz). The small-scale *Paris* was a 195-performance success on Broadway, and it provided the first showcase for one of Porter's most famous songs, the mildly suggestive ''Let's Do It (let's fall in love)'' which was developed into a much more pointed piece in its subsequent reincarnation as a cabaret number than it was in the theatre—even in the throat of perky Mlle Bordoni.

Porter was now in his late thirties, and, after promising so much so early, his musical comedy career had really only just begun. But now, after the happily gallivanting dilettantism of the past decade, he became a regular contributor to the Broadway musical stage. The 1929 C B Cochran London revue *Wake Up and Dream* (263 performances, ''I'm a Gigolo'') transferred to Broadway (136 performances) later in the same year, by which time, again under the management of Goetz (who had also been the first, as producer of *Hands Up,* to use a Cole Porter song on Broadway), the composer had seen his first full-sized book musical since *See America First* produced on the New York stage. *Fifty Million Frenchmen* (''You've Got That Thing,'' ''You Do Something to Me''), composed to a Herbert Fields libretto, won a tidy success in 254 performances.

Goetz produced another Porter/Fields piece, *The New Yorkers* (''Love for Sale,'' ''I Happen to Like New York''), the following year with a cast that included Jimmy Durante, Ann Pennington, old-time stars Richard Carle and Marie Cahill and Fred Waring and his Pennsylvanians (168 performances), but a third teaming of producer and writers, on a piece called *Star Dust* (1931), with Peggy Wood slated as star, was abandoned without going into rehearsal. However, if, with this abortion, Goetz's career in the musical theatre was over, Porter was only hitting his stride.

His next engagement was on the Dwight Deere Wiman/Tom Weatherly production of *Gay Divorce* in which Fred Astaire, the certified star of *For Goodness' Sake, Lady, Be Good!* and *Funny Face,* was featured for the first time without his sister and up-to-then partner, Adele. The songs that Porter provided for Astaire and his new partner, Claire Luce, included ''Night and Day,'' and the show, the star and the song all won success on Broadway, in London and in Hollywood. One last show for Cochran, a musical stage version of the comic novel *Nymph Errant* (154 performances), produced several openly saucy songs (''Experiment,'' ''The Physician,'' ''Solomon''), to go with the show's innocently saucy text, and *Once Upon a Time,* a commission from Gilbert Miller, went the same way as *Star Dust* when it was aborted before reaching the stage. Next time up, though, Porter topped all his musical comedy efforts to date. *Anything Goes* (1934, ''I Get a Kick Out of You,'' ''You're the Top,'' ''Anything Goes,'' ''Blow, Gabriel, Blow,'' etc) gave him a real and international hit and one that was not just a once-around hit like *Gay Divorce,* but a show that, like few other American pieces of this period, would also become an enduring part of the revivable and revived canon.

Over the next 20 years, and in spite of a 1937 riding accident that confined the songwriter in a life of pain and disability for the rest of his days, Porter made up for his delayed start by providing regular new scores to the Broadway stage, and several more to the screen (*Born to Dance, Broadway Melody of 1940, The Pirate,* etc). Not all of these stage shows were successes, but even the less successful amongst them, such as *Jubilee* (169 performances, ''Begin the Beguine,'' ''Just One of Those Things''), *Red, Hot and Blue!* (183 performances, ''Down in the Depths,'' ''It's De-Lovely''), a remusicalization of Siegfried Geyer's already musicalized *Bei Kerzenlicht* as *You Never Know* (78 performances, ''At Long Last Love''), the revue *Seven Lively Arts* (183 performances, ''Every Time We Say Goodbye'') and the classical burlesque *Out of This World* (157 performances, ''From This Moment On'') brought forth new hit songs to add to the considerable catalogue of popular Porter numbers.

Unlike this group, however, the bulk of Porter's musical shows of the late 1930s and the 1940s had extended runs on Broadway. In just half a dozen years, Vinton Freedley's second vehicle for *Anything Goes*'s comedy pair, William Gaxton and Victor Moore, *Leave It to Me!* (307 performances, ''My Heart Belongs to Daddy,'' ''Most Gentlemen Don't Like Love''), Fields's and Buddy De Sylva's comic fantasy *Dubarry Was a Lady* (408 performances, ''Friendship,'' ''Katie Went to Haiti''), a follow-up vehicle for his most helpful star, Ethel Merman, *Panama Hattie* (501 performances, ''Make It Another Old-Fashioned, Please'') and Freedley's musical farce *Let's Face It* (547 performances, ''Let's Not Talk About Love'') with Danny Kaye starring, all had a first-rate metropolitan success, and if a further Merman vehicle, *Something for the Boys* (422 performances) and the Mike Todd spectacular *Mexican Hayride* (481 performances) produced rather less in the way of extractable song hits than the others, this series of shows each had fine, colorful careers on the American stage.

This period of Porter's career produced so many long-running successes, so many song hits, a number of London productions (*Dubarry Was a Lady, Let's Face It, Panama Hattie, Something for the Boys*), which more than made up for *Fifty Million Frenchmen*'s earlier death on the British road, and several film versions, yet the series of musicals that he and his collaborators turned out in these years in and around the Second World War were, as shows, largely ephemeral, and none of them succeeded in following *Anything Goes* into the list of standards.

In 1948, however, after more than 30 years in the business and at an age when more than 90 percent of composers and musical-comedy songwriters have all their best successes behind them, Porter wrote the show that clinched his place in the musical theatre's pantheon. Even more than *Anything Goes,* which has always seemed the quintessential Porter show, the almost atypical backstage musical comedy *Kiss Me, Kate* proved durable, memorable and revivable—not just its songs, this time, but the show as a whole. After its initial 1,077 performances on Broadway, *Kiss Me, Kate,* with its comical script and panorama of revusical and romantic songs, returned to the stages of the world again and again. It proved an international hit of a kind that had gone out of style, a hit that even carried the Broadway musical back into European houses, which had barely taken notice of an English-language piece since the days of *The Geisha* half a century earlier. And having got there, it stayed. *Kiss Me, Kate* was the very opposite of the ephemeral.

Can-Can (892 performances, ''I Love Paris,'' ''C'est magnifique,'' etc) and *Silk Stockings* (477 performances, ''Paris Loves Lovers'') were further Porter Broadway stage hits in the 1950s, *High Society* (''Who Wants to Be a Millionaire?,'' ''True Love,'' etc) and *Les Girls* gave him further film successes, and in 1958 he composed the score for a television version of *Aladdin* (''Wouldn't It Be Fun (not to be famous?)''), a piece subsequently transferred to the stage. In the wake of the West End success of Rodgers and Hammerstein's *Cinderella, Aladdin* was produced in 1959 (with its short score, Porter's last, made up to full-length by the borrowing of numbers from *Red, Hot and Blue!, Out of This World* and *Mexican Hayride*) on the London stage, where so much of the composer's early work had been first heard and where, in more recent decades, he had provided songs new or borrowed for the Drury Lane spectacular *The Sun Never Sets, The Fleet's Lit Up* (''Its De-Lovely''), the musical play *Somewhere in England* and the revue *Black Vanities.*

Porter was essentially a songwriter, and a songwriter who varied his light and apparently jokey style but little through score after score of numbers whose lyrics bristle with what seems like the entire contents of his address book—from the mayor of New York to Rin Tin Tin—catalogues of the once-famous, many of whom mean as little today as Gilbert's Captain Shaw, but who were both topical and good for a laugh and/or a rhyme in their time. However, his elegantly knowing command of words and music—the one fitted into the other as only a solo writer can do—coupled with a kind of period pout that belongs to an attractive-seeming era somewhere between the days when ''a glimpse of stocking was looked on as something shocking'' and these days, when ''anything goes,'' have given his songs a fervent following. This following, in its turn, resulted in his work being pushed back into the theatre in the 1980s and 1990s in varying if often unfortunate and/or unflattering forms.

An early Porter compilation, under the title *The Decline and Fall of the Entire World as Seen Through the Eyes of Cole Porter,* was played at New York's Square East Theater (30 March 1965), and another patchwork show, *Cole* (ad Alan Strachan, Benny Green), was mounted at London's Mermaid Theatre (2 July 1974), with considerably more success than an attempt at a Broadway musical version of the play *Holiday* with a Porter pasticcio score (*Happy New Year,* arr Buster Davis/Burt Shevelove, Morosco Theater 27 April 1980). A remade version of *You Never Know,* which reblended Porter's songs with more than before of Robert Katscher's original Continental score for *Bei Kerzenlicht,* was produced at New York's Eastside Playhouse (12 March 1973), whilst London has been given compilations of Porter material tacked loosely on to the libretti and part-scores of *High Society* (Victoria Palace 25 February 1987) and *Can-Can* (Strand Theatre 26 October 1988). Further abortive attempts to put versions of *High Society* on stage without Sinatra, Crosby, Kelly and Armstrong were tried in Australia (ad Carolyn Burns, Playhouse, Melbourne 31 December 1992) and in America (St James Theater 27 April 1998, ad Arthur Kopit, 144 performances). Almost every production of *Anything Goes* has also, if with rather more consideration for the original, raided Porter's songbook for extra musical icing.

A Hollywood biomusical that did to Porter's life pretty much what musicals and musical films had been doing to composers for decades was issued in 1946 under the title *Night and Day.* The very much alive Porter was doubtless pleased to be played by Cary Grant, even if the story told about him was pretty fictional. He wasn't around when Holland's Pieter van de Waterbeemd devoted a slanted-to-songs-and-homosex stage biomusical to him in 1995 (*You're the Top*).

1915 **Hands Up** (w William Daly, et al/E Ray Goetz /Edgar Smith) Shubert Theater, New Haven 7 June

1916 **See America First** (T Lawrason Riggs) Maxine Elliott's Theater 28 March

1928 **Paris** (Martin Brown) Music Box Theater 8 October

1929 **Fifty Million Frenchmen** (Herbert Fields) Lyric Theater 27 November

1930 **The New Yorkers** (H Fields) Broadway Theater 8 December

1932 **Gay Divorce** (Dwight Taylor) Ethel Barrymore Theater 29 November

1933 **Nymph Errant** (Romney Brent) Adelphi Theatre, London 6 October

1934 **Anything Goes** (Guy Bolton, P G Wodehouse ad Howard Lindsay, Russel Crouse) Alvin Theater 21 November

1935 **Jubilee** (Moss Hart) Imperial Theater 12 October

1936 **Red, Hot and Blue!** (Lindsay, Crouse) Alvin Theater 29 October

1938 **You Never Know** (ad Rowland Leigh) Winter Garden Theater 21 September

1938 **Leave It to Me!** (Bella Spewack, Sam Spewack) Imperial Theater 9 November

1939 **Dubarry Was a Lady** (H Fields, B G De Sylva) 46th Street Theater 6 December

1940 **Panama Hattie** (H Fields, De Sylva) 46th Street Theater 30 October

1941 **Let's Face It** (H Fields, Dorothy Fields) Imperial Theater 29 October

1943 **Something for the Boys** (H Fields, D Fields) Alvin Theater 7 January

1944 **Mexican Hayride** (H Fields, D Fields) Winter Garden Theater 28 January

1946 **Around the World [in 80 Days]** (Orson Welles) Adelphi Theater 31 May

1948 **Kiss Me, Kate** (B Spewack, S Spewack) New Century Theater 30 December

1950 **Out of this World** (Taylor, Reginald Lawrence) New Century Theater 21 December

1953 **Can-Can** (Abe Burrows) Shubert Theater 7 May

1955 **Silk Stockings** (George S Kaufman, Leueen McGrath, Burrows) Imperial Theater 24 February

1959 **Aladdin** (S J Perelman ad Peter Coke) London Coliseum 17 December

Biographies, etc: Ewen, D: *The Cole Porter Story* (Holt, Rinehart Winston, New York, 1965), Hubler, R: *The Cole Porter Story* (World, Cleveland, 1965), Eells, G: *Cole Porter: The Life That Late He Led* (Putnam, New York, 1967), Kimball, R, Gill, B: *Cole* (Holt, New York, 1971), Schwartz, C: *Cole Porter: A Biography* (Dial Press, New York, 1977), Grafton, D: *Red, Hot and Rich!* (Stein & Day, New York, 1987), McBrien, W: *Cole Porter: A Biography* (Knopf, New York, 1998), etc

DIE PORTRÄT-DAME, or Die Profezeinungen des Quiribi Komische Oper in 3 acts by F Zell and Richard Genée. Music by Max Wolf. Theater an der Wien, Vienna, 1 March 1877.

One of Zell and Genée's lesser-known works, set by the lesser-known Max Wolf, *Die Porträt-Dame* was produced at Vienna's Theater an der Wien in 1877. The piece was set in the late 17th century and featured Albertina Stauber (most recently the Cunégonde of the theatre's *Le Voyage dans la lune*) as the 18-year-old Friedrich-August, future monarch of Saxony, and Bertha Steinher as Charlotte, the daughter of the schoolmaster of the little town of Plowirz (Jani Szika), who was apparently the lady in the case. Herr Binder was Quiribi, the prophesying magician of the subtitle, Alexander Girardi played the comedy role of Hofmarschall Graf von Loos and Georgine von Januschowksy was his daughter Amalie, in yet another tale of the early amours of the aristocracy.

Die Porträt-Dame was played only five times at the Theater an der Wien, but it was picked up for production later the same year at Berlin's Friedrich-Wilhelmstädtisches Theater and was played widely around Germany for the next decade. During that time it was also given a German-language production in New York, with Marie König as Charlotte, Kuster as a non-travesty Friedrich-August, Frln Holzapfel as Amalia, and Max Lube and Gustav Adolfi in the other principal roles.

Germany: Friedrich-Wilhelmstädtisches Theater 1877; USA: Thalia Theater 20 September 1880

POSFORD, [Benjamin] George [Ashwell] (b Folkestone, 23 March 1906; d Worplesdon, 24 April 1976).

Law student turned composer Posford began his musical-theatre career with some additional songs for Robert Courtneidge's touring musical *Lavender* (1930), before turning to writing for the radio. There, he hit an unexpected bonus when he collaborated with the powerfully placed Eric Maschwitz on a radio operetta, *Good Night Vienna.* When the broadcast of his piece was delayed, Maschwitz negotiated a film version that, with Jack Buchanan and Anna Neagle starred, gave a nationwide airing to the young composer's title song, as sung to success by Buchanan, and score. Posford collaborated on another radio musical with Herbert Farjeon (*One Day in Summer,* 1934), and continued his work with Maschwitz on a touring stage musical *The Gay Hussar.* In the wake of the first of Ivor Novello's romantic operetta successes, that piece was remade on Novello-esque lines as *Balalaika,* and Posford's title song (''At the Balalaika'') became a considerable song success within the success of the show itself.

A follow-up, *Paprika / Magyar Melody,* was a quick flop, as were an attempt to go where Cole Porter had failed in giving a score to Romney Brent's *Nymph Errant* libretto, as *Evangeline,* and a Maschwitz musicalization of the famous play *The Ghost Train.* However, Posford's principal score for the Cicely Courtneidge and Jack Hulbert show *Full Swing* was an adjunct to a sizeable musical-comedy success, and a further pairing with Maschwitz on the musical adaptation of the play *Brewster's Millions, Zip Goes a Million,* as a vehicle for comedy singing star George Formby (''I'm Saving Up for Sally'') had a fine run, even after the star was forced to retire from the production.

Posford provided music for a number of British films (*The Good Companions, Invitation to the Waltz, The Gay Desperado, Café Colette*) and scored song successes in 1941 with ''The London I Love'' and ''The Song of the Clyde.''

1933 **The Gay Hussar** (Eric Maschwitz) Manchester 2 October

1936 **Balalaika** revised *The Gay Hussar* w Bernard Grün Adelphi Theatre 22 December

1938 **Paprika** (later *Magyar Melody*) (w Grün/Harold Purcell/ Maschwitz, Fred Thompson, Guy Bolton) His Majesty's Theatre 15 September

1942 **Full Swing** (w Harry Parr Davies/Archie Menzies, Arthur Macrae, Jack Hulbert) Palace Theatre 16 April

1946 **Evangeline** (w Harry Jacobson/Maschwitz/Romney Brent) Cambridge Theatre 14 March

1946 **Goodnight Vienna** (Purcell/Maschwitz) Pavilion Theatre, Bournemouth 22 July

1951 **Zip Goes a Million** (Maschwitz) Palace Theatre 20 October

1954 **Happy Holiday** (Maschwitz) Palace Theatre 22 December

LE POSTILLON DE LONGJUMEAU Opéra-comique in 3 acts by Adolphe de Leuven and Brunswick. Music by Adolphe Adam. Théâtre de l'Opéra-Comique, Paris, 13 October 1836.

Adam's opéra-comique *Le Postillon de Longjumeau* was one of the pre-Offenbach pieces that remained in the repertoire of international light-operatic companies after the opéra-bouffe craze had wiped the majority of older pieces from their slates. Its libretto told the tale of the coachman Pierre Chappelou (Chollet), who abandons his rustic wife (Zoë Prévost) on their wedding night to go to Paris and become an operatic star. He meets trouble when he falls in love with and weds a fashionable lady, but the lady turns out to be his Madeleine, who has used the 10 years in between as profitably as he. The keystone of Adam's score is the song of the Postillon de Longjumeau, with its fabled top Ds, which causes the singing coachman to be operatically discovered at the top of the first act, but, like much of Adam's music, the remainder of the score happily straddled the gap between the operatic and the opéra-bouffe.

Hugely successful in France, the piece was given in an English-language version (ad Gilbert a' Beckett sr) in London five months after the Paris premiere, and it was played in several German versions in the principal central European cities before the end of that same year. Thereafter it was regularly performed in all three languages (and less frequently in several others) by repertoire houses and companies. It was given a major commercial revival by John Hollingshead in London in 1886 under the title *A Maiden Wife* (Empire Theatre, August), with Henry Walsham and Mlle Devrient in the leading roles, was produced at the Vienna Volksoper in 1908 and again in 1964, and in 1989 was seen at the Grand Théâtre de Genève.

A film version made in Vienna under the title in 1939, with Willi Eichberger in its title role, took the usual filmland liberties with the stage show.

UK: St James's Theatre *Postillion!* 13 March 1837; Germany: 3 June 1837; Hungary: (Ger) 30 September 1837, Magyar Királyi Operaház *Longjumeau postakocsis* 29 November 1904; Austria: Hoftheater 14 October 1837; USA: Park Theater 30 March 1840

Film: Carl Lamac 1936

Video: (Geneva) 1989

DIE POSTMEISTERIN Operette in 3 acts by August Neidhart. Music by Leon Jessel. Centraltheater, Berlin, 3 February 1921.

Following the European triumph of *Schwarzwaldmädel,* Jessel and Neidhart made several attempts to repeat that success with similarly flavored pieces. If *Die Postmeisterin* did not quite come up to the earlier show, it nevertheless put up a good showing.

Neidhart's story—set in a Hessian village of 1806—involved Magdalene, the postmistress (post as in carriage-post) of his story, in an adventure with Prince Louis Ferdinand of Prussia that had but little of the adventure of that more famous post-office lady, *Der Vogelhändler's* Christel von der Post, about it, and rather more of those of all the Princes who had been busy over the past operettic decade or two falling in love with village maidens. This Prince is unusual in that he's not out gallivanting but actually running away from Napoléon's army, and the lady dresses him up as the postmaster whilst her postboy lover, Fritz, pretends to be the Prince. The French Captain Virvaux—who sees the "postmaster" making love to pretty Pauline Wiesel, and his "postmistress" Magdalene with Fritz, and has to be put off with the excuse that the locals are practicing French-style wife swapping—finally winkles his Prince out, but the Prussians attack in timely fashion and prepare the ground for a happy ending.

If Pauline got the Prince, Magdalene got the bulk and best of the music including an opening solo "Wenn ich Mädel war," a second-act number "Vis-à-vis von mir" with the Capitain and chorus, a Storch-duo with the Prince ("Ja, ja der Storch, das ist ein Vieh"), a Slowaken-duo with Fritz ("Röckchen fliegen") and share in the waltz Quartet (w Pauline, Fritz, Ferdinand) "Reich mir die Lippen, reich mir den Mund," which was the evening's big tune.

Die Postmeisterin had a good Berlin career. It passed its 100th night on 13 September before being taken off to allow the production of Jessel and Neidhart's next piece, *Das Detektivmädel,* and it then moved on to Vienna, where, with Paul Kronegg (Louis Ferdinand) and Rosy Werginz (Magdalene) featured, it played nearly three months (81 performances) at Oskar Fronz's Bürgertheater. It returned to Berlin in 1927 for a revival at the Theater des Westens (15 February, 20 performances).

Austria: Wiener Bürgertheater 29 September 1922

POTTER, Paul M[eredith] [MacLEAN, Walter Arthur] (b Brighton, 3 June 1852; d New York, 7 March 1921).

Son of the rector of King Edward's School, Bath, briefly a member of the civil service in India, Potter, forced to flee Britain following a threatened homosexual scandal, became a journalist and sometime newspaper editor in America. There he authored a number of successful plays, the most notable being the stage adaptations of Gerald du Maurier's *Trilby* (1895) and Ouida's *Under Two Flags* (1901), but he also supplied the libretti for several musical pieces ranging from a series of musical farce comedies, including a song-studded adaptation of Tom Taylor's *The Overland Route* for Crane in the

1890s, to Leslie Stuart's successful London musical comedy, *The School Girl* (1903). He also wrote the libretto for Broadway's *The Queen of the Moulin Rouge,* a piece that illustrated a prince's night spent in the Parisian underworld—complete with Apache dance—when he fails to get amorous satisfaction from his princess. Lambasted by the critics—''a conglomeration of noise, vulgarity and commonplace idiocy'' (*New York Dramatic Mirror*), ''degrades the stage'' (*Theatre*)—it was (like several others of Potter's works) talked about and publicized as being slightly scandalous, and consequently it ran up a fine series of 163 performances.

There have been numerous attempts to musicalize the stage version of *Trilby,* beginning with one by Potter himself, who announced in 1897 a forthcoming comic opera by himself and Leoncavallo in which opera diva Emma Calvé was to play Trilby. It didn't happen anymore than other announced or mooted versions by Harry B Smith and Reginald De Koven (1909, when producer Hammerstein was scared off by Potter's threats of lawsuits), Leslie Stuart and Harry B Smith, Victor Herbert, Isidore de Lara, Viktor Holländer and Herr Prasch, Hubert Bath and Haddon Chambers and, more recently, Britain's Master of the Queen's Music, Malcolm Williamson. An American version, *The Studio Girl* (1927, Will Ortmann/J Kiern Brennan), which actually did make the stage, with Jeanette MacDonald starring folded pre-Broadway. In 1955 (30 July) an NBC television version featuring Basil Rathbone and Carol Channing was, for obvious reasons, entitled *Svengali and the Blonde* (although Trilby was never blonde). Britain's Kidderminster Playhouse staged its version in 1962 and, when it again became an obvious target for the unoriginal following the success of that other singing-girl-and-magnetic-teacher piece, *The Phantom of the Opéra,* several other attempts were made to get a *Trilby* off the ground. She seems, however, to defy musicalization. Only one country seems to have got a musical Trilby to the stage in recognizable condition: Hungary. Károly Clement put out a musical version that was mounted at the Városi Színház in 1922 (19 May).

Trilby also came in for much parody at the time of its production, in spite of manager A M Palmer's threats to sue the burlesquers. It was parodied both in song (''Trilby Will Be True,'' etc) and in stage burlesque in Britain (*Twillbe, or seven-gall-eye on the Hip, A Modern Trilby, A Trilby Triflet, A Dumaur'alised Trilby*), on Broadway (Richard Mansfield's production of *Thrilby*) and even in Australia (*Trilby Burlesque* Edwin Finn, music arr George Pack Theatre Royal, Melbourne 4 December 1897), where Maggie Moore starred as the heroine.

Another Potter stage success, *The Conquerors,* which—after billing it as ''original'' he eventually admitted was an adaptation from de Maupassant and Sardou's *La Haine*—was also burlesqued, as *The Con-Curers* (1898), by Weber and Fields.

1889 **The City Directory** (W S Mullaly and pasticcio) Utica, NY 1 May; Opera House, Chicago 28 May; Bijou Theater 10 February 1890

1889 **The Fakir** (Charles E Bergman/w Harry L Hamlin) Arcade Theater, Kankakee, Ill 22 August, Grand Opera House; Chicago 25 August; Columbus Theater, Harlem 9 February 1891

1890 **The World's Fair** (E E Rice) Broad Street Theater, Philadelphia 9 September

1894 **The Pacific Mail** (uncredited) Star Theater 22 October

1895 **A Stag Party, or A Hero in Spite of Himself** (Herman Perlet/w William Nye) Park Theater, Boston 14 October; Garden Theater 17 December

1898 **Fun on the Pacific Mail** (various) 14th Street Theater 21 March

1903 **The School Girl** (Leslie Stuart/Charles H Taylor/w Henry Hamilton) Prince of Wales Theatre 9 May

1908 **The Queen of the Moulin Rouge** (John T Hall/Vincent Bryan) Chestnut Street Opera House 18 November; Circle Theater 7 December

1912 **Half Way to Paris** (Arthur J Lamb/Hall) Court Square Theater, Springfield, Mass 19 April; Majestic Theater, Boston 23 April

1913 **The Man with Three Wives** (*Der Mann mit den drei Frauen*) American version w Harold Atteridge, Agnes Morgan (Weber and Fields' Theater)

POUCHE Opérette in 3 acts by Alphonse Franck adapted from a play by René Peter and Henri Falk. Music by Henri Hir(s)chmann. Théâtre de l'Étoile, Paris, 18 February 1925.

One of Hirschmann's more successful attempts at a modern musical comedy, *Pouche* was written to a text adapted by producer Alphonse Franck, manager of the Théâtre de l'Étoile, from a comedy of two seasons earlier (Théâtre de la Potinière 8 February 1923). Discovering that the young widowed Marquise de Poulignon (Mlle Vioricia) is planning secretly to look him over as a prospective husband, the miffed Gaston la Fajolle (Gaston Gabaroche) determines to put her off and gets his friend Jacques Bridier (Henri Defreyn) to hire a little dressmaker, Pouche (Yo Maurel), to pose as his mistress. The Marquise discovers the ruse and takes Pouche's place, and the plot begins to roll towards its predestined denouement.

Hirschmann's score included the catchy ''J'ai Pippo dans la peau,'' performed by the real Pouche and her Alfred (Robert Pizani), and ''Ah! les femmes, comm' ça change'' delivered with ease by Gabaroche, as well as some slightly more soigné pieces that shifted *Pouche* just a little away from the most popular musical-comedy genre. The show had a good Parisian run and subsequent touring life.

The play—seemingly its original rather than Franck's musicalization—was very loosely adapted for America by Avery Hopwood as a "romantic song-farce far from the French" under the title *Naughty Cinderella* (Lyceum Theater 9 November 1925) and produced by E Ray Goetz and Charles Frohman as a vehicle for Irene Bordoni (Mrs Goetz). Hirschmann's score was dispensed with, and the musical selection performed by Miss Bordoni included Paul Rubens's aging "I Love the Moon," Goetz's setting of Henri Christiné's "L'Homme du dancing" as "Do I Love You?," a Messager/Sacha Guitry song and the A L Keith/Lee Sterling "That Means Nothing to Me." Henry Kendall was Gerald Grey (ex- Gaston), Evelyn Gosnell played Claire Fenton (ex-Marquise) and Mlle Bordoni, in the role of the Cinderella who was supposed to be naughty, was called Chouchou Rousselle. The show served its star for 121 Broadway performances and for further use around America until her next vehicle was ready. It also temporarily scared the Shuberts' production of Straus's *Riquette* (which claimed, by way of excuse, to be based on the same original *Pouche* text) away from Broadway.

LA POULE BLANCHE Opérette in 3 acts by Antony Mars and Maurice Hennequin. Music by Victor Roger. Théâtre Cluny, Paris, 13 January 1899.

Chapitel (Hamilton) has just married Angèle Bardubec (Blanche Marie) when he hears he has inherited a fortune in Corsica. The newlyweds go off to honeymoon where their money is, only to find that they have been tricked. Chapitel's mild little uncle, Tromboli (Prévost), needs his only nephew to wed Frisca (Mlle Leblanc), the daughter of his friendly neighbor Quiquibio (Gravier jr), so that they can officially end the vendetta that has been raging between their two families since an episode over a white hen, ages and ages ago. The unhappy Chapitel is bigamously wed to the unwilling Frisca, and the complications increase when he helplessly puts Angèle in the kindly charge of a fellow (Rouvière) who just happens to be a passionate former suitor of the as yet unbedded bride. The expert comic writing of Mars and Hennequin carried their characters through plenty of colorful quiproquos on the way to a happy ending.

In spite of playing only 32 performances at the Théâtre Cluny, *La Poule blanche* was quickly exported both to Germany, where a vernacular version (ad Heinrich Bolten-Bäckers) was produced at Berlin's Viktoria Theater, and to Hungary (ad Emil Makai, Gyula P Zempléni).

In 1907 *The White Hen* (Casino Theater 16 February) turned up on Broadway, but Roderic Penfield's piece, which also dealt with a man married to two women simultaneously, had a Viennese setting (it had started off being called *The Girl from Vienna*), a score by Gustave Kerker, Penfield and Paul West, and gave no credit to the French authors but rather claimed nebulously to be taken from something German. Since "The White Hen" was a Tyrolean hotel and the first act was set in a Viennese marriage brokery, there may have been no lien of parentage with the older piece. Ralph Herz, Louis Mann, Lotta Faust and Louise Gunning starred for a cheerful 94 New York performances.

Hungary: Népszínház *A fehér csirke* 28 April 1899; Germany: Viktoria-Theater *Die weisse Henne* 11 September 1899

POUNDS, Courtice [POUNDS, Charles Curtice] (b Pumlico, London, 30 May 1862; d Surbiton, 21 December 1927). Short, boyishly pudgy tenor who went from star roles in comic opera to a career as Britain's best senior singing comedy actor.

The son of a sometime vocalist, Mary [Ann Jane] Curtice, and her builder husband, Pounds did his first singing as a boy soprano, being a choir soloist at St Stephens, South Kensington at the age of 11. He subsequently studied at the Royal Academy of Music and—after a brief turn in the building trade—won his first professional singing job at 19 in the chorus of D'Oyly Carte's *Patience.* He rose through the Savoy ranks, acting as understudy to Durward Lely and Rutland Barrington, playing in forepieces at the Savoy, then moving to leading-manship with the Carte touring companies (Tolloller, 1883, etc) and as New York's first regular Nanki-Poo (*The Mikado*), Hilarion (*Princess Ida*) and Richard (*Ruddigore*). During his American stay, from 1885 to 1887, he also took the tenor roles in the Broadway productions of Lacome's *Jeanne, Jeannette et Jeanneton* (*The Marquis,* Prince de Soubise) and Lecocq's *La Petite Mademoiselle* (*Madelon,* Jolivet).

He returned to Britain in 1888 and replaced Durward Lely as principal tenor of the Savoy company, creating the roles of Colonel Fairfax in *The Yeomen of the Guard* (1888, "Is Life a Boon?"), Marco in *The Gondoliers* (1889, "Take a Pair of Sparkling Eyes"), Indru in *The Nautch Girl* (1890), Sandford in the revised *The Vicar of Bray* and John Manners in *Haddon Hall,* before leaving Carte's company in 1892 to appear in the London version of *Ma mie Rosette* (Vincent).

In 1893 he staged three one-act operettas with a company of his own on the pier at Brighton, but, after appearing fairly briefly as Ange Pitou in a revival of *La Fille de Madame Angot,* in the disastrous *Miami* (1893) with Violet Cameron, and as the heroic Mark Mainstay in the short-lived *Wapping Old Stairs,* he returned to the Savoy to appear as Vasquez in *The Chieftain* (1894). He subsequently went to Australia for a six-month season (Louis Pomerol in *La Belle Thérèse,* Marco, Fairfax) and, on his return, now noticeably plumper, he was cast with great

Plate 312. **Louie Pounds** *(right) with Constance Drever in* Dorothy, *and brother* **Courtice Pounds** *as Ali Baba in* Chu Chin Chow.

success in the juvenile comedy/tenor role of Lanclot in *La Poupée* (1896). *The Royal Star* and *The Coquette* for the same management were less successful, a London revival season of *Dorothy* (playing the role made popular by Ben Davies) was briefer than a subsequent tour, and Pounds then moved away from the musical theatre to spend a period playing supporting roles (with the occasional song) in productions of the classics with Beerbohm Tree (*Twelfth Night,* Touchstone in *As You Like It, The Last of the Dandies, The Merry Wives of Windsor,* etc).

He returned to the musical theatre briefly in 1901, playing Box (*Cox and Box*) in a triple bill at the Coronet, and more substantially in 1903, as the extravagant King in a revival of *Chilpéric,* then, over more than a decade, took a long series of varying singing character roles in a long run of popular musicals, often stealing the show from the nominal stars with his mixture of fun and fine singing: *The Duchess of Dantzic* (1903, Papillon, London and New York), *The Cherry Girl* (1903, Starlight), *The Blue Moon* (1905, Major Callabone), *The Belle of Mayfair* (1906, Hugh Meredith), *Lady Tatters* (1907, Dick Harrold), *Havana* (1908, t/o Diego de la Concha), *The Dashing Little Duke* (1909, Abbé de la Touche), *The Merry Peasant* (*Der fidele Bauer,* 1909, Mattheus), the little *The Idol's Eyes* (1910, Roger Bellingham), *The Spring Maid* (*Die Sprudelfee,* 1911, Nepomuc), *Orpheus in the Underground* (1911, Orpheus), *Princess Caprice* (*Der liebe Augustin,* 1912, Jasomir), *Oh! Oh! Delphine* (1913, Pomponnet), *The Laughing Husband* (*Der lachende Ehemann,* 1913, Otto Bruckner) in London and on Broadway, *Oh, Be Careful* (*Fräulein Tralala,* 1915, Bruno Richard) and *My Lady Frayle* (1916, Canon of Dorcaster). He also appeared, between times, in the music halls in musical sketches (*Fritz* 1905, *A Very Modern Othello, Charles His Friend* 1907, etc).

The biggest success of the second half of Pounds's career came in 1916, when he created the principal comic role of Ali Baba in *Chu Chin Chow* (''Anytime's Kissing Time,'' ''When a Pullet Is Plump''), a part that he played throughout the whole of the show's record-breaking run. Oscar Asche provided him with a similar role in the show's successor, *Cairo,* but the final great starring success of his career awaited him at the age of 53, when he was cast as Schubert in London's *Lilac Time* (*Das Dreimäderlhaus*). His last appearance on the musical stage was in his sixties, in the Spanish musical *The First Kiss* (1924).

His youngest sister, **Louie POUNDS** [Louisa Emma Amelia POUNDS] (b Brompton, 12 February 1872; d Southsea, 6 September 1970), began as a chorister and understudy with George Edwardes (*Joan of Arc,* Daisy Meadows in *Blue-Eyed Susan,* t/o and tour Lady Gwendoline in *In Town*), who promoted her to a tiny role in *A Gaiety Girl* (1893, Daisy Ormsbury and u/s title role) and a better one in *An Artist's Model* (1895, Amy Cripps) in the UK and America. On her return in 1896 she was featured in the ingenue role of the touring musical *The French Maid* (1897, Dorothy Travers), which subsequently came to London. She appeared in *Hans Andersen's Fairy Tales* (1897) and the flop *Her Royal Highness* (Prince Rollo, 1898), then joined D'Oyly Carte's company at the Savoy to play between 1899 and 1903 in *The Rose of Persia* (Heart's Desire), *The Pirates of Penzance* (Kate), *Iolanthe* (Iolanthe), *Ib and Little Christina* (Christina), *The Emerald Isle* (Molly O'Grady), *A Princess of Kensington* (Joy Jellicoe) and *Merrie England* (Jill-all-Alone), plus the little forepiece *Pretty Polly* (1900).

She continued with Carte's successor, William Greet, in *The Earl and the Girl* (1903, Daisy Fallowfield), took over as one of the ''ugly'' sisters in Seymour Hicks's Cinderella story of *The Catch of the Season* (1904), created the title role in Basil Hood's *The Golden Girl* (1905, Mrs Robinson) on the road, took over in *The White Chrysanthemum* (1906, Cornelia Vanderdecken), then scored a particular personal success playing alongside her brother in Leslie Stuart's *The Belle of Mayfair* (1906, Princess Carl, ''The Weeping Willow Wept,'' ''Said I to Myself''). She paired again with Courtice in *Lady Tatters* (1907, Isabel Scraby), the *Dorothy* revival (1908, Lydia) and *The Dashing Little Duke* (1909, Duchesse de Burgoyne) before, in 1910, going to America, where she appeared on Broadway as the outrageous Olga of *The Dollar Princess.*

She subsequently toured in the star roles of *The Merry Widow, Autumn Manoeuvres* and *The Girl in the Train* and visited South Africa and Australia, mixing straight and musical appearances, these last including the role of the comical Alcolom in Australia's production of her brother's great hit, *Chu Chin Chow.* Her last London musical roles were in *Toto* (1916, Madame Jollette) and *The Island King* (1922), although she was seen on the road in *The Blue Kitten* and *Lionel and Clarissa* in the late 1920s.

Three other sisters, **Lillie POUNDS** [Alice Mary POUNDS] (b Chelsea, 2 October 1864), **Nancy POUNDS** [Fanny Elizabeth POUNDS] (b Chelsea, 20 November 1866) and **Rosie POUNDS** [Rowena Emily POUNDS] (b Greenham, 24 December 1869), also played in comic opera and/or musical comedy, and most particularly with Carte's companies. Lillie married [James] George Mudie (b 11 October 1859; d 28 December 1918), a longtime musical-theatre comic actor and formerly the husband of the successful comic-opera contralto known as Adelaide Newton (d 12 May 1900), whilst Nancy was the wife of Savoy player W H Kemble [William Harold Poole], a nephew of the company's star contralto, Alice Barnett.

Pounds himself was successively married to two singers, both sometime members of the D'Oyly Carte Company: Jessie [Louise] Murray, daughter of the actor Gaston MURRAY [Garstin Parker WILSON], then Millicent Pyne.

LA POUPÉE Opéra-comique in 4 acts by Maurice Ordonneau. Music by Edmond Audran. Théâtre de la Gaîté, Paris, 21 October 1896.

A good many years on from his first great successes with *Les Noces d'Olivette, La Mascotte* and *Gillette de Narbonne,* composer Audran suddenly surfaced, amongst what had become a routine of comfortable Parisian runs and not-so-comfortable failures, with another major international hit in *La Poupée.* If Maurice Ordonneau's libretto was not precisely original in its bases—the doll/girl exchange was a well-worn, but apparently not yet worn out, plot device—it did, however, create some endearing characters, most particularly its pink-cheeked monastic hero, and some amusing and charming scenes around which, and in keeping with which, Audran composed one of his prettiest scores. Times had changed since the brightly colored and fun-packed days of *La Mascotte,* and, without going into the pastel colors of some later opérette successes, *La Poupée* purveyed a kind of comical charm rather than the more vigorous humor of yesteryear.

When his monastery falls on hard times, Father Maximin (Lucien Noël) hits on a plan. The novice monk Lancelot (Paul Fugère) had been promised a vast dowry by his drunken, half-blind old uncle (Paul Bert) on his marriage. So Lancelot shall ''marry''—but his bride shall be one of the dolls from the shop of Maître Hilarius (Dacheux). The one the boy unwittingly chooses, however, is the doll maker's daughter Alésia (Mariette Sully), who has been standing in for a figure she damaged in the dusting. By the time the marriage is done, and Lancelot has taken his doll-bride back to the monastery, he has grown attached enough to her that, when she turns out to be real, he prefers to give up his tonsure than his wife. The lower comedy, alongside the gentler strain in the Lancelot-Alésia scenes, was provided by Madame Hilarius (Gilles Raimbaut), sold as a job lot with her daughter, and courted by old Uncle La Chanterelle under the unsuspecting doll maker's nose.

The music of the show was very largely the province of the two principal players. Alésia described in a waltz the young man with whom she fell in love in church (''Mon Dieu, sait-on jamais, en somme?''), went through her paces as the automaton (''Je sais entrer dans un salon''), attacked Lancelot amorously in duo (''Je t'aime! je t'adore!''), charmed Uncle and his boozy pal in a flowing waltz trio, and the monastery in a 6/8 ''Je suis un petit mannequin,'' whilst Lancelot put his inexperienced nose into the real world in 2/4 time (''Dans les couvents on est heureux''), discovered a liking for womanhood in the little duo ''Que c'est donc gentil,'' and awoke wonderingly at the touch of the ''doll's'' kiss into the waltzing duo ''On dirait comme une caresse de femme'' before coming to his final profession of love (''Qui? la femme donne à l'âme''). Amongst the concerted music, the monks' choral farewell to their brother at the end of the first act was a highlight.

La Poupée had a fine first run in Paris, holding up happily through 121 performances, but it was not immediately snatched up for overseas productions. London's leading producers turned it down and, finally, it was tyro impresario Henry Lowenfeld who took up the rights with the idea of starring comic Arthur Roberts as Hilarius. The adaptation was done by Arthur Sturgess, George Byng fashioned some new numbers from Audran's music, largely to give a good singing role to baritone Norman Salmond as Père Maximin, and the piece was produced at the Prince of Wales Theatre with Courtice Pounds (Lancelot), young Parisian ingenue Alice Favier (Alésia) and not Roberts but Willie Edouin (Hilarius). *La Poupée* turned out to be the most successful musical import to the London stage for many years. It ran in London for 576 performances, the Audran/Byng ''A Jovial Monk Am I'' became a baritone party piece and the skillful and experienced Edouin scored a huge personal hit as the comical doll maker. The show returned to the Prince of Wales in 1898 (13 December) and in 1904 with Edna May as Alésia (12 April), and was seen in London again as late as 1931 (24 December) and 1935 (21 December) with Jean Colin and Mark Lester. It also toured incessantly for many years with Mlle Favier's understudy, Stella Gastelle, making half a career of the role of Alésia. So popular, in fact, was the piece with English-speaking audiences, that it even became the subject for a 1922 five-reel Wardour film, with Flora Le Breton starred in the role of a silent Alésia.

After the British success of *La Poupée* other countries began to show interest in the show. Broadway's *La Poupée* opened eight months after London's, with another Frenchish star, Anna Held, as Alésia alongside G W Anson, Trixie Friganza, Frank Rushworth and Rose Leighton. Oscar Hammerstein's production of Sturgess's version ran 46 nights and returned quickly (15 April 1898), this time under the management of Augustin Daly (who had bought the rights of the show from Hammerstein) and with Virginia Earle at its head alongside James T Powers, Frank Celli and two famous old-timers in gangling comedian Joseph Herbert and Catherine Lewis as the doll's parents, for a second series of 18 performances prior to the road.

In Budapest Klára Küry was *A baba* (ad Ferenc Rajna) to the travesty Lancelot of Aranka Hegyi and the Hilarius of József Németh when the piece was mounted at the Népszínház. This production played its 50th performance on 4 November 1899 and ultimately totaled 82 playings—a figure that put the show into the very top league of operettic hits at Budapest's most important musical house—prior to a number of revivals at other theatres (Városligeti Színkör 1909, Esküteri Színház 1920, etc).

In Berlin, José Ferenczy followed up his Centraltheater hit with *Die Geisha* by starring Mia Werber, who had triumphed in the English piece, as the doll-girl of his German version of *Die Puppe* (ad A M Willner), alongside Schulz (Lancelot) and Emil Sondermann (Hilarius), and scored a second hit (100th performance 16 April 1899). Thereafter *Die Puppe* spread through Germany's theatres at a great rate, outstripping not only all of Audran's earlier works in popularity, but quite simply establishing itself (according to Keller's 1926 tally of all-time performances) as the most played of all French works in Germany, ahead of all the favorite works of Offenbach and even of *Les Cloches de Corneville.* In 1904 Ferenczy's company took their version of *Die Puppe* to New York and played it at the Irving Place Theater in repertoire with *Das süsse Mädel* and *Die Geisha,* whilst a 1919 revival at the Theater am Nollendorfplatz proved the show's enduring popularity by running for over one hundred nights.

Perversely, Vienna did not take to Willner's version of the show in the same way. Produced by Alexandrine von Schönerer with Frln von Naday/Frln Worm (Alésia), Ferdinand Pagin (Lancelot) and Franz Tewele (Hilarius), and with Josef Joseffy (Lorémois) and Therese Biedermann (Heinrich) in supporting roles in an otherwise second-best Theater an der Wien cast, it was played 25 successive times and only a handful more thereafter. It was, however, later produced by Gabor Steiner for a season at Danzers Orpheum in 1902 (12 December), with Mizzi Zwerenz as the false doll, and at his Venedig in Wien summer theatre the following season.

La Poupée returned to the Gaîté in 1898 and was seen again on the Paris stage in 1921, when Mlle Mathieu-Lutz appeared as Alésia in a revival at the Théâtre Mogador (10 September), but it never won the extraordinary favor in its country of origin that it had done in England or, most particularly, in Germany.

UK: Prince of Wales Theatre 24 February 1897; USA: Lyric Theater 21 October 1897; Hungary: Népszínház *A baba* 13 January 1898; Australia: His Majesty's Theatre, Sydney 10 September 1898; Germany: Centraltheater *Die Puppe* 5 January 1899; Austria: Theater an der Wien *Die Puppe* 10 October 1899

Film: Wardour (Eng) 1922

LA POUPÉE DE NUREMBERG Opéra-comique in 1 act by Adolphe de Leuven and Arthur de Beauplan. Music by Adolphe Adam. Théâtre Lyrique, Paris, 21 February 1852.

One of the most popular one-act opéras-comiques in the French repertoire in the pre-Offenbach era, Adam's little piece was played throughout Europe for more than half a century, translated into a dozen foreign-language versions and was one of the few early opérettes to survive, with regular productions, the ''modern'' Offenbach onslaught.

Cornelius, the toymaker of Nuremberg, makes a wonderful doll that he believes, with the help of magic art, he can bring alive as a wife for his beloved son, Benjamin. On the night of the carnival ball, Cornelius's nephew and assistant, the ill-treated Heinrich, dresses up as the devil and ''borrows'' the doll's clothes as a costume for his sweetheart, Bertha. When the toymaker comes home, and believes what he sees, Heinrich realizes how he can manipulate things to his advantage. The ''doll'' misbehaves so terribly that Cornelius smashes it with an axe, and Heinrich then lets him believe he has killed Bertha. With the hush money Cornelius gives him, the two will be able to wed. And Cornelius is happy just not to be a murderer.

The opéra-comique was given its first English-language production by Emilia Rudersdorff and her company at Cork, at Christmas 1860, under the title *Dolly,* with the manageress, Charles Durand and Palmieri heading the cast, and it was later seen on the London stage at both Covent Garden, presented by the Pyne and Harrison company (ad George Linley) under the title *The Toymaker* with Annie Thirlwall (Bertha), Susan Pyne (Maximilian), Henry Haigh (Kloster) and George Honey (Cornelius) and at the Gaiety Theatre (*Dolly* 22 August 1870). The tale also provided the bones for a comic opera *The Miraculous Doll,* ''adapted by Henry Wardroper from a Swedish version of *Dockan*'' but utilizing Adam's music (Theatre Royal, Sheffield 12 July 1886).

The American farce comedy (''with 27 musical numbers'') known as *Jollities, or The Electrical Doll* (J Adahm/Charles F Pidgin, Putnam, Conn 8 November 1880) and its remakes as *The Electric Spark* (1882, with new music by Charles Blake) and *Fun in a Toyshop* (1884) were all re-remakes of *La Poupée de Nuremberg* and a briefly Broadway comic opera, *Ardriell* (Union Square Theater 3 June 1889), since it claimed ''Herr Adahm'' (otherwise J A Norris) as its composer, was presumably a further remake of the same concoction. A West Coast operetta entitled *The Toymaker* played at the San Francisco Tivoli, and later a touring vehicle for sometime Tivoli favorite Ferris Hartman was another version of *La Poupée de Nuremberg,* as was the piece played in the same area as *The Magical Doll.* Benjamin Woolf adapted the show afresh in 1882 for the Boston Comic Opera Company as *The Magic Doll.*

Germany: Friedrich-Wilhelmstädtisches Theater *Die Nürnberger Puppe* 26 November 1852; Austria: Carltheater *Die Nürnberger Puppe* December 1860; UK: Theatre Royal, Cork *Dolly* 26 December 1860, Theatre Royal, Covent Garden *The Toymaker* 19 November 1861, Sheffield *The Miraculous Doll* 12 July 1886; Hungary: Nemzeti Színház *A Bubagyaros* (aka *Bűvös baba, A nürnbergi baba*) 16 May 1863

POUR DON CARLOS Opérette à grand spectacle in 2 acts by André Mouëzy-Éon and Raymond Vincy based on the novel by Pierre Benoît. Lyrics by Raymond Vincy. Music by Francis Lopez. Théâtre du Châtelet, Paris, 17 December 1950.

The first of the Vincy/Lopez opérettes à grand spectacle mounted at the Châtelet by Maurice Lehmann, *Pour Don Carlos* assembled, at the Hôtel des Cimes at Cauterets, a group of characters who might have been borrowed from the theatre's hit of the previous year, *L'Auberge du cheval blanc.* There was the rich industrialist Pommier (Fernand Sardou) with his daughter (Colette Hérent), an anti-Carlist policeman (Jack Claret) and his nephew (Pierjac), and, of course, Don Carlos (Georges Guétary) himself, striving for the throne of Spain. The 1875 action led the star through 16 settings, a drill, a ballet lumineux, two grands ballets, the royal court of King Alfonso, the field, prison, hospital, a half dozen solos (three of which were boléros/rumbas) and duets with his gypsyish leading lady (Maria Lopez, herself equipped with four numbers, one a rumba-boléro) to flight towards America, without a crown but with the leading lady, at the final curtain.

Although some of the music was agreeable enough, and Guétary's ''Je suis un bohémien'' did well outside the show, *Pour Don Carlos* was not vintage Lopez nor certainly vintage Vincy. Nevertheless, with the aid of its star and the grand spectacle, it ran through 420 performances at the Châtelet and went on to a provincial afterlife.

Recording: original cast (Pathé)

POWERS, James T [McGOVERN, James] (b New York, 22 April 1862; d New York, 10 February 1943).

A little man, with a face like a cross between a sandwich machine and a Venus flytrap with the giggles, which predestined him for comedy, ''Jimmy'' Powers began his theatrical career, after a stint in vaudeville in a double act with James Carney, playing in stock (Aberle's 8th Street Co), extravaganza (Policeman in *Evangeline,* 1882) and musical farce comedy. He toured with Willie Edouin in America (1882, Bubbles in *Ripples,* etc) and on his unfortunate venture to Britain with *Dreams*

(Bobby Bibbitty/Chip Cheeky/Policeman 123) and *A Bunch of Keys* (Grimes). He subsequently played in Britain with the Vokes Family (deputizing for the ailing Fawdon Vokes), in pantomime, and in John Hollingshead's revival of *Chilpéric* at the Empire Theatre, before returning to America. There, from 1885, for two years, he toured in Hoyt and Thomas's *Tin Soldier* company, featured in the role of Rats.

Powers played for a period in comic opera at the Casino Theater, appearing in such roles as the little Briolet in *The Marquis* (*Jeanne, Jeannette et Jeanneton*) and Taboureau in *Madelon* (*La Petite Mademoiselle*), as Faragas in *Nadjy* (1888), the sighing tailor, Griolet, in *La Fille du tambour-major,* and as Cadeau to the Ravannes of Edwin Stevens in a revival of *Erminie.* He then returned to farce comedy (*A Straight Tip, A Mad Bargain*) for some years, but he came back to the more legitimate musical stage for what would be the most memorable portion of his career, playing the star comic roles in the New York productions of a series of mostly British musical comedies in the 1890s and 1900s.

Beginning with Arthur Roberts's *Gentleman Joe* (1896), these subsequently included the orientals Wun-Hi in *The Geisha* and Li in *San Toy* (both created at Daly's Theatre by Huntley Wright), Teddy Payne's little-chap comic roles in the Gaiety musicals *The Circus Girl, The Messenger Boy* and *A Runaway Girl,* Pentweazle in *The Medal and the Maid* (1904), Walter Passmore's Moolraj (*The Blue Moon,* 1906), Henry Lytton's Jelf (*A Princess of Kensington,* 1903) and, with particular success, a remade (by himself) version of Alfred Lester's creation, Samuel Nix, in the Leslie Stuart musical *Havana* (1909). He also played Hilarius in *La Poupée* (revival), and appeared in such native musical plays as Oscar Hammerstein's *Santa Maria, The Jewel of Asia* (1903, Pierre Lerouge) and Gustave Kerker's second remake of *Two Little Brides* (*Schneeglöckchen,* 1912, Polycarp Ivanovich).

In his later career Powers appeared mostly in straight theatre (though he repeated his Wun-Hi as late as 1931), but without maintaining the star profile he had won through some 20 years of musical comedy. In 1922 he also ventured into authorship with a musical version of the comedy *Somebody's Luggage* written with Mark Swan. He himself starred in a fine cast including Allen Kearns, Marjorie Gateson and Flavia Arcaro, under the direction of Ned Wayburn, but *The Little Kangaroo* died on the road. Powers was also credited with the lyrics for the occasional song interpolated into his own parts (*Havana, Two Little Brides,* etc).

Powers's wife, **Rachel BOOTH,** an original member of the cast of *The Tin Soldier* (1885, Carry Story), *Natural Gas* (Jimpsy), *A Mad Bargain* (1892, Roose Robinson), etc, later appeared in soubrette roles alongside her husband in several shows (Mimi in *The Jewel of Asia,* etc).

1922 **The Little Kangaroo** (aka *Little Miss Butterfly*) (Werner Janssen/w Mark Swan) Stamford, Conn 23 November

Autobiography: *Twinkle, Little Star* (Putnam, New York, 1939)

PRADEAU [Étienne] (b 1817; d Paris, c20 January 1895).

The celebrated comedian began his career of more than half a century on the Parisian stage singing secondary tenor roles at the Opéra-Comique, but he took his most important step to fame when he left those semi-august halls and appeared, paired with Berthelier, as one of the original ''blind men'' in Offenbach's *Les Deux Aveugles* (1855) on the original bill at the Bouffes-Parisiens. He remained a member of Offenbach's company for some years, playing in such pieces as *Croquefer* (1857, Croquefer), *Le Financier et le savetier* (1856, Belazor), *Pépito* (Vertigo), as one of *Les Deux Pêcheurs* (1857, Gros-Minet) with Gerpré, *Le Docteur Miracle, Tromb-al-ca-zar* (1856, Beaujolais), *La Rose de Saint-Flour* (1856, Marcachu), *Le Rêve d'un nuit d'été* (1855, Mr Gray), *Madame Papillon* (1855, Sophoniste Retapée), *Il Signor Fagotto* (1864, Bacolo), *L'Amour chanteur* (1864, Guillaume), *Le Voyage de MM Dunanan* (1862, Tympanon), *Les Bavards* (1863, Sarmiento) and *Les Géorgiennes* (1864, Rhododenron Pasha).

The burly actor later moved on to less musical employment at the Palais-Royal and the Gymnase (Sancho Pança in Sardou's *Don Quichotte,* etc), but returned to musicals when he joined the company at the Théâtre des Variétés and there created such comic roles as Le Commissaire in *La Boulangère a des écus* (1875), Flochardet in *Le Manoir du Pictordu* (1875, ''he kept the audience in a roar the whole evening, his facial expression as usual being often enough to convulse the house''), in *Le Dada* (1876) and as Van Tricasse in *Le Docteur Ox* (1877), alongside a long list of important creations in plays. He was later seen at the Nouveautés in France's original production of *Fatinitza* (1879, Makouli) and as van Mitten in the unfortunate Verne spectacular *Kéraban le Tétu* (1883) in one of his last appearances on the musical stage.

PRESENT ARMS Musical comedy in 2 acts by Herbert Fields. Lyrics by Lorenz Hart. Music by Richard Rodgers. Lew Fields' Mansfield Theater, New York, 26 April 1928.

Herbert Fields followed up his naval success, *Hit the Deck,* with a marine military piece, and for *Present Arms* he rejoined forces with his habitual partners, Richard Rodgers and Lorenz Hart. He brought with him the star of *Hit the Deck,* Charles King, who was featured in the new piece as a marine who pretends that he is a ranking officer when courting the English Lady Delphine (British supporting actress Flora Le Breton, here getting her big chance), who is also ogled by the rich foreigner Ludwig von Richter (Anthony Knilling). It was another English lass, comedienne Joyce Barbour, however, who teamed with Busby Berkeley (doubling as choreographer and hero's best friend) to put across the song that proved the highlight of an evening that was not up to *Hit the Deck,* when they joined together in ''You Took Advantage of Me.'' *Present Arms* lasted 155 Broadway performances and was not exported.

London did, however, get a *Present Arms* in the form of ''a revusical comedy in 2 acts by Fred Thompson. Additional dialogue by Bert Lee. Lyrics by Frank Eyton. Music by Noel Gay,'' produced at the Prince of Wales Theatre, during the Second World War (13 May 1940). Wylie Watson, George Gee and Billy Bennett comicked through wartime France as three old soldiers who had fond memories of the First World War and of Babette (Phyllis Monkman) in a piece built on the lines of the first war's hit show *The Better 'Ole.* In an ephemeral score, grapeshot through with transatlantic interpolations, American soubrette Evelyn Dall and the Vincent Tildesley Meistersingers harmony group encouraged ''Dig for Victory,'' Miss Dall danced with her partner, Max Wall, to ''Dancing People,'' Miss Monkman was ''Mademoiselle de France'' and Herman Timberg's song tried to make people believe that in spite of everything it was a ''Hap-Hap-Happy Day.'' Tom Arnold and Harry Foster's production provided lively, topical entertainment on a twice-daily format for 225 performances before being chased out of town by disapproving bombs.

LES PRÉS SAINT-GERVAIS Opéra-comique in 3 acts by Victorien Sardou and Philippe Gille based on Sardou's play of the same title. Music by Charles Lecocq. Théâtre des Variétés, Paris, 14 November 1874.

Following his two enormous international successes with *La Fille de Madame Angot* and *Giroflé-Girofla,* Lecocq took a turn in a more opéra-comique direction with his version of Sardou's play (with songs) *Les Prés Saint-Gervais,* a piece written for Virginie Déjazet and originally played and sung by her at the Théâtre Déjazet in 1862 (24 April).

The expanded (by an act) and now thoroughly musical version of Déjazet's role of the young Prince de Conti was written for and to the measure of favorite prima donna Zulma Bouffar, but before *Les Prés Saint-Gervais* could get to the stage Mlle Bouffar had crossed words with the Variétés management, walked out and left the prize role of the latest Lecocq piece to the splendidly voiced but less charismatic Mlle Peschard.

The pubescent young Prince has a hard time getting Harpin (Berthelier), his hypocritical, lecherous old tutor, and the rest of the folks around him—notably the courtly girls—to recognize the fact that he is becoming a man with a man's wants and needs. So, on the day when the people of the quarter hie themselves to the Prés Saint-Gervais for a jolly picnic, the lad slips away and follows. When he tries to join in the fun of the bourgeois folk, he is ridiculed for his courtly ways, and the certain success with women that Harpin has dutifully taught his royal pupil will naturally be his is made a mockery of by a little flowergirl named Friquette (Paola Marié). Events come to the point where he ends up fighting a duel with La Rose (Christian), a sergeant in his own regiment. Although the experienced soldier pinks the boy, he then becomes his champion and helps him to put all his mockers in their place (and to sew his royal wild oat with Friquette) before leading him home, wiser to the ways of a world from which he has been all too shielded before. Two of the bourgeois folk, Angélique and Grégoire, provided some contrasting comedy.

Lecocq's score to *Les Prés Saint-Gervais* was written in a manner suited to its period and classic subject, without the bouffe effects of a *Giroflé-Girofla,* or the entrain of an *Angot,* and although there was some fine soprano singing for the star, jolly moments for the comic folk and a good dash of military music, the *Prés Saint-Gervais* music did not produce anything like the remarkable score that Lecocq would provide, a few years later, for a similar subject in *Le Petit Duc.* Nor, in spite of its attractions did it produce a number like ''La Belle Bourbonnaise'' with which Déjazet had made such a hit in the original play.

Les Prés Saint-Gervais played only 46 nights at the Variétés, but its composer's reputation ensured that it was exported in amazingly quick time. London, avid for the newest Lecocq musical, snapped it up and Robert Reece's English version was mounted at the Criterion Theatre with Pauline Rita (Conti) and Catherine Lewis (Friquette) starred and Alfred Brennir as La Rose, only a fortnight after the Paris premiere. One critic, outraged by opéra-bouffe and the can-can and longing for ''good taste'' and the days of Planché, sighed happily ''[It] might have been written twenty years ago; nevertheless, and in spite of a cast of 60, it ran for 132 performances at its very little house. It doubtless appeared less ''good taste'' when the lively Kate Santley, with her penchant for interpolating saucy songs into her shows, then took it to the provinces.

Nowhere else, however, did the piece win a run like that in London. Vienna's Carltheater production, with Hermine Meyerhoff (Conti), Karoline Finaly (Friquette), Franz Eppich (La Rose), Josef Matras (Harpin) and

Therese Schäfer (Dorette), was played 10 times. The uncredited translation retitled the piece *Prinz Conti,* a title retained for Germany and for Hungary, where it found little more success.

Les Prés Saint-Gervais was first seen in America in 1875 as played by Samuel Colville's ill-fated Julia Mathews company, with Miss Mathews supported by London cast member Albert Brennir, G H MacDermott and Rose Keene. Alice Oates added the piece to her repertoire soon after, and in 1883 another London cast member, Catherine Lewis, ventured a *Prince Conti* with Miss Lewis, now a major star, swapping the role of Friquette for that of Conti alongside her sister, Constance Lewis (Friquette). The company introduced the show in Pittsburgh and played only a few nights of *Prince Conti* at New York's Fifth Avenue Theater (billed as an American premiere) as part of their touring schedule.

UK: Criterion Theatre 28 November 1874; USA: Brooklyn Theater 27 September 1875, Library Hall, Pittsburgh *Prince Conti* 29 February 1883, Fifth Avenue Theater *Prince Conti* 29 March 1883; Austria: Carltheater *Prinz Conti* 10 March 1876; Australia: Prince of Wales Theatre, Melbourne 10 July 1876; Hungary: Budai Színkör *Conti herceg* (*A tizenhat éves ezredes*) 19 July 1877; Germany: Aachen *Prinz Conti* 7 August 1880

PRESTON, Robert [MESERVEY, Robert Preston] (b Newton Highlands, Mass, 8 June 1918; d Santa Barbara, Calif, 21 March 1987).

After a 25-year career in theatre and film, the twinkling, crushed-voiced Preston became a musical-theatre star overnight with his 1957 performance of an era as the roguish Professor Harold Hill in *The Music Man* (''Till There Was You,'' ''Seventy-Six Trombones,'' Tony Award). He subsequently starred on Broadway in the musical *Ben Franklin in Paris* (1964, Benjamin Franklin), alongside Mary Martin in the two-handed saga of American marriage *I Do! I Do!* (1966, Tony Award) and as Mack Sennett in the sorry musical tale of *Mack and Mabel* (1974, ''I Won't Send Roses''). His last musical, *The Prince of Grand Street* (1978), folded on the way to town, a fate that had earlier befallen *We Take the Town* (1962), a musical based on the Ben Hecht play *Viva Villa,* in which Preston appeared as Pancho Villa.

Preston repeated his *Music Man* role on film and also appeared as Beauregard, the honeymooning husband of *Mame,* in the filmed version of that musical.

PRÉVEL, Jules (b Saint-Hilaire de Harcouët, 1835; d Paris, 12 September 1889).

A Parisian journalist and theatre critic, Prével is credited with having invented the theatre gossip column or courrier des théâtres with the rubrique which he began at *Le Figaro* in 1865. The boyish-looking, devotedly ''investigative'' journalist operated in and around the Paris theatre for nearly 25 years, penning his columns with a serious enthusiasm in which an actress's private affairs took on all the importance of affairs of state, and winning himself many enemies in the process.

Prével collaborated on the texts of a number of plays and opérettes, including several successful works in conjunction with Paul Ferrier (notably the very fine and very durable *Les Mousquetaires au couvent*) and with Armand Liorat. His part therein was, however, not accepted by many: ''Ill-natured tongues have asserted, indeed, that, if his name was attached to many plays, he seldom contributed anything else to them, and that without writing a line of the text he acquired a share of the author's dues in return for the valuable publicity at his disposal. This charge has been often repeated, but never proved.''

Prével dropped dead suddenly at the age of 54, as he walked into his bachelor flat after a month's holiday in the Pyrénées. Rumor had it for a while that someone had got their revenge, but apparently it was only Mother Nature.

1861 **Marianne** (Théodore Bennet-Ritter) 1 act Opéra-Comique 17 June

1863 **Une paire d'anglais** (Charles Domergue/w Alexis Bouvier) 1 act

1866 **La Vipérine** (Jean-Jacques de Billemont/w William Busnach) 1 act Théâtre des Folies-Marigny 19 October

1869 **La Romance de la rose** (Jacques Offenbach/w Étienne Tréfeu) 1 act Théâtre des Bouffes-Parisiens 11 December

1869 **Tul'as voulu** (Samuel David/w Émile Abraham) 1 act Théâtre des Bouffes-Parisiens 12 September

1874 **Le Cerisier** (Jules Duprato) 1 act Opéra-Comique 15 May

1879 **Le Grand Casimir** (Charles Lecocq/w Albert de Saint-Albin) Théâtre des Variétés 11 January

1880 **Les Mousquetaires au couvent** (Louis Varney/w Paul Ferrier) Théâtre des Bouffes-Parisiens 16 March

1882 **Attendez-moi sous l'orme** (Vincent d'Indy/w Robert de Bonnières) 1 act Opéra-Comique 11 February

1882 **Fanfan la Tulipe** (Varney/w Ferrier) Théâtre des Folies-Dramatiques 21 October

1884 **Mam'zelle Réséda** (Gaston Serpette) 1 act Théâtre de la Renaissance 2 February

1884 **Babolin** (Varney/w Ferrier) Théâtre des Nouveautés 19 March

1885 **Les Petits Mousquetaires** (Varney/w Ferrier) Théâtre des Folies-Dramatiques 5 March

1887 **L'Amour mouillé** (Varney/w Armand Liorat) Théâtre des Nouveautés 25 January

1887 **La Chatte blanche** (Émile Jonas/Cogniard brothers ad w Émile Blavet) Théâtre du Châtelet 2 April

1890 **Ma mie Rosette** (Paul Lacome/w Liorat) Théâtre des Folies-Dramatiques 4 February

PRICE, Michael P[aul] (b Chicago, 5 August 1938). Executive director and guiding light of America's Goodspeed Opera House.

Michael Price has, at the time of writing, spent some 30 years at the helm of the Goodspeed Opera House, in East Haddam, Connecticut, establishing it as the English-speaking theatre's one and only important producing house "dedicated to the heritage of the musical" through a long and effective series of new productions of versions of favorite American musical comedies of earlier years. A number of the most successful of these revivals have made their way to Broadway and/or to the American touring circuits, including *Very Good Eddie* (1975), *Going Up* (1976), *Whoopee* (1979), *The Five o'Clock Girl* (1981), *Little Johnny Jones* (1982), *Take Me Along* (1985), *Oh, Kay!* (1990), *The Most Happy Fella* (1992) and *Gentlemen Prefer Blondes* (1995).

In parallel to this long run of new-old musicals, he has also produced at Goodspeed a regular and substantial series of new musical plays from which the 1974 *Shenandoah* and the 1976 *Annie* both went on from their original productions to become major hits. The smaller-scale *Something's Afoot* (1973) and *The Great American Backstage Musical* (1982) and the musequel *Annie 2 (Annie Warbucks)* also went on to productions further afield.

Other Goodspeed-born musicals have included *After You, Mr Hyde* (1968), *Tom Piper* (1969), *The King of Schnorrers* (1970), *Hubba Hubba* (1971), *Cowboy* (1975), *The Red Blue-Grass Western Foyer Show* (1977), *A Long Way to Boston* (1979), *Zapata* (1980), *The Little Rascals* (1987), *Paper Moon* (1996), *Houdini* (1997) and *Lucky in the Rain* (1997).

In 1984 he founded a second, associate theatre at Chester, Connecticut (Goodspeed-at-Chester, Norma Terris Theater), which has subsequently been devoted expressly to the production of new works. Since the opening of this center, two, three or four new shows have been mounted each season, giving Goodspeed the distinction of being America's busiest producer of new works. Several pieces initially tried at Chester have subsequently been given main house productions—*Arthur: The Musical* (1990), *Swinging on a Star* (1994), *Mirette* (1998)—and both the biomusical *Harrigan and Hart* (1984) and *Swinging on a Star* progressed from Chester to New York.

In more recent years a small number of less-than-large musicals that originated outside America have also been given Goodspeed showings, including the 1920s *Mr Cinders,* as revived by the King's Head Theatre in London, the revamped Lloyd Webber/Ayckbourn *By Jeeves* from Scarborough and the oft-tried Kipling musical, *Just So,* produced in London by Cameron Mackintosh.

In association with the Goodspeed operation, he also established the Goodspeed Library of the Musical Theatre, an archive and research center devoted to the musical stage.

PRIMROSE Musical comedy in 3 acts by George Grossmith and Guy Bolton. Lyrics by Desmond Carter and Ira Gershwin. Music by George Gershwin. Winter Garden Theatre, London, 11 September 1924.

Following his productions of two Anglo-American musicals with Jerome Kern scores (*The Cabaret Girl, The Beauty Prize*), it was rumored that George Grossmith and his producing partner Pat Malone would next bring out at the Winter Garden Theatre a piece on which the young British songwriter Noël Coward would collaborate. However, Grossmith, opted instead for a young American songwriter named George Gershwin whose music had recently been heard in the revues *The Rainbow* and *The Punch Bowl* and who had just premiered a piece called "Rhapsody in Blue."

Grossmith and Guy Bolton's book had parts made to suit the Winter Garden cast of favorites. Leslie Henson was aristocratic and silly Toby Mopham, who has promised more than he should to common but attractive Pinkie Peach (Heather Thatcher) and who uses the author Hilary Vane to help him get out of his commitment. As a result, Hilary's ingenue, Joan (Margery Hicklin), gets upset and makes rash promises to foolish Freddie (Claude Hulbert). Toby's mother (Muriel Barnby) follows the example of the Merry Widow and turns her stately home into a nightclub to keep Toby indoors, and it is there that all the pairings are finally sorted out. Grossmith, the comic who always had a yen for romantic roles, had the part of Hilary Vane mapped out for himself, rather than the more suitable one of Freddie, but Gershwin objected and asked for a proper singer in the part. He got Percy Heming, a staunchly operatic baritone, and Grossmith limited himself to directing.

Heming got new songs, topped by the ballad "This Is the Life for a Man," which sounded as if it had come from the same parlor piano as "Wandering the King's Highway" and other such British yo-ho ballads, Henson had three comedy songs that (particularly one regretting "Wasn't It Terrible What They Did to Mary, Queen of Scots") were more English olde-time musick-hall than anything seen on the London stage in years and, even though a delightfully lyricked little piece for the ill-matched heroine and Freddie, "Berkeley Square and Kew," proved one of the prettiest musical moments of the night, most of the best material came from Gershwin's trunk. He sounded much more at home in the jaunty "Wait a Bit, Susie," the vampy "Boy Wanted" (ex-*A Dangerous Maid*) and "Naughty Baby" and the lilting "Some Far Away Someone" (ex- *Nifties of 1923*) than in the effortfully English tones of the custom-made songs.

Primrose was a well-tailored Winter Garden show and, even without Grossmith, and soon without the clever and popular Miss Thatcher, it had a well-tailored run of 255 performances. That was just about it. It was picked up for an Australian production and mounted by J C Williamson Ltd with Maud Fane and Albert Frith featured for two and a half months in Melbourne and then, with Hugh Steyne replacing Frith at eight minutes' notice on opening night, for just under two months in Sydney (Her Majesty's Theatre 29 August 1925), but although it was announced for Broadway with Basil Durant and Kendall Lee as stars for the 1925–26 season, it never appeared.

Australia: Her Majesty's Theatre, Melbourne 11 April 1925

Recording: original cast (WRC)

PRINCE, Hal [PRINCE, Harold Smith] (b New York, 30 January 1928). Vastly successful Broadway producer turned even-more-successful director of musicals on both sides of the Atlantic.

Originally a stage-management assistant with George Abbott, Prince moved into the production of musical plays at the age of 26 in partnership with co–Abbott worker Robert E Griffith and Freddie Brisson. The trio began with two considerable hits, *The Pajama Game* (1954) and *Damn Yankees* (1955), and drew ambivalent results with the musicalized Eugene O'Neill *New Girl in Town* (1957) before Prince and Griffith took up a project that would turn into an even more significant triumph than their two initial hits: *West Side Story* (1957).

The pair followed up with another hit in *Fiorello!* (1959) and the same authors' less attractive *Tenderloin* (1960). Following Griffith's death in 1961, Prince continued as a producer alone. His first solo venture was yet another hit: *A Funny Thing Happened on the Way to the Forum* (1962), and in an amazing run of fine shows—which only very occasionally included a miss—he followed up with *She Loves Me* (1963), *Fiddler on the Roof* (1964), *Flora, the Red Menace* (1965), *It's a Bird . . . It's a Plane . . . It's Superman* (1966), *Cabaret* (1966), *Zorba* (1968), *Company* (1970), *Follies* (1971), *A Little Night Music* (1973), *Candide* (1973 w Chelsea Theater Group) and *Pacific Overtures* (1976).

By this point, established as one of the most important and certainly one of the very most successful producers on the postwar Broadway musical stage, Prince had also established himself amongst the leading American directors of musicals. His close association with Abbott meant that in his early days as a producer it was the experienced and effective elder statesman of the New York theatre who had been responsible for the staging of Prince's shows, even though Prince had been a ''creative'' producer, providing artistic input as well as cash. It was not until 1962 that he was responsible for the physical staging of a musical, and then it was not one of his own productions but Andrew Siff's *A Family Affair*, a piece that numbered amongst its authors the young John Kander. *A Family Affair* was a 65-performance flop, but Prince moved into the director's chair more happily the following year when he staged his own production of *She Loves Me*.

Plate 313. **Hal Prince.** *The director with lyricist-composer Stephen Sondheim.*

After one more step aside, to direct Alexander Cohen's Sherlock Homes show *Baker Street* (1965), Prince directed all of his own productions, creating memorable stagings for such pieces as *Cabaret, Company* (Tony Award), *A Little Night Music* and the new, multi-stage version of *Candide* (Tony Award). He also took half a third Tony award for his co-staging (w Michael Bennett) of *Follies*.

In the last years of the 1970s, Prince devoted himself to directing rather than to producing, and he scored fresh success with the remarkable mountings of two pieces of widely different kinds in 1978: the operetta burlesque *On the Twentieth Century* for Broadway and *Evita*, the record-turned-stage-show that most of theatrical London had said couldn't be put onto a stage. Both pieces of staging remain classics of the genre.

Thereafter, things went a little less well for the man who had stood so long under the shower of success. The oversized Broadway mounting of *Sweeney Todd* (1979) proved a misjudgment, and three projects for which he again donned a co-producer's hat, *Merrily We Roll Along* (1981), *A Doll's Life* (1982) and *Grind* (1985), were swift failures. But success returned in 1986 when Prince mounted the extravagant, romantic production of London's *The Phantom of the Opéra,* a staging that was, in the manner of modern musical productions, subsequently re-created in the long series of reproductions staged all around the world.

Subsequent projects as a musical-theatre director, amongst a series of operatic productions since 1978, have included *Roza* (1986–87), *Kiss of the Spiderwoman* (1992), off-Broadway's *The Petrified Prince* (1994), the pre-Broadway closed *Whistle Down the Wind* (1996), *Parade* (1998) and revivals of a fiddled-about-with *Show Boat* (1994, with the director more or less credited for the fiddling-about-with) and of what didn't quite look like his definitive *Candide* (1997).

Prince's daughter, Daisy Prince, appeared in the original cast of the musical *Merrily We Roll Along* and in a number of other musicals, including *The Petrified Prince.*

Autobiography: *Contradictions: Notes on 26 Years in the Theatre* (Dodd Mead, New York, 1974); Biographies: Hirsch, F: *Harold Prince, and the American Musical Theatre* (CUP, New York, 1989), Ilson, C: *Harold Prince from* Pajama Game *to* Phantom of the Opéra (UMI Press, Ann Arbor, 1989)

LE PRINCE DE MADRID Opérette à grand spectacle in 2 acts by Raymond Vincy. Lyrics by Jacques Plante. Music by Francis Lopez. Théâtre du Châtelet, Paris, 4 March 1967.

Favorite French tenor Luis Mariano returned to the Paris stage in 1967 to play (in his early fifties) the role of the painter Goya in a spectacularly staged Spanish romance that had as little to do with the real Goya as Lehár's libretti had with their nominal subjects. This Goya got involved with an ingenue named Florécita (Janine Ervil) and the amorous Duchesse d'Albe (Maria Murano), thus invoking the jealous rivalry of a basso matador (Lucien Lupi) and of the ducal Captain of Guards (Jean Chesnel), who plots to have him brought before the Inquisition. Maurice Baquet and Eliane Varon were tacked into the tale as the traditional soubrets of the Vincy/Lopez opérette in a piece that, whilst sticking minutely to the formula they had so successfully established, did not, particularly in its music, rise to the level of the best of the team's previous work. However, Mariano, singing to "España" and "Florécita," enjoying "La Feria de Séville," acclaimed as "Le Prince de Madrid," or sighing "Toi, mon seul amour" in a piece where the rest of the cast took a very secondary musical place, ensured that Marcel Lamy's production lasted 554 performances at the Châtelet prior to serving its time on the road. It thus became well enough established that whilst better Vincy and/or Lopez pieces are little seen it still wins regional revivals.

Goya and the Duchess of Alba had gamboled rather more briefly across the Broadway stage a couple of decades earlier in a kind of Spanish *Dubarry Was a Lady* called *The Duchess Misbehaves* (Adelphi Theater 13 February 1946). He was Joey Faye and she was Audrey Christie, just five times.

Recording: original cast (Pathé)

THE PRINCE OF PILSEN Musical comedy in 2 acts by Frank Pixley. Music by Gustave Luders. Tremont Theater, Boston, 12 May 1902; Broadway Theater, New York, 17 March 1903.

Luders and Pixley had established themselves amongst the most enjoyable American writers of musical comedy of their time with *The Burgomaster* and *King Dodo*; with *The Prince of Pilsen,* their best and most successful show, they confirmed themselves at the very top of their profession.

Pixley's book gave the opportunity for a jolly display of the popular low "Dutch" comedy of the day by making its central character one Hans Wagner, a Cincinnati brewer, of a very obviously "deutsch" background, equipped with the accent that flagged him as a comical person. At Nice's International Hotel, Wagner (John W Ransome, a comedian known for his impersonations of politico "Boss" Crocker) is—thanks to a misunderstanding to do with a mention of Pilsener beer—mistaken for the secretly expected and thoroughly incognito Prince of Pilsen. He wins wonderful attentions from the hotel staff, the slightly disappointed advances of the pretty and wealthy widow Mrs Crocker (Dorothy Morton), who was once rescued from a horse-riding accident by the Prince and had been looking forward to improving on the acquaintance, and the enmity of Artie, the impoverished Earl of Somerset (Maurice Darcy), who is after the millions of Mrs Crocker. While Hans blithely and unwittingly plays royalty, the real prince, Carl Otto (Arthur Donaldson), happy to keep his planned incognito, uses the freedom thus won to woo and win little Nellie Wagner (Ruth Peebles), so that when Artie, after all sorts of beastly tries at discrediting Hans, is able to expose his "pretense," Carl Otto is able to announce that Nellie will after all be, as all had thought her, the Princess of Pilsen. The genuinely funny plot also managed ingeniously to get a foxhunt (with "Tally-ho!" chorus), a subplot with secret documents, a duel, a billiard table and the once-famous Nice Bataille des fleurs into the action.

Luders's score decorated the comedy with some delightful songs in a range of the usual styles, of which a traditionally rousing and partially unaccompanied Stein Song for the Prince and his pals, the pretty "Tale of a Sea

Plate 314. **The Prince of Pilsen.** *A duel on the hills overlooking what is now Nice airport. Tom Wagner (Harry Fairleigh) and the incognito Prince (Arthur Donaldson) come mistakenly to blows under the eyes of Artie Shrimpton (Victor Morley), bellboy Jimmie (Eva Westcott) and Nellie Wagner (Ruth Peebles).*

Shell'' for Carl Otto, and another romantic piece, the waltz ''The Message of the Violet,'' which fell to the number-two juvenile couple (Ivey Anderson, Mabel Pierson), proved the take-away hits. The production numbers included Mrs Crocker's song about ''The American Girl,'' and a piece subtitled ''the Song of the Cities,'' which plugged various towns—Baltimore, ''where the oysters thrive and the streets are alive and the lobsters are fresh and frisky''; St Louis, which boasted ''ginger and push and Anheuser Busch''; Chicago, where ''the stockyards so fair perfume the air''; and New York, where ''the news is so hot they're printing asbestos papers''—to the accompaniment of musical quotes from ''My Maryland,'' the cake-walk, *King Dodo* and ''Yankee Doodle,'' and a parallel parade of feminine beauty. This item ultimately proved so popular that it was toured round the vaudeville theatres by ''Truly Shattuck and the Prince of Pilsen City Girls.''

After a brief run-in at Malden, Mass, Henry Savage's production was introduced to Boston and scored a decided success, but the producer showed no haste to take it to New York. It was 10 months and many touring dates later that Broadway finally got *The Prince of Pilsen.* Helen Bertram was now the widow, Lillian Coleman played Nellie, and Albert Parr and Anna Lichter sang about the violet, and *The Prince of Pilsen* ran through 143 Broadway performances before moving on. It returned as part of an incessant touring program during each of the next four years for further seasons (Daly's Theater 4 April 1904, 32 performances; New York Theater 3 April 1905, 40 performances; New York Theater 2 April 1906, 16 performances; Academy of Music 6 May 1907, 32 performances). It also traveled to London, where the American company moved into the Shaftesbury Theatre, the old home of *The Belle of New York,* for a run.

The Prince of Pilsen was a much superior piece to its predecessor, but it had not the attraction of novelty that that show had had, and a respectable 160 performances was its lot. The show was considerably boosted, however, by a different kind of novelty. One of its chorus girls, the minutely waisted Camille Clifford, who represented New York as ''the Gibson Girl'' in the ''Cities'' number, became a gawker's phenomenon. The stare of the season. When the rest of the cast went home, she stayed in Britain to briefly become a top-of-the-bill name, and almost an actress, before hooking her nobleman and retiring.

Having made it to London, *The Prince of Pilsen* then went on to become one of the few American musicals of the era to go into Europe when the Isola Brothers introduced it as one of a handful of foreign musical plays that they presented at l'Olympia (ad Victor de Cottens), with London's Fred Wright (Artie) and American singer May de Souza starred and the English Fuller troupe of dancers glamorously featured. Wright caused a sensation, the show became the must of the Parisian nightlife circuit, and, while Savage rattled on about all the other shows he was going to bring to Paris, it ran on to top a one hundred nights in its first run. It also went to Australia, under the management of J C Williamson. Charles A Loder (Hans) George Whitehead (Carl Otto), Olive Goodwin (Mrs Crocker), Myles Clifton (Artie) and Amy Murphy (Nell) featured in a six-week season in Sydney before *The Prince of Pilsen* gave way to another American musical, *The Red Mill,* in the Williamson repertoire.

The Prince of Pilsen hung on as a perennial favorite on American stages for a good many years, and it was given a brief reprise on the Broadway stage amongst the Shuberts' series of old favorites that were mounted at the Jolson Theatre in 1930 (13 January). Al Shean played the role of Hans.

UK: Shaftesbury Theatre 14 May 1904; France: Olympia *Le Prince de Pilsen* 14 December 1907; Australia: Theatre Royal, Sydney 30 May 1908

Recording: selection (AEI)

LA PRINCESSE DES CANARIES Opéra-bouffe in 3 acts by Henri Chivot and Alfred Duru. Music by Charles Lecocq. Théâtre des Folies-Dramatiques, Paris, 9 February 1883.

Following his split with Victor Koning and the Théâtre de la Renaissance, Lecocq had scored a double triumph at the Nouveautés with *Le Jour et la nuit* and *Le Coeur et la main.* His next show took him back to the authors of some of his earliest pieces, Chivot and Duru, now as famous as he, but with whom in the years since their early success with *Les Cent Vierges* the composer had come together only once, on *Le Pompon,* the show no one except the Hungarians liked, for the Folies-Dramatiques. Authors and composer did decidedly better with their new effort for the same house, *La Princesse des Canaries,* a piece that presented the particularity of being a two-headed star vehicle for two young girls.

Juliette Simon-Girard had won her star's stripes several years back in *Les Cloches de Corneville,* but Jeanne Andrée, who took the second role à tiroirs of *La Princesse des Canaries,* was a beginner. In a plot that offered something of the opportunities of Mme Simon-Girard's other great triumph, *Madame Favart,* multiplied by two, the girls played foster sisters, Pépita (Mme Simon-Girard) and Inès (Mlle Andrée), who, aided by Uncle General Bombardos (Lepers), cavalcaded through a series of disguises on their undercover mission to win back the throne for whichever one of them is the real Princess of the Canaries. Their rural husbands, Inigo (Simon-Max) and Pédrille (Dekernel), kept in the dark, have to be stopped time and again from scuppering the venture. When Pépita is proclaimed Queen, the incumbent General Pataquès (Delannoy) has her arrested, but, of course, it is all a red herring and at the final curtain Inès (who is the ingenue and has been singing the top soprano line all evening, so we should have known) turns out to be the real monarch.

Lecocq's score was another delightful one, highlighted by its pretty duo music for the two girls, a particularly enjoyable two-faced comic encounter for the rival generals (''Bonjour, Général'') and such happy irrelevancies as the tale of Cupid and Psyche, sung as a ronde for the first-act finale, and the Toréador song, which was part of the very large soubrette role of Pépita. Mme Simon-Girard's role allowed her to run the gamut, from impersonation—in the servant girl's song ''Comm' tout's les femmes''—to *Grande-Duchesse*–style comedy in her political declaration of intent (Chanson de la Princesse des Canaries), a plan that—a couple of years before *The Mikado*'s appearance—included a list of nuisances to be suppressed (the Chambre des Deputés, the police and anyone who takes liberties with her), to some moments of genuine sentiment (''J'étais contente de mon sort''). Mlle Andrée, whilst not lacking sparky moments, had the corner on the loving ones, notably in her first-act romance (''De mon coeur vous êtes le maître''), and the pretty ones, as in her last-act Flowergirl's number (''Les fleurs que nous admirons'').

La Princesse des Canaries was a tidy success at the Folies-Dramatiques, playing for nearly three months, returning after the summer break to pass its 100th performance on 7 September and finally totaling 139 showings in its first year. Oddly, however, it seems not to have returned to the Paris stage, and, equally oddly, its career abroad was mostly undistinguished.

Germany's production of *Die Canarien-Prinzessin* aroused no particular interest, Vienna simply passed on Lecocq's latest work and Budapest's Népszínház played *Kanari hercegnő* (ad Lajos Evva, Béla J Fái) a fair but scarcely outstanding 14 times. Maurice Grau introduced the piece to New Yorkers in the original French with Marie Aimée (Pépita), Mlle Angèle (Inez), Mezières (Pataquès), Duplan (Bombardos), Lary (Inigo) and Mlle Delorme (Catarina) without featuring it extensively in his repertoire, but the piece finally found an altogether more cheering success when it was produced in the English language.

A British version, *Pepita* (ad ''Mostyn Tedde,'' ie, Edward Paulton), directed by Harry Paulton and starring Fanny Wentworth (Pepita), Maude Albert (Ines) and producer Horace Lingard (Inigo), trouped the provinces for some four hundred performances before venturing a season in London, starring Tillie Wadman and Frank Wyatt, then returned to the out-of-town scene, touring interminably under the management of the durable Lingard, eventually to tot up a longer British life than any other Lecocq work bar *La Fille de Madame Angot* had ever achieved. Paulton sr was sufficiently impressed by all this to take the show further. Four and a half years after Aimée's performances, he brought what was now billed as his own, rather than his son's, adaptation of *La Princesse des Canaries* to Broadway under the title *The Queen's Mate.* After the double-meaning original title and the primadonna-pleasing second one, this third referred to none other than the buffeted-about Inigo, scarcely the chief character of the piece, but here played by Harry Paulton. Camille D'Arville was Anita (ex- Pépita), Lillian Russell played Inez and J H Ryley was Pataquès, and the anglicized show was a hit. It played for two months in New York before moving out of town (30 June) for the height of the summer, then came right back in again (13 August) to continue its run—with Miss Russell now playing Anita—until 10 September before heading again for the country. On 7 January 1889 *The Queen's Mate* had a third Broadway season, this time with Lilly Post (Anita) and Marie Halton (Inez) starred. And the rest of the country got a proportionate dose of the piece as well.

Quite how much difference there was between the father's and the son's English versions of *La Princesse des Canaries,* or which was the better (if indeed they were not the same), cannot now be fathomed, but Australia opted for the younger generation and mounted *Pepita* in 1889. Nellie Stewart (Pepita), Fanny Liddiard (Inez), W H Woodfield (Inigo), Walker Marnock (Bombastes) and William Elton (Pataquès) headed the cast. It did well enough to be retained in the repertoire until 1891.

Germany: Viktoria-Theater *Die Canarien-Prinzessin* 13 May 1883; USA: Fifth Avenue Theater (Fr) 10 September 1883, Broadway Theater *The Queen's Mate* 2 May 1888; Hungary: Népszínház *Kanari hercegnő* 19 October 1883; UK: Royal Court Theatre, Liverpool *Pepita* 30 December 1886, Toole's Theatre, London *Pepita* 30 August 1888; Australia: Princess Theatre, Melbourne *Pepita* 9 February 1889

LA PRINCESSE DE TRÉBIZONDE Opéra-bouffe in 2 acts by Charles Nuitter and Étienne Tréfeu. Music by Jacques Offenbach. Baden-Baden, 31 July 1869. New version in 3 acts Théâtre des Bouffes-Parisiens, Paris, 7 December 1869.

Originally produced at Baden-Baden during the summer season, with the young Mdlle Périer in its principal travesty role, *La Princesse de Trébizonde* proved successful enough that Offenbach and his librettists subsequently expanded it into a full evening's entertainment and, later in the same year, at the same time that *Les Brigands* was being mounted at the Théâtre des Variétés, *La Princesse de Trébizonde* Mark II was staged at the Bouffes-Parisiens. Tréfeu and Nuitter's libretto made use of the already over-used doll-girl motif, but they surrounded that motif with such jolly characters and scenes as to make it seem less stageworn. As a result, the piece survived, alongside the ballet *Coppélia* and Audran's *La Poupée,* as the happiest example of that eternal 19th-century plot on the musical stage.

Sparadrap (Édouard Georges), the eagle-eyed tutor of the pubescent Prince Raphaël (Anna van Ghell), allows him to visit the waxworks run by Cabriolo (Desiré), unaware that the mountebank's daughter Zanetta (Mlle Fonti) is standing in for a broken doll. When Cabriolo wins a chateau in the fair's lottery, and Raphaël's family turn out to be their new neighbors, the prince's ultra-careful father, Prince Casimir (Berthelier), is delighted to see that his son's youthful passions are limited to the next-door folks' doll, and he promptly takes the waxworks and its proprietors back to court. When Casimir discovers that his son has known for an act and a half that Zanetta was not made of wax, the boy brings out his dad's old and indiscreet diaries, which he has been using as his guidelines to growing up, and the father is obliged to mutter away into consent. Céline Chaumont starred as Zanetta's sister, Régina, in love with the aristocrat-turned-servant Trémolini (Bonnet), who becomes first the company's fair-barker and then (because of his knowledge of aristocratic etiquette) their butler, and Mlle Thierret played the plum female comedy role of Cabriolo's sister, Paola, who suffers from delusions of royal relationships.

In line with its libretto, the score of *La Princesse de Trébizonde,* although fashionably labeled as opéra-bouffe, had a little less of the zany freedom of music of Offenbach's earliest and genuine opéras-bouffes. Some touches of the burlesque element were still there—the first-act finale, with Cabriolo and his family bidding farewell to their old sideshow (''Adieu, baraque héreditaire'') in one of the happiest pieces of the score was a direct parody of Rossini's *Guglielmo Tell*—but the fun and Offenbachian melody in Casimir's smoke-from-the-ears description of his easily fired temper (''Me maquillé-je comme on dit''), Régina's song about her tightrope act (''Quand je suis sur la corde raide''), Zanetta's Ronde de la Princesse de Trébizonde, and in Raphaël's repeated raptures, both with and over his ''doll,'' was often rather less ''bouffe'' than elsewhere.

The success of *La Princesse de Trébizonde* was barely overshadowed by that of *Les Brigands,* and it stayed at the Bouffes for some four months as a first run. It was revived there, after the interruptive Franco-Prussian War, in 1875 (14 February) with Louise Théo as Régina, again in 1876 (September) with Daubray as Cabriolo and Paola Marié as Régina, and was given a new production at the Théâtre des Variétés in 1888 (15 May) with a cast headed by Mily-Meyer, Mary Albert, Cooper and Christian. The record thus established was a highly satisfactory one, in the terms of any other composer, yet *La Princesse de Trébizonde* remained and remains a little in the shadow of the more celebrated Offenbach works in France, where it has been rarely heard from since that last Paris revival.

Something of the same thing happened in London, where the show, nevertheless, had a fine first production (ad Charles Lamb Kenney) under John Hollingshead's management, at the Gaiety Theatre. Nellie Farren was Régina and J L Toole ad-libbed freely as Cabriolo, at the head of a cast that included Robert Soutar (Casimir), Constance Loseby (Raphaël) and Annie Tremaine (Zanetta). The show stayed in the bill for a little under three months, was brought back later in the same year, was toured and then played again at the Gaiety in 1872 (19 April) in Toole's repertoire. The British provinces actually saw as much or more of *The Princess of Trébizonde* as of any other Offenbach piece, for in 1871 the enterprising Henry Leslie of Liverpool's Prince of Wales Theatre sent out a touring company, led by Augusta Thomson, Edward Chessman and the young Henry Bracy, and that company toured almost nonstop round the country for years. Later (1876) Chessman took the show out himself, followed in 1881 by Joseph Eldred, and more than a decade down the line the Leslie production (with some of its original cast!) was still spottable on the British road. In 1879 the show was given a spectacular revival at the Alhambra with Charles Collette (Cabriolo), J Furneaux Cook (Casimir), Miss Loseby (Raphaël), Alice May (Zanetta) and Emma Chambers (Régina), and an "Automatic Ballet" of wax dolls introduced in the final act. But the 1880s seemingly saw the show out. Other pieces from the era survived into further reproductions, and even up to the presentish day, but this one didn't.

La Princesse de Trébizonde was introduced to America in Kenney's English version in a production at Wallack's Theater that presented the unusual feature of starring the famous burlesquer Lydia Thompson (Régina) in a French opéra-bouffe role. Lydia admitted that the piece had been "rewritten and adapted from" the original, and she went so far as to introduce music from *La Belle Hélène* into the action, but much of what was seen seems to have been the real thing. Camille Dubois played Zanetta, Carlotta Zerbini was Raphaël and Harry Becket took the role of Cabriolo, but in true burlesque fashion Willie Edouin played Manola (ie, Paola) in travesty, as did Hetty Tracy as Tremolina [*sic*]. New York quickly pronounced that it preferred blonde Lydia in traditional burlesque. Aimée appeared in French breeches as Prince Raphaël in 1874, but, in spite of its rather curious beginning, the piece prospered in America in translation rather than in the original French. It was added to the Alice Oates repertoire in 1878, produced at the Casino Theater (5 May 1883) with a top cast including John Howson, Lillian Russell, Digby Bell and Laura Joyce, played in German at the Thalia-Theater (14 December 1882), again at the Casino with Marie Jansen and Francis Wilson (15 October 1883), at Koster & Bial's—decorated with acts—in 1886 (22 February) and, in a heavily revised version, with Pauline Hall and Fred Solomon starred, at Harrigan's Theater in 1894 (5 March). In 1898 Milton Aborn's company produced it in summer season under the title *The Circus Clown.* And then America, too, cried enough.

Die Prinzessin von Trapezunt also won a good reception in Germany, but it was in Austria that the piece found most particular favor. Produced at the Carltheater (ad Julius Hopp) with a very strong cast headed by Pepi Gallmeyer (Régina), Hermine Meyerhoff (Zanetta), Karoline Tellheim (Raphaël), Josef Matras (Casimir), Karl Blasel (Cabriolo), Wilhelm Knaack (Sparadrap) and Therese Schäfer (Paola) and conducted by Offenbach himself, it was immediately seen to be one of the theatre's biggest-ever successes. It was played 53 times between March and May, came back in the spring to reach its 72nd night by the new year, passed its 100th in repertoire on 24 June 1873, its 125th on 13 September 1874, and reached its 141st on 28 May 1878. It was given for 10 performances at the Theater an der Wien in 1885 (17 January) with Ottilie Collin (Raphaël), Blasel, Friese (Casimir), Rosa Streitmann (Zanetta) and Maria Theresia Massa (Zanetta), it was revived at the Carltheater, with Blasel, Knaack, Anna von Boskay and Frln Tornay in 1892, played in 1899 at the Jantschtheater and in 1905 at the Theater in der Josefstadt. However, unlike elsewhere, *Die Prinzessin von Trapezunt* did not then disappear. It was played at the Berlin Opera in 1932, and has been seen in Vienna at the Theater an der Wien (12 May 1966) and at the Wiener Kammeroper in the 1980s. Berlin's Theater des Westens hosted a revival in 1904 (8 April), with Wellhof and Frln Döninger featured.

In Budapest (ad Endre Latabár), where it was first seen in 1871, the show was later taken briefly into the repertoire of the Népszínház (18 May 1876, 5 performances). It was also played in many other European centers (Brussels, Naples, Copenhagen, Stockholm, Prague, Bucharest, Zagreb, etc), as well as in Australia, where

William Lyster introduced it in 1874, but it seems to have survived best and only where the taste for the less extravagantly burlesque operettic works is the strongest.

UK: Gaiety Theatre *The Princess of Trébizonde* 16 April 1870; Austria: Carltheater *Die Prinzessin von Trapezunt* 18 March 1871; Germany: Friedrich-Wilhelmstädtisches Theater *Die Prinzessin von Trapezunt* 30 June 1871; USA: Wallack's Theater 11 September 1871; Australia: Prince of Wales Theatre, Melbourne 22 June 1874; Hungary; Budai Színkör *A Trapezunti hercegnő* 17 September 1871

PRINCESS FLAVIA Musical play in 2 acts by Harry B Smith based on *The Prisoner of Zenda* by Anthony Hope. Music by Sigmund Romberg. Century Theater, New York, 2 November 1925.

The Shubert/Romberg follow-up to *The Student Prince* was another romantic operetta set in a Germanic neverland and dealing with the problems of royalty. The piece was originally intended as a vehicle for tenor Walter Woolf in the role of Rudolf Rassendyl, the sosie of the Prince of Ruritania who doubles for the monarch and in doing so falls in love with his bride, the Princess Flavia. However, the production lost first its star, then two titles (*Zenda, A Royal Pretender*), and then its leading lady when Marguerite Namara, who had already walked out of *The Love Song,* dropped out of this one as well. British baritone Harry Welchman and soprano Mary Mellish took over the roles, the latter being replaced before Broadway by Evelyn Herbert, who was even gratified with the title role when the show became *Princess Flavia.* All the troubles proved in vain, for *Princess Flavia,* regarded as a pale imitation of *The Student Prince* both musically and textually, played for 152 performances without establishing itself as in any way memorable, and then sent one company on the road to join the nine *Student Princes* currently touring.

Some 40 years later, the San Francisco Light Opera under Edwin Lester produced another *Prisoner of Zenda* musical, *Zenda* (Vernon Duke/Lenny Adelson, Sid Kuller, Martin Charnin/Everett Freeman, Curran Theatre, San Francisco 5 August 1963), with Alfred Drake and Anne Rogers as its leading characters. This one didn't even get as far as Broadway.

The London musical *The Happy Day* produced at Daly's Theatre in 1916 by Robert Evett was originally announced as being based on *The Prisoner of Zenda.* But then it apparently changed its mind.

PRINCESS IDA, or Castle Adamant Respectful operatic perversion in 2 acts and a prologue (later 3 acts) of Tennyson's *The Princess,* being a revised version of *The Princess* by W S Gilbert. Music by Arthur Sullivan. Savoy Theatre, London, 5 January 1884.

Never one to waste his own (or other people's) ideas, W S Gilbert reused parts and plots of several of his early works in later pieces, but *Princess Ida* was the only example of his taking and remaking an entire musical show. It was also the only example in his mature works of a burlesque of a specific work of literature, in this case Tennyson's poem *The Princess.* The original of *Princess Ida* was the 1870 burlesque *The Princess* (Olympic Theatre 8 January 1870), a piece written in meter and affecting the fashionable wordplay of mid-19th-century burlesque, and equipped with a pasticcio score that included such melodies as Rossini's ''Largo al factotum,'' *La Périchole*'s Trois Cousines trio and Auber's *Manon Lescaut* laughing song. For the remake, Gilbert took portions of his old text and spaced them out with fresh dialogue and lyrics, which, being written in the modern Gilbert style in which puns and metric dialogue had given way to the kind of stylish wit to which his name has become attached, did not always blend as happily as they might have. Similarly, on this occasion, what had become the Savoy ''team'' of performers did not have roles made to their measure, as had become their habit.

After the rehearsal-time sacking of Lillian Russell, it was ingenue Leonora Braham—originally intended for a lesser role—who played Princess Ida, a bluestocking who has renounced men and set up a university where the male sex is not permitted, nor anything that reeks of the masculine. However Ida's father, King Gama (George Grossmith), had betrothed her at a childish age to Hilarion (Henry Bracy), the son of King Hildebrand (Rutland Barrington), and that grumpy king now threatens inconveniences if the contract is not carried out. Hilarion and his friends Cyril (Durward Lely) and Florian (Charles Ryley) get into the university in female disguise, and the whole institution soon crumbles as much under the influence of the randy laddies inside its walls as of Hildebrand's armies without.

Sullivan's score for *Princess Ida* was also of a dual nature. There were the now expected ''Savoy-style'' songs: two magnificently brittle, wordful patter songs for Grossmith as the misanthropic Gama—a role originally conceived as a direct burlesque of Tom Taylor's Tribouht in *The Fool's Revenge*—(''I Can't Think Why,'' ''Whene'er I Spoke Sarcastic Joke''), a delightfully clever solo for the Prince (''Ida Was a Twelvemonth Old'') which argued, that, since he was two when she was one, ''husband twice as old as wife argues ill for married life,'' Cyril's joyously tipsy ''Would You Know the Kind of Maid,'' and the boys' anticipatory ''Expressive Glances.'' Alongside these, there were less-expected pieces. Ida's numbers (''O Goddess Wise,'' ''I Built Upon a Rock'') were not in the light, nigh-on soubrette style of the Savoy's usual soprano music: they were wholly serious, both lyrically and musically, whilst Richard Temple, cast peripherally as one of Hildebrand's avenging sons, had a mock-Handelian aria, "This Helmet I Suppose," which came straight from the world of operatic burlesque.

Princess Ida won a rather mixed reaction and, truth be told, it sat a little uncomfortably at the Savoy. The performers were, by and large, not suited to their roles as well as in the earlier shows, the comedy was less prominent and the show's hybrid nature could not be overlooked. But the show was still Gilbert and Sullivan, with many parts that were up to their best work, and it found itself a willing audience for 246 performances. If this was short of the previous shows' totals, it was, nevertheless, superior to just about anything else around: *Princess Ida* was no failure. New York was less interested in the piece and an ill- and mostly undercast production with Cora Tanner (Ida) and J H Ryley (Gama) in the lead roles was taken off after 48 performances. Producer John Stetson did bring the show back, several years later, with a better cast including Geraldine Ulmar, Joseph W Herbert and Courtice Pounds, for a second brief season. A simultaneous American opening night in Boston featured Janet Edmonson (Ida) and George W Wilson (Gama).

In Australia, Colbourne Baber (Ida) and William Elton (Gama) headed J C Williamson's production at Melbourne, whilst Sydney was treated to original star Leonora Braham and minstrel veteran Edwin Kelly (Hildebrand) the following year. Williamson brought out *Princess Ida* at intervals thereafter, but London did not see the piece again until it was brought back into the D'Oyly Carte repertoire in 1919 and New York saw it again for the first time only in 1925 (Shubert Theater 13 April, 40 performances). The piece has remained a minor part of the Gilbert and Sullivan canon, but in recent years its apparently feminist (or, more accurately, anti-feminist) tale and sub-operatic star music have given it a newly fashionable air. A version was produced at Hagen (ad Stefan Trossbach) in 1986, and another—tricked out in 1960s junk-theatre gimmickry—at the English National Opera in 1992.

USA: Boston Museum and Fifth Avenue Theater 11 February 1884; Australia: Princess Theatre, Melbourne 16 July 1887

Recordings: complete (Decca, HMV), etc

Video: Brent-Walker 1982

A PRINCESS OF KENSINGTON Comic opera in 2 acts by Basil Hood. Music by Edward German. Savoy Theatre, London, 22 January 1903.

Having proven themselves the most likely inheritors of Gilbert and Sullivan's position in the British musical theatre with their *Merrie England,* Hood and German followed that piece with one that delved into Gilbert's favorite fairyland. Teased eternally by the sprite Puck (Walter Passmore), Fairy Prince Azuriel (Ernest Torrence) has nursed jealousy for a thousand years over the love once shared by the fairy Kenna (Constance Drever) and the long-dead mortal Prince Albion. Finally—forgetting about such things as mortal men's mortality—he decides that he will force Albion to wed someone else. Puck and Kenna choose William Jelf of the *S S Albion* (Henry Lytton) and Joy Jellicoe (Louie Pounds) to perform the charade. Since he is engaged to zealous Nell Reddish (Rosina Brandram) and she to tenorious Lieutenant Brook Green (Robert Evett), there are many complications to be hurdled before the testy fairy is calmed and the mortals can get back to normality.

German's score was a model piece of light opera, with some rich ensembles and lovely fairy music, topped by a charming ballad for the tenor ("My Heart a Ship at Anchor Lies") and by a genuine hit song in the jolly male quartet "We're Four Jolly Sailormen," a piece that became a favorite parlor and concert number for more than half a century. The show itself, however, was not a success. It had a highbrowish flavor to it that the more comical *Merrie England* had not had, and although it was much liked by hard-core light opera-goers, it attracted the general public for only 115 performances. Manager William Greet gave up the Savoy Theatre and, after an indifferent tour, switched the company to musical comedy productions. The famous Savoy era was effectively over.

A Princess of Kensington was, nevertheless, picked up for Broadway, where Dora de Fillipe (Kenna), James T Powers (Jelf), Edward Martindel (Azuriel) and William Stephens (Puck) featured in John C Fisher's production for a 41-performance run.

USA: Broadway Theater 31 August 1903

THE PRINCESS PAT Comic opera in 3 acts by Henry Blossom. Music and lyrics by Victor Herbert. Cort Theater, New York, 29 September 1915.

The Princess Pat was an Irish lass, but unlike the series of her sisters who would soon take over the Broadway stage she was neither poor nor in search of a princely husband to wed at the final curtain. Patrice O'Connor (Eleanor Painter) has already got a prince, for she is wed to Prince Antonio di Montaldo (Joseph Letora) when the curtain goes up. He is, however, not as attentive as a princely husband might be, now that they are married. As a little encouragement to some flattering jealousy, and in order to help out a friend (Eva Fallon), Pat pretends to elope with the aging and comical Anthony Schmalz (Al Shean). Her plan succeeds on both counts, and she goes back to her revived prince whilst friend Grace marries a more suitable and junior member of the Schmalz family (Robert Ober).

The show suffered a nasty setback when the actress originally cast as Grace was murdered by a jealous boyfriend on the eve of the production. Miss Fallon saved the day, and John Cort's production, mounted at the little theatre named for him, was able to open as planned. Blossom's above-average talents as a writer of dialogue and an attractive Herbert score, which included the heroine's pretty ''Love Is Best of All'' (amongst some Irishy bits), her Italian husband's ''Neapolitan Love Song'' (amongst some Italiany bits) and the comic's amusing and tuneful longing ''I Wish I Were an Island in an Ocean of Girls,'' aided by the talented Miss Painter and the comical Shean, assured a Broadway run for *The Princess Pat.* The show ran for a good 158 performances and toured most profitably without, however, finding itself a significant afterlife or an export license.

PRINCESS TOTO English comic opera in 3 acts by W S Gilbert. Music by Frederic Clay. Theatre Royal, Nottingham, 26 June 1876; Strand Theatre, London, 2 October 1876.

When Kate Santley, who had previously commissioned Frederic Clay's *Cattarina* as a vehicle for herself with some success, went on the road again in 1876, she ordered another new piece from the composer. This time, she got a rather superior one, as Clay collaborated on *Princess Toto* not with burlesque's Robert Reece, but with the young librettist and lyricist W S Gilbert.

Miss Santley was Princess Toto, a chronically forgetful and bizarrely romantic royal with a crush on a local brigand named Barberini. When her betrothed Prince Doro (Guillaume Loredan) appears to have vanished, she agrees to wed Prince Caramel (Joseph E Beyer), but he is late for the wedding and Doro turns up so she takes him after all. The piqued Caramel disguises himself as Barberini and whisks the princess off for a jolly bandit life, but her father (John Wainwright) leads his court (including J H Ryley and W S Penley) to the rescue, all of them disguised as Red Indians, and lures her back with their bizarreries. In the end, the dizzy lady settles down with the man she has actually married.

Clay provided a fine opéra-bouffe score that gave the prima donna opportunities for the sentimental (''Like an Arrow from Its Quiver (comes my love to marry me)'') to the comical (''The Pig with the Roman Nose''), whilst Prince Doro had a similar combination in his apostrophe to his unknown bride (''Oh, Bride of Mine, Oh, Baby Wife'') and the lightly topical (''There Are Brigands in Every Station''). There was less of the topsy-turvy humor of the libretto in the lyrics than would later become usual in Gilbert's writing, but the piece was a fine one and quickly proved the most popular item in its producer's repertoire. In October it was brought to London, with Claude Marius (Doro), J G Taylor (Caramel) and Harry Cox (Portico) supporting Miss Santley, but some unrecorded backstage strife occurred that resulted in its being pulled off after just 48 performances. A later report made mention of ''an unfortunate quarrel between the then collaborators, Messrs Clay and Gilbert, and the efforts made by the latter to destroy all copies of the work.''

Bad management also hit an American production, with Leonora Braham as Toto, which was put on poorly prepared and ran only 22 performances in New York (''a decided success artistically but it failed to draw,'' ''its humour is somewhat too quiet and dry to appeal to the general taste'') before going on to other cities, but apparently Gilbert got over his irritation and, following his rise to fame with *HMS Pinafore* and *The Pirates of Penzance,* he succeeded in persuading John Hollingshead to remount a revised version of *Princess Toto* (Opera Comique 15 October 1881). This time, instead of the flamboyantly sexy Miss Santley, the title role was cast with operatic vocalist Annie Albu and baritone Richard Temple was given the role of Portico. But it still ran just 65 performances and spawned a not very successful Australian production with Robert Brough repeating his London performance as Zapeter alongside Annette Ivanova (Toto), Armes Beaumont (Doro) and Edwin Kelly (Portico).

Princess Toto was also produced by ''Fatty'' Crossy at the Philadelphia North Broad Street Theatre (23 February 1880), played in Boston by the Broadway company (1880) and, after the vast success of *The Mikado,* toured by H B Mahn's company in 1886 with Charles J Campbell, W H Montgomery, Alice May, Tellulah Evans and Edward Connell in the cast. Philadelphia's reviewer remarked that ''the opera was supposed to have been finally buried and Mr Gilbert consequently did not hesitate to borrow from his own libretto much of the material that enriches the libretto of *The Mikado* nor did Sir Arthur Sullivan deem it beneath his dignity closely to study Mr Clay's muisc.'' The show was given a number of other productions around America in the late nineteenth century, and in a last reported sighting Barry Jackson exhumed the forgotten piece for a showing at the Birmingham Repertory Theatre in 1935.

USA: Standard Theater 13 December 1879; Australia: Opera House, Melbourne 12 June 1886

PRINTEMPS, Yvonne [WIGNOLLE, Yvonne] (b Ermont, 25 July 1895; d Paris, 19 January 1977). Individually styled actress and vocalist who made herself a star on every kind of stage.

Mlle Printemps began her stage career at the age of 12, and played at first largely in revue, making her earliest appearances in opérette as Prince Charmant in *Les Contes de Perrault* (1913) at the Gaîté, alongside Henri Defreyn in *Le Poilu* (1916, Suzanne Letillois) at the

Palais-Royal, and in *La Petite Dactylo* (1916) at the Gymnase. She abandoned the musical stage when she joined Sacha Guitry (soon to become her husband) for a series of plays that made them into one of the outstanding items in the Paris theatre, but in 1923 she appeared with Guitry in his exquisite and musical *L'Amour masqué* (''J'ai deux amants'') and, thereafter, music took an important part in many of their plays: *Mozart* (1925), in which Printemps appeared as the boy composer, a revival of *Jean de la Fontaine* into which were slipped several songs by Lully and one by Gilles Durant, and *Mariette* (1928), which allowed its heroine the luxury of appearing as a 100-year-old woman (as well as a young one).

Printemps played *Mozart* in London and New York, *Mariette* in London, and then, following the break-up of her marriage, went again to London to create the role of Melanie in *Conversation Piece,* written to her measure by Noël Coward, partly in English, partly in French (''I'll Follow My Secret Heart''). She played the same role in New York, before returning to Paris, where she next appeared in a version of the German Operette *Drei Walzer* specially remade to suit her and her new partner, Pierre Fresnay. *Les Trois Valses,* which had evoked only minor interest in its original form, was an enormous success with Printemps in the three generations of its starring role, and she repeated it, under her own management, when she subsequently took control of the Théâtre de la Michodière, and again in Ludwig Berger's celebrated film version. Thereafter, in a long and always starry career, she confined herself to the non-musical theatre, although she was seen on the screen as Hortense Schneider to the superb Offenbach of Fresnay in *Valse de Paris.*

An impishly winning actress with a mastery of comic timing both in her acting and in the songs that she put across in a clear, accurate and very individual soprano, she was a phenomenon of the musical stage to which, because of the non-singing men in her life, she returned only intermittently.

Biography: Dufresne, C: *Yvonne Printemps* (Perrin, Paris, 1988)

PRINZ METHUSALEM Operette in 3 acts by Karl Treumann adapted from a libretto by Victor Wilder and Alfred Delacour. Music by Johann Strauss. Carltheater, Vienna, 3 January 1877.

Franz Jauner of the Vienna Carltheater commissioned a French libretto from Victor Wilder (the co-author of the remaking of Johann Strauss's *Indigo* as *La Reine Indigo*) and Alfred Delacour to tempt Strauss to abandon the Theater an der Wien and compose an Operette for his theatre instead. Strauss, who had had a happy experience working on the French *Indigo* and considered its libretto much superior to the Viennese original, was duly tempted and, although the composer's French was minimal, much of the work was already composed before Karl Treumann, the longtime adaptor of Offenbach's works for the Vienna stage, put *Prinz Methusalem* into German.

Herzog Cyprian of Riccarac (Wilhelm Knaack) and Sigismund, Fürst von Trocadero (Josef Matras) are signing a military treaty, to be sealed dynastically by the marriage of Prince Methusalem of Riccarac (Antonie Link) and Pulcinella (Karoline Finaly), daughter of the ruler of Trocadero. The marriage has taken place, but the treaty is not yet signed when news comes that Cyprian has been deposed. Sigismund, who is offered his neighbor's crown by the revolutionaries, tries to stop the consummation of the unfortunate marriage, but the young folk are in love and they not only consummate but, by the end of the evening, end up replacing both their tricky fathers as the much-loved rulers of a coalition of both countries. Therese Schäfer was Cyprian's comical wife, Sphisteira, Franz Eppich played Trombonius, the court composer, and the tenor Ausim was the Lord Chamberlain, Vulcanio, in which role he inherited one of the show's happiest songs, ''Du schöner mai, du liebelei.'' The hit number of the piece, however, was the comical number performed by Matras, ''Das Tipferl aus dem i.''

Jauner got 54 performances out of his Strauss Operette before the end of 1877, and another eight, with Lori Stubel as the Prince Methusalem, in the first five months of 1878, before he threw in his managerial hand. When Franz Tewele took over he gave the piece another five showings, and intermittent performances took it up to its 89th on 19 September 1881. In 1904 (13 April) it appeared for a week at the Theater an der Wien with Phila Wolff starred, but, although it was occasionally played thereafter, it never became a part of the generally revived Strauss canon.

Prinz Methusalem duly had a German production, at Berlin's Friedrich-Wilhelmstädtisches Theater, which was followed by a number of others (it returned to Berlin, played at the Theater des Westens in a made-over version from Dresden, as late as 1932), and New York also saw its first performances in German when the piece was mounted at the Thalia with Marie König (later Franziska Raberg) as the Prince. Although San Francisco and other centers soon saw vernacular *Prince Methusalem*s of more or less fidelity to the original, it was several years more before the piece was played in New York in English, but when it was it appeared almost simultaneously both at the Cosmopolitan (ad Leo Goldmark) with Catherine Lewis (Methusalem) and J H Ryley (Cyprian) starring and, a few days later—with the earlier production having already folded—at the Casino Theater (9 July ad Sydney Rosenfeld) with Mathilde Cottrelly in the title role and Lilly Post (Pulcinella), A W Maflin (Cyprian) and Francis Wilson (Sigismund) in support. This latter production proved popular enough for producer John McCaull to bring it back for a second brief season at the Casino the following year (15 December 1884), and again, in 1888, to Wallack's Theater (16 July) with Marion Manola, De Wolf Hopper and Jefferson de Angelis featured. It stayed a month, apparently partly due to Hopper's interpolation, à propos of nothing, of what was to become his celebrated party piece, the recitation of the poem ''Casey at the Bat.''

If New York more or less liked *Prince Methusalem* (or just ''Casey''?), and American touring and summer theatres repeated it on a surprising number of occasions, London, which had seen it a month earlier than New York in another English version (ad H S Leigh), had shown very firmly that it did not. Tenor W S Rising played a non-travesty Prince, Camille Clermont and Ethel Pierson headed the ladies and Phil Day the comedy, to one of the most thundering thumbs-downs London had seen in years. The show did not last a week. It was bundled off, and the music of Strauss was replaced on the stage of the Folies Dramatiques by that of the urging New Zealander Luscombe Searelle as heard in *Estrella.* In Australia, where prima donna Emilie Melville presented herself as the Prince, alongside Gracie Plaisted (Pulcinella) and a score ''for a considerable portion of whose music Strauss is not responsible,'' which included everything from music-hall songs to a Christy Minstrel quartet, the show did little better. Similarly, in Budapest (ad György Verő), where Strauss's *Die Fledermaus* had been a considerable success, *Prinz Methusalem* with the tiny Sarolta Tarnay in her first (and only) lead role as Pulcinella, played just seven times. Paris, never much dazzled by the Strauss name, let it pass, in spite of the piece's French genesis and the original intention of giving it simultaneous premieres at the Carltheater and the Théâtre de la Renaissance, and they were probably right as, although the show had won many mountings, it had played remarkably few performances in most of them.

Germany: Friedrich-Wilhelmstädtisches Theater 21 January 1878; USA: Thalia Theater (Ger) 29 October 1880, Bush Street Theater, San Francisco *Prince Methusalem* 18 August 1880, Cosmopolitan Theater (Eng) 26 June 1883; UK: Folies Dramatiques *Prince Methusalem* 19 May 1883; Hungary: Népszínház *Metuzalem herceg* 5 September 1884; Australia: Princess Theatre, Melbourne 22 September 1883

PROMISES, PROMISES Musical in 2 acts by Neil Simon based on the screenplay *The Apartment* by Billy Wilder and I A L Diamond. Lyrics by Hal David. Music by Burt Bacharach. Shubert Theater, New York, 1 December 1968.

A one-and-only stage musical by popular songwriters Burt Bacharach and Hal David, whose decade of collaboration had brought forth such hit numbers as ''The Story of My Life,'' ''Magic Moments,'' ''Twenty-Four Hours from Tulsa,'' ''Anyone Who Had a Heart,'' ''There's Always Something There to Remind Me,'' ''What's New, Pussycat?,'' ''Trains and Boats and Planes,'' ''What the World Needs Now,'' ''Do You Know the Way to San José?'' and a bookful of others, *Promises, Promises* maintained its writers' high-success profile by becoming a very large and international hit. It was, on the other hand, by no means a one-and-only hit for its librettist, Neil Simon, already the author of two splendid musicals in *Little Me* and *Sweet Charity* and here called upon, as with *Sweet Charity,* to turn a film script into a libretto.

Chuck Baxter (Jerry Orbach) isn't noticed much at work until middle management discover he has a bachelor apartment. Middle management are sufficiently grateful for the use of that apartment for Chuck to get an appointment with J D Sheldrake (Edward Winter), head of personnel. Chuck gets a promotion, Sheldrake gets an exclusive on the apartment and all is well until the boy discovers that ''the branch manager from Kansas'' whom Sheldrake meets at his home is Fran Kubelik (Jill O'Hara), the girl he has sighed over so long. But it has been and is a rocky affair, and one night the desperate Fran inconsiderately takes an overdose in Chuck's apartment. Fortunately, the next-door neighbor is a doctor, and by the end of the act a happy ending has been arranged. At the final curtain it is clear that the apartment won't be available to anyone any more except its two inhabitants.

The show's set of songs duly turned out a Bacharach/David hit in the simple, guitar-accompanied promise of the recovering Fran, ''I'll Never Fall in Love Again'' (an on-the-way-in addition to the score), and its highlight was a jolly office party scene where the tiddly truths and sexual jockeyings were contrasted with a memorably zippy Michael Bennett song-and-dance routine to ''Turkey Lurkey Time'' for a featured trio of girls (Adrienne Angel, Barbara Lang, Donna McKechnie), who had lost their second number when the hit solo was added.

David Merrick's production of *Promises, Promises* was a 1,281-performance hit on Broadway, and the show repeated its success when it was reproduced in London by Merrick and H M Tennent Ltd whilst Broadway's version ran on. Tony Roberts (later to take over on Broadway), Betty Buckley and James Congdon featured, and the show ran 560 performances in the West End. Australia followed quickly behind, with a production featuring Orson Bean, Ann Hilton, Bruce Barry and Nancye Hayes through a rather disappointing 10 weeks in Melbourne and a short season in Sydney.

A German version, which returned to the film title (aka *Das Schlusselkarussell*), was later produced at Munich and at Berlin's Theater des Westens (ad Werner Wollenberger, Charly Niessen), and again in a localized version (ad Gerhard Bronner) at Vienna's Theater an der Wien where, with Peter Fröhlich as Willy Draxler and Marianne Mendt as Franzi Kubelik, and the song ''She Likes Basketball'' transmuted (for a country where basketball isn't exactly hot) into ''Sie hat Fussball gern,'' it played a season of 72 performances. Italy hosted *Promesse, Promesse,* and Switzerland played *Das Appartment,* as the musical got worldwide coverage. The show then rather disappeared from the repertoire, but in the 1990s, when its definite period of style had at last become nostalgiable, it returned in several regional and/or small-house productions in both America and Britain.

UK: Prince of Wales Theatre 2 October 1969; Germany: Theater des Westens *Das Appartment* 16 April 1970; Australia: Her Majesty's Theatre, Melbourne 15 August 1970; Austria: Theater an der Wien *Das Appartment* 3 November 1973

Recordings: original cast (UA), London cast (UA), Italian cast (CGD/FGS), etc

PRUETTE, William (b Washington, DC, 22 September 1863; d Liberty, NY, 15 July 1918). The ''Field Marshal of Comic Opera'' in America.

Baritone Pruette made his first ventures on to the stage singing grand opera at McVicker's Theater in Chicago under the name Signor Pruetti and went on to perform in Paris, and on tour with Emma Abbott's Opera Company, before making his first appearance in opéra-bouffe as Mourzouk in *Giroflé-Girofla.* In 1891 he played with the Lamont company and W T Carleton's company, and sang the role of Alfio in some of the first American performances of *Cavalleria rusticana.* He subsequently appeared with Henry Dixey's Company as a rather (vocally) overweight Pippo to the Bettina of Camille D'Arville in *La Mascotte* (1892) and at the Casino Theater as Picasso in *The Lion Tamer* (*Le Grand Casimir*), Lothair in *The Child of Fortune* (*Das Sonntagskind*), as Vulcan in Gounod's *Philemon and Baucis* and King René in Julian Edwardes's *King René's Daughter* (1893), on tour as Cardamon in *The Tar and the Tartar* (1893) and as Mars in *Prince Kam* (1894). In 1894 he also created the title role in De Koven's highly successful *Rob Roy,* and the following year introduced the part of Prince Chic in *Ollamus* at St Louis and succeeded Julius Steger in the Broadway cast of *In Gay New York.* He then switched temporarily to the vaudeville circuits, playing a *Carmen* burlesque with Marie Bell in variety houses, but was back on Broadway in 1897 playing the Duc du Bouillon in Julian Edwardes's *The Wedding Day* (1897) alongside Jeff de Angelis and Lillian Russell. He appeared during 1898–99 in the opera and comic opera repertoire at San Francisco's Tivoli Opera House—playing Henry Ashton in *Lucia di Lammermoor* or Valentine in *Faust* or Telramund in *Lohengrin* one week and creating a dame role in the Christmas entertainment *The Yellow Dwarf* another—then for the next couple of seasons with the Castle Square Opera Company, with whom he took part in the American premiere of Spinelli's *A basso porto* (1900, Ciccilio), before going on to be seen as the Prime Minister in the original cast of Chicago's *King Dodo* (1901) as Admiral Hi Lung in *A Chinese Honeymoon* (1902), appearing with De Wolf Hopper and Madge Lessing in a revival of *Wang* (1904, Colonel Robert Fracasse) and as Henry VIII to the Mary Tudor of Lulu Glaser in *A Madcap Princess* (1904).

Now established as one of the musical stage's best ''fathers,'' he won his finest new role to date when he appeared as the grouchy Comte de Saint Mar in Victor Herbert's *Mlle Modiste* (1905), introducing ''I Want What I Want When I Want It.'' He appeared as The Rajah of Rangapang in *The Tourists* (1906, Gopal Ram), took over as Abdallah in *The Tattoed Man* (1907), played the Governor General in *Algeria* (1908, General Petipons) and Diego de la Concha in the hit production of *Havana* (1909), and although now tipping the scales at some 200 lbs, he found himself in his element with the arrival in America of the fashion for Viennese Operette. He scored one of his greatest successes as Colonel Popoff in *The Chocolate Soldier* (1909) and—after a turn into a non-singing role in *The Lady from Lobster Square* (1910, Feydeau's *Un Fil à la patte*), he appeared as Pish-Tush and Pooh-Bah in the Casino Theater's star-studded *Mikado* of 1910, in *The Slim Princess* with Elsie Janis (t/o), played in *Doctor De Luxe* (1911, Colonel Houston), *The Kiss Waltz* (*Liebeswalzer,* 1911, Count Arthur Wildenberg) and, in his last Broadway appearances, in *The Red Petticoat* (1912, Big Regan), Oscar Straus's *My Little Friend* (*Die kleine Freundin,* 1913, Barbasson) and *Madame Moselle* (1914, Kerazzo). He then turned again to the vaudeville stage, appearing first with ''the Pruette Quartet'' and later in a ''miniature comic opera'' *A Holland Romance* (1915) in the final part of his fine career in the twilight of which he could still pull ''half a dozen encores'' with his rendition of ''I Want What I Want'' in a guest appearance in a summer season production of *Mlle Modiste* (Washington, 1915).

LES P'TITES MICHU Opéra-comique in 3 acts by Georges Duval and Albert Vanloo. Music by André Messager. Théâtre des Bouffes-Parisiens, Paris, 16 November 1897.

In a busy, varied career in which his musical-theatre writings had often received more connoisseur's praise than profitable runs, Messager had not succeeded in being party to a genuine, full-scale hit of international proportions since his very first opérette venture, completing the score of the late Firmin Bernicat's *François les bas-bleus,* 14 years earlier. With *Les P'tites Michu* not only was that omission thoroughly remedied, but the show's combination of a gently charming libretto, full of enjoyable characters, and a musical score of refinement and beauty as well as of considerable gaiety, produced one of the most elegantly attractive opérettes of the pre-war French theatre.

The little Michu sisters, Blanche-Marie (Odette Dulac) and Marie-Blanche (Alice Bonheur), are not really sisters. One of them was confided to Madame Michu (Mme Vigoureux) and her shopkeeping husband (Regnard) as a baby, and is really the aristocratic child of General des Ifs (Barral). However, as Michu once bathed the babes without due attention, they now have no idea which is which. When des Ifs returns to claim his child from the foster mother, so that she may wed his handsome lieutenant, Gaston Rigaud (Manson), sweet little Blanche-Marie insists that her more extrovert sister, who has fallen madly for Gaston, must be nominated. Blanche-Marie will marry the Michu's shop boy, Aristide (Maurice Lamy). But Marie-Blanche finds the proprieties of aristocratic life unbearably constricting, and Blanche-Marie is just hopeless in the shop. It is clear that blood will out. When the positions are reversed, everyone is much happier.

The gems of Messager's score began with the little sisters' introductory duet (''Blanche-Marie et Marie-Blanche''), the bouncing trio (''Michu, Michu, Michu'') of their first schoolgirlish meeting with Gaston and Marie-Blanche's frank appreciation of his qualities (''Sapristi, le beau militaire''). They continued with Aristide's puzzled light tenor attempt to make his choice between the two girls (''Blanche-Marie est douce et bonne''), and with the girls' second-act discovery of their position (''Ah quel malheur'') and their double prayer to Saint-Nicolas: each sister praying she isn't the one picked to wed the unknown lieutenant and, after they've realized who the bridegroom is to be, each praying that she is. The appearance of the senior Michus, the General's explosive nonsense, Gaston's smooth baritonic vocalizing and some superior ensembles all went with these to make up a truly model opérette score.

Les P'tites Michu was a fine Paris success. It ran for more than 150 nights in its first series, was briskly taken up by the theatres of France and was soon exported first to Hungary (ad Ferenc Rajna), then to Germany (ad Heinrich Bolten-Bäckers), where the Frls Worm and Fischer were Anne-Marie and Marianne and top comic Guido Thielscher led the fun, and then to Vienna's Carltheater. Franz Jauner's production cast Betty Stojan and Aurélie Révy as the two sisters, Louis Treumann was Aristide, and Siegmund Natzler the General through 24 performances before the arrival of Sarah Bernhardt removed them from the stage. In Paris, Mariette Sully and Mary Lebey appeared in an 1899 revival at the Folies-Dramatiques, but although the show appeared in Lisbon and in Prague in the following years, its record outside France was a disappointing one and it seemed that the perhaps rather too wink-and-nodless *Les P'tites Michu* would go no further. But it did.

Plate 315. **Les P'tites Michu.** *London's Michu twins—who aren't twins—were Mabel Green and Adrienne Augarde.*

George Edwardes had decided, after the evident drop displayed in quality of his Daly's Theatre entertainments with *The Cingalee* (not to mention the annoyance of its contiguous lawsuit), that a change was needed at that theatre. Given the great success of his recent production of Messager's *Véronique,* he reached back for the composer's earlier piece and produced an English adaptation of *The Little Michus* (ad Henry Hamilton, Percy Greenbank) at Daly's Theatre. The choice proved a fine one. With Adrienne Augarde and Mabel Green as the two little girls, Willie Edouin as General des Its, Amy Augarde stealing a scene as Madame Michu, the ever-versatile W Louis Bradfield as Aristide and Bobbie Evett as a tenor Gaston, the show took off for a splendid run of 401 London performances, a run in line with what a Daly's show expected and even intrinsically better than the slightly longer life secured by *Véronique* at the smaller Apollo Theatre. The piece moved on from there not only to the provinces but to the colonies, and Florence Young and Margaret Thomas were featured as the little semi-lost Michus, supported by Reginald Roberts (Gaston), George Lauri (Ifs), W S Percy (Aristide) and Clara Clifton (Mme Michu), in an Australian production that played a fine seven weeks in Sydney before moving on to the rest of the country.

Last of all, *The Little Michus* got its showing in America. But J C Duff's production, with Alice Judson and Ruth Julian as the girls, and with British comedian George Graves splattering excesses all over the stage as a General des Ifs with a wooden leg, flopped in 29 under- and over-done performances. The piece was later performed on the road (1907) and in American stock as *Two Little Girls.*

The show returned to Paris's Trianon-Lyrique in 1909 (27 September), and to Berlin's Schiller-Theater in 1910 (August) but whilst *Véronique* prospers to this day, this piece—arguably a better one, if less thoroughly romantic—has been seen only spasmodically since.

Hungary: Magyar Színház *Michu lányok* 19 February 1898; Germany: Metropoltheater *Die kleinen Michu's* 25 December 1898; Austria: Carltheater *Die kleinen Michu's* 16 September 1899; UK: Daly's Theatre *The Little Michus* 29 April 1905; Australia: Her Majesty's Theatre, Sydney *The Little Michus* 2 June 1906; USA: Garden Theater *The Little Michus* 31 January 1907

Recordings: complete (Gaîté-Lyrique), selections (EMI-Pathé)

PUFFERL Operette in 3 acts by Ignaz Schnitzer and Sigmund Schlesinger. Music by Edmund Eysler. Theater an der Wien, Vienna, 10 February 1905.

On a hint from Girardi as to the sort of role and scene(s) that he, the biggest star of the Viennese Operette stage, would like to play in his next piece, Schnitzer and Schlesinger built up a musical comedy around the character of the hairdresser, Pufferl, a figure taken from a set of old Vienna tales.

Pufferl's hairdressing shop on the Graben is a great place for gossip and intrigue, and the hairdresser gets the usual kind of coiffeurial confidences from his clients. The Graf Dreyschatten (Adalbert Minnich) is anxious to get his hands on some land owned by the family of Ewald, Fürst von Limenau (Karl Meister), and Pufferl suggests to him that he get the young man to make an unsuitable marriage, thus forfeiting his property. Dreyschatten enlists Pufferl to his aid with the promise of promotion to "Hoffriseur," and the crafty fellow decides to entrap Limenau into an alliance with the singer Poldi, a wench who is a perfect double for the eccentric Countess Christine Rottek (Gerda Walde) with whom Ewald fell in love when rescuing her from a carriage accident. Although Pufferl thinks the Countess is on his side, she falls for her "prey" during the course of the events, and when Pufferl and Dreyschatten think they have tricked Limenau into marrying Poldi, it turns out that it wasn't Poldi at all, but her "double." A third act sorts everything out, gets Pufferl his title and his girl, Mali (Mila Theren), pairs his hopeful housekeeper, Kathi (Sarolta von Rettich-Birk) off with his assistant (Franz Glawatsch), and gets Dreyschatten out of a sticky spot. Director Siegmund Natzler completed the principal cast as Mali's father.

Eysler's typically Viennese score supplied Girardi with his obligatory big number, the waltzing Kirschenlied (on the forbidden-fruit theme), at the head of a catchy score also marked by a lively dialect march trio "Geh'n ma, Freunderl." Leading lady Gerda Walde, however, had her best number cut at the star's behest after she scored altogether too well with it on the opening night.

Pufferl clearly had the making of a good success in it, but it was not to be allowed to run. Girardi's jealousies went beyond his fellow actors, and he could not bear being directed by Karl Wallner, once a supporting actor and now in charge at the Theater an der Wien. He was as troublesome as he could be and, as soon as his minimum contract was up, he abandoned the Theater an der Wien and *Pufferl,* which, as of 31 March, had played just 51 performances. The show had to be withdrawn.

Pufferl later turned up in Italy under the title of *Amor di Principi,* and the Italian version was briefly played in New York by a touring company, but at home it had committed suicide, leaving just its Kirschenlied behind.

PUGNO, [Stéphane] Raoul (aka "Franz [or Max] Richard") (b Montrouge, Seine, 23 June 1852; d Moscow, 3 January 1914).

After a notable career at the Paris Conservatoire (first prize in organ, etc), Pugno began his career as a composer with classic works, including an oratorio, *La Résurrection de Lazare* (1879). He later wrote the scores for several opérettes as an adjunct to a more appreciable career as a virtuoso pianist and organist and, from 1862, as a professor at the Conservatoire.

His stage pieces had mostly a limited success, although his first opérette, *Ninetta* (16 performances), was staged with a brilliant cast featuring Jeanne Granier, Mily-Meyer, Daubray and Marie Desclauzas, and with much hope and hype. The two vaudeville-opérettes *La Vocation de Marius* and *La Petite Poucette* (a spectacular vehicle allowing Mily-Meyer to play a female Tom Thumb) each had something of a run, with the latter being subsequently produced in Hungary (*Hüvelyk Kató* ad Adolf Mérei, Magyar Színház 26 March 1904), but Pugno never established himself in the world of light music-theatre in the way that he did as a classic performer.

Pugno's other stage works included an opera *Tai-Tsoung* (Marseille 1894), the ballets *Viviane* (1886) and *Le Chevalier aux fleurs* (1897 w Messager), a mimodrama *Pour le drapeau* (1895) and the music for Xavier Roux's short comedy *Trop tard* (1893).

1877 **A qui la trompe?** (as "Max Richard"/Hans de Sartem) 1 act Asnières 13 December

1881 **La Fée Cocotte** (w Léon Bourgeois/Gaston Marot, Édouard Philippe) Palace Théâtre 26 January

1882 **Ninetta** (Alexandre Bisson, Alfred Hennequin) Théâtre de la Renaissance 26 December

1887 **Le Sosie** (Albin Valabrègue, Henri Kéroul) Théâtre des Bouffes-Parisiens 8 October

1888 **Le Valet de coeur** (Paul Ferrier, Charles Clairville) Théâtre des Bouffes-Parisiens 19 April

1889 **Le Retour d'Ulysse** (Fabrice Carré) Théâtre des Bouffes-Parisiens 1 February

1890 **La Vocation de Marius** (Carré, Émile Dehelly) Théâtre des Nouveautés 29 March

1891 **La Petite Poucette** (Maurice Ordonneau, Maurice Hennequin) Théâtre de la Renaissance 5 March

PUPPCHEN Musical comedy (Posse mit Gesang und Tanz) in 3 acts by Kurt Kraatz and Jean Kren. Lyrics by Alfred Schönfeld. Music by Jean Gilbert. Thalia-Theater, Berlin, 19 December 1912.

Puppchen followed behind *Autoliebchen* in Jean Gilbert's run of Berlin hits at the Thalia-Theater and rendered nothing to its predecessor in the way of success or of song hits. Comedian Arnold Rieck played Hänschen Schulze-Bosdorf, the "little doll" of the title, a fellow who pretends to be still a young boy and takes advantage of the liberties this allows him with the ladies. The ladies in this case are the four Briesekorn nieces: Hortense (Eugenie della Donna), Lore (Elsa Grünberg), Marie (Ellen Dalossy) and Hilde (Frl Wallis). Hortense is married to lawyer Blankenstein (Paul Beuchert), but it is her flirtation with the pilot Egon von Hallersdorf (Fritz Junkermann) that sets off many of the complexities of the action. By the end of the evening, Puppchen and Hortense have both reformed, and all four sisters are neatly mated. Theodore Stolzenberg played American Fred William Black, at one stage taken for Puppchen's guardian and ultimately paired with Marie, whilst Emil Sondermann as Brisekorn and Lotte Reinecker (Dörthe) supplied the rest of the comedy.

Gilbert's score was made up largely of waltzes ("Das kann ein Herz nur, welches liebt") and marches, of which the two-steppable duet "Puppchen, du bist mein Augenstern" was the show's oversized hit. The ensemble "Gehn wir mal zu Hagenbeck!" and a gavotte ("Lorchen, wo hast du deine Ohrchen?") were amongst the other favorite numbers.

Puppchen had passed its 250th performance and almost reached the 300th when it was replaced on 4 October by Gilbert's next piece, *Die Tango-Prinzessin*. The Thalia-Theater was, however, only a starting point in these days for Gilbert's works, for *Autoliebchen* had joined *Die keusche Susanne* and *Die Kino-Königin* on the international musical stage, and *Puppchen* was set to do the same. *Buksi* (ad Zsolt Harsányi), with the young Juci Lábass as its female star, opened with more than a little success in Budapest before the Berlin run was done, and George Edwardes bought up the British rights. London was set to be the take-off point to the rest of the world for the show. But then there was war. Edwardes junked

Plate 316. **Puppchen**

all his German shows, *Puppchen* (for which he had paid out £1,000 in advance) the first, for its hit march tune had quickly become a German troop song.

Hungary: Király Színház *Buksi* 16 August 1913

DAS PUPPENMÄDEL Vaudeville in 3 acts by Leo Stein and A M Willner based on the play *Miquette et sa mère* by Robert de Flers and Gaston de Caillavet. Music by Leo Fall. Carltheater, Vienna, 4 November 1910.

The doll-girl of *Das Puppenmädel* was not, like so many of her predecessors, a stand-in for a doll herself, but merely a little lass who finds her doll better company than the local boys. The librettists turned the "Miquette" of de Flers and de Caillavet's successful Paris comedy (Théâtre des Variétés 2 November 1906) into an Yvette, Yvette Prunier (Lisa Weise), who is whisked off from her country home in Picardy to Paris by a kindly, middle-elderly but definitely amorous Marquis (Richard Waldemar) who equates love with "a mansion, buttons like millstones, a 60-horse-power car, a pretty house in Trouville, dresses from Worth and a bank account." But Yvette, like Miquette, has a mother (Dora Keplinger) who is soon hot-foot on the train to Paris, closely followed by her friend, the Marquis's love-struck nephew Tiborius (Hubert Marischka), who ultimately wins the girl after sending her flowers and verses under the pseudonym of René Brion. The Marquis has to resign himself to being loved "wie ein Papa." Mizzi Zwerenz featured (heavily) as a phony Spanish danseuse named Rosalillja, Josef König was theatre director Romuald Talmi and the aged Karl Blasel appeared in a non-singing role as Buffon.

Fall's score was written, in vaudeville style, practically wholly for the play's six principals, and it contained some charming music. Yvette sang a little Ländler to her doll confiding "look at every man twice before you count on him, thrice before you trust him, four times before you love him, and five before you wed," yodeled out a Picard song, joined Tiborius in a clever railway number ("Es war am fünfzehnten Mai") and gave out with the brisk tale of "Die kleine Adele," while Tiborius sang forth his love in waltz time in "Du kleine Fee im Pavilion" and, jubilantly, in the final act's "Sie liebt den, der ihr Blumen schickt," and Rosalillja spread unconvincing Spanish through her "Ach, wie bist du süss, Amigo" and her seductive dance duo with Talmi.

Sigmund Eibenschütz's production (with "architect Joseph Urban" co-credited on the designs) was well received and played for 104 performances at the Carltheater, but, oddly, the piece did not receive the overseas attention that might have been expected for a successor to the enormously successful *Die geschiedene Frau.* Budapest's *Babukska* (ad Andor Gábor) was played some 30 times, and Berlin's production lasted 76 nights, but in Britain, which had stormed to *The Girl in the Train,* and in France, which loved *La Divorcée,* the show remained unproduced. When Charles Frohman mounted *The Doll Girl* (ad H B Smith) in America, he gave the Marquis's role to comedian Richard Carle, cast Hattie Williams as an Irish-Spanish Rosalilla, alongside Dorothy Webb and London's Robert Evett as the young folk, and—in spite of having signed a contract that expressly forbade interpolations—filled up the score with additional bits of music from all over the place: one number from Eysler's *Der Frauenfresser,* another by Henri Christiné, a thumping Walter Kollo song insisting "Come on, Over Here," and several Jerome Kern numbers of which a wistful "Will It All End in Smoke?" was, at least, not incompatible with Fall's melodies. *The Doll Girl* played 88 performances on Broadway and, if that was more than such other top quality imports of the season as *Der liebe Augustin, Leányvásár, Filmzauber, Der lachende Ehemann* and *Das Fürstenkind,* it was still something of a disappointment. The publishers of the interpolated songs ended up in court being sued for $50,000. I don't suppose they got it.

Germany: Theater des Westens 26 November 1910; Hungary: Király Színház *Babuska* 24 February 1911; USA: Globe Theater *The Doll Girl* 25 August 1913

PURCELL, Charles (b Chattanooga, Tenn, 1883; d New York, 20 March 1962).

Purcell was the creator of many richly singing baritonic heroes in American musicals between 1908 and 1933. He appeared on the road as the naval hero of the extravaganza *The Isle of Spice* (1907), on Broadway as Count Androssy in *The Golden Butterfly* (1908), took over in the West Coast spectacular *The Tik-Tok Man of Oz* (1913), played Forest Smith in *The Pretty Mrs Smith* (1914), Prince Nicholas Demidoff in *Flora Bella* (1916), Captain Poildeau in *My Lady's Glove,* John Moore in *The Melting of Molly,* Edmond Dantès in *Monte Cristo Jr,* Beppo Corsini in Romberg's *The Magic Melody,* Bill Pemberton in *Poor Little Ritz Girl,* Victor in *The Rose Girl* and Jack Lethbridge in *Judy.* However, the bright-eyed and boyish singing star had his most successful moments as the hero of Romberg's *Maytime* (1917), introducing "Will You Remember" with Peggy Wood, as John Copeland in Rodgers and Hart's *Dearest Enemy* ("Here in My Arms" w Helen Ford) and in the title role of several reproductions of *The Chocolate Soldier.* He also appeared opposite Beatrice Lillie in Vincent Youmans's *Oh, Please!* (1926) , took over the leading roles in *The Right Girl* (1921) and *Sky High* (1925), played opposite Helen Kane in *Shady Lady* (1933, Richard Brandt) and made his last Broadway appearance, in 1946, in a character role in Arthur Schwartz's short-lived *Park Avenue.*

PURCELL, Harold [Vousden] (b Lewisham, 9 December 1907; d Worthing, 28 May 1977).

A schoolmaster and journalist, Purcell made his first contribution to the musical stage by supplying some lyrics to Eric Maschwitz's megaflop *Magyar Melody.* Undaunted by this unpromising beginning, he subsequently wrote lyrics for a long list of London revues (*Diversion, Rise Above It, The New Ambassadors Revue, Orchids and Onions, Apple Sauce, Hulbert Follies, Big Top, Here Come the Boys, The Shephard Show, The Glorious Days*) and also for the series of very successful and long-running musical comedies starring Cicely Courtneidge (*Full Swing, Something in the Air, Under the Counter, Her Excellency*).

Purcell had his biggest success when he provided both book and lyrics for the wartime musical melodrama *The Lisbon Story,* a piece that also produced his major song success, "Pedro, the Fisherman." He subsequently worked on the highly successful musical farce *Blue for a Boy* as well as supplying lyrics for a short-lived Offenbach pastiche, for an equally unfortunate remake of *The Red Mill* and the spectacular but unsatisfactory *Rainbow Square.*

Purcell also worked for film, writing lyrics for *Spring in Park Lane* and the screenplay for *The Lady Is a Square.*

1939 **Magyar Melody** (George Posford, Bernard Grün/w Eric Maschwitz/Maschwitz, Fred Thompson, Guy Bolton) Her Majesty's Theatre 20 January

1942 **Full Swing** (Posford/Arthur Macrae, Archie Menzies, Jack Hulbert) Palace Theatre 16 April

1943 **The Lisbon Story** (Harry Parr Davies) London Hippodrome 17 June

1943 **Something in the Air** (Manning Sherwin/w Max Kester/ Macrae, Menzies, Hulbert) Palace Theatre 23 September

1944 **Jenny Jones** (Parr Davies/Ronald Gow) London Hippodrome 2 October

1945 **Under the Counter** (Sherwin/Macrae) Phoenix Theatre 22 November

1946 **Goodnight Vienna** (Posford/Maschwitz) Pavilion Theatre, Bournemouth 22 July

1949 **Her Excellency** (Sherwin, Parr-Davies/w Kester/w Menzies, Kester) London Hippodrome 22 June

1950 **Music at Midnight** (Offenbach arr/Guy Bolton) His Majesty's Theatre

1950 **Blue for a Boy** (Parr Davies/ad Austin Melford) His Majesty's Theatre 30 November

1951 **Rainbow Square** (Robert Stolz/w Bolton) Stoll Theater 21 September

PURLIE Musical comedy in 2 acts by Ossie Davis, Peter Rose and Peter Udell based on the play *Purlie Victorious* by Ossie Davis. Lyrics by Peter Udell. Music by Gary Geld. Broadway Theater, New York, 15 March 1970.

A musical version of Davis's successful and winning 1961 play, *Purlie* (the ''Victorious'' part was his middle name, as well as the result of the play's action) followed its hero (Cleavon Little) in his battles to hornswoggle some cash he is sort of owed out of the double-hornswoggling old Cap'n Cotchipee (John Heffernan) so that he can rebuild the Big Bethel Chapel and take up preaching there. Little Lutiebelle (Melba Moore), Purlie's girl, is the secret weapon with which they intend to trick the old man, but she blows it and, ultimately, it is the Cap'n's own son, the gormless Charlie (C David Colson), who double-crosses his father and secures the church for Purlie.

The story was accompanied by some vibrant and often moving musical pieces, from the stirring opening sounds of the church choir and its soloist (Linda Hopkins) singing the soul of the Cap'n—who dropped dead at his son's treachery—up to Heaven (''Walk Him Up the Stairs'') to Lutiebelle's all-stops-out recital of her love for Purlie in ''I Got Love'' and a ringing title song, the man's jaunty description of himself as ''A New Fangled Preacher Man,'' and the joyously wry comedy of ''The Bigger They Are, the Harder They Fall.'' Purlie's weaselly brother's procrastinating ''(There's more than one way of) Skinnin' a Cat'' and Charlie's running-joke attempts to write a folksong, ending, after his momentous betrayal, in success with ''The World Is Comin' to a Start,'' were other unthumpingly funny moments.

Purlie marched victoriously through 689 Broadway performances, was toured and later televised (1981), all without convincing any other musical-theatre centers to share its enjoyments.

Recording: original cast (Ampex/RCA)

Q

THE QUAKER Comic opera in 2 acts by Charles Dibdin. Theatre Royal, Drury Lane, London, 7 October 1777.

One of the few 18th-century ''ballad farcical operas'' that survived into productions in the mid-19th century, *The Quaker* was seen as late as 1870 (5 September) in the repertoire of London's Gaiety Theatre, with Nellie Farren starring as Lubin, the village lad who returns from finally getting himself well enough established to marry pretty Gillian, only to find that her parents have betrothed her to the Quaker, Mr Steady. While the wise and kindly Quaker does all he can to win sulky Gillian's love, Lubin plots to make use of that kindness to make his rival humiliate himself before the whole village. Mr Steady, however, is way ahead of him, but instead of turning the situation against the boy, he sagely resigns the lass. The action was decorated with 14 musical numbers, mostly solo songs but including a quintet and two duets, written and arranged by the author.

USA: Charleston Theater *The Quaker, or The May Day Dower* 13 February 1793; Australia: Albert Theatre, Hobart 29 March 1842

THE QUAKER GIRL Musical play in 3 acts by James T Tanner. Lyrics by Adrian Ross and Percy Greenbank. Music by Lionel Monckton. Adelphi Theatre, London, 5 November 1910.

When George Edwardes took over the Adelphi Theatre to add to his Gaiety and Daly's at the center of the musical-comedy activity of London, he delegated James Tanner, the constructor-in-chief of Edwardes's musicals through their palmiest years, and Lionel Monckton, co-composer of so many Gaiety shows, to write the first musical for the new house in his string. Monckton's wife, Gertie Millar, the star of the Gaiety, insisted on going where her husband went, and in consequence *The Quaker Girl* was written to feature Miss Millar in its title role.

The star played Prudence Pym who, whilst helping the runaway marriage of the Bonapartist Princess Mathilde (Elsie Spain) and the English Captain Charteris (Hayden Coffin), is caught sipping a little celebratory champagne and thrown out of the Family by the uncompromising elders of the Quaker group. Mathilde's friend Madame Blum (Mlle Caumont), a Paris couturier, takes her up and before the second act is long under way, Prudence's little gray dress and bonnet have become the rage of the Parisian fashion world, and she has attracted the attention of the lupine Prince Carlo (Georges Carvey). This doesn't please her American admirer, Tony Chute (Joe Coyne), but Tony is handicapped by an old and jealous mistress, Diane (Phyllys LeGrand), who tries to make herself a point by giving Prudence a bundle of what she thinks are his old love letters. They turn out to be love letters from a French Minister of State and, when Prudence tactfully returns them to him, she earns both the safety of Mathilde and Charteris and a final curtain with Tony.

Miss Millar's Prudence had some of the prettiest songs Monckton had made for his wife over the years: the dainty title song, her wide-eyed appreciation of ''Tony from America'' and, later, a sweet solo about her ''Little Grey Bonnet,'' as well as the shared tale of ''The Good Girl and the Bad Boy'' with Coyne, whose light-comedy role was not overweighted with singing. Jimmy Blakeley as a comical Quaker and Gracie Leigh, as a jokey maid, had the humorous moments, and Miss Spain had a delightful soprano waltz song, ''Time,'' but the gem of the score actually fell to Carvey, the libidinous Prince, as he tried to persuade the Quaker girl to ''Come to the Ball.''

The Quaker Girl was the biggest hit of a season that included *The Chocolate Soldier* and *The Girl on the Train* amongst its other big successes. It played 536 performances at the Adelphi, was swiftly on the road, and, in June 1911 played 13 guest performances at Paris's Théâtre du Châtelet (which had, the previous week, been scandalized by the premiere of *L'Après-midi d'un faun*), with Phyllis Dare as Prudence. This season provoked a delighted response and, as a result, in 1913 *La Petite Quaker* (ad Paul Ferrier, Charles Quinel) was produced in French at the Olympia with Alice O'Brien starred and the young Alice Delysia as Diane. It was later also played at Brussels's Théâtre de la Gaîté, with Marthe Lenclud as its star, and brought back in 1920 to Paris's Ba-ta-clan.

In the meanwhile, Broadway had also welcomed the show enthusiastically. Ina Claire (Prudence), Clifton Crawford (Tony), F Pope Stamper (Charteris), Percival Knight (Jeremiah), Maisie Gay (Mme Blum) and May Vokes (Phoebe) headed the cast of Henry B Harris's production, which—with its score interpolated into only by two numbers by leading man Crawford—stayed on Broadway for an exceptionally good run of 246 performances before going to the country. J C Williamson's Australian production was another singular success: Blanche Browne (Prudence), Leslie Holland (Tony), Bertie Wright (Jeremiah), former Gaiety starlet Grace Palotta (Mme Blum) and Jessie Lonnen (Phoebe, from the British touring company) featured, Miss Vera Pearce performed a champagne dance, and the show played 90 performances in Sydney before moving on for its next date.

The Quaker Girl remained a favorite in English theatres for many years and returned to London in a barely professional production in 1934, then in an Emile Littler ''revised'' version in 1944. This production, intended to star Jessie Matthews, was instead mounted with Celia Lipton (Prudence), Billy Milton (Tony) and Ivy St Helier (Mme Blum), and it turned out such a success that, despite being interrupted by bombs, it was given two London seasons of two months apiece as well as the long tour that had been its original goal.

France: Théâtre du Châtelet (Eng) 20 June 1911, L'Olympia *La Petite Quaker* 1 October 1912; USA: Park Theater 23 October 1911; Australia: Her Majesty's Theatre, Sydney 13 January 1912

QUATRE JOURS À PARIS Opérette in 2 acts by Raymond Vincy. Music by Francis Lopez. Théâtre Bobino, Paris, 28 February 1948.

Whilst Vincy and Lopez established the standards for postwar Parisian opérette à moyen-to-grand spectacle with *La Belle de Cadix* and *Andalousie,* they also collaborated on some pieces for smaller stages, of which *Quatre Jours à Paris* was one of the most successful. It also boasted far and away the best libretto that Vincy ever wrote, in the hilariously complex and farcical story of what happens as the result of Gabrielle Montaron (Ginette Catriens) spending four days in Paris.

Whilest in town, Gabrielle steals the heart of dashing Ferdinand (Andrex), the star attraction of the beauty parlor run by Monsieur Hyacinthe (Orbal), and Ferdinand abandons his hair dryers to follow her to her home in the country. This maddens both Hyacinthe, who needs Ferdinand to ''look after'' a prize client, the fiery Brazilian chanteuse, Amparita Alvarez (Nelly Wick), and the manicurist Simone (Marguette Willy), who has her own feelings about Ferdinand, and these three, along with the singer's husband (René Bourbon), Simone's adoring little Nicolas (Henri Gènes) and the vast Clémentine (Wally Winck), who is mad about Nicolas, all end up tracking Ferdinand to the rural home of chicken-loving Montaron (Duvaleix). There, among pretenses, disguises, chickens, a game of chess and a fair amount of unsuccessfully lustful cavalcading, in which Montaron's exceedingly plain maid Zenaïde (Jeannette Batti) manages to get herself involved, the farce begins. It carries on when the characters all troop back to Paris and, ultimately, to an incredibly de-complicated happy ending.

Lopez's jolly score illustrated the comedy effectively with numbers such as Ferdinand's work-song (''Un petit coup par-ci''), the reminiscence of what can be done in ''Quatre jours à Paris,'' Zenaïde's comical admission of seeing things (''J'ai des mirages''), and, most successfully, a Samba Brésilienne, which brought the first act to its curtain in a display of lively inconsequentiality.

Quatre Jours à Paris played for a year at the Bobino, after which it went into the film studios (ad Vincy, André Berthomieu) with Luis Mariano taking top billing and the central role (rechristened Mario for the occasion), alongside Roger Nicolas (Nicolas), Genevieve Kervine, Orbal, Fernand Sardou, Gisèle Robert, Jackie Rollin and Jane Sourza. Four songs survived from the score alongside a couple of drearies staged in a revue theatre (Mario's abandoned love was now a revue star rather than a working girl) and several more for the star. Mlle Sourza was a comical rather than a fatale Mme Alvarez and original star Andrex, who was tacked in as a local policeman who helped to tie up the ends of a plot that was cut off at about Act I 1/2 and thus missed almost all Vincy's cleverest complexities, provided a touch of comic class.

The show returned to the Paris stage in 1960 (Théâtre de l'ABC 19 February) in a ''revised version'' in which Andrex and Orbal from the original cast, back in their original roles, teamed with Mlle Kervine from the screen, Ginette Baudin (Mme Andrex) and Jean-Marie Proslier. Thoroughly played in the provinces, and televised in 1979 in a now heavily distorted version with Georges Guétary featured, it remains—in its pristine version—one of the slickest French comedy musicals of the postwar period.

Film: Lyrica 1955

Recording: television version (Festival)

QUEEN HIGH Musical comedy in 2 acts by Lawrence Schwab and B G De Sylva based on Edward Peple's play *A Pair of Sixes.* Lyrics by De Sylva. Music by Lewis E Gensler. Ambassador Theater, New York, 9 August 1926.

A lively comedy musical, based on a 1914 play and illustrated with songs in the style of the period, *Queen High* told the tale of two unhappy business partners who no longer see eye to commercial eye. One of them has to go. A game of cards decides that George Nettleton (Frank McIntyre) gets to run the firm, whilst T Boggs Johns (Charles Ruggles) has to act as his butler for the duration. Johns is not a very adept butler, and the conflict and the comedy increase until little Miss Nettleton (Mary Lawlor) and little Master Johns (Clarence Nordstrom) bring about a reconciliation by finding that the younger generation of the warring dynasties are made for each other. Gensler's score, which included a nod to Anita Loos in a song called ''Gentlemen Prefer Blondes,'' threw up one number, a loping little piece called ''Cross Your Heart,'' which became a hit.

Mounted in Providence in April, *Queen High* was not taken straight to Broadway. As Schwab's previous year's piece, *Captain Jinks,* had done, it went instead to Philadelphia and there it won the same sort of enthusiastic reception as its predecessor. Adjectives such as ''sensational'' were flung about, and London's Alfred Butt, mindful of the way Clayton and Waller had snapped up *No, No, Nanette* out of town, quickly bought up the British rights to *Queen High.* The show's Philadelphia summer season stretched to 21 weeks, and ''Cross Your Heart'' made its way into the best-seller list, before Schwab, perhaps mindful of the Broadway disappointment of *Captain Jinks,* announced it would go on to Chicago and not to New York.

In the event, it did both. A new company, headed by Julia Sanderson and Frank Crumit, opened *Queen High* in Chicago, whilst the Philadelphia company moved to Broadway. This time there was no disappointment. *Queen High* was a fine success, continuing the rise of producer-librettist Schwab—for whom it was the first of five consecutive Broadway hits—and giving composer Lewis Gensler his one moment of success. It ran for 378 Broadway performances.

Meanwhile, Alfred Butt had got his London production on to the stage. Joseph Coyne (Johns) and A W Baskcomb (Nettleton) played the partners, Sonnie Hale and Anita Elson the youngsters, and Joyce Barbour (Florence) and Hermione Baddeley (Coddles) supported. *Queen High* did not give him a *No, No, Nanette,* but it ran through 198 performances in the little Queen's Theatre, then toured in 1927–28, and ensured that Butt was first in line to import Schwab's next piece to London. *The Desert Song* did better.

In Australia, however, *Queen High* turned out an unmitigated flop. J C Williamson Ltd's production—with R Barrett-Lennard (Johns) and Cecil Kellaway (Nettleton) heading the comedy and Josephine Read and Alfred Hugo, billed as ''the famous dancers from the Folies Bergère,'' Irene North (Polly) and Leyland Hodgson in support—played a forced five-week season in Melbourne and was left there.

Plate 317. **Quatre Jours à Paris.** *Out for a wicked weekend, Andrex gets cornered by the particularly plain maid of his sweetheart's household.*

UK: Queen's Theatre 2 November 1926; Australia: Theatre Royal, Melbourne 24 December 1927

QUINSON, Gustave (b Marseille, 23 January 1863; d Paris, 1 August 1943). Dominating Parisian producer of the years between the wars.

In his early working years Quinson practiced as a photographer in Marseille, but he moved to Paris in 1900 and there operated in turn the Théâtre de la Tour Eiffel and the tiny Théâtre Grévin before making his fortune by inventing the ''billet Quinson.'' This was a fashion of selling cheap theatre tickets for plays in difficulty in a city in which such things were normally done only in obvious desperation—a system almost identical to the modern cut-rate ticket booths. The ''billet Quinson'' was, however, available to Quinson's ''subscribers'' only, and he thus touched not only 10 percent on his ticket sales but also his subscriptions.

In 1910 Quinson took over the Palais-Royal, and he succeeded in making it pay handsomely enough for him to become involved singly or in partnership in several other Paris theatres. In 1913 he paired with Alphonse Franck at the Théâtre du Gymnase, then with Porel at the Vaudeville, and he took over the Bouffes-Parisiens on his own before spreading to another half-dozen venues during the war years. In 1921 he built the Théâtre Daunou and in 1925 the Théâtre de la Michodière, becoming, in the process, probably the most influential single person in the Parisian theatre.

The vast level of production needed to fill all of these houses meant that Quinson soon moved from producing only plays to including musical pieces in his output. One of these was *Phi-Phi* (1918), which launched the fashion for the small-scale Jazz Age musical in France, a fashion that Quinson maintained with his subsequent productions of pieces such as *Ta bouche* and *Là-haut.* Discovering late in life the desire to be considered a dramatist, Quinson came to agreements with several prominent authors, notably Albert Willemetz and Yves Mirande, which effectively guaranteed his name on their shows (for a greater or, inevitably, a much lesser contribution) as co-author and which in turn guaranteed those shows house room in the Quinson theatres.

In later years, he gradually decreased his enormous activity, taking on partners at the Bouffes-Parisiens (Edmond Roze, Willemetz, Meucci) and ultimately ceding it to Willemetz, but he continued to direct the Palais-Royal, his mascot theatre, alone until the end of his life.

R

RAGTIME Musical in 2 acts by Terrence McNally. Lyrics by Lynn Ahrens. Music by Stephen Flaherty. Ford Center, Toronto, 8 December 1996; Ford Center, New York, 18 January 1998.

Ragtime was a musical based on the whimsically surrealistic 1975 novel by E L Doctorow, a book which supremely successfully mixed a band of happily half-burlesqued fictional characters with a selection of equally humorous fictionalized versions of a whole range of historical people—from Houdini to Henry Ford to every mittel-European-American film producer of the era—and with a bunch of hopeless Harriganesque negroes in a story of merry, iconoclastic complexity with never a dull moment. Doctorow's creation might have provided the opportunity for the creation of a magnificently humorous opéra-bouffe, but librettist McNally surprisingly (given his lively track record) opted instead for sentimentality and political correctness (''a Marxist cartoon . . . a virtual musical conjured up out of an ideologically driven text'') and a consequent ''rearrangement'' of the book's characters, motivations and values, not to mention of America's veritable history.

The story centers on the family of a flag- and firework-maker (cum intermittent polar explorer) from New Rochelle: looming Father (Mark Jacoby) and devoted Mother (Marin Mazzie) and mother's rather unsettling Younger Brother (Steven Sutcliffe) who works for Father in his novelties business until his mental and personal oddities get the better of him. Alongside them, we meet such characters as the poor immigrant silhouette artist Tateh (Peter Friedman) and his Little Girl (Lea Michele), and the sullen, pregnant and abandoned Sarah (Audra MacDonald), who is taken into the family home by foolishly softhearted Mother. Things rise to comical tragedy when Sarah's loose-brained piano-player lover, Coalhouse Walker jr (Brian Stokes Mitchell), turns terrorist in pique at the scratching of his Model-T Ford, and finds an effective ally in that unhinged explosives expert, Younger Brother. Through Doctorow's tale, and woven seamlessly into its progression, came the ''real'' characters: journalist and escapologist Harry Houdini (Jim Cort), carman Ford (Larry Daggett), chorus girl Evelyn Nesbit (Lynnette Perry), agitator Emma Goldman (Judy Kaye), et al.

McNally tatted the various strands of the tentacular novel into a neatly comprehensible libretto, but what came out in the end was a *Ragtime* dipped in chocolate: there was no place in this complacent text for such Monty Pythonesque Doctorow moments as the imprisoned Harry Thaw flapping his penis through the bars of his cell at a stunned, half-escapologized Houdini.

Although composer Flaherty showed the same skill with sparingly used ragtime rhythms that he had with the Caribbean ones of *Once on This Island*, the show's music followed the same trend as the book, being weighted down with the sentimental, or the monumental, and the score flashed to life only in such pieces as a bouncy number for a throughly fictionalized Evelyn Nesbit about ''The Crime of the Century,'' a duo for Evelyn and Houdini ''The Show Biz,'' or a patter song for Tateh (''Buffalo Nickel Photoplay Inc''). Elsewhere in a score dominated by the now vastly overparted Coalhouse, and including a fortissimo lullaby for Sarah (''Your Daddy's Son''), a statement ballad for Mother (''Back to Before'') and very little for anyone else, a little piece for Tateh and Mother about ''Our Children'' made its point the best.

First produced by the soon-to-be-ill-fated Livent Ltd at Toronto, the show was subsequently played in Los Angeles (June 1997) before moving the following year to Broadway's new Ford Center. It provoked some of the more pompous reviews of the time (''a living, breathing social commentary,'' ''a show with a social conscience,'' ''the regeneration of the Broadway musical''), as well as others less complimentary (''a pretentious bore''), but was by and large greeted enthusiastically, being liberally Tonied (although knocked off by *The Lion King* for the season's top award) before settling in for what seemed as if it would be a solid run. Its future was somewhat put on hold when Livent imploded under the weight of some creative accounting, but in any case the Broadway edition stopped living and breathing after an insufficient two years and 861 performances, having regenerated nothing, and leaving behind but a touring company doing the usual rounds, plus regrets that the opportunity for a stinging piece of Gelbart 'n' Coleman style opéra-bouffe had been let slip past in favor of sentimentality and scenery.

Recordings: pre-production recording (RCA Victor), original cast (RCA Victor)

RAIMANN, Rudolf (b Veszprém, Hungary, 7 May 1861; d Vienna, 26 September 1913).

A child performer as pianist, Raimann studied in Vienna and, after beginning a career as a conductor at Oldenberg, Graz, Cologne and then at Gróf Eszterházy's personal theatre (the job had once and long been held by Haydn), he was occupied over an extended period as conductor and musical director at a series of Viennese theatres, including the Carltheater, the Theater an der Wien, the Venedig in Wien summer theatre in the Prater and, most notably, at the Theater in der Josefstadt.

Raimann wrote all kinds of theatre music from an early age, including, at 20, a comic-opera version of *The Three Musketeers* which was played in Germany and at Pest's German Theatre, an operatic *Szinán basa* (*Haroun el Raschid*) produced in Tata in 1890, and a pair of one-act operas, *Imre Király* and *Enoch Arden,* produced at Budapest's Magyar Királyi Operaház in 1894 and subsequently played in several Austrian cities.

He provided part of the score, with his compatriot Béla Szabados, for the vaudeville *Die Küchenkomtesse* (a botched version of Szabados's 1897 *A kuktakisasszony*) at the Theater an der Wien (18 performances) and complete scores for a number of Possen, mostly at the Theater in der Josefstadt, scoring a fine success with the musical comedy *Er und sein Schwester,* produced at the Theater in der Josefstadt in 1902 with producer's wife and musical-comedy megastar Hansi Niese and the town's most celebrated musical comic, Alexander Girardi, in its leading roles, and later seen throughout central Europe. Amongst the other vehicles he provided for Frln Niese, were the Operette *Das Wäschermädl,* which played 38 nights at the Josefstadter Theater before going on to be seen in Germany, then as *A szoknyahős* at Budapest's Városligeti Nyári Színház (15 June 1906) and as played by the Josefstädter company in 1913 in a Gastspiel at the Johann Strauss-Theater; *Die Tippmamsell* (played in Hungary as *A gepirókisasszony,* ad Aurél Föld, Városligeti Színkör 15 May 1908); and *Der Schusterbub* (1906), which again paired the favorite soubrette with Girardi with great success.

1881 **D'Artagnan** (*Die drei Musketiere*) (Victor Léon) Carl-Schultze Theater, Hamburg 18 September

1887 **Das Ellishorn** (Bernhard Buchbinder, Felix Philippi) Theater am Gärtnerplatz, Munich 7 May

1898 **Die Küchenkomtesse** (*A kuktakisasszony*) additional music to Béla Szabados's score/ad Buchbinder, Theater an der Wien 15 March

1900 **Unsere Gustl** (Franz von Radler) Theater in der Josefstadt 9 February

1900 **Der schönste Zeitvertreib** (*Joli Sport*) (ad Otto Eisenschitz) Theater in der Josefstadt 9 October

1901 **'s Muttersöhnerl** (Theodore Taube) Theater an der Wien 7 November

1902 **Tarok** (Léon) Raimundtheater 8 February

1902 **Er und seine Schwester** (Buchbinder) Theater in der Josefstadt 11 April

1902 **Der Burengeneral** (Emil Norini, Ernst Baum) Jantschtheater 10 May

1903 **Der Verwandlungskünstler** (Emil Golz, Arnold Golz) Jantschtheater 9 January

1903 **Der Musikant und sein Weib** (Buchbinder) Theater an der Wien 12 April

1903 **Der Gummiradler** (Rudolf Österreicher) Raimundtheater 22 December

1904 **Wie du mir . . .** (Friedrich Eisenschitz, Siddy Pal) Raimundtheater 16 February

1904 **Port Arthur** (w R Laubner/Julius Wilhelm) Venedig in Wien 1 June

1904 **Der kleine Märchenhaus** (Emil Görg) Theater in der Josefstadt 11 December

1905 **Das Wäschermädel** (Buchbinder) Theater in der Josefstadt 31 March

1906 **Der Schusterbub** (Buchbinder) Theater in der Josefstadt 16 January

1906 **Zur Wienerin** (Richard Skowronnek, Leo Walther Stein ad Ottokar Tann-Bergler) Lustspieltheater 7 April

1907 **Sie und ihr Mann** (Buchbinder) Raimundtheater 5 April

1907 **Der Eintagskönig** (Buchbinder, Hans Liebstöckl) Lustspieltheater 15 May

1908 **Die Tippmamsell** (Wilhelm Frieser, Karl Georg Zwerenz) Danzers Orpheum 28 January

1909 **Paula macht alles** (Buchbinder) Theater in der Josefstadt 23 March

1910 **Chantecler in Wien** (*G'schichten aus dem Hühnerhaus*) (''Fanfaron'') 1 act Carltheater 24 February

1911 **Im Frauenparlament** (Julius Horst) 1 act Apollotheater 1 March

1911 **Die Frau Gretl** (Buchbinder) Theater in der Josefstadt 7 April

1912 **Der Jungfraubrunnen** (Oskar Friedmann) 1 act Wiener Colosseum 1 February

1912 **Unser Stammhalter** (Buchbinder) Lustspieltheater 15 November

Other titles attributed: *Der Pauakönig, Das Damenregiment* (1890)

THE RAINBOW GIRL Musical comedy in 3 acts by Rennold Wolf based on *Fanny and the Servant Problem* (aka *The New Lady Bantock*) by Jerome K Jerome. Music by Louis A Hirsch. New Amsterdam Theater, New York, 1 April 1918.

Jerome K Jerome had shown little talent as a librettist for the musical stage, but his luck changed when his internationally popular play *Lady Fanny and the Servant Problem* was given a Broadway going-over to serve as a libretto for the musical *The Rainbow Girl.*

Mollie Murdock (Beth Lydy) is starring in *The Rainbow Girl* at the Frivolity Theatre when she meets and marries Robert Dudley (Harry Benham)—both times in the theatre green room. It turns out that her new husband is Lord Wetherell, and Mollie is transported to Wetherell Hall (near Manchester, England) where a curious surprise awaits her. The staff of her new stately home, from the butler (Sydney Greenstreet) to the laundry and scullery maids, are all from one family. Hers. She tries to get rid of the embarrassment by sacking them, by getting the comedian from the Frivolity (Billy B Van) to pretend to be her uncle, but ultimately the truth has to come out: Lord Wetherell has married his butler's niece. It takes a third act to straighten things out happily.

Louis Hirsch's score was one which had all the attractions of his *Going Up* music. The central number was the prettily lilting ''I'll Think of You (and maybe you will think of me),'' introduced in the second act by Harry Delf and Leonora Novasio, as the footman and the housemaid, meaningfully reprised by Mollie as a farewell at the end of the act, and by everyone as half of the finale. The other half of the finale was the show's title song, a swinging paean to ''The Rainbow Girl'' which had been plugged as early as the show's opening, sung there by Mollie as part of the show-within-a-show, before getting a more expansive performance as a love song for the star pair. Their other big duet, ''Just You Alone,'' was a more conventional waltz, whilst ''Love's Ever New'' was backed by angel voices. Robert had a curious, cavalier piece telling a bunch of girlies ''Call Around Again (in a month or two)'' when he might have tired of monogamy, and Mollie begged his ancestress's picture, in waltz time, to give her some advice on how to cope with her situation. Alongside these pieces there were several novelty numbers: ''The Alimony Blues'' (''I've got the alimony blues from paying matrimony dues . . .'') as sung by Van, a second duo for Delf and Novasio, ''Soon We'll Be Upon the Screen'' which dropped the names of Pickford, Bushman and Chaplin, and took some digs at the ''amateurs engaged in faking'' in a business where ''talent cuts no ice,'' and a pajama number for the soubrette (Laura Hamilton) and ladies' chorus.

Klaw and Erlanger's production was well received, but somehow, in spite of all its charms, *The Rainbow Girl* did not take off in the way that *Going Up* had done. It ran for 160 performances at the New Amsterdam Theater and duly toured happily without establishing itself as a prospect for a trip around the world in the way the earlier piece had.

A German musical comedy based on Jerome's play and entitled *Lady Fanny* (Theo Mackeben/Erik Ernst, P Holl) was produced in Berlin (Deutsches Künstlertheater 16 February 1934) and, following the composer's expatriation, in London (Duke of York's Theatre, 1939, ad A Dyer, H Risseley, Reginald Long) where it collapsed messily in its first week.

RAISIN Musical in 2 acts by Robert Nemiroff and Charlotte Zaltzberg based on the play *A Raisin in the Sun* by Lorraine Hansberry. Lyrics by Robert Brittan. Music by Judd Woldin. 46th Street Theater, New York, 18 October 1973.

The musical *Raisin* featured Virginia Capers in the role, originally played on the straight stage by Claudia McNeil, of Lena Younger (''Mama''), a Chicago ghetto dweller whose longings to move up a neighborhood are threatened by her self-centered son, who spends most of her widow's insurance windfall on trying to make himself a big man in business. Joe Morton took the part of the selfish son, Walter Lee (portrayed in the original play by Sidney Poitier), Ernestine Jackson played his unfortunate wife, Ruth, and Debbie Allen was his more intelligent and striving sister, Beneatha.

Mama gave forth with her dreams for a better life in ''A Whole Lotta Sunlight'' and made excuses for her son in ''Measure the Valleys,'' whilst Beneatha and her boyfriend (Robert Jackson) headed a sort of African Dance (''Alaiyo'') which was the highlight of the entertainment.

Co-author Nemiroff (the husband of the play's late author) produced *Raisin* on Broadway, and the musical and its leading lady were both awarded the season's Tony Award in a season which included *Candide, Seesaw* and *Gigi. Raisin* went on to run for 847 performances. It was later toured in Europe (Stadttheater, St Gallen, Switzerland 3 February 1979) in an English-language production.

Recordings: original cast (Columbia), European tour cast (Stadttheater St-Gallen)

RAITT, John [Emmet] (b Santa Ana, Calif, 19 January 1917). Broadway baritone leading man who made his mark in a brace of top roles.

Raitt made his first stage appearances in the chorus of the Los Angeles Civic Light Opera Company and subsequently played several operatic roles before (re)-entering the musical theatre as the first takeover of the role of Curly in the national tour of *Oklahoma!* (1944). The following year he found stardom when he created the role of the shiftless carnival barker Billy Bigelow in Rodgers and Hammerstein's next musical, *Carousel,* introducing the celebrated Soliloquy and ''If I Loved You.''

He appeared as the leading man of Wright and Forrest's Villa-Lobos musical *Magdalena* (1948), played re-

Plate 318. **John Raitt** *as Billy Bigelow, with Jan Clayton (Julie Jordan) on the* Carousel.

gionally as the heroes of *Rose Marie* and *The New Moon,* and created the roles of Jamie in *Three Wishes for Jamie* (1952) and The Duke in the quickly departing *Carnival in Flanders* (1953) on Broadway, but it was not until nearly a decade after his first great success that he found himself a second fine starring role, with a long run as Sid Sorokin in *The Pajama Game* (''Hey There'').

Raitt subsequently appeared around America in a number of productions of *The Pajama Game* (which he also filmed with Doris Day in 1957), *Oklahoma!* and *Carousel* as well as in *Destry Rides Again, On a Clear Day You Can See Forever, Zorba, Annie Get Your Gun, Camelot, Seesaw* and *Kismet,* but he returned to Broadway only for the folksy and fast-gone *A Joyful Noise* (1966).

He was seen in television productions of *Knickerbocker Holiday* (ABC, 1950, Broem Broeck) and of *Annie Get Your Gun* (NBC, 1957).

LE RAJAH DE MYSORE Opéra-comique in 1 act by Henri Chivot and Alfred Duru. Music by Charles Lecocq. Théâtre des Bouffes-Parisiens, Paris, 21 September 1869.

One of the most popular of Lecocq's short works, *Le Rajah de Mysore* told of a dissatisfied Rajah, Madapolam (Désiré), who, desiring immortality, is given a brew by his court physician which is supposed to do the trick. He wakes to find himself apparently 18 years on, bereft of wife and friends, and promptly wishes himself back as he was. Nothing is easier than for the physician to undo the deception.

First produced in Paris at the Bouffes-Parisiens, *Le Rajah de Mysore* was later seen in Vienna played under Geistinger and Steiner (ad Josef Weyl) at the Theater an der Wien, and at London's Alexandra Theatre as *Eighteen Years in One Hour* (ad G M Layton). It got a second London showing at the Surrey Theatre (*The Court Physician*) later the same year and a third version, also by Layton, was mounted at the Gaiety Theatre (13 May 1878), played on a program with the burlesque *Little Don Caesar de Bazan,* and subsequently at the Crystal Palace (16 February 1880). The plot of the piece was largely taken over for the British comic opera *The Punch Bowl* (Novelty Theatre 18 June 1887).

Austria: Theater an der Wien 9 July 1871; UK: Alexandra Theatre *Eighteen Years in One Hour* 15 February 1875

RÁKOSI, Jenő (b Acsád, 12 November 1842; d Budapest, 8 February 1929).

Celebrated Hungarian journalist, political editor, poet and dramatist, theatrical producer and director, the author of the hugely successful *Aesopus* (1866), the tragedy *Magdolna* (1883) and *Endre és Johanna* (1885) and the translator of Shakespeare into Hungarian, Rákosi also began and maintained a long connection with the musical theatre from the time that he took up the management of the newly built Budapest Népszínház (15 October 1875). Under his management, in the first six years of its operation, the theatre became the most important musical house in Budapest, without in any way compromising its eminent position in the production of non-musical plays.

Amongst the 158 productions mounted during Rákosi's management were included many of the works of the French opéra-bouffe and -comique stage (a number of which he adapted himself) of which *La Fille de Madame Angot* (48 performances), *La Boulangère a des écus* (28 performances), *Le Pompon* (29 performances), *La Petite Mariée* (35 performances), *Kosiki* (41 performances), *La Marjolaine* (56 performances), *Les Cloches de Corneville* (205 performances), *Le Petit Duc* (42 performances), *Niniche* (55 performances), *La Camargo* (25 performances), *Madame Favart* (34 performances), *Les Mousquetaires au couvent* (37 performances), *La Mascotte* (62 performances) and *Les Noces d'Olivette* (25 performances) all did well. He also mounted a number of Austrian pieces of which *Boccaccio* (129 performances) and *Der Seekadett* (48 performances) were the big successes, as well as Sullivan's *HMS Pinafore* (4 performances) and a number of original Hungarian works including the famous play with music *A falu rossza,* Elek Erkel's *Székely Katalin* (1880) and Ferenc Puks's *Titilla hadnagy* (1880), for which he authored the libretto.

When Rákosi resigned from the Népszínház in favor of his sometime collaborator Lajos Evva in order to devote himself more fully to his other activities, he continued to write occasionally for the house, supplying both adaptations and original texts for Hungarian operetts, amongst which were a musical version of Shakespeare's *Pericles, Prince of Tyre* under the title *A fekete hajó* ("the black ship"), and another based on a Labiche source (*Az első és a második*).

1876 **A talléros pékné** (*La Boulangère a des écus*) Hungarian version (Népszínház)

1876 **A kis menyecske** (*La Petite Mariée*) Hungarian version (Népszínház)

1877 **Kapitánykisasszony** (*Der Seekadett*) Hungarian version (Népszínház)

1877 **Kosiki** Hungarian version (Népszínház)

1877 **Kisasszony feleségem** (*La Marjolaine*) Hungarian version (Népszínház)

1877 **Nanon csaplárosné** (*Nanon*) Hungarian version (Népszínház)

1878 **Ancsi sír, Jancsi nevet** (*Jeanne qui pleure et Jean qui rit*) 1 act Hungarian version (Népszínház)

1878 **Szenes legény, szenes lány** (*Les Charbonniers*) 1 act Hungarian version (Népszínház)

1878 **A kis néma** (*La Petite Muette*) Hungarian version (Népszínház)

1878 **A Cornevillei harangok** (*Les Cloches de Corneville*) Hungarian version (Népszínház)

1878 **A kis herceg** (*Le Petit Duc*) Hungarian version (Népszínház)

1878 **A csillag** (*L'Étoile*) Hungarian version (Népszínház)

1879 **A zengő angyalok** (Elek Erkel/Roderich Fels ad) Népszínház 19 April

1879 **Koko** (Coedès, et al/Clairville, Eugène Grangé, Alfred Delacour ad) Hungarian version of French play with added songs Népszínház 16 May

1880 **Titilla hadnagy** (Ferenc Puks) Népszínház 27 February

1880 **Fatinitza** Hungarian version (Népszínház)

1880 **Az utszéli grófkisasszony** (*La Marquise des rues*) Hungarian version (Népszínház)

1880 **A kétnejű gróf** (*Der Graf von Gleichen*) Hungarian version (Népszínház)

1881 **Dragonyosok** (*Les Dragons de Villars*) Hungarian version w Lajos Evva (Népszínház)

1881 **Apajune, a vizitündér** (*Apajune der Wassermann*) Hungarian version w Evva (Népszínház)

1881 **Az üdvöske** (*La Mascotte*) Hungarian version (Népszínház)

1881 **A Pannifor kapitánya** (*HMS Pinafore*) Hungarian version (Népszínház)

1881 **Szép Ilonka** (Erkel) 1 act Népszínház 22 May

1882 **Szélháziak** (Erkel) Népszínház 16 March

1883 **A fekete hajó** (György Banffy) Népszínház 26 January

1883 **Tempefői** (Erkel) Népszínház 16 November

1883 **Az Afrikautazó** (*Die Afrikareise*) Hungarian version w Evva (Népszínház)

1884 **A kék madár** (*L'Oiseau bleu*) Hungarian version w Arpad Berczik (Népszínház)

1886 **A Mikádó** (*The Mikado*) Hungarian version w Jenő Molnár (Népszínház)

1887 **Világszépasszony Marcia** (Lajos Serly) Népszínház 25 February

1887 **Uff Király** (revised *L'Étoile*) (Szidor Bátor, Béla Hegyi) Népszínház 21 May

1890 **A négy király** (Béla Szabados) Népszínház 10 January

1891 **Az első és a második** (Szabados) Népszínház 8 April

1892 **A koronázás emléknapja** (Szabados) 1 act Népszínház 6 June

1893 **Indigo** (*Indigo und die vierzig Räuber*) Hungarian version (Népszínház)

1898 **A bolond** (Szabados) Magyar Színház 29 December

RALEIGH, Cecil [ROWLANDS, Abraham Cecil Francis Fothergill] (b Nantyglo, Monmouthshire, 27 January 1856; d London, 10 November 1914). British playwright and librettist.

"Fog" Rowlands apparently began his theatrical life touring in an opéra-bouffe chorus, before moving in his mid-twenties (and now rechristened as Cecil Raleigh) first from the stage to front-of-house, as business manager for Kate Lawler at the Royalty Theatre (1881), and then out of the house to journalistic jobs with *Vanity Fair, The Lady,* and as drama critic of *The Sporting Times* (as "Sir Walter"). He is also said to have spent a period—somewhere between the chorus-line bit and the Royalty bit—as a racehorse trainer.

In the late 1880s he began writing for the stage, notably in collaboration with George R Sims, and the pair scored a fine musical-theatre success with the burlesque *Little Christopher Columbus.* However, Raleigh found his principal fame in a series of dramas for Augustus Harris and later Arthur Collins at the Theatre Royal, Drury Lane (*The Derby Winner, Cheer Boys Cheer, White Heather, The Great Ruby* w Henry Hamilton, *Hearts Are Trumps, The Great Pink Pearl, The Pointsman,* etc). He returned to the musical stage with an inept vehicle for *Little Christopher Columbus* star May Yohé as *The Belle of Cairo* and to collaborate with Seymour Hicks on the book for his alleged adaptation of the Armenian comic opera *Leblébidii Hor-Hor* as *The Yashmak,* but only the latter-day Gaiety musical *The Sunshine Girl,* on which he shared a book credit with Paul Rubens, approached his first musical hit in success.

Raleigh was married, for a period, to novelist Effie Rowlands [Effie Adelaide HENDERSON], daughter of producer Alexander Henderson.

1889 **The New Corsican Brothers** (Walter Slaughter) Royalty Theatre 20 November

1893 **Little Christopher Columbus** (Ivan Caryll/w George Sims) Lyric Theatre 10 October

1896 **The Belle of Cairo** (F Kinsey Peile) Court Theatre 10 October
1897 **The Yashmak** (Napoléon Lambelet, et al/w Seymour Hicks) Shaftesbury Theatre 31 March
1912 **The Sunshine Girl** (Paul Rubens/Arthur Wimperis, Rubens/w Rubens) Gaiety Theatre 24 February

RANDOLPH, Elsie [KILLICK, Elsie Florence] (b London, 9 December 1901; d Worthing, 15 October 1982). Dancing comedienne who starred in several musicals with Jack Buchanan.

Miss Randolph appeared on the stage as a chorister in *The Girl for the Boy* (1919), *The Naughty Princess* (1920), *My Nieces* (1921), *His Girl* (1922) and *Battling Butler* (1923) before being given her first supporting role as the comic soubrette, Folly, in Jack Buchanan's *Toni* (1924). She subsequently succeeded to the role of Madeleine in *Madame Pompadour* at Daly's Theatre and then followed up in further light comedy roles in *Boodle* (1925, Clematis Drew), *Sunny* (1926, Weenie) and *Peggy-Ann* (1927, Alice Frost) before cementing the dance-and-comedy partnership with Buchanan, begun in *Toni* and *Boodle,* in the first of a series of musical comedies, *That's a Good Girl* (1928, Joy Dean).

In a Jack-and-Elsie musical, the ingenue was swept to the side as Buchanan and Miss Randolph took the stage for their song-and-dance routines and their wisecracking dialogue, and she returned only in time to lead the leading man to the altar before or after the final curtain. Miss Randolph appeared in *Follow Through* (1929, Ruth Vanning) and *The Wonder Bar* (1930, Inez) without the otherwise-engaged Buchanan, but they came together again for *Stand Up and Sing* (1931, Ena), *Mr Whittington* (1934, Betty Trotter) and *This'll Make You Whistle* (1936, Bobbie Rivers) in a pairing which, in just over a decade of stage performances, and two films, *That's a Good Girl* (1933) and *This'll Make You Whistle* (1935), thoroughly captured the public's imagination.

After some subsequent appearances in comedy, she appeared in the soubrette role of Vittoria in the 1942 revival of *The Maid of the Mountains* at the London Coliseum and came back together one last time with Buchanan for *It's Time to Dance* (1943, Marian Kane) in her last appearance on the London musical stage.

RANKEN, Frederick M (b Troy, NJ, ?1870; d New York, 19 October 1905).

Originally a linen salesman and partaker of amateur theatricals, Ranken had his first taste of the professional stage when he joined Frank Perley on rewriting a piece called *The Sporting Duchess* which the pair then mounted and sent out on the road themselves. He joined Kirk La Shelle to write the libretto and lyrics for the musical *The Ameer,* and had a piece called *The Smugglers of Badoyez* produced, with an utter lack of success, by the Bostonians, but soon found his niche when he became a popular choice as a musical-play doctor, working on such pieces as *The Runaways, The Smugglers, The Isle of Spice* and *Nancy Brown* (''The Glowworm and the Moth'' w Max S Witt) and rewriting Harry Paulton's *Winsome Winnie* to such an extent that by the time it got to town Paulton's name had been replaced on the bill by Ranken's. He also wrote text and/or lyrics for several shows of his own, including the merrily touring fairy-tale spectacular *The Gingerbread Man,* the comic opera *The Student King* and what was billed as Chicago's first hometown revue, *All Round Chicago* (McVickers Theater 30 April 1905). Ranken had been signed by Henry Savage to work on a series of musicals with Reginald De Koven when he died of typhoid at the age of 35.

1899 **The Ameer** (Victor Herbert/w Kirk La Shelle) Lyceum Theater, Scranton, Pa 9 October; Wallack's Theater 4 December
1899 **The Smugglers of Badayez** (Giacomo Minkowsky) Jacques Opera House, Waterford, Conn 19 October
1901 **The Chaperons** (Isidore Witmark) Middlesex Theater, Middletown, Conn 28 September; New York Theater 5 June 1902
1903 **The Jewel of Asia** (Ludwig Englander/Harry B Smith) Criterion Theater 16 February
1903 **Nancy Brown** (Henry K Hadley/w George H Broadhurst) Bijou Theater 16 February
1903 **Winsome Winnie** (Gustave Kerker/Harry Paulton ad) Casino Theater 1 December
1904 **The Isle of Spice** (Paul Schindler, Ben Jerome/w Allen Lowe, George E Stoddard) revised version Majestic Theater 19 September
1905 **Happyland** (ex- *Elysia*) (Reginald De Koven) Lyric Theater 2 October
1905 **The Gingerbread Man** (A Baldwin Sloane) Liberty Theater 25 December
1906 **The Student King** (De Koven/Stanislaus Stange) Lyceum Theater, Rochester, NY 17 May; Garden Theater 25 December

RANZATO, Virgilio (b Venice, 7 May 1883; d Como, 20 April 1937). One of the handful of Italian composers who made a significant contribution to a brief flowering of musical plays in the Italian theatre of the early 20th century.

Ranzato spent the earliest part of his career as a concert and chamber-music violinist, but the bulk of his work as a composer was directed towards the light musical theatre where he had two enduring successes with operettas written in collaboration with the liveliest bricoleur of the Italian musical stage, Carlo Lombardo. The pretty, rustic ''navy-in-town'' musical *Il paese dei campanelli,* with its mixture of traditional elements and tango and fox-trot rhythms and his setting of Lombardo's version of another oft-used subject, the East-meets-West tale of *Cin-ci-là,* both became oft-played parts of the small basic Italian operetta repertoire.

1911 **Velivolo** Teatro Balboa, Turin 28 January
1912 **Yvonne** Teatro Apollo, Rome 16 November
1916 **La Leggenda delle arance** Teatro Diana, Milan March
1919 **Quel che manca a sua altezza** (Gioacchino Forzano) Teatro Quirino, Rome 8 May
1922 **Il paese dei campanelle** (Carlo Lombardo) Teatro Lirico, Milan 23 November
1924 **Luna Park** (Lombardo) Teatro Lirico, Milan 26 November
1925 **Cin-ci-là** (Lombardo) Teatro dal Verme, Milan 18 December
1927 **Zizi** (Carlo Ravasio) Teatro Lirico, Milan 13 April
1927 **La città rosa** (w Lombardo/Ravasio) Teatro Lirico, Milan 13 April
1928 **Cri-cri** (Lombardo) Teatro dal Verme 28 March
1928 **La danze del globo** Politeama, Genoa 30 October
1928 **I Merletti di Burano** (w Lombardo/Lombardo, Ravasio) Teatro Lirico, Milan 22 December
1929 **Lady Lido** (D Marchi) Teatro Nazionale 31 July
1930 **Fuoco fatuo** Teatro Savoia, Messina 16 March
1930 **I Monelli fiorentini** (Luigi Bonelli) Teatro Nazionale, Palermo 13 July
1930 **La Duchessa di Hollywood** (Lombardo) Teatro dal Verme, Milan 31 October
1932 **Re Salsiccia** (Giulio Bucciolini) Politeama, Florence 29 January
1932 **Prigioni di lusso** (Lombardo, Ravasio) Odeon, Milan 26 March
1936 **A te voglio tornar** (Giovanni Maria Sala) Teatro Municipale, Alexandria 24 February
1936 **Briciolina** (M Tibaldi-Chiesa) Teatro Arcimboldo, Milan 7 December

Other title attributed: *Valentina* (G M Sala, 1936)

RASCH, Albertina (b Vienna, 19 January 1891; d Woodland Hills, Calif, 2 October 1967). Broadway choreographer with leanings to the balletic.

Miss Rasch trained and worked as a dancer in Austria (Hofoper, etc) before being taken to America by the Shuberts in 1909 as principal dancer for the Hippodrome. She appeared there in the Ballet of the Jewels in *A Trip to Japan* (1909, Cupid) and with Vincenzo Romeo in R H Burnside's *The Legend of Niagra* in *The International Cup* (1910, Ioneta) and subsequently at the Winter Garden (w Mlle Reyo in the Louis Ganne *Nel Giappone* in *The Revue of Revues*), with the Century and Chicago Opera and in vaudeville at the Capitol before beginning a career as a choreographer in revue, notably for *The George White Scandals of 1925.*

Her training predisposed her to a ballet-based style of dance, at this stage less current on the Broadway stage after many years in which popular dance routines, both solo and chorus, set to modern ballroom-dance music, had been the mode. This solid ballet background was in evidence in her dances for the spectacular *Rio Rita* (1927, "Spanish Shawl," etc), dances which scored her a major personal success within the show's success. She was subsequently engaged for the dances of a number of other Broadway revues (*Three's a Crowd, The Band Wagon,* two editions of the *Ziegfeld Follies,* etc) and for a long list of musical plays amongst which were included *The Three Musketeers* (1928), *Sons o' Guns* (1929), *Princess Charming* (1930), *The Pajama Lady* (1930), *The Cat and the Fiddle* (1931), *The Great Waltz* (1934), *Jubilee* (1935), *Very Warm for May* (1939), *Lady in the Dark* (1941) and Kálmán's *Marinka* (1945). She visited Britain to choreograph Hassard Short's Theatre Royal, Drury Lane production of the hugely spectacular *Wild Violets* (*Wenn die kleinen Veilchen blühen*) and she also worked in the Paris theatre.

From 1929 Miss Rasch choreographed a number of film musicals including the celluloid versions of *The Cat and the Fiddle* (1934), *Rosalie* (1936), *The Firefly* (1937) and *Sweethearts* (1938), as well as *The Rogue Song, The Girl of The Golden West* and *The King Steps Out.*

DER RASTELBINDER Operette in a Vorspiel and 2 acts by Victor Léon. Music by Franz Lehár. Carltheater, Vienna, 20 December 1902.

The first major success of Franz Lehár's career, *Der Rastelbinder* opened at the Carltheater just a month after his debut piece *Wiener Frauen* had been staged at the Theater an der Wien so that, briefly, the two maiden Operetten of the young composer held the boards at the same time in Vienna's two principal musical houses. *Der Rastelbinder* was in a different vein from the other piece, being a Volksstück, or peasant-piece, in its subject matter and presenting as its main characters a Slovakian tinker and an old Jewish onion-seller—both strongly delineated and accented roles which gave fine opportunities to the theatre's principal character actor/singers.

The 12-year-old orphan Janku, who has been raised by tinkers, is about to set out on the road to begin to earn his living selling mousetraps. Before he goes, he must by tradition become betrothed and the girl chosen is eight-year-old Suza, the daughter of his "parents." Suza must send him on his way with the gift of a silver gulden, but her family have no money and, finally, she borrows it (at 5 percent) from the poor Jewish onion-seller Wolf Bär Pfefferkorn (Louis Treumann). A dozen years pass, and hard-working Janku (Willy Bauer), no longer a tinker, has risen to a good job in Vienna. He is betrothed to his

Plate 319. **Der Rastelbinder.** *Herta Freund, Erich Donner and Toni Niessner in the Raimundtheater revival of Lehár's first big hit.*

employer's daughter Mizzi (Therese Biedermann) and his future is assured. Suza (Mizzi Günther) is in love with the rich farmer's son, Milosch Blacek (Karl Streitmann), now a soldier in Vienna, and she persuades the ambulant Pfefferkorn to take her with him on his next visit to the city. Pfefferkorn, believing she is going to the capital to find Janku, delivers her to his door and the old betrothal is remembered. In the final act, they all go to the Uhlan camp in search of Milosch. The girls end up disguised in uniforms, and Janku and Pfefferkorn—his beard and hair shorn and forced on to a horse—are taken as reservists before everything is sorted out and the juvenile betrothal annulled in favor of grown-up preferences.

The book was a strong one, the cast included many of the city's best performers, and both profited from a Lehár score made up of waltzes and polkas and other dancing music—including a quadrille and a duo-gavotte—tinted with Slavonic tones. Louis Treumann—a few years later to be Lehár's Danilo—had a superb role as Pfefferkorn, a comic role which was musically topped by his introductory number in the show's prologue (''Ä, jeder Mensch, was handeln thut'') to which he also provided the summing-up (Die einfache Rechnung) which would return as the curtain piece of the main part of the show. He also led a Remembrance Trio with Janku and Suza in the first act and joined Suza in the four-part quadrille. The lyric music was in the hands of the young people, and it was from here that the show's favorite number emerged in the shape of a second-act duettino for Milosch and Suza, ''Wenn zwei sich lieben.'' In the short list of solos, Janku declared ''Ich bin ein Wiener Kind'' and told the tale of ''Die beiden Kamaraden'' whilst Suza looked forward to her reunion with Miloch in ''Ach endlich, endlich heut'.''

Der Rastelbinder was a big success for the Carltheater. It ran up its 100th performance before the summer break (13 April 1903), passed the 150th in September and the 225th just before it was replaced on the bill by

Lehár's next work, *Der Göttergatte,* a few weeks more than a year after its premiere. In the meanwhile, it had been widely played in central Europe. It became highly popular in Germany, following its first showing at the Centraltheater in the hands of Steinberger, Mia Werber and Frln Stuart, and won another great success in Budapest (ad Adolf Mérei, György Ruttkay) with Kornél Sziklay in the role of Pfefferkorn, playing a magnificent 150 performances in its first year at the Magyar Színház, but it did not attract takers in English-speaking areas where theatrical attention was taken up with such pieces as *Florodora* and *A Chinese Honeymoon,* nor in France. New York saw the show only in a pair of German-language productions in 1909 and 1910 (Irving Place Theater 10 October), and it was left to the ever enterprising Tivoli in San Francisco to introduce *The Mousetrap Peddler,* with Ferris Hartmann, Thomas Persse and Edith Mason featured, in 1904. It was pronounced ''one of the best things we have had in the musical line for some time'' and ran beyond its slot. The piece also proved a remarkable success when it was played at Chicago's Ziegfeld Theater in 1909 by Leon Berg's Viennese company with Emil Berla as Pfefferkorn, running for two months straight and, as a result, the show was subsequently produced with considerable success in a fresh English version at Chicago's Colonial Theater. Berla (15 April 1909 at the Deutsches Theatre, Madison Avenue) and, later, the Irving Place Theatre (10 October 1910 with Adolf Kühns and Georgine Neuendorff) also gave some New York performances in German. But it stopped there.

In Vienna, however, *Der Rastelbinder* remained a frequently played favorite. It was maintained in the repertoire—and played every year—at the Carltheater for more than 20 years, with Friedrich Becker and Ernst Rollé supplementing Treumann in the star role. It was played for the 300th time on 2 December 1908, the 400th time on 13 April 1918 with Treumann again in his great role, and on 28 June 1920 it played its 500th performance at the Carltheater under Lehár's baton with Karl Blasel still in his original role of Gloppler alongside Willy Bauer, now playing Pfefferkorn, Hubert Marischka, Dora Keplinger and Viktor Robert. Treumann played his role again in a handful of performances at the Theater an der Wien in 1923, and there was a new Hungarian production at the Fővárosi Operettszínház the following year (19 September) but, in spite of the great popularity the piece enjoyed in central Europe during the first decades of the century, it subsequently slipped from the repertoire in favor of Lehár's later and more fulsomely romantic works.

A burlesque of *Der Rastelbinder* written by C Karl and Carl Strobl and composed by Karl Josef Fromm was produced at the Jantschtheater (23 April 1904) under the title *Wolf Bär Pfefferkorn auf Reisen.*

An earlier *Der Rastelbinder,* subtitled ''oder Zehntausend Gulden,'' a Posse in 3 acts written by Friedrich Kaiser and composed by Adolf Müller, was produced at the Carltheater, 12 April 1858.

Germany: Centraltheater 19 November 1903; Hungary: Magyar Színház *A Drótostót* 21 April 1903; USA: Tivoli Opera House, San Francisco *The Mousetrap Peddler* 10 October 1904, Ziegfeld Theater, Chicago (Ger) 21 November 1909

RÁTKAI, Márton (b Budapest, 18 October 1881; d Budapest, 18 September 1951).

One of the mainstays of the company at Budapest's Király Színház from 1905 through some three decades, Rátkai created during that period comic roles in a large number of the most important new Hungarian musicals. Amongst these were included, in the earlier years, the parts of the eunuch Zülfikár in Huszka's *Gül Baba* (1905), Nurza in Jacobi's *Tüskerózsa* (1907), Fritz in his *Leányvásár* (1911) and Poire in his *Szibill* (1914), Roth in Aladár Rényi's *A kis gróf* (1911) and the title role in Zsigmond Vincze's *Limonádé ezredes* (1912), and later Manó Csóllan in Károly Komjáti's *Pillangó főhadnagy* (1918), Alois Stühlmüller in Mihály Nádor's *Fanny Elssler* (1923), the comedy lead of Zerkovitz's *Árvácska* (1924), Ribizli in Vincze's *Aranyhattyú* (1927) and Rudolf Rezeda in Zerkovitz's *A legkisebbik Horváth lány* (1927). He also played in many of the operetts of Albert Szirmai—*A Mozikirály* (*Filmzauber*), the title role of *Mágnás Miska* (1916), Gróf Kereszthy in *Gróf Rinaldo* (1918), Buhu in *Mézeskalács* (1923), Achilles Kelemen in *Éva grófnő* (1928), Károly in *Alexandra* (1925), in *A Ballerina* (1931)—as well as such overseas-Hungarian works as those of Kálmán (Pali Rácz in *Cigányprimás* (1913), Bóni in *Csárdáskirálynő* (1916), Napoléon in *Die Bajadere* (1922), Zsupán in *Gräfin Mariza* (1924), Toni in *Die Zirkusprinzessin* (1926, etc) and of Lehár (Pfefferkorn in *Der Rastelbinder* (1908), Basil Basilowitsch in *Der Graf von Luxemburg,* Dagobert Millefleurs in *Eva,* etc).

Rátkai also appeared in the very many other musical and non-musical works produced at the Király Színház or reprised in the house's repertoire, ranging from roles such as Ménélas (*Belle Hélène*), Célestin (*Mam'zelle Nitouche*) and Gaspard (*Les Cloches de Corneville*) to Dom Gil de Tenorio in *Die ideale Gattin* (1913), Fridolin in *Die Rose von Stambul* (1917), Rettenetes Tamás (ie, Hard-Boiled Herman) in *Rose Marie* (1928) and Kristóf in *Mersz-e-Mary?* (1927), and to the aged comicalitites of the French King in *János vitéz,* but also played in Shakespeare and the rest of the comic and dramatic repertoire. In 1920 he appeared as Offenbach in the successful *Dreimäderlhaus*-style pasticcio operett on the French composer's life and works.

In the 1930s and early 1940s he continued as a major musical-comedy star through increasingly characterful and/or ''older'' roles in such pieces as *A csalódott Szerelmesek klubja, Vihar a Balatonon, Hajrá Hollywood, Ő felsége frakkja* (1931), as Giesecke in Hungary's *Im weissen Rössl* (1931), as Jim-Boy in *Die Blume von Hawaii* (1932), *Éjféli tangó* (1932), *Amikor a kislányból nagylány lesz* (1932), *Manolita* (1932), *Zsákmabamacska* (1932), *A Sok szerencsét, Sültgalamb* (1933), *Kék Duna, Ördöglovas* (1934, *Der Teufelsreiter*), *Montmartrei ibolya* (1935, *Das Veilchen vom Montmartre*), *A fenséges asszony* (*Eine Frau von Format*), Benatzky's *Párizsi nő* (1937), *Legyen úgy, mint régen volt* (1938), *Kavé habbál, Ki gyereke vagyok én?* (1939), *Tokaji aszú* (1940) and *Angóramacska.*

Latterly Rátkai played more in drama and less in musical theatre, and in his sixties, having created a sensation with his performance as Tartuffe, had a second starring career as a senior comedy actor in classic plays with the National Theatre in Budapest.

He was married at one stage to the star operett soubrette Juci Lábass.

Biography: Szomory, G: *Rátkai, Márton* (Muzsák, Budapest, 1988)

RAY, Gabrielle [COOK, Gabrielle Elizabeth Clifford] (b Cheadle, Stockport, 28 April 1883; d Virginia Water, 21 March 1973). Postcard beauty who had supporting roles in a number of London musicals.

The daughter of a Cheadle iron merchant, ''Gabs'' Ray made her first stage appearances as a child, playing in John Hollingshead's production of *Miami* (1893), dancing in Paul Valentine's Blackpool ballet and appearing as Cupid in *Little Red Riding Hood* at Richmond. She graduated to touring companies of *The Belle of New York* and *The Casino Girl* (1901, Dolly Twinkle) and was finally brought to London by George Edwardes to understudy the role created by Gertie Millar in *The Toreador* at the Gaiety Theatre. She was given a small but visible role in the next Gaiety musical, *The Orchid* (1903, Thisbe), then was moved across to the Prince of Wales Theatre to take over the number-three female role in *Lady Madcap,* performing ''La Maxixe'' with Dorothy Craske, but by the time of *The Little Cherub* (1906, Lady Dorothy Congress) she had become one of the most popular picture-postcard beauties of the day, and her role in that piece reflected her new status.

She had good supporting roles in *See See* (1906, So-Hie) and *Les Merveilleuses* (1906, Eglé), and headed the grisettes as Frou-Frou in *The Merry Widow* (1907) before Edwardes cast her up a notch as the soubrette, Daisy, in *The Dollar Princess* (1909). She next appeared alongside Phyllis Dare and Olive May as the feminine portion of the Gaiety Theatre *Peggy* (1911, Polly Polino) before she took her leave of the stage to become, temporarily, a wife. However, she returned to the boards four years later to play in Edwardes's production of *Betty* (1916, Estelle) and in revue at the Hippodrome before fading away into variety and pantomime and, from 1924, a long-lived real retirement.

RAYMOND, Fred[y] [VESELY, Friedrich Raimund] (b Vienna, 20 April 1900; d Überlingen, Germany, 10 January 1954). German songwriter who scored some musical-theatre success under National Socialism.

Vesely began his musical career writing songs and performing them himself in amateur cabaret under the fashionably foreign-sounding name of Fredy Raymond, whilst working daytime in a bank for his living as plain Vesely. Just before his 24th birthday, however, he decided to throw in his ''proper'' job and to become a full-time performer. He made his first professional appearance at Dresden's Regina-Palast, singing and accompanying himself at the piano and, for the next few years, he remained in Germany, where his employment situation was greatly eased by the fact that he had, after a genial success with the song ''Ich hab' das Fräulein Helen baden 'sehn'' (ly: Fritz Grünbaum), produced a veritable hit song for himself. ''Ich hab' mein Herz in Heidelberg verloren'' (1925, ly: Ernst Neubach, Beda) became an international song success under the title ''I Left My Heart in Heidelberg.'' Having sold his song to its publishers outright, Raymond cashed in on his biggest success by using its title as that of his first major stage work, a semi-pasticcio Singspiel staged in 1927 at the Vienna Volksoper, with some considerable success.

Nevertheless, in spite of turning out several more songs which found success in Germany and Austria (''In einer kleinen Konditorei,'' ''Im Mainz am schönen Rhein''), a pair of revues (*Die Welt um Mitternacht, Nur mit dir*) and a regular amount of film music (*Eine tolle Nacht, Delikatessen, Nur am Rhein,* etc) Raymond had no further stage success until he was hired by Heinz Hentschke, the director of Berlin's Metropoltheater, to provide the scores to Hentschke's libretti for what turned out to be a series of popular revusical pieces at that theatre. The most successful of these was the 1937 *Maske in Blau,* a jolly hotchpotch of a piece which boasted some exotic settings and some bouncy melodies which became popular favorites—''Die Juliska aus Budapest'' and ''Ja das Temprament''—and which, in spite of many a failing, has found ready acceptance on other stages over the subsequent half-century.

A split with Hentschke led Raymond to have his next work staged at Kiel. The charming *Salzburger Nöckerln* (aka *Saison in Salzburg,* 1938) benefited greatly from a more adept and attractive libretto than Hentschke had ever been able to concoct, and also from the most attractive score of all Raymond's works, mixing fox-trots and a splendid march with polka, waltz and even Ländler rhythms, and with some easily flowing love songs in a delightfully unpretentious mélange. The 1941 *Die Perle von Tokay* also found a measure of success, and indeed made it to the musical screen in 1954, but the remainder of Raymond's wartime and postwar work produced little beyond the song "Es geht alles vorüber, es geht alles vorbei" (1942) which came up to the popularity of his favorite works.

He died at the age of 54, at his home on Bodensee, leaving his pair of successful prewar works as two of the most popular German-language pieces of the last 50 years, on the fringe of the standard repertoire.

1925 **Garderobe nr 9** (Charles Amberg/Hanns Witt-Ebernitz) Stadttheater, Frankfurt im Oder 26 September

1927 **Ich hab' mein Herz in Heidelberg verloren** (Ernst Neubach/Bruno Hardt-Warden, Fritz Löhner-Beda) Volksoper, Vienna 29 April

1928 **Es kam ein Bursch gezogen** (aka *Es war einmal in Jena*) (Neubach, Ernst Wengraf) Neue Wiener Bühne, Vienna 20 January

1929 **Die Jungfrau von Avallon** (Paul Franck, Peter Herz) Zentraltheater, Dresden 16 June

1929 **In einen kleinen Konditorei** (revised *Die Jungfrau von Avallon*) Schiller-Theater, Hamburg-Altona 30 November

1933 **Der Königsleutnant** (Karl Gutzkow ad Frank, Herz) Neues Operetten-Theater, Leipzig 27 February

1934 **Lauf ins Glück** (Günther Schwenn/Paul Beyer) Metropoltheater 24 September

1935 **Ball der Nationen** (Schwenn/Hentschke, Beyer) Metropoltheater 27 September

1936 **Auf grosser Fahrt** (Schwenn/Hentschke) Metropoltheater 21 August

1936 **Marielu** (Schwenn/Hentschke, Theo Halton) Centraltheater, Dresden 19 December

1937 **Maske in Blau** (Schwenn/Hentschke) Metropoltheater 27 September

1938 **Saison in Salzburg** (aka *Salzburger Nöckerln*) (Max Wallner, Kurt Feltz) Stadttheater, Kiel 31 December

1939 **Das Bett der Pompadour** (aka *Die glücklichste Frau der Welt*) (Wallner, Feltz) Kabarett der Komiker

1941 **Die Perle von Tokay** (Wallner, Feltz) Theater des Volkes, Dresden 7 February

1948 **Konfetti** (Schwenn/Waldemar Frank, Arno Assmann) Flora-Theater, Hamburg 20 February; Theater am Nollendorfplatz 5 November

1949 **Wohin mit die Frau?** (aka *Liebling schwindel' nich, Christian mit Herz*) Stadttheater, Schleswig 3 May

1949 **Flieder aus Wien** (w Hannes Reinhardt, Wallner, Rudi Schmidtthenner/Wallner, Reinhardt) Staatsoper, Kassel 8 November

1949 **Romanze im schloss** (Otto Bielen, Wallner) Deutsches Schauspielhaus, Hamburg 31 December

1951 **Geliebte Manuela** (Just Scheu, Ernst Nebhut, Walter Rothenburg/Scheu, Nebhut) Nationaltheater, Mannheim 12 July

RAYMOND, Hippolyte [REYMOND, Auguste Hypolite] (b Valréas, Vaucluse, 20 February 1844; d Paris, August 1895).

The author of many successful Parisian comedies and vaudevilles, Raymond at first doubled his theatrical work with employment as a clerk, and later sous-chef de bureau at the Crédit Lyonnais. He wrote several plays for the Théâtre du Gymnase, collaborated with Alfred Duru in one of that author's rare ventures without his usual partner, Chivot (*Fille du clown*), and his early ventures into the musical theatre included the text for the Châtelet's spectacular *Le Prince Soleil* and a revised version of the Cogniard brothers' féerie *La Fille de l'air.* The one enduring hit with which he provided the musical stage, however, was not in the field of the musical spectacular, but in that of vaudevillesque comedy: the hilarious military piece *Les 28 Jours de Clairette* (1892). Following this major success, he essayed several other pieces with Antony Mars and Victor Roger, his collaborators on that show, but without approaching the results won by their first work together. Become depressive, Raymond committed suicide in 1895, before the production of his last musical piece, a reconstitution of his highly successful play *Le Cabinet Piperlin* accompanied by the Hervé music which was originally commissioned for it but not previously used.

Several of Raymond's works were remade as musical shows in other countries. His vaudeville *Les Deux Nababs* (w Alphonse Dumas) was produced at the Vienna Carltheater as *Der Kukuk* with a fresh score by Josef Brandl (24 April 1880), *Cocard et Bicocquet* (w Maxime Boucheron) was the basis for F Zell's Viennese Posse mit Gesang *Wolf und Lampel* (Julius Stern/Hoffman) produced at the Theater an der Wien in 1888 (13 October), and *Le Cabinet Piperlin* was given another musical score, in an English version, as *The Antelope* (Hugo Felix/Adrian Ross) for an unsuccessful London production (Waldorf Theatre 28 November 1908). The text for the indifferently successful *Clary-Clara,* however, was turned into a hit when it was borrowed by Hungarian composer Béla Zerkovitz as the text (ad László Szilágyi) for his *Csókos asszony* (Városi Színház 27 February 1926), a piece which survives in the Hungarian repertoire up to the present day.

1873 **Rallye-Champdouillard** (de Polignac) 1 act Palais-Royal 20 June

1877 **La Goguette** (Antonin Louis/w Paul Burani) Théâtre de l'Athenée 13 April

1879 **Les Deux Nababs** (Auguste Coedès/w Alphonse Dumas) Théâtre des Nouveautés 21 January

1880 **Le Voyage en Amérique** (Hervé/w Maxime Boucheron) Théâtre des Nouveautés 16 September

1889 **Le Prince Soleil** (Léon Vasseur/w Burani) Théâtre du Châtelet 11 July

1890 **La Fille de l'air** revised version w Armand Liorat, Paul Lacome Théâtre des Folies-Dramatiques 20 June

1892 **Les Vingt-huit Jours de Clairette** (Victor Roger/w Antony Mars) Théâtre des Folies-Dramatiques 3 May

1892 **La Bonne de chez Duval** (Gaston Serpette/w Mars) Théâtre des Nouveautés 6 October

1893 **Catherinette** (Roger/w Mars) Lunéville 17 July

1893 **Pierre et Paul** (Roger/w Mars) 1 act Lunéville 17 July

1894 **Clary-Clara** (Roger/w Mars) Théâtre des Folies-Dramatiques 20 March

1895 **Nicol-Nick** (Roger/w Mars, Alfred Duru) Théâtre des Folies-Dramatiques 23 January

1895 **Mam'selle Bémol** (Louis Varney/w Alfred Delilia) Théâtre Cluny 7 September

1897 **Le Cabinet Piperlin** (Hervé/w Burani) Théâtre de l'Athenée-Comique 17 September

RAYNER, Minnie [Gray] (b London, 2 May 1869; d London, 13 December 1941).

Minnie Rayner first appeared on the stage as a child, making her musical-theatre debut in the original production of Planquette's *Rip van Winkle* (1882) before, at the age of 17, taking over the role of the little rustic bride, Phyllis Tuppitt, in *Dorothy,* and playing it for several years of the show's record-breaking run. In 1886 she appeared in a small part (Trumpeter) in the spectacle *The Palace of Pearl* at the Empire. For a long while thereafter she toured in plays and musicals in South Africa (Edgar Perkins Opera Co, 1889–93), England (Mrs Privett in *Dorothy* 1893, Molly Joy in *Wapping Old Stairs* 1894, Mrs Smythe in *En Route* 1898, Mitsu in *The Mousmé,* Kate in *Percy the Ladykiller* 1903, etc) and on Maurice Bandmann's Eastern circuits, graduating in her twenties to the character roles which would ultimately bring her back to the West End. The creations of the second half of her London career included the part of Clara the dresser in Coward's *Hay Fever,* Emma in Wyndham's Theatre's *The Rose and the Ring* (1923) and, after nearly half a century away from the London large-scale musical stage, a series of nonsinging roles in Ivor Novello's musicals: Phoebe, the fat ex-chorus-girl dresser to the star of *Glamorous Night;* Mrs Ripple in *Careless Rapture;* the heroine's mother, Mrs Wortle, in *Crest of the Wave;* and Hattie, the jolly innkeeper, in *The Dancing Years* (1939).

READER, Ralph (b Crewkerne, Somerset, 25 May 1903; d Bourne End, Bucks, 13 May 1982). Choreographer and dance-driller who marshaled the choruses of two decades of musicals.

After an early nontheatrical working life spent in America, Reader performed as a dancer in several New York shows (*The Passing Show of 1924, Big Boy, June Days*). He also choreographed several others including *Artists and Models, The Greenwich Village Follies, Yours Truly* with Leon Errol and the Tiller girls and *Sunny Days* (1928), as well as a number—such as *Cynthia* (1926, in which he also appeared as a last-minute replacement), *Miss Happiness* (1926) and *Take the Air* (1927)—which didn't get to town, before returning to his native Britain for the large part of his career. His first job there was as a performer, touring as Tom Marlowe in *Good News,* but thereafter he worked almost wholly as a choreographer and later also a director. He choreographed *Virginia, Merry Merry, Hold Everything!, Dear Love* (UK and USA), *Sons o' Guns,* the spectacular *Silver Wings* and *Little Tommy Tucker* for Herbert Clayton and/or Jack Waller and the large and military *The Song of the Drum* and *Three Sisters* (1934) for Alfred Butt at the Theatre Royal, Drury Lane, and he made his West End debut as a director with the London version of *Viktória* (1931) at the Palace Theatre.

Reader returned to Waller to direct and choreograph the highly successful Binnie Hale/Bobby Howes musical *Yes, Madam?* (1934), its sucessor *Please, Teacher!* (1935), and the less successful *Certainly Sir* (1936) and *Big Business,* and continued his association with Drury Lane when he provided the massed dances for Ivor Novello's *Glamorous Night* (1935) and for the unfortunate Robert Stolz musical *Rise and Shine.* He returned to the stage in the London Hippodrome musical *The Fleet's Lit Up* (1938) for which he also shared the choreographic credit with Frederick Ashton and Harry Dennis, but by this stage his attention had begun to be diverted from the professional theatre by the enormous success which he had had in writing, producing and staging the Boy Scout movement's Gang Shows. He remained involved with these young people's spectaculars, throughout the world, up until the mid-1970s.

In 1950 he returned to the theatre at the head of his own National Light Opera Company which toured *Merrie England, The Lilac Domino* and *Chu Chin Chow* for a season, and in 1956 he came back together with Waller to write (under a pseudonym) and stage the musical *Wild Grows the Heather.* Sabotaged at what should have been a successful opening night by hordes of overapplauding Boy Scouts, the piece failed. Reader subsequently wrote another musical, *Summer Holiday,* produced in Scarborough, but he had more success as a songwriter, notably with the number ''Strolling,'' the anthem of the Flanagan and Allen comedy team. Again, however, he was not named on the bill, for Flanagan took the writing credit.

1956 **Wild Grows the Heather** (Jack Waller, Joseph Tunbridge/Ralph Reader) London Hippodrome 3 May

1960 **Summer Holiday** Open Air Theatre, Scarborough

Autobiographies: *It's Been Terrific* (Laurie, London, 1954), *Ralph Reader Remembers* (Bailey & Swinfen, Folkestone, 1974)

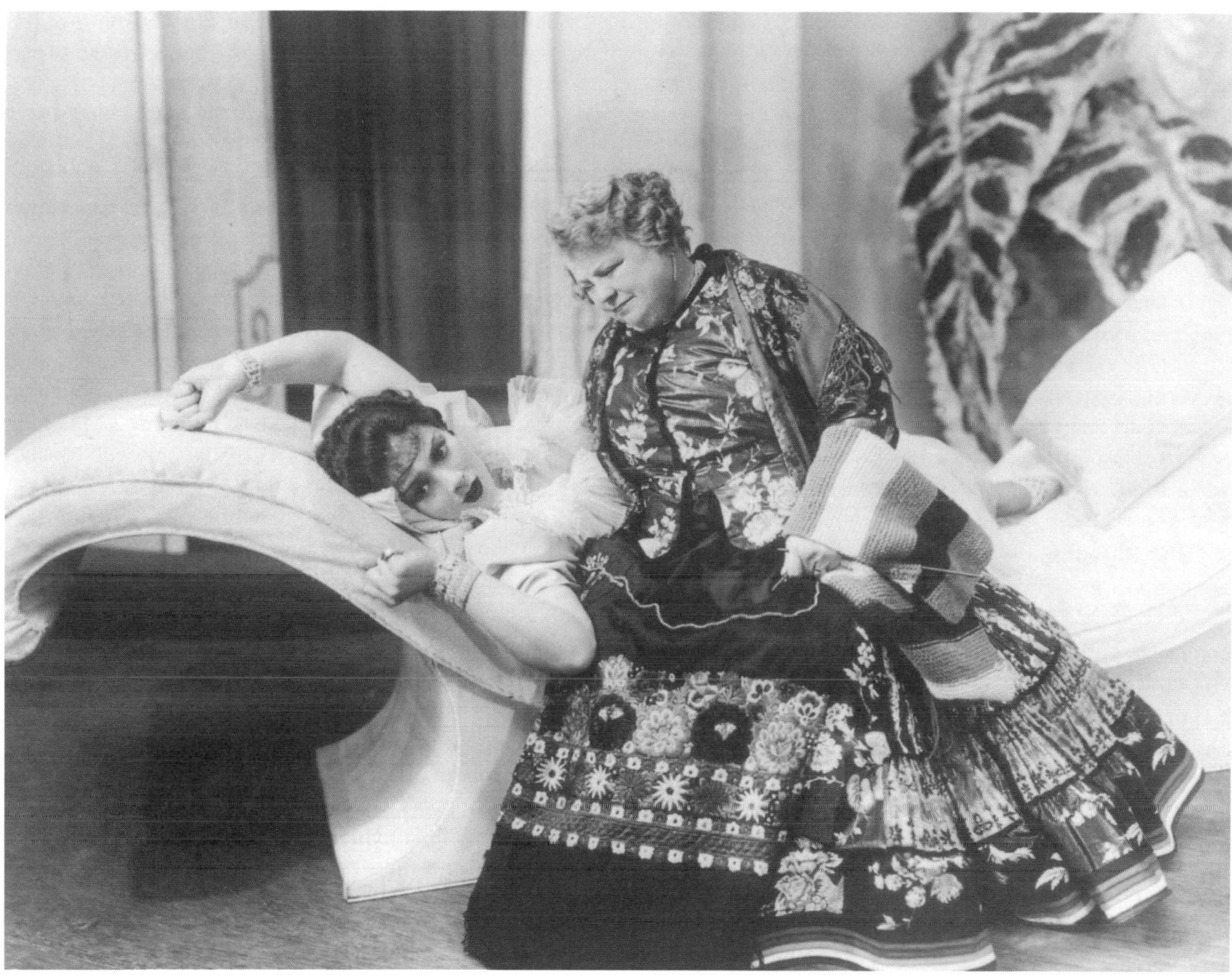

Plate 320. **Minnie Rayner** *(right) was a big lady by the late stage in her career when Ivor Novello cast her in a series of character roles, beginning with the part of the prima donna's duenna in* Glamorous Night.

REDHEAD Musical comedy in 2 acts by Herbert and Dorothy Fields, Sidney Sheldon and David Shaw. Lyrics by Dorothy Fields. Music by Albert Hague. 46th Street Theater, New York, 5 February 1959.

The prototype of *Redhead* was originally conceived by Herbert and Dorothy Fields (and announced as early as 1955 under the title *The Works*) as a mystery tale about a waxworks woman and envisaged as a vehicle for Beatrice Lillie. Having been shelved, the scenario was brought out again in the mid-1950s to be adapted for a rather younger star, Gwen Verdon, and as the piece developed it picked up co-librettist Sidney Sheldon (not yet a best-selling mystery writer), *Plain and Fancy* composer Albert Hague, and then another co-author and two producers who had been working on another piece for the same star.

The result was a period-musical murder-mystery-cum-love story with a London setting which presented Miss Verdon, who had recently starred at the same theatre in *Damn Yankees* and *New Girl in Town,* as Essie Whimple, an ordinary little Victorian girl who makes waxwork figures for a living but who keeps on seeing things. It is thus that she gets mixed up with murder. Essie falls in with music-hall strongman Tom Baxter (Richard Kiley), whose stage partner has been the victim of a mysterious Jack-the-Ripperish strangler, and she even goes on the stage as a dancer at the ill-starred Odeon Music Hall herself, at great risk to her throat, before the murderer is run to ground. The criminial is not the rather obviously red-bearded Sir Charles Willingham (Patrick Horgan), but George Poppett (Leonard Stone), another act on the music hall's bill, who has availed himself of a false red beard to spread a false red herring. The audience might have guessed for, after the two sleuths, Mr Stone had third billing.

The show's score featured Miss Verdon in ''Merely Marvelous'' and '''Erbie Fitch's Twitch,'' Kiley in ''My

Girl Is Just Enough Woman for Me'' and ''I'm Back in Circulation'' and the pair together in ''Look Who's in Love,'' ''I'll Try'' and ''Just for Once'' with Stone, but, under the direction and choreography of Bob Fosse, at the helm for the first time on Broadway, it was not the songs but the dances which were the outstanding feature of *Redhead:* ''The Uncle Sam Rag,'' the ''Pick-Pocket Tango,'' Essie's Vision (Dream Dance) and a Final Chase in the Keystone Kops vein.

Robert Fryer and Lawrence Carr's production of *Redhead* swept the board at the Tony Awards with Miss Verdon, Kiley, the authors, composer and choreographer all taking first prize. It remained on Broadway for over a year for a run of 455 performances, but its success remained there. It did not travel to London (where its very transatlantic ''versions'' of stage cockney and music hall would have fitted ill) and—unlike most Tony laureates of those times—it did not secure itself a regular future. It was, however, revived at the Goodspeed Opera House in 1998 (23 September).

Recordings: original cast (RCA), Mexican cast (RCA), UK studio cast (RCA)

RED, HOT AND BLUE! Musical play in 2 acts by Howard Lindsay and Russel Crouse. Music and lyrics by Cole Porter. Alvin Theater, New York, 29 October 1936.

A thorough-going attempt at a repeat by the authors and composer of *Anything Goes,* Vinton Freedley's production of *Red, Hot and Blue!* was constructed for and scheduled to feature the original stars of the earlier show, Ethel Merman, Victor Moore and William Gaxton. Ultimately (after names from Eddie Cantor to Willie Howard had been ''mentioned'' by the kind of guessing press that ''mentions'' such things) it was not Moore but the much more up-front comedian Jimmy Durante who shared the top billing, and while Gaxton went off to yodel sweet nothings to Kitty Carlisle in *White Horse Inn* the role that would have been his was taken by a funny young man called Bob Hope who had till recently been duetting ''I Can't Get Started'' with Eve Arden in *The Ziegfeld Follies of 1936.*

Miss Merman, the only relict of *Anything Goes,* was cast as the widowed ''Nails'' O'Reilly Duquesne, a former manicurist risen to wealth and social position in Washington; Durante was ''Policy'' Pinky, an ex-(but only just-)convict; and Hope played a young lawyer called Bob Hale whose love-life has been spoiled by the memory of the lost love of his extreme youth. In a plot which managed, in the 1930s let's-play-political mode, to bring both the Senate and the Supreme Court into the action, the search for the missing lass (Polly Walters), identifiable by the imprint of a hot waffle-iron on her posterior, took pride of place. When she is found, however, she proves to be nothing like the little girl of the waffle-iron days, and Hale, his mental blockage cleared away, is left free to stop ''Nails'' being a widow any longer. This time, after having to take second prize in *Anything Goes,* Miss Merman got to have a Happy Ending with the juvenile man.

The score did not turn up the list of perennials that the earlier show had done, but it nevertheless produced one major hit in the duet ''It's De-lovely,'' performed by Miss Merman and Hope, which proved to be a regular successor to ''You're the Top,'' became a Porter standard, and survived beyond *Red, Hot and Blue!* to be heard in the theatre in London's *The Fleet's Lit Up* and both on film and in later, souped-up stage adaptations of *Anything Goes.* Merman had two other fine numbers, the rousing ''Ridin' High'' which closed out the first act in ''Blow, Gabriel, Blow''–style and the comically down-in-the-dumps ''Down in the Depths on the 90th Floor.'' This number had been written and put into the show in double-quick time during the Boston tryout when it was decided that the delicately lovely ''Goodbye, Little Dream'' (which Porter had salvaged from his *Born to Dance* film cutouts) did not fit the bill. Another number, ''You're a Bad Influence on Me,'' was dropped after opening and replaced briefly by the burlesque hillbilly ''The Ozarks Are Calling Me Home.'' Durante introduced the crazy saga of a pregnant sea-captain who admits to being a girl in ''A Little Skipper from Heaven Above,'' Merman asked for melodies that were ''Red, Hot and Blue!,'' and supporting couple Dorothy Vernon and Thurston Crane sang ''Ours'' and ''What a Great Pair We'll Be'' while Grace and Paul Hartman danced.

The result was a musical which, Miss Merman noted, was ''in no way innovative [not even] a slick old-fashioned show'' and, in spite of its star values, its enjoyably over-the-top book and a score which, if it was not *Anything Goes,* contained many good things, *Red, Hot and Blue!* did not score a hit. After 183 Broadway performances it closed, while *White Horse Inn* ran on, and in spite of the general success overseas of the earlier show it found no takers for foreign productions. Perhaps it was the waffle iron.

A revised version of the show (ad Michael Leeds) was given at the Goodspeed Opera House in 2000 (5 November).

Recording: original cast recordings (part record) (AEI)

THE RED HUSSAR Comedy opera in 3 acts by Henry Pottinger Stephens. Music by Edward Solomon. Lyric Theatre, London, 23 November 1889.

After his record-breaking success with *Dorothy* and a good run from its successor *Doris,* the now-very-rich Henry Leslie purchased *The Red Hussar* from composer

Solomon as a third vehicle for his star and mistress, Marie Tempest. *The Red Hussar* had about it much of the layout—if not the tone—of Stephens and Solomon's first (and only) big success, *Billee Taylor,* with its heroine Kitty Carroll (Miss Tempest), who follows her lover Ralph Rodney (Ben Davies) to war in men's clothes, being a close relative of the earlier piece's Phoebe. As in *Billee Taylor,* Kitty sees her beloved tempted by rank and wealth, in the person of Miss Barbara Bellasys (Florence Dysart), but rather than following the comical twist which had given such a lift to the first show's ending, *The Red Hussar* stuck to the romantic and had Kitty discover rank and title and win her man in the most conventional fashion.

The rest of the *Dorothy* team were given roles to suit: comic Arthur Williams was a comical private soldier and baritone Hayden Coffin made an heroic ultimate partner for Miss Dysart, whilst director Charles Harris, choreographer Johnnie D'Auban and conductor Ivan Caryll all repeated their functions on the new show. Amongst the minor players were principal dancer "Birdie" Irving (later to call herself Ethel) and the young Ellis Jeffreys as "a vivandière."

Miss Tempest, naturally, had the largest share of Solomon's attractively straightforward comic-opera score, varying from march rhythms ("Song of the Regiment") to waltzes ("Only Dreams," "The Glee Maiden") in a showy role which demanded considerable vocal resources, and Coffin was supplied with two ballads with which to attempt a follow-up to his huge hit with "Queen of My Heart." However, as in *Doris,* it was the tenor, Davies, who turned out to have the top songs in "When Life and I" and "Guides of the Night." Williams had a comical number called "Variations" which, in an age where the topical and the ad lib in the musical theatre were rife, presented the particularity of using no anachronisms to cut across the period story.

The Red Hussar had a fine London run of 175 performances, went on the road with Effie Chapuy starring, and was exported to America where Miss Tempest scored a great success in 78 performances on Broadway and the first part of a tour which gave out when her voice did. In the meanwhile, however, the show had stayed in the news in England. A piece called *The White Sergeant* (which had been fruitlessly announced for production at Boston's Bijou Theater as long ago as May 1883) had been part of Solomon's assets during a recent bankruptcy and the receiver now claimed that *The Red Hussar* was that same piece and that the royalties belonged to the creditors. There were other claims too, for it seemed that Solomon had previously sold both *The White Sergeant* and a piece called *The Blue Hussar* at least once, and on one occasion to his own cousin, but the composer somehow survived all the legal proceedings as *The Red Hussar* went on to productions in South Africa (Edgar Perkins Co) and on the Eastern circuits, as well as in variously pirated versions in American stock seasons (*The White Hussar* by the Lamont Co, etc). In Britain it continued to surface over the years, being reproduced for touring in a revised version in 1918, played by the Poluskis in 1919, and ultimately put out in variety houses in a chopped-up version under the title *Soldier Girl* under the management of the cousin who had claimed all along that it was his.

USA: Palmer's Theater 5 August 1890

THE RED MILL Musical play in 2 acts by Henry Blossom. Music by Victor Herbert. Knickerbocker Theater, New York, 24 September 1906.

Written by Blossom and Herbert and produced by Charles Dillingham as a vehicle for the comedy team of Montgomery and Stone, *The Red Mill* presented the pair as Kid Conner (Montgomery) and Con Kidder (Stone), a couple of outrageous and impecunious Yankees loose amongst the tulips and windmills of the Netherlandish town of Katwyk-ann-Zee. The two comical fellows get involved in the love affair between Burgomaster's daughter Gretchen van Borkem (Augusta Greenleaf) and a sailor called Doris (Joseph M Ratliff), and they take the side of the lovers against her father (Edward Begley) in a farago of comic events which got them mixed up in moonlit doings in a theoretically haunted mill, and disguised, for a part of the time, as Sherlock Holmes and Dr Watson. Stone had a pretty soubrette called Tina (Ethel Johnson) as a love interest, and there were two subplots—one involving Gretchen's intended husband, the Governor of nearby Zeeland (Neal McCay), with her auntie Bertha (Allene Crater), and a second sparked off by a car crash between a motoring Countess (Juliette Dika) and a British lawyer (Claude Cooper) with a carful of daughters—both of which were unusually neatly tied in to the final denouement of the show.

Blossom's lively libretto gave good opportunities to all the characters, and not just his two nevertheless overwhelming stars, and Victor Herbert's score was a versatile mixture of the music-hally and the light operatic. The two comedians sang of "The Streets of New York," ragged their way through "Go While the Goin' Is Good" and an interpolated (in a Herbert score!) "Good-a-bye, John" (Egbert van Alstyne/Harry Williams), Miss Johnson sparkled out a handful of bright songs ("Mignonette," "Whistle It," "I Want You to Marry Me"), Doris joined his lady-love in "The Isle of Our Dreams" and Miss Crater gave point to "A Woman Has Ways," but the popular gems of the score went to Miss Greenleaf and to McCay. The first-act closing had Gretchen, locked up in the haunted mill to await her unwilling marriage, tak-

Plate 321. *The hero of* **The Red Mill** *is under arrest on the very steps of the titular mill. And not simply because his name is Doris.*

ing the moment—which seemed as good as any—to serenade ''Moonbeams'' in a ballad that was to become a longtime favorite. Only when she was done did the act come to its climax as the two heroes staged the moonlit rescue of the sung-out soprano, Stone dangling from the sails of the mill in an acrobatic attempt to bring Miss Greenleaf down to earth. The other hit came in the second half when the jolly governor bounced out his creed in ''Every Day Is Ladies' Day with Me''prior to settling for the comfy Bertha in ''Because You're You.''

The Red Mill was a big success, and audiences flocked to the show which Dillingham made sure everyone knew about by constructing a moving red mill sign with electric lights on it outside the Knickerbocker Theater. Montgomery and Stone played their roles for 274 performances on Broadway before taking the show on the road for a long stint of touring with most of the cast in their original parts. The run of *The Red Mill* remained a record for a Victor Herbert show on Broadway until 1945 when Stone's daughter, Paula, and Hunt Stromberg jr sponsored a revival of the same piece (Ziegfeld Theater 16 October) in the wake of successful revivals at the San Francisco Light Opera. The libretto was tactfully revised, with new lyrics by Forman Brown; Eddie Foy jr and Michael O'Shea took the comedy roles, Stone's daughter Dorothy was the soubrette, Odette Myrtil and her violin were the motoring Countess (now called Madame La Fleur) and the sailor was understandably rechristened Hendrik instead of Doris. *The Red Mill* was a grand success all over again, and it played for 531 performances before once more heading successfully around the country.

First time round, the show created only a little interest outside America. J C Williamson Ltd picked up *The Red Mill* for Australia, and it was played there in 1908 with Fred A Leslie and John Ford featured alongside Fanny Dango as Tina, but it was another decade before the show was seen in Britain. Alfred Butt eventually took it up for the Empire Theatre and featured the dwarfish variety-comedian Little Tich in Montgomery's role alongside the gangling Ray Kay, Ivy Tresmand (Tina) and Amy Augarde (Bertha). The lead pair failed to attract to a poorly-staged production and the show folded in 64 performances. The success of the Broadway revival prompted a second London attempt with *The Red Mill* in 1947 with variety comedians Jimmy Jewel and Ben Warriss starred, but Emile Littler's £15,000 production lasted only two weeks.

A 1927 film entitled *The Red Mill,* with Marion Davies and Owen Moore starred, had virtually nothing to do with the show, but a 1958 television edition featuring Donald O'Connor, Nichols and May and Shirley Jones had rather more.

Australia: Theatre Royal, Sydney 11 July 1908; UK: Empire Theatre 26 December 1919

Recordings: selections (Capitol, Turnabout, RCA), 1945 revival cast selection (Decca)

REDSTONE, Willy [ROTTENSTEIN, Charles Adolphe Willy] (b Draveil, France ?1883; d Sydney, Australia, 30 September 1949). Conductor and composer for stages on both sides of the world.

The son of Jeanne Baretty—a half-sister of Charles Gounod and a cousin of Albert Carré—and of a Strasbourgeois dentist, Willy Redstone was born while his family was taking refuge in the Paris area from the German attacks of the latest Franco-Prussian warring. He studied at the Paris Conservatoire for six years from the age of 17 and it was during that time that he anglicized his name, allegedly to hide from the authorities the fact that he was breaking the rules by working professionally during his studies.

He began writing short opérettes and revues (*À perte de vue,* 1906, etc) in 1905, and he had some early success with a larger piece, *Mik 1er,* which ran for more than three months in Paris, before striking up a connection with the famous British ballet master John Tiller for whose school and whose northern-England productions he subsequently supplied an amount of musical material. Redstone wed a Tiller pupil, Florence Osborne, and remained in Britain, fathering two children and working at the London Alhambra until the outbreak of war took him into the French army. Invalided out before the Battle of the Marne, he returned home and to his musical activities, taking the baton for the London productions of *Tonight's the Night* (1915), *Theodore & Co* (1916) and *Yes, Uncle!* (1917) and supplying music to such pieces as Sybil Arundale's *All Women* revue (1915), before returning to the front. At the end of the war, he picked up where he had left off, acting as musical director for the highly successful Winter Garden production of *Kissing Time* (1919), supplying music for the revue *Now's the Time,* and composing the principal score for the next Winter Garden show, the internationally successful musical comedy *A Night Out.*

In 1922 Redstone was hired by Hugh J Ward to go to Australia as musical director for his production of *The O'Brien Girl,* and he remained in the southern hemisphere to conduct *Tangerine, The Honeymoon Girl, Little Nellie Kelly, The Rise of Rosie O'Reilly, Battling Butler, The Film Girl, No, No, Nanette, Sunny, Lady, Be Good!, Take the Air, Princess Charming, Whoopee, The Vagabond King* and many other shows.

As his *A Night Out* settled in to a series of revivals as one of Australia's favorite 1920s musical comedies, he also continued to compose, providing the score for a musical version of the farce *Tons of Money* produced by Ward which ran long and strong around Australia (Grand Opera House, Sydney 1 March), and individual numbers for pantomimes and other productions. He also composed the score for a number of Australian movies of the 1930s and 1940s, including First National Films's *The Sea Hawk, The Flying Doctor, That Certain Something, Forty Thousand Horsemen* and films for the Department of Information.

Redstone spent the rest of his life in Australia, where he latterly became director of the Australian Broadcasting Commission's Wireless Chorus and from 1938 Federal Music Editor.

In spite of his success as a musical-theatre man, Redstone did not ever notch up a hit song. However, later in life he laid claim to one. According to him, he had written "If You Were the Only Girl in the World" (without the "if") and sold it for £5 to performer-songwriter Nat Ayer. Ayer took out the top notes (which he couldn't reach), played and published the piece as his own (in the manner of the time) and was—and still is—credited with the hit.

1907 **Le Trou d'Almanzor** (Rip, Wilned) 1 act Théâtre des Arts 9 February; Théâtre des Bouffes-Parisiens 6 April 1908

1907 **Fleur de pétun** (Rip, G P Lafargue) 1 act Tréteau Royale 14 May

1907 **Midas** (Louis Marsolleau, Henri Géroule) 1 act Comédie Royale 22 November

1908 **Le Planteur de Connecticut** (Rip, Georges Arnould) Théâtre Marigny 1 September

1908 **Chanteclairette** (Lafargue, Jean Roby) Scala 9 September

1909 **Nuit sicilienne** (Lucien Meyrargue) mimodrama Théâtre Michel 18 May

1910 **Le Costaud de l'Olympe** (Georges Nanteuil, Léon Miral) La Cigale 11 May

1910 **Baby Pepper** (Lucien Boyer, Max Boyer) 1 act Concert Mayol 2 December

1911 **Baby** (w Adolf Stanislas/L Boyer, Jean Boyer, A Monfred) revised *Baby Pepper* tour

1911 **Mik 1er** (Charles-Antoine Carpentier) Scala 28 September

1912 **Berlingot** (L Boyer, M Boyer, Mlle Mazier) Concert Mayol December

1913 **Les Petits Crevés, ou Henri III et son petit cour** (Rip, Jacques Bousquet) Théâtre des Capucines 24 December

1919 **Aladin, ou La Lampe merveilleuse** (Rip) Théâtre Marigny 21 May

1920 **A Night Out** (Clifford Grey/George Grossmith, Arthur Miller) Winter Garden Theatre 19 September

1921 **Faust on Toast** (w Melville Gideon/Firth Shephard, Adrian Ross) Gaiety Theatre 19 April

1923 **Tons of Money** ("Vaires Louis") New Palace Theatre, Melbourne 27 October

Plate 322. **The Red Widow.** *Chief comic Raymond Hitchcock comes under inspection from the suspicious ''red widow'' (Sophie Barnard) in Broadway's version of the much-musicalized* His Official Wife.

THE RED WIDOW Musical play in 3 acts by Channing Pollock and Rennold Wolf based on the novel *His Official Wife* by Richard Henry Savage. Music by Charles J Gebest. Colonial Theater, Boston, 2 September 1911; Astor Theater, New York, 6 November 1911.

Colonel Savage's enormously successful novel *His Official Wife* was leaped upon by a horde of theatrical adapters, filmed by Hollywood and, with its dramatic ending suitably revamped, successfully musicalized both in Europe and, as *The Red Widow,* in America.

In Pollock and Wolf's version, Raymond Hitchcock appeared as Cicero Hannibal Butts, ''manufacturer of CHB Corsets and a Colonel in the New York State National Guard, USA,'' who gets himself into trouble abroad. At London's Alcazar Music Hall he encounters the glamorous Anna Varvara (Sophye Barnard), who persuades him to let her take his wife's place on a trip to see relatives in St Petersburg. Anna is, however, the nihilist Red Widow of the title, out to shoot the Czar and pursued by Russian Secret Police Ivan Scorpioff (John Hendricks) and Baron Maximilian Scareovich (Joseph Allan). The big denouement is due to come during the White Fête in the Gardens of the Winter Palace, but by then Anna has fallen in love with Captain Basil Romanoff of the Imperial Bodyguard (Theodore Martin) and, when the crucial moment comes, she decides, amid a plethora of top B naturals, that love comes before politics and she ends up joining in a chorus in praise of the ''Soldiers of the Czar.''

Hitchcock described himself as ''A Wonderful Man in Yonkers (but in London nothing at all)'' and schottisched to the rueful ''I Shall Never Look at a Pretty Girl Again,'' whilst Miss Barnard had romantic moments both alone, in the waltz song ''Just for You,'' and in duet with her Basil in the show's effort to duplicate the *Merry Widow* waltz, ''I Love Love.'' The stars were supported by lighter romancing from Butts's son Oswald (Harry Clarke) and his danseuse Yvette (Gertrude Vanderbilt) ("You Can't Pay the Landlord with Love"), and George E Mack had a comical number in the part of a striving nihilist called Popova equipped with some lyrics which yielded some approximate but amusing rhymes (". . . when a King starts out to be a Cromwell, we buy a little bombshell"). The music was by a comparative newcomer to the ranks of Broadway songwriters, Charles J Gebest, who had been an original performing member of George M Cohan's musical-comedy company back in 1901.

George M Cohan and Sam Harris presented Hitchcock in *The Red Widow* through a highly successful tour and a season of 128 performances at Broadway's Astor Theatre between 1911 and 1912, after which the show was taken up by J C Williamson Ltd and produced in Australia and New Zealand with Florence Young (Anna), Phil Smith (Butts) and Reginald Roberts (Basil) featured, beginning its down-under career with three weeks in Melbourne and four in Sydney (Her Majesty's Theatre 3 December 1917). It was later played in South Africa by Wybert Stanford's "London Gaiety Company" headed by Blanche Browne (1917). However, a copyright performance staged in London failed to encourage anyone to produce the piece there and elsewhere folk manufactured their own more-or-less comic versions of *His Official Wife,* notably in Berlin—where Messrs Josef Siegmund and Julius Wilhelm, with musical support from Richard Haller, produced a flop *Die ledige Frau* (Neues Königliches Opernhaus 29 September 1902) which didn't admit to its source but left no one in any doubt—and in Vienna, where Hermann Dostal's *Nimm mich mit!,* which did admit its source, had a successful run at the Theater an der Wien.

A silent film version of the *Red Widow* version of the story starring John Barrymore and Flora Zabelle (Mrs Raymond Hitchcock) was produced by Paramount in 1916.

UK: Ladbroke Hall 31 August 1911; Australia: Her Majesty's Theatre, Melbourne 4 August 1917

Film: (silent) Paramount 1916

REECE, Robert (b Barbados, 2 May 1838; d London, 8 July 1891). One of the busiest writers for the British burlesque stage.

Son of a West Indian planter, Mr Robert Reece of the Hope and Baunatyne Estates in Barbados, and an MA graduate from Balliol College, Robert Reece junior began his working life as a clerk in the emigration department of the Colonial office. He first came to theatrical notice with the texts for a handful of burlesques and operettas written for Fanny Reeves and her husband Eliot Galer and played during their seasons at the Royalty Theatre and went on from there to become one of the most popular writers in the burlesque theatre in the late 1860s and early 1870s.

Reece's Royalty burlesques *Prometheus* and *Ulf the Minstrel* were sufficiently successful, but he aroused livelier interest with his parody of Kotzebue's drama *The Stranger;* entitled *The Stranger—Stranger Than Ever,* which not only had a fine first run at the Queen's Theatre but was reprised two years later at the Royalty. The most enduring of his burlesque works, however, was *Brown and the Brahmins,* an extravaganza based on James Kenney's old musical farce *The Illustrious Stranger, or Married and Buried* (Drury Lane 1 October 1827), a tale suggested in its turn by the Arabian Nights story of Sindbad, and involving the notion of the burying-alive of a relict spouse—later reprised with equal humor by Gilbert in *The Mikado.* The piece ran a remarkable one hundred consecutive performances at the Globe Theatre.

With the coming of opéra-bouffe and opéra-comique Reece began adapting French works for the English stage, writing the libretto for the famous first London production of *Chilpéric* and providing the difficult translation of Lecocq's sexy *Les Cent Vierges* for the Gaiety, and he also authored one of the earliest English attempts at the new-style English comic opera when Kate Santley commissioned him to supply her with the text for the show which became *Cattarina.*

In 1877 Reece began a partnership with the prolific Henry Farnie with whom, through the dozen years before Farnie's death, he wrote a considerable number of extravaganzas, burlesques and further translations from the French and German musical theatre, their most outstanding successes coming with the record-breaking English version of *Les Cloches de Corneville* and the adaptation of *La Mascotte,* two of the longest-running musicals of the early Victorian period. He was at different times chief text-writer for the Alhambra and for John Hollingshead at the Gaiety, he wrote several of Lydia Thompson's successful pieces, and there was little time during the 20 years of his playwriting career when he was not represented by at least one piece on the London stage—yet in the last days of his not over-long life Reece was reduced from a house in Hampstead with a servant to minister to his wife and two daughters, to a state of utter want, and had to survive on handouts from his professional friends.

A sometime composer and songwriter, Reece also supplied individual songs which were used from time to time in his burlesques and in the Alhambra's extravaganzas.

1865 **Castle Grim** (George B Allen) 1 act Royalty Theatre 2 September

1865 **Prometheus, the Man on the Rock** (pasticcio arr Theodore Hermann) Royalty Theatre 23 December

1866 **Love's Limit** (John Elliott Mallandaine) 1 act Royalty Theatre 16 February

1866 **Ulf the Minstrel** (pasticcio arr Hermann) Royalty Theatre 30 March

1866 **The Lady of the Lake, plaid in a new tartan** (pasticcio arr Hermann) Royalty Theatre 8 September

1867 **A Wild Cherry** (Allen) 1 act Reigate 2 September

1867 **Our Quiet Château** (Virginia Gabriel) 1 act Gallery of Illustration 26 December

1868 **Agamemnon and Cassandra, or The Prophet and Loss to Troy** (pasticcio) Prince of Wales Theatre, Liverpool 13 April

1868 **The Stranger—Stranger Than Ever** (pasticcio arr Schöning) Queen's Theatre 4 November

1868 **The Last of the Paladins** (*Croquefer*) English version (Gallery of Illustration)

1868 **The Ambassadress** (*L'Ambassadrice*) English version (St George's Hall)

1869 **Brown and the Brahmins, or Captain Pop and the Princess Pretty-Eyes** (pasticcio arr George Richardson) Globe Theatre 23 January

1870 **Chilpéric** English version w Richard Mansell, F A Marshall (Lyceum Theatre)

1870 **Undine** (Reece, F Taylor, George Martin, pasticcio arr John Winterbottom) Olympic Theatre 2 July

1870 **Whittington Jr and His Sensation Cat** (pasticcio) Royalty Theatre 23 November

1870 **Faust in a Fog** (pasticcio) King's Cross Theatre 7 December

1871 **Perfect Love, or The Triumph of Oberon** (w Thomas Thorpe Pede, George Barnard) Olympic Theatre 25 February

1871 **Little Robin Hood, or Quite a New Beau** (pasticcio) Royalty Theatre 19 April

1871 **In Possession** (Frederic Clay) 1 act Gallery of Illustration 20 June

1871 **Paquita, or Love in a Frame** (Mallandaine) Royalty Theatre 21 November

1872 **The Very Last Days of Pompeii** (pasticcio arr Arthur Nicholson) Vaudeville Theatre February

1872 **The Vampire** (pasticcio) Strand Theatre 15 August

1872 **Ali Baba à la Mode** (Clay, Mallandaine, Richardson, pasticcio) Gaiety Theatre 14 September

1872 **Romulus and Remus** (pasticcio arr Nicholson) Vaudeville Theatre 12 December

1873 **Don Giovanni in Venice** (pasticcio) Gaiety Theatre 17 February

1873 **Martha** (pasticcio) Gaiety Theatre 14 April

1873 **Richelieu Redressed** (pasticcio) Olympic Theatre 27 October

1873 **A Lesson in Love** (T Thorpe Pede) 1 act Alexandra Theatre, Camden Town 10 November

1873 **Moonstruck** (Pede) 1 act Alexandra Theatre 24 November

1874 **Ruy Blas Righted, or The Love, the Ligger and the Lackey** (pasticcio arr Nicholson) Vaudeville Theatre 3 January

1874 **Plucky Parthenia, or A Caution to Ingemar** (pasticcio) Theatre Royal, Portsmouth 26 February

1874 **Cattarina** (Clay) Prince's Theatre, Manchester 17 August; Charing Cross Theatre, London 15 May 1875

1874 **Les Prés Saint-Gervais** English version (Criterion Theatre)

1874 **The Island of Bachelors** (*Les Cent Vierges*) English version (Gaiety Theatre)

1874 **Green Old Age** (pasticcio) 1 act Vaudeville Theatre 31 October

1875 **Spectresheim** (pasticcio arr Georges Jacobi) Alhambra Theatre 14 August

1875 **The Half Crown Diamonds** (pasticcio) Mirror Theatre 27 September

1875 **Toole at Sea** (pasticcio) Gaiety Theatre 3 December

1876 **A Spelling Bee** (pasticccio) Gaiety Theatre 2 February

1876 **Young Rip van Winkle** (pasticcio) Charing Cross Theatre 17 April

1876 **Coming Events** (Procida Bucalossi) 1 act Royalty Theatre 22 April

1876 **William Tell Told Again** (pasticcio) Gaiety Theatre 21 December

1877 **Oxygen, or Gas in the Burlesque Metre** (pasticcio/w H B Farnie) Folly Theatre 31 March

1877 **The Lion's Tale and the Naughty Boy Who Wagged It** (pasticcio arr Nicholson) Globe Theatre 16 June

1877 **Champagne** (pasticcio arr Henry Reed/w Farnie) Strand Theatre 29 September

1877 **Sea Nymphs** (*Les Ondines au champagne*) English version (Folly Theatre)

1877 **Up the River** English version (Folly Theatre)

1877 **La Créole** English version w Farnie (Folly Theatre)

1877 **Wildfire** (pasticcio/w Farnie) Alhambra Theatre 24 December

1878 **Madcap** (*La Chaste Susanne*) (pasticcio arr A J Levey/ad w Farnie) Royalty Theatre 7 February

1878 **The National Question** (pasticcio) 1 act Globe Theatre 17 March

1878 **Pom** (Procida Bucalossi) revised text Park Theatre 2 April

1878 **Les Cloches de Corneville** English version w Farnie (Folly Theatre)

1878 **Stars and Garters** (pasticcio) English version of *L'Étoile* w Farnie, Folly Theatre 21 September

1879 **Carmen, or Sold for a Song** (pasticcio arr Michael Connelly) Folly Theatre 25 January

1879 **Babiole** English version (Prince's Theatre, Manchester)

1879 **The Marionettes** (pasticcio/w J F McArdle) 1 act Haymarket Theatre 16 June

1879 **La Petite Mademoiselle** English version w H S Leigh (Alhambra Theatre)

1880 **Le Voyage en Suisse** English version (Gaiety Theatre)

1880 **The Forty Thieves** (pasticcio) Gaiety Theatre 24 December

1881 **Jeanne, Jeannette et Jeanneton** (aka *The Marquis*) English version (Alhambra Theatre)

1881 **The Half Crown Diamonds** revised version (pasticcio arr Lutz) Gaiety Theatre 14 May

1881 **Welsh Rabbits** (pasticcio/w Knight Summers) Folly Theatre 21 May

1881 **Herne the Hunted** (pasticcio/w Henry Pottinger Stephens, William Yardley) Gaiety Theatre 24 May by amateurs

1881 **La Mascotte** English version w Farnie (Comedy Theatre)

1881 **Aladdin** (pasticcio) Gaiety Theatre 24 December

1882 **Boccaccio** English version w Farnie (Comedy Theatre)

1882 **Little Robin Hood** revised version (pasticcio arr Lutz) Gaiety Theatre 15 September

1882 **On Condition** (Lutz) 1 act Opera Comique 9 October

1882 **The Merry War** (*Der lustige Krieg*) English version (Alhambra Theatre)

1882 **Valentine and Orson** (pasticcio) Gaiety Theatre 23 December

1882 **The Yellow Dwarf** (pasticcio) Her Majesty's Theatre 30 December

1883 **The Flying Dutchman** (pasticcio) Prince of Wales Theatre, Liverpool 12 March

1883 **Our Cinderella** (pasticcio) Gaiety Theatre 8 September

1884 **Our Helen** (pasticcio) Gaiety Theatre 8 April

1884 **Out of the Ranks** (pasticcio) Strand Theatre 3 June

1884 **The Lady of Lyons Married and Claude Unsettled** Royalty Theatre, Glasgow 27 September

1885 **Kenilworth** (pasticcio arr Connelly/w Farnie) Avenue Theatre 19 December

1886 **Keep Your Places** (G B Allen) 1 act St George's Hall 15 February

1886 **Lurline** (pasticcio arr Connelly/w Farnie) Avenue Theatre 24 April

1886 **Robinson Crusoe** (pasticcio/w Farnie) Avenue Theatre 23 December

1886 **The Commodore** (*La Créole*) new English version w Farnie (Avenue Theatre)

1888 **Don Juan Jr** (Edward Solomon/ ''Brothers Prendergast'' ad w Edward Righton) Avenue Theatre 25 August

1889 **La Girouette** English version (Avenue Theatre)

REED, Mrs German [née HORTON, Priscilla] (b Birmingham, 1 January 1818; d Bexleyheath, Kent, 18 March 1895). The multi-talented mainstay of the German Reed company and entertainment.

Miss Horton made her stage debut at the age of 10 playing a gypsy girl in *Guy Mannering* at the old Surrey Theatre under Elliston but, from the beginning of her adult career, she rose swiftly up to important roles in important houses. In 1834 she played at the Victoria Theatre as Kate in Sheridan Knowles's *The Ballad of Bethnal Green,* the following year at the English Opera House in the ballad opera *The Covenanters* and in *Monsieur Jacques,* in 1838 she was seen at Covent Garden as Ariel in *The Tempest* and in 1840 she appeared as Ophelia to the Hamlet and Laertes of Phelps and Macready at the Haymarket. Later the same year she created the role of Georgina Vesey in *Money,* and she continued with a round of Shakespearean engagements with Charles Kean at the Haymarket Theatre.

What was described as ''the finest contralto on the English stage'' was employed in the premiere of Rooke's opera *Amilie* (1837), in Purcell's *King Arthur* and as Acis to the Galatea of Miss Romer in Blow's *Acis and Galatea* (1842) and in a long series of the famous extravaganzas written for the Haymarket Theatre, in which (in between bearing children) she supplemented and/or replaced the celebrated Madame Vestris, mainly in breeches roles: Fortunio in *Fortunio* (1843), Graceful in *The Fair One with the Golden Locks* (1843), Ariel in *The Drama at Home* (1844), Percinet in *Graciosa and Percinet* (1844), Jason in *The Golden Fleece* (1845) to the Medea of Vestris, Princess Linda in *The Bee and the Orange Tree* (1845), The Nightingale in *The Birds of Aristophanes* (1846), Don Leander in *The Invisible Prince* (1846), the title role of *The New Planet* (1847), Rebecca in *The Last Edition of Ivanhoe* (1850), Thaddeus in *Arline* (1851), Fancy in *Camp at the Olympic* (1853) and many others.

In 1854 she virtually put an end to what was potentially a memorable stage career, and she and her husband went on tour with a drawing-room entertainment in which she sang comic songs and performed impersonations to his piano accompaniment. Successful in the provinces, they expanded the entertainment and presented it as ''Miss Priscilla Horton's Illustrative Gatherings'' (''Gatherings from Real Life''), at the St Martin's Hall in Longacre (12 March 1855). The mixture of character sketches and songs gradually developed into more substantial performances, with other artists being engaged to support Mrs Reed, and the solo items being replaced by original sketches and one-act musical plays as the entertainment moved, gathering in popularity, to more permanent premises at the Gallery of Illustration (20 June 1859, *Our Home Circuit, Seaside Studies*) and, eventually, to the larger St George's Hall. The layout for a German Reed program in the later, peak days of the Entertainment consisted most frequently of two short musical plays separated and supplemented by a humorous monologue at the piano, performed in the earlier days by John Parry and, after his retirement, by [Richard] Corney Grain who, along with Mr and Mrs Reed and the second of their children, **Alfred German REED** (b Brompton, c1846; d London, 10 March 1895), made up the backbone of the German Reed company.

Mrs Reed herself was the centerpiece of the English operettas produced by her husband in the middle and later 1860s, creating, amongst other roles, Maggie McMotherly in *Ages Ago,* Mrs Bumpus in *Charity Begins at Home* and Daphne in Gilbert and Clay's *Happy Arcadia* and becoming, arguably, Gilbert's model for the subsequent series of comical elderly contraltos of the Savoy operas. She retired from performing in the entertainment in 1879, but continued for many years to take part in its organization alongside first her husband and later her son.

The status of the Reeds and their standing in the world of entertainment was emphasized when four performers were chosen to represent the performing arts at the wedding of the Prince of Wales and Princess Alexandra in 1863: Jenny Lind was one, Priscilla and German Reed and John Parry were the other three.

In a curious hecatomb, Mrs Reed turned out to be the last survivor of the little group of friends, family and workers. Her son Alfred died on 10 March 1895, followed just a few days later by his friend Grain, and just two days after Grain Mrs Reed also passed away.

Memoir: Williamson, D (ed): *The German Reeds and Corney Grain* (A D Innes, London, 1895)

REED, Michael [Campbell] (b Belstone, 30 April 1953). Conductor, orchestrator and composer for the modern musical stage.

Reed entered on a career as a musical-theatre conductor direct from the Royal College of Music, beginning with the off–West End *Let My People Come* and then, after the rehearsal-time sacking of the original conductor, taking over the baton for Harold Fielding's London Palladium production of *Hans Andersen* (1974). He subsequently conducted 15 years of musicals in the West End (*Irene, On the Twentieth Century, Barnum, Singin' in the Rain,* etc) before becoming Musical Associate to Andrew Lloyd Webber's Really Useful Group for the original productions of *The Phantom of the Opéra* and *Aspects of Love,* the revival of *Joseph and the Amazing Technicolor Dreamcoat, Sunset Boulevard, Whistle Down the Wind* and the series of ''Music of Andrew Lloyd Webber'' concerts. He also oversaw the production of the Vienna musical *Tanz der Vampire* (1997).

Reed composed additional material for several London musicals (*Irene, The Biograph Girl*) and for the film (later turned stage musical) *Victor/Victoria,* arranged the scores of *Mr Cinders, Bitter-Sweet* and *Wonderful Town* for 1980s revivals and that of *The Beggar's Opera* for a touring production with Edward Woodward starred. He also composed the songs for London's only-ever two-evening musical, *Six for Gold,* and for a small-scale piece about J M Barrie played at the Edinburgh Festival.

1984 **Six for Gold** (Warner Brown) King's Head Theatre 5 July

1990 **The House on the Corner** (Brown) Edinburgh Festival, August

REED, Thomas German (b Bristol, 27 June 1817; d East Sheen, Surrey, 21 March 1888). Founder of the famous Gallery of Illustration and its ''German Reed Entertainment,'' and godfather to a whole era of English operetta.

Eldest son of 'cellist Thomas Reed (b Bath c1795; d Fitzroy, Australia, 19 June 1871), the young Thomas German Reed (the ''German'' was his mother's maiden name) became musical director at the Theatre Royal, Haymarket, at the age of just 22 and he spent the bulk of his theatrical career, there (1838–1851) and later at the Olympic Theatre, conducting the orchestra and composing and arranging music for their various plays and pasticcio entertainments. The most notable such products at these two houses, both of which were amongst the most important producers of musical extravaganzas in London, were the long series of twice-to-thrice yearly burlesques written by J R Planché, and the pieces of Charles Mathews.

In 1844 Reed married the vocalist and actress Priscilla Horton with whom, following his retirement from the Olympic, he toured and played London seasons with a drawing-room entertainment. They were seen in London at Sadler's Wells and at the Olympic Theatre. Subsequently, the Reeds made their London base at the Gallery of Illustration, in Regent Street, where they continued to purvey a program made up of songs, impressions and sketches performed by Priscilla Reed, her versatile turned-light-comedian husband, and pianist-entertainer John Parry. Their sketches included pieces by the Brough brothers, H F Chorley, Edmund Yates, Shirley Brooks, Tom Taylor, Andrew Halliday and other successful writers, amongst which were *A Visit to Holly Lodge, A Month from Home, My Unfinished Opera, The Enraged Musician, After the Ball, The County Assizes, Our Ward's Governess, Our Home Circuit, The Seaside, Our Card Basket, The Rival Composers, The Family Legend or Heads and Tails, A Charming Cottage, The Pyramids* and a piece called *The Bard and His Birthday* which permitted Mrs Reed to pull out her repertoire of Shakespearean characters. Most of these pieces were illustrated by songs written and composed by German Reed.

In 1863 Reed extended the program at the Gallery by mounting opera di camera productions alongside his and Mrs Reed's performances. Between 1863 and 1865 he produced MacFarren's *Jessy Lea* (2 November 1863) and *The Soldier's Legacy* (19 October 1964), Balfe's *The Sleeping Queen* (1 September 1864), Virginia Gabriel's *Widows Bewitched* (14 August 1865) and English versions of Offenbach's *Too Many Cooks* (*La Rose de Saint-Flour* 1 September 1864), *A Happy Result* (*Lischen et Fritzchen* 3 November 1865) and *Ching-Chow-Hi* (*Ba-ta-clan* 14 August 1865), played with casts featuring such top artists as Elizabeth Poole and Augusta Thomson alongside himself and his wife, and a range of rising young vocalists. His production of *Ba-ta-clan* was the first production of an opéra-bouffe in English.

In 1867 Reed took the St George's Hall and attempted a season of larger works. His initial thought was to introduce to London the hit of the Paris season, Offenbach's *La Grande-Duchesse*— but in the end he fell back on three older established French pieces, Auber's *L'Ambassadrice* and Offenbach's little *La Chatte métamorphosée en femme* and *Ba-ta-clan* and retained his daring for a wholly new piece: Sullivan's first full-length work, and the first full-sized English opéra-bouffe, *The Contrabandista.* However, the economics of the enterprise beat him (would they have, had he staged *La Grande-Duchesse?*) and he returned to staging chamber musicals. The opera di camera productions were, however, now replaced by English musical comedies, in which the Reeds—father (until 1871), mother and later, in his father's stead, son Alfred—themselves took part at the head of a more or less fixed little team of players. They had particular success with the productions of Sullivan's short *Cox and Box* (1869, with German as Cox) and the Clay/Gilbert *Ages Ago* (1869, Ebenezer Tare), as well as good seasons with Gilbert's *Our Island Home* (1870, himself) and *A Sensation Novel* (1871, Sir Ruthven Glenaloon) and the B C Stephenson/Alfred Cellier *Charity Begins at Home* (1872) at the head of a series of whimsical, character-based comic musical plays which gave their performers plenty of opportunity for impersonations and songs of the drawing-room variety, for a number of years set to music by Reed himself. These programs became enormously popular and made themselves a regular audience for their comic but wholly clean parlor-style entertainment amongst a middle-class of music- and theatre-lovers for whom a visit to the regular theatre held too many moral perils. Reed moved the performances from the Gallery of Illustration to the larger St George's Hall in 1874 and later the works which were played stretched first to two acts and finally to full length. They only declined in popularity in the late 1880s with the retirement of Mrs Reed, the death of her husband and the arrival of a general acceptance of at least certain areas of the theatre by the kind of middle-class audiences which had been the backbone of their support.

At both the Gallery of Illustration and St George's Hall, Reed was instrumental in giving early opportunities to some of the most important English composers and librettists of the time—Frederic Clay, Arthur Sullivan, Edward Solomon, Alfred Cellier, Charlie Stephenson, W S Gilbert—as well as to a number artists of distinction including Emily Pitt, Robertine Henderson, Emmie d'Este, Susan Galton, Leonora Braham, Fanny Holland, Alice Barth, Thomas Whiffen, Edward L Connell, comic Willie Worboys, Alfred Bishop, Arthur Cecil, Richard Mansfield and Wallace Brownlow.

1864 **Too Many Cooks** (*La Rose de Saint-Flour*) English version (Gallery of Illustration)

1867 **A Dream in Venice** (Tom Robertson) Gallery of Illustration 19 March

1868 **Inquire Within** (F C Burnand) 1 act Gallery of Illustration 2 August

1869 **No Cards** (W S Gilbert) 1 act Gallery of Illustration 29 March

1870 **Our Island Home** (Gilbert) 1 act Gallery of Illustration 20 June

1873 **Mildred's Well** (F C Burnand) 1 act Gallery of Illustration 6 May

1874 **He's Coming** (Burnand) 1 act St George's Hall 17 May

1874 **The Three Tenants** (Gilbert a' Beckett) 1 act St George's Hall 26 December

1875 **Ancient Britons** (a' Beckett) 1 act St George's Hall 25 January

1875 **Eyes and No Eyes, or The Art of Seeing** (Gilbert) 1 act St George's Hall 5 July

1875 **A Spanish Bond** (a' Beckett) 1 act St George's Hall 1 November

1876 **An Indian Puzzle** (a' Beckett, Arthur a' Beckett) 1 act St George's Hall 28 February

1876 **The Wicked Duke** (a' Beckett) 1 act St George's Hall 9 June

1876 **Matched and Mated** (Burnand) 1 act St George's Hall 6 November

1877 **A Night Surprise** (Arthur Law) 1 act St George's Hall 12 February

1877 **Number 204** (Burnand) 1 act St George's Hall 7 May

Memoir: Williamson, D (ed): *The German Reeds and Corney Grain* (A D Innes, London, 1895)

REEVE, Ada [ISAACS, Amy Mary Adelaide] (b London, 3 March 1874; d London, 25 September 1966). Music-hall and musical-comedy soubrette of the turn of the century.

Daughter of the actor Charles Reeves [né Samuel Isaacs] and dancer Harriet Saunders [née de Saundres], Miss Reeve[s] began performing with Fred Wright's company at the age of six and won her first notice in the musical theatre playing a little boy in a touring melodrama with variety turns called *Jack in the Box.* She played in pantomime (*Sinbad the Sailor* 1883, Fairy Sweetlove in *Jack the Giant Killer* 1885, etc), drama (Tom Tit in *Hoodman Blind,* 1886, etc), and had some considerable success as a singing, wisecracking music-hall artist before making her first appearance in the musical theatre as Haidée, alongside Teddy Payne and Katie Seymour, in the touring company of the Gaiety burlesque *Don Juan.*

Plate 323. **Ada Reeve** *in* The Shop Girl.

In 1894 George Edwardes brought her to London to create the title role of his celebrated musical comedy *The Shop Girl,* but she quit the show soon after its opening to take up a pantomime engagement and did not return. She subsequently interleaved other up-front, top-billed musical theatre performances (t/o from Sylvia Grey in *Uncle Célestin, All Abroad,* Julie Bon-Bon in *The Gay Parisienne*) into a career which was operated with a music-hall mentality, a mentality which made her a favorite partner of the unsoberly ad-libbing Arthur Roberts (*Milord Sir Smith*) to whom she was able to respond, when necessary, with off-the-cuff scenes of mostly not-very-new material which returned to the cues only to lead in the songs. She appeared in the burlesque *Great Caesar* in 1899 and returned to Edwardes's management for *San Toy,* the successor to his all-conquering *The Geisha,* but walked out in rehearsal when bested by Marie Tempest over pecking order. She later went back to the show to play not her original comic role but her own music-hally version of Miss Tempest's part, but her tantrum had served her well. In between her exit from and re-entry to *San Toy,* the unexpectedly out of work performer had her biggest musical-comedy success when she was snapped up by producer Tom Davis and tacked instead into the original production of *Florodora* (1899, Lady Holyrood, "Tact," "An Inkling," "When I Leave Town").

She subsequently appeared for Edwardes in Evie Greene's role of *Kitty Grey,* and in succession to Madge Crichton as Ada (for the role was intended originally for Miss Reeve) in Paul Rubens's *Three Little Maids,* but she had less luck in the star comedy role of Davis's *The Medal and the Maid* (1903) and with two touring musicals which she commissioned and produced for herself (*Winnie Brooke, Widow, The Adventures of Moll*). However, she had one further London success on the musical stage in her own mounting of a charming remake of Locke's *The Palace of Puck* as *Butterflies* (1908, Rhodanthe). Thereafter she devoted herself largely to music hall, revue and overseas touring, especially in Australia (where she played in *Winnie Brooke, Widow* in 1918) and South Africa, for the latter part of a long career. Her last appearance in the musical theatre was in 1947 when she appeared at the Prince's Theatre as Madame Sauterelle to the *Dubarry* of Irene Manning.

One of her husbands, **Bert GILBERT** [Gilbert Joseph HAZLEWOOD] (b Wolverhampton, 1873), a descendant of a well-known theatrical family which included the barnstorming playwright Colin Hazlewood of Britannia Theatre fame, was a comedian and dancer in the musical theatre in Britain (Pedrillo in *Don Juan* tour 1894, *The Blue Moon* 1906, etc), America (Van Green in *Maids of Athens,* 1914) and Australia (*In Town, Don Juan, The French Maid,* etc), who showed promise of becoming a successor to the famous Fred Leslie before frittering away into a minor career, leaving his sometime understudy, Teddy Payne, to win the Gaiety's chief comic spot. Another husband, theatre manager A[lbert] Wilfred Cotton (b Birmingham, 1873), sent himself bankrupt producing her shows. Her daughter, Goody Reeve (b 1897) also appeared briefly on the musical stage, notably as Suzette in *The Better 'Ole* (1917) in London, and in the soprano role of Virginia in *My Lady Frayle* (1919) in Australia.

Autobiography: *Take It for a Fact* (Heinemann, London, 1954)

REICHE MÄDCHEN Operette in 3 acts by Ferdinand Stollberg. Music by Johann Strauss. Raimundtheater, Vienna, 30 December 1909.

When Alfred Cellier and H B Farnie's *Nell Gwynne* closed out of town, it reproduced, amoeba-like. The libretto went one way, got attached to a Planquette score, and became *Nell Gwynne* Mark II, whilst the now left-over score—the unloved half—went another way, joined up with a new book, and became the record-breaking *Dorothy.*

Virtually the same thing happened in Vienna. Alfred Maria Willner, Bernhard Buchbinder and Johann Strauss's Operette *Die Göttin der Vernunft* was, however, seen in town. It was produced by Alexandrine von Schönerer at the Theater an der Wien (13 March 1897) with Annie Dirkens (Mathilde), Therese Biedermann (Susette), Julie Kopácsi-Karczag (Ernestine), Karl Blasel (Bonhomme), Josef Joseffy (Oberst Furieux) and Carl Streitmann (Capitaine Robert) heading its megastarry cast, and played there for 32 consecutive performances and four later matinées before going on to be seen at the Bellevue-Theater, Stettin (15 July 1897) and Berlin's Theater Unter den Linden (20 January 1898). It was, without question, a flop, but its bits lived on.

Both halves of *Die Göttin der Vernunft* reappeared on the Vienna stage within just weeks of each other, more than a decade later. The libretto, revised by Willner and Robert Bodanzky, turned up at the Theater an der Wien on 12 November 1909, now attached to a Lehár score and called *Der Graf von Luxenburg* [*sic*]. It was the Raimundtheater, however, which had pulled the big names. It had Strauss's skimmed-off score, now attached to a libretto called *Reiche Mädchen,* and the star of the piece was the city's biggest musical-comic personality, Alexander Girardi, who was to introduce the new Strauss Operette during a Girardi Gastspiel which also included performances of his most famous plays (*Der Verschwender, Mein Leopold*) and Operetten (*Der Zigeunerbaron, Bruder Straubinger*).

Girardi played Michael Karinger, a millionaire manufacturer with a social-climbing wife and a pair of daughters with aristocratic marital ambitions. Karinger had hoped that one of his children would marry Stefan, the son of his business associate Falkenberg, but the title-crazy women are not interested—they are busy being taken in by the gold-digging Marquis de los Puntos-Torrenos and his ally Countess Ramsatoff. Stefan has to pretend to be a Count even to get near to his beloved Marie. When Michael loses his money, and thus his wife, second daughter Fanni—who had won herself the Baron Bronningen fair and square—helps him to start over, and there is a happy ending when Marie finds that Stefan, if not an aristocrat, is at least a helpfully wealthy husband.

The score featured the regulation amount of waltz music—''Hand in Hand,'' ''Kein Vergnügen diesem gleicht''—whilst Blasel's best number from *Die Göttin der Vernunft* became ''Geh' zahl!, geh' zahl!'' for Girardi. The duo ''Liebe allein macht nicht satt'' and the song ''Das liebe Geld'' were the other principal numbers of the score.

Gerda Walde, Genie von Grössl, Luise Lichten, Ludwig Herold and Gustav Werner supported the star through 82 performances of *Reiche Mädchen* to 18 March, and Girardi threw in a few more performances on his next visit (14 October 1910), before the show went on to win itself a goodly number of performances around Germany, but *Reiche Mädchen,* for all its big guns and all its productions, never looked like becoming the enduring hit that the show built on the libretto—that libretto originally blamed for all of *Die Göttin der Vernunft*'s woes—did. Just as in the case of *Nell Gwynne,* it was the less-prized half of the collaboration which made up into the great hit, and not the one with the more shining name attached to it.

Germany: Theater am Gärtnerplatz, Munich 28 August 1910

REICHERT, Heinz [BLUMENREICH, Heinrich] (b Vienna, 27 December 1877; d Hollywood, Calif, 16 November 1940). Viennese librettist whose most far-reaching hits came with the pasticcii *Dreimäderlhaus* and *Walzer aus Wien.*

Heinz Reichert was educated in Vienna, but left his home city to become an actor in Berlin. He soon threw in acting and became for a while a journalist with the *Ullstein Verlag* before returning to Vienna in 1906 and turning his attention to writing for the stage. He had his first taste of success in his new career with a Berlin piece, Rudolf Nelson's Scottish musical comedy *Miss Dudelsack* (1909), which went on from Germany to productions in several other countries, and in the next decade he turned out a regular stream of musical-theatre scripts, at first in collaboration with Fritz Grünbaum and subsequently with two other choice partners—A M Willner and Victor Léon—for various stages throughout Germany and Austria. He found regular success, particularly in Vienna, and it was there in 1916 that he scored the greatest triumph of his career with his text (w Willner) to the international hit of the era: *Das Dreimäderlhaus.*

Das Dreimäderlhaus's enormous success was, however, seconded by a number of others, lesser but nevertheless significant, on the Vienna and central European stages. *Drei arme Teufel* (1916) was played in Vienna a number of years after its original German production (Bürgertheater, 1923, 51 performances), *Die schöne Saskia* (1917) ran through 131 performances at the Carltheater, the *Dreimäderlhaus* follow-up *Hannerl* (1918) totted up a better run than most such musequels, and the adaptation from its Hungarian original of Lehár's *Wo die Lerche singt* (*A pacsirta*) scored a genuine hit at the Theater an der Wien. The Posse *Hol mich der Teufel* which ran up 159 nights at the Bürgertheater and *Der Herzog von Reichstadt* (1921) which totaled 183 performances in two seasons at the Carltheater, gave him two further successes.

During the same period, Reichert collaborated on the text for Puccini's venture into light opera with *La Ron-*

dine (1917), which was premiered in an Italian translation, but, unlike most writers, he had the rest of his most important successes in the final part of his career.

In 1922 he collaborated on the making of Pierre Louÿs's *La Femme et le pantin* into the Spanish tale of *Frasquita* for Lehár, then worked on the confection of the Russian lost-love story of *Der Zarewitsch* from Gabryela Zapolska's piece of the same name, and, finally, on the texts for Leo Fall's posthumously completed and staged *Rosen aus Florida* and for the extremely successful Johann Strauss pasticcio *Walzer aus Wien,* the starting point for all the *Great Waltz*–style Strauss biomusicals of subsequent stage and screen.

With the rise of Hitler, Reichert left Europe and in 1938 settled in America, ending his days soon after, in Hollywood.

Reichert was for some years a director of the Austrian performing rights society.

1908 **Madame Flirt** (Anselm Götzl/w Fritz Grünbaum) Neues Operetten-Theater, Hamburg 25 December

1909 **Das Himmelbett** (Fritz Lehner/w Franz Wagner) Jantschtheater 27 March

1909 **Miss Dudelsack** (Rudolf Nelson/w Grünbaum) Neues Schauspielhaus, Berlin 3 August

1910 **Der ledige Gatte** (Gustav Wanda/w Grünbaum) Residenz-Theater, Dresden 28 October

1910 **Die teuerste Frau von Paris** (Leo Schottländer/w Grünbaum) Bellevue-Theater, Stettin 13 November

1910 **Don Quichotte** (Richard Heuberger/w Grünbaum) 1 act Hölle 1 December

1912 **Der Frechling** (Carl Weinberger/w Grünbaum) Wiener Bürgertheater 21 December

1913 **Die Prinzenjagd** (Ludwig Friedmann/w Grünbaum) Residenztheater, Dresden 4 April

1915 **Man steigt nach!** (Oscar Straus/w Victor Léon) Carltheater 2 May

1915 **Papa wider Willen** (Ernst Pfau/Wagner) Stadttheater, Zürich 2 December

1916 **Das Dreimäderlhaus** (Franz Schubert arr Heinrich Berté/w A M Willner) Raimundtheater 15 January

1916 **Drei arme Teufel** (Weinberger/w Rudolf Österreicher) Theater am Gärtnerplatz, Munich 11 March

1917 **La Rondine** (Giacomo Puccini/w Willner ad G Adami) Monte Carlo 27 March

1917 **Wiener Kinder** (Josef Schrammel arr Oskar Stalla/w Léon) Johann Strauss-Theater 16 May

1917 **Die schöne Saskia** (Oskar Nedbal/w A M Willner) Carltheater 16 November

1918 **Hannerl** (Franz Schubert arr Karl Lafite/w Willner) Raimundtheater 8 February

1918 **Wo die Lerche singt** (*A pacsirta*) German version w Willner (Theater an der Wien)

1918 **Eine einzige Rettung** (Gustav Benedict/w Grünbaum) Bellevue-Theater, Stettin 30 July

1920 **Hol mich der Teufel** (Leopold Reichwein/w Léon) Bürgertheater 29 October

1921 **Der Herzog von Reichstadt** (Peter Stojanovits/w Léon) Carltheater 11 February

1922 **Frasquita** (Lehár/w Willner) Theater an der Wien 12 May

1923 **Glück bei Frauen** (Bruno Granichstaedten/w Léon) Carltheater 4 December

1925 **Donna Gloria** (Nedbal/w Léon) Carltheater 30 December

1927 **Der Zarewitsch** (Lehár/w Béla Jenbach) Deutsches Künstlertheater, Berlin 21 February

1928 **Ade, du liebes Elternhaus** (Oskar Jascha/w Willner) Volksoper 5 January

1929 **Rosen aus Florida** (Fall arr E W Korngold/w Willner) Theater an der Wien 22 February

1930 **Walzer aus Wien** (Johann Strauss arr Julius Bittner, [Korngold]/w Willner, Ernst Marischka) Wiener Stadttheater 30 October

1933 **Ein Liebestraum** (Károly Komjáti/Ferenc Martos, László Szilágyi ad) Theater an der Wien 27 October

LA REINE JOYEUSE Opérette in 3 acts by André Barde. Music by Charles Cuvillier. Théâtre des Variétés, Marseille, 31 December 1912; L'Olympia, Paris, 6 February 1913 (as *La Reine s'amuse*); revised version Théâtre Apollo, Paris, November 1918.

The first version of the opérette which made its name as *La Reine joyeuse* was initially produced by Charles Montcharmont at Marseille in 1912, under the title *La Reine s'amuse,* with Angèle Gril featured in its title role. It won a considerable success on the Mediterranean coast, and Montcharmont brought it to his Théâtre des Célestins at Lyon (20 January 1913) before launching it on Paris the following month. There, with Mlle Gril sharing the limelight with revue artist Régine Flory, comedian Polin, Mme Martens, Dorville and Morton, it was housed in the Olympia music hall and given a production by glamor-revue specialist Jacques-Charles which used such revusical staging tricks as the passerelle over the front stalls and entrances through the auditorium. Even under these odd (for a reasonably book-based show) conditions it still confirmed its provincial promise. *La Reine s'amuse* then returned to the touring circuits where (without a passerelle) it passed the war, but its career was far from finished. In November 1918 it was reproduced in Paris in a revised version, under its new *joyeuse* title, not at a music hall but at the Théâtre Apollo, the Parisian home of the *Veuve joyeuse.* Jane Marnac starred alongside Albert Brasseur, Aimé Simon-Girard and Beauval, and this time, amongst the celebrations of the armistice, the show was more thoroughly noticed.

Barde's lively Ruritanian libretto was set in the Kingdom of Panoplie where the aging King (Sulbac/Polin), realizing that his young wife (Mlle Gril) is ripe for a love affair, orders his nephew Boléslas (Armand Franck/Max Capoul) to fill the bill . . . up to a point. Boléslas ''carries off'' the Queen to Paris—chaperoned by the Countess Katisch (Lucy Blémont/Mme Martens) and followed incognito by the king and his court—and after the young pair have danced through the Cabaret du Perroquet and the Quat'z'Arts Ball, got involved with the soubret pair (Mary-Hett, Fabert/Régine Flory, Dorville) and gone as far as the first horrifyingly revelatory kiss, the King decides magnanimously that perhaps it is time for him to head for the divorce court and a consolatory Parisienne.

Cuvillier's score mixed the comical and the romantic in classic doses. The King worried about his people's habit of dethroning their monarchs with a ''Ping, Pan, Vlan!'' and Katisch pointedly wondered when the Queen was going to get a ''Coquerico!'' out of her royal husband, and recommended her mother's recipe of a pretty aide de camp as a remedy for frustration (''Voilà ce que faisait ta mère''), but the hit of the evening came when the heroine moved into waltz rhythm with the aroused ''Ah! la troublante volupté.'' As in so many cases before and after, this waltz was not in the original show, but made up part of Cuvillier's revisions: it proved a revision well done and gave him the biggest single song hit of the French part of his career.

At the height of Cuvillier's popularity in Britain, following the enormous success there of *The Lilac Domino,* London's Grossmith and Laurillard picked up *La Reine joyeuse / s'amuse* and, reangling its title and text once again as *The Naughty Princess* (for British consumption, the heroine was no longer a married woman, which made it all right to be naughty), produced it at the Adelphi Theatre in a version by J Hastings Turner and Adrian Ross. Played by star comedian W H Berry (Michel), Grossmith (who cast himself as the hero, Ladislas), Lily St John (Sophia) and Amy Augarde (Kittisch), with young Yvonne Arnaud as soubrette, and featuring a front line including Heather Thatcher, Elsie Randolph and Sylvia Leslie in the bit part created by the young Alice Delysia, it ran for seven and a half months. *The Naughty Princess* was subsequently produced in Australia, with Gladys Moncrieff starring alongside Jack Cannot (King), George Gee (another comical Ladislas), Ethel Morrison (Kittisch), Hugh Steyne and Gracie Lavers through six weeks in Melbourne. However, before its Sydney season it was again rearranged. The lighter-voiced Kitty Reidy replaced Moncrieff as the Princess and certified operettic baritone Howett Worster took over from comic Gee as Ladislas in a lineup much more like that of the French original as the piece duly ran through its six weeks.

La Reine s'amuse was revived at the Théâtre Marigny under the management of Léon Volterra in 1929 with a cast headed by Mlle L Welcome (Sophia), Charles Prince (Michel), Louis Arnoult (Boléslas) and with former Cuvillier prima donna Anna Tariol-Baugé moving into duenna roles as Katisch.

UK: Adelphi Theatre *The Naughty Princess* 7 October 1920; Australia: Her Majesty's Theatre, Melbourne *The Naughty Princess* 29 July 1922

REINHARDT, Heinrich (b Pressburg, 13 April 1865; d Vienna, 31 January 1922). The composer of sizeable hits on both sides of the Atlantic without actually making himself a rememberable name.

Reinhardt studied music in Pressburg and at the Gesellschaft der Musikfreunde in Vienna and his earliest compositions, in the field of piano and vocal music, were written whilst he ran a parallel career as a musical journalist. His first attempts at theatre work, in collaboration with author Hans Koppel, were in opera (*Die Göldner*) and in ballet-pantomime (*Künst und Co*), but in 1901 he produced the score to Landesberg and Stein's light-hearted and happily folksy Operette *Das süsse Mädel,* a pretty, dancing piece of uncomplicated musical writing in a style far from that of the Suppé, Millöcker and Strauss Operetten of the declining (or declined) ''golden era'' of Viennese musical theatre. *Das süsse Mädel* won a very considerable success at Vienna's Carltheater and throughout Europe and confirmed its composer in a career in the light musical theatre.

The success of *Das süsse Mädel* was followed by another piece in the same genre, *Der Generalkonsul* (1904), and in 1909 by his most widely played overseas success, the pretty, spa-town tale of *Die Sprudelfee.* As played in a 1910 American version written by the Smith brothers and titled *The Spring Maid, Die Sprudelfee* made a great hit on Broadway and around America, and although its London life was considerably shorter, Reinhardt was brought brightly to the attention of the English-speaking world. Broadway welcomed a second Reinhardt piece, under the title *The Purple Road,* in 1913, in which the original score for the composer's shapely *Napoléon und die Frauen* had been dotted with extra numbers by the unexceptional William Frederick Peters, and London's Tivoli music hall staged what it called a ''leap-year comedy Operette in one act,'' *The Daring of Diane* (*Die süssen Grisetten,* ad Arthur Anderson, 22 January 1912), in the period during which it was fashionable to feature Viennese operettas on variety bills. *The Daring of Diane,* in fact, went further afield than any other Reinhardt work, for it was played by Hilda Vining in Australia (Her Majesty's Theatre, Melbourne 12 July 1913) as part of an Adeline Genée ''Imperial Russian Ballet'' program.

The 1913 *Prinzess Gretl* proved more popular than any of these nevertheless well-received works in Germany and also won a French-language production in Belgium (*Princesse Marguerite* Alhambra, Brussels 15 October 1913), whilst Hungary, which had welcomed both *Das süsse Mädel* (*As édes lányka*) and *Der Generalkonsul* (*A főkonsul,* Király Színház), as well as *Prinzess Gretl* (*Diákhercegnő,* Fővárosi Nyári Színház), showed its preference for the 1915 *Die erste Frau* (*Az első feleség,* Budapesti Színház 1917).

Most of Reinhardt's Operetten earned a pleasing reception in Vienna—*Prinzess Gretl* (156 performances) and *Die erste Frau* (101 performances) being the most long-running after *Das süsse Mädel*—and a representation elsewhere in Europe, but the coming of *Die lustige Witwe* and the brightest of the early Lehár, Eysler, Fall and Oscar Straus pieces rather submerged the composer's agreeable and always light-handed work, and *Das süsse Mädel,* which had not had to put up with such tough concurrence, remained Reinhardt's single most successful work in his home country and in the rest of central Europe.

1895 **Die Minnekönigin** (Hans Koppel) 1 act

1901 **Das süsse Mädel** (Alexander Landesberg, Leo Stein) Carltheater 25 October

1902 **Der liebe Schatz** (Landesberg, Stein) Carltheater 30 October

1904 **Der Generalkonsul** (Landesberg, Stein) Theater an der Wien 29 January

1906 **Krieg im Frieden** (Julius Wilhelm) Carltheater 24 January

1907 **Die süssen Grisetten** (Wilhelm) 1 act Hölle 1 December

1908 **Ein Mädchen für Alles** (Heinrich von Waldberg, A M Willner) Theater am Gärtnerplatz, Munich 8 February

1909 **Die Sprudelfee** (Willner, Wilhelm) Raimundtheater 23 January

1909 **Die siamesischen Zwillinge** (Louis Windhopp, Ernst Ress) 1 act Hölle 16 March

1910 **Studentenhochzeit** (Reinhardt) 1 act Kleines Schauspielhaus 1 October

1910 **Miss Exzentrik** (Alexander Engel, Armin Friedmann) 1 act Apollotheater 31 October

1912 **Napoléon und die Frauen** (Reinhardt) Volksoper 1 May

1913 **Prinzess Gretl** (Willner, Robert Bodanzky) Theater an der Wien 31 January

1915 **Die erste Frau** (Willner, Rudolf Österreicher) Carltheater 22 October

1916 **Der Gast des Königs** (Friedmann) Volksoper 9 January

1922 **Der Glückstrompeter** (Gustav Beer, Friedmann) Komödienhaus 7 December

1928 **Grisettenliebe** (Wilhelm) Rolandbühne 23 March

REINKING, Ann (b Seattle, Washington, 10 November 1949). Impressively stylish dancing actress with a career of 30 years on the Broadway stage.

Dancer Ann Reinking began her performing career in the chorus of a touring *Fiddler on the Roof,* and appeared in the line at the Radio City Music Hall before making her first appearance in a Broadway musical as a Kit-Kat Girl in the original production of *Cabaret* (1969). She subsequently appeared in the chorus of *Coco* (1969), of the one-night flop *Wild and Wonderful* (1971) and of *Pippin,* before getting thoroughly noticed in a supporting part in the Andrews Sisters musical *Over Here* (1974, Maggie). She moved to the top lines of the bill as a glamorous Joan of Arc to the *Goodtime Charley* (1975) of Joel Grey, and was thereafter seen succeeding to major roles in *A Chorus Line* (1975, Cassie) and *Chicago* (1975, Roxie Hart). She was largely featured in the long-running Bob Fosse dance revue *Dancin'* (1978), took the title role in the 1986 revival of *Sweet Charity* and in 1991 top-billed in tanden with Tommy Tune in a touring revival of *Bye Bye Birdie* which she subsequently choreographed for television (1995).

In 1996 she appeared as Roxie Hart in the acclaimed revival of *Chicago,* a production which she rechoreographed in the style of Fosse, both for Broadway and for subsequent international productions. She subsequently co-choreographed the revusical compilation of her mentor's works, *Fosse* (1999).

She was seen on musical film as Grace in *Annie* (1982) and both as a character and a performer in the Fosse biopic *All That Jazz* (1979, Kate Jagger).

RENT Musical in 2 acts by Jonathan Larson. New York Theater Workshop, New York, 26 January 1996; Nederlander Theater, 29 April 1996.

Following the production of 1990s musicals based on the libretti of *Madama Butterfly* and *Tosca,* the fashion for taking stories formerly deemed of the weight for opera seria as the bases for works of the lighter musical stage continued with the newest musical-theatre version of Murger's *La Vie de Bohème. Rent,* however, treated the tale decidedly differently from the most successful *Bohème* remake of earlier times, Ferrier and Hirschmann's fairly faithful 1905 *La Petite Bohème* (which had willingly announced its ''petite'' treatment of the subject in its title), setting it in the New York East Village of the 1990s, contemporizing and coarsening both the original's characters and such parallel events from their story as were employed, and using them as the vehicles for as much and many ''up-to-date'' variations on sex, drug and drop-out themes and for as many striving-to-slightly-shock moments as possible, so that, in fact, the show's principal ancestor seemed to be much less *La Vie de Bohème* and much more that last youth-orientated sex-drugs-and-naughty-words hit, the end-of-the-1960s *Hair.*

Unlike *Hair,* however, *Rent* (thanks to its bit of *Bohème* backbone) sported a reasonably connected if sometimes splayed story line. Murger's Mimi and Rodolphe

Plate 324. **Rent.** *Singalong time.*

are still there, though this Mimi is a 19-year-old drug addict and prostitute with AIDS, and her Rodolphe (here, less romantically, called Roger), who is also dying of the disease, is a dead-ended blocked musician. They come together in a version of the traditional candle scene, she duly leaves him for the piece's representative of frowned-upon-by-the-author working-world prosperity, and returns in time for a final curtain death. In parallel (since this is the 1990s, and we know it is because answerphones are called ''voice mail''), Mark (a sort-of filmmaker, and the equivalent of Murger's Marcel) loses his ''Musetta'' (here Maureen) to a Joanne, and just to keep things equisexual, the other two ''bohemians,'' once Schaunard and Colline and now a street musican called Angel and Tom Collins, are depicted as an AIDS-struck gay couple, one of whom preempts Mimi's death by succumbing during the second act. As in *Hair,* the adults of the show, or anyone with a sense of responsibility, a stable life or a position of authority, is represented as a fool or worse, and the idea of getting a real job in the real world is suggested to be copping out (instead of conventional morality's the other way round). The landlord in the affair, who is due the titular rent (the heroes allegedly don't have the money to pay him, but turn up with costly drugs, champagne, film for a movie camera, etc) is blackened unmitigatedly. However, none of the ''bohemians'' except the lovingly drawn Angel and Collins come out as anything like likeable either, even though the audience's sympathy is evidently supposed to be on their side.

The parallels with *Hair* were to be heard throughout (''The Bed'' scene was one item ''reproduced'') both in the text, with its repeated ''carpe diem'' motto, and also in the show's music, which was written in the modern pop-music style (though not disdaining the holiday-camp sing-along number for its final curtain) and delivered with a degree of amplification painful to many of the over-15s. However *Rent*'s most cheerful parallel with its predecessor came not in its substance but in its singular success. Its often ingenuous youthfulness, its use of the of-the-moment preoccupations of the teenaged as its raison d'être, and its simple, loud songs proved to be enormously attractive to precisely the same audience which had made such a huge hit of *Hair*—the young, the striving to stay young and the longing-to-be-shocked by the young—and the piece went swiftly from a New York Theater Workshop production off-off-Broadway (12 performances), and 56 performances (from 13 February 1996) off-Broadway, to a berth at Broadway's Nederlander Theater. The original cast including Adam Pascal (Roger), Anthony Rapp (Mark), Jesse L Martin (Collins),

Wilson Jermaine Heredia (Angel), Daphne Rubin-Véga (Mimi) and Idina Menzel (Maureen) repeated their roles, and *Rent* settled in for what looks at the time of writing like being a *Hair*-sized success.

Already, the show has outdone its long-lived ancestor in one way. Thanks to the change in attitudes in the quarter of a century or so between the production of the two shows (and also, it has to be admitted, to the wholesale shrinkage in competition), *Rent* picked up a whole hatful of the awards *Hair* had been denied. In fact, where the earlier award-givers had been chary the 1996 ones were extravagantly munificent. The show's text was given a Pulitzer Prize above all the not inconsiderable plays of the season. Sadly, the young author of what looked like becoming one of the most lucrative new shows to originate in New York for years did not get to share in the accolades, success and money won by his musical. Larson died of an aneurism between the dress rehearsal and the Workshop's opening night.

While the acclamation was still warm, *Rent* productions popped up in all parts of the world. Toronto welcomed the first, in November 1997, followed by a British mounting in which Rapp, Pascal, Heredia and Martin from the original cast repeated their roles, another in Australia, and a first foreign-language version in Germany (ad Heinz Rudolf Kunze) where John Partridge (Roger), Alex Melcher (Mark), Peti van der Velde (Mimi) and Irina Alex (Maureen) played 10 weeks in Düsseldorf before setting out on tour. However the well-stoked euphoria built up around the piece died somewhat when the London mounting foundered and closed after less than 18 months' run, and *Rent* suddenly started to look altogether less likely to achieve the status of a *Hair.*

The title *Rent,* without its willful double entendre, was notably used in 1881 for M A Manning's drama on the Irish land question.

UK: Shaftesbury Theatre 12 May 1998; Australia: Theatre Royal, Sydney 4 November 1998; Germany: Capitol Theater, Düsseldorf 25 February 1999, Freien Volksbühne, Berlin 3 September 1999

Recordings: original cast (Dreamworks), German cast (Sony), Japanese cast (ESCB), Korean cast (Synnara)

RÉNYI, Aladár (b Kolozsvár, 9 September 1885; d in a concentration camp, 1944).

Rényi studied at the Budapest Zeneakadémia and had his first operett produced at the Király Színház at the age of 26. *A kis gróf* had a great success and it went on to be produced the following year at the Carltheater in Vienna under the title *Susi,* returning to the Király Színház in its German version during the Carltheater company's visit to Budapest in 1913. *Susi* was successfully played in Germany and staged on Broadway (Casino Theater, 1914) before Rényi's second work, *Tiszavirág,* was produced in Budapest. He wrote two further operetts, as well as chamber music, songs and piano music, but without again finding the success of his first stage work.

1911 **A kis gróf** (Ferenc Martos) Király Színház 9 September

1915 **Tiszavirág** (István Bródy, László Vajda) Király Színház 27 March

1917 **Vandergold kisasszony** (Sándor Hevesi, Zsolt Harsányi) Városi Színház 24 October

1926 **Kitty és Kató** (Martos) Király Színház 30 April

RETURN TO THE FORBIDDEN PLANET Musical in 2 acts by Bob Carlton. Cambridge Theatre, London, 18 September 1989.

A product of the tiny but adventurous Bubble Theatre (the bubble came from the fact that they perform in a bubble-tent), *Return to the Forbidden Planet* was a burlesque for the TV age. The story burlesqued was that of Shakespeare's *The Tempest,* which was reset in a *Star Trek* kind of situation with a hero, Captain Tempest (John Ashby), who is a spaceship captain, and with Prospero (Christian Roberts), Miranda (Alison Harding) and Ariel (Kraig Thornber) the inhabitants of a lost planet called D'Illyria.

The bill, however, sported plenty of other well-known names alongside Shakespeare's. The score for the show was made up of versions of such pop favorites of earlier years as Jerry Lee Lewis's chart-topping ''Great Balls of Fire'' (Hammer/Blackwell), Marty Wilde's ''A Teenager in Love'' (Pomus/Shuman), ''Telstar'' (Joe Meek) and The Animals' ''We've Gotta Get Out of This Place'' (Mann/Weill), the space-age special effects were by Gerry Anderson of *Thunderbirds* fame, and there was an ''appearance'' by telly-skywatcher Patrick Moore.

Taken to the West End, *Return to the Forbidden Planet* surprised by putting up a run of over three years (1,516 performances) before going on to be seen in America, Australia and Europe. In America, it played off-Broadway for 245 performances whilst in Germany, where it was rechristened advisedly *Shakespeare and Rock'n'Roll,* its original mounting provoked a number of further productions.

Australia: Theatre Royal, Sydney 27 June 1991; USA: Variety Arts Theatre 13 October 1991; Germany: Musical Theater, Berlin *Shakespeare and Rock'n'Roll* 16 September 1993

Recordings: original cast (Virgin), Australian cast (Festival), German cast (Lighthouse)

REVILL, Clive [Selsby] (b Wellington, New Zealand, 18 April 1930).

Revill's early career was in the non-musical theatre, including a period at Britain's Ipswich Repertory Theatre and another at the Shakespeare Memorial Theatre, Stratford-on-Avon. His first musical appearances were in children's pieces—Pearson in *Listen to the Wind* (1955) and Ratty in Fraser-Simson's *Toad of Toad Hall*—and his first great musical-theatre success his portrayal of the bar-owner/narrator Bob le Hotu in the English and American productions of *Irma la Douce* (1957–61). He appeared with the opera company at Sadler's Wells Theatre as a memorable Ko-Ko in their production of *The Mikado* (1962) and returned to Broadway to take the role of Fagin in the American production of *Oliver!* (1963). He subsequently starred as Sheridan Whiteside in *Sherry!*, the unsuccessful musical version of *The Man Who Came to Dinner* (1967), but has devoted himself since to the non-musical theatre and to film.

He appeared, however, on television in 1977 in a Mitch Leigh musical *Once Upon a Brothers Grimm* (CBS) and on video in 1982 as John Wellington Wells in *The Sorcerer.*

REVOIL, Fanély (b Marseille, 25 September 1910).

A charming ingenue, with an attractive and accurate soprano voice, Mlle Revoil was one of the principal stars of the French opérette theatre of the 1930s.

She had her earliest experience at Nimes, at Mulhouse (where in 1930 she played Lisa in the French premiere of *Comtesse Maritza*) and at the Théâtre du Havre where, the following year, she created the the title role of the French version of Lehár's *Frasquita.* She was hired by Maurice Lehmann for the Théâtre de la Porte-Saint-Martin in 1933, made her Paris debut as Lecocq's *Petit Duc* and, a few months later, stepped in as a late replacement for the star of the Paris premiere of *La Dubarry.* She was seen over the next three seasons as the Countess in *Valses de Vienne,* la Guimard in Pierné's *Fragonard,* in *Véronique* (Hélène), *Les Mousquetaires au couvent* (Louise), *Le Domino noir, Chanson d'amour* (Carlina), *Mam'zelle Nitouche* (Denise), *La Mascotte, Gillette de Narbonne* (Gillette), *Le Petit Faust* (Méphisto), *La Fille de Madame Angot* (in each of the two lead roles), *Rêve de valse, La Fille du tambour-major* (Stella), and *Les Dragons de Villars* (Rose Friquet), and as Sonia in a made-over version of *Der Zarevitsch* played in Paris as *Rêve d'un soir.*

Mlle Revoil appeared alongside Mistinguett in Yvain's *Un coup de veine* (1935) and, again under Lehmann's direction, at the Théâtre du Châtelet in *Au soleil du Mexique* (1935, Juanita). She was seen in *La Belle Traversée* at the Alhambra (1936), and then moved to the Opéra-Comique where she played in, amongst others, *Le Testament de Tante Caroline* and *La Chambre bleu,* took the role of Lazuli when Chabrier's *L'Étoile* was admitted to the Salle Favart, and appeared as Hahn's *Ciboulette* and as la Guimard in *Fragonard.*

After the Second World War she again appeared on the commercial stage, playing *Rose-Marie* at the Châtelet (1945), and creating the title roles of a 1946 opérette based on the life of the actress *Virginie Déjazet* and of a Châtelet spectacular on *Madame Sans-Gêne* (1948). Thereafter she appeared largely in concert and on radio before turning to teaching, ultimately spending more than a decade at the head of the opérette class of the Paris Conservatoire.

LA REVOLTOSA Zarzuela in 1 act by Carlos Fernández Shaw and José Lopez Silva. Music by Ruperto Chapí y Llorente. Teatro Apolo, Madrid, 25 November 1897.

The most successful of Chapí's "genero chico" zarzuelas, *La Revoltosa* was a typically colorful little picture of everyday Madrid and its characters, the chief of whom was the unruly lass of the title, Maria-Pépa (Isabel Brú). Maria-Pépa puts herself around amongst the men in her apartment block, and even the policeman Candelas (José Mesejo) falls for her when he should be keeping her from causing trouble. The women of the block get their revenge on festival night when, taking a leaf out of the book of the ladies of *Les Dominos roses,* they fake invitations to each of their men to meet Maria-Pépa after the dancing. When all the men end up knocking at her door at midnight, the women spring their trap and the frightened girl takes refuge in the arms of the genuine Felipe (Emilio Mesejo), her lesson learned.

The music accompanying the tale was spread amongst both principal and subsidiary characters and featured a seguidilla which proved the evening's favorite musical moment.

La Revoltosa has been several times filmed for cinema and television.

Films: Florian Rey (1925), Jose Diaz Morales 1949 and 1963, TVE 1968

Recordings: complete (Alhambra/Columbia, Montilla/Zafiro, EMI, Hispavox, Edigsa)

REYNOLDS, Dorothy [Marjorie] (b Birmingham, 26 January 1913; d London, 7 April 1977).

Miss Reynolds joined the Bristol Old Vic company as an actress in 1952 and during her engagement there collaborated with another company member, Julian Slade, in writing revue and small-scale musical comedy for their colleagues. Their first efforts, the Christmas revue *Christmas in King Street* (the Bristol Theatre Royal is situated in King Street) and *The Merry Gentleman* (ie, Santa Claus), were genuine local successes, and their third seasonal piece, the ingenuous, revusical *Salad Days,* became a theatrical phenomenon when it transferred to London's Vaudeville Theatre for a record-breaking run, with Miss Reynolds herself appearing in one of the most comical of the show's revusically composite roles and introducing the mock-cabaret song ''Sand in My Eyes.''

She wrote four further works with Slade, appearing in three—*Free as Air* (1957, Miss Catamole), *Hooray for Daisy* (1959, Georgina Cosens) and *Wildest Dreams* (1960, Harriet Gray)—but not in the revised *Christmas in King Street,* which played London as *Follow That Girl* (1960). In 1962 she played the role of Elinor Spencer-Bollard in the London version of Noël Coward's *Sail Away* before returning to exclusively straight theatre.

1953 **The Merry Gentleman** (Julian Slade) Theatre Royal, Bristol 24 December

1954 **Salad Days** (Slade) Vaudeville Theatre 5 August

1957 **Free as Air** (Slade) Savoy Theatre 6 June

1959 **Hooray for Daisy** (Slade) Theatre Royal, Bristol 23 December; Lyric Theatre, Hammersmith 20 December 1960

1960 **Follow that Girl** (Slade) Vaudeville Theatre 17 March

1960 **Wildest Dreams** (Slade) Everyman Theatre, Cheltenham 20 September; Vaudeville Theatre 3 August 1961

RICE, E[dward] E[verett] (b Brighton, Mass, 21 December 1847; d New York, 16 November 1924). Busy American producer-songwriter of the 19th century whose troupes covered the country with the kind of fare which pulled 'em in in the boondocks, yet who also manufactured several large Broadway hits.

Originally an actor, then an advertising printer and copywriter in Boston, the 23-year-old Rice made his first profitable connection with the theatre when he wed Clara Rich, daughter of Isaac B Rich, one of Boston's principal theatre managers. Two years later, whilst earning his daily bread working in the Cunard Company office in Boston, he took his first step towards theatrical success in another way when—in spite of having a musical background consisting of one year's piano lessons at the age of eight—he combined with the young librettist Cheever Goodwin to compose the songs for an extravagant burlesque of Longfellow's *Evangeline,* a piece modeled on the burlesques which had been so successfully purveyed around America at the turn of the 1870s by Lydia Thompson and her company. Previewed musically in Boston, and (according to Rice) initially produced in his home town of Cambridge, Mass, *Evangeline* showed sufficient potential to win a subsidized-by-the-authors production at New York's Niblo's Gardens. It was a quick failure, but Rice did not give up. He revised and then re-produced the piece himself in Boston the following season, and this time it took off, beginning a career that would make it into one of the most popular and successful American burlesques of all time.

Rice followed up *Evangeline* with a *Le Petit Corsair* (an adaptation of Brough's *Conrad and Medora*) and a *Hiawatha* burlesque, and before long found himself being acclaimed as the inventor of nice, clean (which it was prudishly supposed that Lydia's were not), American (which she and hers certainly were not) extravaganza. ''He has revolutionized a department of the stage,'' gushed one contemporary journal exaggeratedly, forgetting that John Brougham and others had produced extremely effective ''American'' burlesque years previously.

Rice continued in the years that followed to compose (with the aid of a writer-down and an orchestrator) and to produce (with the financial backing of Isaac Rich) loose-limbed extravaganza entertainments for the popular touring circuits. He turned out text (w George Fawcett Rowe), lyrics and music for the easy-going *Pop* (''For Goodness' Sake Don't Say I Told You''), put his name to a version of Rowe and John Sheridan's *Fun on the Bristol*—into which he had bought hard on the heels of its Rhode Island opening in 1879—for his Rice's Travestie Company and, like everyone else, jumped on the *HMS Pinafore* bandwagon and put out a company which played the Lyceum in 1879. In Rice's version Gilbert's sophisticated burlesque became an unsophisticated one with George Fortescue playing Buttercup in travesty and Lizzie Webster doing similarly as Ralph in good old-fashioned burlesque style.

In 1879 Rice founded a group which he called Rice's Surprise Party, taking on board a number of players from Lydia Thompson's latest burlesque company, and he toured this ''Party'' successfully for many years playing a repertoire of burlesques, extravaganza and the kind of low-comedy-with-variety-items shows which became known as ''farce comedy.'' Amongst the early and often long-lived successes played by the troupe were *The Babes in the Wood, Horrors, or The Maharajah of Zogobad* (aka *Prince Achmet*), *Hiawatha, Robinson Crusoe, Revels* and *Pop*—into several of which he had more or less authorial input.

In 1880, alongside his multifarious touring activities, Rice took on New York's Fifth Avenue Theater (w Jacob Nunnemacher) to produce a version of Genée's Operette *Der Seekadett.* It flopped in one week, but he then moved decidedly upmarket and joined with Richard D'Oyly Carte to produce the American edition of Solomon's *Billee Taylor* (1881) under the ''Rice-Goodwin Lyric Company'' banner. He subsequently toured the same company in *Cinderella at School* (1881), took ''Rice's Bijou Opera Company'' on the road with the New York Bijou's English drawing-room operetta repertoire of *Charity Begins at Home, Ages Ago* and *The Spectre Knight* (1880–81), and he even ventured the production of a trio of original American comic operas, Calixta Lavelle's *The Widow* (St Louis's Pickwick Theater 16 July

1881), *The Lightkeeper's Daughter* (Chas D Blake, Geo Vickers) mounted at Boston's Casino in June 1882 and Benjamin Woolf's *Pounce & Co* (Bijou Theater, Boston 19 April 1883 w Collier). Around this time, he was declared bankrupt, owing large amounts of wages to Willie Edouin and Henry Dixey, royalties to D'Oyly Carte, and with everything he owned mortgaged.

Although he ventured with further touring Carte productions (*Billee Taylor, Patience, Iolanthe*) and produced Solomon's *Polly* (1885 w J C Scanlan) on Broadway, Rice thereafter mainly stuck to the area he knew best—extravaganza and farce comedy—and his companies were regular visitors to towns and cities, large and small, across America. He even ventured at times to Britain (indifferently with *Adonis,* and more successfully with *Fun on the Bristol*) and—disastrously—to Australia (1891, *Evangeline, The Corsair*).

Alongside repeated reruns of *Evangeline,* he produced, directed and/or composed music for a remake of his *The Corsair* burlesque, the farce comedies *A Bottle of Ink* and *Circus in Town,* the extravaganzas *1492, The Seven Ages* and *Excelsior Jr,* and a badly battered version of Lecocq's *Fleur de thé* staged burlesque-fashion and with some success as *The Pearl of Pekin.* He had his greatest successes as a producer, however, with Willie Gill's burlesque extravaganza *Adonis* (1884)—a vehicle for the Surprise Party's Henry Dixey and one of the longest-running Broadway shows of its era (603 performances)—and with a virtual variety-show version of the British burlesque *Little Christopher Columbus* (1894).

With the displacing of burlesque by English musical comedy, Rice shifted with the fashion and imported several pieces of the kind from Britain, having sizeable successes with *The Girl from Paris* (1896, *The Gay Parisienne*) and *The French Maid* (1897), less with *Monte Carlo* (1898) and very little with *The Ballet Girl* (1897). Into several of these he interpolated additional or replacement songs of his own writing, and he continued throughout his producing career to pen for touring stars and companies the kind of material in which he had specialized in his earlier days (*Captain Kidd USN* for Ernest Hogan, etc). Some of his numbers even turned up in such unlikely places as Seymour Hicks's London musical comedy *The Yashmak* or Alice Atherton's little show *Blackberries* (''Bees Among the Clover'').

After *The French Maid,* however, success became harder to find. He produced the little negro musical *Clorindy, or The Origin of the Cakewalk* (1898) during a two-season stint running the Casino Theater roof garden (''Rice's Summer Nights''), winning a small summertime success, but a subsequent period as manager of the Madison Square's roof garden ended when his principals went broke (1899). He put together several vaudeville acts, including *The Singing Watermelon* for Alice Atherton (Pleasure Palace, May 1898), and several other ventures with un- or little-tried material. *The Show Girl* (aka *The Cap of Fortune,* 1902) and the disastrous *King Highball* (1902) were, like the imported *Mr Wix of Wickham* (1904), *When We Are Forty One* (1905) and *The Merry Shop Girls* (1905, ex- *Mr Wix*), all quick failures. *Lolita, or the Irish Cavalier* (1907), a musical comedy by Richard F Carroll and Fred Eustis, seems to have been his last attempt at a musical-theatre production. In the years that followed, with the kind of show in which he had most succeeded having now become almost a thing of the past, Rice's name slipped out of the chronicles. In 1911 he was sighted taking a 35-minute condensed *Cinderella* round the vaudeville circuits, and issuing promises to follow up with a condensed *Corsair, Fun on the Bristol* and a potted *Adonis* with Dixey's famous role played burleycue fashion by a girl. It seems he didn't. In 1913 he was to be found promoting himself at the head of the People's Moving Picture and Amusement Company (incorporated in Delaware) and announcing film versions of *Evangeline, Adonis, Excelsior, The Corsair, Hiawatha, Horrors, Revels* and even *Robinson Crusoe.* But soon there was silence.

1874 **Evangeline, the Belle of Acadia** (J Cheever Goodwin) Niblo's Gardens 27 July

1877 **Le Petit Corsair** (w John J Braham/William Brough ad Goodwin) Boston Museum 30 July

1878 **Hiawatha [and Minnehaha]** (Nathaniel Childs) Boston Museum 29 July; Standard Theater 21 February 1880

1882 **Pop, or The Fortunes of a Dramatic Author** (George Fawcett Rowe) Academy of Music, Baltimore 25 September; 14th Street Theater, New York 21 May 1883

1884 **Adonis** (William Gill) Hooley's Theater, Chicago 6 July; Bijou Theater, New York 4 September

1884 **A Bottle of Ink** (w others/Gill, George H Jessop) Bijou Theater, Boston 3 November; Comedy Theater, New York 6 January 1885

1887 **The Corsair** revised *Le Petit Corsair* (w John Braham) Bijou Theater 18 October

1889 **The Seven Ages** (w Braham/w Gill) Standard Theater 7 October

1890 **The World's Fair** (Paul Potter) Broad Street Theater, Philadelphia 9 September

1892 **1492** (Carl Pflüger/w R A Barnet) Globe Theater, Boston 16 May; Palmer's Theater, New York *1492 Up to Date or Very Near It* 15 May 1893

1895 **Excelsior Jr** (w A Baldwin Sloane, George Lowell Tracy/Barnet) Hammerstein's Olympia 29 November

1899 **Around New York in 80 Minutes** (w John Braham/Goodwin/James T Waldron, Edward Fales Coward, Richard Carle) Koster and Bial's Music Hall 6 November

1899 **Little Red Riding Hood** (w Fred Eustis/Harrison Ward/Charles F Dennee) Boston Museum 24 December; Casino Theater 8 January 1900

RICE, Tim[othy Miles Bindon] (Sir) (b Amersham, 10 November 1944). Innovative British lyricist of the rock-opera era whose short list of credits nevertheless produced some of the most appreciable shows of the 1970s and 1980s.

In the early 1970s, in collaboration with composer Andrew Lloyd Webber, lyricist Rice pioneered a breakaway from the long popular scenes-and-songs style of musical show which had, in the postwar years, rarely shaken off the classic operetta-without-ensembles layout represented most prominently and recently in the works of Rodgers and Hammerstein and their followers. Rice and Lloyd Webber returned to a cantata form, a sung-through text with no intervening dialogue, scarcely used in the musical theatre since Gilbert and Sullivan's *Trial by Jury,* for their first work, *Joseph and the Amazing Technicolor Dreamcoat* (1968–72). In this little piece, the composer's mixture of modern popular and classical elements was blended with Rice's individual and contemporary verse style, part speech-patterned, part lyrical and combining everyday language with occasional more fanciful flights and an enjoyable and youthful comic sense in a style that was new to the modern British stage. This combination was developed further in the pair's more serious *Jesus Christ Superstar* (1972), subtitled a rock opera, and in *Evita* (1978), two works which became internationally the most successful musical stage shows of the 1970s. By and large, other writers failed to encompass the style and method of these shows, which could have been expected to encourage a rich generation of sung-through, dramatic modern musical shows, but Rice, in a disappointingly rare return to the theatre, secured a further London success in the same mode with the thoroughly up-to-date *Chess* (1986) written in collaboration with Björn Ulvaeus and Benny Andersson, former members of the Swedish pop group Abba.

He subsequently adapted the French/Canadian teeny-musical *Starmania* for an English-language recording under the title *Tycoon,* and found a different kind of success when his song ''A Whole New World'' (w Alan Menken) in the Disney film *Aladdin* took the 1992 Academy Award. He picked up a second Oscar with a tacked-in tune in the film version of *Evita* (''You Must Love Me''), but the 1990s saw the outstanding theatre lyricist of the two earlier decades settle down to churning out songwords for the newest series of Disney cartoon musicals, both as played on the cinema screen and on stage, as the studio launched its bid for the world domination of spectacular musical stage.

A version of *Wuthering Heights* played by Cliff Richard as a concertish piece on the British tour circuits in 1996, to public enthusiasm and critical condemnation, and a 1997 cantata on the biblical story of *King David* with music by Disney partner Menken, performed as the opening attraction at the Disney organization's New Amsterdam Theater (15 May, 5 performances) were the nearest Rice came to producing a new musical for the world's stages in the last 15 years of the century before turning out a pop-musicked lasers-and-hydraulics version of Verdi's *Aida.* Hurriedly removed for revamping after its initial tryout, it ultimately made its Broadway bow under Disney management in the year 2000, to critical distaste but bulging houses.

1971 **Jesus Christ Superstar** (Andrew Lloyd Webber) Mark Hellinger Theater, New York 12 October

1972 **Joseph and the Amazing Technicolor Dreamcoat** (Lloyd Webber) Haymarket Ice Rink, Edinburgh 21 August; Young Vic Theatre, London 16 October

1973 **Jacob's Journey** (Lloyd Webber) 1 act Albery Theatre 17 February

1978 **Evita** (Lloyd Webber) Prince Edward Theatre 21 June

1983 **Blondel** (Stephen Oliver) Old Vic 9 November

1986 **Chess** (Bjørn Ulvaeus, Benny Andersson) Prince Edward Theatre 14 May

1993 **Beauty and the Beast** (Alan Menken/w Howard Ashman/ Linda Woolverton) Palace Theater 18 April

1996 **Heathcliff** (John Farrar) Birmingham 16 October; Labatt's Apollo Theatre 22 January 1997

1997 **The Lion King** (Elton John/Irene Mecchi/Robert Allers) New Amsterdam Theater 13 November

1998 **Elaborate Lives: The Legend of Aida** (John/Woolverton) Alliance Theater, Atlanta, Ga 8 October; revised version as *Aida* Palace Theater 23 March 2000

Autobiography: *Oh, What a Circus* (Hodder, London, 1999)

RICHEPIN, [François Denis] Tiarko (b Paris, 9 March 1884; d Kremlin Bicêtre, 12 October 1973).

The younger son of [Auguste] Jean Richepin, author and librettist (*Le Chemineau, Le Carilloneur,* the 1907 féerie *La Belle au bois dormant* w Henri Cain, and apparently of the source for Anna Held's Broadway show *Mamselle Napoléon*), Tiarko Richepin made his earliest theatre ventures in an eclectic variety of areas: incidental music for Paul Vérola's four-act dramatic poem *Nirvana* and for the five-act tragedy *Dalila* (1908); a little burlesque opérette with another son of a famous father, Sacha Guitry, for the tiny Théâtre Mévisto; a one-act Bohemian ballet *Rômi-Tchávé* for the opening program at the newly reconstructed Folies-Bergère (1909); incidental music for the verse play *Le Minaret* (1913) written by his elder brother, Jacques (the author of the successful play *Xantho et les courtisanes*); and, in 1914, a three-act ''conte lyrique'' *La Marchande d'allumettes,* written by Mme Edmond Rostand and produced by the Isola brothers at the Opéra-Comique.

Wounded during the First World War, he returned to the lyric stage in 1919, but there was to be no return to the Opéra-Comique. Several conventionally sized opérettes were failures and, in a career which included songwriting (''Il n'y a qu'un Paris,'' ''Si tu reviens,'' etc) and film music, he ultimately found his only success in the theatre with the scores or part-scores for a series of opérettes à grand spectacle of which *Venise,* originally composed with the Opéra-Comique in mind, and a collaboration with Henri Christiné on the Châtelet spectacular *Au temps des merveilleuses* proved the most successful.

1909 **Tell père, Tell fils** (Sacha Guitry) 1 act Théâtre Mévisto 17 April

1914 **La Marchande d'allumettes** (Rosemond Gérard) Opéra-Comique 25 February

1919 **Rapatipatoum** (Albert Willemetz) Théâtre Édouard VII 7 April

1927 **Venise** (Willemetz/André Mouëzy-Éon) Théâtre Marigny 25 June

1929 **Le Renard chez les poules** (Mouëzy-Éon, Alfred Machard) Théâtre Michel 31 January

1932 **La Tulipe noire** (Willemetz/Mouëzy-Éon) Théâtre de la Gaîté-Lyrique 19 March

1934 **Au temps des merveilleuses** (w Henri Christiné/ Willemetz, Mouëzy-Éon) Théâtre du Châtelet 25 December

1936 **Yana** (w Christiné/Willemetz, Mouëzy-Éon, Henri Wernert) Théâtre du Châtelet 24 December

1941 **L'Auberge qui chante** (Georges Hirsch, André de Badet) Théâtre de la Gaîté-Lyrique

RICHINGS, Caroline [REYNOLDSON, Mary Caroline] (b Richmond, Surrey, c1827; d Philadelphia, 14 January 1882).

The daughter of English playwright J P Reynoldson, Caroline was brought up in Philadelphia where she was adopted and trained for the stage by the successful actor Peter RICHINGS [Peter PUGET] (b Kensington, 19 May 1798; d Media, Pa 18 January 1871). She made her first appearance with the Seguin Opera Company as Marie in *La Fille du régiment* in 1852 (Walnut Street Theater 9 February), and went on to be seen later the same year on Broadway, alongside Richings, in James Gaspard Maeder's early American musical *The Peri, or The Enchanted Fountain* (Fluvia) and in Balfe's *The Enchantress.* For the remainder of her career, Caroline Richings traveled America, at first in co-starring bills with her father, singing star roles in both English and Italian opera and in comic opera, more often than not under the banner of her own company. Among her most successful ventures were the Broadway production of enlarged versions of *The Enchantress* (1862, Stella) and Auber's *La Sirène* (1862, Zerlina). In 1869 she introduced her own English adaptation of Kreutzer's *Das Nachtlager von Granda* (Boston 11 March).

Miss Riching's company did more than any other of its time to promote the then small and struggling native American musical theatre, and she long featured the works of Eichberg (*The Doctor of Alcantara, A Night in Rome, The Two Cadis, The Rose of Tyrol*) in her repertoire. She also promoted other such English-language works as *The Desert Flower* and *The Lily of Killarney,* as well as the more familiar *The Bohemian Girl, Satanella* and *Maritana.*

The company was dissolved in 1871, but Richings continued to perform with other English opera companies, appearing in such roles as Adalgisa, Azucena, Leonora in *Il Trovatore* on the one hand, and as Little Buttercup (*HMS Pinafore*) on the other. She also continued her relationship with the striving native American musical up till her last days, starring in William Furst's *The Electric Light* in Philadelphia in 1879 (25 August) and in her husband's little *The Duchess* in 1881 (Richmond, Va 30 July).

Miss Richings was married to the principal tenor of her troupe, **Pierre Bernard**, in 1867.

RIDEAMUS [OLIVEN, Fritz] (b Breslau, 10 May 1874; d Porto Alegre, 30 June 1956). German lyricist and librettist whose work was blessed with the occasional enjoyably unconventional touch.

Oliven moved to Berlin as a child and studied there until he became a practicing doctor of law. At the same time, he successfully doubled as a writer of revue material, song lyrics and plays, under the gently learned pseudonym of ''Rideamus'' (Lat: ''let us laugh'').

''Rideamus'' made an early venture into the musical theatre as the author of the burlesque *Die lustigen Nibelungen,* and collaborated with composer Oscar Straus on a second and equally imaginative piece for the Carltheater, *Hugdietrichs Brautfahrt,* but he found his most considerable success when, abandoning this kind of high-comic opéra-bouffe, he joined author-producer Hermann Haller as lyricist for a series of romantic musical plays and revues at the Theater am Nollendorfplatz. In the years during and after the Great War, Oliven lyricked and Haller produced such pieces as Kollo's *Quality Street* musical *Drei alte Schachteln,* which ran for nearly five hundred performances, and a series of five Operetten composed by Eduard Künneke, of which *Der Vetter aus Dingsda* was the highlight and which filled the theatre, with only one interruption, for more than three years.

''Rideamus'' later provided the German adaptations of the French *Ta bouche* and of the American *Rose Marie,* and wrote revue material for Haller for his Admiralspalast revues before joining the exodus of virtually all that was talented (and some that was not) in the German theatre in the early 1930s.

1904 **Die lustigen Nibelungen** (Oscar Straus) Carltheater 12 November

1906 **Hugdietrichs Brautfahrt** (Straus) Carltheater 10 March

1917 **Drei alte Schachteln** (Walter Kollo/Haller) Theater am Nollendorfplatz 6 October

1919 **Der Vielgeliebte** (Eduard Künneke/w Haller) Theater am Nollendorfplatz 17 October

1920 **Wenn Liebe erwacht** (Künneke/w Haller) Theater am Nollendorfplatz 3 September

1921 **Der Vetter aus Dingsda** (Künneke/w Haller) Theater am Nollendorfplatz 15 April

1921 **Die Ehe im Kreise** (Künneke/w Haller) Theater am Nollendorfplatz 2 November

1922 **Verliebte Leute** (Künneke/w Haller) Theater am Nollendorfplatz 15 April

1922 **Dein Mund** (*Ta bouche*) German version w Haller (Theater am Nollendorfplatz)

1928 **Rose Marie** German version (Admiralspalast)

1930 **Majestät lässt bitten** (Kollo) Komische Oper 5 April

1933 **Die Männer sind mal so** (Kollo/w Theo Halton) Schillertheater 4 January

RIEGEN, J *see* BOHRMANN, HEINRICH

RIGBY, Harry (b Pittsburgh, Pa, 21 April 1925; d New York, 17 January 1985).

Co-producer of *Make a Wish, John Murray Anderson's Almanac,* the Broadway version of *Half a Sixpence, Hallelujah, Baby!* and *I Love My Wife,* Rigby is remembered mostly as the guiding genius behind the brief series of 1970s revivals of classic American musicals which resulted in *No, No, Nanette* (not very altered) and *Irene* (considerably altered) being given a fresh lease of life and a fresh trip round the world's stages. A third attempt with *Good News* failed to make the same sort of impact. In 1982 Rigby also mounted the Schmidt/Jones *Colette* with Diana Rigg, Robert Helpmann and John Reardon heading a starry cast to closure out of town.

RING, Blanche (b Boston, 24 April ?1871; d Santa Monica, Calif, 13 January 1961). One of the brightest Broadway stars of the first decades of the 20th century.

Born into a theatrical family—her father may have been a fishmonger, but her grandfather, Jimmy Ring, was for 25 years manager of the Boston Museum—Blanche Ring began performing at an early age. After a number of youthful years touring with James Hearne, Nat Goodwin, Chauncey Olcott (Lady May Tyrrell in *Mavourneen*) and other barn- and region-storming companies, and a first attempt at operetta, along with her sister, Mina, in *Two Jolly Cooks* (Keith's, Boston 8 March 1897), Miss Ring introduced her mega-watt personality and bright, permeating singing voice to Broadway in the 1902–3 season. She opened her metropolitan career in *The Defender* (1902, Millie Canvas) performing the interpolated and not quite new ''In the Good Old Summertime,'' and made herself a name which guaranteed her spots, later the same season, in *Tommy Rot* (introducing ''The Belle of Avenue A''), *The Jewel of Asia* and *The Blonde in Black* (the cakewalking Flossie Featherly with ''The Yankee Girl''). The following year, she was back, equipped with another hit song, Jerome and Schwartz's ''Bedelia,'' in *The Jersey Lily* (1903, Liliandra) and she then visited England where she appeared in variety, and caused a sensation singing Lotta Faust's Broadway hit ''Sammy'' in George Grossmith's youthful but otherwise unremarkable musical *The Lovebirds.*

In 1904 she toured in the comedy *Vivian's Papas* (interpolating ''Bedelia'' and ''The Belle of Avenue A''), in 1905 she played the sprightly Lady Bickenhall in Broadway's version of Liza Lehmann's London musical *Sergeant Brue,* fitted out with several interpolated numbers including the soon-to-be-hit ''My Irish Molly O'' and, in an unlikely piece of casting, she succeeded Marie Cahill in the lead of Victor Herbert's *It Happened in Nordland.* Like Cahill, she was ultimately asked to leave for interpolating her own songs into Herbert's score. She appeared in the Chicago musical *The Pink Hussars* (1905, Katrinka), in a short-lived vehicle called *His Majesty* (1906, Mrs Brown) and, obviously forgiven by Herbert for her *Nordland* vagaries, on the road in an ''improved version'' of Lulu Glaser's role in *Miss Dolly Dollars* (1906, Dorothy Gay), scoring a hit ''especially in the musical numbers that had been rearranged to suit her personality.''

She subsequently reprised *His Honor the Mayor* (1906, which had started life as *The Pink Hussars*), performing her latest song success, ''Waltz Me Round Again, Willie,'' to considerable success; played in the revusical *About Town* (1906, Countess de Rectori) and its companion burlesque *The Great Decide* (Ruth Jordanmarsh), and in *The Great White Way* (1907, Mrs Dane); and took over the title role in the burlesque of *The Merry Widow and the Devil* (1908) for Joe Weber, bringing another of her most successful numbers, ''Yip-I-Addy-I-Ay,'' to add to the piece's musical part.

In 1909 she played in *The Midnight Sons* (Mrs Carrie Margin), performing ''I've Got Rings on My Fingers,'' which she also popped into the following year's *The Yankee Girl* (1910, Jessie Gordon), and followed up in *The Wall Street Girl* (1912, Jimmy Green, ''I Want a Regular Man'') and in a virtual pasticcio called *When Claudia Smiles* (1913–14, Claudia Rogers), into which she inserted—as she had done in several of her other shows—several of her old hit numbers to top up the half-dozen songs (''Wagner Couldn't Write a Ragtime Song,'' ''It's a Grand Old Life,'' etc) with which Jerome & Schwartz had musicalized her comedy vehicle *Vivian's Papas.* She subsequently toured vaudeville houses in the sketch *Oh,*

Papa! (1914) with her husband Charles Winninger, but returned soon to the theatre to play Adele Rowland's role of ''Tony'' Miller in *Nobody Home* in Los Angeles, Madame Nadine (otherwise Jane O'Day) in A H Woods's production of *Broadway and Buttermilk* (which had started out in Chicago as *Jane O'Day from Broadway* without songs) and in the unsuccessful tryout of the Harry Tierney musical *What's Next?* (1917, Angie).

Thereafter, she played in revue, in classic comedy (Mistress Quickly) and in regional shows, one of these last being the out-of-town tryout of *No, No, Nanette* in which she was brought in to play Lucille (''Where Has My Hubby Gone Blues'') in the Chicago company which established the show. Winninger was cast as Jimmy Smith, a role he retained when Blanche ''moved on'' (after some acrimony) to another job and thus missed the show's delayed Broadway transfer. She later appeared with John E Hazzard in his *The Houseboat on the Styx* and, in 1930, trouping on, though no longer the big-drawing star she had been, she played a character role in the Broadway production of Gershwin's *Strike Up the Band* (Mrs Grace Draper). In 1938 she returned one last time to the musical stage to appear in *Right This Way* (Josie Huggins) at the age of nearly 70.

One of the great musical-comedy personalities of her period, Blanche Ring combined an attractive star presence and a brazen, attacking delivery which were responsible for making many of the songs she performed into durable hits.

Her sisters Frances and Julie Ring, and a brother Cyril, all also appeared on the musical stage.

Plate 325. **Blanche Ring,** *longtime star of the American musical stage, as* The Yankee Girl.

THE RINK Musical in 2 acts by Terrence McNally. Lyrics by Fred Ebb. Music by John Kander. Martin Beck Theater, New York, 9 February 1984.

A small-cast musical play following the ups and, mostly, downs of the lives of Anna Antonelli (Chita Rivera, Tony Award) and her daughter, Angel (Liza Minnelli). After a life of drudgery running a seaside fairground skating-rink, Anna is finally selling up and getting out. She will be able to relax for the first time in memory. Then her daughter, who walked out years ago to enjoy sex, marijuana and no responsibility in the West Coast 1960s, turns up, expecting things to be all colored lights and childhood again. A confrontation develops, the self-centered Angel holding it over her mother that she pretended the girl's father was dead when he was only departed, but by the end, aided by the fact that Angel finally reveals that she has a fatherless child of her own to bring up, the two come together in some kind of reconciliation. The characters (male and female) who featured in the flashbacks which made up much of the piece were all played by a gang of a half-dozen men, the wrecker's men sent to pull down the rink, who were put on roller skates.

Kander and Ebb's songs included Anna's recital of her life as ''Chief Cook and Bottle Washer'' and her youthful encouragement to her cracked-up husband (''We Can Make It''), a piece for Angel dreaming of the ''Colored Lights'' that represent the childhood where everything is done and paid for you, and a piece in which the two paired in a druggy decision that they have something in common (''The Apple Doesn't Fall Very Far from the Tree'').

The Broadway production of *The Rink,* sponsored by a half-dozen producers, played for only 204 performances, but in spite of this failure the reputations of its writers and its economical size made it a candidate for further productions. In Britain, the Manchester Library Theatre's *The Rink* featured Josephine Blake and Diane Langton in a staging which was sent on, without success, to the West End, but in Germany the piece, rolling in on the increased fashion for English and American musical plays, followed up its initial German-language showing at Bielefeld with a number of others, at first in Germany and then also in Austria. Hungary followed suit when Annamária Bede-Fazekas and Ági Voith featured in a production at the Arizona Színház. London got a second glimpse at the Orange Tree Theatre in 1998 (21 May). A version of *The Rink* revised by the authors was staged at Washington's Signature Theater in 1999.

Nat Goodwin had had a much less heart-rending time almost exactly one hundred years earlier with his musical comedy *The Skating Rink.* Goodwin gave his sweetheart's father a half interest in his rink in exchange for the girl. But happy endings weren't considered unsophisticated in the 19th century.

Germany: Städtische Bühnen, Bielefeld *Die Rollschuhbahn* 8 March 1986; UK: Forum Theatre, Wythenshawe, Manchester 29 September 1987, Cambridge Theatre, London 17 February 1988; Austria: Landestheater, Salzburg 8 April 1990; Hungary: Arizona Színház *A görkorcsolyapálya* 23 January 1993

Recordings: original cast (TER), London cast (TER)

RIO RITA Musical comedy in 2 acts by Guy Bolton and Fred Thompson. Lyrics by Joseph McCarthy. Music by Harry Tierney. Ziegfeld Theater, New York, 2 February 1927.

Rio Rita was the show with which Florenz Ziegfeld opened the new Broadway theatre named after himself, and it was produced with all the extravagance and style for which the showman and his designer Joseph Urban were celebrated. The libretto was a conventional romantic-swashbuckling one with echoes of Hollywood to it, but its south-of-the-border setting and its high-country heroics were well adapted to the spectacular treatment for which it was constructed. Texas Ranger Captain Jim Stewart (J Harold Murray) is simultaneously pursuing a bandit who is known as the Kinkajou and the love of the fair Rio Rita Ferguson (Ethelind Terry). His enemy on both accounts is General Romero Joselito Esteban (Vincent Serrano), who not only tries to alienate Jim from Rita by telling her that the ranger suspects her brother (Walter Petrie) of being the bandit, but who is actually the chief criminal himself. Bert Wheeler as Chick Bean and Robert Woolsey as lawyer Ed Lovett were the comedy and Ada May in the role of Dolly, a cabaret girl, provided the soubretteries which aerated the romantic plot.

The score of the show was by the writers of *Irene,* but it bore little resemblance to the charmingly up-to-date set of songs which had scored them their biggest success. *Rio Rita* was written in a wholly different range of colors, designed for the very different set of voices which were used in a piece which was laid out more on the *Rose Marie* plan than that of *Irene.* The South American rhythms of the baritone title song, the distinctly operettic sentiments of ''If You're in Love You'll Waltz,'' and the masculinities of the Rangers' Song—a direct descendant of its equivalents in *Naughty Marietta* and *Rose Marie*—were all housed in strong pieces, each soon to be popular, which were well made for the needs of an opérette à grand spectacle. One of the more unlikely moments of the evening had the villain's nickname (apparently actually that of a small but vicious local rodent) turned into the cue for a Charlestonny dance routine, ''The Kinkajou,'' which was much more a challenge to ''Totem Tom-Tom'' in its scope rather than to the ''Tickle-Toe'' of *Going Up.*

Rio Rita's colorful production, tale and score won it a year-long Broadway success (494 performances) and a quick sale to RKO for whom it became one of the earliest sound musical films. The ''radio picture screen operetta'' had Bebe Daniels as Rita, John Boles as her Captain and Wheeler and Woolsey repeating their comedy of the stage version alongside ''1,000 others'' and two new Tierney/McCarthy numbers (''Sweetheart, We Need Each Other,'' ''You're Always in My Arms''). The film was seen in London early in 1930, and soon after, at the Prince Edward Theatre, Lee Ephraim opened his stage version of *Rio Rita,* featuring Edith Day and Geoffrey Gwyther (who interpolated a song written by himself) and comics George Gee and Leslie Sarony. It was poorly received, and Ephraim called in popular playwright and novelist Edgar Wallace to effect running repairs, but after 59 performances the show was taken off and replaced by the film *Song of My Heart.* The effects of films in general—and the film of the show in particular—on shows in general and *Rio Rita* in particular, became a hot topic for a few weeks, but it seemed to have little relevance to this case as the film version of *Rio Rita* had proved no more to London's taste than the stage one. The show was toured in Britain later in 1930 and into 1931.

If London didn't like *Rio Rita* on celluloid or stage, Australia conversely took to it with all the will in the world. It took to the lavish production the Fuller management gave the show, to its eight little Gringos, to the black and white dance and the lovely Spanish Shawl routine choreographed originally by Albertina Rasch, but mostly it took to the country's favorite prima donna, Gladys Moncrieff—Our Glad—in her first appearance back in Australia after some time in London. Glad was known and loved for her gypsyish heroines of *The Maid of the Mountains* and *A Southern Maid,* and *Rio Rita* gave Australia the chance to again see her as it preferred her. With Charley Sylber, Janette Gilmore and John Valentine/Les Pearce in support, Gladys and *Rio Rita* made their way from a season of more than six months in Sydney to four more months in Melbourne (Princess Theatre 22 December 1928) and then around Australia and New Zealand for a total of some two years, popularizing the show's songs in those areas more than in perhaps any other part of the world. When the film arrived, the ground was prepared. But the film came and went, and the stage version of *Rio Rita* remained a revivable feature of the Australian theatre scene, mostly with Gladys but occasionally even without her in its lead role. And there are still Australians of a certain age around who can hum you ''The Kinkajou.''

Plate 326. **Rio Rita.** *Guy Robertson and Leonard Ceeley starred in the St Louis Muny production of Guy Bolton and Fred Thompson's South-American tale of skull-thuggery.*

In 1942 the piece was brought to the screen a second time, as a vehicle for the comedy team of Abbott and Costello whose fun became more important than Kathryn Grayson's Rita.

Australia: St James Theatre, Sydney 28 April 1928; UK: Prince Edward Theatre 3 April 1930

Films: RKO 1929, MGM 1942

Recordings: selections (WRC, RCA Victor)

RIP [THENON, Georges] (b Neuilly-sur-Seine, 28 February 1884; d Paris, 25 May 1941).

The busiest and the most successful Parisian revue author of the peak years of the 20th-century French revue theatre, the former cartoonist ''Rip'' began his career in the genre with *Le Cri de Paris* at the Théâtre des Capucines in 1907 and thereafter wrote or, more often, cowrote over one hundred such pieces—part-evenings or full evenings—for the Paris stage. At the same time, he also penned a regular supply of plays and of opérettes, as well as a number of pieces which straddled the line between revue and opérette, though usually tending more to the former. His unbelievable prolificity, however, was very largely due—especially in later days—to his keeping of a large stable of usually young and underproven ghostwriters, who provided much of the texts for which Rip's reputation had won the commissions.

Several of his revusical pieces progressed beyond France: *Plus ça change* (1915) was adapted for the British and American stages as *As You Were,* whilst his *Les Fils Touffe sont à Paris* (billed as an opérette-revue) was adapted, with fresh music, into the British revue hit *The Bing Boys Are Here.* His most successful musical plays, the comical trainboard *P.L.M.* and the romantic *Brummell,* found favor, however, only in France.

1907 **Le Trou d'Almanzor** (Willie Redstone/w Wilned) 1 act Théâtre des Arts 9 February

1907 **Fleur de pétun** (Redstone/w G Lafargue) 1 act Tréteau Royale 14 May

1908 **Le Coq d'Inde** (Claude Terrasse) Théâtre des Capucines 6 April

1908 **Le Planteur de Connecticut** (Redstone/w Arnould) 1 act Théâtre Marigny 1 September

1912 **Les Fils Touffe sont à Paris** (Fernand Malet/w Jacques Bousquet, Lucien Richemond) Théâtre Fémina 10 April

1913 **Les Petits Crevés, ou Henri III et son petit cour** (Redstone/w Bousquet) Théâtre des Capucines 24 December

1915 **Plus ça change** (Édouard Mathé) 1 act Théâtre Michel 7 September

1918 **Le Cochon qui sommeille** (Terrasse/w Robert Dieudonné [ie, Robert Sorre]) Théâtre Michel 24 December

1919 **Aladin, ou La Lampe merveilleuse** (Redstone) Théâtre Marigny 22 May

1920 **Gigoletto** (Albert Chantrier/w Dieudonné) La Cigale February

1924 **Spartagas** (Léo Pouget/w Paul Briquet, Yoris de Hansewick) La Pie-qui-chante 15 February

1925 **P.L.M.** (Henri Christiné) Théâtre des Bouffes-Parisiens 21 April

1927 **Comme le temps passe** (w Alfred Savoir) Théâtre des Capucines 10 October

1931 **Brummell** (Reynaldo Hahn/w Dieudonné) Folies-Wagram 17 January

1931 **Le Roi Bobard** (arr Xavier Rogé/w Régis Gignoux) tour

1934 **Les Grandes Manoeuvres** (Vincent Scotto) Paris 27 October

RIP VAN WINKLE Comic opera in 3 acts by H B Farnie, Henri Meilhac and Philippe Gille based on *Rip van Winkle* by Washington Irving and the play taken therefrom by Dion Boucicault, and on *The Legend of Sleepy Hollow,* also by Irving. Music by Robert Planquette. Comedy Theatre, London, 14 October 1882.

The overwhelming success of Planquette's *Les Cloches de Corneville* in Britain had made the composer famous there, and when Alexander Henderson, the London producer of the earlier show, and his librettist crony H B Farnie envisaged an adaptation of Dion Boucicault's play *Rip van Winkle* as a comic-opera vehicle for the young comedian Fred Leslie, the French composer was approached to write the score. Farnie, known more as an adapter than an original author, was teamed with the experienced French librettists Meilhac and Gille who, it is reasonable to suppose, would have laid out the scenario on which Farnie then wrote the English dialogue and lyrics. The plot differed more than slightly from that of the 1820 Washington Irving version of the old *Ziegenhirt* tale and the play which Joseph Jefferson had made famous.

The layabout Rip van Winkle (Leslie) and his wife Gretchen (Violet Cameron) are to be thrown out of their home by their creditor, the burgomaster Derrick von Hans (W S Penley), but just in time Rip returns one day from the mountains with pocketsful of gold. Suspected by the townsfolk of having betrayed them to the British, he flees their anger back into the mountains and during the stormy night that ensues he goes through a terrible encounter with the ghostly Captain Henrik Hudson whose long-hidden hoard of gold he has plundered. Returning to his home on what he thinks is the next day, Rip finds that 20 years have passed overnight, he is forgotten, and his Gretchen has wed Derrick. But all is a dream and when Rip really awakes and returns home, he finds that Gretchen is still his lovely, young wife and that their money problems are over—she has sold their home for a vastly inflated price to the British. Worked into this tale were comical roles for the landlord Nick Vedder (Lionel Brough) and his adored serving wench Jacintha (Constance Lewis), and romantic ones for young Peter van Dunk (Louis Kelleher) and Katrina Vedder (Sadie Martinot).

Planquette moved to London, installing himself at the home of expatriate French costumier Charles Alias, and there wrote the score of *Rip van Winkle* to order for the chosen stars of Henderson's production. Leslie sang "O Where's My Girl," and appeared with two little children to sing "These Little Heads Now Golden," and the composer even supplied him with some musical yodeling when he learned that the actor had such a talent. The bulk of the lyric music fell to Miss Cameron, the Germaine of London's *Cloches de Corneville,* who had the musical highlights of the evening in "The Legend of the Katskills," a Letter Song and the pretty "Twilight Shadows." Planquette also provided a varied and lengthy divertissement for the central dream sequence which included a basso chanty for Hudson (S H Perry), a travesty soprano Ninepins number (Miss Lewis), a duo serenade for two other sailors (W S Rising, Clara Graham), a ballet suite with a Rhine Fay's dance which became one of the show's most popular take-out musical items, and a choral finale.

Rip van Winkle was a major success in London and it established Leslie as a regular star whilst also giving the composer his best references since *Les Cloches de Corneville.* It played at the Comedy Theatre for over a year (328 performances) at a time when such runs were rare, and it only closed when Leslie left the cast after being unable to negotiate himself a large enough raise to renew for a second year. Without him, the show no longer had the same attraction, even though his replacement was opera-singer-turned-favorite-actor J A Arnold, who had made himself a name playing the non-musical *Rip van Winkle.* The musical was snapped up by Richard D'Oyly Carte for America and it bowed on Broadway as part of a Carte repertoire season with *Manteaux Noirs* and *Iolanthe* shortly after its London opening. The American production boasted a cast almost as starry as the London one—William T Carleton (Rip), Selina Dolaro (Gretchen), Richard Mansfield (Nick), J H Ryley (Peter), Arthur Wilkinson (Hugh) and Lyn Cadwaladr (First Lieutenant)—but it had but a four-week life, as it had to be removed to allow *Iolanthe* to debut simultaneously with its London opening.

Shortly after the end of the London season, as the piece began a decade of provincial touring, *Rip van Winkle* began to show itself around Europe. Camillo Walzel presented *Rip-Rip* (ad Eduard Jacobsen, Ferdinand Gumbert) at the Theater an der Wien with Josef Joseffy playing Rip, Frln Grünner as Lisbeth (ex- Gretchen) and Carl Adolf Friese (Derrick) and Carl Lindau (Nick) in the principal comic roles. It ran for a month, before its initial run was broken by the production of *Gasparone.* It was later revived and eventually totaled 48 Viennese performances. This total was far outrun in Budapest where the Népszínház version (ad Lajos Evva, Béla J Fái), with Pál Vidor (Rip) and Ilka Pálmay (Lisbeth) starring, was a great hit. It had 53 performances in its first year, was revived 22 October 1886 and passed its 100th performance on 5 September 1888, by which time most of the principal provincial theatres of Hungary had taken it up. Thereafter it became a Budapest regular, playing again at the Népszínház (28 May 1903), at the Népopera (7 February 1914 with Gáspár Szántó and Ilona Szoyer), at the Városi Színház (26 April 1919), at the Revü-Színház (14 May 1921) and at the Fővárosi Operettszínház (22 April 1949).

The first German performance was given in Dresden, and there were productions in Prague (14 April 1884), Stockholm and Australia before the show was finally given in its composer's homeland. Australia's production, mounted under the management of Alfred T Dunning, presented the British comedian Thomas Bilton Appleby as Rip, with Annette Ivanova (Gretchen), Annie Leaf (Katrina) and Howard Vernon (Vedder) in support, and it too found success, being featured by Dunning's company through several repertoire seasons.

For its French production, the show which had had so much international success was heavily rewritten. Meilhac did over the libretto, making the piece less of a comedy and more of a light opera, and Planquette gave his score a heavy rewrite, making the lead role into a big-singing romantic baritone part instead of the light comic one it had been originally. Some of the music was redistributed—the Katskills Legend became a number for Rip called "Vive la Paresse," which was one of the hits of the new *Rip!,* and, in return, the leading lady got a new version of "Oh, Where's My Girl" called "Quel chagrin, hélas!"—and some, including much of the splendid dream divertissement, was cut. Planquette also supplied some fresh pieces including a Chanson de Jeunesse which, set alongside the echo song and drinking song of the second act, became one of the highlights of Rip's role and the show. Brémont (Rip), Mme Scalini (Nelly, ex-Gretchen), Simon-Max (Ichabod, ex- Hans) and Mily-Meyer (Kate) were amongst the cast, and the new, more vocal *Rip!* proved to be as much to the taste of French audiences as the lighter original had been to London, Sydney and Budapest. It entered the basic repertoire, much as the piece had done in Hungary, and it was subsequently reprised at its original house in 1889 with a "simplified" libretto, a little extra music and Gobin, Huguet and Albertine Leriche featured. It was given a major revival at the Gaîté-Lyrique with Soulacroix starring, and repeated there in 1900, 1902 and 1915—each time with Lucien Noël as Rip—in 1913 with Dézair and in 1924 with Robert Jysor. In 1920 Ponzio appeared as Rip at the Théâtre Mogador, and André Baugé played the role in

1933 at the Porte-Saint-Martin and again at the Gaîté-Lyrique in 1938. Over a century after its premiere, *Rip* is still to be seen on occasions in the French regions.

The piece also remained long in the revivable repertoire in its German version, and a major revival was mounted at Berlin's Theater des Westens in 1903 (21 November) with Julius Spielmann featured as Rip, Mary Hagen as Lisbeth, Wellhof as Derrick and Frln von Martinowska as Kate.

An Italian version, premiered at Genoa in 1885, with the young Mascagni as conductor, was repeated 10 years later at Florence with considerable success.

The first version of *Rip van Winkle* to be seen on the musical stage, was an 1855 "American opera" composed by George F Bristow to a text by J H Wainwright and produced by the British Pyne and Harrison company at Niblo's Gardens, New York (27 September) with Mr Stretton as Rip. It was followed by several British burlesques—a *Rip van Winkle, or Sonnambulistic Knickerbockers* (Newcastle 13 June 1866), *Young Rip van Winkle* by Robert Reece (Gaiety Theatre 18 May 1876) and *Rip van Winkle, or A Little Game of Nap* by H Savile Clarke (Portsmouth 29 March 1880)—and by several further American pieces: a burlesque played by the Zavistowski sisters in the late 1860s, a spectacular but unsuccessful burlesque written by Willie Gill for Henry Dixey (Columbia Theater, Chicago 23 July 1890), a comic-opera version by Jules Jordan played briefly by the Bostonians with Henry Barnabee as Rip (Providence, RI, 1897), and a three-act folk opera by Percy Mackaye (text) and Reginald De Koven (music) (Chicago 2 January 1920)—all of which stopped short of Broadway—and a featherweight *Ripples,* written to feature end-of-career comedian Fred Stone as a kind of a Winkle, which was seen in New York in 1930. Another romantic operatic version written by Franco Leoni was played at London's His Majesty's Theatre in 1897 (4 September). Mr van Winkle was also featured in two much-used if incidental musical-theatre hit songs: "Rip van Winkle Was a Lucky Man" (Jean Schwartz/William Jerome, *The Sleeping Beauty and the Beast, The Cherry Girl*) and "Who Paid the Rent for Mrs Rip van Winkle (when Rip van Winkle was away)?" (Alfred Bryan/Fred Fisher, sung by Al Jolson in *The Honeymoon Express,* in *The Belle of Bond Street* and in the *Ziegfeld Follies*).

Washington Irving's works have been used as the bases for several other musical-theatre works. His 1828 *History of the Life and Voyages of Columbus* provided the plot for the early American romantic opera *The Peri, or the Enchanted Fountain* (James Gaspard Maeder/J S Burr, Broadway Theatre 13 December 1852), produced during Irving's lifetime. Later, his *The Legend of Sleepy Hollow* was made into a light opera by Max Maretzek (Academy of Music, New York 25 September 1879) and a short-lived 1948 musical, *Sleepy Hollow* (St James Theater 3 June), and his *Tales from the Alhambra* went into the making of the Ladislaw Tarnowksi opera *Achmed der Pilger der Liebe,* as well as of Albert Smith's British burlesque *The Alhambra, or The Three Moorish Princesses* (Princess's Theatre, 1851) and H J Byron's often-played *The Pilgrim of Love,* first produced at the London Haymarket Theatre in 1860, and subsequently seen in America, Australia and other English-language theatres. The piece was also credited as a source for the Chicago musical *The Rose of the Alhambra* (Lucius Hosmer/Charles Emerson Cook, Majestic Theater 4 February 1907). Irving's *Father Knickerbocker's History of New York* went into the making of Maxwell Anderson's 1938 musical comedy *Knickerbocker Holiday,* in which Irving was represented on stage as narrator, in the person of actor Ray Middleton. The *Knickerbocker Papers* were also quoted as being the source of the H B Smith libretto to *The Knickerbockers* (Tremont Theatre, Boston 5 January 1893, Garden Theater 29 May 1893).

USA: Standard Theater 28 October 1882; Austria: Theater an der Wien *Rip-Rip* 22 December 1883; Hungary: Népszínház 28 December 1883; France: Théâtre des Folies-Dramatiques *Rip!* 11 November 1884; Germany: Residenztheater, Dresden 3 May 1884, Walhalla-Theater 13 November 1886; Australia: Opera House, Melbourne 1 January 1884

Recording: selection in French (EMI-Pathé)

RIQUETTE Operette in 3 acts by Rudolf Schanzer and Ernst Welisch. Music by Oscar Straus. Deutsches Künstlertheater, Berlin, 17 January 1925.

First produced by Heinz Saltenburg at the Berlin Deutsches Künstlertheater, *Riquette* starred Käthe Dorsch as the Parisian telephone-girl of the title. Riquette is a poor lass with a young brother to support, so when she gets a proposition from well-off young Gaston, she says "yes." The proposition is, however, an odd one. Riquette is to be a "beard," his mistress only in appearance, to cover up his affair with the married Clarisse. Clarisse sets off for a holiday in colorful parts (a second act must take place in colorful parts, and this time it is a spa in the Pyrénées) and Gaston and Riquette follow at an almost discreet distance, but the lady's husband is not wholly fooled. He hires the little telephone attendant Picasse to follow Madame. Picasse disguises himself as an Albanian Prince for the purpose, only to discover, as the fun starts to fizz, that there is a vengeful and real Albanian on his heels. Needless to say, by the end of the evening, Riquette has replaced Clarisse in Gaston's affections.

Riquette had a goodish Berlin run of three and a half months before giving over the Deutsches Künstlertheater stage to Hugo Hirsch's *Monsieur Trulala* and then to

Straus's *Teresina* with the other major star of the Berlin musical stage, Fritzi Massary, at its head, but thereafter it had a rather curious career. It doesn't seem to have headed right away for Vienna, yet it was promptly produced in both Britain and in America, albeit with rather strange results.

The American version (ad Harry B Smith) was originally announced to star Britishers Stanley Lupino and June, but in the event it was Vivienne Segal who was in the title role when the show opened at Detroit, only to be replaced by Mitzi as *Riquette* wended towards Broadway. It wended slowly, for E Ray Goetz was taking the same route with *Naughty Cinderella* (a version of the French musical comedy *Pouche*) and the two pieces were said (although it is difficult to see any more than the already well-used fake-girlfriend motif in common) to be based on the same original. Since the musical content of *Naughty Cinderella* was limited to Irene Bordoni's usual handful of songs, however, Goetz's production was adjudged a play and the "musical" rights held by the Shuberts were apparently not infringed. The Shuberts retorted by making their *Riquette* into a *Naughty Riquette* (even though she didn't seem to do anything naughty), but they kept her away from Broadway, playing lucrative dates such as Philadelphia, until more than a year had passed. Once the now "naughty" show arrived in New York, with Straus's score by this stage decorated with extra numbers by Al Goodman and Maurie Rubens, it was in a state to play for 11 weeks.

In Britain, Jimmy White produced the show (ad Gertrude Jennings, Harry Graham) with Annie Croft in the title role and Jay Laurier heading the comedy, with a run at Daly's Theatre in view. Unconvinced by a pre-London Christmas season played in Scotland, he abandoned *Riquette* in the frozen north, but comedian Billy Merson picked it up, chopped it up, and put such pieces of it as he fancied into a show which he called *My Son John* (ad Graham John, Desmond Carter, Graham, add nos Vivien Ellis), which, with Miss Croft again featured, eventually played for 255 performances at the Shaftesbury Theatre (17 November 1926).

Hungary got a production at the Városi Színház (ad Jenő Hoppe) which seems to have been more faithful.

USA: Detroit 17 August 1925, Cosmopolitan Theater 13 September 1926; Hungary: Városi Színház *Rikett* 4 December 1925; UK: Kings Theatre, Glasgow 21 December 1925; Austria: Raimundtheater 1927

RISCOE, Arthur [BOORMAN, Arthur] (b Shelburne-in-Elmet, Yorks, 19 November 1896; d London, 6 August 1954). Comic actor on the postwar London musical stage.

A concert-party player in his teens, Riscoe served through the war in the Australian army before making his stage debut as a musical comedian touring Britain in *The Lilac Domino* (Norman) and *Irene* (Madame Lucy). He covered Joe Coyne in the London production of *Dédé* but, although he made several other London appearances (the revue *Sky High,* as a takeover in *The Bamboula*), it was in the British provinces that he became a firm favorite touring in Jack Buchanan's starring role of *Battling Butler,* and billed above the title in *No, No, Nanette* (Billy), *Princess Charming* (Albert Chuff), *The Girl Friend* (Jerry), *Virginia* (Nicholas), *Hold Everything!* (Spike) and *Follow Through* (Jack Martin).

With *Nippy* (1930, Albert Crumpet) he began a London career which continued with *For the Love of Mike* (1931, Conway Paton) and leading comic roles in *Out of the Bottle* (1932, Tom Oakland), *The One Girl* (1933, Slick Sam) and, with the greatest success, in *Jill, Darling* (1934, Jack Crawford). He mixed star roles in comedy musicals (Freddy Bax in *Going Places,* Willie Cloppitt in *Wild Oats,* Jeremiah Tuttle in *Sitting Pretty*) and revue during the war years, appearing, notably, opposite his *Jill, Darling* partner, Frances Day, in the comic lead of the London production of *Dubarry Was a Lady* (Louis/King), as Madame Lucy in the 1945 revival of *Irene,* and, under his own management, in a moderately successful revival of his biggest success, *Jill, Darling* (1944). He was touring in *And So to Bed* when his final illness took him.

Riscoe put his name to several songs, amongst which the popular "Goodbye Sally"(w J Borelli) featured in the London revue *Shephard's Pie,* and he also appeared in several films, notably as Chitterlow in the 1941 *Kipps.*

RISQUE, W[illiam] H[enry] (b Chorlton-upon-Medlock, 25 August 1860; d Oxford, 17 August 1916).

At first engaged in the theatre on the production and managerial side, Billy Risque made his debut as a lyricist with the songs to *All Abroad,* one of the first attempts by an outside management to copy the new Gaiety Theatre style of musical comedy. *Shop Girl* star Ada Reeve sang his tale of "The Business Girl," alongside some interestingly adventurous pieces such as a legal document delivered to music ("In re the Trespass") and a musicalized piece of land agent's chat ("This Desirable Residence"). His career thereafter curiously failed to take off. He was involved with success when he wrote the lyrics to Leslie Stuart's follow-up to *Florodora, The Silver Slipper,* but with failure when he turned librettist for the flop *Miss Wingrove,* co-authored the revue *Pot-Pourri* and supplied additional words for George Edwardes's *The New Aladdin* and *The Little Cherub,* and in later days was limited to occasional musical sketches for the music halls.

Risque was married to musical-comedy soubrette **Susie Nainby.**

1895 **All Abroad** (Frederick Rosse/Owen Hall, James T Tanner)

Theatre Royal, Portsmouth 1 April; Criterion Theatre 8 August

1901 **The Thirty Thieves** (Edward Jones) Terry's Theatre 1 January

1901 **The Silver Slipper** (Leslie Stuart/Owen Hall) Lyric Theatre 1 June

1905 **Miss Wingrove** (Howard Talbot/Henry Hamilton) Strand Theatre 4 May

1907 **The Zuyder Zee** (Carl Kiefert) 1 act London Hippodrome 24 June

1913 **La Poupée** new English version (Grand Theatre, Clapham)

1914 **Lucky Miss** (Howard Talbot) 1 act Pavilion 13 July

RISTORI, Gabrielle (b Paris, 26 July 1899; d April 1988). Bright-eyed, big-nosed and beautiful leading lady of the French musical stage between the wars.

Mlle Ristori began her theatrical career at Lyon under the management of Charles Montcharmont and there, amongst roles in a series of revivals and post-Paris productions, she took part in several of Montcharmont's premieres of imported works, playing Ketty in the French version of *Leányvásár, Le Beau Voyage* (1923), and Mariette in *La Bayadère* (1925). Whilst playing at Lyon in a production of Yvain's *Ta bouche* she caught the eye of the composer, who subsequently cast her in her first Parisian role in *Bouche à bouche* (1925, Micheline). She also became his long-term mistress.

She repeated her *Bayadère* performance in the show's metropolitan production at the Théâtre Mogador, and took her most notable early part, at the same theatre, as a delightfully young Lucille Early in the French premiere of *No, No, Nanette* (1926, ''Rose,'' ''Faites danser,'' ''Dis-le moi?''). This success was a prelude to a long series of musical-comedy leads through the 1920s and into the 1930s in such Yvain pieces as *Elle est à vous* (1929, Monique, ''Son Doudou'') and *Kadubec* (1929, tomboy Edith Rabourdin singing ''Ouagadougou'' and ''J'aurais voulu être un garçon''), in *Pépé* (1930, Jacqueline), Yvain and Christiné's *Encore cinquante centimes* (1931, La Reine Stasia), Marcel Lattès's *Xantho chez les courtisanes* (1932, Xantho), and opposite André Baugé in *Le Chant du tzigane* at the Châtelet (1937). She scored her greatest success, however, in another imported musical when she created the role of Josépha in the enormously successful French production of *L'Auberge du cheval blanc* (1932).

After a Second World War effort which involved resistance, arrest and internment, she appeared throughout France in various starring roles, including that made famous by Yvonne Printemps in *Les Trois Valses,* returning in between times to Paris for such revivals as *Le Grand Mogol* (Bengaline) and *Mozart* (Madame d'Épinay) and new pieces such as Louis Beydts's *L'Aimable Sabine* (1947, Olympe). In the 1950s and 1960s she moved on to play character roles, notably at the Opéra-Comique.

RITA, Pauline [GLENISTER, Margaret] (b Bourne End, Bucks, 1 June 1842; d West Kensington, London, 28 June 1920).

For half-a-dozen years a prima donna of the British opéra-bouffe stage, Miss Rita was sometimes criticized (by the same journalists who criticized Kate Santley for being too forward) for being too aloof as a performer. None, however, criticized her singing. Originally a concert vocalist, she was first seen on the stage as a small-part player and understudy in the Italian opera company of Colonel Mapleson, and she made her first appearance on the opéra-bouffe stage ''by permission of Mapleson'' as Frédégonde to the *Chilpéric* of Emily Soldene at Doncaster. She made her London debut as a comic-opera vocalist in 1874 in the travesty role of Jean in Serpette's *The Broken Branch,* attracting considerable attention, and later the same year starred as Prince Conti in Lecocq's opéra-comique *Les Prés Saint-Gervais,* before going on to play Clairette to the Mlle Lange of Cornélie d'Anka in *La Fille de Madame Angot* at the Opera Comique and creating the leading role of Barbara in Alfred Cellier's comic opera *Tower of London* (1875) at Manchester.

In 1876 she starred as Gustave Müller in *The Duke's Daughter* (*La Timbale d'argent*), but withdrew as a result of the first signs of the illness which would dog her life and subsequent career. She was not seen on the London stage again until she was featured as the Plaintiff in the huge, starry production of *Trial by Jury* mounted for the Compton benefit in 1877. She appeared briefly in *The Swiss Cottage* (*Le Châlet*) under Mapleson's management at Her Majesty's Theatre, was hired by Carte to lead the first touring company of *The Sorcerer* (1878, Aline) and succeeded to the role of Josephine in the rebel *HMS Pinafore* at the Imperial Theatre, but she held none of these roles long, and disappeared thereafter from the theatrical scene. In the early 1880s she was seen on the Pacific circuits, billed as ''prima donna of the Criterion Theatre, London,'' touring with John Richardson RADCLIFF (1841–1917), her celebrated flautist (eventual and second) husband in ''Radcliff and Rita's entertainment'' and later in a musical lecture, *Pan to Pinafore,* to which she contributed a song or two. Her last stage appearance seems to have been in Auckland, New Zealand, where she appeared in *Trial by Jury* in a benefit performance in 1885 but, following her return to Britain, she was seen for a number of years on the London concert stage before retiring to teaching.

Several years later it was reported that her continued ill-health had sent her blind but, although handicapped, she lived on to the age of 78.

RITCHARD, Cyril [TRIMNELL-RITCHARD, Cyril J] (b Sydney, Australia, 1 December 1897; d Chicago, 18

December 1977). Dancer and light comedian who formed a famous partnership with his wife on British and Australian stages.

Ritchard joined the theatre at the age of 19, playing in the chorus of J C Williamson's Australian production of *A Waltz Dream,* and for the next seven years he appeared continuously in dancing, light-comedy and juvenile roles in a series of British and American musical comedies on the Australian stage (*Oh Lady!, Lady!!, The Pink Lady, Yes, Uncle!, You're in Love, The Cabaret Girl, So Long, Letty, Kissing Time, Going Up,* etc). He then left Australia for America and for Britain where, after early appearances in revue, he became a feature of the dance-and-comedy musicals of the 1920s and 1930s, appearing with his partner, Madge Elliott, as an elegant juvenile dancing, sort-of-singing and, intermittently (un-Australianish), acting duo in Laddie Cliff's successful productions of *Lady Luck* (1927, Tommy Lester), *So This Is Love* (1928, Peter Malden), *Love Lies* (1929, Jack Stanton), *The Love Race* (1930, Harry Drake) and *The Millionaire Kid* (1931, Aubrey Forsythe).

Ritchard and Miss Elliott then returned to Australia and appeared there for several seasons, playing in *Blue Roses, Hold My Hand, Our Miss Gibbs, The Quaker Girl,* the Australian musical *Blue Mountain Melody, Roberta* (also director), *Gay Divorce* and *High Jinks,* and getting married to each other with enormous public ballyhoo, before making a second visit to Britain in 1936. This time Ritchard appeared largely in revue and comedy but in 1943 he and Miss Elliot paired in a production of *The Merry Widow* and in 1945 he partnered Ruth Naylor as the Eisensteins of *Gay Rosalinda.*

In 1946 the pair appeared in Australia in Noël Coward's *Tonight at 8.30,* and in 1954 Ritchard appeared on Broadway as Captain Hook and Mr Darling to the Peter Pan of Mary Martin in the American musical adaptation of Barrie's play (Tony Award). After Miss Elliott's death, he remained in America where, in his sixties, he appeared characterfully as Don Andrès in the Metropolitan Opera's version of *La Périchole,* in the Offenbach pasticcio *The Happiest Girl in the World* (1961, Pluto), the St Louis Muny's *Around The World in 80 Days* (1962, Phineas Fogg), and as Sir in Anthony Newley's *The Roar of the Greasepaint . . . the Smell of the Crowd* (1965). In his seventies he was seen in *Lock Up Your Daughters* in Florida and as the lovestruck Osgood Fielding jr in the Broadway production of *Sugar* (1972). He subsequently toured as Jimmy in *No, No, Nanette* (1973) and in the narrator's role in the compilation show *Side by Side by Sondheim* (1977).

Ritchard's activities in these American years also extended to directing, and he was responsible for the staging of the Metropolitan Opera's production of *Der Zigeunerbaron,* a revival of *La Périchole,* and the national tour of *Where's Charley?* He also appeared as an extravagant Chitterlow in the film version of *Half a Sixpence* (1967) and on musical-theatre-based television (*Peter Pan, Dearest Enemy,* etc).

RITCHIE, Adele [PULTZ, Adele] (b Philadelphia, 21 December 1874; d Laguna Beach, Calif, 24 April 1930). "The Dresden china prima donna." Leading lady of the early 20th-century Broadway stage.

Born in Philadelphia of French Quaker parents, Adele Ritchie made he first notable stage appearance in Thomas Q Seabrooke's *The Isle of Champagne* (1893, Bridgette). Promoted from a small part to prima donna during its Broadway season, she walked out noisily after two weeks to join the cast of *The Algerian* (Suzette, and u/s Marie Tempest as Celeste). She went on from there to play Yum-Yum in *The Mikado* in Boston and was still only 20 when she won her first major new role as the ingenue of Francis Wilson's production of Jakobowski's *The Devil's Deputy* (1894, Princess Mirane). She played Madge in *The District Attorney* (1895), Little Willie in a Broadway burlesque of *Trilby* (*Thrilby*), appeared in De Koven's *The Mandarin* (1896, Ting Ling), visited Britain to play in Victor Herbert's *The Wizard of the Nile* (1897, Cleopatra), and took a turn in vaudeville, performing "a new operetta imported from Paris called *Au bain* in which she sings partially submerged in a lake" and in a dual role in *Le Rêve* at Koster and Bial's, before launching into a series of lead roles in mostly successful musical comedies: *A Runaway Girl* (1898, in Ethel Haydon's role of Dorothy), the ex-Boston Cadets show *Three Little Lambs* (1899, Beatrice Jerome, "The Men Behind the Guns"), *The Belle of New York* (1900, Violet, tour), *The Cadet Girl* (1900, t/o Marguerite), *The King's Carnival* (1900), *The Toreador* (1902, Dora Selby), as Mrs Pineapple in the young brothers Shubert's Broadway production of *A Chinese Honeymoon* (1902), as leading lady to Vesta Tilley's leading "man" in *My Lady Molly* (1904, Alice Coverdale), in *Glittering Gloria* (1904, Gloria Grant) and in the Chicago success *Fantana* (1904–5, Fanny Everett).

She moved away from ingenues and up to spunkier material to star as Lady Holyrood in a revival of *Florodora* (1905), as the dashing heroine of *The Social Whirl* (1906, Violet Dane) and as the Flora of *Fascinating Flora* (1907) at the Casino Theater but, thereafter, her Broadway appearances were few, although she appeared away from New York in Planquette's *Le Paradis de Mahomet* (1909), *The Girl in the Taxi* (1910), *They Loved a Lassie* (1910) and *The Motor Girl* (1910) in a career spattered with walk-outs, lawsuits and arguments. Her last Broadway musical, an adaptation of a French farce called *All for the Ladies* (1912, Nancy Paturel), in which she supported the comedian Sam Bernard, came two years after a messy bankruptcy and, shortly after, she announced that she was marrying the wealthy Charles Nelson Bell ''for his money.'' She subsequently toured in variety singing wartime songs before her career and marriage both faded away. Her last professional engagement seems to have been in Australia (1918).

Adele Ritchie's biggest headlines, however, were made not in her life but in her death. Having married (1916) and then divorced the successful actor Guy Bates Post, she quit their home in Hollywood for Laguna Beach and its high-society ''bohemian'' colony, where she was active in directing local dramatics. She also became involved with another divorcée, the well-off Mrs Palmer. Their bodies were found at her home. Adele had shot Mrs Palmer in the back before turning the gun on herself. It was at first suggested in court that the killing was due to jealousy over Mrs Palmer supplanting Ritchie at the helm of the local playhouse, then a suicide pact was promoted as motive instead, but when the women's wills and some ''intimate letters'' were introduced into the mystery the court and newspaper reports faded pinkly away into muteness, rather than report the details of what seems to have been nothing but a crime passionel.

RIVERA, Chita [del RIVERO, Dolores Conchita Figueroa] (b Washington, DC, 23 January 1933). Striking star dancer-singer for whom Broadway found a worthwhile role only once a decade.

Miss Rivera made her earliest musical-theatre appearances as a chorus dancer in *Call Me Madam* (1952), *Guys and Dolls* (1953) and *Can-Can* (1954) and took a very visible part in *The Shoestring Revue* (1955) before playing her first named role as Fifi in *Seventh Heaven.* She moved quickly up the bill to appear alongside Sammy Davis jr in *Mr Wonderful* (1956, Rita Romano) and, after standing in for Eartha Kitt in *Shinbone Alley* the following year, broke through to stardom when she created the role of the stormy Puerto Rican Anita in *West Side Story* (''America,'' ''A Boy Like That'').

Miss Rivera repeated her *West Side Story* role on the London stage before winning a second success as ''Spanish Rose,'' otherwise Rose Grant—who is not Spanish and who wants her ambitious man to be ''An English Teacher''—in *Bye Bye Birdie* (1960) both on Broadway and in London. After these two sizeable and personal successes she had to wait curiously long for another. She appeared with Alfred Drake and Anne Rogers in *Zenda,* which died before making it to New York, and top-billed as Anyanka in the less-than-successful *Bajour* (1964), but thereafter she played away from Broadway for a number of years, appearing in a mixture of straight and musical stage-pieces including *Sweet Charity* (in the film of which she appeared as Nicky), *Zorba* and *Kiss Me, Kate,* in the West Coast production of Meredith Willson's *1491,* and in nightclub and cabaret dates, before coming back, 15 years after her last Broadway hit, to score a third immense success as Velma, the dazzling dancing murderess of *Chicago* (1975, ''When Velma Takes the Stand,'' ''I Can't Do It Alone,'' ''Cell Block Tango,'' ''My Own Best Friend'').

The musequel *Bring Back Birdie* (1981) was a quick Broadway flop, but Rivera had a fine run as a partner to the magic tricks of Doug Henning in *Merlin* (The Queen) and a rather less long but more visible one when she paired as mother and daughter with Liza Minnelli in Kander and Ebb's *The Rink* (1985, Tony Award). In 1992 she appeared again in London when she top-billed in the Live Entertainment Corporation of Canada's production of *Kiss of the Spiderwoman* (Spiderwoman/Aurora) prior to repeating that performance in the show's Broadway edition (Tony Award). She has subsequently appeared in concert and in recital (*Chita and All That Jazz*) and played the role of Roxie Hart in the latest round of *Chicagos* (Las Vegas, London), in a career of some half a century which shows no signs of slackening its pace.

RIVIÈRE, Jules [Prudence] (b Aix-en-Othe, 6 November 1819; d Colwyn Bay, 26 December 1900).

Rivière was an orchestral player turned conductor (Casino Paganin, Jardin d'Hiver, Cremorne Gardens, etc) and composer whose long career very rarely brought him into contact with the musical theatre. After he had settled in Britain he was, nevertheless, responsible for the musical side of the first, badly butchered version of *La Belle Hélène* to be played on British soil, and he turned out one of the biggest song hits the young British musical theatre had had to that time when he supplied the treble chorus ''Spring, Gentle Spring'' as part of his portion of the music for the Dion Boucicault spectacular *Babil and Bijou.* If the song—which was an international hit and was interpolated into shows on Broadway (sung by ''The London Madrigal Boys'' in the Kiralfy's *The Naiad Queen,* the 1873 revival of *The Black Crook,* etc) and in Europe (*Le Petit Chaperon Rouge* at Paris's Myer's American Circus, 1876), and was pirated, burlesqued and ground out of a million barrel-organs—is now forgotten, the aged Rivière's book of memoirs remains to provide a colorful glimpse into musical life in the mid-19th century.

Autobiography: *My Musical Life and Recollections* (Sampson Low, Marston & Co, London 1893)

THE ROAR OF THE GREASEPAINT . . . THE SMELL OF THE CROWD Musical in 2 acts by Anthony Newley and Leslie Bricusse. Theatre Royal, Nottingham, 3 August 1964.

Plate 327. **Chita Rivera.** *The merriest murderess of the Cook County jail steps it out with her rival, Roxie Hart (Gwen Verdon).*

The successor to the highly successful *Stop the World—I Want to Get Off, The Roar of the Greasepaint* followed the earlier piece both in its style and in its content. Another small-cast piece with a large central character to its pantomime-style fable, it pitted little Cocky (Norman Wisdom), the epitome of the have-not, against the vast and powerful Sir (Willoughby Goddard), the representative of the ''haves'' who artfully stay on top by continually pulling the rules of the game from under the opposition's feet. If the text proved rather more naive this time, the songs were almost as successful as the hit-parading lot from the previous show.

Bernard Delfont's production, which Newley directed but did not appear in, closed down in the provinces without braving London, but the songs survived. The innocent, bright ''On a Wonderful Day Like Today'' became a holiday-camp and club classic as a cabaret-opening number, and the throbbing torch song ''Who Can I Turn To?'' followed it on to the nightclub circuits, whilst the confidence-filled ''Nothing Can Stop Me Now'' and the self-pitying ''The Joker'' also had a longer life out of the show than in it.

The Roar of the Greasepaint's career was not, however, limited to the abortive British production. David Merrick visited the show on the road in Britain and picked it up for Broadway where Newley himself starred as a rather less victimish little chap, pitted against a rather less vastly imposing rival in Cyril Ritchard. It had a 232-performance run.

The chorus of the British show included Elaine Paige, whilst the New York production introduced choreographer Gillian Lynne to Broadway.

USA: Shubert Theater 16 May 1965; Australia: Marian Street Theatre, Sydney 11 November 1975

Recording: Broadway cast (RCA)

ROBBINS, Jerome [RABINOWITZ, Jerome] (b Weehauken, NJ, 11 October 1918; d New York, 29 July

1998). Choreographer and director of several major musicals of Broadway's bonanza years.

Robbins began his theatre career as a dancer, appearing in the chorus of *Great Lady* (1938), *Stars in Your Eyes* and *The Straw Hat Revue* (1939) before joining the Ballet Theatre where he established himself as a choreographer as well as a performer. He returned to Broadway when he choreographed the Leonard Bernstein musical *On the Town* (1944), a piece which had originated in the ballet *Fancy Free* which the two men had composed and performed and choreographed respectively for the Ballet Theatre the previous year. Thereafter, he devised the dances for a number of musicals (*Billion Dollar Baby, Look, Ma, I'm Dancin', Miss Liberty, Call Me Madam*), winning particular praise for a comic routine parodying the silent films in *High Button Shoes* (1947, Tony Award) and the narrated pantomime "The Small House of Uncle Thomas" in *The King and I* (1951), before sharing the direction (w George Abbott), but not the choreography, of *The Pajama Game* (1954).

He acted as both director and choreographer for a musical-comedy version of *Peter Pan* (1954) and subsequently for *Bells Are Ringing* (1956), and for a remarkably variegated trio of musicals: the contemporary drama of *West Side Story* (1957, Tony Award ch) with its exciting, youthful dancing, the megawoman star-vehicle *Gypsy* (1959), and the warmly characterful tale of a changing world that is *Fiddler on the Roof* (1964, Tony Awards dir and ch). He also co-directed yet another hit in the Fanny Brice biomusical *Funny Girl* (w Garson Kanin).

Robbins's work for the hugely successful *West Side Story,* on the dramatic form of which he had a considerable influence, epitomized his skill at expressing contemporary action in a strong combination of dance and drama, and also showed—against strong proofs to the contrary throughout the history of the musical theatre—that there are possibilities and advantages in the creative pairing of the functions of director and choreographer when neither function is made subsidiary to the other.

For the next 25 years he then devoted himself exclusively to the world of dance before, in 1989, taking a twist on the endless run of songwriter compilation shows of recent years, he returned to the musical theatre and Broadway to mount a musical entertainment which was compiled largely of clips from his earlier shows (*Jerome Robbins' Broadway* Imperial Theater 26 February). It was perhaps a compliment to his style of work that routines which had been memorable examples of musical-theatre dance in their time and in their correct context now seemed very much less so out of both the one and the other. For a Broadway looking nostalgically backwards to its finest hours, however, the evening was a marvelous one. In what was, admittedly, a no-contest season, *Jerome Robbins' Broadway* was awarded 1989 Tony Awards for Best Musical and direction (by the rules it was not eligible for its recreated choreography) and, in spite of its large overheads (including what must be the longest rehearsal period for a recent musical show), the compilation played for 634 performances in New York.

Robbins co-directed and choreographed the screen version of *West Side Story* and choreographed the film of *The King and I.*

Literature: Schlundt, C: *Dance in the Musical Theatre: Jerome Robbins and His Peers* (Garland, New York, 1989)

ROBERTA Musical comedy in 2 acts by Otto Harbach based on the novel *Gowns By Roberta* by Alice Duer Miller. Music by Jerome Kern. New Amsterdam Theater, New York, 18 November 1933.

Abandoning his Continental Operette streak after *The Cat and the Fiddle* and *Music in the Air,* Jerome Kern turned for the inspiration for his 1933 musical *Roberta* to a novel by American authoress Alice Duer Miller, whose *The Charm School* had earlier been the basis for the 1925 Shubert musical *June Days* (Fred J Coots/Clifford Grey/Cyrus Wood, Astor Theater 6 August). *Gowns By Roberta* bore, in fact, a certain similarity to *The Cat and the Fiddle* in that it once again had for its central characters a group of Americans set down in that modern equivalent of the crazy foreign islands of early comic opera, the up-to-date Ruritania of glamorous Europe, and on this occasion Paris, France.

American footballer John Kent (Ray Middleton) inherits a Parisian modiste's shop from his old Aunt Minnie (Fay Templeton) and, with the help of her assistant Stephanie (Tamara), he sets himself to trying to run the business. His American ex-girlfriend (Helen Grey) comes to Paris to make up with him, but by this time he is on his way to a final curtain with Stephanie, even though (and this in 1933!) she turns out to be no shop-girl but a real live wait-for-it Princess. A large helping of incidental comedy was provided by popping into this tale a couple of theatrical folk, played by Bob Hope (Huck Haines) and Lyda Roberti (Clementina Scharwenka).

The score for *Roberta* was altogether less conventional than its story. The heroine's song "Smoke Gets in Your Eyes" (made up from a melody Kern had half-used a couple of times) proved to be one of the most internationally popular and successful songs of the composer's long theatrical career. Alongside it, another remade number, "You're Devastating" (formerly "Do I Do Wrong?" from *Blue Eyes*), was manhandled by Hope before getting a more sincere treatment from Tamara; the aged Fay Templeton crackled out her gentle memories of "Yesterday(s)" to another lovely melody and one of

Harbach's most tortured rhymes; Tamara joined William Hain in "The Touch of Your Hand"; and Miss Roberti provided a flamboyant contrast as she insisted in jaunty style "I'll Be Hard to Handle" (ly: Bernard Dougall). There were also two dance set-pieces, a bundle of impersonations (Fred MacMurray did Rudy Vallee) and a fashion parade.

Max Gordon's production of *Gowns by Roberta* (as it began its life) had problems from the start, problems not lightened when Gordon sacked the director and brought in spectacle-merchant Hassard Short as a replacement. The original director had been Kern. Its patently feeble book—some of Harbach's weakest-ever work—was slammed, and all the fashion parades in the world couldn't compensate. Gordon kept the show running, however, and the popularity of "Smoke Gets in Your Eyes" (and some salary cuts) helped him to stretch its run to 295 Broadway performances before taking it on the road with Tamara, Templeton, Odette Myrtil (Clementina), Middleton and Marty May (Huck) featured. Unsurprisingly, it toured only once, and of the other main theatrical centers, only Australia showed any interest in taking it up. With local megastars Cyril Ritchard (Huck and director) and Madge Elliott (Stephanie) at the top of the bill and Australia's best musical character lady, Ethel Morrison, as Aunt Minnie, it played two months in Melbourne and another two in Sydney (Theatre Royal 16 March 1935) before being replaced, in each city, by the indefatigable *High Jinks.*

Roberta had not long departed from town when Sydney folk got another version of it. For if theatres and theatre audiences had not cared greatly for the show, Hollywood did. In 1935 RKO put out a film version which had Irene Dunne as its heroine and Fred Astaire and Ginger Rogers for the dances and jollies, with five of the original songs plus the newly written "Lovely to Look At" and "I Won't Dance" (a melody salvaged from Kern's flop show *Three Sisters*). The new numbers proved as popular as the very best of the old ones, but even they and their famous performers could not give *Roberta* a new metropolitan stage life. They simply gave it an extended screen life, for in 1952 MGM put out another film version of the show, this time under the title *Lovely to Look At.* Kathryn Grayson was romanced by Howard Keel, Red Skelton was funny, and Gower and Marge Champion danced to a score which brought back a couple of numbers dropped last time round, retained the two newer ones and added two new ones which didn't rate.

The show was twice televised with Hope in his old role (1958, 1969) and regular stock productions—with varying libretti—were seen before efforts were made, in the 1980s, to find a first-class theatre production for a revised version of *Roberta.* However, the libretto (which

Plate 328. *Fay Templeton, as Aunt Minnie, and Sydney Greenstreet in the Broadway production of* **Roberta.**

has proved less of a problem at film-length than at stage-length) remained an insuperable barrier to its revival. *Roberta* joins such pieces as *Mack and Mabel* and *Great Day* on the list of shows that are shows long-remembered songs come from, rather than a piece for the stage.

Australia: Her Majesty's Theatre, Melbourne 22 December 1934

Films: RKO 1935, *Lovely to Look At* MGM 1952

Recordings: selections (Columbia, Decca, Capitol), film soundtrack 1952 (MGM)

ROBERT AND ELIZABETH Musical in 2 acts by Ronald Millar based on *The Barretts of Wimpole Street* by Rudolph Besier. Music by Ron Grainer. Lyric Theatre, London, 20 October 1964.

One of the most outstanding British musical plays of the postwar period, *Robert and Elizabeth* came into being only because of the insufficiencies of an unproduced show. An American legal gentleman with writing aspirations had secured the rights to Besier's famous stage play, *The Barretts of Wimpole Street,* concocted a script, and succeeded (with the help of notes sent out on New York Supreme Court letterhead) in convincing the Associated British Picture Corporation of its potential as a movie musical. The filmmakers—ignoring or ignorant of the fact that MGM held the film rights to the play—arranged

Plate 329. **Robert and Elizabeth.** *Robert Browning (Mark Wynter) encourages Elizabeth Barrett (Gaynor Miles) to try to walk (Chichester Festival Theatre).*

for *The Third Kiss* to be tried in the theatre first. Stage producer Martin Landau, realizing that the show as written was embarrassingly unproduceable, called in a playwright (Ronald Millar), who called in a director (Wendy Toye) who called in a composer (Ron Grainer) and, by the time they had finished, not a phrase of the original adaptation remained. They had written a fresh and fine new *Barretts of Wimpole Street* musical.

Elizabeth Barrett (June Bronhill), an invalid bound to a bed in a house where her widowed father (John Clements) rules his large, young family with a formidable sternness, has established a correspondence with the poet, Browning (Keith Michell). When he, all ebullience and life, walks into her room and her palely loitering life and speaks of love to her, she finds the strength to get up from her bed for the first time in years. However, her father, prey to feelings which border on the incestuous, intervenes. Elizabeth's dream of love and her confidence in her ability to lead a normal life are shattered and she returns to her invalid's bed. The furious Barrett now plans to shift his family out of London, but Browning encourages Elizabeth to hope again, and finally to marry and elope with him to Italy and a new life together.

The deft remake of Besier's play focused firmly on the three central characters, and the bulk of the music was written for the two lovers. The role of Elizabeth, tailored to the extraordinary talents of operetta soprano Bronhill, was demanding and dazzling to a degree rarely seen in the musical theatre, skating from one end of the voice to the other as she longed for ''The World Outside,'' soliloquized sanely but desperately (Soliloquy) over her position, or faced up to her father in a triumphal expression of the right to love (''Woman and Man'') which took the soprano up to an all-vanquishing D in alt to finish. Browning joined his beloved in the less extreme love duet ''I Know Now,'' which became the show's take-away tune, and bounded through the joyous ''The Moon in My Pocket,'' but top-billed Clements's vocal limitations meant that one of his numbers had to be cut. He was still left with the powerful, parlando ''What the World Calls Love.'' Some lighter moments were provided by the young Barretts, equipped with one of the most charming of the piece's songs in their daydreaming over ''The Boys That Girls Dream About,'' and by the parallel romance of Elizabeth's sister, Henrietta (Angela Richards), with the military Surtees Cook (Jeremy Lloyd).

Robert and Elizabeth was a major hit in London. It ran for 948 performances, a total which put it into London's top 10 all-time scorers, went on the road (shorn of its top notes, for actresses with a top D in alt are not legion), and was produced in Australia—with Miss Bronhill starring opposite Denis Quilley and Frank Thring for almost six months in Melbourne prior to a season in Sydney (Tivoli 19 November 1966)—and in South Africa, but not on Broadway. The author of the original adaptation, livid over the success of the show he had not written, went to court to stop *Robert and Elizabeth* playing in America. Given his connections with the judiciary, this was not difficult (or expensive) for him, but the British end of the operation were, as he doubtless intended, frightened out of their rights by the thought of an expensive (for them) American court action.

However, there were those in America prepared to brave the legalistic threats, amongst them the Forum Theater in Chicago, Victoria Crandall's Brunswick Music Theater, and, in 1982, the Paper Mill Playhouse in New Jersey, which mounted the show to open their new theatre. This time, when puffing noises came from the New York courts, the authors decided, at last, to take a stand. They won.

In spite of the multiple acting and singing demands of its female lead role, *Robert and Elizabeth* has continued to find productions. In 1987 the Chichester Festival Theatre staged a revival of a slightly rewritten version into which Millar restored some pieces cut, for cast reasons, in the original, and which eliminated almost completely the obligatory-in-the-'60s dance element, making the piece into an ever-tighter musical play. Gaynor Miles

(Elizabeth, with the top D), Mark Wynter (Robert) and John Savident (Barrett) featured through a highly successful season.

Australia: Princess Theatre, Melbourne 21 May 1966; USA: Forum Theater, Chicago 1974

Recordings: original cast (EMI), Chichester Festival cast (First Night)

ROBERTS, Arthur [ROBERTS, John] (b London, 21 September 1852; d London, 27 February 1933). Star comedian of the British burlesque and musical comedy stage.

A late beginner in the performing world, Roberts spent 10 years working in legal and accounting offices before turning to a early career as a music-hall comic (''If I Were Only Long Enough,'' ''I'd Strike You with a Feather,'' ''Little Isle of Cyprus,'' etc). He moved into the musical theatre in his early thirties when he toured with Lizzie Coote as Frederick of Tellramund in *Little Lohengrin* (1881) and with Emily Duncan in the burlesques *The Miller and His Men* (1883, Ravina) and *Sinbad* (1883, Mrs Sinbad), and he made his first appearance on the London musical stage in a version of *La Vie parisienne* (1883, Joe Tarradiddle) at the Avenue Theatre. He followed up with important comedy roles in *Nell Gwynne* (1884, Weasel), *La Mascotte* (1884 revival, Laurent), *Black-Eyed Susan* (1884, Captain Crosstree), *Le Grand Mogol* (1884, Jugginsee-Lal), *Barbe-bleue* (1885 revival, Bobèche), the pasticcio *Nemesis* (1885 revival, Calino), *Boccaccio* (1885 revival, Pietro) and in several plays, and appeared at the Gaiety Theatre in the burlesque *The Vicar of Wide-awake-field* (1885, Vicar) and a revival of *Billee Taylor* (1885, Ben Barnacle), by which time he had become established as one of the foremost musical comedians in London. He confirmed his reputation in several more burlesques (Sir Rupert the Reckless in *Lurline,* Sir Richard Varney in *Kenilworth,* Crusoe in *Robinson Crusoe,* Lancelot in *Lancelot the Lovely*) and comic operas (Frontignac in *The Commodore,* Matt o' the Mill in Audran's *Indiana,* Charles Favart in a revival of *Madame Favart,* Polydore Poupart in *The Old Guard,* Faragas in *Nadgy*) and, as the fashion changed, made the transition first to new burlesque and then to musical comedy with ease.

He hit trouble, however, when he played Scarpia in *Tra-la-la-Tosca.* Not bothering to learn his rhymed and metred lines, he ad-libbed his way through the entire script, instead of merely taking time out in the course of the show, as he had mostly done before, to do his well-oiled ''off-the-cuff'' turn. The show was as a result a flop, and he took his next burlesque *Guy Fawkes* to the provinces, where audiences were less critical of this free-and-easy ''instant theatre'' (little of which, of course, was original stuff, but simply tipsy rechauffé whose charm was in the telling rather than the material). He returned to London in the George Edwardes burlesques *Joan of Arc* (1891, de Richemont) and *Blue-Eyed Susan* (1892, Crosstree), but took a different version of this latter (*Too Lovely Black-Eyed Susan*) on tour in order to pay less royalties, claiming that, since he didn't speak the lines as written, he shouldn't have to pay for them.

Plate 330. **Arthur Roberts** *as Polydore Poupart in* The Old Guard.

In 1892 he was top-billed as the society pimp Captain Coddington in George Edwardes's early variety musical comedy *In Town,* but he returned to more burlesque parts (Pedrillo in *Don Juan,* Claude in *Claude Du-val*) before taking on the title role in his best-ever musical-comedy vehicle, as the cockney cab-driver in Basil Hood and Walter Slaughter's *Gentleman Joe* (1895, ''The Magic of My Eye''). Several attempts to repeat this impressive success under his own management were failures (John Jenkins in *Biarritz,* Jack Hammersley in *The White Silk Dress,* Smith in *Campano / Milord Sir Smith*) and only *Dandy Dan, the Lifeguardsman,* another Hood/Slaughter piece written to formula, around Roberts and his habits and his failings, had an appreciable London life.

Roberts's alcohol-aided gagging had, by now, become repetitive and tiresome rather than inventive, but he found a welcome still in the music halls (*The Cruise of the Saucy Puss,* 1897) and the provinces still welcomed him gladly in such made-to-measure pieces as *The Cruise of the HMS Irresponsible* (1900, Jim Slingsby) and *Bill Adams, the Hero of Waterloo* (1903, Bill Adams). His last major West End role was in *The School Girl* (1903, Sir Ormesby St Leger), in which he took over the central comedy role previously played by G P Huntley and George Grossmith, but he continued to appear before the public for another 20 years, mostly in variety and revue, making his last musical-stage appearances in a sadly amateurish piece called *Society Ltd* (1920, Count Solomon Dupont) and in C B Cochran's unfortunate version of the French musical comedy *Phi-Phi* (1922). In an attempt to make ends meet, Roberts was still to be found touring with a company called *Veterans of Variety* in his late seventies.

Autobiography: *Adventures of Arthur Roberts [by road, rail and river] Told by Himself* (1895), *Fifty Years of Spoof* (Bodley Head, London, 1927)

ROBERTSON, Guy (b Denver, Colo, 26 January 1892). Dashing leading man of two decades of Broadway musicals.

Originally trained as an engineer, Robertson served in the Great War and made his first stage appearance only at the end of hostilities, playing in Henry Savage's production of *Head Over Heels* in 1919. His handsome physique and fine baritone voice very quickly opened the way to principal roles and to Broadway, and he appeared at the George M Cohan Theater later the same year in another Savage show, *See-Saw* (Billy Meyrick), and in the Ed Wynn musical *The Perfect Fool.* He then spent five years as a juvenile leading man under Arthur Hammerstein's management, creating the roles of Kenneth Hobson in *Daffy Dill* (1922) and Guido in *Wildflower* (1923, "Wildflower"), touring as Jim Kenyon in *Rose Marie,* and pairing with Tessa Kosta as the romantic Russian protagonists of *The Song of the Flame* (1925, Prince Volodya). In 1927 he was hired to create the role of Gaylord Ravenal in Ziegfeld's new musical *Show Boat,* but the postponement of the production led him to take up another romantic lead, as Mister X to the Fedora Palinska of Desiree Tabor in *The Circus Princess* (1927), instead.

Robertson followed up in the Frenchified *Lovely Lady* (1927, Paul de Morlaix) and as Chopin to the Georges Sand of Odette Myrtil in the Broadway version of the Hungarian biomusical *White Lilacs* (1928), and was the hero successively of Busby Berkeley's production of *The Street Singer* (1929, George), of Romberg's South American spectacular *Nina Rosa* (1930, Jack Haines), the Shuberts' Harry Revel/Mack Gordon musical *Arms and the Maid* (1931), of the St Louis Municipal Opera's *Show Boat*—where he finally got to play the role intended to be his first time round—and of the German musical *Marching By* (1932, Franz Almassy). He subsequently visited Chicago to star in a revised version of the *Circus Princess* now called *The Blue Mask,* and played both there and in New York opposite Nancy McCord in *All the King's Horses* (1933, Donald Macarthur), in a West Coast revival of *The Only Girl* and as Johann Strauss jr in the pasticcio *The Great Waltz,* both in San Francisco and New York.

He was later seen regionally in *The Three Musketeers* (D'Artagnan), *Glamorous Night* (in Ivor Novello's role of Anthony Allen), *Music in the Air, Wild Violets* (Paul Gutbier), *Rio Rita* and as Allen Phillips in Frederick Loewe's prematurely killed *Salute to Spring* (St Louis, 1937). His last Broadway appearances were in *Right This Way* (1938, Jeff Doane) and as a replacement in *Very Warm for May* (1939).

Robertson was initially married to Broadway performer **Audrey CHRISTIE** (b Chicago, 27 June 1912; d West Hollywood, Calif, 20 December 1989) (t/o Babe O'Day in *Good News* 1928, t/o Olive in *Follow Thru* 1929, t/o *Of Thee I Sing* 1931, Francine in *Shady Lady* 1933, Anna Murphy in *I Married an Angel* 1938, Mabel in *Banjo Eyes* 1941, etc). She was also seen on musical film as Mrs Mullin in *Carousel,* Mrs McGraw in *The Unsinkable Molly Brown* and Mrs Upson in *Mame.*

ROBESON, Paul [Leroy Bustill] (b Princeton, NJ, 9 April 1898; d Philadelphia, 23 January 1976). Rich-voiced American singer who made his fame in areas other than the musical stage.

Bass-baritone Robeson appeared as a singer in *Shuffle Along* (1921) and in the chorus of the 1922 *Plantation Revue* before making his reputation as an actor both on stage (*The Emperor Jones, Othello*) and on film. Although he performed as a vocalist in concert and on record, his one and only stage-musical role was the part of *Show Boat*'s Joe, created by Jules Bledsoe, which Robeson played at London's Theatre Royal, Drury Lane, and in the Broadway revival of 1932. He played the same role in the *Show Boat* film of 1936, introducing "I Still Suits Me," and appeared in several other films with music, notably the 1933 *Sanders of the River* ("My Little White Dove," Canoe Song), which was later adapted to the stage (with different songs) as *The Sun Never Sets.*

Autobiography: *Here I Stand* (Beacon, Boston, 1971); Biographies: Seton, M: *Paul Robeson* (London, 1958), Hoyt, E: *Paul Robeson, the American Othello* (World, Cleveland, 1967), Gilliam, D: *Paul Robeson: All American* (New Republic, Washington, DC, 1976), etc

ROBIN, Leo (b Pittsburgh, Pa, 6 April 1895; d Los Angeles, 24 December 1984).

Lyricist Robin made an early contribution to Broadway's *Greenwich Village Follies of 1925* and subsequently collaborated with the young Philadelphia composer Richard Myers on a musical adaptation of *Brewster's Millions* mounted in that city. With Cecil Lean, Cleo Mayfield and the young Jeanette MacDonald starring, *Bubbling Over* was well worked over in Philadelphia, but failed to make it to Broadway and songs such as ''Red Hot Cradle Snatchers,'' ''It's All Right with Me,'' ''Snap Out of the Blues'' and ''Bubbling Over'' went down with it. However, two songs, ''True to Two'' and ''I'm a One Man Girl,'' did not. They later turned up in the London musical *Mr Cinders* (1928) where they found a deserved success.

Robin worked on an adaptation of A E Thomas's *Just Suppose* as *Just Fancy* (''You Came Along'' w Joseph Meyer and Phil Charig, later used in London's *Lady Mary*) and another of Mark Swan's play *Judy Forgot,* which forgettably became just *Judy,* and on the Chicago revue *Allez-Oop!* (1927, w Phil Charig) and another Myers effort, a musical comedy built around Fred Waring's Pennsylvanians and called *Hello Yourself,* before he scored a major Broadway hit in his collaboration with Vincent Youmans on *Hit the Deck.*

In 1929 he moved to Hollywood where he teamed with Richard Whiting on such films as Maurice Chevalier's *The Innocents of Paris* (1929, ''Louise'') and *The Playboy of Paris* (1930), and on *Monte Carlo,* featuring Jeanette MacDonald and Jack Buchanan and the song ''Beyond the Blue Horizon'' (w Franke Harling). He subsequently paired with Ralph Rainger for the scores of such films as *The Big Broadcast* (1932), *She Loves Me Not* (1934), *Here Is My Heart* (1934, ''June in January,'' ''Love Is Just Around the Corner,'' ''With Every Breath I Take''), *The Big Broadcast of 1936, Waikiki Wedding* (1937, ''Blue Hawaii'') and *Paris Honeymoon* (1939). In 1938 he and Rainger won an Academy Award for ''Thanks for the Memory'' performed by Bob Hope and Shirley Ross in *The Big Broadcast of 1938.*

After Rainger's death, Robin worked with a variety of composers on such films as *The Girls He Left Behind, Centennial Summer, The Time, the Place and the Girl* (1946), *Something in the Wind* (1947), *Casbah* (1948), *Just for You* (Bing Crosby and Jane Wyman's ''Zing a Little Zong'' w Harry Warren), *Meet Me After the Show* (1950), *My Sister Eileen* (1955), etc. Whilst in Hollywood he also contributed to film versions of several stage musicals: the 1930 Paramount film *The Vagabond King* (''If I Were King'' w Sam Coslow, Newell Chase), the 1936 film of *Anything Goes* (''Sailor Beware'' w Richard Whiting) and 1955 film of *Hit the Deck* (extra song w Youmans).

In 1949, after almost two decades in which his only contribution to the musical stage had been with a quick-flop version of *Sailor Beware* entitled *Nice Goin'* for Lawrence Schwab, Robin returned to Broadway to the same kind of success which he had tasted with *Hit the Deck,* when he supplied the sparkling lyrics for Anita Loos's famous characters in *Gentlemen Prefer Blondes* (''Diamonds Are a Girl's Best Friend,'' ''Little Girl from Little Rock,'' ''Bye Bye Baby,'' etc). He later lyricked the Jule Styne score for a television musical *Ruggles of Red Gap,* but his only subsequent Broadway venture was with the less-than-successful Sigmund Romberg piece *The Girl in Pink Tights.*

1926 **Bubbling Over** (Richard Myers/Clifford Grey) Garrick Theater, Philadelphia 2 August

1927 **Judy** (Charles Rosoff/Mark Swan) Royale Theater 7 February

1927 **Hit the Deck** (Vincent Youmans/w Clifford Grey/Herbert Fields) Belasco Theater 25 April

1927 **Just Fancy** (Joseph Meyer, Phil Charig) Casino Theater 11 October

1928 **Mr Cinders** (Vivian Ellis, Richard Myers/w Grey, Greatrex Newman) Opera House, Blackpool 25 September; Adelphi Theatre 11 February 1929

1928 **Hello Yourself** (Myers/Walter de Léon) Casino Theater 30 October

1939 **Nice Goin'** (Ralph Rainger/Lawrence Schwab) New Haven 21 October

1949 **Gentlemen Prefer Blondes** (Styne/Anita Loos, Joseph Fields) Ziegfeld Theater 8 December

1954 **The Girl in Pink Tights** (Romberg/Jerome Chodorov, Joseph Fields) Mark Hellinger Theater 5 March

ROBIN HOOD Comic opera in 3 acts by Harry B Smith. Music by Reginald De Koven. Opera House, Chicago, 9 June 1890; Standard Theater, New York, 28 September 1891.

The most generally successful comic opera of the 19th-century American musical theatre, *Robin Hood,* like so many other musical shows of its time, had only a little to do with the accepted set of events belonging to its title hero's ''history.'' The libretto to the show was made up by writer Harry B Smith more from the stock characters, comedy turns and plot elements of the classic comic-opera stage than from the ''facts'' of the famous British folk tale about the green-clad chap who robbed his enemies to fund his pals and neatly managed to make it look like some sort of politically correct charity.

The Sheriff of Nottingham (Henry Clay Barnabee) has settled that his ward, Lady Marian Fitzwalter (Marie Stone), is to marry his protégé, Guy of Gisbourne (Peter Lang), whom he intends to elevate to the Earldom of Huntingdon, at the expense of its young heir, Robert (Edwin Hoff). So, Robert runs off to Sherwood forest and there, under the alias of Robin Hood, sets himself up as the big chief of a merrie bande of outlaws. Amorous complications arise when, thinking himself deserted by Marian, he flirts with Annabel (Carlotta Maconda), the sweetheart of the merrie bande's minstrel Allan-a-Dale (Jessie Bartlett Davis) who, as a result, Judasly betrays his captain to the Sheriff. When Act III gets under way, Marian and Annabel are to be forcibly wed to Guy and the Sheriff, but with the help of a trunkful of disguises Robin is freed, the weddings stopped, and King Richard turns up in time for a jolly pageant of an ending.

Although these outlines were not unfamiliar (and there actually was an archery contest in the first act), their content was less so. The chief low-comic role of the Sheriff was all-important: in the first act, after an introductory song on regular comic-opera principles (''I Am the Sheriff of Nottingham''), he machinated over the winning of the Huntingdon earldom and gave Guy a musical lesson in how to woo (''When a Peer Makes Love to a Damsel Fair''); in the second, disguised as a tinker (Tinker's Song), he entered the forest for an encounter with the outlaws which left him drunk and in the clutches of the husband-hunting Dame Durden (Josephine Bartlett), was taken prisoner by the outlaws, stuck in the village stocks, and rescued by Guy in time for the third act. Marian, too, had a versatile role, appearing first in disguise as a page boy (''I Come as a Cavalier''), then as a milkmaid, then in the lincoln green uniform of the merrie bande (''Forest Song'') and finally as Annabel—before actually spending the last act as herself. Amongst the other solos, Allan-a-Dale, disguised as a monk, sang a contralto ''Song of the Bells,'' Will Scarlet (Eugene Cowles), disguised as the forger of Robin's chains, had a fine basso Armourer's Song, Robin serenaded Annabel-Marian with ''A Troubadour Sang to His Love'' and Little John (W H MacDonald) counseled ''Brown October Ale'' for lovesickness, alongside a full book of concerted finales, choruses and ensembles.

Produced by the Bostonians in Chicago, with a top-flight cast taken from their fine list of vocalists, *Robin Hood* instantly became a key part of their repertoire. However, New York being only one stop on the company's permanently traveling rota, the show actually appeared in London's West End before it arrived on Broadway. Produced under the title of *Maid Marian* (in order not to be mistaken for a pantomime) it was again given a top-line cast including baritone Hayden Coffin (Robin), Harry Monkhouse (Sheriff), American soprano Marion Manola (Marian), John Le Hay (Guy), Violet Cameron (Allan), Canadian Attalie Claire (Annabel) and Gaiety veteran Madame Amadi (Dame), as well as a chorus of 60. That casting required some little rejigging of the score, including the beefing-up of the role of the slightly underparted Robin for Coffin, and the star duly got an extra number, a ''romanza'' replacing a quintet in the last act. It was a wedding song, with lyrics by London theatre critic Clement Scott, and its title was ''O Promise Me.'' It has, in the century since, been sung at countless millions of weddings throughout America. In 1981 it was given even wider display when sung by Julie Andrews in the film *S.O.B. Maid Marian* had a run of more than two months in London—a little disappointing given the artillery mustered for the occasion—and dropped a sizeable £6,000.

Soon after this, it made its appearance, under its rightful title, in New York. There are various tales related about ''O Promise Me,'' its genesis and its arrival in the show, most, if not all, not mentioning Coffin, but only Miss Davis and her tantrum over not having a song (which she, surely, did have—see above), and some versions crediting her with having introduced the number prior to the London production. No positive proof to the contrary seems to have emerged, unless it be the unlikelihood of London's very popular and powerful Violet Cameron allowing herself to be deprived of the show's hit number even for Coffin's sake, but neither does there seem to be any affirmative proof. Miss Davis did, in any case, manage to get ''O Promise Me'' transferred from being Robin's song in London to being Allan-a-Dale's song in New York, and it was she rather than Coffin who made it famous (and it did as much for her).

Robin Hood's New York season was the first of many that the show would have, both in the repertoire of the Bostonians (who played the 2,348th performance on the 25th anniversary of their founding in September 1903) and, after their dissolution, in a series of revivals, the last to date in 1944, as it carved itself a classic niche in the American musical theatre. De Koven and Smith subsequently wrote a sequel, *Maid Marian* (Chestnut Street Opera House, Philadelphia 4 November 1901, Garden Theater 27 January 1902), which suffered the fate of virtually all other musequels.

Robin Hood itself was later produced in Australia, by J C Williamson, with Charles Kenningham (Robin), Carrie Moore (Marian), George Lauri (Sheriff), Viola Gillette (Allan), Clara Thompson (Dame Durden), Florence Perry (Annabel) and Howard Vernon (Little John) in the cast, for a season. It also eventually appeared in Hungary (ad Árpád Pásztor), and Smith related in his memoirs that it was similarly scheduled for Vienna's Theater an der Wien, where it ought to have followed the quick flop of Fall's *Der Rebell.* He asserts that owing to the unavailability of an unnamed artist, it was put aside in favor of *Die lustige Witwe.* The truth probably reads something like this: it was one of a number of pieces which had been optioned and was thus available to Karczag when *Der Rebell* failed, but he chose to produce Lehár's. In any case, Vienna never did see *Robin Hood.*

The story of Robin Hood has, in various guises, been long played on the stage since Adam de la Halle's 13th-century *Le Jeu de Robin et Marion* introduced one of the lordly outlaw's literary forebears to an early form of musical theatre. In England, Robin Hood was seen on the stage as early as 1598, as the hero of the masque *Robert, Earl of Huntingdon's Downfall* by Anthony Munday and Henry Chettle, produced at the Bankside Theatre and later at Court. He was later used as the subject for an intermezzo *Robin Hood and His Crew of Soldiers* (1627), for a ''musical entertainment'' by Moses Mendez and Charles Burney (Theatre Royal, Drury Lane 13 December 1750), an opera by William Shield and Leonard MacNally (*Robin Hood, or Sherwood Forest* Covent Garden 17 April 1784) and another, and distinctly successful one by George A Macfarren and John Oxenford produced at Her Majesty's Theatre, 11 October 1860, with Sims Reeves as Robin, Helen Lemmens Sherrington as Marian, Tom Bartleman as Little John, Charles Santley as the Sherrif, J G Patey as Much, William Parkinson as Alan-a-Dale and George Honey as the comical Hugo, the Simpnour. There were also a number of *Robin Hood* burlesques or extravaganzas produced in Victorian times including those by Shirley Brooks, et al (*Robin Hood and Richard Coeur de Lion* Lyceum 4 May 1846), F C Burnand (subtitled *The Forester's Fate* Olympic Theatre 26 December 1862) and Robert Reece, whose *Little Robin Hood, or Quite a New Beau* was produced at the Royalty in 1871 (19 April) and revived at the Gaiety in 1882. Another version, played in America in 1872 under the title *Ribon Hood, or The Maid That Was Arch and the Youth That Was Archer,* allowed Lydia Thompson to show off her form in lincoln-green tights. In 1894 Stanley Rogers and Henry May's *Robin Hood Esq* toured Britain, and in the wake of Lewis Waller's dramatic production of *Robin Hood,* Little Tich played Wal Pink's *Cock Robin Hood* and Arthur Roberts gave Herbert Shelley and Ernest Bucalossi's *Robin Waller A.O.F., or The Maid of the Millard By* on the British halls (1906). In 1965 Lionel Bart was responsible for the last British Robin Hood burlesque to date, the dark-doomed *Twang!!*

The German-language theatre also had its *Robin Hood*s, including one by Reinhard Mosen and Albert Dietrich (Frankfurt, 1879) and another with a score by Moritz Fall, father of Leo, whilst France saw a *Robin des bois,* subtitled an ''opéra fantastique,'' from the pens of Castil-Blaize and Theodore Sauvage in the mid-19th century. In 1978 a Czechoslovakian *Robin Hood* (Petr Zdeněk/Jiři Aplt) was produced in Prague, and in 1992 (16 July) Mexico City welcomed an Alvaro Cerviño/Cesar Balcazar, Carlos Osiris musical of the same title.

Quite early, the character of Robin, often played in travesty and supported by his Maid Marian and a long-legged chorus of merrie ''men,'' appeared as the titular hero of a run of British pantomimes, but today he has become most widely seen tacked, slightly curiously, into the tale of another traditional pantomime, *The Babes in the Wood.*

UK: Prince of Wales Theatre *Maid Marian* 5 February 1891; Australia: Her Majesty's Theatre, Sydney 25 November 1899; Hungary: Király Színház 29 October 1904

Recording: Radio broadcast selection (AEI), Mexican musical (Big Bang)

ROBINSON CRUSOE

Daniel Defoe's shipwrecked hero (1719) and his man Friday seem to have made their first appearance on the musical stage as the subject of a pantomime, *Robinson Crusoe, or Harlequin Friday* (1781), written, so it is said, by no less an author than Richard Brinsley Sheridan. Since that time, Mr Crusoe has remained an intermittently popular feature of the British pantomime season, whilst also serving to animate a number of other musical stage pieces of which the best known is probably Offenbach's opéra-comique version of 1867, written to a text by Hector Crémieux and Eugène Cormon. In spite of being a 32-performance failure at Paris's Opéra-Comique (23 November 1867), the piece was subsequently played in New York (6 September 1875), repeated in a much-altered version as *Robinsonade* in Leipzig (21 September 1930), Zürich and Prague, and ultimately shown in London (ad Don White) at the Camden Festival of 1973.

An earlier Paris opérette, written by William Busnach and composed by Jean-Francis Pillevestre, was played at the Fantaisies-Parisiennes in 1866 (21 February), but Italy had got off the mark much more swiftly with a *Robinson Crusoe,* music by Vincenzo Fioravanti, produced at the Naples Teatro Nuovo as early as 1828. A German musical *Robinson Crusoe* appeared at Berlin's Belle-Alliance Theater on 11 November 1881, Ernest Blum and Pierre Decourcelle produced a pasticco spectacular on the famous castaway—which managed to get Father Christmas into the proceedings—for the Théâtre du Châtelet in 1899 (mus: Marius Baggers, 20 October), Adolf Philipp and Wilhelm Hock, with music by Hans Lowenfeld, supplied a similar piece for Hamburg's Stadttheater (10 December 1901) and Karl Josef Fromm and Alexander Ludwig were responsible for a four-act spectacular produced at Vienna's Kaiser-Jubiläumstheater in 1904 (3 April). Spain's *Robinson Crusoe* (Teatro Circo 18 March 1870), again an opéra-bouffe and following, as so often, where France led, was composed by Francisco Asenjo Barbieri to a text from José F Godoy and Rafael Garcia Santisteban, and lasted a little better than most—it was still on display in Madrid in 1992.

In Britain, outside the pantomime productions, *Robinson Crusoe* appeared in burlesque at the Strand Theatre

(12 May 1845) as depicted by E L Blanchard; as *Crusoe the Second* (Lyceum, 1847) in a piece by J H Stoqueler; in H J Byron's *Robinson Crusoe* (Princess's, 1860), a multiple-authored piece, in which W S Gilbert had a hand (Haymarket, 1867); in an Alfred Thompson piece about *How I Found Crusoe (or a Flight of Imagination from Geneva to Cosmopolis),* which burlesqued Stanley's much-publicized trip to ''find'' Livingstone (1872); H B Farnie's *The Very Latest Edition of Robinson Crusoe* (Folly, 1876), in which Lydia Thompson was the hero and Willie Edouin Man Friday; and in a second piece by the last-named author and Robert Reece produced at the Avenue in 1886. In 1894 a *Crusoe the Cruiser* by J Wilton Jones was seen on the touring circuits.

In Hungary, the Népszínház mounted a spectacular piece taken from the Blum/Decourcelle show, with a musical accompaniment composed and arranged by József Bokor (2 June 1900); in Paris, Victor de Cottens, Robert Charvay, Harry Fragson and Maurel combined to turn out a punning *Robinson n'a pas cru Zoë* (22 December 1899) for the Boîte à Fursy; whilst, in America, a little ''chorale'' piece called *Robinsonade* (A Darr/Nat Childs) ''illustrating the career of Crusoe from the time of his embarkation at Hamburg to his safe return home'' was mounted as a forepiece to America's first sighting of *Die Fledermaus* (Boston 29 March 1880), and an extravaganza, *Robinson Crusoe Jr,* was produced at the Winter Garden Theater, 17 February 1916 (Romberg, James Hanley/Atteridge, Edgar Smith), with Al Jolson starred. This last show included perhaps the most memorable bit of Crusoe-iana: the popular song in which George W Meyer, Sam M Lewis and Joe Young demanded ''Where Did Robinson Crusoe Go (with Friday on Saturday Night)?'' The song was given to Londoners in the revue *Follow the Crowd* (1916) as sung by Ethel Levey.

France, of course, managed to get the girls in on the act, and Paul Ferrier and Louis Varney's *Miss Robinson* (with Vauthier as Crusoe) was produced at the Folies-Dramatiques in 1892 (17 December).

Another Defoe tale made it to the musical stage, long after Robinson had done his lot. A singing, dancing *Moll Flanders* (George Stiles/Paul Leigh) was produced at the Lyric Theatre, Hammersmith in 1993 (23 April).

Recording: Offenbach version (Opera Rara)

ROB ROY, or The Thistle and the Rose Comic opera in 3 acts by Harry B Smith. Music by Reginald De Koven. Herald Square Theater, New York, 29 October 1894.

In his mostly ill-rewarded efforts to produce a new *Robin Hood,* De Koven's most successful work was another comic opera based on (or, at least, titled for) a British folk hero, this time one from north of the border, *Rob Roy.* Harry B Smith provided the book in which the chief comedian, the Mayor of Perth (Richard F Carroll), was as much the hub of the action as the Sheriff of Nottingham had been in the first show. Whilst Rob Roy (William Pruette) and his lieutenant Lochiel (W H McLaughlin) connive at the escape of Bonnie Prince Charlie (tenor Baron Berthald) and his inamorata Flora MacDonald (contralto Lizzie McNichol), the Mayor is busy imitating the more famous Vicar of Bray—changing sides with expediency and promising his daughter Janet (Juliette Corden) in marriage to representatives of whichever team he thinks looks like winning. Janet does not only end up, but has secretly been right from the beginning, Mrs Rob Roy.

The score, if it did not turn out anything which would achieve the popularity of Robin Hood's ''Brown October Ale'' or ''O Promise Me,'' nevertheless featured some persistently heather-flavored music which was well adapted to the style of things, topped by the military ''Prince Rupert's Cavaliers'' and Grenadier's Song, a splendidly basso Turnkey's song (''In Darkness Deep'') which was every bit as good as the previous show's Armourer's Song, and Janet's catchy cautionary tale of ''The Merry Miller'' who married a wild coquette.

Produced at Detroit on 1 October, *Rob Roy* was quickly taken to Broadway where it proved a fine success, running up 253 performances during the 1894–95 season and, in that area at least, easily topping the record of *Robin Hood.* It was played around the country, taken into the repertoire of the Bostonians where Henry Barnabee, the original Sheriff of Nottingham, appeared as the Mayor, returned very briefly to Broadway for a second run of two weeks with Jefferson de Angelis starred and James Stevena as Rob Roy (Liberty Theater 15 September 1913) and was reprised at the St Louis Muny in 1925 with Leo de Hierapolis and Yvonne d'Arle in the leading roles. It did not, however, follow *Robin Hood* beyond American stages and across to Europe.

Britain made more than do—and already had since before de Koven's birth—with its own depiction of Rob Roy MacGregor as seen in the highly successful musical play *Rob Roy MacGregor, or Auld Lang Syne,* written by Isaac Pocock and composed and arranged by J Davy, which was played all round the country for three-quarters of a century and more following its first production at Covent Garden on 12 March 1818 with Macready in the role of the MacGregor (the singing was in the role of Osbaldistone). The arrangement of traditional Scots music (including ''Auld Lang Syne'' and ''My Love Is Like the Red Rose'') which made up the vocal side of affairs was later attributed to Henry Bishop rather than Davy. Along with *The Beggar's Opera, Guy Mannering* and *The Waterman,* this *Rob Roy* became a staple of the star British vocalist's touring repertoire, and while the star and stock system lasted it was a feature of every house's repertoire. Pocock's version was produced in America at the Philadelphia Theater, 1 January 1919, with Henry Wallack (MacGregor), John Darley jr (Osbaldistone) and Cornelia Francis Burke (Diana) featured.

The Scottish hero was also seen in burlesque as *Rob Roy and the rale Sougal Cratur* (Marylebone Theatre 29 June 1867, with Augusta Thomson as Rashleigh) and *Robbing Roy* (F C Burnand, Gaiety Theatre, 1879, etc), in which Edward Terry played the hero to the Francis Obaldistone of Nellie Farren.

France, in its turn, saw the McGregor translated to the musical stage in an 1837 opéra-comique with a score by the young Flotow.

UK: Morton's Theatre, Greenwich 29 September 1894 (copyright performance)

ROBYN, Alfred G (b St Louis, 29 April 1860; d New York, 18 October 1935).

Musician, composer of songs and also of a handful of theatrical scores and the son of William Robyn (b 16 February 1814; d St Louis, 2 March 1905), "the dean of St Louis musicians and the organiser of the first orchestra west of Pittsburgh," "Professor Robyn" had his first "light comic opera," composed to a text by a local matron, mounted in his hometown, during the city's annual summer musical-theatre season, when he was just 23. Letitia Fritsch played the *Manette* of the title. *Manette* did not go far, but apparently one song from it did. Robyn and his matron went to court, four years later, to stop Evans and Hoey performing their song in the context of the famous comedians' loose-limbed touring hit *A Parlour Match.*

Robyn subsequently worked as a pianist with Emma Abbott's opera company and as a church organist before making his debut as a composer on the Broadway stage with a comic opera, *Jacinta.* Produced at the Fifth Avenue Theater by Fred Whitney, with Louise Beaudet cast in the title role opposite Signor Perugini and with Edwin Stevens as chief comic, it lasted but 16 performances. Boston voted it the frost of the year, and it was a further decade before Robyn was again represented on Broadway. This time, however, the result was much more positive. *The Yankee Consul,* with its bristling Henry Blossom book, proved a first-rate vehicle for comedian Raymond Hitchcock, and a second piece in the same vein, *The Yankee Tourist,* was also a long-touring success.

Robyn placed songs in a variety of musical shows in the years that followed (*The Old Town, The Slim Princess, Baron Trenck,* etc) and provided the scores for *All for the Ladies,* a vehicle for another star comedian, Sam Bernard, for a respectable Broadway stay, and for the Los Angeles musical *Pretty Mrs Smith,* which featured Fritzi Scheff in its title role. By the time the show reached Broadway, she was sharing the spotlight with the lanky Charlotte Greenwood and he was sharing the music credit with one Henry James. Robyn continued to compose (a revue, *Let's Go,* was played in Baltimore in 1919) but the latter part of the professor's musical career was spent as a cinema organist at the Rialto and other movie houses.

1883 **Manette** (Hannah D Pittman) Pickwick Theater, St Louis 20 August

1893 **Jacinta, the Maid of Manzanillo** (William H Lapere) Grand Opera House, St Louis 22 May; Fifth Avenue Theater 26 November 1894

1903 **The Yankee Consul** (Henry Blossom) Tremont Theater, Boston 21 September; Broadway Theatre 22 February 1904

1906 **The Princess Beggar** (Edward Paulton) Utica, NY 18 January; Casino Theater, New York 7 January 1907

1907 **The Yankee Tourist** (Max Figman, Joseph Blethen) Elyria Theater, Elyria, Ohio 1 February; Astor Theater 12 August

1908 **My Sweetheart** new music for revised version by Thomas Railey, R A Roberts

1911 **Will o' the Wisp** (Walter Percival) Olympic Theater, St Louis 1 May; Studebaker Theater, Chicago 8 May

1912 **All for the Ladies** (Blossom) Lyric Theater 30 December

1913 **The Modiste Shop** (aka *My Partner's Wives*) potted *All for the Ladies* played in *A Glimpse of the Great White Way* 44th Street Music Hall 27 October

1914 **Pretty Mrs Smith** (w Henry James/Earl Carroll/Elmer B Harris, Oliver Morosco) Burbank Theater, Los Angeles 25 January; Casino Theater, New York 21 September

Other titles credited: *The Gipsy Girl* (1905), *Fortune Land* (1907), *Manzanilla* (1909, w Thomas T Railey), *The Western Girl* (w Railey) (1909)

THE ROCKY HORROR SHOW Rock musical by Richard O'Brien. Theatre Upstairs, Royal Court Theatre, London, 19 June 1973.

An innocently winning musical fantasy made up from elements of the less ambitious kind of science fiction and horror movies, some fashionable post-*Hair* intimations of sex, drugs and violence, and a group of simple 1950s-style pop songs, *The Rocky Horror Show* began its life in a tiny studio theatre, from where it stretched out not only into a very long initial run in London but also into a feature film and a continuing life, around the world, as a novelty show.

Toothpaste-clean Brad (Christopher Malcolm) and Janet (Julie Covington) take refuge on a nasty night in a castle in the American countryside (a castle in America . . . wouldn't you have been suspicious?) where they meet the spidery Riff-Raff (O'Brien), peculiar Magenta (Patricia Quinn) and tap-dancing Columbia (Little Nell), and the transvestite lord of the manor, Frank'n'Furter (Tim Curry). Frank has built himself a perfect man, Rocky

(Rayner Bourton), to assuage his desires, but he takes time off to indulge in Brad and Janet (separately), before their tutor, Dr Scott (Paddy O'Hagan), trundles to the rescue in his wheelchair. Dr Scott knows that all the castle's inhabitants are really Creatures-from-Outer-Space, and he helps Brad and Janet escape as internecine warfare erupts, Frank and Rocky are gunned down, and the other aliens saucer off home. The accompanying songs included Frank's introduction as a "Sweet Transvestite from Transexual, Transylvania," a dance routine called "The Time Warp," a hymn to the "Science Fiction, Double Feature" and an incidental rock 'n' rolling "Whatever Happened to Saturday Night?"

The show emerged as a thoroughly entertaining 80 minutes, endearing in its half-attempts to outrage, innocently unsexy with its black suspenders, crossdressing, tap-dancing and silhouetted grunting, always keeping to the comic-strip and avoiding the campy, and inspiring the same enjoyment as the ghastly/funny films which were its inspiration. Michael White's production moved from its tiny nest in the Royal Court Theatre to first one and then a second atmospherically decrepit cinema in the then-trendy King's Road, and there the show developed into a long-running if (given the auditorium size) not highly profitable operation. White foresaw the dangers of moving the piece from its suitable home into a genuine theatre but, finally, in its sixth year and after 2,358 Chelsea performances, *Rocky* was taken out of its natural habitat and transferred to the West End's Comedy Theatre. It undoubtedly lost something of its special atmosphere in the shift, but nevertheless ran for another 600 performances in its midtown home before closing down.

In the meanwhile, *Rocky* productions had sprung up all round the world. An American production was launched in a nicely scruffy Hollywood ex-nightclub, but when it was moved to Broadway's Belasco Theater it proved totally out of its element and failed quickly. In Australia, producer Harry M Miller caught the then-still-unconfirmed appeal of the piece when he opened his 1974 production with a midnight showing at an elderly cinema in the Sydney suburb of Glebe. The epicene Reg Livermore made a hit and a name as Frank'n'Furter, and the show had long runs both in Sydney and, with Max Phipps succeeding to the star role, through 19 months in Melbourne, prior to regular revivals in the years that followed.

A film version, *The Rocky Horror Picture Show,* with Curry, O'Brien, Quinn and Little Nell featured alongside Susan Sarandon and Barry Bostwick, was also a quick failure, but only a temporary one. It later became a late-night campus favorite and, as the show had done in the King's Road, began to attract regulars. A cult grew up, complete with little audience rituals performed with matches, rice, water and frozen peas and involving chanted responses to the dialogue, as the film found itself a semi-permanent home in a number of specialist cinemas. In Britain, would-be cultists could not find the film, but regional theatres and then the touring circuits took up the stage show and British youngsters transferred the American film liturgy to the stage show. It proved so popular, that soon—in contrast to the lesson learned earlier—the show was playing some of the vaster provincial houses to accommodate the audience demand. Fortunately, they also had the staff to clean up the water, the matches, the unfrozen peas and the soggy rice, but many a *Rocky* musical director bewailed a synth keyboard clogged up by rice between the keys.

Under the influence of all this film-flam, of course, the character of the show as first staged got lost. The performance became like an interactive game, and many of the performers lost the innocently winning tone of the original, which was now replaced by a kind of pantomime silliness. At one stage, in the British provinces, the essentially masculine Frank'n'Furter was played by a female impersonator. But the *Rocky* craze blossomed through the 1980s and it was in those years that the show reached its greatest heights of popularity as an audience participation activity. The boom, however, was past its peak when it was tardily decided to bring the show back to the West End. Produced at the Piccadilly Theatre with television comedy actor Adrian Edmondson featured as Frank, it found less audience than it might have done five years earlier at the Windmill or some other Soho dive, but nevertheless held up for a 412-performance run before going back on the road.

This less-than-total success did not, however, discourage another West End attempt—billed as a "21st Birthday Production"—in 1994 (Duke of York's Theatre 29 June). TV's Jonathon Morris, gameshow-host Nicholas Parsons and original cast member Patricia Quinn featured, and the original Brad, Christopher Malcolm, directed. Britain was Rockied again in May 1995 with Robin Cousins playing Frank, and Australia saw its umpteenth production in 1997 with Jason Donovan as Frank, and yet another and elephantine one, souped up with all the trappings of the pop-concert stage, in its very own Rocky Horror Star City, a venue rather a long way in size (and price) from the Royal Court Theatre Upstairs or, indeed, the New Art Cinema in Glebe. Finally, in 2000, as rumors of a sequel rumbled in theatrical circles, America got its stage version of the interactive *Rocky.* Tom Hewitt (Frank), Alice Ripley (Janet) and Jarrod Emick (Brad) headed a topnotch cast at the Circle-in-the-Square (15 November).

In the 1980s, the show also took its first steps on the Continent, finding ready acceptance in Germany where it wins regular regional productions, a brief English-language showing in France and, finally, a production in Hungarian (ad Ágnes Szabó).

Australia: New Art Cinema, Glebe, Sydney 19/20 April 1974; USA: Roxy, Sunset Strip, Los Angeles, 1974, Belasco Theater, New York 10 March 1975; Germany: Theater der Stadt, Essen (Ger) 20 January 1980; France: Théâtre de l'Union 14 February 1984; Hungary: Vidám Színpad 20 September 1993

Film: Twentieth Century Fox 1976

Recordings: original cast (UA, Telstar), American cast (Ode, Rhino), Australian casts (Elephant, Festival, Columbia), New Zealand cast (Stetson), London revival cast 1990 (Chrysalis), film soundtrack (Ode), Mexican recording (Orfeon), German recording (Ariola), studio cast (Stetson, TER, etc), etc

RODGERS, Richard [Charles] (b Hammel's Station, 28 June 1902; d New York, 30 December 1979). Preeminent Broadway composer who won fame twice over, in two seemingly separate careers, one each side of the war, as half of Rodgers-'n'-Hart and then of Rodgers-'n'-Hammerstein.

The young Rodgers served his musical-theatre apprenticeship writing songs for amateur and college shows, coming together early on in a partnership with lyricist Lorenz Hart which would survive virtually up to the latter's early death. The pair had their first Broadway exposure with a song, "Any Old Place with You," which was interpolated into the already sizeable Malvin Franklin/Robert Hood Bowers score of Lew Fields's production of *A Lonely Romeo* (1919), and a more substantial one the following year when seven of their numbers survived into the Broadway version of the semi-successful *Poor Little Ritz Girl.* This youthful start, however, did not produce further opportunities, and it was not until 1925, when the pair supplied the score for the revue *Garrick Gaieties* ("Manhattan"), mounted by some of the younger members of the Theater Guild company, that they got the impetus of genuine success behind them. That success set Rodgers and Hart off on a steady and prolific Broadway career that would last for 23 shows (plus a small handful for London) over 16 years of a virtually exclusive partnership.

The earliest Rodgers and Hart book musicals did extremely well. The first was *Dearest Enemy* ("Here in My Arms"), a piece with a libretto in a kind of period operetta style to which Rodgers would not return until his collaboration with Hart had ended, and for which the pair had had no success in finding a home until their revue had boosted their profile. Its 286-performance Broadway run was followed by a tour, and before that was over they had done even better with a thorough song-and-dance comedy, *The Girl Friend* ("The Blue Room"). *The Girl Friend* ran up 301 performances in New York and bequeathed part of its score to a London show, which, under the same title, played 421 nights in the West End.

Plate 331. **Richard Rodgers** *watches a rehearsal for the stage version of his* State Fair *at St Louis Muny.*

A commission to write a vehicle for Cicely Courtneidge and Jack Hulbert for the London stage brought forth an unexceptional piece called *Lido Lady* which nevertheless did duty for 259 performances at the Gaiety Theatre and productions in Australia and France, and an updated rewrite of that grand old hit *Tillie's Nightmare* called *Peggy-Ann,* in spite of including nothing to equal the earlier piece's song hit "Heaven Will Protect the Working Girl," also had a fine Broadway life (333 performances) and a London production (134 performances). A 1927 revue for C B Cochran, produced in London as *One Dam Thing After Another,* had a satisfactory run, partly thanks to the success of the song "My Heart Stood Still," and that song also proved one of the hits of the most Broadway-successful of all the team's early shows, a fantasy musical comedy based on Mark Twain's tale of *A Connecticut Yankee* ("Thou Swell").

In less than three years, Rodgers and Hart had had four successes on Broadway, two and a bit in London, and had made themselves not only into one of the foremost and most audible forces in the American musical theatre, but also by that token in London—where the shows of Hirsch, Youmans, Gershwin, Romberg, Kern and Tierney and, not to forget, *Mercenary Mary* had induced a craze for all that was theatrically and musically transatlantic—and even further afield.

Then the pudding sank. The pair had tasted failure when, in the midst of their successes, they had succumbed to the siren song of Florenz Ziegfeld and turned out numbers for a weak piece called *Betsy* which even the interpolation of Irving Berlin's "Blue Skies" and Gershwin's "Rhapsody in Blue" could not boost beyond 39 performances. But now, after three good years, came three very indifferent years in which, if their shows turned out a regular stream of durable songs, the shows themselves proved anything but durable. The Beatrice Lillie vehicle *She's My Baby* flopped in 71 performances, a piece about a potential eunuch called *Chee-Chee* winced through 31, London's production of *A Connecticut Yankee* fell in 43, and a musical called *Heads Up!,* which had managed 144 performances on Broadway, crumbled in just 19 in England. There were better runs for *Present Arms* (155 performances, "You Took Advantage of Me"), *Spring Is Here* (104 performances, "With a Song in My Heart"), the Ed Wynn vehicle *Simple Simon* (135 performances, "Ten Cents a Dance") and a spoof of the silent films, *America's Sweetheart* (135 performances), but the only show which achieved a really decent run was a revusical piece for Cochran entitled *Evergreen* ("Dancing on the Ceiling"), which was played for 254 performances in London before heading for screendom.

It was at this stage that Hollywood, avid for the best of Broadway talent to feed the newly popular musical film, called Rodgers and Hart, and the pair spent four mildly unforthcoming years in and out of filmland, a period from which the score of *Love Me Tonight* ("Isn't It Romantic?," "Lover," "Mimi") emerged as the chief product. Finally, the writers found the will to extract themselves from their celluloid quicksand, returned to the theatre, and, with their return to a Broadway which had passed the worst depression years, they found once again the kind of success that they had known in their earliest days.

Their first assignment was the score for a grandiose circus spectacular, *Jumbo* ("The Most Beautiful Girl in the World"), mounted by Billy Rose with such magnificence as to fold in 233 expensive performances, but in 1936 they turned out the dancing tale *On Your Toes* ("There's a Small Hotel," Slaughter on 10th Avenue, "Glad to Be Unhappy," etc), for which they had themselves invented the book, and scored a fine New York success (315 performances). In London, however, where Rodgers had not been represented on the stage since *Evergreen,* seven years earlier, *On Your Toes* was a failure and, although their songs were used in several revues (*All Clear, Funny Side Up, Up and Doing*) in the years that followed, no further Rodgers and Hart show was played in the London theatre until 17 years later when the Broadway revival of *Pal Joey* sparked a London production.

In America, however, between 1937 and 1940 Rodgers turned out a run of successful scores. First came the let's-do-a-show show par excellence, *Babes in Arms* (289 performances, "The Lady Is a Tramp," "Where or When," "My Funny Valentine"), then one in the series of singing-President shows of the era, *I'd Rather Be Right,* with George M Cohan occupying the White House through 290 performances, the Hungarian fantasy *I Married an Angel* (338 performances), a Shakespearean burlesque, *The Boys from Syracuse* (235 performances, "Falling in Love with Love," "This Can't Be Love"); a less-than-wholly-winning college musical, *Too Many Girls* (249 performances, "I Like to Recognize the Tune," "I Didn't Know What Time It Was," "Give It Back to the Indians"); and the lowlife, off-the-beaten-track *Pal Joey* (374 performances "Bewitched"). And in this time the partners had just one real failure with the misconceived *Higher and Higher.*

In 1941, under the influence of the multi-active George Abbott, Rodgers extended his theatre interests by going into partnership with Abbott as a producer on the musical *Best Foot Forward* and, on his own next musical, *By Jupiter,* he again shared the producing duties. It proved a good move, for *By Jupiter,* a burlesque of antiquity, had the longest Broadway first run of any of the Rodgers and Hart musicals (427 performances). But it was also the last new show the pair would write. Hart's irregular personal habits had put the partnership in peril repeatedly and with increasing frequency, and Rodgers had needfully looked elsewhere for a more professional lyricist. Nevertheless, he worked with Hart on a revamp of their old success *A Connecticut Yankee* ("To Keep My Love Alive") which he himself produced before the partnership was naturally dissolved by Hart's death.

In the meanwhile, Rodgers had not only extended his producing activities (*Beat the Band,* 1942), but had also made a momentous entry onto Broadway with his old friend and new partner, Oscar Hammerstein II. For the same Theatre Guild with which Rodgers and Hart had made their mark as a team with *The Garrick Gaieties,* Rodgers and Hammerstein supplied the score for a musical version of the Guild's play *Green Grow the Lilacs.* A period-costume piece of Americana in flavor not unlike Rodgers and Hart's debut musical, *Dearest Enemy,* it was a naive, romantic tale built on traditional comic-opera lines, full of simple charm and immensely singable songs ("The Surrey with the Fringe on Top," "I Cain't Say No," "People Will Say We're in Love," etc)—a show of a type which had become rather forgotten amongst the dancing President shows and very light, comedy-and-chorus-girl-based spectaculars of the past decade. *Oklahoma!* proved as welcome as lilacs that bloom in the spring and made such a hit as to break Broadway's long-run record with its run of 2,212 performances, whilst going on simultaneously to conquer London and the rest of the English-speaking world.

The traditional style of Broadway songwriting which Rodgers had practiced to good effect in his years with Hart was replaced, in his collaboration with Hammerstein, by a more romantic or operettic kind of writing.

The slick, smart take-away song was replaced by a variety of number which proved every bit as take-awayable, but which was musically more substantial, vocally more demanding, and made for a rather different kind of performer, whether romantic or comic, than its predecessor. It was a style to which the pair would largely stick with remarkable results. The flood of popular songs that came out of *Oklahoma!* was followed by another heap from Rodgers and Hammerstein's next show, and next important hit, the musicalized Molnár play *Carousel* (Soliloquy, ''You'll Never Walk Alone,'' ''If I Loved You,'' etc), a piece which followed *Oklahoma!* from Broadway triumph on to the international circuits. *Carousel* was produced, like its predecessor and like its rather less colorful and less successful successor, *Allegro* (''The Gentleman Is a Dope''), under the aegis of the Theatre Guild, but Rodgers had by no means renounced producing and, whilst *Oklahoma!* and *Carousel* reigned on Broadway, he was responsible for producing the show that would prove their greatest rival for popularity, *Annie Get Your Gun.*

Rodgers joined the functions of producer and author for the first time since the revival of *A Connecticut Yankee* for the fourth Rodgers and Hammerstein musical, *South Pacific* (''Younger Than Springtime,'' ''Some Enchanted Evening,'' ''Bali H'ai,'' ''Once Nearly Was Mine'') and, with that piece and with the following *The King and I* (''Hello, Young Lovers,'' ''Shall We Dance?,'' ''Something Wonderful,'' ''Getting to Know You''), the team scored two further enormous successes to set alongside the vast hits of *Oklahoma!* and *Carousel.* That the writers were not, however, infallible was seen when they abandoned the romantic operetta for a rather humdrum backstage tale in *Me and Juliet* (''No Other Love'') or for the downlife characters and unromantic happenings of *Pipe Dream.* There was altogether more success to be found in the Oriental sweet-and-not-very-sourness of *Flower Drum Song* (''I Enjoy Being a Girl,'' ''A Hundred Thousand Miracles'') but, 16 years after their first epoch-making success, Rodgers and Hammerstein combined on what was to be their last work together and produced what was to be perhaps their most widely and wholly successful work: *The Sound of Music* (''Climb Every Mountain,'' ''Do-Re-Mi,'' ''The Sound of Music,'' ''My Favorite Things,'' etc).

Hammerstein's death ended Rodgers's second long and fruitful collaboration, but their years of work together had produced a body of nine musical shows from which five won worldwide popularity both as stage shows and in the cinema and became established both as an essential part of the American classic repertoire, and as outstanding representatives of the musical theatre of their time.

Rodgers continued to write for the stage, if with less regularity than in his younger days, but the same kind of success would not come again. He provided his own lyrics for his first post-Hammerstein show, *No Strings,* which had a 580-performance run on Broadway (and 135 performances in London). The show added the song ''The Sweetest Sounds'' to his standards catalogue, but it did not have the same appeal nor the same propensity to endure as his best works of the 1940s and 1950s. The composer nevertheless proved excitingly that he had lost none of his writing talent when, at 63 years of age, in collaboration with lyricist Stephen Sondheim, he turned out one of the most appealing romantic-comic scores of his career for *Do I Hear a Waltz?* This time, however, Rodgers the producer did not do his job as well as Rodgers the composer, for *Do I Hear a Waltz?* underwent some wrong-headed decisions on its way to the stage and did not become a success in the theatre.

The shows which followed were not in the same class: a television musical version of G B Shaw's *Androcles and the Lion* (NBC 15 November 1967) and a Noah's ark musical, *Two by Two,* which featured Danny Kaye as the floating refugee of the floods, were followed by a dispiritingly uninviting musical version of the play *I Remember Mama* which Rodgers had himself mounted, without music and with great success, in his early days as a producer, and which now marked his farewell to Broadway more than half a century since his first appearance there.

Rodgers's screen scores for *State Fair* (film) and *Cinderella* (television) were both subsequently used as the musical part of stage musicals put together by other hands.

Rodgers's career in the musical theatre, principally as a composer, but also as a producer, was the most important in the American theatre of his time. During his years of collaboration with Hart, he was one of the most effective of the peloton of popular and successful musical-theatre composers then working on Broadway, and from their partnership a good number of popular songs have survived as standards. However, in spite of the immensely saleable names of their writers, only two shows—*Pal Joey* and *On Your Toes*—have lasted into the stage repertoire of the latter part of the century. It is the group of five famous and substantial musical plays written and, later, produced in tandem with Hammerstein which have survived as the enduring part of Rodgers's work as a theatre composer. In their time, these works encouraged and confirmed a return to the basic tenets of the British and Continental operettas of the late 19th and early 20th century, to their classic combination of the sentimental and the comic, their music orientated towards vocal values rather than dance rhythms or Tin Pan Alley, and dance which came from balletic roots rather than from the ballroom, the gymnasium or the parade ground.

Since then, their appeal has never weakened. They have held their place as five of the most popular and frequently played works of their period, a body of work as impressive as any in the history of the Broadway musical and as memorable as the kernel of the opus of Gilbert and Sullivan, of Offenbach or Lecocq, of Franz Lehár or Emmerich Kálmán.

A Hollywood musical biography of Rodgers and Hart called *Words and Music* (1948) featured Tom Drake as Rodgers to the Hart of Mickey Rooney.

Rodgers's daughter, **Mary RODGERS** (b New York, 11 January 1931), had a notable success as a composer for the musical stage with the score for the fairytale burlesque *Once Upon a Mattress.* She also composed the music for the ABC television musical *Feathertop* (19 October 1961, w Charnin/John Marsh), *Hot Spot* (Martin Charnin/Jack Weinstock, Willie Gilbert, Majestic Theater 19 April 1963) and *The Mad Show* (1966) and contributed to the score of *Working* (1978). She also contributed a third generation composer to the musical theatre in her son **Adam GUETTEL** whose musical *Floyd Collins* (w Tina Landau) was played off-Broadway in 1996 (Playwrights Horizons 3 March). The songs of Mary Rodgers were anthologized in a production called *Hey, Love* played as a nightclub entertainment succesively at 88s and Rainbow and Stars.

1920 **Poor Little Ritz Girl** (w Sigmund Romberg/Lorenz Hart/Lew Fields, George Campbell) Central Theater 28 July

1925 **Dearest Enemy** (Hart/Herbert Fields) Knickerbocker Theater 18 September

1926 **The Girl Friend** (Hart/H Fields) Vanderbilt Theater 17 March

1926 **Lido Lady** (Hart/Guy Bolton, Bert Kalmar, Harry Ruby) Gaiety Theatre, London 1 December

1926 **Peggy-Ann** (Hart/ad H Fields) Vanderbilt Theater 27 December

1926 **Betsy** (Hart/Irving Caesar, David Freedman) New Amsterdam Theater 28 December

1927 **A Connecticut Yankee** (Hart/H Fields) Vanderbilt Theater 3 November

1928 **She's My Baby** (Hart/Kalmar, Ruby) Globe Theater 3 January

1928 **Present Arms** (Hart/H Fields) Lew Fields Mansfield Theater 26 April

1928 **Chee-Chee** (Hart/H Fields) Lew Fields Mansfield Theater 25 September

1929 **Spring Is Here** (Hart/Owen Davis) Alvin Theater 11 March

1929 **Heads Up!** (Hart/John McGowan, Paul Gerard Smith) Alvin Theater 11 November

1930 **Simple Simon** (Hart/Bolton, Ed Wynn) Ziegfeld Theater 18 February

1931 **America's Sweetheart** (Hart/H Fields) Broadhurst Theater 10 February

1935 **Jumbo** (Hart/Ben Hecht, Charles MacArthur) Hippodrome Theater 16 November

1936 **On Your Toes** (Hart/Rodgers, Hart, George Abbott) Imperial Theater 11 April

1937 **Babes in Arms** (Hart/Rodgers, Hart) Shubert Theater 14 April

1937 **I'd Rather Be Right** (Hart/Moss Hart, George S Kaufman) Alvin Theater 2 November

1938 **I Married an Angel** (Hart/ad Rodgers, Hart) Shubert Theater 11 May

1938 **The Boys from Syracuse** (Hart/Abbott) Alvin Theater 23 November

1939 **Too Many Girls** (Hart/George Marion jr) Imperial Theater 18 October

1940 **Higher and Higher** (Hart/Gladys Hurlbut, Joshua Logan) Shubert Theater 4 April

1940 **Pal Joey** (Hart/John O'Hara) Ethel Barrymore Theater 25 December

1942 **By Jupiter** (Hart/Rodgers, Hart) Shubert Theater 3 June

1943 **Oklahoma!** (Oscar Hammerstein II) St James Theater 31 March

1945 **Carousel** (Hammerstein) Majestic Theater 19 April

1947 **Allegro** (Hammerstein) Majestic Theater 10 October

1949 **South Pacific** (Hammerstein/Hammerstein, Logan) Majestic Theater 7 April

1951 **The King and I** (Hammerstein) St James Theater 29 March

1953 **Me and Juliet** (Hammerstein) Majestic Theater 28 May

1955 **Pipe Dream** (Hammerstein) Shubert Theater 30 November

1958 **Flower Drum Song** (Hammerstein/Hammerstein, Joseph Fields) St James Theater 1 December

1958 **Cinderella** (Hammerstein) London Coliseum 18 December

1959 **The Sound of Music** (Hammerstein/Russel Crouse, Howard Lindsay) Lunt-Fontanne Theater 16 November

1962 **No Strings** (Rodgers/Samuel Taylor) 54th Street Theater 15 March

1965 **Do I Hear a Waltz?** (Stephen Sondheim/Arthur Laurents) 46th Street Theater 18 March

1969 **State Fair** (Hammerstein/Lucille Kallen) Municipal Opera, St Louis 2 June

1970 **Two By Two** (Martin Charnin/Peter Stone) Imperial Theater 10 November

1976 **Rex** (Sheldon Harnick/Sherman Yellen) Lunt-Fontanne Theater 25 April

1979 **I Remember Mama** (Charnin, Raymond Jessel/Thomas Meehan) Majestic Theater 31 May

Literature: Appleton, W (ed): *Richard Rodgers: Letters to Dorothy* (1926–1937) (NY Public Library, 1988), Suskin, S: *Berlin, Kern, Rodgers, Hart, and Hammerstein: A Complete Song Catalogue* (McFarland, Jefferson, North Carolina, 1990)

Autobiography: *Musical Stages* (Random House, New York, 1975); Biographies: Green, S: *The Rodgers and Hammerstein Story* (Day, New York, 1963), Ewen, D: *With a Song in His Heart* (Holt, New York, 1957), Taylor, D: *Some Enchanted Evening: The Story of Rodgers and Hammerstein* (Harper, New York, 1953), Marx, S, Clayton, J: *Rodgers and Hart: Bewitched, Bothered and Bedevilled* (Putnam, New York, 1976), Nolan, F: *The Sound of Their Music* (Dent, London, 1976), Mordden, E: *Rodgers and Hammerstein* (Abrams, New York, 1992), Hyland, W G: *Richard Rodgers* (Yale UP, 1997), etc

ROGER, Germaine (d 1975).

Soprano Germaine Roger appeared on the Paris stage in a number of opérettes from the end of the 1920s (*Un soir de réveillon, Un coup de veine, L'Auberge du chat coiffé, Un petit bout de femme, Ma petite amie,* the revamped *Les Cent Vierges, Moineau, Phi-Phi,* etc). After the Second World War, her husband, actor and sometime musical performer Henri Montjoye (né Barbero), took over the management of the large Théâtre de la Gaîté-Lyrique and, in 1950, on his death, Mme Roger-Montjoye succeeded him. Through the 1950s and part of the 1960s she produced a program consisting of a mixture of classic revivals (*Les Mousquetaires au couvent, Les Cloches de Corneville, La Chaste Susanne*), reprises of more modern favorites (*Andalousie, Trois Valses, Le Pays du Sourire, La Belle de Cadix, Chanson gitane*) and a number of new works including *Colorado, Minnie Moustache, Chevalier du ciel* with Luis Mariano, José Padilla's *Romance au Portugal* (1949, Ménina), *Pampanilla,* the unfortunate *Premier Rendez-vous* and the musical comedy *Visa pour l'amour,* in which Bourvil and Annie Cordy danced the twist. In a number of these productions, notably *Pampanilla, Trois Valses* and, eternally as the teenaged heroine of *Mam'zelle Nitouche,* the fair proprietress herself took a leading role.

She was also seen during the 1930s in musical film, appearing in the filmed versions of the Meseillais musicals *Un de la Canebière, Trois de la marine* and *Les Gangsters du Château d'If.*

ROGER, Victor (b Montpellier, 22 July 1853; d Paris, 2 December 1903). Composer of a long list of mostly vaudevillesque scores for the French musical-comedy stage.

Victor Roger studied music at the École Niedermeyer, and thereafter spread his young writing talents through every available area of music-related work: vocal and piano music, dance music for the theatre, musical criticism and a number of small scenes and opérettes for the cafés-concerts, notably the Eldorado. One of these, *Mademoiselle Louloute,* was well enough regarded to be revived, 14 years after its initial production, at the Moulin-Rouge (29 September 1896), by which time Roger had thoroughly established himself as a popular composer for the light musical stage.

His first major success came when he provided the score to the particularly clever Paul Ferrier-Fabrice Carré libretto for the vaudeville-opérette *Joséphine vendue par ses soeurs,* which won a long first run (245 performances) in Paris and went on to a series of foreign productions and adaptations. A repeat success of this kind, however, was not swift to follow, although Roger supplied some typical lighthearted and often charming and comical music for a series of shows over the next decade. Only one musical emerged from his opus as the legitimate successor to *Joséphine* during those 10 years, the military vaudeville *Les 28 Jours de Clairette* which, like its predecessor, had a long Parisian season (236 performances) and a clutch of foreign performances and has remained, even more prominently than the earlier piece, a feature of the French musical-theatre repertoire.

Of Roger's other works, *Cendrillonnette* found the most hometown success (124 performances), with *Mademoiselle Asmodée* (88 performances), *La Dot de Brigitte* (73 performances) and *Le Voyage de Corbillon* (72 performances) all putting up respectable runs, but *Oscarine* (45 performances), *Le Fétiche* (37 performances), *Samsonnet* (29 performances), the delightful *Les Douze Femmes de Japhet* (31 performances, and revival), *Le Coq* (43 performances), *Clary-Clara* (8 performances), *Nicol-Nick* (35 performances) and *Sa Majesté l'amour* (10 performances) did not establish themselves in the French repertoire.

In spite of this, a good number of this group of pieces were taken up outside France, and a number of them (not always with Roger's music still attached) became successful in other centers. Vienna saw *Japhet und seine zwölf Frauen, Le Voyage de Corbillon* (as *Das rothe Parapluie*) and *La Dot de Brigitte* (as *Frau Lieutenant*) at the Theater in der Josefstadt, Berlin's Thalia-Theater also played the latter piece, and Hungary staged *Klári* (*Clary-Clara*), *Brigitta* (*La Dot de Brigitte*), *Jafet 12 feleség̃e* (*Les Douze Femmes de Japhet*), *A babona* (*Le Fétiche*), *Vegye el a lányomat!* (*Nicol-Nick*) and *Corbillon utazása / Az orleansi szüzek* (*Le Voyage de Corbillon*).

The year 1897, however, proved a vintage one for Roger, bringing him two more fine and international successes to add to his so-far tally of two: the jolly, comical *L'Auberge du Tohu-bohu* and the very superior musical comedy *Les Fêtards.* If, in Paris, the former (231 performances) won much longer consideration than the latter (72 performances), that verdict was by and large reversed by the rest of the world, even if some of the rest of the world found it preferable to replace much or all of Roger's *Fêtards* score with home-written songs. Vienna's Theater in der Josefstadt, Berlin's Thalia-Theater (*Tohu-Bohu, Wie man Männer fesselt*), London and Broadway (both for the first, but not the second) and the appreciative Budapest (*A biblias asszony, Őssze-vissza fogadó*) welcomed the shows more or less as written.

Of his remaining shows, those written in the last half-dozen years of the composer's life, none reached the same heights of popularity. *La Poule blanche* was played in both Berlin (*Die weisse Henne*) and in Budapest (*A fehér csirke*) after 32 Paris performances, but *L'Agence*

Crook et Cie was a four-performance flop, *La Petite Tache* was played just 12 times and, although his last work, *Le Jockey malgré lui,* after 33 performances in its initial production, was picked up for an American production (it was produced there as *The Office Boy*), this version, like America's adaptation of *Les Fêtards,* replaced Roger's score with one with a more local flavor. Canada, however, saw *Le Jockey* straight.

Provided, during the 16 effective years of his career, with some exceptionally fine and funny libretti, Roger decorated them with the kind of light, dancing music, often with an amusingly apt burlesque touch, which was most suitable to this brand of comedy-with-songs. If *Les 28 Jours de Clairette* with its popular military setting and antics has survived the best of these on the French stage, *Les Fêtards,* in particular, *Les Douze Femmes de Japhet* and *Joséphine* render it nothing in pure, comic enjoyment and almost certainly owe their comparative eclipse to the modern preference for the romantic and spectacular over the witty and farcical in musical theatre.

1880 **L'Amour quinze-vingt** (Laurencin [ie, Paul-Aimé Chapelle]) 1 act Eldorado 10 August

1882 **Mademoiselle Louloute** (Louis Péricaud, Lucien Delormel) 1 act Eldorado 9 September

1882 **La Nourrice de Montfermeuil** (Péricaud, Delormel) 1 act Eldorado November

1883 **La Chanson des écus** (Armand de Jallais) 1 act Eldorado 19 May

1883 **Mademoiselle Irma** (Fabrice Carré) 1 act Casino de Trouville 18 August

1886 **Joséphine vendue par ses soeurs** (Paul Ferrier, F Carré) Théâtre des Bouffes-Parisiens 20 March

1888 **Le Voyage en Écosse** (Cottin, Maurice Lecomte) 1 act Lille 17 May

1888 **Oscarine** (Charles Nuitter, Albert Guinon) Théâtre des Bouffes-Parisiens 15 October

1890 **Cendrillonnette** (w Gaston Serpette/Ferrier) Théâtre des Bouffes-Parisiens 24 January

1890 **Le Fétiche** (Ferrier, Charles Clairville) Théâtre des Menus-Plaisirs 13 March

1890 **Samsonnet** (Ferrier) Théâtre des Nouveautés 26 November

1890 **Les Douze Femmes de Japhet** (Antony Mars, Maurice Desvallières) Théâtre de la Renaissance 16 December

1891 **Le Coq** (Ferrier, Ernest Depré) Théâtre des Menus-Plaisirs 30 October

1891 **Mademoiselle Asmodée** (w Paul Lacome/Ferrier, C Clairville) Théâtre de la Renaissance 23 November

1892 **Les Vingt-huit Jours de Clairette** (Hippolyte Raymond, Mars) Théâtre des Folies-Dramatiques 3 May

1893 **Catherinette** (Mars) 1 act Lunéville 17 July

1893 **Pierre et Paul** (Mars) 1 act Lunéville 17 July

1894 **Clary-Clara** (Raymond, Mars) Théâtre des Folies-Dramatiques 20 March

1895 **Nicol-Nick** (Raymond, Mars, Albert Duru) Théâtre des Folies-Dramatiques 23 January

1895 **La Dot de Brigitte** (w Serpette/Ferrier, Mars) Théâtre des Bouffes-Parisiens 6 May

1896 **Le Voyage de Corbillon** (Mars) Théâtre Cluny 30 January

1896 **Sa Majesté l'amour** (Mars, Maurice Hennequin) Eldorado 24 December

1897 **L'Auberge du tohu-bohu** (Maurice Ordonneau) Théâtre des Folies-Dramatiques 10 February

1897 **Les Fêtards** (Mars, M Hennequin) Palais-Royal 28 October

1898 **L'Agence Crook et Cie** (Maurice Ordonneau) Théâtre des Folies-Dramatiques 28 January

1898 **La Petite Tache** (F Carré) Théâtre des Bouffes-Parisiens 26 March

1898 **Les Quatre Filles Aymon** (w Lacome/Liorat, Albert Fonteny) Théâtre des Folies-Dramatiques 20 September

1899 **La Poule blanche** (Mars, Hennequin) Théâtre Cluny 13 January

1902 **Le Jockey malgré lui** (Ordonneau, Paul Gavault) Théâtre des Bouffes-Parisiens 4 December

ROGERS, Anne (b Liverpool, 29 July 1933).

Nineteen-year-old Anne Rogers won her first success in novelettish style when she was promoted from the small role of Fay (''It's Never Too Late to Fall in Love'') to principal girl in the original club-theatre production of *The Boy Friend,* creating ''I Could Be Happy with You,'' ''A Room in Bloomsbury'' and ''The Boy Friend.'' She repeated the role of Polly Browne in the next year's expanded version of the show and again when it moved to the West End.

In 1957 she went to America to head the first national tour of *My Fair Lady* and she repeated her Eliza Doolittle, in succession to Julie Andrews, at London's Theatre Royal, Drury Lane, in 1959–61. She starred as Princess Flavia alongside Alfred Drake in a musical version of *The Prisoner of Zenda* (*Zenda*) which failed to reach Broadway and as Amalia Balash in the short-lived London production of *She Loves Me,* played Clarissa in Bickerstaff's *Lionel and Clarissa* at Guildford, toured America opposite Dick Kallman as the tough little heroine of *Half a Sixpence* (1966) and replaced Louise Troy as Maggie Hobson in the musical version of *Hobson's Choice* (*Walking Happy*) at Broadway's Lunt-Fontanne Theatre the following year.

Back in London, she paired with Ian Carmichael for the British production of *I Do! I Do!* and several years later with Teddy Green, delivering ''You Can Dance with Any Girl at All'' and the ''Where Has My Hubby Gone?'' blues as Lucille Early in the Theatre Royal, Drury Lane revival of *No, No, Nanette.* She has subsequently appeared as Guinevere in *Camelot* in San Francisco, succeeded to the role of Dorothy Brock in Broadway's *42nd Street* and appeared as The Ghost of Christmas Past in the Long Beach Light Opera's musical *A Christmas Carol.*

ROGERS, Ginger [McMATH, Virginia Katherine] (b Independence, Mo, 16 July 1911; d Rancho Mirage, Calif, 2 May 1995). The musical screen's most popular dancing heroine, particularly as seen in the arms of Fred Astaire.

After early appearances in vaudeville and as a dancer, Miss Rogers began her musical-comedy career appearing on Broadway in *Top Speed* (1929, Babs Green) and in *Girl Crazy* (1930, Molly Gray), in which she introduced George Gershwin's ''Embraceable You'' and ''But Not for Me.'' She made her first screen appearance later the same year in *Young Man of Manhattan* and, for the next 30 years, had an oustanding career as a dancing-singing light comedienne in musical and comedy films. She played in *Golddiggers of 1933* and in *42nd Street* before being teamed for the first time with Fred Astaire in *Flying Down to Rio* (1933). Thereafter the pair appeared together in a series of 1930s films (*The Gay Divorcee, Roberta, Top Hat, Follow the Fleet, Swing Time, Shall We Dance, Carefree, The Story of Vernon and Irene Castle*) which made them into the foremost representatives of the Hollywood musical film. Her later films were largely in the non-musical sphere, although she starred, notably, in the 1943 movie version of *Lady in the Dark.* She won an Academy Award in 1940 for her performance in *Kitty Foyle.* In 1959 (May 18) she starred on British television, alongside tenor David Hughes, as Lisa Marvin in a version of the Hans May musical *Carissima.*

Miss Rogers returned to the musical stage in 1959 in a Vernon Duke musical, *The Pink Jungle* (Tess Jackson), which closed on the road, toured in *Annie Get Your Gun* and *The Unsinkable Molly Brown,* and retook to the Broadway stage in 1965 to succeed to the role of Dolly Levi in *Hello, Dolly!* which she subsequently toured. In 1969 she recreated the role of *Mame* for its British production at London's Theatre Royal, Drury Lane, and she subsequently toured in the role created by Katharine Hepburn, as Coco Chanel in *Coco* (1971), as part of a continuing performing life which latterly included little theatre work. In 1985 she directed a revival of *Babes in Arms.*

Autobiography: *Ginger, My Story* (Harper Collins, New York, 1991); Biographies: Richards, D: *Ginger Rogers* (Clifton, London, 1969), McGilligan, P: *Ginger Rogers* (Pyramid, New York, 1975), Croce, A: *The Fred Astaire and Ginger Rogers Book* (Galahad, New York, 1972), Faris, J: *Ginger Rogers* (Greenwood Press, New York, 1994), Morley, S: *Shall We Dance* (Weidenfeld & Nicolson, London, 1995), etc

THE ROGERS BROTHERS

ROGERS, Gus [SOLOMON, Gustave] (b New York, 1869; d New York, 19 October 1908).

ROGERS, Max [SOLOMON, Max] (b New York, 1873; d Far Rockaway, 26 December 1932).

A song-and-dance act from their earliest teens (National Theater, 1885), the brothers subsequently switched to playing German-accented knockabout comedy. They appeared at Tony Pastor's in 1889, toured in vaudeville combinations for four years and then formed a company of their own playing, at first, variety bills and later dipping occasionally into something a tiny bit more vertebrate. They appeared in 1897 alongside Richard Carle as Boomps (Gus) and Schrumm (Max) in *A Round of Pleasure,* and in 1899 played in the John McNally variety farce *A Reign of Error,* before far-reaching producers Klaw and Erlanger set them up in a series of musical-comedy shows with which they sought to break, or at least shake, the popularity of the rival and highly successful Dutch-comedy performers and renegade producers, Weber and Fields. The brothers appeared on Broadway successively in *The Rogers Brothers in Wall Street, The Rogers Brothers in Central Park, The Rogers Brothers in Washington, The Rogers Brothers at Harvard, The Rogers Brothers in London, The Rogers Brothers in Paris, The Rogers Brothers in Ireland* and *The Rogers Brothers in Panama.*

The younger brother, Max, was generally acknowledged as the strong half of the act. However, when Gus, the elder brother who had been the business brains of the combination, died from typhoid during the post-Broadway tour of *The Rogers Brothers in Panama,* Max was never able to again reach the heights that he had achieved during their partnership. He appeared in the same kind of roles that he had played in the series in the mediocre and shortlived Max Hoffman/Harry H Williams/Aaron Hoffman piece *The Young Turk* (Atlantic City 10 November 1909, Howe Swift jr), in Lew Fields's *Hanky Panky* (1912, William Rausmitt) and in *The Pleasure Seekers* (1913, Heinrich Brobscloff) before fading out of the musical theatre.

LE ROI CAROTTE Grand opéra-bouffe féerie in 4 acts by Victorien Sardou. Music by Jacques Offenbach. Théâtre de la Gaîté, Paris, 15 January 1872.

Le Roi Carotte, for which Offenbach temporarily left his habitual text-partners to collaborate with the successful, popular (and younger) playwright Victorien Sardou, had little in common either with his great opéras-bouffes or with the hugely successful opéras-comiques with which he would end his career. In both of those areas, Offenbach's scores held an important and even predominant place, but in *Le Roi Carotte* the music was an adjunct not only to a pointedly politico-satirical text but also to a vast physical production, in the vein of *La Biche au bois* and *La Chatte blanche,* the like of which even Paris had rarely seen.

Sardou's libretto, apparently based on an idea from one of E T A Hoffman's tales, and played in four acts and 22 (later 17, later even fewer) spectacular scenes, had been written before the Franco-Prussian War and the horrors of the days of the Commune, and it warned only too accurately of the fate that awaited the Second Empire. However, it required few alterations in view of the events of the past years' hostilities before it was put on the Paris stage in 1872.

The text told the allegorical tale of penniless Prince Fridolin (Masset), who sells his ancestral armor to pay for his wedding to the rich Princess Cunégonde (Anna Judic). The suits rise up magically against him and tell him that his sacrilege means that he will be dispossessed. The evil fairy Coloquinte (Mlle Mariani) brings to life the vegetables of the kitchen garden, headed by the hideous King Carotte (Vicini), and under her enchantment the court and Cunégonde all fall under the vegetable monarch's sway. Fridolin goes into exile, along with the faithful Robin Luron (Zulma Bouffar), the court sorcerer Truck (Alexandre) and pretty Rosée du Soir (Mlle Séveste), and seeks out the magician Quiribibi, who sends him off in quest of a magic ring which is hidden in the ruins of Pompeii. Whilst he is making his way there, via such spectacular venues as the Kingdom of Insects and Monkey Island, the people realize that the new rule is much worse than the old and revolt. The vile Carotte, defeated, goes back to being just a vegetable whilst Fridolin is restored to power with Rosée du Soir at his side.

The spectacle (which was sufficiently important that Offenbach and Sardou gave the chief machinist a percentage of their royalties) and the scenes of the show were supported by a score from which an Air des Colporteurs, "Nous venons du fin fond de la Perse," an ants' chorus and a Fridolin/Cunégonde duo proved the best-liked moments.

There was little doubt that, if not exactly an opérette a clef, *Le Roi Carotte* was making a specific political stand. The exiled Napoléon III in particular and the Empire in general were obviously represented by Fridolin and his friends (the foreign marriage pointed at Napoléon's union with Eugénie), and those characters were drawn markedly more sympathetically than the proletarian vegetable (Lat: radix = radical, etc) rabble and their demagogue King Carotte, who was just as clearly meant to represent the left-wing speechifier Léon Gambetta, who had declared the overthrow of the Empire in 1870. Some committed critics, however, preferred to encourage the readers of their newspapers to believe the reverse.

The show had attracted great attention before its opening as much because of this pointed political content and the whisper that it actually represented the Emperor on stage as for the figures that were being touted about as to its extravagant staging. However, in a way to which Offenbach had shown himself prone in the past, producer Bouvet, who had, with the composer's encouragement, spent 345,000 francs on the gorgeous production at the Gaîté—a production on which the first-night curtain fell at 2:30 AM—had calculated his running costs ill and, although he insisted that he could break even on a 65 percent house (after raising seat prices from 6 to 9 francs), he found, after some time, that even 65 percent of an audience was hard to come by. The piece which had been puffed as the glory of the season was barely making ends meet. Bouvet reduced his tickets to half-price, but it was not enough and *Le Roi Carotte* closed after 149 performances with certainly no profit and, if the truth were known, probably a sizeable loss.

Le Roi Carotte was nevertheless regarded as a success, or enough of a success to be given a number of productions outside France. London's large Alhambra Theatre was the first (ad H S Leigh), with a production whose spectacle lost nothing in comparison with Paris. Harry Paulton (Carotte), Cornelie d'Anka (Cunégonde), Frank Celli (Fridolin), Elisa Savelli (Rosée du Soir) and Anetta Scasi (Robin Wildfire) headed a large principal cast backed up by a chorus of 50, an orchestra of 50 and a ballet of 200 which performed a sabatière, a farandole, the grand ballet of insects and a monkey divertissement, through 184 performances up to the Christmas production of its successor, *Black Crook,* another piece based on a French grand opéra-bouffe féerie. This production of *Le Roi Carotte* was said to have lost the theatre £37,000, but it was given a revival, of nearly two further months, two years later (2 November 1874, with Paulton and Rose Bell as Robin) when a flop left a gap in the Alhambra's program.

Augustin Daly's New York production cut out the bulk of the political allusions and the satire and made do with the fairy tale and the spectacle. Mrs John Wood (Robin), John Brougham (Carotte), Rose Hersee (Rosée du Soir), Robert Craig (Fridolin), Emma Howson (Cunégonde) and Stuart Robson (Truck) headed a stellar cast, supported by the Lauri family of pantomimists and the acrobatic Majiltons, and the show played for nearly three months on Broadway, even though, as in Paris, Daly found it impossible to make ends meet. Years later one of the actors described it as "the most famous 'frost' in American stage history." It was enough of an event on Broadway, however, to spawn several burlesques: Dan Bryant came up with a *King Karrot, or Red Monkey Shines,* the San Francisco Minstrels produced *Raw Carrots,* and the Theatre Comique played *King of Carrots,* without the benefit of extravagant scenery. Both of these parodies were more metropolitan than Britain's burlesques: Frank Green and Alfred Lee's *Carrot and Pasnip* (11 May 1872) began life at the North Woolwich Gardens, and George Thorne's *Le Raw Carrot* was produced at Margate's Theatre Royal (19 September 1873).

In France, the response was *La Reine Carotte* (13 January 1872, Clairville, Victor Bernard, Victor Koning) which, on the little stage of the Théâtre des Menus-Plaisirs and with Thérésa as its star, was intended to burlesque the whole prevalent fashion for the overblown spectacular musical, but ended up doing little more than ape it. The local marionette theatre came out with *Le Roi aux cheveux carottes*.

In Vienna (ad Julius Hopp), with a reduced visual content of 12 scenes, *König Carotte* played as a Christmas entertainment at the Theater an der Wien with Felix Schweighofer (Carrot), Jani Szíka (Fridolin), Alexander Girardi (Truck), Bertha Steinher (Princess Abendroth) and Hermine Meyerhoff (Rubin) for 37 performances under the management of Maximilian Steiner—rather less than the other main Offenbach spectacular, *Le Voyage dans la lune,* had totaled earlier the same year.

Although neither the piece nor any portion of its score has endured as a generally popular item in the 20th century, *Le Roi Carotte* has nevertheless survived into intermittent productions and was most recently revived in Amsterdam in October 1990.

UK: Alhambra Theatre 3 June 1872; USA: Grand Opera House 26 August 1872; Austria: Theater an der Wien *König Carotte* 23 December 1876

LE ROI DE CARREAU Opérette in 3 acts by Eugène Leterrier and Albert Vanloo. Music by Théodore de Lajarte. Théâtre des Nouveautés, Paris, 26 October 1883.

When Leterrier and Vanloo, the preferred librettists of Jules Brasseur at the Théâtre des Nouveautés, presented their *Le Roi de carreau* to the producer, they might have expected to see it confided to Planquette or to Lecocq, but Brasseur chose to commission the score from Théodore de Lajarte. Lajarte (1826–1890), a composer of much dance and march music and a number of comic operas, including a little piece called *Le Portrait* which had recently been received at the Opéra-Comique (lib: Adénis, Laurençin 18 June 1883), and one larger piece *Mademoiselle Marguerite s.v.p.* (lib: Jules Adénis, Francis Tourte Bouffes Saint-Antoine 1 September 1868), was not precisely a young talent, but he was new to the world of the opérette and his setting of *Le Roi de carreau* proved to be elegantly acceptable. A top-notch cast including Brasseur himself as the aged aristocrat La Roche Trumeau, his son Albert as the comical Mistigris, Vauthier and Mlle Vaillant-Couturier in the principal singing roles, Berthelier in the plum part of the thief-king, Tirechappe, and the favorite soubrette Mily-Meyer all starred in this tale of a lost aristocratic child picked up by a vagabond and necromancer and trailed through some 18th-century risings before being restored to her rightful place.

The piece was played 88 times in its first run and revived in 1885 for several further weeks after the flop of Planquette's *La Cremaillère* left the theatre at a temporary loss. It was subsequently played in Hungary and in Germany, but it did not achieve a wide acceptance there any more than a remusicked version did in America. Harry B Smith adapted Leterrier and Vanloo's story as *Half a King* (Knickerbocker Theater 14 September 1896), Ludwig Englander replaced Lajarte's music (''although the score contains but few original numbers''), and Francis Wilson starred as Tirechappe alongside Peter Lang (Mistigris) and Lulu Glaser (Pierette) amongst much more low comedy and much less operettic singing than had been heard in the original. The piece proved good for a couple of seasons of Wilson touring.

Hungary: Népszínház *Tökfilkó* 14 November 1885; Germany: Friedrich-Wilhelmstadtisches Theater *Der Carreau-König* 18 February 1887

RÖKK, Marika [KÖRNER, Marie Karoline Ilona] (b Cairo, 3 November ?1913). Durable Hungarian soubrette whose greatest success came in German films.

Born in Egypt of Hungarian parents, somewhen around 1913, Rökk began her working life as a dancer in a touring circus. She made her first theatrical mark in Budapest where she took the principal soubrette role at the Király Színház in *Sültgalamb* (1931), appeared as the jazz composer Daisy (created by Rózsi Bársony in Berlin) in Hungary's production of *Ball im Savoy* (1932) and then featured at the Pesti Színház as the leading lady of Eisemann's highly successful modern musical comedy *Zsákbamacska* (1932). Over the next years, she moved into films, both in Hungary (*Csókolj meg édes* 1932) and in Germany, whilst still appearing from time to time on the stage in such pieces as Komjáti and Eisemann's *A cirkusz csillaga* (Vígsínház, 1934) and Benatzky's *Egy lány, aki mindenkié* (*Wer gewinnt Colette,* Müvesz Színház 1936), but by the mid-1930s she was thoroughly established as a star of Berlin's UFA musical and revusical films (Rosika in *Leichte Cavallerie* 1935, *Heisses Blut* 1936, Bronislawa in *Der Bettelstudent* 1936, *Und Du, mein Schatz, fährst mit* 1936, Ita in *Gasparone* 1937, etc).

When others were fleeing Germany, Rökk was moving in. She became the favorite film soubrette of the Hitler era and an important part of the German film industry through such pieces as *Hallo Janine* (1939), *Kora Terry* (1940), *Tanz mit dem Kaiser* (1941), *Hab' mich Lieb* (1942) and *Frau meiner Träume* (1944). In the postwar years, now based in Austria she was seen in *Das Kind der Donau* (1950), *Die Csárdásfürstin* (1951, Sylva Varescu), *Die geschiedene Frau* (1953), *Maske in Blau* (1953), *Nachts im grünen Kakadu* (1957), *Bühne frei für Marika* (1958), *Die Fledermaus* (1962, Adele), *Hochzeitsnacht im Paradies* (1962, Ilonka) and others.

In later years, Rökk returned to the stage, appearing at Vienna's Raimundtheater in her old role in *Ball im Savoy* and in *Maske in Blau,* playing Dolly Levi in the German production of *Hello, Dolly!* (1968) and appearing at the Theater an der Wien in the Damon Runyon musical *Die Gräfin vom Naschmarkt* (1978). In 1992 she returned to the Budapest stage to take the role originally constructed for another Hungarian veteran, Hanna Honthy, in *Gräfin Mariza* (Katja).

Rökk was married in 1940 to film director Georg Jacoby (b Mainz, 23 July 1882; d Munich, 21 February 1965), the director of many operetta films through a long career, and is the mother of **Gabriele JACOBY** (b 1944), the Eliza Doolittle of Vienna's *My Fair Lady* and the Raina of *Helden, Helden.*

ROLYAT, Dan [TAYLOR, Herbert] (b Birmingham, 11 November 1872; d Rochdale, 10 December 1927). Acrobatic comedy star of several early 20th-century London musicals.

After an insignificant provincial beginning to his stage career, the young Rolyat was spotted by the George Edwardes organization and put to tour in Teddy Payne's lead comedy role in *The Toreador.* However, that job produced no follow up and instead the young performer went touring with Fred Karno's comedians. He subsequently played in variety before being discovered a second time, by Robert Courtneidge, and given a principal comedy role in his London production of *The Dairymaids* (1906, Joe Mivens).

Courtneidge then cast him in his two most memorable roles, as the pattering barber, Benjamin Partridge, in *Tom Jones* (1907) and as John Smith, alias Simplicitas, the comical hero of *The Arcadians* (1909, ''All Down Piccadilly''). He subsequently played the chief comic role in Courtneidge's *The Mousmé,* toured for him in *Princess Caprice,* and returned to London to play the professionally unemployed loafer Slinks in a revival of *Miss Hook of Holland,* but by this time had become a depressive, suffering from the sequels to a series of stage accidents, including a fall from a chandelier in *The Dairymaids* and another from his horse in *The Arcadians.* He never re-established himself at his *Arcadians* level, attempted suicide, and finally died after some years away from the stage.

Rolyat was for a while married to his *Arcadians* co-star, soprano Florence Smithson, who went through the odd bottled problem herself.

ROMBERG, Sigmund (b Nagykanizsa, Hungary, 29 July 1887; d New York, 9 November 1951). Composer of several of Broadway's most successful romantic musicals of the first decades of the 20th century.

Romberg studied the violin in his youthful years in Hungary, but he was set at first towards an adult career in engineering. However, during his technical studies in Vienna he doubled as a member of the house staff at the Theater an der Wien and the attraction of the musical theatre won out over the more practical career. He moved on to London and then, in 1909, to New York where he took work as a pianist and an orchestra leader in a city restaurant whilst making his first attempts at breaking into the songwriting world. His first theatrical songs were interpolated into Adolf Philipp's English version of his *Das Mitternachtsmädel* in 1913, and he got his first title credit when he provided enough replacement music for Delbert Davenport's production of his own *Little Mary Mack* to merit a co-composer credit.

Romberg's earliest published works caught the eye of Jake Shubert and as a result the young composer joined the Shubert staff to take over from the resigning Louis Hirsch the task of providing the musical piece-work the management required for their heavy turnover of revues and musical plays. He made his entrée on to Broadway as the composer of the score for the 1914 revue *The Whirl of the World* and then in quick succession sputtered out several years' worth of melodies for the splendiditious Shubert revues at the Winter Garden Theatre (*The Passing Show, Dancing Around, Maid in America, A World of Pleasure, The Show of Wonders, The Passing Show of 1917, 1918* and *1919, Doing Our Bit*), as well as for a bundle of soi-disant book musicals, most of which had more than a little of revue about them (*Hands Up*—replacing the tryout score by the young Cole Porter—Al Jolson's *Robinson Crusoe Jr,* Justine Johnstone's *Over the Top,* Jolson's *Sinbad,* and the cheekily titled *Monte Cristo Jr*). He also contributed to the odd play with occasional songs (*Ruggles of Red Gap*) and, more and more frequently as the fashion turned, supplied made-to-order interpolations—often considerable enough to leave little place for the melodies of the original composer—to be stuck into American versions of such Continental musical shows as Eysler's *Ein Tag im Paradies,* Leo Ascher's *Was tut man nicht alles aus Liebe,* Winterberg's *Die schöne Schwedin,* Kálmán's *Der gute Kamarad,* Straus's *Die schöne Unbekannte* and Kollo's *Wie einst im Mai,* or even a homemade piece, such as Zoël Parenteau's *Follow the Girl.*

A number of these shows were distinctly successful and in several it was Romberg's part of the music which produced the tunes that Broadway's audiences favored. *Wie einst im Mai,* rewritten thoroughly as *Maytime,* produced the composer's first significant hit song, ''Will You Remember?'' (better known by its first line, ''Sweetheart, sweetheart, sweetheart,'' as performed by Jeanette MacDonald), but it brought him no improved commissions as a composer from the Shuberts and he therefore departed their employ and attempted to produce his own work himself. Teamed with Max Wilner, he offered as his first production a very *Maytime*ish work called *The Magic Melody* at the Shubert Theater. It lasted 143 performances, displayed little of enduring character, and did not make money, but it had at least the merit of bringing its composer forward as having the potential to be more than the virtual hack he had been used as heretofore. The producing venture, however, did not bring sufficiently immediate fruits of the green and pocket-sized kind, as the partners found problems first with a nonstarter called *Oh! Pat* designed for Pat Rooney, then with another musical, *The Three Kisses*—which actually went into rehearsal, with Vivienne Segal as star and Hassard Short directing, but which was abandoned without even opening in Springfield (January 1921).

While the two then tried their hand at producing rather less expensive non-musical plays, Romberg took a composing assignment, from Lew Fields, to provide some interpolations into an apparently only partly satisfactory score for a show called *Poor Little Ritz Girl* by two young writers called Rodgers and Hart. He returned to producing his own work with *Love Birds,* but the show (105 performances) did not even come up to *The Magic Melody* and Romberg found himself obliged to fold up his managerial activities and turn back to the Shuberts and to hack work.

His first adaptation during part two of Romberg's Shubert career turned out to be his most successful to date. The Franz Schubert pasticcio biomusical *Das Dreimäderlhaus* had been hugely successful wherever it had been played, and the version which Romberg and Dorothy Donnelly concocted from the dismembered parts of the previous versions and named *Blossom Time* confirmed that success in America, becoming a hardy annual of the touring circuits and a Broadway regular. *Bombo,* the new Al Jolson vehicle, for which Romberg provided the basic score, was also a fine success, and even the ragbag revusical *The Blushing Bride* won a run and some praise for the composer, who had replaced the show's songs between its tryout and its Broadway outing. However, when the Shuberts went as far as to water down Leo Fall's outstanding score for *Die Rose von Stambul* with gobbets of Romberg, the limits of that praise were displayed.

More revusical pieces followed—*The Passing Shows of 1923* and *of 1924, Artists and Models,* the Winter Garden shows *The Dancing Girl* and *Innocent Eyes* (for Mistinguett)—along with musicals such as the slim-booked *Marjorie,* but, apart from *Springtime of Youth,* an Americanized version of Walter Kollo's *Sterne, die wieder leuchtet,* the Shuberts took a reef in their production of botched Continental shows. In fact, they would shortly have no need of imported operetta, for by the end of 1924 they had at last discovered that they had an American, or at least a naturalized American, operetta composer very near to hand who was capable of turning out scores which there was no excuse for botching. Romberg, who had just knocked off a considerable part of the score for Florenz Ziegfeld's production of *Annie Dear,* a musical version of Clare Kummer's *Good Gracious Annabelle,* for November, supplied the Shuberts with *The Student Prince in Heidelberg* in December. It had taken a decade, but was swiftly evident that the producers finally had that original operetta hit that Romberg had been trying so long to provide. *The Student Prince* was an enormous success and its songs ''Golden Days,'' ''The Drinking Song,'' ''Deep in My Heart, Dear,'' ''Just We Two,'' ''Come Boys, Let's All Be Gay, Boys'' and the celebrated Serenade became a part of the heart of the American classic operetta repertoire.

Of Romberg's 1925 pieces, neither the musical comedy *Louie the 14th,* a vehicle for Leon Errol, nor the Ruritanian operetta *Princess Flavia,* based on *The Prisoner of Zenda* and all too obviously intended to be as much like *The Student Prince* as possible, came up to the expectations aroused by *The Student Prince* and further whetted by Friml's *The Vagabond King,* but with his next work Romberg confirmed thoroughly. *The Desert Song* teamed him with Otto Harbach and Oscar Hammerstein, who had been responsible for the libretto to Friml's *Rose Marie,* under the management of Frank Mandel and Lawrence Schwab and the result was a second huge and enduring hit and a second bundle of classic songs (''The Desert Song,'' ''The Riff's Song'' ''One Alone,'' ''Romance'').

The next year's bundle of shows were less successful. *Cherry Blossoms* mixed reminiscences of *Die schöne Galathee, The Geisha, David Garrick* and *Madame Butterfly* with a utilitarian score; the Barbara Frietchie musical *My Maryland* was a huge hit in Philadelphia but, in spite of a 312-performance Broadway run, left little mark on the musical world beyond the patriotic song ''Your Land and My Land''; whilst the too-routine *My Princess* and *The Love Call* (an adaptation of Augustus Thomas's *Arizona*) both went under thoroughly.

However, Romberg had proven on previous occasions that he could turn out the most mechanical of music one minute, and then follow it up with a truly fine score the next. He did just that again the following year when, whilst supplying Ziegfeld with some unexceptional numbers to set alongside some rather better Gershwin ones for *Rosalie,* he joined with Oscar Hammerstein for a third grand show and a third great score in *The New Moon* (''Lover, Come Back to Me,'' ''Softly, as in a Morning

Sunrise,'' ''The Girl on the Prow,'' ''One Kiss,'' ''Stout-hearted Men''). This third great hit was, however, to be his last of real and enduring value. A further collaboration with Hammerstein produced the by no means unsuccessful South-American-romantic *Nina Rosa,* whilst *Rose de France,* a piece written for Paris—where Romberg's works had proven highly popular as fodder for the kind of opérette à grand spectacle stagings then beloved in the French capital—had a good career at the Théâtre du Châtelet. At the same huge house, a French adaptation of his *Forbidden Melody,* played as *Le Chant du Tzigane,* subsequently proved more popular than its American original. There was success, too, with the 1945 Broadway production of *Up in Central Park,* but the piece was not on the same level as the three works for which Romberg had become famous, and its 504-performance run did not preface the same kind of afterlife those shows have enjoyed.

Romberg proved his considerable worth with the scores of his trio of outstanding shows, a threesome which, along with Friml's *Rose Marie* and *The Vagabond King* and Kern's *Show Boat,* made up the nucleus of the Broadway-bred romantic operettas of the 1920s. Although his music was solidly founded in the Continental Operette tradition, it yet had a flavor to it which marked it out as being distinctly not of Hungary nor of Vienna. As early as *The Blue Paradise,* Romberg's interpolated pieces, set alongside of those of Edmund Eysler, showed a manner and a tone which contrasted with those of that most warmly Viennese of Viennese composers. It was, perhaps, a measure of his knowledge of his audiences that, although his numbers had not the quality of Eysler's, it was one of his which turned out the popular success of the show. After his and its peak in the 1920s, the fashion for the American romantic operetta passed, and Romberg duly had less success. He attempted to adapt to contemporary tastes in some of his later works, but he was never as happy as in the richly lyrical Americo-European idiom which he had employed in the three shows by which his name endures.

1915 **Little Mary Mack [of Hackensack]** (w Newton Ashenfelder/Delbert E Davenport) Lyceum Theater, Scranton, Pa 19 April

1915 **Hands Up** (w E Ray Goetz/Goetz/Edgar Smith) 44th Street Theater 22 July

1915 **The Dream Girl** (Edwin T Emery) Rorick's Theater, Elmira, NY 2 August

1915 **The Blue Paradise** (*Ein Tag im Paradies*) part-score for revised American version (Casino Theater)

1915 **Ruggles of Red Gap** (Harold Atteridge/Harrison Rhodes) Fulton Theater 24 December

1916 **Robinson Crusoe Jr** (Atteridge) Winter Garden Theater 17 February

1916 **The Girl from Brazil** (*Die schöne Schwedin*) part-score for revised American version (44th Street Theater)

1916 **Follow Me** (*Was tut man nicht alles aus Liebe*) part-score for revised American version w Robert B Smith (Casino Theater)

1916 **[Her] Soldier Boy** (*Az obsitos*) part-score for revised American version w Rida Johnson Young (Astor Theater)

1917 **My Lady's Glove** (*Die schöne Unbekannte*) part score for revised American version w Edward Paulton (Lyric Theater)

1917 **Maytime** (*Wie einst im Mai*) new score for revised American version w Young, Cyrus Wood (Shubert Theater)

1918 **Sinbad** (Atteridge) Winter Garden Theater 14 February

1918 **The Melting of Molly** (Wood/Marie Thompson Davies, Edgar Smith) Broadhurst Theater 30 December

1919 **Monte Cristo Jr** (w Jean Schwartz/Atteridge) Winter Garden Theater 12 February

1919 **The Magic Melody** (Frederic Arnold Kummer) Shubert Theater 10 November

1920 **Poor Little Ritz Girl** (w Richard Rodgers/Alex Gerber, Lorenz Hart/George Campbell) Central Theater 28 July

1921 **Love Birds** (Ballard MacDonald/Edgar Allen Woolf) Apollo Theater 15 March

1921 **Blossom Time** (*Das Dreimäderlhaus*) new arranged score for revised American version w Dorothy Donnelly (Ambassador Theater)

1921 **Bombo** (Atteridge) Jolson Theater 6 October

1922 **The Blushing Bride** (Wood/Edward Clark) Astor Theater 6 February

1922 **The Rose of Stamboul** (*Die Rose von Stambul*) part score for revised American version w Atteridge (Century Theater)

1922 **Springtime of Youth** (*Sterne, die wieder leuchtet*) part score for revised American version w Wood, Woodward (Broadhurst Theater)

1923 **The Dancing Girl** (Atteridge) Winter Garden 24 January

1923 **The Courtesan** (w Jean Schwartz/Atteridge/Atteridge, Harry Wagstaffe Gribble) Parsons' Theater, Hartford, Conn 17 October

1924 **Marjorie** (w Herbert Stothart, Stephen Jones, Philip Culkin/Clifford Grey/Fred Thompson, Atteridge) Shubert Theater 11 August

1924 **Annie Dear** (Grey/Clare Kummer) Times Square Theater 4 November

1924 **The Student Prince [in Heidelberg]** (Donnelly) Jolson Theater 2 December

1925 **Louie the 14th** (Arthur Wimperis) Cosmopolitan Theater 2 March

1925 **Princess Flavia** (ex- *A Royal Pretender*) (Harry B Smith) Century Theater 2 November

1926 **The Desert Song** (ex- *My Lady Fair*) (Otto Harbach, Oscar Hammerstein, Frank Mandel) Casino Theater 30 November

1927 **Cherry Blossoms** (H B Smith) 44th Street Theater 28 March

1927 **My Maryland** (Donnelly) Jolson Theater 12 September

1927 **My Princess** (Donnelly) Shubert Theater 6 October

1927 **The Love Call** (ex- *Bonita, Love Song, My Golden West*) (H B Smith/Edward Locke) Majestic Theater 24 October

1928 **Rosalie** (w George Gershwin/P G Wodehouse, Ira Gershwin/Guy Bolton, William Anthony McGuire) New Amsterdam Theater 10 January

1927 **The New Moon** (Hammerstein, Mandel) Chestnut Street Opera House, Philadelphia 22 December; Imperial Theater (revised version) 19 September 1928

1930 **Nina Rosa** (Irving Caesar/Harbach) Majestic Theater 20 September

1931 **East Wind** (Hammerstein) Manhattan Theater 27 October

1933 **Melody** (Caesar/Edward Childs Carpenter) Casino Theater 14 February

1933 **Rose de France** (Albert Willemetz/André Mouëzy-Éon) Théâtre du Châtelet, Paris 28 October

1935 **May Wine** (Hammerstein/Mandel) St James Theater 5 December

1936 **Forbidden Melody** (Harbach) New Amsterdam Theater 2 November

1941 **Sunny River** (Hammerstein) St James Theater 4 December

1945 **Up in Central Park** (Herbert Fields, Dorothy Fields) Century Theater 27 January

1948 **My Romance** (Rowland Leigh) Shubert Theater 19 October

1954 **The Girl in Pink Tights** (Leo Robin/Jerome Chodorov, Joseph Stein) Mark Hellinger Theater 5 March

Biography: (fictionalized) Arnold, E: *Deep in My Heart* (Duell, Sloane & Pearce, New York, 1949)

ROME, Harold [Jacob] (b Hartford, Conn, 27 May 1908; d New York, 20 October 1993). Songwriter who scored several good postwar Broadway runs.

An architectural draftsman, then a summer-camp officer, Rome won his way into Broadway's eye when he provided the songs for an amateur revue, *Pins and Needles* (''Sing Me a Song with Social Significance''), which, as presented by members of the Garment Workers' Union, proved a novelty hit in a series of ever-largening theatres through more than two seasons. A second, and this time professionally produced, revue *Sing Out the News* (''Franklin D Roosevelt Jones'') did not have the same novelty and lasted but four months.

A period in the wartime army, during which he contributed to the servicemen's revue *Stars and Gripes* (1943), convinced Rome to find his fun in military life and its consequences rather than in ''social significance'' and the result—helped by an (almost) all-troops cast—was a two-year success for a further revue, *Call Me Mister* (''South America, Take It Away''). A return to the socially significant for a book musical *That's the Ticket* (''The Money Song''), produced by Joe Kipness, resulted in an out-of-town closure.

Rome found success again with the love-in-a-summer-camp show *Wish You Were Here* which sported a swimming pool on the stage and a hit-parade ballad in its croony title song, and in the following decade he turned out three more shows which posted up fine to fair runs in New York. A pulpy condensation of Marcel Pagnol's marsellais trilogy into *Fanny* didn't offend those who hadn't heard of Pagnol, and kept on not offending them for 888 performances; a musical version of the endearing film story of *Destry Rides Again* with Andy Griffith as a memorable Destry marked up 472 performances; and *I Can Get It for You Wholesale* returned to the garment business which had started its composer on the road to success for a 300-performance run, which nevertheless landed it in the red.

In 1965 Rome provided the lyrics for the short-lived American version of the French revue *La Grosse Valise* (1965), and saw what would be his last Broadway book show, the South African-Jewish musical play *The Zulu and the Zayda,* played through an indifferent run. However, several years later, he was invited to compose the score for a Japanese production of a version of the celebrated novel *Gone with the Wind* and the resultant piece, produced in Tokyo as *Scarlett,* was sufficiently successful for an English version to be produced at London's Theatre Royal, Drury Lane. Atlanta burned convincingly and Clarke Gable and Vivien Leigh were made to sing, altogether less convincingly, through a profitable London engagement. An attempt to brave Broadway was, however, aborted on the West Coast, and a second burned out in Atlanta.

At his best in the gentle fun of *Destry* or the soupy foolishness of *Wish You Were Here,* Rome was unfortunate elsewhere in being assigned subjects which required much more substantial writing, both musically and lyrically, than he provided. But if *Fanny* and *Gone with the Wind* emerged trivialized from the musicalizing process, they nevertheless found stage room through a good number of performances.

1940 **The Little Dog Laughed** (w Joseph Schrank) Garden Pier Theater, Atlantic City 14 August

1948 **That's the Ticket** (Julius Epstein, Philip Epstein) Shubert Theater, Philadelphia 24 September

1952 **Wish You Were Here** (Arthur Kober, Joshua Logan) Imperial Theater 25 June

1954 **Fanny** (S N Behrman, Logan) Majestic Theater 4 November

1959 **Destry Rides Again** (Leonard Gershe) Imperial Theater 23 April

1962 **I Can Get It for You Wholesale** (Jerome Weidman) Shubert Theater 22 March

1965 **The Zulu and the Zayda** (Howard Da Silva, Felix Leon) Cort Theater 10 November

1970 **Scarlett** (Kasuo Kikuta) Imperial Theatre, Tokyo 3 January

1972 **Gone with the Wind** revised *Scarlett* (Horton Foote) (Theatre Royal, Drury Lane)

ROSALIE Musical comedy in 2 acts and 11 scenes by Guy Bolton and William Anthony McGuire. Lyrics by P G Wodehouse and Ira Gershwin. Music by Sigmund Romberg and George Gershwin. New Amsterdam Theater, New York, 10 January 1928.

A Florenz Ziegfeld vehicle for dancing ingenue Marilyn[n] Miller, *Rosalie* had its star playing a Princess called Rosalie from a Ruritanian country called Romanza (a not-very-subtle reference to Marie of Romania?), who falls in love with a nice American lad-in-uniform called Fay (Oliver McLennan) who airplanes to her side across the Atlantic. Her rank being the obstacle between them, it was obvious from reel one that Rosalie's father (Frank Morgan) would have to abdicate before the final curtain. Lieutenant Fay is quite within his rights to wed ex-Princess Rosalie.

Gershwin popped a couple of outcuts from *Funny Face,* one of which was "How Long Has This Been Going On?" (performed by Bobbe Arnst as soubrette Mary), into a hurriedly compiled score which also included "Oh, Gee! Oh, Joy!" and "Everybody Knows I Love Somebody," as well as some not top-drawer and rather reminiscent bits of Romberg. Staged with lavish splendor, Ruritanian hussars, a ballroom with a ballet (by Urban and Seymour Felix respectively) and any other production value available, *Rosalie* drew for 335 performances on Broadway. It did not export, but MGM subsequently decided that the book was worth filming and a cinematic piece which went under the title of *Rosalie* was produced with a wholly different score (by Cole Porter) and a cast headed by Eleanor Powell, Nelson Eddy, and Morgan repeating a version of his original role.

ROSE, Billy [ROSENBERG, William Samuel] (b New York, 6 September 1899; d Montego Bay, 10 February 1966). Broadway showman.

After a 10-year career as a songwriter which included a lyric credit on such theatrical numbers as "A Cup of Coffee, a Sandwich and You" (*Charlot's Revue of 1926*), "More Than You Know," "Great Day!," "Without a Song" (*Great Day*) and others—some of which were ghosted for him by other less pecunious writers—Rose ventured as a Broadway producer.

He staged several revues, but is largely remembered for his extravagant production of Rodgers and Hart's circus musical *Jumbo* which became *Billy Rose's Jumbo* when filmed. He also produced Oscar Hammerstein's *Carmen Jones* (1943), named the old National Theater after himself, "rescued" the famed Ziegfeld Theater and, after accepting the plaudits, sold it to developers, and was flamboyantly in charge of the Diamond Horseshoe club in the late 1930s and 1940s.

Rose was married for a period to the revue comedienne Fanny Brice.

1929 **Great Day** (Vincent Youmans/w Edward Eliscu/William Cary Duncan, John Wells) Cosmopolitan Theater 17 October

Autobiography: *Wine, Women and Words* (Simon & Schuster, New York, 1948); Biographies: Gottlieb, P: *The Nine Lives of Billy Rose* (Crown, New York, 1968), Conrad, E: *Billy Rose: Manhattan Primitive* (World, Cleveland, 1968), Nelson, S: *Only a Paper Moon: The Theatre of Billy Rose* (UMI Research Press, Michigan, 1987)

ROSE, George [William Rolfe] (b Bicester, 19 February 1920; d Dominican Republic, 5 May 1988). British character actor who became Broadway's standard Englishman.

For a number of years a member of the Old Vic Company and of the company at the Shakespeare Theatre at Stratford-on-Avon, Rose made his first musical appearance in 1959 in the Royal Court Theatre's revue *Living for Pleasure.* He made his Broadway debut in a musical as Henry Horatio Hobson in the Hobson's Choice musical *Walking Happy* (1966) and thereafter became a favorite choice for senior English roles in America. He appeared at the City Center as Doolittle in a revival of *My Fair Lady* and at the Eugene O'Neill Theatre in a combination of English character roles in the British musical of the *Canterbury Tales* (1969), and later the same year had a non-English assignment when he appeared as Louis Greff in *Coco,* a role which he also later toured.

Subsequent musical assignments, interleaved with non-musical roles, included Lutz in *The Student Prince* (1973, tour), a repeat season as Doolittle in a Broadway revival of *My Fair Lady* (1976, Tony Award), Captain Hook to the *Peter Pan* of Sandy Duncan in the Broadway revival of the American musical-comedy version of Barrie's play, the Major General in Broadway's bounced-up *Pirates of Penzance* and the principal comic role in the music-hall mystery *(The Mystery of Edwin) Drood.*

Rose was murdered in the Dominican Republic in 1988.

ROSE, L Arthur [ROSE, Lewis Wolf] (b Edinburgh, 27 September 1887; d Brighton, 16 September 1958). Scots playwright who wrote four British musical-comedy successes.

An actor, and for a period a minor producing manager, Rose began writing plays and sketches for the variety stage in 1911. He had his first experience of the musical theatre when he wrote *Pretty Peggy,* a musical play which was in the nature of an extended variety sketch, with and for comedian Charles Austin. Instead of touring the halls, as originally intended, *Pretty Peggy* was taken up by C B Cochran and shown at the Prince's Theatre for a very respectable and surprising 168 performances.

In spite of this success, Rose's name did not appear on a musical-theatre bill again for 16 years, but when it did he garnered an even greater success than the first time, with a racing farce written to feature another comic, Lupino Lane, as a little chap called Bill Snibson. *Twenty to One* ran 383 performances at the London Coliseum and became a perennial vehicle for Lane. As a result, Rose, in collaboration with Douglas Furber, brought the star out a new Bill Snibson adventure. In fact, Snibson/Lane merely remained the same cheeky cockney character, and the events of the new piece, *Me and My Girl* (1937), were in no way a sequel to the earlier one. *Me and My Girl* had an extended wartime run, was regularly revived thereafter, and ultimately won Rose a posthumous Tony Award for the Broadway reproduction of a British revival half a century on.

Rose did not contribute to the Lane musicals which followed *Me and My Girl,* but returned principally to writing for revue and variety, and collaborated only on one further musical, a vehicle for Jack Buchanan, *It's Time to Dance,* which kept his 100 percent success record intact.

1919 **Pretty Peggy** (Archie Emmett Adams/Douglas Furber/w Charles Austin) Kilburn Empire 25 August

1935 **Twenty to One** (Billy Mayerl/Frank Eyton) London Coliseum 12 November

1937 **Me and My Girl** (Noël Gay/w Furber) Victoria Palace 16 December

1943 **It's Time to Dance** (Kenneth Leslie-Smith, et al/several/w Furber) Winter Garden Theatre 22 July

ROSE DE FRANCE Opérette à grand spectacle in 2 acts by André Mouëzy-Éon. Lyrics by Alfred Willemetz. Music by Sigmund Romberg. Théâtre du Châtelet, Paris, 28 October 1933.

The great success of the works of Sigmund Romberg in France, and notably at the Châtelet where the 237 performances of *Robert le Pirate* (*The New Moon*) had been followed by some 700 of *Nina Rosa,* inspired the theatre's director Maurice Lehmann to commission a new work from the composer, especially for the Châtelet. The libretto, with a title that nicely recalled another American hit in *Rose Marie,* was provided by Lehmann's faithful Mouëzy-Éon and was constructed with a wise eye to the spectacular demands of the big Châtelet stage.

Princess Marie-Louise of France (Danielle Brégis) escapes from the strictures of the court and encounters a young sculptor called Beauval (Roger Bourdin). However, her idyll is betrayed by her lady-in-waiting Athénaïs (Simone Faure) and Beauval, caught in a duel, is condemned to the galleys. When Marie-Louise is sent to Spain, where she is to be diplomatically wed to the King (Pierre Morin), she finds that Beauval is a slave on her ship. The Princess helps him to escape, but he is wounded whilst protecting her in a skirmish in the mountains and, when she steals away from her escort to go to her beloved's side, the King arrives at Burgos to meet his bride. Athénaïs takes her place and, since the King seems content, Marie-Louise lets things remain that way. The ambitious lady-in-waiting will be Queen of Spain and the Princess will wed her sculptor in anonymity.

Whether Romberg's score for *Rose de France* was new, or whether at least some of it was taken from some of the many of his scores unknown in France, it proved more than apt for the occasion. The hits of the show were Mlle Brégis's Marche Militaire ''Quand les soldats vont au pas'' and the big baritone/soprano waltz duet of the evening ''Pour vivre auprès de vous,'' which was supplemented by two further duos, one in tango time (''Rose de France'') and the other another waltz (''Frivolette''). The baritone sang a galley-slave solo and insisted ''Je vous aimerai dans l'ombre,'' the soprano had a letter song, and the light-comedy content was supplied by Bach and Monique Bert, as faithful servants of the Princess, with a couple of one-steps (''Pour fair' le tournedos,'' ''Le Baron de Ragotin'').

Rose de France had all the extras expected in a Châtelet show in plenty: the 15 scenes began with a vista of the Pont Neuf and a lacemakers' ballet, moved to the kitchens where a childrens' little chef ballet was danced, then to ''une fête de nuit au Château de Versailles'' where the première danseuse and her partner performed a divertissement. The royal galley, a storm in the Pyrénées and a Spanish gypsy encampment with a suitable gypsy ballet succeeded each other in supplying the visuals, and the crowning of the Spanish monarch brought the spectacle to its peak. One of the less common features, however, also proved one of the most popular: the performance of the comedian Arnaudy in the travesty role of the Princess's old duenna, the Duchesse de Terra-Nova.

Rose de France proved all that could have been wished and remained at the Châtelet for 476 performances before going into the provinces but, in an era when Romberg was decidedly short on Broadway successes, it did not appear in America.

ROSE DE NOËL Opérette à grand spectacle in 2 acts by Raymond Vincy. Music by Franz Lehár adapted by Paul Bonneau and Miklós Rekä. Théâtre du Châtelet, Paris, 20 December 1958.

At his death, Franz Lehár allegedly left an unused and undated score which had been intended to illustrate a libretto by Károly Kristóf which had curiously never got further than an outline. When this score was brought to light in Budapest, the music and its discoverer, Professor Rekä, were taken to Paris by Maurice Lehmann of the

Théâtre du Châtelet and the 17 pieces of "exhumed" music worked into a score around a libretto written by Raymond Vincy and, so it was said, based on the old scenario.

The plot certainly showed up the age of the scenario. Gadabout Count Michel Andrássy (André Dassary) is ordered to a distant provincial post by an Emperor tired of his excesses. Since Michel is off gadding and cannot be found, his friend Sándor (Henri Chananon) takes his place to spare the young man the imperial thunders. When Michel finally gets to his exile, he lets Sándor carry on his aristocratic masquerade while he falls in love with local Vilma (Nicole Broissin). When all comes out, the girl rejects the well-known rake in horror, but all ultimately turns out all right on the Christmas eve of the show's title. Rosine Brédy was the soubrette, Dominique Tirmont the heroine's father, and Henri Bédex (Popelka) provided the comedy.

The score (which may, or as many believe, may not be genuine Franz) was topped up with several Lehár bonbons including the "Gold and Silver Waltz" for dance music, but tenor Dassary made much of "Déjà" (with violin accompaniment), "Rose de Noël" (with Mlle Broissin), "Mon ciel et ma chanson" and "Rendez-vous d'amour" and *Rose de Noël,* produced with the Châtelet's usual splendor, ran for 415 performances in Paris before going on to a kind of enduring provincial life which had been denied to most of Lehár's other, more legitimate but less glamorously mounted works.

Recordings: original cast (Véga, Decca)

LA ROSE DE SAINT-FLOUR Opérette in 1 act by Michel Carré. Music by Jacques Offenbach. Théâtre des Bouffes-Parisiens, Paris, 12 June 1856.

One of the most generally successful of Offenbach's early rural opérettes, the three-handed *La Rose de Saint-Flour* centered on pretty auvergnate Pierrette (Hortense Schneider) and her two lodgers, the shoemaker Charpailloux (Charles Petit) and the potmaker Marcachu (Pradeau), both of whom sigh after their landlady. On her fete day, each gives her a gift of something that he has made: a pair of dancing shoes from Charpailloux and a stout iron cooking pot from Marcachu. Pierrette puts the pot to good use to make the traditional local cabbage soup, but when the two men begin to fight over her, she takes the side of the shoemaker. The disappointed Marcachu breaks all the crockery and runs off with his pot, full of soup, but finally he returns apologetically bringing some new dishes and the soup and the three dance and eat together. The score consisted of an overture and seven straightforward musical pieces sung in jolly auvergnat dialect: Pierrette's dilemma "Entre les deux mon coeur balance," the practical gift of Marcachu, "Chette marmite neuve" and the frivolous one of Charpailloux "Pour les petits pieds," two duos and two pieces for the threesome, the list ending in a lively bourrée which meant "happily ever after."

Helped on its way in its first performances by the young Hortense Schneider's portrayal of Pierrette, *La Rose de Saint-Flour* confirmed itself as a happy little favorite in Paris before being liberally shown in foreign parts. England's first sighting of the piece seems as if it may have been at Hull, where a piece entitled *Pierrette, or the Village Rivals* was produced in March 1858 with the name of Edward Fitzball attached. Quite whether Offenbach's music was still attached, I have been unable to discover. In London, J A Shaw (Michele), Emmie d'Este Finlayson (Lisette) and Thomas Whiffen (Potatou) appeared in a thoroughly Offenbached *Too Many Cooks* (ad Charles Furtado) at the Gallery of Illustration, but the first regular theatre performance was at the Gaiety Theatre where, as *The Rose of Auvergne* (ad H B Farnie), the piece was the second short Offenbach work, in the wake of the success of *Lischen et Fritzchen,* to be produced by John Hollingshead. Annie Tremaine played Fleurette, with Charles Lyall and Edward Perrini as her lovers, and the opérette was reprised regularly for a number of years as an opening item on the Gaiety bill. It was subsequently played in another English version as *Pot Luck,* and yet another as *Spoiling the Broth*—this version was even played on the vast stage of the Alhambra—and was also seen played in its original French at the Charing Cross Theatre (1870, w *Les Pompiers de Nanterre*).

The New York Théâtre Français performed the original French version of *La Rose de son Saint-Flour* a number of times during the 1860s, and it was also played regularly by Bateman's and by Grau and Chizzola's opéra-bouffe companies, amongst others, in the 1870s. The little English operetta company headed by Susan Galton played *Too Many Cooks* in America in their bills during the late 1860s, whilst Kelly and Leon's Minstrels performed their own English-language version (24 October 1870) with Leon playing a travesty Lisette to the Brown of Kelly and the Smith of S S Purdy, and Henri Laurent's company was also among those many English comic-opera companies who traveled *The Rose of Auvergne* in its repertoire. Kelly and Leon later played their version in Australia (Queen's Theatre 9 March 1878) and New Zealand as well, but the piece had been seen in the colonies as early as 1871.

In Vienna, again, the piece was first introduced in its French original, played by the Bouffes-Parisiens company during their visit to the Theater am Franz-Josefs-Kai in 1861 with Lucille Tostée, Desmonts and Marchand as its cast, but it was also later produced in a German version at the Strampfertheater. An Hungarian version (ad

Plate 332a. **Rose Marie.** *Wanda (Mira Nirska) stabs her drunken lover, Black Eagle (P Parsons) to death under the gaze of machinating Hawley (Brian Gilmour) in London's* Rose Marie.

Ferenc Toldy) was first seen in 1875, but central Europe had different favorites in the repertoire of little Offenbach pieces and *La Rose de Saint-Flour* did not win the same strong popularity there as it did in its French and English versions.

Austria: Theater am Franz-Josefs-Kai (Fr) 6 July 1861, Strampfertheater 19 February 1872; USA: Théâtre Français (Fr) 14 February 1863, Wood's Museum September or Washington Hall, Williamsburgh *Too Many Cooks* 22 September 1868; UK: Hull *Pierrette, or The Village Rivals* 6 March 1858, St James's Theatre (Fr) 10 June 1857, Gallery of Illustration *Too Many Cooks* 1 September 1864, Gaiety Theatre *The Rose of Auvergne* 8 November 1869; Australia: Princess Theatre, Melbourne 30 August 1871; Hungary: Népszínház *A saint-fleuri rósza* 12 November 1875

ROSE MARIE Musical play in 2 acts by Otto Harbach and Oscar Hammerstein II. Music by Rudolf Friml and Herbert Stothart. Imperial Theater, New York, 2 September 1924.

Although the Broadway musical theatre had established itself worldwide with its light-handed song-and-dance shows—*Going Up, Irene, Mercenary Mary, No, No, Nanette, Sally* and their kind—American producers had largely gone for imported shows or composers when the more musically substantial, romantic type of ''operetta'' was required. Since the days of Victor Herbert and *Mlle Modiste* and *Naughty Marietta,* there had been few local successes in the operettic vein, but the enormous triumph of *Blossom Time* (*Das Dreimäderlhaus*) had shown postwar producers that there was a vast audience for a robustly sentimental show on classic light-opera lines, and they reacted accordingly. The show which gave the Broadway musical its first major international success of the kind was *Rose Marie.*

Rose Marie was commissioned by Arthur Hammerstein from his nephew, Oscar II, and from Otto Harbach and composer Rudolf Friml, with both of whom the

Plate 332b. **Rose Marie.** *Totem Tom-Tom at Drury Lane.*

younger Hammerstein had worked regularly since the pair's first collaboration a dozen years earlier on *The Firefly. The Firefly,* built for an operatic diva, had been the last example of a memorable Broadway operetta, since which Harbach and Friml had concentrated on following the fashion for light-comedy and dancing musicals, from the well-named *High Jinks* to the jaunty *Blue Kitten* of two seasons previously. Harbach and Hammerstein had also collaborated, under Arthur Hammerstein's management, on three musicals: Herbert Stothart's *Tickle Me* and *Jimmie* and the previous year's colorfully Ruritalian Youmans/Stothart success *Wildflower.*

Using the producer's suggested Canadian setting as a backdrop, the authors put together a plot which was, perhaps, rather more dramatic than was standard and which had a distinct air (and quite a bit of the plot) of Willard Mack's 1917 play *Tiger Rose* to it. That plot turned on a murder, the murder of a drunken villain by his mistress, and the use of that murder by the woman's ex-lover to entrap his rival for the love of the show's heroine. If the terms in which that tale was told here were less than precisely powerful, if the dramatic facts were rather drowned in romantic considerations and low comedy, and if the murderess in the case was also the entertainment's principal dancer, the killing nevertheless remained as a dramatic spine for what producer Hammerstein referred to mouthfillingly as ''an operatic musical play.''

Rose Marie la Flamme (Mary Ellis), the sister of a French Canadian trapper (Edward Cianelli), is in love with miner Jim Kenyon (Dennis King) rather than the well-off city man Edward Hawley (Frank Greene) whom her brother would have her wed. When Hawley's half-caste ex-mistress Wanda (Pearl Regay) stabs her drunken Indian concubine (Arthur Ludwig) to death, Hawley engineers it that the suspicion falls on Kenyon, and the miner is forced to flee before the Mounties. Blackmailed by her brother, who agrees not to reveal Kenyon's escape route if she will agree to marry Hawley, Rose Marie is gradually persuaded that Jim really is a killer, but Kenyon's comical little friend Hard-Boiled Herman (William Kent) tricks the truth from Wanda. When the guilty girl realizes, rather late, that as a result of her actions she is going to lose Hawley to Rose Marie, she interrupts their wedding with her dramatic revelation. With the air now cleared, Rose Marie and Jim can finally get together. The comic element of the piece was provided by another triangle in which both Herman and the Mountie Captain Malone (Arthur Deagon) battled for the hand of soubrette Lady Jane (Dorothy Mackaye).

The music of *Rose Marie,* and most particularly the romantic music, was one of the show's principal assets. Rose Marie and Kenyon joined together in the Indian Love Call, a song which in later decades would become mocked—for its words rather than its melody—as the representative of old-fashioned musical theatre. The song had nothing of the old-fashioned or even the conventional about it in 1924 and it won an outstanding success as sung by King and Miss Ellis. King had a strong, lilting song (w Deagon) in praise of ''Rose Marie,'' Herbert Stothart combined with Friml on a ringing ensemble for ''The Mounties'' and a pounding stage-Indian ballet (''Totem Tom-Tom''), both of which backed up their spectacular set pieces with unusual strength, and, in contrast, Friml provided a delicately dancing melody for the heroine's song about the ''Pretty Things'' that money and Hawley can buy her—a piece which proved much more popular than the waltz ''Door of My Dreams'' which the composer had thought would be the hit of the evening. Stothart was also responsible for some of the comic numbers, of which Herman's profession of faith, ''Hard-Boiled Herman,'' stood up the best in front of the tidal wave of success that attended the lyric part of the score.

The producer extended his determination that the production was ''operatic'' by announcing that he would not list the numbers separately in the program (a determination echoed 60 years later by Andrew Lloyd Webber's refusal to individually track his cast recordings) as they were part of the action. Of course, the comedy pieces in particular were nothing of the kind. The action surrounding them was as often as not there only to justify the songs, and a piece such as ''Totem Tom-Tom'' with its balletic murderess at its head was inserted solely as incidental spectacle. However, for anyone who cared, many of the numbers were indeed solidly linked to the characters or tale, just as they had been in musical theatre since the days of such ''realistic'' musicals as *Le Mariage aux lanternes* and well before.

Hammerstein also posted up his serious intentions by his lead casting. Rose Marie was played not by an established star, from either the opera or musical stage, but by the young Mary Ellis who had played supporting roles alongside Chaliapin and Caruso at the Metropolitan Opera at a very young age before quitting opera for the straight theatre. Rose Marie was her only musical role in America. Leading man King, like Miss Ellis, had abandoned a lyric career begun in Britain for Shakespeare on Broadway, but it was Miss Ellis who got the big billing, even if it was under the title.

The spectacular part of *Rose Marie* was also contributory to its success. Arthur Hammerstein's Canadian settings as given shape by Gates and Morange were dazzling, the towering cliffs and mountains adding, *Maid of the Mountains*–style, both to the dramatic moments and to the long-distance moments of the romance; the ''gowns and costumes'' of Charles Le Maire no less attractive and very numerous on the backs of the large company; whilst David Bennett's arrangment of the dance of the massed ranks of Red Indian girls who featured in ''Totem Tom-Tom'' was a show-stopper. If Hammerstein had operatic pretensions with *Rose Marie,* he certainly did not allow that to stop him taking out an insurance on success with a lavishly spectacular stage production.

Rose Marie was a huge hit on Broadway. One of the biggest of all time, even if, in cold figures, in the ultimate tot-up its run came to just 557 performances, a figure inferior to those chalked up by *Irene* and such old-time favorites as *Erminie, Adonis* or *A Trip to Chinatown,* but on a par with *Florodora* and *Sally.* The first touring companies were on the road before the Broadway run was six months old. They were joined soon after by others, and these tours continued way beyond the end of the New York run. Alfred Butt took up the piece for London and produced it at the venerable Theatre Royal, Drury Lane, which had been struggling along on a mixture of spectacular drama, pantomime and even films. Another young American performer, Edith Day (the original Broadway and London star of *Irene*), starred opposite patented tenor Derek Oldham and comedian Billy Merson and, once again, the piece found a huge following which resulted in an 851-performance, two-year run and the definitive reorientation of the famous house to musical productions.

In Britain, as in America, the touring companies were on the road whilst the metropolitan production ran on, but London, unlike New York, also subsequently welcomed *Rose Marie* back on several occasions. Miss Day starred in a 1929 revival at Drury Lane (100 performances) and Raymond Newell played Kenyon at the Stoll Theatre in 1942, but a 1960 revival at the Victoria Palace done with neither the conviction nor the means of the original only reinforced the prejudices of those for whom such pieces were by then ''old-fashioned.''

The show was produced by J C Williamson Ltd in Australia with Harriet Bennett (Rose Marie), Reginald Dandy (Jim) and Frederick Bentley (Herman) in the leading roles, and once again it scored a major success through nine months in Sydney and a further six in Melbourne (Her Majesty's Theatre 26 February 1927), but *Rose Marie*'s longest run of all came, wholly surprisingly, in Paris. The Isola brothers who ran the Théâtre Mogador visited London and saw *No, No, Nanette* and *Rose Marie.* They bought both and staged *Nanette* first with such success that they were obliged, eventually, to cut short the show's run in order to stage *Rose-Marie* (ad

Roger Ferréol, Saint-Granier, and with a hyphen between the Rose and the Marie) within their option period. But this time the success was even greater, and by the time *Rose-Marie* closed, the production had created a Parisian long-run record with 1,250 consecutive performances.

Two young performers, Cloë Vidiane and Madeleine Massé, alternated in the title role, the baritone Robert Burnier was Jim, Félix Oudart was Malone and the comic Boucot appeared as Herman, whilst the world-traveling American dancer June Roberts led ''Totem Tom-Tom'' (choreography credited to co-director J Kathryn Scott, so presumably not a copy of Mr Bennett's). The piece was luxuriantly staged—with the individually credited mountain scenes, the Totem Pole Hotel, a maison de couture (with a mannequin parade) and a Quebec ballroom commissioned from four different designers—and decorated by hundreds of costumes, and the music played by an orchestra of 50. There had been spectacular musical plays in Paris for decades and decades, but *Rose-Marie* set off a new fashion for opérette à grand spectacle which would last for many years until it ultimately destroyed itself and the musical theatre in Paris by its excesses.

The Mogador brought back *Rose-Marie* in 1930 (20 January), 1939 (1 June), 1963 (23 November with Marcel Merkès and Paulette Merval) and in 1970 (19 December, starring Bernard Sinclair, Angelina Cristi); it was played at the Châtelet in 1940 (19 December with no less a Rose-Marie than Fanély Revoil) and 1944 (21 October, with Madeleine Vernon), at the Théâtre de l'Empire in 1947 and 1950 (12 May with Merval), and most recently at the Théâtre de la Porte-Saint-Martin (18 February 1981), confirming itself as one of the staples of the musical-theatre repertoire in France.

The show opened almost simultaneously with its Paris production both in Germany (ad Rideamus) where, in spite of Hammerstein's personal supervision, operatic tenor Aagard Oestvig and soprano Margarethe Pfahl Wallerstein did not succeed in making the conventions of the Broadway operetta appeal, and in Hungary (ad Adorján Stella, Imre Harmath), where Irén Biller and Glenn Ellyn starred at Budapest's Király Színház with rather more in the way of response. Prague also picked up on the show quickly (Urania Theater 18 June 1928) and the German version was introduced at the Brussels Stadttheater in 1933 (28 January).

In 1928 *Rose Marie* was also made into a film with Joan Crawford starred as a silent Rose-Marie (apparently with a hyphen!). If the tale without the songs was good enough in 1928, 1936 preferred it the other way round and the libretto was rewritten for a second MGM film in which Jeanette MacDonald, Nelson Eddy, Allan Jones and James Stewart participated. The score was also punctuated with bits of opera, ''Dinah,'' ''Some of These Days'' and two extra Stothart songs. A third version, again rewritten, featured Ann Blyth, Howard Keel, Bert Lahr and Fernando Lamas and four additional songs dubiously credited to the aged Friml (who sat in an office at MGM and magically produced songs without a pen) as well as ''The Mountie That Never Got His Man.''

The question of the hyphen in *Rose(-)Marie* has become a cause célèbre amongst those to whom such things matter. Stanley Green and Gerald Bordman, who must be considered the arbiters in such American matters of life and death, finally reached the compromise at the end of Stanley's life that the stage show had no hyphen (except in France), whilst the film did. So why not.

UK: Theatre Royal, Drury Lane 20 March 1925; Australia: Her Majesty's Theatre, Sydney 29 May 1926; France: Théâtre Mogador 9 April 1927; Germany: Admiralspalast 30 March 1928; Hungary: Király Színház 31 March 1928

Films: MGM 1928 (silent), 1936 and 1954

Recordings: London cast recordings (WRC), selections (Columbia, Capitol, Decca, RCA, WRC, etc), film soundtrack 1936 (Hollywood Soundstage), film soundtrack 1954 (MGM), French version (Pathé, CBS, etc), Russian version (Melodiya), etc

ROSEN AUS FLORIDA Operette in 3 acts by A M Willner and Heinz Reichert. Music by Leo Fall arranged by Erich Wolfgang Korngold. Theater an der Wien, Vienna, 22 February 1929.

Rosen aus Florida was an Americo-Ruritanian musical with a score put together from music left by Leo Fall at his death, and produced by Hubert Marischka at the Theater an der Wien for a run of 216 performances. Set in New York and Palm Beach with a third act in a Paris cabaret of ''Zum lustigen Emigranten'' where titled Russian émigrés work as barman, vocalist and liftboy (a situation ''borrowed,'' shortly after, for the better-known musical *Balalaika*), *Rosen aus Florida* took three acts to bring together the self-made millionaire Goliath Armstrong (Hubert Marischka), who hasn't got time to fall in love, and the lady who makes him change his mind when it is almost too late. She is the Russian Princess Irina Naryschkin (Rita Georg) and she supplies the romantic music in solos (a first-act ''Heimatlied,'' a second-act ''Mir ist, als läg' mein ganzes Glück'') and in duet with Goliath (''Rote Rosen,'' ''Das Schönste der Wunder auf Erden''). It was, however, he who was given the show's catchiest number, ''Wer kann die Frauen je ergründen?'' Dorrit (Ossi Oswalda), the girl Goliath didn't quite wed, helped supply the lighter moments alongside his secretary, Tommy (Fritz Steiner), and another émigré, Fürst Nikifor Wladimirowitsch Urusoff (Fritz Imhoff).

The show's satisfactory run in Vienna didn't encourage any exportation at a time when Fall's name had become a little forgotten in the rage for more up-to-date things.

ROSENFELD, Sydney (b Richmond, Va, 26 October 1855; d New York, 13 June 1931). Broadway ''character'' who got himself involved in several decades of theatrical projects and almost as many Broadway lawsuits.

Journalist, magazine editor, playwright, adapter, an unembarrassed cobbler-together of plays and musical libretti, on occasions himself both producer and director, and even, at one stage, briefly the proprietor of his own classical drama company, the Century Players (1904), Rosenfeld began his colorful (and too often off-colorful) career in the theatre by writing one-act pieces for minstrel shows. His first Broadway script was a burlesque of the play *Rose Michel* (1874), and a stream of all kinds of other pieces followed it on to the New York stage. In 1882 he provided the lyric to the ''Tootsy Wootsy'' interpolated by Lillian Russell into Broadway's revival of *The Sorcerer,* and weeks later he was signed up by John McCaull as house librettist to the newly-opened Casino Theater. His first job was to re-readapt *Das Spitzentuch der Königin,* which had been the theatre's opening attraction.

When he laid his hands on such as Offenbach's *Orphée aux enfers* the result was the transformation of the wit of Halévy and Crémieux's into low comic buffonery, but when the fashion for opéra-bouffe gave way to that for German Operette Rosenfeld proved less inept as an adaptor. An early attempt at such a piece with an adaptation of Genée's *Der Seekadett* as *The Sea Cadet* fared poorly when a much superior version (*The Royal Middy*) beat it to town, but other adaptations from the German, including his versions of Millöcker's *Der Feldprediger* (*The Black Hussar*) and Genée's *Nanon,* were considerable successes. Rosenfeld's theatrical activities ended him in prison when he pirated Gilbert and Sullivan's *The Mikado* and produced it at the Union Square Theatre (1885) and—after taking out and pennilessly stranding a comic opera company in the latter part of the same year—he returned to wreaking his will on the less protesting German works, supplying versions of such as *Der Zigeunerbaron* and *Prinz Methusalem* to a Broadway audience which apparently didn't mind its Operette with its comedy and its tone heftily lowered, whilst at the same time penning such ditties as ''There Never Was a Coward Where There Sailed a Yankee Crew'' (publishers S T Gordon & Son) for the baritone market. When he attempted a version of Audran's *Serment d'amour* he again struck a rival production, but he did very much better with Lecocq's *La Jolie Persane* whose new title, *The Oolah,* highlighted the different emphases given such shows on Rosenfeldian Broadway—the girl lost the title to the all-important low comedian. In San Francisco the local version of the piece was called *The Pretty Persian.* But Rosenfeld's emphases ensured the opérette its longest run anywhere in the world.

Rosenfeld ventured with an original libretto for the first time when he turned the famous short story *The Lady or the Tiger* into a musical for John McCaull's comic-opera company and, with a certain bravado, arranged simultaneous premieres in New York and London (the latter was a matinée at the roughish suburban Elephant and Castle Theatre). It was typical of Rosenfeld that he provided an ending for the celebratedly endless piece, but even that was not enough to make the show more than a half-success. He continued his producing efforts, combining episodically with the marginally more reliable George Lederer, and this association led to his becoming the author of the script for the Casino's *The Passing Show,* generally quoted as being the first genuine American revue of modern times. Many of his subsequent pieces, nominally musicals, also had much of the revue about them (*The Giddy Throng, A Round of Pleasure,* etc), their semi-plots dissolving away into concerts halfway through in the manner of the old British variety musicals, but some, like the romantic southern-American comic opera *The Mocking Bird,* proved that Rosenfeld could, when he wished, turn out material that was better than run-of-the-mill.

For all his easy-going prolificity, his often hurried and shoddy work, Rosenfeld was not wholly devoid of ability, as his adaptations of such straight pieces as *Dr Clyde* and *At the White Horse Tavern* (*Im weissen Rössl*) proved, but eventually his theatrical cheek proved insufficient to get him work and his later years were spent rather pathetically attempting to drum himself up engagements with embarrassingly out-of-date showbizzy extravagance. The attempts at drumming were all the more hopeless in that, down through the years, with what looked like a permanent persecution complex perched on his shoulder, the litigation-mad Rosenfeld had flung Broadway lawsuits at half the producers in town. He'd even just occasionally won one.

Rosenfeld's brother, Monroe H Rosenfeld, also tried his hand in the musical and theatrical world, turning out songs with such titles as ''Those Wedding Bells Shall Not Ring Out!'' and ''With All Her Faults I Love Her Still.''

1876 **Rosemishell, or Oh! My Daughter** (pasticcio) Eagle Theater 24 January

1876 **The Pique Family** (pasticcio) Eagle Theater 13 March

1880 **The Sea Cadet, or The Very Merry Mariner** (*Der Seekadett*) American version (Fifth Avenue Theater)

1880 **Our School Days, or Boys and Girls Again** (pasticcio/w Robert McWade, C P Brown) Academy of Music, Montreal 15 March

1882 **Apajune the Water Sprite** (*Apajune, der Wassermann*) American version (Bijou Theater)

1883 **Orpheus and Eurydice** (*Orphée aux enfers*) revision of Max Freeman's adaptation (Bijou Theater)

1883 **Prince Methusalem** American version (Casino Theater)

1884 **Cyclones, or American Bouffoneries** (pasticcio) Arch Street Theater, Philadelphia 28 January

1884 **Well-Fed Dora** Arch Street Opera House, Philadelphia 28 April; Fifth Avenue Theater 19 May

1884 **The Seamstress** (*Die Näherin*) American version (Haverly's Theater, Philadelphia)

1885 **Ixion** all-female version adapted from Burnand's burlesque, Comedy Theater 4 February

1885 **Die Fledermaus** American version (Haverley's Theater, Philadelphia, Casino Theater)

1885 **Nanon** American version (Casino Theater)

1885 **Amorita** (*Pfingsten in Florenz*) American version w George Goldmark (Casino Theater)

1885 **The Black Hussar** (*Der Feldprediger*) American version (Wallack's Theater)

1886 **The Mystic Isle** (John B Grant) Temple Theater, Philadelphia 2 October

1886 **Those Bells** (Gustave Kerker) 1 act Bijou Theater 11 December

1886 **The Gipsy Baron** (*Der Zigeunerbaron*) American version (Casino Theater)

1886 **The Bridal Trap** (*Serment d'amour*) American version (Bijou Theater)

1888 **The Lady or the Tiger** (Julius J Lyons, [Adolph Nowak]) Bijou Theater, New York and Elephant & Castle Theatre, London 7 May

1889 **The Oolah** (*La Jolie Persane*) American version (Broadway Theater)

1893 **The Rainmaker of Syria** (aka *The Woman King*) (Rudolf Aronson) Casino Theater 25 September

1893 **Fritz in Prosperity** (various) Grand Opera House 23 October

1893 **The Fringe of the Froth of the Crust of Society** 1 act Hermann's Theater December

1895 **The Twentieth Century Girl** (Ludwig Englander) Bijou Theater 25 January

1898 **A Dangerous Maid** (*Heisses Blut*) English version (Casino Theater)

1898 **Lili Tse** 1 act English version (Daly's Theater)

1901 **The King's Carnival** (A Baldwin Sloane) New York Theater 13 May

1901 **The Supper Club** (various) New York Winter Garden Theater 23 December

1902 **The Hall of Fame** (Sloane/George V Hobart) New York Theater 3 February

1902 **The Sweet Girl** (Sloane, et al) 1 act Cherry Blossom Grove 18 August

1902 **The Mocking Bird** (Sloane) Bijou Theater 10 November

1905 **The Rollicking Girl** revised version of *A Dangerous Maid* (W T Francis) Herald Square Theater 1 May

1905 **A Society Circus** (Manuel Klein, Gustave Luders) New York Hippodrome 13 December

1906 **The Vanderbilt Cup** (Robert Hood Bowers/Raymond Peck) Broadway Theater 16 January

1908 **Mlle Mischief** (*Ein tolles Mädel*) English version (Lyric Theater)

1910 **Jumping Jupiter** (Karl Hoschna/w Richard Carle) Cort Theater, Chicago 4 August; Criterion Theater 6 March 1911

1911 **The Happiest Night of His Life** (Albert von Tilzer/w Junie McCree) Criterion Theater 20 February

1912 **The Opera Ball** (*Der Opernball*) American version w Clare Kummer (Liberty Theater)

1912 **The Rose of Panama** (*Kreolenblut*) English version fr trans Maurice Hageman w John L Shine (Daly's Theater)

1913 **Hop o' My Thumb** American version w Manuel Klein (Manhattan Opera House)

THE ROSE OF PERSIA, or The Story Teller and the Slave Comic opera in 2 acts by Basil Hood. Music by Arthur Sullivan. Savoy Theatre, London, 29 November 1899.

The sticky patch through which the Savoy Theatre and Richard D'Oyly Carte had passed in the years since the collapse of the Gilbert and Sullivan partnership finally got a little less sticky when Sullivan teamed up with Basil Hood, the experienced librettist and lyricist of such popular successes as *Gentleman Joe,* to write *The Rose of Persia.* Hood had begun his career writing in a literary and "Gilbertian" style before finding his biggest successes with the more popular brand of musical comedy, and now he returned to the comic-opera manner of his early works with a script for Sullivan which was based on the Arabian Nights tale of Abu Hasan.

The eccentric, rich Hassan (Walter Passmore) holds open house to the scroungers of Baghdad, and one night his uninvited guests include the disguised Sultana Rose-in-Bloom (Ellen Beach Yaw) who has sneaked out for a look at the world and then been unable to get back into the palace. When the Sultan Mahmoud (Henry Lytton) arrives at his door, Hassan drugs himself up to the eyeballs in expectation of immediate execution and, under the influence, declares himself the equal of any Sultan. When he comes to, he finds that he apparently is Sultan. It is Mahmoud's little joke. Hassan's ear-crushing wife Dancing Sunbeam (Rosina Brandram), the trouble-making Abdallah (George Ridgewell), the poor story-teller Yussuf (Robert Evett) and the Sultana's maid Heart's Desire (Louie Pounds) are all mixed up in the divorces, marriages and executions which are bandied about before Hassan uses a little bit of semantics to force the Sultan to pardon everyone and put everything back as it was—even to the devastating and punishing extent of giving him back Dancing Sunbeam.

Sullivan's score was not in quite the same merry burlesque vein as those he had written for the best of the Gilbert shows. It was comic-opera music rather than opéra-bouffe music, music which happily illustrated both the superior romantic poetry which Hood composed for numbers such as Yussuf's "Our Tale Is Told" and the comical songs performed by Passmore in something like regular Savoy style, and also the specialist numbers which Sullivan was obliged to write for his prima donna. Miss Beach Yaw was an American soprano with a famed top register, and her role was written to include some of the top Fs in alt in which she specialized. The experiment proved a bad idea, Miss Beach Yaw soon left the cast to be replaced by her understudy Isabel Jay, the upper extremities were written out of the songs, and both the music and the show gained from the normalization.

The Rose of Persia was a fine critical success and Hood was quickly hailed as the successor of Gilbert (who was doubtless not at all pleased to be seen as needing a successor), but even so, at the height of the fashion for Gaiety musical comedy, the show was only able to last for a fair-to-unprofitable seven months and 220 performances at the Savoy. Carte sent *The Rose of Persia* on tour, and it was duly produced in both Australia and in America. J C Williamson mounted Australia's version with two genuine Savoyards, Wallace Brownlow and Charles Kenningham, appearing as the Sultan and Yussuf alongside George Lauri (Hassan), Dorothy Vane (Dancing Sunbeam) and, in a role which seemed to attract double-barreled names, Ada Winston-Weir as the stratospheric sultana. It did better in Australia than in America where John Le Hay and Ruth Vincent crossed the Atlantic to star in Carte's elsewhere desperately undercast and underpowered Broadway production and remained for only a sad 25 performances.

Hood and Sullivan continued to work in tandem, and were part-way through their next work, *The Emerald Isle,* when the composer died, leaving the author to continue a partnership with Edward German that would carry their style of comic opera through into the earliest part of the 20th century. *The Rose of Persia* was, however, revived in 1935 in the wake of a successful revival of German's *Merrie England.* Helene Raye and Joseph Spree featured, with Desirée Ellinger (Heart's Desire) and Amy Augarde (Dancing Sunbeam) supporting, in a production which again managed only 25 performances.

The Abu Hasan tale has served for many other stage pieces, musical and non-musical, ranging from a successful opera by Weber to burlesques.

Australia: Her Majesty's Theatre, Sydney 21 July 1900; USA: Daly's Theater 6 September 1900

Recording: Amateur cast recording (RRE)

DIE ROSE VON STAMBUL Operette in 3 acts by Julius Brammer and Alfred Grünwald. Music by Leo Fall. Theater an der Wien, Vienna, 2 December 1916.

Although the Turkish potentate Kemal Pascha (Karl Tuschl) is very up-to-date European in some ways, he is still traditional enough to have made a dynastic marriage for his daughter, Kondja Gül (Betty Fischer), with Achmed Bey (Hubert Marischka), the son of his Prime Minister. Kondja Gül has been brought up with much freedom. She has even been given a European education during the course of which she has struck up a warm correspondence with the writer André Lery, an outspoken supporter of Western liberties for Turkish women. However, by law and tradition, she cannot do anything to deny the marriage her father has arranged for her. To delay and discourage the union, she imposes a drawn-out, traditional courtship on Achmed and at the same time she continues a growingly romantic exchange with Lery. What she does not know is that the two are one and the same man. When Achmed finally breaks his silence and his cover, she will not believe him, but, finally, under the spell of a Swiss honeymoon hotel, she realizes that the man she has been made to marry is, in fact, the man she would have chosen to marry.

Plate 333. **Die Rose von Stambul.** *Henrike Hoffmann and Hartmut Schneider try out a step that she never learned in the harem in the Bremerhaven Stadttheater's production of 1986.*

The score of *Die Rose von Stambul* was one of Fall's most outstanding achievements. Richly romantic in its tenor and soprano music, deliciously dancing and laughing in the soubret numbers with which the contrasting comic characters leavened the sentimental main plot, it was a classic example of the Viennese Operette of its period—the period prior to the fashion for the unhappy ending and Big Gloomy Operettes. The role of Achmed Bey was one of the great romantic tenor roles written for the Viennese stage, and his music gave him three ringing solos of wide range: the ecstatic waltz song ''O Rose von Stambul'' as he anticipates meeting the beautiful woman who is to be his wife, his sweet-toned greeting of his wife's handmaidens (''Ihr stillen, süssen Frau'n'') and the third act ''Heut' wär ich so in der gewissen.'' Along with two duets with Kondja—of which the sweeping ''Ein Walzer muss es sein,'' in which he introduces her to the romantic joys of Western dancing in a sort of *The-Princess-and-I* scena, is another highlight in a score of highlights—these tenor numbers form the backbone of the star role and of the music of the Operette.

A third-act solo for the heroine and some fine ensemble music support the main romantic pieces, but it is the light comic portion of the score which is the other great joy of *Die Rose von Stambul.* Fridolin Müller (Ernst Tautenhayn), the little Hamburg million-heir, and his veiled sweetheart Midili (Luise Kartousch) meet in duet (''Als fromme Tochter des Propheten''), discuss smoking in duet (''Ihr süssen Zigaretten'') get engaged and have their first moustachy kiss in duet (''Fridolin, ach wie dein Schnurrbart sticht''), get increasingly more familiar in duet (Schnucki-Duett), and calm Hamburger papa with thoughts of grandchildren in a trio (''Papachen, Papachen''), each number a sprightly song-and-dance. The role of Fridolin was as comical as the star role was romantic, and Tautenhayn had particular success in a scene in which he dressed up in feminine garb in order stay in the Palace near his Midili and then paraded about pretending to be ''Lilli vom Ballett.''

It was, in fact, Tautenhayn and Frln Kartousch who made the biggest personal successes of *Die Rose von Stambul,* but although Fall's demanding score stretched both Marischka and Frln Fischer to their vocal utmost, the Theater an der Wien's two star vocalists came through well, and all four contributed their quota to the greatest success that the Theater an der Wien had had since *Die lustige Witwe.* The show played for 15 virtually unbroken months and 422 performances before moving on to other theatres and to other countries. At Berlin's Metropoltheater Fritzi Massary starred as Kondja Gül for just under a year, whilst Budapest's Király Színház presented the Hungarian version (ad Andor Gábor) with Emmi Kosáry and Ernő Király in the romantic roles and Juci Lábass and Árpád Latabár in the comic ones to equally splendid success.

The piece continued around central Europe and was filmed in 1919 with Massary starred, but it did not go further. Wartime conditions and attitudes forbade it to English and French audiences and, later, when England imported other such central European wartime Operetten as *Das Dreimäderlhaus* and *Die Csárdásfürstin, Die Rose von Stambul* was ignored. In France the music-publishing firm of Max Eschig had a translation done by Léon Uhl, Jean de Letraz and Jean Marietti, but the show failed to find a producer. America ultimately took *Die Rose von Stambul,* but the Shuberts let their in-house remakers Harold Atteridge and Sigmund Romberg loose on it and, as a result, the piece that appeared on Broadway as *The Rose of Stamboul* with baritone Marion Green and prima donna Tessa Kosta in its leading roles proved a sadly mangled one. The bits of Fall which remained were sufficient to win a three-month run but the lesson that Shubertian botching very rarely worked—particularly on such a major hit and such a classy piece of writing as *Die Rose von Stambul*—still didn't sink in.

This ill-managed production undoubtedly killed the future of *Die Rose von Stambul* in America as stone dead as the war had done for its propects in Britain and France and, to this day, the show has never become established outside central Europe. There, however, it remains amongst the still-performed but secondary pieces of the repertoire, even though it has curiously not yet been taken into the Volksoper where Fall's unplugged-by-a-foundation-or-family works seem to be little favored. In 1953 a second, sound film was produced, featuring some very scantily clad Turkish girls and a rather different text (ad Walter Forster, Joachim Wedekind). Herbert Ernst Groh supplied the tenor voice to Albert Lievin's Achmed Bey, Ursula Ackermann sang Kondja Gül for Inge Egger, Hans Richter pranced about as Lili von Ballett and Paul Hörbiger appeared as the 106-year-old Pascha. Stage productions, too, have taken some trendy liberties with Brammer and Grünwald in latter days and one 1980s production modernized the tale to the extent of making André Lery not a poet, but a pop singer.

Germany: Metropoltheater 29 September 1917; Hungary: Király Színház *Sztambul Rózsája* 27 June 1917; USA: Century Theater *The Rose of Stamboul* 7 March 1922

Films: 1919, Karl Anton 1953

Recordings: selections (RCA, Eurodisc, EMI, Polydor), etc

ROSS, Adrian [ROPES, Arthur Reed] (b Lewisham, 23 December 1859; d London, 10 September 1933). The British stage's senior lyricist through several eras of musical theatre.

A King's College, Cambridge, history graduate who had won the Chancellor's Medal for verse, and subsequently a fellow and a history lecturer at Cambridge, the wealthily bred Ross made his first attempt at stage writing with the libretto and lyrics for a burlesque, *Faddimir. Faddimir* got itself a West End showing at a showcase matinée and won sufficient praise for its author and his fellow Cambridge man, Frank Osmond Carr, who had composed the music, to be commissioned to write a burlesque for George Edwardes. Edwardes did, however, take the precaution of pairing his new writer with the experienced comedian John Shine on his first outing. *Joan of Arc* (''I Went to Find Emin,'' ''Round the Town,'' ''Jack the Dandy-O'') was a big success, and Ross and Carr were promptly put to work—this time unaided—on another, slightly different kind of piece for Edwardes. *In Town,* with its cocky tale of backstage and society doings, broke away from the burlesque pattern and helped set the up-to-date style for the famous series of Gaiety musicals which followed. For his early works Ross had worked on both libretto and lyrics but, beginning with his next piece, *Morocco Bound* (''Marguerite from Monte Carlo''), he then limited himself almost entirely to writing lyrics, and his few subsequent ventures into original book writing were the less notable side of an otherwise remarkable career.

During the great days of the Gaiety Theatre, Ross contributed many lyrics to virtually all of that theatre's shows from *The Shop Girl* (''Brown of Colorado'') onwards, sharing in all the greatest international hits of the Edwardes ''Gaiety'' era of musical comedy. Edwardes also put him to writing additional numbers for the shows at Daly's Theatre and, after small contributions to *An Artist's Model* and *The Geisha,* he became a fixed part of the Daly's ''team'' from *A Greek Slave* onwards, a function increased on the death of Daly's Theatre's young lyricist-in-chief, Harry Greenbank. He remained in ''the Guvnor's'' service through the whole Daly's Theatre era of British musicals, and, when Edwardes switched to importing Continental shows, he took over the function of adapting the lyrics of those shows into English. His first such assignment was *Die lustige Witwe,* and his songwords to *The Merry Widow* (''Vilja,'' etc) became the standard English version of that piece, performed throughout the world for many decades and rarely equaled by the many subsequent adaptors. Amongst the other Continental musicals which Ross anglicized were *The Girl on the Train, The Marriage Market, The Dollar Princess* and *The Count of Luxembourg,* all of which had a wide and enduring success in their English versions.

After writing songwords for Edwardes's shows, both original works and adaptations, through more than 20 years, Ross continued, after the producer's death, to supply his successors at the Gaiety, Daly's and the Adelphi, whilst also working for other managements on other successful shows. With the advent of the revue, he even ventured into that area, working with Herman Darewski on *Three Cheers* (1917) and with Monckton on *Airs and Graces,* but revue was no more his field than it was that of Monckton or Jones or Stuart, and he worked only once more on a major London revue when he wrote the lyrics for the Palladium's much later *Sky High.*

In the postwar years, he nevertheless kept up the extremely heavy schedule of his earlier days, collaborating on such hit shows as the musicalized French comedy *Theodore & Co,* the Pinero musical *The Boy,* the memorable musicalization of Booth Tarkington's *Monsieur Beaucaire* (''Philomel'') and, in 1922, supplying both the libretto and the lyrics for the enormously successful English version of *Das Dreimäderlhaus,* produced in Britain as *Lilac Time.* In his late sixties and his seventies he eased his work load, and he contributed his last original work to the London stage in 1927 when he collaborated with Australian composer Dudley Glass on a musical version of W J Locke's *The Beloved Vagabond.* His final farewell came three years later, with the English version of Ludwig Herzer and Fritz Löhner-Beda's libretto to the Lehár Operette *Friederike* and with a musical version of Austin Strong's *The Toymaker of Nuremberg,* played as a Christmas entertainment at the unfavored Kingsway Theatre.

Ross wrote regularly and extensively with all of the most successful British-based composers of his time, from Caryll, Monckton, Lutz and Stuart at the Gaiety to Sidney Jones at Daly's and, in later days, Howard Talbot and André Messager, through more than 40 busy years which included uncountable hit shows and hit songs in and beyond the theatre. If, in the manner of the day, much of what he wrote was ephemeral and banal in its subject and sentiments, it was nevertheless tailored precisely to its producer's needs. Ross never wrote a Gaiety song for Daly's, or vice versa, and the result was a personal success inside the general success of, in particular, the Edwardes shows. His many adaptations were literate and to the point and, in spite of the vast changes in speech patterns during the 20th century, those for the most popular shows are still performed today.

In his non-lyric-making periods, Ross edited French books for the Cambridge University Press, published a small history of Europe, and was an examiner for entrance to the Indian Civil Service. In the 1890s he also penned a number of little operettas for publishers Joseph Williams (*Faust and Gretchen, Lodging to Let, Mary and Sairey, The Robber,* etc) for amateur and drawing room production.

1889 **Faddimir, or The Triumph of Orthodoxy** (F Osmond Carr) Vaudeville Theatre 29 April

1891 **Joan of Arc** (Carr/w John L Shine) Opera Comique 17 January

1892 **The Young Recruit** (*Le Dragon de la Reine*) English lyrics w Harry Greenbank, Harry Nicholls (Newcastle)

1892 **In Town** (Carr/w ''James Leader'') Prince of Wales Theatre 15 October

1893 **Morocco Bound** (Carr/Arthur Branscombe) Shaftesbury Theatre 13 April

1893 **Don Juan** (Meyer Lutz/James T Tanner) Gaiety Theatre 28 October

1894 **Go-Bang** (Carr) Trafalgar Square Theatre 10 March

1894 **The Shop Girl** (Ivan Caryll, Lionel Monckton/w Henry J Dam/Dam) Gaiety Theatre 24 November

1894 **Mirette** revised English version (Savoy Theatre)

1895 **Bobbo** (Carr/w Tanner) 1 act Prince's Theatre, Manchester 12 September

1896 **Biarritz** (Carr/w Jerome K Jerome) Prince of Wales Theatre 11 April

1896 **My Girl** (ex- *The Clergyman's Daughter*) (Carr/Tanner) Gaiety Theatre 13 July

1896 **Weather or No** (Luard Selby/w W Beach) 1 act Savoy Theatre 10 August

1896 **The Circus Girl** (Caryll/w Harry Greenbank/Tanner, Walter Palings) Gaiety Theatre 5 December

1897 **His Majesty, or The Court of Vignolia** (Alexander MacKenzie/w F C Burnand, Rudolf C Lehmann) Savoy Theatre 20 February

1897 **The Ballet Girl** (Carl Kiefert/Tanner) Grand Theatre, Wolverhampton 15 March

1897 **The Grand Duchess** (*La Grande-Duchesse de Gérolstein*) new English lyrics (Savoy Theatre)

1898 **The Transit of Venus** (Napoléon Lambelet/Tanner) Dublin 9 April

1898 **Billy** (Carr/w G Cooper) Tyne Theatre and Opera House, Newcastle 11 April

1898 **A Greek Slave** (Sidney Jones/w H Greenbank/Owen Hall) Daly's Theatre 8 June

1898 **Milord Sir Smith** (ex- *Campano*) (Edward Jakobowski/ad Arthur Roberts, etc) Comedy Theatre 15 December

1899 **The Tree-Dumas-Skiteers** addition to Milord Sir Smith (Comedy Theatre)

1899 **The Lucky Star** (*L'Étoile*) (Caryll/w Aubrey Hopwood/ad J Cheever Goodwin, et al) Savoy Theatre 7 January

1899 **Tempests in Teacups** (Florian Pascal/w C Pirkiss) 1 act St George's Parish Hall, Forest Hill

1899 **San Toy** (Jones/w H Greenbank/Edward Morton) Daly's Theatre 21 October

1900 **The Messenger Boy** (Caryll, Monckton/w Percy Greenbank/Tanner, Alfred Murray) Gaiety Theatre 3 February

1900 **Ordered South** (W Augustus Barratt) sketch St George's Tennis Club 28 July

1901 **The Toreador** (Caryll, Monckton/w P Greenbank/Tanner, Harry Nicholls) Gaiety Theatre 17 June

1901 **Kitty Grey** (Monckton, Talbot, etc/w Paul Rubens/J Smyth Piggott) Apollo Theatre 7 September

1902 **A Country Girl** (Monckton/w P Greenbank/Tanner) Daly's Theatre 18 January

1902 **The Girl from Kays** (Cecil Cook, Caryll, etc/w Claude Aveling/Hall) Apollo Theatre 15 November

1903 **Madame Sherry** English version with Charles E Hands (Apollo Theatre)

1903 **The Orchid** (Monckton, Caryll/w P Greenbank/Tanner) Gaiety Theatre 28 October

1904 **The Cingalee** (Monckton/w P Greenbank/Tanner) Daly's Theatre 5 March

1905 **The Spring Chicken** (Monckton, Caryll/w P Greenbank/ad George Grossmith) Gaiety Theatre 30 May

1906 **The Little Cherub** (Caryll/Hall) Prince of Wales Theatre 13 January

1906 **Naughty Nero, or Episodes in the His-Tree of Rome** (Augustus Barratt) 1 act Oxford Music Hall 8 March

1906 **See-See** (Jones/w P Greenbank/C H E Brookfield) Prince of Wales Theatre 20 June

1906 **The New Aladdin** (Caryll, Monckton/w P Greenbank, et al/Tanner, W H Risque) Gaiety Theatre 29 September

1906 **Les Merveilleuses** (Hugo Felix/Victorien Sardou ad Basil Hood) Daly's Theatre 27 October

1907 **The Girls of Gottenberg** (Caryll, Monckton/w Basil Hood/ Grossmith, L E Berman) Gaiety Theatre 15 May

1907 **The Merry Widow** (*Die lustige Witwe*) English lyrics (Daly's Theatre)

1908 **A Waltz Dream** (*Ein Walzertraum*) English version (Globe Theatre)

1908 **Havana** (Leslie Stuart/w George Arthurs/Graham Hill, Grossmith) Gaiety Theatre 25 April

1908 **The King of Cadonia** (Jones/Frederick Lonsdale) Prince of Wales Theatre 3 September

1908 **The Antelope** (Felix) Waldorf Theatre 28 November

1909 **Our Miss Gibbs** (Caryll, Monckton/w P Greenbank/ Tanner, ''Cryptos'') Gaiety Theatre 23 January

1909 **The Dashing Little Duke** (Frank E Tours/Seymour Hicks) Hicks Theatre 17 February

1909 **The Dollar Princess** (*Die Dollarprinzessin*) English lyrics (Daly's Theatre)

1910 **Captain Kidd** (Stuart/Hicks) Wyndham's Theatre 12 January

1910 **The Girl in the Train** (*Die geschiedene Frau*) English lyrics (Vaudeville Theatre)

1910 **The Quaker Girl** (Monckton/w P Greenbank/Tanner) Adelphi Theatre 5 November

1911 **Castles in the Air** (*Frau Luna*) English lyrics (Scala Theatre)

1911 **The Count of Luxembourg** (*Der Graf von Luxemburg*) English lyrics w Hood (Daly's Theatre)

1912 **Gipsy Love** (*Zigeunerliebe*) English lyrics (Daly's Theatre)

1912 **The Wedding Morning** (Lachlan McLean) 1 act Tivoli 30 September

1912 **Tantalizing Tommy** (Felix/w Michael Morton) Criterion Theater, New York 1 October

1912 **The Dancing Mistress** (Monckton/w P Greenbank/Tanner) Adelphi Theatre 19 October

1913 **The Girl on the Film** (*Filmzauber*) English lyrics (Gaiety Theatre)

1913 **The Marriage Market** (*Leányvásár*) English version (Daly's Theatre)

1913 **The Girl from Utah** (Jones, Rubens/w Rubens, P Greenbank/Tanner) Adelphi Theatre 18 October

1914 **The Belle of Bond Street** revised *The Girl from Kays* (Shubert Theater, New York)

1915 **Betty** (Rubens/w Rubens/Lonsdale, Gladys Unger) Daly's Theatre 24 April

1915 **The Light Blues** (Talbot, Herman Finck/Mark Ambient, Jack Hulbert) Prince of Wales Theatre, Birmingham 13 September; Shaftesbury Theatre 14 September 1916

1916 **The Happy Day** (Rubens, Jones/w Rubens/Hicks) Daly's Theatre 13 May

1916 **Theodore & Co** (Ivor Novello, Jerome Kern/w Clifford Grey/Grossmith, H M Harwood) Gaiety Theatre 19 September

1916 **The Happy Family** (Cuthbert Clarke/w Arthur Aldin) Prince of Wales Theatre 18 December

1916 **Oh, Caesar!** (Nat D Ayer, Arthur Wood/Alexander M Thompson, Max Pemberton) Royal Lyceum, Edinburgh 23 December

1917 **Arlette** English version (Shaftesbury Theatre)

1917 **The Boy** (Talbot, Monckton/w P Greenbank/Fred Thompson) Adelphi Theatre 14 September

1919 **Monsieur Beaucaire** (André Messager/Lonsdale) Prince's Theatre 19 April

1919 **The Kiss Call** (Caryll/w Grey, P Greenbank/Thompson) Gaiety Theatre 8 October

1919 **Maggie** (Marcel Lattès/Thompson, H F Maltby) Oxford Theatre 22 October

1919 **The Eclipse** (Herman Darewski, Melville Gideon/w Davy Burnaby/E Phillips Oppenheim, Thompson) Garrick Theatre 12 November

1920 **Medorah** English lyrics (Alhambra Theatre)

1920 **The Love Flower** (Herman Finck/w James Heard/Robert Marshall) Theatre Royal, Brighton 8 March

1920 **A Southern Maid** (Harold Fraser Simson/w Harry Graham/Graham) Daly's Theatre 15 May

1920 **The Naughty Princess** (*La Reine s'amuse*) English lyrics (Adelphi Theatre)

1921 **Faust on Toast** (Willie Redstone, Gideon/w Firth Shephard) Gaiety Theatre 19 April

1921 **Love's Awakening** (*Wenn Liebe erwacht*) English book and lyrics (Empire Theatre)

1922 **Lilac Time** (*Das Dreimäderlhaus*) English book and lyrics (Lyric Theatre)

1923 **The Cousin from Nowhere** (*Der Vetter aus Dingsda*) English lyrics w Furber, Robert C Tharp (Prince's Theatre)

1923 **Head Over Heels** (Fraser-Simson/w Graham/Hicks) Adelphi Theatre 8 September

1927 **The Beloved Vagabond** (Dudley Glass) Duke of York's Theatre 1 September

1930 **Frederica** (*Friederike*) English version (Palace Theatre)

1930 **The Toymaker of Nuremberg** (Glass/w Austin Strong) Kingsway Theatre 20 December

ROSS, Jerry [ROSENBERG, Jerrold] (b New York, 9 March 1926; d New York, 11 November 1955).

A keen theatre participator from a young age, Ross began writing songs before his college years, but he made no breakthrough until he met up with and began to collaborate with Richard Adler in 1950. The pair attracted the attention of Frank Loesser, had a hit song with ''Rags to Riches,'' broke into Broadway with *John Murray Anderson's Almanac* in 1953 and, in quick time, brought out the scores for two hit musicals, *The Pajama Game* (''Hey There'') and *Damn Yankees* (''Whatever Lola Wants,'' ''Heart''). Ross, who had suffered from serious bronchiectasis for many years, died from the infections caused by that illness at the age of 29.

1954 **The Pajama Game** (w Richard Adler/George Abbott, Richard Bissell) St James Theater 13 May

1955 **Damn Yankees** (w Adler/w Abbott, Douglass Wallop) 46th Street Theater 5 May

ROSSE, Frederick (b Jersey, 1867; d Brighton, 20 June 1940).

A very versatile musical-comedy man, Frederick Rosse took the juvenile lead in the 1894 musical comedy *Go-Bang* (Narain), composed the music for the song ''Hands Off'' which Hayden Coffin featured in *An Artist's Model* (1895), wrote the basic score for James Tanner and Owen Hall's musical farce *All Abroad* (1895), and was conductor for the West End production of *The Gay Pretenders* (1900), for Rutland Barrington's version of *The Water Babies* (1902) for which he also composed the score, for *Sergeant Brue* (add music), *Miss Wingrove* (1905) and for the 1908 revival of *Dorothy*.

1895 **All Abroad** (W H Risque/Owen Hall, James T Tanner)) Theatre Royal, Portsmouth 1 April; Criterion Theatre 8 August

1898 **At Zero** (T Hughes) Reading 4 July

1902 **The Water Babies** (Rutland Barrington) Garrick Theatre 18 December

1904 **Little Black Sambo and Little White Barbara** (w Wilfred Bendall/Barrington) Garrick Theatre 21 December

1910 **A Bedouin Beauty** (w Raymond King/Talbot Hughes) Devonshire Park Theatre, Eastbourne 22 August, Royal Artillery Theatre, Woolwich 29 August

ROSSI, Tino [ROSSI, Constantin] (b Ajaccio, 29 April 1907; d Neuilly-sur-Seine, 27 September 1983). Favorite singing star of postwar French screen and, later, stage.

The short, dark and handsome Rossi began his career in southern France as a singer of the songs of his native Corsica, and subsequently made himself a reputation in the music halls and as a recording artist. His first stage appearance was in revue, the 1934 Casino de Paris *Parade de France*, but he was 48 years old, with a long career as a star of film and radio behind him, before he made his debut in the musical theatre. With Luis Mariano and *The Belle of Cadix* having made the romantic opérette topped by a popular tenor the latest rage, Rossi appeared at the Châtelet in the role of a Corsican singing star in *Méditerranée,* written and composed by the authors of Mariano's piece, and scored a success no less ringing than his younger and svelter rival had done.

He subsequently played in a stage version of his old film *Naples au baiser de feu* (1957) as an amorous Italian, in another Lopez opérette, *Le Temps des Guitares* (1963), and as an eccentric millionaire in *Le Marchand de Soleil* (1969), each of which owed a substantial part of its good run to the presence at the top of its bill of Rossi's name. On the screen, he played Schubert in Marcel Pagnol's version of the *Dreimäderlhaus* tale, *La Belle Meunière* (1948), and starred in the film version of the Alibert/Scotto *Au Pays du soleil* (1951).

Literature: Trimbach, G: *Tino Rossi* (Delville, Paris, 1978)

ROTHOMAGO, or The Magic Watch Grand opéra-bouffe féerie in 4 acts by Adolphe d'Ennery, Clairville and A Monnier adapted into English by H B Farnie. Music by Procida Bucalossi, Edward Solomon, Gaston Serpette and Georges Jacobi. Alhambra Theatre, London, 22 December 1879.

A spectacular pasticcio féerie in the line of the perennially popular *Les Pilules du Diable* and *La Biche au bois,* the original French *Rothomago* (mus: A de Groot) was first played at the Paris Cirque (1 March 1862) and subsequently used to open the new Parisian Théâtre du Châtelet (19 August 1862). Although it was given only a handful of performances on that occasion, it was acclaimed as "one of the masterpieces of its kind," and it went on to be played around France, "borrowed" for Broadway by Laura Keene under the title *Blondette, or The Naughty Prince and the Pretty Peasant* (Laura Keene's Theater 25 November 1862, 42 performances), to be remounted at the Châtelet again in 1863, and to be revived spectacularly by Castellano in 1877 (October, 171 performances)—with a cast headed by Anna van Ghell (Rothomago fils), Tissier (Rothomago), Henri Cooper (Blaisinet) and Mlle Donvé (Princesse Miranda)—and yet again in 1878. As a result of this last production, staged at the height of London's infatuation with grandiose fairy-tale productions, the piece was picked up by the inveterate "adapter" H B Farnie, rewritten, fitted out with an original and rather fuller score by Bucalossi, Serpette, Jacobi and Solomon (one act apiece) and presented by Charles Morton on London's large Alhambra stage.

Harry Paulton played the inefficient court sorcerer Rothomago, and Constance Loseby his son of the same name who is supposed to marry Princess Allegra (Mlle Julic), daughter of reigning monarch Impecunioso (Louis Kelleher). Édouard Georges was the rustic Dodo (the Blaisinet of the French version) who gets hold of the magic watch which gives him power and the princess until—after everyone has spent the evening trying to distract him—he finally forgets to wind it up and loses all. Hetty Tracy was the good fairy Anisette and Annie Bentley the nasty Angostura. The chase after the watch went via bear-infested Freezeland, an escape by balloon, the French countryside (cue for a Wine Ballet) and Egypt (mummies' dance, plus real camels and an elephant) and the happy ending was celebrated in a Porcelain ballet which was one of the evening's highlights. Special effects, broad comedy, not too much dialogue, and a spectacle which lasted four hours kept London entertained for nearly four months.

The Châtelet remounted its version in 1897.

THE ROTHSCHILDS Musical in 2 acts by Sherman Yellen based on a book by Frederic Morton. Lyrics by Sheldon Harnick. Music by Jerry Bock. Lunt-Fontanne Theater, New York, 19 October 1970.

Harnick and Bock, who had triumphed with the Russo-Jewish tale of *Fiddler on the Roof,* tackled a second Jewish subject with a biomusical of the Rothschilds, another family struggling against the problems of being Jewish in period Europe. If the 18th- to 19th-century Rothschilds were a rather less appealing bunch than Tevye and his daughters, it might have been that their aims—financial gain, power and an invitation, even an unwilling one, to the ball—were less sympathetic than those of the famous milkman, but their stage potential was proven: the family, and notably the dowager mother, Gutele Rothschild, had earlier been made the subject of an enormously successful straight play in Karl Rössler's *Die fünf Frankfurter.*

In this musical, Mamma was not the central figure. Hal Linden played Mayer Rothschild, the father of the five sons who help him build up his banking empire and, after his death, get the Frankfurt ghetto and its laws abolished. Leila Martin was his wife, Gutele, and Jill Clayburgh provided a love interest for Nathan Rothschild (Paul Hecht), whilst Keene Curtis had a good time in a multiple role as Prince William of Hesse, Fouché and Metternich. The subject meant that there was no place for the endearing warmth of *Fiddler* in the show's score, which instead leaned towards songs of striving, lightened by some sentimental moments and by a touch of comedy, as in the young Mayer's spiel ("He Tossed a Coin") in selling some antique coins, a sale which makes him early money and rich contacts.

Lester Osterman and Hillard Elkins's production played 507 performances on Broadway, won Linden a

Tony Award, and, although the show did not follow *Fiddler on the Roof* overseas, it was later revived at New York's American Jewish Theater in 1990 (25 February) and played at off-Broadway's Circle in the Square Downtown (27 April 1990) with Mike Burstyn featured as Meyer Rothschild.

An earlier musical on the Rothschilds was produced in Hungary, when an 1860 play *Rothschild ház titka* (''the secret of the Rothschild house'') openly subtitled ''how to get rich,'' was followed by a successful 1932 operett entitled *A Rotschildok* (Lajos Lajtai/István Békeffy/Ferenc Martos, 25 November Fővárosi Operettszínház) in which Gyula Kabos and Vilma Medgyasszay (Mama Rothschild) starred. This version, whilst keeping Mama prominent, took more interest in Jacob (Gábor Kertész)—the son who went to Paris and (in this version, at least) got mixed up with the actress Lageorges (Hanna Honthy) and things Napoléonic—than it did in Nathan and the ghettos.

Recording: original cast (Columbia)

ROTT, Matthias [KOCH, Carl Matthias] (b Vienna, 23 February 1807; d Vienna, 10 February 1876). Viennese comic actor who played important roles in the earliest modern musicals in his hometown.

A teenaged organist at the Church of Maria Geburt, a choirboy at the Vienna Hofoper, a theatre chorister at the old Kärtnertor Theater, a 'cellist in the theatre orchestra at Pressburg, a sometime composer who is said to have written the music to accompany Nestroy's first play, and eventually a comedy actor, Rott spent a decade at the Theater in der Josefstadt, and a short period in Pest, before joining the company at the Theater an der Wien. There, more than two decades later, he was one of the principal comic players in Vienna's early productions of opéra-bouffe, a form which he tasted at its very beginnings with some performances at Karl Treumann's Theater am Franz-Josefs-Kai (Herr Boudinet in *Apotheker und Friseur,* Sarmiento in *Die Schwätzerin von Saragossa,* etc) in one of his rare excursions away from the Theater an der Wien.

Rott was Vienna's original Calchas (*Die schöne Helena*), Frangipani (*Coscoletto*), Alphecibdus (*Die Schäfer*), Pompéry (*Die Reise nach China*), Popolani (*Blaubart*), Grabuche, paired with Blasel as the gens d'armes in *Genovefa von Brabant,* the Mandarin Wau-Wau in *Theeblüthe,* General Bum-Bum to Geistinger's *Grossherzogin von Gérolstein,* Pietro (*Die Banditen*), Carol von Calabrien (*Fantasio*), Meister Fulbert in Litolff's *Heloise und Abälard,* Tokuwaka in Jonas's *Die Japanesin,* and Themistocles in *Madame ''Herzog,''* and also appeared as König Klingerlinging in *Prinzessin Hirschkuh,* the Viennese adaptation of *La Biche au bois.*

He also played in some of the earliest Viennese Operetten—as Jonas in Hopp's *Das Donauweibchen* and Herr von Városházy in Millöcker's version of *Drei Paar Schuhe*—and he created the title role of Johann Strauss's first Operette *Indigo und die vierzig Räuber,* before retiring from ther stage, at the age of nearly 70, after the scenery of *Madame ''Herzog''* fell on his head.

His wife also appeared in minor roles in opéra-bouffe at the Theater an der Wien.

ROUNSEVILLE, Robert [Field] (b Attleboro, Mass, 24 March 1914; d New York, 6 August 1974).

Tenor Rounseville appeared on Broadway in *Babes in Arms* (1934, ''Way Out West,'' ''Imagine''), *The Two Bouquets* (1938), *Knickerbocker Holiday* (1938) and *Higher and Higher* (1941), took the role of Jolidon (Camille) in the 1943 revival of *The Merry Widow* and played in a 1944 *Robin Hood* before creating his first major musical role as Andrew Munroe in *Up in Central Park* (1945). In a career which ranged from the operatic to the nightclubby, he appeared in Gilbert and Sullivan, as Ravenal in the City Center's *Show Boat* and Charlie in their *Brigadoon* and regionally in such roles as Karl-Franz, Camille, Charlie Dalrymple, Danilo, Bumerli, Eisenstein, Nordraak, El Gallo and Macheath, and returned to Broadway in 1956, to create the title role in *Candide,* and again in 1965 to introduce ''To Each His Dulcinea'' in the role of the Padre in *Man of La Mancha.*

Rounseville was also seen on film as Hoffmann in *The Tales of Hoffmann* (1951) and as Mister Snow in the 1956 film version of *Carousel.*

LA ROUSSOTTE Comédie-vaudeville in 3 acts and a prologue by Henri Meilhac, Ludovic Halévy and Albert Millaud. Music by Charles Lecocq, Hervé and Marius Boullard. Théâtre des Variétés, Paris, 28 January 1881.

La Roussotte followed *La Femme à papa* in the hugely successful series of made-for-Judic vaudevilles produced by Eugène Bertrand at the Variétés and, if it were not quite the outsized hit that *Niniche* or *Mam'zelle Nitouche* was, it nevertheless proved to be a grand success, playing through over one hundred performances on its first run and being toured through the world as an oft-played part of Mme Judic's repertoire. For this occasion, Albert Millaud was joined in creating the star's vehicle by none less than Meilhac and Halévy, who created an amusing tale and, most importantly, a first-class role for the lady as the ''redhead''of the title.

The gambling Comte Dubois-Toupet (Baron) once had a fling with the English wife (Anna Judic) of a sea captain and of that fling were born a pair of little red-headed children who were tactfully brought up by a foster-priest (Léonce). But one day the Comte overgambled and was obliged to set off east to refill his purse by selling opium to the Chinese. By the time he returned home, re-enriched, both the priest and the English lady were dead, and his children had vanished. The devious quasi-lawyer Gigonnet (Lassouche) whom Dubois-Toupet employs to find them tracks down the daughter, la Roussotte (Mme Judic again), working in an inn and he determines to wed her and her fortune before she is aware she has a fortune. When she turns him down in favor of his assistant, Médard (José Dupuis), Gigonnet revengefully announces that Médard is her lost brother. Back at the Dubois-Toupet château the two find co-existence as brother and sister unbearable, but a happy ending is ensured when the real Édouard (Didier), a red-headed gambling chip off the old green baize, turns up.

The score for *La Roussotte* was to have been written by Lecocq, but his illness prompted Bertrand to turn first to Hervé and then to the reliable Marius Boullard, who had obliged under similar circumstances on *Niniche,* to finish the half-done music. Most of the 11 numbers of the score were, of course, for the star who had three songs in Act I, three in Act II and the only one in Act III, alongside a little romance for Dupuis, plus a jolly introduction for Léonce and one song and a fragment for Baron in the prologue. The star opened with an unblushing reminiscence of her first meeting with her man (''Attendez, je m'rappelle maint'nant''), threw off the story of her love life in Boullard's Couplets des amoureux, and tossed a warning at the would-be compromiser Gigonnet (''Ah! n'fait's pas ça!''). She comically depicted a waitress's life (''Un peu d'silence''), pleaded with her papa against wedding a toff (''Sans Médard'') and, finally, showed off her new aristocratic talents as a horsewoman in waltz time, admitting, alas!, to riding astride. Her big song success of the piece, however, was popped in as a ''come on, la Roussotte, give us a song'' number. Hervé's cheeky Chanson de la Fille du Peintre en Bâtiment, better known by its chorus noise ''Piiii-ouit!,'' gave Judic another big, saucy hit, to follow the famous Chanson du Colonel from *La Femme à papa.*

Like *La Femme à papa* and *Niniche, La Roussotte* was seen in its original state virtually only when Judic took it around the world, and in Paris reprises in 1885 and 1889. Didier, now upped to Dupuis's role, Vois (Gigonnet) and Malard (Dubois-Toupet) supported the star in this second reprise, and the famous old pantomimist Paul Legrand made a hit with a small scene as a lone diner in a restaurant.

Elsewhere, it seemed deemed obligatory to replace the French score with locally written music. Vienna's Theater an der Wien produced the piece as *Ein süsses Kind* (ad Franz von Schönthan, 1 April 1882) with a score by Millöcker attached, Rosa Streitmann as Anne Marie (no longer doubling as her own mother), Girardi as Médard and Friese as Gigonnet; Berlin saw *Rotkäppchen,* described as a Vaudeville-Posse, with book and music both credited to Genée (Thomas-Theater 6 February 1882); whilst Budapest's version was played as *Piròk és Piróska* (ad Emil Kürthy, Népszínház 22 February 1890) with music by Oskar Feith.

Conversely, ''Piiii-ouit!'' went traveling without its play, and it was heard in America as part of Louise Théo's performance in *La Jolie Parfumeuse* in the 1882–83 season, a good two years and more before Broadway had had a chance to hear Judic and the whole of *La Roussotte.*

USA: Star Theater (Fr) 6 April 1885; Austria: Theater an der Wien (Fr) 19 December 1900

LA ROUTE FLEURIE Opérette in 2 acts by Raymond Vincy. Music by Francis Lopez. Théâtre de l'ABC, Paris, 19 December 1952.

Written by the pair of the moment of the Parisian musical theatre, Vincy and Lopez, who had lined up the successes over half a dozen years with *La Belle de Cadix, Andalousie, Le Chanteur de Mexico* and *Quatre Jours à Paris, La Route fleurie* was a piece more in the mode of the last-named of the group rather than in the opérette à grand spectacle style of the other three. It was, however, like the bigger pieces, and in contrast to the more book-orientated and farcical *Quatre Jours à Paris,* written around a star tenor role, which was taken in the original production by Georges Guétary.

Guétary played a Montmartre composer called Jean-Pierre who writes a film score and then gallivants pennilessly off to the Côte d'Azur to stay in a rich aunt's house with his friends Raphaël (Bourvil) and Lorette (Annie Cordy) and the mannequin Mimi (Claude Arvelle) for whom he sighs, in order to write a screenplay to go with his songs which will satisfy the powers that produce. Unfortunately the servants, who are used to letting the house on the side whilst madame is away, have booked in a crazy scientist called Poupoutzoff, and Jean-Pierre has also double-booked the place to his incipient film-producer and his star (Annie Dumas). The comic and romantic ins-and-outs of the preparations, the trip and the house party made up an evening's entertainment and, in the denouement, also the material for the plot's required screenplay. The whole was illustrated by some lively Lopez songs of which Mlle Cordy's soubrette/comic ''Tagada-Tsoin-Tsoin,'' Bourvil's poeticizing over ''Les Haricots,'' a pretty rhapsody, ''Une dinette,'' which recalled Guétary's London hit with ''A Table for Two'' (*Bless the Bride*) and the tenor's tale of the ''Jolie Meunière'' were amongst the happiest.

Producers Mitty Goldin and Léon Ledoux lined up a bill which proved to be a real winner. Guétary's value was known (and valued at 100,000 francs a performance), but that of the other two stars was not. Bourvil was in the doldrums after some successful years playing gormless peasant roles, mostly on film, and the young Mlle Cordy was playing third on a music-hall bill when they were cast—and valued at 15,000 and 5,000 francs respectively. Mlle Arvelle, a beauty contest winner, was scarcely in the same league with a trio which turned out to be the most remarkable team on the Paris musical stage in years. *La Route fleurie* was a major hit, filling its smaller house for three and a half years until mid-1956 and remaining a success even after its three stars had moved on to other successes. It was subsequently played liberally through France and was revived in 1980 at the Théâtre de la Renaissance (25 October).

Recordings: original cast (Pathé), revival cast (Vogue), selection (TLP)

Plate 334. *Annie Cordy and Bourvil set off for a happy song and dance on the Cote d'azur via* **La Route fleurie.**

ROUTLEDGE, [Katherine] Patricia (b Birkenhead, 17 February 1929). Atlantic-hopping character lady of the straight and musical stages through 40 years in search of a memorable new musical role.

After an early career in repertory theatre, Miss Routledge made her first London appearances in musical plays—the Bristol Old Vic's Julian Slade version of *The Duenna* (1954, Carlotta) and the same composer's comic opera version of *A Comedy of Errors* (1956). In 1957 she appeared in the short-lived *Zuleika* (Aunt Mabel), in 1959 in the even-shorter-lived Molière with music, *The Love Doctor* (Henrietta), and in 1960 played Susan Hampshire's mother in Slade's charming *Follow that Girl* (''Waiting for Our Daughter''). In 1962 she appeared in the title role of the British production of *Little Mary Sunshine* and the following year played Berinthia in the musical version of *The Relapse, Virtue in Danger* (1963), before returning to the non-musical theatre for several years.

Amongst a list of stage and television (Megaera in Richard Rodgers's *Androcles and the Lion,* 1967) credits which produced some memorably characterful performances as the years went by, Miss Routledge returned regularly to the musical stage. She gave London a *Grande-Duchesse de Gérolstein* which was spoken of with enthusiasm for decades after and, in 1968, she starred as Alice Challice in the unsuccessful Broadway musical *Darling of the Day,* a performance which nevertheless won her a Tony Award. She played Queen Victoria in a musical tale of that monarch's *Love Match* with Prince Albert which closed pre-Broadway, and in 1976 visited America again to play the President's wives in Leonard Bernstein's short-lived *1600 Pennsylvania Avenue.* In 1981 she appeared as Veta Louise Simmons in *Say Hello to Harvey,* an unsuccessful musical version of *Harvey* in Canada, in 1989 succeeded to the role of the Old Lady in Scottish Opera's production of *Candide* for its London season, and in 1992 appeared as Nettie Fowler in Britain's National Theatre mounting of *Carousel.*

If a worthwhile new musical-theatre role proved elusive, however, television proved kinder. In the 1990s Miss Routledge became British TV's favorite over-the-top upwardly-striving matron in such roles as Hyacinth Bucket of *Keeping Up Appearances* and Hetty Wainwright of *Wainwright Investigates.*

ROXY UND IHR WUNDERTEAM Vaudeville-Operette in 3 acts by Alfred Grünwald adapted from an original by Lászlό Szilágyi and Dezső Kellér. Lyrics by Grünwald and Hans Weigl. Music by Pál Ábrahám. Theater an der Wien, Vienna, 25 March 1937.

Composed by a Pál Ábrahám who was on the run from Nazism and already falling away from the finest moments he would know as a composer with *Viktória, Die Blume von Hawaii* and *Ball im Savoy,* this Vaudeville-Operette was a jolly, up-to-date, flag-waving show about a Scots girl—the titular Roxy—who goes mad over the entire Hungarian national football team. All things considered, this is a fairly natural kind of crush, for in the Operette the Hungarians hand out a thrashing to the once footballmighty English.

Produced by Artur Hellmann at a Theater an der Wien also in the days of its decline, with Rózsi Bársony starred as Roxy alongside her partner Oszkár Dénes and Max Brod, *Roxy und ihr Wunderteam* lasted 59 performances. However, portions of it resurfaced in Paris, to where Ábrahám continued his flight, two years later and two months before the outbreak of war. Maurice Lehmann staged a piece at the Théâtre Mogador under the title *Billy et son équipe,* an ''opérette a grand-spectacle en 10 tableaux'' credited to Mouëzy-Éon and Albert Willemetz for the text and to Michel Emer and ''Jean Sautreuil'' (ie, Maurice Yvain) for the music. Ábrahám was noted as having supplied ''airs additionels,'' but Urban, who starred alongside Coecilia Navarre, Félix Paquet and Arnaudy, got in the ''Lambeth Walk'' as well. The new football show did no better than its Hungaro-Viennese prototype, leaving America's sporting musicals at the top of the medal-list.

THE ROYAL VAGABOND Cohanized opera comique in 3 acts by Stephen Idor Szinnyey and William Cary Duncan. Lyrics by Duncan. Music by Anselm Goetzl. Cohan and Harris Theater, New York, 17 February 1919.

The Cohanized element of *The Royal Vagabond* (for which the canny gentleman pulled a royalty of 5 percent) was the element that made it into a novelty success. *Cherry Blossoms* was the work of the expatriate mid-European musician Anselm Götzl, who had been responsible, amongst others, for the score of Prague's *Frau Lebedame* (1907). This time, however, he did not have a Sardou libretto to work with, but the most conventional tale of Prince and milliner and Ruritanian antics concocted by William Cary Duncan and one Count Stephen Szinnyey.

Cohan took the conventional work, redid most of the lyrics, popped in a couple of his own, and the result was an operetta in which Frederic Santley as Prince Stephan of Bargravia and Tessa Kosta as Anitza Chefcheck, the milliner, still sang their hearts out about ''When the Cherry Blossoms Fall,'' but did it after an opening chorus which has confided ''tra-la-la, the lyric would make you laugh, ha-ha, for that we pay the royalties, they sing it in fifty different keys . . .'' and introduced each of the main characters and their aching conventionalities. When the heroine then sang that her heart was bleeding and his lips had thrilled her, it was difficult, without looking at the program, to know whether one was listening to Cohan or Duncan (it was Duncan). But you knew it was all for hoots. Cohan and Harris produced, Julian Mitchell and Sam Forrest directed, Dorothy Dickson and Carl Hyson danced, the audiences laughed, and *The Royal Vagabond* (as the piece had been renamed) ran 208 Broadway performances. Only a few of them had been played when the 48-year-old Szinnyey was buried in the Bronx, presumably not as a result of a broken heart at the guying of his ''serious'' work.

Goetzl and Duncan later tried again for success with a piece called *The Rose Girl* which traveled from Wilkes-Barre, Pa, to Broadway (11 February 1921). Un-Cohanized, it nevertheless gave them a second good, if more modest, run.

LE ROYAUME DES FEMMES Opérette à grand spectacle in 3 acts by Hippolyte Cogniard and Desnoyers, adapted by Ernest Blum, Paul Ferrier and others. Music composed and arranged by Gaston Serpette. Eldorado, Paris, 24 February 1896.

One of the earliest of the run of highly successful musical spectaculars originated by the Cogniard brothers in the mid-19th century, *Le Royaume des femmes* was first produced in 1833 in a version by Hippolyte Cogniard and Desnoyers. For some reason, it was banned during the reign of Louis-Philippe and the Empire, but it resurfaced in 1866 (1 September), in a new version, done over by Cogniard and Ernest Blum, and was mounted at the Variétés with Couder, Mme Alphonsine and Mlle Vernet featured and with considerable success. In 1889 Blum and the habitual collaborator of his later years, Raoul Toché, revised the piece once more, with a pasticcio score which mixed the music of Offenbach, Gounod, Massé, Planquette and Lecocq with the music-hall songs of Paulus, and Brasseur staged it at the Théâtre des Nouveautés during the Exhibition, with a splendid cast topped by Brasseur père and fils, Guy, Mme Macé-Montrouge, Jane Pierny, Marguerite Ugalde and Juliette Darcourt. In 1896 it was given a final going-over, this time by Blum and Paul Ferrier, for a fourth production, in a fourth version, at the Eldorado. The piece had by this stage come quite a way from its origins, but the bones of the tale, now decorated with a half-new/half-old score from Gaston Serpette, who had proven his skill at musicking grandiose scenic pieces, were much as they had been originally.

Baron Frivolin (Juliette Simon-Girard) and Vicomte Citronnet (Berthaut) are carried away in a balloon, and land on an island where women rule. They not only rule, but they also behave like Parisian men, particularly in their affairs with the opposite sex. Queen Suavita (Marie de l'Isle) takes a fancy to Frivolin, whilst General Trombolinette (Mlle Simier) treats Citronnet like a grisette, an attitude which upsets that gentlemen's macho-Parisian amour propre something proper. Meanwhile the Commanderess-in-Chief, Xéressa (Mily-Meyer), is pursuing the gentle Alcindor (Sulbac), a lad who has been kept to the virtuously straight and innocent path by his aunt, Prudhomma (Mme Mathilde), and when he proves sexually shy she simply has him carried bodily off to her apartments. Ultimately, the visiting men provoke a revolt and everything in this upside-down world is turned back to 19th-century normal.

The island of women, with its topsy-turvy habits, gave the opportunity for much spectacle, not least the parade of the women's army, clad in suitably ''active'' clothing.

Le Royaume des femmes made its way through Europe, several times, in its various forms and under varying titles such as ''the topsy-turvey world'' and ''the island of women,'' Berlin took it twice, both in its 1889 version (*Das Paradies der Frauen* Metropoltheater 3 September, mus: Einödshofer, B Sänger, ad Julius Freund) and then again in its 1896 version (*Die verkehrte Welt* Metropoltheater 25 December 1899, add mus Einödshofer, ad Freund). Vienna's Danzers Orpheum (22 February) and Venedig in Wien both played a *Die verkehrte Welt* (1901) credited to Lindau and Krenn with Karl Kappeller for music, but the *Paradies der Damen* (30 January 1901) mounted at the Theater an der Wien was not a rip-off of the Parisian spectacular, but a wholly different show: in this case the ''women's Heaven'' was a couturier's shop called the Salon Frippon. In Hungary, the 1866 version was played at the Deutsches Theater, Pest, in 1869 with a musical score by the young Carl Millöcker under the title *Die Fraueninsel,* and the Blum/ Ferrier version, with Serpette's music still attached, was played as *Felfordult világ* (ad Ferenc Molnár, Emil Makai) at the Fővárosi Nyári Színház (22 August 1900). The English-language theatre passed.

ROYCE, E[dward] W[illiam] [REDDALL, Edward William] (b Woburn (Eversholt), Beds 11 August 1841; d London, 24 January 1926). Burlesque star of the Gaiety days.

Teddy Royce was, for a good decade, a dancer and comic actor in the provinces (''first low comedian, ballet master and principal dancer'' at the Glasgow Colosseum 1869, Disney Roebuck's Co 1870, *Little Amy Robsart* with Joe Eldred, etc) until John Hollingshead spotted him and brought him to the Gaiety Theatre in 1873 (stage manager, Gaiety touring company, etc). At first he was seen in London—at the Gaiety and at other theatres (*Conrad and Medora* at the St James's 1875, etc)—largely in comedy, and he also directed both plays and musicals, staging amongst others London's perversion of *La Timbale d'argent, The Duke's Daughter* (1876, also played Grand Duke Ulric), but in August 1876 he was promoted to become (with Nellie Farren, Edward Terry and Kate Vaughan) one of the four-cornered star group of Gaiety burlesque players who were to be the figureheads of the first great era of Gaiety burlesque. Over the next years he played for Hollingshead in *Young Rip van Winkle* (1876, Derrick), *Little Don Caesar de Bazan* (1876, Don José), *The Bohemian G'yurl* (1877, Count Smith), *Our Babes in the Wood* (1877, Sir Guy Fox), *Little Doctor Faust* (1877, Valentine), *Il Sonnambulo* (1878, Elvino), *Young Fra Diavolo* (1878, Giacomo), *Pretty Esmeralda*

Plate 335. **Edward Royce** *(and friend). Choreographer and/or director for a generation of British and American musicals.*

(1879, Quasimodo), *Handsome Hernani* (1879, Don Carlos), *Gulliver* (1879, Smuggins), *Robbing Roy* (1879, The Dougal Creature), *Trovatore or Larks with a Libretto* (1880, Ferrando), The *Corsican Brothers & Co Ltd* (1880, the brothers), *The Forty Thieves* (1880, Hassarac), *Whittington and his Cat* (1881, Mynheer van der Skuttle), *Aladdin* (1881, So-Sli), *Very Little Hamlet* (Claudius), *Mazeppa* (Laurinski), *Bluebeard* and many others such pieces, until his health broke down and he was forced to leave both the theatre and, after a brief essay at starting over (Conrad the Corsair in *Cherry and Fairstar,* 1885), the country.

In 1886 he made his way to the more sanitary climate of Australia where he worked at first for Brough and Boucicault and later for other managements, appearing in comedy (Medway in *Turned Up,* etc), burlesque (*Young Fra Diavolo,* Blueskin in *Little Jack Shepperd,* Hassarac in *The Forty Thieves,* etc), drama (*The Silver King, The Silver Falls, Human Nature, The Pointsman, Formosa,* etc) and comic opera (Jack Joskins in *Dick,* Coquelicot in *Olivette*) and adapting, directing and playing in pantomime for Sam Lazar at Sydney's Theatre Royal.

Restored by his stay in the colonies, he returned to Britain in 1892, and returned also to the London stage, playing in the burlesque *Atalanta,* at the Gaiety in *Don Juan* (1893, Sultan of Turkey) and the 1894 revival of *Little Jack Sheppard* (Mr Wood), and in the comic opera *The Bric-à-brac Will* (1895, Barnaba). He also appeared on the road as Gaspard in *Les Cloches de Corneville*—a role he retained for many years—and in *The Black Squire*

(1896, Septimus P Chipmunk), and intermittently directed and choreographed (*The Ballet Girl,* etc) as well. As late as 1908 he appeared on the West End stage, playing Old Jacques in *The Belle of Brittany,* and he survived to a ripe 84.

ROYCE, Edward [REDDALL, James William] (b Bath, 14 December 1870; d London, 15 June 1964).

The son of E W Royce, Edward Royce was originally trained as a scenic artist, and then as a dancer, but went on to make himself a memorable career as a choreographer and a director on both sides of the Atlantic.

He staged pantomime dances in Dublin as early as 1893, but his earliest West End credits, under the management of producer William Greet, included the dances for the original production of *Merrie England* at the Savoy Theatre, for *A Princess of Kensington* (1903), *The Earl and the Girl* (1903), *Little Hans Andersen* (1903) and *The Talk of the Town* (1905) and for the Charles Frohman/Seymour Hicks shows *The Catch of the Season* (1904), *The Beauty of Bath* (1906), *My Darling* (1907) and *The Gay Gordons* (1907). Royce doubled direction and choreography for the first time on the 1905 revival of *Bluebell in Fairyland,* and he fulfilled the same double function on the tour of *The Girls of Gottenberg* and the Gaiety Theatre's *Havana* (1908) for George Edwardes. He subsequently served Edwardes on *Our Miss Gibbs* (1909), *The Dollar Princess* (1909), *The Girl in the Taxi* (1910), *A Waltz Dream, Peggy, The Count of Luxembourg* (1911), *Gipsy Love* (1912) and *The Marriage Market* (1913).

Royce visited America to work for Frohman on his production of *The Doll Girl* (1913), following which he repeated his *Marriage Market* for Broadway and mounted the American version of *The Laughing Husband,* before returning to London for *The Country Girl* and the revue *Bric-à-Brac.* In 1916 he went to America a second time to direct the Gaiety Theatre musical *Betty* for Charles Dillingham, and this time he remained there, becoming one of the most sought-after and successful directors and choreographers on Broadway. He directed *The Century Girl* (w Leon Erroll) for Dillingham and Ziegfeld, and was then put under contract by F Ray Comstock and Morris Gest for whom in the years that followed he staged *Oh, Boy!* (1917 w Robert Milton), *Leave It to Jane* (1917), *Oh! Look* (1918 w Milton), *Oh, Lady! Lady!!* (1918, w Milton), *Oh My Dear* (1918, w Milton) and *See You Later* (1919). He was, however, loaned out regularly to mount such pieces as Louis Hirsch's highly successful *Going Up* (w James Montgomery) with its famous ''Tickle Toe'' dance, *Kitty Darlin'* (1917), *Have a Heart* (1917), *Rockabye Baby* (1918), *The Canary* (1918, w Fred Latham), *Come Along* (1919 w Frank Jackson), *She's a Good Fellow* (1919, w Latham), *Apple Blossoms* (1919), *Irene* (1919), *Honeymoon Town* (1919) and *Lassie* (1919–20). His popularity ultimately became such that he had to rush from one engagement to the next and at one stage Elisabeth Marbury sued him for abandoning A H Woods's sinking Avery Hopwood musical *Dodo / I'll Say She Does* to hurry on to assignments on *The Ziegfeld Follies, Kissing Time* (1920) and *Sally* (1920).

In the 1920s he pulled back to a slightly less demential schedule. In 1921 he directed and choreographed a second *Ziegfeld Follies, The Love Letter* and Jerome Kern's successful *Good Morning, Dearie,* and the following year he turned producer to stage *Orange Blossoms* (1922). Its so-so career was followed by a genuine flop with a second production, *Cinders,* and Royce abandoned producing and returned solely to staging. He mounted the comedy musicals *Kid Boots* and *Louie the 14th, Marjorie* (1924), the musical comedy *Annie Dear,* and was the original stager of *No, No, Nanette,* until Harry Frazee took a bottle in both hands and fired him. Thing went less well thereafter. *Ziegfeld's Palm Beach Girl* wandered through several titles in a disappointing life and the *Brewster's Millions* musical *Bubbling Over* (1926 also producer) failed to make it to town, and Royce slipped away to Australia where he staged the hugely successful local production of *Katja, the Dancer.* Back in America he had Broadway flops with *She's My Baby* (1928) and *Billie* (1928), mounted Los Angeles's *The Rose of Flanders* and San Francisco's *Bambina,* choreographed a couple of 1929 movies (*Married in Hollywood, Words and Music* w Frank Merlin) and then, after 20 years' absence, he went back to London.

There, he directed a revival of *A Waltz Dream* at the Winter Garden, and the following year his name was attached to the libretto of a romantic musical called *Fritzi* (for which he was not connected with the staging). The end of his 30-plus-year career seems to have been marked by his arrangement of the dances for a ''musical-comedy travelogue'' called *George Ahoy,* mounted by Tom Arnold as a vehicle for provincial comic George Clarke and Dan Leno jr in 1936.

ROYSTON, Roy [CROWDEN, Charles Roy] (b Hampstead, London, 5 April 1899; d Surbiton, 7 October 1976). Durable juvenile leading man of the song-and-dance stage.

Royston made his first appearances on the stage as a child performer in London, in Liverpool and in Birmingham, where he took part in Basil Dean's production of the fairy musical *Fifinella* (1912, Olly). He made his London musical debut as the dude boy David in *Betty* (1915) at Daly's Theatre, and he subsequently appeared in both plays and in revue before going into active service in the war. He returned to the stage in 1919, taking over the role of the boy Hughie in *The Boy* at the Adelphi Theatre, then appeared in the London production of *Fifinella* in an adult role and starred opposite Evelyn Laye as the hero of the Gaiety Theatre's revival of *The Shop Girl* (1920, Charlie Appleby).

There followed a series of lead juvenile roles in the musicals *Now and Then* (1920, Henry Bablock-Hythe), *The Lady of the Rose* (1922, Adrian Beltramini), *The Cousin from Nowhere* (1923, Adrian van Piffel) and *Little Nellie Kelly* (1923, Jack Lloyd) and a season in the revue *Snap!* before Royston crossed to America to take up a similar line of juvenile leads in rather less appreciable shows: *Peg o' My Dreams* (1924, Jerry), *Marjorie* (1924, Brian Valcourt) and *June Days* (Austin Bevans). Back in London, in 1925 he took the lead juvenile roles in three American musicals, *The Blue Kitten* (Armand du Velin), *Happy-Go-Lucky* (ex- *When You Smile,* Wally King) and the *Kitty's Kisses* version of *The Girl Friend* (Robert Mason) and, thereafter, he hopped backwards and forwards between Broadway and Britain playing *Ups-a-Daisy* (Roy Lindbrooke) in America, *Lucky Girl* (King Stephan) and *Meet My Sister* (René Fleuriot) on the road in England, *Cochran's Revue* and *Blue Roses* (Jimmy Mallowes) in London, and then the Fred Stone *Smiling Faces* (Robert Bowington) in America.

Back in London once more he took the juvenile lead in the American import *The One Girl* (ex- *Smiles*) and played in revue and in pantomime, and then joined the company at the Gaiety Theatre where between 1935 and 1939 he was to create his best run of roles, paired with American dancer Louise Browne as the straight love interest of the comedy musicals which featured the Leslie Henson, Fred Emney and Richard Hearne comedy team: *Seeing Stars* (Ken Carraway), *Swing Along* (Paul Jerome), *Going Greek* (Leander) and *Running Riot* (Richard Vane). He went once again into uniform for the duration of the Second World War, and emerged in 1943 to return to the stage as Billy in a tour of *No, No, Nanette.* He subsequently appeared in London and Australia (1950) alongside Arthur Askey in *The Love Racket,* in the West End as Stanislaus in *The Bird Seller* (*Der Vogelhändler*) and on the road in *No, No, Nanette, The Quaker Girl* and *The Chocolate Soldier,* until well after his juvenile days.

ROZE, Edmond

A little, round-faced character actor, Roze appeared in Paris before the First World War in comedy, in revue and in musical pieces (Gilfain in *Florodora,* etc) and took his first steps as both a stage director (*Cocorico* at the Apollo, etc) and an administrator under the wing of the all-powerful Gustave Quinson who appointed him as administrator/secretary general—whilst he continued as an actor—at the Palais-Royal. After his demobilization, he resumed his multiple career as a performer, mostly in supporting parts but occasionally in sizeable roles, director and administrator. He was, however, never considered an outstanding actor, and it was as a director that he made his mark on the postwar Paris stage.

After staging the opening revue at Quinson's little wartime L'Abri, Roze directed the original production of the show which had been scheduled to follow it. The vast success of *Phi-Phi*—ultimately mounted at the Bouffes-Parisiens—set him off on a busy career as a director, and thereafter he staged many of the most important Parisian musical comedies of the era including *Dédé, Ta bouche, Madame, Là-haut, Gosse de riche, Troublez-moi, En chemyse, Nonnette, P.L.M., Passionnément, J'aime, Lulu, J'adore ça!, L'Eau à la bouche, Yes, Trois jeunes filles . . . nues!, Zou!* and *Rosy.* Yvain described him as "petit, frétillant, doué d'une patience d'ange et d'une rare diplomatie, il se dépensait frénétiquement. Arrachant des mains sa brochure à l'artiste ânnonnant, il se substituait à lui, jouant la scène, prenant, par mimétisme, sa voix et ses tics. L'acteur éberlué n'avait qu'à répéter servilement ce qu'il avait entendu . . ."

He also directed such imported musical comedies as *Tip-Toes* and *Mercenary Mary* (in which he appeared as Christophe) and latterly also directed some less book-based, more visual shows such as the period piece *Brummell* and Ralph Benatzky's extravagant *Deux sous de fleurs.*

He was, at various periods, co-manager of Théâtre des Nouveautés with Benoît-Léon Deutsch, co-director with Quinson at the Bouffes-Parisiens, and later sole director of the Folies-Wagram.

RUBENS, Paul [Alfred] (b London, 29 April 1875; d Budock, Falmouth, 4 February 1917). Songwriter and scribe of the very lightest kind of material for the Victorian and Edwardian musical stage.

The younger son of an exceedingly wealthy and social Berlin-born stockbroker, Rubens had no formal musical training, but began his career as a composer as a student at Oxford by writing a score (w Nigel Playfair) for a production of an *Alice in Wonderland* on which Lewis Carroll himself collaborated. He took part in university dramatics while continuing to write songs and music, and at the age of 19 he saw his work displayed in the professional theatre for the first time when his "The Little Chinchilla" was performed by Ellaline Terriss in *The Shop Girl* at the Gaiety Theatre. He went on to provide songs for Arthur Roberts in *Dandy Dan, the Lifeguardsman,* the revised version of *A Modern Don Quixote* (1898, "There's Just a Something Missing")

Plate 336. **Paul Rubens**

and *Milord Sir Smith;* for *Little Miss Nobody* (''Trixie of Upper Tooting,'' ''A Wee Little Bit of a Thing Like That'' with his stockbroker brother, **Walter (Emil) RUBENS** [b London, 1877; d Boulevard Cimiez, Nice 14 December 1920], ''We'll Just Sit Out,'' ''The People All Come to See Us''); and for George Edwardes's *San Toy* (1899, ''Me Gettee Outee Velly Quick''). At the same time he made his first and unsuccessful venture as a dramatist with the play *Young Mr Yarde* (1898, w Harold Ellis) and another, equally shortlived, as the co-author and co-composer of a burlesque, *Great Caesar,* produced in the West End with a fine cast but a feeble reception.

Rubens continued songwriting with contributions to two Tom Davies productions, *L'Amour mouillé* (again with brother Walter and with Landon Ronald) and, most importantly, to *Florodora* where he managed to get not only lyrics but a number of tunes tacked into the angry Leslie Stuart's score (''Inkling,'' ''Tact,'' ''When I Leave Town,'' ''I Want to Marry a Man,'' ''When an Interfering Person,'' ''Queen of the Philippine Islands,'' ''When We're on the Stage''). In the wake of his decided success as a supplementary songwriter, George Edwardes put Rubens under contract for ''additional material'' for his wide-ranging schedule of productions, and he used numbers from the young writer's pen in *The Messenger Boy* (1900, burlesque ''Tell Me Pretty Maiden,'' ''How I Saw the CIV,'' ''A Perfectly Peaceful Person''), *The Toreador* (1901, ''Everybody's Awfully Good to Me''), *A Country Girl* (1902, ''Two Little Chicks,'' ''Coo''), *The Girl from Kays* (1902, ''I Don't Care'') and *The Cingalee* (1904, ''Sloe Eyes,'' ''Make a Fuss of Me,'' ''She's All Right,'' ''You and I and I and You,'' ''Gollywogs,'' ''Something's Devilish Wrong''), many with considerable success. Rubens also interpolated pieces during the same period in Tom Davis's *The Medal and the Maid* (1902, ''Consequences'') and *The School Girl* (1903). On a different level, he also provided incidental music for the 1901 His Majesty's Theatre *Twelfth Night.*

Finally, Rubens authored a musical all his own, a piece in which most of the book as well as all of the lyrics and music were his work. *Three Little Maids* was a breeze-weight piece of thoroughly English material, written to order for Edwardes to feature Ada Reeve, Edna May and Hilda Moody. Like its heroines, it was alternately music-hally, pretty, pale, mildly suggestive, slightly soprano and successful. It ran 348 performances in London prior to an international career. A second piece in a similar vein, *Lady Madcap,* also did well, as did *The Blue Moon* for which Rubens supplied some catchy little numbers with which to contrast Howard Talbot's more substantial songs and ensembles.

In spite of their success, both *Three Little Maids* and *Lady Madcap* were pieces of little substance or sense, but in 1905 Rubens turned out the musical which, if not his most generally successful, was almost certainly his best. *Mr Popple of Ippleton* had a genuine libretto, which gave every sign of being modeled on the style if not the substance of a French vaudeville, it had delightful characters and much less of the schoolboy-sniggery tone for which Rubens always showed such a wearying propensity in his lyrics. Bedeviled by theatre arrangements, *Mr Popple* had only a medium London career (173 performances), but it left behind a couple of Rubens's most adult and delightful songs (''Rabbits,'' ''Dear, Sweet Clumsy Old Thing'').

A merry hotchpotch called *The Dairymaids* and the happy Dutch ''musical incident'' *Miss Hook of Holland,* decorated with what the composer-author disarmingly but nonetheless accurately called his ''jingles and tunes,'' gave him further successes, the latter proving ultimately to be the most enduring of all his works. There was less success with a musical version of Tristan Bernard's *La Soeur,* made over as *The Hoyden* for Elsie Janis on Broadway—where Rubens's songs had been already heard as interpolations in several shows including Anna Held's *A Parisian Model* as well as productions of his British shows—and similarly little with attempts at French Riviera and Danish follow-ups to *Miss Hook* (*My*

Mimosa Maid, Dear Little Denmark). However Frank Curzon's production of *The Balkan Princess,* a Ruritanian imitation of the successful *King of Cadonia,* gave the composer a rather surprising success in a type of show—the costume romantic musical—which seemed far from the most suited to him ultra-lightweight style of writing.

The departure of Ivan Caryll to America and the unreliability of Leslie Stuart as a chief composer subsequently gave Rubens the opportunity to take over as the main musical supplier to George Edwardes. Thereafter, the Edwardes houses and their stars helped the composer, as he helped them, to further successes and semi-successes with *The Sunshine Girl, The Girl from Utah* (w Sidney Jones), *After the Girl, Tina* and *Betty.* His best and most enduringly popular piece from this period, however, was Fred Thompson's adaptation of the famous farce *Les Dominos roses, Tonight's the Night.* Supplied, as he had been in *The Balkan Princess,* with an infinitely better libretto than those which he confected for himself, and limited to writing melodies (this was all he ever supplied musically, the rest had to be written for him) and some of the lyrics, Rubens proved, with a singular success, that this kind of illustration of a sound comic text was what he did best. However, just as an era of such pieces was beginning in the British theatre, Rubens, who had suffered severe ill-health through virtually his whole career, died of tuberculosis at the age of 41.

His songs were still to be heard, interpolated into shows in London and New York, for several years thereafter, and as late as 1924 his ''The Gondola and the Girl'' was used, alongside pieces by Padilla, Gershwin and E Ray Goetz as part of the score of Irene Bordoni's *Little Miss Bluebeard* (1924).

Walter Rubens composed the music for the children's musical *Shock-Headed Peter* (lib: Philip Carr, Nigel Playfair) produced at the Garrick Theatre on 26 December 1900 and again for Christmas the following year.

1899 **Great Caesar** (w Walter Rubens/w George Grossmith jr) Comedy Theatre 29 April

1900 **The Nineteenth Century** duologue St James's Theatre 3 December

1902 **Three Little Maids** (w Howard Talbot/w Percy Greenbank) Apollo Theatre 20 May

1904 **The Blue Moon** (w Talbot/P Greenbank/Harold Ellis) Theatre Royal, Northampton 29 February; Lyric Theatre, London 28 August 1905

1904 **Lady Madcap** (w P Greenbank/Nathaniel Newnham-Davis) Prince of Wales Theatre 17 December

1905 **Mr Popple of Ippleton** Apollo Theatre 17 March

1906 **The Dairymaids** (w Frank E Tours/w Arthur Wimperis/ Robert Courtneidge, A M Thompson) Apollo Theatre 14 April

1907 **Miss Hook of Holland** (w Austen Hurgon) Prince of Wales Theatre 31 January

1907 **The Hoyden** (w Tours, John Golden, Robert Hood Bowers/ ad Cosmo Hamilton, et al) Knickerbocker Theater, New York 19 October

1908 **My Mimosa Maid** (w Hurgon) Prince of Wales Theatre 21 April

1908 **The Fly-by-Night** 1 act Palace Theatre December

1909 **Dear Little Denmark** Prince of Wales Theatre 1 September

1910 **The Balkan Princess** (w Wimperis/Frederick Lonsdale, Frank Curzon) Prince of Wales Theatre 19 February

*1910 **The Genius** (Vincent Bryant/William de Mille, Cecil de Mille) Shubert Theater, St Paul, Minn 16 October

1911 **The Balky Princess** (Charles Brown) 1 act Weber's Theater 17 April

1912 **The Sunshine Girl** (w Wimperis/Cecil Raleigh) Gaiety Theatre 24 February

*1912 **A Mix-Up at Newport** (Lew Kelly, Fred Wyckoff, Lon Hascall) 1 act Columbia Theater, New York 21 October

*1912 **A Rube in Chinatown** (Lew Kelly, Fred Wyckoff, Lon Hascall) 1 act Columbia Theater, New York 21 October

1912 **The Boss of the Show** (Wimperis) sketch

1913 **The Girl from Utah** (w Sidney Jones/w Ross, P Greenbank/Tanner) Adelphi Theatre 18 October

1914 **After the Girl** (w P Greenbank) Gaiety Theatre 7 February

1914 **Tonight's the Night** (w P Greenbank/Fred Thompson) Shubert Theatre, New York 24 December

1915 **Betty** (w Adrian Ross/Lonsdale, Gladys Unger) Daly's Theatre 24 April

1915 **Tina** (w Haydn Wood/w Harry Graham, P Greenbank) Adelphi Theatre 2 November

1915 **The Miller's Daughters** revised *Three Little Maids* (w P Greenbank) Prince's Theatre, Manchester 24 December; London Opera House 15 May 1916

1916 **The Happy Day** (w Sidney Jones/w Ross/Seymour Hicks) Daly's Theatre 13 May

* The publicity for these two 1912 pieces insists that Paul Rubens is ''a bandmaster from Schenectady'' (the British Library says ''from Troy''). If there were indeed two Paul Rubenses, *The Genius,* a ''song comedy'' version of the de Mille brothers' successful play, mounted by Mort Singer for Henry Woodruff, may also be the work of this mysterious bandmaster, especially as it was remarked that ''Rubens did not do himself justice'' in such pieces as ''I'd Like to Pose for You'' and ''An Ocean of Love.''

RUBY, Harry [RUBENSTEIN, Harold] (b New York, 27 January 1895; d Los Angeles, 23 February 1974).

Initially a composer, Ruby had his name appear on a musical theatre bill for the first time in Chicago, bracketed in fourth place behind Ted Koehler, William Mills and Paul Church as the supplier of music to the Marigold Gardens revue *Arabian Knights* (3 April 1922). His lyricist for the occasion was Bert Kalmar with whom he would be linked throughout a career which saw them active not only as Broadway and Hollywood songwriters, but also as librettists for musical comedy, and sketch-writers for revue.

Their early Broadway experience included the songs for the unfortunate Kaufman and Connelly *Helen of Troy, New York;* sketches for *The Music Box Revue* (1924, 1925); three cracks at a piece which, ultimately called *No Other Girl,* went under in 52 performances; and a rush job rewrite on the libretto of Will Ortmann's Continental Operette *Frühling im Herbst,* to star Orville Harrold and his daughter Patti. They also supplied songs for a much longer-running comedy vehicle for Bobby Clark and Paul McCullough, *The Ramblers* (289 performances), which produced them a hit number in "All Alone Monday," provided some additional scenes and songs for Louis Werba's production of *Twinkle Twinkle;* and had a share in the scenes and songs of *Lucky,* a musical collaboration with Jerome Kern and Otto Harbach which did not live up to its name (71 performances). At the same time, a libretto which they had written but not used was picked up by Jack Hulbert and Paul Murray and, after some remaking, became the basis for the London musical *Lido Lady.* The songs, on this occasion, were mostly by Rodgers and Hart.

Philip Goodman, the producer of *The Ramblers,* engaged Kalmar and Ruby as songwriters for *The Five o'Clock Girl,* which was first mounted in 1927. This found considerably more success around the world than their next project, Charles Dillingham's Beatrice Lillie vehicle *She's My Baby,* on which they joined Guy Bolton as librettists to the songs of Rodgers and Hart, but *Good Boy,* on which they shared the songwriting with Herbert Stothart, had a good run and launched one of their biggest song successes in the squeakily delivered "I Wanna Be Loved by You." The Marx Brothers show *Animal Crackers* gave them another good run, but their own production of *Top Speed,* for which they provided both songs and, with Bolton, the text, arrived just as New York was teetering on the edge of its Wall Street windowsills, and its run was an indifferent one.

This was a good moment to leave town, and Ruby and Kalmar did just that. They went to Hollywood where the film of *Animal Crackers* prefaced the Marx Brothers *Horse Feathers* and *Duck Soup,* as well as *The Kid from Spain* ("What a Perfect Combination" w Harry Akst), *Do You Love Me?* and, in 1946, *Wake Up and Dream* ("Give Me the Simple Life" w Rube Bloom). They returned only once to Broadway, for the nostalgic *High Kickers* in 1941.

Hollywood put out a Kalmar and Ruby biopic called *Three Little Words* in which Ruby was portrayed by Red Skelton (to the Kalmar of Fred Astaire) whilst he himself appeared in the film in a small role.

A revue of Kalmar and Ruby songs was staged at the Manhattan Theater Club on 9 June 1981 as *Harry Ruby's Songs My Mother Never Sang* (Michael Roth, Paul Lazarus).

1923 **Helen of Troy, New York** (w Bert Kalmar/George S Kaufman, Marc Connelly) Selwyn Theater 19 June

1924 **The Town Clown** (w Kalmar/Aaron Hoffman) Illinois Theater, Chicago 6 January

1924 **The Belle of Quakertown** revised *The Town Clown* Stamford, Conn July

1924 **No Other Girl** revised *The Belle of Quakertown* Morosco Theater 13 August

1925 **Holka Polka** (*Frühling im Herbst,* ex- *Spring in Autumn*) American version w Kalmar, Gus Kahn, Raymond Egan (Lyric Theater)

1926 **The Fly-by-Nights** (w Kalmar/Guy Bolton) Werba's Theater, Brooklyn 30 August

1926 **The Ramblers** (ex- *The Fly-by-Nights*) (w Kalmar/Guy Bolton) Lyric Theater 20 September

1926 **Lido Lady** (Richard Rodgers/Lorenz Hart/w Guy Bolton, Kalmar, Ronald Jeans) Gaiety Theatre, London 1 December

1927 **Lucky** (w Jerome Kern/w Otto Harbach) New Amsterdam Theater 22 March

1927 **The Five o'Clock Girl** (Bolton, Fred Thompson) 44th Street Theater 10 October

1928 **She's My Baby** (Rodgers/Hart/w Bolton) Globe Theater 3 January

1928 **Good Boy** (w Herbert Stothart/Oscar Hammerstein II, Harbach, Henry Meyers) Hammerstein's Theater 5 September

1928 **Animal Crackers** (Kaufman, Morrie Ryskind) 44th Street Theater 23 October

1929 **Top Speed** (w Bolton) 46th Street Theater 25 December

1941 **High Kickers** (w George Jessel) Broadhurst Theater 31 October

RUDDIGORE, or The Witch's Curse Supernatural comic opera in 2 acts by W S Gilbert. Music by Arthur Sullivan. Savoy Theatre, London, 22 January 1887.

The Savoy Theatre's successor to *The Mikado* reverted to the burlesque of melodrama which Gilbert and Sullivan had so successfully practiced in *The Pirates of Penzance* and, like the earlier piece, it also slipped in a recyclable bit of material borrowed from its author's Gallery of Illustration days, in this case a scene taken from the long-running *Ages Ago.*

Ruthven Murgatroyd (George Grossmith) has run away from a baronetcy which, because of a witch's curse, obliged him to commit a crime every day, and he lives a happy life disguised as a pure and blameless village lad called Robin Oakapple. Unfortunately, when he falls in love with Rose Maybud (Leonora Braham), his jealous foster brother Richard Dauntless (Durward Lely) feels moved to reveal his true identity. Sir Despard Murgatroyd (Rutland Barrington), who has inherited the horrid baronetcy, is thus freed from his obligation to daily crime and weds his victim, Mad Margaret (Jessie Bond), whilst Ruthven, hoist to his rightful place and its obligations, squeamishly finds every way he can to avoid his doomful duty. His angry ancestors descend from their picture hooks and demand that he honor his horrid responsibilities, but Ruthven emerges with a spotless piece of complex logic which allows him to baffle the old curse and tie up a happy ending with his Rose.

Sullivan produced a delightful melodrama-burlesque score, from which Richard Temple's sub-operatic solo as the chief of the ghostly ancestors, ''The Ghost's High Noon,'' nautical Richard's breezy ''I Shipped y'see in a Revenue Sloop'' and Magaret's burlesque mad scene stood out, alongside an *Il trovatore*-ical legend for Rosina Brandram as the ghost's aged sweetheart, several pretty soprano pieces and some typically nifty patter from which a truly dazzling flat-out trio for Grossmith, Barrington and Miss Bond was the outstanding moment.

Ruddigore had all the elements necessary for success, but it also had one fault: most of the brilliance came in the first act, which was followed by a second which, apart from the picture-gallery scene, was rather uneventful, and as a result the show was compared unfavorably with *The Mikado* by a press not averse to seeing Gilbert have a failure. The papermen also squealed maidishly over the title (originally *Ruddygore,* but hypocrisy was silenced by replacing the ''y'') and accused the author of cribbing pieces of his piece from places ranging from John Brougham's *The Crimson Mask* to J H Ryley's old ''dancing quaker'' musical-hall act. The public, however, supported *Ruddigore* through 288 West End performances.

Although Carte then sent it on tour, *Ruddigore*'s life thereafter was less happy. Carte's Broadway production, with Courtice Pounds (Richard), Geraldine Ulmar (Rose) and George Thorne (Ruthven), played only 53 performances, John McCaull's productions in other American main centers disappointed, and *Ruddigore* soon vanished from the Carte repertoire. It was 1920 before it was reintroduced and, in the following years, it was played again in America and, for the first time, in Australia—with Charles Walenn and Strella Wilson featured. In spite of sporadic productions thereafter, however, and in spite of its undeniable if uneven merits, it never became a favorite member of the Gilbert and Sullivan canon.

A revival at London's Sadler's Wells Theatre in 1987 which featured Marilyn Hill Smith (Rose), Harold Innocent (Despard) and Gordon Sandison (Robin) gave London a fresh look at *Ruddigore* and, in an age when *The Crimson Mask* and J H Ryley were long forgotten, the piece showed no obvious lack of originality—merely a saggy second act.

In spite of the much-less-than-usual popularity of *Ruddigore* compared to other works of the Savoy canon, it was one of the very few Gilbert and Sullivan works to provoke a British burlersque. John L Toole was the culprit, the piece was called *Ruddy George* (Toole's Theatre 19 March 1887) and it found little favor.

USA: Fifth Avenue Theater 21 February 1887; Australia: Theatre Royal, Adelaide 23 June 1927

RUDOLZ, Hartwig (aka Hardy RUDOLZ) (b Börsen, 26 August 1955). One of central Europe's foremost musical performers of the 1990s.

Hartwig Rudolz began his stage career in Hamburg (1976, *West Side Story, Chicago,* etc) and subsequently played seasons at Bad-Hersfeld and Würzburg before taking the role of Bill in a St Gallen production of *Kiss Me, Kate* (1979). In the years that followed, he appeared at Berlin's Theater des Westens in a series of musicals (Riff in *West Side Story, Barnum, Oh! What a Lovely War,* Freddy in *My Fair Lady,* Bobby in *A Chorus Line*). He appeared in 1982 in the Paris Lido show *Cocorico,* in 1993 in *Hello, Dolly!* (Ambrose) at the Vienna Volksoper and in Switzerland in *West Side Story,* and in 1985 returned to the Theater des Westens for a season including *Peter Pan* (Starkey), *Jesus Christ Superstar* (Pilate, Herod), *Guys and Dolls* (Benny) and *Die Csárdásfürstin* (Boni).

Rudolz took the part of Munkustrap in the original Hamburg cast of *Cats* in 1986, and in 1987 appeared as Jean-Michel in the Theater des Westens production of *La Cage aux folles,* as well as in that theatre's *Cabaret* (Ernst Ludwig) and *Chicago.* He then appeared at several theatres including the Berlin Metropol as Tony in *West Side Story,* before, in 1990 taking up the role of Raoul in the Germany production of *The Phantom of the Opéra.* He subsequently succeeded to the role of the Phantom.

He was seen in Berlin in *Cabaret* (Cliff) and *Anything Goes* (Billy Crocker), in Essen in *Kiss Me, Kate* (1992) in Hamburg in *I Do, I Do* (1994), and in several revues (*UFA Revue* in Germany and America) and touring shows, before in 1996 creating the role of Javert in the German version of *Les Misérables,* a role he later played in the London production before returning to Duisburg to succeed to the role of Jean Valjean in the same production. In 1999 he appeared in Berlin as Guido Contini in *Nine* and as Amos Hart in *Chicago.*

In 1998 he voiced the role of King Ramses in the German version of the cartoon *Prince of Egypt.*

Rudolz has also worked as a choreographer and director in the musical theatre.

RUFFELLE, Frances [RUFFELL, Frances J] (b London, 29 August 1965).

Daughter of a stage-school family, Frances Ruffelle began her theatre and television career as a juvenile, appearing on the West End stage in *The King and I, Gavin and the Monster* (1981, Debbie) and as the narrator in the incessantly touring *Joseph and the Amazing Technicolor Dreamcoat* (1982). In 1984 she created the role of Dinah, the dining car, in *Starlight Express* (''U.N.C.O.U.P.L.E.D.''), before going on to an international success in the role of Éponine (''On My Own'') in the English-language version of *Les Misérables* (1985, London, New York, Tony Award). She subsequently had leading roles in two less successful pieces: *Apples* (1989, Delilah) and *Children of Eden* (1991, Yonah) and, after some time out devoted to a busy career in pop music and recording, in 1997 she reappeared on the musical stage playing in *Lucky Stiff* at the Bridewell Theatre.

RUGANTINO Musical by Pietro Garinei and Sandro Giovannini. Additional scenes by Festa Campanile and Massimo Franciosa. Music by Armando Trovaioli. Teatro Sistina, Rome, 15 December 1963.

The only Italian musical of recent times to have been seen on Broadway, *Rugantino* was one of the most successful of the long series of shows written and produced in Italy by Garinei and Giovannini. Set in 1830s Italy, it presented Nino Manfredi as Rugantino, a cocky layabout who prides himself on his sex appeal and pimps for his primary mistress Eusebia (Bice Valori) to keep himself in food and comforts. Gallivanting through a series of picturesque situations, he chases after a certain Rosetta (Lea Massari) and, when her spy husband Gnecco is murdered, finds himself convicted and condemned to death. The aristocratic Marta Paritelli (Franca Tamantini) who could give him an alibi prefers not to become involved, and Maestro Titta (Aldo Fabrizi), Eusebia's latest touch, but also the local executioner, has the job of ridding the world of Rugantino.

Rugantino had two fine seasons in Rome, and was taken to America by Alexander H Cohen where Manfredi, Ornella Vanoni and Fabrizi played the show in its original Italian with surtitles. It then went on to South America and was later twice revived at the Sistina—15 years after its first staging, with Enrico Montesano in the title role, Fabrizi and Bice Valori repeating and Alida Chelli as Rosetta, and, with great success, again in 1998 and 1999 (21 December).

USA: Mark Hellinger Theater 6 February 1964

Recordings: original cast (Orizzonte), American cast (Warner Bros), revival cast (Cam, 2 records)

A RUNAWAY GIRL Musical comedy in 2 acts by Seymour Hicks and Harry Nicholls. Lyrics by Aubrey Hopwood and Harry Greenbank. Music by Ivan Caryll and Lionel Monckton. Gaiety Theatre, London, 21 May 1898.

George Edwardes followed up the great success of *The Circus Girl* at the Gaiety Theatre with an even more successful piece in *A Runaway Girl,* a slip of a show written by Harry Nicholls and by Seymour Hicks, an ex-Gaiety star himself and the husband of ingenue Ellaline Terriss for whom the piece's title role was constructed. The other favorite players of the Gaiety team were also well fitted out.

Winifred Grey (Miss Terriss) is a ''runaway'' from her Corsican convent and she has run so that she won't have to wed the unseen nephew of old Lord Coodle (Fred Kaye). In her flight, she joins up with a band of wandering minstrels-cum-bandits whose other temporary recruits include handsome Guy Stanley (W Louis Bradfield), and Coodle servants Flipper (Edmund Payne) and Alice (Katie Seymour). Intrigues and disguises intervene when the ''minstrels'' turn nasty, but finally all the English escape back to England where it turns out that Guy is Lord Coodle's nephew and Winifred can stop running. Harry Monkhouse shared the chief comedy as Lay Brother Tamarind, and infringed occasionally on the story line.

The songs were in the now-established Gaiety tradition. Miss Terriss waltzed to an admission to a craving for nicotine (''The Sly Cigarette'') and scored a hit with Monckton's ''The Boy Guessed Right,'' Connie Ediss, cast as Carmenita, a Hispano-Corsican brigand from London's East End, sighed glutinously over her dreams of being in ''Society'' and gave her phony version of being Spanish in ''Barcelona''; Teddy Payne and Katie Seymour performed their expected duet, this time in blackface (a disguise to escape the Corsicans) as ''Piccaninnies''; operatic vocalist John Coates as the chief brigand had a ringing ballad in praise of ''My Kingdom''; and Ethel Haydon, Willie Warde, Fred Wright, Robert Nainby, Grace Palotta, Lawrance d'Orsay, Fritz Rimma and others, all cast as a group of Cooks tourists, wandering in and out of the story, joined together to explain why one should ''Follow the Man from Cook's.'' The hit of the night, however, fell to Miss Haydon, with Monckton's merry ''Soldiers in the Park,'' a march melody which turned out to be the most long-surviving number from any of the original group of Gaiety musical comedies.

The show ran on, with new songs being constantly added, and even an official ''second version'' being announced, until it had reached 593 performances and taken the Gaiety Theatre into the 1900s. In the meanwhile, it had already set out on its travels. Augustin Daly, who had done a superior job with the Gaiety's previous *The Circus Girl* on Broadway, took up the new show and produced it at his New York Daly's Theater, without subjecting the piece to the low-comedy rewrites and local interpolations which had marred so many imports in the hands of other producers. Virginia Earle was Winifred with James T

Powers (Flipper), Mabelle Gilman (Alice), Paula Edwardes (Carmenita), Herbert Gresham (Tamarind) and Cyril Scott (Guy) in support, and the tasteful producer and his show were rewarded with a very fine 216 performances on Broadway, before heading for the road. *A Runaway Girl* was even revived in 1900, this time by Daniel Frohman, for a return season on Broadway (40 performances), and in 1902 another major tour was sent out with George Leslie (Flipper) and Louise Willis (Winifred) starred.

In Vienna, *Ein durchgeganges Mädel* (ad Carl Lindau, Leopold Krenn) starred American soubrette Marie Halton alongside such eminent locals as Karl Streitmann as the bandit leader, Josef Joseffy as Tamarind, Karl Blasel as Jaromir Spindel (ex- Flipper) and Therese Biedermann as Pampeluna (ex- Carmenita), and adapter Lindau appeared as the heroine's father through 37 performances, whilst in Budapest *A kis szökevény* (''the little runaway,'' ad Géza Kacziány, Emil Makai) scored a major hit at the Népszínház. Klára Küry played Winifred, accompanied by Aranka Hegyi, József Németh, Imre Szirmai, Mihály Kovács, Sári Blaha and Mihály Kiss through an excellent 79 performances. In Berlin, where the heroine and title became *Daisy* in C M Roehr's adaptation for his Lessing-Theater, the young Lina Abarbanell starred through 41 consecutive summer-season performances before *Daisy* was replaced on the Lessing Theater stage by a revival of another Edwardes show, *The Geisha.*

Back in Britain the show was quickly on the road, and the colonial companies soon followed—South Africa in 1901, Australia in 1902 with Florence Young running away from Charles Kenningham, and George Lauri (Flipper), Carrie Moore (Alice), May Beatty (Carmenita) and Grace Palotta from the London cast (Dorothy) amongst the pursuers—as *A Runaway Girl* established itself around the world as internationally the most successful of all the Gaiety Theatre musical comedies.

USA: Daly's Theater 25 August 1898; Austria: Theater an der Wien *Ein durchgeganges Mädel* 2 April 1899; Hungary: Népszínház *A kis szökevény* 11 November 1899; Germany: Lessing-Theater *Daisy* 19 May 1900; Australia: Her Majesty's Theatre, Melbourne 15 February 1902

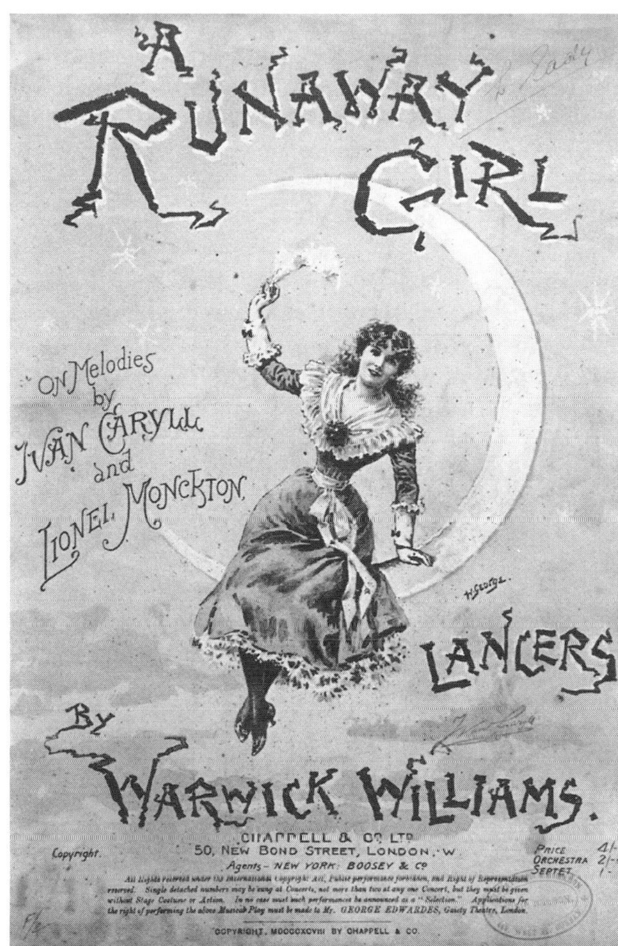

Plate 337. **A Runaway Girl**

RUND UM DIE LIEBE Operette in 3 acts by Robert Bodanzky and Friedrich Thelen. Music by Oscar Straus. Johann Strauss-Theater, Vienna, 9 November 1914.

A wartime hit at Vienna's Johann Strauss-Theater, *Rund um die Liebe* ran up a fine sequence of 375 consecutive performances in just over a year in its initial production, and it remained in the repertoire at the Johann Strauss-Theater until 1924, by which time it had been seen more than 450 times.

The journey ''all around love'' to which ''marriage is the terminus'' didn't take any unusual routes in Thelen and Bodanzky's book. Fritz Werner was the Baron Hans, traveling incognito whilst his chauffeur Vincenz (Josef König) temporarily borrows his title, Mizzi Günther was Countess Stella von Hempel-Heringsdorf with whom he spends a slightly tipsy night in the garden of the Four Seasons restaurant, and Käte Ehren was Steffi Bachmayer, daughter of the enthusiastically nouveau-riche Florian (L Strassmeyer) who thinks he is getting a Baron for a son-in-law when Vincenz and Steffi fall for each other. Florian is disabused in the second-act finale, leaving the third act for the pairs to get tidily together with their socially right partner.

Straus's attractive score gave fine chances to the soprano, topped by a tipsy waltz-song, ''Ein Schwipserl,'' and a buffo-duo with Vincenz which was a patent follow-up to that of *Ein Walzertraum* with its musical intrumental imitations. She also duetted in less staunchly romantic fashion than some with her Baron in ''Schau mein Schatz,'' and ''Es gibt Dinge, die muss man vergessen,'' saving the real moment of musical romance for their final clinch. Hans was equipped with a pair of tidy waltzing tenor solos: ''Ich weiss schon, was ich möcht''' and ''Sie red't nichts, lic sagt nichts'' and partook of a march trio (''Kinder, so ein Mädel''), whilst the soubret pair of Vincenz and Steffi had a choice of soubret numbers, alongside a jolly introduction for Florian, a topical piece about being a reservist performed by Max Brod, and a set of finales that simply rattled with reprises.

In spite of its Vienna success and a good life in Germany, where it initial Berlin production played for 50 nights, *Rund um die Liebe* had, however, little exposure elsewhere. Hungary welcomed a version (ad Andor Gábor) to the Király Színház for 40 performances but, probably at least partly because of wartime conditions, the show did not travel west. It was seen again in Vienna in 1945, but has slipped from the repertoire sufficiently for the Volksoper to scalpel out ''Ein Schwipserl'' and tack it fairly incongruously into its production of *Ein Walzertraum.*

Germany: Theater des Westens 30 January 1915; Hungary: Király Színház *Legénybucsu* 23 September 1915

RUNNIN' WILD Musical comedy by Flournoy Miller and Aubrey Lyles. Lyrics by Cecil Mack. Music by James P Johnson. Additional numbers by Jo Trent and Porter Grainger. Colonial Theater, New York, 29 October 1923.

A successor to the successful *Shuffle Along* which represented Miller and Lyles in their characters of Steve Jenkins and Sam Peck through a further series of scenes of low comedy and high spirits and a handful of songs and dances. The piece played 213 performances at the out-of-the-mainstream Colonial Theater, and introduced the dancing world to ''The Charleston'' for the first time.

Recording: instrumental selection (Columbia)

RUPERT, Michael [RUPPERT, Michael] (b San Marino, Calif, 23 October 1951).

Rupert began in the theatre as a young teenager and appeared on Broadway as the boy Bibi Bonnard in *The Happy Time* at the age of 16. He worked as a young adult as a singer and a television actor, and returned to Broadway to take over the title role of *Pippin* (1976). He appeared in *Shakespeare's Cabaret* in New York, *Damn Yankees* and *Working* regionally, in the shortlived *Festival* (1979) at the City Center, and made a particular success in creating the role of Marvin in *March of the Falsettos* in New York (1981) and in Los Angeles (1982). He subsequently played on Broadway in the *Sweet Charity* revival of 1986 (Oscar, Tony Award), and as Alex in his own musical *Mail* (1988), and succeeded to the role of Stine in *City of Angels* before reprising his Marvin in *Falsettoland* (1990) and then in the Broadway double-header of Marvin musicals produced in 1992 as *Falsettos.* He appeared in 1995 at Chicago's Goodman Theater in *Another Midsummer's Night* (Larry) and in 1997 featured as Norman Papermann in Herman Wouk's musical *Don't Stop the Carnival* at Miami's Coconut Grove Playhouse.

Alongside his acting career, Rupert has also composed the scores for two musicals, the first of which, *Three Guys Naked from the Waist Down,* was mounted off-Broadway in 1985. *Mail,* originally produced at the Pasadena Playhouse, was brought to Broadway in 1988 (48 performances).

1985 **Three Guys Naked from the Waist Down** (Jerry Colker) Minetta Lane Theater 5 February

1988 **Mail** (Colker) Music Box Theater 14 April

RUSSELL, H Scott [RUSSELL, Harold Henry] (b Malvern, 25 September 1868; d Malvern, 28 August 1949). Vocalist and actor, who took part in several eras of the musical theatre.

After an early career as an engineer, Russell made his first appearance on the stage at the age of 22 in the chorus of *Paul Jones* with Agnes Huntington. Three years later, having visited America to play with Miss Huntington in *Captain Thérèse* (1892, Vadreuil) and *Paul Jones* (Bicoquet), he joined the D'Oyly Carte company at the Savoy Theater where he appeared in the Gilbert and Sullivan repertoire and created the roles of Lord Dramaleigh in *Utopia (Ltd),* Bertuccio in both versions of Messager's *Mirette,* Pedro Gomez in *The Chieftain,* Dr Tannhäuser in *The Grand Duke* and Count Cosmo in *His Majesty,* taking time out from the Savoy to appear as Gustave in *Baron Golosh* (*L'Oncle Célestin*) at the Trafalgar Theatre.

He took over Charles Ryley's role in *The Yashmak* after that actor died on stage, played hero Dick Darville in *The Dandy Fifth* (1898) at the Duke of York's, and then joined George Edwardes's company at Daly's Theatre where he succeeded to the tenor role of Katana in *The Geisha* before going on to play in *A Greek Slave* (1898, Archias), *A Gaiety Girl* (revival, in Hayden Coffin's original role) and *San Toy* (1899, Fo Hop). After a further period with the D'Oyly Carte company, touring in the principal tenor roles, he returned to Edwardes to play in *Véronique, The Geisha* (revival) and *Les Merveilleuses,* appeared with Thomas Beecham's Light Opera Company, played in some of the earliest prewar London revues (*Everybody's Doing It, All the Winners*) and took the role of Gilfain in a wartime revival of *Florodora* before moving on to war duties.

In 1920 he appeared as Lockit in the celebrated Lyric, Hammersmith revival of *The Beggar's Opera,* a part he reprised on several occasions whilst taking several other roles, musical and straight, under the same management. The musical roles included parts in *Lionel and*

Clarissa (Colonel Oldboy), a hacked-up *La Vie parisienne, The Fountain of Youth* (Mark Mugwort) and *Derby Day* (1932, John Bitter). During the 1930s he played in Ann Croft's comic opera *Prudence* (1932, Innkeeper), and took the burlesque role of The Bloody Pirate with George Robey in *Jolly Roger* (1933), and he played Rocco in Herbert Farjeon's pasticcio *An Elephant in Arcady* (1938) at the age of 70, before retiring from the stage after nearly half a century of activity.

RUSSELL, Lillian [LEONARD, Helen Louisa] (b Clinton, Iowa, 4 December 1860; d New York, 5 June 1922). America's queen of comic opera in the last decades of the 19th century and a buxom beauty of early 20th-century Broadway burlesque.

One of the five daughters of a profitable printer, Charles E Leonard (of Knight & Leonard), and of Mrs Cynthia Leonard (d Rutherford, NJ, 9 April 1908), a well-known women's rights campaigner, the young Miss Russell was convent-educated in Chicago and went to New York at the age of 16 to study singing with Erminia Rudersdorff. Before long she was appearing in the chorus of E E Rice's touring *HMS Pinafore* (with which she played a single week on Broadway) and *Evangeline* companies and married (briefly) to Harry Braham, the company's musical director. The shapely young soprano soon won engagements as a solo vocalist, and appeared at Tony Pastor's variety theatre as a ballad singer with a success which soon merited her the leading roles in the house's burlesque production of *The Pie-Rats of Penn Yann* (1881, Mabria, ie, Mabel), *Oily-Vet* (1811, Olivette), *Billee Taylor* (a burlesque Phoebe) and so forth.

She left Pastor to go on tour with Willie Edouin's farce-comedy company and when she returned to New York it was under the management of John McCaull, newly launched at the Bijou Theater with the intention of becoming the city's only and/or best musical theatre producer. McCaull starred the 19-year-old Miss Russell as the snake-charming Irma (here called Djemma) opposite Selina Dolaro in his production of Audran's *Le Grand Mogol* (*The Snake Charmer*) and she compounded this success as Bathilde in a production of *Les Noces d'Olivette* (*Olivette*) before returning to Pastor's in January 1882 for more *Patience* and more *Billee Taylor.* She departed again to organize her own production of *Patience* (June 1882) with McCaull at Niblo's Theatre. *Patience* was a 92-performance success for the popular young star, already hailed as "The Queen of the Dudes," and she and her producer followed it with another good run with *The Sorcerer* (Aline, 1882). However, just when she should have been ready to follow up her English operetta sucesses with a piece written specially for her by the composer of *Billee Taylor,* the dashing Teddy Solo-

Plate 338. **Lillian Russell,** *as Giroflé and Girofla, dips into the punch. She well might. She's just married two men in two minutes.*

mon, she fell ill. The illness caused a furor in dudeland, and as the newspapers daily chronicled the fair prima donna's slow progress to health, the production of *Virginia,* without its prima donna, ran through five Broadway weeks.

Miss Russell made her return to the theatre in breeches as Prince Raphaël in *La Princesse de Trébizonde* (Casino Theater), but she walked out after three weeks, in an early example of the cavalier attitude to contracts which was to speckle and damage her career, to follow Solomon to Britain and escape her forthcoming contractual obligations to the Standard Theater. After some characteristic lack of legal cooperation between the British and American courts, she was permitted to appear in *Virginia* (retitled *Paul and Virginia*) at the Gaiety Theatre, but although she won some nice personal notices, the show was quickly over. She then signed to appear in comic opera for Alexander Henderson but was released by him to create the role of *Princess Ida* for Carte. However, her unwillingness to rehearse and her generally unprofessional attitudes resulted in her being dumped by the no-nonsense Savoy.

This time it was she who squealed "contract," but to no avail, and before long she and Solomon were off to Europe with a tour of *Billee Taylor.* They dropped out after a few weeks, leaving the tour to wander on and become stranded, and came back to Britain where, later in the year, they at last had success together as star and composer of *Polly, the Pet of the Regiment.* When Lillian played Solomon's version of *Pocahontas* they were less successful, and the duo promptly switched their field of action back to America. There they did rather better with *Polly* and another new piece, *Pepita,* before coming to a dramatic breakup in their ''married'' life when it was revealed that the composer—whose attitude to contracts was pretty much the same as that of his ''wife''—was a bigamist.

Solomon went back to face charges in a British court (he was sent to prison), Lillian remained in America to play for John Duff, appearing in her ex-almost-husband's *The Maid and the Moonshiner* (1886, Virginia), in the title role of *Dorothy,* as Inez (and later Anita) in *The Queen's Mate,* as Princess Etelka in *Nadgy,* Fiorella in *The Brigands,* in the title role of *The Grand-Duchess,* as Harriet in Broadway's version of *Poor Jonathan* and as Pythia in *Apollo* (*Das Orakel*). She starred in the American production of Audran's *La Cigale* and as Teresa in *The Mountebanks,* and took out her own touring company with these last two pieces, before returning to Broadway to play *Giroflé-Girofla* and the role of Rosa in the American comic opera *Princess Nicotine.*

Miss Russell made her first return to England since her ''divorce'' to play at the Lyceum in a specially organized production of Edward Jakobowski's Austrian success *Die Brillantenkönigin* (1894, *The Queen of Brilliants,* Betta) which was using London as a springboard to Broadway, but the show was a failure and—in spite of the announcement of all kinds of new and original musical vehicles, including a Ludwig Englander piece which would have starred her as Cleopatra—she returned to the safety of Offenbach to star on Broadway in another Hortense Schneider role as *La Périchole.* Over the next few years she also appeared in revivals of *Le Petit Duc, Patience* and *La Belle Hélène,* but a series of new homemade musicals (*The Tzigane, The Goddess of Truth, An American Beauty, The Wedding Day*) did not find her the original role which had eluded her throughout a long and otherwise remarkable career.

After appearing in a revival of *Erminie* she turned, with the century, back to burlesque, and the last part of her career, with the exception of a 1904 sally forth to appear as *Lady Teazle* in a comic opera of that name, was spent at Weber and Fields's place of entertainment, appearing in the revusical concoctions produced there (*Whirl-I-Gig, Fiddle-Dee-Dee, Hoity-Toity, Twirly Whirly, Whoop de doo, Hokey Pokey*). If these naturally did not produce the elusive role, *Twirly Whirly* did produce the only song since Solomon's ''The Silver Line'' (which she had, in any case, not created) to which Miss Russell's name would stay attached—John Stromberg's ''Come Down Ma Evenin' Star.'' Her appearance in *Hokey Pokey* in 1912 was her last on the Broadway musical stage, except for an ''appearance'' in song in the 1914 *The Beauty Shop* when Anna Orr gave out with Charles Gebest's ''I Want to Look Like Lillian Russell.'' Presumably she meant the Lillian Russell of a year or two earlier in time.

Lillian Russell—or what she represented—has been portrayed on stage and film a number of times. A London rewrite of *Sally* (1942) managed to introduce her into the proceedings in the person of the buxom Linda Gray (soon after to be Queen Elizabeth I in *Merrie England* and later London's Domina in *A Funny Thing . . .*), but Hollywood devoted an entire 1940 film to her in which she was portrayed by Alice Faye. Andrea King (*My Wild Irish Rose*) and Binnie Barnes (*Diamond Jim*) were other screen Lillians.

Miss Russell's sister, Suzanne Leonard, played in minor roles in her company in the 1890s.

Biographies: Morell, P: *Lillian Russell: The Era of Plush* (Random House, New York, 1940), Burke, J: *Duet in Diamonds* (Putnam, New York, 1972), Schwarz, D R, Bowbeer, A A: *Lillian Russell: A Bio-Bibliography* (Greenwood, Westport, Conn, 1995), Fields, A: *Lillian Russell* (McFarland, New York, 1999)

RUY BLAS AND THE BLASÉ ROUÉ Burlesque in 2 acts by ''A C Torr'' (Fred Leslie) and Herbert F Clark. Music by W Meyer Lutz. Gaiety Theatre, London, 21 September 1889.

Constructed for the Gaiety Theatre's overwhelmingly popular star team of Fred Leslie and Nellie Farren by Leslie himself, *Ruy Blas and the Blasé Roué* continued the almost unbroken run of first-rate successes which the house had produced since the innovation of the ''new burlesque'' and the partnership between the two performers. Victor Hugo's 1838 verse drama about the phony Prime Minister who wins the love of the Queen of Spain underwent the usual kind of perversion, ending up as a jolly romp in which Ruy (Nellie Farren), Don Caesar (Leslie) and Donna Cristina (Sylvia Grey) spent their time plotting to get back some incriminating papers and the Queen's jewels in the midst of a mass of songs and dances for the two stars and for such other principals as Marion Hood (Queen), Letty Lind and Fred Storey.

The songwords had been written by Leslie, bit by bit, as Fred and Nellie toured their previous burlesques in America, and had been posted back to Edwardes to be set by a variety of composers. The result (with interpolations) was a bevy of contrasting numbers. If there was no resounding hit, the score nevertheless turned up its ration of popular songs from Fred's advice to ''Stick to the Whisky You're Used To,'' to his dressed-up duos with Nellie as a silly sister act (''Ma's Advice''), in a parody of the Christy Minstrels (''Johnny Jones and his Sister Sue'') or with a range of topicalities (''I've Just Had a Wire to Say So,'' ''Don't Know''). There was also a Whistling Lullaby, Fred Bowyer's encouragement to ''Razzle Dazzle,'' Marion Hood's soprano ''Españita'' (mus: Antonio Mora) and a shoeful of dances. One of these last was a burlesque of the Gaiety's own great success, the *Faust Up-to-Date* pas de quatre performed by four men made up as famous actors. One of the four burlesquees involved, the apparently humorless Henry Irving, called in the Lord Chancellor to forbid Leslie thus to ridicule him. Edwardes inherited some splendid publicity from this cause-not-very-célèbre, and the actor more ridicule than if he had simply kept quiet.

Ruy Blas filled the Gaiety for 282 performances before it had to be taken off to go on the road in regular Gaiety fashion. That road actually stretched as far as Australia, where the Gaiety Company presented their show with Leslie, Farren, Grey and Storey supplemented by Grace Pedley as the Queen, Florence Levey in Letty Lind's dance spot, and the young Sidney Jones conducting. Back home, the show continued round the touring circuits for two years during which it did well even without the stars around whom it had been constructed, before being put away in favor of the next Gaiety burlesque.

Ruy Blas and the Blasé Roué wasn't played in America, but ''I've Just Had a Wire'' found its way out of the show and, along with *Cinder-Ellen Up Too Late*'s ''Teaching McFadyen to Dance'' and Teddy Solomon's ''The Silver Line,'' into champion pilferer Paul Potter's farce comedy *The City Directory* (1890).

The Ruy Blas story had been previously burlesqued by Robert Reece in *Ruy Blas Righted* (Vaudeville Theatre 3 January 1874) and by W S Gilbert in his first, published but unproduced attempt at the burlesque genre (1866), as well as being given a serious musico-dramatic treatment in operas by William Howard Glover (Covent Garden 24 October 1861) and Filippo Marchetti (La Scala, Milan 3 April 1869).

Australia: New Princess Theatre, Melbourne 27 June 1891

RYLEY, J[ohn] H[andford] [RILEY, John] (b England, c1841; d Edgeware, Mddx, 28 July 1922). America's preeminent Gilbert and Sullivan comedian of the 19th century.

''Jack'' Ryley began his performing life as a ''comique'' in the music halls where he formed a successful partnership with his first wife, **Marie BARNUM** [Maria Elizabeth CROME] (''the world renowned comic duettists and dancers''), performing a mock-serious routine as the ''Dancing Quakers'' to a selection of Offenbach music. However, he found more significant and sustained success when he switched, in his mid-thirties, to the musical theatre and after a busy and sought-after few years performing in Britain, he established himself as an outstanding comic-opera comedian in America.

Ryley made his earliest appearances in the musical theatre in the burlesque *Ali Baba à la mode* (1872) at the Gaiety, performing his act as known, on tour with the Gaiety company (*A Mere Blind* w Fred Sullivan 1873), with Emily Soldene's company at the Opéra Comique (u/s and t/o Trénitz in *La Fille de Madame Angot, Le Leçon de Chant,* 1873), alongside Marie—in her theatre debut as Angélique—in *Melusine the Enchantress* (1874, *Les Chevaliers de la table ronde*) at Holborn, with Kate Santley in *Cattarina* (1875, Fernando), Lecocq's *Le Prés Saint-Gervais* (Nicole), Gilbert and Clay's *Princess Toto* (Zapeter) and, alongside W S Penley and Florence Trevallyan, in *Madame l'Archiduc* (1876). He was subsequently engaged at Manchester's Prince's Theatre as first low comedian, and appeared there in comedy with Toole (Bungs in *Tottle's,* etc), in pantomime with Mrs John Wood, in *The Sultan of Mocha* (Flint), as Amen Squeak in Cellier's *Nell Gwynne* and as the Foreman in *Trial by Jury,* taking time out to take over as Flint in the London production of *The Sultan of Mocha* (1876). At Easter 1877 he joined the company at the Alhambra to play in *Orpheus in the Underworld* (Mercury), *King Indigo* (Babazouk) and *Wildfire* (Baron Hey Derry Downe) and it was from there that he went on to D'Oyly Carte (1878) to play the principal comic roles (John Wellington Wells, then later Judge, Joseph Porter) in Carte's first touring company in the British provinces. Following what was to be a last British Christmas playing Dame at Leeds, he was then taken across to America with Carte's company to play Porter in the ''official'' Broadway production of *HMS Pinafore* (1879).

Thereafter, Ryley spent most of his time in America, performing there frequently as Carte's principal comedian, and introducing to Broadway such British characters as the Major General (*Pirates of Penzance,* 1879), Flapper (*Billee Taylor,* 1881, 1885), Blood-Red Bill (*Claude Duval,* 1882), Bunthorne (*Patience,* 1882), Lord Chancellor (*Iolanthe,* 1882), The King, then Don José (*Manteaux Noirs*), King Gama (*Princess Ida,* 1884), John Wellington Wells (*The Sorcerer* Boston, 1885), Ko-Ko (*The Mikado,* 1885), General Bangs (*Polly,* 1885) and Jack Point (*The Yeomen of the Guard,* 1888). He also appeared as Laurent (*La Mascotte,* 1882), Cyprian (*Prince Methusalem,* 1883), as the King in both Broadway versions of *Le Coeur et la main, Micaëla* and *Hand and Heart* (1883), as von Folbach in *Falka* (1883), Frimousse in *Le Petit Duc* (1884), Fanfani Pasha in *A Trip to Africa*

(1886), Chow-Chow/The Magician in *The Arabian Nights* (1887) and as General Pataquès in *The Queen's Mate* (1887) in a high profile career as a classy comic-opera comedian.

He toured with Duff's company and Lillian Russell in 1887 (*Gasparone, A Trip to Africa, Iolanthe,* etc) and with Aronson's company as Cadeaux in *Erminie* in 1888–89, but was seen less frequently in the 1890s, playing Baron Otto von Piffleseltzer in the unfortunate *The Robber of the Rhine* (1892), Sir Lionel Ravenswood in the Boston musical *Westward Ho!* (1894) and *Zip* (1894–95), in Broadway's version of Messager's *La Basoche* and in the ''romantic comic opera'' *Leonardo* (1895, Fra Patchouli), before returning to Britain for some less exacting engagements and what turned out to be a long retirement.

He was seen in the 1913 silent film of *Hamlet* as the Gravedigger.

His second wife **Madeleine LUCETTE** [Madeleine Matilda BRADLEY] (b London, 26 December 1858; d Hampstead, London, 17 February 1934) had a career in the musical theatre both in Britain—appearing with Ryley as a teenaged chorister with Kate Santley, at the Alhambra in *Orpheus in the Underworld* (Vesta) and *King Indigo* (Zobeide) and with D'Oyly Carte—and, with much more success, in America where she was seen on Broadway as Susan in *Billee Taylor,* Constance in *The Sorcerer,* Regina in *La Princesse de Trébizonde,* in *Princess Toto,* as Hilaria in McCaull's production of *The Lady or the Tiger* (1888) and in the leading feminine role of Amorita in the American version of *Pfingsten in Florenz* at the Casino. She also went round the country as leading lady with McCaull (Aline in *The Sorcerer* 1885, etc) and with George Lederer's *The Maid of Belleville* company (1887), in Charles Ford's musical company (1881, Patience, etc), in the title role of *Virginia* (1883) and as *Madame Boniface* and *Niniche.* She was, however, voted ''too refined'' for the ''spiciness'' of the French pieces. She then turned her attention wholly to a highly successful career as a playwright, under the name Madeleine Lucette Ryley, and, in what seems to have been her only musical venture (an announced adaptation of Tobin's *The Honeymoon* to be set by Julian Edwards having apparently not been produced), she adapted Messager's *La Basoche* for the American stage.

The first Mrs Ryley who, more than a decade after the fact, came to America and raised a great newspaper scandal over her husband's defection (she finally accepted a cash settlement in lieu of him, and then came back for a second bite a few years later), ended up teaching ''physical culture, deportment, dancing and poetry of motion'' in New York.

RYSKIND, Morrie (b New York, 20 October 1895; d Washington, DC, 24 August 1985). One of the main instigators of Capitol-Hillarity in the Broadway musical of the 1930s.

Ryskind made his first entrance into the theatre writing sketches for the revues *The 49ers* (1922), *The Garrick Gaieties* (1925) and both sketches and lyrics for *Merry Go Round* (1927) before his first musical-comedy assignment, on the words for an out-of-town flop with music by Charles Rosoff (composer of ''Don't Let 'em Take the Blue and White Out of the Red, White and Blue'') and Harold C (''This Little Piggie Went to Market'') Lewis called *Pardon Me.* He did better next time up, in collaboration with George S Kaufman, on the libretto of the Marx Brothers musical *Animal Crackers,* which (like the brothers' earlier *The Cocoanuts* and their *A Night at the Opera*) he later wrote into a screenplay.

He provided further revue material to *Americana* and *Ned Wayburn's Gambols* (1929) and rejoined Kaufman for three musicals without the Marx Brothers, but with George Gershwin and with a political tinge: *Strike Up the Band* (rewrite), *Of Thee I Sing* and *Let 'em Eat Cake.* A fourth piece which found its characters in the world of politics brought him into partnership with another famous name when he scripted the successful *Louisiana Purchase,* set to songs by Irving Berlin.

Ryskind also directed the musical *The Lady Comes Across* (1942).

1927 **Pardon Me** (Charles Rosoff, Harold C Lewis/Ralph Murphy/w Murphy) Apollo Theater, Atlantic City 20 September; Colonial Theater, Boston 26 September

1928 **Animal Crackers** (Bert Kalmar, Harry Ruby/w George S Kaufman) 44th Street Theater 23 October

1930 **Strike Up the Band** (George Gershwin/Ira Gershwin/w Kaufman) Times Square Theater 14 January

1931 **The Gang's All Here** (Lewis Gensler/w Russel Crouse, Oscar Hammerstein II) Imperial Theater 18 February

1931 **Of Thee I Sing** (G Gershwin/I Gershwin/w Kaufman) Music Box Theater 26 December

1933 **Let 'em Eat Cake** (G Gershwin/I Gershwin/w Kaufman) Imperial Theater 21 October

1940 **Louisiana Purchase** (Irving Berlin) Imperial Theater 28 May

Autobiography (w Roberts, J): *I Shot an Elephant in My Pyjamas* (Huntington House, 1994)

S

SACKS, Joseph L[eopold] (b Russia, 17 February 1881; d Johannesburg, South Africa, 19 May 1952).

Born in Russia, buried in South Africa, Joe Sacks wreaked most of his theatrical career on the London theatre where he produced several outstanding hits, more than once took advantage of the laws of bankruptcy, was banned from business, but bounced back irrepressibly from the depths of disgrace to the brink of dishonesty in a couple of decades of activity.

Sacks began his connection with the theatre as a fruitseller in a circus and, ever unable to read or to write English, he launched himself first upon some theatrical ventures in South Africa before appearing in London during the First World War (rich, allegedly from staging shows for the troops) to mount a revue called *Three Cheers.* It was, however, his unlikely second choice, his first musical play, which launched him to prominence and temporary prosperity, when the elsewhere and up-to-then only mildly successful *The Lilac Domino* scored a huge London success. He confirmed that success with another import, Broadway's *Going Up,* in the same year before burning his fingers badly on two further transatlantic pieces—a spectacular written by music publisher Isidore Witmark called *Shanghai* and an inane *Nobody's Boy*—neither of which had been tried at home.

Sacks had a further blockbusting success, however, with yet another import, *Irene,* and he also invested significantly in Jimmy White's fine production of *Sybil,* but had less luck with two other quality pieces: Broadway's pretty *Mary,* and a version of Kálmán's *Das Hollandweibchen* with no less a star than Maggie Teyte top-billed. He subsequently took a thorough tumble with his attempt to create his own *Irene,* a feebly imitative piece called *Jenny.* A second attempt at an original piece, *The Bamboula,* also flopped and when Friml's *Katinka* (108 performances) and a version of Lehár's *Libellentanz* (*The Three Graces,* 121 performances) also disappointed, Sacks ended up in bankruptcy court.

Thereafter his appearances on the London theatre scene were sporadic, and (although he admitted to "an interest" in *The Blue Kitten* and in the super-flop *The Girl from Cook's*) his only further musical forays—with *The One Girl* (ex- *Smiles*) in 1932 and a feeble piece called *Royal Exchange,* which attempted to give film star Ramon Novarro a stage musical vehicle—were as fast and hefty failures as his three big hits had been winners.

SADDLER, Frank (b Franklin, Pa, 9 September 1864; d Albany, NY, 25 March 1921). Classic orchestrator of the dance-age Broadway musical.

Originally a musical director for touring shows, Saddler subsequently became an arranger and orchestrator for the publishing firm of Witmark. Working, for the most part, neither as a composer nor as a theatre conductor, as did the majority of his most important orchestrating colleagues, but as a full-time orchestrator and arranger, he became, at a time when virtually all composers did not or could not write full scores for their music, very largely responsible for the orchestral sound of the Broadway musical comedies of the 1910s. It was a sound which, making use of a more limited number of pit players than had mostly been the case in earlier years, provided a closely textured accompaniment both attractive and, when necessary, sufficiently expansive-sounding in itself and which was, in the pre-amplification age, also supportive of the singers, rather than drowning them out.

Amongst the many shows—from *Follies* spectaculars to *Passing Show* revues, to a vast list of musical comedies of all kinds and weights—for which Saddler supplied the scoring were *Sergeant Kitty* (1904), *Piff! Paff! Pouff!* (1904), *Lady Teazle* (1904), *The Midnight Sons* (1909), *The Jolly Bachelors* (1910), *The Summer Widowers* (1910), *The Bachelor Belles* (1910), *The Three Romeos* (1911), *The Man from Cook's* (1912), *The Honeymoon Express* (1913), Jerome Kern's *The Red Petticoat* (1912), *Oh, I Say!* (1913), *Nobody Home* (1915), *Cousin Lucy* (1915), *Very Good Eddie* (1915), *Have a Heart* (1917), *Love o' Mike* (1917), *Oh, Boy!* (1917), *Oh, Lady! Lady!!* (1918), *The Night Boat* (1920) and *Sally* (1920), *The Dancing Duchess* (1914), *Hands*

Up! (1915), *Robinson Crusoe Jr* (1916, w Oscar Radin), *Step This Way* (1916), Gershwin's maiden *La La Lucille* (1919), Dillingham's Hippodrome extravaganzas, and such other Dillingham shows as *Watch Your Step* (1914), *Stop! Look! Listen!* (1915), *Jack o' Lantern* (1917) and *Tip Top* (1920).

SAGAN, Leontine [SCHLESINGER, Leontine] (b Austria, 1889; d Pretoria, South Africa, May 1974).

A former actress, the South African–bred Sagan made her name with her direction of the cult play *Mädchen in Uniform* and, in the musical theatre, as the director of Ivor Novello's romantic musical spectaculars (*Glamorous Night, Careless Rapture, Crest of the Wave, The Dancing Years, Arc de Triomphe*) and their Eric Maschwitz spinoffs *Balalaika* and *Paprika.* She also directed the British production of Stolz's *Venus in Seide* and the 1940s remakes of two of Strauss's works as *A Night in Venice* and *Gay Rosalinda,* and traveled to Australia to direct *The Dancing Years.* For the screen, she was responsible for the film *Gaiety George* (1946) which alleged that it was ''inspired'' by the career of George Edwardes. In spite of her successes, she is largely recalled today as a bullish, militaristic director who took an apparent pleasure in reducing actresses to tears.

SAGER, Carole Bayer (b New York, 8 March 1946).

Lyricist Sager made her first appearance on a Broadway bill with the four performances of the 1970 musical *Georgy,* but returned a little short of a decade and a good many hit songs (''Nobody Does It Better,'' ''Through the Eyes of Love,'' etc) later to write the numbers, with Marvin Hamlisch, for *They're Playing Our Song,* an enormously successful musical play apparently based on the relationship between herself and the composer. Which must make her the only lyricist to have authored an autobiographical musical-comedy hit.

1970 **Georgy** (George Fischoff/Tom Mankiewicz) Winter Garden Theater 26 February

1979 **They're Playing Our Song** (Marvin Hamlisch/Neil Simon) Imperial Theater 11 February

SAIDY, Fred [SAIDY, Fareed Milhelm] (b Los Angeles, 11 February 1907; d Santa Monica, Calif, 14 May 1982).

Originally a journalist, Saidy wrote revue sketches, a pair of film scripts (w Sig Herzig) and television material before entering the musical theatre with the libretto for one of the earliest attempts to clone an *Oklahoma!* in *Bloomer Girl.* It cloned exceedingly happily through 652 performances, but it was topped by a second collaboration between the librettist and lyricist Yip Harburg on the fantasy *Finian's Rainbow* (725 performances).

When Saidy went into production with the comedy musical *Flahooley* the results were less happy, but a fourth collaboration with Harburg produced yet another good run when the pair manufactured a vehicle for Lena Horne which, as *Jamaica,* played more than five hundred Broadway performances. Like his earlier hits, however, *Jamaica* found its success only at home and no takers outside the United States. His final Broadway offering (after a remake of the flop *Darling of the Day* which he authored did not come to the stage) was *The Happiest Girl in the World,* a piece which did unkind things to the works of Aristophanes and Offenbach simultaneously, and which played 97 performances in 1961.

1944 **Bloomer Girl** (Harold Arlen/E Y Harburg/w Sig Herzig) Shubert Theater 5 October

1947 **Finian's Rainbow** (Burton Lane/Harburg/w Harburg) 46th Street Theater 10 January

1951 **Flahooley** (Sammy Fain/Harburg/w Harburg) Broadhurst Theater 14 May

1952 **Jollyanna** revised *Flahooley* w William Friml, Curran Theater, San Francisco 11 August

1957 **Jamaica** (Arlen/Harburg/w Harburg) Imperial Theater 31 October

1961 **The Happiest Girl in the World** (Jacques Offenbach arr/Harburg/w Henry Myers) Martin Beck Theater 3 April

SAIL AWAY Musical comedy in 2 acts by Noël Coward. Broadhurst Theater, New York, 3 October 1961.

Sail Away was the nearest thing that Noël Coward ever wrote to the witty, revusical kind of musical play which his enormous success as an author of comedies and revue material might have led public and producers to expect from him, rather than the romantic musical plays with which he persisted following his success with *Bitter-Sweet.* But it was not originally designed as such. *Sail Away* was constructed for the American stage. Named for a song from his earlier London musical *Ace of Clubs* which had been tacked into the new score, the show was set on a Cunard cruise liner and its action followed the *Love Boat*–style amours of the passengers, most especially those of middle-aged Verity Craig (Jean Fenn, equipped with two numbers from another London failure, *Pacific 1860*) and the younger John van Mier (John Hurst). It didn't follow them for long, for soon after the Boston opening major revisions were put into action and Verity Craig, her miserable love life and her lovely songs, went under the knife. A secondary character, the comical cruise hostess Mimi Paragon (Elaine Stritch, who had won the best of the applause in Boston), became John's new love, and she and the bevy of comically drawn Coward characters who peopled the cruiser became the center of the piece. With no soprano, no love duets, no soul-searching, the accent was now very largely on comedy and the *Sail Away* that reached Broadway was a very different show from the one that had opened in Boston.

Plate 339. **Sail Away.** *Elaine Stritch as cruise hostess Mimi Paragon digs out some ''Useless Useful Phrases'' from one of those books.*

The comedy songs provided many funny moments: Miss Stritch doing things to one of those foreign-language books that dispense ''Useless Useful Phrases'' or bewailing ''Why Do the Wrong People Travel (and the right people stay back home)?,'' or Charles Brasewell in uniform instructing the ship's stewards that ''The Passenger's Always Right'' and later as an Arab pimp repeating, to the same tune, instructions to a horde of guides on how to please and skin the arriving hordes (''Compel him, sell him anything from sex to dynamite . . .''). The romantic songs took a definite second place, as in all the best revues.

The show opened strongly on Broadway and looked set for success but, suddenly, its audience ran out. It closed after 167 performances. But Miss Stritch, who had had a definite personal success, was not finished with Mimi Paragon. Three months later she opened in *Sail Away* in Britain. Harold Fielding's production included several of the Broadway cast and also one new number: ''Bronxville Darby and Joan,'' which had been cut out of town in America. The aging star of *Irene,* Edith Day, paired with Sydney Arnold to bicker ''We're a dear old couple, and we hate one another . . .'' and grumble another classic into the Coward song book. However, once again *Sail Away,* after a brilliant opening, found that its audience, if enthusiastic, was limited. From fine houses the attendance vanished to a half virtually overnight. The production closed after 252 performances. The following year Maggie Fitzgibbon gave her Mimi Paragon to Melbourne and Sydney (Her Majesty's Theatre 19 July 1963), after which, having given the world a tantalizing glimpse of the musical Coward didn't feel inclined to write, *Sail Away* was folded away for more than three decades.

In 1998 it was given its first showing since, by the Just-the-Ticket Theater Company at the Rhoda McGaw Theater, Woking (2 September). A second British mounting, in 1999, of a ''revised'' *Sail Away* (ad Barry Day) hacked up Coward's libretto, perforated it with a collection of extraneous songs, and sank to the sound of indignant protests from Coward fans and musical-theatre lovers alike.

UK: Savoy Theatre 21 June 1962; Australia: Her Majesty's Theatre, Melbourne 24 May 1963

Recordings: original cast (Capitol), London cast (HMV), composer performing (Capitol)

SAINT-ALBIN, Albert de (b Paris, 1843; d Paris, 1901).

Journalist (*Figaro,* sometime editor of *Jockey*) and playwright (*Le Train de plaisir, Monsieur l'Abbé, Leurs gigolettes, Les Grandes Manoeuvres*) Saint-Albin won his way through to theatrical success in spite of some politically-inspired attempts to stop him. A left-wing demonstration was staged in the auditorium on the opening night of his maiden musical at the Folies-Dramatiques with the aim of sabotaging a show that was the work of an avowed anti-socialist writer. However, although this burlesque of *Ruy Blas* was duly and swiftly removed, the blind whistling and booing brought paragraphs of ridicule against the demonstrators and evoked sympathy for their target, and Saint-Albin went on to a fine and full theatrical career.

In the musical-theatre part of that career, a part comprising just a handful of shows, the playwright collaborated with the four greatest musical-theatre musicians of the era—Offenbach, Planquette, Lecocq and Hervé—albeit, it has to be said, not on their greatest successes. His single most successful piece was the vaudevillesque *Le Grand Casimir* in which Céline Chaumont encouraged the mode for the vaudeville-opérette instigated by Judic and *Niniche,* but Planquette's *Panurge* was a fine Parisian success and Hervé's *La Belle Poule,* evolved as a Hortense Schneider vehicle, also won sightings from London to Sydney. Both Serpette's *Le Manoir du Pic-Tordu* and Offenbach's *La Foire Saint-Laurent,* in spite of failures at home, were also exported. His *Mam'zelle Gavroche,* a vehicle for Jeanne Granier, played 56 Parisian performances.

Saint-Albin also put his name to a number of revues and ballet scenarii.

1872 **Le Ruy Blas d'en face** (uncredited/w Émile Blavet, Henri Chabrillat) Théâtre des Folies-Dramatiques 13 April
1875 **Le Manoir du Pic-Tordu** (Gaston Serpette/w Arnold Mortier) Théâtre des Variétés 28 May
1875 **La Belle Poule** (Hervé/w Hector Crémieux) Théâtre des Folies-Dramatiques 29 December
1877 **La Foire Saint-Laurent** (Jacques Offenbach/w Crémieux, Ernest Blum) Théâtre des Folies-Dramatiques 10 February
1879 **Le Grand Casimir** (Charles Lecocq/w Jules Prével) Théâtre des Variétés 11 January
1885 **Mam'zelle Gavroche** (Hervé/w Blum, Edmond Gondinet) Théâtre des Variétés 24 January
1895 **Panurge** (Robert Planquette/w Henri Meilhac) Théâtre de la Gaîté 22 November

SAINT-BONNET, Jeanne [SAINT-BONNET, Bianca] (b Lyon).

Lovely Parisian Jazz Age musical comedy leading lady ''à la voix fraiche et naturellement mélodieuse.''

Mlle Saint-Bonnet, who worked early on under the name of Jane Fréda, began her career in small theatres in her native Lyonnaise region playing the classic theatre repertoire. In 1907 Montcharmont engaged her at Lyon's Théâtre des Célestins and she appeared both there, and the following season in Brussels, in comedy and in drama. She made an early Paris appearance at the Capucines in the musical *Yette* and in a revue, played at the Gaîté-Rochechouart, at the Cigale, and appeared in 1913 at l'Olympia in the cast of the French version of *Les Arcadiens.* During the First World War, she appeared in Britain (*High Jinks,* etc), and she later played further English pieces in Paris (Prudence in *La Petite Quaker,* Kate in *Rip* for the opening of the Théâtre Mogador in 1920) as well as in such local pieces as *Le Roi de l'air* (1917) at the Variétés, *Béguin des dames* (1918, l'Abri), *La Folle Escapade* (1919, Cecily Palmer) alongside Polin, Victor Alix's *Princesse Lily* and various classic revivals including *La Petite Bohème* (1921, Mimi) and *La Mascotte* (Fiametta). However, she came to the fore thoroughly when she created the role of Eva, the lass with a penchant for practicing for her wedding night before the event, in *Ta bouche* (1922).

She starred thereafter in the juvenile leading roles of several other 1920s musicals—*Elle ou moi* (1925, Conrad), as Lotte in *Trois jeunes filles . . . nues!* (1925, ''Quand on ne dit rien'') and as Ketty, who is both herself and her grandmother, in *Passionnément* (1926, ''Ah! pourquoi les bons moments''), whilst also being seen in further classic roles, such as Diana in the Mogador's starry *Orphée aux enfers* revival (1931) and Pauline in their *La Vie parisienne* (1931).

Mlle Saint-Bonnet was the wife of star musical comedian and director Max Dearly.

SAINT-GRANIER [de GRANIER de CASSAGNAC, Jean Adolphe Alfred] (b Paris, 27 May 1890; d Neuilly sur Seine, 25 June 1976). Highly popular songwriter-performer of the Parisian revue, cabaret and musical-comedy stages.

Saint-Granier studied for the Government service exams, but he threw it in before the test date and instead dabbled at first in the stock exchange, and then in journalism. During this time, he began to write and privately perform songs and he ultimately provided and directed a full revue, *Tais-toi, c'est fou,* for the Little Palace. During the rehearsals for this piece, his own ''performance'' was sufficiently noted for him subsequently to cross the footlights and take to the stage as a performer, at first at the Porc-épic at Saint-Mandé and then at the Parisian Moulin de la Chanson, where he found himself top-billed in *La Revue des Folies-Bergère.* Thereafter, he made himself a successful career as a performer in music hall and revue (''Attends moi sous l'horloge,'' ''Pardon mam'selle,'' ''Ma p'tite canne à la main,'' ''J'ai fait ça,'' ''Pour t'écrire que je t'aime,'' ''Je vous fais mes voeux,'' ''Marchéta,'' ''Dinah,'' ''Ah! Suzanne,'' ''Ça, c'est bien français,'' ''So Blue,'' ''Pour une chanson d'amour,'' ie, ''In a Little Spanish Town,'' etc) at the Pie-qui-chante, the Théâtre Michel (*Plus ça change*), Le Perchoir, the Scala, the Folies-Bergère, the Théâtre Réjane, etc, until it could be claimed, at the end of the 1920s, that he was ''second to Chevalier in popularity'' on the Parisian variety stage. Saint-Granier mixed an attractive light baritone singing voice and an elegant appearance with a knowingly sophisticated style which eventually proved equally as usable on the book-musical stage (*Katinka,* Christiné's *La Madone du promenoir,* etc) and on the screen as in revue.

Alongside his career as a performer he had an even more active and successful one as a revuist and lyricist, writing more than 40 revues in the first decade of his career, as well as a long list of popular songs, a number of which were heard in the composite selections of old and new material which were the musical meat of the Parisian large-scale revue stage. These were often concocted in collaboration with such fellow-lyricists as Albert Willemetz and Jean le Seyeux and with composers of the ilk of Christiné (''Avec mes lunettes'' for Chevalier) and Scotto (''C'est bête de faire ça,'' etc), or in the form of French adaptations of foreign hits by writers from Walter Kollo (''Quand on revient'') to De Sylva, Brown and Henderson (''So Blue'').

In 1916 Saint-Granier was responsible, with Jean Bastia, for founding ''Le Perchoir,'' and in 1919 he built and, for its first unprofitable 15 months of operation, managed the 250-seater Théâtre de la Potinière. There he made some early essays, teamed with Gaston Gabaroche and Rip, in both writing and producing revue (*Vas-y-voir, Danseront-ils?,* etc), but he made his first substantial effort as a writer for the book musical theatre in collaboration with Christiné and Willemetz on the successful musical comedies *J'adore ça* and *J'aime.* However, as could be seen by his frequent choice of transatlantic songs as performance material, Saint-Granier had a decided lean to the west, and his biggest theatrical triumphs as an author came with his adaptations of Broadway musicals for the Paris stage—*Rose-Marie, The Desert Song, Hit the Deck* and whatever it was of De Sylva, Brown and Henderson's work that was turned into *Miami* for Paris.

1920 **Je t'adore** (Gaston Gabaroche) 1 act Théâtre de la Potinière 1 December

1925 **J'adore ça** (Henri Christiné/w Albert Willemetz) Théâtre Daunou 14 March

1926 **J'aime** (Christiné/w Willemetz) Théâtre des Bouffes-Parisiens 22 December

1927 **Rose-Marie** French version w Roger Ferréol (Théâtre Mogador)

1929 **Boulard et ses filles** (Charles Cuvillier/w Jean le Seyeux/ Louis Verneuil) Théâtre Marigny 8 November

1929 **Halléluia** (*Hit the Deck*) French version w Ferréol (Théâtre Mogador)

1930 **Le Chant du désert** (*The Desert Song*) French version w Ferréol (Théâtre Mogador)

1930 **Au temps des valses** (*Bitter-Sweet*) French version (Théâtre Apollo)

1930 **Miami** French lyrics (Théâtre des Ambassadeurs)

1933 **Deux Sous de fleurs** (Ralph Benatzky/Paul Nivoix) Théâtre de l'Empire 6 October

1948 **Les Pommes d'amour** (Louiguy/w Pierre Varennes) Théâtre des Variétés 27 March

ST HELIER, Ivy [AITCHISON, Ivy Janet] (b St Helier, Jersey, 1887; d London, 8 November 1971).

The diminutive actress, singer and songwriter made her first appearance on the West End musical stage in a comedy role in the Seymour Hicks/Ellaline Terriss flop *Captain Kidd* (1910, Aggie Shrubb). She toured South Africa and the wartime front with the Hickses, played in comedy and in variety houses in such short musical pieces as Hicks's *The Model and the Man* (1910, the low comedy slavey, Marguerita) and Leo Fall's *Darby and Joan* (*Brüderlein fein*) (1911, Toni Dreschler), and featured in a number of revues, notably in one of the earliest of the American-influenced pieces, *Everybody's Doing It,* at the Empire and the Apollo in *Samples, Three Cheers* and in *Johnny Jones and His Sister Sue.*

In 1921 Miss St Helier appeared in *Ring Up,* a revue for which she had also supplied the songs, at the Royalty; in 1925 she took a comedy role in the musical *Patricia* (t/o Miss Smythe); and in 1929 she created the part of her career when she was cast as the little cabaret vocalist Manon la Crevette in Noël Coward's *Bitter-Sweet,* introducing ''Bonne Nuit, Merci'' and ''If Love Were All.'' She subsequently played in the Ralph Benatzky circus musical *The Flying Trapeze* (1935, La Directrice) with Jack Buchanan, on tour in 1938 in the role written for Fritzi Massary in *Operette* and as Madame Blum in Emile Littler's successful revival of *The Quaker Girl* (1944), in between engagements in revue and the straight theatre.

As a songwriter, she supplied additional material for a number of book shows including *His Girl* (1922), Harold Fraser-Simson's *The Street Singer* (1924) and the London versions of Friml's *The Blue Kitten* and Robert Stolz's *Mädi* (1927, *The Blue Train*), as well as for many a revue. In *The Quaker Girl* she interpolated a number of her own making, ''It's the Profit That Makes It Dear.'' Her most successful single number was ''Coal Black Mammy'' written with Laddie Cliff for *The Co-Optimists* (1921).

Miss St Helier also appeared on musical film, notably repeating her Manon la Crevette alongside Anna Neagle and Fernand Graavey in the British film version of *Bitter-Sweet.*

Plate 340. **Florence St John.** *Victorian London's ''queen of comic opera'' as the Carmen of the Gaiety Theatre's* Carmen Up-to-Data.

ST JOHN, Florence [GREIG, Margaret Florence] [aka Florence LESLIE] (b Plymouth, 8 March 1855; d London, 30 January 1912). London's unchallenged ''queen of comic opera'' throughout the Victorian era.

Florence St John, equipped with a splendidly strong and true soprano and all the taste and talent needed to use it to best effect, had a career of 40 years in the musical theatre during which she was unflaggingly the darling of the public and the critics through a royal register of the musical shows of her time. The daughter of a Scottish army man, a member of the South Devon militia, she made her first appearances as a singer at a young age at Plymouth's St James's Hall. She began her adult career at 17, touring as a vocalist with Mr Thomas's diorama of ''America [and Canada]'' and then N S Hodges's diorama of ''Ireland'' (''Miss Florence Leslie . . . a pretty ballad singer''). During this time, she married the company's pianist, Alfred St John (''solo pianist, harmonium and accompanist''), and—although he survived the marriage less than four years—it was his name that she took thereafter as her stage name. Later in life she would claim that she was ''the daughter of a musician,'' ''married at 14 years and 7 months'' and ''the widow of a naval officer.'' Quite why, unless she thought it sounded better than the true story, is a mystery.

She moved on to join an operetta company run by the same N S Hodges, touring in Offenbach's *The Rose of Auvergne* and *Breaking the Spell,* and she also appeared on music halls as a ballad singer. When she played the Oxford Music Hall (still as Florence Leslie) in 1875, her singing of Sullivan's ''Meet Me Once Again'' won her a four-week engagement.

She moved into the operatic world when she was hired by Charles as a supporting contralto and made her first appearance with them, at Preston, as one of the ugly sisters in Rossini's *La Cenerentola.* She subsequently sang with the Blanche Cole Opera Company, with Henry Walsham's Company (1876) in a selection of roles ranging from Lazarillo, Cherubino, Maritana and Arline to Azucena, and in the Rose Hersee Company (1877, goatherd in *Dinorah,* Lazarillo, Donna Carmen in *The Rose of Castile,* etc) before making her musical theatre debut touring as Germaine in Alexander Henderson's *Les Cloches de Corneville.* She subsequently took over the role in his long-running London production. The following year when Henderson produced Offenbach's *Madame Favart* at the Strand Theatre she got her big chance. The originally cast Fanny Josephs dropped out of the show's title role, and the producer called in the young ''Jack'' St John. She made a veritable sensation in the part and the show and, from then on, one star role followed another: the title role in another huge hit, *Olivette* (*Les Noces d'Olivette*), and more *Madame Favart* at the Avenue Theatre, where she subsequently appeared as Girola in *Manteaux Noirs,* as Olivette again, as Lurette in Offenbach's posthumous *Lurette* (*Belle Lurette*), Boulotte in *Barbe-bleue* and as Nell Gwynne in Planquette's piece of that name. *Nell Gwynne* transferred to the Comedy Theatre and its star remained there at the end of the run to play Bettina in a revival of *La Mascotte* and Djemma in *The Grand Mogul* (accompanied by a live snake). She went briefly to the Empire Theatre to star in the spectacular *The Lady of the Locket* (1885), but returned quickly to the Comedy Theatre and there late in 1885 she created the title role of Paulton and Jakobowski's hugely successful *Erminie* with its soon-to-be-famous lullaby.

She subsequently appeared as Jacquette in the London version of Messager's *La Béarnaise,* repeated her *Madame Favart* and, after a period out through illness, returned to the stage not in comic opera but in burlesque at the Gaiety Theatre, playing Marguerite in the hugely successful *Faust Up-to-Date* (1888). She toured with this piece to America for a season and returned to the Gaiety to appear in the showcase of *Dick Turpin II* (1889) and to create the role of Carmen in *Carmen Up-to-Data* (1890). She played her Carmen in London and on the road before taking a quick turn at the slightly unlikely title role of the teenage *Miss Decima* (*Miss Helyett*). She then toured opposite Auguste van Biene in *Rip van Winkle,* returned to the Gaiety for a season of *Faust Up-to-Date* and, in October 1892, was top-billed there alongside Arthur Roberts in George Edwardes's new kind of Gaiety entertainment, the musical comedy *In Town.* The show was a huge success, and ''Jack'' held her own thoroughly in the battle-of-the-stars against the difficult but enormously popular Roberts.

She subsequently played further revivals of *Madame Favart* and *La Mascotte* and appeared for a while in the burlesque *Little Christopher Columbus* but, with her always highly admired voice sounding if anything better than ever as she headed into her forties, she tended back towards more substantial singing and, rather than continuing on into more musical comedy with Edwardes, she went instead to the Savoy Theatre where she starred in the title role of Carte's Messager musical *Mirette* and as Rita in *The Chieftain.* She went lucratively into the insufficient comic opera *The Bric-á-Brac Will* at the request of a failing management but she refused to allow the management to transfer her contract when the piece closed and thus, instead of going into the musical comedy *The New Barmaid,* she first succeeded Annie Dirkens as *The Little Genius* (*Der Wunderknabe*) before returning to opéra-bouffe to appear in the West End as a loudly praised *La Périchole* and then as *La Grande-Duchesse* in a major revival sponsored by Carte.

In 1900 she took over from Evie Greene in the starring role of *Florodora* but thereafter she began playing regularly in non-musical vehicles, although she reappeared on the musical stage in 1902, at the closure of the old Gaiety Theatre, to play Marguerite in *Faust Up-to-Date* once more, at nearly 50 years of age. The straight theatre scene seemed to suit her less well, but when she returned to singing, as Catherine in *Madame Sherry,* the piece was a failure. She later appeared on the music halls with a piece called *My Milliner's Bill,* and in 1909 returned for the last time to play the supporting role (with the show's favorite song) of Red Lizi in *The Merry Peasant* at the Strand Theatre as a full-stop to a remarkable career which had taken in opéra-bouffe, Savoy comic opera, musical comedy and burlesque all with equivalent success.

''Jack'' St John was married four (or it may have been five) times, the third (or was it the second?) of her husbands being the six-foot-four musical-comedy actor **Lithgow JAMES** [JAMES SMITH] and the fourth (or third?) the Frenchman Claude Marius [Claude Marius DUPLANY]. The last was wealthy.

Her sister, **Edith St JOHN** [Edith Thornhill GREIG] (b Plymouth, 7 June 1856) also played lead roles on the provincial musical stage, while her dentist brother, Donald St John, took time off from teeth to play reasonable comedy roles in a couple of years of musicals.

ST LOUIS WOMAN Musical play by Arna Bontemps and Countee Cullen based on Bontemps's novel *God Sends Sunday.* Lyrics by Johnny Mercer. Music by Harold Arlen. Martin Beck Theater, New York, 30 March 1946.

When the jockey Little Augie (Harold Nicholas) hits a winning streak he also succeeds in attracting the attentions of Della Green (Ruby Hill), the easy-going, self-pleasing St Louis woman of the title. But Della is the woman of the local bar-owner, Biglow Brown (Rex Ingram), and Brown takes his revenge for this betrayal by beating Della up. Augie goes for his gun, but he is beaten to the shot by Lila (June Hawkins), Brown's rejected mistress. The villain dies cursing Augie. The curse hangs over the jockey and he begins to lose races, and Della, who believes she is handicapping him, decides to leave. Finally both Augie's racetrack touch and Della return.

Harold Arlen and Johnny Mercer provided the score for *St Louis Woman,* a score which was one of the most remarkable of its time and which won a remarkable performance from its original cast. The number which proved to be the most popular outside the show was ''Come Rain or Come Shine'' delivered by Augie and Della during their first blissful thoughts of marriage, but there were half a dozen others of equal power and beauty: Della's loping, off-handed, yet red-hot ''Any Place I Hang My Hat Is Home''; the two cheerfully comical songs of the barmaid Butterfly (Pearl Bailey in her Broadway debut), the one demanding that her man (Fayard Nicholas) ''Legalize My Name'' before getting his way with her, the other reminding him that ''It's a Woman's Prerogative (to change her mind)''; Augie's whoopingly joyous ''Ridin' on the Moon''; and the two dramatic pieces performed by Lila, the despairing ''I Had Myself a True Love'' and the revengeful, hopeless ''Sleep Peaceful (Mr Used-to-Be).'' On top of this exceptional string of numbers came two equally powerful ensembles—the lively closing to the first act with ''Cakewalk Your Lady'' and the second act funeral scene, ''Leavin' Time''—both whipped up vocally as well as visually under the direction of *Porgy and Bess* director Rouben Mamoulian.

In spite of such advantages, *St Louis Woman* played only 113 performances on Broadway. The libretto took the blame. Countee Cullen had died before the show reached town, and the text had never been satisfactorily completed. After its closure Arlen reworked his music, making it up into a more substantial folk-opera style of piece which he called *Blues Opera* and, subsequently, into an orchestral suite which was premiered by the New

York Philharmonic Orchestra in 1957. After further false starts, the show was metamorphosed into a ''blues opera'' now called *Free and Easy* and produced in Amsterdam (December 1959) and in Paris, but the experiment was not considered worth pursuing, and *St Louis Woman* did not make it back to Broadway, as it had been hoped it would. It remains one of that handful of musicals which have left a spectacular legacy of individual songs without leaving a stageworthy show in which to display them.

St Louis Woman was given a New York concert staging by the Encores management in 1998 (City Center 7 May).

Recordings: original cast (Capitol), New York concert (DRG), *Blues Opera* suite (Columbia/EMI)

SAISON IN SALZBURG Revue-Operette in 2 acts and 5 scenes by Max Wallner and Kurt Feltz. Music by Fred Raymond. Kiel, 31 December 1938.

The jolly story of *Saison in Salzburg* follows the efforts of Toni Haberl, owner of Salzburg's ''Zum blauen Enzian'' inn, to buy up the failing old ''Zum Salzburger Nockerl'' as well and there to install little Vroni, the waitress who cooks the best nockerln in town, as manageress and also, hopefully, as his wife. Opposition emerges in the shape of the old owner's daughter, Steffi, and an incognito millionaire, Frank Rex, who has fallen for her. When it turns out that Steffi is an even better cook than Vroni, things get all muddled up. Halfway through the evening, everyone is engaged to the wrong person for all the wrong reasons, but when Steffi comes to understand the situation she gives Vroni her nockerl recipe and soon after things come to a happy ending amongst ribbons and gingerbread in the joyful atmosphere of a little country fete.

In a score of winning charm, Raymond mixed the lively and countrified melodies of pieces such as the rousing hymn to ''Salzburger Nockerl,'' the hopeful little love duet ''Wenn der Toni mit der Vroni'' and the rhythmic march of the ''Blaue Enzian'' with some slightly more towny pieces, notably the smoothly tuneful romancing of Frank and Steffi in ''Warum denn nur bin ich in dich verliebt?,'' and some up-to-date dance melodies as featured in Toni and Vroni's ''Und die Musik spielt dazu.''

Saison in Salzburg, which had—undoubtedly intentionally—something of the tuneful and picturesque ingenuousness of *Im weissen Rössl* in it, was a splendid success both in Germany (Theater am Rudolf-Wildeplatz, Berlin 8 June 1946) and then in Austria where it played an enthusiastically received initial season at the Raimundtheater and was subsequently revived (Titania-Theater 1 July 1946). A first film version, sporting only two of the show's songs, but rather more of its music, was made soon after the premiere under the title of the song hit *Und die Musik spielt dazu,* whilst a second, unsuccessful, one made by Ernst Marischka in 1952 attached eight numbers to a completely different story which had an out of work actor (Adrian Hoven) romancing a Salzburger innkeeper (Gretl Schörg) amongst the Austrian scenery. Marischka helmed a second *Saison in Salzburg* film in 1961 in which Peter Alexander and Waltraud Haas sang a half-dozen Raymond songs as well as some that weren't.

The show was subsequently played in Belgium in a French translation (*Vacances au Tyrol* ad André Mouëzy-Éon, Henri Wernert, 1 April 1967) and its music is still featured in record-shop windows in Salzburg where, without reaching the same international renown, it is (or, at least, tries to be) to Salzburg what *Im weissen Rössl* is to the neighboring Salzkammergut.

Austria: Raimundtheater *Salzburger Nockerln* 20 December 1940

Films: *Und die Musik spielt dazu* 1943, Wien Film/Ernst Marischka 1952, Sascha Films/Ernst Marischka 1961

Recordings: selection (Polydor, Elite Special, Amadeo)

SALAD DAYS Musical entertainment in 2 acts by Julian Slade and Dorothy Reynolds. Music by Julian Slade. Theatre Royal, Bristol, 1 June 1954; Vaudeville Theatre, London, 5 August 1954.

The post-(second-)war repertory theatre system in Britain (which, in fact, was not based on companies with a repertory of pieces but only on permanent acting companies with a consecutive series of plays) originally concentrated entirely on performing straight theatre pieces but, during the 1950s, several enterprising repertory-theatre directors began to include small-scale musical productions in their schedule. The most notable of these was the Bristol Old Vic Company under Denis Carey which produced, at first, versions of Shakespeare's *Two Gentlemen of Verona* and Sheridan's *The Duenna* with original music by company member Julian Slade, as well as a Christmas revue (*Christmas in King Street*) and a festive musical, *The Merry Gentleman,* before launching a revusical end-of-term romp called *Salad Days* written by another company member, Dorothy Reynolds, and by Slade.

Topical and localized, the lightweight framework of *Salad Days* followed the progress of two young Bristol University Students, Timothy (John Warner) and Jane (Eleanor Drew), from graduation into the real world of work, reponsibility and marriage. Urged on by his parents, Timothy visits a series of Uncles trying to find himself a congenial job, whilst Jane is pushed vivaciously towards marriage at all costs by her social mother. The results of all these efforts made up the series of scenes

Plate 341. **Salad Days.** *Dorothy Reynolds complains torchily of ''Sand in My Eyes.''*

that comprised the entertainment with, in revue fashion, each of the dozen actors playing several of the many roles involved. Miss Reynolds was a wordless beautician battering Yvonne Coulette (Jane's mother) into shape whilst her customer carries on a nonstop telephone conversation in the most unlikely positions, later a sultry nightclub singer (''Sand in My Eyes'') seducing the beastly Minister of Pleasures and Pastimes, and then a hopeless model displaying extravagant clothes at danger to limb if not life. Eric Porter was a deeply ''Hush, Hush'' Diplomatic uncle and a nightclub manager with revusical tendencies, Alan Dobie a tramp who gives Timothy a job looking after a piano called Minnie which sets the world dancing, Norman Rossington a PC with ballet shoes in his back pocket, Bob Harris (in a role custom-fitted to his mime talents) was an appealing comic mute, and Pat Heywood a crotchety Aunt one minute and a perky soubrette the next.

The songs which Slade composed for the piece were necessarily musically unambitious, for only Miss Drew of the Bristol company had any skill as a singer. She was in consequence given the whole lyric part of the piece, singing sweetly ''I Sit in the Sun'' as she mulled over her mother's list of eligible gentlemen, duetting with her Tim that ''We Said We Wouldn't Look Back,'' and celebrating adulthood in the show's loveliest melody ''(I'm having) The Time of My Life,'' whilst the other members of the company enjoyed the light comedy of such pieces as ''We Don't Understand Our Children,'' the nightclub number ''Cleopatra,'' and the simple tunefulness of ''It's Easy to Sing a Simple Song'' or ''Look at Me, I'm Dancing.''

The Bristol production won a fine reception and, before its three-week run was over, it had won itself a transfer to London's Vaudeville Theatre under the management of the firm of Linnit and Dunfee and Jack Hylton. Although some cast changes had intervened, the piece was largely what had been seen in Bristol, and London, which according to *The Times* was ''reacting sharply against the hard-hitting, hard-boiled American musical'' gave it a welcome if anything more enthusiastic than Bristol had done. Certainly, its mixture of fantasy, revue, youthful and innocent fun and jovial tunefulness proved to be the apt combination for the time and place. *Salad Days* remained at the Vaudeville Theatre for five and a half years (2,283 performances), becoming in the process the longest-running West End musical to date, before going on to be played in virtually every provincial theatre in Britain and in several overseas venues as well.

Australia saw *Salad Days* in the slightly larger (than the Vaudeville) Princess Theatre in Melbourne for 10 weeks before it was bundled off to Sydney's Elizabethan Theatre (30 January 1958). It was bundled back again when *Bells Are Ringing* didn't go, and played two more Melbourne months, before being moved on again to allow *Free as Air,* the next Slade/Reynolds show, to move in. Through all this curious management, it nevertheless established itself as a success. The same could not quite be said for an attempt to interest New York in *Salad Days.* A Canadian production was brought to the off-Broadway Barbizon-Plaza for 80 apparently too soft-boiled performances in 1958.

Back in Britain, however, *Salad Days* proved that it was not just a one-run hit. After that first huge run, and a thorough provincial exposure, it returned to London on several occasions: for seasons at the Prince's Theatre (26 December 1961) and the Lyric, Hammersmith (18 August 1964); again, in a production transferred from the Theatre Royal, Windsor, for 113 performances at the Duke of York's Theatre (14 April 1976); and in a ''fortieth anniversary production'' at the Vaudeville Theatre in 1996 (18 April), with the comedy team of Kit and the Widow featured. A badly cut television version was produced in 1983, and an ''all-star'' version (which cut the doublings which are the joy of *Salad Days,* rendering it starry but ordinary) broadcast by Radio 2 in 1994.

The first adult musical comedy to move to London from the now virtually vanished British ''repertory'' theatre system, *Salad Days* still remains, more than 40 years later, the most successful.

Australia: Princess Theatre, Melbourne 13 November 1957; USA: Barbizon-Plaza 10 November 1958; France: Théâtre en Rond 1957

Recordings: original cast (Oriole), studio cast with members of 1976 revival (TER), Australian cast (Planet 45 rpm), 1996 revival cast (First Night), studio cast (EMI), etc

SALLY Musical comedy in 3 acts by Guy Bolton. Lyrics by Clifford Grey. Additional lyrics by P G Wodehouse, B G De Sylva and Anne Caldwell. Music by Jerome Kern. Ballet music by Victor Herbert. New Amsterdam Theater, New York, 21 December 1920.

One of the line of popular Cinderellery musicals which followed the manners of the hugely successful *Irene, Sally* was ordered by Florenz Ziegfeld as a vehicle for Marilyn[n] Miller, the lovely blonde dancing star of his 1918 and 1919 *Follies.* Originally to have been a collaboration between Bolton, Kern and P G Wodehouse, and based on a piece called *The Little Thing* on which the three had worked together several years previously, it was ultimately written by Bolton alone, when Wodehouse preferred to spend the time on another project, and another British lyricist, Clifford Grey, replaced him as author of the show's songwords.

Little orphan Sally (Miss Miller) is a dishwasher in Greenwich Village, and like all orphaned blonde dishwashers she harbors the ambition to become a star in the *Follies.* Her co-worker, Connie (Leon Errol), is the exiled Grand Duke Constantine of Czechogovinia who carries on a high social life on the one hand and earns a living as a waiter on the other. Theatrical agent Otis Hooper (Walter Catlett) has been engaged to supply the entertainment for a party given by the father of wealthy Blair Farquar (Irving Fisher) and, when he loses the exotic foreign dance star who was to have been his chief attraction, Sally is disguised to take her place. The party ends in disaster and quarrels, but between the end of Act II and Act III Sally makes it to that star dressing room at the *Follies* in record time and by the end of the act she has netted Blair as well.

Although the part of Connie had been specially written in to feature Errol, Miss Miller was the show's consuming star and her dancing talents in particular were extensively displayed. She performed two first-act numbers, including a solo routine plotworthy enough to bring her to Otis's notice as a danseuse; a slavic dance in her disguise at the party; and a *Follies* Butterfly Ballet in the last act—but she also had a voice in the two most enduring songs in the show, ''Look for the Silver Lining,'' which she shared with Fisher in the first act, and her admission in the second act that she is ''The Wild Rose'' (as opposed to a primrose). She also had a share in another pretty duo, ''Whip-poor-Will'' (ly: De Sylva). Errol had a comical number about the thankless and naked courtesan who leapt from his palace bedroom window and swam the river ''Schnitza-Komisski,'' leaving him to be deposed alone, and Catlett joined with Mary Hay (Rosalind) in the one piece brought forward from *The Little Thing,* ''The Church 'Round the Corner.'' A second piece from that unfinished show also intended for *Sally* did not make it to opening night, but ''Bill'' would surface half-a-dozen years on and make itself famous in another setting. Other, produced shows provided fodder for *Sally*'s score as well: ''The Lorelei'' (ly: Anne Caldwell) had been in *The Night Boat* and the title song, sung by

Plate 342. **Sally.** *The Butterfly Ballet, the apotheosis for the orphaned dishwasher (Dorothy Dickson)—she is starring in the Ziegfeld Follies.*

Fisher, was a remake of a number Kern had inserted into the British musical *King of Cadonia* many years previously.

Staged with truly Ziegfeldian production values, *Sally* was an immediate and great Broadway success. Miss Miller starred for a run of 570 New York performances before taking the show on tour where it continued to collect handsomely, and whilst the Broadway version continued its run, Grossmith and Laurillard opened the show at London's Winter Garden with the theatre's resident stars Leslie Henson (Connie) and Grossmith himself (Otis) featured alongside American dancer Dorothy Dickson as Sally. Once again it was a splendid success (387 performances) and went on to become a touring circuit regular. Proportionately, however, perhaps the biggest success that this hugely popular piece found was in Australia. Dancer Josie Melville was starred as Sally alongside George Lane (Connie, equipped with a variation on George Graves's old routine, ''Olga the Hen''), George Baker (Blair), George Gee (Otis), Gracie Lavers (Rosalind) and William Valentine (Jimmy). It opened to a dazzling reception—it cannot wholly have been a coincidence that Ada Reeve, star of neighboring *Spangles,* suffered a nervous breakdown the same night and abandoned her show—and it established itself at Her Majesty's Theatre for a run of 26 weeks, topping all but the monster Australian record held by *Our Miss Gibbs.* In Melbourne (Theatre Royal 15 September 1923), its success was equally remarkable—another 26 weeks, fairly qualifying the show as the most popular production ever to have played in Australia.

The show later returned to the Australian circuits and also both to Broadway and to London. A 1948 Broadway revival featuring Bambi Linn, Willie Howard and Jack Goode blew up the score with a couple of extra numbers from *Leave It to Jane* and a baker's half-dozen of other Kern pieces and the text with some low comedy and was gone after 36 performances, but a London revamp (ad Richard Hearne, Frank Eyton), produced as *Wild Rose* (Prince's Theatre 6 August 1942) with Jessie Matthews in a rare musical-comedy appearance as Sally did rather better (205 performances). Hollywood, too, tried *Sally,* originally as a silent film with Colleen Moore and with Errol repeating his stage creation (and the music played as an accompaniment) and then again in 1930 when Miss Miller put her part on screen to rather better effect with the help of sound and Joe E Brown at the head of the comedy.

An Eddie Dowling vaudeville sketch which burlesqued the rather overused Cinderella theme in the musical theatre of the time was, in 1922, turned into a full-length musical by its author and presented on Broadway by the Shuberts under the title *Sally, Irene and Mary* (4 September Casino Theater). The joining together of the names of Broadway's three favorite little heroines of recent years persuaded the public to give the show, which had little or no merit, a 112-performance run. Jean Brown was the not-very-burlesqued Sally.

UK: Winter Garden Theatre 10 September 1921; Australia: Her Majesty's Theatre, Sydney 6 January 1923

Films: First National 1925, Warner Brothers 1930

Recordings: London cast (WRC/Monmouth Evergreen), studio cast (WRC)

LES SALTIMBANQUES Opéra-comique in 3 acts by Maurice Ordonneau. Music by Louis Ganne. Théâtre de la Gaîté, Paris, 30 December 1899.

The most commercially successful of Louis Ganne's operéttes, *Les Saltimbanques,* with its picturesque circus atmosphere, is one of the few French pieces of its period which have remained in the repertoire in its native country, where it is regularly played in the provinces to this day.

Nasty Malicorne (Vauthier) and his wife (Mme de Mérengo) run a little circus in which strongman Grand Pingouin (Lucien Noël), the sad, amorous clown Paillasse (Paul Fugère), Suzon (Jeanne Saulier) and Marion (Lise Berty) are engaged. Little Suzon, the Malicorne's foster child, is particularly hard done by and, after an episode involving the handsome soldier André de Langéac (Émile Perrin), she runs away. She and her circus friends roam the country pursued by the now rather circus-less Malicornes until Suzon finally finds her wealthy (if unmarried-to-each-other) parents, André and true happiness.

Ganne's score was in the basic and colorful strain of Ordonneau's text, which was one of much less craft and literary merit than usual on the part of an author with some fine credits to his name. It rang with the march music which the composer always handled with especial felicity (notably André's ''Va, gentil soldat'') and also included some pretty sentimental moments, such as Paillasse's plea of love for Suzon, ''La nature a pour ses élus,'' Marion's gentle reply, ''Mon pauvre Paillasse,'' and a catchy waltz introduced by Marion and Pingouin (''C'est l'amour'') to close the first act, amid a predominance of lively and bouncy pieces.

Les Saltimbanques was played for more than one hundred performances at the Théâtre de la Gaîté in 1899–1900, and was thereafter regularly reprised there: in 1902 with Jeanne Petit starring; with Angèle Gril in 1913, 1914 and 1915; in 1921 and 1922; and once more in 1945. It was also performed at the Apollo in 1911, at the Mogador in 1941 with André Baugé as Pingouin and at the Théâtre de la Porte-Saint-Martin in 1968. Its principal and enduring career, however, has been in the provinces.

Outside France, the piece was played in several other languages, but with lesser effect. In Vienna, where Louis Treumann appeared as Paillasse, Mizzi Günther as Suzon and Therese Biedermann as Marion, it was a four-performance disaster, and Emil Makai's Hungarian version had an indifferent career at the Magyar Színház. England's only taste of the show was in the form of a 1902 production (ad Arthur Sturgess, Dennis Downing, George Mudie) in which Stella Gastelle (Suzon), Pacie Ripple (Pingouin), George Mudie (des Etiquettes) and Tom A Shale (Paillasse) featured briefly on the touring circuits, and the show made what seems to have been its only American appearance in a 1911 performance by a visiting Italian troupe. Canada got the French original from Paul Cazeneuve's repertoire company in 1905.

A film version was produced in 1930, with Käthe Nágy, Nicolas Colline (Paillasse) and Suzanne Gouts (Marion) featured. It was issued in French, German and Italian versions.

Austria: Carltheater *Circus Malicorne* 20 April 1901; Hungary: Magyar Színház *A csepűrógók* 28 December 1901; UK: Opera House, Northampton *Les Saltimbanques, or The Bohemians* 24 March 1902; Canada: Théâtre Français, Montreal 11 September 1905; USA: Majestic Theater *I Saltimbanchi* 24 April 1911

Film: Nero Film/Robert Land 1930

Recordings: complete (Decca, EMI), selection (EMI-Pathe), etc

SAMUEL, Fernand [LOUVEAU, Fernand] (d Cap d'Ail, 22 December 1914). Celebrated straw-hatted French producer and director of the turn-of-the-century decades.

When Fernand Louveau decided to go into the theatre he also decided to change his name. In a reversal of the usual procedure, he swapped his gentile name (to which, apparently, he had no more claim than that it was the name of his mother's husband . . . who was not his father) for a Jewish one, on the theory that it would help him to get on. He got his first footing in Paris when he took over the management of the Cercle Pigalle, but he soon moved upmarketwards when in 1884 (14 October) he took over the Théâtre de la Renaissance, the once-great opérette house which had been recently stumbling along through a series of short-lived and inexperienced managements.

He presented a program of almost entirely non-musical productions through his years at the Renaissance (the few musical offerings included *Miette, La Gardeuse d'oies, Les Douze Femmes de Japhet, La Petite Poucette*), but that was soon to change. On 1 January 1892 Samuel moved on to take over from Eugène Bertrand at the head of the Théâtre des Variétés. Over the years that followed Baron, Brasseur, Vauthier, Dupuis, Guy, Prince, Max Dearly, Anna Judic, Jeanne Granier, Marguerite Ugalde, Ève Lavallière, Marie Magnier, Anna Tariol-Baugé, Juliette Méaly, Jeanne Saulier, Germaine Gallois, Mariette Sully, Henri Defreyn, Paul Fugère and a long list of other stars of the period played under Samuel's management in a mixed series of new and classic plays, operéttes and revues, mounted in a vastly splendid fashion under his own stage direction, as the new manager brought back to the Variétés something like the glory it had known in the heyday of Offenbach. The musical portion of his programs included: *Un lycée de jeunes filles, La Vie parisienne* (1892), *Les Brigands* (1893), *Lili* and *Mam'zelle Nitouche* with Judic and Dupuis (1894), *Le Carnet du Diable, La Femme à papa* with Judic, *Chilpéric, La Chanson de Fortunio, La Périchole* with Granier (1895), *Le Carillon, L'Oeil crevé, La Vie parisienne* (1896), *Le Pompier de service, Le Petit Faust* (1897), *Les Petites Barnett* (1898), *La Belle Hélène* (1899), *Le Carnet du Diable, Les Brigands, Mademoiselle Georges* (1900), *Niniche* with Judic (1901), a famous production of *Orphée aux enfers* (1902), *Le Sire de Vergy, Chonchette* (1903), *La Chauve-Souris,* and, following the announcement in 1904 of an entirely musical repertoire, *Barbe-bleue, La Fille de Madame Angot, Monsieur de la Palisse, Les Dragons de l'Impératrice, L'Oeil crevé* (1904), *La Petite Bohème, Miss Helyett* (1905), *L'Âge d'or* (1905), *Le Paradis de Mahomet* (1906) and *Geneviève de Brabant* (1908).

With the passing of classic French opérette in favor of *La Veuve joyeuse* and her sisters, Samuel rather abandoned his policy of end-to-end musical productions in favor of plays and the inevitable end-of-year revue, and in the final five years of his famous management, up to his death in 1914, only further revivals of *La Vie parisienne* (1911) and *Orphée aux enfers* (1912) and a Paris production of London's *Les Merveilleuses* (1914) were played at the Variétés.

SANDERSON, Julia [SACKETT, Julia] (b Springfield, Mass, 27 August 1887; d Springfield, 27 January 1975).

The delicately beautiful Julia Sanderson was one of the most durable stars of the American musical theatre in the 1910s and 1920s, and her china-doll features, pretty but never pale personality and fine light soprano saw her through more than 15 years of starring in what were mostly soubrette roles.

Daughter of stock actor Albert H Sackett, she began in the theatre very young and, after appearing with her father in Philadelphia's Forepaugh Theatre Stock company, made her first adult appearances on the musical stage in the chorus of *A Chinese Honeymoon* (1903) and, later the same year, in the chorus role of Lady Maude whilst understudying Paula Edwardes as *Winsome Winnie.* She played a couple of out-of-town dates deputizing for Adele Ritchie in the leading role of *A Chinese Honeymoon* (Mrs Pineapple) the following year, played a season in breeches alongside De Wolf Hopper as Mataya in a Broadway revival of *Wang,* and then joined the Chicago cast of *Fantana* in a minor role as cover again to Miss Ritchie. She soon moved on to improving Broadway roles in *The Tourists* (1906, Dora, ''It's Nice to Have a Sweetheart'') and in Carrie Moore's soubrette role of Peggy (''The Sandow Girl'') in the Broadway version of *The Dairymaids* (1907) before she made a first trip to Britain to play opposite G P Huntley in the shortlived *The Hon'ble Phil* (1908, Suzanne). The journey, however, proved worth the making for, when the show failed, producer Charles Frohman promptly exported both Miss Sanderson and Huntley to Broadway as the stars of a production of the established hit *Kitty Grey,* giving 21-year-old Julia, as Kitty, her first regular star role in New York.

She was hurried back to Britain to try (unsuccessfully) to boost the Ellaline Terriss musical *The Dashing Little Duke* (1909 t/o Césarine de la Noce) by replacing Coralie Blythe in the soubrette role, but her next Broadway roles confirmed her new star status: Eileen, the ''girl with the brogue'' in *The Arcadians;* Lolotte, opposite Donald Brian, in Frohman's production of Leo Fall's *The Siren;* and principal soubrettes in two musicals from London's Gaiety Theatre, *The Sunshine Girl* (Delia Dale) and *The Girl from Utah* (Una Trance), in which she introduced respectively ''Honeymoon Lane'' and ''They Didn't Believe Me,'' Jerome Kern interpolations which Phyllis Dare and Ina Claire had not performed in the same roles in London.

Miss Sanderson toured America in *The Girl from Utah,* and then returned to Broadway in 1916 in a very different role, the romantic-comedy and strongly singing title role of Victor Jacobi's Hungarian operett *Sybil.* Another less fine Jacobi piece, *Rambler Rose,* followed and in 1918 she paired for the last time with Joseph Cawthorn (her regular comic co-star for the past five years) in Ivan Caryll's *The Canary.* After a long period touring with that show, she ventured into revue in *Hitchy Koo* (1920), then went on to Broadway and touring assignments as the still-juvenile star of the highly successful *Tangerine* (1921, Shirley Dalton) and of *Moonlight* (1924, Betty Duncan).

Now rising 40, she went on the road in *No, No, Nanette* (1925, Lucille), *Oh, Kay!* (Kay) and *Queen High* (1926, Florence), and saw out the last years of her stage career in revue (*Crazy Quilt, Sweet and Low*) and in vaudeville before retiring after some 30 active years to a new kind of stardom, hosting a popular radio series with her husband, ukelele singer and sometime revue and musical-comedy player **Frank CRUMIT** (b Jackson, Ohio, 26 September 1889; d Longmeadow, Mass, 7 September 1943), through more than a decade.

In private life, Miss Sanderson was for a period (1907) wife to the newsworthy jockey [James] Tod[hunter] Sloane, before her marriage to Crumit, with whom she appeared in a number of her later shows.

SANTLEY, Joseph [MANSFIELD, Joseph] (b Salt Lake City, Utah, 10 January 1890; d Los Angeles, 8 August 1971). Longtime leading man of American musicals.

A member of a family of actors, Santley was put on the stage by his mother, Mrs Lorene Santley, as a young child under the name ''Little Joey.'' He toured as a boy soprano in vaudeville, played child's parts in stock companies (*Little Lord Fauntleroy,* etc), made his debut at the ''age of ten'' (he was thirteen) as a juvenile star in the touring melodrama *A Boy of the Streets* (1902, ''a curious mixture of melodrama and vaudeville'') and had a song hit at 13 with Feist and Baron's ''She's the Pride and the Pet of the Lane'' in *Rags to Riches.* He toured the country in a series of like pieces before turning in his later teens to musical comedy. He made his first Broadway appearance in *The Queen of the Moulin-Rouge* (1909, King Sacha) and the following year played the juvenile lead, Dick Allen, alongside De Wolf Hopper in *A Matinée Idol.* He then continued through a long series of light song-and-dance lead roles in musical comedies, starring with Marie Cahill in *Judy Forgot* (1910, Dixie Stole), in Lew Fields's *The Never Homes* (1911, Webster Choate), Chicago's *The Modern Eve* (1912), the Broadway version of Eysler's *Der Frauenfresser* (*The Woman Haters,* 1912, Camillo) and top-billed in the unexceptional but touringly durable *When Dreams Come True* (1913, Kean Hedges, also dance arrangements). Appearances in vaudeville and revue intervened before he returned to semi-musical comedy in his own tour of *All Over Town* (1915), as Van Courtland Parke in Irving Berlin's *Stop! Look! Listen!* (1915, singing ''The Girl on the Magazine Cover'') and in the role of Gerard in the Broadway version of the Daly's Theatre musical *Betty* (1916) opposite his wife, Ivy Sawyer.

In 1917 he toured in the lead role of *Oh, Boy!,* returning to New York for *Oh! My Dear* (1918, Bruce Allenby) at the Princess Theater, and the Jerome Kern/Anne Caldwell *She's a Good Fellow* (1919, Robert McShane) at the Globe, in which he introduced ''The First Rose of Summer'' with Miss Sawyer. After two further musicals in a similar light vein, *The Half Moon* (1920, Charlie Hobson) and the out-of-town part of *It's Up to You* (1921, Ned Spencer), he moved into the *Music Box Revue* with which he played in New York and London for two years, before returning to the musical theatre for a further series of roles in his established line: the Shuberts' Eduard Künneke musical *Mayflowers* (1925, Billy Ballard), Friml's *The Wild Rose* (1926, Billy Travers) opposite Desirée Ellinger, the impressive flop *Lucky* (1927, Jack Mansfield) and in the part of the Prince of Wales in *Just Fancy,* for which he also took a part-author's credit.

At this stage, with 17-year-old stardom starting to wear just a little thin, Santley moved to Hollywood where he began writing and directing films, including such musical pieces as the Marx Brothers' *The Cocoanuts, Treasure Girl* and *Swing High.* However, after a few years, he returned to the theatre, playing in New York in *Heigh Ho, Everybody* and taking over Fred Astaire's role in *Gay Divorce* for the end of its Broadway season and the road. He subsequently backtracked to Hollywood where he worked as a director through the later 1930s and 1940s (*Swing, Sister, Swing, Brazil, Make Believe Ballroom, Yokel Boy, Dancing on a Dime, Rookies on Parade, Ice-Capades, Earl Carroll's Vanities,* etc), bringing his screen-musical tally to some 30 films by 1950.

Santley seems to have had a hand in the writing of several unsuccessful musicals, but the co-existence of songwriter Joseph H Santly, composer of the successful song ''Hawaiian Butterfly,'' can lead to a little confusion over credits.

Santley's wife, **Ivy SAWYER** [Elsie SAWYER] (b London, 13 February 1898; d Irvine, Calif, 19 November 1999), began her career as a London child starlet. She appeared for a number of years as *Alice in Wonderland,* originally (1906) as the dormouse, the first oyster and the cornflower (with two solo dances) and later as Alice (1909–1914), played in the chorus of Seymour Hicks's *My Darling* (1907), and for George Edwardes as the midshipman in *The Marriage Market* (1913) before, aged 20, she went to America to appear in the title role of Edwardes's *Betty.* She married her co-star, stayed, and they became an on-stage as well as off-stage pair appearing together in the *Oh, Boy!* tour (1917, Mrs Budd), *Oh! My Dear* (1918, Hilda Rockett), *She's a Good Fellow* (1919, Jacqueline Fay), *The Half Moon* (1920, Grace Bolton), *It's Up to You* (1921, Harriet Hollister), three *Music Box Revues*, *Mayflowers* (Elsie Dover), *Just Fancy* (in which she played an American girl, Linda Lee Stafford, whilst her American husband played the English Prince), and *Lucky* (Grace Mansfield), in which Miss Sawyer appeared for once with, but not opposite, her husband.

Santley's elder brother, **Frederic SANTLEY** [aka Freddie MANSFIELD] (b Salt Lake City, Utah, 20 November 1887; d Hollywood, Calif, 14 May 1953) also had a kiddie-onward stage career, playing in nearly two decades of musicals (*Queen of the Moulin-Rouge, Jumping Jupiter, When Dreams Come True, The Cohan Revue of 1916, Have a Heart, The Royal Vagabond, Glorianna, Poor Little Ritz Girl, Two Little Girls in Blue, Up She Goes, Topsy and Eva, Dew-Drop Inn, Sitting Pretty, Kiss Me, Happy, Present Arms, Funny Face, Hello, Daddy*) on the road and in New York.

1915 **All Over Town** (Silvio Hein/Harry B Smith) Shubert Theater, New Haven 26 April; Garrick Theater, Chicago 30 April

1925 **The Daughter of Rosie O'Grady** (Cliff Hess/Edgar Allen Woolf) Walnut Street Theater, Philadelphia 14 September

1926 **Shamrock** (Hess) 1 act RKO/Keith Vaudeville circuit

1927 **Just Fancy** (Phil Charig, Joseph Meyer/Leo Robin/A E Thomas ad) Casino Theater 11 October

SANTLEY, Kate [von HEIDT, Evangeline Estella Gazina] (b Charleston, Va, 29 August ?1837; d Hove, 18 January 1923). One of the great and influential personalities of the early days of the modern British musical theatre.

Born in Virginia, the daughter of a German planter named Frederick Jacob John Herman von Heidt, and educated in South Carolina, Miss Santley ''went on the stage in early childhood as a fairy queen in pantomime'' but, like so many contemporary actresses, only—according to her later description of her beginnings—considered the stage as a career when her parents lost their all in the Civil War. My first professional sighting of her is indeed as fairy queen in pantomime, but it is at Christmas 1864 in *Puss in Boots* at the Theatre Royal in Manchester, England, where she is billed under the name of ''Eva Stella'' (the contraction of her first names under which she originally worked). She also played a bit part in the same theatre's stock *Robert Macaire,* in which the title role was taken by the yet unrisen Henry Irving. She went on from Manchester to employment as ''walking lady and burlesque'' at the Birmingham Prince of Wales (where she supported the visiting Ada Mencken in *Mazeppa*), to a season at Margate, and then to J B Howard's fine stock company at the Theatre Royal in Edinburgh where, during 1866, a vast variety of weekly roles, including such musical ones as a Singing Witch in *Macbeth,* Daphne in *Midas,* Diana Vernon in *Rob Roy* (''too tame'')—was topped by an Ophelia, not to the Hamlet of Charles Kean as she would later claim (he brought his own leading lady), but to the more modest one of the local Mr Talbot. When she took herself a Benefit at the end of the season, she was noticed especially for her playing of a pianoforte fantasia.

The following year, however, as the music-hall boom reached its lucrative peak, ''Eva Stella'' went into retirement and, just days after her final performance at Edinburgh, ''Kate Santley'' surfaced, working in a rather different field: at London's Oxford Music Hall performing the song ''The Bells Go a-Ringing for Sarah'' and the sketch ''Good-for-Nothing Nan'' which allowed her to display her talents as a pianist. She scored a decided hit and was soon playing her way round the best halls in London, hailed as one of the town's merriest seriocomics.

Soon after, with her name thoroughly established, ''Kate Santley'' moved back into the theatre, and made her first regular theatre appearance in London in burlesque, at the Queen's Theatre, playing in breeches as Peter in Reece's *The Stranger—Stranger Than Ever* (1868, ''her saucy style, resonant voice and skill at breakdown dancing are prominently displayed''), and in skirts in the Christmas entertainment *The Gnome King* (Princess Beatrix). The following year she played at the Liverpool Alexandra, and appeared with the Vokes family in the Drury Lane pantomime *Beauty and the Beast,* but her career in the theatre got fully under way in 1870 when she was hired by the Swanboroughs for the Strand Theatre and appeared there in leading roles in the burlesques *Sir George and a Dragon* (Princess Sabra), *Kenilworth, The Field of the Cloth of Gold, The Idle Prentice* (with Harry Paulton) and *Coeur de Lion* (Sir Kenneth, with Paulton and Edward Terry).

It was while she was at the Strand that the operatic manager Colonel Mapleson took an interest in her and arranged for her to have singing lessons with Pauline Viardot-Garcia. However, the experiment proved a failure—the young woman cracked vocally and mentally, and returned to America. Her confidence returned, however, and she had not long ventured again into the theatre before she was given the chance to appear at Niblo's Garden as Stalacta in a revival of *The Black Crook* (December 1871). She had sufficient success to follow up in the title role of *The Naiad Queen* (February 1872), winning herself a small following and pushing ''the Santley girdle,'' a black velvet belt pointed at the waist and embroidered with a matching sash, to popularize her name as she moved on to play Stalacta in Boston (March 1872).

She then returned to Britain and took over the role of Cunégonde in *Le Roi Carotte* at the Alhambra, winning a significant popularity which was only increased when she was starred in the chief soubrette role of the locally-made spectacular *Black Crook,* introducing the popular ''Nobody Knows as I Know.'' She remained at the Alhambra, where she consolidated her new stardom as Hélène in *La Belle Hélène* (1873), Haidée in the extravaganza *Don Juan* (1873) and Rose Michon in *La Jolie Parfumeuse* (1874), playing in each case opposite the French prima donna Rose Bell. The juxtaposition of these two very different ladies—the soubrette and the soprano—went so far as to provoke street fights between their partisans which culminated in a court case brought by Miss Santley against her rival's claque.

Kate left the Alhambra to make her debut as a producer with an original English comic opera which she commissioned for herself from Robert Reece and the composer of part of *Black Crook,* the young Frederic Clay. She toured as *Cattarina* in the later part of 1874 and, after returning to the Alhambra to star in the title role of Offenbach's specially commissioned *Whittington* (1874) for Christmas, introduced her musical to London. It did very well and, with the cachet of a London season behind her, Miss Santley promptly toured it again, in repertoire with *Les Prés Saint-Gervais,* before returning to town to appear in breeches alongside Emily Soldene's *Madame l'Archiduc* (1876, Fortunato) and as Clairette to Soldene's Lange in *La Fille de Madame Angot* at the Opera Comique.

In the summer she again went touring, taking with her a repertoire including a rather battered *Orphée aux enfers, Cattarina, Madame l'Archiduc* and another new English comic opera commissioned from Freddie Clay. This one was called *Princess Toto* and it starred its manageress as a forgetful little royal invented by the young librettist W S Gilbert. Miss Santley's commission gave its author the opportunity to write his first full-length comic opera. *Princess Toto* was successful enough to be brought to London's Strand Theatre, but strife of some kind arose between those involved and it was closed prematurely.

Kate left the Strand and moved instead to the Royalty Theatre where she produced her version of *Orphée aux enfers,* a version with, as was her wont, cockney point numbers, topped by her all-time favorite number ''Awfully Awful,'' interpolated for herself in the role of Eurydice. She then took a long lease on the unloved little Royalty and, in the years that followed, she presented herself there in a series of often broadly staged musical pieces—Lecocq's saucy *La Marjolaine* (1877), the pasticcio *Madcap, La Belle Hélène, La Jolie Parfumeuse, Little Cinderella, Tita in Thibet* (1878)—in the seasonal months, whilst taking herself and her shows to the country in the summer. She let her theatre to others whilst she went to the Globe to take over as Serpolette in *Les Cloches de Corneville,* played principal boy in the pantomime at the Theatre Royal, Drury Lane, or toured in *La Mascotte* (1882), but she took up residence again to present her third new Clay musical, *The Merry Duchess,* in 1883.

With Kate starring as the (ultimately reformed) villainess of the piece, *The Merry Duchess* found a pretty success and a Broadway production, but her subsequent productions, versions of Audran's *Gillette de Narbonne* and Hervé's *La Cosaque,* were less fortunate. She persisted with French works and staged Bernicat's *François les bas-bleus* (*François the Radical*) but that too failed, and once again she let the Royalty and took to the road, first in another commissioned musical, the English comedy with songs *Chirruper's Fortune,* and then in a piece called *Vetah* for which she herself claimed an authorial credit and Bernicat (who was dead) was credited with the score. She toured again, in 1887, in *Vetah* and in Audran's *Indiana,* but now her performing career was entering its final stages and her producing life was virtually at an end.

In the meanwhile, her Royalty Theatre hosted a hotchpotch of shows of which the best were the regular visits of French dramatic companies, but the controversy which Kate seemed to court struck again when she let her theatre to the Independent Stage Society to produce Ibsen's *Ghosts* (1891). It caused a small scandal. Shortly after making her last appearances on the stage in the operetta *Penelope* (1894, Penelope) and *A Night on the Town* (1894), she sublet the theatre to Arthur Bourchier, but although she retired to Hove and a very long retirement as Mrs Lieutenant-Colonel Lockhart Mure Hartley Kennedy, she maintained the lease on the Royalty Theatre up to her death at the age of 86. In 1902 she produced there her own version of Sardou and de Najac's play *Divorçons* (already performed in Britian in a more safely adapted version) under the title *Mixed Relations.*

One of the great figures of the British musical stage during the earliest years of its modern period, Miss Santley was adored by the public as a performer (if often lambasted for vulgarity by the same press which had once called her ''too tame''), whilst as a producer she was both amongst the earliest and most important to encourage British authors and composers to challenge the might of Offenbach and the French opéra-bouffe, and an expert discoverer of new acting talent.

SAN TOY, or The Emperor's Own Chinese musical comedy in 2 acts by Edward A Morton. Lyrics by Harry Greenbank and Adrian Ross. Music by Sidney Jones. Additional music by Lionel Monckton. Daly's Theatre, London, 21 October 1899.

Following the success of *The Geisha* and that, slightly lesser, of *A Greek Slave,* at Daly's Theatre, George Edwardes continued with more of the same in *San Toy*—an exotically set costume piece which, like *The Geisha,* set picturesque Eastern and nattily dressed Western civilizations up against each other to the tune of some richly romantic love songs and a barrage of comic scenes, songs and dances. For *San Toy,* however, instead of sticking with the extremely reliable (quality-wise) bookwriter

Plate 343. **San Toy** *was one of the handful of English-language musicals of the 19th and early 20th centuries to be widely played through Europe. It made it from Leicester Square to Russia.*

''Owen Hall,'' Edwardes accepted instead a libretto written by ''Edward Morton,'' a well-known and influential journalist who had not to date succeeded in breaking through into the theatre. Sidney Jones was again composer, but Harry Greenbank who had written the lyrics for the earlier Daly's successes died, aged only 33, with the work incomplete and was replaced by the experienced Adrian Ross. However, if it did not come from the same team, *San Toy* was, by the time it reached the stage, much the mixture as before.

Mandarin's daughter San Toy (Marie Tempest) has been brought up as a boy to avoid the draft in a country where the Emperor's troops are female. In time, this brings problems, especially when she falls in love with English Captain Bobby Preston (Hayden Coffin) and then when a new and horrider law drafts mandarin's sons as well. San Toy goes to court as a girl, joins the Emperor's guard, fends off his passes and finally comes to a happy ending amongst a barrage of misunderstandings and comedy scenes. What was left of Morton's rather substantial and uncomic book by the time Edwardes's comedy stars had also been fitted with roles—Rutland Barrington as Yen How, the heroine's father, with his six little wives, Huntley Wright as another comical Chinee, Li, and Ada Reeve as the comedy maid Dudley, in place of Letty Lind who had left Daly's for solo stardom—made up into a distinctly jolly if rather wandering text.

It was illustrated by some fine Sidney Jones songs, of which Barrington's description of his ''Six Little Wives'' and his topical ''I Mean to Introduce It into China'' stood alongside Wright's comparison of soldiers of different nations, told in Daly's Theatre pidgin (''Chinee Sojeman''), and Lionel Monckton's soubrette tale of ''Rhoda and Her Pagoda'' at the head of the fun. In the more lyrical moments Coffin scored with the pretty ''Love Has Come from Lotus Land'' and the lilting ''The One in the World'' and Miss Tempest sang of ''The Petals of the Plum Tree,'' all with considerable success.

San Toy had a famously hard birth. Whilst Morton's libretto was being to all intents rewritten in rehearsal to sound more like Owen Hall, it became clear that Ada Reeve and Marie Tempest did not combine as the latter had so happily done with Letty Lind, and sparks flew until Reeve cried enough and walked out. Gracie Leigh replaced her two weeks before opening and began a career as a star comedienne. Then, during the show's run, Miss Tempest (who had already brought in her own frocks, to the disgust of designer Anderson, and a stinging notice in the *Star*) engineered a crisis by cutting up a pair of violet satin duchess trousers to make them more leg-showing and, to a shower of publicity, walked out when reprimanded, conveniently breaking her long contract with Edwardes (and her connection with the musical theatre) in order to begin a second career on the straight stage. *San Toy* survived all the dramas unshakeably. It was one of the greatest successes of the Victorian musical stage, whether with Tempest or with the quickly promoted Florence Collingbourne as San Toy or even, later, with Reeve who returned to take up the star role she had wanted from the start and then promptly altered it to be a more in line with her talents, with three new music-hally songs (''It's Nice to Be a Boy Sometimes,'' ''All I Want Is a Little Bit of Fun,'' ''Somebody''). Other artists also got fresh songs, notably Coffin, the specialist of the interpolated song, who patriotically gave both L S Potter's ''Tommy Atkins'' and Lionel Monckton's ''Sons of the Motherland''as the Boer War raged, and Wright, who had an almost-plot song, ''Me Gettee Outee Velly Quick,'' by young Paul Rubens, added to his part.

San Toy ran 14 months and 778 performances at Daly's Theatre, the longest tally of any of the great group of musicals which made that theatre's fame, and, well before that run was over, it set off round the world. New York proved particularly welcoming, coming out with splendid notices and hosting four seasons of the show in a five-year period: an original run of 65 performances with James T Powers (Li) and Marie Celeste (San Toy) starring, and 385-pound George Fortescue as Yen How; a quick revival (4 March 1901) by the same Daniel Frohman company for a further 103 performances; and short return seasons in 1902 (Daly's Theater 7 April) with Sam Collins replacing Powers, and in 1905 (Daly's Theater 17 April) with Powers now paired with Florence Smith.

In Vienna, Louis Treumann, soon to be famous as the hero of *Die lustige Witwe,* played Li in a version translated for the Carltheater by composer Hugo Felix for a fine first run of 53 performances alongside Therese Biedermann (Dudley), Franz Glawatsch (Yen-How) and America's remarkable international soubrette Marie Halton, who continued her multi-lingual triumph around the world's musical stages by going on to appear in the show's title role in both Berlin and Budapest. If it did not score the overwhelming Continental success that *The Geisha* had, *San Toy* nevertheless did as well as or better than any other English-language musical of the 19th century, barring its famous predecessor and *The Mikado* (three oriental shows!), winning hundreds of performances all around central Europe in the early days of the new century, and being revived into the 1920s.

Australia, too, echoed the British success when the piece was mounted there in 1901 with Carrie Moore in the title role alongside George Lauri (Li), Grace Palotta (Dudley) and Charles Kenningham (Bobby), and *San Toy* followed its Melbourne introduction with visits to Adelaide, Perth, Brisbane and Sydney (Palace Theatre 9 August 1902). In Britain, meanwhile, the piece was toured solidly, at one stage in multiple companies, for many years, then more intermittently for several decades more, and it even returned to London for a brief season in 1932 (Daly's Theatre 22 February) with Jean Colin starring and Leo Sheffield as Yen How.

USA: Daly's Theater 1 October 1900; Hungary: Népszínház 10 October 1900; Austria: Carltheater *San Toy (Der Kaisers Garde)* 9 November 1900; Germany: Centraltheater 2 March 1901; Australia: Her Majesty's Theatre, Melbourne 21 December 1901

S.A.R. (*Son Altesse Royale*) Comédie musicale in 3 acts by Léon Xanrof and Jules Chancel taken from their play *Le Prince Consort.* Music by Ivan Caryll. Théâtre des Bouffes-Parisiens, Paris, 11 November 1908.

Xanrof and Chancel's delicious ''comédie fantaisiste'' *Le Prince Consort,* originally decorated vaudeville-style with a handful of songs with music by Paul Marcelles, and with Augustine Leriche and Lefaur introducing its two memorable star comedy roles, scored a first-rate success in Abel Deval's production at the Théâtre de l'Athénée in 1903 (25 November). It had further success in England—where it played (without its songs) at the Comedy Theatre under the title of *His Highness My Husband* (ad William Boosey, Cosmo Gordon-Lennox)—and in Germany, but rather less in Liebler and Co's American mounting (*The Prince Consort,* New Amsterdam Theater 1905, 28 performances) with Henry E Dixey and Kate Phillips starred. It was, however, in Paris that the piece was seen by and won the interest of Ivan Caryll, who persauded the authors to let him turn it into a musical.

Xanrof and Chancel made their own book revisions and added a more extended lyrical contribution of some considerable wit for Caryll's full-scale musical version—an early one in the composer's long and important series of musical comedies manufactured from French stage plays—which, although originally announced for an English debut in 1905, was ultimately produced at the Théâtre des Bouffes-Parisiens in 1908.

The government ministers of her country are anxious that young Queen Sonia of Concornie (Suzanne Dumesnil) should be married as quickly as possible to assure the dynasty and thus dampen a nasty republican movement which is threatening their privileged positions. Sonia's exuberant maiden aunt Xénofa (Marguerite Deval) selects the excessively male Prince Cyrill (Henri Defreyn), son of the ex-King of Ingra (Tournis), for the purpose, and all works out splendidly when the two young folk fall in love at first sight. After the marriage, however, Cyrill proves unable to cope with the court routine which prevents him having a private life with his wife, and with her protocolic duties and position above him. He gets moody and tetchy and ends by withdrawing the only thing he can withdraw. Things go from bad to worse, divorce is threatened, and Sonia finally forces the government to offer her decorative husband a share of the throne—for the sake of the child she is bearing. The principal love story was adeptly paralleled by the comical and unsuccessful efforts of Xénofa to add a pretty virgin soldier called Sándor (Robert Hasti) to her long list of military bedmates before being herself checkmated by the charming, opportunist ex-King.

Although greater than Gaiety-weight in its music, Caryll's score was certainly more in the vein of his more substantial works for the London stage than in the traditional and now slightly tired French opérette mold, with both Deval and Defreyn, who were the effective stars of the piece, working through their amusing numbers in an unforcedly sung and light-comically played style whilst the principal lyrical music was entrusted to the role of Sonia. *S.A.R.* scored a fine success at the Bouffes-Parisiens and it was later reprised at the Trianon-Lyrique, in 1924 (12 March), with Jane Ferny starring as Xénofa alongside René Rudeau and Marcelle Evrard.

The show's career outside France, at least, was undoubtedly handicapped by the fact that Oscar Straus's highly successful *Ein Walzertraum* (1907) shared (some would say had pilfered) its main plot premise, but this did not prevent it from being seen and published in Germany (ad Erich Moss) nor from having its plot, if not Caryll's score, taken up by Hollywood for the 1930 Ernst Lubitsch musical film *The Love Parade* (Victor Schertzinger/Clifford Grey/ad Ernst Vajda, Guy Bolton) in which Jeanette MacDonald, Lilian Roth, Lupino Lane and Maurice Chevalier starred. Xanrof and Chancel got some recognition from the *Walzertraum* folk by being allotted the task of doing the French version of the work which was specifically stated to be based on a much older source.

Le Prince Consort was given another musical treatment in Hungary in 1904 when *A királynő férje* (László Kun/Jenő Heltai) was produced at the Vígszínház (8 April) for a good run of 23 performances.

Germany: Altes Stadttheater, Leipzig *Die kleine Königin* 27 August 1910

SARDOU, Victorien (b Paris, 7 September 1831; d Paris, 9 November 1908).

In a long and successful career as a playwright which led to his being regarded as the doyen of the French stage, Sardou wrote comparatively little deliberately for the musical stage. His first musical work was an adaptation of Damaniant's much adapted *La Guerre ouverte* set by Vaucorbeil, later director of the Paris Opéra, but it was his forceful and satirical libretto for Offenbach's *Le Roi Carotte,* an adaptation of the play *Les Prés Saint-Gervais*—which he had written for Virginie Déjazet—into a comic opera composed by Lecocq, and the preparation of the libretto to *Les Merveilleuses,* based on his 1873 play, for George Edwardes (played only in Basil Hood's English version and, in France, in a retranslation by Paul Ferrier) which were his main contribution to the lighter end of the musical theatre. These were complemented by the libretti for such more operatic pieces as Paladilhe's opera *Patrie* (Opéra 20 December 1886), Pierné's *La Fille du Tabarin* (Opéra-Comique 20 February 1901), Saint-Saëns's *Les Barbares* (Opéra 23 October 1901) and Amherst Webber's one-act *Fiorella* (w G B Gheusi, Waldorf Theatre, London 7 June 1905).

A number of his other stage works were, however, adapted by other writers both for the operatic and the lighter musical stage. On the operatic front, *La Haine* became the Russian opera *Kordeliya* (P K Bronnykow, St Petersburg 24 November), *Fédora* became Giordano's successful opera of the same name (Milan 17 November 1898) and another by Xavier Leroux (Monte Carlo 1907), whilst *La Tosca* was the stuff of the even more successful Puccini work (14 January 1900). An operatic version of *Gismonda* composed by Février was produced in Chicago in 1919.

In a lighter vein, his *Piccolino* (w Charles Nuitter) became the basis for Mme de Grandval's opera (Italiens 5 January 1869), Strauss's *Carneval in Rom* and, subsequently, for Guiraud's opéra-comique *Piccolino* (Opéra-Comique 11 April 1876), whilst his delightful dramatic-comic *Madame Sans-Gêne* (w Émile Moreau) proved enormously popular worldwide as a source for musical pieces. It was used as the basis for Ivan Caryll's highly successful musical *The Duchess of Dantzic* (Lyric Theatre, London 17 October 1903), for an Operette by Bernhard Grün, an Italian piece called *Cri-Cri* (1928), a Bulgarian *Madame Sans-Gêne* by Paraskev Chadziev, Paris's Châtelet spectacular *La Maréchale Sans-Gêne* (Pierre Petit/Albert Willemetz/Maurice Lehmann, 17 February 1948) and a Czech musical by Eugen Drmola and Milos Vacek, and also given in an operatic version with a score by Giordano (New York, 1915). He was also credited as "librettist" for the musical comedy *Marita* played in America by Marie Aimée (28 September 1886, mus: Théo Benedix).

Plate 344. **Sardou's** Divorçons *became a musical in Germany. Eva-Bettina Schöninger (Cyprienne) and Wilfried Weschke (de Prunelles) featured.*

The comedy *Divorçons* (w Émile de Najac) was made into a musical play in 1907 by Anselm Götzl, Rudolf Bernauer and Alexander Pordes-Milo as *Frau Lebedame* (Neues Deutsches Theater, Prague 31 December) and again in 1966 by the German author/composer Gerhard Jussenhoven as *Cyprienne* (Theater am Dom, Cologne 2 December), whilst Sardou's *Fernande* shared with Bulwer-Lytton's *The Lady of Lyons* (and, according to some sources, ''an old French vaudeville'') the distinction of being the basis for one of the best Viennese Operette libretti, *Der Bettelstudent.* Victor Léon's libretto to Oscar Straus's 1909 Operette, *Didi,* was credited as based on Sardou's play *La Marquise,* whilst another Viennese piece, *Schottenfeld und Ringstrasse* (Theater an der Wien, 1869, Millöcker/Berla), acknowledged an unnamed piece by Sardou as its source. And in 1995 even *La Tosca* became the meat for a musical play when, with the rise in the fashion for the romantic and dramatic as opposed to the comic in musical theatre, a version of Sardou's tale set in Nazi Germany was produced at Newbury's Water Mill Theatre under the title *Laura* (Michael Heath 25 July 1995).

The success of Sardou's plays also led to a number of them being used as the butt of burlesques. In Paris *Fernande* was done over as *Fernandinette, ou la rosière d'en face* at the Palais-Royal and as *Ferblande, ou l'abonnée de Montmartre* at the Variétés; London's F C Burnand burlesqued *Théodora* in *The O'Dora, or the wrong accent* (Toole's 1885), *Dora* as *Dora and Diplunacy or a Woman of Uncommon Scents* (Strand 1878), the Bancrofts' production of *Fedora* as *Stage-Dora* (Toole's 1883) and *La Tosca* as *Tra-la-la Tosca* (Royalty 1890); whilst Broadway hit *Fédora* even lower with an 1884 piece called *Well-Fed Dora* (5th Avenue Theatre). The Kiralfys staged a short-lived but spectacular musicalish version of the serious *La Patrie* at Niblo's Gardens in 1888 which was not intended as a burlesque, even though some thought it came out like one.

Sardou actually made as appearance on the Operette stage—as a character—when he managed to get mixed up in the story line of the *Dreimäderlhaus*-like piece made up around the love and life of *Offenbach* when it was turned from its original Hungarian into Shubertian for Broadway by Harry B Smith. J W Hull portrayed the writer.

1863 **La Bataille d'amour** (Auguste Vaucorbeil/w Charles Daclin) Opéra-Comique 13 April

1864 **Le Capitaine Henriot** (François Gevaert/w Gustave Vaëz) Opéra-Comique 29 December

1865 **Les Ondines au champagne** (Charles Lecocq/ as ''Jules Pélissié'' w Hippolyte Lefèbvre, Merle) 1 act Folies-Marigny 5 September

1872 **Le Roi Carotte** (Jacques Offenbach) Théâtre de la Gaîté 15 January

1874 **Les Prés Saint-Gervais** (Charles Lecocq/w Philippe Gille) Théâtre des Variétés 14 November

1878 **Les Noces de Fernande** (Louis Deffès/w Émile de Najac) Opéra-Comique 19 November

1906 **Les Merveilleuses** (Hugo Felix/w Basil Hood) Daly's Theatre, London 27 October

SARI *see* DER ZIGEUNERPRIMÁS

SATURDAY NIGHT FEVER Musical in two acts based on the film screenplay by Norman Wexler. Book by Nan Knighton. Songs by The Bee Gees. London Palladium, 5 May 1998.

The umpteenth stage version of an aging motion picture musical to hit the world's stages in the last decades of the 20th century, *Saturday Night Fever* was an understandable follow-up by producers Paul Nicholas, David Ian and Robert Stigwood to their long-running success with the mega-revival of Stigwood's other blockbuster teenyfolk movie of the 1970s, *Grease.*

Unlike *Grease,* however, *Saturday Night Fever* was—at the movie's inception in 1977—not a gently smiling parody of a rapidly receding time, but a here and now picture about a lowlife American boy with a yen for the dance. Its score, mostly written by Barry, Robin and Maurice Gibb of the Bee Gees, was written in the then-popular ''disco'' style, and no less than four of its songs became hit parade successes (''How Deep Is Your Love,'' ''Stayin' Alive,'' ''More Than a Woman,'' ''You Should Be Dancing''). John Travolta's performance as the piece's central character confirmed his star-shooting effort in *Grease* and he, the songs and the film became tremendously successful.

The stage *Saturday Night Fever* was a smoothed down affair, a disco dancing show (dir/ch: Arlene Phillips) for young folk played by young performers, and its score, in the manner of the majority of shows of the period, was a pasticco one, the best of the film songs being topped up with other Bee Gees favorites (''Tragedy,'' etc). Australian dancer Adam Garcia played John Travolta, the reviewers shrugged, but *Saturday Night Fever* proved a viable addition to the undemanding set of pasticcio and/or from-the-film shows filling London's theatres through some 18 months at the Palladium, before moving on to tackle Broadway—to similar press reaction, similar public response and a 14 months' run—and the European Continent. The first performance in Germany was played at Cologne, with a German text and the songs performed in English, and with London's Michael Rouse playing Travolta.

Germany: Dom Theater, Cologne 11 September 1999; USA: Minskoff Theater 21 October 1999

Recording: London cast (Polydor)

SAVAGE, Henry W[ilson] (b New Durham, NH, 21 March 1859; d Boston, 29 November 1927).

Harvard-educated Savage was well established as a real-estate operator in Boston when a combination of circumstances led him to switch careers and take over the proprietorship of the failing Castle Square Opera Company, a would-be permanent resident company which played a repertoire of comic and light opera in English. He turned the group's fortunes around, running one company through two solid years (1896–98) at Philadelphia's Grand Opera House and installing another at New York's American Theater (1897) for an extended and highly successful run.

The company's repertoire included, on the one hand, operas such as *Aida, The Barber of Seville, Rigoletto, Carmen, Il trovatore, Cavalleria rusticana, Romeo and Juliet, The Merry Wives of Windsor, Martha, I Pagliacci, Mignon, La Gioconda,* the English-language staples *Lurline, Maritana, The Bohemian Girl* and *The Lily of Killarney* and pieces as diverse as *Die Meistersinger* and *Lohengrin* or *La Fille du régiment* and *Fra Diavolo.* On the other hand, they also performed an interesting mixture of English versions of lighter Continental works (*Die Afrikareise, Boccaccio, Der Feldprediger, Der Zigeunerbaron, Nanon, Das Spitzentuch der Königin, La Grande-Duchesse, Les Cloches de Corneville, Les Noces d'Olivette*), British comic opera (*Dorothy, Billee Taylor, Patience, The Mikado, The Pirates of Penzance, Iolanthe, HMS Pinafore, Paul Jones*) and a handful of homegrown pieces including De Koven's *The Fencing Master,* Julian Edwards's *Madeleine* and Harry B Smith's burlesque *Sinbad.* Amongst the company, for varying periods, such musical-theatre artists as young comedians Raymond Hitchcock and Frank Moulan, British tenor Charles J Campbell and sopranos Marie Celeste and Attalie Claire played a sometimes surprising range of roles.

Savage's success at the American Theatre encouraged him to venture further in the theatre and over the following two decades he introduced to Broadway a number of successful plays (*The County Chairman, The College Widow, Madame X,* etc) and some fine musicals. His first musical-comedy venture was Luders and Pixley's previously shunned *King Dodo,* for which he made the most effective bid following the team's success with *The Burgomaster,* and his subsequent productions included some of the happiest early American comic operas: *The Sultan of Sulu* (1902), in which he starred his Castle Square comedian Moulan; the highly successful Luders/Pixley *The Prince of Pilsen* (1903); George Ade's *Peggy from Paris;* his successful collaboration with Luders on *The Sho-Gun* (1904); and *The Yankee Consul* (1904), starring Savage's other Castle Square comedy favorite, Raymond Hitchcock. Luders and Pixley's *Woodland* (1904), the revusical science-fiction musical *The Man from Now* (1906) and Reginald De Koven's Ruritanian *The Student King* (1906) were less impressive, but Hitchcock's follow-up to his *Yankee Consul* success in *The Yankee Tourist* (1907) did better.

Savage had his biggest success, however, when in 1907 (now, curiously, calling himself "Colonel" Savage) he introduced *The Merry Widow* to Broadway. Its enormous success led him virtually to abandon the American musicals which he had so diligently fostered up to this time, and most of his subsequent productions were imports. Unlike London's *Merry Widow* man, George Edwardes, however, he failed to pick the right ones. Whilst other producers snapped up *Die Dollarprinzessin* and *Der tapfere Soldat,* Savage had mixed fortunes with Edward German's *Tom Jones;* with Kálmán's *Tatárjárás* (*The Gay Hussars*); with *The Love Cure,* a piece fabricated from the scores of Eysler's *Johann der Zweite, Das Glücksschweinchen* and *Künstlerblut,* which he announced as a second *Merry Widow* but which, of course, wasn't; and with Henri Berény's *Lord Piccolo* (*Little Boy Blue*), which, at least at the time, went much further towards being another *Widow*—but he notched up a full-sized disaster with the one-week run of Luders and Pixley's last work, *Somewhere Else.*

Europe at last gave him a second significant hit when he presented the little Hungarian soubrette Mitzi Hajós in a version of Kálmán's *Der Zigeunerprimás,* played on Broadway as *Sári* (1914), but thereafter success proved harder to find. Lehár's *Das Fürstenkind* (*The Maids of Athens*), Hugo Felix's remake of Hungary's *Csibészkirály* as *Pom-Pom* (1916) and the homegrown musicals of Jerome Kern (*Have a Heart, Toot-Toot!, Head Over Heels* with Mitzi Hajós) and Louis Hirsch (*See-Saw*), and yet a further vehicle for the tenacious Mitzi called *Lady Billy* (Harold Levey/Zelda Sears) did, at best, adequately and, at worst, very badly, and although he got a six-month run out of a gently feminist piece by Sears and Levey called *The Clinging Vine* (1922), a further show, *The Magic Ring* (again with Mitzi), failed.

His final musical production, on which Miss Sears teamed with Vincent Youmans, was *Lollipop* (1924), a show which allowed the man who had produced so many fine pieces in his early days, and two enormous successes in *The Merry Widow* and *Sári* in his middle years, to go out with at least a respectable run.

SAY, DARLING Comedy about a musical in 2 acts by Richard and Marian Bissell and Abe Burrows. Lyrics by Adolph Green and Betty Comden. Music by Jule Styne. ANTA Theater, New York, 3 April 1958.

A comical backstage musical of some novelty, *Say, Darling* was co-written by Richard Bissell, the author of the novel *7 1/2 Cents* and co-author of the musical libretto *The Pajama Game* which was based on that novel. *Say, Darling* itself was based on a subsequent novel which Bissell had written about the turning of the other/another novel into a hit musical and all the trials and tribulations that went with it. Jule Styne and Lester Osterman produced the piece, which called itself "a comedy about a musical" and eschewed an orchestra, which was instead replaced by two pianos to accompany the songs—many of which represented the score of the fictitious musical of which *Say, Darling* followed the creation. A cast, which was as à clef as you liked it to be, headed by David Wayne, Vivian Blaine, vocalist Johnny Desmond and Robert Morse as Ted Snow (who either was or wasn't *Pajama Game* producer Hal Prince, depending on whether you were a lawyer or a musical-theatre buff), had a lot of fun with a lot of theatrical in-jokes and out-jokes and, with some help from the two pianos, *Say, Darling* played for 10 months and 332 performances on Broadway, followed by a three-week revival at the New York City Center the next season.

Recording: original cast (RCA)

THE SCARLET FEATHER *see* LA PETITE MARIÉE

SCHÄFER, Therese [née BRAUNECKER] (b Vienna, 3 April 1825; d Iglau, 8 March 1888).

One of the most important Viennese prima donnas of the earliest days of the opéra-bouffe and Operette period, Therese Braunecker-Schäfer (later known simply as Frau Schäfer) began her career as a popular vocalist and then as an actress and singer at the German theatres in Pest and Prague. She was a leading member of the Johann Nestroy company at the Carltheater during the period in which Karl Treumann masterminded his first and influential Vienna productions of the works of Offenbach and other French composers and she appeared as Annemarie (ie, Fanchette) in the Carltheater's landmark production of *Hochzeit bei Laternenschein* (1858). She was Marguerite in *Das Mädchen von Elisonzo* (1858), Susette in *Der Ehemann vor der Tür* (1859) and the first German-language Eurydice in *Orpheus in der Unterwelt* (1860) at the Carltheater, before moving with Treumann to his Theater am Franz-Josef-Kai where she played Fé-an-nich-ton in *Tschin-Tschin* (*Ba-ta-clan*), Magellone (ie, Geneviève) in *Die schöne Magellone* (1861, *Geneviève de Brabant*), Madame Fortunio in *Meister Fortunio und sein Liebeslied,* Madame Balandard in *Salon Pitzelberger* (Monsieur Choufleuri), etc.

In the late 1860s she began a second and even more prominent career as a low-to-lowish comedy singer/actress in Operette, appearing at the Carltheater in, at first, a mixture of good comic character and not-too-juvenile soubrette roles, and even some which bordered on being bit parts, in a long list of pieces: *Die schöne Weiber von Georgien* (Zaida), *Tulipatan* (Aloë), *Pariser Leben* (Madame Quimper-Karadec), *Meister Fortunio* (now as Babette) *Kakadu* (Mademoiselle Paturelle), *Die Jungfrau von Dragant* (Gertrude), *Die Prinzessin von Trapezunt* (Paola), *Angot die Tochter der Halle* (the lusty market-woman Amaranthe with her swingeing expository song), *Cassis Pacha, Die schöne Bourbonnaise* (Gervaise), Delibes's *Confusius IX* (Frau von Moppeldorf), Suppé's ill-fated *Die Frau Meisterin* (the nurse, Petronella), *Hundert Jungfrauen* (Kaca), *Schönröschen* (Julienne), *Prinz Conti* (Dorette), etc. She moved smoothly from this series of roles into a major career as Vienna's foremost Operette "komische Alte," playing mostly at the Theater an der Wien as the voluminously bossy Aurore in *Giroflé-Girofla* (1875), the storyteller Wassildschi in *Fatinitza* (1876), Madame de Parabés in *Margot die reiche Bäckerin* (1877), Sphisteira in *Prinz Methusalem* (1877), as man-hungry Peronella in *Boccaccio* (1879), Donna Olympia in Suppé's *Donna Juanita* (1880), the Marquise von Villereal in *Das Spitzentuch der Königin* (1880), Heloise in *Apajune, der Wassermann* (1880), Javotte Bergamotte in *Die Jungfrau von Belleville* (1881), Sister Opportune in *Musketiere in Damenstift* (1881), the battle-chief Countess Artemisia Malaspina in *Der lustige Krieg* (1881), Madame Victor in Millöcker's *Ein süsses Kind* (1882), Hermine von Tricasse in Offenbach's *Doctor Ox,* the grotesque Buccametta of *Die Afrikareise,* the splendidly comico-aristocratic Palmatica, Gräfin Nowalska in *Der Bettelstudent* (1882), Agricola Barbaruccio in Vienna's revised *Eine Nacht in Venedig* (1883), the duenna Zenobia in *Gasparone* (1884), the housekeeper Barbara in *Der Feldprediger* (1884), Mirabella in *Der Zigeunerbaron* (1885) introducing Strauss's happily comical description of feminine fate in wartime, "Just sind es vier und zwanzig Jahre," written particularly for her) and Donna Candida de Quesada y Mendizabal in *Der Viceadmiral* (1886). She also appeared in Brandl's *Die Mormonen* (Mutter Snow), *Zwillinge* (Pomponne Sarazin) and several other less successful pieces, and reprised her role of Paola in *La Princesse de Trébizonde* at the age of 60.

In the course of this decade and more of comic roles she established herself as one of the town's most popular musical players, and, as was seen in the case of *Der Zigeunerbaron,* her presence in the Theater an der Wien company influenced the writing-in of suitably substantial comic dame roles and songs into the new shows of her time. Frau Schäfer was forced by illness to retire from the stage in 1886 after a remarkable career of some 30 years in which she had an important hand in the emergence of Operette in Vienna and, above all, established the low-comedy female role in 19th-century Viennese Operette in the same way that Marie Desclauzas had in France and Priscilla German Reed had in Britain.

SCHANZER, Rudolf (b Vienna, 12 January 1875; d Fiume, 1944). Librettist and lyricist of a number of standard German Operetten.

Vienna-born Schanzer spent his early working years as a journalist and was for a number of years based in Paris where he worked as secretary to a well-off gentleman. When gentleman and secretary moved to Berlin, Schanzer began to contribute to several newspapers and then tried his hand at writing for the theatre. His first full-sized piece was an adaptation of H G Wells's *The Time Machine* entitled *Der Sonnenvogel* on which he collaborated with Georg Okonkowski and composer Holländer. It was toured by Julius Spielmann's Wiener Operetten Ensemble, and subsequently seen at Berlin's Centraltheater, but although this piece was a by no means negligible start, his first real success came with the internationally played *Lord Piccolo* (1910), with whose composer, Henri Berény, Schanzer then went on to write two further Operetten.

Later the same year he successfully collaborated with the Berliner Theater's director Rudolf Bernauer to turn out an adaptation of the classic Posse *Auf eigenen Füssen* as *Bummelstudenten,* and they subsequently teamed with considerable success on other pieces for Bernauer's theatre—the burlesque *Die Grosse Rosinen* and the musical comedy *Filmzauber*—before Schanzer became officially installed as dramaturg and stage director at the Berliner. Beginning with the highly successful *Wie einst im Mai,* Bernauer, Schanzer and principal composer Walter Kollo thereafter turned out a five-year series of musical plays which entertained wartime Berlin and, occasionally, other countries staunchly.

In 1918 Schanzer teamed up with another Berliner Theater man, Ernst Welisch, and the two quickly established themselves as Berlin's most successful librettists, turning out texts for Jean Gilbert (*Die Frau im Hermelin*), Leo Fall (*Madame Pompadour*), Oscar Straus (*Riquette, Die Teresina*) and Ralph Benatzky (*Casanova, Die drei Musketiere*) with considerable national and international success. In the early 1930s this pair moved on, along with most of the rest of Jewish and/or operettic Germany, and in the years that followed they wrote for Vienna and Switzerland rather than Berlin, but Schanzer did not flee Hitler sufficiently fast or far. He ended his own days when he committed suicide in the face of the Gestapo.

1900 **Der schwarze Mann** (Oscar Straus/Gustav von Moser, Thilo von Trotha ad) 1 act Colberg; Secession-Buhne, Berlin 28 December 1901

1903 **Atelier Edgar** (Robert Leonhard) 1 act Kurtheater, Bad Liebenstein 4 August

1903 **Der Sonnenvogel** (aka *Der Phönix*) (Viktor Holländer/w Georg Okonkowski) St Petersburg (Wiener Operetten Ensemble) 22 August; Centraltheater, Berlin April 1904

1908 **Der Sterndeuter** (Leonhard) Neues Operetten-Theater, Leipzig 16 May

1910 **Lord Piccolo** (Henri Berény/w Carl Lindau) Johann Strauss-Theater, Vienna 1 September

1910 **Bummelstudenten** (Bogumil Zepler, Willi Bredschneider/Emil Pohl, Heinrich Wilken ad w Rudolf Bernauer) Berliner Theater 31 December

1911 **Sein Herzensjunge** (Walter Kollo/w August Neidhart) Thalia-Theater, Elberfeld 1 April

1911 **Das Mädel von Montmartre** (Berény) Neues Theater 26 October

1911 **Der verbotene Kuss** (*Tilos a csók*) German version w I Pasztae (Centraltheater, Dresden)

1911 **Die grosse Rosinen** (*Berlin hat's eilig*) (Leon Jessel, Zepler, Bredschneider, et al/w Bernauer) Berliner Theater 31 December

1912 **Filmzauber** (Kollo, Bredschneider/w Bernauer) Berliner Theater 19 October

1912 **Eine kitzliche Geschichte** (Hugo Hirsch/w Erich Urban) Lustspielhaus, Düsseldorf 31 October

1913 **Mein Mäderl** (Berény/w Eugen Burg, Lindau) Raimundtheater, Vienna 21 January

1913 **Die beiden Husaren** (Jessel/w Wilhelm Jacoby) Theater des Westens 6 February

1913 **Wie einst im Mai** (Kollo, Bredschneider/w Bernauer) Berliner Theater 4 October

1914 **Tanzfieber** (*Tangofieber*) (Hirsch/w Max Heye, Theo Halton/Urban) Walhalla-Theater 15 January

1914 **Extrablätter** (Kollo, Bredschneider/w Heinz Gordon) Berliner Theater 24 October

1915 **Wenn zwei Hochzeit machen** (Kollo, Bredschneider/w Bernauer) Berliner Theater 23 October

1916 **Auf Flügeln des Gesanges** (Kollo, Bredschneider/w Bernauer) Berliner Theater 9 September

1917 **Die tolle Komtess** (Kollo/w Bernauer) Berliner Theater 21 February

1918 **Blitzblaues Blut** (Kollo/w Bernauer) Berliner Theater 9 February

1918 **Sterne, die wieder leuchten** (Kollo/w Bernauer) Berliner Theater 6 November

1919 **Die Frau im Hermelin** (Gilbert/w Ernst Welisch) Theater des Westens 23 August

1919 **Bummelstudenten** revised version (Zepler, Bredschneider/w Bernauer) Berliner Theater 2 October

1920 **Der Geiger von Lugano** (Jean Gilbert/w Welisch) Wallner Theater 25 September

1920 **Die spanische Nachtigall** (Leo Fall/w Welisch) Berliner Theater 18 November

1921 **Die Braut des Lucullus** (Gilbert/w Welisch) Theater des Westens 26 August

1921 **Prinzessin Olala** (Gilbert/w Bernauer) Berliner Theater 17 September

1922 **Madame Pompadour** (Fall/w Welisch) Berliner Theater 9 September

1923 **Die Damen von Olymp** (Rudolf Nelson/w Welisch) Nelson-Theater May

1923 **Der süsse Kavalier** (Fall/w Welisch) Apollotheater, Vienna 11 December

1925 **Riquette** (Oscar Straus/w Welisch) Deutsches Künstlertheater 17 January

1925 **[Die] Teresina** (Oscar Straus/w Welisch) Deutsches Künstlertheater 11 September

1925 **Das Spiel um die Liebe** (Gilbert/w Welisch) Theater des Westens 19 December

1926 **Jugend im Mai** (Fall/w Welisch) Zentraltheater, Dresden 22 October; Städtische Oper, Berlin, 1927

1927 **Eine Frau von Format** (Michael Krasznay-Krausz/w Welisch) Theater des Westens 21 September

1928 **Casanova** (Johann Strauss arr Benatzky/w Welisch) Grosses Schauspielhaus 1 September

1929 **Die drei Musketiere** (Benatzky/w Welisch) Grosses Schauspielhaus, Berlin 28 September

1929 **Die erste Beste** (Straus/w Welisch) Deutsches Theater, Prague 19 October

1930 **Das Mädel am Steuer** (Gilbert/w Welisch) Komische Oper 17 September

1932 **Der Teufelsreiter** (Emmerich Kálmán/w Welisch) Theater an der Wien, Vienna 10 March

1932 **Der Studentenprinz** (*The Student Prince*) German version w Welisch (Grosses Schauspielhaus)

1933 **Die Lindenwirtin** (Krasznay-Krausz/w Welisch) Metropoltheater 30 March

1935 **Maya** German version w Welisch (Theater an der Wien, Vienna)

1936 **Dreimal Georges** (Paul Burkhard/w Welisch) Stadttheater, Zürich 3 October

SCHEFF, Fritzi [JÄGER, Anna Friederike] (b Vienna, 30 August ?1879; d New York, 8 April 1954). Ex-opera soprano who became a Broadway leading lass.

The daughter of an opera singer, Hortense Scheff, the young Fritzi was trained as a vocalist in Dresden and

Frankfurt and made her operatic debut at 19 as Flotow's Martha, as Juliette in Gounod's *Roméo et Juliette* and as *La Fille du régiment* in Munich. She remained in Munich, appearing in a variety of operatic roles (Marguerite, Santuzza, Mimi, Mignon) until 1901, before going to America on contract to Maurice Grau for the Metropolitan Opera House. There she took the lighter soprano roles of the operatic repertoire (Marzelline, Musetta, Zerlina, Cherubino, Nedda, Papagena, and alongside Sembrich and Bispham in Paderewski's new *Manru,* 1902) over a period of some two years, before abandoning opera to make her first appearance on the light musical stage, under the management of Charles Dillingham, in the title role of the little letter-writer who becomes a prima donna in Victor Herbert's *Babette* (1903).

Miss Scheff subsequently created the part of Rose Decourcelles in *Two Roses* (1904, a musical version of *She Stoops to Conquer*) and appeared at the Broadway Theater, New York, during 1905 in the starring roles of a series of classic Continental Operetten—*Fatinitza, Giroflé-Girofla* and *Boccaccio*—but she had her most significant success when she introduced the role of the tiny, sparkling hat-shop demoiselle, Fifi, in Herbert's *Mlle Modiste* (1906, ''Kiss Me Again''), a vehicle which served her for several seasons on the road. She had less success when cast in another Herbert piece whose title insisted fatally (it has always been unlucky) that she was *The Prima Donna* (1908, Mdlle Athénée).

She appeared as a suitably tiny Yum-Yum to Sam Bernard's Ko-Ko and the Pitti Sing of Lulu Glaser/ Christie MacDonald in the Casino Theater's starry 1910 revival of *The Mikado,* but her fourth Victor Herbert vehicle, *The Duchess* (1911, Rose Boutonnière), was a quick Broadway failure. It was also her last Herbert vehicle, as the lady's notoriously difficult temperament got the better of the composer in the same way as that of his other operatic star, Emma Trentini, had done and he wrote for her no more.

In 1912 she appeared on tour in *The Night Birds* (*Die Fledermaus*) and in *The Love Wager,* a piece adapted from an Hungarian play and featuring its star as the fourth of its titular *Seven Sisters*—inevitably called Mitzi—to a score by her protégé Charles J Hambitzer, which did not make it to Broadway and, indeed, sent its self-producing star bankrupt. *The Pretty Mrs Smith* (1914, Drucilla Smith) did make it to Broadway, even though the nominal star had to battle for her laurels with the up-and-coming Charlotte Greenwood's comical dancing. But that dancing helped *The Pretty Mrs Smith* to a tidy success. Several years of vaudeville, (silent!) film work (*The Pretty Mrs Smith*) and an out-of-town closure in the musical *Husbands Guaranteed* (1916) intervened before Miss Scheff returned to success in the musical theatre, touring for John Cort in the role created by Eleanor Painter in *Glorianna* (1919, ''Miss Scheff is wearing auburn hair this season''). Thereafter, however, things went less well. She disappeared from the casts of *The O'Brien Girl* and *Bye Bye Bonnie* before those shows made Broadway; she was announced to lead the Broadway cast of *No, No, Nanette* following the sacking of Blanche Ring, but didn't; and in the end she was not seen in New York again in a singing role until she repeated her one genuine Broadway hit, *Mlle Modiste,* in a 1929 revival, at the age of 50.

Miss Scheff continued to perform, however, appearing in musicals in regional theatres (Frieda in *Music in the Air,* etc), latterly often in supporting roles, for a number of years thereafter. In 1946 she was seen at the Diamond Horseshoe in cabaret, and as late as 1948 was still to be seen occasionally on the stage, a half century after her debut.

DER SCHELM VON BERGEN Operette in 3 acts by Carl Loewe and Carl Lindau. Music by Alfred Oelschlegel. Theater an der Wien, Vienna, 29 September 1888.

Heinrich Heine's narrative poem *Der Schelm von Bergen* is better known for the Operetten it didn't become than for that which it did. At the suggestion of Johann Strauss, Ignaz Schnitzer, the author of *Der Zigeunerbaron,* wrote him a libretto based on this tale of the rogue of Bergen, which was intended to allow the composer, who had jealously noticed the recent success of Nessler's *Der Trompeter von Säkkingen,* to sneak a little further away from the Operettic genre with what he now regarded as its insufficient singers, and a little closer to the romantic opera which he was anxious to write. However, having prematurely accepted the libretto and, indeed, written music for much of one act, Strauss finally reneged on the excuse that the central character of the tale bore too close a resemblance to Ko-Ko, the comic executioner of Gilbert's *The Mikado* which had recently premiered in Austria. Strauss went to work instead on Victor Léon's *Simplicius,* taking over some of the *Schelm von Bergen* music for use in that piece, and Schnitzer subsequently handed his orphaned libretto to the young and unproduced Edmund Eysler. Eysler composed a full score, *Der Hexenspiegel,* to it, which won the interest of publisher Josef Weinberger but was never staged, and Eysler, like Strauss, then cannibalized his score for his hugely successful *Bruder Straubinger* whilst Schnitzer's text once again went back on the shelf.

Although Schnitzer's adaptation was never produced, Heine's Bergen-scamp did make it to the stage. The Theater an der Wien clearly did not share Strauss's worries about *The Mikado,* and they produced an operettic version of *Der Schelm von Bergen* composed by Alfred Oelschlegel in 1888, the same year in which they played a significant series of performances of . . . *The Mikado.* It was played 17 times. Subsequently, another *Schelm von Bergen* by A Camillo Grans and Gustav Niehr was produced at Dessau (13 March 1900) and Ignaz M Welleminsky and Oskar Ritter wrote an operatic libretto on the same tale, set by Kurt Atterberg, and produced at Stockholm under the title *Fanal* (27 January 1934).

Author Heine also eventually got his operettic ''due'' when his fictionalized life was decorated with a pasticcio score taken from the works of Mendelssohn and put on the musical stage under the title *Dichterliebe* (arr Ernst Stern/Julius Brammer, Alfred Grünwald). In Vienna, Heine was impersonated by Hubert Marischka, owner and director of the Theater an der Wien.

SCHMIDSEDER, Ludwig (b Passau, 24 August 1904; d Munich, 21 June 1971). Composer for the wartime German and postwar Austrian theatre.

After a youth spent playing as a pianist in a trio, first in South America and then around the world, Schmidseder returned in 1930 to his native Germany and worked as a bar pianist whilst beginning a career as a songwriter. He turned out a series of popular songs which soon led the way into both the theatre and the film worlds. He wrote three Operetten for the Berlin Metropoltheater of which *Die, oder keine* proved the most successful, and after the war combined with Hubert Marischka on a biomusical of Marie Geistinger, produced in Vienna under the title *Die Walzerkönigin,* and a romantic period piece called *Abschiedswalzer,* again set in the Viennese good old days, both of which, with their librettist starring, had good runs. *Die Walzerkönigin,* with its Viennese star Elfie Meyerhofer repeating, was played in Paris in 1949 (*La Reine des valses* Théâtre des Champs Élysées) and subsequently in the French provinces.

1937 **Die verliebte Frau, Viola** (Günther Schwenn/Paul Beyer) Neues Operetten-Theater, Leipzig 22 January
1938 **Melodie der Nacht** (Schwenn/Heinz Hentschke) Metropoltheater 21 September
1939 **Die, oder keine** (Schwenn, Hentschke) Metropoltheater 20 September
1940 **Frauen im Metropol** (Hentschke) Metropoltheater 27 September
1942 **Heimkehr nach Mittenwald** (Günther Resee) Landestheater, Linz 26 August
1943 **Vorsicht Diana** (Resee) Fürth 19 March
1944 **Linzer Torte** (Ignaz Brantner, Aldo Pinelli/Hans Gustl Kernmayer) Landestheater, Linz
1948 **Die Walzerkönigin** (Hubert Marischka, Pinelli) Bürgertheater 11 October
1949 **Abschiedswalzer** (Marischka, Rudolf Österreicher) Bürgertheater 8 September
1952 **Mädel aus der Wachau** (Jorg Bartner, Pinelli) Landestheater, Linz 26 April

Other titles attributed: *Glück in Monte Carlo* (Salzburg, 1947), *Arm wie eine Kirchenmaus* (1947)

SCHMIDT, Harvey [Lester] (b Dallas, Tex, 12 September 1929).

Schmidt made up a team with songwriting partner Tom Jones during university days and the pair made their earliest stage ventures in college shows. He then began a career as a commercial artist in New York whilst simultaneously carrying on his writing efforts, and the pair placed songs in such revues as Julius Monk's *Demi-Dozen* and *Pieces of Eight, The Portfolio Revue* and *Shoestring '57* before their first stage musical *The Fantasticks* (''Try to Remember'') was brought to the stage. The immense success of this little piece won Schmidt and Jones the opportunity to work on a very much larger show, the adaptation of the play *The Rainmaker* into the musical *110 in the Shade,* but, although the piece had a certain success, they intelligently returned to what they recognized they did best and produced another intimate piece, the two-handed musical adaptation of Jan de Hartog's The Fourposter as *I Do! I Do!* The result was another long-running hit, not in a tiny house like that which housed *The Fantasticks,* but on a regular Broadway-sized plateau. Thereafter, however, success deserted the pair and several attempts at a biomusical on the French writer and music-hall artist *Colette,* a small-scale allegoric piece with multiple echoes of *The Fantasticks* and many more of its 1960s era entitled *Celebration,* a classical burlesque, *Philemon,* and a musical version of Thornton Wilder's *Our Town* failed to confirm the popularity established by their first three shows.

1960 **The Fantasticks** (Tom Jones) Sullivan Street Playhouse 3 May
1963 **110 in the Shade** (Jones, N Richard Nash) Broadhurst Theater 24 October
1966 **I Do! I Do!** (Jones) 46th Street Theater 5 December
1969 **Celebration** (Jones) Ambassador Theater 22 January
1970 **Colette** (Jones/Elinor Jones) Ellen Stewart Theater 6 May
1975 **The Bone Room** (Jones) Portfolio Studio 28 February
1975 **Philemon** (Jones) Portfolio Studio 8 April
1982 **Colette** revised version 5th Avenue Theater, Seattle 9 February
1983 **Colette Collage** revised version of *Colette* York Players 31 March
1987 **Grover's Corners** (Jones) Marriott Lincolnshire Theater, Chicago 29 July
1996 **Mirette** (Jones/Elizabeth Diggs) Goodspeed Opera House, Chester 1 August

SCHNEIDER, Hortense [Catherine] (b Bordeaux, 30 April 1833; d Paris, 5 May 1920). The six-year shooting star of Offenbach's Théâtre des Variétés series whose dazzling career declined at the same time as that of the French Empire of which she was such a visible feature.

Hortense Schneider made her first theatrical appearance in her native Bordeaux in the play *Michel et Christine* at the age of 15, and then moved on to play in Agen where she appeared in everything from farce to opera, as ingenue or pageboy or ''amoureuse.'' She was out of her teens by the time she got to Paris, where she soon got to know the comedian Berthelier and, with his help, auditioned for Hippolyte Cogniard (unsuccessfully) and for Offenbach, with whom Berthelier had scored a great hit a few weeks earlier in *Les Deux Aveugles.* Offenbach, at that stage still running his first little summer Bouffes-Parisiens house, was obviously more impressed by the pretty little actress than Cogniard had been, and she was given the female role, opposite her useful boyfriend, in the next Offenbach one-acter, *Le Violoneux* (31 August 1855). Offenbach's regular soprano, Marie Dalmont, created *Ba-ta-clan* later in the year, but the new little starlet, fresh from her personal success in the distinctly successful little rustic opérette, moved with Offenbach's company to the new house in the Passage Choiseul and there created the more lively part of the actress of *Tromb-al-cazar* (1856, Simplette), appeared in Adam's *Les Pantins de Violette* (reportedly to the delight of the composer), and triumphed in the delightful little three-cornered battle of *La Rose de Saint-Flour* (1856, Pierrette).

Cogniard now changed his mind about the young actress who was winning such delighted reviews for her charming performances and he whisked Hortense off to his Théâtre des Variétés where she opened a few weeks later in *Le Chien de garde.* From the Variétés she moved on to the Palais-Royal and over the next years, through a long series of the vaudevilles à couplets and other varied entertainments which made up the programs of that house (*Le Violoneux, La Poularde de Caux,* Hervé's *Les Toréadors de Grenade* etc), her reputation, both on and off the stage, grew apace.

It was nearly a decade since her first appearance in Paris in *Le Violoneux* when Schneider, now something of a star, returned to Offenbach to create the title role of *La Belle Hélène* at the Variétés (1864). The success of the piece, and of Hortense Schneider in the piece, were only equaled by those of its successors as the star followed up her burlesque Helen of Troy with the rough-and-tough but infinitely sexy last wife of *Barbe-bleue* (1866, Boulotte), the pubescent teenaged *Grande-Duchesse de Gérolstein* (1867) with her famous Sabre Song and her insinuating ''Dites-lui,'' and (in spite of difficult beginnings) the street-singer heroine of *La Périchole* (1868, Letter song). This series filled the Variétés for the best part of four seasons and during the off-season Hortense, at the height of her enormous fame, took her vehicles and ''her'' company to other venues, notably across the channel to London, Dublin, Glasgow and other British centers, where she appeared in her Variétés shows through several summers with great popularity and vast profit to her bank account. It was said that Raphaël Félix paid her £7,000 for 96 performances in Britain in 1869.

Plate 345. **Hortense Schneider.** *The grande-duchesse of Parisian opéra-bouffe.*

Always difficult, perpetually walking out and usually returning, and avid over-salary even though her royal and rich off-stage admirers made such cares unneccesary, Schneider became only more so as she became more successful. She was persuaded to appear as little more than her famous self in Offenbach's *La Diva* (1869), but the piece turned out a failure and even her popularity could not save it. She turned down the role written for her in *Les Brigands* and left the Variétés, having created her last Offenbach role. Several years later, after the Franco-Prussian War and after another truncated run—at a whopping 300 francs a night—last-minute replacing Augustine Déveria in Hervé's *La Veuve du Malabar* (1873, Tata-Lili), she agreed to return to the Variétés to appear in an enlargened version of her old role in *La Périchole* and again to play Margot, the titular baker's wife in *La Bou-*

langère a des écu—the newest piece written by the authors of her greatest successes. Before the first night of this delicious new vehicle, however, she had again walked out (or been dropped, depending which version you believe). Instead, she played Hervé's *La Belle Poule* (1875, Poulette) with only mediocre results and found herself on the end of several tart comments about playing her age.

Schneider had no intention of playing her age. She had been the reigning queen of the Paris stage for a good half-dozen years, and she had no intention of now being its queen mother. She had seriously threatened, more even than just threatened, to quit the theatre before and she had no compunction about doing so now. With *La Belle Poule* the curtain came down on one of the most dazzling—if not extended—careers of the musical stage, and for the 45 years of life remaining to her, Hortense Schneider lived a life of respectability at utter odds with the gay and gallivanting years of her theatrical heyday when she had been known, not with a little admiration, as ''le passage des Princes.''

A character bearing little resemblance to Schneider but given her name and even a love affair with Offenbach was portrayed on the screen by Yvonne Printemps in the film *Valse de Paris.* A different romance for the composer—apparently with Empress Eugénie!—was proposed by the Hungarian author of the composer's biomusical *Offenbach* (1920), but both real-life wife Herminie and Hortense appeared in the piece, the diva originally played by Juci Lábass. In the Vienna production she was portrayed by Olga Bartos-Trau, on Broadway by Odette Myrtil.

Biographies: Rouff, M, Casevitz, T: *Hortense Schneider* (Tallandier, Paris, 1930), Bonami, J-P: *Hortense Schneider, la Grande-Duchesse du Second Empire* (Hérault, Paris, 1995)

SCHNITZER, Ignaz [Manuel] (b Pest, 20 December 1839; d Vienna, 18 June 1921). Author of one major Viennese hit in each century of his activity.

A Budapest journalist who, after a late beginning, made a theatrical career in Vienna, Schnitzer was given his earliest exposure on the operatic stage when his text to Bachrich's *Muzzedin* was heard at the Vienna Opera in 1883. He had, however, already cast his eyes in the direction of the lighter musical theatre and, in 1882, had sent an Operette synopsis to Johann Strauss. This had led to a collaboration on a piece about *Salvator Rosa* (already in 1874 the subject of a fine opera by Gomez) being announced. *Salvator Rosa* never appeared, but it was in collaboration with Strauss that, three years later, Schnitzer wrote his first Operette to make it before the Viennese footlights: the musical stage adaptation of fellow Hungarian Mór Jókai's novel *Sáffi* as *Der Zigeunerbaron* (1885). Schnitzer later prepared a second libretto for Strauss, based on Heinrich Heine's *Der Schelm von Bergen,* but part way through setting it Strauss abandoned the work.

In 1885 Schnitzer adapted Jókai's play *Az aranyember* for the Theater an der Wien as *Der Goldmensch* and in 1889 he had another operatic piece, *Der Königsbraut* (mus: Fuchs) produced, as well as a second Operette, a piece of classical antiquity called *Das Orakel,* based on the work of another famous Hungarian author, Gergely Csiky, and set to music by Hellmesberger. Produced at the Theater an der Wien it lasted only 13 performances, but nevertheless won a production in America under the title *Apollo.* He turned Csiky's famous *Nagymama* into *Die Grossmama* for the German-language stage in its without-music version, but yet another Hungarian-based Schnitzer libretto, taken from Csepreghi's equally celebrated play *A piros bugyelláris,* was set to music by Hugo Felix. *Husarenblut* was played just 20 times.

A second attempt to get his *Schelm von Bergen* script produced, this time with a score by the young Edmund Eysler (*Der Hexenspiegel*), also failed, but the connection with Eysler proved highly fruitful, for a further collaboration between the two on *Bruder Straubinger* not only made the stage at the Theater an der Wien but also turned out to be a major hit. The pair, and Schnitzer's new writing partner Sigmund Schlesinger, subsequently provided a second fine vehicle for *Bruder Straubinger* star Alexander Girardi as the olde Viennese hairdresser *Pufferl,* but the piece's promising run was decapitated by the star's departure from the theatre.

Three subsequent Operetten, all written with Schlesinger, found less success. The conventional Neapolitan-signorina-meets-Indian-sorcerer piece *Zur Indischen Witwe,* set musically by Oscar Straus, struck no sparks in Berlin, a piece called *Der Elektriker,* with Ferdinand Pagin in the title role, played just eight performances at the Carltheater, and *Tip-Top,* a musical based on the stories of Bret Harte and with a cast including Louis Treumann and Luise Kartousch, foundered in 25 nights at the Theater an der Wien. A collaboration with Emmerich von Gatti on the text for *Kreolenblut* was a little more profitable, for Heinrich Berté's Operette went on from its Hamburg premiere to be seen, albeit not for long, on Broadway and also in the French provinces.

1884 **Raffaela** (Max Wolf/Eugène Scribe ad w Adolf Schirmer) Theater am Gärtnerplatz, Munich March

1885 **Der Zigeunerbaron** (Johann Strauss) Theater an der Wien 24 October

1889 **Das Orakel** (Hellemsberger) Theater an der Wien 30 November

1891 **Hand in Hand** (Franz Roth/w Friedrich Gustav Triesch) Deutsches Volkstheater 7 April

1894 **Husarenblut** (Hugo Felix) Theater an der Wien 10 March

1903 **Bruder Straubinger** (Edmund Eysler/w Moritz West) Theater an der Wien 20 February

1905 **Pufferl** (Eysler/w Sigmund Schlesinger) Theater an der Wien 10 February

1905 **Zur Indischen Witwe** (Oscar Straus/w Schlesinger) Centraltheater, Berlin 30 September

1906 **Der Elektriker** (Karl-Josef Fromm/w Schlesinger) Carltheater 23 February

1907 **Tip-Top** (Josef Stritzko/w Schlesinger) Theater an der Wien 5 October

1910 **Kreolenblut** (Heinrich Berté/w Emmerich von Gatti) Neues Operetten-Theater, Hamburg 25 December

1914 **Anno 1814** (Paul Eisler/w Hugo H Regel) Festspieltheater im Kaisergarten 1 May

SCHÖNBERG, Claude-Michel (b Vannes, 6 July 1944). Composer of the operettic version of *Les Misérables.*

A popular music producer at Pathé-Marconi for a number of years, Schönberg had his first contact with the musical theatre when he composed the score for *La Révolution française,* a ''rock-opera''–style musical pageant of the events surrounding that well-publicized event, which was issued as a double-disc recording. The piece subsequently followed the *Jesus Christ Superstar* path by transferring from disc to a stage production at Paris's Palais des Sports in 1973, with Schönberg himself appearing as Louis XVI.

Two years later, Schönberg issued his own first recording as a performer, and he went on to find considerable succes purveying his own material to the hit parades of France. A second alliance with *Révolution française* writer Alain Boublil and with the poet Jean-Marc Natel then resulted in the production of a second recorded musical, *Les Misérables.* This piece, too, found its way to the Paris stage in a spectacular Robert Hossein production. However, it then went further. It was taken up by British producer Cameron Mackintosh and, after considerable rewriting by both adapter and composer, it was produced first in London and then around the world, going on to become one of the most oustandingly successful musical plays of the second half of the 20th century.

In 1989 Schönberg composed a second, this time made-to-order, musical for Mackintosh and the West End and Broadway stages, to a libretto resituating the *Madame Butterfly* story in the Vietnam War. Although it lacked disappointingly the vigorously exciting musical score which had been such a solid part of the success of his first two works, *Miss Saigon,* given an opérette-à-grand-spectacle mounting, profited from the backing of the most successful production organization in the world to win itself extended runs in Britain and America, and a series of further productions in Japan, Germany, Australia and elsewhere.

A second attempt at a made-for-Britain musical play with the 1996 *Martin Guerre* found the composer well and truly back in the exciting musical form of *Les Misérables,* but his sizzling and soaring score was handicapped by libretto and production problems and, in spite of heroic efforts by its producer, the show failed to find its feet at the West End's Prince Edward Theatre. A revised edition subsequently mounted at Leeds's West Yorkshire Playhouse was better liked, but the afterlife that it had seemed *Martin Guerre* might have won seemed compromised when its American production ground to a halt in Los Angeles in early 2000.

A theatre musician in the mode established by the musicals of Andrew Lloyd Webber, blending popular music strains with solid operettic and classic values in the composition of sung-through scores, Schönberg proved in his first two record-to-stage works that he had abilities second to none amongst modern writers for the musical theatre, treating dramatic, romantic and comic situations with equal effectiveness, and his most recent piece proved excitingly that 25 years after the first attempt, there was still much powder in his horn.

1973 **La Révolution française** (w Raymond Jeannot/Jean-Max Riviére, Alain Boublil) Palais des Sports

1980 **Les Misérables** (Boublil, Jean-Marc Natel) Palais des Sports 17 September

1985 **Les Misérables** revised English version ad Herbert Kretzmer, Barbican Theatre, London 8 October

1989 **Miss Saigon** (Boublil, Richard Maltby jr) Theatre Royal, Drury Lane, London 20 September

1996 **Martin Guerre** (Edward Hardy, Stephen Clark/Boublil) Prince Edward Theatre, London 10 July

1998 **Martin Guerre** revised version West Yorkshire Playhouse, Leeds 8 December

DIE SCHÖNE GALATHEE Comic mythological opera in 1 act by ''Poly Henrion.'' Music by Franz von Suppé. Meysels Theater, Berlin, 30 June 1865.

The most enduringly successful of the early short Operetten written, under the influence of the French opéra-bouffe, for the Viennese stage.

One of the moving forces behind the making of the *Die schöne Galathee* was the actor and producer Karl Treumann, who had not only been largely reponsible for bringing the works of Offenbach to the German-speaking public, but also for encouraging the composer, Franz von Suppé, whose *Zehn Mädchen und kein Mann* and *Flotte Bursche* he had produced during his management of the Theater am Franz-Josefs-Kai, to write this kind of piece for the theatre. The other was the favorite actress Anna Grobecker who had been a huge success in the earlier Suppé pieces, and for whom a fine and typical ''boy'' part was prepared in the new work.

The text, by ''Poly Henrion,'' otherwise actor and author Leopold Karl Dietmar Kohl von Kohlnegg (b 13

Plate 346. **Die schöne Galathee.** *A very schöne Galathee hits the bottle in the Wiener Kammeroper's production of 1990.*

December 1814; d Salfeld, Thuringia, 1 May 1876), was very closely modeled on that written by Jules Barbier and Michel Carré for Victor Massé's successful French opéra-comique *Galathée.* It had the same four characters and a chorus, and it not only followed the same plot but even copied situations, scenes and song ideas. The Cypriot sculptor Pygmalion (Telek) has made a statue of a lovely woman, Galatea (Amalie Kraft), which bewitches the art critic Midas (Treumann) by its beauty and prompts the longing sculptor to pray to the gods to bring her to life. When they do, however, Galatea proves to be a liability. She over-indulges in food and wine, prefers the attentions of the studio-boy Ganymede (Anna Grobecker) to those of the passionate Pygmalion and the rich Midas, and finally Pygmalion has to beg Venus to turn her safely back to stone.

Suppé's score was a delightfully lighthearted one, from its set-piece overture with its broad waltz theme, through Midas's comic relating of his pedigree (''Meinem Vater Gordios''), Ganymede's ancient Greek topical song (''Wir sind Griechen''), Galatea's tipsy aria (''Hell im Glas'') and her kissing duet with the boy (''Ach, mich zieht's zu dir'').

The piece got its first showing not in Vienna, but in Berlin, on the occasion of Grobecker's Benefit during her summer season at Woltersdorff's little Meysels Theater, sharing a spectacle coupé program with Zaytz's *Fitzliputzli* and the comedy *Ein Gläschen Tokayer.* Two months later, the star and her producer mounted the show back at home base. It won a fine success, remained more than a decade in the Carltheater repertoire, and was later played at many other Viennese theatres, entering the Theater an der Wien in 1872 and the Volksoper in 1909, whilst spreading itself thoroughly through German-speaking houses abroad, including those in Hungary and in America, where Theodore and Hedwig L'Arronge, Friedrich Herrmann and Laura Haffner first introduced the piece in 1867. An Hungarian version (ad Endre Latabár) quickly followed the first German performances in Budapest and it won repeated productions, but it was not until 1872, following a performance of the show by a visiting German company in London, that an English-language version was produced. John Hollingshead staged an anonymous adaptation at the Gaiety Theatre with Constance Loseby (Galatea), Nellie Farren (Ganymede), Frank Wood (Pygmalion) and Fred Sullivan (Midas) in the principal roles. The minstrel team of Kelly and Leon brought an English-language *schöne Galathee* to Broadway in 1876. Female impersonator Leon played Galatea (apparently with the rangy music quasi-complete), whilst Kelly played Midas, his son Edwin Lester was Ganymede and the minstrel midget known as ''Japanese Tommy'' made an appearance as Bacchus, in what seems to have been a slightly original (not to mention black-faced) version. In spite of the announcement of a Philadelphia production in English (ad Julius Frankel) in 1879, it seems that America waited another decade before getting a rather more straightforwardly cast version, when Tony Pastor mounted an English version at his music hall with Pauline Hall (Ganymede) and Pauline Canissa (Galatea) featured, on a double bill with *Trial by Jury.* Koster & Bial followed in 1889 with a *Lovely Galatea* with house burlesque queen Jennie Joyce in the title role. In the meanwhile Kelly and Leon had treated Australia to its first Galatea.

Unsurprisingly, the piece did not venture to France, where Massé's work was still popular, but in spite of the virtual disappearance of the short Operette from the musical stage, it has remained a perennial in Austrian and German houses where, mostly in altered and expanded versions made to turn it into a full-length entertainment, it is regularly produced to the present day.

The Pygmalion and Galatea story was, in the wake of Massé's and Suppé's shows, used as material for a number of other musicals: notably, the burlesques *Pygmalion, or The Statue* (pasticcio, Strand Theatre 22 April 1867) and William Brough's *Galatea, or Pygmalion Re-Versed* (H Pottinger Stephens, Gaiety Theatre 26 December 1883) and such pieces as the Bostonians *Pygmalion and Galatea*—based on W S Gilbert's play, with music ''adapted from the French of Ambroise Thomas'' by Oscar Weil (Academy of Music, Buffalo 24 November 1888)—*Adonis, One Touch of Venus* and, at one step removed, *My Fair Lady.*

Versions of *Die schöne Galathee* have been several times telecast in Germany and Austria, notably in a 1967 version from the Salzburg Festival and another from the Vienna Kammeroper.

Austria: Carltheater 9 September 1865; Hungary: Budai Színkör *Die schöne Galathea* 15 July 1867, Budai Népszínház *A szép Galathea* 24 August 1867; USA: Stadttheater (Ger) 6 September 1867, Kelly and Leon's Opera House *Galatea, or The Black Statue* 10 May 1870, Tony Pastor's Music Hall *The Beautiful Galatea* 14 September 1882; UK: Opera Comique (Ger) 6 November 1871, Gaiety Theatre *Ganymede and Galatea* 20 January 1872; Australia: Queen's Theatre, Sydney *Galatea* 2 March 1878

Recordings: RCA, Saga

SCHÖNERER, Alexandrine von (b Vienna, 5 June 1850; d Vienna, November 1919).

From 1 September 1884 to 30 April 1900, Frau von Schönerer was the owner and, either in partnership or alone, the manager of the Theater an der Wien, at that stage one of the two most important and productive of Vienna's musical houses. In 1884 she joined Camillo Walzel, Franz Jauner (director of the Carltheater) and, briefly, the actor Girardi, as a 23 percent part of a consortium to run the theatre which had for the previous decade been operated by Maximilian Steiner and his son Franz. When Walzel, who had been the active artistic director, also withdrew in 1889, she continued as ''Eigenthümerin und Direktorin'' in partnership with Jauner (to 1895) and then, for the last five years of her management, alone.

Amongst her musical productions during the decade in which she actively ran the theatre were Dellinger's *Capitän Fracassa* and Hellmesberger's *Das Orakel* (1889); two considerable successes in *Der arme Jonathan* and *Mam'zelle Nitouche* as well as *Die Gondoliere* in 1890; the triumphant *Der Vogelhändler, La Cosaque* and *Miss Helyett* in 1891; Millöcker's *Das Sonntagskind,* the long-running musical Posse *Heisses Blut, La Fille de Fanchon la vielleuse, Der Millionen-Onkel* and Czibulka's *Der Bajazzo* (1892); Strauss's *Fürstin Ninetta* and the Posse *Ein armes Mädel* (1893); *Der Obersteiger, Jabuka* and *Der Probekuss* (1894); Dellinger's *Die Chansonette, Die Karlsschülerin* and *Waldmeister* (1895); von Taund's *Der Wunderknabe, Nordlicht,* Weinberger's *Der Schmetterling* and Verő's Hungarian operett *Der Löwenjäger* in a poor 1896; and Strauss's *Die Göttin der Vernunft* and Weinberger's *Die Blumen-Mary* in an even less profitable 1897, redeemed by the 1898 production of Heuberger's *Der Opernball.* In 1899 she mounted another Heuberger work, *Ihre Excellenz,* without equivalent success, and won fair runs with the British pieces *Ein durchgeganges Mädel* (*A Runaway Girl*) and *Der griechische Sklave* (*A Greek Slave*) and the French *Die Puppe* (*La Poupée*), as well as lesser ones with the homemade *Fräulein Präsident* and *Die Strohwitwe.* Her final two productions—another Heuberger piece, *Der Sechs-Uhr-Zug,* and Messager's *Véronique* (rechristened *Brigitte*)—did not improve matters and she renounced her managership, the latter days of which had, unfortunately, coincided with the fading days of the first prime period of Viennese Operette which had so profited her earlier years. She, nevertheless, sold the theatre for almost double what she had paid for it.

During the latter period of her management, Frau von Schönerer directed a number of the pieces staged at her theatre. Theatre-bills began only in the 1890s to credit stage directors, but she is credited with the original staging of *Der Opernball* as well as of *Die Blumen-Mary, La Poupée* and *Der griechische Sklave* amongst others.

DIE SCHÖNE RISETTE Operette in a Vorspiel and 3 acts by A M Willner and Robert Bodanzky. Music by Leo Fall. Theater an der Wien, Vienna, 19 November 1910.

When the 11th-century King of Burgundy's courtiers drowned his shepherdess mistress, Risette, as a witch so that he would marry and beget an heir, the monarch had his ''democratic'' revenge by enacting a law whereby, every 17 years, 17 17-year-old maidens from the village of Beauséjour could come to court and choose themselves an aristocratic ''husband.'' After three months' trial, during which the men had to live on the land, the marriage could be confirmed. Fifteenth-century King Pierre (Adolf Lussmann), full of himself and fresh from university, ignores the tradition and goes off hunting on ''Schöne Risette-Day,'' so to palliate his absence his friend Edgar de la Tourelle (Max Willenz) stands in as King. The shepherdess Jeanette (Grete Holm) chooses the handsome and late-come huntsman as her ''husband,'' and Princess Margot (Luise Kartousch) of neighboring Aquitaine, having cheated a little to become a Risette, takes a look at the ''king'' to whom she is betrothed and takes him. The men find life on the land hard, but both fall in love with their ''brides'' before King Thomasius II of Aquitaine (Ernst Tautenhayn) comes in search of his missing daughter and all is exposed. When Jeanette hears that her ''Philippe'' is the King, she runs away, but after an act of song and suffering, she returns for a happy royal ending.

Fall's score was composed very largely in march and waltz rhythms (although the first genuine waltz did not come till part way through the first-act finale) and had the peculiarity that, amongst its 14 musical numbers, it included only one song for its hero (''Wisst Ihr, was Grisetten sind?''), a bright 3/8 number illustrating his preference for city grisettes over country maids, and one for its heroine—an entry song about ''Schöne Risette''—both early in the first act. Thereafter the score was made up of duets and ensembles and a substantial first-act finale, all featuring the two lead pairs, plus a comic duet for Thomasius and his Adjutant (Franz Glawatsch). The final act featured only a march quintet and the little musical scene in which Jeanette/Risette returns to her King.

Die schöne Risette had a fine run in Franz Glawatsch's production at the Theater an der Wien, being played one hundred times in the 12 months following its premiere (as well as a Gastspiel at the Raimundtheater) and lifting Ernst Tautenhayn into the star bracket. It went on to be produced with indubitable success in Germany and in Spain (*La bella Riseta* Teatro de la reina Victoria 8 November 1916), and was also played in Paris by the Theater an der Wien company during their 1911 guest season at the Théâtre du Vaudeville.

Germany: December 1910; France: Théâtre du Vaudeville (Ger) 1911

DIE SCHÖNE SCHWEDIN Operette in 3 acts by Julius Brammer and Alfred Grünwald. Music by Robert Winterberg. Theater an der Wien, Vienna, 30 January 1915.

The Stockholm banker Sven Liverstol (Ernst Tautenhayn) is in secret money troubles and anxious to marry his beloved daughter Hilma (Luise Kartousch) to the apparently rich young German Baron Heinz von Reedingen (Hubert Marischka). He is offered a large loan by Torkel (Karl Tuschl) and Schnorkel (Kurt Mikulski) on condition that the marriage takes place, but he is flung into desperate straits when his biggest customer, a dazzling lass from Brazil called Edith Lloyd (Betty Fischer), turns up and won't wait to withdraw her funds. And so there is no marriage, no Torkel-Schnorkel money, and when Edith goes off back to Brazil, with the actually underfunded Heinz as her secretary, she leaves the Liverstols thoroughly in the Swedish soup. In Act III, however, Edith finds her business in trouble through growing competition from one Sr Camberito. It turns out that Camberito is none other than the financially recovered Liverstol, and all can end with Hilma and Heinz at last together and with the money-marketing Edith and Liverstol joining hands and fortunes.

Die schöne Schwedin proved a disappointment at the Theater an der Wien and it was withdrawn after its 50th performance (16 March) to be replaced by Granichstaedten's *Auf Befehl der Herzogin,* a good-old-days piece which proved much more to the wartime public's taste than this often unromantic tale of financial dealings. Nevertheless, it went on to other productions. It was produced in Germany, Budapest was given Vilmos Tihanyi's Hungarian version, *A szöke csoda* (''the marvellous blonde''), it was foreseeably snapped up by Albert Ranf for the Stockholm Opera House and the Shuberts took up the American rights. In its American production the piece started out from New Haven, 11 May 1916, under the curious title *A Brazilian Honeymoon* (perhaps a reference to the very first Shubert success, *A Chinese Honeymoon*), but by the time New York was reached, the lovely Swedish lass (played originally by Marguerite Namara, then by Beth Lydy) had given place to *The Girl from Brazil* (statuesque Frances Demarest) as the show's title. Hal Forde was Liverstol, John H Goldsworth played Heinz, and George Hassell had an enlarged comedy role as Torkel (Schnorkel had vanished). The American version was the work of Edgar Smith (book) and Matthew Woodward (lyrics), and Winterberg's ''above average'' score was supplemented by the inevitable Shubert interpolations from the pen of Sigmund Romberg (''Bachelor Girl and Boy,'' ''The Right Brazilian Girl,'' ''Señorita,'' ''Come Back, Sweet Dream''). In spite of agreeable notices the piece remained only 61 performances on Broadway.

Germany: ?1915; Hungary: *A szöke csoda* Budai Színkör 22 May 1915; USA: 44th Street Theater *The Girl from Brazil* 30 August 1916

DIE SCHÖNE UNBEKANNTE Operette in 2 acts and an epilogue by Leopold Jacobson and Leo Walther Stein. Music by Oscar Straus. Carltheater, Vienna, 15 January 1915.

A brightly conventional story of flirtations, secrets and varied mistakes, *Die schöne Unbekannte* (''the fair unknown'') was set in a garrison town, allowing its hero to be a philandering soldier—Oberleutnant Leopold von Höllriegl (Franz Felix)—and composer Straus to introduce a healthy slice of martial music into his score. The ladies of the piece, both of whom seem in turn to be the fair unknown to whom he commits himself, were Elly (Mizzi Günther), the daughter of the local count (Richard Waldemar), and the exotic Lydia Petrowska (Martha Kriwitz), who doesn't put in an appearance until the second act but causes havoc when she does. The young Robert Nästlberger was the number-two man. Alongside the marches ''Servus Kamerad'' and ''Mit Trommeln, Pfeifen and Tschinellen'' came the requisite number of waltzes—notably the song of the ''schöne Unbekannte'' introduced in the first-act finale and ''Die Walzer von heute Nacht,'' but also a polka quartet, a brilliant entrance song for Lydia (''Ausverkauft''), Poldi's ''Die letzte Frist,'' Tanz-Duetten for Elly and Emil Lampl, a salesgirls' chorus and some pantomime and burlesque.

Produced by Sigmund Eibenschütz at the Carltheater, *Die schöne Unbekannte* had a good run of 103 performances and was taken up by those countries which, in this time of war, were still willing to look at the product of the Vienna stage. Thus, whilst England and France were out, the show was seen in Germany, in Budapest where Sári Petráss, recently returned from Broadway, starred as Elly, and in America. The Shuberts' production of *The Beautiful Unknown* proved unsatisfactory in its out-of town tryout and by the time the show reached town the action had been resituated in France, the score peppered with rashers of Romberg and the title changed to *My Lady's Glove.* Vivienne Segal and Charles Purcell played the leads for 16 Broadway nights.

Germany: ?1915; Hungary: Király Színház *A bajós ismeretlen* 29 May 1915; USA: Parsons' Theater, Hartford, Conn *The Beautiful Unknown* 29 January 1917, Lyric Theater, New York *My Lady's Glove* 18 June 1917

SCHÖNFELD, Alfred (b Breslau, 30 March 1859; d Berlin ?9 December 1916). The most prolific and successful lyricist of the German stage in the years prior to the First World War.

Schönfeld began his theatrical life writing Possen, musical and also not-so-musical, for various German theatres, before in 1892 becoming dramaturg at Berlin's Centraltheater under the management of Richard Schultz. It was during his time at the Centraltheater that he first collaborated on texts with actor-turned-playwright Jean Kren. When Schultz began regularly to use Julius Freund and Wilhelm Mannstädt as librettists for his new shows, the pair decided to move on and ultimately they took on their own house, the old Adolf-Ernst-Theater, rebuilt and rechristened the Thalia-Theater, where they began the construction and production of what would be a highly successful run of musical comedies. In their partnership, Kren soon became the bookwriter and business manager while Schönfeld specialized in the writing of the lyrics, and also turned his hand to the job of stage director.

Julius Einödshofer and Max Schmidt were the partners' earliest musical collaborators, and Paul Lincke and Victor Holländer both provided them with scores for several years, but their greatest successes came when they brought Jean Gilbert to the Thalia-Theater to illustrate musically such comedies as *Autoliebchen, Puppchen, Die Tangoprinzessin* and *Blondinchen,* a list of hits which lifted the Thalia into the international league whilst also giving lyricist Schönfeld a bevy of song hits. The success of the Thalia also allowed Kren to spread himself managerially, and the pair had one of their greatest authorial successes when he produced their *Der Soldat der Marie* (mus: Leo Ascher) at the Neues Operettenhaus. This was also their last great success together for, at the height of their prosperity, in 1916, Schönfeld died.

Schönfeld was also the principal of Thalia-Theater Verlag, the publishing company which printed the music and texts of the theatre's pieces.

1892 **Das grosse Los** (Johannes Döbber/w Jean Kren) Tivoli Theater, Bremen 6 August

1892 **Das Sportmädel** (Max Lustig) Alexanderplatz-Theater 12 November

1893 **Berliner Vollblut** (Julius Einödshofer/w Kren) Centraltheater 31 August

1894 **Ein gesunder Junge** (Einödshofer/w Kren) Centraltheater 6 March

1894 **Falstaff** (Georg Schönfeld) Apollotheater 15 July

1894 **Der neue Kurs** (Einödshofer/w Leopold Ely, Kren) Centraltheater

1899 **Leuchtkafer** (Moritz Fall/w Ludwig Fernand) Wilhelm-Theater, Magdeburg 18 February

1899 **Der Platzmajor** (Gustav Wanda/w Kren) Thalia-Theater 9 September

1899 **Im Himmelshof** (Max Schmidt/Kren) Thalia-Theater 23 December

1900 **Der Liebesschlüssel** (Schmidt/Kren) Thalia-Theater 8 September

1900 **Der Amor von heute** (Wanda/w Kren) Thalia-Theater 30 November

1901 **Der Cadetten-Vater** (ex- *Lucinde vom Theater*) (Conradi, Schmidt/Emil Pohl ad Kren) Thalia-Theater 9 March

1901 **Ein tolles Geschaft** (Einödshofer/Kren) Thalia-Theater 7 September

1901 **Die Badepuppe** (Einödshofer/Kren) Thalia-Theater 26 November

1902 **Seine kleine** (Einödshofer/Kren, Ely) Thalia-Theater 18 January

1902 **Die bösen Mädchen** (Einödshofer/Kren, Leopold Ely) Thalia-Theater 23 December

1903 **Der Posaunenengel** (Einödshofer, Schmidt/Kren) Thalia-Theater 24 March

1903 **Der reicheste Berliner** (Einödshofer, Schmidt/Kren) Belle-Alliance-Theater 23 December

1904 **Freut euch des Lebens** (Einödshofer/Wilhelm Jacoby, Robert Stein ad Kren) Belle-Alliance-Theater 14 April

1904 **Kam'rad Lehmann** (Einödshofer, Julius Stern/F Zell ad Kren, Ely) Belle-Alliance-Theater 7 May

1904 **Der Weiberkönig** (Einödshofer/Kren) Thalia-Theater 15 September

1904 **'s Zuckersgoscherl** (Josef Wolffsgruber/Kren ad August Neidhart) Carltheater, Vienna 15 October

1904 **Der grosse Stern** (Einödshofer/Kren) Thalia-Theater 23 December

1905 **Der beste Tip** (Schmidt/Kren) Thalia-Theater 9 February

1905 **Noch einmal so leben** (Schmidt/Kren) Belle-Alliance-Theater 1 April

1905 **Bis früh um Fünfe** (Lincke/Kren, Arthur Lippschitz) Thalia-Theater 26 August

1906 **Hochparterre-Links** (Lincke/Kren, Lippschitz) Thalia-Theater 7 April

1906 **Wenn die Bombe platzt** (Lincke/Kren, Lippschitz) Thalia-Theater 25 August

1906 **Eine lustige Doppel-Ehe** (Lincke/Kraatz) Thalia-Theater 27 November

1907 **Wo die Liebe hinfallt** (Schmidt/Kren, Lippschitz) Thalia-Theater 20 April

1907 **Ihr sechs-Uhr Onkel** (Lincke/ad Kren) Thalia-Theater 25 August

1908 **Immer oben nauf** (Lincke/ad Buchbinder) Thalia-Theater 22 January

1908 **Doktor Klapperstorch** (Schmidt/Kren, Georg Okonkowski) Thalia-Theater 28 March

1908 **Die Brünnennymphe** (uncredited/Heinrich Stobitzer, Max Neal) Thalia-Theater 18 April

1908 **Das Mitternachtsmädchen** (Viktor Holländer/Kren, Lippschitz) Thalia-Theater 14 August

1909 **Meister Tutti** (Holländer/w Kren) Thalia-Theater 15 January

1909 **Wo wohnt sie denn?** (Holländer/Kren, Okonkowski) Thalia-Theater 12 February

1909 **Prinz Bussi** (Holländer/Kren) Thalia-Theater 13 August

1909 **Die ewige Lampe** (Schmidt/Kren) Thalia-Theater 30 October

1909 **Die süsse Cora** (Holländer/Kren, Lippschitz) Thalia-Theater 11 December

1910 **Die lieben Ottos** (Jean Gilbert/Xanrof ad Kren) Thalia-Theater 30 April

1910 **Polnische Wirtschaft** (Gilbert/Okonkowski, Kraatz ad Kren) revised version Thalia-Theater 6 August

1911 **Die moderne Eva** (Gilbert/Okonkowski) Neues Operetten-Theater 11 November

1912 **Autoliebchen** (Gilbert/Kren) Thalia-Theater 16 March

1912 **Puppchen** (Gilbert/Kren, Kraatz) Thalia-Theater 19 December

1913 **Die Millionenbraut** (Döbber/Kren, Kraatz) Wilhelm-Theater, Magdeburg 17 February

1913 **Die Tangoprinzessin** (Gilbert/Kren, Kraatz) Thalia-Theater 4 October

1914 **Wenn der Frühling kommt!** (Gilbert/Kren, Okonkowski) Thalia-Theater 28 March

1914 **Kam'rad Männe** (Gilbert/Kren, Okonkowski) Thalia-Theater 3 August

1915 **Des Kaisers Rock** (Döbber/Kren, Kraatz) Residenz-Theater 19 February

1915 **Drei Paar Schuhe** (Gilbert/Carl Görlitz ad Kren) Thalia-Theater 10 September

1916 **Blondinchen** (Gilbert/w Kraatz, Kren) Thalia-Theater 4 March

1916 **Der Soldat der Marie** (Leo Ascher/w Kren, Buchbinder) Neues Operettenhaus 2 September

1916 **Das Vagabundenmädel** (Gilbert/Kren, Buchbinder) Thalia-Theater 2 December

SCHÖN IST DIE WELT Operette in 3 acts by Fritz Löhner-Beda and Ludwig Herzer, a revised version of *Endlich allein* by A M Willner and Robert Bodanzky. Music by Franz Lehár. Metropoltheater, Berlin, 3 December 1930.

The first version of Lehár's ''mountain musical,'' *Endlich allein* (Theater an der Wien 30 January 1914), had had a reasonably successful and even international career during the Great War, but this did not prevent the composer, who never showed any reticence to reprocess his older scores in lesser or greater remakes, from bringing its music out again. Having already successfully redone *Die gelbe Jacke* as *Das Land des Lächelns* as a vehicle for Richard Tauber, he now handed Willner and Bodanzky's text over to Fritz Löhner and Ludwig Herzer to be similarly made over into a new piece for the popular tenor's benefit.

The ''in the present'' story of the piece was modernized with motor cars and radios, but otherwise there wasn't too much that was modern about the text of *Schön ist die Welt*: the principals were the royal families of the most conventional of Operetten. Tauber was cast as Georg, prince of a significant but unwealthy country, the Hungarian soprano Gitta Alpár was Elisabeth von und zu Lichtenberg, his intended bride and potential source of finance. They meet without knowing who each other is, and spend the second act together out in the mountains where they are trapped overnight by an avalanche. Love blossoms and, as in all the best old tales, the Prince and the Princess end up wanting to marry the very one they are supposed to marry. Leo Schützendorf as the Prince's penniless father, Kurt Vespermann as his adjutant Sascha, and Lizzi Waldmüller, as the latinate dancer the underling has culpably wed without his monarch's permission, provided the rest of the entertainment in the first and third acts.

The two stars had plenty of music, and Tauber's role included a swingeing title song, the whole of the two-handed snowed-in second act with its ''Liebste, glaub' an mich,'' and the lighter moment of ''In der kleinen Bar'' in the final act, whilst his partner had her solo moments in the anticipatory ''Sag, armes Herzchen, sag'' and her lovestruck ''Ich bin verliebt.'' The latinate dancer got to be latinate in a song and dance about ''Rio de Janeiro.''

Tauber, still in fine voice but physically impossible as any kind of a hero, was less well suited as the young Ruritanian prince than he had been as the impassive Chinese one of the previous show, but Alpár was an enormous success as his princess, and the fact that the show's central novelty (which, nevertheless, had an inkling of

Miss Helyett in it) was elsewhere swathed in happy old clichés did not seem to matter. The Rotter brothers' Berlin production of the revamped show did well enough, and it was duly picked up for Vienna where Hans Heinz Bollmann and Adele Kern headed a cast which featured Gustav Charlé as the King and Kálmán Latabár as the adjutant. It played only a disappointing 93 times.

Hungary's version with László Szűcs and Irma Patkós was produced at the Szeged Városi Színház and subsequently played for two weeks by that company at the Király Színház, whilst France gave a large-stage version nebulously entitled *La Chanson du bonheur* (ad André Mauprey) with only a modicum of success. André Burdino (Georges), Georgette Simon (Elisabeth), Roger Tréville (Sacha), Lyne Clevers (Mercedès), Félix Oudart (King) and Nina Myral (Duchesse Marie de Brankenhorst) topped the bill of an ''opérette in 8 tableaux'' which featured a selection of ''attractions chorégraphiques sur glace'' performed by 10 apparently Hungarian lady skaters, a series of dances by 16 English girl dancers, and 12 French ''boys'' choreographed by June Roberts and Max Révol.

On the whole, *Schön ist die Welt* went rather less far and less well than its original had done 15 years earlier, but the tenor bonbons and the second-act duo survived well enough to make it to the odd recording. And to a film, with Rudolf Schock and Renate Holm (playing nothing less than a celebrated singer) Y and with a whole new book. In the end, it came down to just the bonbons.

Austria: Theater an der Wien 21 December 1931; Hungary: Városi Színház, Szeged *Szép a világ* 23 November 1934, Király Színház (Szeged company) *Szép a világ* 24 December 1934; France: Théâtre de la Gaîté-Lyrique *La Chanson du bonheur* 2 November 1935

Recordings: selections (Philips, Eurodisc, EMI Electrola)

THE SCHOOL GIRL Musical play in 2 acts by Henry Hamilton and Paul M Potter. Lyrics by Charles H Taylor. Music by Leslie Stuart. Prince of Wales Theatre, London, 9 May 1903.

A well-made musical comedy of the Edwardian era, *The School Girl* featured all the favorite elements of the genre, beginning with a star ingenue in the person of *The Belle of New York,* Edna May, continuing with a mass of popular comedy and comedians (G P Huntley, George Graves, James Blakeley), a score by the man of the moment, *Florodora* composer Leslie Stuart, and a production by George Edwardes and Charles Frohman, the most liberal and tasteful of London's managers.

The suitably merry and nonsensical plot had Miss May running away from school to a job as a temp at the stock exchange in Paris. There she unmasks a swindle and saves everyone from ruin. The score gave her a trio of pretty numbers of which her invitation to the chorus boys to ''Call Around Again'' was the most fetching. However, it could not compare for popularity with the catchy ''My Little Canoe'' sung by 17-year-old Billie Burke, making her West End debut as an American chorus girl, nor with the more musically substantial ''When I Was a Girl Like You'' sung by the Mother Superior of the convent in the show's prologue. For this brief role the producers lured Violet Cameron, the great star of *Les Cloches de Corneville* and *La Mascotte* a quarter of a century earlier, back to the stage for a final and hugely appreciated appearance.

The School Girl was a fine London success, playing for 11 months and 333 performances at the Prince of Wales Theatre before moving on to the provinces and to New York. There the score was decorated, to Stuart's annoyance, with some additional ditties mostly by Paul Rubens (and including a ''Japanese Medley'' which ended up with ''Auld Lang Syne'') and Miss May appropriated ''My Little Canoe'' (and duly did well with it), but the strong plot lines were maintained along with a number of the London cast. It was some of these—the comic trio of George Grossmith, Fred Wright and Blakeley—who, in fact, proved the most popular part of Broadway's *The School Girl* and helped it to a fine run of 120 performances.

The same title had previously been used by the stage-young (if at least 35-year-old) actress Minnie Palmer for a young/old vehicle made over from the old play *The Little Rebel* by Albert Maurice and George Manchester Cohen (Grand Theatre, Cardiff 2 September 1895, Syracuse, NY 23 December 1895). It cast her as the teenaged Little Miss Loo in what was largely a stand-up performance by its star who got both all the songs and, in spite of competition from her mother, the man. It was played in the British provinces, but not in London, and was also briefly seen in one of its star's brief Broadway seasons (Bijou Theater 30 December 1895). The show later appeared credited to Willie Gill and with the score announced as being by Maurice Denham-Harrison and others.

USA: Daly's Theater 1 September 1904

SCHRÖDER, Friedrich (b Näfels, Switzerland, 6 August 1910; d Berlin, 25 September 1972).

Educated in Münster and Berlin, the Swiss-born Schröder quickly found himself a career writing song and dance music and, at the age of 20, the first of what would ultimately total 43 film scores (*Sieben Ohrfeigen* 1937, *Immer nur du* 1941, *Des Teufels General, Charley's Tante* 1952, the arrangement of Fall's *Die geschiedene Frau* 1953, etc). In 1934 he became assistant conductor to Werner Schmidt-Bölke at the Berlin Metropoltheater, a post which he held through to 1937.

Schröder made his first mark on the musical stage with the production of his 1942 musical comedy *Hochzeitsnacht im Paradies* which was played for more than five hundred performances at the Metropoltheater, then throughout central Europe before, in its turn, going on to become the basis for two films. His second stage work, *Nächte in Shanghai,* produced at the Metropoltheater after the War, brought forth the popular song ''Komm mit mir nach Tahiti'' to add to the successes he had had with various single and film songs (the most famous being the 1937 ''Ich tanze mit dir in den Himmel hinein''), but none of his subsequent shows came near to sharing the success of the first.

1942 **Hochzeitsnacht im Paradies** (Günther Schwenn/Heinz Hentschke) Metropoltheater 24 September

1947 **Nächte in Shanghai** (Schwenn/Waldemar Frank, Leo Lenz) Metropoltheater 1 February

1947 **Chanel Nr 5** (Schwenn/B E Lüthge) Corso Theater, Berlin

1947 **Lucrezia in Stockholm** Berlin

1954 **Isabella** (Schwenn/Frank, Eduard Rogati, Otto Daue) Nationaltheater, Mannheim 20 July

1955 **Die grosse Welt** (Schwenn) Staatstheater, Wiesbaden

1955 **Das Bad auf der Tenne** (Schwenn/Rolf Meyer) Nuremberg-Fürth 26 March

1969 **Die Jungfrau von Paris** (Schwenn) Raimundtheater 19 December

SCHUBERT, Franz [Peter] (b Lichtenthal, 31 January 1797; d Vienna, 19 November 1828).

Schubert's connection with the musical stage in his own lifetime was an eclectic one, ranging from the operatic *Alfonso und Estrella* and *Fierrabras* to music for the ''grand romantic Schauspiel mit Musik'' *Rosamunde, Fürstin von Cypern* (1823), the melodrama *Die Zauberharfe,* the one-act Georg von Hoffmann Singspiel *Die Zwillingsbrüder* mounted at Vienna's Kärtnertor-Theater, and the Lysistratan comic opera *Der Verschworenen, oder der häusliche Krieg* (1823), subsequently played in French as *La Croisade des dames* and as *Les Conjurées, ou la guerre au foyer* and in Hungarian as *Cselre cselt.*

From soon after the composer's death, however, his music became the raw material for pasticcio pieces compiled by other hands. In 1834 Adolf Müller arranged a Schubert score for *Der Erlkönig* (Theater an der Wien 21 February), whilst in 1864 the first Schubert biomusical, the Singspiel *Franz Schubert* written by Hans Max and with a score arranged by Franz von Suppé, was produced at the Carltheater (10 September) with Karl Treumann playing the role of the composer. A grand success, it was revived in 1886, at the Theater an der Wien in 1897 and at the Volksoper in 1922, and also played at Budapest's Budai Színkör in 1867 (28 June). Other pieces such as the Dresden Singspiel *Die vierjährige Posten* (1 act, Robert Hirschfeld, Theo Körner 23 September 1895) followed, but Shubert's greatest success as an Operatic composer came in another biomusical, the famous *Das Dreimäderlhaus* (arr Heinrich Berté, 1916), and in its derivatives, the British *Lilac Time* (arr G H Clutsam), and the two pieces entitled *Blossom Time* (arr Sigmund Romberg and, again, G H Clutsam, respectively).

Following the vast success of *Das Dreimäderlhaus,* Schubert musicals flooded the world's stages. In 1917 Vienna saw *Anne-Marie* (ad Max Egger, lib: Fritz Löhner-Beda, Singspiel 1 act, Ronacher), Magdeburg produced *Fernando* (Albert Stadler, Singspiel 1 act Viktoria Theater 1 August) and Budapest *Tavasz és szerelem* (*Liebe und Lenz,* Berté, Bruno Hardt-Warden, Ignaz M Welleminsky, Városi Színház), whilst in 1918 the Raimundtheater launched a musequel to *Das Dreimäderlhaus* under the title *Hannerl.* Stuttgart put out *Der treue Soldat* (arr Fritz Busch, F D Tovey/Theo Körner, Rolf Lauckner Landestheater 2 July 1922), the Volksoper staged *Der unsterbliche Franz* (Ernst Decsey, Julius Bittner, Julius Bauer, 1928) and Basle saw *Die Freunde von Salamanka* (ad Hermine Moerike, Josef Rainer, 10 May 1934). The little Viennese Theater Auges-Gottes housed a Schubert revue-Operette, *So war's einmal* (Deutsch, E Limé, 1 October) in 1946, whilst in 1955 (7 June) Britain's Liverpool Playhouse turned out a new Schubert biomusical, *Spring Quartet* (Willard Stoker), with tenor Carlos Montes starred.

Schubert's life and putative loves have also made it to the musical screen. Germany's Karlheinz Bohm (*Das Dreimäderlhaus,* Sascha Films, 1958) more or less followed the Operette story, but Jan Kiepura in the Austrian *Schuberts Unvollende Symphonie* (1934) romanced Marta Eggerth as the daughter of Gróf Esterházy, France's Bernard Lancret (*Sérénade* 1939) had his fling with an English dancing girl (Lilian Harvey) and Tino Rossi (*La Belle Meunière,* 1948) was paired with the pretty milleress of the title. Claude Laydu, in 1955 (*Schubert*), had a choice of Marina Vlady and Lucia Bose. But, if they couldn't agree on who the composer was supposed to love, the directors agreed on one thing. All the celluloid Franzes were equipped with varying degrees of fuzzy hairdo and with the obligatory little spectacles.

DIE SCHÜTZENLIESEL Operette in 3 acts by Leo Stein and Carl Lindau. Music by Edmund Eysler. Carltheater, Vienna, 7 October 1905.

When Alexander Girardi decided to part company with the Theater an der Wien, the theatre where he had become a star and lived through years of idolized successes, he did not part company with the composer who had provided him with the substance of his latest hits. Edmund Eysler was, in fact, part of the package which was richly paid for to bring Girardi and his newest vehicle to Andreas Aman's Carltheater, long the chief rival of the Theater an der Wien and much in need of a new musical-comedy success. Eysler was paid 2,000 kronen, and his two librettists the same sum, for *Die Schützenliesel*—sums which, since the departure of such starry authorial names as Strauss, were no longer current in the Viennese theatre. But in spite of this unaccustomed free-handedness, *Die Schützenliesel* turned out to be a good buy for the Carltheater management.

Girardi starred as Blasius Nestel, fresh out of the army and the winner of the local shooting contest, with Mizzi Zwerenz as his Liesel, the daughter of the Bürgermeister Mooshammer (Friedrich Becker), landlord of the ''zur Schützenliesel'' inn, in a little countrified tale set at Gegend-am-See in the Königssee area. Tenor Max Rohr was the intrusive love interest—the forester Konrad Wille—whilst Artur Guttmann and soprano Flora Siding played the local beer-brewer, Hippolyt Zillinger, and his daughter Wilhelmine. Venerable comedian Karl Blasel took the part of the old landowner Daszewski, the key to the evening's troubles and to its happy ending. For the rich old man promises a fine sum of money to his young relatives, Blasius and Wilhelmine, when they wed each other. Their parents are, of course, anxious for the match to go ahead, and although the young folk wish to follow their hearts, they decide to wed, get the money and then, with their fortunes assured, divorce and wed their right partners. The foreseeable misunderstandings and mishaps intervene when Blasius starts setting up the divorce evidence, but (unlike the usual operettic ending which has the forced pairs coming to like their situation) old Daszewski comes along on schedule to give his blessing to a rematching in time for the final curtain. Richard Waldemar (Schlehreba) and Therese Löwe as the star's mother and the cue for his principal song headed the supporting cast.

Once again, Eysler turned out the hit numbers that were needed for his star and even the rest of the cast, numbers that challenged even his *Bruder Straubinger*'s ''Küssen ist keine Sünd'' as all-time favorites. Girardi's ''Mutterl-lied,'' a slow and sentimental waltz lullaby (''Schlaf', mein liebes Büberl, schlaf'') which was a contrast to his livelier and more comical hits, was a no-dry-eye-in-the-house sensation, whilst his Letter Song ''Du süsse, süsse..!'' gave him a second severe hit. Originally this latter piece had not been pointed up as a likely winner, but on the insistence of the singer Willy Bauer, who was present at the dress rehearsal, Eysler made a last-minute rewrite and, cutting a chunk of his carefully built concerted second-act finale, inserted there a big reprise of the Letter Song. Bauer proved right, and ''Du Süsse, Süsse..!'' became a big favorite. There were, of course, further waltz-songs—one for the tenor in praise of ''Wilhelmine,'' a ''Keine Angst, ich bitte sehr'' and a lilting ''Ist jung man wie schäumender Wein,'' as well as a popular march number (''Heut' fahr'ich aus der Haut'') in a score which lived up enthusiastically to the tuneful and appealing standards Eysler had set in his earlier shows.

In spite of the competition of the all-conquering *Die lustige Witwe* at the Theater an der Wien, *Die Schützenliesel* had a fine run. It passed its 100th performance on 15 January 1906 and played its 105th before Girardi left the Carltheater to go to play in *Der Schusterbub* at the Theater in der Josefstadt. It was played again for a few performances when the star returned to the Carltheater in October of the same year, while the next Eysler/Stein/Lindau piece, *Künstlerblut,* was being got ready. *Die Schützenliesel* passed its 120th performance on 6 January 1907, was played again in 1908 and was later seen at the Raimundtheater in 1910 (27 August) with Ernst Tautenhayn playing Blasius. It was restaged at the Carltheater in 1913, with many of its original cast, as a 60th birthday tribute to author Lindau, then at the Johann Strauss-Theater in 1915, at the Carltheater again in 1920 with Blasel repeating his original part, and once more in 1924 with Fritz Imhoff starred. Mizzi Zwerenz was still to be seen in her original role 20 years after its creation, but Girardi found others of the Eysler pieces—*Bruder Straubinger* and *Künstlerblut*—more to his revivable liking. The show was also exported with great success to Germany, where it clocked up 106 nights in its initial Berlin run, as well as to Italy.

In 1954 a Rudolf Schündler/Central-Europa film called *Schützenliesel,* allegedly based on the piece (ad Ernst Nebhut, Fritz Böttger, ly: Günther Schwenn, add mus: Herbert Trantow) was produced with Paul Hörbiger, Herta Staal, Gretl Fröhlich and Peter W Staub taking the principal singing roles, backed by such rural characters as the Four Ping-Pongs, Egon Kaiser and his orchestra and zither-player Anton Karas.

Another musical comedy (Posse mit Gesang) with the same title, written by Leon Treptow and set to music by Ludwig Gothov-Grüneke, was produced at the Carltheater (24 September 1882) and again, adapted by G Görss with music by Gustave Steffens, at Berlin's Centraltheater (25 December 1882).

Germany: Theater des Westens 22 December 1905

Film: Central-Europa 1954

SCHWAB, Laurence (b Boston, 17 December 1893; d Southampton, NY, 29 May 1951). Author and producer of some of the top Broadway shows of the 1920s.

Harvard-educated Schwab worked with the Alf Wilton agency and, after the First World War, with the Floyd

Stoker agency before he made his first venture into producing for the musical stage, at the age of 28, in collaboration with Daniel Kussell on a piece called *Love and Kisses* (1922). An elaboration of a vaudeville act called *A Man of Affairs,* the show was tried out at Atlantic City in June, and finally made its way into New York under the title *The Gingham Girl* three months later. There, with Helen Ford starring in the title role, it proved a sweet little success.

The following season Schwab went out on his own to write and produce another piece with a dear little country girl for a heroine. Publishers Harms provided him with some rising young collaborators in playwright Frank Mandel and composer George Gershwin, but *Sweet Little Devil* did not catch on as the earlier piece had done and the most significant thing to come out of the show was the partnership between Schwab and Mandel. It soon developed into more than a writing partnership, for Mandel joined Schwab in his production business as well and, although Schwab concurrently presented the successful 1926 show *Queen High* alone, in the six years of collaboration which followed the pair produced eight musical shows, as well as a number of plays—a body of work which included a number of memorable hits.

If their promising *Captain Jinks* disappointed slightly on Broadway after being hailed as a major hit on its way to New York, *The Desert Song* (which Schwab did not help write), *Good News, The New Moon* and *Follow Thru* (all of which he did) were all great successes; taking Schwab and Mandel quickly to the forefront of the producing establishment. After five years of success, however, things turned sour in the year of 1931. The partnership's production of the film burlesque *America's Sweetheart* did not come up to their previous successes, *Free for All,* a weak piece which Schwab co-wrote with Oscar Hammerstein and which purported to be about socialism and free love, flopped in just 15 performances (and even the cast turned down the offer to buy it for just its $5,100-a-week running costs); and an attempt to create another *The Desert Song* with a romantic piece called *East Wind* foundered in 23 performances.

Mandel then abdicated from the partnership, wisely, as it turned out, for the handful of pieces Schwab presented after his departure were unexceptional: *Take a Chance* (1932), which managed 243 performances, Romberg and Mandel's preposterous *May Wine* (1935), which lasted 213 nights, and an attempt at a Gilbert and Sullivan biomusical called *Knights of Song* (1938), which survived two weeks on Broadway, were his last representatives in New York, whilst an English version of Robert Stolz's attractive *Venus in Seide* (*Venus in Silk,* 1935) and a musical version of the play *Sailor Beware* produced as *Nice Goin'* (1939 w Lee Dixon) folded without reaching town.

Towards the end of his career as a producer, Schwab also worked for a while in films (*You Can't Have Everything, Ali Baba Goes to Town* 1937).

1924 **Sweet Little Devil** (George Gershwin/w Frank Mandel) Astor Theater 21 January

1925 **Captain Jinks** (Lewis E Gensler, Stephen Jones/B G De Sylva/w Mandel) Martin Beck Theater 8 September

1926 **Queen High** (Gensler/De Sylva) Ambassador Theater 8 September

1927 **Good News** (Ray Henderson/De Sylva, Lew Brown/w De Sylva) 46th Street Theater 6 September

1927 **The New Moon** (Sigmund Romberg/Oscar Hammerstein II/w Hammerstein, Mandel) Chestnut Street Opera House, Philadelphia 22 December; Imperial Theater (revised version) 19 November 1928

1929 **Follow Thru** (Henderson/De Sylva, Brown/w De Sylva) 46th Street Theater 9 January

1931 **Free for All** (Richard Whiting/w Hammerstein) Manhattan Theater 8 September

1932 **Take a Chance** (ex- *Humpty Dumpty*) (Nacio Herb Brown, Whiting/De Sylva) Apollo Theater 26 November

1935 **Venus in Silk** (aka *Beloved Rogue*) (*Venus in Seide*) English version w Lester O'Keefe (Municipal Opera, St Louis)

1939 **Nice Goin'** (Ralph Rainger/Leo Robin) New Haven, Conn 21 October

DAS SCHWALBENNEST

A twice-used title. The first "swallows' nest" appeared in Berlin in 1904 when an opérette in three acts by Maurice Ordonneau adapted into a German version by Maurice Rappaport, with music by Henri Hirschmann, was mounted at the Centraltheater on 9 January 1904. A tale of 18th-century Versailles, with one of those stories which involved a fellow in disguise in a girls' school in search of his sweetheart, it was subsequently played in Budapest (ad Adolf Mérei *Fecskefészek* 28 October 1904 Magyar Színház), then rewritten and reproduced in Belgium as *Les Hirondelles* (Galeries Saint-Hubert, Brussels 17 November 1906) and had a reasonable life thereafter. However, it did not equal the record of its successor, an Alt Wiener Singspiel in three acts by Ernst Marischka and Bruno Granichstaedten, with music by Granichstaedten, produced by Hubert Marischka and Rudolf Beer at the Raimundtheater, Vienna, on 2 September 1926. This *Das Schwalbennest* was set in the Viennese Schloss Rohnsdorff, but it interested itself in the servants of the house rather than the nobles: Franz Glawatsch played the butler, Franz Rettenbacher, with Luise Kartousch and Margit Künl as his daughters, and Ernst Tautenhayn was the coachman, Ferdinand Brakl. However the evening's tenor was to be found upstairs: Prince Karl was played by Victor Flemming. Guess which girl got the Prince.

The original production of the piece was a fine success, playing four and a half months and 134 performances en suite (to 17 January 1927), swapping stages with *Die Zirkusprinzessin* to go through a 30-performance Gastspiel at the Theater an der Wien in January 1927, and returning to base to finally run to its 208th night. It was later seen in Hungary in a version by István Zágon (Király Színház *A fecskefészek* 23 September 1927).

SCHWARTZ, Arthur (b Brooklyn, NY, 4 November 1900; d Pennsylvania, 3 September 1984). Revue and film songwriter who dipped intermittently into the book musical without comparative success.

The son of a lawyer, Schwartz had his first contact with show business playing piano for the silent films. He passed through college and law school and he worked both as a high school teacher and as a lawyer whilst writing songs, at first for college shows and later with professional publication and performance in mind. He placed several numbers in revues (*The Grand Street Follies, The New Yorkers*) and in Broadway musicals (*Good Boy, Queen High* ''Brother, Just Laugh It Off,'' ly: E Y Harburg, Ralph Rainger) without notable success, before in 1928 he joined forces with lyricist Howard Dietz, already the veteran of a Broadway show with no less a composer than Jerome Kern (*Dear Sir,* 1924) but, like Schwartz, looking for the elusive song hit that would fuel a career.

After further similar contributions to *Ned Wayburn's Gambols* and *Wake Up and Dream,* the pair had a first success with their part of the score for the revue *The Little Show* (1929). Dietz successfully relyricked a melody Schwartz had written a number of years before to a Lorenz Hart lyric (''I Love to Lie Awake in Bed'') as ''I Guess I'll Have to Change My Plan'' alongside four other numbers including ''I've Made a Habit of You.'' Schwartz had recently been given his first opportunity to write at least part of a score for a book musical when he combined on the songs for a musical by *Potash and Perlmutter* author Montague Glass, called *Well, Well, Well.* A version of the show did reach Broadway in 1929 as *Pleasure Bound,* but with a rather different book and score from that with which it had started out. By then, Muriel Pollock and Maurie Rubens had the music credit. He had a happier experience later that year, when he combined with lyricist Desmond Carter and with Dietz on the songs for Julian Wylie's production of the touring British musical *Here Comes the Bride* (1930). It was a fairly functional score, subordinate to the highly farcical libretto, but it turned up one prettily lilting piece in ''High and Low,'' which Schwartz later reused in the Broadway revue *The Bandwagon* (1931).

The composer supplied songs to several other London shows of 1930s (*The Co-Optimists, Little Tommy Tucker*) and back in America he contributed to the revue *Three's a Crowd* (''Something to Remember You By'') and to the musical montage which Szirmai's *Princess Charming* (*Alexandra*) had become, but it was the revue *The Bandwagon* (''Dancing in the Dark,'' ''New Sun in the Sky,'' ''I Love Louisa'') which established Schwartz—who had now renounced law for the theatre on a full-time basis—and Dietz as coming men.

The pair had further success with another Broadway revue *Flying Colors* (''A Shine on Your Shoes,'' ''Louisiana Hayride,'' ''Alone Together,'' ''Smokin' Reefers,'' ''Two-Faced Woman,'' ''Fatal Fascination'') the following season, but Schwartz's next book musical was again for London. He provided nine songs to illustrate the German musical farce *Nice Goings On* (''The Devil and the Deep, Blue Sea,'' ''What a Young Girl Ought to Know''), which starred Leslie Henson through 221 performances. A first Broadway musical score, *Revenge with Music* (1934) lasted less time on the stage (158 performances) but housed a more enduring hit number in ''You and the Night and the Music'' as well as the attractive ''If There is Someone Lovelier Than You.'' In between times (1933), Schwartz teamed with Edward Heyman to supply a pair of songs for Dwight Deere Wiman's production of the Howard Lindsay play *She Loves Me Not,* and the following year set a Morrie Ryskind lyric for use in Ryskind and Kaufman's play *Bring on the Girls.*

Schwartz's real successes in the 1930s came in revue, both—on Broadway with *At Home Abroad* (1935, 198 performances) in which Eleanor Powell introduced ''Gotta Brand New Suit'' and Beatrice Lillie performed ''Get Yourself a Geisha'' and in London with *Follow the Sun* (1936, 204 performances) where ''Love Is a Dancing Thing'' emerged from the song-sheet *Stop Press* and *At Home Abroad.* The book musicals fared less well. Of the two premiered in 1937, *Between the Devil,* with Evelyn Laye, Jack Buchanan and Adele Dixon starred, lasted but 93 performances at Broadway's Imperial Theater, but nevertheless introduced ''Triplets'' (popular ever since as a novelty and benefit item) and ''I See Your Face Before Me,'' whilst *Virginia* survived 60 performances and left nothing more memorable than ''You and I Know.''

When Dietz went to Hollywood as a publicist for MGM, Schwartz teamed up with lyricist Dorothy Fields. Their first Broadway show together was *Stars in Your Eyes* which, disemboweled on the road, lasted only marginally longer than the 1937 pieces (127 performances) in spite of a cast headed by Jimmy Durante and Ethel Merman (''This Is It,'' ''The Lady Needs a Change,'' ''Okay for Sound''), after which Schwartz followed Dietz to Hollywood. There he produced the Rita Hayworth film *Cover Girl* and the much less satisfactory Cole Porter biopic *Night and Day,* as well as providing songs for a number of films, most notably *Thank Your Lucky Stars* (1943, "They're Either Too Young or Too Old"), *The Time, the Place and the Girl* (1946, "A Gal in Calico") and also including *Navy Blues, All Through the Night, Crossroads, Cairo* and *Princess O'Rourke.*

Back on Broadway, seven years on, Schwartz paired with Ira Gershwin on the score for the short-lived *Park Avenue* (72 performances) and came together again with Dietz for the successful 1948 revue *Inside USA* ("Rhode Island Is Famous for You," "Haunted Heart"), which he also produced, before teaming again with Miss Fields for two vehicles for star comedienne Shirley Booth. Both *A Tree Grows in Brooklyn* ("I'm Like a New Broom," "Look Who's Dancing," "He Had Refinement") and *By the Beautiful Sea* ("I'd Rather Wake Up By Myself," "Alone Too Long") ran through 270 performances and both found some fond adherents.

The film version of *Bandwagon* (1953) produced Schwartz's most widely famous song, "That's Entertainment," and the screen's *You're Never Too Young* included "Relax-ay-voo" (w Sammy Cahn), but two subsequent stage musicals with Dietz, the uncomfortable Broadway-Viennesy *The Gay Life* (113 performances) and *Jennie,* which featured Mary Martin and one catchy song called "Before I Kiss the World Goodbye" (82 performances), failed.

Schwartz subsequently shifted to Britain, but none of the pieces on which he worked there came to fruition. He withdrew his score for *Nickelby and Me* before production, and a revised English-set version of *By the Beautiful Sea* (for which he composed a number encouraging "Come to Blackpool" to add to a potpourri score of Schwartz/Dietz hits) remained unproduced. Schwartz's success remains chiefly as a writer of revue material and of individual songs for, in spite of the number of his song successes, he did not manage to compose a show score which had qualities of endurance.

1929 **Well, Well, Well** (w Muriel Pollock/Max and Nathaniel Lief/Montague Glass, Jules Eckert Goodman, Harold Atteridge) Chestnut Street Opera House, Philadelphia 7 January

1929 **Here Comes the Bride** (Desmond Carter/Robert P Weston, Bert Lee, et al) Opera House, Blackpool 7 October; Piccadilly Theatre, London 20 February 1930

1933 **Nice Goings On** (Douglas Furber, Frank Eyton/Furber) Strand Theatre, London 13 September

1934 **Revenge with Music** (Dietz) New Amsterdam Theater 28 November

1937 **Virginia** (Albert Stillman/Laurence Stallings, Owen Davis) Center Theater 2 September

1937 **Between the Devil** (Dietz) Imperial Theater 22 December

1939 **Stars in Your Eyes** (Dorothy Fields/J P McEvoy) Majestic Theater 9 February

1946 **Park Avenue** (Ira Gershwin/Nunnally Johnson, George S Kaufman) Shubert Theater 4 November

1951 **A Tree Grows in Brooklyn** (D Fields/Betty Smith, George Abbott) Alvin Theater 19 April

1954 **By the Beautiful Sea** (D Fields/Herbert Fields, D Fields) Majestic Theater 8 April

1961 **The Gay Life** (Dietz/Fay Kanin, Michael Kanin) Shubert Theater 18 November

1963 **Jennie** (Dietz/Arnold Schulman) Majestic Theater 17 October

SCHWARTZ, Jean (b Budapest, 4 November 1878; d Sherman Oaks, Calif, 30 November 1956). Multi-hit songwriter whose numbers often proved the take-away tunes of other fellows' shows of the early 20th century.

Schwartz had his earliest musical education from his sister, a sometime pupil of Liszt, during his youthful days in Hungary. He moved to America with his family at the age of 10 and was soon on the work market, holding jobs in a cigar factory and a turkish bath, amongst others, before his earliest musical engagements as a band pianist at Coney Island, a song-plugger at the Siegel-Cooper store on Sixth Avenue and for the music-publishing house of Shapiro-Bernstein, and, later, as a rehearsal and pit pianist for Broadway shows.

Schwartz formed a songwriting partnership with lyricist William Jerome, and the young team ("a pair who have risen from the obscure variety halls") soon succeeded in getting their songs placed in a number of touring farce comedies (*Topsy Turvy, Andy Lewis, In Spotless Town,* etc) and Broadway shows, notably Weber and Fields's *Hoity-Toity* (1901, "When Mr Shakespeare Comes to Town"), a show for which young Schwartz was employed as an on-stage pianist, and *The Billionaire* (1902, "When the Stars Are Shining Bright"). Their first big song successes came with "Rip van Winkle Was a Lucky Man," sung on Broadway in J J McNally's *Sleeping Beauty and the Beast* (1901) and in London's *The Cherry Girl* (1903); "Mr Dooley," one of several songs interpolated in the Broadway production of *A Chinese Honeymoon* (USA); and "Bedelia" as sung first by Blanche Ring in the short-lived *The Jersey Lily* (1903) on Broadway, then in London by George Grossmith jr (who had done well with "Mr Dooley" on the halls) in the very much more successful *The Orchid.*

The pair provided fresh material for the Americanized version of the English musical *An English Daisy* (1904), they wrote the songs (one of which was "Bedelia") for a vehicle for the Ellmore Sisters, Kate and May, called *Mrs Delaney of Newport* and, shortly after, the now established songwriters were able to show off their first full Broadway score in Fred C Whitney's production of *Piff! Paff! Pouf!* ("Cordelia Malone"), billed as "a musical cocktail," at the Casino Theater. *Piff! Paff! Pouf!* had a fine run of 264 performances, and its composer and his partner were set up to such an extent that they provided or contributed largely to the scores for no less than five musicals—principally the vaudeville-style shows or spectaculars that their frankly popular songs suited best—over the next year. Their biggest song success of that year, however, was again an interpolation: ''My Irish Molly O,'' one of several of their numbers performed by Blanche Ring in *Sergeant Brue.*

Over the next 20 years a vast stream of numbers issued from Schwartz's pen—''Sit Down, You're Rocking the Boat,'' ''I Love the Ladies,'' etc—but his main and most successful activity was still in the theatre. He wrote a large amount of revue material, including the basic musical scores for such pieces as *The Passing Shows of 1913, 1918, 1919, 1921, 1923* and *1924, The Shubert Gaieties of 1919,* the Shuberts' *The Midnight Rounders* and its 1921 edition, *The Whirl of the Town, The Mimic World of 1921, Make It Snappy* (1922), *Artists and Models* (1923), *Topics of 1923* and *A Night in Spain* (1927), as well as providing odd numbers for shows such as the *Ziegfeld Follies of 1907* (''Handle Me with Care'' w William Jerome) and *1908* (''When the Girl You Love Is Loving'').

Over the same period he also supplied scores, both for regular musicals and for shows which ran a fine line between revue and musical comedy, for Blanche Ring (*When Claudia Smiles*), Eddie Foy (*Up and Down Broadway* in which ''Chinatown, My Chinatown'' was first heard, and three songs in *Over the River*), Eddie Cantor (*Make It Snappy*), Julian Eltinge (*The Fascinating Widow*) and Mistinguett (the 1924 revue *Innocent Eyes*), and in collaboration with J J McNally, author of the successful *Rogers Brothers* series of variety musicals, he also wrote the songs for vehicles for the popular blackface duo McIntyre and Heath (*The Ham Tree, In Hayti*) and for Lulu Glaser (*Lola from Berlin*). However, he found the most effective successor to Blanche Ring as champion purveyor of his songs when Al Jolson introduced his ''Rum Tum Tiddle'' (ly: Edward Madden) in *Vera Violetta* (1911). Schwartz subsequently wrote the basic score of the ''spectacular farce with music'' *The Honeymoon Express* for Jolson but, more notably, he supplied him with four songs for the hit-filled *Sinbad* (1918), including the durable ''Rockabye Your Baby with a Dixie Melody'' and ''Hello Central, Give Me No-Mans Land'' (ly: Joe Young, Sam Lewis).

He also, throughout, continued to supply individual numbers and special material for use as interpolations in musicals both imported and native, amongst which were *The Prince of Pilsen* (1903, ''In Cincinnati''), *The Little Cherub* (1906, ''My Irish Rose''), *The Rich Mr Hoggenheimer* (1906, ''Any Old Time at All''), *The Silver Star* (1909), *The Echo* (1909, ''The Newport Glide''), *Modest Susanne* (1910, ''Peaches,'' ''Tangoland Tap''), *A Winsome Widow* (1912), *The Wall Street Girl* (1912, ''Whistle It'' for Blanche Ring), *The Sun Dodgers* (1913), *Hands Up* (1915), *Pom-Pom* (1916), *Betty* (1916), *Oh, My Dear!* (1918), *Tangerine* (1921) and *The Rose of Stambul* (1922, ''Why Do They Die at the End of a Classical Dance?''). In the 1920s, although he continued to turn out happy songs for the Shuberts and other producers, Schwartz generally fared less well, and in 1923 all three musicals for which he provided the score closed during their out of town tryout. His last Broadway score was written in 1928 for the musical *Sunny Days,* in which some of it was favored by the fresh voice of the young Jeanette MacDonald.

Schwartz also paired with Jerome in ''a singing and talking act'' on the vaudeville stage (Hammerstein's, December 1908) and again as a music publisher, and, for a period, with the Hungarian variety artist Jenny Dolly (née Janszieka Deutsch) of the Dolly Sisters as a husband.

1903 **Mrs Delaney of Newport** (William Jerome) Collingwood Opera House, Poughkeepsie, NY 15 September; Grand Opera House 3 November

1904 **Piff! Paff! Pouf!** (Jerome/Stanislaus Stange) Casino Theater 2 April

1905 **The Athletic Girl** (George V Hobart) 1 act Colonial Music Hall 15 February

1905 **A Yankee Circus on Mars** (w Manuel Klein/Jerome/George V Hobart) New York Hippodrome 12 April

1905 **Lifting the Lid** (Jerome/J J McNally) Aerial Gardens, New Amsterdam Theater 5 June

1905 **The Ham Tree** (Jerome/Hobart) Lyceum Theater, Rochester 17 August; New York Theater 28 August

1905 **Fritz in Tammany Hall** (Jerome/McNally) Herald Square Theater 16 October

1905 **The White Cat** (w Ludwig Englander/Harry B Smith, Jerome/ad H B Smith) New Amsterdam Theater 2 November

1907 **Lola from Berlin** (Jerome/McNally) Liberty Theater 16 September

1908 **Morning, Noon and Night** (Jerome/Joseph Herbert) Opera House, Hartford, Conn 31 August; Yorkville Theater 5 October

1909 **In Hayti** (Jerome/McNally) Circle Theater 30 August

1910 **Up and Down Broadway** (Jerome/Edgar Smith) Casino Theater 18 July

1912 **Over the River** (w John Golden/Hobart, H A Du Souchet) Globe Theater 8 January

1912 **The Fascinating Widow** (w F A Mills/Otto Harbach) Chestnut Street Opera House, Philadelphia 3 April

1913 **The Honeymoon Express** (Harold Atteridge) Winter Garden Theater 6 February

1913 **When Claudia Smiles** (Jerome/Leo Ditrichstein) Illinois Theater, Chicago 13 April

1914 **When Claudia Smiles** (revised version by Anne Caldwell) 39th Street Theater 2 February

1918 **See You Later** (*Loute*) new score w William F Peters/ad Guy Bolton, P G Wodehouse Academy of Music, Baltimore 15 April

1919 **Monte Cristo Jr** (w Sigmund Romberg/Atteridge) Winter Garden Theater 12 February

1919 **Hello, Alexander** (revised *The Ham Tree*) (Alfred Bryan/ Edgar Smith, Emily Young) 44th Street Theater 7 October

1920 **Page Mr Cupid** (Blanche Merrill/Owen Davis) Shubert Crescent Theater, Brooklyn 17 May

1923 **The Bal Tabarin** (w Fred J Coots/McElbert Moore/ Moore, Edward Delaney Dunn) Apollo Theater, Atlantic City 30 April

1923 **The Courtesan** (w Romberg/Atteridge/Harry Wagstaffe Gribble, Atteridge) Parsons' Theater, Hartford, Conn 17 October

1923 **That Casey Girl** (Jerome/Hobart, Willard Mack) Lyceum, Paterson, NJ 22 October

1926 **Nancy** (William H Clifford) Mission, Long Beach 16 May

1928 **Sunny Days** (w Eleanor Dunsmuir/Clifford Grey/William Cary Duncan) Imperial Theater 8 February

1928 **Headin' South** (A Bryan, et al/Edgar Smith) Keith's Theater, Philadelphia 1 October

1942 **Full Speed Ahead** (Irving Actman, H Leopold Spitalny/ Rowland Leigh) Forrest Theater, Philadelphia 25 December

SCHWARTZ, Stephen [Lawrence] (b New York, 6 March 1948).

The writer of songs for two long-running musical shows of the early 1970s, *Godspell* (''Day by Day'') and *Pippin* (''Magic to Do,'' ''Corner of the Sky''), which mirrored the attitudes and preoccupations of American youth of the period.

Schwartz had his earliest work—including revue material, title songs to the plays *Butterflies Are Free* and *Little Boxes,* and a first version of *Pippin*—produced whilst still studying theatre and music at college. By the time he was 25 years old, *Godspell* and the revised Broadway version of his early *Pippin* were both playing successfully, he had written additional lyrics to the Roman mass for the Leonard Bernstein Mass (w Bernstein), and had become a recording company executive and producer.

Schwartz had a further long run with the musical score for magician Doug Henning's vehicle *The Magic Show,* but a musical adaptation of the French classic *La Femme du boulanger* as *The Baker's Wife,* in spite of containing his most substantial and adult work to date, folded without making its Broadway opening. He subsequently contributed to the score of the musical *Working,* before venturing once more and with distaste into the large-scale commercial theatre as the lyricist of the short-lived *Rags.*

In 1988, on the initiative of director Trevor Nunn, who had been impressed with songs from *The Baker's Wife* which he had heard in auditions, the show was exhumed, rewritten and produced by Nunn in Britain. But the very long new version seemed to have more faults than the first and the piece failed again. It was, however, followed by a second London enterprise, a collaboration with Nunn's Royal Shakespeare Company colleague John Caird on another biblical musical, *Children of Eden.* Extravagantly staged, it proved to lack the attractions of the simpler *Godspell* and folded quickly. It was later given a production in America.

Schwartz subsequently turned to writing for the animated screen and provided lyrics and/or songs for this Disney cartoons *Pocahontas* (1995) and *The Hunchback of Notre Dame* (1996, theatre version 1999) and for the rival *The Prince of Egypt* (1998).

1971 **Godspell** (John Michael Tebelak) Cherry Lane Theater 17 May

1972 **Pippin** (Roger O Hirson) Imperial Theater 23 October

1974 **The Magic Show** (Bob Randall) Cort Theater 28 May

1976 **The Baker's Wife** (Joseph Stein) Dorothy Chandler Pavilion, Los Angeles 11 May

1978 **Working** (many inc Schwartz) 46th Street Theater 14 May

1986 **Rags** (Charles Strouse/Stein) Mark Hellinger Theater 21 August

1991 **Children of Eden** (John Caird) Prince Edward Theatre, London 8 January

1996 **Snapshots** (w others/David Stern) Westport County Playhouse 3 September

1999 **The Hunchback of Notre Dame** (Alan Menken/James Lapine ad Michael Kunze) Theater des Westens 5 June

DER SCHWARZE HECHT *see* FEUERWERK

SCHWARZWALDMÄDEL Operette in 3 acts by August Neidhart. Music by Leon Jessel. Komische Oper, Berlin, 25 August 1917.

Hans and Richard, two Viennese lads-about-town, come to the little Black Forest town of St Christoph so that Hans can escape the overwhelming attentions of Malwine von Hainau. Amidst the lively dancing, boozing and scrapping of the festivities of St Cecilia's Day, Malwine (who has arrived in hot pursuit) transfers her attentions to Richard, whilst Hans finds happiness with Bärbele, the orphan maidservant of old Blasius Römer (Gustav Charlé), the town organist, who had almost got around to foolishly proposing to her himself.

Jessel's score was a bright and infectious one, full of dancing country melodies of which the most winning, a little waltz called ''Erklingen zum Tanze die Geigen'' and a pretty shadow dance (''Schöner Tänzer, du entschwindest''), both fell to the ingenue playing Bärbele. Richard won the best of the men's numbers with the bouncy title-song ''Mädel aus dem schwarzen Wald'' and his uncomplicated wooing of ''Malwine, ach, Malwine'' whilst that lady and Hans souped things up with their contrastingly big, lyrical tongue-in-cheek duo ''Muss denn die Lieb' stets Tragödie sein.''

As so often happens in troubled times, this piece of good-old-days simplicity with its delightful folksy music proved a singular success when mounted by Gustav Charlé at his Komische Oper in wartime Berlin. Only *Das Dreimäderlhaus,* another piece of simply sentimental and romantic musical theatre, did better than *Schwarzwaldmädel* which passed its five hundredth performance on 30 December 1918, and then its second anniversary before it finally closed on 1 September 1919. The show's success, however, did not limit itself to the war years. Although it was oddly ignored outside its homeland—a production in Buenos Aires and another in the German-language theatre in New York being isolated non-European productions—*Schwarzwaldmädel* went on to play thousands of performances throughout Germany, proving itself there probably the most popular piece ever premiered in Berlin prior to *Im weissen Rössl,* and establishing itself as part of the standard repertoire. It also found its way on to film four times. The first, in 1920, featured a silent Uschi Elleot in its central role, whilst Victor Janson's version of 1929 starred Liane Haid, Walter Janssen, Fred Louis Lerch, Georg Alexander and Olga Limburg. Hans Söhnker and Maria Beling starred in the third version.

The show's career was halted when the Jewish Jessel was declared persona non grata by the Nazis, but after the war and the death of the composer at the hands of the regime, *Schwarzwaldmädel* made its way ineluctably back to the screen in a 1950 filmed version, with Paul Hörbiger as Blasius, onto television, onto the stage, where it remains regularly performed to this day, and onto a number of recordings.

Austria: Neues Wiener Stadttheater 1923; USA: Irving Place Theater October 1924

Films: Luna Film/Arthur Wellin 1920, Victor Jansson 1929, Georg Zoch 1933, Hans Deppe 1950

Recordings: Selections (EMI-Electrola, Ariola-Eurodisc), etc

SCHWEIGHOFER, [Karl] Felix (b Brünn, 22 November 1842; d Blazewitz nr Dresden, 28 January 1912). Comic star of the Viennese musical stage through the peak of the "golden age."

The young Schweighofer spent a colorful decade in theatres of mostly a lower level throughout central Europe, playing everything from comedy and Possen to the roles normally played by travesty sopranos in Operette, in theatres from Odenburg to Odessa and Bucharest, or on tour, before graduating to good comic roles and to the Stadttheater in Graz.

He was engaged briefly at the Theater an der Wien under Strampfer, but after one season he moved on to Brünn, then to Berlin's Friedrich-Wilhelmstädtisches Theater, and guested in leading comic roles at several German and Austrian houses in company with Josefine Gallmeyer, whom he also joined for a period at Vienna's Strampfertheater. He played there in the Offenbach opérettes *Dorothea* and *Paimpol und Perinette,* in *Die Familie Trouillat* and in Jonas's *Der Ente mit drei Schnabeln* (*Le Canard à trois becs*), and introduced the role of *Hammlet* in the burlesque of that title, but he soon moved on again and in the following years he again trod the stages of Europe, this time round in lead roles. At the same time, however, he also began to make himself a place back at the Theater an der Wien, now under the management of Maximilian Steiner.

Plate 347. **Felix Schweighofer.** *The great Viennese comedian dressed for an unidentified role.*

In the mid- and late 1870s he appeared in many Possen on that house's program and also in a long list of opérettes and Operetten: *Die Perle der Wascherinnin* (1875, van der Pruth), *Die Creolin* (1876, De Feuillemorte), *Luftschlosser* (Kasimir Staarl), *Der Seekadett* (Don Januario), *König Carotte* (Carotte), as Frank in the one hundredth performance of *Die Fledermaus,* in *Königin Indigo* (1877, Romadour), *Ein Blitzmädel* (Leo Brüller), *Der galante Vicomte* (Desfontains), *Der Jahrmarkt von St Laurent* (Ramolini), *Die Glocken von Corneville* (1878, Gaspard), *Madame Favart* (1879, Pontsablé), *Gräfin Dubarry* (Novailles), *Blindekuh* (Kragel), *Die hübsche Perserin* (1880, Moka), *Ein Schotte* (*L'Écossais de Chatou,* Hippolyte), *Musketiere in Damenstift* (1881, Abbé Bridaine) and *Lili (*St Hypothèse).

In the early 1880s Schweighofer created a memorable series of comic roles in some of the most important Austrian shows of the time: Graf Villalobos y Rodriquez in Strauss's *Das Spitzentuch des Königin* (1880), the lubricious Prutschesko in *Apajune, der Wassermann* (1880), the little lost tulip-grower Balthasar Groot in *Der lustige Krieg* (1881), the vengeful Colonel Ollendorf in *Der Bettelstudent* (1882, introducing the great waltz song ''Ach ich hab' sie ja nur auf die Schulter geküsst''), Pappacoda in the Viennese version of *Eine Nacht in Venedig* (1883) and the pompous Podesta Nasoni in *Gasparone* (1884), as well as Troupeau in Millöcker's *Der Jungfrau von Belleville* and Oppini in Müller's *Der kleine Prinz,* before quarreling with the management of the Theater an der Wien and quitting it for the rival Carltheater. His one important new role at the Carltheater was that of Don Ranucio di Colibrados in Dellinger's *Don Cesar* (1885). He subsequently left Vienna to make his home in Dresden and to once more run the circuits of the European houses, now as a fully qualified major star.

He returned occasionally for guest appearances in Berlin (Grimminger in *Der Rosen-Onkel,* 1887, etc) and Vienna, and in 1899 he visited New York, appearing for Hans Conried in several popular Possen including *Das Blitzmädel.* He retired from the stage in 1904.

Autobiography: *Mein Wanderleben* (Heinrich Minden, Dresden, 1912)

SCOTT, Clement [William] (b London, 6 October 1841; d London, 25 June 1904).

The most celebrated theatre critic of the British Victorian era, Scott turned out detailed and informative first-night reports in the *Daily Telegraph* between 1871 and 1898 which remain models of the genre. His journalistic career was effectively ended when he cast doubts on the perfect moral purity of members of the theatrical profession in an interview, and was attacked with hypocrital fervor by the theatrical establishment.

Scott wrote a number of stage pieces, having considerable success both with an adaptation of Sardou's *Dora* as *Diplomacy* and with the long-touring musical comedy drama *Jack in the Box* (w George Sims), and he also penned the lyrics to some highly successful songs including the patriotic ''Here Stands a Post,'' introduced at Drury Lane by Charlotte Russell and interpolated by contralto Adelaide Newton in *Wildfire* (Alhambra Theatre), and ''O Promise Me,'' an additional number inserted in the London and New York productions of De Koven's *Robin Hood* which went on to become an American wedding-day standard. His ''Dear Mother England'' (mus: J M Coward) was interpolated into the Gaiety's *The Shop Girl* (1894) and ''Sixty Years Ago, Boys'' (mus: J M Glover) was sung in the musical *The Yashmak* (1897).

1878 **The Little Duke** (*Le Petit Duc*) English version w B C Stephenson (Philharmonic Theatre)

1881 **Many Happy Returns** (Lionel Benson/w Gilbert a' Beckett) 1 act St George's Hall 28 March

1885 **Jack-in-the-Box** (William C Levey, James Glover/w George Sims) Theatre Royal, Brighton 24 August

1886 **The Lily of Léoville** (Ivan Caryll/Félix Rémo ad Alfred Murray) Comedy Theatre 10 May

1898 **Oh, What a Night** (*Eine tolle Nacht*) English lyrics to new score by John Crook (Wakefield)

SCOTTO, Vincent [Baptiste] (b Marseille, 21 April 1874; d Paris, 15 November 1952).

The teenaged Vincent Scotto, Marseille-born of Neapolitan stock, operated as an amateur songwriter and performer in his home town until the famous chansonnier Polin picked up his song ''Le Navigatore'' and, having had it set to fresh lyrics by the established Henri Christiné, made it famous throughout France as ''La Petite Tonkinoise.''

The 19-year-old composer subsequently moved to Paris, and there quickly became one of the favorite songwriters of the new century, supplying, in partnership with such lyricists as Albert Willemetz, René Sarvil, Lucien Boyer, Phylo, Geo Kogler, Audiffred, Léo Lelièvre and many others, what—in a long career—eventually totaled thousands of songs to such stars as Josephine Baker (''J'ai deux amours,'' ''Mon coeur est un oiseau des Îles''), Maurice Chevalier (''Si j'étais papa,'' ''C'est mon petit doigt''), Perchicot (''Mon Paris,'' ''Viva Mussolini'' ly: Lucien Boyer), Milton (''Le Beau Navire'') Raquel Meller (''Adieu, mon rêve''), Damia, Tino Rossi (''Le Marin veille,'' ''Soirs d'Espagne,'' ''Corsica bella,'' ''Dans la nuit, j'entends une chanson,'' ''Le Pousse Pousse,'' ''Si votre coeur vagabonde,'' ''Je vous aime sans espoir'') and Alibert (''Catherine,'' ''Mon Bateau,'' ''Toute la ville danse,'' ''C'est pas mal . . . c'est bien mieux''). A number of his songs made their way beyond France: ''La Petite Tonkinoise'' became ''It's Delightful to Be Married'' as performed by Anna Held in America (and subsequently by Fabienne Guyon as Anna Held in London's *Ziegfeld*) and ''Angelina'' was sung in Britain's *Our Miss Gibbs.*

Scotto also wrote songs and music for nearly two hundred films including *Naples au baiser de feu, Le Roi de la couture, Marseille tire-au-flanc, Embrassez-moi, La Douceur d'aimer* and *Pomme d'amour,* as well as the scores for the majority of the Marcel Pagnol films and, over a period of some 40 years, also turned out a regular supply of stage opérettes. The earliest of these were played in the provinces or in cafés-concerts and other smaller Paris venues without exciting much attention, but in 1931, in collaboration with two other southerners, his son-in-law Henri Alibert and René Sarvil, he launched *Au pays du soleil,* the first of what would become a series of seven marseillais revue-operéttes which, with their cheerful, regional flavor, accented comedy dialogue and lively songs, proved to be the popular musical equivalent of the Pagnol plays. The best of these simple, happy shows—*Au pays du soleil, Trois de la marine, Arènes joyeuses* and *Un de la Canebière* (''Le plus beau tango du monde'')—remained favorites for a number of years, during which time they were toured, filmed, revived and toured again, and they remain part of the French regional repertoire to the present day.

In 1948 Scotto stepped away from the jolly, locally colored style of these small-scale pieces to supply the score for what was to be his most substantial and long-running stage show, the Théâtre Mogador's romantic and glamorous *Violettes impériales,* and, as a result of its success, he ventured two further spectacular pieces for the same theatre: the period romance *La Danseuse aux étoiles* (1950) and the posthumously-produced *Les Amants de Venise* (1953), which won a run of more than five hundred performances.

One of the most memorable French songwriters of his age, he proved with his large-stage works that he could adapt effectively to a lusher style.

In 1983 a compilation show of the *Dreimäderlhaus* kind, loosely based on the composer's (love) life, was played at the Théâtre de la Renaissance under the title *Vincent et Margot,* whilst a Scotto pasticcio, *Le Curé de la Canebière* (ad Michel de Carol) was produced at Sanary 25 July 1986.

1912 **Suzie, ou la petite milliardaire** (Maurice Mareil) Théâtre des Variétés, Toulouse 6 April

1919 **Charlot de la Chapelle** (*La Poupée du faubourg*) (Armand Foucher) Bouffes-Concertantes 24 January

1919 **On y va tous!** (Georges Arnould, Jacques Charles, Espian, Fernand Rouvray) Marseilles 12 February

1919 **Miss Detective** (Tasta) Scala, Bordeaux 5 September

1920 **L'Amour qui rôde** (Michel Carré fils, Albert Acrémant) Eldorado 30 April

1922 **Pan-Pan** (Carré, Acrémant) Ba-ta-clan 19 April

1922 **Zo-Zo** (Bertal-Maubon, Hérault) Eldorado 2 May

1924 **La Princesse du Moulin-Rouge** (Émile Codey, A Denis) Excelsior-Concert 1 February

1924 **Fauves affamées** (Mark) Marseille 8 February

1924 **Coeur d'artichaut** (Codey) Casino, Limoges 12 August

1925 **La Poule des Folies-Bergère** (Codey) Gâite-Montparnasse 31 July

1925 **La Famille Banaste** (M Andrès) Tarascon 13 September

1926 **P'lotons en avant** (Codey, Denis) Casino, Montreuil 15 January

1928 **Pour un baiser** (Danam, G Barthélémy) Nice 20 January

1930 **As-tu vu son grain de beauté?** (Palan, René Pujol, Cuilliez) Le Havre 21 March

1930 **Denise, garde ta chemise** (*La Belle Mexicaine*) (Pierre Chambard) Lyon 21 November

1931 **Garde-moi** (Danam, Barthélémy) Beaucaire 15 November

1932 **C'n'est pas l'amour** (Bertal, Maubon, Héraud) Fantasio 19 August

1932 **Au Pays du soleil** (Henri Alibert/René Sarvil) Moulin de la Chanson 22 October

1932 **Ces messieurs, dames** (Carco, Rieux, Varna, Merry) Studio Paris 19 November

1933 **Pauline** (Marc-Cab, Gévaudan) Nice 6 January

1933 **Nuits de Princesse** (Carricart, Géo Koger) St Denis 6 October

1933 **Trois de la marine** (Alibert/Sarvil) Nouvel-Ambigu 20 December

1934 **L'Aventure de Céline** (Barthélémy, Danam, Gévaudan) Bizerte 30 January

1934 **Les Grandes Manoeuvres** (Rip) Paris 27 October

1934 **Zou! le Midi bouge** (aka *Arènes Joyeuses*) (Alibert/Sarvil, Vincy) Alcazar 8 December

1935 **Nine** (Danam, Barthélémy, Marc-Cab) Eldorado, Nice 10 January

1935 **Un de la Canebière** (Alibert/Sarvil, Vincy) Théâtre des Célestins, Lyon 1 October; Théâtre des Variétés 3 April 1936

1936 **Les Gangsters du Château d'If** (Alibert/Sarvil, Vincy) Théâtre des Célestins, Lyon 10 November; Théâtre des Variétés 19 January 1937

1937 **Ceux de la légion** (Alibert/Sarvil, Vincy) Théâtre Antoine 15 June

1938 **Le Roi des Galéjeurs** (Alibert/Sarvil/Vincy) Théâtre des Célestins, Lyon 16 April; Théâtre des Variétés 12 September

1940 **Le Verre dans le fruit** (Pujol, Koger, J Baurel) Théâtre de la Trianon, Bordeaux 16 February

1940 **Les Compagnons de la vertu** (Koger, Jean Guitton) Dijon 20 February

1940 **Hugues** (Jean Manse) Théâtre des Variétés, Marseille 20 December

1945 **Les Gauchos de Marseille** (Scotto/Sarvil) Théâtre des Célestins, Lyon 18 May; Théâtre des Variétés, Paris September

1948 **Violettes impériales** (Paul Achard, René Jeanne, Henri Varna) Théâtre Mogador 31 January

1950 **La Danseuse aux Étoiles** (Varna, Guy des Cars) Théâtre Mogador 18 February

1953 **Les Amants de Venise** (Marc-Cab, René Richard, Varna) Théâtre Mogador 5 December

Memoirs: *Souvenirs de Paris* (Staël, Paris, 1947)

SCRIBE, [Augustin] Eugène (b Paris, 24 December 1791; d Paris, 20 February 1861).

The most important librettist to the international musical stage of the first half of the 19th century, Scribe au-

Plate 348. **Scribe's** Un Verre d'eau *became a musical at the Staatsoperette, Dresden, in 1978.*

thored or co-authored 120 operas and opéras-comiques, long and short, including 37 for Auber (*La Muette de Portici, Les Diamants de la couronne, Fra Diavolo, Leicester, Léocadie, Le Maçon, La Fiancée, Le Philtre, Gustave III, Le Cheval de bronze, Le Domino noir, La Sirène, La Part du Diable, Haydée, Marco Spada, Manon Lescaut, La Circassienne,* etc), and others for Meyerbeer (*Robert le Diable, Les Huguenots, Le Prophète, L'Étoile du nord, L'Africaine*), Verdi (*Les Vêpres siciliennes* and an adapation of his earlier *Gustave III* as *Un Ballo in Maschera*), Donizetti (*Betly*), Adam (*Le Châlet, Giralda*), Boïeldieu (*La Dame blanche*), Balfe (*Le Puits d'amour*), Halévy (*La Juive, La Tempesta* based on Shakespeare) and Rossini (*Le Comte Ory*). Several of his opéras-comiques, particularly those written with such composers as Hérold or Auber, or those which treated such subjects as Cherubini's *Ali Baba, ou Les Quarante Voleurs,* ran very close to the imaginary line between the ancient and modern musical theatre, a modern theatre to which his direct contribution was limited only by the fact that he died in 1861. He had, however, strayed across the line in collaborating twice with Offenbach, once on a version of his 1827 vaudeville *La Chatte métamorphosée en femme* (already musicalized in Austria by Hauptner) and again on the full-length tale of a dog called *Barkouf.*

The absent Scribe had, however, a strong indirect influence on what followed his era, both as the most important forefather of the late 19th-century opérette libretto, but also, more concretely, through the multiple adaptations of his plays and libretti made not only by countless contemporaries but also by later writers. Undoubtedly the most important of these, in the modern musical theatre, was the remaking of his text to *La Circassienne* as the libretto for von Suppé's highly successful *Fatinitza* (1876). The widow Scribe's objections to this apparently unauthorized (and unpaid for?) reuse did not stop other Austrian writers and composers from plundering the bottomless Scribe catalogue.

Max Wolf set two remade Scribe libretti: *Césarine* (lib: Adolf Schirmer), produced in 1878 at Berlin's Komische Oper and the Vienna Ringtheater, admitted to being based on an unspecified Scribe piece, but the 1884 *Raffaela* (lib: Ignaz Schnitzer) was announced as based on *Le Duc d'Olonne.* Charles Cassmann and Willi Wulff's text for Zumpe's successful *Farinelli* (1888) was based on Scribe's text for Auber's comic opera *La Part du Diable* (already borrowed for a Vienna vaudeville *Carlo Bracci, oder der Antheil des Teufels* by Emil Titl and Franz Xaver Told) mixed with parts of a play called *Farinelli* (Teigmann), whilst Bernhard Buchbinder's book to Alfred Zamara's *Der Sänger von Palermo* was a version of *Ne touchez pas à la Reine,* a piece already musicalized in 1847 (mus: Boisselot) as *Die Königin von Léon* (Theater an der Wien 15 July). *Der Liebesbrunnen* with music by Paul Mestrozzi (Fürsttheater 21 April 1889) was a fresh version of *Le Puits d'amour,* Ludwig Held and Benjamin Schier's libretto for the Eduard Kremser Operette *Der Schlosserkönig* (1889) admitted to being ''nach ein Idee des Scribe'' and Zell and Genée's *Die Dreizehn* (Carltheater 6 February 1887) and *Die Piraten* (Walhalla-Theater, Berlin 9 October 1886) also came from unspecified Scribe sources.

The borrowing did not let up in the 1890s. The text for Franz Wagner's Operette *Der Cognac-König* (Carltheater 20 February 1897) was taken by Held and Léon from *La Frontière de Savoie, Katze und Maus* by the younger Johann Strauss (1898) was based on the famous *La Bataille de dames* (w Ernest Legouvé), *Der Husar* (1898, Ignaz Brüll/Victor Léon) was taken from ''Scribeschen Stoffe'' and *Leuchtkäfer* (Ludwig Fernand, Alfred Schönfeld), composed by Moritz Fall—father of Leo—and produced at the Wilhelm-Theater, Magdeburg (18 February 1899), also nodded towards Scribe without being more precise. A comic opera, *Offizier der Königin,* composed by Otto Fiebach and produced at Dresden (3 May 1900), was based on *Le Verre d'eau* and the Hirschberger/Pohl libretto to Dellinger's *Jadwiga* (Dresden, 1901) again noted that it was ''frei nach Scribe.'' The author's name was also mentioned in connection with Karl Stix's 1861 one-acter *Ein Kapitalist, der einen Dienst sucht* (mus: Suppé, Theater an der Wien 1 June).

Undoubtedly there were many more ''Scribeischen'' borrowings hidden under the admissions (in various forms) that libretti were ''from the French'' but, again, some of these nebulous credits were undoubtedly due to the fact that at certain periods it was considered fashionable (and critic-warning) to be announced as a version of an unspecified Paris success, and the French source involved was in these cases often at least semi-imaginary.

In Hungary Scribe's *La Déesse* became *Az istennő* (Miklós Forrai, Népszínház 6 March 1896) and *La Bataille de dames* got a second musicalization as *Nők harca* (Pesti Színház 19 November 1942 István Zágon/Tibor Hegedűs), whilst in Britain *Le Philtre* was reused by George Macfarren as the basis for his operetta *Jessy Lea* (1863), *Giralda,* already made over as a play by Dion Boucicault, was most successfully remade into *Manteaux Noirs* and that show's composer Bucalossi commandeered a second Scribe piece, *La Frileuse* (ad Frank Desprez), to set as *Delia* (Bristol 11 March 1889). However, by the 20th century both countries had moved on to writing and enjoying a different style of show and Scribe's material was no longer so frequently useful as raw stuff.

Nevertheless, Künneke's opera *Coeur-As* (Emil Tschirsch, Carl Berg, Dresden 31 October 1913) declared itself based on something by Scribe and even the 1920 Broadway musical *Betty Be Good* insisted that its wisp of a plot was ''from a French vaudeville by Scribe.'' Musical versions of *La Bataille de dames* continued to appear, the younger Strauss's version and an Italian operatic one being followed by a pair of Italian operettas (*Battaglia di dame,* Mario Bona/Gigi Mecheletti, La Spezia 19 September 1914 and *Battaglia di dame,* Gea della Garisenda/Luigi Michelotti Teatro Fossati, Milan, 1915), a German one, *Inkognito* (Rudolf Nelson/Kurt Kraatz, Richard Kessler, Kammerspiele 4 June 1918), and most recently an Austrian one (Hans Pero/Arthur Kendall, Kammerspiele Innsbruck 15 September 1961). *Ein Glas Wasser* got a fresh musicalization as ''ein Stück mit Musik'' by Helmut Käutner at the Dresden Staatsoperette in 1978 (8 November).

Scribe's little *L'Ours et le pacha* (1820, w J X B Saintine) was made over many times as a musical piece. Hervé and Audran both cut their composing teeth on versions and Bazin's setting was played at the Opéra-Comique (21 February 1879), whilst in Austria (1820) and Germany (1821), in different musical versions, it became *Der Bär und der Bassa* and in Britain it was made up into the little *Bears not Beasts.*

Scribe's texts, and the successful operas made from them also underwent much burlesquing in the age of burlesque. In Britain, *Les Diamants de la couronne* (*The Half-Crown Diamonds*), *La Muette de portici* (*Mass-en-yell-oh,* etc), *Fra Diavolo* and *L'Africaine* all came under the burlesque-merchants' punny hands, whilst in Vienna *La Dame blanche* became *Die schwarze Frau* (Adolf Müller, 1826).

1853 **La Lettre au bon dieu** (Gilbert Duprez/w Frédéric de Courcy) Opéra-Comique 28 April

1858 **La Chatte métamorphosée en femme** (Jacques Offenbach/w A H J Mélesville) 1 act Théâtre des Bouffes-Parisiens 19 April

1858 **Broskovano** (Louis Deffès w Henri Boisseaux) Théâtre Lyrique 29 September

1858 **Les Trois Nicolas** (Louis Clapisson/w Bernard Lopez, Gabriel de Lurieu) Opéra-Comique 16 December

1860 **Le Nouveau Pourcegnac** (Aristide Hignard/w Charles Gaspard Delestre-Poirson) 1 act Théâtre des Bouffes-Parisiens 14 January

1860 **Barkouf** (Offenbach/w Boisseaux) Opéra-Comique 24 December

1861 **La Beauté du Diable** (Jules Alary/w Émile de Najac) 1 act Opéra-Comique 28 May

Literature: Arvin, N C: *Eugène Scribe and the French Theatre 1815–1860* (Harvard University Press, Cambridge, 1924)

[LA] SCUGNIZZA Operetta in 3 acts by Carlo Lombardo. Music by Mario Costa. Teatro Alfieri, Turin, 16 December 1922.

One of the most successful Italian operettas of its period, the light-footed *La scugnizza* used for its libretto some of the most hard-worked plot and character elements of the past decades, adjoined to an attractive dance-based score. The tale introduced an American millionaire called Toby, his daughter Gaby and his secretary Chic into a nice, normal Italian town where Toby takes a fancy to pretty little Salomè. By the time there has been a costume ball and Gaby has taught Salomè how to do the shimmy, the signorina sensibly decides to stick to her local Toto. Gaby pairs off with Chic, and Toby has to make do with the embraces of Auntie Maria Grazia.

Mario Costa's score duly took in the fashionable dance rhythms of the fox-trot in Salomè's Fox-Trott della Scugnizza (''Napoletana! come canti tu'') and the shimmy in the duetto comico ''Schimmy!,'' and there were sizeable dance breaks to be found in most of the other main numbers of the score—the Quartetto degli Scugnizzi (''Ombre son che nella notte'') for the four young people, the duetti comici ''Salome'' and ''I capelli bianchi!''—with only the occasional pause for a more romantic moment, such as the soprano romanza ''La giovinezza non ritorna più!''

La scugnizza has remained a part of the small list of (intermittently) revivable Italian shows through the three-quarters of a century since its production.

Recordings: selection (EDM), etc

SEABROOKE, Thomas Q[uigley] [QUIGLEY, Thomas James] (b Mount Vernon, NY, 20 October 1860; d Chicago, 3 April 1913). Comic star of the 19th-century American musical stage.

Originally employed as a bank clerk, Seabrooke went on the stage at the age of 20 and had his early theatrical experience touring as a juvenile man in all kinds of pieces from drama to farce comedies and burlesques (with Barry & Fay in *Irish Aristocracy, Aphrodite, A Tin Soldier,* Charles Wells in Barry & Fay's *97 or 79,* Pinkerton Roberts in *Two Bad Men,* 1884, with The Only Leon in *On the Stage* 1886, *Twenty Maidens to One Dude* 1888, etc). He toured in the principal comic role of General Knickerbocker in *The Little Tycoon,* visited Broadway as Deacon Tidd in Charles Hoyt's farce comedy *A Midnight Bell* (1889) and in the quick flop play *The Stepping Stone* (1890, A B C Johnstone), stopped short in the extravaganza *King Cole* (1889, t/o King Cole) and the farce comedy *The Fakir* (1889, Seth Boker) and in 1890 established himself thoroughly as a Broadway musical comic when he shared the comedy of *Castles in the Air* with De Wolf Hopper (Cabalastro). He ran through a series of leading comic roles in musicals in the years that followed, beginning with the title role in *The Cadi* (1891) and, with enormous success, the part of King Pommery in the popular extravaganza *The Isle of Champagne* (1892). In this latter piece he introduced a dance by five little pink-dressed lassies which was later credited with launching the fashion for the American-slim chorine to the detriment of the previously favored ''pink and palpitating heavyweight'' with valiant bust and aggressive-looking thighs.

Seabrooke carried on his blossoming starring career in another Orientalish bit of nonsense called *Tabasco* (1894, Francis) and in the title role of a Fred Gagel/Edgar Smith sequel to that piece which cast him as *The Grand Vizier* (1895, Dennis O'Grady, also producer), before appearing in a couple of plays and crossing to Britain where he appeared in George Musgrove's production of a rehash of Lecocq's *La Petite Mariée* under the title *The Scarlet Feather* (1897, Dr Alphonse). It didn't do too well, and he soon returned home.

Having parted company with the musical *Papa Gougou* (1897, Papa Gougou) when it collapsed on the pre-Broadway road, he took a fresh turn around the country in the insistent *The Isle of Champagne* before joining the company at the Casino Theater. There he appeared in the 1898 extravaganza *Yankee Doodle Dandy* (Hon Gideon Terwilliger), as Calchas in the Lillian Russell revival of *La Belle Hélène* (1899), and as Ravannes to the Cadeau of Francis Wilson and the Erminie of Miss Russell in a revival of *Erminie* (1899) and featured in the chief comic part in the American version of *Les Fêtards,* here called *The Rounders* (1900), as the roguish and sexually striving King of Illyria. The role was turned for his benefit into an low-comic oriental Irish potentate called Maginnis Pasha. In 1901 he toured in the comedy *A Modern Crusoe,* and in 1901–2 he appeared at the Winter Garden in several pieces including *The Supper Club* (1901, Pop Dingtuttle), a disastrous short musical show called *The Belle of Broadway* and a quick revival of *Florodora* (1902, Tweedlepunch), but soon after he found a new hit when he returned to the Casino Theater to star as Mr Pineapple, the unfortunate bridegroom of the British musical comedy *A Chinese Honeymoon,* for the up-and-zooming Shubert brothers.

He followed up as Baron Bulverstrass in the Casino Theater's less successful romantic comic opera *The Red Feather* (1903) and as Augustus Melon in the long-running *Piff! Paff! Pouf!* (1904) and toured as John Doe in the Gustave Kerker musical *The Billionaire,* before temporarily quitting the stage and taking a turn in vaudeville. He had just one further big role on Broadway, as chief comic Johnny Rocks in *Mexicana* (1906), and appeared later the same season as the Grand Inquisitor in Chicago's *The Alcayde* (1906), but although his starring days were done he continued to work in the theatre, vaudeville and in motion pictures in Chicago, virtually up to his death. He died at the age of 52, one month after his latest marriage and a large inheritance, and two weeks after a (resultant?) nervous breakdown.

His first wife was **Elvia Crox [Seabrooke],** who appeared alongside her husband in a number of his shows (Susan in *97 or 79,* Patty Boker in *The Fakir, The Grand Vizier,* Dolly Dimple in *The Little Tycoon,* etc); his last was vaudeville singer Marie Quine [née Mary Martin Shepard].

SEAL, Elizabeth [Anne] (b Genoa, Italy, 28 August 1933). British soubrette who scored a major success as Irma la Douce.

After appearing in the chorus of *Gay's the Word* and *Glorious Days,* Elizabeth Seal made her first significant London appearance as Gladys in the London Coliseum production of *The Pajama Game.* She then replaced the miscast Belita as Lola in *Damn Yankees* before being cast in the role of Irma in the English version of *Irma la Douce.* She had a great success in that part, both in London and in New York (Tony Award), but, like the role's French originator, failed to find another part in which to confirm, and her career disintegrated.

When *A Chorus Line* was taken to London, she was cast as Cassie, but she was replaced in rehearsals and the subsequent outcry in the acting profession resulted in a serious change in the Equity standard contract, preventing a management from altering a cast during the preparatory stages of a production. Her only appearances in the West End after *Irma la Douce* were as a take-over to the role of Sally Bowles in *Cabaret* (1968) and in a multiple role in a revival of *Salad Days* (1976). She subsequently became involved with teaching and directing young performers.

Plate 349. **Elizabeth Seal** *in* Salad Days.

SEARELL[E], [William] Luscombe (b Kingsteignton, Devon, 13 September 1853; d East Molsey, Surrey, 18 December 1907).

One of the most colorful characters of the Victorian musical-theatre scene, British-born and New Zealand-bred Searelle began his career as a pianist, a conductor and a composer in Christchurch, NZ. He left there in the tow of another colorful fellow, Horace Lingard, conducting a pirated version of *HMS Pinafore* and a self-composed "sequel" to Gilbert and Sullivan's show, *The Wreck of the Pinafore,* which had been (re-)produced in Dunedin. (It had been given the previous year in San Francisco credited variously to Mrs Laura Stevenson Church and to Fred Lyster, and with different music, and briskly taken off).

The pair made their way to Australia on a wave of writs and court cases, and Searelle began a career as composer and self-publicist which eventually took him from Australia to America. There he talked the ever adventurous management of the San Francisco Tivoli (where he briefly took the post of musical director) into mounting a production of his *The Fakir of Travancore,* a comic opera dealing with the Prince of Wales's 1878 visit to India which the critics felt looked and sort-of-sounded rather too much like *Aida* ("one of the chorus airs is taken directly from *Aida*"). It was played 17 times. He soon moved on, via Canada as "manager" with the Lin-

Plate 350. **Luscombe Searelle**

gards, to Britain, where he succeeded in getting not only *The Wreck of the Pinafore* (4 performances), but another comic opera, *Estrella* (37 performances, and a brief tour) exceedingly brief showings in London. Searelle did not give up, however. He got *Estrella* staged in America (1883) only to have it burned out of its Broadway theatre almost immediately (3 performances) but, in spite of its being taken up for the provinces by the third-rate Wilbur comic opera company, and in spite of great announcements as to his forthcoming productions sprayed through whatever newspapers he could charm into printing them, he ended up at the last returning to Australia.

There, finally, he found his success. British comedian Phil Day made *Estrella* a small hit with his low-comic antics, and Searelle—now working as a musical director and co-producer with Majeroni and Wilson and/or singer-manager Charles Harding—won productions for his Arabian Nights musical *Bobadil* and for *Isidora,* a vastly melodramatic piece of *Flying Dutchman*nery which did less well. He pushed, chivvied and publicized himself and others into further productions, went loudly bankrupt in 1886, and then eased his way on again to America and to South Africa. There he paused. Having seen what had happened to property and to entertainments in Australia with the discovery of gold, he bought up large, invested in theatre buildings and made (so he said) a fortune. In 1889 he was reported to be proprietor of the Theatre Royal, Johannesburg, and four or five more of the principal theatres in South Africa (although the *Era* had to retract Searelle's exaggerations after printing his freely distributed self-advertising).

He now set out to try again to conquer London, and managed to get *Isidora* produced at the Globe Theatre under the title *The Black Rover.* It didn't conquer, and from that time on, neither did he. After a few years, alongside his brother Ernest, importing all kinds of artists to South Africa, he lost his South African holdings and—in spite of his ''good friend Cecil Rhodes'' for whom (so he said) he had written a national anthem—was chased from the country, allegedly because the rebels found he was hiding guns for the enemy under his theatre's stage. His missionary sister was murdered by the Boxers in China, his brother went to the Klondyke and never recovered, and his announcements, whilst not lessening in bravado, came less and less to fruition. Yet, with typical style, the last Searelle work to appear on the stage was a sacred blank verse drama entitled *Mizpah* founded on the biblical story of Esther, written in collaboration with no less a personality than Ella Wheeler Wilcox, decorated with 22 pieces of music and songs, and produced at the San Francisco before being played around the country, and at New York's Academy of Music (24 September 1906). It was voted ''not the best work of either author'' (which was saying something) but its text was published . . . with each author's contributions printed in a different color.

Searelle's other works included an opera, *The Kisses of Circe,* which he mounted in South Africa, the cantata *Australia,* a published verse epic *The Dawn of Death* and a selection of *Tales from the Transvaal.* His music was eclectic and apparently run-of-the-mill, but he was a master at getting his shows seen and himself into the public eye, and if London rejected its first New Zealand composer with scorn, the Southern hemisphere gave his pronouncements and his works much more credence. In the end, he probably fooled posterity as well, for almost everything we know about Searelle comes from newspaper paragraphs, and there is little doubt as to who supplied those. Since he told the *New York Dramatic News* in 1902 that *Estrella* ''ran at London's Novelty Theatre for 142 nights'' it would seem that if all his statements are taken at 25 percent value they may be about right.

In 1885 Searelle married a Sydney architect's daughter and amateur singer, Blanche Ella Fenton Spencer (aka Blanche de la Fontaine, Blanche Fenton), who then took leading roles in several of his works in Australia, South Africa and also in the London production of *The Black Rover.* She proved insufficient to this last task and was quickly replaced.

1880 **The Wreck of the Pinafore** (W H Lingard and/or Fred

Lyster) Prince of Wales Theatre, Dunedin, New Zealand 29 November

1881 **The Fakir of Travancore** Tivoli Garden Theater, San Francisco 6 June

1883 **Estrella** (Walter Parke) Prince's Theatre, Manchester 14 May; Gaiety Theatre, London 24 May

1884 **Bobadil** Opera House, Sydney 22 November

1885 **Isidora** (aka *The Black Rover*) Bijou Theater, Melbourne 7 July

SECOMBE, Harry (Sir) [SECOMBE, Harold Donald] (b Swansea, 8 September 1921). Greatly popular barrel-chested Welsh comedian and vocalist, best known for his contribution to radio's *The Goon Show* and for having placed a recording of ''Vestia la giubba'' on the British hit parades.

After appearing in revue, straight theatre and in variety, Secombe moved into the musical theatre for the first time when, in the wake of the success of *Oliver!,* he conceived and starred in the London musical *Pickwick* (1963, introducing ''If I Ruled the World''), which he later also played in America (1965). He subsequently starred as D'Artagnan in a Dumas burlesque, *The Four Musketeers* (1967), with rather less success, the strains of the piece leading him to have to—on occasion—mime his singing to a taped track. Thereafter, although he was announced in 1972 to star in a biomusical on anti-Americanist Sydney Smith, he restricted his musical-theatre appearances to pantomime where he was for many years a great favorite, returning only in 1993 to repeat his *Pickwick* at the Chichester Festival.

Secombe appeared as Mr Bumble in the screen version of *Oliver!* (1968) and of *Song of Norway* (1970).

Autobiograpies: *Arias and Raspberries* (Robson, London, 1989), *Strawberries and Cheam* (Robson, London, 1996)

LE SECRET DE MARCO POLO Opérette à grand spectacle in 2 acts by Raymond Vincy. Music by Francis Lopez. Théâtre du Châtelet, Paris, 12 December 1959.

Luis Mariano, backed by 17 of the Châtelet's most magnificent scenes and a cast including Janine Ribot, Pierjac, Rosine Brédy, Claude Daltys and Robert Pizani, and equipped with a scoreful of what by this time had become very routine Francis Lopez songs (''Marco Polo,'' ''Belle,'' ''Viens,'' ''Tiki Tiki Chou,'' ''Cavaliers,'' etc) and duets, played Marco Polo through a series of unlikely and Oriental adventures. He played it for 10 months (268 performances), but both he and it left a general taste of disappointment. The piece was apparently subsequently played in Romania, making it one of the few (if not the only) Lopez piece to have been seen in translation.

On the other side of the Atlantic, Marco Polo was set to music for NBC (14 April 1956) under the title *The Adventures of Marco Polo.* Clay Warnick, Mel Pahl and Eadward Eager supplied the songs and the book was written by William Friedberg and the young Neil Simon.

Recording: original cast (Philips)

THE SECRET GARDEN Musical in 2 acts by Marsha Norman. Music by Lucy Simon. St James Theater, New York, 25 April 1991.

After languishing dustily for many years on the back-bedroom bookshelves of a million well-bred little girls who had long since grown into wives, mothers and grandmothers, Frances Hodgson Burnett's pretty, sentimental novel *The Secret Garden* (1909) shook off its dust and, at first slowly, and later with surprising commercial intent, found its way to the stage and even the screen in several different versions.

The first of the stage musicals surfaced in the early 1980s, from a trio of wives and mothers—Diana Matterson, Sue Beckwith-Smith (words) and Sharon Burgett (music)—in Watford, England. After a libretto-brush-up from TV-writer Alfred Shaughnessy it was produced at Salisbury's Playhouse (28 April 1983), but attempts to promote it further failed. A second version, however, followed soon behind when Dan Crawford's King's Head Theatre in Islington mounted a *Secret Garden* (12 January 1987) with book and lyrics by the experienced Diana Morgan and music by Stephen Markwick. Lucinda Edmonds played Mary through a six-week season.

However, in the earth prepared by these two small-house versions of the tale, a bigger *Secret Garden* grew up, and in 1991 Mrs Burnett, some seventy years after her death, was given her Broadway musical debut in a prettily designed, prettily musicked production which ran to 706 performances.

Orphaned by an epidemic in India, Mary Lennox (Daisy Eagan) is sent back to England to be cared for by her misanthropic, hunchbacked Uncle Archibald Craven (Mandy Patinkin). Craven, whose indifference to the world stems from the death of his lovely young wife, Lily (Rebecca Luker), barely notices the presence of Mary in his house. The child eventually finds her way both to Lily's garden, closed ond overgrown since the accident which cost her life, and to Colin, the Cravens' apparently invalid son (John Babcock), confined to a bed in an equally closed part of the house and, encouraged by the country lad, Dickon (Cameron Mitchell), she brings life back not only to the garden and to the boy, but also to Uncle Archie who is finally able to banish the ghosts of the past in the face of the joys of the present.

The Broadway musical, short of a leading lady in a tale where the heroine is a child, chose to bring the Ghost of Lily into the action to good dramatic and musical effect, but also to play up a passion held by Archie's doctor brother for the same Lily to very much less effect. The score proved at its best in some reaching romantic music—Lily's ghostly sheer-soprano ''Come to my Garden'' and the effective duet climax to the piece (''Where in the World''/''How Did I Know I Would Have to Leave You'') as Archie plunges haplessly round Europe, trying to exorcise his personal ghosts before returning home in a state of mind to accept the happy ending. There were some comedy maid numbers for the comedy maid (Alison Fraser), some countrified numbers for Dickon, plus an unfortunate hoedown for a comedy gardener (a hoedown in 19th-century Britain?) and a rather too obvious and ill-fitting Big Duet for the two brothers, in a score which otherwise illustrated its sentimental tale with charm, melody and appreciably little sugar.

Following its Broadway season the show was taken on tour, and it subsequently appeared in a reproduction in Australia where, cast with local favorites Anthony Warlowe and Philip Quast as the brothers and Marina Prior as Lily, it played decidedly successful seasons in Sydney and in Melbourne, before continuing on to New Zealand (State Opera House, Wellington 3 May 1996). Its first European performance took place in Pforzheim (ad Frank Thannhäuser) in 1994 with Bernhard Gärtner (Archie), Christa Warda (Lily) and Gaby Kuhn as an overaged Mary heading the cast, before, to general surprise, it turned up in 2000 as a commercial venture on the program of the formerly august British Royal Shakespeare Company (28 November).

Mrs Burnett has proved less musicalizable in the past. Both *The Lass o' Lowries* (1877) and *Little Lord Fauntleroy* (1886), though successfully played as straight plays and even as movies, failed to make it in musical form.

Germany: Stadttheater, Pforzheim *Der geheime Garten* 1 February 1994; Australia: State Theatre, Sydney 7 September 1995

Recordings: 1987 King's Head version (Dress Circle), Salisbury version studio recording (Varese), Broadway version (Sony), Australian cast (Polydor)

DER SEEKADETT Operette in 3 acts by F Zell adapted from *Le Capitaine Charlotte* by Jean-François Bayard and Philippe Dumanoir. Music by Richard Genée. Theater an der Wien, Vienna, 24 October 1876. One of the most internationally successful products of the 19th-century Viennese Operette stage, latterly faded from the repertoire in favor of the works of more fashionable ''name'' musicians.

Der Seekadett shared its title with the popular 1835 comic opera by Labarr and Kupelwieser, but Zell's version of Bayard and Dumanoir's well-known story for the newer piece had, in fact, little enough to do with the sea. The actress Fanchette Michel (Hermine Meyerhoff) comes to Lisbon in search of her strayed lover, Lambert de Saint-Querlonde (Jani Szíka), unaware that he has been secretly married to the young Queen of Portugal (Bertha Steinher). Caught in Lambert's apartments with the Queen approaching, Fanchette disguises herself in the uniform of a well-connected due-to-arrive sea cadet. The antics of the real cadet, who goes on the ran-dan when he finds he doesn't have to turn up for duty, lead Fanchette to a duel, the Queen's belief that Lambert is deceiving her leads to her making advances to the false cadet, and complication piles on deception until finally Fanchette changes back into skirts and, leaving Lambert to his consort's position and the Queen to her wonderings, goes off into the sunset with a wealthy Peruvian called Don Januario de Sonza-Silva e Pernambuco (Felix Schweighofer), who has been chasing her sighfully since the first reel. The chief comical moments of the piece were the province of Alexander Girardi cast here as Don Domingos Borgos de Barros, the royal Master of Ceremonies and the husband of the much younger Donna Antonia (Georgine von Januschowsky), the Queen's lady-in-waiting, whose jealousies and suspicions helped set off a good few of the various twists of the plot.

Der Seekadett was a decided success on its production at Maximilian Steiner's Theater an der Wien and it was played 48 times before dropping from the repertoire in 1878. In 1882 it was taken up by Strampfer at the rival Carltheater with Jenny Stubel appearing as Fanchette Michel and Karl Drucker as Don Januario. The Vienna production was swiftly followed up in Berlin, Chemnitz, Riga, Munich and many other German venues, as well as, with outstanding results, in Budapest (ad Jenő Rákosi), where Lujza Blaha starred as Fanchette Michel alongside Erzsi Vidmár (Queen), János Kápolnai (Lamberto) and Elek Solymossy (Don Januario) for 48 performances at the top of a long career in Hungarian theatres.

America, as it was to do so many times and particularly whilst the reasonably unprincipled Sydney Rosenfeld was active, turned out two separate English-language versions, but the law stepped in to stop a duplication of the original German version. The Thalia Theater mounted *Der Seekadett* with Mathilde Cottrelly as Fanchette alongside Frln Fiebach (Queen), Schnelle (Lamberto) and Gustav Adolfi (Januario), and they scored such a vast success that the opposition Germania Theater promptly announced their production of *Der Marine-Kadett.* They were summonsed and stopped, whilst the Thalia production ran on for an unprecedented two months. Augustin Daly's production of the English version, *The Royal Middy* (ad Fred Williams, add mus Edward Mollenhauer), was also a first-rate success and, after a good two-month season on Broadway with Catherine Lewis wearing the breeches, alongside May Fielding (Queen), Hart

Conway (Januario), Alonzo Hatch (Lamberto) and Charles Leclerq (Prolixio) and Ada Rehan playing Antonia, it proved a fine and enduring touring prospect both in America and on the Pacific and oriental circuits where Emilie Melville played the very grateful leading role for some years. Rosenfeld's version, *The Sea Cadet, or the Very Merry Mariner,* produced by E E Rice and Jacob Nunnemacher with Blanche Chapman starred, went under in less than a week in town, which didn't stop Rosenfeld from pirating happily round the country with it. Alice Oates called her out-West version *Fanchette the Gipsy* and, true to form, used such bits of the original as she fancied pasted on to anything else she fancied, while Fay Templeton had an 1892 Edward Paulton version done, in which she led a ''widows' dance'' to the music of ''Ta ra ra boom de ay,'' amongst the remnants of *Der Seekadett.*

London soon picked up news of the American success and Alexander Henderson staged an H B Farnie version of *The Naval Cadets* (plural!) to follow his record-breaking production of *Les Cloches de Corneville* at the Globe. Selina Dolaro was called Cerisette but still dressed up as a boy, Violet Cameron played the Queen, Bill Loredan was a new version of Lamberto called Florio, and Harry Paulton had the largest comic role, but the piece had a hard act to follow and, after a month and a half, Henderson brought back *Les Cloches.* A few months later the conductor of *The Naval Cadets,* Edward Solomon, broke through as a composer with the much-more-successful *Billee Taylor,* a tongue-in-cheek tale of a girl who disguises herself as a sea cadet to go in search of her lover. *The Naval Cadets,* in spite of its less-than-momentous London season, nevertheless went to the British provinces, and Emily Soldene was seen starred in Farnie's version around the country later the same year. Thus encouraged, the piece was brought back to London, again at the Globe Theater (12 March 1881), cast up with slightly heftier voices. Madame Amadi was now Cerisette, Henry Bracy Florio, Loredan now the lighter-voiced Mauritio and Frank Celli Januario. Paulton repeated. It did not break any records.

A French-language version (ad Gustave Lagye) was first heard at Brussels's ever enterprising Fantaisies-Parisiennes (25 January 1880) but, in a period where Germanic works aroused limited interest in Paris, it never reached the French capital.

An Italian operetta, *Il capitano Carlotta* by Raffaele Mazzoni, also based on Bayard and Dumanoir's play, was produced at Città delle Pieve in 1891 (22 April).

Hungary: Népszínház *Kapitánykisasszony* 13 January 1877; Germany: Friedrich-Wilhelmstädtisches Theater 3 March 1877; USA: Thalia Theater 27 October 1879 (Ger), Daly's Theater *The Royal Middy* 28 January 1880, Fifth Avenue Theater *The Sea Cadet* 7 June 1880 (Eng); UK: Globe Theatre *The Naval Cadets* 27 March 1880; France: Rouen *Le Cadet de Marine* 19 April 1881; Australia: Prince of Wales Theatre, Melbourne *The Royal Middy* 1 October 1880

SEESAW Musical in 2 acts originally written by Michael Stewart based on *Two for the Seesaw* by William Gibson, subsequently revised by, and wholly credited to, Michael Bennett. Lyrics by Dorothy Fields. Music by Cy Coleman. Uris Theater, New York, 18 March 1973.

Gibson's 1958 two-handed play *Two for the Seesaw* (Booth Theater 16 January 1958) was a major Broadway success with Henry Fonda starring as the besuited out-of-towner Jerry Ryan, who finds a long-term relationship with the determinedly bohemian New Yorker Gittel Mosca (Anne Bancroft) impossible for more than two acts. The musical version of the play padded out this central story with a second introduction for its hero (Ken Howard): not only did he come to town and find Gittel (Michele Lee), he found New York itself and a whole lot of trendy 1960s-70s theatrical people who are put forward as representative of the city and its good life, and whose antics provided some fill between the pieces of the central story. Choreography was assured by making the most visible of this group a rising young choreographer (Tommy Tune) and period ethnics by popping in a Puerto Rican troupe (Giancarlo Esposito, et al).

The pre-Broadway troubles of *Seesaw* make up one of 1970s show business's longer and less sympathetic sagas. After an unsatisfactory start, the original director was sacked and director-choreographer Michael Bennett was brought in to restage the piece. The result was some severe rewriting and the departure of librettist Michael Stewart, mostly new and up-front choreography, many sackings including star Lainie Kazan, and even a hatful of alterations to the score which had become and would remain the backbone of the show. By the time *Seesaw* opened on Broadway, it was a very different show from that which had begun in tryout, but its dual nature remained: Gibson's warmly intimate tale on one side, and the glitzy, revusical Broadway extras on the other.

The best of the Coleman/Fields songs belonged, significantly, to the love story—Gittel's klutzy ''Nobody Does It Like Me,'' soon to become a cabaret standard, ''He's Good for Me'' and ''Welcome to Holiday Inn''—but the glitz department also came up trumps with the energetic company song ''It's Not Where You Start (it's where you finish),'' which was another number to survive beyond the 296 Broadway performances and subsequent (and again altered) touring version in which Lucie Arnaz and John Gavin starred. The Broadway establishment's kudos, however, went to the show's decorative part. Bennett was awarded a Tony for his choreography and Tune, who had also had a hand in that choreography, took a Best Supporting performance award.

The piece was subsequently seen in small theatres in both Britain, with pop singer Helen Shapiro as Gittel, and Australia.

The same title—though with a gap between the *See* and the *Saw*—had previously been used for another Broadway musical (Louis Hirsch/Earl Derr Biggers), based on Biggers's novel *Love Insurance,* and produced by Henry Savage at the Cohan Theater in 1919 (23 September). A clever plot had a Lord (Charlie Brown) whose rival in love is an American insurance man (Guy Robertson) taking out a policy with that rival against the lady (Elizabeth Hines) refusing his offer of marriage, and the piece ran for 89 performances.

Australia: Marian Street Theatre, Sydney 2 November 1979; UK: Theatre Royal and Opera House, Northampton 3 April 1987

Recording: original cast (Buddah/DRG)

SEE SEE Chinese comic opera in 2 acts by Charles H E Brookfield adapted from the play *La Troisième Lune* by Fred de Grésac and Paul Ferrier. Lyrics by Adrian Ross. Music by Sidney Jones. Additional material by Frank E Tours and Percy Greenbank. Prince of Wales Theatre, London, 20 June 1906.

See See was a 1906 attempt by producer George Edwardes and composer Sidney Jones, in the wake of the success of Edwardes's production of *Les P'tites Michu,* to put a little more substance—textual and musical—back into homemade contemporary musical comedy. The libretto, taken from a Parisian play which had originally sported a score of incidental music by Cuvillier, was set, like Jones's two big hits, *The Geisha* and *San Toy,* in the Orient but it did not follow the standard Daly's patterns in plot and layout.

Wise and beautiful See See (Denise Orme) teams with comical Hang-Kee (Huntley Wright, chief comic of *The Geisha* and *San Toy*) and Mai Yai (Amy Augarde of *Les P'tites Michu*) so to disgust Cheoo (Bill Berry) that he will not allow his son Yen (Maurice Farkoa) to wed unwilling little Lee (Adrienne Augarde, one of the *P'tites Michu*). Things go wrong, however, and See See herself ends up as Yen's wife, leading to a second act in which the bridegroom tames and woos his horrified partner into happiness. This highly starry cast was supplemented by the queen of the postcard girls, Gabrielle Ray, in a travesty role, young Lily Elsie as See See's maid, Fred Emney and Kitty Hanson for some low comedy, and a set of comical wives for Berry which included Sybil Grey, one of Gilbert and Sullivan's original three little maids (*The Mikado*).

The plot gave Wright a bagful of disguises in which to display himself, Miss Orme (a *Les P'tites Michu* take-over) plenty of pretty songs and Miss Ray lots of exposure—including the show's most popular number, a sweet little duo with Wright in which they dressed as and sang about ''Chinese Lanterns.'' The vastly experienced Edwardes had seemingly done everything right, the papers could find no criticisms except to say it was too lush and too long and too full of good things, but *See See* simply refused to catch on. After 152 performances it was closed, leading to one of those periodic floods of newspaper articles declaring the imminent death of the musical (or any other) theatre.

SEGAL, Vivienne [Sonia] (b Philadelphia, 19 April 1897; d Los Angeles, 29 December 1992). Star musical ingenue who made a second career as a wisecracking character lady.

Miss Segal had studied music and appeared in operatic productions in her native Pennsylvania before her debut in the professional musical theatre. The Shuberts, who were producing an Americanized version of Eysler's *Ein Tag im Paradies* under the title of *The Blue Paradise,* had engaged Chapine for the important role of the ingenue who turns out a shrew and it quickly became evident that the lady was not up to the role. Miss Segal's father offered to invest substantially in the show if his daughter was made the replacement. The 18-year-old ring-in leading lady had four days rehearsal, was the hit of the highly successful production, and began her career where she would stay—at the top.

She toured with *The Blue Paradise* following its long Broadway run, and then went on to play further leading roles in *My Lady's Glove* (Oscar Straus's *Die schöne Unbekannte,* 1917, Elly), the revue *Miss 1917,* Jerome Kern's *Oh, Lady! Lady!!* (1918, Molly Farrington), Friml's *The Little Whopper* (1919, Kitty Wentworth), in the tryouts of *Tangerine* (February 1921) and Ivan Caryll's *Little Miss Raffles* (1921) and, most substantially, as Odette Darimonde in the Americanization of Kálmán's *Die Bajadere* as *The Yankee Princess* (1922). She appeared in the title role of the short-lived *Adrienne,* played in *The Ziegfeld Follies of 1924,* and took the title role of Oscar Straus's *Riquette* pre-Broadway until the Shuberts decided to use Mitzi instead, and then took up instead the lead in Earl Carroll's publicity musical (it was backed by and plugged a real-estate corporation), *Oh, You!,* which finally came to Broadway as *Florida Girl* (1925, Daphne). After its quick closure, she went to Chicago to play the lead role in Percy Wenrich's *Castles in the Air* (1925, Evelyn Devine).

Castles in the Air was a huge success through a run of almost a year in that city and Miss Segal later played her role when the show moved to New York. The production was reaching its latter days on Broadway when the cast were asked to take salary cuts. Miss Segal refused, but generously tore up her contract, thus allowing the show's management to recast more cheaply and her to take the job she had been offered in the tryout of a piece called *Lady Fair.* Her judgment proved sound when *Lady Fair* came into town as *The Desert Song* (1926) with Miss Segal as Margot Bonvalet creating "Romance" and "One Kiss." She followed up as Constance Bonacieux in Friml's *The Three Musketeers,* appeared throughout the country as Nadina in a revival of *The Chocolate Soldier* (1931), and subsequently appeared in regional productions of *Music in the Air, The Three Musketeers, No, No, Nanette,* and at Jones Beach as Rosalinde in *A Wonderful Night,* as Ottilie in *Maytime* and Fedora Palinska in *The Circus Princess.*

Ten years after her last Broadway creation as a romantic lead, Miss Segal began a second career as a character lady. She appeared as the wordly-wisecracking Peggy Palaffi of *I Married an Angel* and followed up for the same authors with a memorable performance (aged 43) as man-nibbling Vera Simpson in *Pal Joey,* creating "Bewitched (bothered and bewildered)" and "Take Him." A revival of the Rodgers and Hart *A Connecticut Yankee* (1943) cast her as Morgan Le Fay, equipped with a new number, "To Keep My Love Alive," which was destined to become an anthology piece.

From these wryly comical ladies, it was something of a volte face to the romanticism of the Tchaikovsky pasticcio *Music in my Heart* (1947), and a step down to the weak and unsuccessful *Great to Be Alive,* but another Rodgers and Hart revival—a repeat of her original role in *Pal Joey*—closed out a memorable pair of Broadway careers covering nearly 40 years with a hole in the middle.

Miss Segal also appeared in a handful of musical films, including the cinema versions of *Golden Dawn* (1930, Dawn) and *The Cat and the Fiddle* (1934), and *Viennese Nights* (1930).

SEIDL, Lea [MAYRSEIDL, Caroline] (b Vienna, 22 August 1894; d London, 4 January 1987). Viennese diva who finished her career in London.

Lea Seidl began her career in juvenile roles at the Vienna Carltheater (the child Janku in *Der Rastelinder* revival, etc), and subsequently played adult roles in Zürich (*Boccaccio, Alt-Wien, Tausend und eine Nacht, Die lustige Witwe, Der letzte Walzer, Die keusche Susanne,* etc), Berlin (*Das Mädel von Davos,* Princess Stefanie in *Der Fürst von Pappenheim, Die vertauschte Frau, Tausend süsse Beinchen*) and in Vienna (Dorine in the Berlin Neues Theater production of *Dorine und der Zufall, Der Fürst von Pappenheim,* as "Sie" in the German version of *L'Amour masqué* 1924, Mara Beltramini in Julius Bittner's *Die silberne Tänzerin*) before appearing as *Friederike* to the Goethe of Richard Tauber in the Vienna version of Lehár's Singspiel (1928). She moved to Britain in 1930 to pair with Joseph Hislop in the British production of the *Friederike* and later created the role of Josefa in the English version of *Im weissen Rössl* at the London Coliseum (1931).

Seidl remained in Britain, but apart from a revival of *A Waltz Dream* (1934, Franzi), a short-lived version of May's *Der tanzende Stadt* (1935, Maria Theresia) and the flop *No Sky So Blue* (1938, Adele), she was not seen in the musical theatre thereafter, restricting her appearances to plays and film.

THE SENTIMENTAL BLOKE Musical play in 2 acts by Nancy Brown and Lloyd Thomson based on the poems of C J Dennis. Lyrics by Nancy Brown, Albert Arlen, Lloyd Thomson and C J Dennis. Music by Albert Arlen. Comedy Theatre, Melbourne, 4 November 1961.

C J Dennis's Australian narrative poems *The Songs of a Sentimental Bloke* (1915) went through adaptation into films both silent (1918) and spoken (1932) and as a stage play (1922) before becoming a stage musical in the hands of Sydney husband-and-wife team Albert Arlen and Nancy Brown (one-time leading lady to Richard Tauber and the star of the 1932 film of *The Maid of the Mountains*) and Canberra diplomat Lloyd Thomson.

Originally produced by the amateur Canberra Repertory Company, *The Sentimental Bloke* was subsequently taken up by the then all-powerful J C Williamson Theatres Ltd and, after a tryout and some considerable rewrites designed to make it a more conventional 1950s musical show, it was given a professional production. The original Canberra leading man, Edwin Ride, repeated his performance as Bill, "the sentimental bloke," opposite Patsy Hemingway as his beloved Doreen, and comedy from Frank Ward (best friend Ginger Mick), Alton Harvey (the rival Stror 'At Coot) and Gloria Dawn (his girl Rosie), all re-creating the familiar (to Australians) characters of Spadger's Lane. The tale was illustrated by some pleasant songs, which mostly escaped being stageocker (the Australian equivalent of stage-cockney) and *The Sentimental Bloke* became the most successful Australian musical of its time. It was (and still occasionally is) played throughout that country but, in spite of efforts to find it a production overseas, it was not exported any further than New Zealand.

Arlen, Thomson and Miss Brown were also the authors of *The Girl from Snowy River,* produced in Canberra in 1960.

A second *Sentimental Bloke* musical, with book and lyrics by Graeme Blundell and music by George Dreyfus was produced by the Melbourne Theatre Company in 1985 (The Playhouse 12 December).

Recordings: original cast (Talent City), radio cast (RCA Camden)

THE SERENADE Comic opera in 3 acts by Harry B Smith. Music by Victor Herbert. Knickerbocker Theater, New York, 16 March 1897.

After having tried repeatedly, with a sometimes considerable adventurousness but little luck, to find another work with which to repeat the success of their famous production of *Robin Hood,* The Boston Ideal Comic Opera Company (The Bostonians) got perhaps the nearest that they ever would with *The Serenade.* The piece was written by *Robin Hood* librettist Harry Smith and composed by Victor Herbert to whom, three years earlier, the company had given his first stage opportunity with the underpowered *Prince Ananias.* The basic story of *The Serenade* was barely a fresh one so Smith, aware that his plot line carried uncomfortable resemblances to those of several other recent comic operas, used the time-honored critic-baffling trick of announcing that the libretto was an adaptation of a piece by Goldoni.

The baritone of the Madrid Opera, Alvarado (W H MacDonald), is in love with Dolores (Jessie Bartlett Davis), and he woos her with the serenade of the title, in spite of the efforts of the Duke of Santa Cruz (Henry C Barnabee) to prevent him. Since Dolores was written as a contralto for the Bostonians' senior lady, Mrs Davis, it was the other woman in the affair who had to be the soprano. Yvonne (Alice Nielsen), pursuing Alavardo as having jilted her, finally pairs off much more suitably with Lopez (William Philp, tenor), the secretary of the President of the Royal Madrid Brigandage Society, Romero (Eugene Cowles). Romero is an uncomfortable brigand: on alternate days he puts aside thieving and becomes a monk. Harry Brown appeared as Colombo, a former primo tenore now reduced to playing pantomime devils and giving singing lessons, and another Bostonians stalwart, George Frothingham, played the tailor Gomez, a hopeless suitor for Dolores's hand.

The feature of the score was, of course, the plot-worthy serenade itself, ''I Love Thee, I Adore Thee,'' introduced by Dolores and Alvarado in the first act, and reprised lyrically, chorally by a group of monks and even comically (Colombo trying to teach it to the anxious Gomez) through the course of the evening. Romero had a baritone ''Song of the Carbine'' and the tale of ''The Monk and the Maid,'' Yvonne gave out a bolero (''In Fair Andalusia'') and a waltz (''Cupid and I''), Dolores sang of ''The Angelus'' and the tenor Lopez had a romance, ''I Envy the Bird,'' all alongside a good ration of concerted music.

First tested in Cleveland, Ohio (Euclid Avenue Opera House 17 February), then run in at Chicago's Columbia Theater, *The Serenade* came briskly to Broadway and played there for 79 performances before being taken on the road as a popular part of the Bostonians' repertoire. In spite of its success at home, *The Serenade* did not follow *Robin Hood* to Europe but it did make it to Australia, where it was produced by George Musgrove in 1903. Lillian Slapoffski starred in its soprano role whilst May Beatty (Dolores), J C Piddock (Alvarado), Edward Lauri (Duke), Jack Leumane (Colombo) and Lemprière Pringle (Romero) completed the principal cast of a production which left little mark.

Portions of *The Serenade* were later used, along with some of Herbert's subsequent *The Fortune Teller,* to make up a 1946 portmanteau piece called *Gypsy Lady* (aka *Romany Love,* Robert Wright, George Forrest/Henry Myers) which went from its original production at the San Francisco and Los Angeles Light Opera to short runs on Broadway and in London.

Another piece, originally from Scandinavia, produced as *Serenade* (without the article) in England and advertised as ''the Swedish *Oklahoma!*'' did not seem or behave at all like *Oklahoma!* and folded on the London-bound road.

Australia: Princess Theatre, Melbourne 18 July 1903

SERGEANT BRUE Musical farce in 3 acts by Owen Hall. Lyrics by J Hickory Wood. Music by Liza Lehmann. Additional music by James Tate and Ernest Vousden. Strand Theatre, London, 14 June 1904.

Producer Frank Curzon had scored a record-breaking success with his production of *A Chinese Honeymoon* at the Strand Theatre and, when that show had finished its run of more than one thousand performances, he needed a follow-up piece which would continue to attract the audiences who had been wooed back to the unloved old Strand Theatre. He hired top librettist Owen Hall to write his new show and, in a surprising decision, paired him musically with Liza Lehmann, best known as a composer of drawing-room music (*In a Persian Garden,* etc). The result justified his decision in a fine musical comedy of a certain substance and quality.

Willie Edouin, the star of *Florodora,* made a memorable character of the amiable but not very crookworthy policeman Sergeant Brue who needs to win promotion to the rank of Inspector before he can inherit a fine legacy. He gets a friendly burglar (Arthur Williams) to help him fake a capture, but things go wrong and he gets caught out. However, when he accidentally stumbles upon the magistrate in charge of his case involved in illegal gambling, promotion arrives like lightning, bringing Brue both money and the hand of pretty Lady Bickenhall (Ethel Irving).

Miss Lehmann's songs imitated the popular models classily in pieces like ''The Twopenny Tube'' and ''So Did Eve'' but, to her fury, Curzon diluted her score with American popular songs (''The Sweetest Girl in Dixie,''

''Under a Panama'') and even with British interpolations. It was not, however, any individual song which was the hit of *Sergeant Brue* but the performance of Edouin, and with him at its head the show quickly became a popular success. Unfortunately, Owen Hall was not content. He demanded that the show be transferred to a ''first class theatre'' and Curzon was contractually obliged to respond. *Sergeant Brue* moved to the Prince of Wales Theatre where he remained for the five months the theatre was available and then, in spite of Hall, moved back to the Strand. The show lasted in all for 280 performances which might, without the vanity-salving moves, have been very many more.

A Broadway production with Frank Daniels in the title role and Blanche Ring interpolating ''My Irish Molly O'' (Jean Schwartz/William Jerome) into the role of Lady Bickenhall came from Atlantic City (Savoy Theater 31 March 1905) and Philadelphia to notch up a fair run of 93 performances in New York before going round the country; Rupert Clarke and Clyde Meynell introduced the show to Australia with Edwin Brett (Brue) and Ruth Lincoln (Lady Bickenhall) starred, and *Sergeant Brue* went on to be played throughout the other English-speaking outposts of the musical theatre to good effect. In 1908 a potted version of the show was mounted on the music-hall stage, at the London Empire.

USA: Knickerbocker Theater 24 April 1905; Australia: Criterion Theatre, Sydney 29 January 1910

SERMENT D'AMOUR Opéra-comique in 3 acts by Maurice Ordonneau. Music by Edmond Audran. Théâtre des Nouveautés, Paris, 19 February 1886.

With the far-reaching successes of *Les Noces d'Olivette, La Mascotte* and *Gillette de Narbonne* and, most recently, the Paris production of *Le Grand Mogol,* composer Audran had secured a position close on the heels of, if not quite alongside, Lecocq at the head of the list of the musical theatre's most fashionable composers of the 1880s. *Serment d'amour,* without ever becoming a major success, confirmed those pretensions thoroughly.

Ordonneau's libretto used some well-worn plot parts. A marquise with money in her sights tries to prevent her nephew from wedding the lowly Rosette by deceitfully marrying the girl off to Grivolin, a local peasant. But Grivolin's girlfriend, Marion, substitutes herself under the wedding veil and all ends happily. The score was bright, tuneful and often graceful, with the most popular number being the lively, ingenuous peasant rondo (''Holà, vertinguette! Holà, vertingué!'') sung by the heroine in the first act (on the cue from the hero to ''sing one of the good old songs of our childhood''). Marguerite Ugalde and the baritone Morlet created the parts of the lovers whose ''serment d'amour'' is so tested, with Juliette Darcourt in the soprano role of the machinating Marquise and Albert Brasseur (Grivolin), Mlle Lantelme (Marion) and Berthelier as the comical marquisal steward, Gavadeau, caught in an unwanted duel or drunkenly courting the heroine unawares, providing the comedy.

The show was well received and ran for a very respectable 104 performances in a season where the first run of *Joséphine vendue par ses soeurs* put up strong competition. By and large, however, it drew little attention from other centers, with the notable exception of America. American producers moved enthusiastically for the newest work by the composer of the till-ringing *Olivette* and *La Mascotte,* with the result that two productions, differerently translated as *The Bridal Trap* (by Sydney Rosenfeld) and *The Crowing Hen* (ad Mr & Mrs Erastus Brainerd for John McCaull's Company) opened on Broadway within two days of each other. The two producers waged a battle across the street separating their theatres, with Miles and Barton of the Bijou projecting ''objectionable designs'' onto the facade of Wallack's with a stereopticon until they were dragged to court. The McCaull version kept nearer the original and had the advantage of a cast starring Mathilde Cottrelly, Bertha Ricci and De Wolf Hopper, as well as better orchestrations and production values; the Bijou version, which top-billed Roland Reed, had been ''cleaned up'' (''A French opera book is like a cucumber, the attempt to make it healthy renders it unpalatable'') and thus was deemed more proper. In fact, there proved to be enough cake for two and both productions did exceeding well.

Rosenfeld—who not long before had been involved in a similar two-productions fiasco over *The Mikado*—and his producers left town first, but *The Crowing Hen* was only a week behind, for McCaull's companies only ever played set Broadway seasons before going out to reap the rewards of the road. And in the meantime *Serment d'amours* were proliferating everywhere. Jeannie Winston's company produced *The Golden Hen* at Washington (Albaugh's Theater, Washington, DC 5 July 1886), the star playing André de Flavignac to the Marquise of Blanche Chapman, and the Boston Museum a version by Ben Woolf under the title *Love's Vow* (5 July 1886) with John Howson featured. The San Francisco Tivoli had *The Golden Hen* on stage in no time at all, and the free-pinching Uhrig's Cave summer theatre in St Louis wasn't far behind: just weeks later it came out with what it called *The Golden Goose* with George Olmi and Dora Wiley featured. Maurice Grau's opéra-bouffe companies subsequently gave Canada (October 1887) and New York (Star Theatre) the French original with Mary Pirard and Mezières in the leading roles, and most other corners of America got *Crowing Hens* (notably, for several seasons, from McCaull's company on tour), *Bridal*

Plate 351. **Gaston Serpette**

Traps, *Golden Hen* and *Love's Vows* at least once, as *Serment d'amour* survived its confrontational start to find a home in touring and summer comic opera repertoires for years to come.

USA: Wallack's Theater *The Crowing Hen* 29 May 1886, Bijou Theater *The Bridal Trap* May 31 1886

SERPETTE, [Henri Charles Antoine] Gaston (b Nantes, 4 November 1846; d Paris, 3 November 1904). Able and prolific French composer who never struck the big time.

Gaston Serpette originally studied for the law and qualified as a barrister but, at the age of 22, he put aside barristering and enrolled at the Paris Conservatoire where he studied under, amongst others, Ambroise Thomas. He was awarded the prestigious Prix de Rome for his scène lyrique *Jeanne d'arc* (lib: Jules Barbier) in 1871 but, on his return to France following his scholarship period, he found, like other and more celebrated prize-winners and composers, difficulty in getting his stage works accepted by the moguls of the Opéra-Comique. When his first proper opérette, *La Branche cassée* (1874), was produced and played for more than 40 performances at the Bouffes-Parisiens and then in London, he decided to continue in the field of the light musical theatre and, over the next 30 years, he composed the scores for some 30 full-sized and one-act stage pieces. A number of these had some success in Paris, others were seen throughout central Europe, and a handful even made it further afield, but, unlike such of his comparable contemporaries as Vasseur and Varney, Serpette did not manage to produce one outstanding work which would find itself a place in the permanent repertoire.

Serpette's career and the careers of the shows which he composed were both curiously erratic. Amongst his early pieces, a *Le Chemin des amoureux* (1875, lib: Albert Millaud) was abandoned in rehearsals at the Bouffes, the vaudevillesque *Le Manoir du Pic-Tordu* (1875) failed in 14 well-noticed performances in Paris yet went on to be seen in Berlin (*Schloss Pictordu*), and *La Petite Muette,* after an indifferent run in Paris, was played in both America and in Hungary. There was a considerable success for the spectacular London version of the old féerie *Rothomago* for which Serpette was invited to compose one act and the grandiose *Madame le Diable* (1882) had a fine run at the Théâtre de la Renaissance but, in the manner of the time, when this latter was adapted for the German-language stage (*Des Teufels Weib*), a fresh score by a local composer was substituted for the 22-piece original.

A little one-acter called *La Princesse* proved popular, and was adapted into both German and Hungarian, but *Fanfreluche,* a rewrite of a piece originally produced in Brussels, disappointed in 46 Parisian performances. It nevertheless went on to be produced in America by the Bostonians as *Fanchonette.* The ''opérette fantastique'' *Le Château de Tire-Larigot,* which found Serpette back amongst devils and magic and lashings of stage effects brought another good Paris run which, in spite of its attractive score, cannot have been said to be wholly due to the show's musical attractions, whilst a further collaboration with authors Blum and Toché produced another picturesque piece in *Adam et Ève* which, helped by Louise Théo's appearance in the traditional costume of Ève, was another to have a fairly good Paris run (80 performances) and an export to Budapest. *La Gamine de Paris* (75 performances) also did respectably at the Bouffes-Parisiens and got relocated to Holland for a performance at Amsterdam's Frascati Theatre as *Truytgen von Noorermarkt* (1889 ''with the introduction of some old Dutch melodies''), whilst the fairy-tale *Cendrillonnette* played 120 performances at the same theatre, and Blum and Toché's *Le Petit Chaperon-Rouge,* an up-to-dated version of the Little Red Riding Hood tale (in which the wolf was, of course, a thoroughly human one) went on from it French production to be staged at Brussels's Galeries Saint-Hubert and by both the San Francisco Tivoli (*The May Queen* 17 March 1887) and Marie Greenwood and her company (*Denisette* Port Jervis, NY 31 August 1891) in America.

In the long run, the most successful of Serpette's works came, a little surprisingly, not in the area of the féerie or the spectacular, which had served him best in the first part of his career, but in the field of the vaudeville. Antony Mars and Maurice Desvallières's musical-comedy tale of *La Demoiselle du téléphone* was not only a Parisian success, but traveled throughout Europe and (with its musical score being more and more replaced en route) to Britain, Australia and America. If the large part of the triumph went to his authors rather than to the composer, Serpette nevertheless had his share in the original success.

There was further success and progress to foreign productions for two other musical-comedy pieces, *Cousin-cousine* and *La Dot de Brigitte,* and for the spectacular devil-piece *Le Carnet du Diable* (*Das Scheckbuch des Teufels*), whilst the ancient Roman opérette *Le Capitole* was seen in Germany (*Metella*) and Hungary (*Az erenyes Metella*) and the latest rewrite of the spectacular girlie-show *Le Royaume des femmes,* for which he provided new music, played throughout Europe (*Das Paradies der Frauen, Die verkehrte Welt, Felfordult világ*). Once again, however, as so often in the case of both spectacular pieces and vaudevilles, Serpette's score was often diluted or wholly replaced by local music.

A composer of undoubted skill, Serpette composed much music of unfailing taste and charm, finely orchestrated and apt, and he won a steady livelihood from the productions of his works in a solid and respectable career. It was perhaps the lack of a dash of individuality or imagination, of comic esprit, that prevented him from turning out one particular work which would be remembered beyond his lifetime.

1870 **Lucrèce Orgéat** Le Gaulois 5 April

1874 **La Branche cassée** (Adolphe Jaime, Jules Noriac) Théâtre des Bouffes-Parisiens 23 January

1875 **Le Manoir du Pic-Tordu** (Albert de Saint-Albin, Arnold Mortier) Théâtre des Variétés 28 May

1876 **Le Moulin du Vert Galant** (Eugène Grangé, Victor Bernard) Théâtre des Bouffes-Parisiens 10 April

1877 **Les Poupées parisiennes** (Gaston Marot, Henri Buguet) Théâtre Taitbout 7 February

1877 **La Petite Muette** (Paul Ferrier) Théâtre des Bouffes-Parisiens 3 October

1878 **Le Chat botté** (w de Bourdeau, Auguste Coedès/Ernest Blum, Etienne Tréfeu) Théâtre de la Gaîté 18 May

1879 **Rothomago** (w Georges Jacobi, et al/H B Farnie) Alhambra Theatre, London 22 December

1880 **La Nuit de Saint-Germain** (Gaston Hirsch, Raoul de Saint-Arroman) Théâtre des Fantaisies-Parisiennes, Brussels 20 March

1882 **Madame le Diable** (Henri Meilhac, Mortier) Théâtre de la Renaissance 5 April

1882 **La Princesse** (Raoul Toché) 1 act Casino de Trouville 25 August; Théâtre des Variétés 22 October

1883 **Tige de lotus** (Toché) 1 act Hôtel de la Rochefoucauld May; Casino de Contrexéville 26 July

1883 **The Steeplechase** (Pierre Decourcelle) 1 act London 10 July; St Gratien 22 July

1883 **Insomnie** (de Mayréna, Félix Cohen) 1 act Casino, Deauville 17 August

1883 **Fanfreluche** (Paul Burani, Hirsch, de St-Arroman) revised *La Nuit de Saint-Germain* Théâtre de la Renaissance 16 December

1884 **Mam'zelle Réséda** (Jules Prével) 1 act Théâtre de la Renaissance 2 February

1884 **Le Château de Tire-Larigot** (Ernest Blum, Toché) Théâtre des Nouveautés 30 October

1885 **Le Petit Chaperon-Rouge** (Blum, Toché) Théâtre des Nouveautés 10 October

1886 **Le Singe d'un nuit d'été** (Édouard Noël) 1 act Théâtre des Bouffes-Parisiens 1 September

1886 **Adam et Ève** (Blum, Toché) Théâtre des Nouveautés 6 October

1887 **La Gamine de Paris** (Eugène Leterrier, Albert Vanloo) Théâtre des Bouffes-Parisiens 30 March

1887 **La Lycéenne** (Georges Feydeau) Théâtre des Nouveautés 23 December

1890 **Cendrillonnette** (w Victor Roger/Ferrier) Théâtre des Bouffes-Parisiens 24 January

1891 **La Demoiselle du téléphone** (Antony Mars, Maurice Desvallières) Théâtre des Nouveautés 2 May

1892 **Mé-na-ka** (Ferrier) 1 act Théâtre des Nouveautés 2 May

1892 **La Bonne de chez Duval** (Mars, Hippolyte Raymond) Théâtre des Nouveautés 6 October

1893 **Cousin-cousine** (Maurice Ordonneau, Henri Kéroul) Théâtre des Folies-Dramatiques 23 December

1895 **Pincette** (Raoul) 1 act Théâtre de la Bodinière 4 January

1895 **Chiquita** (Charles Clairville) 1 act Théâtre des Nouveautés 4 February

1895 **La Dot de Brigitte** (w Victor Roger/Mars, Ferrier) Théâtre des Bouffes-Parisiens 6 May

1895 **Le Carnet du Diable** (Blum, Ferrier) Théâtre des Variétés 23 October

1895 **Le Capitole** (Ferrier, Clairville) Théâtre des Nouveautés 5 December

1896 **Le Royaume des femmes** (Cogniard ad Ferrier, Blum) Eldorado 24 February

1896 **Le Carillon** (Ferrier, Blum) Théâtre des Variétés 7 November

1898 **Le Tour du bois** (Jules Oudot, Henri de Gorsse) Théâtre des Variétés 3 June

1899 **Shakespeare!** (Paul Gavault, P-L Flers) Théâtre des Bouffes-Parisiens 23 November

1903 **Amorelle (1810)** (Barton White/Ernest Boyd-Jones) Kennington Theatre, England 8 June

SERRANO, José (b Valencia, 14 October 1873; d Madrid, 8 March 1941).

Son of the conductor of his hometown band, Serrano followed his musical studies by taking on a job as amanuensis for the nearly blind Manuel Fernández Caballero, working on the scoring of *Gigantes y Cabezudos* (1897). He got his first chance as a composer of zarzuela three years later when he was offered the libretto of *El motete* by the Alvárez Quintero brothers. Produced at the Teatro de Apolo (24 April 1900), the piece marked—in the same manner as *Das süsse Mädel* did at around the same time in Austria—the arrival of a new, freely melodic style of composition in the Spanish musical theatre. Serrano went on to become one of the most prolific theatre composers of his time, helping, in the early decades of the 20th century, to lead the genéro chico away from the classic 19th-century style as epitomized by Chapí and Bretón towards a more evidently popular kind of local verismo theatre.

Of Serrano's 50 or so genéro chico zarzuelas, a considerable number have retained their popularity, notably *La reina mora* (11 December 1903), the exotic tragedy *Moros y Cristianos* (27 April 1905), *Alma de Dios* (17 December 1907), *La cancíon del olvido* (17 November 1916) with its well known serenade "Soldado de Nápoli," *Los de Aragon* (16 April 1927), the contemporary sainete madrileño, *Los claveles* (Teatro Fontalba 6 April 1929), and the two-act *La dolorosa* (Teatro de Apolo of Valencia 23 May 1930). His last work, *Golondrina,* was posthumously produced at San Sebastián in 1944.

His other stage works include *La mazorka roja* (1902), *La casita blanca* (1904), *El mal de amores* (1905), *El perro chico* (w Q Valverde 1905), *El amor en sol-fa* (w Chapí 1905), *El mala sombra* (1906), *La noche de reyes* (1906), *El pollo Tejada* (1906), *La suerta loca* (w Chapí 1907), *L'alegría del batallíon* (1909), *El palacio de los duendes* (w Vives 1910), *El trust de los Tenorios* (1910), *El carro del sol* (1911), *El amigo Melquíádes or Por la boca muere el pez* (w Q Valverde, 1914), and *Las hilanderas* (1927).

He also wrote many songs, including the well-known Hymn to Valencia (1909).

SEVENTEEN Musical in 2 acts by Sally Benson based on the play by Stanislaus Stange and Stannard Mears and the novel by Booth Tarkington. Lyrics by Kim Gannon. Music by Walter Kent. Broadhurst Theater, New York, 21 June 1951.

Booth Tarkington's 1916 novel of very young and quite catastrophic love between wide-eyed Willie Baxter (Gregory Kelly) and fluffy, appalling Lola Pratt (Ruth Gordon) was a considerable success as a Broadway stage play (Booth Theater 22 January 1918, 225 performances), was made up into a silent movie starring Jack Pickford and Louise Huff in 1917 and later into a musical, *Hello, Lola* (Broad Street Theater, Newark 16 November 1925; Eltinge Theater 12 January 1926), in an adaptation by Dorothy Donnelly with music by William Kernell. Edythe Baker and Richard Keene starred for some 60 performances. The well-loved tale made it to the cinema screen again in 1940 with Jackie Cooper and Betty Field featured and it was then given a second chance in a musical version, as produced on Broadway by Milton Berle, Sammy Lambert and Bernie Foyer. Another well-established lady writer, Sally Benson, author of the successful magazine tales which became the play *Junior Miss,* was responsible for the adaptation, and the songs were by Kim Gannon—lyricist of a number of 1940s Hollywood songs ("Moonlight Cocktail," title song of *Always in My Heart* w Ernesto Lecuona, "The Lady Who Didn't Believe in Love" w Jule Styne, "It Can't Be Wrong" in *Now Voyager,* etc)—and Walter Kent, composer of Vera Lynn's anthem "The White Cliffs of Dover" (w Nat Burton).

Kenneth Nelson starred as Willie, desperate for a dress suit and for the fluttering eyes and tortured consonants of Lola (Ann Crowley), with Frank Albertson and Doris Dalton as his parents, Harrison Muller as the slick, Yale competition for Lola's favors and Maurice Ellis as the family handyman, in a version which kept the play's homey, sentimental atmosphere whilst topping it up with some more conventional musical-comedy elements and a score which included such titles as "Things Are Gonna Hum This Summer," "Summertime Is Summertime," "After All, It's Spring" and "If We Could Only Stop the Old Town Clock." The musical *Seventeen* ran 182 performances in a disappointing Broadway season.

Recording: original cast (RCA)

1776 Musical in 7 scenes by Peter Stone based on an idea by Sherman Edwards. Music and lyrics by Sherman Edwards. 46th Street Theater, New York, 16 March 1969.

The musical tale of *1776* follows the historical efforts of the secessionist bloc in the American Continental Congress progressively to persuade or purchase each of the undecided or opposing members of the house into signing his name to the Declaration of Independence. For the good of the cause, the abrasive and unpopular John Adams (William Daniels), the unquestioned leader of the movement, is persuaded by the more reasonable Benjamin Franklin (Howard da Silva) to let Virginia's high-spirited Richard Henry Lee (Ron Holgate) put forward the motion for Independency, ultimately formulated into a document by the young Thomas Jefferson (Ken Howard). The voting begins, the tally swings one way and then the next, and the anti-secessionists under John Dickinson (Paul Hecht) lose ground until the whole game is thrown open by the decision that the vote must be unanimous. But, by the final curtain, the document that creates the independent United States of America is being signed.

Plate 352. **1776.** *Martha Jefferson (Cheryl Kennedy) whirls on the hand of Edward Rutledge (David Kernan).*

With little suspense possible about the outcome of the musical's action, the interest of the show resided in the way the famous characters were depicted, how they retained their credibility in spite of bursting into song, and how the long lucubrations of 18th-century politicians could be made both dramatic and interesting. Adams, irascible and unpersuasively bigoted in politics, kept his impatience in check in a series of letters to his wife Abigail (Virginia Vestoff), Jefferson piaffed with impatience to get away from Congress and back to his bright young bride (Betty Buckley), Lee was represented as gauchely enthusiastic, Dickinson as severely dignified and honorable, Franklin—equipped with the trademark bald patch and flowing locks—as a crinkly paterfamilias, amongst a Congress in which each member was individually characterized. The ins and outs of their plotting and voting were contrasted with a handful of outside scenes, notably Jefferson's reunion with Martha and a glimpse of the war against the British as described by a little messenger (''Momma, Look Sharp'').

The show's musical part moved rarely into conventional song in what was, naturally, a male-voice dominated score. Adams soliloquized (''Till Then,'' ''Is Anybody There?''), Lee exuberated (''The Lees of Old Virginia''), Rutledge of Southern Carolina (Clifford David) fulminated against the North's selfish attempt to abolish slavery (''Molasses to Rum''), Congress chattered (''Piddle, Twiddle and Resolve'') and harmonized, whilst Martha Jefferson made the most extractable contribution to the score with the dancing waltz song ''He Plays the Violin,'' describing her husband's attractions with only a twinkle of double meaning.

1776 was a long time coming to the stage. It had originally been written wholly by Edwards, a former history major and teacher, in the early 1960s, and it had since gone through a long series of ''developments,'' but by the time it reached Broadway it was clear that the authors had succeeded in surmounting all and any of the odds against them, and *1776* was in the shape to win a run of 1,217 performances, followed by more than two years of tours, a film in which Daniels, da Silva, Howard and Miss Vestoff repeated their stage performances, and a London reproduction by the Broadway team. Lewis Fiander (Adams), Ronald Radd (Franklin), John Quentin (Jefferson) and Cheryl Kennedy (Martha) were featured, but the subject matter did not have the same interest for Britain and the piece ran for only 168 performances. That did not stop Australia from trying its hand at the show, but a 10-week season in Melbourne, followed by just 4 weeks in Sydney (Theatre Royal 11 September 1971), proved its appeal to be limited there, too.

1776 proved its enduring qualities when, having shown itself successful in a performance at Roundabout (14 August 1997, 109 performances), it was brought back to Broadway (Gershwin Theater 3 December). This production proved to have less éclat than the original and stayed around proportionately less long (224 performances).

The title *1776* had previously been used for an 1884 Broadway musical (Ludwig Englander/Leo Goldmark) produced in German at the Thalia Theater (26 February) with Austria's top musical-comedy star, Marie Geistinger, starred. It was later played again under the title *Adjutant James* and in 1895 revised and revived at the Broadway Theater, in English, as *The Daughter of the Revolution* (27 May).

The signing of the Declaration of Independence, too, had already been made the stuff of an American comic opera, *The Patriots* (ex- *The Liberty Bell*), produced by its authors, Julius Adler and William Carter in Atlanta in 1895 (18 November) and later in Boston and Philadelphia. This one managed to get the Boston tea party into its first act and the battle of Lexington into its second. The actual signing of the Declaration was the stuff of the third act, seen ''through the windows'' of the old State House. A W F McCollin and Marion Singer, touring operettic sturdies of the time, were amongst the cast and the piece played a whole five determinedly embattled weeks in its initial date. In Boston (12 June 1896), it collapsed in four underfunded nights.

The American Revolution had been even earlier depicted on the musical stage in Arditi's operatic version of J Fennimore Cooper's *The Spy* (1821). Written to an Italian libretto (*La Spia*), it was produced at New York in April 1856 with Brignoli and Mme La Grange starred, and sported a finale manufactured from ''Hail, Columbia.''

UK: New Theatre 16 June 1970; Australia: Her Majesty's Theatre, Melbourne 26 June 1971

Film: Columbia 1972

Recordings: original cast (Columbia), London cast (Columbia), New York revival cast (TVT), film soundtrack (Columbia)

70, GIRLS, 70 Musical in 2 acts by Fred Ebb and Norman J Martin based on the play *Breath of Spring* by Peter Coke as adapted by Joe Masteroff. Lyrics by Fred Ebb. Music by John Kander. Broadhurst Theater, New York, 15 April 1971.

Peter Coke's comical play about a group of naughty geriatrics who turn to crime was produced at London's Cambridge Theatre in 1958 with Athene Seyler as Dame Beatrice Appleby and Elspeth Duxbury in memorable support. It had a 430-performance run, was regularly revived, and filmed as *Make Mine Mink* (1959) with the same two stars featured, before being adapted as a Broadway musical.

Resituated in a New York City venue, its characters declassed, and illustrated with some lively, revusical Kander and Ebb songs ranging from a spiritual (''Believe'') to a topical ''Coffee in a Cardboard Cup'' and a regulation New York number (''Broadway, My Street''), the now confusingly retitled *70, Girls, 70* was produced by Arthur Whitelaw with Mildred Natwick and David Burns starring. Burns died before the show reached town, and *70, Girls, 70* survived only a month on Broadway. The popularity of Kander and Ebb's best works meant, however, that it was given further chances. *70, Girls, 70* was subsequently played regionally in America and in 1990 was seen for the first time in Britain in the tented studio theatre adjoined to the Chichester Festival Theatre, with Dora Bryan starred. That production, with Miss Bryan playing merry Oldham with the text in what became virtually a stand-up comedy show, later played a short run in the West End, toured, and mothered a production at Budapest's Fővárosi Operettszínház (ad György Böhm)with senior divas Zsusza Lehoczsky and Marika Németh amongst its old ladies.

UK: Chichester Festival Theatre 27 June 1990, Vaudeville Theatre, London 17 June 1991; Hungary: Fővárosi Operettszínház *Nercbanda* 22 December 1993

Recordings: original cast (Columbia), London cast (TER)

SEYMOUR, Katie [LOWE, Kate] (b Nottingham, 9 January 1868; d London, 7 September 1903). The Gaiety Theatre's ''musical comedy'' soubrette.

The daughter of music-hall comedian and vocalist William John Seymour (né Burchell) and of Phoebe née Towers (d 25 November 1912), a member of the well-known Towers acting and dancing dynasty and widow of Fred Lowe (d Winchester, 14 October 1863) of the celebrated Lauri family, pretty dancing soubrette Katie Seymour first appeared on the stage as a child, playing in the West End in children's pantomimes (Colin in *Goody Two-Shoes* 1876, Corneygrains the miller in *Little Red Riding Hood* 1877, Little John in *Robin Hood and his Merry Little Men* 1877, etc), and working as a tiny seriocomic on the music halls in England and on the Continent. In 1876 she appeared at the Standard Theatre in the music-hall scene in the drama *After Dark*, and danced at the South London Palace (as ''Katie Lauri'') in the ballet *Birds;* in 1877 she played the halls in an entertainment called *Fortune's Frolic* (Pavilion, Sun, Bedford, Marylebone, Middlesex), toured in the comedy-drama *Grateful* (''Miss Katie Towers only five years old . . .'') singing ''The Five Ages of Woman,'' and appeared at the Middlesex as ''Kate Seymour, the little Entertainer'' doing an impersonation of ''Poor Jo'' and singing Harrigan's ''Mulligan Guards'' (''she danced nimbly and prettily and was warmly cheered''). She also played in music-hall sketches with Ambrose Maynard's company, with the brothers Horne and others. In 1880 she made her Broadway debut at Booth's Theater as Fairy Queen to the Prince of Catherine Lewis, in H C Jarrett's operatic spectacle *Cinderella.*

During the 1880s, she worked mostly in the music halls and pantomime in Britain, appearing in the Covent Garden pantomime of 1881 (Sally Waters), but she took over briefly the role of Edgar in Hollingshead's production of the comic opera *Dick* (1884). She also appeared in variety at the Empire (1889) under the baton of Hervé, and played in America for George W Lederer with a troupe called Herman's Transatlantic Vaudevilles alongside Harry Athol (né Hollorand, whom she subsequently married), before, in her early twenties, she began to appear more steadily in the musical theatre. She appeared in the West End for C J Abud in *Blue-Eyed Susan* (1892, Rosy Morn) and for George Edwardes in *Joan of Arc* (1891, Blanche d'Arc), *Don Juan* (1893, Zöe, t/o Donna Julia) and *La Mascotte* (1893, Bianca) before turning herelf into a first-rank West End favorite through her Gaiety Theatre partnership with star comic Edmund Payne. The pair scored the hit of the night in their song and dance ''Love on the Japanese Plan'' in *The Shop Girl* (1894, Miss Robinson), and Miss Seymour remained at the Gaiety thereafter, as principal soubrette-dancer, through *My Girl* (1896, Phoebe Toodge), *The Circus Girl* (1896, Lucille, the wire walker), *A Runaway Girl* (1898, Alice) and *The Messenger Boy* (1900, Rosa), in each of which she was paired with enormous success with the hugely popular little Payne. She made another Broadway appearance when she was added to the cast of the revamped *The Casino Girl* and subsequently interpolated into the 1901 production of *The Strollers,* but on her return to Britain she switched back to the music halls, appearing at the Alhambra and other important houses. She made only one further appearance on the musical stage when she toured to South Africa with a musical-comedy company along with the other confirmed stars John Le Hay and Frank Celli shortly before her death at the age of 35.

SHAKESPEARE! Opérette-bouffe in 3 acts by Paul Gavault and P-L Flers. Music by Gaston Serpette. Théâtre des Bouffes-Parisiens, Paris, 23 November 1899.

The Shakespeare of the title of Serpette's opérette-bouffe was not William, but a dog. A specifically English dog—for the English were both the villains and the buffoons of Gavault and Flers's libretto—and also a dog who had only a little, if crucial, part to play in what was a piece of standard operettic high jinks, of disguises and amorous combinations, set on the island of Gibraltar.

The traveling salesman Brutus (Jean Périer), his wife Éponine (Mariette Sully) and the Spanish dancer Consuéla (Anna Tariol-Baugé) go to Gibraltar to rescue Consuéla's lover, Miguel (Alberthal), who, in attempting to retake the island for Spain has been captured by the Governor (Régnard), but spared from extinction through the intervention of the Governor's amorous wife (Léonie Laporte). The conspirators impersonate Lord Winning-Post (Vavasseur), his niece (Maud d'Orby) who is coming to Gibraltar to wed Jack (Maurice Lamy), and her maid (Evelyne Janney), and when the real English turn up chaos and counter-accusations reign until the real English are recognized by their dog, Shakespeare. A little amorous blackmail, however, secures everyone's release in time for a happy final curtain.

Serpette provided Mme Tariol-Baugé with several Spanish-flavored pieces (''Fleur d'Andalousie''), Périer and Mlle Sully with vivacious numbers to suit their vivacious roles, and the comical pair of Régnard and Mlle Laporte with opportunities to play the low heavies in a score which also offered a good ration of concerted music and which didn't bother standing around singing love songs when there was comedy to be mined.

Shakespeare! was produced at the Bouffes-Parisiens by MM Coudert and Berny and found a ready audience for its gaiety and its starry cast, the principals of whom had recently been the darlings of the town as the stars of the same theatre's triumphant *Véronique. Shakespeare!,* however, did not have the same future as *Véronique.* It closed after 65 performances, and with that closure its 53-year-old composer exited from the Parisian theatre to which he had supplied much happy and successful music without securing the one important hit which might have helped his name endure.

SHAKESPEARE, William (b Stratford-upon-Avon, 26 April ?1564; d Stratford-upon-Avon, 23 April 1616).

The most famous of English-language dramatists borrowed the source material for a large number of his plays from the works of earlier writers, and his own body of work was, in its turn, incessantly plundered both for the operatic and light-musical stage of later years.

The most successful operas based on his works included Purcell's *The Fairy Queen,* Gounod's *Roméo et Juliette,* Ambroise Thomas's *Hamlet,* Verdi's versions of *Othello, Macbeth* and *Falstaff,* Berlioz's *Béatrice et Bénédict,* Otto Nicolai's *Die lustige Weiber von Windsor,* Vaughan Williams's *Sir John in Love,* Charles Villers Stanford's *Much Ado About Nothing* and Benjamin Britten's *A Midsummer Night's Dream. The Taming of the Shrew* was operaticized in half-a-dozen languages, *Much Ado* became *Beaucoup de bruit pour rien* at Paris's Opéra-Comique (Paul Puget 24 March 1899), Spain produced an *Otello y Desdemona* (Manuel Nieto, 1883), Ambroise Thomas and Leoncavallo both tackled *A Midsummer Night's Dream,* and *Twelfth Night* went from being metamorphosed into a *Cesario* in Düsseldorf to a swatch of *Violas* in various other parts of Germany and even a *Malvolio* in Melbourne, Australia. An operatic *The Tempest* by Shadwell put in an appearance as early as 1697 (Dorset Gardens Theatre). However, the adaptation of Shakespeare to the lighter stage, an exercise practiced mostly outside his native Britain (which has largely limited itself to vivisecting his texts and/or gussying them up in gimmicky productions), has by and large proven much less effective.

The very bare skeleton of *Romeo and Juliet,* set in different times and places, was the basis for two hit musicals in *The Belle of Mayfair* and *West Side Story,* whilst a production of a musical version of *The Taming of the Shrew* made up the play-within-a-play of *Kiss Me, Kate* and its parallel framework. *The Comedy of Errors* was used as the raw material for Charles Pidgin's 1888 musical comedy *Miss Fitz* (Proctor's Theater, Lunn 5 November), for the Rodgers and Hart musical *The Boys from Syracuse,* for Julian Slade's London comic opera *The Comedy of Errors* (Arts Theatre 28 March 1956), and for the up-dated *Oh, Brother!* (Michael Valenti/Donald Driver ANTA Theater, New York, 1981). In Britain, a fine musical adaptation of *The Merchant of Venice* produced as *Shylock* at the Edinburgh Festival was destroyed when glossied up into *Fire Angel* for the West End and the play's casket episode was used for the Players' Theatre's *The Three Caskets, or Venice re-Served* (Peter Greenwell/Gordon Snell, 5 November 1956), whilst another *Romeo and Juliet* derivative, *R Loves J,* was launched at the Chichester Festival in 1973 and also produced in Germany.

A rash of mod-musicalized Shakespeare in 1960s-70s America turned out a *Twelfth Night* variant called *Your Own Thing* (1968) and a John Guare/Mal Shapiro/Galt MacDermott *Two Gentlemen of Verona* (1971) on the credit side, and very much more on the debit. There were two further *Twelfth Nights* in *Love and Let Love* (S J Gelber/John Lollos, Don Christopher Sheridan Square Playhouse 1968, 14 performances) and *Music Is* (Richard Adler/Will Holt/George Abbott St James Theater, 1976); *A Midsummer Night's Dream* was metamorphosed into *Babes in the Wood* (Rick Besoyan, Orpheum Theater, 1964); and there were a risible Canadian *Rockabye Hamlet* (aka *Kronborg, Something's Rockin' in Denmark,* Cliff Jones, Charlottetown Festival, Canada, 1974), a one-performance *As You Like It* (John Balamos/Dran Seitz, Tani Seitz) played at the Theater de Lys, yet another shaken-and-stirred *Romeo and Juliet* under the title *Sensations* (Wally Harper/Paul Zakrzewski, New York, 1970), *The Tempest* served up as *Dreamstuff* (Marsha Malamet/Dennis Green/Howard Ashman, WPA The-

Plate 353. **Shakespeare's** The Merchant of Venice *became a musical as* Shylock. *Author Paul Bentley was Shylock in the 1982 production at Manchester's Library Theatre.*

ater, New York, 1976), *A Musical Merchant of Venice* (Jim Smith/Tony Tanner, Roundabout Theater, 1975) which lasted 13 performances and a *King Lear* made, presumably with a straight face, into *Pop* (Donna Cribari/Larry Schiff, Chuck Knull, New York, 1974) which survived only one performance. In spite of its obvious bankruptcy, the trend crept into the 1980s with a piece called *Ta-Dah!* (1981) which quoted *Much Ado About Nothing* as its source. Australia followed the trend with a *Beach Blanket Tempest* (Chris Harriott/Dennis Watkins) produced at Townsville in 1984. A Los Angeles-initiated version of *Othello* (*Catch My Soul,* Ahamson Theater 5 March 1968) went further than any of this group, being later seen in both London and Paris.

In earlier times, Shakespeare was offered as being at the basis of the plots of the successful French opérette *Gillette de Narbonne* and, more surprisingly, the British song-and-dance low comedy *The Dairymaids* (in the latter case a microscope was necessary to find a similarity with *As You Like It,* but Shakespeare's name doubtless looked good in the publicity). In Hungary one of the more unlikely candidates for a musical treatment, *Pericles,* was made into a operett under the title *A fekete hajó* (György Banffy/Jenő Rákosi Népszínház, 1883) and in Germany *Twelfth Night* was used as the basis for *Viola,* a ''comic opera with ballet'' by Richard Genée, music by Adolf Arensen (Stadttheater, Hamburg 16 March 1893); for a comedy opera, *Liebesspiel* (Richard Rosenberg/Willi Aron), produced at Aachen in 1929 (27 May); and again in 1963 for *Was ihr wollt, oder Die Schiffbrüchigen von Illyrien* (Klaus Fehmel/Günther Deicke, Theater der Freundschaft, Berlin 4 October 1963). *The Taming of the Shrew* was musicalized in 1896 for the Spanish stage by J Lopez Silva and Ruperto Chapí under the title *Las bravias,* and America's Oscar Weil proffered a *Pyramus and Thisbe* (29 September 1879) which survived one week in San Francisco.

Other 20th-century derivatives have included a disastrous attempt at *Swingin' the Dream* (1939) in which Erik Charell had a glossy hand, a British provincial piece which decided that the characters of *The Merchant of Venice* were *The Gay Venetians,* a rock opera which insisted there were *Drei Herren aus Verona* (H C Artmann, Nicolas Brieger Städtische Bühnen, Nuremberg 16 June 1972), a French-language version of *Love's Labours Lost* mounted at the Brussels Théâtre de la Monnaie, another *Shylock* which appeared off-Broadway at the York Theater (23 April 1987, Ed Dixon) and *The Merry Wives of*

Windsor, Texas, a Western musical produced by a clutch of writers at Houston's Alley Theater (1 December 1988). The 1990s saw this overworked and unprofitable trend continue with the umpteenth *Twelfth Night* perversion, this one mixed with Duke Ellington music under the title *Play On!* (Brooks Atkinson Theater 20 March 1997); the umpteenth *Taming of the Shrew,* produced in Copenhagen as *Trold kan taemmes* (Gladszaxe Theater 6 March 1999); a synthesized American *Romeo and Juliet* (T V Mann, Jerome Korman, St Paul, Minn 18 August 1999) and a pop-spectacular French one (*Roméo et Juliete* Palais des Congrès 19 January 2001); and a Czechoslovakian *Hamlet* musical, for which W Shakespeare got the book credit and Janek Ledecky the musical one (Kalich Theatre, Prague 1 November 1999).

In 1989 a TV-space-age pastiche of the plot of *The Tempest* and aged pop tunes was brought into London's West End (Cambridge Theatre 18 September) as *Return to the Forbidden Planet.* It caught the upswing of 1950s/1960s nostalgia, and scored a surprise British success before going on to be played in America, Australia and with particular success in Germany (as *Shakespeare und Rock 'n' Roll*).

Given his domination of the serious stage, Shakespeare's works were not too often maltreated by the makers of 19th-century burlesque. *Hamlet* was the play which was given the most attention, its first remake being as Poole's landmark *Hamlet Travestie* (1810) which made the Dane's celebrated soliloquy into a song. There followed an 1849 *Hamlet* from the pen of Francis Talfourd (seemingly produced only at Oxford), a *Hamlet According to Act of Parliament* at the Strand with Hurlstone as the parodied prince and Fanny Reeves as Ophelia (7 November 1853), a *Hamlet à la mode* (G Lash Gordon, G W Anson, Liverpool, 1877), *Hamlet Whether He Will or No* (Alexandra Theatre, Sheffield 2 June 1879), and William Yardley's *Very Little Hamlet* (Gaiety Theatre, 1884), whilst Vienna saw a successful Strampfertheater *Hammlet* (Richard Genée/Julius Hopp) in which Felix Schweighofer appeared as the hero, and on Broadway T C de Leon provided George Fox with a *Hamlet* burlesque (Olympic Theater 14 February 1870) and H Grattan Donnelly and Homer Tourgee came out with a *Hamlet II* (27 May 1895). Broadway's most successful Hamlet travesty, however, was the a vaudeville act which Eddie Foy subsequently incorporated into his musical-comedy vehicle *Mr Hamlet of Broadway.*

Most of the other principal Shakespeare parodies belonged to the earlier age of burlesque. Poole's burlesque of *Hamlet* was followed by an 1830 *Othello, the Moor of Fleet Street* played at the Adelphi Theatre with John Reeves starred, and by Maurice Dowling's highly successful *Othello Travestie* (Liverpool 1834, Strand Theatre 1836, aka *The Nigger's Revenge*). Gilbert a' Beckett tried his hand with a burlesqued *King John* (St James's Theatre, 1837), Dowling followed up with a *Romeo and Juliet* (Strand, 1838) and Andrew Halliday did the same some 20 years later at the same theatre with a *Romeo and Juliet Travestie, or The Cup of Cold Poison* (3 November 1859) in which Marie Wilton played Juliet. The Theatre Royal, Edinburgh, had a decided hit in 1842 with another *Romeo and Juliet* burlesque. *Richard III*—operafied in Russia and in France by Salvayre—was "done" thrice, by Charles Selby and Stirling Coyne in 1844 (*King Richard ye Third or Ye Battel of Bosworth Field,* Strand 26 February), at the Strand in 1854 as *Richard the Third According to Law* (20 April 1854) with George Hodson as an Irish hunchback, and again by F C Burnand (*The Rise and Fall of Richard III, or A new front to an old Dicky,* Royalty 1868, played in America as *Bad Dickey*) and Francis Talfourd did *Macbeth, somewhat removed from the Text of Shakespeare* (Strand 1848). On Broadway, George Fox followed up his *Hamlet* with a *Macbeth* (Olympic Theater 18 April 1870, using Locke's famous incidental music to the play as its musical part).

What seems to have been the first Shakespearean burlesque on the British stage was, however, a *The Mock Tempest, or The Enchanted Castle* mounted by Tom Killegrew at the King's Theatre in 1667 as a response to the production of Davenant and Dryden's version of Shakespeare's play at Lincoln's Inn Field. This one had Ariel singing "Where good ale is there suck I, in a cobbler's stall I lie, while the watch is passing by, then about the streets I fly. . . ." and other such high-class items. Several other tortured *Tempests* followed, and the Brough brothers turned the play into a popular extravaganza, *The Enchanted Isle, or raising the wind on the most approved principles* (Adelphi Theatre, 1848). This piece, introduced by Mr Stewart in the character of the ghost of Shakespeare, featured Priscilla Horton as Ariel and Buckstone as Caliban, burlesquing Lablache, the star of Halévy's operatic version of *The Tempest,* and managed to slide in a parody of *Hamlet* amongst its various burlesques. Later, Broadway saw Charles Gayler's *The Wizard's Tempest, or The King of the Magical Island* (Winter Garden 9 June 1862) with magician "Professor Anderson," otherwise The Wizard of the North, playing himself and bits of *Midsummer Night's Dream* mixed into the action; someone called Matthews Monck followed up with a *Prospero, or The King of the Caliban Islands* at London's Imperial Theatre in 1884; and F C Burnand gave his version of the same piece in *Ariel* (1883, with Nellie Farren as the sprite introducing electric light to the Gaiety stage).

Burnand also tackled *Antony and Cleopatra* (Haymarket 1866, Gaiety Theatre 1873), to which Charles

Selby had earlier turned his pen in 1843 (*Antony and Cleopatra Married and Settled* Adelphi Theatre 4 December).

In 1855 (9 April) Rebecca Isaacs of the Strand Theatre mounted a *King Queer and His Daughters Three* which Mrs Lane reproduced at the Britannia in 1871 as *Kyng Lear and hys Daughters Queer,* and Stuart Robson introduced Boston to Herbert Chose's *King Lear, the Cuss* (Selwyn Theatre 3 April 1869), whilst E L Blanchard initiated *The Merchant of Venice* to the burlesque stage at the Olympic Theatre in 1843 (2 October). Francis Talfourd followed up with a *Shylock* for the same theatre in 1853, imitated in double-barreled style by John Brougham with his transatlantic *The Merchant of Venice Preserved* (Fifth Avenue Theater 28 September 1867) and *Much Ado About a Merchant of Venice* (Brougham's Theater 8 March 1869) and on a lesser scale by Bryant's Minstrels in *Shylock, the Merchant of Chatham Street.* However, perhaps the most successful of the Shakespeare burlesques of this period was William Brough's *Perdita, or the Royal Milkmaid* (Lyceum, 1856), taken from *A Winter's Tale.* From the 1870s onwards, burlesques of Shakespeare were largely limited to the more unsophisticated circuits, and pieces like *Romeo the Radical and Juliet the Jingo* (1882) kept to the touring lists, but in 1899 George Grossmith and Paul Rubens perpetrated a West End piece called *Great Caesar* (Comedy Theatre 29 April 1899) which had as much to do with Shakespeare's play as previous parodies of the tale of the favorite military dictator of ancient Rome had done, and Nat Goodwin gave America a *Bottom's Dream* (John Braham/W T W Ball, Park Theatre, Boston 25 May 1885) which had fun with the mechanicals and fairies of *A Midsummer Night's Dream.* Britain's answer was *Nap, or A Midsummer's Night's Scream* produced at the Theatre Royal, Blyth (G Salom, Martin Adeson/Stanley Rogers 5 April 1890). In 1905 a burlesque of *Hamlet* was played by Pélissier's Follies at the Palace Music Hall.

Shakespeare was also the victim of what may have been the earliest example of a compilation show in the modern musical theatre. London was treated to an Easter show in 1853 which billed itself as "an historical, musical and illustrated entertainment," *Leaves from the Life and Lays from the Lyre of William Shakespeare. Will!* might have been more inviting as a title. Or not. Miss Clara St Casse, sometime child star, gave an Entertainment called *The Songs of Shakespeare* in which she spoke and sang Rosalind, Puck, Phelia, Ariel, Oberon and Hecate assisted by the Shakespeare Glee Union (New Town Hall, Shoreditch) in 1869. More recently the same concept was revived in *Shakespeare's Cabaret* (Bijou Theater 21 January 1981) and, 140 years after *The Life and Lays,* Britain's National Theatre came up with a Shakespearean compilation produced first at the Swan in Stratford, then in a revised version at the Pit (14 August 1995) and the Vaudeville Theatre (3 November 1995).

The playwright himself has appeared only occasionally on the musical stage, but oddly enough not in the only musical which was called, simply, *Shakespeare!* The Shakespeare of Gaston Serpette's 1899 opérette was not an author, but a dog. An English dog, though. Nor, in spite of being a moving element in the plot, was Will an on-stage character in the 1948 musical comedy *The Kid from Stratford.* In Britain, Martin Adeson played Shakespeare in George Edwardes's *The Merry-Go-Round* (1899) which stayed shy of the West End, Miles Malleson was a plump Shakespeare alongside Beatrice Lillie in *Now and Then* (1921), Conway Dixon a baritonically intrusive one in Eddie Knoblock's remake of *Merrie England* (1946), and Derek Godfrey was the burlesqued Bard in *No Bed for Bacon* (1959), whilst in America William Castle was a 19th-century Shakespeare to the Queen Elizabeth I of Emilie Melville in the rather more serious 1877 *A Summer Night's Dream* (Fifth Avenue Theater 15 October) and Hungary's *Will Shakespeare vagy akit akartok* (Madách Színház 21 September 1997) cast Ottó Viczián as its version of the bard in a piece which got Ann Hathaway, Burbage, Kit Marlowe and Queen Bess into the action. In France, de Leuven and Rosier made the playwright a leading character in their opéra-comique *Le Songe d'une nuit d'été* (Opéra-Comique 20 April 1850, mus: Ambroise Thomas), a piece which showed "Queen Elizabeth knocking about with a couple of drunkards, Shakespeare and Falstaff, in taverns and the palace gardens, passing her night disguised either in a domino noir or as a dame blanche." Sadly, the Avonic bard was not impersonated in Lew Dockstader's merry Broadway musical scena *Shakespeare or Bacon—Which?* (17 October 1887), which debated the question minstrel-style.

Shakespeare also found his way into many a song. Jerome Sykes sang topically of "These Words No Shakespeare Wrote" in *Nanon* and in any other show he felt like shoving it into (1892), and Jerome and Schwartz wrote about "When Mr Shakespeare Comes to Town" for Weber and Fields's *Hoity-Toity* (1901)—but the musical theatre's most enduring Shakespearean reference remains a passive one: *Kiss Me, Kate*'s instruction to "Brush Up Your Shakespeare."

Recording: *Shakespeare on Broadway* (Varèse Sarabande)

SHAMUS O'BRIEN, a story of Ireland 100 years ago Romantic comic opera in 2 acts and 3 tableaux by George H Jessop based on the poem by Joseph Sheridan Le Fanu. Music by Charles Villiers Stanford. Opera Comique, London, 2 March 1896.

The Irish-American writer George Jessop had turned out a long run of pieces for the American theatre, including some with an Irish flavor, but nothing of a quality that presaged the agreeable and touching libretto with which he provided the well-considered British composer Charles Villiers Stanford (1852–1924) (*The Canterbury Pilgrims,* etc) for the latter's one attempt at writing for the lighter lyric stage. *Shamus O'Brien* was described as a romantic comic opera, but its central story was a dramatic one. The rebel Shamus O'Brien (Denis O'Sullivan) is betrayed to the British by Mike Murphy (Joseph O'Mara), who then courts his wife, Nora (Kirkby Lunn), with promises of securing her husband's release. When O'Brien escapes, Murphy is killed trying to stop him. That drama was thinned out with a heavy dose of flirting and singing from the soubrette, Kitty (Maggie Davies), who chases the English Captain (William Trevor) while he unwillingly pursues Shamus. Stanford's music steered a course between the operatic and folk-music styles in a score in which the patriotic songs of Shamus (''I've Sharpened the Sword for the Sake of Ould Erin'') and the pert soubrette melodies (''Where is the Man Who Is Coming to Marry Me?'') were contrasted with some truly dramatic moments for the contralto role of Nora, and which did not shrink from quoting genuine Irish folk airs.

Produced by its authors in collaboration with the publishers Boosey & Co, *Shamus O'Brien* was cast with students from the Royal College of Music. All three leading players went on to memorable careers, Miss Lunn in the operatic world, O'Sullivan on the musical stage until an early death, and O'Mara at the head of his own touring opera company. The production was largely well-received and, at the height of the craze for musical comedy, was played 82 times in London before going on to New York where O'Sullivan and O'Mara were teamed with Annie Roberts and G B Shaw's sister, Lucy Carr-Shaw (Kitty), for a 56-performance Broadway season. In 1897 it was toured through America by the Duff Opera Company, with Arthur Cunningham and Marion Mervyn featured, and through Ireland under the management of Ben Greet with Eone Delrita starred, while the following year it was seen on the road in England with the Savoy Theatre's Leonora Braham as Nora, Avalon Collard as Mike and Frank E Tours conducting.

In 1910 *Shamus O'Brien* was played in repertoire by the Beecham Opera Company with Albert Archdeacon, Edith Evans and O'Mara, and it was for many years also seen in the repertoire of O'Mara's own company. In 1930 it was broadcast by the BBC, but in spite of its composer's respected name, it has since been ignored professionally. In 1960 it was played by the BBC Club Operatic Society at St George's Hall (6 October).

USA: Broadway Theater 5 January 1897

SHARMAN, Jim [SHARMAN, James David] (b Sydney, 12 March 1945).

Australian-born director Sharman entered the musical theatre in his own country when he was hired to direct Harry M Miller's Australian versions of *Hair* and *Jesus Christ Superstar.* The success of the latter resulted in his being asked to stage the subsequent record-breaking London version of the show, and he followed this by mounting the original production of another of the 1970s' most enduring London successes, *The Rocky Horror Show.* He repeated his *Rocky Horror Show* assignment in America and on the subsequent cult film, but was thereafter seen rarely in the musical theatre until he directed a partially rewritten version of *Chess* in Sydney in 1989.

SHAW, George Bernard (b Dublin, 26 July 1856; d Ayot St Lawrence, 2 November 1950).

In spite of the fact that his mother was a singer and music teacher and that his sister, Lucy Carr-Shaw, had a respectable career, mostly as a provincial leading lady, in the musical theatre, the writer G B Shaw professed a lofty disdain for the genre. In his career as a critic he rarely had a good word to say for even the most successful musical plays, he rejected an 1895 offer to write a libretto with the comment that star Arthur Roberts was ''better at inventing lines than speaking other folks'' (Jerome K Jerome took the job), and he insisted that it was impossible for any of his own works to be made into an example of the despised genre. By the time *My Fair Lady* demonstrated posthumously just what a perfect musical-comedy-libretto style of writing he had, Shaw had already been healthily proven wrong, in his own lifetime, by librettists Rudolf Bernauer and Leopold Jacobson and composer Oscar Straus with their ''unauthorized'' adaptation of *Arms and the Man* as *Der tapfere Soldat.* It must indeed have hurt the snooty dramatist's feelings to see his plot and dialogue, re-Englished from the German by Liverpudlian-American Stanislaus Stange as *The Chocolate Soldier,* piling up long and successful runs both on Broadway and in London, runs which far outdid those established by his original play.

The success of *My Fair Lady* provoked surprisingly few attempts to musicalize other Shaw works. After a British musical on *Caesar and Cleopatra* (1899), written by Kitty Black and Michael Flanders and composed by Manos Hadzidakis, had failed to get off the drawing board in 1961, another version entitled *Her First Roman* (Lunt-Fontanne Theater 20 October 1968) made it to Broadway for 17 performances. A musical *Androcles and the Lion* composed by Richard Rodgers was restricted to television (NBC 15 November 1967), whilst a version of *The Admirable Bashville* (1903) slimmed to *Bashville* (Denis King/Benny Green) was produced at London's

Regent's Park Open Air Theatre (2 August 1983). The same team of King and Green also musicalized Shaw's *You Never Can Tell* under the title of *Valentine's Day* (lib: Green, David Williams, Queen's Theatre 17 September 1992).

The German-language stage followed up *Der tapfere Soldat* with a comic-opera version of *Great Catherine* (*Die grosse Katharine* Ignaz Lihén/Trebitsch, Maril Staattheater, Wiesbaden 8 May 1932), and a second successful version of *Arms and the Man* called *Helden, Helden* (Udo Jürgens/Eckart Hachfeld, Walter Brandin, Hans Gmür, Theater an der Wien 23 October 1972), whilst *Mrs Warren's Profession* became *Frau Warrens Gewerbe* (Charles Kálmán/Peter Goldbaum) at the Theater am Dom, Cologne (23 December 1974).

In the days of their first currency, Shaw's works occasionally came under the hands of the revue-days burlesquers, and in this way his *Major Barbara* got a going-over in *The Cohan Revue of 1916* with Lila Rhodes portraying the parodied Barbara.

Shaw was portrayed on the musical stage by John Neville when Britain's Nottingham Playhouse mounted a biomusical of the playwright (Johnny Dankworth/Benny Green) under the title *Boots with Strawberry Jam* (28 February 1968).

SHAW, Oscar [SCHWARZ, Oscar] (b Philadelphia, 11 October 1887; d Little Neck, NY, 6 March 1967).

After beginning his career as a chorus boy in revue, dapperly handsome Schwarz went on to a career of nearly 20 years as a Broadway leading man. Early credits in America in *The Girl and the Wizard* (1909, Max Andressen), *The Kiss Waltz* (1911, Albert), and *Two Little Brides* (1912, Deschamps), and in verge-of-wartime (which prompted his change of name) London in revue, prefaced his first important assignments as Dick Rivers, the love-smacked straight man of *Very Good Eddie* (1915, ''Some Sort of Somebody,'' ''If I Find the Girl'') and Stub Talmadge, the football-mad fun of *Leave It to Jane* (1917, ''The Sun Shines Brighter,'' ''A Peach of a Life''). There was less success for him in 47 performances as Tommy Tilson, forced to wed *The Rose of China* for having seen her unveiled (1919), and just one night more as Bradford Adams whose self-made papa doesn't want him to wed society in *The Half Moon* (1920), but he had successes in both Youmans's *Two Little Girls in Blue* (1920, ''Oh Me! Oh My!'') and as socialite hero Billy van Courtlandt in Kern's *Good Morning Dearie* (1920, ''Blue Danube Blues,'' ''Kailua'').

What remained of the role of Bastien in *One Kiss* (1923, ex- *Ta bouche*) and *Dear Sir* (1924, Laddie Munn) were less productive jobs, but 1926 brought him his most memorable creation of all as the beleaguered bridegroom Jimmy Winters in *Oh, Kay!* introducing ''Do, Do, Do'' and ''Maybe'' alongside Gertrude Lawrence's Kay. He followed up as Gerald Brooks, the hero of *The Five O'Clock Girl* (1927, ''Thinking of You''), as Tom Addison in *Flying High* (1930, ''Thank Your Father'') and, finally, as Steve Addison in *Everybody's Welcome* (1931) before, now in his forties, being forced by nature to drop out of the line of juvenile-to-lead men he had played for a decade and a half. He toured alongside Harriette Lake (aka Ann Sothern) in the role of Wintergreen in *Of Thee I Sing* in 1932, but thereafter faded from the scene.

On the musical screen, he appeared as the Brylcreemy juvenile man to the antics of the Marx Brothers in *The Cocoanuts.*

SHEAN, Al [SCHÖNBERG, Albert] (b Dorum, Germany, 12 May 1868; d New York, 12 August 1949).

A popular ''dutch'' vaudeville comedian, who found fame in partnership with Ed Gallagher, Al Shean also appeared in a number of musicals. The first of these (pre-Gallagher) included the 1893 farce comedy *A Trip to the City*, several pieces which teamed him with Charles Warren—George Totten Smith and Harry von Tilzer's inept *The Pan-American Girl* in which he played a millionaire corst-maker (Bergen Beach 15 June 1901, also director) and the vaudeville burlesque pieces *Quo Vadis Upside Down* and *Kidding the Captain* (1901–2)—and others with another ''dutchman,'' Dave Lewis—the Chicago La Salle productions of *Chow Chow, The Paraders* (1902, ''Sara Sunshine''), *Tom-Tom* (1903) and *Rubes and Roses* (1903). He also appeared in von Tilzer's *The Fisher Maiden* (1903, Dullovitch, with Warren as Grimsky) and the touring *The Isle of Bong Bong,* and in 1908 he was seen in New York supporting Joe Welch and performing his *Quo Vadis Upside Down* in the musical farce *Morning, Noon and Night* (Otto Seise, to the Gusty Bunk of Warren). His first musical-theatre engagement of consequence (with Gallagher), was in the highly successful American version of Granichstaedten's *Bub oder Mädel?, The Rose Maid* (1912, Schmuke), in which they appeared (with Eugene Redding and Arthur Laceby) as a quartet of iffy ''loan brokers and bankers'' who have the show's extravagant hero in their comical grip. He subsequently returned to vaudeville and toured in 1914 without Gallagher but instead with his nephews ''the four Marx brothers,'' teamed in his dutch double-act this time with 19-year-old Julius (later to be known as Groucho) Marx, but he returned to the musical stage the following year in Victor Herbert's *The Princess Pat* (1915, Anthony Schmalz) and then in the surprise success *Flo-Flo* (1917, Isidor Moser).

A reconstitution of the partnership with Gallagher brought the famous song ''Mr Gallagher and Mr Shean'' to light and gave the pair the most prominent moment of their careers, performing in the *Ziegfeld Follies of 1922.* After their second and final split, Shean returned to the musical-comedy stage in the shortlived *Betsy* (1926, Stonewall Moskowitz), and starred in one of the best of all Broadway ''dutch'' roles as Hans Wagner in a revival of *The Prince of Pilsen* (1930) and as the genuinely and only gently comical Austrian Dr Walther Lessing in the Broadway strudel-operetta *Music in the Air* (1932). As late as 1946 he appeared on the musical stage as Gramps O'Brien in *Windy City.*

Shean was seen on the musical screen in such films as *San Francisco* (1936), *The Great Waltz* (1938) and *Ziegfeld Girl* (1941).

SHE LOVES ME Musical by Joe Masteroff based on the play *Illatszertár* by Miklós László. Lyrics by Sheldon Harnick. Music by Jerry Bock. Eugene O'Neill Theater, New York, 23 April 1963.

László's 1937 play *Illatszertár,* a piece about two perfume shopworkers who cordially dislike each other but who are unknowingly engaged in a lonely hearts correspondence which leads them to a happy ending, was first produced at Budapest's Pesti Színház (20 March) and was subsequently made into a Hollywood film (*The Shop Around the Corner,* 1940) with James Stewart and Margaret Sullavan starred. A second film version entitled *In the Good Old Summertime* (1949) was equipped with songs.

In 1963 the piece was made into a stage musical. Barbara Cook played Amália Balásh, warm and wonderful, and Daniel Massey was Georg Nowack, quiet and capable. But apparently incompatible. Alongside them in the perfumery work the gleamingly plastic Steve Kodaly (Jack Cassidy), who is currently playing the field with both the wife of the boss (Ludwig Donath) and another of the shop's clerks, Ilona Ritter (Barbara Baxley); the more straightforward Ladislaw Sipos (Nathaniel Frey); and the boy Árpád László (Ralph Williams), who has longings to rise to be a clerk. While Amália and Georg head through a series of the usual kind of misunderstandings towards their happy ending, the boss tries to shoot himself because of nasty Steve, who is ultimately sacked and vanishes from the story leaving Ilona free to become more decently attached. Árpád gets the vacant job.

The songs which accompanied everyone's progress to happiness were a curious mixture, ranging from gentle, pastelly pieces of charm for the heroine (''Ice Cream,'' ''Dear Friend'') and equally ingenuous if neatly brighter ones for her partner (''She Loves Me'') to some harsh and almost crude numbers for Steve and Ilona. There was not a large amount of ensemble music and the show's chorus intruded little.

Harold Prince's production of *She Loves Me,* directed by its producer and advertised slightly curiously or even ungrammatically as ''the happiest new musical,'' played 302 performances on Broadway and it was subsequently produced in London where Anne Rogers (Amalia), Gary Raymond (Georg), Gary Miller (Steve) and Rita Moreno (Ilona) featured through an indifferent 189 performances. It was later telefilmed by Britain's Channel 4 with Gemma Craven as Amalia.

In 1993 a revival of *She Loves Me* was produced by the Roundabout Theater Company (10 June) with Boyd Gaines, Judy Kuhn and Howard McGillin featured, and transferred to Broadway's Brooks Atkinson Theatre (7 November 1993). It had already shuttered unprofitably after 339 performances when London's Michel White surprisingly staged a London revival at the Savoy Theatre (12 July 1994). John Gordon Sinclair and Ruthie Henshall were billed, the critics—especially those with a sweet nostalgia for the songs-and-scenes musical comedy of what now seemed like yesteryear—said ''charming'' and the pretty revival of the pretty piece ran through an insufficient season in the shadow of the city's larger and more profitable spectacles.

On the élan thus provided, however, the show went on to its first production in Europe at Vienna's Établissment Ronacher. Joseph-René Rumpold (Georg) and Christine Rothacker (Amália) featured in Frank Thannhäuser and Nico Rabenald's adaptation for a nine months' run.

UK: Lyric Theatre 29 April 1964; Austria: Ronacher *Sie liebt mich* 19 September 1996

Recordings: original cast (MGM/DRG), London cast (HMV), New York revival cast (Colosseum), London revival cast (First Night), Austrian cast *Sie liebe mich* (Capriccio)

SHENANDOAH Musical in 2 acts by James Lee Barrett, Peter Udell and Philip Rose based on Barrett's screenplay of the same title. Lyrics by Peter Udell. Music by Gary Geld. Alvin Theater, New York, 7 January 1975.

Based not on the successful Bronson Howard play of 1889, but on the equally successful 1965 film featuring James Stewart, the musical *Shenandoah* told the story of Charlie Anderson (John Cullum), a mind-my-own-business farmer in the Shenandoah Valley who is determined not to allow the warmongers of the Confederacy and the Union to drag him and his family—six sons and one daughter—into their civil war. But the warmongers and those they have infected, the young men of each army who yell for their side as if they were at a football match, do not allow anyone not to play their game. Charlie's determinedly neutral family is attacked and his youngest son carried off by the Union soldiers, and the Anderson family have to get involved. It is a long and cruel time

Plate 354. **Shenandoah.** *The young folk of the Shenandoah Valley will soon be torn apart by other people's wars.*

before they can creep, battered and scarred, back to the Shenandoah Valley to rebuild their lives.

The score of the show, written in a warmly countrified vein, had for its backbone a series of soliloquies for Charlie from which his fierce, anti-war ''I've Heard It All Before'' and the ''Meditation'' over the grave of his wife stood powerfully alongside the happy songs of his young family, topped by a delightful country duo for Anne (Penelope Milton) and Jenny (Donna Theodore), ''We Make a Beautiful Pair,'' and a heart-rending solo for a young soldier (Gary Harger) wending his way back in the aftermath of the war to ''The Only Home I Know.''

Originally produced at the Goodspeed Opera House, and staged without glitz or grandeur, *Shenandoah* was greeted by the more self-consciously sophisticated Broadway critics with a gentle sneer, yet its sincere, wholesome characters and their straightforward and moving story put across their anti-war message far more effectively than any of the trendier and more strident love-not-war musicals of the era, and its songs (even if one lyric did generalize on that sadly overworked period word ''Freedom'') illustrated their story most effectively. The public soon made up their own mind about the show, and continued to support it for 1,050 performances and a tour.

In 1989 Cullum reprised the role he had created, and which had earned him the 1975 Tony Award, for a touring production. Launched in Canada, it played a brief return Broadway season (Virginia Theater 8 August, 31 performances) during its tour under the management of Howard and Sophie Hurst and Peter Ingster.

Recording: original cast (RCA)

SHEPHARD, [F] Firth [SHEPHARD, Frederick Edward] (b London, 27 April 1891; d London, 3 January 1949). London producer of the 1920s and 1930s.

Shephard began his working life in an insurance office, but he soon renounced his desk to become a whistler in a concert party at Clacton. He wrote songs and sketches for the concert party and then, during the First World War, began contributing material to London and provincial revues. His first connection with the musical theatre came when he was entrusted with the adaptation of Rida Johnson Young's tale of Mormon marriage, *His Little Widows,* for Bernard Hishin's London production. He subsequently collaborated on the construction of a musical-comedy vehicle for Ethel Levey, *Oh! Julie,* and on the disastrous Gaiety Theatre burlesque *Faust on Toast* before taking his first turn into management, in partnership with Laddie Cliff, on the dance-and-laughter musical *Dear Little Billie* (1925).

Although he ''authored'' Cliff's subsequent musical comedy *Lady Luck* (a libretto which was filched fairly straight from *His Little Widows*), Shephard's own producing ventures for the next few years were in the revue field. However, at the end of the 1920s he teamed with comedian Leslie Henson on the presentation of a series of successful comedies, amongst which the London production of Broadway's *Follow Through* (1929), the musicalized German farce *Nice Goings On* (1933) and the remake of Broadway's *Little Jessie James* as *Lucky Break* (1934), each with Henson starred, represented the musical portion.

Thereafter Shephard once again went it alone, with Henson remaining as star if not co-producer of a run of musicals which relit the sadly tenebrous Gaiety Theatre in no uncertain manner: *Seeing Stars* (1935), *Swing Along* (1936), *Going Greek* (1937) and *Running Riot* (1938). The very loose-limbed *Wild Oats* (1938, for which, like *Running Riot,* Shephard was credited with ''from a plot by'') and *Sitting Pretty* (1939) also contributed to the comedy-musical gaiety of the prewar years. The war, however, effectively put an end both to the Gaiety series and to the budding Prince's Theatre series begun by *Wild Oats* and *Sitting Pretty.*

In 1941 Shephard produced *Wild Rose,* a revamped version of *Sally* as a vehicle for filmland's Jessie Matthews, but he then returned to producing plays (*Arsenic and Old Lace, My Sister Eileen,* etc) until the end of his career.

1919 **His Little Widows** English adaptation (Wyndham's Theatre)

1920 **Oh! Julie** (aka *The Honeymoon Girl*) (H Sullivan Brooke, Herman Darewski/Harold Simpson/w Lee Banson) Shaftesbury Theatre 22 June

1921 **Faust on Toast** (Willie Redstone, Melville Gideon/w Adrian Ross) Gaiety Theatre 19 April

1925 **Dear Little Billie** (H B Hedley, Jack Strachey/Desmond Carter) Shaftesbury Theatre 25 August

1927 **Lady Luck** (Hedley, Strachey/Carter/w Greatrex Newman) Carlton Theatre 27 April

SHERIDAN, J[ohn] F[rancis] (b Providence, RI, 1843; d Newcastle, Australia, 25 December 1908). Internationally famous American dame comedian.

After spending his earliest work days employed in a gun manufactury, Sheridan began his performing career as a young clog-dancer in minstrel shows (12 April 1864) and music hall, latterly as half of the double act, Sheridan and Mack (''Don't Forget the Old Folks,'' ''Scenes from Childhood,'' ''Little Fraud,'' etc). He also appeared in burlesque, notably alongside Lisa Weber (1872). In 1879 he took part in the tryout of George Fawcett Rowe's temperance drama *Ruth, or The Curse of Rum* (Philadelphia 24 November), performing his speciality in an interpolated concert-garden scene, and in that piece accidentally found what would be his way to fame on the musical stage when one night he donned skirts and deputized for an incompetent extra in the role of an old Irish woman. After the (quick) end of *Ruth,* Sheridan and Rowe got together and invented for Sheridan's benefit the character of the Widow O'Brien and the musical-comedy-cum-variety-show *Fun on the Bristol* (1880) of which she was the central feature. After completing a considerable star tour round America in this top-notch travesty role, Sheridan took his ''musical comedy oddity'' to Britain (1882). He scored a singular success in the provinces and more than safely braved a London season at the Olympic Theatre, before setting off in 1884 to introduce the Widow O'Brien to Australia and the southern Asia circuits. During his time in the southern hemisphere he also appeared as Ko-Ko, Robin Oakapple, the Judge and John Wellington Wells in the Gilbert and Sullivan canon, as Lurcher in *Dorothy,* Cadeau in *Erminie,* Laurent in *La Mascotte* and other lead comedy roles in repertoire, but he returned always to his alter ego as the Widow O'Brien. In 1887 he again presented himself at London's Gaiety Theatre and the Opera Comique in the eternal *Fun on the Bristol.*

He subsequently brought out a sequel to his now-celebrated vehicle, *Bridget O'Brien Esq* (''Bright Little Glass''), which he subsequently took (as *Mrs O'Brien Esq*) first to Broadway's Bijou Theater (31 October 1892) for a season, and—rechristened *A Trip to Chicago*—to Britain (Vaudeville Theatre 5 August 1893, Mrs Johanna Murphy). The piece (ad J S Haydon, mus: W C Vernon and F Leaman) was subsequently toured long around the British provinces.

It was on this visit to Britain that he then found himself a second splendid frock part when he took over from heavy lady Adelaide Newton as the Second Mrs Block in London's *Little Christopher Columbus* (1894). He worked the originally minor role up into a major showpiece with above-the-title billing, and the ailing show into a success, and then, in an age where travesty performances outside pantomime were becoming rare, moved on to appear as the lion-taming Lady Fitzwarren (to whom ''I love'' is pronounced ''je tame'') in the same authors' *Dandy Dick Whittington* (1895). He subsequently toured his own company through Britain with a repertoire including *An Artist's Model, Dandy Dick Whittington, The Shop Girl, The New Barmaid* and *A Trip to Chinatown,* and played on the halls in a musical sketch about another member of the O'Brien family, *Shamus O'Brien* (1898), before returning once more to South Africa and to Australia, where he had become a particular favorite, a fact perhaps not unconnected with his reputation as the man who ''wears the tightest trousers in Australia.'' He also played through India, Burma and China.

During his time in Australia, Sheridan continued to appear regularly as the Widow O'Brien and as Mrs Block and briefly attempted a new travesty vehicle as *Mrs Goldstein.* He also toured a selection of musicals under his own management, including *Naughty Nancy* (which allowed him three roles, one female), *A Trip to Chicago,* and personal versions of *The New Barmaid, The Lady Slavey* (Roberts), *King Dodo* (Dodo) and *The Earl and the Girl* (Cheese). He was also seen in further male comedy roles in such more traditional pieces as *Dorothy* (Lurcher), *Erminie* (Cadeau), *Rip van Winkle* (Rip), in the Gilbert and Sullivan repertoire and as Con in Boucicault's *The Shaughraun.* He remained in Australia, regularly taking the Widow O'Brien around the country, until his death at the age of 61. He was buried in his adopted homeland under a stone bearing his catchphrase ''It's sorry I'm here, I am.''

Sheridan collaborated on the authorship of several theatre pieces, including his last vehicle, and undoubtedly less officially on most of his variety musicals.

His first wife was the male impersonator Alecia Jourdain (d Cincinnati, 25 May 1880) who appeared in the original cast of *Fun on the Bristol,* and he subsequently married another perfomer, Gracie Whiteford.

1887 **Bridget O'Brien Esq** (aka *A Trip to Chicago*) (J A Robertson, et al/Bert Royle/w Fred Lyster) Opera Comique, London 29 October

1902 **Mrs Goldstein** (aka *Mrs Dooley's Joke*) (F Weiterer/w Pat Finn) Criterion Theatre, Sydney 29 September

SHERWIN, Manning (b Philadelphia, 4 January 1903; d Hollywood, Calif, 26 July 1974).

Journeyman composer Sherwin had songs used in the revues *Bad Habits of 1926, Merry-Go-Round* (1927), *Crazy Quilt* (1931) and the musical *Everybody's Welcome* (1931) before moving to Hollywood where he worked as a songwriter for the early sound films for some six years. In 1938 he moved again, this time to London, where his first West End song was interpolated into the Eric Maschwitz flop *Magyar Melody.* Over the next decade he provided the scores for a series of revues including *Shephard's Pie* (''Who's Taking You Home Tonight?'' w Tommy Conner), *Up and Doing, Rise Above It II, Fun and Games, Fine and Dandy* (w Eric Blore), *Magic Carpet* and *Here Come the Boys,* as well as for a number of musical comedies. The first of these, *Sitting Pretty,* was cut short by the outbreak of war, but he had successes with George Black's long-running cabaret-mystery musical *Get a Load of This* (''Wrap Yourself in Cotton Wool'') and with three sturdy comedy vehicles for Cicely Courtneidge, each of which had a fine London run and one of which, *Under the Counter,* was taken to America and to Australia as well.

His most successful single song was ''A Nightingale Sang in Berkeley Square'' originally sung by Judy Campbell in *New Faces.*

1939 **Sitting Pretty** (Douglas Furber) Prince's Theatre 17 August

1941 **Get a Load of This** (Val Guest/James Hadley Chase, Arthur Macrae) London Hippodrome 19 November

1943 **Something in the Air** (Harold Purcell, Max Kester/Macrae, Archie Menzies, Jack Hulbert) Palace Theatre 23 September

1945 **Under the Counter** (Purcell/Macrae) Phoenix Theatre 22 November

1948 **The Kid from Stratford** (Barbara Gordon, Basil Thomas) Prince's Theatre 30 September

1949 **Her Excellency** (w Harry Parr Davies/Kester, Purcell, Menzies) London Hippodrome 22 June

SHEVELOVE, Burt[on George] (b Newark, NJ, 19 September 1915; d London, 8 April 1982).

Shevelove made his first appearance in the theatre as the co-lyricist and director of the revue *Small Wonder* (Coronet Theater 15 September 1948) and three years later combined again with composer Albert Selden on a musicalization of Victor Wolfson's play *Excursion* as *A Month of Sundays.* Nancy Walker topbilled, and it folded pre-Broadway. He directed a revival of *Kiss Me, Kate* at the City Center and finally hit success when he coauthored the Plautian pastiche *A Funny Thing Happened on the Way to the Forum* with Larry Gelbart.

He subsequently found Broadway success also as a director with *Hallelujah, Baby!* and the 1971 revival of *No, No, Nanette,* but was unable to rescue disaster from disaster when he took over the staging of London's *Twang!!* (1965) from Joan Littlewood. As a writer he again went to classic literature when he teamed with Stephen Sondheim for a novelty on-the-water piece, *The Frogs,* but met with an unhappy ending when he arranged Philip Barry's play *Holiday* as a musical with a selection of secondhand Cole Porter numbers as its musical part.

He also wrote the libretto for an ABC television version of Oscar Wilde's *The Canterville Ghost* (2 November 1966) with songs by Jerry Bock and Sheldon Harnick.

1951 **A Month of Sundays** (Albert Selden/w Ted Fetter) Shubert Theater, Boston 25 December

1962 **A Funny Thing Happened on the Way to the Forum** (Stephen Sondheim/w Larry Gelbart) Alvin Theater 8 May

1974 **The Frogs** (Sondheim) New Haven, Conn 20 May

1980 **Happy New Year** (Cole Porter arr Buster Davis) Morosco Theater 27 April

SHINE, John L[loyd Joseph Aloysius] (b Manchester, 28 May 1856; d New York, 17 October 1930). Comic actor and would-be producer of the British musical stage.

John Shine began his career as an actor in Manchester and toured and played in stock before reaching London in 1880. He made his first appearance there with the Hanlons in their pantomime *La Voyage en Suisse,* played in several comedies at the Gaiety and then went into management for the first time, touring a company with a repertoire including the burlesque *Don Juan.* He made his initial attempt at West End management with Sydney Grundy's play *The Glass of Fashion.* The piece failed utterly, dropping £10,000, but Shine continued, in partnership with the Gaiety manager John Hollingshead, with the production of the comic opera *Dick* (1884) at the Globe. The piece, in which he himself took the chief comic role (Fitzwarren), had a certain success but, along with Hollingshead and the money of financier Henry O'Hagan (who had also been behind the financing of much of the Gaiety's early production), he had also taken on the management of the new Empire Theatre, and it soon proved a difficult house to make viable.

An opening with a lavish revival of *Chilpéric* was followed by a transfer of *Dick,* another of Lillian Russell in Teddy Solomon's *Polly,* the production of a new Solomon work, *Pocahontas,* and of the super-lavish *The Lady of the Locket,* and a revival of Solomon's *Billee Taylor* before the management went under. Impoverished, Shine had, however, done well as an actor with principal roles in *Pocahontas* (Sir Hector Van Trump), *The Lady of the Locket* (Oblivio) and *Billee Taylor* (Ben Barnacle).

The following year he produced a rewritten version of the old extravaganza *Piff Paff* (ex- *Le Grand Duc de Matapa*) under the title of *Glamour* (1886) and toured it with himself and his brother in the lead comic roles, but management again proved his downfall and at one stage he ended up in Holloway jail for a debt of £12 to Allen's, the poster-printers. In 1888 he appeared at the Avenue Theatre as Bobèche to the Boulotte of Florence St John in a revival of *Barbe-bleue.*

Shine finally threw in his manager's hand and returned instead to acting in plays. In 1891, however, he co-authored a burlesque of *Joan of Arc,* otherwise commissioned by George Edwardes from a promising new pair called Adrian Ross and Osmond Carr. He was unable to join in the management side this time, as his previous producing activities had brought him face to face with the bankruptcy courts, and, of course, *Joan of Arc* was a singular hit. He had not even the consolation this time of the lead comic role, for Edwardes had cast Arthur Roberts at the top of the bill and Shine had to be content with playing the Dauphin. In 1892 he starred alongside Tillie Wadman in the provincial production of *The Young Recruit* (*Les Dragons de la reine,* Captain Jeremiah Cornelius de Bang).

The coming of musical comedy brought Shine a number of juicy star comedy roles including Spoofah Bey in *Morocco Bound* (1893 and 1901), Dam Row in *Go-Bang* (1894) and William White in *The New Barmaid* (1896), but he could not prevent himself getting mixed up in production again, and he suffered his worst battering yet when he was involved with a feeble burlesque called *All My Eye-van-hoe* (1893), in which he starred and which ended him up once more in the debtors' courts.

The larger part of his later career was spent in the straight theatre where in 1904 he created the role of Larry Doyle in Shaw's *John Bull's Other Island* at the Court Theatre. He ventured not again as a producer, although as a writer he adapted Berté's *Kreolenblut* as *The Rose of Panama* (aka *Jacinta*) for John Cort in America, where he spent the last of his years, apparently much to the relief of his long-suffering relations.

His brother **[Edwin] Wilfred SHINE** (b Manchester, 12 July 1862; d Kingston-on-Thames, 14 March 1939) appeared from 1879 on both the musical and straight stages, spending a period, in his twenties, touring with the D'Oyly Carte companies (Bunthorne, Major General, Judge, Wells) and playing in London for his brother in *Dick* (Alderman Fitzwarren) and *Polly* (t/o Pipeclay). He toured in burlesque for George Edwardes, in John's production of *Glamour* (1886, Count Inferno do Penseroso), with Horace Lingard in *Falka* and *Pepita,* and made further musical appearances in London in the tryout of Adrian Ross and Osmond Carr's first musical *Faddimir* (1889), and in *Miss Decima* (t/o Flannagan). However, he had his most considerable success in Australia and on the Eastern circuit, particularly in his brother's role of Spoofah Bey in *Morocco Bound.* He later toured Britain in the title role of Harry Monkhouse's *Pat* and as Micky O'Dowd in *My Lady* Molly (1904), and played in the musical comedy *Nana* (1902) at Birmingham.

A second brother, **Harry SHINE** [William Henry SHINE] (b Manchester, 24 May 1870; d Sydney, Australia, 11 September 1909), also had a successful career, mostly in Australia, as a musical comedian. The companion of Australian music-hall star Florrie Forde, he died—apparently from persistent liquid intake—before they could legalize their attachment.

Wilfred's son, **Bill Shine** [Wilfred William Dennis SHINE] (b London, 20 October 1911), carried on in the family business, making a handful of musical appearances (Squeezum in *Lock Up Your Daughters,* Boganovich in *The Merry Widow,* Lord Littlehampton in *Maudie!,* etc) in a very long career as an actor.

1891 **Joan of Arc** (F Osmond Carr/Adrian Ross) Opera Comique 17 January

1912 **The Rose of Panama** (*Kreolenblut*) English version (Daly's Theatre, New York)

SHIP AHOY Comic opera in 3 acts by H Grattan Donnelly and Fred Miller jr. Altoona, Pa, 27 November 1890; Standard Theater, NY, 8 December 1890.

This loose-limbed extravaganza shipwrecked a musical comedy manager called Mapleson Mulberry (Tom Ricketts) on a West Indian island with his prima donna, Mlle Auburni Ernani (Bertha Ricci), contralto Georgia Carolini (Edith Sinclair) and soubrette Lulu Lalla (Carrie Tutein). The ladies take over the island, only to have their matriarchal ambitions wrecked by the arrival of the *US Cuckoo* with its complement of naval men under Commodore Columbus Cook (Edward M Favor). All that happened in Act I, and the next two acts were mostly spent in having Mulberry and Cook swap places (and in a would-be *HMS Pinafore* way, Mulberry thus takes charge, for the Commodore's authority is vested only in the uniform he wears) and the ladies romance various men of the sea (Walter H Ford, Newton Brown), with a bundle of semi-pasticcio songs (32 in all) and specialities, before everyone heads back to Washington to claim the island for the ladies.

Run in in Philadelphia to a merry response, the piece got automatically kicked by the more xenophobic critics of New York, but it was in general voted bright and whistleable and stayed in town for five weeks, winning more than a few friends, before setting off to Boston and then on the road in duplicate. The management announced that they would bring it back to the Union Square Theater (April 16) "for a run," but when it returned to New York is was at the same Standard Theater (18 May 1891) with Jerome Sykes, Wallace McCreery and T J Cronin at the head of a slightly upmarketed cast, and only briefly. Over the years that followed, however, *Ship Ahoy* was seen regularly in comic-opera seasons around America.

THE SHO-GUN Comic opera in 2 acts by George Ade. Music by Gustave Luders. Studebaker Theater, Chicago, 4 April 1904; Wallack's Theater, New York, 10 October 1904.

The Sho-Gun was a musical show in a strict line of descent from half a century of such successful Oriental pieces as *Ba-ta-clan, Dick, The Mikado* and *A Chinese Honeymoon,* combining all kinds of comical highjinks with a cast of the sort of colorful barbarians with burlesquey names who get you mixed up with their royals and then either put you on a throne or do unspeakable things to you with an axe or a stake. In George Ade's version of the tale the intruder was one William Henry Spangle (Christopher Bruno), an American chewing gum magnate, who makes his way to Kachoo, "an imaginary and secluded island in the Sea of Japan, between Japan and Corea . . . untouched by modern civilisation," to introduce his wares and his American ways (including labor unions and advice on how to treat them) to the Sho-Gun, Flai-Hai (Edward Martindel). There he becomes involved with as many complications as the entire cast of *A Chinese Honeymoon* put together, as well as with Princess Hunni-Bun (Anna Wilson), little Moozo-May (Adeline Sharp), lusty Omee-Omi (Trixie Friganza) and the aptly named Hi-Faloot (Florence Morrison), not to mention ballad-singing Tee-To (Clyde McKinley) and the royal astrologer, Hanki-Pank (Étienne Girardot). By the end of it all, Yankee enterprise has won Spangle both girl and crown.

Gustave Luders's score was in a photo-fit Victorian musical-comedy vein, with Spangle heading affairs describing himself in march rhythms as "The Irrepressible Yank" ("a regular touring board of trade, and a two-legged sort of a bank . . .") and wooing Omee-Omi with a number about ill-matched couples ("Love, You Must Be Blind") and an anthropomorphic piece about bunny-rabbits ("She's Just a Little Different from the Others That I Know"). The girls sang the pretty numbers, Tee-To provided the tenor romancing, one Ensign Beverly (N E Daignault) turned out the stirring stuff with a nautical song about "The Jackie," and the Sho-Gun described himself ("The Sho-Gun of Kachoo") in the same way that every English comic-opera potentate had done for more than two decades.

First produced in Chicago by Henry Savage—after the traditional run-in at Milwaukee's Davidson Theater (31 March)—*The Sho-Gun* was a splendid success and it quickly found its way east. New Yorkers were as little worried as their western neighbors over the piece's derivative nature, and they gave an equally warm welcome to its fooleries and melodies and to a mostly new cast including Charles E Evans (Spangle), Georgia Caine (Omee-Omi) and Christie MacDonald (Hunni-Bun). The show played for 120 performances at Wallack's Theater, proving itself one of the most popular homebred shows of its time, before taking again to the road for the next of a number of tours. It did not return to Broadway nor did it ever appear in Britain but, by a combination of circumstances which are now sadly undecipherable, *A Sogun* appeared in 1906 on the stage of Budapest's Király Színház (which had hosted *Robin Hood* two years previously), oddly billed as "an Amerikai operett by Clyde McKinley." "Flutter, Little Bird" became "A gyönge pillanat" and "Wistaria, My Bride" was delivered as "Köszöntelek bájos holdvilág" and, curious billing or not, it proved well-liked. It ran for nearly two months, a run given something of a boost three weeks into the season when Maud Allen arrived in town and, with little care for geography, inserted her "Greek dance" and "Salomé" into the piece's second act.

In November 1990 a musical spectacular based on the successful novel *Shogun* by James Clavell, and using that title (with "the musical" added in explanation) was mounted briefly on Broadway. Hungary passed on that one.

Hungary: Király Színház *A Sogun* 15 December 1906

THE SHOP GIRL Musical farce in 2 acts by Henry J W Dam. Music by Ivan Caryll. Additional numbers by Adrian Ross and Lionel Monckton. Gaiety Theatre, London, 24 November 1894.

The Shop Girl is one of those shows which has been lumbered, in the past, by being dubbed "the first musical comedy" by some of the theatre's more facile commentators. It was, of course, nothing of the kind, any more than were George Edwardes's earlier productions *A Gaiety Girl* and *In Town* or Fred Harris's *Morocco Bound*—whose author, Arthur Branscombe, became a figure of fun with his conversational gambit "when I invented musical comedy . . ."—and *Go-Bang,* or even the touring phenomenon *The Lady Slavey* which also preceded it. *The Shop Girl* merely marked a change in style at London's Gaiety Theatre where it was the first of a series of successful modern-dress musical productions (many retaining the "girl" element of its title) which confirmed that theatre as the most popular light musical house in the West End during the turn-of-the-century years.

The death of Fred Leslie and the illness of Nellie Farren, the two most important Gaiety stars of recent years, helped to put an end to the era of New Burlesque which George Edwardes had fostered with such huge international success at his theatre, and the success of his *In Town* and *A Gaiety Girl,* up-to-date pieces full of smart, topical chat and dressed in fashionable modern clothes—both produced at other London theatres—led him to commission a like piece for the Gaiety to follow the indifferent burlesque *Don Juan.* For some reason, he went for his text not to *A Gaiety Girl*'s Owen Hall but to an obscure American journalist and small-time playwright, Henry Dam, and for his score to Ivan Caryll, recently triumphant with *Little Christopher Columbus,* rather than to the Gaiety's house composer, Meyer Lutz, the writer of so many celebrated burlesque scores for him. He also put together an almost wholly fresh company, with only comic Edmund Payne, dancers Katie Seymour, Topsy Sinden and Willie Warde and character lady Maria Davis remaining from the *Don Juan* principals.

The book which Dam concocted was not precisely original in its plot elements. Wealthy, expatriate John Brown (Colin Coop) is searching for his little lost daughter-cum-heiress and the search has been narrowed to the girls employed at the store run by Mr Hooley (Arthur Williams). When it seems that plumply pouting Ada Smith (Lillie Belmore) is she, Hooley swiftly proposes and Ada dumps her little fiancé, shopwalker Miggles (Payne), for a quick tie-up with the boss, only for the pair to discover that the real heiress is not Ada but soubrette Bessie Brent (Ada Reeve). Bessie marries her upper-class Charlie (Seymour Hicks) and Miggles consoles himself with duets with the pretty Miss Robinson (Katie Seymour). If the content of the libretto was old hat, it was, however, told in the style of the moment—crisp, modern dialogue with none of the wordplay or pantomime jokes of burlesque. Hicks and the music hall's Miss Reeve played their juvenile roles with bantering light comedy and without even one of those soulful duetting moments that were usually the province of the "romantic leads" of a musical play, and the whole piece came out as decidedly smart and up-to-date.

The show's score of songs gave all the artists a chance to shine: Payne and Miss Seymour came out perhaps the best with a little oriental duo called "Love on the Japanese Plan," George Grossmith in the incidental role of a mashing dude described himself in a Lionel Monckton number as "Beautiful, Bountiful Bertie," Coop narrated his rise to millionaire status in the soon-popular "Brown of Colorado," Lillie Belmore comically invented an early life for herself as "The Foundling" and American soubrette Marie Halton, in a wholly incidental role called Dodo, supplied a slightly more sentimental moment with the soprano waltz song "Over the Hills." The most successful single song, however, was one interpolated by Seymour Hicks. Felix McGlennon's "Her Golden Hair Was Hanging Down Her Back" had been sung in the British music halls by Alice Leamar and subsequently pirated in America where Hicks heard it and, given the copyright laws of the time, annexed it for himself. Adrian Ross wrote new lyrics, and Hicks scored a great hit with the slyly suggestive song. The hit cost, however, for when "Her Golden Hair" turned out be a British, and not a "free" American, song, McGlennon and Miss Leamar had to be heavily paid off for the privilege of its use. During the run the ever-changing cast interpolated many other successful songs (Leslie Stuart's "My Lousiana Lou," Fay Templeton's "I Want Yer My Honey," Paul Rubens's debut song "The Little Chinchilla") but "Her Golden Hair" and "Love on the Japanese Plan" remained the two biggest song successes of the evening.

The Shop Girl was an enormous success at the Gaiety. "Shares in the 'Gaiety Limited' which could be had readily for five shillings each a few months back are now quoted at seventeen shillings and the stock is still going up," reported one trade paper amazedly soon after the show's opening. The show ran for 18 months and 546 performances and established itself as the model for the next decade of internationally popular Gaiety musicals. But *The Shop Girl* itself remained a favorite in spite of the popularity of its successors, touring long and late in the British provinces, and playing virtually every English-speaking theatre town from Calcutta to Johannesburg to Sydney and New York.

Edwardes sent his own company to America—a very starry affair with Hicks, Grossmith, Ethel Sydney and his new discovery, Connie Ediss (Ada), at its head—where it played 72 performances on Broadway as part of a national tour, and another to Australia where Harry Monkhouse, Louis Bradfield, Fred Kaye and Decima Moore played the show in a Gaiety repertoire season. *The Shop Girl* found sufficient success in this visit for J C Williamson to mount his own Australian production a decade later. Florence Young played Bessie and helped herself to ''Over the Hills,'' leaving soprano Margaret Thomas (Dodo) to re-equip with a Teresa del Riego number called ''The Man in the Moon,'' whilst George Lauri (Miggles), Rose Musgrove (Miss Robinson) and W S Percy (Bertie) supplied the fun and Clara Clifton as Ada borrowed ''Class'' from *The Silver Slipper* in a score which was something of a paste-up job of hits from London musical comedies.

The Shop Girl, however, went further than the round of English-speaking stages. *La Demoiselle de magasin* accomplished the rare exploit for an English-language show of being produced in France, at the Olympia Music Hall, where café-concert diva Mlle Micheline starred as Bessie alongside Messieurs Berville (Houley), Maréchal (Migles) and Danvers (Charley) in a spiced-up version by Maurice Ordonneau which gave ''Love on the Japanese Plan'' to Bessie and Charley, and introduced a ''Chrysanthemum Dance'' divertissement for the big 16 of the Olympia's ballet. This production was followed by a *Die Ladenmamsell,* at Vienna's Theater in der Josefstadt (ad Carl Lindau). Frln Dworak was Bessie, Herr Rauch played Miggles, Otto Maran was Hooley, Viktoria Pohl-Meiser was Ada (now called Eva), Karl Pfann was rich Charley and there was a Puppenlied, a Cancan-Duette and a 10-part Tanz-Ensemble all composed by musical director Karl Kappeller added to the now rather bulging entertainment.

The most sizeable subsequent production of *The Shop Girl,* however, was back in London, at the new Gaiety Theatre. After Edwardes's death, Seymour Hicks and Alfred Butt produced a revised *Shop Girl* (25 March 1920, ad Arthur Wimperis) with the score infiltrated by a bundle of new Herman Darewski songs and with Evelyn Laye (Bessie) and Alfred Lester (Miggles) starring. The show proved popular all over again, a quarter of a century and many, many more musicals in the same vein after its first appearance, and the new production added another 327 performances to the show's West End tally.

USA: Palmer's Theater 28 October 1895; Australia: Princess Theatre, Melbourne, 25 May 1895; France: L'Olympia *La Demoiselle de magasin* 4 June 1896; Austria: Theater in der Josefstadt *Die Ladenmamsell* 5 February 1897

SHORT, [Hubert Edward] Hassard (b Edlington, Lincs, 15 October 1877; d Nice, France, 9 October 1956). British actor turned director with a flair for the musical spectacular.

Originally an actor, at first, from the age of 18 in Britain (tours of *The Old Guard, The Chorus Girl,* etc), and then from 1901 in America, Short created the roles of Alaric in *Peg o' My Heart* and James Potter in *East Is West* and also made just a handful of musical-theatre appearances as (non-singing) Teddy Bacon, alongside Grace La Rue in the 1911 *Betsy,* and on the road as Baptiste Boubillon in *The Belle of Brittany* (1909). He retired from performing in 1919 and moved definitively into directing.

His earliest productions included several revues, notably the *Music Box Revue* series, but also an indifferent set of book musicals—*Honeydew* (1920), Nora Bayes's *Her Family Tree* (1920), Anselm Götzel's self-produced *The Rose Girl* (1921), the musicalized *Peg o' My Heart* known as *Peg o' My Dreams* (1924) and Harold Levey and Zelda Sears's *The Magnolia Lady* (1924)—before he struck seriously lucky as the director of Charles Dillingham's production of the Jerome Kern musical *Sunny* (1925).

An announced move into management with a version of Reynaldo Hahn's opérette *Ciboulette* did not materialize, and in the next years, although Short turned out some successful revue productions (*Three's a Crowd, The Band Wagon*), he did not again find the same fortune in his musical plays (*Oh, Please!, Lucky*). However, he found a fresh upturn in fortune when he returned to London to direct the vast, double-cast challenge to the movies that was Sir Oswald Stoll's London production of the Viennese Strauss pasticcio *Walzer aus Wien* (*Waltzes from Vienna*) at the Alhambra. He took a filmish ''scenario by'' credit along with Desmond Carter which did not interfere with Carter's bookwriting credit, and was also billed above the title in larger letters than Stoll, Strauss or anyone else connected with the production. The next year he took a double credit as director and co-adaptor on London's vast Drury Lane production of Robert Stolz's *Wenn die kleinen Veilchen blühen* (*Wild Violets*) before returning to America and a series of substantial musical shows.

In 1933 he directed the revue *As Thousands Cheer* and a third Kern musical, *Roberta,* in 1934 the American version of *Walzer aus Wien* (*The Great Waltz*), in 1935 Cole Porter's *Jubilee,* in 1937 the American versions of Lehár's *Frederika* and Oscar Straus's *Drei Walzer* and the homemade *Between the Devil* and, in 1939, Mike

Todd's bowl of souped-up Gilbert and Sullivan, *The Hot Mikado,* and Jerome Kern's last musical, *Very Warm for May. Lady in the Dark* (1941) gave him one of his most memorable successes, but the same season's *Banjo Eyes* had only a short run.

There followed further successes with the Ethel Merman vehicle *Something for the Boys* (1943), Oscar Hammerstein's Bizet rehash *Carmen Jones* (1943), Cole Porter's *Mexican Hayride* (1944), the revue *Seven Lively Arts* (1944) and the 1946 revival of *Show Boat,* which overshadowed the failure of the Ruritanian *Marinka* (1945) and a Tchaikovsky pasticcio, *Music in My Heart* (1947), which did not do for the composer what *Das Dreimäderlhaus* had done for Schubert. He had further revue successes with *Make Mine Manhattan* (1948) and *Mike Todd's Peep Show* (1950), but his last musicals, produced when he was well into his seventies, were not as successful. The musical version of *Seventeen* (1951) had a fairish run, but an Americanized *Aida* called *My Darlin' Aida* (1952) tied up a long and effective career with one of the director's few real latter-day flops.

SHOW BOAT Musical play in 2 acts by Oscar Hammerstein II based on the novel by Edna Ferber. Lyrics by Oscar Hammerstein II. Music by Jerome Kern. Ziegfeld Theater, New York, 27 December 1927.

One of the most successful romantic musical plays of the 1920s, *Show Boat* endured into the quasi-sophisticated fin-de-siècle years much better than librettist Hammerstein's other memorable successes of the period, *Rose Marie* and *The Desert Song,* there to be acclaimed as the masterpiece of the American musical theatre. A large amount of that enduring power has been derived from the show's very basis, Edna Ferber's successful novel, the outlines of which Hammerstein and composer Kern followed fairly closely in their construction of the show, whilst eschewing some of its darker and more unpleasant endings.

Unlike *Rose Marie* and *The Desert Song,* the musical play *Show Boat*—although it held to many of the basic tenets of standard operetta—was not laid out with a traditional cast of predictable romantic comic-opera characters, a soprano and baritone/tenor destined to be mated at the final curtain, a villain thwarted, a couple of soubrets with a romance pursued in parallel to the vocalists' one, and so forth. *Show Boat* had no real ''villain,'' the soprano and baritone were wedded at the end of the first act (and the soubrets in the first interval), the ''hero''—probably the most anti-heroic hero in a major musical since Billee Taylor and Ange Pitou—fell to his own weakness, and the heroine suffered misery that was not just temporarily losing her boyfriend, even if she did, like Sally and her sisters, rise operetta-conventionally in the final reel to join the vast number of musical-play heroines crowding out the star dressing-rooms of Broadway. It also had two further unconventional elements to its libretto: the genuinely dramatic sub-plot of the mixed-blood actress whose life is ruined by the laws of miscegenation, and the colorful background to the Mississippi scenes provided by a group of negro principals and choristers who were not just mammy-lingoed minstrels and low comic relief.

Cap'n Andy Hawkes (Charles Winninger) and his wife, Parthy Ann (Edna May Oliver), run a show boat on the Mississippi river. Amongst their employees are leading lady Julie La Verne (Helen Morgan) and her husband Steve Baker (Charles Ellis), soubrets Frank Schultz (Sammy White) and Ellie May Chipley (Eva Puck), and negro maid Queenie (Aunt Jemima). Whilst the boat is berthed at Natchez, the exposure of Julie's mulatto blood forces her and Steve to flee the state and the Hawkes's daughter Magnolia (Norma Terris) and the handsome riverboat gambler Gaylord Ravenal (Howard Marsh) take their places in the company. Soon the young pair are wed, and leave the river. But Ravenal's luck as a gambler is intermittent and he is unwilling or unable to find a stabler employ. The good days soon pass, and the gambling husband, knowing himself a burden to his wife and young daughter, finally leaves them. Thanks to an abnegative gesture by Julie, Magnolia finds work and success as a singer in a club and she goes on from there to Broadway fame. In the years that follow, daughter Kim follows her mother's steps to stardom and Frank and Ellie, too, end up rich and happy, but Julie dwindles to a sad off-stage end. Nothing is heard of Ravenal until one day he runs into Magnolia's father and is persuaded to return to the show boat, where his wife has taken her retirement, and there on the Mississippi river—where nothing ever changes—30 years after their first meeting, the pair are reunited in time for the final curtain.

The score which illustrated this tale was very much more substantial musically than the song-and-dance scores which Kern had supplied for the musical comedies of the previous decade. It mixed the tones of comic opera, in the romantic music for the lovers (''Make Believe,'' the waltz duet ''You Are Love'') and some dashingly insouciant solos for Ravenal (''Where's the Girl for Me?,'' ''Till Good Luck Comes My Way''), with the regular soubret brand of numbers for Frank and Ellie (''I Might Fall Back on You,'' ''Life on the Wicked Stage'') in classic style and added to these a variety of negro-flavored pieces from a beautiful baritone hymn to the Mississippi, ''Ol' Man River,'' sung by Queenie's shiftless man, Joe (Jules Bledsoe), to a searing ballyhoo (''C'mon Folks'') and the superb ensemble ''Can't Help Lovin' That Man.'' This all in the first act. The second, somewhat in

Plate 355. *Roland Friederich (Cap'n Andy), Bianca Fink (Ellie) and Michael Greif (Frank) entertain in the Coburg Landestheater production of* **Show Boat.**

the style of the old variety musicals, rather tailed away in so far as important new songs were concerned. It consisted principally of a number of acts, some of which used Kern's own material, others of which (in the manner which he had shown himself effectively willing to use in earlier shows) he selected from the successes of an earlier period, the period in which the show was set. Amongst these were Charles K Harris's *A Trip to Chinatown* hit, ''After the Ball,'' performed by Magnolia as her nervous club debut, and Joe Howard's infectious ''Goodbye, My Lady Love,'' given as an item by Frank and Ellie. Julie's stand-up song, however, was an older number by Kern himself which he had been unsuccessfully trying to place in a show for some time. ''Bill'' found itself a home worth waiting for in the second act of *Show Boat.* The other ''variety'' items included a variable selection illustrating the entertainment at the World's Fair, several dances, and a series of impersonations performed by Miss Terris in the character of Kim. Apart from ''Bill,'' only the jaunty ''Why Do I Love You?'' and Queenie's ''Hey, Feller!'' added to the list of new Kern numbers in the show's second half.

Show Boat was produced by Florenz Ziegfeld. It had a false start when, with leading players Elizabeth Hines (Magnolia), Guy Robertson (Ravenal) and Paul Robeson (Joe) announced, it had to be postponed to allow its authors more time to complete their work, but it ultimately opened (without those three players), directed by Hammerstein, at Washington's National Theater on 15 November 1927. It was instantly successful, but there were nevertheless alterations made in the half-dozen weeks prior to the Broadway opening. Several pieces of music were removed and ''Why Do I Love You?'' was added. The Broadway opening confirmed the out-of-town reception and the production went on to play 575 performances on its first New York run.

London's production, under the management of Alfred Butt and the Theatre Royal, Drury Lane, starred Edith Day (Magnolia), Howett Worster (Ravenal), Marie Burke (Julie), Leslie Sarony (Frank), Dorothy Lena (Ellie), Cedric Hardwicke (Hawkes) and Paul Robeson in the role of Joe for which he had been originally slated. In spite of the difficulties engendered by the mixed-race cast (blacks and whites had to dress on opposite sides of the stage, Robeson not excepted) it had a good run of 350 performances. Australia's J C Williamson production of *Show Boat* also had a good, if unexceptional, run. Glen Dale (Ravenal), Gwynneth Lascelles (Magnolia), Muriel

Greel (Julie), Bertha Belmore (Parthy Ann), Leo Franklyn (Frank), Frederick Bentley (Andy), Madge Aubrey (Ellie) and the blacked-up Colin Crane (Joe) and June Mills (Queenie) played 80 nights in Melbourne and rather less in Sydney (Her Majesty's Theatre 2 November 1929). This was, however, a better record than the disappointing 115 nights achieved by a French adaptation (ad Alexandre Fontanes, Lucien Boyer) mounted by Fontanes and Maurice Lehmann in the vastness of the Théâtre du Châtelet with British soprano Desirée Ellinger as Magnolia and American baritone Harvey White cast as Joe alongside locals Bourdeaux (Ravenal) and Jacqueline Morrin (Julie).

If *Show Boat* did not follow *Rose Marie* further into Europe, it nevertheless established itself firmly at home. In spite of the iffy financial conditions of the early 1930s, it was toured, filmed in 1929, and brought back to Broadway at the Casino Theater (19 May 1932) with Dennis King (Ravenal) and Robeson alongside Misses Terris and Morgan and Winninger (180 performances) prior to another tour and a second film, with Winninger, Robeson and Miss Morgan featured alongside Irene Dunne (Magnolia) and Allan Jones (Ravenal). London reprised the show during the Second World War (Stoll Theater 17 April 1943, 264 performances) with a cast headed by Gwynneth Lascelles (Magnolia), Bruce Carfax (Ravenal), Pat Taylor (Julie), Leslie and Sylvia Kellaway (Frank, Ellie) and blacked-up basso Malcolm McEachern (Joe), and three years later it again played Broadway's Ziegfeld Theater (5 January 1946, 418 performances) with Jan Clayton (Magnolia), Charles Fredericks (Ravenal) and Carol Bruce (Julie) and toured yet again.

In 1951 a third film version (Kathryn Grayson, Howard Keel, Ava Gardner, Joe E Brown, Marge and Gower Champion, William Warfield) made its way to the screen, in 1954 the show was taken into the New York City Opera, in 1970 it made its first appearance on the German-language stage, and in 1971 it had its longest-running production to date, in London. Harold Fielding's mounting (29 July) starred Frenchman André Jobin (Ravenal) alongside Americans Lorna Dallas (Magnolia), Thomas Carey (Joe) and Kenneth Nelson (Frank) and locals Cleo Laine (Julie) and Jan Hunt (Ellie) and played 910 performances at the Adelphi Theatre.

In 1990, on the heels of the issue of a major EMI recording—and with the black casting which had originally been such a problem now a grand and politically correct plus—it appeared once more in Britain and in London (London Palladium 25 July) in a production sponsored by Opera North and the Royal Shakespeare Company (but including barely a member of either company) and featuring Karla Burns (Queenie) and Bruce Hubbard (Joe) of the recording's cast, and in 1994 a fiddled-even-further-than-usual with version (which program-noted that it was a combination of three stage versions and one of the films, but included alterations not noticeable in any of them) was brought from Canada to Broadway (Gershwin Theater 2 October). Mark Jacoby (Ravenal), Rebecca Luker (Magnolia) and John McMartin (Andy) featured, and the revival totted up a healthy run of 949 performances, followed by a fresh tour, and got showings in both Australia—where the production opened the new Lyric Theatre (7 April 1998), with Peter Couzens, Marina Prior and Barry Otto featured and Nancye Hayes as Parthy, to less than impressive effect—and in Britain (Prince Edward Theatre 20 April 1998), where a ''Broadway cast of 57'' was boasted on ads that billed director Hal Prince large . . . but never mentioned Hammerstein or Kern. And most of the audience were unaware they were watching a Cibberized classic.

Show Boat has become widely accepted and promoted as the foremost American romantic musical-theatre work of its period. In the modern English-speaking world (if not elsewhere) it is today surely the most performed. It has had an entire book devoted to it, American (and even other) commentators write of it with awe and never a pejorative adjective, even if American (and other) producers and directors nevertheless see fit endlessly to fiddle with and ''improve'' it. There is little question that its canonization is at least in part justified, and that there is nothing (give or take a bit of a sag late in Act II) to be pejorative about. There is, however, less justification for investing the show with ''significance.'' Certainly it has more breadth, depth and verisimilitude in its story line and even its characters than a *Rose Marie* or even a *Desert Song,* but these qualities were not innovations. In the same way, its avoidance of many of the more popular operettic clichés of its era is a quality, but those clichés had been avoided many times before, by those who had wanted (and most didn't) to avoid them. Bordman (*Jerome Kern, His Life and Music,* OUP) calls the show ''the first truly, totally American operetta . . . identifiable American types sang American sentiments in an American musical idiom.'' There is no question over any word there except ''first'' and, even then, the ''truly,'' the ''totally'' and the ''operetta'' narrow the field, but something like the same comments could surely have been applied in their time to such older period American musical plays as *Naughty Marietta, The Mocking Bird* or the Civil War piece *Johnny Comes Marching Home,* in spite of the Irish, German and English blood in the pedigree of their writers. *Show Boat* stood (and stands) out among the best of the romantic musicals of the later 1920s and 1930s not because it was innovatory (for a poor show may be innovatory), but because it was excellent, with the kind of excellence which endures.

UK: Theatre Royal, Drury Lane 3 May 1928; France: Théâtre du Châtelet *Mississippi* 15 March 1929; Australia: Her Majesty's Theatre, Melbourne 3 August 1929; Germany: Städtische Bühne, Freiburg 31 October 1970, Theater des Westens 10 October 1979; Austria: Volksoper 1 March 1971

Recordings: complete (EMI, 3 records), London cast recordings (WRC), 1946 revival (Columbia), 1966 revival (RCA), London revival (Stanyan), 1994 Toronto revival (Quality), film soundtrack ASI (CBS/MGM), selections (TER, Columbia, RCA Victor, HMV, Decca), selection in Swedish, etc

Literature: Kreuger, M: *Show Boat: The Story of a Classic American Musical* (OUP, New York, 1977)

SHOW GIRL Musical by William Anthony McGuire based on the novel of the same title by J P McEvoy. Lyrics by Gus Kahn and Ira Gershwin. Music by George Gershwin. Ziegfeld Theater, New York, 2 July 1929.

Ruby Keeler played Dixie Dugan, the "show girl" heroine of Florenz Ziegfeld's 1929 production, struggling like so many of her contemporaries towards that poor girl's nirvana: a star dressing room in a Ziegfeld show. On the way, she sang "Liza (all the clouds'll roll away)," and stood aside whilst Jimmy Durante (equipped with three songs written by himself) and Eddie Foy jr purveyed the comedy of the evening. However, neither this starry lineup (with the intermittent assistance of Al Jolson, singing "Liza" from the audience to "help" his wife), nor a sumptuous Ziegfeld production featuring an Albertina Rasch ballet to Gershwin's "American in Paris" music could make *Show Girl* into a success. It lasted just 111 performances.

An earlier piece under almost the same title (it had a *The* attached), produced by E E Rice with Frank Lalor and Paula Edwards starred, was a 1902 adaptation of a Boston Cadets amdram show originally called *The Cap of Fortune* and written by the unstoppable Boston pair of R A Barnet and H L Heartz. It was added to by Edward Corliss and interpolated into by Jerome and Schwartz ("In Spotless Town") before it got to Broadway, where it remained for 64 performances. A later piece, which sent the title round once again, was a vehicle written by Charles Gaynor to feature Carol Channing. It played one hundred nights at the Eugene O'Neill Theater in 1961 (12 January).

SHUBERT, Messrs

SHUBERT, J J [SZEMANSKI, Jacob] (b Shervient, Lithuania, 29 August 1879; d New York, 26 December 1963).

SHUBERT, Lee [SZEMANSKI, Levi] (b Shervient, Lithuania, 15 March ?1873; d New York, 25 December 1953).

SHUBERT, Sam S [SZEMANSKI, Samuel] (b Shervient, Lithuania, ?1876; d Pennsylvania, 11 May 1905).

The most productive and powerful musical-theatre managers of the first half of Broadway's 20th century.

Brought from their native Lithuania to Syracuse, NY, in 1882, the Shubert boys began their connection with the theatre as youngsters, working in the local houses in a variety of jobs. Sam, who was professedly the youngest (only the Shervient births, deaths and marriages officer knows for sure, and he's not telling), became a box-office manager and before long he and his brother Lee began their careers as theatrical producers by sending out a touring company of the successful Charles Hoyt farce comedy *A Texas Steer* (1894).

It took them half a dozen years to make it from Syracuse to Broadway. There, as independent producers, they leased the Herald Square Theater and slowly—at first with a small man's alliance with the giant Theatrical Syndicate—began to make their way with a schedule of both plays and musicals. Their first production was a play, *The Brixton Burglary* (1901), their first musical the record-breaking London hit *A Chinese Honeymoon* (1902). Although the masthead for the production credited Sam Shubert and Nixon and Zimmerman as producers, *A Chinese Honeymoon* was, in fact, the production of Sam and Lee Shubert. Nixon and Zimmerman were the representatives of the Syndicate who controlled this independent production on the organization's behalf.

A Chinese Honeymoon was a fine success, running 376 performances at Broadway's Casino Theater and going on to a profitable life on the road, and it was the beginning of great things. Over the 40 years that followed, the Shubert name would be attached to some two hundred musicals on Broadway and a vast number—including Giacomo Minkowsky and Curtis Dunham's homegrown *Philipodia,* announced to follow *A Chinese Honeymoon*—which didn't make it that far. The team, however, did not remain the same through those four decades. Third brother Jacob (known as J J—although the second J apparently had no meaning) soon joined Sam and Lee, but in 1905 Sam, the most active of the team, was killed in a train crash, effectively leaving Lee to guide the firm's destiny through the decades of their greatest success.

Having succeeded in securing the rights for London's biggest-ever hit in *A Chinese Honeymoon,* Sam Shubert followed up by securing those for the latest of the Savoy operas. If the kudos was still there, however, he was this time a little late. *The Emerald Isle* was the tail end of the Savoy product, and there was no *Mikado* type of run to be had from it. Billed as the production of "the Jefferson de Angelis Opera Company," it played 50 nights at the Herald Square before moving on to the country.

In 1903 Sam Shubert produced his first native-bred musical when he imported the Chicago Orpheum's burlesque extravaganza *Chow Chow* (still "with Nixon and

Zimmerman'') to Broadway, under the title *The Runaways.* It ran for 167 performances, and Shubert pursued the line of homemade musicals a little further when he launched his first own such pieces later the same year. *Winsome Winnie,* a new musical by the English authors of the famous *Erminie,* proved unsatisfactory when mounted at Baltimore's Academy of Music and Sam—starting out as the Shuberts would notoriously go on—had the whole piece remade by Frederick Ranken and Gustave Kerker before taking it to Broadway. It was ushered out again after 56 nights. The ''Sam Shubert and Nixon and Zimmerman'' production of the semi-pasticcio *The Girl from Dixie,* for what was intended to be a musical stock company, did even less well, not helped by ending up in the center of a confrontation between Shubert and Zimmerman and the Syndicate's powerful Abe Erlanger.

The continued backward-looking part of Sam's policy followed the work of the *Erminie* men with a revival of the old favorite *Wang* and a comic opera on *Lady Teazle* for old-time star Lillian Russell; his forward looking led him to take a trip to scout out a theatre in London where, with no ''Syndicate'' to provoke eternal battles and problems, he might produce in profitable peace. Sam Shubert's last Broadway musical production was one of his most successful. Launched in Chicago under the ''Jefferson de Angelis Company'' banner, *Fantana*—which billed Sam Shubert as co-author (much to the fury of real author Robert Smith, who had been forced to use Sam's ''ideas'')—was a firm success, and Sam announced it to open the new London Waldorf Theatre which he had leased. But, by the time the Waldorf opened, he was dead.

With Lee at the firm's head, fighting a continuing and ultimately victorious war against Erlanger and his allies for control of as large a slice of the American theatrical action as was possible, the schedule of musical productions continued at the rate of a regular half-dozen or so per year: a mixture of imports and new shows. The year 1905 continued with the American fantasy *Happyland,* the London hit *The Earl and the Girl,* and an English pantomime, *The Babes and the Baron,* on Broadway, and a tour of the Chicago *The Royal Chef* as part of the company's growing touring operations; the year 1906 brought the homemade *Mexicana* and *The Tourists,* the British *My Lady's Maid* (ex- *Lady Madcap*) and *The Blue Moon* and the revusical *The Social Whirl,* as well as *Pioneer Days,* the first Shubert production at the vast New York Hippodrome which Lee had taken over as the brothers' sphere of influence grew.

Their 1907 list included *The Orchid* and *The Girl from Kays* from the top of the London hit parade, the Stanislaus Stange/Julian Edwards comic opera *The Belle of London Town* and Reginald De Koven's unfortunate *The Snowman / The Girls of Holland* from home, and a new spectacular for the Hippodrome; their 1908 schedule featured productions of the operetta *Marcelle,* the children's show *The Pied Piper,* Eddie Foy's *Mr Hamlet of Broadway* and—having missed *The Merry Widow*—a first attempt with a Continental Operette with *Miss Mischief* (*Ein tolles Mädel*), with Lulu Glaser starred. Although the Shuberts stuck a little longer with the old habit of importing shows from the once-rich supply made in Britain—*Havana* and *The Belle of Brittany* in 1909, *King of Cadonia* in 1910 and *The Balkan Princess* in 1911—their regular diet soon switched to being a mixture of homemade musical comedies, revusical spectaculars and Operetten imported from the Continent. By the time these last made their appearance on the Broadway stage, however, they were often barely recognizable. Frequently—but, oddly, not always—souped up with spectacle, girls and low comedy and their musical scores sprayed with ''easy'' songs, they ended up very different in character from the pieces they had begun as, and very many of them failed. Yet in spite of this failure rate the policy of ''botching'' was apparently never questioned.

Amongst the new musicals which the Shuberts produced before and during the First World War were included *The Girl and the Wizard* starring Sam Bernard, *Old Dutch* with and starring Lew Fields (1909), the Rida Johnson Young/William Schroeder *Just One of the Boys, He Came from Milwaukee* with Bernard (1910), Victor Herbert's *The Duchess* with Fritzi Scheff starred, the Julian Edwards *The Wedding Trip* (1911), *The Red Petticoat,* another Bernard vehicle *All for the Ladies* (1912), Jolson's *The Honeymoon Express,* the musical version of the Anglo-French farce *Oh, I Say* (1913), Mrs Young's *Lady Luxury* (1914), *Hands Up* (1915), Jolson in *Robinson Crusoe Jr,* Bernard's remade *The Girl from Kays, Step This Way* (1916), *Love o' Mike* (1917), the Philip Bartholomae/Frank Tours *Oh Mama! / Girl o' Mine,* Jolson's *Sinbad, Little Simplicity, The Melting of Molly* and a musical version of Daly's old hit, *A Night Off* (1918).

It was a list which included little that was durable, little outside the Al Jolson and Bernard vehicles which was notably successful, and it was much less interesting than the list of bought-in-and-botched shows mounted by, or partly by, the Shuberts in the same period: *Madame Troubadour, Die Förster-Christl* (*The Girl and the Kaiser*), *Liebeswalzer* (*The Kiss Waltz*), *Vera Violetta, Schneeglöckchen* (*Two Little Brides*), *Die Fledermaus* (*The Merry Countess*), *Der Mann mit den drei Frauen* (*The Man with Three Wives*), *Der liebe Augustin, Filmzauber* (*The Girl on the Film*), *Polenblut* (*The Peasant Girl*), *Ein Tag im Paradies* (*The Blue Paradise*), *Endlich allein* (*Alone at Last*), *Die schöne Schwedin* (*The Girl from Brazil*), *Was tut man nicht alles aus Liebe* (*Follow*

Me), *Az obsitos* (*Her Soldier Boy*), *Die schöne Unbekannte* (*My Lady's Glove*), *Wie einst im Mai* (*Maytime*) and *Der Sterngucker* (*The Star Gazer*). If this was an impressively long list, it was nevertheless one which was the result of significant weeding. In one season, the Shubert office announced such mostly provincial German pieces as Robert Leonhard's *Der Sterndeuter,* Berté's *Der Glücksnarr* (*The Fortunate Fool*), Gustav Wanda's *Der ledige Gatte,* Weinberger's *Die Primaballerina,* Albini's *Die Barfüsstänzerin,* Kollo's *Die Königin der Nacht* (announced as being by Lehár), Karl Kappeller's *Der blaue Klub,* Anselm Goetzl's *Madame Flirt,* the Millöcker pasticcio *Cousin Bobby,* Lehár's *Juxheirat,* Ziehrer's *Der Schatzmeister* and a number of other pieces by such composers as Snaga none of which ever found their way onto the American stage. And some, such as Fritz Korolanyi's Leipzig piece *Der Liebesschule* (1909), which did, did not get further than such tryout venues as Wilkes-Barre, Pa.

The big successes of the Shubert production arm (as opposed to their ever-growing theatre-owning arm) in the wartime period were *The Blue Paradise* and *Maytime,* and the Continental stage was to bring them further hits in the 1920s, the greatest of which was their remake of *Das Dreimäderlhaus* as *Blossom Time.* Other great European hits—and by now the Shuberts, who had missed out on most of the best early German, Austrian and Hungarian hits, were culling virtually all the cream—fared rather less well. Of *Der letzte Walzer, Drei alte Schachteln* (*Phoebe of Quality Street*), *Die Rose von Stambul, Die Frau im Hermelin, Sterne, die wieder leuchten* (*Springtime of Youth*), *Der Vetter aus Dingsda* (*Caroline*), *Der Tanz ins Glück* (*Sky High*), *Riquette* (*Naughty Riquette*), *Gräfin Mariza,* Hungary's *Offenbach* (*The Love Song*) and *Chopin* (*The Charmer/White Lilacs*), *Katja* (*die Tänzerin*), *Die Zirkusprinzessin,* France's *Un bon garçon* (*Luckee Girl*), *Musik im Mai,* and in the 1930s, *Drei arme kleine Mädchen, Das Land des Lächelns, Meine Schwester und ich* (*Meet My Sister*), *Die Wunder-Bar,* Benatzky's *Cocktail, Hotel Stadt-Lemberg* (*Arms and the Maid / Marching By*), *Liebe im Schnee* and the last Shubert imports to Broadway, *Friederike, Drei Walzer* and *Bei Kerzenlicht,* more, much more, or in some cases less tampered with, barely a single one lived up to the run or the reputation that it had gained in Europe, even though some served reasonable periods in New York and longer ones on the American road.

Alongside this heavy schedule of Continental operetta productions, the Shuberts also staged a large number of revue productions in the years between the wars, and their quota of homebred book shows lowered a little. Jolson's later shows, *Bombo* and *Big Boy,* verged on being revue, *The Blushing Bride*—when it finally got to Broadway—verged on being a variety musical, *Sally, Irene and Mary* was little more than an up-to-date burlesque, and the genuine musical comedies, such as the Ivan Caryll *The Hotel Mouse* (*Little Miss Raffles*), *June Days, Hello Lola, Ain't Love Grand / Lovely Lady* or *The Madcap* didn't actually do so very well. The biggest hit that the firm found during this period was one which followed frankly in the *Wie einst im Mai / Das Dreimäderlhaus* tradition of European operetta: *The Student Prince (in Heidelberg).* Given this, it was understandable that they persevered with their versions of Continental hits, revivals of classic successes and, now, with homemade romantic operetta: *Princess Flavia, Mayflowers* (mus: Eduard Künneke), *Cherry Blossoms, My Maryland, The Love Call, Nina Rosa, Cyrano/Roxane.* However, another *Student Prince* was not forthcoming.

From 1938 on the Shubert brothers' musicals became fewer and the handful of book shows produced amongst the revues and revivals did not bring any successes. Pieces like the unrecognizably altered *Bei Kerzenlicht* (*You'll Never Know*), the mock-European *Night of Love* or Romberg's unhappy *My Romance* were quick failures.

Dominant as producers and theatre-owners on the Broadway stage for four decades, the Shubert brothers nevertheless initiated only a small handful of worthwhile new American musicals, and only one—*The Student Prince*—which has stood the test of time and entered the basic repertoire of Broadway shows. All the best and most internationally successful of the flood of both the romantic musicals—*The Desert Song, Rose Marie, New Moon, Show Boat* and their like—and the dancing musical comedies of the age—*Irene, No, No, Nanette, Mercenary Mary, Sally, Going Up* and their fellows—which flowed from America during the years between the wars came from other managements. And yet the Shuberts mounted two hundred musical shows. And flourished.

The Shubert organization continued after the deaths of the two brothers who ran it for so long. Today it exists principally as a theatre-owning company, although it also operates as a producing interest, often in order to supply product—or to secure the best product amongst what is currently available—for its theatres. Thus, the Shubert name which has topped so many playbills and fronted so many theatre marquees across America since the beginning of the 20th century is still very much in evidence as the 21st century gets under way.

Biographics: Stagg, J: *The Brothers Shubert* (Random House, New York, 1968), McNamara, B: *The Shuberts of Broadway* (OUP, New York, 1990), Hirsch, F: *The Boys from Syracuse* (Southern Illinois UP, Carbondale, Ill, 1998)

SHUFFLE ALONG Musical comedy in 2 acts by Flournoy Miller and Aubrey Lyles. Lyrics by Noble Sissle. Music by Eubie Blake. 63rd Street Theater, New York, 23 May 1921.

Nearly 20 years after *In Dahomey,* another negro musical entertainment, effectively mixing cheerfully un-hung-up, high-energy comedy and ''coon'' vaudeville turns in a similar style to its predecessor, was produced on Broadway. Again, as in the case of *In Dahomey,* much of the material for this show was provided by members of the cast.

In a tale which was an expansion of an old variety sketch, vaudeville team and authors Flournoy Miller (Steve Jenkins) and Aubrey Lyles (Sam Peck) featured themselves as a couple of untrusting partners in a small-town grocery store. Both of the men are running for the post of Mayor of Jimtown, and each suspects the other of rifling the till to finance his campaign. Each hires a private detective to catch the other out. The show's choreographer, Larry Deas, played Jack Penrose—the one detective hired, unwittingly, by both competitors. Lyricist Noble Sissle appeared as Tom Sharper, campaign manager to Jenkins, equipped with an impressive box of dirty tricks which help to win the day, especially as Peck's suffragette wife (Mattie Wilks) proves a right handicap to him. Sharper ends up with the job of Chief of Police, until both the scallywags are routed and regular Harry Walton (Roger Matthews) takes over at the head of Jimtown's affairs. Lottie Gee was fitted in as the show's leading lady, Gertrude Saunders was soubrette, the local Board of Aldermen supplied the close harmony singing (shades of *The Music Man*), and composer Eubie Blake, the other half of Sissle's act, climbed up from his position in the pit to join his partner in a singalong in the second act.

Sissle and Blake's score threw up one thoroughly enduring number, ''I'm Just Wild About Harry,'' alongside such pieces as ''Bandana Days,'' ''If You've Never Been Vamped by a Brownskin,'' ''Love Will Find a Way'' (a very different number from that of the same title heard just a few years previously in *The Maid of the Mountains*), ''The Baltimore Buzz'' and the piece's title song. The second enduring piece of the score, however, was an interpolation: during their act, Sissle and Blake performed Walter Donaldson's razzly ''How Ya' Gonna Keep 'em Down on the Farm'' amongst a series of what were otherwise mostly their own numbers (w James Reese Europe).

If Broadway had rejected *In Dahomey* it had other ideas about *Shuffle Along.* The verve, energy and enthusiasm of the players zipped the show to popularity in New York just as it had done for the earlier show in London and *Shuffle Along* remained on Broadway for 504 performances.

An attempt to repeat the success with a *Shuffle Along of 1933* (note the revusical title) didn't take off, and a revival of the original show (Broadway Theater 8 May 1952) with fresh added material written by Sissle and Blake and additional numbers by Joseph Meyer, Floyd Huddlestone and Dean Elliot, foundered in just four performances.

A number of the songs from *Shuffle Along,* however, got almost as long a showing as they had first time around when they were included in a successful compilation show made from the songs of composer Blake and entitled *Eubie!* (Ambassador Theater 23 September 1978).

Shuffle Along has, like a number of other shows, suffered in recent years from being burdened with ''significance,'' such extravagant tags as ''a record-breaking, epoch-making musical comedy'' (what record? what epoch?) and such silly claims as ''the first negro show on Broadway.'' What it was was simply a particularly lively New York hit of its moment, which provided one spanking new candidate for the standards song-list, without going out into the international theatre or proving the stuff of which revivals are made.

Flournoy Miller authored several other musical comedies including *The Mayor of Dixie* (27 August 1906), produced as the initial musical-comedy offering at Chicago's ex-vaudeville house, the Pekin Theatre, *The Husband (?)* originally played in Chicago and subsequently at the Harlem Music Hall (mus: Joe Jordan, James T Brymm 19 August 1907), *The Oyster Man* (Ernest Hogan, Willian Vodery/Harry S Creamer, Yorkville Theater 25 November 1907) and *Dr Night* (mus: Brymm, H Lawrence Freeman, Pekin Theater, Chicago 26 January 1908), and, in the post–*Shuffle Along* period, *Running Wild* (Colonial Theater 29 October 1923), and *Shuffle Along of 1932* (later *1933*).

Recordings: compilation with original cast members (New World Records), selection with 1952 revival cast members (RCA Victor)

SIDONIE PANACHE Opérette a grand spectacle in 2 acts by Albert Willemetz and André Mouëzy-Éon. Music by Joseph Szulc. Théâtre du Châtelet, Paris, 2 December 1930.

Alexandre Fontanes and Maurice Lehmann presented *Sidonie Panache* at the Châtelet with all the splendor which was both the trademark of that theatre and the key to the success of the series of pieces played there. Nevertheless, the management took care to go for quality in the other values of their shows. It was no less a star than Edmée Favart who top-billed in the title role of *Sidonie Panache* as a little blanchisseuse who goes to the Arab wars, in male disguise, in place of the artist Armand des Ormeaux (Géo Bury). After some dramatic complications, during which Sidonie is captured, then saved by an Arab spy to whom she had shown kindness, she leads the

French general to the Arab camp and thus sets up the victory which wins Algeria for France. The star of Paris's *No, No, Nanette,* Loulou Hégoburu (Rosalie), was chief soubrette opposite the Châtelet's favorite comic, Bach (Chabichou).

The score was the work of Joseph Szulc and, although it maintained the dancing rhythms of his small-scale musical-comedy scores in such pieces as Mlle Hégoburu's fox-trot "C'est Rosalie," it also allowed itself moments both more romantic, as in Mlle Favart's charming "À quoi bon aimer," or military, as in her Marche des Zouaves. However, although all its elements were at least satisfactory, the key to the year-long run of *Sidonie Panache* was to be found in its production values: 16 scenes of grand spectacle including the Bal Mabille, a panorama of "les grands boulevards 1840" and a series of desert scenes highlighted by a cavalry charge of soldiers, on live horses, galloping at full tilt towards the footlights.

In spite of these demands—and presumably with them reduced—*Sidonie Panache* found itself a home in the French provinces after its five hundred Paris nights.

Film: Henry Wuschleger 1935

DIE SIEBEN SCHWABEN Volksoper (Operette) in 3 acts by Hugo Wittmann and Julius Bauer. Music by Carl Millöcker. Theater an der Wien, Vienna, 29 October 1887.

Die sieben Schwaben (the title taken from a Brothers Grimm fairy tale) was a mixture of politics, magic and romance set in medieval Stuttgart which followed the efforts of the war hero Junker Otmar von Mannsperg (Karl Streitmann) to win the heart and hand of Käthchen (Ottilie Collin), the daughter of his political opponent, the Burgermeister Stickel (Herr Adam), and, with his other hand, to defeat the Swabian Alliance. Aided and abetted by Dr Theophrastus Bombastus Paracelsus (Siegmund Stelzer), he sets up a helpfully heroic manifestation at the tower of the witch, Die schwarze Grete (Regina Stein), to whom the girls go for advice on their love lives, but when Käthchen finds him out it takes a whole act of heroics and politics, and a timely appearance by the seven Swabians of the title, for Otmar to win both his bride and the war. The prominent comedy element of the piece was largely provided by Alexander Girardi, in the role of Spätzle, Paracelsus's servant, who romanced his Hannele (Therese Biedermann), made a mess of being a sorcerer's apprentice, and performed the show's two most popular numbers "Um halber Neune" and the heftily dialected "Wart' a bissele, halt a bissele, sitz a bissele nieder."

The piece, written by the authorial team of Wittmann and Bauer who had successfully supplied the Theater an der Wien with *Der Hofnarr* earlier in the year, was described as a Volksoper without musically differing largely from Millöcker's earlier works. It had a reasonable success at the Theater an der Wien, where it was well enough considered to be brought back a dozen years later during the last year of the management of Alexandrine von Schönerer, with Streitmann repeating as Otmar, Marie Ottmann as Käthchen, Josef Joseffy as Paracelsus, Seibold (Spätzle) and Guste Zimmermann (Hannele), to top up its total to 63 performances. It was performed with some success in Germany, at St Petersburg, Prague and in many other middle European venues, and returned to Vienna in 1910 when Ernst Tautenhayn appeared as Spätzle in a production at the Raimundtheater (30 September).

An American German-language production with Streitmann (Otmar) and Frln Zimmermann (Käthchen) starred was well-received and, in consequence, a translated version was produced for the American stage by John McCaull's Comic Opera Company, starring Chauncey Olcott (Otmar), Lilly Post (Katherine), William Blaisdell (Spätzle), Annie Meyers (Hannele) and Mathilde Cottrelly (Black Grete). It got no closer to Broadway than the Harlem Opera House. Years later, however, it resurfaced at Philadelphia's German stock theatre (4 May 1908).

Germany: Friedrich-Wilhelmstädtisches Theater 22 December 1887; USA: Amberg Theater (Ger) 12 February 1890, Harlem Opera House *The Seven Swabians* 1 September 1890

DIE SIEGERIN Musikalische Komödie in 3 acts by Oskar Friedmann, Fritz Lunzer and Béla Jenbach. Music by Josef Klein arranged from the works of Piotr I Tchaikovsky. Neues Wiener Stadttheater, Vienna, 7 November 1922.

The most successful of the line of attempts at a Tchaikovsky pasticcio musical, Herbert Trau's production of *Die Siegerin* not unreasonably took an early 18th-century Russian subject as its basis. The "siegerin" of the show was the Empress Catherine (the first, not the Great), although when she is first seen she is simply a serf called Marta (Erika Wagner). She sings all her duets with the tenorious Fieldmarshal Alexander Mentschikoff (Robert Nästlberger) but she nevertheless ends up as the Empress of Peter the Great (Rudolf Teubler). Josef König as Wassili Bronin and producer-director's wife Olga Bartos-Trau (Sonja) were the soubrets, and the production went after a little deep-north authenticity by engaging the Russian Wassilow-Truppe as a speciality.

Following its successful Vienna run (150th performance, 23 March 1923), *Die Siegerin* was produced in Budapest (ad Zsolt Harsányi) and was secured by London's Robert Evett as a vehicle for José Collins with which to follow her first success under his management as Vera Lisaweta in *The Last Waltz* (*Der letzte Walzer*).

The original makers of the piece were barely mentioned on Evett's playbill, the libretto being credited to adaptors Reginald Arkell and Fred de Grésac, and the score worked over by Evett himself with Klein's name tacked limply on to the end of the credits. Miss Collins sang "I Am but a Simple Maid" and scored the success of the show with "Star of Fate" as she made her way to the throne of all the Russias. Robert Michaelis (Mentschikoff) shared three duets with the star, and sang about "The Life of a Soldier," Amy Augarde and Billy Leonard supplied the light relief with a duo in each of the three acts, and Bertram Wallis played the non-singing Czar through a good run of six months and 217 performances.

Although Emmi Kosáry apparently sang a performance of *Die Siegerin* somewhere in America, Broadway never saw it. F C and B C Whitney fabricated what they claimed as their own Tchaikovsky musical called *Natja* (Knickerbocker Theater 16 February 1925) with a different-Catherine script by Harry B Smith and a score arranged by Hungarian conductor Karl Hajós. Madeleine Collins was the lassie of the title who gets dressed up as a pretty boy to win the attention of Catherine the Great and, having thus got her ear, air the griefs of Crimea. Since she was pleading to a woman, Natja was spared the fate of Marta of having to wed where her heart was not, and was thus able to be paired off with H-B-Smithian conventionality to her tenor. This may or may not have had something to do with the fact that *Natja* lasted only four weeks.

In an era where, in the wake of *Das Dreimäderlhaus,* romantic biomusicals of composers had become almost exhaustingly fashionable, European writers seem to have shied off subjecting Tchaikovsky's equivocal (lack of) love life to such a treatment, but America didn't. A San Francisco piece, *Song without Words,* written by Frederick Jackson and musically adapted by Franz Steininger for a production in the 1945–46 season, starred Margit Bokor and John Maxwell Hayes and invented for the poor composer a romance with a French singer. The piece was subsequently rewritten and presented on Broadway as *Music in My Heart* (ad Franz Steininger/Forman Brown/Patsy Ruth Miller, Adelphi Theater 2 October 1947) for a run of 124 performances. Robert Carroll was Tchaikovsky and Martha Wright his putative beloved.

Hungary: Városi Színház *A diadalmas asszony* 27 April 1923; UK: Gaiety Theatre *Catherine* 22 September 1923

IL SIGNOR FAGOTTO Opérette in 1 act by Charles Nuitter and Étienne Tréfeu. Music by Jacques Offenbach. Bad Ems, 11 July 1863.

A pointed little burlesque of musical styles, *Il Signor Fagotto* had the pretentious Bertolucci (Désiré) and the overblown Caramello (Édouard Georges) put in their places by the valet Fabricio (Lucille Tostée) who, disguised as the sort of Italian by whose music-making they swear, knocks spots off their overblown operaticky trilling with something more lively. Zulma Bouffar was the leading lady, Moschetta, and Pradeau completed the comical cast of five as Bacolo. First produced at Offenbach's preferred spa-town of Ems, *Il Signor Fagotto* was staged at the Bouffes-Parisiens the following year and a few weeks later by the Vienna Carltheater.

France: Théâtre des Bouffes-Parisiens 13 January 1864; Austria: Carltheater 11 February 1864

SILK STOCKINGS Musical comedy in 2 acts by George S Kaufman, Leueen McGrath and Abe Burrows based on the screenplay *Ninotchka* by Charles Brackett, Billy Wilder and Walter Reisch and suggested by *Ninotchka* by Melchior Lengyel. Music and lyrics by Cole Porter. Imperial Theater, New York, 24 February 1955.

Having got into Paris with a certain success in *Can-Can,* Cole Porter—this time aided by Mr and Mrs George S Kaufman—remained there for his next musical, *Silk Stockings.* The libretto was based on Ernst Lubitsch's 1939 comedy film *Ninotchka,* in which Greta Garbo had appeared as the ice-cube, hard-line Russian of the title, melted ("Garbo Laughs!") by her contact with Melvyn Douglas and Paris. Hildegarde Neff took Garbo's role in the musical, traveling to Paris to remove the happily defecting composer Peter Boroff (Philip Sterling) from the comfy arms of capitalism and of movie star Janice Dayton (Gretchen Wyler) and drag him back to Moscow. Boroff's agent, Steve Canfield (Don Ameche), and the sights of Paris weaken her resolve, but she duly takes her composer back home. Not for long, though. By the end of the evening not only have Ninotchka and Boroff closed the iron curtains behind them, but the heroine's boss, the Commissar of Art (George Tobias), and his lady friend have followed them to freedom.

Porter's songs were in his by-now-traditional mold, although, in the final score, there were only three names dropped (all in the same song) and the references to sex were both fewer and more romantic than nudgy. Ameche suggestively hymned the effects of the French capital in "Paris Loves Lovers" whilst Miss Neff dropped succinct showerlets of cold water on his warmth, dismissing human attraction as "chemical reaction, that's all" before they got to the genuine sentiment of "All of You" (him), "Without Love" (her) and "As on Through the Seasons We Sail" (them). The title song had Ameche reminiscing over the silk stockings Ninotchka leaves behind, the symbol of her lapse from doctrine, when she returns to Russia. Three thoroughly lapsed Russians (Leon Belasco, David Opatoshu, Henry Lascoe), agents unsuccessfully sent out on the same quest before Ninotchka, indulged in several swipes at the restrictions of communism (''Siberia,'' ''Too Bad''), whilst the revusicalest numbers of the show fell to Miss Wyler, happily detailing the necessity of the latest inventions, including ''Stereophonic Sound,'' to the movie industry, and of ''Satin and Silk'' underwear for a girl's morale, as well as relating in oddly coarse tones the attractions of ''Josephine.''

Feuer and Martin's production of *Silk Stockings* had a sticky start, and *Can-Can* librettist Abe Burrows moved in to make major changes in the text on the road to Broadway. Large amounts of the original score were dropped and replaced, so that there was ultimately as much of Porter's material not used in the show as finally remained to make up the definitive score. By the time *Silk Stockings* got to New York, however, it was in condition to stay there for 478 performances.

The musical was later made into a movie, with Cyd Charisse and Fred Astaire featured, and, although London did not take the show up, it did make it overseas, surfacing at the Landestheater in Linz and the Staatstheater in Kassel (ad Johanna von Koczian) following the great success of *Kiss Me, Kate* in German-language theatres. In 1995 it even got a Berlin showing, in a new adaptation by Joachim Franke, with Ines Rabsilber and Fritz Hille in the lead roles.

Austria: Landestheater, Linz *Seidenstrumpfe* 5 October 1974; Germany: Staatstheater, Kassel 5 November 1975, Metropoltheater 30 November 1995

Film: MGM 1957

Recordings: original cast (RCA), film soundtrack (MGM/CBS)

SILLY, Léa

Tall, dark, suggestively handsome and extravagant, Mlle Silly began her career in the Parisian theatre as a chorus girl at the Théâtre des Variétés at a time when choristers were choristers and principals, even in their early teens, began as principals. She nevertheless, with a little help from her apparently not-uninfluential gentlemen friends, managed the unusual exploit of getting out of the chorus and into employ as a principal, and that at the very same theatre. Silly established herself as a Parisian personality by sporting a monocle and smoking cigars, thus making herself an obvious choice for the travesty roles of the period which, in comparison to the feminine leads, allowed the performer to appear in costumes which were low above and short below, and of which she took advantage to considerable effect. She also established a fierce and public rivalry with Hortense Schneider, the Variétés leading lady, and was said to have been the one to have acidly if aptly christened that queen of opéra-bouffe ''la passage des Princes'' because of her numerous royal ''visitors.''

Plate 356. **Léa Silly** . . . *in female clothes.*

Silly had her first role at the Variétés as the slave girl Busa in Hervé's *Le Joueur de flûte* (1864) and later the same year had her most memorable success when she created the part of Oreste in *La Belle Hélène* (''Au cabaret du Labyrinthe''), a part from which she was ultimately sacked when the battle between herself and Schneider got too hot. Schneider proved powerful enough to keep her rival off the Variétés stage thereafter, but Silly continued a top-billed career—and had some revenge when, in a revue of 1867, she gave a much talked-of burlesque of Hortense Schneider which actually caused a theatrical riot. In 1869 she appeared at the Gaîté in *La Chatte blanche.*

She played a New York season in 1870 (Méphisto, Grande-Duchesse, etc), made a short American tour under James Fisk's management in tandem with Marie Aimée, fulfilled an ill-fated engagement in San Francisco (1871, Périchole, Hélène, Grande-Duchesse) and a more lucrative one at Saint Petersburg at the announced salary of 25,000 francs a month in 1872, before returning to Paris. Silly kept at it usefully to the end of the decade and beyond—in *La Revue en ville* (1872), as Margot in *Les Griffes du diable* (1872) and Risette in *Les Bibelots du Diable* (1874), in the title role in a *La Reine Indigo* revival (1877), as the comical cook in *Fleur d'Oranger* (1878), in *Les Deux Nababs* (1879), *La Cantinière* (1880, Victoire, ''full of life and comicality and makes the utmost of what remains of her voice, if she ever had any'') in the title role of the slightly musical vaudeville *La Champenoise* (1883) and as Lucrèce de Bonnebonne in *Fanfreluche* (1883)—being seen as late as 1888 in a revival of

Coco (''we seldom see her of late years'') and in 1889 as Penelope to the Ulysses of Dekernel in Pugno's *Le Retour d'Ulysse,* without ever getting near another new role of the quality of Oreste. Quite what happened to her after that, history does not relate.

SILVERS, Phil [SILVER, Philip] (b Brooklyn, NY, 12 May 1911; d New York, 1 November 1985).

A confident, old-style comedian with a face like a surprised sausage, Silvers appeared on the Broadway musical stage in his youth as Punko Parks in the unimpressive *Yokel Boy* (1939). Later in his career, after garnering considerable success in the film world, he returned to the musical theatre to appear in star roles as the fast-talking fall-about Harrison Floy in *High Button Shoes* (1947) and as Jerry Biffle in the variety-based telly-mocker *Top Banana* (1951). With his famous creation of television's Sergeant Bilko behind him, he came back once more to Broadway in 1960 to play get-rich-quick Hubie Cram in *Do Re Mi,* helping by his star presence to stretch the show's run considerably but, as in the case of *Top Banana,* not long enough to get it into the black.

In 1966 he appeared as Marcus Lycus in the film version of *A Funny Thing Happened on the Way to the Forum,* and six years later made his last Broadway appearance playing the role of Pseudolus—which he also played in Britain—in revival of the same show (Tony Award). He was seen on television in the musical *Keep in Step* in 1959.

Autobiography: (w Saffron, R): *The Laugh Is on Me* (Prentice-Hall, Englewood Cliffs, NJ, 1973)

THE SILVER SLIPPER New modern extravaganza in 2 acts by Owen Hall. Lyrics by W H Risque. Additional lyrics by Leslie Stuart, Charles H Taylor and George Rollitt. Music by Leslie Stuart. Lyric Theatre, London, 1 June 1901.

Producer Tom Davis, author Owen Hall and composer Leslie Stuart combined on *The Silver Slipper* in the wake of their enormous worldwide success with *Florodora.* Hall provided a libretto which was notably different from that for the earlier work—a fantasy in which a young Venusian maiden (Winifred Hare) slyly drops her slipper from the skies and is bound to descend to earth to retrieve it. There she meets *Florodora* star Willie Edouin as a dubious bookmaker, Gaiety star Connie Ediss as his housekeeper, matinée-idol vocalist Henri Leoni, all-purpose leading man Louis Bradfield and soubrette Coralie Blythe as a girl in boy's clothes. Stuart's score had, on the other hand, many reminiscences of *Florodora*—notably a double sextet ''Come, Little Girl and Tell Me Truly'' which was a colorable imitation of ''Tell Me, Pretty Maiden'' and a piece called ''A Glimpse-impse-impse'' which was a close relative of ''An Inkling''—even though it attempted fresh things elsewhere, as in a light operatic ''Invocation to Venus'' for the ladies' chorus and soprano solo. It was, however, Connie Ediss's comical musings on ''Class'' and Leoni's parlor ballad ''Two Eyes of Blue'' which proved the most popular pieces of *The Silver Slipper*'s score.

The show was received indifferently on opening night, with Owen Hall's sometimes vicious society cracks often missing their mark, and Davis hurried into action. The piece was pruned and patched and before the advance engendered by *Florodora* was gone, it had established itself nicely. *The Silver Slipper* played six and a half months (197 performances) at the Lyric Theatre, went briskly into the provinces, and the following year was staged on Broadway. By the time it opened in New York, it had undergone some further changes since its Shaftesbury Avenue season. The book had been ''adapted'' by Clay Greene, and Stuart, who loathed foreign interpolations, had provided some new songs. However he was still unable to stop Arthur Weld grabbing his traditional conductor's perk of slipping in several pieces of his own. Sam Bernard played the bookmaker, Edna Wallace-Hopper his boyish daughter and Josie Sadler sang ''Class,'' but it was Harry B Burcher from the London *Florodora* sextet, who here restaged Sidney Ellison's choreography, who was largely responsible for the show's success. A dance routine, ''The Champagne Dance,'' in which the girls danced with waiters with little trick tables between them, caused a sensation. *The Silver Slipper* and its Champagne Dance became as big an attraction as Ellison's arrangement of the *Florodora* double sextet had been, and *The Silver Slipper* ran for 165 New York performances before going out to dazzle the regions with ''the most wonderful dance we have ever seen.''

The Silver Slipper also traveled in the opposite direction, being played in Berlin at the Neues Königliches Opernhaus (ad Wilhelm Mannstädt) in repertoire with no less classics than *Der Zigeunerbaron* and *Der Bettelstudent,* and it was also mounted in Budapest (ad Jenő Heltai) with the town's favorite musical star Klára Küry in the lead. It did well enough in both venues, but did not find extended success in either.

Germany: Neueliches Königliches Opernhaus *Der silberne Pantoffel* 1 July 1902; USA: Broadway Theater 27 October 1902; Hungary: Népszínház Az *ezüstpapucs* 8 January 1904

SIMON, [Marvin] Neil (b New York, 4 July 1927).

The most successful comic playwright of the post-war Broadway era, Simon has intermittently contributed a libretto to the musical stage. Each of his first four essays in the field, all comic-based and yet all different, was an international success, and his work has combined with

Left: Plate C-35. Oh! Oh! Delphine. *The parrot gives the warning cry.* **Below: Plate C-36. Der Orlow** *was a diamond.*

Plate C-37. Orphée aux enfers. *Wilhelm Knaack as Styx and Johann Nestroy as the fly Jupiter in Vienna's* Orpheus in der Unterwelt.

Clockwise: Plate C-38. Elaine Paige, *the original Grizabella, in* Cats. **Plate C-39. Le Petit Duc.** *Jeanne Saulier as the little Duke in a revival of Lecocq's opérette.* **Plate C-40. The Pink Lady** *was Hazel Dawn.*

CLOCKWISE: Plate C-41. The Pirates of Penzance. *George Grossmith, Rutland Barrington and Marion Hood in the original London production of Gilbert and Sullivan's comic opera.* **Plate C-42. Yvonne Printemps** *in one of her most successful shows.* **Plate C-43. The Rocky Horror Show.**

Above: Plate C-44. Rose Marie. *Totem Tom-Tom in Paris.*
Right: Plate C-45. A Runaway Girl. *Sheet music cover for "Soldiers in the Park."*

CLOCKWISE: Plate C-46. La Scugnizza. *Fox-trott Italian style.* **Plate C-47. The Shop Girl.** *"Love on the Japanese Plan" sung and danced by Teddy Payne and Katie Seymour.* **Plate C-48. The Spring Chicken.** *Who hired that poster artist?*

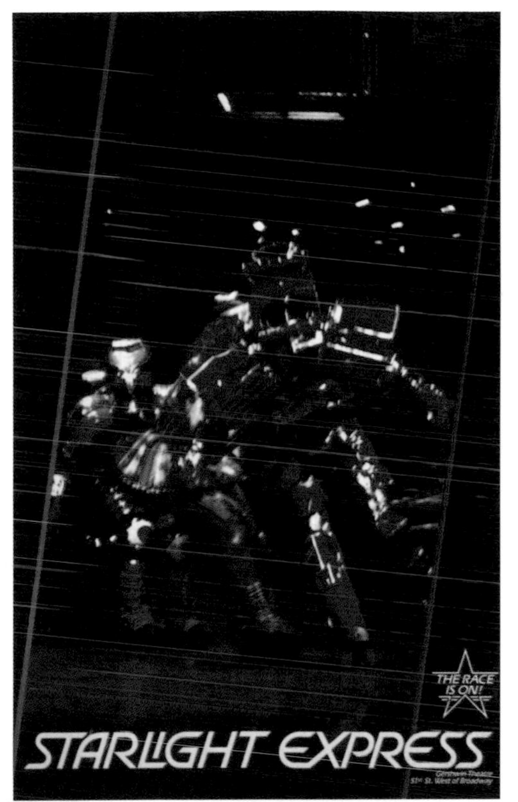

Clockwise: Plate C-49. Starlight Express. *The race is on!* **Plate C-50. Sunny.** *The sheet music got to Europe, where Jerome Kern was billed as "the composer of 'Who?'," but the show didn't go further east than London.* **Plate C-51. Sunset Boulevard.** *Glenn Close takes her turn in the row of stars who donned the gown and toque of Norma Desmond.*

Clockwise: Plate C-52. Tanz der Vampire. *Steve Barton gets ready to sink his teeth.* **Plate C-53. La Vie parisienne.** *Sketches from the original production.* **Plate C-54. Der Vogelhändler.** *Alexander Girardi as the bird-seller of the title.*

that of writers such as Larry Gelbart to keep alive and prominent the genuinely comic element of a genre which used to be called ''musical comedy'' before classy comic writing became too difficult for librettists.

Simon began writing for radio and television, and contributed texts to several television musicals for NBC-TV (w William Friedberg) in the mid-1950s (*Satins and Spurs* 1954, *Heidi* 1955, *The Adventures of Marco Polo* 1956, *Paris in Springtime* 1956, and a TV reduction of a *Naughty Marietta* 1955), while also making contributions to the revues *Catch a Star* (1955) and *New Faces of 1956,* before scoring a major success with his first Broadway play, *Come Blow Your Horn.* The following year he succeeded in translating the orange-flavored witticisms of Patrick Dennis's tale of Belle Poitrine to the musical stage in the crisply funny libretto to *Little Me,* and he combined again with that show's composer, Cy Coleman, on a second outstanding piece when he adapted the screenplay *Nights of Cabiria* as the libretto for the warm and kookily funny 1966 hit *Sweet Charity.* Another screenplay, *The Apartment,* was the basis for the hit Burt Bacharach/Hal David musical *Promises, Promises,* but the virtually two-handed *They're Playing Our Song,* a triumph of realistic and contemporary comedy writing, was an original script, which had for its basis, apparently, only the relationship between its songwriters, Hamlisch and Bayer Sager.

Simon's 100 percent scoresheet got its first blot 30 years after his first great success with a musicalization of a further screenplay, *The Goodbye Girl.*

1962 **Little Me** (Cy Coleman/Carolyn Leigh) Lunt-Fontanne Theater 17 November

1966 **Sweet Charity** (Coleman/Dorothy Fields) Palace Theater 29 January

1968 **Promises, Promises** (Burt Bacharach/Hal David) Shubert Theater 1 December

1979 **They're Playing Our Song** (Marvin Hamlisch/Carol Bayer Sager) Imperial Theater 11 February

1993 **The Goodbye Girl** (Hamlisch/David Zippel) Marquis Theater 4 March; revised version Albery Theatre, London 1997

Autobiographies: *Rewrites* (Simon & Schuster, New York, 1996), *The Play Goes On* (Simon & Schuster, New York, 1999)

SIMON-GIRARD, Juliette [née GIRARD, Juliette Joséphine] (b Paris, 8 May 1859; d Nice, ?1954).

Juliette Girard was the daughter of theatrical parents—the actor-author Lockroy (Joseph Philippe Simon, 1803–91), co-author of *Les Dragons de Villars,* and the Opéra-Comique dugazon soprano Caroline Girard who had created the role of Georgette in *Les Dragons de Villars* and played in the premieres of *Robinson Crusoe* and *Vert-Vert*—and she was trained at the Conservatoire as an actress. She apparently made her debut at the age of

Plate 357. **Juliette Simon-Girard** *in the title role of Messager's* La Fauvette du Temple.

18—though announced as being 16—at the Théâtre des Folies-Dramatiques in the role of Carlinette in Offenbach's short-lived *La Foire Saint-Laurent,* allegedly after only a few weeks of singing lessons. She scored a personal success and was promptly given the role of Serpolette in the theatre's next new show, *Les Cloches de Corneville.* This second performance made her a star, a status thoroughly confirmed when she subsequently created the large title role à tiroirs of *Madame Favart* (1878) and then that of Stella in *La Fille du tambour-major* (1879) for Offenbach.

Having wed her *Cloches de Corneville* co-star, Simon Max, she was now known as Mme Simon-Girard (which, given her father's name, she would seem to have had a right to do all along) and she continued to be so known even after her newspaper-stirring divorce, in 1894, and her remarriage, four years later, to another star of the Paris stage, **Félix HUGUENET** (b Lyon, 1858; d 19 November 1926), who bested the betrayed and vengeful husband in a duel at the Saint-Lazare railway station.

A long list of starring roles followed Mlle Simon-Girard's brilliant beginnings, but few would come near in quality or success to the three great parts which the young diva had created before the age of 21. Over the next 20 years she created leading roles in *La Mère des compagnons* (1880, Francine Thibault), *Le Beau Nicolas* (1880, Camille), *Les Poupées de l'Infante* (1881, l'Infante), *Le Petit Parisien* (1882, Prince de Bagneux), *Fanfan la Tulipe* (1882, Pimprenelle), *La Princesse des Canaries* (1883, Pépita), *La Vie mondaine* (1885, Georgette), *La Fauvette du Temple* (1885, Thérèse), *La Chatte blanche* (1887, Pierrette), *Le Dragon de la reine* (1888, Sedaine), *La Petite Fronde* (1888, Madame Jabotin), *Le Voyage de Suzette* (1890, Suzette), *Mademoiselle Asmodée* (1891, Rosette), *Cendrillon* (1891, Cendrillon), *La Femme de Narcisse* (1892, Estelle), *Miss Robinson* (1892, Eva), *Mam'zelle Carabin* (1893, Olga), *Le Bonhomme de neige* (1894, Ariella), *Les Forains* (1894, Olympia), *L'Enlèvement de la Toledad* (1894, la Toledad), *La Duchesse de Ferrare* (1895, Nadège), *La Belle Épicière* (1895, Nicette), *La Dot de Brigitte* (1895, Brigitte), *La Biche au bois* (1896, Prince Souci), *Le Royaume des femmes* (1896, Frivolin), *Les Soeurs Gaudichard* (1899, Cécile and Clara), *Mademoiselle George* (1900, Mademoiselle George) and *Le Chien du régiment* (1902, Jacquotte), as well as playing the classic repertoire (both Clairettes, Hélène, Thérèse in *La Cigale,* etc), reappearing in her own great roles—including a Serpolette as late as 1908—and latterly playing also in straight theatre. She was seen on the London stage in 1886 when she appeared at Her Majesty's Theatre as Wanda to the Grande-Duchesse of Mary Albert.

It is recounted that Mme Simon-Girard lived to be over a hundred. However, the *état civil* at Nice fails to confirm this, possibly because her second husband, Félix Huguenet, seems to have operated under a nom de théâtre.

Huguenet, originally best known as a straight actor (*L'ami Fritz, Monsieur Bretonneau,* Dartez in *L'Animateur, Le Roi,* Denis Roulette in *Sire,* etc) nevertheless spent many years on the musical stage, making a famous success as the bullfighter, Puycardas, in *Miss Helyett* and often playing alongside Mme Simon-Girard. He appeared on the musical stage as Gustave Bridoux in *La Noce à Nini,* Briancourt in *La Duchesse de Ferrare,* in *Le Brillant Achille,* as Van Gluten in *Le Bonhomme de neige,* Antonio in *L'Enlevèment de la Toledad,* Narcisse in *La Femme de Narcisse,* Englebert in *Les Trois Devins,* as Fortuné Pomerol in *Le Saint-Valentin,* Riquet in *Riquet à la Houppe,* Colonel de Castel-Brillant in *La Dot de Brigitte,* Paul Vaubert in *Les Forains,* Adolphe in *Mam'zelle Carabin,* Lieutenant de Police in Berger's *Le Chevalier d'Éon* (1908), etc.

Mme Simon-Girard's son, **Aimé SIMON-GIRARD** (1889–1950), after starting life as a lawyer's clerk and as the author of several amateur revues, also made a career, from 1913 on, in the musical theatre, in French and British revue and in both silent and spoken films. His musical-theatre appearances included *Les Petits Crevés* at the Capucines (1913, Raoul de Trémouillac), *Mam'zelle Boy Scout* (1915, the English soldier Tommy, billed as Aimé Simon), *L'Archiduc des Folies-Bergère* (1916), *Carminetta* (1917, Don José to the Carminetta of Lavallière), *La Reine joyeuse* (1918) at the Apollo, *Hello!! Charley* (1919), *Princesse Carnaval* (1920), *La Belle du Far West* (1920), Cuvillier's *Annabella* (1922), *Épouse-la!* (1923, André Montrachet), *Le Diable à Paris* (1927), *Un soir de réveillon* (1933), *Érosine* (1935) and London's *No Sky So Blue* (1938, the French Count Paul Ravel). On film, the dapper, dark moustachioed actor was, notably, the silent d'Artagnan of *Les Trois Mousquetaires* (1921).

SIMON-MAX [SIMON, Nicolas Marie] (b Reims, 24 October, 1847; d Paris, 1923). Light-comic vocalist who created a long series of roles in 19th-century French opérettes.

Simon-Max began his career in cafés-concerts before moving from the Alcazar to join the company at the Théâtre des Folies-Dramatiques under Louis Cantin. He made his first appearance there as Quillenbois in a revival of *Les Cent Vierges* and created his first important stage role as the gently comic and tenorious Poulet, opposite the Poulette of Hortense Schneider in her last stage performances in *La Belle Poule* (1875). He took character tenor roles in *Fleur de Baiser* (1876, Gaston) and a *Le Petit Faust* revival (1876–77, Faust) and at 24 created his best role to date as Briolet, the comical little sweetheart (eventually) of the Jeanne of *Jeanne, Jeannette et Jeanneton* (1876).

He later took over as Janio in *La Reine Indigo* at the Renaissance (1876) but returned to the Folies-Dramatiques for Offenbach's indifferent *La Foire Saint-Laurent* (1877, Nicolas Curtius) before winning a run of three memorable shows and roles, cast alongside Juliette Girard—soon to be Mme Simon-Girard—which would be the highlights of his career. He created, in succession, the part of the rural wide-boy Jean Grénicheux in *Les Cloches de Corneville* (1877, ''Va, petit mousse''), the young Hector in *Madame Favart* (1878) and the longing little tailor, Griolet, in *La Fille du tambour-major* (1879).

Other fine new roles, more often than not alongside his wife, followed in *La Mère des compagnons* (1880, Gaston de Champrosé), *Le Beau Nicolas* (1880, Criquet), *Le Petit Parisien* (1882, Cottinet), *Fanfan la Tulipe* (1882, Michel), *La Princesse des Canaries* (1883, Inigo), *Rip* (1884, Ischabod), *Les Petits Mousquetaires* (1885, Planchet), *La Fauvette du Temple* (1885, Joseph Abrial), *La Chatte blanche* (1887, Petitpatapon), *Le Dragon de la reine* (1888, Pamphile), *Le Mariage avant la lettre* (1888, Prosper), *Le Voyage de Suzette* (1890, Pinsonnet), *Mademoiselle Asmodée* (1891, Florestan), the Châtelet's *Cen-*

drillon (1891), *La Femme de Narcisse* (1892, Saint-Phar) and *Miss Robinson* (1892, Capédiou), and he also made regular appearances in both his famous roles and other classic parts (Pomponnet, etc).

By the time the pair divorced, Simon-Max was leaning away from the tenor-with-comic-flair roles to the stocky-to-plump comedian-who-sings parts, and he spent the next decade in such pieces as *Rivoli* (1896), *L'Auberge du Tohu-Bohu* (1897, Bel-Oeil), *Les Quatre filles Aymon* (1898), *Miss Helyett* (1900, Smithson), *Madame la Présidente* (1902, Don Géranios), *L'Armée des vierges, Le Jockey malgré lui* (1902, Godefroy), *Florodora* (1903 Plum-Quick, ie, Tweedlepunch), Berény's *Miss Chipp* (1903, Morin), Lecocq's late *Rose Mousse* (1904, Gilbert Duterroir) and as Barbemuche in a *La Petite Bohème* revival, without ever again finding a role quite like those of his youthful character tenor days.

SIMONS, Moïses (b Havana, 24 August 1888; d Madrid, 28 June 1945).

Songwriter Simons, the son of a Spanish musician, made his fame with the song ''El Manisero'' (known in L Wolfe Gilbert and Marion Sunshine's English version as ''The Peanut Vendor'') and he and it were partly responsible for the spread of the craze for South American rhythms, particularly the rumba, in the postwar years. Simons also wrote for the theatre, composing zarzuelas for the Barcelona theatre and later winning a major Parisian success with the musical comedy *Toi c'est moi* (''Sous les palétuviers''), the second act of which, set in his native Caribbean, allowed the composer to indulge in a festival of rumba, samba and conga rhythms. In *Le Chant des Tropiques,* two years later, he returned to the same part of the world as the setting for a tale of hidden treasure, ultimately discovered by the island's Irish pastor, O'Patt (Morton), after a score of rumbas, blues, a fire dance, a paso doble, and something called a Cubanacan, and songs from stars romantic—Hélène Regelly (''Mon coeur est un oiseau perdu''), Roger Bourdin and Jean Sablon—and comic (''Ah! y'en a bon le doudou''), without hitting the same kind of lightning rod that he had first time up.

''The Peanut Vendor'' was seen performed by a certain Sr Machin in the very briefly-lived Broadway revue *Fast and Furious* in 1931.

1934 **Toi c'est moi** (Henri Duvernois/Bertal, Maubon, Chamfleury) Théâtre des Bouffes-Parisiens 19 September

1936 **Le Chant des Tropiques** (Sauvat, Chamfleury) Théâtre de Paris 4 October

SIMPLE SIMON Musical entertainment by Ed Wynn and Guy Bolton. Lyrics by Lorenz Hart. Music by Richard Rodgers. Ziegfeld Theater, New York, 18 February 1930.

A Florenz Ziegfeld vehicle for comedian Ed Wynn—''the perfect fool''—*Simple Simon* followed the kind of fairy-tale layout of which Montgomery and Stone had made such a success, introducing Wynn as a newspaper-seller with a passion for fairy tales whose daydreams took him off into all sorts of adventures with characters such as Cinderella and Snow White, amongst a dazzling series of Joseph Urban stage pictures. The more successful of Rodgers and Hart's songs for the piece included two made-over pieces from their recent flop *Chee-Chee* (''Send for Me,'' ''I Still Believe in You''), as well as one based on Wynn's lisped catchphrase ''I Love the Woods'' and another encouraging (as London's *Mr Cinders* had done just shortly before) ''On with the Dance.'' Two other songs, ''He Was Too Good for Me'' and ''He Dances on My Ceiling,'' were cut by the producer before the show reached town. The second of these the writers subsequently remodeled for use in the London revue *Evergreen* where it became a hit for Jessie Matthews. The big song success of the night was, conversely, a number written and inserted during the show's pre-Broadway weeks to fit into a comedy scene Wynn had devised. He pedaled onstage on a novelty piano-bicycle with a girl perched on top and accompanied her on his keyboard as she delivered a piece called ''Ten Cents a Dance.'' When the song's original performer was sacked for being drunk on stage, Ziegfeld hired the young Ruth Etting to replace her. The artist made a personal success with her unusually low-life number, launching it on a career as a standard.

In spite of Wynn's proven drawing power, *Simple Simon* turned out to be slow to take off. Ziegfeld made further alterations and cuts in the piece (including the removal or replacement of four more numbers), but finally took the show off after 135 performances and sent it on the road.

SIMPLICIUS Operette in a Vorspiel and 2 acts by Victor Léon taken from Hans Jakob Christoffel von Grimmelhausen's novel *Der abenteuerliche Simplicissimus* (*Simplicius Simplicissimus*). Music by Johann Strauss. Theater an der Wien, Vienna, 17 December 1887.

The musical version of Grimmelhausen's 1669 novel was cannily written by the young Léon with every appearance of providing a splendid vehicle for the reigning king of the Viennese musical theatre, Alexander Girardi. The part of Simplicius, a seeming peasant boy caught up picaresquely in the Thirty Years War and in one of those identity crises which were standard operettic fare at the time, gave him a drawerful of guises and complications to go through before ending up as the long-lost son of the equally long-lost Graf von Grübben.

In fact, the nub of Léon's reduction of the plot had little enough to do with the Thirty Years War. It largely concerned the search for this strayed Graf von Grübben, a young man who is supposed to be getting dynastically married to Hildegard von Bliessen-Wellau, daughter of the Colonel of the regiment in which Simplicius has, through slightly Candide-type circumstances, become enrolled. The apparent heir to the title, Melchior, and Hildegard's beloved Arnim, who impersonates him awhile, are eventually both displaced by Simplicius, but since it turns out that the unsuspecting younger von Grübben's father is actually still alive, and has been lurking about on the fringes of the show's plot most of the night disguised as a hermit, the boy—Graf or no Graf—is still able to wed his beloved Tilly and let Hildegard pair off with her Arnim. Melchior is left with the danseuse with whom he started out.

Strauss displayed an enormous enthusiasm for this project, which he saw as providing him with some moments in which he could write music of a less frivolous kind than that with which he had his greatest triumphs, but this enthusiasm for writing something more resembling a light opera than an Operette did not prevent him from using bits of music left over from *Der Zigeunerbaron* and from his recently aborted comic opera on another respected piece of German literature, *Der Schelm von Bergen,* in making up his score.

Simplicius, as is signaled in its overture, did include some more serious musical moments, but it was nevertheless presented at the Theater an der Wien with a cast of the finest Operette performers in Vienna: Girardi, in the role destined for him, playing alongside Josef Joseffy (Hermit), Karl Streitmann (Arnim), Ottilie Collin (Tilly), Antonie Hartmann (Hildegard), Therese Biedermann (Lisbeth), Alois Pokorny (Wellau) and Siegmund Stelzer. However, Strauss's score did best when it stayed staunchly in waltz time, and the two most liked pieces from Simplicius turned out to be the obligatory Girardi waltz—here shared with his Tilly—''Dummer Bub,'' and, even more so, Joseffy's last-act waltz romance ''Ich denke gern zurück.''

The show was not a success. It played but 29 performances at the Theater an der Wien and an attempt to revise it, with its libretto, which had—as ever when a Strauss Operette was in trouble—taken the bulk of the brickbats, remade by Ludwig Dóezi, lasted only 12 nights when produced at the Budapest Népszínház (ad Sándor Lukácsy, Ferenc Rajna). *Simplicius,* however, proved to be one of those pieces which, in spite of repeated failures, folk will try to revise and revive over and again. It was given a hopeful third try at the Theater an der Wien in 1894 with the libretto revised by Karl Lindau, and Fräulein Stein cast as a travesty Simplicius alongside Streitmann, Joseffy, Frln Pohlner (Tilly), Therese Biedermann, Frln Frey (Hildegard) and the adaptor himself as Melchior. It lasted this time for a meagre 11 showings.

A fourth and happier revision was not just a revision but a thorough rewrite done by Léon himself. He altogether junked the book. The new piece, produced under the title *Gräfin Pepi,* interleaved better-liked bits of the *Simplicius* score with numbers from another of Strauss's less-than-long-running works *Blindekuh* (arr Ernst Reiterer), and the resulting piece was staged by Gabor Steiner at the Venedig in Wien summer theatre on 5 July 1902 with Mizzi Zwerenz in the role of Pepi. This version was subsequently played in Germany (Centraltheater 27 February 1903).

The various Strauss pasticcio musicals have helped themselves to such bits of *Simplicius* as they fancied, the best-known being the remake of ''Der Frühling lacht, es singen die Vöglein ein'' as ''Sei mir gegrüsst, du holdes Venezia'' in one of the more souped-up versions of *Eine Nacht in Venedig.*

Hungary: Népszínház (revised version by Dóczi) 7 February 1889

Recording: complete (EMI) (Zürich cast 1999)

SIMS, George R[obert] (b Kennington, London, 2 September 1847; d London, 4 September 1922). Journalist and stage author with a winning touch for the popular.

Educated in Eastbourne and Bonn, Sims found fame as a journalist (Lunatic Laureate in *Fun,* Dagonet of *The Referee*), a crusading pamphleteer (*How the Poor Live*), a poet (''The Dagonet Ballads,'' ''Ballads of Baylon'') and as a dramatist. His first play, *One Hundred Years Old,* an adaptation, was produced at the Olympic Theatre in 1875 and he had his first big success with the comedy *Crutch and Toothpick* (1879), following up with a series of successful plays including *The Mother-in-Law* (1881), *The Member for Slocum* (1881) and *The Gay City* (1881) before launching with *The Lights of London* (1881) and *The Romany Rye* (1882) on the run of dramas which were to bring him the best of his theatrical fame.

His name first appeared on a London burlesque bill in 1881 when his *The Of-Course-Akin-Brothers, Babes in the Wood* was mounted at the Royalty Theatre, and he made his first serious venture into the musical theatre with the comic opera *The Merry Duchess* produced by and starring the inimitable Kate Santley at that same house. *The Merry Duchess* won a fine London run, a tour and productions in America and Australia. A second happy collaboration with composer Frederic Clay on the fairy-tale spectacular *The Golden Ring,* a Christmas show for the Alhambra, indicated that the composer—W S Gilbert's pre-Sullivan partner—had very likely found the new book-and-lyrics collaborator he needed. When Clay suffered a stroke that ended his career shortly after, Sims effectively abandoned the made-for-London comic-opera style they had shared, and the run of musical-theatre successes which he produced over the next 15 years in parallel with such straight theatre hits as *Harbour Lights* (1885), *The Trumpet Call* (1891) and *Two Little Vagabonds* (1896) fell into two different and separate areas. On the one hand, he co-authored some of the most successful examples of the ''new burlesque'' genre instituted by George Edwardes at the Gaiety Theatre, whilst on the other he wrote book and lyrics for several of the most successful touring musicals of the time.

The earliest Gaiety burlesques (*The Vicar of Wideawake-field, Little Jack Sheppard*) of the new era had been co-written by Sims's cousin and fellow journalist William Yardley, and both the team of ''Richard Henry'' and the Gaiety's star Fred Leslie had then taken their turns at constructing the new kind of song-and-dance shows which were the rage of the town. Sims and his *Harbour Lights* colleague Henry Pettitt, however, brought the new burlesque to its peak with two shows for Edwardes—*Faust Up-to-Date* and *Carmen Up-to-Data*—which not only brought the expression ''up-to-date'' into the language as a synonym for modernity, but which gave all concerned two worldwide hits. Both these pieces retained the old burlesque notion of a parody of their subject—the operas of Gounod and Bizet respectively—but a third burlesque hit, *Little Christopher Columbus,* followed the way of fashion and had very little to do with its nominal subject. It did, however, after a certain amount of remaking, fit public tastes to a nicety and its Ivan Caryll/Sims score produced several hit songs (''Lazily, Drowsily,'' ''Oh Honey, My Honey'') which helped long runs in London and New York.

These three large-sized hits were more than equaled by three provincial Methusalems. The tuppence-colored ''musical variety drama'' *Jack-in-the-Box* written with another respected critic, Clement Scott, was a hugely popular piece of sentimental drama decorated with songs and dances for its personality heroine which had years of touring life; *Skipped by the Light of the Moon* was a musical adaptation of his early touring comedy *A Gay City* which trouped virtually nonstop through the three English-speaking continents for a decade and more; whilst *The Dandy Fifth* was an old French hearts-and-uniforms comic opera which contained some of the best songwords of Sims's career (''Tommy's Tournament,'' ''The Sprig o' Horringe Blossom'').

The Dandy Fifth was a regular feature of the British touring scene for many years, and Sims tried two more musicals with its composer, Clarence Corri: a Spanish piece, *Miss Chiquita,* which did fairly well, and a vehicle for Dan Leno, *In Gay Piccadilly,* which didn't.

In his elderly days Sims continued to write for the stage, and he supplied the text for the Drury Lane pantomime of 1911 as well as for a number of songs and musical playlets for the music halls and variety theatres. His success owed much to his ability to judge aright the level at which to pitch his pieces, both musical and non-musical, without any condescension, to appeal to the large popular audience.

Sims also authored one of the most readable and apparently accurate books of theatrical memoirs to have come from the British stage.

1874 **The Field of the Cloth of Gold** (revival) new lyrics (Strand Theatre)

1879 **A Dress Rehearsal** (Louis Diehl) 1 act Langham Hall 30 October

1881 **The Of Course-Akin-Brothers, Babes in the Wood** Theatre Royal, Hull 19 March

1881 **The Girl He Left Behind Him** (Max Schröter) 1 act Vaudeville Theatre 29 November

1883 **The Merry Duchess** (Frederic Clay) Royalty Theatre 23 April

1883 **Skipped by the Light of the Moon** (comp/arr George Pack, Henry W May/Percy Marshall, et al) Rand's Opera House, Troy, NY 24 September; Fifth Avenue Theater, New York 14 April 1884

1883 **The Golden Ring** (Clay) Alhambra Theatre 3 December

1885 **Jack-in-the-Box** (William C Levey, James Glover, et al/w Clement Scott) Theatre Royal, Brighton 24 August; Strand Theatre 7 February 1887

1888 **Faust Up-to-Date** (Meyer Lutz/w Henry Pettitt) Gaiety Theatre 30 October

1890 **Carmen Up-to-Data** (Lutz/w Pettitt) Gaiety Theatre 4 October

1892 **Blue-Eyed Susan** (F Osmond Carr/w Pettitt) Prince of Wales Theatre 6 February

1893 **Little Christopher Columbus** (Ivan Caryll/w Cecil Raleigh) Lyric Theatre 10 October

1894 **The Yaller Girl** (Caryll) 1 act Moore and Burgess Minstrels 31 December

1895 **Dandy Dick Whittington** (aka *The Circus Boy*) (Caryll) Avenue Theatre 2 March

1895 **Uncle Tom's Cabin** (Caryll) tableaux vivants Moore & Burgess Minstrels, St James's Hall 7 October

1898 **The Dandy Fifth** (Clarence C Corri) Prince of Wales Theatre, Birmingham 11 April; Duke of York's Theatre 16 August

1897 **La Beigneuse** (Caryll) 1 act Palace Theatre

1899 **A Good Time** revised *Skipped by the Light of the Moon* Opera Comique 27 April

1899 **Miss Chiquita** (later *Dancing Girl of Spain*) (Corri) Prince of Wales Theatre, Birmingham 7 August

1899 **My Innocent Boy** (various) Collingwood Opera House, Poughkeepsie 18 September

1899 **In Gay Piccadilly** (Corri) Theatre Royal, Glasgow 9 October

1906 **In Sunny Spain, or The Troubles of a Tourist** (Herman Finck/w Charles Fletcher) 3 scenes Winter Gardens, Blackpool 9 July

1909 **Beauty and the Burglar** sketch

Autobiography: *My Life: Sixty Years Recollections of Bohemian London* (Eveleigh Nash, London, 1917)

SIM-VIVA [VIVA, Simone] (b ?1903; d 1982). Bobbed, pretty-voiced and unforced ingenue of the 1920s and 1930s.

Sim-Viva made early appearances on the musical stage in revivals of Planquette's posthumous *Le Paradis de Mahomet* and Terrasse's *Cartouche* (1922) at the Trianon-Lyrique and subsequently played there in *Sylvie* (1923), but her career was largely made in the Jazz Age musical comedies which were the joy of the Parisian musical theatre of the 1920s. During those years, she introduced the roles of Lilette, one of the ladies referred to in the title of *Trois jeunes filles . . . nues!* (1925), of Nicole in Henri Christiné's *J'aime* (1926, ''C'est pas ça le bonheur''), Jenny in the French version of *Mercenary Mary* (1927), Magali who gets the man from soubrette Christiane Dor in Szulc's *Zou!* (1930, ''J'aime'') and the title role of *Rosy* (1930, ''Quand j'ai promis, j'y tiens''). She moved into a slightly different area when she appeared as Peggy, the little lost laundress love of the British Beau in Reynaldo Hahn's *Brummell* (1931) and when she took the title role of the vast production of *Nina Rosa* (1932) at the Châtelet, but she returned to musical comedy in Christiné's *La Madone du promenoir* (1933), *Miss Cocktail* (1934), *L'Auberge du chat coiffé* (1935) and *Un p'tit bout de femme* (1936). She also appeared in several early to mid-1930s films including a version of the opera *Martha* (1935, Lady Harriet) and *Moulin Rouge* (Mimi).

Through the more-than-a-decade that she starred in jeune fille roles, she never changed her publicity and program photograph, but the ingenue roles nevertheless finally stopped coming.

Her husband **Géo BURY** began a career as a bright-eyed singing juvenile man in a tiny featured role in *Dédé* (1921, Le Commissaire), took the lead role in *Le Beau Voyage* (*Leányvásár*) at Lyon (1923, Jack Grims) and came to light in *Trois jeune filles . . . nues!* (1925), before going on to create the role of Robert Perceval, the American hero of *Passionnément,* lending a ringing baritone to Messager's title waltz. He paired with his wife again as Gaston in Christiné's *J'aime* (1926, ''Quand on est 'de'''), took over as Jim Kenyon in *Rose Marie* (1927), shared ''Je suis tour à tour'' (''Sometimes I'm Happy'') with Coecilia Navarre in *Hallelujah!* (*Hit the Deck,* 1929, Bill Smith), played the jeune premier role of the artist, Armand, in *Sidonie Panache* with Loulou Hégoburu and Edmée Favart (''Le jour de la blanchisseuse'') and appeared at the Théâtre de l'Étoile in *Érosine* (1935). Between times he was seen in lead juvenile roles in musical comedy on the roads of France, and on the musical screen.

SINBAD Musical extravaganza in 2 acts and 14 scenes with dialogue and lyrics by Harold Atteridge. Music by Sigmund Romberg. Additional numbers by George Gershwin, Irving Caesar, B G De Sylva, Jean Schwartz, Joe Young, Walter Donaldson, Gus Kahn, Sam Lewis, Al Jolson, et al. Winter Garden Theater, New York, 14 February 1918.

If the Messrs Shubert's production of *Sinbad,* which ran for 164 performances at the Winter Garden Theater in 1918, goes down as statistically the most successful of the musical theatre's tales of the Arabian Nights sailor, it must be admitted that this was not because of the old tale, to which this extravaganza's resemblance was fairly incidental. In this *Sinbad,* Al Jolson was the star, performing in his regular blackface, down on one knee on a thrust stage, and giving forth with ''Swanee,'' ''Rock-a-Bye Your Baby with a Dixie Melody,'' ''My Mammy,'' ''Chloe,'' ''Dixie Rose,'' ''Hello, Central, Give Me No-Man's-Land'' and others of the same un-Arabian ilk in the middle of Sigmund Romberg and Harold Atteridge's attempts to be at least reasonably eastern with ''A Thousand and One Arabian Nights,'' ''The Raglad of Baghdad'' and ''A Night in the Orient.'' Jolson was undoubtedly a bigger draw than the rather submerged sailor.

The story of Sindbad or Sinbad the Sailor was a less popular theatrical one in Victorian times than its companions *Aladdin, Ali Baba* and *Prince Camaralzaman,* but it nevertheless found its way with reasonable frequency to the spectacular and musical stages, most particularly at pantomime time. Sinbad seems to have made his first musical-theatre appearance (after several dramatic plays had preceded it) as the hero of a Royalty Theatre pantomime in 1805 (*Sinbad the Sailor, or The Spanish Clown*) and he returned as such regularly afterwards, affubled with a variety of subtitles such as *Sinbad the Sailor, or Old Bob Ridley and Davy Jones Locker,* but he did not so much as rate a major burlesque in Britain, although a minor one by Frank Green was produced at Edinburgh in 1879, and another toured in the early 1880s by Emily Duncan's company. In America, he did a little better, becoming the hero of *Sinbad, or The Maid of Balsora,* written by Harry B Smith and played under the management of David Henderson at the Opera House, Chicago (11 June 1891)—with Edie Foy as its chief (apart from the scenery and machinery)—attraction, and later at the Garden Theater, New York (27 June 1892).

Having almost wholly disappeared from the stage in the 20th century, *Sinbad* made a slight comeback as a British pantomime subject in the 1970s and 1980s, in a tiny reaction against the sad shrinkage of the Christmas repertoire to a half dozen over-and-over-repeated titles.

Plate 358. **Singin' in the Rain.** *Danielle Carson, Tommy Steele, Sarah Payne and Roy Castle in London's long-running hit.*

SINGIN' IN THE RAIN Musical in 2 acts by Tommy Steele adapted from the screenplay by Adolph Green and Betty Comden. Songs by Arthur Freed and Nacio Herb Brown. London Palladium, 30 June 1983.

A Chicago lawyer named Rosenfield, having persuaded from MGM the rights to use the story and songs of the milestone movie musical *Singin' in the Rain* in a stage show, took the package to Britain and to producer Harold Fielding to get it made up into a stage musical and put into the theatre. Fielding called in the cockney musical star Tommy Steele who penned the stage adaptation, whilst his office organized replacement songs for some from the film which had suddenly—when it came to the point—become ''unavailable,'' and the resultant piece was produced at the London Palladium, with Steele not only starring as movie star Don Lockwood, but also directing. Roy Castle (Cosmo) performed ''Be A Clown'' (instead of ''Make 'em Laugh'') and tapped out ''Fit as a Fiddle'' and ''Moses Supposes'' with the star, and soubrette Danielle Carson played, sang and danced the role which Debbie Reynolds had danced and mimed (''Would You,'' ''Good Morning'' and ''I Can't Give You Anything But Love'' replacing ''All I Do Is Dream of You'') and planted a cream cake in the face of glamorous Sarah Payne (Lina Lamont) who, in this version, got to sing a corncrake version of ''Temptation,'' which had been only briefly heard, unsung, in the movie. Steele, attempting neither an American accent nor any kind of Gene Kelly imitation, scored on all fronts, whether pounding out the low comedy, tapping with Castle, duetting with Carson, crooning ''You Are My Lucky Star'' or flinging himself into a very individual and very wet reproduction of the famous rain scene and title song.

Singin' in the Rain broke all records for a musical at the London Palladium, closing only when Steele finally cried enough after 894 nights of being drenched to the skin. It was then only a matter of time before the show went to Broadway. However, without reference to his

British partners, Rosenfield announced a Broadway production solo, simultaneously slapping out Broadway lawsuits in the direction of even peripheral members of the London team which kept them busy too long to fight back. And so, *Singin' in the Rain* opened on Broadway in a different stage version and a very different production (Gershwin Theater, New York 2 July 1985). It closed after appalling notices, a very forced run of 367 performances, and what was rumored, following an amazingly—even for the musical theatre—masochistic determination to throw good backers' money after bad, to be the biggest deficit in Broadway history. A touring production which followed hired the London production's choreographer and stayed alive a little longer and less painfully.

Fielding, having subsequently succeeded in recouping the songs his colleague had ''lost'' and replacing them in the show's score, revived his London version with Steele for two British provincial seasons, a season in Tokyo and a return season at the London Palladium (1989, 156 performances), whilst sub-licensing a subsequent tour with Paul Nicholas in the central role (1995) and the first foreign-language production in Hungary (ad György G Denes, Mihály Batkai), South Africa and Italy. The world's amateur societies, however, and many a professional house who knew not better as well, got lumbered. When they applied for permission and performance materials for *Singin' in the Rain* they had the flop Broadway version (with a Lina Lamont who dropped her corncraking to perform an elaborate song-and-dance routine!) pressed upon them. Dresden's Staatsoperette, which introduced the piece to Germany, was—unlike Budapest—amongst them. So was France. An uncredited version with French text but lyrics in English was produced by the Opéra Royal de Wallonie at Liège (17 December 1999) with Isabelle Georges and Joel Mitchell featured, and it subsequently made its way south to be seen around France. And so, amazingly, was Britain's National Theatre which hosted what it insisted was an amateur performance (only the original version being licensed for professional production in Britain) from the West Yorkshire Playhouse for five summer weeks on the stage of the Olivier Theatre in 2000 (22 June). Paul Robinson and Rebecca Thornhill were the leading ''amateurs.''

Hungary: Fővárosi Operettszínház *Ének az esőben* 24 March 1989; Germany: Staatsoperette, Dresden 15 April 1994; France: Opéra, Avignon 22 January 2000, Théâtre de la Porte-Saint-Martin 17 January 2001

Recordings: original cast (Safari), US tour cast (JAY)

SIRAUDIN, [Pierre] Paul [Désiré] (b Paris, 19 December 1812; d Enghien-les-Bains, 8 September 1883).

A fashionable confectioner in Paris's Rue de Paix (''for twenty years one of the instutions of Paris, [he] rivalled with Boissier's in the production of sweetmeats and those elegant caskets containing them that are bought up at such extravagant prices for New Year's Eve''), and an assiduous Parisian first-nighter, Paul Siraudin was also the author, or normally the co-author (for he was reputedly an ideas man rather than a dialoguist) of examples of every kind of theatrical piece, and he ended up with his name attached to two of the most memorable theatrical pieces of his time: the drama *Le Courrier de Lyon* (w Eugène Moreau, Alfred Delacour) and the Charles Lecocq opéra-comique *La Fille de Madame Angot* (w Clairville, Victor Koning).

His other credits, in a playwriting career spanning nearly 60 years, ranged from comedies for the Palais-Royal and drama at the Châtelet (*Le Deluge universal* w Clairville) or the Ambigu (*Canaille et cie* w Clairville), to contributions to the Thérésa féeries (*La Cocotte aux oeufs d'or, La Reine Carotte*), revue (Hervé's *La Revue pour rien* with its burlesque *Roland à Rongeveaux, Paris Revue* at the Châtelet, *La Revue en ville, La Revue n'est pas au coin du quai* at the Variétés) and burlesque (*Paul faut rester!,* burlesque of *Paul Forestier*), to vaudevilles, large and small, comedy and to opérette where, alongside his one huge success, he also teamed with Jules Moinaux on the splendidly comical tale of *Le Voyage de MM Dunanan père et fils* for Offenbach.

In spite of these two memorable musical-theatre successes, however, Siraudin contributed little to the regular opérettic stage after *La Fille de Madame Angot,* collaborating only on the enjoyable *La Marquise des rues* and, after his retirement from confectionery to a richly luxurious bachelor life between the rue Clichy and Enghien-les-Bains, on the vaudevillesque *Fla-Fla,* on each occasion in league with writer Gaston Hirsch and composer Hervé.

1846 **Le Veuf du Malabar** (Alexandre Doche/w Adrien-Robert Basset) 1 act Opéra-Comique 27 May

1861 **Le Jardinier galant** (Ferdinand Poïse/w Adolphe de Leuven) Opéra-Comique 4 March

1862 **Le Voyage de MM Dunanan père et fils** (Offenbach/w Jules Moinaux) Théâtre des Bouffes-Parisiens 23 March

1862 **La Fanfare de Saint-Cloud** (Hervé/w Ernest Blum) 1 act Délassements-Comiques 30 May

1866 **Le Barbier de Molarido** (Victor Robillard) Palais-Royal 5 April

1867 **Malbrough s'en va-t-en guerre** (Georges Bizet, Léo Delibes, Isidore Legouix, Émile Jonas/w William Busnach) Théâtre de l'Athénée 15 December

1868 **Paul faut rester!** (Robillard/w Marc Leprévost) 1 act Palais-Royal 22 February

1871 **El Señor Inigo** (Robillard) 1 act Folies-Bergère 24 December

1872 **La Fille de Madame Angot** (Charles Lecocq/w Clairville, Victor Koning) Fantaisies-Parisiennes, Brussels 4 December

1879 **La Marquise des rues** (Hervé/w Gaston Hirsch) Théâtre des Bouffes-Parisiens 22 February

1879 **Jean qui pleure et Jean qui rit** (Franz) 1 act Ba-ta-clan 15 March

1886 **Fla-Fla** (Hervé/w Hirsch) Théâtre des Menus-Plaisirs 4 September

LE SIRE DE VERGY Opéra-bouffe in 3 acts by Robert de Flers and Gaston de Caillavet. Music by Claude Terrasse. Théâtre des Variétés, Paris, 16 April 1903.

The production of *Le Sire de Vergy* under the management of Fernand Samuel at the Théâtre des Variétés in 1903 marked the most substantial and successful staging of a genuine opéra-bouffe since the palmy days of Hervé and Offenbach three decades earlier. The team of authors de Flers and de Caillavet and composer Terrasse had already embarked into the burlesque area with the classical *Les Travaux d'Hercule* (1901), and this time they followed the same path taken by Offenbach (*Orphée* to *Geneviève de Brabant*) and moved from Ancient Greece to medieval France—an area which Terrasse had already visited in his recent *Au temps des croisades*—with a burlesque of the savage tale of Gabrielle de Vergy, operaticized in all its horror by Carafa (1816) and Mercadante (1828) and previously burlesqued, although only in one act, by Hector Monréal and Henri Blondeau, to music by Demarquette, in 1871 (Folies-Marigny 11 November).

Whereas the original Vergy killed his wife's lover and served up his heart for her dinner, the opéra-bouffe Vergy (Guy) lives quite contentedly with his philandering lady (Anna Tariol-Baugé) and her boyfriend, Coucy (Albert Brasseur). Coucy, however, is embarrassed at being such a comfy cuckolder, so he persuades Vergy to leave his nice home and go off to the crusades with his energetic neighbor Millepertuis (Claudius), entrusting the key of Mme Vergy's chastity belt to him. By the time Vergy returns, the Coucy-Gabrielle affair is on the rocks, but the absent husband has had a grand time. Like his *Geneviève de Brabant* forebears, he stopped off at a party on the way to the crusades and has been having a ball with the sumptuous Mitzy (Ève Lavallière) whom he has brought home, disguised as a Saracen captive, along with a couple of friends (Prince, Max Dearly). Millepertuis, however, seems determined that the story shall have its proper ending. All is dramatically revealed, but Coucy has no more wish to be eviscerated than Vergy has to carry out the operation and all ends as cosily as it started, with a bit of beef from the butcher replacing the fatal dinner.

Terrasse's score supported the burlesque brio of the book happily, with Brasseur reaping one of the comic highlights with his "Je suis l'sire de Coucy-Couça" and Prince and Dearly, ludicrous and laden down with chains, scoring with a comical prisoners' duo, whilst Mlle Lavallière knocked all eyes out with a version of a belly dance which moved every part of her anatomy.

Produced in a period when the French musical theatre was in a veritable trough of despond, *Le Sire de Vergy* brought forth not only a good deal of critical enthusiasm but also of public interest. It was played for 110 performances at the Variétés, and thereafter in the provinces, but it failed to travel very effectively. In 1904 it was produced at Budapest's Király Színház (as "Me, You, He"), with József Németh in the role of Vergy, and in Milan, and the following year, rather surprisingly, it appeared under the management of Tom Davis, in the West End of London. Arthur Sturgess had the unenviable job of making the wholly sexual tale acceptable to the moral dragons of the British press and letters-to-the-editor columns, and musical director Theo Wendt was allowed to botch the score. John Le Hay (Vergy) starred opposite the Hungarian actress Aurélie Révy (Gabrielle), Aubrey Fitzgerald (Coucy) and comedienne Gracie Leigh (Mitzy) in what was one of the quickest failures of the era (7 performances).

The piece has continued to be well thought of by commentators and that-kind-of-music lovers, and a successful small-scale revival was staged in Paris in 1952 (Théâtre Labruyère 31 October) with comedians Roger Pierre and Jean-Marc Thibault starred and without the expensive orchestra before the piece returned to the big time, in 2000, when a new production, with Bernard Alane and Fabienne Guyon featured, was mounted at the Bouffes-Parisiens (21 April).

Hungary: Király Színhaz *Én, te, ő* 13 May 1904; UK: Apollo Theatre *The Gay Lord Vergy* 30 September 1905

DIE SIRENE Operette in 3 acts by A M Willner and Leo Stein. Music by Leo Fall. Johann Strauss-Theater, Vienna, 5 January 1911.

The famous Parisian police-chief Philippe Aristide Fouché (Max Brod) sets Lolotte Boncourt, the siren of the title (Mizzi Günther) and a member of his private band of feminine spies, to entrap Armand de Ravaillac (Louis Treumann), who has been writing satirical letters against the Emperor. Lolotte succeeds, by the end of the second act, both in fulfilling her mission and in falling in love with her victim, but Fouché's jubilant unmasking of Armand gives away his spy's identity and she thus loses her love for the length of the third act.

Die Sirene played 67 times at Vienna's Johann Strauss-Theater and, although it did not follow its composer's *Der fidele Bauer, Die Dollarprinzessin* and *Die geschiedene Frau* on to major international triumph, it was nevertheless successfully staged in Germany and in America. Charles Frohman's Broadway production was mounted in style. Donald Brian, hero of *The Merry Widow,* was Armand, lovely Julia Sanderson played Lolotte and Frank Moulan as Baron Siegfried Bazilos, ex-Fouché—for the piece had for some reason been reset in Vienna!—headed the comedy with Elizabeth Firth from the cast of London's *Merry Widow* as his errant wife. The 14 numbers of Fall's score were, inevitably, augmented with extraneous songs, a list which included the Arthurs/David music-hall song "I Want to Sing in Opera" made famous by Wilkie Bard (and here sung by Will West), and pieces by Howard Talbot, Egbert van Alstyne and Jerome Kern. America's *The Siren* ran for a very respectable four months before going out touring.

The title *La Sirène* had previously been used for Auber and Scribe's opéra comique of 1844.

USA: Knickerbocker Theater *The Siren* 28 August 1911; Germany: Carl-Schultze Theater, Hamburg 25 October 1911

SISSY Singspiel in 2 acts by Ernst and Hubert Marischka based on a play by Ernst Decsey and Gustav Holm. Music by Fritz Kreisler. Theater an der Wien, Vienna, 23 December 1932.

The celebrated violinist Fritz Kreisler had ventured successfully into the world of the musical theatre with a share of the score for the 1919 Broadway musical *Apple Blossoms* (Globe Theater 6 October, 256 performances) during the decade, during and following the War, which he had spent in America. It was more than another decade, however, before he wrote his only other theatre score, for Hubert Marischka and the Theater an der Wien.

Marischka and his brother, Ernst, adapted their libretto from a play which had embroidered a conventional and fictionalized version of the lead-up to the historical marriage of the Empress Elisabeth ("Sissy") and the Emperor Franz Josef. The monarch had originally been—in this version of the "facts"—intended as the husband of Sissy's sister, Helena, who in any case preferred the Prince von Thurn und Taxis. To this piece of period romance, Kreisler provided a score part of which was worked around the themes of some of his most successful compositions, principally for the violin. The Caprice Viennoise was turned into "Ich glaube das Glück hält mich heute im Arm," the Liebeslied became another duet "Dein Küss hat mir den Frühling gebracht," whilst the melody which was to become "Stars in Your Eyes" (and which had already done duty in *Apple Blossoms*) this time made up into Sissy's solo "Ich wär' so gern einmal verliebt."

Paula Wessely starred as the young Empress-to-be, with Hans Jaray as Franz Josef, Hubert Marischka in the role of Herzog Max of Bavaria, Maria Tauber as Helena, and Erika Wagner (Erzherzogin Sophie), Charlotte Waldon (Ludovika, Max's wife), Otto Maran (Thurn und Taxis), Fritz Imhoff (von Kempen) and Irene Ziláhy (Ilona Varady, ballet dancer) amongst the other principals. Ludwig Itznegg, Hanns Schöbinger and Egon von Jordan succeeded to the role of the Emperor, Hilde Schulz and Anny Coty to that of Sissy and Ernst Tautenhayn, Kurt Lessen and Imhoff all played Max as the show compiled a straight 289-performance run, followed by a quick reprise three years later (25 October 1935) of a further 24 performances (300th, 7 November), all making up the best record of any new piece produced at the Theater an der Wien in the last decade of Hubert Marischka's management. It went on from that success to periodic revivals in Austria up to the present day.

Although *Sissy* was not played on Broadway, it was picked up by Hollywood where it was used as the basis for the film *The King Steps Out,* a version which again used a partial Kreisler score and allowed Grace Moore to sing "Stars in your Eyes." It was a different film, however, that got *Sissy* its most considerable exposure. A series of non-musical films about Elisabeth of Austria made in the 1950s with Romy Schneider starring were (and are) highly popular in France, and as a result Henri Varna of Paris's Théâtre Mogador ventured a production of *Sissy,* turned into an opérette à grand spectacle in the habitual style of the house. Varna himself, publisher Jean Marietti, librettist Marc-Cab and René Richard all had book credits whilst Gil Vidal and Françoise Doué appeared as hero and heroine for a slightly forced 11-month run which, nevertheless, established the piece in France.

The romanticized-for-ever Sissy appeared on the French opérette à grand spectacle stage again, at the Théâtre Mogador, when she was portrayed by Raymonde Devarennes as a supporting character to a fictional romantic pair (Marcel Merkès, Paulette Merval) in the 1967 musical *Vienne chante et danse,* whilst in 1991 a *Sissi* with music by Francis Lopez was produced at Paris's Eldorado (Nadine Rotschild, Claude Dufresne, Daniel Ringold, 8 September), and in 1992 Vienna turned out yet another and highly successful variation on the theme (*Elisabeth,* Sylvester Levay/Michael Kunze Theater an der Wien 3 September), confirming the Empress Elisabeth, this time impersonated by Pia Douwes, as a well-established cliché of the romantic operettic stage. *Elisabeth* ran for more than 1,300 nights in Vienna and was subsequently seen in Hungary (ad Péter Sziámi Müller Szeged 17 August 1996), Scandinavia, Germany and in all all-women version in Japan (16 February 1996).

An Austrian musical entitled *Sissi und Romy,* produced at the Mörbisch lake theatre in 1991 (Roland Baumgartner/Daniel Pascal 13 July), was based on the films and attempted to point parallels between the life of the Empress and the life of the actress who played her on film. Claudia Dallinger portrayed the actress/empress.

France: Théâtre Mogador *Sissi, futur imperatrice* 14 March 1959

Recordings: selection in French (Philips), *Sissi und Romy* original cast members (Polydor)

SISTERS Operett in 3 acts and 7 scenes by István Békeffy. Music by Lajos Lajtai. Király Színház, Budapest, 10 January 1930.

Rózsi Bársony and Ilona Titkos played the parts of Rózsi and Anni, two little orphan girls from Pest who are taken in by the Müller family, father (Árpád Latabár sr), mother (Ella Gombaszïgi) and daughter Ildiko (Magda Kun). The girls follow in their departed mother's footsteps and take up dancing. They dance so well that by Act II, spurred on by Anni's disappointment at the engagement of her farmer swain Gábor (József Sziklai) to Ildiko, they have left Pest behind, and become a sister act at the Paris Moulin-Rouge. Gábor follows, and sees Anni courted by the rich and easy Parisians, and almost wed to the Baron Radványi (Kornél d'Arrigó), before she listens to his professions of love, snaps out of her Parisian daydream and flees from the bright lights and barons back to Hungary. Rózsi and her Tommy (Oszkár Dénes) follow close behind and, as the temptations of an American tour swirl round the "Sisters," they sit back to take count of what happiness is.

The show's score was very dance-heavy. In the first scene Anni and Rózsi's schoolgirl chums set things rolling, and the sisters, deciding to be "like mama," launched into an up-to-date fox-trot as an extension to each of two duets. In the second act, the performance of the sister act allowed the girls to go through a Hawaiian routine, an English dance and an Hungarian csárdás, and the tango. The fox-trot, the slow-fox-trot, and a good old-fashioned march were all featured in the finale of a piece where every number was stretched by a considerable dance break. In the final act, Anni had a little song and dance with a bundle of kiddies.

Sisters proved a decided success in Budapest, and within months it had moved up to Vienna (ad Béla Jenbach) where it was produced at Erich Müller's Johann Strauss-Theater with Irén Biller and Grete Hornik starred as the two girls, Robert Nästlberger (Gábor) and Ernst Tautenhayn (Tommy) as their boys, and Richard Waldemar (Müller), Felix Donbrowski (Radvány) and Daisy Solms (Ildiko) amongst the other principals. It stayed for a good run of two months.

Austria: Johann Strauss-Theater 22 October 1930

SKIPPED BY THE LIGHT OF THE MOON Musical farcical comedy in 2 acts adapted from *A Gay City* by George R Sims. Lyrics by Percy Marshall. Music by George Pack and Henry W May. Rand's Opera House, Troy, NY, 24 September 1883; Fifth Avenue Theater, New York, 14 April 1884.

Skipped by the Light of the Moon was a latter-day farce-comedy, in the line of the American shows of Charles Hoyt and his contemporaries, which toured incessantly and with singular success in English-speaking countries in the last part of the 19th century. The history of its development began in 1881 when Charles Majilton commissioned a play for his famous family troupe from the master of the provincial comedy, George Sims. The resulting piece, *A Gay City* (Nottingham 8 September 1881), a lively imbroglio involving a pair of husbands on the loose, mistaken identities and pursuing wives, with a lost baby thrown in for good measure, proved absolutely to the taste of the kind of rural and provincial city dates in which the Majiltons prospered and it remained in their repertoire for many years. One night, at Carlisle, two gentlemen sat in the front row with hats on their laps. As the play progressed, they scribbled the dialogue onto a pile of visiting cards, dropping the filled cards into the hats, and finally walked out of the theatre with *A Gay City* on, rather than in, their heads.

The two gentlemen went home to America and, not long after, a pirated version of *A Gay City,* decorated with popular songs and the odd speciality in a notably less haphazard way than the standard American farce-comedy of the period, and retitled *Skipped by the Light of the Moon,* appeared on the stage at Troy, NY, under the management of and starring Louis Harrison (Felix Crackle) and Johnnie Gourlay (Obadiah Dangle). Emma Schultz (Sarah), Josie Batchelder (Myra Dangle) and Ed Morris (Garnishee McIntyre) as the pursuing policeman of the affair headed the supporting cast, and the press marveled "it has some plot worth mentioning and does not lack continuity. It has plot and continuity enough to make the dialogue and situations extremely ludicrous and keep and audience in a laugh for two hours and a half. . . ." *Skipped by the Light of the Moon* duly proved as popular on the American touring circuits as the parent show had been in England and it trouped solidly for a decade through America and onto the Pacific circuit with an ever-varying musical content, songs being pilfered and pasted in to its running-order en route with the same abandon that the original play had been. John Gourlay introduced *Skipped by the Light of the Moon* to Australia in 1887 and he played it there for many years, being joined in 1893 by Harry Shine and George Walton, both members of well-known British families of comedians who had come out to try their luck on the other side of the world. Walton and Gourlay kept the piece going around Australia for a number of years, in repertoire with such pieces as *Milky White* and George Sims's *Corsican Brothers* burlesque.

It was Walton who ultimately took *Skipped by the Light of the Moon* back to Britain. Billed as "the electrical musical comedy," with Sims given his author's due (and, having long since sued to regain his property, his royalties) and the music credited to the Australian musical director George Pack and to Walton's own conductor Henry W May (but including numbers by such composers as Ivan Caryll, R G Knowles, Milton Wellings and the ballad composer Harry Trotère), it opened at Reading and, 15 years behind the original play, set off on a very long and lucrative career in the provinces. Both the book and score were regularly updated with topicalities and new tunes, and its success was such that in 1899 an inexperienced producer brought it into London under the title *A Good Time* (27 April). The music was now credited to Caryll, May and to Alfred Ketélby. The piece was certainly not London fodder, and it quickly returned to the provinces to see out a second decade of prosperity in its natural habitat.

Australia: Bijou Theatre, Melbourne 23 April 1887; UK: Royal County Theatre, Reading 24 August 1896, Shaftesbury Theatre *A Good Time* 27 April 1899

SKYSCRAPER Musical comedy in 2 acts by Peter Stone based on the play *Dream Girl* by Elmer Rice. Lyrics by Sammy Cahn. Music by James van Heusen. Lunt-Fontanne Theater, New York, 13 November 1965.

Based rather distantly on the 1945 play *Dream Girl* (the leading character rather than the plot survived), *Skyscraper* was a musical made up largely of a series of day-dream sequences, the escapist musings of antique-shopkeeper Georgina Allerton (Julie Harris) who is refusing to sell her home to Bert Bushman (Dick O'Neill), a chap who wants to demolish it to build a skyscraper. She does, however, accept an invitation to dinner with his architect brother, Tim (Peter L Marshall), who tries to explain modern urban beauty to her. Georgina's shop-assistant Roger (Charles Nelson Reilly), who has been bought by the Bushmans, proposes to her to get her to leave the building but she snaps out of her dreaming and opts instead for Tim and demolition.

Cahn and van Husen's score had the advantage of being able to spread itself over reality and dreamland, but it was reality which brought up the most successful song of the score, Tim's "Everybody Has the Right to Be Wrong," and also the most amusing production number, an incidental piece choreographed by Michael Kidd in which a construction foreman forces two indifferent site workers to keep up the uncouthly macho image of their genre by whistling and jawing at passing girls.

Feuer and Martin's production of *Skyscraper* went through a fair if slightly forced run of 248 performances without becoming a genuine success.

Recording: original cast (Capitol)

SLADE, Julian [Penkivil] (b London, 28 May 1930). Composer of several fresh and unpretentious musical scores for the English stage of the 1950s and 1960s, amongst which was one record-breaking hit.

Julian Slade studied at the Bristol Old Vic drama school and joined the Old Vic company at that city's Theatre Royal in 1951. He appeared briefly on the stage, but soon turned his attention to writing and, in collaboration with two other company members, supplied the Old Vic with the highly successful Christmas revue *Christmas in King Street* (1952). He provided the incidental music for a production of *The Duenna,* which subsequently transferred to London, for local productions of *Love for Love* and *She Stoops to Conquer,* and for *The Merchant of Venice* at Stratford-on-Avon (1953), and collaborated with Dorothy Reynolds on a first musical play, a piece about Santa Claus called *The Merry Gentleman,* as a successor to the previous year's seasonal revue. A comic-opera version of *The Comedy of Errors* was produced on BBC-TV in 1954, but it was a second Slade/Reynolds musical, *Salad Days* ("I Sit in the Sun," "We're Looking for a Piano," "The Time of My Life"), written later the same year as an end-of-term romp for a company who had been playing largely more serious things, which hit the jackpot. Following its brief Bristol season, it moved to London where it became the longest-running musical play in the West End's history up to that time.

Slade co-wrote and composed four further works with Miss Reynolds, the slightly more substantial *Free as Air* (1957), another seasonal piece, *Hooray for Daisy* (1959), a version of *Christmas in King Street* stiffened with an amusing libretto and entitled *Follow That Girl* (1960, "Follow That Girl") and *Wildest Dreams* (1960), before teaming with playwright Robin Miller and Alan Pryce-Jones on his largest venture to date, a musical adaptation of *Vanity Fair.* This was not a success, and Slade returned to writing for smaller stages with incidental music for Shakespeare plays at Bristol and London's Regents Park Open Air Theatre, and musical play adaptations of *The Knight of the Burning Pestle* as *Nutmeg and Ginger,* of Nancy Mitford's *The Pursuit of Love,* and of Pinero's *The Schoolmistress,* under the title *Out of Bounds.* He also arranged Fraser-Simson's *The Hums of Pooh* with some additional music of his own into a children's musical (*Winnie the Pooh*) which was played a number of times as a seasonal entertainment in London and also in Germany (*Pu—der Bär* ad James Krüss).

Another Pinero adaptation, a musical version of the romantic *Trelawny of the Wells* (*Trelawny*), initially staged at Bristol, followed the *Salad Days* trail into the West End but, although it showed up as perhaps Slade's most substantial and accomplished piece, it had a reasonable rather than a fine run there. This was perhaps partly because *Trelawny* appeared in London in the same year as *Jesus Christ Superstar.* The passing of an era which

Plate 359. **Julian Slade's** Vanity Fair *featured Frances Cuka as Becky Sharp and Sybil Thorndike, in a rare musical appearance, as Miss Crawley.*

that ''meeting at the crossroads'' represented meant that Slade's style of work was thereafter less in demand than before. Although *Salad Days* continues to be revived, and 1991 saw a reprise of *Nutmeg and Ginger* at London's Orange Tree Theatre, the composer's most recent works, a féerique musical version of J M Barrie's *Dear Brutus* (w Kit Hesketh Harvey/Veronica Flint-Shipman) and of Nancy Mitford's *Love in a Cold* Climate (w Eden Phillips), remain, to date, unproduced.

1953 **The Merry Gentleman** (Dorothy Reynolds) Theatre Royal, Bristol 24 December

1954 **Salad Days** (Reynolds) Vaudeville Theatre 5 August

1956 **The Comedy of Errors** (Lionel Harris, Robert McNab) Arts Theatre 28 March

1957 **Free as Air** (Reynolds) Savoy Theatre 6 June

1959 **Hooray for Daisy** (Reynolds) Theatre Royal, Bristol 23 December; Lyric Theatre, Hammersmith 20 December 1960

1960 **Follow That Girl** (Reynolds) Vaudeville Theatre 17 March

1960 **Wildest Dreams** (Reynolds) Everyman Theatre, Cheltenham 20 September; Vaudeville Theatre 3 August 1961

1962 **Vanity Fair** (Robin Miller, Alan Pryce-Jones) Queen's Theatre 27 November

1963 **Nutmeg and Ginger** (Slade) Everyman Theatre, Cheltenham 29 October; Orange Tree Theatre 13 June

1967 **The Pursuit of Love** (Slade) Theatre Royal, Bristol 24 May

1970 **Winnie the Pooh** (Harold Fraser-Simson ad/Slade) Phoenix Theatre 17 December

1972 **Trelawny** (w Aubrey Woods, George Rowell) Theatre Royal, Bristol 12 January; Sadler's Wells Theatre 27 June

1973 **Out of Bounds** (Slade) Theatre Royal, Bristol 26 December

SLAUGHTER, Walter [Alfred] (b London, 17 February 1860; d London, 2 March 1908). Successful Victorian composer of musical comedy, comic opera and children's shows.

Brought up in London, Slaughter studied music under Georges Jacobi, musical director of the Alhambra, and was both organist at St Andrews Church and a 'cellist and pianist at the South London and other music halls prior to becoming a musical director in a series of West End theatres. He spent three years at the Theatre Royal, Drury Lane, under Sir Augustus Harris (1887–90), and also held engagements at the Prince's, the St James's under George Alexander (1890), the Avenue, the Vaudeville and, in his last days, as the first musical director for Oswald Stoll at the London Coliseum (1904–6).

He composed some ballet music for the South London Theatre and some individual songs, including the popular ''Dear Homeland'' (1894) for the Moore and Burgess Minstrels, and found his first theatre success as a lyric composer with the score for the little all-women operetta *An Adamless Eden* (1882), played in Britain and in America by Lila Clay's ladies' company and their imitators. He confirmed that success with a pretty score for what is, a century and many shows later, still the most successful musical version of *Alice in Wonderland* to have been produced (1886).

He had some more substantial success with the score to the medieval comic opera *Marjorie* produced by the Carl Rosa Light Opera Company (1890), and contributed to the Gaiety Theatre's *Cinder-Ellen Up Too Late* (1891), but he achieved his greatest success when he paired with Basil Hood to produce the outstanding musical comedy *Gentleman Joe* as a vehicle for low comic Arthur Roberts. Of his further collaborations with Hood, *The French Maid* gave him a second and even longer-lived international success, *Dandy Dan, the Lifeguardsman* proved a second happy vehicle for Roberts and *Orlando Dando* did similar if less long service for for Dan Leno. *An English Daisy,* written with Seymour Hicks, won a Broadway production (if not a London one), but the most successful of his subsequent works was another children's piece, *Bluebell in Fairyland,* produced by Charles Frohman and played by Hicks and Ellaline Terriss. Slaughter provided the basic score, subsequently riddled through with interpolations, for what was to turn out to be the most popular Christmas entertainment of its time. A show written with the visiting American comedian and playwright Richard Carle under the title *Little Miss Modesty* seems to have remained unproduced.

Slaughter also contributed to the score of the 1899 revue *A Dream of Whitaker's Almanac* (w Florian Pascal, Walter W Hedgecock) and composed much incidental music for plays, notably those produced at the St James's during his employment there—Walter Frith's *Molière,* Quinton and Hamilton's *Lord Anerley,* Haddon Chambers's *The Idler* (1891), the original production of Wilde's *Lady Windermere's Fan* (1892), Henry James's *Guy Domville* (1895) and *The Prisoner of Zenda* (1896)—and Mrs Langtry's *Enemies* at the Princess's (1886).

His wife **Louisa [Elizabeth] LOWE** (''Mlle Luna'') (b Southwark, 30 August 1861) was the elder of the two well-known dancing daughters of **John Lauri** [John George LOWE], longtime music-hall and pantomime dance star, and ballet-master at the Alhambra Theatre, who, as Mlles Stella [Stella LOWE] (b Haverstock Hill, 12 July 1863; d 17 September 1907) and Luna, appeared as featured soloists in many of the Alhambra spectaculars, and later at Drury Lane, the Princess's and other London houses. Her brother, **George LAURI** [John George LOWE] (d Sydney, 4 January 1909), after playing as a musical-comedy comedian in Britain and, in tandem with his wife, soubrette **Marietta NASH**, in America, made himself a fine career in Australia, being for many year's the colony's foremost comic star of musical comedy before cutting his throat when he feared his fame was faltering.

Slaughter's daughter Marjorie Slaughter, the composer of a number of songs, also wrote the score for the operetta *The Constable and the Pictures* (1 act Arthur Wimperis, Godfrey Turner Devonshire Park Theatre, Eastbourne, 1907) played at the Tivoli by Agnes and Alec Fraser and M R Morand, and supplemented her father's music for a two-act comic opera *A Tangerine Tangle,* staged for one copyright performance after his death at the age of 48 from dropsy.

1880 **Change Partners** (''Lewis Clifton,'' Joseph J Dilley) 1 act tour

1882 **An Adamless Eden** (Henry Savile Clarke) 1 act Opera Comique 13 December

1882 **His Only Coat** (J J Dallas) 1 act Gaiety Theatre 22 May

1883 **Sly and Shy** (A R Phillips) 1 act Princess Theatre, Edinburgh 21 May

1885 **The Casting Vote** (Walter Helmore) 1 act Prince's Theatre 7 October

1886 **Sappho** (Harry Lobb) 1 act Opera Comique 10 February

1886 **Alice in Wonderland** (Savile Clarke) Prince of Wales Theatre 23 December

1889 **The New Corsican Brothers** (Cecil Raleigh) Royalty Theatre 20 November

1890 **Marjorie** (Dilley, Clifton) Prince of Wales Theatre 18 January

1890 **The Rose and the Ring** (Savile Clarke) Prince of Wales Theatre 20 December

1892 **Donna Luiza** (Basil Hood) 1 act Prince of Wales Theatre 23 March

1893 **The Crossing Sweeper** (Hood) 1 act Gaiety Theatre 8 April

1893 **Peggy's Plot** (Somerville Gibney) 1 act St George's Hall 20 December

1894 **A Big Bandit** (T Malcolm Watson) 1 act St George's Hall 30 April

1894 **Melodramania** (Watson) 1 act St George's Hall 27 December

1895 **Gentleman Joe** (Hood) Prince of Wales Theatre 2 March

1896 **The French Maid** (Hood) Theatre Royal, Bath 4 April; Terry's Theatre 24 April 1897

1896 **Belinda** (B C Stephenson, Hood) Prince's Theatre, Manchester 5 October

1897 **Dandy Dan, the Lifeguardsman** (Hood) Belfast 23 August; Lyric Theatre, London 4 December

1897 **The Duchess of Dijon** (Hood) Theatre Royal, Portsmouth 20 September

1897 **Hans Andersen's Fairytales** (Hood) Terry's Theatre 23 December

1898 **Orlando Dando** (Hood) Grand Theatre, Fulham 1 August

1898 **Her Royal Highness** (Hood) Vaudeville Theatre 3 September

1900 **A Sporting Knight-Mayor** (Frederick Bowyer/C Clark, Murray King) sketch Theatre Royal, Bournemouth 13 April

1901 **You and I** (Aubrey Hopwood/Seymour Hicks) 1 act Vaudeville Theatre 24 April

1901 **Bluebell in Fairyland** (Hopwood, Charles H Taylor/Hicks) Vaudeville 18 December

1902 **An English Daisy** (Hicks) Royal County Theatre, Kingston 11 August

1903 **Little Hans Andersen** (Hood) Adelphi Theatre 23 December

1905 **Hamlet** burlesque (Herbert Shelley) sketch London Coliseum 7 May

1905 **The Princess and the Troubadour** (Roland Carse) sketch London Coliseum 7 May

1905 **Pleasure Before Business** (Carse) sketch London colisuem 11 June

1905 **Fritz** (Rutland Barrington) sketch London Coliseum 3 July

1905 **Queah Keschna, or The Safe Cure** (J Hickory Wood) burlesque sketch London Coliseum 3 July

1905 **The Wishing Girl** (J Hickory Wood) sketch London Coliseum 17 July

1905 **The Charioteers, or a Roman Holiday** (Carse) London Coliseum 27 November

1905 **In Bells and Motley** (Carse/Rita Strauss, Thomas F G Coates) sketch London Coliseum 18 December

1905 **The Hooligan Band** scena in *Bluebell in Fairyland* (Aldwych Theatre)

1906 **S'Nero, or a Roman Bank Holiday** (Roland Carse/ Christopher Davis) 1 act London Coliseum January

1906 **The Troubles of Tuffin** (Carse/Arthur Shirley) sketch London Coliseum 12 March

1907 **Lady Tatters** (Carse/Herbert Leonard) Shaftesbury Theatre 31 August

1909 **A Tangerine Tangle** (w Marjorie Slaughter/Norman Slee) Vaudeville Theatre 2 July (copyright performance)

Other titles attributed: *Marie's Honeymoon* (1885), *The King and the Abbot* (1904), *The Cruise of the Great Britain*

SLEEP, Wayne (b Plymouth, 17 July 1948).

For a number of years a principal dancer with Britain's Royal Ballet, the diminutive Sleep moved into the musical theatre as Oblio in *The Point* (1976) and to create the role of Mister Mistoffolees/Quaxo in *Cats* (1980). He subsequently created the principal role in the ''Dance'' half of the entertainment *Song and Dance* (1982), played in pantomime, toured and televised with his own dance show (*The Hot Shoe Show*), and appeared in London as the MC in a revival of *Cabaret* (1986). He has subsequently masterminded and performed in several other dance performances and in 2000 choreographed a British tour of *Carousel.*

Autobiography: *Precious Little Sleep* (Boxtree Macmillan, 1996).

SLEZAK, Walter (b Vienna, 3 May 1902; d New York, 22 April 1983).

The son of the celebrated opera tenor Leo Slezak (who himself ventured into opéra-bouffe as Offenbach's *Barbe-bleue,* et al, and on to the operettic screen in *Der Vogelhändler, Gasparone,* et al), Walter Slezak came to the theatre after false starts in medicine and as a bank clerk. He began his career in Berlin where, in his twenties, he appeared as juvenile man in several musical plays. He subsequently visited Vienna (December 1928) to play Teddy Vandermeere in Oscar Straus's *Hochzeit in Hollywood* and Weyland in *Friederike* at the Johann Strauss-Theater and then succeeded to the role of Roger in *Meine Schwester und ich* in Berlin. Allegedly, he was hired to repeat his role in *Meine Schwester und ich* on Broadway by error—one Shubert brother saw original cast star Oskar Karlweis, the other hired replacement Slezak—but he went and he made a fine impression, laying the foundations for what would be the main part of his career, on the American stage and screen.

After *Meet My Sister* (1930, Eric Molinar), he went back to Europe and played alongside Fritzi Massary in her return to the musical stage in *Eine Frau, die weiss, was sie will* (1932) at the Berlin Metropoltheater. However, he soon joined the exodus from Germany and returned to America where he created the role of village schoolmaster Karl Reder (who ultimately gets the ingenue) in *Music in the Air* (1932) and, after a brief experience in the road-folding *Love! Out of the Window,* was cast in further mittel-European roles as the psychoanalyst Professor Volk in the unfortunate *May Wine* (1935) and the angel-marrying banker Harry in *I Married an Angel* (1938).

After a number of years in Hollywood, Slezak came back to the Broadway musical stage to star alongside Ezio Pinza as Panisse in the homogenized Pagnol show, *Fanny* (Tony Award). When the Metropolitan Opera House dipped into Operette with a version of *Der Zigeunerbaron* he appeared as Zsupán, and he later played regionally as Fagin in *Oliver!* and as Frosch in *Die Fledermaus.* Slezak committed suicide at the age of 80.

Amongst his musical film credits are *The Pirate* (1948), and the screen version of *Call Me Madam* (1953, Tantinnin).

Autobiography: *What Time's the Next Swan?* (Doubleday, Garden City, 1962)

SLOANE, A[lfred] Baldwin (b Baltimore, 28 August 1872; d Red Bank, NJ, 21 February 1925). Supplier of mostly utilitarian music to a generation of Broadway shows.

Interested by the musical theatre from a young age, ''Baldy'' Sloane was instrumental in the formation of an amateur musical group, the Paint and Powder Club, in his hometown, and he nominated himself as the composer of their 1894 show, *Mustapha,* and followed up with a *Midas* produced (21 February 1895) at Albaugh's Lyceum by the local Rouge et Blanc Club. When producer Edward Rice came to town with his *1492* company, the young composer succeeded in selling him some of his work and, as a result, he won his first professional stage exposure with some songs for the score for the ex-Boston amateur extravaganza *Excelsior Jr.* When the extravaganza was ultimately given a full-scale Rice production on Broadway it was a considerable success, and the facile and versatile young composer soon found opportunities coming from all sorts of sources. He composed the whole score for two further pieces by *Excelsior*'s prolific librettist, R A Barnet, the juvenile extravaganza *The Strange Adventures of Jack and the Beanstalk,* produced by Klaw and Erlanger at the Casino Theater, and another piece in the same vein, *Simple Simon,* which was introduced by the enterprising Boston Cadets, an amateur group for whom Barnet supplied shows with notable success over many a year. He contributed several numbers to the Anna Held vehicle *Papa's Wife,* and in the course of one year supplied much of the music for the revusical-spectaculars *Broadway to Tokio* and *A Million Dollars* and for the entertainment *The Giddy Throng* which had both a ''burlesque review'' and a ''musical sketch'' enclosed in its meanderings, and composed a burlesque of *Nell Gwynne* and also the score for the farce-comedy *Aunt Hannah* (''Ma Tiger Lily'').

Over the following years Sloane wrote or contributed to a large number of further such half-revue, half-musical comedy pieces, and had song successes with ''When You Ain't Got No Money, Well, You Needn't Come Around'' (ly: Clarence Brewster) as performed by May Irwin in America and Annie Wunsch in Vienna (''Wer Kein Gelt hat, der bleibt z' Haus''), and with the ''spectacular song'' ''My Rainbow Coon'' as delivered by Miss Mildred Claire. However, he also turned out the appreciable and charming score for the comic opera *The Mocking Bird* and for an old-fashioned girl-goes-to-costume-period-war piece called *Sergeant Kitty,* hailed by one journal (of obviously limited perspicacity) as ''a capital example of a real comic opera of the Strauss-Suppé-Millöcker school.'' George R White's production of Sloane's comic opera lasted but 55 performances on Broadway. The musician's most memorable credit—although the show's success cannot truthfully be said to be attributable to its score—was his composing credit on the original stage version of the fairy-tale spectacular *The Wizard of Oz* for which he supplied half the basic score (''In Michigan,'' ''Niccolo's Piccolo,'' etc). A score which, of course, is not the one that has come down the Yellow Brick Road to the 21st century.

With *Lady Teazle,* a 1904 comic-opera vehicle for Lillian Russell as Sheridan's *School for Scandal* heroine, Sloane reached the high point of his ambitions, and after its 57-performance pretty-much-failure, he devoted himself simply to turning out a stream of unexceptional musical scores for light entertainments of a mostly easygoing structural nature. He supplied the score for Chicago's advertisedly first-ever local revue, *All Round Chicago* (McVickers Theater 30 April 1905), provided Weber and Fields with music for their revusical *Hokey Pokey* (8 February 1912), *Hanky Panky* (5 August 1912) and *Roly Poly* (21 November 1912 w Goetz/Edgar Smith), and the little set-piece burlesques featured in those shows, and later wrote for Lew Fields's series of successful tired-businessman-and-his-wife-'n'-kids ''summer musicals.'' After a period ''out,'' during which he worked as a professional exhibition dancer, he returned to the musical stage with another musical—20-plus years on—for the Paint and Powder Club (*Dear Dorothy,* 1916), and contributed to John Murray Anderson's revue *Venus on Broadway* (Palais Royal 1 October 1917), to *The Greenwich Village Follies* in 1919 and 1920, and to something called *Fantastic Fricassée* produced in Greenwich Village in 1922. Amongst all this forgettable material, he did however turn out one hit song, ''Heaven Will Protect the Working Girl,'' as sung by Marie Dressler in the fantasy comedy *Tillie's Nightmare.*

For his last work, Sloane returned to what was labeled (by them) ''operetta,'' in the company of two of the more prolific junk librettists of his time, Harry Cort and George Stoddard, but although their show's Broadway run was short its composer did not see its last night. He had died shortly after the opening. Lambasted right and left, virtually from the beginning of his career, as a hack, Sloane rarely if ever won critical appreciation for his music, but he nevertheless seems to have held the confidence of producers, for his output was huge and his presence on Broadway, with at least one show at any time, was fairly continuous through nearly two decades. He proved, in the best of his pieces, that he was not without ability, but by and large he worked as a journeyman musician without much ambition, and with rare highlights.

1895 **Excelsior Jr** (w E E Rice, George Lowell Tracy/R A Barnet) Hammerstein's Olympia 29 November

1896 **The Strange Adventures of Jack and the Beanstalk** (Barnet) Casino Theater 2 November

1897 **Simple Simon** (Barnet) Tremont Theater, Boston 8 February (amateur)

1897 **The Marquis of Michigan** (Glen MacDonough, Edward Townsend) Collingwood Opera House, Poughkeepsie 26 August; Bijou Theater 21 September 1898

1899 **The Queen's Fan** (George Totten Smith) 1 act Proctor's Music Hall 6 March

1900 **Broadway to Tokio** (w Reginald de Koven/George V Hobart, Louis Harrison) New York Theater 23 January

1900 **Aunt Hannah** (Clay Greene/Matthew J Royal) Bijou Theater 22 February

1900 **A Million Dollars** (Hobart, Louis Harrison) New York Theater 27 September

1900 **Nell-Go-In** (Hobart) 1 act New York Theater 31 October

1900 **After Office Hours** (Hobart) sketch in *The Giddy Throng* (Sydney Rosenfeld) New York Theater 24 December

1901 **In a Japanese Garden** (William Gill) 1 act Casino Theater 3 May

1901 **The King's Carnival** (Hobart/Sydney Rosenfeld) New York Theater 13 May

1901 **Fun on the Beach** (Hobart) 1 act Cherry Blossom Grove 4 August

1901 **Supper at Sherry's** (Hobart) 1 act New York Theater September

1901 **The Liberty Belles** (w others/Harry B Smith) Madison Square Theater 30 September

1902 **The Hall of Fame** (Hobart/Rosenfeld) New York Theater 3 February

1902 **The Belle of Broadway** (w others/Hobart/W H Post) 1 scene New York Winter Garden 17 March

1902 **The Sweet Girl** (w others/Rosenfeld) 1 act Cherry Blossom Grove 18 August

1902 **Mr O'Reilly** (Hobart) Lyceum Theater, Elmira 29 September

1902 **The Mocking Bird** (Rosenfeld) Bijou Theater 10 November

1903 **The Wizard of Oz** (w Paul Tietjens/Glen Macdonough/Frank Baum) Majestic Theater 20 January

1903 **Sergeant Kitty** (R H Burnside) Montauk Theater, Brooklyn 16 November; Daly's Theater 18 January 1904

1904 **Lady Teazle** (John Kendrick Bangs, Roderic Scheff) Casino Theater 24 December

1904 **Cupid and Company** (Ambrose, Rankin, Mason, E Tracy Sweet/Sweet, [Edward Temple]) Lyceum Theater, Scranton, Pa 6 June

1905 **Mama's Papa** (Joseph Hart) Grand Opera House, Salem 1 February, Casino Philadelphia 6 February

1905 **Coming Thro' the Rye** (w J Sebastian Hiller/Hobart) Casino Theater, Philadelphia 25 May; Herald Square Theater 9 January 1906

1905 **A Four-Leaf Clover** (Martha Morton) Parsons Theater, Hatford, Conn 3 October

1905 **The Gingerbread Man** (Frederick M Ranken) Liberty Theater 25 December

1906 **Seeing New York** (Hart/Hart, Clifton Crawford) 1 act New York Theater Roof 5 June

1907 **The Mimic and the Maid** (Allen Lowe) Bijou Theater 11 January

1907 **Cupid at Vassar** (Owen Davis, Totten Smith) Poli's Theater, Waterbury, Conn 23 August

1907 **Happy Days** (Al Leech/H Hilbert Chalmers) Middlesex Theater, Middletown, Conn 30 September

1908 **Li'l Mose, or A Night in Venice** (Charles H Brown/Fred G Nixon Nirdlinger) Atlantic City 20 April

1909 **Lo** (Franklin P Adams/''O Henry'') Davidson Theater, Milwaukee 29 August

1909 **The Girl from the States** (w Raymond Hubbell/Glen MacDonough) Adelphi Theater, Philadelphia 11 October

1910 **Tillie's Nightmare** (Edgar Smith) Great Northern Theater, Chicago 10 January; Herald Square Theater 5 May

1910 **The Prince of Bohemia** (E Ray Goetz/J Hartley Manners) Hackett Theater 14 January

1910 **The Summer Widowers** (MacDonough) Broadway Theater 4 June

1911 **The Hen Pecks** (Goetz/MacDonough) Broadway Theater 4 February

1911 **The Never Homes** (Goetz/MacDonough) Broadway Theater 5 October

1912 **Bunty Bulls and Strings** (w others/Goetz/E Smith) 2 scenes Broadway Theater 8 February

1912 **Hokey-Pokey** (w W T Francis, John Stromberg/Goetz, Edgar Smith/E Smith) Broadway Theater 8 February

1912 **Hanky Panky** (Goetz/E Smith) Broadway Theater 5 August

1912 **Roly Poly** (Goetz/E Smith) Weber and Fields' Music Hall 21 November

1912 **Without the Law** (Goetz/E Smith) 1 act Weber and Fields' Music Hall 21 November

1912 **The Sun Dodgers** (Goetz/E Smith) Broadway Theater 30 November

1917 **We Should Worry** (Charles Hoyt ad Henry Blossom) Apollo Theater, Atlantic City 25 October

1918 **Look Who's Here** (H B Smith) Trenton, NJ 30 August

1918 **Ladies First** (H B Smith) Broadhurst Theater 24 October

1925 **When Summer Comes** (Jack Arnold) Poli's Theater, Washington, DC 15 February

1925 **The China Rose** (Harry L Cort, George Stoddard) Martin Beck Theater 24 December

Other (unproduced?) titles attributed: *The Mountain Girl* (1909, George Collin Davis, Addison Burkhart), *Pretty Polly* (1908, A M Holbrooke)

SMILES Musical comedy in 2 acts by William Anthony McGuire (with others). Lyrics by Harold Adamson and Clifford Grey. Additional lyrics by Ring Lardner. Music by Vincent Youmans. Ziegfeld Theater, New York, 18 November 1930.

Florenz Ziegfeld commissioned *Smiles* (originally entitled *Tom, Dick and Harry*) as an extravagant vehicle for his preferred but slightly passée star Marilyn[n] Miller, whom he wished to team up with the Astaires, brother and sister, following the pair's fine successes on both sides of the Atlantic in *Stop Flirting, Lady, Be Good!* and *Funny Face*. From a story line allegedly suggested by Noël Coward, McGuire produced a text in which Smiles

(Miss Miller), a French war orphan brought back to America and godfathered by four soldiers, grows up to be a Salvation Army lassie, equipped with a song photocopied from Edna May's famous ''They All Follow Me,'' and meets up with rich, bored Bob Hastings (Fred Astaire) and his sister Dot (Adele Astaire). In McGuire's original script she married him, but in rehearsal Ziegfeld changed the ending so that she paired instead with dashing doughboy Dick (Paul Gregory).

The show hit trouble and lawsuits on the road, Youmans suing Ziegfeld to stop him sacking his selected conductor, Paul Lannin, and threatening to walk out with the music. Ziegfeld won that particular court case and opened *Smiles* on Broadway to largely negative notices from which the Astaires emerged better than Miss Miller who, in turn, emerged better than either the book or the music. Ziegfeld ordered changes, but relations with Youmans still being sticky, he ultimately inserted two replacement numbers by Walter Donaldson. It was in any case too little and too late, and *Smiles* closed in failure after 63 performances.

Oddly enough, that was not the end of the show nor its scorned score. Fred Astaire occasionally reused his ''Say, Young Man of Manhattan,'' but it was another *Smiles* song which was responsible for the show's getting a second opportunity. The Prince of Wales took a fancy to ''Time on My Hands,'' sung in the original show by Paul Gregory, and began requesting it from British dance bands. The New Mayfair Dance Orchestra, Eddie Duchin, Ray Noble and the Mills Brothers recorded the Prince's preferred melody, and finally someone thought to look up the show that it came from. And so, in 1933, a revised version of *Smiles* adapted by Frank Eyton, Clifford Grey and Herbert Sargent, with additional songs by Melville Gideon and entitled *The One Girl,* opened at the London Hippodrome under the management of hustling Joe Sacks. It had a fine cast including Gaiety dancing ingenue Louise Browne and her habitual partner Roy Royston in the roles created by the Astaires, French musical-comedy star Mireille Perrey as the little French heroine, hero Dennis Noble (replaced by Guy Middleton), and a bevy of comics including Lupino Lane, Robert Hale and Arthur Riscoe. Apart from ''Time on My Hands,'' ''Say, Young Man of Manhattan,'' ''Be Good to Me,'' ''Carry on, Keep Smiling'' and the Chinese ballet music, the original *Smiles* score seemed to have disappeared under a welter of new and nearly new numbers of which Youmans's now title tune (salvaged from the flop *Rainbow*) proved most popular. The show did not, and folded on April Fools' Day after a five-week run.

UK: London Hippodrome *The One Girl* 24 February 1933

SMITH, Edgar [McPhail] (b Brooklyn, NY, 9 December 1857; d Bayside, NY, 8 March 1938). Actor turned all-purpose penman through a long career in the musical theatre.

Educated at Pennsylvania Military Academy, Edgar Smith began his association with the theatre as an actor at the age of 21, and had his first experience as a dramatist when he wrote a comedy-drama, *Love and Duty* to be played by a touring company called Dickson's Sketch Club of which he was a member. His first musical piece was a burlesque, *Little Lohengrin,* adapted from an English original for Alice Harrison and the Chicago Casino, but—after a first taste of Broadway honors with the song ''Once in a Thousand Years'' interpolated into the short-lived Boston show *The Pyramid* (1887)—he was quickly plunged into the very center of America's musical theatre activity when he was engaged as resident dramaturg and sometime supporting actor at the Casino Theater. He held this position for more than six years, assisting German-born house director Max Freeman and others in the adaptation of the French opéras-comiques and Austrian Operetten which were the theatre's main fare, and intermittently appearing in them as well (Dimoklos in *Apollo,* Grog in *La Grande-Duchesse,* Clampas in *The Drum Major,* Notary in *The Marquis, The Talisman,* Nowalksy in *Der arme Jonathan,* etc).

After leaving the Casino, Smith appeared with Thomas Q Seabrooke in *Tabasco* (1894), as a result of which he authored a sequel to that successful vehicle for its star under the title *The Grand Vizier.* It was not successful. He also provided the text for the Casino Theater's successor to its revusical *Passing Show,* a part-revue part-burlesque called *The Merry World,* and for an extravaganza, *Miss Philadelphia,* staged with great success in Philadelphia, before taking on a new position—far from the refinements of Continental comic opera—as house writer to the Weber and Fields organization.

Over the next six and a half years, Smith turned out outlines, sketches and scenes for the part-revue, part-burlesque entertainments which were the characteristic productions of Weber and Fields. The basic entertainment was one which allowed for movable parts and regularly, during the run of a piece, an entire one-act or two-scene burlesque of a currently popular play would be inserted. These, too, Smith was more often than not called upon to write, in collaboration with composer John Stromberg (*Onions* on *Carrots, Sapolio* on *Sappho, Waffles* on *Raffles, Trilby, Arizona* etc). Amongst the songs which emerged from the collaboration there was one that lasted: ''Ma Blushin' Rosie.''

At the same time Smith continued to work for other producers, adapting—or rather Americanizing—Ivan Caryll's *The Gay Parisienne* as *The Girl from Paris* (including the lyrics to new songs by Nat D Mann), the enormously successful English musical *The French Maid* and

Harry Greenbank's *Monte Carlo* for the voluminously importing E E Rice, and doing what seems to have been a major rewrite on the French vaudeville-opérette *L'Auberge du Tohu-bohu* for American consumption. He also worked on two original musical plays, *The Little Host* and *Sweet Anne Page,* which, in spite of starring Della Fox and Lulu Glaser respectively, failed to catch on, and on the ''hypnotic musical farce comedy'' *Bimbo of Bombay* which although judged ''above the average of the musical farce comedies'' didn't go far.

In 1903, at the break-up of the association of Weber and Fields, Smith went with Weber, and for two seasons performed his old job for Weber's Music Hall, a job which included a collaboration with Victor Herbert on *The Dream City* and, 20 years after the first time, a second *Lohengrin* burlesque, *The Magic Knight.* However, he did not give up the connection with Fields for whom he remanufactured one of his finest roles, Henry Pecksniff in the Americanized version of the British musical *The Girl Behind the Counter* (1907). In 1910 he turned out what would remain his most famous lyric: the words to Baldwin Sloane's ''Heaven Will Protect the Working Girl'' as performed by Marie Dressler in Fields's production of *Tillie's Nightmare.*

When Weber and Fields came back together again, Smith resumed his old position and supplied them with *Hokey-Pokey, Hanky-Panky* and *Roly Poly,* but the bulk of the work of his latter days was for the Shuberts for whom he ended his career as he had begun it, adapting Continental musical shows for the American stage with the same kind of hand with which he had written for Weber and Fields. The last work to which his name was attached, 45 years after his first show, was an American version of *Das Land des Lächelns* which closed out of town.

1886 **Little Lohengrin** American version of the burlesque by Frederick Bowyer with new music by Fred Solomon, Casino Theater, Chicago 13 September

1887 **The Pyramid** additional material (Star Theater)

1887 **Madelon** (*La Petite Mademoiselle*) American version (Casino Theater)

1888 **Nadjy** (*Les Noces improvisées*) American version of English version (Casino Theater)

1889 **Les Brigands** American version w Max Freeman (Casino Theater)

1889 **The Drum Major** (*La Fille du tambour-major*) American version w Freeman (Casino Theater)

1890 **Poor Jonathan** (*Der arme Jonathan*) American version (Casino Theater)

1890 **The Brazilian** (Francis Chassaigne ad Gustave Kerker) American version of William Lestoq and Max Pemberton's English version, adapted from a text by H B Farnie (Casino Theater)

1890 **Apollo** (*Das Orakel*) American version w Helen F Tretbar (Casino Theater)

1890 **The Grand-Duchess** (*La Grande-Duchesse de Gérolstein*) American adaptation of C H Kenney's English version (Casino Theater)

1890 **La Fille de Madame Angot** American adapatation of English version (Casino Theater)

1890 **You and I** (later *U & I*) (w Richard Carroll) New Worcester Theater, Worcester, Mass 22 August; Globe Theater, Boston 25 August; Standard Theater 2 May 1891

1891 **Fleurette** (Emma Steiner/w Mrs C Doremus) Standard Theater 24 August

1895 **The Grand Vizier** (Frederick Gagel) Grand Opera House, Decatur, Ill 9 January; Harlem Opera House 4 March

1895 **Nancy Lee** revised version of Fred Miller's libretto (People's Theater, Cincinnati)

1896 **Miss Philadelphia** (Herman Perlet, [Gagel]) Park Theater, Philadelphia 27 April; Star Theatre 27 December 1897

1896 **The Girl from Paris** (*The Gay Parisienne*) American version (Herald Square Theater)

1897 **Under the Red Globe** (John Stromberg) 1 act Weber and Fields' Music Hall 18 February

1897 **Bimbo of Bombay** (pasticcio) Star Theater, Elizabeth, NJ 11 September

1897 **Pousse-Café** (Stromberg/w Louis de Lange) Weber and Fields' Music Hall 2 December

1897 **The Worst Born** (Stromberg/w Louis de Lange) Weber and Fields' Music Hall 2 December

1897 **The Wee Minister** (Stromberg) burlesque in *Pousse-Café* Weber and Fields' Music Hall 2 December

1897 **The Way-High-Man** (Stromberg) burlesque in *Pousse-Café* Weber and Fields' Music Hall 20 December

1897 **The French Maid** American version (Herald Square Theater)

1898 **The Con-Curers** (Stromberg/w de Lange) burlesque in *Pousse-Café* Weber and Fields' Music Hall 17 March

1898 **Monte Carlo** American version (Herald Square Theater)

1898 **Hurly Burly** (Stromberg/w H B Smith) Weber and Fields' Music Hall 8 September

1898 **Hotel Topsy Turvy** (*L'Auberge du Tohu-bohu*) American adaptation of Arthur Sturgess's English version (Herald Square Theater)

1898 **Cyranose de Bric-á-Brac** (Stromberg) burlesque in *Hurly Burly* Weber and Fields' Music Hall 3 November

1898 **The Heathen** (Stromberg) burlesque in *Hurly Burly* Weber and Fields' Music Hall 3 November

1898 **The Little Host** (W T Francis, Thomas Chilvers/w de Lange) Herald Square Theater 26 December

1899 **Catherine** (Stromberg/w H B Smith) burlesque in *Hurly Burly* Weber and Fields' Music Hall 19 January

1899 **Helter Skelter** (Stromberg/H B Smith) Weber and Fields' Music Hall 6 April

1899 **Mother Goose** (ex- *Bo-Peep*) (Gagel, Fred Eustis/George Bowles ad w de Lange) 14th Street Theater 1 May

1899 **Zaza** (Stromberg) burlesque in *Helter Skelter* Weber and Fields' Music Hall

1899 **The Girl from Martin's** (Stromberg/H B Smith) burlesque in *Whirl-I-Gig* Weber and Fields' Music Hall 21 September

1899 **Whirl-I-Gig** (Stromberg/H B Smith) Weber and Fields' Music Hall 21 September

1899 **The Other Way** (Stromberg/H B Smith) burlesque in *Whirl-I-Gig* Weber and Fields' Music Hall 26 October

1899 **In Gay Paree** revised version Casino Theater 6 November

1899 **Barbara Fidgety** (Stromberg/H B Smith) burlesque in *Whirl-I-Gig* Weber and Fields' Music Hall 7 December

1900 **Sapolio** (Stromberg/H B Smith) burlesque in *Whirl-I-Gig* Weber and Fields' Music Hall 8 March

1900 **Fiddle Dee Dee** (Stromberg) Weber and Fields' Music Hall 6 September

1900 **Quo Vass Is!** (Stromberg) burlesque in *Fiddle Dee Dee* Weber and Fields' Music Hall 6 September

1900 **Arizona** (burlesque) (Stromberg) burlesque in *Fiddle Dee Dee* Weber and Fields' Music Hall 18 October

1900 **Sweet Anne Page** (W H Neidlinger/w de Lange) Manhattan Theater 3 December

1900 **Exhibit II** (comprising *The Royal Family* and *The Gay Lord Quex* burlesques) (Stromberg) Weber and Fields' Music Hall 20 December

1901 **Captain Jinks** (burlesque) (Stromberg) burlesque in *Fiddle Dee Dee* Weber and Fields' Music Hall 4 April

1901 **Hoity Toity** (Stromberg) including burlesques on *Madame Butterfly* and *Diplomacy* Weber and Fields' Music Hall 5 September

1901 **De Pleurisy** (Stromberg) burlesque in *Hoity Toity* Weber and Fields' Music Hall 5 September

1901 **Home, Sweet Home** (various) Academy of Music, Jersey City 30 September

1901 **A Man from Mars** (Stromberg) burlesque in *Hoity Toity* Weber and Fields' Music Hall 14 November

1902 **The Curl and the Judge** (Stromberg) burlesque in *Hoity Toity* Weber and Fields' Music Hall 9 January

1902 **Du Hurry** (Stromberg) burlesque in *Hoity Toity* Weber and Fields' Music Hall 20 March

1902 **Twirly Whirly** (Stromberg, Francis) Weber and Fields' Music Hall 11 September

1902 **I, Mary McPain** (Stromberg) burlesque in *Twirly Whirly* 11 September

1902 **[Humming Birds and] Onions** (W T Francis) burlesque in *Twirly Whirly* Weber and Fields' Music Hall 6 November

1902 **The Stickiness of Gelatine** (Francis) burlesque in *Twirly Whirly* Weber and Fields' Music Hall 18 December

1903 **The Big Little Princess** (Francis) burlesque in *Twirly Whirly* Weber and Fields' Music Hall 26 February

1903 **Whoop-Dee-Doo** (Francis) Weber and Fields' Music Hall 24 September

1903 **Looney Park** (Francis) burlesque in *Whoop-de-Doo* Weber and Fields' Music Hall 24 September

1903 **Waffles** (Francis) burlesque in *Whoop-de-doo* Weber and Fields' Music Hall 10 December

1904 **An English Daisy** American version (Casino Theater)

1904 **Higgledy Piggledy** (Maurice Levi) Weber's Music Hall 20 October

1905 **The College Widower** (Levi) burlesque in *Higgledy Piggledy* Weber's Music Hall 5 January

1906 **Twiddle Twaddle** (Levi) Weber's Music Hall 1 January

1906 **The Squaw Man's Girl of the Golden West** (Levi) burlesque in *Twiddle Twaddle* Weber's Music Hall 26 February

1906 **The Little Cherub** American adaptation of English text (Criterion Theater)

1906 **The Dream City** (Victor Herbert) 1 act Weber's Music Hall 25 December

1906 **The Magic Knight** (Herbert) 1 act Weber's Music Hall 25 December

1907 **The Girl Behind the Counter** American version (Herald Square Theater)

1907 **Hip! Hip! Hooray!** (Gus Edwards) Weber's Music Hall 10 October

1908 **The Merry-Go-Round** (G Edwards/Paul West) Circle Theater 25 April

1908 **The Mimic World** (Ben Jerome, Seymour Furth) Casino Theater 9 July

1908 **Mr Hamlet of Broadway** (Jerome/Edward Madden) Casino Theater 23 December

1909 **Philpoena** (part of *Higgledly Piggledy*) (Levi) 1 act Aldwych Theatre, London 27 February

1909 **Les Collegettes** (Levi) revised *The College Widower* Aldwych Theatre, London 27 February

1909 **Old Dutch** (Victor Herbert/w George V Hobart) Herald Square Theater 22 November

1910 **Tillie's Nightmare** (A Baldwin Sloane) Great Northern Theater, Chicago 10 January; Herald Square Theater 5 May

1910 **Up and Down Broadway** (Jean Schwartz/William Jerome) Casino Theater 18 July

1910 **He Came From Milwaukee** (Ben Jerome, Louis Hirsch, Melville Ellis/Edward Madden/Mark Swan) revised version Casino Theater 21 September

1911 **La Belle Paree** (Jerome Kern, Frank Tours) Winter Garden 20 March

1911 **A Certain Party** (Robert Hood Bowers) Wallack's Theater 24 April

1911 **The Kiss Waltz** (*Liebeswalzer*) American libretto (Casino Theater)

1912 **Hokey-Pokey** (Sloane, Francis) Broadway Theater 8 February

1912 **Bunty Bulls and Strings** (Sloane/E Ray Goetz) 2 scenes Broadway Theater 8 February

1912 **Hanky-Panky** (Sloane/Goetz) Broadway Theater 5 August

1912 **Roly Poly** (Sloane/Goetz) Weber and Fields' Music Hall 21 November

1912 **Without the Law** (Sloane/Goetz) burlesque in *Roly Poly* Weber and Fields' Music Hall 21 November

1912 **The Sun Dodgers** (Sloane/Goetz) Broadway Theater 30 November

1913 **Lieber Augustin** (aka *Miss Caprice*) (*Der liebe Augustin*) American version (Casino Theater)

1913 **The Pleasure Seekers** (Goetz/Goetz) Winter Garden Theater 3 November

1915 **The Peasant Girl** (*Polenblut*) American version w Herbert Reynolds, Harold Atteridge (44th Street Theater)

- 1915 **Hands Up** (Cole Porter, William Daly, et al/Goetz) Shubert Theater, New Haven, Conn 7 June; revised version (w Sigmund Romberg/Goetz, William Jerome/Goetz) 44th Street Theater 22 July
- 1915 **The Blue Paradise** (*Ein Tag im Paradies*) American version w add music by Sigmund Romberg (Casino Theater)
- 1915 **Alone at Last** (*Endlich allein*) American version w Joseph W Herbert, Matthew Woodward (Shubert Theater)
- 1916 **Robinson Crusoe Jr** (Romberg, James Hanley/Atteridge) Winter Garden Theater 17 February
- 1916 **Step This Way** revised *The Girl Behind the Counter* w Goetz, Bert Grant (Shubert Theater)
- 1916 **The Girl from Brazil** (*Die schöne Schwedin*) American version w Matthew Woodward, Sigmund Romberg (44th Street Theater)
- 1916 **Lieutenant Gus** (*Wenn zwei sich lieben*) American version w Woodward (44th Street Theater)
- 1917 **My Lady's Glove** (ex- *The Beautiful Unknown*) (*Die schöne Unbekannte*) American version w Edward Paulton, Romberg (Lyric Theater)
- 1917 **The Golden Goose** (Silvio Hein/Herbert Reynolds, Schuyler Greene) Apollo Theater, Atlantic City 29 November
- 1918 **Fancy Free** (Augustus Barratt/w Dorothy Donnelly) Astor Theater 11 April
- 1918 **The Melting of Molly** (Romberg/w Cyrus Wood) Broadhurst Theater 30 December
- 1919 **Oh! What a Girl** (ex- *Oh! Uncle,* ex- *The Wrong Number*) (Charles Jules, Jacques Presburg/w Edward Clark) Shubert Theater 28 July
- 1919 **Hello, Alexander** revised *The Ham Tree* (Jean Schwartz/Alfred Bryan) 44th Street Theater 7 October
- 1921 **The Whirl of New York** revised *The Belle of New York* w Sidney Mitchell, Al Goodman, Lew Pollock, Leo Edwardes (Winter Garden Theater)
- 1922 **Red Pepper** (Albert Gumble, Owen Murphy/Howard Rogers, Murphy/w Emily Young) Shubert Theater 29 May
- 1928 **Headin' South** (J Schwartz/A Bryan, et al) Keith's Theater, Philadelphia 1 October
- 1929 **The Street Singer** (Niclas Kempner, Sam Timberg/Graham John) Shubert Theater 17 September
- 1930 **Hello Paris** (aka *So This Is Paris*) (Charles D Locke, Frank Bannister/Russell M Tarbox, Michael Cleary) Shubert Theater 15 November
- 1930 **Prince Chu Chang** (*Das Land des Lächelns*) American adaptation w Henry Clarke (Shubert Theater, Newark)

SMITH, Harry B[ache] (b Buffalo, NY, 28 December 1860; d Atlantic City, NJ, 2 January 1936). The most prolific librettist, lyricist and adapter of the Broadway stage over nearly half a century of writing in the decades round the turn of the century.

The name of Harry Bache Smith permeates the American musical theatre from the late 1880s until the early 1930s. Intelligent, prolific, though rather too often facile, he was able swiftly to turn his hand to anything from comic-opera plots and songwords to the Weber and Fields style of burlesque, music-hall material or a Rogers Brothers song, from the kind of adaptations from the English, the French or the German (as the importing fashion turned) which were thought to be what the American public wanted (and that ''thought'' was often fairly insulting to its public's tastes) to the modern postwar style of revue and musical comedy. From his very earliest days—his early *Rosita* dealing with ''the wholesale capture of Chilian beauties by a band of bold bandits'' was a blatant pinch from *The Pirates of Penzance*—he rarely attempted anything which smacked of originality, being content to rework familiar elements in more or less new guises and in a variety of different dresses, helping himself, in the manner of H B Farnie and the other most successful bricoleurs of musical theatre texts of the past, to plot-pieces and characters from the multitude of sources which his wide theatrical experience and even wider reading exposed him. Few of Smith's principal original libretti were credited with being direct adaptations: most preferred to take a familiar name or title and decorate it with a lively mixture of traditional comic-opera doings. Thus his list of early comic-opera credits included a Begum, a Caliph, a Mandarin, a Tzigane, a Highwayman, a Fencing Master, a Student King and so forth, as well as such earcatching names as Robin Hood, Don Quixote, Rob Roy, Ali Baba, Peg Woffington and their well-to-overused fellows.

Smith's earliest work to make it to the stage was produced by John Templeton's touring musical-theatre company, as a vehicle for the manager's little daughter Fay, and—whilst hanging on to his day job, as dramatic and musical critic for Chicago's *Evening Journal*—he subsequently wrote texts for a handful of pieces for the Milwaukee theatre. The turning point came when he teamed up with composer Reginald De Koven, whom he met when the musician sold the young ex-clerk, ex-chorus-singer, ex-concert agent, ex-theatre critic a little Chicago newspaper he had started. Their first effort together, the *Mikado*-ish *The Begum,* was given a major East Coast production by the powerful John McCaull and the young pair were on their way. This first success was soon followed by one very much more considerable when the Boston Ideal Opera Company produced their *Robin Hood.* It was a success in which Smith's neatly constructed libretto—which had little enough to do with Robin Hood, but involved a great deal of the disguises, mistaken identities and low comedy traditional in British and French comic opera—played a considerable part. Thereafter, he was established at the head of his profession, and in the decades that followed he collaborated with the best Broadway had to offer in the way of comic-opera composers. By the time he was done—and that kind of comic opera was done as well—he had provided 16 libretti to

De Koven (of which *Rob Roy* was the next most successful) and worked on 14 shows with Victor Herbert, as well as collaborating with Julian Edwards, with Ludwig Englander and on one occasion with Sousa. And when the new, romantic style of comic opera surfaced in the 1920s Harry Smith was still around to supply texts to such as Sigmund Romberg.

From the earliest years of his career, Smith also engaged in adaptations of foreign works. Suppé's *Die Jagd nach dem Glück* and Dellinger's *Capitän Fracassa* were amongst the earliest, but when the fashion abandoned French and Austro-German Operette in favor of the product of the British stage, he was still at hand to ''Americanize'' such London products as *The Toreador, The Belle of Mayfair, The Girl from Kays* and *The Sunshine Girl,* and when the first French vaudevilles began to be borrowed as the texts for Broadway shows, Smith was there to cobble together *Mam'zelle Nitouche* and *La Femme à papa* to make up an Anna Held show, to take the dazzling comic shower of *Les Fêtards* and turn it into *The Strollers* with Ludwig Englander, or transform the vaudeville *Le Jockey malgré lui* into *The Office Boy.*

However, it was the coming of the modern Viennese Operette which set him on his most solid swag of adapting. Something like half of his work from 1910 onwards was in compiling American versions of Continental hits, and the final assignments of his long career included two attempts to make Benatzky's *Hotel Stadt-Lemberg* into a Broadway piece, and a short-lived try at making Rudolf Lothar's *The Phantom Ship* into a musical for George Lederer as *The Pajama Lady.*

Smith's contribution to the lighter forms of musical theatre was less than that to the ''comic-opera'' style of piece, but it was by no means negligible. In his early days he wrote burlesque and pantomime scripts and songs, he supplied lyrics to John Stromberg for Weber and Fields and to Maurice Levi for the Rogers Brothers, and he authored the Casino Theater's attempt to write its own Gaiety Theatre musical with *The Casino Girl* and did it well enough that the show did very nicely on the Gaiety's home ground in London. He wrote a children's fairy-tale spectacular with Herbert, material for the *Ziegfeld Follies,* the revusical sketch *Gaby* for after-dinner roof-garden entertainment, revamped a couple of Charles Hoyt plays as libretti, took part in the writing of musical comedies of a more or less vertebrate nature with such composers as Ivan Caryll, Jerome Kern and Irving Berlin, and supplied Ned Wayburn with the texts for revue at the Century Music Hall. On one occasion he even wrote a musical-comedy script which he asserted was based on no less venerable a source than Eugène Scribe. And all this time, he kept steadily turning out romantic operetta texts, more or less ''original'' or, latterly, more often than less adapted.

One thing, however, emerges from the long list of Smith's credits. Although a number of his adaptations did extremely well—*Die Sprudelfee, Der lila Domino, Szibill*—and many of his pieces served their purpose through a month or two on Broadway and a solidly profitable touring life, virtually only the best pieces of his earliest years—*Robin Hood,* and the three Herbert pieces *The Wizard of the Nile, The Serenade* and *The Fortune Teller*—proved to be of the stuff that revivals and exports are made. In the 35 years of constant writing that followed this group, only *The Casino Girl* (1900) and the revusical Irving Berlin piece *Watch Your Step* (1914) were given a much wider life, and only the Victor Herbert operetta *Sweethearts* (1913), with its incoherent Ruritanian libretto, was judged worthy of revival at home. From being one of the flag-bearers of the American musical theatre in the first decade of his writing career, at a period when the products of America's musical theatre were just reaching out towards giving rather than taking on the international scene, Smith faded into being a utilitarian writer. Whilst others were writing the musical comedies and operettas of the 1910s and 1920s which would establish the American musical theatre around the world, Smith, still producing texts and lyrics at a great rate, turned out only a mass of often too facile material for home consumption, quickly consumed.

When his theatrical writing days were all but done, Smith turned out one of his most enjoyable pieces of writing in the form of a friendly, amusing—if occasionally factually forgetful—set of memoirs, which has sadly now become a rarity.

Smith was married to the actress and singer **Irene BENTLEY** (b Baltimore, 23 May 1870; d Allenhurst, NJ, 3 June 1940), who appeared on the Broadway stage as a chorus girl in *Little Christopher* (1895), *Hamlet II* (1895, Osric), *Thrilby* (1895), *The Merry World* (1895), *The Belle of New York* (1898 and London, Gladys Glee, a bridesmaid) and in Koster & Bial's *In Gotham* (1899, Bella Donna) before being upped to better roles by George Lederer in a revival of *The Rounders* (1900, Angélique, t/o Stella) and *The Belle of Bohemia* (1900, Geraldine McDuffy), then paired at the top of the comedy with Francis Wilson as Bertha Lump in Smith's adaptation of *Die Landstreicher* as *The Strollers* (1901). She had good roles in *The Wild Rose* (1902, Rose Romany), *The Girl from Dixie* (1903, Kitty Calvert), *It Happened in Nordland* (1905, tour), *The Belle of Mayfair* (1906, Princess Carl) and the revue *The Mimic World* (1908, the Merry Widow). Her brother, Wilmer Bentley, worked in the theatre as a striving performer (Mucki in *The Strollers,* etc), director and sometime writer, for some nine years on the staff on George Lederer's office, and in the early 1920s in Australia.

Smith's brother, Robert Bache Smith, followed Harry into the theatre and also had a long career there as, principally, a lyricist.

A collected edition of Harry Smith's lyrics was published by R H Russell in 1900 under the title *Stage Lyrics*. He seems to have been the first musical-theatre lyricist thus to have been honored.

1884 **Rosita, or Cupid and Cupidity** (George Schlieffarth/Matthew C Woodward) Foster's Opera House, Des Moines 16 March; Criterion Theater, Chicago 1 April; Park Theater, Brooklyn 30 April

1884 **Amaryllis** (Henry H Thiele) Academy of Music, Milwaukee 1 May (by amateurs)

1884 **Prince Chow Chow** (Thiele) Schlitz Park Summer Theater, Milwaukee 11 June

1887 **The Begum** (Reginald De Koven) Fifth Avenue Theater 21 November

1888 **Fort Caramel** (Thiele) New Academy, Milwaukee 13 April

1888 **The Crystal Slipper, or Prince Prettywitz and Little Cinderella** (Fred J Eustis/w Alfred Thompson) Opera House, Chicago 18 June; Star Theater, New York 26 November

1888 **The Scarecrow** (pasticcio ad George Bowlon/w Robert B Peattie) Myers' Opera House, Janesville, Wis 22 August

1889 **Don Quixote** (De Koven) Boston Theater, Boston 18 November

1889 **Clover** (*Die Jagd nach dem Glück*) English version (Palmer's Theater)

1889 **Captain Fracasse** (*Capitän Fracassa*) American version (Opera House, Chicago)

1890 **Robin Hood** (De Koven) Chicago 9 June; Standard Theater, New York 28 September 1891

1891 **The Tar and the Tartar** (Adam Itzel jr) Palmer's Theater 11 May

1891 **Sinbad, or The Maid of Balsora** (comp & arr William Henry Batchelor) Opera House, Chicago 11 June; Garden Theater, New York 27 June 1892

1892 **Jupiter, or The Cobbler and the King** (Julian Edwards) Palmer's Theater 2 May

1892 **Ali Baba, or Morgiana and the Forty Thieves** (Batchelor/w Franklyn W Lee, John Gilbert) Opera House, Chicago 2 June

1892 **The Fencing Master** (De Koven) Star Theater, Buffalo 26 September; Casino Theater 14 November

1893 **The Knickerbockers** (De Koven) Tremont Theatre, Boston 5 January; Garden Theater 29 May

1893 **The Algerian** (De Koven) Garden Theater 26 October

1893 **Africa** (Randolph Cruger/Clay M Greene, J Cheever Goodwin) revised text Star Theatre, New York 25 December

1894 **Rob Roy** (De Koven) Herald Square Theater 29 October

1895 **The Tzigane** (De Koven) Abbey's Theater 16 May

1895 **Little Robinson Crusoe** (Gustave Luders, Batchelor) Schiller Theater, Chicago 15 June

1895 **The Wizard of the Nile** (Victor Herbert) Casino Theater 4 November

1896 **The Caliph** (Ludwig Englander) Broadway Theater 3 September

1896 **Half a King** (*Le Roi de carreau*) American version w music by Englander, Knickerbocker Theater 14 September

1896 **The Mandarin** (De Koven) Herald Square Theater 2 November

1897 **The Serenade** (Herbert) Knickerbocker Theater 16 March

1897 **Gayest Manhattan, or Around New York in Ninety Minutes** (Englander) Koster and Bial's 22 March

1897 **The Paris Doll** (De Koven) Parsons' Theater, Hartford, Conn 14 September

1897 **Peg Woffington** (Herbert) Lyceum Theater, Scranton, Pa 18 October

1897 **The Idol's Eye** (Herbert) Broadway Theater 25 October

1897 **The Highwayman** (De Koven) Hyperion Theater, New Haven, Conn 28 October; Broadway Theater 13 December

1898 **Hurly Burly** (John Stromberg/w Edgar Smith) Weber and Fields' Music Hall 8 September

1898 **The Little Corporal** (Englander) Broadway Theater 19 September

1898 **The Fortune Teller** (Herbert) Wallack's Theatre 26 September

1898 **Cyranose de Bric-à-Brac** (Stromberg/w E Smith) burlesque in *Hurly Burly* Weber and Fields' Music Hall 3 November

1899 **Catherine** (Stromberg/w Edgar Smith) burlesque in *Hurly Burly* Weber and Fields' Music Hall 19 January

1899 **The Three Dragoons** (De Koven) Broadway Theater 30 January

1899 **Helter Skelter** (Stromberg/E Smith) Weber and Fields' Music Hall 6 April

1899 **The Rounders** (*Les Fêtards*) American version with score by Englander Casino Theater 12 July

1899 **Cyrano de Bergerac** (Herbert/Stuart Reed) Knickerbocker Theater 18 September

1899 **Whirl-I-Gig** (Stromberg/w E Smith) Weber and Fields' Music Hall 21 September

1899 **The Girl from Martin's** (Stromberg/ E Smith) burlesque in *Whirl-I-Gig* 21 September

1899 **The Singing Girl** (Herbert/Stanislaus Stange) Casino Theater 23 October

1899 **The Other Way** (Stromberg/E Smith) burlesque in *Whirl-I-Gig* Weber and Fields' Music Hall 26 October

1899 **Papa's Wife** (De Koven) Manhattan Theater 13 November

1899 **Barbara Fidgety** (Stromberg/E Smith) burlesque in *Whirl-I-Gig* Weber and Fields' Music Hall 7 December

1900 **Sapolio** (Stromberg/E Smith) burlesque in *Whirl-I-Gig* Weber and Fields' Music Hall 8 March

1900 **The Viceroy** (Herbert) Columbia Theater, San Francisco 12 February; Knickerbocker Theater 13 March

1900 **The Casino Girl** (Englander) Casino Theater 19 March

1900 **The Cadet Girl** (*Les Demoiselles de Saint-Cyriens*) American version w Cheever Goodwin and new music by Englander Herald Square Theater 25 July

1900 **The Belle of Bohemia** (Englander) Casino Theater 24 September

1900 **Foxy Quiller** (De Koven) Broadway Theater 5 November

1901 **The Prima Donna** (Aimé Lachaume) Herald Square Theater 17 April

1901 **The Strollers** (*Die Landstreicher*) American version with new music by Englander, Knickerbocker Theater 24 June

1901 **The Rogers Brothers in Washington** (Maurice Levi/J J McNally) Knickerbocker Theater 2 September

1901 **The Liberty Belles** (A Baldwin Sloane, John Bratton, Lachaume, Alfred E Aaarons, Englander, et al) Madison Square Theater 30 September

1901 **The Little Duchess** (*Niniche*) American version with new score by De Koven, Casino Theater 14 October

1901 **Maid Marian** (De Koven) Chestnut Street Opera House, Philadelphia 4 November; Garden Theater 27 January 1902

1902 **The Wild Rose** (Englander/w George V Hobart) Knickerbocker Theater 5 May

1902 **The Billionaire** (Gustave Kerker) Daly's Theater 29 December

1903 **The Jewel of Asia** (Englander/Frederick Ranken) Criterion Theater 16 February

1903 **The Blonde in Black** (Kerker) Knickerbocker Theater 8 June

1903 **The Office Boy** (*Le Jockey malgré lui*) American version with new score by Englander, Victoria Theater 2 November

1903 **Babette** (Herbert) Broadway Theater 16 November

1903 **The Girl from Dixie** (C F Dodgson, et al) Madison Square Theater 14 December

1904 **A Madcap Princess** (Englander) Knickerbocker Theater 5 September

1904 **The Sambo Girl** revised *The Blonde in Black* Nesbitt Theater, Wilkes-Barre, Pa 5 September

1904 **A China Doll** (Alfred Aarons) Majestic Theatre 19 November

1904 **Fatinitza** new American version (Broadway Theater)

1905 **The Belle of the West** (Karl Hoschna) Lyceum Theater, Harrisburg, Pa 28 August; Great Northern Theater, Chicago 29 October; Grand Opera House 13 November

1905 **Miss Dolly Dollars** (Herbert) Knickerbocker Theater 4 September

1905 **The White Cat** (Englander/Arthur Collins, Arthur Wood ad) American version, New Amsterdam Theater 2 November

1906 **The Three Graces** (Stafford Waters) Chicago Opera House 2 April

1906 **The Free Lance** (John Philip Sousa) New Amsterdam Theater 16 April

1906 **The Rich Mr Hoggenheimer** (Englander) Wallack's Theater 22 October

1906 **The Parisian Model** (Max Hoffman) Broadway Theater 27 November

1907 **The Tattooed Man** (Herbert/w A N C Fowler) Criterion Theater 18 February

1907 **The Rogers Brothers in Panama** (Hoffman) Broadway Theater 2 September

1908 **The Paradise of Mahomet** (*Le Paradis de Mahomet*) American version (Lyric Theatre, Philadelphia)

1908 **The Soul Kiss** (Levi) New York Theater 28 January

1908 **Nearly a Hero** (several) Casino Theater 24 February

1908 **The Golden Butterfly** (De Koven) Broadway Theater 12 October

1908 **Little Nemo** (Herbert) New Amsterdam Theater 20 October

1908 **Miss Innocence** (Englander) New York Theater 30 November

1909 **The Silver Star** (Robert Hood, Bowers, Raymond Hubbell, Hoschna, Jean Schwartz, et al) New Amsterdam Theater 1 November

1909 **The (Hot) Air King** (Hubbell) Star Theater, Buffalo 22 November; Colonial Theater, Chicago 28 November

1910 **The Girl on the Train** (*Die geschiedene Frau*) American version (Globe Theater)

1910 **The Bachelor Belles** (Hubbell) Globe Theater 7 November

1910 **The Spring Maid** (*Die Sprudelfee*) American version w R B Smith (Liberty Theater)

1911 **The Paradise of Mahomet** (*Le Paradis de Mahomet*) new American version w R B Smith (Herald Square Theater)

1911 **The Duchess** (ex- *The Rose Shop, Mlle Rosita*) (Herbert/w Joseph Herbert) Shubert Theater, Boston 20 March; Lyric Theater 16 October

1911 **Little Miss Fix-It** (various/w William J Hurlbutt) Globe Theater 3 April

1911 **Gaby** (Bowers/w R B Smith) Folies-Bergère 27 April

1911 **The Red Rose** (Bowers/w R B Smith) Bijou Theater 22 June

1911 **The Siren** (*Die Sirene*) English version (Knickerbocker Theater)

1911 **Gypsy Love** (*Zigeunerliebe*) American version w R B Smith (Globe Theater)

1911 **The Enchantress** (Herbert/w Fred de Grésac) New York Theater 19 October

1911 **The Wedding Trip** (De Koven/w de Grésac) Knickerbocker Theater 25 December

1912 **Modest Susanne** (*Die keusche Susanne*) American version w R B Smith (Liberty Theater)

1912 **A Winsome Widow** (*A Trip to Chinatown*) (Hubbell/ Charles Hoyt ad) Moulin Rouge 11 April

1912 **The Rose Maid** (*Bub oder Mädel?*) English version w R B Smith (Globe Theater)

1912 **The Girl from Montmartre** (*Das Mädel von Montmartre*) English version (Criterion Theater)

1912 **The June Bride** (*Johann der Zweite*) English version (Majestic Theater, Boston)

1912 **My Little Friend** (*Die kleine Freundin*) English version w R B Smith (Studebaker Theater, Chicago, New Amsterdam Theater)

1913 **The Doll Girl** (*Das Puppenmädel*) English version (Globe Theater)

1913 **Sweethearts** (Herbert/R B Smith/w de Grésac) Academy of Music, Baltimore 24 March; New Amsterdam Theater, New York 8 September

1913 **Oh, I Say!** (Jerome Kern/Sydney Blow, Douglas Hoare) Casino Theater 30 October

1914 **The Lilac Domino** (*Der lila Domino*) American version w R B Smith (44th Street Theater)

1914 **The Débutante** (Herbert/w R B Smith) New Nixon Theater, Atlantic City 21 September; Knickerbocker Theater 7 December

1914 **Papa's Darling** (Ivan Caryll) New Amsterdam Theater 2 November

1914 **The Laughing Husband** (*Der lachende Ehemann*) American version (Knickerbocker Theater)

1915 **90 in the Shade** (Kern/Guy Bolton) Knickerbocker Theater 25 January

1915 **All Over Town** (Silvio Hein/Joseph Santley) Shubert Theater, New Haven 26 April; Garrick Theater Chicago 30 April

1916 **Sybil** (*Szibill*) American version from Harry Graham's English version (Liberty Theater)

1916 **The Masked Model** (Carl Woess/Frederick Herendeen/w R B Smith) National Theater, Washington, DC 7 February

1916 **Molly O!** revised *The Masked Model* (Woess/w R B Smith) Cort Theater 20 May

1916 **Girls Will Be Girls** (Kern/''Thomas Sydney'' [Augustus Thomas jr, Sydney Smith]) Lyric Theater, Philadelphia 20 November

1917 **Love o' Mike** revised *Girls Will Be Girls* Shubert Theater 15 January

1917 **The Masked Model** new revised version with score by Harold Orlob, Johnstown, Pa 17 April

1917 **Rambler Rose** (Victor Jacobi) Empire Theater 10 September

1918 **Look Who's Here** (Sloane) Trenton, NJ 30 August

1918 **Ladies First** (Sloane/Hoyt ad) Broadhurst Theater 24 October

1918 **The Canary** (Caryll/Wodehouse, Caldwell/ Louis Verneuil ad) Globe Theater, New York 4 November

1919 **A Lonely Romeo** (Franklin, Bowers/w R B Smith, Lew Fields) Shubert Theater 19 January

1919 **Angel Face** (Victor Herbert/R B Smith) Knickerbocker Theater 30 December

1920 **Betty Be Good** (Hugo Riesenfeld) Casino Theater 4 May

1920 **Florodora** revised libretto (Century Theater)

1922 **The Springtime of Youth** (*Sterne, die wieder leuchten*) American version w Cyrus Wood (Broadhurst Theater)

1923 **Caroline** (*Das Vetter aus dingsda*) (ex- *Virginia*) American version w Edward Delaney Dunn (Ambassador Theater)

1923 **Peaches** (Max R Steiner/w R B Smith) Garrick Theater, Philadelphia 22 January

1925 **The Love Song** (*Offenbach*) American version (Century Theater)

1925 **Natja** (Tchaikovsky arr Karl Hajós) Knickerbocker Theater 16 February

1925 **Princess Flavia** (Sigmund Romberg) Century Theater 2 November

1926 **Sweetheart Time** (Walter Donaldson, Joseph Meyer/ Ballard MacDonald) Imperial Theater 19 January

1926 **Naughty Riquette** (*Riquette*) American version (Cosmopolitan Theater)

1926 **Countess Maritza** (*Gräfin Mariza*) American version (Shubert Theater)

1927 **Cherry Blossoms** (Romberg) 44th Street Theater 28 March

1927 **The Circus Princess** (*Die Zirkusprinzessin*) American version (Winter Garden Theater)

1927 **Half a Widow** (Shep Camp/w Frank Dupree) Waldorf Theater 12 September

1927 **The Love Call** (ex- *Bonita,* et al) (Romberg) Majestic Theater 24 October

1928 **White Lilacs** (*Chopin*) American version (Shubert Theater)

1928 **The Red Robe** (*Das Weib im Purpur*) American version w Edward Delancy Dunn, Shubert Theater 25 December

1930 **Three Little Girls** (*Drei arme kleine Mädels*) American lyrics (Shubert Theater)

1930 **Prince Chu Chang** (*Das Land des Lächelns*) American lyrics (Shubert Theater, Newark)

1930 **Arms and the Maid** (*Hotel Stadt-Lemberg*) American version w Ernest Clarke (Chestnut Street Opera House, Philadelphia)

1930 **The Pajama Lady** (Phil Charig, Richard Myers/w John Mercer/R B Smith, George Lederer) National Theater, Washington, DC 6 October

1932 **Marching By** (*Hotel Stadt-Lemberg*) revised American version (46th Street Theater)

Autobiography: *First Nights and First Editions* (Little, Brown, Boston, 1931)

SMITH, Oliver [Lemuel] (b Wawpawn, Wis, 13 February 1918; d Brooklyn, NY, 23 January 1994).

The set designer for a long list of important Broadway musicals from the mid-1940s to the mid-1960s (*On the Town, Brigadoon, Gentlemen Prefer Blondes, Pal Joey* revival, *My Fair Lady, Candide, West Side Story, The Sound of Music, Camelot, Hello, Dolly!,* etc), gathering in the process a clutch of Tony Awards, Oliver Smith was also for a time active as a musical-theatre producer, notably on the original productions of *On the Town* and *Gentlemen Prefer Blondes,* as well as the less-successful *Billion Dollar Baby, Juno, Show Girl,* and *Bonanza Bound* (w Paul Feigay, Herman Levin), a number of non-musical plays and a signifcant amount of dance productions.

SMITH, Queenie (b New York, 8 September 1899; d Burbank, Calif, 5 August 1978). Button-bright dancing star of the dance-age musical comedy.

Originally a member of the corps at the Metropolitan Opera House, the little dancer left the ballet at the age of 17 to go on the musical-comedy stage where she soon won featured dancing roles in John Cort's production of *Roly Boly Eyes* (1919, Ida Loring), the Shuberts' first attempt to get what became *The Blushing Bride* off the ground as *The Girl in the Private Room* (1920) and in

Friml's indifferent *June Rose* (1920, Tiny Golden). Carrying on an end-to-end schedule, she played in an Earl Carroll mounting of a musical called *Just Because* (1922, Syringa), written by two lady amateurs and backed by their society friends to the tune of $75,000, in *Orange Blossoms* (1922, Tillie), *Cinders* (1923, Tillie Olsen) and in George S Kaufman and Marc Connelly's *Helen of Troy, New York* (1923, Maribel). She then appeared as Gertrude Bryan's twin sister in *Sitting Pretty,* singing "Shufflin' Sam," and in a second Kaufman/Connelly musical, *Be Yourself* (1924, Tony Robinson), before winning the role of her career as the titular lassie of *Tip-Toes* (1925), creating "Looking for a Boy," "These Charming People" and "That Certain Feeling."

She followed up in the title role of the flop *Judy* (1927), succeeded Louise Groody as the star of *Hit the Deck* (1927) and toured in that part the following season, before taking the leading role of Busby Berkeley's production of *The Street Singer* (1929). The Shuberts' *Hearts in Repair* (Brighton Beach 17 August 1931) went down the drain, and her last musical appearance on Broadway was in 1932 as Dixie in *A Little Racketeer,* but from 1935 she found herself a second career as a film actress—memorably as a delicious Ellie May in *Show Boat*—and she remained active for 30 further years in often sizeable film and television roles as a character and comedy actress.

SMITH, Robert B[ache] (b Chicago, 4 June 1875; d New York, 6 November 1951). Lyricist to a long era of less than top-notch Broadway musicals.

Originally a reporter on the *Brooklyn Eagle,* Robert Smith soon followed his brother, Harry B Smith, into the theatre, initially as a press representative for the Casino Theater. His first writings included a comic opera, *The Shah of Persia* (mus: Harry T McConnell), produced by military amateurs at the Brooklyn Academy of music (April 1896), sketches and songs for vaudeville and burlesque houses (*The Bachelor and Belles* 1901 w Harry MacConnell, songs in *The Stickiness of Gelatine* w W T Francis 1902, etc), and his initial book pieces, a "more or less unhappy" burlesque on the Casino's own *The Casino Girl* and another on *L'Aiglon* for a new stock burlesque company mounted in imitation of Weber and Fields at the Theatre Comique. It lasted, like the company, just one week. His career was given its direction, however, when he supplied the lyrics for the Weber and Fields burlesque *Twirly Whirly* and came out with one of the biggest song hits of the period, Lillian Russell's "Come Down, Ma Evenin' Star." Smith's principal activity over the next two decades was as an enormously prolific lyricist, but he also worked on libretti and adaptations for a number of shows, often in collaboration with his brother. Amongst the songs for which he wrote the words are included Victor Herbert's "Sweethearts" for the show of the same name and "I Might Be Your Once in a While" (*Angel Face*).

1900 **The Casino Boy** (Harry T McConnell) burlesque Casino Roof Garden 31 July

1900 **L'Ongleg** (McConnell) 1 act Theatre Comique 24 December

1902 **Twirly Whirly** (John Stromberg/Edgar Smith) Weber and Fields' Music Hall 11 September

1904 **Fantana** (Raymond Hubbell) Garrick Theater, Chicago 9 October; Lyric Theater, New York 14 January 1905

1904 **A China Doll** (Alfred Aarons/w H B Smith) Majestic Theatre 19 November

1905 **When We Are Forty-One** (Gus Edwards) burlesque New York Roof Garden 12 June

1905 **Breaking into Society** (Gus Edwards, Leo Edwards, et al/w Lee Arthur) National Theater, Rochester, NY 4 September; West End Theater 2 October

1905 **The Babes and the Baron** (Herbert E Haines, et al/ Alexander M Thompson, Robert Courtneidge, et al) Lyric Theater 25 December

1906 **Mexicana** (Hubbell/w Clara Driscoll) Lyric Theater 29 January

1906 **Mam'selle Sallie** (Hubbell) Poli's Theater, Waterbury, Conn 15 October; Grand Opera House 26 November

1907 **[The Girl from] Yama** (Aarons/George Totten Smith) Walnut Street Theater, Philadelphia 4 November

1907 **Knight for a Day** revised *Mam'selle Sallie* Wallack's Theater 16 December

1908 **The Hotel Clerk** (Aarons) Walnut Street Theater, Philadelphia 27 April

1908 **The Girl at the Helm** (Hubbell) La Salle Theater, Chicago 5 September

1908 **The Girl of the Great Divide** (Hubbell) sketch in *Western Life* 125th Street Theater 26 October

1909 **The Girl and the Wizard** (Julian Edwards/J Hartley Manners) Casino Theater 27 September

1910 **The Spring Maid** (*Die Sprudelfee*) American version w H B Smith (Liberty Theater)

1911 **The Paradise of Mahomet** (*Le Paradis de Mahomet*) American version w H B Smith (Herald Square Theater)

1911 **Gaby** (Robert Hood Bowers/w H B Smith) Folies-Bergère 27 April

1911 **The Red Rose** (Bowers/w H B Smith) Bijou Theater 22 June

1911 **Gypsy Love** (*Zigeunerliebe*) American version w H B Smith (Globe Theater)

1912 **Modest Susanne** (*Die keusche Susanne*) American version w H B Smith (Liberty Theater)

1912 **The Rose Maid** (*Bub oder Mädel?*) English version w H B Smith, Raymond W Peck (Globe Theater)

1912 **The Girl from Montmartre** (*Das Mädel von Montmartre*) English version w H B Smith (Criterion Theater)

1913 **My Little Friend** (*Die kleine Freundin*) English version w H B Smith (Studebaker Theater, Chicago; New Amsterdam Theater)

1913 **Sweethearts** (Herbert/H B Smith, Fred de Grésac) New Amsterdam Theater 8 September

1914 **The Lilac Domino** (*Der lila Domino*) American version w H B Smith (44th Street Theater)

1914 **The Débutante** (Herbert/w H B Smith) New Nixon Theater, Atlantic City 21 September; Knickerbocker Theater 7 December

1916 **The Masked Model** (Woess /Frederick Herendeen/w H B Smith) National Theater, Washington, DC 7 February

1916 **Molly O!** revised *The Masked Model* (Carl Woess/H B Smith) Cort Theater 20 May

1916 **Follow Me** (*Was tut man nicht alles aus Liebe*) American version w Romberg (Casino Theater)

1917 **The Masked Model** (revised version with new score by Harold Orlob) Johnstown, Pa 17 April

1919 **A Lonely Romeo** (Malvin Franklin, Bowers/w H B Smith, Lew Fields) Shubert Theater 19 January

1919 **Angel Face** (Victor Herbert/H B Smith) Knickerbocker Theater 30 December

1920 **Oui, Madame** (Herbert/w ''G M Wright'') Little Theater, Philadelphia 22 March

1920 **The Girl in the Spotlight** (Herbert/as ''Richard Bruce'') Knickerbocker Theater 12 July

1923 **Peaches** (Max R Steiner/w H B Smith) Garrick Theater, Philadelphia 22 January

1923 **Sunbonnet Sue** (G Edwards) Illinois Theater, Chicago 7 October

1930 **The Pajama Lady** (Phil Charig, Richard Myers/w John Mercer/H B Smith, George Lederer) National Theater, Washington, DC 6 October

SMITHSON, Florence [Annette] (b Leicester, 13 March 1884; d Cardiff, 11 February 1936). Soprano star whose career wasted away too soon.

The elfin-pretty, dark-eyed little daughter of Will Smithson, manager of the Theatres Royal, Preston and Merthyr, was bundled on to the stage for the first time at the age of three, and had an early ''education'' in pantomime, drama and farce-comedy before attending the London College of Music and graduating to jobs in a minor touring opera company and in the provincial music halls. She made her first appearance in the musical theatre in Robert Courtneidge's tour of *The Cingalee,* created the role of the Indian singing maid Chandra Nil in the same manager's *The Blue Moon* at Northampton and then repeated that role in London when the intended ''name'' dropped out of the production prior to opening. The wispy 21-year-old with the sweet, high soprano voice won fine notices, and Courtneidge cast her next as the ingenue of *The Dairymaids* (1906, Hélène) and sent her on tour as Sophia in *Tom Jones* before allotting her the creation of the role of Sombra in his production of *The Arcadians* (1909, ''The Pipes of Pan''). Along with the show, Florence Smithson became famous.

The composers of that piece wrote the star role of its successor, *The Mousmé* (''My Samisen''), to suit her exceptionally high and fluid voice, but thereafter her career (marred by a drinking problem) was spent largely in variety and in pantomime in Britain, Australia and South Africa. She was married for a period to another Courtneidge star, the ill-fated comedian Dan Rolyat.

Plate 360. **Florence Smithson**

LE 66 Operette in 1 act by Philippe Pittaud de Forges and ''Laurençin'' (Paul-Aimé Chapelle). Music by Jacques Offenbach. Théâtre des Bouffes-Parisiens, Paris, 31 July 1856.

A three-handed piece in the warmly rustic vein of *Le Mariage aux lanternes* and *Le Violoneux, Le 66* told the tale of tyrolean Frantz (Gertpré) who wins 100,000 florins in a lottery with the ticket number 66. He promptly borrows money from the pedlar Berthold (Guyot) and goes on a fatuous spending spree until he discovers with horror that his ticket is actually number 99. But the pedlar turns out to be a long-lost and wealthy relation, so all ends happily for Frantz and his pretty cousin Grittly (Mlle Maréchal). The score, which began unusually with a duo sung offstage, included a particularly popular tyrolienne (''Dans mon Tyrol'') and romance (''En apprenant cette détresse'') for Grittly, a jolly air for the pedlar (''Voilà le colporteur'') and a happy trio in which the three discover that they are all related (''Ah! quel bonheur se trouver ensemble'').

Le 66 was one of nine one-act pieces which Offenbach produced at the Bouffes-Parisiens during the year 1856, whilst still bound by the laws limiting the number of characters which could be used in his operéttes, and along with *La Rose de Saint-Flour, Tromb-al-ca-zar, La Bonne d'enfants* and *Le Savetier et le financier* it won a fine success. It remained in the Bouffes repertoire, and was played by the company on their 1862 summer visit to Vienna, where it had, by that time, already been seen in Karl Treumann's Carltheater version as *Die Savoyarden* (1859). That German version was also played in Budapest before a Hungarian one (ad Pál Madarassy) was produced. I haven't been able to pinpoint the first German showing, but the show was being revived in Berlin as late as 1895 at the Alexanderplatz Theater (27 October).

A potted English version of the piece (containing all the music) was first heard at London's Oxford Music Hall in 1865, and thereafter all round the music halls of Britain, but the complete piece first got a theatre showing as toured by Louisa Pyne's little operetta company in 1867–68 in a repertoire of short pieces. It was later played in the West End by Albert Brennir, Edith Percy and Norman Kirby as a curtain-raiser to *The Marble Heart.* Susie Galton, Louisa's cousin and a member of her company, subsequently introduced the piece to America, in her 1868–69 season at Wood's Museum as part of a large repertoire of short pieces, which also included *Lischen and Fritzchen, Le Mariage aux lanternes, Too Many Cooks* (ie, *La Rose de Saint-Flour*) and MacFarren's *Jessy Lea.* She, her sister Blanche, and Tom Whiffen were the performers, and Susie interpolated ''Home, Sweet Home'' into the proceedings.

The opérette's most recent appearance on the Paris stage was in 1984, played in a double bill with Offenbach's *Pépito* (Studio Bertrand 24 July).

Austria: Carltheater *Die Savoyarden* 24 November 1859, Theater am Franz-Josefs-Kai (Fr) 4 June 1862; Hungary: Budai Színkör *Die Savoyarden* 29 June 1860, Budai Népszínház *A 66-os szam* 7 December 1863; Germany: *Loterielos No 66* np nd; UK: Operetta House, Edinburgh *Sixty-Six* 2 December 1867, Charing Cross Theatre 4 July 1876; USA: Wood's Museum *Sixty-Six, or Fortune's Chance* 31 August 1868

DER SOLDAT DER MARIE Operette in 3 acts by Bernhard Buchbinder, Jean Kren and Alfred Schönfeld. Music by Leo Ascher. Neues Operettenhaus, Berlin, 2 September 1916.

Along with *Hoheit tanzt Walzer, Der Soldat der Marie* was the most successful of all Ascher's Operetten, and the best of his pieces to have been premiered in Berlin.

Buchbinder and Kren's libretto told the rakish tale of the philandering Prince Kurt von Hansendorf who courts two of the three daughters of the dispossessed dancer-turned-miller Theodor Mumme at one and the same time: in his lordly guise he makes love to Mariann whilst he worms his way into the heart of Marie (Käthe Dorsch) dressed as a simple soldier. When he is discovered, the sensible Marie realizes that she is much better off with the sincere Hans Wonneberger, leaving the Prince, suddenly aware of the depth of his feelings, to offer title and marriage to Mariann. Amongst this plethora of Ms, the littlest sister, Mariett, goes off and becomes a famous dancer as . . . Maria Mirabelli.

Ascher's score was dominated by dance rhythms: the broad waltzes ''Ach liebste ich halt dich'' and the mirror song (''Spieglein, Spieglein in meiner Hand''), the March-gavotte ''Mit Parapluie und Pompadour,'' the polka ''Ach Theo—Theo—Theodor!,'' the marching Trommellied (''Ja, ja im jeden Städtchen'') and ''Wenn die Veilchen wieder spriessen,'' all of which together, along with the romantic serenade ''Du bist meine Freunde,'' made up the most popular part of the music.

Produced as Jean Kren's initial offering as manager at Berlin's Neues Operettenhaus (ex- Montis Operetten Theater), the sweetly old-fashioned *Der Soldat der Marie* scored a considerable success with a typical wartime public avid for good-old-days entertainment, and it was soon being staged throughout central Europe. In Oscar Fronz's Vienna production, Otto Storm (Kurt), Ida Russka (Marie), Grete Holm (Mariann), Ludwig Herold (Hans) and Leopold Strassmeyer (Mumme) headed the cast for a season of 112 performances, whilst in Budapest *A Marcsa katonája* was played happily at the Városi Színház for a good run. However, any wider life the show might have had was stifled by the very wartime conditions which had first helped it to success.

Austria: Wiener Bürgertheater 19 January 1917; Hungary: Városi Színház *A Marcsa katonája* 28 December 1918

SOLDENE, Emily [?LAMBERT, Emily] (b Clerkenwell, 30 September 1838; d Bloomsbury, 8 April 1912). One of the most memorable characters of the English and international stage of the 19th century.

Emily Soldene, happily equipped with a generously rounded figure and a very fine mezzo to soprano voice, began her career singing ballads, arias and potted operas, opéras-bouffes (*Orphée aux enfers*) or opérettes (*M et Mme Denis, The Market Girls, Tromb-al-ca-zar*) in the music halls under the name of Miss FitzHenry, whilst performing in more sedate concert and oratorio surroundings, alongside the great operatic names of the era, under her own name. She made her first appearance on the opéra-bouffe stage deputizing for Julia Mathews as *La Grande-Duchesse* (1869) and she followed up as Offenbach's Boulotte (*Barbe-bleue,* 1869) and on tour as the

Duchess before making her West End debut as Marguerite to the Faust of Hervé in the London production of the composer's *Le Petit Faust* (1870) at the Lyceum. She later deputized for a few performances for Hervé at the Lyceum in his more famous role as *Chilpéric,* toured Britain in the same role, and appeared at the Islington Philharmonic Music Hall in potted opéra-bouffe (also director) before shooting to stardom at the same house in the star role of the little pastry cook, Drogan, in the theatre-world-shaking London version of *Geneviève de Brabant* (1871).

She subsequently appeared in tights again in a season of Delibes's *Fleur-de-Lys* (1873, *La Cour du Roi Pétaud,* Prince Hyacinth), scored a further major London success at the Gaiety and the Opera Comique as Mlle Lange in *La Fille de Madame Angot* (1873) and, now established at the very top of her profession, presented herself at the Lyceum in *La Grande-Duchesse* and as Mlle Lange before taking the "Soldene Opéra-Bouffe Company," under the management of Messrs Grau and Chizzola, off to America. The repertoire which she played there, at Broadway's Lyceuym and then round the country, included her inevitable *Geneviève de Brabant, La Fille de Madame Angot, Chilpéric, La Grande-Duchesse* and Offenbach's new *Madame l'Archiduc,* of which the title role of Marietta became another Soldene regular.

The success of this experiment meant that in the following years Soldene was continually on the move, playing both in London and on Broadway, and touring in Britain and in America before, in 1877, making a first trip to Australia and New Zealand. She was rapturously received there ("a fine actress in comic opera. She never loses a point and all her by-play is telling, while she takes care that the idea of the character is carried consistently through the opera") and her company, especially the distinctly buxom and lightly clad supporting ladies whom their manageress chose with particular care, became legends. Her now celebrated basic repertoire was supplemented, at various times, by *La Belle Poule, La Jolie Parfumeuse, La Belle Hélène, Trial by Jury, Barbe-bleue, La Périchole, Les Cloches de Corneville, Giroflé-Girofla* and *The Waterman* but Drogan, Lange (into which role she was not above inserting her rendition of "Silver Threads Among the Gold"), Chilpéric and, for a while and a notch below, Marietta long remained her staple roles.

One her return to Britain in 1878 she starred in a reprise of *Geneviève de Brabant,* the four-act *La Périchole* and Thérésa's famous vehicle *La Poule aux oeufs d'or* at the Alhambra, and the following year became the British provinces' first vernacular Carmen. She toured her production of Bizet's opéra-comique, with Durward Lely as her José, for two years with notable success—even bring-

Plate 361. **Emily Soldene**

ing it to the East End (the West End was forbidden, for Carl Rosa held exclusive London rights) to extraordinary acclaim. However, after the good and great times, during which she had been toasted as the musical theatre's most outstanding star, the bad ones came. During the 1880 panto season at Glasgow her husband suffered a stroke, and when, the following year, she took a (rather less good than before) company to America, under amateurish management, the enterprise fell messily to pieces, leaving her to troupe the American outbacks with a shoestring outfit which finally ground to a halt in Cincinatti. However, she finally made it back to Britain and the following year she was up and going again, trouping around Britain with her hardy annuals. In 1883 she eventually stopped her racing round the world and took on the management of the Gaiety Theatre, Hastings. However, before long her theatre produced cash-flow problems and Soldene was quickly back playing Drogans and Langes and singing opéra-bouffe arias on the music halls to raise money. There is little doubt that she was one of those artists to whom money will not stick, and as a result she stuck to the stage.

In 1885 she went back on the road, touring for the first time in years as an employee rather than a manager (Bathilde in *Olivette,* Lange, Princess Machinstoff in *La Cosaque*), before in 1886, now decidedly buxom, she abandoned her traditional roles and moved up to a comedy-character part in an unfortunate piece called *Frivoli* at Drury Lane. By chance, she was spotted in the short-lived *Frivoli* by John McCaull, and a few weeks later she found herself back on Broadway, starring as Madame Jacob in *Joséphine vendue par ses soeurs.* She played for McCaull in *Don César* (Dona Uraca) and *Lorraine* (1887, Oudarde) but found herself without a job when the producer's empire started to shrink. She continued, however, to work in America, touring a highly successful "Soldene Burlesque Company" through the nation's variety houses (the entertainment included a potted *Geneviève de Brabant,* too many years on), appearing on Broadway in musicals (Broken Arrow in *Dovetta,* Barbara in *The Black Crook*) and in the French melodrama *La Porteuse de pain* (*Jeanne Fortier, the Bread Carrier,* also adaptor, director); going on tour with the Mestayer-Vaughan company in the variety musical *The Tourists* (Aunt Pamelia); and, in 1890, joining the company at San Francisco's Tivoli Theatre as resident character lady. She appeared as the Duchess in *La Fille du Tambour-major,* Public Opinion in *Orphée aux enfers,* Olympia in *Donna Juanita,* The Duchess in *The Gondoliers,* with great success in her old role in *Geneviève de Brabant,* and in breeches again (aged 52) as Stenio Strozzi in Lecocq's *The Red Bird.* A benefit mounted for her at the Tivoli at the end of her season featured a sparring bout between Jim Corbett and McCord. She returned to San Francisco the following year for a similar engagement at the Orpheum (Duchess of Plaza Toro, Gipsy Queen in *The Bohemian Girl,* Princesse de Gramponneur in *Erminie,* Katisha in *The Mikado,* Marchioness in *The Queen's Lace Handkerchief,* Manola in *La Prinmcesse de Trébizonde,* Barbara in *The Back Hussar,* Little Buttercup, etc), but the company subsequently foundered in the backblocks of Oregon, and she returned to San Francisco.

She didn't stay there long, however, but set off south towards the scene of some of her greatest triumphs, Australia. There she mounted productions of *La Fille de Madame Angot* and *Geneviève de Brabant* with a locally picked-up company (including several of her "own" who had stayed behind), but the season quickly foundered and Emily Soldene's career on the stage was done.

However, she had a second career to come. An old newspaperman admirer from her younger days got her a job as a music and drama critic on a Sydney paper, and before long she was back in Britain working as the heavily bylined social correspondent of the Sydney *Evening News.* It was a job she retained, first for the *News* and later, poached, for the brand new Sydney *Sun,* up till the day of her death, as she made herself a huge personality on the Australian front, and a familiar figure, in her black dress and inevitable hat, wherever something royal, racing, theatrical or political, or just plain interesting or gossipworthy was happening in London.

One feature of her newspaper columns was a tendency to reminisce, and she brought up many an old theatrical tale, and many an "I knew him when . . ." paragraph, until finally she put them together (she had always kept a detailed diary) and brought out her memoirs. The book, which caused a huge kiss-and-tellish scandal in society at its publication, remains one of the classic theatre books of all time, the most outstanding and warming (and, for a theatre book, remarkably accurate—if personally discreet) picture of the theatre of her age.

She remained, too, a symbol of the glittering days of opéra-bouffe, a rather more visible and good-fun one than Hortense Schneider in Paris, and when, in 1906, a benefit matinée was given for her at London's Palace Theatre, the crisp result proved that Madame Soldene was still fondly remembered by Victorian musical theatregoers . . . and Victorian high society gents.

Soldene's younger half-sister, **Clara VESEY** [Clara Ann SOLDEN] (b St Luke's, 8 May 1850; d ?Colombo, Ceylon), appeared in the Soldene company for many years, mostly playing roles which allowed her to show off her legs and her cutely wisecracking sense of comedy rather than her smallish soprano voice (Riccardo in *Madame l'Archiduc,* Oswald in *Geneviève de Brabant,* Bacchis in *La Belle Hélène,* Hermia in *Barbe-bleue,* Plaintiff in *Trial by Jury,* Wanda in *La Grande-Duchesse,* etc). Clara's daughter Kate Emily Hoffmeister (b London, 8 January 1882; d Brighton, 20 December 1967) appeared for more than 20 years on the variety and musical comedy stage in Britain and Australia, under the name of **Katie VESEY** (solo dancer in *The Lucky Star* 1899, *The Messenger Boy* 1900 at the Gaiety, Miss Enid Gibson in *The Catch of the Season* 1904, *The Golddiggers* 1906, etc), before retiring to Veylon and the British south coast as Lady Forrest Garvin. Soldene's son Edward, who worked under the name **E Soldene POWELL** (b London, 27 February 1863; d New York, 7 April 1915) also had a career as a minor actor and stage manager in mostly straight theatre, and mostly in America, where he was a member of the original cast of William Gillette's *Sherlock Holmes.* He also appeared unsingingly in a couple of musical shows on Broadway (*Miss Dynamite, The Sunshine Girl,* etc).

Autobiography: *My Theatrical and Musical Recollections* (Downey & Co, London, 1897)

SOLOMON, Edward (b Lambeth, London, 25 July 1855; d London, 22 January 1895). Victorian composer whose irresponsibilites eventually won him more notice than a rather wasted musical gift.

The son of music-hall pianist and musical director Charles Solomon (b London, c1819; d London, 16 May

1890), Edward was brought up in the rough-and-ready atmosphere of the Winchester and Middlesex Music Halls where both he and his brothers gained a colorful and varied early musical experience and where the young Edward officiated as an accompanist to the variety of singers and other acts from an early age. He appeared (as ''Edward Lewis'') at the Haymarket at Christmas 1866 as one of 20 ''Living Miniatures,'' playing Captain Needlegun, a volunteer exquisite, in *Littletop's Christmas Party* alongside his brothers Fred (as Littletop) and Bowers (as Mr Grumblegudgeon Mite), and as Dame Fatty in the burlesque *Sylvus*, then in the Drury Lane pantomime of 1867 and in concert with Mackney as a boy singer. He officiated as ''solo pianist'' at Vance's Variety in Bayswater in 1873, and was still a teenager when he won his earliest position as a theatre musical-director at the Alexandra Palace. After moving on to similar posts at the St James's Theatre and then at the Royalty in March 1876, he took over the desk at the Globe Theatre, where he became musical director of Alexander Henderson's record-breaking production of *Les Cloches de Corneville*. In 1879 he was musical director for Charles Wydham at the Criterion Theatre. During this period, he provided incidental music and arrangements for the plays and burlesques produced at these theatres and made his first attempts at composing original scores with some small operettas which won favorable notice.

In 1879 he won his most important commission to date when he supplied the whole of the music to the first act of the Alhambra's spectacular opéra-bouffe féerie *Rothomago*—the other three acts being written by Procida Bucalossi, Gaston Serpette and musical director Georges Jacobi—and his first solo full-length work came the following year when a collaboration with journalist Henry Pottinger Stephens resulted in the comic opera *Billee Taylor*. *Billee Taylor* combined a neatly written, tongue-in-cheek libretto with attractive and catchy songs (''All on Account of Eliza'') and, as staged by Charles Harris, proved both a critical and a popular success, favorably compared by many critics with Sullivan's contemporaneous *The Pirates of Penzance*. A decided success in Britain, it went on, however, to become an enormous favorite throughout America, being played by dozens of companies all round the country for several years.

After this maiden success, Solomon continued to work with Stephens on a series of comic operas based on ballad subjects but although *Claude Duval* (1881) did well enough, the successors of *Billee Taylor* did not live up to the hopes, too easily kindled, that the pair would become a combination to rival Gilbert and Sullivan, and ultimately their partnership broke up.

Over the years which followed, the darkly dashing Solomon was a colorful figure in theatrical circles on both sides of the Atlantic and his gaudily irresponsible private life, which led him frequently into the courts for both debt and also once for bigamy, often overwhelmed his professional life. His bigamous marriage to the American singer Lillian Russell led to her appearing in several of his works in Britain, America and on the Continent but, following Solomon's arrest and trial, she kept the Atlantic Ocean between them.

Plate 362. **Edward Solomon**

The half-success of *Claude Duval* and the failures of *Lord Bateman* (1882, ''The Silver Line'') and the original version of *The Vicar of Bray* (1883) in London led Solomon to try his luck in America, where *Billee Taylor* was still a prime reference. His *Virginia* (1883) was staged in New York by John McCaull without adding to his reputation, but Solomon brought both the piece and Miss Russell back to Britain. When *Virginia* was staged at the Gaiety Theatre, the actress had more success than the piece, but Solomon and James Mortimer supplied her with a more efficient vehicle in *Polly* the following year at the Novelty and Empire Theatres. A third vehicle which featured the Iowa-born star as the Indian maiden *Pocahontas* was a flat failure, and the pair, having now gone through the ''marriage'' which was to cause all the trouble, left Britain to take their shows to America. *Polly* proved a fair success on Broadway, but of two new Solomon pieces, *Pepita*—with Miss Russell starred—did only moderately well and *The Maid and the Moonshiner,* with Tony Hart in its central role, was a failure.

Only a few weeks after the production of *The Maid and the Moonshiner,* Solomon was back in Britain and in jail. The bigamy case took some time to be cleared up and Teddy suffered badly from his spell in prison. His health never wholly recovered, but his theatrical fortunes were soon on an improving bent. Henry Leslie, who had made his fortune with Cellier's comedy opera *Dorothy,* bought Solomon's *The Red Hussar,* a comic opera which he had originally written in happier times to be played by Lillian, as a vehicle for *Dorothy* star Marie Tempest and the piece proved a fine success in both Britain and America. However, much of the well-known fire seemed to have gone out of the little composer and, although he turned out several handfuls of songs, including some for the Gaiety Theatre new burlesques, and music for a few short theatre pieces, it seemed as if the ebullient composer of *Billee Taylor* had seen his day.

The break-up of the Gilbert and Sullivan partnership, however, proved Solomon's chance for a second coming. When D'Oyly Carte, bereft of his standard authors, was left at a loss for a new show for the Savoy Theatre in 1891 he chose to produce Solomon's *The Nautch Girl. The Nautch Girl* was a fine piece and a fine success, and once again Solomon found himself being compared to Sullivan and on the edge of a major career. Carte followed the two hundred performances of *The Nautch Girl* with a revival of Solomon's 1882 piece, *The Vicar of Bray,* and subsequently sent both pieces on the road in repertoire, but when Sullivan supplied him with *Haddon Hall* the Savoy once again billed its favorite composer and Solomon's moment was over.

Although he continued to work, in spite of now seriously bad health, and his bottom drawer piled up collaborations with F C Burnand and with Bill Yardley, he had no more London productions. He had individual numbers included in a whole array of musicals and continued to work, from time to time over the next few years, as a theatre conductor, but his career as a composer was virtually done. In January 1895 he was working as conductor of a dreadful piece called *The Taboo* when he was taken seriously ill and died. He had not made it to his 40th birthday.

Teddy Solomon had no formal musical training. He was a product of a musical background wholly different from that of Arthur Sullivan, yet he produced music which in its time was considered by some to be comparable in value to that of the Savoy operas, and Sullivan himself went on record as saying that Solomon had it in him to have been the British Bizet. In the versatile manner of the day, he was able to switch from writing a comic song, like his famous ''All on Account of Eliza'' in *Billee Taylor,* to a complicated piece of ensemble work or a finale, but his more substantial work held the same catchiness which made his comedy songs so popular and his comedy songs had something of the substance which characterized his ensemble writing, to the advantage of both.

If most of Solomon's works did not live on after their original productions, it was not largely the fault of the composer. It was perhaps a weakness in him that he suffered so clearly and so often from poor libretti but, in the wake of *Billee Taylor,* although he had successes with *Polly* (1884), *The Red Hussar* (1889) and above all *The Nautch Girl* (1891), George Dance's highly skillful and humorous book for the last-named gave him his only really satisfactory libretto and lyrics since *Billee Taylor.* The work proved wholly worthy of the famous theatre which played it.

Solomon's first wife, Jane ISAACS (d London, 15 July 1898), was a successful music-hall artist under the name of **Lily GREY**, and their daughter, Clara Jessie Elizabeth SOLOMON (b London, 21 December 1873; d London, 21 December 1964), became a musical-theatre and variety performer in her turn. As Claire Solomon she played Eliza Bangs in her father's *Polly* at the age of 10 (1884) and in *Erminie* (1885, Rosalie) at 12, and later appeared at the Gaiety in the chorus of *Cinder-Ellen Up Too Late* and as an understudy to Cissie Loftus and Katie Seymour in *Don Juan* (1893, Zoë). She also took over the role of the callboy, Shrimp, in *In Town* on tour (1894) and later played it in Broadway's season of the show (1897), and she understudied Ada Reeve in the title role of *The Shop Girl.* She became **Claire ROMAINE** after her marriage to Edgar Romaine Keddie and went on to play in *The Maid of Athens* (1897, Ina) and in the title role of the successful touring musical *The Gay Grisette* (1898, Babette), and was taken back to the Gaiety to deputize for Connie Ediss as the heavy lady of *The Messenger Boy* (1901, t/o Mrs Bangs) and *The Toreador* (Mrs Malton Hoppings). On the verge of the big time, she blew it when her husband chose to have a row with George Edwardes over his wife's material. She only played once in a London musical after that: in the heavy-lady role of the short-lived *Amorelle* (1904). She visited Australia where she billed herself as the ''idol of London'' on the Australian halls, and ended up a useful touring character lady in revue and in such pieces as *Toni* (1924, Camille), *Lady Letty* (1926, The Cook) and *Peggy-Ann.* Her last chances of a return to the West End were poleaxed when she was replaced for London by Viola Tree in the role of Bessie Bunting in *Jill Darling* (1933), and when the British production of Vincent Youmans's *Two Little Girls in Blue,* in which she was cast as Hariette Neville, closed on the pre-London road.

Solomon's daughter by Lillian Russell, known as **Dorothy RUSSELL** (Lillian SOLOMON, b London, 10

May 1884; d New York, 1954), also took uneventfully to the musical stage (*The Girl from Kays* 1903, Lillian Saddart in *The Mimic and the Maid* 1907, *The White Hen* 1907, etc).

Solomon's second ''wife''—somewhere between Lily and Lillian—was the successful actress and musical-theatre player Edith Blande. After the Lillian episode he married yet another popular musical theatre actress, **Kate EVERLEIGH** [Catherine Priscilla JONES] (d St John's Wood, 8 February 1926). And before too long she too was suing, for maintenance.

1876 **Crotchets** (Frederick Hay) 1 act Strand Theatre 7 June

1876 **A Will with a Vengeance** (Hay) 1 act Globe Theatre 27 November

1877 **Contempt of Court** (Arthur Matthison) 1 act Folly Theatre 5 May

1878 **Neptune's Trust, or This Was the Charter** (Frank Hall) sketch London Pavilion, and Middlesex Music Hall 30 September

1879 **Venus, or the gods as they were and not as they should have been** (aka *Vulcan*) (pasticcio arr/Edward Rose, Augustus Harris) Royalty Theatre 27 June

1879 **Another Drink** (Henry Savile Clarke, Lewis Clifton) 6 scenes Folly Theatre 12 July

1879 **The Happy Man** (Tyrone Power) new score 1 act Globe Theatre 6 September

1879 **Balloonacy** (pasticcio arr/H Pottinger Stephens, F C Burnand) Royalty Theatre 1 December

1879 **Rothomago** (H B Farnie) 1st act of 4 Alhambra Theatre 22 December

1880 **Popsy Wopsy** (Sydney Grundy) 1 act Royalty Theatre 4 October

1880 **Billee Taylor** (Stephens) Imperial Theatre 30 October

1881 **Claude Duval** (Stephens) Olympic Theatre 24 August

1881 **Quite an Adventure** (Frank Desprez) 1 act Olympic Theatre 7 September

1882 **Lord Bateman, or Picotee's Pledge** (Stephens) Gaiety Theatre 29 April

1882 **Through the Looking Glass** (Stephens) 1 act Gaity Theatre 17 July

1882 **The Vicar of Bray** (Sydney Grundy) Globe Theatre 22 July

1883 **Virginia and Paul, or Changing the Rings** (aka *Virginia*) (Stephens) Bijou Theater, New York 8 January

1884 **The Little Cricket** (James Mortimer) Avenue Theatre 24 May

1884 **Polly, the Pet of the Regiment** (Mortimer) Novelty Theatre 8 November

1884 **Pocahontas, or The Great White Pearl** (Grundy) Empire Theatre 26 December

1885 **Round and Square** (Desprez) 1 act Theatre Royal, Manchester 6 April

1886 **Pepita, or The Girl with the Glass Eyes** (Alfred Thompson) Union Square Theater, New York 16 March

1886 **The Maid and the Moonshiner** (Charles Hoyt) Standard Theater, New York 16 August

1888 **Don Juan Jr** (''Brothers Prendergast'' ad Robert Reece, Edward Righton) Avenue Theatre 25 August

1888 **Penelope** (comp & arr/Stephens) Star Theatre, New York 15 October

1889 **The Real Truth About Ivanhoe, or Scott Scotched** (E C Nugent) Theatre Royal, Chelsea Barracks 1 February

1889 **Pickwick** (F C Burnand) 1 act Comedy Theatre 7 February

1889 **Penelope** (George Proctor Hawtrey) 1 act Comedy Theatre 9 May

1889 **Tuppins & Co** (Malcolm Watson) 1 act St George's Hall 24 June

1889 **The Tiger** (Burnand) 1 act Old Stagers, Canterbury August; St James's Theatre 3 May 1890

1889 **The Red Hussar** (Stephens) Lyric Theatre 23 November

1890 **Domestic Economy** (Burnand) 1 act Comedy Theatre 7 April

1890 **A Swarry Dansong** (Barrington) Criterion Theatre 5 June

1890 **In and Out of Season** (Watson) 1 act Lecture Hall Ipswich 16 October

1890 **Claude Duval** (Frederick Bowyer, R Morton) 1 act Alhambra 27 October

1891 **Incompatibility of Temper** (Barrington) 1 act private performance

1891 **Killiecrumper** (Watson) 1 act St George's Hall 30 March

1891 **Robinson Crusoe Esq** (William Yardley) Theatre Royal, Chelsea Barracks 11 April

1891 **The Nautch Girl** (Desprez/George Dance) Savoy Theatre 30 June

1891 **Pat** (w John Crook, Alfred Lee, Fred Eplett/Mark Ambient, Frederic Wood/Harry Monkhouse,George Roberts) Royal Artillery Theatre, Woolwich 16 November; revised version w add mus Edward Jakobowksi Aquarium, Yarmouth 1 August 1892

1892 **The Vicar of Bray** (revised version) Savoy Theatre 28 January

1893 **Robinson Crusoe Up-to-Date** revised *Robinson Crusoe Esq* Theatre Royal, Preston 16 October

1893 **Sandford and Merton** (Burnand) 1 act Vaudeville Theatre 20 December

1894 **Polly** (Malcolm Watson) sketch West London Theater 18 November

1895 **The Professor** (Barrington) 1 act St George's Hall 15 July

1896 **On the March** (w John Crook, Frederic Clay/Yardley, B C Stephenson, Cecil Clay) Prince of Wales Theatre 22 June

SOLOMON, Fred[erick Charles] (b London, 31 August 1853; d New York, 9 September 1924).

''Fritzy'' Solomon ultimately had a career in the musical theatre which was no less notable, and both longer and more varied, than his more up-front brother's. During a colorful career of nearly half a century in the theatre he worked as an author, director, composer and musical director, on Broadway and in London, but the heart of his work was in a highly successful career as a comic-opera comedian.

Fred, too, benefited from the eclectic show business upbringing which their father's life imposed on them, becoming adept on a multiplicity of musical instruments during his life around the Winchester Music Hall. He began a career as a singer as a child (as "Frederick Charles"), being strongly featured in Thomas Coe's Living Miniatures (Dubup in *Sylvus,* Little Top in *Littletop's Christmas* Party 1866), taking children's spots at Drury Lane (*Faw Fee Fo Fum* 1867, Bluebottle in *Grimalkin the Great,* 1868, singing "The Bay of Biscay"—and making "the hit of the evening" in Chatterton's 1868 Ash Wednesday concert with "The Village Blacksmith," with 12-year-old Teddy at the piano), appearing with his father's juvenile troupe and in the famous children's chorus in *Babil and Bijou* (1872). He subsequently went to study at the School of Military Music in Chatham, Kent, and became a bandmaster in the Volunteer Cadets, but through the later 1870s and earliest 1880s he worked largely on the halls, first as "Fred Charles, the military comique" and later with a sketch called *Wagnermania.* He turned from the halls to the theatre when his brother's pieces began to be produced and, in the early part of his adult theatrical life, he followed in Edward's traces, appearing at the Royalty in 1879 (Rémy in *Nicette,* Jupiter in *Venus,* Charley Maloni in *A Will with a Vengeance*) and making his first hit when he played the role of Ben Barnacle in *Billee Taylor* (1880), introducing the show's top song "All on Account of Eliza." Over the years that followed, he reprised this role around Britain and in 1884 through Europe. He also created the comic roles of Edward's *Quite an Adventure* and *Claude Duval* (1881, Blood-Red Bill), appeared with Lotta at the Royalty Theatre, conducting her performances as *Nitouche* and appearing as a performer in *Wagnermania* as an afterpiece, and he played Dominie Sampson in Sims Reeves' first production of *Guy Mannering* at the Brighton Theatre Royal in 1884. In the same year he went on the road as conductor of the Alexander Henderson production of *Nell Gwynne.* He also composed music for some musical stage pieces.

In 1885 Fritzy emigrated to America where he made a good career as a comic actor in musicals, making his debut as General Bang in Edward's *Polly* at Cleveland, Ohio (1885) and in his famous role in *Billee Taylor* on the road, and continuing with Broadway appearances in his *Pepita* (1886, Curasao) and *The Maid and the Moonshiner* (1886, Rev Mr Thayer) and a stint with his own company touring the musical farce *Inside Out* in 1886. He subsequently took over as Cadeaux in *Erminie* from Francis Wilson (1886, then two years on the road and a reappearance in 1915) at the top of what would be a six-year stint as a leading comedian at the Casino Theater. He was the original American Shadbolt in *The Yeomen of the Guard* (1888) and appeared, amongst other works in *Nadjy* (Margrave), *Les Brigands* (1889, Pietro), *The Brazilian* (1890, Daniel), *La Fille de Madame Angot* (1890, Larivaudière), *La Grande-Duchesse* (1891, t/o General Boum), *The Tyrolean* (Baron Weps), *Nanon* (Abbé La Plâtre), Pauline Hall's *Puritania* (1892, the witchfinder John Smith, "the real success of the piece" also director), *La Tzigane* (General Buguslav Schlemvitchikoff) and *Le Petit Duc* (Frimousse).

He subsequently spent two periods writing, directing and playing in operetta and burlesque at Koster and Bial's music hall, but he came to grief in Rome, NY, when he sent out his own starring tour in the autumn of 1893. In the years that followed, he went on to tour with Lottie Collins in her "Troubadours" company (1894, *The Fair Equestrienne, The Devilbird* principal comedian and stage director), played Don Andrès to the Périchole of Lillian Russell (1895) and got into skirts to play the Directrice in her production of *Le Petit Duc* (1896). He played with the Whitney-Mapleson company, appeared as Jonathan in *Der arme Jonathan* and in *The Whirl of the Town* (1897), directed Oscar Hammerstein's *Mrs Radley Barton's Ball* (1897) at the Olympia, played in E E Rice's productions of *Evangeline* (1896, Le Blanc) and *The Ballet Girl* (1897, Baton Blanc), starred as Cadeau in Aronson's attempt to relaunch *Erminie* (1897), appeared at Madison Square Garden in the West Coast musical *Captain Cook* (1897, Koko Bola) and went again on the road with the Cummings Opera Co as Lurcher in *Dorothy* (1898). Between these performing assignments he worked as a conductor both in the British and American provinces. In 1898 he became connected with the Witmark Musical Library, and his appearances in the theatre became for a time less frequent, but in 1900 he conducted the Casino Theater production of *The Cadet Girl* and appeared as Yellowplush in *The Belle of Bohemia* (1900), after which he joined the Klaw and Erlanger organization as musical supervisor and conductor of the shows at the New Amsterdam Theater. He held that position for some 14 years, taking a Broadway baton on such productions as *A Little of Everything* (1904), *Forty-Five Minutes from Broadway* (1906), *The Pink Lady* (1911) and *Oh! Oh! Delphine* (1912), but also for such non-K&E pieces as *The Ziegfeld Follies of 1908* and *1909,* and the Werba and Luescher production of *Little Miss Fix-It* (1911). As late as 1917 he was seen on Broadway playing in *The Rainbow Girl* (Clergyman).

Fritzy's youngest brother, **Sol[omon] SOLOMON** (b London, 18 November 1871; d USA) followed him to America and appeared alongside him at Koster and Bial's. He later played at Koster & Bial's under the name of Sol Mirandoli and in comic roles in such musicals as Fred's *King Kalico* (1892), *The Brownies* (1894–96), *Captain Cook* (1897, Buntline), the Casino's *La Belle*

Hélène (1899, Ajax II), *The Rounders* (1899, Schlitz then Ludwig Dollar), *The Casino Boy* (1900, Dennie), *The Belle of Bohemia* (1900, USA and UK, Arris), and *The Chaperons* (1901, Signor Stumpiani), *Comin' thro the Rye* (1905, Ouioui), *The Little Cherub* (1906, Ethelbert), *Captain Careless* (1906), on the halls in Kerker's *Very Grand Opera or Burning to Sing* (1907), in an Aborn revival of *Erminie* (1908, Simon), *The Goddess of Liberty* (1909, Lord Jack's tailor), with Aborn Comic Opera Co as Pozzo in *El Capitan* (1909) and, in a last recorded appearance, in *His Little Widows* (1917).

Fred Solomon also composed a number of popular songs (''Everybody Smiled,'' etc), additional material for a variety of Broadway shows including *Dorcas* (1896, ''A Cup of Tea''), *The Man in the Moon* (1899, ''Rastus Loves Me Truly''), *A Little of Everything* (1904, ''Turn Those Eyes Away''), *Three Million Dollars,* etc, as well as for pasticcio and song-and-speciality burlesques and extravaganzas for such groups as The Bowery Burlesquers and May Howard's Extravaganza Company (''spicy burlesques''), and even composed a full-scale Broadway musical, *King Kalico,* as well as adapting the musical part of several British pantomimes for their Broadway productions.

He married first the British serio-comic and burlesque actress **Flora PLIMSOLL** (Sarah NATHAN, of the famous costumery family), later Mamie Sutton, a chorus lady from the Casino Theater, and fathered children by several other theatrical paramours, including performer Clara Becque. One of his daughters went on the stage under the name of Justine Grey, and a son Edward Becque became a scenic designer in Britain's northern theatres.

1881 **The Good Young Man Who . . .** 1 act His Majesty's Theatre, Aberdeen 30 May

1883 **Captain Kidd** (Charles Harrie Abbott) Prince of Wales Theatre, Liverpool 10 September

1885 **The Fairy Circle** (Frederick Bowyer) 1 act Grand Theatre, Islington 27 May

1885 **A Seaside Holiday** 1 act Harry White's Minstrels 10 September

1886 **A-Donis** (w H M Pitts) 1 act Koster & Bial's Music Hall 8 February

1886 **Little Lohengrin** (new score for Frederick Bowyer's burlesque ad Edgar Smith) Casino Theater, Chicago 13 September

1888 **Black Sheep** Hyde and Behman's Theater, Brooklyn 10 September

1888 **Terry, the Swell** (C L Graves, Harry B Bell ad George Clarke) Corinne Lyceum, Buffalo, NY 12 November; Howard Athenaeum, Boston 19 November

1889 **Banditti, or Lamb'd in Corsica** 1 act Koster & Bial's Music Hall 29 July

1889 **Young Don Juan** 1 act Koster & Bial's Music Hall, New York 2 December

1890 **Prince Lavender's Reception** 1 act Koster & Bial's Music Hall 20 January

1890 **The Chandeliers, or Venice in New York** 1 act Koster & Bial's Music Hall 17 February

1890 **Our Belle Helene** 1 act Koster & Bial's Music Hall 31 March

1890 **[The Bijou Edition of] La Fille de Madame Angot** (burlesque) 1 act Koster & Bial's Music Hall 30 June

1890 **The Isle of Red** (w Harry Morris) 1 act Olympic Theater, Harlem 30 August

1890 **The Dumb Girl of Sevilla** 1 act Koster & Bial's Music Hall 30 October

1890 **The Clemenceau Case** (burlesque) (William J Rostetter) 1 act Koster & Bial's Music Hall 10 November

1890 **O'Nero or the Lady of the Lions** 1 act Koster & Bial's Music Hall 22 December

1891 **The Dashing Dragoons** 1 act Koster & Bial's Music Hall 23 February

1891 **Adam's Temptation, or The Birds of Paradise** 1 act Koster & Bial's Music Hall 30 March

1891 **Ye Olden Times** 1 act Koster & Bial's Music Hall 29 June

1891 **Dick Whittington and His Cat** 1 act Koster & Bial's Music Hall 10 August

1891 **Carmen Up Too Late, or the Bold Toreador** 1 act Koster & Bial's Music Hall 19 October

1892 **Joan of Arc, or the Merry Maid of Orleans** 1 act Koster & Bial's Musc Hall 4 January

1892 **Fra Diavolo** 1 act Koster & Bial's Music Hall 7 March

1892 **King Kalico** (w R L Scott/Frank Dupree) Broadway Theater 7 June

1892 **Robin Hood** (burlesque) 1 act Koster & Bial's Music Hall 12 September

1892 **Bluebeard** (with music from *Barbe-bleue*) 1 act Koster & Bial's Music Hall 4 November

1892 **The Rendezvous** (''by Offenbach'') (?*La Permission de dix heures*) 1 act Koster & Bial's Music Hall 11 November

1893 **The Miller's Daughter** (''from an original by Delibes'') 1 act Koster & Bial's Music Hall 6 January

1893 **Orpheus** potted *Orphée aux enfers* Koster & Bial's Music Hall 6 January

1893 **La Fille de Madame Angot** potted version Koster & Bial's Music Hall 20 March

1893 **Billee Taylor** potted version Koster & Bial's Music Hall 9 May

1893 **Paul's Dilemma** (Planché ad) Koster & Bial's Music Hall 16 May

1893 **La Belle Hélène** potted version Koster & Bial's Music Hall 19 June

1893 **The Admiral** (Morton) 1 act Koster & Bial's Music Hall 30 June

1897 **Mr Paris at Niagara** 1 act Kernan's Lyceum Theater, Washington 1 September

1897 **The Maid from Paris** (aka *The Naughty French Girl*) 1 act Pleasure Palace 6 September

1897 **The Three Lost Brothers** 1 act Pleasure Palace 6 September

- 1898 **Slumming** (Loney Haskell) 1 act Miner's Bowery Theater 20 August
- 1899 **The Maid in the Moon** (Richard Carle) 1 act Casino Roof 31 July
- 1901 **The Sleeping Beauty and the Beast** (w J M Glover/J Hickory Wood, Arthur Collins ad Cheever Goodwin, J J McNally) Broadway Theater 4 November
- 1903 **Mr Bluebeard** (Wood, Collins ad Goodwin) Knickerbocker Theater 21 January
- 1903 **Mother Goose** (w others/George V Hobart/Wood, Collins ad McNally) New Amsterdam Theater 2 December
- 1904 **Humpty Dumpty** (w Bob Cole, J Rosamund Johnson, et al/Wood, Collins ad McNally) New Amsterdam Theater 14 November

SO LONG, LETTY Musical farce in 2 acts by Oliver Morosco and Elmer Harris, based on Harris's play *Your Neighbour's Wife.* Music and lyrics by Earl Carroll. Morosco Theater, Los Angeles, 3 July 1915; Shubert Theater, New York, 23 October 1916.

Following the success won by comedienne Charlotte Greenwood in his production of *Pretty Mrs Smith,* producer Oliver Morosco quickly bundled the actress into a star-billed role as Letty Robbins in *So Long, Letty.* Miss Greenwood had been Letitia (Letty) Proudfoot in *Pretty Mrs Smith,* but *So Long, Letty* was the first of what would become a series of comical "Letty" musicals fabricated around her. This one, written by Morosco and Elmer Harris on the bones of Harris's 1913 *Your Neighbour's Wife* (Morosco Theater, Los Angeles 28 September), had her involved in a bit of husband-swapping. Tommy Robbins (Sydney Grant) and Harry Miller (Walter Catlett) covet the comfy and sensual qualities, respectively, of each other's wives, Letty (Miss Greenwood) and Grace (May Boley). So they swap spouses and go through an evening of comedy before returning to the status quo. Vera Doria was Mrs Cease, a wealthy aunt, caught up in the whole thing in the way that wealthy aunts always are in such affairs. Earl Carroll provided a lightweight score, topped by its title duo, "Here Come the Married Men," "All the Comforts of Home" and "On the Beautiful Beach," as an accompaniment to the comedy.

The show was a considerable success when Morosco mounted it at his base in Los Angeles, but the producer did not hurry it east. Whilst Miss Greenwood was deployed into a damply splashy Ned Wayburn revue *Town Topics,* the musical moved first to San Francisco's Cort Theater (11 October) and then off round the rest of the country. It was another year before *So Long, Letty* touched down—complete with its original star—in New York.

The show played but 96 performances on Broadway, but it was soon back on the road to continue a long touring life, as Morosco readied the next of the series of like shows which would follow it, and it also found itself a really appreciative home in Australia. The show was first produced there, in Sydney, as a wartime Christmas entertainment before it had even made its way from its original American West Coast production to Broadway. It was advertised by the banner "when husbands exchange wives they sing 'So Long, Harry, Gracie, Tommy, Letty'!" Dot Brunton was Australia's Letty (equipped with an interpolated "They Didn't Believe Me"), the Gaiety star Connie Ediss was Grace, and ex-Savoyard C H Workman (Tommy), Alfred Frith (Harry) and Ethel Morrison as the aunt completed a strong cast which played an outstanding 113 performances in Sydney before going on to two months in Melbourne (Her Majesty's Theatre 22 April 1916). The show's marked success encouraged the Williamson firm to pick up the next Morosco/Carroll piece, the less worthy *Canary Cottage,* but what was lost on that venture was more than made up by repeat seasons of *So Long, Letty* which remained an oft-reprised Australian favorite for many years.

In 1928 the piece was finally taken up for Britain by producer Laddie Cliff. Rewritten by Austin Melford, equipped with a new and equally weightless score by Billy Mayerl and Frank Eyton, it was sent on the road with the producer's wife, Phyllis Monkman, starred as Letty (Theatre Royal, Birmingham 22 October). When it proved ineffective, it was again rewritten by Stanley Lupino as *Oh, Letty!* and failed again. Another producer, H Wellesley Smith, then took up the now-orphaned show, had it done over yet again as *Change Over* (8 April 1929), and put it out yet again with Renée Reel starred. It toured this time for two and a half months and left it at that. Wife-swapping, last glimpsed in the West End in *Oh! Oh!! Delphine!!!* in the 1910s, didn't get back there until *I Love My Wife* came along more than half a century later.

A film version of the piece was produced in 1930 with Miss Greenwood featured alongside Charles Roach.

Australia: Her Majesty's Theatre, Sydney 26 December 1915

SOMETHING FOR THE BOYS Musical comedy in a prologue and 2 acts by Herbert and Dorothy Fields. Music and lyrics by Cole Porter. Alvin Theater, New York, 7 January 1943.

A wartime musical put together by producer Mike Todd for the frequently proven *Anything Goes* combination of Ethel Merman (star) and Cole Porter (songwriter), *Something for the Boys* featured its cheerful leading lady as Blossom Hart, a chorus girl become war worker who inherits a share in a broken-down ranch. She and her cousins (Paula Laurence, Allen Jenkins) fit the place out as a rendezvous for the wives of men at a nearby base but, when Blossom gets too matey with airman Rocky Fulton

(Bill Johnson), his girl Melanie Walker (Frances Mercer) casts loud doubts on the morals of the place and gets it closed down. Blossom becomes a heroine when (thanks to the fillings in her healthy white teeth) she turns out to be a human radio-receiver and saves an aeroplane from disaster, so her house is rehabilitated and she, of course, gets herself Rocky.

The delightfully zany final twist redeemed a script that was more like a wartime film scenario than anything else, but the role of Blossom gave Miss Merman sufficient to get her energetic (radio-receiving) teeth into and she lit into Porter's ''Hey, Good Lookin''' with Johnson, ''He's a Right Guy,'' ''The Leader of a Big-Time Band,'' and a revusical Indian duo with Miss Lawrence about bigamous doings ''By the Mississinewa'' with her usual all-conquering vibrancy. But, all in all, Porter's score was a little disappointing. Johnson had an attractive ballad in ''Could It Be You?'' but there was little else to compare with the songwriter's more popular work. Nevertheless, Miss Merman, a splendid physical production and that wartime effect which encourages long runs for happy shows, proved more than sufficient to keep *Something for the Boys* at the Alvin Theater for 422 performances.

A British Bernard Delfont production was opened in Glasgow in December 1943 with Evelyn Dall (Blossom), Jack and Daphne Barker, and Leigh Stafford (Rocky) starring and, in March 1944, it came into the London Coliseum. There it ran for three months until an onslaught of enemy bombs compounded the effect of already less-than-full houses and Delfont called it a day.

UK: London Coliseum 30 March 1944

Recordings: San Francisco revival cast 1997 (Moon Company), selection (AEI)

SOMETHING IN THE AIR Musical play in 2 acts by Arthur Macrae, Archie Menzies and Jack Hulbert. Lyrics by Max Kester and Harold Purcell. Music by Manning Sherwin. Palace Theatre, London, 23 September 1943.

A successor to the two hugely successful Cicely Courtneidge/Jack Hulbert musical comedies *Under Your Hat* and *Full Swing, Something in the Air* was very much cooked to the same recipe: the two comical stars, here called Jack Pendelton and Terry Porter, spent the evening chasing about in a series of disguises trying to foil the machinations of a German spy. This time a third comedian, Ronald Shiner, took part in the fun as an upstart officer who, under war conditions, is the superior of the wealthy Jack in his own co-opted house. The fun and the stars were the thing, but on this occasion the Manning Sherwin/Purcell/Kester score also came up with a couple of numbers which were superior to anything from the previous episodes of this see-Cis-and-Jack-beat-the-Germans series of shows. Both went to the lady, who announced comically ''The Airforce Didn't Want Me (but they got me)'' and crackled warmly through the heart-strung ''Home Is the Place Where Your Heart Is.'' Hulbert also scored with a war-orientated piece, as he looked forward to the outbreak of peace in ''It'll Take a Lot of Getting Used To.''

Something in the Air was quickly established as a hit and by the time of the bombing excesses which closed down the other *Something—Something for the Boys*—in the first week of July 1944 it had been played 336 times at the Palace Theatre. *Something in the Air*, however, didn't close. It moved out of London to take in some provincial dates and, three months later when things had calmed down, it returned to its London home. It happily achieved the difficult task of starting over again, and played another four and a half months and 163 performances.

SOMETHING'S AFOOT Musical in 2 acts by James MacDonald, David Vos and Robert Gerlach. Additional music by Ed Linderman. Goodspeed Opera House, East Haddam, Conn, 20 August 1973; Lyceum Theater, New York, 27 May 1976.

A small-scale burlesque of the Agatha Christie murder-mystery genre, *Something's Afoot* took the tale of the ''Queen of Crime's'' enormously successful novel and play *Ten Little Niggers* and pummeled it into an hilariously exaggerated series of unlikely deaths perpetrated in a storm-bound English country house under the beady little eyes of the bemused Miss Tweed. As the audience tried to guess which of the guests was the murderer through a preposterous series of ''accidents,'' the characters took time off to confide their thoughts in such songs as the sleuthly lady's ''I Owe It All to Agatha Christie,'' the dastardly-seeming nephew's claim to be ''The Legal Heir,'' the suspiciously awakened title song or some moon-in-June romancing for a pair of tongue-in-a-chocolate-box juveniles.

First produced at the Goodspeed Opera House, and then at Los Angeles's Huntingdon Hartford Theater (19 February 1975), the show was given a Broadway production the following year with bulky British variety performer Tessie O'Shea brought in to appear as Miss Tweed in a cast made up mostly of members of the West Coast production: Neva Small (Lettie), Gary Beach (Nigel Rancour), Willard Beckham (Geoffrey), Barbara Heuman (Hope), Liz Sheridan (Grace Manley Prow), Sel Vitella (Clive), Gary Gage (Col Gillweather), Marc Jordan (Flint) and Jack Schmidt (Dr Grayburn). *Something's Afoot* lasted only 61 performances at the Lyceum Theatre, but a West End production in London's little Ambassador's Theatre with a cast featuring a number of performers from the Player's Theatre, Britain's home of Victorian burlesque productions, did altogether better (232 performances) and helped establish *Something's Afoot* as a favorite piece for small and limited-resources theatres.

Australia: Marian Street Theatre, Sydney 3 February 1977; UK: Ambassador's Theatre 17 June 1977

SOMETIME Musical comedy in 2 acts by Rida Johnson Young. Music by Rudolf Friml. Additional lyrics by Ed Wynn. Shubert Theater, New York, 4 October 1918.

Henry Vaughan (Harrison Brockbank) was engaged to marry actress Enid (Francine Larrimore), his now wife, when the exuberantly voluptuous Mayme (Mae West), who had other ideas, got Henry in a situation which caused Enid to call the wedding off. Or, rather, to postpone it for five years with Henry on a good-behavior bond. The story, in line with its title (which purposely tried to recall that of mega-hit *Maytime*), was told in a flashback as Enid related the story of her love life to her girlfriends, and it went in for some film-style switchbacks in the plot before reaching the point where the lovers were reunited and Mayme left to vamp alone. The love story was supplemented by comedy from top-billed Ed Wynn, who had been brought in to the show in tryout (Atlantic City 26 August) as a replacement for Herbert Corthell in order to give the piece some star value. Wynn had rewritten the libretto and supplied some (very weak) lyrics for himself, but basically he swanned through the evening doing his own thing in the characters, variously, of the props man of Enid's show and a theatrical landlord.

The musical part included a ''Baby Doll'' for Enid, a title-waltz, ''Picking Peaches'' for Vaughan, and a ''Keep on Smiling'' and ''The Tune You Can't Forget'' for Frances Cameron as supporting Sylvia. Wynn gave out with his own ''Oh, Argentine'' and a Spanish singer delivered ''Spanish Maid'' in a set of South American songs and dances during a plot turn which took everyone to the Argentine. Mae West did the ''Shimmy Schwabble'' and ''bowled them over with her dance after 'Any Kind of a Man' . . . with the assistance of a well-placed claque.''

Sometime did well, but it hit a problem when it had to shift from the Shubert to the Casino. Wynn was given the star dressing room and Miss Larrimore objected. When producer Arthur Hammerstein sided with Wynn and he installed himself, the lady took all the comic's things, turfed them out on to the stage, and moved in. Not for long, as Hammerstein sacked her. The show, nevertheless, totted up a fine 238 performances before going on the road.

A London production with Desirée Ellinger and Joe Farren Soutar triumphing over Bibi Delabere, and without a star comedian, lasted for just 28 performances.

UK: Vaudeville Theatre 5 February 1925

SONDHEIM, Stephen [Joshua] (b New York, 22 March 1930).

Stephen Sondheim had an early connection with the musical theatre through a family friendship with the Oscar Hammersteins, and began his own contribution by writing college shows. He studied music, but had his first show-business work writing scripts for television's Topper before providing incidental music for plays *The Girls of Summer* (1956) and *Invitation to a March* (1961).

It was, again, not as a composer that he broke through into the Broadway musical establishment. As a result of Arthur Laurents hearing some lyrics he had written for a nonstart show called *Saturday Night* he was brought in to work on *West Side Story,* supplying the lyrics the now too-busy Leonard Bernstein was originally to have done. The vigor and variety of the show's ''Something's Coming,'' ''America,'' ''I Feel Pretty,'' ''A Boy Like That,'' ''Officer Krupke'' and ''Tonight'' gave the young writer a memorable launch. He followed up by combining with Laurents again, and with composer Jule Styne, on a second assignment as a lyricist on *Gypsy* (''Everything's Coming Up Roses,'' ''All I Need Is the Girl,'' ''Let Me Entertain You,'' ''If Mama Was Married,'' ''You Gotta Have a Gimmick,'' ''Rose's Turn''), before, in 1962, offering his first score—lyrics and music—to Broadway in the classical burlesque *A Funny Thing Happened on the Way to the Forum.* The show's inherently comic nature gave endless possibilities for lyric wit, if little for expansive musical writing, and those possibilities were hilariously fulfilled in a set of songs which helped the piece to a position alongside the great classical burlesques of the past, from *Orphée aux enfers* to *Phi-Phi*: ''Comedy Tonight,'' ''Lovely,'' ''Everybody Ought to Have a Maid,'' ''Impossible,'' ''I'm Miles Gloriosus,'' etc.

A third collaboration with Laurents on a sour, extravagant piece called *Anyone Can Whistle* proved a curious misfire all round, but Sondheim returned to form with a vengeance in a collaboration with Richard Rodgers on the score to Laurents's adaptation of his own *The Time of the Cuckoo* as *Do I Hear a Waltz?* Composer and lyricist combined to produce a musically and lyrically rangy score which was as good as anything they had ever or would (to date, in the case of the lyricist) ever write. ''Someone Woke Up,'' ''This Week Americans'' ''Take the Moment,'' ''Moon in My Window,'' ''Here We Are Again,'' ''We're Gonna Be All Right,'' ''Stay'' and their fellows made up a remarkable and remarkably shapely score in the traditional Broadway mold. But *Do I Hear a Waltz?,* manhandled in production, was not a success.

It was also the last time (to date) that Sondheim would supply lyrics to another composer's show score.

In the more than 25 years and nine shows that have followed—apart from a lyrical contribution to the 1974 revisions of Leonard Bernstein's *Candide*—he has written both lyrics and music, although oddly enough never a libretto, to each of the shows with which he has been involved.

The first of these was *Company,* a revusical piece which paraded through a sharply observed series of sketches and songs which exposed the little pretensions, vanities and impossibilities of a group of married, middle-class New Yorkers. ''Another Hundred People,'' ''Barcelona,'' ''Getting Married Today,'' ''You Could Drive a Person Crazy,'' ''The Little Things You Do Together'' and ''The Ladies Who Lunch'' each sketched a story or personality to fine revusical effect, and *Company* won its songwriter the first of what would become a bundle of Tony Awards in the years to come, a good Broadway run, and the first of the fervent followers who would soon become legion.

Company was followed by another piece on similarly revusical lines. *Follies,* however, exchanged the everyday New Yorkers for a parade of everyday ex-Follies girls. Once again, as in Company, the audience had to look hard to find a warmly drawn or sympathetic character amongst the mostly foolish, egotistical folk who peopled the evening's parade of characters, but those people gave the songwriter fine opportunities to display his talents in a number of fairly friendly parodies of the song styles of past days: the pattering of the comedian's ''The God-Why-Don't-You-Love-Me-Oh-You-Do-I'll-See-You-Later Blues,'' the charming old Vienna ''One More Kiss,'' the dance routine of overgrowing-up ''Who's That Woman?,'' the sweetie-pie duo ''Rain on the Roof,'' and the creaky self-serenade of an elderly ''Broadway Baby.'' Some of the burlesques ran close enough to the real thing to be taken for the real thing, and the blowtorch song ''Losing My Mind'' went on to join the show's catalogue of a tough life, ''I'm Still Here,'' as a nightclub favorite. But the Broadway production of *Follies,* like *Do I Hear a Waltz?* was not a genuine success, although it played over five hundred nights on Broadway, gave Sondheim his second successive Tony award, and produced several enduring numbers.

An adaptation of the Ingmar Bergman film *Smiles of a Summer Night* was a different kind of project to the two previous pieces on which Sondheim had worked. For the first time since *Do I Hear a Waltz?* he was dealing with ''real'' people set in a story with a beginning, an end and a development, characters who, for all that many of them were again foolish folk, were without exception likeable and interesting. It was a piece which required painting in different colors, and this time Sondheim the composer surfaced with as many trumps as the previously superior Sondheim the lyricist. The waltzing score of *A Little Night Music* was both an homogenous score, rather than a collection of songs, and as melodious as it was witty, and it remains for many the most appreciable achievement of Sondheim the composer-lyricist. The score produced a hit song in ''Send in the Clowns,'' but that piece was only one high spot of a score which mixed the wryly funny, the wordfully funny and the musically funny, but never the harshly or cruelly funny in such pieces as the three-part dilemma expressed in ''Soon,'' ''Now,'' and ''Later''; in the characters' horrid premonition about a ''Weekend in the Country'' which they wouldn't miss for the world; in the aged ex-plaything of a king reminiscing about the devalued status of ''Liaisons''; in a husband telling his ex-mistress ''You Must Meet My Wife''; or in two rivals for a lady's bed joining (separately) in regretful wishes (''It Would Have Been Wonderful'').

A Little Night Music found fond friends from one end of the world to the other as it went on to a round of continuing productions in a multitude of languages. In the meantime, however, Sondheim had switched dramatically from Sweden, warmth and waltzes, to Japan, cardboard cutout figures and a slow-paced tale of exploitation in *Pacific Overtures.* There were moments that were recognizably the Sondheim of *A Little Night Music* or of *A Funny Thing* in the new show, but by and large *Pacific Overtures* was a piece apart, from which such ''items'' as a Gilbert and Sullivan parody (''Hello, Hello'') and a plotfully witty murder (''Chrysanthemum Tea'') emerged to remind the listener of the author's earlier work. Some of its lyrics seemed to have taken of the succinct opaqueness of the haiku style: they were difficult to comprehend and the show and its songs were, all in all, not made to appeal to those who had loved the sweet and worldly sophistication of *A Little Night Music.*

Pacific Overtures was a failure. But with that show the composer reached a position from which he was rarely to retrench. There were to be no more *A Little Night Music*s. Having proved the qualities of warmth and wit were not only compatible but hugely effective in his hands, Sondheim put aside subjects which called for such treatment. And, bit by bit, he began what can only have been an intentional series of attempts to stretch various parameters of the established style and structure of the contemporary musical play, both textually and musically, as he had done in *Pacific Overtures.* The literate lyrical style, both comic and sentimental, which he had developed in his earlier shows with a skill unequaled in the modern musical theatre became refined in such a fashion that it often led to a lack of accessibility or clarity that was incompatible with general popularity. But if that general popularity was frankly renounced, a fervent minority following of the kind and strength usually reserved for the works of the best-plugged dead composers quickly became his.

This following was given an early boost by the production, in Britain, of a compilation show of songs from Sondheim's musicals under the title *Side by Side by Sondheim.* Britain, which had given Sondheim's works a limited appreciation, suddenly discovered the wit and wonder of his songwords in this evening which displayed the numbers naked, without the often irritating characters who had originally delivered them in their various plays. The entertainment was a major London success, and its pocket size (five characters, no scenery) helped it to be toured and produced throughout the country in regional theatres, spreading the composer's work far and wide in a way that London's productions of *A Funny Thing* and *Company* or, latterly, *Gypsy* had not done. With *Side by Side by Sondheim* Britain suddenly woke up to the works of Stephen Sondheim. The little show then went on to Broadway and round the English-speaking world, continuing its missionary work, and creating happy zealots wherever it went.

Sondheim's next Broadway work was another curious one. It was not that it was in any way recherché—it was, rather, a musical melodrama mostly in the two-dimensional grand guignol style, grandly dressed up. *Sweeney Todd* was peopled with almost burlesque characters, allowing the songwriter to have much fun with the broad humor of songs describing the meat in a human pie or burlesquing a British parlor ballad, but also to include a mixture of the powerful, the high-romantic and the hyper-dramatic in a score which sometimes teetered on the verge of the tongue-in-cheek. Sunk by overproduction on its original mounting on Broadway and in London, *Sweeney Todd* nevertheless earned yet another Tony for its composer-lyricist and became a perennially revived piece in a cut-down version which placed heavier emphasis on the grand guignol and less on the scenery, as it angled for the same audiences who once patronized Tod Slaughter and now wallow in *The Texas Chain-Saw Massacre.*

An attempt to musicalize George S Kaufman and Moss Hart's bitter tale of youth disillusioned, *Merrily We Roll Along* (1981), was a failure, but there was, on the other hand, a reasonable Broadway run and some special kudos for Sondheim's next work, *Sunday in the Park with George* (1984). This time, both librettist and songwriter purposefully went once again down the path established in *Pacific Overtures.* The former supplied a two-part text which followed what was virtually a one-act operetta about the artist Seurat with an actful of dissertation on artistic matters. The latter illustrated it with a meandering, impressionistic score from which, as in *Pacific Overtures,* only the occasional set piece of wit or charm emerged. Those who had mumbled ''pretentious'' at *Pacific Overtures* now said it out loud, those who had enthused over the former work now enthused doubly. Many a theatregoer was on the first list; the second list included the Pulitzer Prize committee and Britain's National Theatre. The Sondheim legend was now becoming well fixed in place, and it was being orientated towards the refined rather than towards the popular.

Into the Woods (1988) proved a little more generally popular than its predecessor, largely because its once-more sour and sombre tale was dressed up in the clothes of a fairy-tale burlesque, encouraging the composer to variants on his early burlesque material which showed up clearly his change in style: the clear and clever humor of his early song lyrics was now largely replaced by something much more in a vein of contemporary poetry. It was a style which sometimes fitted well (when, like much modern poetry, it could be comprehended) and on other occasions was less effective. And it was paired with a musical style which took the same track, rarely going in for frank melody in the traditional style of the musical theatre on the one hand, nor yet for the kind of ensemble work, so effectively achieved in *A Little Night Music,* which might have taken the piece into the light operatic area. It was quite clear, however, that established ''areas'' were of little interest to Sondheim and his collaborators and, as a result, these works remain of interest largely to connoisseurs.

However, after another venture into the grand guignolesque with a revusical small-house piece bringing together the *Assassins* whose victims have been American presidents, Sondheim returned, for the first time in 20 years, to a subject and a libretto which featured real people, with real feelings and a real end-to-end story. The musical *Passion,* however, had nothing of the rueful comedy of *A Little Night Music* to it. In line with its title it was a story of powerful and painful emotion, the kind of story which in earlier years would have been used as the text for an opera rather than a piece of musical theatre. The composer-lyricist echoed the passion of the tale in the score with which he set it, and the result was a darkly effective chamber opera which, however, failed to find itself an audience amongst a musical-theatre public thoroughly and apparently exlusively now hooked on spectacle and romance.

In 40 years of contributing to the musical stage, in an era when the popular mainstream has gone from the well-made musical plays of Rodgers and Hammerstein to the musically lush romantic and speciality shows of Andrew Lloyd Webber, Sondheim has moved steadily away from that mainstream. In doing so he has disappointed many who were thrilled by his pre–*Pacific Overtures* work, but he has established a firm and truly enthusiastic following for his new styles which have ensured even his commercially unsuccessful works repeated productions throughout the world in non-commercial circumstances.

1957 **West Side Story** (Leonard Bernstein/Arthur Laurents) Winter Garden Theater 26 September

1959 **Gypsy** (Jule Styne/Laurents) Broadway Theater 21 May

1962 **A Funny Thing Happened on the Way to the Forum** (Burt Shevelove, Larry Gelbart) Alvin Theater 8 May

1964 **Anyone Can Whistle** (Laurents) Majestic Theater 4 April

1965 **Do I Hear a Waltz?** (Richard Rodgers/Laurents) 46th Street Theater 18 March

1970 **Company** (George Furth) Alvin Theater 26 April

1971 **Follies** (James Goldman) Winter Garden Theater 4 April

1973 **A Little Night Music** (Hugh Wheeler) Shubert Theater 25 February

1973 **Candide** revised version w Wheeler Chelsea Theater Center 18 December; Broadway Theater 8 March 1974

1974 **The Frogs** (Shevelove) New Haven, Conn, 20 May

1976 **Pacific Overtures** (John Weidman, Wheeler) Winter Garden Theater 11 January

1979 **Sweeney Todd, the Demon Barber of Fleet Street** (Chris Bond ad Wheeler) Uris Theater 1 March

1981 **Merrily We Roll Along** (Furth) Alvin Theater 16 November

1984 **Sunday in the Park with George** (James Lapine) Booth's Theater 2 May

1987 **Into the Woods** (Lapine) Martin Beck Theater 5 November

1991 **Assassins** (Weidman) Playwrights Horizons 27 January; Donmar Warehouse, London 22 October 1992

1994 **Passion** (Lapine) Plymouth Theater 9 May

1997 **Saturday Night** (Julius J Epstein) Bridewell Theatre, London 17 December

Biographies: Zadan, C: *Sondheim & Co* (Macmillan, New York, 1974, 1986), Gordon, J: *Art Isn't Easy* (Southern Illinois University Press, 1990), Banfield, S: *Sondheim's Broadway Musicals* (University of Michigan Press, Ann Arbor, 1993), Gottfried, M: *Stephen Sondheim* (Abrams, New York, 1993)

SONG AND DANCE Concert for the theatre in 2 parts with music by Andrew Lloyd Webber. Lyrics by Don Black. Palace Theatre, London, 26 March 1982.

This ''concert for the theatre'' consisted of a semi-staged and slightly expanded version of Lloyd Webber's 50 minute solo song-cycle ''Tell Me on a Sunday,'' originally sung, televised and issued as a top-10 record by vocalist Marti Webb, and a performance of his ''Variations'' (on a theme of Paganini), written for and recorded by his 'cellist brother, Julian, and here reorchestrated and used as the basis for a series of dance scenas.

The song cycle, which followed a middle-aging English woman in New York through a series of unfortunate love affairs with wry optimism and melodious humor, was played by Miss Webb on a small stage-within-a-stage set between the two halves of the orchestra and in front of an effective series of projections of American skylines. The ups and (mostly) downs of her relationships brought forth some unexaggerated and highly effective modern songs, peaking in ''The Last Man in My Life'' and ''Nothing Like You've Ever Known,'' dipping into humour in ''Capped Teeth and Caesar Salad'' and linked throughout by recurring fragments of the hopeful ''It's Not the End of the World.'' The dance part, choreographed by Anthony van Laast, formerly of the London Contemporary Dance Theatre, brought together an eclectic team of eight dancers including ballet's Wayne Sleep, jazz dancer Jane Darling, contemporary dance's Linda Gibbs and acrobatic Paul Tomkinson in a dance entertainment which mixed technical brilliance with a stylish sense of fun and a kaleidoscope of styles in a colorful and audience-pleasing piece.

Originally envisaged as a limited-season production, John Caird's mounting of *Song and Dance* soon proved to have the potential to be more than that. The Cameron Mackintosh/Really Useful Group production ultimately ran for two years (781 performances) at the Palace Theatre, was toured and retelevised (BBC 27 August 1984 with Sarah Brightman) and later returned to London for a second season at the Shaftesbury Theatre with its original stars (25 April 1990, 149 performances). An Australian production, with Gaye Macfarlane at its head as an Australian girl abroad, won fine notices but failed to catch on in seasons in Sydney and Melbourne (Her Majesty's Theatre 21 October 1983), whilst a German one (ad Michael Kunze) turned its heroine (Angelika Milster) into a German girl and did rather better.

For Broadway, the ''Dance'' section was rechoreographed and the ''Song'' part rewritten to an extent which no successful foreign musical had suffered since the bad old days of botching, three-quarters of a century earlier. The whole immensely believable character of the little piece's deeply ordinary and real heroine was metamorphosed into a campy kook, several numbers were excised and a linking piece, written to the theme of the ''Dance'' part and unhappily inserted late in the London run, made prominent. Bernadette Peters and Christopher d'Amboise were featured, and the resulting show ran 474 performances without ever looking like repeating the London success.

Song and Dance, in its original form, has remained an attraction and, alongside its British remountings, it was toured through Europe, in a production by van Laast, in 1997.

Australia: Theatre Royal, Sydney 4 August 1983; USA: Royale Theater 18 September 1985; Germany: Deutsches Theater, Munich 10 October 1987

Plate 363. **Song and Dance.** *The dance part.*

Recordings: original song cycle (Polydor), original cast (Polydor), television cast (RCA), American cast (RCA), German cast (Global), etc

SONGBOOK A tribute to Mooney Shapiro in 2 acts by Monty Norman and Julian More. University of Warwick Arts Centre, Warwick, 2 May 1979; Globe Theatre, London, 25 July 1979.

A burlesque of the endless stream of songwriter-based compilation shows which had engulfed British theatres since the production of *Cole* and *Cowardy Custard, Songbook* followed the musical and personal fortunes of the fictitious Mooney Shapiro (Bob Hoskins/David Healey) through a life and career of endless opportunity and professional mediocrity, illustrated by songs which gleefully parodied various musical clichés of the century. Diane Langton out-Cicelied Miss Courtneidge in a cheery wartime ''Bumpity-Bump'' and joined Gemma Craven in demolishing the sociopolitical musical comedy in ''I Accuse,'' whilst Anton Rodgers smoked his way through a parody of the French chanson and the full cast of five joined in a selection from *Happy Hickory,* a winsomely identifiable musical full of outback innocence which umpteen years later provides Shapiro with his biggest hit when its ghastliest song is revamped as a blazing pop number.

Originally conceived as a small-theatre cabaret-style piece, allegedly for the National Theatre, *Songbook* was first presented by the Cambridge Theatre Company before being brought to London by Stoll Moss Theatres. It won a fine reception, but was taken off after only 208 performances in a climate of boardroom battling at Stoll Moss. Its future was downhill thereafter. A New York version produced by Stuart Ostrow as *The Mooney Shapiro Songbook* was criticized as too unsophisticated for Broadway and folded after one performance, and the show failed to find the place it might have expected in small and provincial theatres.

USA: Morosco Theater *The Mooney Shapiro Songbook* 3 May 1981

Recording: original cast (PYE)

SONG OF NORWAY Operetta in 2 acts by Milton Lazarus adapted from a play by Homer Curran and based on the life of Edvard Grieg. Lyrics and musical adaptation from the works of Edvard Grieg by Robert Wright and George Forrest. Imperial Theater, New York, 21 August 1944.

Song of Norway was a biomusical in the *Das Dreimäderlhaus* tradition, illustrating a romantic incident allegedly taken from the life of a famous composer—this time Grieg rather than Schubert—with a score fabricated from his own melodies. It proved one of the happier examples of its kind and succeeded in its aims much better than most of the slather of such pieces which had tumbled such composers as Offenbach, Chopin, Tchaikovsky and Johann Strauss onto the world's stages in the nearly 30 years since Schubert's story and songs had set the bandwagon careering.

Initiated by San Francisco theatre-owner and writer Homer Curran, and musically created by filmland's Robert Wright and George Forrest, the piece had the young Grieg (Walter Cassel) plucked from his homely Norwegian hills by the man-eating diva Louisa Giovanni (Irra Petina) and carried off towards fame and fortune, leaving behind him Nina (Helena Bliss), the girl he was to have wed, and Nordraak (Robert Shafer), the poet friend with whom he had dreamed one day of writing the great Norwegian lyric work. Louisa promotes Grieg in the high places of the musical and social world, and it takes Nordraak's death to bring him to the realization that he has been led away from his real purposes. He returns to Norway, to Nina and to his friend's text, and finds both fame and happiness.

Amongst the musical items, the theme of the A-minor piano concerto (the setting of the Nordraak poem) and "Ich liebe dich" both got a virtually straight performance, whilst a Norwegian Dance was twinklingly turned into "Freddy and His Fiddle," and "Wedding Day at Troldhaugen" and a nocturne were melded together into the expressive "Strange Music." The comic moments were provided by Louisa and her little husband, and she had an enjoyably extravagant soprano moment in another piece made up from two Grieg sources, "Now."

The show was lavishly produced by Edwin Lester for the Los Angeles and San Francisco Civic Light Opera (July 1944), with the Ballet Russe de Monte Carlo choreographed by Georges Balanchine providing the dance element alongside the notably strong legitimate vocal part of the show. It won a fine West Coast success and was duly transferred to Broadway's Imperial Theater, with Lawrence Brooks replacing Cassel in the role of the composer. Once again it won a splendid reception, as well as an 860-performance run. Emile Littler's 1946 London production did almost as well. Splendidly staged with a singing cast featuring John Hargreaves (Grieg), Halina Victoria (Nina), Janet Hamilton-Smith (Louisa) and Arthur Servent (Nordraak), and with Robert Helpmann and Pauline Grant in charge of the dances, it notched up a very fine 526 performances at the Palace Theatre. Australia saw *Song of Norway* in 1950 with Charles Dorning (Grieg), Marjorie Cooke (Nina), Doreen Wilson (Louisa) and Henrik de Boer (Nordraak) featured for four months in Melbourne and for three and a half in Sydney (Theatre Royal 15 December).

A large-scale revival was mounted at Jones Beach in 1958, and in 1970 a version of the show, considerabley rewritten by Wright and Forrest, was filmed by Cinerama with Toralv Maurstad, Florence Henderson, Frank Poretta and Christina Schollin featured. In 1981 *Song of Norway* was played by the New York City Opera.

UK: Palace Theatre 7 March 1946; Australia: Her Majesty's Theatre, Melbourne 17 July 1950

Film: Cinerama 1970

Recordings: original cast (Decca/MCA), Jones Beach cast (Columbia), film soundtrack (ABC), studio casts (TER, HMV etc), etc

SONG OF THE FLAME Romantic opera in a prologue, 2 acts and an epilogue by Oscar Hammerstein II and Otto Harbach. Music by George Gershwin and Herbert Stothart. 44th Street Theater, New York, 30 December 1925.

Russian aristocrat Aniuta (Tessa Kosta) takes the side of the local revolutionaries against her own people, and goes into action dressed in a dramatic red dress which earns her the soubriquet "the flame." Without suspecting that Aniuta and "the flame" are one and the same person, Prince Volodyn (Guy Robertson) falls in love with her, but it is not until the fall of Russia that the two can come together as émigrés in Paris.

After the fleeting melodies of *Lady, Be Good!* and *Tip-Toes,* which had opened just two nights before *The Song of the Flame*'s premiere, it was something of a surprise to find Gershwin's name attached to the score of what was a distinctly Rombergian romantic operetta, even in a collaboration with that operettic sturdy Herbert Stothart. However, the score of *Song of the Flame* turned out to be thoroughly in the spirit of the tradition which had, in that same season, turned out *The Vagabond King* and *Princess Flavia,* even if it produced none of the enduring numbers which Friml's show did. The richly voiced Miss Kosta had the score's best moments in the title song and a Cossack Love Song ("Don't Forget Me"), whilst a group called the Russian Art Choir performed a selection of interpolated Russian folk songs.

Lavishly produced by Arthur Hammerstein, *Song of the Flame* had a 219-performance run on Broadway and, though not exported, was later used as the basis for a First National technicolor film starring Bernice Claire, Alexander Grey and Noah Beery. It was billed as "The talking screen's answer to The Volga Boatmen" (who probably weren't aware they were asking for an answer) and put out with the warning "children not admitted" attached, a veto which was doubtless not because the remnants of the original score were supplemented by new songs by Grant Clarke and Harry Akst.

Film: First National 1930

DAS SONNTAGSKIND Operette in 3 acts by Julius Bauer and Hugo Wittmann. Music by Carl Millöcker. Theater an der Wien, Vienna, 16 January 1892.

A Viennese piece with a British setting, *Das Sonntagskind* began at the Schloss Rockhill in Scotland, and ended up in the dungeons of Damkirk. Ilka Pálmay was Lady Sylvia Rockhill, Regina Stein her sister Betty Parnell (known as ''Miss Droll''), and they were teamed with the royal register of the Theater an der Wien's male staff: Alexander Girardi as Tristan Florival, artist-turned-photographer, Siegmund Stelzer as Rolf Butterfield, Rudolf del Zopp as the guardsman Sir Edgar Lanimor, Josef Joseffy as his colleague, Sir Lothar, and Carl Lindau as the Sheriff Plunkett. The ''Sunday's child'' of the title was Florival, who believes he was born under a lucky star because of his good fortune with women.

Lady Rockhill is a dashing young widow, and Butterfield, Lothar and Edgar (who being a tenor is the favored one) are amongst the pretenders to her hand. Butterfield, the late lord's chief creditor and mortgage-holder, presses his suit by bringing in the Sherrif and announcing that whoever marries Sylvia will be thrown in prison for debt. So Betty comes up with a plan. Sylvia shall marry Florival, get him thrown in jail, then when the money has been raised and the creditors paid off she can divorce him and marry Edgar. However, Butterfield gets wise to their game, and when the marriage has taken place he tears up the mortgage papers. Fortunately, it turns out that Florival is the long-lost brother of Sylvia's late husband, so the marriage is invalid. The complex amorous doings of these Austro-tartan folk were illustrated by an attractive Millöcker score from which an Echo Song proved the plum.

Das Sonntagskind was a fine success at the Theater an der Wien, running for 62 performances between January and 17 March, and establishing itself thoroughly before going on to productions in Germany and in Hungary (ad Béla J Fái, Ferenc Rajna) and in America, where an initial two-month season in English (ad Helen F Tretbar) at the Casino Theater with Lilly Post (Sylvia), Annie Meyers (Betty), Henri Leoni (Hannibal), Harry Macdonough (Rolf), William Pruette (Lothair) and Jefferson de Angelis (Florival) featured was followed by a German-language production by Hans Conried's company at the Amberg Theater.

Although it did not establish itself in any of those countries, *Das Sonntagskind* nevertheless got a fresh showing in Vienna. A major revival was mounted at the Johann Strauss-Theater on 17 March 1922 with Fritz Werner starred, and it actually played longer than the original production had done, running through until 24 May.

A fairy-tale piece by Albert Dietrich and Heinrich Bulthaupt under the same title had been previously given at Bremen in 1886.

Germany: ?1892; USA: Casino Theater *The Child of Fortune* 18 April 1892, Amberg Theater (Ger) 2 March 1893; Hungary: Népszínház *A serencsefia* 20 September 1892

SON P'TIT FRÈRE Opérette légère in 2 acts by André Barde. Music by Charles Cuvillier. Théâtre des Capucines, Paris, 10 April 1907.

This nine-handed libretto by the young, and as yet unknown, Barde was—a decade before *Phi-Phi*—a delighfully comical and classically Grecian one in which, as in its more famous successor, the accent was firmly on wit and on sparkling sexual comedy, leavened with a good deal of puns and jokes on classical words and names. Barde's story centered on the fading Ancient Greek courtesan Laïs (Marguerite Deval), abandoned by her lover and become unfashionable where it counts, who inveigles the prettiest, richest and most innocent newcomer in town, the aptly named Agathos (Henri Defreyn), to her house by pretending to be his long-lost sister. Before too long she is very happy to admit to her ''little brother'' that she lied. Polin appeared as the comical and grubby parasite of Laïs's household, Eukratés, and Lucienne Delmay had the other principal role as Xantho.

Cuvillier's score, written to be accompanied only by a piano (the pianist at the Capucines at this stage was none other than composer Albert Chantrier), echoed Barde's intimate and tongue-in-cheek comicality in the dancing rhythms of the pre-thé dansant age, and if his melodies were scarcely deathless, his music had the merit of holding up and cleanly displaying the cleverest lyrics the Parisian theatre had heard in years. Eukratès lauded the virtues of having a Parasite round the house (''Être parasite, ah! le bon métier!'')—a house philosopher is a family luxury, like having a mother but less expensive and ''cela remplace un petit chien''—and encouraged Laïs towards the cult of pleasure (''Laïs laicisons!'') apparently for the pure joy of the song's opening pun. The lady began affairs by justifying letting herself go, after years of keeping up her figure and her athleticism for the benefit of her customers—''a quoi bon soigner les décors, puisqu'il n'y a plus de spectacteurs . . .''—before lurching into a big burlesque love duo on her meeting with Agathos and launching her little deception in the Couplets du petit frère. Faced with real love, however, the courtesan loses all her amorous skills and tells us about it in song (''Oui j'ai tout appris auprès d'Aphrodite''). The Duo du frisson saw Agathos—introduced in the first act protesting, like Aspasie in *Phi-Phi* (not to mention Meilhac and Halévy's Baronne Gondremarck), ''je suis encore tout étourdi''—go, via fear and madness, to ''amour'' and, in the second-act finale to alarm: ''j'étais si vertueux, et je deviens incestueux!'' Eukratés, always there with a bon mot, is around to comment ''L'inceste c'est comme le pal, ça commence bien et finit mal.'' Another jolly moment of the second act was a musical Ancient-Greek tea party with distinctly modern Parisian overtones (''les ten o'clock c'est vraiment bien moins toc et mieux assorti que le five o'clock tea . . .'').

The production of *Son p'tit frère* at the little Théâtre des Capucines was a fine small-house success and the show went on to have a substantial provincial life, was played in Brussels by its two original stars, and was revived at the Theatre Édouard VII a decade later (18 January 1917). In 1930 it was enlarged into a three-act opérette and played on tour by the Opéra-Comique's Geneviève Vix, Guy Ferrell and Julien Carette under the title *Laïs, ou la courtisane amoureuse.*

Thanks to the West End successes of *The Lilac Domino* and *Afgar,* Cuvillier became a name to reckon with in postwar London, and as a result what purported to be a version of *Son p'tit frère* was produced by André Charlot at the Comedy Theatre in 1920 as *The Wild Geese.* It had a text by Ronald Jeans, however, which involved neither courtesans nor ancient Greece. Jack Buchanan and Phyllis Monkman were amongst the cast, Amy Augarde played one Dame Agatha Boot, and it ran for 112 performances whilst less heavy-handedly inflated small shows, led by *Irene,* prospered more thoroughly in the public favor.

UK: Comedy Theatre *The Wild Geese* 12 February 1920

SONS O' GUNS Musical comedy in 2 acts by Fred Thompson, Jack Donahue and Bobby Connolly. Music and lyrics by Fred J Coots, Benny Davis and Arthur Swanstrom. Imperial Theater, New York, 26 November 1929.

A spectacular Connolly and Swanstrom production with Urban sets, Charles le Maire costumes, a Connolly mounting, Albertina Rasch dances and a Hollywood leading lady (Lili Damita), *Son o' Guns* followed the fortunes of co-author Jack Donahue in the role of devil-may-care Jimmy Canfield, ill-fittingly drafted into the wartime army along with his peacetime manservant (William Frawley). Donahue gamboled with ''rough-hewn grace'' through a serious of low-comic adventures to accidental heroism and to Mlle Damita (as a mademoiselle called Yvonne), winning the war in the traditional Old Bill style which *The Better 'Ole* had so happily exploited a decade earlier. The score was made up of lightly reminiscent numbers with titles such as ''Why?,'' ''It's You I Love,'' ''Cross Your Fingers'' and ''I'm That Way Over You'' which served their purpose in the show, became dance-band fodder, and were otherwise not remembered.

A reviewer announced that ''the war has been refought with spendthrift prodigality'' as *Sons o' Guns* and its ''pawky, homespun humours'' found itself a cheerful and lighthearted Broadway success for 295 performances. It was subsequently and elaborately produced in London by Jack Waller and Herbert Clayton with equally happy results. Bobby Howes and Robert Hale took the comedy roles, the Parisian musical-comedy star Mireille Perrey played French Yvonne, and the piece lasted 211 performances at the London Hippodrome before going on the road.

Australia, too, enjoyed the show with Gus Bluett (Jimmy), Leo Franklyn (Hobson), Bertha Riccardo (Yvonne) and Elsie Prince (Bernice) featured in a J C Williamson Ltd production which resituated the events of the evening in Australia. It played through 10 weeks in Sydney and 9 in Melbourne (Theatre Royal 5 February 1931).

UK: London Hippodrome 26 June 1930; Australia: Her Majesty's Theatre, Sydney 4 October 1930

Film: 1929

THE SORCERER Comic opera in 2 acts by W S Gilbert. Music by Arthur Sullivan. Opera Comique, London, 17 November 1877.

The first full-length comic opera from the Gilbert and Sullivan partnership, following their collaborations on *Thespis* and *Trial by Jury, The Sorcerer* was produced in London by budding manager Richard D'Oyly Carte who, as business manager for Selina Dolaro, had been responsible for the first staging of *Trial by Jury.* Carte formed the Comedy Opera Company with investors' capital and took a lease on the unpopular old Opera Comique to stage the new work by the pair who had caused such a stir with their one-act dramatic cantata. He advertised the piece as a well-mannered English comic opera, in the vein of the pieces played at the German Reeds' Entertainment, in a deliberate contrast to the colorful but suspiciously naughty opéras-bouffes which were currently filling London theatres.

Like *Trial by Jury, The Sorcerer* was based on a magazine story which Gilbert had written for the *Graphic,* but it was less straightly satirical than its predecessor. It told the story of one John Wellington Wells (George Grossmith), a professional sorcerer, who is hired by philanthropic young Alexis (George Bentham) to distribute a love potion to the inhabitants of his rural hometown on the occasion of his betrothal to lovely Aline (Alice May).

The potion has unintended effects, throwing Alexis's aristocratic father (Richard Temple) into the arms of the common pew-opener Mrs Partlett (Harriette Everard), separating her daughter Constance (Giulia Warwick) from the curate she adores (Rutland Barrington), and setting the dragonistic Lady Sangazure (Mrs Howard Paul) onto Wells himself. The sorcerer has to give himself up to the spirits of the underworld to undo the effects of his necromancing.

Sullivan's music followed the vein set up at the German Reeds' establishment and in *Trial by Jury,* eschewing the extravagant gaiety and big burlesque effects of opéra-bouffe and—while not failing to evoke burlesqued memories of *Der Freischütz, Robert le diable* and other favorite ever-so-grand operas—remaining merrily and wittily melodious within the normal bounds of English operetta. The score included several pieces which became drawing-room favorites, notably the comedian's patter song "My Name Is John Wellington Wells," Barrington's reminiscences of the days when he was "A Pale Young Curate" and the soprano solo "Happy Young Heart," and Gilbert turned out some sharply funny lyrics for pieces such as the duo in which Temple manfully resisted the amorous advances of Mrs Paul ("Hate Me!").

The Sorcerer was well received ("refined, finished, exquisitely humorous and altogether admirable . . . a triumph") and well attended, but Carte soon had to fight with his investors who, having quickly recouped, were soon anxious to close the show before they lost what they had won. They were, apart from anything else, having to pay Gilbert and Sullivan six guineas' royalty a performance, and that on top of the £200 the writers had earned on delivering the script and score. Carte fought hard enough to keep the show on for 175 performances, closing only in time to stage the new piece which Gilbert and Sullivan had written to follow it, *HMS Pinafore.* The new piece would be much more, and much more widely, successful, but *The Sorcerer* had not only laid the foundations for that success by both putting the production structures in place and introducing the public to the brand of show they would see at the Opera Comique, but also by putting together the basis of the company—Grossmith, Miss Everard, Temple, Barrington—which would help make the Gilbert and Sullivan operas what they became.

The Sorcerer did not attract attention outside Britain until later, when *HMS Pinafore* had made Gilbert and Sullivan internationally famous. Then—after a scramble of announcements from various New York theatres and managers in the throes of Pineuphoria—it was flung on for 20 undercast, under-rehearsed performances at the Broadway Theater with Horace Lingard in the role of John Wellington Wells. It was later seen again on Broadway as played by a company from Philadelphia's Arch Street Theater which had premiered their production at their home base the same night as the Broadway attempt, by which time Adah Richmond had got her *Pinafore* company playing it in Boston, the "Saville English Opera Co" was offering it to smaller centres, and approximate versions were being carried by several other companies along with their equally approximate versions of *Pinafore.* However, *The Sorcerer* later had a rather less harum-scarum New York run in 1882 when John McCaull produced a version with John Howson (Wells), Laura Joyce (Sangazure), Digby Bell (Daly) and Lillian Russell (Aline, interpolating Jesse Williams's "Tootsy Wootsy"!) featured which played for 92 performances at his Bijou Theater and returned for three further weeks at the Casino the following year. In 1892 it was again played at Palmer's Theater by Henry Dixey's Company.

Five months after the first Broadway performances, Lingard and his wife Alice Dunning (Aline) introduced Australia to *The Sorcerer* in a version in which the music was boasted as having been "specially arranged" (presumably from the piano-vocal score) by expatriate French conductor Charles van Ghele.

The Sorcerer returned to London in 1884 when Carte staged a major revival of the piece, revised by its authors for the occasion, at the Savoy Theatre. Temple, Barrington and Grossmith repeated their original roles with Rosina Brandram, Mrs Paul's erstwhile understudy, as Sangazure and tenor Durward Lely and soprano Leonora Braham as the lovers. It played for 150 performances in a bill with *Trial by Jury.* The Savoy Theatre hosted a further 102 performances in 1898 (still with Temple and Miss Brandram) and the piece subsequently became an undeservedly minor part of the repertoire of the D'Oyly Carte Company, perching slightly politely alongside its writers' later and often more colorful shows, through the remaining part of the company's existence.

The Sorcerer does not appear to have had a full-scale professional production in mainland Europe, but in May 1886 a double bill of *The Sorcerer* and Gilbert's earlier *Creatures of Impulse,* directed by former opera diva Mme Lemmens-Sherrington, was mounted at Brussels's Théâtre Molière. The cast included Mlle Wieniawska, daughter of the celebrated violinist.

USA: Broadway Theater 21 February 1879; Australia: Academy of Music, Melbourne 28 July 1879

Recording: complete (Decca)

Video: Brent-Walker 1982

SOROZÁBAL, Pablo (b San Sebastián, 18 October 1897; d Madrid, 26 December 1988).

A juvenile performer on the piano and violin, Sorozábal made his living playing in cinemas, cafés and fairgrounds, before the success there of his first orchestral compositions gave him the oportunity to go to study in Leipzig and Berlin. He returned to Madrid to make a career as a conductor. As a composer, he turned out orchestral works, song cycles and choral music, but his first zarzuela, the two-act *Katiuska* (Victoria Theatre, Barcelona, 27 January 1931), brought him a significant success and thereafter he produced a steady stream of theatre works, the most successful of which were *La del manojo de rosas* (13 November 1934) and *La tabernera del puerto* (16 May 1936). Other successes include *Black, el payaso* (21 April 1942), *Don Manolito* (24 April 1943) and a version of the Don Juan story, *Los burladores* (10 December 1948). His final work was *Las de Caín* (23 December 1958). With his death in 1988 the last chapter in the creative history of the zarzuela apparently came to an end.

His other works include *La guitarra de Figaro* (1931), the ''opera chica'' *Adios a la Bohemia* (1933), *La isla de las perlas* (1933), *El alguacil Rebolledo* (1934), *Sol en la cumbre* (1934), *No me olvides* (1935), *Cuidado con la pintura* (1941), *La Rosario* or *Rambla fiun de siglo* (1941), *La eterna cancíon* (1945), *Entre Sevilla y Triana* (1950), *Brindis, Jai-Alai, La casa de las tres muchachas, La opera de mogollon* and *Maria—matricula de Bilbao.*

Autobiography: *Mi vida y mi obra* (Fundación Banco Exterior, Madrid, 1986)

SO THIS IS LOVE Musical play in 2 acts by Stanley Lupino and Arthur Rigby. Lyrics by Desmond Carter. Music by ''Hal Brody.'' Winter Garden Theatre, London, 25 April 1928.

The first solo production of producer-performer Laddie Cliff, *So This Is Love* crystallized the dancing-comedy format which he had so successfully used in the recent *Lady Luck* and *Dear Little Billie.* Comedian Leslie Henson directed, ubiquitous choreographer Max Rivers did the dances, Australian dancers Cyril Ritchard and Madge Elliott were given the romantic leads, acrobatic Australian Reita Nugent (as a character called Cherry Carleton, with a number called ''Dance'') was in support, the chorus was the John Tiller Girls, and eccentric dancer-comedian Cliff paired with co-author and comedian Lupino at the head of the fun.

Ritchard was rich Peter who pretends to become poor in order to woo his proud and penniless secretary, Pamela (Miss Elliott), Cliff played a brash and bespectacled Yankee called Hap J Hazzard, who got Peter's rejected but rich Kitty (Sylvia Leslie), and Lupino was Potiphar Griggs, a newly married man with a buxom and suspicious wife, Minnie (Connie Emerald). The comedy was fairly continuous, the dancing bright and varied and the whole accompanied by suitable music which was not, as Cliff tried to pretend, by a fashionably transatlantic composer but by a bundle of English ones, including H B Hedley and Jack Strachey, hidden under a portmanteau pseudonym. On one of the rare occasions on which the music was not meant to be danced to, Sylvia Leslie got to give a pretty ballad, ''Lazy Father Time (can't you see I'm finding you too slow),'' and Lupino had a go at the craze for thrillers in the comical ''Hats off to Edgar Wallace.''

So This Is Love hit the mood of the moment precisely and racked up 321 performances at the Winter Garden before going on the road for the next three seasons whilst Cliff and his team carried on turning out more shows on the same successful lines.

In spite of its lively British success, the show scarcely seemed like an export prospect, but that was reckoning without the world's most cosmopolitan musical-theatre cities. Budapest, having gone through the products of the new French musical-comedy genre and dipped briefly into Broadway, cast a glance at London and *Ez hát a szerelem!* (ad István Békeffy) turned up at the Fővárosi Operettszínház the year after the London production. The following year Melbourne and, a year further on, Sydney (Grand Opera House 7 November 1931) also welcomed *So This Is Love.* The White-Edgeley production company featured Clem Dawe (Potty), Betty Eley (Pamela), Rita McLean (Minnie) and Bobby Gordon (Hap) in a pairing of *So This Is Love* and the later *Love Lies,* and George Marlow presented the former piece in Sydney where Eric Edgeley renounced his producing credit but instead starred as Hap Hazzard alongside his partner, Dawe, and John Wood as Peter.

Hungary: Fővárosi Operettszínház *Ez hát a szerelem!* 24 September 1929; Australia: King's Theatre, Melbourne 10 May 1930

THE SOUND OF MUSIC Musical in 2 acts by Howard Lindsay and Russel Crouse. Lyrics by Oscar Hammerstein II. Music by Richard Rodgers. Lunt-Fontanne Theater, New York, 16 November 1959.

The Sound of Music was the last and arguably the greatest success of the famous team of Rodgers and Hammerstein. It put the button on the memorable set of five romantic musical plays which the pair turned out in their 16 years as the most successful musical-theatre writers and producers on Broadway, and with which they marked not only American stages, but the rest of the English-speaking musical-theatre and cinema world as well.

The story of Maria von Trapp and her stepchildren, who together formed the singing group known as the Trapp Family Singers, and the episode of the family's escape from Nazi Germany were originally used as the subject for a German film. It was a proposal to make a Hollywood film based on that German film which tossed

Plate 364. **The Sound of Music.** *The von Trapp family, headed by the Captain (Theodore Bikel) and Maria (Mary Martin), do their act.*

the subject into currency in America in the 1950s. The idea was taken to Mary Martin, the project furthered by her husband, Richard Halliday, and Leland Hayward, and Howard Lindsay and Russel Crouse were signed by them to write a libretto into which it was primitively intended to introduce examples of the material sung by the Trapp Family Singers. When it was decided to supplement that material with some more up-to-date songs, Rodgers and Hammerstein were approached and the result was that the original idea went out the window and *The Sound of Music* became a Rodgers and Hammerstein project with the pair both writing the show's score and acting as co-producers.

Maria Rainer (Miss Martin) is a fledgeling nun in the abbey at Nonnberg, but her natural exuberance seems to fit her ill for a life of walled devotion and the Abbess (Patricia Neway) decides to send her as governess to the widowed Captain von Trapp (Theodore Bikel). Maria wins the confidence and friendship of the seven motherless von Trapp children, but when she awakens romantic feelings in the Captain—and something she does not quite understand in herself—she flees back to Nonnberg. The children are distressed, the more so as von Trapp is to wed the wealthy and not very loveable Elsa Schräder (Marion Marlowe), but the Abbess, refusing to let Maria hide from life behind a wimple, orders her to return to her duties and, as a result, she shortly becomes the Baroness von Trapp. When von Trapp's aggressively nationalistic and anti-German stance threatens to make trouble for his family, they are obliged to flee Austria and, with the help of the nuns, they make their way over the mountains of Maria's youth to Switzerland and safety.

The score for the piece fell largely to Maria, beginning with a rhapsodic hymn to the hills in "The Sound of Music," continuing with a set of tuneful and sweet numbers with, since most of them were addressed to children, a suitably innocent air to them ("My Favourite Things," "Do-Re-Mi," "The Lonely Goatherd"), and returning to things adult to sing with the Captain of being "An Ordinary Couple." The singing of the children was displayed in "So Long, Farewell" and of the Captain in the folky "Edelweiss," whilst eldest daughter Liesl (Lauri Peters) and her teenage boyfriend (Brian Davies) romanced ingenuously to "Sixteen Going on Seventeen." Elsa and the parasitic but plotworthy impresario Max Detweiler (Kurt Kasznar) supplied the more sophisticated/cynical element ("How Can Love Survive," "There's No Way to Stop It") and a quartet of sub-operatic nuns discussed the problems posed by ''Maria'' in a delightfully comic number, but the evening's hit number proved to be the most substantial bit of singing in the score, the last in the series of throbbing feminine hymns which had become a feature of the Rodgers and Hammerstein shows. After ''Bali H'ai,'' ''You'll Never Walk Alone'' and ''Something Wonderful'' came ''Climb Every Mountain,'' the soaring homily with which the Abbess sent Maria from the Abbey to face life, and which returned to speed the escaping family on their way at the play's end.

The Sound of Music, directed by Vincent Donehue—the man who had brought the idea to Miss Martin in the first place—initially won a few dismissive critical comments for its pink-ribbon ingenuity, but the public made its positive feelings felt in no uncertain way, driving the show to a 1,443-performance Broadway run, parallel to a long tour in which Florence Henderson was the first Maria. Fine though that record was, however, it was only the beginning. London's edition, in spite of being cast without any of the star values of the Broadway version, turned out to be the most successful production of a Broadway musical ever to have played London. Jean Bayless (Maria), Roger Dann (von Trapp) and opera's Constance Shacklock (Abbess) headed a reproduction which played for 2,385 performances in the West End. Australia's production, with June Bronhill as a Maria with much more substantial vocal qualifications than the usual soubrette casting, followed, before *The Sound of Music* moved into another dimension with the issue of its film version in 1965.

It was a film version with a difference, for whereas the earlier Rodgers and Hammerstein filmed musicals had been slimmer but fairly faithful versions of the stage shows, on this occasion the score underwent significant changes between stage and screen. Rodgers (Hammerstein was now dead) wrote two fresh songs—the bubbling, characterful ''I Have Confidence'' and the sublimely and foolishly happy ''Something Good''—with which to give Maria's role a little more breadth and a little less of the soubrette, and ''An Ordinary Couple'' and the Max/Elsa pieces were cut. One of the triumphs of modern-day musical-film casting—that of Julie Andrews (soubrette neither in personality nor voice) as Maria—compounded by shots of some of the world's most beautiful mountain scenery helped turn *The Sound of Music* into what must be, in real terms, the most successful motion-picture version of a stage musical ever made. Christopher Plummer (von Trapp, with the voice of Bill Lee), Peggy Wood and the singing voice of Margery McKay (Abbess) and Eleanor Parker (a plum performance as a dewy-voiced Elsa) took the other principal roles.

The vast success of the film had a dual effect on the show. It turned its songs into even greater hits than they already were and it was ultimately responsible for the show being adapted into both German and French (and probably other languages), but it presented a problem for a major revival. How to cast Julie Andrews and how to reproduce those mountains? It was a challenge that Broadway declined to pick up, but London's Ross Taylor was less chary. Using a neatly revised text and score which incorporated ''I Have Confidence,'' a design which went remarkably far towards reproducing the main pictorial elements of the film, and with former child actress and pop vocalist Petula Clark as a pleasingly gentle, folksy Maria—quite different from, but just as appealing as, Miss Andrews—he produced a version (Apollo Victoria Theatre 17 August 1981) which satisfied almost everyone. It ran 444 performances, prompted a decade and more of fresh touring and provincial productions and an Australian revival (Princess Theatre, Melbourne 25 May 1983), with Julie Anthony (Maria) and Anthea Moller (Abbess) featured, and proved that there was still a life on stage for *The Sound of Music* even without Julie Andrews and those mountains. The show visited London once again, in 1992, when a touring production featuring Christopher Cazenove and Liz Robertson stopped off at Sadler's Wells Theatre as part of its tour, and Australia got another round in 1999 (Lyric, Sydney 2 November).

Unlike most of the Rodgers and Hammerstein opus, *The Sound of Music* also made some headway in Europe. The Opéra Royal de Wallonie, Belgium's specialists in French-language versions of American musical plays, introduced *La Mélodie de bonheur* in Liège in 1973 (22 December) with Pierrette Delange as Maria, Guy Fontagnère as von Trapp, Maria Murano (Abbess), Madeleine Vernon (Eva) and Hubert Meens (Max). It had a great success, and was regularly reprised there (1974, 1977, 1981, 1986), whilst making its way thence into the provincial theatres of France. The first German production (ad Ute Horstmann, Eberhard Storch) followed in 1982, but the piece did not establish itself in its German-language version in the same way that it did in the French and the only sighting of the piece on the Vienna stage has been a clever-dick mounting (the children played by adults, etc) shoestrung together at the Schauspielhaus in 1993. The Fővárosi Operettszínház introduced the piece in Hungarian (ad Mihály Bátki) in 1992 with Erika Pápai and Bálint Farkas featured.

The Sound of Music continues to flourish around the world, but the piece has also received repeated revivals at home. It was produced under the aegis of the New York City Opera (8 March 1990, 54 performances) with Debby Boone starred as Maria alongside Laurence Guittard (von Trapp) and Claudia Cummings (Abbess), and

Marie Osmond and Guittard headed a touring company round America in 1993, before the show finally returned to Broadway in 1998 (Martin Beck Theater 12 March). Rebecca Luker played Maria, with Michael Siberry as Captain von Trapp and the piece had an ultimately rather disappointing run of 532 performances before taking again to the road with Richard Chamberlain now as a startlingly overaged von Trapp.

UK: Palace Theatre 18 May 1961; Australia: Princess Theatre, Melbourne 20 October 1961; Germany: Stadttheater, Hildesheim *Die Trapp Familie* 9 March 1982; Hungary: Fővárosi Operettszínház 11 December 1992; Austria: Schauspielhaus 27 February 1993

Film: Twentieth Century Fox 1965

Recordings: original cast (Columbia), London casts (HMV, Epic), Australian casts (HMV, EMI, BMG), Mexican cast (Orfeon), Netherlands casts (Philips, Columns), Israeli cast (Disneyland), film soundtrack in English, French and Spanish (RCA), Swedish cast (BMG), New York revival cast (BMG/RCA Victor), Japanese cast (Toshiba), selection (Telarc), etc

SOUSA, John Philip (b Washington, DC, 6 November 1854; d Reading, Pa, 6 March 1932).

The American ''march king'' was as yet uncrowned, and still touring as a musical director with comic opera companies when he made his first produced attempt to break into the theatre as a composer. His *The Smugglers,* written to a libretto ''borrowed'' from F C Burnand's book for *The Contrabandista* and produced by the Gorman's Church Choir *HMS Pinafore* Company (which he was currently conducting), had a couple of short lives. The following year, as conductor of F F Mackay and Louise Sylvester's Comedy Company, he supplied ''all the solos, duets, trios, choruses, etc'' sung in their three-act traveling farce comedy, *Our Flirtations.* It was most unusual for such a show to have a complete score of new music, but the trade press was not impressed with this originality, remarking ''the music with the exception of two numbers is not likely to become popular,'' qualifying ''not because it is not good, but because it is too good.''

A piece called *Catherine* written to a libretto by Wilson J Vance, ''who has charge of the Indian affairs in the Department of the Interior, Washington, DC'' does not appear to have got to the stage, but another comic opera, *Desirée,* a musicalization of J Maddison Morton's 1856 *Our Wife, or The Rose of Amiens,* first produced in Washington during Sousa's time as leader of the local Marine Band, was taken up briefly by John McCaull. It was produced at Haverly's Theater, Philadelphia (10 November 1884) with De Wolf Hopper in its chief comic role, but Boston gave it a firm thumbs down and it was promptly dropped from the McCaull repertoire. In the same season Sousa supplied the music for the wildish-Western songs featured in Joaquín Miller's stagecoach melodrama *Tally Ho!* with equally little success. However, several tries and more than a decade later, and this time allied with a good, professional librettist in Charles Klein, he ultimately produced what would be his one genuine musical-theatre hit in *El Capitan.*

Having written some of his own lyrics to *El Capitan,* Sousa ventured to write his own libretto for his next piece, *The Bride Elect,* but the negative results that emerged encouraged him to go back to Klein and then to such favorite Broadway librettists as Glen MacDonough and Harry Bache Smith for his later comic operas. *The Charlatan* (1898), a custom-made vehicle for Hopper, had a short Broadway life (40 performances), but served its star well on the road and as far afield as London (as *The Mystical Miss* 13 December 1899), whilst *Chris and the Wonderful Lamp,* an *Aladdin* derivative, proved happier through 57 performances than his earlier attempt at a children's piece with *The Queen of Hearts.*

However, in spite of *El Capitan*'s success, Sousa's career as a composer of comic opera did not flourish in the 20th century. Several of his pieces remained unproduced, and on another occasion he priced himself out of a job. When Francis Wilson wanted the libretto of the French opérette *Babolin* reset, Sousa's financial demands proved too much for him and it was Edward Jakobowski who wrote *The Devil's Deputy.* The handful of Sousa scores which did make it to the stage in later days did so for very short and unprofitable seasons and *El Capitan* and, to a lesser extent, *The Charlatan* remained Sousa's sole musical-theatre references.

In 1987 his music was used as the basis for the score of a musical about the American presidential Roosevelt family entitled *Teddy and Alice* (arr Richard Kapp/Hal Hackady/Jerome Alden, Minskoff Theater 12 November 1987, 77 performances).

1879 **The Smugglers** (Wilson J Vance/F C Burnand ad Archibald Gordon, Charles Gayler) Jersey City 7 December; revised version Chestnut Street Opera House, Philadelphia 27 March 1882

1880 **Our Flirtations** (James Bird Wilson) Park Theater, Philadelphia 30 August

1884 **Desirée** (Edward M Taber/J Maddison Morton ad) National Theater, Washington, DC 1 May

1886 **The Queen of Hearts, or Royalty and Roguery** (Taber) 1 act Washington, DC 12 April

1896 **El Capitan** (w Tom Frost/Charles Klein) Broadway Theater 20 April

1897 **The Bride Elect** (Sousa) Hyperion Theater New Haven 28 December; Tremont Theater, Boston 3 January; Knickerbocker Theater, New York 11 April

1898 **The Charlatan** (Klein) Academy of Music, Montreal 29 August; Knickerbocker Theater 5 September

1899 **Chris and the Wonderful Lamp** (Glen MacDonough) Hyperion Theater, New Haven 23 October; Victoria Theater 1 January 1900

1906 **The Free Lance** (Harry B Smith) New Amsterdam Theater 16 April

1913 **The Glassblowers** (Leonard Liebling) Shubert Theater, Rochester, NY 27 January

1913 **The American Maid** (revised *The Glassblowers*) Broadway Theater 3 March

Autobiography: *Marching Along* (Hale, Cushman, Boston, 1928); Biographies: Berger, K: *The March King and His* Band (Exposition, New York, 1957), Bierley, P E: *John Philip Sousa: American Phenomenon* (Prentice Hall, Englewood Cliffs, NJ, 1973), etc

SOUTAR, J[oseph] Farren (b Greenwich, 17 February 1870; d Cookham, 23 January 1962).

The son of the famous Nellie Farren and her husband, Gaiety Theatre actor and director Robert Soutar, J Farren Soutar (as he was ever billed) went on the stage at the age of 16. He became a successful musical-comedy leading man in the prewar part of a long and varied stage career, which effectively began under George Edwardes at Daly's Theatre (t/o Bobbie Rivers in *A Gaiety Girl,* Algernon St Alban in *An Artist's Model*) and, subsequently, included the juvenile lead in the Little Tich musical *Billy* (1898, Reggie Neville), the early revue *Pot Pourri* (1899), the Broadway production of *The Girl from Up There* (1900, Jack Hemingway) and its London transfer, and the juvenile leads of London's *A Chinese Honeymoon* (1902, t/o Tom Hatherton), *Sergeant Brue* (1904, Michael Brue), *Miss Wingrove* (1905, Frank Leyland), and *The Belle of Mayfair* (1906, Raymond Finchley), in which he was Romeo to the Juliet of Edna May.

He toured in America, played in music hall, straight theatre, revue (Owen Deed in *Oh! Indeed,* 1908, etc) and the short-lived musical play *The Antelope* (1908) in Britain but, after his appearance in the juvenile role of *Peggy* (1912, Bendoyle) on Broadway and war service, he had less luck with his choice of musicals (Sydney Heap in *The Eclipse,* Amarak el Deeb in *Almond Eye,* Hank Vaughan in *Sometime,* Dodo in *Riki-Tiki*) until he appeared as Baron Chamard in *The Dubarry* (1932) in the twilight of his career.

He was married to musical-comedy actress **May HOBSON** (b London 12 January 1889), who played in London in supporting parts in *The Belle of Mayfair* (1906, Lucille), *The Merry Widow* (1907, Zo-Zo), *The Dollar Princess* (1909, Lady Dorothy), *A Waltz Dream* (1911, Mitzi) and *The Count of Luxembourg* (1911, Amélie), and toured in the lead roles of *The Merry Widow* and *The Dollar Princess.*

A SOUTHERN MAID Musical play in 3 acts by Dion Clayton Calthrop and Harry Graham. Lyrics by Harry Miller. Additional lyrics by Adrian Ross. Music by Harold Fraser-Simson. Additional music by Ivor Novello. Prince's Theatre, Manchester, 24 December 1917; Daly's Theatre, London, 15 May 1920.

A Southern Maid was commissioned by Robert Evett for Daly's Theatre, and designed as a follow-up to the enormously successful *The Maid of the Mountains.* Its title role was made to measure for the darkly dramatic heroine of the earlier piece, the theatre's adored new prima donna, José Collins. If *A Southern Maid*'s Dolores was as like as could be to *The Maid of the Mountains*'s Teresa, this time the brigand beauty's amorous tendencies went the opposite way. Dolores was in love with the apparently cruel governor of the piece's "southern" country, Sir Willoughby Rawdon (Claude Flemming, tenor), and she helped him to escape the assassination planned by her gypsy lover (Frederick Ross). If the show's score did not have a basketful of songs destined for the popularity of *The Maid of the Mountains*'s music, it nevertheless turned up one genuine hit, Miss Collins's sultry "Love's Cigarette," a hymn to nicotine which outpointed the number "Dark Is the Sky" which was billed as "The Great Waltz Song" and clearly intended to be the "Love Will Find a Way" of the new show.

The Maid of the Mountains had been running for 10 months when Evett took Miss Collins out of the cast, put understudy Dorothy Shale on, and sent his star to Manchester for a Christmas tryout season of *A Southern Maid.* He intended to follow the same plan which had worked so well with the first piece—Christmas in Manchester, then in to Daly's in February—but, in spite of the overwhelming reception that Manchester gave to the new piece, it was obvious that *The Maid of the Mountains* still had too much life left in it to be removed. Miss Collins was thus rerouted back to *The Maid of the Mountains* and *A Southern Maid* was sent on tour, with Gracie Sinclaire starring, to await its moment. It waited for two further years, returning for a second Manchester Christmas season the following year, before Miss Collins had finally had more than she could take of *The Maid of the Mountains* and demanded a change. *A Southern Maid* moved into Daly's two and a half years after its original tryout with Flemming and *Maid* stars Bertram Wallis (Francesco) and Mark Lester (Wex) teaming with Miss Collins in the lead roles. If its quality was something less than its predecessor, it nevertheless had all of "the mixture as before" in the right doses and it proved a first-class vehicle for its star, running through 1920 (306 performances) until, with Miss Shale again holding the fort, the star went back to Manchester to prepare its successor, *Sybil.*

A Southern Maid continued its already-long touring life during and after the London production, and it was also produced in Australia with Miss Collins's down-under double, Gladys Moncrieff, scoring as big a success there as her model had done in London. The initial Melbourne run, with Claude Flemming back on home ground repeating his original role, Arthur Stigant, Robert Chisholm and Reginald Purdell supporting and Daly's Theatre's other Australian, Asche, directing, topped one hundred consecutive Melbourne performances—a rare feat at this time—and a Sydney season later the same year (Her Majesty's Theatre 27 October) added another two and a half months to its fine record.

In 1933 *A Southern Maid* was made into a film starring Bebe Daniels, Harry Welchman, Clifford Mollison and comedian Lupino Lane.

Australia: Theatre Royal Melbourne 27 January 1923

Film: BIP 1933

SOUTH PACIFIC Musical play in 2 acts by Oscar Hammerstein II and Joshua Logan adapted from *Tales of the South Pacific* by James Michener. Lyrics by Oscar Hammerstein II. Music by Richard Rodgers. Majestic Theater, New York, 7 April 1949.

Director Joshua Logan was pointed towards Michener's *Tales of the South Pacific* by a filmland friend, and he tied up successively with producer Leland Hayward and with Rodgers and Hammerstein in adapting a combination of the book's stories for the musical stage. Logan's original idea was to center on the story ''Fo' Dolla,'' the love story of American officer Joseph Cable and the island girl Liat, but in his scenario Hammerstein made this tale a secondary one and focused the main attention on another love story, as related in ''Our Heroine,'' featuring the middle-aging French planter Émile de Becque and a bright little nurse from Arkansas. Other elements were taken in from other stories to make up the actual plot line of the libretto.

Nellie Forbush (Mary Martin) is quite enjoying being away from Arkansas and stationed out on a wartime Pacific island. She knows how far she has come from Little Rock when she falls in love with the older, foreign De Becque (Ezio Pinza). However, she has not come far enough, for when she finds out that he is not just a widower, but that his wife was a Polynesian and he is the father of two half-caste children, she is revolted. But if Nellie cannot throw off the effects of her upbringing, the young lieutenant Cable (William Tabbert) can. Inveigled by the venal Asian peddler Bloody Mary (Juanita Hall) into the arms of her lovely young daughter, Liat (Betta St John), he quickly finds both love and the determination to drop his old values. The disappointed De Becque agrees to join a dangerous American spying mission to a neighboring island, and only when she realizes that she may not see him again does Nellie comprehend the depths of her feelings. Émile escapes the Japanese attack and returns to a final-curtain happy ending, but there is no such happy ending for Joe Cable and his island girl. Cable is killed in the attack, and Liat is left alone. The love stories of the evening were flavored with comedy from Bloody Mary, and from her equally venal American counterpart, the sailor Luther Billis (Myron McCormack)—a sticky-fingered gob who is always trying to get a bit of business going amongst the boys—and his lively pals.

The role and the soubrette songs of Nellie Forbush were written with Mary Martin in mind—her declaration of intent ''A Cockeyed Optimist,'' the bouncing hymn to her ''Wonderful Guy,'' her later determination that ''I'm Gonna Wash That Man Right Outa My Hair,'' her amateur-dramatics number describing the mincing Billis as ''Honey Bun''—and the casting of the role of Émile de Becque had an even more important effect on the score. Edwin Lester at the San Francisco and Los Angeles Light Opera Company had contracted the Metropolitan Opera's Ezio Pinza for a two-year stint, and had nothing to put him into. *South Pacific*'s producers took over that contract, and Rodgers and Hammerstein wrote Émile's songs around the voice of the great basso. The falling-in-love ''Some Enchanted Evening,'' the glorious, deep-toned waltz of regrets ''This Nearly Was Mine,'' and the Twin Soliloquies between Émile and Nellie (the nearest they got to a duet, as Miss Martin not unwisely didn't fancy doing battle with that voice) were some of the finest pieces that the composer and lyricist would ever write.

The hits of the evening were not, however, channeled only into the star roles. Cable fell in love to ''Younger Than Springtime'' (a melody taken from an *Allegro* outcut), the sailors declared raucously that ''There Is Nothing Like a Dame'' and serenaded ''Bloody Mary,'' and that lady wove her matchmaking between Cable and Liat in the delicate ''Happy Talk,'' but it was another big, romantic number rather than one of the comic or lively pieces which proved to be, along with ''Some Enchanted Evening,'' the most enduringly favorite part of this enduringly favorite score. Little Bloody Mary took up where Nettie Fowler of *Carousel* had left off, with one of Rodgers's big-voiced, sweeping feminine solos, singing the praises of the island of ''Bali H'ai.''

South Pacific put Rodgers and Hammerstein back on the romantic musical play trail they had begun to follow with *Oklahoma!* and *Carousel,* but strayed from in *Allegro,* and it also put them back on the trail of oversized success. The show settled in for a 1,925-performance run on Broadway, as the first national tour (April 1950) with Janet Blair, Pinza's erstwhile understudy Richard Eastham and Ray Walston (Billis) at its head, went out for what would be more than four years of traveling. Miss Martin left the Broadway production to open the show in London, where it arrived at the Theatre Royal, Drury Lane, dressed out with more pre-publicity than had ever

Plate 365. **South Pacific.** *Gemma Craven as Nellie Forbush touts the charms of her ''Honey Bun'' (Johnny Wade) in a London revival production.*

before been seen in the West End. Betta St John from the original cast and Walston from the tour were teamed with American baritone Wilbur Evans (Émile), Muriel Smith (Mary) and Peter Grant (Cable) and the show effortlessly bucked its advance oversell, going on to become another fine hit through 802 performances in the theatre which had already housed *Oklahoma!* and *Carousel* through a combined total of some two thousand performances.

Australia's J C Williamson Ltd followed up the next year with a production which, similarly, imported its leading players—Swede Richard Collett (Émile), Americans Mary La Roche (Nellie), Leonard Stone (Billis) and Virginia Paris (Mary), Briton David Welch (Cable)—and similarly scored a massive success: 333 performances in Melbourne alone, before going on to Sydney (Empire 9 July 1953).

In 1958 *South Pacific* followed *Oklahoma!* and *Carousel* into the film studios. Logan, who had directed both the original and the London productions was again at the helm. In contrast to the earlier Rodgers and Hammerstein films, *South Pacific* was not made with singer-actors. Although film soubrette Mitzi Gaynor was cast as a bubbling little Nellie, and Walston repeated his tour and London Billis, the rest of the cast were dubbed. Handsome Rossano Brazzi was given the voice of Giorgio Tozzi, Miss Hall got to play her original role but when she sang it was London's Miss Smith who was heard, and John Kerr's Cable gave over "Younger Than Springtime" to the voice of Bill Kerr. The film also had the unfortunate luck to arrive at a time when one of those periodic bigger-'n'-better-size-shape-and-color processes was going on in Hollywood, and in consequence some of the visual results—such as the infamous rainbow-sky accompaniment to "Bali H'ai"—were a little curious.

South Pacific, like the rest of its fellows, made its impression almost entirely and solely on the English-speaking theatre, but in that area it was a major hit. Its songs became entrenched in the classic show-song repertoire, and it was given regular regional productions over the decades that followed. The show was seen at New York's State Theatre in 1967 with Giorgio Tozzi and Florence Henderson featured (12 June, 104 performances), and the New York City Opera mounted a *South Pacific* in 1987, but it has yet to have a regular Broadway revival. London, on the other hand, welcomed the show back in 1988 when a touring production moved into the Prince of Wales Theatre, with a cast headed by Émile Belcourt, Gemma Craven and Bertice Reading (Mary) for a fine run of 413 performances, and Australia followed suit with its first major revival, starring Bernard Alane and Paige O'Hara, in 1993 (Adelaide Festival Centre 23 June).

A French-language version (ad Marc-Cab, André Hornez) was launched in 1974 by the ever-Broadway-orientated Belgian Opéra de Wallonie (*Sud-Pacific* Verviers 8 November) with Guy Fontagnère (Émile), Caroline Dumas (Nellie), Line May (Mary) and Willy Fratellini (Billis) featured, and half a century down the line a German-language production was put on the boards at Hildesheim where it was introduced by Piet Bruninx (Émile) and Ingrid Barth (Nellie).

UK: Theatre Royal, Drury Lane 1 November 1951; Australia: His Majesty's Theatre, Melbourne 13 September 1952; Germany: Stadttheater, Hildesheim 13 February 1999

Film: Twentieth Century Fox 1958; TV film: ABC 2001

Recordings: original cast (Columbia), London cast (Columbia EP), revival cast 1967 (Columbia), London revival 1988 (First Night), film soundtrack (RCA), studio casts (CBS, Warner Bros, Jay, Decca, WRC, etc)

SPEND, SPEND, SPEND Musical in 2 acts by Steve Brown and Justin Green. Music by Steve Brown. West Yorkshire Playhouse, Leeds, 23 May 1998; Piccadilly Theatre, 5 October 1999.

Subtitled "The Legend of Viv Nicholson," this modest-sized musical play told the newspaperworthy story of the Yorkshire miner's wife of that name, a 1961 British football-pools winner who, when asked what she was going to do with her huge windfall replied quotably: "spend, spend, spend." The tabloid papers thereafter gleefully charted the high-and-lowlights (and there were ultimately more of the latter than the former) of Viv's life, as she and her husband Keith splashed their cash haplessly around in an effort to find what they imagined might be happiness or even enjoyment. Things were already on the downslope when Viv lost her already-lost husband to a car crash, and she ultimately ended up, virtually penniless, working in a hairdressing shop. In this version of the tale, when she revisits her old home, the place where she had lived before the money came in, she surprisingly backtracks on her live-it-up philosophy and retreats into sentimentality. "We had it all," she lies to herself.

Already the subject of a well-liked Jack Rosenthal television play of the same title (1977), and of a stage pasticcio musical adaptation (Half Moon Theatre, 1984), Viv's story was here turned into a full-scale musical which was produced initially at Leeds's West Yorkshire Playhouse. The tale was set with a plangent series of songs and ensembles by Steve Brown from which a set piece in the "Miner's Arms" on Viv and Keith's awkward return to their old surroundings, and such pieces as the raucous tale of the time they spent "Drinking in America" rather than dare to go outside their hotel room, the post-mortem duet for Viv and her younger self, "Who's Gonna [*sic*] Love Me," and Keith's gently significant little piece about a "Canary" proved the most natural and effective.

The initial Leeds production, with Rosemary Ashe as Viv, Sophie-Louise Dann as her younger self, and Nigel Richards as Keith, was well received, and subsequently a version of the show was brought to the West End's Piccadilly Theatre. Barbara Dickson now appeared as the older Viv, alongside Rachel Leskovac (young Viv), Steven Houghton (Keith), Jeff Shankley (father George), and a supporting cast of 13. Once again the piece was well received, but it won only a ''small'' musical's London run, closing after some 10 months in town.

Recording: London cast (Garforth)

SPENSER, Willard (b Cooperstown, NY, 7 July 1852; d St David's, Pa, 16 December 1933).

The son of a wealthy New York family, Spenser studied music with serious intent and, settling in Philadelphia, there began writing for the musical theatre. Beginning with the merrily very long-running *The Little Tycoon* (1886), which credited Spenser only as composer and which he insisted had been written and copyrighted some three years before *The Mikado* gave a new impulse to things oriental, his shows were highly successful in his adopted hometown and also in other parts of the United States. When the first two were, in spite of already good records round the country, scornfully attacked by the New York press—always intolerant of successes brewed anywhere else but hometown—Spenser not only hit back at the jealous journalists; he took the simple way out and happily excluded New York thereafter from the healthily profitable itinerary of his shows.

In fact, Spenser's musicals, if fairly conventional comic operas in their substance, were as good as or better than most of what New York had to offer in the way of original musical-theatre entertainment at the time, and *The Little Tycoon,* introduced by comic R E Graham and later played by more famous names; *Princess Bonnie,* originally directed by no less a luminary than Richard Barker and starring Frank Daniels; and *Miss Bob White,* which featured top comic Raymond Hitchcock and Merry Widow-to-be Ethel Jackson at the head of its cast, racked up amongst them several thousands of performances on the American circuits around the turn of the century.

1886 **The Little Tycoon** (''Zisko'') Temple Theater, Philadelphia 4 January; Standard Theater, New York 29 March

1894 **Princess Bonnie** Chestnut Street Theater, Philadelphia 26 March; Broadway Theater, New York 2 September 1895

1901 **Miss Bob White** Chestnut Street Theater, Philadelphia 15 April

1906 **Rosalie** (w Helen Louise Burpee) Chestnut Street Theater, Philadelphia 23 April

1912 **The Wild Goose** Lyric Theater, Philadelphia 22 April

SPEWACK, Sam[uel] (b Bachmut, Russia, 16 September 1899; d New York, 14 October 1971).

Continental-born, but American-educated, Sam Spewack and his wife **Bella SPEWACK** [née COHEN] (b Bucharest, 25 March 1899; d New York, 27 April 1990) both ran careers in journalism, including a four-year stint in Europe as foreign correspondents for the *New York World* (1922–26), prior to beginning a play- and screenwriting collaboration which produced several successful Broadway shows (*Boy Meets Girl, My Three Angels,* etc). They made their first musical venture when adapting their 1932 play *Clear All Wires* as a libretto for Cole Porter's *Leave It to Me!,* and in their only other foray into that field, paired with the same composer, scored their biggest single hit with the internationally successful *Kiss Me, Kate.*

Sam, who also directed *Leave It to Me!* and the London production of *Kiss Me, Kate,* later teamed with Frank Loesser to manufacture the libretto for Loesser's unsuccessful period piece *Pleasures and Palaces,* a musical based on an equally unsuccessful Spewack play, *Once There Was a Russian.* Catherine the Great hired John Paul Jones to help her fight the Turks, but she didn't get to do it on Broadway.

1938 **Leave It to Me!** (Cole Porter/w Bella Spewack) Imperial Theater 9 November

1948 **Kiss Me, Kate** (Porter/w B Spewack) New Century Theater 30 December

1965 **Pleasures and Palaces** (Frank Loesser/w Loesser) Fisher Theater, Detroit 11 March

DAS SPITZENTUCH DER KÖNIGIN Operette in 3 acts by ''Bohrmann-Riegen'' and Richard Genée. Music by Johann Strauss. Theater an der Wien, Vienna, 1 October 1880.

Following the notable success of *Die Fledermaus,* Johann Strauss had fared less well with *Cagliostro in Wien* and *Prinz Methusalem* and disastrously with *Blindekuh* and he was constantly on the lookout for a winning libretto for, although he had been enthusiastic about each when setting it, it was inevitably the libretto that was ultimately blamed for his half- or whole-failures. The secretary of the Stadttheater unter Laube, Heinrich Bohrmann, who, with his partner Julius von St Albino Nigri, dit Riegen, had ambitions as librettists, had written a piece around a supposed adventure of the poet Cervantes which they hoped to have set by Suppé. But Strauss, hearing of this, summoned Bohrmann to his presence and, having listened to him read his play, took it for himself. Aware that it was not wholly stageworthy, he passed it to the Theater an der Wien's Richard Genée (and also, apparently, to a number of other folk, judging by the legal wrangles which later arose) for improvements, and the finished piece appeared on that theatre's stage in October 1880.

The underaged King of Portugal (Eugenie Erdösy) is kept away from both affairs of state and from his young

Queen (Karoline Tellheim) by the regent Villalobos (Felix Schweighofer) who is plotting a coup, but the poet Cervantes (Ferdinand Schütz) and his sweetheart Irene (Hermine Meyerhoff) secretly prepare the King to announce his majority and thus end the hated regency. Villalobos uses the handkerchief of the title, dangerously but innocently inscribed by the lonely Queen with the words "A Queen loves you, though you are not a King," to turn the King against his wife and Cervantes, and back to reliance on himself, but a bit of disguise and a few opportune explanations round off the final act and the action happily. Therese Schäfer played the Marquise de Villareal, the Queen's duenna, and Alexander Girardi supported as the King's tutor, Don Sancho d'Avellaneda.

The similarities of Bohrmann's starting point with the very recent *Le Petit Duc* and the handful of reminiscences of *La Grande-Duchesse* seemed to worry no one, and *Das Spitzentuch der Königin* was well received. Strauss's score turned in several numbers which became popular, the King's waltzing Trüffel-Couplet "Stets komm mir wieder in den Sinn" remembering—with further Offenbachian reminiscence, this time of *Geneviève de Brabant*—the delicious pie his new wife served him on their wedding night, and the waltz poem "Wo die wilde Rose erblüht," sung by Cervantes to open the second act, winning special favor. Although neither is now remembered as a song, their melodies are well known as the principal themes of Strauss's concert piece "Rosen aus dem Süden."

Franz Steiner's production at the Theater an der Wien played through the month of October, and the piece was subsequently brought back for additional performances in repertoire, playing its 55th night on 13 February 1883. It was revived by Wilhelm Karczag in 1901 with Julie Kopácsi-Karczag as the King and Carl Streitmann as Cervantes, and again in 1911 with Ida Russka (King), Poldi Rizek (Queen) and Max Rohr (Cervantes), at both the Theater an der Wien and the Raimundtheater, ultimately bringing its tally up to one hundred performances at its original home.

Berlin followed the original production of what looked like being Strauss's most successful piece since *Die Fledermaus* quickly, but although the Friedrich-Wilhelmstädtisches Theater had the rather uninspiring libretto revised by Julius Rosen, the show did not prove overly successful. Similarly, György Verő's Hungarian version, with Ilka Pálmay (King) and Célia Margó (Irene) starring, was only reasonably received in a delayed Budapest production, where it had the misfortune to open just after the highly successful local piece *Az eleven ördög.* Neither Paris nor London took the piece on and the show ultimately had its best career, in spite of an unpromising start, in America.

The Queen's Lace Handkerchief (ad Randolph T Pursy) was selected by Rudolf Aronson and John McCaull to initiate their grand new musical theatre, the Casino Theater. It opened, with John Perugini (Cervantes), Lilly Post (the Queen), Louise Paullin (the King), Joseph Greenfelder (Villalobos), Jennie Reiffarth (Marquise) and Mathilde Cottrelly (Irene) in the leading roles, only to be met by a storm of protest. The theatre was not sufficiently finished to be comfortable. The producers closed at the end of the week, sent the company off to Philadelphia's Broad Street Theatre and to Chicago, and brought them back (with William Carleton now Cervantes and the young Francis Wilson in Girardi's role) a month later (30 December). This time, in a new and well-appointed house and with a new and improved adaptation (by Sydney Rosenfeld), they were a hit, running 113 consecutive performances followed by a quick return (11 June 1883) when a following production, *La Princesse de Trébizonde,* was sabotaged by one of Lillian Russell's contract-breaking walk-outs. The piece was subsequently produced at the Thalia Theater (1 October 1883) in its original German with Schütz playing his original role alongside Frlns Seebold (King), Engländer (Queen) and Schatz (Irene). It did well in the country, was revived in the German theatres, played in many of the country's summer comic-opera seasons and musical repertoire houses, won the honor of a burlesque, *The Queen's Safety-Pin* (1889), and, when all was said and totted up, actually played more performances in America than in any other area. It was also, throughout the 19th century, far and away the most popular of Johann Strauss's stage works in the United States.

The English-language version was also seen, though much more briefly, in Australia where it was introduced by soprano Clara Merivale (Irene) and her English Comic Opera Company, featuring Knight Aston (a tenor King), W H Woodfield (Cervantes), Katharine Hardy (Queen) and Edwin Kelly (Villalobos) through a short season.

In 1931 a revised version of the show written by Rudolf Österreicher and Julius Wilhelm, which kept the title but replaced the characters and the plot with a tale which was now set in Vienna, Salzburg and Munich in 1842, was played at the Johann Strauss-Theater in Vienna. Hans Heinz Bollmann was Nikolaus von Tomba, Mizzi Zwerenz the Fürstin-Mutter, Anny Coty played Rosette Falcari and the music was "fur die Bühne musikalisch neuarbeitet" by Karl Pauspertl. But things didn't go any better with a conventional new libretto than they had with a conventional old one, and *Das Spitzentuch der Königin* remained in only a mid-list position amongst the successes and slight successes of Strauss's Operetten.

Germany: Friedrich-Wilhelmstädtisches Theater 24 November 1880; USA: Casino Theater *The Queen's Lace Handkerchief* 21 October 1882; Hungary: (Ger) 21 February 1881, Népszínház

A királyné csipkekendője 29 December 1885; Australia: Theatre Royal, Melbourne *The Queen's Lace Handkerchief* 12 August 1893

SPORTING LOVE Musical horse play in 2 acts by Stanley Lupino. Additional dialogue by Arty Ash and Arthur Rigby. Lyrics by Desmond Carter and Frank Eyton. Music by Billy Mayerl. Gaiety Theatre, London, 31 March 1934.

The fourth in the successful series of Laddie Cliff/Stanley Lupino shows staged at the Gaiety Theatre in the 1920s and 1930s, *Sporting Love* followed the other three happy comedy musicals at a distance of three years and did as well as they (and better than anything else around) with a 10-month, 302-performance town run, a good touring life and a film which omitted the songs but in which Cliff and Lupino repeated their stage roles with great success.

Lupino's libretto was a farcical hotchpotch of well-used musical-comedy elements ranging from mistaken identities and impersonations to rich aunts, topped by the inevitable curtain-time pairing-off, and settings including the Derby (being used as an incident for the third time in a year in a London musical) and a shipboard scene, which served merely to give Cliff and Lupino as many comic opportunities as possible and to introduce some dance-and-song pieces by pianist-composer Billy Mayerl mostly written for the no fewer than four pairs of dancing-singing young folk in the cast (''Have a Heart,'' ''You're the Reason Why'').

Film: Hammer 1936

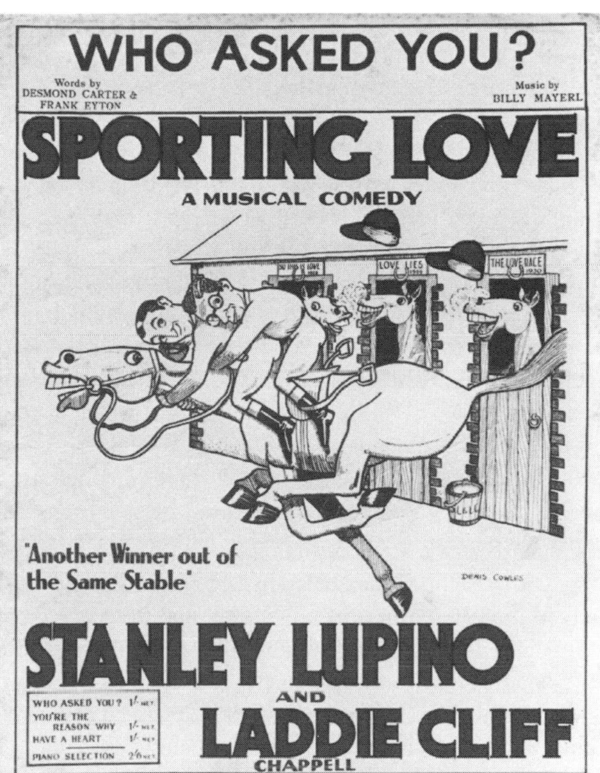

Plate 366. **Sporting Love**

THE SPRING CHICKEN Musical play in 2 acts by George Grossmith based on the play *Coquin de printemps* by Adolphe Jaime and Georges Duval. Lyrics by Adrian Ross and Percy Greenbank. Music by Ivan Caryll and Lionel Monckton. Gaiety Theatre, London, 30 May 1905.

The Gaiety musical comedy, as exemplified by the very lightly plotted, song-and-dance filled pieces which had reigned supreme in London over the dozen years and more from *The Shop Girl* to *The Orchid,* underwent something of a change in character with the advent of *The Spring Chicken.* George Edwardes had sensed that change was due, and had turned—as he would do several times—to France for inspiration. Daly's Theatre, the bulwark of the English musical play, now held his production of Messager's *Les P'tites Michu,* the same composer's *Véronique* was a hit at the Apollo, and on top of all this Gallic entertainment Edwardes announced a new English musical comedy for the Gaiety which would be ''based on'' an established French farce, part-written by Georges Duval, one of the librettists of the two Messager works. It was the first time that a Gaiety musical had been genuinely based on the text of a modern farce with all that meant in the way of problems—those same problems encountered by the old opéra-bouffe adapters, trying to translate French ''indecencies'' into English ''seeming decencies''—as well as of unaccustomed plot intricacy and vertebracy.

Every year the lawyer Babori (librettist George Grossmith), a faithful husband for most months, gets wanderlusty when spring arrives. This year his attack of below-the-belt fever sets him making eyes and passes at one of his clients, the Baronne Papouche (Kate Cutler), whose divorce he is handling. Just to complicate things, the parents of his English wife Dulcie (Olive Morrell) choose this moment to arrive in Paris. Papa Girdle (Edmund Payne) promptly experiences the same kind of fever—a little more indiscriminately—but the enterprising Mama Girdle (Connie Ediss) leaps into action and leads the ladies in getting everyone back, undamaged and almost uncompromised, to the status quo by the final curtain.

If the construction and the workings of even this thinned-down version of Jaime and Duval's sprightly farce was rather more substantial than usual fare for the Gaiety's audiences, there was no stinting on the Gaiety's accompanying specialities: the spectacle, the girls, the fun and the songs and dances. The fun was headed by Payne, a ludicrous little Englishman abroad trying to chat up the countrified French Rosalie (Gertie Millar), reminiscing over ''The Delights of London,'' swapping thoughts with Grossmith on the advantages of being ''Under and Over Forty'' or disserting blithely on the eternally ghastly attributes of ''The British Tourist,'' and by Connie Ediss who had the hit of the show with her plump and pointed accusations of family philandering in ''I Don't Know, But I Guess.'' Caryll and Monckton's songs and dances, if producing no standards, were nevertheless as bright and apt as ever, and the girls and dances were legion. Miss Millar, in the evening's principal soubrette role, had a number of songs by her husband, Monckton, and a little interpolated march, named after her character, which had been written by the young Jerome Kern.

The extra bit of substance in *The Spring Chicken* dismayed the Gaiety patrons not a whit, and the piece spent a splendid 14 months in London (401 performances) before heading out to the provinces and overseas. Richard Carle snapped the show up for America and he presented himself on Broadway in the role created by Payne, as ''Americanized'' by himself, with Bessie McCoy in Miss Millar's role and Emma Janvier as Connie Ediss. He also interpolated several songs partly or wholly his own (''A Lemon in the Garden of Love,'' ''All the Girls Love Me,'' ''Marching,'' ''No Doubt You'd Like to Cuddle Up to Baby'') and billed the show ''Richard Carle presents himself and his songs in George Edwards [*sic*] success of two London seasons.'' The American *Spring Chicken* succeeded splendidly, chalked up 91 performances in town and returned for a repeat season (24 performances) the following year during the long touring run through the better dates of the American circuits which was Carle's most lucrative activity.

Coquin de printemps, which in its original vaudeville version had taken in several songs by Fauchey, served as the basis for another musical play, the Josef Strauss pasticcio *Frühlingsluft* produced with considerable success in Vienna (Venedig in Wien 9 May 1903) before going on to be played in Germany, Hungary and America. It also shared a title, but seemingly little else, with a French musical *Coquin de printemps* (Guy Magenta/Fernand Bonifay/Jean Valmy, Marc-Cab, Théâtre de l'Européen 30 January 1958) which, with a cast headed by Henri Gènes, Brigitte Mars, Orbal, Jeannette Batti and Fernand Sardou, ran up an excellent initial run in Paris, soon followed by a second season (September 1959, Théâtre de l'ABC) with Luc Barney, Padquaim, Aglaë and Mathé Altéry in the cast, and a long touring and provincial life.

USA: Daly's Theater 8 October 1906; Australia: Her Majesty's Theatre, Melbourne 3 November 1906

SPRING IS HERE Musical comedy in 2 acts by Owen Davis adapted from his play *Shotgun Wedding.* Lyrics by Lorenz Hart. Music by Richard Rodgers. Alvin Theater, New York, 11 March 1929.

A commission from producers Alex Aarons and Vinton Freedley, *Spring Is Here* paired Pulitzer Prize–winning author Owen Davis, whose comedy *The Nervous Wreck* had been made into the successful musical *Whoopee* the previous year, with songwriters Richard Rodgers and Lorenz Hart, whose most recent Broadway shows (*She's My Baby, Present Arms, Chee-Chee*) had not been too successful, but who had had a fine run with their musical version of *A Connecticut Yankee* in 1927.

The show's tiny story covered the attempts of its heroine, Betty Braley (Lilian Taiz), to get herself wed to a fellow called Stacy Haydon (John Hundley) of whom her father disapproves. Daddy wins out and boneheaded Betty realizes that there has been better in the person of Terry Clayton (Glenn Hunter) around all the time. Since the Hollywooden Hunter (*Smilin' Through, Merton of the Movies*) had a negligible singing voice, the score's big ballad, ''With a Song in My Heart,'' was taken away from the show's hero and given to Hundley, who thus got the hit if not the girl, leaving Hunter to tiptoe his way parlando through the letter-song ''Yours Sincerely'' with Miss Taiz and to effuse ''What a Girl!'' Miss Taiz joined with Inez Courtney, in the role of her sister, Mary Jane, in the show's other favorite song ''Why Can't I?''

Spring Is Here was well enough received, but it survived only 104 performances on Broadway before going on to be made into a film with Frank Albertson, Lawrence Grey and Bernice Claire featured and Miss Courtney repeating her original role. ''With a Song in My Heart,'' however, survived to be heard in London's Cochran revue of 1930, and in a long series of musical films which culminated in the Jane Froman biopic which used the song's title as its own (Twentieth Century Fox, 1952).

Film: First National 1930

DIE SPRUDELFEE Operette in 3 acts by A M Willner and Julius Wilhelm. Music by Heinrich Reinhardt. Raimundtheater, Vienna, 23 January 1909.

Wilhelm Karczag and his partner, Karl Wallner, had taken over the ailing Raimundtheater in 1908, and there they found themselves obliged to fight a battle against a lease which bound them to stage only the classic German-language repertoire—and no musical pieces. It was not long before they had that discriminatory clause struck out, and their second new Operette production, following Ziehrer's *Liebeswalzer,* was the latest work of Heinrich Reinhardt, still haloed with the success of *Das süsse Mädel.*

Die Sprudelfee (''the mineral-water fairy'') was set at the Carlsbad springs in the year of 1830 and followed the flirtations of Fürst Aladar von Marosházy (Ludwig Herold), a nobleman whose taste in ladies leads him towards the girls who serve at the water fountains rather than towards Princess Bozena (Betty Seidl), daughter of the lofty but ill-financed Fürst Nepomuk Wrzbrzlicky (Franz Glawatsch). Bozena temporarily puts her rank away and becomes a Sprudelfee until she has hooked her Hungarian. The comedy of the piece was boosted by Karl Göstl as a matinée idol, sighed after by a married lady (Gisela Wurm) and pursued by a policeman (Karl Matuna), and the romance profited from the gallivantings of pretty Annamirl (Rose Karin-Krachler), daughter of the local innkeeper (Luise Lichten), and the other Sprudelfeen who paired off neatly in number with a male chorus of more Barons and Grafs than there would seem to have been room for even in Carlsbad in the summer.

Reinhardt's score was in the same catchingly sweet and unpretentious style as that of his biggest success and the piece's principal waltz once again proved the hit of the evening, but *Die Sprudelfee,* in a post–*Die lustige Witwe* era brimming with new hits, did not pull the same reaction in Vienna as *Das süsse Mädel* had done. However, if the show was overwhelmed by the competition on its home ground, it was that very competition which finally resulted in it winning a success . . . in America. American producers, frantically searching for another *Merry Widow,* were snatching up Austrian and German musicals by the often fairly indiscriminate handful and the young partnership of Louis F Werba and Mark A Luescher got *Die Sprudelfee* as part of their booty. Adapted by Harry and Robert Smith as *The Spring Maid* (spring as in fountain, not as in season), musically fiddled with by Robert Hood Bowers, expanded with a danced ''divertissement depicting the legend of the discovery of Carlsbad Springs,'' and cast with Christie MacDonald (Bozena), Lawrence Rea (Aladar), William Burress (Nepomuk) and Tom McNaughton (Roland, a famous English tragedian, equipped with a music-hall recitation ''The Three Trees'') it turned out a singular hit. Whilst versions of Continental mega-hits *Die Förster-Christl* and *Die geschiedene Frau* did only fairly, the pretty *The Spring Maid* ran through 194 performances on Broadway and saw its waltz (now called ''Day Dreams'') become a top-notch hit, before going triumphantly on to the road, with Mitzi now starring in its title role, for the first of many tours.

F C Whitney, reveling in the riches brought to him by *The Chocolate Soldier,* introduced an anglicized version of the show (ad C H E Brookfield) to London the following year at his Whitney (ex- Waldorf) Theatre with Tom McNaughton repeating his role alongside Paris's Marise Fairy (Bozena), Walter Hyde (Aladar), Julia James (Annamirl) and Courtice Pounds (Nepomuk). London was less enthusiastic about the piece than Broadway, and 64 performances put an end both to Britain's *The Spring Maid* and to the Whitney Theatre.

Germany: Neues Operettentheater 9 June 1909; USA: Liberty Theater *The Spring Maid* 26 December 1910; UK: Whitney Theatre *The Spring Maid* 30 September 1911

STAND UP AND SING Musical play in 2 acts by Douglas Furber and Jack Buchanan. Lyrics by Douglas Furber. Music by Vivian Ellis and Phil Charig. London Hippodrome, 5 March 1931.

Stand Up and Sing was constructed as a vehicle for the favorite comedy-with-dance team of Jack Buchanan and Elsie Randolph, returning to the London stage where they had triumphed in 1928–29 with *That's a Good Girl.* As with the previous show, Douglas Furber was the author and American songwriter Phil Charig shared the musical score, this time with local composer Vivian Ellis, and once again the accent was on the fun and the dancing. These were set in a minimal tale which had Buchanan as layabout Rockingham Smith taking employment as a valet in order to gain the good graces of his young lady and, as a result, being put in a position to win back some frightfully important papers for her originally disapproving father. Buchanan's partner, Miss Randolph—firmly labeled comedienne, and thus unable to play the heroine—instead appeared as her maid, whilst a chorus dancer called Marjorie Robertson was given the ingenue role. She changed her name to Anna Neagle and from there moved on to an impressive career on film and stage.

A fine display of scenery included one of the currently inevitable shipboard scenes, an English country house and a visit to Cairo, whilst the songs followed the established patterns from the earlier Buchanan shows, featuring a new tipsy song for the star, a ballad ''There's Always Tomorrow'' as performed by Buchanan and Miss Neagle, and a comedy number, ''It's Not You,'' for him to sing and dance with Miss Randolph, as well as a jolly title song. There was also a big, bright dance finale tacked on to the end of the show, apropos of nothing at all, to climax the routines, straight and comical, which Buchanan performed with his respective ladies and with the lushly comical Vera Pearce, here cast as an Egyptian Princess. When the stars were not on, handsome Richard Dolman did his number-two song-and-dance spot, Anton Dolin performed more classical dance, the Seven Hindustanis did acrobatics and soprano May Tomlinson performed a Vivian Ellis vocalise called ''Cairo,'' all adding their bit to to the highly revusical entertainment.

Stand Up and Sing was, unusually, produced out of town and played in several provincial cities, including a six-week Christmas season in Glasgow (without Miss Randolph, who didn't tour), before coming to London. There it remained for eight and a half months (325 performances) before rounding off in the suburbs after a total of some six hundred performances.

STANGE, Stanislaus [STANGE, Joseph William Henry] (b Chorlton-upon-Medlock, 1 November 1860; d New York, 2 January 1917).

Lancashire-born Stange, the son of an American confectioner, worked as a young man in his father's business, but in 1881 he returned to America where he worked at first as an actor and subsequently, through more than a decade, turned out a solid run of comic-opera libretti for pieces designed, by and large, for the more musically ambitious end of the market. Several of these—notably the fairy-tale light opera *Madeleine,* an adaptation of Garrick's *The Country Girl* as *Dolly Varden* and the not-unoriginal American Civil War musical *When Johnny Comes Marching Home,* each written with his habitual musical partner, fellow expatriate Englishman Julian Edwards—did well, touring for several years around the country after their initial productions, but Stange compiled his best Broadway records when he dropped his sights a little. The spectacular extravaganza *The Man in the Moon* (the attraction of which was scarcely in its libretto) and the farcical-comical *Piff! Paff! Pouf!* (where it, conversely, was) were both long-running hits to place alongside their author's highly successful (non-musical) dramatization of the novel *Quo Vadis?* (1900).

Stange had the concourse of some big names in his comic operas: his musical version of *She Stoops to Conquer* (*Two Roses*) starred Fritzi Scheff, *The Singing Girl* had Alice Nielsen singing Stange's lyrics to Victor Herbert's music and *Love's Lottery* boasted the operatic diva Ernestine Schumann-Heink as its star, but although these more ambitious pieces toured strongly round America, none of them performed as well in New York as his two more ''popular'' shows.

The librettist's greatest success, however, came when the new fashion for Continental Operetten hit America and Stange was given the job of turning the Germanized George Bernard Shaw of *Der tapfere Soldat* back into English. It was reported that he had ''evolved a book of subtle humour, literary nicety and consequential interest'' for the piece that became known through thousands of performances as *The Chocolate Soldier* (what Shaw thought is not reported). In the process, he invented the lyric to ''My Hero,'' the song which remained his most enduring contribution to the musical theatre, and he also directed Broadway's production of the show for producer F C Whitney.

Stange did not, however, follow up his biggest hit with others in the same line. He turned out the musical comedy *The Kissing Girl* which toured a couple of season, with Texas Guinan latterly starred, without braving Broadway, and adapted Anthony Mars's hit play *Fils à papa* for a semi-musical Broadway production as *The Girl in the Taxi* (not to be confused with the British production of the same title), and then in 1910—in the selfsame week that his partner of always, Edwards, died—whilst directing the London version of *The Chocolate Soldier* he suffered a stroke. His upcoming *The Pet of the Petticoats* was never finished, and in the remaining half-dozen years before his death he provided no more texts to the Broadway musical stage.

His stage adaptation (w Stannard Mears) of Booth Tarkington's novel *Seventeen* became the basis for the musicals *Hello, Lola* (1925) and *Seventeen* (1951).

1893 **Friend Fritz** (Julian Edwards) Herrmann's Theater 26 January

1894 **Madeleine, or The Magic Kiss** (ex- *Baron Grim*) (Edwards) Tremont Theater, Boston 30 July; Bijou Theater, New York 25 February 1895

1896 **The Goddess of Truth** (Edwards) Abbey's Theater 26 February

1896 **Brian Boru** (Edwards) Broadway Theater 19 October

1897 **The Wedding Day** (*La Petite Fronde*) English version w new music by Edwards, Casino Theater

1898 **The Jolly Musketeer** (Edwards) Broadway Theater 14 November

1899 **The Man in the Moon** (Ludwig Englander, Gustave Kerker, Reginald De Koven/w Louis Harrison) New York Theater 24 April

1899 **The Singing Girl** (Victor Herbert) Casino Theater 23 October

1901 **Dolly Varden** (Edwards) Princess Theater, Toronto 23 September; Herald Square Theater 27 January 1902

1902 **When Johnny Comes Marching Home** (Edwards) Opera House, Detroit 6 October; New York Theater 16 December

1904 **Piff! Paff! Pouf!** (Jean Schwartz/William Jerome) Casino Theater 2 April

1904 **The Two Roses** (Englander, Kerker) Cleveland, Ohio 20 August; Broadway Theater 21 November

1904 **Love's Lottery** (Edwards) Broadway Theater 3 October

1906 **The Student King** (De Koven/w Frederick M Ranken) Lyceum Theater, Rochester, NY 17 May; Studebaker Theater, Chicago 21 May; Garden Theater 25 December

1907 **The Belle of London Town** (Edwards) Lincoln Square Theater 28 January

1907 **The Snowman** (De Koven) Majestic Theater, Boston 18 March

1907 **The Girls of Holland** (revised *The Snowman*) (De Koven) Lyric Theater 18 November

1908 **The Magic Bottle** (De Koven) 1 act American Theater, St Louis 23 November

1908 **The Patriot** (Edwards) 1 act Keith's Theater, Providence, RI 14 September; Fifth Avenue Theater 30 November

1909 **The Chocolate Soldier** (*Der tapfere Soldat*) American version Lyric Theater

1909 **The Kissing Girl** (Harry von Tilzer/Vincent Bryan) Cort Theater, Chicago 25 October

1910 **The Girl in the Taxi** (various) Astor Theater 24 October

STANISLAUS, Frederic (b Kidderminster, ?December 1844; d Hammersmith, London, 22 November 1891). Conductor and composer for the 19th-century British stage.

Originally a member of the CCC Minstrels, later accompanist for Louisa Pyne's operetta group (1867–68), later again an operatic conductor in the British provinces, Stanislaus subsequently worked as a theatrical musical director in Dublin, Manchester and London. In a very full and top-flight career at the baton, he toured with Julia Mathews in Mrs Liston's *Giroflé-Girofla* company (1875), and in her ill-fated American season (1875), was musical director at Sadler's Wells (1880), and conducted Broadway's *Pirates of Penzance* and the first British tour of the show for Carte (1880–81), as well as London's *Princess Toto* (1881) and *Dick* (1884) for Hollingshead. He was musical director for Brough and Boucicault's new burlesque productions in Australia (1886), for the Carl Rosa light opera company in *Paul Jones* (1889) and *Marjorie* (1890), and for the burlesque *Joan of Arc* (1891) for George Edwardes, supplying such occasional songs and music as were needed along the way. He also ventured into production, putting out a tour of *Little Jack* Sheppard in 1890 with his wife in the star role. His last job, before his premature death, was as musical director for the London production of *Miss Decima* (1891).

His one major stage work as a composer was the comic opera *The Lancashire Witches,* produced in Manchester to some considerable praise. In spite of this success, however, Stanislaus did not follow it up with any further pieces of equal significance.

Stanislaus was married to burlesque actress and principal boy **Fanny ROBINA** [Fanny COOPER] (b London, 22 December 1861; d Nottingham, 13 February 1927), the daughter of top-flight music-hall duettists George Newman [George John COOPER] (d Southwark, 2 November 1871) and Miss Mortimer (née Margaret Jones, d London, 10 December 1874), who appeared in a number of musicals both in Britain (notably as the original Faust in the Gaiety's *Faust Up-to-Date* and on tour as *Little Jack Sheppard*) and in Australia (*Young Fra Diavolo, Dick, Little Jack Sheppard,* Ganem in *The Forty Thieves*) before continuing a career in the music halls.

1867 **The Lady Volunteers** (Andrew Campbell) Waterloo Opera House, Edinburgh 2 December

1873 **Little Tom Tug, or The Fresh-Water Man** (comp and arr/F C Burnand) Opera Comique 12 November

1879 **The Lancashire Witches** (R T Gunton) Theatre Royal, Manchester 20 October

1884 **Im-Patience** (comp, sel & travestied/Walter Browne) 1 act Prince of Wales Theatre, Liverpool 25 August

1884 **Called There and Back** (comp and arr/Herman C Merivale) Gaiety Theatre 15 October

1886 **The Palace of Pearl** (w Edward Jakobowski/Alfred Murray) Empire Theatre 12 June

STARLIGHT EXPRESS Musical in 2 acts with lyrics by Richard Stilgoe. Music by Andrew Lloyd Webber. Apollo Victoria Theatre, London, 27 March 1984.

Composer Andrew Lloyd Webber and director Trevor Nunn followed up their success with *Cats* (1981) with another musical show which, like its predecessor, presented a set of anthropomorphic characters in a series of loosely linked songs and choreographic routines. Where *Cats* had presented felines, *Starlight Express* featured trains, and the characters of the piece—the macho-mechanical Greaseball (Jeff Shankley), the country-and-western dining car called Dinah (Frances Ruffelle), the two-faced little red caboose (Michael Staniforth), soul-singing Poppa (Lon Satton) and the androgynous electric train—were brought together around a simplistically improbable plot line in which a good old steam train called Rusty (Ray Shell) beats all modern opposition in some kind of railway challenge and wins himself a coupling with a pretty carriage called Pearl (Stephanie Lawrence).

Lloyd Webber's score for *Starlight Express* was a purposefully youth-orientated one with the songs mostly written and orchestrated in a forceful, modern pop idiom varied occasionally with some burlesques of older song styles, and Nunn's production—which put all the performers on roller skates—was equally youthful and also probably the most technically complex and spectacular ever seen on the West End stage. To accommodate this wheelie concept and John Napier's settings for the series of skated races which comprised the backbone of the show's action, the entire interior of the Apollo Victoria Theatre, an ugly big cinema of the 1920s, was gutted and rebuilt with a network of wooden tracks, encircling the auditorium, rising to the level of the dress circle, and meeting at a mobile, hydraulically operated bridge suspended high above the stage area. In order that the public could watch the races, minutely timed to a musical accompaniment, even when they were taking place above or behind them, pop-concert style television screens were installed at the front of the auditorium.

Unlike *Cats, Evita* and *Jesus Christ Superstar, Starlight Express* produced no hit parade singles. The principal ballad "Only He Has the Power to Move Me" and the electric train's "AC/DC" performed by the pop world's Jeffrey Daniels did not catch on and, in the show, it was the burlesques, such as Frances Ruffelle's plaintive country version of "U.N.C.O.U.P.L.E.D." and the droopily comical "One Rock and Roll Too Many" which proved the most popular individual pieces, alongside such lively skated ensembles as "Freight." In spite of some adverse criticism from journalists who belonged to another world and/or time and/or entertainment industry from *Starlight Express,* the show itself caught on decidedly.

On 23 November 1992, the show broke a record all of its own when, without being taken from the London stage, it was given a £1/2 million overhaul, with all its original creative team returning to restage and rechoreograph a revised version of the show in the kind of "second edition" not seen on the London stage since the days of George Edwardes's running remakes of his Gaiety Theatre hits. Several new songs ("Crazy," "Next Time You Fall in Love") were added, several others remade, two characters vanished (with their numbers), the plot was slimmed vigorously, the music reorchestrated in line with 1990s sounds, and the now dated pop references and styles updated, as the "new" *Starlight Express* rolled on towards its first decade on the London stage.

At the time of writing it has been playing for more than 15 years and 6,000 performances (6,000th 12 August 1998) in London, notching itself into second place on London's "all-time" list of runs.

A Broadway production, with the show slightly reorganized with several new musical pieces and the addition of a clever explanation of the piece's naive action as taking place on a child's train-set layout, played for 761 performances in 1987–89 prior to touring America, whilst a highly successful German production and another, less successful, played in Japan and Australia both opened the piece up as something more approaching an arena entertainment rather than a stage show. The German production has, like the London one, proved to be a long-running fixture and is running on into its 12th year at its custom-made Starlighthalle at the time of writing. In 1993 (14 September) a version of the show was staged in the Show Room at Las Vegas's Hilton Hotel.

USA: Gershwin Theater 15 March 1987; Australia: Sydney Showground 24 January 1988; Germany: Starlighthalle, Bochum 12 June 1988

Recordings: original cast (Polydor), German casts (Stella, Polydor, CBS, Steel Street), touring cast (EMI), American selection (MCA), new London version (Polydor)

STARMANIA Rock opera by Luc Plamondon. Music by Michel Berger. Palais des Congrès, Paris, 16 April 1979.

A Franco-Canadian attempt at an answer to everything from *Jesus Christ Superstar, West Side Story* and *Hair* to *Batman, The Rocky Horror Show, Metropolis* and the less imaginative American comic strips, *Starmania* is a strange compound which hovers between being a burlesque and a calculated aim at a pre-puberty crowd weaned on TV, computer games and comics and a belief in the power of "naughty"words. If its writing tends, *Rocky Horror Show*–style, towards being a parody of the sci-fi strip material that is its content, its performance has tended to indicate that it is actually taken for real by those who play it and watch it.

Starmania is a kind of science-fiction melodrama, illustrated by songs whose titles point up the level of its ambition: "Sex shops, cinéma pornos," "Ce soir on danse à Naziland," "Un enfant de la pollution," "Le Monde est stone." It takes place in a futuristic city called Monopolis, and its chief characters are the black-leather-clad Sadia (Nanette Workman), head of the terrorist "Black Stars" who are actively led by one Johnny Rockfort (Daniel Balavoine) in trying—unsuccessfully—to stop the millionaire businessman Zéro Janvier (Étienne Chicot) becoming President of the Western World on a law-and-order ticket. In the course of affairs Johnny falls in love with the TV-child's equivalent of the Princesses of operetta, a television presenter called Cristal (France Gall). She dies in his arms during a bombing attack on Janvier's offices. The other main characters include film star Stella Spotlight (Diane Dufresne), the fiancée of Janvier; Marie-Jeanne (Fabienne Thibeault), the waitress at the automat which the Black Stars use as their rendezvous; and Ziggy (Grégory Ken), the androgynous young person over whom Marie-Jeanne sighs.

First produced, *Superstar*-style, as a two-record concept disc, the piece threw up one number—Janvier's "Les Blues du Business-Man"—which found its way to the pop charts, and the show was duly put on stage in Paris, under the management of Roland Manuel and the direction of *Superstar* and *Hair* director Tom O'Horgan, in a vast, colorful, gimmicky production sponsored by the radio station Europe 1 and, of all unlikely backers, Perrier mineral water. France's *Superstar* star Balavoine was the leading man, alongside some of the choicer French/Canadian female pop vocalists. *Starmania* played a season of 25 performances but, if its Parisian stage life was short, it outdid even *Superstar* by spawning a four-record cast album.

Starmania, however, continued to be energetically pushed and promoted by those behind it. It was played in Montreal, toured in Canada and in 1988 a new version of the piece, revised into a very much reduced size physically, orchestrally and in all personnel departments (the original had boasted a cast of 70, the new a dozen), was remounted in Paris (Théâtre de Paris 15 September) with a cast headed by Norman Groulx (Johnny), Maurane (Marie-Jeanne), Martine St-Clair (Cristal) and Renaud Hantson (Ziggy). Directed this time by its writers, without the frills and sillies of the first mounting, and with the comic-strip humor replaced by a certain earnest belief (or pretended belief) in the material, it won sufficient success to transfer to the Théâtre Marigny (14 January 1989) for a further five months, returning after the summer for a further season of six weeks before going on tour and to the television screen. In 1993 (28 September) it was again reprised in Paris, at the Théâtre Mogador, by which time it had become established in the minds of the French public (which around the same time was rejecting the outstanding *Les Misérables*) as the most successful French-language musical of recent decades. A tour and yet another Paris appearance in 1995 (Palais de Congrès 20 October) prefaced yet another tour, in 1996 (which took in performances at Eurodisney), another in 1998, and yet another return to Paris (Casino de Paris 28 October 1998). In 1999 (Casino de Paris 22 October) it played a "20th anniversary" season.

In 1992 a German-language version (ad Jürgen Schwalbe, Gerulf Pannach) was mounted at Essen with Andrea Weiss (Marie-Jeanne), Erwin Brühn (Janvier), Paul Kribbe (Johnny) and Annika Bruhns (Cristal) featured and an English-language *Tycoon* (ad Tim Rice) was issued as a recording and put on trial at Andrew Lloyd Webber's Sydmonton Festival without, in spite of London-bound announcements, progressing further. But in the otherwise modern-musical-theatre desert that is France, *Starmania* somehow lives on. And on. And on.

Germany: Aalto Theater, Essen 14 February 1992

Recordings: pre-production recording, original cast recording (Warner Brothers), revival cast recording (Apache), 1993 revival recording (WEA), 20th anniversary recording (WEA), English language recording (Epic)

STARS IN YOUR EYES Musical play in 2 acts by J P McEvoy. Lyrics by Dorothy Fields. Music by Arthur Schwartz. Majestic Theater, New York, 9 February 1939.

Originally conceived as a satire on left-wing doings in Hollywood, *Stars in Your Eyes* was intended to feature Ethel Merman as Jeanette Adair, a film star pursuing a lefty, boy-wonder screenwriter called John Blake (Richard Carlson) with the aid of a union man (Jimmy Durante) and a bookful of nibbling songs lyricked by Dorothy Fields. However, bit by bit, through the planning stages, the politics went out the window, dancer Tamara Toumanova was inserted as a rival for Merman in her chase after the now apolitical Blake and, under the guidance of director Joshua Logan, the piece finally turned into a sex-and-films one instead of a politics-and-films one, even though odd traces of the original orientation remained in the songs.

Without the political focus, which had not been replaced by anything else, the show lacked much in the way of individuality, and even its starry credits could not keep Dwight Deere Wiman's production on Broadway more than 127 performances. Amongst the songs provided for the star were "This Is It," "It's All Yours," "A Lady Needs a Change" (replacing the union-ridiculing "My New Kentucky Home") and "Just a Little Bit More," none of which feature amongst either Schwartz's or Miss Merman's enduring credits.

Recording: selection (AEI)

Plate 367. **Tommy Steele** *as Hans Andersen in his own musical-play version of the Frank Loesser film.*

STEELE, Tommy [HICKS, Thomas] (b London, 17 December 1936).

Seaman turned Britain's first and foremost rock idol, Steele was reorientated towards the musical stage when he was starred as Buttons in a stage version of Rodgers and Hammerstein's television musical *Cinderella* in 1958. His success in this piece encouraged producer Harold Fielding to commission a musical play vehicle for him, and the resultant *Half a Sixpence* (1963), in which Steele played H G Wells's Artie Kipps ("Half a Sixpence," "If the Rain's Got to Fall," "Flash, Bang, Wallop"), established him as one of Britain's top musical-theatre names.

He repeated *Half a Sixpence* on Broadway (1965) and for the screen but it was a decade before, in a carefully dosed career, he returned to the West End in a second Fielding production, the stage adaptation of Frank

Loesser's *Hans Andersen* (1974, "The Ugly Duckling," etc). This piece served him for a year's run, two tours and a second London run before, once again, he returned to television, concert and a record-breaking West End one-man (with dancers) stage show at the Prince of Wales Theatre. In 1983 he appeared in his third West End musical, again under Fielding's management, playing Don Lockwood in a stage version of *Singin' in the Rain* which he had himself adapted and for which he also acted as director. It gave him a third success, with a two-year run, two tours, a Japanese season and another return to London.

In 1991 he authored, directed and starred in another film-based musical, *Some Like It Hot,* using elements of the film script and (of contractual necessity) much of its earlier musical adaptation, *Sugar.* After an extensive British tour, the show was taken to London in March 1992, but it failed to give its star a fourth consecutive musical hit.

In 1978 Steele appeared as Jack Point in the production of *The Yeomen of the Guard* mounted in the moat of the Tower of London on the occasion of the building's 900th anniversary. The production was later reproduced in a television film (ATV, 1978).

1974 **Hans Andersen** (Frank Loesser, Marvin Laird/w Beverley Cross) London Palladium 17 December

1983 **Singin' in the Rain** (Arthur Freed/Nacio Herb Brown) London Palladium 30 June

1991 **Some Like It Hot** revised version of *Sugar* Churchill Theatre, Bromley 17 June; Prince Edward Theatre 17 March 1992

STEIN, Joseph (b New York, 30 May 1912). Librettist of several Broadway hits of the 1950s and 1960s.

Stein's earliest contributions to the stage were made in the world of revue where he supplied material for such pieces as *Inside USA, Lend an Ear, Alive and Kicking* and the *Ziegfeld Follies of 1956.* His first venture into writing a musical play was with *Plain and Fancy* (w Will Glickman), a piece which brought him a considerable success with its tale of the results of the interference of some worldly folk into the well-ordered lives of the Amish community. The pair had a further good Broadway showing with *Mr Wonderful,* a show-business tale without a difference set up as a vehicle for the young Sammy Davis jr. After three less-than-successful shows in the years that followed, Stein then turned out two of the most impressive libretti of 1960s Broadway with his adaptation of Sholem Aleichem's tales as the book for *Fiddler on the Roof* (Tony Award) and the remaking of the warmly passionate tale of Zorba the Greek, already famous on the screen, as the musical play *Zorba.*

A rewrite of a rewrite of the libretto to the classic musical comedy *Irene,* whilst going rather far from the original, provided a winning text for a 1970s 1919 musical and it was rewarded with a long run, but an adaptation of his own 1963 play *Enter Laughing* as the musical *So Long, 174th Street* was a failure. Several further adaptations, the Pagnol/Giono *La Femme du boulanger* as *The Baker's Wife,* another screenplay as *King of Hearts,* and yet another, *Buona Sera, Mrs Campbell,* as *Carmelina* failed to bring another success, and the Charles Strouse/Stephen Schwartz musical *Rags* was seen for only four nights on Broadway. While it came and went, *Fiddler on the Roof* and *Zorba* continued to be played worldwide.

More than half a century after his first contributions to the theatre, Stein returned with one further adaptation, the remake of Thornton Wilder's *The Skin of Our Teeth* as the libretto for the Kander/Ebb *Over and Over.*

1955 **Plain and Fancy** (Albert Hague/Arnold B Horwitt/w Will Glickman) Mark Hellinger Theater 27 January

1956 **Mr Wonderful** (Jerry Bock, Larry Holofcener, George Weiss/w Glickman) Broadway Theater 22 March

1958 **The Body Beautiful** (Bock/Sheldon Harnick/w Glickman) Broadway Theater 23 January

1959 **Juno** (Marc Blitzstein) Winter Garden Theater 9 March

1959 **Take Me Along** (Bob Merrill/w Robert Russell) Shubert Theater 22 October

1964 **Fiddler on the Roof** (Bock/Harnick) Imperial Theater 22 September

1968 **Zorba** (John Kander/Fred Ebb) Imperial Theater 17 November

1973 **Irene** adaptation w Harry Rigby, Hugh Wheeler Minskoff Theater 13 March

1976 **So Long, 174th Street** (Stan Daniels) Harkness Theater 27 April

1976 **The Baker's Wife** (Stephen Schwartz) Dorothy Chandler Pavilion, Los Angeles 11 May

1978 **King of Hearts** (Peter Link/Jacob Brackman/w Steve Tesich) Minskoff Theater 22 October

1979 **Carmelina** (Burton Lane/Alan Jay Lerner/w Lerner) St James Theater 8 April

1986 **Rags** (Charles Strouse/Stephen Schwartz) Mark Hellinger Theater 21 August

1999 **Over and Over** (Kander/Ebb) Signature Theater, Washington 9 January

STEIN, Leo [ROSENSTEIN, Leo] (b Lemberg, 25 March 1861; d Vienna, 28 July 1921).

A railway official turned playwright and librettist, Stein collaborated—at first mostly with Alexander Landesberg, Julius Horst or Alexander Engel, and later with Victor Léon, Carl Lindau and Béla Jenbach—on a large number of successful plays and, most particularly, of Operetten during the most fruitful years of the Viennese theatre.

His first piece, *Lachende Erben,* produced with a cast headed by Wilhelm Knaack and Karl Blasel, was played 32 times at the Carltheater and was subsequently produced both at Berlin's Theater Unter den Linden (15 January 1893) and as *A Nevető őrökösök* in Budapest (Budai Színkör 2 April 1893). Two further pieces for the Carltheater, *Die Königin von Gamara* (27 performances) and *Lady Charlatan* (37 performances), did only fairly, but his first piece for the Theater an der Wien, *Der Wunderknabe* (36 performances), topped its Vienna run by making it to the London stage (*The Little Genius*). *Die Blumen-Mary* (41 performances), *Der Dreibund* (23 performances) and *Der Blondin von Namur* (31 performances) all performed just adequately, before Stein's first major success with a first collaboration with Victor Léon on the libretto for the slow-starting but eventually popular Johann Strauss pasticcio *Wiener Blut* (1899).

Two seasons later, Stein scored an even more considerable hit with the Heinrich Reinhardt Operette *Das süsse Mädel,* and thereafter the hits began to come with more regularity. He combined again with Léon on the text for the so-so classical burlesque *Der Göttergatte* set by Franz Lehár, teamed with Carl Lindau and Edmund Eysler on the highly successful rustic *Die Schützenliesel* as a vehicle for Girardi, and returned to Léon and Lehár for his greatest hit of all, the adaptation of the French play *L'Attaché d'ambassade* as the text for *Die lustige Witwe.*

Stein and Léon did not team again for a number of years after their world-shaking hit. Although they were originally announced to share the writing of Lehár's Das *Fürstenkind* as a team, in the end Léon went it alone. This apparent divorce was not because of any breach, but simply because the authors of *Die lustige Witwe* found themselves deluged with offers of work, and realized they could cash in better on their success by each separately taking a bundle of what was offered.

Stein's partnership with Eysler, on the other hand, continued fruitfully, bringing forth further international hits in *Künstlerblut, Vera Violetta, Der Frauenfresser* and *Ein Tag im Paradies,* but Stein, haloed with his success as the author of the most successful Operette of the age in *Die lustige Witwe,* supplied texts to virtually all of the outstanding composers of his period and harvested hits, national and/or international, in tandem with each of them. His name appeared on Leo Fall's *Das Puppenmädel* and *Die Sirene,* Oskar Nedbal's *Polenblut* and *Die Winzerbraut,* Oscar Straus's *Die kleine Freundin,* Kálmán's vastly successful *Die Csárdásfürstin* and *Das Hollandweibchen,* Lehár's long-running Vienna hit *Die blaue Mazur* (curiously, his only subsequent work with the composer of *Die lustige Witwe*), and Robert Stolz's *Mädi.*

Stein's body of work, which ranged from such featherlight pieces as the delightful *Das süsse Mädel* and the sentimental musical comedies written for Girardi to Operetten more richly romantic than comic, gave him a place amongst the most important of all the Operette writers of his age. If *Die lustige Witwe* and, to a lesser extent, *Die Csárdásfürstin* are largely responsible for his continuing presence on the world's stages, *Das süsse Mädel, Künstlerblut, Ein Tag im Paradies, Polenblut* and others were major successes of their time, and both the last-named and *Wiener Blut* also continue to be performed nearly a century after their initial performances.

Stein was active, much of his career, parallel to an almost homonym: **Leo Walther STEIN** (b Gleiwitz, 10 August 1866; d Berlin, 3 January 1930), whose libretto and lyrics credits included *Die Herren Söhne* (1903 Rudolf Nelson), *Zur Wienerin* (1906, Rudolf Raimann/w Richard Skowronnek), *Der blaue Reiter* (1914, Friedrich Bermann/w Ludwig Heller), *Die schöne Unbekannte* (1915, Oscar Straus/w Leopold Jacobson), *Die Dose seiner Majestät* (1917, Jean Gilbert/w Presber), *Der Hoflieranten* (1917, Hugo Hirsch), *Der Liebesdiplomat* (1921, Franz Dorffe/w Presber), *Ein Prachtmädel* (1921, Rudolf Nelson), *Die beiden Nachtigallen* (1921, Bredschneider/w Presber), *Die Scheidungsreise* (1922, Hugo Hirsch), *Der Gauklerkönig* (Gilbert/w Presber, Hans Hellmut Zerlett), *Sonja* (1925, Leo Ascher/w Presber) and the Singspiel *Chopin* (w Presber), as well as a source credit (w Oskar Walther) in the 1920 musical *Zwei tipp-topp Mädel* (Friedrich Schmidt/Curt Lauermann). Following his suicide in 1930 he had a posthumous credit on a musical version of the British farce *Tons of Money* produced as *Geld wie heu* at Berlin's Neues Theater am Zoo in November of that year.

1892 **Lachende Erben** (Carl Weinberger/w Julius Horst) Carltheater 24 October

1893 **Münchener Kind'l** (Weinberger/w Alexander Landesberg) Theater Unter den Linden, Berlin 7 November

1894 **Die Königin von Gamara** (Alexander Neumann/w Julius Nigri, Richard Genée) Carltheater 27 October

1894 **Lady Charlatan** (Adolf Müller jr/w Paul von Schönthan) Carltheater 29 November

1895 **Die Lachtaube** (Eugen von Taund/w Landesberg under ps "Otto Rehberg") Carltheater 14 April

1896 **Der Pumpmajor** (Neumann/w Horst) Theater in der Josefstadt 11 January

1896 **Der Wunderknabe** (von Taund/w Landesberg) Theater an der Wien 28 March

1896 **Der Pfiffikus** (Muller/w Horst) 1 act Raimundtheater 18 April

1896 **Der Löwenjäger** (*Az oroszlánvadász*) German version (Theater an der Wien)

1897 **Die Blumen-Mary** (Weinberger/w Landesberg) Theater an der Wien 11 November

1898 **Der Dreibund** (von Taund/w Landesberg) Theater an der Wien 28 April

1898 **Frau Reklame** (Louis Roth/w Horst) Venedig in Wien 6 August

1898 **Der Blondin von Namur** (Müller/w Horst) Theater an der Wien 15 October

1899 **(Die) Gräfin Kuni** (*Der Minnesänger*) (F Baumgartner/w Paul von Schönthan) Theater an der Wien 11 March

1899 **Wiener Blut** (Johann Strauss arr/w Victor Léon) Carltheater 26 October

1899 **Der griechische Sklave** (*A Greek Slave*) German version (Theater an der Wien)

1899 **Die wahre Liebe ist das nicht** (Fritz Skallitzky/w Horst) Raimundtheater 9 November

1900 **Der Sechs-Uhr-Zug** (Richard Heuberger/w Léon) Centraltheater, Berlin 17 January

1900 **Man lebt nur einmal** (w Horst) Raimundtheater 14 November

1901 **Das süsse Mädel** (Heinrich Reinhardt/w Landesberg) Carltheater 25 October

1902 **Das gewisse Etwas** (Weinberger/w Léon) Carltheater 15 March

1902 **Der liebe Schatz** (Reinhardt/w Landesberg) Carltheater 30 October

1902 **Clo-Clo** (Ferdinand Pagin/w Landesberg) Danzers Orpheum 23 December

1904 **Der Göttergatte** (Franz Lehár/w Léon) Carltheater 20 January

1904 **Der Generalkonsul** (Reinhardt/w Landesberg) Theater an der Wien 29 January

1904 **Das Garnisonsmädel** (*Huszárvér*) (Raoul Mader/w Landesberg) Theater an der Wien 29 October

1904 **Eduard, der Herzensdieb** (w Alfred Schick von Markenau) Raimundtheater 17 December

1905 **Der Schnurrbart** (*A bajusz*) German version w Carl Lindau (Carltheater)

1905 **Die Schützenliesel** (Edmund Eysler/w Lindau) Carltheater 7 October

1905 **Die lustige Witwe** (Lehár/w Léon) Theater an der Wien 30 December

1906 **Tausend und eine Nacht** (Johann Strauss arr Reiterer/w Lindau) Venedig in Wien 15 June

1906 **Künstlerblut** (Eysler/w Lindau) Carltheater 20 October

1907 **Der selige Vincenz** (Mader/w Landesberg) Carltheater 31 January

1907 **Vera Violetta** (Eysler) 1 act Apollotheater 30 November

1907 **Weiberlaunen** (*Leányka*) German version (Frankfurt am Main)

1908 **Das Glücksschweinchen** (Eysler/w Lindau) Venedig in Wien 26 June

1908 **Johann der Zweite** (Eysler/w Lindau) Carltheater 3 October

1910 **Lumpus und Pumpus** (Eysler) 1 act Apollotheater 21 January

1910 **Das Puppenmädel** (Leo Fall/A M Willner) Carltheater 4 November

1911 **Die Sirene** (Fall/w Willner) Johann Strauss-Theater 5 January

1911 **Die kleine Freundin** (Oscar Straus/w Willner) Carltheater 20 October

1911 **Der Natursänger** (Eysler/w Jenbach) 1 act Apollotheater 22 December

1911 **Der Frauenfresser** (Eysler/w Lindau) Wiener Bürgertheater 23 December

1912 **Die Premiere** (Josef G Hart/w Béla Jenbach) 1 act Apollotheater 10 August

1912 **Der fliegende Rittmeister** (Hermann Dostal/w Jenbach) 1 act Apollotheater 5 October

1913 **Polenblut** (Oskar Nedbal) Carltheater 25 October

1913 **Der Nachtschnellzug** (Leo Fall/w Léon) Johann Strauss-Theater 20 December

1913 **Ein Tag im Paradies** (Eysler/w Jenbach) Wiener Bürgertheater 23 December

1915 **Die—oder keine** (Eysler/w Jenbach) Wiener Bürgertheater 9 October

1915 **Die Csárdásfürstin** (Emmerich Kálmán/w Jenbach) Johann Strauss-Theater 13 November

1916 **Die Winzerbraut** (Nedbal/w Julius Wilhelm) Theater an der Wien 11 February

1918 **Bloch und co** (Robert Stolz/w Ernst Wengraf) 1 act Budapester Orpheum 5 April

1920 **Das Hollandweibchen** (Kálmán/w Jenbach) Johann Strauss-Theater 30 January

1920 **Die blaue Mazur** (Lehár/w Jenbach) Theater an der Wien 28 May

1923 **Mädi** (Stolz/w Grünwald) Berliner Theater, Berlin 1 April

Biography: Herz, P: *Die Librettisten der Wiener Operette: Leo Stein* (Weinberger, Vienna, 1973)

STEINER, Max[imilian] (b Buda, 27 August 1830; d Vienna, 29 May 1880).

At first a shopworker, then an actor and stage director in the German theatres at Temesvár, Arad and Hermannstadt under Friedrich Strampfer, Max Steiner was one of those who followed their director to Vienna when he took over the management of the Theater an der Wien. When Strampfer moved on, Steiner, who had already taken a secretarial role in the running of the house, took over and became lessee and manager of the theatre in his place. He remained at the house's head, in partnership with prima donna Marie Geistinger, from 1869 up to 1875, and then alone, until his death in 1880.

During his management the fashion for French opéra-bouffe, which had been fostered at the theatre by Strampfer, continued, and Steiner produced the Viennese versions of such pieces as *Les Brigands* (*Die Banditen*), *Le Petit Faust* (*Doktor Faust Junior*), *Fantasio, Les Braconniers* (*Die Wilderer*), *La Créole* (*Die Creolin*), *Le Voyage dans la lune* (*Die Reise in den Mond*), *Le Roi Carotte* (*König Carotte*), *La Foire Saint-Laurent* (*Der Jahrmarkt Saint Laurent*), *Madame Favart, La Fille du tambour-major* (*Die Tochter des Tambour-Majors*) and, most successfully of all, *Die Glocken von Corneville,* as well as Offenbach's original Viennese piece *Der schwarze Korsar.* It was, however, his productions of local musical comedies and Operetten with which he left his mark. He introduced Johann Strauss to the musical stage with *Indigo und die vierzig Räuber* (on which he took a book credit to cover the fact that the hotchpotch text had been put together by a mass of contributors and rewriters), and subsequently produced his *Carneval in Rom, Die Fledermaus* and *Cagliostro in Wien.* He staged Genée's two international hits *Der Seekadett* and *Nanon,* and Millöcker's most important early venture into Operette, *Das verwunschene Schloss,* as well as such successful musical plays as *An der schönen blauen Donau, Schottenfeld und Ringstrassen, Der deutsche Bruder, Der Pfarrer von Kirschfeld, Drei Paar Schuhe, Abenteuer in Wien, Durchgegangene Weiber, Ihr Korporal, Der barmherzige Bruder, Ein Blitzmädel, Der Gypsfigur* and *Die Näherin.*

The eldest of Steiner's four sons, **Franz STEINER** (b Temesvár, 1855; d Berlin, February 1920) took over the running of the theatre during his father's final illness and succeeded him as manager through four further successful seasons, during which time he produced Strauss's *Das Spitzentuch der Königin, Der lustige Krieg* and the revised *Eine Nacht in Venedig,* Millöcker's *Apajune, der Wassermann, Die Jungfrau von Belleville, Der Bettelstudent* and *Gasparone,* Suppé's *Die Afrikareise* and the German versions of *La Mascotte, Rip van Winkle* and the French spectacular *L'Arbre de Noël* remusicked with a new local score. In 1884, when the lessee of the theatre, Franz Jauner, sold out to Alexandrine von Schönerer, Steiner was replaced as artistic director of the house and left Vienna for Berlin, accompanied by the former Frau Lili Strauss with whom he had been all too obviously linked, to the detriment of the theatre's relations with Vienna's most famous composer. In Berlin, he took over the running of the Walhalla-Theater and successfully mounted Dellinger's *Don Cesar* (1885) there, but he returned two seasons later to Austria to take over the Carltheater from Carl Tatartzy. His productions there (*Rikiki, Die Dreizehn, Der Glücksritter, Der Sänger von Palermo, Don Cesar, Ein Deutschmeister, Der Freibuter, Farinelli, Colombine, Die Jagd nach dem Glück*) were not particularly successful, and after three years he handed over the house to Carl Blasel. He ultimately returned to Berlin where for some dozen years he managed the Wintergarten.

Another son **Gabor, [Christian] STEINER** (b Temesvár, 1858; d Hollywood, Calif, 9 September 1944), also spent his career in the theatre world, partaking of almost every kind of activity it had to offer. He was at one time an agent, another a publisher and, ultimately, a director specializing in extravagant and spectacular productions with a variety element. He worked as secretary to Carl Tatartzy during his mangagement of the Carltheater, ran the Residenztheater in Hanover and the Residenztheater in Dresden, and supported his brother during his reigns at both the Theater an der Wien and the Carltheater, before, in 1895, setting up the summer theater, Venedig in Wien, in the "Englischer Garten im Praterstern," the pleasure gardens at the Prater with their celebrated Riesenrad, or Ferris wheel (1897). There he produced a program which included a good percentage of the foreign imports which always appealed to him, including the German versions of Broadway's *The Belle of New York* and *The Girl from Up There,* of Britain's *Miss Hook of Holland,* Berlin's *Venus auf Erden,* Paris's *La Poupée,* Madrid's *La gran vía* and also an original Operette, *Der Reise nach Cuba,* composed by London's Ivan Caryll. He also mounted a number of successful pasticcio shows based on the music of favorite composers, including *Jung Heidelberg, Gräfin Pepi, Der schöne Rigo,* the highly successful *Frühlingsluft* and *1001 Nacht.* His most notable production, however, was an original piece, Carl Michael Ziehrer's *Die Landstreicher,* which he both produced and directed.

The success of the summer theater led him to open a winter counterpart, Danzers Orpheum, in 1900 and he ran the two houses together, sometimes sharing productions, and continuing with his bias to the imported with such pieces as *Trial by Jury,* the Gaiety Theatre's *The Circus Girl* and *The Messenger Boy,* a visit by the Berlin Apollo Company (*Frau Luna, Lysistrata, Im Reiche des Indra*), Paris's *Le Carnet du Diable, Le Fils prodigue* and *Paris ou le bon juge,* as well as burlesque, revue and semi-variety programs. In 1908 he moved to the rebuilt 3,000-seater Établissement Ronacher, an entertainment house built and run with a purposely Parisian air, which he operated until 1912. Once again, he favored English productions (*Our Miss Gibbs, A New Aladdin, The Arcadians,* etc), which he himself directed, often on a program where they were surrounded with variety items. He also took an author's credit on a revamped version of Offenbach's *La Belle Hélène* (*Die schöne Helena von heute* [Offenbach arr Ludwig Gothov-Grüneke/w Leopold Krenn] Ronacher, 1911).

His son, **Max[imilian Raoul Walter] STEINER** (b Vienna, 10 May 1888; d Hollywood, Calif, 28 December 1971), ventured into the musical theatre from his earliest days, and produced an amount of music that got a hearing in the provinces (*Ein Kosestündchen,* 1903) or at his father's houses—additional music for the Viennese versions of Serpette's *Das Scheckbuch des Teufels* (*Le Carnet du Diable,* 1906) and a Berlin burlesque of *Die lustige Witwe* (*Der lustige Witwer,* 1907), the mime scene *Bei Ihr* (1906), and the score for the two-act Lucien

Boyer vaudeville *Die schöne Griechen* (20 December 1907), which played for three weeks at Danzers Orpheum on a double bill with the burlesque *Eine Sensation.* He won intermittent jobs conducting variety programs in Britain and France before, in 1914, moving on to try his luck in America. There he continued his theatrical activity not as a composer but as an arranger and orchestrator of other folks' music and as a conductor for mostly touring musical shows. In 1929 he moved on again, this time to the newly sound-conscious Hollywood, and there he finally found success. He became at first a screen conductor and then a highly successful composer of film music (*Gone with the Wind, A Star Is Born, Now Voyager, Since You Went Away, Mildred Pierce,* etc, 3 Academy Awards). Steiner impinged intermittently on the musical theatre with scores for such piece as the flop George Lederer musical production *Peaches* (1923 w R B Smith, H B Smith), without ever finding a success in any way comparable to that which he found in the film world.

A third of the four sons of the elder Max Steiner, Alexander Steiner, familiarly known as ''Doc,'' was for a long time employed on the American Keith vaudeville circuit.

STEPHENS, Henry Pottinger [Lygon] (aka Henry BEAUCHAMP) (b Belgrave, Barrow-on-Soar, Leicestershire, 21 September 1851; d London, 11 February 1903).

The well-bred, well-connected, ex-Etonian nephew of the celebrated soldier and diplomat Sir Henry Pottinger (1789–1856), ''Pot'' Stephens—thoroughly ''bohemian'' and inevitably and all his life penniless—worked, when he did work, as a journalist (*Daily Telegraph, Tit Bits,* first editor of *Topical Times*) and made his first appearance as a dramatic author under the aegis of the German Reed management at St George's Hall. He subsequently wrote lyrics for F C Burnand's *Robbing Roy* burlesque at the Gaiety and collaborated with Burnand on a couple of other burlesques before, in the wake of *HMS Pinafore,* joining up with composer Teddy Solomon on a comic opera. Their *Billee Taylor* appeared in the same year as *The Pirates of Penzance,* won a major success and favorable comparison with Gilbert and Sullivan's piece, and caused its authors to be hailed briefly as the equals of Carte's prized writers. Carte had his associate, Michael Gunn, get the pair under contract, but they failed to come up with a second piece at the same level. Stephens returned to burlesque, and he had an important effect on the London theatre when his *The Vicar of Wide-awake-field* and *Little Jack Sheppard* set in motion George Edwardes's management at the Gaiety Theatre and the fashion for the ''new burlesque.''

However, other authors provided the later scripts for the Gaiety, and Stephens had just one more success, like the first in tandem with Solomon, when a piece they had written several years before was produced under the title *The Red Hussar.* Since Solomon was involved, law suits were also the order of the day, but the show had a good international career, giving Stephens his third major stage hit.

He also authored novels, plays, a revue (*A Dream of Whittaker's Almanack* w Walter Slaughter, Florian Pascal, Georges Jacobi, Walter Hedgecock, Crystal Palace 5 June 1899) and pantomimes, in one of which he was appearing at Brighton at the time of his death.

1879 **Back from India** (Cotsford Dick) 1 act St George's Hall 25 June

1879 **Robbing Roy, or Scotched and Kilt** (pasticcio arr Meyer Lutz/F C Burnand) Gaiety Theatre 11 November

1879 **Balloonacy, or A Flight of Fancy** (pasticcio arr Edward Solomon/w Burnand) Royalty Theatre 1 December

1880 **Cupid, or Two Strings to a Beau** (pasticcio arr Barrow/w Charles Harris [uncredited]) Royalty Theatre 26 April

1880 **The Corsican Brothers & Co Ltd** (pasticcio w Burnand) Gaiety Theatre 25 October

1880 **Billee Taylor** (Solomon) Imperial Theatre 30 October

1881 **Herne the Hunted** (pasticcio/w William Yardley, Robert Reece) Gaiety Theatre 24 May

1881 **Claude Duval** (Solomon) Olympic Theatre 24 August

1882 **Lord Bateman, or Picotee's Pledge** (Solomon) Gaiety Theatre 29 April

1882 **Through the Looking Glass** (Solomon) 1 act Gaiety Theatre 17 July

1883 **Virginia and Paul, or Changing the Rings** (aka *Virginia*) (Solomon) Bijou Theater New York 8 January

1883 **Galatea, or Pygmalion Re-Versed** (pasticcio) 1 act Gaiety Theatre 26 December

1885 **Hobbies** (George Gear/w Yardley) 1 act St George's Hall 6 April

1885 **The Vicar of Wide-awake-field, or the Miss-Terryous Uncle** (Florian Pascal/w Yardley) Gaiety Theatre 8 August

1885 **Little Jack Sheppard** (Meyer Lutz, et al/w Yardley) Gaiety Theatre 26 December

1888 **Penelope** (comp & arr Solomon) Star Theatre, New York 15 October

1889 **The Red Hussar** (Solomon) Lyric Theatre 23 November

1896 **The Black Squire, or Where There's a Will There's a Way** (Pascal) Royal Theatre & Opera House, Torquay 5 November

STEPHENSON, B[enjamin] C[harles] (aka Bolton Rowe) (d Taplow, 22 January 1906).

The nephew of General Sir Frederick Stephenson, and the son of Sir William Stephenson KCB, ''Charlie'' Stephenson began his working life in government service, holding secretarial posts with Gladstone and Sir George Cornewall Lewis, before moving on to occupy himself with the stock exchange. During these years he turned out a number of song lyrics and several little dramatic texts, collaborating with the young composer Frederic Clay on three one-act musicals—*The Pirate's Isle, Out of Sight* and *The Bold Recruit*—but his first notable success came two years after this, when he provided the libretto for Alfred Cellier's little operetta *Charity Begins at Home,* produced by the German Reeds at their Gallery of Illustration (1870). Another short comic piece, *The Zoo,* set by Arthur Sullivan, brought his name further to the front.

Stephenson's first full-scale successes came when he collaborated with Clement Scott on the English versions of Sardou's plays *Nos intimes* (as *Peril*) and *Dora* (*Diplomacy*) and the English text for Lecocq's opérette *Le Petit Duc,* but his most notable was his libretto for a first full-length musical, the comedy opera *Dorothy,* manufactured around Alfred Cellier's secondhand *Nell Gwynne* score. Much criticized on its first production, Stephenson's text was subjected to all sorts of serious scholarly analysis after *Dorothy* became the hit of the century, and its initially despised plot was traced carefully back to the Restoration playwrights, Garrick and Aphra Behn. Although the pair—bohemian, chattery Cellier and the fussy, health- and money-conscious Stephenson—made up an unlikely pair, together they continued to prosper and another Cellier remake, *Doris,* also had a good run. However a collaboration with Arthur Goring Thomas on another staunchly period comedy piece, *The Golden Web,* in spite of some appreciative critical nods, was short-lived and Stephenson did not again find a musical-theatre success.

1859 **The Pirate's Isle** (Clay) played by amateurs

1861 **Out of Sight** (Frederic Clay) 1 act Bijou Theatre 8 July

1868 **The Bold Recruit** (Clay) 1 act Theatre Royal, Canterbury 4 August; Gallery of Illustration 19 July 1870

1872 **Charity Begins at Home** (Alfred Cellier) 1 act Gallery of Illustration 7 February

1875 **The Zoo** (Arthur Sullivan) 1 act St James's Theatre 5 June

1878 **The Little Duke** (*Le Petit Duc*) English version w Clement Scott (Philharmonic Theatre)

1881 **The Masque of Pandora** (Cellier) Boston Theater, Boston 10 January

1886 **Dorothy** (Cellier) Gaiety Theatre 25 September

1888 **Warranted Burglar Proof** (Ivan Caryll, H J Leslie) 1 act Prince of Wales Theatre 31 March

1889 **Doris** (Cellier) Lyric Theatre 20 April

1892 **The Young Recruit** (*Le Dragon de la reine*) English version w Augustus Harris, et al (Newcastle)

1893 **The Golden Web** (Arthur Goring Thomas/w Frederick Corder) Lyric Theatre 11 March; revised w Charles Thomas 5 April 1893

1893 **The Venetian Singer** (aka *The Improvisatore*) (Edward Jakobowski) 1 act Court Theatre 25 November

1896 **On the March** (John Crook, Edward Solomon, Clay/w William Yardley, Cecil Clay) Prince of Wales Theatre 22 June

1896 **Belinda** (Walter Slaughter/w Basil Hood) Prince's Theatre, Manchester 5 October

STEPPING STONES Musical comedy in 2 acts by Anne Caldwell and R H Burnside. Lyrics by Anne Caldwell. Music by Jerome Kern. Globe Theater, New York, 6 November 1923.

The seventh in the series of Fred Stone children-of-all-ages shows staged by Charles Dillingham, *Stepping Stones* was an ingenuous piece based not very heavily on the Red Riding Hood story. Prince Silvio (Roy Hoyer) is in love with little Rougette (Dorothy Stone), but that villainous robber of the woods, Otto de Wolfe (Oscar Ragland), wants his daughter Lupina (Evelyn Herbert) to have that royal title. Stone was Peter Plug, a plumber, whose various comic machinations helped the lovers to a happy ending.

Jerome Kern's functional score included little to rate amongst his best music, but the pretty trio ''Once in a Blue Moon'' and the jaunty ''Raggedy Ann'' emerged as enjoyable numbers. Another lilting tune, ''In Love with Love,'' was reused after *Stepping Stones* was gone, reappearing in the London musical *Lady Mary* (1928) set to a fresh Graham John lyric as ''If You're a Friend of Mine.'' Alongside the original songs, there was plenty of dance music for the Tiller Sunshine Girls and the first act highlighted a selection of old ''Rose'' favorites (as Kern's score to *The Night Boat* had done with ''river'' songs) ranging from ''Ma Blushin' Rosie'' to ''The Last Rose of Summer.'' Stone's daughter Dorothy, making her stage debut billed above the title as Rougette, performed a duet, ''Wonderful Dad,'' with Fred, the connotations of which went clearly beyond the show's context. Another famous musical-theatre-man's daughter was seen in the smaller role of Radiola—Primrose Caryll, daughter of the late Ivan who had composed the earlier Fred Stone shows.

Stepping Stones was immediately popular, and it had reached its 241st Broadway performances (in spite of higher than usual ticket prices) when it was closed by an actors' strike. Stone later took it on the road with equal success.

STERK, Wilhelm (b Budapest, 28 June 1880; d Theresienstadt, c1943–44).

A prolific writer of Operetten and revues for Austrian and German theatres for 30 years, Sterk provided material for a number of smaller and provincial theatres, but also intermittently and particularly in his later days for some of the principal houses. His most successful piece was the small-scale musical comedy *Dorine und der Zufall,* set to music by Jean Gilbert, and he also had several productions out of Robert Stolz's *Der Favorit* and Jessel's *Des Königs Nachbarin.* He was deported to Theresienstadt during the war and not seen again.

1906 **Casanova** (Karl Kapeller/w Tandler) Centraltheater, Berlin 10 March

1907 **Odysseus Heimkehr** (Hans Albert Cesek) 1 act Hölle 1 October

1907 **Ein tolles Mädel** (Carl Michael Ziehrer/Kurt Kraatz, Heinrich Stobitzer) Walhalla-Theater, Wiesbaden 24 August; Danzers Orpheum, Vienna 8 November

1908 **Die Wunderquelle** (Heinrich Berté/w Emmerich von Gatti) 1 act Hölle 1 November

1909 **Herr und Frau Biedermann** (Ziehrer pasticcio) 1 act Lustspielhaus, Munich 10 January; Kleine Bühne 5 October 1910

1910 **Die schlaue Komtesse** (Béla Laszky) 1 act Kleine Bühne 18 November

1910 **Champagner** (Karl Stigler) 1 act Wiener Colosseum 1 December

1911 **Ball bei Hof** (Ziehrer) Stadttheater, Stettin 22 January

1911 **Der flotte Bob** (Stigler/w A M Willner) Altes Theater, Leipzig 8 April

1912 **Die klingende Mühle** (Cesek) 1 act Hölle 1 October

1914 **Der Gott der Kleinen** (Laszky) 1 act Künstlerspiele 1 January

1914 **Das dumme Herz** (Ziehrer/w Rudolf Österreicher) Johann Strauss-Theater 27 February

1914 **Der Märchenprinz** (Berté/w Willner) Schauburg, Hanover 28 February

1914 **Der Kriegsberichterstatter** (many/w Österreicher) Apollotheater 9 October

1914 **Das Mädchen im Mond** (Stigler/w Österreicher) Carltheater 7 November

1916 **Der Favorit** (Robert Stolz/w Fritz Grünbaum) Komische Oper, Berlin 7 April

1916 **Mein Annerl** (Georg Jarno/w Grünbaum) Carltheater 7 October

1916 **Servus, Mädel** (Stolz) 1 act Wintergarten, Budapest December

1919 **Wiener Leut—einst und heut** (Arthur M Werau) 1 act Künstlerspiele Pan 30 December

1920 **Das verbotene Fräulein** (Werau) 1 act Künstlerspiele Pan January

1920 **Der Filmstern** (Fritz Lehner) Lustspieltheater 21 July

1920 **Eine tolle Sache** (Werau) Künstlerspiele Pan 1 October

1920 **Wer hat's gemacht** (Eysler) 1 act Variété Réclame 1 October

1920 **Der Herr Oberst** (Károly Hajós) 1 act Hölle 1 November

1920 **Ein nobler Herr** (Werau) Rolandbühne 1 November

1921 **Die 1000ste Jungfrau** (Lehner) Femina 1 January

1921 **Eine feine Nummer** (Hajós) 1 act Olympia Variété 1 February

1922 **Dorine und der Zufall** (Jean Gilbert/w Grünbaum) Neues Theater am Zoo, Berlin 15 September

1923 **Des Königs Nachbarin** (Leon Jessel/w Grünbaum) Wallner-Theater, Berlin 15 April

1923 **Pusztaliebchen** (Michael Krasznay-Krausz) Johann Strauss-Theater 19 December

1924 **Agri** (Ernst Steffan/w A M Willner) Wiener Bürgertheater 30 January

1926 **Ich hab' dich lieb . . . !** (Leo Ascher) Raimundtheater 16 April

1926 **Ich und Du** (Lamberto Pavanelli/w Grünbaum) Neues Deutsches Theater, Prague 28 November

1927 **Meine Tochter Otto** (Jessel/w Grünbaum) Rolandbühne 5 May

1927 **Rosen aus Schiras** (Frank Stafford/w Grünbaum) Johann Strauss-Theater 24 June

1927 **Yvette und ihre Freunde** (Krasznay-Krausz/w Österreicher) Wiener Bürgertheater 18 November

1929 **Der lustige Krieg** revised libretto (Johann Strauss-Theater)

1930 **Eine Woche Glück** (Max Niederberger) Opernhaus, Graz 25 January

1930 **Die verliebte Eskadron** (Ziehrer arr Karl Pauspertl) Johann Strauss-Theater 11 July

1930 **Der König ihres Herzens** (Offenbach arr Pauspertl) Johann Strauss-Theater 23 December

1933 **Tango um Mitternacht** (*Éjféli tangó*) German version (Volksoper)

1933 **Die Schönste im Dorf** (Friedrich Smetana arr J Orel) Volksoper 24 March

1934 **Wiener G'schichten** (Josef Hellmesberger ad Oskar Jascha) Volksoper 27 October

1936 **Die goldene Mühle** (Jessel/Hugo Wiener, Karl Costa ad) Städtebundtheater, Olten, Switzerland 29 October; Volksoper, Vienna 2 March 1937

STERN, Ernst (b Bucharest, 1876; d London, 28 August 1954). Set designer whose name became synonymous with large and lavish in Germany, and then wherever *Im weissen Rössl* was staged.

In 1906 Stern joined the staff of Max Reinhardt at the Deutsches Theater in Berlin and there, over a period of 15 years, designed a variety of productions, mostly of classic plays, but also (in spite of being described by one journal as ''Reinhardt's spare set designer,'' with the ''spare'' certainly not describing his style) his versions of *Orphée aux enfers* and *La Belle Hélène.* He subsequently designed for Ernst Lubitsch for film and for Hermann Haller at the Theater am Nollendorfplatz (*Wenn Liebe erwacht,* etc) before being picked up by Erik Charell to design his spectacular Berlin musical productions. He contributed much, by his elaborate stage pictures, to such productions as Charell's expanded *Madame Pompadour,* the disastrously jazzed-up *The Merry Widow* with its purposely grotesque design, his mincemeat *Mikado,* to the much happier productions of Benatzky's *Casanova* and *The Three Musketeers* (''the most exceptional dictator of colour and line in the international theatre'') and, most famously, to the first production of *Im weissen*

Rössl. Versions of his designs were repeated for *White Horse Inn* and *L'Auberge du cheval blanc,* spreading Stern's reputation for everything-that-moves design throughout the world.

Stern subsequently left Germany and moved to London where his musical credits included *Bitter-Sweet* (1929 w Gladys E Calthrop), *White Horse Inn* (1931) and *The Song of the Drum* (1931, scenery and costumes), *The Lilac Domino* revival (1944) and *The Bird Seller* (1947, *Der Vogelhändler*).

Autobiography: *My Life, My Stage* (Gollancz, London, 1951)

DER STERNGUCKER *see* LIBELLENTANZ

STEWART, Michael [RUBIN, Michael Stewart] (b New York, 1 August 1929; d New York, 20 September 1987). Librettist for some sizeable hits of Broadway's postwar heyday.

Stewart made his way into the musical theatre by way of writing for summer shows and for revue, supplying lyrics and sketches for such pieces as the *Shoestring Revue* (1955) and comedy material for Sid Caesar before joining songwriters Strouse and Adams, who had followed a similar route to Broadway, as the librettist of the rock-and-roll parody musical *Bye Bye Birdie.* The piece gave its writers a highly successful introduction to the musical stage, and Stewart soon built on that success with two fine adaptations, teaming with songwriter Bob Merrill on the delightful and successful *Carnival,* a musical based on the film *Lili* and its original story by Paul Gallico, and then with Jerry Herman on the blockbusting triumph of *Hello, Dolly!,* a musical version of *The Matchmaker* and its German-language model.

After this memorable start to his career, things quietened down for a decade. *How Do You Do, I Love You* pulled up before Broadway, and if a pasticcio biomusical on *George M!* Cohan had a good Broadway run, an adaptation of Pinero's play *The Amazons,* produced in Britain, also failed to find a metropolitan showing and Stewart's original adaptation of the play *Two for the Seesaw* as the text for the Cy Coleman musical *Seesaw* (1973) was dollied up and around by Michael Bennett and a handful of other folk before the show's New York presentation. The following year, a second collaboration with *Hello, Dolly!* composer Herman, on a vaguely biographical musical on silent filmland's Mack Sennett and Mabel Normand (*Mack and Mabel*), folded in 66 performances.

The indifferent results of Stewart's post–*Hello, Dolly!* years gave way to renewed success with the small-scale musical comedy *I Love My Wife,* a piece based on a Continental on-the-verge-of-sex farce, for which Stewart provided this time both text and lyrics. A fine metropolitan success in New York and in London, the show found a lively life thereafter. In 1979 Stewart paired with fledgling writer Mark Bramble to adapt the successful play *Jacobowsky and the Colonel* to the musical stage and though neither this nor their musical version of Maxwell Anderson's *Elizabeth the Queen* proved successful, the pair had a major success third time around with the circus-filled biomusical *Barnum,* on which Stewart was credited with lyrics and Bramble with the libretto.

A second substantial hit followed when the pair adapted the celebrated film *42nd Street* to the musical stage, but the show was to be Stewart's last success. *Bring Back Birdie,* an attempt at a musequel to his first hit, failed to connect, a *Harrigan and Hart* pasticcio biomusical on *George M!* lines, and a new musical version of Robert Louis Stevenson's *Treasure Island* were failures, and his last work, a fresh musicalization of the famous farce *Nothing But the Truth* (w Coleman, Bramble), remained unproduced at the time of his death, in the wake of an operation, in 1987.

A writer of great freshness and vigor, his great successes, after the original *Bye Bye Birdie,* were with adaptations (*Carnival, Hello, Dolly!, I Love My Wife, 42nd Street*) but his infrequent excursions into lyric-writing (*I Love My Wife, Barnum*) encouraged regrets that he had not ventured more frequently into that field.

1960 **Bye Bye Birdie** (Charles Strouse/Lee Adams) Martin Beck Theater 14 April

1961 **Carnival** (Bob Merrill) Imperial Theater 13 April

1964 **Hello, Dolly!** (Jerry Herman) St James Theater 16 January

1967 **How Do You Do, I Love You** (David Shire/Richard Maltby jr) Shady Grove Music Fair, Gaithersburg 19 October

1968 **George M!** (George M Cohan/w John and Fran Pascal) Palace Theater 10 April

1971 **The Amazons** (John Addison/David Heneker) Playhouse, Nottingham, UK 7 April

1974 **Mack and Mabel** (Herman) Majestic Theater 6 October

1977 **I Love My Wife** (Cy Coleman) Ethel Barrymore Theater 17 April

1979 **The Grand Tour** (Herman/w Mark Bramble) Palace Theater 11 January

1980 **Elizabeth and Essex** (Doug Katsaros/Richard Engquist/w Bramble) South Street Theater 24 February

1980 **Barnum** (Coleman/Bramble) St James Theater 30 April

1980 **42nd Street** (Harry Warren, Al Dubin pasticcio/w Bramble) Winter Garden Theater 25 August

1981 **Bring Back Birdie** (Strouse/Adams) Martin Beck Theater 5 March

1985 **Harrigan and Hart** (Max Showalter, David Braham/Peter Walker, Edward Harrigan) Longacre Theater 31 January

1985 **Pieces of Eight** (Jule Styne/Susan Birkenhead) Citadel Theater, Edmonton 27 November

STEWART, Nellie [TOWZEY, Eleanor Stewart] (b Sydney, 20 November 1858; d Sydney, 18 June 1931).

The daughter of a well-known Australian actor and actress—father **Richard STEWART** [Richard Stewart GZECH otherwise TOWZEY] (b England ?1826; d Melbourne, 24 August 1902) had been Australia's first Jupiter and Bobèche with Lyster and Cagli, and mother, **Theodosia YATES** [née MacINTOSH; aka Mrs GUERIN] (b Ireland, ?1815; d Melbourne, 19 July 1904), had been the first Arline of *The Bohemian Girl* in Australia—the young Nellie performed with her half-sisters, Maggie and Docie, children of Theodosia's earlier marriage, in the Stewart family's entertainments. These included a specially written program called *Rainbow Revels,* which Richard took as far afield as London's Crystal Palace in 1866, a hotchpotch entitled *If, or an old gem reset* and a pirate production of *HMS Pinafore* (1878) with Nellie playing as Ralph Rackstraw to Docie's Josephine, which tactfully became a burlesque, *HMS Pinnacle,* with Nellie playing Jack Jackstraw, when legal furies threatened.

Hired as a replacement by George Musgrove during the run of his record-breaking Australian production of *La Fille du tambour-major,* she made a personal success when she succeeded Jessie Grey to the normally tenor role of the little tailor Griolet, and subsequently went on to play such parts as Suzanne (*Madame Favart*), Bathilde (*Les Noces d'Olivette*) and Serpolette (*Les Cloches de Corneville*) before the sudden departure of prima donna Emilie Melville allowed her to take over the star parts in the company's repertoire.

Over the next five years she became Australia's favorite native musical star, appearing for Musgrove (with whom she developed what was to be a lifelong liaison) and with his partners J C Williamson and Arthur Garner in a long series of comic operas: *Olivette* (Bathilde, Olivette), *Madame Favart* (Suzanne, Mme Favart), *La Fille du tambour-major* (Stella), *Les Cloches de Corneville* (Serpolette), *La Petite Mademoiselle* (Countess Cameroni), *The Merry Duchess* (Duchess), Searelle's *Estrella* (Estrella), *Billee Taylor* (Phoebe), *La Mascotte* (Fiametta), *The Sorcerer* (Aline), *HMS Pinafore* (Josephine), *The Pirates of Penzance* (Mabel), *Patience* (Patience), *Iolanthe* (Phyllis), *The Mikado* (Yum-Yum), *La Fille de Madame Angot* (Clairette), *Pepita* (*La Princesses des Canaries,* Pepita), *Dorothy* (Dorothy), *Ma mie Rosette* (Rosette), *Mam'zelle Nitouche* (Denise), etc. In 1888 Alfred Cellier persuaded her to attempt *Faust,* and in 1890 Musgrove financed the Nellie Stewart Comic Opera Company which played *Paul Jones, Boccaccio* and *Chilpéric* successfully, around its star, in Australia and New Zealand.

Miss Stewart made several trips overseas, appearing in New York in *An Artist's Model* (Adèle) and in London in the title role of *Blue-Eyed Susan* (1892) and for two weeks as a replacement in the lead role of Princess Micaëla in the English version of *Le Coeur et la main* (*Incognita*), but Cellier's attempts to persuade D'Oyly Carte to take her on foundered when she walked out on the role of Hollee Beebee in *The Nautch Girl* after having a number cut. Later, during an extended London stay whilst Musgrove was running the Shaftesbury Theatre, she starred in a specially made new boy-role in his *The Scarlet Feather* (*La Petite Mariée*) and also played principal boy in the 1899 Drury Lane pantomime, but she never achieved the same success outside Australia that she did at home.

From 1902 she renounced the musical stage and found new success, most notably as *Sweet Nell of Old Drury,* on the straight stage.

Docie STEWART [Theodosia GUERIN] (b Sydney, 1849) also played for many years on the Australian musical stage, before retiring to (third-time-round) married life as Mrs Pierre Chamboissier of the Savoy Hotel, Market Street, Sydney. She was earlier the wife of actor-manager H R HARWOOD [né Jack BIGGS] (b London, 19 October 1830; d Melbourne, 16 April 1898) of the Melbourne Theatre Royal.

Maggie STEWART [Margaret E GUERIN] (b Sydney, 1852; d Melbourne, 28 September 1903) also made up part of the family act.

Autobiography: *My Life's Story* (John Sands, Sydney, 1923)

STIGWOOD, Robert (b Adelaide, 15 April 1934). Highly successful musical-theatre and film producer who made his pile, shot off to spend it, but ultimately returned to the fray.

A pop-music man with as many downs as ups to his career—one of the principal ups being his management of the Bee Gees—Robert Stigwood zoomed to the forefront in London's musical theatre when his cleverly calculated purchase of the English rights of *Hair* (he guessed rightly that the censor was about to be abolished) gave him a long-running London hit. He hit the gold again when he mounted the American and British productions of *Jesus Christ Superstar,* followed up with the less-successful London seasons of *Pippin, Joseph and the Amazing Technicolor Dreamcoat* (w Michael White), *Jeeves* (w White) and an Off-Broadway *Sergeant Pepper's Lonely Hearts Club Band* (1974), and then put a full-stop to his theatre career with another vast hit, *Evita.*

He did not yet get out of the business, but instead moved on into the film world. He had already been responsible for the films of *Jesus Christ Superstar* (1973) and *Tommy* (1975), now he followed up with *Bugsy Malone* and then with the two oversized teeny-hits of their age—*Saturday Night Fever* and *Grease*—and with *Sergeant Pepper's Lonely Hearts Club Band* (1978), *Times Square* (1980), *Gallipoli* (1981), *The Fan* (1981), a *Grease 2* (1982) and *Staying Alive* (1983).

Then, with a common sense which few producers have been able to show, he folded up his account books and went off to enjoy himself on the proceeds of so much intelligently run entertainment business. After more than a decade away, however, he returned to the theatre, to take part in the management of the 1990s stage productions of his big films, *Grease* and *Saturday Night Fever* (w Paul Nicholas, David Ian), subsequently taking the latter to America and Europe (w Michael Brenner, Thomas Krause) as well. He also returned to the film world with the film version of *Evita* (1996).

STOJANOVITS, Petér [Lázár] (b Budapest, 6 September 1877; d Belgrade, 12 September 1957). Composer of two Operette hits from two tries in a career devoted to other areas of music.

Stojanovits studied composition and violin in Hungary, Vienna and Bonn, and subsequently first taught violin, then worked as an inspector of violin teaching in both Vienna and Budapest, before establishing his own school for violinists in Vienna in 1913. Parallel to his teaching and to some performing, he also composed for the concert hall (violin music, sonatas, chamber music) and for the stage, and his one-act opera *A tigris* was produced at Budapest's Magyar Király Operaház when he was 18 years of age. However, he found his most important success as a theatrical composer, a dozen years on, with a pair of Operetten produced at the Vienna Carltheater.

Liebchen am Dach, written and directed by Victor Léon, had an excellent first run of 183 performances and was subsequently produced in Hungary (*Padlásszoba* Városi Színház 30 November 1917) and in Germany, and its successor, *Der Herzog von Reichstadt,* a period piece with Hubert Marischka and Mizzi Zwerenz starred as the son of Napoléon and ballerina Fanny Elssler respectively, was played 111 times in its initial season and brought back later in the year for a further 75 performances before going on to a like career (*A reichstadti herceg* Városi Színház 14 October 1921).

In 1925 Stojanovits became director of the Belgrade conservatoire, and although he continued a career as a concert violininst he did not, in spite of the success of his two Vienna Operetten, again return to the lyric stage.

1917 **Liebchen am Dach** (Victor Léon) Carltheater 19 May

1921 **Der Herzog von Reichstadt** (Léon, Heinz Reichert) Carltheater 11 February

STOLZ, Robert [Elisabeth] (b Graz, 25 August 1880; d Berlin, 27 June 1975). The composer of three-quarters of a century of music for the Viennese operettic stage.

Robert Stolz began his theatrical career as a répétiteur and a conductor in his hometown, then worked as Kapellmeister in Marburg (Maribor), Salzburg and Brünn

Plate 368.

before being engaged at the Theater an der Wien in 1907. There he conducted the premieres of such pieces as *Tip-Top* (1907) and *Der schöne Gardist* (1908), and performances of some of the most important European Operetten of the time—*Die lustige Witwe, Der tapfere Soldat, Der Graf von Luxemburg, Ein Herbstmanöver*—which then made up part of the theatre's repertoire.

During this period Stolz composed both Viennese songs (''Servus Du'') and theatre scores, and his first Viennese premiere, with *Die lustigen Weiben von Wien,* took place at the Colosseum in 1908, followed by a Budapest first with an Hungarian version, *A trabucói herceg,* 12 months later. His first full-sized metropolitan Operette, *Das Glücksmädel,* produced in 1910 at the Raimundtheater, played 52 performances with no less a star than Alexander Girardi in its central role, *Die eiserne Jungfrau* made some 40 nights with another favorite local star, Hansi Niese, at the top of the bill, whilst *Der Favorit,* first produced in Berlin, was later played at Vienna's Apollotheater and in Budapest (ad Zsolt Harsányi) and brought forth, if not a long run, a popular song in ''Du sollst der Kaiser meiner Seele sein.''

During the war years and after, Stolz produced a mixture of short stage pieces and musical plays, popular songs (''Im Prater blühn wieder die Bäume,'' ''Salomé,'' ''Hallo, du süsse Klingelfee'') and a one-act opera *Die*

Rosen der Madonna (1920), before he had his first significant international success with the Operette *Der Tanz ins Glück. Der Tanz ins Glück* was played for two hundred performances at the Raimundtheater before being exported to a widespread series of foreign productions (*Whirled into Happiness, Sky High, Szerencsetánc, La Danza di fortuna*) in a variety of remade shapes and musical forms.

Die Tanzgräfin, first produced in Berlin, went on to play a splendid 204 performances at Vienna's Johann Strauss-Theater (but flopped pre-Broadway when lavishly produced in America as *The Dancing Duchess*), and if *Eine Sommernacht*'s two-month run and the 68 performances of *Die Liebe geht um!* were not in the same league, the pretty tale of *Mädi,* produced at the Berliner Theater for a fine run and later at the Vienna Apollotheater and London's Prince of Wales Theatre (*The Blue Train*), gave him a third success to round off this most productive period of his stage-writing life.

A costly divorce and the equally costly failure of an attempt to become a theatre director led him to leave Vienna, but he resurfaced with the coming of the film musical, scoring a hit with his score for *Zwei Herzen im Dreivierteltakt* (1930) near the beginning of more than a decade of prewar film writing which included such movie musicals as *Das Lied ist aus* (1930, ''Adieu, mein kleiner Gardeoffizier''), a screen version of his *Der Hampelmann* (1931) with Max Hansen starred, *Liebeskommando* (1931), *Sein Liebeslied* (1931), Géza von Bolvary's *Die lustigen Weiber von Wien* (1931), *Der Liebling von Wien* (1933), *Frühjahrsparade* (1934), *Der Himmel auf Erden* (1935), *Herbstmanöver* (1935) and *Husaren, heraus* (1938) in Germany and *Spring Parade* (ex- *Frühjahrsparade,* ''Waltzing''), *My Heart Is Calling* (1935), *The Night of the Great Love* (1937) and *It Happened Tomorrow* (1943) in Hollywood.

At the same time that this second career was beginning, Stolz also turned out what were to be his most famous stage songs, two of the many interpolations inserted in Ralph Benatzky's score for *Im weissen Rössl* (''Mein Liebeslied muss ein Walzer sein,'' ''Die ganze Welt ist Himmelblau''), later supplemented by the song from *Das Lied ist aus,* made over famously by Harry Graham as ''Goodbye,'' and by ''Auch du wirst mich einmal betrügen'' (''You Too''), borrowed from *Zwei Herzen im Dreivierteltakt,* when the show's score was expanded in London. Parallel to his film career, he continued to produce Operetten, making a success with the pretty *Wenn die kleinen Veilchen blühen,* initially produced in the Netherlands; with the romantic period piece, *Venus in Seide,* and *Grüezi,* both mounted in Zürich; and with a stage version of *Zwei Herzen im Dreivierteltakt.*

Stolz's musical hand subsequently moved far and wide as he provided additional music for Paris's *Balalaika* and Yves Mirande's *Saisissez-moi,* had a fast London flop with the Drury Lane production of the very indifferent *Rise and Shine* (44 performances) and, during a six-year stay in America, contributed rather less happily to the stage than to the screen. *Night of Love,* a Shubert operetta about operetta folk taken from the successful 1930 play *Tonight or Never,* lasted just one week on Broadway, whilst an umpteenth attempt to write an operetta about Johann Strauss, decorated this time not with a pasticcio score but one by Stolz, had a life of just 12 performances.

Back in Vienna, after the Second World War, Stolz turned out further pieces for the stage, including a remake of Nestroy as *Drei von der Donau,* and for the screen (*Die Deutschmeister,* etc), and in his eighties saw *Frühjahrsparade* transferred to the stage and several other earlier pieces remade for the modern Operette theatre as he continued a career as a conductor in concert and the recording studio. In the still remarkably active years up to his death at the age of 94, Stolz, who had throughout his life composed music in the lightest and most Wienerisch style, became the epitome of old-world Vienna and its waltzing music, not only to the world in general, but to Vienna itself where his monument, in the heart of Vienna, is today as prominent as that of Johann Strauss.

His music was used by Italian pasticcio writer Carlo Lombardo as the basis for a score illustrating Hennequin and Veber's Parisian farce *La Présidente* (*La Presidentessa*).

1901 **Studentenulke** (Theodor Haller) Stadttheater, Marburg 21 March

1903 **Schön Lorchen** (A Moisson [ie, Hans Kleindienst]) Stadttheater, Salzburg 3 March

1906 **Manöverliebe** (Karl Waldeck, Gustav Bondi) Stadttheater, Brünn 15 April

1908 **Die lustigen Weiber von Wien** (Julius Brammer, Alfred Grünwald) 1 act Wiener Colosseum 16 November

1909 **Die Commandeuse** (Egon Dorn) 1 act Wiener Colosseum 1 September

1910 **Grand Hotel Excelsior** (Fritz Friedmann-Friedrich) Auenkeller-Theater, Erfurt 28 August

1910 **Das Glücksmädel** (Robert Bodanzky, Friedrich Thelen) Raimundtheater 28 October

1911 **Der Minenkönig** (Ernst Marischka, Gustav Beer) 1 act Apollotheater 3 October

1911 **Die eiserne Jungfrau** (Léon) Raimundtheater 11 November

1913 **Du liebes Wien** (aka *Komm, Mädel und tanze . . . !*) (Otto Hein, Kurt Robitschek) 1 act Intimes Theater 24 January

1913 **60 Meilen in 60 Minuten** (Fritz Schönhof/Herbert Emmerson) 1 act Ronacher 1 September

1915 **Das Lumperl** (revised *Die eiserne Jungfrau*) Operntheater, Graz 4 April

1915 **Die Variété-diva** (revised *Du liebes Wien*) 1 act Ronacher 1 December

1916 **Die schöne Katharin** (Ludwig Hirschfeld, Hein) 1 act Ronacher 11 January

1916 **Pension Schraube** (Hein, Ernst Wengraf) Ronacher 27 February

1916 **Der Favorit** (Fritz Grünbaum, Wilhelm Sterk) Komische Oper, Berlin 7 April

1916 **Mädel, kusse mich!** (Hardt-Warden, Emil Schwarz) Lustspieltheater 29 April

1916 **Servus, Mädel** (Sterk) 1 act Wintergarten, Budapest December

1916 **Die anständige Frau** (Hein) 1 act Budapester Orpheum 16 December

1917 **Die Bauernprinzessin** (Anton Aldermann, Fritz Lunzer) Volkstheater, Munich 3 March

1917 **Eine einzige Nacht** (Hein, Wengraf) 1 act Budapester Orpheum 15 March

1917 **Lang, lang ist's her** (Bruno Hardt-Warden) Lustspieltheater 18 March

1917 **Dolores** (Robitschek) 1 act Budapester Orpheum 1 September

1917 **Die Familie Rosenstein** (Hein, Wengraf) 1 act Budapester Orpheum 12 October

1918 **Die Hose des Tenors** (Willy Berg, Hein) 1 act Budapester Orpheum 1 January

1918 **Muschi** (aka *Die Kuckucksuhr*) (Fritz Löhner-Beda) Gartenbau 1 January

1918 **Brautersatz** (Gutbach) 1 act Gartenbau 1 March

1918 **Bloch und Co** (aka *Die schöne Maske*) (Wengraf, Hein) 1 act Budapester Orpheum 5 April

1918 **Leute von heute** (w Eysler, Arthur M Werau/Lunzer, Arthur Rebner) Bundestheater 22 June

1918 **Das Busserlschloss** (Grünbaum) 1 act Ronacher 1 August

1918 **Muzikam** (Hein, Wengraf) 1 act Budapester Orpheum 2 September

1919 **Dagobert, wo warst du?** (Hein) 1 act Wintergarten, Budapest 19 January; Rolandbühne, Vienna 8 August

1919 **Funserls Entdeckung** (Hein) 1 act Rolandbühne 1 November

1920 **Ein toller Tag** (Robitschek) 1 act Rolandbühne 1 January

1920 **Das Sperrsechserl** (Robert Blum, Grünwald) Komödienhaus 1 April

1920 **Das Mädel vom Variété** Hölle April

1920 **Das Haus des Schreckens** (Hein, Wengraf) 1 act Künstlerspiele Pan 1 May

1920 **Die fidele Pension** (Hein, Wengraf) 1 act Hölle May

1920 **Die schönste Frau** (Hein) 1 act Variété Réclame 1 October

1920 **Der Tanz ins Glück** (Bodanzky, Hardt-Warden) Raimundtheater 23 December

1921 **Kirikiri** (Hein, Fritz Löhner-Beda) 1 act Rolandbühne 1 January

1921 **Das Vorstadtmädel** (Hein, Adolf Klinger, Otto Taussig) 1 act Hölle February

1921 **Die Tanzgräfin** (Jacobson, Bodanzky) Wallner-Theater, Berlin 18 February

1921 **Eine fesche Landpartie** 1 act Rolandbühne 1 March

1921 **Eine tolle Nacht** (Hein) 1 act Hölle 1 October

1921 **Eine Sommernacht** (Bodanzky, Hardt-Warden) Johann Strauss-Theater 23 December

1922 **Die Liebe geht um** (Bodanzky, Hardt-Warden) Raimundtheater 22 June

1923 **Mädi** (Alfred Grünwald, Leo Stein) Berliner Theater, Berlin 1 April

1923 **Der Hampelmann** (Gustav Beer, Fritz Lunzer) Komödienhaus 9 November

1924 **Ein Ballroman** (*Der Kavalier von zehn bis vier*) (Fritz Rotter/Österreicher, Alfred Maria Willner) Apollotheater 29 February

1924 **Das Fräulein aus 1001 Nacht** (*Ein Rivieratraum*) (Karl Farkas, Hardt-Warden, Rotter) Robert Stolzbühne 6 October

1925 **Märchen im Schnee** (Robitschek, Morgan) 1 act Kabarett der Komiker 1 December

1926 **Der Mitternachtswalzer** (Willner, Österreicher) Wiener Bürgertheater 30 October

1927 **Eine einzige Nacht** (expanded 3-act version) (Leopold Jacobson, Österreicher) Carltheater 23 December

1928 **Prinzessin Ti-Ti-Pa** (Beer, Lunzer) Carltheater 15 May

1930 **Peppina** (Österreicher) Komische Oper, Berlin 22 December

1932 **Wenn die kleinen Veilchen blühen** (Hardt-Warden) Princess Theater, The Hague 1 April

1932 **Venus in Seide** (Grünwald, Ludwig Herzer) Stadttheater, Zürich 10 December

1933 **Zwei Herzen im Dreivierteltakt** (aka *Der verlorene Walzer*) (R Gilbert/Paul Knepler, Ignaz M Welleminsky) Stadttheater, Zürich 30 September; revised version Centraltheater, Dresden 26 December

1934 **Gruezi** (aka *Servus, Servus, Himmelblaue Träume*) (Robert Gilbert/"Georg Burkhard," ie, Gilbert, Armin Robinson) Stadttheater, Zürich 3 November

1935 **Zum goldenen Halbmond** (Fritz Koselka) Deutsches Nationaltheater, Osnabrück 21 March

1936 **Rise and Shine** (aka *Darling You*) (w others/Gilbert ad Desmond Carter/Franz Arnold ad Harry Graham) Theatre Royal, Drury Lane, London 7 May

1936 **Gloria und der Clown** (Julius Horst, R Gilbert) Stadttheater, Aussig 31 December

1937 **Der süsseste Schwindel der Welt** (Weys) Scala Theater 21 December

1937 **Die Reise um die Erde in 80 Minuten** (R Gilbert, H Gilbert, Wiener Volksoper 22 December

1941 **Night of Love** (Rowland Leigh) Hudson Theater, New York 7 January

1945 **Mr Strauss Goes to Boston** (Robert B Sour/Leonard L Levinson) Century Theater, New York 6 September

1946 **Schicksal mit Musik** (Farkas) Apollotheater 24 November

1947 **Drei von der Donau** (R Gilbert/Johann Nestroy ad Österreicher, R Gilbert) Wiener Stadttheater 24 September

1948 **Lied aus der Vorstadt** (Dora Maria Brandt, Georg Fraser) Deutsches Volkstheater 19 April

1949 **Frühling im Prater** (Ernst Marischka) Wiener Stadttheater 22 December

1949 **Fest in Casablanca** (Günther Schwenn, Waldemar Frank) Städtische Bühnen, Nuremberg 27 March

1951 **Das Glücksrezept** (Hugo Wiener/Raoul Martinée, Wiener) Wiener Bürgertheater 1 May

1951 **Rainbow Square** (Guy Bolton, Harold Purcell) Stoll Theatre, London 21 September

1953 **Mädi** revised version (Stadttheater, Zürich)

1955 **Signorina** (Per Schwenzen, R Gilbert) Städtische Bühnen, Nuremberg-Furth 23 April

1956 **Der kleine Schwindel in Paris** revised *Der süsseste Schwindel der Welt* (R Gilbert) Theater in der Josefstadt 25 December

1958 **Hallo! das ist die Liebe?** (revised *Der Tanz ins Glück* Wiener) Raimundtheater 4 January

1959 **Kitty und die Weltkonferenz** (aka *Die kleine und die grosse Welt*) (R Gilbert/Kurt Nachmann, Peter Preses) Theater in der Josefstadt 4 February

1960 **Joie de vivre** (Paul Dehn/Terence Rattigan) Queen's Theatre, London 14 July

1960 **Wiener Café** revised *Zum goldenen Halbmond* ad Willy Werner Göttig Städtische Bühnen, Dortmund 15 October

1962 **Trauminsel** revised *Signorina* Seebühne, Bregenz 21 July

1963 **Ein schöner Herbst** (Hans Weigel) Theater in der Josefstadt 5 June

1964 **Frühjahrsparade** (Marischka, H Wiener) Volksoper 25 March

1968 **Wohl dem, der lügt** (Weigel) Theater in der Josefstadt 4 June

1969 **Hochzeit am Bodensee** revised *Gruezi* Seebühne, Bregenz 23 July

Biographies and literature: Holm, G: *Im Dreiveirteltakt durch die Welt* (Ibis Verlag, Linz, 1948), Brümmel, W, van Booth, F: *Robert Stolz, Melodie eines Lebens* (Marion von Schröder Verlag, Hamburg, 1967), Herbrich, O: *Robert Stolz: König der Melodie* (Amalthea Verlag, Vienna, 1975), Làng, A: *Melodie aus Wien: Robert Stolz und sein Werk* (Jugend und Volk, Vienna, 1980), Stolz, R, Stolz, E: *Servus Du* (Blanvalet Verlag, Munich, 1980), Bakashian, A (ed): *The Barbed Wire Waltz* (1983), Pflicht, S: *Robert Stolz:Werkverzeichnis* (Katzbichler, Munich, 1981), Eidam, K: *Robert Stolz: Biographie eines Phänomens* (Lied der Zeit, Berlin, 1989), Bredschnetder, F: *Robert Stolz in Holland* (Gooise Uitgeverij, Bussum, 1980), etc

STONE, Fred [Andrew] (b Denver, Colo, 19 August 1873; d Hollywood, Calif, 6 March 1959). Long-loved comic star of the American musical-comedy stage.

Topeka-raised Fred Stone first appeared on stage at the age of 11 and worked as a teenager at first in variety, then along with his younger brother, Edward (d Jersey City, 22 August 1903), as an acrobat, clown and general all-purpose lad with the Sells-Renfrew Circus, before he took his first steps in the theatre, making an early appearance as Topsy in Dick Sutton's touring production of *Uncle Tom's Cabin.* In 1894 Stone teamed up with another young comedian, minstrel David Montgomery, and the pair began working the variety theatres as a double act. They made their first appearance as a pair at Keith's Theater, Boston and in 1900 they crossed to London for an engagement at the Palace Theatre.

They made their musical theatre debuts when they were engaged by Charles Frohman to appear as a pair of comical pirates in his production of *The Girl from Up There,* both at New York's Herald Square Theater (1901) and again in the London transfer of the show (Duke of York's Theatre, 1901), and went on from there to play in pantomime in Liverpool, but they achieved their first memorable success when they were featured as the Scarecrow (Stone) and the Tin Man (Montgomery) in Fred Hamlin's spectacular production of *The Wizard of Oz* (1903).

The pair confirmed themselves as public favorites with their extravagant clowning in Charles Dillingham's production of *The Red Mill.* In the roles of Con Kidder (Stone) and Kid Connor (Montgomery), two cocky, loud-mouthed, down-in-the-pocket Yankees, stranded in the land of windmills and tulips amongst a plotful of plots and a handful of girls, the two men indulged in a festival of fall-about, broadly cracking, full-of-disguises comedy which took time off only for some bright Victor Herbert songs, their most successful of which, ''The Streets of New York,'' almost out-Cohaned George M Cohan.

After three years milking the fun and profit from this great success all around America, the pair came back to Broadway with their 1909 touring piece *The Old Town* (1910). This time they were presented as a pair of circus performers in an elastic libretto which allowed them to ease in their versions of popular low-comedy routines and dances, and although neither the characters, the text nor the score came up to *The Red Mill,* the piece served the now-famous pair as a vehicle through two seasons on the road. They got the next two seasons, including 232 performances at the Globe Theatre, out of a version of the Cinderella tale called *The Lady of the Slipper.* Stone was Spooks, Montgomery was Punks and together they helped the little lady of the title (Elsie Janis) to get to the ball to the accompaniment of a Victor Herbert score which threw them no lasting songs but which served its purpose as an adjunct to the comedy and to a lavish Dillingham production.

Another fairy-tale subject, Aladdin, served as a basis for their 1914 vehicle, *Chin-Chin,* in which the pair, served up with their best vehicle since *The Red Mill,* cavorted through a story which hadn't too much to do with the traditional one as a pair of loopy coolies, Chin Hop Hi (Stone) and Chin Hop Lo (Montgomery), in various disguises and unchanging style, singing about ''Ragtime Temple Bells'' and ''A Chinese Honeymoon.''

After Montgomery's death in 1917, Stone continued on alone in custom-built shows of the same kind which they had played together. Producer Dillingham and the writing team of *Chin-Chin* (Ivan Caryll, Anne Caldwell, R H Burnside) had confected the pair another of the semi-pantomime, semi-comedy spectacular shows which had been their speciality ever since *The Wizard of Oz,* and it was revised to allow Stone to star at the Globe (1917) in a vaguely *Babes in the Woodsical* piece as the good little assassin, *Jack o' Lantern.* This show turned up Stone's most successful single song hit, "Wait Till the Cows Come Home," and gave him three further seasons of touring.

Tip Top (1920, Tip Top), in which he appeared as a little handyman, supported by the variety duo the Duncan Sisters, and *Stepping Stones* (1923, Peter Plug), which featured him in a similar character mixed up in a version of the Little Red Riding Hood tale, alongside his daughter Dorothy, both served for good seasons on Broadway and similar touring lives. *Criss-Cross* (1926, Christopher Cross), another piece built on the now very familiar model, also obliged if with a little less éclat than before, but illness obliged Stone to drop out of his next piece, *Three Cheers* (1928), before its opening on Broadway. He was back again, however, in 1930 teamed with his daughter as Rip and Ripples van Winkle in *Ripples,* but this time the overripe formula went wrong. The show had only a short Broadway season before being turned out into the country.

For *Smiling Faces* (1932, Monument Spleen) the recipe was changed, and the old fantasy-comedy line exchanged for a straighter musical comedy which cast Stone—now nearly 60, and no longer as limberly acrobatic as before—as a curious old movie-director. This piece proved even less successful than its predecessor, and Stone gave up the round which he had followed for 30 years. He appeared on the stage intermittently thereafter, but his outstanding decades as the most durably popular comedian of America's musical theatre were over.

Stone's wife, **Allene CRATER** (b St Paul) appeared in *Aladdin Jr* in Chicago (1894), and was seen on Broadway in *A Parlour Match* (revival, 1896, Ralph), in a supporting role in *Very Little Faust* (1897, Jess Tryon), in E E Rice's *The Ballet Girl* (1897, Violette), in Oscar Hammerstein's *War Bubbles* (1898, Niblette) and in *Miss Simplicity* (1901, Rosalie), and toured to Australia with Hoyt's comedians (Mrs Guyer in *A Trip to Chinatown,* Hattie in *A Stranger in New York* 1899). She subsequently appeared alongside Stone in his shows, being seen as Cynthia Cynch in *The Wizard of Oz,* Bertha in *The Red Mill* ("A Widow Has Ways"), Ernestine Bilwether in *The Old Town,* Romnyea in *The Lady of the Slipper,* Widow Twankey in *Chin-Chin,* Vilanessa in *Jack o' Lantern,* Mrs Hood in *Stepping Stones,* etc.

His elder daughter, **Dorothy STONE** (b Brooklyn, NY, 11 June 1904; d Montecito, Calif, 24 September 1974), made her first appearance on the stage, with above-the-title billing, opposite her father (and playing her mother's daughter) as Rougette Hood in *Stepping Stones* (1923). She paired with him a second time in *Criss-Cross* (Dolly Day); played with his replacement, Will Rogers, in *Three Cheers* (Princess Sylvia); and herself replaced Ruby Keeler in *Show Girl* (1929), before again teaming with Fred for *Ripples* and *Smiling Faces.* After his retirement she appeared in a number of shows outside New York, and on Broadway in the revue *As Thousands Cheer* (vice Marilyn[n] Miller), in *Sea Legs* (1937, with her husband, Charles Collins) and as Tina in a 1945 revival of *The Red Mill* co-produced by her sister Paula.

Paula STONE (b Brooklyn, NY, 20 January 1912; d Sherman Oaks, Los Angeles, 23 December 1997), who had in earlier days also worked as a performer with her father and who appeared with Dennis King in his short-lived *She Had to Say "Yes,"* later also produced (w Mike Sloane) a revival of *Sweethearts* (1947), the 1951 *Top Banana* and the 1957 musical *Rumple,* a piece reminiscent of her father's old vehicles (Alvin Theater, 45 performances).

Fred's brother, **Edward STONE** (d Jersey City, NJ, 22 August 1903), a partner in the vaudeville team Williamson and Stone, created the role of the cow in *The Wizard of Oz.*

Autobiography: *Rolling Stone* (Whittlesey House, New York, 1945)

STONE, Peter [H] (b Los Angeles, 27 February 1930).

Playwright Stone had his first stage work, a dramatization of Dostoevsky's *Friend of the Family,* produced in St Louis's Crystal Palace in 1958 and made his debut in the Broadway musical theatre with the libretto to Wright and Forrest's musicalization of the Jean-Paul Sartre play *Kean,* before going on to make a mark in the film world with the screenplays for such movies as *Charade* (1963) and *Father Goose* (1964, Academy Award).

In a career embracing film, television and stage he adapted a number of other well-known works to the musical theatre. Elmer Rice's *Dream Girl* became *Skyscraper,* Clifford Odets's *The Flowering Peach* was made into *Two By Two* for a run of 343 Danny-Kaye-oed performances, whilst two shows adapted from screenplays also had long and international lives: *Some Like It Hot* under the title of *Sugar,* and *Woman of the Year.* He combined with Sherman Edwards on the final, highly successful version of Edwards's Declaration of Independence musical, *1776,* and 30 years after his first entrance onto Broadway he had further stage success with the libretti to the

Tony Award–winning musicals *The Will Rogers Follies* and *Titanic*.

Stone also adapted *Sweet Charity* (1968) and *1776* (1972) for the screen, and his musical version of *Androcles and the Lion,* with a score by Richard Rodgers, was produced for television.

1961 **Kean** (Robert Wright, George Forrest) Broadway Theater 2 November

1965 **Skyscraper** (James van Heusen/Sammy Cahn) Lunt-Fontanne Theater 13 November

1969 **1776** (Sherman Edwards) 46th Street Theater 16 March

1970 **Two by Two** (Richard Rodgers/Martin Charnin) Imperial Theater 10 November

1972 **Sugar** (aka *Some Like It Hot*) (Jule Styne/Bob Merrill) Majestic Theater 9 April

1981 **Woman of the Year** (John Kander/Fred Ebb) Palace Theater 29 March

1983 **My One and Only** (Gershwin pasticcio/w Timothy S Mayer) St James Theater 1 May

1991 **The Will Rogers Follies** (Cy Coleman/Betty Comden, Adolph Green) Palace Theater 1 May

1997 **Titanic** (Maury Yeston) Lunt-Fontanne Theater 23 April

1999 **Annie Get Your Gun** revised libretto (Marquis Theater)

STOP FLIRTING *see* FOR GOODNESS' SAKE

STOP THE WORLD—I WANT TO GET OFF Musical in 2 acts by Anthony Newley and Leslie Bricusse. Queen's Theatre, London, 20 July 1961.

In 1961 impresario Bernard Delfont hired successful pop singer and actor Anthony Newley for a summer season at the Brighton Hippodrome but, when he was subsequently offered the potentially more lucrative Max Bygraves for the same date, he approached Newley to stand down. Newley agreed to do so, and made it a condition that, in return, Delfont produce a small-scale musical which he had written for himself. The bargain was struck and, for an outlay of £2,000, Delfont staged *Stop the World—I Want to Get Off* at the Queen's Theatre.

Stop the World told the story of the life of Littlechap (Newley) in a revusical journey from his birth to his death via ambition, accomplishment, marriage, infidelity, fatherhood and disillusion. A kind of a biographical harlequinade with a strong flavor of the 1960s to it, the piece mixed brief, spiky sketches with broad ballads in which Newley—intermittently supported by one actress (Anna Quayle) playing his wife, Evie, and all his other incidental women, and very occasionally by a pair of identical twins (Baker twins) as his daughters and a small group of choristers dressed as clowns—performed what was virtually a stand-up routine in the middle of a circus ring.

The naivety and the rather pretentious simplicity of the piece and its production were counterbalanced by the curious, appealing character that Newley created at its center, and also by a score which produced an enduring group of successful hit singles. Newley sang strivingly of how "I'm Gonna Build a Mountain" as he set off to turn his boss's most unpromising area office into a model of successful enterprise, launched emotionally into "Just Once in a Lifetime," and looked back sadly and selfishly, demanding "What Kind of Fool Am I? (who never fell in love)." Each number fitted its place in the show, but each also became hit-parade and cabaret material par excellence. The star howled out a youthful "I Wanna Be Rich," bewailed getting "L.U.M.B.E.R.E.D." with a pregnant girlfriend-wife, and later gently wondered how a creep like him had been lucky enough to be paired with "Someone Nice Like You," whilst Miss Quayle made a personal success with Evie's "Typically English" (later repeated by her as each of Littlechap's multinational concubines in her own national character).

The show proved a popular success and, aided by its reasonable break-figure and costs, ran through 16 months and 478 performances at the Queen's Theatre. Shortly before its end, Newley, Miss Quayle and the Bakers departed the cast to repeat their assignments in David Merrick's New York production and there, again, *Stop the World* proved to have an undeniable appeal. Newley, and subsequently Joel Grey, headed the piece through 555 performances. In Australia, however, without Newley and with Jackie Warner and Evelyn Page featured, it had uneven fortunes, playing three months in Melbourne, but only five weeks in Sydney (Theatre Royal 13 May 1964).

The piece's manageable size, hit songs and vast leading role won it not only a good touring life but also numerous productions in regional theatres and further international showings in both English and in translation. Vocalist Sammy Davis jr, who particularly affectioned the show and the role, played it on a number of occasions including on a brief visit to Broadway (State Theater 3 August 1978) and in an unreleased film, whilst in 1989 Newley made a short-lived return to London (Lyric Theatre 21 August) with a piece which, although it remained his most successful show, proved to be too marked by its era to succeed for a second time.

A German version was produced in Berlin (ad Mischa Mleinek) with Harald Juhnke and Violetta Ferrari starred and the mendacious boast of one thousand London performances attached to its advertising.

A 1966 Warner Brothers film which starred London takeover Tony Tanner and Millicent Martin was released, but was not a success.

USA: Shubert Theater 3 October 1962; Australia: Tivoli, Melbourne 7 February 1964; Germany: Der Komödie *Halt die Welt an—ich mochste aussteigen*

Film: Warner Bros 1966

Recordings: original cast (Decca), Broadway cast (AM), Broadway revival cast w Sammy Davis (Warner Bros), German cast (Philips), film soundtrack (Warner Bros), etc

THE STORKS Musical fantasy in 2 acts by Richard Carle and Guy F Steely. Lyrics by Steely. Music by Frederic Chapin. Dearborn Theater, Chicago, 18 May 1902.

Written and directed by rising comedian Richard Carle, in the style of the recently successful Chicago musicals of Gustave Luders and Frank Pixley, *The Storks* starred its author in the comic role of The Bungloo of Baktaria who is turned into a stork by a miffed magician (Henry Norman). The poundmaster's daughter, Violet (Harriet Standon), is made an owl for trying to help him turn back, but all eventually ends happily after two acts of picturesque fantasy and merry songs. Steely's lyrics ran through such titles as ''Tootsie Wootsie,'' ''Flirty Little Gertie,'' ''The Cuckoo and the Pussy Cat'' and ''The Terrible Puppy Dog,'' whilst Chapin's pleasantly ordinary score included a jolly patter song for the magician declaring ''I Did It!,'' some romantic parlor-ballady pieces for the magician's son (Edmund Stanley) and Violet (''Sorrow Is Mine''), and a picnic ensemble which was faintly reminiscent of the era's biggest hit song, ''Tell Me, Pretty Maiden.''

The Storks was a great success in Chicago, running right through the summer months (traditionally, at this era, empty of touring companies) and beyond, and helped encourage the burgeoning Chicago theatre to continue to develop a highly successful musical tradition of its own. It also encouraged Carle, soon a major star, to base himself there artistically. *The Storks* did not bother to take in New York, which, given the mostly unappreciative attitude taken to Chicago shows there in later days, probably saved its producers some of the profits they made in 17 Chicago weeks and a road tour.

STOTHART, Herbert P[ope] (b Milwaukee, Wis, 11 September 1885; d Los Angeles, 1 February 1949). Musical director, arranger and composer for the stage and screen.

Stothart left a teaching career (''professor of dramatic art at the University of Wisconsin'') while still in his twenties to try his luck as a composer and conductor of musical plays, and he had his first contact with the professional musical theatre in Chicago, where he combined with Joe Howard on the songs for a 1912 musical with a book written by ex–Wisconsin University student-turned-journalist Theodore Stempfel. One of two other pieces written with Stempel, *The Manicure Shop*, got a showing in St Louis, but their first attempt together, *Alpsburg*, seems to have not made it beyond the college precincts.

Stothart moved on from these small beginnings to become a Broadway musical director and to supply songs for a decade of Broadway musicals. All but one of his Broadway shows were mounted under the management of Arthur Hammerstein, whose own attempts at lyric writing he set to music when the producer's 1918 show *Somebody's Sweetheart* needed some hurried pretown revamping. His first four works for the New York stage, including three in one year, were composed alone, but although *Tickle Me,* with the help of the antics of popular comedian Frank Tinney, lasted 207 performances on Broadway, they were indifferent pieces, notable in retrospect only for having introduced Oscar Hammerstein II to the Broadway stage for the first time.

Thereafter, Stothart worked musically in a series of partnerships, being teamed with Vincent Youmans, Rudolf Friml, Emmerich Kálmán and George Gershwin on further shows for Hammerstein, often in collaboration with the young Oscar Hammerstein and Otto Harbach as librettist(s) and/or lyricist(s). He contributed six numbers (though not the hits) to the score of the successful Vincent Youmans piece *Wildflower;* ''Hard-Boiled Herman,'' ''Why Shouldn't We?,'' ''Only a Kiss'' and much of the incidental and concerted music to what has become generally thought of as Friml's *Rose Marie* (although Stothart had equal billing) and to what is similarly called Gershwin's *Song of the Flame;* and shared an all-in credit with Kalmar and Ruby on *Good Boy* with its boop-de-doop song ''I Wanna Be Loved By You.''

In 1930 Stothart joined MGM as a staff composer and conductor and, during the years that followed, he supplied songs for a long list of films, including additional and/or replacement numbers for the screen versions of *I Married an Angel* (w Wright and Forrest), *New Moon, Rose Marie* and *Sweethearts* (''Summer Serenade'') and supervised the musical devastation of *Zigeunerliebe* as *The Rogue Song* for Lawrence Tibbett and the ''adaptation'' of Lehár for the 1934 film of *The Merry Widow.* He composed an imaginary operetta *Czarita* to be used in *Maytime,* and scored his most particular successes with the title song for *Cuban Love Song* (w McHugh, Fields), also for Tibbett, and ''Sweetheart, Darling'' (w Gus Kahn) in the film *Peg o' my Heart.* He remained at MGM, as musical director, until shortly before his death. He was awarded an Academy Award for his orchestrations for *The Wizard of Oz.*

1912 **Frivolous Geraldine** (w Joe Howard/Theodore Stempfel) Olympic Theater, Chicago 22 December

1913 **A Broadway Honeymoon** (w Howard/George Collin Davis/Davis, Thomas T Reilley) Joe Howard's Theater, Chicago 3 October

1914 **The Manicure Shop** (w Howard/Stempfel) Suburban Garden, St Louis 29 June

1915 **The Girl of Tomorrow** (w Howard/Joseph Knowles) La Salle Theater, Chicago 18 October

1920 **Always You** (ex- *Joan of Ark-ansaw*) (Oscar Hammerstein II) Central Theater 5 January

1920 **Tickle Me** (Otto Harbach, Hammerstein, Frank Mandel) Selwyn Theater 17 August

1920 **Jimmie** (Harbach, Hammerstein, Mandel) Apollo Theater 17 November

1922 **Daffy Dill** (Hammerstein/Guy Bolton, Hammerstein) Apollo Theater 22 August

1923 **Wildflower** (w Vincent Youmans/Harbach, Hammerstein) Casino Theater 7 February

1923 **Mary Jane McKane** (w Youmans/William Cary Duncan, Hammerstein) Imperial Theater 25 December

1924 **Marjorie** (w Sigmund Romberg, Stephen Jones, Philip Culkin/Clifford Grey, Fred Thompson) Shubert Theater 11 August

1924 **Rose Marie** (w Rudolf Friml/Harbach, Hammerstein) Imperial Theater 2 September

1925 **Song of the Flame** (w George Gershwin/Harbach, Hammerstein) 44th Street Theater 30 December

1927 **Golden Dawn** (w Emmerich Kálmán/Harbach, Hammerstein) Hammerstein's Theater 30 November

1928 **Good Boy** (Kalmar, Ruby/Harbach, Hammerstein, Henry Meyers) Hammerstein's Theater 5 September

1929 **Polly** (w Phil Charig/Irving Caesar/Guy Bolton, George Middleton, Isobel Leighton) Lyric Theater 8 January

STRACHEY, Jack [STRACHEY, John Francis] (b London, 25 September 1894; d Brighton, 27 May 1972). Composer for a handful of the dancing musicals of the London 1920s.

An education at Marlborough and Oxford University led Jack Strachey to an early career as a pianist in seaside concert parties before he won his first London credits as the composer of revue material for such shows as *The Punch Bowl, Charlot's Revue* and *The Nine O'Clock Revue.* He entered the musical theatre in the early days of the craze for dance-and-comedy shows, sharing the musical credit on Laddie Cliff's early musicals *Dear Little Billie* and *Lady Luck* and then, along with H B Hedley, Stanley Lupino, et al under the pretendedly American umbrella-name of "Hal Brody," on the highly successful *So This Is Love* and *Love Lies.*

He continued to write principally material for revue (*Shake Your Feet, The Bow Wows, Charlot's Masquerade, The Chelsea Follies, The Savoy Follies, Spread It Abroad, All Wave, Moonshine, Swinging the Gate, Apple Sauce, New Ambassadors Revue, Sky High, Sweet and Low, Flying Colours, The Boltons Revue, Pay the Piper,* etc) and had his most notable single song hit with "These Foolish Things."

Two decades after his last West End dance-and-laughter musical, Strachey returned to the musical stage with a rather different type of score for the costume operetta *Belinda Fair* (131 performances) which, although not disgraced, did not find the same success as those light-footed shows of the 1920s.

1925 **Dear Little Billie** (w H B Hedley/Desmond Carter/Firth Shephard) Shaftesbury Theatre 25 August

1926 **Lady Letty** (w Ernest Longstaffe/Sydney Blow, Douglas Hoare) Empire Theatre, Glasgow 18 January

1927 **Lady Luck** (w Hedley/Carter/Shepard) Carlton Theatre 27 April

1928 **So This Is Love** (w Hedley, et al/Carter/Stanley Lupino, Arthur Rigby) Winter Garden Theatre 25 April

1929 **Love Lies** (w Hedley, et al/Carter/Lupino, Rigby) Gaiety Theatre 20 March

1932 **The Compulsory Wife** (w Carter, Collie Knox/C Bailey Hick) tour

1949 **Belinda Fair** (Eric Maschwitz, Gilbert Lennox) Saville Theatre 25 March

STRAMPFER, Friedrich (b Grimma, 23 May 1827; d Graz, 8 April 1890). One of the most influential personalities of the Austrian stage in the years of the infancy of the Operette who thereafter went helplessly downhill.

The son of an actor, Strampfer began his theatrical career in Weimar, but when he—a protestant—wed the catholic prima donna of the theatre, they were forced out of town. He ran a touring theatre company for a number of years and, during the 1850s, moved his operations from Trieste to Temesvár to Hermannstadt, in the early 1860s to Laibach, and then back to Temesvár. In May 1862, he took on the lease of Vienna's Theater an der Wien and there, at a period when the first stirrings of the new style of musical theatre were beginning to be heard, he put together a remarkable troupe of performers—a number of whom had worked with him in his previous theatres—and quickly made his theatre into one of the most important purveyors of musical plays in Vienna. In the wake of Karl Treumann's success with Offenbach's pieces, he made a deal with the French composer which got him a three-year contract for three one-acters and one full-length opéra-bouffe per year and he thus creamed off much of the best of the famous composer's works from his principal rival's theatre. In 1863 he played Offenbach's *Der Brasilianer* and Suppé's *Flotte Bursche,* in 1864 *Eine Künstreiterin* and *Ritter Eisenfrass* (*Croquefer*), but his first major acquisition was *La Belle Hélène.* After having gone to see the show in Paris, he cast the leading role in masterly fashion with the young, Berlin-based Marie Geistinger and produced *Die schöne Helena* in 1865 with enormous success for the theatre and the new star.

Coscoletto, Die Schäfer, Blaubart, Der Zaubergeige (1866), *Orpheus in der Unterwelt, Die Grossherzogin von Gérolstein* (1867), *Genovefa von Brabant* (1868) and *Périchole, die Strassensängerin* (1869) were amongst the other Offenbach pieces which followed, alongside such other imports as *Die Reise nach China* (1866), a version of the Cogniards' immense féerie *La Biche au bois* as *Prinzessin Hirschkuh* (1866), Grisar's *Les Douze Innocents* as *Ein dutzend Naturkind* (1866), Frédéric Barbier's *Les Oreilles de Midas,* Jonas's *Les Deux Arlequins* (1867), Hervé's *L'Oeil crevé* (1868) and Lecocq's *Fleur de thé* (1869) and homemade pieces including *Das Donauweibchen und der Ritter von Kahlenberg* (1866) and Genée's comic opera *Der schwarze Prinz.*

Strampfer left the Theater an der Wien in 1869, after seven highly effective and profitable years, and the following year turned the old Musikvereinsaal into a theatre as the Strampfertheater. He operated there with the same kind of material he had promoted at the Theater an der Wien, but luck seemed to have left him and he had soon to quit his theatre. He did no better, however, when he moved on to try his hand at the Pest Deutsches Theater nor, later, when he took on the Komische Oper in Vienna in partnership with his sister Frau Völkl (1878). He returned to Pest (1881), then for a short period took on the management of his old rival establishment the Carltheater (16 September 1882). Under his direction there were produced there Jonas's *Javotte* (*Cinderella the Younger*), the English comic opera *Drei Schwärzmantel,* Lecocq's *Kosiki* and a revival of *Der Seekadett.*

He later tried his luck in America where he even took to the boards as an actor and reciter and, finally, renouncing the theatre, set up as a backwoods farmer. He returned to Europe in 1888 and tried to set up a theatre school in Graz, before he died, in poverty, two years later.

STRAUS, Oscar [Nathan] (b Vienna, 6 March 1870; d Bad Ischl, 11 January 1954). One of the most important composers for the 20th-century Viennese and Berlin stages.

The young Oscar Straus spread his composing and conducting activities through all areas of musical and theatrical life, but he at first concentrated principally on a career as a theatre conductor and worked in several houses in Berlin and in the German provinces during the 1890s. In the earliest years of the 20th century, when he began to turn his attention more to composing for the theatre, rather than conducting in it, he turned out such diverse works as the comic opera *Der schwarze Mann,* the pantomime *Pierrots Fastnacht* (w Leo Held, Secession Bühne, Berlin 13 January 1901), a one-act opera, *Colombine,* a version of Erich Korn's *Bajazzade* produced at the Theater des Westens in 1904 (lib: Arthur Pserhofer 13 February), some five hundred Überbrettlgesänge and duets with such collaborators as Rudolf Volker and Paul von Schönthan (''Krabbel-Krabbel,'' ''Der Piccolo,'' ''Lied von der höhern Tochter,'' ''Wiener Corso,'' etc) and, most importantly, the burlesque *Die lustigen Nibelungen,* his first step towards the mainstream world of Operette.

Plate 369.

In the wake of the success of *Die lustige Witwe,* Straus was one of the first and most effective new-come composers to follow Lehár into the new era of Viennese Operette, and the first to win a comparable triumph. The piece which won him that triumph was *Ein Walzertraum.* Produced at Vienna's Carltheater, where his *Die lustigen Nibelungen* had previously been introduced to Vienna and where his merry and imaginative *Hugdietrichs Brautfahrt* had played 88 times the previous year, it turned out to be a huge success, running virtually uninterrupted for more than 450 performances in its first series, launching the duo ''Leise, ganz leise klingt's durch den Raum'' as one of its composer's most popular-ever melodies, and establishing itself as one of the classic Austrian pieces of its time before setting off to play other areas of the world.

His next full-length Operette, an adaptation of G B Shaw's Arms and the Man as *Der tapfere Soldat* (1908), played only 60 performances at the Theater an der Wien, but it more than solidified Straus's international fame when, adapted in Stanislaus Stange's English-language version under the title *The Chocolate Soldier,* it proved considerably more popular in America and Britain than in Europe, introducing the popular waltz song ''My Hero'' into the canon of Operette standards and ultimately becoming the basis of a Hollywood film.

Straus's next efforts were less successful. An adaptation of Sardou's *La Marquise* (a plot perhaps rather too reminiscent of *Der Graf von Luxemburg*) as *Didi,* with Mizzi Zwerenz starred, failed at the Carltheater (26 performances), *Mein junger Herr,* with Girardi featured, lasted only some 30 nights at the Raimundtheater, *Die kleine Freundin,* also with Zwerenz top-billed, was gone in 55 performances, and if the richly written *Das Tal der Liebe* provoked considerable praise from musicians, the show itself did not turn out to be a success on the scale of his two earliest triumphs. All the last three pieces were tried in America, in the wake of the success of *The Chocolate Soldier* (*Boys Will Be Boys, My Little Friend, Das Tal der Liebe*), but none took.

Straus ventured two pieces on the London stage, one, *Eine vom Ballet,* being played at first by a German touring company in German, then recast to be played in English, and neither time with success, the other (*Love and Laughter,* 65 performances) composed to a British libretto, with disappointing results, but he encountered some kind of success once more when, in wartime Vienna, he took up the kind of good-old-days libretto which inevitably succeeds at such times, and told the tale of the much theatrically maltreated ballet dancer Fanny Elssler in the Operette *Die himmelblaue Zeit.*

Major success, however, soon came round once more with a second wartime Operette. *Rund um die Liebe* gave its composer an even longer first run than had been achieved by *Ein Walzertraum,* tenanting the Johann Strauss-Theater for a year and a half and 533 performances. However, the same wartime circumstances which boosted its run also lopped off its overseas prospects, and the show did not ever establish itself in the standard repertoire. It remains, nevertheless, nominally Straus's longest-running show on the Viennese stage. At the Carltheater the Operette *Die schöne Unbekannte* played 103 performances prior to going on to foreign productions, but the Posse mit Gesang *Man steigt nach!* saw Straus abandon the regular Operette format which had been his since *Ein Walzertraum* with a piece which included such diverse items as a two-act film parody (*Opfer der Sünde*) and "sensationelle Naturaufnahme Strasse in Bombay," described as "a glimpse at deepest India." It ran for five weeks.

After the fair run of the more conventional *Liebeszauber* at the Bürgertheater (77 performances), Straus turned briefly to management and took on the running of the Établissement Ronacher where he produced a revival of his own *Die lustigen Nibelungen* with Mizzi Freihardt as Brünnhilde and his newest piece, the Singspiel *Nachtfalter* (later played at the Theater an der Wien, to its 99th performance), as well as Ralph Benatzky's *Liebe im Schnee,* both with Mizzi Günther starred, before getting out of his producer's shoes and handing over the management to Egon Dorn.

Another new piece composed at this time, *Die Marmorbraut,* received its first performance in Budapest prior to being given in its original German, as Straus continued to turn out a regular supply of agreeable and often successful Operetten. Both *Eine Ballnacht* and *Dorfmusikanten* (166 performances), tuneful if now perhaps rather conventional, pleased Vienna and Berlin for good runs, but it was Berlin which mounted the composer's next major success, *Der letzte Walzer,* a mixture of power politics and sex illustrated by one of the composer's most outstanding musical scores. *Der letzte Walzer* gave Straus his first truly international showing, and his first truly international success, since his two initial hits more than a decade earlier.

Straus subsequently based himself in Berlin and there he turned out several further scores for Fritzi Massary, the beloved star of *Der letzte Walzer—Die Perlen der Cleopatra, Die Königin, Teresina*—and one for Berlin's other major Operette star, Käthe Dorsch, as *Riquette,* in a continuing and regular list of mostly successful pieces. But from the late 1920s he led a peripatetic existence which was reflected in his credits. He composed the score for Sacha Guitry's successful *Mariette,* a vehicle for Yvonne Printemps which was first produced in Paris before being souped up with extra sentiment and songs for Berlin and Vienna productions; he turned an eye to the filmland fashion of the time with *Hochzeit in Hollywood,* which played eight weeks at Vienna's Johann Strauss-Theater and was duly metamorphosed into a Hollywood film; and he had pieces produced in Magdeburg and in Prague, at the Theater an der Wien, and, for the last time, in Berlin—with a final and highly successful vehicle for Fritzi Massary, an adaptation of a Louis Verneuil play entitled *Eine Frau, die weiss, was sie will* (which became an equally fine vehicle for Alice Delysia in the English language). At the same time he also supplied Hollywood with film music for such celluloid pieces as *One Night with You* (1932), alongside screen versions of *Hochzeit in Hollywood* (*Married in Hollywood*), *Ein Walzertraum* (*The Smiling Lieutenant*) and *Der tapfere Soldat* (*The Chocolate Soldier*).

In 1935 he assembled and composed the best of the many Strauss pasticcio shows with which the stages of Europe had been invested even before the waltzing Johann's death, the nostalgic *Drei Walzer,* before he pointed his definitive departure from Germany and from Austria by taking out French nationality. It was in France that *Trois Valses* established itself as an enduring favorite, and in France, in his 70th year, that Straus composed the score for one of his last musical plays, *Mes amours,* a musical version of Edward Childs Carpenter's successful play *Bachelor Father,* but he returned, after the Second World War, to Austria where, in his eighties, he worked on revised versions of *Drei Walzer, Eine Frau* and *Ein Walzertraum* and added one more memorable credit to a list stretching back half a century, with the theme song for the film *La Ronde.*

As skilled and tuneful a writer of light theatre music as any of his contemporaries, Straus's quality is evidenced by the way his original music stands up alongside the Strauss melodies which comprise the rest of the *Drei Walzer* score, and his versatility by the way different countries have retained different of his works as favorites—*Ein Walzertraum* still goes best in Vienna, *The Chocolate Soldier* is still the favorite of the English-speaking world, whilst *Trois Valses* holds pride of place in France. Until the day when someone listens again to such first-rate pieces as *Hugdietrichs Brautfahrt, Der letzte Walzer* or *Das Tal der Liebe,* or dips into the delicious mixture of Guitry and Straus that makes up the original *Mariette.*

1894 **Die Waise von Cordova** (Max Singer) 1 act Pressburg 1 December

1900 **Der schwarze Mann** (Rudolf Schanzer) 1 act Colberg 24 August; Secession Bühne, Berlin 28 December 1901

1904 **Die lustigen Nibelungen** (Rideamus) Carltheater 12 November

1905 **Zur indischen Witwe** (Ignaz Schnitzer, Sigmund Schlesinger) Centraltheater, Berlin 30 September

1906 **Hugdietrichs Brautfahrt** (Rideamus) Carltheater 10 March

1906 **Mam'zell Courasch** (Erich Korn) 1 act Lustspieltheater 16 March

1907 **Ein Walzertraum** (Felix Dörmann, Leopold Jacobson) Carltheater 2 March

1907 **Der Frauenmörder** (Victor Léon) 1 act Danzers Orpheum 8 November

1908 **Der tapfere Soldat** (Rudolf Bernauer, Jacobson) Theater an der Wien 14 November

1909 **Little Mary** (Léon ad Auguste Germain, Robert Trébor) 1 act Comédie-Royale, Paris 9 January

1909 **Didi** (Léon) Carltheater 23 October

1909 **Der tapfere Kassian** (Arthur Schnitzler) 1 act Stadttheater, Leipzig 30 October

1909 **Venus im Grünen** (Rudolf Lothar) 1 act Stadttheater, Leipzig 30 October

1909 **Das Tal der Liebe** (Lothar) Kaiser-Jubiläums-Stadttheater (Volksoper) and Komische Oper, Berlin 23 December

1910 **Mein junger Herr** (Ferdinand Stollberg) Raimundtheater 23 December

1911 **Der andere Herr war nicht so** (aka *Die anderen Herren sind nicht so*) (Léon) 1 act Hölle 1 February

1911 **Die kleine Freundin** (Leo Stein, A M Willner) Carltheater 20 October

1912 **Eine vom Ballet** (Julius Brammer, Alfred Grünwald) London Coliseum 2 June

1913 **Love and Laughter** (Frederick Fenn, Arthur Wimperis) Lyric Theatre, London 3 September

1914 **Die himmelblaue Zeit** (Paul Wertheimer, Richard Batka) Volksoper 21 February

1914 **Rund um die Liebe** (Robert Bodanzky, Friedrich Thelen) Johann Strauss-Theater 9 November

1915 **Die schöne Unbekannte** (Jacobson, Leo Walther Stein) Carltheater 15 January

1915 **Man steigt nach!** (Léon, Heinz Reichert) Carltheater 2 May

1916 **Liebeszauber** (Léon) Bürgertheater 28 January

1917 **Nachtfalter** (Jacobson, Bodanzky) Wiener Stadttheater (Ronacher) 13 March

1917 **Die Marmorbraut** (*A márványmenyasszony*) (Oskar Blumenthal ad Jenő Heltai) Vígszínház, Budapest 19 April; as *Niobe* Lessing-Theater, Berlin 1 June

1918 **Eine Ballnacht** (Jacobson, Bodanzky) Johann Strauss-Theater 11 October

1919 **Die galante Markgräfin** revised *Das Tal der Liebe* (Dörmann) Volksoper 24 January

1919 **Dorfmusikanten** (Jacobson, Bodanzky) Theater an der Wien 29 November

1920 **Der letzte Walzer** (Brammer, Grünwald) Berliner Theater, Berlin 12 February

1921 **[Das] Nixchen** (Willner, Rudolf Österreicher) Wallner-Theater, Berlin 10 September

1923 **Die törichte Jungfrau** ("Florido," ie, Heinz Saltenburg) Grosses Schauspielhaus, Berlin 13 January

1923 **Die Perlen der Cleopatra** (Brammer, Grünwald) Theater an der Wien 17 November

1924 **Der Tanz um die Liebe** (Jacobson, Saltenburg) Deutsches Künstlertheater, Berlin 25 September

1925 **Riquette** (Schanzer, Ernst Welisch) Deutsches Künstlertheater, Berlin 17 January

1925 **[Die] Teresina** (Schanzer, Welisch) Deutsches Künstlertheater, Berlin 11 September

1926 **Die Königin** (Ernst Marischka, Bruno Granichstaedten) Deutsches Künstlertheater, Berlin 5 November

1928 **Mariette, ou comment on écrit l'histoire** (Sacha Guitry) Théâtre Édouard VII, Paris 1 October

1928 **Hochzeit in Hollywood** (Jacobson, Hardt-Warden) Johann Strauss-Theater 21 December

1929 **Herzdame** (Richard Kessler, Willi Steinberg) Centraltheater, Magdeburg 26 February

1929 **Die erste Beste** (Schanzer, Welisch) Deutsches Theater, Prague 19 October

1931 **Der Bauerngeneral** (Brammer, Gustav Beer) Theater an der Wien 28 March

1932 **Eine Frau, die weiss, was sie will** (Grünwald) Metropoltheater, Berlin 1 September

1933 **Zwei lachende Augen** (Österreicher, Ludwig Hirschfeld) Theater an der Wien 22 December

1935 **Das Walzerparadies** (Grünwald) Scala Theater 15 February

1935 **Drei Walzer** (Paul Knepler, Armin Robinson) Stadttheater, Zürich 5 October

1940 **Mes amours** (Léopold Marchand, Albert Willemetz) Théâtre Marigny, Paris 2 May

1948 **Die Musik kommt** (Knepler, Robinson) Stadttheater, Zürich 6 November

1950 **Ihr erster Walzer** (revised *Die Musik kommt* ad Robert Gilbert) Theater am Gärtnerplatz, Munich 31 March

1952 **Bozena** (Brammer, Grünwald) Theater am Gärtnerplatz, Munich 16 May

Biographies: Grün, B: *Prince of Vienna* (W H Allen, London, 1955), Mailer, F: *Weltbürger der Musik* (Österreichische Bundesverlag, Vienna, 1985)

STRAUSS, Johann [Baptist] (b Vienna, 25 October 1825; d Vienna, 3 June 1899). The Viennese ''Waltz King'' of the middle years of the 19th century whose ventures into the musical theatre produced several major hits and much more frustration.

For the first 25 years of his career as a composer and conductor of the orchestral dance music which was the chief entertainment of his time, Johann Strauss had little to do with the theatre. He composed a set of dance variations on themes from Offenbach's *Orphée aux enfers* following the piece's production at the Vienna Carltheater in 1860 (Orpheus-Quadrille op 236) and in 1862 he married Henriette Chalupetzky, otherwise known as Jetty Treffz, a successful singer. It was apparently she, who for the rest of her days organized much of her husband's life, who was foremost in encouraging him to write for the musical stage. His beginnings were halting. A *Die lustigen Weiber von Wien,* composed to a text by Josef Braun—the author of Suppé's popular *Flotte Bursche*—which was destined as a vehicle for Josefine Gallmeyer at the Theater an der Wien did not come to fruition. Not for the last time, Strauss failed to get to grips with a score. It was actually several years and several subjects later before the first Strauss Operette finally made it to the stage, and then it made it only with a struggle. The piece was a fairy-tale one, based partly on the Arabian Nights story of Ali Baba and partly on a compote of French opéra-bouffe elements, and theatre-manager Maximilian Steiner's name on the librettist's side of the bill only veiled the fact that the text of the show had gone through all kinds of writers and rewriters in an effort to get the composer to complete his work. There is little doubt, however, that the main midwife to *Indigo und die vierzig Räuber* was not so much Steiner, nor indeed Jetty Treffz, but Richard Genée, the multi-talented resident author and composer at the Theater an der Wien.

Indigo had an indifferent reception and an indifferent career in Vienna, but its music went round the town, and the show was nevertheless picked up for productions in many of the other musical centers where Strauss's name was a potent one. When it ultimately reached France, the libretto was given a major rewrite rather than just an adaptation and Strauss wrote some additional music to fit the remodeled text. He liked *La Reine Indigo* (Théâtre de la Renaissance ad Victor Wilder, Adolphe Jaime 27 April 1875) altogether better than he did *Indigo und die vierzig Räuber* and, thus, it was put back into German and reproduced in Vienna as *Königin Indigo* (ad Josef Braun, Theater an der Wien 9 October 1877). It was the first of many attempts, both in the composer's lifetime and after, to make a theatrical success out of an unremarkable libretto and a Strauss score which sounded better out of a show than in one.

Strauss persevered in his new career and two years later the Theater an der Wien produced his second Operette, *Carneval in Rom.* There was nothing wrong with the libretto of this one. And it was a text much more suited to the composer's style of writing. Braun had come up with a lively adaptation of Victorien Sardou's *Piccolino*—a piece which was successfully set just three years later in French by Guiraud—which mixed country scenes and Roman festive gaiety with both a genuine and a frisky love story. *Carneval in Rom,* again with the theatre's co-director and star, Marie Geistinger, in the lead role, did somewhat better than the muddly *Indigo* but it certainly didn't set the Danube alight.

It was the trusty Genée who supplied the text for the piece that did. Another French play, the comedy *Le Réveillon,* provided the starting point for the libretto of *Die Fledermaus,* a piece which was all women, wine and frivolity. No longing love story such as that of the little Swiss maiden and her untrue painter in *Carneval in Rom,* it was just fickle, bright comedy from end to end to end. Here Strauss found himself in his element, and the result was the triumph that the world had been expecting from him since his first piece. *Die Fledermaus* went round the world, beginning the career which would ultimately (if slightly unfairly) lead it to be the one really great survivor of the 19th-century Viennese Operette stage, the familiar representative of its era to the later part of the 20th century.

Having hit the tone so rightly with *Die Fledermaus,* Genée and Strauss then missed it with their next collaboration. *Cagliostro in Wien* abandoned the French gaiety of the earlier piece for a lumpen tale of chicanery and romance which its Viennese carnival-time setting could not alleviate. Once again, the music was glued to the piece rather than going with it, and once again the results were indifferent. Strauss later cannibalized *Cagliostro in Wien*'s music and used his favorite bits, along with more of *Die Fledermaus,* to make up the score of his Paris pasticcio piece *La Tzigane* (lib: Wilder, Alfred Delacour, Théâtre de la Renaissance 30 October 1877).

The Carltheater's Franz Jauner, anxious to challenge the Theater an der Wien with his own Strauss Operette, commissioned a libretto from Victor Wilder, the author of the French *Reine Indigo* which Strauss had so liked, with which to tempt the composer. If the tempting succeeded, the piece he got—*Prinz Methusalem*—proved to be another indifferent one, although its composer's fame once again ensured that it got both a certain run and a certain, if not very happy, overseas life. *Prinz Methusalem* was, however, a triumph compared to Strauss's next stage piece, *Blindekuh.* This one played just 16 performances.

After some eight years in the musical theatre, Johann Strauss had composed six original Operetten and he had had just one genuine success. Compared with Offenbach—and people insisted on making the comparison—it was a feeble average. However, the next few years brought a singular improvement: between 1880 and 1885 the composer produced four more Operetten, a group of four which—after his monumental hit with *Die Fledermaus*—would comprise the principal valuable bulk of his stage opus. *Das Spitzentuch der Königin,* a so-so tale of amorous highjinks in period Spain, nevertheless worked reasonably well in the theatre, and Strauss's score worked pretty well with it, but *Der lustige Krieg* was a different matter altogether. Genée and his co-writer "F Zell," turned out a version of another merry French text which was fun from top to bottom—with barely a pause for a lush, romantic moment, although with some charming ones for a little pathetic sentiment—and Strauss pulled out some of his most magical melodies to fit this "merry war" and its laughable characters. The piece was a stinging success, and Strauss was able once more to taste—after more than a half-dozen years of trying—the kind of triumph he had found so far only with *Die Fledermaus.*

For *Eine Nacht in Venedig* Zell and Genée dug up another French text, and one with the composer's apparently preferred Italianate setting. If the result was not an Operette as thoroughly good as its predecessor, the show produced some charming numbers and, after some revisions on its way from its Berlin premiere to Vienna, it did well enough to establish itself as one of the favorite targets for Strauss-remakers of the future. It was the fourth of the set, however, which brought Strauss the biggest and most enduring triumph. Having split with Zell and Genée over what he regarded as the insufficient libretto of *Eine Nacht in Venedig,* Strauss turned instead to a novel by Hungary's respected Mór Jókai, which was adapted into a libretto by Hungarian-born librettist Ignaz Schnitzer, an author with whom he had had one of his false starts on another project several years previously.

Der Zigeunerbaron was a piece of a different color altogether from anything the composer had yet tackled. Based on a thoroughly romantic Hungarian tale of gypsies and lost treasures and princesses, it had not a champagne bubble in it anywhere. It was a text seemingly suited to one of the more vigorous Hungarian composers than to the Viennese waltz king. Yet the composer whose talent had always seemed to be based in the gay, in the comic, in the frivolous, found an inspiration in the highly colored sentimental melodrama of this tale, and produced a score which was rangy and powerful enough to override the wandering banalities of the libretto. *Der Zigeunerbaron* gave the composer the third major hit of his career.

Strauss now became determined to compose further stage pieces in a musically more substantial manner. Whether a result of that decision or not, because of his dissatisfaction with the musical voice of *Die Fledermaus* and *Der lustige Krieg* and his wish to write operatic music, in the 10 years and six more musical plays that remained of his career Johann Strauss never had another success.

Five Operetten and his one attempt at an operatic piece, a show based on another Hungarian original, *Ritter Pásmán* (lib: Lajos Dóczi, Opernhaus 1 January 1892), were all failures, even though *Fürstin Ninetta* was played 76 times at the Theater an der Wien, *Jabuka* 57 and *Waldmeister* 88, and all were given further productions. The libretti got the blame each time: yet Victor Léon and A M Willner, two of the "culprits," were to become two of Vienna's finest musical stage writers, and each would total many more hits than the composer in his career. Willner even, later, took back the unloved libretto to the final Strauss flop, *Die Göttin der Vernunft,* remade it, presented it to Lehár and got no less a hit than *Der Graf von Luxemburg* from it. What was more likely as a reason for Strauss's failure was that text and music were out of sympathy with each other. Strauss—whose music was often, in any case, vaguely "untheatrical"—did not have, or could not retain interest and/or enthusiasm in his texts. He considered, and so many people told him, that they had let him down so often.

If Strauss wrote no more for the Operette stage after the quick failure of *Die Göttin der Vernunft,* he did at least concur in the making of the first of what would later became an avalanche of pasticcio shows fabricated from his music. *Wiener Blut,* written to a libretto by Léon and Stein, its music arranged by the younger Adolf Müller, did not get to the stage, however, until a few months after the composer's death. On its production at the Carltheater on 25 October 1899 it did not prove popular, and it was soon put away, but it was later remounted at the Theater an der Wien, and this time it won a rather different reaction. The success of *Wiener Blut,* and the magic of the name of Strauss, which survived whilst the *Blindekuh*s and *Simpliciuse*s were forgotten, soon led to many, many more such paste-ups and a number of remakes. Julius Hopp arranged a Strauss score for a *Das Narrenhaus* (Centraltheater, Berlin 3 May 1906); Gabor Steiner mounted two remakes amongst his series of pasticcio works—*Gräfin Pepi* (Venedig in Wien 5 July 1902) with music from *Blindekuh* and *Simplicius* arranged by Ernst Reiterer and *Tausend und eine Nacht* (Venedig in Wien 15 June 1906, arr Reiterer), yet another piece trying to make something out of the *Indigo* score—whilst the *Die Göttin der Vernunft* score was put to a new text by Ferdinand Stollberg under the title *Reiche Mädchen* (mus arr Reiterer, Raimundtheater 30 December 1909).

In 1928 Ralph Benatzky turned a bit of *Blindekuh* into the Nuns' Chorus as part of a Strauss pasticcio score to the Berlin spectacular *Casanova* (lib: Schanzer, Welisch 1 September 1928) and in 1930 the Wiener Stadttheater launched a *Dreimäderlhaus*-style biomusical of the composer. Willner, Reichert and Marischka's libretto to *Walzer aus Wien* (arr Julius Bittner, E W Korngold, Stadttheater 30 October) had a Johann Strauss struggling against his father's wishes that he become a composer, wooing a local maiden, winning his musical spurs with the aid of a sexy countess, and indulging a little bedroom-farcery before heading on to fame and fortune. In its essentials, their book crystallized the Johann Strauss myth that would be handed down through many a remake of this almost wholly fictional, conventional operettic tale. Others would have a go at the accompanying pasticcio, but by and large the tale stuck to the same story line through a series of *Great Waltzes, Valses de Vienne* and a bevy of other such stage and screen soft-soap Strauss-stories with music.

Walzer aus Wien also pulled out the stopcock on a gusher of homogenized Strauss musicals. Another Korngoldized piece, *Das Lied der Liebe,* mounted at the Berlin Metropoltheater later the same year (23 December 1931) with Richard Tauber starred proved an expensive flop, but the Volksoper followed up with a *Freut euch das Lebens* (arr Grün/Wilhelm, Herz 22 December 1932), Nuremberg mounted an *Eine Nacht am Bosporus* (arr Ernst Schlieppe/Gustav Heidrich, 30 August 1936), Hanover produced a *Ballnacht in Florenz* (Eugen Müri, Edwin Burmester, Mellni Theater 21 January 1939) which went on to be seen at Berlin's Theater des Volkes (24 January 1941), and the Neues Wiener Stadttheater hosted a Strauss Revue-Operette, *An der schönen blauen Donau* (arr Tiller, 21 December 1939).

The Strausses' family life got another going over in a piece called *Die Straussbuben* which used music by both Johann Strauss and his brother Josef for its score (arr Stalla/Marischka, Weys Raimundtheater 20 October 1946), but it was another shared score which produced the best of all the Strauss remakes—Oscar Straus's three-eras tale, *Drei Walzer* (arr Oscar Straus/Paul Knepler, Armin Robinson Stadttheater, Zürich 5 October 1935), which used Johann Strauss I music for its first act, Johann II for the second act and Straus's own for the third in a wholly winning combination.

Father Strauss, in fact, also supplied the entire score for another successful Operette, a biomusical on the actress Therese Krones who, as portrayed by Betty Fischer at the Raimundtheater in 1913 (21 November), was called *Die tolle Therese* (ad Otto Römisch/Krenn, Josef von Ludaffy). The piece ran for more than 150 nights. The same Römisch also later arranged the score for a piece called *Lanner und Strauss* (1937) which gave theatregoers a chance to see father Strauss depicted as something other than the spoilsport of the *Walzer aus Wien* story.

Perhaps surprisingly, it was brother Josef, who never wrote a note for the musical stage, who proved to be the family's real musical-theatre winner years after his death. The ever-arranging Ernst Reiterer organized a pasticcio of his music as the score to an adaptation of the famous French play *Coquin de printemps* and, produced at Venedig in Wien under the title *Frühlingsluft* (lib: Lindau, Wilhelm, 9 May 1903), it became a serious hit. Josef was made to serve again for Steiner's 1905 *Frauenherz* (*Die kleine Milliardärin*) (Danzers Orpheum, Lindau 29 September), the Raimundtheater's *Das Schwalberl aus dem Wienerwald* (ad Fritz Sommer/E Berger, Louis Taufstein, 31 March 1906) and the little *Das Teufelsmädel* (arr Siebert/J S Chifford, Apollotheater 2 March 1908), before having his life done over in the 1942 Singspiel *Walzerträume* (ad Bruno Uher/Tilde Binder, Ernst Friese).

From 1908 onwards Vienna had a theatre in the Favoritenstrasse which devoted itself to Operette and which was named after the composer of *Die Fledermaus, Der lustige Krieg* and *Der Zigeunerbaron.* The Johann Strauss-Theater opened with *Tausend und eine Nacht,* and played each of the composer's main works, as well as versions of *Eine Nacht in Venedig* and *Das Spitzentuch der Königin,* during its some 25 years of existence. It later became first shabby and second-class and then the Scala Theater.

Portrayed interminably on both stage and screen in various versions of *Walzer aus Wien* by such (mostly much better looking) performers as Hubert Marischka, Robert Halliday, Esmond Knight, André Baugé, Guy Robertson, Fernand Graavey and Edmund Schellhammer, Johann Strauss has become a cliché of the old-days-Vienna storytelling of the 20th century, his name attached to all sorts of dashing juvenile men with a waltz to play and a girl to win. The fact is that, even though he and his music can fairly be considered a major representative of the Viennese world of entertainment in the second part of the 19th century, it was in entertainment in general—the world of balls and concerts and so forth—that he shone brightest. His work for the theatre was neither the happiest nor the most successful part of his musical life, and he was never a comfortable man of the theatre. But he still left to posterity the scores of *Die Fledermaus, Der lustige Krieg* and *Der Zigeunerbaron*—a musical-theatre contribution greater than that produced by many nevertheless talented writers who spent the whole of their lives and all their efforts on a career in Operette.

1871 **Indigo und die vierzig Räuber** (Maximilian Steiner) Theater an der Wien 10 February

1873 **Carneval in Rom** (Josef Braun) Theater an der Wien 1 March

1874 **Die Fledermaus** (Carl Haffner, Richard Genée) Theater an der Wien 5 April

1875 **Cagliostro in Wien** (F Zell, Genée) Theater an der Wien 27 February

1877 **Prinz Methusalem** (Victor Wilder, Alfred Delacour ad Karl Treumann) Carltheater 3 January

1878 **Blindekuh** (Rudolf Kneisel) Theater an der Wien 18 December

1880 **Das Spitzentuch der Königin** (Bohrmann-Riegen, Genée) Theater an der Wien 1 October

1881 **Der lustige Krieg** (Zell, Genée) Theater an der Wien 25 November

1883 **Eine Nacht in Venedig** (Zell, Genée) Friedrich-Wilhelmstädtisches Theater, Berlin 3 October

1885 **Der Zigeunerbaron** (Ignaz Schnitzer) Theater an der Wien 24 October

1887 **Simplicius** (Victor Léon) Theater an der Wien 17 December

1893 **Fürstin Ninetta** (Hugo Wittmann, Julius Bauer) Theater an der Wien 10 January

1894 **Jabuka** (*Das Apfelfest*) (M Kalbeck, Gustav Davis) Theater an der Wien 12 October

1895 **Waldmeister** (Gustav Davis) Theater an der Wien 4 December

1897 **Die Göttin der Vernunft** (A M Willner, Bernhard Buchbinder) Theater an der Wien 13 March

Biographies and literature: Kemp, P: *The Strauss Family* (Baton Press, Tunbridge Wells, 1985), Eisenberg, L: *Johann Strauss: Ein Lebensbild* (Breitkopf & Härtel, Leipzig, 1894), Decsey, E: *Johann Strauss: ein Wiener Buch* (Deutsche Verlag-Anstalt, Stuttgart, 1922), Loewy, S: *Johann Strauss, der Spielmann der blauen Donau* (Wiener Literarische Anstalt, Vienna, 1924), Jacob, H E: *Johann Strauss und das 19 Jahrhundert* (Querido Verlag, Amsterdam, 1937), Prawy, M: *Johann Strauss: Weltgeschichte in Walzertakt* (Ueberreuter Vienna, 1975), Mailer, F: *Das kleine Johann Strauss Buch* (Residenz Verlag, Salzburg, 1975), *Johann Strauss (Sohn): Leben und Werk in Briefe und Dokumenten* (Hans Schneider, Tutzing, 1983), Endler, F: *Johann Strauss: Um die Welt im Dreivierteltakt* (Amalthea, Vienna, 1998), Dachs, R: *"Was geh' ich mich an?"* (Styria, Graz, 1999), Brusatti, O: *Johann Strauss* (Bonechi Verlag Styria, Graz, 1999), Dieman-Dichtl, K: *Freut euch des Lebens: Die Strauss-Dynastie und Niederösterreich* (NP Buchverlag, St Pölten, 1999), Mailer F: *Johann Strauss: Kommentiertes Werkverzeichnis* (Pichler, Vienna, 1999), Mayer, F: *Johann Strauss: A Nineteenth Century Pop-Idol* (Böhlau, Vienna, 1999), Sinkovicz, W, Knaus, H: *Johamn Strauss* (Verlag Holzhausen, Vienna, 1999), etc

STREET SCENE Dramatic musical [an American opera] in 2 acts by Elmer Rice taken from his play of the same name. Lyrics by Langston Hughes. Music by Kurt Weill. Adelphi Theater, New York, 9 January 1947.

Street Scene, advisedly described as a "dramatic musical," was an attempt to straddle the apparent gap between the operatic form and the popular theatre in the same style that such pieces as *Porgy and Bess* had done, and as Gian-Carlo Menotti would do regularly with such pieces as *The Medium, The Telephone* (1947), *The Consul* (1950) and other works.

Elmer Rice's 1929 play, a memorable Broadway success at the Playhouse Theater (10 January, 601 performances), was closely adapted by its author, retaining the many characters who make up the atmospheric population of the street where the adulterous Mrs Maurrant is murdered by her husband one hot afternoon. The lyrics were written by Langston Hughes, poet and the successful author of the play *Mulatto* (1935), and the score composed by Kurt Weill, recently successful on Broadway with *Lady in the Dark* and *One Touch of Venus.* The natural yet stark drama of the text and the mostly colloquial poetry of the songwords were matched by the composer with music which was in the same mode—darkly and operatically dramatic in Mrs Maurrant's aria "Somehow I Never Could Believe," warmly light-operatically chatty in such pieces as the young father to-be's "When A Woman Has a Baby," and ranging from the lyrical-gossipy to the almost burlesque operatic in the chatter of the folk on the block ("Ain't It Awful the Heat," "The Woman Up There," "Get a Load of That"). The darker moments of the piece were contrasted with plenty of lighter ones—an ice-cream septet, the jitterbugging "Moon-faced, Starry-eyed"—and only in the lightly jazzy "Wouldn't You Like to Be on Broadway?" did the musical mix falter a little as the "Broadway" dominated the "opera" rather than combining with it as elsewhere.

The piece was purposely aimed for the Broadway market rather than for an opera-house production. Weill insisted that opera houses were museums, and that living, popular theatre should be seen under commercial-theatre conditions. It also, of course, stood to make considerably more money under such conditions. After some tergiversation, the show was produced by the Playwrights Company and Dwight Deere Wiman. Polyna Stoska from New York's City Center Opera played Mrs Maurrant, operatic vocalist-turned-Hollywood-actress Ann Jeffreys and Joseph Sullivan, recently come to Broadway from opera, were the juveniles, and Metropolitan Opera basso Norman Cordon was the murderer in a cast where legitimate singing was foremost.

Street Scene had a disastrous out-of-town tryout, but its reception on Broadway was much more encouraging and for a while there was hope that a commercial-theatre audience might accept the sombrely ending local tragedy as a complement to the newly opened and definitely successful fantasies of *Brigadoon.* However, with the first fine flush of enthusiasm over, *Street Scene*'s audience began to dwindle. In spite of protests from the authors who had, after all, wanted a commercial production, Wiman began to advertise, but it was in vain and after 148 performances the show closed in failure.

It was subsequently given a German production (ad Lys Bert) in 1955, but Weill's efforts to interest European opera houses in the work did not have the hoped-for result.

However, with the powerful support of the cast recording of its original production, *Street Scene* continued, after its closure, to have strong partisans and, aided by the strong promotion of Weill's works in the 1970s and 1980s, ultimately it found its way back to the stage in the very opera houses to which Weill had originally insisted (before revising his opinion and dubbing the published work ''an American opera'') it did not belong. The New York City Opera produced *Street Scene* in 1978 (State Theater 27 October 1979) and, after its first British stage presentation in a single performance benefit in 1987, it was seen at both the Scottish Opera (1989) and the English National Opera (12 October 1989).

Germany: Städtische Bühnen, Düsseldorf *Die Strasse* 26 November 1955; UK: Palace Theatre 26 April 1987

Recordings: original cast (Columbia), studio casts (Decca, TER)

THE STREET SINGER Musical play in 3 acts by Frederick Lonsdale. Lyrics by Percy Greenbank. Music by Harold Fraser-Simson. Additional numbers by Ivy St Helier. Lyric Theatre, London, 27 June 1924.

A romantic costume piece from the pens of Freddy Lonsdale and his *Maid of the Mountains* partner Harold Fraser-Simson, the old-fashioned *The Street Singer* was a splendid West End success in an era full of revue hits, of Viennese musicals and of up-to-date dancing melodies which, before *The Street Singer* had ended its run, would find their most successful expression in the production of *No, No, Nanette.* Phyllis Dare, no longer the youngest of ingenues, purchased *The Street Singer* from the authors and arranged for Daniel Mayer to produce the show for her. It opened at Birmingham in February 1924 with Miss Dare starring as the Duchess of Versailles who anonymously buys her beloved Bonni's garret paintings on the one hand, and woos and is wooed by him (Arthur Pusey), disguised as a little street singer, on the other. Sam Wilkinson headed the comedy as misogynistic François, tracked down to marriage by a merry little widow (Julie Hartley-Milburn).

The show played 16 weeks on the road before opening in London, with Harry Welchman now taking the romantic lead and A W Baskcomb the comedy one, and there it was greeted with critical bouquets for the well-written book—which had, after all, been provided by the author of some of the town's most popular light comedies—and for its merrily romantic Fraser-Simson score, of which Baskcomb's furious ''Ow I 'ate Women'' and the love duet ''Just to Hold You in My Arms'' were the most popular single pieces. These were topped off by three songs by Ivy St Helier which contrasted with the main music as effectively as Jimmy Tate's songs had done in Fraser-Simson's basic score for *The Maid of the Mountains,* but a misguided attempt to pop George Gershwin's ''Virginia'' into the score of this period French romance later in the run was quickly reversed.

The Street Singer played for 10 months and 360 performances in London to such effect that Lee Shubert made an offer to Mayer to export the whole production and cast bodily to New York. But leading man Welchman was preparing one of his periodic ventures as producer/star of a fourth-rate light opera, and that and other factors sunk the proposal. *The Street Singer* headed, instead, for the British provinces and there over the next half-dozen years it kept up a fairly constant presence in the face of the first famous barrage of Broadway musicals, a barrage which had probably already helped shorten its town life. It also followed the bulk of the most successful shows from both sides of the Atlantic to Australia where Gladys Moncrieff was starred as Yvonne alongside Arthur Stigant (François), Noël Leyland (Bonni) and Claude Flemming (Armand). It moved out of Sydney after a good seven weeks to make way for Gershwin's *Primrose,* and made its way to Melbourne (Theatre Royal 24 October 1925) where it played for two months as part of a satisfactory Australian life.

In America the show was not seen, only its title. The title *The Street Singer* had been previously used for a 1905 touring musical drama of the sentimental type, and it was now used again, in 1929, for a musical written by Edgar Smith, Graham John and composers Niclas Kempner and Sam Timberg (Shubert Theater, New York 17 September 1929) in which for the umpteenth time in recent years the heroine of the title (Queenie Smith) ended up a theatre star. For once, this time, it wasn't at the *Ziegfeld Follies* but rather the Folies-Bergère. The Busby Berkeley production emphasized dancing and glamor in a show which, like its English equivalent, was rather after its time but which nevertheless had a good run of 191 performances.

Australia: Her Majesty's Theatre, Sydney 4 July 1925

STREISAND, Barbra [ROSEN, Barbara Joan] (b Brooklyn, NY, 24 April 1942). Protean woman of the entertainment world whose early career included stage and film musicals.

First seen on the New York revue stage in the 1961 off-Broadway *Another Evening with Harry Stoones* and on the musical-comedy stage as the secretary, Miss Marmelstein, in the musical *I Can Get It for You Wholesale,* the soon-to-be-celebrated recording star had a major Broadway hit playing the role of comedienne Fanny Brice in *Funny Girl* (''People,'' ''I'm the Greatest Star,'' etc). A London repeat, cut short by pregnancy, marked Miss Streisand's last musical-stage appearance.

She subsequently appeared on film in the starring roles of *Funny Girl* (1968, Academy Award), *Hello, Dolly!* (1969) and *On a Clear Day You Can See Forever* (1970), followed by a series of both comedy films (*Funny Lady,* etc) and more dramatic roles (*A Star Is Born, Yentl*) featuring some music, prior to turning her hand with notable success to film directing.

Biographies: Jordan, R: *I'm the Greatest Star* (Putnam, New York, 1975), Spada, J: *Barbra: The First Decade, the Films and Career of Barbra Streisand* (Citadel, Secaucus, NJ, 1974), Spada, J: *Streisand, Her Life* (Crown, New York, 1995), Zec, D, Fowles, A: *Barbra* (St Martin's Press, New York, 1981), Considine, S: *Barbra Streisand* (Delacorte Press, New York, 1985), Carrick, P: *Barbra Streisand* (Hale, London, 1991), Kimbrell, J: *Barbra: An Actress Who Sings* (2 vols) (Branden, Boston, 1999), etc

STREITMANN, Carl (b Vienna, 8 May 1858; d Vienna, 29 October 1937). Strapping-voiced tenor singer and actor who had a memorable career in the musical theatre.

Carl Streitmann studied medicine before turning to the stage and becoming an actor at Pressburg, at the Wiener Stadttheater and in small musical roles at the Carltheater (Affaroth in Suppé's *Der Teufel auf Erden,* de Mérignac in *Der kleine Herzog* 1878, t/o Pomponnet in *La Fille de Madame Angot* 1878, Josef, Casimir's butler in *Der grosse Casimir* 1879, Scharbel in *La Marjolaine* 1879, t/o Briddidick in *Hundert Jungfrauen* 1879, Riflos in *Der Gaskogner* 1881, etc). He followed this with a further Operettic engagement in Meiningen before being engaged, at the age of 24, as an opera singer in Prague.

The operatic episode did not last. In 1885 Streitmann returned to Vienna and, in August of the year, he made his debut at the Theater an der Wien, taking over as Caramello in *Eine Nacht in Venedig.* He quickly became the theatre's leading tenor, creating a handful of new roles in each of the next three seasons (Sándor Barinkay in *Der Zigeunerbaron,* Henri de Villeneuve in *Der Viceadmiral,* Prinz Julius in *Der Hofnarr,* Armin in *Simplicius*), to add to star parts in the reprises of the theatre's most successful pieces (Eisenstein from 1887, when still in his twenties, Umberto in *Der lustige Krieg,* Symon in *Der Bettelstudent,* etc). In 1888 he left the Theater an der Wien and moved once more to the Carltheater to appear as Rudolf in Suppé's *Die Jagd nach dem Glück,* and he played there as Baron Hellborn in *Ein Deutschmeister,* Oscar de Morande in *Colombine,* Nanki-Poo in *Der Mikado,* the Brazilian in *Pariser Leben* and Azalea in *Tulipatan* before again moving on, this time to make an extended visit to America.

There, between 1889 and 1891 he was starred at the German-language Amberg Theater—where he was seen as Barinkay, Symon, Eisenstein, de Villeneuve, Caramello, Rudolf and Nanki-Poo as well as in *Mignon, Die sieben Schwaben* (Otmar), Julius Hopp's *Morilla,* Zamara's *Der Doppelgänger,* et al—and in the other German houses of the union (Grand Opera House, Chicago, etc). In 1891–92 he made a single appearance on the English-language stage when he took the role of Chevalier Franz von Bernheim in the highly successful Broadway production of Audran's *La Cigale et le fourmi.*

On returning to Vienna he once again joined the company at the Theater an der Wien and, apart from a period spent at the Carltheater between 1902 and 1905, he played there and at the same management's Raimundtheater for virtually all of the next 20 years, repeating his famous roles and playing such other or new parts as Fodor in *Der Millionen-Onkel* (1892), Ferdinand in *Fürstin Ninetta* (1893), Bryk in a revival of *Carneval in Rom,* Armin in the revised *Simplicius,* Fürst Roderich in *Der Obersteiger* (1894), Mirko von Gradinaz in *Jabuka* (1894), Prinz Dietrich von der Pfalz in *Der Probekuss* (1894), Rodolfo in *Die Chansonette* (1895), Jim in *Der goldene Kamerad* (1895), Botho von Wendt in *Waldmeister* (1895), Gaston Catusse in *General Gogo* (1896), Graf Edward in *Der Wunderknabe* (1896), Émile Previllier in Verő's *Der Löwenjäger* (1896), Egon in Leo Held's *Die Schwalben,* Erwin von Sleiwitz in *Die Blumen-Mary,* Capitaine Robert in *Die Göttin der Vernunft* (1897), Graf Julius Hardt in *Die Küchen-Comtesse* (1898), Dr Oskar von Pendl in *Der Dreibund* (1898), Otmar in a revival of *Die sieben Schwaben,* St Raymond in *Der Blondin von Namur* (1898), Georges Duménil in *Der Opernball,* Henri in *Katze und Maus* (1898), Anatole de Beaupersil in *Ihre Excellenz* (1899), Leonello in *Ein durchgeganges Mädel* (*A Runaway Girl*), Raleigh in *Die Strohwitwe* (1899, Berlin 1900), Prinz von Cypern in *Die Stiefmama* (1900), Hermann in a revival of *Leichte Kavallerie* and Florestan in *Brigitte* (*Véronique,* 1900).

In his period at the Carltheater his new roles included Milosch in *Der Rastelbinder* (1902), Meridan in *Der*

Glückliche (1903), Manolle Ritschano in the revived *Apajune der Wassermann* (1903), Léonardo y Gomez in *Madame Sherry* (1903), Metello in *Der Mameluck* (1903), Amphytrion in *Der Göttergatte* (1904), Fred in *Der Schätzmeister* (1904) and Rafael Garrucci in *Der Polizeichef* (1905), before he returned to the Theater an der Wien, picking up as Jimmy Blackwell in *Vergeltsgott* and as Nicola in *Der Rebell* (1905).

He succeeded for a long period to the role of Camille de Rosillon (*Die lustige Witwe*) and later to Louis Treumann's part of Fredy in *Die Dollarprinzessin,* introduced Adhemar Ricardon in *Der Mann mit den drei Frauen* (1908) and Major Alexius Spiridoff in *Der tapfere Soldat* (1908) and appeared at the Raimundtheater and/or Theater an der Wien as Eisenstein, Barinkay, Symon and Pluto (*Orphée aux enfers*), as well as playing repeats of his Camille and Fredy. In 1909, past the age of 50, he celebrated his 1,000th performance in the role of Barinkay at the Raimundtheater, and he continued there in *Die arme Lori, Jabuka* (Mirko), *Die schöne Galathée* (Pygmalion) and *Das süsse Mädel* (Hans), before moving to the Bürgertheater to take over the part of Hubertus von Murner in *Der Frauenfresser* from Fritz Werner at its 148th night.

He continued through the following years to play Barinkay, Camille de Rosillon and Eisenstein, took a turn at playing Schubert in *Das Dreimäderlhaus* (1916) during the long run of that piece, created *Bruder Leichtsinn* (1917, Graf Fabrice Dunoir) and *Die schöne Mama* (1921) at the Bürgertheater, took over in *Die Herzogin von Chicago* in 1928 and celebrated his 74th birthday by appearing as Eisenstein at the Raimundtheater. The Theater an der Wien marked his 80th birthday as well, with a performance of *Die Fledermaus,* but this one was posthumous.

His sister **Rosa STREITMANN** (b Vienna, 21 February 1857; d Vienna, 30 July 1937) made her debut in the theatre as a ballet dancer, but her small well-produced voice and attractive personality soon won her principal roles and she went on to establish herself as one of the most important soubrette performers of her time. She made her debut as a singing actress in 1876 as Rose Michon in a revival of *Schönröschen* (*La Jolie Parfumeuse*) at the Carltheater, and played thereafter in *Flotte Bursche* (Brand), *Leichte Kavallerie* (Dorothea), *Margot die reiche Bäckerin* (1877, the page Ravannes), as Spadi in *Prinz Methusalem,* Isabella in Suppé's *Der Teufel auf Erden,* Jeannette in *Jeanne, Jeannette et Jeanneton* and Hanne in Brandl's short comic opera *Der verfallene Mauer* (1878). Her status as ''principal girl'' was confirmed when she was featured in Gallmeyer's role of Regina in a revival of *La Princesse de Trébizonde* (1878), as Caroline in *Niniche* (1878) and as the Herzogin von Parthenay in *Der kleine Herzog* (*Le Petit Duc,* 1878) and she appeared as Ninetta in *Der grosse Casimir,* as Aveline in *Marjolaine,* created the leading juvenile roles of Fiametta in *Boccaccio* (1879) and René Dufaure in *Donna Juanita* (1880) and starred in Judic's role of Anna in *Papas Frau* before departing to join the opposition Theater an der Wien.

There, she was given some fine roles (in mostly fine shows) including Louise in *Musketiere in Damenstift,* Else in *Der lustige Krieg,* Virginie in *Die Jungfrau von Belleville* (1881), Beatrix in *Tag und Nacht,* Anne Marie in *Ein süsses Kind* (1882), Ciboletta in the Viennese production of *Eine Nacht in Venedig* (1883), Sora in *Gasparone* (1884), the page, Jerome, in *Der Marquis von Rivoli* (1884), Rosette in *Der Feldprediger* (1884), Clapotte in *Zwillinge* (1885), Rosita in *Gillette de Narbonne* and Regina in the 1885 revival of *La Princesse de Trébizonde* before, though not yet 40, disappearing from the Viennese playbills.

STRIKE UP THE BAND Musical play in 2 acts by Morrie Ryskind based on a libretto by George S Kaufman. Lyrics by Ira Gershwin. Music by George Gershwin. Times Square Theater, New York, 14 January 1930.

Strike Up the Band was a preliminary attempt by Kaufman and the Gershwins to get into the openly burlesque-political stride which they hit more accurately soon after in *Of Thee I Sing.* An anti-war, anti-politics, anti-business, anti-anyone-rich-or-in-power saga, it followed what happens when Switzerland and America go to war over import duties on cheese: everyone makes such a nice profit on both sides that, when it is all over, the Americans arrange another fun war against Russia. The score included lots of comi/bitter and eye-pecking pieces—including the martially mocking title song—as well as the reused and very contrasting ''The Man I Love,'' originally included in the out-of-town score of *Lady, Be Good!* and subsequently dance-band fodder around the world.

The show was produced at Long Branch, New Jersey, under the management of Edgar Selwyn on 27 August 1927, directed by R H Burnside, designed by Norman Bel Geddes, with a company including Herbert Corthell (Fletcher), Vivian Hart (Joan), Roger Pryor (Jim), Lew Hearn (Colonel Holmes), Jimmie Savo (George Spelvin) and Edna May Oliver (Mrs Draper) and with Max Hoffman jr leading the title number as Timothy Harper. After two weeks it was abandoned.

Selwyn, however, did not give up on the show and in the 1929–30 season he remounted a rewritten version, still under the title of *Strike Up the Band.* Kaufman's libretto had had its bitterest bits sandpapered down with comedy by Morrie Ryskind, who had framed the whole piece as a dream, and it now pinpointed the rather more frivolous product of chocolate as the cause of war. Half a dozen numbers retained from the old score (including the title march, but not ''The Man I Love'' which had by now become too well known) were supplemented by a baker's dozen of new ones by the brothers Gershwin, including ''I've Got a Crush on You'' rescued from the flop *Treasure Girl.*

Chocolate manufacturer Horace J Fletcher (Dudley Clements) tries to persuade America to go to war with Switzerland to boost his business, and even offers to pay for the war as long as it is named after him. Jim Townsend (Jerry Goff) who is engaged to Joan Fletcher (Margaret Schilling) finally blackmails the businessman into turning pacifist, but America is already at war and, with the Swiss defeated, is happily preparing to have a caviar war against Russia as the curtain falls. Popular comedian Bobby Clark as ''The Unofficial Spokesman'' (a faceless politician who prefigures Throttlebottom in *Of Thee I Sing*), singing gleefully about ''If I Were President,'' and a megastar of earlier days, Blanche Ring, were included in the cast in less plotworthy roles; Doris Carson and Gordon Smith sang ''I've Got a Crush on You'' and the principal juveniles did prettily with ''Soon,'' a number developed from a couple of lines in *Strike Up the Band* Mark I; whilst Red Nichols's Band, including a lineup of jazz royalty from Benny Goodman and Gene Krupa to Glenn Miller, Jimmy Dorsey and Jack Teagarden, gave their all to the title number.

Strike Up the Band lasted 191 performances and then called it a day, but it is regularly recalled to memory by those commentators who go mad for a mention of anything just a whiff political in their musical theatre. Its title song remains the one original piece of the score in the current repertoire, where it is now performed, like Gilbert's ''When Britain Really Ruled the Waves,'' with every ounce of its satiric intent washed away, as a genuine, patriotic march.

The show, subtitled *Cheese!,* was given a tardy European showing in 1999 (14 May, ad Stefan Bachmann, Franz Wittenbrink) at the Theater Basel. The improvements made to Gershwin's lines included an exhortation to ''piss on the Swiss.''

Recording: complete (Elektra-Nonsuch)

STRITCH, Elaine (b Detroit, Mich, 2 February 1925). Comico-musical belter who belted herself into an interesting rasp in later years.

Miss Stritch had her first Broadway assignments in the revue *Angel in the Wings* (1947, ''Civilization'') and as the newspaperwoman, Melba, in the 1952 revival of *Pal Joey,* before she took over the role of Mrs Sally Adams in the national tour of *Call Me Madam.* She returned to New York to play Peggy Porterfield in the 1954 revival of *On Your Toes,* played her first straight Broadway role in *Bus Stop* (1955), and created her first Broadway musical role as musical-comedy-star-turned-film-actress Maggie Harris in *Goldilocks* (1958).

She had a personal success when she was upped from second lead to star as part of the on-the-road rewriting of Noël Coward's *Sail Away* (1961), and she went on to deliver ''Why Do the Wrong People Travel?'' and ''Useless Useful Phrases'' to Broadway and London in the character of cruise-hostess Mimi Paragon. She subsequently appeared as Anna Leonowens (*The King and I*), Ruth (*Wonderful Town* City Center, 1967) and as Vera Charles and later Mame Dennis in *Mame,* in a schedule which mixed musical- and straight-theatre appearances, before creating her next major role as the loud, nailfile-tongued Joanne in *Company* (1970), performing ''The Ladies Who Lunch'' in what were now becoming corncrake tones.

Ms Stritch settled for some time in London, appearing in the West End theatre in Neil Simon's *The Gingerbread Lady* and Tennessee Williams's *Small Craft Warnings* and top-billed with Donald Sinden in a successful British television series, *Two's Company,* but she introduced no further musical roles to add to the three she had created in America, before returning there in 1985. She appeared as Hattie in the gala concert performance of *Follies* in New York in 1985, and was seen on the Broadway stage again only in 1993 as a parted-up Parthy Ann in *Show Boat.*

STROUSE, Charles [Louis] (b New York, 7 June 1928). The most prolific musical-stage composer of the modern age who hit it good and even very good on several occasions.

After a thorough schooling in classical music, Strouse began a songwriting collaboration with lyricist Lee Adams in 1950, a collaboration which led first to a series of published songs, special material for television and nightclub performers and, from 1954, contributions to revue. From writing for a summer resort in the Adirondacks, they progressed to supplying their efforts to New York where they placed additional material in Ben Bagley's *The Littlest Revue* (1956) and *Shoestring '57,* in *The Ziegfeld Follies of 1956* and *Catch a Star* before joining a third young habitué of summer camp and the off-Broadway revue, Michael Stewart, to write a full-scale musical.

Bye Bye Birdie (1960), which kidded the newish rock-'n'-roll craze, won its authors a Tony Award, rucked up a 607-performance Broadway run, and proved a sizeable and enduring international success (''Kids,'' ''Put on a Happy Face,'' ''A Lot of Livin' to Do''). Strouse and Adams followed up with the scores for seven further musicals over the next two decades or so. Of these, *Applause,* a musicalization of the film *All About Eve* and its source novel, which starred Lauren Bacall in a first-rate Broadway-Big-Momma role, proved the most generally successful (Tony Award), whilst New York also welcomed a musical version of the play *Golden Boy* with Sammy Davis jr featured as a black singing version of Clifford Odets's ill-fated Italian boxer.

All American (1962), with a libretto by Mel Brooks and a cast headed by Ray Bolger, and a musical version of the Superman comic strips (predating the widely publicized modern films of the same subject) both found some adherents but insufficient audiences, but an effort to bring a singing, dancing Queen Victoria to the London stage in *I and Albert* (something that the censor had forbidden Rodgers and Hammerstein to do) foundered nastily. Their later shows, including an attempt to mount a sequel to *Bye Bye Birdie,* were first-week failures.

In the meanwhile, however, Strouse had provided the music to the lyrics of Martin Charnin for what would turn out to be his most successful show and score to date, the musical version of the Little Orphan Annie comic strip, *Annie* (''Tomorrow,'' ''You're Never Fully Dressed without a Smile,'' ''Easy Street,'' ''Little Girls''). Niftily pitched at just the right level between ahhh! and yrrchh!, *Annie* proved to be one of the most internationally successful musical plays of its period, but in spite of a regular series of new shows (and several pieces, such as a musical about Bojangles Robinson and a new piece based on Anouilh's *Thieves' Carnival,* which were announced but which did not make it to the stage) in the years that followed, Strouse did not succeed in finding another success.

An affecting musical version of the Daniel Keyes novel *Charlie and Algernon,* originally mounted in Edmonton, Canada, failed to find appreciation either in Britain or America, a collaboration with Alan Jay Lerner on an awkwardly updated musical version of *Idiot's Delight* was a quick failure, whilst a ''cabaret musical'' based on the life and the autobiography of New York mayor Ed Koch played 198 performances off-Broadway and 70 on. Another full-sized Broadway musical, *Rags,* lasted but four performances. There was no more success for a children's piece about a crocodile called *Lyle,* based on Bernard Waber's already musicalized *The House on 88th Street,* which faded away in disarray at London's Lyric, Hammersmith. The same house had earlier given an almost metropolitan home to a little Strouse operetta, *The Nightingale,* a version of the Hans Andersen *The Emperor's Nightingale,* previously produced at Buxton and in a juvenile theatre in New York.

Undeterred by the failure of *Bring Back Birdie,* Strouse also collaborated on a musequel to his other principal success, *Annie,* which was christened movie-style as *Annie 2.* It failed to reach Broadway at its first attempt and was later brought back, rewritten bootlessly, to try again. In the meanwhile he had seen *Nick and Nora,* a musical based on the *Thin Man* films and yet another piece with all the right names attached to it, also go down as a quick flop, leaving *Bye Bye Birdie* and *Annie*—and, one notch down, *Applause*—to represent Strouse in the list of enduring musicals.

In 1978 Strouse mounted a compilation show of his own material at off-Broadway's Ballroom-off-Broadway under the title of *By Strouse* (1 February) which played for a run of 156 performances.

Strouse and Adams also authored a television musical *Alice in Wonderland, or What's a Nice Kid Like You Doing in a Place Like This* (1966).

1960 **Bye Bye Birdie** (Lee Adams/Michael Stewart) Martin Beck Theater 14 April
1962 **All American** (Adams/Mel Brooks) Winter Garden Theater 19 March
1964 **Golden Boy** (Adams/Clifford Odets, William Gibson) Majestic Theater 20 October
1966 **It's a Bird . . . It's a Plane . . . It's Superman** (Adams/David Newman, Robert Benton) Alvin Theater 29 March
1970 **Applause** (Adams/Adolph Green, Betty Comden) Palace Theater 30 March
1971 **Six** Cricket Playhouse 12 April
1972 **I and Albert** (Adams/Jay Presson Allen) Piccadilly Theatre, London 6 November
1977 **Annie** (Martin Charnin/Thomas Meehan) Alvin Theater 21 April
1978 **Flowers for Algernon** (David Rogers) Citadel Theater, Edmonton, Canada 12 December; Queen's Theatre, London 14 June 1979
1978 **A Broadway Musical** (Adams/William F Brown) Lunt-Fontanne Theater 21 December
1981 **Bring Back Birdie** (Adams/Stewart) Martin Beck Theater 5 March
1982 **The Nightingale** First All Childrens Theater 25 April
1983 **Dance a Little Closer** (Alan Jay Lerner) Minskoff Theater 11 May
1985 **Mayor** (Warren Leigh) Top of the Gate 13 May
1986 **Rags** (Stephen Schwartz/Joseph Stein) Mark Hellinger Theater 21 August
1988 **Lyle** (Bernard Waber ad) Lyric Theatre, Hammersmith, London 3 December
1989 **Charlotte's Web** Wilmington, Del 17 February
1990 **Annie 2** (Charnin/Meehan) Kennedy Center, Washington, DC 4 January
1991 **Nick and Nora** (Richard Maltby jr/Arthur Laurents) Marquis Theater 8 December
1992 **Annie Warbucks** (revised *Annie 2*) Marriott's Lincolnshire Theater, Chicago 9 February

STUART, Leslie [BARRETT, Thomas Augustine] (b Southport, 15 March ?1863; d Richmond, Surrey, 27

March 1928). British songwriter who made his musical-comedy mark as the composer of *Florodora.*

The son of an Irish cabinet-maker, the young Leslie Stuart spent some of his earliest professional musical moments as a pianist at Manchester's Ship Inn and then, from the age of 14, for seven years as church organist at St John's Roman Catholic Cathedral in Salford and a further seven at the Church of the Holy Name in Manchester. At the same time, he gradually became known as a writer of popular songs, ranging from such heroic stuff as "The Bandolero" for the popular baritone who called himself Signor Foli, to a veritable flood of the then-popular coon songs, many of which were introduced by Eugene Stratton, the supreme blackface singer of the time. The most successful and enduring of these was "Lily of Laguna," but Stuart had notable successes with "Little Dolly Daydream," "Sweetheart May," "Is Your Mamie Always with You?" and with a song fabricated from a march which he had written to celebrate the opening of the Manchester Ship Canal and later relyricked under the title "Soldiers of the Queen." Stuart also became for a while a concert impresario in the Manchester area, presenting Paderewski in his first British appearances and opera's Fanny Moody in concert.

His earliest theatrical writing was done for the Manchester theatre, where he provided songs and incidental music for the local pantomimes which boasted some of the biggest British names in their bills. In the 1896 Liverpool *Aladdin* he supplied Lottie Collins with "The Girl on the Rand-dan-dan," "I Went with Papa to Paris" and "Is Your Mamie Always with You?" In the late 1890s Stuart also had individual numbers interpolated into a number of West End and touring musicals. The most notable was the highly successful "Lousiana Lou," which had already been published by Francis, Day and Hunter (who would remain Stuart's publishers throughout his career) and performed on the music halls before being picked up by Ellaline Terriss and inserted into the original production of *The Shop Girl* at the Gaiety Theatre, alongside Stuart's "The Little Mademoiselle."

When the *Trilby* craze hit London during the run of George Edwardes's *An Artist's Model* (1895, "The Military Model"), Stuart wrote and composed "Trilby Will Be True" for Maurice Farkoa to perform at Daly's Theatre, and he subsequently had songs used in *Baron Golosh, The Circus Girl* (1896, "She May Not Be That Sort of a Girl" for Louis Bradfield), the London version of the American musical *A Day in Paris* (1897, "The Goblin and the Fay"), Kiefert's *The Ballet Girl* (1897, "She's an English Girl," "I Never Saw a Girl Like That," "De Baby am Crying, Mommer Come"), *The Yashmak* (1897, "The Silly Old Man in the Moon") and the "American musical comedy" *The Muddle Up* (1900,

Plate 370. **Leslie Stuart**

"special musical numbers by"). He also provided the music-halls scenas *The Willow Pattern Plate* and *The Lily of Laguna* (1898) for the variety team the Sisters Hawthorne (Koster & Bial's Music Hall, etc), but it was not until 1899 that he completed his first full musical-comedy score.

Florodora, written in collaboration with London's most fashionable librettist, Owen Hall, and produced by neophyte producer Tom Davis at the Lyric Theatre in Shaftesbury Avenue, was a musical-comedy sensation. Its famous double sextet, "Tell Me, Pretty Maiden," became the most successful show tune of its time and the show itself, for which Stuart had provided a score ranging from the most traditional and beautiful of waltzes ("The Silver Star of Love," "The Fellow Who Might") to the more quirkily rhythmic and long-lined numbers which were his trademark, was a worldwide success, earning its composer an international theatrical reputation to add to that already secured by his songs.

Davis followed *Florodora* at the Lyric Theatre with a second Stuart/Hall musical *The Silver Slipper.* If its musical content seemed to be molded rather closely on the *Florodora* score, it nevertheless fulfilled the ''more of the same'' requirements opened by the extravagant success of the earlier show and *The Silver Slipper* had good runs in the West End and on Broadway, as well as being played in Hungarian in Budapest and in German in Berlin, where it was mounted at the Neues Königliches Opernhaus in repertoire with no less pieces than *Der Zigeunerbaron* and *Der Bettelstudent.* The composer had further show-successes in London, New York and on the national and international touring circuits with *The School Girl* (1903, ''My Little Canoe''), *The Belle of Mayfair* (1906, ''Come to St George's,'' ''In Montezuma'') and *Havana* (1908, ''Hello, People, Hello'') and George Edwardes, always on his toes to keep one step ahead of public taste, decided that Stuart was the man to replace the well-loved and well-used Ivan Caryll/Lionel Monckton combination at the Gaiety Theatre.

However, Stuart did not in the end turn out a Gaiety musical to follow *Havana,* but instead wrote the score for *Captain Kidd,* a Seymour Hicks piece which the scavenging actor had adapted from the American farce *The Dictator.* His undistinguished songs added nothing to a weak piece which lasted but a month on the stage, in spite of the drawing power of Hicks and his wife, Ellaline Terriss, and Stuart was faced with his first and only flop, a flop so complete that his publishers did not even print up the score.

1911 saw his return to the Gaiety with the reasonably successful *Peggy,* and in the same year he finally composed his one and only Broadway score—something which had been announced by American managers on a number of occasions since *Florodora* had become the hottest hit on the New York stage—with a useful if hardly out-of-the-ordinary vehicle for Elsie Janis as *The Slim Princess,* an anorexic Ruritanian lass who goes to America for a husband because slim girls are fashionable there. The score to *The Slim Princess* was, in true Broadway fashion, dotted with non-Stuart interpolations, but by this stage the composer was no longer in a position to object to a practice which he had fought energetically and sometimes legally throughout the 10 years of his time at the theatrical top, ever since he had discovered Paul Rubens's songs being shoveled into his very first show, *Florodora,* at an early stage of preparation.

Sometimes, at the time when he had the weight of his *Florodora* fame behind him, Stuart had succeeded in stopping this time-dishonored practice—a practice which was not dictated simply by artistic motives but often by financial ones, as publishers and wealthy second-rate songwriters would pay producers for exposure for their songs, especially in a show by a ''hot'' composer like Stuart. Similarly, he had succeeded from time to time in parts of his fight in Britain and in America against music piracy and on behalf of firmer national and international copyright laws. But, by 1911, his personal and, most particularly, his financial life were in the doldrums and later the bankruptcy courts, the days of his style of music were rapidly coming to an end under the influence of more modern dance rhythms and, at the age of 45, his career in the musical theatre had effectively come to an end.

Stuart interpolated a number into Broadway's *The Queen of the Movies* (*Die Kino-Königin,* ''Whistle'') and another into *The Kiss Waltz* (*Liebeswalzer,* ''Belle of Vienne'') and composed some unexceptional songs for a 1915 revival of *Florodora,* but his last contributions seem to have been, against all his expressed principles, songs for the provincial manager Mark Blow to interpolate into his tour of *Toto* (1919), and for the short-lived *Jenny* (1922) at the Empire Theatre. In his later years he continued to write, and although he would not show his final work, *Nina,* to anyone, both it and *The Girl from Nysa* were mooted for production both before and after his death without ever coming to the stage. When his gambling debts outweighed his royalties from the still-lively *Florodora,* Stuart appeared in variety performing his most famous songs at the piano.

Stuart's stage works fell somewhere between the very light song-based shows of the Gaiety Theatre and the more substantial fare played at Daly's, but although the concerted music of his shows—in which he was aided by the West End's master journeyman musician, Carl Kiefert—was highly effective, the greatest success of each and every one of them was in their individual songs, many of which became widely and enduringly popular.

His brother, Stephen BARRETT (b Manchester 1855), originally a cabinet-maker but later ''entertainer, songwriter, singer and businessman'' and the manager of the artistes department at the publishing house of Francis, Day and Hunter, wrote songs under the name of **Lester BARRETT,** while his daughter, **May Leslie STUART** [Mary Catherine BARRETT] (b Salford, 4 December 1886), appeared on the musical stage as Beauty in *Pinkie and the Fairies* (1909), in *The Count of Luxembourg* (1911, Jacqueline) and *A Country Girl* revivals, and as a last-minute replacement for Ada Reeve as Lady Holyrood in the 1915 *Florodora* before seeing out her career in variety. The first of her husbands was musical-comedy actor Cecil Cameron, son of the celebrated Violet Cameron.

1899 **Florodora** (Ernest Boyd-Jones, Paul Rubens/Owen Hall) Lyric Theatre 11 November

1901 **The Silver Slipper** (W H Risque/Hall) Lyric Theatre 1 June

1903 **The School Girl** (Charles H Taylor/Henry Hamilton, Paul Potter) Prince of Wales Theatre 9 May

1906 **The Belle of Mayfair** (Basil Hood, Charles H E Brookfield) Vaudeville Theatre 11 April

1908 **Havana** (Adrian Ross/Graham Hill, George Grossmith jr) Gaiety Theatre 25 April

1910 **Captain Kidd** (Ross/Seymour Hicks) Wyndham's Theatre 12 January

1910 **The Slim Princess** (Henry Blossom, George Ade) Star Theater, Buffalo 5 September; Globe Theater, New York 2 January 1911

1911 **Peggy** (C H Bovill/Grossmith) Gaiety Theatre 4 March

A STUBBORN CINDERELLA Musical comedy in 3 acts by Frank R Adams and Will M Hough. Music by Joseph E Howard. Princess Theater, Chicago, 1 June 1908; Broadway Theater, New York, 25 January 1909.

Adams, Hough and Howard, the most successful purveyors of musical comedy to the turn-of-the-century Chicago stage, carried on their run of unbroken success with this curiously straggly piece in which an aristocratic Scots lady (Sallie Fisher) gets together with a sculptor called Mac (John Barrymore) who tells her the tale of Cinderella whilst their train is landlocked by a slip. Howard and his clever lyricists provided several pretty and imaginative songs including the waltz finale ''When You First Kiss the Last Girl You Love,'' an Anna Held-ish piece declaring ''Don't Be Cross with Me (for I'm having lots of trouble with my smile),'' another in which the hero addressed the heavens with ''Don't Be Anybody's Moon But Mine,'' booking the moon to shine on his smooching, and a comical ''What's the Use (of sleeping, when there's things to do instead).'' There were several incidental ballets, scenes set in California and including an orange fête, and a lot of pre-production buzz about the new young leading man, and the Princess Theater company kept the piece on stage for more than three hundred performances in their hometown before producer Mort Singer took them east. *A Stubborn Cinderella* ran 88 performances on Broadway, the most New York would ever allow one of the ''foreign'' musicals from the Chicago team, but it toured happily and long enough thereafter to compensate for Broadway's disdain of its charms and those of the young John Barrymore.

STUBEL, Lori (b Vienna; d Vienna, 21 June 1922). Well-traveled Viennese soubrette who matured into a good character lady.

The career of Lori Stubel is a little hard to decipher in retrospect, largely due to the fact that she had a sister, **Jenny STUBEL** (b Vienna; d Kierling, 19 August 1893), who led a parallel career in often similar roles, and who had a similar penchant for travel. It seems, however, that it was Lori who worked as a dancer in the corps de ballet of the Hofoper, then from 1867 as a dancer and singer at the Harmonietheater, and who subsequently became a member of the company at the Carltheater where she won good soubrette roles, taking over from Gallmeyer as Regina in *Die Prinzessin von Trapezunt* (1872), playing Clairette in *Cannebas* (1872) and Prinz Leo in *Confusius IX* (1872), Eglantine in *Hundert Jungfrauen* (1873), Cascadetto in *Der Seufzerbrucke* (1873) and Annette in *La Jolie Parfumeuse* (1874). She then, apparently, began her travels, playing in Germany (Countess Cameroni in *La Petite Mademoiselle*) and with her own company throughout Italy (Florence, Rome, Genoa, Naples, Milan, Venice, Trieste), returning (it seems) to Vienna to take over the title role in *Prinz Methusalem* at the Carltheater before in 1882 turning up in London (this was definitely her) where she was cast alongside Constance Loseby, Henry Walsham and Allen Thomas in what was claimed to be ''her original role'' (it wasn't) as Else in *The Merry War.* Her comedy proved a little near the knuckle for the Alhambra audience, and when they shouted her ''vulgar'' antics down she thumbed her nose at them. She vanished ''ill'' from the Alhambra cast list shortly afterwards and a few weeks later the theatre burned down. At some stage, too, (she says) she appeared in France. ''Frln Stubel'' next turned up in 1884 playing Possen at the Theater in der Josefstadt, but she (Lori, specified) was soon on the move again, and in 1885 she made her first appearance in America (16 November) appearing at the Thalia Theater in the title role of *Boccaccio,* as Pauline in Mannstädt and Brandl's Posse *Der Walzerkönig* and as Fanchette Michel in *Der Seekadett,* all pieces from Jenny's repertoire at the Carltheater.

Eventually both the soubretting and the traveling came to an end, and in 1894 Lori Stubel (the playbills had, at last, started giving full names—unnecessarily in this case, for Jenny was now dead) joined the Theater an der Wien company as a character lady. Over the next four years she appeared in *Der Obersteiger* (1894, Elfriede, announced as her house debut), *Husarenblut* (1894, Frau Kendler), *Kneisl & Co* (1894, Frau Stowasser), *Der Probekuss* (1894, Die Obersthofmeisterin), *Die Chansonette* (1895, Miss Box), *Der Bettelstudent* (t/o Palmatica), *Die Karlsschülerin* (1895, Generalin von Papperitz), *Waldmeister* (1895, t/o Malvine), *General Gogo* (1896, Miss Kopkins), *Der Löwenjäger* (1896, Dorothee), *Die Blumen-Mary* (1897, Bessie Thomson), *Die Schwalben* (1897, Emitschka), *Die Küchen-Comtesse* (1898, Miss Nelly), *Der Dreibund* (1898, Sabine von Drachenfels) and *Der Opernball* (1898, Madame Beaubuisson), before retiring from the stage.

Jenny Stubel had the shorter but seemingly better-quality career of the two sisters. It is probably she who is the ''Frln Stubel'' who appeared in what were simply chorus tights-roles as Fernand in *Die Wilderer,* Sigefroi in *Heloïse und Abälard* (1873) and as a Japanese chorine, Cili, in *Die Japanesin* (1874) before winning promotion to the title role of Wilhelmine in *Die Perle der Wascherinnen* (1875). It is undoubtedly she who was—several years before her elder sister—playing at New York's Thalia Theater in 1881–82 as Haiderose (Serpolette) in *Die Glocken von Corneville,* Bettina in *La Mascotte,* Natalitza in *Apajune der Wassermann,* Regerl in *Das verwunschene Schloss,* in *Die Fledermaus,* as Fanny Rehborstl in *Der Chevalier de San Marco* and as the vocally demanding Violetta in *Der lustige Krieg.* Jenny Stubel then went home to join the Carltheater company as principal soubrette and between 1882 and 1883 she played title roles in *Javotte* and *Kosiki,* Girola in *Drei Schwarzmantel,* in *Boccaccio* and as Fanchette Michel in *Der Seekadett* under the short management of Friedrich Strampfer, before she went off with her boyfriend, tenor Karl Drucker, to Germany. She was engaged as lead soubrette at the Walhalla-Theater for a couple of seasons, where she appeared (though some journals credited it to Lori) in the house's triumphant production of Genée's *Nanon,* then moved back to the Carltheater to play Danilowna in *Der Jagdjunker* and Eurydice in *Orphée aux enfers* (1886), before returning to Germany (1887) to take up a post at the head of the company at Berlin's Friedrich-Wilhelmstädtisches Theater. There she appeared as *Madame Favart,* Manuela in *Farinelli,* Frau von Bonton in *Berlin in Wort und Bild,* Tarcha in Louis Roth's *Die Lieder des Mirza Schaffy,* (1887), Arsena in *Der Zigeunerbaron,* as Meta (ie, Phoebe) in *Der Königsgardist* (*The Yeomen of the Guard*), as the Tessa of Berlin's original *Die Gondoliere,* as Nanon and in other leading roles until 1892, her final illness and death the following year.

Just to make things even more indecipherable, there was a third singing Stubel sister, Ludmilla or Emilie (known as Milly), who also went on the operettic stage. She didn't travel about, she made a career apparently entirely in Berlin (unless, that is, she was the ''Frln Stubel'' with the legs at the Theater an der Wien in the early 1870s)—but she outdid her sisters thoroughly in newsworthiness. She was the companion of ''Johann Orth,'' otherwise Johann Nepomuk Salvator the abdicated Archduke of Austria and Prince of Tuscany, when he set out from Hamburg on a post-abdicatory yacht trip around the world in 1890. The lovers were never seen or heard from again. Millie also beat her two more talented sisters out in one other way, for she became the heroine of an opérette, the French pasticcio spectacular *Vienne chante et danse* (Théâtre du Châtelet, 1933), in which she was impersonated, in a grotesquely fictionalized version of her archducal love story, by Paulette Merval.

A fourth sister, Marie, apparently stuck to the nonmusical stage before becoming longtime wardrobe mistress at the Theater an der Wien.

THE STUDENT PRINCE [IN HEIDELBERG] Musical play in 2 acts by Dorothy Donnelly based on *Old Heidelberg* by Rudolf Bleichmann, a version of *Alt-Heidelberg* by Wilhelm Meyer-Förster. Lyrics by Dorothy Donnelly. Music by Sigmund Romberg. Jolson Theater, New York, 2 December 1924.

The well-known and long-loved *The Student Prince* was not the first musical to be based on Meyer-Förster's 1901 Studentenstück *Alt Heidelberg* (Berliner Theater 22 November). Lázsló Kun added a selection of student songs to the piece when it was produced as *Díakélet* at Budapest's Vígszínház (29 October 1904, ad: Miksa Marton; ly: Jenő Heltai), and a first full-scale musical, written by Alberto Collantuoni and composed by Ubaldo Pacchierotti, was produced in Milan in 1908 (*Eidelberga mia!*) and subsequently played at Vienna's Kaiser-Jubiläums-Stadttheater (Volksoper 12 February 1909).

The original play had been an international success, notably in America where, in spite of having a very limited Broadway life both as *Old Heidelberg* (1902) and as *Prince Karl* (1903), it became both a long-touring vehicle for popular actor Richard Mansfield as the Prince Karl-Heinrich who was to become ''the student prince'' and a 1915 D W Griffith film featuring Wallace Reid as the prince alongside Dorothy Gish, Erich von Stroheim and Karl Formes jr.

Dorothy Donnelly's American musical version stuck closely to the lines of the well-known play as the Prince, now called Karl-Franz (Howard Marsh), accompanied by his tutor Dr Engel (Greek Evans) and his pompous valet Lutz (George Hassell), left the cloistered life of his home court and headed off to Heidelberg University for an education in Latin and in life. We see little of the Latin, but his life quickly includes pretty Kathi (Ilse Marvenga), a waitress at his lodgings, to whom he vows eternal love before even a term is over. But Karl-Franz has presumed on his liberty. He is recalled home to the deathbed of his grandfather and ordered, for reasons of state, to wed Princess Margaret (Roberta Beatty). He tries desperately to hold off the end of the only brief period of youthful freedom he has known, but in the end he has to bid farewell to Kathi and follow his duty.

This Leháresque plot provided Romberg with many opportunities for romantic music, but the setting also gave him the chance to include any amount of virile Continental student songs and marches, and, indeed, the score of *The Student Prince* was made up almost entirely of these two styles of music, the traditional comic element of operetta being relegated to a very subsidiary place. It was, in fact, the masculine music of the piece which was its greatest triumph: Dr Engel reminiscing soaringly over the ''Golden Days'' of youth, Karl-Franz serenading the skies in what was to become perhaps the best-known Serenade since Schubert's (''overhead the moon is beaming . . .''), and the students raising their voices in the equally famous Drinking Song (''Drink, drink, drink''). Kathi had a lively showpiece, trilling above the massed male voices in ''Come Boys, Let's All Be Gay, Boys,'' and joined with Karl-Franz in the evening's big duet ''Deep in My Heart, Dear,'' a piece which was echoed in the gentler strains of the duo ''Just We Two'' shared by Margaret and Tarnitz, the man she would really have liked to marry had dynastic considerations not interfered.

The Student Prince had a difficult road to the stage. The Shuberts, for whom most of Romberg's previous work had been on flimsily built revusical pieces and botchings of foreign shows, had not expected their house composer to turn their old play into a big, florid operetta which featured a sad ending and a big, singing male chorus instead of wedding bells, a walk-down and a female and dancing chorus. At first Romberg got his way. The show went into production with his score intact, the unhappy ending intact and with the 40-strong male chorus he had demanded, all in matching costumes. It also went into production with Patti Harrold, a former *Irene* star, as its female lead.

Miss Harrold caused the first problem. One day she came to rehearsal and heard some other soprano singing her music. She apparently didn't wait to find out that Elsa Ersi was both Austrian and unavailable; she flamed, said her bit and she walked. The next contretemps came the moment the piece went on stage at the Apollo, Atlantic City, and Jake Shubert actually saw and heard those men, that music and the ending without a clinch. He started to try to fiddle with the show. When Romberg protested, a row ensued which ended with Shubert taking the composer's name off the billing and Romberg going to law. He won his suit in time to get back on the billboards before *The Student Prince* opened on Broadway to become not only the biggest success the Shuberts had had in years, but far and away the most important original musical they had or would ever produce.

The original production of *The Student Prince* ran for 608 performances and, before it closed, Shubert was already on the road with the first of what would soon become multiple, long-running touring companies. For some 20 years *The Student Prince* was a permanent fixture on the tour circuits in America and it remained a perennial favorite for decades thereafter. It reappeared on Broadway in 1931 (Majestic Theater 29 January) and again in 1943 (Broadway Theater 8 June) and in 1980 it was produced by the New York City Opera (29 August), which organization has been subsequently responsible for keeping the piece in view, most recently in its revival of 1993 (17 August).

In spite of its enormous success, however, the piece failed to export with the same success that the other two comparable hits of the era, *The Desert Song* and *Rose Marie,* achieved. France, where Meyer-Förster's *Vieil Heidelberg* had for many years been a favorite in the repertoire at the Odéon, and which welcomed the other two pieces largely, did not take up this work by a composer who otherwise found a wide welcome in the Paris theatre. A production at Berlin's Grosses Schauspielhaus in 1932 left little trace, and England rejected the show not once but twice. Produced at His Majesty's Theatre in London with several of the original cast, including Miss Marvenga who was starred opposite Allan Prior as Karl-Franz, it was poorly received and closed after three months and 96 performances whilst *Rose Marie* continued its triumphant progress at Drury Lane. A road tour convinced producer Edward Laurillard that the show had been unlucky, and he brought it back to the Piccadilly Theatre (7 November 1929) with Donald Mather now starring. This time it lasted 60 performances.

Australia, however, gave *The Student Prince* a much warmer welcome than Britain had done. The show played for nearly three months in Sydney, after which the Dutch soprano Beppi de Vries (Kathy) and James Liddy (Karl-Franz) featured in a splendid four-month Melbourne run (Her Majesty's Theatre 5 November 1927), before the show returned for a revival season in Sydney the following year (Her Majesty's Theatre 15 September 1928). It got a further showing in Melbourne in 1929 when it shared the public's attention with a concurrent run of a film version starring Ramon Novarro and Norma Shearer, and it was brought out again in 1940 by the ''New Royal Comic Opera Company,'' confirming a success which the show had found nowhere else outside America.

In 1944 the show was tried yet again, and yet again fruitlessly, in the West End (Stoll Theatre 23 May), and England, like the rest of the world, got its most appreciated glimpse of *The Student Prince* via the medium of film—the 1954 MGM picture in which the dashing Edmund Purdom and the voice of Mario Lanza at its peak at last established the show, the title and Romberg's score (botched with three numbers by Nicholas Brodszky) internationally.

Through the years, endless and often cheap tours of the popular operetta slightly tarnished the title of *The Student Prince* in America, much in the same way that they did with *Blossom Time* and *The Desert Song* and with the works of Ivor Novello in Britain. But John Hanson, the darkly tenor hero of many such British tours, had proved he could be a draw in the West End when a 1967 stopgap revival of *The Desert Song* had turned into a profitable long run, and he selected *The Student Prince* as his next vehicle. This sadly botched 1968 revival gave *The Student Prince* (with additional songs by Hanson) its longest London season, but it confirmed a creak-and-tat image for it which effectively finished it off as a revival prospect.

In 1974 the Heidelberg Festival produced a version of *The Student Prince,* with American tenor Erik Geisen starring, in the courtyard of Heidelberg castle, overlooking the well-preserved streets of the University city where the action of the play takes place. It has subsequently been performed regularly there, during the summer months.

Although it let such obvious libretto material as *Alt-Heidelberg* slip past, the Austrian musical theatre did, however, provide a before-the-Romberg-event musical-play sequel to *The Student Prince. Jung Heidelberg,* with a text by Carl Lindau and Leopold Krenn and a pasticcio score taken from the works of Carl Millöcker by Ernst Reiterer, followed the son of Karl-Franz to a happier ending with a suitable Princess in a production which top-billed Mizzi Zwerenz and Max Brod at Gabor Steiner's Venedig in Wien (9 July 1904). *Jung Heidelberg* was seen the following season both in Germany (Neues Königliches Opernhaus, Theater des Westens 1 July 1905) and in America, where it was played in the German-language theatre with Curt Weber and Mariesa Verena in the lead roles and Lina Abarbanell in breeches as Lieutenant Vogel.

UK: His Majesty's Theatre 3 February 1926; Australia: Empire Theatre, Sydney 16 July 1927; Germany: Grosses Schauspielhaus *Der Studentenprinz* 1932

Films: MGM 1927, 1954

Recordings: British tour/revival cast (Philips), Heidelberg cast recording (Kanon), film soundtrack (RCA), complete (TER), selections (Columbia, Capitol, RCA, Pye, Philips, WRC, etc)

STUDHOLME, Marie [LUPTON, Caroline Maria] (b Eccleshill, 10 September 1872; d London, 10 March 1930). Postcard beauty who played 20 years of musical-comedy juveniles.

After early appearances in *La Cigale, The Mountebanks* (1892, chorus) and *Haste to the Wedding* (1892, Anna Maria Maguire), pretty teenaged Marie Studholme rose up the cast list to take, take over and/or tour in good roles in some of the earliest Victorian musical comedies. She played Rhea Porter and covered Jenny McNulty as the Comtesse before taking over Violet Cameron's role of Ethel Sportington in *Morocco Bound* (1893), then took the tiny role of Gladys Stourton in *A Gaiety Girl* (1893) before being promoted to succeed Maud Hobson in the show's title role. She continued under George Edwardes's management, creating the small role of Jessie and succeeding star soubrette Letty Lind as Daisy in *An Artist's Model* (1895) in London and America (1896), toured as Molly in Edwardes's number one *Geisha* company (1896–97), played Gwendoline in *In Town* on the road and on Broadway (1897), toured as Dora in *The Circus Girl* (1898) and as Iris in *A Greek Slave* (1898–99) and returned to London to repeat her Alma in Edwardes's *Gaiety Girl* revival (1899). She then succeeded Violet Lloyd as the soubrette (Nora) of *The Messenger Boy* at the Gaiety, and had her first major London creation there in the leading juvenile role of Dora Selby in *The Toreador* (1901).

During the course of the run, she was succeeded by the rising Gertie Millar, which may have been why she ended up back on the road playing the title role of *San Toy* (1903), but she then returned to London to create the second juvenile role of Cicely Marchmont, alongside Edna May, in *The School Girl,* replaced Ethel Sydney as Josephine Zaccary in *The Orchid,* repeated her Molly in *The Geisha* revival and succeeded to the title role of *Lady Madcap* (Lady Betty). In 1906 she appeared as Alice in a revival of *Alice in Wonderland* at the Prince of Wales Theatre and then starred in *My Darling* in place of Ellaline Terriss (1907, Joy Blossom). She later played the title roles in such pieces as *Miss Hook of Holland* (1907–8 and 1909) and *My Mimosa Maid* (1908–9) on the road and appeared on the musical stage in South Africa before the approach of her 40th year ended an ingenue career of nearly 20 years which had spawned a vast number of picture postcards.

STYNE, Jule [STEIN, Julius Kerwin] (b England, 31 December 1905; d New York 20 September 1994).

The British-born Styne, who moved to America with his family at the age of eight, had a juvenile career as a classical pianist, but in his young adult years he switched his attention to dance-band music, playing piano and, during his university years in Chicago, leading his own group. He later worked as a vocal coach and arranger in New York and then in Hollywood, and gradually began placing songs in films. He had his first success, still as Julius Stein, with the number "Sunday" (w Chester Conn, Ned Miller, Benny Krueger) in 1926, but his next decade was spent largely as a piano player, both accompanying and coaching the new stars of Hollywood's singing films, rather than in writing.

His songwriting career did not take off until he had given up the piano playing and taken a post, first with Republic Pictures and then with Paramount, specifically as a composer. Now metamorphosed into Jule Styne, he teamed with lyricist Frank Loesser to produce a series of songs including "Since You" (*Sailors on Leave,* 1941) and "I Don't Want to Walk without You" as sung by Betty Jane Rhodes in *Sweater Girl* (1942), and then with Sammy Cahn for a prolific period which produced, amongst other successful numbers, "I've Heard That Song Before" (*Youth on Parade,* 1942), "The Victory

Polka'' (*Jam Session,* 1944), ''Thinking About the Wabash,'' ''There Goes That Song Again'' (*Carolina Blues,* 1944), ''I'll Walk Alone'' (*Follow the Boys,* 1944), ''And Then You Kissed Me,'' ''Come Out, Come Out Wherever You Are'' (*Step Lively,* 1944), Frank Sinatra's ''Saturday Night Is the Loneliest Night of the Week'' (1944), ''Can't You Read between the Lines,'' ''I Fall in Love Too Easily,'' ''What Makes the Sunset'' and ''The Charm of You'' (*Anchors Away,* 1945), ''Let It Snow!'' (1945), ''It's Been a Long, Long Time'' (*I'll Get By,* 1945), ''Five Minutes More'' (*Sweetheart of Sigma Chi,* 1946), ''The Things We Did Last Summer'' (1946), Sinatra's ''Time After Time'' and ''It's the Same Old Dream'' (*It Happened in Brooklyn*) and ''It's Magic'' (*It's Magic*).

Cahn and Styne made a first attempt at a theatre show with the songs for David Wolper's production of *Glad to See You,* a 1944 musical which starred Eddie Foy jr and Jane Withers, but they had more success with a second venture, *High Button Shoes,* three years later. A jolly, old-fashioned piece of musical comedy with a cast headed by top comedian Phil Silvers and set alight by some energetic dancing, *High Button Shoes* ran for some two years and put in evidence such numbers as ''I Still Get Jealous'' and ''Papa, Won't You Dance with Me?'' as performed by Nanette Fabray and Jack McCauley.

From this time on, Styne devoted most of his attentions to the theatre. He followed *High Button Shoes* with another successful musical comedy, *Gentlemen Prefer Blondes* (1949), which, if its score was not necessarily its most attractive attribute, nevertheless produced ''Diamonds Are a Girl's Best Friend'' and ''A Little Girl from Little Rock,'' and in 1951 he turned producer to collaborate with Alexander H Cohen and Harry Rigby on the Hugh Martin musical *Make a Wish* (Winter Garden Theater 18 April, 102 performances). In the same year he underwent a first stage collaboration with lyricists Betty Comden and Adolph Green on the revue *Two on the Aisle,* a collaboration which would be repeated often, although only surprisingly occasionally with success, over the following 15 years.

Through the 1950s Styne continued to mix composing and producing on Broadway, whilst still turning out single songs, of which the title song to the film *Three Coins in a Fountain* (Academy Award, 1954) was the most memorable. His productions included the 1952 revival of Rodgers and Hart's *Pal Joey* (w Leonard Key, Anthony Brady Farrell), Jerry Bock's *Mr Wonderful* (1956 w George Gilbert, Lester Osterman), a vehicle for the young Sammy Davis jr, and his own 1958 musical about the making of a musical, *Say, Darling* (w Osterman), all of which found success, and finally a musical version of *Pride and Prejudice, First Impressions* (1959), which did not, and folded in 84 performances.

The composing front, too, brought mainly success for, if *Hazel Flagg* (1953) had only a mild career (190 performances) and a collaboration with Comden, Green and Moose Charlap on a musical comedy version of *Peter Pan* (152 performances) had to wait until a 1979 revival to win a substantial stage run, the lively *Bells Are Ringing,* the love story of an answer-service girl, produced a long run (924 performances), overseas performances, a film and two hit songs, ''Just in Time'' and ''The Party's Over.'' Another musical written around an overwhelming central female role also proved successful, if not quite as long-running, when Styne composed the music to Stephen Sondheim's lyrics for *Gypsy* (1959). Ethel Merman made ''Everything's Coming Up Roses'' into a hit, whilst other pieces of the score (''All I Need Is the Girl,'' ''If Momma Was Married,'' ''Some People'') also found popularity.

Do Re Mi, another vehicle for Phil Silvers, had a 400-performance run in 1960–61, and *Subways Are for Sleeping* (1961) lasted a little more than half of that time, but Styne had one further hit show to come. A return to the vehicle for a big female star, an area for which he had proven himself particularly adept at writing, brought forth *Funny Girl* (1964) in which Barbra Streisand played a version of the life story of comedienne Fanny Brice, and for which Styne composed the melodies to Bob Merrill's lyrics for ''People,'' ''Don't Rain on My Parade,'' ''I'm the Greatest Star,'' ''If a Girl Isn't Pretty'' and ''You Are Woman.'' *Funny Girl* gave Styne his longest Broadway run as well as a highly successful film.

The year 1964 also saw Styne's debut as a director in the musical theatre when he helmed the short-lived *Something More* (Sammy Fain/Marilyn and Alan Bergman/Nate Monaster) for his old partner Lester Osterman, but it also marked the peak of his career in the musical theatre. He continued to compose theatre scores for 15 further years, teaming again with Cahn on *Darling of the Day* and finding a limited success with *Hallelujah, Baby!* (Tony Award) and a good run with a musical version of *Some Like It Hot* entitled *Sugar* which topped five hundred Broadway performances in spite of its score rather than because of it, but there were no more *Funny Girl*s or *Gypsy*s, no more megastars and no more successful songs. Styne's last works, a disastrous musical adaptation of a successful television play, *Bar Mitzvah Boy,* for London and the 1980 *One Night Stand* which closed on Broadway without playing its opening night were shows too feeble to come from a man who was not chary of going into print to rubbish other people's work. His final work was an equally ill-starred (3 performances) adaptation of the film *The Red Shoes.*

In the composer's 84th year a ''new'' Styne musical was produced off-off-Broadway: *The Dangerous Games of Red Riding Hood* was an adaptation of a 1965 television score of an updated version of the fairy tale (*The Dangerous Christmas of Red Riding Hood* ABC 28 November). Other television musicals included *Ruggles of Red Gap* (NBC 3 February 1952 w Leo Robin, David Shaw*),* the animated *Mr Magoo's Christmas* (18 December 1962 w Merrill, Barbara Chain), *I'm Getting Married* (w Comden, Green), broadcast in 1967 and the little *The Night the Animals Talked* (9 December 1970 w Cahn).

Styne's other credits included the 1964 World's Fair revue *Wonder World,* and a score of incidental music for the very brief 1963 Broadway revival of *Arturo Ui.*

1944 **Glad to See You** (Sammy Cahn/Fred Thompson, Eddie Davis) Shubert Theater, Philadelphia 13 November

1947 **High Button Shoes** (Cahn/Stephen Longstreet) New Century Theater 9 October

1949 **Gentlemen Prefer Blondes** (Leo Robin/Anita Loos, Joseph Fields) Ziegfeld Theater 8 December

1953 **Hazel Flagg** (Bob Hilliard/Ben Hecht) Mark Hellinger Theater 11 February

1954 **Peter Pan** (w Moose Charlap/Betty Comden, Adolph Green, Carolyn Leigh) Winter Garden Theater 20 October

1956 **Bells Are Ringing** (Comden, Green) Shubert Theater 29 November

1958 **Say, Darling** (Comden, Green/Richard and Marion Bissell, Abe Burrows) ANTA Theater 3 April

1959 **Gypsy** (Stephen Sondheim/Arthur Laurents) Broadway Theater 21 May

1960 **Do Re Mi** (Comden, Green/Garson Kanin) St James Theater 26 December

1961 **Subways Are for Sleeping** (Comden, Green) St James Theater 27 December

1964 **Funny Girl** (Bob Merrill/Isobel Lennart) Winter Garden Theater 26 March

1964 **Fade Out—Fade In** (Comden, Green) Mark Hellinger Theater 26 May

1967 **Hallelujah, Baby!** (Comden, Green/Laurents) Martin Beck Theater 26 April

1968 **Darling of the Day** (E Y Harburg/Nunnally Johnson, Keith Waterhouse, Willis Hall) George Abbott Theater 27 January

1970 **Look to the Lilies** (Sammy Cahn/Leonard Spigelgass) Lunt-Fontanne Theater 29 March

1971 **Prettybelle** (Merrill) Shubert Theater, Boston 1 February

1972 **Sugar** (aka *Some Like it Hot*) (Merrill/Peter Stone) Majestic Theater 9 April

1974 **Lorelei** revised *Gentlemen Prefer Blondes* (ad Kenny Solms, Gail Parent) Palace Theater 27 January

1978 **Bar Mitzvah Boy** (Don Black/Jack Rosenthal) Her Majesty's Theatre, London 31 October

1980 **One Night Stand** (Herb Gardner) Nederlander Theater 20 October (previews only)

1985 **Pieces of Eight** (Michael Stewart/Susan Birkenhead) Citadel Theater, Edmonton 27 November

1989 **The Dangerous Games of Red Riding Hood** (Merrill) TADA Theater December

1993 **The Red Shoes** (Marsha Norman, Bob Merrill [as ''Paul Stryker'']) Gershwin Theater 16 December

Biography: Taylor, T: *Jule* (Random House, New York, 1979)

SUBWAYS ARE FOR SLEEPING Musical in 2 acts by Adolph Green and Betty Comden adapted from a novel of the same name by Edmund G Love. Music by Jule Styne. St James Theater, New York, 27 December 1961.

An uneventful musical about people who do nothing, *Subways Are for Sleeping* saw two professional drifters (Sydney Chaplin, Orson Bean), court, respectively, a journalist who is doing an article on drifters (Carol Lawrence) and a down-and-out dolly (Phyllis Newman), in a modern New York atmosphere which just occasionally, in its more revusical moments, recalled the zany joys of *On the Town* (not the least in a museum scene). Comden and Green's lyrics sparked best when Bean serenaded Miss Newman, clad in nothing but a bath towel to avoid eviction, with ''I Just Can't Wait (to see you with your clothes on).''

When the show reaped poor notices, producer David Merrick published quotes from members of the public with the same names as the critics, winning outraged publicity that helped his show to a nevertheless largely insufficient 205 performances.

Recording: original cast (Columbia)

SUGAR Musical in 2 acts by Peter Stone based on the screenplay *Some Like It Hot* by Billy Wilder and I A L Diamond. Lyrics by Bob Merrill. Music by Jule Styne. Majestic Theater, New York, 9 April 1972.

The 1959 film *Some Like It Hot,* an all-time favorite as interpreted by Jack Lemmon, Tony Curtis, Marilyn Monroe and Joe E Brown, was an adaptation of an original story by Robert Thoeren made by Wilder and Diamond, the authors who would come up with *The Apartment* the following year. Like their later screenplay, *Some Like It Hot* was natural fodder for a transfer to the musical-comedy stage, and a French version of the tale, *La Polka des lampions,* came out in 1961 (Théâtre du Châtelet, Paris 20 December). However, after the splendid and successful results achieved by Neil Simon, Hal David and Burt Bacharach on the transformation of *The Apartment* into *Promises, Promises,* another *Some Like It Hot* musical appeared, this time on Broadway.

Musicians Joe (Tony Roberts) and Jerry (Robert Morse) witness a gangland killing and are obliged to ''disappear.'' They do this by getting themselves dressed up in frocks, and joining an all-girl band run by Sweet Sue (Sheila Smith) which is heading out of town for an engagement in the summer sunspots. Their travesty leads the boys into all sorts of troubles. Joe—or Josephine—

gets sweet on a fellow band-member called Sugar (Elaine Joyce), whilst Jerry—otherwise Daphne—attracts the attentions of millionaire Osgood Fielding jr (Cyril Ritchard). Morse and Roberts sang about the attractions of "Sugar" and of themselves in "The Beauty That Drives Men Mad" and Ritchard had a "November Song," but the score did not bring out anything that looked like eclipsing the screenic memories of Miss Monroe singing "I Wanna Be Loved By You."

Produced by David Merrick, directed by Gower Champion, *Sugar* simply wasn't in the same class as *Promises, Promises* and it didn't raise a blink at the Tony Award prize-giving, but that didn't stop it running through 505 performances on Broadway and netting itself not only regional productions but also a number of overseas ones, especially in South America and Mexico and in central Europe. However, the show had to wait 20 years to reach London. British star Tommy Steele, who had had a singular success with his adaptation of *Singin' in the Rain,* lit on *Some Like It Hot* as a next vehicle for himself. He then discovered it had two stage scores already. Rejecting strong advice to take the French one, he instead went for the English-language one, only to find that—unlike with *Singin' in the Rain*—the songwriters had the power to forbid interpolations. They did—particularly of "I Wanna Be Loved By You"—and the score was instead bolstered with several songs taken from other shows of theirs. With the libretto reorganized and the original film title restored (at a price, although the Hungarians had done it without even asking), *Some Like It Hot* was played with some success in the British provinces and with considerably less in London (108 performances). The piece was subsequently seen in Germany—where any musical that allows a man to get into a frock seems particularly favored—in Denmark (*Ingen Er Fuldkommen*), Czechoslovakia (*Nedko to rád horké*), Austria and given a fresh run in Budapest, this time at the Fővárosi Operettszínház (8 March 1997) which had done so well with *Singin' in the Rain.*

A further, Australian musicalization of *Some Like It Hot* saw stagelight at Sydney's Bankstown Town Hall Theatre Restaurant in 1983 (8 February).

The title *Sugar* was earlier used for a little musical piece (Louis Jerome/George Arthurs/Lauri Wylie, Alfred Parker) produced at London's Oxford Theatre in 1917 (15 July).

Hungary: Vidám Színpad *Van aki forrón szereti* 19 March 1987; UK: Prince Edward Theatre *Some Like It Hot* 17 March 1992; Germany: Metropoltheater 23 March 1989; Austria: Vereinigte Bühnen, Graz 28 February 1997

Recordings: original cast (United Artists), Mexican recording (Daff), London cast *Some Like It Hot* (First Night)

SULLIVAN, Arthur [Seymour] (Sir) (b London, 13 May 1842; d London, 22 November 1900). The most successful composer of the English opéra-bouffe and -comique stage.

Plate 371. **Arthur Sullivan**

Educated at the Chapel Royal, the Royal Academy of Music and Leipzig Conservatory, Arthur Sullivan was intended for a serious musical career. Indeed, he was regarded, after his earliest orchestral, choral and instrumental compositions—including a first theatrical venture with incidental music to Shakespeare's *The Tempest*—as one of the white hopes of the British musical establishment. However, even early on he had expressed a liking for lighter forms of music, and had also looked towards the musical stage, making an attempt at an unstaged piece—probably a light opera—called *The Sapphire Necklace* when in his earliest twenties.

It was Sullivan's friendships in musical and theatrical London that ultimately led him to take his first steps in the world of the musical theatre. An acquaintance with draper and amateur actor-singer Arthur Lewis, the leading light in a group called "The Moray Minstrels" which had recently performed Moinaux and Offenbach's *Les Deux Aveugles,* resulted in Sullivan being asked if he would compose another, similar piece for the group's members to play. F C Burnand, another acquaintance, was seconded for the text and, to his adaptation of Maddison Morton's favorite farce *Box and Cox,* Sullivan wrote his first musical-comedy score. At first played privately, then at a memorial benefit, *Cox and Box* was taken up by Thomas German Reed two years later and given a long run at his Gallery of Illustration.

By this time, however, Sullivan had stepped fully into his new career. He and Burnand went on to compose a full-length comic opera for the enterprising Reed, whose entertainments had been successful enough that he was preparing to launch himself onto more substantial things. He took the St George's Hall for a season, hired a full orchestra and chorus and, amongst his Offenbach and Auber productions, he produced *The Contrabandista, or The Law of the Ladrones. The Contrabandista* was an interesting piece: a full-scale comic opera with more than a touch of the new French ''bouffe'' flavor which the experienced Burnand, an inveterate and vastly successful burlesque writer since his earliest days in the theatre, had encountered as recently as the previous year in adapting Meilhac and Halévy's text to Offenbach's *La Belle Hélène* for the British stage. Sullivan, who might have been expected to compose in the style of those English classics *The Bohemian Girl, Maritana* and *The Lily of Killarney,* instead turned out a matching score which had a decided quantity of the bubble of the French musical theatre amongst its English strains. The buffo song ''From Rock to Rock'' gave the composer his first show-song success as it headed for parlor pianos on the one hand, and was also ''borrowed'' by the makers of overseas pasticcio entertainments on the other.

The Contrabandista was played 72 times, a very fine record for a contemporary comic opera, and it went on to be played in America, pilfered—textually and even musically—in both America and Australia and, many years later, actually revised and revived in London. It was not, as has been so many times written, a failure. It was removed to allow the other part of Reed's advertised season to be played, and only dropped from his repertoire when he found the finances of a full-scale company beyond his means and returned to the piano/harmonium and one-act operetta formula and to his old base at the Gallery of Illustration. There Reed took up *Cox and Box,* played on a double bill with a piece composed by Reed himself and entitled *No Cards.* The author of *No Cards* was barrister and burlesque-writer W S Gilbert.

Actively advertised by Messrs English and Blackmore, agents, *Cox and Box* went the rounds while Sullivan returned to his more serious work. A couple of months after the closure of *Cox and Box* at the Gallery, the Philharmonia was performing his *In Memoriam* and *The Prodigal Son.* It was not too long, however, before Sullivan ventured back into the musical theatre. This time—after a parlor operetta and an English comic opera—he ventured with the score for a Christmas extravaganza for the Gaiety Theatre. *Thespis, or The Gods Grown Old* was the work of Gilbert, who had supplied the opening-night burlesque for the Gaiety's manager, Hollingshead, and although it was only part of the Gaiety program it was indeed a full-length work. The first performance ran over three hours. The score that Sullivan (''our most distinguished English composer'') provided included some fine comical pieces, and also a ballad, ''Little Maid of Arcadee,'' which found some popularity as a single. *Thespis* was played 64 times before the Gaiety moved on to its next change of program.

More than three further years passed, however, before the collaboration between Sullivan and Gilbert was repeated. Richard D'Oyly Carte, searching for a filler piece to go with Selina Dolaro's production of *La Périchole,* got the pair to get up a ''dramatic cantata'' which Gilbert had prematurely intended as a vehicle for the late Mme Parepa Rosa. As *Trial by Jury* the little piece, with its witty words and laughing score, proved a sensation. A second little piece (''after the pattern of the agreeable entertainments given by Mrs German Reed''), *The Zoo,* written to a text by B C Stephenson, followed (''recollections of Mozart, Auber and Donizetti, blended with Mr Sullivan's own ideas''), but, although it was reported in June 1876 that Sullivan and Gilbert ''have been engaged in arranging as a comic opera *The Wedding March* of La-Tour Tomline'' (ie, Gilbert's version of *Le Chapeau de paille d'Italie*) and then that Arthur's brother, Fred Sullivan was taking the Globe Theatre to produce a new work by the pair, the nearest the musician got to another stage work was the interpolation of his song ''Once Again'' into J A Cave's Christmas production, *Lord Bateman,* at the Alhambra for contralto Adelaide Newton. It was left to Carte, launching himself as a producer after a number of years managing for others, to bring Sullivan and Gilbert firmly together on their first full-length comic opera.

The Sorcerer put the first significant seal on the British comic-opera tradition which had been developing in the decade since *The Contrabandista,* and his score to the show placed Sullivan swiftly alongside and even ahead of his friends Cellier and Clay, who had been leading the field in the production of local musical plays up to this time. But it was left to the writers' second work together for Carte to confirm worldwide what *The Sorcerer* had shown only to those able to believe their ears. *HMS Pinafore* was the international musical hit of its era in the English-speaking theatre, and the Gilbert and Sullivan partnership was launched.

Eight further Sullivan and Gilbert comic operas followed *HMS Pinafore* on to the stage in the next decade or so, and almost all were major international successes, establishing the partnership as the English-speaking world's most important and popular writers of musical theatre. However, ceaselessly chivvied by a section of the press, who had never forgiven Sullivan for becoming merely the country's most popular writer of light theatre music, the composer still hankered after writing an opera. Carte, too, was not indifferent to the plan, and between them they nurtured an *Ivanhoe* into production at Carte's newly built Royal English Opera House. Though *Ivanhoe* was no disgrace, it was no *Iolanthe* either. It failed, the Opera House failed, and Carte and Sullivan ended up back at the Savoy. But they ended up back there without Gilbert. Whether because of the fact that the other two had been off playing operas without him, or whether because of some other reason, a breach had grown between the author and his producer and composer. Gilbert departed the Savoy, and Carte, after filling in with some non-Sullivan works, instead teamed the composer with the author of one of these, the respected playwright Sydney Grundy. Their *Haddon Hall* reeked more of old English not-very-comic opera than the joyous burlesques which Sullivan had composed with Gilbert, but it had a fair run in town and country.

The breach between author and composer was mended, and Gilbert and Sullivan came back together for two more comic operas. *Utopia (Limited)* and, especially, *The Grand Duke* were not up to their earlier works and, after the last-named, the collaboration lapsed once again. Gilbert moved away, Sullivan stayed with Carte. An attempt to pair the composer with Pinero and J Comyns Carr on *The Beauty Stone,* a curious medievally fantasy with undertones of *Ivanhoe* to it, which was all too painfully an effort not to compete with or copy the style of the Gilbert comic operas, was a failure. Although the Victorian age was coming to an end, there was still a place in the English theatre for Victorian comic opera and Sullivan was still as well- if not better-equipped than anyone else to provide it. The answer was, however, not a medieval romantic opera.

The answer turned out to be a librettist from the lowly world of musical comedy. Apparently there was at one time question of Sullivan writing a work with ''Owen Hall,'' the most successful author of contemporary musical libretti from *A Gaiety Girl* to *The Geisha* and *A Greek Slave,* but temporarily displaced at Daly's Theatre by Edwardes's need to humor a powerful journalist by using his text for what became *San Toy.* A Daly's Theatre musical by Arthur Sullivan and Owen Hall? It would have been a curious combination, worth hearing, the only problem being that the pair—both super-extravagant gambling men—might have spent their time playing cards rather than writing. As it turned out, Sullivan got the second most successful musical-comedy librettist of the time, the author of *Gentleman Joe* and *Dandy Dan, the Lifeguardsman,* Basil Hood. Hood provided his composer with the best libretto he had seen in years: a spendidly crafted version of the Arabian Nights Abu Hasan tale, written in a witty comic-opera style which differed from Gilbert's only in eschewing that ultimate air of cockeyed burlesque. Sullivan rose to the script with a score in the same style, and *The Rose of Persia* was a splendid success, scoring a fine run of 213 performances in a London where comic opera had definitely given over its place as a favorite entertainment to the products of the Gaiety and Daly's Theatres and their ilk.

Sullivan and Hood began work on a second piece together, an Irish musical comic opera called *The Emerald Isle.* It was clever, it was fun, it was tuneful—though not quite as attractive as its predecessor, perhaps—but it was also unfinished. Sullivan died in November 1900 with *The Emerald Isle* still in the writing, and it was completed by Edward German for its production and a thoroughly respectable run at the Savoy Theatre.

During his life as Britain's most popular composer of comic opera, Sullivan did not wholly neglect the areas of more serious music in which it had been originally thought that he would make his career. Although the flow of individual songs, hymn tunes and orchestral and instrumental works which he had composed in the 1860s and 1870s largely dried up once he became devoted to the theatre, he composed two important choral works (*The Golden Legend, The Martyr of Antioch*), the latter of which was later reworked as a staged opera (ad T H Friend, Theatre Royal, Edinburgh 25 February 1898), several sets of incidental stage music (*Macbeth, King Arthur, The Foresters*) and a ballet for the Alhambra Theatre (*Victoria and Merrie England*), as well as continuing a celebrity conducting career.

Sullivan's music for the Victorian British theatre struck precisely the right note for its time and place. It was a little less extravagant than that of the overly French Offenbach, just as Gilbert's text held back from the extreme burlesque of a Hervé, but it mixed grace, melody and sufficient, but never low or vulgar, humor in almost the same measure as the author did with his texts. Sullivan's comic-opera scores were not only good music and attractive music, they were nice. They could be played and sung in any decent household, and they have been now for well over a century whilst almost every other bit of British writing of the period has slipped away into oblivion or rarity. And their composer stands up today in his home country as the only representative of the Victorian musical theatre, and in popular terms—give or take a music-hall song or two—of Victorian music to have stood the test of time with an almost undiminished appeal.

Sullivan's brother, **Fred[eric Thomas] SULLIVAN** (b London, 25 December 1837; d London, 18 January 1877), was for many years an architect and surveyor, but he turned to the stage late in his short life for a brief but high-profile career ended by his death at the age of 39.

Fred appeared on the stage first as Bouncer (1869) and later as Cox (1871) in *Cox and Box,* played in burlesque with Henrietta Hodson at the Royalty Theatre (1870, Trombonius in *F N Julius Cnaesar*) and as Punch in W C Levey's operetta *Punchinello* (July 1871), before mounting ''Mr Sullivan's Operetta Company'' in several provincial venues for performances of *Cox and Box, The Rose of Auvergne* and *Breaking the Spell* (August 1871). He repeated *Cox and Box* at the Alhambra Theatre (October 1871), and took a supporting role in Arthur's next work, at the much more demanding Gaiety Theatre, as Apollo in *Thespis* (1871) with sufficient success to be cast with the theatre's stars, Nellie Farren and Connie Loseby, as Midas in the four-handed *Ganymede and Galatea* (*Die schöne Galathee*).

He played *Cox and Box* and *A Mere Blind (Les Deux Aveugles)* at the Gaiety, appeared in repertoire with the Gaiety touring company (1872, *Robert the Devil, The Princess of Trébizonde,* etc), returned to the Gaiety for the operetta *Fleurette* (1873, Marquis Beaurivage) and repeated both *Cox and Box* and *Die schöne Galathee* at Crystal Palace (1874) before he tried his hand again at management, presenting *Cox and Box* and *The Contrabandista* for fortnights at the Prince's, Manchester (11 May) and Birmingham (25 May) with Cellier as conductor and a cast including Ella Collins, Adelaide Newton, Frank Wood, Edward Connell and himself as Grigg and Cox. When things went poorly he added Fred Evans's comic ballet *Fra Diavolo* and Offenbach's *Lischen and Fritzchen.* The agent for the season was one Mr D'Oyly Carte.

Fred returned to performing in *Ixion* at the Opera Comique (1874) and as the Duke of Rodomont in *Melusine the Enchantress* (1874) at Holborn, played the principal comic role of the Viceroy in London's first *La Périchole* (1875) and had his biggest success of all when he created the role of the Judge in *Trial by Jury* (1875) and played it at the Royalty, on the road and at the Opera Comique (1876) with no less than three different main pieces. During this run he was taken ill and *Trial by Jury* was suspended till his return. He subsequently toured as the Judge, Pomponnet (*La Fille de Madame Angot*) and Cocorico (*Geneviève de Brabant*) with Emily Soldene, and it was announced that he would further his producing activities by staging the first full-length work by his brother and W S Gilbert the following season at the Globe Theatre. However, *The Sorcerer* was ultimately produced by Richard D'Oyly Carte at the Opera Comique some months after his death.

He is largely remembered today through the song ''The Lost Chord'' which Sullivan composed in mourning for his brother.

1867 **Cox and Box, or The Long Lost Brothers** (F C Burnand) 1 act Adelphi Theatre 11 May; Gallery of Illustration 29 March 1869

1867 **The Contrabandista** (Burnand) St George's Opera House 18 December

1871 **Thespis, or The Gods Grown Old** (W S Gilbert) Gaiety 26 December

1875 **Trial by Jury** (Gilbert) 1 act Royalty 25 March

1875 **The Zoo** (B C Stephenson) 1 act St James's Theatre 5 June

1877 **The Sorcerer** (Gilbert) Opera Comique 17 November

1878 **HMS Pinafore, or The Lass That Loved a Sailor** (Gilbert) Opera Comique 25 May

1880 **The Pirates of Penzance, or The Slave of Duty** (Gilbert) Fifth Avenue, New York 31 December

1881 **Patience, or Bunthorne's Bride** (Gilbert) Opera Comique 23 April

1882 **Iolanthe, or The Peer and the Peri** (Gilbert) Savoy Theatre 25 November

1884 **Princess Ida, or Castle Adamant** (Gilbert) Savoy Theatre 5 January

1885 **The Mikado, or The Town of Titipu** (Gilbert) Savoy Theatre 14 March

1887 **Ruddigore, or The Witch's Curse** (Gilbert) Savoy Theatre 22 January

1888 **The Yeomen of the Guard, or The Merryman and His Maid** (Gilbert) Savoy Theatre 3 October

1889 **The Gondoliers, or The King of Barataria** (Gilbert) Savoy Theatre 7 December

1892 **Haddon Hall** (Sydney Grundy) Savoy Theatre 24 September

1893 **Utopia (Limited), or The Flowers of Progress** (Gilbert) Savoy Theatre 7 October

1894 **The Chieftain** revised *The Contrabandista* Savoy Theatre 12 December

1896 **The Grand Duke, or The Statutory Duel** (Gilbert) Savoy Theatre 7 March

1898 **The Beauty Stone** (Arthur Wing Pinero, J Comyns Carr) Savoy Theatre 28 May

1899 **The Rose of Persia, or The Storyteller and the Slave** (Basil Hood) Savoy Theatre 29 November

1901 **The Emerald Isle, or The Caves of Carric-Cleena** (w Edward German/Hood) Savoy Theatre 27 April

Biographies: Jacobs, A: *Arthur Sullivan, a Victorian Musician* (OUP, Oxford, 1984), Lawrence, A H: *Sir Arthur Sullivan* (James Bowden, London, 1899), Findon, B W: *Sir Arthur Sullivan, His Life and Music* (James Nisbet, London, 1904) revised as *Sir Arthur Sullivan and His Operas* (Sisley's, London, 1908), Sullivan, H, Flower, N: *Sir Arthur Sullivan* (Cassell, London, 1927), Young, P M: *Sir Arthur Sullivan* (Dent, London, 1971), Dunhill, T: *Sullivan's Comic Operas* (Edward Arnold, London, 1928), Saxe Wyndam, H: *Arthur Seymour Sullivan (1842–1900)* (Kegan Paul, Trench, Trübner, London, 1926), etc, etc

SULLY, Mariette (b Belgium, 9 December 1878).

Mlle Sully was first seen on the Paris stage in 1894, playing Kate in Planquette's *Rip,* and she subsequently appeared in leading opérette roles at most of Paris's principal musical houses in a career of more than 40 years. During this period, which was far from the most productive of the French musical stage, she created several of the most important new prima donna roles available: the doll-girl Alésia in Audran's *La Poupée* (1896), the title role of Messager's *Véronique* (1898), and another doll-girl, Lisbeth, in Louis Ganne's *Hans, le joueur de flûte* (1906).

Amongst her other creations were included *Le Bonhomme de neige* (1894, Edwige), *Les Forains* (1894, Clorinde), *Panurge* (1895, Caterina), *Les Quatre Filles Aymon* (1898, Michelene), *Shakespeare!* (1899, Éponine), *La Demoiselle aux caméllias* (1899, Césarine), *Le Petit Chaperon rouge* (1900, Nichette), *Princesse Bébé* (1902, La Princesse Maia), *La Bouquetière du Château d'Eau, Les Dragons de l'Imperatrice* (1905, Cyprienne), *Oeil de Gazelle, Madame Marlborough, Rhodope* (1910), *Les Maris de Ginette* (1916, Ginette), *La Fiancée du lieutenant* (1917) and, as late as 1935, *La Nuit est belle.* At the same time she appeared on the Paris stage in such classic roles as Miss Helyett, Serpolette, Rose Michon, Marie-Blanche, Suzette (*Le Voyage de Suzette*), Musette (*La Petite Bohème*) and Missia (*La Veuve joyeuse*).

Mlle Sully appeared in *La Poupée* in Brussels, in the French version of *A Country Girl* in Paris, and in London both as Pervenche in *Les Merveilleuses* (1906) and as Juliette—the role created for another Miss Helyett, Juliette Nesville—in George Edwardes's 1906 revival of *The Geisha.* She also played in the zarzuela *La Rose de Grenade* at the Olympia, appeared in a number of operéttes, both new and revived, in Monaco, and repeated her most famous role of Véronique for over 20 years.

THE SULTAN OF MOCHA Comic opera in 3 acts by ?Albert Jarret (uncredited) and others. Music by Alfred Cellier. Prince's Theatre, Manchester, 16 November 1874; St James's Theatre, London, 17 April 1876.

The Sultan of Mocha was one of the earliest British musicals of the modern era both to have a significant career at home and to win overseas productions. It was first produced at the Prince's Theatre, in Manchester, by Charles Calvert, the actor-manager who with his wife had become known for their superior productions of Shakespeare, and who accepted a text supplied by "a local gentleman of some literary attainment" which he had set to music by the young musical director of his theatre, Alfred Cellier.

Dolly (Bessie Emmett) is in love with handsome sailor Peter (Robertha Erskine), but she is whisked away from such nautical temptations by her horrid slave-trading uncle, Captain Flint (Henry M Clifford), and carried off to Mocha where she is pounced upon by the amo-

Plate 372. **The Sultan of Mocha**

rous Sultan (John Furneaux Cook). Rescued by Peter, recaptured by the falsity of another jealous suitor, Sneak (Fred Mervin), Dolly finally escapes becoming a Sultana by disguising a more ambitious member of the Sultan's harem in her wedding veil.

Well in the tradition of such popular nautical yarns as *Black-Eyed Susan* and of pantomime extravaganza, with its staunchly British hero and heroine, comical villains and exotic second-act location, the tale was told in some naive and sometimes punning dialogue which nevertheless sufficiently supported a well-made and tuneful score in a similar tradition. Cellier's music took little or no notice of the French opéra-bouffe style which had been dominant in Britain's musical theatres for the past years and which had featured in such French-composed British musicals as *Aladdin II* (Hervé), *Cinderella the Younger* (Jonas) and *Whittington* (Offenbach) and the spectacular *Black Crook* and *Babil and Bijou.* Following instead the tones of Sullivan's *Contrabandista* and Clay's *The Gentleman in Black* and *Cattarina,* Cellier's music for *The Sultan of Mocha* helped establish the kind of English comic-opera score which would find its apogée in the Savoy operas and his own *Dorothy.*

Amongst the solos, Peter had a delightful ballad in an old English mode ("Twas Sad When I and Dolly Parted"), and a Yawning Song which, like Dolly's Slumber

Song, became a popular recital piece. Dolly also had a number which made no bones about ''Women's Rights'' (''woman strongminded is not to be blinded by man when he's minded to make her his slave''), Sneak listed the contents of his shop (''The Telescope'') to dazzle the heroine and the Sultan described himself (''Sultan Am I'') in multiple rhymes and traditional style alongside a series of lively choruses of which the finale ''We'll Sail Away with Peter'' was particularly well received.

In the manner of the time, the piece was produced first, and worked on after, and it was worked up and added to with new jokes and songs to such good effect that it was still running after five weeks when it was time for Calvert to mount the annual pantomime. As soon as Christmas was over, the theatre's homemade musical was hurried back to the Prince's stage with Catherine Lewis now as Dolly and a tenor instead of a travesty Peter, and it was brought back again after another pre-booked season had intervened, and yet again the following year. Finally Manchester's musical was produced in London by Mrs John Wood, 18 months and five series after its first appearance. Constance Loseby (Dolly), Alfred Brennir (Peter) and Henri Corri (Sultan) headed the cast, the book was sharpened up (and its Mancunian references cut), and a chorus of 70 engaged to boom out Cellier's finale, but in spite of some good notices 47 performances were its lot.

The Sultan of Mocha continued to win provincial productions, however, and in December 1878 it was even given a showing in San Francisco by the indefatigable Alice Oates. However, just weeks earlier *HMS Pinafore* had struck in Boston, and it was already showing signs of being a blockbuster. Alice quickly shelved *The Sultan* and flung a version of *Pinafore* into rehearsal instead. Two years later, American vocalist Blanche Roosevelt, who had encountered Cellier whilst singing Josephine (*HMS Pinafore*) at London's Opera Comique, got John McCaull to stage Cellier's piece for her ''Blanche Roosevelt Comic Opera Company'' in New York. Poorly and hastily produced, it folded quickly.

After the vast success of Cellier's *Dorothy, The Sultan of Mocha* was given a brush-up, a fresh book and a new West End production under the management of Lydia Thompson (Strand Theatre 21 September 1887). Violet Cameron and Henry Bracy starred, and the piece won a fine reception and 114 performances, following which Bracy took up the Australian rights. He produced the show in Melbourne in 1889 and at Sydney's Criterion Theatre the following March. The producer again played Peter to the Dolly of Lilian Tree, with John Forde (Sneak), Knight Aston (Sultan), Flora Granpner (Lucy) and William Stevens (Flint) supporting. After 15 colorful years of life, during which it had been seen from one side of the globe to the other, *The Sultan of Mocha* was then left at rest.

USA: Bush Street Theater, San Francisco 9 December 1878, Union Square Theater 14 September 1880; Australia: Alexandra Theatre, Melbourne 9 November 1889

THE SULTAN OF SULU Comic opera in 2 acts with lyrics by George Ade. Music by Alfred G Wathall. Additional music by Nat D Mann. Studebaker Theater, Chicago, 11 March 1902; Wallack's Theater, New York, 29 December 1902.

The Islamic Philippine island domain of Ki-Ram, Sultan of Sulu (Frank Moulan), is an idyllic place where ''we have no daily papers to tell of Newport capers, no proud four hundred to look down on ordinary folk, no French imported liquors, no stock exchange and tickers, to fill one full of rosy hopes and someday land him broke.'' One day Sulu is annexed by America which, in the persons of Arkansas Colonel Budd (William C Mandeville), baritonic Lt William Hardy (Templar Saxe) and the bigoted Judge Jackson (1870s Gilbert and Sullivan star Blanche Chapman), promptly decides that it is time to civilize—that is to say, Americanize—both island and Sultan.

Thirty years before Ira Gershwin won fulsome praise for equating war with trade in musical-comedy terms in *Strike Up the Band,* Englishman Templar Saxe marched on to the stage singing George Ade's softly stinging backhander ''But though we come in warlike guise and battle-front arrayed, It's all a business enterprise, we're seeking foreign trade.'' Education arrived in the shape of four schoolma'ams (''from the land of the cerebellum where clubs abound and books are plenty we come to teach this new possession all that's known to a girl of twenty'') and new experience in the disastrous form of cocktails which led poor, innocent Ki-Ram to end up intoning a splendidly comical post-drinking song of ''R.E.M.O.R.S.E.'' After a busy evening of song and dance in which the blithely satirical was mixed with such popular items as a hoe-down for the Colonel (''Ol' Jay Bird''), a Irish number (''Rosabella Clancey''), a topical trio (''Oh, What a Bump!''), several marching routines, a fashionably croony Nat Mann two-step (''My Sulu Lulu Loo''), a coon song (''Delia'') for Gertrude Quinlan as the Sultan's Number One Wife and some jolly ensembles, Ki-Ram and Sulu escape their dreadful fate on a legal technicality.

Commissioned by Henry Savage from the well-established journalist and author Ade and from a 22-year-old English musician, Alfred Wathall, who was a teacher at Chicago's North Western School of Music, *The Sultan of Sulu* was produced in Chicago under the auspices of Savage's Castle Square Opera Company, which had branched out after several successful years playing operatic and light-operatic repertoire seasons. After a sticky start, it became a major success. With a score constantly growing (''The Puzzled Man,'' ''Money, Money, Money,'' ''The Cuckoo and the Clock''), and a libretto perked up with fresh topicalities for the occasion, the show moved to Broadway. Perhaps because the Castle Square company had so long been installed in New York, the piece was apparently not regarded as a Chicago musical and it was both well reviewed and a fine success. It ran up two hundred performances at Wallack's Theater and put the final stardust on Frank Moulan's reputation before continuing a strong career around the country for a number of seasons.

The Sultan of Sulu was a jolly mixture of plot notions which had done duty for years on the English comic opera stage (with ''Americanization'' here replacing the ''anglicization'' of such pieces as *Dick* and *Utopia Ltd*), and some of which had had a particularly happy recent showing in Britain, America and around the world in the record-breaking *A Chinese Honeymoon.* But Ade had done his librettist's and lyricist's jobs with skill and humor and the piece's singular success was no accident. That success helped revive the favorite old musical-theatre hometown-boy-in-exotic-foreign-places theme with its preposterous Rurarabian monarchs and harum-scarum plots for the joy of another generation of Americans, but it did not encourage this particular show to travel beyond its native borders.

SUNDAY IN THE PARK WITH GEORGE Musical in 2 acts by James Lapine. Music and lyrics by Stephen Sondheim. Booth Theater, New York, 2 May 1984.

Sunday in the Park with George presented the peculiarity of being a musical drawn not from a text, but from a painting: Georges Seurat's well-known pointilliste *Un dimanche d'été á l'île de la Grande Jatte.* The libretto that James Lapine constructed around, or rather drew from, the work of art fell into two loosely linked halves, which gave the impression of being a one-act musical play followed by a modern commentary on that play.

In the first act the artist, George (Mandy Patinkin), is seen gathering together the material and the people who will ultimately make up the subject matter of his painting, and the audience gets to know who the soldiers, the girls, the boatman, the child, and the memorably straight-backed couple with a monkey are, before they are all frozen onto canvas together in the artist's imaginative, rather than factual, rearrangement at the end of the act. Parallel to the construction of the painting, the act follows the ups and (mostly) downs of the failing relationship between George and his mistress, Dot (Bernadette Peters). The second act moves on from the period setting of the first to modern times. The modern George (Patinkin again) is the illegitimate great-grandson of the first, and Marie, the child borne to the first George by Dot (and played by the same actress), is now an elderly woman. This George is an artist as well, and in contrast to his ancestor's painting, he produces a Chromolume, a piece of mechanical performance art, the display of which is used by the authors to give the audience their comments on art patronage and criticism.

The musical score illustrating this pair of acts was not made up of ''numbers'' in the traditional sense, but rather seemed to take on the flavor of the artistic techniques with which the show deals, building up its ''modern art'' score from repeated fragments and conversational pieces rather than extended solo pieces. Its most generally accessible parts come in the first act, notably in a monologue for Dot where Sondheim the lyricist produces some amusing moments as he collects the thoughts going through her brain as she models uncomfortably for her artist, and the act comes effectively to an end in its picture to the strains of ''Sunday.''

Highly regarded in some quarters, and the recipient of several awards, *Sunday in the Park with George*—and in particular its second act—nevertheless proved incomprehensible and/or uninteresting to the bulk of theatregoers and it finished its New York run of 604 performances in the red. The show was subsequently played for a season at Britain's Royal National Theatre with Philip Quast (George) and Maria Friedman (Dot) in the principal roles. A German version was premiered in 1989 at Kaiserslautern, but a French production announced for 1992 at the Opéra-Comique was ultimately canceled and replaced by an evening of zarzuelas.

The piece was televised with its Broadway cast in 1986.

Germany: Pfalztheater, Kaiserslautern *Sonntags im Park mit George* 30 September 1989; UK: Lyttelton Theatre 15 March 1990

Recording: original cast (RCA)

SUNNY Musical comedy in 2 acts by Oscar Hammerstein II and Otto Harbach. Music by Jerome Kern. New Amsterdam Theater, New York, 22 September 1925.

Sunny was commissioned by producer Charles Dillingham as a vehicle for ex-Ziegfeld star Marilyn[n] Miller, and it was built around her and a series of scenic considerations with rather less expertise than might have been expected, given the famous names which were attached to the show's book. Since a circus setting had been decided upon, Miss Miller was cast as Sunny Peters, the daughter of a lovable old German-accented circus man (written to type for aging star ''dutch'' comic Joseph Cawthorn), and herself a circus rider. The circus element had nothing to do with what little plot there was, but it allowed Dillingham to fill the stage with circus acts. Similarly, the circus was situated in Britain, which allowed that little plot to step sideways for a hunting scene even more ridiculously unsuitable than the infamous one tacked into *Dorothy* 40 years earlier. The second act (apparently not written when rehearsals began) got the principals on an ocean liner—a fashionable setting of the time—heading for America, and the plot had Sunny married, because of American entry laws (in one version), to the wrong man (in one version) before, ultimately, getting the right one (in one version). Jack Donahue (Jim), Paul Frawley (Tom) and Clifton Webb (Harold) were the men in the piece, Mary Hay (Weenie) the soubrette, and—for a while—Ukelele Ike, who had gone down so well in *Lady, Be Good!* the previous season, was another item on the bill.

Jerome Kern's score for *Sunny*—which also underwent heavy overhauling pre-Broadway—shared its most popular songs amongst the principals. Miss Miller and Frawley joined together in ''Who (stole my heart away)?,'' Frawley serenaded his ''Sunny'' who, in turn, demanded ''Do You Love Me?,'' and Webb and Miss Hay soubretted in song and dance about ''Two Little Bluebirds'' (which had begun life, less romantically, as ''Two Total Losses''). All these soon-to-be-favorites came in the first act, and the second, which introduced only three fresh (or made-over) Kern songs, plus a lot of dances, Ukelele Ike's spot, another for Pert Kelton, and George Olsen and his Music, was less productive.

Sunny's run-in to New York was hair-raising. Whilst frantic writes and rewrites went on, Dillingham announced to the press that the problem was simply that they had discovered that their plot was very similar to that of a Raymond Hubbell/Anne Caldwell piece called *Miss Liberty* which Abe Erlanger was producing. The same excuse was able, at a pinch, to cover the wholesale replacement of the second act by a fresh one, but not the sacking of choreographer Julian Alfreds, replaced by veteran Julian Mitchell. Rumor was floated that the show was costing $250,000, Miss Miller being on a vast guarantee of $2,000 per week and Donahue and Webb on $1,000 apiece, and it looked like a bad investment. However, in just two weeks between opening at Philadelphia's Forrest Theater and bowing on Broadway, *Sunny* was turned into a hit. Miss Miller, Donahue, the spectacle and Kern's successful and singable songs earned the show some splendid reviews, 517 Broadway performances, a tour, and a London production under the auspices of Moss' Empires, Lee Ephraim and Jack Buchanan. *Miss Liberty* didn't ever show, but Dillingham's excuses and cover-ups were soon forgotten.

Binnie Hale (Sunny), Jack Buchanan (Jim), Jack Hobbs (Tom) and Elsie Randolph (Weenie) featured in the London *Sunny* which ran up a fine 363 performances of a version that took in four additional numbers, did without Ike and his ''Paddlin' Madelin' Home,'' and even—goodness knows why—altered the ending to give the heroine her final curtain with the other young man of the piece. Australia, too, proved fond of *Sunny,* as produced by Rufe Naylor at Sydney's Empire Theatre with Wyn Richmond in the little heroine's role supported by Fred Heider (Jim), Queenie Ashton (Weenie), Fred Bluett (Siegfried) and Jack Morrison (Tom). A good Sydney run was followed by a Melbourne season (Princess Theatre 15 July 1927) of three months, the whole accompanied by some of the most over-the-top advertising of the period. The advertising did not, however, encourage Australia to support *Sunny* to the grand extent it had done *Sally.*

Sunny was metamorphosed twice into a film. The first starred Miss Miller, repeating her original role alongside the Tom of Lawrence Grey and the papa of O P Heggie, whilst Jim Donahue, brother of her recently deceased partner, Jack, was given the role of Jim. A decade later, a second *Sunny* featured Anna Neagle in the title role. Each time the three principal numbers of the stage show's score were retained. But not much else.

UK: London Hippodrome 7 October 1926; Australia: Empire Theatre, Sydney 27 February 1927

Films: First National 1930, RKO 1941

Recordings: London cast compilation (WRC, Stanyan) (part-record)

SUNNY RIVER Musical in 2 acts by Oscar Hammerstein II. Music by Sigmund Romberg. St James Theater, New York, 4 December 1941.

First produced at the St Louis Muny under the title of *New Orleans,* the show headed for Broadway with its title altered to the less precisely geographical *Sunny River.* That river was the Mississippi, and the show's tale was a period piece set in early-19th-century New Orleans and stretched over the 10 years between the first attempt of the little singer Marie Sauvinet (Muriel Angelus) to win lofty Jean Gervais (Robert Lawrence) away from his intended Cécile Marshall (Helen Claire), and a second and equally unsuccessful try after she returns as a famous prima donna Marie got the main part of the musical action both in solo (''Call It a Dream,'' ''Can You Sing?'') and duo with Jean (''Along the Winding Road,'' ''Let Me Live Today,'' ''Time Is Standing Still'') whose own principal solo was in praise of ''My Girl and I.'' The show's title song fell to a supporting character.

The Mississippi did not yield another *Show Boat* nor New Orleans another *Naughty Marietta* and Max Gordon's Broadway production drew only enough public to last for five weeks. However, London's Emile Littler (''by arrangement with Max Gordon of New York City'') picked the piece up for Britain and produced it with a strong cast headed by Evelyn Laye (Marie) and Dennis Noble (Gervais) and with older stars Edith Day (Lolita, with the title song) and Bertram Wallis (George Marshall) amongst the character players. It was many years since Romberg's music had been heard in the West End, but *Sunny River* could not interest a wartime public who preferred Jack Buchanan, Cicely Courtneidge, Palladium revue or, for heavier stuff, the topical romance of *The Lisbon Story.* The show closed after little more than two months.

UK: Piccadilly Theatre 18 August 1943

SUNSET BOULEVARD Musical in 2 acts by Christopher Hampton adapted from the screenplay by Billy Wilder, Charles Brackett and D M Marsham jr. Lyrics by Don Black. [Book and lyrics by Christopher Hampton and Don Black.] Music by Andrew Lloyd Webber. Adelphi Theatre, London, 29 June 1993.

After the indifferent international showing of the small-but-beautiful *Aspects of Love,* Andrew Lloyd Webber sagely returned for his next show to the formula which had proved so extravagantly profitable in *The Phantom of the Opéra*—the combination of a large-stage spectacular musical with the title of a famous, verging-on-a-cult movie, and a melodramatic tale with an oversized and grotesque central character.

The cinema's *Sunset Boulevard* was the work of screenwriter-director Billy Wilder (others of whose screenplays had been mostly successfully brought to the musical stage as *Promises, Promises, La Polka des Lampions* and *Sugar*) and two collaborators, and it starred Gloria Swanson in the role of the faded film star, Norma Desmond, whose attempt at a too-late comeback ends in madness and murder. Swanson's queen-sized performance as the grand guignolesque actress was an anthology one, to be ranged alongside Claude Rains's Phantom, Bette Davis's Baby Jane and Klaus Kinsky's Nosferatu in the hit parade of great grotesques of the cinema, yet in its tale and place it fitted the bill without seeming either risible or over-the-top.

A number of efforts were made over the years to transmute *Sunset Boulevard* into a stage piece, not least one written by Miss Swanson herself which changed the ending so that Joe stayed alive and continued his love affair with Norma. Amongst the songs of her musical was one (not for Norma) called ''Hand It to the Glands.'' This version got as far as being turned into a concept album under the title *Boulevard* but it was not until a good few years on that *Sunset Boulevard* (thankfully not subtitled ''the musical'') made it to the stage.

The text for the piece was arranged, with frequent use of the film's almost sacrosanct lines, by Don Black—whose previous collaborations with Lloyd Webber had been on those of his works sporting relatively normal folk as their characters (*Tell Me on a Sunday, Aspects of Love*)—and the patented playwright Christopher Hampton, most recently seen to advantage with his new adaptation of *Les Liaisons Dangereuses.* Strangely, their respective special talents did not shine through trademarkedly in the finished work, in which the film's originally claustrophobic atmosphere had to be foresaken to allow for the required stage display. An unecessarily complex scene change which hoisted the whole principal set above stage level seemed to be there only to allow a complex scene change, and the feel of the piece often became that of an intimate musical blown up like the frog who wanted to be a cow.

Joe Gillis (Kevin Anderson), an out-of-work screenwriter, is escaping some heavy creditors when he runs his car down a Hollywood drive. It is the grandiose but shabby house where Norma Desmond (Patti LuPone), a once famous star of the silent screen, lives under the protective care of Max, her one-time director and husband (Daniel Benzali). Introduced mistakenly into the household, Joe soon finds himself entwined in Norma's plans to return to the screen in a vast unwieldy film about the young Salomé. He plays along, is moved in house, but then finds Norma falling in love with him. When the outside world, and particularly the friendly Betty Schaefer (Meredith Brown) intervene, Norma ''attempts'' suicide and drags him back. Finally, however, Joe snaps and turns on the deluded woman, pouring out the truth from which Max has so long shielded her. She can never come back. She is finished. When the police come to take her away, Joe's body is floating in the swimming pool, and Norma's mind is gone forever.

The score with which the drama was set featured one of Lloyd Webber's most richly romantic songs in Norma's description of her art ''With One Look (I can break your heart),'' as well as a second touching and self-deluding aria, ''It's As If We Never Said Goodbye,'' as the one-time star looks over the sound-stage to which she thinks she will return. Joe had his moment in a sour look at the glories ''Sunset Boulevard'' never brought him. The handful of other characters were less well served, however, and some intermediate passages suffered from longueurs and exaggerated thematic repetition.

The range and power of the music allotted to the role of Norma made that role an enormous casting problem and, not for the first time, the Really Useful Company found itself in trouble over star casting. Patti LuPone was selected to create the part in London, and the result was a superbly sung rendition which lacked the stature and star-quality needed to make the character credible. When it came to casting for America, the values were reversed and filmland's Glenn Close introduced the show, laden with stature but underpowered vocally. Replacement casting didn't go without hiccups either—Miss LuPone had to be paid off for not getting the Broadway job, and Faye Dunaway had to be paid off for not getting to the stage in Los Angeles—but replacement stars Betty Buckley, Elaine Paige and Petula Clark proved that the role was not only castable but playable. What, however, it never became was sympathetic. Unlike the Phantom of the Opéra, Norma Desmond and her egocentric states of mind seemed to evoke more irritation than compassion.

Sunset Boulevard was only a partial success. It ran for 1,529 performances in London, 977 on Broadway (after a pre–New York run of 369 performances in Los Angeles, and the award of a swatch of Tonys in another of the no-contest years of recent times), and some eight months in an Australia production mounted in Melbourne with Debbie Byrne in the role of Norma and Hugh Jackman as Joe. In Canada Diahann Carroll was Norma to the Joe of Rex Smith and the Max of Walter Charles, in Germany (ad Michael Kunze) Helen Schneider starred opposite Uwe Kröger and Norbert Lamla in a production which ran through two and a half years. And everywhere it ended in the red. Yet its principal numbers remain royally to take their place in the Lloyd Webber songbook, and the thought lingered—was there a successful small and claustrophobic few-handed musical play lurking in there among the hydraulics and longueurs? The thought apparently lingered profitably, for a revised, cut-down version of *Sunset Boulevard* was toured in America in 1998 with Petula Clark repeating her Norma Desmond.

In the wake of *Sunset Boulevard,* off-Broadway was visited by a piece in the most iconoclastic tradition of the burlesque stage. Mesopotamian Opera mounted a musical called *Sunset Salomé* (Max Kinberg/Peter Wing Healey 5 April 1996) which purported to be a musical version of the script written by Norma Desmond for her screen comeback. Norma gets to play her Salomé in Palm Springs's Whispering Sands Hospital for the Criminally Insane. Perhaps that was the treatment the story needed all along.

USA: Shubert Theater, Los Angeles 9 December 1993, Minskoff Theatre 17 November 1994; Australia: Regent Theater, Melbourne 26 October 1996; Germany: Rhein-Main-Theater, Niedernhausen 8 December 1995

Recordings: original cast (Polydor), American cast (Polydor), Canadian cast (Polydor), German cast (Polydor)

Literature: Perry, G: *Sunset Boulevard: From Movie to Musical* (Pavilion, New York, 1994)

THE SUNSHINE GIRL Musical comedy in 2 acts by Paul Rubens and Cecil Raleigh. Lyrics by Paul Rubens and Arthur Wimperis. Music by Paul Rubens. Gaiety Theatre, London, 24 February 1912.

In the twilight of the great musical-comedy years at the Gaiety Theatre, a new (or, rather, new-old) team of writers took a turn at supplying the famous house with what they thought the contemporary theatregoer, whisked along on the brand new wave of syncopated rhythms and revue, might best appreciate. Far from taking anything resembling a turn for the modern, however, Rubens, Raleigh and Wimperis moved in a distinctly backward direction. They threw out the noticeably more vertebrate musical-comedy form which the theatre's previous piece, the George Grossmith/Leslie Stuart *Peggy,* had ventured and, far from constructing their musical play on an established comedy as that piece had done, they simply put together a show to the very old Gaiety days formula of minimal plot and maximum star exposure.

The Sunshine Girl had a skeletal story in which soap-factory worker Delia Dale (Phyllis Dare) wins the heart and hand of her workmate Vernon (Basil Foster) who is—in good 19th-century fashion—really the factory's owner in disguise. George Grossmith was the hero's best friend, Teddy Payne and Connie Ediss were an East End pair who spot the deception, Mabel Sealby was soubrette and the beautiful Olive May, soon to quit the stage to join the British peerage, paired with Grossmith at the head of the usual line of Gaiety belles.

The piece was staged in the habitually attractive Gaiety style and illustrated with a bundle of the simplistically suggestive but catchy songlets which Rubens purveyed so successfully. Miss Ediss pulled the best of these, describing "Brighton" and relating how "I've Been to the Durbar," Miss Dare simpered pinkly "Take me for—!" and Grossmith clipped out a jaunty and decidedly catching "Little Girl, Mind How You Go" alongside the score's rare tentative try at things new in the form of Miss Dare and Grossmith performing "a new dance from South America" called the tango, and the show filled the bill very well. The favorite stars had plenty to do (the unimportant Vernon was quickly pushed aside to allow the top-of-the-bill folk to do their thing) and they did it with gusto for a 12-month run (336 performances), confirming the fact that Grossmith's attempts to turn Gaiety musicals into something more substantial were not really necessary.

The Sunshine Girl even proved capable of existing without Payne, Grossmith, Connie Ediss and their fellows. It had a fine life in the British provinces, and Charles Frohman took it to Broadway where Gaiety stage manager Pat Malone directed the equally potent local stars Julia Sanderson and Joseph Cawthorn (who interpolated a song of his own, "You Can't Play Every Instrument in the Orchestra"), Eva Davenport (who didn't go to the Durbar, but instead insisted "I've Been to America"), Vernon Castle and Alan Mudie (who tangoed with

Plate 373. **The Sunshine Girl.** *George Grossmith fends off the embraces of Connie Ediss whilst Teddy Payne and the juveniles of the piece look on unamused and/or bemused.*

Miss Sanderson) in a suitably Americanized version which played for a fine 101 nights in New York before going on the road. Amongst the supporting cast was Edward Soldene Powell, the son of the great London prima donna of opéra-bouffe days.

J C Williamson Ltd, continuing their association with the Gaiety Theatre, duly took *The Sunshine Girl* to Australia, where she was seen in seasons in Sydney and in Melbourne (Her Majesty's Theatre 17 May 1913) with Jessie Lonnen—daughter of the former Gaiety star E J—in the soubrette role, and the following year the show was mounted in Budapest, where the product of the London stage had been, for a number of years, receiving unusual attention. The Gaiety had furnished *A Runaway Girl* and *The Circus Girl* to Hungarian stages some while previously, and Edwardes had memorably provided the oft-revived *The Geisha* and *San Toy* to Europe at the turn of the century, but recently it was Paul Rubens who had been winning the most attention from Budapest. Both *Miss Hook of Holland* (1908) and *The Balkan Princess* (1910) had been produced at the Király Színház, and now *Napsugár kisasszony* (ad Jenő Heltai) followed them. It evidently did well enough, for the same theatre also subsequently purchased Jones and Rubens's *The Girl from Utah* from the Gaiety management.

Australia: Her Majesty's Theatre, Sydney 19 January 1913; USA: Knickerbocker Theater 3 February 1913; Hungary: Király Színház *Napsugár kisasszony* 3 June 1914

SUPPÉ, Franz von [SUPPÉ, Francesco Ezechiele Ermenegildo von] (b Spalato, 18 April 1819; d Vienna, 21 May 1895). The first major composer to emerge in the budding Viennese Operette tradition.

A descendant of a Belgian family who had settled in Italy, Francesco von Suppé was born in Spalato, Dalmatia (the modern Split) where his parents were working as civil servants. After the death of his father in 1835, his mother left Italy and moved her family to her native Vienna where the young Suppé continued the general musical and composition studies which he had already pursued in Italy at the Vienna Konservatorium and, at the age of 21, took up his first professional post as third conductor at the Theater in der Josefstadt, under the management of Franz Pokorny. There, in the manner of the time, the young Kapellmeister helped supply such songs and incidental music as the theatre's productions required, and his first full score appeared the following year, attached to a Volksstück called *Jung lustig, im Alter traurig.* It was well received, and quickly followed by a second fine success with the music to Schickh's *Die Hammerschmiedin* which went on to be seen in Budapest (14 April 1844) and later at the Theater an der Wien (23 September 1846). Thereafter Suppé provided regular full scores for the Theater in der Josefstadt—including one for the same vaudeville, *Marie, die Tochter des Regiments* (*La Fille du régiment*), which Donizetti had used as the basis for his opera four years previously—as well as for the other suburban and provincial theatres which Pokorny also managed.

When Pokorny took over the Theater an der Wien in 1845, his young conductor and composer moved with him. He provided an original occasional overture for the opening program under the new regime, and then moved into the same conducting/composing routine that he had pursued in the Josefstadt, between 1846 and 1848 alongside Albert Lortzing of *Waffenschmied* and *Zar und Zimmermann* fame, and then, for the rest of his long period at that theatre, with Adolf Müller as a colleague. In the first year, of the half-dozen pieces for which he was called on to supply music and songs, one ran just a single performance and only Kaiser's Charakterbild *Sie ist verheiratet* (43 performances) compiled a good run. The following year two pieces cleared the 20-performance mark, but the overture which Suppé composed for one of these, Karl Elmar's *Dichter und Bauer* (*Poet and Peasant*), was to have a much longer life than the 22 performances the play lasted: it went on to become a concert classic with a century and a half of life in it.

In 1847 Suppé covered seven new shows, but he also posted up his ambition to write something more substantial when he combined with Elmar to write an opera, *Das Mädchen vom Lande.* It was Suppé's third completed opera, but his first to be produced (Theater an der Wien 7 August) and it was played just eight times. Opera for the moment put behind him, he returned to the normal run of his duties and provided the scores the following year for the usual run of comedies with songs as well as for a full-scale Alois Berla burlesque of von Flotow's *Martha* and incidental music for a five-act drama.

In his years at the Theater an der Wien, the most immediately successful pieces with which he was involved were the long-running Possen *Des Teufels Brautfahrt, Gervinus* and *Wo steckt der Teufel?,* but the most noteworthy was the little one-act Operette *Das Pensionat,* produced in 1860 with considerable success and played for a series of 34 performances. *Das Pensionat* is generally quoted as the first significant local attempt to follow the Offenbachian operettic fashion which had been imported to Vienna in the previous few years, and its success set first Suppé, and then Millöcker, Strauss and others on the road to building what would become the 19th-century tradition of Viennese Operette.

The success of *Das Pensionat* encouraged Suppé to go where his career as a composer of such pieces would be best appreciated and, in consequence, he left the Theater an der Wien, after more than 15 years in residence, and took up the position of conductor and composer at the little Theater am Franz-Josefs-Kai, run by Karl Treumann, the most effective producer of the works of Offenbach and other musical theatre of the kind in contemporary Vienna. Treumann mounted several Suppé Operetten at his little riverside theatre and, after an initial flop with *Die Kartenschlägerin,* the composer scored two further successes with the little *Zehn Mädchen und kein Mann* and the part-fresh, part-pasticcio *Flotte Bursche.*

After the destruction of the Kai-Theater, Suppé moved with Treumann back to the producer's old base at the Carltheater. There, whilst still turning out scores for the usual run of Possen—including the musical biography *Franz Schubert* (with Treumann as Schubert), and burlesques such as *Dinorah* (on Meyerbeer's opera)—he produced a line of further short Operetten of which *Die schöne Galathee,* in 1865, proved the high-water-mark of the new Viennese tradition up to that time. His other principal pieces at this period included *Leichte Kavallerie*—another piece which used some existing popular music in its score but which rendered up an original overture to posterity which would be no less popular than his *Dichter und Bauer*—and *Banditenstreiche.*

In 1868 Suppé first ventured with a three-act Zauberposse, a version of the famous old British musical *The Devil to Pay* under the title *Die Frau Meisterin,* which was produced with a stellar cast including Pepi Gallmeyer, Franz Tewele, Josef Matras, Wilhelm Knaack and Therese Braunecker-Schäfer, and was followed in 1870 by a full-length opéra-bouffe, *Die Jungfrau von Dragant,* which benefited from Matras, Karl Blasel, Knaack, Albin Swoboda, Frau Schäfer and Anna Grobecker as its leading players. Neither was successful, and (though *Die Frau Meisterin* was briefly seen in Germany) they were put away after a handful of performances whilst the little *Die schöne Galathee, Leichte Kavallerie* and *Flotte Bursche* remained in the repertoire and were brought back on a regular basis. However, Strauss's triumph in 1874 with *Die Fledermaus* convinced Suppé to have another try. Utilizing a well-proven French libretto by no less a playwright than Eugène Scribe, a libretto already once used by Auber for his opéra-comique *La Circassienne,* he turned out, to the words of Zell and Genée, the Operette *Fatinitza* (1876), which was produced by Franz Jauner, by this time the manager of the Carltheater.

The enormous success of *Fatinitza* re-placed Suppé alongside Strauss at the forefront of the Viennese Operette. Able, as a result, to put aside forever the virtual hack composing that had been so long his lot, he concentrated, from that time, on a 10-year series of full-sized Operetten, almost all staged at the Carltheater, from which he was able comfortably to take retirement as a conductor in 1882. *Der Teufel auf Erden* had only a limited success (20 performances), but his next work, *Boccaccio* (1879), not only confirmed but topped the success of *Fatinitza* and, in the opinion of Suppé and of most of posterity, marked the acme of his career as a theatre composer.

There was further, if not quite equivalent, success with his third Zell-Genée piece *Donna Juanita* (1880) and, to a lesser extent, with the Eugène Sue-based *Der Gascogner* (1881) and his one piece written for his old house, the Theater an der Wien, the lively, comical *Die Afrikareise* (1883) which had a fine worldwide career, but his other works were not immune from lesser or greater degrees of failure. *Herzblättchen,* which came between *Der Gascogner* and *Die Afrikareise,* proved the most ephemeral. In spite of a cast headed by Pepi Gallmeyer, Josef Joseffy and Karl Blasel, it survived only four performances. His two last works also had limited first runs. *Bellman* lasted two and a half weeks at the Carltheater whilst *Die Jagd nach dem Glück* played for just a month and, although both won further and overseas productions, and the latter's music was as substantial stuff as the composer's best, neither was a success in the image of *Fatinitza, Boccaccio, Donna Juanita* or *Die Afrikareise.* The posthumous *Das Modell* (completed by Alfred Zamara and Julius Stern) did somewhat better, beginning with a six-and-a-half week run at the Carltheater, followed by a brief revival and a very reasonable career in Germany and Hungary, but it was far from finding a place in the permanent repertoire.

Suppé shared his life in later years between Vienna and a little estate in Kampthal in Lower Austria where he worked on a regular plan—writing from 6:30 AM to 1 PM, sleeping till 5 PM, and relaxing in the evening. It was under these agreeable conditions that the now-famous and courted composer turned out the last items of a half-century of writing life in which he had composed the scores for more than two hundred Operetten, Possen, burlesques, Singspiele and other stage pieces, including several further unsuccessful operas (*Paragraph drei, Des Matrosens Heimkehr,* the unproduced *The Corsican*), as well as over a thousand other musical works ranging through church music, overtures, symphonies, orchestral music, and songs and choral pieces both in the serious and light vein.

Boccaccio and *Die schöne Galathee* alone remain to represent Suppé in the very limited "Golden Age" repertoire that is still played, often in a sadly savaged state, today, even though his overtures fill many a gramophone record. *Donna Juanita* has retained some place in Eastern Europe, but, amazingly, the once enormously popular *Fatinitza,* in particular, has disappeared. However, in spite of this limited appreciation of his work in the late 20th century, Suppé's reputation and position as "the father of the Viennese Operette" remains intact.

Although he has not yet had the misfortune to have his life and loves transmogrified into an opérette à grand spectacle, Suppé has crept onto the musical screen alongside his contemporaries, Strauss and Millöcker. In Willy Först's film *Operette* he was portrayed by no less an artist than Leo Slezak, and in 1953 he was given the glorious technicolor treatment in a Schonbrünn/Farbe film, *Hab ich nur deine Liebe,* in which Johannes Heesters, Gretl Schörg, Margit Saad, Helmut Qualtinger and Pepi Glöckner featured and his music was "arranged" by Rudolf Kattnigg.

1841 **Jung lustig, im Alter traurig** (*Die Folgen der Erziehung*) (C Wallis) Theater in der Josefstadt 5 March

1841 **Die Wette um ein Herz** (*Künstlersinn und Frauenliebe*) (Karl Elmar) Theater in der Josefstadt 10 March

1841 **Stumm, beredt, verliebt** (Franz Xaver Told) Ödenburg 1 May; Theater an der Wien 15 July 1856

1841 **Die Bestürmung von Saida** (w Carl Binder, Anton Emil Titl/Told) Theater in der Josefstadt 10 September

1841 **Der Pfeilschütz im Lerchenfeld** (Josef Kilian Schickh) Theater in der Josefstadt 27 October

1841 **Der Komödiant** (Eine Lektion in der Liebe) (Elmar) Theater in der Josefstadt 14 December

1842 **Das grüne Band** (Elmar, et al) Theater in der Josefstadt 2 July

1842 **Das Armband** Theater in der Josefstadt 8 September

1842 **Die Hammerschmiedin aus Steiermark** (*Folgen einer Landpartie*) (Schickh) Theater in der Josefstadt 14 October

1844 **Ein Morgen, ein Mittag und ein Abend in Wien** Theater in der Josefstadt 26 February

1844 **Die schlimmen Buben** (*Der Teufel in allen Ecken*) (w Witt/ Anton von Klesheim) Theater in der Josefstadt

1844 **Nella, die Zauberin** (*Der Maskenball auf Hochgiebel*) (Elmar) Theater in der Josefstadt 11 May

1844 **Marie, die Tochter des Regiments** (ad Friedrich Blum) Theater in der Josefstadt 13 June

1844 **Ein Sommersnachts-Traum** (Straube) Theater in der Josefstadt 31 August

1844 **Der Mörder in Einbildung** (aka *Der Kramer und sein Kommis*) (Friedrich Kaiser) Theater in der Josefstadt 28 September

1844 **Dolch und Rose** (*Das Donaumädchen*) (Told) Theater in der Josefstadt 5 November

1844 **Zum ersten Mal im Theater** (Kaiser) Theater in der Josefstadt 31 December

1845 **Die Champagner-Kur** (*Lebenshass und Reue*) (K Gruber) Theater in der Josefstadt 20 February

1845 **Die Müllerin von Burgos** (Josef Kupelwieser) Theater in der Josefstadt 8 March

1845 **Der Preussische Landwehrmann und die französischen Bäuerin** (Kaiser) 1 act Theater in der Josefstadt 22 April

1845 **Die Preussen in Österreich** (Landmädchen, Volontair und Trompeter) (Elmar) Theater in der Josefstadt 29 April

1845 **Der Nabob** (Karl Haffner) Theater in der Josefstadt 9 May

1845 **Die Industrie-Ausstellung** (*Reise-Abenteuer in London*) (Kaiser) Theater in der Josefstadt 1 August

1845 **Des Wanderers Ziel** (Karl Meisl) 1 act Theater an der Wien 30 August

1845 **Reich an Gelt und arm an Schlaf** (Told) Theater an der Wien 17 September

1845 **Das Lustspiel in Hietzing** (Blum) Theater an der Wien 26 September

1845 **Sie ist verheiratet** (Kaiser) Theater an der Wien 7 November

1846 **Die Gänsehüterin** (ad G Ball) Theater an der Wien 11 February

1846 **Der Sohn der Haide** (Kaiser) Theater an der Wien 15 June

1846 **Dichter und Bauer** (Elmar) Theater an der Wien 24 August

1847 **Die Karikaturen** (Kaiser) Theater an der Wien 8 February

1847 **Die Reise nach Grätz mit dem Landkutscher** (*Die Raüber auf dem Semmering*) (Schickh) Theater in der Josefstadt 24 February

1847 **Das Menschenherz** (Lang) Theater an der Wien 15 March

1847 **Liebeszauber, oder Ein Wunder in den Bergen [in der Schweiz]** (Elmar) Theater an der Wien 21 April

1847 **Zwei Pistolen** (Kaiser) Theater an der Wien 8 May

1847 **Ein Feenmärchen** (Kupelwieser) Theater an der Wien 25 May

1847 **Das Mädchen vom Lande** (Elmar) Theater an der Wien 7 August

1847 **Tausend und eine Nacht** (w Anton Storch/Told) Theater in der Josefstadt 20 August

1847 **Die Schule des Armen, oder Zwei Millionen** (Kaiser) Theater an der Wien 26 October

1847 **Was eine Frau einmal will, oder der Friedrichsdor** (w Heinrich Proch/Heinrich Börnstein) Theater an der Wien 23 November

1847 **Hier ein Schmidt, da ein Schmidt, noch ein Schmidt und wieder ein Schmidt** (Elmar, Heinrich Mirani) Theater an der Wien 30 December

1848 **Männer-Schönheit** (Kaiser) Theater an der Wien 6 February

1848 **Unter der Erde, oder Freiheit und Arbeit** (*Arbeit bringt Segen*) (Elmar) Theater an der Wien 30 May

1848 **Eine Petition der Bürger einer kleinen Provinzstadt, oder Theolog, Jurist und Techniker** (aka *Bauer, Bürgermeister, Gutsherr*) (Josef Böhm) Theater an der Wien 12 July

1848 **Wie die Reaktionäre dumm sind!** (Elmar) 1 act Theater an der Wien 3 August

1848 **Ein Traum—kein Traum, oder Die letzte Rolle einer Schauspielerin** (Kaiser) Theater an der Wien 2 December

1848 **Martl** (*Der Portiunculatag [*or *Der Tanzboden] in Schnabelhausen*) (Alois Berla) Theater an der Wien 16 December

1848 **Nacht und Licht** (Kaiser) 1 act Theater an der Wien 31 December

1849 **Des Teufels Brautfahrt, oder Böser Feind und guter Freund** (Elmar) Theater an der Wien 30 January

1849 **Ein Fürst** (Kaiser) Theater an der Wien 17 March

1849 **Gervinus, der Narr vom Untersberg** (*Ein patriotischer Wunsch*) (Berla) Sommer-Theater in Fünfhaus/Theater an der Wien 1 July

1849 **Der Edelstein** (Berla) Sommer-Theater in Fünfhaus

1849 **Ein Blatt von Weltgeschichte** (Beethoven arr/Otto Prechtler) Theater an der Wien 3 October

1849 **Unterthänig und unabhängig** (*Vor und nach einem Jahre*) (Elmar) Theater an der Wien 13 October

1849 **'s Alraunl** (Klesheim) Theater an der Wien 13 November

1850 **Die Philister-Schule** (Elmar) Theater an der Wien 17 January

1850 **Die Künst zu lieben** (*Gentil Bernhard*) (w Adolf Müller/Ida Schuselka-Brünning) Theater an der Wien 26 February

1850 **Liebe zum Volke** (Elmar) Theater an der Wien 18 March

1850 **Die Assentirung** (aka *Bürger und Soldat, oder Liebe zum Vaterland*) (w Adolf Müller/V W Niklas ad Böhm) Theater an der Wien 26 April

1850 **Die beiden Fassbinder** (*Reflexionen und Aufmerksamkeiten*) (Leopold Feldmann) Sommer-Theater in Fünfhaus 16 May

1850 **Der Dumme hat's Glück** (*Er muss tolle Streiche machen*) (Berla) Sommer-Theater in Fünfhaus 29 June

1850 **Der Mann an der Spitz, oder Alles aus Freundschaft** (Anton Bittner) Sommer-Theater in Fünfhaus 19 August

1850 **Der Vertrauensmann, oder Wahrheit und Lüge** (Berla) Theater an der Wien 19 September

1851 **Dame Valentine, oder Frauenräuber und Wanderbursche** (Elmar) Theater an der Wien 9 January

1851 **Fliegende Blätter** (pasticcio comp and arr w Müller) Theater an der Wien 22 May

1851 **Waldmärchen** (Berla) Sommer-Theater in Fünfhaus 30 July

1851 **Angeplauscht** (L Wysber) Sommer-Theater in Fünfhaus 20 August

1852 **Die Jungfer Mahm von Gmunden** (Nikola) Sommer-Theater in Fünfhaus 20 May

1852 **Ein Filz als Prasser** (Leopold Feldmann, Theodor Flamm) Sommer-Theater in Fünfhaus 30 June

1852 **Pech!** (Berla) Sommer-Theater in Fünfhaus 31 July

1852 **Das Beispiel** (Nissl, Sigmund Schlesinger) Theater an der Wien 2 October

1852 **Der Grabsteinmacher** (Wysber) Theater an der Wien 6 November

1853 **Die Heimkehr von der Hochzeit** (Feldmann) Theater an der Wien 8 January

1853 **Der Baum des Lebens, oder Österreichs Eiche** (Feldmann) 1 act Theater an der Wien 13 March

1853 **Hansjörge** (Karl von Holtei) Theater an der Wien 20 April

1853 **Die Irrfahrt um's Glück** (Elmar) Theater an der Wien 24 April

1853 **Die weiblichen Jäger** (*Die Jägermadchen oder Eine moderne Diana*) (Feldmann) Sommer-Theater in Fünfhaus 30 July

1854 **Die Bernsteinhexe** (Heinrich Laube) Theater an der Wien 6 January

1854 **Durcheinander** (pasticcio arr/Wilhelm Grüner) Theater an der Wien 5 February

1854 **Trommel und Trompete** (Elmar) Theater an der Wien 1 April

1854 **Im Bauernhaus—im Herrenhause** (J L Deinhardtstein) 1 act Theater an der Wien 25 April

1854 **Der Biberhof** (Feldmann, Marzroth) Sommer-Theater in Fünfhaus 28 June

1854 **Wo steckt der Teufel?** (Eduard Breier ad Johann Grün) Sommer-Theater in Fünfhaus 28 June

1854 **Mozart** (Alois Wohlmuth) Theater an der Wien 23 September

1854 **Nur romantisch!** (Kaiser) Theater an der Wien 18 November

1854 **Bum! Bum!, oder Zwei Schlauköpf und ein Dummkopf** (Bittner) Theater an der Wien 9 December

1855 **Das Bründl [Schuster] bei Sievring** (*Ein Blick in die Zukunft*) (Hugo Merlin) Theater an der Wien 14 April

1855 **Der Teufel hol die Komödie** (Merlin) Sommer-Theater in Fünfhaus 17 May

1855 **Der Höllenross** (Karl Bruno) Sommer-Theater in Fünfhaus 23 May

1855 **Die G'frettbrüder** (Bittner, Berla) Theater an der Wien 28 June

1855 **Märchenbilder und Geschichten für kleine und grosse Kinder** (*Prinz Lilliput und das Schneiderlein*) (Klesheim) Theater an der Wien 20 October

1855 **Judas im Frack** (*Ein Judas von Anno neune*) (w Müller/ Langer) Theater an der Wien 20 December

1856 **Nur keine Verwandten** (Feldmann) Theater an der Wien 12 April

1856 **Ein Musikant, oder Die ersten Gedanken** (Ludwig Gottsleben) Theater an der Wien 7 June

1856 **Die Wahrheit auf Reisen** (Berg) Sommer-Theater in Fünfhaus 22 June

1856 **Die Weingeister** (Alois Blank, J Bernhofer) Sommer-Theater in Fünfhaus 10 August

1856 **Eine ungarische Dorfgeschichte** (Bittner, Berla) Sommer-Theater in Fünfhaus 31 August

1856 **Die schöne Leni** (Julius Findeisen) Theater an der Wien 4 October

1856 **Die Kreuzköpfeln** (Berg, Grün) Theater an der Wien 22 October

1856 **Vertrauen** (Moritz A Grandjean) Theater an der Wien 22 November

1856 **Ein gefährlicher Mensch** (Der Bücher-Hausirer) (Wilhelm Tesko) Theater an der Wien 7 December

1857 **Der Faschingsteufel** (Berla) Theater an der Wien 23 February

1857 **Eine Schlange** (Karl Gründorf) Theater an der Wien 18 April

1857 **Kopf und Herz** (Flamm) Theater an der Wien 9 May

1857 **Der Komet vom Jahre 1857** (Feldmann, Weyl) Theater an der Wien 23 May

1857 **Ein desparater Kopf** (Karl) Sommer-Theater in Fünfhaus 20 June

1857 **Die Wäschermädeln** (*Ritter Bomsen und seine schauderliche Mordthau*) (aka *Die Hellseherin von Thury*) (Berg) Theater an der Wien 29 June

1857 **Eine Landpartie** (Findeisen) Sommer-Theater in Fünfhaus 17 July

1858 **Die Mozart-Geige, oder Der Dorfmusikant und sein Kind** (Elmar) Theater an der Wien 27 February

1858 **Das tägliche Brot** (Berla) Theater an der Wien 13 March

1858 **Der Werkelmann und seine Familie** (Langer) Theater an der Wien 17 April

1856 **Die Firmgold** (Elmar) Sommer-Theater in Fünfhaus 21 May

1858 **Die Kathi von Eisen** (Berla) Sommer-Theater in Fünfhaus 15 August

1858 **Nach der Stadterweiterung** (Gans, Schlesinger) Theater an der Wien 11 December

1859 **Ein Faschings-Gugelhupf** (w Müller/Langer) Theater an der Wien 5 March

1859 **Etwas zum lachen, oder Keine Politik** (Feldmann) Sommer-Theater in Fünfhaus 9 July

1859 **Eine Wienerin** (Flamm) Sommer-Theater in Fünfhaus 23 July

1859 **Über Land und Meer** (w Müller/Blank) Sommer-Theater in Fünfhaus 21 August

1859 **Eine Judenfamilie** (Mirani) Theater an der Wien 22 October

1859 **Die Zauberdose, oder Um zehr Jahre zu spät** (Elmar) Theater an der Wien 19 December

1860 **Meister Winter** (Berla) Theater an der Wien 13 March

1860 **Das Pensionat** (C K) 1 act Theater an der Wien 24 November

1860 **Mein ist die Welt** (Kaiser) Theater an der Wien 16 December

1861 **Ein Loch in der Hölle** (Johann Schonau) Theater an der Wien 1 February

1861 **Ein Faschingsdonnerstag in Venedig** (J Golinelli) (pantomime divertissement) Theater an der Wien 9 March

1861 **Ein Kapitalist, der einen Dienst sucht** (aka *Ein Ratzelhafter Freund, oder Kapitalist und Kammerdiener*) (Scribe ad Carl F Stix) 1 act Theater an der Wien 26 May

1861 **Der politische Schuster** (Berg) Sommer-Theater in Fünfhaus 1 June

1861 **Der Höllen-Kandidat** (Bernhofer, Blank) Sommer-Theater in Fünfhaus 26 July

1861 **Wiener Nachtfalter** (Gottsleben) Theater an der Wien 3 October

1861 **Ein Schwindler** (Mirani) Theater an der Wien 12 October

1861 **Die Wunderkinder aus Californien** (Elmar) Theater an der Wien 29 November

1862 **Ein Mann dreier Weiber, oder Ein alter Tarockspieler** (w Müller/Blank, J L Harisch) Theater an der Wien 22 April

1862 **Die Kartenschlägerin** 1 act Theater am Franz-Josefs-Kai 26 April

1862 **Zehn Mädchen und kein Mann** (W Friedrich) 1 act Theater am Franz-Josefs-Kai 25 October

1862 **Baedeckers Reisenhandbuch** (w C F Conradin/G Belly) 1 act Theater am Franz-Josefs-Kai 27 December

1862 **Werners Vergnügungszügler** 1 act Theater am Franz-Josefs-Kai 27 December

1863 **Der Herr Vetter** (Berla) Theater am Franz-Josefs-Kai 28 February

1863 **Flotte Bursche** (Josef Braun) 1 act Theater am Franz-Josefs-Kai 18 April

1863 **Überall Geister** (Langer) 1 act Carltheater 23 September

1864 **Das Corps der Rache** (Harisch) 1 act Carltheater 5 March

1864 **Franz Schubert** (Schubert arr/Hanns Max) 1 act Carltheater 10 September

1864 **Der Schweigerpapa aus Krems** (Langer) Carltheater 19 November

1864 **Das Christkindl** (Langer) Carltheater 26 December

1865 **Dinorah, oder Die Turnerfahrt nach Hütteldorf** (Friedrich Hopp as "Julius Cäsar") Carltheater 4 May

1865 **Die schöne Galathee** ("Poly Henrion") 1 act Meysels Theater, Berlin 30 June

1865 **Der Ehemann in der Baumwolle** 1 act Carltheater 4 November

1865 **Die alte Schachtel** (Berg) 1 act Carltheater 2 December

1866 **Leichte Kavallerie** (Karl Costa) Carltheater 21 March

1866 **Die Tochter der Puszta** 1 act Carltheater 24 March

1866 **Der letzte Gulden** (Berg) Carltheater 18 August

1866 **Ein patriotische Dienstbote** Carltheater 18 August

1866 **Theatralische Ausverkauft** Carltheater 25 August

1866 **Es wird annektiert** 1 act Carltheater 20 September

1866 **Die Freigeister** (Costa) Carltheater 23 October

1867 **Banditenstreiche** (B Boutonnier) 1 act Carltheater 27 April

1868 **Die Frau Meisterin** (Costa) Carltheater 20 January

1868 **Schlechte Mittel, gute Zwecke** (Kaiser) Carltheater 5 March

1868 **Tantalusqualen** 1 act Carltheater 3 October

1869 **Isabella** (J Weyl) 1 act Carltheater 6 November

1870 **Vineta, oder Die versunkene Stadt** Theater im Gärtnerplatz, Munich 10 February

1870 **[Lohengelb, oder] Die Jungfrau von Dragant** (Nestroy ad [Costa], M A Grandjean) Stadttheater, Graz 23 July; Carltheater 30 November

1871 **Centifolie** (Langer) Carltheater 9 February

1871 **Eine schöne Wirtschaft** (Flamm) Carltheater 15 November

1872 **Ein weibliche Dämon** (Langer) Carltheater 13 April

1872 **Cannebas** (Josef Doppler) 1 act Carltheater 2 November

1873 **Tricoche und Cacolet** (Henri Meilhac, Ludovic Halévy ad Treumann) Carltheater 3 January

1873 **Wolfgang und Constanze** (Mozart arr/Langer) Carltheater 3 May

1875 **Fräulein Schwarz** (Langer) Carltheater 11 March

1875 **Die Reise um die Erde in 80 Tagen** (Jules Verne, Adolphe d'Ennery ad Karl Treumann) Carltheater 28 March

1876 **Fatinitza** (F Zell, Richard Genée) Carltheater 5 January

1876 **Zahnarzt und Magnetiseur** (A Reichenbach) 1 act Carltheater 4 February

1876 **Nach dem Mond und unterm Meer** (Verne ad Adolphe L'Arronge, Zell) Carltheater 25 March

1876 **Die Frau Baronin vom Ballet** (Berg) 1 act Carltheater 2 December

1876 **Die treulose Witwe** (Berg) 1 act Carltheater 2 December

1877 **Unsere Handwerk** (Berg) 1 act Carltheater 1 April

1878 **Der Teufel auf Erden** (Julius Hopp, Carl Juin) Carltheater 5 January

1879 **Boccaccio** (Zell, Genée) Carltheater 1 February

1880 **Donna Juanita** (Zell, Genée) Carltheater 21 February

1880 **Die Schwestern** (Held) Carltheater 19 October

1881 **Der Gascogner** (Zell, Genée) Carltheater 22 March

1882 **Das Herzblättchen** (Karl Tetzlaff) Carltheater 4 February

1883 **Die Afrikareise** (Moritz West, Genée) Theater an der Wien 17 March

1887 **Bellman** (West, Ludwig Held) Theater an der Wien 26 February

1887 **Joseph Haydn** (Haydn arr/Franz von Radler) Theater in der Josefstadt 30 April

1888 **Die Jagd nach dem Glück** (Genée, Bruno Zappert) Carltheater 27 October

1895 **Das Modell** (Victor Léon, Held) Carltheater 4 October

1898 **Die Pariserin** (Léon, Held) revised *Die Frau Meisterin* Carltheater 26 January

Biographies: Keller, O: *Franz von Suppé, der Schöpfer der deutschen Operette* (Richard Wöpke, Leipzig, 1905), Schneidereit, O: *Franz von Suppé: ein Wiener aus Dalmatien* (VEB, Berlin, 1977)

SURCOUF Opéra-comique in a prologue and 3 acts by Henri Chivot and Alfred Duru. Music by Robert Planquette. Théâtre des Folies-Dramatiques, Paris, 6 October 1887.

The tale of *Surcouf* was (very) loosely based on that of the Captain Kidd of French popular history, the sea captain Robert Surcouf (1773–1827) who plied the Indian Ocean at the turn of the 18th century, pillaging English trading vessels, before settling down in his native Saint-Malo to become a rich commercial shipowner and, eventually, a Baron under the Empire. Chivot and Duru's libretto built upon this well-known personality a traditional comic tale of misunderstandings and revelations, topped up with a romance and a particularly colorful dose of stage spectacle. If the libretto occasionally took a breath for some slightly labored exposition, it nevertheless turned up a very superior bunch of comical characters of whom the two slangy Breton mariners, big papa Gargousse and his little friend Flagéolet, were classics of the genre.

The action begins with a prologue, in which young Robert (Louis Morlet) is sacked by businessman Kerbiniou (Montrouge) and joins up with a corsair ship, vowing to return rich within four years and wed Kerbiniou's niece, Yvonne (Mlle Darcelle). The four years pass, the war with England is over, but Surcouf, who has been rumored dead, does not come, and the new Madame Kerbiniou (Juliette Darcourt) makes plans for Yvonne to wed the English Captain Thompson (Marcellin). But Robert, who has only been injured, arrives in time to foil the marriage, just as war with the English breaks out once more. Mme Kerbiniou is visiting her uncle MacFarlane (Duhamel) in seaside England when Surcouf is captured, but she realizes that he is the man who once saved her from a crocodile, and so she bullies her husband into "admitting" that he is himself the real corsair. Finally, Surcouf escapes and, with Gargousse (Gobin), Flagéolet (Guyon fils) and Yvonne—who have all come to the rescue disguised as Italian nobility—and the Kerbinious, heads back to France pursued by MacFarlane and Thompson. By cunning and bravery his little ship defeats them both and all ends with a "vive la France!"

Planquette's score was tuneful, stirring and comical in turn, with "père Gargousse" particularly well served with a joyous opening duo with his little companion "Moi, j'suis Gargousse," with "Et moi, Flagéolet," another comical duo in their Italian disguise which contained some frenetic above-the-stave falsetto (to A in alt); and with a jauntily martial 6/8 song ("Dedans l'Inde") in the last act. The fun was also well served by Mme Kerbinou's history of her encounter with the crocodile (Couplets du Caïman), whilst the romance was highlighted by a lovely prayer for Yvonne ("En ce jour, avec confiance") and her duets with Surcouf, and the patriotic fervour by the hero's final, poundingly triumphant Air de la navire ("Mon navire si beau").

Surcouf was produced by Henri Micheau and Jules Brasseur at the Folies-Dramatiques and was an instant success. It was played for 135 consecutive nights in its first season and brought back for a further showing in the next two seasons, quickly passing its 200th performance. In the meanwhile, it traveled promptly to Hungary (ad Béla J Fái, Andor Kozma) and to Austria (ad Richard Genée, Bruno Zappert) where Adolf Brackl played the title role and Flagéolet was played by a girl in travesty, but it paused before making its debut on British soil. There was, of course, a problem with the libretto, in which the British were depicted as the baddies and, if not necessarily cowardly, at the best both buffoonish and as being sunk by a Frenchman outnumbered 10 to 1. That problem, however, soon disappeared. Planquette, who had found an audience for his works even greater in Britain than in France, was too much in demand and too anxious to be demanded to allow something of this nature to stand in the way of success. In H B Farnie's version, Robert Surcouf simply became Paul Jones, a swashbuckling Britisher, and the buffoonish enemy was Spain.

Paul Jones was produced by the newly formed Carl Rosa Light Opera Company, an outfit with which the endlessly touring operatic producer hoped to capitalize on the lucrative fashion for comic opera. Planquette went to Britain to remodel his score on "English" lines (as he had done with enormous success with Farnie on *The Old Guard / Les Voltigeurs de la 32ème*), adding a considerable amount of new music for the benefit of Rosa's cast. The show opened in Bolton with 10 original numbers included in its score. By the time it reached London even more was new, but it was effective and so was its new leading "man." *Paul Jones* was played by the Errol-Flynnish American contralto Agnes Huntington, whose performance caused the biggest musical-theatre sensation in years. Harry Monkhouse and Albert James were the comical Bouillabaisse and Petit-Pierre (with an interpolated number by md Frederic Stanislaus), with another American singer, Tillie Wadman, as Yvonne and the old favorite Phyllis Broughton as the crocodile lady.

If anything, *Paul Jones* proved even a bigger hit even than *Surcouf.* The London production ran for a year (370 performances) and toured widely and long, and Farnie's version was subsequently produced in both America—where Miss Huntington starred alongside Marguerite van Breydell (Yvonne), Fanny Wentworth, Hallen Mostyn and James for a month at the Broadway Theater—and, with great success, in Australia where it launched the Nellie Stewart Opera Company with that lady playing Yvonne to the pirate of Mme Marion Burton ("the lady baritone") and the comicals of G H Snazelle and George Leitch. Almost simultaneously with the Broadway production of *Paul Jones,* San Francisco's Tivoli Opera House mounted *The Privateer,* an independent adaptation of *Surcouf.* That enterprising outfit also later mounted their own and wholly new Paul Jones musical in the form of "an American nautical opera" called *An American Hero* (6 June 1898).

In France, *Surcouf* was revived at the Théâtre de la Gaîte in 1893 (20 December) in a more spectacular version with the baritone Jacquin as the show's hero; and again at the Château d'Eau in 1901 (2 December) with Guillot as Jones alongside Vauthier and Mlle Esquilar, and it remained on the provincial schedules for some time thereafter. During the Second World War the German administration decided to revive the show, with its anti-British sentiments, in Paris, but the publisher claimed that he had accidentally mislaid the scores and scripts (they had apparently been hastily buried in someone's garden) and this propagandizing revival did not take place.

Robert Surcouf (Jean Maugendrez), another opérette having Surcouf as its hero, was produced in Mauritius on 22 August 1978.

Hungary: Népszínház *A kalózkirály* 28 February 1888; Austria: Carltheater *Der Freibuter* 1 September 1888; UK: Prince of Wales Theatre *Paul Jones* 12 January 1889; USA: Tivoli Opera House, San Francisco *The Privateer* 22 September 1890, Broadway Theater *Paul Jones* 6 October 1890; Australia: Opera House, Melbourne *Paul Jones* 27 March 1890

SUSI *see* A KIS GRÓF

DAS SÜSSE MÄDEL Operette in 3 acts by Alexander Landesberg and Leo Stein. Music by Heinrich Reinhardt. Carltheater, Vienna, 25 October 1901.

Graf Balduin Liebenburg (Karl Blasel) comes to town to take his nephew Hans (Willy Bauer) back to the family estate to wed his niece, Lizzi (Helene Schupp). He finds him in the gaudy company of what the boy insists is a charity committee, and so the old man invites Lola Winter (Mizzi Günther), the süsse Mädel of the title, who is really Hans's girlfriend, and the artist Florian Lieblich (Louis Treumann) to join them in the country. Florian's jealous little Fritzi (Therese Biedermann) follows secretly. Neither Hans nor Lizzi wishes to wed the other and, after some antics at a ball, an untimely interruption by Fritzi—who Liebenburg becomes convinced is his illegitimate child—and various other quiproquos, everyone weds whom they wish. To put the icing on the ending, Balduin's long-lost love child turns out to be not a girl child at all, but Lizzi's boyfriend, Prosper Plewny (Ferdinand Pagin).

Reinhardt's first attempt at a full-length Operette score produced a bundle of light, dancing Viennesey melodies, strong on waltzes and country rhythms, from which Lola's opening number ''So g'waschen wie a Bamerl'' (Lied vom süssen Mädel) turned out to be a huge popular hit. Hans's waltz ''Launische Dame, Glück ist dein Name'' and several pretty duets—Lola and Hans's ''Geh' sag mir nicht, dass du mich liebst,'' a farewell duo, ''Warum verziehst du deinen Mund'' (which had the particularity of a gramophone accompaniment), and Florian and Lizzi's burlesque of an English musical-comedy duet—also stood out, and helped the show to, to the surprise of some, a great success.

In spite of criticisms, particularly of its ''unsubstantial'' music, from those who regretted the passing of the ''Golden Age'' style of Operette, director Andreas Aman's production of *Das süsse Mädel* turned out to be the most successful piece to have been put up by a Viennese composer in years. It was played 140 times in succession and eventually ran up its total to more than 200 performances at the Carltheater (200th performance, 18 April 1905) before returning at the Raimundtheater in 1909 with a cast headed by Genie von Grossl (Lola), Gerda Walde (Fritzi), Marie Trethan (Lizzi), Carl Streitmann (Hans) and Franz Glawatsch (Prosper). The show found a similarly enthusiastic response in Germany (Otto Keller's survey of 1925 rated it all-time number 30 amongst Viennese Operetten for the number of performances given in Germany) and went on to productions in Hungary (ad Gyula Komor) and throughout central Europe. A German-language production by José Ferenczy's Berlin Centraltheater company, which played at New York's Irving Place Theater with Mia Werber as Lola, Edmund Loewe as Florian, Sigmund Künstadt as Hans, Therese Delma (Lizzi), Henny Wildner (Fritzi), Rudolf Ander (Balduin) and Carl Knaack (Prosper), was again a great hit, lasting for over a month in its first run and causing Sam Shubert to take up the English-language rights. However, no Shubert production forthcame on American soil, the German version being reprised in 1910 with Lucie Engelke starred (19 April) and again in 1912 (25 January) without finding the piece a vernacular production. Britain's 1906 English-language production (ad A Demain Grange, William Caine, Herbert Cottesmore, add mus K Ernest Irving), mounted by Charles Hamilton, London agent for the Shuberts, to feature leading lady Claudia Lasell and mooted for the Shaftesbury Theatre, did not make London.

The success of *Das süsse Mädel* has been pointed up as a turning point in the Viennese musical theatre, one which signaled the end of that ''Golden Age'' which had been marked by the works of such composers as Suppé, Strauss and Millöcker. By turning in a direction which followed and embraced the more folksy elements of works such as Zeller's *Der Vogelhändler* and *Der Obersteiger,* but which yet lightened them into an up-to-date and frothy musical score and story, Reinhardt and *Das süsse Mädel* helped lay the first foundations for the ''Silver Age'' of 20th-century musical theatre in Vienna.

Germany: Centraltheater 19 December 1901; Hungary: Fővárosi Nyári Színkör *Az édes lányka* 26 April 1902; USA: Irving Place Theater (Ger) 10 March 1903; UK: Kennington Theatre 29 November 1902 (copyright), Theatre Royal, Nottingham *The Sweet Girl* 27 August 1906

SWANBOROUGH Family

The Swanborough family was a prominent and important one in the world of the London musical theatre in the third quarter of the 19th century. For many years they ran the old Strand Theatre as a home for some of the best and brightest burlesque entertainments in town, launching many pieces which went on from their initial London runs to performances all round the English-speaking theatre world, and taking the technical honor of being the producers of the ''first English opéra-bouffe'' when F C Burnand and the Strand's house musical director Frank Musgrave wrote, and they staged, the original musical burlesque *Windsor Castle.*

Their era began when father ''Swanborough,'' a former accountant, took up the lease of the decrepit and out-of-favor Strand Theatre in January 1858. He overhauled it and launched it on a diet of multiple-bill burlesque and comedy productions, intermittently putting at the head of the bill as proprietor, for reasons which apparently had something to do with financial liabilities, variously the name of his son, his wife—the soon-to-be-''famous'' Mrs Malaprop of the West End theatre establishment—or his elder daughter, Louisa, known simply for the stage as ''Miss Swanborough'' and already established as a leading burlesque actress at the Olympic and the Haymarket (Alphonse in *Masaniello,* Princess Young and Handsome in *Young and Handsome,* Hero in *Much Ado,* etc).

Musical pasticcio burlesques played a major part in the entertainment at the Strand and many of them—at first largely from the pen of H J Byron (author of the house's two previous burlesques, and who was said to be ''behind'' and well as ''with'' the Swanborough régime), later from other top burlesque authors including Burnand and Farnie—were major successes. The list of their original productions, which continued through the death of father Swanborough (he committed suicide amid much gossip and whispering about deeds unrecorded, but the official reason for his rash act was that he had gone deaf) without any change in policy, included *Fra Diavolo Travestie* (5 April 1858), *The Bride of Abydos* (31 May 1858), *The Maid and the Magpie* (11 October 1858), *The Very Latest Edition of the Lady of Lyons* (11 July 1859), *The Miller and His Men* (9 April 1860), *Cinderella* (26 December 1860), *Aladdin, or The Wonderful Scamp* (1 April 1861), *Esmeralda, or The Sensation Goat* (28 September 1861), *Puss in a New Pair of Boots* (26 December 1861), *Pizzaro, or The Leotard of Peru* (21 April 1862), *Ivanhoe* (26 December 1862), *Ali Baba, or The 39 Thieves* (6 April 1863), *The Motto* (16 July 1863), *Patient Penelope* (25 November 1863), *Orpheus and Eurydice* (26 December 1863), *Mazourka* (27 April 1864), *The Grin Bushes* (26 December 1864), and *Windsor Castle* (5 June 1865).

These shows, and their style of management, proved to be successful enough that in 1865 the Swanboroughs were able to upgrade their theatre, reopening with further bills in the same style on which featured such burlesques as *L'Africaine* (18 November 1865), *Paris, or Vive Lemprière* (2 April 1866), *The Latest Edition of Kenilworth* (revival), *Der Freischütz* (8 October 1866), *Guy Fawkes* (26 December 1866), *Pygmalion and the Statue Fair* (20 April 1867), *William Tell with a Vengeance* (5 October 1867), *The Caliph of Baghdad* (26 December 1867), *The Field of the Cloth of Gold* (11 April 1868), *Joan of Arc* (29 March 1869), *The Pilgrim of Love* (revival, 30 August 1869), *Ino* (30 October 1869), *The Flying Dutchman* (2 December 1869), *Sir George and a Dragon* (31 March 1870), *Kenilworth* (revival, 30 May 1870), *The Field of the Cloth of Gold* (revival, 20 June 1870), *The Idle Prentice* (10 September 1870), *Coeur de Lion* (December 1870), *Eurydice* (24 April 1870), *My Poll and Partner Joe* (6 May 1871), *The Three Musket-Dears* (1871), *Arion* (20 December 1871), *The Vampire* (15 August 1872) and *The Lady of the Lane* (31 October 1872).

Keeping within reach of the same kind of entertainment, the theatre moved on in the 1870s to play a mixture of pasticcio musical comedies, extravaganzas which only occasionally put themselves up as regular burlesques, and revivals of old favorites. Amongst the new pieces were the hugely successful *Nemesis* (17 April 1873), *Eldorado* (19 February 1874), *Loo* (28 September 1874), *Intimidad* (8 April 1875), *Flamingo* (18 September 1875), *Antarctica* (26 December 1875), *The Lying Dutchman* (21 December 1876), *Champagne* (29 September 1877), *An Ambassador from Below* (1878), *Dora and Diplunacy* (14 February 1878) and *The Desperate Adventures of the Baby* (1878). Mrs Swanborough then sublet the house to Alexander Henderson, the newly rich producer of *Les Cloches de Corneville,* for his French opéra-comique productions. In 1882 the Strand Theatre was once again rebuilt, but by 1887 the Swanboroughs were in financial difficulties, Mrs Swanborough was adjudged bankrupt, and the theatre was finally ceded to J S Clarke, thus ending the most famous era of its existence.

Alongside the ''Swanborough'' parents, William [Henry Valentine SMITH] (d Kilburn, London, 31 May 1863) and his wife Mary Ann, née Swanborough and always billed just as **Mrs (H V) SWANBOROUGH** (b Somerset, 7 May 1804; d London, 6 January 1889), five of their offspring worked at the Strand Theatre. The youngest, **Ada SWANBOROUGH** [Marianne Ada Hannah SMITH] (b London, 29 October 1845; d London, 12 December 1893), was the most prominent. The ''handsome, tall and graceful'' actress took leading roles in the theatre's burlesque productions from her teens—William in *Puss in a New Pair of Boots,* Hardress Cregan in *Eily O'Connor,* Lady Rowena in *Ivanhoe,* Eurydice to the Orpheus of Marie Wilton in *Orpheus and Eurydice,* Amy Robsart in *The Latest Edition of Kenilworth,* Geraldine in *The Grin Bushes,* Agnes in *Der Freischütz,* Penelope in *Patient Penelope,* Lord Mounteagle in *Guy Fawkes,* Venus in *Paris,* William Tell in *William Tell with a Vengeance*—but latterly left the burlesque plums to others and appeared mainly in the comedy parts of the bill.

In the earliest Swanborough days at the Strand the team included Ada's sister, Louisa Maria Sporle Smith (b London, 1833) known as plain **Miss SWANBO-**

ROUGH, who—after playing lead roles at the Haymarket and the Olympic—starred at the Strand until her marriage and retirement in 1860, and her brothers, **William H[enry] Swanborough** (b London, 1830; d Liverpool, 17 December 1886), **Arthur [Henry Kent] Swanborough** (b London, 1837; d London, 22 December 1895) and **Edward Swanborough** (b London, 14 April 1841; d London, 21 December 1908).

William—the original ostensible manager of the Strand—had been previously in the company at the Lyceum and he appeared on the stage at the Strand playing such roles as Beppo in the *Fra Diavolo* burlesque. He was subsequently billed as ''acting manager'' of the house and also directed a number of the shows (a job which was later taken by his mother), before expanding his theatrical interests both at other London houses and in the provinces. He was responsible for the construction of the Prince of Wales Theatre, Birmingham.

Arthur was treasurer at the Prince of Wales, Birmingham, manager of the Royalty, and held the post of front-of-house manager at the Strand for a number of years before becoming manager of the Royal Music Hall in Holborn, whilst Edward managed the Strand's box office and, after the collapse, moved on to become manager of the London Pavilion, and later of the Chelsea Palace.

The two younger brothers also married prominent actresses of the burlesque stage. Arthur was the husband of **Eleanor BUFTON** (b Wales, ?1840; d London, 9 April 1893) and Edward of [**Mary Ann**] **Fanny HUGHES** (b London, ?1842; d London, 12 January 1888). William was married to the dancer Kate Kirby (d Rochester, 4 December 1862).

SWEENEY TODD, the Demon Barber of Fleet Street Musical thriller in 2 acts by Hugh Wheeler based on a play by Chris Bond. Music and lyrics by Stephen Sondheim. Uris Theater, New York, 1 March 1979.

Sweeney Todd, the demon barber of Fleet Street, first saw daylight in Chapter One of a tale called *The String of Pearls,* written by one Fred Hazleton Esq (''author of *Edith the Captive, Charley Wag,* etc'') and published in a magazine called *The People's Periodical and Family Library* in 1846. The character of the barber who ''tilted his customers out of the shaving chair through a trap-door into a cellar, where he pickled them and made them into pork pies'' quickly caught the public imagination and he and it appeared on the stage at the Britannia Theatre early the next year (*Sweeney Todd, or The Fiend of Fleet Street* by George Dibdin Pitt, 8 March 1847). Hazleton's name was attached to a rival version played at the Bower Saloon as *Sweeney Todd, the Barber of Fleet Street, or The String of Pearls,* the Grecian mounted a *The String of Pearls* in 1861, a Whitechapel melodrama subtitled *The Life and Death of Sweeney Todd* was produced the following year and a Matt Wilkinson drama came out in 1870. *Sweeney Todd* was repeated regularly on the British stage for more than half a century, and other versions, including one by Andrew Melville, gave the early ones concurrence in the period in which the character of the bloody barber came to the height of his fame on the British stage, in the hands of grand guignol specialist Tod Slaughter.

Although the demon barber might have seemed obvious meat for the operatic stage, he apparently did not ever make it there. On the other hand, he did make several appearances with musical accompaniment on the British stage, notably in 1959 when Donald Cotton and Brian Burke's *The Demon Barber* was mounted at the Lyric, Hammersmith (10 December) with Roy Godfrey as Todd and one Barry Humphries, né Dame Edna Everage, as Jonas Fogg. Todd's musical apotheosis came, however, as the result of a 1973 mounting of a version of *Sweeney Todd* written and staged by Chris Bond at London's suburban Half Moon Theatre. This version's difference was that it presented Todd not as a twisted maniac, but as a cruelly-done-by fellow whose murders were part of/a result of his revenge against his (upper-class) oppressor(s), and therefore either all right or, at the worst, comprehensible. This Sweeney was the hero rather than the villain of his piece, and this production, in its turn, inspired Wheeler and Sondheim's more substantial, and musical *Sweeney Todd.*

Sweeney Todd (Len Cariou) returns to London city, after 15 years of prison exile, with nothing but revenge in his heart. For once upon a time he was a barber with a pretty young wife and a little daughter, but a lecherous judge lusted after the barber's wife and so he had her husband transported on a trumped-up charge, raped the woman and kept her child. Todd sets up shop in Fleet Street, above a pie-shop run by a common widow called Mrs Lovett (Angela Lansbury) who soon becomes his ally. He establishes a reputation for his barbering skill and determines to lure the hated Judge Turpin (Edmund Lyndeck) to his barber's chair and under his barber's blade. His plans go wrong when the efforts of his young friend Anthony (Victor Garber) to run off with Todd's daughter Johanna (Sarah Rice), a pale little prisoner whom the Judge has planned to wed himself, are exposed.

His prey escaped, Todd sets off instead on a mindless round of murders. And the corpses of his victims go to make the fillings for Mrs Lovetts pies. Eventually the Judges turn comes, but the horror is not at an end yet. Todd discovers that a crazed beggar-woman who has fallen to his blade was his wife—not dead as Mrs Lovett had pretended, but turned witless from her rape. In revenge he hurls the widow into her own oven before he himself

Plate 374. *Leon Greene as the demon barber of Fleet Street in the Manchester Library Theatre's 1985 production of* **Sweeney Todd.**

is cut down by her brain-addled shop boy, Tobias (Ken Jennings). After a hecatomb to challenge *Hamlet* only the juveniles are left standing to provide a happy ending of sorts.

The melodrama was illustrated by a large score, framed in the broadsheet-style ''Ballad of Sweeney Todd,'' a score which was threatening in color, dissonant in tone one moment, and grotesquely comical the next, with the comic moments sometimes proving the most truly horrid. Mrs Lovett admitted to selling ''The Worst Pies in London,'' chuckled with Todd over the prospect of much tastier man-meat ones in the music-hally ''A Little Priest'' and sang horribly flirtatious parlour music at the barber (''By the Sea'') between murders, whilst Todd duetted with the judge over ''Pretty Women'' as he prepared to slit his victim's throat. Elsewhere the barber thundered out his maddened ''Epiphany,'' Anthony serenaded his ''Johanna,'' a rival Italian barber (Joaquin Romaguera)—soon to be Todd's first victim—vaunted his wares in burlesque operatic tones (''Pirelli's Miracle Elixir''), and in a rare moment of sensibility Mrs Lovett cuddled her frightened little shop boy to assure him ''(No one's going to harm you) Not While I'm Around.''

Hal Prince's original production of *Sweeney Todd* encased this fairly straightforward grand guignol story in a welter of meaningful scenery in the most extravagant opérette à grand spectacle style. There were looming grey walls and a roof representing an industrial-revolutionized British factory, all heavy with implications of social (dis)order. There was a pipe organ on the proscenium arch. There was also a razor which spurted blood in the best traditions of the grand-guignol stage as each victim's throat was sliced. The production provoked mixed reactions, but for many the verdict was that somewhere the amongst the scenery, and underneath the sometimes rather pretentious sentiments that had been pasted on top of the story, there was a fine show.

Sweeney Todd took its season's Tony Award as Best Musical and played 557 performances at Broadway's Uris Theater, but a reproduction of the New York staging at London's Theatre Royal, Drury Lane, with Denis Quilley (Todd), Sheila Hancock (Mrs Lovett), Austin Kent (Judge), Andrew C Wadsworth (Anthony) and Michael Staniforth (Tobias) proved a quick failure (157 performances). The show was taken on tour in America, with Lansbury and Lyndeck repeating their original performances alongside takeover Todd, George Hearn, and this production was filmed for television (1982) before, in 1984, *Sweeney Todd* was produced by the New York City Opera.

However, whilst the musical headed for what had always seemed its story's natural home on the operatic stage, it also began to find itself a second life on another level, in another area. It was produced in Britain in a severely cut-down version—no factory, no pipe organ, no large chorus and orchestra, just the savage story of Sweeney Todd, told in music (and with the Judge's role musically restored to its full length after having been cut in New York previews). Bond mounted this stark and spare version back at the Half Moon, with Leon Greene as Todd, and the piece began to find an audience in Britain which it had not attracted at Drury Lane. Provincial productions proliferated, and *Sweeney Todd* became established in the repertoire in a manner which had looked wholly unlikely after its unfortunate first London production.

In 1987 the show was mounted in Australia by the Melbourne Theatre Company with Peter Carroll and Geraldine Turner featured, subsequently playing a season in Sydney (Her Majesty's Theatre 6 January 1988, 28 performances), and in 1989 a similarly reduced-size version (length and breadth) was mounted at New York's Circle in the Square with Bob Gunton and Beth Fowler in the featured roles (14 September, 189 performances). Gathering impetus all the time, an impetus fueled by the growing cult for Sondheim's works, particularly in the subsidized sector of the theatre, *Sweeney Todd* appeared in 1992 on the Hungarian stage, in 1993 on the studio stage of Britain's National Theatre, with Julia Mackenzie as Mrs Lovett, and in 1998 it was played in repertoire by Opera North (Grand Theatre Leeds 17 January) as it spread itself throughout the theatrical spectrum—from small dramatic theatres to opera houses—in a way accomplished by few other pieces.

UK: Theatre Royal, Drury Lane 2 July 1980; Australia: Playhouse, Melbourne 1 October 1987; Hungary: Erkel Theater *Nyakfelmetsző* 5 June 1992

TV film: RKO/Nederlander 1982

Recordings: original cast (RCA), concert recording 1999 (NY Philharmonic)

SWEET ADELINE Musical in 2 acts by Oscar Hammerstein II. Music by Jerome Kern. Hammerstein's Theater, New York, 3 September 1929.

Sweet Adeline was evolved by Hammerstein and Kern as a vehicle for the talents of Helen Morgan, who had recently created the role of Julie in *Show Boat* for them. An historical setting was chosen—1890s Hoboken—and Miss Morgan was cast as beer-garden-proprietor's daughter who is unlucky in love (an uncomplicated romantic tale for the deliciously suffering Miss Morgan would have been entirely inept) but instead becomes a Broadway star, with a different man (Robert Chisholm) at her side. Her sister Nellie (Carly Bergman) gets the much-loved sailor (Max Hoffman jr) who caused Addie's misery.

The enduring song from this score, performed first by the sweetly sad-soprano Miss Morgan and subsequently outside the show by more torchy vocalists, was the broadly broken-hearted "Why Was I Born?" Miss Morgan's other numbers ("Here Am I," "Don't Ever Leave Me") shared the same flavor, leading Gerald Bordman in his biography of Kern to catalogue them nicely as "three sweet, long-faced sisters." This tendency to misery gave the carefully constructed period operetta a rather downbeat feeling which was only partially alleviated by such pieces as the bright, waltzing "The Sun About to Rise" and the interpolations written and/or performed by Irene Franklin as an incidental Hoboken starlet.

Arthur Hammerstein's production of *Sweet Adeline* made a fine start on Broadway, but had its prospects shattered when the Wall Street crash occurred just a few months into the run. 234 performances in such an ambiance were better than most shows managed. But in spite of this the show did not travel beyond America. It did however make it to celluloid. Kern went to Hollywood to supply extra numbers for a Warner Brothers film version, starring Irene Dunne, which bore more resemblance to its original than many other such films. Alongside seven of the show-score songs, one number ("Lonely Feet") taken from his London failure *Three Sisters,* and three fresh ones, there was however also found place for the well-known and definitely lively von Tilzer/Bryan "Down Where the Wertzberger Flows."

Sweet Adeline was given a revival at the Goodspeed Opera House in 1977 (26 April), and a concert showing in New York in 1997 (13 February) in which Patti Cohenour sang Miss Morgan's role.

Film: Warner Bros 1935

Recording: film soundtrack (part-record) (JJA)

SWEET CHARITY Musical comedy in 2 acts by Neil Simon based on the screenplay *Nights of Cabiria* by

Plate 375. *Juliet Prowse as London's* **Sweet Charity.**

Federico Fellini, Tullio Pinelli and Ennio Flaiano. Lyrics by Dorothy Fields. Music by Cy Coleman. Palace Theater, New York, 29 January 1966.

The adaptation of Federico Fellini's film *Nights of Cabiria* into what eventually became *Sweet Charity* was originally done by director/choreographer Bob Fosse in the form of a one-act, half-of-an-evening musical comedy. However, the other half of the project eventually faded away and Neil Simon came in to develop the *Sweet Charity* half into a full-length musical comedy. In the process, he considerably softened down the cruel and rather gaudy colors of the original dramatic film. The heroine of that film had been a prostitute, but Charity Hope Valentine (as her name suggested) was a dancing hostess in a seedy New York ballroom where you got the impression that some of the girls ''did'' and some of them ''didn't.'' Not unless they were in love, anyway. Cabiria, as created by Guilietta Masina, was a simple, willing girl who cannot keep a ''protector,'' who is the unkind joke of her fellow workers, and who is so unhappy that she attempts to drown herself. When Charity Hope Valentine falls into the water, it is accidentally and for laughs.

Falling is Charity's problem—or, rather, falling in love. She seems to do it every moment that she's not already done it, but always with the wrong kind of feller. She gets dumped as regularly as she is picked up, but she always comes back, hopeful as ever, and falls in love with the next man who asks. Her adventures during the course of the show include an accidental encounter with a Continental film star, Vittorio Vidal (James Luisi), who has had a stormy bust-up with his girl and who just uses Charity until the bust is mended, and an another with shy, deeply sincere Oscar (John McMartin) whom she meets in a stuck lift in the 92nd Street YMCA. Oscar actually gets round to proposing, but although he says that the equivocal nature of Charity's employment and the unequivocal nature of her past don't worry him, they do, and at the end of the evening Charity is back to picking herself up and starting over again.

The role of Charity was created by Gwen Verdon, accredited star of Fosse's productions of *Damn Yankees, New Girl in Town* and *Redhead,* and star and character came together perfectly in one of Broadway's most memorable performances of the era. Charity dreamed and hoped her way through a series of songs: the self-deluding ''You Should See Yourself,'' a jubilant ''If My Friends Could See Me Now'' as she found herself in the company of the film star, an encouraging ''I'm the Bravest Individual'' to the lift-shy Oscar, a dizzy ''Where Am I Going?'' as she quit her dance-hall job, and an explosive ''I'm a Brass Band'' on her receipt of her first proposal. The show's biggest single song successes, however, came not from the star's solo lineup but from two rather tongue-in-cheek numbers. Charity's sisters-in-work, Nickie (Helen Gallagher) and Helene (Thelma Oliver), led a tartily over-the-top encouragement to a ''Big Spender'' to be their partner for the evening, and a visit to Oscar's ''church,'' the Rhythm of Life Church, turned up a parody of such institutions as the leader of the group, Johann Sebastian Brubeck (Arnold Soboloff), let rip with his creed in song and dance (''The Rhythm of Life''). Both songs, taken from their context, suffered the ''When Britain Really Ruled the Waves'' fate of being later taken at face value and performed without the slightest satirical intent.

If the presence in the season's lists of *Man of La Mancha* and *Mame* limited the show's Tony Award takings to just a prize for Fosse's choreography, *Sweet Charity* was nevertheless a first-class Broadway hit, playing 608 performances before setting off on the road with Chita Rivera in the role of Charity. Australia was quickly off the mark with a production of the show, and *Sweet Charity,* with Nancye Hayes as Charity supported by Peter Adams (Oscar), Judith Roberts (Nickie) and Alec Novak (Vidal), opened there 12 months into the Broadway run. It played four months in Sydney and 2 1/2 in Melbourne (Her Majesty's Theatre 6 May 1967). Harold Fielding and Bernard Delfont mounted London's version of *Sweet Charity* later the same year with Juliet Prowse as its leading lady alongside Rod McLennan (Oscar), Josephine Blake (Nickie), Paula Kelly (Helene) and Fred Evans (Brubeck), and the show marked up another hit through a run of 476 performances.

A film version of the show put out in 1969 featured Shirley Maclaine as Charity, alongside McMartin, Miss Rivera, Ricardo Montalban (Vidal) and Sammy Davis jr (Brubeck). It included the main numbers from the original score, but added a couple more and replaced the original title song with another under the same name. And all the time *Sweet Charity* continued its way around the world. In 1970 the piece was seen in Paris, traditionally shy of Broadway material, when Arthur Lesser mounted a version (ad Albert Husson, Jacques Plante) at the Théâtre de la Gaîté-Lyrique with Magali Noël playing Charity alongside Jacques Duby (Oscar), Sidney Chaplin (Vidal), Dominique Tirmont (Brubeck), Florence Arnell and Corinne Marchand, and in Germany. Germany's first *Sweet Charity* (the title survived, as it had in France), production was staged at Wiesbaden (ad Victor Bach, Marianne Schubart) with Dagmar Koller as Charity and subsequently at the Theater des Westens (51 performances), and the following year this version made its first appearance on the other side of the then Wall when it was mounted at the Dresden Staatsoperette (29 April 1971).

Sweet Charity maintained a place in the standard repertoire through the years after its first productions, and in 1986 it made a return to Broadway. Fosse again directed and choreographed a version which had been slightly fiddled with musically—the Mark II title song held its place—and Debbie Allen, the heroine of the television series *Fame,* starred as Charity alongside Michael Rupert (Oscar), Bebe Neuwirth (Nickie), Allison Williams (Helene), Mark Jacoby (Vidal) and Irving Allen Lee (Brubeck). Produced at the Minskoff Theater by the now-normal clutch of producers (four were billed) on 27 April, it this time picked up four Tony Awards from the now rather more extended selection available to be shared amongst many less and lesser contenders, and it ran for 386 performances. In 1992 another major revival was mounted at Berlin's Theater des Westens (24 January, 71 performances) with Michelle Becker starred, as *Sweet Charity* passed her first quarter-century as a hardy perennial, and both Australia and Britain (Victoria Palace, 1998) also took a fresh look. Former child star Bonnie Langford played the role of Charity in London's edition.

Australia: Her Majesty's Theatre, Sydney, 21 January 1967; UK: Prince of Wales Theatre 11 October 1967; France: Théâtre de la Gaîté-Lyrique 1970; Germany: Staatstheater, Wiesbaden 7 February 1970, Theater des Westens 4 September 1970

Film: Universal 1969

Recordings: original cast (Columbia), London cast (CBS), French cast (CBS), German cast (Decca), New York revival cast (EMI), Dutch cast (Philips), film soundtrack (Decca), studio cast (TER), etc

SWEETHEART MINE Musical comedy in 2 acts by Lauri Wylie and Lupino Lane based on the play *My Old Dutch* by Albert Chevalier. Lyrics by Frank Eyton. Music by Noel Gay. Victoria Palace, London, 1 August 1946.

The fourth and last of the long-running series of Lupino Lane ''little cockney chappie'' musicals produced at the Victoria Palace, *Sweetheart Mine* did not find the same success as *Twenty to One* or *Me and My Girl,* but it nevertheless filled the house which he had made his own through eight months and 323 performances in the year after the war.

In a tale taken from Albert Chevalier's successful play (based in its turn on the famous song of the same title), Lane, surrounded by mostly the same company of family and friends as had worked with him in the earlier shows, starred as the layabout 'Arry 'Awkins whose ''old dutch'' Liza (Barbara Shotter) wins a fortune and spends it trying vainly to make something of her husband. The score, in the jolly drop-your-aitches cockney vein, featured such Noel Gay numbers as the ''The Missus, the Moke and Me,'' '''Appy 'Ampstead'' and ''It's all a Blooming Lot of La-di-da,'' but the highlight of the show's musical part was Lane's eleven o'clock performance of Chevalier's original song: ''We've been together now for forty years, and it don't seem a day too much.''

SWEETHEARTS Operetta in 2 acts by Harry B Smith and Fred de Grésac. Lyrics by Robert B Smith. Music by Victor Herbert. Academy of Muic, Baltimore, 24 March 1913; New Amsterdam Theater, New York, 8 September 1913.

Victor Herbert wrote a great deal of highly attractive music in his career, Fred de Grésac wrote the delicious light comedy *La Passerelle* and Harry B Smith the neat comic opera libretto of *Robin Hood,* amongst a long list of others. They also got together and wrote *Sweethearts.*

Princess Sylvia of Zilania (Christie MacDonald) has been stolen away from her home as a baby to keep her safe from a revolution, and boarded with an unobtrusive family of working folk in a far-off country. No, this is not *The Gondoliers,* it is not burlesque . . . it is for real, and it's 1913. Sylvia's foster-family aren't gondoliers, however, because they live in Bruges and she's a girl. They are laundry-folk. Dame Paula (Ethel Du Fre Houston) runs a washing-shop called ''The White Geese.'' Back home in Zilania, with the Princess given up for lost, a distant cousin called Prince Franz (Thomas Conkey) is more or less about to ascend the throne, but he comes to Belgium, just happens to wander into the washing shop, falls in love with the laundry maid, and after a couple of acts of ups and downs they get round to true love and half-a-crown apiece. Tom McNaughton played Mikel Mikelovicz, the Prime Minister who originally stole the princess and brought her to Bruges and left her gaily prattling, Hazel Kirke was soubrette Liane who disguises herself as one of the White Geese girls to fake a disappearance and gets mistaken for the Princess, and Edwin Wilson was Karl, over whom Sylvia sighed even for a little while after she knew he was a rotter, before getting round to falling for Franz.

Herbert's score was not up to those for most of his comic operas. There was a dainty little number, ''Cricket in the Hearth,'' for the heroine, who also had a more soulful one singing about ''The Angelus'' and a title duo to share with her Prince, whilst he in his turn had a stridingly baritonic number declaring that ''Every Lover Must Meet His Fate.'' Perhaps strangely, the prettiest moment of the score came in a nicely silly little Belgian number for the soubrette all about ''Jeanette and Her Little Wooden Shoes.''

Louis Werba and Mark Luescher's production of *Sweethearts* had a slow start, and following its Baltimore opening the piece was put thoroughly under the knife. But in the end it did very nicely. If it did not come up to their last production with Miss MacDonald, *The Spring Maid* (*Die Sprudelfee*), or to their second Smith brothers adaptation, *The Rose Maid* (*Bub oder Mädel?*), in terms of its first run of Broadway performances, it nevertheless totted up 136 nights in New York—when it finally got there—before going back on the road. But it went without Lou-nephew-of-Erlanger Werba and Mark Luescher, for a month into the production they had gone noisily bankrupt. Miss Macdonald promptly claimed the show as her own to save it from the creditors.

Oddly enough, in spite of everything, *Sweethearts* survived. The Shuberts produced it as part of their revival series at the Jolson Theater in 1929 with Gladys Baxter as Sylvia (21 September), it gave its title and a handful of its songs to a 1938 Jeanette MacDonald and Nelson Eddy film (for which, understandably, it was thought wiser to scrap the libretto entirely), and it returned to Broadway in 1947 in a production co-sponsored by Paula Stone and Michael Sloane, by which time its songs had become familiar and, ergo, ''favorites.''

Miss Stone had done splendidly with a revival of her father Fred's old vehicle *The Red Mill,* starring comedian Bobby Clark, two years earlier. She now looked around for another Victor Herbert piece for Clark and, out of all the jolly comical musicals available she chose *Sweethearts* . . . and had a comedy role written in (ad John Cecil Holm). Or, rather, up. Clark played Prime Minister Mikel, and when the second act arrived the hoary old plot went out of the window in the good old 19th-century fashion and the comedian just got to do his thing. Gloria Story as Sylvia also profited, as the soprano ballad ''The Land of My Own Romance'' was lifted from Herbert's score for *The Enchantress* and added to the score, along with *Angel Face*'s ''I Might Be Your Once in a While.'' June Knight was Liane, Marjorie Gateson played Dame Paula, Mark Lawson was Franz, and *Sweethearts* comedy-model stayed a fine 288 performances at the Shubert Theater (21 January). Which seemed to signify, in statistical terms, that it was twice as good without half its plot. Regional companies in America have, however, preferred not to take this reductio ad logicam to its end, and versions of *Sweethearts* still appears from time to time on amateur and professional stages. Some shows are simply survivors.

Recordings: selections (RCA, MMG etc), 1944 radio broadcast (Pelican)

SWEET YESTERDAY Musical romance in 3 acts by Philip Leaver. Lyrics by Leaver, James Dyrenforth and Max Kester. Music by Kenneth Leslie-Smith. Adelphi Theatre, London, 21 June 1945.

A musical with a message, *Sweet Yesterday* was written and composed for BBC Radio (26 January 1941 Home Programme) to push home to the public that ''careless talk costs lives.'' It was subsequently enlarged to stage size and produced by Lee Ephraim with radio vocalists Anne Ziegler and Webster Booth starring in its tale of love and sacrifice, set in the Napoléonic wars and leading up to the British victory at Trafalgar.

The tale was set with an attractive if unexceptional romantic operetta score of the kind which gave Miss Ziegler and Booth plenty of legato things to sing and Doris Hare and Mark Daly, in the chief comedy roles, some light relief, and *Sweet Yesterday* found some success in the atmosphere prevailing in immediately postwar London. But if the War in Europe was over, war backstage was the order of the day. *Sweet Yesterday*'s preparation was full of sackings and unpleasantness and, after 196 West End performances, the stars refused to renew their contracts and the show was withdrawn.

SWING ALONG Musical show in 2 acts by Guy Bolton, Fred Thompson and Douglas Furber. Lyrics by Graham John. Music by Martin Broones. Gaiety Theatre, London, 2 September 1936.

Following the success of the revusical *Seeing Stars* at the Gaiety Theatre, producer Firth Shephard ordered another vehicle for Leslie Henson and company from the team which had written the earlier show. This time Henson was cast as little Maxie Mumm, stranded in nasty foreign Europe, and mixed up in the fearsome war between the ''Yellow Shirts'' and the ''No Shirts.'' In disguises which ranged from an impersonation of the Yellow Shirt leader to a lady in a Gainsborough hat and party frock, frog-faced Henson and his confederates—big, monocled, cigar-chomping Fred Emney and gangling, acrobatic Richard Hearne—went through a variety of comic routines including a burlesque of radio broadcasting, a parodied cancan, and a ladies' trio (for which Emney retained his monocle and cigar), whilst juveniles Roy Royston and Louise Browne repeated their song-and-dance assignment of the earlier show: she danced an interpolated ballet scena, and London's most esoteric baddie, Gavin Gordon, stalked and bullied little Maxie through the various phases of the plot.

A merry, ephemeral score featured ''Another Dream Gone Wrong'' for Miss Browne, the more lively ''Like a Tin Can Tied to a Puppy Dog's Tail'' performed by Zelma O'Neal in one of the incidental soubrette roles in which she specialized, and the grotesque, revusical trio ''Let's Be Ladies'' performed by the three frocked-up stars.

The layout, one not too distant from the old-style Gaiety entertainments of the turn of the century, worked well. *Swing Along* proved even more successful than *Seeing Stars,* played 311 performances at the Gaiety, and then toured, whilst the company began the next in the series of musicals in the same vein with which they would enliven London during the late 1930s.

Swing Along was also mounted in Australia where a cast headed by George Gee, Valerie Hay, Donald Burr, Percy Le Fre, Lois Green and John Dobbie played four weeks at Sydney's Theatre Royal and five in Melbourne (Her Majesty's Theatre 19 February 1938).

Australia: Theatre Royal, Sydney 13 November 1937

SWOBODA, Albin (b Neustrelitz, 13 November 1836; d Dresden, 4 August 1901).

The son of opera singers, Swoboda first appeared on the stage in the chorus at the Theater in der Josefstadt at the age of 16. He later worked in several provincial and suburban theatres before, in 1857, joining Nestroy's company at the Carltheater. There, playing alongside such stars as Karl Treumann, Wilhelm Knaack and Therese Braunecker Schäfer, he soon began to make himself popular. He moved to the Theater an der Wien in 1859 and there his youth, handsome looks, large and rich performance and fair tenor voice won him good roles in comedy and in Operette. After making his debut in the little French opérette *Singspiel am Fenster* (4 February 1859), he created the jeune premier role of Karl in *Das Pensionat* (1860), appeared in Conradin's *Liebchen am Dach* (1861, Serafin), played Raimund to the *Therese Krones* of Gallmeyer, and introduced many of Offenbach's comic tenor roles to Vienna: Paris opposite *Die schöne Helena* of Geistinger, *Blaubart* to her Boulotte, Piquillo to her *Périchole*, Policarpo (*Coscoletto*), Pyramus (*Die Schäfer*) and Siegfried (*Genovefa von Brabant*), as well as Henri in *Die Reise nach China* and Pinsonnet in *Theeblüthe*.

Swoboda left the Theater an der Wien in 1870 and teamed with Knaack and Röhring as the three red knights in Suppé's short-lived *Die Jungfrau von Dragant* at the Carltheater (1870, 5 performances), but he returned as a guest artist to create the role of Janio in Strauss's *Indigo und die vierzig Räuber* (1871), to play Ugolino in Offenbach's *Fantasio* (1872) and Kipfelbäck in his *Die Theaterprinzessin* (1872) and to create Millöcker's *Abenteuer in Wien* (Friedrich Bendel, 1873). He introduced a second Strauss role when he appeared as the original Arthur Bryk in *Carneval in Rom* (1873) and took up another memorable character as Marasquin in Vienna's version of *Giroflé-Girofla* (1874). In 1875 he appeared at the Carltheater in *La Fille de Madame Angot, Giroflé-Girofla* and *La Jolie Parfumeuse.* In 1877 he took over the role of Eisenstein in the Theater an der Wien's production of *Die Fledermaus* and was Vienna's first Henri in *Die Glocken von Corneville,* and in 1879 he created Nauticus in Genée's *Die letzten Mohikaner* and Hellmuth Forst in Strauss's *Blindekuh,* and played Falkenbach in Offenbach's *Der Brasilianer.* In a career that latterly leaned ever away from singing roles, he subsequently played in Russia, in Berlin and in Dresden before largely retiring from the stage in 1888.

Swoboda made two attempts to move into theatrical management, first at the ill-fated Vienna Komische Oper (Ringtheater) in 1877, and later, with barely better results, at Budapest's German-speaking theatre.

SYLVANE, André [GERARD, Marie Paul Émile] (b L'Aigle, Orne, 27 March 1851; d 1932).

A commissaire-priseur by profession and a playwright and play doctor as a hobby, Sylvane wrote or collaborated on many plays with such authors as Alexandre Bisson (*Disparu*), Maurice Ordonneau (*L'Article 214*) and later André Mouëzy-Éon (*Tire-au-flanc!*), as well as on the texts of a number of musical plays, mostly in the vaudevillesque vein, and often without his name appearing on the bill. He apparently had an uncredited hand in Bisson's highly successful *Un lycée de jeunes filles* (1881) and in the Antony Mars-Maurice Desvallières libretto for the even more widely traveled *La Demoiselle du téléphone* (1891), but his name was officially attached to the texts for Audran's *Madame Suzette* (74 performances), *Mon prince!* (85 performances) and *Les Petites Femmes,* as well as to the vaudeville *Patart, Patart et Cie* (48 performances), which was later produced at the Theatre an der Wien as *Kneisl & Co* (ad Theodor Taube, Isidor Fuchs).

Tire-au-flanc!, adapted as a libretto by no less an author than the young Ferenc Molnár, became *Gyöngyélet* (Ferenc Bekési/Adolf Mérei, Magyar Színház 21 April 1906) on the Hungarian musical stage.

1889 **Mam'zelle Pioupiou** (William Chaumet/w Alexandre Bisson) Théâtre de la Porte-Saint-Martin 31 May

1892 **Nini Fauvette** (Edmond Missa/w Charles Clairville) Théâtre des Nouveautés 16 January

1893 **Madame Suzette** (Edmond Audran/w Ordonneau) Théâtre des Bouffes-Parisiens 29 March

1893 **Patart, Patart et Cie** (Louis Gregh/w C Clairville) Théâtre des Folies-Dramatiques 9 October

1893 **Mon prince!** (Audran/w C Clairville) Théâtre des Nouveautés 18 November

1897 **Les Petites Femmes** (Audran) Théâtre des Bouffes-Parisiens 11 October

SZABADOS, Béla (b Budapest, 3 June 1867; d Budapest, 15 September 1936).

The younger brother of the composer and conductor Károly Szabados (1860–1892), Béla Szabados studied from the age of 14 at the Budapest Zeneakadémia and had his first symphonic and stage music (including the incidental music for Béla Hetényi's *Csicsóné* 18 July 1884) played whilst he was still a student. He subsequently became a professor of music, and had his first operetts, to texts by Jenő Rákosi, played at the Népszínház in 1890 and 1891. However, in spite of being favored with this conjunction of one of the country's best librettists and its most important musical theatre on his very first stage

Plate 376.

works, his first important success came only several years later, after he had taken up a teaching post at the Zeneakadémia, when the same theatre presented his 1895 operett *Rika* (25 performances).

The musical plays *A három Kázmér* (41 performances) and *A kuktakisasszony* (27 performances), the second later played in a revised version at Vienna's Theater an der Wien as *Die Küchenkomtesse* (15 March 1898), the ''song legend'' *A bolond* and *Szép Ilonka* gave him further successes, during a period in which he also composed both operatic scores (the one-act comic opera *Alszik a nagynéni,* 1895, *Mária* w Árpád Szendy/Géza Béri Magyar Király Operaház 28 February 1905) and incidental theatre music, as well as symphonic and chamber works.

Szabados subsequently held several high posts in the Budapest musical establishment, and returned only rarely to the musical theatre.

1890 **A négy király** (Jenő Rákosi) Népszínház 10 January

1891 **Az első és a második** (Labiche ad Rákosi) Népszínház 8 April

1892 **A koronázás emléknapja** (Rákosi) 1 act Népszínház 6 June

1895 **Rika** (József Márkus) Népszínház 23 November

1896 **A három Kázmér** (László Béothy) Népszínház 25 January

1897 **A kuktakisasszony** (J Márkus) Népszínház 23 November

1898 **A bolond** (Rákosi) Magyar Színház 29 December

1904 **Felsőbb asszonyok** (Károly Lovik) Népszínház 26 March

1904 **A múmia** (Vilmos Kaczér) Magyar Színház 9 April

1905 **Sportlovagok** (Gyula Déry) Fővárosi Nyári Színház 19 May

1906 **Szép Ilonka** (Gyula Szávay, Géza Vágó) Király Színház 20 October

1922 **Bolond Istók** (Ede Sas, Ákos Bihari) Városi Színház 22 December

1923 **Menyasszonyháború** (Sas) Városi Színház 7 December

1927 **Fanni** (Jenő Mohácsi) Magyar Király Operaház 16 February

SZIBILL Operett in 3 acts by Miksa Bródy and Ferenc Martos. Music by Viktor Jacobi. Király Színház, Budapest, 27 February 1914.

Szibill, first produced in Budapest at the dawn of the War years, was the peak achievement of the short career of composer Viktor Jacobi. The young musician, who had known little but success from the very beginning of his composing career, had made an international hit with *Leányvásár* (*The Marriage Market*) in 1911, and *Szibill* followed up some three years later, his last work for Budapest before leaving for America, disillusion and a premature death.

Lieutenant Petrov (Jenő Nádor) has deserted his regiment for love of the diva Sybil Renaud (Sári Fedák) and is in hiding in her hotel at provincial Bomsk. The local Governor, charged with capturing the runaway, mistakes Sybil for the Grand-Duchess Anna Pavlovna and, to give her lover the chance to escape, she takes up the pretense. Before the pair can get away, however, Sybil is forced to attend a reception in the Duchess's honor and there she finds herself faced with—the Duke (Ernő Király). He, delighted with the possibilities offered by this new ''wife,'' amusedly goes along with her deception, but both are taken aback when the real Grand-Duchess (Mici Haraszti) arrives and announces herself as Mme Renaud. Jealousies flare back and forth until Sybil is able to explain all to the angry Duchess, reunite her with her husband, and win a pardon for Petrov.

Jacobi's score mixed the romantic and the comic in impeccable measures. The romantic music rose to its height with the long-lined, pregnantly pausing duet between the Duke and Sybil as he, only half teasingly, asks her to imagine a sentimental idyll for two (''Illuzió a szerelem''), whilst Sybil's opening letter-song, as she writes to her Petrov, little knowing he is on his way to her, proved another highlight. The comic side of affairs was provided by Sybil's manager Poire (Márton Rátkai) and his wife Sarah (Juci Lábass), and Jacobi served them with some outstandingly lively duos in well-accented dance rhythms, topped by the energetic mazurka

''Gombhaz, sej, hogyha leszakad'' and the light-footed ''Van valami,'' whilst Poire's merrily bouncing duo with Sybil provided another memorably rhythmic moment (''Félre csapom a kalapom'').

The First World War prevented *Szibill* from following its Budapest triumph with what would normally, in the wake of the success of *Leányvásár,* have been a quick appearance on international stages. However, war or none, America soon picked up the show that was the rage of in-fashion Budapest, and *Sybil* was produced on Broadway with Julia Sanderson and Donald Brian as the diva and the duke and Joseph Cawthorn (Poire) paired with British revue comedienne Maisie Gay (Margot) at the head of the comedy. Jacobi, who had seen *The Marriage Market* plugged full of mostly substandard interpolated songs, was on hand to provide new numbers as and when required, to fit with Harry Graham and Harry B Smith's version of the book.

The most successful of these additions was a solo for Sybil herself, ''The Colonel of the Crimson Hussars.'' A blatantly simple and march-rhythmically sticking number, made to measure, it was not, however, of the same quality as the piece it replaced (''Volt egy hercegnő''). Several of Jacobi's best lighter, rhythmic numbers also went under the knife, and Cawthorn performed a number (''I Can Dance with Everybody But My Wife'') which he had himself written with John Golden. But *Sybil* proved indestructible enough to be received with raves (''an instantaneous success,'' ''it exhausts commedatory adjectives,'' ''the best musical production in five years,'' etc) and proved a considerable success in Charles Frohman's production at Broadway's Liberty Theater (168 performances), on the road, and in a quick revival at the Empire (28 August 1916).

After Fedák and Sanderson, another of the most outstanding stars of the contemporary musical theatre took up the role of Sybil when the first German-language performances (ad Robert Bodanzky) appeared after the war. Fritzi Massary and Guido Thielscher introduced the piece in Berlin and the diva then took it to Vienna, where it was performed for a successful season at the Wiener Stadttheater with Massary (and later Ida Russka) playing alongside Hubert Marischka as the Duke, Viktor Flemming as Petrov and Emil Guttmann as Poire. The show was later given a further 26 performances at the Theater an der Wien.

If Britain was slow in producing *Sybil,* it was not wholly because of anti-German feeling in the wake of the war, but also because of a logjam of success. Robert Evett had bought the rights to the piece early on in order to star José Collins as Sybil, and Harry Graham had duly prepared his adaptation, but the continuing popularity of Miss Collins's current vehicles, *The Maid of the Mountains* and *A Southern Maid,* retarded the show's production in London, and thus Graham's version was seen on Broadway long before Evett was able to find it stage room in England. When *Sybil* did finally arrive at Daly's Theatre, in what now looked like a revised version of the American version, some seven years after the original Budapest production, it showed it had been worth the wait. It proved a magnificent vehicle for Miss Collins and ran from February to Christmas (347 performances) being removed only to allow a farewell season of *The Maid* prior to Evett and Miss Collins's departure from Daly's.

Miss Collins's Australian ''double,'' Gladys Moncrieff, was Sybil in her native country, with Claude Flemming, Leslie Holland, Robert Chisholm, Arthur Stigant (performing Cawthorn's song), Ethel Morrison and Clarice Hardwick supporting through an excellent original run of 11 weeks in Melbourne and a further 10 in Sydney (Her Majesty's Theatre 8 February).

In Hungary, *Szibill* has remained in the standard repertoire and has been produced at Budapest's Fővárosi Operettszínház in 1932 (23 April), 1945 (21 December), and in 1972 (21 January) as well as, most recently, at Győr (1992), Tatabánya (1993), Pécs (1994), Szolnok (1994), Kecskemét (1996) and Debrecen in 1997.

USA: Liberty Theater *Sybil* 10 January 1916; Austria: Wiener Stadttheater 12 February 1919; Germany: Metropoltheater October 1919; UK: Prince's Theatre, Manchester 26 *Sybil* December 1920, Daly's Theatre, London 19 February 1921; Australia: Theatre Royal, Adelaide *Sybil* 9 June 1923, Her Majesty's Theatre, Melbourne 23 June 1923

Recording: selection (Qualiton)

SZIKA, Jani [SZÍKA, János] (b Pest, 7 February 1844; d Vienna, 20 October 1916). The original Eisenstein of *Die Fledermaus* and the star of a long run of Viennese musicals.

After being originally destined for a medical education, Jani Szika began his stage career, at the age of 18, at the Deutsches Theater in his native Pest. In 1864 Friedrich Strampfer hired him for the Theater an der Wien as an actor, but soon after he found himself cast in such musical pieces as Bazin's *Die Reise nach China* (Maurice Fréval), in the spectacular *Prinzessin Hirschkuh* (*La Biche au Bois,* Mesrour), and as Prince Saphir in Offenbach's *Blaubart.* During the run of *Die Grossherzogin von Gerolstein,* Szika stepped in to substitute for Albin Swoboda in the lead tenor role of Fritz, and coped so admirably with the part that his career from then on took a quite different turning, and he went on to make his name as a leading man in opéra-bouffe and Operette.

In 1868 Szika appeared as Charles Martel in *Genovefa von Brabant,* and in 1871 he was seen as Flink in

Drei Paar Schuhe, Marzas in Lecocq's *Le Rajah de Mysore* and Falsacappa in Offenbach's *Die Banditen,* and also created the lead light-comedy role of Ali Baba in Johann Strauss's maiden work, *Indigo und die vierzig Räuber.* In 1872 he was Spark in Offenbach's *Fantasio* and Emil Falkner in *Die Theaterprinzessin* (*La Diva*), in 1873 he created the part of Benvenuti Raphaeli in Strauss's *Carneval in Rom* and played Abälard in Litolff's *Abälard und Heloise* and Marcassou in Offenbach's *Die Wilderer* (*Les Braconniers*). In 1874 he appeared as Gstettner in Jonas's *Die Japanesin* and took time out briefly to attempt to run the ill-fated Komische Oper (later the Ringtheater, and the site of Vienna's worst ever theatre fire) before returning to the Theater an der Wien to create the most famous role of his career as Gabriel von Eisenstein to the Rosalinde of Marie Geistinger in *Die Fledermaus.*

In the following years he played Giletti in Offenbach's *Madame "Herzog"* (1875) and Albert von Graff in Varney's *Die Perle der Wascherinnen* (1875, *La Blanchisseuse de Berg-op-Zoom*), created Graf Stefan Fodor in Strauss's *Cagliostro in Wien* (1875), appeared as Frontignac in *Die Creolin* (1876, *La Créole*) and Prinz Qui-Passe-Par-La in *Die Reise in den Mond* (1876, *Le Voyage dans la lune*), created the part of Lambert de Saint-Querlonde in *Der Seekadett* (1876), and was the Fridolin of *König Carotte* (1876), Cornelius in *Die Porträt-Dame* (1877) and the first Marquis d'Aubigny in *Nanon* (1877), before ending his 10-year tenure with the Theater an der Wien.

In 1878 he returned as a guest artist to create the role of Sepp in *Das verwunschene Schloss* and in 1879 he appeared as Loisl in *Das Versprechen hinter'n Herd* with Geistinger, but he was engaged in Berlin in 1880 and he made his career during the 1880s largely in Germany. There he created the role of Caramello in Strauss's *Eine Nacht in Venedig* in 1883, and appeared as Sauritz Sonsen in *Der Doppelgänger* (1887), Graf Neckar in Adolf Neuendorff's *Waldmeisters Brautfahrt* (1887) and Giuseppe in *Incognito* (1887) at the Walhalla-Theater, but he spent an increasing amount of time acting in non-musical plays. In 1891 he went to Frankfurt where he completed his retransformation back to being the straight actor that he had begun, and he spent his later years playing in classic drama and comedy, from Shakespeare to Schiller.

SZILÁGYI, László (b Budapest, 2 October 1898; d Budapest, 6 September 1942).

One of the foremost librettists of the Hungarian stage of his era, Szilágyi wrote the texts for a considerable body of successful shows for the Budapest musical theatre, notably in collaboration with the composers Béla Zerkovitz and Mihály Eisemann. Few of them, however, were seen outside Hungary.

His first full-length piece, the musical comedy *Levendula,* was played more than 75 times at the Várszínház and the Lujza Blaha Színház, the operett *Régi jó Budapest* ran over 125 performances, both his adaptation of the French *Clary-Clara* as the text for *Csókos asszony* and the even further westward-looking *Miss Amerika* passed the 75 performance mark first time up, and his Hungarian version of Broadway's *Good News* also topped 100 performances—a figure which marked a major success at the time. Amongst his later pieces, collaborations with the young Eisemann on the up-to-date musical comedy *Zsákbamacska,* which played some 250 performances at the Pesti Színház in 1932–33 with the young Marika Rökk as soubrette, and with the elderly Jenő Huszka on *Mária főhadnagy* both brought major local successes, whilst such pieces as Zerkovitz's *Eltörött a hegedüm,* Buday's *Csárdás* and several other Eisemann musicals also had good local runs.

Zsákbamacska was produced in Vienna as *Katz im Sack* with Trude Berliner, Magda Kun and Steve Geray starred, and also seen briefly in Britain as *Happy Weekend* (1934), whilst Zerkovitz's *Csókos asszony* was played in Prague, *Miss Amerika* in Germany and Vincze's *Aranyhattyú* is said to have been played on the New York stage. His libretto to another successful piece, *Eltörött a hegedüm,* was later used as the basis for an early Hollywood sound film. The Komjáti operett *Ein Liebestraum* was produced in Vienna in a German translation, with Marta Eggerth starred, for 49 performances.

Szilágyi's output also included both non-musical plays and screenplays.

- 1923 **Levendula** (Frigyes Friedl/Sándor Somló) Várszínház 16 February
- 1923 **A kék póstakocsi** (Dénes Buday) Várszínház 22 December
- 1924 **Amerika lánya** (Gyula Kiszely/Zsolt Harsányi) Városi Színház 17 May
- 1925 **Régi jó Budapest** (József Radó) Király Színház 20 May
- 1926 **Csókos asszony** (Béla Zerkovitz) Városi Színház 27 February
- 1926 **Muzsikus Ferkó** (Zerkovitz) Budai Színkör 18 June
- 1927 **Aranyhattyú** (Zsigmond Vincze) Király Színház 15 January
- 1927 **A legkisebbik Horváth lány** (Zerkovitz) Király Színház 21 May
- 1928 **Eltörött a hegedüm** (Zerkovitz) Király Színház 3 November
- 1929 **Miss Amerika** (Mihály Eisemann) Fővárosi Operettszínház 12 January
- 1929 **Pesti család** (Radó/Adorján Stella) Király Színház 5 September
- 1929 **Tommy és Társa** (Pál Tamássy/Ernő Anday) Király Színház 11 October
- 1929 **Diákszerelem** (*Good News*) Hungarian version (Király Színház)

1930 **Alvinci huszárok** (Eisemann) Király Színház 9 April

1931 **Gróf Romeo** (Tividar Szántó) Fővárosi Operettszínház 28 January

1932 **Zsákbamacska** (Eisemann) Pesti Színház 3 September

1932 **Pillangó** (József Kóla/w Andor Kardos) Fővárosi Operettszínház 25 September

1932 **Kadétszerelem** (Pál Gyöngy/w István Békeffy) Fővárosi Operettszínház 23 December

1933 **Ein Liebestraum** (Károly Komjáti/w Ferenc Martos ad Heinz Reichert) Theater an der Wien 27 October

1934 **Én és a kisöcsém** (Eisemann) Fővárosi Operettszínház 21 December

1935 **Ezüstmenyasszony** (Eisemann) Royal Színház 20 December

1936 **Pármai ibolya** (Béla Dolecskó) Városi Színház 9 April

1936 **Meseáruház** (Eisemann) Fővárosi Operettszínház 11 April

1936 **Csárdás** (Buday) Budai Színkör 16 June

1936 **3:1 a szerelem javára** (Ábrahám/Harmath/w, Dezső Kellér) Royal Színház 18 December

1937 **Gólyaszanatórium** (Eisemann/w Dezső Kellér) Márkus Park Színház 25 June

1937 **Éva a paradicsomban** (Tamás Bródy/w Kellér/Endre Solt) Városi Színház 22 October

1938 **Nem leszek hálátlan** (Alfred Márkus) Andrássy-uti Színház 19 March; Magyar Színház 3 May

1938 **Szomjas krokodil** (Márkus/Imre Harmath) Márkus Park Színház 21 June

1939 **Erzsébet** (Jenő Huszka) Magyar Színház 5 January

1939 **Pusztai szerenád** (Szabolcs Fényes/w István Békeffy) Fővárosi Operettszínház 29 September

1939 **Pozsonyi lakodalom** (Miklós Beck) Fővárosi Operettszínház 17 November

1940 **Handa-Banda** (revised *Macskazene*) (Eisemann/Gyula Halász, Károly Kristóf ad) Fővárosi Operettszínház 26 January

1940 **Tokaji aszu** (Eisemann) Magyar Színház 15 March

1940 **Három huszár** (Buday/w Gyula Halász) Fővárosi Operettszínház 12 April

1940 **Angóramacksa** (Eisemann) Vígszínház 26 April

1941 **Gyergyói bál** (Huszka) Magyar Színház 4 January

1942 **Vén diófa** (Fényes) Magyar Színház 26 March

1942 **Mária főhadnagy** (Huszka) Fővárosi Operettszínház 23 September

1943 **Die verliebte Station** (Dolecskó) Nuremberg 6 March

1943 **Egy boldog pesti nyár** (Buday, Eisemann, Fényes/w Attila Orbók) Fővárosi Operettszínház 14 April

SZIRMAI, Albert [aka SIRMAY] (b Budapest, 2 July 1880; d New York, 15 January 1967). Top-flight Hungarian composer whose career faded when he left home.

Szirmai studied at the Budapest Zeneakadémia and subsequently worked as musical director at the Modern Színpad whilst producing all types of music for Hungarian theatres, concert halls and cabaret houses. His output included instrumental music, ballet scores, chamber music, a pair of so-called comic operas (*Balkirálynő* 1908, *Harangvirág,* 1918), a large number of songs and, most notably, a long string of operetts and musical comedies, the first of which, *A sárga dominó,* was produced by Raoul Mader at the Népszínház-Vígopera in 1907 (18 performances).

Szirmai had several fine early successes, amongst which were included the musical comedy *Naftalin* (still to be seen on the Budapest stage in 1990) and the operett *Táncos huszárok* (played in Austria and Germany as *Tanzhusaren,* Venedig in Wien 30 April 1909, Theater des Westens ad Rajna, Motz 30 April 1910), and he got a wider exposure for the first time when the local version of the German musical comedy *Filmzauber* (*A mozikirály*) for which he had supplied a fair amount of additional music, went on to an international career as *The Girl on the Film.* He had his greatest success to date with the wartime operett *Mágnás Miska,* later played in the German-speaking world as *Der Pusztakavalier* and subsequently regularly revived in Hungary, repeated successfully with *Gróf Rinaldo* (*Rinaldo* at Vienna's Johann Strauss-Theater 1 March 1921) and with *Mézeskalács* which ran over a one hundred nights in its first season in Budapest, and scored his most international hit with the 1925 Ferenc Martos operett *Alexandra* (played in English as *Princess Charming*).

Szirmai subsequently shifted his base to Britain and wrote the basic scores for two musical plays produced on the London stage. The old-fashioned Ruritanian *The Bamboula* was a failure but *Lady Mary,* for which the remainder of the score was put together from a mixture of American sources (Kern, Charig, Richard Myers), won a respectable run at Daly's Theatre through 181 performances in the wake of the London success of *Princess Charming.* Sirmay (as he now spelled himself) then moved on from Britain to America where he settled in the late 1920s. There he contributed to the score for the disappointing Fred Stone musical comedy *Ripples* (w Oscar Levant), but his appealing Hungaro-French style of writing apparently made little mark on a Broadway more tuned to up-to-date dance music, and, although his *A balerina* (which sported a touch of American influence—it included a song called ''Óh Zsuzsánna'') played successfully in Budapest the following year, Sirmay never again recaptured the success he had known in his earlier days. Like Victor Jacobi, he seemed to have had his spark extinguished by his self-chosen, ambitious exile.

In New York, Sirmay became a backroom musical man, administering and arranging rather than composing, and he spent most of his American years as chief music editor at the firm of Chappell. Few of those who encountered the delightfully dutiful ''Doc'' Sirmay, as he pursued his job of putting often less able men's music into sellable shape, were aware that, as Albert Szirmai, he had been one of the most successful Hungarian operett composers of the most prosperous period of that country's musical theatre.

In his old age he visited Budapest on a number of occasions and wrote two further scores which were produced in Budapest theatres.

Mágnás Miska remains in the standard Hungarian repertoire nearly a century on, but others of Sirmay's works such as *Naftalin* and *Gróf Rinaldo* (Békéscsaba 1994) also still get occasional showings.

1907 **A sárga dominó** (Adolf Mérei) Népszínház-Vígopera 4 October

1908 **Naftalin** (Jenő Heltai) Vígszínház 6 June

1909 **Táncos huszárok** (Ferenc Rajna) Király Színház 7 January

1911 **A Ferencvárosi angyal** (Ferenc Molnár, Heltai) Royal Orfeum 31 December

1912 **A mexikói lány** (Andor Gábor/Ferenc Rajna) Király Színház 11 December

1912 **Filmzauber** (w Willi Bredschneider, Walter Kollo/Rudolf Bernauer, Rudolf Schanzer) additional music

1914 **Az ezüstpille** (Franz Arnold, Ernst Bach ad Andor Gábor) Vígszínház 9 May

1916 **Mágnás Miska** (Károly Bakonyi) Király Színház 12 February

1918 **Kék orgonak** (Gábor) 1 act Belvárosi Színház 2 May

1918 **Gróf Rinaldo** (Bakonyi, Gábor) Király Színház 7 November

1919 **Kutyuskám** (Ferenc Martos) 1 act Andrássy-uti Színház 12 December

1922 **Breton legenda** (Tamás Emöd) 1 act Andrássy-uti Színház 10 September

1923 **Mézeskalács** (Emöd) Király Színház 15 December

1925 **The Bamboula** (w Harry Rosenthal/Douglas Furber, Irving Caesar/Harry M Vernon, Guy Bolton) His Majesty's Theatre, London 24 March

1925 **Alexandra** (Ferenc Martos) Király Színház 25 November

1928 **Éva grófnő** (Martos) Király Színház 3 February

1928 **Lady Mary** (Harry Graham/Frederick Lonsdale, J Hastings Turner) Daly's Theatre, London 23 February

1928 **Enyém az első csók** (Heltai) Andrássy-uti Színház 16 May

1930 **Ripples** (w Oscar Levant/Caesar, Graham John/William Anthony McGuire) New Amsterdam Theater, New York 11 February

1931 **A balerina** (Martos) Király Színház 7 March

1957 **Tabáni legenda** (Károly Kristóf) Deryne Színház 1 January

1964 **A tündérlaki lányok** (Jenő Heltai ad Ernő Innocent Vincze) Fővárosi Operettszínház 29 January

Other title attributed: *A kaloz* (1933)

SZTOJANOVITS, Jenő (b Pest, 4 April 1864; d Pest, 28 January 1919).

Plate 377.

Organist, maître de chapelle, teacher, administrator and critic, Sztojanovits also covered a wide area in his composing activities which ranged from religious music to several ballets (*Uj Romeo* 1889, *Csárdás* 1890, *Tous les trois* 1892), operas (*Ninon* 1898, *Othello mesél* 1917) and other theatre music, as well as the scores for several operetts and musical plays. The first of these, the successful *Peking rózsája,* was based on the Turandot tale, nearly 40 years before Puccini's operatic version, and the second, *A kis molnárné,* on Scribe's libretto for Adolphe Adam's *Giralda,* previously used for the successful British show *Manteaux Noirs.* The most successful of the remainder of the group was the 1908 fairy-tale piece *A csókkirály.* None, however, seems to have been played outside Hungary.

1888 **Peking rózsája** (Carlo Gozzi ad Miksa Ruttkay) Népszínház 7 April

1892 **A kis molnárné** (Antal Radó) Népszínház 29 January

1903 **A kis kofa** (*Phryné*) (Richard Falk) Magyar Színház 20 November

1905 **A portugál** (Adolf Mérei) Magyar Színház 3 January

1906 **A papa lánya** (Gyula Molnár) Népszínház 4 October

1908 **A csókkirály** (Dezső Orbán) Fővárosi Nyári Színház 16 July

1910 **A sziámi herceg** (Pál Péter) Fővárosi Nyári Színház 27 July

1915 **Karikagyürü** (Dezső Urai, László Zsoldos) Király Színhaz 13 November

Other titles attributed: *Családi szentely* (1895, Ede Sas), *Lengyel legionarius*

SZULC, Joseph [SZULC, József Zygmunt] (b Warsaw, 4 April 1875; d Paris, 10 April 1956). One of the happiest musical contributors to the French musical-comedy stage between the wars.

Born into a family which boasted three generations of eminent Polish musicians, Szulc studied piano and composition at the Warsaw conservatory and at first attempted a career as a concert pianist. He moved to France to further his studies in 1899, and remained there, eking out a living as a piano teacher whilst he concentrated on trying to make a career in composition and conducting. His work as a theatre conductor took him to Stuttgart, then in 1903 back to Paris, to the Théâtre de la Monnaie in Brussels and finally once more, in 1908, to Paris, but his first attempts at composition, both with pieces in a serious vein and lighter works for the theatre, failed for a long time to find homes.

He placed a ballet, *Nuits d'Ispahan,* in Belgium and in 1913 the tide finally—if painfully slowly—began to turn for him when the Brussels Alhambra mounted his musical comedy *Flup..!* Slowly, *Flup..!* made its way first to Lyon (1917) and finally, seven years on, to Paris (1920). In the meanwhile, the composer had provided the music for only one other piece which had succeeded in getting a showing, an adaptation of Pierre Veber's hit comedy *Loute* which was produced in Marseille. *Loute* moved more quickly than *Flup..!,* for although it did not make it to Paris, it was taken up by producer A H Woods for America (where *Loute* the play had done well under the title *The Girl from Rector's*) and, done over by P G Wodehouse and Guy Bolton, produced under the title *See You Later.* It opened at Philadelphia, but was soon seen to be in trouble and Woods dropped it amongst a welter of lawsuits from Veber and London would-be-producer G B McLellan. *See You Later* ultimately resurfaced in Chicago (La Salle Theater 16 January 1919) in a production by Elliot, Comstock and Gest, with Victor Moore starred and with a score credited to Jean Schwartz and William Peters (although a bit of Szulc seems to have remained). It did not, however, move east and New York thus narrowly missed what might have been the only example of a French provincial musical which never played Paris making its way to the Broadway stage.

The Parisian success of *Flup..!* at the Théâtre Ba-ta-clan finally launched Szulc on a career as a popular theatrical composer, and he followed it up with a second lively musical comedy full of dance melodies later the same year at the same theatre. After Dranem as Flup, the new piece featured Polin as *Titin,* a comical nouveau-riche marseillais who purchases a Pacific Island and, if the second show did not outshine the earlier one, it certainly confirmed it. Szulc had another major hit in 1923 with *Le Petit Choc,* contributed to the six-handed score of the Potinière's successful *Mon vieux* and scored further long-running hits with the up-to-date comedy musical *Quand on est trois* and the delightful small-scale *Mannequins* at the little Théâtre des Capucines. He also produced two more happy comical pieces, *La Victoire de Samothrace* and *Vivette,* for the Belgian stage in tandem with his *Flup..!* collaborator, Dumestre, as the rage for Jazz Age dancing musical comedies continued. In 1929 he scored yet again with the featherweight *Flossie* before being tempted, like such other stars of the small-scale musical comedy as Christiné and Yvain, into writing for the larger houses with their larger potential for income.

Szulc made his very-big-stage debut with the score for the Théâtre du Châtelet's production of the military spectacular *Sidonie Panache* and found himself connected with a fine success which was not unconnected with the theatre's hugely lavish staging of the piece. He supplied some or all of the score for two further opérettes à grand spectacle (*Mandrin, Le Coffre-fort vivant*), but he nevertheless continued to write for the smaller stages which had seen the bulk of his real success. If he had been slow to start, he compensated by staying on late, and his last piece was mounted in his 70th year.

Like most of his French contemporaries, Szulc found that his success was limited almost entirely to France and Belgium, but he also found a vogue in Hungary where, in the mid-1920s *Le Petit Choc* was mounted as *Jolly Joker* (Belvárosi Színház 29 September 1928), *Mannequins* as *Párisi kirakat* (Magyar Színház 9 April 1926) and *Quand on est trois* as *Hármacskán!* (Vígszínház 4 September 1925). *Mannequins* also got a showing in Vienna and Italy's Carlo Lombardo, in habitual fashion, borrowed much of the score of *Flup..!* for the score to his successful *Madama di Tebe,* but after the *Loute* episode Broadway left Szulc alone.

1913 **Flup..!** (Gaston Dumestre) Théâtre de l'Alhambra, Brussels 19 December

1914 **Loute** (Pierre Veber, Maurice Soulié) Théâtre du Châtelet, Marseille February

1918 **See You Later** (revised English version of *Loute* by P G Wodehouse, Guy Bolton) Adelphi Theater, Philadelphia 13 May

1920 **Titin** (Dumestre, Roger Ferréol) Ba-ta-clan 2 October

1923 **La Victoire de Samothrace** (Dumestre) Forum, Liège 11 February

1923 **Le Petit Choc** (P-L Flers) Théâtre Daunou 25 May

Plate 378. **A szultán.** *Sári Fedák and Grete Freund in Vero's first and most famous operett.*

1924 **Vivette** (Dumestre) Forum, Liège 31 October

1924 **Mon vieux** (w others/André Birabeau, Battaille-Henri) Théâtre de la Potinière 18 December

1925 **Quand on est trois** (P Veber, Serge Veber, Willemetz) Théâtre des Capucines 20 April

1925 **Mannequins** (Jacques Bousquet, Henri Falk) Théâtre des Capucines 30 October

1926 **Divin Mensonge** (Hugues Delorme/Alex Madis, P Veber) Théâtre des Capucines 12 October

1929 **Couchette No 3** (Albert Willemetz/Madis) Théâtre des Capucines 6 February

1929 **Flossie** (Marcel Gerbidon, Charles L Pothier) Théâtre des Bouffes-Parisiens 9 May

1930 **Zou!** (Jean Boyer/Félix Gandéra) Folies-Wagram 2 May

1930 **Sidonie Panache** (Willemetz, Mouëzy-Éon) Théâtre du Châtelet 2 December

1933 **Le Garçon de Chez Prunier** (André Barde, Michel Carré) Théâtre des Capucines 19 January

1934 **Mandrin** (André Rivoire, Romain Coolus) Théâtre Mogador 12 December

1935 **L'Auberge du chat coiffé** (Alfred Lavauzelle) Théâtre Pigalle 18 December

1938 **Le Coffre-fort vivant** (w Maurice Yvain ps ''Jean Sautreuil'' Henri Wernert /Georges Berr, Louis Verneuil) Théâtre du Châtelet 17 December

1945 **Pantoufle** (Willemetz, Léopold Marchand) Théâtre des Capucines 28 February

A SZULTÁN Operett in 3 acts (prologue and 2 acts) by György Verő based on *Les Trois Sultanes* by Charles Favart. Népszínház, Budapest, 19 October 1892.

Thirty-five-year-old Verő, a conductor at the Népszínház and a sometime playwright, had been leading a busy career in the musical theatre, principally as a translator of Viennese Operetten for the Hungarian stage, when he was given the opportunity, in the wake of the success of such local composers as József Konti, to write the score for an operett for his theatre.

His first work, for which he wrote not only the music but also the book and the lyrics, was *A szultán,* a piece based on Charles Favart's verse comedy *Les Trois Sultanes, ou Soliman II,* originally played in Paris with a musical score by Gilbert (Italiens 9 April 1761). Since then,

Les Trois Sultanes had been through the musical mill, being set to original scores by several Italian operatic composers (*Le tre sultane, Solianno II*), by Vienna's Francis Xaver Süssmayer (*Soliman II,* Kärtnertor Theater 5 October 1799), and by Swedish and Danish composers, and being played in Paris, London (Bickerstaff's *The Sultan, or A Peep in the Seraglio,* 1775, et al) and in New York in variegated forms of its various operatic forms. Amongst a further bevy of adaptations and musicalizations it was also produced as a Singspiel under the title *Roxelane* (*Die drei Sultaninnen*) in a version by J Perinet at Vienna's Freyhaus-Theater (18 July 1799), given in a new version by Lockroy at Paris's Théâtre des Variétés in 1853, with Delphine Ugalde starred as Roxelane, and featured at the Comédie français (18 August 1892), with all its ''antique'' musical sections intact, with Albert Lambert.

Verő's version of the famous tale of a traveling mademoiselle who gets caught up in a sultan's harem and ends up subduing and marrying the mighty man was illustrated by a delightful if vocally demanding score which mixed the rhythms and harmonies of the Viennese Operette with some more particularly Hungarian ones and also with a definite but unclichéd flavor of the East. If the Sultan's waltz rondo ''Szeretlek Roxelánom'' proved the hit of the show, there were plenty of other fine and funny musical moments: a delicious laughing song, with nothing but ''ha-ha-ha'' lyrics, which twittered up to rows of top B-natural acciacaturas, a lively galop trio, a splendidly unsoppy romance for the number-two lady, a drinking song in waltz time, littered with trills and cadenzas, the Sultan's tricky Oriental Serenade and some flavorful ensembles, all of which made repeated use of the area above the stave in their vocal writing.

The Népszínház's established musical star Aranka Hegyi created the trousers role of Selim, the Sultan, whilst the newest addition to Budapest's stellar register, plumply pretty Klára Küry (who had just made a hit as the heroine of Varney's *La Fille de Fanchon la vielleuse),* was cast as little French Roxeláne, with Népszínház comedians Vidor Kassai, József Németh, József Ferenczy and Adolf Tollagi and the composer's wife, Célia Margó (Délia), in support. Helped just a little by the newfound popularity of Küry, *A szultán* was a major success. It was played no fewer than 84 times, almost equaling the record of Konti's *A suhanc,* the Népszínház's most successful local piece to date. If this was not the equal in terms of run to such all-time Budapest favorites as *Les Cloches de Corneville, Der Vogelhändler, Mam'zelle Nitouche, Der Zigeunerbaron, Boccaccio* or *Rip,* it nevertheless allowed *A szultán* to place itself firmly on the second rung alongside *The Mikado, Le Petit Duc* and *Der Bettelstudent* in the Népszínház's annals and, like them, it remained for many years a favorite in Hungary, being given a major revival at the Király Színház in 1911.

Later, when Verő ventured abroad, *Der Sultan* (ad Verő, Carl Lindau) was staged in Vienna—an achievement shared by few other Hungarian operetts of the period—with Sári Fedák starred in the title role and Grete Freund as Roxelane (46 performances).

Austria: Johann Strauss-Theater *Der Sultan* 27 March 1909

T

TABBERT, William [Henry] (b Chicago, 5 October 1919; d New York, 19 October 1974).

After early appearances with the Chicago Civic Light Opera Company, Tabbert made his Broadway debut as Sergeant Dick Benham in *What's Up?* (1943). He appeared in *Follow the Girls* and *The Seven Lively Arts* (1944), played Rocky Barton in *Billion Dollar Baby* (1945) and toured in *Three to Make Ready* before winning the role of his career as Lieutenant Joseph Cable in *South Pacific* (''Younger Than Springtime''). In 1954 he paired again with *South Pacific* co-star Ezio Pinza, playing singing version of Pagnol's Marius to the older man's César in the musical *Fanny*.

He subsequently had his own show on ABC-TV and led the remainder of his career in television and the nightclub world, appearing only occasionally in regional musical theatre.

TA BOUCHE Opérette in 3 acts by Yves Mirande. Lyrics by Albert Willemetz. Music by Maurice Yvain. Théâtre Daunou, Paris, 1 April 1922.

One of the first and most frothily delightful of the French Jazz Age musical comedies, this spicy nine-hander takes the form of a three-part serial about sex, money and sex at second-best seaside resorts. Whilst the unmoneyed Monsieur Pas de Vis (Guyon fils) and the phony Countess (Jeanne Cheirel) prowl about in search of married wealth for their children—and, not incidentally, themselves—those starry-eyed children, her daughter Eva (Jeanne Saint-Bonnet) and his son Bastien (Victor Boucher), are out practicing premarital sex together. Just to make sure that they will be compatible when they are married. Circumstances lead the two pairs and their pragmatic servants (Mary Hett, Gabin) through an hilariously farcical series of unfortunate marriages and multi-colored affairs before Eva and Bastien finally arrive at the wedding night they've been rehearsing for three acts.

Maurice Yvain's irrepressible title song, the comical duo in which the parents each explain their lack of ready cash by assuring the other that their fortune is bound up in ''Des terres et des coupons,'' the heroine's wish for ''Un petit amant'' for every girl in the world, La Comtesse's roguishly reminiscing ''De mon temps,'' young Bastien's ruefully jaunty ''Ça c'est une chose'' and his admission that he takes his life, and especially his love life with his rich wife, ''Machinalement,'' the backbiting ensemble ''Puisqu'un heureux hasard,'' and the young people's discovery that ''La seconde étreinte'' is even better than the first, were all unqualified hits. In fact, they became popular to such an extent that the old British pantomime trick of dropping a song sheet from the flies to allow the audience to join the players in the refrains was finally put into action at the Théâtre Daunou.

Ta bouche had a first run of over a year in Paris and its composer was launched, alongside Henri Christiné, as one of the heroes of the new style of Parisian musical theatre as his rhythmic, up-to-date show tunes became some of the most popular dance melodies of the ''années folles.'' The show also set in motion a series of opérettes which used ''bouche'' in their titles to show that they were in a similar vein (*Pas sur la bouche, Bouche à bouche, Eau à la bouche,* etc). *Ta bouche* itself returned to Paris on several occasions: in 1924 at both the Ba-ta-clan (14 January) and the Variétés (18 June), at the Théâtre de la Michodière, in 1944 at the Mogador (12 August) with Daniel Clérice, Marcelle Garnier, Edmond Castel and Germaine Charley, and at the Théâtre Antoine in 1980 (29 May) with Daniel Demars, Arièle Semenoff, Caroline Cler, Bernard Lavalette, Patrick Préjean and Perette Souplex.

Its extremely French style and its irreverently enjoyful and pragmatic attitudes to sex and marriage limited the show's overseas productions. C B Cochran had his proposed London production banned by the Lord Chamberlain, but Charles Dillingham ventured a 1923 Broadway production with Louise Groody, Oscar Shaw, Ada Lewis and John E Hazzard featured amongst the cast of a deeply sanitized version (ad Clare Kummer) with a new and less sexy story made up of ''conventional bits of old musical comedy plot,'' and an expanded principal cast

Plate 379. **Ta bouche** *was a ''grand succès'' in Paris, a ''egnagyobb sikere'' in Budapest and would have gone on to other such triumphs had not the moral pretensions of the age meant that it got emasculated as it traveled.*

and chorus. It ran 95 performances. However, French-speaking New Yorkers had a change to see the unexpurgated and unfattened version in 1929 when a French touring musical-comedy company headed by Servatius (Pas de Vis), Jane de Poumeyrac (Countess), Georges Foix (Bastien) and Sonia Elny (Eva) played the piece in its repertoire during a season at the Jolson Theater (14 March).

Herman Haller and Rideamus adapted *Dein Mund* for an 109-performance run at Berlin's Theater am Nollendorfplatz, and Budapest's Vígszínház mounted a fearless Hungarian version (ad Jenő Heltai) for a splendid 80 performances prior to a 1930 revival (3 May) and *Ta bouche* was regularly revived in the French provinces, both before and after its Paris revivals, remaining one of the most popular and representative (and best) shows of its era of musical theatre.

Germany: Theater am Nollendorfplatz *Dein Mund* 30 August 1922; Hungary: Vígszínház *Cserebere* 8 September 1922; USA: Fulton Theater *One Kiss* 27 November 1923

Recordings: original cast selection on *L'Opérette française par ses créateurs* (EPM), selection (Decca)

EIN TAG IM PARADIES Musikalische Posse in 3 acts by Leo Stein and Béla Jenbach [and Carl Lindau]. Music by Edmund Eysler. Wiener Bürgertheater, Vienna, 23 December 1913.

A cheerful and cosily unpretentious musical play illustrated with the joyously tuneful kind of Viennesey score for which Eysler had become known and loved, *Ein Tag im Paradies* gave the composer his fourth major hit (after *Der unsterbliche Lump, Der Frauenfresser* and *Der lachende Ehemann*) in as many years at the prewar Bürgertheater. The musical was played for 167 performances on its first run, passed its double century on 16 April 1916, and was played again to open the 1916–17 season, finally totaling some 220 nights in its initial production.

The libretto by Stein and Jenbach (and, apparently, an uncredited Carl Lindau) gave a fine, almost Girardiesque central role to Louis Treumann as Tobby Stöger, an expatriate Viennese who comes back home after 20 years away and parks himself at the Ringhotel, determined to have a wonderful time, cost what may. But ''home'' turns out to be not quite what it was 20 years ago, and the fondly remembered Mizzi of his youth is not only married but has turned out something of a shrew. However, not all is disappointment. By the end of his holiday he has attracted the attentions of an American widow, Gladys Wyne (Emmy Petko), who serenades him with ''Ahoy, my boy, reich mir die Hand, und komm mit mir in Dollarland . . . !'' Mizzi Eisenhofer played young Gaby, the girl who makes him think of what Mizzi was, and tenor Vincenz Bauer was Hans Walther, a painter, who is destined—when fantasy time is over, and Tobby has stopped mooning over Gaby and come down to earth—to be her young and logical partner.

The most popular individual numbers in a score that brimmed over with waltzing music were the waltzes ''Im Herzen da klingt eine Saite so fein'' and ''(Das ist) der Walzer der Saison,'' the march quartet ''Servus Wien,'' which returned repeatedly through the night and finally brought down the third-act curtain, the title song Das Lied vom blauen Paradies (''Im Liebhartstal im Garterl'') and the duo ''Nur eine Witwe''—a piece expressing the ''widows are wonderful'' sentiment. There was also a merry burlesque scena in the second act which was made up of a Viennese duet, a Berliner song and an ''English-Wienerische G'stanzlen,'' and a jolly entrance number for Gladys explaining ''Mein father war Amerikanische, meine mother war aus Wien'' and insisting that American women ''haben die Hosen an,'' as well as much in the way of dance music, from an Alt Wiener Tanz to a parody Polka.

Following its splendid success in Vienna, *Ein Tag im Paradies* pursued its career happily through central Europe, being produced with equal success in Germany and in Hungary (ad Andor Gábor), but the outbreak of war rather clipped its prospects further afield. An American version appeared, however, produced by the Shuberts at the Casino Theater under the title *The Blue Paradise* (ad Edgar Smith, Herbert Reynolds, [Blanche Merrill]) with Cecil Lean (Rudolph Stöger), Frances Demarest (Mrs Gladys Wynne) and the young Vivienne Segal (Mitzi/Gaby, replacing the sacked Chapine pre-Broadway) in the cast. It had, of course, undergone the usual kind of Shubertization. The play had gained a flashback start, and Eysler's score of 13 and some bits numbers was bulked up and watered down with local interpolations, including three numbers by Leo Edwards and one ''up-to-date'' little dance piece by leading man Lean. Fortunately, the remainder of the new numbers were by the Hungarian Sigmund Romberg who was much more at home imitating Eysler than writing songs to order for the usual Shubert compilations and the result was a pretty and reasonably homogenous score which contributed much to a superb run of 360 Broadway performances. But if Eysler's ''The Waltz of the Season'' and ''I'm Dreaming of a Wonderful Night'' still stood out as the gems of the musical part of the entertainment, it was little Miss Segal and Romberg's interpolated ''Auf Wiederseh'n'' number which got the public's vote as the hits of the show.

The Blue Paradise was one of the most successful of all the botched Continental Operetten to appear on the Broadway stage in the entire history of Continental Operetten and botching, but even a success on this scale did not encourage the Shuberts to pay their bills. Counting on the War to protect them, they sent not a cent to Eysler and his producer, Oscar Fronz, until the Austrians were able to mount a lawsuit against them, at which point they shruggingly settled. They had, however, given Eysler—after the indifferent record of Henry Savage's well-considered but untriumphant *The Love Cure* (*Künstlerblut*), the short-lived *The June Bride,* their own fairly successful production of a very botched version of *Vera-Violetta* and the more-or-less-flop of *Der Frauenfresser* (*The Women Haters*)—his most successful American show. Even if it wasn't quite all his.

Germany: ?1914; Hungary: Király Színház *Cserebogár* 11 December 1914; USA: Casino Theater *The Blue Paradise* 5 August 1915

TAKE A CHANCE Musical in 2 acts by Laurence Schwab. Lyrics by B G De Sylva. Music by Nacio Herb Brown and Richard Whiting. Additional music by Vincent Youmans. Apollo Theater, New York, 26 November 1932.

Author-producer Schwab, cold from the quick failures of *East Wind* and *Free for All* and the break-up of his once-triumphant partnership with Frank Mandel, produced a conventional backstage musical comedy called *Humpty Dumpty* at Pittsburgh in September 1932. In spite of a score by co-producer Buddy De Sylva and Nacio Herb Brown, and the casting of the rising Ethel Merman and Eddie Foy jr, it was a full-sized frost and was taken off after its first awful week. Schwab, who had rescued *The New Moon* after a similarly unpromising beginning, pulled in Vincent Youmans to do seven extra songs (five of which made it to opening night) and revamped and rewrote his book, and the piece resurfaced less than two months later as *Take a Chance.*

Jack Haley and Sid Silvers played two comically crooked gents who back a revue, Jack Whiting was their less worldly wise associate and June Knight their girl pal who proves to be really straight enough to be allowed to get the handsome Whiting at the final curtain. Miss Merman was still there, playing Wanda Brill, a performer in the revue-within-a-musical and, if she had nothing much to do with the plot, she had the most durable number of the evening in the walloping ''Eadie Was a Lady,'' a piece expressing similar sentiments to the later ''Cabaret.'' She also delivered two other numbers which went on after the show had finished: Youmans's ''Great Day''-ish ''Rise 'n' shine,'' which subsequently appeared in, and gave its title to, a short-lived London musical (Theatre Royal, Drury Lane 7 May 1936) and, with Whiting, ''You're an Old Smoothie,'' later reused in London's *Nice Goings On.*

Even if the show was no *New Moon,* Schwab and De Sylva undoubtedly pulled off their rewrite, for *Take a Chance* proved decidedly popular fare, ran for 243 performances on Broadway and was then metamorphosed into a Paramount film with original cast member June Knight starred alongside Cliff Edwards, James Dunn and Lillian Roth. Only two of the show's numbers survived in this new transformation (''Eadie'' was one), but one of the replacements was Harold Arlen's ''It's Only a Paper Moon.''

Film: Paramount 1933

TAKE ME ALONG Musical comedy in 2 acts by Joseph Stein and Robert Russell based on Eugene O'Neill's play *Ah, Wilderness!* Music and lyrics by Bob Merrill. Shubert Theater, New York, 22 October 1959.

The musical version of Eugene O'Neill's popular play (Guild Theater 2 October 1933, 289 performances), a work acclaimed by George Jean Nathan as ''the tenderest and most amusing comedy of boyhood in the American drama,'' followed the lines of the original play closely. Its focus was, however, by reason of star values, shifted somewhat from the tale of the painful growing-up of young Richard Miller (Robert Morse), his pangs of po-

Plate 380. **Take Me Along.** *Gene Kelly in the St Louis Muny production.*

litical naiveté and his passions for classic prose and capitalist's daughter Muriel McComber (Susan Luckey), towards the subsidiary romance of the drink-sodden Sid (top-billed Jackie Gleason) and Auntie Lily (Eileen Herlie). The third above-the-title star of the musical was Walter Pidgeon as Nat Miller, the small-time newspaper proprietor who is father to the young non-hero of the piece, whilst Una Merkel completed the principal line-up as Mrs Goodwin.

Merrill was seemingly on more promising musical-theatre ground with O'Neill's one and only comic play than he had been with his previous adaptation from the author's dramatic opus (*New Girl in Town,* 1957, from the drama *Anna Christie*), but oddly, in spite of the song-writer's practically permanent residence in the hit parades of the period, *Take Me Along* did not produce any individual numbers which became generally popular. Amongst the most enjoyable moments were a comic duet for Gleason and Miss Herlie, ''I Get Embarrassed,'' a piece about ''Staying Young'' for Pidgeon (at first refusing to admit he needs to, and in reprise acknowledging he can't) and a duo version for Pidgeon and Gleason of the show's title song. The conventional musical-comedy dance quota of the period was satisfied by Onna White's nightmare ballet (''The Beardsley Ballet''), which put young Richard's pubescent problems into dance.

David Merrick's production of *Take Me Along* (a title in the vein of the meaningless catchphrase names so favored two decades earlier) was played for 448 performances over more than a year at New York's Shubert Theater. However, the box office collapsed when Gleason left the cast and, in the summing-up, the show did not either make money for its Broadway investors or provoke any overseas productions. It did win a revival at East Haddam's Goodspeed Opera House some 25 years on, and that revival was taken to New York's Martin Beck Theater where it opened on 14 April 1985. Like the same company's recent Broadway transfer of the very different

Little Johnny Jones, it played just one performance before shipping out.

Recording: original cast (RCA)

TALBOT, Howard [MUNKITTRICK, ?Richard Lansdale] (b New York, 9 March 1865; d Reigate, England, 12 September 1928). The composer of two of the new century's greatest hits.

Born in New York and brought up from the age of four in London, Howard Talbot studied medicine at King's College before switching to the Royal College of Music to pursue a musical education and career. He had a slow and difficult start to his life as a composer and musician, succeeding in the first years only in placing the occasional song and, although it was floated as early as 1890 that the young man was "collaborating with Fred Broughton on a piece for New York," his first staged work was a one-act operetta played at the Albert Hall Ice Carnival, his second a musical setting of a complex little piece, diligently based on a game of chess by its authoress, the Hon Albinia Brodrick, and produced by amateurs at Oxford and at King's Lynn. King's Lynn, however, ultimately provided the venue for Talbot's first full-sized professional production, the comic opera *Wapping Old Stairs,* which was well enough received locally to earn it a London season in 1894 with a cast including D'Oyly Carte stars Jessie Bond, Courtice Pounds and Richard Temple. The show had, however, only 35 performances in London, and no afterlife, and Talbot found further ill fortune when his contribution as composer and musical director to the quick-flop burlesque *All My Eye-van-hoe* led him into court, suing the producers for nonpayment of his earned dues of £42 1s 10d.

Talbot did his principal work in these early days of his career as a musical-theatre conductor, notably behind the baton for the long-touring *The Lady Slavey,* and although his next produced show, *Monte Carlo* (1896), did considerably better than the first, both in Britain and in America, it did not lift him into the top category of London writers. He continued to be just a supplier of additional material here and there whilst earning his living conducting a series of London shows: the play *The Sorrows of Satan* at the Shaftesbury (1897), both *Dandy Dan, the Lifeguardsman* (1897, into which he interpolated the successful "Someone Ought to Speak to Millie Simpson") and *Milord Sir Smith* (1898) for Arthur Roberts, the flop burlesque *Great Caesar* (1899) and George Edwardes's *Kitty Grey* (1900–1901), a show which included another charming Talbot song, "Mademoiselle Pirouette," in its score. However, during this time, a little provincial touring show for which he had composed the bulk of the music was brought to town, and Talbot at last found very genuine success.

A Chinese Honeymoon, equipped with a list of songs including Talbot's quickly popular "Martha Spanks the Grand Pianner" and "The à la Girl," became the first musical in theatre history to run up one thousand consecutive metropolitan performances and, as it went round the world, its composer's name and fortune were made. He continued to work as a conductor, spending a short time at the Gaiety with *The Toreador,* and then helming *Three Little Maids* for which, although Paul Rubens took sole music credit, he actually composed the whole of the concerted music, and as a composer he turned out over the next eight years the scores for six further musicals, most of which he also conducted. He scored comfortable West End successes with *The Blue Moon, The White Chrysanthemum, The Girl Behind the Counter* and *The Belle of Brittany,* each of which went on to be played throughout the English-speaking theatre world, but had unmitigated flops with *Miss Wingrove* and *The Three Kisses.* He also contributed regular individual numbers to other composers' scores including the coon song "Smiling Sambo" and "Bob and Me" in *The Girl from Kays* and numbers for pieces ranging from Leslie Stuart's *The School Girl* ("One of the Boys") and Ada Reeve's *Winnie Brooke Widow* to the Gaiety Theatre's *The Sunshine Girl* ("You and I Together") and the London piece that passed for Kálmán's *Tatárjárás* (*Autumn Manoeuvres*).

In 1909 he had the second major success of his career when he combined with Lionel Monckton on the score of *The Arcadians.* Ten years after his first major triumph, he again hit the international heights with his contributions ("I've Got a Motter," "I Like London," "Half Past Two," the beautiful ensemble "The Joy of Life" and the quintet "Truth Is So Beautiful") to the most successful musical of the Edwardian era. Although its successor, *The Mousmé,* proved an overproduced failure, its music, notably Talbot's pretty high soprano "My Samisen," molded to the talents of the show's star, Florence Smithson, was not at fault. There was also much of quality in both *The Pearl Girl* and the interesting but unlucky *My Lady Frayle,* but each of these pieces was written and composed in an idiom which was on its way out, and it was noticeable that the song success of Talbot's sprightly modern musical comedy *Mr Manhattan* was not one of his numbers, but a lively secondhand American number interpolated for the show's American star.

Talbot supplied music for several of the newly popular musical playlets produced around this time in the variety theatres and then, at a point when it might have been thought that he would gently fade away, along with the other composers of his era who were unable or unwilling to adapt to the new rhythms and styles invading the musical theatre, Talbot put his name on his third long-running hit. In 1916 the composer contributed some additional material to the London wartime production of the American musical *High Jinks* which Alfred Butt was pretending wasn't by the German-sounding Rudolf Friml as he revamped it as a vehicle for comedian Bill Berry at the Adelphi, and he and Monckton were subsequently hired to write the full score for the comedian's next musical. *The Boy,* an adaptation of Pinero's *The Magistrate,* was a major hit, and even if the bulk of the favorite numbers were Monckton's, Talbot once again fulfilled more than a supporting role, supplying both solos and the bulk of the concerted music. Talbot—paired this time with the young Ivor Novello—repeated with the score for a second Pinero musical, *Who's Hooper?,* which proved almost as big a success at the first, but when he went it alone on a third, *My Nieces*—not only without Monckton or Novello but, perhaps more importantly, without Berry as its very box-officeable star—it proved less happy.

My Nieces was his last West End show. Talbot retired to the south of England and, although he continued to compose, his last works were for amateur companies: *His Ladyship* (w Percy Greenbank, Dorothy Langton, Scala Theatre 24 April 1928) and *The Daughter of the Gods* (1929). His earlier *Athene* (1911) was written for another amateur group, the Hunstanton Operatic Society, where he had taken his first steps as a theatre composer.

Talbot's nephew, **Howard [Ellis] CARR** (b Manchester, 26 December 1880, d Kensington, 10 November 1960), was a prominent musical-theatre conductor and arranger in Britain and Australia.

1889 **Thisbe and Pyramus** (Robert S Hickens/Mrs Aylmer Gowing) 1 act Albert Hall 15 March

1892 **A Musical Chess Tournament** (Albinia Brodrick) New Theatre, Oxford 28 October

1894 **Wapping Old Stairs** (Stuart Robertson) Theatre Royal, King's Lynn 4 January; Vaudeville Theatre 17 February

1896 **Monte Carlo** (Harry Greenbank) Avenue Theatre 27 August

1898 **One of the Boys** (Wal Pink) sketch Alhambra 11 April

1899 **A Chinese Honeymoon** (George Dance) Theatre Royal, Hanley 16 October; Royal Strand Theatre, London 5 October 1901

1900 **Kitty Grey** (w Augustus Barratt, Lionel Monckton, et al/ Adrian Ross/J Smyth Piggott) Bristol 27 August; Apollo Theatre, London 7 September 1901

1902 **Three Little Maids** (w Paul Rubens/Percy Greenbank/ Rubens) Apollo Theatre 20 May

1904 **The Blue Moon** (w Rubens/P Greenbank, Rubens/Harold Ellis) Theatre Royal, Northampton 29 February; Lyric Theatre, London 28 August 1905

1905 **Miss Wingrove** (W H Risque) Strand Theatre 4 May

1905 **The White Chrysanthemum** (Arthur Anderson/Leedham Bantock, Anderson) Criterion Theatre 31 August

1906 **The Girl Behind the Counter** (Anderson/Bantock, Anderson) Wyndham's Theatre 21 April

1907 **The Three Kisses** (P Greenbank/Bantock) Apollo Theatre 21 August

1908 **The Belle of Brittany** (P Greenbank/Bantock, Percy J Barrow) Queen's Theatre 24 October

1909 **The Arcadians** (w Lionel Monckton/Arthur Wimperis/ Mark Ambient, Alexander M Thompson, Robert Courtneidge) Shaftesbury Theatre 28 April

1911 **Athene** (R T Nicholson) Theatre Royal, King's Lynn 6 February

1911 **The Mousmé** (w Monckton/Wimperis, Greenbank/A Thompson, Courtneidge) Shaftesbury Theatre 9 September

1913 **The Pearl Girl** (w Hugo Felix/Basil Hood) Shaftesbury Theatre 25 September

1913 **A Narrow Squeak** (F J Whitmarsh) sketch Hippodrome, Manchester 26 May; London Coliseum 16 June

1913 **Simple 'Earted Bill** (Barrow, Huntley Wright) sketch London Coliseum 1 December

1914 **Lucky Miss** (Risque) sketch London Pavilion 13 July

1915 **The Light Blues** (w Finck/Adrian Ross/Ambient, Jack Hulbert) Prince of Wales Theatre, Birmingham 13 September; Shaftesbury Theatre 14 September 1916

1915 **Vivien** (w Herman Finck/Wimperis/Max Pemberton, Wimperis) Prince of Wales Theatre, Birmingham 27 December; Shaftesbury Theatre as *My Lady Frayle* 1 March 1916

1916 **Mr Manhattan** (w Philip Braham, Frank E Tours)/C H Bovill, Fred Thompson) Prince of Wales Theatre 30 March

1917 **The Boy** (w Monckton/Ross, Greenbank/F Thompson) Adelphi Theatre 14 September

1919 **Who's Hooper?** (w Ivor Novello/Clifford Grey/F Thompson) Adelphi Theatre 13 September

1921 **My Nieces** (Greenbank) Queen's Theatre 19 August

DAS TAL DER LIEBE Musical play in 3 acts by Rudolf Lothar taken from *Das Tal des Lebens* by Max Dreyer. Music by Oscar Straus. Volksoper, Vienna, 23 December 1909.

The folk of the ''valley of love'' are famed as wet nurses, and when the elderly Markgraf Waldemar (Herr Aschner), piqued by his failure to produce an heir, appoints a chastity officer and decrees that only married couples may pursue such a calling, the young folk of the valley rebel. Hans Stork (Herr Zigler), elected their representative, gets himself a post as a castle guard, eventually at the young Markgräfin's (Frl Ritzinger) bedroom door. Nine months later the Markgraf has his heir, the chastity commission is forgotten, and Hans—the King Nurse—settles down with his Lisbeth (Emmy Petko) for a happy ending.

Straus's score was a most musicianly one, much more tuneful and catching than some he had recently turned out. The evening began with a melodious overture filled with rural refrains, and these jolly tones were echoed in the opening duo for Hans and Lisbeth (''Komm! Komm! der Pfarrer wartet schöne'') before being brought back repeatedly throughout the evening in what proved to be the show's most appealing musical moments. Little

Lisbeth disappeared after her first duet until the last act, when her part was graced with a doleful, high tessituraed little lay about having lost her husband (''So lacht nur eine'') but Hans went on to share the lushest part of the music with the Markgräfin, a part from which their duet ''Ei, ei wie sonderbar'' was the principal morceau. The Markgräfin, the prima donna of the piece, led a tuneful waltz ensemble (''Wir haben gesiegt''), joined a canzone and bolero with the contralto and a minuet of sterile formality with her husband, and delivered a wishful little romanze about a Princess who went out into the world disguised as a peasant girl and had a good time.

In spite of its many attractions, *Das Tal der Liebe* was not a genuine success either in Vienna or in a simultaneous production in Berlin, and an attempt to get a production off the ground in America went no further than a handful of performances by C E Schmid's Cincinnati stock company. But the show's music was, in particular, warmly praised and, over the following years, regretted in print a number of times, so it was little surprise when the piece was ultimately revised and reproduced in 1919 as *Die galante Markgräfin* (Volksoper 24 January ad Felix Dörmann). The new version, however, did not succeed in making its way into the repertoire any more than the old one had, and some of Straus's most charming music went to waste.

An earlier *Das T(h)al der Liebe* by Karl Haffner, music by Anton Titl, was produced at Vienna's Theater an der Wien 20 April 1846.

Germany: Komische Oper 23 December 1909; USA: Grand Opera House, Cincinnati 9 October 1913

TALFOURD, Francis N[oon] (b London, ?1824; d Menton, 9 March 1862). Popular burlesque writer of the mid-19th century.

The son of Justice Sir Thomas Noon Talfourd, author of the successful tragedy *Ion,* and educated at Eton and Oxford, Frank Talfourd began his working life as a barrister on the Oxford circuit. However, an early attempt at a burlesque, a parody of *Macbeth* initially produced at the Henley regatta in 1847, was picked up for transfer to the professional theater and thereafter he quickly made himself a reputation as an author of burlesques through a fine career ended by his premature death at the certified age of 37. A number of his favorite pieces were on the classical themes with which his education had made him familiar (Alcestis, Thetis and Peleus, Atalanta, Pluto and Proserpine, Electra), but he also mined Shakespeare, English legends, faerie and the Arabian Nights in the tradition established by Planché, and proved one of that author's most effective followers. His versions of *Ganem, Shylock* and *Atalanta,* in particular, proved revivable over a number of seasons, and were seen in several English-language countries.

1847 **Macbeth, Somewhat Removed from the Text of Shakespeare** (pasticcio) Henley-on-Thames; Strand Theatre 1848

1848 **Sir Rupert the Fearless** (pasticcio) Strand Theatre 24 April

1849 **Hamlet**

1850 **Alcestis, the Original Strong Minded Woman** (pasticcio) Strand Theatre 4 July

1850 **The Princess in the Tower, or A Match for Lucifer** (pasticcio) Olympic Theatre 2 September

1850 **La Tarantula, or The Spider King** (pasticcio/w Albert Smith) Adelphi Theatre 26 December

1851 **Godiva, or Ye Ladye of Coventrie and Ye Exyle Fayre** (pasticcio/w William P Hale) Strand Theatre 7 July

1851 **Thetis and Peleus** (pasticcio/w Hale) Strand Theatre 27 October

1851 **The Mandarin's Daughter, or The Story of the Willow Pattern Plate** (pasticcio/w Hale) Punch's Playhouse 26 December

1852 **The Bottle Imp, or Spirits in Bond** (pasticcio/w Hale) Grecian Saloon 12 April

1852 **Ganem, the Slave of Love** (pasticcio) Olympic Theatre 31 May

1852 **Leo the Terrible** (pasticcio/w Stirling Coyne) Haymarket Theatre 26 December

1853 **Shylock, or The Merchant of Venice Preserved** (pasticcio) (US: *Shylock, or a Jerusalem Hearty-Joke*) Olympic Theatre 4 July

1854 **Abon Hassan, or The Hunt after Happiness** (pasticcio) St James's Theatre 26 December

1857 **Atalanta, or The Three Golden Apples** (pasticcio) Haymarket Theatre 13 April

1858 **Pluto and Proserpine, or The Belle and the Pomegranate** (pasticcio) Haymarket Theatre 5 April

1859 **Electra in a New [Electric] Light** (pasticcio) Haymarket Theatre 25 April

1859 **King Thrushbeard, or The Little Pet and the Great Passion** (pasticcio) Lyceum Theatre 26 December

1859 **Tell!, and the Strike of the Cantons, or The Pair, the Meddler and the Apple** (pasticcio arr Ferdinand Wallerstein) Strand Theatre 26 December

1860 **The Miller and His Men** (pasticcio/w H J Byron) Strand Theatre 9 April

LE TALISMAN Opéra-comique in 3 acts by Adolphe d'Ennery and Paul Burani. Music by Robert Planquette. Théâtre de la Gaîté, Paris, 20 January 1893.

A lavishly produced Versailles opérette, in which an elderly Louis XV (Lacressonière), having been served up the pretty peasant Michelette (Juliette Méaly) as a potential bedtime replacement for Madame Dubarry by the ambitious Valpinçon (Louis Morlet), is checked in his libertine designs by the talisman of the title. The ''lucky'' ring had been given by Renée de Chavannes (Armande Cassive) to her superstitious favorite cousin Georges

(Émile Perrin) in an attempt to get him to believe in his prospects, but it was originally a gift from the King himself to the beloved of his far-off youth. That beloved turns out to have been the young folks' grandmother. Paul Fugère was the rustic swain of the rustic maid, heading the comedy which was the highlight of the piece before pairing off with his lass at the final curtain, at the same time as Renée and her loving cousin. Planquette's score decorated the tale and its scenery with his habitual charm and *Le Talisman* proved a 133-performance success at the Gaîté.

Oscar Hammerstein produced an English version of *The Talisman* (ad A R Schade) at his Manhattan Opera House with Bianca Lescaut (Michelette), Max Freeman (Louis XV), Richard F Carroll (Nicolas), Marguerite La Mar (Renée) and J Aldrich Libby (Valpinçon) heading the cast. It was not a success and proved the last blow to Hammerstein's tottering enterprise, and his "Opera House" was soon metamorphosed into Koster & Bial's Music Hall. Budapest, on the other hand, gave a warm welcome to *A várazsgyürü* ("the magic ring," ad Gyula Komor) which was played 36 times at the Népszínház in spite of immediate competition from the Hungarian version of *La Poupée.*

The title *The Talisman* (*Il talismano, Le Talisman*) has been much used over the years, notably for operas by Salieri (1788) and Balfe (1874), and an opéra-comique by Josse (1850).

USA: Manhattan Opera House *The Talisman* 21 June 1893; Hungary: Népszínház *A várazsgyürü* 17 December 1897

TAMIRIS, Helen [née BECKER, Helen] (b New York, 24 April 1905; d New York, 4 August 1966).

Miss Tamiris began her theatrical career as a dancer, originally with the Metropolitan Opera Company and ultimately with her own company, before coming to the musical theatre for the first time, in 1944, as the choreographer of the short-lived *Marianne.* She was subsequently responsible for the dances for *Up in Central Park* (1945 w Lew Kessler), the 1946 revival of *Show Boat,* the original production of *Annie Get Your Gun* (1946) and the revue *Inside USA* (1948), and less successfully for *Park Avenue* (1946), *Bless You All* (1950), *Great to Be Alive* (1950), *Flahooley* (1951) and *Carnival in Flanders* (1953). Her choreography for the revue *Touch and Go* (1950) won her a Tony Award, and she had further successes in the book musicals *Fanny* (1954), *By the Beautiful Sea* (1954) and *Plain and Fancy* (1955). In 1947 she staged the London production of *Annie Get Your Gun.*

TANGERINE Musical comedy in 2 acts by Guy Bolton and Philip Bartholomae, adapted from a play by Bartholomae and Lawrence Langner. Lyrics by Howard Johnson. Music by Monte Carlo and Alma Sanders. Casino Theater, New York, 9 August 1921.

In the midst of the craze for the *Irene* and *Sally* style of musical show, Guy Bolton and Philip Bartholomae suddenly and surprisingly presented 1921 Broadway with a theoretically out-of-style piece with which they had been fiddling about on the road since it had set out from Atlantic City with the young Vivienne Segal in its central role half a year earlier. *Tangerine* was surprising in that it was a violent quarter-century throwback to such 19th-century French entertainments as *Le Royaume des femmes* (whose plot it took over fairly intact), or to the earliest days of the modern musical comedy when such shows as *Go-Bang* and *Morocco Bound* ruled the stage and South Seas monarchs turned out to be hometown gents (as they had been doing at least since *Ba-ta-clan*) and their islands the setting for unbridled highjinks and song-and-dance concerts.

The island in this latter-day 19th-century show, which its authors saw fit to dub "a satire of the sexes," was actually called Tangerine, and its King (John E Hazzard) was an ex-sailor called Joe Perkins who rules a society where women go to work and men stay home. A bundle of exported Americans with marital problems finds this inversion of what they consider the natural order not at all to their taste and, after the American women—obliged by law to support their husbands—have caused chaos by setting up fashion shops and salons and finally going into rebellion and deposing King Joe, everyone is returned to the status quo and the US of A at the end of the evening.

Carlo and Sanders's blow-away score included pieces with titles like "Tropical Vamps," "It's Great to Be Married (and lead a single life)" and "There's a Sunbeam for Every Drop of Rain," but it was the interpolated "Sweet Lady" (David Zoob, Frank Crumit), performed by Julia Sanderson and Crumit, which proved the nearest thing to a popular success in the show's musical part. *Tangerine* did not depend on its songs, however, and the old-fashioned fun of the book, Hazzard's comicalities, and the delicious Miss Sanderson were much more responsible than the show's tunes for the unexpected run of 337 Broadway performances which the production racked up prior to going back on to the road and to further success.

Tangerine's success was not even limited to America. Although London did not join the takers, the piece did splendidly in Australia where Hugh J Ward chose it to follow his initial venture with the hugely successful *The O'Brien Girl* at Melbourne's New Princess Theatre. It ran precisely half as long as its predecessor, but still managed a decidedly non-negligible 101 performances in Melbourne. In 1925 Ward also showed it in Sydney (Grand Opera House 28 March) with Mark Daly starred as Joe, and Mamie Watson, May Beatty and dancer June Roberts amongst the ladies, for a fine eight weeks.

Australia: New Princess Theatre, Melbourne 9 June 1923

DIE TANGOKÖNIGIN *see* DIE IDEALE GATTIN

DIE TANGOPRINZESSIN Posse mit Gesang und Tanz in 3 acts by Jean Kren and Kurt Kraatz. Lyrics by Alfred Schönfeld. Music by Jean Gilbert. Thalia-Theater, Berlin, 4 October 1913.

The fashion for the tango in Europe in the years before the First World War was spurred on and reflected by its performance first in the Paris revue theatres and then by its featuring on the London stage, notably as performed by George Grossmith jr and Phyllis Dare in the Gaiety musical comedy *The Sunshine Girl* and shown off in the glitzy Albert de Courville dance revue *Hullo, Tango* (Hippodrome 23 December 1913, with Ethel Levey singing "My Tango Girl"). On Broadway, Arthur Stanford interpolated Jean Schwartz's "Tangoland Tap" into *Die keusche Susanne,* Julia Sanderson and Alan Mudie repeated the *Sunshine Girl* routine, Joseph Santley danced what he called "The Santley Tango" in *When Dreams Come True,* George Grossmith enquired "Tommy, Won't You Teach Me How to Tango?" in *The Girl on the Film, The Laughing Husband* told of what happened "Since Grandpa Learned to Tango" and the grotesque version of *Die Fledermaus* staged as *The Merry Countess* also sported a decidedly incoherent tango tacked into its already made-incoherent proceedings. By the time of the 1913 *Ziegfeld Follies* the craze was already exhausting enough for a group billed as the Tangomaniacs to present their "Tangoitis" alongside "Turkish-Trottishness" (the Turkey-Trot was the other current dance fashion) and "Classicxentrique" in a featured dance section. Tangos flooded the dance floors and sheet-music market throughout Europe, and the dance soon made its way not only into musical-comedy scores, but into their titles.

Germany surfaced with Jean Gilbert's *Die Tangoprinzessin,* a piece which featured the obligatory dance in a number called "Ich tanz so gern den Tango." However, the novelty number was backed up by a solid score of tried-and-true song styles: the waltzes "Das Glück kommt über Nacht," "Ich bin verrückt" and "Komm' doch bloss mal runter schatz," the two-step "Ja, wenn das Petrus wüsste," and a whole series of marches ("In Hi-Ha-Hellerau," "Ja das war früher mal," "Willst du mein Kind?," etc).

Die Tangoprinzessin followed the two splendidly successful Jean Gilbert musical comedies *Autoliebchen* and *Puppchen* into Berlin's Thalia-Theater in late 1913, and it did almost as well as they. It played through the winter and spring, a regular season of nigh on six months, before giving way to the next Gilbert piece, *Wenn der Frühling kommt!,* in March. The show was duly purchased for a London production by George Edwardes, but the outbreak of the war led to all German-tainted plans being abandoned and *Die Tangoprinzessin*'s international progress was stopped short.

The tango hung around for a while, as a vaguely exotic symbol of South Americanness, and song titles such as "A Tango Dream" (*The Girl Who Didn't*) or "A Tango Melody" (*The Cocoanuts*) were legion. It also snuck into the titles of such shows as the South American rewrite of Lehár's *Die ideale Gattin* as *Die Tangokönigin* (Apollotheater, Vienna, 1921) and Komjáti's Budapest operett *Éjféli tangó* (1932) later seen in Leipzig (1932) and Vienna as *Tango um Mitternacht* (Volksoper, 1933). In later days, however, the dance became associated with exaggerated vampery and was, more often than not, presented on the musical stage as a parody of sexuality rather than anything near to the real thing.

TANNER, James T[olman] (b London, 17 October 1858; d London, 18 June 1915). Architect-in-chief of the George Edwardes musical comedies.

In his earliest years in the theatre Tanner ("a dark, Japanese-looking young man") worked with Alice Dunning-Lingard as a scene-painter and actor, and he subsequently toured with Horace Lingard and with Auguste van Biene's companies, first as a performer (Volteface in *The Old Guard,* etc), and later as company manager and stage director. In 1892 he added the function of playwright-by-appointment to this list when he provided the dramatically inclined 'cellist who was his employer with a vehicle that would allow him to wring withers and to play his instrument in the same evening. The play that Tanner turned out, *The Broken Melody* (Lyceum Theatre, Ipswich 26 July 1892), was an enormous success on the touring circuits, and van Biene duly trouped this musical weepie for many, many years from Blackpool to Broadway to Brisbane.

By the early 1890s van Biene had becomer more than just a 'cellist with dramatic ambitions. He was touring number-one road versions of the Gaiety Theatre's burlesque productions and, in 1892, his *Faust Up-to-Date* company (directed by Tanner) was popped briefly into the Gaiety to fill a gap in the house schedule. George Edwardes's eye fell on the obviously useful Tanner, who soon exchanged touring for a place in Edwardes's organization. He retained that place through two decades, becoming one of the most important members of the Edwardes establishment as constructor of the libretti for his shows, stage director, and all-round ally and confidant to the great producer.

Tanner's first West End directing credit was on the shortlived *The Baroness,* but soon after Edwardes entrusted him with the construction (billed as ''James Leader'') and staging of his new-style musical play *In Town* (1892). He next had Tanner provide the outline on which Owen Hall would construct *A Gaiety Girl* (1893), and gave him the unfinished burlesque of *Don Juan,* which the late Fred Leslie had begun, to complete and stage as a vehicle for Arthur Roberts. Tanner directed the original Gaiety production of *The Shop Girl* (1894) and Daly's Theatre's *An Artist's Model* (1895), as well as *A Modern Trilby* (1895) for Nellie Farren. Thereafter, however, although he directed his own *The Ballet Girl* for Broadway (w Frederick Leon) in 1898, he mostly left the staging to Edwardes's other principal aide, J A E (''Pat'') Malone, and concentrated largely on evolving the outlines and libretti of the shows with which Edwardes conquered the theatrical world in the Victorian and Edwardian eras.

1892 **In Town** (F Osmond Carr/w Adrian Ross) Prince of Wales Theatre 15 October

1893 **Don Juan** (Meyer Lutz/Ross) Gaiety Theatre 28 October

1895 **All Abroad** (Frederick Rosse, et al/w Owen Hall)) Theatre Royal, Portsmouth 1 April; Criterion Theatre 8 August

1895 **Bobbo** (F O Carr/Ross) 1 act Prince's Theatre, Manchester 12 September

1896 **The Clergyman's Daughter** (F O Carr/Ross) Theatre Royal, Birmingham 13 April

1896 **My Girl** revised *The Clergyman's Daughter* Gaiety Theatre 1 December

1896 **The Circus Girl** (Caryll, Monckton/Ross, Harry Greenbank/w Walter Palings) Gaiety Theatre 5 December

1897 **The Ballet Girl** (Carl Kiefert/Ross) Grand Theatre, Wolverhampton 15 March

1898 **The Transit of Venus** (Napoléon Lambelet/Ross) Theatre Royal, Dublin 9 April

1900 **The Messenger Boy** (Caryll, Monckton/Ross, H Greenbank/w Alfred Murray) Gaiety Theatre 3 February

1901 **The Toreador** (Caryll, Monckton/Ross, Percy Greenbank/w Harry Nicholls) Gaiety Theatre 17 June

1902 **A Country Girl** (Monckton/Ross, P Greenbank) Daly's Theatre 18 January

1903 **The Orchid** (Caryll, Monckton/Ross, P Greenbank) Gaiety Theatre 28 October

1904 **The Cingalee** (Monckton/Ross, P Greenbank) Daly's Theatre 5 March

1906 **The New Aladdin** (Caryll, Monckton/Ross, P Greenbank, et al/w W H Risque) Gaiety Theatre 29 September

1909 **Our Miss Gibbs** (Monckton, Caryll/Ross, P Greenbank/w ''Cryptos'') Gaiety Theatre 23 January

1910 **The Quaker Girl** (Monckton/Ross, P Greenbank) Adelphi Theatre 5 November

1912 **The Dancing Mistress** (Monckton/Ross, P Greenbank) Adelphi Theatre 19 October

1913 **The Girl on the Film** (*Filmzauber*) English libretto (Gaiety Theatre)

1913 **The Girl from Utah** (Sidney Jones, Paul Rubens/Ross, P Greenbank, Rubens) Adelphi Theatre 18 October

TANNER, Susan Jane (b Manchester, 3 September 1947).

At first a dancer and singer in regional theatres (Nancy in *The Boy Friend,* Tessie Tura in *Gypsy,* Miss Lynch in *Grease,* Miss Lewisham in *Worzel Gummidge*) and shipboard productions (Nickie in *Sweet Charity,* Irene in *Irene,* Alice in *John, Paul, George, Ringo and Bert*), Susan Jane Tanner had her first major role in the musical theatre when she succeeded Barbara Windsor in the title role of *Calamity Jane* in Britain's first production of the show-of-the-film.

In 1980 she originated the roles of Jellylorum/Lady Griddlebone in *Cats* (''In questa tepida notte''), winning special notice amongst all the dancing for her abilities as a comedienne, and moving from there to join the company at the Royal Shakespeare Theatre where she appeared in a number of plays (Mopsa in *A Winter's Tale,* Ostrich in *Peter Pan,* etc) and in the musical *Poppy.* She subsequently appeared regionally as Mrs Lovett in *Sweeney Todd* and as Miss Hannigan in *Annie,* before, in 1985 returning to the Barbican to introduce the role of Madame Thénardier in the original English production of *Les Misérables.*

In a career thereafter largely angled to the non-musical theatre, she appeared as Mrs Peachum in the RSC production of *The Beggar's Opera* (1992), in 1996 initiated the role of Madame de Rols in *Martin Guerre* and in 1998 played the role of Miss Pross in a new musical based on *A Tale of Two Cities* at Birmingham.

She repeated her original *Cats* role in the 1998 video version of the show.

TANNHÄUSER-PARODIE Zukunftsposse in 3 acts (mit vergangener Musik und gegenwärtigen Gruppirungen) by Johann Nestroy (after H Wollheim). Music by Karl Binder. Theater in der Leopoldstadt (Carltheater), Vienna, 31 October 1857.

Produced just two months after Wagner's opera had been given its Viennese premiere at the Thalia-Theater, Nestroy's *Tannhäuser-Parodie* was one of the most successful of Vienna's regular supply of popular operatic burlesques. The newest work by the ''composer of the future'' was parodied in a rhyming-coupletted ''play of the future . . . with music from the past and staging from the present,'' which presented Venus as a Weinkeller temptress, and Elisabeth as the daughter of the Landgraf Purzel, an over-the-top Musikenthusiast who loathes the ''music of the future.'' The second act, which takes place in a Wartburg where all the furniture is made in the shape of musical instruments, features a musical contest at which all the greats of classical opera, from Robert le Diable and Norma to Figaro and la muette de Portici, appear. In the contest, however, Tannhäuser shows himself up as a disciple of the dreaded modern music, and he is banished, and told not to come back until he's lost his voice. But even though the hero keeps on singing modern music, it doesn't ruin his voice, so, when Elisabeth commits suicide, he decides he might as well go back to the Venusburg nightclub. The ''goddess'' appears to bring the dead to life and tie up a happy ending. Alongside Nestroy's parody of the text, pieces of the Wagnerian score also got the burlesque treatment, with Wolfram delivering a song to the evening star which began ''Guter Mond, du goldene Zwiebel'' and Elisabeth's greeting at the opening of the second act being paralleled by a ''Dich Harfenisten Kampplatz grüsse ich.''

The *Tannhäuser-Parodie* was played throughout the German-speaking theatre world and it was revived on a number of occasions over the years, including seasons at the Berlin Central-Theater in 1904 (1 September), at Vienna's Theater in der Josefstadt in 1915 (*Tannhäuser oder Die Keilerei auf der Wartburg* 22 May), at the Theater an der Wien 19 March 1927 and in a short season of new production mounted at the Wiener Bürgertheater, 2 June 1928.

Given the often scornful attitude taken to Wagner's works on their first productions, and their eminently burlesquable subject matter and style, the ''music of the future'' did not come in for as much parody as might have been expected. Alongside Nestroy's *Tannhäuser* came several French burlesques launched hot on the heels of the opera's first Paris showing (*Panne-aux-airs* Frédéric Barbier/Clairville 30 March 1861, *Ya-mein-herr* Clairville, Delacour,Thiboust 6 April 1861), whilst *Lohengrin* became *Lohengelb,or Die Jungfrau von Dragant* in the hands of Nestroy in Austria (Franz von Suppé/Moritz A Grandjean 30 November 1870) and America (Germania Theater 30 March 1874), *Little Lohengrin* in both London (Frederick Bowyer, Theatre Royal, Plymouth 14 March 1881, Holborn Theatre 16 August 1884) and in America (ad Edgar Smith, Chicago, 1886) and *Lohengrin in a Nutshell* (Academy of Music, Melbourne, 1878) in Garnet Walch's Australian perversion. *Der fliegende Holländer* was done over in Vienna as *Der fliegende Holländer zu Füss* (Müller/Nestroy Theater in der Leopoldstadt 4 August 1846) and in Britain as *The Flying Dutchman* (William Brough, Royalty Theatre, 1869) and *The Lying Dutchman* (Alfred Lee/Arthur Clements, Frederick Hay, Strand Theatre 21 December 1876), whilst *Die Meistersinger von Nürnberg* and its musical contest were parodied during the action of Hervé's *Le Petit Faust*. The Brussels Alcazar perpetrated a *La Petite Valkyrie* in 1887. In more recent years, the Nibelung saga got a going over in the American burlesque *Das Barbecü* (Seattle Opera, 1991). It is, however, Rideamus and Oscar Straus's 20th-century Viennese version of a bit of the Ring cycle, *Die lustigen Nibelungen,* which shares with the *Tannhäuser-Parodie* the record of being the most successful among the musical theatre's Wagnerian burlesques.

Plate 381. **Susan Jane Tanner.** *A very original cat.*

Hungary: Budai Színkör (Ger) 1 June 1863

TANTIVY TOWERS Comic opera in 3 acts by A P Herbert. Music by Thomas F Dunhill. Lyric Theatre, Hammersmith, 16 January 1931.

The best of the group of original light operas produced under Nigel Playfair's management at London's Lyric, Hammersmith, *Tantivy Towers* was an enjoyable attempt at a sung-through comic opera which aspired to lines of wit—and often achieved them—in a ridiculous little story of love not leveling all ranks. Chelsea's pretentiously artistic Hugh Heather (Trefor Jones) comes to grief when he moves out of his natural habitat and tries to outshine aristocratic Captain Bareback (Harvey Braban) for the hand of Lady Ann Gallop (Barbara Pett-Fraser) on her home ground at Tantivy Towers. He is damned for all time when he commits the solecism of shooting the fox during a hunt and has to settle for joining the Savage Club whilst the aristocrat gets the girl.

The respected serious composer Thomas Dunhill provided a suitably and strongly English score to illustrate a piece which, in spite of some happy moments, lacked the crazy sparkle of the Gilbert and Sullivan genre, but still found sufficient audience to run through two and a half months at the Lyric before transferring to the West End's New Theatre for another two months. It was revived at the Lyric by Claud Powell in 1935 with Maggie Teyte starred as Ann alongside Steuart Wilson (Hugh) and Frank Philips (Bareback).

TANZ DER VAMPIRE (Das Musical) Musical in 2 acts by Michael Kunze based on the film screenplay *The Fearless Vampire Killers, or Pardon Me But Your Teeth Are in My Neck* by Gérard Brach and Roman Polanski. Music by Jim Steinman. Raimundtheater, Vienna, 4 October 1997.

The vast success of *The Phantom of the Opéra* provoked a tidal wave of musicals with twisted (mentally and/or physically), melodramatic heroes ranging from the Dracula, Frankenstein and Mr Hyde of classic literature to a bunch of murderers and lynch-merchants and a usually absolutely straight-faced selection of werewolves, hunchbacks and vampires. It was something of a relief, therefore, to see arrive a musical which treated the genre with a tongue-in-cheek grin, a piece which treated the wicked world of vampiredom with a toothy smile on its face.

The libretto was based on the 1967 spoof horror film *The Fearless Vampire Killers* in which director-co-author Roman Polanski (Alfred) had starred alongside Sharon Tate (Sarah), Ferdy Mayne (von Krolock) and Jack MacGowran (Ambronsius). Shyly gormless Alfred (Aris Sas) is the ''hero'' of the affair. He is the inexperienced assistant to vampire-seeking Professor Ambronsius (Gernot Kranner), and in this story he goes out to Transylvania with his boss on a bloodsucker-hunt. There he meets lovely Sarah (Cornelia Zenz), the innkeeper's daughter, a lass with a fetish for bath-taking, and his mind veers to things other than vampires. But Sarah is captured by the vampirical Count von Krolock (Steve Barton) and carried off to his lairical castle, a suitably spooky place inhabited also by the obligatory Hunchback (Torsten Flach) of such castles, and the count's perilously gay son (Nik). Things come to their peak at the annual Vampire Ball. But, when all is said and sung, Alfred rescues Sarah, they embrace at last and . . . well, you knew that even all those baths couldn't keep a girl clean in this castle. It's vampire time.

If the story was a comical one, there were nevertheless moments in it which verged on pure melodrama or the heights of horror movie, and the score, by rockman Jim Steinman (''Total Eclipse of the Heart'') reflected this double edge. There were some ringing numbers for the Vampire (''Gott ist tot,'' ''Die unstillbare Gier''), including a big-sing duo of Steinman's big hit song (''Totale finsternis''), which burlesqued from time to time the style of the big-sing duos of *The Phantom of the Opéra* and its kind, some delicately tuneful pieces for Alfred both alone (''Für Sarah'') and with Sarah (''Draussen ist Freiheit''), a vocal showpiece for the maid, Magda (''Tot zu sein ist komisch''), a vampire-pop-spectacular-dream-sequence with the delicious title of ''Carpe noctem,'' an Offenbachian patter-song in the pure tradition of the opéra-bouffe for Ambrosius (''Wahrheit''), A Vampire March (''Ewigkeit''), and a final song-and-dirty-dance ''Tanz der Vampire,'' as highlights in a melodiously melodramatic score whose music and lyrics both rang with burlesque brightness.

The tale, the fun, the music and the spectacle all came together in what was undoubtedly the most complete and effective musical to have come out of central Europe in half a century.

Directed by Polanski, with a virtually all-English production team, *Tanz der Vampire* was immediately established as a hit on its production in Vienna. With the traditional breaks for the hot summer weeks, it ran on until the production was shifted to Stuttgart as the first stop on what looks like will be a considerable voyage.

Germany: Musical Hall, Stuttgart 31 March 2000

Recording: original cast (Polygram)

DIE TÄNZERIN FANNY ELSSLER Operette in 3 acts by Hans Adler. Music taken from the works of Johann Strauss, arranged by Oskar Stalla and Bernhard Grün. Deutsches Theater, Berlin, 22 December 1934.

The dancer Fanny Elssler, whilst furthering her career, sidesteps the lascivious and devious statesman von Gentz and the Herzog von Reichstadt, the son of Napoléon, through three acts, postponing a happy ending with her childhood friend, Baron Franz Fournier, only until she has conquered the world with her dancing. The score for the piece was made up of clips from the works of Johann Strauss.

First produced in Berlin, the show was also played with some success in Italy, where it proved one of the more popular Strauss pasticcii, but elsewhere had to give way to such pieces as the superior *Drei Walzer* or the bio-musical *Walzer aus Wien.*

Fanny Elssler (b Vienna, 23 June 1810; d Vienna, 27 November 1884) was a real person, an Austrian ballerina who had a notable career both in Europe and in America, but in the hands of the central-European mythmakers she became simply the archetypal 19th-century star and her name was given—like poor Nell Gwynne and Empress Elisabeth and other theatrically mythologized ladies of history—to the heroines of several stage pieces with more or, more often, less to do with her real story and character. Having at first been the ''subject'' of an Hungarian play, succinctly titled ''Viennese dancer'' (*Bécsi táncosnő* 8 January 1916), she later served as the title and heroine for the Hungarian musical *Fanny Elssler* or, since it was in Hungarian, *Elssler Fanny* (Mihály Nador/Jenő Faragó, Király Színház 20 September 1923) in which Hanna Honthy played Fanny. She also got involved with the Herzog von Reichstadt a second time in August Pepöck's successful Operette *Hofball im Schönbrunn,* a third time in the person of Mizzi Zwerenz in Reichert and Léon's 1921 Carltheater Operette *Der Herzog von Reichstadt* (mus: Stojanovits) and appeared, played by Fräulein Engel, as a character in Oscar Straus's Operette *Die himmelblaue Zeit* (Volksoper 21 February 1914). As enduring as Mistress Gwynne and Empress Sissi and the rest of the operettic cliché ladies, she has come back for more right up to the present day and was seen on the Viennese stage as the heroine of a very unfortunate new ballet at the Volksoper as recently as 1990.

DER TANZ INS GLÜCK Operette in 3 acts by Robert Bodanzky and Bruno Hardt-Warden. Music by Robert Stolz. Raimundtheater, Vienna, 23 December 1920.

The most internationally successful of Robert Stolz's extremely long list of Operetten, *Der Tanz ins Glück* was played around the world in some very diverse versions after its highly successful Viennese premiere at the Raimundtheater at Christmas 1920. Franz Glawatsch played Sebastian Platzer, a former music-hall attendant turned valet, who ends up accidentally unmasking the high-society charade of his employer, Fritz Wendelin (Robert Nästlberger), a hairdresser who, with the help of an identifying blue edelweiss, has been masquerading as a count in order to win the hand of hatmaker's daughter Lizzi Mutzenbacher (Anny Rainer). But Fritz is the evening's tenor, so all ends happily and conjugally when he wins a hairdressing championship. The real Count Hans-Joachim von Bibersbach (Eduard Fritsch) goes back to the arms of glamorous music-hall star Desirée Viverande (Klára Karry), who has been the object of the extramarital desires of Lizzi's socially ambitious father (Josef Egger).

Stolz's score for this comedy musical tripped along in the popular dance rhythms of the world's theatres of the time. The one-step (''Halloh, was das für Mädeln sind!,'' ''Ich hab' kein Geld,'' ''Kakadu'' quintet) and the fox-trot (''Guter Mond, schau uns nicht zu!'') were mixed in with some Viennesey songs (the waltz ''Einmal im Mai,'' ''Brüderlein, Brüderlein!'') and the usual dose of catchy marches (''Heut' geht's los!,'' ''Wenn es zehn wird, geht man nicht zu Bett!'') in a pleasing combination that added to the evening's gaiety.

Karczag's production of *Der Tanz ins Glück* ran for a straight two hundred performances, but it had then to be removed when the Raimundtheater struck its eternal barrier to viableness as a theater—its stage had to be ceded for an equitable amount of time to co-manager Rudolf Beer and his money-losing serious plays. So the Raimundtheater lost its big hit which was brought back in the autumn at the Komödienhaus (18 October 1921) instead. It reappeared briefly at the Bürgertheater in 1927 with Glawatsch featured alongside Hilde Schulz (Lizzi) and Walter Swoboda (Fritz), was seen for a handful of performances at the Theater an der Wien between 1928 and 1930, and was revived at the Raimundtheater in 1949. In 1951 a Viennese film version was made (scr: Fritz Koselka, Lilian Belmont) with Waltraut Haas, Fritz Imhoff, Johannes Heesters, Josef Egger and Ursula Lingen amongst the cast, and three of the show's songs in its score.

An Hungarian version (ad Miksa Bródy) opened before the Vienna run was done, playing first at the Városi Színház and later (29 May 1922) at the Fővárosi Nyári Színház, by which time Miksa Preger at Berlin's Theater des Westens had also produced the show (67 performances) and a London version (ad Harry Graham, add ly: Graham John) had been mounted by James White as a ''George Edwardes production.'' Billy Merson starred in *Whirled into Happiness* as valet Matthew Platt, Tom Walls was Horridge, the hatmaker, whose daughter Florence (Winnie Melville) duetted with Derek Oldham as hairdresser Horace Wiggs, and Mai Bacon was Delphine de Lavallière of the music halls. Conductor Arthur Wood and Archie Emmett Adams supplied an extra number apiece, and the show ran a useful 244 performances (only the lavish *Wild Violets* of Stolz's shows did better in Britain) before going on the road.

It also went on to Australia where Alfred Frith (Platt), Kitty Reidy (Florence), Madge Elliott/Winnie Collins (Delphine), Harry Pearce (Wiggs) and Cecil Kellaway (Horridge) featured in ''a pot-pourri of drollery and dancing'' performing ''Robinson Crusoe's Isle'' (ex-''Kakadu''), an unfamiliar ''Somebody's Wrong'' and ''Once in a While I Love You'' (''Einmal im Mai'') and apparently not very much more of Stolz through two months in Melbourne and a fine 10 weeks in Sydney (Her Majesty's Theatre 6 September 1924).

The basics of *Der Tanz ins Glück* or, more accurately, of *Whirled into Happiness* went into the making of the Shuberts' Broadway show *Sky High,* a piece put together by Harold Atteridge (the billing read, ''a new musical play by Harold Atteridge and Captain Harry Graham'') to feature the talents of the much-loved fun-maker Willie Howard as the comical valet/hero, who was now called Sammy Myers. Plenty of spectacle, some impersonations, ballet specialities, two spots for a chorus girl called Marjorie Whitney, a section called ''Broadcasting'' in which Howard, Ann Milburn (Aggie), Vannessi (Delphine) and John Quinlan (Horace) all got to do their thing, and a Shubert-sized chorusline (35 girls, 12 boys, 3 speciality girls and 6 ponies) all went to build up a show that featured ''added numbers'' by Alfred Goodman, Maurie Rubens and Carlton Kelsey, James Kendis and Hal Dyson, additional lyrics by Clifford Grey, and ''Give Your Heart in June,'' advertised as ''music by Victor Herbert—his last waltz'' as performed by the juveniles. Of Stolz's score there apparently remained just Florence's two solos, ''Hello, the Little Birds Have Flown'' (''Halloh, was das für Mädeln sind'') and ''Somewhere in Lovers' Land,'' which had been ''Somewhere in Fairyland'' in London, and ''Sonntag komm' ich zu dir'' (lyric by Fritz Grünbaum, and anyway not in Vienna's *Tanz ins Glück* originally) the duo Letter Song and some concerted and orchestral moments. Whatever *Sky High* was, however, it was still a descendant of *Der Tanz ins Glück*—if perhaps a slightly distant one—and it kept up the show's good record by running for 220 performances on Broadway before going out to tour.

Der Tanz ins Glück was revised as a 33-scene spectacular (ad Hugo Wiener) and produced in 1958 at the Vienna Raimundtheater under the title *Hallo, das ist die Liebe.* The principal numbers of the original score (''Einmal im Mai,'' ''Ich hab' kein Geld,'' ''Guter Mond,'' ''Wenn es zehn wird'') were supplemented by several new pieces with lyrics by Wiener. But this time their music was by Stolz.

Hungary: Városi Színház *Szerencsetánc* 14 May 1921; Germany: Theater des Westens 20 January 1922; UK: Lyric Theatre *Whirled into Happiness* 18 May 1922; Australia: Theatre Royal, Melbourne *Whirled into Happiness* 24 June 1924; USA: Shubert Theater *Sky High* 2 March 1925

Film: Mundus-Film/Farbfilm 1951

DIE TANZGRÄFIN Operette in 3 acts by Leopold Jacobson and Robert Bodanzky. Music by Robert Stolz. Wallner-Theater, Berlin, 18 February 1921.

Coming hard on the heels of Robert Stolz's Viennese triumph with *Der Tanz ins Glück, Die Tanzgräfin,* first mounted in Berlin, helped to make 1921 into the most memorable year of the composer's career.

The Gräfin Colette Planterose goes out to fete the Mardi Gras in Montmartre in disguise, gets acclaimed the festive queen of the affair, and then vanishes, leaving a lovestruck Marine-Lieutenant Octave Dupareil behind her. She is supposed to marry the unpleasant Marquis Philippe Villacroix in Act II, but Act III sees her sailing off with her sea captain on the aptly named good ship ''Porte-bonheur'' at the final curtain.

The tale was accompanied by a scoreful of dance-rhythmed music—waltzes (''Irgend was ist mit mir heut' los,'' ''Mädelchen von Montmartre,'' etc), one steps (''Du, nur du,'' etc), fox-trots (including the evening's top tune ''Faschingsnacht, du Zeit der Liebe''), a polka and even a paso doble that encouraged ''Zieh an den seidenen Pyjama.''

Die Tanzgräfin played for six months at Berlin's Wallner-Theater, and it was reprised for further performances between the end of the run of its successor, Straus's *Nixchen,* and the opening of the next new piece, Goetze's *Die Spitzenkönigin.* This success was more than repeated in Vienna, where *Die Tanzgräfin* was produced by Erich Müller at the Johann Strauss-Theater, with Ida Russka (Colette), Karl Bachmann (Octave) and Max Ralf-Ostermann (Villacroix) featured. This production gave Stolz one of his most substantial Viennese successes, with a run of 204 performances in seven months, before the show moved on to score a further success in Budapest where the ''dancing countess'' became the ''little grisette'' in Miksa Bródy's adaptation. Emmi Kosáry and Ernő Király headed the romance through a fine initial 53 performances, and the production was later restaged at the Fővárosi Operettszínház (8 April 1923).

With the Broadway success of *Sky High* (*Der Tanz ins Glück*) fresh in memory, Paul M Trebitsch gave his American *The Dancing Duchess* (ad J J Garren) a hugely lavish production at Boston's Wilbur Theater. Gertrude Land and Glen Dale starred alongside a workforce of 150 personnel (including a male chorus of 24), but a weekly nut of $28,000 proved much too much for it to recoup and the show folded after five weeks without moving out of Boston.

The heroine became *La Contessa delle danze* in Angelo Nessi's Italian adaptation, mounted in Milan in 1924.

Austria: Johann Strauss-Theater 13 May 1921; Hungary: Vígszínház *A kis grisett* 11 June 1921; USA: Wilbur Theater, Boston *The Dancing Duchess* 6 September 1926

DER TAPFERE SOLDAT Operette in 3 acts by Rudolf Bernauer and Leopold Jacobson based on George Bernard Shaw's play *Arms and the Man.* Music by Oscar Straus. Theater an der Wien, Vienna, 14 November 1908.

Der tapfere Soldat (''the brave soldier'') was based on the main plotline of G B Shaw's *Arms and the Man,* with much of the subsidiary action cut away, and the almost too-operetta-to-be-true character of the maid, Louka, eliminated in favor of a family cousin called Mascha, who was inserted to allow the rejected Alexius

Plate 382. *Gustav Matzner (Bumerli) climbs through the bedroom window of buxom Marie Ottmann (Nadina) in Berlin's* **Der tapfere Soldat.**

(ex- Sergius) a suitably operettic pairing-off at the final curtain.

The Swiss soldier Bumerli (Gustav Werner), a mercenary in the Serbian army, takes refuge in flight in the bedroom of Nadina (Grete Holm), the daughter of the enemy Bulgarian Colonel Kasimir Popoff (Max Pallenberg). Nadina is engaged to wed the exorbitantly dashing Alexius Spiridoff (Karl Streitmann), whom she devotedly perceives as everything that is heroic, but the practical Bumerli undeceives her over the glories of war and wins not only her heart but those of the other lonely ladies of the house: Frau Oberst Aurelia Popoff (Mizzi Schütz) and cousin Mascha (Luise Kartousch). When the men come home from the war, a bit of business with some lovingly signed photographs and an overcoat stirs up feelings, and Alexius threatens a duel before all is calmed over and Nadina is promised to her "Praliné-Soldat."

Straus's score was a delightful one, with Nadina's waltz-song "Komm', komm'! Held meiner Träume," sighed starrily over the portrait of her long-absent "hero," being the evening's solo gem. Amongst the ensembles, however, there were several other charming numbers: Nadina and Bumerli's duo "Ach, du kleiner Praliné-Soldat," a first-act finale trio for the three women ("Drei Frauen sassen am Feuerherd") and a comic sextet over the wretched overcoat, a garment which each of the women wants to get back from Popoff in order to rescue from its pocket the incriminatingly dedicated photo of herself, and the Colonel just wants to put comfortably on to his back ("Ach, es ist doch ein schönes Vergnügen").

Karczag and Wallner's original production of *Der tapfere Soldat* at the Theater an der Wien was, in spite of its very fine cast, a disappointment. It played just 60 initial performances before being removed from the evening bill two weeks into the new year to allow what was to be the triumphant production of Kálmán's *Tatárjárás* (*Ein Herbstmanöver*). A German production was mounted six weeks after the Vienna one at Berlin's Theater des Westens with Gustav Matzner (Bumerli), Marie Ottmann (Nadina), Julius Donath (Popoff), Albert Kutzner (Alexius), Vilma Conti (Mascha) and Fr Gaston (Aurelia) (99 performances), and Miksa Preger's German company introduced the piece to Budapest, in German, during a guest season of three weeks and nine shows at the Vígszínház in 1912 before the show was eventually given an Hungarian showing (ad Andor Gábor) at the Népopera in 1916, with Ilona Dömötör as Nadina and Straus himself directing. Its title showed where the impetus had come from, for it was called *A csokoládé-katona.*

If central Europe showed no particular liking for *Der tapfere Soldat,* the English-speaking world, on the contrary, gave it a huge welcome. An adaptation by the Anglo-American writer Stanislaus Stange was produced on Broadway by Fred C Whitney, one of the many American producers who had joined the frantic grabbing for new Continental musicals, both successful and unsuccessful, in the dollar-green euphoria created by *Die lustige Witwe.* Whitney proved to have grabbed either more cleverly or more luckily than most. With Jack E Gardner (Bumerli), Ida Brooks Hunt (Nadina), William Pruette (Popoff), George Tallmann (Alexius) and Flavia Arcaro (Aurelia) featured, *The Chocolate Soldier* proved a splendid success through 296 performances at Broadway's Lyric Theatre, and Nadina's waltz song, anglicized as ''My Hero,'' was launched as an all-time soprano bonbon.

As *The Chocolate Soldier* set off round America to reap its rewards in the first of many, many tours, Whitney went into partnership with London's Philip Michael Faraday to mount a production of his hit in the West End. Britain brought forth an even more enthusiastic reaction to the show. Ex-Savoyards C H Workman and Constance Drever (France's veuve joyeuse) played Bumerli and Nadina with Roland Cunningham as Alexius and veteran Amy Augarde as Madame Popoff and *The Chocolate Soldier* played no fewer than five hundred performances at London's Lyric Theatre before going on the road and out to the other English-speaking parts of the Empire. It was quickly back, playing a further London season in 1914, and was seen again in the West End in 1932 and 1940. New York, however, solidly topped that record by welcoming the show back to Broadway in 1910, 1921, 1930, 1931, 1934, 1942 and 1947 (ad Guy Bolton, Bernard Hanighen). None of these reasonably faithful revivals, however, had the inflated kudos of a Los Angeles Light Opera production, which boasted—as well as John Charles Thomas as its hero—''four new Oscar Straus songs'' in its score.

Australia kept up the impressive record of Stange's version of the piece when Clarke and Meynell's production of *The Chocolate Soldier* was mounted in Melbourne. Winifred O'Connor sang ''My Hero'' for 52 nights before its producers merged their company with the great white shark of Australian entertainment, J C Williamson Ltd. Thus *The Chocolate Soldier* played its Sydney season the following year under the new banner, with Florence Young and J Talleur Andrews—who were also paired as Karel and Gonda in *Die keusche Susanne* and René and Angèle in *Der Graf von Luxemburg*—in the leading roles. The show did well enough, playing in repertoire alongside these two fine favorites, and *The Chocolate Soldier* established itself in Australia in the same way it had done on the other side of the world, being revived as late as 1954 with Nancie Grant and Desmond Paterson featured.

Similarly spurred on by the Broadway and then the London successes of *The Chocolate Soldier,* Charles Montcharmont followed up with productions of *Le Soldat de chocolat* (ad Pierre Veber) at Brussels (8 September 1911) and at his Théâtre des Célestins in Lyon. Raoul Villot, Angèle van Loo and Fabert introduced the French version, before Alphonse Franck at the Théâtre Apollo—the home of *La Veuve joyeuse* and *Le Comte de Luxembourg*—took the show up for Paris. His Danilo, Henri Defreyn, was cast in the role of Bumerli alongside Brigitte Régent and Villot repeated his Popoff through a run of two and a half months. This was neither a record to challenge Franck's other Viennese imports nor the kind of success the piece had had in its English version, but *Le Soldat de chocolat* nevertheless got a Parisian rehearing more than 20 years later when it was played in the repertoire of the Trianon-Lyrique (1 March 1935).

Behind the success of *The Chocolate Soldier* there was a bitter little twist. A tale of a gesture which rebounded on the author of *Arms and the Man,* who had had to suffer the indignity of seeing the unconsidered Stange's re-Englished version of his work far outrun not only the original play but any and all of his plays to date. Shaw, who had sneered consistently at the musical theatre through his life and his career as a critic, had always insisted that it was not possible to musicalize his works. When permission was sought for the making of an Austrian musical of *Arms and the Man* he consented, but refused to take any royalties and postulated that a disclaimer be printed apologizing for the liberty taken in ''burlesquing'' his play. His principles were clearly hurt when he saw the money made by *The Chocolate Soldier* and he discarded them in typical fashion when permission was sought to make the show into a film. This time he demanded big money. But he didn't get it. All MGM needed was the title and ''My Hero,'' neither of which belonged to Shaw, so they took these and pasted them into a version of Ferenc Molnár's *A testőr* instead. Nelson

Eddy and Risë Stevens starred in a 1941 film that had virtually nothing of *Der tapfere Soldat* or *The Chocolate Soldier* about it. But no one knew that till they got into the cinema. In 1955 Stevens starred in an NBC-TV production which stuck closer to the real thing.

There had, actually, been a previous *Chocolate Soldier* film, one which followed closer on the original production of the musical but which also lacked part of the theatrical show. This time it was not the story but the music. Whitney—who lacked no enterprise in cashing in on his hit—and the Daisy Film Company turned out a silent film called *The Chocolate Soldier,* featuring Tom Richards (Bumerli), William H White (Popoff), the producer's sister-in-law Alice Yorke (Nadina) and former comic-opera soprano Lucille Saunders (Aurelia). Apparently Shaw didn't know about that one.

Germany: Theater des Westens 23 December 1908; USA: Lyric Theater *The Chocolate Soldier* 13 September 1909; UK: Lyric Theatre 10 September 1910; France: Théâtre des Célestins, Lyon *Le Soldat de chocolat* 1911, Théâtre de l'Apollo, Paris 7 November 1912; Australia: Theatre Royal, Melbourne *The Chocolate Soldier* 26 August 1911; Hungary: Vígszínház (Ger) 24 May 1912, Népopera *A csokoládé-katona* 7 October 1916

Films: Daisy Film Co (silent) 1914, TV film (NBC) 1955

Recordings: complete in English (RCA), selections in English (RCA, Columbia, World Records)

THE TAR AND THE TARTAR Comic opera in 2 acts by Harry B Smith. Music by Adam Itzel jr. Chicago Opera House, 15 April 1891; Palmer's Theater, New York, 11 May 1891.

The Tar and the Tartar was the first production by the once proud McCaull Opera Company following McCaull and Madame Cottrelly's sell-out of their business to Harry Askin. It was a rather lesser quality piece than those that McCaull had purveyed in his heyday, but—no little thanks to being built neatly around large roles for McCaull's longtime stars, Mrs and Mrs Digby Bell—that did not stop it becoming decidedly more popular than some of its more upmarket predecessors.

The Harry B Smith book was a tacked-together compound of the tales of several older French pieces, notably *Le Rajah de Mysore,* and following into town not too far behind Philadelphia's *Ship Ahoy* it gave New York its second concurrent musical of the season to start, *Ba-ta-clan*-ishly, with a shipwreck on a strange-folked island.

Shipwrecked Muley Hassan (Digby Bell) floats ashore on an island off the coast of Morocco. In line with local custom, the tar is made sultan (the local one having apparently committed suicide) and takes over his palace and his harem of 400 wives with 1,313 children. There he meets the tartar, chief wife Alpaca (Laura Joyce Bell), a lady who is none other than his own wife, on account of whom he fled to become a sailor. There is a nephew of the old sultan (Hubert Wilke) who longs for the throne so that he may wed his sweetheart (Helen Bertram) who is only interested in a man with a title, there is a soubrette with similar ambitions who gives her hand to whichever royal physician is currently in power, and there is a physician who is on hand to provide the Tar sultan with the magic potion that will make him immortal (that was the *Rajah de Mysore* bit). Anyway, in a rather feeble ending the original sultan comes back, and Muley goes off to be admiral of the fleet. But the ending wasn't really the point. This was a summer musical, a laugh-a-lot-and-simple-tunes sort of show. And Mr and Mrs Bell were a class act.

The striving young Baltimore composer Adam Itzel jr provided the music for the show. It was supposed to be all brand spanking new, but his partner on his first ever piece, *Jack Sheppard* (Baltimore Academy of Music 28 November 1885), surfaced at an embarrassing moment, and complained loudly that Itzel had reused the tunes from their show for the score of *The Tar and the Tartar.*

The Tar and the Tartar had an encouraging (if unprofitable) run-in in Chicago, then moved swiftly to New York for its summer-season run. It went well, in spite of the over-enthusiastic young conductor getting carried away on opening night and leading his band with ''more vigor than discretion,'' and settled in for a standard summer run of 122 hot New York nights with sufficient success to provoke J H Smith's ''Henry Burlesque Company'' to a burlesque *The Ta and the Ta Ta* (mus: Max Sturm), and Askin to an attack of ''nervous prostration,'' which necessitated his disappearance to the Adirondacks, before setting out on the road. And on the road it proved itself to be just a touch more than a typical summer musical. It kept on touring, and when it was done touring it got picked up by the repertoire troupes and summer-season companies who usually liked to play more substantial stuff. Itzel, up to this time with a lot of publicity but few credits on his belt, looked set for a good career. But it didn't happen. He died just two years later, aged 24, of consumption. Harry Smith, of course, wrote hundreds more musicals.

TARIOL-BAUGÉ, Anna [née TARRIOL, Anne Rose] (b Veyre-Mouton, Puy de Dôme, 28 August 1871; d Asnières, 1 December 1944). Favorite prima donna of the Paris stage.

Anna Tariol-Baugé made her stage debut at Bordeaux playing opéra-comique, and she worked in the provinces and in Russia before making her first appearances in Paris. There she became one of the most popular opérette stars in the last years of the old century and the first decades of the new, appearing in many of the great roles of the classic repertoire (Boccaccio, Fiorella, Gab-

Plate 383. **Anna Tariol-Baugé**

rielle, Boulotte, Dindonette, Serpolette, the Josephine who was ''vendue par ses soeurs,'' etc) and, in a career of over 30 years, creating a long list of new parts, of which the most important were the flighty Agathe in *Véronique,* the tempestuous Spaniard, Manuela, in *Miss Helyett* and Gabrielle, the wife of Claude Terrasse's *Le Sire de Vergy.* Amongst the other new pieces in which she introduced roles were *La Dame de trèfle* (1898, Loia), *Shakespeare!* (1899, Consuélo), *La Demoiselle aux camellias* (1899, Lison), Lecocq's *La Belle au bois dormant* (1900, Aurore), *L'Âge d'or* (1905, Reine Margot) and *Les Rendez-vous Strasbourgeois* (1908, Berthe). She also played on a number of occasions at the Parisiana (*Les Poupées americaines, Cabriole,* etc), at the Folies-Bergère and at the Moulin-Rouge in both opérette and in revue, sharing bills with Liane de Pougy and other luminaries of the variety stage, and visited Brussels to play in revue (1902, *Paris-Ostend*).

In 1908 she appeared in London in the title roles of *La Fille de Madame Angot* and *La Fille du tambour-major,* but soon after this she began to orientate her career towards the straight theatre. She returned to the musical stage in the 1920s to repeat her Agathe and then to appear in character roles in several other musical shows (*Le Mariage de Pyramidon, La Reine joyeuse,* as the Directrice in *Le Petit Duc*), including a group (*Le Diable à Paris, Venise, Vouvray*) alongside her son, André Baugé, himself one of the most prominent opéra-comique and opérette leading men of the period.

TATÁRJÁRÁS Operett in 3 acts by Károly Bakonyi. Lyrics by Andor Gábor. Music by Emmerich Kálmán. Vígszínház, Budapest, 22 February 1908.

The military operett *Tatárjárás* revealed to the world in general for the first time the talents of the 25-year-old Imre (soon to be Emmerich) Kálmán, strikingly displayed in a refreshingly tuneful scoreful of Hungarian-flavored waltzes and marches which illustrated what was to be the internationally most successful Hungarian musical play up to its time.

The regiment of Fieldmarshal Lohanyay (Ferenc Vendrey) is on maneuvers near the castle of the widowed Baroness Riza (Juliska Keleti) who duly entertains the officers at her home. Lieutenant Lőrenthy (Gyula Hegedűs) does not join them, for not only was the castle where the baroness is installed once the home of his family, but in earlier and blither days he had himself been in love with Riza. By the end of the play's three acts, enlivened by the Jewish fooleries of the reservist Wallerstein (Aladár Sarkadi) and the chase of the little volunteer Mogyoróssy (Berta Kornai) after the Fieldmarshal's daughter, Treszka (Ilonka Komlóssy), a lass who had been intended by her father as a bride for Lőrenthy, the operettically expected happy ending has been tied up all round.

The romantic leads were supplied, as was only normal, with waltz music, and it was waltz music of a specially flavored strain. The principal waltz theme of the piece, originally introduced by Lőrenthy (''War einst verblendet'') and then duetted by tenor and soprano, and by soprano and ingenue, and finally given as a serenade by the chorus in the last act, needed no such plugging to remain irresistibly in the mind. It was a winner. Riza had a second superb waltz, ''Mir is so bang,'' and a third, ''Tanzen sich wiegen,'' with which to score in a role that was a prima donna's delight. But, in spite of this, *Tatárjárás* was not Riza's show, any more than it was Lőrenthy's show. It was the travesty soubrette role of the lovelorn little volunteer and that of the foolish, comical Wallerstein which proved the plum parts of the evening. Mogyoróssy made his entrance with the bright little ''Ich bin ein kernig fester Soldat,'' marched with the chorus to ''Ziehen die Husaren ein,'' won a triumph with his Küsslied (''Die kleine Gretl'') and danced a lightly comical love duo with his Treszka. There were two comical numbers for the foolish Wallerstein as well, but his moments came in his comedy rather than in his songs.

The original production of *Tatárjárás* at Budapest's Vígszínház was a fine success, running up one hundred performances in the house's repertoire by 1 October 1909 and being revived there on 11 January 1913. The piece went on to be played throughout the country, the Népopera mounted a new production in August 1916 and in 1923 the Vígszínház production was played at the newly opened Fővárosi Operettszínház (14 January). In the meantime, however, *Tatárjárás* had already made the tour of the world, beginning with a phenomenally successful production under the management of Wilhelm Karczag and Karl Wallner at Vienna's Theater an der Wien where Robert Bodanzky's German-language version, *Ein Herbstmanöver,* replaced the disappointing *Der tapfere Soldat* on the theatre's schedule. Grete Holm—who had just introduced ''Held meiner Träume'' and now got Riza's role full of waltzes—and Otto Storm took the romantic roles, Max Pallenberg put aside the Bulgarian Colonel Popoff to take up the Jewish comedy of Wallerstein and Luise Kartousch got one of the most outstanding roles of her outstanding career as the little Mogyoróssy (now called Marosi).

Ein Herbstmanöver was an immediate and enormous success—the biggest the theatre had had since *Die lustige Witwe* three years earlier—and the show ran on at the Theater an der Wien, with guest performances at the Raimundtheater, through to the close of the season in late June (150 performances). It reopened the new season and continued to its 226th performance before giving way to *Der Graf von Luxemburg* in November. It was seen again at both theatres the following year, passing its 300th performance on 8 November 1910 with Holm still in her original role alongside Alexander Haber (Lorenty), Mizzi Parla (Marosi) and Kurt Mikulski (Wallerstein), and being reprised in the repertoire at one or both theatres in 1914, 1916, 1920, in 1924 with Richard Tauber, Holm and Storm, and again in 1934.

Two months after the Vienna premiere, Bodanzky's version was produced by Bendiner in Hamburg, and the following month the Hamburg company brought their production to Berlin as the first foreign-language versions began to appear in such cities as Moscow (30 April 1909), Stockholm (6 September 1909), Copenhagen (17 February 1910), Trieste (1 March 1910) and at Rome's Teatro Apollo (25 September 1910) as the piece spread through Europe with huge success. The English-language versions, however, did not come up to the mark. After the Shuberts had prematurely announced a production under the title *The Dancing Dragoons,* Henry Savage, the American producer of *The Merry Widow,* took what he called *The Gay Hussars* (ad Maurice Brown Kirby, Grant Stewart) to Broadway with a cast including Muriel Terry (Marosi), Edwin Wilson (Lorenty), Anna Bussert (Risa), Bobby North (Wallerstein) and Florence Reid (Treszka). One critic praised ''saner, livelier music and more jollity with a basis of reason than any number of our native

Plate 384. **Tatárjárás.** *Luise Kartousch made a huge hit as the little cadet Marosi in Vienna's production of* Ein Herbstmanöver, *alongside Grete Holm as the leading lady of the piece.*

hodge-podges,'' but worried that ''the element of humorous satire on army conditions in Hungary could hardly be conveyed.'' Another thrilled, ''To say the least, *The Gay Hussars* belongs to *The Merry Widow* class.'' It was, apparently, more the underpar casting and flung-together staging of the piece, hurried on to beat out the Shuberts, which led to its leaving town after just 44 performances.

George Edwardes's London production of *Autumn Manoeuvres* (ad Henry Hamilton, Percy Greenbank) was anglicized into a setting at ''Ambermere Park'' with Huntley Wright playing comical Captain Withers of the Broadshire Territorials, Gracie Leigh replying to him as Lady Larkins, and Robert Evett (Captain Frank Falconer) and Phyllys LeGrand (Alix Luttrell) singing the romantic bits of a cooperative score which included only two and a half Kálmán numbers. Herbert Bunning (three pieces), Howard Talbot (four and the other half), Carl Kiefert, Hamish MacCunn and Lionel Monckton (one apiece) contributed music to a show which was scarcely *Tatárjárás* and would probably have run much more than its 75 performances if it had been.

Manoeuvres d'automne became the first Hungarian operett to be produced in France when Pierre Veber's version, an odd hybrid which had half British characters and half Hungarian ones, not to mention an Irish servant called Pat, was staged by Montcharmont at Lyon in 1914. Maguy Warna and Claude Arnés shared the role of Risa alongside Edmond Tirmont (Lorenty), Marthe Lenclude (Marosi) and Urban as Waltebled (ex- Wallerstein), but the career of the show was hobbled by the outbreak of war: Paris of 1914–15 was not about to welcome a joyous musical about the enemy's military.

Tatárjárás is still played intermittently in Hungary, but rather less than the same composer's big-name and more romantically inclined Operetten.

Austria: Theater an der Wien *Ein Herbstmanöver* 22 January 1909; Germany: Neues Operetten-Theater, Hamburg *Ein Herbstmanöver* 20 March 1909, Berliner Theater, Berlin 24 April 1909; USA: Knickerbocker Theater *The Gay Hussars* 29 July 1909; UK: Adelphi Theatre *Autumn Manoeuvres* 25 May 1912; Australia: Her Majesty's Theatre, Sydney *Autumn Manoeuvres* 26 June 1913; France: Théâtre des Célestins, Lyon *Manoeuvres d'automne* 24 March 1914

TATE, James W[illiam] (b Wolverhampton, 30 July 1875; d Stoke-on-Trent, 5 February 1922). Songwriter and conductor for revue and musical theatre of the early 20th century.

The elder brother of Margaret Tate, who was to become internationally known as the opera and operetta singer Maggie Teyte, Jimmy Tate was also the second husband of Lottie Collins, the famous singer of ''Ta-ra-ra-boom-di-ay,'' and thus stepfather to her three eldest daughters. The first, José Collins, was to have a career to more than rival her mother's.

Tate began his career as a musician (after a youthful start in the brewing trade) with ambitions in the operatic field but he soon turned himself rather towards popular songwriting and to intermittent work in the musical theatre. In 1898 he went on tour as conductor with Miss Collins in the musical comedy *The White Blackbird,* and he later went into management to stage the musical *The Dressmaker* in which his wife appeared briefly at the Islington Grand in 1902. In 1903 he toured with the musical *All at Sea,* but his principal activity over the two following decades was as a popular songwriter (''Don't Forget Tonight,'' ''When I Marry a Millionaire,'' etc) and a compiler of scenas for variety houses (w John P Harrington). He had numbers interpolated in shows from *Sergeant Brue* (1904, ''Instinct,'' ''And So Did Eve'') to *High Jinks* (1916), scored song hits with ''If I Should Plant a Tiny Seed of Love'' (1909, ly: Ballard MacDonald) and the enduring ''I Was a Good Little Girl Till I Met You'' (1914, w Clifford Harris), and found his theatrical metier with the arrival of the fashion for the variety revue just before the First World War.

Tate put together the scores for the Palladium revue *I Should Worry* (1913) and the Victoria Palace's *A Year in an Hour* (1914), shared the musical credit for the more successful *Samples* (1916) with Herman Darewski and Irving Berlin and came out of this last show with the evening's hit song, ''Broken Doll.'' The Vaudeville Theatre revue *Some* produced another successful song, ''Ev'ry Little While,'' but a revue built around his variety-theatre act with his second wife, **Clarice MAYNE** [Clarice Mabel DULLEY, 1886–1966], *This and That* (1916) (''That'' was Tate, off-handedly referred to at his seat at the piano by his comedienne spouse), lasted only 48 performances.

His biggest success came about almost by accident. During the pre-London run of *The Maid of the Mountains* at Manchester he happened to be on hand when Robert Evett decided that Harold Fraser Simson's score needed some strengthening. Thus, Tate was called in to provide, firstly, the waltz song ''My Life Is Love'' for his now ex-stepdaughter José and the duet ''A Paradise for Two'' for Miss Collins and Thorpe Bates. After the notable success of these two pieces a third song, for Bates—''A Bachelor Gay Am I''—followed them into the show's score. These comic-operatic numbers, far distant in style from ''Broken Doll'' and ''I Was a Good Little Girl,'' proved to be Tate's biggest successes, and ''A Bachelor Gay Am I'' became one of the most popular baritone songs in the British concert repertoire.

He subsequently wrote the score for the revusical wartime piece *Lads of the Village* and another revue-musical, *The Beauty Spot,* created for Régine Flory and produced by Parisian revue specialist P-L Flers at the Gaiety Theatre, without any of his material winning equivalent notice. He continued, however, to turn out popular songs (''Somewhere in France with You'' w Arthur Anderson and Valentine, ''Give Me a Cosy Little Corner'' w Clifford Harris, etc) and provided the scores for his most successful revues, *Peep Show* and *Round in 50* (w Herman Finck) at the London Hippodrome, in the postwar years, but the musical which it was persistently paragraphed that he would write for his famous sister never eventuated. He did not venture again into the field of the book musical where his memorable contribution to *The Maid of the Mountains* remains his only real reference.

1904 **The Belle of the Orient** (w Paul Knox/Clifford Harris, George Arthurs, J B Peterman) 3 scenes Islington Empire 18 July

1906 **Skyland** (w J P Harrington) 1 act Palace Theatre 18 June

1907 **Two's Company, Three's None** (Harrington) scena Palace, Camberwell March

1909 **The Roll Call** (George Arthurs) monologue Oxford Music Hall 25 October

1915 **Very Mixed Bathing** (Clifford Harris, Lawrence Wright/P T Selbit) 3 scenes Palace Theatre, Bath 26 April

1915 **Kiss Me, Sergeant** (Harris/Lauri Wylie, Alfred Parker) 1 act Leicester Palace 2 August

1917 **Lads of the Village** (Harris, Valentine) 1 act Oxford Theatre 11 June

1917 **The Beauty Spot** (Harris, Valentine/Arthur Anderson, P-L Flers) Gaiety Theatre 22 December

1921 **Swindell's Stores** (Valentine) 1 act Finsbury Park Empire

TAUBER, Richard [SEIFFERT, Ernst] (b Linz, 16 May 1891; d London, 8 January 1948). Much-loved tenor singer whose voice was the inspiration for some of the main romantic roles of postwar Viennese Operette.

The son of the manager of the Stadttheater, Chemnitz, tenor Richard Tauber was orientated at first towards an operatic career, but although he found considerable success at the lighter end of the operatic repertoire, it was as the hero of a line of romantic Operetten that he was to win his greatest fame.

He made early appearances in Operette when he appeared at Berlin's Komische Oper in the German version of Ubaldo Pachetti's pre–*Student Prince* musicalization of *Alt-Heidelberg* and at the Theater an der Wien opposite Betty Fischer as Barinkay in *Der Zigeunerbaron* (1921) and, in succession to Hubert Marischka and Harry Bauer, in the tenor role of *Frasquita* (1922). He subsequently took over Marischka's roles in both *Der Bacchusnacht* and *Der letzte Walzer,* teamed with Marischka and Fischer in a version of *Eine Nacht in Venedig* (1923), and appeared opposite Fritzi Massary as Victorian Silvius in *Die Perlen der Cleopatra* and alongside Grete Holm in a revival of *Ein Herbstmanöver* (1924).

After this run of Viennese engagements, Tauber based himself in Berlin where he played in Benatzky's *Ein Märchen aus Florenz* and in another revival of *Eine Nacht in Venedig* before taking up the role of the romantic violinist *Paganini,* originally played in Vienna by Carl Clewing, for the German production of Lehár's Operette. He continued a fruitful collaboration and friendship with the show's admiring composer thereafter, creating his first Lehár hero in the title role of *Der Zarewitsch* (1927), and drawing both an adoring public and the kind of notices which would beset his career (''Richard Tauber is one of the best tenors Germany possesses today, and perhaps the best voice found in operetta anywhere. Unfortunately he looks like a butcher''). He introduced the role of Goethe in the romanticized tale of the poet's love for *Friederike* (1928) equipped with Lehár's first Tauber bonbon, the lilting ''O Mädchen, mein Mädchen,'' and made perhaps his finest success to date with a third Lehár hero, the rewritten version of the Chinese Prince Sou-Chong originally played by Marischka in *Die gelbe Jacke,* in the show's remake as *Das Land des Lächelns* (1929). He drew delighted applause for his performance of Lehár's tenorious ''Dein ist mein ganzes Herz'' and rather less for his ''ponderous attempts at matinée idol mannerisms.'' Another rewritten piece of Lehár cast him somewhat improbably opposite the beautiful Gitta Alpár as the dashing mountain-climbing princeling of *Schön ist die Welt* (1931). As ever, he deliverered the show's (re)made-to-measure music superbly but proved dramatically unconvincing with his ''heavy trunk on limbs twisted with gout.''

Tauber played his Sou Chong at the Theater an der Wien on the occasion of Lehár's 60th birthday celebrations, but he had an unaccustomed flop when he appeared again at the Berlin Metropoltheater in *Das Lied der Liebe* (1931), a pasticcio piece with a Korngoldized Strauss score which was quickly done away with. He had further disappointments with two attempts to establish *The Land of Smiles* in London, where he also played Schubert in a version of *Das Dreimäderlhaus* (in German) at the Aldwych Theatre (1933), before he returned to Vienna and the stage of the Staatsoper to create perhaps the most demanding of Lehár's custom-made series of overwhelming tenor roles in the short-lived first run of *Giuditta* (1934). Later the same year he appeared in some of the 89 performances of his own Operette, *Der singende Traum,* at the Theater an der Wien.

Soon after this, Tauber joined the exodus from Germany and Austria, settled in Britain and in 1940 he became a British subject. In this period he interleaved concert work with occasional ventures into both opera (Tamino, Belmonte, Don Ottavio, etc) and the musical theatre, where his appearances included English versions of *Paganini* and *Das Land des Lächelns,* an unsuccessful *Dreimäderlhaus* remake called *Blossom Time* (Schubert) and a determinedly romantic period piece called *Old Chelsea,* for which he again composed much of the score. Although in his fifties and seemingly squatter than ever, he cast himself in the juvenile romantic lead through 95 London performances. If the show was not quite a success, it did, however, produce one of his best-known songs as a composer, the soaring ballad ''My Heart and I.'' In 1946 he was seen briefly on Broadway in another version of *Das Land des Lächelns,* and he made his last stage appearance the following year.

Tauber also appeared in a number of musical films including *Blossom Time* (1934), *Heart's Desire* (1935), *Land without Music* (1936) and *I Pagliacci* (1936) and performed solo spots in the screen versions of the British musicals *Waltz Time* (1946) and *The Lisbon Story* (1946, ''Pedro, the Fisherman'').

Tauber's memorable singing career was, of course, the main part of his professional life, but his broad musical education led him both into composing and also an intermittent career as a conductor. He led several performances at the Bürgertheater in 1924, conducted matinée performances of *Marietta* at the Theater an der Wien at the same time that he was appearing there in his *Der singende Traum,* and later conducted performances of both *Gay Rosalinda* and *The Bird Seller* in London.

Tauber had an important influence on the course of the German-language musical theatre in the late 1920s and early 1930s, the kind of influence rarely wielded to such an extent by a performer. His voice and his popularity encouraged Franz Lehár to develop the whole line of lush, romantic Operetten with large leading tenor roles in which Tauber starred with such considerable success in Berlin and/or Vienna and which became the enduring classics of their time. But if the star served his composer well, that service was mutual, for nowhere else did Tauber find such music and such shows. His non-Lehár vehicles were, by and large, poor stuff and quickly gone, and outside the German and Austrian theatre, although his concert work was highly appreciated, he did not find the same success as an operettic hero.

Tauber was portrayed on the screen by Rudolf Schock in the film *Du bist die Welt für mich.*

1934 **Der singende Traum** (Ernst Marischka, Hermann Feiner) Theater an der Wien 31 August

1942 **Old Chelsea** (w Bernard Grün/Fred Salo Tysh, Walter Ellis/Ellis) Birmingham 21 September; Prince's Theatre, London 17 February 1943

Biographies: Ludwig, H (ed): *Richard Tauber* (Otto Elsner Verlagsgesellschaft MBH, Berlin, 1928), Napier, D: *Richard Tauber* (Arts & Educational Publishers, London, 1949), Korb, W: *Richard Tauber* (Vienna, 1966), Castle, C: *This Was Richard Tauber* (W H Allen, London, 1971), Schneidereit, O: *Richard Tauber: Eine Leben—eine Stimme* (VEB Lied der Zeit. Musikverlag, Berlin, 1976), Pot, C: *Richard Tauber: Zanger Zonder Grenzen* (Deboektant, Den Haag, 1988), Jürgs, M: *Gern hab' ich die Frau 'n geküsst: Die Richard-Tauber-Biografie* (List Verlag, 2000), etc

TAUND, Eugen von (b Hausmannstetten, Steiermark, 17 July 1856).

Eugen von Taund, whose principal occupation seems to have been in the retail trade, did not appear on the Operettic scene until he was in his mid-thirties, when he had two Operetten mounted in Graz, but he flourished as a musician in his forties, in the later 1890s, when he had three further Operetten produced with some success in Vienna's principal theatres.

Die Lachtaube, played for 51 performances at the Carltheater with Julie Kopácsi-Karczag and manager Karl Blasel topping the bill, was also produced at Berlin's Theater Unter den Linden (20 August 1895) and, with Kopácsi-Karczag in her original role, at New York's Irving Place Theater (4 November 1898), whilst *Der Wunderknabe,* mounted at the Theater an der Wien with Annie Dirkens and Girardi for 36 performances, also progressed to the Theater Unter den Linden (5 May 1897) and to London's West End, where it was played under the title *The Little Genius. Der Dreibund,* with Ilka Pálmay starred, was the least successful of the three, being played 23 times at the Theater an der Wien, and marking von Taund's last appearance on a Viennese playbill.

1890 **Der Gouverneur** Stadtparktheater, Graz 18 October

1891 **Die Murnixen** Stadtparktheater, Graz 18 February

1895 **Die Lachtaube** (''Otto Rehberg,'' ie, Alexander Landesberg, Leo Stein) Carltheater 14 April

1896 **Der Wunderknabe** (Landesberg, Stein) Theater an der Wien 28 March

1898 **Der Dreibund** (Landesberg, Stein) Theater an der Wien 28 April

TAUSEND UND EINE NACHT Fantastic Operette in a Vorspiel and two acts by Leo Stein and Carl Lindau. Music by Johann Strauss arranged by Ernst Reiterer. Venedig in Wien, Vienna, 15 June 1906.

One of the series of remakes and pasticcio Operetten mounted by Gabor Steiner at his summer theatre, Venedig in Wien, in Vienna's Prater, *Tausend und eine Nacht* was the house's third raking-over of the Strauss family oeuvre following *Gräfin Pepi* (a musical mix of *Simplicius* and *Blindekuh*) and the highly successful *Frühlingsluft* (music from Josef Strauss). Unlike the latter, *Tausend und eine Nacht* did not take an established and successful play as its backbone, but instead simply tacked much of Strauss's *Indigo und die vierzig Räuber* score on to a suitably Arabian Nights-like dream-tale of romance and mistaken identity. Willy Bauer played Prince Suleiman who, in the dream-within-an-Operette, swaps places for a day with a fisherman so that he can romance the fisherman's wife, Leila (Phila Wolff). Fella Schreiter was Viennese Wally, the flirtatious representative of things Western, equipped with the evening's most successful musical piece, the waltz ''Ja, so singt man,'' and paired with Adolf Rauch as the Prince's secretary.

The show did well enough in its summer season to be taken up the following year by the Volksoper (27 October) and then by the Johann Strauss-Theater (1908 with Karl Grünwald and Therese Krammer) and to be played in both Germany and Hungary. It has been revived at the Volksoper on several occasions, and its potential for spectacular staging has made it a favorite at the Bregenz Seebühne where it has been mounted as part of several seasons.

An English version was played at London's Rudolf Steiner Hall in 1936 (29 January) by the amateur Alan Turner Opera Company.

The title has been used many times, notably for the Parisian spectacular *Les Mille et une nuits* first produced in Paris in 1881 (Théâtre du Châtelet 14 December).

Germany: Centraltheater 15 September 1906; Hungary: Népszínház-Vígopera *1001 éj* 8 May 1908

Plate 385. *Light comedian* **Ernst Tautenhayn** *donned skirts for his imitation of a harem-girl in* Die Rose von Stambul.

Recording: two-record set (Urania)

TAUTENHAYN, Ernst (b Vienna, 3 April 1873; d Zlabing, 30 August 1944).

One of the most outstanding light comedians of the Viennese musical stage of the 1910s and 1920s, Tautenhayn created a long run of roles, mostly at the Theater an der Wien, and often in a hugely popular partnership with soubrette Luise Kartousch.

He began his metropolitan career at the Carltheater in the mid-1890s, creating small-to-supporting roles in such pieces as *Das Modell* (Emmanuel Foresti, an officer), *Bum-Bum* (Edgar) and *Der Cognac-König* (Lt Dorn), and playing the light-to-comic tenor Landry in *König Chilperich,* Prinz Saphir in *Blaubart,* Pedro in *Die Schwätzerin von Saragossa* (*Les Bavards*) and Ein Schildwache (the sentry) in *Herr Gouverneur* (W S Gilbert's *His Excellency*) before moving on to take larger roles in provincial theatres.

In 1910 he returned to the big time when he joined the company at the Theater an der Wien and appeared there first of all in *Schneeglöckchen* (Polycarp Wasiliewitsch) before making a personal hit in the role of Thomasius II, the comical King of Aquitania, in *Die schöne Risette.* Over the following years he appeared in leading roles in a number of classic pieces at that house and its companion Raimundtheater (Blasius in *Die Schützenliesel,* Spätzle in *Die sieben Schwaben,* Matthaeus in *Der fidele Bauer,* Orpheus *in Orpheus in der Unterwelt,* Paul Aubier in *Der Opernball,* Fleck in *Flotte Bursche,* etc) and at the same time created a decade-long series of new roles and works: *Ihr Adjutant* (Trendelberg), Dagobert to the Pipsi of Kartousch in *Eva,* Jonny Burns in *Die keusche Barbara* (1911), *Der blaue Held* (Enzerich), *Der kleine König* (1912, Huck), *Prinzess Gretl* (Felix Hirschfeld), *Die ideale Gattin* (1913, Don Gil Tenorio de Sevilla), *Endlich allein* (Graf Willibald Splenningen), *Gold gab' ich für Eisen* (1914, Rabenlechner), *Die schöne Schwedin* (Sven Liverstol), *Auf Befehl der Herzogin* (Toni), *Wenn zwei sich lieben* (1915, Baron Géza von Steinbach), *Der Sterngucker* (Franz Höfer), *Die Winzerbraut* (Franjo Svecak), the memorable Fridolin to the Midlili of Kartousch in the very long run of *Die Rose von Stambul* (1916), the Austrian *Wo die Lerche singt* (1918, Török Pál), *Nimm mich mit!* (1919, Franz Xaver Edelbrunner), *Die blaue Mazur* (Adolar), *Dorfmusikanten* (1920, Peterl) and *Die Frau im Hermelin* (1921, Suitangi).

He then left the Theater an der Wien and later in 1921 he created the plum role of the comical Marquis Napoléon St Cloche in *Die Bajadere* at the Carltheater. He played there again in *Die Brasilianerin* (Tobias Taube), as Calicot to the *Madame Pompadour* of Fritzi Massary, as Matthaeus in *Der fidele Bauer* and in *Glück bei Frauen* (1923, Jakob Vollaczek), before going on to play at the Wiener Stadttheater in the Anton Profès Operette *Glück muss man haben* (1923, Bacherer). He created the parts of Severin to the Cloclo of Kartousch in *Cloclo* (1924) and Tomasoni in *Revanche* (1924) at the Bürgertheater, was Abilio in *Donna Gloria* (1925) at the Carltheater, and played star comedy roles in *Ich hab' dich Lieb* (1926, Emil Schick), *Das Schwalbennest* (1926, Ferdinand Brandl), *Riquette* (1927) and *Musik in Mai* (1927) at the Raimundtheater and alongside Kartousch in *Eine einzige Nacht* (Wolfgang Schöbel) at the Carltheater. He paired with Kartousch again in *Die Lady vom Lido* (1927, Pfefferminz) at the Johann Strauss-Theater where he went on to repeat his St Cloche and to star in a revival of *Der lustige Krieg* and also took part in the premieres of *Das Veilchen vom Montmartre* (1930)—in the role of the composer Hervé—*Der verliebte Eskadron* (1930, Dr Siegfried Apfelbaum), the Viennese version of *Sisters* (1930, Thomas Pirk) and the pasticcio *Der König ihres Herzens* (1930, Don Rodrigo del Carmona). He later succeeded to the role of Herzog Max in *Sissy* at the Theater an der Wien and in 1933 returned to the Johann Strauss-Theater to play President Philippe Peron in the musical comedy *Dame Nr 1 rechts.*

In 1937 Tautenhayn ill-chose his moment to try to turn manager and opened a ''Deutsche Bühne'' at the Raimundtheater. The project was a disastrous failure, and the adored comic of two generations of musical-theatregoers eventually committed suicide at the age of 71.

TAUTIN, Lise [VAISSIÈRE, Louise Émilie Victorine] (b Yvetot, 31 January 1834; d Bologna, May 1874). Leading lady of Offenbach's earliest large-scale operas-bouffes.

Born into a theatrical family—great-niece of a stage director of the Palais-Royal and daughter of artist and actor **Jacques Adolphe VAISSIÈRE** *dit* **TAUTIN** (b Paris, 24 September 1804)—Lise Tautin made her first stage appearances at the Galeries Saint-Hubert in Brussels in 1850. She went from there to the Brussels Théâtre du Vaudeville, played for three seasons at the Grand Théâtre de Lyon (1854–57) and made her debut in Paris at the Théâtre des Bouffes-Parisiens as Aspasie in Offenbach's *Une demoiselle en loterie* (1857). She spent virtually all of the remainder of her short career and life playing under the composer's aegis. She created the roles of Catherine in the original production of *Le Mariage aux lanternes* (1857), Minette in *La Chatte métamorphosée en femme* (1858), Croûte-au-pot in *Mesdames de la Halle* (1858), Rosita in *Un mari à la porte* (1859) and Les Bouffes-Parisiens in *Le Carnaval des revues* (1860), and she found substantial fame as the original Eurydice of *Orphée aux enfers* (1858).

Mlle Tautin created three other major Offenbach roles after her Eurydice: the outstanding travesty role of Drogan in the original two-act version of *Geneviève de Brabant,* the dramatically beset Catarina Cornaro of *Le Pont des soupirs* (1861) and the vocally florid Ernestine, who pretends to be Henriette Sontag, in the one-act *Monsieur Choufleuri restera chez lui le . . .* (1861).

She visited Vienna and Budapest with the Bouffes-Parisiens troupe in the summer of 1861, appearing in *Le Pont des Soupirs, Un mari à la porte, Orphée aux enfers* and the rest of the theatre's repertoire, then moved on to join the company at the Variétés in 1862. She returned to the Bouffes the following season and subsequently created further Offenbach roles in *Les Bergers* (1865, La Sincère) and, back at the Variétés, the new version of Catarina in the extended four-act version of *Le Pont des soupirs* in 1868, and succeeded Schneider in the title roles of *La Grand-Duchesse* and *La Belle Hélène.* In 1869 she starred at the Bouffes in the first revival of Lecocq's *Fleur de thé.* In 1873 she appeared on the London stage (24 April) for a fortnight in a French plays season.

She died of the smallpox in 1874 whilst returning home from an engagement in Constantinople.

Her father was also a member of the Bouffes-Parisiens company, alongside his daughter, creating small roles in *Orphée aux enfers* (Cerbère), *Geneviève de Brabant* (Savant), *Les Vivandières de la grande armée* (Ramponneau), *Le Carnaval des revues* and *Le Pont des soupirs* (Gibetto).

TAYLOR, Charles H[enry] (b Manchester, 21 July 1859; d London, 27 June 1907). Lyricist for a busy few years on the London stage.

Taylor began his working life alongside his father in the silk trade, but he operated in parallel as a comic writer for the Manchester papers and a friendship with producer Robert Courtneidge led to his supplying some topical verses for pantomimes at Courtneidge's Prince's Theatre in Manchester and, eventually, for other Courtneidge ventures. He finally gave up silk and moved to London to pursue a career as a lyricist and there, after at first concentrating on songs for the popular market (''The Wide World,'' ''Little Sou Chong,'' ''Through the Telephone,'' ''The Lonesome Coon,'' ''Bother the Belle of New York,'' etc), and the management of the publishing firm of Moon & Co, he made his first incursion into the world of West End musical comedy with some additional lyrics for Tom B Davis's production of fellow-Mancunian Leslie Stuart's *The Silver Slipper* (1901).

Taylor quickly became one of the most sought-after lyricists of the London stage and, in the two years that followed, he contributed to Sidney Jones's comedy opera *My Lady Molly* and to George Edwardes's production of *The Girl from Kays,* shared the lyric-writing credit of Seymour Hicks's extremely successful *Bluebell in Fairyland,* and wrote all the songwords for Davis's disappointing *The Medal and the Maid* and for Leslie Stuart's *The School Girl.* Following the success of *Bluebell,* he became lyricist-in-chief to the Seymour Hicks/Charles Frohman organization, and between 1904 and 1907 he supplied the lyrics to Herbert Haines's music for the four shows that the team wrote and produced, scoring a major success with *The Catch of the Season* (''Cigarette,'' ''The Charms on My Chain'') and a fine run with *The Beauty of Bath.* His most enduring work, however, came in his one London show with Courtneidge, *Tom Jones* (1907).

To an Edward German musical score of more lasting substance than those written by Haines, Taylor provided the words for such pieces as the celebrated waltz song ''For Tonight,'' the charming tale of ''The Green Ribbon'' and the lusty ''West Country Lad.'' *Tom Jones* proved, however, to be his last show. He was working on his first musical-comedy libretto when he died at the age of 47. His last song had been played very shortly before, as a special addition to the score of *Tom Jones* for the 100th night of its run. It is that song, ''Dream o' Day Jill,'' which has survived through nigh on a century as his most popular single number.

1901 **A Busy Day** (Herbert Evelyn Baker/w W A Brabner) Theatre Royal, Blackburn 22 April

1901 **Bluebell in Fairyland** (Walter Slaughter/w Aubrey Hopwood/Seymour Hicks) Vaudeville Theatre 18 December

1902 **My Lady Molly** (Sidney Jones/w Percy Greenbank, G H Jessop/Jessop) Theatre Royal, Brighton 11 August; Terry's Theatre, London 14 March 1903

1903 **The Medal and the Maid** (Jones/Owen Hall) Lyric Theatre 25 April

1903 **The School Girl** (Leslie Stuart/Henry Hamilton, Paul M Potter) Prince of Wales Theatre 9 May

1904 **The Catch of the Season** (Herbert Haines, Baker/Hicks, Cosmo Hamilton) Vaudeville Theatre 9 September

1905 **The Talk of the Town** (Haines/Hicks) Lyric Theatre 5 January

1906 **The Beauty of Bath** (Haines/Hicks, Hamilton) Aldwych Theatre 19 March

1907 **My Darling** (Haines, Baker/Hicks) Hicks Theatre 2 March

1907 **Tom Jones** (Edward German/Alexander M Thompson, Robert Courtneidge) Apollo Theatre 17 April

TELLHEIM, Karoline [BETTELHEIM, Karoline] (b Vienna, 1842; d ?Vienna, 13 December 1925).

Karoline Tellheim first appeared at the Carltheater at 19 years of age and made a success in J B Klerr's one-act operetta *Das war ich* (1862). She subsequently played in Berlin and then again briefly at the Carltheater before joining the company at the Vienna Hofoper where for nine years she sang soubrette roles in opera (Zerlina, Ännchen, Papagena, etc). In 1871—now Frau Tellheim-Kanitz, the wife of a banker—she returned to the Operette stage to play Prince Raphaël in *La Princesse de Trébizonde* at the Carltheater, in Budapest and elsewhere, and she later played Prince Caprice in Berlin's version of *Le Voyage dans la lune* (1876), introduced the travesty role of Fortunato in the German version of *Madame l'Archiduc* at the Theater an der Wien, appeared as Adele in *Die Fledermaus* (1877) and created the parts of Mirzl in *Das verwunschene Schloss* and of the Queen in *Das Spitzentuch der Königin* (1880). She then left the stage for the international concert platform where she saw out her career.

TELL HER THE TRUTH Musical play in 2 acts by R P Weston and Bert Lee based on *Nothing But the Truth* by James Montgomery. Music by Jack Waller and Joseph Tunbridge. Saville Theatre, London, 14 June 1932.

One of the successful series of comedies with songs produced at the Saville Theatre by Jack Waller and starring little-chap comic Bobby Howes, *Tell Her the Truth* followed closely the tale of the well-known farcical play *Nothing But the Truth* in which the hero is bound by a bet to tell no lies, no matter how white, for 24 hours. Telling the truth about an ugly hat or frock is minor as compared to facing up to his boss's wife about her husband's attachment to a chorus girl or to a demanding client over an iffy business deal, but after hoursful of humorous situations all ends happily and little Bobby wins both his gamble and his girl.

In the very short score (six numbers) supplied by Waller and Tunbridge, Howes joined in duet with the girls of the piece, and again with the bullet-headed character actor Alfred Drayton in the role of his challenger and employer (''Hoch! Caroline''), but the favorite musical moments came from the bristling Wylie Watson as the innocent amateur-choir-singing Yorkshireman (''I'm a child in business'') on whom Bobby's firm has palmed off some dud land. He stole the song honors with his comical Boy Scout exhortation to ''Sing, Brothers'' and in the mock oratorio scena ''Horrortorio,'' a pastiche of favorite oratorio bits in which he vents his fury at having been robbed.

Tell Her the Truth was closed after 239 West End performances when Howes decided he preferred the high life of the South of France to work, and a Broadway production starring Jack Sheehan jr was a quick flop, but the show had a good British touring life, still appearing on the provincial schedules more than a decade after its production.

Nothing But the Truth was also used as the basis for the Broadway musical *Yes, Yes, Yvette* and for a musical by Michael Stewart, Mark Bramble and Cy Coleman, at the time of writing unproduced.

USA: Cort Theater 28 October 1932

TELL ME MORE! Musical in 2 acts by Fred Thompson and William K Wells. Lyrics by Ira Gershwin and B G De Sylva. Music by George Gershwin. Gaiety Theater, New York, 13 April 1925.

Prolific librettist Fred Thompson and his partner Wells didn't trouble their heads too much about the libretto for *Tell Me More!* The tale was just about as significant as the title. But that didn't matter: what mattered was the content—the dancing, the fun, the girls and, hopefully, the songs. Veteran producer Alfred Aarons, whose son Alex had produced the last George Gershwin musical, *Lady, Be Good!,* with such success, provided most of those ingredients, the Gershwins and Buddy De Sylva came up with a useful if not durable score and Aarons was able to get a one hundred-performance run on Broadway out of the mixture.

The plot was the usual mixture of everyday amours. Jeune premier Kenneth Dennison (Alexander Grey) falls for the once wealthy shop girl Peggy Vandeleur (Phyllis Cleveland), goofy Monty Simpkin (Lou Holtz) falls for the wealthy Jane Wallace (Esther Howard), and simple Billy (Andrew Tombes) falls for the passionate shop girl Bonnie (Emma Haig). And (in 1925!) there was even the next best thing to a baby-swap. Peggy turns out to be Billy's long-lost sister. From the 14 numbers of the score, the lively intimation that one should be ''Kickin' the Clouds Away'' surfaced as the evening's jolliest musical moment in a set of songs (including bits by William Daly and others) which weren't marked out as memorable. One song had a title that would become memorable, however: it was called ''My Fair Lady.''

Oddly enough, *Tell Me More!* had a better life outside America than it did at home. George Grossmith, who had given Gershwin one of his earliest chances as a stage writer with *Primrose,* picked up *Tell Me More!* and mounted it at his Winter Garden Theater, where *Primrose* had just closed, a few weeks after the New York opening. He added a couple of extra songs with local lyrics, cast the show up with Leslie Henson (Monty), Claude Hulbert (Billy, plus one lyric), Arthur Margetson (Kenneth), Vera Lennox (Bonnie), Heather Thatcher (Jane) and Elsa MacFarlane (Peggy) and the piece even overran *Primrose*'s already good record by totaling 263 West End performances. Such a run ensured that *Tell Me More!* followed *Primrose* to the colonies.

J C Williamson Ltd's Australian production featured George Gee (Monty), Leyland Hodgson (Kenneth), Gus Bluett (Billy), Marjorie Hicklin (Peggy) and Dorothy Lena/Maud Fane (Jane), with Freddie Carpenter as principal dancer and Harry Woods's ''Paddlin' Madelin' Home,'' which had somehow got out of its second-hand spot in Broadway's *Sunny* and into the score of this show on the way, as the evening's musical highlight. The piece ran a good three months in Melbourne and six weeks in Sydney.

UK: Winter Garden Theatre 26 May 1925; Australia: Theatre Royal, Melbourne 17 July 1926

TEMPEST, Marie (Dame) [ETHERINGTON, Susan Mary] (b London, 15 July 1862; d London, 14 October 1942). Singer and actress who was London's favorite comic-opera soubrette until she decided she preferred not to sing.

Convent-educated in Belgium, the young Miss Etherington studied music in Paris and at London's Royal Academy of Music and made her first professional stage appearance at the age of 21 in the role of Fiametta in a revival of *Boccaccio.* She was next hired by hopeful singer-manageress Agnes de la Porte to appear alongside that lady in the juvenile role of the dramatic *The Fay o' Fire* and, after making a personal success, followed the piece's quick closure by taking over the title role of *Erminie* from Florence St John for the last part of that show's run at the Comedy Theatre.

Miss Tempest appeared as ingenue Rosella opposite Rose Hersee (and alongside now senior prima donnas of the quality of Soldene and Kate Munroe) in a short-run piece called *Frivoli* at the Theatre Royal, Drury Lane, and took the second lead (to Miss St John) in a finely cast production of Messager's *La Béarnaise* at the new Prince of Wales Theatre, but it was a further takeover, in the title role of *Dorothy,* which finally established the young vocalist as a star. When Henry Leslie took over the management of the unwanted show and transferred it to the Prince of Wales Theatre, he replaced the coolly elegant Marion Hood with the more personality-laden Miss Tempest, from the cast of the outgoing *La Béarnaise,* and the piece and its new star helped each other to memorable success through a very long run.

The new star's personal life hit the headlines when her husband divorced her, naming Leslie as co-respondent, but her popularity only increased as she continued on to play the title roles of *Doris* and *The Red Hussar* for the producer of the moment, repeating the latter role with great success in New York where one journal acclaimed her as ''a Lotta with a prima donna voice.'' After dropping out of the tour of *The Red Hussar* with vocal problems (it was a big sing) and breaking up with Leslie under dramatic circumstances, she took further engagements in America. Over a period of several years, she toured with J C Duff's comic-opera company (Dorothy, Carmen, Mignon, Mabel in *The Pirates of Penzance,* Arline in *The Bohemian Girl*), and appeared as a travesty Adam in a version of *Der Vogelhändler* (1891), as the girl raised as a boy in De Koven's *The Fencing Master* (1892), as the heroine of Genée's *Nanon* and as the operatic Countess of De Koven's *The Algerian* (1893) before returning to Britain in 1895.

On her return, George Edwardes hired her as prima donna for Daly's Theatre and had a role specially written into *An Artist's Model* (1895, Adèle) for her. She scored her biggest London success yet as the enriched model whose artist ex-lover is now chary of resuming their relationship, and confirmed dazzlingly as the heroine of *The Geisha* (1897, O Mimosa San), in which she introduced "The Amorous Goldfish," "Love, Love" and "A Geisha's Life," of *A Greek Slave* (1898, Maia) and of *San Toy* (1899, San Toy), the series of shows which established Daly's Theatre as the bulwark of substantial modern musical theatre.

During the run of *San Toy* she brought about a situation which allowed her to break her contract with Edwardes, calculatedly ending her career in the musical theatre in order to begin what turned out to be a second and equally outstanding career as a light-comedy actress. She sang little thereafter, appearing in concert and, in 1906, for what she insisted was a lot of money, at the Palace Music Hall. She sang a little in the 1912 *Art and Opportunity,* took a turn on the American Keith vaudeville circuit in 1916 ("in a special setting designed by Elsie de Wolfe") in a twosome with pianist Melville Ellis, and made her last appearance in a musical show with the 1924 play *Midsummer Madness,* which mixed some fragments of Clifford Bax music with its sentimental harlequinade of a story.

In spite of the fact that her musical career lasted only some 15 years, compared with the lifelong activities of such as Florence St John, the combination of a strong unaffected soprano and a superior acting talent made Tempest arguably the finest of all the romantic musical theatre's leading ladies of the later Victorian era.

Biography: Bolitho, H: *Marie Tempest* (Cobden-Sanderson, London, 1936)

TEMPLE, Richard [COBB, Richard Barker] (b London, 2 March 1846; d London, 19 October 1912). Longtime member of the original Savoy Theatre company.

Temple made his first appearance on the stage in May 1869 as Count Rodolfo in a performance of *La Sonnambula* at the Crystal Palace and spent most of his early career as a baritone vocalist in touring opera (Stanley Betjeman's Co, Crystal Palace Co, Rose Hersee's National Opera Co at the St James's Theatre and tour, premiere of T Luard Selby's *Adela,* etc) playing Figaro, Conte di Luna, Mephistopheles, Devilshoof and other such roles. He also appeared in comic opera, at the Alfred Theatre (*Lost and Found,* 1871), in Manchester (Levey's *Punchinello* 1871, Marquis), with Fred Sullivan's touring company (1871) in *Cox and Box, The Rose of Auvergne* and *Breaking the Spell,* and in opéra-bouffe first in the provinces (Cocorico in *Geneviève de Brabant* at Liverpool) and then in London (*Le Roi Carotte* [1872, t/o Pippertrunk], *L'Oeil crevé* [1872, Geromé]). In 1873 he toured with Julia Mathews and the Gaiety Theatre company, and got his best London opportunity to date when he played Larivaudière in the original English production of *La Fille de Madame Angot.* The following year he stepped up from the part of Larivaudière temporarily to take over as Ange Pitou (from the tenor Edward Beverley) during an emergency in Emily Soldene's production at the Opera Comique.

Temple subsequently appeared in the burlesque *Ixion Rewheeled* (1874, Jupiter) at the same house, played Rhododendron Pasha in the Islington production of Offenbach's *Les Géorgiennes* (1875), directed and played in Sullivan's *The Zoo* on the same program, appeared as the Sultan in *The Sultan of Mocha* at Liverpool (1876), as Buckingham in Cellier's *Nell Gwynne* at Manchester and as Carlo Maloni in Solomon's *A Will with a Vengeance* (1876) at the Royalty, and toured with François Cellier's opéra-bouffe company performing his own adaptation of *Geneviève de Brabant* and *Cox and Box* (Prince of Wales Theater, Liverpool, March 1877).

Later that same year he joined Richard D'Oyly Carte's Comedy Opera Company to create the role of Sir Marmaduke Pointdextre in Gilbert and Sullivan's *The Sorcerer* (1877). He remained with Carte to create the part of Dick Deadeye in *HMS Pinafore* (1878) and to appear as London's first Pirate King in *The Pirates of Penzance* ("The Pirate King") and Colonel Calverly in *Patience* ("When I First Put This Uniform On"), but when Carte moved his operations to the new Savoy Theatre Temple stayed at the Opera Comique to play for Hollingshead in his revival of Gilbert's *Princess Toto* (1880, Portico) and thereafter at the Gaiety in Solomon's *Lord Bateman* (Ephraim MacDallah).

He returned to Carte's company, however, to create further Gilbert and Sullivan roles as Strephon in *Iolanthe* (1882) and as Arac, with his mock Handelian aria, in *Princess Ida* (1884), and to play the title role of *The Mikado* (1885, "A More Humane Mikado"), the ghostly Sir Roderic in *Ruddigore* ("The Ghosts' High Noon") and Sergeant Meryll in *The Yeomen of the Guard* (1888). When it came to *The Gondoliers,* however, he declined the limp role of Luis which had been written for him and, after more than a decade of playing little else than the works of Gilbert, attempted, with no more success than his fellow departing members of the company, to take his Savoy popularity into other fields.

He appeared in the operetta *The Silver Trout* (1889, Jack Lacy) at a benefit, then made an attempt at management by taking out a tour of Gounod's *The Mock Doctor* starring Effie Chapuy in 1890. It was an expensive failure, and his later ventures as a performer and director similarly held few highlights: he played in the disastrous *Miami* (1893), succeeded Colin Coop as Sid Fakah in the variety musical *Morocco Bound* (1893), directed and played Dick Fid in Howard Talbot's maiden *Wapping Old Stairs* (1894) and performed in *The Geisha* in St Petersburg. He later directed the touring musical *The Red Spider* (1898), toured as John Ironsides in an khaki-updated *Fille du Tambour-Major* (1900), appeared as Henry VII in the unfortunate *The Gay Pretenders* (1900), played in the children's musical *Little Hans Andersen* (1903), and made his final West End appearance in 1906 as Mr Burchell in Liza Lehmann's comic-opera version of *The Vicar of Wakefield.* In the later part of his career he also did some teaching, but in his last years he became an invalid, and he ended his days in Charing Cross Hospital in ''dire poverty.''

In his young days (1872), Temple married the very rising young comic-opera soprano **Bessie EMMETT** [Elizabeth Ellen EMMETT] (b London, 3 August 1846; d Peckham, 9 May 1875), who appeared alongside him in touring opera, provincial operetta and as second soprano with Rose Hersee's National Opera Company at the St James's Theatre and on tour (Lisa, Lazarillo, Gipsy Queen, Nancy in *Martha*) before joining Julia Mathews's company to play Wanda to the star's *La Grande-Duchesse.* She came to town in 1873 as Eurydice in *Orphée aux enfers,* and as a replacement Clairette in the original *La Fille de Madame Angot,* a role she then played in the West End opposite Emily Soldene. In 1874 she toured with Hersee as Leonora in *Il Trovatore* and Eily in *The Lily of Killarney,* played Polly Peachum to the Macheath of Sims Reeves and created the lead role of Dolly in *The Sultan of Mocha* at Manchester, before her death at the age of 28 ''from peritonitis.''

Their son, **Richard TEMPLE jr** [Richard William Emmett COBB] (b Camberwell, 25 October 1872), later known as Dick Temple, made a career in the musical theatre in Britain (original Tom Everleigh in *The Gay Parisienne* [1894], *En Route* [1896, Ted Stanford], *Billy* [1898, Sir Richard Neville], *Geisha* tour [1898, Fairfax], *The New Barmaid* tour [1897–98, Lovebury], *The Prince of Borneo* [1899, Paul Bennett]) and later in America where he appeared in *Winsome Winnie* (1903, Lord Poverish), *Moonshine* (1905, Hon Lionel Longacre), *The Blue Moon* (1906, Bobbie Scott), *The Naked Truth* (1908, Johnnie MacIntosh), *The Queen of the Moulin Rouge* (1909 t/o), *The Pirates of Penzance* (1911, Samuel), *HMS Pinafore* (1913, Sir Joseph), *Oh, I Say!* (1913, Baptiste), *Iolanthe* (1915, Mountararat), *The Hotel Mouse* (1922, Caesar), *Sons o'Guns* (1929, General Harper), *Let 'em Eat Cake* (1933, John P Tweedledee), etc. He also wrote the occasional song (''My Girl'' in *The Yashmak, Winsome Winnie,* ''Any Old Tree'' in *Smiling Island,* ''Daisy, I'm Crazy'' in Chicago's *The Earl and the Girl* and one complete comic opera, a *Three Musketeers,* which he himself produced at the Manhattan Opera House for five performances in 1921 (19 May). Temple also played D'Artagnan to his then wife's Anne of Austria.

TEMPLETON, Fay [TEMPLETON, May] (b Little Rock, Ark, 25 December ?1865; d San Francisco, 3 October 1939). Buxom comedienne and vocalist of the burlesque and musical-comedy stage.

Daughter of actor-manager John Templeton (sometime of De Give's Opera House, Atlanta and the Charleston Theater, SC, b 1838; d New York, 10 December 1907) and his actress wife, Alice Vane [née Van Est], Miss Templeton first appeared on the stage as a very small child and was seen featured in her parents' Southern-states touring company as ''the petite songstress May the Fay'' as early as 1869, going on after the performances of drama by her parents and her aunt Isabel, to give imitations of current stars as an afterpiece, at what was advertised as five years of age. She was subsequently seen in New York as Shakespeare's Puck (Grand Opera House 18 August 1873, billed as ''Little May Templeton'') to the Oberon of Annie Kemp Bowler, provoking the *Clipper* to acclaim her ''the best child actress we ever saw,'' and as Romeo to the Juliet of the equally precocious Bijou Heron (5th Avenue Theater). She played the title roles in the operatic farces *Parepa Rosa* (1874) and *Lucca's Farewell* (1874) at Niblo's and interpolated her specialities into the spectacle *The Twelve Temptations* at the Grand Opera House (1875, ''Queen of the petites''), but went ever back on the road, traipsing one-to-three-night stands at the head of what was now called ''Fay Templeton Star Alliance'' playing as Meenie in *Rip van Winkle,* in *The New Magdalen, East Lynne* (1876) and, later, such pieces as *Prince Napoleon or the Fatal Field in Zululand* or appearing as Topsy in *Uncle Tom's Cabin.* At the age of 14 she toured round the country with a juvenile comic-opera troupe playing Gilbert and Sullivan's Ralph Rackstraw, and in the next couple of years appeared with her father's Fay Templeton Opera Company as Serpolette (*Les Cloches de Corneville*), in the title roles of *Giroflé-Girofla, La Mascotte* (whilst her mother played Fiametta and her father Pippo!), *Patience, Olivet-*

te, Billee Taylor and *La Grande-Duchesse* and in *Good Luck.*

She added to her repertoire over the years that followed a hacked up version of *Gilette de Narbonne* called *La Belle Coquette* and a piece called *Rosita, or Cupid and Cupidity* (1884) by the untried Harry Bache Smith, and then at the age of 19 made her first adult Broadway appearance as Gabriel in a revival of the favorite burlesque *Evangeline* (1885). She played in further burlesques (*The Corsair,* etc) on the road, in America and also in London, where she was hired at the not inconsiderable salary of £15 per week for a supporting part in *Monte Cristo Jr* at London's Gaiety Theatre, performing the song ''I Like It, I Do.'' She was sacked from this job for impenitently lowering the neckline and raising the trunks of her costume, sued in a blaze of publicity, and lost. She did not play the Gaiety again, but nearly a decade later she nevertheless had a success there when the coon song ''I Want Yer My Honey,'' which she had written was introduced by Ellaline Terriss into *The Shop Girl.*

Back in America, she returned to the kind of burlesque which encouraged low necks and short trunks, appearing in the breeches title role of the short-lived burlesque *Henrik Hudson* (1890) before going on the road in the title role of Russell's Comedians' *Miss McGinty of the Comédie Française* (1890). By this stage, the once well-built performer had grown distinctly buxom, but this proved to be no bar to an increasing popularity and she won herself a further following playing comic opera in summer season at Philadelphia's Park Theater (1892, Drogan in *Geneviève de Brabant,* Fanchette Michel in *The Royal Middy, La Grande-Duchesse,* Javotte in *Erminie,* etc), touring the country as *Madame Favart* (1893) and in the burlesque *Excelsior Jr* (1895), and particularly when she moved for two seasons to Weber and Fields's burlesque house, appearing as a revived Cleopatra in *Hurly Burly* (1898), as Roxy to the *Cyranose de Bric-à-brac* of Fields (1898), impersonating Ethel Barrymore in *Carrots,* as Mary Mannering in *The Stickiness of Gelatine,* Mrs Leslie Carter in *Du Hurry,* Annie Russell in *Catherine* (singing her own song ''What, Marry Dat Man?'') and as the sleepwalking star of *Helter Skelter* (1899). In *Broadway to Tokio* (1900) she repeated her impersonation of Cleopatra before she returned to Weber and Fields to share starry billing with Lillian Russell, De Wolf Hopper and David Warfield in *Fiddle-dee-dee* (1900), in which she introduced ''Ma Blushin' Rosie'' and impersonated Lythia to the Petrolius of Hopper, in the burlesque *Quo Vass Iss?* (''Come Fetch Your Baby Home'') and in *Hoity-Toity* (1901), in which she played Minnie in the *A Message from Mars* burlesque.

Miss Templeton appeared at the Casino Theater and around the country in *The Runaways* (1903 t/o), and in spite of the announcements that the Shuberts would star her in a musical called *The Infant Prodigy,* by no less an playwright than Clyde Fitch, and conversely that Aubrey Boucicault would be the author of her next vehicle, she next co-starred with Peter F Dailey as Mrs Aurora Daye Knight in the loose-limbed vaudeville *A Little Bit of Everything* (1904). She then took the top of the bill again as Mamselle Fleurette in *In Newport* (1904, with her own song ''Nobody But You'') and took over in *Lifting the Lid* at the Aerial Gardens (1905)—before making her biggest success, teamed with Victor Moore and Donald Brian, as the devoted Mary Jane Jenkins (''Mary'' [it's a grand old name], ''So Long Mary'') in George M Cohan's *Forty-Five Minutes from Broadway* (1905–6). This piece, in which she toured for a long period, was supposed to be her last major stage appearance, for at the end of the tour, in May 1907, she announced her retirement from the theatre. She returned, however, for several special occasions, appearing in the Weber and Fields reunion show *Hokey-Pokey* in 1912 (Peachie Mullen, and Bunty in *Bunty, Bulls and Strings,* ''Alexander's Bagpipe Band''), as Little Buttercup in a spectacular and highly successful ''all-star'' revival of *HMS Pinafore* and, finally, at nearly 70 years of age, as Aunt Minnie in *Roberta* (1933), introducing Jerome Kern's enduring ballad ''Yesterdays.''

She was seen on film in the 1933 *Broadway to Hollywood,* and was impersonated in the Cohan biopic *Yankee Doodle Dandy* by Irene Manning.

Beyond her *Shop Girl* song, Miss Templeton wrote and composed a number of other numbers, mostly of the coon variety, several of which found their way into musical comedies (''My Oneliest One,'' ''My Poppy Belle'' in *Hoity Toity,* ''Nobody But You'' in *Lifting the Lid,* ''My Hindoo Belle'' in *The Runaways,* etc).

Her first (and exceedingly brief) husband was William H West (né Flynn) of the well-known Primrose and West Minstrel combination.

LA TEMPRANICA Zarzuela in 1 act (3 scenes) by Julián Romea. Music by Geronimo Giménez. Teatro de la Zarzuela, Madrid, 19 September 1900.

The tale of ''la tempranica,'' the precocious girl, moved away from the favorite setting of many of the other most successful zarzuelas, the suburbs of the city, to the Spanish countryside and to a tale slightly more in the conventions of the rest of European musical theatre. The noble Andalucian Don Luis, Count of Santa Fe (Pepe Sigler), once had a hunting accident in the mountains and was nursed back to health by the peasant girl María (Concha Segura). During the days of his recovery a strong feeling grew up between the two young people, but Don Luis returned to his home and to his own way of life. The two meet again when Luis is leading an English guest through the mountains, but María finally agrees to marry her village Miguel. When Don Luis turns up at the celebrations she is tempted to renounce Miguel, but her little brother, Grabié, brings her the news—Luis is married. María has to see for herself. She and Grabié go to Granada and, watching outside Luis's home, she sees him, his wife and his child together. Then she returns to her home, her people and to Miguel who will be her husband.

Although the music of the show included some colorful ensembles, including the village betrothal fete, and a virtual stand-up solo for the boy (''La tarantula é un bicho mu malo''), presented as such, the backbone of the score was in the romantic music for the two central characters, their duo of reminiscence ''Te quiero . . . poque eres güeno,'' and María's showpiece ''Sierras de Granada.''

Recordings: complete (Columbia/Alhambra, Montilla/Zafiro)

THE TENDERFOOT Musical play in 3 acts by Richard Carle. Music by Harry L Heartz. Dearborn Theater, Chicago, 12 April 1903; Daly's Theater, New York, 22 February 1904.

Richard Carle's self-made vehicle of 1903 presented him as Professor Zachary Pettibone LLD, BA, wandering the wild spots of the West, from the ranch of heiress Marion Worthington (May de Sousa) to the Indian camping ground presided over by Big Bluff (William Russell). Honest John Martin (gambler and soubret), Reckless Reddy (cowboy), White Pill (medicine man), Abe Splicer (parson), Flora Jane Fibby (authoress and soubrette), a bunch of Texas Rangers headed by hero Paul Winthrop (Edmund Stanley) and number-two comic Bill Barker (Gilbert Gregory), and a gaggle of Gibson Girls were included in the personnel of an entertainment which rolled up 20 weeks in Chicago before the Dearborn management sent it on the road.

Carle made a hit everywhere singing about ''My Alamo Love'' whose eyes outshone the rising moon, described himself as ''A Peaceable Party'' and joined in trio to sing about ''The Tortured Thomas Cat,'' whilst the girls' chorus imitated Gilbert and Sullivan's policemen with a ''tantara'' chorus, the rangers chorused to ''rataplan,'' the hero baritoned an ''Adios'' and the heroine serenaded ''Fascinating Venus'' (the planet). ''Noise, numerous pistol shots, jumping-jack business, and some old-fashioned comedy'' were mixed with ''streaks of beauty and romance and moments of true dramatic power'' in a piece ''with a Spanish-American-cowboy-cavalry flavoring,'' which Chicago found agreeably recalled *The Mocking Bird* in its picturesque olde American setting. A New York season of what was there noted as being little more than a series of variety sketches, linked by ''song and dance specialities and knockabout galore'' lasted a good (for a ''foreign'' show) 81 performances.

Perhaps a little suprisingly, *The Tenderfoot*'s afterlife included, beyond its touring seasons in America and a full-scale revival by and with Carle in the autumn of 1909, a production in Australia. A producer called George Willoughby launched a company in Sydney in 1914 with Carrick Major in Carle's role supported by Booby Woolsey, Don Hancock, Myrtle Jersey, Eva Olivotti, George M Bogues, Grace Ellsworth and J Monte Crane, and a repertoire of *The Tenderfoot* (11 April) and *The Mayor of Tokio* (2 May). Of the two, *The Tenderfoot* did better, but the enterprise was not a lengthy one.

Australia: Adelphi Theatre, Sydney 11 April 1914

TENDERLOIN Musical comedy in 2 acts by George Abbott and Jerome Weidman based on the novel by Samuel Hopkins Adams. Lyrics by Sheldon Harnick. Music by Jerry Bock. 46th Street Theater, New York, 17 October 1960.

Following the success of their *Fiorello!*, the team of writers Jerome Weidman, George Abbott, Sheldon Harnick and Jerry Bock and producers Robert E Griffith and Harold S Prince followed up with another New York period piece, this one set in the dirty underbelly of the city known as the *Tenderloin.* Maurice Evans starred as the Reverend Andrew Brock, out to wipe up and out the worst immoralities and corruptions of the area (which, of course, involved showing them on stage). Those immoralities are headed and personified by prostitute Nita (Eileen Rodgers), the corruption by police lieutenant Schmidt (Ralph Dunn), and the minister's ally of circumstance is a reporter Tommy Howatt (Ron Husmann) who is out to win the church choir belle, Laura (Wynne Miller). It is Tommy's court evidence which wins the day and stonkers Schmidt. Nita marries church choirman Joe (Rex Everhart), and the other wiped-out girls of the Tenderloin go off to set up the best little whorehouse in the West.

A jolly score, topped by a first-rate burlesque of the damper kind of Victorian ballad, ''Artificial Flowers,'' sung by Tommy as his audition for Brock's choir, and a singalong expose of ''How the Money Changes Hands'' (a relation of *Fiorello!*'s ''Little Tin Box''), illustrated the costume girlie tale happily, if unprofitably, through a Broadway run of 216 performances. The show was played for a season at the Equity Library Theater in 1975 (6 November).

Recording: original cast (Capitol), concert cast (DRG), etc

TENNENT, H[enry] M[oncrieff] (b Eltham, 18 February 1879; d London, 10 June 1941). London play producer whose organization also imported a number of successful musicals.

After working initially for piano manufacturers and music publishers Broadwood, Harry Tennent moved to the managerial side of the theatre business and ultimately became General Manager of Moss' Empires and Howard and Wyndham's Tours and of the Theatre Royal, Drury Lane. In this position, he was responsible for booking many musicals into the chain of theatres under his control, and he was credited by Ivor Novello with having commissioned *Glamorous Night* for Drury Lane over a luncheon table.

In 1936, in partnership with **Hugh (''Binkie'') BEAUMONT** [Hugh Griffiths MORGAN], (b London, 28 March 1908; d London, 23 March 1973), he founded his own theatrical-management firm, H M Tennent Ltd. The pair scored an early major success with the play *French without Tears* (1936) and, from then until Beaumont's death 37 years later, H M Tennent Ltd held a place as the dominant play-producing organization in London. Although Tennent had produced a number of revues in the 1910s, and had even written songs, including the successful ''My Time Is Your Time,'' for them, the firm did not become involved in producing musicals until well after his death.

In 1945 Noël Coward persuaded Beaumont to produce his revue *Sigh No More,* and its comparative success led to Beaumont venturing into a number of other successful revues (*The Lyric Revue, The Globe Revue, At the Lyric*). He also made rare incursions into the musical theatre with Coward's ill-fated *After the Ball,* and, more successfully, Sandy Wilson's *The Buccaneer* and the London production of Frank Loesser's *Where's Charley?* (1958).

Beaumont secured an option on the British rights of *My Fair Lady* as part of canny piece of showbusinessmanship over the availability of Rex Harrison. When Harrison was eagerly wanted for the role of Higgins, he was playing for Tennent's in *Bell, Book and Candle.* Beaumont purposely kept the fading play resolutely on (and Harrison, thus, resolutely unavailable) until he had won himself a splendid deal which included London's *My Fair Lady.* Following the enormous success of this production, he had a second success with the French musical *Irma la Douce* and a third with a musical which nobody wanted and which its publishers had virtually to pay him to produce—*West Side Story.*

Amongst a heavy schedule of play production, Tennent's staged and/or managed a number of other imported musicals, some like *The Most Happy Fella, Bye Bye Birdie, Promises, Promises, Godspell* and, after a very sticky start, *Hello, Dolly!,* with success, others (*Do Re Mi, Carnival, I Do! I Do!, On the Town, No, No, Nanette* revival) with less or none. Beaumont, who was not particularly interested in the musical theatre, made little attempt to produce untried musicals after the musical version of Terence Rattigan's *French without Tears,* produced as *Joie de Vivre* (1960), folded in four performances, and otherwise backed only a West End transfer of another classic adaptation, the richly cast *Virtue in Danger,* from the Mermaid Theatre, again without success.

The one success which the firm had with an original musical came shortly after Beaumont's death, before Tennent's had begun to seriously decline from its predominant position in the West End, when the company produced (w Peter Witt) the musical version of *Billy Liar, Billy,* at the Theatre Royal, Drury Lane, with Michael Crawford (succeeded by Roy Castle) starring for 904 performances.

[DIE] TERESINA Operette in 3 acts by Rudolf Schanzer and Ernst Welisch. Music by Oscar Straus. Deutsches Künstlertheater, Berlin, 11 September 1925.

Schanzer and Welisch's libretto for *Teresina* brought out that favorite operettic hero, Napoléon Bonaparte, one more time. This time he started off in Fréjus, on his way to take power in Paris, gathering on his way the allegiance of the çi-devant Comte de Lavalette who has engaged to wed a little theatre girl, Terésa, to comply with the ''equality'' decrees of the Directoire. But Lavalette is called suddenly to the road and she is abandoned. By Act II Napoléon is in power, Lavalette is a Maréchal and Terésa has become the fabulous diva, La Terésina, sighed after by the whole male world, including the emperor. It takes till the end of the third act for the reasons for Lavalette's mysterious disappearance from Fréjus to be cleared up and the pair to be reunited. The comic characters of the piece were Terésa's barber brother, Daniel, taken up by the foolish Prince Borghese to supply him with healthy, son-producing blood transfusions, and by the Princess Borghese for altogether more agreeable reasons and ways of achieving the same object. The bulk of the score fell to the prima donna, as played by Fritzi Massary in the Berlin premiere, and to her Count, with the Borgheses and Daniel providing the lighter musical moments. The role of Napoléon (Johannes Riemann) was a non-singing one.

A useful success through four months in Berlin, *Teresina* was subsequently given in the provinces and exported to Budapest (ad Zsolt Harsányi), where Sári Fedák took the title role and Hanna Honthy played Pauline Borghese, to Vienna's Ronachers Operetten-Theater where Luise Kartousch starred as Terésa, and to Nantes and subsequently Paris (ad Léon Uhl, Jean Marietti), with Léo Bovy (Terésa), Harlé (Lavalette) and Davenay (Napoléon).

Hungary: Fővárosi Operettszínház *Terezina* 30 December 1925; Austria: Ronacher 6 March 1926; France: Théâtre Graslin, Nantes 19 November 1927, Folies-Wagram, Paris 25 May 1928

TERRASSE, Claude [Antoine] (b L'Arbresle, 27 January 1867; d Paris, 30 May 1923). The musical illustrator of de Flers and de Caillavet's much-admired prewar opéras-bouffes, whose works (now as then) seem to be more talked-of than played.

Terrasse studied at the Conservatoire de Lyon and the École Niedermeyer and, after periods spent as an orchestral trumpeter, a provincial piano teacher and a church organist in Paris, he found his way into the theatre through his friendship with Alfred Jarry, for whose play *Ubu Roi* (1896) he composed the incidental music. He provided scores for a handful of plays and short opérettes, as well as for Courteline's ''fantaisie'' *Paris-Courcelles* at the Grand Guignol, and the sparkling and burlesque extravagance of his composing talent, helped by an equal talent for attracting first-class friends and collaborators, ensured him in the first days of the new century a success in a genre—the genuine opéra-bouffe—which had been largely submerged since the days of Hervé, Crémieux, Meilhac and Halévy.

La Petite Femme de Loth (1900), written to a libretto by Tristan Bernard, and *Les Travaux d'Hercule* (1901), a collaboration with Robert de Flers and Gaston de Caillavet, provoked connoisseurs, in a fallow period for French opérette, to hopeful comparisons with the greatest writers of 19th-century burlesque. Those comparisons were fueled by the successes of the same team's crazily risqué *Le Sire de Vergy* (1903) and *M de la Palisse* (1904), the topsy-turvy classicisms of *Paris, ou le bon juge* (1905) and even by the tiny and non-burlesque *Chonchette* (1902) and Terrasse had a further success with another little classical burlesque, *Eglé* (1907), a piece whose heroine was the baby born of Jupiter's bovine dalliance with the nymph Io, and who here somehow got mixed up with the Golden Fleece and Jason's famous quest.

Terrasse went apparently upmarket with *Le Mariage de Télémaque* (1910), written to a text by two Academicians, produced by Albert Carré at the Opéra-Comique, and revived there in 1913. This piece called itself simply a ''comédie'' and, indeed, it lacked the bouffe spirit of the earlier works, its post–Trojan-War tale of Telemachus' infatuation with Helen, and her rather unimaginative plot to disillusion him, comparing poorly with Meilhac and Halévy's *La Belle Hélène.* However, the now celebrated team with de Flers and de Caillavet was not re-formed and the composer never again found the same level of praise or popularity that he had with his most effective collaborators. The musical comedies *Les Transatlantiques,* which mixed Americanisms with old-world aristocracy, and *Miss Alice des PTT* were at best half-successes, and of his later full-scale works only the costume opérette *Cartouche* (1912), produced at the Trianon-Lyrique, came near equaling the quality and success of the works of the composer's best years. His last shows returned to the one-act formula, which he had earlier practiced with more success. They also inclined to lesser venues, and the composer's last full-scale piece, *Frétillon,* a period opérette written to an Albert Carré libretto based on *Les Chansons de Béranger,* was produced posthumously in Strasbourg.

Terrasse's other works included a number of revues (*Paris tout nu* at the Ambassadeurs, 1908, etc), such pieces as the ballet-pantomime *La Mariée de la Rue Brisemiche* (1909, Courteline, Marsolleau) and the ballet *Strella* (1911), both produced at the Folies-Bergère, and the little divertissement *Les Lucioles* played at a matinée at the Opéra-Comique, 28 December 1910.

The composer's favorite opéras-bouffes were given a good number of showings in other languages and other countries, and several of his little pieces also traveled—*Chonchette* did the rounds, *La Fiancée du scaphandrier* was seen in Germany under the title of *Elisa, die Taucherbraut* (ad Maurice Rappaport, Intimes Theater, Berlin 3 September 1902) and the one-act vaudeville *Le Tiers porteur* was exported to Vienna's Apollotheater (1914, *Checkvekehr*)—but his best works were always handicapped in foreign lands by the ''necessity'' of making considerable alterations in the happily scabrous de Flers and de Caillavet libretti to suit the moral standards of the early years of this century. However, Terrasse and his best works have always enjoyed a high reputation amongst commentators in his own country and his opéras-bouffes have won several revivals there, often under non-commercial circumstances.

1900 **L'Heure du berger** (Rosenval) 1 act Théâtre Aphration 23 May

1900 **L'Amour en bouteille** (Bonis-Charancle) 1 act Folies-Parisiennes 19 June

1900 **La Petite Femme de Loth** (Tristan Bernard) Théâtre des Mathurins 10 October

1901 **On demande des chanteurs** 1 act Royan 6 March

1901 **Les Travaux d'Hercule** (Gaston de Caillavet, Robert de Flers) Théâtre des Bouffes-Parisiens 7 March

1902 **La Fiancée du scaphandrier** (Franc-Nohain [ie, Maurice Étienne Legrand]) 1 act Théâtre des Mathurins 8 January

1902 **Chonchette** (de Caillavet, de Flers) 1 act Théâtre des Capucines 11 April

1902 **Au temps des croisades** (Franc-Nohain) Pavillon de Flore, Liège 21 December

1903 **La Botte secrète** (Franc-Nohain) 1 act Théâtre des Capucines 27 January

1903 **Le Sire de Vergy** (de Caillavet, de Flers) Théâtre des Variétés 16 April

1903 **Péché véniel** (Franc-Nohain) 1 act Théâtre des Capucines 14 November

1904 **M de la Palisse** (de Caillavet, de Flers) Théâtre des Variétés 2 November

1905 **Le Manoir de Cagliostro** (aka *Le Manoir enchanté*) (Alfred Jarry, Eugène Demolder) 1 act (privately) 10 January
1906 **Paris, ou le bon juge** (de Caillavet, de Flers) Théâtre des Capucines 18 March
1907 **Le Chant de muezzin** (Franc-Nohain) Monte-Carlo January
1907 **Eglé, ou l'enfant de la vache** (Emmanuel-Philippe Moreau, Charles Clairville, Ernest Depré) Théâtre du Moulin-Rouge 7 May
1907 **L'Ingénu libertin** (Louis Artus) Théâtre des Bouffes-Parisiens 11 December
1908 **Le Coq d'Inde** (Rip) Théâtre des Capucines 6 April
1908 **Le Troisième Larron** (Henri Gauthier-Villars) 1 act Folies-Pigalle 13 April
1910 **Le Mariage de Télémaque** (Jules Lemaître, Maurice Donnay) Opéra-Comique 4 May
1911 **Pantagruel** (Jarry, Eugène Demolder) Grand Théâtre, Lyon 30 January
1911 **Le Relai** (Jarry, Demolder) Salle Rostand March
1911 **Les Transatlantiques** (Abel Hermant, Franc-Nohain) Théâtre de l'Apollo 20 May
1912 **Cartouche** (Hugues Delorme, Francis Gally) Trianon-Lyrique 9 March
1912 **Le Tiers porteur** (Jean Kolb, André de Fouquières) 1 act Théâtre Michel 27 April
1912 **Miss Alice des PTT** (Maurice Vaucaire/Bernard) La Cigale 14 December
1913 **L'Amour patriote** (Gally, Jean Kolb) 1 act Royan 12 August
1916 **La Farce du poirier** (Ferdinand Hérold) 1 act Théâtre des Bouffes-Parisiens 29 July
1918 **Le Cochon qui sommeille** (Rip, Robert Dieudonné [ie, Robert Sorre]) Théâtre Michel 24 December
1919 **Le Muphti** (Paul Millet) 1 act Monte-Carlo 10 April
1920 **Un Mari sans sa femme** (Édouard Adénis) 1 act Alhambra 1 November
1923 **Chamouche** (de Féraudy) 1 act Alhambra 23 March
1924 **Faust en menage** (Albert Carré) 1 act Théâtre de la Potinière 5 January
1927 **Frétillon** (A Carré) Théâtre Municipal de Strasbourg 5 March

TERRIS, Norma [ALLISON, Norma] (b Columbus, Kans, 13 November 1900; d Lyme, Conn, 15 November 1989). Singing actress whose one major role was never followed up.

Miss Terris first appeared on the stage as a teenaged dancer in *The Midnight Frolics,* and had her first speaking role in the musical comedy *Queen o' Hearts* (1922, Grace). She toured in vaudeville with her first husband, Max Hoffman jr, in the title role of George M Cohan's *Little Nellie Kelly* and again in the George S Kaufman/Marc Connelly musical *Be Yourself,* and returned to Broadway in the revues *A Night in Paris* and *A Night in Spain.*

In 1927 the pretty, dark performer won the role of her career when she created the part of Magnolia Hawkes in *Show Boat,* introducing "Why Do I Love You," "Make Believe" and "You Are Love" in partnership with leading man Howard Marsh (Gaylord Ravenal). She made her greatest success, however, in the final part of the show in which she returned as Magnolia's modern-day daughter, Kim, performing a series of vaudevillesque impersonations of celebrities.

This success was to remain an isolated one. Although Miss Terris again played Magnolia in a revival of *Show Boat* in 1932, she appeared only in two further Broadway musicals, both of which counted their runs in days: as the heroine of the naive 1930 *The Well of Romance* and in the 1938 *Great Lady.* She later appeared at the St Louis Muny in her *Show Boat* role as well as in the star roles of *Bitter-Sweet,* Ivor Novello's *Glamorous Night* and Fall's *Madame Pompadour,* and in various stock companies in both straight and musical roles.

Miss Terris also appeared on the musical screen alongside J Harold Murray and Reginald Dandy as the heroine of *Married in Hollywood,* the Hollywood film version of Oscar Straus's *Hochzeit in Hollywood.*

The Goodspeed Opera House in Connecticut named its second, smaller house in Chester for Miss Terris, a longtime resident of the area.

TERRISS, Ellaline [LEWIN, Mary Ellaline] (b Stanley, Falkland Islands, 13 April 1871; d Richmond, Surrey, 16 June 1971). Sweetheart of London's turn-of-the-century musical comedy stage.

Miss Terriss, daughter of the favorite actor William Terriss (né Lewin), made her teenaged appearances on the stage in non-musical pieces with Beerbohm Tree and, over a period of three years, with Charles Wyndham. In 1892 she took an engagement at the Court Theatre which brought her both her first singing roles, in the little operettas *A Pantomime Rehearsal* and *His Last Chance,* and a husband in the person of fellow actor, Seymour Hicks. Over the years that followed, Hicks and Miss Terriss were to become the most famous married couple in the West End musical theatre.

The pair were taken to the Gaiety Theatre by George Edwardes for a stopgap revival of *Little Jack Sheppard* in 1894, Hicks to fill the lead comedy role, and his wife to play the ingenue role created by Marion Hood, with whose cool elegance and coloratura soprano the prettily voiced light-comic actress had nothing in common. Edwardes next cast her as Jessie Bond's sister in Gilbert's *His Excellency* (1894) where she also played in the fore-piece, *Papa's Wife,* for which she composed the little bit of accompanying music, and, after Ada Reeve, Kate Cutler and Eva Moore had all done their time as the heroine of *The Shop Girl,* he brought her back to the Gaiety to take over the role of Bessie Brent.

When the next Gaiety musical was prepared, Hicks refused his role and parted company with Edwardes, but Mrs Hicks stayed and starred as May, *The Clergyman's Daughter,* in a piece which was renamed for town *My Girl* (1896). She followed up—opposite her returned husband/partner—as the sparkily ingenue heroine of *The Circus Girl* (1896, Dora Wemyss) and here she introduced her first major hit song with Lionel Monckton's "A Little Bit of String." *A Runaway Girl* (1898) was another huge success for the Gaiety Theatre and for musical comedy's favorite ingenue, cast here as the "runaway" Winifred Grey and equipped with another popular song, "The Boy Guessed Right." Miss Terriss then left the Gaiety for a brief return to comedy before moving on with her husband to take up a long and lucrative association with Charles Frohman.

In the years that followed, Miss Terriss played no more musical-comedy ingenues, but she had a particular success in the play *Quality Street* and also played in several juvenile musicals that had a wider than juvenile appeal, notably as Alice in *Alice in Wonderland,* as Bluebell in the 1901 *Bluebell in Fairyland*—in which she performed "The Honeysuckle and the Bee" and "The Sunflower and the Sun," jaunty up-to-date versions of the kind of song popularized by Letty Lind at Daly's in the previous decade—and in a far from unsuccessful attempt to repeat this same formula in 1903 as *The Cherry Girl.*

Hicks and Frohman next organized a piece intended to present the star pair in musical comedy once more, as a modern Cinderella and Prince Charming, but, before *The Catch of the Season* (1904) made it to the stage, its intended heroine had become pregnant. Zena Dare was given the part until Miss Terriss was fit to return to take over, after which she toured the piece throughout Britain before returning to London to revive *Bluebell* and to open the pair's new vehicle, *The Beauty of Bath* (1906, "My Little Hyacinth"). During the run of the show they transferred to the new Hicks Theatre, named in their honor by Frohman.

After *The Beauty of Bath* came another fine success with *The Gay Gordons* (1907, "Humpty and Dumpty") before Hicks conceived the odd idea of putting his wife into breeches as the young hero of *The Dashing Little Duke* (1909) in a style which had long gone out of fashion, and now reeked somewhat of pantomime time. *The Dashing Little Duke* worked much less well than the previous shows, but when Hicks returned to pair with his wife in a musical adaptation of the play *The Dictator* called *Captain Kidd* (1910) they were faced with an utter and unprecedented flop. The bubble had burst. The pair abandoned the world of musical comedy and took to the lucrative music halls for several years and their subsequent West End vehicles were more often comedy than musical. However, Miss Terriss took over the juvenile role of Elphin Haye in a wartime revival of *The Earl and the Girl,* repeated *Bluebell in Fairyland* under family management at Prince's Theatre in 1916 and, in a final West End musical appearance, featured in Hicks's indifferent *Cash on Delivery* at the Palace Theatre.

During the Hickses' heyday in the musical theatre, Miss Terriss composed a number of fairyweight songs which were interpolated into London shows including *The Yashmak* (1897), *The Merry-Go-Round* (1899) and *The Talk of the Town* (1905).

1895 **Papa's Wife** (Seymour Hicks, F C Phillips) 1 act Lyric Theatre 26 January

1898 **The Lady Wrangler** (Hicks) 1 act Duke of York's Theatre 4 March

Autobiographies: *Ellaline Terriss, By Herself and Others* (Cassell, London, 1928), *A Little Bit of String* (Hutchinson, London, 1955); Biography: Hicks, S: *Me and My Missus* (Cassell, London, 1939)

TERRY, Ethelind (b Philadelphia, 14 August 1901; d Fort Lauderdale, Fla, March 1984). Darkly lovely musical-theatre soprano whose voice and career did not last.

Miss Terry made her first Broadway appearance at the age of 20 when she took over from Eleanor Painter in the leading soprano role, as the Latin Dolores, in Jake Shubert's revival of *Florodora.* She subsequently appeared in Ephraim Zimbalist's musical *Honeydew* (1920, Muriel) and in two editions of *The Music Box Revue* before, in 1923, creating the part of Carmen Mendoza in *Kid Boots.* After touring the country in this role for several years, she was cast as yet another South Americanate lady, again equipped with songs by Harry Tierney and Joseph McCarthy, when she created the title role in their *Rio Rita* (1927). Amongst the songs which she introduced in the part were "Rio Rita" and Tierney's own favorite of his works, "If You're in Love, You'll Waltz."

This second success was followed by an unsuccessful attempt at a musical film (*Lord Byron of Broadway*) and by a slightly more mitigated success as the heroine of Romberg's *Nina Rosa,* a show and a role that she repeated at London's Lyceum Theatre. She subsequently toured America as French Yvonne in *Sons o' Guns* in 1931–32, took part in a puree of Lehár's *Zigeunerliebe* perpetrated in Boston under the title *The Moon Rises,* and in 1935 visited Australia to play in Ernest Rolls's homemade musical *Flame of Desire.* Her voice was noted as being in a shabby state and she was quickly replaced by local star Strella Wilson. Back in America, she closed out of town in *Cocktail Bar* (1937, Princess Pierotti), and was not seen again on Broadway.

TÊTE DE LINOTTE Opérette in 2 acts by Raymond Vincy. Music by Francis Lopez. Théâtre de l'ABC, Paris, December 1957.

A first top-of-the-bill vehicle for comedienne Annie Cordy, who starred opposite Jean Richard and Pierre Miguel as the "featherbrain" of the title, singing "Jojo la fleur bleue," "Tête de linotte," "C'est estraordinaire" and "Le Rhythme des tropiques" for three seasons at Paris's Théâtre de l'ABC.

Recording: Annie Cordy selection (Pathé-Marconi)

TEWELE, Franz (b Vienna, 29 July 1843; d Bad Ischl, 10 September 1914). Celebrated Viennese musical comedian of the 19th century.

The son of a Viennese court official, Tewele abandoned technical college for acting studies and worked in theatres in Brünn, Pressburg and Graz, appearing in sometimes heavy dramatic roles, before being engaged in 1864 at the Hoftheater in Munich. There he was first cast in the kind of comedy roles—with or without music, but always with ad-libbing and burlesque effects—for which he would become famous. In 1865 he joined the company at the Vienna Carltheater under Karl Treumann where he was cast as the first Viennese Gardefeu in *Pariser Leben.* During the rest of his almost 50 years on the stage he played largely in the principal Viennese theatres, including three periods at the Carltheater (between 1878 and 1882 as the manager of the house), two substantial periods at the Wiener Stadttheater (1872–78, 1883 sq) and, at the end of his career, at the Deutsches Theater. His two significant periods away from Austria came in 1882, when he toured America and appeared at New York's Thalia Theater with Josefine Gallmeyer and Wilhelm Knaack and, later, with a stay of three years in Berlin.

Tewele's one important musical creation was the part of Pietro in *Boccaccio,* but amongst his other musical roles were included comedy parts in such pieces as *Niniche* (Grégoire), *Der grosse Casimir* (Casimir), *Die Mormonen* (King of the Sandwich Islands), *Der Kukuk* (Theobald von Falibourde), *Papas Frau* (Aristides/Florestan), *Die Puppe* (Hilarius), *La Prima Ballerina* (Tamponin), *Die Pariserin* (Karl Durer), *Die Näherin* and *Der griechische Sklave* (Heliodorus). Under his management of the Carltheater the productions included *Der kleine Herzog, Der grosse Casimir, Papas Frau, Marjolaine, Die Mormonen, Der Kukuk, Olivette, Die Carbonari* and Genée's *Nisida* and *Rosina.*

Tewele also won a different kind of renown as one of Vienna's first intrepid bicyclists, becoming the city's first cycle casualty when he broke his leg in a velocipedic accident in 1869.

TEXAS, LI'L DARLIN' Musical comedy in 2 acts by John Wheldon and Sam Moore. Lyrics by Johnny Mercer. Music by Robert Emmett Dolan. Mark Hellinger Theater, New York, 25 November 1949.

An American state for a title and a title song, a tale of politics and shenanigans (not to mention love), a GI hero and a big business villain—all these favorite elements of the moment went into the making-up of the musical comedy *Texas, Li'l Darlin'.*

Publisher Harvey Small (Loring Smith) chooses Texan senator Hominy Smith (radio megastar Kenny Delmar) to be molded into a candidate for high and helpful office. The opposition, headed by a group of ex-GIs, puts up one of their own, Easy Jones (Danny Scholl), against Smith. After an act and a half of infighting, Small sees the way things—including his daughter Dallas (Mary Hatcher)—are going, and he switches his backing to what is clearly going to be the winning team. Smith walloped out the praises of his state in the title song and duetted with his sponsor on "Politics" whilst Jones stuck to the more nice 'n' homely with "Hootin' Owl Trail" and the quasi-revivalist "The Big Movie Show in the Sky" and duetted with his Dallas over "A Month of Sundays."

The show got through 293 performances of easy, prejudice-patting entertainment for Studio Productions and Anthony B Farrell without ever looking like going any further.

Recording: original cast (Decca/Columbia)

TEYTE, Maggie [TATE, Margaret] (b Wolverhampton, 17 April 1888; d London, 27 May 1976).

Sister of the songwriter James W Tate, Miss Teyte made the most important part of her career in opera where she won particular fame as Debussy's Mélisande (*Pelléas et Mélisande*) whilst still in her twenties. In 1910 she appeared with the Beecham Opera Company as Melka in Edmond Missa's opéra-comique *Muguette* but it was in her thirties that she turned towards the lighter musical theatre and made a notable appearance in London as Lady Mary Carlisle in Messager's *Monsieur Beaucaire* (1919, "Philomel"). She subsequently played Princess Julia in Kálmán's *A Little Dutch Girl* (1920, *Das Hollandweibchen*) at London's Lyric Theatre and appeared as Mrs Fitzherbert in an unfortunate and short-lived piece called *By Appointment* (1934). In 1935 she took part in a revival of Dunhill's *Tantivy Towers* at the Lyric, Hammersmith.

Autobiography: *Star on the Door* (Putnam, London, 1958); Biography: O'Connor, G: *The Pursuit of Perfection* (Gollancz, London, 1979)

THAT'S A GOOD GIRL Musical comedy in 2 acts by Douglas Furber. Music by Phil Charig and Joseph Meyer. London Hippodrome, 5 June 1928.

That's a Good Girl set in motion the series of dance-and-laughter musicals in which Jack Buchanan and Elsie

Randolph starred over a period of 15 years as one of London's favorite musical-comedy teams. On this occasion, what there was of a plot had her as a detective called Joy Dean pursuing Bill Barrow (Buchanan) from the Royal Opera House, Covent Garden to the South of France, with the employment of a succession of disguises and predictable results. On the way, they encountered baritone Raymond Newell, soubrette Maidie Andrews, the comical and operatic Sunya Berata (Vera Pearce), Victorian musical star Kate Cutler playing rich Aunt Helen, speciality dancers from the modern to the balletic, Debroy Somers and his band, and every kind of topical rhythm and dance-step imaginable.

The music to which all this was set was a last-minute affair, ordered by Buchanan shortly before rehearsals started from the New York office of Chappell. The fashionably American score which resulted was a self-effacing one from which the happiest tune was the pretty duo for the leads, ''Fancy Our Meeting.'' The same pair also sang and danced (in slow motion) about ''The One I'm Looking For'' and Newell scored with a contrastingly straight baritone ''A Marching Song.'' However, the principal elements of the show were its fun (directed by Buchanan) and its dances (choreographed mostly by Buchanan), and these went down splendidly. *That's a Good Girl* ran for 363 performances in London and toured widely, establishing the Buchanan/Randolph partnership at the top of the heap, before they moved on to their next vehicle. In 1933 they filmed a version of the show, with original cast members Kate Cutler and Vera Pearce repeating their stage roles.

Film: British and Dominion 1933

THATCHER, Heather [Mary] (b London, 3 September 1896; d Hillingdon, 15 January 1987). Tall, attractive comedienne-who-sang who briefly took the limelight in 1920s London.

After working first as a walk-on in films and as a takeover in a London comedy, Miss Thatcher moved into the musical theatre in the small role of Katie Muirhead in the Adelphi Theatre production of *The Boy* (1917). She won quick promotion to a considerably larger role in the revue *Buzz Buzz* before running up a series of progressively better comedy roles in London musicals of the 1920s. She played Salomé in *The Naughty Princess* (*La Reine joyeuse*), and a travesty Valentine in the short-lived attempt at a return to burlesque with *Faust on Toast* (1921) and then joined Grossmith and Laurillard at their Winter Garden Theatre where, between 1921 and 1925, she played a run of musico-comical roles that lifted her to almost-star status: Rosalind Rafferty in *Sally,* Little Ada in *The Cabaret Girl,* the common Lovey Toots in *The Beauty Prize,* Victoria in the revival of *Tonight's the Night,* Pinkie Peach in *Primrose* (introducing ''Boy Wanted'' to London) and Jane Wallace in *Tell Me More!*

Over the next decade she appeared largely in non-musical pieces, but she returned to the musical stage in the mid-1930s to play the colorful gossip Sophie Otford in Coward's *Conversation Piece* (1934) and to appear once more with former Winter Garden star Leslie Henson in *Lucky Break* (1934), the farcical anglicization of Broadway's *Little Jessie James.* Her subsequent career in films and straight plays faded away without her rereaching the heights of her Winter Garden days.

THÉO, Louise [PICOLO, Anne Louise] (b Paris, 20 April 1850; d Paris, 24 January 1922). One of Offenbach's most successful discoveries.

The illegitimate daughter of Mlle Anne-Gertrude Picolo, proprietor of the Café l'Horloge on the Champs Elysées, and from an early age the wife of Monsieur Théophile Vachier, chief cutter in a Parisian clothing house, the little, blonded Louise Théo (her stage name taken from her husband's first name) worked as a teenager at the El Dorado and other Parisian cafés-concerts. Quickly hailed as the successor to Judic (who had started out at the El Dorado as well) she was snapped up to play at the Exhibition Theatre in Vienna, before being taken by Offenbach to the Bouffes-Parisiens to create the title role in the little opérette *Pomme d'api* (1873) at the age of 19. She shot to stardom when she created the role of the rabidly pursued little shopkeeper, Rose Michon, in the same composer's *La Jolie Parfumeuse* (1873) and thereafter, in spite of the fact that she never got another role as good, she maintained a firm place at the top of her profession. She played in the Bouffes-Parisiens revue *Les Hannetons* (1875, ''she is as round and bulky as a barrel'') teaming with Mme Peschard to burlesque the famous gens d'armes of *Geneviève de Brabant,* and featured as Régina in a revival of *La Princesse de Trébizonde* (1875), but flopped, alongside Paola Marié and Lucien Fugère, when she appeared as the gallantly helpful Francine in Offenbach's *La Boîte au lait*—even though she caused something of a sensation by her ability genuinely to handle a rapier. Neither *Le Moulin du Vert-Galant* (1876, Toinette) nor Coedès's *Fleur d'oranger* (1878, Flora) did her any better service, and she missed a third flop when she rejected the title role of Vasseur's *La Sorrentine* (1877), but she had better luck when she created the titular Mercedès, the lass who loses her voice without sex, in Serpette's *La Petite Muette.* She then put aside new roles, essayed Judic's famous parts in *La Timbale d'argent* (1878) and *Madame l'Archiduc* in Paris revivals, appeared (''a handsome fat little woman'') as Cinderella in the Porte-Saint-Martin's vast *Cendrillon* (1879) and then moved on to play the established repertoire in Brussels (*Giroflé-Girofla* 1880, *Madame l'Archiduc* 1881, etc), Russia and further afield and even to deliver private concerts in the salons of the British aristocracy (1880). In 1881 she appeared back at the Variétés in a revival of the revusical *Le Tour de Cadran.*

In 1882–83 she visited America for Maurice Grau. She was scheduled as the opening attraction for the new Casino Theater but, since the theatre was not ready, she played instead at the Fifth Avenue Theater before going on to tour America with considerable success, carrying a proven repertoire including *La Jolie Parfumeuse, Madame l'Archiduc, Les Cloches de Corneville, La Marjolaine, La Périchole, La Mascotte, La Fille de Madame Angot* and *Le Grand Casimir.*

Back in Paris, Théo finally found herself another fine new role as the heroine of Paul Lacome's *Madame Boniface* (1883, Friquette)—a piece and character almost too like *La Jolie Parfumeuse* to be true—and she included that show in her repertoire when she returned to America for a second season in 1884 along with *François les bas-bleus, Le Jour et la nuit, La Fille du tambour-major, Giroflé-Girofla, La Petite Mariée, La Timbale d'argent,* et al. A subsequent visit to Mexico reportedly netted her some $50,000.

In 1886 she created the role of Ève in Serpette's *Adam et Ève* (her appearance in ''the costume of Eve'' did more for the box office than her rapier duel), and she subsequently appeared at the Nouveautés in *Ninon* (1887, Ninon), at the Gaîté in Varney's *Dix Jours aux Pyrénées* (1887, Zoë Chaudillac), starred in revivals of *La Mascotte* (1889) and *Le Droit du seigneur* (1889) at the Bouffes, and featured in the production of Pugno's *La Vocation de Marius* (1890, Estelle) and alongside Félix Huguenet as Rose in the vaudeville *Le Brillant Achille* (1892). In 1894 she appeared at Monte Carlo alongside Grisier-Montbazon in *La Timbale d'argent,* after which her performing career seems to have become lighter in its schedules.

In 20 years as a star of the opéra-bouffe and opérette stage, little Mlle Théo's very light soprano never got any bigger, but her charm didn't lessen either, and so no one worried.

Monieur Vachier having quit this earth in 1884 at the age of just 38, she ultimately went into retirement as the wife of a well-off New York art dealer.

Plate 386. **Louise Théo**

THEODORE & CO Musical play in 2 acts by H M Harwood and George Grossmith taken from the play *Théodore et Cie* by Marcel Nancey and Paul Armont [here credited to Paul Gavault]. Lyrics by Adrian Ross and Clifford Grey. Music by Ivor Novello and Jerome Kern. Gaiety Theatre, London, 19 September 1916.

Producers Grossmith and Laurillard, having established themselves at the Gaiety Theatre of the post-Edwardes era with the highly successful *Tonight's the Night,* followed up by using the same company on a musical adaptation of another French farce, Armont [and/or Gavault?] and Nancey's *Théodore et Cie* (Théâtre des Nouveautés 29 September 1909). Pony Twitchin (Leslie Henson), Theodore Wragge (George Grossmith), Fudge Robinson (Peggy Kurton) and their friends convince Bompas, the Earl of Shetland (Davy Burnaby), that it was not his daughter Pansy (Madge Saunders) who was photographed in compromising company by having Pansy dress up and pretend to be an actress who is supposed to be her double. Henri Leoni played an incidental Continental vocalist and Julia James the Hon Sapphire Blissett.

The score, originally to have been written by the dying Paul Rubens, was instead shared between the young composer of the hit song ''Keep the Home Fires Burning,'' 23-year-old Ivor Novello, and the experienced Jerome Kern. The honors were fairly even. Novello's share was topped by the comedy song ''My Friend John'' with which Henson scored the success of the evening, but the other top number, a jaunty comic waltz duo called

''365 Days,'' performed by Henson and Burnaby, was Kern's. Alongside the nominal authors and composers, several of the performers apparently had a hand in the text and Melville Gideon, Phil Braham, Eric Blore, Burnaby and others, including Rubens (one song), also contributed to the score. The potpourri which resulted proved—no little thanks to the great and growing popularity of Henson, and to Grossmith's all-round expertise as performer and producer—a 15-month and 503-performance success, sharing the limelight in the second half of the war years with two pieces of a very different kind, the romantic spectaculars *Chu Chin Chow* and *The Maid of the Mountains.*

An Australian production was mounted for a two-month season in Melbourne in 1919 with a cast including Maud Fane (Fudge), Reginald Roberts (Legallos), Gladys Moncrieff (Pansy), Leslie Holland (Theodore), Sidney Sterling (Earl), Theodore Leonard (Pony) and Florence Young (Sapphire), but the show did not win the same kind of extreme popularity as in Britain and did not get a Sydney showing until 1921 (Theatre Royal 22 October), with Maud Fane and W S Percy featured. America simply passed.

Australia: Theatre Royal, Melbourne 29 November 1919

Recording: original cast recordings on *Jerome Kern in London* (WRC)

THÉRÉSA [VALLADON, Eugénie Emma] (b La Chapelle Gouet, Eure et Loire, 25 April 1837; d Neufchâtel-en-Saosnois, Sarthe, 15 May 1913).

Already in her mid-thirties and more than a little portly, the bosomy, bulldog-featured Mlle Thérésa had made herself into one of the biggest names in the world of the café-concert (''la diva de la choppe'') with her often more-than-risqué songs (''La Femme à la barbe,'' ''Rien n'est sacré pour un sapeur,'' ''C'est dans l'nez qu'ça m'chatouille,'' ''Le bon gîte,'' etc) before she ventured back onto the musical stage where she had taken her first, unnoticed steps as a teenaged chorister years before. Most of her appearances on the musical stage were made in the field of the spectacular féerie where, more often than not, she was able to simply insert a selection of her own material. Pieces like the Gaîté's *La Chatte blanche* (1869, Fanfreluche), Armand de Jallais's productions at the Menus-Plaisirs of *Le Puits qui chante* (1871) and *La Reine Carotte* (1872) and the Gaîté's *La Poule aux oeufs d'or* (1872, Fanfreluche), in which she delivered no fewer than eight numbers amongst the festival of scenic effects which made up the backbone of the entertainment, were typical Thérésa theatre engagements.

She later starred opposite Paulin Ménier at the head of Vasseur's disappointing opérette *La Famille Trouillat* (1874, Mariotte), appeared in Offenbach's Gaîté revival of *La Chatte blanche* (1875), featured in the expanded five-act version of Offenbach's *Geneviève de Brabant* (1875) in which a new role, Briscotte, with new Offenbach songs was specially added for her, and—at a rumored salary of a vast 300 francs a night—starred in the title role of the revamped version of the same composer's *La Boulangère a des écus* (1876), where her boundless personality almost succeeded in making the unlucky piece into a first-class success. She returned to the féerie to play Regaillette in *Les Sept Chateaux du Diable* (Théâtre du Châtelet, 1876–77) equipped, again, with her repertoire of café-concert songs, but she also played in revue at the Menus-Plaisirs, and in 1880 took the title role of the vaudeville *Madame Grégoire* at the former Menus-Plaisirs (now the Théâtre des Arts) singing eight numbers by such composers as Planquette, Serpette and Coedès. ''Thérésa and her songs constitute the whole piece,'' remarked a critic. In 1881 she starred in the title role of Varney's *La Reine des Halles* at the Comédie-Parisien.

Having already once temporarily retired, to marriage as Mme Guilloreau, in 1878, Thérésa retired definitively from performing in 1893 and spent the last 20 years of her life in respectable retirement in the Sâone.

Two books of memoirs—not written by the star, although said to have been ''recounted'' by her—turned out to be slightly spicy semi-fiction rather than autobiography.

Memoirs: Blum, W: *Mémoires de Thérésa* (1865), Morel, H: *Nouveaux Mémoires de Thérésa* (1868); Biography: Blanche, J: *Thérésa* (La Fresnaye-sur-Chedouet, 1981)

THESPIS, or The Gods Grown Old Original grotesque opera in 2 acts by W S Gilbert. Music by Arthur Sullivan. Gaiety Theatre, London, 26 December 1871.

The first collaboration of Messrs Gilbert and Sullivan, this two-act ''grotesque opera'' was produced as the 1871 Christmas entertainment at the Gaiety Theatre, where manager John Hollingshead had the previous year initiated the practice of staging an operatic extravaganza with an original score of music for the festive season with his production of Alfred Thompson and Hervé's highly successful *Aladdin the Second.*

Gilbert's tale (apparently borrowed from the old Viennese Posse *Die Schauspieler-Gesellschaft in Olymp,* Theater in der Josefstadt 13 December 1825) had the aged Gods of Olympus temporarily giving over their places to an Athenian troupe of actors whilst they descend to earth for a quick look-around. The mortals make a real mess of their mountain-sitting job, and after many jollities they are sent scurrying back to earth. The previous year's stars were well in evidence again: last year's Aladdin, Nellie Farren, played Mercury the ''celestial drudge'' and Johnnie Toole was Thespis, the manager of the theatricals, whilst Connie Loseby (Nicemis), the composer's brother Fred Sullivan (Apollo), Annie Tremaine (Daphne), Mlle Clary (Sparkeion) and the Payne family of pantomimists were also featured in a part-extravaganza, part-burlesque, part-fairy play, part-pantomime entertainment which—even if it was occasionally a touch sophisticated for some of the Gaiety audience—was just the ticket for Christmas.

Of Sullivan's score, the ballad "Little Maid of Arcadee" proved the take-away song, whilst Nellie Farren scored roundly with a number describing her job, "It's the Way of the World," and Toole launched patteringly into a cautionary tale which asserted "I once knew a man who discharged a function on the North South Eastern Diddlesex Junction" and had as little to do with Ancient Greece as most of the entertainment.

Thespis ran to almost three hours at its first performance, but it was subsequently cut to more like two—a necessity, as it shared the program with other pieces, including, at one stage, Suppé's *Die schöne Galathee.* It proved less successful than *Aladdin II,* but nevertheless played 63 times and was revived for an extra benefit performance in April the following year. The show was never given a full-scale revival, although D'Oyly Carte considered remounting it as a Christmas piece in 1875, and the musical score was at some stage lost, so that Sullivan's assertion that he plundered it for tunes for his later works cannot be substantiated.

Several efforts have been made to stage the show with Gilbert's lyrics set to replacement music.

Literature: Rees, T: *Thespis: A Gilbert & Sullivan Enigma* (Dillons University Bookshop, London, 1964)

Plate 387. **Thérésa** *decked out for an over-the-top role as a medieval maid in* Geneviève de Brabant.

THEY'RE PLAYING OUR SONG Musical comedy in 2 acts by Neil Simon. Lyrics by Carol Bayer Sager. Music by Marvin Hamlisch. Imperial Theater, New York, 11 February 1979.

A virtually two-handed musical play, allegedly based on the relationship between its composer and lyricist, *They're Playing Our Song* was one of the few musicals of its era which put the comedy back into the genre that had once been freely called musical comedy, favoring a high-class comic libretto as its basis rather than the extravaganza of visual elements emphasized in many contemporary shows.

The highly successful songwriter Vernon Gersch (Robert Klein) is in need of a new lyricist, and what he gets is Sonia Walsk (Lucie Arnaz). She sweeps crazily into his life and turns out to be the most neurotic, unreliable, impossible little collaborator he could have chosen. But she can write lyrics. By the end of Act I they are lovers, and she has sent her even more neurotic ex, Leon, on his way. By the beginning of Act II she has moved in with Vernon and they actually get down to some work. But Leon keeps ringing up whenever he has one of his crises, and his omnipresence eventually results in Vernon and Sonia's partnership—professional and personal—breaking up. However, Leon (who is never seen) finally gets his life in order and, by the final curtain, Vernon and Sonia are back together again.

A number of the show's nine songs were displayed as the product of Vernon and Sonia's work together—the ballad "I Still Believe in Love," the lively "Workin' IT Out," "Fallin'"—and, thus, they were written in a style that adapted popular-music tones and conventions (including the half-dozen backing singers who made up the rest of the cast as the hero and heroine's alter egos) to stage considerations. The remainder, topped by the rhythmic and gently tongue-in-cheek title song, a pensive and plotworthy "If (S)He Really Knew Me" and the romantic "When You're in My Arms" and "Just for Tonight," took up the same tone, in a short score which illustrated

THE GAIETY PROGRAMME.

Sole Lessee and Manager ... Mr JOHN HOLLINGSHEAD.

MR. J. L. TOOLE

EVERY EVENING

To commence at 7 with HENRY J. BYRON'S Popular Three Act Drama,

DEARER THAN LIFE

Michael Garner .. (his Original Character) ... Mr J. L. TOOLE
Uncle Ben ... ... Mr JOHN MACLEAN
Bob Gassitt ... ... Mr J. G. TAYLOR
Charles ... ... Mr W. RIGNOLD
Bolter ... (with a Song) ... Mr F. SULLIVAN
Mr Kedgley ... ... Mr SYDNEY DYNELEY
Lucy Garner ... ... Miss ADA CAVENDISH
Mrs Garner Mrs H LEIGH Mrs Pellet Miss ANNIE TREMAINE
Mrs Mingle ... ... Miss JOLLY

At 9.15, an entirely Original Grotesque Opera, in Two Acts, entitled

THESPIS.

Or The Gods Grown Old.

Written by W. S. GILBERT. Music Composed by ARTHUR SULLıVAN.

Jupiter ... Aged Olympians ... Mr JOHN MACLEAN
Apollo ... ... Mr F. SULLIVAN
Mars ... . Mr WOOD
Diana ... ... Mrs H. LEIGH
Mercury ... . Miss E. FARREN

Other Aged Deities by Members of the Company.

Thespis ... (Manager of a Travelling Theatrical Company) .. Mr J. L. TOOLE
Sillimon .. (his Stage Manager) ... Mr J G. TAYLOR
Timidon ... Thespians .. Mr MARSHALL
Tipseion ... ... Mr ROBERT SOUTAR
Preposteros ... ... Mr H. PAYNE
Stupidas ... .. Mr F. PAYNE
Sparkeion ... ... Mdlle CLARY
Nicemis ... ... Miss CONSTANCE LOSEBY
Pretteia ... ... Miss BEREND
Daphne ... ... Miss ANNIE TREMAINE
Cymon .. ... Miss L. WILSON

Ballet, Chorus, and Increased Band.

ACT I Ruined Temple of the Gods on Mount Olvmbus. | ACT II. The Tembie on Olvmbus restored

In Act First, A GRAND BALLET.

Principal Dancers, Mdlle. ESTA, Misses L. WRIGHT, SMITHERS, & the Gaiety Corps de Ballet.

NEW DRESSES. NEW SCENERY BY MR. GORDON.

Plate 388. **Thespis.** *Gilbert and Sullivan’s names together on the Gaiety Theatre’s program for the first time.*

the endlessly comic dialogue and action of the piece to a nicety.

They’re Playing Our Song was a first-class Broadway success, running for 1,082 performances in New York before setting out for an overseas career which included productions in places that few other recent English-language musicals had got anywhere near. John Waters and Jacki Weaver starred in an extremely successful Australian production, which spawned both revivals and tours, Tom Conti and Gemma Craven were featured in a slightly undercooked London staging which nevertheless played 667 performances before the show was taken up by provincial venues, Gaby Gasser and Harald Juhnke introduced a German version of *Sie spielen unser Lied* in Berlin and Michaela Rosen and Peter Fröhlich starred in a Viennese production (ad Jurgen Wöffler, Christoph Busse). Luigi Proietti and Loretta Goggi featured in Italy’s production of *Stanno suonando la nostra canzone* at Milan’s Teatro Nuovo (11 November 1981 ad Roberto Lerici, Carla Vistarini), Mauricio Herrera and Macaria played *Están tocando nuestra canción* (ad Sanchez Navarro-Fresan) in Mexico’s Spanish-language version, and Marianne Weber and Jachen Janett introduced the piece to Switzerland at St Gallen (Kellerbühne 29 December 1990).

The show’s economic size, allied to its ubiquitous success, encouraged a proliferation of productions in theatres and on circuits with limited resources (although the original production effortlessly encompassed a large stage and a by no means inexpensive setting), and *They’re Playing Our Song*’s mixture of bright, modern comedy and music meant that its crazy but loveable pair of rib-squeezingly real Jewish New Yorkers, their comical lines and their songs, went down a treat all round the world. Few theatres felt obliged to sink to the gimmickry of one sad Salzburgian production which desperately piled all the campy clichés and accessories this musical so refreshingly avoided back in, and pictured Vernon as Groucho Marx and Sonia as Marilyn Monroe.

Australia: Theatre Royal, Sydney 23 August 1980; UK: Shaftesbury Theatre 1 October 1980; Germany: Theater am Kurfürstendamm *Sie spielen unser Lied* 1981; Hungary: Fővárosi Operettszínház *A mi dalunk szól* 26 October 1984; Austria: Wiener Kammerspiele *Sie spielen unser Lied* 1985

Recordings: original cast (Polydor), London cast (TER), Australian cast (Festival), Italian cast (Polydor), Austrian cast (Stage), Mexican cast (Polydor), German cast (Kontra-Kreis-Theater), etc

THIS’LL MAKE YOU WHISTLE Musical show in 2 acts by Guy Bolton and Fred Thompson. Music and lyrics by Maurice Sigler, Al Goodhart and Al Hoffman. King’s Theatre, Southsea, 16 December 1935; Palace Theatre, London, 15 September 1936.

The third Jack Buchanan–Elsie Randolph star vehicle, following the successes of their pairings in *That’s a Good Girl* and *Mr Whittington, This’ll Make You Whistle* relied, as had the first of their pieces, very largely on some farcical and funny scenes (directed by Buchanan) and the dancing of the two favorites (ch: Buddy Bradley). Buchanan played Bill Hopping, who pretends to be a dreadfully unproper person in order to disgust the rich and puritanical Uncle Sebastian (Charles Stone) of his now unwanted fiancée Laura (Sylvia Leslie) into forcing her to break off the engagement. Uncle, however, is not in truth so very puritanical and it is Bill’s beloved Joan (Jean Gillie) who gets upset, until all comes right for the final curtain. Miss Randolph was featured as Bobbie Rivers, encouraged into disguise as a French tart as part of the plan.

It was a well-used plot, illustrated by a bundle of unexceptional songs (one of which, apparently straight-faced, actually rhymed ‘‘spoon,’’ ‘‘June’’ and ‘‘moon’’), and when the show was produced out of town Buchanan decided that it was not ready for a London showing. He toured it for four months, closed, cut and rewrote, and relaunched the piece at Blackpool in September of the following year. A week later it came to town, spit-and-polished by its touring experience, and won a happy reception for its favorite pair and their routines. After four months at the Palace Theatre it transferred to Daly's for its last weeks, and closed after 190 performances. During that time, the stars had taken time off to record a film version and that film actually opened in London during the last week of the show's stage run, so that Jack and Elsie were visible simultaneously in the West End on celluloid (79 minutes) and in the flesh (full-length) for a short while.

Film: 1936

THOMAS, John Charles (b Meyerdale, Pa, 6 September 1887; d Apple Valley, Calif, 13 December 1960). A tall, fair, blue-eyed and rich-voiced American baritone, best remembered for his recordings of ballads and devotional songs.

Thomas came to the stage via church choirs, Baltimore's medical school and Peabody College to begin his career as a musical-theatre singer touring in Gilbert and Sullivan with De Wolf Hopper. He made his first appearance on Broadway in *The Passing Show of 1913* (Inspector Burke, with a solo ''Strongheart'') at the age of 25, and soon rose to take good roles alongside Emma Trentini in *The Peasant Girl* (1915, *Polenblut,* Bolo Baránski), as the mountain-climbing Baron Franz von Hansen wooing Marguerite Namara in the successful American production of *Alone at Last* (1915, *Endlich allein*), in the revusical *Step This Way* (1916, Charlie Chetwynd), in *Her Soldier Boy* (1916, *Az obsitos,* Alain Teniers), Lehár's *The Star Gazer* (1917, *Der Sterngucker,* Arthur Howard) and in the title role of a revival of De Koven's *The Highwayman* (1917, Dick Fitzgerald). He toured in the principal role of Romberg's *Maytime* (Richard Wayne) played on Broadway by Charles Purcell, and then returned to New York to score his biggest stage success opposite Wilda Bennett as the hero of the Jacobi/Kreisler musical *Apple Blossoms* (1919, Philip Campbell, ''You Are Free''). He also starred in Victor Jacobi's last work *Love Letters* (1921), the unsuccessful musicalization of Molnár's celebrated *A farkas.*

Thomas spent several years at Brussels's Théâtre de la Monnaie (1925–28) and later sang at Covent Garden and the Metropolitan Opera, making his career largely in opera, concerts, recording and broadcasting, but he ultimately returned, after 15 years' absence, to the musical theatre and made a series of appearances on the American West Coast during the late 1930s and early 1940s, playing Schubert in *Blossom Time,* Barinkay in a badly perverted version of *Der Zigeunerbaron* which presented him as a strolling lion tamer, in *HMS Pinafore,* as Bumerli in *The Chocolate Soldier* and in *Music in the Air.*

Plate 389. **This'll Make You Whistle.** *Jack Buchanan and Jean Gillie did—on-stage as well as off.*

THOMPSON, Alexander M[attock] (b Karlsruhe, 9 May 1861; d London, 25 March 1948). British librettist of the early 20th century.

Manchester-based socialist writer and journalist and founder of the left-wing journal *Clarion,* Thompson also worked as a theatre critic under the pseudonym ''Dangle.'' He came to the theatre slowly, making his first notable stage appearances with the texts for pantomimes for his crony Robert Courtneidge, manager of the Prince's Theatre in Manchester. Courtneidge was, thereafter, the provider of virtually all of Thompson's theatrical work, to which his own name was also sometimes appended as co-writer.

Thompson began his connection with English musical comedy when he reorganized the text of Walter Ellis's *The Blue Moon* before Courtneidge brought it to town after its author's death, and he then supplied the hotchpotch of a libretto (allegedly, but not evidently, based on Shakespeare's *As You Like It*) for Courtneidge's successful musical piece *The Dairymaids.* In real contrast to this piece of jobbery, he next expertly fulfilled the task of slimming and resituating Henry Fielding's *Tom Jones* as the libretto for the enduring comic opera of the same name, but he had his biggest success in fleshing out Mark Ambient's ideas for a fantastical musical as *The Arcadians.*

His first all-original text, the comic and romantic Japanoiseries of *The Mousmé,* was a costly failure for his producer friend, but Thompson and Courtneidge had another success together with the London version of Leo Fall's *Der liebe Augustin,* adapted and produced as *Princess Caprice.* Having enjoyed Courtneidge's high days with him, Thompson continued to supply scripts for his later and less-fortunate ventures. A revusical piece of Ancient Roman foolery called *Oh, Caesar!* failed to make it to town, whilst the cloak-and-swashbuckle *The Rebel Maid* with its durable paean to "The Fishermen of England" survived largely with choral societies after 114 London performances.

His autobiography was amusingly if tellingly titled *Here I Lie.*

1897 **Toto and Tata** (*Toto*) English version w lyrics by J J Wood, E Boyd Jones (Grand Theatre, Leeds)

1903 **Chilpéric** new English version w Richard Mansell (Coronet Theatre)

1905 **The Blue Moon** revised version Lyric Theatre 28 August

1906 **The Dairymaids** (Paul Rubens, Frank E Tours/Rubens, Arthur Wimperis/w Robert Courtneidge) Apollo Theatre 14 April

1907 **Tom Jones** (Edward German/Charles H Taylor/w Courtneidge) Apollo Theatre 17 April

1909 **The Arcadians** (Howard Talbot, Lionel Monckton/Wimperis/w Ambient) Shaftesbury Theatre 28 April

1911 **The Mousmé** (Talbot, Monckton/Wimperis, Percy Greenbank/w Courtneidge) Shaftesbury Theatre 9 September

1912 **Princess Caprice** (*Der liebe Augustin*) English version (Shaftesbury Theatre)

1916 **Oh, Caesar!** (Nat D Ayer, Arthur Wood/Adrian Ross/w Max Pemberton) Royal Lyceum Theatre, Edinburgh 23 December

1921 **The Rebel Maid** (Montague Phillips/Gerald Dalton/w Bertrand Davis) Empire Theatre 12 March

Autobiography: *Here I Lie* (Routledge, London, 1937)

THOMPSON, Alfred [JONES, Thompson Ernest] (b England, c1831; d Barnegat Park, NY, 31 August 1895). Librettist and designer for some of the best-written and -designed early British musicals.

Tall, elegant and handsome Alfred Thompson was educated at Rugby and Cambridge and began a military career in the Eniskillen Dragoons. However, having risen to the rank of Captain, he renounced the army to study art in Munich and Paris and there "caught the continental style of illustration, associated with the name of Grévin." On returning to Britain he took up journalism, becoming sometime co-editor of *The Mask* with Leopold Lewis of *The Bells* fame, and he got his first chance in the theatrical world when John Hollingshead took him on as a design coordinator and house author at the new Gaiety Theatre. His contribution to the theatre's opening bill was an adaptation of *L'Escamoteur* as *On the Cards* and the design of the costumes for Gilbert's burlesque *Robert the Devil.*

Over the next three years, Thompson took charge of the designing at the Gaiety, giving a care to the costuming of burlesques such as Gilbert's *Thespis* and Offenbach's *La Princesse de Trébizonde* not usually associated with that form of entertainment—"for delicate and harmonious combinations of colours, mostly half-tints, he was quite unrivalled . . . the old coarse costume combinations—strong reds, strong greens, strong blues and strong yellows—were doomed from the hour that Thompson's dresses appeared before the footlights." Hollingshead wrote, "Alfred Thompson was very clever and tricky with his costumes. He was the first man to utilize upholstery cretonnes for dresses, and this cheap material, at a distance, under the glamour of stage lights, looked like the most expensive tapestry products of Lyons. His embroideries, to use the theatrical slang, were 'faked.' On a groundwork of white satinette he stencilled patterns, with brown 'smudge,' rubbed across a perforated piece of paper. When the paper was removed the pattern was visible on the satin and had the appearance on the stage of elaborate needlework. Alfred Thompson could not only design a dress, but like M Worth of Paris, if necessary, he could 'fit' and make one. He ought to have started a fancy millinery business, and made a fortune."

Thompson's talents, however, were not limited to those of a dressmaker, or even a watercolorist. He also supplied the scripts for the Gaiety burlesques *Columbus* and *Linda di Chamouni,* translated Hérold's opéra-comique *Zampa* into a new English version for Hollingshead and provided the texts for the Gaiety's two original operas-bouffes, *Aladdin II* and *Cinderella the Younger,* which he also designed. Although Hollingshead seems to have considered him a better artist than a writer, his scripts for *Aladdin II* and for *Cinderella the Younger,* in particular, were as good as anything of their kind produced in the English language up to the time, and both his burlesques were subsequently revived.

Thompson's success at the Gaiety led to his services, notably as a costume designer, becoming called for elsewhere and he was summoned by Boucicault to design the multitude of clothes for the superspectacular *Babil and Bijou* at Covent Garden, and by the Alhambra to outfit their newly commissioned, very own Offenbach spectacular *Whittington,* their English/French *The Demon's*

Plate 390. **Alfred Thompson's** *Columbus burlesque for the Gaiety Theatre sketched by the* London Illustrated News.

Bride and a number of other productions, whilst the go-ahead Kate Santley had him both design her *Cattarina* (1874) and also write her a forepiece. As *The Three Conspirators* that little piece of quick-change foolery proved a hugely successful vehicle for the fair manageress. Thompson also designed the grandiose Covent Garden pantomime *Sleeping Beauty,* Lydia Thompson's version of *Le Grand Duc de Matapa, Piff-Paff* (1876), Lauro Rossi and Frank Marshall's production of their five-act opera *Bjorn* (1877) and a long list of other productions ranging from Shakespeare to burlesque.

In the late 1870s Thompson became for a time the manager of the Manchester Prince's Theatre and Theatre Royal and under his management were produced there Cellier's *Belladonna* (for which he authored the libretto), Stanislaus's *The Lancashire Witches* (1879) and John Crook's *The King's Dragoons* (1879). In the early 1880s he created the ballets *Hawaia* (1880) and *Cabul* (1882), mounted at the Alhambra by Katti Lanner.

In the mid-1880s Thompson moved on to America, and there his monocled figure became a well-known one in theatrical circles as he worked as author, director and set and above all costume designer for the New York and Chicago theatres. He authored the comic opera *Pepita,* composed by Teddy Solomon for his ''wife,'' Lillian Russell, and he worked with considerable success as author-director, on a series of fairy-tale musicals written, designed and staged for producer David Henderson at the Chicago Opera House. *The Crystal Slipper* totted up 858 nights in two runs, and *The Arabian Nights* 492 in one. The two finally fell out over Henderson's creative accounting, and Thompson walked out. He directed a number of other spectaculars around the country and was reponsible for the direction of an 1885 revival of *A Comedy of Errors,* into which he managed to introduce an Amazon March and a 16-coryphée ballet, and of a *Romeo and Juliet* decorated with ''characteristic dances'' and also staged the opening of the Madison Square Garden Amphitheater in 1890.

Thompson designed *The Seven Ages* (1889), Henry Dixey's unfortunate *Rip* (1890), the clothes for De Wolf Hopper's *Wang* (1891), Digby Bell's *Jupiter* (1892), *Miss Helyett* (1892), the highly successful *The Isle of Champagne* (1892), Marie Tempest's *The Fencing Master* (1892), Rice's *1492* (1893), *Panjandrum* (1893) and *Le Voyage de Suzette* (1893), and provided costumes for a number of other visually based productions, musical and otherwise. On the authorial front, he wrote a pantomime, *Pierrot the Painter,* mounted at the Berkeley Lyceum in 1893, and a sketch, *Around the Operas in Twenty*

Minutes, played in *The Passing Show of 1894,* which seems to have been his last produced show.

In his last years Thompson fell into financial problems, and shortly before his death the profession mounted a benefit for him.

His son (b London, 6 December 1869; d Toronto, 20 March 1900) worked as an actor under the name of Ernest Tarleton.

1867 **The Bird of Paradise** (comp/arr Henry Tissington) New York Theater 29 January

1867 **The Lion's Mouth** (Virginia Gabriel) Gallery of Illustration 31 May

1869 **Columbus, or The Original Pitch in a Merry Key** (arr Meyer Lutz) Gaiety Theatre 17 May

1869 **Linda of Chamouni, or Not a Formosa** (arr Lutz) Gaiety Theatre 13 September

1870 **Zampa** English version (Gaiety Theatre)

1870 **Aladdin II, or An Old Lamp in a New Light** (Hervé) Gaiety Theatre 23 December

1871 **Cinderella the Younger** (aka *Javotte*) (Émile Jonas) Gaiety Theatre 23 September

1872 **How I Found Crusoe, or A Flight of Imagination from Geneva to Crusopolis** (pasticcio arr Frederic Stanislaus) Olympic Theatre 28 December

1874 **Calypso, or The Art of Love** (pasticcio) 1 act Royal Court Theatre 6 May

1874 **The Three Conspirators** (pasticcio) 1 act Theatre Royal, Belfast 16 October; Charing Cross Theatre 12 July 1875

1876 **Orphée aux enfers** new English version (Royalty Theatre)

1878 **Belladonna, or The Little Beauty and the Great Beast** (Alfred Cellier) Prince's Theatre, Manchester 27 April

1878 **The Yellow Dwarf** (pasticcio /w Robert Reece) Theatre Royal, Manchester 6 December; Her Majesty's Theatre 30 December 1882

1886 **Pepita, or The Girl with the Glass Eyes** (Edward Solomon) Union Square Theater, New York 16 March

1887 **Aladdin, or The Wonderful Lamp** (various) Grand Opera House, Chicago 4 June

1888 **The Arabian Nights** (revised *Aladdin, or the Wonderful Lamp*) Standard Theater, New York 12 September

1888 **The Crystal Slipper, or Prince Prettywitz and little Cinderella** (Fred Eustis/w Harry B Smith) Grand Opera House, Chicago 18 June; Star Theater, New York 26 November

THOMPSON, Fred[erick James] (b London, 24 January 1884; d London, 10 April 1949). Prolific librettist for the musical stage on both sides of the Atlantic.

Thompson began his working life articled to an architect before taking his draftsmanship to the *London Opinion* and a job as a theatrical caricaturist. He moved on to work on several other newspapers before throwing drawing in altogether and for a while taking employment as an actor. It was at this stage that he made his first attempts at writing for the theatre. He wrote lyrics for a number of music-hall sketches and songs (''For a Woman's Honour'' for Millie Hylton, 1910, etc) and made his first significant inroad when he contributed to George Grossmith's script for the revue *Eightpence a Mile* (1913), and it was Grossmith again who gave him his first opportunity to work on a major musical by entrusting him with the adaptation of the famous farce *Pink Dominoes* as the libretto for the successful musical comedy *Tonight's the Night.*

Thompson subsequently wrote the text for Phil Braham's little variety-house pieces *Alice Up-to-Date* (w Eric Blore), *Violet and Pink* and *Sugar and Spice,* for the Frank Tours revue *The Merry-go-Round* and Nat Ayer's *Pell Mell* (w Morris Harvey) and *Look Who's Here,* and worked again with Grossmith first on the adaptation of the French revue *Les Fils Touffe sont à Paris* into the highly successful *The Bing Boys Are Here* and later on its successors *The Bing Girls Are There* (w Grossmith), *The Other Bing Boys* and *The Bing Boys on Broadway* (w Howard Vernon). His later work, however, was largely in the way of libretti for book musicals.

Following his debut success at metamorphosing a French farce into a musical, Thompson moved on to an even greater triumph with a similar operation on a couple of English ones, adaptating Pinero's plays *The Magistrate* and *In Chancery* as *The Boy* and *Who's Hooper?* for the Adelphi Theatre and comedian Bill Berry. He also accomplished the adaptation of the tricksy French sex tale of *Afgar* into an English version for Cochran with such skill that the British (and comparatively undersexed) version clearly outran the original, but the same skill deserted him on the even more tricksy/sexy text of *Phi-Phi* and the piece as staged by Cochran proved to have had the fun quite murdered out of it. In the year 1919, Thompson dominated the West End musical theatre, being billed with a share in the credits of no less than six libretti.

In 1924 he moved his base to America and over half a dozen years furthered his musical-theatre success with libretti for a string of musicals, the majority of which were decided successes—*Lady, Be Good!, Tip-Toes, Rio Rita, Funny Face, The Five o'Clock Girl, Sons o' Guns*—before returning to Britain at the dawn of the 1930s. His most significant contribution to the West End musical stage in the following years was, in collaboration with his frequent Broadway partner Guy Bolton, in constructing the comical vehicles with which Leslie Henson, Fred Emney and Richard Hearne brought the Gaiety Theatre back to its former place at the head of London's musical theatre—*Seeing Stars, Swing Along, Going Greek*—but he also worked on vehicles for the other top teams of the musical-comedy moment: Jack Buchanan and Elsie Randolph's *This'll Make You Whistle, Hide and Seek* for

Bobby Howes and Cicely Courtneidge, and *Going Places* for Arthur Riscoe and company.

Thompson subsequently spent a second period in America, and had his last hit at the age of 60 when he worked on the libretto for the comical, if old-fashioned, *Follow the Girls.* He was last represented on Broadway when an original story of his went into the making of the very shortlived 1945 musical *The Girl from Nantucket* (mus: Jacques Belasco, Adelphi Theater).

One of the very best comic librettists of the interwar period when light and often farcical comedy rather than sentiment or spectacle was the keynote of the most popular musical plays, Thompson had considerable successes on both sides of the Atlantic, and over 30 years lined up a list of hit credits which few other bookwriters equaled.

1908 **The Little Jockey** sketch

1911 **Freddie's Flat** (Cecil Cameron/H E Garden) 1 act Alhambra 4 September

1913 **Alice Up-to-Date** (Philip Braham/w Eric Blore) 1 act London Pavilion 29 December

1914 **Violet and Pink** (Braham) East Ham Palace 4 May, London Pavilion 11 May

1914 **Tonight's the Night** (Paul Rubens/Rubens, Percy Greenbank) Shubert Theater, New York 24 December

1915 **The Lady Birds** (J M Glover/w Luri Wylie, Alfred Parker) 3 scenes Theatre Royal, Plymouth 9 August

1915 **The Only Girl** English adaptation (Apollo Theatre)

1916 **Mr Manhattan** (Howard Talbot, Braha, Frank E Tours/w C H Bovill) Prince of Wales Theatre 30 March

1916 **Houp-La!** (Nat D Ayer/Greenbank, Hugh E Wright/w Wright) St Martin's Theatre 23 November

1917 **The Boy** (Talbot, Lionel Monckton/Adrian Ross, P Greenbank) Adelphi Theatre 14 September

1919 **Who's Hooper** (Talbot, Ivor Novello/Clifford Grey) Adelphi Theatre 13 September

1919 **Afgar** English version w Worton David (Adelphi Theatre)

1919 **Baby Bunting** (Ayer/Grey/w David) Shaftesbury Theatre 25 September

1919 **The Kiss Call** (Ivan Caryll/Adrian Ross, P Greenbank, Grey) Gaiety Theatre 8 October

1919 **Maggie** (Marcel Lattès/Ross/w H F Maltby) Oxford Theatre 22 October

1919 **The Eclipse** (Herman Darewski, Melville Gideon, et al/ Ross/w E Phillips Oppenheim) Garrick Theatre 12 November

1921 **The Golden Moth** (Novello/w P G Wodehouse) Adelphi Theatre 5 October

1922 **Phi-Phi** English version w Grey (London Pavilion)

1923 **The Cousin from Nowhere** (*Der Vetter aus Dingsda*) English libretto (Prince's Theatre)

1924 **Marjorie** (Sigmund Romberg, Herbert Stothart, Stephen Jones/Grey, Harold Atteridge) Shubert Theater, New York 11 August

1924 **Lady, Be Good!** (George Gershwin/Ira Gershwin/w Guy Bolton) Liberty Theater, New York 1 December

1925 **Tell Me More!** (G Gershwin/I Gershwin, B G De Sylva/w William K Wells) Gaiety Theater, New York 13 April

1925 **Tip-Toes** (G Gershwin/I Gershwin/w Bolton) Liberty Theater, New York 28 December

1927 **Rio Rita** (Harry Tierney/Joseph McCarthy/w Bolton) Ziegfeld Theater, New York 2 February

1927 **The Five o'Clock Girl** (Harry Ruby/Bert Kalmar/w Bolton) 44th Street Theater, New York 10 October

1927 **Funny Face** (G Gershwin/I Gershwin/w Paul Gerard Smith) Alvin Theater, New York 22 November

1928 **Here's Howe** (Roger Wolfe Kahn, Joseph Meyer/Irving Caesar/w Gerard Smith) Broadhurst Theater, New York 1 May

1928 **Treasure Girl** (G Gershwin/I Gershwin/w Vincent Lawrence) Alvin Theater, New York 8 November

1929 **Sons o' Guns** (Arthur Swanstrom, et al/w Jack Donahue, Connolly) Imperial Theater, New York 26 November

1931 **The Song of the Drum** (Vivian Ellis, Herman Finck/ Desmond Carter/w Bolton) Theatre Royal, Drury Lane 9 January

1932 **Out of the Bottle** (Ellis, Oscar Levant/w Grey) London Hippodrome 11 June

1935 **Seeing Stars** (Martin Broones/Graham John/w Bolton) Gaiety Theatre 31 October

1936 **Swing Along** (Broones/John/w Bolton, Douglas Furber) Gaiety Theatre 2 September

1936 **This'll Make You Whistle** (Maurice Sigler, Al Goodhart, Al Hoffman/w Bolton) Palace Theatre 14 September

1936 **Going Places** (Ellis/w Bolton) Savoy Theatre 8 October

1937 **Going Greek** (Sam Lerner, Goodhart, Hoffman/w Furber, Bolton) Gaiety Theatre 16 September

1937 **Hide and Seek** (Ellis, Lerner, Goodhart, Hoffman/w Bolton, Furber) London Hippodrome 14 October

1938 **The Fleet's Lit Up** (Ellis/w Bolton, Bert Lee) London Hippodrome 17 August

1938 **Bobby Get Your Gun** (Jack Waller, Joe Tunbridge/Grey, Lee, Carter/w Bolton, Lee) Adelphi Theatre 7 October

1939 **Magyar Melody** (George Posford, Bernard Grün/Harry Purcell/w Eric Maschwitz, Bolton) His Majesty's Theatre 20 January

1940 **Present Arms** (Noel Gay/Frank Eyton) Prince of Wales Theatre 13 May

1942 **The Lady Comes Across** (Vernon Duke/John Latouche/w Dawn Powell) 44th Street Theater, New York 9 January

1944 **Follow the Girls** (Phil Charig/Dan Shapiro, Milton Pascal/w Bolton, Eddie Davis) Century Theater, New York 8 April

1944 **Glad to See You** (Jule Styne/Sammy Cahn/w Davis) Shubert Theater, Philadelphia 13 November

1945 **The Girl from Nantucket** (Jacques Belasco/Kay Twomey/w Bern Giler) Forrest Street Theater, Philadelphia 9 October

THOMPSON, Harlan (b Hannibal, Mo, 24 September 1890; d New York, 26 October 1966). Librettist to some happy little Broadway shows of the 1920s.

A chemistry teacher, a reporter for the *Kansas Star,* a drama critic, a First World War artillery lieutenant and air force commanding officer, Thompson did not get around to writing significantly for the theatre until he returned from overseas service at the end of the War. He essayed at first in the field of vaudeville, but he found success with his first real venture in the musical theatre, paired with songwriter Harry Archer on the farcical musical comedy *Little Jessie James* (''I Love You'').

The pair became hailed as the natural successors to the team of Kern and Bolton in the production of an intimate, book-based style of musical comedy, as they turned out a four-year, four-show series of similar pieces for the Broadway stage. *Little Jessie James* proved to be the most widely successful, being played in varying versions all around the world, but Thompson's libretto to *Merry, Merry* also found its way to Britain, where, adapted by Bert Lee and R P Weston, it was attached to a new score by Jack Waller, Joe Tunbridge and Harris Weston for a reasonable West End run (Carlton Theatre 28 February 1929, 131 performances) under the same title.

Thompson subsequently went on to Hollywood where, over a decade, he wrote screenplays and lyrics for a number of Paramount films (the lyrics to Oscar Straus's music for *Married in Hollywood, The Phantom President, I'm No Angel, Here Is My Heart, Rose of the Rancho,* etc), and also worked as a film producer (*College Holiday, The Big Broadcast of 1938, Romance in the Dark, Paris Honeymoon, The Road to Singapore*).

In 1940 he attempted a return to the theatre, but his first new play closed on the road, and he was never to make it back to Broadway.

1923 **Little Jessie James** (Harry Archer) Longacre Theater 15 August

1924 **My Girl** (Archer) Vanderbilt Theater 24 November

1925 **Merry, Merry** (Archer) Vanderbilt Theater 24 September

1926 **Twinkle, Twinkle** (Archer) Liberty Theater 16 November

THOMPSON, Lydia [THOMPSON, Eliza Hodges] (b London, 19 February 1838; d London, 17 November 1908).

Lydia Thompson is one of the theatre's ''legends,'' and as in the case of other such legendary figures, the truth of her life and career has become, down the years, fictionalized to a stage where it was rather difficult to exhume the truth. But here it is. ''Lydia'' was (in spite of all that has been written to the contrary) born in the parish of St Paul's, Covent Garden, the second daughter of Cumberland-born Philip Thompson, sometime publican of London's ''Sheridan Knowles'' public house in the now defunct Brydges Street, other-times an account agent, other-times probably something else, and his wife Eliza née Cooper, previously the widow Griggs. Mythology says that mother Eliza was ''a Quaker lady who was fond of the stage.'' She was, in fact, whether Quaker or not, a pub landlady. Mythology also says, with meaningful whiffs of a gentlewoman in tight straits, that ''Lydia went on the stage after her father died.'' Well, that she certainly did, for Philip Thompson gave up the ghost in 1842, when Eliza junior was just 4 years old. Mother Eliza, however, with enormous promptitude, tied herself up with another publican, Edward Hodges of the Canonbury Tavern. Whose surname makes you wonder just whose child Lydia (like her younger brother, Alfred Hodges Thompson) really was. But the young Lydia wasn't so precocious as to hit the stage at 4. She was actually quite 14 years old (and not 10 or 11 as often related) when she joined the dancing chorus at Her Majesty's Theatre in 1852.

She appeared thereafter with the kiddie-show the ''Living Marionettes'' at the Linwood Gallery (1853), but she first won critical and public notice playing the part of Little Silverhair (with pieces of silver thread woven into her hair) in the pantomime *Harlequin and the Three Bears* at the Haymarket Theatre at Christmas that year. In 1854 she featured at the Haymarket as a solo dancer in the Grand Oriental Spectacle of *Mr Buckstone's Voyage Round the Globe,* before going on to play a season at the St James's Theatre where her appearances included the burlesques *Ganem, the Slave of Love* and Charles Selby's *The Spanish Dancers* in which she caused a small sensation with her imitation-cum-parody of the extraordinary Spanish dancer Perea Nina. At Christmas, she returned to the Haymarket in the title role of the pantomime *Little Bo Peep.*

In 1855 she crossed to Europe and for more than three years performed her speciality dances before audiences which, if the reports are to be believed, included both Russian and German students who pulled her unhorsed carriage through the streets of Moscow and Berlin, respectively, in homage to her talent and sex appeal. Billed as ''first danseuse of the Drury Lane Theatre, London,'' she had obvious success both as an act and also as an interpolated item in such theatre pieces as Karl Gross's *Eine kleine Kur* in Hungary (Budai Színkör), Russia (where she was ''personally introduced to the Emperor'' and the St Petersburg Theatre burned down publicity-worthily during her stay), Germany (Berlin went mad for her ''saylorboys dance''), Austria (where the Theater an der Wien produced a Schwank called *Miss Lydia* in memoriam), France and Scandinavia—''Miss Lydia Thompson the danseuse formerly well known in London has after a most wonderfully brilliant tour of Germany, visited Copenhagen (Casino), Stockholm (King's), and lately astonished the good people of Riga, Finland, with her

Highland fling, hornpipe &c. She is a favourite wherever she goes but Germany appears to be her trysting place . . .''—and as far afield as Constantinople, before eventually returning to London.

There she was re-engaged at the St James's Theatre under Chatterton, where her roles included ''a Mysterious Stranger'' in Lester Buckingham's *Virginus* burlesque; Valentine, the magician's son (''who will introduce a Sailor's Hornpipe, les Juinea, grand Pas Seul, and Pas Demon'') in the hugely successful ballet-farce *Magic Toys;* Dolly Mayflower in the drama of *Black-Eyed Susan;* and Young Norval in the ballet-burlesque *My Name Is Norval.* In 1860 she appeared at the Lyceum where she played again in her favorite vehicle, *Magic Toys;* as Abdallah, Captain of *The Forty Thieves* in the Savage Club burlesque, in the farce *The Middy Ashore* (''in the course of which she will dance her famous sailor's hornpipe''); as Fanchette in George Loder's *The Pets of the Parterre* (*Les Fleurs animées*); in the drama *The House on the Bridge of Notre Dame;* and at Christmas as Mephisto in the fairy extravaganza *Chrystabelle, or The Rose without a Thorn.* In 1861 the Lyceum cast her in a soubrette role in the drama *Woman, or Love Against the World,* in a comedy-with-dance-solo role in *The Fetches,* and as Blondinette in *Little Red Riding Hood,* and in 1862 she mixed the dances and the plays with an appearance in the Brough burlesque *The Colleen Bawn Settled at Last* but, having married in 1863, she then took a little time off from the stage to give birth to the daughter who was to become the actress Zeffie [Agnes Lydia] Tilbury. She was widowed 15 months after her marriage when, whilst she was playing in *The Alabama* at Drury Lane, her riding-master husband was rolled on by his horse in a steeplechasing accident.

By that time, however, she was already back on the stage. In the years that followed, Lydia mixed London engagements with appearances, most often in burlesque, in the major (and some not so major) provincial towns. She made what would prove the most far-reaching such appearance at the Theatre Royal in Birkenhead in 1864, playing the burlesques *Perdita* and *Ixion* for manager Alexander Henderson. She subsequently played at Henderson's new Liverpool Prince of Wales Theatre in a series of roles including Brough's *Ernani* alongside the Iago of Lionel Brough (1865), the title role of the new burlesque *Papillionetta* and Mercury in *Paris* (1866). She returned to the West End at the famous Prince of Wales Theatre under Marie Wilton performing a ''Rifle Dance'' as Max in the burlesque of *Der Freischütz* (1866), and in pantomime and as Sophonisba in Drury Lane's production of Delibes' *Wanted Husbands for Six* (*Six Demoiselles à marier*), but for Christmas 1867 she again visited Henderson's theatre in Liverpool where she appeared as Prince Buttercup in *The White Fawn,* Massaroni in the burlesque *The Brigand* and Prince Florizel in *Perdita.*

Plate 391. **Lydia Thompson,** *the famous burlesque actress in her costume for* Robinson Crusoe.

In early 1868 she created the role of Darnley in the burlesque *The Field of the Cloth of Gold* at the Strand Theatre. The show was a remarkable hit, but Lydia did not stay with it till its end. After 104 nights she quit the cast, and three days later she left England for America. Along with her went manager Alexander Henderson (to whom she was subsequently married), a trio of British burlesque actresses and a chief comedian, all of whom who within weeks would be famous.

After a well-publicized arrival, Lydia Thompson made her first appearance on the American stage, on 28 September in Burnand's burlesque *Ixion,* under the management of local manager Samuel Colville and of Alexander Henderson, at Wood's Museum and Metropolitan Theater, New York. She made an enormous effect with her extremely sexy (but never vulgar) comic performances, her dazzling dancing, and her extraordinary merry and warm stage presence, and Wood's Museum became the hottest ticket in town and what had been intended to be a six-month tour eventually developed into one of more like six years. Within nights, Lydia Thompson became the unquestioned burlesque queen of her period, leading her company of ''British Blondes'' (several of whom were not one or the other) around the country—with frequent returns to Broadway—playing pieces such as *Ixion, The Forty Thieves, Bluebeard, Aladdin, Robin Hood, Kenilworth, Mephisto, Lurline, Sinbad, La Sonnambula, Robinson Crusoe, Ivanhoe,* a burlesque *La Princesse de Trébizonde* and *Pippin* (ie, Byron's *The Yellow Dwarf).* If the blondes' trademarks were short trunks and shapely thighs, many of them were, however, by no means devoid of talent and several, including Pauline Markham, Alice Atherton, Camille Dubois, Carlotta Zerbini, Eliza Weathersby, Alice Burville and Rose Coghlan went on to fine careers. Amongst the male members of her company were such top comic talents as Harry Beckett, Bill Cahill, John L Hall, Willie Edouin and Lionel Brough. Nevertheless, the company thrived—to begin with, at least—on a slightly scandalous reputation which Lydia's managers fostered finely, winning nationwide publicity with the tales of her ''lesbian attacker'' and of her public horsewhipping of the ungentlemanly proprietor of the *Chicago Times* who had published a piece reflecting on the virtue of the ''blondes.''

In 1874 she returned to Britain and played in London and the provinces in *Bluebeard, Robinson Crusoe, Piff-Paff* (*Le Grand Duc de Matapa*), *Oxygen, The Lady of Lyons, Pluto!, Carmen* and other burlesque entertainments, but in the years to come she made regular return trips to America, where she remained a hugely popular and always newsworthy figure in the musical theatre.

Her days of playing in burlesque were done when in 1887 she took a turn in direction and mounted a revival of Alfred Cellier's comic opera *The Sultan of Mocha* in London, but her voice proved far from up to the task when she starred in the French vaudeville-opérette *Babette* (1888, Antonio), and in later days she found herself in no position to produce, and jobs harder to come by. Although she appeared in America in 1894 as an actress in *The Crust of Society,* and George Edwardes, hearing of her plight, used her briefly the following year in *An Artist's Model,* she was badly enough off in 1899 for a benefit to be staged for her at the Lyceum Theatre. She made her last stage appearance in 1904.

A phenomenon in the American theatre, where she gave general popularity to a superior brand of song and dance show with extravagant comedy which remained popular for many years, at home she was—although recognized at her peak unqualifiedly as the ''queen of burlesque''—just one of a number of fine leading burlesque actresses of the period. However, her skillful management, the adept casting of her troupe, her knack for publicity, her own exceptional charms and talents and the fact that she spent the most blooming of her blooming years on the American stage, built a special place for her in American theatre history.

Lydia's half-sister, **Clara THOMPSON** [Clara Rose HODGES], one of the children of Edward Hodges and Eliza née Cooper, ex-Griggs, ex-Thompson, made a very considerable career as a vocalist and actress both under her own name and under her married name of ''Mrs Bracy'' (she was the wife of tenor ''Henry Bracy'' né DUNN), in Britain, Australia and America. Daughter Zeffie Tilbury played mostly in the non-musical theatre, but can be seen in a supporting role as the Princess in the Hollywood version of *Balalaika* (1939).

Several other theatrical Thompsons claimed, over the years, to be related to the meteoric Lydia, but it seems that Clara was the only genuine sibling to go on the stage.

THOMSON, Augusta (b Glasgow, 11 December 1836; d Pimlico, London, 14 March 1877).

The daughter of Glasgow musician and teacher Andrew D Thomson, Augusta Thomson studied at the Paris Conservatoire and graduated therefrom with the coveted Premier Prix in 1858. She made her first appearance in London at the Philharmonic concerts (16 May 1859), singing Auber's ''Reviens, ma noble protectrice'' under the baton of Sterndale Bennett and caused a veritable sensation. In no time she was summoned to sing before the Queen at Buckingham Palace.

However, in spite of the predictions of a stunning career that were made for the dazzling young soprano, she stagnated as a concert vocalist for several years, before being hired by Offenbach to return to Paris and become the first and only anglophone member of his Bouffes-Parisiens company. She created the ingenue role of Inès in *Les Bavards* (1863) there, but soon returned to Britain where, in September 1864, she made her British stage debut in drama (with songs) at Ryde. She played in pantomime, sang at Liverpool in *Les Noces de Jeannette,* and then caused a fresh sensation when she appeared at Drury Lane as Sabrina in a production of Milton's *Comus* 1865 (17 April 1865). However, with a perversity which would characterize her career, she then moved into performing drawing-room operetta, playing first in the provinces with her own Royal English Opera Comique Company in Balfe's *The Sleeping Queen,* Glover's *Once Too Often* and *Les Pantins de Violette* and *La serva padrona* as adapted by herself, and then at the German Reeds' Gallery of Illustration, where she delivered *Widows Bewitched, La serva padrona,* and *Too Many Cooks* (*La Rose de Saint-Flour*) and became Britain's first prima donna of opéra-bouffe when she sang the role of Fe-an-nich-ton in *Ching Chow Hi* (*Ba-ta-clan*).

She followed up in that year's Drury Lane pantomime, but then sidled off into burlesque and plays at Liverpool and at the Princess's Theatre, and in 1867, with a girlfriend, took the Marylebone Theatre for a season, presenting themselves in a fairly lowbrow selection of dramas and burlesques. However, when opéra-bouffe truly hit Britain, with John Russell's Covent Garden production of *La Grande-Duchesse,* Augusta was cast as Wanda, and in the years that followed—although she continually took time out to run companies of her own in which she performed unsophisticated material (with sophisticated arias) in unsophisticated places, or to play in burlesque, plays and pantomime—she made a good career as an opéra-bouffe prima donna.

She introduced the role of Cyril in Gilbert's *The Princess,* appeared as Boulotte in *Barbe-bleue,* Zanetta in *La Princesse de Trébizonde* and Frédégonde in *Chilpéric* on tour, starred at the St James's Theatre as Catarina Cornaro in *Le Pont des soupirs* (1872) and at the Gaiety as principal boy in *Snae Fell.* She subsequently played the Grand Duchess, Clairette (*La Fille de Madame Angot*) and Eglantine (*Les Cent Vierges*) and toured with the Gaiety Theatre's opéra-bouffe company, repeatedly reaping amazed reviews for her singing, and in 1875 appeared again as Wanda at London's Opera Comique. But then she faded away yet again into a series of little operetta companies before joining another opéra-bouffe star of previous years, Rose Bell, as the leads of the 1976 Whitechapel pantomime *Open Sesame.* Within weeks of the closing of the panto, she was dead, in an obscure Pimlico boarding house run by someone who didn't know her age or her marital status or even what she did for a living. Her death certificate cited ''brain disease (one month & 14 days) and paralysis (seven days).''

In her heyday Augusta Thomson also adapted several French and Italian pieces (*La serva padrona,* etc) for the English stage.

THREE LITTLE MAIDS Musical play in 3 acts by Paul Rubens. Additional music by Howard Talbot. Additional lyrics by Percy Greenbank. Apollo Theatre, London, 20 May 1902.

The first full show to be written by the rising Paul Rubens, *Three Little Maids* was originally conceived as a vehicle in an old English light-operatic vein for three top West End leading ladies: soprano Evie Greene, pretty Edna May and comedienne Ada Reeve. However, the choice of Rubens as author and composer meant that the light operatic was wholly improbable, and what he turned out was a whisper-light piece of froth set with the most simple of songs (Talbot supplied the ensembles), often catchy and only occasionally—in the manner which would blight his whole career—in a rather childish bad taste. Only Miss May of the three intended stars made it to opening night. Miss Greene, starring for producer Edwardes in *A Country Girl* and *Kitty Grey,* was deputized for by Hilda Moody and Miss Reeve was replaced in rehearsal by Madge Crichton as the third of the countrified Branscombe sisters who take a whole evening to win partners (Bertram Wallis, Maurice Farkoa, G P Huntley) away from a trio of town ladies (Millie Legarde, Betty Belknap, Ruby Ray). Tiny George Carroll was the comedy and Lottie Venne the class.

Rubens's numbers included a pretty piece for the six ladies about ''The Town and Country Mouse,'' Huntley had a nifty comic number about ''Algy'' who was ''simply, awfully good at algebra'' and the three girls danced and sang the ''Tea and Cake Walk'' to good effect, but there were also some shabby pieces that, perversely, were the ones which became popular: ''She Was a Miller's Daughter'' of whom, like so many of Rubens's boringly two-faced country maidens, it was said ''there were flies on the water, but she was flier still,'' a witless tirade against ''Men'' and an inanity called ''Sal.''

The show's muslin-and-cherries simplicity, in an era of highly colored and up-to-date shows, aided by the star and production values supplied by Edwardes and Charles Frohman, won *Three Little Maids* an excellent London life of 348 performances at the Apollo, and later the Prince of Wales, Theatres. The show proved distinctly popular on the road, too, and it even scored a success on Broadway, to where the producers exported a British cast including Miss Crichton, Huntley, Farkoa, Carroll and London takeover Delia Mason for a broken run of 129 performances. These stars continued further south to appear in an Australian season of the show the following year, as *Three Little Maids* covered the English-speaking world, making money for all and setting its author-songwriter on his way to a substantial career.

USA: Daly's Theater 1 September 1903; Australia: Princess Theatre, Melbourne 14 May 1904

THE THREE MUSKETEERS Musical play in 3 acts by William Anthony McGuire based on *Les Trois Mousquetaires* by Alexandre Dumas. Lyrics by P G Wodehouse and Clifford Grey. Music by Rudolf Friml. Lyric Theater, New York, 13 March 1928.

Alexandre Dumas's famous musketeers and their cavaliering quest to save the honor of the barely naughty Queen of France have been the subject of a long list of stage and musical adaptations since they first appeared on the printed page in 1844 and in the theatre the following year (Théâtre l'Ambigu, Paris 27 October 1845 w Auguste Maquet).

Amongst their musical stage appearances have been included two operatic ones—the first, by Reginald Somerville and Herbert Whitney, produced by the National Grand Opera Company at Liverpool (Royal Court Theatre 24 March 1899) with Roland Cunningham as D'Artagnan and Marie Titiens as Queen Anne; the second, Lsidoore de Lara's *Les Trois Mousquetaires,* appearing at Cannes 3 March 1921 and subsequently played in Britain—and a number of operettic ones as well. A spectacular *D'Artagnan* (''Bétove''/Mouëzy-Éon) was produced at Paris's Théâtre de la Gaîté-Lyrique (18 November 1945) under Henri Montjoye with some success, and others of the same title in Italy (Romeo Simonesi, Genoa, July 1888) and in Germany, where Victor Léon supplied the text for a Rudolf Raimann Operette, *D'Artagnan [und die drei Musketiere]* mounted at Hamburg's Carl-Schultze Theater (18 September 1881).

The musketeers were Francis Lopezzed in a *Les Trois Mousquetaires* curiously described as an ''opérette western'' (Théâtre du Châtelet, February 1974, Daniel Ringold/René Jolivet), whilst Ralph Benatzky composed and arranged the score of ''Musik von gestern und heute'' (''[he has] collected some American hits and sandwiched in a sentimental waltz or two of his own'') for a spectacular-comical *Drei Musketiere* produced at Berlin's Grosses Schauspielhaus in 1929 (libretto ''nach Motiven von Dumas'' by Ernst Welisch, Rudolf Schanzer, 28 September). Alfred Jerger as D'Artagnan, Max Hansen (Aramis) and Sig Arno (Porthos) were the ''three'' of the title (Athos had been done away with on the principle that the title always has been misleading), featured alongside Gosta Ljungberg (Queen), Trude Hesterberg (Leona, a spy) and one Josef Schmidt, in a story which forgot all about the Queen's jewels and instead concentrated on a plot about a marriage with the Infanta of Spain . . . and on no less than 10 ballets. The show did well enough to be taken to Vienna's Theater an der Wien (16 October 1931) with Jerger teamed with Anny Coty (Queen), Max Brod (Porthos), Max Willenz (Aramis) and Rosl Berndt (Leona), and to Budapest where it was produced at the Városi Színház (17 October 1930) in a version by Jenő Faragó.

There have been further versions of the tale in recent decades from Russia and again from Germany (*Die drei Musketiere* Jaro Dlouhy/Ursula Damm-Wendler, Horst-Ulrich Wendler, 17 June 1966), whilst France's modern-day specialists of the spectacular remake of much-to-over-remade stories, MM Lecocq and Dunoyer Segonzac, churned out their version, *Les Trois Mousquetaires, ou le petit D'Artagnan,* at Nanterre in 1995 (Espace Chorus 15 November) and Hungary contributed its musical *A három testőr* (Zoltán Papp /Szabolcs Várady) at the Pécs Nemzeti Színház in 1994 (11 February). A British *The Three Musketeers* (George Stiles/Peter Raby) went to Switzerland (Stadttheater, St Gallen 26 February 2000) for its premiere.

In Britain, a jolly musketeers-in-the-round was produced at the Royal Exchange, Manchester (Derek Griffiths/Braham Murray 25 June 1979) with Robert Lindsay as its athletic hero, but British musketeers have normally been burlesque ones, ranging from the days of Joseph and Harry Paultons's *Three Musket-Dears and a Little One In* (Strand Theatre 1871, mus arr John Fitzgerald)—which featured Tilly Wright as D'Artagnan, with two equally feminine fellow musketeers, Paulton as Athos and Edward Terry as Lady de Winter—up to a large-scale *The Four Musketeers* (Laurie Johnson/Herbert Kretzmer/ Michael Pertwee, Theatre Royal, Drury Lane 5 December 1967) in which bulky Harry Secombe frolicked through 462 performances as Dumas's young Gascon.

Broadway had its first *The Three Musketeers* in the form of a light opera by Richard W Temple (son of the Savoy baritone), produced by its author at the Manhattan Opera House for five performances in 1921 (19 May), but it was its second one, produced just shortly before the Grosses Schauspielhaus extravaganza, which has been the only really successful attempt at turning Dumas's flamboyant foursome into the heroes of a romantic musical play. Following on behind the romancing success of *Rose Marie* and the swashbuckling triumph of *The Vagabond King,* Willam Anthony McGuire and Rudolf Friml's *The Three Musketeers* (all four of them) romanced and swashbuckled simultaneously whilst keeping pretty much to both the central story and the characters of the original book. D'Artagnan (Dennis King) supported by his companions-in-arms, Athos (Douglass Dumbrille), Porthos (Detmar Poppen) and Aramis (Joseph Macauley) set off for England to recover the jewels embarrassingly given to the Duke of Buckingham (John Clarke) by the Queen of France (Yvonne d'Arle), whilst the romance was supplied by innkeeper's daughter and royal lady-in-waiting, Constance Bonacieux (Vivienne Segal), and the baddies were represented by Reginald Owen (Richelieu) and Vivienne Osborne (Milady). The score was in a suitably stirring light-operatic vein, but The March of the Musketeers did not come up to The Song of the Vagabonds in public favor, and although the virile ''My Sword (and I)'' and the romantic ''Ma Belle'' (Aramis), ''My Dreams'' (Queen) and ''Your Eyes'' (D'Artagnan and Constance) did well enough in the show, none of them survived to the popularity gained by Friml's two earlier successes.

Florenz Ziegfeld's lavishly staged production, with settings by Urban, ballets by Albertina Rasch and, rather curiously, a brigade of Tiller Girls in support, ran for a good but untriumphant 319 performances. In London, where the show followed *Show Boat* and *The New Moon* on to the stage of the Theatre Royal, Drury Lane, the result was much the same. A very fine cast, headed by

King, Raymond Newell (Aramis), Robert Wollard (Porthos), Jack Livesey (Athos), Adrienne Brune (Constance), Webster Booth (Buckingham), Lilian Davies (Queen), Arthur Wontner (Richelieu) and Marie Ney (Milady) played the piece for 240 performances under Alfred Butt's management, without approaching the grand totals achieved by Friml's two big successes. *The Three Musketeers* remained a relative success.

In 1984 a revised version of the show (ad Mark Bramble) was produced on Broadway. Michael Praed was the D'Artagnan of an all-action *Three Musketeers* which failed to please for more than a handful of nights (Broadway Theater 11 November).

UK: Theatre Royal, Drury Lane 28 March 1930

Recording: London cast recordings on *Rudolf Friml in London* (WRC)

THE THREEPENNY OPERA *see* DIE DREIGROSCHENOPER

(THE) THREE TWINS Musical comedy in 2 acts by Charles Dickson (and Isidore Witmark) based on *Incog* by Mrs Romualdo Pacheco. Lyrics by Otto Harbach. Music by Karl Hoschna. Herald Square Theater, New York, 15 June 1908.

The play *Incog* (Grand Opera House, Indianapolis 21 August 1891), written by the wife of the Governor of California, Mrs Pacheco, and played in Britain by Charles Hawtrey as *Tom, Dick and Harry,* was brought to publisher Isidore Witmark with the "suggestion" that he might like to have it turned into a musical comedy. Witmark took the "suggestion" and, having himself reorganized the play into a libretto form, set a team of writers to work on completing the transformation. He allotted the musical side to his young employee, Karl Hoschna, who had written the scores for three touring musicals without breaking into Broadway, and he accepted Hoschna's suggestion that he bring in as lyricist an advertising man called Hauerbach with whom he had been working on an unproduced show. Hauerbach was paid $100 for the opportunity to have his lyrics heard on Broadway.

The title that they gave to Mrs Pacheco's story had rather more significance than its original. Tom Stanhope (Clifton Crawford), the disinherited heir to the fortune of his dyspeptic General father (Joseph Allen), disguises himself—for good and proper reason—as one of the Winters twins, Harry (Willard Curtiss) and Dick (George S Christy), to the deep confusion of the former's sweetheart (Bessie McCoy) and the latter's wife (Frances Kennedy) until, after two acts of mistaken identities, problems, songs and dances, things are sorted out and he can be restored to parental favor and his own sweetheart, Kate (Florence Willarde).

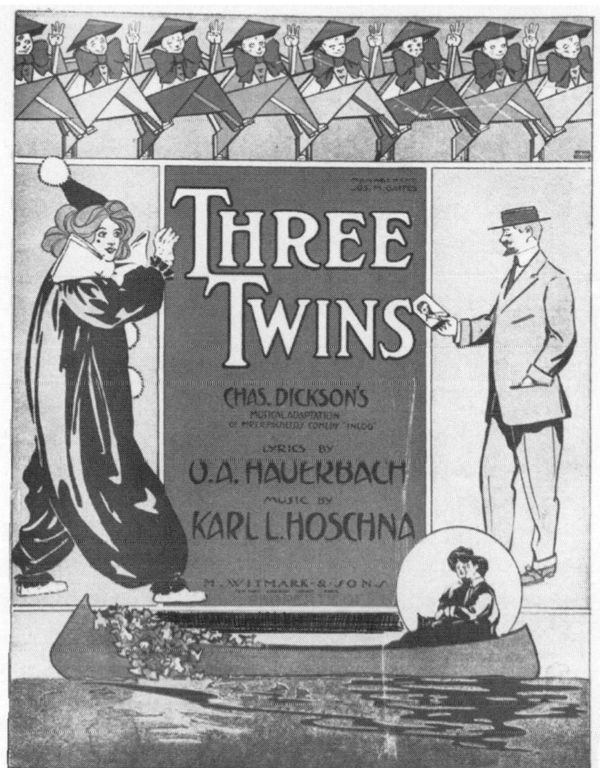

Plate 392. **Three Twins**

The nine songs (plus two opening choruses and two finales) which illustrated the piece included two which became first-class favorites, Miss Willarde's encouragement to her beloved to "Cuddle Up a Little Closer, Lovey Mine" (a piece originally written for a vaudeville act and transported into the show by its writers) and a jaunty, naive little number about the child-scaring "Yama-Yama Man," a number very much in the line of the famous "Hush, the Bogie," which was added to the score during rehearsals for the benefit of Miss McCoy. A pretty, swooping waltz duo, "Good Night, Sweetheart, Good Night" for Crawford and Miss Willarde, the waltzed praises of "The Little Girl Up There," a novel laughing and crying duet for Misses Kennedy and McCoy, and a rouser claiming "We Belong to Old Broadway" also contributed to an enjoyable musical part and to the splendid success of Joseph M Gaites's Broadway production.

Three Twins stayed in New York for 288 performances, in spite of being burned out of the Herald Square Theater and being forced to take a break before re-establishing itself at the Majestic. Victor Morley (Tom), Bessie Clifford (Molly) and Eva Fallon (Kate) led out a West Coast company, and *Three Twins* was toured healthily thereafter throughout America. In spite of a showcase presentation mounted by Witmark in London,

Plate 393. *Sheet music cover for* **Harry Tierney's** Rio Rita.

it did not succeed in finding itself a production there, but it was picked up for an Australian season. Dorothy Brunton (later Maud Fane) was Kate and Harry Wooton (later director Harry B Burcher) played Harry, with Alfred Frith (Dick), William Greene (Tom) and the Gaiety star Connie Ediss as Mrs Dick. The show, however, met some indignant opposition, its ''travesty of mourning and grief'' in wartime being considered ''ill-timed'' and ''disfiguring,'' and an illumination showing an apparently nude lady as an accompaniment to the song ''Bachelor Days'' was voted objectionable. *Three Twins* was bumped from Melbourne after only a fortnight, and played just four weeks in Sydney (Her Majesty's 1 June 1918) the following year.

UK: Victoria Hall, Westbourne Grove 3 March 1908; Australia: Her Majesty's Theatre, Melbourne 26 May 1917

TIERNEY, Harry [Austin] (b Perth Amboy, NJ, 21 May 1890; d New York, 22 March 1965). Broadway songwriter whose music accompanied both the comic and romantic-spectacular.

Born into a musical family, Tierney studied music in New York before appearing on the concert stage in both America and Europe as a juvenile pianist. He subsequently became a song-plugger in England, notably at Harrod's department store in London, and it was apparently through his playing of other people's songs in this capacity that he ultimately came in contact with C B Cochran and was given the opportunity himself to write for the stage.

Tierney contributed numbers to the potpourri scores of the Alhambra revues *Keep Smiling* (1913) and *Not Likely* (1914) for André Charlot, along with other fashionably foreign composers such as France's Willie Redstone and American Melville Gideon, and apparently also to some for Cochran, without catching too much attention, before he returned to America. There he had his first significant show assignment when, with lyricist Alfred Bryan, he supplied a half-dozen songs for what had once been a Leo Ascher musical, *Was tut man nicht alles aus Liebe,* but had now been metamorphosed into a Shubert Anna Held vehicle as *Follow Me* (1916). His contribution included ''The Girls Are Getting Wiser Every Day,'' ''Happyland,'' ''It's a Cute Little Way of My Own,'' ''It's the Little Things That Count,'' ''How Would You Like to Bounce a Baby on Your Knee?'' and Miss Held's memorable ''I Want to Be Good (But my eyes won't let me).'' He interpolated ''Sometime'' into *Betty;* the score for *Hitchy-Koo* (1917) included his hit number ''M.I.S.S.I.S.S.I.P.P.I.'' (ly: Bert Hanlon, Benny Ryan), later used in London's Gaiety Theatre musical *The Beauty Spot; The Passing Show of 1917* used ''My Yokohama Girl''; and in the same year he turned out his first full-scale musical score for the American stage. However, *What's Next?,* produced in Los Angeles by Oliver Morosco, with no less a star than Blanche Ring topping the bill, stopped short of a Broadway opening.

Tierney continued over the years that followed to provide additional numbers for the other folks' musicals, including the anglicized French musical *Afgar* (''Why Don't You?,'' etc) and the ''Cohanized'' comic opera *The Royal Vagabond,* as well as for the revue *The Broadway Whirl* and from 1919 for the *Ziegfeld Follies* (''They're So Hard to Keep When They're Beautiful,'' ''Where Do the Mosquitos Go?,'' ''Take, Oh Take Those Lips Away''). In 1924 when he and his partner Joseph McCarthy supplied seven numbers they were credited for the entertainment's basic score. In the meantime, however, Tierney had achieved that one stage hit necessary to shift a composer into the classic class. The musical comedy *Irene,* produced on Broadway in 1919, introduced the most memorable of the mostly subsequent gaggle of mostly Irish Cinderella-type heroines to the New York musical stage, equipped with Tierney and McCarthy's ''Alice Blue Gown'' and two handfuls of other charming songs. The show was a major international hit, scoring from Sydney to Budapest to London, and establishing its writers at the forefront of their craft.

Tierney had another, if less than international, success with a musical version of Frank Craven's *Too Many*

Cooks, produced by William A Brady under the title *Up She Goes.* On this occasion, the comedy was more important than the agreeable if not particularly outstanding score, but the combination was good for 256 Broadway performances. The same success did not, however, attend a second go at a Cinderella piece with *Irene*'s author, James Montgomery. *Glory* failed to take, and closed after 64 performances leaving behind only ''The Saw Mill River Road'' as a briefly popular number.

The following year Tierney and McCarthy provided the songs for the comedy musical *Kid Boots,* and once again found a by no means first-rate score carried to success by a lively comedy and a popular star, not to mention an interpolated number (''Dinah'') which gave the piece the genuine song hit they had not turned up. For their next musical, however, the pair did not go for another comedy libretto, but instead supplied the songs for the spectacular romance *Rio Rita.* The spectacle undoubtedly had as much to do with *Rio Rita*'s fine Broadway success as the comedy and the star had with that of *Kid Boots,* but this time the score—including ''Following the Sun Around,'' ''Rio Rita,'' The Rangers' Song, ''If You're in Love You'll Waltz'' and ''The Kinkajou''—more than did its bit towards that success.

Thereafter, however, Tierney's career faltered and faded. A 1928 musical *Cross My Heart* played itself out in eight weeks, a period in Hollywood, which included the film version of *Rio Rita* and such movies as *Dixiana* and *Half Shot at Sunrise,* was unproductive and a subsequent return to the musical stage did not reach out as far as Broadway.

1917 **What Next?** (Alfred Bryan/Oliver Morosco, Elmer B Harris) Majestic Theater, Los Angeles 24 June

1919 **Irene** (McCarthy/James Montgomery) Vanderbilt Theater 18 November

1922 **Up She Goes** (McCarthy/Frank Craven) Playhouse 6 November

1922 **Glory** (w Maurice de PackhMcCarthy, James Dyrenforth/Montgomery) Vanderbilt Theater 25 December

1923 **Kid Boots** (McCarthy/William Anthony McGuire, Otto Harbach) Earl Carroll Theater 31 December

1927 **Rio Rita** (McCarthy/Guy Bolton, Fred Thompson) Ziegfeld Theater 2 February

1928 **Cross My Heart** (McCarthy/Daniel Kusell) Knickerbocker Theater 17 September

1933 **Beau Brummell** (Edward Eliscu, Raymond Egan/Gladys Unger) Municipal Opera, St Louis 7 August

TILLEY, Vesta [POWLES, Matilda Alice] *see* DE FRECE, LAURI

LA TIMBALE D'ARGENT Opéra-bouffe in 3 acts by Adolphe Jaime and Jules Noriac. Music by Léon Vasseur. Théâtre des Bouffes-Parisiens, Paris, 9 April 1872.

Jaime and Noriac's ''timbale d'argent'' is the prize in a rustic singing contest. The village of Grog-et-l'eau-de-seidlitz is desperate to beat the neighboring village of Feldkirch, and the local judge, Raab (Désiré), has offered his daughter's hand to the man who can bring off a victory. Young Müller (Mme Peschard) from over Feldkirch way crosses villages to win the prize and the girl, but the choirmaster and local gaoler, Pruth (Édouard Georges), who has himself had designs on Molda (Anna Judic), first on behalf of his nephew Fichtel (Marguerite Debreux) and then on his own, discovers that the invincibility of the Feldkirch vocalists comes from an oath of sexual abstinence and calls Müller to hold to his troth, even on his wedding night. The men of Grog-et-l'eau-de-seidlitz take to abstinence and winning trophies, there is a women's rebellion, and Molda seduces her husband from his vow in time for a lively and happy ending.

Vasseur's happily lightsome score was largely shared between the artists playing Molda and Müller. The soprano hero introduced himself with a showy serenade (''Pendant que sur la nappe blanche'') and won his timbale in jolly tyrolienne, but it was the piece's leading lady who turned *La Timbale d'argent* and its music into a major success. The 22-year-old Judic opened proceedings with the not entirely unsuggestive Couplets de la Timbale (''V'la qu'ça glis-se!''), enlivened the wedding scene with the Chanson du Postillon with its ''clic! clac! hop! hop!'' refrain and seduced her husband in the Couplets de Coquetterie with a winsome sexuality, making the simple lyrics into songs of swingeing but sweet suggestiveness which took away the breath of even the delighted Paris public of 1872. Judic and *La Timbale d'argent* both became the hottest things in town—thanks to it, she was hoisted to instant stardom and, thanks very largely to her, the show proved almost as popular as *La Fille de Madame Angot* as it totted up some three hundred Parisian performances in just two seasons. The censors, who had missed the intent of the double entendres preproduction, got into the act later in the run, and a new song introduced for Judic (''in which she has full scope for her archness, and keeps up her reputation as an artiste to whom even the most risky double-entendre can be entrusted'') had its final verse amputated as being beyond the pale.

The show also produced an early example of what, a century later, was to become one of the plagues of the musical stage: merchandising. A confectioner of the Boulevard des Italiens produced an electroplated cup, bearing a picture of Judic en medaillon, and filled with sweets. He did splendid business. And since electroplate lasts better than some modern merchandise, maybe there is an example of this 19th-century ''souvenir mug'' still lurking in a French cupboard.

Inevitably, such a hit was soon exported. Brussels quickly got not one but two productions when, in spite of the fact that the Galeries Saint-Hubert had paid out 5,000 francs for the rights, *Angot* producer Eugène Humbert at the Alcazar ignored what he claimed as the invalid copyright and got in first with his version. The Galeries riposted by bringing Judic and Désiré from Paris for their production. However, outside France, *La Timbale d'argent* never seemed likely to challenge the success of Lecocq's work nor even to equal the popularity it had found at home. America took its *Timbale* in French and was treated to Marie Aimée not in the role created by Judic, which was played by Léontine Minelly, but as Müller. Produced in the Grau and Chizzola opéra-bouffe season in 1874 it earned more pursed lips than untied purses, even in French, and it was not persevered with. However, several years later, when Louise Théo visited America, she featured *La Timbale d'argent* prominently in her repertoire for several years.

In Britain the only way a piece which *The Era* gasped was ''so saturated with indecent suggestions'' could be staged was in a severely rewritten form. G M Layton used the score and as much as he dared of the original text to make up a piece called *The Duke's Daughter, or Sold for a Song,* still set in the village of Grogandseidlitz in the Duchy of Duffendorff, in which Pauline Rita was leading man, Alice Burville principal girl and Rachel Sanger, in a lesser role, was billed in the program as having ''kindly consented to play the part.'' Various rehashings and recastings were tried as the cleaned-up piece moved from the Royalty to the Globe and the Charing Cross in search of a popularity which did not come and after a peripatetic two-month life it closed.

More regular versions were staged in Italy and South America (in French), in Vienna in German (for just three nights) and in St Petersburg in Russian (1874). The show even got an English-language production in America when the Norcross touring company produced a version, with a much altered and uncredited libretto—which, however oddly enough, maintained the ''total abstinence'' bit!—and a disguised title which claimed that the show's hero was ''the Tyrolean,'' at St Louis in 1883, during their seasonal travels. British soprano Lizzie St Quinten starred as Müller and the show and the company fell to pieces after eight nights. Germany apparently didn't get a production. A Berlin impresario applied for the rights and, so the story goes, was told by the French publishers he could have them in return for the restoration of Alsace and Lorraine (annexed by Prussia in the recent war) to France.

The real success of *La Timbale d'argent* was won, and won again and again, solely in France. There the show was reprised at the Bouffes-Parisiens in 1876, with Judic teamed with Paola Marié (Müller), Daubray (Raab) and Pescheux (Pruth), 1878 (this time with Théo starring alongside Mme Peschard and Daubray as Raab) and 1887, when neophyte Mlle Andrée, cast for Molda, broke down on the first night and doomed the production. In 1889 it was mounted by a cooperative of the Bouffes company, following the collapse of the current management, and succeeded in setting their ''management'' off on a good footing, which nevertheless did not last. It reappeared again at the Théâtre des Menus-Plaisirs in 1893 and at the Folies-Dramatiques in 1897 when Blanche-Marie (Molda), Jane Pierney (Müller) and Gardel (Raab) topped the bill. ''It seems quite innocent . . .'' wondered more than one critic, on this occasion, a quarter of a century after all the fuss.

Austria: Theater an der Wien *Der Silberbecher* 16 November 1872; USA: Lyceum Theater (Fr) 24 August 1874, Pickwick Theatre, St Louis *Le Tyroléan* 16 July 1883; UK: Royalty Theatre *The Duke's Daughter* 10 January 1876

THE TIME, THE PLACE AND THE GIRL Musical comedy in 3 acts by Will M Hough and Frank R Adams. Music by Joseph E Howard. La Salle Theater, Chicago, 20 August 1906; Wallack's Theater, New York, 5 August 1907.

The most successful of the bundle of successful musical comedies written by the team of Hough, Adams and Howard for the Chicago theatre of the earliest years of the 20th century, *The Time, the Place and the Girl* was a jolly romp which thoroughly fulfilled its description of ''musical comedy.'' The tale on which the fun and the songs were draped had dashing young hero Tom Cunningham (George Anderson) and his comical pal Johnny Hicks (Cecil Lean/Arthur Deagon) fleeing from Boston after having done some damage to the cranium of a card-cheat with a bottle. They choose for their hideout a sanatorium in the nearest mountains and there Tom meets up with his old sweetheart, Margaret Simpson (Florence Holbrook/Violet McMillan). Johnny falls for the pretty nurse, Molly Kelly (Georgia Drew Mendum/Elene Foster), whose name unfortunately shows that she is none other than the sister of the belligerent chap (Thomas Cameron) with the dented cranium. Revenge is kept at bay, however, when the sanatorium is close-quarantined. By the time the all clear is given, the only bells to be heard are wedding ones.

The songs which the team provided to illustrate their tale were as lively and well-made a lot as was being produced anywhere on the East Coast. The waltz ''The Waning Honeymoon'' (''Honeymoon, honeymoon, why do you set so soon?'') proved the favorite and enduring part of the score, alongside the winning ''Blow the Smoke Away,'' a jaunty ''Dixie, I Love You,'' ''Thursday Is My Jonah Day'' and ''I Don't Like Your Family,'' all of which did the rounds in Chicago, and further afield, for many years.

Chicago welcomed *The Time, the Place and the Girl* for a vast run of some four hundred performances, and with that success attached to its title it set out, in the tracks of the earlier Hough-Adams-Howard hits, to tour the country. Like its predecessors, it did splendidly, and did it long. Experience might have told the managers to skip New York, but they didn't. *The Time, the Place and the Girl* not only braved New York, but braved it in the heat of the summer. One journal reported, ''Chicago liked it last season, Boston accorded it a welcome last spring, and New York may grow to be fond of it, if New York can be brought to liking anything it has not conceived itself'' before going on to opine that it might prove ''a little too heavy for a hot weather show,'' which was a slightly strange thought, given that the Chicago musicals were usually attacked as being spineless and weightless. New York, however, could not be persuaded to like it, and Ned Wayburn and Arthur Evans's production went back on the road after four weeks at Wallack's to continue its very long touring life.

The show later became a popular choice in American dramatic stock companies, where musical pieces were rarely played, during the early decades of the 20th century, and time eventually saw it peep into Broadway again, in 1942, when it was brought back—with the aged Howard actually appearing in the cast himself—for a brief run at the Mansfield Theatre (21 October).

A Hollywood film which used the title *The Time, the Place and the Girl* was a campus affair which used nothing else of the stage piece but its name. As for the song ''The Time, the Place and the Girl,'' it belonged not to this show but to the previous year's *Mlle Modiste.*

TINA Musical play in 3 acts by Paul Rubens and Harry Graham said to be based on a play called *Kitty.* Lyrics by Paul Rubens, Percy Greenbank and Harry Graham. Music by Paul Rubens and Haydn Wood. Adelphi Theatre, London, 2 November 1915.

The play *Kitty* on which this piece was said to be based remains an (unproduced?) mystery, but there were fragments or reminiscences of a number of other favorite shows, ranging from Rubens's own *Miss Hook of Holland* to *Ein Walzertraum* and back, to be found in the make-up of the very slim book of *Tina.* Phyllis Dare was Tina, a little Dutch cocoa heiress (the show was prematurely titled *Cocoa-Tina*) anxious to make a romantic runaway match with a dashing violinist. The one she chooses, however, turns out to be the impecunious Duke of Borgolese (Godfrey Tearle) in disguise, and she is disappointed for a whole act before the obvious ending is firmed up. Bill Berry played Tina's wealthy manufacturing father, delighted at getting a Duke in the family and mostly occupied flirting with a lady musician (Yvonne Reynolds), and there was supporting comedy from Mabel Sealby and George Gregory.

If the libretto was minimal, however, the songs which decorated it were some of Rubens's most attractive. The Violin Song, in which Tina throbbed over her lover's playing with a vocal imitation of the sound of a fiddle, proved a popular hit, and there were several other attractive pieces (''Something in the Atmosphere,'' ''Let Me Introduce You to My Father,'' ''A Self-Made Man'') to support it. The romance and the comedy, too, were supported by a dance feature from Jan Oyra and Dorma Leigh (''Billstickers' Dance'') and by a fine production so that *Tina* won a run of 277 London performances before going on the British road. But it didn't go further. Australia, that yardstick of international taste, showed why: it was busy around this time with *High Jinks, So Long, Letty, Tonight's the Night* and *The Pink Lady*—book-strong shows with dancing tunes. *Tina* belonged to yesterday rather than to today and tomorrow.

TIP-TOES Musical comedy in 2 acts by Guy Bolton and Fred Thompson. Lyrics by Ira Gershwin. Music by George Gershwin. Liberty Theater, New York, 28 December 1925.

Another musical comedy in the Cinderella-superstar series of which *Sally, Mary* and *Irene* had been the favorite examples, *Tip-Toes* was, like them, named after its heroine (Queenie Smith), a little lady from the lesser ranks of the music halls. Having, all unawares, captured the heart of a glue millionaire called Steve Burton (Allen Kearns) who has gone slumming in search of true love, then forfeited his regard by being so rash as to appear in a beauty contest to win money to pay an hotel bill, she sticks by her man when it seems he is ruined and Society and rich Sylvia (''Jeannette'' [*sic*] MacDonald) shun him, and thus earns herself a happy ending. The dozen songs which made up the Gershwins' score did not include any of their biggest and/or best-traveling hits, but Tip-Toes's pretty confidence that she is ''Looking for a Boy,'' the lovers' description of ''That Certain Feeling,'' the jaunty enquiry ''When Do We Dance?'' put out by Steve and a couple of accompanying damsels (Gertrude McDonald, Lovey Lee), the lilting ''These Charming People'' as delivered by Tip-Toes and her music-hall partners (Andrew Tombes, Harry Watson jr) and the up-to-date ''Sweet and Low-Down'' all proved at least locally popular, and enduringly pleasing.

Pretty *Tip-Toes* appeared in the same Broadway season as her sisters *No, No, Nanette, Sunny* and *The Girl Friend* and, although she had a lesser stay in town they they did, she notched up a respectable 192 performances before moving on to the road. In London, the show was presented at the Winter Garden Theatre with Dorothy Dickson starring opposite Kearns and with a supporting cast including Laddie Cliff and Vera Bryer. Its lifespan did not come up to the runs of Gershwin's earlier pieces in London, nor indeed to *Lady, Be Good!,* simultaneously on stage at the Empire, but it played a more than respectable 182 London performances before moving out of the Winter Garden and leaving it to the more resonant tones of *The Vagabond King.*

Australia's Tip-Toes was Elizabeth Morgan, and her pals were played by Gus Bluett, Ole Olsen and Chick Johnson through fair showings in Sydney and Melbourne (Theatre Royal 13 August 1927) and the show was also honored with a Parisian production (ad André Mauprey, Robert de Mackield, Serge Veber) with Loulou Hégoburu and Adrien Lamy, the juvenile stars of France's hugely successful production of *No, No, Nanette,* in the leading roles.

Having had her moment, *Tip-Toes* tiptoed on, but she came briefly to life again when a 1978 revival was staged at the Goodspeed Opera House with Georgia Engel and Russ Thacker featured (11 April), followed by a short tour and a season in Brooklyn.

UK: Winter Garden Theatre 31 August 1926; Australia: Her Majesty's Theatre, Sydney 7 May 1927; France: Folies-Wagram 27 April 1929

Recording: London cast recordings on *George Gershwin in London* (WRC)

TITANIC Musical in two acts by Peter Stone. Music and lyrics by Maury Yeston. Lunt-Fontanne Theater 23 April 1997.

The entertainment world's fin de siècle era of dubious taste pinned another black rosette on itself when it decided that—dinosaurs, serial murderers, the Holocaust and AIDS having been (almost) milked of their entertainment value—1997–98 would be *Titanic* season. Hollywood (forgetting perhaps that Hitler himself had backed a *Titanic* film as anti-allies propaganda in 1941) churned out a mediocre movie which publicized itself towards a (disaster!, not *quite* record) row of Oscars and a vaunted ''biggest-box-office-gross-of-all-time,'' Christie's auctioned off the ship's 85-year-old distress signals to a collector of sick memorabilia for a six-figure sum, another collector paid out a vast amount of money for one of the ship's boarding passes, and Broadway joined in the game with a sing-the-sinking-ship show which, in parallel to the screenic piece, duly came out with a handful of the dignified nation's prize-ribbons on it.

The author of the piece was Peter Stone, who had handled (rather further-in-the-past) history with such skill and to such fine effect in *1776,* and the songs were the work of Maury Yeston whose music for *Nine* had presaged exciting things, but who had since been in search of a subject of his own apt to his art. *Titanic* was his first score to an original rather than an adapted text.

The piece focused on the facts of the now heavily mythologized story of the sinking of the *Titanic,* concentrating on the ship itself, and the why and wherefore of its sinking, rather than on the hundreds of personal tragedies that the event involved. It used some fictional characters alongside some not-yet-far-enough-in-the-past-to-be-historical ones, and stood back far enough from both lots so that it did not scratch too deeply things that should not be scratched. Like other people's tragedies. It also forebore to spectacularly feature that most traditionally unlucky of theatrical elements, the sinking of the ship. Having chosen a bad taste subject, the writers treated it in a less than bad taste way. Had they chosen to call the ship by another name, they might have still had a show . . . but, of course, none of the brand-name recognition. So they called it *Titanic.*

John Cunningham (E J Smith) captained the ship built by David Garrison (J B Ismay) for Michael Cerveris (Thomas Andrews), and the passengers included Larry Keith and Alma Cuervo as Isidor and Ida Strauss and William Youmans as J J Astor among the mélange of real and fictional folk who went through the show's *Chorus Line*–style ''test'' . . . which of them would survive and which would not?

The musical part of the show, very often expository, bulging with words, and including much sometimes expansive ensemble work, rarely got frankly lyrical either in word or melody and rendered up little in the way of take-awayable parts. Among the more extractable moments were a trio for the Irish girls looking forward to a new life in a new land (''A Lady's Maid''), the voluminous farewell at the lifeboats, ''We'll Meet Tomorrow,'' and a gentle duo for the elderly Strauses, ending their lives together on the sinking ship (''Still'').

Vastly boosted, the show still failed to tot up the sort of run needed to ticket a show a success, closing its Broadway run after less than two years.

A French version (ad J-L Grinda, S Laporte) was produced at Liège at the end of 2000.

The *Titanic* actually made its way to the stage hard on the heels of the tragedy. One Edward Dorking, a survivor, went on the American halls doing an act which consisted of describing his experience (''it's the quickest way I can repay mother the money I owe, which went down with the *Titanic*'' was his excuse), while Messrs Charles and John Poole touted their ''immortal tale of simple heroism'' *The Loss of the Titanic* round the British music halls in 1913. The ship also went down on the musical stage, without the backing of Hollywood, in the

1960 musical *The Unsinkable Molly Brown.* Not to mention (deeply disguised and in impeccably operatic good taste) as the *Gigantic,* in *Little Me.*

Another *Titanic* musical, this one burlesquing the bandwagon-jumping of the other, was produced in Sydney, Australia under the aegis of ''The Tilbury Team.'' Tony Harvey, Genevieve Lemon, Colli Salter and Gary Scale featured in a Maiden Voyage Production, under the lipsmacking banner ''Don't Go Down on Anything Else This Christmas'' (Cambridge Park Inn 24 November 1997).

And to think, in kinder days, Vincent Freedley had *Anything Goes* rewritten (or so he said) because his sensibilities were aroused by the wreck of the *Morro Castle.*

France: Opéra Royal de Wallonie 15 December 2000

Recording: original cast (RCA)

Literature: Stone, P, Yeston, M: *Titanic* (Applause, New York, 1999)

TOCHÉ, Raoul (b Bougival, 1850; d Chantilly, 17 January 1895). Comic playwright and librettist to the Parisian fin de siècle stage.

Son of a familiar Parisian first-nighter, the young man who went under the nom de Bohème of Toché—''mince, élégant, assez timide, a qui son nez un peu long donnait un air à la fois étonné et narquois''—eagerly put himself about in theatrical circles until he became a happy member of the Parisian literary and musical late-nighters of his time. He began his own writing career on the one hand as a theatrical columnist under the pen name ''Frimousse,'' and on the other as a revuist, providing the texts for a number of such pieces, notably the *Revue des Variétés* and the extremely successful *Paris en actions* staged by Brasseur at the Théâtre des Nouveautés. Before long he moved on to more ambitious areas, and turned out a series of highly successful and widely played comedies and vaudevilles including *La Maison Tamponin, Le Parfum, Madame Mongodin* and *Monsieur Coulisset,* as well as the famous ''vaudeville-pantomime'' *Le Voyage en Suisse,* long toured throughout the world by the Hanlon Lees group of pantomimists, and also a number of opérettes, many of which were written in collaboration with Ernest Blum. In the journalistic world, he moved on simultaneously to pen the ''Soirées Parisiennes'' of *Le Gaulois.*

The first of Toché's full-length musical works was set with a score by the aged Offenbach, the last work of the celebrated composer, but thereafter the larger and easily the most significant part of his musical-theatre work was written with Gaston Serpette. If none of their works became a standard, the little *La Princesse* and the saucy *Adam et Ève* found several overseas productions, *Le Petit Chaperon-Rouge* made it to America (as *Denisette), Le Château de Tire-Larigot* won undeniable success in Paris, and his adaptation of the latest adaptation of the Cogniard *Le Royaume des femmes* attracted the lovers of a saucy spectacle during the Paris Exhibition before going on to be staged throughout Europe. He also contributed to the texts of the Châtelet spectaculars *Le Testament de M Crac* and *Madame L'Amiral.*

However, although his professional life was going well, the ''gay, inoffensive'' Toché messed up his private life. He inherited money, married—apparently unwisely—more money, and embarked on a crazy spree of extravagant, away-from-home living. When he had run through his own cash, he borrowed. When the usurers became too pressing, he put a bullet through his head, in a field near Chantilly, at the age of 44.

Toché's non-musical works extended his list of musical-theatre credits quite considerably in the hands of other folk. His play *La Maison Tamponin* (Palais-Royal 22 March 1893 w Blum) was used as the basis for the Carl Weinberger/Hugo Wittmann Operette *Prima Ballerina* (Carltheater 23 November 1895) and its revised version for Weinberger's 1901 *Auch so eine* (Theater in der Josefstadt 18 October), whilst his *Madame Mongodin* (Théâtre du Vaudeville 17 December 1890) was turned into the American musical comedy *Mary's Lamb* by actor-author-manager Richard Carle (New York Theater 25 May 1908). The vaudeville, *Le Parfum* (Palais-Royal 20 October 1888 w Blum), was also given a German-language musical version at the Theater in der Josefstadt under the title *Im Pavillon* (ad Ludwig Fischl, Alexander Landesberg, mus: Karl Kappeller, March 1896).

Between 1882 and 1892 Toché published seven volumes of *Soirées parisiennes* in book form.

1877 **Chanteur (chanteuse) par amour** (Paul Henrion/w Georges Vibert) 1 act Casino d'Étretat 20 August; Théâtre des Variétés 1 September

1879 **Le Voyage en Suisse** (uncredited/w Ernest Blum) Théâtre des Variétés 30 August

1880 **Belle Lurette** (Jacques Offenbach/w Blum, Édouard Blau) Théâtre de la Renaissance 30 October

1882 **La Princesse** (Gaston Serpette) 1 act Casino de Trouville 25 August; Théâtre des Variétés 22 October

1883 **Le Premier Baiser** (Émile Jonas/w Émile de Najac) Théâtre des Nouveautés 21 March

1883 **Tige de lotus** (Serpette) 1 act Casino de Contrexéville 26 July

1884 **Le Château de Tire-Larigot** (Serpette/w Blum) Théâtre des Nouveautés 30 October

1884 **Le Diable au corps** (Romuald Marenco/w Blum) Théâtre des Bouffes-Parisiens 19 December

1885 **Le Petit Chaperon-Rouge** (Serpette/w Blum) Théâtre des Nouveautés 10 October

1886 **Les Aventures de M Crac** (uncredited/w Toché) Théâtre du Châtelet 19 April

1886 **Adam et Ève** (Serpette/w Blum) Théâtre des Nouveautés 6 October

1888 **[La] Divorcée** (Louis Varney) 1 act Cabourg 11 August

1889 **Le Royaume des femmes** (Serpette/Cogniard, Blum ad w Blum) Théâtre des Nouveautés 28 February

1892 **Madame l'Amiral** (uncredited/w Blum) Théâtre du Châtelet 17 September

1893 **Madame Satan** (pasticcio/w Blum) Théâtre des Variétés 26 September

1896 **La Biche au bois** revised version w Blum (Théâtre du Châtelet)

TODD, Michael [GOLDBOGEN, Avrom Hirsch] (b Minneapolis, 22 June 1907; d New Mexico, 22 March 1958).

American showman who, after cashing-up large in real estate and in the sale of soundproofing for movie sound stages, switched his attention to theatrical production where he specialized in the flamboyant and the spectacular in much the same way that he led his life.

Todd produced *The Hot Mikado* (1939), *Star and Garter* (1942), *Something for the Boys* (1943), *Mexican Hayride* (1944), *Up in Central Park* (1945), *As the Girls Go* (1948) and *Mike Todd's Peep Show* (1950), finding some success, some good runs and some distinctly forced good runs, but mounting nothing of enduring quality. At the same time, he continued his interest in whatever was most oversized and spectacular in the film world: he was behind the development and promotion of the wide-screen Todd-AO and Cinerama processes and he married Elizabeth Taylor. He was killed in an airplane crash in New Mexico at the age of 50.

In 1988, amidst the continuing passion for biomusicals, a musical (Mitch Leigh/Lee Adams/Thomas Meehan) was made out of his life, and produced by Cyma Rubin under the title *Mike* (without an exclamation point) at the Walnut Street Theater, Philadelphia, 26 March. Todd was impersonated by Michael Lembeck. It did not go any further until 1993 when, retitled *Ain't Broadway Grand* and with Mike Burstyn portraying Todd, it appeared briefly on Broadway.

Autobiography: *The Nine Lives of Mike Todd* (Random House, New York, 1958); Biography: Todd, M jr, Todd, S: *A Valuable Property* (Arbor House, New York, 1983)

TOI C'EST MOI Opérette in 2 acts by Henri Duvernois [ie, Henri Schwabacher] (and Albert Willemetz and André Mouëzy-Éon). Lyrics by Bertal-Maubon and Chamfleury. Music by Moïse Simons. Théâtre des Bouffes-Parisiens, Paris, 19 September 1934.

Bob Guibert (Jacques Pills) has been leading an extravagantly debauched life in the night-spots of Paris, sponsored by the check book of indulgent and not-fully-comprehending Aunt Honorine (Pauline Carton). But when Aunt Honorine finally does comprehend, she cries enough and banishes penniless, dependent Bob to her plantation in the Antilles, equipped with a sealed letter to the director, Pedro Hernandez (René Koval), ordering him to overwork the young cretin into something resembling a man. The cretin is smart enough to steam open the letter, and takes with him on the ship his inseparable, bludging pal, Pat Duvallon (Georges Tabet), whom he convinces to change places with him. Hernandez puts Pat to backbreaking work in the sugar fields, whilst Bob, pretending to be the "unstable" heir's doctor, is free to romance the director's child-of-nature daughter, Maricousa (Simone Simon). Lyne Clevers played Viviane, daughter of the colonial official Robinet (Duvaleix), whose close relationship with the Colonial Minister gets her father transferred anywhere she wants to chase a man; Numès fils was Honorine's crooked secretary; and Ginette Leclerc doubled as a Parisian vamp and her smart Caribbean equivalent—all mixed up in a tale which had most of the cast getting laid and engaged (in that order) in the final act, amongst such good-humored dialogue and scenes that it didn't even seem conventional.

The show's score, written by Cuban composer Simons, had a genuine Caribbean tone to it, introducing the rumba ("À l'ombre calme des grandes palmes"), the samba and even the unheard-of conga ("C'est ça, la vie, c'est ça l'amour"), alongside a series of light-comic numbers in a more conventional style which included Bob and Pat's "Toi c'est moi" and the hit of the evening, Honorine and Pedro's loopy duet "Sous les palétuviers."

Toi c'est moi was produced by Albert Willemetz and Louis Meucci at the Bouffes-Parisiens, after Willemetz and Mouëzy-Éon had (without credit) revamped the original libretto and, cast by Willemetz with some of the most attractive comic names of the period, headed by the popular double act of Pills and Tabet, the musical turned out a great success. It played a full year in Paris and was subsequently exported and translated into both English and Hungarian.

In London (ad Reginald Arkell), Charlotte Greenwood starred as Aunt Isabel alongside David Hutcheson (Bob), Clifford Mollison (Pat), Gina Malo (Vivienna) and Clare Luce (Maricousa), and the remnants of Simons's score were peppered with other folks' music, amongst which James Hanley's "Zing, Went the Strings of My Heart" and Martin Broones's (Mr Charlotte Greenwood) "It Happened in the Moonlight." However, Miss Luce's demonstration of the rumba remained the highlight. The show was well received, but after two months producer Lee Ephraim greedily shifted it from the Gaiety to the vastness of the London Coliseum—almost twice as large both in stage and auditorium—and after eight weeks' further run in its oversized surroundings it withered away. In the same year the Hungarian version (ad János Vaszary, Andor Szenes) was produced at Budapest's Andrássy-uti Színház.

In 1936 a French film version was made, with Pills and Tabet playing their original roles alongside Claude May and Junie Astor.

Hungary: Andrássy-uti Színház *Egyszer vagyunk fiatalok* 20 February 1935; UK: Gaiety Theatre *The Gay Deceivers* 23 May 1935

Film: René Guissart 1936

Recording: original cast selection on *L'Opérette française par ses créateurs* (EPM)

LA TOISON D'OR Opérette à grand spectacle in 2 acts by Raymond Vincy based on the novel by Pierre Benoît. Music by Francis Lopez. Théâtre du Châtelet, Paris, 18 December 1954.

An opérette about oil, or rather about those once opérette-worthy romantic lands of the East which have now suddenly become financially desirable property. Stanislas Monestier (André Dassary) has to fight to retain his Middle Eastern lands in the face of some comical plotting bankers, an unhelpful basso priest (Lucien Lupi) and a power-crazy Regent. When his beloved turns out to be the local Princess (Colette Riedinger) in disguise (oh, no!), Stanislas helps out in a revolt against the Regent and ends up as Prince Consort of Asterabad.

The show's ''à grand spectacle'' physical production—including a scene in which Stanislas blows up a burning oil well—and Lopez's agreeably illustrative score, in which a basso title prayer for the Priest and the romantic ''L'Étoile bleue'' and ''Jamais je n'aurais d'autre amour'' were the most notable numbers, were elements in ensuring the show a solid run of 419 performances in Paris and an occasional provincial afterlife.

Recording: original cast (Pathé)

DIE TOLLE KOMTESS Operette in 3 acts by Rudolf Bernauer and Rudolf Schanzer. Music by Walter Kollo. Berliner Theater, Berlin, 21 February 1917.

One of the most successful of the series of Walter Kollo Operetten produced at the Berliner Theater in the seven-year period surrounding the First World War, *Die tolle Komtess* did not, partly because of that war, find the same international success as *Filmzauber* (*The Girl on the Film*) or *Wie einst im Mai* (*Maytime*). It did, however, have a fine run of 350 performances in Berlin during the War, and was revived at the Berliner Theater in 1919.

The crazy countess of the title was a 17-year-old whose husband-seeking mama passes her off for 13. The girl revenges herself by getting up to all sorts of childish mischief, and finally gets herself engaged to the butler. Fortunately, the butler turns out to be a nice young nobleman who was just fulfilling his wealthy uncle's orders that he prove himself capable of holding down a job for three months.

Kollo's score again favored the march rhythms featured in his previous pieces (''Edelweiss-Marsch,'' ''Die Kinderchen, die braven''), but there was also a regular helping of waltz music (''Du ahnungloser Engel'') and a brisk polka, and the hero and heroine sang staunchly of being ''Dein auf ewig'' (''yours forever'') in time-dishonored soupy fashion while the lighter musical moments included the tale of Aunt Carola who played the pianola. It was, however, the song ''Junges Herz lass die Liebe ein'' that proved the hit of the evening and that has endured through the more than 80 subsequent years as a favorite.

EINE TOLLES MÄDEL Vaudeville Operette in 2 acts and a Vorspiel by Kurt Kraatz and Heinrich Stobitzer. Lyrics by Wilhelm Sterk. Music by Carl Michael Ziehrer. Walhalla-Theater, Wiesbaden, 24 August 1907.

A piece in the vaudevillesque tradition exemplified by such contemporaneous musicals as *Les 28 Jours de Clairette* and *Toto, Eine tolles Mädel* existed largely to allow the show's female star, as the ''madcap maid'' of the title, to gallivant through the evening in a role that got her into masculine garb, into the army, and into as many comical situations as possible, all as the result of a bet that she can get away with impersonating a soldier for a day. These antics were accompanied by a brightly tuneful Carl Ziehrer score from which the waltzes ''Manderl'' and ''Gib acht!'' and the just-a-kiss-in-the-dark number ''Küsse im Dunkeln'' proved the favorites.

First produced at Wiesbaden, the show moved quickly on to be seen at Dresden and in other German houses and then to Austria. Wilhelm Sterk adapted the libretto for Vienna, where veteran Karl Tuschl, the former stage director/comedian of Danzers Orpheum who had taken over the management from Gabor Steiner, mounted the show on a program with Léon and Straus's ''melodramatische szene'' *Der Frauenmörder*. With Gerda Walde starred as the all-consuming Rosette alongside Rauch, Mizzi Gribl, Greissnegger, Frau Berger and Josef König, the bill played 42 straight performances and a handful of subsequent matinées. The Austrian version was then picked up both for Budapest (ad Adolf Mérei) and for New York (ad Sydney Rosenfeld). In the post *Merry Widow* era on Broadway, Lulu Glaser starred as Rosette, alongside veteran W T Carleton and Alexander Clark, in the Shubert brothers' production of *Mlle Mischief* (the intended title, *The Girl Who Dared,* was considered too daring) in Philadelphia, for 66 performances at the Lyric Theater, then transferred to the Casino for a further three

Plate 394. **Tom Jones.** *Many chapters of Fielding's novel Tom Jones are reduced into one scene in the inn at Upton. Hayden Coffin (Tom Jones, far right), Dan Rolyat (Partridge) and Ambrose Manning (Squire Western) (both center) and Dora Rignold (Lady Bellaston, up center).*

weeks, before taking her show on to a good life on the road and in the suburbs. When Miss Glaser had finished being *Mdlle Mischief* another popular touring star in Corinne took the piece around one more time (1909).

Austria: Danzers Orpheum 8 November 1907; Hungary: Fővárosi Nyári Színház *Fuzsitus kisasszony* 15 August 1908; USA: Lyric Theater *Mlle Mischief* 28 September 1908

TOLLE WIRTSCHAFT *see* POLNISCHE WIRTSCHAFT

TOM JONES Comic opera in 3 acts by Alexander M Thompson and Robert Courtneidge based on the novel by Henry Fielding. Lyrics by Charles H Taylor. Music by Edward German. Apollo Theatre, London, 17 April 1907.

The comic opera version of Fielding's famous novel was brought out by producer Robert Courtneidge on the occasion of the 200th anniversary of its author's birth. Courtneidge and Alexander Thompson slimmed the original novel wisely, not attempting to take in the whole panorama of town and country depicted by Fielding, but simply following the amorous adventure of the apparently orphaned and obviously attractive Tom (Hayden Coffin) with the rampant Lady Bellaston (Dora Rignold) on his way to the finding of a family, social acceptance, and the hand of his truly beloved Sophia (Ruth Vincent). The character of the village schoolmaster, Benjamin Partridge, was rewritten to make it a traditional star comedy role (Dan Rolyat) and Sophia's canny maid, Honor (Carrie Moore), was the soubrette, teamed with yokel Gregory (Jay Laurier), all of them involved in the amorous goings-on gathered together from the book's pages by the librettists and effectively reset in a wayside inn on the London road.

Edward German was an ideal choice of composer for this most English of old English subjects, and his score for *Tom Jones* turned out to be one of the best ever written for a British period light opera. Sophia's waltz song ''For Tonight,'' a soprano showpiece par excellence, has become a standard in the concert repertoire, Rolyat had a fine pattering piece describing himself as ''Benjamin Partridge, person of parts'' and Miss Moore a delightful ballad telling what a country girl will do ''all for a green ribbon to tie in her hair.'' Coffin had a handful of stout baritone songs, the yokels drank to the ''Barley Mow,'' and Ambrose Manning as the Somerset Squire Western rousted along ''On a Januairy Morning in Zummerzetshire.'' During the run, the score was stiffened with several further numbers, including Sophia's long-since popular ''Dream o' Day Jill'' and Honor's delicious ''I Knew That He Looked at Me,'' but in spite of a delighted reception the show played only 110 performances in London before being sent on the road. It was musical-comedy time, and a comic opera, beautifully made though it might be, with no pretty, scanty girls, no glitz, no dance and no glamor had the same limited audience then as it does nowadays. *Tom Jones* did not even make it to the total knocked up by its fellow light opera *The Rose of Persia,* a few years earlier.

Henry Savage mounted a production of *Tom Jones* in New York, with Van Rensslaer Wheeler (Tom), Louise Gunning (Sophia), Gertrude Quinlan (Honor) and William Norris (Partridge) starred, and a score expanded with ''King Neptune'' from *Merrie England* and even an interpolated number ''The Road to Yesterday'' (Clare Kummer). As in London, the show won superb reviews but failed to find sufficient audience for more than 65 performances. In spite of these disappointing first runs, however, *Tom Jones* and its favorite songs became and remained a firm part of the English repertoire whilst those less substantial and ephemerally popular shows which prospered around it disappeared.

Several other *Tom Jones*es have been written to libretti bearing more or less relation to Fielding's novel. Easily the most successful of them was Philidor's French comic opera, a piece which was played throughout Europe following its introduction at Versailles in 1765 (20 March). The tale was seen again in France, at the Théâtre de Paris in 1974. André Jobin played Tom and Georges Guétary Squire Western in a piece entitled *Les Aventures de Tom Jones* (Jacques Debronckart/Jean Marsan) which included rather more ''belles dames volcaniques'' in its tale than even Fielding or certainly Edward German imagined . . . and omitted Miss Western (and thus, presumably, the keystone of the plot) entirely!

In Britain, a comic-opera version written by Joseph Reed, imitating Philidor and using some small parts of his libretto, was produced at the Theatre Royal, Covent Garden, in 1769 (14 January) whilst some two centuries later, in America, one version was played at Stamford, Connecticut in 1976 (Barbara Damaschek/Larry Arrick, Hartman Theater), and another, billed as ''the musical version of *Tom Jones*'' (as if there were no other), appeared in record form.

USA: Astor Theater 11 November 1907; Australia: Theatre Royal, Melbourne 1 October 1910

Recording: selection (EMI)

TOMMY Rock opera with music and lyrics by Pete Townshend, John Entwhistle, Keith Moon and Sonny Boy Williamson. Derby Playhouse, England, 15 May 1975; Queen's Theatre, London, 6 February 1979.

A dramatically incoherent piece with a score of contemporary rock music, *Tommy* has a deaf and dumb (but singing) hero who suffers all sorts of humiliations and interferences at the hands of the little people in his young life before temporarily becoming a 1960s pop messiah. The songs ''Pinball Wizard'' and ''I'm Free'' both made it to the hit parades.

Performed by the pop group The Who in a concert form, issued on record, lavishly praised by some who (erroneously, as it turned out) saw here the musical theatre/theatre music of the future, it was subsequently made into a film (1975, with Roger Daltrey, Elton John, Tina Turner, Ann-Margret, Jack Nicholson, et al). Highly popular for many years, *Tommy* was played in various versions as a staged concert or a stage show before a first genuine theatre version was mounted at Derby in 1975. It was played at several British provincial theatres thereafter before a production from the Queen's Theatre, Hornchurch, was brought to London in 1979. In spite of the popularity of both the disc and the film, the rather-too-late-coming show—which boasted none of the starry names of the two earlier manifestations of the piece—failed in 118 performances.

In 1993, with nostalgia for the 1960s raging hilariously, a new version of the piece was brought out on Broadway under the title *The Who's Tommy.* The book was credited to Townsend and Des McAnuff, additional music to Entwhistle and Moon, and Michael Cerveris featured in the title role. Produced on a much more lavish and special-effective scale than the earlier attempts, it was duly more successful, playing through nine hundred performances in New York, being sent on the American road, and subsequently playing on the Continent, where Cerveris was teamed with Helen Hobson (mother) and Romi Bruno (Acid Queen), and in London's West End (Shaftesbury Theatre 5 March 1996) with Paul Keating (Tommy) and Kim Wilde (mother) featured. London gave it the thumbs down in 11 expensive months.

A German-language version (ad Anthony Gebler) was given a showing at Lübeck in 1999 (2 July) with Sven Olaf Denkinger in the title role.

USA: St James Theater 22 April 1993; Germany: Musical-Theater-am-Goethestrasse, Offenbach-am-Main 28 April 1995

Film: Columbia 1975

Recordings: original concept recording (Polydor), Broadway cast recording (BMG), etc

Literature: *The Who's Tommy: The Musical* (Pantheon Books, New York, 1993)

TONIGHT AT 8.30 Plays in 1 act by Noël Coward. Phoenix Theatre, London, 9 January 1936.

Of the group of nine (and one reject) one-act playlets which made up the three ''nights'' of this entertainment, four included musical numbers. Noël Coward and Gertrude Lawrence sang ''We Were Dancing'' as the victims of an ephemeral mutual attraction under the tropical moon in the play of the same name, gave out with ''Then,'' ''Play, Orchestra Play'' and ''You Were There'' in the fantastical half-dream of divorce that is *Shadow Play* and performed the music-hall ''Has Anybody Seen Our Ship'' and ''Men About Town,'' as a declining variety act called *The Red Peppers,* and the melodies from a music box in the post-funeral scene of *Family Album.* Several of the plays have been revived either as a group or singly since the show's first production, and two of the non-musical ones were made into films.

USA: National Theater 24 November 1936; Australia: Theatre Royal, Sydney 2 July 1938

Recordings: songs included on HMV, WRC, RCA Victor, etc

TONIGHT'S THE NIGHT Musical play in 2 acts by Fred Thompson based on *Les Dominos roses* by Alfred Hennequin and Alfred Delacour. Lyrics by Paul Rubens and Percy Greenbank. Music by Paul Rubens. Shubert Theater, New York, 24 December 1914.

Tonight's the Night was a new musical version of the enormously successful French comedy *Les Dominos roses,* which had already been turned into a musical comedy in both Austria (*Der Opernball*) and in Hungary (*Három légyott* József Bokor, Népszínház 22 October 1897). The show was written and cast in Britain, but probably as a result of some theatrical infighting between George Grossmith and Alfred Butt—who was anxious to squeeze his rival out of the Gaiety Theatre—rather than on account of the war, it was not produced there. Producers George Grossmith and Edward Laurillard linked up with the Shubert brothers and transported the show, which had been originally intended and announced for the Gaiety, across to New York. George Grossmith (Hon Dudley Mitten), Davy Burnaby (Robin Carraway), James Blakeley (Montagu Lovitt-Lovitt) and Lauri de Frece (Henry) headed the men out for a spree at a masked ball, and Emmy Wehlen (June), Iris Hoey (Beatrice), Fay Compton (Victoria) and Gladys Homfrey (Angela Lovitt-Lovitt) played their respective partners. Miss Compton scored with the jolliest song of the evening, ''I'd Like to Bring My Mother,'' Grossmith encouraged ''I Think I Could Love You if I Tried,'' whilst Blakeley launched into the show's title song and joined de Frece and Grossmith in going ''Dancing Mad.'' Maurice Farkoa as a spivvy tango teacher crooned over ''Pink and White'' and Burnaby and Emmy Wehlen joined in ''Round the Corner'' in the other main musical moments of the evening.

The show had a fine run of 112 Broadway performances after which the producers took it back to London, opening at the Gaiety in April 1915. Grossmith, Blakeley and Miss Homfrey were now teamed with Vernon Davidson, promoted understudy Leslie Henson, Haidée de Rance (briefly, then Madge Saunders), Julia James and Moya Mannering, and Max Dearly was the tango teacher. Henson joined Miss Mannering in ''I'd Like to Bring My Mother'' and scored the hit of the evening, whilst Grossmith slipped in a concert-party number by Greatrex Newman—a tipsy confession of a mass of unlikely ''Murders'' with which Leslie Henson had bolstered his little part in New York—and joined in two freshly added Jerome Kern songs brought back from America: ''They Didn't Believe Me'' (from Broadway's version of *The Girl from Utah*) and ''Any Old Night'' (ex- *Nobody Home*). *Tonight's the Night* was a major hit in London, staying at the Gaiety for 460 performances as productions headed first to the British countryside and then throughout the English-speaking world.

In 1924 (21 April) Grossmith and his new partner, Pat Malone, revived the show at the Winter Garden. Since he was now a major star, Henson had his role as the schoolboy, Henry, enlarged to put him on a par with Grossmith, the score was remade (a good half of the original survived with ''additional lyrics by Desmond Carter''), and, with a cast including Heather Thatcher (Victoria) and Adrienne Brune (June), the old piece ran for another 139 performances. The show was still to be seen touring the British provinces in the 1940s.

In 1916 J C Williamson Ltd produced *Tonight's the Night* in Australia. Charles Workman (Montagu), Alfred Frith (Dudley), Connie Ediss (Victoria), Dorothy Brunton (June), Daisy Yates (Beatrice), Maud Fane (Angela), Fred Maguire (Henry) and Field Fisher (Robin) headed the cast which played six weeks in Melbourne and seven in Sydney (Her Majesty's Theatre 23 September 1916) in what was basically a repertoire season. However, the piece proved to have remarkable stickability, and it was brought back on a number of occasions in years to come, proving itself in the process one of the staple musical comedies of its period on the Australian stage.

UK: Gaiety Theatre 28 April 1915; Australia: Her Majesty's Theatre, Melbourne 8 July 1916

TOOLE, J[ohn] L[aurence] (b St Mary Axe, London, 12 March 1830; d London, 30 January 1906).

One of the greatest British comic actors of the Victorian era, ''Johnnie'' Toole, like most of the other top comedy performers of his time, moved happily in and out of the musical productions which were often staged as one part of a two-or three-part program, from the earliest part of his career. In 1853 he appeared in burlesque at the St James Theatre (*Ganem, Abon Hassan,* etc) in his first London engagement, in 1859 he played Asmodeus in the burlesque *Asmodeus, the Devil on Two Sticks* at the Adelphi, in 1866 he was London's first Agamemnon in *La Belle Hélène* and Popinoff in *Jeanne qui pleure et Jean qui rit,* and whilst engaged at the Gaiety Theatre in the early 1870s he introduced the role of Cabriolo in the English premiere of *La Princesse de Trébizonde,* played Ko-kil-ko in *Aladdin II* and the title role in *Thespis,* and appeared in such burlesques as *Guy Fawkes* (Fawkes), *Ali Baba à la Mode* (Ali Baba), *Don Giovanni* (Giovanni), *William Tell Told Again* (1876), *Toole at Sea* (1876) and *Our Babes in the Wood* (1877, Tommy to the Polly of Nellie Farren). He later played Professor Muddle in the musical farce *A Spelling Bee* (interpolating ''The Two Obadiahs''), included the one-act operetta *Mr Guffin's Elopement* with its comical song ''The Speaker's Eye'' in his repertoire and produced and played in the ''dramatic and musical absurdity'' *Welsh Rabbits* (1881) at the Folly. During his subsequent tenancy of the tiny Toole's Theatre he also mounted and played in the extravaganza *The Great Taykin* and a number of burlesques (*Paw Claudian, The O'Dora, Stage Dora,* as Mephistoolepheles in *Faust and Loose* 1886, et al).

Autobiography: w Hatton, J: *Reminiscences of J L Toole Related by Himself* (Hurst and Blackett, London, 1889)

TOO MANY GIRLS Musical comedy in 2 acts by George Marion jr. Lyrics by Lorenz Hart. Music by Richard Rodgers. Imperial Theater, New York, 18 October 1939.

Too Many Girls was, in spite of its title, a college musical set—like all good college musicals—around that most important element of college life, a football game. Its footballing leading lad (Richard Kollmar), however, was not what he seemed: he was really one of the four bodyguards (Desi Arnaz, Eddie Bracken, Hal LeRoy) infiltrated into Pottawatomie College by rich and influential Harvey Casey to keep an eye on his wayward student daughter, Consuelo (Marcy Westcott). When Consuelo finds she has fallen in love with her father's stool pigeon, she threatens to leave town on the day of the big match duly followed, in the course of their bodyguarding duty, by four all-important parts of the school's team. But true love and Pottawatomie are, naturally, both finally triumphant.

Rodgers and Hart's bookful of songs for this unpretentious and lightweight show brought up a handful of winners including the leading pair's pretty ''I Didn't Know What Time It Was,'' the comical-topical rubbishing of New York in ''Give It Back to the Indians'' and an enduring cry against those so-called arrangers who tear a composer's work to ribbons, ''I'd Like to Recognize the Tune.''

Too Many Girls ran 249 Broadway performances and was subsequently filmed with Bracken, Arnaz and LeRoy backing up Richard Carlson, Lucille Ball and Ann Miller but, in spite of using seven of the show's songs, without ''Give It Back to the Indians'' or ''I'd Like to Recognize the Tune.''

Film: RKO 1940

Recording: selection (Painted Smiles)

TOP BANANA Musical comedy in 2 acts by Hy Kraft. Music and lyrics by Johnny Mercer. Winter Garden Theater, New York, 1 November 1951.

Phil Silvers was the ''top banana'' (American burlesque lingo for chief comedian) of this musical show about show business, which was constructed around, and existed in order to feature, a series of tried and true variety and burlesque routines. The tiny story which framed these routines cast Silvers as Jerry Biffle, burlesque star turned television comedian, who loses the girl (Judy Lynn) picked to star alongside him in the Blendo Soap show to the handsome young singer of the affair (Lindy Doherty), and (temporarily) also drops his top spot to the appealing young couple.

Johnny Mercer supplied the songs, allowing Silvers to explain what it was to be a ''Top Banana,'' to encourage his new partner that ''You're OK for TV,'' to vaunt the advantages of a snappy sell for Blendo (Slogan Song) or burble cheerfully through the speciality number ''A Word a Day.'' The romantic musical moments fell to the juvenile pair (''Only if You're in Love,'' ''That's for Sure'') and there was a heroine's-best-friend (Rose Marie) to wallop out a comical ''I Fought Every Step of the Way'' and head the production number ''Sans Souci.''

Paula Stone and Mike Sloane's production ran for 350 performances on Broadway, but the show did not prove to be a money-maker. A film version of a reduced version of the stage show was made, but the made-for-Silvers *Top Banana* did not have a theatre afterlife beyond regional revivals with Silvers (1964) and Milton Berle (1963) featured.

Film: United Artists 1954

Recording: original cast (Capitol)

TOPOL [Chaim] (b Tel Aviv, Israel, 9 September 1935).

The Israeli actor known simply as "Topol" had a considerable success in the role of Tevye in the London production of *Fiddler on the Roof* (1967) and later in the film version (1971) of the same musical, but his subsequent ventures into the musical theatre (Aimable in *The Baker's Wife,* The General in *R Loves J,* and, improbably, replacing Len Cariou in the title role of *Ziegfeld*) were less successful. He reprised his *Fiddler* role on the stage on a number of occasions, making a late Broadway debut as Tevye in 1990.

In 1974 Topol directed the Israeli musical play *Dominos* at London's Shaw Theatre (30 April).

THE TOREADOR Musical comedy in 2 acts by James T Tanner and Harry Nicholls. Lyrics by Adrian Ross and Percy Greenbank. Music by Ivan Caryll and Lionel Monckton. Gaiety Theatre, London, 17 June 1901.

The last musical to be produced at the original Gaiety Theatre, *The Toreador* was also one of the most successful. Constructed by the tried and hugely successful Gaiety team of writers (plus newcomer Percy Greenbank, having his first full Gaiety credit with this show) for the tried and hugely successful Gaiety team of performers, *The Toreador* featured top comic Teddy Payne as Sammy Gigg, a little "tiger" who gets mixed up with a luscious señora (Queenie Leighton) and a Carlist conspiracy in deepest Spain. Also on the Spanish roads were juvenile lady Dora Selby (Marie Studholme) and the fake husband (Florence Collingbourne as best friend Nancy) she sports to avert a blind marriage to Augustus Traill (Lionel Mackinder), the voluminous Mrs Malton Hoppings (Claire Romaine) with her toreador fiancé (Herbert Clayton) and his angry rival for her charms, animal dealer Pettifer (Fred Wright), not to mention man-about-town Sir Archie Slackitt (George Grossmith), soubrette Susan (Violet Lloyd) and the massed forces of the Gaiety Girls.

Payne got into toreador costume to help Donna Teresa in her naughty political mission and ended up facing bulls and bombs as the plot thickened comico-dramatically between the songs. Amongst the musical numbers, Grossmith scored well with a couple of typical dude-y numbers, "Everybody's Awfully Good to Me" and "Archie," Clayton had a baritonic Toreador's Song, Miss Romaine sighed comically "I'm Romantic" and Miss Collingbourne sang the wry soprano "The Language of the Flowers," but the hit of the evening was a little character number given to the young Gertie Millar, in a tiny role, telling the boys to "Keep Off the Grass."

Miss Millar's role soon expanded to take in other songs ("Captivating Cora," et al) as the show rolled on to success, and the score underwent further alterations when Connie Ediss arrived back at the Gaiety and took over the role of Mrs Malton Hoppings which had been made to her measure. In April 1902 Edwardes even announced a "new edition" and, by the time the show and the famous old theatre closed down *The Toreador* had been played 675 times. The Gaiety run was, however, only the beginning of the success of what would ultimately be one of the internationally most successful of all the Gaiety musicals. The show was quickly out into the provinces and the colonies, and London's triumph was repeated on Broadway when Nixon and Zimmerman mounted a version of *The Toreador* with Francis Wilson in Payne's role alongside Adele Ritchie (Dora), Melville Ellis (Traill), Christie MacDonald (Nancy) and Joseph Coyne (Archie), and little in the way of interpolated music, for a season of 121 performances prior to touring. In Australia J C Williamson presented the piece with George Lauri starred in the principal comic part and Carrie Moore (Susan), Lulu Evans (Nancy) and Maud Chetwynd (Dora) heading the female team, in South Africa Myles Clifton and Victor Gouriet featured, and *The Toreador* even made it to Gibraltar.

Gabor Steiner's Viennese successes with the Gaiety's *The Circus Girl* and *The Messenger Boy* undoubtedly encouraged Karczag and Wallner at the Theater an der Wien to snap up *The Toreador* ahead of him. Their production of Richard Wilde's version—advertised as a "spectacular Operette"—featured Siegmund Natzler as Archie, Franz Glawatsch as the Governor of Villaya, Dora Keplinger (Dora, provided with a Siegmund Eibenschütz "English" number called "Shoking!"), Louise Robinson (Nancy, equipped with a real English interpolation, W Wesley Wells's "Singe, singe, Vöglein") and Carlo Böhm (Gigg, interpolating a Will Marion Cook song called "Liebesabentuer"). However, *Der Toreador* proved no match for the theatre's other main novelty of the season, Eysler's *Bruder Straubinger* with Girardi starred in its title role, and the English piece was played only 25 times. It nevertheless continued on to Hungary (ad Andor Letzkó) where it was mounted at Budapest's Király Színház.

In France, however, the show had a triumph on a par with its English one. The enormous success of *The Belle of New York* at the Moulin-Rouge prompted the management to stage further foreign musical comedies there and, amongst those which followed, *Le Toréador* (ad Arnold Fordyce, Jacques Bousquet) was the most successful, outdoing even its famous predecessor in popularity. With comics Prince and Claudius heading the fun, and Ellen Baxone (Nancy), Jeanne Yannick (Cara Pansy) and Miss Campton (Teresa) providing the glamor, it proved so successful that the supporting music-hall program was annulled and the show extended (with such music-hall extras as Harry Tate's automobile sketch *La Panne*) to virtually the whole night's entertainment. *Le Toréador* ran for half the year and was brought back again the following season (9 April 1905) for a second run.

Back home, *The Toreador* toured happily for a number of seasons after its London run but, like the others of its equally successful fellow Gaiety musical comedies since *The Shop Girl,* it was never taken back to London.

USA: Knickerbocker Theater 6 January 1902; Australia: Her Majesty's Theatre, Melbourne 11 October 1902; Austria: Theater an der Wien 19 September 1903; Hungary: Király Színház *A Toreador* 26 February 1904; France: Théâtre du Moulin-Rouge *Le Toréador* 18 June 1904

TOSTÉE, Lucil[l]e [Emilie] (b Paris 19 December 1837) French opéra-bouffe star who led the export of the genre to America.

Although Lucile Tostée was to make the most famous part of her career in America, she began her life on the stage in France, becoming one of Offenbach's principal interpreters at the Théâtre des Bouffes-Parisiens at a young age. Amongst her assignments at the Bouffes, she played Scipionne in *Les Vivandières de la grande armée* (1859), L'Étoile in *Le Roman comique* (1861) and the original version of the page, Amoroso, in his *Le Pont des soupirs* (1861). She donned skirts to play Béatrix in the Parisian version of *Les Bavards* (1863) but went back into travesty in the role of Fabricio in *Il Signor Fagotto* (1864). She also appeared with the Bouffes company at Vienna's Theater am Franz-Josefs-Kai in 1861 (Crouteau-pot in *Mesdames de la Halle,* Fanchette in *Une nuit blanche,* Pierrette in *La Rose de Saint-Flour,* Atala in *Vent du soir*) and in 1862 (Dorothée in *La Bonne d'enfants,* etc). Following the advent of Zulma Bouffar in his life and theatre, Tostée apparently found less favor in Offenbach's eyes, but her career did not by any means go downwards as a result.

In 1867 Lucile Tostée headed a troupe exported from Paris under the management of H L Bateman to play French opéra-bouffe at New York's Théâtre Français. On 24 September she opened in America as Offenbach's *Grande-Duchesse de Gérolstein* and she took the town by storm, launching at the same time the craze for opéra-bouffe which was to sweep the country over the following years. One critic rhapsodized "The new opéra-bouffe's a brilliant success, the music most sparkling, allow us to state, man, and while they've Miss Tostée to play 'La Duchesse,' there's no grounds for fearing the crowds will a-Bate-man."

She toured throughout the United States in that season and the next in a variety of such pieces, appearing in *La Belle Hélène, Lischen et Fritzchen,* as Eurydice in *Orphée aux enfers* and in her original role from *Les Bavards,* sharing the top billing in later days with Mlle Irma—who had been starring in an opposition production of *Barbe-bleue* and who amalgamated her forces with Bateman's to reinforce a company which was by that time being challenged for opéra-bouffe supremacy by a team brought out by Jacob Grau and headed by Rose Bell, Marie Desclauzas and Gabel.

Equipped with some fairly dubious advertising—Tostée's Eurydice was described as "her original rôle played by her 300 nights in Paris"—the pair continued, increasing their repertoire with such pieces as *Monsieur Choufleuri* (with Tostée in the vocally demanding role of Ernestine), *Le Mariage aux lanternes, La Chanson de Fortunio* (Valentin) and Maillart's *Les Dragons de Villars.* When Tostée left America after less than two years, the flood that she and *La Grande-Duchesse* had begun continued in the hands of such other French artists as Irma, Marie Aimée, Léa Silly, Céline Montaland, Marie Desclauzas, Coralie Geoffroy, Louise Théo and Paola-Marié, as well as their English-language followers. And Tostée herself? She went home, and there apparently just vanished from theatrical annals.

TOTO Opérette in 3 acts by Paul Bilhaud and Albert Barré. Music by Antoine Banès. Théâtre des Menus-Plaisirs, Paris, 10 June 1892.

Banès's one great international success, *Toto* was a vaudevillesque piece with a splendid dual-sex lead role to its tale of an identical (well, not altogether identical) twin brother and sister, Toto and Tata Bernard, who find it useful to swap places temporarily. Tata (Rosalia Lambrecht) elopes with her preferred gentleman, Gaston Ferrier, disguised in Toto's army uniform, whilst Toto (also Mlle Lambrecht), dressed up in Tata's skirts, takes it into his hands to get rid of the unwanted suitor, Cabestan, who has been wished on her by the interfering director of his military academy, Dupalet, and his busybody sister Aurélie. Toto stands in for Tata at her betrothal as the girl takes flight. Everyone winds up in a Railway hotel in the final act—Gaston and Tata waiting for their train to safety, Cabestan with Césarine Bassinet, the little bit of fluff whom he had got a job as nurse at the academy, Dupalet and papa Bernard chasing the runaways, as well as a lubricious old Academy inspector called Blanchart, and, of course, Toto (when Tata isn't on, anyhow) who presides over the inevitable happy ending. Mlle Derly, Fanny Génat, Charpentier, André Simon, Vandenne and Saint-Léon completed the cast and *Toto* found a real success in Paris, running through 130 performances in its initial run at the Théâtre des Menus-Plaisirs, before going on to the provinces and to productions around the world.

In Vienna, *Tata-Toto* was the first opérette staged under the management of J Wild at the Theater in der Josefstadt (ad F Zell, Victor Léon) and, with Frln Dworak starring, supported by such performers as Carl Adolf

Friese (Bernard), Otto Maran (Blanchard) and Viktoria Pohl-Meiser (Aurélie), it proved an enormous success, running up a quite outstanding 100 successive nights, 16 further performances in repertoire, and encouraging the management to repeat the experiment of, in particular, French vaudeville-opérettes over a number of years. *Les Petites Brebis, Le Voyage de Corbillon* and *Le Papa de Francine* brought them further successes, but only the vast and international triumph of the Josefstädter Theater's *Les Fêtards* ever outdid the record set up there by the hugely popular *Toto.*

The Vienna version was smartly picked up for a German production at Hamburg's ever-interesting Carl-Schultze Theater, with Frln Bergère in the title role and manager José Ferenczy subsequently took the show to Berlin. It proved such a success that the Neues Theater was kept open for the entire summer and *Tata-Toto* alone was played through until the opening of the new season. This version was also heard at the German-language Irving Place Theater in New York, with Elly Bender in the title roles, and Adolf Link as Blanchart, whilst Budapest's Népszínház followed on with a good 30-performance season of Klára Küry playing *Toto és Tata* (ad Emil Makai) in an Hungarian adaptation. *Tata-Toto* returned to Berlin for a run at the Friedrich Wilhelmstädtisches Theater in 1900.

The show did less well, however, in what appear to have been some underpowered English-language versions. A first British adaptation (ad A M Thompson, J J Wood, E Boyd-Jones) was produced by Willie Edouin in Leeds in 1897 with Marie Montrose starred alongside E J Lonnen (Cabestan), Roland Cunningham (Gaston) and Alys Rees (Cezarine). It visited the suburban Metropole Theatre in Camberwell before it fizzled out on the road, but nine years later Edouin tried again. He had the piece revised, and mounted it under the unfortunate pantomime-sounding title of *Jack and Jill* (ad Barton White) at Manchester's Gaiety Theatre with Stella Gastelle starred. Again, it did not find its way to central London. In America a heavily revised version, with Banès's score replaced by some pieces by the ex-Austrian Alfred Müller-Norden, was produced by Nathaniel Roth in 1904 (Princess Theater 30 September) under the title *The West Point Cadet.* Della Fox featured in the dual lead role, supported by Joseph Herbert in the role of Washington Graft (a name which gives some idea of the style of the adaptation) for just four Broadway performances of a show which was ultimately a rip-off, rather than a production, of *Toto.*

Another musical play called *Toto* was produced in Britain in 1916 (Duke of York's Theatre 19 April). Written by Gladys Unger with lyrics by Arthur Anderson and music by Archibald Joyce and Merlin Morgan, it was a musical adaptation of Alfred Capus's *Les Deux Écoles* and its Toto (Mabel Russell) was a little Parisian person who set married men in a whirl. She lasted only 77 performances in London, but she toured happily for several years and the show even got itself produced in Budapest (Lujza Blaha Színház 7 April 1922, ad Zsolt Harsányi).

The title *Toto* was also used in Austria for the local adaptation of Meilhac, Halévy and Offenbach's *Le Château à Toto,* produced at the Carltheater in 1869.

Austria: Theater in der Josefstadt *Tata-Toto* 28 September 1894; Germany: Carl-Schultze Theater, Hamburg *Tata-Toto* 25 December 1894, Neues Theater, Berlin 18 May 1895; Hungary: Népszínház *Toto és Tata* 5 April 1895; USA: Irving Place Theater 11 February 1897; UK: Grand Theatre, Leeds *Toto and Tata* 23 August 1897, Gaiety Theatre, Manchester *Jack and Jill* 29 October 1906

TOULMOUCHE, Frédéric [Michel] (b Nantes, 4 August 1850; d Paris, 20 February 1909).

A composer for his own pleasure rather than with any career thoughts in mind, Toulmouche studied music under Massé in Paris and thereafter contributed scores to the opérette stage for some 30 years, winning some agreeable success with some attractive work, but without ever penning the one major work which might have brought him full-scale success. His first full-length opérette, *Le Moutier de Saint-Guignolet,* was produced in Belgium with sufficient positive notice for it to be taken up for Paris where, revised, and produced under the title of *La Veillée de noces,* it had a good run of over 50 nights at the Menus-Plaisirs. It was subsequently produced in London as *The Wedding Eve* (Trafalgar Square Theatre September 1892). His *Mademoiselle ma femme* was played for 72 Parisian performances with Rosalia Lambrecht in the central role, whilst *Tante Agnès,* first seen at the Paris Olympia, was later played in Budapest as *Ágnes Néni* (ad Dezső Vidor, Magyar Színház, September 1899).

Toulmouche's other stage works included the ballets *Les Deux Tentations* (1895) for the Nouveau Théâtre, *Pierrot au Hammam* (1897) for the Olympia and *Madame Malbrouck* (1898 w H José) for the Casino de Paris.

He was, for a period, director of the Théâtre des Menus-Plaisirs.

1882 **Ah! le Bon Billet** (Bureau-Jattiot [ie, E Bureau, F Jattiot]) 1 act Théâtre de la Renaissance 6 December

1885 **Le Moutier de Saint-Guignolet** (Bureau-Jattiot) Galeries Saint-Hubert, Brussels 5 May

1888 **La Veillée de noces** revised *Le Moutier de Saint-Guignolet* ad Alexandre Bisson Théâtre des Menus-Plaisirs 27 November

1892 **La Belle au coeur dormant** 1 act Le Clou 25 January

1892 **L'Âme de la patrie** (Lionel Bonnemère) 1 act St Brieuc 9 July

1893 **Mademoiselle ma femme** (Maurice Ordonneau, Octave Pradels) Théâtre des Menus-Plaisirs 5 May

1894 **La Chanson du roi** (Bonnemère) 1 act Fougères 7 January

1895 **La Perle du Cantal** (Ordonneau) Théâtre des Folies-Dramatiques 2 March

1895 **La Saint-Valentin** (Ordonneau, Fernand Beissier) Théâtre des Bouffes-Parisiens 28 March

1896 **Le Lézard** (Armand Liorat, William Busnach) 1 act Scala 29 August

1896 **Tante Agnès** (Maxime Boucheron) Olympia 27 October

1899 **La Rêve de Madame X** (Louis Lagarde, Georges Montignac) 1 act Carillon 25 March

1899 **Les Trois Couleurs** (Georges Arnould, H de Vrécourt) 1 act Olympia 29 March

1904 **Auto-Joujou** (Félix Puget) 1 act Théâtre des Capucines 24 September

1908 **La Môme Flora** (Ordonneau, Pradels) Théâtre de la Scala 26 December

1909 **Chez la sonnambule** (Bisson) 1 act Théâtre Grévin 24 March

1910 **La Demoiselle du Tabarin** (w Edmond Diet, Edmond Missa/Ordonneau, André Alexandre) Théâtre du Château d'Eau 25 March

1911 **La Marquise de Chicago** (Ordonneau, Beissier, Louis Hérel) Enghien 26 September

THE TOURISTS Musical comedy in 2 acts by R H Burnside. Music by Gustave Kerker. New Lyric Theatre, Philadelphia, 21 May; Daly's Theater, New York, 25 August 1906.

In the course of 24 hours in Rangapang in the Hindustan, a young American, John Duke (Alfred Hickman), who has escaped the not-very-eagle eye of his hopeless tutor, Timothy Todd (Richard Golden), gets mixed up with a rajah (William Pruette) and a princess (Vera Michelena); a Yankee multi-millionaire called Benjamin Blossom (Phil Ryley) toting five marriageable daughters headed by Dora (Julia Sanderson), all of whom he destines for titled gentlemen; their governess (Della Niven); and a bandit (Albert Froom) impersonating the Boojam of Bangalore. Since John is a ''Duke'' it is safe betting that the eldest Blossom daughter will be his by the time the comical complications of two acts have been ironed out. The Princess, who was supposed to marry the (real) Boojam of Bangalore, gets the Captain of the Guard (Howard Chambers) with whom she has been singing about ''A Game of Hearts.'' W H Denny, formerly of D'Oyly Carte's Savoy Theatre company and the original Grand Inquisitor of *The Gondoliers*, played Loofah, the owner of the Hotel Oriental, and George A Schiller was the ex-court physician.

Both the book and the score of *The Tourists* showed that their writers had studied—and borrowed from—many of the more successful musical comedies of the recent years, as well as a few comic operas from further back. Kerker's score included a traditional entry song for the Rajah, some pattering pieces for Timothy Todd, a waltz declaring ''Love Is a Wonderful Thing,'' a *Florodora*-style double quartet (''Which One Shall We Marry?''), the latest in the endless line of songs hymning ''Dear Old Broadway'' (with a verse for Philadelphia as well) and a dance speciality called ''The Gnomes.''

If originality was not precisely rife, the combination was nevertheless jolly enough to please, and Sam and Lee Shubert's production of *The Tourists* ran for a more than useful 124 performances on Broadway before continuing its life on the road.

The Tourists was a title already well known on the American circuits, for the variety farce comedy *The Tourists in a Pullman Car* (Pittsburgh, Pa 8 September 1879), a combination of low comedy, songs and speciality acts written and led by Will A Mestayer, was for many years one of the most popular of such entertainments in the country's outerbacks. Although the ''Pullman Car'' remained officially in the title, Mestayer's troupe were fondly known as ''The Tourists.'' Mestayer had died just months before the comic opera borrowing ''his'' title hit the stage.

TOURS, Frank E[dward] (b Hammersmith, London, 1 September 1877; d Los Angeles, 2 February 1963). Conductor, arranger, orchestrator and sometime composer to the musical stage on both sides of the Atlantic.

The son of the well-known conductor, composer and arranger W Berthold Tours (d London, 11 March 1897), Frank Tours studied music at London's Royal College of Music and was employed thereafter, for many years, as a theatre conductor. At the age of 21 he was musical director for Marie Lloyd's tour of Granville Bantock's musical comedy *The ABC*, and over the next 20 years he conducted shows in a series of London theatres (*Lady Madcap, The Little Cherub, The Gay Gordons, The Dashing Little Duke, Captain Kidd, Irene,* et al) and, from 1912 and increasingly thereafter, in American houses (*The Kiss Waltz, The Wedding Trip, Robin Hood* and *Rob Roy* revivals, *Tonight's the Night, Step This* Way, *Follow Me, Irene, Love o' Mike, The Highwayman* revival, *Rock-a-Bye Baby, The Lady in Red, Mecca,* several editions of the *Ziegfeld Follies, Smiles, Face the Music, As Thousands Cheer, Jubilee,* the *Music Box Revues*, *Red, Hot and Blue!*, etc). He was also, for a period, musical director at the Plaza picture theatre in London.

As a composer, he made an early attempt at comic opera with a musical version of *The Lady of Lyons,* but he was best known as an adept of the additional number, composing songs or part-scores for such pieces as *Mr Wix of Wickham, The Dairymaids, The Little Cherub, See See, The New Aladdin,* Broadway's semi-British *The Hoyden* and *The Gay Gordons.* He actually turned down the opportunity to write the full score for the last-named piece, but he did write the whole music for Seymour Hicks's subsequent *The Dashing Little Duke,* only to find it perforated with Jerome Kern numbers in the course of the run. After the limited success of this piece, he returned to composing piecework and wrote individual songs for a number of further shows, including *Miss Information* (1915), *Mr Manhattan* (1916), *Follow Me* (1916), *Mayflowers* (1925) and *Blue Eyes* (1928), as well as for the music halls (''Beyond the Sunset,'' ''Red Rose,'' ''In Flanders Fields''). His only other full score was that for the musical comedy *Girl o' Mine* (including a ''song entitled ''Silver Lining''), produced by Elisabeth Marbury and the Shuberts for 48 performances in 1918 and then taken around America as *The Victory Girl.* In later years he readapted the music for the British adaptation of *Walzer aus Wien* for Broadway and spent six years working for Paramount Pictures in Britain and in America (*The Cocoanuts,* etc).

In spite of his long period as a contributor to the musical stage, Tours's most successful single song was not a show number but his setting of Rudyard Kipling's ''Mother o' Mine'' as performed by Richard Crooks, et al.

1901 **Melnotte, or The Gardener's Bride** (Arthur Anderson/Herbert Shelley) Coronet Theater 30 September

1902 **Mr Wix of Wickham** (w Frank Seddon, George Everard, Herbert Darnley/Darnley) Borough Theatre, Stratford East 21 July

1905 **The Lady Bankrupt** (Owen Hall) 1 act Empress, Brixton 24 November; Oxford Music Hall 2 July 1906

1906 **The Dairymaids** (w Paul Rubens/Rubens, Arthur Wimperis/Alexander M Thompson, Robert Courtneidge) Apollo Theatre 14 April

1907 **The Hoyden** (w Rubens/Tristan Bernard ad Cosmo Hamilton) Knickerbocker Theater, New York 19 October

1907 **A Dress Rehearsal** (w ''A Lotte''/Seymour Hicks, A C Robatt) 1 act Tivoli 2 December

1909 **The Dashing Little Duke** (Adrian Ross/ Hicks) Hicks Theatre 17 February

1910 **Cook's Man** (Tours) 1 act London Coliseum 4 April

1910 **Little Johnnie Jones** (Preston Wayne/H M Vernon) 1 act Tottenham Palace 9 May

1910 **The Model and the Man** (C H Bovill/Hicks) 1 act London Hippodrome 22 August

1910 **Lady at Large** (Hicks) 1 act King's Theatre, Southsea 10 October

1911 **La Belle Paree** (w Jerome Kern/Edward Madden/Edgar Smith) Winter Garden, New York 20 March

1912 **O-Mi-Iy** (w Herman Finck/Hicks) 1 act London Hippodrome 25 March

1918 **Girl o' Mine** (aka *Oh Mama!*) (w Augustus Barrétt/Philip Bartholomae) Bijou Theater, New York 28 January

1918 **The Victory Girl** revised *Girl o' Mine* (ad Alex Sullivan, Lynn Cowan) Syracuse, NY 16 November

1920 **Mimi** (w Adolf Philipp/Edward Paulton/Paulton, Philipp) Shubert Belasco Theater, Washington, DC 13 March

TOVARICH Musical comedy in 2 acts by David Shaw based on the play by Jacques Deval [ie, Jacques Boularan] as adapted by Robert E Sherwood. Lyrics by Anne Crosswell. Music by Lee Pockriss. Broadway Theater, New York, 18 March 1963.

A musical adaptation of the successful 1933 French play (subsequently played widely in translation and filmed with Claudette Colbert and Charles Boyer in its lead roles), *Tovarich* featured Vivien Leigh (Tony Award) and Jean-Pierre Aumont as a Russian émigré couple, Grand Duchess Tatiana Petrovna and Prince Mikhail Alexandrovitch Ouratieff, who are reduced to taking jobs as servants in the Parisian household of Pennsylvania businessman Charles Davis (George S Irving). The younger members of the Davis household (Byron Mitchell, Margery Gray) are very taken with their new servants, but the pair are of even more substantial interest to the financial community as they are caretaking a vast sum of money entrusted to them by the murdered Czar. By the end of the play that trust has been betrayed: they have not taken the cash for themselves, but they have been conned by communist Commissar Gorotchenko (Alexander Scourby) in giving it to him to help ''feed the starving peasants in Russia.'' The Grand-Ducal pair remain servants.

The musical part of *Tovarich* was provided by Anne Crosswell and Lee Pockriss, a pair who had earlier made an off-Broadway musical out of *The Importance of Being Earnest,* and the piece was produced on Broadway by Abel Farman and Sylvia Harris for a 264-performance run, a run largely boosted by Miss Leigh's presence and performance. A German adaptation by Gert Wilden sr and jr was produced at Aachen in 1981.

Germany: Stadttheater, Aachen *Towarischtsch* 23 February 1981

Recording: original cast (Capitol/EMI)

TOYE, Wendy [TOYE, Beryl M Jessie] (b Hackney, London, 1 May 1917).

Originally a dancer, Miss Toye appeared in the musical theatre as the child, Marigold, in Fraser-Simson's *Toad of Toad Hall* (1930), in the spectacular *The Golden Toy* (1934), *Tulip Time* (1935) and *Follow the Girls* (1945) and played the role of Winnie in the London production of *Annie Get Your Gun* (1948). She had, by this time, already developed a considerable career as a choreographer and a director, arranging the dances for a long list of revues and for such musicals as *The Lisbon Story, Panama Hattie, Jenny Jones, Gay Rosalinda* and *Follow the Girls,* and staging C B Cochran's productions of *Big Ben* and *Bless the Bride.*

Plate 395. **Wendy Toye's** *ballets for the wartime* The Lisbon Story *mixed balletic steps with musical-theatre dance to great effect.*

She subsequently directed a long series of London musical productions including *Tough at the Top, And So to Bed, Wild Thyme, Lady at the Wheel,* the famous Sadler's Wells production of *Orpheus in the Underworld* and its fellow versions of *La Vie parisienne* and *Die Fledermaus, Virtue in Danger,* the long-running *Robert and Elizabeth, On the Level,* the Theatre Royal, Drury Lane version of *The Great Waltz* and the 1971 revival of *Show Boat,* as well as the Chichester Festival musicals *R Loves J* and *Follow the Star,* the revue *Cowardy Custard,* and musicals, operas and light operas from Newbury (*Once Upon a Mattress*) to Turkey (*The Mikado*) in a career of more than 60 years in the theatre.

LES TRAVAUX D'HERCULE Opéra-bouffe in 3 acts by Gaston de Caillavet and Robert de Flers. Music by Claude Terrasse. Théâtre des Bouffes-Parisiens, Paris, 7 March 1901.

Following Terrasse's first opéra-bouffe success with *La Petite Femme de Loth* (1900), the composer joined with the playwriting couple who were generally agreed to be the most ''spirituel'' of all Parisian comic writers, de Flers and de Caillavet, on another burlesque of things ancient in *Les Travaux d'Hercule.* In their version of mythology, we learn that it was not, after all, the lazy, cowardly, barely potent demigod Hercules (Abel Tarride) who accomplished the famous 12 labors, but the owner of those infamous stables which were the object of one of the labors, Augias, King of Elis (Colas). This extravagantly physical and energetic fellow not only zooms around doing labors, he also borrows Hercules's neglected wife, Omphale (Amélie Diéterle), and labors over her. However, in the end, she finds all this energy and enthusiasm rather more than she can take and, labors or no labors, she goes back to her more peaceful and passive demigod who has somehow ended up getting the credit for everything Augias has done. Amongst the supporting cast Victor Henry ''made a hit'' as Palémon, a demi-demigod, and Léo Demoulin was the amazonian Erichtona.

Produced by André Lénéka and Tarride at the Bouffes-Parisiens, *Les Travaux d'Hercule* won delighted praise from those who welcomed the return of ''Offenbachian'' opéra-bouffe, but its first run was limited to little more than 80 performances. It was subsequently produced in Hungary (ad Adolf Mérei, Ernő Keszthelyi) and in Germany, and it was revived in Paris in 1913 (3 October) at the Théâtre Fémina with Gabriel Signoret (Hercule), Henri Fabert (Augias) and Edmée Favart (Omphale) featured, in a version revised by the composer which provided the female star with a new Laughing Song. Like the bulk of the Terrasse/de Flers and de Caillavet works, it remains more talked-about than performed, but it was briefly seen at Saint-Maur in 1994 (9 April).

The same title was used for a piece with music and text by Antoine Duhamel produced at the Opéra de Lyon in 1981.

Hungary: Magyar Színház *Herkules Munkái* 25 April 1902; Germany: Neues Operetten-Theater, Leipzig *Die Arbeiten des Herkules* 28 March 1908

Recording: complete (Gaîté-Lyrique)

A TREE GROWS IN BROOKLYN Musical play in 2 acts by Betty Smith and George Abbott based on the novel of the same name by Betty Smith. Lyrics by Dorothy Fields. Music by Arthur Schwartz. Alvin Theater, New York, 19 April 1951.

A highly successful novel, then a film, then a stage musical, Betty Smith's gentle, downbeat tale of unexceptional Brooklyn folk, as remade with songs, followed the amorous misfortunes of sisters Katie (Marcia van Dyke) and Cissy (Shirley Booth) through a decade and a half of the early years of the 20th century. Sincere, faithful Katie is unlucky enough to put her trust in the charming but weak and downfallen-by-drink Johnny Nolan (Johnny Johnston) who is unable to keep a job and brings her little but sorrow, whilst flippant Cissy goes from one beau to another, christening each one Harry after the fondly remembered first (Albert Linville) until that first returns and turns out a disappointment. By the finale, widowed Katie has put her hopes in daughter Francie (Nomi Mitty) and Cissy has settled for her latest beau (Nathaniel Frey). The score of the show ranged from the comical, as in Cissie's memories of her first love (''He Had Refinement'') to the lively in Johnny's ''I'm Like a New Broom'' and the polka-ed wedding ensemble ''Look Who's Dancing,'' and to Katie's heartfelt ''Make the Man Love Me,'' set alongside a group of ballads and a rather pasted-in (but, for the period, obligatory) Halloween ballet.

George Abbott and Robert Fryer's production won many friends, Miss Booth and her endearingly comic performance, which had become (in contrast to book and film) the center of the evening, won more, but *A Tree Grows in Brooklyn* failed to establish itself and its 270 Broadway performances and a tour, led by Joan Blondell (who had been Cissy in the novel's 1945 film version), did not encourage anyone else to take it up.

Recording: original cast (Columbia)

TRÉFEU [de TRÉVAL], Étienne [Victor] (b Saint-Lô, 25 September 1821; d Paris, June 1903).

A prolific songwriter for the Parisian cafés-concerts, Tréfeu moved into the musical theatre with the rise of the small comic opérette in the mid-1850s. He wrote or co-wrote the texts for a large number of such short pieces, amongst the earliest of which the crazy medieval *Croquefer,* set by his friend Offenbach, and *Les Petits Prodiges* with a score by Émile Jonas, were successfully played at Offenbach's Théâtre des Bouffes-Parisiens. It was, however, his first full-length work, a further but much more substantial piece of medieval burlesque, *Geneviève de Brabant,* which gave Tréfeu his first big international success, a success which was repeated a few years later when, after the unsuccessful *Die Rheinnixen, Coscoletto* and some further happy one-act pieces (*Jeanne qui pleure et Jean qui rit, Il Signor Fagotto, Le Soldat magicien*), he again combined with Offenbach and with Charles Nuitter on the greatly successful comic opera *La Princesse de Trébizonde.*

Thereafter, although he adapted the libretti of *Javotte* (from Alfred Thompson's English original), *Boule de neige* (with music from the unsuccessful *Barkouf*) and *Le Chat du Diable* (from H B Farnie's original *Whittington*), he co-authored only one further original full-length work of any significance, the Émile Jonas *Goldchignon / Chignon d'or* which, although produced in Vienna in translation and in Brussels, was never played in Paris. His output in these later years of his writing life was mainly limited to little pieces for those cafés-concerts where he had begun his writing career and for the salons of Paris.

Tréfeu apparently also had a hand in the first draft of the text for Offenbach's *Le Violoneux,* but he received no credit alongside MM Chevalet and Mestépès on the finished work.

1854 **Les Echos de Rosine** (Alphonse Thys) 1 act Paris Salon 13 October

1855 **Le Rêve d'une nuit d'été** (Jacques Offenbach) 1 act Théâtre des Bouffes-Parisiens 30 July

1855 **Les Trois Troubadours** (Julien Nargéot) 1 act Folies-Nouvelles 19 December

1857 **Croquefer, ou Le Dernier des paladins** (Offenbach/w Adolphe Jaime) 1 act Théâtre des Bouffes-Parisiens 12 February

1857 **Les Petits Prodiges** (Émile Jonas/w Jaime) Théâtre des Bouffes-Parisiens 19 November

1859 **Geneviève de Brabant** (Offenbach) Théâtre des Bouffes-Parisiens 19 November

1863 **Il Signor Fagotto** (Offenbach/w Charles Nuitter) 1 act Ems 11 July

1864 **Die Rheinnixen** (Offenbach/w Nuitter) Hofoper, Vienna 4 February

1864 **Le Soldat magicien** (aka *Le Fifre enchanté*) (Offenbach/w Nuitter) 1 act Ems 9 July

1864 **Jeanne qui pleure et Jean qui rit** (Offenbach/w Nuitter) 1 act Ems 19 July; Théâtre des Bouffes-Parisiens 3 November 1865

1865 **Coscoletto** (Offenbach/w Nuitter) Ems 24 July

1867 **Geneviève de Brabant** 3-act version w Hector Crémieux Théâtre des Menus-Plaisirs 26 December

1868 **En manches de chemise** (Étienne Ettling/w Émile Mendel) 1 act Alcazar 2 April

1868 **Un bal à la Sous-Préfecture** (A de Villebichot) 1 act Alcazar

1868 **L'Invalide à la tête de bois** (Maximilien Graziani) 1 act Odéon 3 April

1869 **La Princesse de Trébizonde** (Offenbach/w Nuitter) Baden-Baden 31 July

1869 **La Romance de la rose** (Offenbach/w Jules Prével) 1 act Théâtre des Bouffes-Parisiens 11 December

1871 **Javotte** (*Cinderella the Younger*) French version w Nuitter (Théâtre de l'Athénée)

1871 **Boule de neige** revised *Barkouf* w Nuitter Théâtre des Bouffes-Parisiens 14 December

1872 **Der schwarze Korsar** (Offenbach/w Nuitter) Theater an der Wien 21 September

1872 **Le Nain** (Ettling) 1 act Café Tertulia 19 November

1873 **Le Tigre** (Ettling) 1 act Café Tertulia 5 April

1873 **Der Goldchignon** (*Chignon d'or*) (Émile Jonas/w Eugène Grangé) Strampfertheater, Vienna 20 May; Théâtre des Fantaisies-Parisiennes, Brussels 17 October 1874

1874 **L'Oeil de M Expert** (Ettling) 1 act Eldorado 21 November

1878 **Le Chat botté** (de Bourdet, Gaston Serpette, Coedès/w Ernest Blum) Théâtre de la Gaîté 18 May

1880 **Monsieur de Floridor** (Théodore de Lajarte/w Nuitter) 1 act Opéra-Comique 11 October

1889 **Le Marché aux domestiques** (Luigi Bordèse) 1 act Le Creuzot

1892 **Chien et chatte** (G Bornier/de Forges ad w Hubert) 1 act Eden-Concert 21 May

1893 **Le Chat du Diable** (*Whittington*) French version w Nuitter (Théâtre du Châtelet)

1897 **La Gaudriole** (Albert Vizentini/w Nuitter) Aix-les-Bains 12 September

TRELAWNY Musical in 2 acts by Aubrey Woods, George Rowell and Julian Slade taken from *Trelawny of the Wells* by Arthur Wing Pinero. Book by Aubrey Woods. Music and lyrics by Julian Slade. Theatre Royal, Bristol, 12 January 1972; Sadler's Wells Theatre, London, 27 June 1972.

Pinero's pretty period tale told of actress Rose Trelawny (Hayley Mills), who leaves her profession to move to Cavendish Square and become affianced to Arthur Gower (John Watts), the son of the lofty Sir William Gower (Timothy West). Stiflingly unhappy in this new world, she runs back to the theatre only to find that her acting abilities have deserted her. But in the new, naturalistic play written by the ever-faithful Tom Wrench (Ian Richardson), Rose is cast opposite a new actor—Arthur has come to join his beloved Rose in her world. Slade's score turned out some truly touching numbers—Rose's thoughts of ''The One Who Isn't There,'' Arthur's letter to his sympathetic aunt, the old ballad ''Ever of Thee I'm Fondly Dreaming'' and the rapprochement scene between Rose and Sir William (''Two Fools'')—as well as some, like Wrench's philosophy of ''Life,'' forceful and some—particularly the joyous pantomimic ''The Turn of Avonia Bunn''—colorfully theatrical, and all illustrating the filleted Pinero book effectively.

Originally produced at Bristol, *Trelawny* was taken up by Veronica Flint-Shipman and the young Cameron Mackintosh and brought to London's Sadler's Wells Theatre with Richardson and Watts joined by Gemma Craven (Rose), Max Adrian (Sir William) and Joyce Carey (Miss Gower) at the head of the cast. It did well enough there to be taken to the West End proper (Prince of Wales Theatre 3 August 1972), but after four months it was obliged to quit the house and, no other theatre being available, closed after an all-in total of 177 London performances.

Recording: original cast (Decca)

TRENTINI, Emma (b Mantua, 1878; d Milan, 12 April 1959). Diminutive operatic soprano who zoomed into the musical theatre, then pouted her way out.

Trentini made her first stage appearances in opera in her native Italy before she was taken to America by Oscar Hammerstein in 1906. There she appeared in the lightest roles of the soprano repertoire (Nedda, Frasquita, Musetta, Antonia, etc) until Hammerstein's operatic endeavor collapsed and he transferred her to the starring role in his alternative venture into the musical theatre. The role was that of ''naughty'' Marietta d'Alténa in Victor Herbert's *Naughty Marietta* (1910) and Trentini scored an outstanding success with the character of the Italian countess disguised as a casket girl and then as a boy, as she introduced Herbert's ''Naughty Marietta,'' the Italian Street Song and, with Orville Harrold, ''Ah! Sweet Mystery of Life.'' When Herbert refused to write again for the ill-behaved soprano, Rudolf Friml was given the opportunity to provide the score for *The Firefly* (1912), another piece that allowed the star to play an Italian and to get into boy's clothes for a good part of the evening before emerging as a full-blown prima donna. Trentini scored a second major hit, notably with the Neapolitanate serenade ''Giannina Mia'' and ''Love Is Like a Firefly.''

She next took the role of Helena in a made-over Broadway version of the Austrian hit *Polenblut* called, at first, *The Ballet Girl* and then *The Peasant Girl,* and seemed to be in line for a third hit. However, anxious to go off and pursue a love affair with Friml, she refused to extend her Broadway contract beyond its initial eight weeks and had to be replaced. In spite of her skills and attractions, her frequent displays of unprofessionalism finally rendered her all but unemployable and, although she later played in vaudeville and appeared in London in

Plate 396. **Ivy Tresmand** *trips across a decreasing row of chairs with Ray Kay in London's* The Red Mill.

the revue *The Whirl-I-Gig* (1919), she ultimately went back home to Italy and oblivion.

TRESMAND, Ivy (b London, 15 December 1898; d South Africa, 2 November 1980). British soubrette of the 1920s and 1930s.

After early appearances in the chorus of the revue *Shell Out* (1915) and in small parts in the musical *Houp-La!* (1916, Betty) and the revue *Bubbly,* Ivy Tresmand was cast at the age of 21 in the role of Tina in London's version of *The Red Mill.* She subsequently appeared in the revue *Just Fancy,* took over the comic role of Margot in *Sybil* from May Beatty and featured as Sophie Lavalle in *The Lady of the Rose* (*Die Frau im Hermelin*), both at Daly's Theatre, then played Frou Frou in a revival of the *Merry Widow* and Patricia in *Katja the Dancer,* prior to starring in a series of late 1920s West End musical comedies at what proved the peak of her career: Yvonne in *Yvonne,* Looloo in the British version of *Hit the Deck,* Lora Moore in *Follow Through* and Thomasina Tucker in *Little Tommy Tucker* (1930).

She later toured as Bobby Carr in *The Compulsory Wife,* flopped out of town in *On the Air* (1934), played with the Co-Optimists and toured Britain in the leading role of *Careless Rapture* (1936) and then South Africa with Leslie Henson (*Going Greek, Swing Along*). She remained in South Africa, appearing in concert parties and in plays, and although she ultimately returned to spend some time in Worthing, she did not thereafter return to the London musical stage.

TREUMANN, Karl (b Hamburg, 22 July 1823; d Baden bei Wien, 18 April 1877). Midhusband to the Viennese Operette tradition.

Born in Germany, while his father was working at the Stadttheater in Hamburg, Karl Treumann began his own theatrical career at the age of 18, alongside his brother Franz in the chorus at the Deutsches Theater in Pest. He soon rose to be a popular member of the company, playing major roles, until the theatre was destroyed by fire in 1847. However, thanks to a recommendation from a fellow singer (one story says it was Suppé) who had found an engagement at the Theater an der Wien, Franz Pokorny engaged Treumann for that theatre as first comedian for comedies and musical pieces. In 1851, unhappy under the management of Pokorny's son and sucessor, Treumann moved on to the Carltheater. There he was cast in often supporting comedy roles in all kinds of musical and non-musical pieces, forming with Nestroy and

Scholz a memorable trio at the head of the theatre's comic forces.

The visit of Pierre Levassor, the French actor, in 1856 suggested to him a new direction in which he might strike out. The Palais-Royal comedian played the Carltheater with a repertoire including musical vaudeville, burlesque and the first Offenbach piece, *Les Deux Aveugles,* to be seen in Vienna. Treumann set out to imitate his style of performance—a performance not unlike those purveyed by the Howard Pauls or the German Reeds in Britain—in German. He performed in programs made up of comic songs (''Der Jungg'sell,'' ''Les Deux Gendarmes'') and scenes (*Der Wiener Poldl vom Burgtheater, Die Leiden eines Choristen, D'Froschmirl, Der Hans und sein Basle, Wiener Sommervergnügen, Schicksal einer Böhmischen Köchin,* etc), sometimes with such partners as Gallmeyer or Frln Zergraf. Then in October 1858, as part of his benefit bill he translated, adapted, directed and starred as Peter in *Die Hochzeit bei Laternenschein,* a Viennesed version of *Le Mariage aux lanternes* and the first Offenbach work to be played in Vienna in German. Offenbach protested at the unauthorized adaptation, but soon went quiet when it proved a considerable success. Treumann thereafter adapted and/or appeared in a number of other Offenbach pieces for the Carltheater and its manager Johann Nestroy, and he also introduced Offenbach's works to Hungary with German-language performances of *Hochzeit bei Laternenscheine, Das Mädchen von Elisonzo* and *Die Zaubergeige,* guest-played at the Budai Színkör in May/June 1859.

In October 1860 Nestroy ended his management of the Carltheater, and Treumann moved on. He had previously applied for permission to build a theatre of his own and, no little thanks to some friends in high places, he had been granted royal permission to construct and operate a sixth Vienna theatre. Unfortunately he found the time too short to raise sufficient cash to build the solid edifice he had in mind, and the Theater am Franz-Josefs-Kai which resulted was a fairly flimsy building. That didn't stop it from quickly becoming decidedly popular. Treumann opened his house the day after Nestroy handed over the Carltheater to Gustav Brauer, with many of the old Carltheater company, including Wilhelm Knaack and Anna Grobecker, amongst his players and Franz von Suppé from the Theater an der Wien as musical director. He staged mostly spectacles-coupés consisting of heavily adapted versions of the opérettes of Offenbach and other French composers such as Caspers, Adam, Massé and Poise and including *Tschin-Tschin* (Peter Gix), *Meister Fortunio und sein Liebeslied, Daphnis und Chloë, Herr und Madame Denis* (Sergeant Bellerose), *Salon Pitzelberger, Tromb-al-ca-zar, Häuptling Abendwind* (*Vent du Soir*), *Die Damen vom Stand* (*Mesdames de la Halle*), *Die verwandelte Katze, Zwei arme Blinde, Herr von Zuckerl* (*MM Dunanan*) and a variety of short comedies, also often taken from the French. In many cases the adaptations were uncredited, in other cases (*Daphnis und Chloë,* etc) Treumann's name eventually appeared as author . . . even though someone else had sometimes been originally credited.

Treumann also ventured into larger works with the production of *Die schöne Magellone,* his version of Offenbach's original *Geneviève de Brabant* (played Sifroy), *Die Seufzerbrücke* (*Le Pont des soupirs,* Cornarino, with ''original melodies by Franz von Suppé'' inserted) and *Die Schwätzerin von Saragossa* (*Les Bavards,* Roland). Even more enterprisingly, he also initiated performances of home-brewed musical theatre, producing the first performances of *Zehn Mädchen und kein Mann*—Suppé's follow-up to his successful *Das Pensionat,* in which the manager appeared as Herr von Schönhahn, the father of the 10 titular maidens—the same composer's equally successful *Flotte Bursche* (Fleck), and *Die Kartenschlägerin.* He thus earned himself in retrospect the honor of being the principal assistant at the birth of what was to become the Viennese Operette tradition.

The Theater am Franz-Josefs-Kai (familiarly known as the Treumanntheater or Kaitheater) got the Offenbach seal of approval when the company of the Théâtre des Bouffes-Parisiens introduced their Parisian repertoire (*Le Pont des soupirs, Vent du soir, Un mari à la porte,* etc) there to such Viennese as could comprehend them in 1861 and 1862, and the composer himself conducted several of his works during the season. He also gave a cello concert on the Kaitheater stage. Nestroy played several good seasons in Treumann's little theatre as well, scoring a notable hit as Pan in *Daphnis und Chloë.* In mid-1863, after three lively and successful years of operation, Treumann was able to make plans, as he was obliged to, to replace his wooden theatre with a stone one. But one June night the Theater am Franz-Josefs-Kai was struck by fire, and overnight Treumann and his company were homeless. There was no time to rebuild and yet carry on the season, so Treumann moved his operations to the Carltheater, which was again empty. He continued as before, playing the most successful items of his repertoire and introducing new Offenbach pieces (*Der Regimentzauberer, Hanni weint,* etc), but his position as unofficial Vienna agent and adapter for Offenbach was dented when Strampfer at the Theater an der Wien made a lucrative contract with Offenbach which secured him not only a great success with *La Belle Hélène* but also a regular supply of the works over which Treumann had previously held sway.

In 1866 Treumann handed over the direction of the Carltheater to Anton Ascher, but he continued to play there from time to time, taking part in what was now only a share of the Offenbach goldmine: whilst Ascher produced Treumann's version of *Pariser Leben* (1867, Prosper/Frick/Brazilian) and Julius Hopp's of *Die Prinzessin von Trapezunt* (1871), the opposition played *Blaubart* (1866) and *Die Grossherzogin von Gérolstein* (1867). Amongst the local pieces in the house's repertoire, Treumann also played Piffard in Zaytz's successful *Mannschaft an Bord,* the old balletmaster in Suppé's *Das Korps der Rache* and Schubert in the pasticcio Operette *Franz Schubert* (1864), and created the role of the comical art critic, Midas, in Suppé's *Die schöne Galathee* (1865).

In parallel to his acting career, progressively hampered by ill health in later years, he continued to write, turning out many further adaptations from the French, including the Viennese versions of Offenbach's *La Jolie Parfumeuse,* Hervé's *Le Joueur de flûte,* Lecocq's *La Petite Mariée* and *Kosiki* and of the Parisian spectacle made of Jules Verne's *Le Voyage autour du monde en 80 jours,* as well as turning the French libretto prepared by Victor Wilder and Alfred Delacour for the Carltheater into the German *Prinz Methusalem* for Johann Strauss. His last work was a spectacular adaptation of *Der Kurier der Zar.*

An all-around man of the theatre of wide and considerable talents and great enthusiasms, Treumann, particularly by virtue of his imaginative venture at the Theater am Franz-Josefs-Kai, established himself as one of the major characters of the earliest part of the modern history of Viennese theatre, which he helped to shepherd through the years which led its musical theatre from its first experience of Offenbach, through Suppé's ground-breaking Operetten, to the days of Johann Strauss and the "Golden Age" of Austrian Operette.

Treumann was represented on the stage as a character in Paul Knepler's *Josefine Gallmeyer* (1921) in which he was played by August Nietl.

1858 **Die Hochzeit bei Laternenscheine** (*Le Mariage aux lanternes*) German version wirh music ad Karl Binder (Carltheater)

1858 **Das Mädchen von Elisonzo** (Pépito) German version (Carltheater)

1859 **Jungfer Nachbarin** (*Bonsoir voisin*) German version w music ad Carl Krottenthaler (Carltheater)

1859 **Schuhflicker und Millionär** (*Le Savetier et le financier*) German version (Carltheater)

1859 **Die Zaubergeige** (*Le Violoneux*) German version (Carltheater)

1859 **Die Savoyarden** (*Le 66*) German version (Carltheater)

1859 **Der Ehemann vor der T(h)üre** (*Un mari à la porte*) German version (Carltheater)

1860 **Tschin-Tschin** (*Ba-ta-clan*) German version (Carltheater)

1861 **Die Tante schlaft** (*Ma tante dort*) German version (Theater am Franz-Josefs-Kai)

1861 **Ein Nase für 1000 Pfund** (Carl Binder) 1 act (Theater am Franz-Josefs-Kai)

1862 **Die Schwätzerin von Saragossa** (*Les Bavards*) German version (Theater am Franz-Josefs-Kai)

1864 **Die schönen Weiber von Georgien** (*Les Géorgiennes*) German version (Carltheater)

1867 **Pariser Leben** (*La Vie parisienne*) German version (Carltheater)

1868 **Urlaub nach Zapfenstreich** (*La Permission de dix heures*) German version (Carltheater)

1869 **Der Flötenspieler von Rom** (*Le Joueur de flûte*) German version (Carltheater)

1872 **Der Dorfadvokat** (Robert von Hornstein) 1 act Munich

1873 **Zwei Hochzeiten und ein Brautigam** (*Les Deux Noces de M Boisjoli*) German version with music by Carl Ferdinand Conradin (Carltheater)

1873 **Fünfundzwanzig Mädchen und kein Mann** expanded version of *Zehn Mädchen und kein Mann* (Franz von Suppé) Hofoper 15 April

1873 **Tricoche und Cacolet** German version w music by Suppé (Carltheater)

1874 **Schönröschen** (*La Jolie Parfumeuse*) German version (Carltheater)

1875 **Die Reise um die Erde in 80 Tagen** (*Le Voyage autour du monde en 80 jours*) German version w music by Suppé

1876 **Graziella** (*La Petite Mariée*) German version (Carltheater)

1877 **Prinz Methusalem** German version of unproduced libretto by Victor Wilder and Alfred Delacour (Johann Strauss) Carltheater 3 January

1882 **Kosiki, der Sohn der Sonne** (*Kosiki*) German version (Carltheater)

TREUMANN, Louis [POLLITZER, Ludwig] (b Vienna, 1 March 1872; d Theresienstadt, during 1942). Versatile light-comic leading man who became a major star of the Vienna stage.

Treumann began his working life in business rather than the theatre, his main connection with the dramatic art being his membership of the claque at the Carltheater. He used this connection to make useful acquaintances and finally the chorus-leader of the theatre helped him to get a job in a minor theatre in Budapest. He moved on to Laibach and Trieste, singing in choruses, then graduated to light comedy/light baritone roles in the German, Swiss and Austrian provinces. In 1899 he ended up back at the Carltheater, this time on the stage, playing Josef in *Wiener Blut,* the sweetly gormless Aristide in *Die kleinen Michus,* Izzet Pacha (*Fatinitza*), the comical Wun Hi (*Die Geisha*), Menelaus (*Die schöne Helena*), Li (*San Toy*) and Lambertier in the flop musical *Die Primadonna.*

In 1901 he played alongside top-billed Mizzi Günther in Ziehrer's *Die drei Wünsche,* as Paillasse to her Suzon in a version of *Les Saltimbanques* and Philippe to her Hortense in *Der Opernball,* and he appeared thereafter as Der Marchenkönig in *Die verwunschene Prinzessin,* Jan in *Der Bettelstudent,* Geiersberg in *Das verwunschene Schloss,* in the title role of *Der Damenschneider* and in the role of Florian alongside the Lola of Günther in the hugely successful *Das süsse Mädel.* The following season he played alongside another choice prima donna in Ilka Pálmay as Aristide Limonard in *Das gewisse Etwas* and as Sylvester Morelli in *Der liebe Schatz* before winning his most significant role to date as the onion-seller Wolf Bär Pfefferkorn in Lehár's *Der Rastelbinder.* This time he was not only the equal of his leading lady, but rated star billing on his own, and when (after a three-performance flop called *Der Glücklichste*) he and Frln Günther came together as a genuine star pair in a revival of *Apajune, der Wassermann* (Prutschesko), the partnership which had been hovering for the two years they had been together at the Carltheater gelled.

The Carltheater schedule meant that each still played without the other: Treumann played Anatole McSherry to the *Madame Sherry* of Marie Halton and Poldl in *Das Marktkind* whilst Günther appeared on between nights with Karl Streitmann in *Der Mameluck,* but they came back together again in Lehár's *Der Göttergatte* (Sofias), as husband and wife in Hellmesberger's successful *Das Veilchenmädel* (Stiebel) and again in the German musical comedy *'s Zuckersgoscherl* (Amadeus Herzig) and Ziehrer's *Der Schätzmeister* (John Botterbroad). The Hungarian operett *Der Schnurrbart* (Graf Otto Plechnitz) and Ujj's *Kaisermanöver* (1905, Czapás) were failures and, as the Carltheater took in Alexander Girardi following his walkout from the Theater an der Wien, Treumann, soon followed by Günther, abandoned the Carltheater and went the opposite way—to the Theater an der Wien.

The pair's first vehicle at the an der Wien was Leo Ascher's *Vergeltsgott* (Bogumil, Graf Karinsky) and Treumann then appeared alone in Leo Fall's *Der Rebell* (Franzl Obrowitsch) before they were cast as the lightly comic hero and heroine of the newest Lehár Operette, *Die lustige Witwe.* Treumann played Danilo Danilowitsch for the large part of *Die lustige Witwe*'s immense run, and then took his now megastardom on to the role of Top in Stritzko's short-lived Bret Harte musical *Tip-Top* before pairing with Günther again as the hero of a further major hit in *Die Dollarprinzessin* (Fredy Wehrburg). *Der schöne Gardist* (Peter) was less successful, but *Der fidele Bauer* gave Treumann another fine role, as the old peasant Matthaeus Scheichelroither, before he moved on to the newly opened Johann Strauss-Theater to star in Granichstaedten's successful *Bub oder Mädel?* (Fürst Fritz Ragan), in the title role of a revival of *Der arme Jonathan* and, joined once more by Günther, as Hadschi Stavros in Lehár's next, *Das Fürstenkind.*

In 1910 Treumann and Günther brought out *Apajune* again, Treumann starred as the detective Arsène Dupont

Plate 397. **Louis Treumann.** *The original Danilo of* Die lustige Witwe.

in *Lord Piccolo,* and the pair came back together for the 74 performances of *Das erste Weib* (Alphonse, Graf Dyllenau von Dyllendorf), the 67 nights of Fall's *Die Sirene* (Fouché) and the 73 of Weinberger's *Die romantische Frau* (Fürst Egon) to end their Johann Strauss-Theater interlude.

They returned to the Theater an der Wien for the 1911–12 and 1912–13 seasons, starring together in *Der Graf von Luxemburg* (René), *Das Fürstenkind, Die schöne Helena* (Menelaus), the 500th *Die lustige Witwe, Pariser Leben* (Frick/Brasilien) and *Der Rastelbinder* and introducing Lehár's *Eva* (Octave Flaubert), the Strauss pasticcio *Der blaue Held* (Prince Balthasar) and Kálmán's *Der kleine König* (der König). Treumann then departed to the Bürgertheater to take on the star role of Tobby Stöger in Eysler's *Ein Tag im Paradies,* to play Célestin to the *Mam'zelle Nitouche* of Annie Dirkens, and to lead the cast of Eysler's newest and less-successful *Frühling im Rhein* (Moritz Frühling).

In 1916 he went to the Carltheater for 106 performances of *Der Weltenbummler* (Hans Hölle) and 131 of *Die schöne Saskia* (Adrian von Rudder) as well as a major revival of *Der Rastelbinder* in which he once more took up his famous role. He re-paired with Mizzi Günther for the first time in several years for *Der Millionendieb*

(1918, Tangua) at Ronacher and in 1920 directed and starred in a revival of *Der Hofnarr* (Carillon) and reprised *Das Fürstenkind* at the Apollotheater. He had further starring roles in the successful *Die Frau im Hermelin* (1921, Oberst Paltitsch) and as the romantic Prince Radjami in *Die Bajadere* (1921), in the title role of the biomusical of *Offenbach* (1922) and in *Mädi* (1923, Anatole), played more *Rastelbinder*s and appeared as Lord Durham in *Agri* (1924), but from this stage, after a solid quarter of century almost nonstop in front of the Viennese public, most of it as a major star, his schedule slowed down.

In 1927 he took over as President Nikola Tonitscheff in *Die Königin* at the Theater an der Wien where in 1931, at nearly 60 years of age, he repeated the role of the Ambassador, John Cunlight, which he had played in the German production of *Viktoria und ihr Husar* the previous year, alongside Rita Georg and Ernst Nadherny in the piece's Viennese production. In 1933 he directed the Vienna production of *Rosen im Schnee.*

A singing, dancing, light-comic leading man of elegance and charm, Treumann had a remarkable career as a musical comedy star of the ''Silver Age.'' If it is as the creator of Lehár's Danilo that he is best remembered today, it was his Pfefferkorn in *Der Rastelbinder* which nevertheless remained his most outstanding, and more-often-repeated role amongst the many successful parts which he created in successful and memorable shows.

TRIAL BY JURY Dramatic cantata in 1 act by W S Gilbert. Music by Arthur Sullivan. Royalty Theatre, London, 25 March 1875.

The libretto for *Trial by Jury* was developed by Gilbert from a comic ballad he had written for the magazine *Fun* (11 April 1868) and was originally submitted to manager-composer Carl Rosa as a possible vehicle for his wife and company. Madame Parepa Rosa died, and the libretto sat in a drawer until D'Oyly Carte asked Gilbert and Sullivan for a replacement forepiece for Selina Dolaro's production of *La Périchole.* Quite what form the piece took before its eventual production is a mystery (it was advertised first as being in two acts and as set to star Selina Dolaro and Nellie Bromley—although the final piece has but one feminine role) but Sullivan quickly produced the comical score which was to be the forerunner of so many others, and after a short postponement *Trial by Jury*—in one act—was produced at the Royalty.

Pretty, greedy Angelina (Nellie Bromley) is suing Edwin (Walter Fisher) for breach-of-promise before an all-male jury and a drooling Judge (Frederic Sullivan) who are not at all interested in the defendant's admirable explanations of how a fellow can change his mind. He tries to show what a rotten husband he would make, she weeps prettily to influence the award and objects when it is suggested he is got drunk to see if he would, in fact, beat her when in his cups. The Judge solves the whole affair by deciding to marry the clever little creature himself. The score, with its pattering number for the Judge (''When I, Good Friends, Was Called to the Bar'') and its singing tenor solos (''When First My Old, Old Love I Knew,'' ''Oh, Gentlemen Listen, I Pray''), all encased in the body of a sung-through little cantata, was the most sophisticated piece of English comic opera to hit the British stage in memory.

Acclaimed by the critics, and an instant hit with the public, *Trial by Jury* was given for two seasons by Dolaro's company, and soon snapped up by dozens of other companies, notably by Emily Soldene who took it through Britain, America and the colonies, and the Swanboroughs who mounted it on burlesque territory at the Strand Theatre. When the length of Offenbach's *Madame l'Archiduc* meant that audiences for its London production were asked to forego the afterpiece, *Trial by Jury,* the public revolted and the management was forced to cut a chunk out of Offenbach's piece instead.

The little piece was quickly seen on other continents. America's Alice Oates soon had a rather approximate version on the stage in Philadelphia, with herself playing the Plaintiff to the Defendant of Henri Laurent and the Judge of John Howson, and several weeks later *Trial by Jury* made its first appearance in New York in a flung-together production by some stranded members of Julia Mathews' English troupe in which G H MacDermott played the Judge. The ''as directed by the authors'' *Trial by Jury,* however, only got an American showing a little later when Emily Soldene's troupe arrived with the little piece featured in its repertoire. And this time it hit the mark.

Henry Bracy and his wife Clara Thompson appeared as defendant and plaintiff at Melbourne's Opera House in Australia's first professional production of the piece, Soldene and Lydia Howard's troupe both took the show round that country and New Zealand, and it became a thorough-going favorite in every corner of the English-speaking world.

The show had an important London revival (1878) at the Opera Comique, as an afterpiece to *The Sorcerer,* with George Grossmith appearing as the Judge, and it was paired again with that piece on its first revival by Carte at the Savoy Theatre in 1884 with Rutland Barrington playing the chief comic role, and the participants made up to resemble Lord Garmoyle and the lawyers who had taken part in the recent front-page breach-of-promise suit taken by Savoy bit-parter May Fortescue. It returned again in 1898 with Henry Lytton featured as the Judge, and remained thereafter a fixture in the D'Oyly Carte

Plate 398. **Trial by Jury.** *Anthony Warlowe (Defendant) comes face-to-face with the court Usher (John Germain) in the Australian Opera's 1984 production.*

company's repertoire. It was also a favored piece on the program of benefit performances, and was featured at the Theatre Royal, Drury Lane, on the programs for Nellie Farren (1898) and for Ellen Terry (1906) with Gilbert himself playing the Associate on each occasion alongside juries and bridesmaids composed of the theatrically famous.

Trial by Jury was played as a forepiece to *The Mikado* on the D'Oyly Carte company's European tour of 1886, and subsequently got played in two different German versions.

Varying versions of the piece (ranging from 25 minutes to 50) have been televised and/or filmed. A 1950 CBS-TV version features Patricia Morison as Angelina, a shorter version from 1953 has Martyn Greene starred, and the most recent, in the Brent-Walker series of Gilbert and Sullivan recordings, has Frankie Howerd as the Learned Judge.

USA: Arch Street Theater, Philadelphia 22 October 1875, Eagle Theater, New York 15 November 1875; Australia: Prince of Wales Theatre/Opera House, Melbourne 24 June 1876; Germany: Wallner-Theater (Eng) 14 June 1886; Austria: Carltheater *Im Schwurgericht* 14 September 1886, Danzers Orpheum *Das Brautpaar vor Gericht* 5 October 1901

Film: World of Gilbert & Sullivan 1974

Recordings: complete (Decca), etc

Video: Brent-Walker 1982

A TRIP TO CHINATOWN Idyll of San Francisco (musical trifle) in 3 acts by Charles H Hoyt. Music written and arranged by Percy Gaunt. Powers' Grand Opera House, Decatur, Ill, 18 September 1890; Madison Square Theater, New York, 9 November 1891.

A Trip to Chinatown rates arguably as the most popular American-made show of the 19th century. As far as statistics go, it had the longest single Broadway run of any homebred musical show—657 straight performances in its initial New York run in 1891–93, not counting a return visit of seven weeks in 1894 (Madison Square Theater 12 February)—but it was its additional and widespread life as a touring piece, both in America and abroad, which made it such a phenomenon. In fact, the show took its time to come to Broadway. It was first produced a whole year prior to arriving at the Madison Square Theater, and it made its real first New York appearance as part of those 12 months of touring when it was played, as a stop on a regular road schedule, at the combination house known as the Harlem Opera House (8 December 1890) with Anna Boyd and Harry Conor in its featured roles.

A Trip to Chinatown was one of those loose-limbed farcical comedies with often haphazardly introduced, and intermittently replaced, revised and moved-around songs and dances which had become highly successful in the popular American theatre in the second half of the 19th century. Its author, Hoyt, the most generally skillful practitioner of this chimeric kind of low-comedy-plus-variety-show entertainment, had a series of successes with like pieces, but in *A Trip to Chinatown* he brought together a splendid bunch of comical characters in a simple and hilarious, if derivative, plot which, decorated with several very successful nearly new songs, made the entertainment into something more than the run-of-the-mill farce comedy.

The basic story of the show (much embroidered upon as the years went by) had two young men and their girls (Mattie Hornby, Irene Murphy) ostensibly going out on a "trip to Chinatown." As in Labiche and Delacour's famous *Voyage en Chine,* they don't actually go there at all. This cultural(!) trip is a blind for the benefit of strict papa, Ben Gay (George A Beane jr), and the young folk are really off to have a high old time at a dance. They are, however, nice young people—in spite of the boys being called Rashleigh Gay (Louis Finniger) and Wilder Knights (Ed S Metcalf)—and they are taking a chaperone with them, a pretty widow called Mrs Guyer (Lena Merville). Unfortunately Mrs Guyer's letter arranging to meet the young folk at the "Balloon" restaurant goes to Ben by mistake, and the old fellow hurries off excitedly for this unlooked-for rendezvous with a charming lady. At the restaurant he ends up both lady-less and then embarrassedly unable to pay his bill as the comedy gambols on towards a forgiving and happy ending.

The other, incidental characters of the piece were headed by a variant of another favorite stock character, the imaginary invalid, here called Mr Welland Strong (Harry Conor), "a man with one foot in the grave." Strong's role developed, eventually, into the major comic part in the show, alongside humorous vignettes from such supporting characters as the regularly crushed servant, Slavin Payne, (pronounced "slayv-in," of course) (Harry Gilfoil), Flirt the maid (Ollie Archmere), the lad Willie Grow ("proposed at the Bohemian Club" . . . and played by a girl) and Noah Heap, the waiter at the Restaurant (also Gilfoil).

The songs were, in the tradition of such shows, moveable and changeable, but a number of those in *A Trip to Chinatown* became such favorites that they remained a fixed part of the show over the many years of its life. Percy Gaunt's "Reuben and Cynthia," "The Pretty Young Widow" and "On the Bowery" (to the old English tune, "Down in the Coalmine" aka "The Harem"), all originally written and/or arranged from familiar melodies for the show, were the backbone of a score which, towards the end of the show's third year read: Act I: "The Pretty Widow," "Out for a Racket,"

African Cantata: ''Love Me Little, Love Me Long,'' ''Crisp Young Chaperone'' (mus: Barton); Act II: Trio—burlesque of Italian opera; Medley including ''There Will Never Be Another Like You,'' ''Naughty Sporty Boys,'' ''I Will Be True,'' ''Reuben and Cynthia,'' ''Amorita Waltz,'' ''Whistling Extraordinary,'' ''You Did That''; Act III: Toe dance and Flower girl by première danseuse, ''On the Bowery.''

''Push Dem Clouds Away'' was a popular early addition to the score, but it was a slightly later one, a number already seen in another production, which proved the biggest success. Charles K Harris's ''After the Ball'' became one of the enduring elements of the show, along with ''The Bowery'' (which Hoyt, who claimed to have written four hundred to five hundred extra verses for it, averred had been ''heard in America, England and Australia . . . translated and sung in German, French, Italian, Danish and Swedish [and is] now the rage in St Petersburg'') and ''Reuben and Cynthia'' (''Reuben, Reuben, I've been thinking . . .'').

Hoyt covered his show with a program note attempting to defuse any attempt to see sense in the entertainment: ''In extenuation, the author begs to say that whatever the play may be, it is all that is claimed for it.'' He also claimed, second time into major dates that ''playwright Hoyt has made many alterations to his skit, adding new and witty lines here, and unique business there, until the *Trip* is almost a new play.'' Whilst undoubtedly an exaggeration, it is certain that alterations and additions came with a will. The largest alteration came after Hoyt's death when a whole new version of the piece entitled *A Winsome Widow* was produced by Florenz Ziegfeld in 1912. It was a singular flop.

In Britain, the show was preempted by Jonnie Sheridan's swiftly retitled *A Trip to Chicago* (ex- *Bridget O'Brien Esq* Vaudeville Theatre 5 August 1893) but, nevertheless, when the real thing arrived its pitch was not spoiled. Played with a local cast headed by R G Knowles, Herman de Lange and Edith Bruce, *A Trip to Chinatown* had a good 125-performance run at the tiny Toole's and the larger Strand Theatres (with Alice Atherton now as Mrs Guyer) and a very long touring life around the British provinces. Australia did not, on the other hand, cast the piece locally and, in fact, saw the show with some of its original creators when Hoyt sent a company to the south Pacific in 1896. Harry Conor, J Aldrich Libby (Rashleigh), Frank Lawton, Amelia Stone and Bessie Clayton played the show in repertoire with Hoyt's *A Milk White Flag* in Sydney, Adelaide and Melbourne (Princess Theatre 29 August 1896). Australia later got the *Trip to Chicago* piece as well, billed as the work of Fred Lyster and its star John F Sheridan (Theatre Royal, Melbourne 15 September 1900), who trouped it a while in his repertoire alongside his more favored pieces.

UK: Toole's Theatre 29 September 1894; Australia: Lyceum, Sydney 27 June 1896

TROIS DE LA MARINE Opérette-revue in 2 acts by Henri Alibert. Lyrics by René Sarvil. Music by Vincent Scotto. Theatre Nouvel Ambigu, Paris, 20 December 1933.

The second of the series of successful Marseillais-flavored opérettes written and played by Henri Alibert in the 1930s, *Trois de la marine* was as good as its title. Its heros were three sailors, jeune premier Antonin (Alibert) and his comical mates Papillotte and Favouille (Rellys), and the plot—when it wasn't being amorous—concerned a spy and some mysterious stolen papers. The suspect is the gorgeous Dorah who has been casting her spell over impressionable Antonin, but Dorah turns out to be a French agent chasing the real spy and, after the exposures have all been made, Antonin comes back to his little local Rosette (Gabys Sims) in time for the final curtain.

Scotto's jolly score was topped by the three men's rousing valse-musette ''Sur le plancher des vaches'' and the march ''À Toulon.'' Papillotte had fun with the chanson arabe ''Viens dans ma kasbah,'' Rosette fox-trotted a pretty piece about being a laundress with ''De l'eau, du savon, du soleil'' and joined her man in a tango declaring ''L'amour est une étoile,'' whilst Alibert got romantic over a pair of slow fox-trots (''Je ne sais pas ce qui m'attire,'' ''Depuis . . . j'ai peur de tout'').

Trois de la marine repeated the success won by *Au pays du soleil,* and after a fine Paris season set out for a long life on the road. It was filmed by Charles Barrois with Alibert, Rellys and Mlle Sims in support in their original roles and Germaine Roger, reprised at the Théâtre des Variétés in 1945 and refilmed in 1957 with Paulette Merval and Marcel Merkès, and still wins provincial productions in France to the present day.

Films: Metropa Films 1934, 1957

Recording: selection (TLP)

TROIS JEUNES FILLES . . . NUES! Comédie musicale in 3 acts by Yves Mirande and Albert Willemetz. Music by Raoul Moretti. Théâtre des Bouffes-Parisiens, Paris, 3 December 1925.

The three nice, well-brought-up jeunes filles in Mirande and Willemetz's libretto (like the musketeers, there are, in fact, four) do not quite go naked, but they take part in a revue—which is just about as shocking. Modest, Cinderella-like Lotte (Jeanne Saint-Bonnet) and her sisters Lilette (Sim-Viva), Lola (Eliane de Creus) and Lulu (Renée Varville) live in the country under the care of their aunt, Mme Duclos (Mlle Allems), and their good tutor, Hégesippe (Dranem). But Lotte's sisters decide that sitting sweetly in Garches isn't going to get them a husband in these up-to-date days, and in order to show off their advantages to three attentive marine officers (Géo Bury, Gustave Nellson, Adrien Lamy) they decide to take part in a show at the Folies-Bocagères. After they (and Hégesippe and Lotte who have gone in pursuit) have all been seen in roles lightly clad enough to justify the show's title, they are all transported to the battleship *Espadon* where they are happily paired off, Lotte with the rich Lord Cheston (Raymond de Boncour) and her sisters with their trio of officers. Director Edmond Roze played Patara, a comic sailor, Jean Gabin sr was the commander of the ship in question, whilst his soon-to-be-celluloid son also appeared in the show, succeeding to Nellson's role.

The musical's score was in the modern dancing mode, fox-trots to the fore, as Dranem demanded comically ''Est-ce que je te demande (si ta grand'mèr' fait du vélo)?'' in a lecture against curiosity which proved the hit of the evening, Mlle Saint-Bonnet delivered ''Quand on ne dit rien,'' Roze mused ''Quand on n'en a pas on s'en passe'' and Colette Etcherry (later Christiane Dor) as Miss Tapsy hurtled forth ''Raymonde.'' During the course of affairs, the Charleston also found its way into the entertainment.

Trois jeunes filles . . . nues! scored a bull's-eye, Dranem's song and Roze's comic number both put catch-phrases in the French language, the La Cigale end-of-season revue was soon frantically declaring that it housed *Cent jeunes filles . . . nues!,* and ultimately played for a few weeks over a year at the Bouffes-Parisiens. It thoroughly confirmed the composer of the previous season's *Troublez-moi!* as a man of the musical moment, and it took to the road, with Pauley and Ginette Winter featured, with vigor. One of the many roads the show took in the following years led to Canada and then to New York where a repertoire company headed by Servatius (Hégesippe) played the piece in French during a season at the Jolson Theater.

A film version of the piece was subsequently made, and the opérette has maintained itself in the just-sometimes-seen category in France up to the present day.

USA: Jolson Theater 4 March 1929

Film: Robert Boudrioz 1929

TROIS VALSES *see* DREI WALZER

TROMB-AL-CA-ZAR, ou Les Criminels dramatiques Bouffonnerie musicale in 1 act by Charles Dupeuty and Ernest Bourget. Music by Jacques Offenbach. Théâtre des Bouffes-Parisiens, Paris, 3 April 1856.

Tromb-al-ca-zar was one of the earliest short pieces written by Offenbach after the widening of his license allowed him to present one-act comic operas with up to four speaking/singing characters. Tromb-al-ca-zar is a famous brigand, and it is with fear of his horrid depredations that the actress Gigolette and her two friends, Beaujolais and Vert-Panné, suitably and ludicrously disguised, come revengefully to taunt the cowardly Ignace, her innkeeper cousin who abandoned her as a child. The piece, bristling with extravagant parodies both of specific (and more serious) musical works and of the brigand element in opera and comic opera generally, included some merry burlesque numbers, notably Gigolette/Simplette's super-Spanish boléro ''La gitana, ah! croyez bien'' and the comical Trio du jambon de Bayonne.

The show was given a choice first production with the young Hortense Schneider as Simplette teamed with top comedians Pradeau (Beaujolais) and Léonce (Vert-Panné) and Rubel as Ignace, and it won a considerable success, leading to a regular continuing life in France, its most recent performance in Paris being in 1985 (Éspace Marais 15 June).

Outside France the show was at first regularly musically disemboweled to provide melodies for pasticcio burlesques, but it also received several proper productions. Paul Juignet played it in his French theatre season in New York in 1864 and Jacob Grau included it alongside pieces by such as Adam, Auber and Massé in his New York opéra-comique season of 1866, Karl Treumann staged a German version at his Vienna theatre with himself, Louis Grois and Helene Weinberger as the theatricals and Wilhelm Knaack as the innkeeper, and in London, after a sizeable potted version had been heard at the Oxford Music Hall (9 June 1866) and the Canterbury Music Hall, John Hollingshead produced the piece (ad Charles Henry Stephenson) on a program with *La Poupée de Nuremberg* and *Bluebeard,* and later with *Zampa,* at London's Gaiety Theatre. Julia Mathews, John Maclean and Charles Lyall did the frightening of J D Stoyle. However, it seems that the only contemporary English language-version to have been played in America was that produced by Offenbach's principal American ambassador of these early years, Susan Galton, with her little troupe—John Howson, J A Arnold, Alfred Kelleher—at the San Francisco Alhambra in 1873.

Austria: Theater am Franz-Josefs-Kai *Tromb-al-ca-zar, oder Die dramatischen Verbrecher* 19 March 1862; USA: Théâtre Français (Niblo's Saloon) 12 January 1864; Alhambra, San Francisco 22 September 1873; UK: Gaiety Theatre 22 August 1870

Recording: TLP

LE TRÔNE D'ÉCOSSE [et la difficulté de s'asseoir dessus] Opéra-bouffe in 4 acts by Hector Crémieux and Adolphe Jaime. Music by Hervé. Théâtre des Variétés, Paris, 17 November 1871.

Following their burlesques of Goethe's *Faust* (*Le Petit Faust*) and Racine's *Bajazet* (*Les Turcs*), the Crémieux/Jaime/Hervé team switched to things Scottish (always popular in France) as the subject for their next extravagantly ridiculous burlesque opera.

There is a conspiracy going on in Scotland, under the leadership of one ambitious MacRazor, to replace Queen Jane (Anna van Ghell) with a descendant—any descendant—of Robert the Bruce. Since one can't be found, the conspirators light upon a certain Robert Mouton (José Dupuis), a commercial traveler in wines, who apparently bears a certain resemblance to the all-but-deified Bruce, as their candidate. Mouton duly ends up marrying the Queen, but when the French envoy arrives and finds his sometime wine-merchant is now King of Scotland he is livid. Things wind up to a furious and farcical height—with Queen Jane winding up the highest in a flamboyant parody of an operatic mad scene—before, finally, a genuine Bruce is found hidden in a cupboard and brought out to claim the throne and the lady. Léonce played a flashy, sexy Duke of Buckingham, Baron was the lofty Baron des Trente-six Tourelles and Céline Chaumont featured as Flora. Alice Regnault was a character called Julia Good-Morning in a cast list where the other ladies included Fanny Hyde-Park, Ann Charing-Cross and Eva Thank-You.

Hervé's score, written whilst he sheltered in appreciative London from the problems of the Franco-Prussian War across the channel, quoted happily and humorously from other operas—notably and naturally Boïeldieu's Scottish *La Dame blanche*—as it made its bubbling burlesque way through the tale. Flora's song "Dans mes chimères les plus sottes," the Queen's mad scene and her third-act song, and the comical gentlemen's numbers were all as lively as the best of Hervé, but *Le Trône d'Écosse* proved less popular than *Le Petit Faust* and it never established itself for any more than its initial run of 70 nights in Paris. Hervé promptly recycled one number for his next show in London, *Babil and Bijou,* where it appeared as the decidedly unburlesque tenor solo "To Her Who Owns My Heart's Devotion" as performed by Joseph Maas. The rest of what seems to have been a splendidly bouffe opéra-bouffe, however, slipped into oblivion.

TROUBLEZ-MOI! Opérette-vaudeville in 3 acts by Yves Mirande. Music by Raoul Moretti. Théâtre des Bouffes-Parisiens, Paris, 17 September 1924.

Following his first, if limited, success with *En chemyse,* the composer Moretti provided another bright, dancing score as an adjunct to an Yves Mirande libretto called *Troublez-moi!* which, like the earlier show, featured the comedian Dranem at the top of its bill. Here the star was cast as the nouveau-riche Picotte whose little secrets from the taxman, Goulichon (Gabin), can apparently only be resolved by allowing his daughter, Suzy (Renée Duler), to wed Goulichon fils, a lad who is unfortunately christian-named Pollux (Adrien Lamy). Suzy, however, has other ideas, and he is called Robert (Jean Poc). As for the naughty Picotte, in good Parisian middle-class fashion, he has not only a wife (A Beylat) but a mistress who goes by the give-away name of Cri-cri (Christiane Dor) and whose mother (Louise Danville) is a concièrge. He also, fortunately, has a second daughter, Arlette (Mlle Davia), to whom the dashing, comical Pollux has more appeal.

Dranem gallivanted through the comedy of the show, appearing now in a toreador's outfit (on the excuse of a visit to the Bal de l'Opéra), now in nightclothes for his night of extramarital pleasure—taken whilst Cri-cri is deputizing for her mama and interrupted incessantly by the clanging of the concièrge's bell—and performing a series of songs including "Ernestine," "J'ai eu tort," "Cordon, s'il vous plaît," "Le petit revenez-y" and "Ah! les p'tits poissons." Alongside some fine ensembles, the two girls culled the best of the rest of the solo music, with Davia explaining "Ce sont des choses qu'on dit, mais on ne fait pas," describing the efforts made to make herself beautiful "Pour un homme" whom she has never met, and, after the coup de foudre, assuring naïvely "Je sais ce que c'est maintenant" as she bewailed her first 20 years, passed without a grand passion. Mlle Duler sang sweetly of "La jolie bétise" and joined Poc in the waltz duo "Peut-être."

A splendid musical-comedy success, *Troublez-moi!* played seven months in Paris before going on the road, and confirmed Moretti as one of the musicians to be reckoned with in the dance age of the French musical comedy.

TRUEX, Ernest (b Kansas City, Mo, 19 September 1889; d Fallbrook, Calif, 26 June 1973). Little character man who had some fine roles through more than half a century in the theatre.

Truex went on the stage as a five-year-old "prodigy," at the beginning of a busy theatre, film and television career in which the dapper little actor embraced a variety of comic and character roles including a number in musical shows. He appeared on Broadway in *Girlies* (1910, Billy Murray) and *Dr De Luxe* (1911, Dennis), and on the road in *The June Bride* (1912) before creating his most successful musical role as the diminutive Eddie Kettle in *Very Good Eddie* (1915), introducing "When You Wear a Thirteen Collar" and "Babes in the Wood" (w Alice Dovey).

In 1919 he had star billing in the Shubert's *Page Mr Cupid,* which closed after one week's tryout, but he subsequently appeared on musical Broadway in *Pitter Patter*

(1920, Dick Crawford) and as wealthy George Wimbledon in Romberg's *Annie Dear* (1924) before going on to score London successes as Johnnie Quinlan in the play *The Fall Guy,* as P G Wodehouse's Bill Paradene in *Good Morning Bill,* and in the role of Gerald Brooks, created on Broadway by Oscar Shaw, in the London Hippodrome production of the musical *The Five o'Clock Girl* (1929). Truex later co-starred with Beatrice Lillie in the revue *The Third Little Show,* played the part of Lenz in Broadway's version of Lehár's *Frederika* (1937), was a mini-Menelaus in *Helen Goes to Troy* (1944), the business mogul B G Bigelow in the brief run of *Flahooley* (1951) and featured alongside Frank Sinatra in a television musical version of Thornton Wilder's *Our Town* (NBC 1955) as part of a career largely spent in the non-musical theatre.

TUCKER, Sophie [KALISH, Sonia] (b Russia, 13 January 1884; d New York, 9 February 1966).

A vaudeville, burlesque and cabaret performer (''Some of These Days,'' ''My Yiddishe Momma''), who billed herself from early in her career as ''the last of the red hot mamas,'' Miss Tucker appeared on the Broadway stage in *The Ziegfeld Follies* in 1909, but then sidelined to vaudeville (''The Cubanola Glide,'' ''My Southern Rose,'' ''Carrie and Harry,'' ''The Wild Cherry Rag''). ''Seldom is such a vivacious, intense and entertaining personality found in one body,'' sighed a critic—''she has a very powerful voice, of the coon shouting variety, which she uses to such good advantage that the harshness of it is soon forgotten . . . but it isn't her voice, it's her ability to act . . . but that gown! Whoever designed it must have thought the main idea is to get everything into the trimming of one gown.'' ''Musical comedy will undoubtedly soon take her away from the variety stage,'' he concluded. It did, but only for a while. After a turn in Gus Edwards's *Song Revue* at Brighton Beach (1911) when another critic dubbed her ''the Mary Garden of ragtime,'' she moved on to make her first musical-theatre appearances in Chicago where she played in *Merry Mary* (1911, singing ''The Land of Bombaloo'') and Ben Jerome's *Louisiana Lou* (1911, Jenny Wimp). She was seen on Broadway in *The Shubert Gaieties* in 1919, and in the same year made her first appearance there in a book musical playing Aunt Kitty in the long touring McIntyre and Heath show *Hello Alexander* (ex- *The Ham Tree*). In an international career of which only a small part was spent in the theatre, she starred in London in a custom-built piece called *Follow a Star* (1930), which cast her as a cabaret vocalist and in which she spent much of the second act performing the act as known, and on Broadway as the pushy wife of the deliberately clumsy diplomat in Cole Porter's *Leave It to Me!* (1938), returning thereafter only to play herself in Kalmar and Ruby's vaudeville musical *High Kickers* in 1941.

In 1963 she was the subject of a fictionalized biomusical (*Sophie* Winter Garden Theater 15 April Steve Allen/Philip Pruneau) in which she was portrayed by Libi Staiger for a run of one week.

Autobiography: w Giles, D: *Some of These Days* (Doubleday, New York, 1945)

TULIP TIME Musical comedy in 2 acts—based on the play *The Strange Adventures of Miss Brown* by Robert Buchanan and Charles Marlowe (ie, Harriet Jay)—by Worton David and Alfred Parker. Lyrics by Bruce Sievier. Music by Colin Wark. Alhambra Theatre, London, 14 August 1935.

Vocalist-turned-manager Anne Croft was the force behind the musical *Sweet Seventeen,* produced at the Theatre Royal Brighton in 1933 (31 July) but quickly abandoned. The abandonment was only temporary, however, for after some rewrites Miss Croft put the show back on the stage in her home town of Hull and the rechristened *Tulip Time* finally made its way to the West End's Alhambra as a cheap-price, twice-daily entertainment. Bernard Clifton, George Gee and Hungarian comic Steve Geray played airmen disguised in frocks looking for the first-named's young wife (Jean Colin) in a girl's school to the accompaniment of a brightly colored production (including three practical windmills), some simple songs and a lot of energy, all aimed at a music-hall audience. The aim was good, for *Tulip Time* ran 427 performances and toured for three seasons thereafter.

TUNBRIDGE, Joseph A[lbert] (b London, 21 January 1886; d Bromley, 27 December 1961). Musical director and amanuensis to Britain's producer/songwriter Jack Waller.

The young Joe Tunbridge worked originally as a pianist, an accompanist and as a member of a pierrot show, whilst at the same time editing and arranging music for the Star Music Company, a purveyor of cheap printed popular music, and subsequently for the more upmarket B Feldman Ltd. The first of his own compositions to get exposure were heard in pierrot shows, concert parties and touring revues, the most lasting of which were the long-running minor circuit shows produced by Harry Day (*Sparkles, Rockets, Jingles,* etc). He had his greatest single song success in 1919 with ''Mademoiselle from Armentières'' (w Harry Carlton), and moved definitively into the theatre in 1926 when he conducted and composed the basic score (which was more interpolations than score) for C B Cochran's musical version of the famous farce *Turned Up.* Soon after, he teamed up with another graduate of the pierrot and concert party world, Jack Waller, the neophyte producer of London's *No, No, Nanette.* From then on, for more than 20 years, Tunbridge worked with Waller and his organization as musical director, amanuensis and as part-composer (and writer-down/arranger of Waller's part) of many of the long list of musical plays which the producer mounted, both in partnership and alone.

The musical *Virginia* (1928) had a good West End run and produced the song ''Roll Away Clouds,'' written in imitation of ''Ol' Man River'' and actually recorded by Paul Robeson, and others of their shows such as the spectacular *Silver Wings,* the farcical series of Saville Theatre musicals (*For the Love of Mike, He Wanted Adventure, Tell Her the Truth*) and the highly successful Hippodrome shows (*Mr Whittington, Yes, Madam?, Please, Teacher!*) had good-to-splendid successes in Britain without proving particularly exportable.

Tunbridge continued to tour as a musical-theatre conductor into his sixties, but in the 1940s his composing activity decreased and his later work was limited to additional music for Waller's productions of such pieces as *The Kid from Stratford* (1948) and *Caprice* (1950). The score of the musical version of *The Little Minister,* mounted as *Wild Grows the Heather* in 1956, was largely put together from Waller's trunk of their unused music.

1926 **Turned Up** (Stanley Lupino/Arthur Rigby) New Oxford Theatre 11 January

1928 **Billy Blue** (w Fred Elkin/Harold Dayne) Empire Theatre, Newcastle 6 August

1928 **Tipperary Tim** (w Max Miller/Arthur Field, George Arthurs) Alhambra Theatre, Bradford 6 August

1928 **Virginia** (w Jack Waller/Herbert Clayton, Douglas Furber, R P Weston, Bert Lee) Palace Theatre 24 October

1929 **Merry Merry** (w Waller, Harris Weston/Weston, Lee, et al) Carlton Theatre 28 February

1929 **Dear Love** (w Waller, Haydn Wood/Clayton, Dion Titheradge, Lauri Wylie) Palace Theatre 14 November

1930 **Silver Wings** (w Waller/Titheradge, Furber) Dominion Theatre 14 February

1931 **For the Love of Mike** (w Waller/Clifford Grey, Sonny Miller/Grey) Saville Theatre 8 October

1932 **Tell Her the Truth** (w Waller/Weston, Lee) Saville Theatre 14 June

1933 **He Wanted Adventure** (w Waller/Weston, Lee) Saville Theatre 28 March

1933 **Command Performance** (w Waller/Grey/C Stafford Dickens) Saville Theatre 17 October

1933 **Mr Whittington** (w Waller, John W Green/Grey, Greatrex Newman, Furber) Alhambra, Glasgow 30 November; London Hippodrome 1 March 1934

1934 **Yes, Madam?** (w Waller/Weston, Lee, K R G Browne) London Hippodrome 27 September

1935 **Please, Teacher!** (w Waller/Weston, Lee, Browne) London Hippodrome 2 October

1936 **Certainly, Sir!** (w Waller/Weston, Lee) London Hippodrome 17 September

1937 **Big Business** (w Waller/Lee, Browne, Desmond Carter) London Hippodrome 18 February

1938 **Bobby Get Your Gun** (w Waller/Grey/Guy Bolton, Fred Thompson, Lee) Adelphi Theatre 7 October

1943 **Hearts Are Trumps** (w Waller, Leon Carroll/Ian Grant, Robert Fyle/Fyle) Theatre Royal, Birmingham 19 October

1956 **Wild Grows the Heather** (w Waller/Ralph Reader/Hugh Ross Williamson) London Hippodrome 3 May

TUNE, Tommy [TUNE, Thomas James] (b Wichita Falls, Tex, 28 February 1939). Award-winning performer, choreographer and director who was instrumental in leading Broadway back towards a revusical and dance based style of staging in the 1980s and 1990s.

The very tall and slim dancer studied at the universities of Texas and Houston, and subsequently led a dual career as a performer and a choreographer. His earliest major performing assignments were as a chorus dancer in *Baker Street* (1965), *A Joyful Noise* (1966), *How Now Dow Jones* (1967) and *State Fair* (1969, St Louis Muny) and his earliest choreographic credits in regional productions of classic musicals.

In 1973, having joined the production of *Seesaw* as assistant choreographer, he ended up having his first significant role when he took over the part of David during the Detroit tryout. He created the number ''It's Not Where You Start, It's Where You Finish'' and collected his first Tony Award for his performance.

Tune's first New York directorial assigment was with the ''musical diversion'' *The Club* produced in 1976 at the Circle in the Square, and he subsequently choreographed and co-directed (w Peter Masterson) the expanded version of *The Best Little Whorehouse in Texas* (1978) with its memorable Aggie Dance for its productions on Broadway and in London's West End. His choreography for the New York edition of the British revue *A Day in Hollywood—A Night in the Ukraine* (1980) won particular praise and he won further praise when he directed *Nine* (1982), decorating the piece's inherently inactive libretto with a lively series of character pieces and song-and-dance routines. He took another Tony Award when he both starred in and co-choreographed the 1983 Gershwin pasticcio *My One and Only.*

Brought in to try to salvage *Grand Hotel* (1989) on the road, he enlivened it with some picturesque dances, including a genuinely show-stopping legmania spot for one character, which earned him further awards, before going on to confirm himself as the modern master of glamorous staging in 1991's *The Will Rogers Follies* (Tony Award). The attempt at a sequel to *The Best Little Whorehouse in Texas* foundered quickly, but what was billed as ''The Tommy Tune production'' of *Grease* proved a nationwide winner.

At the same time, Tune continued the other side of his high-profile career by leading out a highly successful

Plate 399. **Tommy Tune** *in* My One and Only.

touring revival of *Bye Bye Birdie,* and launching a *Tommy Tune Tonite!* at Broadway's Gershwin Theater (27 December 1992). A proposed *Busker's Alley* (1995), a rewrite of an aging though unproduced British piece, was abandoned, but Tune returned to the stage in 1999 when he succeeded to the role created by Michael Crawford in the spectacular *EFX* at Las Vegas.

He was seen on the musical screen in the film version of *The Boy Friend.*

Autobiography: *Footsteps* (Simon & Schuster, New York, 1997)

LES TURCS Opéra-bouffe in 3 acts by Hector Crémieux and Adolphe Jaime. Music by Hervé. Théâtre des Folies-Dramatiques, Paris, 23 December 1869.

A burlesque of Racine's *Bajazet* written by the authors who, earlier in the same year, had given Hervé the libretto for his enormously successful *Le Petit Faust, Les Turcs* was produced at the same house which had been so successful with the former piece, under the management of Moreau Sainti, the producer of Hervé's triumphant *L'Oeil crevé.*

Augustine Devéria, a French diva who had been successful in St Petersburg, returned home to play the lovely Roxane, in love with Bajazet (Marcel), whom she saves from being murdered by his beastly brother. They run away from Stamboul to Babylon where Roxane turns out to be the long-lost daughter of the King and everything can conclude happily. Needless to say, in the hands of Hervé and the librettists of *Le Petit Faust* the well-known tale was told neither as simply nor as seriously as that, but *Les Turcs,* all the same, was not quite as "bouffe" as its predecessors. At the head of the comedy, Milher, the Geromé of *L'Oeil crevé* and the Valentin of *Le Petit Faust,* played Ababoum. Hervé's score included a Marche Turc, a Valse des houris and . . . a chorus of mutes!

Although it was well received by press and public, *Les Turcs* did not go on to equal the runs of its predecessors. It was, however, taken on tour by Eugène Meynadier's company with Mme Matz-Ferrare as Roxane, Juteau as Bajazet and Christian as Ababoum, a tour which found its way as far afield as Vienna. It was also played in the repertoire of the Halleck French opéra-bouffe company in Canada and the USA. But quite why and how *A törökök* finally turned up in Budapest (ad Gyula Zempléni) in 1901—years after it had last been played anywhere else—remains to be explained. But it did.

Austria: Theater an der Wien 27 June 1872; Canada: Theatre Royal, Montreal November 1880; Hungary: Városligeti Színkör *A törökök* 23 August 1901

TURNED UP Musical farcical comedy in 2 acts by Arthur Rigby (and Stanley Lupino) adapted from the play of the same title by Mark Melford. Lyrics by Stanley Lupino, Stanley J Damerell, Robert Hargreaves, Eric Valentine, R P Weston and Bert Lee. Music by Joseph Tunbridge. Additional numbers by Isham Jones and Jack Melton, Lupino, Sydney Clare and Cliff Friend. New Oxford Theatre, London, 28 January 1926.

Willie Edouin's famous old touring farce *Turned Up* (Vaudeville Theatre 27 May 1886), long a feature of the British provincial circuits, was given music 40 years on by a battery of folk under the eye of producer C B Cochran and musical director Joe Tunbridge. Lupino Lane was starred as young George Medford, all anxious to organize the vital meeting between his mother (Ruth Maitland) and his beloved (Nancie Lovat) whilst all hell is breaking loose around their home. The cause of the problem is that, since the death of her husband, Mrs Medway has married the prospecting undertaker Carraway Bones (Leo Franklyn)—but now Medway (Henry N Wenman) has ''turned up''! The hotchpotch score, of which the basic music was the first West End show for provincial revue composer Tunbridge, did its job tidily but turned up nothing more memorable than a piece called ''My Castle in Spain'' delivered by a female character stuck irrelevantly into the tale for nothing more then girlie value and the song.

Turned Up was shunted out of the Oxford Theatre when the building was sold during its run, and after 87 performances it went off to the provinces. It also went to Australia, where Australian Franklyn repeated his role alongside Gus Bluett (George), Bertha Belmore (Mrs Medway), Edwin Brett, Mary Lawson, Molly Fisher and Cecil Kellaway for six Christmas weeks in Melbourne, and the following festive season in Sydney with Franklyn now replacing the ill Bluett as George, Phil Smith as Bones and Maidie Hope as Mrs Medway (Her Majesty's Theatre 20 December 1930).

Broadway also saw a musical version of *Turned Up* when Nat Goodwin mounted his production of what was, in theory, the play, but decorated it liberally with songs and dances (Bijou Theater 11 December 1887). Goodwin himself played Bones, with Jeannie Weathersby as Mrs Medway. A second American musicalized version of the play, this one authored by Harry Sheldon White, was produced at Chicago's Whitney Theater in 1911 (15 April) under the title *Merry Mary*, with the youngish Sophie Tucker amongst the cast.

Australia: Theatre Royal, Melbourne 26 December 1929

TURNER, J[ohn] Hastings (b London, 16 December 1891; d Fakenham, 29 February 1956).

The author of a considerable list of successful plays and revues (*Bubbly, Tails Up, Hullo! America, Jumble Sale, The Fun of the Fayre, Mayfair and Montmartre, Wake Up and Dream, Follow the Sun*, etc) in the years between the wars, Turner also adapted several Continental musicals to the English stage. However, he had his principal musical-theatre success with the well-regarded *Betty in Mayfair*, a musical adapted from his own play *The Lilies of the Field*, which played 193 performances in the West End with Evelyn Laye starred in its title role. *Merely Molly*, a second self-adaptation, taken from his novel *Simple Souls* and produced by the same Daniel Mayer management with the same star, was less successful (85 performances), but the musical *Lady Mary*, on which he collaborated with another highly rated writer of the period, Freddie Lonsdale, had a satisfactory 181-performance run in London.

1920 **The Naughty Princess** (*La Reine s'amuse*) English version (Adelphi Theatre)

1921 **Now and Then** (Philip Braham/Reginald Arkell/w George Graves) Vaudeville Theatre 17 September

1925 **Cleopatra** (*Die Perlen der Cleopatra*) English version (Daly's Theatre)

1925 **Betty in Mayfair** (Harold Fraser-Simson/Harry Graham) Adelphi Theatre 11 November

1926 **Merely Molly** (Herman Finck, Joseph Meyer/Graham) Adelphi Theatre 22 September

1928 **Lady Mary** (Albert Szirmai/Graham/w Frederick Lonsdale) Daly's Theatre 23 February

1937 **Venus in Silk** (*Venus in Seide*) English version (tour)

TWAIN, Mark [CLEMENS, Samuel Langhorne] (b Florida, Mo, 30 November 1835; d Redding, Conn, 21 April 1910).

The works of American novelist Mark Twain have been regularly delved into as a source of musical libretti over the years and the world. Perhaps unsurprisingly, the most successful results have been achieved in his native America where the 1985 adaptation of *The Adventures of Huckleberry Finn* as *Big River* (Eugene O'Neill Theater 25 April), and the Fields, Rodgers and Hart musical version of his *A Connecticut Yankee (at King Arthur's Court)* (Vanderbilt Theater 3 November 1927) both became considerable successes. A third success came when *The Diary of Adam and Eve* (Jerry Bock/Sheldon Harnick) was used as one of the three one-act pieces which made up the entertainment *The Apple Tree* (Shubert Theater 18 October 1966).

As early as 1872, Augustin Daly made what was more or less an early attempt at presenting musicalized Twain, when he presented an extravaganza called *Roughing It* (18 February). The Twain elements—the title apart—were apparently fairly limited. Other attempts to musicalize the Mississippi novels have included *Livin' the Life* (Jack Urbont/Bruce Geller, Dale Wasserman Phoenix Theater 27 April 1957), the off-Broadway *Downriver* (John Braden/Jeff Tamborino, 1975), London's *Tom Sawyer* (Tom Boyd, Theatre Royal, Stratford East 26 December 1960) and the televised *The Adventures of Huck Finn* (Frank Luther, Ann Crosswell, Lee Pockriss CBS 20 November 1957). Off-Broadway also hosted a version of *The Prince and the Pauper* (George Fischoff/Verna Tomasson, 1963) and in the same year a *The Man Who Corrupted Hadleyburg* (Daniel Paget/Lewis Gardner) was produced at New York's Minor Latham Playhouse (6 August).

In France the 1925 Albert Chantrier/Jean Bastia musical comedy *Elle ou moi,* which had definite echoes of *L'Île de Tulipatan* and *San Toy* in its tale of children brought up as the opposite sex, was subtitled in English "the right man in the right place" and given out as based on "une nouvelle de Mark Twain" (Théâtre Daunou 29 August 1925), whilst in Hungary *The Million Pound Note* became *Egymillió fontos bankjegy* (1962, Zdenkó Tamássy/István Kallai/János Erdődy), described as a "revü komédia," and Otto Vincze supplied the score for another piece of Hungarian Twain in Miklós Vidor's radio musical *Szőzek városa.*

In 1992 Twain even got a biomusical when Walt Stepp's *Lightin' Out* was produced at off-Broadway's Judith Anderson Theater (3 December), and he appeared again as a character in Jim Post's one-man (and two-musician) musical entertainment *Mark Twain and the Laughing River* (Northlight Theater, Evanston, Ill 28 February 1996).

Autobiography: Paine, A B (ed): *Mark Twain's Autobiography* (Harper & Bros, New York, 1924); Biography: Paine, A B: *Mark Twain: A Biography* (Harper, New York, 1912), etc

TWENTY TO ONE Musical sporting farce in 2 acts by L Arthur Rose. Lyrics by Frank Eyton. Music by Billy Mayerl. London Coliseum, 12 November 1935.

Twenty to One, the musical which marked the move into management by comedian Lupino Lane, was a racing farce which cast him as a cocky little chap called Bill Snibson who helps one Timothy Quaintance (Clifford Mollison), a member of the anti-gambling league, to settle his affairs and win his Mary (Betty Norton) by the helpful measure of getting him on a cert at 20 to 1. Joyce Barbour featured as Miss Lucretia Harbottle, head of the aforementioned league.

First produced at Glasgow with Lane supported by Barry Lupino, Rita Cooper and Renée Reel, the piece had a tour of a half-dozen dates before Lane took it off and had it done over and worked up into a twice-nightly vehicle for himself for the London Coliseum. The juveniles sang and danced to "How Do You Like Your Eggs Fried?," Miss Harbottle got tipsy and fell all over the comedian gushing "I've Never Felt Like This Before," Lane went through all the acrobatic, cheeky comicalities that were his trademark and the piece proved worthy of 383 performances in six months in the West End. When *Twenty to One* ended its London run, and began what was to be a long provincial life, the persona and name (if not the character) of Bill Snibson moved on with Lane into his next musical play, *Me and My Girl.*

Following the great success of that piece, Lane brought *Twenty to One* back to London (Victoria Palace 10 February 1942) and, again reorganized and with new numbers by *Me and My Girl*'s Noel Gay added to the score, it did even better than it had first time round, playing there for 10 months and 408 performances. The show remained a provincial favorite for many years and Lane himself played *Twenty to One*'s Bill Snibson, as well as the more famous one of *Me and My Girl,* right on into the 1950s.

The title *Twenty to One* had—with rather different connotations—been previously used in America by comedian-manager Will Mestayer for his (doubled-in-size) adaptation of Suppé's *Zehn Mädchen und kein Mann* (1887).

TWO BY TWO Musical in 2 acts by Peter Stone based on *The Flowering Peach* by Clifford Odets. Lyrics by Martin Charnin. Music by Richard Rodgers. Imperial Theater, New York, 10 November 1970.

Clifford Odets's 1954 play *The Flowering Peach* was a sincere and willfully meaningful retelling of the legend of the devout Noah and his deluge. The musical version, which cast Danny Kaye in the role of Noah (from 90 to 600, or the other way round), had a rather different flavor, as the comedian plugged his part full of home-made and borrowed vaudeville tricks and ad libs which did nothing to maintain the flavor which the authors had tried to impart to their show. However, the low-comedy festival which resulted (Kaye even played in a wheelchair after an accident) proved popular enough to keep Rodgers's production of *Two by Two* on the stage for 343 performances, a total it is doubtful that it would have reached if it had been played straight. The show's best musical moment came in a number for youngest son, Japheth (Walter Willison), telling his brother's wife, Rachel (Tricia O'Neil), "I Do Not Know a Day I Did Not Love You."

The piece was given a Kaye-less and reasonably straight provincial production in Britain in 1991, a deluge-orientated year which had aleady seen a Noah musical, *Children of Eden,* go under in the West End. Colin Farrell (Noah) and Geoffrey Abbott (Japheth) featured in the Ipswich mounting of the older show. The piece was also produced in Germany, where it went on to several further provincial productions, one under the 1960s-ish title of *Noah! Noah!*

Noah and his flood featured in a much earlier piece, *La Tour de Babel* (Paul Fauchey/Pierre Eléazar, Auguste Paër) produced at Paris's Théâtre de la Renaissance in 1889 (29 May). This one featured a dipsomaniac, post-deluge Noah (M de Beer), paralleled the construction of the Eiffel Tower with the Tower of Babel, and explained the story of the dove and the olive branch in purely human terms. There was no ark. The ark, on the other hand, was thoroughly featured in the Italian musical *Aggiungi un posto alla tavola* which treated of a second, modern-days deluge.

UK: Wolsey Theatre, Ipswich 4 April 1991; Germany: Staatstheater, Bielefeld 23 January 1993

Recording: original cast (Columbia)

TWO GENTLEMEN OF VERONA Rock musical by John Guare and Mel Shapiro based on the play by William Shakespeare. Lyrics by Guare. Music by Galt MacDermot. Delacorte Theater, New York, 27 July 1971; St James Theater, 1 December 1971.

Two Gentlemen of Verona was Shakespeare metamorphosed into a 1970s post-*Hair* American musical play with post-*Hair* music by the composer of *Hair* and some for-the-people chunks of look-how-naughty-we-little-boys-can-be vulgarity mixed in with bits of Bard. This otherwise unaggressively modern and rather long version of *Two Gentlemen of Verona* developed from what was intended as a reasonably normal production of the play for the New York Shakespeare Festival. Withdrawn after a fortnight of free performances at the Delacorte Theater, it was transferred to Broadway later in the year where, in a season which included *Follies* amongst its novelties, it picked up the Tony Awards for Best Musical and Best Libretto that the same voters hadn't been game to give to *Hair*. They weren't the only ones who liked it either for, although no longer free, *Two Gentlemen of Verona* proved itself a worthy successor to its famous predecessor on Broadway, totting up a run of 614 performances before going out on the road.

Raul Julia played Proteus, who betrays both his friend Valentine (Clifton Davis) and his lady, Julia (Carla Pinza/Diana Davila), in chasing after Silvia (Jonelle Allen), daughter of the Duke of Milan (Norman Matlock), whilst the comic element was, as in Shakespeare, in the hands of the servant, Launce (Jerry Stiller/John Bottoms). On the road, Larry Kert played Proteus alongside Davis and Miss Allen.

A London production under the management of Michael White and Robert Stigwood, with Ray C Davis as Proteus and Brenda Arnau making a personal success as Silvia, played 237 performances at the Phoenix Theatre without finding enough folk interested simultaneously in Shakespeare and pop music to make it profitable. Australia's production did not make the normal move from Melbourne to Sydney.

UK: Phoenix Theatre 26 April 1973; Australia: Her Majesty's Theatre, Melbourne 31 March 1973; Hungary: Ódry Színpad *Veronai fiúk* 17 December 1993

Recordings: original cast (ABC/MCA), London cast (Polydor), Swedish cast *Tva gentleman fran verona* (CAM)

U

UDELL, Peter (b Brooklyn, NY, 24 May 1934).

Udell worked in a songwriting partnership with composer Gary Geld that produced such 1960s hits as "I Ain't Gonna Wash for a Week," "Ginny Come Lately" and "Sealed with a Kiss" before the pair moved into the musical theatre. Geld provided the music and Udell the lyrics and, in collaboration, the libretti for two fine musical plays of the 1970s, an upliftingly vigorous musical version of Ossie Davis's play *Purlie Victorious* ("I Got Love," "Purlie," "Walk Him Up the Stairs," "The Bigger They Are," etc) and a movingly unpretentious piece based on the Civil War screenplay *Shenandoah* ("We Make a Beautiful Pair") featuring some warmly written soliloquies for its leading man. Both pieces had long Broadway runs, but a third adaptation, a version of Ketti Frings's successful but downbeat play *Look Homeward, Angel* (Ethel Barrymore Theater 28 November 1957, 564 performances), proved a failure when put to music.

Udell then collaborated with Philip Rose, his co-writer on each of the other shows, and composer Garry Sherman on two other musicals. A sort of Harlemized *A Christmas Carol* produced under the title *Comin' Uptown* with Gregory Hines as a modern Scrooge failed in 45 performances, and a musical *Amen Corner,* based on the play by James Baldwin, went under in 29 performances in spite of a roof-raising score of gospelly music.

1970 **Purlie** (Gary Geld/w Ossie Davis, Philip Rose) Broadway Theater 15 March

1975 **Shenandoah** (Geld/w James Lee Barrett, Rose) Alvin Theater 7 January

1978 **Angel** (Geld/w Ketti Frings, Philip Rose) Minskoff Theater 10 May

1979 **Comin' Uptown** (Garry Sherman/w Rose) Winter Garden Theater 20 December

1983 **Amen Corner** (Sherman/w Rose) Nederlander Theater 10 November

1997 **Sing a Christmas Song** revised *Comin' Uptown* George Street Playhouse, New Brunswick 6 December

UFF KIRÁLY *see* L'ÉTOILE

UGALDE, Delphine [née BEAUCÉ] (b Paris, 3 December 1829; d Paris, 19 July 1910). Star Parisian vocalist turned producer and teacher.

Delphine Ugalde made her debut at the Opéra-Comique at the age of 19 in *Le Domino noir* and subsequently became a major star at the Salle Favart, creating the role of Massé's *Galathée* (1852) and playing in such pieces as Adam's *Le Toréador, La Fée aux roses* and *Le Songe d'un nuit d'été.* In 1862, with her voice just slightly used by a dozen young years of lead roles, she left the Opéra-Comique and turned her attention to opérette. She played Eurydice in *Orphée aux enfers* at the Bouffes-Parisiens, and followed this by creating the role of the chattering Roland both at Baden and in the full-sized Paris edition of *Les Bavards.* She later created another major Offenbach role as Feroza in *Les Géorgiennes* (1864). She also appeared on the spectacular stage, playing the Prince in the 1867 production of *La Biche au bois* at the Porte-Saint-Martin.

When the Société Hanapier, which had taken over the running of the Bouffes-Parisiens a couple of seasons earlier, decided to give it up, following the flop of *Les Bergers* in 1865, Varcollier, whom Madame Ugalde had married after her first husband's death in 1858, took up the lease on the theatre, and for the next two years his wife effectively ran the house. The Varcolliers produced Hervé's *Les Chevaliers de la table ronde* (1866, with Mme Ugalde starred) and Frédéric Barbier's *Légendes de Gavarni* (1866) and revived *Orphée aux enfers* (1867) with Mme Ugalde as Eurydice and the famous bit of casting of the English courtesan "Cora Pearl" as Cupid. This production played with great success (but without Ms Pearl) through the Exposition, and Mme Ugalde then took it and the Bouffes repertoire to Brussels. *Les Bavards,* Flotow's *La Veuve Gratin,* Adam's *Les Pantins de Violette,* Jonas's *Les Petits Prodiges,* Duprato's *M Landry,* Offenbach's *Daphnis et Chloë* (with Mme Ugalde as Daphnis), Léonce's little pochade *Une femme qui a perdu son clef, Nicaise* (1867) and other short pieces were also played in the repertoire at the Bouffes under the Varcollier regime.

Mme Ugalde went back to the Opéra-Comique in 1870, and made one last success there in *Déa,* but she departed again in the following year, and made further appearances on the opérette stage, notably in the title role of Jonas's *Javotte* (otherwise London's *Cinderella the Younger*) at the Théâtre de l'Athénée at Christmas 1871, before taking on the management of the little Folies-Marigny in the middle of the gardens of the Champs-Élysées in the winter of 1872. She opened with a spectacle-coupé featuring Adrien Talexy's opéra-comique *La Fête aux lanternes.*

She later largely devoted herself to a third career as a singing teacher, but in 1885 she once again went into management at the Bouffes. She produced Messager's *La Béarnaise,* had a triumph with *Joséphine vendue par ses soeurs* and featured her daughter in the leading roles of Lecocq's *Les Grenadiers de Mont-Cornette* and Serpette's *La Gamine de Paris* (1887). She also mounted Pugno's unhappy *Sosie* (1887) and the vaudeville *Le Microbe* (1887) before handing over the direction to an English lady with theatrical ambitions and that lady's manager, Broadway's Carlo Aquila Chizzola, and finally quitting the game.

Mme Ugalde composed an opérette, *La Halte au moulin* (lib: Constant Jarry), in which she played at the Bouffes-Parisiens in 1867 (11 January), and later a one-act opéra-comique *Le Page de Stella* (lib: Charly, Théâtre Bodinière 4 January 1895).

Her daughter, **Marguerite UGALDE** [Marie VARCOLLIER] (b Paris, 30 June 1862; d Paris, 6 July 1940), taught by her mother, made her Parisian debut at the Opéra-Comique on 19 April 1880 as Marie in *La Fille du régiment* and appeared there as Mnazile in *Le Bois,* Nicklausse in *Les Contes d'Hoffmann,* etc. She soon found her way into the more congenial world of the light musical theatre, and there she became one of the favorite leading ladies of her era.

Her first ''outside'' venture was perhaps her most successful of all, for she went straight from the Opéra-Comique to Brasseur's Théâtre des Nouveautés to create the role of Manola in *Le Jour et la nuit* (1881). Amongst the other new shows that followed this famous first were *Le Droit d'aînesse* (1883), in which she created the role of Falka, *Le Premier Baiser* (1883, Suzel), *L'Oiseau bleu* (1884, Stenio Strozzi), *La Nuit aux soufflets* (1884, Hélène), *Les Petits Mousquetaires* (1885, D'Artagnan), *Le Petit Chaperon rouge* (1885, Denisette) and, the most successful of this set, *Serment d'amour* (1886, Rosette). She left the Nouveautés to star for her mother in *Les Grenadiers de Mont-Cornette* (1887, Tonio) and *La Gamine de Paris* (1887, Titine Pépin).

She later played in Russia and in Brussels, appeared as Joveline in the 1889 version of the spectacular *Le Royaume des femmes,* starred in the French production of Suppé's *Donna Juanita* (1891, René Belamour) and had the most successful new role of her career since *Le Jour et la nuit* when she created the very different part of Clairette, who gets herself into military disguise and all sorts of comic situations in the vaudeville-opérette *Les 28 Jours de Clairette* (1892). Thereafter, when she appeared on the musical stage it was largely in revivals of the classic repertoire (Fragoletto, Frédégonde, Clairette), although she was yet to be seen, still in comely travesty, as the Prince of Styria in Hennequin and Mars's *Sa Majesté l'amour* as late as 1896.

UJJ, [Adalbert Franz Maria] Béla [von] (b Vienna, 2 July 1873; d Vienna, 1 February 1942).

The son of a Major in the Hungarian lifeguards, von Ujj (the ''von'' came simply from the Austrian habit of sticking particles onto perfectly ordinary Hungarian names) lost virtually all his sight at the age of seven, but this handicap did not prevent him from first studying and then practicing music as a career.

He made his debuts in the theatre with two shows, the opera *Der Bauernfeind* (1897) and the musical play *Die beiden Truminger* (1898), written for the theatre at Baden bei Wien. A revised version of the second piece gave him a more substantial credit when it transferred the following year to the uptown Jantschtheater. His next work, *Der Herr Professor,* written to a text by Victor Léon that was calculatedly built around a role for Alexander Girardi, the star of the Theater an der Wien, was produced there in 1903 with the famous comedian starred (37 performances), and repeated six months later at Berlin's Neues Königliches Opernhaus (18 June 1904) with Mia Werber and Gollwig featured.

Over the following decade, the blind composer, with his extravagantly waxed mustaches and sporting a dramatic black eye patch over his left eye, cut an unmissable figure in the Viennese music and theatrical world, where he produced regular if rarely very successful scores for the stage. The Operette *Kaisermanöver* was played just 16 times at the Carltheater in spite of being led by Mizzi Günther and Louis Treumann, and *Die kleine Prinzessin* was outshone by *Miss Hook of Holland* and *Frühlingsluft* in the 1907 season at Venedig in Wien, but *Der Müller und sein Kind,* first produced in Graz, was well enough considered to be later given a showing at the Volksoper. He supplied the music for the ''Wiener Stück'' *Der Dumme hat's Glück* produced at the Raimundtheater in 1911 and in 1914 collaborated with Carl Lindau on *Teresita,* a pastiche Operette for which he arranged melodies by Émile Waldteufel as a score.

Ujj's one widely traveled piece was a burlesque of Rostand's farmyard play *Chantecler,* which went on from its original production at Ronacher to be seen in America, with Jeff de Angelis starred as *A Barnyard Romeo* (1910) and in London as *Chanteclaire, or Hicockalorum* (ad Joe Peterman, mus arr Frank Leedham, Oxford Music Hall 20 June 1910).

1898 **Die beiden Truminger** (Reitler) Stadttheater, Baden bei Wien

1899 **Die Stellvertreterin** revised *Die beiden Truminger* (M A Reitter [ie, Emil Arter]) Jantschtheater 26 October

1903 **Der Herr Professor** (Victor Léon) Theater an der Wien 4 December

1905 **Kaisermanöver** (Léon) Carltheater 4 March

1907 **Die kleine Prinzessin** (Carl Lindau, F Antony) Venedig in Wien 5 May

1907 **Der Müller und sein Kind** (Karl Schreder, Robert Prosl) Stadttheater, Graz 1 November; Volksoper, Vienna 30 October

1907 **Eine Sensation** (Lindau, Anthony) 1 act Danzers Orpheum 20 December

1909 **Drei Stunden Leben** (Lindau, Anthony) 1 act Apollotheater 1 November

1910 **Chantecler, oder Die Sehnsucht nach dem Hahn** (Leopold Krenn, Lindau) Ronacher 24 February

1910 **Die schwarze Mali** (*Ma gosse*) (w pasticcio arr Maurice Jacobi) 1 act Apollotheater February

1910 **Der Dumme hat's Glück** (Krenn, Lindau) Raimundtheater 10 September

1912 **Der Türmer von St-Stephan** (H Roffan, Prosl) 1 act Intimes Theater 13 September

1914 **Teresita** (Émile Waldteufel arr/Lindau) Venedig in Wien 27 June

ULMAR, [Annie] Geraldine (b Charlestown, Mass, 23 June 1862; d Merstham, England, 13 August 1932).

The daughter of a Boston jeweler, pretty, dark-eyed Geraldine Ulmar started a concert career as a young teenager and became a leading lady with the Boston Ideal Opera Company in 1879. She made her first appearance with what was then regarded as the country's best light opera company as Josephine in *HMS Pinafore* at New Bedford, Mass, and appeared thereafter throughout the country, during some five years, in roles as diverse as Bettina in *La Mascotte,* Beatrice in *Boccaccio,* Germaine in *Les Cloches de Corneville,* the title role in *Giroflé-Girofla,* Constance in *The Sorcerer,* Arline in *The Bohemian Girl,* Marie in *The Musketeers,* Mabel in *The Pirates of Penzance,* Bathilde in *Olivette,* Giralda in *Giralda* and Susanna in *The Marriage of Figaro.* In between her Bostonian engagements, she played Josephine with "The Peerless *Pinafore* Company" in Chicago (1880), with Flora E Barry's comic opera company (1880, Josephine in *Pinafore,* Rita in *The Contrabandista,* etc), with the Boston Opera Company (*Betsy Baker,*

Plate 400. **Geraldine Ulmar** *as Yum-Yum in America's* The Mikado.

1881) and with the Grayson Opera Company (1881), before, in 1885, she announced her retirement to marry. However, she dropped such connubial plans when she was offered the role of Yum-Yum in John Stetson's official Broadway production of *The Mikado.*

She subsequently appeared in New York in the title role of *Princess Ida* and as Rose Maybud in Richard D'Oyly Carte's *Ruddigore* (1887), and when Leonora Braham left the London cast of the latter show to go to Australia, Miss Ulmar was moved by Carte to Britain to take over as leading lady at the Savoy. She remained there for the subsequent revival of *HMS Pinafore* and to create the roles of Elsie Maynard in *The Yeomen of the Guard* (1888, " 'Tis Done, I Am a Bride," "I Have a Song to Sing, O") and Gianetta in *The Gondoliers* (1889).

Although she then left the Carte company, she spent the rest of her career in Britain. In 1890 she starred as Marton in the highly successful London version of Audran's *La Cigale et la fourmi,* in 1892 she introduced the leading feminine role of Teresa in Gilbert and Cellier's *The Mountebanks* and she subsequently took over the title role in Haydn Parry's light romantic opera *Cigarette* when it was recast for a first-class London run. She also made a surprise shift to lighter things when she appeared for a while as the juvenile heroine of the burlesque *Little Christopher Columbus* (1894). In 1896 she starred as O Mimosa San in George Edwardes's first tour of *The Geisha,* but she was not seen again in the West End until she was persuaded out of retirement in 1904 for a disastrously amateurish piece called *Ladyland.*

In later life (''a mountain of pale blue hair and a staggering cascade of bosom''), she became a singer teacher at the Wigmore Hall, numbering among her pupils such coming stars as José Collins, Binnie Hale and Evelyn Laye, but she was forced from her work by blindness before her death at the age of 70.

Married, between 1891 and 1903, to Ivan Caryll, she later wed Jack Thompson, a less high-profiled performer and composer.

ULVAEUS, Bjørn (b Gothenburg, Sweden, 15 April 1946).

A member of the Swedish singing group, Abba, Ulvaeus collaborated with fellow member Benny Andersson on the composition of the group's many hit songs (''Waterloo,'' ''Dancing Queen,'' ''Take a Chance on Me,'' ''The Winner Takes All,'' etc) during Abba's decade at the forefront of the popular-music scene. Their music was first heard as a musical-theatre score when *Abbacadabra,* a pasticcio children's show based on their songs, was transferred from a concept disc to the stage, and Ulvaeus and Andersson subsequently collaborated with Tim Rice on the successful musical *Chess* (''I Know Him So Well,'' ''One Night in Bangkok,'' ''Heaven Help My Heart''), on the impressive Swedish musical *Kristina fran Duvemala* and—on the wave of the Abba nostalgia boom of the last years of the century—on another compilation piece, *Mamma mia!*

1983 **Abbacadabra** (w Andersson/Don Black/Alain Boublil, Daniel Boublil ad David Wood) Lyric Theatre, Hammersmith 8 December

1986 **Chess** (w Andersson/Tim Rice) Prince Edward Theatre 14 May

1995 **Kristina fran Duvemala** (w Andersson/Carl-Johan Seth) Storan Malmö Music Theater 7 October; Cirkus Teater, Stockholm 14 February 1998

1999 **Mamma mia!** (w Andersson/Catherine Johnson) Prince Edward Theatre 6 April

Literature: Oldham, Calder, Irwin: *Abba: The Name of the Game* (Sidgwick & Jackson, London, 1975), etc

THE UMPIRE Musical comedy in 2 acts by Will M Hough and Frank R Adams. Music by Joseph E Howard. La Salle Theater, Chicago, 2 December 1905.

One of the earliest great successes of Chicago's Hough-Adams-Howard combination, *The Umpire* had a record-breaking first season run of more than 300 performances at the little La Salle Theatre, helping to launch a splendid decade of prosperity in the musical theatre there. It then toured merrily around America for several seasons, without visiting Broadway, establishing itself everywhere as a jolly regional favorite.

The show's text took an enjoyably original turn on the musical-comedy formulae then in use, using for its hero the baseball umpire of the title (Cecil Lean) who gets himself into trouble by making a bad on-field decision. Fleeing town, he then ends up in the picturesque Oriental locations beloved of contemporary musical-comedy second acts, where he discovers not only football but also love when the local team's star player takes off his helmet, shakes out his hair and turns out to be called Maribel Lewton (Florence Holbrook, the real-life Mrs Lean).

Hough, Adams and Howard's songs included several with plotful baseball and football references—''The Umpire's a Most Unhappy Man,'' ''The Quarterback''—as well as a lively run through the gamut of popular styles from coon song (''The Sun That Shines on Dixie,'' ''Clorinda Jackson''), to military (''The Drums of the Fore and Aft''), to the ''Hush the Bogie'' style (''The Big Banshee''), the jolly (''Let's Take a Trolley'') and the brightly romantic (''I Want a Girl Like You,'' ''Cross Your Heart'').

The Umpire was, in fact, not America's first baseball musical. That honor goes to a rather less successful piece entitled *Angela, or the Umpire's Revenge,* written by Paul Eaton and produced at Philadelphia's Grand Opera House 29 June 1888. The revenge was taken by Mr Moberly, umpire at the New York Baseball Club, upon pitcher Eli Yale, as the price of an imagined slight. Moberly made Eli miss his wedding to the lovely Angela, but was confounded when it turned out that the substitute groom was a girl, and the loving couple were able to get together at the final curtain. The opening scene took place at the baseball club's grounds. *Angela* was swiftly followed by a farce comedy called *A Game of Ball,* mounted in Dubuque, Iowa (Duncan & Waller's Opera House 17 November 1888), in which author J L Mackey starred as ''His Royal Nibs, principal catcher and all-round player of the burg'' to the accompaniment of ''numerous songs'' apparently by one Mr Mayes. It was altogether less professional and altogether less successful. Ernest Howard's *A Baseball Crank* produced at Chelsea, Mass, in 1891 (2 July) professed to be ''a satire on our national game'' equipped with ''several new baseball songs,'' but came out more like the standard musical farce comedy. The author starred opposite the rising Josephine Hall.

UN DE LA CANEBIÈRE Opérette in 2 acts by Henri Alibert. Lyrics by René Sarvil. Music by Vincent Scotto. Théâtre des Célestins, Lyon, 14 October 1935; Théâtre des Variétés, Paris, 3 April 1936.

One of the most popular of the successful group of opérettes marseillaises produced by Alibert, Sarvil and Scotto in the early 1930s, *Un de la Canebière* once again had three joyful southern lads—fishermen, this time—as its central characters. These fishermen, Toinet (Alibert),

Pénible (Rellys) and Girelle (Gorlett), spend the evening chasing Francine (Mireille Ponsard), Malou (Marguette Willy) and Margot (Mlle Gerlatta) and the dream of a factory where they can can their own fish. A few amorous fibs, the odd contretemps and a series of catchy, dancing songs headed by Alibert's enduring tango chanté "Le plus beau tango du monde," his slow-fox declaration that "J'aime la mer comme une femme," the fox-trotted "Les Pescadous" and the men's hymn to the "Cane-, Canebière" made up an entertainment that began its success in Lyon, made its way to Paris's Théâtre des Variétés for an eight-month season, was put on to film, then took itself back to the provinces, where it is still happily played more than half a century later. It returned to Paris for fresh seasons in 1952 (Théâtre Bobino 18 October) and in 1980 (Théâtre de la Renaissance 14 June).

A 1938 film version featured Alibert, Rellys and Sarvil alongside Germaine Roger and Jenny Hélia.

Film: René Pujol 1938, *Trois de la Canebière* 1956

Recordings: selections (Vega, TLP, etc)

UNDER THE COUNTER Comedy with music in 3 acts by Arthur Macrae. Lyrics by Harold Purcell. Music by Manning Sherwin. Phoenix Theatre, London, 22 November 1945.

A flimsy but funny vehicle for the West End's favorite auntie-comedienne, Cicely Courtneidge, who appeared as actress Jo Fox, an enterprising Englishwoman-in-wartime, dipping her fingers into government postings and the black-market whilst simultaneously rehearsing her new show (in her living room, to save on *Under the Counter*'s wartime budget for scenery). The five songs used in the show, numbers from the show-within-the show, included a winning ballad, "The Moment I Saw You," a fashion parade and an opening chorus for the girls, a ballad for leading man Thorley Walters, and a burlesque song and dance for the star.

A huge hit in end-of-the-wartime London, Emile Littler, Tom Arnold and Lee Ephraim's production of *Under the Counter* ran for 665 West End performances (Florence Desmond briefly spelling the holidaying star) and, whilst a British touring company went on the road, Miss Courtneidge took a company including Walters and Wilfrid Hyde White to Broadway—the first such cross-Atlantic venture in a decade. Broadway wasn't interested, and after three weeks Miss Courtneidge packed up and headed for Australia. There, the tale was very different, for in spite of a very sticky beginning when weeks of performances had to be canceled because of her illness, the star, accompanied by Walters, Aileen Bilton (Zoë) and Claude Horton (Mike), trouped her show through the antipodes for an entire year.

USA: Shubert Theater 3 October 1947; Australia: Theatre Royal, Sydney 3 January 1948

Plate 401. **Under Your Hat.** *Jack Hulbert and Cicely Courtneidge impersonate Mr and Mrs Sheepshanks from Poona.*

UNDER YOUR HAT Musical comedy in 2 acts by Archie Menzies, Arthur Macrae and Jack Hulbert. Music and lyrics by Vivan Ellis. Palace Theatre, London, 24 November 1938.

Under Your Hat brought Jack Hulbert and Cicely Courtneidge back to the West End stage, starred as a pair of film stars, Jack Millet and Kay Porter, chasing after a carburetor that was apparently absolutely vital to national security. Jack sets out on the track of the glamorous thief-spy Carol Markoff (Leonora Corbett), and Kay follows on the track of Jack, until nasty Russian Boris (Frank Cellier) is thoroughly outwitted and Britain triumphs. Disguises were legion, from Kay's impersonation of an extravagantly red-headed waitress to the pair's portrayal of the Rajer-than-Raj Colonel and Mrs Sheepshanks from Poona, and Vivian Ellis's score gave Jack and Cis all the musical opportunities they needed, whether singing about being "Together Again" or rehearsing for a film in "Rise Above It." Miss Courtneidge burlesqued the French cabaret in "La Danse, c'est moi!" and scored the hit of the evening delivering the hooting "The Empire Depends on You" in her guise as the lady of the colonial East.

Quickly hailed as the biggest West End hit in a decade, Lee Ephraim's production of *Under Your Hat* was

Plate 402. **Die ungarische Hochzeit.** *Anneliese Mucke as Frusina and Sigi Kurzweil as Stuhlrichter in the Kaiserslauten Pfalztheater production of 1985.*

clobbered by the war, and after 10 months it had to be taken off when London's theatres were closed. Ephraim remounted the show out of town and brought it back to the Palace Theatre when things quieted down a bit (31 October 1939). It lasted another six months and more, closing after 512 West End performances. It was later produced by J C Williamson Ltd in Australia with Marjorie Gordon and Edwin Styles taking the lead roles, filmed in Britain with its stage stars, and sent on the road, but some of the larger and more transatlantic plans originally announced for it did not eventuate.

Australia: Her Majesty's Theatre, Melbourne 9 September 1939

Film: Grand National 1940

DIE UNGARISCHE HOCHZEIT Operette in a Vorspiel and 3 acts by Hermann Hermecke based on the novel by Koloman Mikszáth. Music by Nico Dostal. Staatstheater, Stuttgart, 4 February 1939.

Following the success of his *Monika* at the Stuttgart Staatstheater, Dostal wrote this second Operette for the same house. Its story dealt with what was superficially the same topic as Lecocq's long-loved *Les Cent Vierges*—the organization of a supply of brides to a group of settlers. However, this being 1939, there was not a hint of the crazy fun of the older show in Hermecke's limpish libretto, which was firmly in the conventional operettic style of its time. When the lush-living Count Stefan Bárdossy (Karl Mikoray) is ordered by his Empress to take charge of the bride business, he off-handedly sends his valet Árpád to do the work instead, and complications sprout thick and fast. Etelka, who thinks she is wedding a Count, gets a valet, and Bárdossy, who falls in love with Janka (Paula Kapper), daughter of the local President, is tricked by her into marrying a maidservant. The Empress herself arrives in the third act to annul virtually everything and to pair off tenor and soprano. The Hungarian flavors of the piece and of Dostal's music were very much more convincing than the cowboy–South American text and songs of his first success, *Clivia,* and the score of *Die ungarische Hochzeit* contained some of his better writing.

Die ungarische Hochzeit was played in a number of German provincial theatres, produced in Czechoslovakia and, in 1981, mounted at the Vienna Volksoper with Kurt Schreibmayer (Stefan), Mirjana Irosch (Janka), Kurt Huemer (Árpád) and Elisabeth Kales (Etelka).

Austria: Volksoper 6 March 1981

Recordings: selections (Eurodisc, Philips, EMI, Telefunken)

UNGER, Gladys B[uchanan] (b San Francisco, 16 September 1882; d New York, 25 May 1940).

Granddaughter of Robert Buchanan, a Wild West sheriff who was—so the story goes—shot dead by the bandit Murietta, Miss Unger studied art in Paris, and other things in Hampstead, before taking up a theatrical pen while still in her teens. For some 30 years from the production of her first play, *Edmund Kean,* in 1903, she operated as a prolific Atlantic-hopping stagewriter and, particularly, as a translator of French and German originals (*Inconstant George, The Goldfish, The Werewolf,* etc) for the American and British theatre. She made her first incursion onto the musical stage in Britain with an adaptation of Johann Strauss's *Die Fledermaus,* under the odd title *Nightbirds,* an adaptation that had respectable runs in London (138 performances), on Broadway (retitled even more curiously as *The Merry Countess,* Casino Theater 20 August 1912, 129 performances), and in Australia (Criterion Theatre, Sydney 13 June 1912).

She had two fine successes at London's Daly's Theatre in the years before the First World War, the first when she Englished the Hungarian musical *Leányvásár* for George Edwardes as *The Marriage Market* and then when she collaborated with Freddie Lonsdale on the libretto for the long popular *Betty.* Alongside these, the musical comedy *Toto,* adapted from her own version (*Better Not Enquire*) of Alfred Capus's French play *Les Deux Écoles,* had a reasonable touring life, but an attempt at an original Persian musical with composer-of-the-moment Charles Cuvillier produced only a short run and a short-lived marriage to her Persian co-author K K Ardaschir.

Miss Unger's last musical credits were her only ones in her native land. The first was an adaptation of Régis Gignoux and Jacques Théry's saucy *Le Fruit vert,* musicalized as a vehicle for diminutive Hungarian star Mitzi under the title *The Madcap,* the second a version of André Birabeau's *Un Dejeuner de soleil* (which she had already adapted for the screen) made over for the Shuberts to star filmland's Edna Leedom under the title *Ain't Love Grand.* By the time it reached town it was called *Lovely Lady* and Miss Leedom had jumped ship to marry a brewery millionaire, but the indefatigable Mitzi came in to save the situation and the show ran up 164 performances on Broadway.

A musical version of Elinor Glin's notorious *Three Weeks* commissioned by the Shuberts did not eventuate, and thereafter, except for a version of the *Beau Brummell* tale mounted at the St Louis Muny, Miss Unger concentrated on non-musical pieces and on seven busy Hollywood years as a screenwriter (*Daughter of Shanghai, The Mystery of Edwin Drood, Marianne, Madam Satan, Music Is Magic, Rendezvous at Midnight,* etc).

1911 **Nightbirds** (aka *The Merry Countess*) (*Die Fledermaus*) English version w Arthur Anderson (Lyric Theatre)

1913 **The Marriage Market** (*Leányvásár*) English version (Daly's Theatre)

1915 **Betty** (Paul Rubens/Adrian Ross, Rubens/w Frederick Lonsdale) Daly's Theatre 24 April

1916 **Toto** (Archibald Joyce, Merlin Morgan/Anderson) Duke of York's Theatre 19 April

1920 **The Sunshine of the World** (Charles Cuvillier/James Heard/w Kai Kushrou Ardaschir) Empire Theatre 18 February

1927 **Lovely Lady** (ex- *Ain't Love Grand*) (Harold Levey, Dave Stamper/Cyrus Wood/w Wood) Sam H Harris Theater, New York 29 December

1928 **The Madcap** (Fred J Coots, Maurie Rubens/Clifford Grey/w Gertrude Purcell) Royale Theater, New York 31 January

1933 **Beau Brummell** (Harry Tierney/Edward Eliscu, Raymond Egan) Municipal Opera, St Louis 7 August

THE UNSINKABLE MOLLY BROWN Musical in 2 acts by Richard Morris. Music and lyrics by Meredith Willson. Winter Garden Theater, New York, 3 November 1960.

The heroine of *The Unsinkable Molly Brown* (Tammy Grimes)—a lass who actually existed in real life—was a brassy little prewar broad from out-of-town, determined to make herself wealthy and social in the big city of Denver. Marrying the attractive young miner Johnny Brown (Harve Presnell) doesn't seem too promising a start, but Johnny proves to have a habit of digging up silver. However, even when she gets seriously rich, Molly finds social position can't be bought in Colorado. So she tries Europe instead, and finds she goes down much better in translation. Unfortunately, Johnny is only happy back home, and when she finds that he is more important to her than her social position, she catches the ship back to America. The ship is the *Titanic.* In the disaster she turns out a heroine, and after that society and Johnny both love her.

Like the show's characters and tale, Willson's score had rather less light and shade about it than his great hit

The Music Man. Molly howled forth her ambitions in ''I Ain't Down Yet,'' headed a rousing cry to a saloonful of miners to ''Belly Up to the Bar, Boys,'' went fund-raising with the revivalist ''Are You Sure?'' and turned polyglot in ''Bon Jour,'' whilst Johnny wooed her baritonically in ''I'll Never Say 'No.''' Mitchell Gregg played Prince de Long, one of the attractive faces of Europe with a title to offer the heroine, whilst Edith Meiser (Mrs McGlone) headed the rejecting battalions of Denver society and Oliver Smith was responsible for putting the sinking of the *Titanic* on the stage. Already.

The Theatre Guild and Dore Schary (who also directed) mounted *The Unsinkable Molly Brown* for a fine Broadway run of 532 performances. However, although the show found subsequent productions around America, and also proved to be well suited for transformation into a lively and colorful film, in which Presnell starred alongside Debbie Reynolds, it did not follow *The Music Man* to productions further afield and to classic status.

Film: MGM 1964

Recordings: original cast (Capitol), film soundtrack (MGM/CBS)

DER UNSTERBLICHE LUMP Altwiener Stück in 3 acts by Felix Dörmann based on a novel by Jakob Wassermann. Music by Edmund Eysler. Wiener Bürgertheater, Vienna, 15 October 1910.

Oskar Fronz, manager of the Vienna Bürgertheater, had always avoided producing musicals at his theatre, on the grounds that they were far too costly. However, in 1910 he allowed himself to be convinced by publisher Josef Weinberger to change this policy and to produce the Felix Dörmann/Edmund Eysler musical *Der unsterbliche Lump.* Fronz hired an orchestra and chorus, brought in three guest principals in Otto Storm, Mimi Marlow and Gisela Marion for the chief singing roles, himself directed the show with his brother, Richard, conducting and was rewarded with a hit that resulted in the Bürgertheater becoming, for a period, one of Vienna's most prosperous musical houses. *Der unsterbliche Lump* played 192 consecutive performances in its first run and returned to pass its 250th performance on 25 May 1913 alongside two other Eysler hits that had since made the fortune of the house—*Der Frauenfresser* and *Der lachende Ehemann.* The show was given further performances in 1914, and brought back again in a fresh production in 1920 with Josef Viktora starred alongside Vinzenz Bauer and Rosa Koppler (17 September).

Burghausen's young village schoolteacher, Hans Ritter (Storm), dreams of fame as a composer, and of lovely local Anna Reisleitner (Gisela Marion) as a wife. Since he has for rival the Burgermeister's son, Florian (Vinzenz Bauer), Hans leaves his schoolhouse and goes off to Vienna, determined to win fame, fortune and thus Anna. While he is away, Anna's parents marry her to Florian. The distraught Hans becomes a vagabond, wandering the world until he finds friendship and redemption working, under a new name, as a pianist at the ''Blaue Flasche'' coffeehouse. The singer there is a girl named Luisl Freitag (Mimi Marlow), the same girl to whom, with her old wandering harpist father, he had one night given shelter in the Burghausen schoolhouse years before. Slowly, under Luisl's care, Hans puts his life back together, and when he revisits Burghausen he goes unrecognized—Hans Ritter, the vagabond, is dead, and the new Hans Ritter is ready to start a new life.

Eysler's score was full of Wienerische melodies, with waltzes and marches as ever to the fore. The waltzes included a Hans/Anna duet, ''Ja nur du,'' and a solo for the travel-weary Luisl (''Blätter rauschen'') in the first act, a jolly piece for Viktoria Pohl-Meiser, the komische Alte of the piece, to introduce the second (''Sich so im Tanz zu drehn'') and Hans and Luisl's duo ''Das ist das Glück,'' whilst the march melodies were headed by the rousing ''Blaue Flaschen-Marsch'' and Luisl's Brettellied (''Tröpferl zum trinken''). Other features of the score included a children's chorus (''Lieber guter Sonnenschein'') and Hans's principal solo Trutzlied (''Weise dem Leben die Zähne'').

The libretto of *Der unsterbliche Lump* was subsequently used as the basis for two films, neither of which used Eysler's music. The first (1930), in which Gustave Fröhlich played Hans and Liane Haid Anna, had a score by Ralph Benatzky, the second by Bert Grund and Robert Gilbert.

UP IN CENTRAL PARK Musical play in 2 acts by Herbert and Dorothy Fields. Lyrics by Dorothy Fields. Music by Sigmund Romberg. Century Theater, New York, 27 January 1945.

Mike Todd's wartime production of *Up in Central Park* bore some fine names on its bills: his own, guaranteeing your money's worth of spectacle, and those of Sigmund Romberg, Herbert Fields and Dorothy Fields, each of which had been attached to some of the happiest shows of the past decades. Only Todd truly lived up to the promise of the marquee, turning out a splendid physical production that was highlighted by a skating ballet routine (Currier and Ives ballet) set in Central Park and choreographed by Helen Tamiris in the image of a period print. The show's story was yet another featuring an all-American hero gallantly exposing the crimes of a nasty politician whilst simultaneously getting himself a girl.

The hero, in this case, was an ambitious young ''investigative'' journalist named John Matthews (Wilbur Evans), the villains were the historical Boss Tweed Gang and Tammany Hall, and the girl was Rosie Moore (Maureen Cannon), daughter of one of our hero's victims. When John starts attacking her father in print, Rosie goes off and marries one of Moore's friends, but she has weakened enough by the time that she discovers her ''husband'' is already married to go back to John in time for the final curtain. Romberg's period-flavored score featured a romantic duo for John and Rosie, ''Close as Pages in a Book,'' which won particular popularity alongside a pretty ''April Snow,'' but, in spite of the show's fine run of 504 performances, none of the numbers joined the old Romberg favorites in his list of standards.

A 1947 film version featured Deanna Durbin and some of the stage score, plus an oh-she-shouldn't-have chunk of *Forza del destino.* Vincent Price was Boss Tweed (what would the Boss have said to that?) and Dick Haymes the romantic interest.

Film: Universal International 1947

Recordings: selections (Decca, RCA)

URBAN [André] [URBIN, Alphonse Antoine] (b Le Bouscat, Gironde, 4 December 1884; d Paris, 28 October 1947). Light comedy leading man of the French musical comedy stage.

At first an employee in the ''contributions indirectes'' office in Bordeaux, Urban made his first attempts as a performer in a local café-concert and left town playing a servant in a touring company of *Ruy Blas.* In 1903 he reached Paris and, after an early career as a singer of comic songs (Bousquet-Concert, la Grande Roue, l'Époque, Petit Casino, and from 1904 to 1909 at the Pepinière), he switched first to revue at La Cigale and then, under the management of Charles Montcharmont at the Théâtre des Célestins in Lyon, to the musical stage. His first big musical comedy success came when he was engaged in Belgium to play the principal comic role in Josef Szulc's new opérette, *Flup..!* He subsequently appeared in the French premiere of Emmerich Kálmán's *Tatárjárás* at Lyon (1914), playing the role of the Jewish volunteer that had helped launch Vienna's Max Pallenberg to fame, at the Marseille Gymnase, in *L'Orgie à Babylone* at the Olympia, in the wartime revival of *The Belle of New York* at the Variétés, reprised his role in *Flup..!* at Lyon and—after a period in uniform—appeared in revue at the Vaudeville and in *La Fausse Ingénue* at the Théâtre Fémina (1918, Sageret). However, the success that would make his name came as the war ended, when he created the title role of the naughty Greek sculptor in the memorable *Phi-Phi* (''Les petits païens,'' ''C'est une gamine charmante,'' ''Vertu, Verturon, Verturonette''). Alongside the show, Urban triumphed in a role that he would repeat at intervals for some 30 years.

Now at the forefront of the modern musical comedy's range of stars, he featured in Goublier's *La Sirène* (1920, Le Vicomte de Kernichet) and in *Titin* in Brussels (1921), then took up the title role of Christiné's next opérette, *Dédé* (''Elle porte un nom charmant,'' ''Tous les chemins menent à l'amour''), sharing top billing with Maurice Chevalier. After playing the comical Baron, alongside Sacha Guitry and Yvonne Printemps, in Guitry's exquisite musical play *L'Amour masqué* (1923, ''Tango chanté,'' La Chanson des Bonnes), appearing alongside Yvette Guilbert in *Les Amants légitimes* (1924) and making a return visit to Lyon to play Napoléon to the Marietta of Gabrielle Ristori in the French premiere of Kálmán's *La Bayadère* (1925), he followed up with leading roles in a series of successful Parisian musical comedies: *Un Bon garçon* (1926, Pontavès), *Comte Obligado* (1927, ''Mio Padre,'' ''Le petit oiseau des îles''), *Elle est à vous* (1929, Jouvencel ''Elle est à vous''), *Louis XIV* (1929, Le Comte) and *Bégonia* (1930, ''Simplement,'' ''Que l'amour est traître'').

With the passing of the best of the musical comedies of the era, his opportunities declined. He appeared in the less successful *Femme de minuit* (1930, Verdurier), played the role of the Commandant in the 1934 Josephine Baker revival of *La Créole,* appeared in the Johann Strauss *Les Jolies Viennoises* (1938) and in the Paul Ábrahám remake, *Billy et son équipe* (1939) at the Mogador. In the last-named show he performed the Lambeth Walk. In the 1940s, he appeared in the revival of *Les Cent Vierges* (1942) and in 1945 took up his old part in *On cherche un roi* (ex- *Louis XIV*). But he returned, always, to Phidias and *Phi-Phi,* reappearing in his famous role at the Bouffes-Parisiens just months before his death.

He also appeared on the musical screen, notably in the film version of *Ciboulette* (1933).

Urban was the husband of Lily Zévaco [Blanche Laurence ZÉVACO] who appeared alongside him in *Louis XIV.*

URBAN, Joseph (b Vienna, 26 May 1872; d New York, 10 July 1933).

Austrian architect, decorator and theatrical designer, whose eclectic career in his homeland ranged from town planning and constructing and decorating castles to illustrating fairy tales. His work appeared on the Viennese stage in such pieces as the Carltheater *Das Puppenmädel* (1910, billed as ''architect Joseph Urban'') and the 1911 *Alt-Wien,* in Berlin, Munich and Hamburg—but mostly in opera houses—before he moved definitively to America in 1911. He was engaged at the Boston Opera Company for several years and later designed scenery for James Hackett's Shakespeare productions, but he became best known in the musical theatre, where his name remains particularly attached to the spectacular settings he designed for Florenz Ziegfeld and his series of *Follies* (from 1915).

Amongst the Broadway musicals for which, amongst a bundle of revue productions, he designed the scenery and ''decorations'' were Henry Savage's production of *Pom Pom* (1916), *Flora Bella* (1916), Klaw and Erlanger's *Miss Springtime* (1916), *The Riviera Girl* (1917), *Jack o'Lantern* (1917), *Glorianna* (1918), *Apple Blossoms* (1919), *The Rose of China* (1919), *Sally* (1920), the 1921 revival of *The Merry Widow, The Love Letter* (1921), *The Yankee Princess* (1922), *Sunny* (1925), *Song of the Flame* (1925), *The Wild Rose* (1926), *Betsy* (1926), *Rio Rita* (1927), *Yours Truly* (1927), *Golden Dawn* (1927), *Show Boat* (1927), *The Three Musketeers* (1928), *Rosalie* (1928), *Treasure Girl* (1928), *Whoopee* (1928), *Polly* (1929), *Show Girl* (1929), *Sons o' Guns* (1929), *Ripples* (1930), *Simple Simon* (1930), *Flying High* (1930), *Princess Charming* (1930), *Smiles* (1930), *Hot-Cha!* (1932), *Music in the Air* (1932) and *Melody* (1933). He was also the designer of New York's Ziegfeld Theater and several other theatres in a parallel career as an architect.

URGEL, Louis

Madame Urgel, a comfortably-off amateur musician and composer who chose, so she said, to take a male pseudonym so as not to have to write in the polite, parlory fashion considered apt for lady writers, composed the scores for a group of period opérettes that were played in Paris during the 1920s at the height of the fashion for Jazz Age musical comedy. If her music won little in the way of appreciation from the professionals, being criticized for looking too reminiscently back to the world of Lecocq and Audran at the same time that certain critics were bemoaning the passing of traditional opérette, it nevertheless proved pleasing enough to the public, who gave her works a more than respectable hearing.

The first piece, the Louis XVIII–era *Monsieur Dumollet,* had Edmée Favart as a royalist spy engaged in helping a conspirator (Félix Oudart) to escape from the house of her natural father (Vilbert), who is faced with the problem of explaining this premarital child to his new wife (Mme Cebron-Norbens). After some 200 Parisian performances, it continued on to the provinces, with Andrée Le Dantec and Javerzac starred, whilst Mme Urgel's second piece, *Amour de princesse,* was produced in town. Vilbert again starred alongside comic Morton, baritone Robert Jysor, Germaine Gallois, Germaine Charley and Flore Mally, and the show won another critically cool reception and a reasonable run amongst the Théâtre de la Gaîté-Lyrique's program of classic revivals.

The most successful of the three pieces was, however, the third. *Qu'en dit l'abbé?* was an 18th-century ''opérette galante'' of potential musical beds that had ambitious Rose Pinchon (Mlle Vioricia), to whom a title is the price of a tumble, wed off to the young and excessively innocent Vicomte de Castel-Bidon (Robert Burnier) for the carnal purposes of the lecherous Duc de Roquelaure (Harry Baur/Abel Tarride). Honorine de Pompignan (Nina Myral), the Duc's mistress, battles trick for trick with him to prevent him from claiming his prize until the young spouses end up in each other's arms and the curtain comes down. The Abbé (Gaston Gabaroche/Paul Ville) was reasonably incidental, the title a catchphrase, and the music strove occasionally away from the period of the play towards more modern dance rhythms. *Qu'en dit l'abbé?* topped 150 performances at the Théâtre de l'Avenue, was subsequently revived at the Théâtre Édouard VII later the same year and had a lively life in the French provinces.

Mme Urgel wrote a considerable number of songs (''Le Poulailler,'' ''Trois petits garçons,'' etc) and also several ballets, one, *Lumière et Papillons,* produced at the Opéra-Comique in 1916, another, *Le Loup et l'agneau,* at Monte Carlo and subsequently at the Paris Gaîté.

1922 **Monsieur Dumollet** (Hugues Delorme/Victor Jeannet) Théâtre du Vaudeville 25 May

1923 **Amour de princesse** (Delorme/Jeannet) Théâtre de la Gaîté-Lyrique 25 October

1925 **Qu'en dit l'abbé?** (Battaille-Henri) Théâtre de l'Avenue 22 May

1928 **Une nuit au Louvre** (Henri Duvernois, Charles Dorin) Théâtre des Bouffes-Parisiens 13 October

1931 **Vieux Garçons** (Michel Carré) 1 act Théâtre de la Gaîté-Lyrique 21 February

UTOPIA (LIMITED), or The Flowers of Progress

Comic opera in 2 acts by W S Gilbert. Music by Arthur Sullivan. Savoy Theatre, London, 7 October 1893.

The reunification of the Carte-Gilbert-Sullivan team, some three years after its angry dissolution, for a new comic opera at the Savoy Theatre, brought forth *Utopia (Limited),* a piece more brittle and harsh in tone than its authors' earlier works. Gilbert's targets—Parliament, the ridiculous institution of government by party, big business and British traditions in general—were hammered in a much less subtle and less humorous fashion than before, and much of Sullivan's music also strayed from the old opéra-bouffe mode.

King Paramount of Utopia (Rutland Barrington), a monarch kept under the little fingers of his advisers Scaphio (W H Denny) and Phantis (John Le Hay), has sent his daughter Zara (Nancy McIntosh) to be educated amid what he believes to be the utter perfection of the institutions of Britain. When she returns, she brings with her the Flowers of Progress, a group representing those institutions: the army (Charles Kenningham), the navy (Lawrence Gridley), the law (H Enes Blackmore), local government (Herbert Ralland), big business (R Scott Fishe) and the woolsack (H Scott Russell). Their reforms threaten the smooth and natural running of Utopia with a painful perfection, but this is avoided by introducing party politics, thus allowing the reintroduction of interest, graft and squalor. Rosina Brandram played an English governess, and Walter Passmore was Utopia's Exploder, a mixture of executioner and heir to the impotent crown.

Several individual pieces of the score were on Gilbert's cleverest level: a dissertation on Company practice from businessman Mr Goldbury (''Some seven men form an Association''), a comic song in a music-hall vein for the army's Captain Fitzbattleaxe describing the disastrous effects of love on a tenor's top notes (''A tenor, all singers above'') and a funny piece for Barrington, in the vein of its author's earliest Bab Ballads (''First you're born'').

Utopia (Limited) won a fine reception and ran for 245 performances at the Savoy, longer than any other West End comic opera since the pair's last collaboration on *The Gondoliers.* It went on the road in four companies, and it was restaged on Broadway by director Charles Harris, whilst the London production still ran, with J J Dallas (Paramount), Clinton Elder (Fitzbattleaxe), John Coates (Goldbury) and Isabel Reddick (Zara) featured (55 performances). After 1902, however, *Utopia Limited* (the parentheses disappeared from the title) was dropped from the Carte repertoire. In 1906 J C Williamson Ltd in Australia, which had not picked up the show originally, mounted it, with Kenningham in his original role alongside Howard Vernon (Paramount), Frank Wilson (Goldbury) and Dolly Castles (Zara), but the show did not establish itself among the Gilbert and Sullivan favorites in Australia any more than it did, despite its reasonable early life, elsewhere.

USA: Broadway Theater 26 March 1894; Princess Theatre, Melbourne 20 January 1906

Recordings: complete (Decca), etc

V

THE VAGABOND KING Musical play in 4 acts by Willmarth H Post and Brian Hooker based on the romance *If I Were King* by Justin McCarthy. Lyrics by Brian Hooker. Music by Rudolf Friml. Casino Theater, New York, 21 September 1925.

One of the many variants on the Abu Hasan "king for a day" tale, Justin McCarthy's play *If I Were King* (Garden Theater 14 October 1901) was—in spite of the cold statistics of its first run of just 56 Broadway performances—a considerable success, with Edward Sothern starring as the historical ruffian poet François Villon who, in McCarthy's version (based on R H Russell's novel), is made king for a week, defeats Burgundy and wins a royal bride.

In 1922 the young Richard Rodgers and Lorenz Hart wrote a musical version of *If I Were King* that was produced in an all-girl amateur performance with the equally young Dorothy Fields as Villon. It evoked the interest of producer Russell Janney, but he was unwilling to take a chance with these unknown writers and he subsequently hired a better-known composer to write a score for a version of the play as adapted by W H Post and Brian Hooker. The composer he chose was Rudolf Friml, then basking in the enormous success of the previous season's *Rose Marie*.

Dennis King played Villon, a swaggering thief and versifier, who has been sending love poems to the courtly Katherine de Vaucelles (Carolyn Thompson), and who boasts in the presence of the disguised King of France (Max Figman) himself that he, Villon, would make a more effective leader in the war against Burgundy. To take a personal revenge on haughty Katherine, the King gives the arrested Villon 24 hours as Grand Marshal of France, and the mission to make good his boast to win his lady as a bride by the morrow or lose his life. Villon has the court make ostentatious revelry and at the same time organizes the beggars and vagabonds of Paris into an army that defeats the besieging Burgundians. He is saved from the gallows when the 24 hours are up, when Katherine freely gives her hand to the man she now knows is only a vagabond. A traditional comic element, represented by Villon's little friend Guy Tabarie (Herbert Corthell), was tacked in alongside the main plot, but the dramatic character of Huguette (Jane Carroll), who sacrifices her life to save Villon from a plotter's dagger, was retained, helping to keep a thoroughly dramatic core to the piece.

Friml's score was in the most vigorously romantic vein, more richly colored than his *Rose Marie* music and ideally suited to the subject in hand. Villon's virile call to the people of Paris, the Song of the Vagabonds, was one of the most stirring marches ever to have come from the Broadway theatre, and his duet with Katherine, "Only a Rose," one of the most thoroughly romantic of love songs. The star was well equipped with further romantic numbers ("Tomorrow," "Love Me Tonight") to place alongside his martial song, and these were supported by two fine numbers for Huguette ("Love for Sale," Huguette Waltz), an atmospheric Scotch Archer's Song, which set the scene for the second act with great effect, and a comic serenade featuring Tabarie.

The Vagabond King ran for 511 performances on Broadway, and it confirmed this appeal on the other side of the Atlantic when Janney mounted his show at London's Winter Garden Theatre with Derek Oldham starred as Villon alongside Winnie Melville (Katherine), Mark Lester (Tabarie) and Norah Blaney (Huguette). It ran for 480 London performances before touring and later returned to London on three occasions: in 1929 Alec Fraser played Villon (Adelphi Theatre 14 October), in 1937 Harry Welchman starred (London Coliseum 18 March) and in 1943 Webster Booth and Anne Ziegler featured back at the Winter Garden (22 April). In Australia, J C Williamson Ltd's production starred Strella Wilson, James Liddy, Arthur Stigant and Mabel Gibson for a season of more than 100 nights in Sydney, but although it proved less popular than *The Desert Song,* which preceded it, and *The Student Prince,* which was brought back to replace it in Melbourne, it did well enough to cement the show's popularity, and the popularity of its songs, in another area of the English-speaking world.

In spite of the fact that it was indubitably a better made piece than its famous predecessor, *The Vagabond King* did not, however, follow *Rose Marie* to the long list of more distant, foreign-language stages that had made the earlier piece such a remarkable musical-theatre phenomenon. It did, however, turn up at Amsterdam's Theater Carré in 1932, where the rising Johannes Heesters, Mimi Lebrat, Nelly Gerritse and Oscar Tournaire featured in a rare foreign-language production.

A Paramount film was released in 1930 with King repeating his original role alongside Jeanette MacDonald. O P Heggie was the King, Lilian Roth played Huguette and Warner Oland was the treacherous Thibault, and a song entitled "If I Were King" was interpolated. A second attempt was made at filming the show in 1956 when Maltese tenor Oreste Kirkop and Kathryn Grayson were paired in a version that used four new pieces, credited to Friml and Johnny Burke, alongside half a dozen pieces of the original score.

François Villon was earlier the eponymous hero of a French opera written by Foussier and Got, composed by Edmond de Membrée, and produced at the Paris Opéra in 1857 (20 April), and more recently of an Hungarian rock musical *Villon és barátai* (Máté Victor/György Kardos/Dezső Mészöly, Esztergomi Várszínház 29 July 1994) and a Germany *Villon* (Bühnen der Landeshauptstadt, Kiel 1 June 1996).

UK: Winter Garden Theatre 19 April 1927; Australia: Her Majesty's Theatre, Sydney 27 October 1928

Films: Paramount 1930, Paramount 1956

Recordings: London cast recordings on *Rudolf Friml in London* (WRC), 1956 film soundtrack (RCA), selections (RCA, WRC, Pye, etc)

DER VAGABUND Operette in 3 acts by Moritz West and Ludwig Held based on a theme of Émile Souvestre. Music by Carl Zeller. Carltheater, Vienna, 30 October 1886.

Although the title of the piece was a singular one, the tale of *Der Vagabund* dealt, in fact, with the stories of two vagabonds, Alexis (Herr Detschi) and Ossip (Adolf Brackl). These wandering fellows are in Tiflis—in 1812 under Russian domination—and Alexis has cast his eyes on the lovely Marizza (Frl Peschi), daughter of the crooked local Russian police chief, Ivan the Ghastly (Wilhelm Knaack). When the pair interfere in the plans of General Gregor Gregorovitch (Alexander Guttmann) and Gräfin Prascowia (Fr Hart) to take Marizza to the Grand Ducal court as a lady-in-waiting, they end up in prison, but, since Ivan thinks Alexis is his illegitimate son, only Ossip gets sentenced. The influential fortune-teller, Dyrsa (Marie Schwarz), gets into the act too, and it finally turns out, after two acts of red herrings, that Ossip is Prascowia's lost child and Alexis the by-blow of none other than the Grand Duke himself. He gets Gregor's generalship and the girl whilst Ossip pairs off with the fortuneteller.

Produced by Carl Tatartzy at the Carltheater, *Der Vagabund* was, like the rest of his productions, not a big success. It played 34 performances through November and closed, but it nevertheless had a future. A week after its Vienna closure it opened under the management of Franz Steiner at Berlin's Walhalla-Theater; the following month Budapest's Budai Színkör mounted Lajos Makó's Hungarian version. Other German language productions followed, and, in 1887, the show was seen as far afield as America, played by a cast including Max Lube, Sophie Offeney, Cora Cabella, Ferdinand Schütz and Adolf Link at the Thalia Theater. It was later revived in repertoire at Amberg's Terrace Garten with a cast including Adolf Philipp.

Germany: Walhalla-Theater 10 December 1886; Hungary: Budai Színkör *A Csavargó* 23 January 1887; USA: Thalia Theater (Ger) 3 February 1887

VAILLANT-COUTURIER, Mlle

Mlle Couturier started her young career with much publicity when it was discovered that, in spite of the rule stating that Conservatoire pupils must hold themselves ready to be directed into employment as a form of payment for their study (a much-breached rule), she had signed a contract to go direct from her studies to Brussels and the Théâtre de la Monnaie. In spite of the fuss, she actually did go to Belgium and caused quite a stir there, before returning to Paris, the poorer by the 15,000 francs awarded against her by the Paris courts, to appear at the Opéra-Comique (where she made the short list for the creations of the title roles of both *Carmen* and *Manon*) and in opérette, where she created the vocally demanding role of Princess Micaëla in *Le Coeur et la main* (1882, "Un jour, Perez le capitaine") as well as prima donna roles in *Le Roi de carreau* (1883, Benvenuta) and *Babolin* (1884, Elverine). On the last occasion it was remarked that her acting was rather "provincial" and that she was perhaps not suited to opérette. She seems to have taken the remark to heart and went back to the Opéra-Comique, where "provincial" (by which the critic presumably meant unsophisticated) acting was apparently all right.

VALLI, Valli [nee KNÜST] (b Berlin, 11 February 1882; d London, 3 November 1927).

Brought up in London, with her two sisters Lulu Valli and Ida Valli, Valli Valli had a career as a child performer that included an appearance (with Lulu) at Berlin's Theater Unter den Linden in a British production of

Morocco Bound (1895; ''a notable feature was the remarkably clever song and dance of two talented children, the sisters Valli''), another as Alice in *Alice in Wonderland,* and the creation of the part of Mundel in Bach's opera *The Lady of Longford* at Drury Lane in 1896 (''a very youthful operatic vocalist'') amidst a number of otherwise straight dramatic engagements. Although she continued in later life to play in non-musical pieces, her adult career favored the musical theatre, beginning with a small role in *Véronique* in London (replacing sister Lulu) and in New York (1905–6, Denise) and continuing through London takeovers in *A Waltz Dream* (Franzi) and *The Merry Widow* (Sonia), through a period in revue (Mrs Merry in *Oh Indeed!* 1908, Empire) to another George Edwardes role, this time in New York, the part of Lady Binfield created for Edna May in *Kitty Grey* (1909).

She appeared in further Edwardes pieces in America (Alice in *The Dollar Princess*) and in Paris (title role in *La Veuve joyeuse* revival) and also in vaudeville and the British music halls (*After the Honeymoon* w Seymour Hicks, Lincke's *Am Hochzeitsabend* as *In a Mirror* w Pope Stamper Palace Theatre 3 May 1909), but after her marriage to American music publisher Louis Dreyfus, she made the later part of her career in America. There she was seen in a botched version of Jean Gilbert's *Polnische Wirtschaft* called *The Polish Wedding* (1912, Marga), which failed to make it to Broadway, in Weber and Fields's *Roly-Poly* (1912), *The Purple Road* (1913, Empress Josephine, later Wanda), *The Queen of the Movies* (*Die Kino-Königin,* 1914, Celia Gill), *The Lady in Red* (*Die Dame in Rot,* 1915, Sylvia Stafford) and *Miss Millions* (1919, ingenue Mary Hope). She was also seen on Broadway in *The Cohan Revue of 1916* (1916, Jane Clay).

Sister Lulu, who was seen as early as 1894 in *The House That Jack Built* (Miss Truth) at the Opera Comique, appeared as an adult as Miss Yost and deputized for Marie Studholme as Cicely in London's *The School Girl* (1903) and later took over Billie Burke's role of Mamie and played it on Broadway (1904, without its big song, ''My Little Canoe,'' which had been appropriated by the star), as well as appearing in such diverse pieces as *The Silver Slipper* (1902, tour), *The Orchid* (1905, t/o Thisbe) at the Gaiety, *The Maid and the Motor Man* (1907, Kate Wicks) and *Véronique.*

As for little Ida [Maude Ida Fredrika KNÜST], who had done so well as a child when she appeared as Mr Hook in Frank Curzon's children's production of *Miss Hook of Holland,* in *Little Black Sambo and Little White Barbara* (1904, Topsy) and in the Gaiety Theatre's *Two Naughty Boys* (1906, Agnes), she muddied the waters by changing her name to ''Phyllis Maude'' when she reached years of discretion, and as Phyllis Maude she apparently worked in America in supporting roles.

VALMOUTH Musical in 2 acts by Sandy Wilson adapted from the works of Ronald Firbank. Lyric Theatre, Hammersmith, 2 October 1958; Saville Theatre, London, 27 January 1959.

Commissioned from the author-composer of *The Boy Friend* by Oscar Lewenstein and the Royal Court Theatre as a vehicle for American actress and vocalist Bertice Reading, the musical *Valmouth* was ultimately not produced by the English Stage Company, but by the young Michael Codron. Miss Reading starred as Mrs Yajnavaikya, the ambivalent and outrageous negro masseuse of Ronald Firbank's *Valmouth* at the center of a libretto crafted with great skill from the somewhat diffuse elements of the novellaist's quirky and esoteric universe.

At the English spa town of Valmouth we meet the eccentrically papist and centenarian lady of the manor, Mrs Hurstpierpoint (Barbara Couper), the unquenchably lustful and equally aged Lady Parvula Panzoust (Fenella Fielding), the plebeian 120-year-old Granny Tooke (Doris Hare) and Mrs Thoroughfare (Betty Hardy), whose seafaring son, Captain Dick (Alan Edwards), provokes the events of the evening by abandoning his bosom pal, Lieutenant Whorwood (Aubrey Woods), for the charms of the dusky Niri-Esther (Maxine Daniels). Nemesis falls on the arcane mysteries of Valmouth when the defrocked and debauched Cardinal Pirelli (Geoffrey Dunn) is summoned to celebrate the young pair's nuptials, and from the ensuing cataclysm only Mrs Yaj, Niri-Esther and her now illegitimate baby escape.

Wilson, having arranged these recondite folk into a shapely story, equipped them with some suitably special songs, which were eased into more natural English than Firbank's greenly jeweled prose. Lady Parvula sighed brazenly over the thighs of a teenaged shepherd (who had just been naively querying ''What Do I Want with Love?''), preparing to leap into the hay ''Just Once More'' and apostrophized her late husband's shade apologetically with a history of her indiscretions (''Only a Passing Phase''); an incidental nun (Marcia Ashton) under a vow of silence for 364 days of the year burst forth with a veritable ejaculation of ecstatic chatter on ''My Talking Day''; Cardinal Pierelli described the joys of ''The Cathedral of Clemenza''; the two sailors sang (with rather different feelings) of ''Niri-Esther''; and the three old beldames looked back in creaking harmony to their far-off youth when ''All the Girls Were Pretty (and all the men were strong).'' Mrs Yaj's songs glittered just a little less than these, but her bouncy ''Big Best Shoes'' proved the show's easier-to-eat take-away number.

On its production in Hammersmith, *Valmouth,* not unexpectedly, drew some outraged reviews and customers and some that and who were simply thrilled. A West End transfer was delayed and, as a result, when *Valmouth*

Plate 403. **Valmouth.** *Doris Hare, Fenella Fielding, Bertice Reading, Peter Gilmore and Barbara Couper caricatured by Keith Mackenzie.*

opened at the Saville Theatre, Cleo Laine deputized for the otherwise engaged Miss Reading. The show got a similarly bipartite reception, but even the enthusiasm of its fans could not win it more than 102 West End performances to add to the 84 clocked up in Hammersmith.

Gene Andrewski mounted the show at New York's York Playhouse the following year with Miss Reading starred alongside Anne Francine (Hurstpierpoint), Constance Carpenter (Parvula) and Alfred Toigo (Dick), but there the show died away in just 14 performances. For many years after, *Valmouth* remained remembered by connoisseurs of its generation as a lost masterpiece of the musical theatre, and the next generation were given their opportunity to agree when the Chichester Festival mounted a revival of the show in 1982 (17 May). Misses Reading, Fielding, Ashton and Hare repeated their original roles alongside Judy Campbell (Hurstpierpoint), Jane Wenham (Thoroughfare), Mark Wynter (Dick) and Sir Robert Helpmann (Cardinal Pirelli) in a memorable production by John Dexter that started all the discussions over again. The show's evident minority appeal, however, meant that it did not transfer from its festival location to the commercial theatre of London.

USA: York Playhouse 6 October 1960 Recordings: original cast (Pye), Chichester Festival cast (TER)

VALMY, Jean (b Bordeaux; d 1989).

Valmy began his theatrical career writing for intimate revue in the southwest of France and then in Paris, and his earliest work in the field of the book musical was on a similarly smaller scale. The musical comedy *Baratin* (1949), a star vehicle for comedian Roger Nicolas, was a long-running comedy hit at the little Theatre l'Européen, whilst *Les Pieds nickelés,* staged at the Bobino with Jacques Pills, Irene Hilda and the Frères Jacques heading the cast, also held the stage for some two years.

Valmy's most important play success, *J'y suis, j'y reste,* was produced for the first time in 1950, but he returned to the musical theatre with a second comic vehicle for Nicolas, *Mon p'tit pote* (1954), which proved yet another long-running success, remaining at the Européen for three and a half years, after which it was succeeded by what was supposed to be (but doesn't read like) a musical version of the classic play *Coquin de printemps.* This piece had neither Nicolas (who returned in 1961 to play *À toi de jouer* without creating the same kind of extended run) nor the same very long Parisian life, but it was successful enough to have a number of out-of-town revivals over the following decades.

In 1958 Valmy collaborated with the aged Maurice Yvain on the composer's last work, *Le Corsaire noir,* and in 1969 moved to the opposite end of the theatrical scale to that in which he had found his greatest successes to collaborate on the indifferent Châtelet spectacle *La Caravelle d'or.* His last new work, an adaptation of Tristan Bernard's *Le Petit Café* (previously musicalized for Broadway by Ivan Caryll as *The Little Café* and by Ralph Bentazky for Vienna), returned to the musical-comedy genre.

1943 **Les Debrouillards de la Garonne** (Guy Lafarge/w Robert Valaire) Théâtre de la Trianon, Bordeaux

1947 **On a volé une étoile** (Georges Ulmer/w Yves Bizos) Théâtre Bobino 22 March

1949 **Baratin** (Henri Betti/André Hornez) Théâtre l'Européen 18 March

1949 **Les Pieds nickelés** (Bruno Coquatrix/w Hornez, Jean Lanjin) Eldorado 23 December

1951 **Le Leçon d'amour dans un parc** (Lafarge/w Lafarge/w André Birabeau) Théâtre des Bouffes-Parisiens 20 December

1954 **Les Chansons de Bilitis** (Joseph Kosma/w Marc-Cab) Théâtre des Capucines 30 January

1954 **Mon p'tit pote** (Jack Ledru/w Cab) Théâtre l'Européen 29 September

1958 **Coquin de printemps** (Guy Magenta/Fernand Bonifay/w Cab) Théâtre l'Européen 31 January

1958 **Le Corsaire noir** (Maurice Yvain) Opéra, Marseille 24 February

1959 **Bidule** (Ledru/w Cab) Théâtre l'Européen 27 November

1961 **À toi de jouer** (Ledru/w Cab) Théâtre l'Européen 24 November

1962 **Farandole d'amour** (Ledru/w Cab) Casino, Enghien 21 July

1968 **L'Auberge du cheval blanc** new French version w Marcel Lamy (Théâtre du Châtelet)

1968 **My Fair Lady** French version (Geneva)

1969 **La Caravelle d'or** (Francis Lopez/w Jacques Plante) Théâtre du Châtelet 19 December

1980 **Le Petit Café** (Lafarge, Ledru/w Lafarge) Opéra du Rhin 14 December

1982 **Balalaïka** new French version (Saint-Étienne)

VALVERDE, Joaquín (b Badajoz, 27 February 1846; d Madrid, 17 March 1910).

The elder Joaquín Valverde and his son Joaquín Valverde Sanjuán [*alias* Quinito] (b Madrid, 2 January 1875; d Mexico City, 4 November 1918) between them kept the name of Valverde to the forefront on the zarzuela stage and, more than any other composer(s) of the Spanish musical theatre, on the international musical stage during some four decades.

Valverde sr had his most considerable success with the internationally played and enduringly popular *La gran vía,* composed in collaboration with Federico Chueca (lib: Martinez Felipe Perez, Teatro Felipe 2 July 1886), and the pair worked together on the music for a number of other pieces, including *Las ferias* (1878), *La canción de Lola* (1880), *Fiesta nacional* (1882), *De la noche a la mañana* (1883), *Caramelo* (1884), *Vivitos y coleando* (1884), *Cadiz* (1886), *Le magasin de musique* (1889) and *Majas y torero* (1901).

His other works for the stage included *El centenario en la aldea* (1881), *Los Puretanos* (1885 w Tómas Lopez Torregrosa), *Pasar la raga* (1886 w Julian Roméa y Parra), *Niña Pancha* (1886 w Roméa), *Las grandes potencias* (1890 w Roméa/Burgos), *La paraja francesa* (1890), *El director* (1891), *Retolondron* (1892), *La de vámonos* (1894 w Felipe Perez y Gonzales), *Los coraceros* (1896), *Padre Benito* (1897), *La obra de la temporada* (1904), *Sangre moza* (1907), *El gallo de la pasión* (1907 w Joaquín Quirito Valverde y San Juan, Chapí) and *La Chanteuse* (w Torregrosa).

La gran vía was seen throughout the world in various guises, whilst others of his works also got a hearing further afield, notably *Majas y toreros,* which was played at Vienna's Danzers Orpheum by a visiting zarzuela company in 1902.

The younger Valverde made his first appearance on a playbill at the age of 21, turning out *Y de la niña ''que?,'' La Zingara, La fuente de los milagros, La fantasia de Carmen* and *La marcha de Cadiz,* all in 1896, and in the 22 remaining years of his life a vast number of scores for the theatre, mostly in Spain, but also abroad. He was represented on Broadway by the revusical pasticcio *The Land of Joy* (Park Theater 1 November 1917) and a second, less successful revusical piece *A Night in Spain* (6 December 1917), and also supplied several pieces for the French-language theatre including *L'Amour en Espagne* (Alévy, Eugène Joullot, Maurice Mareil, Parisiana 20 August 1909; Moulin-Rouge 21 October 1910), *La Rose de Grenade* (Hanneaux, Fredoff, Théâtre des Variétés, Brussels, March 1911; Olympia, Paris, 1912), *La Reluquera* (Joullot, Adams, Théâtre l'Européen 17 November 1911) and *La Belle Cigarière* (Joullot, Benjamin Rabier, Moulin-Rouge 20 March 1913).

His list of zarzuela credits included *La torre de babel* (1897), *El primer reserva* (1897, w Torregrosa), *El alcade de Corneja* (1898) *Los novicios* (1898), *Las niñas de Villagarda* (1898, w Torregrosa), *Toros del saltillo* (1898), *La Castafieras picadas* (1898, w Torregrosa), *La batalla de Tetuan* (1898), *Las campesina* (1898) *La chiquita de najera* (1898), *El sueño de una noche de verano* (1898), *La estatua de Don Gonzalo* (1898), *La magra negra* (1898 w Caballero), *Los tres gorriones* (1898),

Bettia (1899), *Le Mari-Juana* (1899), *Citrato? der ver serà* (1899 w Caballero), *El trabuco* (1899, w Torregrosa), *Concurso universal* (1899, w Calleja), *Los camarones* (1899 w Torregrosa), *Los cocineros* (1899, w Torregrosa), *Instantáneas* (1899 w Torregrosa), *Las buenas formas* (w Rubio, 1899), *Los flamencos* (1899 w Torregrosa), *La reina de la fiesta* (1899), *El ultimo chulo* (1899 w Torregrosa), *Los besugos* (1899), *La señora capitana* (1900 w Tómas Barrera), *El fondó del bául* (1900 w Enrico Cleto, Marcellino Barrera y Gomez), *La tremenda* (1901), *Los niños Llorones* (1901 w Barrera, Torregrosa), *El genero infimo* (1901 w Tómas Barrera), *El debut de la Ramirez* (1901 w Torregrosa) *Plantas y flores* (1901 w Torregrosa), *Chispita* (1901 w Torregrosa), *La casta Susana* (1902), *San Juan de Luz* (1902 w Torregrosa), *El trébol* (1904 w Serrano), *La inclusera* (1904 w Caballero), *Las estrellas* (1904 w Serrano), *El pobre Valbuena* (1904 w Torregrosa), *Pasa-calle* (1905) *La mulata* (1905), *La Galerna* (1905 *), Y no es noche de dormir* (1905) *El Perro chico* (1905 w Serrano), *La reya de la Dolores* (1905 w Serrano), *El iluso Cañizares* (1905 w Calleja), *El vals de las sombras* (1906), *El moscón* (1906), *La peña negra* (1906 w Toregrosa), *El gallo de la pasión* (1907 w Joaquín Valverde), *La isla de los suspiros* (1910), *La suerta loca* (1910 w Serrano), *El principe casto* (1912), *El fresco de Goya* (1912), *La ultima Pelentia* (1913 w Torregrosa), *Las mujeres guapas* (1914 w Luis Foglietti), *Feria de Abril* (1914 w Foglietti), *La gitanada* (1914 w Foglietti), *Caralimpia* (1914 w Foglietti), *El tango argentino* (1914), *Serafina la Rubiales, o una noche en el juzgao* (1914 w Foglietti), *A versicuidas de Amalia* (1914 w Foglietti), *El potro salvaje* (1914 w Pablo Luna), *El amigo Melquiades* (1914 w Serrano), *Las pildoeas de Hercules* (1914 w Foglietti), *El principe carnaval* (1920 w Serrano), *El estuche de monerias, La guitarra, El Paraíso de los niños, La chanteuse* (w Torregrosa), *El Recluta* (w Torregrosa), *San Juan de Luz* (w Torregrosa), *Los Granujas* (w Torregrosa), *Los chicos de la escuela* (w Torregrosa), *Colorin colorao* (w Torregrosa), *El terrible Pérez* (w Torregrosa), *El puesto de flores* (w Torregrosa), *La muerte de Agripina* (w Torrerosa), *La Cocotero* (w Torregrosa), *Congreso feminista, La grandes cortesanas, Los nenes, Viva Córdoba, El corenta de la partida, El Pollo Tejada* (w Serrano), *El noble amigo* (w Calleja), *Biblioteca popular* (w Calleja), *La ola verde* (w Calleja) and *La casa de la juerga* (w Gay).

VAN BIENE, Auguste (b Holland, 16 May ?1849; d Brighton, 23 January 1913). Performer, conductor, producer and a colorful contributor to Victorian musical theatre.

Auguste van Biene studied music in Brussels and played in the Rotterdam Opera House orchestra at the age of 15 before moving to Britain, where, for lack of connections, he found himself forced to go busking with his 'cello in the streets of London. He related frequently how he played for nine or 10 weeks in this way, in order to keep body and soul together, before he was noticed by the celebrated conductor Sir Michael Costa and given a job at the Covent Garden Theatre. Aided by an extravagant personality, his musical skills were in any case sufficient for him to rise quickly through the orchestral ranks to become a concert soloist.

He subsequently began a second career as a musical director and was engaged by D'Oyly Carte as conductor on the first *HMS Pinafore* tour (1878) before defecting to the ''rebel'' production of *HMS Pinafore* staged by the Comedy Opera Company after their dispute with Carte (1879) and to their following production *Marigold* (Vasseur's *Le Droit du seigneur,* 1879). Having burned his bridges as far as the D'Oyly Carte organization was concerned, in 1881 he joined Alexander Henderson at the Comedy Theatre and acted as musical director for his productions of *La Mascotte, The Grand Mogul, Rip van Winkle* and *Falka,* but he picked the wrong horse again when he left Henderson and went off to Europe with the ill-fated *Billee Taylor* tour of 1884. He returned, however, to a job at the Comedy Theater under Violet Melnotte's management, and there conducted the original London productions of *Erminie* (1885), *The Lily of Léoville* and *Mynheer Jan,* before again shifting on to take the baton for Julia Woolf's comic opera *Carina.*

In 1881 he began a career as a theatrical manager, touring opera in the British provinces with a company including such top performers as Blanche Cole, Annette Albu, Michael Dwyer and Arabella Smythe and the young Julian Edwards as chorus master and assistant conductor. He later moved into musical comedy, at first in partnership with Horace Lingard, touring *Falka,* to which Henderson had ceded him the provincial rights, and later *Rip van Winkle.* From 1890 to 1895 van Biene was given the number one touring rights on George Edwardes's enormously popular Gaiety burlesque productions, a right that made him one of the most significant musical-comedy impresarii in the country. Amongst the Gaiety pieces that he toured were the burlesques *Faust Up-to-Date, Carmen Up-to-Data, Ruy Blas and the Blasé Roué, Cinder-Ellen Up Too Late, Blue-Eyed Susan* and the musical comedy *In Town.*

Van Biene always had a yen to perform as an actor, and on one emergency occasion he took over the star role in Lingard's *The Old Guard* on the road, calling himself ''Henri Tempo'' for the occasion. He later featured himself in the title role of a tour of *Rip van Winkle,* and in 1892 he commissioned the sentimental musical drama *The Broken Melody,* and starred himself (and his instrument) overwhelmingly as the dramatically weepie-effective old 'cellist, Paul Borinski, whom James Tanner had created for him. He played this piece with enormous success in the British provinces, at the Prince of Wales Theatre and on overseas touring circuits, for more than 6,000 performances before commissioning a sequel, *The Master Musician.* He played this second piece, and a duologue, *van Biene's Dilemma* (Metropolitan Music Hall 15 August 1909), written for him by his second son, Edward, in theatres and then on the halls literally up to his death, for this most flamboyant of showmen died on stage at the Brighton Hippodrome. Slumping back in his chair at the end of his performance in the second house, apparently simply exhausted, he had died, his 'cello still in his hand.

Van Biene was married to the vocalist Rachel de Solla.

VAN GHELL, [Céline] Anna (b ?1844; d Paris, January 1926).

Recognized as one of the best vocalists amongst the leading ladies of the French opéra-bouffe stage, Anna van Ghell created a number of important roles in Paris in her twenties and thirties. She made her first successes in Brussels, and came to notice in Paris when she became prima donna at William Busnach's striving Théâtre de l'Athénée, making her debut in de Rillé's *Le Petit Poucet* (October 1868) and playing there also in *Les Horreurs de la guerre* (1868) and Legouix's *Le Vengeur* (1868). Her performances in these less-than-memorable pieces did not, however, go unnoticed, and the shapely young soprano was soon creating much better roles.

Her first big success came when she introduced the role of Méphisto in Hervé's *Le Petit Faust* (1869), and she compounded that with another travesty role, as the original Raphaël in Offenbach's *La Princesse de Trébizonde* (1869). She reprised the role of the chattering Roland, famously created by Delphine Ugalde in *Les Bavards* (1870) and that of Fiorella in *Les Brigands* (1872), returned to Hervé to create the part of the extravagantly zany Queen Jane of Scotland, equipped with a spectacular burlesque operatic mad scene, in *Le Trône d'Écosse* (1871). She was also the first Parisian Gabrielle in *Les Cent Vierges* (1872), but she threw away the chance to create the star role in Offenbach's *Les Braconniers,* refusing to work opposite the scene-stealing Céline Chaumont. She went off instead to the Opéra-Comique and played *Les Dragons de Villars* (1873).

She played the role of Alaciel in *La Fiancée du roi de Garbe* and Bertrase in a revival of *Heloïse et Abélard* at the Folies-Dramatiques (1874), appeared in the 1874 revival of *La Vie parisienne,* and had a further fine creation, again in travesty, when she was cast opposite Anna Judic as René in the first production of Offenbach's *La*

Plate 404. **Anna van Ghell**

Créole (1875). She subsequently took a turn as Clairette in the long-running *La Fille de Madame Angot,* Guillemine in Vasseur's *La Blanchisseuse de Berg-op-Zoom* (1875) and played Toinon in the Brussels production of *La Boulangère a des écus* (1876), but she found less joy with Offenbach's *La Foire Saint-Laurent* (1877, Bobèche). Later in 1877 she appeared at the Châtelet as Young Rothomago in the féerie *Rothomago,* in 1879 she was Prince Charmant to the Cendrillon of Théo in the Porte-Saint-Martin *Cendrillon,* and in 1880 she was in Brussels, playing at the Eden Théâtre as Régaillette in *Les Sept Châteaux du diable,* after which her name seems to slip from the Parisian bills.

She died in the Baron Taylor Foundation Home for old artists in Paris at the age of 81.

VANLOO, Albert [Guillaume Florent] (b Brussels, 10 September 1846; d Paris, 4 March 1920). One of Paris's top librettists of classic opérette through a long and productive career.

Vanloo was at first destined for the law, but during his legal studies he fell in with another young man, the four-years-older Eugène Leterrier, who shared his ambitions to write for the stage, and the pair began to immerse themselves in the Parisian theatre world. They succeeded in placing several of their short pieces in various Paris houses (including the Bouffes-Parisiens) and one full-length opérette, the Tom Thumb musical *Le Petit Poucet,* which was produced by William Busnach at the Théâtre de l'Athénée, but, in spite of incursions into the straight theatre in collaboration with such celebrated writers as Labiche and Eugène Grangé, it was some years before the pair finally found genuine success. Thanks to a friendship struck up with Charles Lecocq in everyone's struggling days at the Athénée, Vanloo and Leterrier got the opportunity to write the libretto for the successor to the composer's enormously successful *La Fille de Madame Angot.* Their sparklingly funny *Giroflé-Girofla* turned out a triumph, and its librettists were thoroughly launched.

The pair collaborated on a long series of subsequent opérettes with Lecocq, turning out the texts for a number of the composer's series of works mounted at the Théâtre de la Renaissance—the exceptionally classy comic book of *La Petite Mariée,* the sexy and successful *La Marjolaine* and the rather more conventional but nevertheless joyous *La Camargo* and *La Jolie Persane*—as well as the spectacular féerie tale of *L'Arbre de Noël* for the Porte-Saint-Martin and the complex and comical imbroglio of *Le Jour et la nuit* for the Nouveautés, all in a period of just six seasons. Later, Vanloo provided another successful script (w Busnach) for Lecocq with his version of the *Ali Baba* tale and, as late as 1900, the librettist and composer worked together on a version of *La Belle au bois dormant* for the great stage of the Gaîté.

During their Lecocq years, Vanloo and Leterrier also produced the text for Offenbach's fantasy spectacular *Le Voyage dans la lune* and the libretto of *L'Étoile,* which was set by the young Emmanuel Chabrier in a style that did not appeal as it might have to the audiences of its time. However, the libretto was found so superior that it was later reused throughout the world set by other composers. It became *The Merry Monarch* in America (mus: Woolson Morse), *The Lucky Star* in Britain (mus: Ivan Caryll) and *Uff király* in Hungary (mus: Béla Hegyi and Szidor Bátor), and has still survived to the present day as *L'Étoile.* Their libretto to *La Gardeuse d'oies,* set in France to a score by Paul Lacome, underwent a similar borrowing process when it was turned into the musical play *Papa Gougou* (*A Normandy Wedding*) in the hands of American composer William Furst, whilst the book of *L'Arbre de Noël,* stripped of Lecocq's music, was reset by Louis Roth in Austria (Theater an der Wien *Der Weihnachtsbaum*), Germany and in Hungary (Népszínház *A karácsonyfa*), and their libretto to *Le Roi de carreau,* deprived of its Lajarte score in favor of one by Ludwig Englander, became *Half a King* in America.

The pair provided libretti for several other, if less notable successes, such as Francis Chassaigne's *Le Droit d'aînesse* (a huge hit, nevertheless, in English as *Falka*) and André Messager's *La Béarnaise,* as well as for the occasional revue, and won a percentage rate of hits to failures that was quite remarkable given the size of their output.

After Leterrier's death, Vanloo worked with several different collaborators, producing the texts for all kinds of stage pieces, including a handful of spectacular musical shows on the lines of *L'Arbre de Noël,* of which *Le Bonhomme de neige* (w Chivot), musically set by Antoine Banès in its Parisian version and subsequently taken up for Britain (*The Snowman*), was the most successful. Major success had to wait, however, until he found himself a real replacement for Leterrier, and that replacement turned out to be a neighbor. Georges Duval had an apartment in the same block as Vanloo, and they were able to communicate from window to window.

It was with Duval that Vanloo confected the texts for Messager's two great fin de siècle opérettes, *Véronique* and *Les P'tites Michu.* These "gentille" turn-of-the-century pieces were much more sweetly conventional than the best and most farcically funny of the Vanloo/Leterrier opérettes—decidedly different, indeed, in flavor from such shows as the spicily hilarious *La Petite Mariée* and *Le Jour et la nuit*—but they were a stylish mixture of sentiment and gentle comedy that suited their composer ideally, and the result was a pair of notable and international hits. Vanloo's last Parisian opérette libretto, *Les Dragons de l'Imperatrice,* was also written with Duval and for Messager, letting him end a career of nearly 40 years during which he had been one of the brightest stars of two eras of Parisian and international musical theatre in the best company.

Amongst the other musical-theatre adaptations of Vanloo's works was a German piece titled *Frau Lohengrin,* apparently taken from his vaudeville *L'Oncle Bidochon* (w Chivot, Roussel Théâtre Cluny 2 March 1894), written by Eduard Jacobson and Wilhelm Mannstädt, with lyrics by G Görss and music by Gustav Steffens, and produced at Berlin's Adolf Ernst Theater on 21 December 1895.

In his retirement, Vanloo authored a book of memoirs, *Sur le plateau,* which gives a highly enjoyable look at the Paris stage of the later years of the 19th century and which has repeatedly been mined as take-it-for-a-fact source material by 20th-century theatre writers.

1868 **Le Petit Poucet** (Laurent de Rillé/w Eugène Leterrier) Théâtre de l'Athénée 8 October

1869 **Madeleine** (Henri Potier/w Leterrier) 1 act Théâtre des Bouffes-Parisiens 10 January

1869 **La Nuit du 15 Octobre** (Georges Jacobi/w Leterrier) 1 act Théâtre des Bouffes-Parisiens 25 October

1871 **Nabucho** (A de Villebichot/w Leterrier) Folies-Nouvelles 13 September

1874 **Giroflé-Girofla** (Charles Lecocq/w Leterrier) Théâtre des Fantaisies-Parisiennes, Brussels 21 March

1875 **Le Voyage dans la lune** (Jacques Offenbach/w Arnold Mortier, Leterrier) Théâtre de la Gaîté 26 October

1875 **La Petite Mariée** (Lecocq/w Leterrier) Théâtre de la Renaissance 21 December

1877 **La Marjolaine** (Lecocq/w Leterrier) Théâtre de la Renaissance 3 February

1877 **Madame Clara, sonnambule** (Isidore Legouix/w Leterrier) 1 act Palais-Royal 15 March

1877 **L'Étoile** (Emmanuel Chabrier/w Leterrier) Théâtre des Bouffes-Parisiens 28 November

1878 **La Camargo** (Lecocq/w Leterrier) Théâtre de la Renaissance 20 November

1879 **Une education manquée** (Chabrier) 1 act Cercle Internationale de la Presse 1 May

1879 **La Jolie Persane** (Lecocq/w Leterrier) Théâtre de la Renaissance 28 October

1880 **L'Arbre de Noël** (Lecocq/w Leterrier, Mortier) Théâtre de la Porte-Saint-Martin 6 October

1880 **Le Beau Nicolas** (Paul Lacome/w Leterrier) Théâtre des Folies-Dramatiques 8 October

1881 **Mademoiselle Moucheron** (Offenbach/w Leterrier)1 act Théâtre de la Renaissance 10 May

1881 **Le Jour et la nuit** (Lecocq/w Leterrier) Théâtre des Nouveautés 5 November

1883 **Le Droit d'aînesse** (Francis Chassaigne/w Leterrier) Théâtre des Nouveautés 27 January

1883 **Le Roi de carreau** (Théodore de Lajarte/w Leterrier) Théâtre des Nouveautés 26 October

1883 **Juanita** (*Donna Juanita*) French version w Leterrier (Galeries Saint-Hubert, Brussels)

1885 **Le Petit Poucet** (André Messager/w Leterrier, Mortier) Théâtre de la Gaîté 28 October

1885 **La Béarnaise** (Messager/w Leterrier) Théâtre des Bouffes-Parisiennes 12 December

1887 **La Gamine de Paris** (Gaston Serpette/w Leterrier) Théâtre des Bouffes-Parisiens 30 March

1887 **Ali-Baba** (Lecocq/w William Busnach) Alhambra, Brussels 11 November

1888 **La Gardeuse d'oies** (Lacome/w Leterrier) Théâtre de la Renaissance 26 October

1890 **L'Oeuf rouge** (Edmond Audran/w Busnach) Théâtre des Folies-Dramatiques 14 March

1890 **La Fée aux chevres** (Louis Varney/w Paul Ferrier) Théâtre de la Gaîté 18 December

1892 **Le Pays de l'or** (Léon Vasseur/w Henri Chivot) Théâtre de la Gaîté 26 January

1894 **Le Bonhomme de neige** (Antoine Banès/w Chivot) Théâtre des Bouffes-Parisiens 19 April

1897 **Les P'tites Michu** (Messager/w Georges Duval) Théâtre des Bouffes-Parisiens 16 November

1898 **Véronique** (Messager/w Duval) Théâtre des Bouffes-Parisiens 10 November

1900 **La Belle au bois dormant** (Lecocq/w Duval) Théâtre des Bouffes-Parisiens 19 February

1905 **Les Dragons de l'Imperatrice** (Messager/w Duval) Théâtre des Variétés 13 February

Memoir: *Sur un plateau* (Ollendorf, Paris, nd)

VAN PARYS, Georges *see* PARYS, GEORGES VAN

VAN STUDDIFORD, Grace [née QUIVE, Gracia] (b North Manchester (Lafayette), Ind, 8 January 1873; d Fort Wayne, Ind, 29 January 1927). Vocally superior Broadway prima donna of the American stage of the early 20th century.

After making early appearances in *The Black Hussar* (*Der Feldprediger*) in Chicago, with the Bostonians, and on tour with Jefferson de Angelis in *The Jolly Musketeer* (1889), Miss Quive moved on to the world of opéra-comique and appeared at the Metropolitan Opera House in the soprano roles of the lighter repertoire—*Martha* (Lady Harriet), *Carmen* (Micaëla), *Faust* (Marguerite), *Esmeralda* (Fleur-de-Lys), *HMS Pinafore* (Josephine)—and as Leonora in *Il trovatore.* She subsequently played with the St Louis Opera and the Schiller organization, and returned to the musical theatre to play with the Bostonians as Anita in *In Mexico* (1897). She later—now Mrs Van Studdiford, wife of a St Louis society gentleman—appeared in St Louis's Uhrig's Cave summer season (1900) and in 1903 created the title role of Reginald De Koven's musequel to *Robin Hood, Maid Marian.* She was subsequently seen in the comic operas *The Red Feather* (1903, Countess Hilda von Draga) and *Lady Teazle* (1905) before making her first appearances as a vocalist in variety.

In 1908 she launched herself as "the Grace van Studdiford Amusement Company" with a capital stock of $15,000, and the company brought her back to Broadway as the star of *The Golden Butterfly* (1908, Ilma Walden). She subsequently divorced her traveling salesman husband, but kept his name when she toured in *The Bohemian Girl* (1909), played Bengaline in the Broadway version of *Le Paradis de Mahomet* (aka *The Bridal Trap,* 1910) and went bankrupt. She later toured in the Chicago musical *Louisiana Lou,* in the title role of *Oh! Oh! Delphine,* alongside Howard Marsh in *Maytime* and, during the war years, visited military camps playing Mrs Guyer in a version of *A Trip to Chinatown.* She died after an operation at the age of 54.

Her sister, Mary Quive, also appeared in the musical theatre, notably in the title role of *Louisiana Lou* (1911).

VARNA, Henri [VANTARD, Henri Eugène] (b Marseille, 31 October 1887; d Paris, 10 April 1969). Parisian manager and director with a special flair for the revusical and spectacular in the musical theatre.

After studies at Aix-en-Provence and Marseille, Varna worked first as an actor, playing at the Théâtre des

Célestins at Lyon in 1909 and continuing in supporting roles at various Paris theatres. He soon found his vocation as a director and producer and from 1910, when he directed a revue at the Château d'Eau, he expanded his career in that direction, writing and staging the starry variety shows at the Ambassadeurs and the Concert Mayol, then producing and directing the spectacles at the Bouffes du Nord, the Palace, the Empire and, from 1929, at the Casino de Paris, which he was to head for 40 years.

In 1939 Varna took over both the famous Théâtre de la Renaissance, menaced with demolition, and the Théâtre Mogador, which he reopened as a home for revivals of the classics of opérette, staged in the luxurious manner with which his name had become synonymous in the world of variety. Beginning with *Les Cloches de Corneville* in March 1940 (in which he took to the stage as Gaspard), he continued with *Les Mousquetaires au couvent, Les Saltimbanques* (also playing Malicorne), *La Fille de Madame Angot, La Veuve joyeuse, Véronique, La Mascotte* and after the end of the war *Ta bouche, No, No, Nanette* and *Rêve de valse,* as well as mounting the Paris premiere of Georges Sellers's *La Vie de Château* (1945), which ran for more than 12 months. From 1948, with the modern opérette now finding its feet in the wake of the success of *La Belle de Cadix,* Varna began to produce a good ration of new works, most of which bore his own name as coauthor. Over the next decade, between periodical revivals of *La Veuve joyeuse,* he gave spectacular productions to Vincent Scotto's *Violettes imperiales* (1948), *La Danseuse aux étoiles* (1949) and *Les Amants de Venise* (1953) for long runs, made over the elderly *The Belle of New York* as *Belle de mon coeur* and Fritz Kreisler's *Sissy* as *Sissi, futur Imperatrice,* and starred Merkès and Merval in *Les Amours de Don Juan* (1955) and Tino Rossi in *Naples au baiser de feu* (1957). He presented Géori Boué as *La Belle Hélène,* Merval as *Rose-Marie,* and featured Merkès and Merval again in a scenic musical version of the old Châtelet favourite *Michel Strogoff* (1964), a reprise of *Les Amants de Venise* in which he took to the stage one last time to play the aged Cardinal, and in *Vienne chante et danse* (1967), his last production before his death in 1969.

In his early café-concert days, Varna coauthored a number of small pieces for such houses as the Concert Mayol and the Folies-Belleville (*Le Mariage de Pépita* [1915], *Le Voyage du Prince M'amour* [1916], *Le Droit de la cauchage* [1919], *Le Couvent des caresses* [1920], *Le Coucher de la Pompadour* [1921], *Vive la femme!, Yo t'aime* [Palace, 1925], etc).

VARNEY, [Francis] Louis (b New Orleans, 30 May 1844; d Paris, 20 August 1908). Composer of one major hit and many other works for the 19th-century opérette stage.

Louis Varney was the son of **[Pierre Joseph] Alphonse VARNEY** (b Paris, 1 February 1811; d Paris, 7 February 1879), conductor at and sometime manager of the Théâtre des Bouffes-Parisiens, director of the Bordeaux conservatoire and composer of a number of short opéras-comiques and opérettes (*Le Moulin joli, La Quittance de minuit, La Ferme de Kilmour, L'Opéra au camp, La Polka des sabots, Un fin de bail, Un leçon d'amour*). The younger Varney was born in America, during his father's engagement there with a French opéra-comique company, and he lived in Louisiana until the age of seven.

He ultimately followed his father into the musical theatre and in 1876 became musical director at Paris's Théâtre de l'Athénée-Comique, under the management of Montrouge, conducting and supplying the various music required for such of the theatre's productions as the revues *De bric et de broc* (Clairville, Armand Liorat, 5 February 1876) and *Babel Revue* (Paul Burani, Édouard Philippe, 10 January 1879) or the drame-bouffe *Il Signor Pulcinella* (Beauvallet, Marc Le Prevost, 26 September 1876). Following these first essays at composing for the stage, he won a more significant opportunity when the ever-adventurous Louis Cantin of the Théâtre des Bouffes-Parisiens commissioned from him a full-length score to a libretto by Paul Ferrier and Jules Prével. The resulting opérette, *Les Mousquetaires au couvent,* proved an outstanding success, playing more than 200 performances in its first run and establishing itself as one of the most popular of contemporary Parisian favorites through regular revivals over the succeeding seasons. It also won itself a wide series of international productions and hoisted the 36-year-old neophyte composer immediately to the top of his profession.

If his appearance as a noticeable composer had been rather a tardy one, Varney more than made up for that tardiness by a very high rate of productivity in the years that followed. In the 25 years after the first production of *Les Mousquetaires au couvent* he composed the scores for nearly 40 opérettes and vaudevilles. If he did not ever repeat the enormous triumph of his first work, a good percentage of his pieces nevertheless had successful initial runs in Paris and in the 1890s when, with the age of Offenbach and Lecocq over, French works were becoming less fashionable on the international stage; Varney was one of the few French composers to find a regular market for his shows both elsewhere in Europe and even overseas.

The first of his post-*Mousquetaires* shows were not very successful, even though the composer's new reputation found them occasional further productions: *La Reine des Halles* was a flop in London as *Gibraltar* and as *Madam Rose* (Haymarket Theatre 6 August 1881), and

Coquelicot was produced briefly, after its 40 Paris performances, at Budapest's Népszínház as *A pipacs* (ad Lajos Evva) and in English at the San Francisco Tivoli (7 August 1882) and St Louis's Schnaider Gardens summer theatre (July 1889). The composer found more success, however, with a musical version of the tale of *Fanfan la Tulipe* and with a little piece for Anna Judic titled *Joséphine,* which she played as a forepiece or part-program on her tours in Austria and America as well as at home.

Between 1884 and 1887, on the other hand, Varney had a good run of success, with four consecutive pieces reaching the 100-performance mark, which, in the Paris of that time, guaranteed success. The success of the comical *Babolin* (100 performances), the picturesque and farcical *Dix Jours aux Pyrénées* (128 performances) and, above all, the perversion of Dumas written—with care to its title—by the same authors as his first great hit as *Les Petits Mousquetaires* (150 performances), was contained in France, but the saucy *L'Amour mouillé* followed its Paris run by winning productions in London, Vienna and Budapest.

La Japonaise (13 performances), *La Vénus d'Arles* (21 performances) and *Riquet à la houppe* (40 performances) were failures, but the more farcically comical *La Fille de Fanchon la vielleuse* went on from its 110-performance run at the Folies-Dramatiques to be seen in both Austria and Hungary. The vaudevillesque *Le Brillant Achille,* less successful at home (48 performances), also traveled, playing in Austria and Germany as *Die eiserne Jungfrau* (Theater in der Josefstadt 7 April 1895, Centraltheater 7 November 1894), as did the circus musical, *Les Forains* (*Olympia die Muskelvenus* in Austria, *Olympia* in Germany, *Komédiások* in Hungary) and, above all, another comical musical, *Les Petites Brebis,* which was played throughout Europe and in Britain (*Die kleine Schäfen, A bárányak, The Little Innocents*) and proved a particular hit in its German adaptation. Other pieces, such as *Miss Robinson* (116 performances) and *Cliquette* (93 performances), did well at home without being seen elsewhere.

The year 1896 brought Varney's two most successful works since his first big success. The two were quite different in character, the ghost story *La Falote* being in the old-fashioned *Cloches de Corneville* comic-opera style, whilst *Le Papa de Francine* was a thorough musical comedy piece with a touch of the spectacular revue to it. Both had fine Paris runs of nearly 200 performances, and both were produced in other countries in a series of languages and adaptations. These two pieces represented the last peak in Varney's career, for although *Le Pompier de service, Les Demoiselles de Saint-Cyriens* (US: *The Cadet Girl*), *Les Petites Barnett* and, in particular, the 1902 piece *La Princesse Bébé* of his later works found audiences in and beyond France, none were in the same league as his greatest hits.

The composer of much delightfully melodious and happy music, including several further revues and a ballet, *La Princesse Idéa* (1895), produced at the Folies-Bergère, Varney proved himself able to illustrate all types of musical pieces—from classic opérette to musical comedy—that came and went in and from fashion in the last two decades of the 19th century. His first and most famous piece assured him a place in the very narrow repertoire of 19th-century pieces that have survived as standards a century later and, if his other works particularly those that were based on comic and vaudeville libretti—have proven more ephemeral, the same can be said for all but a few of his contemporaries' works as well.

1879 **Les Amoureux de Boulotte** (P Albert, P Calixte) 1 act Folies Marigny 1 October

1879 **Les Sirènes de Bougival** (Armand de Jallais) 1 act Alcazar 8 November

1880 **Les Mousquetaires au couvent** (Paul Ferrier, Jules Prével) Théâtre des Bouffes-Parisiens 16 March

1881 **La Reine des Halles** (Alfred Delacour, Victor Bernard, Paul Burani) Comédie Parisienne 4 April

1882 **Coquelicot** (Théodore Cogniard, Hippolyte Cogniard ad Armand Silvestre) Théâtre des Bouffes-Parisiens 2 March

1882 **La Petite Reinette** (William Busnach, Clairville) Galeries Saint-Hubert, Brussels 11 October

1882 **Fanfan la Tulipe** (Ferrier, Prével) Théâtre des Folies-Dramatiques 21 October

1883 **Joséphine** (Albert Millaud) 1 act Casino de Paramé (Trouville) 10 August; El Dorado 23 September; Théâtre des Variétés 16 March 1884

1884 **Babolin** (Ferrier, Prével) Théâtre des Nouveautés 19 March

1885 **Les Petits Mousquetaires** (Ferrier, Prével) Théâtre des Folies-Dramatiques 5 March

1887 **L'Amour mouillé** (Prével, Armand Liorat) Théâtre des Nouveautés 25 January

1887 **Dix Jours aux Pyrénées** (Ferrier) Théâtre de la Gaîté 22 November

1888 **Divorcée** (Raoul Toché) 1 act Cabourg 11 August

1888 **La Japonaise** (Émile de Najac, Millaud) Théâtre des Variétés 23 November

1889 **La Vénus d'Arles** (Ferrier, Liorat) Théâtre des Nouveautés 30 January

1889 **Riquet à la houppe** (Ferrier, Clairville) Théâtre des Folies-Dramatiques 20 April

1890 **Peau d'âne** new score (Théâtre du Châtelet)

1890 **La Fée aux chevres** (Ferrier, Albert Vanloo) Théâtre de la Gaîté 18 December

1891 **La Fille de Fanchon la vielleuse** (Liorat, Busnach, Albert Fonteny) Théâtre des Folies-Dramatiques 3 November

1892 **La Femme de Narcisse** (Fabrice Carré) Théâtre de la Renaissance 14 April

1892 **Le Brillant Achille** (Charles Clairville, Fernand Beissier) Théâtre de la Renaissance 21 October

1892 **Miss Robinson** (Ferrier) Théâtre des Folies-Dramatiques 17 December

1893 **Cliquette** (Busnach) Théâtre des Folies-Dramatiques 11 July

1894 **Les Forains** (Maxime Boucheron, Antony Mars) Théâtre des Bouffes-Parisiens 9 February

1894 **La Fille de Paillasse** (Liorat, Louis Leloir) Théâtre des Menus-Plaisirs 20 April

1895 **Les Petites Brebis** (Liorat) Théâtre Cluny 5 June

1895 **Mam'zelle Bémol** (Alfred Delilia, Hippolyte Raymond) Théâtre Cluny 7 September

1895 **La Belle Épicière** (Pierre Decourcelle, Henri Kéroul) Théâtre des Bouffes-Parisiens 16 November

1896 **La Falote** (Liorat, Maurice Ordonneau) Théâtre des Folies-Dramatiques 17 April

1896 **Le Papa de Francine** (Victor de Cottens, Paul Gavault) Théâtre Cluny 5 November

1897 **Le Pompier de service** (de Cottens, Gavault) Théâtre des Variétés 18 February

1897 **Pour sa couronne** (Arnold Fordyce) 1 act Théâtre des Bouffes-Parisiens 17 April

1898 **Les Demoiselles de Saint-Cyriens** (de Cottens, Gavault) Théâtre Cluny 28 January

1898 **Les Petites Barnett** (Gavault) Théâtre des Variétés 8 November

1900 **Le Fiancé de Thylda** (de Cottens, Robert Charvay) Théâtre Cluny 26 January

1900 **Frégolinette** (de Cottens) 1 act Théâtre des Mathurins 25 April

1900 **Mademoiselle George** (de Cottens, Pierre Veber) Théâtre des Variétés 1 December

1902 **La Princesse Bébé** (Decourcelle, Georges Berr) Théâtre des Nouveautés 18 April

1902 **Le Voyage avant le noce** (de Cottens, Charvay) Trianon-Lyrique 19 December

1902 **Le Chien du Régiment** (Decourcelle) Théâtre de la Gaîté 24 December

1905 **L'Age d'or** (Georges Feydeau, Maurice Desvallières) Théâtre des Variétés 1 May

VASSEUR, Léon [Félix Augustin Joseph] (b Bapaume, Pas-de-Calais, 28 May 1844; d Paris, 25 May 1917). Successful and prolific Parisian 19th-century composer.

The son of an organist, Vasseur moved to Paris at the age of 12 to study music at the École Niedermeyer, and he subsequently began his musical career, aged 20, as organist at the Cathedral of Saint-Symphorien in Versailles. In 1872 he made his debut in the world of opérette with an unsuccessful one-act piece produced at the Alcazar, but later the same year his first full-length piece, *La Timbale d'argent,* hastily composed to a Jaime and Noriac libretto to fill a gap in the schedule at the Théâtre des Bouffes-Parisiens, propelled him into the limelight. *La Timbale d'argent* was an enormous Parisian success. The show's overseas career was limited by the fact that its libretto was based entirely on matters explicitly sexual, but it established Vasseur thoroughly as a popular composer—or at least as the composer of a popular hit—in his home country.

Attempts to repeat the formula with another musical for *Timbale d'argent* starlet Anna Judic with *La Petite Reine* and *Les Parisiennes* were not a success, but over the next quarter of a century the composer kept up a steady stream of pleasantly characteristic stage scores for the Paris theatres. He scored a couple of solid successes with another pair of saucy opérettes, *La Cruche cassée* at the little Théâtre Taitbout and *Le Droit du seigneur* at the Fantaisies-Parisiennes, and he won several other respectable runs with both legitimate opérettes, such as *Le Billet de logement* and *Mam'zelle Crénom* (110 performances), and with his scores to a number of spectacular productions, such as the adaptation to the musical stage of Dumas's *Le Mariage au tambour,* the partly fresh-composed and partly pasticcio *Le Voyage de Suzette* (227 performances) the Châtelet's *Le Prince Soleil* (173 performances) and the Gaîté's globe-trotting *Le Pays de l'or* (126 performances). None of these won him the kind of success and notoriety that his first great hit had done, but they served him as the basis for a well-furnished career with sufficient substantial runs to earn him a good rank amongst 19th-century French opérette composers.

That rank and reputation were, however, made and held virtually entirely in France. Following the disappointing career of *La Timbale d'argent* in other centers, those of Vasseur's later pieces to win productions beyond home territory did not do particularly well. *La Famille Trouillat,* a failure in Paris in spite of a cast headed by Paulin Ménier and Thérésa, was produced in London by Alexander Henderson as *La Belle Normande* (ad Alfred Maltby, Richard Mansell, add mus Greve, Globe Theatre 26 January 1881) for 40 performances, *La Blanchisseuse de Berg-op-Zoom* appeared at the Theater an der Wien (14 November 1875) as *Die Perle der Wäscherinnen* (ad Julius Hopp) for 17 performances and later at Essegg and Berlin's Woltersdorff-Theater, *La Cruche cassée* became *Der zerbrochene Krug* at Vienna's Ringtheater (2 February 1881), *Mam'zelle Crénom* played Budapest's Népszínház eight times as *Szedtevette nagysám* (ad Lajos Evva, Béla J Fái, 27 September 1888), *Le Droit du seigneur* failed in some three weeks at London's Olympic Theatre as *Marigold* (ad Arthur Matthison, 29 October 1879), whilst an English version of *Madame Cartouche,* produced at Leicester (21 September 1891), did not make it to London.

The spectaculars fared better than the sauce, with *Le Mariage au tambour* being played in Germany and in Hungary and varying versions of *Le Voyage de Suzette* (not always with Vasseur's music attached) seen in several countries, but the composer did not establish himself away from home in the same fashion that, strongly aided by regular revivals of *La Timbale d'argent,* he did in the Paris theatre.

1872 **Un fi, deux fi, trois figurants** (Adolphe Jaime) 1 act Alcazar 1 April

1872 **La Timbale d'argent** (Jaime, Jules Noriac) Théâtre des Bouffes-Parisiens 9 April

1872 **Mon mouchoir** (Jaime) 1 act Théâtre des Bouffes-Parisiens 9 May

1873 **La Petite Reine** (Jaime, Noriac) Théâtre des Bouffes-Parisiens 9 January

1873 **Le Grelot** (Victor Bernard, Eugène Grangé) 1 act Théâtre des Bouffes-Parisiens 20 May

1873 **Le Roi d'Yvetôt** (Henri Chabrillat, Émile Hémery) Galeries Saint-Hubert, Brussels 25 October; Théâtre Taitbout, Paris 3 April 1876

1874 **Les Parisiennes** (Jules Moinaux, Victor Koning, [Ernest Blum]) Théâtre des Bouffes-Parisiens 31 March

1874 **La Famille Trouillat** (Hector Crémieux, Blum) Théâtre de la Renaissance 10 September

1875 **La Blanchisseuse de Berg-op-Zoom** (Henri Chivot, Alfred Duru) Théâtre des Folies-Dramatiques 27 January

1875 **La Cruche cassée** (Moinaux, Noriac) Théâtre Taitbout 27 October

1877 **La Sorrentine** (Moinaux, Noriac) Théâtre des Bouffes-Parisiens 24 March

1877 **L'Oppoponax** (William Busnach, Charles Nuitter) 1 act Théâtre des Bouffes-Parisiens 2 May

1878 **Le Droit du seigneur** (Paul Burani, Maxime Boucheron) Fantaisies-Parisiennes 13 December

1879 **Le Billet de logement** (Burani, Boucheron) Fantaisies-Parisiennes 15 November

1882 **Le Petit Parisien** (Burani, Boucheron) Théâtre des Folies-Dramatiques 16 January

1884 **Royal Amour** (P Lagrange, Christian de Trogoff) 1 act Alcazar d'Hiver 10 November

1885 **Le Mariage au tambour** (Burani) Théâtre du Châtelet 4 April

1886 **Madame Cartouche** (Pierre Decourcelle, Busnach) Théâtre des Folies-Dramatiques 19 October

1887 **Ninon** (Émile Blavet, Burani, Émile André) Théâtre des Nouveautés 23 March

1888 **Mam'zelle Crénom** (Jaime, Georges Duval) Théâtre des Bouffes-Parisiens 19 January

1889 **Le Prince Soleil** (Hippolyte Raymond, Burani, Charles Lauri) Théâtre du Châtelet 11 July

1890 **Le Voyage de Suzette** (Chivot, Duru) Théâtre de la Gaîté 20 January

1891 **La Famille Vénus** (Charles Clairville, R Bénédite) Théâtre de la Renaissance 2 May

1892 **Le Pays de l'or** (Chivot, Albert Vanloo) Théâtre de la Gaîté 26 January

1892 **Le Commandant Laripète** (Armand Silvestre, Burani, Albin Valabrègue) Palais-Royal 3 March

1893 **La Prétentaine** (Paul Ferrier, Bénédite) Nouveau Théâtre 10 October

1894 **La Corde** (Lucien Puech) Théâtre des Célestins, Lyon June

1896 **Au premier hussards** (Maurice Hennequin) 1 act Casino, Saint-Malo 6 August

1896 **Le Royaume d'Hercule** (Charles Quinel, Ernest Dubreuil) 1 act La Cigale 20 November

1897 **La Souris blanche** (w de Thuisy/Chivot, Duru) Théâtre Déjazet 9 November

1897 **Au Chat qui pelote** (Jules Oudot, Henri de Gorsse) 1 act Scala 28 August

1898 **Dans la plume!** (Pierre Kok) 1 act Eldorado 17 November

1899 **Excéllente Affaire** (w de Thuisy/Clairville, Henri Bocage, C Worms) Théâtre des Folies-Dramatiques 18 February

VAUCAIRE, Maurice (b Versailles, 2 July 1865; d February 1918).

The author of a variety of plays and libretti, Vaucaire turned out such pieces, alone or in collaboration, as *Le Carrosse du Saint-Sacrement, Valet de coeur* (1893), *La Petite Famille, Petit Chagrin, L'Amour quand-même* (1899), *Le Fils surnaturel, Amoureuse Amitié* (1901) and *Souper d'adieu* (1902), as well as a number of operatic texts. He wrote a new version of Leoncavallo's libretto to *Chatterton,* an adaptation of *La Femme et le pantin*—the piece that served Lehár as libretto to *Frasquita*—as a libretto for Zandonai's *Conchita* (1911 w Carlo Zangarini), and supplied the French libretti for Puccini's *Manon Lescaut* and *La fanciulla del West,* Mascagni's *Iris* and Zandonai's *Il grillo del focolare* and *Francesca da Rimini.* He also combined with ''J Burgmein,'' otherwise Giulio Ricordi of the publishing firm, on a piece called *Tapis d'orient.*

In the musical theatre he scored two significant successes, the first as the author of the popular Pied Piper musical *Hans, le joueur de flûte,* and the second as the French adaptor of *Die geschiedene Frau* as *La Divorcée.* His play (w Ernest Grenet d'Ancourt) *Le Fils surnaturel* was used as the basis for Ivan Caryll's Broadway musical comedy *Papa's Darling* (2 November 1914) and for the Hungarian *A törvénytelen apa* (Király Színház 14 October 1904), whilst *Petit Chagrin* (Gymnase 13 November 1899) became *L'Amante ideal* in the hands of Italy's Alberto Randegger.

Vaucaire was the lyricist for Edith Piaf's celebrated songs ''Je ne regrette rien'' and ''Mon Dieu'' (mus: Charles Dumont).

1905 **Au temps jadis** (Justin Clérice) Monte Carlo 16 April

1906 **Hans, le joueur de flûte** (Louis Ganne/w Georges Mitchell) Opéra, Monte Carlo 14 April; Théâtre Apollo 31 May 1910

1910 **Malbrouck s'en va t'en guerre** (*Malbruck*) French version (Théâtre Apollo)

1911 **La Divorcée** (*Die geschiedene Frau*) French version (Théâtre Apollo)

1912 **Pavillon de fleurs** Liège 7 December

1912 **Miss Alice des PTT** (Claude Terrasse/w Tristan Bernard) La Cigale 14 December

Other work credited: *Fra Angelico* (mus: Paul Hillemacher) (1924)

VAUGHAN, Kate [CANDELIN, Kate Alice] (b Holloway, London, 16 August 1855; d Braamfontein, South Africa, 21 February 1903). Victorian London's graceful dancer, the ''reviver of the skirt dance'' and star of the Gaiety burlesques.

One of the several dancing and/or singing daughters of James Matthias Candelin, an orchestral musician at the old Grecian Theatre, and trained as a performer from her earliest childhood, Kate Vaughan made her first stage appearances as a child, playing the title role in *Little Nell* (Manchester and tour, 1871) and Little Emily under her real name of Candelin. By the age of 18 she was already established as a principal dancer in the music halls, appearing (now as Kate Vaughan) ''with her celebrated troupe in the enchanting ballet entitled *Elysium.* ''The graceful sisters Vaughan'' (one was sister Susie, the other two ''sisters'' were not) appeared at the Metropolitan (1873) and the Royal Surrey Gardens, at the Gaiety Theatre interpolated into the burlesque *Ali Baba* (August 1873) and in pantomime (Goblina the dark fairy in *Jack in the Box,* Drury Lane, Christmas 1873). She made a first appearance in opéra-bouffe at the Holborn Theatre in October 1873, dancing The Spirit of Darkness in the Ballet of the Furies in a version of *Orphée aux enfers,* and in comic opera dancing the role of one of the daughters in Suppé's *Ten of 'em* (1873) at Drury Lane. She also danced in the dramas *Amy Robsart* and *Richard Coeur de Lion* (a pas de deux with comic dancer Fred Evans) and a divertissement at the same house, and appeared at the Adelphi in Lydia Thompson's old vehicle, *Magic Toys.* At some stage here she is also said to have made her burlesque debut at the Royal Court Theatre, under Marie Litton.

She took some time off to bring into the world a pair of daughters to her aristocratic lover, Arthur Wellesley, heir to the Duke of Wellington, and when she reappeared on the stage it was in Paris, where she was featured alongside Léonce and Pradeau in the ''folie-vaudeville'' *Le Dada* at the Variétés (February 1876).

Shortly after, she was engaged by Hollingshead for the Gaiety Theatre, and there, in August 1876, she began the series of burlesque performances that culminated in her becoming established as one-quarter of the most famous contemporary foursome of British burlesque players. In a virtual end-to-end parade of shows she appeared alongside ''boy'' Nellie Farren, Edward Terry and E W Royce in such principal girl roles as Maritana in *Little Don Cesar de Bazan* (1876), Arline in *The Bohemian G'yurl* (1877), Miss Jenny Merton in *Our Babes in the Wood* (1877), Margaret in *Little Doctor Faust* (1877), Amina in *Il Sonnambulo* (1878), Zerlina in *Young Fra Diavolo* (1878), Esmeralda in *Pretty Esmeralda* (1879), Doña Sol in *Handsome Hernani* (1879), Pretty Polly of Plymouth in Gulliver (1879), Diana Vernon in *Robbing Roy* (1879), Leonora in *Trovatore or Larks with a Libretto* (1880), Emily de l'Esparre in *The Corsican Brothers & Co Ltd* (1880), Morgiana in *The Forty Thieves* (1880), Alice in *Whittington and His Cat* (1881), Badroulbadour in *Aladdin* (1881), Fatima in *Bluebeard* and Lili in *Bluebeard, or The Hazard of the Dye* (1883).

In 1883 she left the Gaiety and went to Drury Lane to play the title role in the pantomime *Cinderella* (1883). She followed up at the Novelty in the title role in *Lallah Rookh* (1884) and in the spectacle *Round the World* (1886) at the Empire, but soon after she quit the musical stage in order to play in comedy. Although her considerable name value won her good roles, particularly on the road, she nevertheless proved to be less adept and less popular in her new career. She toured Australia and, in particular, South Africa and made an ill-starred attempt to return to the West End alongside Terry in the 1894 musical comedy *King Kodak,* but she ultimately went back to non-singing/dancing roles and the touring circuits. Thereafter, life went sour for the woman who had been the darling of London's young theatregoing men for so many years, and who had briefly hit the very top of the scandal pages when she won and ultimately (in 1884, following his divorce) wed Wellesley. By 1896 she was ill and poor enough for a theatrical benefit to be mounted, raising £1,000 to send her on a restorative sea voyage, and in 1897 she was in the divorce courts. She left Britain for South Africa, but she survived only another half-dozen years and died on the very day that *The Linkman,* a piece put together by George Grossmith reviving the great days of the Gaiety, was produced at that theatre, with the young Gertie Millar performing Miss Vaughan's most famous number, Morgiana's skirt dance from *The Forty Thieves.*

Her sister **Susie VAUGHAN** [Susan Mary Charlotte CANDELIN] (b Hoxton, 21 February 1853; d Redhill, Surrey, 17 April 1950) appeared first with Kate and later alone, in music-hall, pantomime and provincial burlesque, before moving into character roles—mostly as heavy ladies—at an unusually early age. Her principal musical credits in a long career that also included the creation of roles in such plays as Burnand's *The Colonel* (1887, Lady Tompkins) and Jerome K Jerome's *Miss*

Hobbs (1899, Susan Abbey), included comical roles in such pieces as *Little Carmen* (1884, Don Jose), *Polly* (1884, Lady McAsser), *Lallah Rookh* (1884, Plumjhama), *The Lady of the Locket* (1885, Cantancarina), *Round the World* (1886), *The Palace of Pearl* (1886, Queen Amaranth), *Glamour* (1886, Queen Palmyra Jane), *Babette* (1888, Countess Iphigenia), *Airey Annie* (1888), *Incognita* (*Le Coeur et la main,* 1892, Doña Inesilia), *The Magic Opal* (1893, Olympia, then Martina) and *The Bric-a-Brac Will* (1895, Chiara). She returned to the West End musical stage in later years in *The Cinema Star* (1914, Mrs Clutterbuck) and toured in *Tonight's the Night* (1915, Mrs Lovitt Lovitt). She also spent time in Australia both with Brough and with Williamson, appearing there in such roles as Miss Pyechase in *The Dairymaids* and the Duchess in *King of Cadonia,* and in 1924 in *The Cabaret Girl,* and also toured for a period on the oriental circuits in the middle part of a life of 97 years in length.

A second of her other seven (at least) sisters, who worked simply as ''Miss Vaughan'' and, later, as Florence Vaughan, also appeared in burlesque and opéra-bouffe, including the original London *Geneviève de Brabant* (1871, Brigitte).

VAUTHIER, Eugène Victor (b Auxerre, 28 September 1843; d Cassis, 11 November 1910).

One of the most popular male stars of the Parisian musical theatre of the last decades of the 19th century, the vocalist and actor known simply as Vauthier used his fine and strong bass-baritone singing voice to great effect in what were, from the beginning, mostly character roles. In 1872 he featured as van Ostebal in *Le Canard à trois becs,* Merlin in *Les Chevaliers du table ronde,* Siegebert in *Chilpéric* and the Marquis in *L'Oeil crevé* at the Folies-Dramatiques; he also visited London with the theatre's company in the summer to play their repertoire at the Globe Theatre. In 1873 he played at the Athénée, scoring a personal hit in the title role of *Monsieur Polichinelle,* but it was in 1874, when he joined the company at the Théâtre de la Renaissance, that he came seriously to the fore. He made a splendid success as the rampaging moorish Morzouk in *Giroflé-Girofla* (1874), took the role of Romadour in one Strauss rewrite, *La Reine Indigo* (1875), and shared that of Mathias in another, *La Tzigane* (1877). He created the part of the revengeful Podesta, Rodolfo, in Lecocq's *La Petite Mariée* (1875), played in the Paris version of *La Filleule du roi* (1875, Camescas) and created further Lecocq roles in *La Marjolaine* (1876, Annibal) and *Kosiki* (1876, Namitou). He scored another major hit as the rough-and-ready soldier Montlandry in *Le Petit Duc* (1877, Chanson du petit bossu), starred opposite Jeanne Granier as the brigand, Mandrin, who kidnaps *La Camargo* (1878) and as the disguised Manicamp who gets *La Petite Mademoiselle* (1879), played the comical Moka in *La Jolie Persane* (1879), took the central role in the Brussels production of de Rillé's *La Princesse Marmotte* (1880) as well as appearing in Offenbach's posthumous *Belle Lurette* (1880, Campistrel), as Latignasse in the unsuccessful *Janot* (1881), as Geromé in a new version of *L'Oeil crevé* (1881) and as the Caliph in the disastrous *Le Sais* (1881). In 1881 he visited London with the Renaissance company.

Vauthier followed Lecocq from the Renaissance to the Nouveautés and was rewarded with one of his most successful roles when the composer made the jeune premier of his *Le Coeur et la main* (1882, Gaétan) a baritone rather than a tenor, and he remained at the Nouveautés to appear in *Le Droit d'aînesse* (1883, Boléslas), *Premier Baiser* (1883, Johann), *Le Roi de carreau* (1883, Agénor de la Cerisaie), *L'Oiseau bleu* (1884, César) and *La Nuit aux soufflets* (1884, Candolle). He then moved on to create further roles in such pieces as *Le Mariage au tambour* (1885, Sergeant Lambert), *La Béarnaise* (1885, Perpignac), *Madame Cartouche* (1886, Labretèche), *Dix Jours aux Pyrénées* (1887, Piperlin), *Le Mariage avant la lettre* (1888, Baron de Botferdum), *Mam'selle Piou-Piou* (1889, Papillon), the title role of Grisart's *Le Bossu* (1889, Lagardère) and *La Fée aux chèvres* (1890, La Crémade), whilest appearing in parallel in the roles of the established repertoire (Jupiter in *Orphée aux enfers* 1887, Monthabor in *La Fille du Tambour-Major* 1889, etc).

By the later 1890s his voice was not quite the stentorian instrument it had been at the peak of his career but, in spite of apparently limited acting abilities, he continued a steady career for many more years, creating important character roles in such pieces as *La Cocarde tricolore* (1892, La Cocarde), *Les 28 Jours de Clairette* (1892, Gibard), *Miss Robinson* (1892, Robinson Crusoe), *Jean Raisin* (1893, Francoeur), *Patatart, Patatart et cie* (1893, Patatart), *Clary-Clara* (1894, Rio Santo), *La Fille de Paillasse* (1894, Paillasse), *La Fiancée en loterie* (1896, Lopez), *Madame Putiphar* (1897, Pharaon) and *Les Soeurs Gaudichard* (1899, Gaudichard), playing Athos in a revival of *Les Petits Mousquetaires* (1893) and Siegebert in the Variétés revival of *Chilpéric* (1895), as well as reviving some of his early successes (Montlandry, etc) and taking the older roles in some of the classic repertoire (Louchard, Monthabor, Pontcourlay, etc). Vauthier worked on into the 1900s, playing in a revival of *Surcouf* (1901), Sombrero in Paris's *Capitaine Thérèse* and creating roles in *La Bouquetiere du Château d'Eau, Le Sire de Vergy* (1903, Alcofribas), *M de la Palisse* (1904, Beni Zou-Zou) and Varney's *L'Age d'or* (1905) at the Variétés, his last appearance before a comfortably off retirement to his native Yonne, after 45 years in the theatre and more than 30 famous years of Parisian opérettes.

His niece, Aline Vauthier, also had a good career on the musical stage (Thérèse Courtalin in *Cousin-cousine* 1893, etc).

VEBER, Pierre [Eugène] (b Paris, 15 May 1869; d Paris, 21 August 1942).

An eclectic and eminently successful Parisian novelist, playwright and journalist, Veber was editor of and/or a contributor to papers and revues ranging from *Le Journal* and *La Vie parisienne* (editor) to *The New York Herald* and *The New York Times* (critic). Beginning in 1897, he also produced a regular supply of plays for the French stage, sometimes solo, sometimes with collaborators such as Courteline, Victor de Cottens and Léon Xanrof and, later, most often with Maurice Hennequin. Amongst these were included *Que Suzanne n'en sache rien, La Main gauche, La Dame du Commissaire, Mariette, Loute, L'Amourette, Chambre à part, Florette et Patapon, Qui perd gagne, La Gamine, Madame et son filleul, Vingt jours à l'ombre* and, his biggest successes, *La Présidente* and *Vous n'avez rien a declarer?,* as well as the occasional revue and also a handful of musical-theatre pieces.

The most substantial of Veber's early musicals were *Mademoiselle George,* composed by Louis Varney and played at the Théâtre des Variétés, and Henri Hirschmann's Les Petites Étoiles; the most extravagant was a fantaisie-opérette called *Son Altesse l'amour,* which featured Gaby Deslys and the British comedian Fred Wright at the Moulin-Rouge, but perhaps the most widely played was *La Plus Belle,* a little piece written for the Casino de Paris that had a subsequent life in German-speaking venues as *Die schöne Vestalin* (ad Heinrich Bolten-Bäckers, Apollotheater, Berlin 22 December 1906, Apollotheater, Vienna 31 October 1907). His musical play *Le Poilu* (w Hennequin) also got overseas exposure, being played in America, in its original French, under the Shubert management (Garrick Theater 9 October 1916).

Later, Veber won longer runs with the Jazz Age musical comedies *Épouse-la!* and *Quand on est trois,* and joined with his son Serge on the musical tale of the ruined banker who sold his soul to the devil (*L'Homme qui vendit son âme au Diable*), and then, with the help of little Lola the stenographer, had to spend the evening working out how to avoid the consequences of his deal. He also had a considerable success with his translations of foreign musicals for the French stage. In this field he was responsible, notably, for the French versions of *Der tapfere Soldat, Die Bajadere* and of Frederick Lonsdale and Adrian Ross's text to the enduring *Monsieur Beaucaire.*

In France, his play *La Gamine* (1911 w Henri de Gorsse) was later used as the source for the opérette *Sans tambour ni trompette* (1931), with music composed by Henri Casadesus, and the 1902 *Loute* (highly popular in Paul Potter's American version as *The Girl from Rector's*) was given a musical score by Josef Szulc and played in France as *Loute* and in America as *See You Later. Madame et son filleul* (1916, w M Hennequin, de Gorsse) was made into *The Girl Behind the Gun* for Broadway and *Kissing Time* for the English stage (Ivan Caryll/ad Guy Bolton, P G Wodehouse) with singular success, whilst the farce *Le Monsieur de cinq heures* (w Hennequin, Palais Royal 1 October 1924), successfully played in America as *A Kiss in a Taxi,* was musicalized for Broadway's Hassard Short under the title *Sunny Days* (Jean Schwartz/Clifford Grey/William Cary Duncan Imperial Theater 8 February 1928).

Problems arose when two Broadway-bound musicals that were announced as being based on his *La Presidénte* both surfaced in 1926. In fact, the source was not very evident in either case, but *Cheerio,* later renamed *Oh, Kay!,* with Gertrude Lawrence starred, went on to Broadway and success, whilst *Oh, Please!,* featuring Beatrice Lillie, stayed on the road a while longer, allegedly to try and iron away the announced similarities. Italy's musical version of the play, *La Presidentessa* (Robert Stolz arr/Carlo Lombardo), had no such concurrence.

Another of his works became the 1938 Budapest musical *A hölgy hozzám tartozik,* adaptation by Adorjan Stella and István Békeffy and music by Mihály Eisemann (Andrássy Színház 29 January), whilst the German musical *Angst vor der Ehe* (Emil Reznicek/Erich Urban, Louis Taufstein, Frankfurt 28 November 1913) was similarly announced unspecifically as based on one of Veber and Hennequin's plays.

1900 **Mademoiselle George** (Louis Varney/w Victor de Cottens) Théâtre des Variétés 1 December

1901 **Le Puits d'amour** (Louis Gibaux/w L Bannières) Théâtre Cluny 26 December

1906 **La Plus Belle** (Viktor Holländer/w Léon Xanrof) 1 act Casino de Paris 29 October

1908 **Son altesse l'amour** (Maurice Jacobi, pasticcio/w de Cottens) Théâtre du Moulin-Rouge 24 March

1909 **Léda** (Antoine Banès/w Lucien Augé de Lassus) Monte-Carlo 17 April

1911 **Le Soldat de chocolat** (*Der tapfere Soldat*) French version (Galeries Saint-Hubert, Brussels)

1911 **Les Petites Étoiles** (Henri Hirschmann/w Xanrof) Théâtre Apollo 23 December

1914 **Manoeuvres d'automne** (*Tatárjárás*) French version (Théâtre des Célestins, Lyon)

1914 **Loute** (Joseph Szulc/w Maurice Soulié) Théâtre du Châtelet, Marseille February

1916 **Le Poilu** (Maurice Jacquet/w Maurice Hennequin) Théâtre du Palais-Royal 14 January

1916 **La Charmante Rosalie** (Hirschmann) 1 act Opéra-Comique 18 February

1923 **Épouse-la!** (Hirschmann) Théâtre Fémina 15 February

1925 **Quand on est trois** (Joseph Szulc/Albert Willemetz/w Serge Veber) Théâtre des Capucines 20 April

1925 **Monsieur Beaucaire** French libretto (Théâtre Marigny)

1925 **La Bayadère** (*Die Bajadere*) French version w Bertal, Maubon (Théâtre des Célestins, Lyon)

1925 **Le Péché capiteux** (René Mercier) L'Étoile 18 September

1926 **L'Homme qui vendit son âme au Diable** (Jean Nouguès/w S Veber) Théâtre de la Gaîté March

1926 **Divin mensonge** (Szulc/Hugues Delorme/w Alex Madis) Théâtre des Capucines October

VEBER, Serge (b Paris, 2 September 1897; d Paris, 1975).

The son of Pierre Veber, Serge Veber also ventured into most fields of the theatre—from the grand guignol to revue—but, unlike his father, he made his principal mark in the musical comedy theatre. He formed a profitable team with the songwriters Georges van Parys and Philippe Parès that produced several Paris successes, and he also later supplied several long-running comedy musicals to smaller houses.

Amongst his works, *Quand on est trois* and *Lulu* were given a showing in Hungary, while *Une femme par jour* was produced in Britain (ad Ray Allen, Guy Elmes, add ly Stanley Lloyd, add mus Frederick Chapelle) by Morris Chalfen, in a largely remusicked version that stopped short of London.

Veber also worked as a scenarist, lyricist and director in the cinema.

1925 **Quand on est trois** (Joseph Szulc/Albert Willemetz/w Pierre Veber) Théâtre des Capucines 20 April

1926 **L'Homme qui vendit son âme au Diable** (Jean Nouguès/w P Veber) Théâtre de la Gaîté March

1927 **Lulu** (Georges van Parys, Philippe Parès) Théâtre Daunou 14 September

1928 **L'Eau à la bouche** (van Parys, Parès) Théâtre Daunou 5 September

1929 **Tip-Toes** French version w André Mauprey, Robert de Mackiels (Folies-Wagram)

1929 **Louis XIV** (*On cherche un roi*) (van Parys, Parès) Théâtre de la Scala

1937 **Ma petite amie** (van Parys) Théâtre des Bouffes-Parisiennes 31 January

1943 **Une femme par jour** (van Parys/Jean Boyer) Théâtre des Capucines

1946 **La Bonne Hôtesse** (Bruno Coquatrix/Jean-Jacques Vital) Théâtre Alhambra 26 December

1947 **Le Maharadjah** (Coquatrix/Vital) Théâtre Alhambra 19 December

1950 **Il faut marier maman! . . .** (Guy Lafarge/Lafarge, Marc-Cab/w Marc-Cab) Théâtre de Paris 15 September

1950 **L'École des femmes nues** (Henri Betti/J Boyer) Théâtre de l'Étoile 22 September

1951 **Trois faibles femmes** (Coquatrix) Bobino 22 December

1953 **Mobilette** (Betti/w André Hornez) Theatre l'Européen 23 December

1958 **Le Moulin sans-souci** (van Parys, Parès/w Marc-Cab) Strasbourg 24 December

DAS VEILCHENMÄDEL Operette in a Vorspiel and 2 acts by Leopold Krenn and Carl Lindau. Music by Josef Hellmesberger. Carltheater, Vienna, 27 February 1904.

Hellmesberger's most successful Operette, *Das Veilchenmädel* was first produced by Andreas Aman at the Carltheater in the wake of the indifferent runs of *Madame Sherry, Das Marktkind* and *Der Mameluck* and the half-success of *Der Göttergatte* and, in a production directed by co-author Lindau, it turned the house's luck back to good.

Krenn and Lindau's libretto featured Louis Treumann as Stiebel, a wandering prestidigitator, and tenor Willy Bauer and Ernst Greisnegger as his performing companions, singer Hans Muck and acrobat Rovelli. Sheltering overnight in an hotel, courtesy of a kindly housemaid (Therese Biedermann) who has taken a shine to the acrobat, they see the ghost of the miser Flaps (Rudolf Hofbauer) counting and hiding his gold. In the morning, the gold is there, hidden just where the dead man left it, and with it is a note proving it has been left in his care for one Hänschen Muhlbach. Hänschen turns out, after two acts of plot, not to be a little boy but a little girl—the very little flower girl, Johanna (Helene Merviola), over whom Hans has been sighing since the prologue. Events were enlivened by the antics of Stiebel's newly rediscovered wife, Flora (Mizzi Günther), a lively piece of soubrettery who gets herself mixed up with the old Graf Willy Sickendorf (Karl Blasel). Sickendorf pays the conjurer a vast sum to divorce her, then finds his wedding with ''an artiste'' vetoed by his even-more-aged Papa (Theodore Mannel). Friedrich Becker played the agent Siebenschein who is mixed up in all these money businesses.

The prettiest moment of Hellmesberger's score was the violet maiden's longing waltz ''Einmal nur möcht' ich mich schwingen im Tanz,'' and the tenor had his happiest music in the first-act song ''Ich hab' ihr in's Auge, in's dunkle geblickt'' and its ensuing waltz duo with the heroine (''Für dich will gern ich betteln geh'n''). But the stars of this show were not the juveniles but Treumann and Günther, and they were, not surprisingly, the best supplied when it came to songs. Flora bounced out ''Ein Ball ist ein schönste Vergnügen,'' played a comedy duet with the old Graf (''Ach, liebste Flora'') and topped the last act with a song-and-dance duo with Treumann, ''Es liebt den Hugo Melanie,'' whilst he, apart from joining with his two comperes in some lovely ensembles, had a show-off song with a waltz tag at the end of the first act (''Ich sehne mich nach Bühnenluft''). The show's Schlussgesang, instead of being the usual jolly reprise, in this score ended up with a merry couplet refreshingly agreeing (in the face of the favorite operatic dogma that starving in a Montmartrish attic is simply wonderful, n'est-ce pas?) that ''money is the great cure-all.''

Das Veilchenmädel played 63 consecutive performances up to the end of the season, reopening the theatre after the summer break for a further 21 nights, and then being played in repertoire with the Posse *'s Zuckersgoscherl* and Straus's *Die lustigen Nibelungen* to the end of the year. It was reprised intermittently thereafter, passing its 100th performance at the Carltheater on 4 October 1906. Two nights later an Hungarian adaptation (ad Adolf Mérei) opened in Budapest. A tongue-in-cheek ''brother-show,'' *Der Veilchenkavalier,* written by Krenn and with music by Hellmesberger, was played at Ronacher in a double bill with *Im Schilderhaus,* directed by and featuring Karl Tuschl, in 1911. The original piece reappeared in Vienna as late as 1925, when it was revived at the Johann Strauss-Theater.

Hungary: Magyar Színház *Az Ibolyaslány* 6 October 1904

DAS VEILCHEN VOM MONTMARTRE Operette in 3 acts by Julius Brammer and Alfred Grünwald. Music by Emmerich Kálmán. Johann Strauss-Theater, Vienna, 21 March 1930.

Brammer and Grünwald, the authors of so many bright libretti, supplied Kálmán with a rather curious, not to say clichéd, text for *Das Veilchen vom Montmartre.* It was a sort of sub– *La Bohème* affair, set in the everybody-be-jolly-in-poverty Paris of belle époque Montmartre attics and cafés and featuring as its characters no less personalities than the composer Hervé (portrayed by Ernst Tautenhayn), the *La Vie de Bohème* poet Henri Murger (Robert Nästlberger) and the painter Delacroix (Walter Jankuhn) alongside a Musette-ish model named Ninon (Anny Ahlers) and the inevitable street singer, Violetta Cavallini (Adele Kern), who ends up in the third act starring at the Théâtre du Vaudeville in a strictly unhistorical opérette written by Murger and Hervé (who, in any case, never starved in a garret anywhere). Eugen Neufeld played the Baron Jacob Rothschild, who, of course, finds before the finale that Violetta is a long-lost child of the aristocracy. Needless to say, she also gets herself the artist, over whom she has sighed since Act I, when he was preoccupied with Ninon. Ninon herself has tied up with a useful government minister.

Kálmán did his best to swap his vibrant Hungarian-to-Austrian tones for something approaching what he perceived as the French, but the result was more than a touch Kálmán and rose water (one critic complained, ''it swims languidly along in lukewarm internationalism''). The three friends jollied along in march time (''Warum sollen wir nicht fröhlich sein,'' Künstlermarsch: '''raus aus dem Quartier''), Violette introduced herself floridly in traditional soprano style (''Ich sing' mein Lied im Regen und Schnee''), indulged in a bootblack number (Schuhputzerlied), adopted more romantic tones for numbers both alone (''Warum weiss dein Herz nicht von mir?'') and with Delacroix, joined Hervé for the duet ''Ein Kuss im Frühling,'' and had her happiest moment in the Moon Song ''Du, guter Mond, schaust zu'' of the Act I finale. In contrast, Ninon tossed off a ''Carrambolina-Carramboletta!'' and also duetted with Hervé and Delacroix in turn, if in a rather different tone.

Vienna's production of *Das Veilchen vom Montmartre,* mounted under the management of Erich Müller at the less than spick-and-span Johann Strauss-Theater, did well enough. Marta Eggerth succeeded the Staatsoper's Frln Kern in the title role as the show ran up 109 performances to the end of the season (10 July). The authors, who apparently thought their piece deserved better, had further and more upmarket plans for it, however. Two weeks after closing at the Johann Strauss-Theater (25 July), *Das Veilchen vom Montmartre* resurfaced at the Theater an der Wien, recast and restaged with Otto Maran (Raoul), Ado Darian (Murger), Paula Brosig (Ninon), Grete Philipsty (Violette) and Ernst Nadherny (Jacob Rothschild) featured. This second production proved to have another two months and 61 more performances in it.

The newest Kálmán show was naturally picked up with international enthusiasm, but although it was mounted in most of the main centers the results were not what might have been hoped. Gitta Alpár appeared as Violette and Karl Joken as Raoul in a production at the Berlin Metropoltheater that broke no records, whilst in America a version produced by Lillian Albertson and her husband, Louis Owen MacLoon, in San Francisco as *Paris in Spring* (ad Albertson, John Mercer), with Allan Prior and Lilli Segrena featured, did not win sufficient success to encourage it to make its way eastwards. A second English version (ad L du Garde Peach) sprinkled with musical additions by one Herbert Griffiths was mounted at London's Alhambra as *A Kiss in Spring.* Billy Milton (Hervé), Eric Bertner (Delacroix), Kenneth Kove (Murger), Eileen Moody (Violette) and Sylvia Welling (Ninon) all thankfully had their historical names replaced with simple forenames, and Rothschild became the Baron Goldstein in an Oswald Stoll production that featured danseuse Alicia Markova in a full-sized Ballet of Spring as part of its operetta within an operetta. London couldn't be persuaded to patronize it for more than seven weeks.

France witnessed Max Eddy and Jean Marietti's adaptation first at Marseille, with Marthe Ferrare and André

Gaudin starring, before Maurice Lehmann took it up for the troubled Théâtre de la Porte-Saint-Martin. Lotte Schoene and Miguel Villabella headed his cast, but, once again, the show failed to take, and the Porte-Saint-Martin became even more troubled than before. Budapest saw *Montmartrei ibolya* in 1949 when Marika Németh, Judith Hódossy, Zoltán Szentessy, József Antalffy and Róbert Rátonyi appeared in a production at the Fővárosi Operettszínház, and it has since held its place in the repertoire, being still played regularly in the 1990s (Győr 5 March 1994, Zalaegerszeg 25 November 1994, Ódry Színpad 16 December 1994, Debrecen 7 April 1995, Szekszárd 2 May 1996, Tatabánya 15 March 1997, Eger 2 May 1997, Székesfehérvár 27 June 1997) and being given a major revival at the Fővárosi Operettszínház in 1997 (29 November). Otherwise, it seems that the piece found its best reception in Eastern Europe, where it has been preferred to some of Kálmán's more typical and virile works.

Germany: Stadttheater, Karlsbad 31 May 1930, Metropoltheater, Berlin 1930; UK: Alhambra Theatre *A Kiss in Spring* 28 November 1932; France: Théâtre des Variétés, Marseille *Violette de Montmartre* 1932, Théâtre de la Porte-Saint-Martin 20 December 1935; USA: Hollywood Playhouse, Los Angeles *Paris in Spring* 26 February 1931; Hungary: Fővárosi Operettszínház *Montmartrei ibolya* 24 November 1949

Recording: complete in Russian (Urania)

VENISE Opérette à grand spectacle in 3 acts by André Mouëzy-Éon based on a story by Paul de Musset. Lyrics by Albert Willemetz. Music by Tiarko Richepin. Théâtre Marigny, Paris, 25 June 1927.

A piece set in the richly picturesque and theatrically popular venue of 18th-century Venice, *Venise* was spectacularly staged at Léon Volterra's Théâtre Marigny by director Paul Clerget and designers Deshayes and Arnaud (sets) and Jean le Seyeux (costumes) and, in spite of the competition provided by the overwhelming popularity of *Rose-Marie,* it proved a fine success.

Mouëzy-Éon's libretto mixed a touch of humor with its colorful romance as the musician Gianetto (André Baugé) strove, against the enmity of the self-seeking Marcantonio (Jean Deiss), to win the consent of the unkind notary (Raimu) to the hand of his daughter Stella (Danielle Brégis). When the honest Gianetto returns a jewel that an old man has dropped in the street, he is given a seal that he is promised will fulfill all his desires. Aladdin-like, he uses the seal to win the palace, fortune and jewels demanded by Stella's father as prerequisite to marriage, only to find out in Act IV, after losing both the seal and Stella in Act III, that the talisman is not magic but the signet of the rich Turk Ali-Mahmud (Gilbert Moryn), whose money helps put all to right by the final curtain. Jane Pierly (Jacomina) played Marcantonio's thieving accomplice, the aging diva Anna Tariol-Baugé (Marietta), mother of the leading man, had a substantial role as the leading man's foster mother, and the most famous of all Parisian dance captains, Elsie Skidmore, headed 16 (English) Marigny Girls in some not very Venetian dances.

Richepin had had little theatrical success in nearly 20 years of composing, and *La Marchande d'allumettes,* produced at the Opéra-Comique 13 years earlier, still remained his best credit. He had originally intended *Venise* as a piece of the same genre and ambitioned its production at the Salle Favart but, finding his seriously crafted work rejected at the Opéra-Comique, he took it back and rearranged it, removing some of the more obviously opéra-comique elements and replacing them with something more purely popular in appeal to make up the score of the piece as staged at the Marigny. The mixture proved the right one, and *Venise* turned out to be the greatest success the composer would have. The romance "Un beau soir" as sung by the bass-baritone Moryn was the take-away hit, but several other numbers—Gianetto's first-act Serenade and Chanson de l'étoile, Marietta's Chanson du Bambino and "C'est si bon," and the duo Barcarolle du Rialto (Gianetto/Jacomina)—also won favor and lasted better than almost anything else of their composer's work.

Venise played through the season at the Marigny, was revived in 1929 at the Trianon-Lyrique (24 May) and was thereafter consigned to the provinces, where it has been intermittently played since, and as recently as 1989 (Rochefort 28 May).

Successful and/or significant works with Venetian settings have come from virtually all the principal countries where musical theatre is created. Amongst the most notable have been Offenbach's *Le Pont des soupirs,* Gilbert and Sullivan's *The Gondoliers,* Johann Strauss's *Eine Nacht in Venedig* and pasticcio *Casanova,* Arthur Laurents and Richard Rodgers's *Do I Hear a Waltz?* and the British musical comedy *Grab Me a Gondola,* along with such mostly less favored pieces as *The Lady of the Locket, Estrella, The Gay Venetians, Fioretta, The Venetian Twins, Les Amants de Venise* and *The Bric-a-Brac Will.* Other works have used the city of canals as a romantically picturesque venue for the traditional last-act visit to somewhere with a colorful setting (Serge Veber's *Lulu, Hochzeitsnacht im Paradies, Carissima,* etc) or even, as in *Kiss Me, Kate,* for a show-within-a-show, and, as in *Le Voyage de MM Dunanan,* for a phony Venice within a show. All in all, Venice has had more than its share of operettic visitors.

The title, *Venice,* was also used in London for a Charles Searle version of *Le Pont des soupirs* produced at the Alhambra Theatre (5 May 1879), and a German *Venezia* written by Herman Hermecke and composed by

Arno Vetterling was produced in 1934 (Grenzland-Theater, Görlitz 18 November).

VENNE, Lottie [VENN, Charlotte Hannah] (b London, 28 May 1852; d London, 16 July 1928). One of Victorian London's favorite comedy and musical-comedy players.

Lottie Venne made her first metropolitan stage appearance at the Gallery of Illustration in Tom Robertson's *A Dream in Venice* (1867) and she soon established herself in the provinces (Nottingham, Cheltenham, Brighton, etc) as a popular soubrette in comedy, burlesque (*Aeneas or Dido Done,* Earl of Leicester in *Kenilworth,* etc) and pantomime, before winning herself an even greater reputation in London. She made her first London stage appearances in comedy at the Theatre Royal, Haymarket, and as Cupid in Talfourd's burlesque *Atalanta* (1870), toured in Farnie's *The Idle Prentice,* and returned to town to play Polly Twinkle in the same author's anglicized version of *La Vie parisienne* and Franz in *Dr Faust* (*Le Petit Faust*) at Holborn. In two seasons at the Court Theatre she was seen in the burlesques of *Christabel* (1872, t/o) and *Zampa* (1872), as Cupid in Ixion (1873), Zayda in Gilbert's controversial *The Happy Land* (1873) and as principal boy in his *Creatures of Impulse* (1872, Peter). She then moved on from the Court and appeared as Zerlina in the Christmas extravaganza *Don Juan* at the Alhambra (1873).

In 1874 Lottie Venne joined the Swanboroughs' famous burlesque outfit at the Strand Theatre. She remained there for more than four years, appearing in the title role of Louisa in the highly successful musical comedy *Loo* (1874, *Le Carnaval d'un merle blanc*), in *Intimidad* (1875, Cachuca), a revival of *Nemesis* (1875, Rosalie Ramponneau), *Patient Penelope* (1875, Penelope), *Flamingo* (1875, Normanda Pippina), *Antarctica* (1875, Madeleine Bastille), revivals of *The Field of the Cloth of Gold* (1876–77 and 1879 Lady Constance) and *The Maid and the Magpie* (1877, Ninette), *Dan'l Traduced, Tinker* (1876, Dolly), the prose burlesque *Champagne* (1877, Bobinette), *The Latest Edition of the Red Rover* (1877, Gertrude), *Dora and Diplunacy* (1878, Countess Zicka) and *The Baby* (1879, Dodlinette), as well as in a long list of plays and in the several original English musicals produced there. She played the soubrette role of Jelly in Gilbert and Clay's *Princess Toto* (1876), the Plaintiff in *Trial by Jury* (1877) and featured as Coraline Coalscuttle in Alfred Lee's *The Lying Dutchman* (1876).

In 1879 the Swanboroughs and burlesque gave place to Alexander Henderson and comic opera, and when Henderson mounted *Madame Favart,* Miss Venne moved on. In the following decade she found her best roles in comedy, creating the role of Amy in *Crutch and Toothpick,* the title role of the long-running *Betsy* and later appearing as Agatha Poskett in *The Magistrate* and Honour in *Sophia,* but she also made several musical appearances, notably in Sullivan's *The Zoo* (1879, Eliza Smith), as Fiametta in *La Mascotte* (1882 t/o), at the Avenue in *Lurette* (Marcelline) and *Barbe-bleue* (Fleurette), and she played Katrina in the first provincial tour of Planquette's *Rip* (1883). She also appeared as Mrs Bardell in Solomon's operetta *Pickwick* and Pauline Marsher in the burlesque *The Scalded Back* (1884), and returned to musical comedy in the 1885 revival of *Nemesis.*

The musical portion of her career seemed as if it were in the past when Lottie Venne returned and made her biggest-ever hit in the musical theatre. After a season at the Comedy Theatre playing Mrs Earlybird in the burlesque *The Poet and the Puppets* (1892), she created the star role of Lady Virginia Forrest in George Edwardes's *A Gaiety Girl* (1893) and she followed up this personal triumph with a second equivalent part as Madame Amélie in *An Artist's Model* (1895). However, she did not remain with the Daly's Theatre company, and she did not better these roles when cast as similarly attractive middle-aged ladies in *Monte Carlo* (1896, Mrs Carthew), *The Mermaids* (1897, Lady Barker), *The Royal Star* (1898, Lady Horton), *Three Little Maids* (1902, Lady St Mallory) or *The Lovebirds* (1903, Fatima Wilson West). In another two decades of a distinguished career she appeared rarely on the musical stage, returning only in 1911 to play Mrs Grundy (L'Opinion Publique) in Tree's revival of *Orphée aux enfers* and, in her final appearance, in the Lyric, Hammersmith production of *Lionel and Clarissa* in 1925 (Lady Mary Oldboy).

Lottie Venne was the wife of the actor and vocalist **Walter Henry FISHER** (b Bristol, 1845), creator of the role of the Defendant in *Trial by Jury* and London originator of the roles of Marasquin in *Giroflé-Girofla,* Piquillo in *La Périchole* and Henry Sandford in Edward Solomon's *The Vicar of Bray* (1882). Originally a concert vocalist, Fisher made his stage debut in his native Bristol as Henry Bertram in *Guy Mannering* (April 1866). He played with the stock companies at Plymouth and Brighton, and although he took part in provincial burlesque and opéra-bouffe productions (Chilpéric in *Chilpéric,* 1871, etc), he became first and foremost a light comic actor. He was several years at the Court Theatre, where he was involved in the scandal over W S Gilbert's burlesque *The Happy Land* (Fisher's imitation of Gladstone was one of the reasons for the scandal). In 1874 he made his mark in the musical theatre when he appeared in *Giroflé-Girofla,* and for a decade thereafter he was one of Britain's most popular musical leading men. He took over as Grénicheux in the long run of *Les Cloches de Corneville* (1878), toured as Ange Pitou, Robert in *La Fille du tambour-major,* Billee Taylor, Fritz in *La Grand-Duchesse,*

Giletti in *Madame l'archiduc,* Captain Corcoran, etc, as part of a highly successful career in all areas of theatre.

Their daughter, **Audrey FORD** [Amy Richmond FISHER], (b Stroud, 23 August 1873), also had a career on the musical stage.

VENT DU SOIR, ou L'Horrible festin Opérette-bouffe in 1 act by Philippe Gille. Music by Jacques Offenbach. Théâtre des Bouffes-Parisiens, Paris, 16 May 1857.

The Parisian coiffeur Arthur (Tayau), who has been shipwrecked on a cannibal island, is served up by chief Vent du Soir (Desiré) as a meal for his neighbor, Chief Lapin Courageux (Léonce), in spite of his having a distinct and noncomestible appeal for the Princess Atala (Mlle Garnier). She is fascinated by Arthur's chiming watch, which plays the national hymn of Lapin Courageux's tribe. There is, of course, a reason for this. Arthur is the chief's long absent son, sent off to study hairdressing in London—and Vent du Soir has just served him up to his papa in a pie. Actually, he hasn't, for although the watch can be heard chiming post-prandially and patriotically in Lapin's stomach, Arthur has swapped places with the Sacred Bear of the tribe.

Offenbach's musical accompaniment to this extravagant tale comprised a fine storm overture and seven numbers—four of which are trios—and a finale, amongst which Atala's couplets ''Petit bébé,'' Arthur's couplets ''Je suis coiffeur'' and the plotworthy national anthem of the Papa-Toutou tribe were the highlights.

Written in the thoroughly ''bouffe'' style of a *Ba-ta-clan, Vent du Soir* did not find quite the same kind of success as its crazy predecessor. It nevertheless remained in the Bouffes-Parisiens repertoire for some years, and was introduced to Vienna by Offenbach's company during their 1861 visit to the Kai-Theater with Desiré repeating his original role alongside Lucille Tostée (Atala), Jean Paul (Arthur) and Duvernoy (Lapin Courageux). Johann Nestroy subsequently provided the same theatre with a German version in which he starred alongside Karl Treumann, Louis Grois and Helene Weinberger in one of his last appearances. It did not find the same popularity as his earlier efforts, such as *Daphnis und Chloë,* and its curiously disappointing career apparently ended there.

Britain got a brief glimpse of the piece when Alice Barth, Theodore Distin, Henry Guy and Fred Russell featured in a handful of performances of *The Howling Wind* (ad uncredited) at Crystal Palace in 1874.

Austria: Theater am Franz Josefs-Kai (Fr) 22 June 1861, *Hauptling Abendwind* 1 February 1862; UK: Crystal Palace *The Howling Wind* 22 September 1874

VENUS AUF ERDEN Operette in 1 act by Heinrich Bolten-Bäckers. Music by Paul Lincke. Apollotheater, Berlin, 6 June 1897.

One of the first of the successful short but showy Operetten written by Bolten-Bäckers and Lincke to be played on the program at the Berlin variety house the Apollotheater, *Venus auf Erden* was designed as a mixture of spectacle, girls, comedy and song in the best big-variety-house style. The story on which all this entertainment was tacked had an every-dreamaday Berliner named Fritz Leichtfuss, who fancies a fling with Venus, being summoned to Olympus, where his description of the jollities and pleasures of Berlin encourages the Olympian family to come down and see for themselves. Fritz takes them to a masked ball where everyone has a good naughty time, and he himself chats up Venus when he can get the local lechers out of the way. Of course, in the end he wakes up.

The piece did well enough that, when Lincke returned to Berlin and the Apollotheater after his two-season interlude at the Paris Folies-Bergère, the series was continued, producing such similarly constructed pieces as the highly successful *Frau Luna* and *Lysistrata.*

Venus auf Erden's popularity in Berlin won it a showing in similar circumstances in Vienna, where it was produced as the opening attraction at Gabor Steiner's Danzers Orpheum. It was ''freely adapted'' for Vienna by Carl Lindau with musical interpolations by Ernst Reiterer and Karl Kappeller, and lavishly mounted by Steiner with Flora Siding as Venus, Eduard Lunzer as Jupiter and Karl Tuschl as Theodor (ex- Fritz). It ran for 77 straight performances before Steiner took it on to his summer theatre, Venedig in Wien, where, with Frln Carena and Lunzer featured, it passed its 100th performance on 15 July 1901. Only the huge success of Steiner's second production, *Die Landstreicher,* kept it from being brought back to the Orpheum for more than 11 further performances. *Venus auf Erden* remained in Steiner's repertoire and was given by his company for a handful of performances at the Theater an der Wien in 1902. The show was given a Budapest production, several years later, under similar circumstances, following *Frau Luna* and *Nakiris Hochzeit* on to the program at the Royal Orfeum. Paris, which saw a French version of *Frau Luna* at the Olympia in 1904, didn't take *Venus auf Erden.* Instead, MM Moreau, Verdellet and Quinel manufactured their own *Venus à Paris,* in which Venus's daughter comes down to earth in Brother Cupid's automobile (a direct steal from *Frau Luna*) for a lively time amongst the nightlives of Paris. The piece was staged at the Parisana in August 1904.

Immortals on earth was one of the oldest themes in the dramatic book, even if Venus was not the most frequent visitor. However, a Venusian maiden visited earth just a few years later in London in search of *The Silver Slipper,* whilst an Anatolian version of the lady herself turned up to cause havoc on Broadway in *One Touch of Venus* a few decades later.

Austria: Danzers Orpheum 30 October 1900; Hungary: Royal Orfeum *Venusz a földön* 1 November 1905

VENUS IN SEIDE Operette in 3 acts by Alfred Grünwald and Ludwig Herzer. Music by Robert Stolz. Stadttheater, Zürich, 10 December 1932.

Grünwald and Herzer's "Venus in Silk" was the Princess Jadja Milewska-Palotay whose intended fiancé is kidnapped on his way to their wedding and whose castle is visited instead by two fine strangers. One is the prince Stefan Teleky, the rightful heir to Jadja's castle, and the other is the famous bandit Sándor Rósza. The first is after Jadja's heart, the second is more interested in her heirlooms, and it is only after the pair have spent two acts conveniently mistaken for each other that Teleky, at least, succeeds in his aims.

Stolz illustrated this romantic comic opera text with a more unpretentiously melodic score of light music than it might have been given by other hands, thus taking some of the mostly chocolatey Ruritanianism off the tale, and the resultant Operette, produced in Zürich, was one of his most artistically successful works. It did not, however, prove very happy when produced further afield. An American version (ad Laurence Schwab, Lester O'Keefe) was produced at the St Louis Muny, with Nancy McCord and Robert Halliday starred, under the title *Beloved Rogue,* and the piece was subsequently toured by Schwab (1 October 1935), with Miss McCord and J Harold Murray in the leading roles, without braving Broadway. Similarly, in Britain, Lee Ephraim and Carl Brisson's production of another version (ad John Hastings Turner, Graham John), advertised as a "world premiere," and starring Brisson opposite Helen Gilliland, started out from Glasgow but also failed to make it to the metropolis.

In 1970 the Vienna Volksoper produced a version that introduced *Venus in Seide* to Austria, and in 1997 the show made it to Germany.

USA: Municipal Opera, St Louis *Beloved Rogue* 22 July 1935; UK: Alhambra Theatre, Glasgow 26 October 1937; Austria: Volksoper 4 March 1970; Germany: Leipzig 23 March 1997

Recording: selections (Eurodisc)

VERA VIOLETTA Vaudeville in 1 act by Leo Stein. Music by Edmund Eysler. Apollotheater, Vienna, 30 November 1907.

The first essay by composer Eysler at writing a piece for a variety house, *Vera Violetta* was a little piece of amorous nonsense set in a Paris palais de glace. Polly Koss starred as the lady of the title, alongside Flora Siding and Carlo Böhm (who found the opportunity during the proceedings to get into a frock and impersonate a music-hall lady) and a bundle of typically tuneful Eysler melodies, including the Vera Violetta waltz, the Adele Polka, "Sapristi! Ein Käfer" and "Paris, Paris wie bist du süss!"

Written for and produced by Ben Tieber at the Vienna Apollotheater, the piece was played there as an important part of the bills of the 1907–8 season, running up 128 performances in its first year, being brought back again the following autumn to run up its 200th and yet again in the autumn of 1909. When it came back for a further run in 1913 it was billed as having passed its 350th night on the Viennese stage. The Paris Olympia produced a French version (ad Jacques Redelsperger) with a cast including Baron, Feréal, Sinoël, Girier, Marion Winchester, Maud d'Orly and Mathilde Gomez, whilst in America (ad Leonard Liebling and Harold Atteridge) *Vera Violetta* was featured on a Shubert Winter Garden program, sharing the bill with the swimmer Annette Kellerman and a comedy. Amongst bits of Eysler and Stein, Gaby Deslys and Harry Pilcer did Louis Hirsch's "Gaby Glide," José Collins as Mme von Grunberg performed her mother's old hit "Ta-ra-ra-boom-de-ay," and Al Jolson as the waiter, Claude, gave Schwartz and Madden's "Rum Tum Tiddle" and George M Cohan's "That Haunting Melody" through a run of 112 performances. Along with most of Eysler's music, a young lady named Mae West was replaced before opening night.

France: Olympia 7 November 1908; USA: Winter Garden 23 November 1911; Hungary: Royal Orfeum 31 December 1914

LA VERBENA DE LA PALOMA, o El Boticario y las chalupas (y celos mal reprimidos) Sainete liricio in 1 act by Ricardo de la Vega. Music by Tomas Bretón. Teatro Apolo, Madrid, 17 February 1894.

One of the most popular of the "genero chico" zarzuelas, *La verbena de la paloma* has been regularly performed in Spanish-language theatres in the century since its production, and has, like few others of its species, also been given occasional performances in translation.

The piece's little contemporary slice-of-life tale centered on lovelorn print-worker Julián (Emilio Mesejo), who is moping because his beloved, Susana (Luisa Campos), has said she cannot go 4ith him to the last-night celebrations of the Festival of the Virgin of Paloma. And Julián has seen Susana and her sister Casta (Irene Alba) driving with the flirtatious old chemist Don Hilarión (Manuel Rodriguez)—it is he who is taking the girls and their Aunt Antonia (Pilar Vidal) out for the night. That evening the boy causes a scene at the dance, and things get to a state where the police are called, but Susana ultimately leaves her old beau for her young lover and all ends happily amongst the sounds of the festival.

The story wound its way through three scenes that were, in the best zarzuela tradition, peopled by folk of the area who were mostly quite incidental to the plot line and to whom a number of the evening's musical pieces were allotted: the innkeeper's wife, Rita (Leocadia Alba); Hilarión's compere Sebastián and his wife, Mariquita; their niece Teresa and some of their friends; the janitor and his wife (''El niño está dormido''); a nightwatchman (''¡Buena está la política!''); and a flamenco singer in a café (''En Chiclana me crié''). The bulk of the little piece's music, however, was the portion of Julián sighing over Susana (''También la gente del pueblo''), wondering how to win his suit with her (''Y escucha, que hablo yo'') or confronting her on her doorstep on the arm of Hilarión (''¿Donde vas con mantón de Manila?''), while Don Hilarión sang with light comicality of his profession (''Hoy las ciencias adelantan'') and of his prospects for the evening (''Una morena y una rubia'').

A two-act piece called *Fiesta in Madrid* (ad Tito Capobianco), produced at New York's City Center in 1969 (28 May), admitted to being based on *La verbena de la paloma,* but it included in its score numbers lifted from the works of Chapí, Chueca and Valverde, Lleó, Serrano and Gimenez that made up some 50 percent of its considerable score, whilst an entertainment toured in France in 1992 as *Zarzuela: historia de un patio* also quoted Bretón's zarzuela as its basis. The show was revived at the Teatro de la Zarzuela in 1997 and subsequently played at Britain's Edinburgh Festival.

Several film versions have been issued in Spain.

Films: Jose Buchs 1921, Benito Pwerojo 1935, de Heredia 1963

Recordings: complete (Auvidis Valois, Philips, Alhambra/Columbia, EMI, Montilla/Zafiro, Hispavox, Edigsa, Blue Moon)

VERDON, Gwen [VERDON, Gwyneth Evelyn] (b Culver City, Calif, 13 January 1926; d Woodstock, Vt, 18 October 2000). One of the Broadway musical's most attractive stars of the postwar era.

Miss Verdon studied dance with choreographer Jack Cole, and she later assisted him on several assignments in the theatre. She made early musical comedy appearances dancing in the choruses of *Bonanza Bound* (1947) and *Magdalena* (1948), appeared in the short-lived revue *Alive and Kicking* (1950) and worked as a dancer in four films between 1951 and 1953 (*The Merry Widow,* etc). She broke through to stardom with her performance as the dancer Claudine in *Can-Can* (1953) when, in spite of her role's being aggressively slimmed when she threatened to run away with the show, her mixture of dance and comic talents let her run away with it anyhow. Those talents found an even more effective vehicle when she was next cast as the devil's ultimate seductress, Lola, in *Damn Yankees* (1955, Tony Award), singing and dancing her way through ''Whatever Lola Wants'' on Broadway and the screen.

Miss Verdon subsequently worked with (and married) choreographer/director Bob Fosse, starring for him in the musicalized version of Eugene O'Neill's *Anna Christie* as *New Girl in Town* (1957, half a Tony Award), in the mystery music-hall musical *Redhead* (1959, Tony Award) and in her two most memorable roles, mixing an irresistible vulnerability and swingeing dancing as *Sweet Charity* (1966, ''If My Friends Could See Me Now,'' ''Where Am I Going?'') and as the kookie, butter-melting murderess Roxie Hart in *Chicago* (1975).

VERGELTSGOTT Operette in 2 acts and a Nachspiel by Victor Léon. Music by Leo Ascher. Theater an der Wien, Vienna, 14 October 1905.

Like the recent *Der arme Jonathan* and *Der Schätzmeister,* Leo Ascher's first full-scale Operette presented the peculiarity (for the time) of being set in New York, though given its action and its carnival opening—so reminiscent of other closer-to-home pieces—it might just as easily have been set anywhere. Its tale, however, was rather more original than was usual. Bogumil, Graf Karinsky (Louis Treumann), has gone through his patrimony and now, stranded in New York, is about to put a bullet through his head when he falls in with a band of beggars headed by Slippel (Oskar Sachs) and his daughter Jessie (Mizzi Günther) and discovers that he has a lucrative talent after all—as a beggar! When Bogumil falls in love with Malona (Phila Wolff), daughter of Police Inspector Stephenson (Siegmund Natzler), jealous Jessie and the journalist Jimmy Blackwell (Karl Streitmann) of the *New Yorker Stundenblatt* get together to fake a newspaper article exposing the ''beggar count'' and the horrified Malona sends him away. Six years and a child intervene before she herself turns beggar, to beg him to return for a happy ending.

The favorite moment of Ascher's score was the march duo ''Es kommt nicht jeder reich zur Welt'' sung by Jessie and Bogumil in the second act and reprised as the Schlussgesang of the evening. Elsewhere, Bogumil came out the best served, with a comical entrance, revolver to his head (''Das ist ein Revolver''), and a song that took him through the gamut of rhythms from waltz to march (''Ist denn ein Wunder da geschehn''), as well as duets with each girl and a final scene with his six-year-old son (''Fang mich, Bübchen''). Jimmy had a tenor waltz song (''Hab' nur Geduld''), Malona a soprano one (''Tage gehen, Tage kommen'') and the police chief had a scene and song with a bunch of kiddies, but somewhat surprisingly apart from her March duo the star soubrette role of Jessie was limited to duos and a comical trio with Jimmy and Slippel imitating poor Quakers.

Vergeltsgott ran 42 performances at the Theater an der Wien before being removed to allow the production of Leo Fall's *Der Rebell* and, after the quick flop of that piece, it came back to run through to its 60th night (26 December), whilst a new replacement was prepared. When that replacement turned out to be *Die lustige Witwe, Vergeltsgott* didn't get much more of a look-in.

A month later it was mounted in Budapest (ad Adolf Mérei), with its title changed to *A koldusgróf* (the beggar count), and there it proved very much of a hit. It ran past its 100th night (25 August 1906) as it proved itself the most popular new piece mounted on the Magyar Színház program for some time. In May 1907, whilst the Lessing-Theater company occupied their stage, the Theater an der Wien company presented the show in Berlin under the Hungarians'' more obvious title, *Der Bettelgraf.* Glawatsch now played Stephenson and Frln Wirth was Malona. The show was seen in Budapest as late as 1931 in a revival at the Városi Színház (21 March).

Hungary: Magyar Színház *A koldusgróf* 26 January 1906; Germany: Lessing-Theater *Der Bettelgraf* 9 May 1907

VERNE, Jules (b Nantes, 8 February 1828; d Amiens, 24 March 1905).

The celebrated science-fiction author (who had begun his writing life with a series of vain attempts to get plays produced) wrote 63 novels between *Five Weeks in a Balloon* in 1863 and his death more than 40 years later. A number of these were adapted for the spectacular stage in his lifetime, often by the author himself in collaboration with Adolphe d'Ennery, or with Michel Carré and composer Aristide Hignard, and Verne's name duly appeared on the programs for a good number of often long-running pieces, both very large and sometimes less large (*Le Colin-Maillard, Les Compagnons de la Marjolaine, M de Chimpanzé, Le Page de Mme Malborough, L'Auberge des Ardennes, Michel Strogoff, Le Voyage à travers l'impossible,* etc). However, on the one occasion that he attempted to go it alone, with the spectacular but vacuous *Kéraban le tétu* (Gaîté, 1883), the result was a gigantic failure.

The most famous of the Verne stage pieces, a spectacle with musical accompaniment rather than an opérette, was the adaptation the author made of his *Le Tour du monde en 80 jours* (w Adolphe d'Ennery, mus: Marius Baggers) produced at the Théâtre de la Porte-Saint-Martin on 7 November 1871 and played for 415 performances there, thousands more later in a long series of revivals at the Châtelet, as well as in Hungary (Népszínház *Utazás a föld körül 80 nap alatt* 27 December 1875), Germany (Viktoria-Theater, Berlin 350 performances by 1876), Britain and in America, where it was for many years a regular production of the spectacle specialists, the Kiralfys. In each of these versions, the physical production and the action it contained were shot through with various amounts of musical scenes and pageants, speciality acts, songs and massed dance routines. So much in the way of extras was ladled into one production of d'Ennery's adaptation, at Berlin's Carl-Weiss Theater in 1904, that the show ran for five and a quarter hours.

Julius Freund and Jean Gilbert cut the time in half when they produced a *Die Reise um die Erde in 40 Tagen* at Berlin's Metropoltheater (13 September 1913), but it is more recent times that, with the overwhelming return of the fashion for the spectacular stage, have led to a flood of musical shows based on Verne's work. Orson Welles and Cole Porter collaborated on one that appeared at New York's Adelphi Theater on 31 May 1946 for 75 performances, with Welles himself starred as ''Dick Fix'' to the Fogg of Arthur Margetson and, after the 1956 film, with its famous title song and David Niven's Fogg, came a St Louis Muny version (11 June 1962), with Sammy Fain supplying additional music to Victor Young's film score and a libretto arranged by Sig Herzig. It was subsequently staged as a Jones Beach Marine Theater epic (22 June 1963), with Fritz Weaver and Dom DeLuise starred and repeated there the following season. The subsquently famous directorial name of Trevor Nunn was attached to a piece on the same theme produced in Coventry, England, in 1963, and a New Zealand *Around the World in 80 Days* spectacular was announced as part of a Christchurch Commonwealth Games better remembered for its pre-steroid-days mile race between Filbert Bayi and John Walker.

The tale has continued right up to the present day to appeal to producers and directors with more thought for scenic considerations than anything else, and versions of Verne's novel have continued to flow. Jerome Savary mounted a version with music by Joachim Kuntzch at Hamburg (Deutsches Schauspielhaus 26 November 1978), whilst in France, following a television musical (1975) composed by Gerard Calvi and written by Jean Marsan and Jean Le Poulain, there came a stage version written by Jean-Marie Lecoq and Louis Dunoyer de Segonzac, mounted at Chambéry on 10 October 1987 and subsequently seen at Paris's Théâtre Déjazet. This was followed by further efforts in America (*80 Days* by Snoo Wilson, music and lyrics by Ray Davies, La Jolla Playhouse, San Diego, 1988) and Britain (Chris Walker/Mary Stewart-David/Roberta Hamond, Buxton, 1990). Like the earlier musicals, none looked like even approaching the success of Verne's original.

Offenbach's *Le Docteur Ox,* based on Verne, spawned the H B Farnie pasticcio *Oxygen* (1877), which was played through Britain and America by Lydia Thompson and Australia by others, but although the same composer's *Le Voyage dans la lune* shared some ideas with Verne's work, it was not an adaptation—the moon had, after all, long been a favorite fairyland of stage writers. An actual and admitted burlesque of Verne's moon story was produced in 1877 at the Parisian Vaudeville in New York, with its author J J Wallace in the leading role.

Versions of Verne's *Les Enfants du Capitaine Grant,* on the other hand, appeared on the spectacular musical stage with regularity. Following Verne and d'Ennery's Parisian mounting of their own version, local remakings turned up in Spain (*Los sobrinos del Captain Grant*), in Boston (*Voyages in the Southern Seas* ad Eugene Tompkins, mus: Jean-Jacques de Billemont, Boston Theater 26 October 1880) on Broadway (Booth's Theater 21 March 1881), and above all in Vienna, where *Die Abenteuer des Seekapitäns* (Julius Hopp/Arendt Theater in der Josefstadt 27 September 1878) and the rival *Die Kinder des Kapitän Grant* (Kleiber/Bayer Fürsttheater 26 September 1878) were followed the next year by yet another, under the same title, with music by Louis Roth at the Theater an der Wien (25 September 1879).

Amongst other Verne derivatives may be numbered an Hungarian *Kin-Fu, vagy egy kinai ember kalandjai* (Jenő Faragó/Géza Márkus, mus: Izsó Barna, 31 May 1902 Népszínház), a Viennese *Die Reise nach Sibirien* set to music by Millöcker (Theater an der Wien 21 April 1877), a *Michel Strogoff,* following another enormously successful non-musical Parisian spectacular dating from 1880, composed by Jack Ledru and written by Henri Varna, Marc-Cab and René Richard and produced at the Théâtre Mogador in 1964 (5 December), and a German *Der Kurier des Zaren* (Döbeln 2 November 1940, ad Ernst Hans Richter).

VERNEUIL, Louis [COLLIN du BOCAGE, Louis Jacques Marie] (b Paris, 14 May 1893; d Paris, 3 November, 1952). Parisian playwright, occasional librettist and effective source of material for the musical stage.

Louis Vernueil began his theatre career writing small-house revues before going on to establish himself as one of Paris's most successful playwrights (*Monsieur Beverley, Pour avoir Adrienne, Ma cousine de Varsovie,* etc). He wrote several more substantial revues in tandem with the Parisian master of the genre, Rip (*1915, La Nouvelle Revue 1915,* etc), and subsequently made his first entry into the world of the musical theatre in collaboration with his friend Ivan Caryll, who had successfully adapted the play *Le Satyre,* written by Verneuil's sometime collaborator, Georges Berr, for Broadway as *The Pink Lady.* Their first effort together, *Le Coffre-Fort Vivant,* an adaptation of a novel by Frédéric Mauzens, was produced in America as *The Canary* and topped 150 nights before going on the road. Verneuil subsequently adapted *The Pink Lady* for the French stage, and later collaborated on a fresh version of *Le Coffre-Fort Vivant* for Paris (mus: Szulc, ''Sautreuil'').

Verneuil's stage works were the source for two highly successful musicals during a decided flush of adaptations in the late 1920s and the early 1930s. Alfred Grünwald's libretto for Oscar Straus's *Eine Frau, die weiss, was sie will* (1932), based on his 1923 play *Le Fauteuil,* proved a major international hit, whilst Ralph Benatzky's *Meine Schwester und ich* (1930), a musical version of his *Ma soeur et moi* (1928, w Berr), also found success around the world. The rest did a little less well. Vienna's *Das Walzerparadies* (Oscar Straus/Grünwald, Johann Strauss-Theater 15 February 1935, then Bürgertheater), based on an uncredited Verneuil play, did not prove up to *Eine Frau,* whilst in America, where one of his (unspecified) plays had inspired *Oh Mama! / Girl o' Mine* aka *The Victory Girl* as early as 1917, a Shubert brothers version of his *Mademoiselle ma mère* (Théâtre Fémina 24 February 1920), made over as *Boom Boom* (Casino Theater 28 January 1929, Werner Janssen, Mann Holiner, J Kiern Brennan/Fanny Todd Mitchell) and played by Jeanette MacDonald and Cary Grant, was a Broadway failure (72 performances). His *Ma cousine de Varsovie* was musically played as *One More Night* (1931), a ''new intimate musical divertissement'' fabricated for Irene Bordoni by Russell Medcraft and composer Herman Hupfeld, but didn't make it to New York and, if his 1924 *Pile ou face,* remade for Broadway under the title *First Love* in a version illustrated with interpolated songs (Booth Theatre 8 November 1926), did make it, it was hardly a hit. Another unidentified Verneuil piece was adapted to the Hungarian musical stage as *Megcsallak, mert szeretlek* (ad István Zágon, mus: Ralph Ervin, Andrássy-uti Színház, 1930), and *Mademoiselle ma mère* was again musicalized in Germany as *Fräulein Mama* (Hugo Hirsch/Willi Kollo/Kessler, Deutsches Schauspielhaus, Hamburg 1 July 1928).

Verneuil left Paris in 1940, three days before the German army invaded the city, and settled in America, where he wrote one successful Broadway play, *Affairs of State,* adapted *La Vie parisienne* for a new American production and authored a splendid volume of reminiscences. Sadly, the announced second and third volumes did not appear, for Verneuil returned to Paris and, at the age of 59, slit his throat in his bath.

1918 **The Canary** (Caryll/P G Wodehouse, Caldwell/ad H B Smith) Globe Theater, New York 4 November

1921 **La Dame en rose** (*The Pink Lady*) French version (Théâtre des Bouffes-Parisiens)

1929 **Boulard et ses filles** (Charles Cuvillier/Saint Granier, Jean Le Seyeux) Théâtre Marigny 8 November

1938 **La Féerie blanche** (Mitty Goldin, Oberfeld) Théâtre Mogador 5 January

Plate 405. *Comic* **Jerry Verno** *and hero Donald Mather in* El Dorado.

1938 **Le Coffre-Fort vivant** revised version of *The Canary* (Joseph Szulc, Maurice Yvain ps Sautreuil/Henri Wernert/w Georges Berr) Théâtre du Châtelet 17 December

1941 **La Vie parisienne** new American version w Felix Brentano (City Center, New York)

Autobiography: *Rideau à neuf heures* (Éditions des Deux-Rives, Paris, 1943)

VERNO, Jerry (b London, 26 July 1894; d London, 29 June 1975). British comic who spent half a century on the variety and musical comedy stages.

Verno made his first stage appearances as a child vocalist in vaudeville and thereafter mixed variety and touring revue with comedy. After the war he joined Maurice Bandmann's company touring musical comedy on the oriental circuits, and he did not make his first London appearance until 1925, when he appeared as the comical Alf in the play *Alf's Button.* He appeared in the musical *Song of the Sea* at His Majesty's Theatre (1928, Wilkins) and thereafter spent much of his stage career playing comedy roles in such musical pieces as *The Three Musketeers* (1930, Planchet), *Eldorado* (1930, the crooked Mr Budwell), *The Maid of the Mountains* revival (1930, Tonio), *Wild Violets* (1932, Hans Katzen), *That's a Pretty Thing* (1933, Billy Blake), the 1940–41 revival of *Chu Chin Chow* (Ali Baba), *A Night in Venice* (1944, Pappacoda), *The Dubarry* (1947, de la Marche), *Belinda Fair* (1949, Peregrine), *The Merry Widow* (1952, Popoff) and *The Water Gipsies* (1955, Albert Bell). He toured in 1954 in George Formby's role of Percy Piggott in *Zip Goes a Million* and appeared as late as 1968 in the British provinces in a musical *Lysistrata* perversion called *Liz.*

His film credits included the 1932 English-language version of *Der Bettelstudent.*

VERŐ, György [HAUER, Hugo] (b Igal, 31 March 1857; d Budapest, 12 March 1941).

Successful as a playwright, composer, author, conductor and director, György Verő was one of the outstanding and most versatile men of the Budapest theatre in the period when a significant native musical theatre tradition was beginning to blossom in Hungary.

Verő had originally studied law, but at the age of 23 he turned his attentions to the theatre, at first briefly as an actor and then as a writer. He made his earliest ventures translating some of the Viennese Operetten that were currently all the rage for the Hungarian stage, but at the same time he began another career, as a conductor, at the theatre in Miskolc. It was there that his first original play, *A mükedvelők,* was produced. In 1885 he supplied some translations to Budapest's principal musical theatre, the Népszínház, and the following year he joined the staff there as musical director and conductor, a position he held for the next 15 years.

In 1892, after a period in which he devoted himself to conducting rather than writing, he turned out an operett written and composed to a text taken from Favart's old opéra-comique *Les Trois Sultanes. A szultán* (1892) was a first-class success at the Népszínház, and it quickly assured itself a place at the top of the Hungarian native repertoire, a landmark between the earlier works of such composers as József Konti and the real opening-out of the Hungarian musical theatre that would soon follow. He had a second success at the Népszínház with *A virágcsata,* which merited his third operett, *Der Löwenjäger,* the opportunity of being taken up for production by Alexandrine von Schönerer at the Theater an der Wien even before it had been staged in Hungary. If it lasted but 17 performances there, it won a better reception on its return to the Népszínház (1897). Verő wrote and composed one further operett, *Kleopatra* (later staged by Max Reinhardt at Berlin's Deutsches Theater as *Die Bettelgräfin* 8 June 1908), as well as the scores for several musical spectaculars (*Ezer év, Hadak útja, A pesti ucca*), before moving to the Nemzeti Színház and, for two seasons, exchanging his baton for a pen in the post of dramaturge.

In the years that followed, he wrote pieces of all kinds ranging from full-scale tragedy to cabaret material and revue, not only for the Nemzeti Színház but for many of the other principal Budapest houses. His output included the tragedy *Kain* (1902), the allegorical *Bölcső és koporsó* (1902), the play *A nép* (1907), the Singspiel-revue *Göre Gábor Budapesten* (1907) and three one-act musicals played at the Népszínház under the title *Menyecskék* (1903), as well as three full-scale musical pieces: the Hungarian musical comedy *A bajusz* (the mustache, 1903), the operett *Doktorkisasszony* (1903) and the musical comedy *Leányka* (1906). All three were successful, and the production of *A bajusz* (*Der Schnurrbart*) at Vienna's Carltheater (20 January) and Berlin's Neues

Plate 406.

Königliches Opernhaus in 1905 (10 June) was followed a few years later by a Vienna production of *Der Sultan* (1909), which was also revived in Budapest in 1911. *Leányka* was played in a German version as *Weiberlaunen* (ad Carl Lindau, Leo Stein) at the Schumann-Theater, Frankfurt-am-Main in July 1907.

Following the production of the musical comedy *Falusi madonna* in 1907, Verő returned largely to playwriting with pieces such as the one-act comedy *Leánynéző* (1914), *A mennyország* (Király Színház, 1915) and *Az ellenség* (Vígszínház 27 February 1915), but he also collaborated on the libretto for a German Operette, *Das geborgte Schloss,* composed by Herman Dostal, before turning full circle to end as he had begun with the translation of Robert Stolz's *Mädi* for the Hungarian stage.

In 1926 Verő authored the history of the Népszínház (*Blaha Lujza es a Népszínház*).

Verő's wife was the prominent musical-theatre contralto **Célia Margó** (1865–1942), who played at the Vár színház and then at the Népszínház, where she appeared, amongst others, in the local versions of *Das Spitzentuch der Königin* (Donna Irene), *Gasparone, The Mikado* (Katisha), *Der Gascogner* (Cascarita), *Nell Gwynne* (Margot), *Der Ziegunerbaron* (Czipra), as the Vicomte de Letorrières in Konti's *Az eleven ördög* and variously as Delia and Roxelane in her husband's most continuously popular piece, *A szultán.* She retired from the stage in 1904.

1881 **Mathuzsálem herceg** (*Prinz Methusalem*) Hungarian version (Budai Színkör)

1883 **A gascognei nemes** (*Der Gascogner*) Hungarian version w Ivan Relle (Budai Színkör)

1883 **Ördög a földön** (*Der Teufel auf Erden*) Hungarian version w Viktor Rákosi (Budai Színkör)

1885 **Tökfilkó** (*Le Roi de carreau*) Hungarian version (Népszínház)

1885 **A királyné csipkekendője** (*Das Spitzentuch der Königin*) Hungarian version (Népszínház)

1886 **Esketés dobszóval** (*Le Mariage au tambour*) Hungarian version w Béla J Fái (Népszínház)

1886 **Százszorszép** (*La Jolie Parfumeuse*) Hungarian version w Fái (Népszínház)

1887 **Bellman** Hungarian version (Népszínház)

1892 **A szultán** (Verő) Nepszínház 19 November

1894 **A virágcsata** (Verő) Nepszínház 28 April

1896 **Ezer év** (Verő) Népszínház 17 April

1896 **Az oroszlánvadász** (*Der Löwenjäger*) (Verő ad Paul Schönthan, Leo Stein) Theater an der Wien, Vienna 1 November

1898 **Hadak utja** (Verő) Népszínház 15 March

1900 **Kleopatra** (Verő) Magyar Színház 6 March

1900 **A pesti ucca** (Ferenc Rajna) Magyar Színház 14 November

1903 **A bajusz** (Verő) Magyar Színház 6 February

1903 **Menyecskék** (Verő) three 1-act musical plays Népszínház 27 November

1903 **Doktorkisasszony** (Verő) Magyar Színház 19 December

1904 **Csak tréfa** (Adolf Mérei) Magyar Színház 10 September

1906 **Leányka** (Verő) Népszínház 17 January

1907 **Göre Gábor Budapesten** (w Zsigmond Vincze, Imre Kálmán, Béla Zerkovitz) Király Színház 25 May

1907 **Falusi madonna** (Verő) Király Színház 6 November

1911 **Das geborgte Schloss** (Hermann Dostal/w Carl Lindau) Stadttheater, Leipzig 15 May

1924 **Huncut a lány** (*Mädi*) Hungarian version (Király Színház)

VÉRONIQUE Opéra-comique in 3 acts by Albert Vanloo and Georges Duval. Music by André Messager. Théâtre des Bouffes-Parisiennes, Paris, 10 December 1898.

The most enduring of Messager's opérettes, *Véronique* also gave its composer the largest international success of his long career as a composer of light musical theatre in the years immediately following its first production.

As in *Les P'tites Michu,* their previous and very happy collaboration with the composer, Vanloo and Duval's libretto used well-worn plot elements in its construction but treated them with the slightly genteel elegance that was now fashionable in opérette. The aristocratic Hélène de Solanges (Mariette Sully) is to be wed, by royal command, to the wild oat–sowing Vicomte Florestan de Valaincourt (Jean Périer). Florestan takes the grim news of this dowdy-sounding match to his mistress, the florist Agathe (Anna Tariol-Baugé), and he is overheard by Hélène who just happens to be in that very shop, shopping for flowers. She disguises herself as a flower girl, Véronique, and, during a jolly lunch party at Romainville, completely wins her intended husband's heart. When Agathe spills the beans, Florestan pretends proudly to refuse Hélène for love of Véronique, but the pretense only serves to stretch the third act to a little more length. The comedy of the affair was provided by Agathe's pouter-pigeon of a husband, Coquenard (Regnard), Hélène's sporty aunt, Ermerance (Léonie Laporte), who joins her in her escapade, the impecunious aristocrat Loustot (Maurice Lamy), who has been royally deputized to get Florestan to his betrothal in one piece, and the principals of a rural wedding (Brunais, Madeleine Mathyeu, Mme Bonval) laid waste by Florestan's pursuit of his ''Véronique.''

If the material was not new, the librettists nevertheless deployed it with a great deal of charm and refined humor, and Messager set their lyrics with some of his most delightful and elegant music. Two pieces, in particular, became worldwide favorites: the little duet sung by Florestan and Hélène on their way, by donkey, to Romainville (''De çi, de là'' or, in English, ''Trot Here, Trot There'') and their idyllic Swing Song, ''Poussez, poussez l'escarpolette.'' Agathe led a lively hymn to the country pleasures of Romainville (''Au Tourne, Tourne, Tournebride''), Ermerance plucked a harp in soulful romance (''De magasin la simple demoiselle''), Hélène spat out her indignation at hearing her future husband calling her a ''Petite Dinde!'' and Loustot rambled on about what life was like ''Quand j'étais Baron des Merlettes'' in some of the score's varied highlights.

Véronique was a fine success, running for some 200 performances at the Bouffes-Parisiens, and following up with a number of productions outside France. The Theater an der Wien mounted the piece (ad Heinrich Bolten-Bäckers) with the heroine's nom de bataille changed to *Brigitte.* Frln Worm and Carl Streitmann headed the romance, with Frln Milton and Josef Joseffy as the floral couple, but they did it for just 11 performances. Budapest got *Veronka* and, two years later, Bolten-Bäckers's version was seen in Berlin, but the English-singing world seemed disinterested in the piece. However, Messager had influential friends in Britain from his days at the head of the Covent Garden Opera House and one of them, Lady Gladys de Grey, promised the composer she would find him a production. When she failed, she and her brother put up the money for a showcase performance by a Parisian cast headed by Mlle Sully, Adolphe Corin and Regnard.

The performance was well enough liked that, when the surefire *Madame Sherry* flopped horribly, George Edwardes decided to put a version of *Véronique* (ad Henry Hamilton, Lilian Eldée, Percy Greenbank) into the unexpectedly empty Apollo Theatre. Ruth Vincent (Hélène), Lawrence Rea (Florestan), Kitty Gordon (Agathe), George Graves (Coquenard) and Rosina Brandram (Ermerance) headed the cast, and the show turned out a major hit, playing 495 performances in London prefatory to a long touring and colonial life, and a wartime West End revival (Adelphi Theatre 3 April 1915, 59 performances). Misses Vincent and Gordon and Rea later headed a company that took the piece to America, but *Véronique*'s pretty elegance appealed more to the New York press than its public, and the show ran only 81 performances on Broadway before being put on the road under the title *The Flower Girl,* with Louise Gunning as its heroine. Australia, on the other hand, proved quite partial to the piece when J C Williamson's company presented it in Melbourne with Margaret Thomas (Hélène), Florence Young (Agathe), Clara Clifton (Ermerance), John Doran (Florestan), George Lauri (Coquenard) and Claude Flemming (Octave) in the cast, and the piece was brought back a number of times in the Williamson repertoire thereafter.

Véronique was revived in Paris in 1909 (Folies-Dramatiques 30 January) with Mlle Sully and many of the original cast, and again in 1920 (Gaîté-Lyrique 1 March) with Edmée Favart featured alongside Périer and Mlle Tariol-Baugé, repeating yet again more than 20 years after their creation of their roles. These revivals confirmed and even increased the popularity of the show in France, and it subsequently became a member of the basic repertoire of opérettes, even being played at the Opéra-Comique in 1925 with Mlle Favart and André Baugé as Florestan whilst his mother repeated her Agathe (thus playing his mistress!). It was remounted in Paris in 1936 and 1943, filmed in 1949 with Marina Hotine, Gisèle Pascal and Jean Desailly, and played at the Opéra-Comique again in 1978 and 1980.

A new English-language adaptation (ad Charles Kondek) was produced by America's Ohio Light Opera in 1997 (July).

Austria: Theater an der Wien *Brigitte* 10 March 1900; Hungary: Magyar Színház *Veronka* 21 April 1900; Germany: Stadttheater, Cologne 28 October 1900, Neues Königliches Opernhaus 12 September 1902; UK: Coronet Theatre (Fr) 5 May 1903, Apollo Theatre (Eng) 18 May 1904; USA: Broadway Theater 30 October 1905; Australia: His Majesty's Theatre, Melbourne 11 November 1905

Film: 1949

Recordings: complete (EMI, Decca), selections (EMI-Pathé, etc), English (Newport Classics)

Video: Opéra-Comique 1979

VERT-VERT Opéra-comique in 3 acts by Henri Meilhac and Charles Nuitter. Music by Jacques Offenbach. Opéra-Comique, Paris, 10 March 1869.

One of the rare Offenbach works to be accepted by the musically lofty gentlemen of the Opéra-Comique, *Vert-Vert* was not a success in its production there.

Meilhac and Nuitter's story, based on a de Leuven and Desforges vaudeville that had been played by Déjazet some years before (but also apparently on a 1733 piece by Gresset), was set in a girls' school and the characters included Mlle Paturelle (Mlle Revilly), a deputy headmistress secretly wed to the dancing master Baladon (Couderc), and a couple of pupils (Mlle Moisset, Mlle Tual) more or less affianced to a couple of dragoons (Sainte-Foy, Ponchard). The Vert-Vert of the title (Capoul) is the headmistress's nephew, thus christened after the popular parrot of the establishment, recently deceased. He is amorously pursued by another pupil, Mimi (Marie Cico), who disguises herself as a dragoon and follows him out of bounds to an inn, where he is seen drinking with the singer La Corilla (Caroline Girard). With the help of the real dragoons, she gets him drunk, back to school, and, having uncovered her teacher's secret marriage, she has no qualms about using that knowledge to get the required permission for a little wedlock of her own.

Vert-Vert's song "Oui, l'oiseau reviendra dans sa cage" and the Air du coche proved to be the best-liked numbers of Offenbach's score. Yet, even when the piece was revised by its composer after a sticky start, it still didn't go, and *Vert-Vert* had to be written off as a flop. However, it was an Offenbach flop, and that meant that it still found foreign theatres willing (or precommitted) to take it up. The show was produced in German at the Carltheater (ad Julius Hopp) in 1870 with the richest of Carltheater casts—Therese Schäfer, Hermine Meyerhoff, Karl Blasel, Josef Matras and Wilhelm Knaack—and was played 21 times in that season and twice more the following year. The German version was played in Berlin the same year, and an Hungarian version appeared several years later. Offenbach played pieces of the show's score in his concerts when he visited America in 1875, announcing the performance as the "first time in this country." It wasn't—the German *Kakadu* had been given a performance at the Stadttheater in 1870.

A piece produced in London as *Vert Vert* (ad Henry Hermann, Richard Mansell) was an under-rehearsed, ill-cast and cut-about fiasco, apparently flung together in 48 hours and sporting Offenbach music culled from half a dozen of his works. It got sufficient scandalous notice for an under-dressed dance called the Riperelle to win it an eight-week run. When the journal *Vanity Fair* was sued by the management for announcing ''the worst orchestra, some of the flattest singing and one of the most indecent dances in London,'' they won their case. The criticism, it was adjudged, was justified. An altered and recast version tried again at the Globe Theatre later the same year (26 September) and somehow added another seven London weeks to the run of a show that was scarcely Offenbach's *Vert-Vert.*

Holland saw the piece as *Kakatoe* and with success at the Frascati Theatre, Amsterdam, in 1888.

Austria: Carltheater *Kakadu* 3 February 1870; Germany: Friedrich-Wilhelmstädtisches Theater *Kakadu* 4 June 1870; USA: Stadttheater *Kakadu* 31 October 1870; UK: St James's Theatre 2 May 1874; Hungary: Budai Színkör *A Papagáj* 7 August 1875

DAS VERWUNSCHENE SCHLOSS Comic Operette in 3 acts by Alois Berla. Music by Carl Millöcker. Theater an der Wien, Vienna, 30 March 1878.

The folk of the Tyrolean village situated alongside the estate of the Graf von Geiersburg (Carl Adolf Friese) keep well away from his castle, for strange nightly lights and noises have convinced them it is inhabited by the devil. When the young dairyman Sepp (Jani Szíka) says he doesn't believe in ghostly things, the farmer Grosslechner (Liebwerth), to whose daughter Mirzl (Karoline Tellheim) he is engaged, throws him out for impiety. Sepp and his goasbua Andredl (Alexander Girardi) take to the hills, and from the hut of old Traudl (Frl Herzog) and her mahm, Regerl (Josefine Gallmeyer), they look down on the lights in the castle. When they go to investigate, it turns out that the Count is simply having a bawdy party, but the devilishly masked guests are enough to curdle Andredl's blood. However, when the attractive Sepp is drugged and taken back to the castle, Andredl leads Regerl to the rescue. The Count's naughty excesses are displayed to the village, and he is only saved from the anger of the locals when his little mistress, Coralie (Berthe Olma), assures them that it is their wedding they are celebrating. The gratitude of the new Countess earns Sepp a fine reward to add to the hand of Mirzl, whilst Andredl and Regerl make up a third final-curtain pair.

Of the musical numbers written for the piece—described as a ''komische Operette''—it was the heavily accented dialect-comedy pieces performed by the top-billed Gallmeyer (the second act opener ''Schirlingskraut beim Mondschein g'hohlt,'' the hit ''S' is a Bisserl Liab' und a Bisserl Treu'') and by Girardi (the hugely popular ''Dalkata Bua!''), and the tacked-in Lied in Österreichisches Mundart (''O, du himmelblauer See'') performed by Andredl and Sepp, as entertainment for the Count's party, that proved the most popular items. The comic folk also had one of the most substantial ensembles, the trio ''Wie glanzt der grüne Wald,'' as well as a ghostly ''Gespenster, gespenster.'' Mirzl was given a ballad with which to open the proceedings, but the role of Coralie proved rather the more grateful of the soprano roles with its solo ''Ihr edlen Cavaliere'' and some showy coloratura in the third-act trio and finale that rocketed her up to D in alt.

Berla and Millöcker's friendly, jolly piece was a lively success in a season that also featured several other hits: Gallmeyer's introduction of the Costa/Millöcker *Ihr Korporal,* Berla and Millöcker's *Plausch net Pepi* and the first performances of *Die Glocken von Corneville,* with Girardi as Grénicheux. If *Das verwunschene Schloss*'s initial performance figures were limited, as a result, the show and its songs nevertheless proved their popularity by an extraordinary durability. The piece was played at the Theater an der Wien again in 1881, given a full-scale revival there in 1893, with Girardi teamed with Therese Biedermann in Gallmeyer's role, Lili Lejo (Coralie), Josef Joseffy (Geiersberg) and Julius Spielmann (Sepp) (19 performances), and seen again in 1894, 1901 and 1909. It had meanwhile found its way into other Viennese theatres, being played, notably, at the Carltheater in 1901 (27 May), with Franz Glawatsch and Biedermann, Mizzi Günther as Coralie and Louis Treumann as Geiersberg, and in 1910, with Streitmann again as Sepp. The Johann Strauss-Theater mounted *Das verwunschene Schloss* in its first months of operation in 1908 and again in 1913, the Bürgertheater in 1916 with Gerda Walde as Coralie and again in 1924, and it was also seen at the Raimundtheater in 1921.

The success that the show found in Austria was repeated in Germany, where *Das verwunschene Schloss* compiled a record second only to *Der Bettelstudent* amongst Millöcker's works, but the show did not run very much further afield. However, Marie Geistinger was not averse to picking up her great rival's fine role, and she introduced Regerl to American audiences (in German) on several occasions between 1881 and 1883. The German version was repeated at the Amberg Theater as late as 1890, but the show does not appear to have ever been translated into English. It was, however, put into Hungarian (ad Béla J Fái, Ferenc Rajna) for a late production in Budapest. Mounted in 1890 after the huge Hungarian success of *Der arme Jonathan,* it did even better than the composer's big latter day success with a run of 55 performances at the Népszínház.

A revised version by Gustav Quedenfeldt and Walther Brügmann was produced at the Nationaltheater, Munich, 4 February 1934.

Germany: Brünn 13 September 1878; USA: Thalia Theater 3 November 1881; Hungary: Népszínház *A Boszorkanyvár* 3 October 1890

VERY GOOD EDDIE Musical comedy in 2 acts by Philip Bartholomae and Guy Bolton based on Bartholomae's play *Over Night.* Lyrics by Schuyler Greene. Music by Jerome Kern. Princess Theater, New York, 23 December 1915.

Following their first venture at a non-(very-)girlie, non-(very-)glossy and comparatively intimate musical comedy with their adaptation of the British musical play *Mr Popple of Ippleton,* Bessie Marbury and F Ray Comstock purchased the rights to the successful comedy *Over Night* (Hackett Theater 2 January 1911, 162 performances) and commissioned its author, Philip Bartholomae, to adapt it as a similar kind of musical comedy for the little Princess Theater. Miss Marbury's client Jerome Kern, who had provided the songs for the earlier *Nobody Home,* was booked for the music in tandem with his current lyric-writing partner, Schuyler Greene. The show was mounted in Schenectady, with a cast headed by Ernest Truex (who had toured four years earlier in the original play) and Florence Nash in the lead roles, but the producers were unhappy with the result and it was taken off, revamped by *Nobody Home* librettist Guy Bolton, and fitted out with some additional Kern songs taken from his bottom drawer. Two and a bit of these had even been used in Broadway's *Miss Information* earlier the same year. Alice Dovey, heroine of *Nobody Home,* took over the top feminine role, and just a fortnight after the out-of-town closure the piece reopened in Cincinnati (28 November) prior to moving to New York.

Very Good Eddie (the title, which puzzled even contemporary playgoers, was a current Fred Stone catchphrase from the show *Chin-Chin,* and the leading comic character was named accordingly) took place on and along the Hudson River. When circumstances lead to Georgina (Helen Raymond), the hectoring new wife of little Eddie Kettle (Truex), and Percy (John Willard), the new husband of Elsie Darling (Miss Dovey), missing the honeymoon steamer, their partners are forced, for reasons explained, to pretend to be husband and wife and to pass the night almost together in the honeymoon hotel. At the end of the night little Eddie proves able to handle his suspicious wife with unsuspected firmness. Parallel to this little adventure ran the efforts of Dick Rivers (Oscar Shaw) to win himself Elsie Lilly (Anna Orr), whilst extra comedy was the lot of Ada Lewis as that young lady's eccentric singing teacher, Madame Matroppo, and of patented comedian John E Hazzard (Al Cleveland).

The show's songs included several that would become popular, notably Truex and Miss Dovey's naive little "Babes in the Wood," the warm duo for Shaw and Miss Orr, "Some Sort of Somebody" (which hadn't clicked in *Miss Information* but now did), and a delightful piece of comedy material for Truex called "(When You Wear a) Thirteen Collar." Shaw (who dominated the evening's singing quotient) also joined Miss Orr in hula rhythm to sing à propos of nothing about "On the Shore at Le Le Wei" (another *Miss Information* cut-out) and in waltz time for "Nodding Roses."

Plate 407. **Very Good Eddie.** *Ernest Truex and Alice Dovey.*

Very Good Eddie did very nicely for its producers. Between its run at the Princess and subsequent tactical transfers first to the larger Casino Theater (more cheap seats for a show that had run its first fine flush), then to the 39th Street Theater, followed by a brief return to base, it ran up 341 New York performances, prior to setting out on a touring schedule that extended its life for a further couple of seasons. After that, like a number of its contemporaries, it was potted into a 45-minute version and sent out on the vaudeville circuits. It was also smartly picked up by the rising young Tait Brothers for an Australian production, and it was mounted, as the first of what would be their very many musical comedy productions, at Sydney's Palace Theatre. Barry Lupino was cast as Eddie alongside Fayette Perry (Elsie), Emily Fitzroy (Georgina), Andrew Higginson (Dick) and Lillian Rucker (Elsie Lilly) through 10 weeks in Sydney and five further at Melbourne's King's Theatre (21 April 1917).

A British production in 1918 did less well. Produced under the management of André Charlot and Guy Bragdon, it featured diminutive revue actor Nelson Keys as Eddie, Nellie Briercliffe as Elsie Darling and Walter Williams as Dick Rivers, and it opened in the same week as the local version of another Broadway success, *Going Up.* London audiences gave their vote to the latter in no uncertain terms: by 574 performances to 46.

A 1975 revival, produced at the Goodspeed Opera House (8 July), dropped a handful of pieces of the original score and replaced them with eight numbers taken from other of Kern's shows. Two of the best (''Good Night Boat,'' ''Left All Alone Again Blues'') came from the equally river-based *The Night Boat* and the sparky ''Katy-Did'' was plucked from *Oh, I Say!* David Christmas and Cynthia Wells played Dick and Elsie, whilst Charles Repole and Virginia Seidel profited from the increased score as Eddie and the other Elsie. A Broadway transfer of this made-over version played 304 performances at the Booth Theater (21 December 1975) and provoked a new London run (Piccadilly Theatre 23 March 1976). Robert Swann, Mary Barrett, Richard Freeman and Prue Clarke featured in a production that profited from a theatre anxious to stay lit to stretch its run to 411 performances.

Australia: Palace Theatre, Sydney 10 February 1917; UK: Palace Theatre 18 May 1918

Recording: 1975 revival cast (DRG)

VESTRIS, Madame [Eliza] [BARTOLOZZI, Lucy Elizabeth] (b London, 3 January 1797; d London, 8 August 1856).

The young Eliza Vestris (she had married at 16 into the famous dancing family) worked as a vocalist and actress in London (debut as Proserpina in von Winter's opera *Il ratto di Proserpina* 1815, *Zaira, Una cosa rara,* Susannah in *Le nozze di Figaro*) and in Paris before she made her name in the title role of the extravaganza *Don Giovanni in London* at the Theatre Royal, Drury Lane, in 1820. Over the following decade she established herself as a public favorite in opera (Fatima in *Oberon, Semiramide, Zelmire, The Siege of Belgrade, Cosi fan tutte, Il Seraglio, Artaxerxes* often in male roles), ballad opera (Macheath, Diana in *Lionel and Clarissa, The Duenna,* etc), comic opera (Adela in *The Haunted Tower, The Castle of Andalusia, The Lord of the Manor, The Pirate, Jean de Paris, Fra Diavolo,* etc), and burletta (Apollo in *Midas, The Invincibles,* etc), as well as in all kinds of dramas and comedies, often decorated with interpolated songs for her benefit.

In 1831 she became manageress of the Olympic Theatre, and there she launched what was to become a famous series of extravaganzas and burlesques authored by J R Planché and beginning with *Olympic Revels,* a burlesque of the Pandora myth with herself starred as the overcurious nymph. During nine years at the Olympic, and subsequently, with her second husband, Charles Mathews, at Covent Garden (September 1839 to April 1842) and the Lyceum (1847), Madame Vestris (no little aided by a sexually scandalous gutter press) fostered a highly popular line in burlesque and extravaganza as an important part of her repertoire, a line that provided a backbone for the freer kind of musico-comical theatre of the time and that led directly to the burlesque tradition of the later part of the 19th-century British stage.

Biographies: Pearce, C E: *Madame Vestris and Her Times* (Paul, London, 1923), Williams, C J: *Madame Vestris: A Theatrical Biography* (Sidgwick & Jackson, London, 1973), Appleton, W: *Madame Vestris and the London Stage* (Columbia, New York, 1974)

DER VETTER AUS DINGSDA Operette in 3 acts by Herman Haller and ''Rideamus'' based on a comedy by Max Kempner-Hochstädt. Music by Eduard Künneke. Theater am Nollendorfplatz, Berlin, 15 April 1921.

If *Der Vetter aus Dingsda* was far from the longest-running piece to play Berlin's Theater am Nollendorfplatz under Herman Haller's management in the 1910s and 1920s—its 200 performances paled beside the more than 650 of the wartime *Immer feste druff!* and the nearly 500 of *Drei alte Schachteln*—it was, nevertheless, qualitatively the best of the series of Operetten that Eduard Künneke composed for the house and the most enduring amongst all of Haller's musical-theatre ventures. Whilst the other Haller pieces are forgotten, it has survived through 80 years into the repertoire of modern European theatres in a way that very few other German Operetten have done.

Pretty Dutch Julia (Lori Leux) longs for the day when her beloved cousin Roderich will come home from ''nowhere'' in the East Indies. As a result, she refuses the attentions of local Egon and is not inclined to fall in with the plans of her Uncle Josse (Gottfried Huppert) that she should wed his brother's son, August. One day a handsome stranger (Johannes Müller) arrives at the house, and Julia is delighted when, in response to her hopeful prodding, he says he is Roderich, and then devastated when it eventuates that he is not. When the real Roderich (Eugen Rex) does come, however, he is aghast to find that Julia has kept a candle alight for him all the years since their childhood, and she, in her turn, regrets having turned the false Roderich away. But she will keep her dream: to her, August—for the stranger is none other than he—will take the place of the Roderich she dreamed of, and best friend Hännchen (Ilse Marvenga) will be very happy with a Roderich she never dreamed of.

Künneke's score to this little, 24-hour-span, nine-handed Operette ranged from some sweetly natural

Plate 408. **Der Vetter aus Dingsda.** *Uncle and Auntie (Horst Schafer, Elvira Beitler) settle down to their supper unaware of the shock to their daily routine that is on its way from ''nowhere'' (Stadttheater, Darmstadt, 1986).*

scenes set around the family table, to a beautiful spun-soprano ''Strahlender Mond'' in which Julia asks the moon to carry her love to her cousin on the other side of the world, to the plaintive musical line of the stranger's mysterious answer to the girl's persistent questioning: ''Ich bin nur ein armer Wandergesell,'' as well as to such up-to-date strains as the boston, the tango and the fox-trot.

Haller's production of *Der Vetter aus Dingsda* played at the Theater am Nollendorfplatz from April to its 200th night on 24 October, before making way for the next Haller-Künneke piece, *Die Ehe im Kreise,* then headed out to other German-language houses. It reached Vienna the following October, playing at the Johann Strauss-Theater under the management of Erich Müller for a little under three months with Lola Grahl (Julia), Karl Bachmann (August), Fritz Imhoff (Roderich), Gisa Kolbe (Hännchen) and Georg Kundert (Josse) in the leading roles.

The show was taken up for America by the Shuberts, but, before it was seen by Broadway, it underwent a most curious transformation. It was now, thanks to Harry B Smith, called *Caroline* (after having tried out in Wilmington as *Virginia*), it was set in the American Civil War, and Künneke's svelte score had been dotted with extra bits by Al Goodman. Tessa Kosta played the eponymous heroine, whilst Harrison Brockbank and J Harold Murray were the men in the affair, and the mixture pleased for 151 performances. London's version (ad Douglas Furber, Adrian Ross, Fred Thompson, R C Tharp), which opened a few weeks later, treated the original more kindly. But the Prince's Theatre production, with Helen Gilliland (Julia), Walter Williams (August), Cicely Debenham (Hannchen) and Roy Royston (Egon, worryingly renamed Adrian van Piffel) did not win the favor it might have hoped for in the West End. It closed after three months and 105 performances prior to what nevertheless turned out to be a good tour.

J C Williamson Ltd's Australian production also went through a few vicissitudes. The management decided to make a star out of a local amateur vocalist whom they renamed ''Jill Manners'' and cast her as Julia alongside Claude Flemming (Stranger), Arthur Stigant (Josse), Marie La Varre (Wimpel), Gus Bluett (Adrien, ie, Egon), Charles Brooks (Roderich) and ''the twelve tulips, a dozen of Australia's most beautiful girls'' who were dressed in white, blue and pink in successive acts. Jill Manners was a dreadful disappointment, and Marie

Burke had to be hurried in to replace her for two months in Sydney. When Miss Burke went on to make a huge hit in *Wildflower, The Cousin from Nowhere* was put away, but it reemerged at Christmas two years later to play a two-month Melbourne season with Maud Fane in the lead role (Her Majesty's Theatre, Melbourne 18 December 1926).

A new English version, *The Cousin from Batavia,* was produced at the Ohio Light Opera in 2000 (26 July).

If the show's overseas record was just a little disappointing, however, *Der Vetter aus Dingsda* remained a strong favorite on home ground where, helped by the reasonable size of its (12-tulip-less) cast, it has remained a regularly produced item in German-language houses to this day. It was twice filmed, first by Georg Zoch in 1934 with Lizzi Holschuh, and a second time in 1954 in a version in which Künneke was credited as co-musical director, and one of the screenplay authors was a (but not the) Haller. Vera Molnár (Julia), Gerhard Riedmann (Hans), Joachim Brennecke (Roderich) and Ina Halley (Hannchen) featured.

Austria: Johann Strauss-Theater 13 October 1922; USA: Ambassador Theater *Caroline* 31 January 1923; UK: Prince's Theatre *The Cousin from Nowhere* 24 February 1923; Australia: Theatre Royal, Sydney *The Cousin from Nowhere* 27 September 1924

Films: Georg Zoch 1934, Central-Europa/Karl Anton 1953

Recordings: complete (RCA), selections (Eurodisc, Fontana, etc)

THE VICAR OF BRAY English comic opera in 2 acts by Sydney Grundy. Music by Edward Solomon. Globe Theatre, London, 22 July 1882.

The successful playwright Sydney Grundy turned librettist and lyricist for the first time on *The Vicar of Bray,* inventing a story around the character of the famous vicar of song and fable whose byword was "expediency" and who changed his denomination as quickly as circumstances demanded it. He mixed this character with Thomas Day's almost as well known nursery-tale pair of idealized 18th-century schoolboys—rich and horrid Tommy Merton and angelic farmer's lad Henry Sandford—and came out with a libretto in which the two fellows (the latter now a curate rather than a farmer, and both grown up) court the vicar's daughter, Dorothy (Lizzie Beaumont). The vicar (W J Hill) scares off impecunious Henry (Walter H Fisher) by turning high church, suffers along with his chorus of students the celibacy such a change incurs, but hurriedly goes "low" again when the bishop intervenes, allowing Dorothy to have her Henry and himself to take to wife the wealthy widowed Mrs Merton (Maria Davis). Tommy (H Cooper Cliffe) is paired off in good aristocratic fashion with danseuse Nellie Bly (Emma d'Auban). Gently Gilbertian, though set firmly in the Britain that encouraged composer Solomon to his most natural style of music, *The Vicar of Bray* seemingly suffered from its lack of demonstrativeness. It was revised and partly recast after an indifferent opening, but ended after 69 performances, and one week on Broadway in an ill-staged production with Marie Jansen (Dorothy), Harry Allen (Vicar) and the D'Oyly Carte's Lyn Cadwaldr (Sandford) in the leading roles.

However, a decade later, after Solomon's *The Nautch Girl* had very much more than satisfactorily filled the gap left by the Gilbert-Sullivan split at the Savoy Theatre, D'Oyly Carte revived *The Vicar of Bray.* Savoy stars Rutland Barrington (Vicar), Courtice Pounds (Sandford) and Rosina Brandram (Mrs Merton) headed the cast, and the show ran through five months and 143 performances before going on to tour merrily throughout Britain in the Carte repertoire companies for several seasons. On the wings of this classy revival, *The Vicar of Bray* also won a production in Australia with Joseph Tapley (Sandford), George Lauri (Vicar), Sydney Deane (Merton) and Clara Thompson (Mrs Merton) at the head of its cast.

USA: Fifth Avenue Theater 2 October 1882; Australia: Princess Theatre, Melbourne 20 May 1893

DER VICEADMIRAL Operette in a Vorspiel and 3 acts by F Zell and Richard Genée. Music by Carl Millöcker. Theater an der Wien, Vienna, 9 October 1886.

Henri, Comte de Villeneuve (Karl Streitmann), who is viceadmiral of the French-Spanish fleet fighting against Britain in the year of 1804, is obliged to get wed within 48 hours or lose a large inheritance. He heads for Cádiz to the home of Don Mirabolante, Count of Miraflores y Villalar Bermudez (Siegmund Stelzer), dressed, by his admiral's orders, as a simple sailor, to take his pick between the don's daughters Serafina (Antonie Hartmann) and Sybillina (Regina Stein). But Henri disdains the ordered disguise, and whilst the foolish "prewarned" Mirabolante and his daughters make a great fuss of the common sailor, Punto (Alexander Girardi), the nobleman, gets to know the family Cinderella, Gilda (Ottilie Collin). When Punto chooses Sybillina, Serafina plots with the interfering Donna Candida (Therese Schäfer) to upset things, replacing the mayor and notary with the old lady's disguised sons (Carl Lindau, Herr Horwitz) for the wedding ceremony. Then the English capture the phony viceadmiral, the Spanish come to his rescue and the plotters are aghast when the ultimately victorious Henri, revealed in his true position, chooses Gilda as his bride, leaving the sulky sisters no option but to pair off with Candida's sons.

Millöcker's score was marked by some particularly happy ensembles: the wooing trio of the two daughters and Punto ("Geh'n wir in den Garten, atmen Blüthenduft"), the introduction of Henri and Gilda in duet, a song and dance for Punto and Sybillina in the second act, and a sextet amongst the four plotters and the unwittingly unmarried bride and her father in the final act being among the evening's choice pieces.

Der Viceadmiral did not have a dazzling Viennese career. It played its 25th performance on 3 November, then appeared intermittently in the repertoire up to its 30th on 26 March 1887, but in the meanwhile, it had been taken up widely in other European cities. Berlin's production at the Friedrich-Wilhelmstädtisches Theater launched the show on a successful career in German houses, Budapest saw it first in German and subsequently (ad Emil Makai, Albert Kövessy) in Hungarian, and St Petersburg (8 December 1886) and later Sweden, Finland, Switzerland, Romania, Mexico, Yugoslavia, Italy and Spain all saw productions, but Britain (perhaps because the British were the ''enemy'' in the tale, or perhaps just continuing its general ignoring of Millöcker's works) did not.

Der Viceadmiral did, however, get an English-language production. After Duff's Opera Company had announced one in 1888, but canceled it in the light of the success of their production of *Der Seekadett,* it turned up at San Francisco's Tivoli Opera House with Edwin Stevens in the role of Mirabolante. New York's Amberg Theater introduced the show in German with a cast headed by Streitmann in his original role, Carl Adolf Friese and the Fräuleins Englander and von Varndal, and some three years later the Casino Theater followed their two months of Millöcker's *Das Sonntagskind* with a version of the earlier *The Viceadmiral* (ad John P Jackson). Jefferson de Angelis (Punto), Annie Meyers (Sybillina), Villa Knox (Gilda), Jennie Reiffarth (Candida), Harry MacDonough (Mirabolante) and Charles Bassett (Henri)—mostly from the earlier show's cast—got almost another three months out of Millöcker.

Der Viceadmiral remained around. It was given in a French adaptation by Armand Lafrique, under the title *Gilda* at Geneva in 1895 (9 March), revived in Hungary in 1903 (Budai Színkör 22 August) and played for a few performances at Vienna's Johann Strauss-Theater from 13 February 1909, but in more recent years it has been seen only in botched versions, such as those produced in Germany as *Der Herzog von Mirenza* (ad F Giblhauser, F Neupert, Fürth 4 January 1936) and *Das Heiratsnest* (A Mette-Neumann, Regensburg 25 January 1936).

The most durable portion of *Der Viceadmiral,* however, turned out to be the waltz ''Geh'n wir in den Garten,'' which was metamorphosed from a gently comic trio into a robustly romantic solo as ''Dunkelrote Rosen,'' the hit number of the rehashed, and still performed, version of Millöcker's *Gasparone.*

Germany: Friedrich-Wilhelmstädtisches Theater 29 October 1886; Hungary: (Ger) 29 November 1886, *A Viceadmiralis;* USA: Tivoli Theater, San Francisco 21 February 1889, Amberg Theater, New York (Ger) 24 October 1889, Casino Theater *The Viceadmiral* 18 June 1892

VICTOR/VICTORIA Musical in 2 acts by Blake Edwards. Lyrics by Leslie Bricusse. Music by Henry Mancini. Additional music by Frank Wildhorn. Marquis Theater, New York, 25 October 1995.

One of the relentless series of Leslie Bricusse remakes of remakes that invested the world's stages in the last decade(s) of the twentieth century, *Victor/Victoria* was a stage musical version of a tale that had—in its present form—begun its career in the Continental cinema with Reinhold Schünzel's *Viktor und Viktoria* of 1933, with Renate Müller, Hermann Thimig and Anton Wallbrook starred (mus: Fritz Doelle). This original screenplay was subsequently given a 1957 remake and was most recently used as the basis for a 1982 American musical film.

The conceit of a man (or woman) falling in love with someone disguised as the sex that they are not has been endlessly (over)used in the theatre—whether for pathos or for humor—down through the years. On the non-musical side *Twelfth Night* is amongst the favorite examples, and the 19th-century musical theatre bulges with travesty love affairs, often concocted not just for their situation comedy but also to allow the ladies of the show to get into ''masculine'' tights. And the men into frocks.

This particular tale (which favored a comely top hat and tails rather than tights) concerned a young female vocalist in Paris who, unable to get work, disguises herself—with the help of a kindly gay companion—as a dashing young man with an amazing soprano voice. Victoria becomes Victor. And no one guesses. Then a big, butch gangster finds himself falling in love with this creature and begins to wonder about himself. (This is the humorous part.) The 1982 film version included musical numbers by Bricusse and (give or take a Michael Reed) Mancini and starred Robert Preston and Julie Andrews.

Miss Andrews was the raison d'être of the film's transformation into a stage musical, allegedly after the umpteenth refusal of the Travers estate to allow what Miss Travers called the ''ghastly'' *Mary Poppins* film, in which the star had been so charming, to be made into a stage show. She was also the raison d'être for what turned out to be a good run on Broadway. If the critics loathed *Victor/Victoria* (''lyrics . . . pathetic,'' ''background music,'' ''nothing to generate any excitement,'' ''utterly joyless''), they—and the public—loved Miss Andrews, and in spite of an unfortunate time-out for illness, which had everyone concerned with the production running to their lawyers, insurers and brokers, she established the show on Broadway before crying enough. She was spelled by Liza Minnelli and succeeded by Raquel Welch for the final part of the 788-performance run. Tony Roberts played the part of her companion in charms, Michael Nouri was the gangster and Rachel York was the conventionally loud and tarty girlfriend whose company he drops for his ''boyfriend.'' A subsequent bus-and-truck tour, featuring Toni (the Captain and) Tennille, did less well.

The show was given a European presentation at Dresden (ad Stefan Huber) with Marianne Larsen playing Julie Andrews.

Germany: Staatsoperette, Dresden 3 July 1998

Recording: original cast (Philips)

DER VIELGELIEBTE Operette in 3 acts, based on an old work, by Herman Haller. Lyrics by ''Rideamus.'' Music by Eduard Künneke. Theater am Nollendorfplatz, Berlin, 17 October 1919.

One of a number of musical adaptations of the celebrated French play *Le Vicomte de Letorrières,* earlier set with considerable success as *Az eleven ördög* by Hungarian composer József Konti, this German version shifted the tale into a Germanic setting. The hero became Hans, Graf von Liebenstein (Eduard Lichtenstein), a penniless but sexy aristocrat, struggling against his horrid cousin Nicodemus for the hand of pretty Annette and the family money. In the course of a party at the home of the lofty Graf von Wildammer, Hans lives up to his reputation as ''der Vielgeliebte'' (the much-loved one), wooing and manipulating the ladies and, through them their men. After swords have been drawn, wine flowed and flirtations succeeded flirtations, Hans ends up with both money and girl. Claire Waldoff took the principal soubrette role as the tailor's daughter, Kläre, who is Hans's companion in poverty and who ends up wedding his servant, Franz.

Künneke's score featured—not surprisingly—a ''Frauen-Walzer'' and a ''Lieblich und hold ist die Nacht'' alongside a Vogelstellerlied, ''Ein kleines bisschen so'' and ''Ach, ich tat's nur für dich'' amongst its favorite moments.

Produced at the Theater am Nollendorfplatz by adapter Haller, *Der Vielgeliebte* was the first of a series of musical plays on which the director/author collaborated with lyricist ''Rideamus'' and composer Künneke. It ran for six months, to 29 April 1920, before ceding place to Bromme's *Eine Nacht im Paradies,* then to its Haller/Künneke successors *Wenn Liebe erwacht* and *Der Vetter aus Dingsda.* It was subsequently produced around Germany without attracting attention in the other main centers.

Virtually the same title (but in the feminine) was given to an Operette produced in Stralsund, and also to another piece that found success in Germany—Rudolf Köller, F Maregg and Nico Dostal's 1934 *Die Vielgeliebte* (Centraltheater, Leipzig 23 December 1934, Schillertheater, Berlin 5 March 1935). On this occasion the ''much-loved'' heroine was the Garboish film star Dena Darlo, portrayed by the composer's wife, Lillie Claus. Precisely the same title had also been given to another piece mounted just a few months earlier in Königsberg (Manfred Nussbaum, Erich Walter/Karl Winter, 1 March).

LA VIE PARISIENNE Opéra-bouffe in 4 (originally 5) acts by Henri Meilhac and Ludovic Halévy. Music by Jacques Offenbach. Palais-Royal, Paris, 31 October 1866.

In the midst of Meilhac, Halévy and Offenbach's dazzling series of successes with the earliest of their famous opéras-bouffes—*La Belle Hélène* (1864), *Barbe-bleue* (1866), *La Grande-Duchesse de Gérolstein* (1867)—the team collaborated on an equally successful non-burlesque work (which they, nevertheless, on the wings of the current fashion described as an ''opéra-bouffe''), which was produced by Plunkett at the Palais-Royal. That house and its company were not in the business of producing opérette, the members of the resident company (only slightly reinforced for the occasion) were not experienced singers, only actors, and the piece—a farcical comedy of manners which did not make extravagant vocal demands on most of its performers—was written (and rewritten, for it was reduced from five acts to four shortly after its premiere) accordingly.

Bobinet (Gil-Pérès) and Gardefeu (Priston) are a pally pair of men-about-Paris who have suffered some amour-properly bruising treatment in their affairs with the women of the demi-monde, notably the saucy Métella (Mlle Honorine). As a result, they have decided to opt for an affair with a femme du monde instead. Gardefeu poses as a tour guide and picks up the visiting Swedish Baron (Hyacinthe) and Baroness (Céline Montaland) de Gondremarck and, in his attempt to seduce the lady, takes the pair to his own home, pretending it is an hotel. The Baron is hoping for a good Parisian time, and indeed has a letter of introduction to Métella, so Gardefeu gets Bobinet to arrange a jolly party—with all his servants and their friends dressed up as cavorting aristocratic guests—to keep the husband happy whilst he chats up the Baroness. However, the Baron has no luck with Métella, who instead provides him with a masked friend as company whilst she turns her charms back on to Gardefeu. When the mask finally comes off, the Baron finds he has been charmed by his own wife. As for Bobinet and Gardefeu, they are back where they started.

Jules Brasseur had a triple role as an extravagant Brazilian (Acts I and IV) out to spend a fortune on a fling in Paris, as a bootmaker, disguised as an army major for the Act II party, and as a butler (Act III); Elvire Paurelle was the pretty maidservant, Pauline, who catches the Baron's eye at the party; and Zulma Bouffar—added to the cast at Offenbach's insistence to give some vocal values—played Gardefeu's little glove maker, Gabrielle, who partakes of all the fun and impersonations and ends up on the arm of the Brazilian as everyone prepares to live it up at the isn't-Paris-wonderful final curtain.

Offenbach provided a glitteringly light-fingered musical score to go with the wittily concocted high-jinks of the text. The Brazilian gabbled out his joy at being back in Paris all over the railway station (''Je suis brésilien''), the Baron declared gluttonously ''Je veux m'en fourrer jusque-là!,'' Gabrielle trilled into her upper-class disguise (''Je suis veuve d'un colonel'') and described sexily how ''Sa robe fait frou, frou,'' whilst Métella had a showpiece letter song—the letter in question being the ''recommendation'' of the Baron's once-lucky friend to show the hungry Swede an extremely good time (''Vous souvient-il, ma belle'')—all as part of a score that never left off laughing from beginning to end.

In spite of a lack of confidence prior to opening, *La Vie parisienne*—soon shorn of a fourth act showing what the Baroness is up to whilst her husband is partying with Bobinet—was an enormous success, occupying the Palais-Royal for an entire year whilst the show began to spread to other parts of the world. Vienna's Carltheater was first off the mark, opening its version of the five-act version (ad Karl Treumann) three months to the day after the Palais-Royal premiere. Josef Matras (Bobinet), Franz Tewele (Gardefeu), Wilhelm Knaack (Gondremarck), Karl Treumann (Brazilian/Prosper/Frick), Josefine Gallmeyer (Gabrielle), Anna Grobecker (Pauline), Marie Fontelive (Baroness) and Anna Müller (Métella) took the leading roles, and the piece became an instant favorite. It remained in the theatre's repertoire for many years, being played 126 times (to 11 August 1876) in its first decade, and was brought back in a new production in 1889, with Knaack in his original role alongside Emma Seebold (Métella) and Karl Streitmann (Brazilian), which was played for the next four seasons. A major Viennese revival was mounted at the Theater an der Wien in 1911 (28 October) with Louis Treumann (Brazilian, etc), Mizzi Günther (Gabrielle), Luise Kartousch (Pauline), Paul Guttmann (Baron), Victor Flemming (Bobinet), Ludwig Herold (Gardefeu) and Ida Russka (Métella) featured through 43 performances.

Berlin, which followed Vienna in maintaining the five-act version, followed just months behind the Austrian capital, and, although it never became the favorite that *Blaubart* or *Die schöne Helena* did, the show did well enough that it was still to be seen on the Berlin stage in 1906 (13 December), when it was produced at the Komische Oper with Karl Pfann (Gardefeu), Brose (Bobinet), Frln Hofmann (Gabrielle) and Frln von Martinowska (Métella) featured.

New York first saw the piece, in French, two years after Vienna, with Rose Bell, Marie Desclauzas and Paul Juignet heading the cast of the four-act version. *La Vie parisienne* was subsequently played by Marie Aimée and by other opéra-bouffe companies throughout the country, but the first English-language version (ad F C Burnand) was seen not in New York but in London. Burnand considerably altered, resituated and generally anglicized the script, and the result, which he even titled *La Vie Parisienne in London,* in spite of being played by such actors as Lionel Brough (Baron), Harriet Coveney (Baroness) and Lottie Venne (Polly Twinkle), was not long-lived. But the lesson of the flop was not learned. H B Farnie turned out another English adaptation which called itself simply *La Vie* (all things Parisian having been again deleted), which was mounted by Alexander Henderson with great fanfare at the Avenue Theatre in 1883 (3 October), with Brough again starred alongside Arthur Roberts, Camille D'Arville and Lillian La Rue. It again proved to be a hamfistedly anglicized and altered version and, again, it was a failure, although the production was kept doggedly on for 116 performances. This version was later sent to the country, in a production that reeked more of variety show than of opéra-bouffe, and it was also produced on Broadway—duly Americanized and its comedy even more roundly lowered—with Richard Mansfield as Baron von Wienerschnitzel (the name more or less typified the tone of the adaptation) and Fannie Rice as Gabrielle. However, even more disastrous than these was an effort by A P Herbert and A D Adams to ''improve'' Meilhac and Halévy (and Offenbach) with a feeble patchwork mounted at the Lyric, Hammersmith, in 1929 (29 April). England had to wait until 1961 (24 May) and Geoffrey Dunn's witty version for the Sadler's Wells Opera Company to hear an English *La Vie parisienne* that approximated the original French one. The most recent British production was given in the 1990s by the resuscitated D'Oyly Carte Opera Company.

Budapest first saw *Pariser Leben* in its German version, but Endre Latabár's *Párizsi élet* followed, and it won much the same success that the French and German versions had. Swedish, Spanish, Polish, Russian, Danish and Czech versions were amongst those that followed. However, it was in France that *La Vie parisienne* won and maintained its greatest popularity. The show was taken into the repertoire at the Théâtre des Variétés in 1875 (25 September), where Mlle Bouffar repeated her creation alongside such seasoned musical performers as José Dupuis (Baron), Berthelier (Brazilian, etc) and

Cooper (Gardefeu), and Paris saw regular performances thereafter. Dupuis, Mlle Bouffar and Cooper repeated their performances in 1883, with Baron now appearing as Bobinet and Mary Albert as Métella. In 1889 (18 September) at the Variétés Jeanne Granier was Gabrielle alongside Dupuis and Baron.

The Opéra-Comique received the piece in 1931, and the Jean-Louis Barrault and Madeleine Renaud company revived it at the Palais-Royal in 1958, with its principals appearing as the Brazilian (etc) and the Baroness, respectively. A revised version (ad Jean Marsan, Raymond Vogel) was produced at the Opéra-Comique in 1974, whilst, in the desert of musical productions that Paris became in the 1980s, it was nevertheless produced twice (Théâtre du Châtelet 4 November 1980, Théâtre de Paris 16 October 1985). In 1990 further performances were given at the Opéra-Comique (4 December).

The characters of the Baron de Gondremarck, Bobinet and Gardefeu were reprised by Victor de Cottens and Robert Chavray in their 1899 *Le Fiancé de Thylda* in which the fiancé of the title, longing to taste the naughty world before marriage, dreams himself into a whirl around Paris with the folk of Meilhac and Halévy's tale.

An important vertebra of the French musical theatre repertoire, the show is played regularly and still retains popularity throughout the world in varying forms—the German-language theatre, for example, still favors the five-act version and now, apparently, others are also casting eyes towards it—but in the English-language theatre *La Vie parisienne* has never wholly recovered from its initial poor adaptations and the unfavorable impression they left behind.

English and French versions of an inevitably messed-about-with version were filmed in 1935, with Max Dearly featured, and a slightly less cavalier version in 1977. A trendy, underfunny production from Lyon was videofilmed in 1991.

Austria: Carltheater *Pariser Leben* 31 January 1867; Germany: Friedrich-Wilhelmstädtisches Theater *Pariser Leben* 22 May 1867; USA: Théâtre Français (Fr) 29 March 1869, Bijou Theater (Eng) 18 April 1884; Hungary: (Ger) 25 May 1867, Budai Színkör *Párizsi élet* 1 July 1871; UK: Holborn Theatre *La Vie Parisienne in London* 30 March 1872, Avenue Theatre *La Vie* 3 October 1883

Films: Robert Siodmak 1935, Christian Jacque 1977

Recordings: complete (EMI), complete in German (Philips, Klang Forum), complete in Russian (Melodiya), revival cast 1974 (Carrère), revival cast 1958 (Paris), selections (Pathé, Philips, etc), English cast recording (HMV)

Video: CDN 1991

VIKTÓRIA Operett in a prologue and 3 acts by Emmerich Földes. Lyrics by Imre Harmath. Music by Pál Ábrahám. Király Színház, Budapest, 21 February 1930.

The first and most successful of Pál Ábrahám's three hit operetts of the early 1930s, *Viktória* relied a little less than the two later pieces—*Die Blume von Hawaii* and *Ball im Savoy*—on the composer's characteristic mixture of traditional Operette and jazzy up-to-date dance elements. This was partly due to the show's story, which was a particularly strong-backed and dramatic one, flavored with some of the easternness of the recent *Das Land des Lächelns* but using a more measured exotism in its settings and also eschewing the other piece's trendy unhappy ending.

The Hungarian hussar captain Stefan Koltay (Ferenc Kiss) and his batman Janczi (József Sziklai), who have been sentenced to death for their part in the Russian counterrevolution, bribe their way to escape and flee from Siberia to Tokyo, where they are given refuge in the American Embassy. When it turns out that the wife of Ambassador John Cunlight (Dezső Kertész) is Viktória (Juci Lábass), the woman he had loved before the war came between them, Koltay accepts Cunlight's offer to accompany them to his new posting in St Petersburg, in spite of the danger he runs in returning to Russia. Viktória tries to put her feelings behind her and remain faithful to her kindly husband, but when Cunlight discovers the truth he both protects Koltay from the Russians who surround the embassy and, ultimately, steps out of the picture so that Viktória can be reunited with the lover she had thought dead in the war. The romantic story was thoroughly filled out by the more lightly colored romances of two other couples: Viktória's brother, Count Ferry Hegedűs (Oszkár Dénes) and his little Japanese bride Lia San (Rózsi Bársony), and Janczi and Riquette (Teri Féjes), the extremely "French" maid who is actually not French at all, but Hungarian.

Both the romantic and soubret sides of the score produced a bundle of attractive and popular numbers. Cunlight and Viktória remember his first proposal to her in "Pardon, Madame," Viktória reflects on her days in Japan as epitomized by "Rote Orchideen," and first Koltay ("Reich mir zum Abschied noch einmal die Hände") and then Cunlight take their leave of the lady with a gentle "Good Night." In a brighter vein, Lia San explains her international personality—she is half-Japanese and half-French—in the sprightly "Meine Mama war aus Yokohama," and Riquette and Janczi sing of the Hungarian charms of the big, brass "Honvéd-Banda" and of compatibility ("Ja, so ein Mädel, ungarisches Mädel"). However, by far the biggest hit of the evening came in Lia San and Ferry's giggling little song-and-dance duo "Mausi, süss warst du heute Nacht," a piece that would go on to become an international favorite.

Within months of the production at the Király Színház, the wheeler-dealing impresario-director Miksa Pre-

Plate 409. **Viktória.** *Janczi (István Mester) chats up the French maid, Riquette (Klara Krasznoi) –only to find she isn't French at all, but a good Hungarian girl from Budapest! (Pecs, 1978).*

ger, who had picked up the German-language rights, found a home for *Viktoria und ihr Husar* (the gentleman got into the title in Alfred Grünwald and Fritz Löhner-Beda's German version) in Leipzig. The show caused a sensation there, and instantly the Berlin houses, which had previously turned Preger and his production away, began to court the man who owned this new and red-hot Hungarian musical. Preger was able to choose his terms as he brought his show to the Rotter brothers and the Metropoltheater, where Anny Ahlers starred as Viktória alongside Fritz Steiner (Koltay) and Louis Treumann, and Dénes paired with Lizzi Waldmüller for the famous duet. *Viktoria und ihr Husar* triumphed all over again in Berlin. It was hailed as "an undeniable success . . ." its book praised as being "as water-tight as its music," and its Metropoltheater career launched it as a classic of the German-language musical stage. Later the same year, it was mounted by Preger at the Theater an der Wien with Rita Georg (Viktória), Treumann (Cunlight) and Otto Maran (Koltay), and with Dénes and Waldmüller repeating their duet. It played a three-month season and was later reprised with Betty Fischer as Viktória, bringing its Viennese total to 121 performances.

The Hussar stayed in the title when *Viktória* made its first appearance on the English-language stage (ad Harry Graham), and Dénes gave his Ferry and "Mausi" in a third different language as he paired with the Lia San of Barbara Diu, alongside Margaret Carlisle (Viktória), Harry Welchman (Cunlight) and Roy Russell (Koltay) in Alfred Butt's production at London's Palace Theatre. The show was greeted as "a musical comedy with a melodramatic plot rather than an Operette" as it played 100 performances before going out to tour. This and the German success were, oddly, not enough to provoke a production on Broadway, although America ultimately did see *Viktória* a decade later when productions were mounted in St Louis, with Helen Gleason (Viktória),

Lansing Hatfield (Koltay) and Robert Chisholm (Cunlight), and in Los Angeles. However, Australia's J C Williamson Ltd took up both *Victoria and Her Hussar* and the ubiquitous Dénes. The Hungarian actor—actually taken to Australia to play in the later *Ball at the Savoy*—notched up his fourth major production of *Viktória* when he took over his earlier part from Cecil Kellaway for *Viktória*'s Melbourne season, teaming this time with local soubrette Sylvia Kellaway, alongside Sylvia Welling (Viktória), John Mayer (Stefan), Jack Kellaway (Janczi), Sydney Burchall (Cunlight) and Nellie Barnes (Riquette). Sydney's six-week season and seven weeks in Melbourne (Her Majesty's Theatre 20 April 1935) were not, however, the only chance Australians had to see *Viktória.* Although there was some critical grumbling over the fact that—most unoperettically—you didn't know which of the two chaps you were supposed to side with, the show proved a solid success, and it was later brought back to the Australian circuits as a vehicle for the country's musical-comedy megastar, Gladys Moncrieff (1945).

The show's French version (ad André Mauprey, René Coëns) was staged at the rather unlikely venue of the Moulin-Rouge, which had for many years devoted itself to revue before sinking into cinema. Grazia del Rio, Lilli Palmer, Colette Fleuriot, Mercier, Peraldi and Marcel Lamy featured in Maurice Catriens's production and, although that initial production was not a success, *Victoria et son hussard* was still to be seen on the French stage in the 1990s.

The Hungarian and German *Viktórias* have been maintained in the repertoire since their creation, and both are still regularly played to this day. What passed for versions of the show were also put twice on film. The first (1931), produced by Richard Oswald, adapted by Fritz Friedmann Friedrich and featuring Michael Bohnen, Friedel Schuster and Iwan Petrovich, stayed fairly close to the story, but introduced some Ábrahám dance numbers not used on the stage (''Du bist mein Glück, du bist mein Frühling!,'' ''Da sag' ich sehr gern: Igen!''); the second, some 20 years later (International-Films, 1954), had poor Viktória becoming ''ein Revuestar des Broadway'' and went ludicrously on from there. Eva Bartok was the ''Revuestar,'' Frank Felder her hussar, and that was about all—apart from the title—of the original that remained.

Germany: Stadttheater, Leipzig *Viktoria und ihr Husar* 7 July 1930; Austria: Theater an der Wien *Viktoria und ihr Husar* 23 December 1930; UK: Palace Theatre *Victoria and Her Hussar* 17 September 1931; France: Théâtre du Moulin-Rouge *Victoria et son hussard* 16 December 1933; Australia: Theatre Royal, Sydney, *Victoria and Her Hussar* 22 December 1934; USA: Municipal Opera, St Louis *Victoria and Her Hussar* 21 August 1937

Film: Richard Oswald 1931

Recordings: selections (Eurodisc, Telefunken, Fontana, etc), selection in French (TLP), selection in Swedish (Telestar), selection in Italian (Vesuvius), selection in Polish (Muza), etc

VINCENT, Ruth [BUNN, Amy Ruth] (b Runham, Great Yarmouth, 22 March 1874; d London, 8 July 1955). D'Oyly Carte soprano who went on to further successes on the musical and operatic stages.

Daughter of a Yarmouth butcher, Miss Vincent began her career at the Savoy Theatre as a small part player (1894, *Mirette*) and leading lady understudy in *The Chieftain* and *The Grand Duke* (1896, Gretchen). She fulfilled similar functions in *The Mikado* revival of 1895, *His Majesty* (1897), *The Yeomen of the Guard* revival (1897, Kate, then Elsie) and *The Grand Duchess* (1897), before being cast as Casilda in the company's 1898 revival of *The Gondoliers.* She then played Princess Laoula in *The Lucky Star* (1899), took the lead juvenile soprano role in the production of Sullivan's *The Beauty Stone* (Laine) and played Aline (*Sorcerer*) and Josephine (*HMS Pinafore*) before walking out of *The Rose of Persia* in rehearsals and retiring to marriage.

Miss Vincent returned to the stage in 1903 to play in the unfortunate musical comedy *The Medal and the Maid* (Merva Sunningdale), but she found the role she needed to make her a star the following year when George Edwardes cast her in the title role of the London production of *Véronique* (1904). Having made her name in London, she then went on to repeat her success in the same role in America. She appeared for Edwardes again in the indifferent *The Girl on the Stage* (1906, Molly Montrose) before finding her two most memorable new roles as the comic opera Princess of *Amasis* (''Little Princess, Look Up'') and as Sophia Western in Edward German's *Tom Jones* (''For Tonight,'' ''Today My Spinet''). These two parts and shows established her as the reigning queen of London comic opera, but after further London appearances as the star of *The Belle of Brittany* (1908, Babette) and the unsuccessful *A Persian Princess* (1909, Princess Yolene), she departed the light musical stage and moved into the opéra-comique, creating Vrenchen in Delius's *A Village Romeo and Juliet* (1910) at Covent Garden and appearing in such lighter roles of the operatic repertoire as Gretel, Micaëla, Antonia (*Tales of Hoffmann*), Missa's Muguette, Dorabella and Zerlina. In later years she performed in variety, retiring in 1930.

Her sister **Madge VINCENT** [Margaret BUNN] (b Great Yarmouth, 1876) was also a member of the D'Oyly Carte Company from 1899 and had small and sometimes larger roles in such musical comedies as *San Toy, The Toreador, Three Little Maids, The Medal and the Maid, Véronique, Amasis, The Gay Gordons* and *The Merry Peasant* in Britain, and larger ones in the Far East with Maurice Bandmann's company.

VINCY, Raymond (b Marseille, 23 February 1914; d Marseille, 26 May 1968). The librettist of the most important successes of the postwar French musical stage.

The Marseillais librettist and songwriter known as "Raymond Vincy" made his first incursions into the musical theatre on the jolly wave of Henri Alibert/Vincent Scotto opérettes before the Second World War, but his career in the Parisian musical theatre took off in 1945, when he was invited to dig in his bottom drawer in a hurry and supply a libretto for a six-week filler opérette for the Casino Montparnasse. *Mariage à l'essai* became *Mariage gitane,* which became *La Belle de Cadix,* which became the hit of its time, and Vincy began a 20-year collaboration with composer Francis Lopez, which, at its beginning, produced some of the best postwar French musicals, both in the field of romantic opérette à grand spectacle (*Andalousie, Méditerranée, Le Chanteur de Mexico*) and occasionally and especially in the vaudevillesque line (*Quatre Jours à Paris*).

Vincy, more than any other author, set the style of the French musical theatre of the postwar period, supplying many shapely libretti not only to the service of composer Lopez but also to such singing stars as Luis Mariano, Tino Rossi and Georges Guétary, and—more demandingly—to such comic ones as Annie Cordy and Bourvil. He crystallized the layout of the French romantic musical, with its overwhelmingly central male singing star, its often somewhat discreet soprano heroine and its supportive light comic couple, all mixed up in mildly dramatic and amorous events in colorful places, and he kept that kind of musical play fresh for a surprisingly long time before it sombered into rather repetitive formulae and less imaginative shows in later days. When Lopez and others attempted to follow his lines after his death, the genre plummeted into absolute vacuity, and the quality of Vincy's work became all the more evident.

Vincy also scripted a number of the Alibert/Scotto musicals for the screen, and remade a number of his own (*La Belle de Cadix, Andalousie, Quatre Jours à Paris,* etc) as film musicals. However, undoubtedly his most enduring credit is for the lyrics to Henri Martinet's melody for France's favorite Christmas song, the "Petit papa Noël" made famous by Rossi.

1935 **Un de la Canebière** (Scotto/w René Sarvil/Henri Alibert) Théâtre des Célestins, Lyon 14 October; Théâtre des Variétés 3 April 1936

1945 **La Belle de Cadix** (Francis Lopez/Maurice Vandair/w Marc-Cab) Casino Montparnasse 24 December

1947 **Andalousie** (Lopez/Albert Willemetz) Théâtre de la Gaîté-Lyrique 25 October

1948 **Quatre Jours à Paris** (Lopez) Théâtre Bobino 28 February

1949 **Symphonie portugaise** (aka *Romance au Portugal*) (José Padilla/w Marc-Cab) Théâtre de la Gaîté-Lyrique 9 October

1949 **Monsieur Bourgogne** (Lopez/w Jean-Jacques Vital) Théâtre Bobino 12 March

1950 **Pour Don Carlos** (Lopez/w André Mouëzy-Éon) Théâtre du Châtelet 17 December

1951 **Le Chanteur de Mexico** (Lopez/w Henri Wernert/w Félix Gandéra) Théâtre du Châtelet 15 December

1952 **La Route fleurie** (Lopez) Théâtre de l'ABC 19 December

1953 **Soleil de Paris** (Lopez/as "Henri Villard") Théâtre Bobino 7 March

1954 **À la Jamaïque** (Lopez) Théâtre de la Porte-Saint-Martin 24 January

1954 **La Toison d'or** (Lopez) Théâtre du Châtelet 18 December

1955 **Méditerranée** (Lopez) Théâtre du Châtelet 17 December

1957 **Maria-Flora** (Lopez, Henri Betti) Théâtre du Châtelet 18 December

1957 **Tête de linotte** (Lopez) Théâtre de l'ABC December

1958 **Rose de Noël** (Franz Lehár arr Miklós Rekaï, Paul Bonneau) Théâtre du Châtelet 23 December

1959 **Le Secret de Marco Polo** (Lopez) Théâtre du Châtelet 12 December

1960 **Dix millions cash!** (revised *Monsieur Bourgogne*) Théâtre de la Porte-Saint-Martin 10 December

1961 **Visa pour l'amour** (Lopez) Théâtre de la Gaîté-Lyrique December

1963 **Cristobal le Magnifique** (Lopez) Théâtre de l'Européen December

1963 **Le Temps des guitares** (Lopez/w Marc-Cab) Théâtre de l'ABC October

1967 **Le Prince de Madrid** (Lopez/Jacques Plante) Théâtre du Châtelet 4 March

1967 **Pic et pioche** (Darry Cowl/Jacques Mareuil) Théâtre des Nouveautés

VINCZE, Zsigmond (b Zombor, 1 July 1874; d Budapest, 30 June 1935).

Trained in Budapest, Vincze subsequently led a successful career as a theatre conductor and composer in his own country. In the first of these capacities he was, in turn, musical director at Debrecen, at Budapest's Király Színház (where he conducted the premiere of *Gül Baba*) and Vígszínház, at Szeged and at the metropolitan Belvárosi Színház. As a composer, he made a memorable success with his first full-scale operett, *Tilos a csók* (the forbidden kiss), which was produced at the Király Színház in 1909 and subsequently played in Germany as *Der verbotene Kuss* (ad Rudolf Schanzer, I Pasztae, Centraltheater, Dresden 24 June 1911). *Limonádé ezredes,* a musical version of a German comedy by Julius Horst and Arthur Lippschitz, confirmed this first success, scoring a big success at the Király Színház, getting an airing at the Vienna Carltheater (11 May 1913) and being regularly revived thereafter.

Vincze subsequently composed the incidental music for the Hungarian adaptation of Frances Hodgson Burnett's *Little Lord Fauntleroy* and musicalized Kéroul and

Barré's play *Le Portrait de ma tante* as *Léni néni,* but he was not heard from again until after the First World War when he added to his list of hit shows with *A cigánygrófné* (the gypsy countess), played for over 100 consecutive nights at the Király Színház in 1920.

A hamburgi menyasszony, a musical version of Gyula Pekár's 1914 *A kölcsönkért kastély,* which was produced at the Városi Színház a couple of years later, proved equally popular, giving Vincze his biggest single song success with "Szép vagy, gyönyörű vagy Magyarország," and running through its first 100 performances in two years in the repertoire before going on to revivals at the Várszínház (1922) and the Fővárosi Operettszínház (1926). Another adaptation of a Pekár work as *A gárdista* was less successful, and Vincze then moved sideways to compose a one-act opera, *Az erősebb,* produced at the Magyar Királyi Operaház (1924), to arrange the music for the posthumous Jacobi operett *Miami* and for a piece based on the music of Robert Volkmann, whilst also, at the other end of the musical scale, contributing to revue. When he returned to operett, however, it was to add yet another success to his list with *Aranyhattyú,* played more than 50 times at the Király Színház and reprised thereafter.

Amongst his later stage works, which ranged from musical plays to operett, only *Huszárfogás* proved to be as substantial as his most successful works with which, in a career of some 15 effective years, he had achieved a high hometown hit percentage without winning an international reputation. His music was heard in London's West End, however, when Eric Maschwitz and his composers posthumously borrowed one of his songs to give a little verisimilitude to their disastrous Hungarian-set *Paprika* (aka *Magyar Melody*) in 1939. It proved the show's most successful number.

1909 **Tilos a csók** (Miksa Bródy, József Pásztor) Király Színház 8 October

1912 **Limonádé ezredes** (Julius Horst, Arthur Lippschitz ad Zsolt Harsányi) Király Színház 15 September

1914 **Léni néni** (*Le Portrait de ma tante*) Hungarian version with songs Magyar Színház 2 May

1920 **A cigánygrófné** (Ferenc Martos, Ernő Kulinyi) Király Színház 13 March

1922 **A hamburgi menyasszony** (Kulinyi) Városi Színház 31 January

1923 **A gárdista** (Kulinyi) Városi Színház 15 February

1925 **Anna-bál** (Robert Volkmann arr/Kulinyi/Martos) Király Színház 30 September

1927 **Aranyhattyú** (László Szilágyi) Király Színház 15 January

1927 **Kiss és kis** (László Bús-Fekete, Kulinyi) Városi Színház 22 January

1927 **Az aranypók** (Imre Harmath) Andrássy-uti Színház 14 October

1929 **Az aranyszőrű bárány** (Ferenc Móra) Szeged 15 November

1930 **Huszárfogás** (Rezső Török, Harmath) Fővárosi Operettszínház 4 April

1930 **Jobb, mint otthon** (Adorján Stella, Harmath) Nyári Operettszínház 5 July

LES 28 JOURS DE CLAIRETTE Vaudeville-opérette in 4 acts by Hippolyte Raymond and Anthony Mars. Music by Victor Roger. Théâtre des Folies-Dramatiques, Paris, 3 May 1892.

One of the most successful examples of the endlessly popular (in France) military vaudeville, here given an operettic turn, *Les 28 Jours de Clairette* (the 28 days were the government military-service requirement) was a major hit in Paris in the 1890s and won revivals for several decades.

Clairette Vivarel (Marguerite Ugalde) is going to visit her aunt whilst her husband (Guyon fils) does his 28 days, unaware that his old flame, Bérénice (Mlle Stelly)—who has no idea that he has married—has pursued him to the barracks. Auntie is not home, so Clairette goes instead to the barracks, where she is met by her husband's helpful friend, Gibard (Vauthier), who assumes that—since the obviously loving Bérénice must be Vivarel's new wife—she is his mistress. The arrival of everyone's superior officer forces the out-of-bounds Clairette into disguise in a missing soldier's uniform. While Vivarel stews horribly, she gets into a duel with the dumb recruit Michonnet (Guy), into all sorts of complexities with sleeping arrangements, and is finally arrested for insubordination for punching a superior—her husband, whom she suspects of irregularities with Bérénice. Michonnet helps her escape, and the fourth act winds up to farcical heights until the truth comes out and marital bliss is restored. Gibard gets Bérénice as consolation.

The bulk of the numbers fell to the star, displaying the martial arts taught to her by a father who wanted a boy ("En tierce, en quarte, en quinte, en prime"), going on menacingly about infidelity ("Avec moi, c'est tout ou rien"), doing her imitation of a recruit ("Je suis Benoît, le réservisse") and topping the second-act finale with a famous call to the saddle ("Trotte, trotte, trotte, cocotte"), another sporting art at which she is adept. The star did not have the whole musical evening to herself, however. There were first-rate songs for each of the other principals, as well as a cameo for a gormless peasant girl who brought low comedy to the sleeping-quarters episode ("Eh! donc, si le coeur vous en dit"), and some lively choruses and ensemble music.

Les 28 Jours de Clairette had a splendid first run of 236 Parisian performances, with Mlle Ugalde triumphant in the big star role. It was brought back the following year for another 92 (during which Juliette Simon-Girard was seen as Clairette), produced at the somewhat larger Théâtre de la Gaîté (5 September 1895) in a suitably expanded form with lots of dancing and Mariette Sully, Paul Fugère and Lucien Noël top-billed, and at the Bouffes-Parisiens with Mily-Meyer (1900). It was thereafter repeated regularly in Paris, into the 1920s, while simultaneously making itself a home in provincial theatres. In 1927 an Italian silent film version was issued, and in 1935 Mireille was starred in a French one with sound. The show was more recently mounted at Grand Théâtre, Bordeaux in 1988 (18 March), with Mireille Laurent as Clairette.

The military vaudeville being perhaps less enjoyed in other countries than in France, *Les 28 Jours de Clairette* did not travel as it might have. However, its inviting central role won it a production in London (ad Charles Fawcett), where it was produced by Willie Edouin as a vehicle for his wife, Alice Atherton. It played just over a month. A German version was produced at Berlin's Adolf-Ernst-Theater, with Gisela Fischer, Frln Schlüter and Alexander Klein featured, but in America, where a local adaptation was mounted to feature the waning star Della Fox, *The Little Trooper* (ad Clay Greene) was given a new musical score by conductor William Furst (Casino 30 August 1894). Jeff de Angelis played Gibard, Charley Campbell was Michonnet and Paul Arthur was the heroine's husband. It did just reasonably well (68 performances), and put in the occasional reappearance around the country over the next 15 years. New Orleans got the real show, a couple of years later, played in repertoire by a French company alongside *La Navarraise* and *Guillaume Tell.*

UK: Opera Comique *Trooper Clairette* Prince of Wales Theatre, Liverpool 31 October 1892, 22 December 1892; Germany: Adolf-Ernst-Theater *Lolottes 28 Tage* 8 September 1894; USA: New Orleans (Fr) 17 January 1897

Films: Eugenio Perego *I 28 giorni de Claretta* 1927, André Hugon 1935

VIOLETTES IMPÉRIALES Opérette à grand spectacle in 2 acts by Paul Achard, René Jeanne and Henri Varna based on the screenplay by Henri Roussel. Music by Vincent Scotto. Théâtre Mogador, Paris, 31 January 1948.

The romantic period tale of the successful film(s) *Violettes impériales* (silent in 1923, talky in 1932) was adapted to the Théâtre Mogador's musical stage in the wake of the success of *La Belle de Cadix,* and composer Vincent Scotto, better known for his popular songs and, theatrically, for his cheerful music for the marseillais opérettes of the years between the wars, supplied a suitably romantic-spectacular score, dotted with conventional soubretteries, which followed at least partly in the style that the earlier show had made de rigeur.

Don Juan, Comte d'Ascaniz (Marcel Merkès), is in love with Seville flower girl Violetta (Lina Walls), but his mother intends that he shall wed Eugénie de Montijo (Raymonde Allain). Violetta is devastated when she sees the two have been betrothed, but Eugénie, discovering the truth of the situation, roundly renounces her new fiancé. She wins not only the girl's tearful thanks but an Hispanic prophecy: by losing this fiancé, she has gained a throne. Two years later, Eugénie is the wife of Napoléon and Empress of France. She brings the lovers back together, but there is a Spanish conspiracy against the Emperor in the air, and Don Juan is almost involved. Violetta impersonates the Empress and attracts a conspirator's bullet before all ends happily. The lighter moments of the evening were provided by the heroine's mother, Serafina (Marcelle Ragon), the girl's elderly suitor, Picadouros (Fernand Gilbert), a comic detective named Estampillo (Robert Allard) and a soubret couple (Pierjac, Annie Alexander) whose love affairs and interferences popped persistently in and out of the main story.

Violette's role featured a soprano ''Mélancolie,'' two numbers about violets (''Qui veut mon bouquet de violettes,'' Valse des violettes) and a song set around a Spanish shawl. The hero serenaded his beloved with ''Ce soir, mon amour'' and swore his faith in the first act in ''Il n'y a pas de Pyrénées'' and all over again, two acts later, in ''Tu peux croire à mon amour.'' The bright songs were topped by Serafina's lusty ''Quand on a de c'sang là'' and a silly spy ensemble, ''C'est un secret d'état.''

Violettes impériales proved to be what the public wanted. It ran for just over two years at the Mogador and was reprised in 1952 (28 June) with largely the same cast, and again in 1961 when Merkès teamed with Rosita, each time with further success. In 1952 the musical that had been made from a film was turned back into a film—a musical one this time. However, Scotto's score was discarded and at the behest of the star, Luis Mariano, who was cast as Don Juan opposite the Violetta of the beautiful Carmen Sévilla, a new supply of distinctly tenor songs was provided by Francis Lopez. The resultant film, distinctly popular, was thus more a fresh musical film than an adaptation of the stage show.

On the stage, *Violettes impériales* continued its life into and around the French and Belgian provinces, where this most plumbingly ''romantic'' of romantic opérettes à reasonably grand spectacle is still to be seen from time to time, and from where it emerged to pay return visits to Paris in 1981 (Théâtre de la Porte-Saint-Martin, September) and 1991 (Casino de Paris 18 January).

Recordings: selections (Véga, Odéon, CBS), film soundtrack (HMV)

LE VIOLONEUX Légende bretonne (opérette) in 1 act by Eugène Mestépès and Émile Chevalet [and Étienne Tréfeu uncredited]. Music by Jacques Offenbach. Théâtre des Bouffes-Parisiens, Paris, 31 August 1855.

Plate 410. **Violettes Impériales.** *Marcel Merkès and Rosita in one of the lush revivals of Scotto's opérette.*

Rustic Pierre (Berthelier) and Reinette (Hortense Schneider) would like to marry, but he has been called up for the army and they are too poor to pay a substitute. Reinette asks the poor fiddler Père Mathieu (Capoul/Darcier) to help them, but, when he goes off to try to find the money, the superstitious Pierre, who suspects the old man of witchcraft and his violin of harboring black magic, breaks the instrument. When Mathieu comes back, bringing the money he has persuaded from the daughter of the local overlord, he finds in the belly of the broken instrument a letter telling him that he is the rightful heir to the surrounding lands. But his masters have proved their goodness, and Mathieu prefers to remain what he has always been, a poor fiddler. The foolish, repentant Pierre promises to mend the violin.

The little seven-piece score to the tale included songs for each of its three actors. Pierre cursed his call-up in the Couplets du conscrit, Reinette proposed to the boy in a jolly duettino (''J' sais bien que ce n'est pas l'usage''), and Mathieu sang of his life in the ronde ''Le violoneux du village,'' and cried sadly and angrily over his smashed fiddle (''Je t'apportais ta délivrance'') before the evening finished on a hopeful couplet ''Donnons-leur la richesse, et gardons les bons coeurs.''

Le Violoneux was produced two months after the opening of Offenbach's first little Bouffes-Parisiens, on the second change of program. It was the occasion of Hortense Schneider's debut under his management, and her success and the piece's success were happily mingled. The little opérette became one of the most favored of the rural—as opposed to the burlesque—one-acters of Offenbach's early years, and it has been revived regularly since.

Le Violoneux was one of the earliest Offenbach works to be exported around Europe. Vienna had never seen one of the composer's works when, in 1856, Levassor, the comedian from the Paris Palais-Royal, visited the Carltheater with four colleagues and appeared as Père Mathieu to the Reinette of Mlle Teissière and the Pierre of M Fauvre in *Le Violoneux,* and in *Les Deux Aveugles.* Again, when Karl Treumann began staging his versions of Offenbach's works at the same theatre, *Die Zaubergeige*—with himself as Mathieu—was fourth on his list of productions. It was played there again as late as 1914. Treumann also played his version at his own Theater am Franz Josefs-Kai, with Anna Grobecker appearing in breeches as the lad, Antoine, to the Georgette of Anna Marek, and later on tour in Hungary. Another German-language version was played under the title *Martin der*

Geiger in Germany and in the German theatre in New York, whilst an Hungarian version (ad Kálmán Szerdehelyi) came out two seasons later, being first played at the Nemzeti Színház with Ida Huber and Ilka Markovics featured. It was played widely thereafter throughout the country, and it was revived at the Magyar Színház in 1902 (16 September) and the Dunaparti Színház in 1920 (6 March).

Offenbach's Bouffes-Parisiens company played *Le Violoneux* in London during their visit in 1857 with Guyot (Mathieu), Mesmacre (Pierre) and Mlle Mareschal (Reinette) in its three roles, but it was not until 1868 that an English version, *The Village Fiddler,* was seen, played in the touring repertoire of Louisa Pyne's Royal English Comic Operetta Company. A different version, *Breaking the Spell* (ad H B Farnie), was the first played in London, as a forepiece to the Lyceum production of *Le Petit Faust,* with Selina Dolaro and Aynsley Cook featured. It subsequently did duty on a number of occasions as a part-program or curtain raiser, being revived as late as 1904 by Arthur Bourchier at the Garrick Theatre (26 April) as a forepiece to the play *The Arm of the Law.* Australia first saw this English version as a part of a program in Fannie Simonsen's entertainment, with the prima donna teaming with Messrs Daniels and Barry O'Neill, and it was played there thereafter on several other occasions in the 1870s, 1880s and 1890s. Another English version, entitled *The Chelsea Pensioner,* was played at Melbourne's People's Theatre on 15 January 1881 with C Florence (Peter), Maud Walton (Jenny Wood) and T R Brown (Old Matthew).

Louisville, Ky, apparently saw the first American *Le Violoneux*—in French—in 1860, but New York got it both in French, as one of the earliest items played by Paul Juignet's company at Niblo's Saloon, and later in German (*Martin der Geiger*), as played by Minna von Berkel, Hubsch and Klein at the Stadttheater. The first English-language performances seem to have been those given at New Orleans by Susie Galton's company of the *The Village Fiddler* version. *Breaking the Spell* also got American performances at a later date, including one from Fred Zimmerman's company with Fanny Wentworth (Jennie), Paul Vernon (Peter Bloom) and J H Poulette (Matthew) at the Metropolitan Alcazar in 1882.

Austria: Carltheater (Fr) 17 April 1856, Carltheater *Die Zaubergeige* 30 April 1859; Germany: *Die Zaubergeige, Martin der Geiger;* Hungary: Budai Színkör *Die Zaubergeige* 8 June 1859, Nemzeti Színház *A varázshegedű* 14 March 1861; USA: Louisville, Kentucky (Fr) 1860, Niblo's Saloon (Théâtre Français) 11 February 1864, Stadttheater *Martin der Geiger* 19 May 1865, Academy of Music, New Orleans *The Village Fiddler* 13 November 1869, Metropolitan Alcazar *Breaking the Spell* 25 September 1882; UK: St James's Theatre (Fr) 27 May 1857, tour *The Village Fiddler* May 1868, Lyceum *Breaking the Spell* 2 May 1870; Australia: St George's Hall, Melbourne *Breaking the Spell* 18 November 1871

Recordings: complete (Bourg, Anna)

VIRGINIA Musical comedy in 2 acts by Herbert Clayton, Douglas Furber, R P Weston and Bert Lee. Music by Jack Waller and Joseph Tunbridge. Palace Theatre, London, 24 October 1928.

In the midst of the craze for the dance-and-laughter musical comedies of the 1920s, Jack Waller and Herbert Clayton bucked the trend and produced a picturesque-to-spectacular musical play. The buck wasn't all that great, for *Virginia* (which was both the heroine's name and the setting of Act II), although its producers loudly denied it, was clearly aimed at copying as much of *Show Boat* as was delicate. Its plot, which Waller long insisted was of fashionably American composition, was actually not comparable, relying on the eons-old tale of a rich American (John Kirby) trying to marry his daughter (Emma Haig) to an English lord (Harold French). He doesn't know that she has secretly wed the little comic (George Gee) and the lord is already paired off with the soprano (Marjorie Gordon, replacing Ursula Jeans before London). It was the incidentals that bore the similitudes, notably the tacking-in of two black characters, Lizzie (Cora le Redd) and Uncle Ned (Walter Richardson), the latter of whom led the number that was clearly intended to be *Virginia*'s "Ol' Man River," "Roll Away, Clouds." If it didn't reach that level, the song nevertheless provided a huge spectacular centerpiece to the show, with its lavishly staged representation of cotton-pickin' darkies slogging away under a spectacular display of thunder, lightning and clouds, and went on to become a hit outside it. It was even recorded by Paul Robeson.

Jolly songs and dances for Gee and Miss Haig ("I Love You More than You Love Me," "All Mine"), more soulful ones for the baritone and soprano ("Dreams of Yesterday"), some more spectacle, and a Ralph Reader chorus drilled into the kind of parade ground maneuvres popular in large-stage musicals at the time, all made *Virginia* into a perfectly good show (especially if you hadn't seen *Show Boat*), which remained for 227 performances in the West End and toured for two seasons thereafter.

The title *Virginia* had already been used several times on the musical stage. Edward Solomon and "Pot" Stephens's English musical *Virginia, or Ringing the Changes* was produced in America in 1883 (8 January), but its title had to be changed to *Virginia and Paul, or Changing the Rings* when it went home to Britain (16 July), because of the existence of a recent opera entitled *Virginia* by the Welsh composer Joseph Parry. Both pieces were well and truly forgotten by the time the Shuberts launched a *Virginia* in Wilmington in December 1922. Since this remake of the German *Der Vetter aus*

Dingsda switched to being *Caroline* before hitting Broadway, no one had to forget it to make way for Waller and Tunbridge. Virginia, the state, was the star of yet another American musical, again called *Virginia,* a further decade on. This time Laurence Stallings, Owen Davis and Arthur Schwartz were the writers, but the period romantico-dramatic piece, mounted at the Center Theater, fizzled out in 60 performances.

On the song level, Ethel Levey hymned ''Virginia'' (Ethel Levey's Virginia Song) in the 1906 musical *George Washington Jr.*

VISA POUR L'AMOUR Comédie musicale (opérette gaie) in 2 acts by Raymond Vincy taken from an original by Louis Sapin. Music by Francis Lopez. Théâtre de la Gaîté-Lyrique, Paris, December 1961.

A vehicle for a pair of Paris's top musical-comedy stars, tenor Luis Mariano and comedienne Annie Cordy, *Visa pour l'amour* presented him as an over-advanced Paris architect and her as an Italian diplomat's daughter whose social position means she cannot marry him. However, she accompanies papa to Paris for an international peace conference and uses the occasion to elope. The eloping pair end up in the American embassy and on the front pages of the papers before the happy ending. Constructed as a lively and up-to-date entertainment, it had its heroine going in for ''Le genre américaine,'' taking part with her man in ''Twist, contre twist!,'' and joining him in several other jolly numbers, whilst he reveled in the tenor ballading of such numbers as a serenade to a ''Fontaine romaine'' and ''Juliette et Roméo.'' The show proved accurately tailored to the public's taste and, no little thanks to the pulling power of its two stars, stayed at the Gaîté-Lyrique for some 600 performances.

Recording: original cast (Pathé)

VIVA NAPOLI Opérette à grand spectacle in 3 acts by René Jolivet. Lyrics by Daniel Ringold. Music by Francis Lopez. Lille, 20 December 1969; Théâtre Mogador, Paris, 4 September 1970.

Probably the best of the later, post–Raymond Vincy musical shows written by the already fading Francis Lopez, *Viva Napoli* was produced in Lille and subsequently made its way to Paris's Théâtre Mogador for a season of 100 performances before going back to the provinces and well-earned popularity.

The piece starred Rudi Hirigoyen as Gino, a Neapolitan water seller, who is the double of Napoléon Bonaparte and who stands in for the emperor in a diversionary kind of I-was-Monty's-double situation, to allow him to beat the English and head on to fame and ill-fortune. The love interest was Maria Scarlettina (Angelina Cristi), an attendant of Queen Caroline of Naples, plotting to assassinate Bonaparte but falling in love with him in his plebeian disguise, whilst the good-for-little Beppo (Jean-Louis Blèze/Henri Gènes) and his bossy Pépina (Arta Verlen) provided the usual ration of comical and song-and-dance moments.

A score that had as many reminiscences of every other Lopez opérette as the plotline had of the early work of his late librettist, Vincy, nevertheless produced some fine songs: a stirring march for Bonaparte (''Soldats, je suis content de vous''), a pretty entrance song for Maria (''Les fleurs d'Italie''), some lively duos for the comics (''Les Italiennes,'' ''La Mandoline a du bon'') and a comical scaredy-cat ''Aie! Mamma mia!'' for Beppo, as well as an interpolated waltz for the Queen of Naples, written by Madame Lopez in perfect imitation of her husband's style.

Recording: original cast (Philips)

VIVES, Amadeo (b Collbato, 18 November 1871; d Madrid, 1 November 1932).

Spanish teacher and the composer of a long list of musical pieces for the theatre, ranging from the tragic and operatic in such works as the early *Artus* and the ''comedia lirica'' *Don Lucas de Cigarral* to the ''ecloga lirica'' *Maruxa* (lib: Luis Pascual Frutos) and André Bisson's ''comedia dramatica'' *El rosario* on the one hand and to the most folky of zarzuelas on the other. Vives's most considerable success on the zarzuela stage came with the full-length *Doña Francisquita* (lib: Federico Romero, Guillermo Fernández Shaw, Teatro Apolo 17 October 1923), written in the latest stages of his career, whilst the most important of his shorter works proved to be *Bohemios* (lib: Guillermo Perrín, Miguel Palacios, Teatro de la Zarzuela 24 March 1904), a piece that he later rearranged and enlarged.

His other musical theatre credits included *La preciosilla* (1899), *La luz verde* (1899), *Frutta del tiempo* (w Mateos, 1899), *El rey de la Apujurra* (1899), *El Escalo* (1900), *Viage de instrucción* (1900), *La balada de la luz* (1900), *Polvoriela* (1900), *Eude d'uriach* (1900), *La Buenaventura* (1901), *La Gitaniela* (1901), *Doloretes* (w Quislant, 1901), *El coco* (1901), *La nube* (1902), *El tivador de palomas* (1902), *Lola Montes* (1903), *El General* (w Gerónimo Giménez, 1903), *El húsar de la guardia* (1904, w Giménez), *La gatita blanca* (1905 w Giménez), *La cancion del naufrago* (1905), *La mascera duende* (1905), *La Veladura* (1905), *La libertad* (w Giménez, 1905), *La favorita del rey* (1905), *El alma de pueblo* (1905), *La marche Real* (w Giménez, 1906), *¡El golpe de estado!* (w Giménez, 1906), *El guante amarillo* (w Giménez, 1906), *El arte de ser Benita* (w Giménez, 1906), *Sangre torera* (*La caprichiosa,* 1906), *La rabalera* (1907), *Las tre cosos de Jerez* (1907), *El Róllo de la perla* *negra* (1908), *Pepe Botella* (1908), *Episodios nacionales* (w Vicente Lléo, 1908), *La orden del dia* (1908), *El talisman prodigioso* (1908), *La mujer de Boliche* (1908), *Abreme la puerta* (1909), *La muela del rey Fanfan* (1910), *Juegos malabares* (1910), *Agua de Noria* (1910), *La casa de los duendes* (w Joaquín Serrano, 1911), *Anita la risveña* (1911), *Los viajes de Gulliver* (1911), *La canción española* (w Barrera, 1911), *La generala* (1912), *La veda del amor* (1912), *El Pretendiente* (1913), *Miss Australia* (1914), *La cena de los husares* (1915), *Los pendientes de la Trini, or No hay mal que por bien no venga* (1916), *El señor Pandolfo* (1917), *El tesoro* (1917), *Todo el mundo contra mia* (1918), *Trianerias* (1919), *Balada de carnaval* (1919), *Pepe conde* (1920), *El Duqesido* (*La corte de Versailles,* 1920), *El parque de Sevilla* (1921), *El sinverguenza* (1921 w Pablo Luna), *La Villana* (1927), *Los flamencos* (1928) and *Talismán* (1932).

Biographics: Llado, J M: *Amadeo Vives* (Orfeó Català, Montserrat, 1988), Girbal, F H: *Amadeo Vives: el musico e el hombre* (Ediciones Lira, Madrid, 1971), Burgete, S: *Amadeo Vives* (Espasa-Calpe, Madrid, 1978)

DER VOGELHÄNDLER Operette in 3 acts by Moritz West and Ludwig Held based on the comedy *Ce qui deviennent les roses* by Charles Varin and de Biéville [ie, C H Edmond Desnoyers]. Music by Carl Zeller. Theater an der Wien, Vienna, 10 January 1891.

The most outstanding and enduring product of the Viennese stage of the 1890s, Carl Zeller's warmly endearing and melodious musical play carried on the local Operettic tradition established in the best works of Strauss, Suppé and Millöcker to great effect. The libretto developed by West and Held, if not bristling with original ideas, gave fine opportunities both to the composer and to the star comedian Alexander Girardi, cast in the title role of Adam, the little bird-seller from the Rhineland Pfalz.

Jolly, boyish Adam is anxious to marry the village postmistress, Christel (Ilka Pálmay), who would be able to give up her job if he could land the secure position of Royal Menagerie Keeper. When the Prince comes to town on a hunting trip, Christel boldly goes to his private pavilion to speak to him about the job, but the circumstances arouse Adam's jealousy and, believing his sweetheart untrue, he impulsively promises himself to a pretty stranger named Marie (Ottilie Collin). In fact, the Prince is not the Prince but one fairly shabby Count Stanislaus (Rudolf del Zopp) masquerading as royalty, and Marie is not a villager but the real Prince's wife, out enjoying the Pfalz without her crown on. When she gets back to court, she is able to tax her husband with naughty behavior, until she hears the innocent truth of the encounter from Christel. The deceptions are unmasked, but Adam takes a whole act to come around to believing that if Christel gave his betrothal bouquet to Stanislaus, it was only to win him a steady royal job, so they might be able to marry.

Zeller's score was the most consistently melodious to have been heard in Vienna in years, and hit followed hit as the show progressed. Girardi, who had a marvelously sympathetic role as the sincere, bruised innocent, and only slightly silly bird-seller, entered to a vigorously tenor, country-accented ''Grüss enk Gott, alle miteinander,'' wrung hearts with his waltzed description of the serious significance of a gift of roses to a Tyrolean (''Schenkt man sich Rosen in Tirol'') in the first-act finale, had a jolly time describing the amorous antics of an ancestor (''Wie mein Ahnl zwanzig Jahr'') and gave forth with a heartfeltly homesick little ''Kom' ih iazt wieder ham.'' Christel's introductory song (''Ich bin die Christel von der Post'') proved to be the soubrette number of the century, and Princess Marie was blessed with two outstanding numbers, her fiendishly difficult, driving waltz in praise of ''Fröhlich Pfalz'' and the warm, long-lined reminiscing of ''Als geblüht der Kirschenbaum.'' There were numbers, too, for Stanislaus and his comical Uncle Weps (Sebastian Stelzer), as well as an incidental comedy routine par excellence for two crazy, harmonizing examiners, sent to test Adam for aptitude for the menagerie post (''Ich bin der Prodekan'').

Der Vogelhändler was played 50 times at the Theater an der Wien in January and February before Girardi went off for a month's vacation. When he returned on 1 April, *Der Vogelhändler* went back into the repertoire, and it passed its 100th performance on 26 November with Frln Baviera now playing Marie. The 125th was played 4 November 1892, and the show was maintained in the repertoire until 1898. It was subsequently seen for more or less performances in the basic repertoire of the other main Viennese musical houses including the Carltheater (1900), the Bürgertheater (1917–20), Johann Strauss-Theater (1910–12), the Raimundtheater (1909, 1927, 1933 revival w Josef Graf, Lizzi Holdschuh and Lya Beyer) as well as at the Theater an der Wien (1902 w Edmund Loewe, Betty Seidl, Mary Hagen, 1904, 1935 w Karl Ziegler), and more recently at the Volksoper in 1974 (21 October) as it became established throughout the German-speaking world as one of the favorite pieces from its era.

Introduced to Germany at the Friedrich-Wilhelmstädtisches Theater whilst the original Viennese production was still in its first run, *Der Vogelhändler* won as many friends there as it did in Austria, topping its 100th night in early September and continuing to such effect that Keller's survey of 1925 rated it all-time fifth amongst 19th-century Operetten in the tally of the number of performances played in Germany (behind *Die Fledermaus, Die Geisha, Der Zigeunerbaron* and *Der Bettelstudent*).

In Hungary, the Népszínház production of *A madarász* (ad Béla J Fái) proved the biggest hit the theatre had had since *Mam'zelle Nitouche* four years earlier, and it played for 106 performances with Pál Vidor as Adam and Julie Kopácsi-Karczag as Christel prior to becoming a regular part of the repertoire in theatres throughout the country.

Several German-language film versions of the Operette have also been made, amongst which an E W Emo version (scr Max Wallner) with Wolf-Albach-Retty, Maria Andergast and Lil Dagover, a version by Géza von Bolvary (scr Ernst Marischka, music composed and arranged by Franz Grothe) featuring Hans Holt (Adam), Elfriede Datzig (Christel) and Marte Harell (Countess), with Johannes Heesters and Leo Slezak in support, another, directed by Rabenalt (scr Curt Johannes Braun), including Gerhard Riedmann, Eva Probst and Ilse Werner in its cast, and a fourth, ''freely adapted'' by Géza von Cziffra to include views of the Bavarian castles of Linderhof and Nymphenburg and the town of Alsfeld, top-billing Albert Ruprecht, Conny Froboess and Maria Sebalt.

Away from central Europe *Der Vogelhändler* prospered rather less. Perhaps it was simply that the name of Zeller was less fashionable than a Strauss or a Millöcker, but only America really gave the show a full-scale contemporary production. And then Helen F Tretbar's American version had—of all things—Marie Tempest cast as a travesty Adam alongside Annie Meyers (Christel), Anna Mantel (Marie) and Fred Solomon (Weps), with Jeff de Angelis playing one of the professors. *The Tyrolean* compiled a run of 100 performances, in two editions (''extended with some new songs for the principals,'' 7 December), before the show was mounted by the usually nippier German-language Amberg Theater with Carl Schultz as Adam. The German theatres of New York repeated the show several times thereafter, but *The Tyrolean* only got a handful of repeats in provincial summer season and repertoire companies. It has, however, been seen in recent years (1993, 1994) in a new version at the ever enterprising Ohio Light Opera.

It was a long time before Britain saw *Der Vogelhändler* in anything but its original language. Its first German glimpse came when the visiting Saxe-Coburg company played the show at the Theatre Royal, Drury Lane (with Pálmay repeating her original Christel), and it was 50 years before Bernard Delfont, Tom Arnold and Emile Littler introduced an English *The Birdseller* (ad Austin Melford, Rudolf Bernauer, Harry S Pepper) at the Palace Theatre. James Hetherington was Adam, Irene Ambrus and Adele Dixon his two ladies, and Richard Tauber conducted through a brief run.

The indifference of the English- (and French-) speaking world, however, has not dented the popularity of *Der Vogelhändler* in the German and Hungarian languages, and, a century after its first run, the show remains a regularly produced part of the central European repertoire—the only Viennese ''Golden Age'' work apart from the Operetten of the ''top'' trio of Suppé, Strauss and Millöcker so to be.

Germany: Friedrich-Wilhelmstädtisches Theater 20 February 1891; Hungary: Népszínház *A madarász* 12 September 1891; USA: Casino Theater *The Tyrolean* 5 October 1891, Amberg Theater (Ger) 26 December 1892; UK: Theatre Royal, Drury Lane (Ger) 17 June 1895, Palace Theatre *The Birdseller* 29 May 1947; Belgium: Brussels 21 October 1896 and subsequently in France as L'Oiseleur

Films: Majestic Films/E W Emo 1935, Géza von Bolvary *Rosen in Tirol* 1940, Berolina/Arthur Maria Rabenalt 1953, Gloria Films 1962

Recordings: 2-record set (EMI), complete (Philips), complete in Russian (Melodiya), selections (Telefunken, Eurodisc, Philips, etc), selection in Danish (Polyphon), selection in Hungarian (Qualiton), selection in Swedish (Telestar), etc

VOKES Family

The celebrated Vokes family of Victorian musical-comedy performers were the children of costumier **Frederick M[ortimer] T[hwaites] Vokes** (d London, 4 June 1890) and his wife, Sarah Jane, and included **Fred[erick Mortimer] Vokes** (b London, 22 January 1846; d London, 3 June 1888), husband of [Martha Isa]Bella [née Moore] (d Battersea, 9 January 1913), the daughter of ''Pony'' Moore of the Moore and Burgess Minstrels, his sisters **Jessie [Catherine Biddulph]** (b London, 1849; d London, 7 August 1884), **Victoria [Rosaline Sarah]** (b London, 1853; d London, 2 December 1894) and **Rosina [Theodosia]** (b London, 1854; d Babbicombe, 27 January 1894) and **Herbert Fawdon** (d 1904), who took the name Vokes on joining their act.

The family played a broad, swift mixture of comical scenes, songs and dances made up into such pieces as the famous below-stairs ''original, musical, saltatorial, operatic, comic and tragic extravaganza'' *The Belles of the Kitchen* (Theatre Royal, Drury Lane 5 August 1869), *Fun in a Fog* (Theatre Royal, Drury Lane 7 October 1872), *Phoebus's Fix,* E L Blanchard's *Bunch of Berries* (Adelphi Theatre 8 May 1875), *The Wrong Man in the Right Place,* and the later and celebrated *In Camp* (Academy of Music, Buffalo 12 June 1883, Prince of Wales Theatre, Liverpool 24 September 1883), a tale of amateur dramatics and soldiery, which won them a vast following all around the English-speaking theatre world and which were the vaudeville-style forerunners of the more substantial musical comedies of later years. They also performed their own versions of such classics as Buckstone's remade *La Fille du régiment* (in which Victoria took the part of Josephine, with Donizetti's music and Fred as Pumpernickel), or the remade-to-measure drama *A Rough Diamond.* The Vokes family starred for many years in the pantomimes at Drury Lane, and they made 10 visits to the United States, where their popularity was as high as it was at home.

On the stage as a team for nearly a quarter of a century from 1861, when (after separate beginnings as child performers) they played together at Rotherhithe St Helena Gardens and at Edinburgh's Operetta House, the Vokes Family retired from the stage after the marriage of Rosina to Cecil Clay, the brother of composer Frederic. All four Vokeses died in their prime, and, after their deaths, *In Camp* (credited somewhat tactically to Victoria as author) was expanded into a full-length ''legitimate'' musical called *On the March* (Prince of Wales Theatre 22 June 1896), which played 77 performances in London.

VOLGA Opérette à grand spectacle in 2 acts by Claude Dufresne. Lyrics by Jacques Plante. Music by Francis Lopez. Additional music by Anja Lopez. Théâtre du Châtelet, Paris, 26 November 1976.

Volga was 18 scenes of Châtelet Russian spectacle arranged around a story about Colonel Boris Gorsky (José Todaro), who goes off to crush some anti-Tsarist rebels but falls in love with the pretty innkeeper (Maria Candido), who is the head of the rebellion. The jealous local Governor (Claude Calès) gets the pair condemned to death, but they escape through the best bits of the scenery and, thanks to a friendly Tsarina (Lena Oliviera), all ends happily.

The show's musical axis was heavily towards the principal tenor (six solo numbers) singing to his ''Anja,'' to ''Ma troïka,'' ''Volga'' and ''Ma Russie,'' all in similarly throbbing tones, whilst the soprano gave ''Les Cloches de St Petersbourg'' and ''J'ai pleuré'' in what had become traditional Lopez style. There was also the regular baritone number, but there was one distinctly pleasant variation to the usual Lopezzery in the inclusion of a quintet (''La loi du destin'').

The show ran for 18 months at the Châtelet and was subsequently seen in the provinces.

Recordings: original cast (CBS), replacement cast (Ibach)

LES VOLTIGEURS DE LA 32ÈME Opéra-comique in 3 acts by Georges Duval and Edmond Gondinet. Music by Robert Planquette. Théâtre de la Renaissance, Paris, 7 January 1880.

Les Voltigeurs de la 32ème had a difficult start to life, and a long road to follow before it marched ultimately to a large and long success. After the by-and-large failure of Lecocq's *La Jolie Persane* at the Théâtre de la Renaissance, Victor Koning decided that a military opérette was the thing that would catch the public, so he dug out a script that had been previously submitted by the young Georges Duval, which he handed to the experienced Edmond Gondinet for rubbing-up, and to Planquette, a hot property after *Les Cloches de Corneville,* for its music. He found himself legally pursued by Cantin of the Folies-Dramatiques, who claimed to have first option on both the piece and the composer, but he won out and got *Les Voltigeurs de la 32ème* to the stage, only to find that in spite of largely favorable reactions it was unable to hold up for more than 73 performances.

When Napoléon Bonaparte decides to set up an artificial new class by ordering the mixture by marriage of the old aristocracy and his parvenu class, the Marquis des Flavignolles (Ismaël) decides to trick him. He has the goatherd Nicolette (Jeanne Granier) pose as his daughter and plans to marry her off to the bourgeois Lieutenant Richard (Marchetti). However, his real daughter Béatrix (Marie Gélabert) turns up, decides her father's choice is, bourgeois or not, indeed to her taste, and Nicolette is able to go back to her country César (Lary). Marie Desclauzas played Dorothée, the oversized and comical village May queen, and the young Mily-Meyer appeared in travesty as little sergeant Flambart.

The score (to the distaste of those who sneered at Suppé and Strauss for basing their scores on dance-rhythms) was ''a superabundance of waltzes and polkas'' in a style ''carefully elaborated, light and gay'' from which it was noticed that ''the morceaux most applauded were not those which the composer had most finished, but the simpler ones such as he formerly gave in *Les Cloches.*'' They were topped by the airs ''Ah, la rosière joyeuse et fière'' and ''Aux temps des muguets'' and by the piece's march finale.

Following its disappointing Paris run, the show was seen in Budapest (ad Lajos Evva, Ferenc Nemes) as ''the goatherd marchioness,'' the Renaissance company, which had played a handful of further performances during 1881 (Planquette added a new song for Granier, ''La Chanson des Biquots,'' for the occasion), gave some performances in their summer season at London's Gaiety Theatre, and in America the ever-enterprising Tivoli Theater in San Francisco produced an English version, but it then faded away. It was, however, not gone. Six years later, following the London success of *Rip van Winkle,* librettist H B Farnie combined with Planquette to do a remake of *Les Voltigeurs.* The resultant (English) piece, *The Old Guard,* which contained a certain amount of fresh Planquette music, was constructed to English tastes, featuring a wholly incidental, but large (and expandable) principal comic role—Polydore Poupart—in which Arthur Roberts, recently so successful in a similar part in Farnie's *Indiana,* could woo the public.

Otherwise the bones of much of the tale were the same, with J J Dallas as the Marquis d'Artémac, Marion

Edgecumbe playing the phony daughter, now called Fraisette, Joseph Tapley the beloved Gaston de la Rochenoir, Wilford Morgan the marriageable Marcel, Fanny Wentworth as Murielle (ex- Béatrix), and with Phyllis Broughton largely featured in what seemed to be a reductio ad feminam of Mily-Meyer's part as a vivandière named Follow-the-Drum. Roberts sang of being "The Dashing Militaire" and joined with Dallas in a topical duet about "When We Were Young," whilst Gaston's "The Lover's Hour," Marcel's "Only a Moment Love Was Mine," and Fraisette's "Fare Thee Well!" proved the pick of the romantic numbers.

Things went quite the reverse to what they had in Paris. *The Old Guard* got mediocre reviews for everything except its comic performances, and it ran for an outstanding 300 performances plus a quick revival (1 October 1888) at the Avenue Theatre, whilst Farnie and Planquette went promptly to work on a similar adaptation of the composer's *Surcouf.* Auguste van Biene and Horace Lingard took up the touring rights, and, with Lingard taking Roberts's role, the show began what was to become a very long life in the British provinces and colonies. Australia launched its production four years later, with William Elton playing Poupart alongside Ida Osborne (Fraisette), Flora Graupner (Follow-the-Drum) and Jack Leumane (Gaston), and the show was revived there as late as 1915, when Ethel Cadman appeared as Fraisette. In Britain, similarly, a good 20 years on, *The Old Guard* was still to be seen trouping determinedly around the provinces, year in, year out, long after France had forgotten all about *Les Voltigeurs de la 32ème.*

Hungary: Népszínház *A kecskepásztor markiné* 28 May 1880; UK: Gaiety Theatre (Fr) 23 July 1881, Avenue Theatre *The Old Guard* 26 October 1887; USA: Tivoli Opera House, San Francisco *The Voltigeurs* 19 June 1882; Australia: Princess Theatre, Melbourne *The Old Guard* 11 April 1891

LE VOYAGE DANS LA LUNE Opéra-féerie in 4 acts by Eugène Leterrier, Albert Vanloo and Arnold Mortier. Music by Jacques Offenbach. Théâtre de la Gaîté, Paris, 26 October 1875.

Three years and eight major shows after the splenditious production of *Le Roi Carotte,* Offenbach returned to the world of the grand opéra-bouffe féerie with the spectacular *Le Voyage dans la lune.* Allegedly planned by its librettists after a revue at the Théâtre du Château d'Eau had featured the moon as a venue, but nevertheless helping itself to an idea or two from the works of Jules Verne and several more from those of the brothers Cogniard, the show—for all that the novelist was said to be cross about it—really did have much more of the revusical and the fantastical than the science fiction to it.

Prince Caprice (Zulma Bouffar), bored with earthly things, decides he wants to go to the moon. The court sage, Microscope (Grivot), makes a cannon that shoots the prince, his father, King V'lan (Christian), and himself to the lunar surface. There they encounter their equivalent in the way of royal families, King Cosmos (Tissier), Queen Popotte (Adèle Cuinet) and Princess Fantasia (Mlle Marcus). On the moon, everything is the reverse of that which it is on earth, and, amongst other reversals, love is considered a malady. That malady is spread by some apples the travelers have brought with them, and love and its physical expressions wreak havoc on the moon, ultimately leading the cosmonaughty earth folk to be entombed in a lunar volcano from which they only escape thanks to an eruption. Finally, when all the spectacular incidents and scenes are done, the union of earth and moon occurs—Caprice weds Fantasia.

As in *Le Roi Carotte,* Offenbach's score played second fiddle to the glories of the stage-machinist's and painter's art, and to the ballets—above all the evening's most admired moment, a Snow Ballet with a corps of little snowflakes and a featured quartet of petit-sujet swallows. However, there were still many attractive numbers for the Gaîté stars, headed by Mlle Bouffar, who cried melodiously for the moon ("Papa, je veux la lune!") and ran through both waltz and madrigal moments, whilst her father introduced himself in comical style ("V'lan, v'lan, je suis V'lan") and the Princess ran from coloratura to boléro, alongside a staunch scoreful of choruses and ensembles.

Although Offenbach had originally refused to stage *Le Voyage dans la lune* at his Théâtre de la Gaîté, or even to compose the score for what he regarded as too costly a piece to succeed, the show was mounted at that very theatre by musical director Albert Vizentini, who had taken over the management of the house from the musician. It was a distinct success, and played for 185 performances. During the run it was regularly spruced up and, in its later days, even benefited from an appearance by café-concert queen Thérésa, for whom Offenbach composed some additional music. When it closed, the Gaîté closed too, reopening in the autumn as the Théâtre Lyrique. Vizentini was still in charge, but the fare was somewhat loftier. In the meanwhile, *Le Voyage dans la lune* began its trips abroad, being quickly seen in both London and Vienna.

The big Alhambra Theatre, which had produced Britain's *Le Roi Carotte,* mounted the new spectacle in London (ad H S Leigh) with all its usual lavishness. Rose Bell (Caprice), Kate Munroe (Fantasy), J D Stoyle (King Clashbang), Emma Chambers (Popette), Edmund Rosenthal (Microscope) and Harry Paulton (Cosmos) headed the company, the snow ballet danced by Mlle Pitteri and some imported Parisian swallows again turned out to be the highlight of the night, and the piece again proved elastic enough to allow the insertion of the odd music-hall act, such as the Girards acrobatic speciality (mus: Georges Jacobi), into the final act. *Le Voyage dans la lune* was ideal Alhambra fare, and it ran there for an initial five and a half months, being brought back after the failure of the following piece (11 November) to play five additional weeks until the London premiere of *Die Fledermaus* was ready.

In Vienna, Maximilian Steiner directed his own production (ad Julius Hopp) of 12 scenes of phantastisch-burlesk Ausstattungs-Operette "with the original scenery from the Gaïté," at the Theater an der Wien with Bertha Steinher (Caprice), Albertina Stauber (Fantasia), Carl Adolf Friese (Vlan), Herr Grün (Cosmos), Alexander Girardi (Microscope) and Frln Zimmermann leading the two grand ballets. It proved a regular success through 67 performances and prompted Steiner to try (less happily) *Le Roi Carotte* later in the year. Yet Budapest, which had apparently less taste for the spectacular, passed on *Le Voyage dans la lune* as it had done on *Le Roi Carotte,* and America, which had given a good hearing to *Le Roi Carotte,* could just not be persuaded to be interested in *A Trip to the Moon.* The Kiralfys gave the piece (Leigh's version ad J J Wallace) their inevitably glamorous to over-the-top production (also their inevitable under-the-top casting), and the show still closed after less than a fortnight of Broadway performances. They nevertheless took the whole huge production to San Francisco's California Theater and then on the road the following season (Haverly's, Chicago 1 April 1878), with Alice Harrison (Caprice), Gracie Plaisted (Fantasy) and W A Mestayer (Kosmos) and a ballet of 200 billed large (and the librettists names nowhere). The local critic commented that, among the insect and snow dances, the interpolated trained dogs and the Kiralfy's own routines it was a bit hard to find any trace of Verne or Offenbach, but voted it "a capital extravaganza."

Le Voyage dans la lune was well enough liked to come around again in its most favored venues. London saw *A Trip to the Moon* again in 1883 (26 March), when F C Leader produced a revival at Her Majesty's Theatre with a cast headed by Anna Barnadelli (Caprice), Annie Albu (Fantasy) and Lionel Rignold (Cosmos). Consuelo de la Bruyère headed the snow ballet, in which a spot was made for the famous aerialist Mlle Aenea as "the flying dove" amongst the swallows. A Paris revival was mounted 21 March 1892 at the Théâtre de la Porte-Saint-Martin with Dailly (Vlan), Jeanne Granier (Caprice) and Germaine Gallois (Fantasia) in the leading roles. However, the heavy and costly scenic content of the show militated against it thereafter until the return, in the 1970s, of the fashion for heavily spectacular theatre. A version of the show (ad Jerome Savary) was mounted in 1979 in Berlin, repeated at Geneva's Grand Théâtre in 1985 (12 December) with Joseph Evans as a male Caprice, Michel Trempont as Vlan and Marie McLaughlin as Fantasia, and was subsequently seen in Belgium (7 February 1986) and at the Opéra-Théâtre de Massy (31 December 1993).

UK: Alhambra Theatre 15 April 1876; Austria: Theater an der Wien *Die Reise in den Mond* 16 April 1876; Germany: Viktoria-Theater *Die Reise in den Mond* 18 March 1876; USA: Booth's Theater 14 March 1877

LE VOYAGE DE MM DUNANAN PÈRE ET FILS

Opéra-bouffe in 2 acts by Paul Siraudin and Jules Moinaux. Music by Jacques Offenbach. Théâtre des Bouffes-Parisiens, Paris, 23 March 1862.

Le Voyage de MM Dunanan père et fils, composed and produced by Offenbach during the period of his triumph with his series of full-length works in the genuinely burlesque opéra-bouffe mold, was something of an oddity. It was a piece set in the present, with up-to-date protagonists in modern dress, farcical in a vaudevillesque manner in its action and, in spite of taking in some parodies in its musical part and some extravagances in its tale, neither a burlesque proper nor—in the manner of so many of the composer's shorter pieces—a rural romance. In something like the vein of *La Vie parisienne,* produced four years later, it was a full-scale modern musical comedy in the true sense of those words, individually and together, and as such something of a novelty.

The parallel with *La Vie parisienne,* in fact, went further, for the story of the Messrs Dunanan—father Adolphe (Desiré) and son Patrocle (Léonce)—who are whipped away from their provincial home in Macon to visit the romantic fleshpots of Venice, took something of the same turn as the adventurous awaydays of the Baron and Baroness Gondremarck in the later piece. The wayfaring Tympanon (Pradeau), Astrakan (Duvernoy) and Lespingot (Potel) fool father and son into thinking they have made the trip to Italy, although they have actually got no further than Paris. There, with the assistance of their disguised friends—a group of cleaning ladies—the jolly fellows present the Dunanans, in a virtual revue or variety show, with a Venice equipped with barcarolles, romances, masks and murderers, not to mention a children's ballet, much scenery and a massed cast of extras, all of which is as phony but as temporarily effective as Raoul de Gardefeu's house-turned-hotel, and all without leaving France. The excuse for the whole charade is that the fellows want to stop Dunanan junior being engaged to the lady that one of them loves, and they succeed in their aim when not only does Patrocle pair off with Paméla (Mme Geraldine), the most soprano of the cleaning ladies, but papa recognizes in Léocadie (Mlle Beaudoin), who has been deputized to impersonate the intended bride, an old and distinctly recyclable flame of his own.

The phony Venice gave Offenbach, just 10 months after the premiere of *Le Pont des soupirs,* the occasion for a goodly amount of fake Venetian music. The burlesque barcarolle ''O Venezia la bella'' with its refrain of ''Youp, la Catarina!'' (to be used with equal effect many years later in Hugo Felix's *Madame Sherry*), a four-part Sérénade des Guitares, a valse-mazurka ''La Perle de l'Adriatique,'' boasting a cadenza full of high Cs for Paméla, and a quartet in which Lespingot and Tympanon pretend to be assassins (''J'escoffie'') were amongst the jolly moments of the pseudo-Italian scenes, whilst Tympanon also had a stand-up number about being a one-man band and Dunanan and his Léocadie joined in a pleasingly sincere little duo (''C'était en l'an de grâce 1839''), safely ''home'' after all the hurly-burly was done.

Offenbach introduced *Le Voyage de MM Dunanan* at the Bouffes-Parisiens, where it passed its time happily, but without causing too much stir, and, three months later, during the summer break, the Bouffes company took the piece to Vienna for a season at the Theater am Franz-Josefs-Kai. Manager Karl Treumann promptly produced a German version, *Herr von Zuckerl, Vater und Sohn,* the following year. It had little chance to prosper, as five weeks later the Kaitheater burned. By this time, however, the first Hungarian production, in a version by Pál Tarnay, and starring Károly Simonyi as father Dunanan alongside József Szép, Béla Szilágyi, József Vincze, Emma Harmath and Sarolta Krecsányi, had already been mounted at the Budai Népszínház. And this time, the bull's-eye was hit. The piece was an enormous success. It ran for over 100 nights, a vast run for the time and place and one that broke all records in Budapest, leading to a whole series of further stagings for the piece in its Hungarian version. It was played at the Budai Színkör in German (*Zuckerl und Sohn* 4 June 1865) and in Hungarian (14 July 1867), and it was the first Operette to be produced at Budapest's new center of musical theatre, the Népszínház, on 5 November 1875. An Hungarian company even took their production to Vienna in 1866. Another German-language version, entitled *Venedig in Paris* (ad Georg Ernst), was produced first in Germany and played subsequently at the Theater an der Wien in 1903.

Although it was long popular in central Europe, where it was periodically revived over a long period, the show had a more uneventful reception at home, and it did not officially reach English-speaking territories. However, in 1874 F C Burnand turned out a piece called *The Great Metropolis, or The Wonderful Adventures of Daddy Daddles and His Son in Their Journeying from Stoke-in-the-Mud to Venice (via London)* at the Gaiety Theatre (6 April), decorated with a pasticcio score arranged by Meyer Lutz. George Honey played Mr Daddles, J G Taylor was his son Peregrine, Charles Lyall (Robert Rumble), Nellie Farren (James Gilter) and Edward Perrini (Frank Flittermore) were the three tricksters, and Elizabeth Leigh (Mme Mantilla) and Connie Loseby (Flora Sorbetto) headed the ladies. Its origins were not difficult to trace, although no one seems to have done so at the time and, certainly, no one gave MM Siraudin and Moinaux any credit. Interestingly enough, producer John Hollingshead in his memoirs claimed this ''burlesque in plain clothes'' as ''a pioneer'' almost two decades before *In Town* and its ilk set off the fashion for modern-dress musicals in the London and international theatre. He may have had a point. *Le Voyage de MM Dunanan* certainly belongs to the vaudeville and musical-comedy tradition, rather than to that of the burlesque or the romantic opéra-comique, and as such it would, in 1862, have been able fairly to be accounted, at least, one of the earliest genuine ''musicals'' of the modern era of musical theatre.

Austria: Theater am Franz-Josefs-Kai (Fr) 25 June 1862, *Herr von Zuckerl, Vater und Sohn* 21 March 1863, Theater an der Wien *Venedig in Paris* 5 September 1903; Hungary: Budai Népszínház *Dunanan apó és fia utazása* 17 January 1863; Germany: *Herr von Zuckerl und Sohn* (aka *Zuckerl Vater und Sohn*)

LE VOYAGE DE SUZETTE Pièce à grande spectacle in 3 acts by Henri Chivot and Alfred Duru. Music by Léon Vasseur. Théâtre de la Gaîté, Paris, 20 January 1890.

A piece of musical-theatre spectacle, signed nevertheless by a pair of top-rank authors in Chivot and Duru, *Le Voyage de Suzette* passed through 11 different tableaux during the course of its evening of visual display: from a Persian palace to a Barcelona hovel, to a Spanish seaport, to Athens, a brigand camp, a mountain fiesta, the harem of Omar Pacha and an English pantomime-style display called ''the butcher's shop,'' ending its round of scenic art and variety acts in the ''grand cirque américain.''

The linking story for the scenery and the acts had Suzette (Juliette Simon-Girard), the daughter of the poor Verduron (Mesmaecker), traveling to wed André (Alexandre), son of her father's now vastly rich foster brother, Blanchard (Fournier), via many perils, much spectacle and plenty of musical numbers—some of which were written by Vasseur, some selected from amongst the works of other composers. Marie Gélabert was Suzette's maid and Simon-Max (Pinsonnet) André's servant, whilst one Don Giraflor (Bellot) and the amorous slave Cora (Mlle Burty) represented the opposition to the marriage. The scenery, songs and a whole series of costumed parades (including a Barnum circus parade) did duty for a splendid run of 227 performances on the big Gaîté stage, and the piece followed in the successful line of French spectacular entertainments exported to other areas of the world.

Vienna's Carltheater saw a 10-scene *Susette, oder zweihundert Millionen* (ad Zell, Richard Genée) reproduced from the Paris staging by régisseur Epstein with Marie Schwarz (Susette, with an interpolated ''Blaue Auge'' by A Krakauer), Karl Blasel (Pinsonnet) and Wilhelm Knaack (Verduron) and ballerina Rosa Hrozsy ''from the Royal Opera of Budapest'' featured for a splendid 61 performances in 1890. New York's version (ad C A Byrne, Louis Harrison), produced at the American Theatre three years later 23 December 1893, had voluptuous Sadie Martinot as Suzette but none of Vasseur's music. Jesse Williams and Charles Puerner were credited for the music to which the large and long ballets that replaced the songs were danced to for the 31 nights the piece lasted. The show was, however, later seen in more pristine condition in the repertoire of a touring French opera company. Presumably without the circus.

Austria: Carltheater *Zweihundert Millionen (Susette)* 6 September 1890; USA: California Theater, San Francisco (Fr) March 1897

Plate 411. **Le Voyage de Suzette**

LE VOYAGE EN CHINE Opéra-comique in 3 acts by Eugène Labiche and Alfred Delacour. Music by François Bazin. Opéra-Comique, Paris, 9 December 1865.

Like the heroes of *Le Voyage de MM Dunanan* on their trip to Venice, and like the folk of *A Trip to Chinatown* and other later shows, the characters of *Le Voyage en Chine* didn't actually go there. Marie Pompéry (Marie Cico) has secretly married the marine officer Henri de Kernoisan (Montaubry), and now the young people have to persuade her father (Couderc) to give his consent to their union, without telling him of the fait accompli. Unfortunately, Henri and Pompéry are involved on the opposite sides of a carriage accident, and the pig-headed Pompéry takes an unmoving stance against the young man, proposing instead to wed Marie to the stuttering Alidor de Rosenville (Sainte-Foy). Things come to a head when Henri follows the Pompéry family to their vacation hotel in Cherbourg. Pistols and épées are drawn, and Alidor tries to trick Henri away by a false telegram ordering him to sail for China. It is another trick, however, that works—and it is Henri who is behind it. When the Pompérys go to pass an instructive morning looking over a ship in Cherbourg harbor, they suddenly find themselves at sea, under Henri's captaincy, headed for China! Faced with such a horrible abduction, Pompéry ultimately gives in on all points, but only after he has staged an abortive mutiny and his son-in-law has condemned him to hang on the high seas. Then the old man finds that the ship has never left Cherbourg. Ponchard as Maurice Frével courted the younger Pompéry sister, Berthe (Mlle Gontier), whilst Prilleux appeared as a ubiquitous comical notary, Bonneteau, and Mme Révilly completed the principal cast as mother Pompéry.

The libretto, by confirmed comic playwrights Labiche and Delacour, was illustrated with a series of ballads (several presented as drawing-room numbers) and ensembles composed by the successful composer of *Maître Pathelin,* and the show, like *MM Dunanan* a veritable musical comedy, was produced with very considerable success at the Opéra-Comique. Thereafter, it was quickly mounted throughout Europe. The Theater an der Wien staged a German version (ad J C Grünbaum) with Albin Swoboda (Henri), Matthias Rott (Pompéry), Jani Szíka (Maurice), Friederike Fischer (Marie), Wilhelm Knaack (Alidor) and Carl Adolf Friese (Bonneteau) featured, which was played 21 times in half a dozen years in the repertoire, Berlin's Wallner-Theater followed suit, and in 1870 an Hungarian version (ad Endre Latabár) appeared at Budapest's Budai Színkör.

The ''first complete adaptation in English'' was billed at London's newly upmarketed Garrick Theatre in Whitechapel in June 1879 (ad William Yardley) and again in November of the same year, but America seems to have seen the piece only in the French original, as played by Quercy (Henri), Debeer (Alidor) and Mlle Minelli (Marie) at the Park Theater in 1875. Versions of *Le Voyage en Chine* were played in Scandinavia, variously in Swedish and Danish, in the Netherlands and in South America, but its chief and enduring popularity was in

France, where it continued to be played for many decades after its original production.

Le Voyage en Chine proved the inspiration, both stylistically and in its story, for a number of later shows, and the London paste-up piece *The Black Prince* even lifted a large chunk of Labiche and Delacour's tale for its libretto.

Austria: Theater an der Wien 12 May 1866; Germany: Wallner-Theater 2 July 1867; Hungary: Budai Színkör *Utazás Kinába* 12 May 1870; UK: Royalty Theatre (Fr) 13 February 1873, Garrick Theatre *A Cruise to China* 5 June 1879; USA: Park Theater (Fr) 11 January 1875

Recording: complete (Gaîté-Lyrique)

WALDBERG, Heinrich von (Baron) (b Jassy, ?2 March 1860; d Theresienstadt, ?1942). The co-author of one major Viennese hit and several other musical-theatre successes in an appreciable career as a librettist.

In the late 1880s and 1890s the Baron von Waldberg collaborated on a number of plays, adaptations and libretti for German and Austrian theatres, mostly in tandem with the highly successful Victor Léon. After beginning with a Schwank, *Die Rheintochter,* for Teplitz (1886), they found a modest success with the vaudeville *Die Chansonette,* played after its Dresden premiere in both Vienna (Theater an der Wien 16 February 1895) and Berlin (Theater Unter den Linden 22 August 1895), then a major one with an adaptation of the famous farce *Les Dominos roses* as a libretto for the Operette *Der Opernball.*

Waldberg subsequently adapted a number of other French plays as libretti without the same success. He teamed with Léon to remake *Niniche* as *Ihre Excellenz* and the vaudeville *La Dot de Brigitte* as *Frau Lieutnant,* and later with A M Willner to transform *Le Mari de la débutante* into *Die Debütantin,* first produced in Munich and then at Vienna's Carltheater (4 October 1901, 10 performances), as well as making over the English farce *The Magistrate* as *Das Baby* (17 performances). It was another adaptation, however, this time from the American, which brought him his other principal success. *Nimm mich mit!,* a lighthearted adaptation of Colonel Savage's famous *His Official Wife,* produced at the Theater an der Wien at the end of the First World War, had a fine Viennese run. Edmund Eysler's *Die schöne Mama,* first produced in Italy and later for 111 performances in Vienna, gave him further success. The Baron von Waldberg's career in the theatre had been some years ended when he joined the long list of musical-theatre authors declared missing and presumed dead during the Second World War.

1890 **Der bleiche Gast** (Alfred Zamara, Josef Hellmesberger/w Victor Léon) Carl-Schultze Theater, Hamburg 6 September

1890 **Erminy** (*Erminie*) German version w Léon (Carltheater)

1892 **Der Bajazzo** (Alfons Czibulka/w Léon) Theater an der Wien 7 December

1894 **Die Chansonette** (Rudolf Dellinger/w Léon) Residenztheater, Dresden 16 September; Theater Unter den Linden, Berlin 22 August 1895

1895 **Die Doppelhochzeit** (Hellmesberger/w Léon) Theater in der Josefstadt 21 September

1896 **Toledad** (*L'Enlèvement de la Toledad*) German version w Léon (Theater in der Josefstadt)

1898 **Der Opernball** (Richard Heuberger/w Léon) Theater an der Wien 5 January

1899 **Ihre Excellenz** (aka *Die kleine Excellenz*) (Heuberger/w Léon) Centraltheater, Berlin 17 January

1899 **Die Strohwitwe** (Albert Kauders/w Léon) Theater an der Wien 4 November

1900 **Frau Lieutnant** (*La Dot de Brigitte*) German version w Léon (Theater in der Josefstadt)

1901 **Die Debütantin** (Zamara/w A M Willner) Theater am Gärtnerplatz, Munich 17 January; Theater des Westens 20 September

1902 **Das Baby** (Heuberger/w Willner) Carltheater 3 October

1908 **Ein Mädchen für alles** (Heinrich Reinhardt/w Willner) Theater am Gärtnerplatz, Munich 8 February

1908 **Die Frauenjäger** (Zamara/w Hans Liebstockl) Theater an der Wien 16 October

1911 **Die vertauschte Braut** (Zamara/w Felix Ujhély) Theater am Gärtnerplatz, Munich 20 January

1913 **Dorette** (Bruno Hartl/Julius Wilhelm) Theater am Gärtnerplatz, Munich 7 February

1919 **Nimm mich mit!** (Hermann Dostal/w Willner) Theater an der Wien 1 May

1921 **Die schöne Mama** (*La bella mammina*) (Edmund Eysler/w Bruno Hardt-Warden) Teatro Nazionale, Rome 9 April; Wiener Bürgertheater 17 September

1922 **Fräulein Frau** (Max Niederberger/w Hardt-Warden) Wiener Bürgertheater 23 December

1926 **Das Amorettenhaus** (Leo Ascher/w Hardt-Warden, Max Steiner-Kaiser) Carl-Schultze Theater, Hamburg January

WALDMEISTER Operette in 3 acts by Gustav Davis. Music by Johann Strauss. Theater an der Wien, Vienna, 4 December 1895.

The least unsuccessful of Johann Strauss's later Operetten, *Waldmeister* was composed to a feather-light libretto that might have been written half a century earlier, had it not been that it was actually set in the present, albeit in a little provincial town in Saxony. The plot, such as it was, hinged on the favorite old magic-potion trick. This one was a concoction made with something called ''Waldmeister'' (apparently the herb woodruff), which was administered to the guests of the lofty Christof Heffele (Herr Kernreuter) in the place of a linden-blossom brew, and resulted in a happy ending for the juveniles of the piece: Heffele's daughter Freda (Frln Pohlner) gets the woodsman, Botho von Wendt (Karl Streitmann), she wanted, instead of having to marry the head forester, Tymoleon von Gerius (Josef Joseffy). Alexander Girardi had the chief comic role as the John Wellington Wells-ish botanist responsible for the drink, Annie Dirkens played a prima donna caught in the rain and mistaken, in her borrowed dry clothes, for a miller's wife, and Therese Biedermann played her companion, pairing off with Girardi for the final-curtain roundup. The 70-year-old Strauss wrote an attractive light score, topped by the waltz ''Trau,' schau,' wem!'' of the under-the-influence second-act finale, the march ''Es war so wunderschön'' and Botho's waltz song ''Im Walde, wo die Buchen rauschen,'' without drawing forth a hit number.

Waldmeister was played 55 successive times under Alexandrine von Schönerer's management during December and January, and it put in an occasional appearance in the Theater an der Wien's repertoire during 1896 and 1897, passing its 75th performance on 14 April 1897. It reappeared on the schedule in 1908 for a few performances, to bring its performance total there to 88, although it had, in between times, had another Viennese showing at the Jantschtheater in 1901. Berlin's Lessing-Theater hosted a production in 1896, New York's German-language Irving Place Theater mounted the piece the following year, with Julie Kopácsi-Karczag as Pauline, an Hungarian version (ad Ferenc Reiner, Zsigmond Sebők) was produced, under the more comprehensible title of ''May Wine'' at the Népszínház for 10 performances in the same year, and Berlin took a second look when the Theater des Westens brought the show back in in 1914 (5 December, 33 performances). In 1951 Ralph Benatzky wrote a fresh libretto around the *Waldmeister* score.

Germany: Lessing-Theater 2 May 1896; Hungary: Népszínház *Májusi bor* 15 May 1897; USA: Irving Place Theater 29 November 1897

WALKER, George W [MYERS, George] (b Lawrence, Kans, 4 June 1872; d Central Islip, NY, 6 January 1911). The more sharply comical and well-dressed half of the Williams and Walker cakewalk-dancing team that became a popular musical-theatre pairing of the turn-of-the-century American stage.

Walker worked at first in western minstrel companies and joined up in a double act with the tall, gaunt Williams when he was 18 years old to perform in variety and minstrelsy as ''The Two Real Coons.'' The partnership was to last 16 years, up to Walker's death. The duo first appeared on the Broadway stage when they were interpolated into a few performances of the quick-folding Victor Herbert musical *The Gold Bug* (1896), but they went on to increase their audiences playing in variety at Koster and Bial's Music Hall (''a cakewalk act and songs of the coon order'') and, billed as the ''Tabasco Senegambians,'' at Keith's Union Square, and one of their songs ''You Ain't So Wahm'' [*sic*], became a catch of the town. They failed, however, to find the same reception when they crossed to England and returned home after just two weeks on the bill at the Empire. They subsequently returned to the musical theatre to tour unsuccessfully ''with two score of Georgia rosebuds'' in the Ernest Hogan's summertime musical sketch *Clorindy* (*The Senegambian Carnival*). After more variety-house appearances with their company playing an act called *A Lucky Coon* (1899), they took another turn into the book-musical show when they appeared under the Hurtig and Seamon management in the musical comedy *The Policy Players* (1899, Happy Hotstuff). ''The plot does not figure largely and is frequently lost sight of; this however does not detract from the entertainment which consists of the best sort of Ethiopian fun and music,'' judged a trade paper. The pair followed up, under the same management, with *Sons of Ham* (1901, Harty Lafter) and *In Dahomey* (1902). In this last-named and most successful of their shows, which they played with particularly happy notoriety in Britain, Williams was characteristically cast as ''Shylock Homestead'' (''Shy, to his friends'') misused and misdirected by the natty, close-to-the-wind Rareback Pinkerton (his personal friend and adviser), as portrayed by the slicker Walker.

The pair split from their managers before *Abyssinia* (1906, Rastus Johnson USA, ''Let It Alone''), an attempt to repeat the same formula in a fairly plotless piece about a group of colored tourists going from Kansas to Jerusalem, via Africa, with disastrous results. Their mangement company sank, with $10,000 in debts in September 1906. In court it was stated that they had had only ''one profitable week in the season.'' The pair persisted, however, but during the run of their next show, *Bandana Land* (1908, Bud Jenkins, ''Late Hours'') Walker was forced to retire, suffering from the onset of the paresis from which he died the following year. On 31 March 1908 the two staged a special performance of *Bandana Land,* with the third act replaced by a retrospective of their performances together, to mark their 16 years as a duo, and soon after Walker was gone.

Walker was married in 1899 to the successful musical-theatre performer **Aida Overton WALKER** [née Ada OVERTON] (b New York, 17 February 1880; d New York, 11 October 1914), the soubrette and choreographer of the Williams and Walker company (Kioka in *The Policy Players,* Caroline Jenkins in *Sons of Ham,* Rosetta Lightfoot in *In Dahomey,* Miriam in *Abyssinia,* Dinah Simmons in *Bandana Land,* etc) and later a member of the Smart Set (*His Honor the Barber,* 1911, etc).

A biomusical show, *Williams and Walker,* was played at off-Broadway's American Place Theater 9 March 1986.

1899 **The Policy Players** (Bert Williams, et al/W Jesse A Shipp) Star Theater 16 October

1900 **Sons of Ham** (Williams, et al/Stephen Cassin, Shipp) Star Theater 15 October

WALKER, Nancy [SWOYER, Anna Myrtle] (b Philadelphia, 10 May 1922; d Studio City, Calif, 25 March 1992). A favorite Broadway comedienne in the musical and non-musical theatre.

The small-sized, funny-faced Nancy Walker made her earliest New York musical appearance in a supporting role in *Best Foot Forward* (1941) before she created the part of the energetic cabdriver Brunhilde Esterházy in *On the Town,* insisting that her passenger ''Come Up to My Place'' and, once there, that ''I Can Cook Too.'' She appeared in the 1947 *The Barefoot Boy with Cheek* (Yetta Samovar) and starred as Lily Malloy, the brewery lady who goes ballet, in *Look Ma, I'm Dancin'* (1948), but she closed on the road with *A Month of Sundays,* a musical version of Victor Wolfson's *Excursion* (1951, Shirley Harris). Walker then replaced Helen Gallagher as Gladys in the successful 1952 revival of *Pal Joey* and was briefly seen in police-force low comedy in *Copper and Brass* (1957, Katie O'Shea) before she co-starred as the wife of Phil Silver's Herbie Cram in *Do Re Mi* (1960). It was her last role on a Broadway that, with its general abandonment of the comic musical in favor of the romantic and/or spectacular one, no longer seemed to have a place for a genuine low comedienne.

Although she played Domina in the 1971 revival of *A Funny Thing Happened on the Way to the Forum* on the West Coast, she did not move east with the production and made her later success largely in television, made notably as the mother of Valerie Harper's *Rhoda.*

WALKING HAPPY Musical comedy in 2 acts by Roger O Hirson and Ketti Frings based on the play *Hobson's Choice* by Harold Brighouse. Lyrics by Sammy Cahn. Music by James van Husen. Lunt-Fontanne Theater, New York, 26 November 1966.

Following the success of their musicalized *Charley's Aunt, Where's Charley?,* producers Feuer and Martin turned to another British classic, Harold Brighouse's celebrated English north-country comedy *Hobson's Choice,* which had been a 143-performance success on its Broadway production in 1915 and a 246-performance hit the following year in London, as musical-mix.

Like its predecessor, *Hobson's Choice* was subjected to some surprising changes in both plot and character in its transformation into the curiously titled *Walking Happy,* which featured Norman Wisdom, London star of *Where's Charley?,* as the exceedingly simple shoemaker, Will Mossop, who is taken in marriage by his boss's organizing daughter, Maggie (Louise Troy), as a business proposition. When Maggie's boozy father (George Rose) objects, the pair set up in competition to him, but all is sweetness and light by the end of the evening, and Will is set to become a proper husband. Ed Bakey appeared as George Beenstock, a temperance man opposed to Hobson, but who nevertheless lets his sons (James B Spann, Michael Berkson) tidily wed the bootmaker's remaining two daughters (Gretchen van Aken, Sharon Dierking) by the end of the show.

The largest part of the score fell to the two principals. He pondered ''How D'Ya [*sic*] Talk to a Girl?'' after the surprise order to wed, she determined that ''I'll Make a Man of the Man'' and they concluded ''I Don't Think I'm in Love'' before he decided that a wife is a wife and ''It Might as Well Be You.'' There was also a title song. The musical comedy Maggie and Mossop played 161 performances on Broadway, and toured briefly to the West Coast, where Anne Rogers was seen as Maggie.

Recording: original cast (Capitol/EMI)

WALLER, Jack (b London, 2 April 1881; d London, 28 July 1957).

Producer, songwriter and all-round showman-of-the-theatre, Waller began his life in the business working the music halls. In 1910 he formed the concert party ''The Butterflies'' (whose members included Wylie Watson), and he toured the company for many years around the Pacific circuits. In the southern seas, he also ventured for the first time as an impresario and presented the revue *Look Who's Here* (1917), in conjunction with Sydney James, at Sydney's Palace Theatre, ''Jack Waller's Company of Comedians'' in *Vanity Fair* at the Tivoli (1918) and a new edition of *Look Who's Here* the following year.

Soon after this he returned to Britain, the concert party broke up, and Waller went on to play in several revues (*Robey en Casserole, The Little Revue Starts at Nine*) before starting up a managerial partnership with Herbert Clayton, whom he had met when Clayton had booked what was left of the Butterflies for the Chelsea Palace in 1920. The pair began writing and touring revues and musical comedies like those Waller had purveyed to the Australians on the minor British theatre and music-hall circuits (*Archie, Tilly*), but they were shot to the forefront of the big league soon after in fairy-tale style. On a trip to America's out-of-town venues to pick up some fashionably American pieces to mount on the British circuits, the pair purchased the British rights to the musicals *So Long, Letty, The Kiss Burglar* and *Canary Cottage.* Their fourth purchase was the first to be staged, however, and they eventually mounted it not on the road but in London. *No, No, Nanette,* their first West End production, gave them the hit of the era.

They didn't get their other three purchases to the London stage, but Waller and Clayton followed up with West End versions of several other, and more tried-and-tested, American musical comedies—*Mercenary Mary, Kitty's Kisses* (as *The Girl Friend*), *Hit the Deck* and *Good News*—as well as the Hungarian *Princess Charming* (*Alexandra*) and a number of plays (including *Abie's Irish Rose*) before they launched their own, homemade *Virginia* (1928), a piece that Waller tried to pretend was not homemade at all, but fashionably American. It did very nicely, but thereafter—in spite of some reasonable or even good-looking runs—neither their imports (*Merry, Merry, Hold Everything!, Sons o' Guns*) nor their original shows (the sub-operatic *Dear Love,* the expensively spectacular *Silver Wings*) came financially good, and their partnership fizzled out in 1930.

Waller, however, continued. He co-composed and mounted a series of musical comedies featuring comedian Bobby Howes (*For the Love of Mike, Tell Her the Truth, He Wanted Adventure, Yes, Madam?, Please, Teacher!*) that proved highly successful, and he even contributed half a score to another hit musical, the Jack Buchanan vehicle *Mr Whittington,* in a period in which, of all his productions, only a further attempt at a romantic musical with the adaptation of C Stafford Dickens's *Command Performance,* and a George Robey show, *Certainly, Sir!,* proved flops. After this last piece, however, things again went rather more consistently less well: *Big Business, Oh! You Letty* and *Bobby Get Your Gun* all failed, and a London staging of the Broadway success *Let's Face It,* produced in collaboration with Tom Arnold, didn't do sufficiently well to compensate. Waller went uncharacteristically quiet, and when he reemerged it was with a provincial musicalization of the play *The Best People,* which he had produced in London in 1925.

This *Hearts Are Trumps* stayed intentionally in the provinces, but Waller's attempt at a major comeback with a production of Broadway's *By Jupiter,* which also stopped short of London, had not been supposed to. Waller, nevertheless, battled on. He mounted a revival of *Merrie England,* a new musical called *The Kid from Stratford* with Arthur Askey (1948) and a tour of the first musical by the young Sandy Wilson, *Caprice* (1950), but it was a play picked up from a repertory theatre, the Worthing-mounted *Sailor Beware,* that restored his fortunes and his credibility for his last years in the theatre. Those years included only one musical, a last attempt at a romantic piece with his own name and that of his musical helpmate, Joe Tunbridge, hidden under a pseudonym as the composers of a score taken piecemeal from the vast tin trunk of un- or underused music that the producer kept in his office. *Wild Grows the Heather,* an adaptation of J M Barrie's *The Little Minister,* was not a success, but Waller kept going and he was still talking and planning productions up to the day of his death.

A monstre sacré of the West End theatre, sailing often near to the wind of legitimacy, and a familiar of the bankruptcy courts in the best tradition of the theatrical impresario, Waller was nevertheless responsible for many fine West End productions and hits. As a composer, he turned out much lively music, all of it written in collaboration with (and written down by) efficiently trained musicians such as Haydn Wood and Tunbridge, which, if it did not prove enduring, more than served the needs of the moment.

1923 **Our Liz** (w Pat Thayer/Herbert Clayton, Con West) Hippodrome, Southampton 13 August

1923 **Suzanne** (w Haydn Wood/Clayton, West) Palace Theatre, Plymouth 31 December

1924 **Tilly** (w Wood/Bert Lee, R P Weston/Clayton, West) Empire, Leeds 21 July; Alhambra 3 November

1924 **Archie** (w Wood/George Arthurs, Worton David) Grand Theatre, Hull 28 July

1928 **Virginia** (w Joseph A Tunbridge/Lee, Weston, Clayton, Douglas Furber) Palace Theatre 24 October

1929 **Merry Merry** (w Tunbridge, Harris Weston/Weston, Lee, et al) Carlton Theatre 28 February

1929 **Dear Love** (w Tunbridge, Wood/Dion Titheradge, Lauri Wylie, Clayton) Palace Theatre 14 November

1930 **Silver Wings** (w Tunbridge/Titheradge/Titheradge, Furber) Dominion Theatre 14 February

1931 **For the Love of Mike** (w Tunbridge/Clifford Grey, Sonny Miller/Grey) Saville Theatre 8 October

1932 **Tell Her the Truth** (w Tunbridge/Weston, Lee) Saville Theatre 14 June

1933 **He Wanted Adventure** (w Tunbridge/Weston, Lee) Saville Theatre 28 March

1933 **Command Performance** (w Tunbridge/Grey/C Stafford Dickens) Saville Theatre 17 October

1933 **Mr Whittington** (w Tunbridge, John W Green/Grey, Furber, Greatrex Newman) Alhambra, Glasgow 30 November; London Hippodrome 1 February 1934

1934 **Yes, Madam?** (w Tunbridge/Weston, Lee, K R G Browne) London Hippodrome 27 September

1935 **Please, Teacher!** (w Tunbridge/Weston, Lee, Browne) London Hippodrome 2 October

1936 **Certainly, Sir!** (w Tunbridge/Weston, Lee) London Hippodrome 17 September

1937 **Big Business** (w Tunbridge/Carter, Lee, Browne) London Hippodrome 18 February

1938 **Bobby Get Your Gun** (w Tunbridge/Carter, Lee, Grey/ Guy Bolton, Fred Thompson, Lee) Adelphi Theatre 7 October

1943 **Hearts Are Trumps** (w Tunbridge, Leon Carroll/Ian Grant, Robert Fyle/Fyle) Theatre Royal, Birmingham 19 October

1956 **Wild Grows the Heather** (w Tunbridge/Ralph Reader/ Hugh Ross Williamson) London Hippodrome 3 May

WALLIS, Bertram [Harvey] (b London, 22 February 1874; d London, 11 April 1952). Handsome actor and singer who became a longtime London leading man.

Wallis began his theatre career playing in classical drama, but he soon shifted to George Edwardes's management, playing initially supporting parts (Manlius in *A Greek Slave* tour 1898) and later the Hayden Coffin star baritone roles on tour before being brought to town to cover the same star in *The Country Girl* and to play one of the beaux to Paul Rubens's *Three Little Maids* (1902, Lord Grassmere). He appeared in *The Love Birds* (1904, Alec Rockingham) in London, then visited Broadway, where he created roles in *A Madcap Princess* (1904, Charles Brandon) and *The Princess Beggar* (1907, Prince Karl) and played in the American editions of *The Little Cherub* (1906, Lord Congress) and *Miss Hook of Holland* (1907, Adrian Papp) before returning to Britain.

Frank Curzon starred him in the title role of the successful *King of Cadonia* alongside Isabel Jay in London, then with Alice Venning on the road, and he followed this up by teaming with the same leading lady (Miss Jay) and the same management in *Dear Little Denmark* (1909, Conrad Petersen) and *The Balkan Princess* (1910, Sergius). In 1911 he moved back to George Edwardes's management to star with Lily Elsie in the title role of London's *The Count of Luxembourg* (René), and he later appeared as leading man in Oscar Straus's unsuccessful *Love and Laughter* (1913, King Carol) and the British version of *Autoliebchen* (1914, *Joy Ride Lady,* Édouard Morny). He subsequently revived the Musketeers concert party under his own management (Herbert Clayton, Frederic Norton and Nelson Keys were amongst the players), and played for several years in plays, revue and pantomime, before returning to the musical theatre to take over as the non-singing hero, Baldasarre, opposite José Collins in *The Maid of the Mountains.* He played the role for a large part of that show's long run and later starred opposite Miss Collins in *A Southern Maid* (1920, Francesco del Fuego) and in two other vocally limited roles in *The Last Waltz* (1922, Prince Paul) and *Catherine* (1923, Peter the Great). He later returned to Daly's Theatre to play King Louis to the *Madame Pompadour* of Evelyn Laye, appeared in the short-lived *Nicolette* (1925, Pan Fulano), in London's *The Blue Mazurka* (1927 Clement, Baron von Reiger) and as the Duke of Cumberland to Miss Laye's *Blue Eyes* (1928).

Wallis went on to tour again as Baldasarre and as King Louis, and his transition from handsome and gloriously singing leading man to handsome not-singing-much older gentleman continued in the musical comedy *Lucky Break* (t/o William J Pierce), alongside Leslie Henson, as King Joachim in a revival of *A Waltz Dream* (1934) and Count Hédouville in *Paganini* (1937). At 70 he played in *Blossom Time* (1942, Pierre) and the Chopin pasticcio *Waltz without End* (1942, The Stranger), and he went on to appear in the London version of *Sunny River* (1943, George Marshall) and on the road in *Betty* (1945) before ending a career of over 50 almost nonstop years in the theatre.

WALLS, Tom [Kirby] (b Kingsthorpe, Northants, 18 February 1883; d Ewell, Surrey, 27 November 1949).

Best known for his appearances in the series of farces produced at the Aldwych Theatre in the 1920s and early 1930s—and as the owner-trainer of a Derby winner (April the Fifth)—Walls had spent most of his previous stage career in musical theatre. He began in pantomime and concert parties, played comedy roles in the British music hall (Captain Jack Jermyn in the Adeline Genée ballet *The Belle of the Ball* 1907, A Constable in the revue *Oh! Indeed* 1908) and in musical comedy in Australia (Doody in *The Arcadians,* Marquis in *The Belle of Brittany,* Mr Hook, etc), and in his early thirties took a number of supporting comedy roles under George Edwardes's management in England: *The Sunshine Girl* (1912, Hodson), *The Marriage Market* (1913, Bald-Faced Sandy), *A Country Girl* revival (1914, Sir Joseph), *Véronique* revival (1915, Coquenard). He subsequently replaced George Huntley in the principal comedy part of Edwardes's production of *Betty* (Lord Playne), played in London's version of *High Jinks* (1916, Colonel Slaughter), created roles in *The Beauty Spot* (1917, Paul Prince) at the Gaiety and *Kissing Time* (1919, Colonel Bollinger) at the Winter Garden, succeeded Davy Burnaby as General Zonzo in *Oh! Julie* (1920) and appeared as Mephistopheles in the ill-fated *Faust on Toast,* before the production of the comedy *Tons of Money* changed his career. His last musical appearance was in the central role of *Whirled into Happiness* (Albert Horridge) in 1922, but he dabbled briefly in the production of provincial musicals (*Our Liz, Suzanne*) with the emerging Jack Waller and Herbert Clayton before finally turning his attention full-time to farces and films.

Plate 412. **Tom Walls** *with Teddy Payne and Robert Nainby in the Gaiety Theatre's* The Sunshine Girl.

WALZER AUS WIEN Singspiel in a Vorspiel and 3 acts by A M Willner, Heinz Reichert and Ernst Marischka. Music taken from the works of Johann Strauss I and II arranged by Julius Bittner (?and/or Erich Wolfgang Korngold uncredited). Wiener Stadttheater, Vienna, 30 October 1930.

One of the many Operetten manufactured from the music of the Johann Strausses, *Walzer aus Wien* was constructed on *Dreimäderlhaus* lines, as a fictionalized biomusical of its composer. The young Johann Strauss (Hubert Marischka) wants to follow in his father's footsteps and become a conductor and composer, but the elder Strauss (Willy Thaller) will not hear of it. However, the seductive Countess Olga Baranskaja (Betty Fischer) takes an interest in the young man, and arranges it so that he gets a chance to conduct his father's orchestra in one of his own waltzes before a packed house at Dommayers. His name is made and, as Olga sweeps on from Vienna on the arm of Prince Gogol (Ludwig Herold), and whilst his beloved Resi (Paula Brosig), the daughter of the baker Ebeseder (Fritz Imhoff), is promised instead to the tailor's son Leopold (Karl Gottler), Johann junior is reconciled with his father and heads on to fame and, presumably, the three wives he really and historically had. Amongst the show's supporting cast was former star soubrette Mizzi Zwerenz, now playing character roles, as Frau Kratochwill.

The selection and arrangement of the score—which did not shrink from using some of the more obvious Strauss bonbons that other pasticheurs had modestly sidestepped—was credited to Julius Bittner. However, it has been recounted that it was in fact Korngold (billed only as ''musical director'') who was responsible for assembling and revamping the music, and that he had his out-of-luck friend's name included in the credits so that he might share the royalties in the work. Maybe. Those royalties were, in fact, to turn out to be considerable, for although *Walzer aus Wien* did not establish itself in the repertoire of its country of origin as the earlier and slightly less musically naive pasticcio *Wiener Blut* had done, it was used as the basis for a whole series of Strauss bio-musicals around the world.

Hubert Marischka's Vienna production—which originally ran some four hours in length—played a regular season at the Stadttheater and was later seen for 19 performances at the Theater an der Wien (17 May 1931) before it was done, without attracting the attention of its nearest neighbors. However, if Germany and Hungary bypassed the piece, it was picked up by Oswald Stoll and presented at London's Alhambra Theatre (ad Hassard Short, Desmond Carter, Caswell Garth) under the title of *Waltzes from Vienna,* "a love story of music." The Strausses were credited, but Bittner and Korngold's names only appeared on the program in minuscule letters alongside the rather larger credit for G H Clutsam and Herbert Griffiths, who had, it seems, done a new arrangement of a score that now started off with the Radetzky March and ended on the "Blue Danube." *Waltzes from Vienna* was lavishly staged (spectacle-director Hassard Short's name was splashed above the title in larger type than the Strausses) and presented as a twice-daily entertainment with Robert Halliday and Esmond Knight alternating the role of young Strauss, Evelyn Herbert, Adrienne Brune and Borghild Bodom sharing Resi, Marie Burke as Olga, Dennis Noble as Leopold, and C V France as Strauss sr. It played for almost a year, alongside the spate of early 1930s mega-productions that were crowding London's stages (*White Horse Inn, Helen!, Cavalcade, Nina Rosa,* etc), totting up 607 performances at its double-paced rate prior to closing. Soon after, an English film version was made with Knight featured alongside Edmund Gwenn, Fay Compton and Jessie Matthews. In Australia, the Alhambra/Clutsam version was mounted with John Moore (Strauss), Shirley Dale (Resi), Miriam Sabbage (Olga) and Aubrey Mallalien (Strauss sr) in the lead roles, and it played three months in Melbourne prior to a season in Sydney (Her Majesty's Theatre 15 April 1933).

A French version (ad André Mouëzy-Éon, Max Eddy, Jean Marietti) put considerable further changes, both textual and—via Eugène Cools—musical, into a piece that had now gone further from its original than even the various versions of *Dreimäderlhaus* had done. For *Valses de Vienne* it was also decided to add the conventional soubret element that had been avoided in the original. A baker's assistant called Pepi was added to the script, supplied with a subplot and a duet, and allowed to pair off with Leopold at the final curtain whilst—with all history thrown to the winds and the most conventional of opérettic conventions reigning supreme—Strauss for-goodness-sake now married Resi! But, history or no history, and conventional as it was, it was the jolly *Valses de Vienne* that proved the most durable version of the Strauss family musical. Maurice Lehmann's production, with André Baugé (Strauss jr), Pierre Magnier (Strauss sr), Fanély Revoil and Lucienne Tragin starred and settings by the famous artist Marie Laurençin, was a thorough success, prefatory to a long line of Parisian large-stage revivals (Théâtre du Châtelet 1941, 1947, 1957, 1958, 1964, 1974, Théâtre Mogador 1975, 1977) and an unceasing presence in French provincial houses to the present day.

In America, Moss Hart took his turn at the libretto (a revision of the London one), and Frank E Tours and Robert Russell Bennett put their hands into the score for what was now called *The Great Waltz.* Guy Robertson and H Reeves Smith played the Strausses, Marion Claire was the baker's daughter and Marie Burke repeated her London performance as the sexy Maecenas of the piece. The vast Center Theater was filled with Short's Viennesey spectacle, and the show clocked up 298 Broadway performances. Four years later, Hollywood contributed its version of the Strauss story with Fernand Graavey, Miliza Korjus and Luise Rainer in the principal roles and a slim new score of Strauss pieces (ly: Oscar Hammerstein) that turned *Der Zigeunerbaron*'s Dompfaff duo into "One Day When We Were Young" alongside the "Blue Danube," "Tales from the Vienna Woods" and "I'm in Love with Vienna."

Whilst France—understandably, given its success—stayed true to its first-time version, in America those bits that remained of *Walzer aus Wien* were recycled interminably. A freshly fabricated Strauss-purée piece called *The Waltz King,* masterminded by Paramount Pictures music man Boris Morros, was mounted twice on the West Coast—in 1943 (13 September), with Richard Bonelli and Irra Pettina starred and, revised, in 1944 (28 August)—and flopped twice. But when, in the wake of the success of *Song of Norway,* pasticcio was all the rage on the Pacific seaboard, and that show's authors, Robert Wright and George Forrest, took a turn at a Strauss show, they returned to the basis established in *Walzer aus Wien.* Film star Korjus featured as the real-life Jetty Strauss in a less improbable *The Blue Danube* in 1949, but the Los Angeles Light Opera brought out its version of *Walzer aus Wien* (lib: readapted by Milton Lazarus, add ly: Forman Brown) the same year, with Walter Slezak as the older Strauss, and again in 1953, and it was dusted off and given yet another rewrite (lib re-readapted by Jerome Chodorov) for a revival in 1965 (14 September) as *The Great Waltz,* with Giorgio Tozzi starred. By this time, the complicated credits included no less than 13 different writers' names. The 13-handed mixture, however, proved a successful one, for this production was exported to Lon-

Plate 413. **Ein Walzertraum.** *The lights are glistening, the ladies' band is playing, and the café seems a much more welcoming place to homesick Niki than his new wife's palace (Volksoper, Vienna).*

don's Theatre Royal, Drury Lane, where, under the management of Harold Fielding and Bernard Delfont, and with Hungarian Operette star Sári Bárábás (Olga) featured, it rolled up a fine 706-performance run. The success prompted another MGM film, based on this version, with Kenneth McKellar and Mary Costa featured, which was not a success, and the Strauss fairy tale was then put away, except, of course, in France.

UK: Alhambra Theatre *Waltzes from Vienna* 17 August 1931; Australia: Theatre Royal, Melbourne 24 December 1932; France: Théâtre de la Porte-Saint-Martin *Valses de Vienne* 21 December 1933; USA: Center Theater 22 September 1934

Films: Gaumont *Waltzes from Vienna* 1934, MGM *The Great Waltz* 1938, 1972

Recordings: 1970 London cast recording (Columbia), complete in French (Connoisseur Society), selections in French (Decca, Pathé, Pomme, Columbia), etc

EIN WALZERTRAUM Operette in 3 acts by Felix Dörmann and Leopold Jacobson based on the story *Nux der Prinzgemahl* from Hans Müller's *Buch der Abenteuer.* Music by Oscar Straus. Carltheater, Vienna, 2 March 1907.

The first major Operette success to follow *Die lustige Witwe* out of Vienna, with all that meant in the way of impetus behind it, Oscar Straus's *Ein Walzertraum* had already won an enormous pre-export success on home ground. Unlike its famous predecessor, it did not then go on to sweep the world's stages with success, but it nevertheless established itself firmly in both the German- and French-speaking repertoires for the rest of the century.

Viennese Lieutenant Niki (Fritz Werner) has been married to Princess Helene of Flausenthurn (Helene Merviola), but he quickly finds the strictures of court etiquette and his consort's position impossible to take. On his wedding night he slips out with friend Montschi (Rudolf Kumpa) to relax at a local restaurant where a Viennese ladies' band is playing, and there he falls romantically in with pretty Franzi Steingrüber (Mizzi Zwerenz), the conductor of the orchestra. King Joachim (Karl Blasel) and his cousin Lothar (Arthur Guttmann), anxious that Niki is not thinking about perpetuating their dynasty on his wedding night, follow him, and soon Helene and her lady-in-waiting Friederike (Therese Löwe) arrive worriedly on the spot as well. Franzi is ready to fight the newcomer for her newfound man, but then she realizes who she is. It is Franzi, in the end, who saves the apparently doomed royal marriage. She helps Helene reorganize her quarters Viennese-style, with everything that might make Niki feel more at home and at ease, before heading off home with her orchestra, leaving the Flausenthurn dynasty hopefully to perpetuate itself in the approved fashion.

Straus's score glittered with good things, from which the longing waltz duet for Niki and Montschi, "Leise, ganz leise klingt's durch den Raum," tempting the new prince from the castle to the place where the orchestra is playing, proved to be the major hit. A comic duo for Franzi and cousin Lothar, with him tootling on a piccolo and her accompanying him on the violin ("Piccolo! Piccolo! Tsin-tsin-tsin"), was another musical highlight, alongside the comical trio in which the future of the dynasty is debated ("Ach die arme Dynastie"), another for the three ladies on "Temp'rament! Temp'rament!" and the lively chorus march "Mädel, sei net dumm!"

Ein Walzertraum was the biggest hit the Carltheater had ever had. It played 261 consecutive performances in 1907 and provoked the Wiener Colosseum to a burlesque, *Polkatraum,* before running on unbroken to the end of the next season, 15 June the following year, by which time it had been seen 427 times, and the cast was now headed by Willie Strehl (Niki), Dora Keplinger (Franzi), Frln Mödl (Helene) and Richard Waldemar (Joachim). It remained in the Carltheater's repertoire for almost two decades thereafter, passing its 600th performance there on 24 May 1913, and was subsequently taken up in other Viennese houses, playing its 1,000th Viennese performance during a revival (20 January 1927) at the Johann Strauss-Theater on 15 February 1927, with Robert Nästlberger and Gisela Kolbe in the leading roles.

Whilst the original run was still playing, most of the other major musical-theatre centers brought *Ein Walzertraum* to the stage. Budapest was the first (ad Adolf Mérei) with a production at the Király Színház that featured Ákos Ráthonyi, hero of the Hungarian *Die lustige Witwe,* as Niki alongside Gitta Ötvös (Franzi), Sári Petráss (Helene), József Németh (Joachim) and Sándor Pápi (Lothar). The piece repeated its Viennese success and passed its 100th night on 26 February 1908 before going out to other theatres and to regular revivals (Városi Színház 1926, Király Színház 1 February 1936, etc). Berlin's Theater des Westens followed suit soon after with similar results (351 performances).

It was in the English-language sector that the piece was to prove something of a disappointment. In America, actor-author Joseph W Herbert made the English version (with just two interpolated numbers) and took the role of Lothar in a production that was mounted at Philadelphia's Chestnut Street Opera House in January 1908. Sophie Brandt (Franzi), Edward Johnson (Niki), Magda Dahl (Helene) and Charles A Bigelow (Joachim) were the other principals in Frank McKee's Interstate Amusement Co production. Three weeks later it opened on Broadway. Vera Michelena and Frank Rushworth took over as Helene and Niki, and the show did well enough through 111 performances without ever looking like approaching the status of *The Merry Widow.* Miss Brandt teamed with Armand Kalisz for a subsequent tour in which the part of Montschi was boosted by the addition of an Ivan Caryll song called "The Prater."

In London, however, even though the show was given a star-sprinkled production under George Edwardes and Charles Frohman's management, *A Waltz Dream* (ad Adrian Ross) was frankly a flop. Gertie Millar (Franzi), Robert Evett (Niki), George Grossmith jr (Lothar) and the great comic Arthur Williams (Joachim) starred, and there was a piece, featuring the members of the ladies' band alongside Joachim and Lothar, about "The Big Bass Drum," which allowed the girls the extra opportunities Lehár had provided for his grisettes in London's *Die lustige Witwe,* but *A Waltz Dream* just didn't and wouldn't appeal. It closed after 146 determined performances (Miss Millar had already gone, being replaced by Denise Orme in an attempt to up the show's rating from undersung to adequately sung), whilst such pieces as *Butterflies, Havana* and *The Gay Gordons* prospered. All sorts of excuses were advanced to account for its poor showing, and Edwardes remained convinced the show had been unlucky, so in 1911 he remounted it (ad Basil Hood) at Daly's Theatre (7 January), the home of *The Merry Widow,* with the "widow," Lily Elsie, starred alongside Robert Michaelis and W H Berry. But once again, with what looked like all the trumps on its side, it failed to go. Edwardes closed it after 106 performances and produced *Der Graf von Luxemburg* instead. In 1934 Lea Seidl, Bertram Wallis, Carl Esmond and Berry starred in a three-week revival at the Winter Garden (20 December).

In spite of the less than happy results won in Britain and America, Australia's J C Williamson duly produced *A Waltz Dream* (English version) in 1910. The Sydney season lasted only a month, and the show did not become a favorite, but it was nevertheless brought out again in 1917 with Dorothy Brunton as Franzi, William Green as Niki, C H Workman as Joachim and Connie Ediss as drummer Tschinellen-Fifi, again in 1936 with Strella Wilson and Marie Bremner featured, and yet again in 1939. Williamson's, you see, had the costumes and the band parts and never wasted anything.

If France was slower than other countries to stage its version of the show that was supposed to be the best thing out of Vienna since *La Veuve joyeuse, Rêve de valse* (ad Léon Xanrof, Jules Chancel)—in spite of the noted similarities of its libretto to the adapters' *Le Prince Consort* and Ivan Caryll's musical version thereof (not to mention inter alia Hennequin and Bilhaud's *Nelly Rozier*)—did very much better there than anywhere else. Produced by *La Veuve joyeuse*'s producer, Alphonse Franck, at the same Théâtre Apollo with Paris's Danilo, Henri Defreyn, as Niki alongside Alice Bonheur (Franzi), Alice Milet (Helene), Saturnin Fabre (Joachim) and Paul Ardot (Lothar), it was played with great success for three months and was subsequently revived both there and later at the Folies-Dramatiques (8 December 1922), the Porte-Saint-Martin (11 June 1934), and on several occasions at the Mogador (22 March 1947, 24 February 1962, 31 July 1976), remaining to this day one of the most frequently seen of the short list of Viennese Operetten still played in the French provinces.

A regular part of the German-language repertoire, *Ein Walzertraum* has also been revived on a number of occasions in Vienna, notably at the Stadttheater in 1945, at the Raimundtheater in 1954 and at the Volksoper (9 February 1974), where, the lesson of the English productions unlearned, both the script and the score had been uncomfortably and incongruously tinkered with to boost the role of the romantic Helene (notably with the addition of *Rund um die Liebe*'s ''Ein Schwipserl'') above that of soubrette Franzi in importance.

A Hollywood film, *The Smiling Lieutenant,* developed by Ernst Vajda and Samuel Raphaelson from *Ein Walzertraum* and, allegedly, from Müller's novel, featured Maurice Chevalier (Niki), Claudette Colbert (Franzi) and Miriam Hopkins (Anna) in a tale in which the Princess was a frumpish creature, Niki's marriage to her forced and Franzi was behind turning the royal lady into a pretty person. In Germany Mady Christians and Willi Fritsch featured in a silent 1925 film, whilst a sound version with the voice of Fritz Wunderlich as Niki was produced for German TV in Cologne in 1960.

Hungary: Király Színház *Varázskeringő* 26 November 1907; Germany: Theater des Westens 21 December 1907; USA: Chestnut Street Opera House, Philadelphia 6 January 1908, Broadway Theater *A Waltz Dream* 27 January 1908; UK: Hicks Theatre *A Waltz Dream* 7 March 1908; Australia: Her Majesty's Theatre, Sydney *A Waltz Dream* 18 February 1910; France: Théâtre Apollo *Rêve de valse* 3 March 1910

Recordings: 2-record set (EMI), in Italian (RAI), selections (Period, Telefunken, Fontana, EMI-Electrola), in English (HMV), in French (EMI-Pathé, CBS, Vega, Decca, etc)

WANG Comic opera by J Cheever Goodwin. Music by Woolson Morse. Broadway Theater, New York, 4 May 1891.

Described more than a little loosely as a comic opera, *Wang* mixed elements of burlesque and extravaganza with a tale that showed the influence of, yet contrasted starkly with, its author's previous piece: an adaptation of Vanloo and Leterrier's libretto to *L'Étoile.* Once again the tale was set in picturesque faraway lands—this time, Siam—where the crafty, comical and horribly impecunious regent of Siam, Wang (De Wolf Hopper), is plotting to lay his hands on the missing fortune left by his late royal brother. The young heir, Prince Mataya (Della Fox), is interested only in making love to Marie (Jeannette St Henry), the daughter of the late French consul. Through a little skulduggery, Wang finally discovers that the treasure was left in the care of that very same Frenchman, a chest now guarded by Marie's mother, the widow Frimousse (Marion Singer), until the day of Mataya's coronation, when all will be handed over to its rightful owner. The action of the evening centered on Wang's attempts to get his hands on the chest. Alas, when he does, on the very day that Mataya is to be crowned, it is empty. Mama has sewn the treasure into the folds of the Prince's coronation robes. Tiny Alfred Klein played Pepot, the royal elephant keeper, and a bit of romantic vocalizing was supplied by another French daughter, Gillette (Anna O'Keefe), and her baritonic cavalier, Jean Boucher (Edmund Stanley).

Woolson Morse's score borrowed freely from the music used in his recent failure *King Cole II,* and the favorite songs included ''The Man with an Elephant on His Hands,'' the topical trio ''Ask the Man in the Moon'' and Mataya's ''Some Other Fellow.'' There were even five children who—in a direct pinch from the repertoire of Lydia Thompson's burlesque troupe—sang nursery rhymes to up the aaah-quotient of the evening.

Wang, with its ''gay and graceful music, picturesque dresses and scenes, abundance of wit and elephantine byplay,'' proved a hot-weather favorite in the summer of 1891, running 151 performances through the season and providing itself with fine credentials for the touring circuits, whilst at the same time giving both Hopper—a comical sensation as the excessively tall, plumbingly basso regent—and pretty Miss Fox the last boost to above-the-title stardom. Hopper toured *Wang* for two seasons, bringing it back to Broadway for a month in May 1892, again from 15 August (when its ''450th performance'' was announced) and for a further week in November. When Hopper moved on to other shows and roles, Edwin Stevens took a turn at playing Wang, but the original star came back to Broadway in a show that became his most durable and perennial warhorse as late as 1904 (Lyric Theater 18 May, 57 performances), under the Shubert management with Madge Lessing and Julia Sanderson as his leading ladies, and he was still playing *Wang* on the road as much as 20 further years on.

An Australian season of *Wang* was played by Josephine Stanton's company, which toured to the South Pacific with that piece and another American ''comic opera,'' Richard Stahl's *Said Pasha,* in 1901. Miss Stanton was Mataya to the Wang of George Kunkel, with Henry Hallam as Boucher.

Australia: Criterion Theatre, Sydney 9 November 1901

WARDE, Willie [REDBOURN(E), William James] (b Great Yarmouth, 17 June 1857; d London, 18 August 1943). Dancer, choreographer, and lucky "mascot" to producer George Edwardes.

Willie Warde was the son of William Warde [né REDBOURN(E)] sr (b London, c1811; d Wandsworth, London, 21 November 1859), newsvendor, comic singer and songwriter and for 17 years chairman and manager at the Surrey Music Hall, and the brother of **John [Edward] WARDE** [John REDBOURN] (b Christ Church, 24 November 1841; d London, 23 June 1892) and Emma Warde [Mrs D'Auban], music hall duettists and sometime members of the D'Auban and Warde dance combination. This team's families produced, in Willie jr and John D'Auban, the two most successful choreographers of the Victorian and Edwardian musical theatre.

Willie made his earliest stage appearances as a dancer in the music halls before being engaged by John Hollingshead at the Gaiety in 1877. He spent some 30 years there as ballet master choreographer under the managements of Hollingshead and Edwardes, whilst spreading his work around other managements and theatres as well. In later years he designed the dances for the large part of Edwardes's productions. He also appeared frequently in character roles and/or special dancing and pantomime spots in both Gaiety and Daly's musicals, where Edwardes always ensured him a place, no matter tiny, as a kind of "lucky charm." Warde made himself celebrated in these brief appearances by his ability to draw all eyes merely with a walk or a shrug. When he appeared in the famous farce *Tons of Money* in his mid sixties, his one-word appearances throughout the evening in the role of Giles proved one of the highlights of the production.

In an age when the organizer of a show's dances was not always credited on the program, Warde's confirmed choreography credits included *Dick* (1884), *Little Jack Sheppard* (1885), *The Lily of Léoville* (1886), *Lancelot the Lovely, La Prima Donna, The Gondoliers* (1889), *Captain Thérèse* (1890), *Joan of Arc, Cinder-Ellen Up Too Late* (1891), *Blue-Eyed Susan* (1892), *Don Juan* (1893), *Claude Du-val, The Shop Girl* (1894, "Love on the Japanese Plan"), *Gentleman Joe, Dandy Dick Whittington, A Model Trilby* (1895), *My Girl, The Geisha* ("Chon-kina"), *The Circus Girl* (1896), *In Town* (USA, 1897), *A Runaway Girl, A Greek Slave* (1898), *The Lucky Star, San Toy* (UK and USA), *The Rose of Persia* (1899), *The Messenger Boy, Kitty Grey* (1900), *The Toreador, Bluebell in Fairyland* (1901), *A Country Girl, Three Little Maids, An English Daisy, The Girl from Kays* (1902), *The School Girl, The Duchess of Dantzic* (UK and USA), *The Cherry Girl* (1903), *The Cingalee, Lady Madcap* (1904), *Les P'tites Michu* (1905, UK and USA), *The Little Cherub* (1906), *Butterflies* (1908), *The Quaker Girl* (1910), *The Sunshine Girl* (1912), *The Pearl Girl, The Girl from Utah* (1913) and *After the Girl* (1914). His last West End show as a dance arranger seems to have been *Head Over Heels* (1923).

The London shows in which he played roles included *Il Sonnambulo* (1878, the clerk who dances attendance), *Gulliver* (1879, the gorilla), *The Forty Thieves* (1880, Hassan), *Blue Beard* (1883, Jean de Talons aux ressorts), *Ariel* (1883, Echicidio), *Virginia and Paul* (1883, A Mysterious Photographer), *Camaralzaman* (1884, Li Kwinki), *Mazeppa* (1885, Rudzoloff), *Little Jack Sheppard* (1885, Kneebone), *Billee Taylor* (Black Cook, ie, principal dancer), *Dick* (1884, Hassan), *Don Juan* (1893, Cecco), *The Shop Girl* (1894, Mr Tweets), *My Girl* (1896, Weeks), *The Circus Girl* (1896, Auguste), *A Runaway Girl* (1898, Mr Creel), *The Messenger Boy* (1900, Professor Phunkwitz), *The Toreador* (1901, Bandmaster), *A Country Girl* (1902, Granfer Mummery), *The Cingalee* (1904, Myamgah), *Les P'tites Michu* (1905, Gardener), *Les Merveilleuses* (1906, des Gouttières), *Butterflies* (1908, Paul), *The Dollar Princess* (Sir James McGregor), *The Count of Luxembourg* (waiter), *A Waltz Dream* revival, and the 1914 *Country Girl* revival, in which he repeated perhaps his happiest role as old Mummery. As late as 1924 he appeared in *Patricia* at His Majesty's Theatre (Humphrey). On only one occasion have I spotted him playing anything larger than a bit part—in 1883 when he played Crab in *Billee Taylor* at Bournemouth for a fortnight—for, as all the world knew, Willie didn't, or couldn't, speak a line. Nevertheless, "he invented more funny business for comedians than anyone dreams of," and Seymour Hicks averred "had he been able to carry through a long part in dialogue he would have been the god of our theatre life and a figure very large in the public eye."

Warde also appeared in Vienna ("principal dancer of the Gaiety Theatre") in 1881 in the local production of the féerie *L'Arbre de Noël,* and made a visit to Australia for Brough and Boucicault, for whom he choreographed and performed in burlesque and comic opera for a season (1886, Ben Zouatte in *The Forty Thieves,* Blobbs/choreography in *Dick,* etc).

DAS WASCHERMÄDEL Operette in 3 acts by Bernhard Buchbinder. Music by Rudolf Raimann. Theater in der Josefstadt, Vienna, 31 March 1905.

A musical-comedy vehicle for the popular soubrette Hansi Niese, here cast as Betti, the youngest of three washergirls (the other two are called Wetti and Netti!) in a tale of 1835 Vienna that involved its heroine with the Fürst Josef von Kleben and his son, Prinz Karl, and a whole lot of other lofty folk, not to mention the obligatory lady of the theatre (Irene Leitner, a singer). *Das Waschermädel* played 38 performances at the Theater in der Josefstadt, but it remained in the company's and in Niese's repertoire, and was seen again in Vienna in 1913, when the Josefstadter company played a season at the Johann Strauss-Theater (4 October), with Niese featured alongside Emil Guttmann (Josef), Paul Olmuhl (Karl) and Adele Baum (Irene).

The show was also seen in Germany and in Hungary, but its most significant effect was that it persuaded Josef Jarno of the Theater in der Josefstadt to mount other Buchbinder musical plays for his wife's benefit. In 1906 the author supplied *Der Schusterbub,* in which Niese and Alexander Girardi played an initial 52 performances, then in 1907 he turned out Niese's all-time greatest musical-comedy vehicle, *Die Förster-Christl.*

Germany: ?1905; Hungary: Városligeti Nyári Színház *A szoknyáshős* 15 June 1906

THE WATER GIPSIES Play with music in 2 acts by A P Herbert based on his novel of the same name. Music by Vivian Ellis. Winter Garden Theatre, London, 31 August 1955.

The musical *The Water Gipsies* was an updated version of Herbert's successful 1930 novel, which had previously been filmed with the interpolation of one song written by Ellis and performed by Dora Labette. The central characters were Jane (Pamela Charles) and Lily (Dora Bryan), the daughters of old Albert Bell (Jerry Verno), who live on a barge on the River Thames. Jane is the innocent one who gets engaged to the local communist (Wallas Eaton), falls for a dashing artist (Peter Graves), but ends up, after an innocuous adventure in an hotel room, with her childhood sweetheart (Laurie Payne). Lily is the wise and wisecracking one who doesn't expect more than is available from her flashy chap (Roy Godfrey) and who rescues Jane from the episode in the hotel room.

The song ''Little Boat'' was taken from the film score and sung by Payne, but the most successful moments of the evening came when Miss Bryan let loose with her comedy numbers, bewailing her unsuitable name (''Why Did You Call Me Lily?''), damping her beau's proposals (''It Would Cramp My Style'') or helping her sister through her adventure (''You Never Know with Men''). In spite of poor general notices for the show, Miss Bryan's performance proved a draw, so that when she got pregnant and had to leave the cast, Peter Saunders's production foundered and was ultimately withdrawn after 239 performances.

Recordings: original cast (HMV, WRC)

THE WATERMAN, or The First of August Ballad opera in 2 acts by Charles Dibdin. Music composed, compiled and arranged by Dibdin. Little Haymarket Theatre, London, 8 August 1774.

The most successful and enduring of the works of Charles Dibdin, *The Waterman* was a little story of Thameside love and nagging with a salutory ending. Wilhelmina (Anne Jewell), the daughter of the simple, hagridden gardener Mr Bundle (Richard Wilson) and his pretentious wife (Jane Thompson), is sought in marriage by the waterman, Tom Tug (Charles Bannister), and the dandified Robin (Thomas Weston), whose claims are supported by father and mother, respectively. Robin relies on flowery words, but Tom goes out and wins the Thames watermen's rowing race and dedicates his victory to the girl who is, in the end, sensible enough to prefer deeds to words. Since Bundle finally squashes his ever-nagging wife, the evening can end in a happy quartet.

Dibdin's ballad score, much of it original but partly arranged from popular sea songs, went mostly to the three young folk, with Tom's tenor song ''And Did You Not Hear of a Jolly Young Waterman?'' being the most substantial song in a role that was decorated ad lib with nautical numbers (''The Bay of Biscay'' became a traditional feature of the part). Tom Tug was a part that proved a favorite with many famous performers—notably John Braham, Sims Reeves, Charles Santley and Emily Soldene—in the more than a century that the show enjoyed a popularity second to none (not even *The Beggar's Opera*) amongst English ballad operas. Played endlessly through Britain and its colonies as one part of the multiple-bill theatre programs of the 18th and 19th centuries, *The Waterman* was given its last major revival at the Gaiety Theatre in 1870 (19 November), with Santley as a baritone Tom.

The piece was burlesqued in F C Burnand's 1873 *Little Tom Tug* (Opera Comique 12 November), in which Pattie Laverne starred as Tom to the Wilhelmina of Emily Muir, with Emily Thorne, Charles Lyall and J A Shaw supporting and a score ''composed and selected'' by Frederic Stanislaus.

USA: Northern Liberties Theater, Philadelphia 8 April 1791, John Street Theater 22 May 1793; Australia: Theatre Royal, Sydney 24 May 1834

WATSON, Susan [Elizabeth] (b Tulsa, Okla, 17 December 1938). Top Broadway ingenue of the 1960s.

After playing in American regional productions as a teenager, Miss Watson appeared in London in the imported company playing *West Side Story* (Velma), then, back home, at Mildred Dunnock's Barnard Summer Theater as the girl in the original short version of *The Fantasticks* (1959). She made her first Broadway appearances in revue and had her initial metropolitan musical-comedy role as the teen-dreaming Kim McAfee, the underaged heroine of *Bye Bye Birdie* (''One Boy''). She subsequently toured as Lili in *Carnival,* then replaced Anna Maria Alberghetti in the same role in the show's Broadway production, and took leading ingenue roles in *Ben Franklin in Paris* (1964, Janine Nicolet), *A Joyful Noise* (1966, Jenny Lee) and *Celebration* (1969, Angel), whilst playing in more successful shows away from Broadway (Louise in *Gypsy,* Carrie in *Carousel,* Laurey in *Oklahoma!,* Amy in *Where's Charley?*).

She returned to Broadway in 1971 as Nanette in the highly successful revival of *No, No, Nanette* and saw out her ingenue days in regional productions of *Funny Face, Gigi, Promises, Promises* and *The Music Man* before moving west and into married life and more intermittent adult roles.

WATSON, Wylie [ROBERTSON, John Wylie] (b Scotland, 1889; d Scotland, 3 May 1966). Scots variety performer who found late fame as a character man in musical comedy.

Watson worked for many years as a versatile vocalist, instrumentalist and comic in Jack Waller's ''Butterflies'' concert party in the more far-flung parts of the Empire, and although he had appeared discreetly in the cast of the touring musical *The Wishing Well* as early as 1925 (Sawney Potts), he was in his forties when Waller, now a successful producer, fixed him in a musical-theater career by casting him in a supporting character role in the musical comedy *For the Love of Mike* (Rev Archibald James, 1931). He made a personal hit when he played the comical little Yorkshireman Mr Parkin, ''fourteen years tenor with the Ilkley Parish Church,'' in that show's successor, *Tell Her the Truth* (''Sing, Brothers!,'' ''Horror-torio''), and confirmed himself as a star comedy name as the sour-faced, long-shorted scoutmaster Eustace Didcott in *He Wanted Adventure* (''Smile and Be Bright''), as button manufacturer Peabody in *Yes, Madam?* (Cat's Duet, ''Laugh!'') and as the 'cello-playing schoolteacher Mr Clutterbuck in *Please, Teacher!* (Song of the 'Cello). He later played in Waller's less-successful *Big Business, Oh! You Letty* and *Bobby Get Your Gun,* as his ''usual picture of lugubrious dejection'' in the wartime *Present Arms* (Syd Pottle) and on tour in a showy role in Waller's *Hearts Are Trumps* (1943, Mr Mosscockle).

Most of Watson's later career was angled towards the cinema, where he repeated his stage roles in the film versions of *For the Love of Mike, Yes, Madam?* and *Please, Teacher!,* appeared as Mr Memory in the 1935 film of *The Thirty-Nine Steps,* in the 1945 movie musical *Waltz Time, Whisky Galore* and, in his seventies, *The Sundowners.*

WAYBURN, Ned [WEYBURN, Edward Claudius] (b Pittsburgh, Pa, 8 January 1874; d New York, 2 September 1942). Ubiquitous choreographer and director of the early-20th-century Broadway stage.

The son of a wealthy manufacturer of cloth-cutting machines, Wayburn began his working life in his father's business in Pittsburgh and Atlanta before becoming an assistant hotel manager in Chicago. Out of hours, he also worked as an amateur entertainer, playing ragtime piano and writing his own songs. Ned C Wayburn, ''eccentric character comedian and 'ragtime' pianist,'' went professional in 1896, touring the Hopkins Circuit, and playing Milwaukee, Chicago and the Castle circuit with his speciality *The Dude Brownie.* An introduction to May Irwin resulted in her taking up both one of his songs and the composer as her sometime accompanist and stage director. Thus, Wayburn began his life in the theatre as a pianist—appearing (as Edward Wayburn) on Broadway with Miss Irwin in *The Swell Miss Fitzswell* (1897, Parker) and, cheekily billed as ''the man who invented ragtime,'' in *At Gay Coney Island* and *By the Sad Sea Waves* (1899, General Smiles with piano speciality). ''Comedian, composer and stage manager'' Wayburn tried—and not for the last time—to get his fingers into another piece of the musical pie in 1900, when he joined comedian Dave Reed jr and publisher George L Spaulding in a new music publishing firm. Like most of his ventures, it did not last.

In the end, it was as a choreographer and stage director that he made his name. From staging the routines for a group called ''The Minstrel Misses'' on the New York Theater Roof, he moved on to an engagement as a stage director with Klaw and Erlanger, then with the Shuberts. Often working in collaboration with book-wise Herbert Gresham and later with other stagers more libretto-conscious than he, Wayburn remained widely in evidence through more than 20 heavily packed years of musical shows in America and also, during the revue-time fashion for things American, occasionally in London.

Wayburn allegedly made his directorial debut with *The Swell Miss Fitzswell* (although W H Post is credited) and his earliest productions, including such pieces as *By the Sad Sea Waves, Star and Garter, The Night of the Fourth, The Hall of Fame, Miss Simplicity* (1901), *Circus Day* (1901), *Mother Goose, A Little of Everything, Humpty Dumpty,* the Eddie Foy *Mr Bluebeard,* three of the *Rogers Brothers* musicals, *In Newport* (1904), *The Pearl and the Pumpkin* (1905), *The Ham Tree* (1905), *Fritz in Tammany Hall* (1905), *The White Cat* (1905), *A One Horse Town* (1906), were in the farce comedy, extravaganza and/or variety musical style. However, he had a significant success with Chicago's comical, song-filled *The Time, the Place and the Girl* (w Arthur Evans) in 1907, following which he worked on some more substantial book shows such as Lulu Glaser's protean Viennese *Mlle Mischief,* the Gaiety Theatre imports *Havana* (''entire production staged by . . .'') and *Peggy,* and Victor Herbert's operetta *The Rose of Algeria.* His list nevertheless included a predominance of more free and easy pieces: *The Mimic World* (1908), the Eddie Foy show *Mr Hamlet of Broadway,* a string of the loose-limbed dance and comedy shows that were played as ''summer musicals'' by producer Lew Fields, such road pieces as the Gus Edwards/Aaron Hoffman expanded vaudeville sketch *School Days* (1908) and Chicago's *The Heartbreakers* (1911) and *The Military Girl* (1912), as well as some ''big and expensive vaudeville acts'' such as the one-star, 20-dancer ''Ned Wayburn's Jockey Club'' (1902), ''Ned Wayburn's Side Show'' with Harry Pilcer, ''The Phantastic Phantoms'' (1907) or the 20 pint-sized girls who made up ''Ned Wayburn's Broilers'' (1908).

During this time he continued to write occasional songs for interpolation into stage shows, a number of which insisted on the ragtime theme (''The Ghost of Ragtime'' in *The Girl at the Helm,* etc) and in 1912—on the way back from a resounding 1908 bankruptcy—he himself took to the vaudeville stage, playing a sketch called *The Producer.*

In 1913 Albert de Courville took Wayburn to Britain to stage the short-lived Leoncavallo musical comedy *Are You There?,* but his brash and vigorously precise style proved much better suited to revue. He mounted several successful such shows in London between 1913 and 1919 (*Hullo, Tango!, Zig-Zag, Box o' Tricks, Joy Bells*) whilst scoring equal success back home with half a dozen editions of the *Ziegfeld Follies* and even mounting—with pocket-painfully much less success—his own revue, *Town Topics* (1915). He did not, for all that, wholly abandon the book musical. He was called in to work over Fields's *Poor Little Ritz Girl* after an unpromising Boston opening, and, in the 1920s, he directed several other musical plays, notably the highly successful *The Night Boat* (1920) and *Two Little Girls in Blue* (1921). However, he also suffered a number of quick failures, failing to reach Broadway with James T Powers's *The Little Kangaroo* (1922) and, most dangerously to his already frequently and badly dented bank balance, his own *Town Gossip* (1921), which he billed questionably as a ''musical comedy.''

It took Wayburn several years to pay off the debts incurred on this unfortunate production, but he surfaced again in 1926 with *The Maiden Voyage,* only to have the show fold on the road amongst all kinds of recriminations. He was back in 1929 with *Ned Wayburn's Gambols,* but his show could not compete with *George White's Scandals, Earl Carroll's Sketch Book, John Murray Anderson's Almanac* and the other proprietorially named shows of the time and flopped in 31 performances. His last Broadway assignment was on Ziegfeld's unhappy *Smiles* (1930).

Wayburn opened a dance training school (Ned Wayburn Studios of Dancing) in 1905, taking over an entire house on 45th Street and fitting its second floor up as a theatre. In time-dishonored sell-me-a-job fashion (''Every man or woman who wishes to reach prominence—in the shortest time—needs the training of the wonderful producer . . . in the new *Follies* are . . . 97 Ned Wayburn-made chorus girls'') he drew many dancers from its classes to perform the energetic physical-jerks-in-stage-patterns style of choreography that he favored and that subsequently became much used in early cinema musicals. The ''studios'' later became the Ned Wayburn Institutes of Dancing and went for a wider catchment (''You wouldn't think of neglecting your child's education. How about their bodies? Are you willing to let them grow up physically undeveloped, shy, lacking in personality?''). In 1925 he also authored a book, *The Art of Stage Dancing.*

Like most choreographer-directors before and after him, Wayburn's emphasis was ever on the visual and musical side of his productions rather than on the text. But in many of the shows on which he worked, that text was organized either by his collaborator or, when he had none, by the comedians of the show themselves.

Along with his claim to have ''invented'' ragtime, Wayburn claimed to have invented tap dancing, by replacing the clogs of the traditional clog dancer with shoes equipped with little metal thingummyjigs nailed upside down to the soles. History—and particularly theatre history—has usually shown that folk who make such claims are fibbing, but, even though the ludicrous ragtime statement makes Wayburn stand up as a fairly dubiously veracious claimant, no one else seems to have put in a bid for the title of the creator of the claquettes. So maybe he really did do it.

The first of his wives, Agnes Saye Wayburn, was a dancer who appeared alongside Wayburn in *By the Sad Sea Waves* (1899, Effie Eastman) and who really was a member of the first famous sextette in Broadway's original *Florodora* (Lottie Chalmers).

1921 **Town Gossip** (Harold Orlob/w George Stoddard) Ford's Theater, Baltimore 4 September

WEATHER OR NO In 1 act by Adrian Ross and W Beach. Music by B Luard Selby. Savoy Theatre, London, 10 August 1896.

Weather or No was a tiny one-act piece about a flirtation between the man and the lady on a weather-house, which was first produced at London's Savoy Theatre and played by Emmie Owen and H Scott Russell as a forepiece to six months of *The Mikado*'s original run. With the fashion for such little forepieces rapidly dying away, it did not prove one of the theatre's more durable such sketches, so it was all the more surprising to find it picked up by Continental houses, and played with considerable popularity in Berlin, Hamburg, Vienna and a number of other cities in its German version (ad Hermann Hirschel) and in Hungary in a version by Jenő Faragó.

Germany: Thalia-Theater *Das Wetterhäuschen* 19 November 1896; Austria: Theater an der Wien *Das Wetterhäuschen* 23 January 1897; Hungary: Magyar Színház *Derül-borul* 10 November 1897

WEBB, Clifton [HOLLENBECK, Webb Parmalee] (b Indianapolis, 19 November 1889; d Beverly Hills, Calif, 13 October 1966). A slimly elegant juvenile man of stage and screen.

''Encouraged'' by one of the most (in)famous stage mothers of history, the very presentable Webb survived years as a child actor and an operatic aspirant and put his song-and-dance talents to use in a list of Broadway musicals. He had his first metropolitan role in the American production of Reinhardt's *Napoléon und die Frauen* (*The Purple Road,* 1913, Bosco), played in several revues (*Dancing Around, Town Topics,* etc), appeared discreetly in the Princess Theatre productions of *Nobody Home* and *Very Good Eddie* (t/o), in *See America First* (1916, Percy) and was upped to a supporting dance-and-charm role in *Love o' Mike* (1917, Alonzo Bird, ''Look in the Book''). He was the juvenile gentleman in the successful *Listen Lester* (1918, Jack Griffin), played on Broadway in the revue *As You Were* (1920) and the following year in London in the revue *The Fun of the Fayre* before being cast in the title role of the show that C B Cochran called *Phi-Phi* (1922).

He played and danced the role of the other man in Broadway's *Jack and Jill* (1923, Jimmy Eustace) and, after a loop into some non-musical pieces, returned for a similar role in *Sunny* (1925, Harold Wendell Wendell), introducing ''Two Little Bluebirds.'' He subsequently played in *She's My Baby* (1928, Clyde Parker) and *Treasure Girl* (1928, Nat McNally, ''I've Got a Crush on You'') and in a further series of Broadway revues (introducing ''Easter Parade'' in *As Thousands Cheer*). Webb made one final Broadway musical appearance as Gaston in the revamped musical version of *Bei Kerzenlicht* (*You Never Know*) in 1938 before moving on to some elegant and often English roles in comedy, and to Hollywood and a second successful career of some 20 years as a character actor in films. In the 1952 film *Stars and Stripes Forever* he portrayed composer John P Sousa.

Plate 414. **Lizbeth Webb** *in* Bless the Bride.

WEBB, Lizbeth [WILLS-WEBBER, Elizabeth] (b Reading, 30 January 1926). The outstanding ingenue of the British 1950s stage.

A teenage band and radio vocalist, Miss Webb was hired by C B Cochran as a trainee star and put initially into the cover of the lead role of his production of *Big Ben* (1946). Stardom came earlier than intended, when motherhood overtook the leading lady and the very attractive young soprano succeeded to the role of Grace Green. She subsequently took the lead role of Lucy Veracity Willow in Cochran's next production, the highly successful *Bless the Bride,* creating ''I Was Never Kissed Before'' and ''This Is My Lovely Day'' with George Guétary, then starred alongside Cicely Courtneidge as the juvenile heroine of *Gay's the Word* (1949) and played Sarah Brown in London's production of *Guys and Dolls* (1953). She departed from the unfortunate *Jubilee Girl* (1956) on the road, appeared as Giulietta in the televised version of the musical *Carissima* (1959) and subsequently retired to married life as Lady Campbell. She was seen once more in the West End when she played a season as *The Merry Widow* in 1969.

WEBER, [Morris] Joseph (b New York, 11 August 1867; d Los Angeles, 10 May 1942). The other half of the Weber and Fields vaudeville and burlesque team.

Plate 415. **Weber and Fields**

Polish-parented Weber's career as a music-hall comedian was long linked with that of Lew Fields, with whom he worked in a Dutch-dialect duo and alongside whom he became the manager of the celebrated Weber and Fields burlesque house and the Broadway Theater. The pair produced and appeared in a long list of burlesque/variety musical comedy pieces in which they inevitably played roles that allowed them to perform their heavily accented Germanic low comedy.

When the partnership broke up in 1904, Fields moved on, and Weber continued to run their theatre, producing several shows on the lines of the old Weber and Fields pieces as well as Victor Herbert's *Dream City,* the low-comic *Hip Hip Hooray!* (1907, Julius Grienbacher) and a burlesque of *The Merry Widow* (1908), in which he appeared as Disch to the widow of Lulu Glaser and of Blanche Ring with considerable success. However, the best had been had from the house and its tradition, and Weber soon gave up his theatre and went into independent production, mounting the play *The Climax* (1909) and an English version of Adolf Philipp's musical comedy *Alma, wo wohnst du?,* a slightly scandalous hit at the German-language Terrace Garten the previous year. It was a slightly scandalous hit all over again in English.

Weber joined forces with Fields again in 1912, and the pair attempted to set their old style of show going once more, but the effort was not prolonged, and Weber returned to producing regular musical plays. He had a fine success with Victor Herbert's *The Only Girl,* won esteem with the same composer's Irish operetta *Eileen* and little with his *Her Regiment* (both 1917), and after an even briefer second attempt at getting *Back Again* with Fields, mounted two last musical plays. The ''gay, girly, glad musical farce'' *Little Blue Devil* (1919), an adaptation of the hit German play *Der blaue Maus,* was a disappointment, and Weber hedged by producing the Efrem Zimbalist musical *Honeydew* (1920)—this one based on a French play, *Les Surprises du divorce*—on the earlier show's sets. When the piece showed up strong in tryout, he built a lavish new production for it and was rewarded with a final Broadway musical success (192 performances).

As late as 1940 Weber and Fields appeared performing one of their routines in the film *Lillian Russell.*

Biography: Isman, F: *Weber and Fields* (Boni & Liveright, New York, 1924)

WEEDE, Robert (b Baltimore, 22 February 1903; d Walnut Creek, Calif, 9 July 1972).

Operatic baritone Weede made his name in broadcasting before joining the Metropolitan Opera in 1937. He performed there until 1945, but reached his widest audience when, in 1956, he made his first appearance on Broadway, creating the role of Tony, *The Most Happy Fella* of the title of that show (''The Most Happy Fella,'' ''My Heart Is So Full of You,'' etc). He had a second Broadway success when he paired with another operatic vocalist, Mimi Benzell, for the middle-aged romance of the Jerry Herman musical *Milk and Honey* (1961), but thereafter made only one more Broadway appearance, in the rather less successful *Cry for Us All* (1970, Edward Quinn).

WEHLEN, Emmy (b Mannheim, 1887). Glamorous German singer who abandoned the musical stage for films.

Emmy Wehlen began her career in the musical theatre in Stuttgart, Munich and Berlin, where she was a member of the company at the Thalia-Theater (*Das Mitternachtsmädel,* Magda in *Die Brunnen-Nymphe* 1908) before going to Britain to tour in the title role in George Edwardes's production of *The Merry Widow* (1909). She appeared next as the gold-digging Olga in Edwardes's version of *The Dollar Princess* in London and in the British provinces, then crossed to America to star in Ivan Caryll's *Marriage à la Carte* (1910, Rosalie) and as another fairly merry widow, Mrs Guyer, in Ziegfeld's remake of *A Trip to Chinatown* as *A Winsome Widow* (1912), ''singing 'Reuben, Reuben' as if it were the latest thing from France.'' Scheduled for the star role in Broadway's *The Lilac Domino,* she dropped out with what was said to be appendicitis. She took the role of Winifred in the German musical comedy *The Girl on the Film* both in London and then in New York, replaced Isobel Elsom as the heroine of *After the Girl* at the Gaiety Theatre, then returned to America with the British company that played *Tonight's the Night* there in 1914. Feeling her German nationality, she remained behind when the company returned to wartime Britain, and she soon abandoned the musical stage for the screen, where she became a favorite leading lady of silent films between 1915 and 1921, making her screen debut in Metro's *When a Woman Loves* and appearing in such slightly daring pieces as *The Amateur Adventuress* (''the story of a girl who wanted to know the meaning of the word life!''), the serial *Who's Guilty?, Fools and Their Money* and *The Outsider* (''she determined to become an adventuress . . . she succeeded beyond her wildest dreams!''). Then she vanished from show business annals.

DAS WEIB IM PURPUR Operette in 3 acts by Leopold Jacobson and Rudolf Österreicher. Music by Jean Gilbert. Wiener Stadttheater, Vienna, 21 December 1923.

The ''lady in purple'' is Catherine II of Russia (Margit Suchy), who affirms that royalty cannot afford to fall in love until she meets Lieutenant Michael Michailowitz (Hubert Marischka). She courts him in disguise as the peasant Marinka, until a birthmark gives her away. The lighter moments were provided by the Austrian Ambassador Graf Aladár Gombaty (Fritz Werner) and his wife, Stanzi (Olga Bartos-Treu), a happily married pair who gamboled through happy duets (''Liebling, du hast was,'' ''Jedes neue Jahr'') whilst the Tsarina—in her disguise as ''ein strammes Bauernmädel'' (a strapping peasant lass)—and her lieutenant joined together more expansively to insist ''Bleib' bei mir die heutige Nacht.''

Produced at Wiener Stadttheater, which a year earlier had been watching *Die Siegerin* rise to power at the side of Tsar Peter the Great, *Das Weib im Purpur* had a reasonable if not memorable run. The show was subsequently played in Hungary (ad Ernő Kulinyi) and a new Viennese production was mounted at the Bürgertheater in 1929 (31 October) and played for three weeks, with Ida Russka in the star role.

What started out to be a Broadway production of *Das Weib im Purpur* was barely recognizable as such by the time it arrived in New York. If Edward Delaney Dunn and Harry B Smith's title *The Red Robe* (Shubert Theater 25 December 1928) still had a savor of the original, the savor was all. The ''red robe'' referred to Cardinal Richelieu, and their story was a *Three Musketeers* wannabe. In spite of such notices as ''it approaches being the worst thing the Shuberts have ever done,'' stars Walter Woolf and Helen Gilliland performed a few of Gilbert's tunes—and a lot of others—for 167 Broadway nights.

Hungary: Városi Színház *A bíborruhás asszony* 3 March 1927

WEIDMAN, Jerome (b New York, 4 April 1913).

After the success of his first book, *I Can Get It for You Wholesale,* at the age of 22, Weidman abandoned thoughts of a career in the law and instead authored a long list of further novels before making his first venture into the musical theatre as the co-author of the libretto for the long-running Broadway hit *Fiorello!* (1959). He teamed with Jerry Bock, Sheldon Harnick and George Abbott for a second New York costume musical in the music-hally tale of the *Tenderloin* (1960), and scored again with a stage musicalization of his maiden novel, *I Can Get It for You Wholesale* (1962). Two subsequent musicals were, however, failures—a Faustian piece called *Cool Off!,* which featured the post-*My Fair Lady* Stanley Holloway in a multiple role, closed out of town, and a New Orleans version of the *Blue Angel* story, set to Duke Ellington music under the title *Pousse-Café,* played just three Broadway performances. On film he took a screenplay credit on *The Eddie Cantor Story.*

His son, **John WEIDMAN**, was the author of the libretto for the 1976 musical *Pacific Overtures* (mus/ly: Stephen Sondheim, Winter Garden Theater 11 January) and *America's Sweetheart* (Robert Waldman/w Alfred Uhry, Hartford Stage, Hartford, Conn 5 March 1985), had a hand in the adaptation of *Anything Goes* for its successful revival at the Vivian Beaumont Theater and in lands beyond, and subsequently supplied the texts to a second Sondheim work, *Assassins* (1991), and to *Big* (Maltby/Shire Shubert Theater 28 April 1996).

1959 **Fiorello!** (Jerry Bock/Sheldon Harnick/w George Abbott) Broadhurst Theater 23 November

1960 **Tenderloin** (Bock/Harnick/w Abbott) 46th Street Theater 17 October

1962 **I Can Get It for You Wholesale** (Harold Rome) Shubert Theater 22 March

1964 **Cool Off!** (Howard Blankman) Forrest Theater, Philadelphia 31 March

1966 **Pousse-Café** (Duke Ellington/Marshall Barer, Fred Tobias) 46th Street Theater 18 March

WEILL, Kurt [Julian] (b Dessau, 2 March 1900; d New York, 3 April 1950). German musician who adapted his style to the American commercial and uncommercial stage with some success in a veritable two-part career.

Kurt Weill studied music in Berlin and began his professional life in the theatre as a repetiteur at Dessau and as a conductor in Ludenscheid, before returning to Berlin to study with Busoni (1921–24). In 1922 his first stage work, a children's piece called *Zaubernacht,* was produced at Berlin's Theater am Kurfurstendamm, but he concentrated his composing efforts at this stage principally on orchestral and instrumental writing, and his first adult theatre piece, the one-act opera *Der Protaganist,* written to a text by the celebrated playwright Georg Kaiser, was not produced until 1926. In 1927 a second one-act opera, *Royal Palace* (lib: Yvan Goll), a piece featuring revusical elements, a film sequence and popular music idioms, was mounted in Berlin, and he collaborated with Kaiser on another short piece, *Der Zar lasst sich photographieren* (1928), before making his first entry into the world of the musical comedy with the music for Elisabeth Hauptmann and Bertolt Brecht's purposefully harsh revision of *The Beggar's Opera, Die Dreigroschenoper.* He matched the tone of the show's text with a series of numbers written in tinny, jazzy contemporary tones in which there was rarely place for sentiment or grace, or for humor of any but the bitterest kind (''Seeräuber Jenny,'' ''Moritat,'' Salomonsong, Barbarasong, etc), and the show found a considerable and commercial success throughout Germany, as well as a number of productions abroad.

Hauptmann, Brecht and Weill combined on a second show for the same Theater am Schiffbauerdamm in *Happy End* (''Surabaya Johnny,'' Bilbao song), but, lacking the solid dramatic structure that had been provided by Gay's durable play for their earlier success, this attempt to paste some simplistic politicizing onto a curiously naive little story folded in chaos in just three performances, leaving some fine songs orphaned. Weill returned to the opera with the young people's ''Schuloper'' *Der Jasager* (1930), with *Aufstieg und Fall der Stadt Mahagonny,* first played in its completed state later the same year, *Die Bürgschaft* and, again with Kaiser, in his most substantial work, *Der Silbersee* (1931), before in 1933, with the rise of the Nazi party, he and his wife, Lotte Lenya, joined the mass exodus of Jewish theatrical writers and artists from Germany, ending permanently his connection with the German theatre.

The composer stopped at first in Paris, where his sung dance piece (ballet-chanté) *Die sieben Todsünden* was given its first production, and briefly visited London, where his musical play *A Kingdom for a Cow,* composed to a text by Robert Vambery, dramaturge at the Schiffbauerdamm, was produced at the Savoy Theatre. Another politically orientated piece of whimsy, it folded in two weeks. Before the end of the year Weill had continued on to America.

His first work for the American stage was the score for Paul Green's musical play *Johnny Johnson,* a mildly surrealistic anti-war parable written in a Singspiel style, which was produced by the Group Theatre at Broadway's 44th Street Theater (68 performances), and his second, a collaboration with the respected playwright Maxwell Anderson on a purposefully fictional reworking of early American history, *Knickerbocker Holiday.* Although it survived rather longer than the earlier, less uncompromising and less traditionally ''commercial'' *Johnny Johnson, Knickerbocker Holiday* did not become a Broadway success (168 performances). The show's score, however, brought forth the wistful ''September Song'' which, notably as recorded by Bing Crosby, became one of Weill's most enduring show songs.

Theatrical success, which had avoided Weill since *Der Jasager,* returned with his next Broadway piece. *Lady in the Dark* abandoned the political posturings of the previous works and took a further step towards the standard musical play or, in this case, extravaganza in a piece that included a set of ''dream sequences'' in its brightly well-written text. The musical part of the show was largely contained in those dream sections, which thus took the form of extended, operatic-style musical scenas, and some of the plangent tones of Weill's first hit could be occasionally heard interbred with operatic strains and with traditional Broadway music (''My Ship,'' ''Jenny'') in a score that was none the less attractive for being unusual and interesting. Another fantasy, *One Touch of*

Venus (''Speak Low''), which moved even closer to the traditional American musical-comedy style, confirmed the success of *Lady in the Dark,* but a period piece about sculptor Benvenuto Cellini, which insisted that he was *The Firebrand of Florence,* failed in 43 performances.

In 1947 Weill composed the score for a version of Elmer Rice's successful play *Street Scene,* which was purposely announced under the description of a ''Broadway opera,'' in the vein of *Porgy and Bess.* Here, Weill found himself in the area that clearly suited him best and, given a substantial, dramatic and purely personal story to illustrate he produced an excitingly pictorial modern theatre score that richly bestrode the musical and operatic idioms. If *Street Scene* was unable to encourage the kind of audiences that *Lady in the Dark* or *One Touch of Venus* had done (148 performances), it was, years later, to find itself and its level of composition in the height of fashion, and, whilst other shows of the era were forgotten, to find itself a home in the very opera houses from out of which Weill had hoped to bring this form of musical theatre.

Street Scene was succeeded by two further musicals—a whimsical panorama of *Love Life* (1948), which played an insufficient 252 Broadway performances, and an adaptation of Alan Paton's South African novel *Lost in the Stars* (1949, 281 performances), neither of which proved to have a wide appeal, and by a one-act folk opera, *Down in the Valley,* originally played at Indiana University and subsequently at many other colleges, as well as being broadcast and televised on several occasions, and played professionally in a German stage version (*Drunten im Tal* Staatstheater, Karlsruhe 22 October 1960).

However, Weill's final and most resounding success in his adopted homeland was a posthumous one. Following his death during the run of *Lost in the Stars,* a new version of *Die Dreigroschenoper*—originally unsuccessful in America—was produced at off-Broadway's Theatre de Lys (1954). The production and the piece appealed to the striving anti-establishment feelings of its times much in the same way that *Hair* would do more than a decade later, and it played for more than 2,600 performances, firmly establishing the work and its songs in the English-speaking world, where it has since remained by far the most popular and the most frequently produced of its composer's works.

Weill's other theatrical work included incidental music for several plays, and he also composed the score for Fritz Lang's film *You and Me* (w Sam Coslow, Johnny Burke), as well as the songs performed in the film *Where Do We Go from Here?* (w Ira Gershwin).

The composer proved his versatility in successfully matching his music to styles of lyrics and libretti as diverse as the deep, allegorical *Der Silbersee,* the comic-strip retelling of the tale of *Die Dreigroschenoper,* the wholesale fantasy of *One Touch of Venus* and the three-dimensional drama of *Street Scene.* Most of his theatrical failures came when he teamed with authors whose political and/or social preoccupations infringed unhelpfully on their theatrical ones—but it is those same political/social preoccupations that have subsequently been responsible for several of these pieces continuing to find a place on the world's stages, sometimes in preference to their composer's better and initially more successful shows.

Since the 1970s, powerfully encouraged by a foundation set up in the composer's name by his widow, Weill's music has become both hugely fashionable and seemingly more widely performed than at any time in his life. In particular, those of his show songs that were previously identified with the performance of his wife, on whose scorched-soubrette voice many of them were modeled, have become favorite meat for a stream of torch singers. These, and others of his songs, have gone into a number of concert and compilation shows, notably the 1972 *Berlin to Broadway with Kurt Weill* (Theatre de Lys 1 October 1972).

1928 **Die Dreigroschenoper** (Elisabeth Hauptmann, Bertolt Brecht) Theater am Schiffbauerdamm, Berlin 31 August

1929 **Happy End** (Brecht/Hauptmann [and Brecht uncredited]) Theater am Schiffbauerdamm, Berlin 2 September

1935 **A Kingdom for a Cow** (*Der Kuhhandel*) (Desmond Carter/Robert Vambery ad Reginald Arkell) Savoy Theatre, London 28 June

1936 **Johnny Johnson** (Paul Green) 44th Street Theater, New York 19 November

1938 **Knickerbocker Holiday** (Maxwell Anderson) Barrymore Theater 19 October

1941 **Lady in the Dark** (Ira Gershwin/Moss Hart) Alvin Theater 23 January

1943 **One Touch of Venus** (Ogden Nash/S J Perelman) Imperial Theater 7 October

1945 **The Firebrand of Florence** (I Gershwin/Edwin Justus Mayer) Alvin Theater 22 March

1947 **Street Scene** (Langston Hughes/Elmer Rice) Adelphi Theater 9 January

1948 **Down in the Valley** (Arnold Sundgaard) 1 act University of Indiana 15 July

1948 **Love Life** (Alan Jay Lerner) 46th Street Theater 7 October

1949 **Lost in the Stars** (Anderson, Alan Paton) Music Box Theater 30 October

Biographies, etc: Kowalke, K: *Kurt Weill in Europe* (UMI, Ann Arbor, Mich, 1979), Kowalke, K (ed): *A New Orpheus: Essays on Kurt Weill* (Yale University Press, New Haven, Conn, 1986), Sanders, R: *The Days Grow Short* (Holt, Rinehart & Winston, New York, 1980), Jarman, D: *Kurt Weill* (Bloomington, Ind, 1982), Drew, D: *Kurt Weill: A Handbook* (University of Berkeley, Calif, 1987), Schebera, J: *Kurt Weill: Eine Biographie in Texten, Bildern und Dokumenten* (Deutsche Verlag für Musik, Leipzig, 1990 and Yale UP, New Haven, Conn, 1995), Taylor,

R: *Kurt Weill: Composer in a Divided World* (Northeastern UP, 1992), Kowalke, K, Edler, H: *A Stranger Here Myself: Kurt Weill Studien* (Olms, Hildesheim, 1993), Kilroy, D: *Kurt Weill on Broadway: The Postwar Years 1945–1950* (UMI, Ann Arbor, Mich, 1995), Symonette, L, Kowalke, K: *Speak Low (When You Speak Love): The Letters of Kurt Weill and Lotte Lenya* (University of California, Los Angeles, 1996), Grosch, N, Luchjesi, J, Schebera, J: *Kurt Weill-Studien* (M&P, Stuttgart, 1996), etc

WEINBERGER, Carl [Rudolf Michael] (b Vienna, 3 April 1861; d Vienna, 1 November 1939).

Although his pieces have long dropped from the schedules, even in central Europe, Carl Weinberger's attractive dance-rhythmed scores were heard not only in Vienna but also in Germany, in Hungary, in Italy and as far afield as America, during the last decade of the 19th century and the earliest years of the 20th, and he continued to produce music for the theatre until well after the First World War. If none of his Operetten scored the kind of success that would make it last for half a century, he regularly found respectable runs and only a handful of genuine failures.

His first piece, *Pagenstreiche,* an adaptation of Kotzebue's comedy (set with rather more success in Hungary by József Konti as *A kopé*), was produced by Camillo Walzel at the Theater an der Wien when the composer was 27 years of age, and it won only a dozen performances before being withdrawn, but the second, *Die Uhlanen,* was played 34 times at the Carltheater and again at Berlin's Thomastheater (30 April 1892), whilst the third, *Lachende Erben,* won a genuine success. It followed 33 performances in Vienna with a production at Berlin's Theater Unter den Linden (15 January 1893), another at Budapest's Budai Színkör (*Nevető őrőkősők* 2 June 1893) and was played at New York's German-language Irving Place Theater (25 December 1893) by José Ferenczy's touring Operette company.

Weinberger had a further success with *Die Karlsschülerin,* played 59 times at the Theater an der Wien with Ilka Pálmay adding not a little to its attractions in the role of the leading boy, in Frankfurt, Hamburg and again at Budapest's Népszínház (*Hektor kisasszony* 16 May 1903), but two efforts to make an Operette out of Toché and Blum's French vaudeville *La Maison Tamponin* (Palais-Royal 22 March 1893) were less happy: *Die Prima Ballerina* was played 25 times at the Carltheater and again at Berlin's Thalia-Theater (24 October 1896), whilst *Auch so eine!,* produced six years later at the Theater in der Josefstadt (18 October 1901), managed only 27 nights. However, with *Der Schmetterling* he found another fair success. Produced at the Theater an der Wien, with Julie Kopácsi-Karczag top-billed, it was played 57 times there and was later seen at Berlin's Theater des Westens (29 November 1906, 14 performances) as well as in Italy.

Die Blumen-Mary, the following year, had Ilka Pálmay playing a New York florist, Carl Blasel an American umbrella manufacturer, and a respectable Vienna run (41 performances) before crossing the border (Metropoltheater 17 November 1898), whilst *Adam und Eva,* which featured Girardi and American divette Marie Halton in four scenes of love through the ages (Josef and Mme Putiphar, Quixote and Dulcinea, etc) up to the present day, was played 52 times at the Carltheater. Annie Dirkens was *Die Diva* (the title had been unlucky for Offenbach, too) just 22 times, and Ilka Pálmay showed that she had *Das gewisse Etwas* (otherwise ''it'') for 25 nights before the piece went on to Hungary (*Az izé,* Népszínház ad Jenő Heltai, Miksa Márton, 26 April 1902), where it won a distinct popularity through 31 performances.

Weinberger's name then slipped from the schedules for a number of years, but he returned to the forefront with an adaptation from Wichert called *Die romantische Frau,* which was played by Vienna's *Die lustige Witwe* stars Treumann and Mizzi Günther through a run of 73 nights. However, the composer had his longest Vienna run of all when Oscar Fronz produced *Der Frechling* with Fritz Werner starred for 86 performances at the Bürgertheater. *Drei arme Teufel,* produced in Munich, subsequently came to the Bürgertheater as well (15 June 1923, 51 performances), but after this the composer contributed little more to the metropolitan musical stage, his few remaining theatre pieces being either on a small scale or for regional houses.

Weinberger's other works included an opera, *Das Sonnenkind* (1929), songs, dance music and pantomimes.

1888 **Pagenstreiche** (Hugo Wittmann) Theater an der Wien 28 April

1889 **Der Adjutaut** (A Rupprecht) 1 act Baden bei Wien 13 July; Carltheater 24 September

1890 **Angelor** (Julius Horst) 1 act Troppau 15 January

1891 **Die Uhlanen** (Wittmann) Carltheater 5 December

1892 **Lachende Erben** (Horst, Leo Stein) Carltheater 24 October

1893 **Münchener Kind'l** (Alexander Landesberg, Stein) Theater Unter den Linden, Berlin 7 November

1895 **Die Karlsschülerin** (Wittmann) Theater an der Wien 21 March

1895 **Die Prima Ballerina** (later *Auch so eine!*) (Wittmann) Carltheater 23 November

1896 **Der Schmetterling** (A M Willner, Bernhard Buchbinder) Theater an der Wien 7 November

1897 **Die Blumen-Mary** (Landesberg, Stein) Theater an der Wien 11 November

1899 **Adam und Eva** (*Die Seelenwanderung*) (Wittmann, Julius Bauer) Carltheater 5 January

1900 **Der Wundertrank** (Horst, Benjamin Schier) 1 act Hotel Continental 17 March

1900 **Die Diva** (Buchbinder, Josef Wattke) Carltheater 12 October
1902 **Der Spatz** (Buchbinder) Deutsches Volkstheater 14 January
1902 **Das gewisse Etwas** (Victor Léon, Stein) Carltheater 15 March
1904 **Schlaraffenland** (Mathilde Schurz) Neues Deutsches Theater, Prague 27 March
1911 **Die romantische Frau** (Karl Lindau, Béla Jenbach) Johann Strauss-Theater 17 March
1912 **Der Frechling** (Fritz Grünbaum, Heinz Reichert) Wiener Bürgertheater 21 December
1914 **Die Nachtprinzessin** (Feydeau ad Weinberger) Operetten-Theater, Hamburg 4 April
1916 **Drei arme Teufel** (Rudolf Österreicher, Reichert) Theater am Gärtnerplatz, Munich 11 March
1919 **Paragraph 88** (Edmond Gondinet, P Giffard ad Richard Wilde, M Günther) Stadttheater, Zürich 28 December
1926 **Ein Nachtmanöver** (*Der Nachtfalter*) (Buchbinder, Schurz) Bozen March
1928 **Die Liebesinsel** (Wilde, Schurz) Baden bei Wien 17 November
1936 **Der alte Silbergulden** (Fred Angemeyer-Höft) 1 act Stadttheater 5 April

WELCH, Elisabeth (b New York, 27 February 1904). Vocalist who featured in a handful of musicals.

After an early career in supporting roles in New York black musical comedy (Ruth Little in *Runnin' Wild,* introducing the ''Charleston,'' *The Chocolate Dandies*) and revue (*Lew Leslie's Blackbirds of 1928*), appearances in cabaret in America and Europe, and a takeover of the role of May in *The New Yorkers* (1931) on Broadway, Miss Welch went to Britain, where she had her first engagement in a revue, *Dark Doings* (1933). She was subsequently cast as Haidee Robinson in C B Cochran's production of *Nymph Errant,* scoring a particular success with the song ''Solomon,'' then as an incidental stowaway with a couple of incidental songs in Ivor Novello's first Drury Lane spectacular, *Glamorous Night* (''The Girl I Knew,'' ''Shanty Town''). Thereafter, the theatrical portion of her career was largely in revue, but she had another plot-incidental role in a Novello musical in *Arc de Triomphe* (1943, Josie, ''Dark Music'') and returned to the book-musical stage to play the Soho lowlife Sweet Ginger in the 1959 *The Crooked Mile* and again as the aged Berthe in London's brief run of *Pippin* (1973). She was subsequently seen in compilation shows and in concert into the 1990s, becoming London's most popular I-can-still-do-it artist and the darling of critics and theatricals.

WELCHMAN, Harry [Geth] (b Barnstaple, 24 February 1886; d Penzance, 3 January 1966). Handsome baritone who became the epitomic operetta leading man for several decades of London shows.

Plate 416. **Elisabeth Welch** *with Jack McGowran in* The Crooked Mile.

Welchman was first employed by Ada Reeve, at the age of 18, for the chorus of her touring musical *Winnie Brooke, Widow,* and he toured the British provinces in several musicals and plays before making his first appearance in the West End. He entered London's musical theatre as understudy to Hayden Coffin in the title role of Edward German's *Tom Jones* and, after he had toured the piece in replacement of Coffin, producer Courtneidge cast him, between 1909 and the war, in the baritone hero roles of *The Arcadians* (Jack Meadows, ''Half Past Two,'' ''Charming Weather''), *The Mousmé* (Captain Fujiwara), *Princess Caprice* (Augustin Hofer), *Oh! Oh! Delphine* (Victor Jolibeau), *The Pearl Girl* (Duke of Trent) and *The Cinema Star* (Victor de Brett). In 1915 he toured in *The Miller's Daughters* (Jack Charlton). After the war, he continued to play staunchly singing heros starring opposite Alice Delysia as Don Juan jr in C B Cochran's production of the saucy *Afgar* (1919), in the feather-light *Oh! Julie* with Ethel Levey (1920), as the Grand Duke Constantine to the *Sybil* of José Collins (1921), as Colonel Belacour to *The Lady of the Rose* of Phyllis Dare (1922) and as Bonni to her *The Street Singer* (1924)—four and a half long-running hits in five successive productions.

That average was soon to be spoiled, for Welchman nurtured a continual determination to present himself in a romantic operetta, and over the years he turned down fine London roles as he tried to set up a series of invariably awful pieces under his own steam. *Love's Prisoner* (1925) was the first of these to get to London, but not for long. An attempt in a musical comedy with *The Bamboula* (1925, Jimmy Roberts) did only a little better before he switched back to other folks' romantic operettas. He appeared on Broadway as Rudolf Rassendyl in the musical version of *The Prisoner of Zenda* (Princess Flavia, 1925), a role and a show that had actually been written for Walter Woolf, toured Britain as Karl-Franz in *The Student Prince,* then starred at Drury Lane in *The Desert Song* (1927, Pierre) and, replacing the original Howett Worster, in *The New Moon* (t/o Robert Misson). In between, however, he had another go at actor-management with the ineffectual *The White Camellia* (1929).

Welchman starred in Jack Waller's spectacular *Silver Wings* (Pablo Santos, 1930), toured in *Nina Rosa* and appeared as both leading men—in turn—in London's version of *Viktória* (*Victoria and Her Hussar*). He toured again as *Casanova,* found other weak vehicles as *Beau Brummell* (1933) and as the hero of the touring *Hearts Are Trumps* (1935), returned to London as the star of reprises of *The Desert Song* and *The Vagabond King* and toured in similar vehicles (*The Student Prince, The Maid of the Mountains, Chu Chin Chow*) through the late 1930s and early 1940s.

In 1944 he was seen in London as Macheath in *The Beggar's Opera,* but thereafter his musical appearances were in character roles, and his remaining London shows, *Lucky Boy* (1953) and *The World of Paul Slickey* (1959), were both unmitigated failures.

Welchman appeared on film alongside Nancy Brown as Baldasarre in the 1932 film of *The Maid of the Mountains* and opposite Bebe Daniels as Francesco del Fuego in the 1933 *A Southern Maid.* In 1946 he appeared in the film version of *The Lisbon Story.*

WELISCH, Ernst [JURASCHEK, Ernst Friedrich Wilhelm] (b Vienna, 27 February 1875; d Vienna, 26 March 1941).

Playwright, longtime dramaturge at the Berliner Theater and stage director, Welisch made an early venture into the musical theatre with the libretto for the young Leo Fall's first Operette *Der Rebell* (1905). The show was a quick flop, but Welisch had a hand in its subsequent rewriting as *Der liebe Augustin,* providing him with a first-class success that he followed up with a series of major Operetten written over a period of some 20 years with co-author Rudolf Schanzer and with some of the era's most important composers: Fall, Straus, Jean Gilbert, Kálmán and Ralph Benatzky.

His first significant hit after *Der liebe Augustin* was the Jean Gilbert Operette *Die Frau im Hermelin,* a romantic costume piece that, after a good Berlin run, became one of London's longest-running hits of the 1920s, and, following the respectable showings of the parallel Berlin runs of *Der Geiger von Lugano* (162 performances) and *Die spanische Nachtigall* with Fritzi Massary in its title role (143 performances) and the nearly five months of *Die Braut des Lucullus* at the Theater des Westens (144 performances), he saw his name attached to another major international hit, this time alongside the music of Leo Fall, with the comical tale of the putative love life of *Madame Pompadour.*

There were further Berlin successes with Straus on *Riquette* and the Napoléonic tale of *Teresina* and with Benatzky on the spectaculars *Casanova* and *Die drei Musketiere* (which, nevertheless, drew less than favorable mentions for its text), while Fall's *Der süsse Kavalier,* with a flashback libretto that took in the Chevalier d'Éon and the Queen of England, Gilbert's *Das Spiel um die Liebe,* produced at Berlin's Theater des Westens (80 performances) and Vienna's Stadttheater in 1925–26, and Krasznay-Krausz's *Eine Frau von Format* (56 performances, also dir) all had at least respectable careers in central Europe. Kálmán's *Der Teufelsreiter,* played 148 times at the Theater an der Wien after Welisch had left Berlin to return to his native city in the early 1930s, also did well in its initial showing.

1905 **Der Rebell** (Leo Fall/w Rudolf Bernauer) Theater an der Wien, Vienna 29 November

1912 **Der liebe Augustin** revised *Der Rebell* Neues Theater 3 February

1914 **Jung England** (Fall/w Bernauer) Montis Operetten-Theater 14 February

1919 **Die Frau im Hermelin** (Jean Gilbert/w Rudolf Schanzer) Theater des Westens 23 August

1920 **Frau Ministerpräsident** (Fall/w Bernauer) Residenztheater, Dresden 3 February

1920 **Der Geiger von Lugano** (Gilbert/w Schanzer) Wallner-Theater 25 September

1920 **Die spanische Nachtigall** (Fall/w Schanzer) Berliner Theater 18 November

1921 **Die Braut des Lucullus** (Gilbert/w Schanzer) Theater des Westens 26 August

1922 **Madame Pompadour** (Fall/w Schanzer) Berliner Theater 9 September

1923 **Die Damen von Olymp** (Rudolf Nelson/w Schanzer) Nelson-Theater May

1923 **Der süsse Kavalier** (Fall/w Schanzer) Apollotheater, Vienna 11 December

1925 **Riquette** (Oscar Straus/w Schanzer) Deutsches Künstlertheater 17 January

1925 **[Die] Teresina** (Straus/w Schanzer) Deutsches Künstlertheater 11 September

1925 **Das Spiel um die Liebe** (Gilbert/w Schanzer) Theater des Westens 19 December

1926 **Jugend im Mai** (Fall/ w Schanzer) Centraltheater, Dresden 22 October; Städtische Oper, Berlin 1927

1927 **Eine Frau von Format** (Michael Krasznay-Krausz/w Schanzer) Theater des Westens 21 September

1928 **Casanova** (Johann Strauss arr Ralph Benatzky/w Schanzer) Grosses Schauspielhaus 1 September

1929 **Die drei Musketiere** (Benatzky/w Schanzer) Grosses Schauspielhaus 28 September

1929 **Die erste Beste** (Straus/w Schanzer) Deutsches Theater, Prague 19 October

1930 **Das Mädel am Steuer** (Gilbert/w Schanzer) Komische Oper 17 September

1932 **Der Teufelsreiter** (Emmerich Kálmán/w Schanzer) Theater an der Wien, Vienna 10 March

1932 **Der Studentenprinz** (*The Student Prince*) German version w Schanzer, Grosses Schauspielhaus

1933 **Die Lindenwirtin** (Krasznay-Krausz/w Schanzer) Metropoltheater 30 March

1935 **Maya** German version w Schanzer, Theater an der Wien, Vienna

1935 **Der junge Herr René** revised *Der süsse Kavalier* ad Krasznay-Krausz

1936 **Dreimal Georges** (Paul Burkhard/w Schanzer) Stadttheater, Zürich 3 October

1939 **Die Sacher-Pepi** (Rudi Gfaller) Operetten-Theater, Leipzig 16 September

1941 **Venedig in Wien** (Gfaller) Centraltheater, Chemnitz 29 March

WELLEMINSKY, I[gnaz] M[ichael] (b Prague, 7 December 1882; d Luschetz, 11 December 1941). Librettist to the German stage between the wars.

Originally involved principally in the operatic world, where he found some success as the co-librettist (w Bruno Hardt-Warden) of such pieces as Brandt-Buys's *Glockenspiel* (1912) and *Der Schneider von Schönau* (1916), and of Max Oberleithner's *Der eiserne Heiland* (1917), *La Vallière* (1918) and *Cäcilie* (1920), Welleminsky authored his first Operette script in 1915. By the time it reached the stage, it was in an Hungarian version, set by the violinist and composer Ludwig Gruber as *A főnyeremény-kisasszony,* but the piece and its "jackpot girl" were later seen in Hamburg in the original German. In 1920 he wrote, in tandem with the composer, the libretto to Ralph Benatzky's Operette *Apachen,* and although he subsequently wrote several more opera texts both with Hardt-Warden (Dahn's *Fredegundis,* Brandt-Buys's *Carnevals Ende*) and with Oskar Ritter (an adaptation of *Der Schelm von Bergen* as *Fanal* for Kurt Atterberg), Welleminsky was from then on more prominent in the Operette world, where he developed a profitable partnership with author-composer Paul Knepler. Their *Die Glocken von Paris* played for over two months at the Carltheater, and they had an international hit with their new libretto and lyrics to an arranged version of Carl Millöcker's *Gräfin Dubarry,* which, as *Die Dubarry,* followed Berlin success with a worldwide career. They subsequently found further success when they adapted the film script *Zwei Herzen im Dreivierteltakt* to the Operette stage and provided Eduard Künncke with the backstage libretto for his *Die lockende Flamme.* Welleminsky and Knepler also combined on the libretto for Hans Pero's one-act opera *Belsazar* (1929).

1915 **A főnyeremeny-kisasszony** (Ludwig Gruber/w Hardt-Warden ad Zsigmond Rajna) Pressburg March; Hamburg 9 November 1920

1917 **Tavasz és szerelem** (*Liebe und Lenz*) (Heinrich Berté) Hungarian version Városi Színház 15 September; German version w Hardt-Warden Hamburg 1918

1920 **Apachen** (Ralph Benatzky/w Benatzky) Apollotheater, Vienna 20 December

1921 **A korhély gróf** (Gruber/w Hardt-Warden ad László Fodor) Budai Színkör, Budapest 18 June

1924 **Wenn der Hollunder blüht** (Paul Knepler/w Knepler) Bundestheater (Metropoltheater), Berlin 1 July

1927 **Die Glocken von Paris** (Richard Fall/w Knepler) Carltheater, Vienna 14 October

1929 **Lebenslichter** (Hans Pero/w Hardt-Warden) Stadttheater, Hamburg 12 March

1931 **Die Dubarry** (Carl Millöcker arr Theo Mackeben/w Knepler) Admiralspalast, Berlin 14 August

1932 **Heirat aus Liebe** (Ernst Deloe/w Oskar Ritter) Stadttheater, Krefeld 5 November

1932 **Tanz durchs Leben** (R Düringer/w Paul Knepler) Stadttheater, Danzig 13 November

1933 **Zwei Herzen im Dreivierteltakt** (*Der verlorene Walzer*) (Robert Stolz/Robert Gilbert/w Knepler) Stadttheater, Zürich 30 September; revised version Centraltheater, Dresden 26 December

1933 **Die lockende Flamme** (Eduard Künncke/w Knepler) Theater des Westens, Berlin 25 December

1938 **Die Dubarry** revised version w Hans Martin Cremer, Städtische Bühnen, Breslau

WENN DIE KLEINEN VEILCHEN BLÜHEN Singspiel in 6 scenes by Bruno Hardt-Warden based on *Als ich noch in Flügelkleide* by Albert Kehm and Martin Frehsee. Music by Robert Stolz. Princess Theatre, The Hague, 1 April 1932.

Father Katzensteg (Fritz Hirsch) and his wife, Auguste (Elly Krasser), reminisce in three scenes over a little incident that occurred when Frau Katzensteg was a maidservant in the school run by Frau Gutbier years before. The headmistress's nephew Paul (Paul Harden) disguised himself as a new teacher and got inside the school to claim a kiss from his sweetheart, Liesl (Friedl Dotza), and boys and girls ended up having a champagne party together before being caught. Back in the present (the two scenes that top and tail the show), the Katzenstegs' daughter uses this tiny tale to force the now lofty Paul to let her wed his son. The remaining scene was a ballet.

Plate 417. **Wenn die kleinen Veilchen blühen.** *Robert Stolz's Operette became a large-scale spectacular on the London stage, with a skating scene being featured amongst the extras.*

The songs of this good-old-days piece (set at the turn of the century) were in the good-old-days mode, with such pieces as the scene-setting ''In Bacharach am Rhein,'' the praises of earlier years (''Servus, du gute alte Zeit''), and the student song ''Ich hab' gern ein Mädel,'' all getting several repeats throughout the evening. The young folk had some pretty, very light and less-plugged songs—schoolgirl Trude gave out the title number, and Liesl joined in duo with her Paul in ''Du, du, du, schliess' deine Augen zu,'' whilst Auguste and Katzensteg peeped in Trude's juvenile diary with wonderment in ''Kleine Fee, süsse Fee.''

Produced in The Hague, *Wenn die kleinen Veilchen blühen* went neither to Vienna nor to Berlin, but it turned up later the same year in London, its puffball of a story adapted by Reginald Purdell, Desmond Carter and director Hassard Short (''entire production, including scenic and lighting effects devised and staged by'') as a vast, spectacular musical show for the Theatre Royal, Drury Lane. The six scenes had evolved into 15—now set in picturesque Switzerland with its opportunities for snow and skating scenes rather than homely Bacharach-am-Rhein—there was a chorus of 55, including a half-dozen Albertina Rasch dancers, and the cast was headed by Jerry Verno (Katzen), Charlotte Greenwood (Augusta), John Garrick (Paul), Adele Dixon (Liesl), Esmond Knight (Otto) and Jean Cadell (Mme Hoffmann). ''You, Just You'' (recorded by no less than Heddle Nash) and ''Don't Say Goodbye'' became popular singles as *Wild Violets* ran through 291 performances, giving Stolz his longest West End run, before going on the road. It was later revived, at the Stoll Theatre by Prince Littler (February 1950) with a cast including Ian Carmichael (Otto), Verno (Katzen), Stella Moray (Augusta) and Doreen Duke (Liesl), for a brief season.

Wild Violets also appeared in Australia, where ''the great revolving stage'' manipulated by director Frederick Blackman was—with reason—billed larger than Marie La Varre (Auguste), Cecil Kellaway (Algernon), Dorothy Dunkley (Mme Hoffman) and juveniles Lloyd Lamble, Phillia Dickinson and Diana du Cane.

The English version was also played in America, in St Louis, with Guy Robertson (Paul), Wilbur Evans (Otto), Violet Carlson (Auguste) and George Meader (Hans), without inspiring a New York showing. A tardy French-language premiere (ad Marc-Cab, André Hornez), based on the normal-sized original rather than the big British remake, was seen in Liège in 1973.

UK: Theatre Royal, Drury Lane *Wild Violets* 31 October 1932; Australia: Her Majesty's Theatre, Melbourne *Wild Violets* 26 December 1936; USA: Municipal Opera, St Louis *Wild Violets* 23 August 1937

Recordings: selection (Eurodisc), selection in French (part-record) (TLP), selection in English (HMV)

WENN LIEBE ERWACHT Operette in 3 acts by Hermann Haller based on *Renaissance* by Franz von Schönthan and Franz Koppel-Ellfeld. Lyrics by Rideamus. Music by Eduard Künneke. Theater am Nollendorfplatz, Berlin, 3 September 1920.

One of the run of successful Berlin musicals from the Haller-Künneke combination, *Wenn Liebe erwacht* had a fine run of 218 performances on its original production, but it did not prove to have the same traveling or staying power as its more attractive companion, *Der Vetter aus Dingsda.*

The show's story, set in 19th-century Italy, centered on the reclusive and religious Countess Francesca da Costa (Lori Leux), who brings up her son, Tonio (Grete Freund), away from worldly things, under the tutelage of the well-named Dr Pedantius (Carl Geppert) and the more friendly Chaplain Philippo (Gottfried Huppertz). The household is upset when the painter Lorenzo (Erik Wirl) comes to decorate and obliges with a fresco depicting Venus and Bacchus. By the time Francesca has agreed to pose for the painter as the face of Venus, reclusion and religion have altogether taken a back seat and her son has, at the same time, learned about kissing and so forth from the apprentice artist, Marietta (Agni Wilke).

In Künneke's accompanying score, Francesca had the main waltz number of the evening, ''Es war ein Traum,'' Marietta shared the soubrette moments (''Komm' her, du süsser Lummerl'') with the second soubrette, Nella (Claire Waldoff), and Philippo had the religious but pro-sexual pieces (''Ein Zauber ist . . .'').

The Operette reached its 200th night at the Theater am Nollendorfplatz on 22 March and closed on 12 April, before going on to productions throughout Germany, but, like most of the rest of Künneke's shows, it found few takers abroad. It did, however, find one in Britain, where *Love's Awakening* (ad Adrian Ross) was produced at the Empire Theatre by Edward Laurillard. Juliette Autran and Harry Brindle, from the world of opera, were cast in the leading roles with musical-comedy players Amy Augarde, Vera Pearce, Billy Leonard, Marjorie Gordon and Betty Chester in support for an unsuccessful 37 performances.

UK: Empire Theatre *Love's Awakening* 19 April 1921

WENRICH, Percy (b Joplin, Mo, 23 January 1880; d New York, 17 March 1952). Hit songwriter who rarely hit it in the theatre.

A popular music pianist from an early age, then for 15 years half a variety act with his wife, Dorothy Connolly, Wenrich doubled his nightclub and vaudeville performing with a career as a songwriter that produced a considerable list of hit songs including ''Red Rose Rag,'' ''Silver Bell,'' ''On Moonlight Bay,'' ''Goodbye Summer, So Long Fall, Hello Wintertime'' (ly: Edward Madden), ''Put on Your Old, Gray Bonnet'' (Stanley Murphy), ''When You Wore a Tulip'' (Jack Mahoney), ''By the Campfire'' (Mabel Girling), ''The Shores of Minnetonka'' (Gus Kahn) and ''Sail Along Silvery Moon'' (Harry Tobias).

He made his entry into the musical theatre with some songs for female impersonator Julian Eltinge's touring *The Fascinating Widow* (1912), and thereafter he contributed songs to Eltinge's later *The Crinoline Girl* (1914) and *Cousin Lucy* (1915) and to a number of revues (*Everything, The Greenwich Village Follies, Some Party,* etc) before going into partnership with writer Raymond Peck, with whom he turned out four musical plays. Of the first three, two died on the road and one after a single week on Broadway, but number four, *Castles in the Air,* became a major hit when produced in Chicago, ran up exceptional stays in several centers and finally gave the composer his one Broadway success. A revue, *Who Cares?* (1930), lasted a month at Broadway's 46th Street Theater and marked the end of Wenrich's curiously unproductive Broadway career.

1914 **The Crinoline Girl** (Julian Eltinge/Otto Hauerbach) Knickerbocker Theater 16 March

1916 **The Bride Tamer** (Edgar Allen Woolf) 1 act Colonial Theater 12 June

1920 **Maid to Love** (Raymond Peck) Academy of Music, Baltimore 31 May

1921 **The Right Girl** (Peck) Times Square Theater 15 March

1922 **And Very Nice Too** (Peck) His Majesty's Theater, Montreal May 9

1925 **Castles in the Air** (Peck) Olympic Theater, Chicago 22 November; Selwyn Theater, New York 6 September 1926

WENZEL, Léopold [Vincent François] (b Naples, 23 January 1847; d Asnières, 21 August 1925).

Born in Italy, of French parents, and educated from the age of nine at the Naples Conservatoire of San Pietro Majella, Wenzel was obliged to leave school after four years when his mother died, and he made his living thereafter as a violinist. He wandered around musical Africa, Asia and Europe and, in 1865, arrived in Marseille having—so it is said—hitched a ride from Cyprus with a friendly sea captain. By 1870 he was working as chef d'orchestre at the Alcazar in Marseille. He subsequently became a naturalized Frenchman, moved to Paris and was engaged as musical director of the Alcazar there. During this period he wrote many successful songs (''Le p'tit vin de Bordeaux,'' ''Veux-tu?,'' ''P'tit bleu,'' etc), a large amount of ballet music, including an 1884 piece, *La Cour d'amour,* for the Théâtre de l'Eden, which, lavishly staged, was played some 400 times in spite of indifferent reviews, and a couple of short opérettes for the Alcazar. He subsequently became musical director—and even for a period manager—of the overlarge and always troubled Eden.

In the same year that *La Cour d'amour* brought him good fortune, Wenzel's first full-scale opérette, *Le Chevalier Mignon,* was produced at the Bouffes-Parisiens with a cast headed by Édouard Maugé, Marie Grisier-Montbazon, Marguerite Deval and Paola Marié. It played an indifferent 38 performances. However, with his second such piece, *Le Dragon de la reine,* he did very much better. Produced at Brussels and then, less memorably, in Paris (36 performances), it went on to be played as *Die Dragoner der Königin* at the Viktoria-Theater, Berlin, in the British provinces as *The Young Recruit* and in Budapest as *Királyne dragonyosa.*

Soon after the show's production Wenzel left France for London to take up the post of musical director at the Empire Theatre. He retained that position from 1889 to 1894, during which time he composed 10 ballets for the London house (Katti Lanner's *Brighton* was exported back to Paris and played at the Olympia) whilst also contributing individual songs to several West End musicals (*Cinder-Ellen Up Too Late, Manola,* etc) and the score for one further Parisian musical show, a vehicle for the favorite soubrette Mily-Meyer as *L'Élève de Conservatoire,* produced at the Menus-Plaisirs in 1894.

Wenzel remained in Britain, where he subsequently worked for George Edwardes as conductor and occasional songwriter at Daly's Theatre on *An Artist's Model* (1896) and *The Geisha* (1896), at the Gaiety in 1903 on *The Orchid* (''Le Promenade des Anglais'') and, after a return to the Empire, in 1911 as the original musical director of *Peggy* and of *The Sunshine Girl* (1911–12). He returned to France in his later years.

1875 **Le Neveu du colonel** (w C Wansinck/Paul Burani) 1 act Alcazar 30 September

1876 **Une nuit à Skyros** (de Voisin) 1 act Alcazar 28 October

1884 **Le Chevalier Mignon** (Clairville ad Charles Clairville, Ernest Depré) Théâtre des Bouffes-Parisiens 23 October

1888 **Le Dragon de la reine** (Pierre Decourcelle, Frantz Beauvallet) Théâtre de l'Alhambra, Brussels 25 March; Théâtre de la Gaîté, Paris 31 May

1894 **L'Élève de Conservatoire** (Burani, Henri Kéroul) Théâtre des Menus-Plaisirs 29 November

WEST, Moritz [NITZELBERGER, Moritz Georg] (b 1840; d Aigenschlagel, Upper Austria, 15 July 1904).

In more than 25 years as a librettist/lyricist in the musical theatre, Moritz West contributed to the authorship of a number of the most successful Operetten of his time. He began an early association with the composer Carl Zeller in the 1870s and, if their first collaboration, *Joconde,* had an indifferent Viennese life (20 performances), the pair progressed together through the two versions of *Die Carbonari* (later played in Germany and America as *Capitän Nicol*), to the more successful *Der Vagabund* and finally to their most important works, *Der Vogelhändler* and *Der Obersteiger,* and to Zeller's last, posthumously produced *Der Kellermeister.*

West also worked, in the early part of his career, with both members of Vienna's most famous libretto-manufacturing team, Richard Genée and ''F Zell'' (Camillo Walzel). The three collaborated on the Operette *Nisida,* whilst West and Genée provided the comical libretto, set by Suppé, for Franz Steiner's production of *Die Afrikareise.* West subsequently provided Suppé with a second text, the almost-operatic tale of the Swedish poet *Bellman,* written with the collaborator with whom he would go on to his biggest successes, the playwright and librettist Ludwig Held. It was West's last work, however, written in the year before his death in collaboration with Ignaz Schnitzer, the librettist of *Der Zigeunerbaron,* that gave him his most important success since *Der Vogelhändler. Bruder Straubinger,* which launched the young Edmund Eysler as an Operette composer, brought to a close a particularly consistent and successful career on a particularly high note.

1876 **Joconde** (Karl Zeller/w Moret) Theater an der Wien 18 March

1880 **Nisida** (Richard Genée/w F Zell) Carltheater 9 October

1880 **Die Carbonari** (Zeller/w Zell) Carltheater 27 November

1881 **Capitän Nicol** revised *Die Carbonari* w Hermann Hirschel Friedrich-Wilhelmstädtisches Theater, Berlin 5 November

1883 **Die Afrikareise** (Franz von Suppé/w Genée) Theater an der Wien 17 March

1886 **Der Vagabund** (Zeller/w Ludwig Held) Carltheater 30 October

1887 **Bellman** (Suppé/w Held) Theater an der Wien 26 February

1888 **Gil Blas von Santillana** (Alfons Czibulka/w Zell) Carl-Schultze-Theater, Hamburg 23 November

1889 **Polnische Wirtschaft** (Hermann Zumpe/w Genée) Carl-Schultze-Theater, Hamburg; Friedrich-Wilhelmstädtisches Theater, Berlin 26 November 1891

1891 **Der Vogelhändler** (Zeller/w Held) Theater an der Wien 10 January

1891 **Die Kosakin** (*La Cosaque*) German version w new score by Johann Brandl (Theater an der Wien)

1894 **Der Obersteiger** (Zeller/w Held) Theater an der Wien 5 January

1897 **Die Schwalben** (Leo Held/w Held) Theater an der Wien 12 February

1901 **Der Kellermeister** (Zeller arr Johann Brandl) Raimundtheater 21 December

1903 **Bruder Straubinger** (Edmund Eysler/w Ignaz Schnitzer) Theater an der Wien 20 February

WESTON, R[obert] P[atrick] [HARRIS, Robert] (b London, 7 March 1878; d Brentford, Calif, 6 November 1936).

Songwriter, lyricist, author and adapter, Weston had several song hits to his credit (''What a Mouth,'' ''I'm Henery the Eighth'' w Fred Murray, ''When Father Papered the Parlour'' w F J Barnes, ''I've Got Rings on My Fingers'' w Barnes, Maurice Scott, ''Sister Susie's Sewing Shirts for Soldiers'' w Herman Darewski) before he teamed with Bert Lee to write a long list of hit songs, monologues and, variously, texts and/or songs for an extensive series of often highly successful musical plays.

1924 **Mr Tickle MP** (various/w Lee) Grand Theatre, Blackpool 29 September

1924 **Tilly** (Haydn Wood, Jack Waller/w Bert Lee/Herbert Clayton, Con West) Empire Theatre, Leeds 21 July; Alhambra 3 November

1926 **King Rags** (Harris Weston/w Lee) Empire Theatre, Leeds 23 August

1927 **The Girl Friend** English adaptation of the libretto *Kitty's Kisses* w Lee (Palace Theatre)

1928 **Billy Blue** (w Joseph A Tunbridge, Fred Elkin, Lee/Harold Dayne) Empire Theatre, Newcastle 6 August

1928 **Virginia** (Waller, Tunbridge/w Furber, Lee/Clayton, Waller) Palace Theatre 24 October

1928 **Lucky Girl** (Phil Charig/w Douglas Furber, Lee) Shaftesbury Theatre 14 November

1929 **Merry, Merry** English adaptation and new lyrics w Lee (Carlton Theatre)

1929 **Hold Everything!** English adaptation w Lee (Palace Theatre)

1929 **Here Comes the Bride** (Arthur Schwartz/Desmond Carter, Howard Dietz/w Lee) Opera House, Blackpool 7 October; Piccadilly Theatre, London 20 February 1930

1930 **Sons o' Guns** English lyrics w Lee (London Hippodrome)

1930 **Little Tommy Tucker** (Vivian Ellis/w Desmond Carter, Caswell Garth, Lee) Daly's Theatre 19 November

1932 **Tell Her the Truth** (Waller, Tunbridge/w Lee) Saville Theatre 14 June

1933 **He Wanted Adventure** (Waller, Tunbridge/w Clifford Grey, Lee/w Lee) Saville Theatre 28 March

1933 **Give Me a Ring** (Martin Broones/Graham John/w Guy Bolton, Lee) London Hippodrome 22 June

1934 **Yes, Madam?** (Waller, Tunbridge/w K Browne/w Lee) London Hippodrome 27 September

1935 **Please, Teacher!** (Waller, Tunbridge/w Browne, Lee) London Hippodrome 2 October

1936 **Certainly, Sir!** (Waller, Tunbridge/w Lee) London Hippodrome 17 September

WEST SIDE STORY Musical in 2 acts by Arthur Laurents. Lyrics by Stephen Sondheim. Music by Leonard Bernstein. Winter Garden Theater, New York, 26 September 1957.

Loosely based on the outlines of Shakespeare's *Romeo and Juliet* and set in the urban slums of New York, *West Side Story* used for its modern equivalents of Montagues and Capulets the juvenile gangs of local whites and immigrant Puerto Ricans, battling with a deadly childish seriousness over the streets that they claim as their ''territories.'' The Romeo of the tale is Tony (Larry Kert), once the leader of the white group who call themselves the ''Jets,'' but now in a regular job and on his way to adulthood. It is when he allows himself to be dragged back to help the gang by its new young leader, Riff (Mickey Calin), that he meets his Juliet in the person of Maria (Carol Lawrence), sister of Bernardo (Ken LeRoy), the leader of the rival ''Sharks'' gang. Their games turn to tragedy when Bernardo provokes a knife fight, kills Riff and is then murdered himself by the revenging Tony. Maria prepares to flee the city with Tony, but when Bernardo's girl, Anita (Chita Rivera), tries to help their rendezvous, she is nastily manhandled by the Jet boys, and in revenge tells them that Maria has been shot dead by Chino, the Puerto Rican man Bernardo had intended her to marry. Wild with grief, Tony runs from his hiding place into the streets and is shot down by the marauding Chino. As the play ends, Jets and Sharks join together as they follow Maria behind the corpse of the third victim of their immature foolishness.

The idea of developing the *Romeo and Juliet* theme in such a young, modern and American setting had first been mooted by director/choreographer Jerome Robbins some eight years earlier. Laurents and Bernstein had taken the first steps to following up the idea (at one stage, the working title was *East Side Story* and the conflict was a Jewish-Catholic one), but other projects had intervened. When it was taken up again, the same three collaborators were still involved, but a fourth, the young lyricist Stephen Sondheim, joined the team to provide the words that Bernstein had originally intended to supply himself.

Bernstein gave the show a score that was not quite like any other. Whilst there were conventional love songs for Tony and Maria, and comic numbers of varying degrees, the show also included some of the vocal ensemble work already seen to such advantage in the composer's *Candide* and, most particularly, a large body of the substantial dance music, both orchestral and sung, at which he excelled and which the staging concept of director Robbins called for. If it was the love songs—Tony's hymn to ''Maria,'' Maria's joyously simple declaration that ''I Feel Pretty,'' their rapturously innocent looking forward to their meeting ''Tonight,'' sung in the show over the fateful bragging of the two gangs and over Anita's less innocent thoughts, and the wishful ''Somewhere''—that proved the hit songs outside the show itself, it was the ensemble work and the dance music that gave the show its character and its climaxes.

Plate 418. **West Side Story:** *The Rumble.*

The boy members of the Jets, dancing their way with finger-clicking energy through the Jets' Song, edgily on their toes through their captain's instructions to stay "Cool" and facing up to their "enemy" in the choreographed "rumble" that turns to fatality; Anita and her friends dancing with saucy abandon to their praise of the way of life in "America" and the dance-hall scene that moved from a whirling contest in dance between Jets and Sharks to a dreamy slow motion for the lovers' first meeting, worked the first act up to its climax in a dynamic display of ever-increasing energy. In the second act, with the reality of two deaths hanging over the children, the hectic, youthful tempo of the show takes a pull as the drama rises to its musical climax in the duet scene between Maria and Anita ("A Boy Like That"/"I Have a Love") before moving on to its last fatal pages.

Mounted with a young cast of dancer-actors, who were directed and choreographed by Robbins to enormous effect, Harold Prince and Robert Griffith's production of *West Side Story* had a fine 732-performance run on Broadway before going on the road. It had, in the meanwhile, opened in London, but not without some difficulty. Though there was no quarrel about the quality of the piece, there seemed some difficulty in finding a producer interested in mounting a West End musical with three deaths in it. Finally, Bernstein's publisher, Louis Dreyfus of Chappell & Co, himself put up the money to stage the show and hired H M Tennent Ltd to manage it. His faith in his composer was more than justified. With a cast of young Americans headed by Marlys Watters (Maria), Don McKay (Tony), George Chakiris (Riff) and Miss Rivera and LeRoy of the original cast, the show created rather more of a sensation in London than it had in New York, and the result was a run of 1,039 performances. The same initial resistance was found in Australia, where the country's principal producer of musicals, J C Williamson Ltd, would not take the show on. Instead, Garnet Carroll mounted it in 1960 with a cast headed by

Wendy Waring (Maria), Bob Kole (Tony), Rita Tanon (Anita) and Ben Vargas (Bernardo). It managed only three months in Melbourne, however, prior to a season in Sydney (Tivoli 8 February 1961).

The New York production returned to Broadway after its initial tour and played an additional 249 performances at the Winter Garden Theater, and another American company was sent out to Europe, but the seal was set on the celebrity of *West Side Story* when the film version of 1961 began its travels. Robbins and Robert Wise's transfer of the show to the screen worked dazzlingly, and Richard Beymer (Tony), Natalie Wood (dubbed by Marni Nixon, Maria), Rita Moreno (dubbed by Betty Wand, Anita), George Chakiris (Bernardo) and Russ Tamblyn (Riff) took *West Side Story* and its songs to a new and very wide audience.

New York saw *West Side Story* again in 1968, when, now accepted as a classic, it was produced at the State Theater (24 June) with Kurt Peterson and Victoria Mallory featured, and again in 1980, when the original staging was reproduced for a production at the Minskoff Theater (14 February), whilst London saw a small-budget version brought from the Collegiate Theatre to the Shaftesbury in 1974 (19 December) before it welcomed back the original staging in 1984 (Her Majesty's Theatre 16 May), with Stephen Pacey and Jan Hartley in the leading roles for a run of 589 performances. Yet another revival (cringingly billed by its producers as ''the masterpiece that changed the face of the modern musical'') in which David Habbin and Katie Knight-Adams played the youngsters was seen at the Prince Edward Theatre in 1997 and the Prince of Wales Theatre in 1998–99. Australia saw a full-scale revival in 1983 (Her Majesty's Theatre, Sydney 19 May) and another in 1995.

Outside English-speaking areas, the piece has had a slightly curious career. Although *West Side Story* was one of the most appreciated of all Broadway musicals in the Europe of the later years of the twentieth century, constantly on display throughout the Continent, the majority of its performances there seem to have been in English. A German-language version (ad Marcel Prawy) was produced at the Vienna Volksoper in 1968, and an Hungarian (ad Zoltán Jékely, István Remyi Gyenes) version appeared the following year—neither of which attempted to translate the title—but the continuing presence of *West Side Story* on Continental stages was long assured by companies playing one- or few-night stands in English, and suggesting in their advertising with more or with (much) less accuracy that they had something to do with Broadway and/or the original staging. It nevertheless finds regular Continental productions over 40 years after its first production.

UK: Her Majesty's Theatre 12 December 1958; Australia: Princess Theatre, Melbourne 29 October 1960; France: Alhambra (Eng) 30 March 1961; Austria: Volksoper 25 February 1968; Hungary: Parkszínpad 3 July 1969, Fővárosi Operettszínház 27 September 1969

Film: Mirisch/United Artists 1961

Recordings: original cast (Columbia), Austrian cast (CBS), Japanese cast (Toshiba/HMI), Australian revival cast (K-Tel), Dutch cast (Endemol), Swedish cast (Gazelle), film soundtrack (Columbia), complete (DGG), etc

WHAT MAKES SAMMY RUN? Musical in 2 acts by Budd and Stuart Schulberg based on the book of the same title by Budd Schulberg. Music and lyrics by Ervin Drake. 54th Street Theater, New York, 27 February 1964.

Another in the run of the ''how to succeed in business by stepping on other folk's faces'' musical shows, *What Makes Sammy Run?,* based on a 1941 novel about 1930s filmland, followed two seasons behind the similarly flavored *I Can Get It for You Wholesale.* The tunnel-visioned hero of the show was Sammy Glick (Steve Lawrence), who bluffs, plagiarizes and threatens his way up via the newpaper industry into a place in Hollywood, uses producer Sidney Fineman (Arny Freeman), fellow writers Kit Sargent (Sally Ann Howes), Julian Blumberg (George Coe) and Al Manheim (Robert Alda) and anyone else available to his own ends and weds the tarty daughter (Bernice Massi) of the studio boss on his way to almost the top. Finema is dead, Kit, Julian and Al departed, and his wife faithless when we leave Sammy with one more step to run up, all on his own.

Nightclub and recording star Lawrence won plenty of radio play for the seductive ''A Room without Windows'' and his hymn to back-stabbing Hollywood as ''My Hometown,'' and the show ran longer (540 performances) than its predecessor had done although, like it, to insufficient audiences.

Recording: original cast (Columbia)

WHEELER, Hugh [Callingham] (b Northwood, Mddx, 19 March 1912; d Pittsfield, Mass, 26 July 1987).

At first a writer of detective fiction under the noms de plume of Patrick Quentin and Q Patrick, Wheeler had a success with his first Broadway play *Big Fish, Little Fish* (ANTA Theater, 1961) and, more than a decade later, with his first Broadway musical, the adaptation of Ingmar Bergman's screenplay to *Smiles of a Summer Night* as the libretto for *A Little Night Music* (Tony Award). He subsequently worked on a number of further adaptations, including the highly successful remakes of the 1919 musical *Irene* and the rather more recent *Candide* (Tony Award), and on the development of the London play *Sweeney Todd* as the libretto for the musical of the same title, as well as remaking *A Little Night Music* for the screen.

Reputed as an excellent play doctor, he provided sometimes uncredited assistance on several musical projects for both stage and screen, including *Pacific Overtures* (1976), on which he was credited with ''additional material,'' and the film version of *Cabaret,* where the credit was given as ''research consultant.'' He turned out the severe rewrite of Georg Kaiser's atmospheric script for the New York City Opera production of *Der Silbersee* (State Theater, 20 March 1980), and also authored a musical version of Saint-Exupéry's *The Little Prince and the Aviator,* which folded before opening.

A similar fate befell his one attempt at an original libretto in the 1975 *Truckload,* which did not make it past its Broadway previews.

1973 **A Little Night Music** (Stephen Sondheim) Shubert Theater 25 February

1973 **Irene** revised version w Joseph Stein, Harry Rigby Minskoff Theater 13 March

1973 **Candide** revised version w Sondheim Chelsea Theater Center 18 December; Broadway Theater 8 March 1974

1975 **Truckload** (Louis St Louis/Wes Harris) Lyceum Theater 6 September

1979 **Sweeney Todd, the Demon Barber of Fleet Street** (Sondheim/Chris Bond ad) Uris Theater 1 March

1980 **The Student Prince** revised libretto (New York City Opera)

1982 **The Little Prince and the Aviator** (John Barry/Don Black) Alvin Theater 1 January

WHEN JOHNNY COMES MARCHING HOME American (military) spectacular comic opera in 3 acts by Stanislaus Stange. Music by Julian Edwards. Opera House, Detroit 6 October 1902; New York Theater, New York, 16 December 1902.

The success of Stange and Edwards's *Dolly Varden* gave the encouragement to producer Fred Whitney to mount another of the pair's light operas, and in 1902 the Whitney Opera Company came out with *When Johnny Comes Marching Home.* Stange's script was unusual in that, up to that time, it had not been normal to deal with national historical events in a romantic—rather than burlesque or comic—fashion on the light musical stage. However, otherwise this Civil War musical was barely adventurous, its tale being in the vein of sentimental melodrama and the score—to lyrics of the most thee-and-thouing kind—mixed the military-patriotic and the romantic with local color and some polite comic pieces in standard light-operatic fashion.

In a Civil War where the two sides seem to mix rather freely socially, southern belle Kate Pemberton (Zetti Kennedy) marries Union Colonel John Graham (William G Stewart). When a stolen wallet of army dispatches is found in Graham's possession, he allows himself to be condemned as a spy rather than incriminate Kate and her brother Robert (Julia Gifford). At the end, all is cleared up, and John even proves to be the long-lost son of a southern gentleman (Albert McGuckin). The temporary and phony son, one Jonathan Phoenix (Fred H Perry), is a deserter who sings comic songs. Homer Lind as General William Allen headed the army and was given a middle-aged romance with Kate's aunt Constance (Lucille Saunders), whilst the soubrette moments were assured by the General's daughter, Cordelia (Maude Lambert).

John sang staunchly to the ''Flag of My Country'' and of ''My Own United States'' and serenaded ''Katie—My Southern Belle,'' Kate had a couple of incidental soprano ballads with cadenzas, Phoenix gave the tale of ''Sir Frog and Mistress Toad'' and Constance had a ballad of the drawing-room kind musing that ''Time Leaves No Wrinkle on the Heart.'' The local color was provided by a second act opening with a cotton-picking chorus and dance of darkies ''Heah in de Land ob Coon and Chicken'' and by a character called Uncle Tom (Will Bray) singing of ''My Honeysuckle Girl.'' Edwards also included bits of ''Swanee River,'' ''John Brown's Body,'' ''Good Night Ladies'' and ''I Wish I Was in Dixie'' in his first-act finale.

When Johnny Comes Marching Home received some appreciative notices, and Whitney played it 71 times on Broadway before taking it on the road, where it proved a good touring prospect. The show was considered by many to be the best of Edwards's often rather stiff light-operatic output, ''My Own United States'' was seriously posited by some of the press as a candidate for America's national anthem, and the whole piece was well enough thought of to be given a revival at the New Amsterdam Theater in 1917 (7 May) with Edward Basse as Johnny. Although it was never exported, England heard two of the show's songs when *Dolly Varden* was produced in London. ''Katie—My Southern Belle'' switched nationalities and became ''Dolly, My English Rose,'' whilst the soubrette duo ''It Was Down in the Garden of Eden'' was shifted from Civil War America to Restoration Britain without a word of change being needed.

WHERE'S CHARLEY? Musical comedy in 2 acts by George Abbott based on the play *Charley's Aunt* by Brandon Thomas. Music and lyrics by Frank Loesser. St James Theater, New York, 11 October 1948.

Frank Loesser's first full Broadway score was written to what surprisingly seems to have been the first attempt to make a musical out of Brandon Thomas's celebrated 1892 farce, *Charley's Aunt.* The play, however, underwent some considerable alterations in the process of becoming George Abbott's libretto, the most far-reaching being the combining of two of the three principal male roles to make one top-billable star part. The romantically involved Charley Wykeham—he of the aunt—was rolled into one with the main comic role of Lord Fancourt Babberley—he who impersonates the aunt—and, if the result allowed the artist involved to revel in both the romantic and comical sides of the evening's entertainment, the actual construction of the play and the mass of credible farcical moments that had originally helped win it its fame went very largely out the window.

In this version, Charley (Ray Bolger) gets dressed up as his wealthy aunt, who has been delayed in her expected visit, so that Amy (Allyn McLeerie) and Kitty (Doretta Morrow), who were to lunch with him and his friend Jack (Byron Palmer), won't refuse a chaperoncless invitation. When Kitty's uncle (Horace Cooper) arrives, he woos the phony aunt, and Charley is ultimately able to get him to agree to the marriages of the two young couples before the deception is revealed. The real Donna Lucia d'Alvadorez, who has allowed the masquerade to continue, has meanwhile been happily duetting with Jack's father, Sir Francis (Paul England). Into this now rather anodyne outline were fitted—in the fashion of the time—the opportunities for a Balanchine ballet scena telling of Donna Lucia's doings in Brazil, a ball scene, and a parade by ''The New Ashmolean Marching Society and Conservatory Band.''

However, if the adaptation did—in the cause of things spectacular and starry—some rather fatally painful things to the previously durable *Charley's Aunt,* Loesser decorated it with some pretty and (the Ashmolean Band apart) suitably English-pastiche songs, few of which, however, showed of what the future composer of *Guys and Dolls* and *The Most Happy Fella* was capable. A straightforward little love duet, ''My Darling, My Darling,'' for Jack and Kitty, proved popular, whilst Bolger's song-and-dance performance of the equally simple but more catchy ''Once in Love with Amy'' was a highlight of a singular performance that thoroughly caught the public's imagination. The ensembles ''Better Get Out of Here Quick'' and ''The Gossips'' allowed the songwriter a little more latitude for humor.

Feuer and Martin's Broadway production of *Where's Charley?* and, most particularly, their star (Tony Award), were both an undoubted success. *Where's Charley?* ran for 792 performances on Broadway, visited Boston, then returned to New York (Broadway Theater 29 January 1951) for a further 48 performances before Bolger went on to put his performance down on film in a version that retained the larger part of the musical's score. The show later reappeared on the New York stage at the City Center (1966 w Susan Watson as Amy) and the Circle in the Square (1974 w Raul Julia).

When *Where's Charley?* was mounted in London by Bernard Delfont and H M Tennent Ltd a decade later,

Plate 419. *Brandon Thomas's* Charley's Aunt *has undergone a number of musicalizations. Here Heinz Zimmer stars as Lord Fancourt Babberley in* Die Tante aus Brasilien *at the Dresden Staatsopérette.*

with Norman Wisdom as Charley and Terence Cooper, Pamela Gale and Pip Hinton as his partners, it again had a good run (404 performances). In between, however, a production in Australia, featuring Tommy Fields (''brother of Gracie''), had foundered expensively after some two months in Melbourne. A French-language version produced in Antwerp 20 years later demanded ''Who Is Charley?'' rather than ''where?,'' which seemed to indicate that someone French had seen the original play.

Other musicals based on *Charley's Aunt* have included a number of German adaptations, three produced as *Charleys Tante*—the first by Arthur Rebner and Hugo Hirsch, the next by Robert Gilbert and Max Colpet, with music by Ralph Maria Siegel (Deutsches Theater, Munich 9 March 1967) in which Hans Clarin starred as Fancourt Babberley, and the third by Hertha Roth and Erwin Amend (Staatsheater, Mainz 17 February 1968)—whilst another *Charley's Tante* (Len Praverman, John Hawkins/Ida From, Bent From) was produced in Denmark and found considerable success there. In 1965 Hamburg got a *Charleys neue Tante* (Lothar Olias/Gustav Kampendonck), which, unlike *Where's Charley?,* admitted honestly that it was ''loosely based on some events from''

Thomas's play. An Hungarian musical version by Iván Szenes has also appeared.

The original French production of Brandon Thomas's play, adapted by Maurice Ordonneau as *La Marraine de Charley,* interpolated a number of songs by Ivan Caryll and others into the action.

Australia: Tivoli, Melbourne 4 May 1950; UK: Palace Theatre 20 February 1958; Belgium: Anvers *Qui est Charley?* 28 January 1978

Film: Warner Brothers 1952

Recordings: London cast (Columbia, EMI, Monmouth Evergreen)

WHISTLE DOWN THE WIND Musical in 2 acts by Patricia Knop based on the novel by Mary Hayley Bell. Lyrics by Jim Steinman. Music by Andrew Lloyd Webber. National Theater, Washington, DC, 12 December 1996; revised version, Aldwych Theatre, London, 1 July 1998.

A musicalized version of the long-remembered Hayley Mills film of 1961, *Whistle Down the Wind* was inspired by composer Lloyd Webber's viewing of a British National Youth Theatre production of a stage show (Edinburgh Festival, 1993) based on Willis Hall and Keith Waterhouse's screenplay. However, for this willfully ambitious version of a piece judged ''too English'' for the all-important American market, the setting was shifted from the pious countryside of Lancashire, England, to small-town Louisiana, and since this was the 1990s the central relationship between The Man and the growing girl who is the tale's ''heroine'' was given sexual overtones.

The teenaged Swallow (Irene Molloy), her younger sister (Abbi Hutcherson) and little brother (Cameron Bowen) discover a stranger hiding in the barn of their farm. The Man (Davis Gaines) is, in fact, a dangerous escaped criminal, but a chance expletive leads these motherless children of the Bible Belt country, soaked in revivalist religion and desperate for something to believe in, to become convinced that he is, in fact, Jesus Christ come again to earth. The children and their friends succor the man, but his hiding place is finally revealed. As the police and the folk of the countryside descend on the barn, the man sets the place aflame. When the fire dies, no trace of him is to be found. The other central characters of the piece were motorbiker Amos (Steven Scott Springer), a youngster with a weakness for the blossoming Swallow, and the girlfriend Candy (Lacey Hornkohl) with whom he reckons to quit town for the bright lights. It is Candy who, when Amos—tarrying with Swallow—fails to turn up for their departing date, betrays the children's secret.

First produced in America, the show was poorly received (the title predictably allowed the newspapers some clevernesses), and its Broadway production was canceled. It was subsequently revamped by Lloyd Webber and director Gale Edwards, and the new version, advertised as being 80 percent different (musically, in fact, there were only five fresh numbers), was mounted instead at London's Aldwych Theatre. Lottie Mayor (Swallow), Marcus Lovett (The Man), Dean Collinson (Amos) and Veronica Hart (Candy) took the central roles. If the cutting and pasting that had taken place meant that the piece's first act was rather dispersed and the second required some suspension of disbelief over its time frame, the drama—played out an impressive but also sometimes incoherent motorway/barn setting—nevertheless came powerfully and surprisingly credibly to its peak.

The music of the show mixed dramatic numbers and takeoutable tunes in the composer's regular style, the principal dramatic set piece of the evening being the long and driving two-tenor (plus a little soprano) ensemble ''No Matter What'' (Amos, The Man, Swallow), the favorite takeaway Amos and Candy's motorbiky farewell to small-town life, ''Tire Tracks and Broken Hearts.'' As recorded by Boyzone, the former number went to the top of the British charts, giving Lloyd Webber another number one with a show tune 20 years on from his first with ''Don't Cry for Me, Argentina.'' An appealingly gentle title song, delivered by the children's father, topped the rest of the music, alongside the pop-tenor soliloquy ''The Nature of the Beast'' and a rather curious kiddie piece called ''When Children Rule the World.''

Whistle Down the Wind did altogether better in its second coming, without ever turning itself into a full-sized hit in a London run of two and a half years.

The National Youth Theatre's version of *Whistle Down the Wind* (Richard Taylor/Russell Labey) was given a professional production in 1997 at the Everyman Theatre, Cheltenham (18 July).

Recordings: London cast (Polydor/RUG), studio cast (Polydor/RUG), etc

WHITE, James (b Rochdale, 1878; d Foxhill, Wilts, 29 June 1927). Millionaire who tried, not without some success, to be another George Edwardes but eventually killed himself instead.

Colorful poor-boy-made-good financier White caused some shock waves in theatrical circles when he acquired the control of London's Daly's Theatre in 1922 and straight away showed his intention of keeping artistic control in his own hands. Robert Evett, who had saved the George Edwardes estate's investment from bankruptcy and who had run the theatre since he had put it back on its feet with *The Maid of the Mountains,* soon departed, taking with him the theatre's *Maid of the Mountains* star José Collins. White carried on without them, presenting *The Lady of the Rose* with Phyllis Dare for 514 performances, a revival of *The Merry Widow* with Evelyn Laye and Carl Brisson, Miss Laye as Leo Fall's *Madame Pompadour* (469 performances), a revival of *The Dollar Princess,* and *Katja the Dancer,* which moved to Daly's from White's production at the Gaiety (501 performances). He also did well with *Whirled into Happiness* (*Der Tanz ins Glück*), produced at the Lyric Theatre for 244 performances, and kept a number of companies—billed under the banner ''George Edwardes presents,'' the formula Evett had used—on the road, but Daly's Theatre was his pride and joy.

A spectacular version of Straus's *Die Perlen der Cleopatra* with Evelyn Laye as Cleopatra flopped (110 performances), a new mounting of Edwardes's *A Greek Slave* with José Collins starred closed on the road, and neither a rehash of Jean Gilbert's *Uschi* and *Wenn zwei sich lieben* as *Yvonne* (280 performances) nor Lehár's *The Blue Mazurka* (140 performances) helped refloat the situation at a time when White's dealings in general were at a sticky impasse. He went bankrupt and committed suicide by taking poison in his office at the theatre whilst *The Blue Mazurka* struggled on, leaving behind him a long and explanatory testament that the papers published in full. Sneered at for years by theatre and newspaper-theatre folk as the man who merely provided the money, and who couldn't be expected to know anything about ''the theatre, darling,'' he got his best press from them—including a whole page in *Variety*—at his death. And the bankrupt's will was probated at a vast £83,000.

WHITE, Michael [Simon] (b Scotland, 16 January 1936). London producer with an early taste for the youth-orientated or off-center who later switched to importing proven Broadway hits.

After a period as assistant to producer Peter Daubeny, White began producing on his own account in the early 1960s, often, particularly in earlier days, choosing plays of a striving avant-garde or provocative nature. Amongst others, he introduced London to *Cambridge Circus, The Paper Bag Players, Oh! Calcutta, The Dirtiest Show in Town* and, a little too later, a follow-up erotic-ish revue called *Carte Blanche.*

His musical-theatre ventures, on the whole more mainstream, began with a piece called *The Man from the West,* which played only in East Grinstead, and later included a revival of *The Threepenny Opera* (ad Hugh MacDiarmid), the initial West End showing of *Joseph and the Amazing Technicolor Dreamcoat* (w Robert Stigwood), Lloyd Webber's subsequent *Jeeves* (w Stigwood) and Galt MacDermot's contemporary musicalization of *Two Gentlemen of Verona.* It was, however, his production of *The Rocky Horror Show,* which made its way through several theatres and many more years to win itself the status of an institution, that gave him his first memorable musical success to set alongside such long-running straight productions as *Sleuth.* A second piece by *The Rocky Horror Show*'s author, *T. Zee* (1976), was a fast flop, and another small-scale venture, *Censored Scenes from King Kong,* produced on Broadway in 1980 (w Eddie Kulukundis), also failed.

White subsequently became a filmmaker to produce *The Rocky Horror Picture Show* and, parallel to a subsequent career in the cinema (*Monty Python and the Holy Grail, The Life of Brian,* etc), he has since been responsible for London's reproductions of several major Broadway musicals: *A Chorus Line* (1975), the long-running *Annie* (1978), the New York Shakespeare Festival staging of *The Pirates of Penzance* (1982), *On Your Toes* (1984), *Crazy for You* (1993) and *She Loves Me* (1994). Most of these did decidedly well, which was not the case with a curious arrière-garde Continental mishmash of variety acts called *Y* to which he loaned his name as producer or the lesbian musical *Voyeurz* produced in 1998 at the Whitehall Theatre.

His latest project is a London version of the French entertainment *Notre Dame de Paris,* currently installed at the large Dominion Theatre (2000).

Autobiography: *Empty Seats* (Hamish Hamilton, London, 1984)

WHITE, Onna (b Nova Scotia, Canada, 24 March 1922).

After a career as a chorus dancer in ballet and in Broadway shows (*Finian's Rainbow, Guys and Dolls, Silk Stockings*) during which she acted as assistant to Michael Kidd, Miss White reproduced Kidd's dances for the City Center's 1955 revival of *Guys and Dolls,* choreographed the 1956 revival of *Carmen Jones* and established herself at the front of her profession with her dances for the original production of *The Music Man* (1957). Her subsequent credits include *Whoop Up!* (1958), *Take Me Along* (1959), Broadway's version of *Irma la Douce* (1960), *Let It Ride!* (1961), *I Had a Ball* (1964), Broadway's *Half a Sixpence* (1965), *Mame, Ilya Darling* (1967), *A Mother's Kisses* (1968), *1776* (1969), *Gantry* (1970, also director), *70, Girls, 70* (1971), *Gigi* (1973), London's *Billy* (1974), *Goodtime Charley* (1975), *I Love My Wife* (1974), *Working* (1978), *Home Again, Home Again* (1979), *Elizabeth and Essex* (1984) and the London revival of *Charlie Girl* (1986, w Mike Fields).

She also provided the dances for the screen versions of *The Music Man, Bye Bye Birdie, Oliver!, 1776* and *Mame.*

THE WHITE CHRYSANTHEMUM Lyrical comedy in 3 acts by Leedham Bantock and Arthur Anderson. Lyrics by Anderson. Music by Howard Talbot. Criterion Theatre, London, 31 August 1905.

An unusual venture for its time, *The White Chrysanthemum* was the nearest thing London's West End had seen to an intimate musical since the explosion onto its stages of Gaiety Theatre–style musical comedy, more than a decade previously. *The White Chrysanthemum* was considerably shorter than usual, it had virtually no spectacle nor dancing, and a principal cast of just seven, supported by a chorus of half a dozen girls and half a dozen boys (a *Florodora* double sextet), made up the onstage personnel of Frank Curzon's production at the little Criterion Theatre. Otherwise, however, the show differed little from standard fare, with its tale of out-east Reggie Armitage R N (Henry Lytton), who has to free himself from the wish of his father (Rutland Barrington) that he wed American heiress Cornelia Vanderdecken (Marie George) so that he can pair himself up with his Sybil (Isabel Jay). Sybil bides her time close at hand, disguised as a little Japanese lady, whilst best friend Betty (Millie Legarde) helps events on. Lawrence Grossmith was Reggie's mate who takes over Cornelia when Reggie gets Sybil and father pairs off with Betty, and M R Morand was the seventh principal of a very Savoy Theatre–flavored cast, playing a comical Oriental.

Equipped with a score that was charmingly well written in its sentimental parts, but rather imitative and verging on the vulgar when it tried to supply up-to-date material for Miss George, in particular, *The White Chrysanthemum* nevertheless proved itself to be a well-made little piece. It drew for six months at the Criterion (179 performances) before going on the road, where it featured for several years.

An American version, which had Ethel Jackson/Lina Abarbanell (Sybil), Lawrence Grossmith (Chippy) and Edna Wallace Hopper (Betty) in its cast and the name of Jerome Kern (which hadn't been there before) in its song list, folded without reaching Broadway, but the piece's dimensions made it a good touring prospect. Thus, it was all the more surprising that when it was later produced by John and Nevin Tait in Australia, with a cast including Barry Lupino and Florence Perry, the little piece was dolled up with "a chorus and ballet, superb costumes and magnificent scenic effects" so that it resembled any and every other piece of the time. *The White Chrysanthemum* was also played throughout Asia and the rest of the eastern circuits by Maurice Bandmann's endlessly touring musical comedy company.

USA: Garrick Theater, Philadelphia 25 March 1907; Australia: King's Theatre, Melbourne 2 June 1917

WHITE HORSE INN *see* IM WEISSEN RÖSSL

WHITING, Jack (b Philadelphia, 22 June 1901; d New York, 15 February 1961). Durable Broadway juvenile song-and-dance man who didn't manage to draw too many hits from his long list of original roles.

Young Whiting, whom a Philadelphia paper noted was "of a socially prominent local family," worked as a stenographer before getting a job in the 1922 edition of *The Ziegfeld Follies.* He quickly moved on to roles in musical plays—*Orange Blossoms* (1922, Frank Curran), *Cinders* (1923, Bruce), *Stepping Stones* (1923, Captain Paul), *Annie Dear* (1924, Alfred Weatherly), *When You Smile* (1925, Larry Patton), *Rainbow Rose* (1926, Tommy Lansing)—and returned to his hometown to appear as the live-wire young salesman hero of *Cynthia* at the Walnut Street Theater. *Cynthia* folded after a fortnight, but Whiting went on to the juvenile lead in the successful comedy show *The Ramblers* ("All Alone Monday") and the plum leading role of Bobby Bennett, fated to tell "nothing but the truth," in *Yes, Yes, Yvette* (1927).

A long series of leading juvenile roles followed: alongside Beatrice Lillie and Irene Dunne in *She's My Baby* (1928, Bob Martin), as the boxer Sonny Jim Brooks in *Hold Everything!* (introducing "You're the Cream in My Coffee"), as coastguardsman Jack Mason in *Heads Up!* (1929), as film star Michael Perry in *America's Sweetheart* (1931), and as amateur producer-cum-love-interest Kenneth Raleigh in *Take a Chance* (1932). He visited London in 1934 to star as Billy Crocker to the Reno Sweeney of Jeanne Aubert in the West End's *Anything Goes* and, following that success, was more briefly seen on the London stage in the flop *Rise and Shine* (1936) and as the hero of the unliked West End production of *On Your Toes* (1937).

Back on Broadway, he appeared in *Hooray for What!* (1937), as Johnny Graham in *Very Warm for May* (1939) and as Kitty Carlisle's love interest in *Walk with Music* (1940), got a longer run out of *Hold on to Your Hats* (1940), in which he appeared alongside the aging Al Jolson, and a brief one out of the role of bandleader Damon Dillingham in *Beat the Band* (1942). In his forties, he appeared on Broadway replacing Michael O'Shea in the low-comedy role of Con Kidder in the 1945 revival of *The Red Mill* and toured in both that role (1947) and as Henry Longstreet in *High Button Shoes.* In his fifties he played the supporting role of the Chief Justice in the 1952 revival of *Of Thee I Sing* and the Mayor of New York in *Hazel Flagg* (1953), and his last Broadway appearance was as a soft-shoeing Charybdis in *The Golden Apple* (1954). The 1956 *Strip for Action* (Jack), in which he featured as a song-and-dance man turned soldier, closed out of town, but he was seen in 1958 playing Charlie in the City Center's *Annie Get Your Gun.*

WHITNEY, Frederick C[lark] (b Detroit, 6 January 1861; d Los Angeles, 4 June 1930).

The son of millionaire producer and theatre-owner **Clark J WHITNEY** (b Troy, Mich, 1832; d New York, 21 March 1903) of the Whitney Opera House in Detroit (opened 13 September 1875) and also later of theatres in Toronto, Buffalo and Chicago, Fred Whitney worked as a booker, house and business manager on his father's circuit from his teens. He managed Mrs Scott Siddons's tour ''when little more than a boy,'' and after a timeout from the theatre as treasurer of the new Detroit Organ Co (1882), toured Europe with Dr Carver's spectacular ''Wild America'' show, spent several years mounting Wild West entertainments and cowboy tournaments in Colorado, tried his hand (w Charles J Davis) with The Royal Midget Company (1891), which went bankrupt in Chicago, and finally began producing musical plays in 1892. Some of his earliest efforts included tours of the Chicago-bred shows produced by his brother, Bert C Whitney.

In his early years, Fred Whitney was a staunch supporter and producer of native comic opera, and in his first seasons as a producer he launched both Reginald De Koven's *The Fencing Master* (1892), a Broadway success with Marie Tempest starred, and that lady's next vehicle, *The Algerian* (1893), which did less well. The ''Louise Beaudet Opera Company'' with Alfred Robyn's *Jacinta* (1894) and *The Dragoon's Daughter* proved a brisk disaster, and neither Jakobowski's *The Birth of Venus* nor a piece called *The Bathing Girl* (1895) went beyond a stumbling road season, but De Koven's *Rob Roy,* produced in the same season, gave the composer his best result since *Robin Hood* and the producer one of the longest Broadway runs (253 performances) that he would achieve in a decade of trying. Julian Edwards's Irish light opera *Brian Boru* (1896) and a William Furth rewrite of Vanloo and Leterrier's *La Gardeuse d'oies* as *A Normandy Wedding* (ex- *Papa Gougou*) (1897) were not hits, but two other Edwards pieces, *Dolly Varden* and *When Johnny Comes Marching Home,* both achieved respectable runs in New York and good lives on the road. Edwards's *Love's Lottery,* which featured the opera star Ernestine Schumann-Heink in a single venture into light opera, a Broadway staging of the London success *A Greek Slave* (1899) and Lucius Hosmer's *The Rose of the Alhambra* all performed only indifferently, but Whitney had a fine success when he left comic opera for musical comedy and mounted the nonsensical *Piff! Paff! Pouf!* for a splendid 264 performances on Broadway. If other Chicago and road ventures were sometimes less successful (*The Belle of Newport* 1903, *A China Doll* 1904, *The Baroness Fiddlesticks* 1904, the eventually successful *The Pink Hussars* 1905, etc), he did well enough with Chicago's *The Isle of Spice* and the *The Land of Nod,* and he finally hit the jackpot with a vengeance when he joined the post–*Die lustige Witwe* rush for Continental musicals and staged the Broadway version of *Der tapfere Soldat* (*The Chocolate Soldier*) in 1909.

Whitney later took a hand in the very successful London reproduction of his show and, on the wings of that success, took the West End's Waldorf Theatre and, renaming it the Whitney Theatre, opened it with another Continental piece, Felix Albini's substantial *Baron Trenck.* When that flopped, he replaced it with the American hit version of *Die Sprudelfee* (*The Spring Maid*). When that, too, failed to run, he was forced to withdraw from London in disarray.

Things went less well thereafter. A Broadway mounting of *Baron Trenck* (1912) and the Oscar Straus *My Little Friend* (1913) did only fairly, a piece called *The Innocent Sinner* by one William Parker Chase (1913) played in Pittsburgh and Baltimore didn't go much farther, a 1919 musical called *Suite 16* apparently got no farther than Syracuse, and his last Broadway production was a not-very-memorable Tchaikovsky pasticcio called *Natja,* mounted in partnership with brother Bert in 1925. Whitney nevertheless continued to be active on the West Coast, but in a slightly different register: his final production there was a Los Angeles mounting of Shaw's *Saint Joan.*

His brother, **Bert[ram] C[lark] WHITNEY** (d October 1929), operated theatres in Chicago, Toronto (Princess Theater), Montreal (His Majesty's Theater), Ann Arbor, Ypsilanti, Owosso and Battle Creek as well as, for 30 years, in his native Detroit. Amongst the musical plays and extravaganzas that he mounted or co-mounted, mostly from Chicago, were the successful *A Knight for a Day* (ex- *Mam'selle Sallie*), *The Isle of Spice, The Isle of Bong Bong, Piff!Paff! Pouf!, The Show Girl, The Broken Idol, They Loved a Lassie* (Benjamin Hapgood Burt's 1909 musicalization of the George Arliss farce *There and Back*), Clifton Crawford's *Captain Careless, My Little Friend, Ed Wynn's Carnival, The Perfect Fool, The Chocolate Dandies* and *The Head Waiters.*

WHITTINGTON Grand opéra-bouffe in 3 acts by H B Farnie. Music by Jacques Offenbach. Alhambra Theatre, London, 26 December 1874.

The history of London's very own made-to-order Offenbach opéra-bouffe has become befuddled over the years. Some French commentators have insisted that the libretto to the piece was a French one, written by Nuitter and Tréfeu and subsequently translated for the English stage by Farnie. However, these same commentators (one copying from the other, perhaps?) insist on calling the work variously *W[h]ittington et son chat,* so maybe they are not to be taken too seriously.

Contemporary English accounts reported that the favorite composer of the period was signed by the publishers Wood & Co of Regent Street to compose an original score for which he was to be paid a total of 75,000 francs, apparently then the equivalent of £3,000, the money to be paid to the composer at a rate of £1,000 as each act was handed, completed, to the copyist. The newspapers of the period noted that it was the first time that the composer would set a text in the English language. As it eventuated, the script of *Whittington* as constructed by H B Farnie to fit into the spectacular production designed by Alfred Thompson (he who had authored the splendid book to *Cinderella the Younger* for Jonas and the Gaiety) for the vast Alhambra stage was not one for which the credit was really worth squabbling over (which is possibly one reason more for denying Nuitter and Tréfeu as its authors). The traditional tale of Dick (Kate Santley) and Alice Fitzwarren (Julia Mathews) was squeezed to one side to allow three comical suitors (Harry Paulton, John Rouse, William M Terrott) to vie for the hand of Dorothy, the Cook (Lennox Grey) in Act I, and to try to run the country of Bambouli on ''perfect'' English lines much in the manner later re-proposed by W S Gilbert in *Utopia (Limited)* in Act II, before the bit with the cat and the rats intervened, almost as an afterthought, in time to tie up proceedings.

The score, too, proved disappointing, and the highlight of the evening turned out to be a Grand Barbaric Ballet invented, arranged and produced by ballet master Henri Léopold Dewinne and danced by him with Mlles Erminia Pertoldi, Jeanne Pitteri and Sidonie (the future Mme Eugène Goossens) and the massed forces of the Alhambra corps de ballet. *Whittington* survived through 112 performances, largely on the attractions of the Alhambra's staging, and was then put away.

Eighteen years later, however, it was disinterred, adapted (ad Nuitter, Tréfeu) and mounted at Paris's equally spectacle-orientated Théâtre du Châtelet where it was now billed as a ''féerie.'' No longer was there a leggy travesty soubrette of a Dick, for the hero was played by Alexandre fils, whilst Gardel, the son of Hervé, was cast as King Lallali and Juliette Darcourt played his daughter. The cook (Blanche Miroir) and her suitors were still there, and the cat had made it to the title as *Le Chat du diable*. It was played a goodish 86 times.

France: Théâtre du Châtelet *Le Chat du diable* 28 October 1893

WHOOPEE Musical comedy in 2 acts by William Anthony McGuire based on the comedy *The Nervous Wreck* by Owen Davis. Lyrics by Gus Kahn. Music by Walter Donaldson. New Amsterdam Theater, New York, 4 December 1928.

Owen Davis's play *The Nervous Wreck* (Sam H Harris Theater 9 October 1923) had been a 279-performance hit on Broadway and the basis for a silent film before comedian Eddie Cantor took it to Florenz Ziegfeld as the material for a musical comedy vehicle for himself. The musical was put together by the producer's currently favorite stagewriter, McGuire, and songwriters Donaldson and Kahn, who had provided Cantor with several big song hits in the past. Stanley Green reported, ''By the time he was finished, McGuire had managed to turn an 11-character, three-set play into a 35-character, 11-set song-and-dance spectacle with room enough for cowboys, cowgirls, showgirls, ballet dancers, Indians, gipsies, two automobiles, a heifer, a kitchen stove, Eddie Cantor's blackface routine, and five nude girls on horseback.'' The songwriters had done their bit too: Cantor had a joyously cynical number describing ''Makin' Whoopee!'' and a blackface spot full of jolly numbers; the juveniles had a fine romancing duet in ''I'm Bringing a Red, Red Rose''; and an incidental movie star named Leslie Daw (Ruth Etting), wandering through the plot, insisted that someone who wasn't in the play should ''Love Me or Leave Me.'' Cantor's blackface spot, needless to say, did not remain static throughout the run, and he introduced several more popular numbers into it as time went on.

The story centred on Sally Morgan (Frances Upton), who is about to be made to marry Sheriff Wells (Jack Rutherford) even though she is in love with the Indian Wanenis (Paul Gregory). Since her father harbors anti-Indian sentiments, she runs away. Henry Williams (Eddie Cantor), a professional hypochondriac, is kidded into being her companion in flight, and they gallop through a series of adventures, characters and sets before it turns out that the leading man isn't really and truly an Indian after all, so Sally is allowed to wed him. Henry, most suitably, is left paired with his nurse, Mary Custer (Ethel Shutta).

Whoopee ran for more than seven months, took a break and returned, with movie person Ruth Morgan now paired with Cantor, to run another three and a half months before Ziegfeld took it off to allow United Artists to film a movie version with Cantor, Ethel Shutta, Gregory and Rutherford, with Eleanor Hunt as Sally and with some fresh songs.

The show did not travel to Britain, but it was taken up for Australia by Ernest G Rolls and George Marlow, who produced it at Sydney's Empire Theatre with what they advertised as ''a huge star cast of 100'' topped by comic Charley Sylber (Henry), Genevieve McCormack (Mary), baritone Forest Yernall (Wanenis), Palmer Stone (Wells) and American comedienne Beulah Benson (replaced by Mary Gannon) as Sally, not long after *The Nervous Wreck* had passed across the Sydney stage. The Indians and a Halloween sequence proved the most popu-

Plate 420. **Who's Hooper?** *Star comedian Bill Berry tackled Pinero with music and found himself a fine success. Here, the amnesiac Hooper finds himself with—apparently—two wives (Violet Blythe, Cicely Debenham).*

lar bits of the evening, and the show managed 69 performances after being bumped from the Empire to Frank Neil's Grand Opera House after three weeks of its season. When Neil took it to Melbourne (King's Theatre 31 August 1929), he was gratified with a run of nearly three months.

The show was televised by NBC in 1950 with Johnny Morgan and Nancy Walker featured, and a made-over version was produced at the Goodspeed Opera House in 1978 (20 July) and subsequently taken to Broadway's ANTA Theater for 204 performances. Charles Repole starred as Henry in a version that mixed half a dozen numbers from the original score with one of the additional film numbers, and half a dozen other Donaldson/Kahn pieces.

Australia: Empire Theatre, Sydney 15 June 1929

Film: United Artists 1930

Recording: archive collection (Smithsonian Institution)

WHO'S HOOPER? Musical comedy in 2 acts by Fred Thompson founded on *In Chancery* by Arthur Pinero. Lyrics by Clifford Grey. Music by Ivor Novello and Howard Talbot. Adelphi Theatre, London, 13 September 1919.

The huge success of the musicalized *The Magistrate, The Boy,* at the Adelphi Theatre naturally suggested more Pinero-with-songs as the next vehicle for the earlier piece's town-drawing comedian W H Berry. The adapter of the former musical, Fred Thompson, chose this time to remodel the old Edward Terry hit *In Chancery* (Gaiety Theatre 24 December 1884) for producer Alfred Butt and his star.

Berry was Vincent Hitchens, who has been in a rail accident and has lost his memory. Because of the initials on his bag, he is taken for one Valentine Hooper, a chap who is on the run from the law for having wed a ward-in-chancery. The plot thickens when the owner of the pub where the amnesiac is taken (W H Rawlins) all but inveigles him into matrimony with his daughter (Cicely Debenham); it rethickens when the real newlyweds (Robert Michaelis, Marjorie Gordon) turn up, and thickens all over again when they all run off to hide at a little boardinghouse in Portsea, which turns out to be none other than Hitchens's own home. Each twist gave more opportunities to the comedian, who was also well supplied with songs: a topical drinking song, a burlesque of Tennyson's ''What Are the Wild Waves Saying?,'' and an explanatory ''It Must Be Very Trying to Be Mad.'' Miss Debenham bounced through a Novello-ized version of *Lohengrin'* s "Wedding March" and cooed with the star over "Wonderful Love," but the prettiest piece of the evening went to Violet Blythe as the real Mrs Hitchens, singing of "Day Dreams," the melody of which floated in and out through the play, tugging poor, befuddled Vincent's memory back towards reality.

Who's Hooper? had a fine run, but after seven and a half months it was given a thorough revamp, the whole last act rearranged and seven numbers replaced. The alterations did not give the show anything additional, and it ran on for two more months, closing after 349 performances.

WIE EINST IM MAI Posse mit Gesang (musical comedy) in four scenes by Rudolf Bernauer and Rudolf Schanzer. Music by Walter Kollo and Willy Bredschneider. Berliner Theater, Berlin, 4 October 1913.

The most enduring of Bernauer, Schanzer, Bredschneider and Walter Kollo's run of musicals for the Berliner Theater, *Wie einst im Mai* used the triple-header love-through-the-generations layout that had been so effectively foreshadowed in such pieces as *Lili* and was later to be regularly reused in other successful stage musicals (*Drei Walzer, Perchance to Dream,* etc) and films, allowing the authors and their designers to travel through a sentimental panorama of Berlin from the late days of the Biedermeier era to what turned out to be—although its authors could not have suspected it would be so—the last days of the Kaiser's Germany.

In the first scene, Colonel's daughter Ottilie (Lisa Weise) is prevented by convention from marrying the locksmith Fritz Jüterbog (Oscar Sabo); in the second, 20 years later, she goes to a nightspot to catch out the "suitable" husband her family forced her to take in a dalliance and, instead, meets Fritz again. They part for a second time. By the third scene, Fritz is rich, successful, a grandfather and living in the very house from which the Colonel had turned him out in Scene one. Ottilie comes to see him on behalf of her daughter, Vera, who has attracted the unwelcome attentions of his married son. The old pair share their fond memories of their youth, and part for the last time. In the fourth scene, Vera's daughter, Tilla, and Fritz's grandson, Fred, finally bring the two families together. The four scenes were also linked by the comical exploits of the aptly named Stanislas von Methusalem, flirting and dancing his way through the generations from his youth to his 100th year.

The love story was carried musically through from 1838 to 1913 to the melody of "Das war in Schöneberg im Monat Mai," Ottilie and Fritz's recollection of their first kiss, whilst the comical part was connected by Methusalem's sung and danced "Heissgeliebtes Firlefänzchen," a piece that shifted into a different dance mode for each era of the play. In the other foremost minutes of the score, Ottilie scorned her faithless husband in "Die Männer sind alle Verbrecher" and reminisced over Fritz's little grandson that, had things been different, she might have been his "Grossmama, Grossmama."

By the time authors and stagers had finished, *Wie einst im Mai* came out as a wholly romantic costume piece, rather than the slightly social-commenting "Posse mit Gesang" that had been originally envisaged, and as such it proved to be wholly to its audience's tastes. It had a splendid run at the Berliner Theater, outdoing even the success of the team's previous hit, *Filmzauber,* as it held the stage for nearly a year before being taken off to be replaced by the team's more patriotic and wartimely *Extrablätter.*

The First World War virtually destroyed the international career of *Wie einst im Mai.* Adolf Weisse produced it at Vienna's Deutsches Volkstheater with Kamilla Eibenschütz (Ottilie/Tilla), Anton Edthofer (Fritz/Fred) and Hans Junkermann (Methusalem) starred, and Budapest saw *Egyszer volt* (once upon a time) in Zsolt Harsányi's version, but the other important paths opened up to the team's works by *The Girl on the Film* (*Filmzauber*) were now closed. Britain and its colonies never saw *Wie einst im Mai* as such. America, however, half-did. The Shubert brothers took up the show, but in a manner that they had made particularly their own, they threw out Bredschneider and Kollo's score (which nevertheless got a hearing at the city's German-language Irving Place Theater) and instead decorated Rida Johnson Young's fairly faithful version of Bernauer and Schanzer's tale with nine numbers composed by Sigmund Romberg.

The resultant piece, *Maytime* (Shubert Theater 16 August 1917), now set in New York rather than Berlin, kept much of the feeling and flavor of the original even though Peggy Wood and Charles Purcell as the long-term lovers were allowed to flush rather more (and more often) romantic than before alongside William Norris (Matthew, ex- Methusalem) and his succession of wives. *Maytime* was a resounding success, and the number that did duty for "Das war in Schöneberg im Monat Mai," the duet "Will You Remember?" (better known, perhaps, by its opening line "Sweetheart, sweetheart, sweetheart"), became an all-time Romberg favorite. Amongst the other numbers, a "Jump Jim Crow" replaced the Caribbean polka danced by Methusalem's wife in the second act, the lovers got two more duets ("In Our Little Home Sweet Home," "The Road to Paradise") and the aged Matthew insisted "Dancing Will Keep You Young." The main Broadway production of the piece ran for 492 performances, and *Maytime* proved to be one of the Shubert brothers' most successful productions ever.

The American version of *Maytime* was produced in Australia in 1919 (Criterion Theatre, Sydney 8 March 1919, Her Majesty's Theatre, Melbourne 22 August), with Gladys Moncrieff as Ottilie, Reginald Roberts as her Richard Wayne and Leslie Holland as Matthew, for a season disturbed by an influenza epidemic and later for seven weeks at Melbourne's Her Majesty's (22 August 1919). It did fairly rather than finely. But if Australia was not hugely enthusiastic and Britain didn't even take a look, *Maytime* toured for a number of years on the American circuits, and its fame was considerably increased and even spread abroad to those countries where neither *Wie einst im Mai* nor *Maytime* had previously gone when a 1937 film version starring Jeanette MacDonald and Nelson Eddy engraved ''Will You Remember'' into the consciousness of a generation. This huge and happy success had only one shadow over it: it encouraged the Shuberts in particular and other American managements in general to continue to botch (invariably rather less well than Miss Young and Romberg had done here) an ever-increasing list of further overseas hits, almost always with disappointing results. But *Maytime* was there for a long, long time to prove that it was not impossible to do it and make it work.

The original *Wie einst im Mai* was also filmed silently, in 1926, with Camilla Spira in the cast, and again in 1937 with Charlotte Ander, Paul Klinger, Otto Wernicke and Ilse Füsternberg and, at last, the Kollo and Bredschneider music.

Wie einst im Mai was brought back in Berlin as a spectacular piece of good-old-days entertainment for the next war (Theater des Volkes, Berlin 26 May 1943 w Edith Schollwer and Hubert von Meyerinck). For this occasion, it had been revised into a more scenic eight sections, with an updated final episode, by the composer's son Willi Kollo and Walter Lieck, and the score had been stripped of Bredschneider's contribution, which was replaced by some additional music composed by each of the Kollos (''Es geht doch nischt über Berlin,'' etc). A second update and revision was practiced on the piece for a 1966 production at Braunschweig, starring grandson René Kollo, which was subsequently seen at Berlin's Theater des Westens (5 April 1979, 165 performances), and the piece was given yet another all-Kollo overhaul for a Munich production in 1992.

Austria: Deutsches Volkstheater 23 April 1915; Hungary: Fővárosi Nyári Színház *Egyszer volt* 26 May 1916; USA: Irving Place Theater (Ger) 1916

Films: Willi Wolff (silent) 1926, Ariel Films 1937

Recordings: 1966 version (RCA), complete (EMI Classics)

WIENER BLUT Operette in 3 acts by Victor Léon and Leo Stein. Music taken from the works of Johann Strauss and arranged by Adolf Müller jr. Carltheater, Vienna, 26 October 1899.

Plate 421. **Wiener Blut.** *Sabine Rossert (Gräfin) and Peter Branoff (Ypsheim) in the Salzburg Landestheater production of 1986.*

One of the earliest of the long list of scissors-and-paste Strauss Operetten, *Wiener Blut* has survived over a century in the German-language repertoire. Whilst other countries have preferred other Strauss pasticcii, such as *Drei Walzer / Trois Valses, Valses de Vienne / The Great Waltz, Casanova* or *Die Tänzerin Fanny Elssler,* and whilst other such shows won considerably more popularity on their original production in Vienna, it is *Wiener Blut* that has established itself—in Austria and Germany, at least—as the most frequently played semi-Strauss show, to such an extent that only *Die Fledermaus* and *Der Zigeunerbaron* of the composer's original, untouched-up shows are now more often seen.

Wiener Blut had the particularity of being a pasticcio made with the composer's knowledge and even blessing, although he did not at any time attempt to take part in its making. It was originally intended for the Theater an der Wien, and that theatre's musical director, Adolf Müller jr, was given the job of selecting and adapting the Strauss tunes that would make up the score. Finally, it was the Carltheater under the management of Franz Jauner that mounted the show, but in the meantime Strauss himself had died.

The libretto to *Wiener Blut* centered on Balduin, Count Zedlau (Julius Spielmann), who has a wife, Gabriele (Frln Marker), who has gone home to mother, a mistress, the dancer Franziska Cagliari (Ilonya Szoyer), as well as a potential bit on the side in the seamstress Pepi (Betty Stojan). His wife left him because he was dull and provincial, but now she finds that he has become a veritable and thus, apparently, attractive Viennese rake, whilst he in the course of the evening suddenly rediscovers a preference over the others for the woman he actually married. Count Zedlau's last evening out before returning to married life, booked to be devoted to the seduction of Pepi, goes awry amongst a barrage of mistaken identities and misconceived rendezvous, before Franziska is paired off with the interfering Prime Minister of Reuss-Schleiz-Greiz, Prince Ypsheim-Gindelbach (Eduard Steinberger), and Pepi goes undeflowered(?) back to her Josef (Louis Treumann).

The musical part of the show was composed almost entirely of dance music, preponderantly waltzes—including the popular "Geschichten aus dem Wienerwald," "Morgenblätter" and "Wein, Weib, Gesang"—and polkas ("Wildfeuer," "Stadt und Land," "Leichtes Blut"), some presented as dances at the second-act ball, but otherwise transformed into vocal numbers and into finales to each of the show's three acts.

Wiener Blut was a failure. After 30 performances Jauner was forced to remove it and hurry back his successful production of *Die Geisha* with American soubrette Marie Halton starred until he could get his next new piece, the American operetta *Der kleine Korporal,* ready. When both that and his next production, *Rhodope,* failed, Jauner put a bullet through his head in his Carltheater office. *Wiener Blut* was given a half-dozen extra performances during the runs of these two pieces, then put away. However, it got a second chance when the precipitate departure of megastar Girardi from the Theater an der Wien in 1905 left that theatre with a hole in its schedule. After a handful of performances of Strauss's *Die Fledermaus* and *Prinz Methusalem,* Karczag and Wallner decided to try a revised version of *Wiener Blut.* Mounted with a cast headed by Karl Meister (Balduin), Dora Keplinger (Franziska), Phila Wolff (Gabriele), Siegmund Natzler (Gindelbach), Gerda Walde (Pepi), Carlo Böhm (Josef) and Oskar Sachs (Kagler), the show did rather better than it had first time round. It played three weeks to end the season, came back to open the new season in September, and was played again to launch the following season. Without ever running up a series, it was brought back regularly (1912, 1923, 1925, 1934, etc), and in 30 years perched on the edge of the repertoire it was played 134 times at the Theater an der Wien as well as at the companion Raimundtheater (1910 w Betty Fischer as Franziska, Franz Glawatsch as Kagler, 1911, 1913, etc). This was sufficient to establish it, and in 1928 it was taken into the repertoire at the Volksoper (13 June), where it has been played to this day.

Elsewhere, the reaction to the show was less receptive. Rudolf Aronson took it for Broadway, in spite its initial failure, and mounted it as *Vienna Life* (ad Glen MacDonough), with Ethel Jackson (Gabriele), Charles H Drew (Prince), Thomas Persse (Zedlau), Amelia Stone (Franzi) and Raymond Hitchcock in the chief comic role of Franzi's father, and with Prince Bitowski played Orlofsky-like in travesty. Some hurried rewrites and recasting after a negative opening couldn't keep the show afloat more than 35 performances.

Paris first saw the piece in 1911, played by a visiting company, but in 1934, following the enormous Paris success of *Valses de Vienne,* the enterprising Trianon-Lyrique tried to jump on the bandwagon with *Les Jolies Viennoises* (ad André Mauprey), with a cast headed by Jeanne Guyla, Coecilia Navarre, Janine Delille, Max Moutia and Morton. It did not succeed in approaching the success of its sister piece, and *Les Jolies Viennoises* did not make the revivable repertoire. Another version, *Sang viennois* (ad Marc-Cab), later found its way to the stage without provoking any more attention.

London saw the show in 1955 during the visit of a Viennese company headed by Karl Terkal, Christine von Widmann, Tony Niessner and Fritz Imhoff, but has not witnessed an English version.

A film version was produced in 1942 with Willy Fritsch and Maria Holst in the central roles, and the piece was televised in Germany in 1971 with Rene Kollo and Dagmar Koller featured.

USA: Broadway Theater *Vienna Life* 23 January 1901; France: Théâtre du Vaudeville (Ger) 1911, Trianon-Lyrique *Les Jolies Viennoises* 22 December 1934; UK: Stoll Theatre (Ger) 16 August 1955

Film: Willy Forst 1942

Recordings: complete (Urania, EMI, Eurodisc etc), selections (Fontana, Saga, Philips, etc), selection in French (Radio Bleue), etc

Video: Tautus 1971

WIENER FRAUEN Operette in 3 acts partly "based on a French original" by Ottokar Tann-Bergler and Emil Norini. Music by Franz Lehár. Theater an der Wien, Vienna, 21 November 1902.

Although the first entry of the young Franz Lehár into the world of the Operette was initially announced for Berlin's Centraltheater, and the title of his piece as *Der Klavierstimmer,* the work in question was ultimately mounted as *Wiener Frauen,* and produced under the management of Lehár's fellow Hungarian Wilhelm Karczag and his partner Karl Wallner at the Theater an der Wien.

The piano teacher of the abandoned title is Willibald Brandl (Alexander Girardi), who not only played divinely but also sang a mean waltz song. He is in the past tense, for he went off to America, was rumored lost at sea, and his romantically inclined former pupil, Klara Schwott (Lina Abarbanell), went and married the wealthy confectioner Philipp Rosner (Karl Meister) and more or less forgot about her music master. But one day, when the piano tuner was in, Klara heard that waltz. Willibald was not drowned nor in America, but in her house. Finally, marriage lines prevail, and Willibald is paired off with Klara's maid, Jeannette (Betty Seidl). Oskar Sachs played Johann Nepomuc Nechledil, head of the Musikinstitut Nechledil and the possessor of three daughters named Lini, Tini and Fini, whilst the theatre's resident komische Alte, Sarolta von Rettich-Birk, played Klara's mother. The key number of the score was, of course, the plotworthy waltz tune (Paradies Walzer), which shared the honors of the evening with the so-called Nechledil-Marsch.

Mounted at a theatre that had gone four years without initiating a hit, *Wiener Frauen* came nearer than any piece since *Der Opernball* to fulfilling Karczag's hopes and needs. It ran for 50 straight performances over the Christmas and New Year period, and, if it was little seen after the producer at last found his elusive hit in its successor, Edmund Eysler's *Bruder Straubinger,* it was nevertheless played intermittently in the repertoire up to its 75th performance on 14 September 1905, ''helped'' by the interpolation into its second act of ''Mlle Célia Galley of the Paris Nouveautés in her imitations of Bernhardt, Otéro, Guilbert, Réjane, etc.''

When the show was taken up in Germany, by José Ferenczy, the following year, the original title was reverted to, but in Aurél Föld and Adolf Mérei's Hungarian version the Viennese ladies became *Pesti nők* (women of Pest) and, later, in a revival at the Városligeti Színkör (15 May 1907), they were even (re)juvenated to being *Pesti asszonyok* (girls of Pest).

Lehár's first Operette was also the first of his works to undergo what was to become his habitual process of remaking. In October 1906—less than four years after *Wiener Frauen*'s initial run—the Leipzig Stadttheater produced a rewritten version of the piece entitled *Der Schlüssel zum Paradies.*

Germany: Neues Königliches Opernhaus *Der Klavierstimmer* 27 June 1903; Hungary: Budai Színkör *Pesti nők* 15 August 1903

WILDCAT Musical in 2 acts by N Richard Nash. Lyrics by Carolyn Leigh. Music by Cy Coleman. Alvin Theater, New York, 16 December 1960.

The Broadway debut of composer Cy Coleman, *Wildcat* was a vehicle for film and television comedy megastar Lucille Ball in the role of a bright and brassy little lady by the name of Wildcat Jackson who is out to make good amongst the oilfields of the American South. With nothing but her natural advantages to her name, she bluffs and fibs herself the services and the glances of Joe Dynamite (Keith Andes)—the best foreman around—as well as a drilling crew and a plot of 10 acres for them to drill in. Inevitably at least one lie is found out, and her whole tale starts to topple. When it seems she will lose all of Joe's services, she sadly tips his belongings down the dry well hole. But those belongings include dynamite. In the resulting panic, Joe's feelings for ''Wildy'' finally come to the top around about the same time the dynamite proves that the well hole wasn't dry after all.

The score of *Wildcat* came up with a take-away hit in Wildcat's cheer-up song to her beloved, lame sister (Paula Stewart), ''Hey, Look Me Over.'' Elsewhere, the star leaped into a hoedown over ''What Takes My Fancy'' and took a quieter tone to reason out her ambitions in ''That's What I Want for Janie''; Joe's assistant, Hal (Clifford David), coaxed lame Janie to forget her handicap in ''One Day We Dance''; and the star's faded, foolish-elegant landlady (Edith King) tried to install some ladylikeness into this Annie Oakley of the oil wells in ''Tippy, Tippy Toes.'' An invitation to ''Give a Little Whistle'' had different connotations to the song of the same title made popular in the cartoon film *Pinocchio.*

Wildcat, produced by director/choreographer Michael Kidd and librettist N Richard Nash, did good business until Miss Ball left the cast when it closed after 171 performances. An attempt to mount the show in Australia, with Toni Lamond and Stephen Boyd starred, played two months in Melbourne and did not move on to Sydney.

Australia: Princess Theatre, Melbourne 19 July 1963

Recording: original cast (RCA Victor)

WILDE, Oscar [Fingal O'Flahertie Wills] (b Dublin, 15 October 1854; d Paris, 30 November 1900).

Although, unlike such of his contemporaries as Barrie and Conan Doyle, Oscar Wilde wrote nothing for the musical theatre, other writers have, in recent years, seemed determined to mend the omission. The plays of the celebrated playwright have been grist to the mill of many an adapter-librettist of the 20th century, and it is probably more a comment on the unsuitability of the wordful Wildean style of comedy as the basis for musicalization than a reflection on the abilities of the adapters that the results have been almost entirely, if not egregiously, unsuccessful.

Unsurprisingly, Wilde's most popular play, *The Importance of Being Earnest,* has come under musical attack the most frequently. Broadway was first given *Oh, Ernest!* in 1927 (Robert Hood Bowers/Francis de Witt, Royale Theater 9 May) with Marjorie Gateson as Gwendolen, Hal Forde as John and Flavia Arcaro as Lady Bracknell, whilst Britain saw its first attempt at a musical *Importance of Being Earnest* in 1957 when *Found in a Handbag* (Allan Bacon, Margate 18 November 1957) was played in the provinces. A Vivian Ellis version, *Half in Earnest,* originally mooted for production by C B Cochran on the verge of the play's copyright expiry in 1950 with a stellar cast, instead found its way to the stage at America's Bucks County Playhouse, also in 1957, with Anna Russell as Lady Bracknell and Jack Cassidy as Worthing. That version was played in Britain in 1958 (Coventry 27 March), with Marie Lohr as Lady Bracknell, and later in Australia (Independent Theatre 6 November 1974). America also committed a 60-minute television version *Who's Earnest* (CBS 9 October 1957), which included Savoy veteran Martyn Green in its cast.

Earnest in Tune (John de Grey/Humphrey Tilley, Patricia Lawrence) was played at Canterbury the same year (4 August), *Ernest* (Malcom Sircom/Neil Wilkie/Henry Burke) at Farnham the next (18 May), and *Ernest in Love* (Lee Pockriss/Anne Croswell Grammercy Arts Theater, New York 4 May 1960) kept the limp list growing the next year. A wave of Wilde adaptations in Germany brought forth a *Mein Freund Bunbury* (Gerd Natschinski/Bez, Degenhardt Metropoltheater 2 October 1964) that did alarming things to Wilde—it opened in Victoria station with Chasuble leading a Salvation Army choir in something like ''Follow the Fold,'' moved on to party at Algy Moncrieff's, where everyone dances the ''Black Bottom'' before trotting off to a music hall, and continued in Wilder and Wilder disarray—but nevertheless turned out to be East Germany's most successful musical comedy up to that time. It still wins the occasional production. Another *Bunbury* (Paul Burkhard/Hans Weigel) was played, close on its heels, at the Stadttheater, Basel (7 October 1965). The most recent adaptation, probably because most of the title variations had been already used, called itself simply *The Importance* (Sean O'Mahoney, Ambassador's Theatre, London 23 June 1984) and was the first to make it to London's West End. It played 29 regular performances.

Lady Windermere's Fan was given several thoroughly professional adaptations, most notably in Noël Coward's *After the Ball* (Globe Theatre, London 10 June 1954). There were also an early burlesque, Charlie Brookfield's *The Poet and the Puppets* (Comedy Theatre 19 May 1892) in which Lottie Venne played ''Mrs Earlybird'' and Charles Hawtrey burlesqued Wilde himself, an Italian version, and Karl Farkas and Peter Kreuder turned out a piece in which Zarah Leander as ''Odette'' Erlynne was supposed to be the *Lady aus Paris* opposite co-star Paul Hörbiger's Augustus Lorton (Raimundtheater, Vienna 22 October 1964, Theater des Westens, Berlin 19 March 1965).

If *An Ideal Husband* did not seem ideal libretto fodder, the German interest in Wilde musicals provoked its use as such not once but twice in *Der Ideale Gatte* (Franz Grothe/Hermann Mostar, Hamburger Kammerspiele 3 December 1963) and again in the curiously titled *Piccadilly Circus* (Hary Osterwald, Curt Prina/Hans Schachner, Dick Price, Städtische Bühne, Munster 2 May 1975). Also in Germany, *Lord Arthur Saville's Crime* became *Lord Arthurs pflichtbewusstes Verbrechen* (Bernd Wefelmeyer/Gerd Hornawsky, Theater der Stadt, Plaunen 10 January 1975).

Possibly the first Wilde musical, however, was a version of *The Canterville Ghost,* which became *Das Gespenst von Matschatsch,* a burlesque opera by ''Simplizissimus'' produced at the Munich Theater am Gärtnerplatz on 18 January 1905. Eleven months later Richard Strauss's opera of *Salomé,* based on Wilde's text, was given its premiere in Dresden, followed in 1908 by Mariotte's French version of the same tale. Zemlinsky's operas *Eine florentinische Tragödie* (1917) and *Der Zwerg* (1922, on *The Birthday of the Infanta*) and Kika's Czech *Bily pán* (1929, on *The Canterville Ghost*), later played in Germany as *Spuk im Schloss* (Breslau, 1931), were other operatic works with Wildean origins, whilst Jenő Hubay's Hungarian opera *Az őnzo óriás* (one act, L Márkus, J Mohácsi, 26 February 1936) was written around *The Selfish Giant.*

The central European preoccupation for musicalized Wilde continued in 1990, when an Hungarian ''rock opera'' version of *The Picture of Dorian Gray* (previously operaticized in a more traditional way by Leonid Kreutzer) was successfully mounted at Budapest's Vígszínház (Mátyás Várkonyi/Gunar Braunke ad János Acs 16 July), subsequently adapted for the German stage and also given a brief showing in Britain. Yet another musical version of *The Canterville Ghost* (Marc Berry/Michael Korth) was given a showing in Stralsund in 1996 (Theater Vorpommern 31 August), and the umpteenth at Marburg in 1997.

Another musical based on *Dorian Gray* had been announced—without coming to fruition—as an early project of the young producer Cameron Mackintosh, but by and large Wilde musicals were less frequent on English-language stages. *Dorian Gray* did find its way to off-off-Broadway in 1996 (Gary Levinson/Allan Reiser/Don Price, Reiser Judith Anderson Theater 17 September), and American television put out a 1966 musical version of *The Canterville Ghost,* written by Sheldon Harnick and Jerry Bock. Another stage version of the same piece (Charles Miller/Peter Quilter) was put on the stage in the British provinces in 1998 (Northcott Theater, Exeter 30 April).

Sent on a lecture tour to America by D'Oyly Carte in order that Americans might better appreciate the burlesque of the aesthetic movement (if not originally of Wilde personally) in Gilbert and Sullivan's *Patience,* Wilde ultimately found himself parodied by John Howson, the Bunthorne of one Broadway production. His notoriety (''one of the most successful self-advertisers of the age, who has consistently pursued the principle of making himself conspicuous in order to secure notoriety'') made him an easy target for comedians, and he was subsequently burlesqued in a number of London shows. He was, however, actually portrayed on the Broadway stage in *Knights of Songs* (a piece that proposed itself as a Gilbert and Sullivan biomusical), where Robert Chisholm ''was'' Wilde and sang numbers from *Patience.* The playwright, however, suffered a greater indignity when a piece called *Dear Oscar* (Playhouse 16 November 1972) was swept off Broadway in five nights. Self-publicist or not, how he would have hated that one.

If Oscar Wilde did not himself write for the musical stage, his brother Willie on one occasion did. He was the author of an adaptation of F Anstey's *The Tinted Venus,* produced at the Liverpool Prince of Wales Theatre, 7 September 1885, and subsequently at Boston (Globe Theater 8 October 1885) with Rosina Vokes as its untinted star.

WILDER, Victor (b Wetteren, Belgium, 21 August 1835; d Paris, 8 September 1892).

A journalist and theatrical author in Paris, Wilder contributed mostly to the operatic stage, adapting Wagner's *Ring des Nibelungen* into French and gallicizing Schubert's *Der häusliche Krieg* as *La Croisade des dames* (3 February 1868, Fantaisies-Parisiennes), as well as Mozart's *L'Oie de Caire,* Schumann's *Le Paradis et la Péri,* Paisiello's *Il barbiere di Siviglia,* Ricci's *La Fête de Piedigrotta* and *Une folie à Rome,* Handel's *Judas Maccabaeus* and *The Messiah,* and supplying the text for Weber's *Sylvana* (w Mestépès), Chapuis's *Enguerrand* (w Émile Bergerat) and Rubenstein's *Le Tour de Babel.* However, he was called upon by Victor Koning to work on the replacement libretto for the French production of Johann Strauss's *Indigo,* and as a result he was allotted two other Strauss assignments—the supply of a fresh text to go with a mixture of *Fledermaus* and *Cagliostro in Wien* music to make up another Strauss piece for Koning (*La Tzigane*) and an original tale commissioned by the Vienna Carltheater as a bait to Strauss to compose a work for them (*Prinz Methusalem*).

1875 **La Reine Indigo** (Johann Strauss/w Adolphe Jaime) Théâtre de la Renaissance 27 April

1877 **Prinz Methusalem** (Strauss/w Alfred Delacour ad Karl Treumann) Carltheater 3 January

1877 **La Tzigane** (Strauss/w Delacour) Théâtre de la Renaissance 30 October

1879 **Fatinitza** French version w Delacour (Théâtre des Nouveautés)

WILDFLOWER Musical play in 3 acts by Oscar Hammerstein II and Otto Harbach. Music by Vincent Youmans and Herbert Stothart. Casino Theater, New York, 7 February 1923.

The most successful show of Broadway's 1922–23 season, *Wildflower* was intended by its authors to take the currently fashionable ''Cinderella and her dancing chorus'' kind of musical, epitomized by such pieces as *Irene* and *Sally,* and give it a more substantial, operettic dimension. They began by setting their show not in a mixture of high- and low-life New York, but in the Lombardy sunshine, and continued by picking up that favorite old theatrical theme the musical-comedy will, beloved of authors since the days of London's German Reed establishment and the 19th-century French vaudevillists (and probably other folk before), and mixing it with a good dose of the recently succesful play *Nothing But the Truth.* Their Cinderella, the ever-simmering farmgirl Nina Benedetto (*Irene* star Edith Day), is to inherit a fortune if she can keep her temper for six months. Nasty cousin Bianca (Evelyn Cavanaugh), who is next in line to inherit, naturally pursues Nina from farmyard to fancy villa on the banks of Lake Como and back, intent on irritating her to explosion point, but she doesn't succeed and Nina ends up happily rich and wed to her peasant Guido (Guy Robertson).

The show's 13 songs plus two finales—written about half and half by the two composers—turned out one piece that won huge popularity in the heroine's lively ''Bambalina,'' ''a piquant little staccato melody with a refrain to which the singer stepped with rhythmical sounds, much as in the sabot dances of Holland'' (the Bambalina of the title was actually an old man who played the fiddle for dancing). The hero's apostrophe to his ''Wildflower''—written, like the hit piece, by Youmans, although all were credited jointly—ran it a good second. The comedy was headed by Olin Howard and Esther Howard singing about ''The World's Worst Women.''

Arthur Hammerstein's production of *Wildflower* fulfilled all the hopes placed in it. It ran for 477 performances on Broadway and subsequently toured for more than two seasons whilst going on to productions in both London and Australia. London's version—which arrived in town on the peak of the Broadway-in-London wave as represented by *No, No, Nanette, Rose Marie* and *Mercenary Mary*—featured Kitty Reidy (Nina), Evelyn Drewe (Bianca) and Howett Worster (Guido) with Mark Daly and Julie Hartley-Milburn heading the comedy. It had a bumpy ride, being transferred first to the Adelphi (3 April), then to His Majesty's Theatre (15 May), but it never looked like coming up to the level of the earlier shows in popularity. It closed after 114 performances.

In Australia, however, *Wildflower* was a hit, no little thanks to the young and darkly soprano Marie Burke, plucked from touring variety and cast by J C Williamson Ltd in the leading role. Herbert Browne (Guido), Marjorie Dawe (Bianca), Gus Bluett and Marie La Varre (Lucrezia) completed the team that—again in spite of having to shift theatres in both main centers—made *Wildflower* an all-Australian favorite. The show ran almost five months in its initial Sydney season and two and a half in its first stint in Melbourne (Her Majesty's 7 August 1925), and it was still to be seen in a revival under the Williamson banner as late as 1954.

Australia: Theatre Royal, Sydney 29 November 1924; UK: Shaftesbury Theatre 17 February 1926

Recordings: London cast recordings (part-record) (WRC, Monmouth-Evergreen)

WILDHORN, Frank (b 29 November 1958).

Pop musicwriter Wildhorn (''Where Do Broken Hearts Go?'') came to the musical theatre in 1990 with his score to the Leslie Bricusse version of *Jekyll and Hyde.* He subsequently composed additional pieces for the stage version of the musical film *Victor/Victoria* and found himself well represented on the fin de siècle American stage when both *Jekyll and Hyde* and another primary-colored costume piece, *The Scarlet Pimpernel,* installed themselves for good Broadway runs and a continuing life on the touring circuits.

An attempt to re-create *The Civil War* in musical terms, however, quit Broadway after 63 nights.

1990 **Jekyll and Hyde** (Leslie Bricusse) Alley Theater, Houston 25 May; Plymouth Theater, New York 28 April 1997

1995 **Victor/Victoria** (w Henry Mancini/Bricusse, Blake Edwards) Marquis Theater, New York 25 October

1997 **The Scarlet Pimpernel** (Nan Knighton) Minskoff Theater 9 November

1999 **The Civil War** (Gregory Boyd, Jack Murphy) St James's Theater 22 April

WILHELM [PITCHER, William John Charles] (b Northfleet, 21 March 1858; d London, 2 March 1925).

One of the most celebrated of British Theatre designers, Wilhelm was prominent in the London theatre for some 40 years, for 25 of which he designed the costumes for the famous pantomimes at the Theatre Royal, Drury Lane. He both devised and designed a large number of the ballets at the Empire Theatre (including a *La Camargo* for Adeline Genée), from soon after its opening until the First World War, provided the costumes for many major spectaculars and pantomimes, and was one of the regular designers of clothes for the London musical theatre over nearly half a century.

Amongst his credits were included a long run of the most famous Gaiety Theatre shows (*Cinder-Ellen Up Too Late, In Town, Don Juan, The Shop Girl, My Girl, A Runaway Girl, The Messenger Boy, The Toreador, The Orchid, The Spring Chicken, The New Aladdin*), the original Savoy Theatre productions of *The Mikado* and *Ruddigore,* such early British musicals as *Manteaux Noirs, Rip van Winkle, The Vicar of Bray, Cymbia, The Golden Ring, Marjorie* and *Jane Annie,* and early-20th-century musical comedies including *The Girl from Kays, The Cherry Girl, The Blue Moon, The Dairymaids, Tom Jones, The Gay Gordons, The Arcadians* and *The Mousmé.* Amongst his last assignments were the clothes for J M Barrie's modern musical *Rosy Rapture,* with its clothes-horse star Gaby Deslys, and, in complete contrast, the period comic opera *Young England.*

WILHELM, Julius (b Vienna, 22 February 1871; d Hinterbrühl, 20 March 1941).

For 30 years a librettist for the musical stage, Julius Wilhelm contributed texts and lyrics to several internationally successful Operetten, as well as to a number more that had fine runs on home ground without going further. He had an early and very genuine success when Gabor Steiner mounted *Frühlingsluft,* his adaptation of the French comedy *Coquin de printemps* (w Carl Lindau) to a pasticcio Josef Strauss score, at his summer theatre, and he confirmed that beginning with the text to the little entertainment *Wien bei Nacht,* ''ein Episode aus der Grossstadt,'' a second summer theatre success that, like the earlier one, was played for many seasons in Vienna, right into the 1920s.

He supplied the texts for two highly successful short pieces, Heinrich Reinhardt's *Die süssen Grisetten* and Leo Fall's *Brüderlein fein,* both of which subsequently traveled far (*The Daring of Diane, Darby and Joan*) from their productions at the Theater an der Wien's studio theatre, Hölle, but his first full-length pieces for the major Vienna theatres, an adaptation of Schönthan and von Moser's famous *Krieg im Frieden* (27 performances) and the unfortunate *Mutzi* (6 performances), both failed when mounted at the Carltheater. A further collaboration with Heinrich Reinhardt on *Die Sprudelfee* at the Raimundtheater in 1911 gave him his biggest international success to date, and another pasticcio piece, *Alt-Wien* (1911), this time to the music of Josef Lanner, was a hit at the Carltheater, but it was the creation of the role of the old violinist, Racz, for Alexander Girardi in Kálmán's *Der Zigeunerprimás* that earned Wilhelm his biggest and best single credit, both at home and abroad.

Die Winzerbraut (137 performances at the Theater an der Wien), Hermann Dostal's little *Urschula,* which was played for two seasons on the bill at the Apollotheater and later in Hungary, and a fresh libretto manufactured to go with the music of Suppé's *Donna Juanita* score and played under the title *Die grosse Unbekannte* for 101 performances at the Johann Strauss-Theater were further Viennese successes for the librettist.

Wilhelm also collaborated with A M Willner on the 1914 opera *Der Schuster von Delft* (mus: Benito von Berra, Nationaltheater, Zagreb 26 January) and with Paul Frank on the libretto for Leo Fall's 1920 opera *Der goldene Vogel* (Dresden 21 May).

He was also the author (w Paul Frank) of the comedy *Ludwig XIV* (Theater des Westens 15 March 1918) on which the Broadway musical *Louie the 14th* was based.

1902 **Die ledige Frau** (Richard Haller/w Josef Siegmund) Neues Königliches Opernhaus, Berlin 29 September

1902 **Was ein Frauenherz begehrt** (Ernst Reiterer/w Louis Gundlach) 1 act Danzers Orpheum 2 October

1903 **Frühlingsluft** (Josef Strauss arr Reiterer/w Carl Lindau) Venedig in Wien 9 May

1904 **Port Arthur** (Rudolf Raimann, R Laubner) Venedig in Wien 1 June

1904 **Spiritus** (Philipp Silber)

1904 **Wien bei Nacht** (Josef Hellmesberger/w Lindau) 1 act Venedig in Wien 28 October

1904 **Die Eisjungfrau** (*The Girl from Up There*) German version w Lindau, M Band and add mus by Hellmesberger (Venedig in Wien)

1906 **Krieg im Frieden** (Heinrich Reinhardt) Carltheater 24 January

1906 **Mutzi** (Hellmesberger/w Robert Pohl) Carltheater 15 September

1907 **Die süssen Grisetten** (Reinhardt) 1 act Hölle 1 December

1908 **Die Paradiesvogel** (Silber/w A M Willner) Theater am Gärtnerplatz, Munich 6 June

1908 **Drei kleine Mädel** (Béla Laszky) 1 act Hölle 18 November

1909 **Die Sprudelfee** (Reinhardt/w Willner) Raimundtheater 23 January

1909 **Brüderlein fein** (Leo Fall) 1 act Hölle 1 December

1910 **Eine göttliche Nacht** (Hermann Dostal) 1 act Hölle 1 March

1910 **Schneeglöckchen** (Gustave Kerker/w Willner) Theater an der Wien 14 October

1911 **Alt-Wien** (Josef Lanner arr/Gustav Kadelberg) Carltheater 23 December

1912 **Susi** (*A kis gróf*) German version (Carltheater)

1912 **Der Zigeunerprimás** (Emmerich Kálmán/w Fritz Grünbaum) Johann Strauss-Theater 11 October

1913 **Dorette** (Bruno Hartl/w Heinrich von Waldberg) Theater am Gärtnerplatz, Munich 7 February

1916 **Die Winzerbraut** (Oskar Nedbal/w Leo Stein) Theater an der Wien 11 February

1916 **Urschula** (H Dostal/w Béla Jenbach) Apollotheater 1 September

1919 **Die Verliebten** (Ralph Benatzky) Raimundtheater 29 March

1919 **Die Blume von Tokio** (Laszky) 1 act Hölle 1 July

1923 **Mozart** (Hans Duhan/w Paul Frank) Volksoper 2 June

1925 **1001 Freier** (Hans Zomack/w Frank) Stadttheater, Meissen 7 February

1925 **Die grosse Unbekannte** (Franz von Suppé arr Karl Pauspertl/w Gustav Beer) Johann Strauss-Theater 8 April

1926 **General d'amour** (Julius Bittner/w Frank) Volksoper 3 March

1928 **Grisettenliebe** (Reinhardt) Rolandbühne 23 March

1929 **Pariser Blut** (H Reichart) Rose-Theater, Berlin 23 November

1930 **Böhmische Musikanten** (Bernhard Grün/w Peter Herz) Neues Operettentheater, Leipzig 30 October; Wiener Bürgertheater 18 December 1931

1931 **Das Spitzentuch der Königin** new version w Rudolf Österreicher (Johann Strauss-Theater)

1931 **Der Hochstapler** (Richard Schwarz/w Gustav Heim) Volksoper, Hamburg 18 February

1932 **Freut euch das Lebens** (Josef and Johann Strauss arr Grün/Nestroy ad w Herz) Neues Operettentheater, Leipzig 24 October

1933 **Tango am Mitternacht** (*Éjféli tangó*) German version (Volksoper)

WILKINSON, C[olm] T[homas] (b Dublin, 5 June 1944). Tenor/actor who introduced or played several of the most substantial musical-dramatic roles of the modern musical theatre on both sides of the Atlantic.

At first a member of the cabaret group "The Witnesses," the Irish singer-songwriter made his earliest musical-theatre appearance as Judas in Dublin's production of *Jesus Christ Superstar* (1972), a role he later took over in the show's long-running London production in 1974. Wilkinson initially mixed his theatre performances with periods in variety and cabaret, appearing on the one hand as Barach in the West End musical *Fire Angel* and as Herod in *Rock Nativity* at Reading, and, on the other, representing Ireland in the 1978 Eurovision song contest.

He sang Che on the pre-production recording of *Evita,* repeated the role of Judas in *Jesus Christ Superstar* on tour in Britain (1981), and starred as The Witness in the Irish musical *Voices* (1984), before moving on to create the English-language version of the role of Jean Valjean in *Les Misérables* in London (1985). He subsequently appeared in the same role in New York (1987) and as the *Phantom of the Opéra,* a role that he had initiated in its Sydmonton tryout, in Canada. He later appeared in Canada in his original role in *Les Misérables* (1998).

WILLEMETZ, Albert [Lucien] (b Paris, 14 February 1887; d Marnes-la-Coquette, 7 October 1964). The dominant librettist and lyricist—in quality and quantity—of the French musical stage for several decades between and beyond the wars.

The young Albert Willemetz studied law and, after his graduation, took employment in the offices of the

French Ministry of the Interior. During the war years he was attached to the cabinet office of President Clemenceau's government, whilst at the same time using another and rather different pen to supply sketches and, most particularly, song words to the revue stage.

The reputation that he built up in the world of the revue and the chanson was, however, eventually equaled and even overtaken by a fame second to none as the virtual inventor of, and, with André Barde, the most outstanding practitioner of the postwar Jazz Age musical comedy. Theatre owner and producer Gustave Quinson, who had mounted Willemetz's very first stage piece, the one-act *Le Renseignement,* at the Palais-Royal as early as 1905, and who had since tied the young author to him in one of those "collaborations" for which he was notorious, commissioned and produced the small-scale opérette-bouffe *Phi-Phi,* ultimately on the stage of the Théâtre des Bouffes-Parisiens. *Phi-Phi* ("C'est une gamine charmante," "Les petits païens," "Bien chapeautée," "Ah! tais-toi," etc) became the hit of an era. The intimate, wittily sexy tone of its well-constructed farcical text, and of lyrics that were both revusically pointed and unashamedly but unclichédly sexy in a style that had nothing to do with the opérettes of prewar years, proved wholly to the taste of the audiences of a liberated France, well and truly ready for the good time the "années folles" of one-steps and fox-trots promised. Willemetz's style became the joyously fashionable style of the French postwar musical stage.

Willemetz followed up the triumph of *Phi-Phi* with another, barely lesser, in *Dédé* ("Dans la vie faut pas s'en faire," "Je m'donne," "Si j'avais su," etc), but for the next two pieces in his triumphant series he left the task of the libretto to another of Quinson's team, Yves Mirande, and himself concentrated on the lyrics that were his favorite area of work. With Maurice Yvain he supplied the songs to the dazzling *Ta bouche* ("Ta bouche," "Des terres et des coupons," "Ça, c'est une chose," "La seconde étreinte," "Non, non, jamais les hommes," "Machinalement," "De mon temps," etc) and the Maurice Chevalier-Dranem fantasy *Là-haut* ("C'est Paris," "Si vous n'aimez pas ça," etc), but when allied once more with *Phi-Phi* and *Dédé*'s composer, Henri Christiné, he again provided both book and lyrics for a further success in the delicious little tale of *Madame.*

Thereafter, the successes—in various degrees—rolled out in sequence, rarely interrupted by failure, as Willemetz supplied unfailingly clever song words and, from time to time, libretti or part-libretti to many of the 1920s most popular shows. *En chemyse* returned to the historical burlesque style so successfully practiced in *Phi-Phi,* if without the same triumph, the little *Ri-Ri,* a vehicle for *Le Fruit vert* star Maud Loty, ran for more than 100 nights at the Théâtre Daunou, *Trois jeune filles . . . nues!* ("Est-ce que je te demande?") was a copper-bottomed hit, and the intimate comedy musical *Quand on est trois* had a fine run at the little Théâtre des Capucines. *J'aime,* another piece with Christiné, followed the now-normal course of events, and Willemetz's collaboration with André Messager, the opérette hero of the prewar French musical stage, on an up-to-date musical comedy proved a singular success, with first *Passionnément* and then *Coups de roulis* proving to be enduring hits.

When the fashion for his kind of musical comedy, a species based on a witty farcical text and modern songs and dances, gave way to that for the romantic opérette à grand spectacle, Willemetz went with the tide. He adapted a number of foreign successes to the French stage (*New Moon, Good News, Madame Pompadour, The Dubarry,* etc) and he also authored or co-authored Richepin's spectacular *Venise* and such large-stage Châtelet shows as *Sidonie Panache* and *Au temps des merveilleuses* to scores by his erstwhile partners in the area of the intimate musical.

In 1927, without decreasing his workload as a writer, Willemetz also joined Quinson in the management of the Théâtre des Bouffes-Parisiens, the scene of his first great hit (and a great many since), and there he was involved in the production of such pieces as *Les Aventures du Roi Pausole, Flossie* and *Arsène Lupin banquier.* In 1929, with Quinson's era of dominance beginning to come to an end, he took over the famous theatre and, subsequently partnering with Louis Meucci, continued to run it for some years, scoring a success with the comical *Un soir de réveillon,* winning critical bouquets, at least, for Sacha Guitry's *O mon bel inconnu,* more substantially financial ones for the rumba-musical *Toi c'est moi* and, above all, for his own greatest success of the period, the adaptation (w Léopold Marchand) of the German musical play *Drei Walzer* as a vehicle for Yvonne Printemps and Pierre Fresnay. For two seasons he also joined Quinson at the head of the affairs of the Palais-Royal.

By the Second World War, though still enormously active on both the stage and screen, Willemetz had done most of his best work for the theatre, but he still had a few cartridges to expend. He expanded the libretto of Lecocq's *Les Cent Vierges* for the Théâtre de la Gaîté-Lyrique and disproved the fairly watertight theory that adaptations are necessarily destructive when he produced a book that quite simply outshone the original. A similar attempt on the *Grande-Duchesse* was, however, not successful. Proving his continual adaptability, he also joined the newly prominent Vincy-Lopez school of musical theatre, supplying the lyrics for one of the most successful of their shows, *Andalousie.* He also adapted Irving Berlin's songwords for *Annie du Far-West* (*Annie Get Your Gun*) for the French stage.

In spite of his long and important career, however, it is as the man of the 1920s that Willemetz made his mark. But it was a mark that was almost entirely confined to France, for the ''outrageous'' sexual comedy of his lyrics and libretti made them deeply unsuitable for the polite ears of the English-speaking world, in particular. *Phi-Phi, Dédé* and *Ta bouche* all underwent severe emasculation for their English-language productions and, not surprisingly, failed. Only in Hungary, beyond the borders of France, did his work find the kind of reception that it won at home.

Various figures have been given over the years as to Willemetz's output. It is said that he wrote the lyrics to over 3,000 songs (''Valentine,'' ''Mon homme,'' ''J'en ai marre,'' etc), contributed more or sometimes less to 150 revues and wrote the text and/or lyrics to some hundred opérettes. Even if some or all of these figures have been rounded (severely?) upwards—and the figures are never accompanied by lists—Willemetz still remains one of, if not the most important and enjoyable writers for the musical theatre of his era. Of any era. Anywhere.

Willemetz was for a number of years president of SACEM, the French copyright authority.

1918 **Phi-Phi** (Henri Christiné/w Fabien Sollar) Théâtre des Bouffes-Parisiens 13 November

1919 **Rapatipatoum** (Tiarko Richepin) Theatre Édouard VII 7 April

1921 **Dédé** (Christiné) Théâtre des Bouffes-Parisiens 10 November

1922 **Ta bouche** (Maurice Yvain/Yves Mirande) Théâtre Daunou 1 April

1923 **Là-haut** (Yvain/Mirande, Gustave Quinson) Théâtre des Bouffes-Parisiens 31 March

1923 **Madame** (Christiné) Théâtre Daunou 14 December

1924 **En chemyse** (Raoul Moretti/w Cami) Théâtre des Bouffes-Parisiens 7 March

1925 **J'adore ça** (Christiné/w Saint-Granier) Théâtre Daunou 14 March

1925 **Quand on est trois** (Joseph Szulc/Pierre Veber, Serge Veber) Théâtre des Capucines 20 April

1925 **Ri-Ri** (Charles Borel-Clerc/Mirande, Quinson) Théâtre Daunou 4 November

1925 **Trois jeunes filles . . . nues!** (Moretti/w Mirande) Théâtre des Bouffes-Parisiens 3 December

1926 **Passionnément** (André Messager/w Maurice Hennequin) Théâtre de la Michodière 15 January

1926 **J'aime** (Christiné/w Saint-Granier) Théâtre des Bouffes-Parisiens 22 December

1927 **Venise** (Richepin/w André Mouëzy-Éon) Théâtre Marigny 25 June

1927 **Le Diable à Paris** (Marcel Lattès/w Robert de Flers, Francis de Croisset) Théâtre Marigny 27 November

1928 **Coups de roulis** (Messager) Théâtre Marigny 29 September

1929 **Couchette No 3** (Szulc/Alex Madis) Théâtre des Capucines 6 February

1929 **Good News** French version (Palace Théâtre)

1929 **Robert le pirate** (*The New Moon*) French version (Théâtre du Châtelet)

1930 **Madame Pompadour** French version w Eddy and Marietti (Théâtre Marigny)

1930 **Sidonie Panache** (Szulc/w Mouëzy-Éon) Théâtre du Châtelet 2 December

1930 **Les Aventures du Roi Pausole** (Arthur Honegger) Théâtre des Bouffes-Parisiens 12 December

1931 **Nina Rosa** French version w Mouëzy-Éon (Théâtre du Châtelet)

1932 **La Tulipe noire** (Richepin/Mouëzy-Éon) Théâtre de la Gaîté-Lyrique 19 March

1933 **Rose de France** (Sigmund Romberg/Mouëzy-Éon) Théâtre du Châtelet 28 October

1933 **Florestan 1er, Prince de Monaco** (Werner Richard Heymann/w Sacha Guitry) Théâtre des Variétés 8 December

1933 **La Dubarry** (*Die Dubarry*) French lyrics (Théâtre de la Porte-Saint-Martin)

1934 **Le Bonheur, mesdames!** (Christiné arr/Francis de Croisset, Fred de Grésac ad) Théâtre des Bouffes-Parisiens 6 January

1934 **Au temps des merveilleuses** (Christiné, Richepin/w Mouëzy-Éon) Théâtre du Châtelet 25 December?

1934 **La Créole** new libretto w Georges Delance (Théâtre Marigny)

1935 **Les Joies du Capitole** (Moretti/Jacques Bousquet) Théâtre de la Madeleine 25 February

1935 **Pour ton bonheur** (Marcel Lattès/Leopold Marchand) Théâtre des Bouffes-Parisiens 20 September

1935 **Un coup de veine** (Yvain/w Mouëzy-Éon) Théâtre de la Porte-Saint-Martin 11 October

1935 **Au Soleil du Mexique** (Yvain/w Mouëzy-Éon) Théâtre du Châtelet 18 December

1936 **Simone est comme ça** (Moretti/Mirande, Madis) Théâtre des Bouffes-Parisiens 5 March

1936 **Yana** (Christiné, Richepin/w Mouëzy-Éon, Henri Wernert) Théâtre du Châtelet 24 December

1937 **Trois valses** (*Drei Walzer*) French version w Leopold Marchand (Théâtre des Bouffes-Parisiens)

1938 **Le Flirt ambulant** (Christiné/w Tristan Bernard) Théâtre Michel 13 January

1938 **Les Petites Cardinal** (Jacques Ibert, Honegger/w Paul Brach) Théâtre des Bouffes-Parisiens 12 February

1939 **Billy et son équipe** (Michel Emer, ''Jean Sautreuil'' [Maurice Yvain]/w Mouëzy-Éon) Théâtre Mogador 6 March

1940 **Mes amours** (Oscar Straus/w Marchand) Théâtre Marigny 2 May

1942 **Valses de France** (pasticcio arr Henri Casadesus/Eddy Ghilain) Théâtre du Châtelet 23 December

1942 **Les Cent Vierges** new libretto w Mouëzy-Éon (Théâtre Apollo)

1945 **Pantoufle** (Szulc/w Marchand) Théâtre des Capucines 28 February

Plate 422. **Arthur Williams** *as Lurcher in* Dorothy.

1947 **Andalousie** (Francis Lopez/w Raymond Vincy) Théâtre de la Gaîté-Lyrique 25 October

1948 **La Maréchale Sans-Gêne** (Pierre Petit/Maurice Lehmann) Théâtre du Châtelet 17 February

1948 **La Grande-Duchesse de Gérolstein** new libretto (Théâtre de la Gaîté-Lyrique)

1950 **Annie du Far-West** (*Annie Get Your Gun*) French lyrics (Théâtre du Châtelet)

1956 **La Quincaillere de Chicago** (Louiguy/w Jean Le Seyeux) Théâtre de l'ABC 4 October

1961 **Le Jeu de dames** (Georges van Parys/w Georges Manoir) Théâtre Moderne 2 December

Autobiography: *Dans mon retroviseur* (La Table Ronde, Paris, 1967); Biography: Willemetz, J: *Albert Willemetz, Prince des années folles* (Michalon, Paris, 1996)

WILLIAMS, Arthur [WATTS, Arthur] (b Islington, London, 9 December 1844; d London, 15 September 1915). Top British musical comedian of the Victorian era.

Arthur Williams began his professional life as a legal stationer, and gave his first performance in the theatre at Gravesend in 1861. He performed in "booths, fit-ups and ghost shows," and spent seven years playing in stock companies in the provinces before making his London debut at the St James's Theatre with Mdlle de la Ferté in 1868. He appeared at the St James's in comedy and in burlesque (Baron Factotum in *The Sleeping Beauty in the Wood*) until the management collapsed. In 1870 he appeared in pantomime at the Crystal Palace (Master Sugarplum in *Gulliver*), in 1871 he played for W H C Nation at the Royalty, where the repertoire included the manager's *Nell Gwynne* (Duchess of Cleveland), and he subsequently appeared at the Grecian, the Surrey, the Pavilion and other minor theatres.

It was, however, a full decade decade after his London debut before Williams became prominent in the musical theatre. After appearing in a supporting part in *Venice* (1879, *Le Pont des soupirs*) at the Alhambra, he was cast in the role of the comico-nasty Sir Mincing Lane in the highly successful Solomon/Stephens *Billee Taylor* (1880 and revivals), and he followed up in the same team's next musicals, playing the important comic roles of Sir Whiffle Whaffle in *Claude Duval* (1881), Amurath CVIII in *Lord Bateman* (1882) and Robinson Brownjones in *Virginia and Paul* (1883). He appeared at the Gaiety under Hollingshead in comedy, including the slightly musicalized version of *High Life Below Stairs* (1884, Sir Harry) and in burlesque—*Little Robin Hood* (1882, Richard Coeur de Lion), *Little Don Cesar de Bazan* revival (1884), Menelaus in *Our Helen* (1884)—took over as Brabazon Sikes in *The Merry Duchess* at the Royalty Theatre and took the role of Jack Joskins in the comic opera *Dick* (1884). Williams subsequently toured alongside Willie Edouin and Alice Atherton as Rolland Butter in *The Babes* and made a notable success in the title role of their burlesque *Oliver Grumble* (1886). He returned that same year to the Gaiety Theatre—now under the management of George Edwardes—where his first engagement was the part of the comic bailiff, Lurcher, in *Dorothy*.

Dorothy made Williams a star. He remained with the show through its change of management, change of leading players, changes of theatres, and its two-and-a-half-year run, and continued on into the management's follow-up *Doris* (1889, Dinniver) and *The Red Hussar* (1889, Corporal Bundy) before returning to the Gaiety to play in the later new burlesques. He appeared as Zuniga ("The Villain of the Day") in *Carmen Up-to-Data* (1890) as Sir Ludgate Hill in *Cinder-Ellen Up Too Late* (1892) and as Doggrass in *Blue-Eyed Susan* (1892) before Edwardes's change of policy brought musical comedy to the Gaiety. Williams went on to play more comical nasties as Mr Hooley in *The Shop Girl* (1894) and the ringmaster Drivelli in *The Circus Girl* (1896), before moving on to a career that mixed more straight comedy with the musical comedy. He had further major successes on the musical stage, however, when he took over as Mr Pineapple, the hapless hero of *A Chinese Honeymoon* and played the amenable convict Crookie Scrubbs to the *Sergeant Brue* of Willie Edouin (1904), less when he appeared briefly as Topping in *Miss Wingrove* (1905), and he found yet another hit playing Edna May's father as Sir John Chaldicott in the Romeo and Juliet musical, *The Belle of Mayfair* (1907).

Williams returned to Edwardes management in 1908 to take his place in the next new style of musical theatre, and was cast as the comical King Joachim in *A Waltz Dream* (1908). He repeated the role that had made his fame in a revival of *Dorothy* (1909), then returned to play comedy parts in two further Viennese works: Lopf in *The Merry Peasant* (1909) and the naughty train conductor Scrop in *The Girl in the Train* (1910). This last was his final musical theatre performance, but he remained on the stage until his death in 1915.

Williams's second wife was the vocalist and burlesque player **Emily SPILLER** [Annie Reeve SPILLER] (b Marylebone, 14 November 1859; d Streatham Hill, 14 January 1941), who originated the part of Zolide in the long-touring *Bears Not Beasts* (1880), appeared at the Gaiety in *The Vicar of Wide-awake-field* (1885, t/o Squire Thornhill), as a *Billee Taylor* in breeches at Toole's in 1886, and alongside Williams as Prince Rupert in *Oliver Grumble* (1886). He was also uncle to the comedian Fred Emney, who replaced him briefly in *Dorothy*.

His brother, **Fred WILLIAMS** (?1853–1916), was a well-known music-hall sketch artist.

An inveterate collector, Arthur Williams put together one of the finest collections of theatrical memorabilia in the history of the genre. After his death it passed to George and Alfred Black, and thence to a dealer and a sad and inevitable breakup.

WILLIAMS, [Eg]Bert [Austin] (b Antigua, West Indies, 12 November 1874; d Detroit, Mich, 4 March 1922).

During his early years in the San Francisco minstrel world, Bert Williams made up a partnership with fellow minstrel George Walker. Their cakewalk act won them a Broadway spot in the short-lived Victor Herbert musical *The Gold Bug* (1896), and they moved on from there to play their mixture of comedy, song and dance in variety—in a ''double act'' that employed 16 people in ''the great cakewalk''—and, quickly at the top of the bill, in a series of musical plays. They toured with the sketch *Clorindy, or the origin of the cakewalk* (*The Senegambian Carnival*), then joined the management of Hurtig and Seamon, which produced the musical comedies *The Policy Players* (1899, Dusty Cheapman), *The Sons of Ham* (1901, Tobias Wormwood, ''Zulu Babe'') and the pair's most successful show, *In Dahomey* (1902), before splitting away to more lucrative offers. However, when the management sued to stop them departing it was revealed that the performers' annual share of the profits during the combination had averaged a pretty startling $20,000.

Williams repeated his *In Dahomey* character of the ''awkward, slow-witted darkey'' in *Abyssinia* (1906–7, Jasmine Jenkins) and in *Bandana Land* (1908, Skunkton Bowser) before the dying Walker dropped out of the business, leaving him to star alone in *Mr Lode of Koal* (1909, Chester A Lode), alongside his writers and supports of always, J Leubrie Hill and Alexander Rogers. ''Walker does not seem to be missed to any extent,'' reacted a critic to the first performance. He then joined *The Ziegfeld Follies,* where he became famous through a decade of stand-up comedy performances and songs (notably his well-used ''Nobody'' of 1905). He subsequently appeared in *Broadway Brevities* and took once more to the musical theatre in *Under the Bamboo Tree* (ex- *The Pink Slip*) in 1922, but he collapsed during a performance at Detroit and died in a town hospital 11 days later. *Under the Bamboo Tree* switched its title to *In the Moonlight* and finally struggled to Broadway with James Barton in Williams's role as *Dew Drop Inn* in 1923.

Williams provided himself with individual songs for a number of his own musical comedies and revues (''Constantly,'' ''That's Harmony,'' ''I'm Cured'' in *The Ziegfeld Follies*).

A *Williams and Walker* biomusical was produced at off-Broadway's American Place Theater in 1986 (9 March).

1899 **The Policy Players** (w others/George Walker, Jesse A Shipp) Star Theater 16 October

1900 **Sons of Ham** (w others/Walker/Stephen Cassin, Shipp) Star Theater 15 October

1906 **Abyssinia** (w Will Vodery, Will Marion Cook, et al/Earl C Jones/Shipp, Alex Rogers) Majestic Theater 20 February

Biographies: Charters, A: *Nobody: The Story of Bert Williams* (New York, 1970), Smith E: *Bert Williams* (McFarland & Co, Jefferson, NC, 1992)

WILLIAMS, Hattie (b Boston, 17 March 1870; d New York, 17 August 1942). Broadway star soubrette of comedy and musical comedy.

Hattie Williams first appeared on the stage in 1892 in her native Boston, in E E Rice's extravaganza *1492,* and she moved from the chorus to a small named role (Infanta Catalina) for the Broadway transfer. She subsequently played in several farce comedies (Helen Best in *Courted into Court,* 1896, etc), toured in *The Girl from Paris* (1897, Mabel), appeared on Broadway in *A Day and a Night in New York* (1898, Lura Mann) and with the Rogers Brothers in *The Rigers Brothers in Washington* (1901, Maizi Mahoney) and *The Rogers Brothers in Har-*

Plate 423. **J C Williamson** *and his wife Maggie Moore were emperors of the Australian musical stage for many years.*

vard (1902) and toured in in the title role of the comedy *The Girl from Maxim's* but made her mark in musical comedy when she starred in the Broadway version of *The Girl from Kays* (1903, Winnie Harborough). In the next few years, she took the large and versatile title role of *The Rollicking Girl* (*Heisses Blut*) (1905, Ilona), was starred above the title as the actress Molly Montrose in the highly successful American production of *The Little Cherub* (1906) and played the title role of *Fluffy Ruffles* (1908), a musical based on the *New York Herald*'s cartoon. She then spent several seasons in the straight theatre before returning to play the naughty Praline in Berény's Operette *The Girl from Montmartre* (1912), the musical version of *The Girl from Maxim's.* She made a last Broadway musical appearance as Rosalilla in *The Doll Girl* (1913), America's version of Leo Fall's *Das Puppenmädel,* before retiring from the stage.

WILLIAMSON, J[ames] C[assius] (b Mercer, Pa, 26 August 1844; d Paris, 6 July 1913). Australia's principal producer of musical theatre both during and, through the company he founded, long after his lifetime.

A successful character comedian on the New York and San Francisco stages, Williamson, with his wife, **Maggie MOORE** [Margaret Virginia SULLIVAN] (b San Francisco, 10 July 1851; d San Francisco, 15 March 1926), scored a particular success in Australia, where, from 1874, their Dutch-dialect comedy melodrama *Struck Oil* became an enormous hit. In 1879 Williamson legally secured the rights to the all-pervading *HMS Pinafore* for Australasia, and he appeared as Sir Joseph Porter in the region's ''official'' production, whilst bringing the law to bear on pirated versions. As a result, Gilbert, who had previously had cause to be struck by the man's honesty amid wide and otherwise uncontrollable piracy, ensured that he was allotted similar rights for the other Gilbert and Sullivan comic operas, and his highly successful and high-class productions of these works provided the basis for what was to become Australia's most powerful production company for a period of almost 100 years.

Williamson's Royal Comic Opera Company (operated at various periods in partnership with Arthur Garner and/or George Musgrove) presented a large part of the most successful musical shows from the world's stages to Australia during the 1880s and 1890s. As opposition companies came, went or were swallowed up by ''the firm,'' his business developed into J C Williamson Ltd, which continued to introduce the largest part of the world's musical theatre to 20th-century Australia and New Zealand. Variously run by Sir George Tallis and the four Tait brothers with continuing success, the firm finally fell to pieces under less adept leadership in the 1970s.

Biography: Dicker, I G: *JCW* (Elizabeth Tudor Press, Sydney, 1974)

WILLNER, A[lfred] M[aria] (b Vienna, 11 July 1859; d Vienna, 27 October 1929). One of the busiest and most successful authors for the 20th-century Viennese Operette stage.

Journalist Willner came late to the theatre and made his first appearances on Viennese theatre bills as the author of ballet scenarii: Josef Bayer's *Rund um Wien* (Hofoper 1894) and Harry Berté's 1895 *Amor auf Reisen* (w Gaul, Hassreiter). It was in collaboration with Berté that he essayed his first libretto, the one-act comic opera *Die Schneeflocke,* produced in Prague and later at Berlin's Neues Königliches Opernhaus and the Budapest Operaház (March 1899). Whilst still lingering intermittently in related areas with such pieces as Forster's one-act opera *Tokayer,* he quickly moved on to larger things in the light musical theatre, collaborating with Bernhard Buchbinder on libretti for Carl Weinberger, Josef Bayer and Johann Strauss.

Success was not immediate. Weinberger's *Der Schmetterling* had a fair career after a 57-performance first run, Bayer's *Fräulein Hexe* folded in 11 showings, and the Strauss Operette *Die Göttin der Vernunft* played 32 successive performances and a handful of subsequent matinées in Vienna and was seen in several other central European cities without establishing itself. In fact, Willner's first real success as a librettist came, ultimately, as an adapter when he remade Maurice Ordonneau's libretto for *La Poupée* for its enormously popular German production.

Adaptations of a pair of celebrated comedies, *Le Mari de la débutante* (*Die Debütantin*) and *The Magistrate* (*Das Baby*), as distinctly uncelebrated musicals, and the translation of Robert Planquette's opérette *Mam'zelle Quat' Sous* for Girardi and the Theater an der Wien did not bring further success, but it was the latter house that gave the librettist his first major hit with an original text when it produced Leo Fall's musicalization of the dotty American tale of *Die Dollarprinzessin.*

The author's most fruitful and busy period then followed as Felix Albini's *Baron Trenck* found its way from Leipzig to the stages of the world, and the singular international success of Lehár's *Der Graf von Luxemburg*—a rewrite of the unloved *Die Göttin der Vernunft* libretto—set in motion a series of collaborations with the composer that included the more dramatic *Zigeunerliebe, Eva, Endlich allein* and the adaptation of *La Femme et le pantin* as *Frasquita,* as well as the German versions of his Hungarian operett *A Pacsirta* (*Wo die Lerche singt*) and his Italian revue-operetta *La danza delle libellule* (*Libellentanz*).

In the same period Willner and his collaborators provided Leo Fall with the texts for *Das Puppenmädel, Die schöne Risette* and *Die Sirene,* authored Oscar Straus's *Die kleine Freundin,* Heinrich Reinhardt's *Die Sprudelfee* and *Prinzess Gretl* (156 performances), Eysler's *Wenn zwei sich lieben* (110 performances) and Kálmán's *Die Faschingsfee,* all with success. He adapted the famous *Official Wife* tale as the libretto for Hermann Dostal's *Nimm mich mit!* and supplied Oskar Nedbal with the text for *Die schöne Saskia* for 131 performances at the Carltheater, but his greatest success came when he was teamed once more with the composer of his debuts, Harry Berté, and Heinz Reichert on the Schubert pasticcio *Das Dreimäderlhaus.* This fictional Schubertian love story turned out to be one of Vienna's greatest hits in decades, went around the world thereafter, and even provoked a musequel, *Hannerl,* from the same authors' pen.

The 1920s were mildly less productive. *Frasquita* and *Libellentanz* both had appreciable lives, Ernst Steffan's *Das Milliarden-Souper* had a six-month run at Berlin's Berliner Theater before failing in 28 performances in Vienna, Oscar Straus's *Nixchen* topped 100 performances at the Wallner-Theater and Leo Fall's posthumous *Rosen aus Florida* had a good 244 performances at the Theater an der Wien, but there was one more major success awaiting the librettist. After the success of *Das Dreimäderlhaus,* he had been tempted into another pasticcio show telling the life of *Johann Nestroy* as portrayed by Willy Thaller at the Carltheater, and now, a dozen years on, he turned his attention to Johann Strauss and, in collaboration with the most habitual partner of his later years, Heinz Reichert, embroidered a love-and-fame story onto the bones of the history of Vienna's most celebrated composer. The posthumously produced *Walzer aus Wien* did not outdo *Das Dreimäderlhaus* on home ground but, like it, it became the starting point for a long list of foreign versions, each of which maintained the fictitious romantic situations embroidered by the Viennese authors.

Amongst Willner's other stage works were three operatic libretti for composer Carl Goldmark: the adaptation of Charles Dickens's *A Cricket on the Hearth* as *Das Heimchen am Herd,* the 1902 version of Goethe's *Götz von Berlichingen,* and the Shakespearean *Ein Wintermärchen* (1908). His *Der Eisenhammer* and *Der Schuster von Delft,* set by Benito von Berra, were produced in Zagreb in 1911 and 1914, respectively, whilst the libretto written for Puccini by Willner and Reichert was translated into Italian before being set as *La Rondine.* His name was also attached very posthumously to the Operette *Die kleine Schwindlerin* (mus: Jára Beneš) produced at Vienna's Theater Auges Gottes in 1949 (1 March).

1896 **Die Schneeflocke** (Heinrich Berté) 1 act Prague 4 October

1896 **Der Schmetterling** (Carl Weinberger/w Bernhard Buchbinder) Theater an der Wien 7 November

1897 **Die Göttin der Vernunft** (Johann Strauss/w Buchbinder) Theater an der Wien 13 March

1898 **Fräulein Hexe** (Josef Bayer/w Buchbinder) Theater an der Wien 19 November

1899 **Die Puppe** (*La Poupée*) German version Centraltheater, Berlin

1901 **Die Debütantin** (Alfred Zamara/w Heinrich von Waldberg) Theater am Gärtnerplatz, Munich 17 January; Theater des Westens, Berlin 20 September

1902 **Das Baby** (Richard Heuberger/w Waldberg) Carltheater 3 October

1903 **Die beiden Don Juans** (*Mam'zelle Quat' Sous*) German version w Robert Pohl (Theater an der Wien)

1904 **Die Millionenbraut** (Berté/w E Limé) Theater am Gärtnerplatz, Munich 3 April

1907 **Der schöne Gardist** (Berté/w Alexander Landesberg) Neues Operetten-Theater, Breslau 12 October; Theater an der Wien 4 April 1908

1907 **Die Dollarprinzessin** (Leo Fall/w Fritz Grünbaum) Theater an der Wien 2 November

1907 **Der kleine Chevalier** (Berté) 1 act Centraltheater, Dresden 30 November

1908 **Ein Mädchen für alles** (Heinrich Reinhardt/w Waldberg) Theater am Gärtnerplatz, Munich 8 February

1908 **Baron Trenck [der Pandur]** (Felix Albini/w Robert Bodanzky) Stadttheater, Leipzig 15 February; Kaiser-Jubilaums Stadttheater 29 October 1909

1908 **Die Paradiesvogel** (Philipp Silber/w Julius Wilhelm) Theater am Gärtnerplatz, Munich 6 June

1908 **Der Glücksnarr** (Berté/E Limé ad w Landesberg) Carltheater 7 November

1909 **Die Sprudelfee** (Reinhardt/w Wilhelm) Raimundtheater 23 January

1909 **Der Graf von Luxemburg** (Franz Lehár/w Bodanzky) Theater an der Wien 12 November

1910 **Zigeunerliebe** (w Bodanzky/Lehár) Carltheater 8 January

1910 **Schneeglöckchen** (Gustave Kerker/w Wilhelm) Theater an der Wien 14 October

1910 **Das Puppenmädel** (Fall/w Leo Stein) Carltheater 4 November

1910 **Die schöne Risette** (Fall/w Bodanzky) Theater an der Wien 19 November

1911 **Die Sirene** (Fall/w Stein) Johann Strauss-Theater 5 January

1911 **Der Flotte** Bob (Karl Stigler/w Wilhelm Sterk) Altes Theater, Leipzig 8 April

1911 **Die kleine Freundin** (Oscar Straus/w Stein) Carltheater 20 October

1911 **Eva (das Fabriksmädel)** (Lehár/w Bodanzky) Theater an der Wien 24 November

1911 **Casimirs Himmelfahrt** (Bruno Granichstaedten/w Bodanzky) Raimundtheater 25 December

1913 **Prinzess Gretl** (Reinhardt/w Bodanzky) Theater an der Wien 31 January

1914 **Endlich allein** (Lehár/Bodanzky) Theater an der Wien 30 January

1914 **Der Märchenprinz** (Berté/w Sterk) Schauburg, Hanover 28 February

1914 **Der Durchgang der Venus** (Edmund Eysler/w Rudolf Österreicher) Apollotheater 28 November

1915 **Der künstliche Mensch** (Fall/w Österreicher) Theater des Westens, Berlin 2 October

1915 **Die erste Frau** (Reinhardt/w Österreicher) Carltheater 22 October

1915 **Wenn zwei sich lieben** (Eysler/w Bodanzky) Theater an der Wien 29 October

1916 **Das Dreimäderlhaus** (Franz Schubert arr Berté/w Reichert) Raimundtheater 15 January

1917 **Die Faschingsfee** (Emmerich Kálmán/w Österreicher) Johann Strauss-Theater 21 September

1917 **Die schöne Saskia** (Oskar Nedbal/w Reichert) Carltheater 16 November

1918 **Hannerl** (Schubert arr Karl Lafite/w Reichert) Raimundtheater 8 February

1918 **Wo die Lerche singt** (*A pacsirta*) German version w Reichert (Theater an der Wien)

1918 **Johann Nestroy** (arr Ernst Reiterer/w Österreicher) Carltheater 4 December

1919 **Nimm mich mit!** (Hermann Dostal/w Waldberg) Theater an der Wien 1 May

1921 **Das Milliarden-Souper** (Ernst Steffan/w Hans Kottow) Berliner Theater, Berlin 16 April

1921 **Das Nixchen** (Straus/w Österreicher) Wallner-Theater, Berlin 10 September

1921 **Der heilige Ambrosius** (Fall/w Arthur Rebner) Deutsches Künstlertheater, Berlin 3 November

1922 **Frasquita** (Lehár/w Reichert) Theater an der Wien 12 May

1923 **Libellentanz** (*La danza delle libellule*) revised *Der Sterngucker* German version (Stadttheater)

1924 **Agri** (Steffan/w Sterk) Bürgertheater 30 January

1924 **Ein Ballroman** (*Der Kavalier von zehn bis vier*) (Robert Stolz/w Österreicher, Fritz Rotter) Apollotheater 29 February

1926 **Der Mitternachtswalzer** (Stolz/w Österreicher) Wiener Bürgertheater 30 October

1928 **Ade, du liebes Elternhaus** (Oskar Jascha/w Reichert) Volksoper 5 January

1929 **Rosen aus Florida** (Fall arr Korngold/w Reichert) Theater an der Wien 22 February

1930 **Walzer aus Wien** (Strauss arr Julius Bittner [Korngold]/w Reichert, Marischka) Wiener Stadttheater 30 October

THE WILL ROGERS FOLLIES, a Life in Revue A musical in 2 acts by Betty Comden and Adolf Green. Music composed and arranged by Cy Coleman. Palace Theater, New York, 1 June 1991.

Close behind London's attempt to re-create the world of the glitzy old-time ''revue'' show in *Ziegfeld,*

Broadway's Coleman, Comden and Green came up with something in a very similar style. As the backbone for their show's production numbers and its songs, they used the life story of lariat-swinging humorist Will Rogers (Keith Carradine), who proved to be an altogether more charismatic centerpiece to an evening's entertainment than Mr Ziegfeld, his longtime employer, had been in the earlier show. Here the producer was limited to being an off-stage voice (Gregory Peck).

The score of the show sported a billing once common on programs, but long in disuse: ''composed and arranged by.'' It was the composed part, however, that came up with the evening's best liked number, Rogers's assertion that he ''Never Met a Man I Didn't Like.'' The raison d'être of the show, however, was its production numbers, a series of chorus stage pictures whipped up by the era's favorite ''impresario of glitz,'' Tommy Tune.

They sufficed to win the show a best musical citation for its season (along with another award for Coleman for his score), and a run of 963 performances before this ''deliberately mindless evening'' went on its way, leaving no trace.

Recording: original cast (Columbia)

WILLSON, Meredith [REINIGER, Robert Meredith] (b Mason City, Iowa, 18 May 1902; d Santa Monica, Calif, 15 June 1984). Author and composer of one of Broadway's most memorable postwar musicals.

A flutist in bands and orchestras, including the Sousa band (1921–23) and the New York Philharmonic (1924–29), a musical director for NBC and other radio networks, a songwriter (''May the Good Lord Bless You and Keep You,'' ''I See the Moon'') and composer of band, piano, orchestral and film music (*The Great Dictator* 1940, *The Little Foxes* 1941), Willson was pointed towards the musical theatre by the ever-on-the-ball Frank Loesser when already well into his musical career. His first stage musical, *The Music Man* (1957), was a huge and international success, and he followed up with two other successful pieces, the jolly tale of *The Unsinkable Molly Brown* and the little fantasy, *Here's Love,* a stage musical adaptation of *The Miracle on 34th Street,* both of which had good runs on Broadway (532 and 338 performances, respectively) without looking likely to equal the admittedly virtually unequalable appeal of his first show.

A 1969 piece, *1491,* produced by the San Francisco and Los Angeles Civic Light Opera with a cast headed by John Cullum, Jean Fenn and Chita Rivera, did not move east.

1957 **The Music Man** (Willson) Majestic Theater 19 December

1960 **The Unsinkable Molly Brown** (Richard Morris) Winter Garden Theater 3 November

1963 **Here's Love** (Willson) Shubert Theater 3 October

1969 **1491** (w Morris, Ira Barmak) Dorothy Chandler Pavilion, Los Angeles 2 September

Autobiographies: *And There I Stood with My Piccolo* (Doubleday, Garden City, 1948), *Eggs I Have Laid* (Holt, New York, 1955), *But He Doesn't Know the Territory* (Putnam, New York, 1959)

WILSON, Francis [B] (b Philadelphia, 7 February 1854; d New York, 7 October 1935). Broadway musical low comic of the 19th century.

Wilson first appeared in a song-and-dance act in vaudeville with John B Mackin and in stock in Philadelphia, and made his first appearance on the musical stage for the W C Mitchell Pleasure party in Willie Gill's extravaganzas *Our Goblins* (1880, Alfred Comstock Silvermine) and *A Gay Time at Whymple's* (1882, Mr Oscar Myld). He was subsequently engaged by John McCaull for the comic opera company at the new Casino Theater (1882), where he was given increasing comedy roles in *The Queen's Lace Handkerchief* (t/o Don Sancho), *The Princess of Trébizonde* (t/o Tremolini), *Prince Methusalem* (Sigismund), *The Merry War* (Balthazar Groot), *Falka* (Folbach), *Nanon* (Marquis de Marsillac), *Apajune* (Prutchesko), *Amorita* (Castrucci) and *The Gipsy Baron* (Zsupán) before being cast in the British comic opera *Erminie* (1885) in the role of Cadeau, invented by Harry Paulton for himself and here re-created in an Americanized version under the direction of the author/original star.

The record-breaking success of *Erminie* lifted Wilson into the star class and also into the bigheaded class. In 1889 he was sacked from the role of Faragas in *Nadgy* after his overbearing ways became too much for manager Rudolph Aronson. He promptly mounted ''the Francis Wilson Comic Opera Company'' and attempted to woo away as many of Aronson's company as he could to join him in a heavily botched version of the French opérette *La Jolie Persane* (1889, *The Oolah,* Hoolah Goolah). *The Oolah* did well, and Wilson followed up with further botchings of *L'Étoile* (*The Merry Monarch,* King Anso IV) and *Le Grand Casimir* (*The Lion Tamer,* Casimir), a version of Sullivan's *The Chieftain* (Grigg), an American comic opera *The Little Corporal* (Petipas), in which he impersonated Napoléon, and remade and remusicked versions of France's *Babolin* as *The Devil's Deputy* (Mélissen) and *Le Roi de carreau* as *Half a King* (Tirechappe). He also mounted frequent revivals of *Erminie.* ''For a man that can't sing,'' commented a critic in Milwaukee, ''Wilson is one of the best entertainers in comic opera ever seen here.''

Wilson appeared in the title role of Victor Herbert's unsuccessful *Cyrano de Bergerac* (1899), took the chief comic roles of *The Monks of Malabar* (1900, Boolboom) and George Lederer's production of *The Strollers* (1901,

Plate 424. **Francis Wilson** *in his most famous role: Cadeau in* Erminie.

August Lump), a version of the Austrian hit *Die Landstreicher,* and played Teddy Payne's role of little Sammy Gigg in the Broadway version of the London musical *The Toreador* (1902), in the most successful of his ventures since *Erminie.* He signed off his career as a musical star with a reprise of the inevitable *Erminie* in 1903, but returned in 1921 to play the role that had made his name one last time.

He subsequently authored a book of memoirs that showed either a tendency to distort the truth for the sake of a good story or a good plug, or a distinctly iffy memory.

Wilson was married to comic opera vocalist Myra Barrie (d New York, 18 November 1915).

Memoir: *Francis Wilson's Life of Himself* (Houghton Mifflin, Boston, 1924)

WILSON, Sandy [WILSON, Alexander Galbraith] (b Sale, 19 May 1924). Versatile British author/songwriter who was able to write both a major international hit and a connoisseur's delight before wit and charm went out of fashion.

Wilson made his first impact as a writer and composer in the early 1950s, in the heyday of the small club-theatres into which British revue and musical-theatre writers had retreated under the postwar barrage of big Broadway musicals that were dominating the major West End venues of the period. A youthful venture into lyric writing for a latter-day Jack Waller production aside, his early experiences came principally in the revues staged at the Watergate Theatre (*See You Later, See You Again*) but it was his first musical comedy, *The Boy Friend* (''A Room in Bloomsbury,'' ''It's Never Too Late to Fall in Love,'' ''I Could Be Happy With You,'' etc), produced at the tiny Players' Theatre in 1953, that secured his fame. An affectionate pastiche (without ever being a burlesque) of the *No, No, Nanette* brand of 1920s musical, *The Boy Friend,* for which Wilson wrote book, lyrics and music, was eventually transferred to the West End Wyndham's Theatre, where it became one of the longest-running shows of London theatre history, before going on to a vast and worldwide succession of productions that have continued to the present day at a rate that barely any genuine 1920s musical has achieved.

Before *The Boy Friend* reached the big time, Wilson had written and composed another small-scale piece for the Watergate. Like its predecessor, *The Buccaneer,* a little tale of skulduggery and youth and virtue triumphant set in the world of kiddie comics, moved from its little home into the West End, but it was a another piece, the highly skillful 1958 musical play *Valmouth,* based on the esoteric works of Ronald Firbank, that confirmed its author-composer at the top of his profession. *Valmouth* won as much success with the cognoscenti as *The Boy Friend* had with the public, and although its West End and off-Broadway runs were comparatively brief, it remained and remains a connoisseur's delight such as few exist in the musical theatre.

An attractive 1930s musequel to *The Boy Friend, Divorce Me, Darling* (1964) again progressed from the Players' Theatre to the West End, but Wilson's other works, including two further musicals, a seasonal version of *Aladdin,* and songs for the play *Call It Love,* were confined to the small theatres that best suited his intimate style.

The unaffected simplicity of the *Boy Friend* text and lyrics and the brittle brilliance of those for *Valmouth* indicate Wilson's range as a writer, and the accompanying tuneful, light musical scores throw those words into prominence in the same way that was achieved by and for the best French and American writers of the 1920s.

Wilson has also authored an autobiography (up to and including *The Boy Friend*), and a book on Ivor Novello (London 1975).

1950 **Caprice** (Geoffrey Wright/Michael Pertwee) Alhambra Theatre, Glasgow 24 October

1953 **The Boy Friend** (Wilson) Players' Theatre 14 April

1953 **The Buccaneer** (Wilson) New Watergate Theatre 8 September

1958 **Valmouth** (Wilson) Lyric Theatre, Hammersmith 2 October

1964 **Divorce Me, Darling** (Wilson) Players' Theatre 15 December

1971 **His Monkey Wife** (Wilson) Hampstead Theatre Club 20 December

1978 **The Clapham Wonder** (Wilson) Marlowe Theatre, Canterbury 26 April

1979 **Aladdin** (Wilson) Lyric Theatre, Hammersmith 27 December

Autobiography: *I Could Be Happy* (Stein & Day, New York, 1975)

WIMAN, Dwight Deere [WIMAN, Dwight Erastus] (b Moline, Ill, 8 August 1895; d Hudson, NY, 20 January 1951)

Independently wealthy Wiman followed his dramatic studies at Yale by venturing first into films and then, as a producer, into the theatre. His early productions (w William A Brady jr) were all straight, and often serious, plays until, in 1929, the pair ventured into the area of revue with their production of *The Little Show.* Amongst a regular schedule of play productions in the 1930s, Wiman made his first ventures into the musical theatre. The very first, the Cole Porter/Fred Astaire *Gay Divorce,* was a distinctly successful one, and he followed it up with a version of *Die Fledermaus* entitled *Champagne, Sec* before, in 1936, he began an association with the works of songwriters Rodgers and Hart. During that association he produced five of their shows in six years, almost always with some considerable success: *On Your Toes, Babes in Arms, I Married an Angel, Higher and Higher* and, the longest-running of the group, *By Jupiter* (w Rodgers, Richard Kollmar).

Wiman did less well when he mounted a piece called *Great Lady* (1938) with a score by neophyte composer Frederick Loewe, little better with the indecisive *Stars in Your Eyes* (1939) with Ethel Merman and Jimmy Durante, and disastrously with the Jay Gorney piece *They Can't Get You Down* (w Jack Kirkland), mounted futurelessly in Hollywood in 1941, and if his adventurous 1947 Broadway production of the Elmer Rice/Kurt Weill "Broadway opera" *Street Scene* won more kudos than cash, his final musical offering, the revue *Dance Me a Song,* mounted in the year before his death, was a simple 35-performance failure.

WIMPERIS, Arthur [Harold] (b London, 3 December 1874; d Maidenhead, 14 October 1953). Lyricist and librettist for a quarter of a century of London shows.

Wimperis began his working life as a black-and-white artist, and it was not until after the Boer War, in which he served with Paget's Horse (1899–1902), that he began a writing career. He made his theatrical mark at first as a lyricist, contributing to Robert Courtneidge's production of *The Dairymaids* and to the Seymour Hicks and Ellaline Terriss musical *The Gay Gordons,* before he found major success with his songwords for a second Courtneidge show, *The Arcadians* ("The Pipes of Pan," "'ve Got a Motter," "Arcady Is Always Young," "Half Past Two," etc). He next supplied some replacement lyrics to a rewrite of the in-trouble *The Mountaineers* at the Savoy Theatre (1909) but, with the coming of the Viennese musical, he found a new area of activity. He adapted a number of such pieces to the English stage, winning a major success with *The Girl in the Taxi* (*Die keusche Susanne*) and a second good run with the Hungarian musical *Princess Charming* (*Alexandra*). He also adapted Julius Wilhelm and Paul Frank's German *Ludwig XIV* as the libretto for the lavish American musical *Louie the 14th.*

Several attempts at an original musical libretto, with the clever, Faustian *My Lady Frayle* (130 performances), the pretty *Pamela* (172 performances) and a vehicle for Binnie Hale as a tea-shop *Nippy* (137 performances), did well enough without establishing themselves as genuine hits.

Wimperis provided musical burlesques and lyrics for *The Follies* pierrot show during its period in London, scored two of his most memorable song hits with "Gilbert the Filbert" and "I'll Make a Man of You" in *The Passing Show* (1914) and contributed scenarios, scenes and songwords to a large number of other revues including *By Jingo If We Do . . . , Bric à Brac,* Irving Berlin's *Follow the Crowd, Vanity Fair,* the French *As You Were, Buzz Buzz, Just Fancy, London, Paris and New York, The Curate's Egg* and *Still Dancing.* He also put out a number of plays, most of which were adaptations from French or German originals.

In 1932 Wimperis both made his last contribution to the musical stage with a disastrous version of a piece by *Girl in the Taxi* composer Jean Gilbert (*Lovely Lady,* 3 performances) and had his first great success in the film world with the screenplay for *The Private Life of Henry VIII.* Thereafter, filmland became his chief occupation, and his subsequent screen credits included *Sanders of the River* (1935), *The Four Feathers* (1939), and the wartime *Mrs Miniver* (1942, Academy Award) and *Random Harvest* (1943).

1904 **The Duchess of Sillie-Crankie** (George Byng/w Herbert Fordwych /Fordwych) Terry's Theatre April

1906 **The Dairymaids** (Paul Rubens, Frank E Tours/w Rubens/Alexander Thompson, Robert Courtneidge) Apollo Theatre 14 April

1907 **The Constable and the Pictures** (Marjorie Slaughter/w Godfrey Turner) sketch Devonshire Park Theatre, Eastbourne; Tivoli

1907 **The Gay Gordons** (Guy Jones/w others/Seymour Hicks) Aldwych Theatre 11 September

1909 **The Arcadians** (Lionel Monckton, Howard Talbot/Mark Ambient, Alexander M Thompson) Shaftesbury Theatre 28 April

1910 **The Balkan Princess** (Rubens/w Rubens/Frederick Lonsdale, Frank Curzon) Prince of Wales Theatre 19 February

1910 **Our Little Cinderella** (Herman Löhr/Leo Trevor) Playhouse 20 December

1911 **The Mousme** (Talbot, Monckton/w Percy Greenbank/Thompson, Courtneidge) Shaftesbury 9 September

1912 **The Sunshine Girl** (Rubens/w Rubens/Rubens, Cecil Raleigh) Gaiety 24 February

1912 **The Boss of the Show** (Rubens) sketch

1912 **The Girl in the Taxi** (*Die keusche Susanne*) English version w Frederick Fenn (Lyric Theatre)

1913 **Love and Laughter** (Oscar Straus/w Fenn) Lyric Theatre 3 September

1913 **The Laughing Husband** aka *The Girl Who Didn't* (*Der lachende Ehemann*) English version (New Theatre)

1914 **Mam'selle Tralala** aka *Oh! Be Careful* (*Fräulein Tralala*) English version w Hartley Carrick (Lyric Theatre)

1914 **The Slush Girl** (Herman Finck) 1 act Palace Theatre 14 September

1915 **Vivien** (later *My Lady Frayle*) (Talbot, Finck/w Max Pemberton) Prince of Wales Theatre, Birmingham 27 December; Shaftesbury Theatre as *My Lady Frayle* 1 March 1916

1917 **Pamela** (Frederic Norton) Palace Theatre 10 December

1920 **The Shop Girl** revised version (Gaiety Theatre)

1925 **Louie the 14th** (Sigmund Romberg) Cosmopolitan Theater, New York 2 March

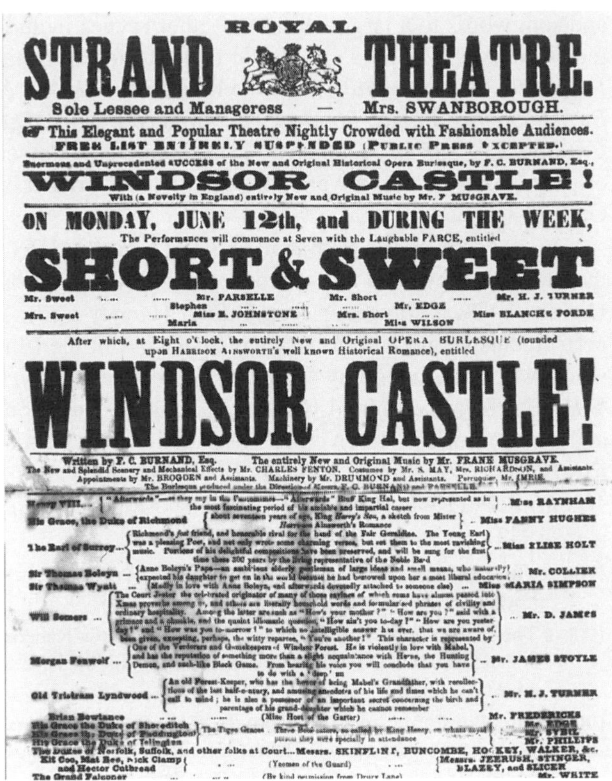

Plate 425. **Windsor Castle.** *"The first English opéra-bouffe"—the playbill and the star, Ada Swanborough.*

1926 **Princess Charming** (*Alexandra*) English version w Lauri Wylie (Palace Theatre)

1928 **Song of the Sea** (*Lady Hamilton*) English version w Wylie (His Majesty's Theatre)

1930 **Nippy** (Billy Mayerl/w Frank Eyton/w Austin Melford) Prince Edward Theatre 30 October

1932 **Lovely Lady** (?*Die grosse Sünderin*) English version Phoenix Theatre 25 February

WINDSOR CASTLE Operatic burlesque in 5 scenes by F C Burnand based on W Harrison Ainsworth's historical romance of the same title. Music by Frank Musgrave. Royal Strand Theatre, London, 5 June 1865.

Claimed by its author, with seemingly every justification, as "the first English opéra-bouffe," *Windsor Castle* differed from its burlesque predecessors, and followed the way led by the Offenbachs and Hervés across the Channel, in one vital area. Whereas previous British burlesques had been decorated with musical scores made up from the melodies of popular songs and borrowed arias, the Swanborough family's 1865 production had a purpose-composed original score as its musical part. The capers evolved by Burnand around King Henry VIII (Polly Raynham), Anne Boleyn (Thomas Thorne), the Dukes of Richmond (Fanny Hughes) and Surrey (Elise Holt), jester Will Somers (David James), evil Morgan Fenwolf (J D Stoyle), poet Thomas Wyatt (Maria Simpson) and the heroine of the piece, Miss Mabel Lyndwood (Ada Swanborough), were of an almost Hervé-style extravagance, and the tunes written by the theatre's musical director, Musgrave, simple and catchy. Anne Boleyn's baritone arietta "La Chevalier et sa belle," a farrago of nonsense French, proved a distinct success, as did a jolly "Tiddley Wink" piece for Herne the Hunter and the jester. The critics were a little taken aback at the exercise, and several pondered as to whether original music was a thing to be desired in a musical comedy entertainment, but *Windsor Castle* played a very respectable 43 performances before being sent to the provinces.

Musgrave's music and the occasion were considered of sufficient interest for the music publishers Metzler & Co to print up a vocal score, so that both the text and the music of the piece, which can make a fair claim to be regarded as the earliest original English-language musical of the modern era, have survived.

Ainsworth's piece was taken as the basis for several other burlesques over the years, including one produced at the Elephant and Castle Theatre in 1882 under the title of *The King, the Ring and the Giddy Young Thing, or Herne the Hunter, Anne Boleyn and the Fair Maid of the River Dee* (George Reeves 8 April).

Plate 426. **Charles Winninger** *as Cap'n Andy entertains the folk on his* Show Boat.

WINNINGER, Charles J [WINNINGER, Karl] (b Athens [Wausau], Wis, 26 May 1884; d Palm Springs, Calif, 19 January 1969). Favorite character man of the musical stage and film who got two of the best roles 1920s Broadway had to give.

Winninger began his career at the age of five, playing in vaudeville as one of the "Five Winninger Brothers." He later worked as a trapeze artist in a circus and on a showboat, before making his first appearance on the legitimate stage in 1908 in a village-storming version of the old warhorse *My Sweetheart.* In the first years of a career that moved amongst all areas of stage and screen performing, he took part in several musicals, including *The Yankee Girl* (1910, Rudolf Schnitzel), *The Wall Street Girl* (1912, John Chester and co-director w Gus Sohlke) and *When Claudia Smiles* (1914, dir Charles D Farnham), each opposite his wife, Blanche Ring. He also appeared, in his thirties, in a number of Broadway revues (*Cohan Revue of 1916,* etc), but his biggest musical-comedy successes came as a character actor, beginning with his performance in Chicago, again alongside Miss Ring, and on Broadway as the generous bible-publisher Jimmy Smith, in the original production of *No, No, Nanette* ("I Want to Be Happy").

Winninger followed this hit with major roles in *Oh, Please!* (1925, Nicodemus Bliss) and *Yes, Yes, Yvette* (1927, S S Ralston) before creating the other most memorable role of his musical theatre career as Cap'n Andy Hawkes, father to the heroine and the proprietor of Oscar Hammerstein's *Show Boat* (1927). He reappeared as Cap'n Andy in the show's 1932 revival and again in the 1936 film version, and it was on film that he subsequently made most of his musical appearances—*Babes in Arms* (1939, Joe Moran), *Little Nellie Kelly* (1940, Michael Noonan), *Ziegfeld Girl* (1941), *State Fair* (1945, Abel Frake), *Give My Regards to Broadway* (1948), etc. He returned to Broadway only to appear as Don Emilio in *Revenge with Music* in 1934 and as Dr Walter Lessing in the 1951 revival of *Music in the Air.*

WINTERBERG, Robert (b Vienna, 27 February 1884; d Berlin, 23 June 1930). Successful tunesmith of the central European theatre in the 1910s and 1920s.

Vienna-born Winterberg had his first pieces played on the musical stages of his home town whilst he was in his mid-twenties and scored a tidy early success with the Operette *Ihr Adjutant,* produced by Karczag and Wallner at the Theater an der Wien with an impressive cast headed by Fritz Werner, Grete Holm, Luise Kartousch and

Ernst Tautenhayn. The piece's run was cut short after six weeks when the great Girardi and the Raimundtheater company moved in to the theatre for a season, and the Theater an der Wien company departed their home stage taking *Ihr Adjutant* and the rest of their repertoire with them for a month at the Raimundtheater. The piece went on to play in Germany and, in Frigyes Hervay's Hungarian version (*Az adjutáns*), at Nagyvárad (22 October 1911) and Budapest's Fővárosi Nyári Színház (23 May 1914).

Winterberg had a second sizeable success when Berlin's Theater des Westens produced his *Die Dame in Rot* later the same year (78 performances). As that piece went on to productions around Germany and in Hungary and America, the composer left Vienna to settle in Berlin. An Operette, *Hoheit der Franz,* produced at Magdeburg did well, and *Die schöne Schwedin* was mounted for 50 nights at the Theater an der Wien and subsequently played in America, Hungary, Germany and, of course, Sweden, but it was a series of musical comedies, composed to texts by Jean Kren and his collaborators, that gave Winterberg his most substantial successes in Germany. *Graf Habenichts* did well enough to be snapped up (but not produced) by Broadway's Henry Savage, *Die Dame vom Zirkus* played for eight months and more than 200 performances at the Thalia-Theater and was revived within a year, and *Die Herren von und zu* also clocked up some 200 Berlin performances in a run of over seven months.

Although he was a melodist by nature, a composer who wrote down a single line and passed it on to an arranger to fill out and orchestrate, Winterberg attempted a rather more substantial piece in the 1921 *Der Günstling der Zarin.* He was gratified by a good reception, but he did not linger in such an area and returned to musical comedy with the tale of *Anneliese von Dessau,* seen after its Berlin run at New York's Yorkville Theater in 1926, with a musical version of Feydeau's *Un fil à la patte* entitled *Der letzte Kuss,* and with a musicalization of the much-adapted American novel *His Official Wife, Die offizielle Frau.*

At one stage, Winterberg doubled his writing with producing, and went into management variously at Berlin's Centraltheater (1926) and at the Residenztheater, but neither venture proved fruitful. In his mid-forties his health gave way, and he retired to his country estate, where he died, aged 46, from pulmonary tuberculosis.

1909 **Die Frau des Rajah** (Paul Wertheimer) Deutsches Volkstheater, Vienna 18 May

1910 **Fasching in Paris** (II Vigny, Louis Windhopp) 1 act Venedig in Wien, Vienna 13 May

1911 **Ihr Adjutant** (Franz von Schönthan, Rudolf Österreicher) Theater an der Wien, Vienna 3 March

1911 **Madame Serafin** (Georg Okonkowski, Bruno Granichstaedten) Neues Operettentheater, Hamburg 1 September

1911 **Die Dame in Rot** (Julius Brammer, Alfred Grünwald) Theater des Westens 16 September

1912 **Die Frauen von Monte-Carlo** (Alfred Deutsch-German) 1 act Colosseum 11 March

1913 **Hoheit der Franz** (Artur Landesberger, Willy Wolff) Wilhelm-Theater, Magdeburg 27 September

1914 **Unsere Feldgrauen** (Alfred Müller-Forster, Josef Bendiner) Friedrich-Wilhelmstädtisches Theater 13 October

1915 **Die schöne Schwedin** (Brammer, Grünwald) Theater an der Wien, Vienna 30 January

1916 **Die Blume der Maintenon** (Reinhard Bruck) Königliches Schauspielhaus 19 August

1917 **Der sanfte Hannibal** (Müller-Forster, Arthur Lokesch) Bellevue-Theater, Stettin 10 August

1918 **Graf Habenichts** (Jean Kren, Bernhard Buchbinder) Wallner-Theater, 4 September

1919 **Circe und die Schweine** (Max Brod) Neues Operettenhaus 4 January

1919 **Der dumme Franzl** (Bruck) Tivoli-Theater, Bremen 16 March; Thalia-Theater 17 October 1920

1919 **Die Dame vom Zirkus** (Kren, Buchbinder) Neues Operetten-Theater 31 May

1921 **Der Günstling der Zarin** (Hermann Feiner, Richard Kessler) Operettenhaus, Hamburg 3 March

1921 **Der blonde Engel** (Kessler, Arthur Rebner) Komödienhaus 18 June

1922 **Die Herr(e)n von und zu . . .** (Kren, Richard Bars) Thalia-Theater 3 January

1924 **Anneliese von Dessau** (Kessler) Berliner Theater 23 December

1925 **Der letzte Kuss** Komödienhaus

1925 **Die offizielle Frau** (Kessler, Max Jungk) Theater am Nollendorfplatz 23 December

1926 **Der alte Dessauer** (Kessler) Thalia-Theater 13 February

1926 **Der Trompeter vom Rhein** (Viktor Nessler arr/August Neidhart, Cornelius Bronsgeest) Centralhalle 23 December

1929 **Schnirps und Knirps** (Grete Filling) Residenztheater 30 March

Other titles attributed: *Ehe auf Befehl, Der Schauspieler des Kaisers, Ausser Betrieb*

DIE WINZERBRAUT Operette in 3 acts by Leo Stein and Julius Wilhelm. Music by Oskar Nedbal. Theater an der Wien, Vienna, 11 February 1916.

Oskar Nedbal followed up his well-spaced successes with *Die keusche Barbara* and the splendid *Polenblut* with a third colorful and popular Operette in *Die Winzerbraut.*

The first act of Stein and Wilhelm's tale was set at a gathering in the castle of Baron Bogdan Lukovac (Robert Nästlberger) in Zagreb. The actress Julia Lella (Betty Fischer), who has arrived straight from the first night of her new play, *Der Schirokko,* relates to her longtime lover

Count Milan Mikolic (Karl Pfann) and the rest of the company the story of the show. Once upon a time there was an actress who had never married her longtime lover. Then, one day, when the sirocco blew, he gave a young woman shelter in the actress's car. And thus she lost him. Fact quickly starts to follow fiction when the nubile Viennese Lisa Müller (Margit Suchy) appears amongst them under very similar circumstances. The second act shifts to a vine-festival at Mikolic's estates (where Julia is the titular ''vine-harvest queen'') and the third to Vienna, as the various romantic pairings—in which Micolic's son Nikola (Gustav Werner), the light-comical Franjo Svecak (Ernst Tautenhayn) and prima ballerina Mizzi Müller (Mizzi Schürz) are also involved—work themselves out.

The show's music was in the same colorful strain as the composer's earlier pieces, with the waltz duet for Milan and Lisa, ''Einmal noch erklingt es,'' proving the gem of the evening. The pair shared a second piece, ''Du kleine Fee vom Donaustrand,'' whilst Julia teamed three times with Franjo (''Kind, Ich bin so musikalisch,'' ''Romeo und Julie,'' ''Liebe, kleiner Wurstelmann'') in a score where double-handed dance numbers dominated.

Produced at the Theater an der Wien by Wilhelm Karczag, *Die Winzerbraut* ran through 108 consecutive performances before giving way to the spring Gastspiele of the Berlin Lessing-Theater's production of *Die Troierinnen* of Euripides and the hit *Die Dreimäderlhaus* from the Raimundtheater. When the autumn season began, however, *Die Winzerbraut* was put back on the program and ran through to its 137th performance (24 September).

In Germany, the show proved the most popular of Nedbal's works after the all-conquering *Polenblut,* and it was played throughout central Europe in the years following its Viennese premiere without following its predecessor further afield.

Germany: 1918

Recording: selection in Czech (Supraphon)

WISDOM, Norman [Joseph] (Sir) (b London, 4 February 1915).

The favorite British little-fellow comic of his time and the star of many popular films, Wisdom appeared on the stage top-billed in three musicals. He starred in the role of Charley, created on Broadway by Ray Bolger, in London's 1958 edition of the *Charley's Aunt* musical *Where's Charley?,* a role made over from the play in a fashion that allowed him both the romance and the female impersonation, and in 1966 he went to Broadway to play the leading role of Willie Mossop in another musicalized classic, the *Hobson's Choice* musical *Walking Happy,* mounted by *Where's Charley?* producers Feuer and Martin.

When *The Roar of the Greasepaint . . . the Smell of the Crowd* (1964) was first produced in the British provinces, pre-London, Wisdom created the central role of Cocky and the songs ''Nothing Can Stop Me Now,'' ''The Joker'' and ''What Kind of Fool Am I?'' The piece was, however, abandoned on the road, and when it did reopen, on Broadway, co-author Anthony Newley himself took the starring role. Although he appeared thereafter in pantomime and featured as Androcles in the 1967 TV musical of *Androcles and the Lion,* Wisdom did not return to the musical stage except to play the lead role in a tryout of a musical about the advertising business, *Jingle-Jangle,* which was not taken up for professional staging.

Wisdom wrote a number of songs, amongst which the successful ''Don't Laugh at Me'' (w June Tremayne) featured in the film *Trouble in Store* (1952).

Autobiography: w Bale, B: *'Cos I'm a Fool* (Breedon, Derby, 1996)

WISH YOU WERE HERE Musical by Arthur Kober and Joshua Logan based on Kober's *Having Wonderful Time.* Music and lyrics by Harold Rome. Imperial Theater, New York, 25 June 1952.

A musical play set in a holiday camp, *Wish You Were Here* won itself celebrity by including a real swimming pool, dug into the stage, as part of its setting. Based on the successful 1937 play *Having Wonderful Time* (Lyceum Theater 20 February, 372 performances), which had in between times been made into a Hollywood film, the musical followed the love life of stenographer Teddy Stern (Patricia Marand) through a fortnight's holiday at Camp Karefree. She throws over Herman (Harry Clarke) for Chick (Jack Cassidy), losing him only temporarily when he thinks she's been up to no good with the medallion man Pinky (Paul Valentine). Sheila Bond played soubrette Fay Fromkin, and Sidney Armus was the comical camp director who rejoiced in the name of ''Itchy.''

The little tale was illustrated by some suitably ''summer holiday'' songs, and it was one of these, the gently lilting title song, that (along with the swimming pool) helped assure the show's success. It needed assuring, for Leland Hayward and Joshua Logan's much ballyhooed production of *Wish You Were Here,* which was mounted directly on Broadway because of the problems of digging up out-of-town stages for the traditional tryout, had had a difficult birth and the opening had been several times postponed as director Logan tried to get the piece into shape. However, the delays allowed Eddie Fisher's happily crooned version of ''Wish You Were Here'' to become popular and, in spite of a poor critical reception, the show galloped on to a run of 598 Broadway performances and a long life in regional theatres.

Logan continued to work on the show after it had opened and, in consequence, a London production mounted by Jack Hylton the following year included several amendments and one song not used at New York's opening. It was also largely de-Judaized, with popular comedian Dickie Henderson playing an anglicized Itchy called "Dickie" and Bruce Trent (Chick), Elizabeth Larner (Teddy, still called Stern) and Shani Wallis (Fay) performing sometimes reorientated lyrics. London's version played 282 performances.

UK: Casino Theatre 10 October 1953

Recordings: original cast (RCA Victor), London cast (Philips/DRG)

WITTMANN, Hugo (b Ulm, 16 October 1839; d Vienna, 6 February 1923).

Journalist, author and stage writer, Wittmann enjoyed two decades of prominence as an operettic librettist, providing seven libretti to Carl Millöcker and several to each of Carl Weinberger and Adolf Müller jr during the 1880s and 1890s.

His first work in the musical theatre was in the field of adaptation and, although his name is now to be found attached, in this field, only to the German-language version of Lecocq's *Le Petit Duc,* it is probable that he provided others amongst the often uncredited adaptations of foreign shows of the 1870s to the Viennese stage. He found success with his first original libretto, Millöcker's *Der Feldprediger,* which went on to an appreciable international life after its initial run at the Theater an der Wien, and followed it up with two further successes at the same house: Adolf Müller's *Der Hofnarr* and Millöcker's *Die sieben Schwaben,* both written with the partner, Julius Bauer, with whom he would collaborate through much of the rest of his career.

The quaint, American tale of *Der arme Jonathan* won the pair their biggest international hit, and two further Millöcker Operetten, *Das Sonntagskind* (74 performances) and *Der Probekuss* (55 performances), a single collaboration with Johann Strauss on *Fürstin Ninetta* (76 performances) and the most successful of the pair's works with Weinberger, *Die Karlsschülerin* (59 performances) and *Adam und Eva* (52 performances), kept Wittmann firmly before the Vienna public through the 1890s. His last pieces for Millöcker, *Nordlicht* (38 performances) and the revised *Der Damenschneider* (11 performances), were not successful, and thereafter he supplied only one further text to the Vienna stage, *Der Kongress tanzt,* mounted by Emil Guttmann at the Wiener Stadttheater in 1918.

Early in his theatre career, Wittmann also wrote libretti for the operas *Heini der Steier* (C Bachrich, 1884) and *Der Papagei* (Anton Rubenstein, 1884), and in 1895 he adapted the text of Sullivan's *Ivanhoe* to the German stage (Königliches Opernhaus, Berlin 26 November 1895).

1878 **Der kleine Herzog** (*Le Petit Duc*) German version (Carltheater)

1884 **Der Feldprediger** (Carl Millöcker/w Alois Wohlmuth) Theater an der Wien 31 October

1886 **Der Botschafter** (Eduard Kremser/w Wohlmuth) Theater an der Wien 25 February

1886 **Der Hofnarr** (Adolf Müller jr/w Julius Bauer) Theater an der Wien 20 November

1887 **Die sieben Schwaben** (Millöcker/w Bauer) Theater an der Wien 29 October

1888 **Pagenstreiche** (Carl Weinberger) Theater an der Wien 28 April

1888 **Der Liebeshof** (A Müller jr/w Oskar Blumenthal) Theater an der Wien 11 November

1890 **Der arme Jonathan** (Millöcker/w Bauer) Theater an der Wien 4 January

1891 **Die Uhlanen** (Weinberger) Carltheater 5 December

1892 **Das Sonntagskind** (Millöcker/w Bauer) Theater an der Wien 16 January

1893 **Fürstin Ninetta** (Johann Strauss/w Bauer) Theater an der Wien 10 January

1894 **Der Probekuss** (Millöcker/w Bauer) Theater an der Wien 22 December

1895 **Die Karlsschülerin** (Weinberger) Theater an der Wien 21 March

1895 **Die Prima Ballerina** (later *Auch so eine!*) (Weinberger) Carltheater 23 November

1896 **General Gogo** (A Müller jr/w Gustav Davis) Theater an der Wien 1 February

1896 **Nordlicht** (*Der rote Graf*) (Millöcker) Theater an der Wien 22 December

1899 **Adam und Eva** (*Die Seelenwanderung*) (Weinberger/w Bauer) Carltheater 5 January

1901 **Der Damenschneider** (Millöcker/w Louis Hermann) Carltheater 14 September

1918 **Der Kongress tanzt** (Karl Lafite/w Bauer) Wiener Stadttheater 9 November

THE WIZ Musical in 2 acts by William F Brown based on *The Wonderful Wizard of Oz* by L Frank Baum. Music and lyrics by Charlie Smalls. Majestic Theater, New York, 5 January 1975.

An immensely energetic modern version of the long-loved *Wizard of Oz* tale, equipped with a driving, jazzy-to-gospelly 1970s score, *The Wiz* followed little Dorothy (Stephanie Mills) on the well-known route from Kansas to the land of Oz and its phony wizard (André de Shields). On the way she meets a dancing Scarecrow (Hinton Battle), a gruff Tin Man (Tiger Haynes) and the scaredy-cat Lion (Ted Ross), the Good Witch Glinda

(Dee Dee Bridgewater) and the howlingly horrid Evillene (Mabel King). Charlie Smalls's songs ranged from the move-it-along ''Ease on Down the Road,'' which set the friends out on what used to be the yellow brick road to the wizard's palace, to the heroine's rangy, soulful thoughts of ''Home,'' a broken-glass-edged ''Don't Nobody Bring Me No Bad News'' for the nasty witch and a warmly hopeful piece in which the lion tries to convince himself and everyone else that ''I'm a Mean Ol' Lion.''

Mounted with an all-black cast, staged with great pace and some eye-catching dance pieces (the tornado was a spankingly threatening dance piece, and the Scarecrow's introduction a thoroughly modern equivalent of the famous Ray Bolger film routine), the show caught on both with the normal Broadway audience and also with a new and inexperienced black audience unused to the Broadway theatre and inclined to arrive at any stage during the evening and to wander in, out and around the theatre during the performance in a manner reminiscent of the Gaiety and Alhambra gentleman patrons of Victorian times. As in those days, the entertainment in the stalls only gave atmosphere to the entertainment on the stage.

The Wiz was a first-rate success. It overcame unanimously negative notices with positive word of mouth and a touch of telly-push, took the year's Tony Award as Best Musical with additional citations for composer Smalls, director Geoffrey Holder and choreographer George Faison, and went on to play 1,672 performances at the Majestic and, later, the Broadway Theaters. The piece, however, did not continue as prosperously as it had begun. A 1976 Australian production, cast on a colorblind basis, fared poorly, running a bare two months in Melbourne and just five weeks in Sydney (Her Majesty's Theatre 1 May 1976), whilst in England, in spite of several attempts, the show was not picked up for an open-ended run. The first British production was seen at Sheffield's Crucible Theatre, which, having succeeded in winning a London transfer with its mounting of *Chicago,* was looking for a second lucrative Broadway piece. Celena Duncan played Dorothy through a regular repertory theatre season, but the production did not go south. It was Miss Duncan, however, who was again Dorothy when the suburban Lyric Theatre in Hammersmith mounted the piece four years later for a Christmas season, which, once again, had no tomorrow. There was also no success for an attempt to mount a Broadway revival in 1984. The production (Lunt-Fontanne Theater 24 May) folded in 13 performances.

A film version, which also featured an all-black cast, including a not-very-juvenile Diana Ross as Dorothy, Michael Jackson, Lena Horne and Richard Pryor, alongside the original cast's Ross and Miss King, supplemented the main parts of the score with some additional pieces by Quincy Jones. It wasn't very successful either, and in the end the swingeing success of the original production was left as the show's only successful outing.

Australia: Her Majesty's Theatre, Melbourne 7 February 1976; UK: Crucible Theatre, Sheffield 3 September 1980, Lyric Theatre, Hammersmith 8 December 1984

Film: Universal 1978

Recordings: original cast (Atlantic), film soundtrack (MCA)

THE WIZARD OF OZ Musical extravaganza in 3 acts by L Frank Baum based on his book *The Wonderful Wizard of Oz.* Music by Paul Tietjens and A Baldwin Sloane. Grand Theater, Chicago, 16 June 1902; Majestic Theater, New York, 21 January 1903.

A fantasy spectacular mounted by producer Fred Hamlin and played as the opening piece at New York's Majestic Theater, *The Wizard of Oz* was adapted to the stage by the original author of the tale, Lyman Baum, as a picturesque extravaganza for the fabled children of all ages. Anna Laughlin played Dorothy Gale, caught up almost peripherally in the story of the deposed King Pastoria (Neil McNeil/Gilbert Clayton) and his girlfriend, Trixie Tryfle (Grace Kimball), who are struggling to regain the throne of Oz from a usurping so-called Wizard (John Slavin/Bobby Gaylor) from the outside world. The King and Trixie are blown into Oz on the same tornado that brings Dorothy and her cow Imogene (Edwin J Stone) there, and Dorothy plods off through the scenery to seek the Wizard who can get her back home. The helpers she picks up en route include a nice witch (Aileen May), King Pastoria's ex-poet laureate, Sir Dashemoff Daily (Bessie Wynn), a scarecrow without a brain (Fred Stone), a cowardly lion (Arthur Hill) and a tin woodsman called Nick Chopper without a heart (Dave Montgomery). In the end, it is the useful witch who forces the issue and gets the now restored King to give Dorothy her ticket home.

The Wizard of Oz was not, as a piece, much thought of. The libretto was a rather rudimentary affair (''the book of the piece is very weak . . . the lines consist almost entirely of old-fashioned puns''), with elements of the old English and French grand opéra-bouffe féerie of 30 years earlier cobbled together into what was little more than an excuse for some songs and scenery, and the songs that illustrated it were unremarkable (''the music is tuneful and there is plenty of it''). Of the pieces by the nominal composers, Sloane's contribution included ''Niccolo's Piccolo,'' ''In Michigan'' (ly: Glen MacDonough) and a medley of all nations (ly: H B Smith), and Tietjens's share was topped by a ballad ''When You Love,'' but the best bits came from the added numbers: ''Hurrah for Baffin Bay'' (written by Vincent Bryan and Theodore Morse of ''Hail, Hail, the Gang's All Here'' fame), Cobb and

Edwards's ''I Love Only One Girl in the Wide, Wide World'' and a later addition, when Lotta Faust succeeded to the leading role of Trixie, O'Dea and Hutchinson's ''Sammy.''

However, if neither the text nor the songs evoked much interest, there were other elements that were enough to ensure *The Wizard of Oz*'s success. The *Dramatic Mirror* reported, ''[T]o say the new piece made a hit is putting it mildly . . . as a production *The Wizard of Oz* has never been excelled in this city.'' Director Julian Mitchell and designer John Young had done their share of the work superbly, and the piece's seven scenes—beginning with the Kansas town and its cyclone, portrayed with the aid of a stereopticon, moving via a transformation scene (again with the help of the aforesaid stereopticon) into Munchkinland in the best style of the Victorian British pantomime, then on to the road in the woods, the poppyfield (''one of the most beautiful ideas ever worked out by a scenic artist'') with chorus girls at first as poppies dressed in green with big red hats, and then transformed by a change of millinery into the same field covered with snow, and finally to the wizard's palace—was a triumph of staging.

That staging was reinforced by two big, traditionally grotesque clown-comedy performances by Stone and Montgomery, performances that, whilst *The Wizard of Oz* and its scenery were superseded by bigger and better productions in the following years, took the two men on to stardom in bigger and better vehicles. But the show was the hit of the 1902–3 season, first in its original birthplace, Chicago (''the biggest hit in years . . . they are selling seats four weeks in advance!''), where it played to packed houses for three months, then in New York, where it ran up 293 performances at the Majestic, prompting, like all big hits, the burlesquers to leap in with such pieces as *The Wizard of Jersey* (Robert Recker, Billy Busch/Ralph Post, Dewey Theater 15 August)—before Hamlin and Mitchell got ready to produce a successor in the same mold. It was, perhaps, the great success of that successor, *Babes in Toyland*, that partly led to *The Wizard of Oz* being a little forgotten, although it returned to Broadway for an additional 72 performances at the Majestic and New York Theaters in 1904 (21 March) and a Christmas season at the Academy of Music at the end of the same year (66 performances).

A production announced by Victor de Cottens for Paris's Olympia in 1908 did not eventuate.

The title and the tale—popular though both were in their time—might have gone the way of most turn-of-the-century children's fiction, but they didn't. *The Wizard of Oz* became internationally famous through the production of a different musical version, with a wholly different score by Harold Arlen, which was put together for the cinema by MGM in 1938. Judy Garland, Ray Bolger, Jack Haley, Bert Lahr, Billie Burke and Margaret Hamilton as a bad witch starred in this third film version (there had been silent ones in 1915 and 1925), which dumped King Pastoria and his soubrette, dumped the cow and the court poet, and concentrated on getting Dorothy to the Wizard of Oz in the company of her tin and straw companions and of the Cowardly Lion, who had been upped from an incidental part in the 1903 version to a much more important character. ''Follow the Yellow Brick Road,'' ''Over the Rainbow,'' ''We're Off to See the Wizard'' and ''If I Only Had a Heart'' gave the show the kind of accompaniment it had not previously had, and the score, along with the film, became a classic of its kind.

The film version was subsequently rewritten into a series of stage shows, the first of which seems to have been that staged at St Louis's Municipal Opera in 1942. This version, with a libretto credited to Frank Gabrielsen, still hung on to some of the original stage score, mixing it with Arlen's songs, but, even though the initial London showing of the piece (Winter Garden 26 December 1946, w Walter Crisham as the Scarecrow and Claude Hulbert as the Lion) puzzlingly credited it as ''a play for children by Paul Tietjens, present version by Janet Green, lyrics by E Y Harburg, music by Harold Arlen,'' later productions abandoned the original music in favor of the new as varying versions of *The Wizard of Oz* went on to be played in theatres ranging from Australia's Tivoli circuit to Britain's Royal Shakespeare Theatre and to the Radio City Music Hall and, in variously star-spangled reproductions, at Madison Square Garden (1997, 1998, 1999, ''America's favourite movie brought magically to life . . .''), as well as in such translations as the odd *Zauberer von Oss* and *Óz, a csodák csodája* (ad Pál Bénes, Győri Nemzeti Színház 9 April 1994).

Other inhabitants of Baum's books have also made it to the stage, both in spectacular stagings such as the American tour pieces *The Woggle Bug* (Frederick Chapin/Baum, Garrick Theater, Chicago 18 June 1905) and *The Tik-Tok Man of Oz* (Louis F Gottschalk/Baum Morosco Theater, Los Angeles 30 March 1913)—both less than successful—or, on a more modest scale, as in the 1988 British piece, *The Patchwork Girl of Oz* (Andy Roberts/Adrian Mitchell, Palace Theatre, Watford 16 December).

Recordings: (Arlen score) original film soundtrack (MGM/CBS), London cast (TER), Madison Square cast (TVT), Belgian cast selections (Decca), etc

THE WIZARD OF THE NILE Comic opera in 3 acts by Harry B Smith. Music by Victor Herbert. Casino Theater, New York, 4 November 1895.

Victor Herbert's setting of the *The Wizard of the Nile,* an opéra-bouffe about a phony rainmaker, brought the rising composer his first Broadway success. Harry B Smith's central plot line was scarcely new. It had been about—even in an Egyptian setting—since Joseph and Pharoah, it had been used for a comic opera called *The Rainmaker of Syria* and its remake as *The Woman King* just a couple of years earlier, and would still be around nearly 60 years later in *110 in the Shade.* But the character of Kibosh, "the wizard of the Nile," was worked up into a splendidly ridiculous role for Frank Daniels, the odd-looking and even more oddly made up comedy star, and Smith added several humorous turns to the low-comedy plot. This wretchedly unsuccessful royal rain-maker gets into even worse trouble when he is unable to stop the rain once it has started, and, in a burlesque of *Aida,* he ends up being entombed alive for his troubles. His tomb mate, however, is no adoring soprano but King Ptolomaeus (Walter Allen) himself, who has somehow got on the wrong side of the sealing-up process. The soprano of the affair was Cleopatra (Dorothy Morton), who was allowed to sing romantically with her music teacher, Ptarmigan (Edwin Isham), but not to wed him for, as all the world knows, history had other things in store for Cleopatra.

Herbert provided a delightful light-operetta score to go with the fooleries of the evening, and Daniels reaped some of the best of it with his merrily pattering assertion that "That's One Thing a Wizard Can Do" and a bouncing celebration of the very un-Egyptian "My Angeline," whilst the pretty music was topped by the waltz quintet "Star Light, Star Bright" and the soprano "Pure and White Is the Lotus." The whole mixture worked splendidly, and Kirk la Shelle and Arthur F Clark's production came from Detroit's Opera House (14 October) to play out a fine 105-performance season on Broadway before going into the country, returning in 1897 (19 April) for a brief repeat run in New York.

Unusually for its time, *The Wizard of the Nile* found takers further afield than the American circuits. It made its way to Europe, and there it ran up a series of productions that has never been equaled by any other of Victor Herbert's works. The first of these was in Austria, where Franz Jauner's production of *Der Zauberer vom Nil* (ad Alexander Neumann) featured Julius Spielmann as Kibatschki, the wizard, Herr Frank in the role of King Ptolomaeus, and Frln Sipos and Herr Bauer as the unconsummated romantic pair alongside no less than three female choruses—an Amazon guard, a bunch of noble ladies and another of dancing girls. *Der Zauberer* was by no means a hit, but it ran for 28 performances before being replaced by a new musical based on Meilhac and Halévy's *La Cigale.* When that did no better, Jauner pushed *Der Zauberer* back on for a few more performances. It was played for Christmas Day and again in the new year, but was dropped from the repertoire after 39 performances. It was well enough noticed, however, to get a production down the river at Budapest (ad Gyula Komor) the following year, and another German version (ad Julius Freund) was later played at Berlin's Metropoltheater. The show was even heard in German in New York, produced by and starring Adolf Philipp at the Terrace-Garten. The owners announced that the famous French baritone Pol Plançon had bought the French rights, in order to mount it for his own benefit at the Bouffes-Parisiens, but a French *Wizard* never appeared.

It was perhaps a simple transatlantic difference in terminology that led London critics to find that the piece "more resembles a burlesque than a comic opera," complaining that there was but a "rudimentary plot" and that the fun was obtained by "detached drollery rather than by a humorously culminating consistent scheme." They conceded, however, that it was "quite up to the standard of burlesque" and praised the "tuneful and spirited" music. London's critics had obviously forgotten the days of opéra-bouffe, but opéra-bouffe and the crazy low comedy it had favored still lay at the basis of what America called comic opera, and *The Wizard of the Nile* was of a very different flavor from the more sophisticated comic/romantic genre of the current hit of the London stage, *The Geisha.* London, however, didn't want to know about the forgotten joys of opéra-bouffe, and, in spite of a cast topped by Adele Ritchie (Cleopatra), J J Dallas (Kibosh), Charles Rock (Ptolemy), Amy Augarde (Simoona), Harrison Brockbank (Ptarmigan) and Ells Dagnall (Cheops), the show played only a few weeks in the West End.

Austria: Carltheater *Der Zauberer vom Nil* 26 September 1896; Hungary: Budai Színkör *A Nilusi Varázslo* 1 August 1897; UK: Shaftesbury Theatre 9 September 1897; Germany: Metropoltheater *Der Zauberer am Nil* 12 May 1900

Recording: live performance (AEI)

WODEHOUSE, P[elham] G[renville] (b Guildford, Surrey, 15 October 1881; d Southampton, NY, 14 February 1975). British novelist, lyricist and sometime co-librettist for a decade of Broadway and London musical comedies that brought forth a couple of jolly, enduring hit shows and a couple more songs to match.

At first a journalist and from his earliest years a comic novelist, Wodehouse at the same time supplied a handful of lyrics to the West End musical comedy stage, adapting, co-writing and occasionally penning original words for songs used in such musicals as *Sergeant Brue* ("Put Me in My Little Cell" w Frederick Rosse), *The Beauty of Bath* (1905, "The Frolic of the Breeze," "Mr Chamberlain" w Jerome Kern, Clifford Harris), *My Darling* (1907, "The Glowworm" w Haines, C H Taylor) and *The Gay Gordons.* As his career as a novelist, boosted by the creation of the comic character of Psmith, and as a journalist flourished, he had less to do with the theatre, although he had an adaptation of one of his books presented on Broadway (*A Gentleman of Leisure*) and a couple of quick flops in London.

All sorts of tales have been touted about concerning the beginning of Wodehouse's theatrical teaming with Guy Bolton (Bolton and Wodehouse told different ones, and even told differing ones themselves at different times). Whenever and however their meeting occurred, its first tangible product came when the two adapted the lyrics and book to the Hungarian musical *Zsuzsi kisasszony* for the New York stage. They followed this up over the next few years with a busy schedule of pieces. On the one, and often less successful, hand there were a number of other adaptations: another Kálmán hit, *Die Csárdásfürstin,* was turned into a flop as *The Riviera Girl,* and the French musical *Loute,* which had been a play hit as *The Girl from Rector's* on Broadway, closed on the way there twice as *See You Later,* but a version of another French hit, *Madame et son filleul,* made up successfully into *The Girl Behind the Gun* (aka *Kissing Time*) to become a hit around the English-speaking world.

Apart from this last piece, the livelier part of their work was in their original musical comedies, on which, although the credits often read ''book and lyrics by Guy Bolton and P G Wodehouse,'' it was known that Wodehouse's department was principally that of songwords and his partner's that of the libretto. The earliest of this group of musical comedies were written in collaboration with Jerome Kern, Wodehouse's songwriting partner of one and a half songs a dozen years earlier, who had also had an assignment as botcher-in-chief on *Zsuzsi kisasszony.* The team began tentatively with *Have a Heart* (78 performances), but had a fine hit with the comical *Oh, Boy!* (463 performances, ''Till the Clouds Roll By''), produced at the small Princess Theatre, where Bolton had previously had a success with Kern with *Very Good Eddie.* It was a hit they didn't quite manage to repeat, for though an adaptation of George Ade's happy college play *The College Widow* as *Leave It to Jane* (167 performances, ''Siren's Song,'' ''Leave It to Jane'') and their second piece for the Princess, *Oh, Lady! Lady!!* (219 performances) proved reasonably successful, the threesome's only other piece together, an attempt at a Ziegfeld revue called *Miss 1917,* did not.

Thereafter composer and authors went in separate directions—directions that would bring them individually together again, but only once more as a fully constituted team. Thus the ''Princess Theatre musicals of Bolton, Wodehouse and Kern,'' which have been so long and so glibly referred to by some commentators, actually come down to a total of two shows: the sizzling *Oh, Boy!* and the less sizzling *Oh, Lady! Lady!!* Or three if *Leave It to Jane,* adapted and conceived in the same style, but staged elsewhere, is counted.

Bolton and Wodehouse went on to write short-lived shows with Louis Hirsch and Armand Vecsey and to the exportable hit of *Kissing Time,* before Wodehouse—now the author of a book about a butler named Jeeves—moved back to center his activities in Britain. He left behind him in America a part-written musical called *The Little Thing* which Bolton and Kern later turned around and into a major hit without him. Wodehouse's songwords for ''The Church 'Round the Corner'' and ''You Can't Keep a Good Girl Down'' survived into the score of what became *Sally.*

Whilst Psmith and Jeeves continued to increase Wodehouse's success and fame quotient, he nevertheless kept in touch with the musical stage. He was involved in an almost-successful attempt to remake the famous 19th-century comic opera *Erminie* as a vehicle for London and comedian Bill Berry under the title of *The Golden Moth* but he found more joy when he was called in by George Grossmith to work on two homemade ''American'' musicals for his Winter Garden Theatre in the wake of the grand success there of *Sally.* A sort of transatlantic collaboration with Kern produced the successful *The Cabaret Girl* (361 performances) and the less successful *The Beauty Prize* (214 performances). Both, however, proved much more popular than the one reunion of the team of Bolton, Kern and Wodehouse: *Sitting Pretty* was a 95-performance failure on Broadway.

Thereafter, Wodehouse's musical-theatrical career was largely limited to adaptation, but the second highlight of that career—a decade after *Oh, Boy!*—was still to come. The Viennese hit *Der Orlow* (set in America!) became a London flop as *Hearts and Diamonds,* and an attempt at a Jenny Lind biomusical to feature Bolton's wife (who then didn't play it) was a Broadway failure, but in the two collaborators' hands the famous French farce *La Présidente* became a deliciously constructed American comedy decorated with endearing George and Ira Gershwin songs and entitled *Oh, Kay!* Wodehouse and Bolton's final text together, some years later, for *Anything Goes,* was (very?) largely replaced before the play was produced.

Over the years, Wodehouse contributed isolated lyrics to a number of other shows, the most famous of which was ''Bill,'' a cut-out from an earlier Wodehouse-Kern show that finally found itself a place in *Show Boat* and also a place as probably the best known of all the writer's songs in later days. He also had a co-lyricist's credits on two Gershwin songs (w Ira Gershwin) in *Rosalie* (''Oh Gee! Oh Joy!,'' ''Say So!'') and (although the printed score does not credit him) for some of the lyrics of Rudolf Friml's *The Three Musketeers* (1928). In later years he also worked on the revamping of the *Oh, Kay!* score for an off-Broadway revival, adapting some lyrics and replacing some from Gershwin songs from other sources.

In 1975—after Wodehouse and his partner Bolton had failed to get their own version to the musical stage—his most famous creations, the butler Jeeves and his master, Bertie Wooster, already famed on screens large and small, made their way onto the musical stage. However, a singing-dancing *Jeeves* (Andrew Lloyd Webber/Alyn Ayckbourn, Her Majesty's Theatre 20 March), revised and retried twenty years later as *By Jeeves* (Duke of York's Theatre, London 2 July 1996) did not bring the characters the same success that they had won in other areas.

His novel *A Damsel in Distress* (1919) remade as a screenplay for an RKO film (1937) was re-remade in 1998 as the book for the latest in the series of reconstituted Gershwin-scored musicals (*A Foggy Day* Norm Foster, John Mueller Royal Gerge Theater, Niagara 3 May 1998).

''Plum'' Wodehouse has, in recent years, become almost a cult figure, particularly amongst book and music collectors, but the details of his life in the theatre, now much pored over, have been, at best, rather muddied. A 1982 biography billed as ''the authorized biography'' does not much interest itself in Wodehouse's work for the musical theatre, and when it touches on it, more than once goes badly wrong. As for Bolton's *Bring on the Girls*—it may look like an autobiography, but to his friends he made no secret of the fact that he'd made up as much of it as he fancied sounded either good or better than the facts . . . which it was a bit much to expect a chap to remember anyway.

1916 **Miss Springtime** (*Zsuzsi kisasszony*) English lyrics (New Amsterdam Theater)

1917 **Have a Heart** (Kern/w Guy Bolton) Liberty Theater 11 January

1917 **Oh, Boy!** (Kern/w Bolton) Princess Theater 20 February

1917 **Leave It to Jane** (Kern/w Bolton) Longacre Theater 28 August

1917 **The Riviera Girl** (*Die Csárdásfürstin*) American version w Bolton (New Amsterdam Theater)

1917 **Kitty Darlin'** (Rudolf Friml/w Otto Harbach) Casino Theater 7 November

1918 **See You Later** (*Loute*) English lyrics (Academy of Music, Baltimore)

1918 **Oh, Lady! Lady!!** (Kern/w Bolton) Princess Theater 1 February

1918 **The Girl Behind the Gun** (aka *Kissing Time*) (Ivan Caryll/w Bolton) New Amsterdam Theater 16 September

1918 **The Canary** (Caryll/w Anne Caldwell/Louis Verneuil ad H B Smith) Globe Theater 4 November

1918 **Oh, My Dear!** (ex- *Ask Dad*) (Louis Hirsch/w Bolton) Princess Theater 26 November

1919 **The Rose of China** (Armand Vecsey/Bolton) Lyric Theater 25 November

1919 **Kissing Time** revised version of *The Girl Behind the Gun* Winter Garden Theatre, London 20 May

1921 **The Golden Moth** (Ivor Novello/w Fred Thompson) Adelphi Theatre, London 5 October

1922 **The Cabaret Girl** (Kern/w George Grossmith) Winter Garden Theatre, London 19 September

1923 **The Beauty Prize** (Kern/w Grossmith) Winter Garden Theatre, London 5 September

1924 **Sitting Pretty** (Kern/w Bolton) Fulton Theater 8 April

1926 **Hearts and Diamonds** (*Der Orlow*) English libretto w Lauri Wylie (Strand Theatre)

1926 **Oh, Kay!** (ex- *Cheerio!*) (George Gershwin/Ira Gershwin, Howard Dietz/w Bolton) Imperial Theater 8 November

1927 **The Nightingale** (Vecsey/w Bolton) Jolson Theater 3 January

1928 **The Three Musketeers** (Rudolf Friml/w Clifford Grey/ William Anthony McGuire) Lyric Theater, New York 13 March

1934 **Anything Goes** (Cole Porter/w Bolton ad Russel Crouse, Howard Lindsay) Alvin Theater 21 November

Literature: Davis, L: *Bolton and Wodehouse and Kern: The Men Who Made Musical Comedy* (James H Heinemann, Inc, New York, 1993), etc

Autobiographies: *Performing Flea* (Jenkins, London, 1953), *Bring on the Girls* (fictionalized) (Simon & Schuster, New York, 1953); Biographies: Jasen, D J: *P G Wodehouse* (Mason & Lipscomb, New York, 1974), *The Theatre of P G Wodehouse* (Batsford Ltd, London, 1979), Green, B: *P G Wodehouse, A Literary Biography* (Pavilion Books, London, 1981), Donaldson, F: *P G Wodehouse* (Weidenfeld & Nicolson, London, 1982)

WO DIE LERCHE SINGT (*A pacsirta*) Operette in 3 acts by Ferenc Martos. Music by Franz Lehár. Király Színház, Budapest, 1 February 1918.

With *A pacsirta,* Lehár returned to his native Hungary to set, for the only time in his career, a libretto written in Hungarian for a show that was produced in Budapest. The tale told by Martos, one of the most experienced and best librettists of the Hungarian stage, was neither his most original nor his most interesting, but it allowed Lehár to write music in which the strains of rural and urban Hungary could be occasionally heard, rather than the unmingled bubbling Viennoiseries of the favorites amongst his previous works.

In a little Hungarian country village live the old peasant Török Pál (Dezső Gyárfás) and his pretty granddaughter, Juliska (Emmi Kosáry), who goes around singing like the carefree lark all day (hence the show's title) until the Budapest painter Sándor Zápolya (Ernő Király) comes to board. While he paints her, they fall in love.

When the two of them go back to the city, Sándor's painting of his "lark" wins a prize and he becomes famous, but now his old girlfriend, the actress Vilma Garami (Juci Lábass/Ilona Dömötör), who was so horribly out of her element in the country, shows up with all the suitable city graces that Juliska can't learn, and before long the country mouse decides she'd better go back to the village and her faithful Pista (Jenő Nádor).

The score, for all its Magyar intentions, was heavy with waltzes. Both Juliska ("Durch die weiten Felder") and Vilma ("Ein Hauch, wie von Blüten") made their first appearances in 3/4, and the final act took place largely in waltz time. One of the most successful numbers, however, was the jauntiest of the march-time pieces, which numbered almost as many as the waltzes, "Schau mich an und frag' nicht lang." The lyric singing of the piece went to Vilma and to Sándor, whilst Juliska was the evening's soubrette and old Török had two numbers, the Marschlied von Temesvár ("Pálikam, Pálikam") and the brisk "Was geh'n mich an die Leute" in croaking comic contrast.

The Budapest premiere was quickly followed by a Viennese one (ad A M Willner, Heinz Reichert) at the Theater an der Wien with Ernst Tautenhayn (Török), Luise Kartousch (Margit, ex- Juliska), Betty Fischer (Vilma), Hubert Marischka (Sándor) and Karl Meister (Pista) in the leading roles. Boosted by those wartime conditions that favor long runs, *Wo die Lerche singt* became a solid 10-month success. Brought back occasionally thereafter in the repertoire, it ultimately played over 400 performances at the Theater an der Wien and, in consequence, has become accepted as a Viennese Operette—its Hungarian origins (like Lehár's, often) quite forgotten.

The Vienna success was paralleled by a fine run in Germany, but there was no rush to take up the latest show of the composer of *Die lustige Witwe* elsewhere. Britain, which wasn't looking to Europe for shows in 1918, ignored it, France passed, and although Max Winter mounted a German-language version at New York's Lexington Opera House in 1920 as a hopeful shop window for a sale to the English-speaking theatre, the show was not taken up there either.

Thanks to its original Vienna success, *Wo die Lerche singt* found its way swiftly to film in a version written and directed by Marischka. He, Tautenhayn and Kartousch all repeated their stage roles alongside Marietta Weber as Vilma. Lehár's music was played as an accompaniment to the film. Nearly 20 years later, however, a sound film was made, with Marta Eggerth featured.

Wo die Lerche singt did not become a repertoire piece in the way that so many of Lehár's other—and even initially less popular—pieces did. However, it was given a major Vienna revival at the Raimundtheater in 1972.

Austria: Theater an der Wien *Wo die Lerche singt* 27 March 1918; Germany: Theater am Nollendorfplatz *Wo die Lerche singt* 21 February 1919; USA: Lexington Opera House *Where the Lark Sings* December 1920

Films: Hubert Marischka 1918, Carl Lamac 1936

Recordings: complete (Bel Age), selection (Mastertone)

WOMAN OF THE YEAR Musical in 2 acts by Peter Stone based on the screenplay of the same title by Ring Lardner jr and Michael Kanin. Lyrics by Fred Ebb. Music by John Kander. Palace Theater, New York, 29 March 1981.

First seen as a 1942 MGM film with Katharine Hepburn and Spencer Tracy in its starring roles, *Woman of the Year* underwent some modernization in its transfer to the musical stage of some 40 years later. Miss Hepburn's role of the upmarket woman of intelligence (a diplomat's daughter and current affairs reporter) was transmogrified into that of a more suitable heroine for the 1980s, a television talk-show hostess, whilst Tracy's rumpled sports-page writer became, less obviously, a cartoonist. The nub of the story, however, remained the same.

When Tess Harding (Lauren Bacall) starts trashing "the funnies" on her TV show, cartoonist Sam Craig (Harry Guardino) gets his own back by inserting a "Tessie-Cat" character into his strip. The two meet, the sparks fly, and they fall in love. After the wedding, it doesn't work. In the course of the evening, Tess and Sam have to learn how to balance their private and professional lives, separately and together. Elvind Harum played a defected Soviet dancer and Marilyn Cooper the ordinary second wife of Tess's first husband, both of whom have something to teach Tess as she struggles to keep her marriage intact and work out why it's going wrong. The Woman of the Year Award, which Tess is seen accepting at the evening's opening, epitomized her worldly success, soon to be contrasted with her home failure.

The score for the show was the work of Kander and Ebb, proven nonpareil experts at outfitting musically a 100 percent above-the-title Broadway star. Miss Bacall declared with gruff determination that—like Lulu Glaser, 70 years earlier—she was one of the girls who's just "One of the Boys," quelled her querulous secretary (Roderick Cook) with no-nonsense imperiousness ("Shut Up, Gerald") and unshakeably announced "When You're Right, You're Right." She also moved momentarily into a more sentimental vein, but it was, uncharacteristically, a duet that proved to be the show's favorite number: Miss Bacall joined with the unspectacular homebody played by Miss Cooper to declare with mutual envy that "The Grass Is Always Greener" in other folks' lives.

Since it was a period when a substantial investment in a show could command a presentation credit, Miss Bacall shared her above-the-title billing with no fewer than six co-producers, the more active of whom ensured the show a slickly staged, eye-catching production that yet did not submerge the play, which was still the heart of the entertainment. The result was a run of 770 performances, for the last of which Miss Bacall was succeeded—to a surprised and pleased critical and public reaction—by another film star, Raquel Welch and, at the end of the run, by Debbie Reynolds.

The show was toured with Miss Bacall at its helm, and played regionally in America, and, although it did not find its way to London or to Paris, *Woman of the Year* did win productions in Budapest (ad István Hajnal), where Ági Voith and János Gávőlgyi starred in *Az év asszonya* at the Thalia Színház, and in . . . Colombia.

Hungary: Thalia Színház *Az év asszonya* 15 December 1989

Recordings: original cast (Arista), Colombian cast *El mujer del año* (private label)

WONDERFUL TOWN Musical comedy in 2 acts by Joseph Fields and Jerome Chodorov based on their play *My Sister Eileen.* Lyrics by Adolph Green and Betty Comden. Music by Leonard Bernstein. Winter Garden Theater, New York, 25 February 1953.

The play *My Sister Eileen,* adapted from a book by Ruth McKinney, was produced by Max Gordon at Broadway's Biltmore Theater in 1940 (26 December, 864 performances) with 42-year-old Shirley Booth and Jo Ann Sayers playing the two out-of-town sisters holed up amongst the endearing and quirky inhabitants of Greenwich Village, New York City, whilst they strive for fame and fortune in the literary and theatrical worlds, respectively. It was one of the longest-running comedy hits of its period, and its Broadway success was followed by a 1942 film that starred Rosalind Russell and Janet Blair.

Slimmed tactfully into a libretto, without the loss of either plot or comedy, by its original authors, the show was set with songs by Betty Comden, Adolph Green and Leonard Bernstein, the trio who had been so successful a decade earlier with another jolly celebration of life in New York City in *On the Town.* Miss Russell, repeating her film role in this New York equivalent of a French Montmartre musical, was a now glamorous and 40-plus Ruth Sherwood comically counting ''A Hundred Easy Ways to Lose a Man,'' leading a basketful of Brazilians in a wild ''Conga'' through the streets of New York, and joining in glum harmonics with her blonde bombshell of a sister, Eileen (Edith Adams), in one of the show's most successful single numbers, wondering why on earth they left their home in ''Ohio'' for an uncomfortable cellar in New York. Eileen had another winning number, assuring herself, to a delicate melody, that she is again ''A Little Bit in Love,'' next-door neighbor Wreck (Jordan Bentley)—an out-of-work football player with a talent for ironing—described his other talent in ''But I Could Pass a Football,'' a jailful of Irish policemen sang their praises of ''Darlin' Eileen'' in burlesque shamrocky harmonies, and the hero mumbled out his liking for ''A Quiet Girl.'' If *Wonderful Town*'s play-based nature meant that Bernstein had fewer opportunities for the orchestral and dance sections, which were one of his particular fortes, he demonstrated his musical skills with a brilliantly babbling ''Conversation Piece'' at an unfortunate, improvised dinner party for the men in the girls' lives (George Gaynes, Dort Clark, Cris Alexander).

Robert Fryer's production of *Wonderful Town* played a fine 559 performances at Broadway's Winter Garden Theater (during which time Carol Channing replaced Miss Russell to give a very different interpretation of the role of Ruth), and the show moved on to London, where Pat Kirkwood and Shani Wallis took the featured roles in the 207 performances played by Jack Hylton's production at the Prince's Theatre. At the same time, Hollywood mounted a fresh version of *My Sister Eileen* (1955), with Betty Garrett and Janet Leigh in its starring roles, but with songs by Styne and Robin rather than Comden, Green and Bernstein.

Wonderful Town won regular regional productions following its initial run, and it returned to New York at the City Center in 1957 (March), with Nancy Walker and Jo Sullivan featured, again in 1963, and for a third time in 1967 (May), with Elaine Stritch (the Ruth of the television series based on *My Sister Eileen*) starred. In 1994 New York City Opera mounted the show with Kay McClelland giving much-more-than-usual vocal values to the role of Ruth and Crista Moore as Eileen. The show was also played on CBS television in 1958, with Miss Russell as an increasingly middle-aged Ruth now paired with Jacqueline McKeever.

London saw the show a second time in 1986 (7 August), when a scaled-down production, sponsored by the King's Head Theatre and starring television actress Maureen Lipman as a gawkily comical young Ruth, was transferred to the West End for a run of 264 performances.

UK: Prince's Theatre 23 February 1955

Recordings: original cast (Decca/MCA), TV soundtrack (Columbia), London 1986 revival (First Night), studio recordings (DGG, TER)

WONTNER, Arthur (b London, 21 January 1875; d Burnham, Bucks, 10 July 1960).

A popular straight-theatre leading man who had played with Lewis Waller, Edward Compton and Beerbohm Tree, appearing on the London stage as Orsino, Laertes, Bassanio, as Raffles in the play of that title, Ben

Plate 427. **Wonderful Town.** *Rosalind Russell gets the attentions of the Brazilian navy.*

Hur, Voysey (*The Voysey Inheritance*), Robert Chiltern, and in many other major roles, Wontner made a side-step into the musical theatre in his early forties. He appeared first as the non-singing hero of Robert Evett's Daly's Theater production of *The Happy Day* (1916), then of his subsequent *The Maid of the Mountains* (1917), creating the part of the songless brigand chief Baldasarre opposite José Collins. After several years back in the straight theatre he teamed with Evett and Miss Collins again, in their new enterprise at the Gaiety Theatre, taking over as Peter the Great opposite Miss Collins's *Catherine* and playing King Charles II to her Nell Gwynne (*Our Nell*). He later played Cardinal Richelieu to the D'Artagnan of Dennis King in the London production of Rudolf Friml's *The Three Musketeers* (1930). After both many more fine stage roles and the later part of a 40-year film career, he appeared one last time in the musical theatre as General Birabeau in a London revival of *The Desert Song* (1943).

WOOD, Arthur [Henry] (b Heckmondwike, 24 January 1875; d London, 18 January 1953).

One of the most popular of British theatre conductors for over 20 years, Wood was assistant to Sidney Jones at the head of the Harrogate Municipal orchestra in the 1890s, and when he led his first London show, at Terry's Theatre in 1903, it was Jones's comedy opera *My Lady Molly*. The following year he was musical director for George Edwardes's production of *Véronique* at the Apollo and in 1905 for the short-lived *The Gipsy Girl* before he joined Robert Courtneidge to conduct *The Dairymaids* (1906). This assignment began a long collaboration between Wood and the producer that saw him acting as musical director for the original production of *The Arcadians* and for *Courtneidge's The Mousmé, Princess Caprice, Oh! Oh! Delphine, The Pearl Girl, The Cinema Star, My Lady Frayle* and *Young England.* When Courtneidge's fortunes declined, Wood also served him as composer and provided the scores for his touring shows

Oh, Caesar!, Petticoat Fair, Fancy Fair and *Too Many Girls.*

Wood succeeded Percy Fletcher as the conductor of *Chu Chin Chow,* acted for several years as musical director at the Gaiety Theatre (*The Beauty Spot, Going Up, The Kiss Call, The Shop Girl, Faust on Toast, The Little Girl in Red*), took over at the head of *A Night Out* at the Winter Garden (1921), and conducted the short-lived London production of *Die Csárdásfürstin* (*The Gipsy Princess*), the flop *Jenny* (Empire) and *His Girl* (Gaiety). He spent several years under Jimmy White at Daly's Theatre conducting the producer's series of Continental musicals (*The Lady of the Rose, Madame Pompadour, Cleopatra, The Blue Mazurka*), and later conducted Stolz's *The Blue Train* (1927) and the London production of *Oh, Kay!* (1928) as well as some less well-made spectacular pieces (*The White Camellia, Eldorado, Kong*). He joined one last time with Courtneidge for the Chopin pasticcio *The Damask Rose* at the Savoy in 1931.

Wood's last West End appearances with the baton were for the vast *Casanova* at the London Coliseum in 1932 and an amateurish revival of *The Quaker Girl* in 1934. He also headed the band for *The Gay Hussar* (later to become *Balalaika*) on its initial 1933 tour.

Wood's light orchestral music was extremely popular in its day, and has in one instance survived thoroughly to modern times, a fragment of his ''My Native Heath'' being used as the theme tune for the long-running radio serial ''The Archers.'' His theatre scores were entirely made for music halls and touring circuits, although he interpolated numbers into several West End shows and was much used as a theatrical orchestrator for the London stage.

1908 **His Living Image** (Stanley Cooke) 1 act Coronet Theatre 23 November

1916 **Oh, Caesar!** (w Nat D Ayer/Adrian Ross/Alexander M Thompson, Max Pemberton) Royal Lyceum, Edinburgh 23 December

1918 **Petticoat Fair** (Robert Courtneidge) Hippodrome, Newcastle 23 December

1919 **Fancy Fair** (G Hartley Milburn/Courtneidge) Hippodrome, Newcastle 14 April

1919 **Too Many Girls** (Hartley Milburn/Jack Hulbert, Harold Simpson, Courtneidge) Hippodrome, Liverpool 22 December

1922 **The Rose Garden** (Arthur Miller, Eustace Baynes) Hippodrome, Boscombe 1 May

1924 **The Sheik of Shepherd's Bush** (Harry Lowther/Arthur Shirley) Brixton Theatre 24 November

WOOD, David [Bernard] (b Sutton, 21 February 1944).

Britain's most successful author of juvenile musical plays, Wood led an early career as an actor (Bingo Little in *Jeeves,* the film *If,* etc) and also had several adult musicals produced (*A Life in Bedrooms, A Present from the Corporation, Maudie, Rock Nativity*). Since the considerable and enduring success of *The Owl and the Pussycat Went to See . . . ,* his regular stream of lively and uncondescending plays with songs have been frequently played in theatres throughout Britain, and later toured under the banner of the Whirligig Theatre Company. The most successful of the group have been *The Owl and the Pussycat Went to See . . .* and *The Gingerbread Man.* He has also authored a number of Christmas fairy-tale shows (*Mother Goose's Golden Christmas, Babes in the Magic Wood, Cinderella, Aladdin, Dick Whittington and Wondercat, Jack and the Giant*) and a children's opera (*The Forest Child* Welsh National Opera 10 July 1998), as well as the Roald Dahl plays *The BFG* (1991), *The Witches* (1992) and *The Twits* (1999), and a large number of children's books.

1967 **A Life in Bedrooms** (w David Wright) Traverse Theatre, Edinburgh 11 April

1967 **A Present from the Corporation** (John Gould/Michael Sadler) Swan Theatre, Worcester 14 November; Fortune Theatre 30 November

1967 **The Tinderbox** Swan Theatre, Worcester 26 December

1968 **The Owl and the Pussycat Went to See . . .** (w Sheila Ruskin) Swan Theatre, Worcester 26 December; Jeannetta Cochrane Theatre, London 16 December 1969

1969 **The Stiffkey Scandals of 1932** revised *A Life in Bedrooms* Queen's Theatre 12 June

1969 **Toytown** (*Larry the Lamb in Toytown*) (w Ruskin) Swan Theatre, Worcester 26 December; Shaw Theatre, London 12 December 1973

1970 **The Plotters of Cabbage Patch Corner** Swan Theatre, Worcester 26 December; Shaw Theatre, London 15 December 1971

1971 **Flibberty and the Penguin** Swan Theatre, Worcester 26 December

1972 **The Papertown Paperchase** Swan Theatre, Worcester 26 December; Sadler's Wells Theatre, London 23 October 1984

1973 **Hi-Jack Over Hygenia** Swan Theatre, Worcester 26 December

1974 **Maudie** (w Iwan Williams) Thorndike Theatre, Leatherhead 12 November

1974 **Rock Nativity** (Tony Hatch, Jackie Trent) Newcastle University Theatre 18 December

1975 **Old Mother Hubbard** Queen's Theatre, Hornchurch 16 December

1976 **The Gingerbread Man** Towngate Theatre, Basildon 13 December; Old Vic, London 13 December 1977

1976 **Old Father Time** Queen's Theatre, Hornchurch 20 December

1977 **Nutcracker Sweet** Redgrave Theatre, Farnham 20 December; Sadler's Wells Theatre, London 14 October 1980

1979 **There Was an Old Woman** Haymarket Theatre, Leicester 25 July

1980 **The Ideal Gnome Expedition** (*Chish 'n' Fips*) Liverpool Playhouse 3 December; Sadler's Wells Theatre, London 13 October 1981

1981 **Robin Hood** (w Dave Arthur, Toni Arthur) Nottingham Playhouse 29 May; Young Vic, London 9 December 1982

1981 **Meg and Mog Show** Arts Theatre 10 December

1983 **The Selfish Shellfish** Redgrave Theatre, Farnham 29 March; Sadler's Wells Theatre 15 November

1983 **Abbacadabra** English version w Don Black (Lyric Theatre, Hammersmith)

1984 **Jack the Lad** Library Theatre, Manchester 23 March

1986 **The See-Saw Tree** Redgrave Theatre, Farnham 18 March; Sadler's Wells Theatre, London 8 December 1987

1986 **The Old Man of Lochnagar** His Majesty's Theatre, Aberdeen 10 September; Sadler's Wells Theatre 11 November

1986 **Dinosaurs and All That Rubbish** (Peter Pontzen) Arts Centre Darlington 20 October; Sadler's Wells Theatre, London 17 November

1988 **The Pied Piper** (w D Arthur, T Arthur) Octagon Theatre, Yeovil 16 November

1990 **Save the Human** Arts Theatre, Cambridge 15 February; Sadler's Wells Theatre, London 11 December

1993 **Rupert and the Green Dragon** Throndike Theatre, Leatherhead 22 January

1994 **Noddy** Wimbledon Theatre 23 September; Lyric Theatre, Hammersmith 14 December

1995 **More Adventures of Noddy** Wimbledon Theatre 27 September

1997 **The Prostitute's Padre** revised *The Stiffkey Scandals of 1932* Norwich Playhouse 10 July

1997 **Babe, the Sheep-Pig** New Victoria Theatre, Woking 18 November

WOOD, Mrs John [née VINING, Matilda Charlotte] (b Liverpool, 6 November 1833; d Birchington-on-Sea, 10 January 1915). Internationally celebrated performer and sometime manager.

A versatile actress of comedy, drama, musical burlesque and pantomime, Mrs John Wood (she was thus billed) spent much of her early career in America, where, from September 1854, she played in such extravaganzas and burlesques as *Shylock, The Corsair* (*Conrad and Medora*), *Cinderella, Fortunio, The Invisible Prince, Hiawatha, Cinderella e la comare,* in the title role of John Brougham's *Pocahontas* (*La Belle Sauvage*) and as America's first Robin Luron in Offenbach's *King Carrot,* proving herself one of the country's foremost and most popular players of musical-comic theatre. She managed theatres in San Francisco and New York (Olympic Theater) and, on her eventual return to her native England, took over London's St James's Theatre, where she performed in several burlesques, including *La Belle Sauvage* (Pocahontas) and *My Poll and Partner Joe* (Pretty Poll of Putney) and produced Alfred Cellier's *The Sultan of Mocha* (1876). Her schedule at this house also included such musical pieces as *Treasure Trove* (*La Mariage aux lanternes*), *Jenny Lind at Last* and the burlesque *Vesta!*

The John Wood of her name was comedian John Wood (d Victoria, VL, 28 May 1863) with whom she originally went to America, but from whom she separated soon after.

Mrs Wood's daughter, Florence Wood, also took to the stage and was seen in London in *The Dashing Little Duke, Mitislaw* and *The Better 'Ole.*

WOOD, Peggy [WOOD, Margaret] (b Brooklyn, NY, 9 February 1892; d Stamford, Conn, 18 March 1978). Soprano and actress who created several important musical roles on both sides of the Atlantic.

Miss Wood made her first stage appearance as "a quadroon belle" in the chorus of *Naughty Marietta* (1910) at the age of 18, and the following year had a small part in the briefly seen *Three Romeos* (Vera Steinway). She subsequently took over a one-solo role in the more successful Eddie Foy musical *Over the River* (t/o Sarah Parke), played in the Montgomery and Stone spectacular *The Lady of the Slipper* (Valerie), a revival of *Mlle Modiste* (1913, Fanchette) with Fritzi Scheff, and in Victor Herbert's *The Madcap Duchess* (1913, Gillette), before rising to her first leading role, touring in the title part of Adolf Philipp's successful *Adele* (1914), created in New York by Nathalie Alt.

She performed a couple of numbers alongside George M Cohan in the revue *Hello, Broadway* (1914, Elsie Workingson, "I Wanted to Come to Broadway," "My Flag"), replaced Elinor Henry as Nina in the Columbia Musical Company's production of *The Firefly* ("instantaneously a notably strong personal and singing success") and in the lead role of *The Girl of My Dreams* (1915) and appeared in the title role of *Naughty Marietta,* before returning to Broadway for a number-three role with a song ("A Little Lonesome Tune") and half a duet ("We'll See" w Alan Edwards) in *Love o' Mike* (1917, Peggy) and then, at 25, her first starring role as the three-generations heroine of *Maytime* (1917, Ottilie), introducing "Will You Remember?" in duet with Charles Purcell.

Miss Wood followed up the Broadway and touring productions of this long-running success as the heroine of *Buddies* (1919, Julie), in the title role of the musicalized *Pomander Walk* as *Marjolaine* (1922), and as Antoinette Allen, the new woman who pretends to be prettily weak, in Henry Savage's production of Zelda Sears's *The Clinging Vine* (1922), before tackling a number of non-musical roles including Candida, Lady Percy, Imogen Parrott, and a Portia to George Arliss's Shylock. She returned to the musical stage in 1926 to play Jenny Lind in a biomusical called *The Nightingale,* originally scheduled for the librettist's wife, Marguerite Namara, but was replaced after the New Haven tryout. In 1929 she created her second major musical role, Sarah Linden, in Noël Coward's *Bitter-Sweet,* in London, introducing "I'll See You Again," "The Call of Life" and "Zigeuner."

Back in America she mixed musical and straight plays, getting away to a false start when E Ray Goetz's *Stardust,* in which she was billed to star, was abandoned in a flurry of lawsuits, but then creating the role of Shirley Sheridan in Jerome Kern's 1932 *The Cat and the Fiddle* ("She Didn't Say 'Yes'"), playing Rosalinde in a version of *Die Fledermaus* christened *Champagne, Sec* (1933) and appearing on the West Coast as Kálmán's *Countess Maritza.* In 1938 she returned to London to play another Coward role as Rozanne Gray, the heroine of *Operette,* but thereafter continued her career in non-musical pieces and, notably, on television, where she played the eponymous heroine of *Mama* from 1949 to 1957.

In 1965 she appeared as the Mother Abbess in the film version of *The Sound of Music,* her voice dubbed by Margery McKay.

Memoirs: *Actors—and People* (Appleton, New York, 1930), *How Young You Look* (Farrar & Rinehart, New York, 1940), *Arts and Flowers* (Morrow, New York, 1963)

WOODS, A[lbert] H[erman] [HERMAN, Aladore] (b Budapest, 3 January 1870; d New York, 24 April 1951).

The picturesque, cigar-chomping, "sweetheart"-ing Woods was the cliché Broadway producer of what ought to have been fiction. Born in Hungary and raised in New York, he at first worked in the theatre as an advance man for a touring company. He began producing on his own account in 1902, at first with road productions of highly colored melodramas (w Paddy H Sullivan, Sam H Harris) of the *The Queen of the White Slaves* and *Dangers of Working Girls* ilk, and subsequently with slightly more sophisticated comedies and with musicals. He first mounted a piece on Broadway in 1909, and thereafter kept up a regular supply of productions, both straight (*Potash and Perlmutter, Up in Mabel's Room, The Trial of Mary Dugan, Twentieth Century, The Green Hat,* etc) and musical, to the New York stage over some 20 years. He also built and operated the Eltinge Theater in New York and ran the Apollo and Adelphi Theaters in Chicago.

Amongst Woods's musical productions were numbered *The Girl in the Taxi,* the Julian Eltinge vehicles *The Crinoline Girl, The Fascinating Widow* and *Cousin Lucy,* the Sam Bernard show *All for the Ladies, Kick-In, Broadway and Buttermilk,* Lehár's *Gipsy Love,* the highly successful *Madame Sherry* (w H H Frazee and George Lederer), *Modest Suzanne* (*Die keusche Susanne* w Frazee), *The Woman Haters* (*Der Frauenfresser*) and *Tantalizing Tommy,* as well as the unfortunate Avery Hopwood *I'll Say She Does, Under the Bamboo Tree* and a hopeless piece called *Naughty Diana* (1923) by the ever-failing Detroit-German composer Ortmann, for which Woods brought Continental star Ilse Marvenga to America. He also presented New York with Sacha Guitry and Yvonne Printemps in *Mozart* in 1926.

Flattened by the onset of the depression, he discovered that his secret cache of rainy-day cash had been rifled by a "friend," and he ended his career on Broadway broke.

WOOLF, Benjamin E[dward] (b London, 16 February 1836; d Boston, 7 February 1901).

Ben Woolf jr, whose grandfather had been "a singer of some celebrity on the London stage," and whose father was sometime leader of the orchestra at the New York Bowery Theater, was brought to America from England in his childhood. He worked first as a theatre violinist, playing in the band at Barnum's Museum at the age of 14, then as a conductor in Boston, Philadelphia and New Orleans and finally, after settling in Boston, music and theatre critic and sometime editor for the *Boston Globe,* the *Saturday Evening Gazette* and, from 1894, the *Herald.* An eclectic talent, he wrote and published poetry, painted to exhibition standards, and composed a considerable amount of chamber music, but he found his most enduring success as a theatrical author. Able, or at least willing, to turn his hand to whatever kind of theatre was à la mode, he was said to have been responsible for "over a hundred dramatic works"—many local, many adaptations, and I suspect many unproduced—of which the most notable efforts were his libretto to Julius Eichberg's *The Doctor of Alcantara,* the first American comic opera to win a production in Britain, and the play *The Mighty Dollar* (1875). His other works included a second comic opera *The Rose of Tyrol,* which was performed by Caroline Richings company; the extravaganza *Hobbies* with which Nat Goodwin launched his Froliques company; the "original, musical and eccentric comedy" *Photos,* a farce comedy with a second-act variety show toured vigorously by Alice and Louis Harrison; a Gilbertian satirical comic opera *Pounce & Co* produced in Boston for a fine run of 52 nights, and an attempt at a thoroughly English musical comedy called *Lawn Tennis.*

In 1894 he was credited not with the book, but with the music for the Boston comic opera *Westward Ho!*

1862 **The Doctor of Alcantara** (Julius Eichberg) Boston Museum 7 April; Théâtre Français, New York 28 May 1866

1863 **The Rose of Tyrol** (Eichberg) Boston Museum 6 April

1878 **Hobbies** (various) Leland Opera House, Albany 22 February; Lyceum Theater 6 October 1879

1880 **Photos** (various) Hooley's Theater, Chicago 23 August; Grand Opera House 9 May 1881

1880 **Lawn Tennis, or Djack and Djill** (Woolf) Park Theater, Boston 13 September; Abbey's Park Theater, New York 20 September

1882 **The Magic Doll** (*La Poupée de Nuremberg*) American version (Grand Opera House, San Francisco)

1883 **Pounce & Co, or Capital versus Labour** Bijou Theater, Boston 19 April

1884 **An Adamless Eden** American version (Oakland Gardens, Boston)

1884 **Fantine** (*François les bas-bleus*) American version w Roswell Martin Field (Boston Museum)

1886 **Love's Vow** (*Serment d'amour*) American version (Boston Museum)

1890 **Fauvette** (*La Fauvette du Temple*) American version (Boston Museum)

1894 **Westward Ho!** (Richard D Ware) Museum, Boston 31 December

Other titles attributed: *The King's Frolic* (1884?), *Elfinella, or The Last of the Fairies, Once on a Time, The Village Orphan* and *Wapping Old Stairs*

WOOLF, Edgar Allen (b Phalanx, NJ, 5 April 1886; d Beverly Hills, Calif, 9 December 1943).

The nephew of Ben Woolf, Edgar Allen had an even more prolific, if decidedly less quality, career than his uncle, at first as an actor (Murray Hill stock company, etc), then as a playwright and librettist, but more specifically as a prolific author of sketches and acts for the vaudeville stage, a director and, with the fading away of that vaudeville field in which he very largely operated, a screenwriter. Woolf had a stinging start to his Broadway career when the opening night of one of his Columbia University shows, *Mamzelle Champagne,* taken up as a professional entertainment for the Madison Square Roof Garden, was the scene of the famous Harry Thaw murder, and the piece became a curiosity for scandal seekers through 60 performances. Its connotations even won it a revival years later. However, although Woolf won considerable success in the vaudeville halls with short pieces such as Amelia Stone and Armand Kalisz's *Mon désir* and Ida Brooks Hunt's vehicle *The Singing Countess,* and although he went on to collaborate with both Jerome Kern and Sigmund Romberg during his musical-comedy career, he did not ever notch up a significant musical-stage hit. However, during his time as a contract scenarist to Metro films he managed to get his name on some rather happier ventures, including *The Wizard of Oz, The Night Is Young, Everybody Sing* and *Ziegfeld Follies of 1939.*

1906 **Mamzelle Champagne** (Cass Freeborn) Madison Square Roof Garden 25 June

1910 **Three Million Dollars** (Anatol Friedland/David Kempner) Atlantic City 25 July; Colonial Theater, Boston 1 August

1911 **Hello, Paris!** (J Rosmund Johnson/J Leubrie Hill) Folies Bergère 15 August

1911 **The Wife Hunters** (revised *Three Million Dollars*) (Friedland, Malvin Franklin/Kempner) Herald Square Theater 2 November

1912 **A Persian Garden** (Friedland) Colonial Theatre 26 February; revised version Wilmington, Del February 1914

1912 **The Prima Donnas' Honeymoon** (later *A Modern Prima Donna*) sketch

1912 **The Woman Who Wants** (Armand Kalisz) 1 scene Tivoli, London

1913 **The Song of the Heart** (Massenet ad Friedland) 1 act Maryland Theater, Baltimore 22 April

1913 **Mon désir** (Kalisz) sketch Norfolk, Va 8 September; Palace 20 October

1913 **The Singing Countess** sketch Maryland Theater, Baltimore 22 September

1913 **Peggy** 1 act Orpheum, Yonkers 25 September

1913 **A Daddy by Express** sketch Keith's Providence 13 October

1914 **Castle Romance** (various) sketch New Brighton Theater 17 July

1914? **Mon Amour** sketch

1916 **The Bride Tamer** (Percy Wenrich) 1 act Colonial Theater 12 June

1917 **The Bride of the Nile** (Friedland) Royal Theater 2 April

1917 **Houp-La** (Jerome Kern) Parsons Theater, Hartford 25 June

1918 **Toot-Toot!** (Kern/Berton Braley) Cohan Theater 11 March

1918 **Rock-a-Bye Baby** (Kern/Herbert Reynolds/w Margaret Mayo) Astor Theater 22 May

1918 **Head Over Heels** (Kern) Cohan Theater 29 August

1919 **What's the Odds?** (Albert von Tilzer/Neville Leeson) Academy of Music, Baltimore 11 September

1919 **Roly Boly Eyes** (Eddy Brown, Louis Grünberg) Knickerbocker Theater 25 September

1921 **Love Birds** (Sigmund Romberg/Ballard MacDonald) Apollo Theater 15 March

1925 **The Daughter of Rosie O'Grady** (Joseph Santley/Cliff Hess) Walnut Street Theater, Philadelphia 14 September

WOOLF, Walter [KING, Walter] (b San Francisco, 2 November 1895; d Beverly Hills, Calif, 24 October 1984). Operetta hero who largely abandoned the stage for the (singing and non-singing) screen.

After first playing in vaudeville, in revue, and in Gilbert and Sullivan in Chicago, Woolf made his Broadway debut in an edition of *The Passing Show* and took his first legit musical role in New York as Abercoed in the Shuberts' 1920 revival of *Florodora.* He subsequently played a series of strong-singing heroes in musically substantial shows, appearing as the star of Broadway's *The Last Waltz* (Jack Merrington), *The Lady in Ermine* (Belovar), *The Dream Girl* (Jack Warren), *Countess Mariza* (Tassilo), the sad *The Red Robe* (Gil de Beraud), the brief *The Duchess of Chicago* (1929) and the ill-fated American production of the London operetta *Dear Love* (1930) before visiting Hollywood for the first time to appear in the film version of Kálmán's *The Golden Dawn* (1930).

Thereafter he mixed film appearances with vaudeville and straight plays, but he renounced the role intend-

Plate 428. **Howett Worster** *was Gaylord Ravenal to the Magnolia Hawkes of Edith Day in London's first* Show Boat.

ed for him in the musical version of *The Prisoner of Zenda* and instead made his return to the singing stage in Romberg's next operetta, the unfortunate *Melody* (1933, George Richards). He subsequently appeared on the West Coast in *Music in the Air,* and in New York (now calling himself, at filmland's behest, Walter Woolf King) in *May Wine* (1935, Baron Kuno). It proved to be his last such appearance, for he then returned to Hollywood, where he appeared in the Marx Brothers' *A Night at the Opera* and *Go West,* as Sibirsky in *Balalaika* (1939) and in a number of other films, increasingly in later years, as a character actor in non-musical movies and television, and limited his stage appearances to the West Coast (Danilo to the *Merry Widow* of Jarmila Novotna, 1940, etc).

WORSTER, [Alexander] Howett (b London, 26 April 1882; d St Mary's, Isle of Scilly, 9 June 1952). Staunchly baritonic hero of 1920s operetta.

A 10-year-old boy soprano in the Westminster Abbey choir, Worster studied music in Belgium and began his musical theatre career as a baritone chorister in George Edwardes's *Les P'tites Michu* and *Les Merveilleuses.* He went on to play in the original *Merry Widow,* as cover to Joe Coyne, appeared as Danilo in South Africa, toured as Fredy in *The Dollar Princess,* then took time out from the theatre to try his hand at acting and directing for the Hepworth Film Company. He returned to singing two years later, joining Maurice Bandmann's company purveying musicals to the Orient.

When the First World War broke out, he spent a period serving in the Indian army's Rattray Sikhs, then, invalided out, worked in the army offices in Simla and Bombay before leaving India for Australia, where he took a post as a singing teacher at the Albert Street Conservatory. When he played Figaro in a student production, he was spotted by a representative of J C Williamson Ltd and, as a result, was cast as the Earl of Essex in the belated first production of *Merrie England* (1921) in Australia. He stayed down under for seven years altogether, playing in such pieces as *Dorothy* (Harry Sherwood), *The Naughty Princess* (Ladislas), the revue *Snap* (1925, producer/performer), *The Maid of the Mountains* (Baldasarre to the Maid of Gladys Moncrieff) and *The Lady of the Rose,* returning to England at the age of 44 to find himself shot quickly to the very forefront of fashionable musical theatre.

His first job was as the male star of London's *Wildflower* (Guido), and he followed up as the Red Shadow in an early revival of *The Desert Song,* as Gaylord Ravenal in London's original *Show Boat* and as the Robert Misson of *The New Moon* at the Theatre Royal, Drury Lane. He was quickly replaced in this last role by the younger and apparently slightly less stiff Harry Welchman, and he went back to the touring circuits as the Red Shadow, disappearing from the West End as suddenly and as wholly as he had come to it.

WRIGHT, Huntley (b London, 7 August 1869; d Penmaenmawr, Caernarfonshire, 10 July 1941). Star comic of the Daly's Theatre series of musicals.

Huntley Wright was the son of stock and touring actor-manager Frederick Wright (b 6 August 1826; d Hampstead, 17 November 1911), who liked to claim in the early part of the new century to be "the oldest living actor in active work." Over a long period of years, Wright senior traveled the roads of Britain with a bulging repertoire of dramas, though when fashion demanded he included such musical productions as *Nemesis* and *La Fille de Madame Angot* in his stock. He was also sometime lessee of the Dover Theatre, the Woolwich Theatre, Edinburgh's Southminster Theatre, the Theatre Royal, Stockton, the Gaiety, West Hartlepool and at one stage of a quarter of the East End's City of London Theatre.

He died, still in the saddle, while on tour as Dr Manette in *The Only Way.*

Huntley Wright worked alongside his father, his mother, [Emma] Jessie Francis (b London, 5 November 1844; d Golder's Green, 21 February 1919) and his brothers and sisters in their stock engagements and touring companies from babyhood, initially under the name of "Walter Huntley." He subsequently won provincial jobs as a comedian, and in 1891 was engaged as chief comedian at Newcastle. He made his first London appearance at the Princess's Theatre, as the cockney bird catcher Sorne in *Fate and Fortune* later the same year, and went on to play the leading part of Captain Bacon in his father's old extravaganza *Merrie Prince Hal, or A Prime Piece of Bacon* at Sadler's Wells (31 August 1891). He appeared in the low-comedy part of Dame Diccory in the trouping *Bonnie Boy Blue* (1893) and made his West End musical-comedy debut in a supporting role in *King Kodak* (1894, Hugh E Foote).

After a spell in the non-musical theatre, he next appeared as the comical waiter in *A Trip to Chinatown* and as a takeover from E M Robson as father Cripps in *An Artist's Model* before joining George Edwardes's company playing musical comedy in South Africa. On his return, he was again engaged at Daly's Theatre. There he created the decade-long series of roles that gave him a star reputation second to none amongst musical comedians of his era: Wun-Hi in *The Geisha* (1896, introducing "Chin Chin Chinaman"), the comical soothsayer Heliodorus in *A Greek Slave,* a second comic oriental, Li, in *San Toy,* Barry in *A Country Girl* ("Me and Mrs Brown"), Chambuddy Ram in *The Cingalee* and Bagnolet in *Les P'tites Michu* (1905).

Annoyed by the propinquity of the by then more successful Willie Edouin in this last piece, he then left Daly's to play in comedy but soon returned (somewhat chastened by less than ringing success) to the George Edwardes management to play yet another comic oriental, Hang-Kee in *See See* and, back at the scene of his great successes, the less than star part of St Amour in *Les Merveilleuses,* before crossing the Atlantic to star for Charles Frohman as Joe Mivens in Broadway's version of *The Dairymaids* (1907). He subsequently created the roles of the terrified King of Alasia in *King of Cadonia* (1908) and of Hans Hansen in *Dear Little Denmark* (1909) for Frank Curzon at the Prince of Wales Theatre, but returned again to Edwardes's management for other good (though no longer star-sized) comic roles in *The Girl in the Train* (Van Eyck), *The Count of Luxembourg* (Grand Duke Rutzinov) and *Autumn Manoeuvres* (Captain Withers) before taking a turn in the halls playing a musical playlet called *Simple 'Earted Bill.*

After the First World War, Wright returned to the West End to appear at the Gaiety in *The Kiss Call* (1919,

Plate 429. **Huntley Wright** *as soothsayer Heliodorus in the comedy of* A Greek Slave.

t/o Dr Thomas Pym) and at his old stamping ground, Daly's, in three comic leads more redolent of his parts of 20 years earlier—as the comical Poire in *Sybil,* Suitangi in *The Lady of the Rose* and Calicot to the *Madame Pompadour* of Evelyn Laye. Thereafter, he appeared more often in the straight theatre than the musical, but he reprised *The Lady of the Rose* and *Madame Pompadour,* played in the unfortunate romantic operetta *The White Camellia* (1928, Odino) and, in his early sixties, appeared as Gaspard in a revival of *Les Cloches de Corneville.* His last musical appearance in a career that had spanned several eras of the musical theatre, from burlesque to interwar musical comedy, came when he replaced Will Fyffe in *Give Us a Ring* (1933).

Wright's brothers **Fred[erick] WRIGHT** (b Dover, 8 March ?1871; d New York, 11 December 1928) and Herbert [Bertie] WRIGHT also appeared as comic actors in the musical theatre, and at one stage all three followed each other in the same role of Wun-Hi (*The Geisha*) at Daly's Theatre. Fred Wright (thanks to his father's longevity, for a good while billed as Fred Wright jr) had an outstanding international career. Having begun, like Huntley, as a child with his father's companies, he toured as principal comedian with *Frivolity* (1887), with Horace Lingard as Pedrillo in *Pepita,* Tancred in *Falka,* Polydore Poupart in *The Old Guard* and St Angénor in *La Fauvette du Temple,* played in stock at the Pavilion (1890), then traveled through Europe with the Fanny Wentworth *Carmen Up-to-Data* (Don José) and *Faust Up-to-Date* (Mephistopheles) company of 1892. He played the title role in the Liverpool musical *Pickles* (1893), Friday in the touring burlesque *Crusoe the Cruiser* (1894), appeared alongside Lillian Russell in London's edition of *The Queen of Brilliants* (1894, Max), in the flop *All My Eye-van-hoe* (1894, Seedie Wreck), at Daly's Theatre in *An Artist's Model* (t/o Cripps) and *The Geisha* (t/o Wun-Hi), in America as Cripps again (1896), in the central comic role of Bidart in the original American musical comedy *Lost, Strayed or Stolen* (Chicago, 1896), and then in major comic roles at the Gaiety in *A Runaway Girl* (1898, Sir William Hake), *The Messenger Boy* (1900, Captain Pott), *The Toreador* (1901, Pettifer) and *The Orchid* (1903, Zaccary). In between times he succeeded Sydney Paxton as Siroco in the Savoy's *The Lucky Star* (1899) and Courtice Pounds as Papillon in *The Duchess of Dantzic* (1904). He then set out on travels that no other musical comedian of the time equaled. He crossed to America to play in *The School Girl* (1904, General Marchmont) and *The Catch of the Season* (1906, Mr William Gibson), returned to London for a revival of *The Geisha* at Daly's (1906, Wun-Hi), a tour in variety, and *Nelly Neil* (1907, t/o Nordheim), then went to Paris to star as Archie in the French production of *The Prince of Pilsen* at the Olympia (1907). In spite of "almost incomprehensible French," he became the toast of the town ("he is in great demand at all social functions and almost necessary when there is anything connected with sport on hand"), and he followed up this first Paris experience with a considerable hit at the Moulin Rouge, performing a burlesque of an English policeman, and duetting with Mistinguette. After a brief return via London for the short-lived *The Antelope* (1908, Bennett Barker), he disappeared back to the Continent, this time to Germany and Berlin's Metropoltheater, where he starred with notable success in *Der oberen Zehntausend* and the local version of *Our Miss Gibbs.* He repeated his Timothy in *Our Miss Gibbs* in Vienna to the Mary of Mizzi Hajós, then in Budapest and finally in America (August 1910). He remained in America to play in *The Pink Lady* (1911, Benévol). The London season of that production took him home again, and he settled into variety and provincial musicals (Cadeau in *Erminie,* Polydore Poupart in *The Old Guard,* etc) for a few years before the war called him abroad again, this time in uniform. He was home by 1916, touring as Tonio in *The Maid of the Mountains,* a role he later repeated in the show's Canadian production. His last appearances in a West End musical were in the spectacle *Shanghai* (1921, Ah Sing) and in *Katinka* (1923, Knopf).

On top of all this activity, Fred Wright jr found the time to become an official Football Association referee, making his debut in 1906 with the cup tie Milwall-Portsmouth.

Bertie WRIGHT, who was "master carpenter and musical director" of the *Merrie Prince Hal* bills, succeeded Huntley both as Wun-Hi and as Li at Daly's Theatre, and starred as Miggles in the Broadway production of *The Shop Girl* (1895), but made the large part of his career in lead comic roles in touring musical comedy in England (Cadeau in *Erminie, The Orchid, Theodore & Co* 1916, etc) and in Australia (Timothy in *Our Miss Gibbs,* 1910, etc), and in such lesser pieces as *The Girl from Over the Border* (1908, Tubby Wiggles).

The Wrights were all married into other theatre familes. Huntley Wright himself was husband to Mary Fraser, sister to Savoy Theatre prima donna Agnes Fraser (herself wife to musical comedian Walter Passmore) and vocalist and actor Alec Fraser. His daughter, **Betty [Jessie] Huntley WRIGHT** (b London 3 December 1911; d London, 1999), also appeared in the musical theatre, being seen in *Bitter-Sweet, Clancarty* and *Six Pairs of Shoes* in London and in *Madame Pompadour* and the title role of *Sally Who?* on the road. Her daughter **Bridget McConnel** was seen in the West End production of *Charlie Girl.*

Fred Wright was first married to **Madge GREET** [Fanny May GREET], who was a member of the pas de quatre in the 1892 Continental new burlesque tour, played in musical comedy (Lucien in *An Artist's Model* on Broadway, t/o Juliette in *The Circus Girl,* Eva Sketchley in *Morocco Bound,* Milistra in *Florodora,* Alison in *My Lady Molly*) in Britain and appeared as Princess Schowenhöhe-Hohenschowen in the American production of *The Catch of the Season.* Her sister, Clare Greet, in a distinguished career as an actress, dipped into the musical theatre in early years (Lady Walkover in *Morocco Bound* tour, etc) and later created the roles of Lisette in *The Duchess of Dantzic* (1904) and Lady Heldon in *My Darling* (1907).

WRIGHT, Robert [Craig] (b Daytona Beach, 25 September 1914). *See* FORREST, GEORGE.

DIE WUNDER-BAR Spiel in Nachtleben in 2 parts by Géza Herczeg and Karl Farkas. Music by Robert Katscher. Wiener Kammerspiele, Vienna, 17 February 1930.

A novelty piece that mixed conventional theatre with the fashionable jazz cabaret of the time, Franz Wenzler's production of *Die Wunder-Bar* was mounted in an auditorium that was done up throughout to represent the cabaret bar of the title, the ''Wunder-Bar'' operated by Sam Wunder (Fritz Wiesenthal). The strong, dramatic and cleverly worked out story of the piece, in which the lead dancer of the club, Harry (Hans Unterkircher), gets himself involved in an unpleasant mess with some effectively stolen jewels and a touch of adultery (Friedl Haerlin), was shot through with opportunities for the various members of the cast to perform cabaret items. Vera Molnár as Harry's partner, star dancer Inez, Dolly the jazz singer played by none other than jazz singer Dolly, Trude Brionne as Elektra Pivonka ''the opening act,'' and the Sid Kay's Fellows as the bar's jazz band were listed on the program along with the casting ''Guests of the Wunder Bar . . . the public'' (those members of the company invited, in their quality as stars, to dance, are requested to resume their seats when finished). But established star Otto Storm, in the role of Louis von Ferring, a flushed out aristocrat out for a last night of entertainment at the bar before committing the suicide no one believes he will, stole much of the limelight. He also provided the clever denouement to the plot.

Die Wunder-Bar was a great success in its initial season at Vienna's Kammerspiele, moved on for five additional weeks to the Johann Strauss-Theater (23 January 1931), and was soon picked up for productions in Munich and in Budapest (ad Zsolt Harsányi), where, with Gyula Kabos (Wunder), Ferenc Delly (Harry), Teri Féjes (Inez) and Ilona Titkos (Erdy) featured, it was again a hit. Whilst the German production continued on to Berlin, London too welcomed the *Wonder Bar* (ad Rowland Leigh), to no less than the once august precincts of the Savoy Theatre. Joseph Greenwald directed the proceedings, Carl Brisson and Elsie Randolph were the dancers, Dorothy Dickson the ''other woman'' Liane, Norah Blaney, Gwen Farrar and Giovanni were ''cabaret turns,'' and Katscher's score was lightly infiltrated with additional numbers. The entertainment proved popular and ran through 210 performances.

Morris Gest had a new version made for his Broadway production (ad Irving Caesar, Aben Kandel), at least partly because the show, subtitled ''a continental novelty of European night life,'' was being used as a vehicle in which to bring Al Jolson back to Broadway, after five years in Hollywood, in the role of the chief of the now Parisian bar. But Jolson, here performing without his famous blackface, was old news, and Broadway theatregoers showed little interest in him or, in spite of Arthur Treacher's Lord Cauldwell (ex- von Ferring) and the dancing of Rex O'Malley and Trini, in the show. It folded in 76 performances.

Farkas and/or Herczeg wrote and Katscher composed several more shows on similarly cabaret-revusical lines, whilst in London a show called *Get a Load of This,* penned by James Hadley Chase as a vehicle for Austrian comic Vic Oliver and produced in the larger London Hippodrome in 1941 (19 November), based itself very closely on the *Wunder-Bar* format and plot and came out with a run of nearly 700 performances.

A film version of *Wonder Bar,* with Jolson featured, also followed the outlines of the original show. It went perhaps unintentionally funny when the cabaret scenes opened out into vast Busby Berkeley numbers, and unintentionally unfunny when everything stopped to allow Jolson to fling out a ration of joey-joey jokes. But when Ricardo Cortez (Harry), Dolores del Rio (Inez), Kay Francis (Liane) and Robert Barrat (Captain von Ferring) were on, the tale and the film moved on incisively. Dick Powell (Tommy) and Jolson—going blackface for a heavenly coon-cum-mule number—had the most of the six Harry Warren/Al Dubin songs which replaced Katscher's score.

Germany: Munich, Berlin; Hungary: Fővárosi Operettszínház Csodabár 15 September 1930; UK: Savoy Theater *Wonder Bar* 5 December 1930; USA: Nora Bayes Theater *Wonder Bar* 17 March 1931

Film: Warner Bros 1934

DER WUNDERKNABE Operette in 3 acts by Alexander Landesberg and Leo Stein. Music by Eugen von Taund. Theater an der Wien, Vienna, 28 March 1896.

The most widely played of von Taund's Operetten, *Der Wunderknabe* was written to a Stein and Landesberg libretto that was set in an original combination of locations: Edinburgh, Ostend and Aberdeen. Josef Joseffy played Patricio Gordoni, a showman about as Italian as his name, pushing a child prodigy violinist named Paolo (Annie Dirkens) through the houses of credulous Edinburgh society. Paolo is, of course, not a 15-year-old boy, but an 18-year-old girl, and, by the end of the evening, has been discovered to be the long-lost daughter of Graf Calmore, Lord von Aberdeen (Carl Lindau). The principal comic role was that of a musician called Tween, played by Alexander Girardi, a plagiaristic composer/pianist chasing after the daughter (Marie Ottmann) of a wealthy Scots mine owner (Wallner), whilst real romance was represented by Karl Streitmann as the young Graf Edward Calmore.

Der Wunderknabe was given 27 times en suite at the Theater an der Wien and brought back for further performances later in the year and early the next to total 36 performances in all. In the meanwhile, it had been played briefly in Berlin and in London, where Sir Augustus Harris produced an English version (ad Harris, Arthur Sturgess) that had to be postponed when its producer died shortly before opening night. Frln Dirkens came from Vienna to play the opening performances of a version that popped in some additional numbers by Landon Ronald and J M Glover, and which featured Arthur Williams (Patricio), Harrison Brockbank (Edward) and E J Lonnen (Tween) in the other leading roles. In one of the busiest and richest London seasons in history, the show found it hard to make an effect. It was revised and recast (Ells Dagnall replaced Williams, Dirkens went home and was replaced by Florence St John); some variety turns, including a quartet from the Moulin-Rouge headed by La Goulue, were popped into the Ostend Kursaal scene, new songs added, a ''second edition'' announced, a group of midgets featured between the acts, and in the end the run stretched to 117 performances.

In Budapest (ad Gyula Komor), without the midgets and La Goulue, the run was rather shorter.

Germany: Theater Unter den Linden 8 May 1897; UK: Shaftesbury Theatre *The Little Genius* 9 July 1896; Hungary: *A csodagyerek* 1896, Budai Színkör 22 May 1897

WYATT, Frank [GUNNING, Francis Nevill] (b Greenwich, 7 November 1852; d London, 5 October 1926). Musical comedian who created two of the best British comico-musical roles of his period.

Son of a Devonshire barrister, and for a number of years an artist and illustrator, Wyatt moved into the theatre in his twenties and made his earliest appearances in small parts in comedy with Charles Wyndham as ''Francis Wyatt.'' His varying musical appearances—Don Pedro in *La Périchole* and the Zola burlesque *Another Drink* (1879, Gouget) with Dolaro at the Folly, the inevitable *La Fille de Madame Angot* with Cornélie d'Anka at Holborn, the burlesques *La Sonnambula* (Notary) and *Don Juan Jr* (1880, Baba) at the Royalty, a Drury Lane pantomime (1880), at the Royalty again in the little operetta *Rosalie* (1881), a tour with the Hanlon-Lees in *Le Voyage en Suisse* in America (1881, Henri d'Escargot), the burlesques *Valentine and Orson* (1882, Hugo), *Ariel* (1883, Sebastian) and *Blue Beard* (1883, Mustafa) at the Gaiety—were interleaved with non-musical assignments. That mixture continued, when, following his first rather expensive musical engagement in a starring role, as Célestin to the *Nitouche* of American actress Lotta (he was also the management and lost £959 13s 6d in the affair), and opposite Lydia Thompson at the Crystal Palace, he went on to play Shakespeare with Irving at the Lyceum (Aguecheek), comedy with the Bancrofts at the Haymarket and comic opera with Alexander Henderson and others (silly-ass Captain Coqueluche in *The Grand Mogul,* Don José in *Manteaux Noirs*).

Then, in November 1885, Wyatt paired with Harry Paulton to create the suave thief to the author's low-comical one in the comic opera *Erminie* (Ravannes). The success he won in that part led to a list of major musical roles over the following years: Alphonso in Paulton's burlesque *Masse-en-Yell-oh* (1886), Alfred Pasha in *Our Diva* (*Joséphine vendue par ses soeurs*), Karl in *Mynheer Jan* (1887), Hippomenes in *Atalanta* (1888), Pedrillo in *Pepita* (1888), Don Trocadero in the Carl Rosa Light Opera's *Paul Jones* (1889), the Duke of Plaza-Toro in the original production of *The Gondoliers* (1889) and Baboo Currie in *The Nautch Girl* (1890) at the Savoy, Arrostino Annegato in *The Mountebanks* (1892) and Woodpecker Tapping in *Haste to the Wedding* (1892) for W S Gilbert, and Bouillon in *Ma mie Rosette* (1892).

The partner of his wife, *Erminie* producer Violet Melnotte, in the building of the Trafalgar Square Theater (later the Trafalgar and now the Duke of York's Theatre), Wyatt appeared there in *Dora, or Diplunacy, Nitouche* (1893, this time opposite May Yohé with his wife as Corinne) and in several of the unsuccessful new musicals produced there (Octopus Sharp in *The Taboo,* Count Acacia in *Baron Golosh*). He also played the title role in Robert Buchanan's *The Pied Piper* (1893), appeared at the Avenue in the little *The Mermaids* (1897, John Doricus) and made a last West End musical appearance in the unfortunate *The Gay Pretenders* (Earl of Oxford) in 1905.

WYLIE, Julian [METZENBERG, Julian Ulrich Samuelson] (b Southport, 1 August 1878; d London, 6 December 1934).

The son of a Prussian refugee tobacconist, Lancashire-born Samuelson began his working life as an accountant, before turning business manager, then theatrical agent, then director and producer. He began his managerial career by touring musical productions through provincial variety houses before moving on to mount first revues and then musical plays in London. Amongst the musicals that he produced or co-produced and directed were the early Weston and Lee piece *Mr Tickle MP* (tour, 1925), the musical version of *Turned Up* (w C B Cochran, J W Tate), the musical melodrama *The Yellow Mask* (w Laddie Cliff), the original pre-London *Mr Cinders* (which he then sold to J C Williamson Ltd for London), Arthur Schwartz's early musical, *Here Comes the Bride* (1929), the Binnie Hale vehicle *Nippy* (1930 w Moss' Empires), *Out of the Bottle* (1932) and the Eric Maschwitz spectacular *The Gay Hussar* (1933, for Moss's Empires and Howard & Wyndham). An indefatigable touring manager and producer of Christmas pantomime, Wylie's directorial style tended towards the latter genre in his love for scenic effects.

WYLIE, Lauri [METZENBERG, Morris Lawrence Samuelson] (b Southport, 25 May 1880; d Brighton, 28 June 1951).

The brother of Julian Wylie, Lauri Wylie worked as a musical-theatre player (Koran Champ in *Jacko* 1898), a music-hall entertainer with a marionette act (Lauri Wylie and his Mannakin) and pantomime comedian (Captain Lee Scupper in *Robinson Crusoe* Kingston 1901, Baron in *Cinderella,* Kingston 1908, etc) before turning to writing. His earliest writings were for the music-hall sketch stage, but he subsequently supplied a long list of revusical pieces and musical sketches to the provincial stage and, subsequently, the London theatre (*Bric à Brac, Vanity Fair, Peep Show, Brighter London, Dover Street to Dixie, Leap Year, Palladium Pleasures, Better Days,* etc). He also adapted a number of Continental musicals, the most successful of which was Albert Szirmai's *Alexandra,* the most unsuccessful a Swedish musical called *Serenade,* announced as the Scandinavian answer to *Oklahoma!,* but which never made it to London. Wylie's own most successful works, however, were the two musical plays that he wrote for (and apparently with) Lupino Lane, which were produced at the Victoria Palace in the aftermath of the triumph of *Me and My Girl.*

1915 **Kiss Me, Sergeant** (James W Tate/Clifford Harris/w Alfred Parker) 1 act Leicester Palace 2 August

1915 **The Lady Birds** (J M Glover/w Fred Thompson, Alfred Parker) 3 scenes Theatre Royal, Plymouth 9 August

1917 **Sugar** (Louis Jerome/George Arthurs/w Parker) 1 act Oxford Theatre 16 July

1918 **Shanghai** English adaptation (Theatre Royal, Drury Lane)

1919 **A Good-Looking Lass** (Herman Darewski/w Leon Pollack) 1 act Chelsea Palace 11 August

1926 **Hearts and Diamonds** (*Der Orlow*) English version w P G Wodehouse (Strand Theatre)

1926 **Princess Charming** (*Alexandra*) English version w Arthur Wimperis (Palace Theatre)

1927 **The Grass Widow** (Vivian Ellis/William Helmore) Empire Theatre, Bristol 8 August

1927 **The Other Girl** (Ellis/Helmore, Collie Knox) Empire Theatre, Bristol 17 October

1928 **Song of the Sea** (*Lady Hamilton*) English version w Wimperis (His Majesty's Theatre)

1929 **Dear Love** (Haydn Wood, Jack Waller, Joseph Tunbridge/w Herbert Clayton, Dion Titheradge) Palace Theatre 14 November

1931 **My Sister and I** (*Meine Schwester und ich*) English version (Shaftesbury Theatre)

1944 **Meet Me Victoria** (Noël Gay/Frank Eyton/w Lupino Lane) Victoria Palace 8 April

1946 **Sweetheart Mine** (Gay/Eyton/w Lane) Victoria Palace 1 August

1948 **Serenade** English version w Eric Maschwitz (tour)

WYNN, Ed [LEOPOLD, Isaiah Edwin] (b Philadelphia, 9 November 1886; d Beverly Hills, Calif, 19 June 1966).

"The Perfect Fool" of the vaudeville stage appeared in tabloid musical comedy in variety houses (*Me Busybody,* 1908, etc) and apparently turned down comedy roles in *The Algerian* (1908) and other musicals in favor of staying in variety before making his first Broadway appearance in a book musical in 1910 in *The Deacon and the Lady* (Jupiter P Slick). It lasted just two weeks. His next theatre appearances were in revues (*Ziegfeld Follies, The Passing Show,* etc), but, in 1918, now established as a comedy star name, he was brought in, during tryout, to play Loney Bright, a throughly incidental highlight of Rudolf Friml's *Sometime.* The piece almost certainly owed some of its subsequent success to his zany performance.

Wynn went on to pay on Broadway in several of his own made-to-measure entertainments (*Ed Wynn Carnival, The Perfect Fool, The Grab Bag,* etc), but ventured further book musicals in *Manhattan Mary* (1927), *Simple Simon* (1930) and *Hooray for What!* (1937) in between those presentations and between radio and, later, television successes. He also appeared in musical films, including the screen's *Manhattan Mary* (1930), and later, during his more celluloidly successful older character period, as the Toymaker in the 1961 version of *Babes in Toyland,* and as Uncle Albert ("I Love to Laugh") in *Mary Poppins* (1964).

Wynn also wrote and composed songs and other material for his own use, and co-wrote the libretto to his 1930 musical *Simple Simon.*

1930 **Simple Simon** (Richard Rodgers/Lorenz Hart/w Guy Bolton) Ziegfeld Theater 18 February

X

XANROF, Léon [FOURNEAU, Léon] (b Paris, 9 December 1867; d Paris, 17 May 1953).

A highly successful Parisian playwright, journalist (courrier des théâtres on *Gil Blas,* etc) and literary figure, Xanrof first came to the notice of his contemporaries during his days as a law student, as the author and performer of some songs "d'une ironie pincée, d'une gaîté un peu âpre [qui] chantaient, sur des modes sautillants, la vie des étudiants, leurs deboires, leurs faciles amours, leur existance insouciante" ("L'Hotel du No 3," "Les Quatre-z-étudiants," etc). He went on to become celebrated as a songwriter with pieces such as "Le Fiacre," "Encombrement" and "Les Trottins," numbering Yvette Guilbert amongst his regular interpreters. He began his career in the theatre writing material for revue (*Paris en bateau* for La Cigale, *Revue intime* 1889, *Paris Nouveautés* 1892, etc), and saynètes and short plays for cafés-concerts and minor theatres, before going on to make a name as the author of such plays as *A Perpète, La Marmotte* and *Pour être aimée,* and also of libretti.

Xanrof's first Parisian opérette, *Madame Putiphar,* won a good run in the French capital (64 performances) and a later production in Budapest (*Putifarné* ad Adolf Mérei, Magyar Színház 27 January 1905), but he had his most important theatrical success with the 1903 play *Le Prince-Consort* (w Jules Chancel, Théâtre de l'Athénée 25 November). After long runs in Paris, Berlin and London (*His Highness, My Husband*), and a production illustrated with songs and incidental music in Hungary (*A királynő férje* ad Jenő Heltai, mus: László Kun, Vígszínház 8 April 1904), the piece was fully musicalized, five years later, by its authors, in collaboration with Ivan Caryll, under the title *S.A.R.* (*Son Altesse Royal*). If the musical piece was less popular than the play, it nevertheless had a good Parisian run and was produced in Germany as *Die kleine Königin.* Xanrof subsequently wrote several other musical scripts, the most enduring of which was his French version of the libretto for *Ein Walzertraum*—the main plot line of which was the same as that of *Le Prince Consort*—but late in life he collected perhaps his best music-based royalties from the song "Le Fiacre," after it was popularized internationally by Jean Sablon, who performed it in the New York revue *The Streets of Paris* (1939).

Plate 430. **Léon Xanrof.** *Proof that the letter X can exist in an encyclopedia.*

His play *L'Amorçage* (w Gaston Guérin) was used as the basis for George Edwardes's London musical *Peggy* (Leslie Stuart/C H Bovill/George Grossmith jr,

Gaiety Theatre 4 March 1911), the text of *Madame Putiphar* was borrowed to become that of the highly successful zarzuela *La corte de Faraon* (1910, Vicente Lleo), whilst another of his works, unspecified, served as the source for the German musical *Die Lieben Ottos* (Jean Gilbert/Alfred Schönfeld/Jean Kren, Thalia-Theater 30 April 1910).

1892 **Cavalcada-Rastaquoera** (Nazy/w Malpertuis) Brussels April

1894 **Le Petit Chasseur alpin** (Pierre Brus) Villers-Cotterets 24 June

1897 **Madame Putiphar** (Edmond Diet/w Ernest Depré) Théâtre de l'Athénée-Comique 27 February

1898 **Feuilles à l'envers** (w Léon Garnier, Fabrice Lemon) 1 act Eldorado 13 October

1906 **La Plus Belle** (aka *Die schöne Vestalin*) (Viktor Holländer/w Pierre Veber) 1 act Casino de Paris 29 October

1908 **S.A.R.** (Ivan Caryll/w Jules Chancel) Théâtre des Bouffes-Parisiens 11 November

1909 **Mam'zelle Gogo** (Émile Pessard/w Maxime Boucheron) Théâtre Molière, Brussels 27 February

1910 **Rêve de valse** (*Ein Walzertraum*) French version w Chancel (Théâtre Apollo)

1910 **Lysis rata** (w H Sère, Ondet) Théâtre des Variétés, Brussels 1 May; Casino de Paris 6 April 1911

1911 **Les Petites Étoiles** (Henri Hirschmann/w Pierre Veber) Théâtre Apollo 23 December

1926 **Souris blonde** (François de Breteuil/w Alain Monjardin) Théâtre des Folies-Dramatiques May

Y

THE YANKEE CONSUL Comic opera in 2 acts by Henry M Blossom jr. Music by Alfred G Robyn. Tremont Theater, Boston, 21 September 1903; Broadway Theater, New York, 22 February 1904.

A vehicle for rising young comedian Raymond Hitchcock, the star of *King Dodo* of two seasons back, *The Yankee Consul*—allegedly inspired by an AP dispatch about revolutionary doings in San Domingo, but with decided flavorings of London's *The Toreador* of the same two years back—presented him as a US diplomat, Abijah Booze (the name said it all), based in the Ruramerican outpost of Puerta Plata. On his way to winning himself the hand of the local wealthy widow, Donna Teresa (Eva Davenport), ''Bi'' (as he is dubiously called) gets himself entangled with an incipient revolution and a lot of throwing into and out of the dungeons. While all this is going on, the evening's ingenue, Teresa's daughter, Bonita (Flora Zabelle), is sweetly persuading the leader of the rebellion to postpone his attack so as not to spoil the governor's ball she has been so looking forward to. Her reward is Lieutenant Commander Jack Morrell of the US gunboat *Vixen* (Harry Fairleigh), who arrives—as the British one had done a couple of seasons back in *A Chinese Honeymoon*—in time to turn that postponement into a cancellation. Jacques Kruger played the befuddled Governor, Rose Botti featured as soubrette, and a good time was had by all.

Hitchcock sang in praise of ''In Old New York'' and ''In Days of Old,'' and queried ''Ain't It Funny What Difference Just a Few Hours Make?'' (with just a few topicalities), and joined with Miss Botti to sing a smart duo about gossip (''The Hammers Will Go Rap, Rap, Rap''). Bonita had an ''Hola!'' entrance number and a piece about a ''San Domingo Maid,'' Jack got into the first act (the tenor couldn't really wait until the denouement to appear!) to sing soupily that ''Cupid Has Found My Heart'' (''a rapture o'er me stealing'') and the male chorus, led by Captain Leopoldo of the Dominican Army (German comic opera baritone Hubert Wilke, no less, giving the evening its vocal values) snarled ''We Come of Castilian Blood.'' A ''San Domingo Dance'' ensemble and military duo for Wilke and Miss Botti were other highlights.

Blossom's book, Hitchcock's comic style and George Marion's direction got some upmarket praise for using ''no horseplay, no local jibes, Rialtoisms or Tenderloin slang,'' and the recipe pleased the general public too. Henry Savage's production of *The Yankee Consul* played a highly successful set Boston season (four weeks) before going on the road. It took in 115 performances on Broadway early the following year, then continued its touring (with a return to Wallack's Theater 24 January 1905 for a further 47 metropolitan performances for a second season) through the three succeeding years.

The ''Yankee'' tag was picked up again by Hitchcock, Robyn and Mrs Hitchcock (Flora Zabelle) when they christened their next piece, a version of Richard Harding Davis's *The Galloper, The Yankee Tourist.* It too did well (103 performances on Broadway and much touring), as did two other Yankees in the next few seasons: *The Yankee Prince* (George M Cohan) and *The Yankee Girl* (Blanche Ring).

A film suggested by *The Yankee Consul* was made in 1924, directed by James W Horne and starring Douglas Maclean and Patsy Ruth Miller.

YARDLEY, William (b Bombay, 10 June 1849; d Kingston-on-Thames, 26 October 1900).

A cousin of George Sims, and a journalist on the *Sporting Times,* where he wrote dramatic criticism under the nom de plume of ''Bill of the Play,'' Yardley was also an occasional writer for the theatre, a sometime amateur performer (under the pseudonyms ''William Courtleigh'' and ''William Wye''), on one occasion—for a revival of his ''inseparable chum'' ''Pot'' Stephens's *Billee Taylor* (Crystal Palace, then Toole's)—a producer, and briefly a theatre proprietor at the Garrick Theatre, Whitechapel. Not to mention a much admired cricketer and an irresponsible and high-night-living bohemian whose appearance in the bankrupcty courts in 1897 was innocently attributed by him to "his expenses having exceeded his income." His principal contribution to the musical stage came when he collaborated with Stephens on the texts for the two burlesques, *The Vicar of Wide-awake-field* and *Little Jack Sheppard,* which were instrumental in beginning the fashion for "new burlesque" that flourished in the hands of George Edwardes, Nellie Farren and Fred Leslie in the late 1880s at the Gaiety Theatre.

1876 **Our Doll's House** (Cotsford Dick) 1 act St George's Hall 26 December

1879 **A Cruise to China** (*Le Voyage en Chine*) English version (Garrick Theatre)

1881 **Herne the Hunted** (pasticcio/w Robert Reece) Gaiety Theatre 24 May

1884 **The Scalded Back, or Comin' Scars** (pasticcio) Novelty Theatre 12 July

1884 **Very Little Hamlet** (pasticcio) Gaiety Theatre 29 November

1885 **Hobbies** (George Gear/w H Pottinger Stephens) 1 act St George's Hall 6 April

1885 **The Vicar of Wide-awake-field, or the Miss-Terryous Uncle** (Florian Pascal/w Stephens) Gaiety Theatre 8 August

1885 **Little Jack Sheppard** (Meyer Lutz, et al/w Stephens) Gaiety Theatre 26 December

1890 **Venus** new version of burlesque by Edward Rose and Augustus Harris (Prince of Wales Theatre, Liverpool)

1891 **Robinson Crusoe Esq** (Edward Solomon) Theatre Royal, Chelsea Barracks 11 April

1892 **The Wedding Eve** (*La Veillée de noces*) English version (Trafalgar Theatre)

1895 **A Model Trilby, or A Day or Two After Du Maurier** (Lutz/w C H E Brookfield) 1 act Opera Comique 16 November

1896 **On the March** (Edward Solomon, Frederic Clay, John Crook/w B C Stephenson, Cecil Clay) Theatre Royal, Sheffield 18 May; Prince of Wales Theatre 22 June

1899 **L'Amour mouillée** (*Cupid and the Princess*) English version w Henry Byatt (Lyric Theatre)

YEAMANS, Annie [née GRIFFITHS] (b Isle of Man, 18 November 1835; d New York, 4 March 1912).

Born into a family of entertainers, Mrs Yeamans began her adult performing life working as a bareback rider in a circus in Australia and on the Pacific circuits ("Madam Yeamans and Mr J L Smith as Diana and Endymion on two horses;" "Madam Yeamans in her wreath and scarf act" "Madame Yeamans in her Danse of all Nations"), a calling she followed until the death of her clown husband, Edward Yeamans, in San Francisco in 1868. She moved into the theatre in New York soon after, and appeared in a variety of entertainments (*Humpty Dumpty, Richelieu of the Period* and *Jack Sheppard* with G L Fox, the musical farce *Roughing It, Under the Gaslight* for Daly, the inevitable *Uncle Tom's Cabin,* etc) until, in 1877, she joined Edward Harrigan's company to play a supporting role in *Old Lavender.* When, the following year, in *The Mulligan Guards' Ball,* Harrigan's Dan Mulligan acquired a wife, little, exuberantly funny Mrs Yeamans became the striving, social-climbing Cordelia Mulligan. Equipped with a red wig and an Irish brogue, she portrayed that lady through the next five years of Mulligan shows, winning a huge personal popularity in the process. In 1883, in one of the most successful of the series, she even made it to the title line of *Cordelia's Aspirations.* When the Mulligan shows were superseded by other Harrigan plays, Mrs Yeamans stayed on, as Harrigan's leading lady and foil, starring in nearly all his musicals until the last, in 1903 (Nancy Delaney to Harrigan's Owen Gillaney in *Under Cover*).

She was also seen in character roles in the musical comedies *The Good Mr Best* (1897, Marion Agnes McAleer), *A Chinese Honeymoon* (1902, Mrs Brown), *The Maid and the Mummy* (1904, Auroria Dubbins), *The Hurdy Gurdy Girl* (1907, Mrs Sarah Otis, the sausage king's wife), *His Honor the Mayor, Li'l Mose* (1908, Mrs Bullfrog Hennessy), *The Candy Shop* (1909, Mrs Montrose Quilligan), and for the last time, at the (probable) age of 74, in *The Echo* (1910).

In 1985 she was portrayed on the Broadway stage (as Mrs Yeamons) by Armelia McQueen in the biomusical *Harrigan and Hart* (Longacre Theater 31 January).

Her daughter **Jennie YEAMANS** [Eugenia Marguerite YEAMANS, b Sydney, Australia, 16 October 1862; d New York, 24 November 1906] followed her mother on to the stage (François in *Richelieu of the Period,* 1871, etc) where she became a favorite player in, most especially, farce comedy (Sally Smiles in *The Electric Spark* 1882–83, Venus Grout in *A Rag Baby* 1884, Miss Innocent Kidd in *A Parlor Match* 1885, Jack in *12 PM* 1892, Adelaide Starr in *The Night Clerk* 1895, etc). She also became, for three years, the wife of producer Charles Dillingham. A second daughter, Lydia, better known as **Lydia YEAMANS-TITUS** (b Camperdown, NSW, Australia, 1857), also had a prominent career as a performer in farce comedy (*On the Road, The New City Directory,* Vestalia in *A Society Fad,* etc) and vaudeville in America, and also played in Britain, where she appeared in burlesque at the Avenue Theatre (Gaff in *Robinson Crusoe*) and on the music halls. The third daughter, **Emily E YEAMANS** (b Newtown, NSW, Australia, 1860; d New York, 29 February 1892), was a minor member of the Harrigan company, alongside her mother.

THE YELLOW MASK Musical comedy drama in 2 acts by Edgar Wallace. Lyrics by Desmond Carter. Music by Vernon Duke. Additional numbers by Harry Acres. Additional lyrics by Eric Little. Carlton Theatre, London, 8 February 1928.

In the midst of the 1920s fashion for dancing-and-comedy musicals, the rising producer Laddie Cliff joined with pantomime- and spectacle-specialist Julian Wylie to mount an unusual "musical comedy drama." Thriller author Edgar Wallace provided the melodramatic tale of a diamond stolen from the crown jewels of Britain by a horrid Chinaman (Malcolm Keen) and the efforts of English John (Wilfred Temple) and Mary (Phyllis Dare) to avoid the yellow perils (Chinaman-specialist Frank Cochrane) and regain the stone. Top-billed Bobby Howes featured as a comical detective.

The songs with which they were provided, however, were the same waltzes, fox-trots, and danced choruses to be found wedded to more suitable subjects in most of the rest of the shows in town, so that one officer of the crown was heard to sing about "Blowing the Blues Away" whilst hero and heroine took time off to fox-trot through "Half a Kiss" between drama in the Tower of London and Chinese tortures. The mixture of "melodrama garnished with the froth and fribble of musical comedy," and most particularly the expanding comicalities of the young Howes, found themselves an audience, but had more difficulties with a theatre. After seven weeks the piece was booted out of the Carlton, which switched terminally to movies, and having found a new home down the street at His Majesty's, was forced out of there three months later. It transferred to the (then) unlikely precincts of variety's London Palladium, and there ran out the last days of its 218-performance London run before going on the road.

A film version of the piece, made in 1930, used Temple and Cochrane in their stage roles and Lupino Lane in Howes's role. It did not use the already forgotten music.

THE YEOMEN OF THE GUARD, or The Merryman and His Maid Opera in 2 acts by W S Gilbert. Music by Arthur Sullivan. Savoy Theatre, London, 3 October 1888.

In spite of the semi-setback of the melodrama burlesque of *Ruddigore,* Gilbert and Sullivan turned back once again to older theatrical forms for the subject matter of their new musical. This time, it was the romantic English opera of the earlier part of the century that provided the librettist with his starting point, but, perhaps surprisingly, not for a burlesque of its conventions. Gilbert took the thread of the *Don César de Bazan* tale, which had been used as the basis for, amongst other, Vincent Wallace's hugely successful *Maritana* and remade it into a libretto that was much more in a conventional light-opera vein than in the very individual opéra-bouffe style that he had developed in his earlier pieces.

Lieutenant Fairfax (Courtice Pounds) has been condemned for witchcraft on the false witness of a relative who seeks to inherit his property. To balk that inheritance, Fairfax persuades the Governor of the Tower of London (Wallace Brownlow) to find him a bride. She will be married a few hours, then become a wealthy widow. Sir Richard agrees, and he chooses Elsie Maynard (Geraldine Ulmar), a strolling player whose partner, Jack Point (George Grossmith), agrees nervously to the exercise for the sake of the money. But after the wedding the Yeomen Sergeant Meryll (Richard Temple) and his daughter, Phoebe (Jessie Bond), help Fairfax escape. He remains in the Tower, however, disguised as Meryll's son, Leonard, whilst waiting for the expected pardon to come, and in his disguise he woos and wins Elsie, who believes the false reports put out by Point and the culpable jailor Wilfred Shadbolt (W H Denny) that her husband was shot while escaping. When she is told that he is, in fact, alive and coming to claim his bride, she collapses, only to find that her lover and her husband are one and the same. And it is poor, silly, greedy Jack Point who, like *Patience*'s Bunthorne, is left alone at the final curtain.

In fact, the difference between Point's and Bunthorne's fate epitomized the difference between *The Yeomen of the Guard* and the earlier Gilbert libretti. In Point, the official comic role of the show, Gilbert wrote a character that was wholly unburlesque. Point had feelings, and whilst Bunthorne's wifeless end was humorous and ridiculous, Point's end was sentimental and even touching. So much so, indeed, that an overenthusiastic touring Jack Point, George Thorne, decided that it would be correct to play the jester's final curtain collapse not as a despairing faint but as nothing less than a broken-hearted death. Elsie, too, a conventional light-opera leading lady, was very different from the tongue-in-cheek star soubrettes of *Patience* or *The Mikado,* and what bitter witticisms there were in the script turned up largely in Point's repertoire of jestering jokes.

Sullivan wrote a score in the English opera style to match the tone Gilbert had taken. It exchanged the burlesque humor of the earlier shows for a straightforward light-opera lyricism, and the soprano and tenor were the chief beneficiaries. Fairfax was equipped with two of the loveliest straight tenor melodies Sullivan ever wrote as he mused "Is Life a Boon?" and wondered on his reckless marriage in "Free from His Fetters Grim," whilst Elsie's tuneful soprano showpiece, "Tis Done, I Am a Bride" urged on into a driving chorus of operatic proportions. Not, as with the dilemma aria of *Pinafore*'s Josephine, a burlesque one, but a for-real one. Elsie also joined with Point in one of the popular highlights of the show, their "act" of *The Merryman and the Maid,* played before the public in the utterly artless "I Have a Song to Sing, O!" Jessie Bond's soubrette number, "Were I Thy

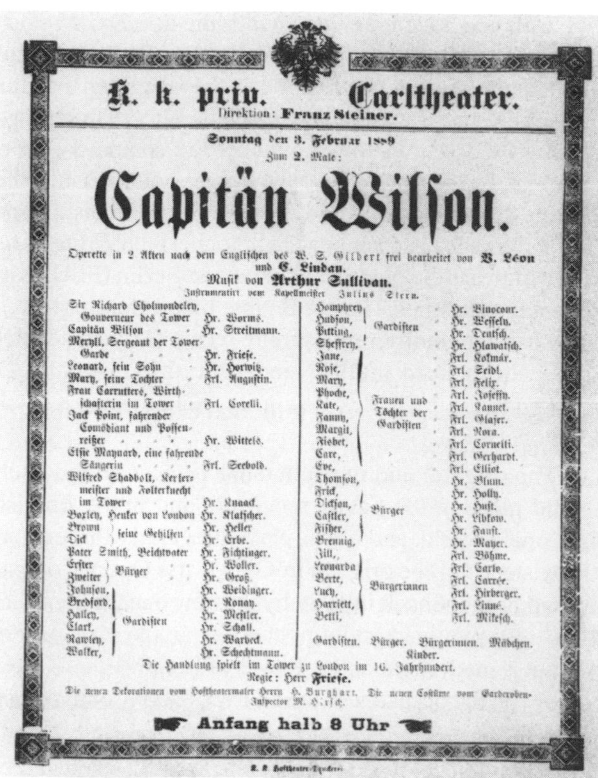

K. k. priv. Carltheater.
Direktion: **Franz Steiner.**

Sonntag den 3. Februar 1889
Zum 2. Male:

Capitän Wilson.

Operette in 2 Akten nach dem Englischen des W. S. Gilbert frei bearbeitet von **V. Léon** und **C. Lindau.**
Musik von **Arthur Sullivan.**
Instrumentirt vom Kapellmeister Julius Stern.

Sir Richard Cholmondeley, Gouverneur des Tower — Hr. Worms.
Capitän Wilson — Hr. Streitmann.
Meryll, Sergeant der Tower-Garde — Hr. Friese.
Leonard, sein Sohn — Hr. Horwitz.
Mary, seine Tochter — Frl. Augustin.
Frau Carrutters, Wirthschafterin im Tower — Frl. Corelli.
Jack Point, fahrender Comödiant und Possenreißer — Hr. Wittels.
Elsie Maynard, eine fahrende Sängerin — Frl. Seebold.
Wilfred Shadbolt, Kerkermeister und Folterknecht im Tower — Hr. Knaack.
Boxley, Henker von London — Hr. Klatscher.
Brown, Dick — seine Gehilfen — Hr. Heller, Hr. Erbe.
Pater Smith, Beichtvater — Hr. Fichtinger.
Erster, Zweiter — Bürger — Hr. Woller, Hr. Groß.
Johnson, Bredford, Halley, Clark, Rawley, Walker, Homphrey, Hudson, Pitting, Sheffrey — Gardisten — Hr. Weidinger, Hr. Ronay, Hr. Meßtler, Hr. Schall, Hr. Warbeck, Hr. Schechtmann, Hr. Vinocour, Hr. Wesselu, Hr. Deutsch, Hr. Hlawatsch.
Jane, Rose, Mary, Phoebe, Kate, Fanny, Margit, Fiebet, Care, Eve — Frauen und Töchter der Gardisten — Frl. Lokmár, Frl. Seidl, Frl. Felix, Frl. Josefin, Frl. Nannet, Frl. Glaser, Frl. Nora, Frl. Cornelli, Frl. Gerhardt, Frl. Elliot.
Thomson, Frick, Dickson, Castler, Fisher, Brennig — Bürger — Hr. Blum, Hr. Holly, Hr. Huft, Hr. Libkow, Hr. Faust, Hr. Mayer.
Jill, Leonarda, Berte, Lucy, Harriett, Betti — Bürgerinnen — Frl. Böhme, Frl. Carlo, Frl. Carrée, Frl. Hirberger, Frl. Linné, Frl. Mikesch.

Gardisten. Bürger. Bürgerinnen. Mädchen. Kinder.

Die Handlung spielt im Tower zu London im 16. Jahrhundert.
Regie: Herr **Friese.**
Die neuen Dekorationen vom Hoftheatermaler Herrn H. Burghart. Die neuen Costüme vom Garderoben-Inspector M. Hirsch.

Anfang halb 8 Uhr

K. K. Hoftheater-Druckerei

Plate 431. **The Yeomen of the Guard** *underwent some changes between the Savoy Theatre and its Austrian staging as* Capitän Wilson.

Bride,'' and Rosina Brandram's heavy dame legend of the Tower (''When Our Gallant Norman Foes'') were in the same vein, whilst the comic pieces—Jack's disquisition on the arts of jesting, his duo with Wilfred inventing the details of the phony death of Fairfax with rather less comical extravagance than the authors had shown in the same situation in *The Mikado*—though predictably excellent, took second place to the romantic tale and its music.

It was thus not surprising that Sullivan won all the praise for *The Yeomen of the Guard* and Gilbert, who had dared to go outside his usual style into something less wittily showy, was less critically appreciated. The public, however, had no doubts, and *The Yeomen of the Guard* was a grand success at the Savoy through 423 performances before going out into the provinces and overseas. On Broadway, too, where local soprano Bertha Ricci played Elsie alongside Englishmen J H Ryley (Point) and Fred Solomon (Shadbolt) and Australian Henry Hallam (Fairfax), there were also initial queries, but New York audiences proved in 100 performances that they were unnecessary ones.

J C Williamson of Australia had *The Yeomen of the Guard* on the stage just six months after its London premiere. Jack Leumane (Fairfax), Nellie Stewart (Elsie), Ida Osborne (Phoebe), Wiliam Elton (Point) and G Walter Marnock (Meryll) headed the cast, and the piece quickly installed itself amidst the Gilbert and Sullivan favorites. In later Australian revivals, Pounds and his fellow Savoyard Charles Kenningham were both seen as Fairfax, and Clara, Henry and Sydney Bracy all took turns in the cast.

On the Continent, however, where *The Mikado* had been a big success, the queries over the nature of *The Yeomen of the Guard* were given a preproduction answer. To Sullivan's fury, the score of *Capitän Wilson* (ad Victor Léon, Carl Lindau) was topped up with a half-dozen pieces from *Patience, Iolanthe, The Mikado* and . . . *Madame Favart*! When he complained, the botching practiced on Viennese Operetten in London was meaningfully pointed out to him. Franz Steiner's production of *Capitän Wilson,* with Karl Streitmann starred as the Captain, Marie Seebold as Elsie, Wilhelm Knaack as Shadbolt, Carl Adolf Friese as Meryll and Herr Wittels as Point, played just over two weeks (2–19 February) and said adieu to Vienna with a matinée the following 10 March. It turned up the following year in Prague (23 November 1890), by which time another version had found its way to Budapest (ad Lajos Evva, ''Imre Ukki'') for seven performances at the Népszínház. Berlin ignored *Capitän Wilson* and mounted a marginally less eccentric version by F Zell and Richard Genée under the title *Der Königsgardist*. The plural "yeomen" had given place to a singular, presumably intended to mean the disguised Fairfax . . . except there was no Fairfax left. The adaptors had switched the setting to "Königstein in Saxon Switzerland" and the period to "the reign of Augustus the Strong," and Fairfax was now one Count Wolski. The production sent its manager Scherenberg bankrupt. The following year the piece was revived in Berlin (Friedrich-Wilhelmstädtisches Theater 8 November), but its reception was again indifferent. A more recent German adaptation was produced in 1972 under the title *Die Gaukler von London* (ad Charles Lewinsky, Stadttheater Kassell 8 October).

The original and unadulterated *Yeomen* found itself a solid place in the Savoy repertoire and in the English light opera world, and it was played regularly throughout the existence of the original D'Oyly Carte Opera Company, and brought back in 1989 by the new one. In between, it was also mounted on four occasions in the (dry, except when it rained) moat at the Tower of London itself, most notably on the occasion of the edifice's 900th anniversary in 1978.

A tiny piece of the first act finale of *The Yeomen of the Guard* was put on film by Cinematophone Singing Pictures in 1907, and the show was later televised both in America (10 April 1957), with a cast headed by Alfred Drake, Barbara Cook and Celeste Holm, and in Britain, where the Tower of London production, with Tommy Steele as Jack Point and Della Jones as Phoebe, was recorded by ITV. *The Yeomen of the Guard* included in the 1982 Brent-Walker series featured Joel Grey as its Jack and Alfred Marks as Wilfred in an otherwise operatic cast.

USA: Casino Theater 17 October 1888; Austria: Carltheater *Capitän Wilson* 2 February 1889; Australia: Princess Theatre, Melbourne 20 April 1889; Hungary: Népszínház *A gárdista* 26 April 1889; Germany: Krolls Theater *Der Königsgardist* 25 December 1889

Recordings: complete (Decca, HMV), etc

Videos: ITV 1970, Brent-Walker 1982

YES Comédie musicale in 3 acts by René Pujol and Pierre Soulaine adapted from *Totte et sa chance* by Soulaine. Additional lyrics by Paul Géraldy. Music by Maurice Yvain. Théâtre des Capucines, Paris, 26 January 1928.

Maxime (Louvigny), son of Gavard (Constant-Rémy), the *roi de vermicelle,* is horrified when his father arranges a useful marriage for him with the Chilean Marquita Negri (Lily Mounet), a little thing who apparently squashed a cobra in her bare hands at the age of five. Convinced that he is to be sacrificed to a vast negress, Maxime can think of only one way out of the marriage. He hurries to London with the little manicurist Totte (Renée Devillers) and for 50 francs gets her to say a quick "yes," which can be undone for another 50 francs when Marquita is safely wed elsewhere. There are many quiproquos to be gone through between Touquet and Paris as father tries to get the marriage undone, but at the final curtain Maxime saves his second 50 francs, for Totte, it eventuates, is about to make him a father. Roger Tréville played a confident dreamboat singer named Roger, whilst alongside the main action Arletty appeared as a kooky maidservant with a hatred for work, and George played a valet who dreams of nothing but standing for political office (he gets a feeble 341 votes when he does).

Yvain's score was in the best modern dance tradition of the times. Totte fox-trotted through the belief that "La vie n'est faite que d'illusions" and went through all the different things that can be meant by the little word "yes" both before and after the one said before the clergyman; Marquita attacked "Je suis de Valparaiso" with Latin vigor, Roger crooned out two pieces written as popular songs, Clémentine the maid asserted "Moi, je cherche un emploi" with assorted conditions attached, and the deflated César, who had put forth his "Profession de Foi" so eagerly in Act I, said goodbye to his 341 voters in a comical Valse d'Adieu in the final act, alongside a selection of rhythmic and highly effective ensembles.

Mounted by Armand Berthez at the tiny Théâtre des Capucines with a cast of 16 actors and a two-piano accompaniment, which was given a featured spot in an apropos-of-nothing song for Roger describing what "Deux pianos" can do, *Yes* proved the hit of its season in a Paris which at that moment in time found much more entertainment in the intimate theatre and its sprightly humor and music than in lavish spectacle.

Like most pieces of its era, *Yes* was denied too much overseas travel by the sexuality of its lyrics and its tale, but Hungary—which alone seemed to share the French ease about such things—had a production (ad Adorján Stella, Imre Harmath) on the stage whilst Paris's *Yes* still ran. Later, during the Second World War, a film version was made, with Suzy Delair and Paul Meurisse starred, under the title *Défense d'aimer.*

Hungary: Magyar Színház 18 May 1928

Film: *Défense d'aimer*

YES, MADAM? Musical comedy in 2 acts by R P Weston, Bert Lee and K R G Browne, based on the novel by Browne. Lyrics by Weston and Lee. Music by Jack Waller and Joseph Tunbridge. London Hippodrome, 27 September 1934.

Browne's novel, already used as the basis of a 1933 British Lion film, proved ideal material as the starting point for a musical comedy vehicle for comedian Bobby Howes, the enormously successful star of a series of musical farces since his singular hit in *Mr Cinders. Yes, Madam?* brought him back together with his co-star of that show, Binnie Hale, as cute little Bill and sweet little Sally, obliged by the conditions of an *Oncle Célestin*–type musical comedy will to go into service for two months before they can inherit. There is, as in all such tales, a nasty cousin, Tony (Billy Leonard), who stands to benefit if he can make them throw it in before the time is up. Yorkshire button manufacturer Peabody (Wylie Watson) and his dragonistic sister (Bertha Belmore) employ the pair, who get themselves into all sorts of scrapes in their disguises. In the principal adventure, Bill is sent by Peabody to retrieve some incriminating love letters from the bosomy Pansy Beresford (Vera Pearce) at great risk to virtue and limb, but Pansy ends up entwined with the terrible Tony as Bill and Sally come through safely to richness and happiness.

Waller and Tunbridge supplied some happy songs to illustrate the tale. Bill and Sally sang sweetly of ''Sitting Beside o' You'' and chirruped ''What Are You Going to Do?,'' Miss Pearce yodeled out her preference for ''Czechoslovakian Love'' and a memorably lusty ''[I'm] The Girl the Soldiers Always Leave Behind,'' and Watson and Howes, locked out when returning from a secret spree, made ghastly noises to a version of Rossini's ''Cat's Duet'' as a signal to Sally to open the door to them. This touch of culture—a recurring item in the Waller shows—was compounded by a ''Shakespearean sextet'' of dubious authenticity.

Yes, Madam? was a full-scale hit. The fine and favorite cast were all fitted with material that suited them splendidly, and Waller's production played at the Hippodrome for 302 performances before going out on the road for two seasons of touring and then into the film studios, where Howes, Watson, Miss Belmore and Miss Pearce repeated their stage roles with Diana Churchill as Sally. Miss Pearce, however, did not return to her home country when *Yes, Madam?* was given its Australian production. Her role was taken by Ethel Morrison, whilst Charles Heslop and Nellie Barnes played Bobby and Binnie, Marie La Varre the heavy lady, and Leo Franklyn, Cecil Kellaway, Robert Coote (who would, two decades later, be *My Fair Lady*'s Pickering) and Lois Green completed the leading players. The show played a satisfactory seven weeks in Sydney and two months in Melbourne.

Australia: Theatre Royal, Sydney 29 August 1936
Film: 1938

YESTON, Maury (b Jersey City, NJ, 23 October 1945). Composer for two Tony-winning musicals.

A member of the staff at Yale University, Yeston had his music heard off-Broadway for the first time when he supplied the incidental music to the play *Cloud Nine* (1981) and on Broadway when he turned out the often adventurous score to the musicalized version of the film *8 1/2,* known as *Nine.* His music won him his first Tony Award, and the show itself won both a fine run and a coterie following. He subsequently provided additional music and lyrics for Wright and Forrest's revamped *Grand Hotel* (Martin Beck Theater, New York 12 November 1989) and rejoined *Nine* librettist Arthur Kopit in the writing of a copycat *Phantom of the Opéra* musical for Texas's Theater Under the Stars. In 1997 he returned to Broadway with the score for another bandwagon-jumping exercise, a musical written around the sinking of the liner *Titanic* (Tony Award).

He is also credited with an *Alice in Wonderland* musical produced at the Long Wharf Theater, New Haven, in 1970, and a Japanese musical *Nukata No Okime.*

1982 **Nine** (Arthur Kopit) 46th Street Theater 9 May
1991 **Phantom** (Kopit) Theater Under the Stars, Dallas, Tex 31 January
1997 **Titanic** (Peter Stone) Lunt-Fontanne Theater 23 April

YES, UNCLE! Musical comedy in 2 acts by Austen Hurgon and George Arthurs based on *Le Truc de Brésilien* by Marcel Nancey and Paul Armont. Lyrics by Clifford Grey. Music by Nat D Ayer. Prince of Wales Theatre, London, 29 December 1917.

Conceived by producers Grossmith and Laurillard as a follow-up to their earlier French farce–based musical hits, *Tonight's the Night* and *Theodore and Co, Yes, Uncle!* was scheduled for the Gaiety Theatre with Leslie Henson again as comic star. A coup d'état at the Gaiety sent them instead to the Prince of Wales Theatre, and the war almost deprived them of Henson, who, anxious to join up, finally agreed to create the principal comedy role of the show before departing.

Henson played Bobby, a typical musical-comedy best friend to the artist, G B Stark (Fred Leslie). Stark goes to a ball disguised as a French Count, and there he woos and wins his own wife, Joan (Margaret Bannerman), whilst disposing of his embarrassingly passionate and operatic model Lolita (Alexia Bassian) to his convenient uncle (Davy Burnaby). Henri Leoni sang tenorish ballads as a dashing Zouave who gets the household's maid (Lily St John), and Julia James was the widow Mabel Mannering who paired off at the final curtain with the bounding Henson. Their songs, written by Nat D Ayer of recent *Bing Boys* fame, included some attractive light pieces in the current dance-rhythmed fashion of which Leoni and Miss James's duet ''Think of Me (when the band is playing)'' proved the much-plugged hit of the evening. Miss James also had the other success of the evening, a coy but catchy ballad insisting that ''Widows Are Wonderful.''

However, as intended, it was Henson who was the key to the entertainment, Henson and his ''working up'' of the part of Bobby with his various bits of comic business. The producers knew this, and even though they knew they could only keep their star a short while, they agreed to pay him a royalty for the run of the show to rehearse and set up his role. Their idea worked, for when Henson handed over his role to his understudy, Norman Griffin, after two weeks of the show's run, the piece was in sufficiently good condition to last out the First World War, with 626 performances in over a year and a half in London prior to going on the road.

J C Williamson Ltd mounted the show in Australia, with Dorothy Brunton (then Gracie Lavers) as Mabel, Cyril Ritchard and Madge Elliott as the Zouave and the maid, Marie Eaton (Lolita) and Alfred Frith in Henson's role. William Greene (Stark) performed Fred Fisher and Joseph McCarthy's ''They Go Wild Over Me,'' Miss Brunton sang Maceo Pinkard and William Tracy's ''Mammy o' Mine'' and joined Frith in Anita Elson's London revue hit ''I'm Getting Tired of Playing Second Fiddle,'' whilst Cecil Bradley (Joan) popped in Victor Jacobi's ''On Miami Shore'' alongside a half-dozen bits of the original score. Even though the show was considered ''considerably short of the level of *Kissing Time,*'' which had preceded it, it (or what was left of it) did duty for a fine nine weeks in Melbourne and 10 weeks in Sydney.

Australia: Theatre Royal, Melbourne 12 June 1920

YOHÉ, May [YOHÉ, Mary Augusta] (b Bethlehem, Pa, 6 April 1869; d Boston, 28 August 1938). One of the more colorful and self-publicizing of the parade of musical-theatre performers who passed across the British and American stages of her era, though certainly not one of the more talented.

May Yohé, ''daughter of a Pennsylvania iron-moulder,'' a darkly pretty lass who claimed intermittently to be bred from Narraganset Indian stock (the Yohé was actually kosher Huguenot), was working in the chorus of a musical in Chicago when someone took a fancy to the very individual sound of ''one of the three notes in her voice'' and decided she deserved to be featured. She began as a chorister in John McCaull's touring comic opera company, appearing in short trunks as the boy, Alphonse, in *Lorraine* and as Zal-am-Boo in *Aladdin* (Chicago, 1888), featured on the bill at the Fifth Avenue Theater and toured as the Princess in the Chicago extravaganza *The Arabian Nights.* She was again seen on Broadway playing in *Natural Gas* at the Bijou (1888, Jeannette), around the country as a principal boy in the Eddie Foy spectacular *The Crystal Slipper* (1888, Prince Prettywitz) and in the original company of *The City Directory* (1889) before, in 1890, she went out to Australia,

Plate 432. **May Yohé** *made up for having only three notes in her voice in other ways.*

billed as a ''baritone,'' performing with a minstrel company cheekily calling itself the Boston Ideal Company. The season was not a success, and May returned to San Francisco, announcing her arrival by having her carriage run away newspaperworthily with her in the local park. She subsequently went touring with ''George Lederer's Players'' in a farce comedy called *U & I* (1891) and appeared as Celia Cliquot in *Hoss and Hoss* (1891).

It was London that decided to make May Yohé, albeit very briefly, a star. She appeared there in a supporting part in the Albéniz comic opera *The Magic Opal,* caught several eyes and, having been swiftly written out of that show, equally promptly got herself starred as *Mam'zelle Nitouche.* This time she walked out, but still got herself a new job—the title role of *Little Christopher Columbus.* She also got a Lord for a (second or third—the US senator she was scheduled to have wed may have escaped) husband. The Lord in question was the very questionable Lord Francis Hope, a weak gambler and womanizer who was heir to the Ducal seat of Newcastle and the infamous Hope Diamond. He was also the chief backer, to the tune of over £5,000, of *Little Christopher Columbus,* in which May herself had invested £1,000. However, even if the actress had bought herself her role, both *Little Christopher* and her performance of the songs written for her, within her wriggle-through range, by Ivan Caryll turned out a genuine hit.

These were May's peak months. The next year she starred in the title role of the London production of the surefire *The Lady Slavey,* which (apparently with more than a little help from her) misfired, and Hope was declared bankrupt. She was cast in *Christopher*'s follow-up, *Dandy Dick Whittington,* with less than happy results, then, her notorious unprofessionalism having made her unemployable, took the Court Theatre to present herself first as *Mam'zelle Nitouche,* then as *The Belle of Cairo.* Then she was gone.

She later turned up in Australia, and in 1900 appeared on the stage in New York again, billing herself as Lady Francis Hope, in the role of Lady Muriel Despair in a piece called *The Giddy Throng* at the New York Theater. She sang two Ivan Caryll songs, was on stage for a total of 12 minutes, and prompted a critic to report, ''When Miss Yohé left here she was said to have three notes in her voice. She has apparently lost two of them in her voyage across the Atlantic.'' She also ended up being sued by producer A H Chamberlyn for breach of contract. By that stage she was lucky to have a contract to break.

In 1902 she eloped to Buenos Aires with a gentleman named Captain Putnam Bradley Strong and was divorced from Hope. Captain Strong—who actually took to the vaudeville stage with his new wife (1905)—lasted 18 months. In 1904 she appeared in London ''in a new song scena assisted by eight ladies with special scenery and effects.'' She tried another comeback in 1907, attempting to add some scandal to her own faded notoriety by appearing as La Folaire in a revival of *Mamzelle Champagne,* the piece of which the opening night had been marked by the Harry Thaw murder. A critic remarked, ''It would be harsh to speak of the efforts of Miss Yohé. It is sufficient to say that she was 'featured.''' She moved from New York to San Francisco, where she found employment singing in a restaurant, then to the vaudeville circuits, and made an attempt to garner the attention she craved by faking a suicide in Central Park. She turned up in Japan, re-remarried (1911, he was called plain F M Reynolds), then hurried back to England for yet another abortive return to the stage in the revue *Come Over Here* (1913), before helping herself to yet a fourth husband, Captain John Smuts, who took her off to a rubber plantation in the South Pacific. Of course, it didn't last. She later worked as a janitress, on a chicken ranch and in a tearoom, and tried yet again to return to the theatre, but her last years were spent working as a clerk in the Works Progress Administration.

A relative of Miss Yohé, David Pursley, has appeared in a number of musicals on the modern Broadway stage with rather more success.

YOUMANS, Vincent [Millie] (b New York, 27 September 1898; d Denver, Colo, 5 April 1946). One of the most effective songwriters of the peak period of the Broadway dancing musical comedy.

The young Youmans got his first musical opportunities during a wartime period in the navy and, on his return home, worked as a song plugger and rehearsal pianist whilst taking his first steps as a songwriter. He placed individual numbers in *Linger Longer Letty* and the E Ray Goetz revue *Vogues and Vanities* and had his first opportunity at a musical-comedy score, in collaboration with Paul Lannin and lyricist Ira Gershwin, on Abe Erlanger's production of *Two Little Girls in Blue.* A modest success through 135 performances on Broadway, but a pre-London flop when mounted in England, *Two Little Girls in Blue* did, however, bring Youmans sufficient Broadway exposure to make the favorite songs from the show (''Oh Me! Oh My! [Oh You!],'' ''Who's Who with You?,'' ''Dolly'') popular and to win him another opportunity, this time with top-drawer collaborators in Otto Harbach and Oscar Hammerstein II.

The show that they wrote together, *Wildflower,* was a fine success and Youmans's song ''Bambalina'' proved the take-away hit of a score written in collaboration with operetta hardy Herbert Stothart. However, its success was nothing compared to that which awaited Youmans's first solo effort as a musical comedy composer. Harry Frazee's production of *No, No, Nanette* opened in Detroit less than three months on from *Wildflower*'s debut on Broadway, and the show soon became a Chicago hit as ''Tea for Two,'' ''I Want to Be Happy,'' ''Too Many Rings Around Rosie,'' ''You Can Dance with Any Girl At All'' and much of the rest of its score became national song favorites. *No, No, Nanette* cleaned up around the country and overseas, establishing itself as one of the greatest hits of its era before it was finally brought to Broadway. In the meantime, two other shows with songs by Youmans had appeared in New York. Neither *Mary Jane McKane* (151 performances) nor *Lollipop* (152 performances) was a disaster, but neither proved to be on *Wildflower*'s level. The latter show, however, did leave behind two songs that did not go down with the ship: ''Take a Little One Step'' was later incorporated into *No, No, Nanette,* and ''Tie a String Around Your Finger'' subsequently did the rounds of Europe, interpolated into the hugely successful *Mercenary Mary.*

Whilst *No, No, Nanette* continued to make its triumphant way around the world, Youmans produced the scores for a remake of the hit London musical version of *L'Hôtel du Libre Échange,* A Night Out—remade so badly that it flopped on the road—and for an unfortunate adaptation of another huge play hit, Veber and Hennequin's *La Présidente,* called *Oh, Please!* (75 performances). Unhappy with this lack of success and with the peremptory treatment handed out by producers, he then went into production himself to mount a musical version of the play *Shore Leave* under the lively title *Hit the Deck. Hit the Deck* gave its composer his third Broadway hit in three years, and "Sometimes I'm Happy" (transferred from *A Night Out*) and "Hallelujah!" (another trunk piece) found their way into the book of Youmans standards as the show followed *Nanette* around the world.

Thereafter, however, things went less well. An attempt to follow the path taken by Hammerstein and Kern in *Show Boat* resulted in a flop called *Rainbow* (29 performances); *Great Day,* in spite of a score that housed several numbers that would endure way beyond its out-of-town closure ("Without a Song," "More Than You Know," "Great Day"), vanished even more quickly; a Florenz Ziegfeld vehicle for Marilyn[n] Miller and the Astaires called *Smiles* ("Time on My Hands") foundered in 63 nights, and an attempt to turn the famous old play *Smiling Through* into a musical, under the title *Through the Years,* lasted just 20 performances. Only a contribution to a remake of the revue-within-a-musical piece, which was ultimately called *Take a Chance,* won the composer an extended Broadway representation (243 performances). "Rise and Shine," the most popular piece from his five-song share in this show's score, was later reused as the title song of a 1936 London flop for which Robert Stolz had the principal music credit, alongside another Youmans number, "Leave It to Love." On tour, the show became *Darling You*—the title of one of Stolz's songs—and Youmans's contribution, his last to the musical stage, was not detailed.

Youmans's last taste of success was in the film world, notably with his score to the 1934 *Flying Down to Rio* ("Orchids in the Moonlight," "Carioca," etc), but precarious health and an inability to get to grips with work meant that for the last decade of a life that ended at the age of 47, no new work came to the stage to add to the three big hits of the earliest years of his career. His name appeared on a bill for the last time as a producer when he mounted a dance compilation piece *Vincent Youmans' Ballet Revue* (Baltimore 27 January 1944) with music by Ravel, Rimsky-Korsakov and Lecuona, some choreography by Massine, and utter failure.

Perhaps because of this narrow period of celebrity, it has been Youmans's fate—like the much more prolific Fall and Eysler in Austria, and Christiné in France—to have seen his reputation fritter away over the years. Although his music is still widely played and *No, No, Nanette* regularly reproduced, he has not come in for the personal publicity and the sometimes exaggerated homage given to the more fashionable Broadway names of the prewar era. But his contribution was considerable, and the songs he gave to the musical theatre remain delightful examples of their genre 60 and 70 years on.

A compilation show of Youmans's works (ad Tom Taylor, Darwin Knight) was staged under the title *Oh Me, Oh My, Oh Youmans* at the Wonderhorse Theater, New York, 14 January 1981.

1921 **Two Little Girls in Blue** (w Paul Lannin/Ira Gershwin/Frederick Jackson) George M Cohan Theater 3 May

1923 **Wildflower** (w Herbert Stothart/Otto Harbach, Oscar Hammerstein) Casino Theater 7 February

1923 **The Left Over** (Zelda Sears, Walter de Leon) Albany 24 September

1923 **Mary Jane McKane** (w Stothart/Hammerstein, William Cary Duncan) Imperial Theater 25 December

1924 **Lollipop** revised *The Left Over* Knickerbocker Theater 21 January

1924 **No, No, Nanette** (Frank Mandel, Harbach, Irving Caesar) Garrick Theater, Detroit 23 April; Palace Theatre, London 11 March 1925

1925 **A Night Out** revised American version (Garrick Theater, Philadelphia)

1926 **Oh, Please!** (Anne Caldwell/Caldwell, Harbach) Fulton Theater 17 December

1927 **Hit the Deck** (Leo Robin, Clifford Grey/Herbert Fields) Belasco Theater 25 April

1928 **Rainbow** (Hammerstein/Laurence Stallings, Hammerstein) Gallo Theater 21 November

1929 **Great Day** (Edward Eliscu, Billy Rose/William Cary Duncan, John Wells) Garrick Theater, Philadelphia 4 June; Cosmopolitan Theater 17 October

1930 **Smiles** (Harold Adamson, Grey/William Anthony McGuire, et al) Ziegfeld Theater 18 November

1932 **Through the Years** (Edward Heyman/Brian Hooker) Manhattan Theater 28 January

1932 **Take a Chance** (w Nacio Herb Brown, Richard Whiting/Buddy de Sylva/Schwab) Apollo Theater 26 November

Biography: Bordman, G: *Days to Be Happy, Days to Be Sad* (OUP, New York, 1982)

YOUNG, Rida Johnson [née JOHNSON, Ida Louise] (b Baltimore, 28 February ?1866; d Southfield Point, Conn, 8 May 1926). Broadway librettist and lyricist who scored a brace of major hits in the romantic musical theatre.

Daughter of a striving Baltimore middle-class family, Rida Johnson graduated from college in 1882 and decided on a career in the theatre. She spent several years as an actress in upmarket companies, but then swapped the stage for a job in the press department at the music publisher Witmark. It was there that she began a career as a theatre writer with a play, *Lord Byron,* produced by her soon-to-be-husband, actor, writer and subsequently film director James Young, at Norfolk, Va, in 1900 (19 January). Mrs Young scored an early success with the play *Brown of Harvard* in 1906, and she made her first moves into the musical theatre with the odd number interpolated into other folks' musical comedies (''A Song of Yesterday,'' mus: A Heindl in *The Sultan of Sulu* 1903, etc), before authoring a slightly musicalized version of the well-known German play *Krieg im Frieden* (1907) and supplying the Shuberts with a text for Lulu Glaser (*Just One of the Boys,* 1911), and Augustus Pitou with a romantic Irish weepie-comedy for the perennial touring star Chauncey Olcott. Amongst the handful of lyrics that Mrs Young provided to composer Ernest Ball to set for the tenor hero of Barry of Ballymore was one that gave her and them an enormous and international hit: ''Mother Machree.''

For several years, she continued to turn out variations on the Irish theme for Pitou and Olcott. Meanwhile, she scored a major hit with her first attempt at a romantic operetta, the picturesque New Orleans tale of *Naughty Marietta,* written with Victor Herbert around the members of Oscar Hammerstein's failed opera company. Along with her libretto, Mrs Young provided the lyrics to a score including ''Ah! Sweet Mystery of Life,'' ''Tramp, Tramp, Tramp,'' ''Neath the Southern Moon'' and ''I'm Falling in Love with Someone.''

The Red Petticoat, a musical adaptation of her unsuccessful play *Next,* won some notice for its refreshingly unconventional choice of an unglamorous mining-town barber as its heroine, and also over the fact that ''a musical comedy with a distinctly American setting is a novelty,'' but there was nothing original about the glitzy *Lady Luxury,* a quick failure at the Casino Theater.

The war years brought the author several more successes. The two happiest of these were adaptations—Americanized versions of the Hungarian military piece *Az obsitos,* and of the romantic Berlin hit *Wie einst im Mai*—and the second, as *Maytime,* gave its author a long-running stage success and yet another song hit with ''Do You Remember?'' An original script for a comical tale about Mormons and multiple marriage, *His Little Widows,* had Broadway and London runs with good rather than great results, but Mrs Young's libretto was well enough thought of by its British adapter, Firth Shephard, for him to borrow it a few years later and attach it to a different score under the title *Lady Luck* (Carlton Theatre 27 April 1927).

The *Maytime* order of things worked less well in another time-shift script for Rudolf Friml's *Sometime,* a piece that nevertheless rode to a good run on its comedy. But a collaboration with British composer Augustus Barratt proved unfruitful, and a fresh teaming with the partner of her first great Broadway success, Victor Herbert, on a musical version of another through-the-ages tale, *The Road to Yesterday,* turned up only medium results for the author's last musical play before her death at the age (although she admitted to much less) of 60.

1907 **The Lancers** (George Spink, Cecilia Loftus, et al/w J Hartley Manners) Daly's Theater 5 December

1908 **Ragged Robin** (Chauncey Olcott, et al/w Rita Olcott) Metropolitan Theater, Minneapolis 23 August; Academy of Music 24 January 1910

1910 **Just One of the Boys** (William A Schroeder) Van Curler Opera House, Schenectady, NY 27 January

1910 **Barry of Ballymore** (Ernest Ball, et al) Broadway Theater, Saratoga Springs 23 August; Academy of Music 30 January 1911

1910 **Naughty Marietta** (Victor Herbert) New York Theater 7 November

1911 **Macushla** (Ernest Ball, C Olcott, et al/J Keirn Brennan, et al) Columbia Theater, San Francisco 11 July; Grand Opera House 5 February 1912

1912 **The Isle of Dreams** (C Olcott, et al) McVickers Theater, Chicago 27 October; Grand Opera House 27 January 1913

1912 **The Red Petticoat** (ex- *Look Who's Here*) (Jerome Kern/Paul West) Daly's Theater 13 November

1913 **Shameen Dhu** (C Olcott, et al) Olympic Theater, Chicago 19 October

1913 **When Love Is Young** (Schroeder) Cort Theater, Chicago 28 October

1914 **Lady Luxury** (Schroeder) His Majesty's Theater, Montreal 5 October; Casino Theater, New York 25 December

1916 **[Her] Soldier Boy** (*Az obsitos*) American version w Sigmund Romberg (Astor Theater)

1917 **Captain Cupid** (Schroeder/w William Cary Duncan) Shubert Theater, Minneapolis 15 April

1917 **His Little Widows** (Schroeder/w Duncan) Astor Theater 30 April

1917 **Maytime** (*Wie einst im Mai*) American version w Romberg (Shubert Theater)

1918 **Miss I-Don't Know** (Augustus Barratt) Stamford, Conn 14 September

1918 **Sometime** (Rudolf Friml) Shubert Theater 4 October

1918 **Little Simplicity** (Barratt) Astor Theater 4 November

1924 **The Dream Girl** (Herbert/w Harold Atteridge) Ambassador Theater 20 August

YOU NEVER KNOW *see* BEI KERZENLICHT

YOU'RE A GOOD MAN, CHARLIE BROWN Musical by John Gordon based on the comic strip *Peanuts* by Charles M Schulz. Music and lyrics by Clark Gesner. Theater 80 St Marks, New York, 7 March 1967.

The songs that made up *You're a Good Man, Charlie Brown* were originally issued on record, as ''an original MGM Album Musical . . . a series of delightful (and meaningful) new songs which portray the ups and downs of Charlie Brown, Lucy, Snoopy, Linus and Schroeder.''

The piece was subsequently expanded—the ultimate cast was six—and made up into a stage show that was produced by Arthur Whitelaw and Gene Persson in a small off-Broadway venue. The favorite comic strip's characters appeared in a series of little strip-like scenes and songs, with Charlie Brown (Gary Burghoff) flying his ''Kite,'' Lucy (Reva Rose) putting on imperious airs as ''Queen Lucy'' and dispensing blithely inaccurate ''Little Known Facts,'' Snoopy the dog (Bill Hinnant)—otherwise the fearless wartime flying ace, ''The Red Baron''—serenading his favorite pursuit of ''Suppertime,'' Linus (Bob Balaban) getting down to the nitty-gritty about ''My Blanket and Me'' and everybody getting tied up in the all-important baseball game with predictable (to the millions of fans of the cartoon strip) results.

A long-running success in its New York production (1,597 performances), the show suffered the same fate as most other off-Broadway pieces mounted in a London with no comparable area of theatre. Even in the tiny Fortune Theatre, Harold Fielding and Bernard Delfont's production could not find the equivalent atmosphere and audience, and it folded in 115 performances. David Rhys-Anderson appeared as Charlie with Don Potter as Snoopy and Boni Enten as Lucy. The producers attempted to publicize their show by approaching a famous greetings card firm with the proposal that they publish ''Peanuts'' greeting cards, but they were turned down with the answer that such a thing could never catch on.

In spite of its West End failure, *You're a Good Man, Charlie Brown* later (with a little help from ''Peanuts'' greeting cards) established itself as a regular favorite in British provincial theatres in the same way that it did in smaller American houses and colleges. It also won productions elsewhere, including several in Australia. Sydney saw a first mounting in 1970, Harry M Miller, Melbourne's Actors' Theatre staged the piece three years later and Sydney's Phillips Street Theatre and Ensemble Theatre followed in 1981.

The show was televised in America in 1972, a German-language version was produced in Hamburg in 1991 with Thomas Borchert (Snoopy), Goetz Fuhrmann (Charlie) and Sabine Steinke (Lucy) featured, and in 1999 (4 February) the little piece came back to New York, to Broadway's Longacre Theatre. Anthony Rapp played Charlie and Roger Bart Snoopy through 150 performances.

Another *Peanuts* musical, *Snoopy—the Musical* (Larry Grossman/Hal Hackady), was mounted in San Francisco in 1982 and subsequently played in New York (Lamb's Theater 20 December 1982, 152 performances) and in London (Duchess Theatre 20 September 1983) prior to winning a similar run of small-house productions.

Plate 433. **You're in Love**

UK: Fortune Theatre 1 February 1968; Australia: Playbox Theatre, Sydney 7 May 1970; Germany: Neues Theater, Hamburg *Du bist in Ordnung, Charlie Brown* 6 March 1991

Recordings: original concept disc (MGM), original cast (MGM), TV cast (Atlantic), revival cast 1999 (RCA)

YOU'RE IN LOVE Musical comedy in 2 acts by Otto Hauerbach and Edward Clark. Music by Rudolf Friml. Casino Theater, New York, 6 February 1917.

You're in Love was a musical comedy that was in many ways as conventional as could be—but it had one or two enjoyable little flavors of an almost French-comedy style of originality about it. It was not, for example, yet the fashion for a musical play to be set on a sea-going yacht (though it was by no means unprecedented), and it was almost always a wealthy uncle with dynastic or financial reasons who was, until minutes from the final curtain, the bar to the marriage of the singing-dancing juveniles. *You're in Love* opened with a chorus of young San Francisco folk getting ready to sail off on a six months' ocean cruise on the SS *High Hopes,* and the whole of the second act was spent on board, three days out of port. And the marriage between Georgina Payton (Marie Flynn) and Hobby Douglas (Harry Clarke) was celebrated before sailing time. It was not on this occasion forbidden—merely surrounded by all sorts of conditions laid down by Auntie Payton (Florine Arnold), the nitty-gritty of which was—no physical contact for a year. By the time Georgina has gone sleepwalking on the ship's railings and on a boom that was swung gasp-makingly out over the audience, Auntie is ready to give in to the inevitable.

The score to the show was in Friml's most light-hearted vein. Georgina went sleepwalking to a shower of harp arpeggios and the song ''I'm Only Dreaming,'' serenaded ''Loveland'' in waltz time, nodded through the pre-wedding quartet explaining ''Things That They Must Not Do'' and commiserated with her Hobby over the fact that, under certain circumstances, ''A Year Is a Long, Long Time.'' The number-two couple, Lacey Hart (Lawrence Wheat) and Dorothy (May Thompson), delivered several bright pieces (''Married Life,'' ''Be Sure It's Light,'' ''He Will Understand''), and Lacey—who bore the brunt of the male music—joined Georgina to explain ''You're in Love.'' Hauerbach and Clark had, however, their best time with the comedy numbers. Principal (and incidental) comedian Mr Wix (Al Roberts) burlesqued ''The Cradle of the Deep'' in the sad tale of how he was ''Snatched from the Cradle (in my sleep)'' to a youthful marriage, and demonstrated the dance the ''Boola Boo,'' whilst Mrs Payton sprayed out her mistrust of the male race in a ''Keep Off the Grass,'' which was much more lyrically juicy than Gertie Millar's famous Gaiety song of the same title: ''I know the brutes, for I've had three, they're all alike as dollars, they differ merely in degree of waistbands, shirts or collars . . . that's why I'm a grass widow, with a sign 'Keep Off the Grass'!''

Arthur Hammerstein's production of *You're in Love* was warmed up in Stamford and Springfield, then moved to Broadway, where it played for a fine 162 performances before heading for the regions dressed in success. In fact, it had further success awaiting it further afield for, although Britain did not take the show up, Australia's J C Williamson Ltd did, and Australia proved to like the show even better than America had. It was first produced in Sydney, understandably billed as ''by the author and composer of *High Jinks,*'' which had been one of the biggest musical-comedy hits of the era in Australia. It wasn't entirely by them by this time for ''Day Dream Isle,'' ''Naughty Times Three'' and several other popular songs of the moment had made their way into the score in typical Williamson fashion. Talleur Andrews, Maud Fane, Field Fisher, Connie Ediss, Alfred Frith, Madge Elliott and William Greene headed the cast as the production moved to Melbourne (3 November–17 December), then back to Sydney after pantomime was done, then back again to Melbourne (7–25 March) as *You're in Love* established itself as a genuine favourite. It was revived in 1921–22 with Frith and Miss Fane again featured, and, if it did not quite join the very favorites of its period—*A Night Out, High Jinks, Kissing Time*—on the revival plan, it ended up holding a position not far behind them.

Australia: Her Majesty's Theatre, Sydney 7 September 1917

YOUR OWN THING Rock musical in 2 acts by Donald Driver suggested by Shakespeare's *Twelfth Night.* Music and lyrics by Hal Hester and Danny Apolinar. Orpheum Theater, New York, 13 January 1968.

A lively, up-to-date tale of pop people in the then ''Now Generation'' that followed the outline of *Twelfth Night* and its tale of sexual ambiguities to a score of contemporary rock-and-roll music. If the girl-as-boy storyline was reminiscent of many Victorian musical plays, the manner of its telling (as reflected in the 1960s lingo of its title) put it squarely into its own time and place.

Sebastian (Rusty Thacker) and Viola (Leland Palmer) are identical pop-singing twins who get separated when they are involved in a shipwreck. The rescued Viola gets a job as a replacement singer in a rock quartet who have lost their vocalist to the draft, and soon afterwards the recovered Sebastian gets the same job. Orson (Tom Ligon), the manager of the group, who has been courting disco owner Olivia (Marian Mercer/Marcia Rodd), finds himself worryingly attracted by the new singer. He's not modern enough to be displeased when it turns out they are not one, but two, that Viola is a girl, and that Sebastian has been using his message-carrying moments between Orson and Olivia to win the disco lady for himself.

Several of the songs in the show were presented as the songs of the pop group (''Somethin's Happ'nin,'' ''Your Own Thing,'' ''What Do I Know?,'' ''The Apocalypse Fugue''), whilst Shakespeare's words were set as lyrics for ''Come Away Death'' (Sebastian in hospital) and ''She Never Told Her Love'' (Viola on Orson).

Zev Bufman and Dorothy Love's off-Broadway production was a 937-performance success at the Orpheum Theater, and the show was subsequently mounted in London, under the same management. Misses Palmer and Rodd and composer Apolinar (who appeared as one of the Apocalypse rock group) from the New York production appeared alongside Gerry Glasier (Sebastian) and Les Carlson (Orson) for a run of six weeks. In Australia the response was equally negative, though better at Sydney's Phillip Street Theatre, where Lynn Rogers, Bunny Gibson, Bryan Davies and Kristen Mann featured, than in a brief subsequent season in Melbourne (Comedy Theatre 8 June 1969). In France, where the trendy title apparently meant nothing, the piece was produced in the 1969–70 season with Arielle Semenoff and Jacques Tadieu featured, under the title *Charlie.*

UK: Comedy Theatre 6 February 1969; Australia: Phillip Street Theatre, Sydney 15 February 1969; France: *Charlie* 1969–70 season; Germany: Theater der Freien Hansestadt, Bremen *Tut was ihr wollt* 5 April 1969

Recording: original cast (RCA)

YVAIN, Maurice [Pierre Paul] (b Paris, 12 February 1891; d Suresne, 28 July 1965). One of the happiest composers of the French interwar musical theatre through a long series of hit plays that mixed sprightly textual comedy with a touch of dance-musical class.

Trained at the Paris Conservatoire, Yvain made his first professional inroads into the world of music as a pianist and accompanist, playing the piano with Louis Ganne's well-respected orchestra in Monte-Carlo until military service called. That military service, however, turned into war, and Yvain's musical career was forcibly postponed. After the war, a friendship struck up with Maurice Chevalier in the earliest days of his eight years in uniform proved highly useful, for the singer introduced Yvain to Albert Willemetz, author of the landmark musical *Phi-Phi,* and the two collaborated soon after on several songs that were performed at the Casino de Paris by Rose Amy (La Légende de la Violette), Dréan (''Cach' ton piano'') and Mistinguett. The last-named's performance of Yvain and Willemetz's ''Mon homme'' proved the breakthrough for the neophyte composer, a breakthrough confirmed, in particular, by the Trio des épiciers in the revue *On peut monter!* Many other successful revue songs also followed: Mistinguett's ''J'en ai marre,'' Chevalier's ''Avec le sourire,'' ''L'Étrange Valse,'' ''Billets-doux,'' ''Le Gri-gri d'amour'' (taken from an aborted opérette and turned into a ''Hawaiian'' revue duo for Mistinguett and Boucot), ''En douce,'' ''Le Java'' and ''La Belote.''

His songwriting success brought Yvain to the notice of wide-handed theatre magnate Gustave Quinson, who had produced Henri Christiné's *Phi-Phi* three years earlier and, in spite of the fact that the composer had not a full score to his name, Quinson signed him up to write three musicals. It took only the first to establish Yvain at the top of the field. The winningly sexy *Ta bouche,* its bounding dance music no little assisted by a delicious Yves Mirande libretto, some amusing Willemetz lyrics and a fine cast of nine, followed behind and rendered nothing in popularity to Christiné's modern musical comedies. And whilst *Ta bouche* continued its Parisian, provincial, and limited (by its subject matter) international career, Yvain followed up with the same collaborators on a second big success, *Là-haut,* with Chevalier and Dranem as stars.

La Dame en décolleté, which leaned slightly less on the popular dance rhythms of the age than its hit predecessors, won more praise than run (three months), but another up-to-date piece, *Gosse de riche,* did much more than a little better, and a collaboration with André Barde—hitherto best known as the librettist to Charles Cuvillier and the author of some superior revues—brought forth Yvain's fourth musical comedy hit in less than three years. In *Pas sur la bouche,* as illustration to another sparklingly sexy libretto, Yvain turned out a fresh selection of numbers in the light, dancing style of *Ta bouche*'s songs, and Benoît-Léon Deutsch's production at the Théâtre des Nouveautés gave the new team an enormous and enduring success both in the theatre and, for Yvain's most popular numbers, outside it. Continuing with the ''bouche'' titles, the pair then wrote *Bouche à bouche,* a piece that took a pot shot at the pretensions of Paris's inevitably noble inflood of Russian emigrés, which managed a round 100 nights, and had a further grand success with another vehicle for that piece's comic star, Georges Milton, *Un bon garçon,* which followed a more than useful Paris career of over a year with provincial and overseas showings.

The small-scale *Yes,* produced at the tiny Théâtre des Capucines with just a two-piano accompaniment, added to the total of successes, *Elle est à vous* and *Kadubec* to the semi-successes. If *Jean V,* a second collaboration with the authors of *Gosse de riche,* was a month and a bit's flop, the very few failures were heavily outweighed by the successes as versions of Yvain's works—their libretti bowdlerized for more maidenly audiences—found their way to the stages of the world. London saw *Pas sur la bouche,* New York *Ta bouche* and *Un bon garçon,* Berlin got a Germanned *Ta bouche* whilst in Budapest where, for a period, the French musical comedy and in particular the works of Yvain and Christiné became all the rage, *Ta bouche, Gosse de riche, Pas sur la bouche, Un bon garçon* and *Yes* were all shown.

Yvain's fine record of the 1920s got a little reinforcement in the 1930s with *Oh! Papa . . .* and the composer's first collaboration with Christiné in a two-handed score for *Encore cinquante centimes*—both pieces successful at home and both subsequently played in Budapest—but other productions, ranging from the Puss-in-Boots fairy tale *La Belle Histoire* to a one-act ''modern féerie'' and the musical comedy *Pépé,* failed to make a mark. The fashion for the French Jazz Age musical comedy of which Yvain had been one of the earliest and most successful purveyors had gone its way, and, in the years that followed, the composer found himself more successful in the world of the cinema and, subsequently, in the newly refashionable opérette à grand spectacle.

Yvain's approach to the large-scale opérette was less conquering than the entrance he had made more than a decade earlier onto the musical comedy stage. He supplied a couple of additional songs to the grandiose production of a De Sylva, Brown and Henderson piece mounted as *Miami* (1930) and found failure with *Un coup de veine* at the Porte-Saint-Martin, but the spectacular and romantic *Au soleil du Mexique* won a good run at the Châtelet before its composer found it advisable to blush behind the pseudonym of "Jean Sautreuil" for a new musical version of Louis Verneuil's *Le Coffre-fort vivant,* which played during the early days of the war, and *Le Beau Voyage d'un enfant de Paris,* which was seen in its last days. The change of name did not, however, save him from being prosecuted and banned for collaborating by permitting his works to be "used" by the invaders.

Yvain returned to his own name for the production of *Monseigneur,* a final effort in the small-scale musical field at the Daunou (a house that had not been lucky for the composer since *Gosse de riche*) before he switched modes again to compose the score for the larger *Chanson gitane* in 1946. Following behind the enormous success won by Raymond Vincy, Maurice Vandair and Francis Lopez with *La Belle de Cadix,* Yvain turned out a lushly romantic and colorful score in the same postwar opérette vein. It was a score that was more than a little "better made" than that of Lopez's landmark show, without perhaps having quite the same unerringly popular ring to it but, just as Yvain had successfully followed *Phi-Phi* with *Ta bouche,* he again took the newest fashion and made his mark on it with a show that proved not only a long-running hit in its first run but that, although it did not follow *Ta bouche* and its sisters abroad, was to have a long and continued life in the French musical theatre.

In spite of this success, Yvain found that there was less of a place for him in the postwar theatre than there had been before the hostilities. Although he was only in his mid-fifties, he had in fact made his last contribution to the Parisian stage. His underexposed talents as a writer of soigné romantic musicals were given one last showing in *Le Corsaire noir,* another colorful costume piece, produced at Marseille and played through the French provinces for a number of years, but denied a Parisian production. Yvain's handful of opérettes à grand spectacle still make regular appearances on French stages, but his principal achievement remains his shapely, rhythmical and sparkling scores to the musical comedies of the années folles, the principal of which stand alongside Christiné's best works as the enduring representatives of a particularly attractive era in musical theatre.

Yvain's film scores included music for such screen pieces as *Paris-Béguin, Sans famille* ("Ma Lola"), *Les Deux Gamines, La Belle Équipe, La Chanson de Paris* with Tino Rossi, Suzy Delair and Milton, *Carthacala* and *La Fausse Maîtresse,* as well as a film version of *Yes* under the title *Défense d'aimer,* again with Suzy Delair. *Ta bouche* and *Pas sur la bouche* were also remade for the screen.

1922 **Ta bouche** (Albert Willemetz/Yves Mirande) Théâtre Daunou 1 April

1923 **Là-haut** (Willemetz /Mirande, Gustave Quinson) Théâtre des Bouffes-Parisiens 31 March

1923 **La Dame en décolleté** (Mirande, Lucien Boyer) Théâtre des Bouffes-Parisiens 22 December

1924 **Gosse de riche** (Jacques Bousquet, Henri Falk) Théâtre Daunou 2 May

1925 **Pas sur la bouche** (André Barde) Théâtre des Nouveautés 17 February

1925 **Bouche à bouche** (Barde) Théâtre de l'Apollo 8 October

1926 **Un bon garçon** (Barde) Théâtre des Nouveautés 13 November

1928 **Yes** (Pierre Soulaine, René Pujol) Théâtre des Capucines 26 January

1929 **Elle est à vous** (Barde) Théâtre des Nouveautés 22 January

1929 **Jean V** (Jacques Bousquet, Henri Falk) Théâtre Daunou 2 March

1929 **Kadubec** (Barde) Théâtre des Nouveautés 12 December

1930 **Pépé** (Barde) Théâtre Daunou 25 October

1931 **Encore cinquante centimes** (w Christiné/Barde) Théâtre des Nouveautés 17 September

1933 **Oh! Papa . . .** (Barde) Théâtre des Nouveautés 2 February

1934 **La Belle Histoire** (Henri-Georges Clouzot) Théâtre de la Madeleine 25 April

1934 **Un, deux, trois** (René Bizet, Jean Barreyre) 1 act Moulin de la Chanson

1934 **Vacances** (Henri Duvernois, Barde) Théâtre des Nouveautés 20 December

1935 **Un coup de veine** (Willemetz, Mouëzy-Éon) Théâtre de la Porte-Saint-Martin 11 October

1935 **Au soleil du Mexique** (Mouëzy-Éon, Willemetz) Théâtre du Châtelet 18 December

1938 **Le Coffre-fort vivant** (w Joseph Szulc, as Jean Sautreuil/ Henri Wernert/Georges Berr, Louis Verneuil) Théâtre du Châtelet 17 December

1944 **Le Beau Voyage d'un enfant de Paris** (as Jean Sautreuil/ Wernert/Ernest Morel) Théâtre du Châtelet 15 January

1945 **Monseigneur** Théâtre Daunou

1946 **Chanson gitane** (Mouëzy-Éon, Louis Poterat) Théâtre de la Gaîté-Lyrique 13 December

1958 **Le Corsaire noir** (Jean Valmy) Opéra, Marseille 24 February

Autobiography: *Ma belle opérette* (La Table Ronde, Paris, 1962)

Z

ZAMARA, Alfred [Marie Victor] (b Vienna, 1863; d 1940).

The musically trained son of a musician—his father was a well-known harpist—Zamara had his first short Operette produced when he was 21 years of age, and his first full-length work two years later. *Der Doppelgänger,* first produced in Munich, was seen soon after both in Berlin and in Vienna (Theater an der Wien 1 October 1887, 15 performances), and subsequently in many provincial German and Austrian theatres as well as in New York's Amberg Theater (27 February 1891). The young composer's next work from *Doppelgänger* librettist Victor Léon was to have been his version of *Simplicius,* but that text was instead given to Johann Strauss, and Zamara turned out *Der Sänger von Palermo* to a version of *Ne touchez pas à la reine* libretticized by Buchbinder. After a fortnight's first run at the Carltheater, it was seen in Budapest and in the regions.

Zamara's subsequent works, all written with collaborators of the quality of Léon, von Waldberg, Genée or Willner, were produced in Munich and in Hamburg, but only *Die Debütantin,* a musical version of the hit comedy *Le Mari de la débutante,* was taken up for Vienna (Carltheater 4 October 1901), where it failed in 10 performances. Zamara's last works, *Die Frauenjäger,* produced at the Theater an der Wien for just 14 performances, and a last piece for Munich, *Die vertauschte Braut,* also had short lives, and the promise of his earliest work was never fulfilled.

Zamara worked with Julius Stern on the completion of Suppé's posthumous *Das Modell* (Carltheater 4 October 1895) and again on the arrangement of the score of *Der Goldschmied von Toledo* (w Stern, lib Karl Georg Zwerenz) from the works of Offenbach.

1883 **Die Königin von Arragon** (Victor Léon) 1 act Moling 30 August; Ronacher, Vienna 1 May 1884

1886 **Der Doppelgänger** (Léon) Theater am Gärtnerplatz, Munich 16 September; Friedrich-Wilhelmstädtisches Theater 9 March 1887

1888 **Der Sänger von Palermo** (ad Bernhard Buchbinder) Carltheater 14 February

1889 **Der Herr Abbé** (Léon, Franz Josef Brackl) Theater am Gärtnerplatz, Munich 10 August

1890 **Der bleiche Gast** (w Josef Hellmesberger/Léon, Heinrich von Waldberg) Carl-Schultze Theater, Hamburg 6 September

1895 **Die Welsenbraut** (Richard Genée, Max Tull) Stadttheater, Hamburg 20 March

1901 **Die Debütantin** (A M Willner, von Waldberg) Theater am Gärtnerplatz, Munich 17 January; Theater des Westens, Berlin 20 September

1908 **Die Frauenjäger** (von Waldberg, Hans Liebstockl) Theater an der Wien 16 October

1911 **Die vertauschte Braut** (von Waldberg, Felix Ujhély) Theater am Gärtnerplatz, Munich 20 January

1919 **Der Goldschmied von Toledo** (Jacques Offenbach arr w Julius Stern/Karl Georg Zwerenz) Nationaltheater, Mannheim 7 February

ZAPPERT, Bruno (b Sechshaus bei Wien, 28 January 1845; d Vienna, 31 January 1892).

A prolific author of Possen and some Operetten for the Viennese stage of the 1870s and 1880s, Zappert had his biggest success with the Gesangsburleske *Ein Böhm in Amerika,* an oft-revived piece that ran some 250 performances in its first decade at the Theater in der Josefstadt. His two principal contributions to the Operette stage, Czibulka's *Der Glücksritter* and Suppé's *Die Jagd nach dem Glück,* both went on to overseas productions, being seen in America as *The May Queen* and *Clover,* respectively.

1878 **Eine Hochgeborene** (Henrik Delin) Theater in der Josefstadt 19 January

1878 **Ninischerl** (Ludwig Gothov-Grüneke) 1 act Theater in der Josefstadt 7 November

1879 **Eine Gumpoldskirchnerin** (*Les Noces de Bouchencoeur*) Theater in der Josefstadt 1 March

1879 **Die Glöckerln von Kornfeld** (Gothov-Grüneke) 1 act Komische Oper 10 October

1880 **Eine Parforcejagd durch Europa** (Julius Hopp) Theater in der Josefstadt 14 February

1881 **Ein Böhm in Amerika** (Gothov-Grüneke) Theater in der Josefstadt 29 January

1881 **Unser Schatzerl** (Josef Reiter/Léon Treptow ad) Theater in der Josefstadt 17 December

1882 **Moderne Weiber** (Gothov-Grüneke) Theater in der Josefstadt 8 February

1884 **Der Herr Dr Schimmel** (Louis Roth) Theater in der Josefstadt 29 March

1885 **Johann Nestroy** (pasticcio) Graz 17 January

1885 **Sein Spetzl** (Franz Roth/Julius Findeisen ad) Carltheater 21 February

1885 **Der Walzerkönig** (Johann Brandl/Wilhelm Mannstädt, Karl Costa) Carltheater 9 October (additional lyrics)

1886 **Die Susi ihr G'spusi** (F Roth/w Bruno Hartl-Mitius) Carltheater 7 May

1886 **Ein gemachter Mann** (L Roth/w Jacobson) Theater in der Josefstadt 8 May

1886 **Das fünfte Rad** (L Roth/Treptow, Louis Herrmann ad) Carltheater 15 October

1887 **Der Glücksritter** (Alfons Czibulka/w Richard Genée, Mannstädt) Carltheater 22 December

1888 **Der Freibuter** (*Surcouf*) German version w Genée (Carltheater)

1888 **Die Jagd nach dem Glück** (Franz von Suppé/w Genée) Carltheater 27 October

1888 **Ein Deutschmeister** (Carl Michael Ziehrer/w Richard Genée) Carltheater 30 November

1891 **Im Fluge um die Welt** (Adolf Gisser) Fürsttheater

1892 **Die Tugendwachter** (Aurel Schwimmer) Odenburg

DER ZAREWITSCH Operette in 3 acts by Béla Jenbach and Heinz Reichert based on the play *A csárevics* by Gabryela Zapolska. Music by Franz Lehár. Deutsches Künstlertheater, Berlin, 21 February 1927.

Perhaps the most thoroughly gloomy of the line of more or less gloomily romantic tales that were elaborated to make libretti for Franz Lehár in the later part of his writing career, *Der Zarewitsch,* whilst purporting to be based on a real incident in the life of the Russian Tsarevitch Alexis, followed the already cliched formula of Lehár's librettists through its blighted love affair between tenor (extremely large role) and soprano (less large role) up to the fashionable unhappy ending.

Aljoscha, an apparently homosexual tsarevitch (Richard Tauber), will have nothing to do with women until, with his marriage and the dynasty needing to be secured, his uncle is forced into a plot to change his tastes. A dancer named Sonja (Rita Georg) is set up as bait. Disguised as a young male athlete, she attracts his attention, surmounts his horror at learning her real sex and wins from him first friendship and then love. However, when it is time for Aljoscha to assume the crown, she has to be renounced in favor of an unknown royal bride. Such lighter moments as the piece held were provided by the tsarevitch's servant, Iwan (Paul Heidemann), and his wife, Mascha (Charlotte Ander). At first kept away from her flirtatious husband by the tsarevitch's anti-women rules, she later becomes the despair of his life when she learns to flirt herself.

The score to *Der Zarewitsch,* tinted with a little balalaika music, was made to the measure of its tenor star. Apart from two or three lighthearted intrusions by the soubret pair (''Schaukle, Liebchen, schaukle,'' the one-step ''Heute Abend komm' ich zu dir,'' ''Ich bin bereit zu jeder Zeit'' / ''Taglich frische, heisse Liebe''), and an optional piece for the Grand Duke, it was devoted almost wholly to the tenor (a great deal) and soprano (quite a lot). Aljoscha waxed lonely in the Wolgalied (''Allein! Wieder allein!''), fell in love (''Herz, warum schlägst du so bang'') and fell in love more thoroughly (''Willst du?,'' ''Ich bin verliebt!''), but still felt depressed—because he's the depressive sort—at the thought that it was too good to go on (Napolitana: ''Warum hat jeder Frühling, ach, nur einen Mai?''). He also joined in a series of duets and sung scenes with the soprano, moving into tango time in the first-act finale as he sang in praise of champagne, but into more standard rhythms for the big duets, the waltzing ''Hab' nur dich allein'' and ''Liebe mich, küsse mich.'' It was to Sonja, however, that the most successful single number fell with a wondering solo ''Einer wird kommen'' in the first act—before her part in the tale and the music became more intense.

Der Zarewitsch was first produced in Berlin, and it was over a year before Vienna mounted its version at the Johann Strauss-Theater with Hans Heinz Bollmann and Emmi Kosáry starred, and with a Russian dance duo speciality, the Original Don-Kosakentruppe, and a Tcherkessentanz billed as large as they. Tauber took over from Bollmann for two weeks, and Sergei Abranowicz then saw the piece through to its 146th performance. A Hungarian-American pop-music piece called *Spektakel* took over and flopped violently, so three weeks later the theatre brought *Der Zarewitsch* back. It went through three more tenors before the 221st performance ended its run. In the meantime, Budapest had seen János Halmos and Hilda Harmath introduce the piece at the Városi Színház (ad Ernő Kulinyi).

The following year *Le Tzarévitch* (ad Robert de Mackiels, Bertal-Maubon) was mounted in France. The Lyon production, which alternated a high baritone and a tenor in the lead role, inspired several other provincial productions, but Paris was not tempted to take it up until 1935, when Maurice Lehmann mounted a version at the Théâtre de la Porte-Saint-Martin. Roger Bourdin continued the French tradition of playing Lehár tenor roles with a baritone, alongside Fanély Revoil as Sonja. It survived less than a month.

If the French version was unfortunate, an English one simply did not take place. In spite of the appeal of

Plate 434. **Der Zarewitsch.** *The heir to the tsardom (Andrea Poddigre) is about to find out that his companion (Eva-Maria Kaufmann) is a girl and not a boy (Bielefeld, 1986).*

the leading role—or, at least, its music—to operatic tenors, *Der Zarewitsch* played neither Broadway nor London. That same tenor appeal has, however, led to the piece being thoroughly represented on record, and it has also been the subject of three film versions. The first, in 1929, was actually a silent version of Zapolska's tale; the second, with Hans Sohnker and Marta Eggerth starred, was produced by Victor Janson in 1933, with a parallel version in French being issued as *Son altesse impériale.* A third, with a rather uncomfortably cast Luis Mariano playing the tsarevitch opposite Sonja Ziemann, was made by Arthur Maria Rabenalt in 1954, and a German television version with Wieslaw Ochmann and Teresa Stratas featured appeared in 1973.

A version of *Der Zarewitsch* was mounted at the Volksoper in 1978 (11 December), with Adolf Dallapozza and Bettina Schoeller featured, and the piece continues to find its way onto German-language stages when a starryish tenor is in need of a vehicle.

Austria: Johann Strauss-Theater 18 May 1928; Hungary: Városi Színház *A csárevics* 25 May 1928; France: Théâtre des Célestins, Lyon *Le Tsarévitch* 16 April 1929, Théâtre de la Porte-Saint-Martin *Rêve d'un soir* 30 January 1935

Films: J & L Fleck 1929 (silent), Victor Janson 1933, *Son altesse impériale* 1933, A M Rabenalt 1954

Recordings: complete (EMI, Eurodisc), complete variant version (Eurodisc), selections (Telefunken, London, Decca, Philips, Amadeo, Polydor, etc), selection in English (Telarc), etc

Video: Taurus 1973

ZAYTZ, Giovanni von [ZAJC, Iván] (b Fiume, 3 August 1831; d Zagreb, 16 December 1914). One of the most successful of the earliest contributors to the Viennese Operette stage.

The son of a military bandmaster, Iván Zajc was musically taught by his father and began composing at a young age, turning out an operatic *Maria Theresia* at the age of 12. He was sent to Milan to study, metamorphosed there from Zajc into Giovanni von Zaytz, and had his first full opera, *La Tirolese,* produced on stage there in 1855 (4 May). He continued to work in the operatic field and another opera, *Amelia,* was produced in Fiume in 1860, but he also ventured into the lighter musical theatre and after moving to Vienna to work as a theatre conductor in 1862 provided two of the most popular of the earliest Viennese Operetten to the Carltheater stage.

Mannschaft an Bord was a little nautical piece in which the composer made effective use of English sea shanties, even though it had a French setting. It held its own amongst the flood of newly popular Offenbach opérettes and other French works, and it was maintained in the repertoire in Vienna for more than a decade as a forepiece and an item in spectacles-coupés. It was also liberally played on Hungarian stages (*Matrozok a fedelzeten*). *Der Meisterschuss von Pottenstein* was scarcely less popular, holding a place in the Carltheater and Theater an der Wien repertoires for many years, whilst the little Zauberposse *Fitzliputzli* was also reprised at the Carltheater for five years after its initial production. Amongst this series of short pieces, Zaytz also composed a three-act romantic opéra-bouffe, *Die Hexe von Boissy,* played both in Vienna and Budapest (*A Boissy boszorkány* ad Endre Latabár, Budai Népszínház 1 February 1868) without it achieving the popularity of the best of his smaller works.

In 1870 he left Vienna and moved to Zagreb, as conductor at the local theatre, and returned to mainly operatic composition. His opera *Nikola Šubíc Zrinjki* (lib: Hugo Badaić, Zagreb 4 November 1876), said to be the first written in the Croatian language, won a number of productions in Yugoslavia. In 1889 he became director of the Zagreb Conservatoire, a post he retained until 1908.

Along with his operettic and operatic work, Zaytz composed incidental music to more than 20 plays, plus a large amount of vocal, instrumental and, particularly, choral music.

1861 **I funerali del karnevale** (Iván Prodan) Teatro Civico, Fiume

1863 **Mannschaft an Bord** (J L Harisch) 1 act Carltheater 15 December

1864 **Fitzliputzli, oder die Teufelchen der Ehe** (''from the French'') 1 act Carltheater 5 November

1865 **Die Lazzaroni von Neapel** (Hans Max) 1 act Carltheater 4 May

1866 **Die Hexe von Boissy** (Karl Costa) Carltheater 24 April

1866 **Nachtschwärmer** (Erik Nessl) 1 act Carltheater 10 November

1867 **Ein Rendezvous in der Schweiz** (Gustav Neuhaus) 1 act Carltheater 3 April

1867 **Das Gaugericht** (Carl Julius Folnes) 1 act Carltheater 14 September

1868 **Nach Mekka** (Nessl) 1 act Harmonietheater 11 January

1868 **Sonnambule** (Nessl) 1 act Harmonietheater 25 January

1868 **Der Meisterschuss von Pottenstein** (Anton Langer) 1 act Carltheater 25 July

1869 **Meister Puff** (Nessl) 1 act Theater an der Wien 22 May

1870 **Der Raub der Sabinerinnen** (Betty Young) Friedrich-Wilhelmstädtisches Theater, Berlin 6 August

1874 **Der gefangene Amor** (Wieland ad) 1 act Vaudeville Theater 12 September

1888 **Afrodita** (Nicola Milan) National Theatre, Zagreb 8 January

1906 **Die Nihilsten** (Wilhelm Otto) National Theatre, Zagreb 15 December

Biography: Pettan, H: *Popis Skladbi Ivana Zajca* (Jugoslavenska Akademija Znanosti i Umjetnosti, Zagreb, 1956)

ZEHN MADCHEN UND KEIN MANN Komische Operette in 1 act by ''W Friedrich'' [ie, Wilhelm Friedrich Riese] based on the libretto *Six demoiselles à marier* by Adolphe Jaime and Adolphe Choler. Music by Franz von Suppé. Theater am Franz-Josefs-Kai, Vienna, 25 October 1862.

Previously set in its original French by Delibes, *Six demoiselles à marier,* first produced in Paris in 1856, had been played at Theater an der Wien (*Sechs Mädchen zu heiraten* ad J F Niemetz) in 1860 (13 October). The borrowed libretto was remade by Riese, and set by Suppé for production at Karl Treumann's Theater am Franz-Josefs-Kai, where it proved a thorough confirmation of his first little work in the same Viennese-French vein, *Das Pensionat.*

Herr von Schönhahn (Treumann) had a son by his first wife. But she went off and left him, and his two subsequent wives provided him with nothing but daughters. Ten of them. Getting this gaggle married off is a problem, and the overly proud father has put up a sign outside the door inviting visitors. If an unmarried man comes in, he is given a tour of the daughters. When the young veterinarian Agamemnon Paris (F Markwordt) ventures in, in pursuit of a pretty girl, he is given the full display, rehearsed to a nicety. Papa has it worked out, and in order to appeal to all probable tastes, each daughter displays her accomplishments in a different national style—Austrian, Castilian, English, Bavarian, Portuguese, Tyrolean, Italian, Mexican, Bohemian and Aragonese. However, the girl Paris is after is none of them but the housekeeper, Sidonia (Anna Grobecker), and since it turns out that he is the long-lost son of Schönhahn's first marriage, the old fellow ends up with 10 daughters . . . and a daughter-in-law.

Suppé had great fun with the score for the little piece, of which the clou was the series of national numbers sung by the daughters, beginning with a Tirolienne for Almina and Maschinka, highlighted by a burlesque Italian aria for

Limonia (Anna Marek), which gamboled up to a D in alt, then an ''Englische Ariette'' for Britta, a dance quartet for four of the less vocal daughters, and (as alternatives and additions, depending on the daughters available) a Holz-und-Stroh Polka, a Trinklied, an Italienisches Volkslied for soprano and alto, a Böhmische Volkslied for two of each, and a Guilleaume Walzer with florid cadenzas. The whole ended up in a massed family concert. Paris did his singing before the concert started, being equipped with a lively entrance song (''Der Frühling ist kommen'') and a duo with Schönhahn in which he performed a lot of laughing on repeated high Bs. Sidonia, too, did her singing in the first part of the night, with a Stiefel-Putzer Lied and a Complimentier-Lied, and the father introduced his daughters and saw the action along in song as well as word.

Zehn Mädchen was a great success. It was played 32 times over the seven months' remaining life of the Kai-Theater, and Treumann took it with him when he removed to the Carltheater, where Karl Blasel and Josef Matras both succeeded to the role of the father, Hermine Meyerhoff had a turn at Limonia but Anna Grobecker retained her part of Sidonia (17 June 1870). The piece later reappeared both there (20 September 1879, 19 December 1873 as *25 Mädchen und kein Mann*) and in other Viennese houses.

One of the earliest Viennese pieces to travel to any extent, *Zehn Mädchen* was quickly played throughout Austria and Germany, and also in Hungary, where Endre Latabár's vernacular version included the son in the title ''ten girls and one man''—instead of no man. Both London and New York first saw the piece in its original German, London as performed by a visiting German troupe and New York from Theodore L'Arronge, who played it during his 1867–68 season at the local German-speaking theatre with Auguste Steglich-Fuchs as Sidonia and Rosa Zerboni as Limonia, and again the following year with his wife, Hedwig L'Arronge, as his daughter, Limonia. The Terrace-Garten also played the piece, which became a familiar part of New York German spectacles-coupés.

An English-language version was played at London's Theatre Royal, Drury Lane (ad Arthur Matthison) in 1874, with Cyril Ashton as Papa, Harriet Coveney as Sidonia, and Cicely Nott, Charlotte Russell, Clara Jecks, and the young Alice Burville and Kate Vaughan amongst a royal register of daughters. It was subsequently toured by Karl Meyder's Operetta Company (1876). The Gaiety Theatre also got in on the act in 1882 (6 March) with an adaptation by Robert Soutar and Meyer Lutz played as *Oh! Those Girls* and featuring the young Connie Gilchrist. Another version was seen in the New York repertoire of the Kelly and Leon Minstrels in which Leon featured as Sidonia, but this prima donna altered things, so that he also performed the Italian aria and a dance routine. This version was the first to be seen in Australia, when Kelly and Leon introduced it there in their repertoire in 1880. Another was played in Chicago in 1883 (and doubtless prior to that) as *Ten Daughters and No Husband,* Koster and Bial's mounted a *Seven Maidens* in November 1884, Will Mestayer played yet another, in 1887, as *Twenty to One* and in 1894 (January) an ''up-to-date'' version of the piece reset in rural America was produced at Broadway's Imperial Theatre (a vaudeville house) under the title *Zeka.* Zeka was the new name given to Sidonia.

The number of daughters in poor (overstrained?) Herr von Schönhahn's family varied from production to production, depending on the number of girls available, or the number wishing to interpolate a national song. The Italians avoided the issue and entitled the piece with a slightly different emphasis as *Le Amazzoni* (ad A Scalvini), whilst a certain A von Bayer and Karl Kleiber produced a contemporary comic-opera-parody in which there were *Zehn Männer und keine Frau.* I wonder what the plot was in that one.

Germany: Friedrich-Wilhelmstädtisches Theater 3 May 1863, Nationaltheater *Vierzehn Mädchen und kein Mann* 12 July 1881; Hungary: Budai Népszínház *Tíz leány, egy férj sem* 20 June 1863, Budai Színkör (Ger) 5 July 1863; UK: Opera Comique (Ger) 7 November 1871, Theatre Royal, Drury Lane *Ten of 'Em* 2 December 1874; USA: Stadttheater (Ger) 24 April 1867; Australia: Opera House, Sydney *Six Brides and No Bridegroom* 25 September 1880

ZELL, F[riedrich] [WALZEL, Camillo] (b Magdeburg, 11 February 1829; d Vienna, 17 March 1895). The most important librettist of the 19th-century Viennese stage.

Born in Magdeburg whilst his mother, the singer Fortunata Franchetti-Walzel, was engaged at the local theatre, Walzel was educated in Leipzig and in Pest and, as a young man, joined the Austrian army, where he rose to the rank of lieutenant. When he resigned his commission he joined the Danube Steamship Company, became a captain, and in that capacity he served in the war of 1866. In the off-sailing season he found plenty of time to indulge his literary and journalistic predilections, and in the early 1860s he began to work intermittently in the theatre, adapting French playlets and opérettes for Karl Treumann at the Theater am Franz-Josefs-Kai and at the Carltheater. As often happened in those days, however, his name did not necessarily appear on the playbills, and it seems not to have been until 1863 that his first credited musical works, a pasticcio burlesque, a one-performance Genrebild ''from the French'' and an adaptation of Offenbach's *Une demoiselle en loterie,* were played at the Theater an der Wien.

Sent to Paris to spy out adaptable material for the Viennese theatre, Walzel became friendly there with a number of prominent theatrical personalities, notably Offenbach, and, as a result, he became thoroughly orientated towards a theatrical rather than a nautical career, and one in which his texts, much like those of H B Farnie in Britain, were very often based—admittedly or not—on ''borrowed'' French originals. He had his first significant success, however, with a piece on which there was no source doubt—collaborating with Julius Hopp on the Viennese version of *La Belle Hélène* for the Theater an der Wien. He subsequently wrote a sequel to Meilhac and Halévy's piece, dealing with the events of the Siege of Troy.

Walzel wrote several burlesques and satires (*Elegante Tini,* the parody of Patti entitled *Abällina, oder Ein Schwager für Alles, Sarah und Bernhardt,* etc) and some straight comedies, and dipped again into the area of opérette with a translation of Lecocq's *Fleur de thé* for the Vienna stage, before he came together with the Theater an der Wien's resident adapter and conductor, Richard Genée, to form a working partnership that would produce both men's most memorable work over a period of some 20 years.

The pair collaborated on both the adaptation of many of the principal imports of the period and the texts for many of the most important Viennese Operetten of the 1870s and 1880s, a number of which were, again, adaptations of French libretti: Suppé's *Fatinitza, Boccaccio* and *Donna Juanita,* Millöcker's *Apajune, der Wassermann, Der Bettelstudent* and *Gasparone,* and Strauss's *Der lustige Krieg, Eine Nacht in Venedig, Cagliostro in Wien,* and *Das Spitzentuch der Königin.* Walzel also supplied the libretti for Genée's own musical compositions, notably his two international Operette successes *Der Seekadett* and *Nanon,* each of which was, once more, a version of an established French text.

Thoroughly established in his ''alternative'' career, he eventually resigned from the Steamship Company in 1883 and devoted himself wholly to his theatrical occupations, often carrying on his collaboration with Genée, who in later days moved away from Vienna to live at Pressbaum, by post, either from Vienna or from his estate at Weissenbach. The division of their labor left much of the plot and dialogue to Walzel and the bulk of the lyric writing to Genée, but such a division was by no means automatic. Both (but Genée in particular) also worked alone or with other partners, and Walzel was responsible, alone, for the adaptation of several French vaudevilles as musical comedies for the Vienna stage, as well as for the straight adaptation of pieces such as the successful comedy *Décoré* (1889).

In 1884 Walzel became part of a syndicate under Alexandrine von Schönerer put together to run the Theater an der Wien, and between 1884 and 1889 he was the effective manager of the house. His management was initiated with the reasonably successful Vienna production of Strauss's revised *Eine Nacht in Venedig,* and during the next five years his most important productions included Planquette's *Rip van Winkle, Gasparone, Der Feldprediger, Der Zigeunerbaron, Der Hofnarr, Die Wienerstadt in Wort und Bild, Die sieben Schwaben, Simplicius* and *Der Mikado.*

Following his withdrawal from the management and the managerial syndicate, Walzel continued to write for the theatre, but the last years of his life did not bring any original works comparable to those of the earlier part of his career. He did, however, see out his career with a final flourish: the extremely successful Josefstadter-Theater production of his version of the French vaudeville *Toto,* produced in the year before his death.

1863 **Abällina, oder Ein Schwager für Alles** (pasticcio) Theater an der Wien 16 May

1863 **Die Schwaben in Wien** (Adolf Müller/J Mery ad) Theater an der Wien 12 August

1864 **Eine Künstreiterin** (*Une demoiselle en loterie*) German version (Theater an der Wien)

1864 **Des Nachbars Äpfel** (*Les Pommes du voisin*) German version w O F Berg and music by Adolf Müller (Theater an der Wien)

1865 **Die schöne Helena** (*La Belle Hélène*) German version w Julius Hopp (Theater an der Wien)

1867 **Die Federschlange** (Carlo di Barbieri) 1 act Deutsches Theater, Budapest 16 February

1869 **Theeblüthe** (*Fleur de thé*) German version (Theater an der Wien)

1872 **Die Theaterprinzessin** (*La Diva*) German version w F Zell (Theater an der Wien)

1873 **Die Wilderer** (*Les Braconniers*) German version w Genée (Theater an der Wien)

1874 **Die Japanesin** (Émile Jonas/Eugène Grangé, Victor Bernard) German version w Genée (Theater an der Wien)

1874 **Angot und der blauen Donau** (Karl Pleininger) Strampfertheater 13 November

1875 **Cagliostro in Wien** (Strauss/w Genée) Theater an der Wien 27 February

1876 **Fatinitza** (Franz von Suppé/w Genée) Carltheater 5 January

1876 **Nach dem Mond und unterm Meer** (Suppé/Verne ad Adolphe L'Arronge ad) Carltheater March

1876 **Der Seekadett** (Genée) Theater an der Wien 24 October

1877 **Die Porträt-Dame** (*Die Profezeiungen des Quiribi*) (Max Wolf/w Genée) Theater an der Wien 1 March

1877 **Nanon, die Wirthin vom "goldenen Lamm"** (Genée/w Genée) Theater an der Wien 10 March

1877 **Im Wunderland der Pyramiden** (Genée/w Genée) Komische Oper (Ringtheater) 25 December

1878 **Die letzten Mohikaner** (Genée) Theater am Gärtnerplatz, Munich 29 September; Theater an der Wien 4 January 1879

1878 **Vom Touristen Kränzchen** (Franz Roth) 1 act Stadttheater 28 November

1878 **Niniche** German version w new music by Brandl (Carltheater)

1879 **Boccaccio** (Suppé/w Genée) Carltheater 1 February

1879 **Die Fornarina** (Karl Zeller/w Genée) Theater am Gärtnerplatz, Munich 18 October

1879 **Gräfin Dubarry** (Carl Millöcker/w Genée) Theater an der Wien 31 October

1879 **Der grosse Casimir** (*Le Grand Casimir*) German version (Carltheater)

1880 **Papas Frau** (*La Femme à papa*) German version w new music by Brandl (Carltheater)

1880 **Die hübsche Perserin** (*La Jolie Persane*) German version w Genée (Theater an der Wien)

1880 **Donna Juanita** (Suppé/w Genée) Carltheater 21 February

1880 **Nisida** (Genée/w Moritz West) Carltheater 9 October

1880 **Die Carbonari** (Karl Zeller/w West) Carltheater 27 November

1880 **Apajune, der Wassermann** (Millöcker/w Genée) Theater an der Wien 18 December

1881 **Der Gascogner** (Suppé/w Genée) Carltheater 22 March

1881 **Jean de Nivelle** German version (Hofopern-Theater)

1881 **Die Jungfrau von Belleville** (Millöcker/w Genée) Theater an der Wien 29 October

1881 **Der lustige Krieg** (Strauss/w Genée) Theater an der Wien 25 November

1882 **Lili** German version (Theater an der Wien)

1882 **Der Bettelstudent** (Millöcker/w Genée) Theater an der Wien 6 December

1883 **Königin Mariette** (Ignaz Brüll/w Genée) Munich 16 June

1883 **Eine Nacht in Venedig** (Strauss/w Genée) Friedrich-Wilhelmstädtisches Theater, Berlin 3 October

1884 **Gasparone** (Millöcker/w Genée) Theater an der Wien 26 January

1885 **Zwillinge** (Genée, Louis Roth/w Genée) Theater an der Wien 14 February

1885 **Die Kindsfrau** (Julius Stern arr/Hennequin ad) Theater an der Wien 7 May

1885 **Der Jagdjunker [der Kaiserin]** (Alfons Czibulka/w Genée) Walhalla Theater, Berlin 3 December; revised version Carltheater 20 March 1886

1886 **Die Novize** (Wilhelm Rab) Theater an der Wien 21 January

1886 **Der Nachtwandler** (Roth/w Genée) Friedrich-Wilhelmstädtisches Theater, Berlin, 25 September

1886 **Der Viceadmiral** (Millöcker/w Genée) Theater an der Wien 9 October

1886 **Die Piraten** (Genée/w Genée) Walhalla-Theater, Berlin 8 October

1887 **Die Wienerstadt in Wort und Bild** (Adolf Müller jr, Julius Stern, et al/w Isidor Fuchs, Julius Bauer) Theater an der Wien 10 April

1887 **Die Dreizehn** (Genée/w Genée) Carltheater 14 November

1888 **Die Hochzeit des Reservisten** (Julius Stern/w Hoffmann, Isidor Fuchs) Theater an der Wien 28 January

1888 **Der Mikado** German version w Genée (Theater an der Wien)

1888 **Wolf und Lampel** (*Cocard et Bicoquet*) (Stern/w Hoffmann) Theater an der Wien 13 October

1888 **Gil Blas von Santillana** (Czibulka/w West) Carl-Schultze Theater, Hamburg 23 November

1889 **Die indische Witwe** (Gustav Geiringer/w Genée) 1 act Theater an der Wien 9 February

1889 **Capitän Fracassa** (Rudolf Dellinger/w Genée) Carl-Schultze Theater, Hamburg 2 March; Theater an der Wien 21 September

1889 **Der schöne Kaspar** (Josef Bayer) Theater am Gärtnerplatz, Munich 6 April

1889 **Der Königsgardist** (*The Yeomen of the Guard*) German version w Genée (Krolls Theater, Berlin)

1889 **Die Piraten** (*The Pirates of Penzance*) German version (Theater an der Wien)

1890 **Die Gondoliere** (*The Gondoliers*) w Genée (Theater an der Wien)

1892 **Wiener Ausstellungs-G'schichten, oder Das Rendezvous der Strohwitwer** (Fritz Lehner) Theater in der Josefstadt 14 October

1892 **Der Millionenankel** (Adolf Müller jr/w Genée) Theater an der Wien 5 November

1893 **Das Mädchen von Mirano** (*La Stupida*) 1 act (Alexander Neumann/w Genée) Carltheater 6 April

1893 **Der Schwiegerpapa** (Alfred Strasser, Max von Wienzierl/w Wilhelm Ascher) Brünn 22 April; Adolf Ernst-Theater, Berlin 10 June

1894 **Fürst Malachoff** (Stern/fr Fr) Carltheater 22 September

1894 **Sein erster Walzer** (Johann Strauss arr) Carltheater 15 October

1894 **Die Königin von Gamara** (Neumann/w Genée) Carltheater 27 October

1894 **Tata-Toto** (*Toto*) German version w Léon (Theater in der Josefstadt)

ZELLER, Carl [Johann Adam] (b St Peter-in-der-Au, 19 June 1842; d Baden-bei-Wien, 17 August 1898). The composer of some of the happiest music of the Golden Age Vienna stage, and of one of its most enduring Operetten.

Carl Zeller led, throughout his working life, two separate careers: one as a civil servant and one as a musician. Having been, from the age of 11, a chorister in the Vienna Boys' Choir, he led parallel studies in law and in music and, on his graduation, took up a post in the civic administration. In 1873 he was made an artistic consultant under the umbrella of the Department of Education.

Although he had already turned his hand to composition, notably of choral and instrumental music, in earlier years, it was not until 1876 that he turned out his first work for the stage, the "comic opera" *Joconde,* produced by Maximilian Steiner at the Theater an der Wien "in collaboration with members of the Gesang-Verein." A Scottish Roundheads-and-Cavaliers piece, with Carl Adolf Friese featured as the 1650s Lord Dunstan Meredith of Killarnock Castle, Bertha Steinher in the title role as the Cromwellian Governor of the area, and young Alexander Girardi in the role of Bob Calladwader [*sic*], the Laird's steward, *Joconde* was played 20 times. It boasted, however, the most remarkable male-voice comic opera chorus ever seen in Vienna: 250 of Zeller's colleagues from the Gesang Verein volunteered.

For his second work, Zeller collaborated with the Theater an der Wien's accredited text writers, Zell and Genée, but the resultant work, *Die Fornarina,* did not make it back to Vienna from its Munich presentation. A much more widespread future, however, was reserved for *Die Carbonari.* Produced at Vienna's Carltheater, it was remounted the following year in a revised version at Berlin's Friedrich-Wilhelmstädtisches Theater under the title *Capitän Nicol,* and that version found its way to other German houses and as far afield as America, where it was given by Marie Geistinger's company with Adolf Link, Emma Seebold and Ernst Schütz at the Thalia-Theater (2 May 1883). The show lasted well enough that it was reproduced in 1891 at New York's Amberg Theater in its original *Die Carbonari* form.

The real breakthrough for Zeller the composer came in 1886, a decade after the first promises of *Joconde,* when the Carltheater produced the first of his collaborations with the new pairing of his faithful Moritz West and Ludwig Held, the successful author of *Die Näherin. Der Vagabund*'s 37 performances at the Carltheater may have looked statistically light, but they were the beginning of a series of productions throughout the world for the Operette, and the foundation of a team that five years later turned out the piece that was the triumph of its times and would become one of the most endearing classics of the 19th-century Viennese repertoire, *Der Vogelhändler* ("Ich bin die Christel von der Post," "Fröhlich Pfalz," "Schenkt man sich Rosen in Tirol," etc). With Alexander Girardi, now the darling of the Viennese theatre public, introducing the starring role of the little bird seller, the show and its glorious folk-tinted music were launched on a career that has kept it to the front of the repertoire to this day.

Zeller, West and Held followed *Der Vogelhändler* with *Der Obersteiger,* which, if it attempted rather openly to reproduce all the winning elements of the previous show, nevertheless turned out to be another delightful and successful musical-comical evening and, with its Girardi waltz, the delicious "Sei nicht bös," it produced the song that would become Zeller's most internationally known number.

At the height of his fame as a musician, Zeller met his downfall in his public position. Convicted of perjury in a damages case, he was sentenced to 12 months in prison. Forced to resign in disgrace from his civil service post, he died soon after, at the age of 56. There was, however, one more Zeller musical produced on the Viennese stage. The uncompleted *Der Kellermeister,* put together from music left by the composer by Johann Brandl, was mounted in 1901 under the management of Ernst Gettke at the Raimundtheater. Girardi appeared as the hotelier, Urban, alongside Toni Braun and Oskar Braun, and the composer won another, posthumous, song hit with the star's "Lass dir Zeit." *Der Kellermeister* was later seen, played in German, in America.

Zeller's son, Karl Zeller jr, also composed for the musical stage (*Das Haremsmädel,* etc).

1876 **Joconde** (Moritz West, Moret) Theater an der Wien 18 March

1879 **Die Fornarina** (West, Richard Genée) Theater am Gärtnerplatz, Munich 18 October

1880 **Die Carbonari** (West, Zell) Carltheater 27 November

1881 **Capitän Nicol** revised *Die Carbonari* by West and Hermann Hirschel, Friedrich-Wilhelmstädtisches Theater, Berlin 5 November

1886 **Der Vagabund** (West, Ludwig Held) Carltheater 30 October

1891 **Der Vogelhändler** (West, Held) Theater an der Wien 10 January

1894 **Der Obersteiger** (West, Held) Theater an der Wien 5 January

1901 **Der Kellermeister** (arr Johann Brandl/West) Raimundtheater 21 December

Biography: Zeller, K W: *Mein Vater Karl Zeller* (St Poltner Zeitungs-Verlag, St Polten, 1942)

ZERKOVITZ, Béla (b Szeged, 11 July 1882; d Budapest, 23 October 1948). Popular songwriter who turned out scores to a large number of musical plays and scored a full ration of hometown hits.

Béla Zerkovitz studied music in his youth, but he paired those studies with more practical ones and qualified as an architectural engineer. Whilst continuing a career in his "proper job," he made his first ventures as a songwriter, and his songs were regularly interpolated into Hungarian musical shows of the early years of the 20th century. His first full score for the musical stage seems to have been that to Adolf Mérei's 1911 *A kék róka,* but in 1913 he successfully supplied the full scores to two operetts, *Aranyeső* and *Katonadolog* (a soldier's tale), written to texts by Izor Béldi, the librettist of Budapest's first 100-performance Operette *Katalin* a decade earlier.

Over the following years, Zerkovitz became hugely popular as a songwriter—the most famous of his many hits being the gently rhythmic 1914 song "Hulló falevél," for which he wrote both music and lyric—and he won himself the reputation of being the "national songsmith of Pest." He ranged from opera to revue in his stage writings, from strongly lyrical music to many pieces that sounded like British music-hall numbers with an intermittent national flavoring, as he turned out a regular supply of songs in particular as house composer for the variegated productions at the Royal Orfeum. However, he won his chief success with the scores for a line of musical comedies produced both in Hungary and in Austria after he had finally retired from his architectural work in 1919 and devoted himself wholly to music.

The highly successful *A csókos asszony,* a reset version of the French libretto to *Clary-Clara* (originally composed in its French version by Victor Roger), and *Aranymadár* (the golden bird) ("Párizsban huncut a lány"), which totaled some 300 Budapest performances, set the scene for their composer to provide the scores for a series of popular musical plays, written with such top local writers as László Bús-Fekete, László Szilágyi and Imre Harmath, a series that gave Zerkovitz a regular run of stage success right through the late 1920s.

With Bús-Fekete he wrote *Árvácska* (pansy), which, with Ilona Vaály in the title role, ran for over 100 consecutive nights on its production at the Budai Színkör and produced a hit with the java "Egyszer volt, hol nem volt . . . ," and *A nóta vége* (the end of the song), a musical adaptation of the playwright's internationally successful 1921 play *Buzavirág* (cornflower), set to a score featuring the fox-trots ("Kaderabek!") and tangos ("Tango d'amour") that were as de rigeur in Budapest as in the rest of the world. *A nóta vége,* similarly, had a fine run at the Budai Színkör before going on to pile up some 300 performances in the repertoire of the Városi Színház.

Harmath's *Póstás Katica* was another success, and a set of four pieces with the young librettist Szilágyi in the late 1920s maintained the composer's career at its peak through its later stages with a fresh lot of fine runs and hit songs: a new version of *A csókos asszony,* with Hanna Honthy and Gyula Kompothy starred, *Muzsikus Ferkó* (Ferkó, the musician), mounted with Ferenc Kiss in the title role alongside Irén Biller, Hanna Honthy and Gyula Kabos for more than 50 performances at the Budai Színkör, *A legkisebbik Horváth lány* (the littlest Horvath girl) and the happy *Eltörött a hegedűm* (the violin is broken), which mixed modern, jazzy dance numbers with traditional Hungarian melodies as illustration to a tale in which Juci Lábass played a country girl who turns vamp to win back a husband tempted by city lights and Oszkár Dénes and Rózsi Bársony tripped through the lighter numbers to triumph.

The 1930 *Meluzina,* a circus musical that had the prima donna performing a rope dance, was the last of his major works, although a 1936 piece *Hulló falevél,* mounted at the Városi Színház, had Hanna Honthy leading the company in its composer's most famous song as a finale. After his death, a score was arranged from his works as a musical accompaniment to Molnár's play *Doktor úr.* First staged in 1957 (Kis Színpad 8 February), it was revived in Budapest in 1990.

Alongside his composing career, Zerkovitz latterly led a second as a theatre manager. In the mid-1920s he became director of the Városi Színház, which in the pre-1917 era, when it was known as the Népopera, had housed his first hits, and in the early 1930s he took over at the head of the Royal Orfeum (1930), the other house that had supplied him with his early work.

Csókos asszony has been seen as recently as 1994 at the Székesfehérvári Nyári Színház and at Veszprém.

1911 **A kék róka** (Adolf Mérei) Royal Orfeum 29 September

1912 **Die schöne Marietta** (Lantsch) 1 act Wiener Kolosseum 1 December

1913 **Finom familia** (*Eine feine Familie*) 1 act Royal Orfeum 31 January

1913 **Aranyeső** (Mérei/Izor Béldi) Népopera 21 February

1913 **Katonadolog** (Mérei/Béldi) Népopera 25 October

1914 **Die Wundermühle** (Bernhard Buchbinder) Theater in der Josefstadt, Vienna 24 March

1915 **Vándorfecskék** (Mérei) Télikert 1 March; Royal Orfeum, Budapest 2 October

1915 **Das Finanzgenie** (Felix Dörmann, Hans Kottow) Apollotheater, Vienna 1 November

1917 **A szegény Golem** (Endre Nagy) Royal Orfeum 2 January

1917 **A mondur fiatalít** (Nagy) Royal Orfeum 1 February

1917 **A porcellán-őrült** (Nagy) Royal Orfeum 31 March

1917 **A Balaton Romeoja** (Béla Szenes) Royal Orfeum 10 August

1917 **Háron Határ Hotel** (Nagy) Royal Orfeum 1 October

1917 **Az utolsó Dankó-nóta** (Nagy) Royal Orfeum 1 November

1918 **Pambu** (Nagy) Royal Orfeum 1 January

1918 **A zsámbéki földesúr** (Nagy) Royal Orfeum 1 March

1918 **Pitypalaty kisasszony** (Jenő Faragó) Royal Orfeum 1 June

1918 **Páratlan menyecske** (Faragó) Royal Orfeum 1 October

1918 **Aranykalitka** (Imre Harmath) Royal Orfeum 1 December

1919 **Beppo** (Harmath) 1 act Royal Orfeum 1 February

1919 **Kalandor kisasszony** (Harmath) Royal Orfeum 2 November

1919 **Százszorszép** (Faragó) Városi Színház 28 November

1920 **Csillagok csillaga** (Harmath) Royal Orfeum 1 January

1920 **Zsuzsu** (Harmath) Royal Orfeum 1 April

1920 **Lucia** (Harmath) Royal Orfeum 1 September

1920 **Csalogánydal** (Harmath) Royal Orfeum 1 November

1921 **Csókos asszony** (*Clary-Clara*) Hungarian version with new songs Eskü Téri Színház 11 March

1921 **Kvitt** (Harmath) Royal Orfeum 2 April

1921 **A 28-as** (László Bús-Fekete) Royal Orfeum 1 October

1921 **A főúr** (Bús-Fekete) Royal Orfeum 1 December

1922 **Aranymadár** (Harmath) 1 act Royal Orfeum 1 April

1922 **A szép Sara** (ad István Zagon) Royal Orfeum 1 October

1922 **A vörös majom** (László Bkeffy) Royal Orfeum 2 November

1923 **A hattyúlovag** (Harmath) Royal Orfeum 1 April

1924 **Árvácska** (Ernő Kulinyi/Bús-Fekete) Budai Színkör 1 July; Király Színház 13 September

1924 **Póstás Katica** (Harmath) Lujza Blaha Színház 19 December

1925 **A nóta vége** (Bús-Fekete, Kulinyi) Budai Színkör 24 June

1926 **A csókos asszony** (new version ad Lazslo Szilágyi) Városi Színház 27 February

1926 **Csuda Mihály szerencséje** (Kulinyi/Bús-Fekete) Magyar Színház 22 May

1926 **Muzsikus Ferkó** (Szilágyi) Budai Színkör 18 June

1927 **Zsiványkirály** (Harmath) Royal Orfeum 1 January

1927 **A legkisebbik Horváth lány** (Szilágyi) Király Színház 21 May

1928 **Balról a harmadik** (Béla Szilágyi) Royal Orfeum 1 January

1928 **Eltörött a hegedűm** (Szilágyi) Király Színház 3 November

1930 **Meluzina** (Harmath, Rezső Török) Városi Színház 12 April

1931 **Falu végén kurta kocsma** (Harmath) Bethlen-Téri Színház 10 April

1936 **Hulló falevél** (Dezső Kellér/Szilágyi, Ernő Andai) Városi Színház 23 December

ZIEGFELD, Florenz jr (b Chicago, 21 March 1867; d Los Angeles, 22 July 1932). Flamboyant Broadway producer of revue and musical plays whose name and fame have, with a little help from Hollywood and some healthy self-publicity, become legend.

Originally a variety producer, Florenz Ziegfeld ventured into the musical theatre when he produced a series of mostly made-over vehicles for his sometime wife, ''French'' soubrette Anna Held. Beginning with a revival of the old Charles Hoyt farce-comedy *A Parlour Match* (1896), into which Miss Held was inserted as a speciality, he followed up with chopped-up versions of the Anna Judic shows *La Femme à papa, Mam'zelle Nitouche* and *Niniche* (*Papa's Wife, The Little Duchess*), a *Mam'selle Napoléon,* which gave Jean Richepin as its source, *The Parisian Model* and *Miss Innocence* (which was not *Mam'zelle Nitouche*). He also mounted vehicles for soubrette Edna Aug (*The Four-Leaf Clover*), the soprano Grace van Studdiford (the romantic comic opera *The Red Feather*) and ballerina Adeline Genée (*The Soul Kiss*), and was involved with Weber and Fields on *Higgledy Piggledy* in what should have been another star outing for Miss Held but from which she (and he) withdrew when it turned out not to be.

In 1907 Ziegfeld produced his first *Follies* variety show, and in the next two decades these ever-more-grandiose mixtures of dance, spectacle, comedy and song comprised the main part of his career as a producer. He did, however, venture a pair of musicals in 1912, of which the variety-based *Over the River* did better than another attempt to revive a Hoyt farce comedy: the transformation of the old-time mega-hit *A Trip to Chinatown* into the flop *A Winsome Widow.*

Ziegfeld had his first real success as a musical-comedy producer in 1920, when he produced *Sally* as a vehicle for his *Follies* star Marilyn[n] Miller, and thereafter book musicals featured much more prominently amongst his works. In the final decade of his producing career, he presented 14 new musicals on Broadway, from which the comical *Kid Boots,* the colorful spectacular *Rio Rita, Show Boat* (1927), *Rosalie* (1928), Friml's *The Three Musketeers* (1928) and *Whoopee* (1928) were all successes.

The name of Florenz Ziegfeld has gone down in Broadway's theatrical history as the epitome of glamour and glitter, of showmanship and show business hype. He was the man who wanted to put a line of up-to-date chorus girls in *Bitter-Sweet.* Yet he was also the producer—and by no means the silent producer—of one piece, *Show Boat,* that has survived through the decades since as a classic of the substantial musical stage, and another, *The Three Musketeers,* that rendered it little in success in its time.

After his divorce from Anna Held, Ziegfeld was married to another leading lady, Billie Burke, who also spent a part of her career on the musical stage.

In 1988 an extravaganza based on the life of *Ziegfeld* was presented at the London Palladium (arr: Michael Reed/Ned Sherrin, Alistair Beaton). Len Cariou, Marc Urquhart and Topol in turn played the part of the producer. A version of the piece was later seen in the American regions. On film, *The Great Ziegfeld* was represented by William Powell.

Ziegfeld's younger brother, W K Ziegfeld, also became a producer, based in Chicago, where he ran for a time Ziegfeld's Theater and produced the musicals *The Girl in the Kimono* (1910), *The Military Girl* (1912), etc.

Biographies: Higham, C: *Ziegfeld* (Regnery, Chicago, 1972), Carter, R: *The World of Flo Ziegfeld* (Elek, London, 1974), Ziegfeld R & P: *The Ziegfeld Touch* (Abrams, New York, 1993), etc

ZIEHRER, Carl Michael (b Vienna, 2 May 1843; d Vienna, 14 November 1922). Composer of much popular Viennese music, including a number of scores for the Operette stage.

Born into a well-off Viennese family, the young Ziehrer studied music in his hometown and was launched, at his family's expense, at the head of his own dance orchestra when only 20 years of age. Throughout a busy, prolific and highly successful career of some 40 years as a composer and conductor of orchestral dance music and military band music, Ziehrer also contributed, at first spasmodically but later more purposefully, to the Operette stage.

His first work for the Carltheater, *Wiener Kinder,* was produced in 1881 and was brought back for further showings in the following season, whilst the subsequent *Ein Deutschmeister,* a military piece allowing the composer to indulge in his now famous march music, played for several weeks at the same theatre, seven years later. A score for a remade Posse, *Wiener Luft,* at the Theater an der Wien was heard 26 times. However, the breakthrough for Ziehrer as a theatre composer finally came in 1898, when Gabor Steiner produced *Der schöne Rigo,* a piece that—in a manner practiced normally only after a composer's death—reused some of Ziehrer's earlier music to make up a score for the libretto by Venedig in Wien house writers Leopold Krenn and Carl Lindau. With Rudolf del Zopp, Arthur Guttmann and Karl Tuschl in the cast, it proved, if scarcely a hit, successful enough to go on to a production in Leipzig (Carola Theater 25 December 1898) and for Steiner to produce another piece from the same writers for the next season.

Die Landstreicher was something different altogether. Not only was it a custom-written piece, it was easily Ziehrer's best stage work up to that time, and would remain one of his best of all time. It was a great summer-season success at the theatre at the Englisch Garten in the Prater, was brought back the following season, played at Steiner's Danzers Orpheum in the winter season, at the Theater an der Wien in 1902, and then beyond Vienna for many years to come.

The success of *Die Landstreicher* opened up top-drawer theatrical opportunities for the composer. He and his librettists had their next piece, *Die drei Wünsche,* mounted at the Carltheater with Mizzi Günther and Louis Treumann heading the cast, and, although it managed a first run of only 27 performances, the following season the Theater an der Wien took up their *Der Fremdenführer.* A 40-night run was prefatory to productions in Germany and Hungary, and the show remained sufficiently alive to be revived at the Raimundtheater in a suitably altered wartime version and, again, in an even more altered state, at the Volksoper in 1978.

Back at the Carltheater, *Der Schätzmeister* saw Günther and Treumann featured in a second Ziehrer piece, but one that once again could manage only an indifferent first run of 31 performances, limited engagements in Germany and Hungary (*A Becsüs,* Budai Színkör 1 May 1906), and a tardy and aborted American tryout by the Shuberts as *Love in Pawn* (ad Howard Jacot) in 1911, and Ziehrer returned to Steiner and his summer theatre with *Fesche Geister.* His second great hit, however, was not mounted in Vienna. In 1907 he supplied the music for Kraatz, Stobitzer and Wilhelm Sterk's *Ein tolles Mädel,* a female star-vehicle musical comedy produced at Wiesbaden, and saw it score the biggest success he had known in his career as it moved on to Steiner's Danzers Orpheum in Vienna and then to productions around the world (*Mlle Mischief, Fuzsitus kisasszony,* etc).

Ziehrer's *Liebeswalzer,* produced by Karczag as the first new Operette under his management of the Raimundtheater in 1908, also did well, being played in repertoire there for more than 150 performances over six years (100th 28 October 1909), and winning a botched Broadway production as *The Kiss Waltz.* Another collaboration with Sterk produced *Ball bei Hof,* which also traveled (*Bal az udvarnal* Budapesti Színház 21 March 1912), but neither *Fürst Kasimir,* played at the Carltheater with Mizzi Zwerenz and the aged Karl Blasel as chief comic (40 performances), nor a revised version of the summertime *Manöverkind* as *Der Husarengeneral,* played at the Raimundtheater with Betty Fischer and Franz Glawatsch featured (51 performances), nor a further collaboration with Sterk on *Das dumme Herz* (68 performances) at the Johann Strauss-Theater proved able to win the same kind of popularity.

Ziehrer's theatre pieces did not find the same success that his dances, marches and Viennese songs did, but even though many of his Operetten had indifferent runs in Vienna most were mounted in Germany, several in Hungary, and even a small handful in America. Today, it is for his non-theatre music that the composer is celebrated in his hometown, where even the most successful of his Operetten remain at best on the fringe of the repertoire.

A would-be biomusical film on Ziehrer, which had him challenging Johann Strauss for the title of waltz king of Vienna, had director Willy Forst as the composer. It was issued in 1949 as *Wiener Mädeln.*

1866 **Mahomeds Paradies** 1 act Harmonietheater 26 February

1872 **Das Orakel zu Delphi** (Karl Costa) Landestheater, Linz 21 September

1875 **Kleopatra** (w Richard Genée/Josef Steinher) Komische Oper 13 November

1878 **König Jérôme** (Adolf Schirmer) Ringtheater 28 November

1879 **Alexander der Grosse** (Costa) Marburg January

1879 **Ein kleiner Don Juan** (Ludwig Ernst Pollhammer) Deutsches Theater, Budapest 21 November

1881 **Wiener Kinder** (Leopold Krenn, Carl Wolff) Carltheater 19 February

1888 **Ein Deutschmeister** (Richard Genée, Bruno Zappert) Carltheater 30 November

1889 **Wiener Luft** (Carl Lindau, Heinrich Thalboth) Theater an der Wien 10 May

1890 **Der bleiche Zauberer** (Isidor Fuchs) 1 act Theater an der Wien 20 September

1898 **Der schöne Rigo** (Krenn, Lindau) Venedig in Wien 24 May

1899 **Die Landstreicher** (Krenn, Lindau) Venedig in Wien 29 July

1901 **Die drei Wünsche** (Krenn, Lindau) Carltheater 9 March

1902 **Der Fremdenführer** (Krenn, Lindau) Theater an der Wien 11 October

1904 **Der Schätzmeister** (Alexander Engel, Julius Horst) Carltheater 10 December

1905 **Fesche Geister** (Krenn, Lindau) Venedig in Wien 7 July

1906 **Die Spottvogelwirtin** (Rudolf Österreicher) Raimundtheater 30 October

1907 **Ein tolles Mädel** (Wilhelm Sterk/Kurt Kraatz, Heinrich Stobitzer) Walhalla Theater, Wiesbaden 24 August; Danzers Orpheum, Vienna 8 November

1907 **Am Lido** (Ottokar Tann-Bergler, Alfred Deutsch-German) Budapester Orpheum 31 August

1908 **Liebeswalzer** (Robert Bodanzky, Fritz Grünbaum) Raimundtheater October 24

1909 **Herr und Frau Biedermann** (Sterk) 1 act Lustspielhaus, Munich 10 January

1909 **Der Gaukler** (Emil Golz, Arnold Golz) 1 act Apollotheater 6 September

1911 **In fünfzig Jahren** (arr/Krenn, Lindau) Ronacher 7 January

1911 **Ball bei Hof** (Sterk) Stadttheater, Stettin 22 January

1912 **Manöverkind** (Oskar Friedmann, Fritz Lunzer) Venedig in Wien 22 June

1913 **Fürst Kasimir** (Max Neal, Max Ferner) Carltheater 13 September

1913 **Der Husarengeneral** revised *Manöverkind* (Friedmann, Lunzer) Raimundtheater 3 October

1914 **Das dumme Herz** (Österreicher, Sterk) Johann Strauss-Theater 27 February

1916 **Im siebenten Himmel** (Neal, Ferner) Theater am Gärtnerplatz, Munich 26 February

1930 **Der verliebte Eskadron** (arr Karl Pauspertl/Sterk) Johann Strauss-Theater 11 July

Biographies: Schönherr, M: *Carl Michael Ziehrer, Sein Werk, Sein Leben, Seine Zeit* (Österreicher Bundesverlag, Vienna, 1974), Diamond, J: *From Gold to Silver: Carl Michael Ziehrer* (1993)

DER ZIGEUNERBARON Comic opera in 3 acts by Ignaz Schnitzer based on the story *Sáffi* by Mór Jókai. Music by Johann Strauss. Theater an der Wien, Vienna, 24 October 1885.

Second only to *Die Fledermaus, Der Zigeunerbaron* has proved itself through the years to be steadily the most popular of Johann Strauss's Operetten both in the theatre and outside it, and it has been played continually on European stages—and occasionally elsewhere—over the century and more since its first production in Vienna.

The genesis of the show apparently came in a meeting in Budapest between Strauss and the respected Hungarian author Mor Jókai, at which the latter suggested—amongst other possibilities—that of his novella *Sáffi* as the basis for an Operette libretto. It was also said to be Jókai who suggested that the Vienna-based Hungarian journalist and stage writer Ignaz Schnitzer, who also did a successful job on his famous *Arányember* (*Goldmensch*), be asked to write the stage adaptation. In contrast to the bubbling comedy of *Der lustige Krieg* and the Italianate pageantry and highish-jinks of *Eine Nacht in Venedig,* the subject matter and principal plotline of *Der Zigeunerbaron* (Jókai suggested the title as well) were in a strongly romantic and sentimental vein, and it was even announced at one stage that Strauss's new piece would be staged at the Vienna Hofoper. However, Schnitzer's adaptation, although it was a little lumpy in some respects, ultimately dosed the romance with just sufficient comedy to keep the show, though still palpably different in tone from its predecessors, safely in the operettic field.

The young Sándor Barinkay (Karl Streitmann) is brought back to Temesvár by the government official, Carnero (Carl Adolf Friese), to have restored to him the lands of which his father was dispossessed. He has barely arrived when his new neighbor, the pig farmer Zsupán (Alexander Girardi), is hustling him into a tactical betrothal with his daughter, Arsena. But Arsena (Karoline Reisser) is in love with Ottokar (Holbach), the son of her governess, Mirabella (Therese Schäfer), and she refuses the match, claiming by way of an excuse that she must have at least a Baron for a husband. Barinkay soon discovers the truth of her refusal and, to the anger of Zsupán and his family, plights himself instead to the gypsy maiden Sáffi (Ottilie Collin). Sáffi and her mother, Czipra (Antonie Hartmann), lead Barinkay to the ruin of his family home, and there they discover the treasure hidden by his fleeing father. Zsupán and Carnero are both anxious to lay claim to the gold, but when the governor, Graf Homonay (Josef Joseffy), comes by to recruit for the war against Spain, Barinkay gives him the treasure towards the war effort. Zsupán and Ottokar unknowingly drink the recruiting wine and are taken for the army, and the distraught Barinkay joins up as well when Czipra reveals that Sáffi is truthfully no child of hers, but the daughter of Hungary's last pasha—a veritable gypsy princess. When the men return, two years later, with Barinkay a real hero and Zsupán a phony one, the young man hands Arsena over to Ottokar and, his scruples over her rank now gone, weds Sáffi.

The romantic backbone of the score centered on the character of Sáffi, who was equipped with a powerful gypsy song, "Habet acht!," and joined rapturously in duet with Barinkay in the bullfinch duet "Wer uns getraut?," justifying their unofficial marriage before the Morality Commission regulations put forward by the

Plate 435. **Der Zigeunerbaron.** *Claus Klincke as Zsupán gathers his pigs about him in the Theater Hof's 1986 production.*

fussy Carnero. Barinkay's own big moment came with his lively introductory ''Als flotter Geist,'' describing the occupations he has gone through since his father's dispossession, whilst a baritone recruiting song for Homonay was another of the strongly sung vocal highlights. The soubret side was represented by Arsena and Ottokar, and the comic headed by Zsupán with a famously farmyard entrance piece (''Ja, das Schreiben und das Lesen'') and by Mirabella, relating to the booming of orchestral cannons, and in the evening's funniest number, the disastrous tale of how she lost her husband in the middle of a war (''Just sind es vierundzwanzig Jahre''). That husband is Carnero, the representative of that overworked Operette convention the Morality Commission, whose tenets are related in a song that was possibly funnier in its time than it is now. Alongside the solo pieces, some fine ensemble music was highlighted by a treasure trio for the two gypsy women and Barinkay (''Ha, seht es winkt'').

Der Zigeunerbaron was produced at the Theater an der Wien with great success. It was played 87 times consecutively in its first series, and it remained a regular part of the theatre's repertoire for many years thereafter, passing its 150th performance on 19 February 1887, and its 300th on 23 October 1903, with Karl Meister and Gisela Noris playing alongside Girardi in his original role. The show was produced at the Raimundtheater in 1908, in the earliest days of Karczag and Wallner's management, played there in repertoire for three years, and it was there that it passed its 1,000th Viennese night on 19 April 1909. In 1915 Streitmann and Girardi—both of whom repeated their roles for very many years—appeared in a new revival there. In 1910 the show entered both the Volksoper (23 March) and the Hofoper (26 December), and it was played in 1925 at the Carltheater, with Albin Mittersheim and Ilona Kelmay. It returned to the Theater an der Wien in 1921 with Richard Tauber and Betty Fischer featured, and again in 1935, and it has been reproduced at the Volksoper in various versions since, being most recently reproduced in 1998 (4 April) with Heinz Zednik (Zsupán), Irina Popova (Sáffi) and Alexandru Badea (Barinkay) featured, and with Renate Holm (Mirabella) and Kurt Schreibmayer (Homonay) amongst the starry support.

In 1886 the show was mounted for the first time in Germany, in Munich and then in Berlin, where it raced to its 200th performance by the end of the year, and also at Budapest's Népszínház, which it had originally been intended should share the premiere of Strauss's ''Hungarian Operette.'' The show (ad Károly Gerő, Antal Rádo) had already been seen in Kolozsvár, with tenor János Kápolnai as Barinkay, but the metropolitan version followed the fashion of travesty casting, and displayed the city's favorite soubrette, Ilka Pálmay, as the gypsy baron to the Sáffi of the city's best vocalist, Aranka Hegyi, and the Zsupán of József Németh. *A cigánybáró* was played a remarkable 42 times in its first year, and 156 times in all, placing it amongst the top shows at Budapest's most important musical house. Like Vienna, Budapest later took the show into its opera house, and in 1905 (27 May), *A cigánybáró* was produced at the Magyar Királyi Operaház with Dezső Arányi as a male Barinkay and Teréz Krammer as Sáffi. The show has remained firmly in the repretoire in Hungary ever since and was most recently remounted at the Thália Színház in 1996 (21 March) with Győző Leblanc and Andrea Zsadon in the leading roles.

New York followed with the first English-language production (ad Sydney Rosenfeld) only a few weeks after these, when Rudolf Aronson produced the show at the Casino Theater. William Castle and the darkly beautiful Pauline Hall played the romantic leads, with Francis Wilson as Zsupán and Billie Barlow playing Ottokar in travesty. New York didn't care for the show as Continental audiences had, and it was soon removed. However, local audiences had a chance to hear the piece in the original German shortly after when the Thalia Theater mounted *Der Zigeunerbaron* with Ernst Schütz and Franziska Raberg for an excellent four-week run. The German house reprised the show through several seasons, and in the 1889–90 season New Yorkers had the opportunity to see Streitmann in his original role. As in Europe, if a little more tardily, the show also made its way into the opera houses, being produced at the New York City Opera in 1944, with William Horne and Polyna Stoska, and, in their usual heavily botched version and with little success, at the Metropolitan Opera in 1959, with Lisa della Casa, Nicolai Gedda and Walter Slezak. There was even less success, however, for an even more embarrassing version produced on America's West Coast in the 1938–39 season (ad George Marion, Ann Ronell), with John Charles Thomas as Barinkay (now a lion tamer, thank you), which squeezed out more than half the score and made up the difference by plugging the piece full of spare Strauss waltzes and additional material by Ms Ronell, author of ''Who's Afraid of the Big, Bad Wolf?'' This nasty bit of botching later called itself *The Open Road* (1944, ad Milton Lazarus).

The show was first seen in Italian in 1890, but it was nearly a decade after the Vienna premiere before a production was mounted in France (ad Armand Lafrique). That production took place in Le Havre, but it clearly did well enough, for later the same year the show was produced at the Paris Théâtre des Folies-Dramatiques, with Monteux (Barinkay), Jane Pernyn (Sáffi), Mlle Paulin (Arsena), Mlle Maya (Czipra) and the comic Paul Hittemans (Zsupán) in the principal roles. One critic noted that it was "tastefully mounted, and in spite of the wretched libretto I shall not be surprised if it becomes popular." It stayed for a run of 60 performances.

Australia bypassed *Der Zigeunerbaron* in the 19th century, and it was not until 1953, in the midst of the blossoming fashion for American musical plays (not to mention a sudden passion for ice shows), that J C Williamson Ltd, for some reason, decided to mount *The Gypsy Baron.* It proved a bad, unprofitable idea and was not long persevered with. Similarly, in England, where Strauss's works had originally created little interest, *Der Zigeunerbaron* failed to find a contemporary production, and, although performances were played by visiting German-language troupes, it was not until 1964 that *The Gipsy Baron* (ad Geoffrey Dunn) was first seen in London professionally performed in English, in a production at the Sadler's Wells Opera, with Nigel Douglas and June Bronhill starred.

A number of German-language films have been made of versions of the work, the first—a silent one—in 1927, a German sound version by Karl Hartl, with Adolf Wohlbruck, Hansi Knotek and Fritz Kampers in the lead roles, and a matching French version with Wohlbruck and Jacqueline Francell. In 1954 Arthur Maria Rabenalt produced simultaneous German and French versions, with Margit Saad (Sáffi) and Harald Paulsen (Zsupán) appearing alongside Gerhard Riedmann for the German version and Georges Guétary for the French, and Kurt Wilhelm put out a further German film in 1962, with Carlos Thompson, Daniele Gaubert and Willy Millowitsch featured. Rabenalt was again at the helm of a German TV version of 1975, which featured Siegfried Jerusalem as Barinkay and Ivan Rebroff as Zsupán.

One of the most popular of all 19th-century Viennese Operetten in central European theatres of both yesteryear and the present day, *Der Zigeunerbaron,* in spite of its composer's saleable name and of a widespread familiarity through recordings, remains today, as it has from the start, altogether less popular in translation.

Germany: Munich January 1886, Friedrich-Wilhelmstädtisches Theater 24 January 1886; Hungary: Kolozsvár 2 March 1886, Népszínház *A cigánybáró* 26 March 1886; USA: Casino Theater *The Gypsy Baron* 15 February 1886, Thalia-Theater (Ger) 1 April 1886; France: Le Havre 9 January 1895, Théâtre des Folies-Dramatiques *Le Baron tzigane* 20 December 1895; Australia: Theatre Royal, Sydney *The Gipsy Baron* 4 July 1953; UK: Sadler's Wells Theatre *The Gipsy Baron* 9 June 1964

Films: Friedrich Zelnik (silent) 1927, Karl Hartl 1935, A M Rabenalt 1954, Kurt Wilhelm 1962

Recordings: complete (Decca, Vanguard, EMI, Eurodisc, etc), complete in Russian (Melodiya), selections in English (HMV, RCA), selections in French (Musidisc, Vega, EMI), selection in Hungarian (Qualiton), selections in Czech (Supraphon, Opus), etc

Video: Taurus 1975

Plate 436. **Zigeunerliebe.** *Zorika (Gudrun Schafer) with the easy-going gypsy Jozsi (Jorg Vorpahl) (Theater Dortmund, 1986).*

ZIGEUNERLIEBE Romantic Operette in 3 acts by A M Willner and Robert Bodanzky. Music by Franz Lehár. Carltheater, Vienna, 8 January 1910.

The era of the bubbling *Die lustige Witwe* and *Der Graf von Luxemburg* put firmly, if not finally, behind him, Lehár turned with the score for the 1910 *Zigeunerliebe* to what was to be his most genuine and substantial romantic Operette. Willner and Bodanzky's passionate Hungarian tale, which was lightened only briefly by some unforcedly amusing moments in a style that had little of the traditional soubret to it, drew from the composer a score of sometimes darkly dramatic power, as it moved on through a plot of more than usual verisimilitude to a positive ending much more convincing than the glum parade of final-curtain partings-for-ever that a self-made fashion and his librettists would later impose on him.

On the day that Zorika (Grete Holm), the daughter of the well-off Dragotin (Karl Blasel), is to be affianced to Jonel Bolescu (Max Rohr) she encounters his gypsy half-brother, Józsi (Willi Strehl). Józsi speaks to her of love in a way that has nothing to do with the well-mannered relationship between Zorika and her husband-to-be, and when the moment comes for the now confused Zorika to commit herself to the betrothal, she refuses. She runs to the river, drinks from the waters, which legend says allow you to see into the future, and she dreams. She sees herself passionately following Józsi to the gypsy life, whilst he plays the field and shares glances with Dragotin's rich neighbor, Ilona von Körösháza (Mizzi Zwerenz), on the very day of the gypsy wedding that should bind him to Zorika. Rejected by her family, longing for a proper church wedding and the other conventional parts of married life that have been shared by her bright little cousin Jolán (Littl Koppel) and the mayor's shy son, Kajétan (Hubert Marischka), Zorika realizes the gypsy life is not for her. She awakes to go thankfully to her betrothal with Jonel. At the same time, Ilona, casting a liberated look at Józsi as he heads insouciantly back to his gypsy folk, brings together the impatient Jolán and the backward Kajétan.

The score to *Zigeunerliebe* showed its intentions from the very start, when the first-act curtain rose on a dramatic storm scene, with a soaring solo for Zorika (''Heissa, heissa!''). The role of Zorika was endowed with a rapturous second-act number ''Gib mir dort vom Himmelszelt,'' and with a series of duos, beginning with the troubling ''Es liegt in blauen Fernen'' with Józsi in the first act and ending with her safe in the arms of Jonel at the show's conclusion. However, the part of Ilona—and Mizzi Zwerenz had the star billing in the original production—was also well equipped, with a set of pieces that ranged from the charming ''Nur die Liebe macht uns jung'' with Dragotin to the lighthearted love lesson ''Zuerst sucht man Gelegenheit.'' In later years, the Lehár song ''Hör' ich Cymbalklänge'' was added to make Ilona's role even more important. The two men—tenors both, as is the third male role of Kajétan—were also well supplied, Jonel reaping one of the gems of the score—and, indeed, of Lehár's oeuvre—in his waltzing dream-plea to Zorika to return to him (''Zorika, Zorika kehre zurück''), and Józsi with his defiant hymn to the a-responsible life, ''Ich bin ein Ziegunerkind.''

Zigeunerliebe was mounted at the Carltheater whilst *Der Graf von Luxemburg* dominated the stage of the city's other main house, the Theater an der Wien, and it gave Lehár a second simultaneous hit. The show ran non-stop through 10 months and 232 performances, and continued in the house's repertoire well into the 1920s. Budapest was swift to pick up this most Hungarian of Lehár's Viennese Operetten, and *Cigányszerelem* (ad Andor Gábor) was produced at the Király Színház with Sári Fedák in the role of Zorika, racing past its 100th performance on 14 February 1911 before confirming itself on the Hungarian stage in such a fashion that it is still to be seen in the Fővárosi Operettszínház repertoire to the present day.

A visit by the Carltheater company to Paris resulted in a French version (ad Jean Bénédict, Henri Gauthier-Villars, ie, ''Willy'') being mounted in Brussels in January 1911 with Germaine Huber starring, but it was a second French version (ad Saugey), produced at Marseille in the same year with Suzanne Cesbron and Louise Mantoue sharing the lead role, that was subsequently played at Paris's modest Trianon-Lyrique with Jane de Poumayrac featured. In Berlin, Marthe Winternitz-Dorda (Zorika), Mary Hagen (Ilona) and Jean Nadolovitch (Józsi) starred in *Zigeunerliebe* at the Komische Oper, whilst the first English-language performance was staged not by Lehár's most effective promoter—George Edwardes—but in New York (ad Harry B Smith, Robert B Smith), under the management of A H Woods. The production was dogged by bad luck that climaxed on the opening night when prima donna Marguerite Sylva broke down during the performance and understudy Phyllis Partington was thrust on. Although she actually knew the role, and acquitted herself well, the evening was not what it might have been, and *Gipsy Love* left town for the touring circuits after 31 performances.

Edwardes gave the piece rather more solid service, although the *Gipsy Love* heard in London was rather different from that which had been played in Vienna. The libretto was vastly rewritten (ad Basil Hood, Adrian Ross), with the role of Ilona reworked as one Lady Babby to feature resident star Gertie Millar in a tale with most of the passion taken out and replaced by more harmless emotions. The score, too, was torn apart. The storm opening vanished, Lady Babby primped about being ''Cosmopolitan'' (possibly to explain what she was doing in Hungary instead of in *Florodora*), and the role of Jonel (Webster Millar) all but vanished. His waltz melody was given to the soprano, Hungarian prima donna Sári Petráss, whose role—now called Ilona—had become decidedly secondary to the ubiquitous Lady Babby. Jolán (Mabel Russell) and Kajétan (Lauri de Frece) were played soubret-comic, Bill Berry made Dragotin low-comic, Józsi (Robert Michaelis) was a baritone, and, with Lehár's assistance on some new musical pieces, *Gipsy Love* was remade as near to conventional musical comedy lines as was thought desirable. However, although this emasculation meant that Britain saw a show that resembled *Zigeunerliebe* only superficially, Edwardes clearly knew his audience. His *Gipsy Love,* without getting anywhere near the success of *The Merry Widow,* did almost as well as *The Count of Luxembourg* with a run of 299 London performances. It then took to the road and also to the Australian stage, being produced by J C Williamson Ltd with a cast including Gertrude Glyn (Lady Babby), Elsie Spain (Ilona), Field Fisher (Dragotin), Phil Smith (Kajétan) and Dorothy Brunton (Jolan) for eight weeks in Sydney prior to Brisbane and Melbourne (Her Majesty's Theatre 5 September 1914).

If London remade *Zigeunerliebe* as a conventional musical comedy, Hungary's Ernő Innocent Vincze preferred to take it diametrically the opposite way: in 1943 an operatic version of *Zigeunerliebe* was mounted at the Budapest opera with Tibor Udvárdy and Julia Orosz starred under the title *Garabonciás diák.* The ''versions'' did not end there either. In some productions the Act II dream was put aside, and its doings depicted as reality in a scenario where Zorika runs away with Józsi, and a 1930 Hollywood film called *The Rogue Song,* allegedly based on *Zigeunerliebe,* used only a little of Lehár's music set to an entirely different story. However, the show's worst fate came in an American production of the 1930s where one Kay Kenny turned out a ''version'' that interpolated both some additional ''comic relief'' and some vaudeville songs. Produced as *The Moon Rises* (Shubert Theater, Boston 14 April 1934), Ms Kenny's piece was an unmitigated and salutory failure.

In an age when it is no longer obligatory for a piece to be either frankly opera or frankly musical comedy, when there are no vaudeville songs to interpolate, and when the romantic Operette is much in style, the rare modern productions of this show—which has undergone a surprising amount of fiddling with when its great initial success is considered—have (''Hör' ich Cymbalklänge'' apart) largely returned to the original script and score.

A German TV version with Jon Buzca, Adolf Dallapozza and Janet Perry featured was produced in 1974.

Germany: Komische Oper 11 February 1910; Hungary: Király Színház *Cigányszerelem* 12 November 1910, revised version as *Garabonciás diák* Opera Színház 20 February 1943; USA: Globe Theater *Gypsy Love* 17 October 1911; UK: Daly's Theatre *Gipsy Love* 1 June 1912; France: Théâtre du Vaudeville (Ger) 22 June 1911, Théâtre de l'Opera, Marseille *L'Amour tsigane* 16 December 1911, Trianon-Lyrique, Paris 1911; Australia: Her Majesty's Theatre, Sydney 13 June 1914

Recordings: two-record set (Urania), in Russian (Melodiya), selections (Ariola-Eurodisc, Amiga), selections in Hungarian (Electrarecord, Qualiton), selection in French (Radio Bleue), etc

Video: Taurus 1974

DER ZIGEUNERPRIMÁS Operette in 3 acts by Julius Wilhelm and Fritz Grünbaum. Music by Emmerich Kálmán. Johann Strauss-Theater, Vienna, 11 October 1912.

Emmerich Kálmán's *Der Zigeunerprimás* (the gypsy violinist) has had a curious career. Highly successful in those centers where it was produced (Vienna, Berlin, New York, Budapest), it was completely ignored elsewhere (London, Paris) and now, whilst others of its composer's works continue to be played, it seems to have wholly slipped from the repertoire even in central Europe.

The story of *Der Zigeunerprimás* purported to be about the famous 19th-century gypsy violinist Pali Rácz

Plate 437. **Der Zigeunerprimás.** *Girardi as Pali Racz.*

and his equally historical son, Laczi, but it had a decided ring to it of the tale used for the Strauss biomusicals—the famous musician father who has no confidence that his son can follow him in his profession, but who is ultimately outdone and replaced by that son. Alexander Girardi played aging Pali Rácz, cared for quietly by his eldest daughter, Sári (Gerda Walde), at loggerheads with his son Laczi (Willy Strehl) over the young man's preference for the music of Wagner, Bach and Handel over the old gypsy melodies that made his father's fame, and itching for a fourth wife in his young niece, Juliska (Grete Holm). Gaston, Count Irini (Josef Victora) persuades the old man to leave his Hungarian home and travel to Paris to play once more before King Heribert VII (Paul Harden). On the big night, however, Rácz misses his cue, and Laczi steps in to replace him to enormous applause. When the old gypsy follows his son's bravura modern performance with his country tunes, he seems old-fashioned. He will return home, retire for good and wed Juliska. But, away from the constraints of his father's home, Laczi has finally found the courage himself to speak his heart to Juliska. With the help of Gaston's grandmother (Alma Sorel), a love of Rácz's youth, the violinist is persuaded ruefully but gracefully to let the young people go into the future together: Laczi and Juliska, Sári and Gaston. As for the comical Cadeau (Max Brod), who has lingered a little too long in his choice of a bride, he will have to wait until the youngest of Rácz's 16 children grows up.

Girardi had the big number of the evening in the gypsy's description of his love for his violin—"Mein alter Stradivari"—in a Hungarian-flavored Kálmán score that included numbers of spirit for Juliska ("Du, du, du, lieber Gott schaust zu") and of gentler charm for Sári ("So ein armes, dummes, kleines Ding vom Land") prior to each becoming romantic with her tenor in duet.

Erich Müller's production at the Johann Strauss-Theater was a hit. Only a handful of performances of another current hit, *Die Förster-Christl,* intervened in an effectively continuous run of 180 performances between October 1912 and 10 April 1913, and the show was still to be seen in the repertoire at the Johann Strauss-Theater in 1924. Budapest's Király Színház production (ad Zsolt Harsányi) starred Antal Nyárai (Rácz), Sári Fedák (Sári), Sári Perczel (Juliska), Márton Rátkai (Gaston) and Jenő Nádor (Laczi), with the great star of earlier years, Ilka Pálmay, as the old countess, and scored a comparable success, being brought back for a second run the following year. In Berlin Gross (Rácz), Frln Alder (Sári), Hansen (Gaston), Kutzner (Laczi) and Frln Schwarz (Juliska) featured at Monti's Operettentheater. In New York, too, the show was a hit. Henry Savage's production of *Sari* (ad C C S Cushing, E P Heath, and initially advertised as *The Gypsy Chief*), with the little Hungarian soubrette Mizzi Hajós taking the title role alongside one-time juvenile leading man van Rensselaer Wheeler as Rácz, J Humbird Duffy as Laczi and Blanche Duffield (Juliska), played 151 New York performances, giving the producer his biggest Broadway success since *The Merry Widow* prior to touring for many years. The show was even brought back to Broadway in 1930 (29 January, Liberty Theater) with a rather older Mitzi (as she was now called) and Duffy repeating their roles.

Given this unsmudged record of success, it must clearly have been wartime considerations that stopped Britain, France and Australia from getting a glimpse of *Der Zigeunerprimás.* But after having missed it first time around, none of these countries thought to look at it a little later, and, apart from the odd song in the heart of an elderly American, it remains virtually unknown outside central Europe.

A silent film version with Ernst Verebes (Laczi), Raimondo van Riel (Pali Rácz), Vera Malinowskaya (Sári) and Margarete Schlegel (Juliska) was put out in 1929.

Hungary: Király Színház *Cigányprimás* 21 January 1913; Germany: Montis Operettentheater 8 March 1913; USA: Liberty Theater *Sari* 13 January 1914

Film 1929 (silent)

Recording: selection in Hungarian (Qualiton)

ZIP GOES A MILLION Musical extravaganza in 2 acts by Eric Maschwitz adapted from the novel *Brewster's Millions* by George Barr McCutcheon, and the play by McCutcheon, Winchell Smith and Byron Ongley. Music by George Posford. Palace Theatre, London, 20 October 1951.

The successful 1906 play *Brewster's Millions* (New Amsterdam Theater, New York 31 December), made up from McCutcheon's novel about a fellow who has to spend a million in order to inherit several, long defied attempts to make it into a musical comedy. Broadway's Comstock and Gest were the first to try, with a piece called variously *Maid o' Millions, Maid of Money* and *Zip Goes a Million,* and written by Guy Bolton, Buddy De Sylva and Jerome Kern. Produced at the Worcester Theater, Worcester, 8 December 1919, it failed to make Broadway. The composer, however, rescued "Look for the Silver Lining" and "Whip-Poor-Will" from the score and reused them with more success in his *Sally.* The story, too, was reused. The second try, this time under the title *Bubbling Over,* had a libretto by Clifford Grey and songs by Richard Myers and Leo Robin. Produced at the Garrick Theatre, Philadelphia with the young Jeanette MacDonald and certified stars Cecil Lean and Cleo Mayfield in its cast (2 August 1926), it ran out a good season and moved on to Chicago, where it expired a fortnight later. Myers rescued the pretty "I'm a One-Man Girl" and "True to Two," which were used in Britain's *Mr Cinders* a couple of seasons later. And still the story went begging.

The third version, put together in Britain a quarter of a century later, had less weighty names attached to it. Producer Emile Littler mounted a jolly, unpretentious version of the tale with the role of Brewster northern-anglicized as little window cleaner Percy Piggott for ukelele-strumming singing star George Formby. Percy went through New York and the South Seas in his attempts to get rid of his million secretly and hurry home to his Sally (Sara Gregory), passing on the way such folk as the shady banker Van Norden (Frank Tilton) and his predatory daughter (Phoebe Kershaw) and a musical-comedy couple (Wade Donovan, Barbara Perry) whose awful show seems like a certain way to lose a fortune. George Posford's songs allowed him to insist "I'm Saving Up for Sally" and that they are "Ordinary People" in the simplest of music-hall style, whilst Donovan and Perry aped Broadway musical comedy (notably the current *South Pacific*) in the show within a show.

Formby was forced to withdraw from the production six months into the run after a heart attack, but comedian Reg Dixon replaced him to good effect, and *Zip Goes a Million* ran for 544 performances in 16 months in London prior to going on the road for several seasons and winning productions in venues as far apart as Norway (Edder-Koppen Theater, 1955) and Australia. Australia's production, mounted by David N Martin, featured Roy Barbour in Formby's role in satisfactory seasons in Sydney and in Melbourne (Tivoli 30 October 1954, two months).

Brewster's Millions was also made over as a musical film (1935) with Jack Buchanan starred.

Australia: Tivoli, Sydney 17 April 1954

Recordings: London cast recordings (Columbia, Encore)

ZIRKUS AIMEE Operette in 3 acts by Kurt Goetze and Ralph Benatzky. Music by Ralph Benatzky. Stadttheater, Basel, 5 March 1932.

Goetze starred in his own show as a well-born army lieutenant, stationed in an out-of-the-way town, who falls in love with little Aimée (Valerie von Martens) from the circus. To be with her, he flings in his commission and joins the circus. His horrified family is won over when they actually come and see the pair in action.

Following behind *Die Dame vom Zirkus, Das Zirkuskind* and *Die Zirkusprinzessin, Aimée* gave further lie to the myth that circus musicals were unlucky, as it followed up its first production in Basel by transferring to the Berlin Metropoltheater for a good run.

DIE ZIRKUSPRINZESSIN Operette in 3 acts by Julius Brammer and Alfred Grünwald. Music by Emmerich Kálmán. Theater an der Wien, Vienna, 26 March 1926.

Prince Sergius (Richard Waldemar) has had his honorable offers rejected by the rich, widowed and beautiful Fedora Palinska (Betty Fischer) and, in revenge, he tricks her into a marriage with a supposed nobleman who is, in fact, the circus star Mister X (Hubert Marischka) in disguise. Sergius is discomforted when it eventuates that Mister X is actually the very aristocratic Fedor Palinski, the young man Fedora disinherited by her first marriage, and after pride has been assuaged all around, the two find they are happy to be wed. The romantic story was counterpointed by the adventures and the winsome wooing of the soubret pair, hotelier's son Toni Schlumberger (Fritz Steiner) and the little circus girl, Miss Mabel Gibson (Elsie Altmann), and the show's third act, which abandoned the aristocratic lovers until it was time to tie up their story, concentrated instead on life at the hotel run by Toni's mother (Mizzi Zwerenz) and contained an extended comic scene for the elderly waiter Pelikan, a role created to fit comedy star Hans Moser, a famous specialist in comic servants and functionaries.

The bonbon of Kálmán's score was the romantic tenor hymn to ''Zwei Märchenaugen,'' a piece that went on to become a recital and recording favorite, and the hero also got to serenade Vienna (''Wo ist der Himmel so blau wie in Wien'') and to join with his lady to murmur romantically ''Mein Darling, Mein Darling,'' but the music of *Die Zirkusprinzessin* also contained a number of distinctly lively pieces ranging from the march song ''Mädel gib acht!'' to a set of bouncing melodies for Toni and Mabel—he slavering over the charms of ''Die kleinen Mäderln im Trikot,'' and joining with her in ''Liese, Liese komm mit mir auf die Wiese,'' as well as a moving little semi-spoken piece for Frau Schlumberger in the final act.

If it did not quite equal the record of *Der Orlow,* its predecessor at the Theater an der Wien, *Die Zirkusprinzessin* was nevertheless a fine Vienna hit, playing 311 performances as Erik Wirl, Ernst Nadherny, Harry Bauer and Karl Ziegler all took a turn behind the hero's mask. It moved quickly to Germany, and was played 75 times in Breslau and 50 in Hamburg before reaching Berlin where it was produced with Wirl repeating the role he had played in Vienna alongside Lori Leux (Fedora), Max Hansen (Toni) and Szőke Szakall—later better known to filmgoers as ''Cuddles''—in the role of Pelikan. In Hungary, the Király Színház production (ad Imre Liptai, Ernő Kulinyi), with Juci Lábass, Márton Rátkai, Tibor Halmay, Jenő Nádor and Vilma Orosz, added further to the run of success.

The Shuberts took up the show for Broadway (ad Harry B Smith) and there, too, it won success, with Guy Robertson sporting the hero's mask in a version that stretched and fiddled with the plot to make it both more explicit and more conventional than the original, alongside Desirée Tabor (Fedora), Ted Doner (Toni), Gloria Foy (Fritzi Burgstaller), George Hassell (Grand Duke Sergius), and Jesse Greer and Raymond Kalges's song ''What D'Ya Say?,'' through 192 performances. A 1931–32 West Coast revival with Robertson again featured called itself *The Blue Mask,* but a Jones Beach production in 1937 went back to being *The Circus Princess.* The show was presented with great success in Milan, but a tardy French version (ad Max Eddy, Jean Marietti), produced at Le Havre, with Vidal and Maguy Dalcy featured, did not make it to Paris, and London failed to see *Die Zirkusprinzessin* at all. Two silent film versions were produced, in 1925, and again in 1928 with Harry Liedtke and Vera Schmitterlow starred. A German television version with Rudolf Schock as Mister X and Ingeborg Hallstein as the heroine was produced in 1969.

Back home, the show was given a 1957 revival at the Raimundtheater, and in 1988 a curiously altered version—which compared unfavorably with that being played simultaneously down the river at the Budapest Fővárosi Operettszínház—was taken into the repertoire of the Volksoper (15 February 1988). The Hungarian company visited Paris in 1991 to give the first Paris performances of *A cirkuszhercegnő* . . . in German, and Budapest and other Hungarian cities saw regular productions through the 1990s (Miskolc 1992, Győr 1996, 1997, Békéscsaba 1996). Perhaps at least partly because of its colorful circus atmosphere, its one big tenor bonbon, and the fine opportunities it gives to its soubret players in particular, *Die Zirkusprinzessin* has remained staunchly in the modern European repertoire alongside Kálmán's *Gräfin Mariza* and *Die Csárdásfürstin,* whilst others of the composer's works that might have been considered more, or at least equally, eligible for revival are rarely if ever seen.

Germany: Breslau, Metropoltheater, Berlin; Hungary: Király Színház *A cirkuszhercegnő* 24 September 1926; USA: Winter Garden Theater *The Circus Princess* 25 April 1927; France: Théâtre du Havre *La Princesse du Cirque* 24 March 1934, Opéra-Comique (Ger) 20 March 1991

Films: Adolf Gartner 1925, Victor Janson 1928

Recordings: complete in Russian (Melodiya), selections (Ariola-Eurodisc, Baccarola, Polydor), selections in Hungarian (Qualiton, Műresz Ház)

Video: Unitel/Taurus 1969

THE ZOO Musical folly (musical absurdity) in 1 act by ''Bolton Rowe'' (B C Stephenson). Music by Arthur Sullivan. St James's Theatre, London, 5 June 1875.

A comical little burlesque piece in which a disguised duke (Edgar Bruce) finds true love with Eliza, the refreshment stall lady at the zoo (Henrietta Hodson), whilst a lovesick pharmacist (Carlos Florentine) tries to commit suicide in the bear pit for love of his Laetitia (Gertrude Ashton). Sullivan's comicalities and intermittent parodies of opera provided a lively accompaniment to the humorous little text, and the show was given several London productions as a forepiece. Pauline Markham, a famous Lydia Thompson blonde, appeared as Eliza, whilst Richard Temple, later of the Savoy, produced, directed and played the duke in a second production, and W S Penley, the original Charley's Aunt, was Laetitia's nasty dad in a third version.

The Zoo was exhumed, published and recorded in the 1980s and has since been staged by a number of groups and colleges. It made its way back to the professional stage in 1999 under the auspices of the Ohio Light Opera.

Recordings: D'Oyly Carte Co (Decca), amateur cast (RRE)

ZORBA Musical in 2 acts by Joseph Stein based on the novel by Nicos Kazantzakis. Lyrics by Fred Ebb. Music by John Kander. Imperial Theater, New York, 17 November 1968.

At first a novel, then the celebrated Michael Cacoyannis film of 1965 in which Antony Quinn played *Zorba the Greek* alongside Lila Kedrova and Alan Bates and the famous bouzouki music of Mikos Theodorakis's ''Zorba's Dance,'' the tale of Kazantzakis's exuberant Greek was finally made into a musical play in 1968 by the author of *Fiddler on the Roof* and the songwriters of *Cabaret.*

Framed within the kind of play-within-a-play setting that *Man of La Mancha* had recently re-repopularized, the tale of Zorba (Herschel Bernardi) was narrated by the leader of a bouzouki group (Lorraine Serabian). That tale begins in a Piraeus café where the ''hero'' of the story encounters young Nikos (John Cunningham), who is on his way to the islands to open up a mine he has inherited. Zorba attaches himself to the venture, and the two men go off to Crete. There Zorba sets himself up with the sweet, aging cocotte, Hortense (Maria Karnilova), whilst Nikos becomes involved with the Widow (Carmen Alvarez). But Nikos's relationship leads to tragedy, when an unstable boy (Richard Dmitri) who fancies himself in love with the woman commits suicide, leading his father revengefully to stab the Widow to death. The mine turns out to be useless, and when Hortense dies, happy with the pretense of a betrothal she has gone through with Zorba, the two men leave the island, each going his separate way on to the next stage of life, that life which, in Zorba's philosophy and that of the islanders, leads uncomplicatedly and inevitably to death.

The score to the show was not made up of obvious ''numbers,'' but the musical part was a strongly effective support to the story and its characters. There were set pieces for the group leader, written in an ethnic style, one musical scene for Nikos and the Widow, a Zorba's Dance, which was not the famous one of the same name, and most effectively in what was essentially a masculine musical some delicate songs for the self-deluding Hortense, whether telling of how she saved Crete by an arrangement between all the wartime admirals who were her lovers (''No Boom Boom''), bidding a temporary farewell to Zorba (''Goodbye Canavaro'') or, in the haze of death, movingly reliving a childish ''Happy Birthday.''

Zorba had a 305-performance run on Broadway in Harold Prince and Ruth Mitchell's original production, and 15 years later it was given a major touring revival under the management of Barry and Fran Weissler and Kenneth-Mark Productions, with Cacoyannis directing the two stars of his film, repeating their performances in the musical version. The convention of the framework was with profit discarded, and an additional song for Zorba added, and this time the show—with a 354-performance Broadway run—made money.

Zorba did not play the West End, a British production with Alfred Marks featured as Zorba stopping short at the Greenwich Theatre, but it found great popularity in central Europe. It was produced (ad Robert Gilbert, Gerhard Bronner) at Vienna's Theater an der Wien—which had staged both *Anatevka* (ie, *Fiddler on the Roof*) and *Cabaret* in the two previous years—with Yossi Yadin (another *Fiddler* star, like Bernardi and Karnilova, following up in *Zorba*) in the title role, alongside Luise Ulrich, Dagmar Koller, Peter Frohlich and Olivia Molina, through a series of 80 performances, and went on from there both to regular performances in German-speaking houses and also to Hungary, where a local version (ad Agnes György) was first produced in 1973 and where it has been played on a good number of occasions since. It was also given in Paris, with Armand Mestral featured in the title role.

UK: Greenwich Theatre 1973; Austria: Theater an der Wien *Sorbas* 28 January 1971; Hungary: Fertőrákosi Barlangszínház 5 July 1973; France: Théâtre de Boulogne-Billancourt 1973; Germany: nd

Recordings: original cast (Capitol), revival cast (RCA), Hungarian cast (Hungaraton), Austrian cast (Preiser)

ZORINA, Vera [HARTWIG, Eva Brigitta] (b Berlin, 2 January 1917).

At first a ballet dancer in Norway and later with the Ballet Russe de Monte Carlo (1934–36), Vera Zorina made her first appearance on the musical stage in the role of the ballerina Vera Barnova in the short-lived London production of *On Your Toes* in 1937. She made her Broadway debut as the Angel of Rodgers and Hart's subsequent *I Married an Angel*—another role with a large dance content—and later appeared as the sexy Marina van Linden in another successful musical, *Louisiana Purchase* (1940) and as a dream-Scheherazade in the very much less successful *Dream with Music* (1944). Each of these productions was choreographed by her sometime husband, George Balanchine.

Miss Zorina appeared in the film versions of *On Your Toes* (1939) and *Louisiana Purchase* (1941), and also in *The Goldwyn Follies, I Was an Adventuress* (1940), *Star Spangled Rhythm* (1943) and *Follow the Boys* (1944) and finally, after a decade's absence from the New York theatre, returned to Broadway to repeat her *On Your Toes* role in the show's 1954 revival, before retiring from the stage.

Miss Zorina was latterly married to Columbia Records executive Goddard Lieberson.

Autobiography: *Zorina* (Farrar, Straus & Giroux, New York, 1986)

ZSUZSI KISASSZONY Operett in 3 acts by Ferenc Martos and Miksa Bródy. Music by Emmerich Kálmán. Vígszínház, Budapest, 27 February 1915.

Plate 438. **Zsuzsi kisasszony.** *Nusi Diosy as the heroine of Kálmán's opérette.*

Emmerich Kálmán's *Zsuzsi kisasszony* did not achieve the same kind of international coverage as the pieces with which he had preceded it (*Az obsitos, Der Zigeunerprimás, Die Csárdásfürstin*) or those with which he followed it (*Das Hollandweibchen, Die Bajadere, Gräfin Mariza,* etc), but there was a reason.

Produced at Budapest's Vígszínház, the story of Miss Susy (Nusi Diósy) who gets all starry-eyed over her village's long-departed most famous inhabitant, the Kammersanger Falsetti, when he returns home for a local festival, only to find the man is a stand-in, was decorated with a typically lively score made up of predominantly waltz and march rhythms. It was well received, passed its 50th performance on 3 May 1915 and finally totaled a very respectable 78 nights. America's Klaw and Erlanger were quickest off the mark as buyers for the newest work by the composer of *Die Csárdásfürstin,* and—after *Miss Rabbit's-Foot,* as adapted by Channing Pollock and Rennold Wolf had proved a non-starter—*Miss Springtime* (ad Guy Bolton, P G Wodehouse) was produced on Broadway with Hungary's Sári Petráss starred 18 months after its Budapest premiere. Susy had become Rosita, Kálmán's score had been infiltrated by three numbers by Jerome Kern, and the resultant show ran for nearly 230 performances before going to the country.

In spite of such success, however, *Zsuzsi kisasszony* went nowhere else. The reason became apparent—so the story goes—when the Viennese hit *Die Faschingsfee* was transported to Hungary. It was due to go into rehearsal when someone recognized one of the tunes. The producer telegraphed Kálmán asking if the music of *Die Faschingsfee* was not that of *Zsuzsi kisasszony,* and the composer blithely telegraphed back that it was. But it had gone much better with its new Viennese libretto. In fact, virtually all the principal numbers of *Zsuzsi kisasszony* had been used either in whole or partially made over for the later work, effectively ending any further life for Susy or for *Miss Springtime. Zsuzsi kiasassony,* however, didn't vanish. It was played in Sopron as recently as 1994 (19 March) and at Zalaegerszeg in 1996 (8 March). And its a long time since anyone saw *Faschingsfee* . . . so, maybe someone misjudged.

France did have a *Mam'selle Printemps* in 1946, but it was a different show with a score by Henri Betti and Maurice Vandair, and it never made it to Paris.

USA: New Amsterdam Theater *Miss Springtime* 25 September 1916

ZUMPE, Hermann (b Oppach [Taubenheim], 9 April 1850; d Munich, 4 September 1903).

Conductor and composer Zumpe was, in the former capacity, associated in particular with the works of Wagner, and in the latter wrote the scores for several operas, including *Des Teufels Anteil, Anahna* (Viktoria-Theater, Berlin 23 December 1881) and *Sawitri* (Hoftheater 8 November 1907), and for three well-considered Operetten that were premiered at Hamburg's Carl-Schultze Theater in the 1880s.

The first of these, *Farinelli,* a textual mix of the Scribe libretto for Auber's *Carlo Broschi* and a Hamburg play called *Farinelli* by Teigmann, had a considerable success, being played throughout Germany and Austria (Carltheater 22 September 1888, 35 performances) and even in the German Amberg Theater in New York (20 December 1888), where Ernst Schütz appeared in the title role, through a successful Christmas and New Year season. The second, *Karin,* does not seem to have progressed far beyond Hamburg, but the third, *Polnische Wirtschaft,* made its way to Berlin's Friedrich-Wilhelmstädtisches Theater in 1891 (26 November).

1886 **Farinelli** (Friedrich Willibald Wulff, Charles Cassmann) Carl-Schultze Theater, Hamburg 28 November; Friedrich-Wilhelmstädtisches Theater 13 August 1887

1888 **Karin** (Wulff, Eduard Pochmann) Carl-Schultze Theater, Hamburg 1 December

1889 **Polnische Wirtschaft** (Moritz West, Richard Genée) Carl-Schultze Theater, Hamburg; Friedrich-Wilhelmstädtisches Theater 26 November 1891

ZWAR, Charles [Joseph] (b Broadford, Vic, 10 April 1911; d Oxford, 2 December 1989). Australian-born composer of revue and musical comedy.

Zwar was not long out of university when he was offered the opportunity to compose the score for the musical play *Blue Mountain Melody,* one of several attempts in the 1930s to find a native musical comedy vehicle for home stars, in this case Cyril Ritchard and Madge Elliott. The show, a piece about a boxer and a dancer, set in Sydney, won certain local attention before Zwar moved on to Britain, where he became pianist/md for the little Gate Theatre, accompanying and supplying music for their memorable run of intimate revues. He subsequently composed the music for a long run of small-scale London revues including *Sweeter and Lower, Sweetest and Lowest, One, Two, Three, Four, Five, Six, À la Carte, The Lyric Revue, The Globe Revue* and *Airs on a Shoestring,* and continued to write for revue long after that form of entertainment had been deflated by television. He also supplied the scores for two West End musical plays, the Arthur Askey comedy piece *Bet Your Life* (w Kenneth Leslie-Smith), which had a good 362-performance run as a twice-nightly entertainment, and a musical adaptation of the successful romantic Scottish play *Marigold* (77 performances). He also composed the songs for a tentatively politico-topical provincial piece titled *The Station Master's Daughter.*

1934 **Blue Mountain Melody** (J C Bancks) Theatre Royal, Sydney 15 September

1952 **Bet Your Life** (w Kenneth Leslie-Smith/Alan Melville) London Hippodrome 18 February

1959 **Marigold** (Melville) Savoy Theatre 27 May

1968 **The Station Master's Daughter** (Frank Harvey) Yvonne Arnaud Theatre, Guildford 11 April

ZWEI HERZEN IM DREIVIERTELTAKT [aka *Der verlorene Walzer*] Operette in 3 acts (8 scenes) by Paul Knepler and Ignaz M Welleminsky based on the screenplay of the same name by Walter Reisch and Franz Schulz. Lyrics by Robert Gilbert. Music by Robert Stolz. Stadttheater, Zürich, 30 September 1933.

One of Robert Stolz's most successful film scores was that for the prettily titled 1930 *Zwei Herzen im Dreivierteltakt* (two hearts in 3/4 time), produced by Géza von Bolvary and richly cast with Gretl Theimer, Walter Janssen, Oscar Karlweis, Willi Först, Szőke Szakall and Paul Hörbiger. Three years later, when the film was adapted to the stage, Stolz composed virtually an entirely new score for the occasion, only the film's two major song hits—the title number and "Auch du wirst mich einmal betrügen" (better known for having been interpolated into London's *Im weissen Rössl* under the title "You Too")—being remade for the occasion.

The lost waltz of the sometime title of the stage show is the tune that composer-star Toni Hofer needs for his new Operette. He also may need a new leading lady, for his co-star/lover Anny Lohmayer is threatening to abandon ship, especially as the Hofer recipe for musical inspiration is apparently a new love affair. His librettists plan to send him a juicily willing soubrette, but their teenage sister, Hedi, takes her place and the result is a winning waltz. It disappears when she does, but returns in time for a happy ending for the new production and the new lovers.

The new score placed several other attractive numbers alongside the film score's hits, several of which were presented as parts of the Operette within the Operette (''Das ist der Schmerz beim ersten Kuss'') and one as a straightforward Heurige number (''Das ist kein Zufall, dass das Glück in Wien wohnt'').

The Zürich premiere (as *Zwei Herzen,* etc) was followed by a production in Dresden of a version given the title *Der verlorene Walzer,* but it was the more familiar and catchy title that was used when the show was produced in Austria, both in its initial showing at the Titania-Theater and at the Volksoper, where it was mounted on 29 March 1975 with Peter Minich (Toni), Sylvia Holzmayer (Anny) and Helga Papouschek (Hedi). An English-language version (ad Dailey Paskman, William A Drake) was staged at the St Louis Muny in 1938 with a cast including Eric Mattson (Toni), Gladys Baxter (Anny), Nancy McCord (Hedi) and the Three Olympics roller-skating speciality. It was repeated there in 1939 and 1946 (without the roller skates) and played again at Los Angeles and at the Greek Theater in Hollywood in 1946, with Kenny Baker, Irene Manning and Pamela Caveness featured.

Germany: Centraltheater, Dresden *Der verlorene Walzer* 23 December 1933; USA: Municipal Opera, St Louis *The Lost Waltz* 11 July 1938; Austria: Titania-Theater 15 May 1948

Recordings: selection (Ariola-Eurodisc, Remington)

ZWERENZ, Mizzi (b Pistyán, Hungary, 13 July 1876; d Vienna, 14 June 1947). Longtime star soubrette of the Vienna stage who matured into a fine second career as a character player.

The daughter of Karl Ludwig Zwerenz, an actor who subsequently became a theatre director in Bucharest and Pressburg, Mizzi made her first stage appearances at Baden bei Wien and at Berlin's Friedrich-Wilhelmstädtisches Theater before joining the company at the Vienna Carltheater in 1901 at the start of what was to be one of the most remarkable careers in the history of the Viennese musical stage. She made her earliest appearances at the Carltheater covering Therese Biedermann and playing in such new pieces as Millöcker's *Der Damenschneider* (1901, Marinka) and *Das gewisse Etwas* (1902, Cascarette Joujou), in the Vienna version of *Der kleine Günstling* (1902, Anita) and as Nelli in *Der Obersteiger,* before moving on to play leading roles in the Operetten at Gabor Steiner's summer theater, Venedig in Wien—

Plate 439. **Mizzi Zwerenz** *as Franzi in* Ein Walzertraum.

Gräfin Pepi (1902, Pepi), *Frühlingsluft* (1903, Hanni), Edna May's role of Olga in *The Girl from Up There* (*Die Eisjungfrau,* 1904), *Jung Heidelberg* (1904), Ziehrer's *Fesche Geister* (1905), *Wien bei Nacht* (1905, Mizzi) and the Parisian *Die Ringstrassen-Prinzessin* (1905, t/o Milli).

Zwerenz had grown to star-billing when she appeared opposite Girardi at the Carltheater in 1905 in the title role of Eysler's hit *Die Schützenliesel,* and she held the top of the bill when she subsequently appeared in the travesty role of von Reif-Reiflingen in Reinhardt's Operette version of the famous comedy *Krieg im Frieden,* then as Fifine in *Mutzi,* Hugdietrich in *Hugdietrichs Brautfahrt* and in the short-lived *Der Rosenjüngling* (1906). She paired with Girardi as Nelli in *Künstlerblut,* and again as Gusti Frohlich in *Der selige Vincenz* (1907), then created one of her most memorable roles when she played the part of the little violinist, Franzi Steingrüber, in *Ein Walzertraum* (1907), introducing the comedy duo ''Piccolo, Piccolo, tsin, tsin, tsin'' with her husband, Arthur Guttmann. She starred in a 1908 revival of Suppé's

Donna Juanita, was billed large above the title in the less fortunate new pieces *Der schwarze Tenor* (Henriette), *Johann der Zweite* (Elly) and *Der Glücksnarr* (Friedel), but found another fine role as the memorable unwronged wife of the major hit that was *Die geschiedene Frau* (Jana).

In 1909 she starred in the title role of Oscar Straus's *Didi* (Lydia Garousse), and a major revival of Genée's *Nanon* featured her in the title role to the Ninon of Dora Keplinger, before, in 1910, she won another memorable role as the high-spirited Ilona von Köröshaza in Lehár's *Zigeunerliebe.* She created the roles of Rosalilla in Fall's *Das Puppenmädel* (1910) and of Granichstaedten's *Majestät Mimi,* played, with notable success, the Viennese version of Jean Gilbert's *Die keusche Susanne* (1911, Susanne), appeared as Lini Stöckl, the little heroine of the Lanner pasticcio *Alt-Wien* (1911), Louison Duval in *Die kleine Freundin* and scored yet another singular hit as Princess Helene, the mixed-up non-Princess of *Der liebe Augustin* (1912).

Later in 1912 she appeared in the title roles of a revival of *Boccaccio* and of the Hungarian operett *Susi* (*A kis gróf*), in Ziehrer's unsuccessful *Fürst Casimir,* and scored again when she created the role of the wily Helena, who wins her raffish Count, in the Viennese production of Nedbal's highly successful *Polenblut* (1913). She played in travesty in the short-lived *Der erste Kuss* (1914, Harry), in a revival of the Posse *Zwei Mann von Hess* with Karl Blasel and appeared as Karl von Stigler's less-than-memorable *Mädchen im Mond* (1914, Hedwig Hübner), as Oscar Straus's *schöne Unbekannte* (1915, Elly) and as Reinhardt's *Die erste Frau* (the little model, Seffi) in the same year. Other wartime roles included the vocally dazzling Princess (otherwise Maria Theresia) in Fall's magnificent *Fürstenliebe,* Lola Brandt in the Posse *Man steigt nicht!,* and the film star Delia Gill in Vienna's version of the Berlin musical *Die Kino-Königin* (1915) before, in 1916, she ended her long-starring run with the Carltheater and moved to the Apollotheater.

There she turned out a further series of leading roles, starring in *Hanni geht tanzen* (Hanni), the title role of *Urschula, Graf Toni* (1916, Fritzi Paradeiser), as Richard Fall's *Die Dame von Welt* and *Die Puppenbaronessen,* in Eysler's *Der Aushilfsgatte* (1917), Granichstaedten's *Walzerliebe,* Lehár's *Rosenstock und Edelweiss,* Jean Gilbert's *Die Fahrt ins Glück* (1918), Stolz's *Der Favorit* (Pauline Villinger), Ascher's *Der Künstlerpreis* (Etelka von Vasarhély) and the Vienna production of *Die Dame vom Zirkus* (1919).

She was back at the Carltheater in 1921 as Josepha Freisinger in *Der Herzog von Reichstadt,* still heading the bill as she had done for 15 years, and the following year was seen in *Die Csárdásfürstin* at the Johann Strauss-Theater, but after some 20 years as a prima donna/soubrette, she now gave way to others.

Her career as a leading lady had been one of the most remarkable in the Viennese Operette, but Mizzi Zwerenz was not finished yet. She was to have a second career, as a character player. Over the next decade she appeared in such komische Alte roles as the splendid Frau Schlumberger in *Die Zirkusprinzessin* (1926), Portschunkula in *Die gold'ne Meisterin* (1927), Die Oberin in *Mam'zelle Nitouche* (1927), the hostess of "Zum Blauen Insel" in a Bürgertheater rewrite of Strauss's *Cagliostro in Wien* (1927), Maria von Kirschstätt in *Prinzessin Ti-Ti-Pa* (1928), Cyprienne in Pál Ábrahám's jazz show *Spektakel* (1928), Jeanette in *Ihr erste Ball* (1929), Frau Kratochwill in *Walzer aus Wien* (1930), Die Fürstin-Mutter in the revised version of *Das Spitzentuch der Königin* (1931) and Madame Labile in *Die Dubarry* (1935) in a career only a little less memorable than her first, before finally going into retirement.

Her son, **Fritz Zwerenz** (b Baden bei Wien, 3 October 1895; d 12 October 1970), was a musical director, for a time at the Raimundtheater.

Illustration Acknowledgments

The illustrations in these volumes are drawn from the British Musical Theatre Collection and from the following sources, who have generously given permission for their reproduction:

Agence de Presse Bernard (Plates 27, 239, 249, 300, 317, 334, 410)

The Australian Opera, photography by Branco Gaica (Plates 24, 152, 256, 301, 398)

Frank-Roland Beenern (Plate 221)

John Bennewitz, Pictorial Associates (Plate 295)

Bettmann/CORBIS (Plates 30, 31, 58, 61, 63, 67, 127, 128, 132, 134, 135, 166, 197, 225, 253, 313, 318)

Billy Rose Theatre Collection, The New York Public Library for the Performing Arts, Astor, Lenox and Tilden Foundations (Plates 73, 108, 119, 126, 156, 161, 167, 188, 205, 210, 213, 226, 231, 240, 287, 289, 294, 295, 308, 324, 327, 354, 364, 399, 427)

Michael Boys (Plates 47, 74)

Martin Büttner (Plate 434)

Wilson H. Brownell (Plate 150)

CORBIS (Plate 136)

Peter Cunningham (Plate 226)

Erwin Döring, Dresden (Plates 212, 277, 344)

W & D Downey (Plate 219)

Fotofleck Presse- und Bühnenfotograf (Plate 333)

Peter Ferman (Plate 137)

Free Library of Philadelphia, Theater Collection (Plates 8, 46, 69, 82, 110, 158, 182, 193, 199, 224, 243, 264, 271, 286, 299, 325, 328)

Friedman/Abeles (Plate 354)

Gordon Frost Organisation, Sydney, Australia (Plates 33, 203)

Vera von Glasner, Trier (Plate 272)

Gold Coast (Plate 203)

Theo Gröne, Wiesbaden (Plate 26)

L. Gutmann, Vienna (Plates 198, 296, 384)

Harrogate Opera House (Plate 270)

Harvard Theatre Collection (Plates 22, 98, 116, 179a, 281, 285, 400)

Ernst Haas (Plate 54)

Klaus Hofman (Plate 435)

Houston Rogers (Plate 14)

Hubert Huber (Plates 138, 421)

Hulton-Deutsch Collection/CORBIS (Plates 1, 29, 140, 178)

Helène Happaille (Plate 176)

Tom Hustler (Plates 93, 162, 276, 339, 341, 375)

Herbert Jäger, Badendorf (Plate 87)

Peter Joslin Collection (Plates 65, 77, 83, 86, 103, 144, 214, 284, 345, 371)

George Karger (Plate 294)

Helga Kirchberger (Plate 436)

Marco Klompalberts (Plate 106)

Gerhard Kolb (Plate 292)

Helmut Koller, Vienna (Plate 129)

Manfred Kortmann (Plate 346)

Andrew Lamb Collection (Plates 97, 404)

Library Theatre Company, photography by Gerry Murray (Plate 374)

Lucas Studios (Plate 299)

Magyar Színházi Intézet (Plates 43a, 113, 121, 123, 172, 190, 194, 273, 297, 378b, 409, 438)

Mander & Mitchinson Collection (Plates 282, 302)

Joan Marcus (Plate C-51)

Joan Marcus/Carol Rosegg (Plate 324)

Angus McBean (Plate 102)

Chris Monoghan (Plate C-27)

National Library of Australia (Plates 322, 417)

Ohio Light Opera (Plate 19)

Palffy, Vienna (Plates 237, 309, 413)

Atelier Parisienne, Budapest (Plate 194)

Michael le Poer Trench (Plates 236, 258)
Ormond Gigli Rapho-Guilliumette (Plate 205)
Rapport Studios (Plate 308)
H Remmer (Plate 44)
Schamll, Berlin (Plate 382)
Günther Schreckenberg, Darmstadt (Plate 408)
Bradley Smith/CORBIS (Plate 45)
St Louis Municipal Opera (Plates 58, 137, 185, 186, 326, 380, 414)
Staatsoperette, Dresden (Plates 80, 90, 212, 277, 419)
Stage Photo Co (Plate 389)
Hans Uhlemann, Freital (Plates 80, 348)
Uwe Stratmann (Plate 153)
Vandamm Studios (Plate 427)
Volksoper, Wien (Plates 32, 207, 233, 309, 413)
Karlheinz Weinmann (Plate 402)
White Studios (Plates 199, 210, 224, 234, 243, 291)
Reg Wilson (Plates 7, 28, 35, 51, 85, 149, 164, 242, 288, 329, 349, 352, 358, 359, 367, 416, C-25, C-30)
Nigel Yates (Plate 230)
Axel Zeininger, Vienna (Plates 32, 207)

Every effort has been made by the Publisher to trace the copyright holder of all the illustrations in this publication. If copyright has been infringed, we will be pleased to make proper acknowledgment, on being satisfied as to the owner's title, in future editions.